T4-AKJ-337

Contemporary Authors

EDITORS' NOTE

Contemporary Authors, Volume 101, introduced two changes in the physical appearance of *Contemporary Authors* original volumes: a new cover design and a new numbering system.

Contemporary Authors, Volume 97-100, published in 1980, is the last volume with a four-unit volume number.

Contemporary Authors, Volume 101 and Volume 102, carry single volume numbers, as will all subsequent original volumes.

The only changes that have been made in *Contemporary Authors* are the cover design and the numbering plan. No change has been made in the amount or type of material included.

Contemporary Authors

A Bio-Bibliographical Guide to
Current Writers in Fiction, General Nonfiction,
Poetry, Journalism, Drama, Motion Pictures,
Television, and Other Fields

FRANCES C. LOCHER
Editor

volume 102

GALE RESEARCH COMPANY • THE BOOK TOWER • DETROIT, MICHIGAN 48226

Copyright © 1981 by
GALE RESEARCH COMPANY

Library of Congress Catalog Card Number 62-52046
ISBN 0-8103-1902-2
ISSN 0010-7468

Preface

The more than 1,300 entries in *Contemporary Authors,* Volume 102, bring to more than 64,000 the number of authors, either living or deceased since 1960, now represented in the *Contemporary Authors* series. *CA* includes nontechnical writers in all genres—fiction, nonfiction, poetry, drama, etc.—whose books are issued by commercial, risk publishers or by university presses. Authors of books published only by known vanity or author-subsidized firms are ordinarily not included. Since native language and nationality have no bearing on inclusion in *CA,* authors who write in languages other than English are included in *CA* if their works have been published in the United States or translated into English.

Although *CA* focuses primarily on authors of published books, the series also encompasses prominent persons in communications: newspaper and television reporters and correspondents, columnists, newspaper and magazine editors, photojournalists, syndicated cartoonists, screenwriters, television scriptwriters, and other media people.

No charge or obligation is attached to a *CA* listing. Authors are included in the series solely on the basis of the above criteria and their interest to *CA* users.

Compilation Methods

The editors make every effort to secure information directly from the authors through questionnaires and personal correspondence. If authors of special interest to *CA* users are deceased or fail to reply to requests for information, material is gathered from other reliable sources. Biographical dictionaries are checked (a task made easier through the use of Gale's *Biography and Genealogy Master Index* and other volumes in the "Gale Biographical Index Series"), as are bibliographical sources, such as *Cumulative Book Index* and *The National Union Catalog.* Published interviews, feature stories, and book reviews are examined, and often material is supplied by the authors' publishers. All sketches, whether prepared from questionnaires or through extensive research, are sent to the authors for review prior to publication.

Informative Sidelights

Numerous *CA* entries contain Sidelights—insights into the authors' lives and writings, personal philosophies, etc., often provided by the authors themselves, as well as material about the critical reception the authors' works have received. Among the authors in this volume who have worked closely with *CA*'s editors to provide lengthy, incisive Sidelights are Olga Franklin, a British writer, who describes her discovery of a previously unknown trip Leo Tolstoy made to London in 1891; Joan Lesley Hamilton, an American author of a book about St. Patrick, *The Lion and the Cross,* who comments on how she came to be a writer; and John

Hollowell, an American educator, who discusses the influence of journalism on what is perceived to be "news."

Equally incisive Sidelights are written by the *CA* editors when authors and media people of particular interest are unable to supply Sidelights material themselves. This volume, for example, includes lengthy Sidelights compiled by the editors on Romare Bearden, Charles Ralph Boxer, Claud Cockburn, Odysseus Elytis, John Hale, Paul Harvey, William Douglas Home, R.W.B. Lewis, Valery Panov, Neil Postman, Jean-Jacques Servan-Schreiber, Liv Ullmann, and Andrzej Wajda.

Exclusive Interviews

Generally, authors' remarks to *CA*'s editors are reserved for the Sidelights sections of sketches. While no limitations are placed on the length of such material, the editors believe that readers might want even more comment from some of *CA*'s authors.

Accordingly, *CA* is now providing such additional primary information in the form of exclusive author interviews. Prepared specifically for *CA,* the never-before-published conversations presented in the section of the sketch headed *CA INTERVIEW* give *CA* users the opportunity to learn the authors' thoughts, in depth, about their craft. Subjects chosen for the interviews are, the editors feel, authors who hold special interest for *CA*'s readers.

Authors and journalists in this volume whose sketches include interviews are Forrest J Ackerman, James G. Bellows, William Bowers, John Keyes Byrne, Mary Gordon, Tom T. Hall, Jane Kramer, Richard Maibaum, David Newman, Jill Robinson, Kathryn Morgan Ryan, and Gordon Sinclair.

Other Writers of Special Interest

In addition to the authors mentioned above under "Informative Sidelights" and "Exclusive Interviews," a number of other prominent authors and media people are sketched in this volume, such as Julian Beck and his wife, Judith Malina, Joel Brinkley, Tim Brooks, James Burke, Charles W. Colson, Richard L. Cramer, Rodney Dangerfield, Jerry Falwell, Norma Farber, Henry Jay Heimlich, Robert C. Stigwood, John Cameron Swayze, Yves Theriault, Egon von Furstenberg, and George Willig.

Since *CA* includes sketches on deceased authors, a great deal of effort on the part of *CA*'s editors also goes into the compilation of full-length entries on deceased authors of current interest to *CA* readers. This volume contains listings on, among others, J.R. Ackerley, Lincoln Barnett, Ilya Ehrenburg, George Gamow, Etienne Gilson, Robert Fleming Heizer, Julius W. Hobson, David Lawrence, John Lennon, Gabriel Marcel, Jean Monnet, Vera Panova, Adam Clayton Powell, Jr., Maurice Samuel, Burton Egbert Stevenson, John Whiting, and Ethel Davis Wilson.

Obituary Notices Make *CA* Timely and Comprehensive

To be as timely and comprehensive as possible, *CA* publishes obituary notices on deceased authors within the scope of the series. These notices provide date and place of birth and death, highlight the author's career and writings, and list other sources where additional biographical information and obituaries may be found. To distinguish them from full-length sketches, obituaries are identified with the heading *OBITUARY NOTICE.*

CA includes obituary notices both for authors who already have full-length sketches in earlier *CA* volumes, thus effectively completing the sketches, and for authors not yet included in the series. Thirty-five percent of the obituary notices contained in this volume are for authors with listings already in *CA*. Deceased authors of special interest presently represented only by obituary notices are scheduled for full-length sketch treatment in forthcoming *CA* volumes.

Cumulative Index Should Always Be Consulted

The most recent *CA* cumulative index is the user's guide to the volume in which an author's listing appears. The entire *CA* series consists of original volumes, containing entries on authors new to the series, and revision volumes, containing completely updated entries on authors with earlier sketches in the series. The cumulative index, which lists all original and revision volume entries, should always be consulted to locate the specific volume containing an author's original or most recently revised sketch.

For the convenience of *CA* users, the *CA* cumulative index also includes references to all entries in three related Gale series—*Contemporary Literary Criticism* (CLC), which is devoted entirely to current criticism of major novelists, poets, playwrights, and other creative writers, *Something About the Author* (SATA), a series of heavily illustrated sketches on juvenile authors and illustrators, and *Authors in the News* (AITN), a compilation of news stories and feature articles from American newspapers and magazines covering writers and other members of the communications media.

As always, suggestions from users about any aspect of *CA* will be welcomed.

CONTEMPORARY
AUTHORS

A

ABEL, Robert H(alsall) 1941-

PERSONAL: Born May 27, 1941, in Painesville, Ohio; son of Robert H. (a textile worker) and Lora Constance (a school bus driver; maiden name, Logan) Abel; married Joyce Keeler (a budget officer), October 31, 1964; children: Charles Robert. *Education:* College of Wooster, B.A. (cum laude), 1964; Kansas State College, M.A., 1967; University of Massachusetts, M.F.A., 1976. *Politics:* "Hopeless Utopiast." *Religion:* "Hopeless idealist." *Home address:* P.O. Box 96, Lake Pleasant, Mass. 01347. *Agent:* Elaine Markson Literary Agency, Inc., 44 Greenwich Ave., New York, N.Y. 10011.

CAREER: Painesville Telegraph, Painesville, Ohio, reporter, 1964-65; Kansas State University, Pittsburg, instructor in English, 1965-67; affiliated with Flint Community Junior College, Flint, Mich., 1967-68; Northern Illinois University, DeKalb, instructor in English, 1968-72; University of Massachusetts, Amherst, creative writing fellow, 1972-75, public affairs writer, 1975-78; writer. Fiction editor for Lynx House Press. Member of Lake Pleasant Volunteer Fire Department. Instructor at Waubonsee Community Junior College, summer, 1973, and Amherst Senior Center, 1975-76. *Member:* Authors Guild. *Awards, honors:* National Endowment for the Arts fellowship, 1978.

WRITINGS: Skin and Bones (stories), Colorado State Review Press, 1979; *Freedom Dues; or, A Gentleman's Progress in the New World* (novel), Dial, 1980; *Curses!* (stories), Panache Press, 1980. Also author of "The Preacher's Wife," a radio play.

Work represented in anthologies, including *Great Lakes Anthology II,* edited by Peter Neuramont, Antioch Press, 1965.

Contributor of about twenty articles, stories, and reviews to literary magazines, including *Poor Richard's Almanac, Midwest Quarterly, Explicator, Epoch, Margins,* and *Kansas Quarterly.* Fiction editor of *Lynx,* 1972—.

WORK IN PROGRESS: Novels; stories; research on the history of the Vietnam War, human sexuality, contemporary teenagers, and China.

SIDELIGHTS: Abel commented to *CA:* "Fiction should be, at its best, about something that matters. My hope, my gamble is: that fiction can help create a contemporary mythology helpful to the survival of the species, that will make it possible to live in peace. I feel the planet is threatened, that writing should attempt to define and respond to this emergency, not with hysteria, but with some vision of a workable, maybe even beautiful future. Who are we? Where are we going? What are our predicaments, and how do people of this age respond to them?

"I have written some science fiction and a somewhat historical novel, 'experimental' and traditional stories, fantasy and slice-of-life. Why not? Whatever works, works. Stylistics are important, but at the moment it is the subject we are slave to, our survival.

"I understand imperfectly, but have been most influenced by J. P. Sartre, Buckminster Fuller, Alan Watts, Paul Goodman, Gregory Bateson, Erich Fromm, among others. Contemporary writers who most excite (and irritate) me include J. C. Oates, Grace Paley, Philip Levine, Galway Kinnell, Chiua Achebe, V. S. Naipul, Gunter Grass, John Updike, William Styron, Norman Mailer, Joan Didion. Who would I most like to meet? Frederick Douglass, Ghandi, Emma Goldman, Margaret Mead, Thomas Jefferson, Carl Jung, and Hitler. And my father (now deceased). Of course."

BIOGRAPHICAL/CRITICAL SOURCES: Colorado State Review, autumn, 1980.

* * *

ABRAHAMS, Gerald 1907-1980

PERSONAL: Born April 15, 1907, in Liverpool, England; died March 15, 1980, in Liverpool, England; son of Harry and Leah (Rabinowitz) Abrahams; married Elsie Krengel, 1971. *Education:* Wadham College, Oxford, M.A. (with first class honors), 1928. *Residence:* Liverpool, England.

CAREER: Called to the Bar, Gray's Inn, England, 1931; practiced law in Manchester and Liverpool, England; WEA lecturer, 1930-33; acting professor of law at University of Belfast, Belfast, Northern Ireland, 1934. *Wartime service:* Lecturer to Her Majesty's Forces, 1940-44. *Member:* Author's Club. *Awards, honors:* Numerous prizes in chess championships, including third prize at British Championship, 1936 and 1946, and second prize at British Championship, 1954.

WRITINGS: The Law Affecting Police and Public, Sweet & Maxwell, 1938; *The Law Relating to Hire Purchase: Being a Digest of the Present State of the Law, Including the Changes Effected by the 1938 Act,* Eyre & Spottiswoode, 1938; *Ugly Angel* (fiction), Eyre & Spottiswoode, 1940;

Retribution, W. H. Allen, 1941; *Day of Reckoning,* W. H. Allen, 1943; *The World Turns Left,* W. H. Allen, 1943; *Conscience Makes Heroes* (fiction), Eyre & Spottiswoode, 1945.

Lunatics and Lawyers (fiction), Benn, 1951; *The Chess Mind,* Pellegrini & Cudahy, 1952; *The Legal Mind: An Approach to the Dynamics of Advocacy,* H.F.L., 1954; *Chess,* Van Nostrand, c. 1955; *According to the Evidence: An Essay on Legal Proof,* Cassell, 1958; *The Law for Writers and Journalists,* H. Jenkins, 1958; *Technique in Chess,* G. Bell, 1961, Citadel, 1965; *The Jewish Mind,* Constable, 1961, Beacon Press, 1962; *Brains in Bridge,* Constable, 1962, Horizon Press, 1964; *Test Your Chess,* Constable, 1963, London House & Maxwell, 1964; *Police Questioning and the Judge's Rules,* Oyez Publishing, 1964; *The Handbook of Chess, for Beginners and Practiced Players,* Barker, 1965; *Let's Look at Israel,* Museum Press, 1966; *Trade Unions and the Law,* Cassell, 1968; *Morality and the Law,* Calder & Boyars, 1971; *Not Only Chess: A Selection of Chessays,* Allen & Unwin, 1974; *Brilliance in Chess,* Pitman, 1977.

Contributor to numerous periodicals, including *Jewish Chronicle, New Law Journal, Encyclopedia Judaica, Philosophy, National Review, Courier,* and *British Chess Magazine.*

SIDELIGHTS: In *The Jewish Mind* Gerald Abrahams explores the motivation and experience of Judaism and its impact on society. He delves into such topics as the problems and effects of anti-Semitism, traditional thinking and its relevance to the modern Jew, Jewish law as it has developed throughout history, and the influence of Judaism on Western thought. "The book is the product of vast subject knowledge, . . . and it should kindle many intellectual sparks for those interested and knowledgeable in the subject area," noted reviewer S. L. Simon. A writer for the *Times Literary Supplement* likewise praised *The Jewish Mind,* pointing out that Abrahams's "learning is sometimes esoteric, sometimes whimsical, he has thought deeply about his subject, and makes challenging and provoking reflections. . . . He has certainly made a fresh and serious contribution to the English literature about Jews."

In addition to his activities as a lawyer, lecturer, and scholar, Abrahams was an amateur chess-master. "He was an amateur in the best sense of the word," recalled the chess correspondent for the *London Times.* "He had a great passion and enthusiasm for the game." Although his most successful period was during the 1930's, he won numerous prizes in national competitions in the 1940's and 1950's. Of his several books on the game, *The Chess Mind* has proven his most popular. In it he probes the inner workings of the player's mind as he is involved in a game. A reviewer for the *San Francisco Chronicle* related that "if you have ever watched a chess player staring down at the board and wondered what is going on in his brain, this book will come as close to telling you as anything in modern chess literature." Theodore Berg of the *Chicago Sunday Tribune,* moreover, commended *The Chess Mind* as a "fresh approach, rich in philosophical and psychological overtones."

BIOGRAPHICAL/CRITICAL SOURCES: Chicago Sunday Tribune, October 5, 1952; *San Francisco Chronicle,* November 9, 1952; *Guardian,* March 16, 1962; *Times Literary Supplement,* March 30, 1962; *Library Journal,* August, 1962.

OBITUARIES: London Times, April 11, 1980; *AB Bookman's Weekly,* June 16, 1980.*

ABRAMS, Linsey 1951-

PERSONAL: Born January 4, 1951, in Boston, Mass.; daughter of Orville C. (a businessman) and Janis (an educational consultant and book distributor; maiden name, White) Abrams. *Education:* Sarah Lawrence College, B.A., 1973; City College of the City University of New York, M.A., 1978. *Residence:* New York, N.Y. *Agent:* Georges Borchardt, Inc., 136 East 57th St., New York, N.Y. 10022.

CAREER: Queens College of the City University of New York, Flushing, N.Y., adjunct lecturer in English, 1978—. Guest faculty member in fiction writing at Sarah Lawrence College, 1980-81. *Awards, honors:* Grant from Creative Artist Public Service, 1980.

WRITINGS: Charting by the Stars (novel), Harmony, 1979.

WORK IN PROGRESS: A novel, completion expected in 1981.

SIDELIGHTS: Abrams told *CA:* "They say that an author's second novel is the most difficult one to write. Whether this is true or not, I don't know, but just in case it is I have been working on my own second novel like there is no tomorrow in hopes of getting the better of it before it gets the better of me. So far, I am winning. I have to this same end attempted to bamboozle myself by doing in this novel things that I *didn't do* in my first: different time relationships, different use of tenses, different person of narration, different plot movement. Perhaps the only aspect that has remained the same from one book to the next is *concerns*—I don't believe that a writer's concerns change; they merely enlarge, and in each new book you look for the structure that will more perfectly encompass them, if not even draw them out. When I finished my last book, I was sure that I had exhausted everything I could think of to say about the world. Happily, this wasn't true. The real eye-opener about a second book (and this is perhaps what it is, finally, that makes them potentially so difficult to write) is that you realize you can write about *anything,* that there are endless stories to tell and endless points of view to be made known. As in life, this is a matter of both consternation and joy."

*   *   *

ABRAMSON, Harold Alexander 1889-1980

OBITUARY NOTICE: Born November 27, 1889, in New York, N.Y.; died of cancer, September, 1980, in Cold Spring Harbor, Long Island, N.Y. Psychiatrist, allergist, research scientist, and author. In addition to being a pioneer in the study of asthma and eczema, Abramson was one of the first Americans to research the effects of LSD, a hallucinogenic drug. He was also involved with the Central Intelligence Agency's experiments with the controversial drug. He was co-founder of the Asthma Care Association, Asthmatic Children's Foundation, and the Asthmatic Publications Society. In 1962 he founded the *Journal of Asthma Research* and remained its editor-in-chief until his death. His writings include *Dimensional Analysis for Students of Medicine, The Patient Speaks,* and *The Use of LSD in Psychotherapy and Alcoholism.* Obituaries and other sources: *Who's Who in America,* 40th edition, Marquis, 1978; *New York Times,* October 1, 1980.

*   *   *

ACHILLES
See LAMB, Charles Bentall

ACKERLEY, J(oe) R(andolph)   1896-1967

PERSONAL: Born in 1896 in Herne Hill, Kent, England; died June 4, 1967; son of Alfred Roger Ackerley (a banana importer). *Education:* Received degree from Magdalene College, Oxford, 1921.

CAREER: Memoirist, dramatist, novelist, poet, and editor. Private secretary to ruler of state in India; British Broadcasting Corp. (BBC), London, England, assistant producer in talks department, 1928-35, editor of *Listener*, 1935-59. *Military service:* Royal Army, 1914-18.

WRITINGS: The Prisoners of War (three-act play), Chatto & Windus, 1925; *Hindoo Holiday: An Indian Journal*, Viking, 1932; *My Dog Tulip*, Secker & Warburg, 1956, Fleet Publishing, 1965; *We Think the World of You* (novel), Bodley Head, 1960; *My Father and Myself* (autobiography), Bodley Head, 1968, Coward, 1969; *E. M. Forster: A Portrait*, McKelvie, 1970; *Micheldever and Other Poems*, McKelvie, 1972; *The Ackerley Letters*, Harcourt, 1975 (published in England as *The Letters of J. R. Ackerley*, Duckworth, 1975).

SIDELIGHTS: J. R. Ackerley's position as editor of the *Listener* placed him at the center of British literary activity. And while he served quietly there for twenty-five years, he wrote candidly of his homosexual relationships with waiters, soldiers, and errand boys far from the literary world. Though his writing output is small, he produced "three or four books which will survive," said Stephen Spender, "if humanity survives."

Ackerley was known as a fair and eclectic editor, and his careful selection of the poems, short stories, and articles that appeared in the *Listener* helped him earn the reputation as "one of the most brilliant editors of his generation." Spender explained some of the reasons behind that reputation: "He cared immensely about what books were reviewed—and by whom—and what poems he published. He encouraged young writers." Ackerley himself was encouraged in his career by a close friend, E. M. Forster, and he acknowledged his debt to him in his short book, *E. M. Forster: A Portrait.*

While Ackerley's career was marked by his success as an editor, his private life was darkened by personal suffering. His enemy, reported Paul Bailey, was "class conscious, puritanical England." Its attitude towards homosexuality particularly troubled him, and even such friends as W. H. Auden and William Plomer, upon reading *My Father and Myself*, were offended by Ackerley's candid discussion of the subject. Ackerley related his need to be frank in a 1955 letter to Spender: "I think people *ought* to be upset, and if I had a paper I would upset them all the time; I think that life is so important and, in its workings, so upsetting that nobody should be spared."

Ackerley's family life, specifically his relationship with his father, was a source of much confusion to him. When Alfred Roger Ackerley's first wife died he took two mistresses and maintained each of them privately. He later married one of them, Ackerley's mother, in 1919—twenty-three years after Ackerley's birth. In the meantime the senior Ackerley had fathered a second secret family of three girls who knew their father only as "uncle." Ackerley undertook the painful task of discussing his family as well as his homosexuality in *My Father and Myself.* As he said upon presenting the book to one of his half sisters: "I don't expect you to like the book, I don't enjoy it myself, but it tries to speak the truth, which is seldom palatable."

Much of Ackerley's writing, whether comic or serious, deals with subjects that many would find disturbing. His play *Prisoner of War*, considered one of the best plays inspired by World War I, contains an undercurrent of homosexuality. *My Dog Tulip* is a tribute to Ackerley's beloved German shepherd, who is said to have represented for him "uncontaminated physical beauty." In his comic novel, *We Think the World of You*, the protagonist gradually redirects his affections from a young thief, Johnny, to Johnny's dog. But throughout his work, Ackerley attracted many readers with his ability to laugh at himself. According to Bailey, "he possessed a talent for self-humiliation."

The many sides of Ackerley are perhaps best revealed in his letters. To Paul Theroux, *The Ackerley Letters* show that "he was a wonderful writer, a man of great gusto, and happily for us, most of his energy went into his letter writing." Even Ackerley's weaknesses are converted to strengths in his letters, as Theroux pointed out: "Though that rather too many of these letters are a repetition of his obsessive dependency on his dog, sometimes amounting to a soppy infatuation, . . . he was able to communicate the passion he felt for the dog and it moved him to write some of his most heart-wrenching prose." Spender, too, admired the collection: "These letters are beautifully done, at times exceedingly funny, and very self-revealing."

"Ackerley wrote little in his long life," reported Bailey. "The act of writing was painful to him and he only wrote when he absolutely *had* to. He lacked, it is fair to say, the gift of invention. What he did instead was to look clearly at the messy, everyday world around him. He described it honestly, 'without fear or favour.' He said some upsetting things about it, and left us in his debt."

BIOGRAPHICAL/CRITICAL SOURCES: J. R. Ackerley, *My Father and Myself*, Coward, 1969; *New Statesman*, January 31, 1975; *Times Literary Supplement*, January 31, 1975; *Spectator*, February 1, 1975, September 6, 1975; *Economist*, March 8, 1975; *New York Times Book Review*, May 25, 1975; *New Yorker*, June 23, 1975.*

*   *   *

ACKERMAN, Forrest J(ames)   1916-

PERSONAL: Born November 24, 1916, in Los Angeles, Calif.; son of William Schilling (a statistician) and Carroll Cridland (Wyman) Ackerman; married Wendayne Wahrmann, June, 1949. *Education:* Attended University of California, Berkeley, 1934-35. *Politics:* Apolitical. *Religion:* Atheist. *Home:* 2495 Glendower Ave., Hollywood, Calif. 90027. *Agent and office:* Ackerman Science Fiction Agency, 2495 Glendower Ave., Hollywood, Calif. 90027.

CAREER: U.S. Civil Service, Los Angeles, Calif., senior typist, 1937; Associated Oil Co., Los Angeles, clerk, 1938; Academy of Motion Picture Arts and Sciences, Hollywood, Calif., chief varitypist, 1939-40; Fluor Drafting Corp., Los Angeles, chief varitypist, 1942; Ackerman Science Fiction Agency, Hollywood, owner and agent, 1947—. Collector and curator of Ackerman Science Fiction Archives, 1926—. Founder of Boys' Scientifiction Club, 1929; lecturer on science fiction and films at schools and universities; guest on commercial and public television programs, including "To Tell the Truth," "Down Memory Lane," "Merv Griffin Show," "PM," "Tomorrow Show," "Today Show," "Mike Douglas Show," and "Good Morning, America"; actor in motion pictures, including "The Time Travelers," 1964, "Queen of Blood," 1966, "Dracula vs. Frankenstein," 1971, "Schlock," 1973, "The Howling," 1981, and "Aftermath," 1981. *Military service:* U.S. Army, 1942-45; became staff sergeant; edited wartime newspaper.

MEMBER: Science Fiction Writers of America, National Fantasy Fan Federation (honorary lifetime member), Science Fiction League (honorary member No. 1), Los Angeles Science Fantasy Society (honorary charter member). *Awards, honors:* Hugo Award from World Science Fiction Convention, 1953, naming him ''Number One Fan Personality''; has subsequently received German, Italian, and Japanese Hugo Awards; Ann Radcliffe Award from Count Dracula Society, 1963 and 1966, for gothic excellence; fan guest of honor at twenty-second World Science Fiction Convention, 1964; guest of honor at Lunacon, 1974, at first annual Famous Monsters of Filmland Convention, 1974, and at science-fiction conventions in England, Germany, Italy, Japan, and Spain; Science Fiction Hall of Fame Award, 1976; Academy of Science Fiction Films Award, 1977; Frank R. Paul Award from Kubla Khanate, 1980, for outstanding achievement in science fiction.

WRITINGS: (Editor with Cliff Lawton) *A Book of Weird Tales*, Veevers & Hensman Ltd. (London), 1958; *James Warren Presents the Best From Famous Monsters of Filmland*, Paperback Library, 1964; *James Warren Presents Famous Monsters of Filmland Strike Back!*, Paperback Library, 1965; *James Warren Presents Son of Famous Monsters of Filmland*, Paperback Library, 1965; *The Frankenscience Monster*, Ace, 1969; (with others) *Science Fiction Worlds of Forrest J Ackerman and Friends*, Powell Publications, 1969; (editor) Alfred Elton van Vogt, *Monsters*, Paperback Library, 1970; (editor) *Best Science Fiction for 1973*, Ace, 1973; *Amazing Forries*, Metropolis Press, 1976; *Souvenir Book of Mr. Science Fiction's Fantasy Museum*, Kodansha, 1978.

(With Philip J. Riley) *London After Midnight Revisited*, Metropolis Books, 1981; (with A. W. Strickland) *A Reference Guide to American Science Fiction Films*, four volumes, T.I.S. Publications, 1981; (with Strickland) *A Book of Great Science Fiction Films*, T.I.S. Publications, 1981; *The Treasure Trove of Imagi-Movies*, Donning, 1981; (contributor) Luigi Cozzi, editor, *Italianthology of Sci-Fi, 1930-35*, Editrice Libra, 1981; (editor with Cozzi) *The Great Science Fiction, 1936-40*, Editrice Libra, 1981; *Gosh! Wow!! Boy-oh-Boy!!! Science Fiction*, Bantam, 1982.

Author and narrator of motion picture ''Science Fiction Films,'' University of Kansas, 1970. Creator and author of comic books ''Vampirella'' and ''Jeanie of Questar.'' Contributor of more than two thousand articles and short stories to magazines, including *Wonder Stories, Thrilling Wonder Stories, Other Worlds, Weird Tales, Authentic Science Fiction* (England), *Vertex Science Fiction, Nebula Science Fiction* (Scotland), *Spaceway, New Worlds* (England), *Hapna!* (Sweden), *Famous Monsters of Filmland, Fantasy Book, Marvel Science Stories, Perry Rhodan, International Science Fiction, Los Cuentos Fantasticos* (Mexico), *Utopia* (Germany), *Fantastic Story, Super Science Stories, After Hours, Penthouse,* and *Science Fiction Digest.*

Editor-in-chief of *Famous Monsters of Filmland,* 1958—; managing editor of Perry Rhodan series, Ace, 1969-79; editor of *The Time Traveller,* beginning 1932, *Voice of the Imagi-Nation,* beginning 1939, *Ft. McArthur Bulletin-Alert* (Army newspaper), 1942-45, *Spacemen,* 1961-64, and *Monster World,* 1964-66.

SIDELIGHTS: Forrest J Ackerman has amassed the largest collection of science-fiction and fantasy artifacts on Earth. Housed in the ''Ackermansion,'' his four-story home in Hollywood, is virtually every fantastic title ever printed, including two hundred editions of *Dracula* and as many *Franken-*

steins. Among row after row of bookcases and shelves that occupy the garages, basement, halls, cupboards, and rooms of the Ackermansion are the books, magazines, manuscripts, correspondence, photographs, paintings, posters, movie props, and assorted memorabilia that define a genre—more than 300,000 items valued at many millions of dollars. Professionally, Ackerman is a writer, editor, and literary agent. Within the science-fiction community, however, he is 4SJ, the ''World's Greatest Science-Fiction Fan.''

Since 1926 the collection and promotion of science fiction have been a way of life for Ackerman. Schoolmates who shared his interest in space flight and otherworldly beings were hard to find in the twenties and thirties, so he organized fan clubs, published newsletters, and developed a correspondence with science-fiction enthusiasts around the world. Magazines at that time were limited to a handful of Hugo Gernsback publications—*Amazing Stories, Science Wonder Stories, Science Wonder Quarterly*—but Hollywood provided other imaginative outlets. Ackerman attended as many as seven films a day, taking in everything from Fritz Lang's classic ''Metropolis'' to low-budget B movies about creatures from outer space. In a short time he added stills, posters, and sound discs to his library, deciding that the major goal of his life would be to ''create and maintain the greatest collection of imaginative memorabilia on this or (hopefully) any other planet.''

Hollywood's impact on the evolution of sci-fi is a prominent part of the collection. It is even part of Ackerman's personality; he adopted the swirling hairstyle of matinee idol Warren William and fashioned his handwriting from an inscribed photograph of actress Kay Francis. But to take the full measure of his film lore, a visitor to the Ackermansion moves to the lower level, the heart of the collection, where galleries of movie monsters, masks, props, posters, and stills are on exhibit. In one section is a full-scale replica of Ultima, the robotrix from ''Metropolis''; in another are five of ''The Seven Faces of Dr. Lao.'' Prehistoric monsters from ''King Kong'' are featured along with the head of Werner Herzog's ''Nosferatu,'' a makeup kit used by Lon Chaney, Sr., and 125,000 stills from pictures like ''Things to Come,'' ''War of the Worlds,'' and ''The Day the Earth Stood Still.''

The hallmark of the collection, however, is its all-inclusiveness. Everything from the supernatural to fantasy to hardcore science fiction is there. For approximately fifty-five years Ackerman has been scanning publishers lists, searching out and purchasing every possible edition, whether he personally likes a book or not. ''It's breathtaking,'' said one Los Angeles librarian. ''Clearly the world's best. Nothing could touch it.'' Tom Nolan, a feature writer for *New West,* gave his impressions of the archives: ''Planetary vistas glow from pastel dust jackets, the little-boy hero of van Vogt's *Slan* peers at a flying saucer in the nighttime sky, the tableau etched in a stylized 1950s woodcut. Here the past breathes. Even to a nonenthusiast, the sight is awesome. For a devotee, viewing The Collection must be akin to a glimpse of the Afterlife.''

Before his fame as ''sweeper of the galactic bestiary, indexer of the sum total of things,'' Ackerman was already a sci-fi celebrity with unique credentials. Beginning with the first issue of *Science Wonder Quarterly* in 1929, he has probably published more fan letters and articles than anyone else in fandom, many of them under pseudonyms like Dr. Acula, Weaver Wright, Claire Voyant, and scores of others. At the first World Science Fiction Convention in 1939, Ackerman was the only one to show up in a futuristic costume, but it set a precedent for future conventions that fans of "Star Trek," "Star Wars," and Tolkien continue to observe. When the highest honor in science fiction, the Hugo Award, was created in 1953, Isaac Asimov presented the very first one to Ackerman, naming him sci-fi's "Number One Fan Personality."

Ackerman's most famous (or infamous) contribution to the science-fiction field came in 1954. The atomic age had by then transformed science fiction from a literary outpost to a popular cultural force, and it was felt that "scientifiction" was too cumbersome a term for current needs. Taking his cue from other hybrids of the day like "hi-fi" and "poly-sci," Ackerman coined the abbreviation "sci-fi," a universally recognized acronym that some authors and fans still wish had never been uttered. "'Sci-fi' is the sound of two crickets screwing," Harlan Ellison complains. Nevertheless, the word is in popular usage worldwide and has found its way into numerous dictionaries.

Ackerman's efforts to boost the popularity of science fiction have taken other forms as well. As a literary agent he represents such writers as A. E. van Vogt, H. L. Gold, Hugo Gernsback, L. Ron Hubbard, Ray Cummings, and Donald F. Glut. His *Famous Monsters of Filmland,* launched in 1958, remains one of the most popular monthlies on the market. He is the author of occasional short stories, a lifelong supporter of Esperanto ("the language of the future"), and a widely-sought guest speaker at schools and universities. But the abiding interest of his life, the occupation that overshadows all others, is the expansion and preservation of his collection.

Lest his life's work should ever be auctioned off in blocks or sealed up in a university vault, Ackerman decided that the archives should remain intact and available to the public. In 1979 he offered his entire collection to the city of Los Angeles with the understanding that it would someday be housed in its own separate facility. In the meantime Ackerman continues to stock his shelves with new acquisitions, despite the mounting, enormous expense. He remains, in Nolan's words, "sole occupant of this remote outpost in space, guardian of the knowledge, wearer of the ring, . . . self-elected 4SJ Aristotle of the asteroids, the cosmic curator, the chief and original and one and only compiler of . . . the Encyclopedia Fanatica."

CA INTERVIEW
CA interviewed Forrest J Ackerman by phone on March 13, 1980, at his home, the Ackermansion, in Los Angeles, Calif.

CA: You became involved in the science-fiction scene when you were nine. What accounted for science fiction's enormous appeal at that age?

ACKERMAN: As far as I can figure out fifty-four years later, it was right around that time that I had seen my first circus, and I was astonished at the life forms. I'd never encountered a giraffe before, or an elephant, or a python. Shortly thereafter, I saw the October, 1926, issue of *Amazing Stories,* and it had an imaginary life form on it—a gigantic crustacean creature up at the North Pole, about three times the size of a human being. I think I had so many visions of zebras and various exotic things in my mind, I didn't even know that that was an imaginary creature; I just wanted to read about it.

So I got the magazine, and when I got inside I was introduced to the imaginations of H. G. Wells and Edgar Allan Poe and Edgar Rice Burroughs and Jules Verne. Looking back on it, I wonder if I understood every other word, because I had never encountered *planets* before or *comets* or *galaxies* or *atoms* or so many of the terms of science fiction, but I had an inquisitive mind and a pair of grandparents who sponsored me in all my interests. If I didn't understand a word, they would explain it to me, or I'd look it up in a dictionary. It set my imagination on fire, and the blaze has never been put out.

CA: So you had a lot of encouragement from home?

ACKERMAN: From my maternal grandparents. Not so much from my parents, although they never really actively opposed my interest. My dad was a solid businessman in the world of oil companies and always figured his son would follow in his footsteps. My mother was a little concerned by the time I was around twelve years old and had my own little den, where I was keeping my science-fiction collection. It couldn't have amounted to much then, because by 1929 there were still only six or seven science-fiction magazines, but I kept them all. So my mother took me aside and said, "Son, do you have any idea how many of these science-fiction magazines you have? I just counted them. You have twenty-seven. If you continue to accumulate at this rate, by the time you're a grown man you might have a *hundred!*" Well, Mother lived with me right here in my home until she passed away when she was nearly ninety-four, and she saw the collection grow to fill a seventeen-room, four-story home with three garages. I call them the Garage-Mahal, son of Taj. Whenever I see a garage sale, I buy another garage. Actually, I have two more garages around town that I'm renting now to hold part of the collection.

CA: I've read that you were considered rather strange at school. Is that true?

ACKERMAN: Yes, in all of high school. When I graduated, I think I was in something like eighth place out of 256 in scholastic standing, and I had only found three boys and one or two girls who in the least fashion shared my interest and my belief that one day we would go to other worlds and atomic power would free the world with energy. It was a kind of sad and lonely thing to be put upon and considered the resident crazy. Although I did early on, in 1931, get some recognition.

I was living in San Francisco, and the Sunday newspaper had one page devoted to children. The paper had a short-story contest and there were about two hundred entries. Mine was a very primitive little tale called "A Trip to Mars," but it had a kind of O. Henry ending to it. That won the prize. So I was invited down to the editorial offices and photographed, and my picture appeared in the paper proudly holding the first issue of *Amazing Stories.* That got me a little prestige in school and around the house. And also when my parents saw a letter by me in print in 1929—I had my first letter published in the first issue of *Science Wonder Quarterly*—they took pride in seeing their son's name in print. I got the message and thought, "Oho! If I have a letter in every one of those magazines I'll be sure to cadge a quarter off of Mom and Pop to buy it."

CA: How have you managed to integrate your roles as writer, editor, publisher, and collector?

ACKERMAN: I think in a way World War II contributed to an ability to juggle half a dozen literary balls in the air at one time. For three years, five months, and twenty-nine days of World War II, I was editing one of the wartime newspapers. There were two thousand military papers during World War

II, and the one I edited was the second most popular each year, the *Ft. McArthur Bulletin-Alert*. Rain or shine, every seven days that popular newspaper had to roll out of my fingers. I had to sit and do it right behind the sound system where, eighteen hours a day, draftees would be coming in, and they would be seeing on film the wonders of war—the rat-a-tat-tat of the machine guns, the grenades and diving airplanes—and hearing lovely lectures on venereal disease.

With all this going on I had to sit there and be creative, including the sad week I got the word that my brother had been killed. He didn't quite make it to twenty-one. He got up New Year's Day, 1945, and wasn't alive that night, courtesy of Hitler and his gang and the Battle of the Bulge in Belgium. But I guess I got disciplined there that the show must go on. So here in this world, where I'm representing 140 science-fiction authors and have written 165 issues of the magazine, *Famous Monsters of Filmland*, where at any moment of the night or day somebody can ring the doorbell or the phone (the phone's been ringing off the hook since my appearance this morning on the ''Today Show''), I leave off one thing and may not get back to it till much later, but I just pick it up and carry on.

CA: When did your interest in movies begin?

ACKERMAN: Before I was six years old I began to remember movies that I saw. My grandparents would take me to as many as seven films in a single day. I once saw 356 in a single year. I was kind of a young critic, I suppose. I would grade them all.

Carl Laemmle, Sr., was the president of Universal Studios in the halcyon days when they were making the great movies of ''Frankenstein,'' ''Dracula,'' ''The Invisible Man,'' and so on. I never met Laemmle, but I started a correspondence with him. As soon as I saw one of his pictures, I would write and tell him what I thought of it. I guess back in the early thirties he thought I was the all-American movie-going boy. Eventually, on his president's stationery, he wrote me a nice carte blanche saying, ''Give this kid anything he wants.'' I was able to take it around to the branch office and get stills and posters and sound scores. It was so early then that sound was on huge discs instead of little squiggles on the side of film as it is nowadays. I got the entire sound scores from ''Frankenstein'' and ''The Mummy'' and ''Murders in the Rue Morgue.''

CA: You were a promoter of Esperanto?

ACKERMAN: Still am. Had I not been so involved in science fiction, Esperanto probably would have been my life. I missed out on becoming an Esperanto instructor by being just three months too young to go into night school and teach it. Then I got diverted into the oil company and later on into the Academy of Motion Picture Arts and Sciences and so on.

I guess Esperanto interests me next best to science fiction; I just don't have time enough for it. But it's always with me, and anywhere in the world I run into a fellow Esperantist, or if I get a letter or somebody sends me something to translate, there's no problem about it. I was an excellent student in French, but I was appalled after four years of it to get to France and find that I couldn't understand anything. In Esperanto, no problem.

A couple of years ago I was in Vienna among two thousand Esperantists, and no matter where in the world we came from, we had nothing in common except that we could talk to each other. Ten different nationalities could sit down at a table and have a conversation. There are about thirty million

people, the last figure I heard, who know Esperanto, but I've become rather disillusioned that it's taking so long for anything sensible to happen. It's a lot like the metric system in the U.S.A.; I guess most of the rest of the world has it, and I'm told it's simpler to get along with than what we have, but we don't seem to be getting very far.

Esperanto to my mind is like arithmetic. You wouldn't think of trying to teach trigonometry to anybody who didn't know that one and one was two, two and two were four, and so on. It seems to me the most sensible thing on earth that every kid who's going to learn another language should start with Esperanto. If they can't learn that, you can jolly well forget about any other language. On the other hand, it gives you a sense of satisfaction when you learn Esperanto, because you really can speak another language. You want me to give you a little sample of it? *Internacia lingvo estas kombinajho franca itala. Por eksemplo: tre komprenas lingvon.* You can see how easily understood it is.

CA: Would you talk about the growth of fandom over the years?

ACKERMAN: In the beginning, when I picked up that 1926 magazine, there was no fandom. I think the science-fiction magazines started the notion of readers' letters, which are so popular today in many magazines. Most of us thought the magazines were put out just for us alone—that there was one copy. We didn't realize until we began to see names and addresses we recognized in New York, Chicago, and so on that there were other people out there.

The first time I ever heard from a fellow science-fiction fan was when I was in high school. I had a bit of a sore throat or something, so Mother kept me home that day, and along came a letter from a Linus Hogenmiller. He had seen several letters by me in print, and he sent me a handwritten letter about eight pages long pouring his heart out to me and enthusing about the things he liked. Being right there in bed and not in school, I wrote him a letter and sent Mother down to the corner mailbox with it. No sooner had I finished that letter than I had another one in my mind. I sent him three letters the first day, and we started quite a correspondence.

I'd been born in Hollywood and used to hang around the studios and get autographs from Marlene Dietrich and Gary Cooper and other greats of the early days. That idea carried over into the science-fiction field. I thought I'd like to have the autographs of Hugo Gernsback (the editor of *Amazing*), Frank R. Paul (the great artist), and various writers I admired; and I thought maybe they would send me a manuscript, as indeed they did. Then I thought, ''Gee, I'd really love that cover; I wonder what happens to it after it's published?'' So I would just write and ask for it, and generally they sent me the artwork.

I guess I had a kind of reportorial instinct early in life, because I found an autograph would lead to a correspondence, and naturally the authors would tell me what stories they were working on. I wanted to share this information, so I first started out with a typewriter and carbon paper and would make a little science-fiction news sheet a couple of pages long and mail it around as a chain letter. Then I discovered the wonders of hectography, where you get some nauseous gelatin and firm it up and put some horrid purple ink on it and run off about fifty illegible copies of something you'd typed. So around 1930 I created a little publication called the *Meteor*, in which I would reproduce the autograph of a science-fiction author and write little things. I knew about what movies were forthcoming and what writers were doing.

About that time I got the notion of forming a correspondence club. I called it the Boys' Scientifiction Club. I had nothing against girls, but they were as rare as dinosaurs' teeth in the early days of science fiction. It didn't even occur to me that there was any use in including the female gender in the title. A number of boys wrote and joined my little club. It was ten cents a month (postage was only two cents then, and we got mail delivery twice a day). When you joined my club, you sent in either one hardcover book—there were no paperbacks at that time—or three issues of a magazine, preferably in chronological sequence. Then I had a mailing library. You were entitled to borrow a book or a magazine for two weeks. But I was a one-man show, and before I knew it I was spending so much time after school wrapping up packages and tramping to the post office and corresponding—I had 117 correspondents by the time I was fifteen years old—that my parents had me cool it. But I had this little club, and other independent clubs started up.

Then the main thing that happened was that in 1932 I was part of the team that created the first of all legitimately recognized science-fiction fan magazines, called *The Time Traveller*. On the first page of the first issue I wrote the first article, giving a list of about thirty-four titles of all known fantasy films. I lumped them all together as science fiction at the time. Although under no circumstances today would I consider "Dracula" to be a science-fiction film, in the beginning we were so starved for anything fantastic that I guess we just lumped everything together as science fiction. *The Time Traveller* branched off after nine issues and became a printed publication called *Science Fiction Digest*.

There was a young man named Charles D. Hornig who, when he was seventeen, was publishing an excellent fanzine called the *Fantasy Fan*. Hugo Gernsback, who at that time (about 1934) was editing the professional magazine *Wonder Stories,* needed a managing editor. A copy of young Hornig's *Fantasy Fan* came into his hands, and he was so impressed by it that he sent for Hornig and was astounded to find a seventeen-year-old boy walking into his office. Nevertheless, he was so impressed by Hornig, in spite of his youth, that he offered him the associate editorship. Charles Hornig's immortal response was, "I'll have to go home and ask my mother and dad if they'll let me." Because Hornig was a big fan at heart, he carried all kinds of fannish notions right into the professional world. And Hugo Gernsback went along with them all. He let him put in a swap column so that fans could sell and trade and advertise freely.

Then Hornig sold Gernsback on the notion of creating what was called the Science Fiction League, which would have chapters all over the United States and in other parts of the world. Here in Los Angeles we were the fourth chapter to be formed, and I went to the first meeting. It's still going on every Thursday night. Over a hundred science-fiction fans come to the meetings of the Los Angeles Science Fantasy Society. I was at the very first meeting in 1934 or so, and there have been over fifteen hundred meetings since.

In the beginning the reason for the science-fiction clubs was for reinforcement, I would say; we weren't quite as crazy as the outside world figured us to be. And also to share information. We would discuss the magazines that had come out and the stories we had read. And particularly in the early days, when there was so little science fiction, we had to seek elsewhere. There were pulp magazines like *Blue Book, Excitement, Topnotch, Argosy;* and every once in a while we'd get lucky and there would be a new H. G. Wells or Sax Rohmer with his Fu Manchu, which was science fiction of a

sort, or we'd discover a magazine like *Doc Savage.* So we would get together to tell each other about these new things.

It was a tremendous thrill when some science-fiction author would come to the club and explain to us how he got his ideas and went about writing his stories. There was a man named Arthur J. Burks who was kind of a fiction factory—he turned out millions of words a year—and I remember when he came to our science-fiction club back in the late thirties. You could toss any word into the air or point to anything and he would instantly start spinning a science-fiction story around it. And a Dr. David H. Keller, who was one of the first men to bring sociology into science fiction. He was the superintendent of an insane asylum in Pennsylvania. He had a very strange childhood; he refused to speak English and created a language all his own, communicated only through his older sister. She died when she was about eight, and that left him incommunicado with humanity.

In the beginning it was all information and the thrill of meeting authors; and when the rare science-fiction film would come along, we would all clan together and go down en masse to see it. Then in 1939 the feeling came that the time had arrived for the first world science-fiction convention. The entire world was certainly welcome, but at that time there were only about 185 of us who could afford the money or the time. I lent Ray Bradbury fifty dollars to get on the Greyhound bus and make the pilgrimage. It was held in New York over the July Fourth weekend. I went, trembling all the way with every clickety-clack of the railroad track; I was such a shy, introverted boy that I was just terrified of the notion that I might be sitting in the audience, minding my own business, and, like on the "Ed Sullivan Show," somebody might notice me and ask me to stand. I got as far as Chicago and had to change trains, and boy did I ever struggle with myself to go on.

I was the only one who came in a futuristic outfit. Nobody else thought to do that, but it caught on, starting the next year. Not that everybody wore costumes all the time, but they did like the idea, and there were twenty-five or thirty who turned up for a masquerade. It became part and parcel of even the lowliest science-fiction convention. There's certainly a change there: in the beginning the costumes appeared only at masquerade time for a couple of hours. Now you walk into a hotel with a science-fiction convention going on and it's masquerade time all during the convention.

We grew from 185 at that first convention to 3,200 fans from thirty countries last August in Brighton, England. And by now it's like a kaleidoscope. In the beginning it was pretty much focused on science-fiction magazines and such few movies as there were. Now you have splinter groups: you have people who are just crazy about Dr. Who, and there are the Trekkies and the "Logan's Run" people and the "Star Wars" fans and the Tolkien people. There's so much for everybody now that it's kind of a three-ring circus; you're faced with constant decisions any hour of the day as to where you're going to spend your time. I wish I could be cloned and about a half a dozen of me go to every convention nowadays.

CA: Is there anything you haven't done that you'd like to try?

ACKERMAN: Absolutely, yes. I would like to take some of my favorites, such as the *Four-Sided Triangle* by William F. Temple or *Slan* by A. E. van Vogt, and turn them into screenplays and be involved with the creative end of it and watch the whole thing come true—to put a couple of classics on the screen and do it right. Or another thing would be to take my great favorite of all time, the film "Metropolis," which in 1926, of course, had to be black and white and silent and small, and do that over again almost frame for frame, but on the giant screen with Sensurround and Dolby stereo and color and the magnificence of futuristic cities. I'd have a world-wide contest for architects to create their impressions of what the world is going to look like a hundred years from now.

Also, I feel like a sponge that's been around in the science-fiction field for fifty-four years now: I should be squeezed while I'm here to get all kinds of information out of me and into print. I've seen "Metropolis" more times than anybody else on earth, I believe, and have more stills from it. I have stills from the personal collection of the woman who wrote it, and from Fritz Lang, who directed it, and from all over the world. I'd like to do a gorgeous, fifty-buck coffee-table book showing and telling everything in the world about "Metropolis." And another project: all our lives we've heard Lon Chaney, Sr., referred to as the man of a thousand faces. I *have* a thousand faces of Lon Chaney. I have the stills, and I would like to share them with the world and put out a book where we see the thousand faces of Lon Chaney.

I feel like kind of a repository of knowledge and an archaeologist of early science fiction. Despite all the anthologies that have appeared, I still remember wonderful stories that have never been brought back into print—whether because the anthologists never read them, or they don't have the magazines, I don't know. I am in the process of doing a book for Bantam, the theme being to turn back the clock to the first ten years that I read science fiction—from 1926 to 1936—and pick out the stories that thrilled me at the time, the seminal science fiction that grabbed my attention and kept me going the first ten years. In conjunction with each story I will reminisce about whatever was going on at the time in the science-fiction world, and there'll be a general introduction to it all. But I feel that there are ever so many books in me that I would love to get into print before I'm gone—not only memoirs, but anthologies.

And the museum plans, now that the mayor of Los Angeles has discovered me, to create an actual futuristic-looking edifice to house my three-hundred-thousand-piece collection. I expect three to five years from now there'll be a ribbon-cutting ceremony, and I'll be curator of my own work as long as I want to carry on with it.

Actually, I'm getting a little enthusiastic now about living a lot longer than I originally figured on. Two routes to go. One, I have long since decided that if I ever get the bad news that I have about six months to live, if I have the funds for it (I think it costs about thirty-five thousand dollars at the present time), I will die out at the University of California where they have a cryogenic set-up and become a human popsicle a few moments after being declared dead. I'll be frozen and hope that in ten, twenty, fifty years—however long it would take to clear up whatever I died of—they would thaw me out and give me a shot of something or other, and there I'd be in the brave new world, if there's anything left of it. To me that would be like the great culminating experiment of my life, like time travel, if I closed my baby-blue eyes in 1998 and woke up in 2050 with no feeling of passage of time, and in an instant half a hundred years had gone by. But if that doesn't happen, I'm still encouraged. I read recently in *Omni* that they seem to feel now that anybody alive in the year 2000 has a very good chance of living another two or three hundred years. I'll be about eighty-four in 2000. If the world could put up with an eighty-four-year-old version of me for another

two or three hundred years, I could go on collecting and anthologizing.

BIOGRAPHICAL/CRITICAL SOURCES: Forrest J Ackerman, *Amazing Forries,* Metropolis Press, 1976; Ackerman, *Souvenir Book of Mr. Science Fiction's Fantasy Museum,* Kodansha, 1978; *Science Fiction and Fantasy Literature,* two volumes, Gale, 1979; *Los Angeles Times,* December 8, 1979; *New West,* January 28, 1980; *Polaris,* spring, 1980; *Glendale News-Press* (Glendale, Calif.), June 23, 1980.

—*Sketch by B. Hal May*
—*Interview by Jean W. Ross*

*   *   *

ADAMS, Arthur Stanton   1896-1980

OBITUARY NOTICE: Born July 1, 1896, in Winchester, Mass.; died November 18, 1980, in Concord, N.H. Author and educator. Arthur Adams, who was president of the University of New Hampshire and provost of Cornell University, headed the American Council on Education from 1951 to 1961. While presiding over the Seminar in American Studies in Salzburg, Austria, Adams was chosen to conduct a study on joint graduate study programs under a grant from the Eugene and Agnes E. Meyer Foundation. He was co-author of *The Development of Physical Thought* and *Fundamentals of Thermodynamics.* Obituaries and other sources: *Time,* May 15, 1950;. *Current Biography,* Wilson, 1951; *American Men and Women of Science: The Physical and Biological Sciences,* 12th edition, Bowker, 1973; *The International Who's Who,* Europa, 1978; *Who's Who in America,* 40th edition, Marquis, 1978.

*   *   *

ADLER, Denise Rinker   1908-

PERSONAL: Born September 18, 1908, in New Rockford, N.D.; daughter of Robert F. and Lydia R. (Messerschmidt) Rinker; married Lloyd F. Adler (a college athletic coach and merchant), June, 1934; children: Bruce Charles. *Education:* Asbury College, B.A., 1932; received M.A. from University of Idaho. *Religion:* Presbyterian. *Home:* 17969 Normandy Ter. S.W., Seattle, Wash. 98166.

CAREER: Writer.

WRITINGS: The Morning Star: God's Gift for Daily Living, Word, Inc., 1974; *Philippians: The Confident, Contented Life in Christ,* Tyndale, 1980; *Five Women: Lessons in Forgiveness and Usefulness,* Tyndale, 1980; *Jonah: Lessons in Obedience and Repentance,* Tyndale, 1980; *Jesus: The Man Who Changes Lives,* Tyndale, 1981. Author of Bible study material.

*   *   *

ADLER, Kathleen
See JONES, Kathleen Eve

*   *   *

AGAR, Herbert (Sebastian)   1897-1980

OBITUARY NOTICE—See index for CA sketch: Born September 29, 1897, in New Rochelle, N.Y.; died November 24, 1980, in Sussex, England. Author, journalist, editor, and Pulitzer Prize-winner for *The People's Choice From Washington to Harding: A Study in Democracy.* He served in London, England, as correspondent for the *Louisville Courier-Journal* and the *Louisville Times,* as director of Rupert Hart-Davis (publisher) and Independent Television

South Wales and West of England, and as American ambassador. He edited the *Courier-Journal* for two years. In 1941, Agar founded Freedom House to stimulate international cooperation. His writings include *The Defeat of Baudelaire, Beyond German Victory, World-Wide Civil War, A Time for Greatness, Abraham Lincoln, An Account of Jewish Survival Since 1914,* and *The Darkest Year: Britain Alone, June 1940-June 1941.* Obituaries and other sources: *New York Times,* November 25, 1980; *Chicago Tribune,* November 26, 1980; *Newsweek,* December 8, 1980; *Time,* December 8, 1980; *AB Bookman's Weekly,* January 19, 1981.

*   *   *

AINSWORTH, Patricia
    See BIGG, Patricia Nina

*   *   *

ALBRAN, Kehlog
    See SHACKET, Sheldon R(ubin)

*   *   *

ALEXANDER, John Kurt   1941-

PERSONAL: Born October 25, 1941, in Vancouver, Wash.; son of Eugene V. (a grocer) and Marta (Tuominen) Alexander; married S. June Granatir (a historian), December 29, 1973. *Education:* Oregon College of Education, B.S., 1964; University of Chicago, M.A., 1965, Ph.D., 1973. *Home:* 3410 Bishop Ave., Cincinnati, Ohio 45220. *Office:* Department of History, University of Cincinnati, Cincinnati, Ohio 45221.

CAREER: University of Cincinnati, Cincinnati, Ohio, assistant professor, 1969-75, associate professor of American history, 1975—. *Member:* American Historical Association, Organization of American Historians, American Association of University Professors.

WRITINGS: (Contributor) Kenneth T. Jackson and Stanley K. Schultz, editors, *Cities in American History,* Knopf, 1972; (contributor) Dennis J. Clark, editor, *Philadelphia, 1776-2076,* Kennikat, 1975; *Render Them Submissive: Responses to Poverty in Philadelphia, 1760-1800,* University of Massachusetts Press, 1980. Contributor to history journals.

WORK IN PROGRESS: Research on popular efforts for price control in the American Revolution and on the media and the movement for creation of the U.S. Constitution.

SIDELIGHTS: Alexander wrote: "Working with Jesse Lemisch at the University of Chicago sparked my interest in the American Revolution. I share his belief that we must study those at the bottom of society as well as those in other ranks. Historians should not, in my view, set out to prove a hypothesis. Rather, they should investigate a topic based on the view that whatever they uncover—whether they like the facts or not—will add to our knowledge of the past. I believe that a university professor's first responsibility is to teaching his or her students, not to doing research and writing."

*   *   *

ALEXANDER, Louis (George)   1932-

PERSONAL: Born January 15, 1932, in London, England; son of George (a doctor) and Mary (Manolas) Ftyaras-Alexandros; married Athena Voyiatzis (a teacher), 1958 (deceased); married Julia Banner-Mendus (a teacher trainer), 1980; children: (first marriage) Mary-Anne, George. *Education:* Attended Aquinas College, Perth, Australia; received B.A. (with honors) from University of London. *Home:* Garden House, Weydown Rd., Haslemere, Surrey, England.

CAREER: Protypon Lykeion Athinon, Athens, Greece, teacher and head of department of English, 1957-65; writer and consultant, 1966—. Member of threshold level committee of Council of Europe, 1973—. *Member:* Society of Authors (chairman of educational writers group, 1975-77).

WRITINGS—All published by Longman, except as noted: *Sixty Steps to Precis,* 1962; *Poetry and Prose Appreciation,* 1963; *A First Book in Comprehension,* 1965; *Essay and Letter-Writing,* 1965; *Detectives From Scotland Yard,* 1966; *First Things First: Practice and Progress, Developing Skills, Fluency in English,* 1967; *Question and Answer,* 1967; *For And Against,* 1968; *Car Thieves,* 1969; *Operation Mastermind,* 1971 *Guided Composition in ELT,* 1971; *Mainline Progress,* Books A-B, 1973; (with Catherine Wilson) *In Other Words,* 1974; *K's First Case,* 1975; *Good Morning Mexico!,* 1975; (with Vincent and Kingsbury) *Mainline Skills A,* 1975; (with W. S. Allen, R. A. Close, and R. J. O'Neill) *English Grammatical Structure,* 1975; (with Kingsbury) *I Think You Think,* 1976; *Operation Janus,* Longman, 1976; *Clint Magee,* Longman, 1976; *Dangerous Game,* 1977; (with Kingsbury) *Mainline Skills B,* 1977; (with Jan van Ek and A. M. Fitzpatrick) *Waystage,* Council of Europe, 1977; *Some Methodological Implications of Waystage and Threshold Level,* Council of Europe, 1977; (with Ed Cornelius) *Comp,* 1978; *Mainline Beginners A,* 1978; *Mainline Beginners B,* 1979.

Juvenile; all published by Longman, except as noted: *The Carters of Greenwood,* 1966; *April Fools Day,* 1966; *Worth a Fortune,* 1967; *Look, Listen, and Learn,* four volumes, 1968-71; *Reading and Writing English,* 1969; (with Alberto Evangelisti) *Language and Life,* Longman/Zanichelli, 1970; *Tell Us a Story,* 1972; (with Janet Tadman and Roy Kingsbury) *Target,* three volumes, 1972-74; (with Karl Preis, Franz Schimek, and Anton Prochazka) *Look, Listen, and Learn for Austria,* four volumes, Langenscheidt-Longman, 1974-78; (with Monica Vincent) *Make Your Point,* 1975; (with Evangelisti and others) *Way In,* 1978.

Joint course designer, with Fitzpatrick, of television series, "Follow Me," broadcast by German television networks, 1979-80.

WORK IN PROGRESS: Survive in French, with Judith Clopeau and Madeleine Le Cunff-Renouard; *Survive in Italian,* with Timothy and Bianca Holme; *Survive in German,* with Antony and Ingeborg Peck; *Survive in Spanish,* with Carolina Haro and Peter Vickers; a series of self-study language courses for home computers.

SIDELIGHTS: Alexander told *CA:* "The mindless time-filling that characterizes a great many language courses has prompted me throughout my professional life to attempt to develop simpler and more cost-effective systems for learning languages. Using English-as-a-foreign-language as a starting point, I have increasingly become concerned with creating blueprint course-designs which can be adapted to the learning of other languages either in the classroom or through self-study systems. For me writing is a habit and I do not feel I have done any true work in a day unless I have written. It is all too easy for a writer who has achieved any success at all to be lured into talking about writing instead of writing. Inspiration, if it exists at all, in my view, is the by-product of habitual application."

*   *   *

ALEXANDER, Michael Van Cleave   1937-

PERSONAL: Born December 24, 1937, in Chapel Hill, N.C.; son of Marion R. (in business) and Mildred (Lasater)

Alexander; married Ann Field, June 12, 1971; children: Michael Van Cleave, Peter Barton. *Education:* University of North Carolina, B.A., 1960, M.A., 1964, Ph.D., 1969. *Home:* 901 McBryde Dr., Blacksburg, Va. 24060. *Office:* Virginia Polytechnic Institute and State University, 510 McBryde Hall, Blacksburg, Va. 24061.

CAREER: Virginia Polytechnic Institute and State University, Blacksburg, assistant professor of history, 1969-76; University of North Carolina, Chapel Hill, visiting associate professor of history, 1976-77; Virginia Polytechnic Institute and State University, associate professor of history, 1977—. *Member:* Conference on British Studies, Southern Historical Association.

WRITINGS: Charles I's Lord Treasurer: Sir Richard Weston, Earl of Portland (1577-1635), Macmillan, 1975; *The First of the Tudors: A Study of Henry VII and His Reign,* Rowman & Littlefield, 1980.

WORK IN PROGRESS: Society and Culture in Elizabethan England: A Study of the Origins and Nature of the English Renaissance, completion expected in 1985; *Early Modern London: A Social and Cultural History,* 1987.

SIDELIGHTS: Alexander wrote: "Trained primarily as a political and constitutional historian, I have become increasingly interested in social and cultural history, on which I intend to concentrate. In my view too few historians of the early modern period pay sufficient attention to this field of inquiry."

*　　*　　*

ALLEN, Leonard 1915(?)-1981

OBITUARY NOTICE: Born c. 1915; died of heart attack, February 5, 1981, in Washington, D.C. Journalist and television executive. Allen joined the National Broadcasting Co. (NBC) in 1942 as a radio newswriter. During his thirty-four years with that company, he held a variety of positions, including manager of television news reporting, director of the news operation for the Washington bureau, and director of public affairs in New York. Allen also served as managing editor of the Radio-Television News Directors Association in Washington, D.C. Obituaries and other sources: *Washington Post,* February 7, 1981.

*　　*　　*

ALLEN, Linda 1925-

PERSONAL: Born May 19, 1925, in West Yorkshire, England; daughter of Harold (an engineer) and Ethel (Wilkinson) Beaumont; married Walter Allen (a college lecturer), December 19, 1953; children: Alexandra Christine, Lesley Elizabeth (Mrs. Paul Andrew Roe), Mark Gideon. *Education:* Attended Huddersfield Polytechnic, 1943-45. *Politics:* "Ecology party." *Religion:* "Not active church member." *Home:* 113 Heath Croft Rd., Sutton Coldfield, West Midlands, England.

CAREER: Secretary in West Yorkshire, England, 1945-53, and West Midlands, England, 1964—; writer, 1974—. *Member:* World Wildlife Fund, National Canine Defense League, Royal Society for the Protection of Birds, Society of Authors, Animals' Vigilantes (life member).

WRITINGS—Juvenile: When the Wind Blows, Abelard, 1974; *Birds of a Feather,* Abelard, 1975; *Flight of Fancy,* Abelard, 1977; *Fly Away Peter,* Abelard, 1979; *Mr. Simkin's Grandma* (picture book), Morrow, 1979; *The Runaway Nest,* Abelard, 1980; *Lionel and the Spy Next Door,* Morrow, 1980; *Mrs. Simkin's Bed* (picture book), Morrow, 1980.

Work represented in anthologies, including *People and Places,* Harcourt, 1979; *A Book of Pig Tales,* Kaye & Ward, 1979; *All Year Round,* Evans, 1980.

Contributor of articles and poems to magazines, including *Good Housekeeping, Cricket, Lady,* and *Fate,* and newspapers.

WORK IN PROGRESS: Cloud Cuckoo Land, a picture book; books on birds; a juvenile novel about "a group of children who become curious about an old grave"; a series of books for nursery teachers.

SIDELIGHTS: Linda Allen told *CA:* "I live in the county of Warwickshire, famous for its leafiness, its witches, and Shakespeare.

"Although my work is unremittingly humorous and designed chiefly to entertain, I find that my books are widely used as 'readers' in schools in England. There is, however, an underlying didactic theme (carefully researched) of bird lore and information which I hope will spark off in my young readers a love of wild creatures—particularly birds. Birds fascinate me, not from a cold-blooded, scientific point of view, but for their sheer beauty, their freedom to move about the world at will. I am deeply concerned about the serious ecological imbalances being produced by man's modern activities, and I believe that it is of the utmost urgency that the decline in wildlife numbers and species should be taken to the very highest international levels of arbitration. Tomorrow may be too late. I also have an abhorrence of factory farming, the fur trade, and vivisection.

"On a lighter note, I have achieved success in the United States with my Mrs. Simkin stories. These stories are written purely for fun, and Mrs. Simkin is my own favorite character. *Lionel and the Spy Next Door* is a totally different type of story, although the humor is still there. I adore my dealings with the United States as I feel Americans appreciate my sense of humor and the ridiculous.

"After the success of my bird stories I was in danger of being typecast as 'the lady who writes the bird stories,' and this I wished to avoid. I find it difficult to channel my inspiration into one type of book. Many themes interest me. I have even found my way into a poetry anthology with a poem on the history of football!"

*　　*　　*

ALLEN, Michael J(ohn) B(ridgman) 1941-

PERSONAL: Born April 1, 1941, in Lewes, England; came to the United States in 1966; married Elena Hirshberg, 1972; children: Benjamin. *Education:* Wadham College, Oxford, B.A., 1964, M.A., 1966; University of Michigan, Ph.D., 1970. *Office:* Department of English, University of California, Los Angeles, Calif. 90024.

CAREER: University of California, Los Angeles, assistant professor, 1970-74, associate professor, 1974-79, professor of English, 1979—, associate director of Center for Medieval and Renaissance Studies, 1979—. *Awards, honors:* Eby Award from University of California, 1977, for distinguished teaching; Guggenheim fellow, 1977-78.

WRITINGS: Marsilio Ficino: The Philebus Commentary, University of California Press, 1975; (with Daniel G. Calder) *The Sources and Analogues of Old English Poetry,* Brewer, Rowman & Littlefield, 1976; (editor with Fredi Chiappelli and Robert L. Benson) *First Images of America,* University of California Press, 1976; *Marsilio Ficino and the Phaedran Charioteer,* University of California Press, 1981. Contributor to philosophy and literature journals.

WORK IN PROGRESS: Research on Renaissance literature and Renaissance Platonism.

* * *

ALONSO, J(uan) M(anuel) 1936-

PERSONAL: Born March 13, 1936, in Argentina; came to the United States in 1948, naturalized citizen, 1952; son of Amado (a professor) and Joan (Canne-Evans) Alonso; married Viola Thomas (a college teacher); children: Marc, Melissa. *Education:* Harvard University, B.A., 1957; Brown University, Ph.D., 1967. *Home:* 14 Remington St., Cambridge, Mass. 02138. *Office:* Tufts University, East Hall, Medford, Mass. 02155.

CAREER: Tufts University, Medford, Mass., instructor, 1961-66, associate professor, 1966-73, professor, 1973—. Visiting professor at New York University, 1970. Consultant to Arthur D. Little, Inc. *Military service:* U.S. Air Force, 1959-65. *Member:* International P.E.N., National Book Critics Circle, Harvard Club of Boston. *Awards, honors:* National Endowment for the Arts grant, 1975.

WRITINGS: The Chipped Wall (novel), Identity Press, 1966, 2nd edition, 1967; *The Passion of Robert Bronson* (novel; first volume of a trilogy), McCall Publishing, 1970; *Althea* (novel; second volume of a trilogy), Fiction Collective, 1976. Contributor to magazines, including *Review* and *Nation.* Editor of *New Boston Review,* 1975-79.

WORK IN PROGRESS: A novel, the third volume of a trilogy; a book of essays on Hispanic literature.

AVOCATIONAL INTERESTS: Travel (Spain and France), playing squash.

BIOGRAPHICAL/CRITICAL SOURCES: Boston Globe, January 17, 1971; *New Boston Review,* January, 1977.

* * *

ALSOP, Mary O'Hara   1885-1980
(Mary O'Hara)

OBITUARY NOTICE—See index for *CA* sketch: Born July 10, 1885, in Cape May Point, N.J.; died of arteriosclerosis, October 14, 1980, in Chevy Chase, Md. Author and composer, best known for her book, *My Friend Flicka.* Alsop achieved fame with *My Friend Flicka,* which she wrote under the name Mary O'Hara. The book was the basis for a movie and television series. As a composer, she wrote a folk musical entitled *The Catch Colt* as well as "Esperan," "May God Keep You," and other songs. Alsop's books include *Let Us Say Grace, Thunderhead, Green Grass of Wyoming, The Son of Adam Wyngate, Novel-in-the-Making, Wyoming Summer,* and *A Musical in the Making.* Obituaries and other sources: *Washington Post,* October 15, 1980; *Chicago Tribune,* October 16, 1980; *Time,* October 27, 1980; *Newsweek,* October 27, 1980.

* * *

AMALRIK, Andrei Alekseyevich   1938-1980

OBITUARY NOTICE: Born May 12, 1938, in Moscow, U.S.S.R.; died in an automobile accident, November 11, 1980, near Guadalajara, Spain. Historian and author. As a result of his dissident views and his anti-Soviet publications, Amalrik was arrested numerous times and spent six years in a Soviet labor camp. Upon his release from prison in 1976, he immigrated to the Netherlands and later came to the United States where he taught at Harvard University, George Washington University, and the Hoover Institution.

His autobiographical writings include *Involuntary Journey to Siberia* and *Notebooks of a Revolutionary.* Obituaries and other sources: *Time,* December 19, 1969, June 1, 1970, November 24, 1980; *Newsweek,* June 1, 1970, November 24, 1980; *New York Times,* July 29, 1973; *Current Biography,* Wilson, 1974; *Publishers Weekly,* November 28, 1980.

* * *

AMARE, Rothayne
See BYRNE Stuart J(ames)

* * *

AMES, Jennifer
See GREIG, Maysie

* * *

ANDERSEN, Richard   1946-

PERSONAL: Born December 27, 1946, in New York, N.Y.; son of Arnold (in sales) and Isabel (a legal secretary; maiden name, Guilfoyle) Andersen; married Deborah Shea (a writer), September 11, 1981. *Education:* Loyola University of Los Angeles (now Loyola Marymount University), B.A., 1968; City University of New York, M.A., 1971; New York University, Ph.D., 1977. *Politics:* None. *Religion:* None. *Home:* 174 Bay State Rd., Boston, Mass. 02215. *Agent:* Zigler, Diskant, Inc., 9255 Sunset Blvd., No. 1122, Los Angeles, Calif. 90069. *Office:* Department of Humanities, Boston University, 871 Commonwealth Ave., Boston, Mass. 02215.

CAREER: High school teacher of English in Brooklyn, N.Y., 1969-72; director of cultural exchange program in New York, N.Y., 1975; Boston University, Boston, Mass., assistant professor of humanities, 1977—.

WRITINGS: William Goldman, G. K. Hall, 1979; *Straight Cut Ditch* (novel), Ashley Books, 1979; *Muckaluck* (novel), Delacorte, 1980; *Robert Coover,* G. K. Hall, 1981. Contributor to magazines, including *Boston Today, Phi Kappa Deltan,* and *University College Quarterly.*

WORK IN PROGRESS: The World's Greatest Runner, a novel; *Heart-Shaped Pubes,* a novel, with wife, Deborah.

SIDELIGHTS: Andersen told *CA:* "I think my main reason for writing is that I enjoy telling stories, but being liked also has something to do with it. Ironically, success as a writer has alienated me further from family and colleagues. In my books I am most interested in narrative techniques and life's ironies."

Andersen described his works in progress as a "fictional biography of Felix Carvajal, a Cuban mailman who, in 1904, ran six hundred miles to compete in the St. Louis Olympics," and a novel about "the relationship between a college student and her married English professor."

BIOGRAPHICAL/CRITICAL SOURCES: Los Angeles Times Book Review, September 9, 1979; *New York Times Book Review,* June 15, 1980; *Boston Globe,* December 14, 1980.

* * *

ANDERSON, Kenneth Norman   1921-

PERSONAL: Born July 10, 1921, in Omaha, Neb.; son of Duncan McDonald (an agronomist) and Letitia Jane (a teacher; maiden name, Steed) Anderson; married Lois Elaine Harmon, January 12, 1945; children: Eric Stephen, Randi Laine, Jani Jill, Douglas Duncan. *Education:* Attended University of Omaha, 1939-41; Oregon State College (now University), B.S., 1944; attended Stanford University, 1944-45, Northwestern University, 1945-46, and University of Chicago, 1958-60. *Home:* 23 McQueen St., Katonah, N.Y. 10536. *Agent:* Rosalie Brody Feder, 52 East 41st St., New York, N.Y. 10017. *Office:* Coffee Information Institute, 60 East 42nd St., New York, N.Y. 10017.

CAREER: Associated with U.S. Army Finance Office, Washington, D.C., in Omaha, Neb., and Fort Peck, Mont., 1941-42; U.S. Army Corps of Engineers, Omaha, engineering aide, 1946; KOIL-Radio, Omaha, news editor, 1946-47; International News Service, bureau manager in Omaha, 1947-51, and Kansas City, Mo., 1951-56; *Better Homes and Gardens,* Des Moines, Iowa, special features editor, 1956-57; *Popular Mechanics,* Chicago, Ill., associate editor, 1957-59; American Medical Association, Chicago, editor of *Today's Health,* 1959-65; Holt, Rinehart & Winston, Inc., New York City, editor, 1965-70; Coffee Information Institute, New York City, executive director, 1970—. Lecturer at New School for Social Research, 1959, New York University, 1960, University of Omaha, 1961, and Rensselaer Polytechnic Institute, 1964. Executive editor of Publishers Editorial Services and president of Editorial Guild, both 1979—. *Military service:* U.S. Army, 1942-46.

MEMBER: National Association of Science Writers, American Association for the Advancement of Science, American Public Health Association, Society of Illustrators, American Institute of Biological Sciences, American Society of Journalists and Authors, Outdoor Writers Association of America, Overseas Press Club of America, New York Public Health Association, New York Academy of Sciences, Sigma Delta Chi. *Awards, honors:* Citation from National Poetry Association, 1946, for "Psychodrama, Act III."

WRITINGS: (Co-author) *Lawyers' Medical Cyclopedia,* Allen Smith, 1962; (with Robert Addison) *The Family Physician,* Greystone, 1963; (with William Baver) *Today's Health Guide,* American Medical Association, 1965; (with Addison) *Pictorial Medical Guide,* Niagara Family Library, 1967; *Field and Stream Guide to Physical Fitness,* Holt, 1969.

(With Bruce Berg, D. Jeanne Collins, Anthony A. Davis, and others) *The New Concise Family Health and Medical Guide,* Doubleday, 1971; (with Paul Kuhne) *Home Medical Encyclopedia,* Fawcett, 1973; (with Berg, Collins, Davis, and others) *Illustrated Encyclopedia of Better Health,* two volumes, Doubleday, 1974; (with Berg, Collins, Davis, and others) *New Complete Medical and Health Encyclopedia,* four volumes, Doubleday, 1977; *Sterno Guide to the Outdoors,* Dorison House, 1977; *Eagle Claw Fish Cookbook,* Dorison House, 1977; *The Newsweek Encyclopedia of Family Health and Fitness,* Newsweek, 1980; (with Walter Glanze) *Bantam Medical Dictionary,* Wiley, 1980; *How Long Will You Live?,* Arlington House, 1981. Contributor to *Funk & Wagnalls Encyclopedia.* Advisory editor of *Nutrition Today,* 1965-74.

WORK IN PROGRESS: A dictionary of psychology, with Robert Goldenson and Walter Glanze, for Longmans; *Liquid Assets,* a book about beverages.

SIDELIGHTS: Anderson commented to *CA:* "I've never considered myself to be a good writer. I admire and envy the really good writers. But I suppose if somebody wanted evidence that it's possible for a person to make a satisfactory living merely by punching typewriter keys with two fingers every day, I might qualify as an example. My original inspiration was something said by Bertrand Russell around 1940, to the effect that the only truly free people in the world are writers."

ANDREWS, James P. 1936(?)-1980

OBITUARY NOTICE: Born c. 1936; died October 19, 1980, in Kansas City, Kan. Editor, publisher, and author. James Andrews, co-founder and editor of Universal Press Syndicate (UPS), began his publishing career at Sheed & Ward. After the 1973 purchase of Sheed & Ward by UPS, Andrews served as both president and editor-in-chief. The company was subsequently renamed Andrews & McMeel. He was also managing editor of *Ave Maria* and the *National Catholic Reporter.* He wrote *The Citizen Christian* and *The Perplexed Catholic.* Obituaries and other sources: *Publishers Weekly,* October 31, 1980.

* * *

ANDRUS, (Vincent) Dyckman 1942-

PERSONAL: Born June 8, 1942, in New York, N.Y., son of Vincent Dyckman and Dorelle Jordan (Moulton) Andrus. *Education:* Yale University, B.A., 1963. *Residence:* Cody, Wyo. *Address:* c/o Charles Scribner's Sons, 597 Fifth Ave., New York, N.Y. 10017.

CAREER: Writer. *Adirondack Daily Enterprise,* Saranac Lake, N.Y., reporter; *New Haven Journal-Courier,* New Haven, Conn., reporter; licensed Wyoming guide. *Military service:* U.S. Army, Infantry.

WRITINGS: Days When the House Was Too Small, Scribner, 1974.

* * *

ANGO, Fan D.
See LONGYEAR, Barry Brookes

* * *

APPADORAI, A(ngadipuram) 1902-

PERSONAL: Born March 16, 1902, in Angadipuram, India; son of Ananthanarayanan and Sita Appadorai; married Lakshmi Viswanathan, January 25, 1930; children: Parvathi Appadorai Vasudevan, Venugopal, Prema Appadorai Sundaram, Vijay Kumar. *Education:* Presidency College, B.A. (with honors), 1923, M.A., 1925; Madras University, Ph.D., 1932. *Religion:* Hindu. *Home:* 8 Central Lane, Bengali Market, New Delhi 110001, India. *Office:* Department of Politics and International Relations, Jawaharlal Nehru University, New Mehrauli Rd., New Delhi 67, India.

CAREER: Loyola College, Madras, India, chief lecturer in political science, 1930-44; Indian Council of World Affairs, New Delhi, India, secretary-general, 1944-55; Indian School of International Studies, New Delhi, professor of international relations and director of school, 1955-64; Union Public Service Commission, India, member of commission, 1964-67; Jawaharlal Nehru University, New Delhi, honorary professor of international relations, 1969—. *Member:* Indian Council of World Affairs. *Awards, honors:* Sankara Parvathi Prize for Indian History from Madras University, 1932; LL.D. from Sri Venkateswara University, 1971; Dadabhoy Naoroji Memorial Prize for Political Science from Dadabhoy Memorial Trust, 1973, for distinguished work in political science.

WRITINGS: Economic Conditions in Southern India, A.D. 1000-1500, two volumes, Madras University, 1936; *Dyarchy in Practice,* Longman's, Green, 1937; *Revision of Democracy,* Oxford University Press, 1940; *The Substance of Politics,* Oxford University Press, 1942, 10th edition, Oxford University Press, 1968; *Collective Security,* United Nations Educational, Scientific & Cultural Organization, 1953; (editor with Maurice Gwyer) *Speeches and Documents on the Indian Constitution, 1921-1947*, two volumes, Oxford University Press, 1957; *The Use of Force in International Relations*, Asia Publishing House, 1958.

Dilemma in Foreign Policy in the Modern World, Institute of Economics and Politics (Poona, India), 1963; *Technology and International Relations*, Viswa Bharati, 1966; (editor) *India: Studies in Social and Political Development, 1947-1967*, Asia Publishing House, 1969; *Essays in Politics and International Relations*, Asia Publishing House, 1969; *Towards a Just Social Order: Based on Contemporary Indian Thought*, Verry, 1970; *Tashkent Declaration*, Institute of Technology (Pilani, India), 1970; *Political Thinking in India in the Twentieth Century From Naoroji to Nehru*, Oxford University Press, 1971; *Essays in Indian Politics and Foreign Policy*, Verry, 1971; (editor) *Documents on Political Thought in Modern India*, Oxford University Press, Volume I, 1973, Volume II, 1976. Editor of *India Quarterly*, 1945-55, and *International Studies*, 1956-64.

WORK IN PROGRESS: India's Foreign Policy and Relations, 1947-72, with a chapter on current developments, publication expected in 1984; *Political Thinking in India From Ancient Times to the Present*, publication expected in 1985.

*   *   *

APPLETON, Jane (Frances)   1934-

PERSONAL: Born December 31, 1934, in Brockton, Mass.; daughter of Louis (a shoe executive) and Rhoda (Orentlicher) Scovell; married William S. Appleton (a psychiatrist and writer), June 1, 1958; children: Amy, Lucy, William. *Education:* Wheaton College, Norton, Mass., A.B., 1956; graduate study at Columbia University, 1958-60. *Home:* 59 Brewster St., Cambridge, Mass. 02138.

CAREER: Newton College of the Sacred Heart, Newton, Mass., lecturer in music, 1964-75; writer. Member of board of directors of Opera Company of Boston, 1973—. President of Massachusetts Mental Health Center Auxiliary, 1963-65.

WRITINGS: (With husband, William Appleton) *How Not to Split Up*, Doubleday, 1978. Author of "Plain Jane," a column in *Boston Herald*, 1976. Contributor to magazines and newspapers, including *Redbook, Cosmopolitan, Saturday Review, Weightwatchers, Ms.*, and *Travel & Leisure*.

WORK IN PROGRESS: Fiction.

*   *   *

ARCHER, Myrtle (Lilly)   1926-

PERSONAL: Born June 14, 1926, in Carp Lake, Mich.; daughter of Henry Wadsworth and Lillian Marie (Craven) Archer; married Howard Spracklen (an electrical engineer); children: Jay Allen. *Education:* Attended University of California, Berkeley. *Home:* 21172 Aspen Ave., Castro Valley, Calif. 94546.

CAREER: Accountant, 1957—. *Member:* National League of American Pen Women (president, 1976-78), California Writers Club (member of board of directors, 1972-74). *Awards, honors:* First prize for fiction from National League of American Pen Women, 1975, for *The Young Boys Gone*.

WRITINGS: The Young Boys Gone (young adult novel), Walker & Co., 1978.

Work represented in anthologies, including *Dance of the Muses*, Young Publications; *I Am Talking About Revolution*, Harper Square Press; *Yearbook of Modern Poetry*, Young Publications. Contributor of poems, stories, and arti-

cles to magazines and newspapers, including *New Directions for Women, Open Road, Christian, Mature Years*, and *Explorer*.

WORK IN PROGRESS: Git Aeoup, My Beauties, a novel about the California gold rush.

SIDELIGHTS: "One of ten children," Myrtle Archer told *CA*, "I was born in Michigan, and spent my childhood in the primitive remoteness of northern Idaho, then moved near San Francisco, where I have since lived. I have been selling poetry, fiction, and articles for twenty years. I taught writing at Alameda Adult School, and as a member of California Writers Club and the National League of American Pen Women I take an active part in the literary community near San Francisco Bay."

She added that her writing career came about because "I always wanted to express myself and never had anyone in my life to listen to me."

AVOCATIONAL INTERESTS: Reading, music, cooking, gardening, hiking, history, art, "all things live or dead."

*   *   *

ARKELL, Anthony John   1898-1980

PERSONAL: Born July 29, 1898, in Hinxhill, Kent, England; died February 26, 1980, in Chelmsford, Essex, England; son of John Norris (a clergyman) and Eleanor Jessy (Bunting) Arkell; married Dorothy Davidson, 1928 (died, 1945); married Joan Margaret Burnell Andrews, 1950; children: (first marriage) one son, one daughter. *Education:* Attended Queen's College, Oxford.

CAREER: Joined political service in Sudan, 1920, assistant district commissioner in Darfur Province, 1921-24, acting resident in Dar Masalit, 1925-26, district commissioner in Kosti (White Nile Province), 1926-29, and in Sennar (Blue Nile Province), 1929-32, acting deputy-governor in Darfur Province, 1932-36; Sudan Government, commissioner for archaeology and anthropology, 1938-48, chief transport officer, 1940-44, editor of *Sudan Notes and Records*, 1945-48, archaeological adviser, 1948-53; University of London, London, England, lecturer in Egyptology at University College, 1948-53, curator of Flinders Petrie Museum of Egyptian Antiquities, 1948-63, reader in Egyptian archaeology, 1953-63; became deacon, 1960, priest, 1961, ordained, 1963, Vicar of Cuddingham, Oxford, England, 1963-71. Member of British Ennedi expedition, 1957; assistant curate at Great Missenden, 1960-63. *Military service:* Royal Flying Corps (now Royal Air Force), 1916-19; received Military Cross, 1918.

MEMBER: Philosophical Society of Sudan (former president; honorary life member), German Archaeological Institute (honorary member), Society of Antiquaries (member of council, 1956-57), Egypt Exploration Society (member of committee), Athenaeum. *Awards, honors:* Member of the Order of the British Empire, 1928; Order of the Nile, 4th class, 1931; D.Litt. from Queen's College, Oxford, 1955.

WRITINGS: Early Khartoum: An Account of an Early Occupation Site Carried Out by the Sudan Government Antiquities Service in 1944-1945, Oxford University Press, 1949; *Shaheinab: An Account of the Excavation of a Neolithic Occupation Site Carried Out for the Sudan Antiquities Service in 1940-1950*, Oxford University Press, 1953; *A History of the Sudan: From the Earliest Times to 1821*, Athlone Press, 1955, 2nd edition, 1961, Greenwood Press, 1974; *Wanyanga, and an Archaeological Reconnaissance of the South-West Libyan Desert*, Oxford University Press, 1964; *The Prehistory of the Nile Valley*, Brill, 1975. Also author of

The Old Stone-Age in the Anglo-Egyptian Sudan, 1949. Contributor to *Encyclopaedia Britannica* and to numerous scholarly journals.

* * *

ARMSTRONG, Judith Mary 1935-

PERSONAL: Born May 18, 1935, in Melbourne, Australia; daughter of George Thomas (an accountant) and Phyllis Ernestine Emerson; married Gregory Armstrong (a university lecturer), May 18, 1957; children: Hugo Dominic, Piers Digby. *Education:* University of Melbourne, B.A. (with honors), 1956, M.A., 1969, Ph.D., 1975. *Home:* 99 Newry St., North Carlton, Melbourne, Victoria 3054, Australia. *Agent:* Curtis Brown Ltd., 1 Craven Hill, London W2 3EP, England. *Office:* Department of Russian, University of Melbourne, Parkville, Melbourne, Victoria 3052, Australia.

CAREER: University of Melbourne, Melbourne, Australia, lecturer, 1974-79, senior lecturer in Russian, 1980—.

WRITINGS: The Novel of Adultery, Harper, 1976; (translator from French) Oscar Comettant, *In the Land of Kangaroos and Gold Mines,* Rigby, 1980; (editor with Rae Slonek) *Essays to Honour Nina Christesen,* Australia International Press, 1980.

WORK IN PROGRESS: A novel of Australia; research on the metaphor, the superfluous man, and nineteenth-century Russian literature.

SIDELIGHTS: Judith Armstrong wrote: "*The Novel of Adultery* explores the history of marriage (from the legal and religious point of view) and consequent attitudes to infidelity in English, French, and Russian society (the English includes America to a limited extent). The literature of adultery is seen to be a literature of punishment, except for the use adultery is put to in Henry James's *The Golden Bowl,* in which adultery is redemptive.

"*Essays to Honour Nina Christesen* is a festschrift marking the respect and admiration in which Mrs. Nina Christesen is held. She was born in St. Petersburg and left Russia with her parents at the time of the Revolution. They settled in Brisbane, and later Nina and her husband moved to Melbourne, where she founded a Russian department in the University of Melbourne that parented all departments of Russian in Australia and New Zealand."

* * *

ARNOLD, Olga Moore 1900-1981

OBITUARY NOTICE: Born January, 1900, near Buffalo, Wyo.; died of cancer, January 9, 1981, in Laramie, Wyo. Author, journalist, and public relations specialist. Olga Arnold was a reporter and columist for newspapers, including the *Denver Post.* She later worked for the U.S. Information Agency in Washington, D.C., for nearly twenty years. In addition to short stories, Arnold wrote *Windswept,* a book about Wyoming, and *I'll Meet You in the Lobby,* an autobiography. Obituaries and other sources: *Who's Who of American Women,* 6th edition, Marquis, 1970; *Washington Post,* January 11, 1981.

* * *

ARONIN, Ben 1904-1980

OBITUARY NOTICE: Born 1904; died August 26, 1980, in Chicago, Ill. Author, Hebrew scholar, and lawyer. Aronin, a Chicago lawyer for more than fifty years, was known as Uncle Ben on the children's television program "Magic

Door," which he created. In 1962 he received a Chicago Emmy Award for the show. For many years Aronin taught Hebrew and Bible classes at the College of Jewish Studies. He was the author of a Hebrew epic entitled *The Abramiad* and of numerous children's books, including *The New Mother Goose Book, Mother Goose and Father Gander,* and *Daily Prayers for Children.* He also wrote books of fantasy, including *Cavern of Destiny, The Moor's Gold,* and *The Lost Tribe: Being the Strange Adventures of Raphael Drale in Search of the Lost Tribes of Israel.* Obituaries and other sources: *Science Fiction and Fantasy Literature,* Gale, Volume 1, 1979; *Chicago Tribune,* August 28, 1980.

* * *

ARPEL, Adrien
See NEWMAN, Adrien Ann

* * *

ATKINS, Meg Elizabeth
(Elizabeth Moore)

PERSONAL: Born in England; married Percy G. Moss (an engineer), June 19, 1976. *Home:* 40 Moseley Rd., Kenilworth, Warwickshire, England. *Agent:* Laurence Pollinger Ltd., 18 Maddox St., London W1R OEU, England.

CAREER: Writer. *Member:* Crime Writers Association.

WRITINGS: The Gemini, Morrow, 1964; *Shadows of the House,* Viking, 1968; *By the North Door,* Harper, 1975; *Samain,* Harper, 1976; *Kestrels in the Kitchen,* W. H. Allen, 1979; *Haunted Warwickshire,* R. Hale, 1981.

(Under pseudonym Elizabeth Moore) *Something to Jump For* (juvenile), Country Life, 1960.

WORK IN PROGRESS: A crime novel.

SIDELIGHTS: Meg Atkins wrote: "For me writing is constructive daydreaming, a voyage of discovery, a means of reworking reality—the door to Never-Never Land standing always, invitingly, half-open."

BIOGRAPHICAL/CRITICAL SOURCES: Books and Bookmen, June, 1969.

* * *

AUGUSTSON, Ernest
See RYDEN, Ernest Edwin

* * *

AURANDT, Paul Harvey 1918-
(Paul Harvey)

PERSONAL: Born September 4, 1918, in Tulsa, Okla.; son of Harry Harrison (a policeman) and Anna Dagmar (Christiansen) Aurandt; married Lynne Cooper, June 4, 1940; children: Paul Harvey, Jr. *Home:* 1035 Park Ave., River Forest, Ill. 60305. *Office:* 360 North Michigan Ave., Chicago, Ill. 60601.

CAREER: Worked as announcer for KVOO-Radio in Tulsa, Okla., as station manager with radio station in Salina, Kan., as special events director with KXOK-Radio in St. Louis, Mo., and as program director with WKZO-Radio, 1941-43; director of news and information for Office of War Information in Michigan and Indiana, 1941-43; American Broadcasting Co., Inc. (ABC), Chicago, Ill., news analyst and commentator, 1944—; syndicated columnist for General Features Corp., 1954—; syndicated television commentator for Paulynne Productions; regular commentator for ABC-

TV's "Good Morning America," 1979—. Lecturer. *Military service:* U.S. Army Air Forces, 1943-44.

MEMBER: Washington Radio and Television Correspondents Association, Aircraft Owners and Pilots Association, Chicago Press Club. *Awards, honors:* Citation from Disabled American Veterans, 1949; radio award from American Legion, 1952; Freedom Foundation awards, 1952, 1953, 1961, 1962, 1964, 1965, 1967, 1968, 1974, 1975, and 1976; certificate of merit from Veterans of Foreign Wars, 1953; Christopher award, 1953; award of honor from Sumter Guards, 1955; citation of merit from American Legion, 1955 and 1957; elected to Oklahoma Hall of Fame, 1955; national public welfare services trophy from Colorado American Legion, 1957; named top commentator of the year by *Radio-TV Daily,* 1962; Great American award from KSEL, 1962; special award from ABC, 1973; Illinois Broadcaster award, 1974; John Peter Zenger award from University of Arizona Department of Journalism, 1975; American of the Year award from Lions International, 1975; named to National Association of Broadcasters Hall of Fame, 1979. Honorary Litt.D. from Culver-Stockton College, 1952, and St. Bonaventure University, 1953; LL.D. from John Brown University, 1959, Montana School of Mines, 1961, Trinity College, 1963, and Parsons College, 1968; H.H.D. from Wayland Baptist College, 1960, Union College, 1962, Samford University, 1970, and Howard Payne University, 1978.

WRITINGS—Under name Paul Harvey: *Remember These Things,* Heritage Foundation, 1952; *Autumn of Liberty,* Hanover House, 1954; *The Rest of the Story,* Hanover House, 1956.

SIDELIGHTS: "Hello, Americans. This is Paul Harvey. . . . Stand by for news!" Those words are familiar to the millions of Americans who listen to Harvey's daily radio programs and telecasts. His programs are broadcast on more than eight hundred radio stations and 120 television stations. In addition, his syndicated column appears in three hundred newspapers. Not only is Harvey one of the most popular news commentators in the United States; he is also one of the richest. Some observers estimate that he earns in excess of $2 million a year.

Arriving at his studio by 4:30 A.M. each day, Harvey spends his early morning hours preparing his scripts, which are a hodgepodge of news, anecdotes, homespun humor, and personal opinion. He does most of the writing himself, although his son Paul, Jr., does write the segments for "The Rest of the Story," an afternoon radio spot about famous people and places in history. Harvey's wife, Lynne, also plays an important part in his career. She serves as his promoter, producer, and business manager as well as editor of his books.

Harvey's style of oratory is immediately recognizable. Descended from five generations of preachers, Harvey delivers his broadcasts with evangelistic fervor. He thunders out his opinions, gesticulates to emphasize his points, and fills his speech with pregnant pauses. William Brashler described him as "more of an entertainer than a journalist; more of a silken-voiced pulpit thumper than a news broadcaster; a latter-day Walter Winchell, not radio's equivalent to Walter Cronkite."

Harvey began his broadcasting career at radio station KVOO in Tulsa, Okla. After garnering experience at several different stations in the Midwest he moved to Chicago and landed a job as network commentator for the American Broadcasting Co., Inc. (ABC). He has remained in Chicago ever since, spurning all suggestions that he relocate to network headquarters in New York City. A move to the big

city, Harvey fears, would put him out of touch with the concerns of grass roots America.

The concerns of grass roots America are very much Harvey's concerns. Dubbed the "Voice of the Silent Majority," he is unabashedly conservative. Divorce, strikes, welfare, drugs, and the Internal Revenue Service have all been the targets of his wrath. During the 1950's he supported the Red hunts led by Joseph McCarthy. He still believes that Richard Nixon was hounded out of office by a hostile press.

In 1951 Harvey's right-wing zeal almost ended his broadcast career. Having often addressed his listeners to the dangers of Communist infiltration, he was naturally interested when some guards at the Argonne National Laboratory (a federal atomic research installation) informed him that security was lax at the facility. Harvey decided to check out the story for himself. On the night of February 6, 1951, he attempted to scale the wall surrounding the laboratory and was caught in the act. Arrested and detained by federal authorities, he had to appear before a federal grand jury. Harvey's line of defense was that he was not looking for a scoop but rather was motivated by concern for his fellow citizens. After a naval intelligence officer testified that Harvey had told him prior to the break-in that he would be testing the security at the facility, the jury decided not to indict the newscaster.

During the course of the grand jury investigation, the FBI uncovered some information about Harvey distinctly at odds with his all-American image. They discovered that under his real name, Paul Aurandt, he had been inducted into the Army Air Corps in 1943. Only three months later he was given a medical discharge. According to some sources, he received the medical discharge because he had deliberately cut himself on the heel with a razor, and Army doctors considered him to be emotionally unstable. Harvey has repeatedly denied these charges, claiming he was wounded on an obstacle course.

Although Chicago press raised quite a furor over the Argonne incident, Harvey managed to salvage his broadcast career. By that time he had attracted a large following of listeners, so ABC was reluctant to fire him. In the ensuing years, he has avoided controversy, except for one incident in 1970. During the 1960's Harvey was a hawk on the Vietnam War, but in a dramatic broadcast on May 1, 1970, he reversed his position. Later he reflected on what led him to change his mind: "I came up under Douglas MacArthur's philosophy—the only excuse for getting into a war was to *win* it. But then it seemed that with Vietnam, much as I advocated drive it or park it, we were determined just to stand there, mark time, and *bleed.* . . . It seemed to me that the *best* we were going to be able to leave them in Vietnam, despite the *worst* we could do, was the perpetuation of another kind of military dictatorship and that the perpetuation of military dictatorship anywhere in the world was not worth the expenditure of one American life." Some of Harvey's critics, however, contended that his abrupt change in position was due to the fact that his only child had reached draft age. Paul Jr. registered as a conscientious objector, a fact his father never reported on the air.

Despite this one departure from right-wing thinking, during the 1970's Harvey's popularity as a spokesman for conservative values continued to grow. One of his favorite themes is the moral disintegration that he sees taking place in the United States. "I think moral decay is the main problem in America," he once said. "I think that's obvious by the amount of mud and blood that we (newsmen) have to handle every day. But it's not singular, every great nation in history has had the same problem. They have a good government . . . they prosper . . . they get fat . . . they get lazy . . . and rot starts to set in. I wish we could learn from history and not make the same mistake again.''

BIOGRAPHICAL/CRITICAL SOURCES: *Newsweek,* December 24, 1962; *Editor and Publisher,* March 23, 1963; *Esquire,* May, 1970, November 7, 1978; *Grand Rapids Press,* July 28, 1974; *Biography News,* Gale, September, 1974; *People,* January 22, 1979.

—*Sketch by Ann F. Ponikvar*

* * *

AUSTIN, K(enneth) A(shurst) 1911-

PERSONAL: Born October 9, 1911, in Ascotvale, Australia; son of James William Ashurst (an estate agent) and Jane Elizabeth (Tymms) Austin; married Fanny Ralton Davies, May 7, 1938; children: John Douglas Ashurst, Margaret Jillian Austin Hunter. *Education:* University of Melbourne, B.A., 1953; Australian College of Theology, Th.A., 1957. *Office:* 12 Earlsfield Rd., Hampton, Victoria 3188, Australia.

CAREER: Bank of New South Wales, Victoria, Australia, clerk, 1928-45; Melbourne Church of England Grammar School, Melbourne, Australia, schoolmaster, 1945-76; writer, 1976—. Tutor at University of Melbourne, 1953-57. Chairman of panel of advisory historians and executive member of Matthew Flinders Bicentenary Citizens' Council, 1973-75. *Military service:* Royal Australian Navy, 1942-45; became lieutenant. Royal Australian Naval Volunteer Reserve.

MEMBER: Australian Society of Authors, National Trust of Australia, Fellowship of Australian Writers, Aviation Historical Society of Australia, Royal Geographical Society (fellow), Royal Historical Society of Victoria, Shiplovers Society of Victoria, Friends of the La Trobe Library. *Awards, honors:* Grant from Literature Board of Australia Council for the Arts, 1973.

WRITINGS: *The Voyage of the Investigator, 1801-1803: Commander Matthew Flinders, R.N.,* Rigby, 1964; *The Lights of Cobb and Co.: The Story of the Frontier Coaches, 1854-1924,* Rigby, 1967, Verry, 1972; *Port Phillip Bay Sketchbook,* Rigby, 1970; *Phillip Island Sketchbook,* Rigby, 1972; *Matthew Flinders on the Victorian Coast,* Cypress Books, 1974; *Gippsland Sketchbook,* Rigby, 1975; *A Pictorial History of Cobb and Co.,* Rigby, 1977.

Work represented in anthologies. Contributor to *Australian Dictionary of Biography* and to academic journals and popular magazines in Australia and the United States, including *Walkabout, Port of Melbourne Quarterly, Carriage Journal, Age, Aircraft,* and *Northern Perspective.*

WORK IN PROGRESS: Research for his autobiography, concentrating on the social backgrounds of his ancestors back to the eighteenth century; continuing research on the life and work of Matthew Flinders.

SIDELIGHTS: Austin told *CA:* ''I was moved to write my first book when I was navigating from Flinders's charts during World War II. My major work has been motivated by a desire to do justice to the man on the job, be he a famous explorer or an unknown worker, to describe the settings and circumstances in which he operates, and to assess his achievements. Another motivation has been an urge to portray the complexity and fascination of the history, geography, and development of important regions which present-day residents take for granted. I am increasingly awed by the mystery resulting from contrasting the view of history as a

continuous process with T. S. Eliot's vision of 'the critical moment which is always now.'

''I have traveled in England, Canada, and Europe and have led several large-scale student excursions to the Great Barrier Reef and Central Australia.''

AVOCATIONAL INTERESTS: Music (classical, light, and popular), travel, exploring old towns.

BIOGRAPHICAL/CRITICAL SOURCES: *Liber Melburniensis,* Centenary Edition, 1958; *Age,* December 19, 1970, March 2, 1974; *Melburnian,* December, 1978.

* * *

AYLEN, Leon (William) 1935-

PERSONAL: Born February 15, 1935, in Vryheid, South Africa; son of Charles (an Anglican bishop) and Elisabeth (Hills) Aylen; married Annette Battam (a musician). *Education:* Oxford University, M.A. (with first class honors), 1959; University of Bristol, Ph.D., 1962. *Religion:* Anglican. *Home:* 71 Chelsham Rd., London S.W.4, England. *Agent:* 118 Tottenham Court Rd., London W. 1, England.

CAREER: BBC-TV, London, England, producer, 1965-70; Fairleigh Dickinson University, Rutherford, N.J., poet-in-residence, 1972-74; writer, 1974—. *Member:* Poetry Society of Great Britain, Writers Guild of Great Britain, British Academy of Film and Television Arts, Association of Film and Television Technicians, Poetry Society of America, Writers Guild of America. *Awards, honors:* Nominated for television directors award from British Academy of Film and Television Arts, 1966; Cecil Day Lewis fellowship from Greater London Arts Association, 1979.

WRITINGS: *Greek Tragedy in the Modern World,* Methuen, 1964; *Discontinued Design* (poems), Venture Press, 1969; *I, Odysseus* (poems), Sidgwick & Jackson, 1971; *Greece for Everyone,* Sidgwick & Jackson, 1976; *Sunflower* (poems), Sidgwick & Jackson, 1976; *The Apples of Youth* (children's opera; first produced in London, England, at Lyric, Hammersmith, February 5, 1981), Chappell, 1980; *Return to Zululand* (poems), Sidgwick & Jackson, 1980.

Author of films for television, including ''1065 and All That,'' first broadcast by BBC-TV, 1966; ''The Drinking Party,'' first broadcast by BBC-TV, 1966; ''Dynamo,'' first broadcast by BBC-TV, 1967; ''Steel Be My Sister,'' first broadcast by HTV, 1976.

Work represented in more than twenty anthologies, including *Tunes on a Tin Whistle, Laugh or Cry or Yawn, Folk and Vision, Open the Door, The Adolescent, It Makes You Think, Bridges, Sport and Leisure, Him and Her, English at Work* and *The Art of English.*

WORK IN PROGRESS: A television film series on the potential of the new scientific revolution; another television series; a musical stage play.

SIDELIGHTS: Aylen wrote: ''As a poet I am concerned that poetry should stop contemplating its own navel and become serious again—in other words, become entertainment like the theatre, attempting to make audiences laugh and cry, attempting to change society. As a scholar I have worked on the Greek dramatists—Aeschylus, Sophocles, Euripides, Aristophanes—who, of all poets, were probably the most concerned with showing their audiences what society could be.

''I have a number of political concerns, but I see my work as more about detailed problems than about joining one British political party. I am concerned that all of us in the western world should understand the potential for human freedom and human enslavement that the new developments in science and technology are bringing out. This preoccupation was shown in 'Poet at Large,' the television program about my work as a poet, first broadcast by CBS-TV in March, 1975.

"I am involved with various projects to help the hungry in the Third World, especially in Zululand where I was born. I am concerned as a poet to work out ways in which we of the First World can live justly with the enormous luxury of our lives, as contrasted with the people of the Third World. More or less my earliest memory is the line of beggars at our door, waiting for a weekly handout of bread. My father did not have the money to buy them bread, but had to earn that specially. I am also working on a project to do with inner-city London.

"Influences? They are many. I have a rough acquaintance with many languages, including Zulu, of course, and the fact that I come from Africa is very important to me. Greece and Greek are important, too, as well as a visit to Iceland, and my awareness of Celtic Britain, being part Welsh. This complicated mixture, with other Western European languages and travels, is my background. The two trips to exotic places which gave me the most were to the Pacific Northwest coast and its native American inhabitants (when I was commissioned to write a film for American television based on a Tsimshian legend) and a visit to Thailand (again for a television film)."

AVOCATIONAL INTERESTS: "Music. I play piano and church organ. I run. I welcome the chance, when possible, to go mountain-walking, though I no longer rock-climb. I have always enjoyed animals, and want to do more to help save the wild places of the world."

BIOGRAPHICAL/CRITICAL SOURCES: Times Literary Supplement, November 21, 1980.

*   *   *

AZUMI, Atsushi 1907-

PERSONAL: Born July 1, 1907, in Tokyo, Japan; son of Yasushi and Etsu Azumi; married wife, Yoshi, May 25, 1937; children: Kunio, Yoko Azumi Sato. *Education:* Attended National Training School of Communication. *Politics:* None. *Religion:* Buddhist. *Home:* 3-4-14 Kakinokizaka, Meguro-ku, Tokyo, Japan.

CAREER: Worked in Ministry of Communications, Tokyo, Japan, 1927-44; Japan Itinerant Theatre League, Tokyo, 1944-45; Governmental Labor Institute, Tokyo, 1949-67; writer, 1967—. *Military service:* Japanese Army, 1945. *Member:* Haiku Poets Association (chief director), Japan Essayists Club. *Awards, honors:* Award from Japan Essayists Club, 1966, for *Shunka-shuto-cho,* Dakotsu Award, 1971, for *Gozen-Gogo,* and Purple Ribbon Medal, 1970.

WRITINGS—In English translation: (With Hiroshi Kaneko) *Tokyo,* Kodansha, 1972.

Other writings; all published in Japan: *Zuihitsu Tokyo saijiki* (addresses, essays, lectures), 1969; *Shisei rekijitsu* (essays), 1971; *Fuyu no haiku* (criticism and poetry), 1973; *Azumi Atsushi kushu* (poems), 1975; *Kiyose,* 1977; *Azumi Atsushi kushu* (poems), 1979. Also author of *Huru kayomi, Rekijitsu-sho, Gozen-Gogo, Shunka-shuto-cho, Zuihitsu-saijiki, Tokyo saijiki,* and *Shinsen haiku saijiki.*

B

BAAR, James A. 1929-

PERSONAL: Born February 9, 1929, in New York, N.Y.; son of A. W. (a stockbroker) and Marguerite (Rascovar) Baar; married Beverly Hodge, September 2, 1948; children: Theodore Hall. *Education:* Union College, Schenectady, N.Y., A.B., 1949. *Politics:* Republican. *Religion:* Episcopalian. *Home:* 113 Williams St., Providence, R.I. 02906. *Office:* Creamer Dickson Basford, Inc., 40 Westminster St., Providence, R.I. 02903.

CAREER: United Press International (UPI), Washington, D.C., correspondent and editor, 1954-59; *Missiles and Rockets,* senior editor, 1959-62; General Electric Co., manager of new bureau operations, 1962-66, manager of European marketing communications operation, 1966-70, president of international marketing communications operation, 1970-72; Lewis & Gilman, Inc. (international marketing communications consultants), Philadelphia, Pa., senior vice-president and director of public relations, 1972-74; Creamer Dickson Basford, Inc., executive vice-president in New York, N.Y., 1974-78, president in Providence, R.I., 1978—. Member of board of directors of Providence Opera Theatre.

MEMBER: International Public Relations Association, International Association of Business Communicators, National Investor Relations Institute (past president), Public Relations Society of America (past member of board of directors; member of counselors section executive committee), American Management Association, National Press Club, Overseas Press Club of America, Aviation/Space Writers Association, Chi Psi, Dunes Club, Mohawk Club, Hope Club (Agawam Hunt).

WRITINGS: Polaris, Harcourt, 1960; (with William E. Howard) *Combat Missileman,* Harcourt, 1961; (with Howard) *Spacecraft and Missiles of the World,* Harcourt, 1962, new and revised edition, 1966; *The Great Free Enterprise Gambit,* Houghton, 1980. Contributor to magazines.

*   *   *

BABSON, Marian

PERSONAL: Born in Salem, Mass. *Address:* c/o Collins Publishers, 14 St. James's Pl., London SW1A 1PS, England.

CAREER: Writer, 1971—. *Member:* Crime Writers Association (secretary, 1976—), Mystery Writers of America, National Book League (member of general council).

WRITINGS—Novels: *Cover-Up Story,* Collins, 1971; *Murder on Show,* Collins, 1972; *Pretty Lady,* Collins, 1973; *The Stalking Lamb,* Collins, 1974; *Unfair Exchange,* Collins, 1974; *Murder Sails at Midnight,* Collins, 1975; *There Must Be Some Mistake,* Collins, 1975; *Untimely Guest,* Collins, 1976; *The Lord Mayor of Death* (Detective Book Club selection), Collins, 1977, Walker & Co., 1979; *Murder, Murder, Little Star* (Detective Book Club selection), Collins, 1977, Walker & Co., 1980; *Tightrope for Three,* Collins, 1978; *So Soon Done For,* Collins, 1979; *The Twelve Deaths of Christmas* (Detective Book Club selection), Collins, 1979, Walker & Co., 1980; *Dangerous to Know,* Collins, 1980, Walker & Co., 1981; *Queue Here for Murder,* Collins, 1980. Contributor to *Woman's Realm* and *Woman's Own.*

WORK IN PROGRESS: Another novel.

*   *   *

BACON, Edward 1906-1981
(Francis Boon)

OBITUARY NOTICE—See index for *CA* sketch: Born July 6, 1906, in Normanby, England; died January 13, 1981, in Suffolk, England. Editor and author. Bacon served as archaeological editor for the *Illustrated London News* for over thirty years. He authored several books on archaeology, including *Digging for History, Archaeology: Discoveries in the 1960's, Archaeology: A Survey,* and *The Great Archaeologists.* Under the pseudonym Francis Boon he wrote novels, including *Lord, What Fools; Ancient and Fishlike;* and *A Cat Among the Rabbits.* Obituaries and other sources: *London Times,* January 20, 1981.

*   *   *

BAIR, Frank E. 1927-

PERSONAL: Born November 22, 1927, in Beckley, W.Va.; son of Frank Peter (a builder) and Cleo (Miller) Bair; married Gloria Frances (in paralegal work), July 3, 1947; children: Mark, Tracey, Kelley. *Education:* Attended Wayne State University, 1954-55. *Home:* 26610 Westmeath Rd., Farmington Hills, Mich. 48018. *Office:* Bobertz, Swaney & Bair, Inc., 33550 Schoolcraft, Livonia, Mich. 48150.

CAREER: U.S. Merchant Marine, merchant seaman, 1945-46; Batten, Barton, Durstine & Osborne (advertising firm), Detroit, Mich., marketing representative, 1954-56; Clark & Bobertz, Inc. (advertising firm), Detroit, copywriter and account executive, 1957-60, vice-president, 1960-62; Bo- bertz & Associates (advertising firm), Detroit, executive vice-president and creative director, 1962-67; Bobertz, Swa- ney & Bair, Inc. (marketing consultants), Livonia, Mich., president, 1967—. Member of mayor's committee on hous- ing, 1979-80. *Military service:* U.S. Army, special agent in counterintelligence, 1952-54. *Member:* Detroit Philosophical Society. *Awards, honors: Biography News* and *Weather Almanac* were both named outstanding reference books by American Library Association, 1974; *Weather Almanac* was also named among one hundred top scientific-technical books, 1975.

WRITINGS: (Editor with James A. Ruffner) *Weather Alma- nac,* Gale, 1973, 2nd edition, 1977; (editor with Frederick G. Ruffner) *Countries of the World and Their Leaders,* Gale, 1974, 6th edition, 1980; (editor) *Biography News,* Volume I, Gale, 1974, Volume II, 1975; (editor with Barbara Nykoruk) *Business People in the News,* Gale, 1976; (editor with Nyko- ruk) *Authors in the News,* two volumes, Gale, 1976; (editor) *International Marketing Handbook,* Gale, 1980; (editor) *Minority Businessman's Almanac,* Gale, 1981.

WORK IN PROGRESS: Interfacing to the More Complex Society, publication by Harcourt expected in 1981 or 1982.

SIDELIGHTS: Bair commented: "My military stint in- cluded training in research techniques for assessing social, technological, and industrial resources of nations. This, and my work in industrial advertising, have helped me develop basic reporting skills. In my youth I studied advertising art (briefly) and did some work as a graphics designer while employed in advertising agencies.

"My hobby is inventing. I am the joint inventor of a patented system employed in the publishing field for assembling indi- vidual typographic 'chunks' into book pages. Currently I am developing an automatic system for creating individual signs and posters. I enjoy working with a home computer and ex- pect to adapt the micro-processor to further automate this sign-making system.

"Philosophy and anthropology are subjects of great interest to me. My forthcoming book, *Interfacing to the More Com- plex Society,* has grown out of the conjunction of these inter- ests. It observes that the bulk of society is lagging at an alarming rate in gaining facility with a new genre of sys- tems—administrative as well as physical ones—which are restructuring the techno-cultural environment."

*   *   *

BAKER, D(onald) Philip 1937-

PERSONAL: Born February 2, 1937, in Hornell, N.Y.; son of Donald Hills and Mildred (Higgins) Baker. *Education:* Alfred University, B.A. (cum laude), 1958, M.S.Ed. (with distinction), 1959; Pratt Institute, M.L.S., 1968; further graduate study at Fairfield University, 1968-69. *Religion:* Episcopalian. *Office:* Instructional Media Programs, Stam- ford Public Schools, 195 Hillandale Ave., Stamford, Conn. 06902.

CAREER: High school history teacher in Bethel, Conn., 1959-60; U.S. Senate, Washington, D.C., research assistant to Senator Jacob Javits, 1960-61; high school teacher of his- tory and social studies in Darien, Conn., 1962-67, director of public school libraries, 1967-71; Stamford Public Schools, Stamford, Conn., coordinator of library media programs, 1971—. Instructor at University of Bridgeport, 1974-78. President of Connecticut Library Foundation, 1976-79; member of Connecticut State Library Advisory Council,

1973-76; member of task force of National Commission on Libraries and Information Science, 1977-79, and national advisory board of Library of Congress's Center for the Book, 1980; speaker at international meetings. Vice-presi- dent of board of directors of New Neighborhoods, Inc., 1971—.

MEMBER: International Reading Association, American Library Association, American Association of School Li- brarians (member of New England board of directors, 1976- 79; president, 1980-81), National Education Association, National Council of Teachers of English, Association for Educational Communications and Technology, Association for Supervision and Curriculum Development, New England Educational Media Association (member of board of direc- tors, 1976-79), Connecticut Education Association, Con- necticut Educational Media Association (member of board of directors, 1975-76), Connecticut School Library Associa- tion (member of board of directors, 1968-74; president, 1974- 75).

WRITINGS: School and Public Library Media Programs for Children and Young Adults, Gaylord Professional Publica- tions, 1977; (contributor) Thomas Galvin and Margaret Kimmel, editors, *Excellence in School Media Programs: Essays Honoring Elizabeth T. Fast,* American Library Asso- ciation, 1979; (contributor) *Issues in Media Management, 1979 Series,* Maryland State Department of Education, 1979; (with David Bender) *Library Media Programs and the Spe- cial Learner,* Shoe String, 1980. Author of "Media Centric," a column in *Wilson Library Bulletin,* 1977-79, and "The Li- brary Media Center," a column in *Instructor,* 1979—. Con- tributor to *American Library Association Yearbook.* Con- tributor of about a dozen articles to library and education journals. Associate editor of *School Media Quarterly,* 1973- 79.

SIDELIGHTS: Baker told *CA:* "My professional career has been spent in education, most recently as a library media specialist and a supervisor of library media programs. The central purpose of my writing is to establish that the library media specialist is a teacher and that the library media pro- gram is a bona fide teaching program with an instructional purpose similar to other educational programs. I am also concerned that the use of media in teaching programs be made as comprehensible and rational as is possible, a natural part of any teaching program."

*   *   *

BAKEWELL, K(enneth) G(raham) B(artlett) 1931-

PERSONAL: Born July 13, 1931, in Dudley, Worcester- shire, England; son of James Arthur and Mabel (Bartlett) Bakewell; married Agnes Lawson (a librarian), June 9, 1956; children: Linda Carol, June Christine. *Education:* Queen's University of Belfast, Northern Ireland, M.A., 1972. *Reli- gion:* Christian. *Home:* 9 Greenacre Rd., Liverpool L25 0LD, England. *Office:* School of Librarianship, Liverpool Polytechnic, Tithebarn St., Liverpool L2 2ER, England.

CAREER: Worked in public and special libraries in England, 1947-66; Liverpool Polytechnic, School of Librarianship, Liverpool, England, lecturer, 1966-69, senior lecturer, 1969- 78, principal lecturer in librarianship, 1978—. Library liaison adviser to Anbar Publications Ltd. *Member:* British Institute of Management, Library Association (fellow), Society of Indexers (chairman, 1976-79, vice-chairman, 1979—). *Awards, honors:* Wheatley Medal from Library Association, 1979.

WRITINGS: How to Find Out: Management and Productiv-

ity, Pergamon, 1966, 2nd edition, 1970; (editor) *Classification for Information Retrieval,* Bingley, 1968; (editor) *Library and Information Services for Management,* Bingley, 1968; *Industrial Libraries Throughout the World,* Pergamon, 1969; *A Manual of Cataloguing Practice,* Pergamon, 1972; *Management Principles and Practice: A Guide to Information Sources,* Gale, 1977; *Classification and Indexing Practice,* Bingley, 1978; (with J. M. Bibby, E. J. Hunter, and V. de P. Roper) *A Study of Indexers' Reactions to the PRECIS Indexing System,* Department of Library and Information Studies, Liverpool Polytechnic, 1978; (with Hunter) *Cataloguing,* Bingley, 1979; (with K.D.C. Vernon, V. Lang, and D. A. Cotton) *The London Classification of Business Studies,* 2nd edition, Aslib, 1979; (with G. M. Dare) *The Manager's Guide to Getting the Answers,* Library Association, 1980.

Contributor to journals, including *Catalogue and Index, Education Libraries Bulletin, Indexer, Journal of Documentation, Library Association Record, Management Decision,* and *Library Resources and Technical Services.*

WORK IN PROGRESS: Research into user reactions to PRECIS indexes.

SIDELIGHTS: K.G.B. Bakewell's reference books have received consistently high praise from reviewers for their thoroughness and readability. A reviewer for the *Times Literary Supplement,* for example, declared that in *How to Find: Management and Productivity,* Bakewell is "readable, in the sense that he is able to explain things clearly, and his definitions and descriptions of individual items make this book much more than an annotated bibliography." Likewise, Hans Wellisch of *Library Quarterly* assessed that another of Bakewell's books, *A Manual of Cataloguing Practice,* is "not a dry-as-dust discussion of the AACR rules but shows the prospective cataloger (or future head of a cataloguing department) how these rules may be applied to the varying requirements of different libraries."

In a review of *Management Principles and Practice,* Ross Shimmon of the *Library Association Record* described the work as "a very useful bibliographical guide to books, periodicals, audio-visual materials, organizations and even some significant periodical articles in the field of management." And Theodore Kunin of *Personnel Psychology* noted: "As with all the Gale Research Information Guides, our readers might find this book a time-saving tool which makes things just a bit easier."

Bakewell commented to *CA:* "I began writing because of the problem of teaching with out-of-date or otherwise unsatisfactory textbooks. My original teaching interest was indexing and I have been stimulated by the contributions of a number of writers and innovators, including S. R. Ranganathan, H. E. Bliss, J. Mills, D. J. Foskett, Seymour Lubetzky, and Derek Austin, whose PRECIS (Preserved Context Index System), was introduced in *The British National Bibliography* in 1974. I regard this as a particularly significant development; I want to know what others think about it, however, and hence my current research. My main teaching area is now library management, but I retain my interest in indexing. Writing and research are pleasurable pastimes for me, as well as work, but I also enjoy reading purely for recreation (my favorite novelist is Graham Greene) and I try not to neglect my family and cat."

AVOCATIONAL INTERESTS: Information retrieval, theatre, cinema, travel (Scandinavia, Germany, Brazil).

BIOGRAPHICAL/CRITICAL SOURCES: Times Literary Supplement, May 18, 1967; *Library Quarterly,* January, 1973; *Personnel Psychology,* summer, 1978; *Library Association Record,* August, 1978.

*   *   *

BAKSHIAN, Aram 1944-

PERSONAL: Born March 11, 1944, in Washington, D.C.; son of Aram, Sr. (a rentier) and Ruth (Yeatman) Bakshian. *Education:* Educated privately. *Politics:* Republican. *Religion:* Presbyterian. *Home:* 3400 Macomb St. N.W., Washington, D.C. 20016.

CAREER: U.S. News and World Report, Washington, D.C., editorial assistant, 1965-66; legislative assistant to U.S. Congressman William E. Brock, Washington, D.C., 1966-69; U.S. Small Business Administration, Washington, D.C., information specialist, 1970; Republican National Committee, Washington, D.C., assistant to chairman, 1971; aide to Presidents Richard Nixon and Gerald Ford, Washington, D.C., 1972-75; Union Carbide Corp., Washington, D.C., communications manager, 1978-79; writer, 1966—. Member of communications advisory board of Republican National Committee, 1977—; assistant editor of 1980 Republican party platform; political speechwriter and corporate consultant. Delegate to Atlantic Assembly, Brussels, Belgium, 1973; accompanied presidential visit to the Soviet Union, 1974; adviser on cultural affairs, Reagan White House transition staff, 1980-81. Television and radio commentator, 1965—. *Member:* National Press Club, Reform Club. *Awards, honors:* Senior North American officer of Sealed Knot, 1968—; fellow of Institute of Politics, Harvard University, 1975-76.

WRITINGS: (With Peter Young) *The War Game,* Dutton, 1972, 2nd edition, 1975; (editor) Robert Stolz, *Servus Du* (memoirs), Blanvalet, 1980; *The Candidates: 1980,* Arlington House, 1980; (co-author) *The Future Under President Reagan,* Arlington House, 1981. Contributor of several hundred articles and reviews to magazines, including *National Review, Washingtonian, History Today, Spectator, Stereo Review, Newsday,* and *Reader's Digest,* and newspapers.

WORK IN PROGRESS: A historical novel, publication expected in 1982 or 1983; two works of nonfiction on contemporary arts and manners, 1982 or 1983; another book in presidential "Candidates" series, Arlington House, 1984.

SIDELIGHTS: Bakshian told *CA:* "A lifelong fascination with the written and spoken word (and a certain facility at using both) made a writing career inevitable. In my experience, the key to successful writing is deceptively simple: write about things that interest you in a way that other people will find interesting as well. To date, the result has been hundreds of articles and a number of books, introductions, and contributions to anthologies published here and abroad in at least ten different languages. My favorite hobbies and pastimes include general and military history, food and drink, travel, biography, politics, music, art, and humor—and these are the things I most often treat in print or on radio and television.

"Through blind good luck and a gradually growing reputation I've been able to collaborate on the memoirs of Vienna's last Waltz King and a former president of the United States, travel extensively throughout Europe, and witness much lively (if occasionally distasteful) history in the making. I can think of no other field of endeavor that would have offered a man of my temperament the same satisfactions and opportunities. As for the periodic frustrations—you can find them in any profession, without the commensurate rewards in good company and interesting conversation. With writing as with music, I believe that the true distinction is between the good and the bad, not the light and the serious. The more complex society and technology become, the greater the need for writers who can explain and entertain lucidly and with at least a little style to a broad general audience. This is what I seek to do, whether my subject of the moment is a picaresque eighteenth-century librettist or the SALT treaty.''

AVOCATIONAL INTERESTS: Dining, conversation, collecting books and military items, reading, broadcasting, public speaking.

*   *   *

BALACHANDRAN, M(adhavarao)   1938-

PERSONAL: Born March 25, 1938, in Madras, India; came to the United States in 1968, naturalized citizen, 1977; son of Seshagiri (a teacher) and Sadhana (Bai) Madhavarao; married Sarojini Ananthakrishnaiyer (a librarian), May 30, 1969. *Education:* University of Madras, B.A., 1957, M.A., 1959; University of Bombay, LL.B., 1967; University of Illinois, J.D., 1971, M.S.L.S., 1972. *Politics:* Independent. *Religion:* Hindu. *Home:* 2113 Burlison, Urbana, Ill. 61801. *Office:* Library, University of Illinois, Urbana, Ill. 61801.

CAREER: Indian Express Newspapers Ltd., Madurai, India, assistant editor, 1959-61; Life Insurance Corp. of India, Bombay, administrative officer, 1962-68; University of Illinois, Urbana, commerce reference librarian, 1972-74, assistant commerce librarian, 1974—, instructor, 1972-74, assistant professor, 1974-77, associate professor of library administration, 1977—. *Member:* American Library Association, American Bar Association, Illinois Bar Association, Beta Phi Mu.

WRITINGS—Editor: *Guide to Trade and Securities Statistics,* Pierian, 1977; (with wife, Sarojini Balachandran) *Reference Book Review Index, 1973-1975,* Pierian, 1979; (with S. Balachandran) *Subject Guide to Reference Books, 1970-1975,* Pierian, 1979; (with S. Balachandran and Linda Mark) *Reference Sources, 1979,* Pierian, 1979; *Regional Statistics: A Guide to Information Sources,* Gale, 1980. Co-editor of series, "Reference Sources," Pierian. Contributor of articles and reviews to library journals.

WORK IN PROGRESS: Investigating composite sources of commodity price information; research on recent trends in corporate social involvement.

SIDELIGHTS: Balachandran told *CA:* "I strongly believe that as an academic reference librarian it is my job not only to help other scholars with their research, but also to keep myself abreast of new developments in my subject area, which is business and economics. This enables me to perform my job with utmost efficiency. Now one of the best ways a reference librarian can achieve this efficiency is to get involved in one's own research activities. This is the reason why I spend a considerable amount of my time surveying the needs of the library users in my area and trying to come up with helpful guidebooks, directories, and indexes that facilitate faster retrieval of needed information. I also believe that research and publication activities are a necessary concomitant of the faculty status bestowed upon most academic librarians in this country."

AVOCATIONAL INTERESTS: Outdoor activities (especially jogging and swimming), travel.

BIOGRAPHICAL/CRITICAL SOURCES: Serials Review, July-September, 1977.

BALACHANDRAN, Sarojini   1934-

PERSONAL: Born May 12, 1934, in Madras, India; came to the United States in 1968, naturalized citizen, 1977; daughter of K.V.A. Iyer (a civil engineer) and Madhurambal Ananthakrishnaiyer; married Madhavarao Balachandran (a librarian), May 30, 1969. *Education:* University of Madras, B.Sc., 1954, M.A., 1958; Indiana State University, M.S., 1970; University of Illinois, M.S.L.S., 1972. *Politics:* Independent. *Religion:* Hindu. *Home:* 2113 Burlison, Urbana, Ill. 61801. *Office:* Library, University of Illinois, 221 Engin Hall, Urbana, Ill. 61801.

CAREER: Bhabha Atomic Research Centre, Bombay, India, scientific officer, 1959-68; University of Illinois, Urbana, cataloger and instructor of library administration, 1972-76, cataloger and assistant professor of library administration, 1976-78, assistant engineering librarian and associate professor of library administration, 1978—. *Member:* American Library Association, American Society for Engineering Education.

WRITINGS—Editor: *Employee Communication: A Bibliography,* American Business Communication Association, 1976; *Airport Planning, 1965-1975,* Council of Planning Librarians, 1976; *Energy Statistics: A Guide to Sources,* Council of Planning Librarians, 1976; *A Selected Bibliography in Home Economics Education, 1966 to 1976,* Department of Vocational and Technical Education, Division of Home Economics Education, University of Illinois, 1977; *Technical Writing,* American Business Communication Association, 1977; (with husband, Madhavarao Balachandran) *Reference Book Review Index, 1973-1975,* Pierian, 1979; (with M. Balachandran) *Subject Guide to Reference Books, 1970-75,* Pierian, 1979; (with M. Balachandran and Linda Mark) *Reference Sources, 1979,* Pierian, 1979; *New Product Planning: A Guide to Information Sources,* Gale, 1980; *Energy Statistics: A Guide to Information Sources,* Gale, 1980. Co-editor of series, "Reference Sources," for Pierian. Contributor of articles and reviews to scientific and library journals.

WORK IN PROGRESS: Research on publishing requirements and opportunities in engineering and related fields.

SIDELIGHTS: Balachandran told *CA:* "As an information professional, most of my recent writings have been influenced by an acute awareness of the needs of academic library users. I think the most important job of any library and information science professional is providing easy access to library materials. It is for this reason I have devoted considerable amounts of time to the preparation of indexes, guidebooks, and literature surveys. The response from my users convinces me of the utility of this type of activity."

AVOCATIONAL INTERESTS: Swimming, jogging, flying small aircraft, travel, professional football and baseball.

BIOGRAPHICAL/CRITICAL SOURCES: Serials Review, July-September, 1977.

*   *   *

BALAKIAN, Peter   1951-

PERSONAL: Born June 13, 1951, in Teaneck, N.J.; son of Gerard (a physician) and Arax (Aroosian) Balakian; married Helen Kebabian, 1980. *Education:* Bucknell University, B.A. (cum laude), 1973; New York University, M.A., 1975; Brown University, Ph.D., 1980. *Home:* 32 Payne St., Hamilton, N.Y. 13346. *Office:* Department of English, Colgate University, Hamilton, N.Y. 13346.

CAREER: Dwight-Englewood School, Englewood, N.J., teacher, 1974-76; Bucknell University, Lewisburg, Pa., teacher and chairman of writing department at Pennsylvania Governors School for the Arts, 1973-79; Colgate University, Hamilton, N.Y., assistant professor, 1980—. *Awards, honors:* Prize from Academy of American Poets, 1974; Phi Beta Kappa prize.

WRITINGS: Father Fisheye (poems), Sheep Meadow Press, 1980. Contributor to *American Quarterly, Nation, Poetry Northwest, New Directions in Prose and Poetry, Carolina Quarterly, Literary Review, Southern Poetry Review,* and *Ararat.* Co-founder and co-editor of *Graham House Review;* member of editorial board of *Ararat.*

WORK IN PROGRESS: Sad Days of Light, poems; editing an anthology of contemporary American poetry, 1960-80, publication by Sheep Meadow Press, expected in 1981; a critical study of Theodore Roethke's poetry.

SIDELIGHTS: Balakian told *CA:* "Family past, the history of Armenia, and the peculiar nature of pluralistic American culture inform my new poems. The retelling of the past that brings history to myth is a starting point."

*   *   *

BALLANTRAE, Bernard Edward Fergusson   1911-1980

OBITUARY NOTICE: Born May 6, 1911, in London, England; died November 28, 1980, in London, England. Author and soldier. Ballantrae, former governor of New Zealand, wrote thriteen books, including military and historical works and two collections of poetry. His writings include *Eton Portrait, The Wild Green Earth, Return to Burma,* and *Captain John Niven.* Obituaries and other sources: *The International Who's Who,* 43rd edition, Europa, 1979; *AB Bookman's Weekly,* January 19, 1981.

*   *   *

BALY, Monica Eileen   1914-

PERSONAL: Born May 24, 1914, in Shirley, Surrey, England; daughter of Albert Frank (an accountant) and Anne Elizabeth (Marlow) Baly. *Education:* St. Hilda's School, London, degree, 1939; Royal College of Nursing, H.V. certificate, 1948; Open University, B.A., 1978. *Home:* 19 Royal Cres., Bath, England.

CAREER: Middlesex Hospital, London, England, nurse training, 1936-39, midwifery training, 1939-40; Foreign Office, Germany, chief nursing officer of Displaced Persons' Division, 1949-51; Royal College of Nursing, London, western area officer, 1951-74; writer, 1972—. Lecturer at Bath Technical College, 1960—, London University, 1962—, and Royal College of Nursing. Examiner, 1975—. *Military service:* Royal Air Force, Nursing Service, 1941-46; mentioned in dispatches. *Member:* Medical Historical Association, Library and Art Gallery Association, Bath Historical Association, Bath Preservation Trust, Royal College of Nursing Historical Association. *Awards, honors:* Essay prize from British Medical Association, 1967, for "The Future of Nursing Education," and 1969, for "Florence Nightingale's Influence on Nursing Today."

WRITINGS: Nursing and Social Change, Heinemann, 1973, revised edition, 1980; *Professional Responsibility,* Medcalf, 1975; *Nursing: Past-Into-Present,* Batsford, 1976, 2nd edition, 1980; (contributor) *Professional and Legal Responsibility,* Churchill Livingstone, 1980; (editor and contributor) *District Nursing,* Heinemann, 1981. Contributor to *Nursing Times.*

WORK IN PROGRESS: Research on the "sick poor" in Bath, 1780-1880.

SIDELIGHTS: Monica Baly described herself as "a nurse, *faute de mieux,* with a historical *manque.* I was pushed into lecturing on the development of nursing for the University of London. Shocked at the lack of a textbook on the subject, I wrote my own, then did a degree in history. Other books are mainly spin-offs."

*   *   *

BANBURY, Philip   1914-

PERSONAL: Born May 15, 1914, in London, England; son of George (a photographer) and Amy Lilian (a governess; maiden name, Motts) Banbury; married Claire Darlington, 1948; children: Peter John, Barbara Anne. *Education:* Attended technical high school in Brighton, England. *Politics:* "Royalist, Conservationist, European, and Commonsense." *Home:* Great Circle, 19 High Ridge, Seabrook, Hythe, Kent CT21 5T6, England.

CAREER: Design draftsman in electrical control gear for Allen West Ltd., 1939-43; fitting out draftsman in submarine and coastal forces craft for Admiralty Signal Establishment, 1943-46; cartographical draftsman for British European Airways, 1946-48; International Aeradio Ltd., Southall, England, cartographer and editor of aeronautical charts, 1948-76; writer, 1971—. *Member:* Royal National Lifeboat Institution, Whitstable Society (honorary member). *Awards, honors:* Certificate of astronavigation from Royal Yachting Association, 1974.

WRITINGS: Shipbuilders of the Thames and Medway From 1500 to 1914, David & Charles, 1971; *Man and the Sea,* Adlard Coles, 1975. Contributor to magazines, including *Aeronautics, Motor Boat, Popular Mechanics, Sea Breezes, Model Shipwright,* and *Yachting Monthly.*

WORK IN PROGRESS: A book on all European ships, shipping, and naval operations, including cargoes and passengers, 1066-1350, publication expected in 1981 or 1982.

SIDELIGHTS: "I come from a North Devon seafaring family," Banbury told *CA. "Shipbuilders of the Thames and Medway* combined an interest in industrial archaeology and ships, and filled a gap in the lore of the London river. I also have a deep interest in aircraft design, which has resulted in study of power/weight/speed ratios of aircraft and ships. And, as an amateur boat designer, I have made dozens of design studies and built three boats. I have traveled to nine countries in search of boat and ship data."

*   *   *

BANCROFT, Iris (Nelson)   1922-
(Andrea Layton, Ingrid Nielson)

PERSONAL: Born May 26, 1922, in Kingchow, China; came to the United States in 1923; daughter of Carl Johann (a minister) and Emma Marie (Anderson) Nelson; married Robert Koenig, July, 1945 (divorced, 1962); married Keith O. Bancroft (a writer); children: William Carl, Walter Daniel. *Education:* Chicago Teachers College, Chicago, Ill., B.Ed., 1945; Northwestern University, M.Ed., 1962. *Residence:* Granada Hills, Calif. *Agent:* H. N. Swanson, Inc., 8523 Sunset Blvd., Hollywood, Calif. 90069.

CAREER: Peterson Industries, Chicago, Ill., bookkeeper, 1945-47; worked as union organizer for Women's Garment Workers in Chicago, 1947-50; teacher in public schools in Elmhurst, Ill., 1957-61, and Chicago, 1961-62; photographer and editor for Elysium Publications and for American Art, Los Angeles, Calif., 1962-77; writer, 1977—. Violist with Burbank Symphony Orchestra and La Mirada Symphony Orchestra. *Member:* Mensa.

WRITINGS—All romances, except as noted: (Under pseudonym Andrea Layton) *Love's Gentle Fugitive*, Playboy Press, 1978; (under Layton pseudonym) *So Wild a Rapture*, Playboy Press, 1978; (under Layton pseudonym) *Midnight Fires*, Playboy Press, 1979; *Love's Burning Flame*, Bantam, 1979; *Rapture's Rebel*, Pinnacle Books, 1980; *Whispering Hope* (fictionalized biography of mother, Emma Anderson Nelson), Pinnacle Books, 1981; (under pseudonym Ingrid Nielson) *Freedom's Daughter*, Pinnacle Books, 1981.

WORK IN PROGRESS: Trudy's Story (tentative title), a sequel to *Whispering Hope*, publication expected in 1982; *Dorothy*, the story of a girl who is the victim of incest, publication expected in 1983; *Take Care of Trina* (tentative title); *The Break in the Circle* (tentative title).

SIDELIGHTS: Iris Bancroft told *CA:* "Like many authors, even when my material is not autobiographical, I gain insights into my own emotions through writing about the emotions of my characters. This effect is magnified when the subject is my mother (as in *Whispering Hope*), or, to some degree, myself (as in *Trudy's Story*). Maybe this introspection is helpful since it does, I believe, contribute to making all the characters in my books become more real. It certainly is helpful to me as a person, since it presents me with insights into cause-and-effect relationships I might otherwise not recognize.

"I was upset by my divorce, even though I initiated it, because I left my sons with my first husband as I wanted them to have the advantage of the schools in Elmhurst, Ill. (since they are far better schools than those in Chicago or Los Angeles). The separation was still very hard for me, however. I felt both pleased as my sons advanced in their educations and guilty because I had left them instead of taking them with me. I wanted to write partly as a cathartic. *Trudy's Story* will deal with that subject. In a way, I wrote the romances as a way to master the skills of writing well enough for me to deal with other, more important matters.

"Another subject close to my heart is incest, not because I personally experience it, but because I knew a child who was a victim. When her mother learned what was going on she called the police, sent her husband to jail, and took the girl, almost twelve at the time, away so she could forget. Since I am convinced that no twelve-year-old child can forget so traumatic a thing, I have worried about that girl ever since. I want to write a book about incest just for her—and for the other children like her whose parental fear of the subject is forcing them to bury what cannot be that easily laid to rest. Toward this goal, I have been doing research for the last five years. I have read books, attended conferences, and interviewed people. And I have continued to write other books (my romances) dealing with human emotions so that I will hopefully have the skill I need to fulfill my aims when I begin my book *Dorothy*.

"I have also done research in preparation for other books, but that is not too far along. In the future somewhere is a book, tentatively entitled *The Break in the Circle*, about a woman's devotion to her children and what it does to her husband, and also a book about family involvement in the illness of one child. This book I have tentatively entitled *Take Care of Trina*.

"As for the basic reason for my writing, I can't say. I do know that as a child I used to take long walks, describing to myself my every step—as if I were writing about me. It was good practice. I have no difficulty dealing with action in my books. I love history—always have. I also love human relationships, and in my writing I try to combine these interests."

BANCROFT, Robert
See KIRSCH, Robert R.

*   *   *

BANG, Betsy   1912-

PERSONAL: Born July 9, 1912, in South Carolina; daughter of Francis Walton (a tax expert) and Estelle (Edwards) Garrett; married Frederick Barry Bang (a physician and professor), June 1, 1940; children: Caroline Bang Moyer, Molly Garrett Bang-Campbell, Alex F. II. *Education:* George Washington University, B.A., 1933; also attended Johns Hopkins University. *Politics:* Independent Democrat. *Religion:* Episcopal. *Home:* 3956 Cloverhill Rd., Baltimore, Md. 21218. *Office:* School of Hygiene and Public Health, Johns Hopkins University, 615 North Wolfe St., Baltimore, Md. 21205.

CAREER: American Museum of Natural History, New York City, illustrator in comparative anatomy, 1935-37; associated with New York Postgraduate Medical School, New York City, 1938-40; Johns Hopkins University, Baltimore, Md., research associate in pathobiology, 1958—, worked at Center for Medical Research, Calcutta, India, 1962-74. Associated with Macausland Orthopedic Clinic, 1938-40. Past president of Maryland Prisoners Aid Association. Member of Baltimore Criminal Justice Commission, police commissioner's advisory panel, and Health and Welfare Council. *Member:* American Association for the Advancement of Science, Marine Biological Association, Maryland Mental Health Association.

WRITINGS: The Old Woman and the Red Pumpkin, Macmillan, 1976; *The Old Woman and the Rice Thief*, Greenwillow, 1977; *Tuntuni the Tailorbird*, Greenwillow, 1978; *The Cucumber Stem*, Greenwillow, 1979; *The Demons of Rajpur*, Greenwillow, 1980. Contributor of about fifty articles to scientific journals.

SIDELIGHTS: Betsy Bang wrote that her main interest is "folk literature and art as representatives of the historic roots of current beliefs and social attitudes."

*   *   *

BANG, Garrett
See BANG, Molly Garrett

*   *   *

BANG, Molly Garrett   1943-
(Garrett Bang)

PERSONAL: Born December 29, 1943, in Princeton, N.J.; daughter of Frederik Barry (a research physician) and Betsy (a translator and scientist; maiden name, Garrett) Bang; married Richard H. Campbell (an acoustics engineer), September 27, 1974; children: Monika. *Education:* Wellesley College, B.A., 1965; University of Arizona, M.A., 1969; Harvard University, M.A., 1971. *Home:* 89 Water St., Woods Hole, Mass. 02543.

CAREER: Author, illustrator, and translator. Doshisha University, Kyoto, Japan, teacher of English, 1965-67; Asahi Shimbun, New York, N.Y., interpreter of Japanese, 1969; Baltimore Sunpapers, Baltimore, Md., reporter, 1970. Editor of *Woods Hole Passage;* member of Woods Hole Community Association (trustee). Consultant for UNICEF in Dacca, Bangladesh. *Awards, honors:* Notable book award from American Library Association, 1977, for *Wiley and the Hairy Man;* Honor Book award from *Horn Book*, 1980, and Caldecott Honor Book award, 1981, both for *The Grey Lady and the Strawberry Snatcher.*

WRITINGS—All for children; all self-illustrated: (Editor) *The Goblins Giggle, and Other Stories* (stories from France, China, Japan, Ireland, and Germany), Scribner, 1973; (under name Garrett Bang; translator and editor) *Men From the Village Deep in the Mountains, and Other Japanese Folktales,* Macmillan, 1973; *The Old Woman and the Red Pumpkin: A Bengali Folktale,* translated and edited by mother, Betsy Bang, Macmillan, 1975; (editor) *Wiley and the Hairy Man* (adapted from American folktale), Macmillan, 1976; (editor) *The Buried Moon and Other Stories* (tales from China, Japan, England, and India), Scribner, 1977; *The Old Woman and the Rice Thief,* translated by B. Bang, Morrow, 1978; *Tuntani, the Tailor Bird,* translated by B. Bang, Greenwillow, 1978; *The Grey Lady and the Strawberry Snatcher,* Four Winds Press, 1980.

* * *

BANK, Mirra   1945-

PERSONAL: Born May 12, 1945, in Miami, Fla.; daughter of Michael L. (in textiles) and Julia (in textiles; maiden name, Oppenheim) Bank. *Education:* Smith College, B.A., 1967; attended HB Studio, 1976. *Home and office:* 347 West Broadway, New York, N.Y. 10013.

CAREER: Free-lance editor and director of motion pictures in London, England, 1967-69, and New York, N.Y., 1969—. Editor of motion pictures, including "Gimme Shelter," 1970, "Harlan County, U.S.A.," 1976, and numerous specials for Public Broadcasting System, including "The Movie Crazy Years," "Hollywood, You Must Remember This," and "The Men Who Made the Movies" (eight parts); producer and director of motion pictures, including "The Fifty First State," "Becoming Tough Enough," and "Anonymous Was a Woman"; also producer and director for Volunteers in Service to America (VISTA). *Awards, honors:* Grants from American Film Institute, 1976, Creative Artists Public Service Program, 1976 and 1980, Corporation for Public Broadcasting, 1977, Women's Fund, 1977 and 1979, National Endowment for the Arts, 1977, 1978, and 1979, and New York State Council on the Arts, 1977, 1979, and 1980; fellow of MacDowell Colony, 1981.

WRITINGS: Anonymous Was a Woman (nonfiction), St. Martin's, 1979; *Reckless Hearts* (nonfiction), St. Martin's, 1981.

WORK IN PROGRESS: "Reckless Hearts," a screenplay adapted from the book by Bank; a motion picture trilogy adapted from the stories by Grace Paley.

SIDELIGHTS: Bank told *CA:* "My 1981 book, *Reckless Hearts,* deals with eccentric, adventurous women outcasts of the American West."

* * *

BANKS, Hal N(orman)   1921-

PERSONAL: Born December 16, 1921, in Pittsburgh, Pa.; son of William March (in repair work) and Florence Marguerite (McKain) Banks; married Virginia Wheeler, September 28, 1946 (divorced July 8, 1971); married Phyllis Eileen Lancaster Davis (an artist and writer), December 24, 1971; children: Kenneth, Jean, Susan, Scott; (stepchildren) Randal, Linda. *Education:* Whittier College, B.A., 1950; San Francisco Theological Seminary, M.Div., 1953; Boston University, S.T.M., 1971; Geneva Theological College, S.T.D., 1976. *Politics:* Independent. *Home and office:* 1016 Crescent Dr., Roswell, N.M. 88201.

CAREER: Ordained United Presbyterian minister, 1953;

youth director at Presbyterian church in Monrovia, Calif., 1948-50; student pastor of Presbyterian church in Moss Beach, Calif., 1952-53; director of Christian education at Presbyterian church in San Anselmo, Calif., 1952-53; minister of Christian education at Presbyterian churches in Pendleton, Ore., 1953-54, Portland, Ore., 1954-55, and Lakewood, Calif., 1955-60; Immanuel United Presbyterian Church, Anchorage, Alaska, minister, 1960-80; writer and lecturer, 1980—. Part-time member of faculty at Alaska Methodist University (now Alaska Pacific University), 1973-76, Chapman College, 1976-78, and University of Alaska and Anchorage Community College, 1976-79. Founder and director of Seminary of the Church (adult education center), Anchorage. Member of ESP Research Associates.

Moderator of Presbytery of the Yukon, 1966-67, past chairman of committees on Christian education and ministerial relations; chairman of Oregon Council of Churches committee on leadership training, 1954-55, Long Beach Council of Churches Division of Christian Education, 1965-67; dean of Christian Leadership School of Greater Anchorage Area Council of Churches, 1961-62, vice-president of council, 1962-66, president, 1966-68. Vice-president of Anchorage Inter-Agency Council, 1961-63; member of board of trustees of Community Presbyterian Hospital, Anchorage, 1962-63, and board of directors of Anchorage Young Men's Christian Association, 1969-74; member of Greater Anchorage Area Borough Library Board, 1969-71. *Military service:* U.S. Coast Guard, 1941-46. *Member:* American Society of Physical Research (fellow), Academy of Religion and Physical Research, Spiritual Frontiers Fellowship. *Awards, honors:* Fellow of College of Human Sciences, International Institute of Integral Human Sciences, Montreal, Quebec.

WRITINGS: Introduction to Psychic Studies, Maverick Publishers, 1976, revised edition, 1980. Writer for "On the Edge of the Unknown," a series broadcast by KBYR-Radio and KEEI-Radio, 1976-77, rebroadcast in Australia and Trinidad. Author of "Between the Cross and the Crossroads," a column in *Anchorage Daily News,* 1966-73. Cofounder and executive editor of *Psychic Spectrum,* 1973; founder and editor of *Barracks Watch.*

WORK IN PROGRESS: Death: A Preface.

SIDELIGHTS: Banks told *CA:* "The foundation upon which a democratic society rests is freedom, with a minimum of restrictions. This inevitably leads to respect for the individual. Thus, the burden of growth to become a mature person rests solely upon the person's own creative efforts. The search for truth, a lifelong adventure, must preclude any authoritarian encroachment. The individual, on the basis of his own personal efforts, makes the ultimate decision as to what is truth for him. It is the person's inner response that is the root of freedom.

"With freedom of the individual as the first principle, my challenge, be it in teaching or in other employment, is to confront a person with choices, both pros and cons. I provide the resources so that the seeker can ultimately become his own authority. This approach permits one to choose from among several alternatives.

"Secondhand information, whether it be from pulpit, lectern in the classroom, or wherever, is usually purely informational and is seldom life-changing. In a relationship I feel free to say what is for me the truth, but I have a responsibility to cite alternatives as well as sources which disagree with what I have stated. So, equipped with the resources, the individual is able to study or research both sides of an issue. He or she then makes his or her own personal decision based upon his or her personality, abilities, and needs."

He added: "My major interests are religion and psychic studies (parapsychology). Within those areas my major interest is survival of the human personality, and its religious and parapsychological implications."

BIOGRAPHICAL/CRITICAL SOURCES: Quarterly Journal of Spiritual Frontiers Fellowship, summer, 1979.

* * *

BARBOUR, Thomas L.
See LESURE, Thomas B(arbour)

* * *

BARCLAY, Ann
See GREIG, Maysie

* * *

BARD, James (Alan) 1925-

PERSONAL: Born June 1, 1925, in Youngstown, Ohio; son of John Linus (a postal worker) and Mildred (Lackey) Bard; children: Jennifer, Christopher. *Education:* University of Pittsburgh, B.S., 1948; Western Reserve University (now Case Western Reserve University), Ph.D., 1953. *Home:* 6811 Mayfield Rd., Mayfield Heights, Ohio 44124. *Office:* 3659 Green Rd., Beachwood, Ohio 44122.

CAREER: Fenn College (now Cleveland State University), Cleveland, Ohio, assistant professor, 1953-58, associate professor, 1958-70, professor of psychology, 1970—. Practicing clinical psychologist. *Military service:* U.S. Navy, 1943-46. *Member:* American Psychological Association, Cleveland Psychological Association, Cleveland Academy of Consulting Psychologists.

WRITINGS: Rational Emotive Therapy in Practice, Research Press, 1980.

WORK IN PROGRESS: Research on faulty reasoning and psychopathology; research on "psychotherapy outcomes if, in fact, there is any such 'treatment' that has any outcome at all."

SIDELIGHTS: Bard commented: "I wrote my book for several reasons, one being my hope that it is possible to convince some graduate students and some interested lay persons that clinical psychology is not all bad (though much is), and secondly to maybe (though not likely) nudge some of my colleagues to consider the possible value in defining and more systematically employing common sense."

* * *

BARE, Colleen Stanley

PERSONAL: Born in Oakland, Calif.; daughter of Carl Jessup (a banker; in feed business) and Harriett (Kirkman) Stanley; married Grant Eugene Bare, June 29, 1947; children: Randall Stanley, Warren Grant. *Education:* Stanford University, A.B., 1946; University of California, Berkeley, M.A., 1950. *Home and office:* 2502 Dorrington Court, Modesto, Calif. 95350.

CAREER: Psychometrist and counselor at public schools in Stanislaus County, Calif., 1946-47; College of Marin, Kentfield, Calif., psychometrist and counselor, 1947-48; freelance writer, 1959—. Creative writing instructor at public schools in Stanislaus County, 1966-70; chairman of Stanislaus County task force on gifted education and Open Enrollment Education Committee, 1974-75. Vice-chairman of Modesto Culture Commission, 1975, chairman, 1976—.

MEMBER: National League of American Pen Women (president, 1964-66), American Association of University Women, California Writers Club, Stanislaus County Psychological Association, Pi Lambda Theta, Delta Kappa Gamma. *Awards, honors:* Prizes from California Writers Club poetry contests, 1966-79, including first prize, 1974, for "What Is Christmas?," and 1979, for "A Lady's Letter to Santa."

WRITINGS: (Also photographer) *The Durable Desert Tortoise* (juvenile), Dodd, 1979; (also photographer) *Ground Squirrels* (juvenile), Dodd, 1980. Contributor of hundreds of poems and articles to magazines, including *Good Housekeeping, Saturday Evening Post, Ladies' Home Journal, Look, McCall's,* and *Christian Home,* and newspapers.

WORK IN PROGRESS: Another children's book, publication by Dodd expected in 1981; light poems; articles.

SIDELIGHTS: Colleen Bare told *CA:* "Writing is my obsession and salvation. Without it life would be much less meaningful. I enjoy the diversity of doing both prose and poetry and am constantly challenged by new directions in my writing. Currently, my travels to areas like the Galapagos Islands have cultivated a new interest in natural and wildlife subjects, particularly for children. My juvenile books reflect this and have given me the opportunity to utilize my lifelong hobby of photography with my writing. Writing is very hard work, and photography is often even harder, so it takes true dedication and motivation to sustain an author."

* * *

BARKER, Dudley 1910-1980(?)
(Lionel Black, Anthony Matthews)

OBITUARY NOTICE—See index for *CA* sketch: Born March 25, 1910, in London, England; died in London, England, c. 1980. Editor, journalist, and author. Barker worked as a news and magazine editor, feature writer, and reporter in London, England, for the *Evening Standard, Daily Herald,* and *John Bull.* He was also an author of both fiction and nonfiction, writing crime novels under the pseudonyms Lionel Black and Anthony Matthews. Barker's books include *The Voice, Laughter in Court, The Young Man's Guide to Journalism,* and *The Man of Principle: A View of John Galsworthy.* Under the name Lionel Black, he wrote *Chance to Die, Two Ladies in Verona, Breakaway,* and *Death Has Green Fingers.* Under the Matthews pseudonym, Barker wrote *Death of Peter Wade, Death By Hoax, Arafat Is Next,* and *The Penny Murders.* Obituaries and other sources: *AB Bookman's Weekly,* January 26, 1981.

* * *

BARKER, Howard 1946-

PERSONAL: Born June 28, 1946, in London, England; son of Sydney Charles (a bookbinder) and Georgina Irene (Carter) Barker; married Sandra Law (an educator), July 24, 1972; children: Thomas. *Education:* University of Sussex, M.A., 1968. *Home:* 57 Freshfield Rd., Brighton, Sussex, England. *Agent:* Judy Daish Associates, Globe Theatre, Shaftesbury Ave., London W. 1, England.

CAREER: Playwright, 1970—; Open Space Theatre, London, England, resident playwright, 1974-75. *Awards, honors:* Arts Council bursary, 1971.

WRITINGS—Plays: "Cheek" (two-act; first produced on the West End at Royal Court Theatre Upstairs, September 10, 1970), contained in *New Short Plays 3*, Methuen, 1972; *Claw and Stripwell* (two plays; "Claw" first produced off the West End at Open Space Theatre, 1975; "Stripwell" first produced on the West End at Royal Court Theatre, 1975),

J. Calder, 1976; *Fair Slaughter* (two-act; first produced on the West End at Royal Court Theatre,1977), J. Calder, 1977; *That Good Between Us* (two-act; first produced at Warehouse Theatre, 1977), J. Calder, 1980; *The Love of a Good Man* (three-act; first produced at Sheffield Crucible Theatre, 1978), J. Calder, 1980.

Unpublished plays: "No One Was Saved" (two-act), first produced on the West End at Royal Court Theatre Upstairs, November 18, 1970; "Edward: The Final Days," first produced off the West End at Open Space Theatre, 1971; "Faceache" (one-act), first produced in London, 1971; "Alpha Alpha" (two-act), first produced off the West End at Open Space Theatre, 1972; "Private Parts" (two-act), first produced in Edinburgh, Scotland, at Traverse Theatre, 1972; "Skipper" [and] "My Sister and I" (two one-act plays), first produced in London at Bush Theatre, 1973; "Rule Britannica" (one-act), first produced in London at King's Head Theatre, 1973; "Bang" (two-act), first produced off the West End at Open Space Theatre, June, 1973; "Wax" (one-act), first produced in Edinburgh, Scotland, at Traverse Theatre, 1976, produced in London at Bush Theatre, 1976; "The Hang of the Gaol" (two-act), first produced in London at Warehouse Theatre, 1978; "The Loud Boy's Life" (three-act), first produced in London at Warehouse Theatre, 1980.

Screenplays: "Made," EMI, 1972; "Aces High," EMI, 1975. Also author of "Rape of Tamar," 1973.

Radio and television plays: "One Afternoon on the North Face of the 63rd Level of the Pyramid of Cheops the Great," British Broadcasting Corp. (BBC) Radio, 1970; "Henry V in Two Parts" BBC-Radio, 1971; "Herman, With Millie and Mick," BBC-Radio, 1972; "Cows," BBC-TV, 1972; "The Chauffeur and the Lady," BBC-TV, December, 1972; "Mutinies," BBC-TV, 1974.

SIDELIGHTS: Barker is one of the new breed of British playwrights who has taken on the role of "investigative reporter as well as moral sharpshooter," reported the *New York Times*. His first play, "Cheek," concerned a lustful young man's hatred for his dying father. Helen Dawson wrote, "Barker has succeeded, very well for a first attempt, in creating a sub-suburban world, where you need 'cheek' to be out of the ordinary, to be noticed."

A *Stage* critic praised Barker's 1973 play, "Bang": "This is a good drama—entertaining, original, probing beneath the surface of our images of ourselves." The theme of the play was "the dangerous similarity between the extremes of anarchy, and law, worked out in terms of a grotesque 1970's-style eternal triangle."

Barker told *CA:* "The popular theatre does not exist. The theatre of the people does not exist. There is only a theatre of some of the people. In this crippled state, to be a popular writer involves writing only of these people, and to be successful commercially is to be successful in describing the lives of these people. Hence the term 'popular' with reference to dramatists is empty and without resonance."

BIOGRAPHICAL/CRITICAL SOURCES: Observer Review, September 13, 1970; *Listener,* September 17, 1970; *Plays and Players,* November, 1970, January, 1971; *Variety,* July 21, 1971, September 13, 1972; *Stage,* December 14, 1972, June 7, 1973; *New York Times,* March 18, 1979, December 7, 1979.

* * *

BARKER, Nicolas (John) 1932-

PERSONAL: Born December 6, 1932, in Cambridge, En-

gland; son of Sir Ernest and Olivia Stuart (Horner) Barker; married Joanna Mary Sophia Nyda Cotton, 1962; children: Emma, Christian, Olivia, Cecilia, Cosmo. *Education:* Received M.A. from New College, Oxford. *Home:* 22 Clarendon Rd., London W.11, England. *Office:* British Library, Great Russell St., London W.C.1, England.

CAREER: Associated with Bailliere, Tindall & Cox, and Rupert Hart-Davis, 1959; National Portrait Gallery, London, England, assistant keeper, 1964; associated with Macmillan & Co., Ltd., 1965; Oxford University Press, production manager, 1972; head of conservation at British Library in London. *Member:* Royal National Institute for the Blind (member of publications board of directors), Bibliographical Society (vice-president), Printing Historical Society, William Morris Society, Amici Thomae Mori (president), Pilgrim Trust, St. Bride's Foundation, London Library, Friends of the National Library, Roxburghe Club.

WRITINGS: (Editor and contributor) Stanley Morison, *The Likeness of Thomas More: An Iconographical Survey of Three Centuries,* Burns & Oates, 1963; *The Publications of the Roxburghe Club: An Essay With a Bibliographical Table,* Roxburghe Club, 1964; (editor) *Portrait of an Obsession: The Life of Sir Thomas Phillips, the World's Greatest Book Collector,* Constable, 1967; (with Douglas Cleverdon) *Stanley Morison, 1889-1967: A Radio Portrait,* W. S. Cowell, 1969; *Politics and Script: Aspects of Authority and Freedom in the Development of Graeco-Latin Script From the Sixth Century B.C. to the Twentieth Century A.D.,* Clarendon Press, 1972; *The Early Life of James McBey: An Autobiography, 1883-1911,* Oxford University Press, 1977; *Bibliotheca Lindesiana,* Quaritch for the Roxburghe Club, 1978; *Essays and Papers of A.N.L. Munby,* Scolar Press, 1978; *The Oxford University Press and the Spread of Learning, 1478-1978: An Illustrated History,* Clarendon Press, 1978. Editor of *Book Collector,* 1965—.

WORK IN PROGRESS: An Enquiry Into the Nature of Certain Nineteenth-Century Pamphlets, publication expected in 1981.

AVOCATIONAL INTERESTS: Collecting books.

* * *

BARNES, Julian 1946-

PERSONAL: Born January 19, 1946, in Leicester, England. *Education:* Magdalen College, Oxford, B.A. (with honors), 1968. *Agent:* A. D. Peters & Co. Ltd., 10 Buckingham St., London WC2N 6BU, England.

CAREER: London Sunday Times, London, England, lexicographer for *Oxford English Dictionary Supplement,* 1969-72; free-lance writer, 1972—.

WRITINGS: Metroland (novel), St. Martin's, 1980. Television critic for *New Statesman,* 1977—, assistant literary editor, 1977-79; contributing editor of *New Review,* 1977-78; deputy literary editor of *London Sunday Times,* 1979—.

WORK IN PROGRESS: Another novel, publication by J. Cape expected in 1981 or 1982.

SIDELIGHTS: Julian Barnes told *CA:* "I don't think writers—especially beginning writers—should either indulge themselves or bore their readers with 'background,' 'influences,' 'critical moments in their writing life,' and so on. Nor on the whole should they be encouraged to be critics of their own work—they're not good enough at it. 'Where you're going' and 'where you've been' as a writer are like two bales of hay to Buridan's ass: you can starve to death contemplating the two of them. Writers should get on with writing, rather than fret about what makes them want to do it in the first place. There'll be plenty of time to turn that over in their minds when they run out of books to write. If such a time never comes, so much the better.''

* * *

BARNETT, Lincoln (Kinnear) 1909-1979

PERSONAL: Born February 12, 1909, in New York, N.Y.; died September 8, 1979, in Pittsburgh, Pa.; son of Leon H. (a mining engineer and inventor) and Jessie (Kinnear) Barnett; married Hildegarde Harris, 1935; children: Timothy Lincoln, Robert Morgan. *Education:* Princeton University, B.A., 1929; Columbia School of Journalism, B.Litt., 1931, M.S., 1933. *Residence:* Westport, N.Y.

CAREER: New York Herald Tribune, New York City, reporter, 1932-37; *Life,* New York City, worked as staff writer, domestic news editor, war correspondent in England and North Africa, Hollywood correspondent, and articles editor, 1937-46, free-lance writer, 1946-79. *Awards, honors:* National Book Award Special Citation, 1949, for *The Universe and Dr. Einstein;* George Westinghouse Science Award from American Association for the Advancement of Science and Benjamin Franklin Magazine Award, both 1953, for "The World We Live In" series, and both 1956, for "The Epic of Man" series.

WRITINGS: The Universe and Dr. Einstein, foreword by Albert Einstein, W. Sloane, 1948, 2nd revised edition, New American Library, 1964; *Writing on Life: Sixteen Close-Ups* (biographical essays), W. Sloane, 1951; *The Treasure of Our Tongue: The Story of English From Its Obscure Beginnings to Its Present Eminence as the Most Widely Spoken Language,* Knopf, 1964.

Editor with editorial staff of *Life* magazine; juvenile; all published by Golden Press unless otherwise noted: *The Wonders of Life on Earth,* Simon & Schuster, 1955, revised edition, Golden Press, 1961; *Prehistoric Animals: Dinosaurs and Other Reptiles and Mammals,* 1958; *The Sea: The Strange Animals and Plants of the Oceans,* 1958; *The Epic of Man,* 1962; *The Wonders of Animal Life: How Animals Adapt for Survival,* 1963; *The Ancient Adirondacks,* Time-Life Books, 1974.

SIDELIGHTS: In 1948 Lincoln Barnett wrote *The Universe and Mr. Einstein,* an explanation of Albert Einstein's theories concerning relativity and the workings of the universe to the average individual. R. F. Humphreys of the *Yale Review* applauded the book as "neither superficial nor erudite; [it] requires no special knowledge to be brought to its reading. It will, however, provide for the layman who is armed with a normal curiosity about the simple physical phenomena around him an experience of stimulating and exciting thought." Waldemar Kaempffert of the *Saturday Review of Literature* also commended the author: "Gifted as he is with a penetrating mind, and a sense of style, [Barnett] interprets what he sees with a simplicity and clarity that few popularizers can match."

BIOGRAPHICAL/CRITICAL SOURCES: Christian Science Monitor, January 20, 1949; *Saturday Review of Literature,* January 22, 1949; *Yale Review,* summer, 1949.*

* * *

BARNEY, Stephen A(llen) 1942-

PERSONAL: Born October 10, 1942, in Rocky Mount, N.C.; son of Marshall Hobart (a social security administrator) and Mary (Swett) Barney; married Cherry Green, September 8, 1962; children: Thomas Baldwin, Peter Greene. *Education:* University of Virginia, B.A., 1964; Harvard University, M.A., 1965, Ph.D., 1969. *Home:* 19 Lansdowne Ave., Hamden, Conn. 06517. *Office:* Department of English, University of California, Irvine, Calif. 92717.

CAREER: Yale University, New Haven, Conn., assistant professor, 1968-75, associate professor of English, 1975-78; University of Virginia, Charlottesville, visiting associate professor of English, 1978; University of California, Irvine, professor of English, 1979—. *Member:* Modern Language Association of America, Mediaeval Academy of America, Early English Text Society, Connecticut Academy of Arts and Sciences. *Awards, honors:* Woodrow Wilson fellowship, 1965; Kent fellowship, 1965-68; Morse fellowship, 1972-73; Elliott Prize from Mediaeval Academy of America, 1973, for "Troilus Bound"; American Council of Learned Societies fellowship, 1975; National Endowment for the Humanities fellowship, 1979-81.

WRITINGS: Word-Hoard: An Introduction to Old English Vocabulary, Yale University Press, 1977; *Allegories of History, Allegories of Love,* Archon, 1979; (editor) *Chaucer's Troilus: Essays in Criticism,* Archon, 1980. Contributor to literature journals.

WORK IN PROGRESS: Editing *Distinctiones Abel* of Peter the Chanter; writing notes on Chaucer's *Troilus,* to be included in 3rd edition of Robinson's *Chaucer,* edited by R. A. Pratt and L. D. Benson, publication expected in 1983; "Allegory," an article to be included in *Dictionary of the Middle Ages,* for Scribner.

SIDELIGHTS: Stephen A. Barney commented to *CA:* "My recent work in *distinctiones* (allegorized dictionaries of biblical and theological terms) arose out of an effort to find specific allegorical meanings in the imagery and events of such secular poets as Chaucer and Langland. But pursuing the *distinctiones* tradition has led me down two more fruitful by-paths: an interest in the theory of textual criticism, and an interest—especially inspired by the work of Richard and Mary Rouse—in the form and order of knowledge in the Middle Ages. I now think that the content of allegory, especially of biblical allegories, is much influenced, if not determined, but the form of its presentation in medieval books. And Chaucer's *Troilus* is the finest work of medieval literature."

* * *

BARR, Jennifer 1945-

PERSONAL: Born July 25, 1945; married Roderick Barr, 1969; children: three sons. *Education:* Western Michigan University, B.A., 1968. *Residence:* Fulton, Md. *Office address:* P.O. Box 201, Columbia, Md. 21045..

CAREER: High school history teacher in Frederick Md., 1969-70; Juan Crespi Junior High School, Richmond, Calif., teacher of history and English, 1971-72; writer. Counselor and member of board of directors of Howard County Rape Crisis Center, 1976—.

WRITINGS: Within a Dark Wood (nonfiction), Doubleday, 1979.

SIDELIGHTS: Jennifer Barr told *CA: "Within a Dark Wood* portrays a rape through the eyes of its victim from its beginning through the final trial. The book describes the rape's shattering effects and the slow process of rebuilding trust, faith, and confidence. I was propelled to write this book when my firsthand experience showed me how little most of us know about rape and how many misconceptions exist in the minds of people who sincerely want to help. The book was designed to fill that faceless void behind the headlines and to continue the movie scenes that depict the violence without dealing with the long aftermath. My writing goal was to portray, as accurately as possible, the events and feelings of that year, limiting creative expression to building characters and filling details not essential to the accuracy of the story. As my first attempt at writing, it was an intensive course in literature.''

BIOGRAPHICAL/CRITICAL SOURCES: Baltimore Sun, September 30, 1979, January 29, 1980; New York Daily News, November 19, 1979; Newspaper Enterprise Association, January 14, 1980; Columbia Flier, February 21, 1980.

*   *   *

BARRON, (Richard) Neil 1934-

PERSONAL: Born March 23, 1934, in Hollywood, Calif.; son of James C. (in sales) and Dorothy (Terrell) Barron; married Dorothy Weiss, 1966 (marriage ended); married Carolyn Ann Goyer (a teaching aide), August 19, 1978; children: Craig R., Felicia A. Education: University of California, Riverside, A.B., 1961; University of California, Berkeley, M.L.S., 1964. Home and office: 1149 Lime Pl., Vista, Calif. 92083.

CAREER: U.S. Peace Corps, worked in libraries in Lahore, Tando Jam, and Peshawar, Pakistan, 1962-63; Queens Borough Public Library, Jamaica, N.Y., librarian, 1964-65; Columbia University Libraries, New York, N.Y., assistant to associate director of libraries and manager of chemistry library, 1965-67; California State University Library, Sacramento, assistant librarian for technical services, 1967-70; Baker & Taylor Co., Somerville, N.J., coordinator of library services, 1970-72; University of South Florida, Tampa, assistant director of technical services, 1972-73; World Book-Childcraft International, Chicago, Ill., sales manager, 1973—. Military service: U.S. Army, 1954-56; served in Germany. Member: Science Fiction Research Association. Awards, honors: Outstanding reference book award from Library Journal and Choice, 1976, for Anatomy of Wonder.

WRITINGS: (Contributor) Jack Williamson, Science Fiction: Education for Tomorrow, Owlswick, 1980; (editor) Anatomy of Wonder: Science Fiction, Bowker, 1976, 2nd edition published as Anatomy of Wonder: A Critical Guide to Science Fiction, 1981. Contributor of articles and reviews to magazines, including Choice. Editor of Science Fiction and Fantasy Book Review, 1979-80.

SIDELIGHTS: Barron commented: ''An active science fiction reader in the early 1950's, my interest in the field is more academic today. Having recognized in the late 1960's that the best science fiction was worthy of more sustained critical attention than it was receiving, I wrote two survey essays for Choice, urging that a retrospective critical guide to the best works be published, later undertaking this myself, aided by several knowledgeable colleagues.''

AVOCATIONAL INTERESTS: Reading, music, archery.

*   *   *

BARROW, Pamela
See HOWARTH, Pamela

*   *   *

BARRY, Roger Graham 1935-

PERSONAL: Born November 13, 1935, in Sheffield, England; came to the United States in 1968; son of Graham

Charles and Winifred (Watson) Barry; married Valerie Tompkin, October 3, 1959; children: Rachel, Christina. Education: University of Liverpool, B.A., 1957; McGill University, M.Sc., 1959; University of Southampton, Ph.D., 1965. Office: Institute of Arctic and Alpine Research, University of Colorado, Boulder, Colo. 80309.

CAREER: University of Southampton, Southampton, England, lecturer, 1960-66 and 1967-68; Department of Energy, Mines, and Resources, Ottawa, Ontario, research scientist in geographical branch, 1966-67; University of Colorado, Boulder, associate professor, 1968-71, professor of geography, 1971—. Director of World Data Center for Glaciology, 1976—.

WRITINGS: (With R. J. Chorley) Atmosphere, Weather, and Climate, Holt, 1970, revised edition, Methuen, 1976; (with A. H. Perry) Synoptic Climatology, Methuen, 1973; (editor with J. D. Ives) Arctic and Alpine Environments, Methuen, 1975; Mountain Weather and Climate, Methuen, 1981. Contributor to professional journals.

SIDELIGHTS: Roger Barry told CA: ''My current research interests relate to the present and past physical environment of the Arctic and Subarctic, and in particular to interactions between the atmosphere and the snow and ice cover. Study of these interactions, using meteorological and satellite data, provides valuable information on climatic variability and change, especially with respect to causes of the ice ages.''

*   *   *

BARTH, Edna 1914-1980
(Edna Weiss)

OBITUARY NOTICE—See index for CA sketch: Born March 13, 1914, in Marblehead, Mass.; died October 1, 1980, in New York, N.Y. Editor and author. Barth served as an editor of children's books at McGraw-Hill and T. Y. Crowell before becoming vice-president of William Morrow and editor-in-chief of Lothrop, Lee & Shepard Co. She also wrote books for children, including Truly Elizabeth, The Day Luis Was Lost, and I'm Nobody: Who Are You?; The Story of Emily Dickinson. Obituaries and other sources: Publishers Weekly, October 17, 1980.

*   *   *

BARTZ, Patricia McBride 1921-
(Patricia McBride)

PERSONAL: Born February 16, 1921, in Australia; daughter of John Duncan (a builder) and Jessie (a teacher; maiden name, Boyes) McBride; married Carl Frederick Bartz (a foreign service information officer), June 11, 1948; children: Ann Bartz Potter, Isobel. Education: University of Melbourne, B.A. (with honors), 1938, diploma in education, 1939, M.A. (with honors), 1943; University of California, Berkeley, Ph.D., 1950. Home: 6242 Cheryl Dr., Falls Church, Va. 22044.

CAREER: University of Melbourne, Melbourne, Australia, lecturer, 1939-46; University of California, Berkeley, lecturer, 1946-50; National University, Seoul, Korea, lecturer, 1969-70. Director of Northern Virginia Soil and Water Conservation District, 1974—. Member: Association of American Geographers. Awards, honors: Award from South Korea's Ministry of Culture for South Korea.

WRITINGS: (Under name Patricia McBride; with G. L. Wood) The Pacific Basin, Oxford University Press, 1940; (contributor; under name Patricia McBride) Wood, editor, Australia: Its Resources and Development, Macmillan, 1947; South Korea, Oxford University Press, 1972.

SIDELIGHTS: Patricia Bartz told *CA:* "I am currently active in public participation and education programs relating to erosion and water pollution prevention in Fairfax County, Virginia."

*   *   *

BASELEY, Godfrey 1904-

PERSONAL: Born October 2, 1904; son of Walter Ernest (a farmer) and Mary (Court) Baseley; married Betty Hartwright (a teacher); children: Jane Baseley Brodie, Helen Baseley Sims. *Education:* Attended secondary school in York, England. *Politics:* "Floating Voter." *Religion:* Society of Friends (Quakers). *Home and office:* Ambridge, Corse Lawn, near Gloucester, England.

CAREER: British Broadcasting Corp. (BBC), England, producer and organizer of rural programs for radio and television, including "The Archers of Ambridge," 1950-51, editor, 1952; BMT Visuals (filmmakers), Birmingham, England, director and scriptwriter, 1960-65; Godfrey Baseley Ltd. (agricultural information consultants), England, chairman, 1962-74. Lecturer and meetings organizer for Ministry of Information during World War II. Host of a gardening program on Associated Television Ltd. *Member:* Guild of Agricultural Journalists, Farmers Club.

WRITINGS: The Archers: A Slice of My Life, Sidgwick & Jackson, 1971; *A Village Portrait,* Sidgwick & Jackson, 1972; *Country Calendar,* Sidgwick & Jackson, 1975; *A Country Compendium,* Sidgwick & Jackson, 1977. Gardening correspondent for *Birmingham Mail.* Contributor to magazines, including *Country Life, Field, Listener, Country Fair,* and *Farmers Weekly,* and newspapers.

WORK IN PROGRESS: The Diary of a Countryman; Another Ambridge; research on the pattern and style of English village life, 1900-1918.

SIDELIGHTS: Baseley commented: "My major interests are concerned with the life and work in rural areas. I created Britain's longest running daily radio serial, 'The Archers of Ambridge' in 1950, and it is still running. I have lectured to overseas students in collaboration with Radio Nederland on the use of the daily serial in agricultural education and I lecture on English rural life to a wide variety of clubs and societies."

*   *   *

BASSETT, George William 1910-

PERSONAL: Born March 26, 1910, in Orange, Australia; son of Francis (a teacher) and Flora (a teacher; maiden name, McPhee) Bassett; married Phyllis A. Breakwell (a teacher), December 29, 1934; children: Anna Bassett Farrelly, Jennifer Bassett Davidson. *Education:* University of Sydney, B.A., 1929, diploma in education, 1930, M.A., 1932; University of London, Ph.D., 1940. *Religion:* Church of England. *Home:* 146 Macquarie St., St. Lucia, Queensland 4067, Australia.

CAREER: Teacher, 1930-42; lecturer at teacher's college in Sydney, Australia, 1943-47; principal at Armidale Teacher's College, 1948-60; University of Queensland, St. Lucia, Australia, professor of education, 1961—. Member of Commonwealth Council for Educational Administration, 1965—, and Queensland Board of Advanced Education, 1971—; president of Australian College of Education, 1968-69; member of council of Darwin Community College, 1977-79.

MEMBER: Australian Institute for Educational Administration, Royal Society of Arts (fellow), Queensland Institute for Educational Administration (fellow), Queensland Institute for Educational Research (president, 1962). *Awards, honors:* Canadian Commonwealth fellowship, 1965; fellow of Australian College of Education, 1978; Member of Order of Australia, 1979; Mackie Medal for education from Australia and New Zealand Association for the Advancement of Science, 1980.

WRITINGS: Headmasters for Better Schools, Queensland University Press, 1963; *Each One Is Different,* Australian Council for Educational Research, 1965; *Teaching in the Primary School,* Novak, 1967; *Innovation in Primary Education,* Wiley, 1970; (editor) *Planning in Australian Education,* Australian Council for Educational Research, 1970; *Primary Education in Australia,* McGraw, 1974; *Individual Differences,* Allen & Unwin, 1978; *Teachers in Australia, 1979,* Australian College of Education, 1980; *Modern Primary Schools in Australia,* Allen & Unwin, 1981.

SIDELIGHTS: Bassett told *CA:* "My books are primarily textbooks. I write them because I like writing, but I regard them as adjuncts to my university teaching, which widen my influence, at least throughout Australia."

He added: "I have always tried to write simply and lucidly, as I dislike unnecessary jargon. I find the use of English in many books in the social sciences, including education, appallingly prolix and pretentious.

"I have been fortunately attracted to primary education, and was greatly stimulated by the revolutionary changes in England during the 1960's and the ferment in America at the same time. The cycle of innovation-reaction-accountability-back to the basics that occurred abroad followed much the same pattern in Australia. I have tried to present a stable view, free of innovation in a bandwagon sense, stressing the need to use modern theory affectively, to cater to individual differences, and to renew the primary school as a community in which children can develop in a protected and stimulating environment.

"My latest study of teachers in Australia has revealed considerable advances in the quality and qualifications of teachers since a similar study that was done in 1963. Whether teachers have improved in professional dedication since that time I could not tell from this research, but they certainly have improved in their capacity for professional behavior."

*   *   *

BATAILLE, Gretchen M. 1944-

PERSONAL: Born September 28, 1944, in Mishawaka, Ind.; daughter of George H. and Adrienne (in sales; maiden name, VanderHeyden) Mueller; children: Marc, Erin. *Education:* Attended Purdue University, 1962-65; California State Polytechnic University, B.S., 1966, M.S., 1967; Drake University, D.A., 1977. *Home:* 1602 Grand Ave., Ames, Iowa 50010. *Office:* 317 Ross Hall, Iowa State University, Ames, Iowa 50011.

CAREER: Iowa State University, Ames, instructor, 1967-77, assistant professor of English and Indian studies, 1977—. Member of Iowa Civil Rights Commission, 1975-79, chairperson, 1977-79; member of advisory council of Iowa Humanities Board and advisory committee on Indian education of Iowa Department of Public Instruction; consultant to U.S. Department of Health, Education and Welfare, 1977-80. *Member:* National Association of Interdisciplinary Ethnic Studies (member of executive council), Modern Language Association of America, Association for the Study of American Indian Literatures (member of executive board), Midwest Modern Language Association.

WRITINGS: (Editor with Charles L. P. Silet and David M. Gradwohl) *The Worlds Between Two Rivers: Perspectives on American Indians in Iowa,* Iowa State University Press, 1978; *American Indian Literature: A Selected Bibliography,* Department of Public Instruction, State of Iowa, 1978; (editor with Silet) *The Pretend Indians: Images of Native Americans in the Movies,* Iowa State University Press, 1980; (with Kathleen Sands) *Native Women in a Changing World: Their Lives as They Told Them,* University of Nebraska Press, 1981. Author of multi-media program, "Inside the Cigar Store." Contributor to journals, including *Women and Film, Poet and Critic, Journal of Popular Film, Quarterly Review of Film Studies,* and *Melus.* Associate editor of *Explorations in Ethnic Studies.*

SIDELIGHTS: Gretchen Bataille told *CA:* "The distortions and misrepresentations of the American Indian which have been perpetuated by mass media and textbooks are of particular concern to me. Most of my research has been aimed at discovering what exists and exposing it. Research on the literature of American Indians is essential to correct the mistaken notions fostered by non-Indian writers and the media."

* * *

BATE, Sam 1907-

PERSONAL: Born December 30, 1907; son of Samuel (a preacher) and Alice (Kirkham) Bate; married Mavis Dorothy Cole, November 6, 1926. *Education:* Attended secondary school in England. *Politics:* Conservative. *Religion:* "Can't decide!" *Home and office:* 16 Bridge St., Illogan, Redruth, Cornwall TR16 4SA, England.

CAREER: Professional actor, 1928—. Playwright, 1958—. Air-raid warden in Coventry, England, during World War II. *Member:* Society of Authors, League of Dramatists, Wild Life Preservation Society.

*WRITINGS—*Plays; all published by Kenyon-Deane, except as noted: *Flora Macdonald's Mission* (one-act), 1956; *Legacy of Ladies* (one-act), 1956; *Grannie Takes Helm* (one-act), 1956; *They Wanted a Leader* (one-act), 1956; *Holiday Haunts* (three-act), 1956; *Rugs and Pewter* (one-act), 1957; *Her Husband's Harem* (one-act), 1958; *Crisis in Clover* (three-act comedy), Walter H. Baker, 1958; *Head of the House* (one-act), Samuel French, 1958; *Well! Well!* (three-act), Walter H. Baker, 1958.

Love and Lavender (one-act), Kenyon House Press, 1960; *Monday's Washing Day* (one-act), 1960; *Wedding Crisis* (one-act), 1961; *Someone Else's Pretty Toys* (three-act), 1961; *Pickle in Paradise* (three-act), 1961; *Black Tulip* (three-act), H.W.F. Deane, 1961; *Mrs. Dooley's Table* (one-act comedy), Walter H. Baker, 1961; *Tarzan's Mother* (one-act), 1962; *Motive for Murder* (three-act), 1962; *A Question of Colour,* Samuel French, 1964; *Wishing Day Welcome* (one-act), 1964; *Christmas Cheer* (one-act), 1964; *End of the Honeymoon* (three-act), 1964; *Right of Way,* Walter H. Baker, 1966; *Hit or Miss* (one-act comedy), Walter H. Baker, 1966; *Christmas Crackers* (one-act comedy), Walter H. Baker, 1967; *Royal Carpet* (one-act), 1969.

Christmas Spirit (one-act), 1973; *Raising the Roof* (three-act), 1973; *Playback* (one-act), Samuel French, 1974; *Honeymoon for One* (one-act), 1977; *Murder at Eight,* Samuel French, 1977; *Decline and Fall* (one-act), Samuel French, 1977; *Stage Door Murder* (one-act), New Playwrights Network, 1979; *South Seas Sighting* (one-act), New Playwrights Network, 1979; *Quiet Places* (one-act), New Playwrights Network, 1979; *Murder at Deem House* (three-act), Samuel

French, 1980; *Dummy Run* (three-act), Toneel Centrale, 1980. Also author of *Rumour* (one-act).

*WORK IN PROGRESS—*Plays: *Double Djinn* (three-act); *Bottom's Up* (three-act); *Unscheduled Stop* (one-act).

SIDELIGHTS: Bate told *CA:* "I am a man of the theatre. I believe people go to the theatre to be entertained. I write to that end—to entertain—and, with the majority of my plays, to give the audience some good laughs. I don't believe in preaching in plays. That is for the church, not the theatre. Social matters are for politicians. If I make people laugh I am doing them more good than church or state.

"Although I have not dramatized any of these things, I am extremely interested in the myths of history—things taken as true by almost everyone but which are completely untrue. There was never a Gunpowder Plot, for instance, and Guido Fawkes never attempted to blow up Parliament. Joan of Arc was never burned at the stake but was alive twenty years later; a peasant girl was burned in her place. Richard III was not a wicked murderer of two princes; he was the only king to be elected by popular vote. The princes were of no danger to him—they had been eliminated from the succession by an act of Parliament—but they were a danger to Henry VII. Macbeth did not murder Duncan—he killed him in battle. Duncan was the wicked king. Macbeth ruled for seventeen years and was a very popular monarch in Scotland."

* * *

BATES, Peter Watson 1920-

PERSONAL: Born June 25, 1920, in New Plymouth, New Zealand; son of Thomas Herbert (an architect) and Emma (Watson) Bates; married Joan Winifred Lewis, September 15, 1945; children: Shirley Joan Bates Oliver, Neville Peter. *Education:* Attended high school in New Plymouth, New Zealand. *Religion:* Anglican. *Home:* 43 Raukawa St., Stokes Valley, Lower Hutt, New Zealand. *Office:* INL Print, Eastern Hutt Rd., Taita, Lower Hutt, New Zealand.

CAREER: Taranaki Herald, Taranaki, New Zealand, reporter, 1938-41 and 1945-52; *Taranaki Daily News,* Taranaki, chief reporter, 1952-54; *Auckland Star,* Auckland, New Zealand, chief reporter, 1954-58; *Church and People,* managing editor, 1958-68; *Hutt News,* New Zealand, editor, 1968-80; *INL Print,* Taita, New Zealand, special publications editor, 1980—. Marriage guidance counselor with Hutt Valley Marriage Guidance Council; publicity director for Stokes Valley Recreation Complex Promotion Group. *Military service:* New Zealand Army, 1941-45. *Member:* Stokes Valley Rotary Club.

WRITINGS: Supply Company, War Histories Branch, Department of Internal Affairs, 1955; *The Red Mountain,* R. Hale, 1966; *Man Out of Mind,* R. Hale, 1968; *Old Men Are Fools,* R. Hale, 1970; *A Kind of Treason,* R. Hale, 1973. Author of columns; contributor to New Zealand newspapers.

WORK IN PROGRESS: Behold, a Cry, a novel; research for a murder mystery.

SIDELIGHTS: Bates commented: "I write because I want to write, and have wanted to almost as long as I can remember. In my plots, I like to work around an idea which is not so much a 'message' as a point of view. The story, or the conflicts of the story, tend to be secondary to the working out of conflict—the story is the vehicle for achieving this, and must be strong enough to hold interest, yet be subsidiary to the central purpose.

"Other interests are art, photography, and physical fitness.

My wife is a painter and I am an exponent of black and white, so we share an interest and tend to view the world from the point of view of its potentiality as a picture. I'm a mildly fanatical swimmer and runner, and I guess this and art together tie in with my love of the outdoors. On reflection, I suppose this shows up in my work, which tends toward the outdoors. I have trouble trying to work out a story entirely indoors—I like room to move. We live on a half-acre section, backing on bush.''

AVOCATIONAL INTERESTS: International travel, collecting pictures and photographs of travels.

* * *

BATTEN, James Knox 1936-

PERSONAL: Born January 11, 1936, in Suffolk, Va.; son of Eugene Taylor (an agronomist and farmer) and Josephine (Winslow) Batten; married Jean Elaine Trueworthy, February 22, 1958; children: Mark Winslow, Laura Taylor, Taylor Edison. *Education:* Davidson College, B.S., 1957; Princeton University, M.P.A., 1962. *Religion:* Presbyterian. *Home:* 8125 Southwest 52nd Ave., Miami, Fla. 33143. *Office:* Knight-Ridder Newspapers, Inc., One Herald Plaza, Miami, Fla. 33101.

CAREER: Washington bureau correspondent for Knight Newspapers (now Knight-Ridder Newspapers), 1965-70; *Detroit Free Press,* Detroit, Mich., editorial staff member, 1970-72; *Charlotte Observer,* Charlotte, N.C., executive editor, 1972-75; Knight-Ridder Newspapers, Inc., Miami, Fla., vice-president, 1975-80, senior vice-president, 1980—. Presbyterian deacon, 1967-70. *Military service:* U.S. Army, 1958-60; became first lieutenant. *Member:* American Society of Newspaper Editors. *Awards, honors:* George Polk Memorial Award, 1968, for regional reporting; award from Sidney Hillman Foundation, 1968.

WRITINGS: Arms Control and the Problem of Evasion (monograph), Center of International Studies (Princeton, N.J.), 1962. Contributor of numerous articles to periodicals, including *New York Times Magazine, New Republic, Reporter,* and *Presbyterian Survey.*

* * *

BAUER, Malcolm Clair 1914-

PERSONAL: Born March 19, 1914, in Enterprise, Ore.; son of John Jacob (a grain broker) and Lucille (Corkins) Bauer; married Roberta Moody, July 11, 1937; children: Bette, Mary, Kent, Jean. *Education:* University of Oregon, B.S., 1935; graduate study at Harvard University, 1950-51. *Home:* 1641 Southwest Englewood Dr., Lake Oswego, Ore. 97034. *Office:* 1320 Southwest Broadway, Portland, Ore. 97201.

CAREER/WRITINGS: Eugene Register Guard, Eugene, Ore., reporter and news editor, 1935-36; *Pendleton East-Oregonian,* Pendleton, Ore., news editor, 1936; *Oregonian,* Portland, Ore., began in 1936, became city editor, 1941-51, associate editor, 1951-79, book editor, 1951-79, and editorial page editor, 1977-79. Oregon correspondent for *Christian Science Monitor* and *London Economist.* Lecturer in journalism, Portland State College, 1956—; Oregon commissioner of Education Commission of the States, 1966-81. Member of board of directors of Reed College; chairman of Oregon Mental Health Board, 1972—; trustee of Mills College. *Military service:* U.S. Army; served during World War II; became colonel; received Bronze Star Medal, Legion of Merit with Oak Leaf Cluster, and Order of British Empire. *Member:* American Society of Newspaper Editors, Oregon

Historical Society (past president), Phi Delta Phi, Phi Beta Kappa, Phi Delta Theta.

* * *

BAZELON, Irwin 1922-

PERSONAL: Born June 4, 1922, in Evanston, Ill.; son of Roy and Jeanette (Green) Bazelon; married Cecile Gray (a painter), 1960. *Education:* De Paul University, B.A., 1944, M.A., 1945; attended Mills College, 1946-48. *Home and office:* 142 East 71st St., New York, N.Y. 10021.

CAREER: Composer. Composer-in-residence at Wolftrap, Va., 1974, and at University of Akron, 1979. Guest conductor of National Symphony Orchestra, Detroit Symphony Orchestra, National Symphony of France, and Kansas City Philharmonic. *Member:* American Society of Composers, Authors, and Publishers. *Awards, honors:* MacDowell Colony fellowship, 1949-50 and 1952; Yaddo fellowship, 1969.

WRITINGS: Knowing the Score: Notes on Film Music, Van Nostrand, 1975.

Published compositions: *Piano Suite in Two Volumes,* Southern Publishing, 1950; *Five Pieces for Piano,* Weintraub, 1951; *Five Pieces for Cello and Piano,* Weintraub, 1951; *Sonatine for Piano,* Weintraub, 1952; *Short Symphony,* Boosey & Hawkes, 1965; *Brass Quintet,* Boosey & Hawkes, 1965; *Symphony No. 5,* Boosey & Hawkes, 1973; *Propulsions,* Boosey & Hawkes, 1978; *Churchill Downs Concerto,* Boosey & Hawkes, 1978; *Double Crossings for Trumpet and Percussion,* Boosey & Hawkes, 1978; *A Quiet Piece,* Boosey & Hawkes, 1979; *Duo for Viola and Piano,* Novello, 1981; *Imprints for Piano,* Novello, 1981; *Partnership,* Novello, 1981; *De-Tonations,* Novello, 1981. Also composer of *Symphony No. 7.* Composer of film scores.

Recordings: ''Short Symphony,'' Louisville Records, 1967; ''Symphony No. 5,'' CRI Records, 1973; ''Brass Quintet,'' CRI Records, 1975; ''Churchill Downs Concerto,'' CRI Records, 1975; ''Propulsions,'' CRI Records, 1975; ''Duo for Viola and Piano,'' CRI Records, 1977; ''Woodwind Quintet,'' Orion Records, 1979.

SIDELIGHTS: Originally shy, withdrawn, and beset by a hearing impairment, Bazelon's early studies included a short time with composer Paul Hindemith at Yale University. Bazelon then left New England for the less restrictive environment of California. Surgery corrected his hearing problem, and the dynamic personality change that followed is evident in such musical compositions as ''Testimony to a Big City,'' which uses drums, gongs, cowbells, wood blocks, maracas, xylophones, glockenspiels, and tubas.

Bazelon supported himself primarily by his compositions which, at the beginning, included music for television commercials. He moved on to television films and music for documentary films, finally becoming secure enough financially to devote all of his time to symphonic music.

Bazelon composed the incidental music for the American Shakespeare Festival Theatre productions of ''Taming of the Shrew'' in 1958 and ''Merry Wives of Windsor'' in 1959. He wrote the music for ''What Makes Sammy Run?,'' first broadcast by the National Broadcasting Company, Inc. (NBC-TV) in 1959, and for ''Wilma,'' broadcast by NBC-TV in December, 1977. ''De-Tonations'' for brass quintet and orchestra, commissioned by the National Endowment for the Arts, was first performed in New York City at Carnegie Hall in April, 1979.

He commented to *CA:* ''I suspect I am an old-fashioned composer because I believe that music is a rhythmic-emotional experience. The intellectual aspect of how a composer puts a piece together is a personal matter and I do not have to share my 'secrets' with the public or private sector of my musical life.

"Music to me is not a competitive race or an artistic contest; it is a love affair, a marriage. I have always felt this way, and still do. Music does not describe anything, neither heroic proportions nor philosophical intent. Those composers claiming these meanings in their music are involved in artistic obfuscation.

"The world does not owe an artist a living because he or she wanted to be a composer, writer, or painter. The world cares little for the serious artist. The biggest enemy of the free-lance artist in America is the Internal Revenue Service.

"My background has allowed me to enter the world as a practical, functioning musician, composing and conducting live musicians and sustaining myself through these efforts. It has taught me to become a professional composer. I write music quickly, rely on my ear and technique, hear it played immediately by the best performers in the world, and do the conducting myself. It is the total musical experience."

BIOGRAPHICAL/CRITICAL SOURCES: Time, May 20, 1966.

* * *

BEADELL, Len 1923-

PERSONAL: Born April 21, 1923, in Pennant Hills, Australia; son of Fred Algernon (an orchardist) and Viola Pearl (Mackay) Beadell; married Anne Rosalind Matthews, July 1, 1961; children: Connie Sue, Gary, Jacqueline. *Education:* Attended grammar school in Sydney, Australia. *Politics:* Liberal. *Religion:* Church of England. *Home:* 15 Fleet St., Salisbury, South Australia 5108. *Office:* Weapons Research Establishment, Salisbury, South Australia 5108.

CAREER: Affiliated with Sydney Water Board, Sydney, Australia, 1949; Weapons Research Establishment, Salisbury, Australia, range reconnaissance officer, 1950-65, graphic illustrator, 1966—. Lecturer on central Australia. *Military service:* Australian Army, warrant officer, 1941-48. *Member:* Australian Society of Authors, Savage Club. *Awards, honors:* British Empire Medal, 1958, for work on rocket range.

WRITINGS: Too Long in the Bush, Rigby, 1965; *Blast the Bush,* Rigby, 1967; *Bush Bashers,* Rigby, 1971; *Still in the Bush,* Rigby, 1975; *Beating About the Bush,* Rigby, 1976; *Outback Highways,* Rigby, 1978.

WORK IN PROGRESS: Back to the Bush, completion expected in 1982.

SIDELIGHTS: Beadell first studied surveying as a boy, with his scoutmaster. His career began with a military mapping program in northern New South Wales in the early stages of World War II. A year later he joined the Australian Army's Survey Corps, serving in New Guinea until the end of the war.

While still in the army, he worked as a surveyor on the first combined scientific expedition of Commonwealth Scientific and Industrial Research Organisation into the Alligator River country. Next he carried out initial surveys for the establishment of the rocket range at Woomera.

His work as a civilian has involved camping, surveying, exploring, and road building. His efforts were responsible for opening up for the first time two-and-one-half million square kilometers of the Gibson, Great Sandy, and Great Victoria

deserts. He also discovered and laid out the first atomic bomb site in Australia, at Emu, and the site for the succeeding atomic tests at Maralinga.

Since building the Gunbarrel Highway, which was the first sixteen hundred kilometers of the east-west road link across central Australia, he has made available an additional six thousand kilometers of desert roads.

Beadell told *CA:* "Having been born in the bush, my natural tendency was to work in the outback. I studied under a dedicated bush surveyor I had met as a boy and accepted desert assignments. I consider myself fortunate to have been selected to start the rocket range at Woomera and open up a million square miles of central Australia, and I have found it satisfying to share my experiences through books and about eight hundred lectures."

BIOGRAPHICAL/CRITICAL SOURCES: Guinness Book of Records, Australian Supplement, Trowbridge & Esher, 21st edition, 1974.

* * *

BEARDEN, Romare (Howard) 1914-

PERSONAL: First name is pronounced *Rome*-ery; born September 2, 1914, in Charlotte, N.C.; son of Richard Howard (a sanitation inspector) and Bessye (a newspaper editor; maiden name, Johnson) Bearden; married Nanette Rohan, September 4, 1954. *Education:* New York University, B.S., 1935; studied at Art Students League under George Grosz, 1936-37; attended Boston University, Columbia University, 1943, Sorbonne, University of Paris, 1950-51, and University of Pittsburgh. *Home:* 357 Canal St., New York, N.Y. 10013.

CAREER: Artist. Worked as political cartoonist for *Baltimore Afro-American;* Department of Social Services, New York City, caseworker, 1938, 1946-49, and 1952-66; art director for Harlem Cultural Council, 1964—; Cinque Gallery, New York City, co-founder and director, 1969—. Member of board of directors of New York State Council on the Arts; charter member of advisory committee of Community Gallery of the Brooklyn Museum. Visiting lecturer in African and Afro-American art and culture at Williams College, 1970. Designer of sets and costumes for play, "Bayou Fever," 1979. One-man exhibitions of paintings held at G Place Gallery, Washington, D.C., 1943, Kootz Gallery, New York City, 1945-47, Duvuloy Gallery, Paris, 1945, Barone Gallery, New York City, 1955, Michael Warren Gallery, New York City, 1960, Cordier-Ekstrom, New York City, 1964, 1967, and 1973-75, Corcoran Gallery, Washington, D.C., 1965, and Museum of Modern Art, 1971. Paintings shown in group exhibits at Harlem Art Center, 1937 and 1939, Institute of Modern Art, Boston, 1943, San Francisco Museum of Art, 1969, New Jersey State Museum, 1970, and Pace Gallery, New York City, 1972. Work represented in permanent collections, including Musuem of Fine Arts, Museum of Modern Art, Newark Museum, and Albright Museum, Buffalo. *Military service:* U.S. Army, 1942-45; served with 372nd Infantry Regiment; became sergeant. *Member:* American Academy and Institute of Arts and Letters, Black Academy of Arts and Letters, Spiral Group. *Awards, honors:* National Institute of Arts and Letters award, 1966; American Academy of Arts and Letters purchase award, 1970; Guggenheim fellowship, 1970-71; Ford Foundation grant, 1973.

WRITINGS: (With Carl Holty) *The Painter's Mind: A Study of the Relations of Structure and Space in Painting,* Crown, 1969; (with Harry Brinton Henderson) *Six Black Masters of American Art,* Doubleday, 1972; (illustrator) Samuel Allen,

Poems From Africa, Crowell, 1973; (author of foreword) Elton Clay Fox, *Black Artists of the New Generation,* Dodd, 1977.

SIDELIGHTS: Although the art of Romare Bearden draws primarily upon the experiences of his early childhood in the South and his formative years in Pittsburgh and Harlem, the artist also incorporates styles from diverse artistic sources into his work. Recognizable in his pictures are elements of early Byzantine mosaics, African sculpture, Chinese watercolors, and Dutch masters such as Vermeer, Ter Borsch, and de Hooch. *Horizon*'s Bruce Duff Hooton declared that Bearden "has recycled . . . these influences into an American idiom that reflects the simple virtues of rural life and the driving tempo of urban jazz."

While Bearden lived in Harlem during the 1920's, the area was in the midst of an exciting revival due to the large influx of Southern blacks in search of jobs. Jazz bands played everywhere; writers and artists flourished, and many took an active role in politics. Bearden was exposed to much of Harlem's bustling society through his mother who was involved in many political pursuits, such as serving on school boards, founding the Negro Women's Democratic Association, and working as the New York editor of the *Chicago Defender.* The vitality of Harlem life during this time is often reflected in Bearden's art.

Bearden moved to Pittsburgh in 1925, and it was there that he first considered becoming an artist. One day he and his friends met a boy suffering from polio. The boy, Eugene, had braces on both legs and lived in the bordello where his mother worked. Eugene eventually showed Bearden some drawings he had done. Bearden recounted the incident: "He'd done one drawing of a house of prostitution not far from where we lived, run by a woman named Sadie. . . . Eugene had drawn Sadie's house with the facade cut off, so you could see in all the rooms. And somebody had shot off a pistol, and the bullet was going all through the house. Women were on top of men, and the bullet was going through them, into the next room and the next, until it came down through the ceiling into the front parlor, and Sadie had her pocketbook open, and the bullet had turned into coins and was dropping into her pocketbook. I said to Eugene, 'You did this? Can you teach me to do it?' He said, 'Sure.' So I started taking drawing lessons from Eugene. . . . That was the first time I ever thought about drawing—and then for years I forgot about it."

After finishing high school in Pittsburgh, Bearden played semi-professional baseball in Boston for a short time and then returned to New York City to attend New York University. Planning to one day become a doctor, Bearden majored in mathematics, but also began contributing cartoons to a number of magazines, including *College Humor, Life,* and *Judge,* and worked as a regular political cartoonist for the *Baltimore Afro-American.*

At this time the Depression was in full swing, and many black artists could for the first time devote themselves seriously to their work with the support of the federally-funded Works Progress Administration (WPA). Although ineligible for this assistance, Bearden was enthused with the project that "gave minority artists what they could never have afforded otherwise." As a result, he joined the Art Students League after graduating from New York University in 1935. Studying under the German artist George Grosz for a year and a half, Bearden was exposed to the works of the great masters. He decided to become an artist instead of a doctor.

Since he could not support himself solely through painting,

Bearden took a job as a caseworker with New York's Department of Social Services, a position he held off and on for nearly thirty years. This enabled him to rent his own studio, but the fledgling artist found himself unable to paint. "I was truly trying to find myself," Bearden recalled. "I put this sheet of brown paper up and it laid there for months. Brown paper was cheaper than canvas, it was in the midst of the Depression. I didn't know what to paint." During this time, Bearden met a very homely woman endeavoring to make a living as a prostitute. He told her she was in the wrong business and with the help of his mother, Bearden got her a job as a cleaning woman. In gratitude, the woman cleaned the artist's studio once each week. "One day she asked if it was the same piece of paper [that had been there for so many weeks], and I told her that it was—that I didn't have my ideas together. She said, 'Why don't you paint me?' Well, the way I must have looked at her she could see what was going through my mind. 'I know what I look like,' she said. 'But when you can look through me and find what's beautiful in me, then you're going to be able to do something on that paper of yours.'" Bearden reflected that "this was as good a lesson for me as all my studying with Grosz."

When the artist began to paint again, his work was more abstract than most of the art of that time. He did not paint in the popular style of social realism. Charles Alston, a fellow artist, revealed that Bearden's "approach to art is more intellectual. He's read a great deal all his life, and he's been intensely curious about many different kinds of art." Bearden commented, however, that "some people have looked at my work and said it was Surrealism. But these things were all around me all the time. The things I saw every day—the people, the music, the dancing. My models were as great as Lautrec's." In 1940 Bearden's work was shown in his first one-man exhibition in Harlem. After that, he participated in a number of exhibitions and slowly began to establish his name in the art world. World War II intervened, though, and the artist served in the army for three years.

On his return to New York City in 1945 Bearden found Harlem a changed place. Many of his friends were gone and the exciting atmosphere of the area had vanished due to the outbreak of a race riot in 1943. Bearden felt isolated. This feeling was exacerbated by the unexpected death of his mother. Consequently, the paintings of this period took on a somber mood. They usually derived their themes from Biblical or literary sources, and displayed such titles as "The Passion of Christ" and "Lament for Ignacio Sanchez Mejias."

In 1950 Bearden journeyed to Paris to study at the Sorbonne under the G.I. Bill. He found in the French capital all the verve that Harlem lacked. "Paris was just wonderful for me," he asserted. "I liked everything about it." The artist fell into the company of such well-known figures as James Baldwin, Richard Wright, and Constantin Brancusi. Nonetheless, in Paris Bearden did not paint. "I couldn't *ever* do a painting in Paris," he remarked.

After staying in France for six months, Bearden returned to New York and found that he could not resume his painting. Instead, he turned to songwriting. Twenty of his tunes were recorded, and one of them, "Seabreeze," became very popular. "I just turned away from painting," Bearden explained. "And meanwhile the years were going by." When a couple of his friends scolded him for forsaking his true vocation of painting, Bearden became confused. He conceded that "when you're serious about something, you don't really like doing it. Painting is so difficult; the canvas was always saying no to me." Eventually, Bearden suffered a nervous breakdown. The experience made him realize that "I just had to be a painter, that was it."

Part of Bearden's inability to paint at this time arose from his painful awareness of his lack of training in art. The year and a half with Grosz was his only formal education. To overcome this feeling of inadequacy, he began to copy the works of the old masters. He would enlarge a black and white photograph of a painting and copy it using his own choice of colors and textures. For three years Bearden trained himself in this manner to regain his confidence.

In the early 1960's Bearden began experimenting with collage. He glued pictures from magazines on a wooden board and filled in the empty spaces with his own drawings. He also superimposed other materials onto the work's surface. This new style sold well and Bearden seemed to have found his niche. A colleague, Ernest Crichlow, on seeing the collages, commented to Bearden, "It looks like you've come home." Crichlow further observed that: "It was not only an aesthetic but an emotional breakthrough for [Bearden]. . . . There was something entirely fresh about them, about that vision."

Bearden's collages deal primarily with images of black life. Hooton noted that Bearden is "squarely in the tradition of American artist-reporters, and he continues to share that tradition with other living artists, including Andrew Wyeth, Jack Levine, Andy Warhol, James Rosenquist, George Segal, and the new group of photorealists." A number of critics agree that Bearden's combination of classical and modern techniques, his use of interior space, the cubist approach with rectilinear overlapping planes, and the documentary feeling summoned by the photographs, give the artist's work tension and rhythm. Hooten asserted that "with the renewed interest in figurative painting, Romare Bearden has finally gained the recognition he has justly earned."

While Bearden's individual success has done much to promote black art, he has also been aggressive in the encouragement of minority artists. In the early 1960's he was a founding member of the Spiral Group whose purpose is to help black artists. In addition, Bearden helped found the Cinque Gallery, which shows only the work of minority artists. The artists receive the entire proceeds of any work they sell; the gallery takes no percentage. Cinque's first administrative director, Chris Shelton, declared that Bearden's "success is maybe more of an influence than his work. [Younger artists] see one black man who's made it, and that makes them think they have a chance, too. . . . [Bearden] sees them all. When he gets home from his own studio at night, his phone never stops ringing. He spends most of his free time now helping other artists."

BIOGRAPHICAL/CRITICAL SOURCES: Time, October 27, 1967; *Romare Bearden: Paintings and Projections* (exhibition catalog), Art Gallery, State University of New York, Albany, 1968; *School Arts,* April, 1969; *Newsweek,* April 5, 1971; *Romare Bearden: The Prevalence of Ritual* (exhibition catalog), Museum of Modern Art, 1971; Elton Clay Fox, *Seventeen Black Artists,* Dodd, 1971; *The Art of Romare Bearden* (collection of paintings), Abrams, 1973; *New Yorker,* November 28, 1977; *Art News,* February, 1979; *Horizon,* August, 1979.*

—*Sketch by Anne M. Guerrini*

*   *   *

BEATTS, Anne Patricia 1947-

PERSONAL: Born February 25, 1947, in Buffalo, N.Y.; daughter of Patrick Murphy Threipland and Sheila Elizabeth Beatts. *Education:* McGill University, B.A., 1966. *Residence:* New York, N.Y.

CAREER: Worked as advertising copywriter in London, England; free-lance writer, 1970—. *Member:* Writers Guild, American Federation of Television and Radio Artists. *Awards, honors:* Emmy Awards from Academy of Television Arts and Sciences, 1976, 1977, and awards from Writers Guild, 1976, 1980, all for "Saturday Night Live."

WRITINGS: (Editor with Deanne Stillman) *Titters: The First Collection of Humor by Women,* Macmillan, 1976; (editor with John Head) *Saturday Night Live,* Avon, 1977. Writer for television series, "Saturday Night Live," 1975—. Editor of *National Lampoon,* 1970-74.

*   *   *

BEAUMAN, Katharine (Burgoyne) Bentley 1902-

PERSONAL: Born September 30, 1903, in Leeds, England; daughter of Frank Wolstencroft (a solicitor) and Mary Catherine (Rattenbury) Miller Jones; married Eric Bentley Beauman (a wing commander in Royal Air Force), June 22, 1940; children: Christopher Burgoyne Bentley. *Education:* Lady Margaret Hall, Oxford, M.A. (with honors), 1925; studied voice in Vienna, Austria. *Politics:* Conservative. *Religion:* Church of England. *Home:* 59 Chester Row, London S.W.1, England.

CAREER: Conservative Party, London, England, women's organizer in London, Yorkshire, and Durham, 1927-29; *Yorkshire Post,* Leeds, England, women's editor, 1929-31; free-lance writer, 1931-50; St. Michael's Secondary School, Westminster, England, governor and historian, 1950-77; Grey Coat Hospital, Westminster, governor, 1977. Member of headquarters staff of Women's Royal Voluntary Service, 1957-67. Chairman of Lady Margaret Hall Settlement, 1969-72, vice-president, 1972—. Concert soloist in London and Leeds; artist, with exhibits. *Military service:* Women's Auxiliary Air Force, public relations officer, 1939-41; became flight officer. *Member:* International P.E.N., British Federation of University Women (chairman of Crosby Hall library committee, 1980), University Women's Club, London Library. *Awards, honors: Green Sleeves* was named British Ambassador book by English Speaking Union, 1978.

WRITINGS: Wings on Her Shoulders, Hutchinson, 1943; *A Short History of St. Michael's, Chester Square Church of England Secondary School,* Greaves, 1959; *Partners in Blue: The Story of Women's Service With the Royal Air Force,* Hutchinson, 1971; *Green Sleeves: The Story of Women's Voluntary Service/Women's Royal Voluntary Service,* Leo Cooper, 1978. Also author of *A History of Lady Margaret Hall Settlement,* 1982. Writer for British Broadcasting Corp. Contributor to journals, including *RAF Quarterly,* and newspapers.

SIDELIGHTS: Katharine Beauman told *CA:* "My lifelong interest in politics, social work, and education of women for citizenship is reflected in my current work with schools and settlements.

"I am also interested in music and art. I studied singing in Vienna in 1932 and gave recitals in London and Leeds. I played the viola for several years with the Royal Amateur Orchestral Society in London, and have exhibited with the Chelsea Arts Club and Services Arts Society."

AVOCATIONAL INTERESTS: Travel (United States and Europe).

BIOGRAPHICAL/CRITICAL SOURCES: Economist, June 5, 1971; *New Statesman,* June 18, 1971; *British Book News,* June, 1978.

BECK, Julian 1925-

PERSONAL: Born May 31, 1925, in New York, N.Y.; son of Irving (in business) and Mabel Lucille (a teacher; maiden name, Blum) Beck; married Judith Malina (a writer, actress, producer, and director), October 30, 1948; children: Garrick Maxwell, Isha Manna. *Education:* Attended Yale University, 1942-43, and City College of New York (now of City University of New York), 1946-49. *Politics:* "Pacifist Anarchist." *Religion:* Jewish. *Home:* 800 West End Ave., New York, N.Y. 10025. *Office:* Living Theatre, Via Gaeta 79, Rome, Italy 00185.

CAREER: Living Theatre, New York, N.Y., and Europe, 1947—, co-founder, 1947; stage designer of plays for Living Theatre, including "The Thirteenth God," 1951, "The Marrying Woman," 1960, "In the Jungle of Cities," 1960, "The Brig," 1963, "The Maids," 1965, "Frankenstein," 1969, and "Masse Mensch," 1980; actor in plays for Living Theatre, including "Childish Jokes," "He Who Says Yes and He Who Says No," "Dialogue of the Young Man and the Manikin," "The Heroes," 1952, "The Age of Anxiety," 1954, "The Spook Sonata," 1954, "Orpheus," 1954, "The Idiot King," 1954, "Tonight We Improvise," 1955, "Phaedra," 1955, "In the Jungle of Cities," 1960, "Many Loves," 1961, "The Apple," 1961, "The Connection," 1962, "The Maids," 1965, and "Frankenstein," 1967; director of plays for Living Theatre, including "Ladies Voices," 1952, "Tonight We Improvise," 1955, "The Young Disciple," 1955, "Many Loves," 1959, "The Cave at Machpelah," 1959, "The Women of Trachis," 1960, "Man Is Man," 1962, "Mysteries and Smaller Pieces," 1965, "Frankenstein," 1965, and "Prometheus," 1968. Actor in motion pictures, including "Narcissus," 1957, "Living and Glorious," 1965, "Amore, Amore," 1966, "Agonia," 1967, "Oedipus Rex," 1967, "Le Compromis," 1968, "Etre Libre," 1968, and "Paradise Now," 1969.

AWARDS, HONORS: Lola D'Annunzio Award, 1959, for outstanding contribution to Off-Broadway theatre; Page One award from Newspaper Guild, 1960; Obie Award from *Village Voice*, 1960, for "The Connection," 1964, for direction and production of "The Brig," 1969, for acting in "Antigone," 1969, for best new play for "Frankenstein," 1975, for sustained achievement; Creative Arts Theatre Citation from Brandeis University, 1961; Grand Prix de Theatre des Nations, 1961; Paris Critics Circle medallion, 1961; Prix de L'Universite, 1961; New England Theatre Conference award, 1962; Olympio Prize, 1967, for "Antigone"; Maharam Award for stage design, 1969, for "Frankenstein."

WRITINGS: Songs of the Revolution: One to Thirty-Five (poems), Interim, 1963; *Revolution and Counterrevolution,* Nuovi Argumenti, 1968; *Twenty-One Songs of the Revolution* (poems), April Verlag, 1969; *Conversations With Julian Beck and Judith Malina,* edited by Jean-Jacques Lebel, Belfond, 1969; (with wife, Judith Malina, and Aldo Rostagno) *We, the Living,* Ballantine, 1970; (with Malina) *Paradise Now: A Collective Creation of the Living Theatre,* Random House, 1971; (with Malina) *The Legacy of Cain: Three Pilot Projects; A Collective Creation of the Living Theatre,* Belibaste, 1972; (with Malina) *Frankenstein: A Collective Creation of the Living Theatre,* La Fiacola, 1972; *The Life of the Theatre,* City Lights, 1972; (with Malina) *Seven Meditations on Political Sado-Masochism: A Collective Creation of the Living Theatre,* Fag Rag, 1973; *Songs of the Revolution: Thirty-Six to Eighty-Nine* (poems), Union Generale d'Editions, 1974; (contributor) John Lahr and Jonathan Price, editors, *The Great American Life Show,* Bantam, 1974.

Plays, all with Malina: "Frankenstein"; "Paradise Now"; "Six Public Acts"; "The Money Tower."

WORK IN PROGRESS: Living in Volkswagen Buses and Other Songs of the Revolution, publication expected in 1981; *Meditations on Theatre,* publication expected in 1982; *Living in the Streets,* with Malina, publication expected in 1982.

SIDELIGHTS: The Living Theatre, founded in 1947 by Beck and his wife, Judith Malina, is the forerunner of avant-garde theatre in the United States. The company's use of unconventional methods, nudity, and profanity have made the Living Theatre a controversial group and has attracted the wrath of governments in the United States, Europe, and South America. While performing in Brazil in 1971, the entire company was arrested and jailed for more than a month. The Living Theatre's aim, to heighten the "conscious awareness among the poorest of the poor," was not appreciated by the Brazilian dictatorship. Beck, however, did not view his incarceration as a total loss. He exclaimed in his cell that "*this* is theatre!" His wife disagreed: "We came to help the cause of liberation in the third world and got put into jail. We came to perform for the arts festival, and our only scene was our exit."

BIOGRAPHICAL/CRITICAL SOURCES: Yale/Theatre, spring, 1969; Renfreu Neff, *The Living Theatre USA,* Bobbs-Merrill, 1970; *The Living Book of the Living Theatre,* Greenich House, 1971; *Newsweek,* August 16, 1971; Pierre Biner, *The Living Theatre,* Horizon Press, 1972; Karen Malpede, *People's Theatre in Amerika,* Drama Books, 1972.

* * *

BEER, Vic
See BIRD, Vivian

* * *

BEERS, Paul Benjamin 1931-

PERSONAL: Born November 13, 1931, in Homestead, Pa.; son of Charles Mortimer (a teacher) and Leonore (a teacher; maiden name, Hart) Beers; married Joan Shoemaker, July 29, 1957 (divorced, 1978); children: Philip Benjamin. *Education:* Wilkes College, A.B., 1953; Columbia University, M.S., 1956; further graduate study at Stanford University, 1967. *Religion:* Protestant. *Home:* 2313 Valley Rd., Harrisburg, Pa. 17104. *Office:* Harrisburg Patriot-News, P.O. Box 2265, Harrisburg, Pa. 17105.

CAREER: Harrisburg Patriot-News, Harrisburg, Pa., associate editor and author of column, 1957—. Member of board of trustees of Harrisburg Area Community College. *Military service:* U.S. Navy, 1953-55. *Awards, honors:* Nominated for Pulitzer Prize, 1974; newspaper awards include seven citations from Pennsylvania Newspaper Publishers Association.

WRITINGS: The Pennsylvania Sampler, Stackpole, 1970; *The Republican Years,* Harrisburg Patriot-News, 1971; *Profiles From the Susquehanna Valley,* Stackpole, 1973; *Profiles in Pennsylvania Sports,* Stackpole, 1975; *Pennsylvania Politics: Today and Yesterday,* Pennsylvania State University Press, 1980.

* * *

BEGG, A(lexander) Charles 1912-

PERSONAL: Born February 28, 1912, in Wellington, New Zealand; son of Charles Mackie (a surgeon) and Lillian Helen (a musician; maiden name, Treadwell) Begg; married Margaret A. Birks (a medical practitioner), February 1,

1941; children: Eleanor Margaret Begg Anderson, Katharine Elizabeth Begg Malcolm, Alastair Charles, Barbara Helen Begg Anglem, Janet Lillian. *Education:* University of Otago, M.B., Ch.B., 1935, D.D.R., 1946; University of New Zealand, M.D., 1946. *Home:* 107 Braeview Cres., Maori Hill, Dunedin, New Zealand.

CAREER: Dunedin Hospital, Dunedin, New Zealand, resident medical and surgical officer, 1936-37, diagnostic radiologist, 1941-56; Otago Hospital Board, Dunedin, director of diagnostic radiology, 1956-77; writer. Lecturer at University of Otago, 1946-71, associate professor, 1971-77; Costello Memorial Lecturer at Royal Australian College of Radiologists, 1966. *Member:* New Zealand Medical Association, Royal Society of New Zealand, Royal Forest and Bird Protection Society of New Zealand, Royal Australasian College of Radiologists (fellow). *Awards, honors:* Nuffield traveling scholarship from Nuffield Foundation, 1949-50; Rouse traveling fellowship from Royal Australian College of Radiologists, 1962; Hubert Church Award from P.E.N., 1967, for *Dusky Bay;* J. M. Sherrard Award from Historical Association, Canterbury, New Zealand, 1972-73, for *Port Preservation.*

WRITINGS—All with brother, Neil C. Begg: *Dusky Bay,* Whitcombe & Tombs, 1966, 3rd edition, 1975; *James Cook and New Zealand,* Government Printer (Wellington, New Zealand), 1969; *Port Preservation,* Whitcombe & Tombs, 1973; *The World of John Boultbee,* Whitcoulls, 1979.

Contributor: Alastair Campbell, editor, *School Journal,* Department of Education (Wellington, New Zealand), 1969; Ray Knox, editor, *New Zealand's Heritage,* Hamlyn, 1971. Contributor to medical journals.

SIDELIGHTS: Begg commented to *CA:* "Ever since I was at school and university I have derived great enjoyment from exploring the wild and rugged fiord country in the southwest of the South Island of New Zealand and Stewart Island. I have always carried a camera and been interested in photography and natural history. Since I retired in 1977 I have traveled with my brother along the route taken by John Boultbee 150 years ago in Tasmania, Bass Strait, Eastern Australia, the South Island, Foveaux Strait, and Stewart Island in New Zealand. John Boultbee kept a diary of his wanderings, which has recently come to light in England. It is the only eye-witness account of sealing made by a literate man, and gives an unrivaled view of the sealing trade carried out at the beginning of the settlement of Australia and New Zealand when Europeans first came into contact with the native races. Our 1979 book is based upon Boultbee's diary and our reconstruction of his observations and the places and events he so accurately described."

AVOCATIONAL INTERESTS: "Since retiring I have begun a course in ceramics and am thoroughly enjoying the challenge of trying to throw a worthwhile pot."

*   *   *

BEGG, Neil Colquhoun   1915-

PERSONAL: Born April 13, 1915, in Dunedin, New Zealand; son of Charles Mackie (a surgeon) and Lilian Helen (a musician; maiden name, Treadwell) Begg; married Margaret Milne McLean (a librarian), April 11, 1942; children: Michael James, Alison Margaret, John Graham, Elizabeth Ann. *Education:* University of Otago, M.B., Ch.B., 1941. *Home:* 86 Newington Ave., Dunedin, New Zealand.

CAREER: Dunedin Hospital, Dunedin, New Zealand, resident physician, 1941-42; Royal Masonoc Hospital, London,

England, resident medical officer, 1946-47; Queen Elizabeth Hospital for Children, London, clinical tutor, 1948; Dunedin Hospital, pediatrician, 1949-56; University of Otago, Dunedin, senior lecturer in pediatrics at Medical School, 1949-77. Director of medical services for Plunket Society of New Zealand, 1956-77; member of Child Health Council, 1958-64; member of New Zealand Historic Places Trust, 1970—, chairman, 1978—; chairman of Home Safety advisory council, 1976-79. Consultant to American Foundation for Maternal and Child Health. *Military service:* New Zealand Army, 1942-46; served in the Middle East and Italy; became major; mentioned in dispatches.

MEMBER: Royal College of Physicians (fellow), Royal College of Physicians (Edinburgh; fellow), International P.E.N., Royal Society of New Zealand, New Zealand Medical Association (fellow), New Zealand Pediatric Society (honorary member), American Association of Maternal and Child Health (honorary member). *Awards, honors:* Hubert Church Award from International P.E.N., 1966, for *Dusky Bay;* Member of Order of the British Empire, 1973; J. M. Sherrard Award from New Zealand Historical Society, 1973, for *Port Preservation.*

WRITINGS: The Child and His Family, Whitcoulls, 1970, revised edition, 1974.

With brother, A. Charles Begg: *Dusky Bay,* Whitcome & Tombs, 1966, 3rd edition, 1975; *James Cook and New Zealand,* Government Printer (Wellington, New Zealand), 1969; *Port Preservation,* Whitcome & Tombs, 1973; *The World of John Boultbee,* Whitcoulls, 1979.

Contributor: Ray Knox, editor, *New Zealand's Heritage,* Hamlyn, 1971; Frances Porter, editor, *Historic Buildings of New Zealand: South Island,* Cassell, 1982.

SIDELIGHTS: Begg told *CA:* "From my study of children's illnesses came an interest in the prevention of these illnesses; then came the realization that, though *treatment* was in the hands of the medical professionals, only the parents and those associated with healthy children could *prevent* sickness and accident. The best way to reach these people is through such voluntary parents' associations as the Plunket Society and the American Association of Maternal and Child Health. It is a pleasure to meet parents both in New Zealand and the United States through these organizations. Parallel to my medical work has always been an interest in the history of New Zealand and the Pacific."

*   *   *

BELL, Adrian (Hanbury)   1901-1980

OBITUARY NOTICE—See index for *CA* sketch: Born October 4, 1901, in England; died September 5, 1980, in England. Farmer, novelist, essayist, and designer of crossword puzzles. Bell's novels and essays reflected his thoughts on English farm life. His essays were featured weekly in an *Eastern Daily Press* column entitled "Countryman's Notebook." In 1930 Bell designed the first *London Times* crossword puzzle and contributed puzzles regularly until his death. Among his books are *Corduroy, Silver Ley, The Cherry Tree, The Budding Morrow, A Suffolk Harvest, A Countryman's Notebook,* and *The Green Bond.* Obituaries and other sources: *London Times,* September 6, 1980; *AB Bookman's Weekly,* January 26, 1981.

BELLAMY, Harmon
  See BLOOM, Herman I.

                    *   *   *

BELLOWS, James G(ilbert) 1922-

PERSONAL: Born November 11, 1922, in Detroit, Mich.; son of Lyman Hubbard (a business executive) and Dorothy (Gilbert) Bellows; married first wife, Marian, 1950 (divorced, 1963); married Maggie Savoy (a journalist), March 7, 1964 (died, 1970); married Keven Ryan (a business executive), July 1, 1971; children: Amelia, Priscilla, Felicia, Michael, Justine. *Education:* Kenyon College, B.A., 1946. *Home:* 115 South Rockingham Ave., Los Angeles, Calif., 90049. *Agent:* Sterling Lord Agency, 610 Madison Ave., New York, N.Y. 10021. *Office:* Los Angeles Herald Examiner, 1111 South Broadway, Los Angeles, Calif. 90015.

CAREER: Columbus Ledger-Inquirer, Columbus, Ga., reporter, 1947; *Atlanta Journal,* Atlanta, Ga., news editor, 1950-57; *Detroit Free Press,* Detroit, Mich., assistant editor, 1957-58; *Miami News,* Miami, Fla., managing editor, 1958-61; *New York Herald Tribune,* New York, N.Y., editor, 1962-66; *Los Angeles Times,* Los Angeles, Calif., associate editor, 1965-74; *Washington Star,* Washington, D.C., editor, 1975-78; *Los Angeles Herald Examiner,* Los Angeles, editor, 1978—. Trustee of Kenyon College. *Military service:* U.S. Navy, 1942-46; became lieutenant junior grade. *Member:* Psi Upsilon, Delta Chi. *Awards, honors:* L.H.D. from Kenyon College, 1965.

WRITINGS: (Author of annotation, with Richard C. Wald) Jimmy Breslin, *The World of Jimmy Breslin,* Viking, 1967; (editor) *Anyone Who Enters Here Must Celebrate Maggie: A Collection of Writings About Maggie, and by Maggie,* [Los Angeles], 1971.

SIDELIGHTS: Known as a savior of struggling newspapers, Bellows has been called on to lift three of the nation's most depressed dailies back to respectability. In each of his editing posts he has fought against a formidable opponent. At the *New York Herald Tribune* Bellows had to compete against the *New York Times.* He accepted the job at the *Washington Star* while the city's premier paper, the *Post,* sat at the height of its Watergate fame. And in 1978 he took the helm of the *Los Angeles Herald Examiner,* regarded as "the worst urban daily newspaper in America." In a market dominated by the *Los Angeles Times,* the *Herald Examiner* was given little chance of surviving. "To call the pair rivals," reported *Time* in 1977, "is an overstatement."

Bellows has brought to his papers a flair for innovation, an eye for the exciting, and a willingness to gamble. The *Herald Tribune* became known as a "haven for literary freedom" during Bellows's reign, featuring the writing of Tom Wolfe, Jimmy Breslin, Dick Schaap, Judith Crist, Richard Reeves, and Pete Axthelm, among others. At the *Washington Star* he added a front-page interview column and a writer-in-residence column. Bellows also played to the Capitol's love of gossip by originating the frequently quoted column "The Ear." In short, "he turned a newsprint morgue into a laboratory of editorial innovation," reported *Time.* Many of these same features followed Bellows to the *Herald Examiner,* where he made further changes by firing more than half the staff and openly raiding other publications for talent. Bellows also promised to challenge his former employer, the *Los Angeles Times.* "They are so thin-skinned over there," he said. "This is going to be fun. What we are trying to do is get into the same pond with the big fella, and if he won't come in, we'll have to lure him."

The question many observers ask is why has Bellows repeatedly forsaken success and security for the challenge of rebuilding big-city newspapers. "What made him think he could save the self-destructive *Los Angeles Herald Examiner* after a decade of abysmal editorial and financial failure?," asked *Esquire*'s Mary Murphy. "What made him think he could turn it into a weapon with which to attack the most profitable newspaper in the history of post-World War II journalism, the *Los Angeles Times?* Some say it was the money . . . ; some say it is Bellows's need to 'walk uphill through life carrying a heavy load on his shoulders'; some say that death would be more comfortable to Bellows than life without risk; and some say that the sound you hear as Bellows loads his guns may be the sweet sound of his own private revenge."

CA INTERVIEW

CA interviewed James Bellows at his *Los Angeles Herald Examiner* office on June 11, 1980.

CA: How deep in the trenches are you day to day?

BELLOWS: We just keep busy with the whole paper all day, and I enjoy that.

CA: So you're actually out there where the stories are breaking, deciding what weight to give a story, which way to cover it, totally, with ten fingers on every aspect of it.

BELLOWS: Well, I try to. Sometimes I need eleven or twelve.

CA: How has the role of the newspaper in our lives changed?

BELLOWS: Television has changed it. Most people get their first information from television and radio, but that is only a fragment. Really the newspaper, the print medium, is the one that you count on for the full information that really makes sense out of the little fragment you've heard on the radio or watched on television. A paper makes sense out of the news and helps people make sense out of their daily lives.

We're trying to tell people how to look at the world, and we're trying to make the telling interesting. We give a guide as to how to think, not just what to think about. Thus, to take a recent example, when President Carter made his Sunday night fighting speech, we tried to give it a special perspective. We didn't just report on what he said—the whole world knew that already. Our headline was, "We've got a new president." That was how to look at it. We didn't just report on the Proposition Thirteen victory. Our headline was, "California's message . . . By a landslide, the people won't take it anymore." That was how to look at it.

CA: You said that a newspaper tells you how to look at the news?

BELLOWS: There is a certain amount of opinion in the paper, and there isn't that much opinion on television. Television is much straighter in that way. Our value is to shoulder some of the complication for our readers and to give them more than the facts, more than the welter of details. It is to give them a steady, sometimes humorous, always informed way of looking at the world that will make it seem a little less complex, a little more understandable—a guide that makes the world human.

If we go back fifty years, newspapers provided sensation—they were probably more emotion than reason. Then TV came along, and, as the *New Yorker* said during the last paper strike, it has become our eyes and ears and our public meeting place, but print continues to be our memory. Now TV pictures provide the sensationalism, the emotion, and we must provide the reason. Newspapers speak to the way we think, in concepts and words, not necessarily in pictures. Print has to look for the connective tissue; TV does not have memory.

CA: In speaking of that, how do you establish a point of view for a newspaper in a city as diversified as Los Angeles?

BELLOWS: We try to create a personality in the newspaper. In other words, a newspaper ought to be like an old bathrobe or a friend. It ought to have some anger and some sadness, so it isn't just as inanimate object that appears on the front porch. It is a part of your household and your family. That's the ideal situation.

CA: But there's such diversity in Los Angeles.

BELLOWS: Well, that's true, but I'm not sure that even in that diversity there aren't some unifying forces that run through it. It is the only horizontal city known to man, at least that I know of, and it does not have a center—not only geographically, but it really doesn't have a center in industrial force or in bureaucracy. But there is an ambience of the southern Californian that I think is certainly different than the ambience of the Washingtonian, New Yorker, or Chicagoan.

CA: Some people criticize the Los Angeles Times *for being sterile and narrow in point of view. Do you feel that the* Herald Examiner, *with such columnists as Tony Castro, Ben Stein, Mary McGrory, Joseph Benti, and Carl Rowan, speaks to the diversity of Los Angeles?*

BELLOWS: We have a lot of different things, different elements, because I just don't think southern California is as platonic and placid a place as the *Los Angeles Times* would have you believe. And I think there is more going on here than they would want you to get involved in. There is almost an establishment point of view that the *Times* has that we do not have. We are broader in the different things we cover or just feel free to say, whether it's in a movie review, an editorial, or whatever.

CA: In the 1950's, didn't the old Herald Examiner *have a reputation for printing yellow journalism?*

BELLOWS: To me that was what was wrong with the image of the *Herald Examiner.* We've had to change considerably, and we're still working on that because we've had to build up respect and credibility, and that takes a lot of time.

CA: This is still a Hearst paper, isn't it?

BELLOWS: It's still owned by the Hearst Corporation. The Hearst Corporation, in fact, used to be completely family-owned and family-run. Now it is family-owned, but it is not run by the family. It has business managers who are running the corporation.

CA: So you're not getting daily phone calls from William Randolph Hearst, Jr., telling you what to put on page one and how to cover a story?

BELLOWS: No. He certainly makes some suggestions, but he doesn't run the papers like the old chief used to.

CA: Not back to the days of Adela Rogers St. Johns at all?

BELLOWS: No. And there is an effort, really, to make quality newspapers out of all those papers. It takes a lot of time

to overcome the image they had of the sensational newspapers. There's no question about it. We've still got some time to overcome that.

CA: Some people might say that compared to the Times, *the* Herald *is really a fighting, feisty paper that wants to say something to Los Angeles.*

BELLOWS: It's got to be irreverent, rash, feisty, and really care about the city and the people here in southern California more than the other newspapers do, not in the sense of a San Gabriel, or Pasadena, or Santa Monica, or Valley News does. It has to really somehow capture the essence of the whole place. We do not have that small, geographical base; we're dealing with all of southern California. And not only do we have to do a good job, but we have to be sophisticated enough and have a good enough quality product that it will be recognized as one of two Los Angeles newspapers in a very different way than the *Los Angeles Times* is.

CA: You worked at the Times *for eight years?*

BELLOWS: Yes.

CA: And then you were in a very competitive market in Washington, D.C.?

BELLOWS: Well, I've truly spent most of the years with underdog, competitive, big-city newspapers, so that certainly gave me a good background.

CA: Did your work experience at the Times *help you in coming to this job? Surely you know how they operate, how they think, after eight years.*

BELLOWS: Well, I don't think that's the important thing. I think I understand enough about this city and the area to be able to figure out a different approach than the *Los Angeles Times,* which is one of smug success.

CA: You have a broad coverage of professional women; the Herald's *women's section addresses the diversity of today's women very successfully.*

BELLOWS: Nowadays newspapers are getting out of the old macho sexist ways, and they ought to. In the Los Angeles area especially there are more women who are in executive positions than in any other big city in the country. I think there is a hell of a role for a newspaper that really cares more about those young career women who are twenty-five, thirty, or thirty-five, and we need to get more of that audience. We have a managing editor who's thirty-three, and she's a woman. It helps our thinking at this point. And then my wife Maggie, who died in 1970, was the women's editor at the *L.A. Times* when I was there, and that certainly helped me understand the function and coverage of a women's section.

CA: Now women have become over the last ten years a newly opened topic. Do you see another area like that coming up?

BELLOWS: No. I just think the newspapers have got to do a better and better job because television is going to do a better and better job on the news. Consumer news, and all that it implies, is going to be bigger and bigger in the coming years, as ''Sixty Minutes'' has shown, and newspapers are going to have to do more and more of that to be able to prove their worth in comparison with TV.

CA: Are you talking about picking up those many stories

that don't hit the wires, that don't make the big news?

BELLOWS: What we've got to do is stop talking at the public and start talking *with* the public. And it's poetry we need to see more of in newspapers. Poetry has lost its power in men's minds, and I expect we journalists are accountable in our minute-by-minute recording, photographing, interpreting, analyzing, and arranging of every last detail of every news event in columns. It's a pity. You see, TV has the numbers, no question about that. We've got to have the quality audience, and only the quality content with quality writing and editing will win us that.

CA: There was an interesting article in your paper the other day on an FBI agent, a woman, the first woman of theirs to be killed in the line of duty. In covering the funeral you ran a picture of the funeral and a picture of a man who did not attend the funeral but was alive today because a few years ago this woman saved his life. And that was a totally unexpected point of view.

BELLOWS: It was a human, personal story; I think too many papers deal with *issue* stories and not the human, personal stories that really can connect with the readers. I think that one way to pull this whole diverse area of southern California together is with personal stories, so that people understand how other people work out their problems.

BIOGRAPHICAL/CRITICAL SOURCES: Newsweek, December 30, 1974, August 11, 1975, March 6, 1978; *Time,* July 28, 1975, December 5, 1977; *Esquire,* August 1, 1978.

—*Interview by Judith Spiegelman*

*   *   *

BENDER, David R(ay) 1942-

PERSONAL: Born June 12, 1942, in Canton, Ohio; son of John Ray and Mary (Witmer) Bender; married Harriet Posgay, August 12, 1967 (divorced, 1979); children: Robert, Scott, Lori Jo. *Education:* Kent State University, B.S., 1964; Case Western Reserve University, M.S., 1969; Ohio State University, Ph.D., 1977. *Politics:* Republican. *Religion:* Episcopalian. *Home:* 444 Bedford St., Stamford, Conn. 06901. *Office:* Special Libraries Association, 235 Park Ave. S., New York, N.Y. 10003.

CAREER: Head librarian at high school in Willoughby, Ohio, 1964-68; Lakeland Community College, Mentor, Ohio, instructor in library science and head of technical aides program, 1968-69; Ohio Department of Education, Columbus, consultant in school library services, 1969-70; Maryland State Department of Education, Division of Library Development and Services, Baltimore, chief of School Library Media Services Branch, 1972-79; Special Libraries Association, New York, N.Y., executive director, 1979—. Reference librarian at Mentor Public Library, 1965-67; visiting professor at Towson State University, autumn, 1976; lecturer at Rutgers University, summer, 1978. Member of National Commission on Libraries and Information Science task force on the role of the school library program in networking, 1977-78; chairperson of public relations committee of Council on Library Technology, 1970; member of National Standards Institute subcommittee, 1977-78; consultant to National Center on Educational Media and Materials for the Handicapped.

MEMBER: American Library Association (second vice-president of Young Adult Services Division, 1972-73; member of President's Commission, 1976-77), American Association of School Librarians (member of executive board and second vice-president, 1975-76; vice-chairperson, 1978-79;

chairperson, 1979-80), American Society of Association Executives, National Association of State Educational Media Professionals, Association of Educational Communications and Technology, Special Libraries Association, State School Library Media Supervisors Association (president, 1973-74; member of board of directors, 1974-75), Maryland Library Association, Maryland Educational Media Organization (honorary member; member of executive board, 1976-79), Archons of Colophon, Phi Delta Kappa, Beta Phi Mu, Kappa Sigma. *Awards, honors:* Grant from National Institute of Education, 1978; distinguished service award from Maryland Educational Media Organization, 1980.

WRITINGS: (Contributor) G. Estes and J. Hannigan, editors, *Media Center Facilities Design,* American Library Association, 1978; *Learning Resources and the Instructional Program in Community Colleges,* Shoe String, 1980; (with D. Philip Baker) *Library Media Programs and the Special Learner,* Shoe String, 1980.

Author of multi-media sets "If Not Now, When?: Media Center Development in Ohio Secondary Schools," Ohio Department of Education, 1970, and "Media Technology in Maryland," School Media Services Office, Division of Library Development and Services, Maryland State Department of Education, 1976-77. Co-editor of "Monograph Publication Series," American Association of School Librarians, 1977—. Author of "Reviews: Books for Professionals," a column in *Media Review.* Contributor to *Bowker Annual* and *Educational Media Yearbook.* Contributor of more than twenty articles to library and education journals. Member of advisory board of *Media Review.*

WORK IN PROGRESS: Research on services and program activities of special libraries and information centers.

SIDELIGHTS: Bender told CA: "In order to write or to excel in any chosen field, one must know what is happening. Reading, traveling, listening, and speaking are important and necessary skills required for me to accomplish my career goals. One must remain flexible and open to change, therefore, living in the present, remembering the past, and dreaming and planning for the future. Weaving all of this into my own life pattern provides me with a rewarding personal and professional life."

BIOGRAPHICAL/CRITICAL SOURCES: Special Libraries, August, 1979.

*   *   *

BENHAM, Mary Lile 1914-

PERSONAL: Born October 8, 1914, in Winnipeg, Manitoba, Canada; daughter of William D. and Gussie (Drewry) Love; married Hugh A. Benham (an investment consultant), October 16, 1935; children: Patricia Joan Benham Porth, Hugh John, William Drewry, Donald Bruce. *Education:* University of Manitoba, B.A., 1935. *Religion:* Anglican. *Home:* 249 Waverley St., Winnipeg, Manitoba, Canada R3M 3K4.

CAREER: Writer, 1971—. Worked in public relations division of National War Finance Committee, Winnipeg, Manitoba, 1943-45. *Member:* Writers' Union of Canada, Canadian Authors Association, Canadian Society of Children's Authors, Illustrators, and Performers, Penhandlers, Junior League of Winnipeg.

WRITINGS—Published by Fitzhenry & Whiteside, except as noted: *Winnipeg,* City of Winnipeg, Manitoba, 1974; *The Manitoba Club: One Hundred Years, 1874-1974,* Manitoba Club, 1974; *Nellie McClung* (biography), 1975; *Paul Kane* (biography), 1977; *La Verendrye* (biography), 1980.

Author of radio plays and puppet plays, including "Heather and Feather" (three-act children's play), first produced in Winnipeg, Manitoba, at Playhouse Theatre, 1951. Contributor of articles and poems to magazines, including *Harlequin, Style, Branching Out, Pierian Spring, Manitoba Business,* and *Canadian Hotel and Restaurant.*

WORK IN PROGRESS: A one-hundred-year history of St. George's Church, in Winnipeg, Manitoba, publication by St. George's Church expected in 1982.

SIDELIGHTS: Benham wrote: "I have always done some writing, but mainly confined my activities to volunteer work until my last child started at the university in 1971. Then I started writing in earnest for markets.

"I am strongly committed to 'The Canadians' series published by Fitzhenry & Whiteside. Primarily designed for school libraries, the books have steady sales in book stores as adults, too, like these easy-reading, profusely illustrated, biographies which weave the contemporary scene into the story of one mover-and-shaker in Canada.

"With a semi-retired husband, I travel a great deal—so much that I don't have time to write travel articles! We spend summers on a tiny island near Keewatin, Ontario, an island shaped like a Chianti bottle, which may someday sink into the lake under the sheer weight of Benhams, as our offspring and their offspring join us in the sun."

*   *   *

BENNETT, Neville   1937-

PERSONAL: Born July 25, 1937, in Bradford, England; son of Stanley (an engineer) and Gladys (Welch) Bennett; married Susan Gail Umney (a social worker), March 18, 1961; children: Neil Stephen, Louise Gail, Sara Jane. *Education:* University of Lancaster, B.Ed. (with first class honors), 1969, Ph.D., 1972. *Politics:* None. *Religion:* None. *Home:* Kiln Croft, Bilsborrow Lane, Bilsborrow, near Preston, Lancastershire, England. *Office:* Department of Educational Research, Cartmel College, University of Lancaster, Bailrigg, Lancastershire, England.

CAREER: International Marine Radio Co., Croydon, England, radio officer, 1956-61; British Aerospace, Warton, England, radio and radar engineer, 1961-65; University of Lancaster, Bailrigg, England, research officer, 1969-70, lecturer, 1970-76, senior lecturer, 1977-78, professor of educational research and director of Centre for Educational Research and Development, 1978—, head of department of educational research, 1981-84. *Member:* British Educational Research Association (member of executive council, 1975-78), British Psychological Society, American Educational Research Association.

WRITINGS: Teaching Styles and Pupil Progress, Harvard University Press, 1976; (with David McNamara) *Focus on Teaching,* Longman, 1979; *Open Plan Schools: Teaching, Curriculum, and Design,* National Foundation for Educational Research, 1980. Assistant editor of *British Journal of Educational Psychology,* 1974—; co-editor of *British Educational Research Journal,* 1975—.

WORK IN PROGRESS: Research on aspects of school and classroom organization.

SIDELIGHTS: Neville Bennett told *CA:* "I came to academic life late, after spells in the Merchant Navy and in industry. Recognition came from my research on educationally sensitive topics. The material covered in my book *Teaching Styles and Pupil Progress* is one such area. The situation in Britain at the time the book was written was that the teaching profession was divided on the best way to teach children. Most felt that progressive, or 'open,' approaches were the best, although this view was based on ideology rather than evidence. Our research indicated that this was not the case; in general, traditional methods were found to be associated with improved achievement.

"These findings triggered an emotional furor. Proponents of progressive methods were incensed, and as a result the book attracted a great deal of criticism from this quarter. On the other hand, teachers using traditional methods sat back and smiled knowingly. This controversy eventually resulted in government action, a precurser to the current teacher accountability debate.

"'Open Plan' schools are architectural manifestations of the progressive education ideology. Of interest, however, is that in our national inquiry into such schools there was little evidence of open education practices. This is just one of the many paradoxes to be found in the education world.

"I have no particular preferences regarding teaching styles or types of school buildings. The ultimate aim of my research is to improve teaching irrespective of the style or building in which it is taking place."

AVOCATIONAL INTERESTS: Cycling, gardening, photography, painting, squash, sport parachuting.

*   *   *

BENSON, Daniel
See COOPER, Colin Symons

*   *   *

BENSON, Rolf Eric   1951-

PERSONAL: Born May 31, 1951, in Madison, Wis.; son of Leonard Axel (a minister) and Noreen (a nurse; maiden name, Obright) Benson. *Education:* St. Olaf College, B.A., 1973. *Home:* 1425 Taylor Ave., St. Paul, Minn. 55104.

CAREER: Prospect Foundry, Minneapolis, Minn., laboratory technician, 1974-78; Stillwater State Prison, Stillwater, Minn., instructor in music, 1977-80; Olson Boat Co., Wisconsin Dells, boat pilot, 1973—.

WRITINGS: Skydiving, Lerner, 1978.

SIDELIGHTS: Benson commented: "I have had a three-year involvement with skydiving. I hold a 'C' license and jumpmaster rating with two-hundred-fifty jumps. I also earned the SCR and SCS relative work awards for free-fall activities. SCR stands for Star Crest Recipient, which requires a person to be one of the first seven in an eight-person or larger formation. SCS is the Star Crest Solo, which means a jumper has entered eighth or later on such a formation during relative work. They indicate the level of relative work ability, the latter being more difficult to get.

"Relative work is difficult to describe since it involves weightlessness, the huge expanse of the sky, and the illusion that one is flying, not falling. Different body positions induce different falling speeds and different glide angles, allowing jumpers to rendevouz during free-fall periods that may last a minute and a half. The perceptions and skills take several hundred jumps to master. The feeling of sharing a very special feeling with other jumpers is incredible."

*   *   *

BERESFORD, Elisabeth

PERSONAL: Born in Paris, France; daughter of J. D. (a novelist) and Evelyn (Roskams) Beresford; married Maxwell

Robertson (a broadcaster), 1949; children: Kate, Marcus. *Home:* St. Anne's House, Alderney, Channel Islands. *Agent:* A. M. Heath Ltd., 40-42 William IV St., London WC2N 4DD, England; and David Higham Associates, 5/8 Lower John St., Golden Sq., London W.1, England.

CAREER: Writer; free-lance journalist, beginning 1948; radio broadcaster. *Wartime service:* Radio operator in Women's Naval Service during World War II.

WRITINGS—For children: *The Television Mystery*, Parrish, 1957; *Flying Doctor Mystery*, Parrish, 1958; *Trouble at Tullington Castle*, Parrish, 1958; *Cocky and the Missing Castle* (illustrated by Jennifer Miles), Constable, 1959; *Gappy Goes West*, Parrish, 1959; *Tullington Film-Makers*, Parrish, 1960; *Two Gold Dolphins* (illustrated by Peggy Fortnum), Constable, 1961, Bobbs-Merrill (illustrated by Janina Domanska), 1963; *Danger on the Old Pull'n Push*, Parrish, 1962, White Lion Publishers, 1976; *Strange Hiding Place*, Parrish, 1962; *Diana in Television*, Collins, 1963; *The Missing Formula Mystery*, Parrish, 1963; *The Mulberry Street Team* (illustrated by Juliet Pannett), Friday Press, 1963 (also see below); *Awkward Magic* (illustrated by Judith Valpy), Hart-Davis, 1964, Granada Publishing, 1978; *The Flying Doctor to the Rescue*, Parrish, 1964; *Holiday for Slippy* (illustrated by Pat Williams), Friday Press, 1964 (also see below); *The Magic World* (illustrated by Domanska), Bobbs-Merrill, 1964.

Game, Set, and Match, Parrish, 1965; *The Hidden Mill* (illustrated by Margery Gill), Benn, 1965 (also see below), Meredith Press, 1967; *Knights of the Cardboard Castle* (illustrated by C. R. Evans), Methuen, 1965, revised edition (illustrated by Reginald Gray), 1976; *Travelling Magic* (illustrated by Valpy), Hart-Davis, 1965, published as *The Vanishing Garden*, Funk, 1967, Granada Publishing, 1977; *Peter Climbs a Tree* (illustrated by Gill), Benn, 1966; *The Black Mountain Mystery*, Parrish, 1967; *Fashion Girl*, Collins, 1967; *Looking for a Friend* (illustrated by Gill), Benn, 1967; *More Adventure Stories* (contains "The Mulberry Street Team," "Holiday for Slippy," and "The Hidden Mill"), Benn, 1967; *The Island Bus* (illustrated by Robert Hodgson), Methuen, 1968, revised edition (illustrated by Gavin Rowe), 1977; *Sea-Green Magic*, Hart-Davis, 1968, revised edition (illustrated by Ann Tout), 1976; *The Wombles*, Benn, 1968, revised edition (illustrated by Margaret Gordon), Meredith Press, 1969 (also see below); *David Goes Fishing* (illustrated by Imre Hofbauer), Benn, 1969.

Gordon's Go-Kart (illustrated by Gill), McGraw, 1970; *Stephen and the Shaggy Dog* (illustrated by Robert Hales), Methuen, 1970; *Vanishing Magic* (illustrated by Tout), Hart-Davis, 1970; *The Wandering Wombles* (illustrated by Oliver Chadwick), Benn, 1970 (also see below); *Dangerous Magic* (illustrated by Chadwick), Hart-Davis, 1972; *The Invisible Womble and Other Stories* (illustrated by Ivor Wood), Benn, 1973; *The Secret Railway* (illustrated by James Hunt), Methuen, 1973; *The Wombles at Work* (illustrated by Gordon), Benn, 1973, revised edition (illustrated by B. Leith), 1976 (also see below); *The Wombles in Danger*, Benn, 1973; *Invisible Magic* (illustrated by R. Gray), Hart-Davis, 1974; *The Wombles Go to the Seaside*, World Distributors, 1974; *The Wombles to the Rescue* (illustrated by Gordon), Benn, 1974 (also see below).

Orinoco Runs Away (illustrated by Gordon), Benn, 1975; *The Snow Womble* (illustrated by Gordon), Benn, 1975; *Snuffle to the Rescue* (illustrated by Gunvor Edwards), Harmondsworth, 1975; *Tomsk and the Tired Tree* (illustrated by Gordon), Benn, 1975; *Wellington and the Blue Bal-*

loon (illustrated by Gordon), Benn, 1975; *The Wombles Book* (contains "The Wombles" and "The Wandering Wombles"), Benn, 1975; *The Wombles Gift Book* (illustrated by Derek Collard and Gordon), Benn, 1975; *The Wombles Make a Clean Sweep*, Benn, 1975; *Bungo Knows Best* (illustrated by Gordon), Benn, 1976; *The MacWombles' Pipe Band* (illustrated by Gordon), Benn, 1976; *Madame Cholet's Picnic Party* (illustrated by Gordon), Benn, 1976; *Tobermory's Big Surprise* (illustrated by Gordon), Benn, 1976; *The Wombles Go Round the World* (illustrated by Gordon), Benn, 1976; *The Wombles of Wimbledon* (contains "The Wombles at Work" and "The Wombles to the Rescue"), Benn, 1976; *The World of the Wombles* (illustrated by Edgar Hodges), World Distributors, 1976; *The Wombles Annual, 1975 to 1978*, four volumes, World Distributors, 1974-77; *Beginning to Read Storybook*, Benn, 1977; *Secret Magic* (illustrated by Caroline Sharpe), Hart-Davis, 1978; *Toby's Luck* (illustrated by Doreen Caldwell), Methuen, 1978; *Wombling Free* (illustrated by Hodges), Benn, 1978; *The Treasure Hunters*, Elsevier, 1980; *The Four of Us*, Hutchinson, 1981.

For adults; novels; all published by Hale, except as noted: *Paradise Island*, 1963; *Escape to Happiness*, 1964; *Roses Round the Door*, 1965; *Islands of Shadows*, 1966; *Veronica*, 1967; *A Tropical Affair*, 1968; *Saturday's Child*, 1969; *Love Remembered*, 1970; *Love and the S.S. Beatrice*, 1972; *Pandora*, 1974; *Thunder of Her Heart*, Dale Books, 1978; *Tropical Affairs*, Dell, 1978; *The Steadfast Lover*, 1980; *The Silver Chain*, 1980.

Plays: "The Wombles," produced in London, 1974; (with Nick Renton) "Road to Albutal," produced in Edinburgh, Scotland, 1976. Also author of screenplay, "The Wombles," 1977, and more than sixty television scripts.

Contributor of short stories to magazines.

SIDELIGHTS: Elisabeth Beresford has achieved her greatest success as a writer through the creation of her "Womble" series for children. These tales, which number over twenty-five, explore the fantasy world of the Womble family, made up of numerous peculiar creatures, such as Tomsk, Bungo, and Wellington, who are based on film puppets designed by Ivor Wood. Most of the books are colorfully illustrated to depict Wood's originations. The endearing Wombles uphold old-fashioned virtues and are concerned with conservation. They constantly seek other uses for worn-out items, in accordance with the family motto: "Make good use of bad rubbish."

Some of Beresford's other publications for children are also set in a fantasy world. Several of these stories, including *Secret Magic*, *Invisible Magic*, and *Travelling Magic*, tell of characters journeying through time. The main character of *Secret Magic* is a talking cat who is actually an ancient sphinx. In *Invisible Magic* a young boy encounters a princess from another era while bicycling in a park. A girl and her younger brother befriend a magician from ancient Britain in *Travelling Magic*.

Beresford told *CA*: "As my father was the novelist J. D. Beresford and two of my brothers are writers, I grew up in a world of books, and it was inevitable that I should follow in their footsteps, although I began work as a radio reporter for the BBC. In the last twenty-four years I've written seventy-nine books and started on my eightieth in January, 1981. I hate typing the dreaded words 'Chapter One' as I find writing very hard work and will think up a dozen good reasons for *not* sitting down at the typewriter. But one of the great bonuses is getting letters from children all over the world who sometimes just put 'The Wombles. England' on the envelope.

"My daughter, Kate, has had four children's books published; my son Marcus is a sports journalist; and my husband, Max Robertson, who is a BBC sports commentator, is just finishing a book on the history of the Wimbleton Tennis Championships. So sometimes the house does feel a bit like a book factory.

"My pet peeve is the people who say, 'Of course I could write a book if I had the time.' If I had a sunny day for every time that's been said to me I should live in a world of perpetual sunshine. My ambition is to get so far ahead of the tax/gas/electric/oil bills that I can write the book I *really* want to write. It would be about family life, along the lines of Betty Macdonald's wonderfully funny *The Egg and I*. But by the way things are going at the moment, it'll probably be about book number one hundred and one."

AVOCATIONAL INTERESTS: Reading, photography, surfing, breakfast in bed.

*   *   *

BERGMAN, Bernard A(aron)   1894-1980

PERSONAL: Born July 8, 1894, in Chillicothe, Ohio; died April 11, 1980, in Philadelphia, Pa.; son of Eleazer and Carrie (Weiler) Bergman; married Frances Dellar, March 17, 1933 (died October, 1965). *Education:* Ohio State University, B.A., 1916. *Politics:* Democrat. *Religion:* Jewish. *Home:* 226 West Rittenhouse Sq., Philadelphia, Pa. 19103.

CAREER/WRITINGS: Worked in public relations in New York City, 1919-31; *New Yorker,* New York City, managing editor, 1931-33; editor of "March of Events Page" for Hearst Newspapers, 1933-35; *Philadelphia Record,* Philadelphia, Pa., 1935-42, began as Sunday editor, became feature editor and executive editor; *New York Post,* New York City, feature editor, 1938; editor of *Pageant* (magazine), 1946; director of public relations for Publicker Industries, Inc., 1947-55; *Philadelphia Daily News,* Philadelphia, editor and director, 1955-58; *Jewish Exponent,* Philadelphia, editor, 1958-61; *Philadelphia Bulletin,* Philadelphia, editor of Sunday magazine, 1961-66, editor of book division, 1966-69, book editor, 1970-80, book columnist, 1977-80. Special instructor in journalism at University of Pennsylvania, 1951-52, lecturer, 1960. Author of book with Philip Wylie, *The Smiling Corpse,* 1935. *Military service:* Served with U.S. Army during World War I; became sergeant major. Served with U.S. Army Air Forces during World War II; became lieutenant colonel. *Member:* Philadelphia Public Relations Association, Phi Beta Kappa, Sigma Delta Chi, Zeta Beta Tau, Franklin Inn (Philadelphia, Pa.).

SIDELIGHTS: In 1974 the *Philadelphia Bulletin* established the B. A. Bergman Award for outstanding literary achievement in Greater Philadelphia.*

*   *   *

BERKSON, William Koller   1944-

PERSONAL: Born June 17, 1944, in Urbana, Ill.; son of Ralph (an orthodontist) and Ruth (Koller) Berkson; married Isabelle Tsakok (an economist), October 31, 1970; children: Aaron, Eve. *Education:* University of Illinois, B.A., 1965; London School of Economics and Political Science, London, M.Sc., 1967, Ph.D., 1970. *Home:* 11414 Orchard Lane, Reston, Va. 22090.

CAREER: Polytechnic, London, England, part-time lecturer in philosophy, 1966-67; Enfield Technical College, Middle-sex, England, part-time lecturer in philosophy, 1967-68; University of London, London School of Economics and Political Science, London, part-time lecturer in philosophy, 1968-69; Hofstra University, Hempstead, N.Y., instructor of philosophy, 1970; Boston University, Boston, Mass., part-time lecturer in philosophy, 1971-72; Northeastern University, Boston, part-time lecturer in philosophy, 1972; Emerson College, Boston, part-time lecturer in philosophy, 1972; William Patterson College, Wayne, N.J., assistant professor of philosophy, 1973; Bridgewater State College, Bridgewater, Mass., assistant professor of philosophy, 1973-76; freelance writer, 1976—. *Member:* Philosophy of Science Association, Washington Independent Writers.

WRITINGS: Fields of Force: Development of a World View From Faraday to Einstein, Routledge & Kegan Paul, 1974; (with John Wettersten) *Lernen durch Irrtum* (title means "Learning From Error: The Significance of Karl Popper's Psychology of Learning"), Hoffmann & Campe, 1981. Contributor to scholarly journals, including *Inquiry.*

WORK IN PROGRESS: Drawing the Line, a self-help book on problem-solving.

SIDELIGHTS: Berkson told *CA:* "In my first book, *Fields of Force,* my main accomplishment was to show that Faraday had a view of the physical world that was distinct from both Einstein's and J. C. Maxwell's—a view in which contemporary physicists might still find inspiration. My book on Popper as a psychologist was the result of a marathon argument with my co-author, John Wettersten—an argument which we decided to write down and develop. We point out in the book that Popper's work provides new insights—beyond those of Piaget and Gestalt psychology—into how we learn.

"*Drawing the Line,* my forthcoming book on personal problem solving, was born of both my technical ideas on rationality and my own struggles in life. In it I have tried to translate the philosophical ideas into practical methods for solving personal problems and communicate these methods to the reader who is not so much interested in philosophy as in living a happier life. Trying to make my philosophy practical and accessible to the general reader has proved the greatest challenge I have yet faced either as a thinker or as a writer. To what extent I have succeeded the public will, I hope, soon be able to judge."

*   *   *

BERRY, Jo(celyn)   1933-

PERSONAL: Born July 17, 1933, in El Dorado, Kan.; daughter of Fred (a grocer) and Inez (Stebbins) Gladfelter; married George Berry (an aerospace engineer), January 30, 1955; children: Brenda Jean, Cathy Lynn, Brian Fredric. *Education:* Attended University of Kansas, 1952-55; University of Southern California, B.S., 1960. *Politics:* Republican. *Religion:* Presbyterian. *Home and office:* Center for Creative Ministries, 12739 Deon Pl., Granada Hills, Calif. 91344.

CAREER: Elementary school teacher and reading specialist in Los Angeles, Calif., 1960-69; Grace Community Church, Sun Valley, Calif., director of children's and women's ministries, 1972-76; David C. Cook Publishing Co., Elgin, Ill., writer and consultant, 1973-80; Center for Creative Ministries, Granada Hills, Calif., founder and director, 1979—. Writer and educational consultant for Glenco Publishing Co. in Encino, Calif. Teacher at Forest Home Women's Auxiliary, 1976-78; public speaker. *Member:* Christian Writers Guild.

WRITINGS: *The Happy Home Handbook*, Revell, 1976; *Can You Love Yourself?*, Regal Books, 1978; *Growing, Sharing, Serving*, David Cook, 1979; *Alcoholism: The Way Back to Reality*, Regal Books, 1980; *Proverbs for Easier Living*, Regal Books, 1980; *Beloved Unbeliever*, Zondervan, 1981. Contributor to magazines, including *Christianity Today*, *Family Life Today*, *Working Woman*, and *Family Circle*.

WORK IN PROGRESS: A book for families and children of alcoholics; a series of children's books for Macmillan.

SIDELIGHTS: Jo Berry told *CA*: "The Center for Creative Ministries is designed for the woman who wants to explore possibilities about becoming more effective in her home, community, and church, and be trained to set up biblically-oriented women's ministries in her local church.

"We do not teach doctrine or theology. Our seminars are motivational and present a storehouse of ideas from both the scriptures and personal experiences that each participant can draw upon as a resource for use in her own life and her local church."

She added: "I am especially concerned, in my writing and teaching, with helping women of *all* ages reach their full potential. I am convinced that poor self-image is at the root of their problems, so many of my seminars are on that subject.

"My book *Can You Love Yourself?* is a special pleasure to me. It is being used in women's prisons and in psychological counseling centers throughout the United States. I also distribute tapes of the seminars all over the world."

AVOCATIONAL INTERESTS: Travel, sewing, collecting country-western music, the Los Angeles Dodgers.

* * *

BERRY, Paul 1919-

PERSONAL: Born December 25, 1919, in Weston-by-Welland, England; son of Philip Kendall (a farmer) and Mabel Hannah (Fisher) Berry. *Education:* Attended grammar school in Kettering, England. *Politics:* Socialist. *Religion:* Church of England. *Home:* Bridgefoot Cottage, Stedham, Midhurst, Sussex, England. *Office:* Department of Secretarial Studies, Kingsway-Princeton College for Further Education, London W.C.1, England.

CAREER: Free-lance writer, 1947—; Kingsway-Princeton College for Further Education, London, England, lecturer, 1956-73, senior lecturer in secretarial studies and deputy head of department, 1973—. *Military service:* British Army, Royal Engineers, 1940-46; became corporal. *Member:* Royal Society for Literature.

WRITINGS: (With Renee Huggett) *Daughters of Cain* (biographical accounts), Allen & Unwin, 1956; *By Royal Appointment: A Biography of Mary Ann Clark, Mistress of the Duke of York, 1803-1807*, Femmina Books, 1970; (author of introduction) Vera Brittain, *Testament of Experience*, Virago, 1979.

WORK IN PROGRESS: *Testament of Faith* (tentative title), a biography of Vera Brittain, publication expected in 1982.

SIDELIGHTS: Berry commented to *CA*: "My mother's influence has led to my being deeply interested in the progression and emancipation of women, which is reflected in my writing. As a lecturer to sixteen- to nineteen-year-olds I am concerned with the development and difficulties of young people. As a close friend (for twenty-eight years) of Vera Brittain, and also as her literary executor and literary executor for Winifred Holtby, I am deeply involved in the recent renaissance of their works, and in their lives.

"Being a private person, I derive much sustenance from the countryside and rural surroundings, gardening, and tennis fanaticism. My burning obsession is to see world peace and goodwill to all people, which I believe can only be achieved by a change of heart by all individuals, and not through national or international politicking."

* * *

BERRY, Thomas Edwin 1930-

PERSONAL: Born September 19, 1930, in Illinois; son of Thomas Edison and Lillian (Dietz) Berry; married Kira Vladimirovna Kalichevsky, December 15, 1965. *Education:* Southern Illinois University, B.S., 1952; Syracuse University, diploma, 1953; University of Illinois, M.A., 1956; University of Texas, Ph.D., 1965. *Home:* 6919 Carleton Ter., College Park, Md. 20740. *Office:* Slavic Department, University of Maryland, College Park, Md. 20742.

CAREER: Ford Administration, Chicago, Ill., administrator, 1957-58; University of California, Irvine, professor of Russian, 1966-68; University of Maryland, College Park, professor of Russian, 1969—. Interpreter for International Parachute Championships, 1962.

WRITINGS: *The Seasons in Russian Literature*, Burgess, 1969; *A. K. Tolstoy: Russian Humorist*, Bethany Press, 1972; *Plots and Characters in Major Russian Fiction: Pushkin, Lermontov, Turgenev, Tolstoi*, Archon Books, 1977; *Plots and Characters in Major Russian Fiction: Gogol, Goncharov, Dostoevskii*, Archon Books, 1979; *Russian for Business*, Birchbark Press, 1979; *Russian Poetry: An Intermediate-Level Manual for Literary Discussion*, Terrace Press, 1979; *Russian-English Sports Dictionary*, Welt Publishing, 1979; *Information Peking (Beijing)*, Welt Publishing, 1980; *Spiritualism in Tsarist Society and Literature*, Nordland, 1981.

* * *

BEST, Marc
See LEMIEUX, Marc

* * *

BEVERIDGE, George David, Jr. 1922-

PERSONAL: Born January 5, 1922, in Washington; son of George David and Lillian Agnes (Little) Beveridge; married Betty Jean Derwent, June 6, 1944; children: Barbara J., Deborah A., David C. *Education:* Attended George Washington University, 1939. *Home:* 9302 Kingsley Ave., Bethesda, Md. 20014. *Office:* 225 Virginia Ave., Washington, D.C. 20003.

CAREER/WRITINGS: *Washington Star*, Washington, D.C., reporter, 1946-63, editorial writer, 1963-74, assistant managing editor, 1974-75, senior assistant managing editor and ombudsman, 1976—. *Military service:* U.S. Army, 1942-46; became lieutenant. *Awards, honors:* Pulitzer Prize, 1958, for reporting in local news category.

* * *

BEWES, Richard 1934-

PERSONAL: Born December 1, 1934, in Nairobi, Kenya; son of T.F.C. (a missionary) and Sylvia (a missionary) Bewes; married Elisabeth Jaques, April 18, 1964; children: Timothy, Wendy, Stephen. *Education:* Emmanuel College, Cambridge, B.A., 1958, M.A., 1961. *Home:* 3 Gatehill Rd., Northwood, Middlesex HA6 3QB, England. *Office:* Emmanuel Church, High St., Northwood, Middlesex, England.

CAREER: Ordained minister of Church of England, 1959; assistant minister of Church of England in Beckenham, England, 1959-65; vicar of Church of England in Harold Wood, England, 1965-74; Emmanuel Church, Northwood, England, vicar, 1974—. Host of "Orange and Lemon Club," a program on BBC-Radio, 1969-74. Public speaker.

WRITINGS: God in Ward Twelve, Lutterworth, 1974; *Advantage Mr. Christian*, Lutterworth, 1975; *Talking About Prayer*, Falcon, 1979; *John Wesley's England*, Hodder & Stoughton, 1981; (with Robert F. Hicks) *Explaining Bible Truth*, Pioneer International Publishing, 1981; *A Movement Is Born*, Mowbrays, 1981. Author of "Quest," a weekly column, syndicated by Church of England Newspaper to Christian newspapers.

WORK IN PROGRESS: Explaining Bible Truth, a series of nine books to be published collectively as *The Pocket Handbook of Christian Truth* (tentative title).

SIDELIGHTS: Bewes told *CA:* "*John Wesley's England* gave me great pleasure in producing—partly because of my admiration for Wesley, and also because the book is very attractive; it has over two hundred etchings and prints of Old England, and some fascinating excerpts from Wesley's journals. Most of my writing is in the realm of Christian experience. I work fast, and usually at night, because of my duties as a church pastor. *Talking About Prayer* was a joy to write, and I was delighted that Billy Graham was able to write the foreword."

AVOCATIONAL INTERESTS: Travel (Kenya, Tanzania, Germany, Spain, Switzerland, Belgium).

*   *   *

BEY, Isabelle
  See BOSTICCO, (Isabel Lucy) Mary

*   *   *

BEYNON, John
  See HARRIS, John (Wyndham Parkes Lucas) Beynon

*   *   *

BHARTI, Ma Satya   1942-
  (Jill Jacobs, Jill Safian)

PERSONAL: Born January 12, 1942, in New York, N.Y.; daughter of Lewis (a physician) and Jean (Becker) Jacobs; married Kenneth Safian (a securities analyst), November 18, 1960 (divorced, 1969); children: Nancy, Patricia, William. *Education:* Attended Brown University, 1959-60, and New York University, 1960; Sarah Lawrence College, B.A., 1970. *Politics:* "Presently apolitical; formerly a liberal Democrat with radical leanings." *Religion:* "Sannyasin, a disciple of Bhagwan Shree Rajneesh." *Home and office:* 17 Koregaon Park, Poona, Maharastra, India.

CAREER: Free-lance writer, 1960-69; yoga teacher in Westchester County, New York, 1969-72; Rajneesh Foundation, Poona, India, editor and publishing coordinator, 1972—.

WRITINGS: The Ultimate Risk, Wildwood House, 1980, published as *Drunk on the Divine*, Grove, 1981; *Death Comes Dancing*, Routledge & Kegan Paul, 1981; *In Meditation* (novel), Grove, 1982.

Editor—All by Bhagwan Shree Rajneesh: *Come Follow Me*, Volume I, Rajneesh Foundation, 1976, Harper, 1981, Volume II, Rajneesh Foundation, 1977; *Meditation: The Art of Ecstasy*, Harper, 1976; *I Am the Gate*, Harper, 1977; *The*

New Alchemy: To Turn You On, Rajneesh Foundation, 1978; *The Psychology of the Esoteric*, Harper, 1979; *The Eternal Quest*, Orient, 1980; *The Great Challenge*, Anubhuti Verlag, 1980; (also translator) *Bhakti Sutra*, Rajneesh Foundation, 1981; (also translator) *The Odyssey Within*, Rajneesh Foundation, 1981; (also translator) *The Gateless Gate*, Rajneesh Foundation, 1982. Political speech writer, 1972. Contributor of poems to magazines, under names Jill Jacobs and Jill Safian.

WORK IN PROGRESS: The Confessions of a Disciple, a diary, completion expected in 1981; *Beyond Relationship*, 1981; *The Master's Work: A New Phase*, 1981.

SIDELIGHTS: Ma Satya Bharti's books have been published in Dutch, Italian, German, Portuguese, Japanese, Spanish, and French.

She wrote: "Since taking initiation from an enlightened master, Bhagwan Shree Rajneesh, in 1972, the vast amount of my writing has been concerned with Bhagwan's revolutionary work. If I can be said to have any goals at all beyond my own continual evolution, they are to indicate in every and all possible ways, to as many people as possible, the miracle that is happening around Bhagwan—to extend an invitation to all to come and join in this unique experiment: a community where God can descend, an opportunity for each to attain his or her own Buddhahood."

BIOGRAPHICAL/CRITICAL SOURCES: Ma Prem Divya, *In My Master's Garden*, Part I, Rajneesh Foundation, 1982.

*   *   *

BIBBY, Violet   1908-

PERSONAL: Born February 18, 1908, in Newport Pagnell, Buckinghamshire, England; daughter of James Wilson (a manager) and Theresa (Hall) Richardson; married Edmund Bibby, July, 1937; children: two sons. *Education:* Whitelands College, teaching diploma, 1928; attended Central School of Art, London, 1928-30. *Home:* One Cumberland Rd., Angmering, Sussex BN16 4BG, England. *Agent:* Murray Pollinger, 4 Garrick St., London WC2E 9HB, England.

CAREER: Teacher of English and arts and crafts in England, 1928-42, part-time teacher, 1942-69; writer, 1950—. Artist, with paintings exhibited in major galleries in southern England. Lecturer at writers' conferences, schools, colleges, and libraries; appeared on radio programs in England, Australia, and the United States. *Member:* Association of Sussex Artists.

WRITINGS—Juvenile: Saranne, Penguin, 1969; *The Mirrored Shield*, Penguin, 1970; *The Wildling*, Penguin, 1971; *Many Waters*, Faber, 1974, published as *Many Waters Cannot Quench Love*, Morrow, 1975; *Tinner's Quest*, Faber, 1977, Merrimack Book Service, 1978; *Phantom Horse*, Kaye & Ward, 1979.

Contributor of articles to periodicals, including *London Times* and *Manchester Guardian*.

SIDELIGHTS: Bibby's books are generally set in past centuries and feature characters with occupations such as stonemason, glass worker, and engineer. *Tinner's Quest*, for example, centers on the tin miners of Cornwall during the eighteenth century. This tale follows the adventures of a young boy working a mine recently reopened after having been flooded fifteen years earlier. The boy's father had been suspected of flooding the mine and was transported to Australia. Encouraged by his uncle, the lad convinces his mother to travel there in search of his father. *Times Literary Supplement* critic Ros Francy said that in "this well-constructed story, Violet Bibby combines detail from much careful research with a clear and fast-moving narrative."

Bibby told *CA:* "All of my books have been set among small, enclosed communities: the canal folk, the forest glassblowers, the tinners, the fen-dwellers. They show loyalty, divided loyalty, courage, and compassion. An awareness of the rhythms of the seasons, and an acute sensitivity of the earth and its creatures is most often the driving force in my work."

BIOGRAPHICAL/CRITICAL SOURCES: Times Literary Supplement, March 25, 1977.

*   *   *

BIGELOW, Robert Sydney 1918-

PERSONAL: Born April 26, 1918, in Canning, Nova Scotia, Canada; son of Scott Sidney (a builder) and Amy (Chisolm) Bigelow; married Moyra Frances Hale, January 15, 1946; children: John Christopher, David Robert, Neville Scott. *Education:* McGill University, B.Sc., 1950, Ph.D., 1954. *Home:* 14 Head St., Sumner, Christchurch 8, New Zealand.

CAREER: McGill University, Montreal, Quebec, assistant professor, 1953-59, associate professor of entomology, 1959-62; University of Canterbury, Christchurch, New Zealand, reader in zoology, 1962-78; writer. *Military service:* Canadian Army, Armoured Corps, 1941-46; served in Europe.

WRITINGS: The Grasshoppers of New Zealand, University of Canterbury Press, 1967; *The Dawn Warriors,* Little, Brown, 1969; *Stubborn Bear,* Little Brown, 1970; *A New Approach to Human Evolution,* Behavioral Sciences Tape Library, 1972.

SIDELIGHTS: Bigelow told *CA:* "I extend my thanks to other authors, especially historical writers and biographers, for providing me with so many hours of enjoyment, and my apologies for spending so much time reading and so little time writing."

*   *   *

BIGG, Patricia Nina 1932-
(Patricia Ainsworth)

PERSONAL: Born March 20, 1932, in Adelaide, Australia; daughter of William Alfred (a company director) and Una (Lovell) Luckman; married Robert Bigg (a credit manager), March 26, 1955; children: Grant Robert, Justin Glen. *Education:* Attended technical high school in Adelaide, Australia. *Home:* 5-A Way Ave., Myrtle Bank, South Australia 5064. *Agent:* John Farquharson Ltd., Bell House, Bell Yard, London WC2A 2JU, England.

CAREER: Commonwealth Trading Bank, Adelaide, Australia, secretary, 1948-51; G. & R. Wills & Co. Ltd. (warehouse firm), Adelaide, secretary, 1952-55; writer, 1967—. *Member:* Australian Society of Authors.

WRITINGS—All novels under pseudonym Patricia Ainsworth; all published by R. Hale: *The Flickering Candle,* 1968; *The Candle Rekindled,* 1969; *Steady Burns the Candle,* 1970; *The Devil's Hole,* 1970; *Portrait in Gold,* 1971; *A String of Silver Beads,* 1972; *The Bridal Lamp,* 1975; *The Enchanted Cup,* 1980.

WORK IN PROGRESS—All novels under pseudonym Patricia Ainsworth: *The Sword and the Rose; A Scabbard for the Sword; The Larkspur Mountain.*

SIDELIGHTS: Patricia Bigg wrote: "I have always had the need to write in order to be a complete person. My abiding interest has always been the underestimated role in history

played by women through family life. In the last two years I have visited Canada, the United States, Great Britain, and Europe, and I really enjoy the research necessary to write my books, which I would describe as historical romance, the emphasis on historical. My periods are the seventeenth century at the time of the English civil war and nineteenth-century Australia."

AVOCATIONAL INTERESTS: Reading detective novels, classical music, international events, walking.

*   *   *

BILLINGTON, Michael 1939-

PERSONAL: Born November 16, 1939, in Leamington Spa, England; son of Alfred Robert (an accountant) and Patricia (Bradshaw) Billington; married Jeanne Bradlaugh, December 12, 1978; children: Natasha Alexandra. *Education:* St. Catherine's College, Oxford, B.A., 1961. *Home:* 15 Hearne Rd., London W.4, England. *Agent:* A. P. Watt Ltd., 26/28 Bedford Row, London WC1R 4HL, England. *Office:* Guardian, 119 Farringdon Rd., London EC1 3ER, England.

CAREER: London Times, London, England, deputy drama and film critic, 1965-71; television critic, 1968-70; *Guardian,* London, drama critic, 1971—. Presenter of "Kaleidoscope" and "Critics' Forum" on British Broadcasting Corp. (BBC-Radio). *Member:* Critics' Circle. *Awards, honors:* Named critic of the year by International Press Corp., 1974.

WRITINGS: The Modern Actor, Hamish Hamilton, 1973; *How Tickled I Am: A Celebration of Ken Dodd,* David & Charles, 1977; (editor) *Performing Arts,* Macdonald & Co., 1980; *The Guinness Book of Facts and Feats: Theatre,* Guinness Superlatives, 1982; *Alan Ayckbourn,* Macmillan, 1982. Film critic for *Illustrated London News* and *Birmingham Post,* 1968—. Contributor to *TV Guide* and *New York Times.*

SIDELIGHTS: Billington told *CA:* "I am principally a drama critic; I feel the job chose me as much as I chose it. I feel an ungovernable urge to set down my impression of plays and performances that I have seen. But it can be a very monastic profession. Therefore I enjoy the exposure to other arts that comes from doing a monthly film column and from doing radio arts programs which give me a chance to discuss books, television, opera, and ballet."

*   *   *

BINDOFF, Stanley Thomas 1908-1980

OBITUARY NOTICE—See index for *CA* sketch: Born April 8, 1908, in Brighton, East Sussex, England; died December 23, 1980, in England. Educator, author, and editor. Bindoff taught history at the University of London for nearly forty years, retiring in 1975. He wrote and edited numerous books on history. Among his writings are *The Scheldt Question to 1839; Ket's Rebellion, 1549; Tudor England;* and *The Fame of Sir Thomas Gresham.* Obituaries and other sources: *London Times,* December 29, 1980.

*   *   *

BIRD, James Harold 1923-

PERSONAL: Born June 9, 1923, in London, England; son of Frederick Thomas (a grocer) and Kate Bird; married Olwen Joyce Sturge, September 6, 1955. *Education:* University of London, B.A. (with honors), 1951, Ph.D., 1953. *Home:* 95 Lakewood Rd., Chandler's Ford, Eastleigh, Hampshire SO5 1AD, England. *Office:* Department of Geography, University of Southampton, Southampton SO9 5NH, England.

CAREER: University of Southampton, Southampton, England, assistant lecturer, 1953-54; University of London, King's College, London, England, assistant lecturer, 1954-57, lecturer, 1957-62; University of New England, Australia, visiting lecturer, 1963; University of London, University College, London, reader in geography, 1964-67; University of Southampton, Southampton, England, professor of geography, 1967—, deputy vice-chancellor, 1978—. *Member:* Royal Institute of Geographers (member of council, 1970-73; president, 1980), Geographical Association, Institute of British Geographers (member of council, 1971-74, 1977—). *Awards, honors:* Social Science Research Council grant, 1978-80.

WRITINGS: The Geography of the Port of London, Hutchinson, 1957; *The Major Seaports of the United Kingdom,* Hutchinson, 1963; *Seaport Gateways of Australia,* Oxford University Press, 1968; *Seaports and Seaport Terminals,* Hutchinson, 1971; *Centrality and Cities,* Routledge & Kegan Paul, 1977. Contributor to learned journals.

WORK IN PROGRESS: A historical novel "exploring the idea of societal change."

SIDELIGHTS: Bird told *CA:* "My specialized research output has been on the economic geography of seaports. *Centrality and Cities* welded the development of seaports onto the general development of cities. It included the gateway concept, whereby regions are sometimes developed and then certainly sustained by links with other areas in the home territory and overseas by gateways, many of which are seaports.

"This theme is continued in the presidential address to the Institute of British Geographers, 'The Target of Space and the Arrow of Time,' delivered in January, 1981, where the general theme of change as it affects an academic subject like geography focused on the necessity for a constant process of comparison, a word that is finally explored in its very varied manifestations in arts and science methodologies."

*   *   *

BIRD, Vivian 1910-
(Vic Beer)

PERSONAL: Born October 31, 1910, in Warwick, England; son of John Allsebrook (a publican) and Rose (Weaver) Bird; married Edith Drew, November 27, 1937; children: Michael Arthur, Molly Deirdre Bird Langridge and Jennifer Ann (twins). *Education:* Received certificate in education from Alsager Teachers Training College. *Politics:* "Very right, non-party." *Religion:* Atheist. *Home:* 486 Shirley Rd., Hall Green, Birmingham 28, England. *Office: Post and Mail,* Birmingham 4, England.

CAREER: Writer. *Post and Mail,* Birmingham, England, special feature writer, 1951-75, author of "Sunday Mercury," a weekly column, and "Warwickshire and Worcestershire Life," a monthly column. Broadcaster for British Broadcasting Corp. President of Sparkbrook Junior Imperial League, 1927-33. *Military service:* British Army, gunner in Royal Artillery, 1940-45.

WRITINGS: Bird's-Eye View: The Midlands, Roundwood Press, 1969, 3rd edition, 1973; *Portrait of Birmingham,* R. Hale, 1970, 3rd edition, 1979; *The Sunset Coasts,* Roundwood Press, 1970; *Warwickshire,* Batsford, 2nd edition, 1973; *Staffordshire,* Batsford, 1974; *Short History of Warwickshire and Birmingham,* Batsford, 1977; *Exploring the West Midlands,* Batsford, 1977. Contributor to *Orkney Blast,* under pseudonym Vic Beer.

SIDELIGHTS: Bird wrote: "My books have been written with my feet—as a walker. The most satisfying thing I have done in my life is to have walked fifty miles on my fiftieth birthday, in seventeen-and-a-quarter hours; the most useful thing is to have put on the map of Britain the thirty-five-mile Six Shropshire Summits Walk, now one of the great one-day stamina tests.

"My main literary interest now is the essay. Other interests which have grown out of and contribute to my journalism are epitaphs, heraldry, names of anything (particularly houses), saints and their emblems, and (despite my atheism) anything to do with churches except their basic architecture."

*   *   *

BIRKSTED-BREEN, Dana 1946-
(Dana Breen)

PERSONAL: Born July 12, 1946, in Maryland; daughter of Julian and Mary (Lurie) Breen; married Ian Birksted (an art dealer); children: Sasha, Noah. *Education:* Institut des sciences de l'education, Geneva, Switzerland, Propedeutique, 1965; Sorbonne, University of Paris, Lic. es Lettres, 1967; University of Sussex, Ph.D., 1972. *Home:* 57 Wood Lane, London N. 6, England. *Agent:* Deborah Rogers Ltd., 5-11 Mortimer St., London W1N 7RH, England.

CAREER: University of Sussex, Brighton, England, research fellow at Student Health Center, 1970-72, psychotherapist, 1972-74; private practice of psychotherapy and psychoanalysis in London, England, 1974—.

WRITINGS—Under name Dana Breen: *The Birth of a First Child: Towards an Understanding of Femininity,* Tavistock Publications, 1975; (contributor) Susan Lipshitz, editor, *Tearing the Veil,* Routledge & Kegan Paul, 1978; *Talking With Mothers,* Jill Norman, 1981.

SIDELIGHTS: Dana Birksted-Breen told *CA:* "I have always been interested in how people change. This has led me to my work as a psychoanalyst (I qualified at the Institute of Psychoanalysis in London) and to my research on psychological changes in women with the birth of a child, which also arose out of my interest in understanding femininity. My first book endeavored to show that pregnancy is not a temporary illness to be recovered from, but that the birth of a first child is a time of potential growth. *Talking With Mothers,* my second book, is less academic and is the 'story' of the experience of having a baby."

In *The Birth of a First Child* conventional concepts of femininity and motherhood, held by both women and psychiatrists, are the main targets of inquiry. Rachel Chazan, reviewing the book for the *Israel Annals of Psychiatry and Related Disciplines,* observed that "Breen centres her research on self-concept. The way in which the woman sees herself in relation to other important persons in her life, in early and late pregnancy and after the birth of her child." Breen's study contends that the traditional view of the "good mother"—unselfish, self-sacrificing, emotional—is rooted in a false definition of femininity. "We see that the conventional concepts of motherliness and femininity become less and not more evident after childbirth," Chazan wrote. "Activity, even assertiveness are found in practice to be important."

According to Breen, pregnancy is not a hurdle to overcome on the way back to health. Naseen Khan wrote in *New Society:* "[Breen] subscribes to the more attractive idea of 'the person as actor, as involved in a continual process of reappraisal and change, of reorganisation and adaptation.' In this context, pregnancy is obviously a powerful catalyst. It involves a change in status, in responsibilities, in relationships with husband, parents and the outside world. How women deal with that—whether positively or negatively—and what influence current cultural stereotypes of 'motherhood' have is central to the book.''

Breen is especially critical of Freud and others who assert that passivity, masochism, and narcissism are among the essential traits of femininity. Chazan commented: ''The assumption used to be that women with traditionally 'masculine' attitudes encounter problems; this is fallacious. It is more likely that the women with stereotyped 'feminine' attitudes will encounter problems. Dr. Breen suggests that, to avoid confusion, femininity should be defined on a biological basis. 'Femininity refers to the qualities which make for a good adjustment to the female biological role, the bearing of young.'

''In summary,'' said Chazan, ''the women best adjusted to childbearing are found to be those who had honest, differentiated appraisals of self and others, who did not over-idealize motherhood. They recalled a good mother of their own; they did not experience themselves as passive.... The beautiful drawings by Nan Lurie are in keeping with the tenor of this unusual work, the reading of which is a fascinating and thought-provoking experience.''

BIOGRAPHICAL/CRITICAL SOURCES: New Society, July 17, 1975; *Israel Annals of Psychiatry and Related Disciplines,* December, 1978.

* * *

BIRN, Raymond Francis 1935-

PERSONAL: Born May 10, 1935, in New York, N.Y.; son of Saul Albert (a machinist) and Celia (Markman) Birn; married Randi Marie Ingebrigtsen (a university professor), July 18, 1960; children: Eric Stephen, Laila Marie. *Education:* New York University, B.A., 1956; University of Illinois, M.A., 1957, Ph.D., 1961. *Home:* 2140 Elk Ave., Eugene, Ore. 97403. *Office:* Department of History, University of Oregon, Eugene, Ore. 97403.

CAREER: University of Oregon, Eugene, instructor, 1961-63, assistant professor, 1963-66, associate professor, 1966-72, professor of history, 1972—, head of department, 1971-78. *Military service:* U.S. Army, 1959-60. *Member:* American Historical Association, American Society for Eighteenth Century Studies, Society for French Historical Studies, Institut d'Etude du Livre, Phi Beta Kappa. *Awards, honors:* Fulbright fellow in France, 1968-69; National Endowment for the Humanities senior fellow, 1976-77.

WRITINGS: Pierre Rousseau and the Philosophes of Bouillon, Institut et Musee Voltaire, 1964; *Crisis, Absolutism, Revolution: Europe, 1648-1789/91,* Holt, 1977. Contributor to professional journals. Advisory editor of *Eighteenth Century Studies,* 1974—; member of board of editors of *French Historical Studies,* 1977—.

WORK IN PROGRESS: Research on the book trade, publishers, and authors in France in the early eighteenth century.

SIDELIGHTS: Birn told *CA:* ''I see the history of books as a central theme in the development of modern civilization. In my research I try to fuse together the ideas of authors, economic motivations of publishers, and censorship patterns of state officials into a cohesive narrative-analysis. The history of a book can inform us, in microcosm, of the texture of a civilization. I am particularly interested in the origins of the

French enlightenment, and it is through the history of early eighteenth-century French books that I am developing my knowledge of this important movement.''

* * *

BIRNBAUM, Phyllis 1945-

PERSONAL: Born May 27, 1945, in Bronx, N.Y.; daughter of Louis (in business) and Ruth (a teacher; maiden name, Kreisel) Birnbaum; married Ashok Trimbak Modak (an engineer), September 24, 1971. *Education:* Barnard College, B.A., 1967; University of California, Berkeley, M.A., 1972. *Residence:* Watertown, Mass. *Agent:* A. L. Hart, Fox Chase Agency, Inc., 419 East 57th St., New York, N.Y. 10022.

CAREER: University of Tokyo Press, Tokyo, Japan, editor, 1966-69. Fellow of Translation Center, Columbia University, 1979. *Member:* National Book Critics Circle.

WRITINGS: An Eastern Tradition (novel), Seaview Books, 1980. Contributor of articles, translations, and reviews to magazines.

WORK IN PROGRESS: Rabbits, Crabs, Etc., a collection of translations of short stories by Japanese women writers, publication expected in 1981; a novel, *In the Year of the Monkey,* publication expected in 1981.

* * *

BLACK, Brady Forrest 1908-

PERSONAL: Born July 31, 1908, in Lawrence County, Ky.; son of Fred Nixon and Melissa (Cornwell) Black; married Edra Dailey, September 17, 1930; children: Brenda Gayle, Brady Brent, Lisa Anne. *Education:* Attended public schools in Ashland, Ky. *Politics:* Republican. *Religion:* Presbyterian. *Home:* 1009 Park Crest, Park Hills, Ky. 41011.

CAREER: Ashland Independent, Ashland, Ky., sports editor, 1927-38, city editor, 1938-40, author of column, ''Freelance Sports,'' 1928-39; *Cincinnati Enquirer,* Cincinnati, Ohio, copyreader, 1940-42, reporter, 1943, political writer, 1944, assistant city editor, 1945-46, Kentucky correspondent, 1946-48, Ohio correspondent, 1948-56, managing editor, 1956-57, editor of editorial page, 1957-59, author of columns on national and international affairs, 1957-75, executive editor, 1959-64, vice-president and editor, 1964-75; Kiplinger Professor at Ohio State University, Columbus, 1975-76; Black, Black & Seitz (advertising and marketing firm), Cincinnati, president, 1976-80. Member of board of trustees of Behringer-Crawford Museum; director of Covington Trust Bank, 1976-79; past vice-president of Ohio Chamber of Commerce; past member of national board of trustees of Citizens Conference on State Legislatures. *Member:* Inter American Press Association (past member of board of directors), American Society of Newspaper Editors (past member of board of directors), Sigma Delta Chi (president of Central Ohio Chapter, 1955-56).

WRITINGS: Fighters, Lovers, and Others, Ohio State University School of Journalism, 1977. Author of column syndicated by Black, Black & Seitz, 1976-80, personally syndicated, 1980—.

SIDELIGHTS: Black told *CA:* ''My imagination was fired, as a teenager, by fictional reading to such a degree that I wrote and wrote in longhand. This led to writing for my high school newspaper in Ashland, Kentucky, and an immediate transition from high school to the staff of the local newspaper. Coverage of a National Labor Relations unfair labor practices hearing in 1938-39 led me to the staff of the *Cincinnati Enquirer,* and a transition to writing on politics and government, and writing with extensive research in later years on international affairs.

"Journalism to me was a continuing education and development. It opened doors and led me to national and world leaders whose special insights gave me perspectives on problems and issues about which I could write. My book was a gleaning from all these writings that offered insights on history as it happened over about two decades. In that period I was in and wrote about issues on five continents. I have seen and written about, for example, the evolvement of the energy problems; the decline of United States power and influence as the Soviet Union expanded; and the spread of inflation (I felt a smugness that our country wasn't like that when I encountered severe inflation in South America in 1962, but our's was to come)."

* * *

BLACK, Clinton Vane De Brosse 1918-

PERSONAL: Born August 26, 1918, in Kingston, Jamaica; son of Thomas Henry and Violet (Bogle) Black; married Olive Mellor, February 6, 1951. *Education:* Attended University of London. *Religion:* Anglican. *Home:* 5 Avesbury Ave., Kingston 6, Jamaica. *Office:* Jamaica Archives, Spanish Town, Jamaica.

CAREER: Associated with West Indian Reference Library, Jamaica, 1945-48; Jamaica Archives, Spanish Town, archivist, 1949—. Justice of the peace and game warden. *Member:* International P.E.N. (member of Jamaica executive committee; past president), International Council on Archives, Jamaica Historical Society, Jamaica Library Association, Society of Antiquaries (fellow), British Records Association. *Awards, honors:* Commander of Order of Distinction, 1974.

WRITINGS: Tales of Old Jamaica, Pioneer Press, 1952, 2nd edition, 1956; *History of Jamiaca,* Collins, 1958, 4th edition published as *The Story of Jamaica From Prehistory to the Present Day,* 1965; *Spanish Town: The Old Capital,* Parish Council of St. Catherine, 1960; *Port Royal: A History and Guide,* Bolivar Press, 1970. Also author of *Jamaica Guide,* 1973, and *A New History of Jamaica,* 1973. Author of "Words," a column in *Daily Gleaner,* Kingston, Jamaica. Contributor to periodicals in Jamaica and abroad.

WORK IN PROGRESS: A book on Montego Bay; a book on the history of architecture in Jamaica.

* * *

BLACK, Lionel
See BARKER, Dudley

* * *

BLACKSTONE, Tessa Ann Vosper 1942-

PERSONAL: Born September 27, 1942, in London, England; daughter of Geoffrey Vaughan (a fire officer) and Joanna (a medical secretary; maiden name, Vosper) Blackstone; married Tom Evans, 1963 (divorced, 1975); children: Benedict, Liesel. *Education:* London School of Economics and Political Science, London, B.Sc., 1964, Ph.D., 1969. *Home:* 11 Grazebrook Rd., London N. 16, England. *Office:* Institute of Education, University of London, 59 Gordon Sq., London W.C.1, England.

CAREER: University of London, London School of Economics and Political Science, London, England, assistant lecturer, 1966-69, lecturer in social administration, 1969-75; Cabinet Office, London, adviser on Central Policy Review

Staff, 1975-78; University of London, Institute of Education, professor of educational administration, 1978—. Fellow of Centre for Studies in Social Policy, 1972-74. Member of Hackney Community Health Council, 1976-78. Member of educational advisory council of Independent Broadcasting Authority, 1973—. Member of Labour party's national executive committee on education, 1974-75, 1978—. *Member:* Royal Institute of Public Administration, British Educational Administration Association, Fabian Society (member of executive committee, 1979—), Hackney and Islington Housing Association (member of management committee, 1978—).

WRITINGS: (With Roger Hadley, Kathleen Gales, and Wyn Lewis) *Students in Conflict,* Weidenfeld & Nicolson, 1970; *Education and Day Care for Young Children in Need: The American Experience,* Bedford Square Press, 1973; (with Gareth Williams and David Metcalf) *The American Labour Market: Economic and Social Aspects of a Profession,* Elsevier, 1974. Contributor to magazines and newspapers, including *New Society.*

WORK IN PROGRESS: Research on educational policy and inequality, testing in the schools, and implementation of programs for the young unemployed.

SIDELIGHTS: Blackstone commented: "I am interested in the relationship between educational policy and other areas of social policy, and how the two interact with respect to creating equality. I am in favor of extending educational provision so that a wider range of the population is able to benefit from the opportunities it offers. This includes preschool education at one end of the system and continuing education for adults at the other. Much of my writing explores ways in which this expansion could be achieved."

* * *

BLACKWOOD, Paul Everett 1913-

PERSONAL: Born July 12, 1913, in Talmo, Kan.; son of Charles Everett and Florence (Pettyjohn) Blackwood. *Education:* Kansas State University, B.S., 1935; Columbia University, M.A., 1941, Ed.D., 1953. *Politics:* Democrat. *Religion:* Protestant. *Home:* 4000 Cathedral Ave. N.W., Washington, D.C. 20016.

CAREER: Central Washington State College, Ellensburg, instructor, 1941-42, assistant professor, 1942-43, associate professor of science, 1944-45; Ohio State University, Columbus, assistant professor of education, 1945-47; U.S. Department of Health, Education & Welfare, Office of Education, Washington, D.C., science specialist, 1947-65, chief of instructional services section and Division of State Agency Cooperation, 1966-73, chief of program operations and equal education opportunities, 1973-78. Writer, 1959—. *Member:* American Association for the Advancement of Science (fellow), National Council on Elementary Science (president, 1952-53), National Science Teachers Association, National Association for Research in Science Teaching, Educational Leadership Council of America, Association for Supervision and Curriculum Development, Association for the Education of Science Teachers, Phi Delta Kappa, Kappa Delta Phi.

WRITINGS: (With Margaret M. Stevens) *The World and Its Wonders* (young adult), Child's World, 1949; *How Children Learn to Think,* U.S. Office of Education, 1951; *Push and Pull: The Story of Energy* (young adult), Whittlesey House, 1957; (with Paul F. Brandwein, F. G. Watson, and others) *Teaching High School Science: A Book of Methods,* Harcourt, 1958; *Science Teaching in the Elementary Schools,* U.S. Office of Education, 1965; (with Brandwein, Elizabeth

Cooper, and others) *Concepts in Science* (elementary school textbook), six volumes, Harcourt, 1966, 5th edition, 1980; (with Brandwein and Brenda Lansdown) *Teaching Elementary Science Through Investigation and Colloquium,* Harcourt, 1971. Contributor to education journals.

SIDELIGHTS: Blackwood commented to *CA:* "Most of my writing has been in the field of science for children and teachers of children. Throughout these articles and books the emphasis has been on the importance of involving children in science through activities, experimenting, observing, exploring, thinking, and the multiple other ways that persons reach an understanding of the methods and concepts of science."

*   *   *

BLAKE, Sally
See SAUNDERS, Jean

*   *   *

BLAKEBOROUGH, Jack Fairfax
See FAIRFAX-BLAKEBOROUGH, John Freeman

*   *   *

BLAKEBOROUGH, John Freeman Fairfax
See FAIRFAX-BLAKEBOROUGH, John Freeman

*   *   *

BLANCH, Lesley 1907-

PERSONAL: Born in 1907 in London, England; married Romain Gary (a writer), 1945 (divorced, 1963). *Home:* Roquebrune Village, 06500 Cap Martin, France.

CAREER: Writer. *Member:* Royal Society of Literature (fellow).

WRITINGS: The Wilder Shores of Love (biography), Simon & Schuster, 1954; *The Sabres of Paradise* (biography), Viking, 1960; *Under a Lilac-Bleeding Star* (travel book), J. Murray, 1964; *The Nine Tiger Man* (novel), Collins, 1965; *Journey Into the Mind's Eye* (autobiography), Atheneum, 1968; *Pavillions of the Heart* (biography), Weidenfeld & Nicolson, 1974; *Farah Shabanou of Iran* (biography), Collins, 1978.

WORK IN PROGRESS: A biography of Pierre Loti.

*   *   *

BLANPIED, Pamela Wharton 1937-

PERSONAL: Born April 15, 1937, in Washington, D.C.; daughter of George Brewster and Thalia (Oliphant) Wharton; married John Warren Blanpied (in housing rehabilitation; a Shakespearean scholar), September, 1960; children: Michael, Thomas. *Education:* Mount Holyoke College, B.A. (cum laude), 1959, M.A., 1974. *Residence:* Rochester, N.Y. *Agent:* Jean Rosenthal, J & R Literary Agency, 28 East 11th St., New York, N.Y. 10003.

CAREER: Free-lance researcher and writer, 1969—. Tutor at Susquehanna University, 1967-69, and State University of New York, 1980—. Director of day-care center for migrant children in Susquehanna, Pa., 1970.

WRITINGS: Dragons: An Introduction to the Modern Infestation, Warner Books, 1980. Contributor to *Book Forum.*

WORK IN PROGRESS: A novel.

SIDELIGHTS: Pamela Blanpied told *CA:* "I wrote *Dragons* as a strictly private exercise in sanity and delight. Publica-

tion came serendipitously. Since I wrote for my own pleasure and curiosity, to my own taste and sense of humor, it is an odd book, and resists classification into any one genre. I see it as an exploration of the relationship between truth and the search for truth; as a satire of the apparatus we mistake for knowledge; and finally as pure play, free imagination—a kind of joy I thought I had lost when I crossed the boundary to the adult world."

In a review of *Dragons,* Jill Merrill of the *Smithsonian* described it as "a lively, witty satire of those anthropological studies that reduce human (and other animal) habits to infuriating abstractions.... With a brusque precision that would do Margaret Mead proud, Blanpied sets forth the latest findings in dragonology." *Village Voice* reviewer Barry Yourgrau declared: "To her credit, Blanpied academizes convincingly, covering a lot of the genre's nuances.... But the real strength of *Dragons* lies in its first-person narrative sections (Blanpied can turn a crisply intelligent, drily elegant phrase whenever she wants) and in the charm and ingenuity of some of the details, the touches."

BIOGRAPHICAL/CRITICAL SOURCES: Smithsonian, June, 1980; *Village Voice,* July 30, 1980; *Toronto Globe and Mail,* August 23, 1980.

*   *   *

BLASHFORD-SNELL, John Nicholas 1936-

PERSONAL: Born October 22, 1936, in Hereford, England; son of Leland John (a minister of Church of England) and Gwendolyn (Sadler) Blashford-Snell; married Judith Frances Sherman; children: Emma, Victoria. *Education:* Attended Royal Military Academy, Sandhurst, 1955-57. *Religion:* Church of England. *Home address:* c/o Lloyds Bank Ltd., 9 Broad St., St. Helier, Jersey, Channel Islands. *Office:* Scientific Exploration Society, Mildenhall, Marlborough, Wiltshire, England.

CAREER: British Army, Royal Engineers, career officer, 1955—, instructor at Royal Military Academy, Sandhurst, and organizer of adventure training, beginning in 1963; present rank, lieutenant colonel. Member of council of Outward Bound Trust. *Member:* Scientific Exploration Society (chairman, 1969—), Explorers Club (fellow). *Awards, honors*—Military: Member of Order of the British Empire; named man of the year by British Army, 1972. Other: Exploration awards include gold medal from Darien Action Committee, 1972; Livingstone Medal from Royal Scottish Geographical Society, 1975; Segrave Trophy from Royal Automobile Club, 1975.

WRITINGS: (With G. R. Snailham) *The Expedition Organisers Guide,* Daily Telegraph, 1969; (with Tom Wintringham) *Weapons and Tactics,* Penguin, 1974; *Where the Trails Run Out,* Hutchinson, 1974; *In the Steps of Stanley,* Hutchinson, 1975; (with Alistair Ballantine) *Expeditions: The Experts' Way,* Faber, 1977; *The Official Books of Operation Drake,* W. H. Allen, Volume I, 1980, Volume II, 1981; *In the Wake of Drake,* W. H. Allen, 1980.

SIDELIGHTS: Blashford-Snell's army service has taken him all over the world, and in his capacity as instructor at Royal Military Academy, Sandhurst, he launched sixty expeditions for students in adventure training.

In 1968 he led the Great Abbai Expedition, a team of civilians and military personnel that made the first descent and exploration of the Blue Nile, and in 1979, at the request of the Ethiopian government, he led the Dahlak Quest Expedition, which explored an archipelago of the Red Sea.

In 1974 he led an international group of explorers, soldiers, and scientists in an attempt to navigate the Congo, following the path of H. M. Stanley's 1874 expedition. Using a fleet of large inflatable craft, with jet boats and air support, they started at the source and, after three-and-one-half months, navigated almost every rapid that Stanley had been forced to portage around, and reached the Atlantic Ocean in 1975. There were many casualties, but no deaths; boats were destroyed in cataracts and one was eaten by a hippopotamus.

Blashford-Snell was off to Panama's Darien Gap in 1976 where, with the backing of the Explorers Club, he searched for the remains of the abandoned seventeenth-century Scots colony of New Caledonia. His team discovered the site and what seemed to be evidence of the lost Spanish city of Acla. While there, Blashford-Snell was bitten by a vampire bat and underwent anti-rabies injections.

In 1978, with the encouragement of Charles, Prince of Wales, he launched a mammoth expedition to inspire challenge for young people. Their flagship, *Eye of the Wind,* set out from Plymouth, England, to carry teams of soldiers, scientists, and young people around the world on a voyage of discovery. As director of operations, Blashford-Snell led the explorers through the Panama jungle, to the crater of Mount Soufriere shortly before it erupted, to Papua New Guinea, Africa, and the Mediterranean.

AVOCATIONAL INTERESTS: Jogging, fishing for giant perch, shooting, Scotch whisky, wine, seafood, Peter Sellers films.

*   *   *

BLEAKLEY, David (Wylie) 1925-

PERSONAL: Born January 11, 1925, in Belfast, Northern Ireland; son of John Wesley (a bricklayer) and Sarah (Wylie) Bleakley; married Winifred Wason, August 5, 1949; children: Brian, Desmond, Peter. *Education:* Ruskin College, Oxford, diploma in economics and political science, 1949; Queen's University, Belfast, Northern Ireland, B.A. (with honors), 1951, M.A., 1955. *Politics:* Democratic socialist. *Religion:* Church of Ireland. *Home:* 8 Thorn Hill, Bangor, County Down, Northern Ireland. *Office:* Irish Council of Churches, 48 Elmwood Ave., Belfast BT9 6AZ, Northern Ireland.

CAREER: Worked at Belfast Shipyard, Belfast, Northern Ireland, 1940-46; Belfast Further Education Centre, Belfast, principal, 1955-58; Northern Ireland General Assembly, Belfast, Labour member of Parliament for Victoria, 1958-65; Kivukoni College, Dar-es-Salaam, Tanzania, lecturer in industrial relations, 1966-69; Methodist College, Belfast, head of department of economics and political studies, 1969-71; Government of Northern Ireland, Belfast, minister of community relations, 1971; Northern Ireland General Assembly, Labour member of assembly for East Belfast, 1973-74; Methodist College, head of department, 1974-79; Irish Council of Churches, Belfast, chief executive and general secretary, 1980—. Privy Councillor to Queen Elizabeth II. Irish delegate to Anglican Consultative Council, 1971; delegate to World Council of Churches. Chairman of British Government Advisory Commission on Human Rights, 1980—. Tutor at Open University and Workers Educational Association. Commentator on current affairs in education for British Broadcasting Corp. and Independent Television. *Member:* Amnesty International, Fellowship of Reconciliation, Fabian Society, Anglican Conservative Council. *Awards, honors:* M.A. from Open University, 1975.

WRITINGS: (With J. C. Beckett and T. W. Moody) *Ulster Since 1800,* BBC Publications, 1955; *Young Ulster and Religion in the Sixties,* Churches Industrial Council, 1964; *Peace in Ulster,* Mowbray, 1972; *Faulkner: Conflict and Consent in Irish Politics,* Mowbray, 1974; *Saidie Patterson: Irish Peacemaker,* Blackstaff Press, 1980; *The Second Industrial Revolution in Britain and Ireland,* S.C.M. Press, 1981. Contributor to journals.

SIDELIGHTS: Bleakley commented: "My background has been Irish industrial working class with strong Christian associations. Adult education enabled me to become involved with academic work. My life to date has been a fusion of these themes: I have sought to make people more aware of the impact of industrial pressures on all our lives; I have sought also for methods of political reconciliation; and, in Ireland, to turn peace theory into practice; and always within the framework of Christian principles."

*   *   *

BLOODSTONE, John
See BYRNE, Stuart J(ames)

*   *   *

BLOOM, Herman Irving 1908-
(Harmon Bellamy, Barry Hart)

PERSONAL: Born October 14, 1908, in Springfield, Mass.; son of Meyer and Anne (Hurwitz) Bloom; married Julia Prosansky, March 2, 1942 (died April 13, 1954); married Nellie Korsakov, January 13, 1957; children: (first marriage) Miriam Ellen Bloom Chaiklin and Muriel Joan Bloom Bruskin (twins). *Education:* Attended Northeastern University (now Western New England College), 1925-29. *Politics:* "Was Independent, switched to Republican, may return to Independent." *Religion:* Jewish. *Home:* 85 Pinewood Dr., Longmeadow, Mass. 01106. *Office:* Bloom's Photo Supply, Inc., 211 Worthington St., Springfield, Mass. 01108.

CAREER: Evening News, Newark, N.J., reporter, 1930-31; worked as an editor, 1931-34; Bloom's Photo Supply, Inc., Springfield, Mass., founder and treasurer, 1934-74; Zeppo Marx Agency, Hollywood, Calif., agent, 1938-39. Trustee of Rona-Mel Realty Trust, 1954—; treasurer of Good-Block Realty Corp., 1955-77. Member of Meals on Wheels program, Springfield, Mass. *Military service:* U.S. Army, 1942-45, served in American theater. *Member:* Mystery Writers of America, Disabled American Veterans, Jewish War Vets, Crestview Country Club.

WRITINGS: (Published anonymously) *The Seventh Commandmant,* G. Howard Watt, 1932.

Under pseudonym Harmon Bellamy: *The Transgressor,* G. Howard Watt, 1933; *Bedmates,* Godwin, 1934; *Skin Deep,* Godwin, 1934; *Bodies Are Different,* Godwin, 1935; *Struggle,* Godwin, 1935; *Sacrifice,* Godwin, 1936; *Leap Year Madness,* Hillman-Curl, 1937; *Sweet and Lovely,* Gramercy, 1938; *A Fine Romance,* Hillman-Curl, 1938; (editor) *Let's Read* (anthology), Henry Holt, 1939; *Tune in on Love,* Gramercy, 1940.

Also author of two films. Author of newspaper column, "The Book Nook," for thirty years. Contributor of more than one hundred articles and stories to magazines, sometimes under pseudonym Barry Hart, including *Detective Fiction Weekly, Black Mask, Boy's Life, St. Nicholas, The Writer,* and *Author and Journalist.*

WORK IN PROGRESS: A mystery novel; a short "whodunit"; book and theatre reviews; an article series on the heyday of pulp magazines for Trident Publications.

BODMER, Walter Fred 1936-

PERSONAL: Born January 10, 1936, in Frankfurt am Main, Germany (now West Germany); son of Ernest Julius (a physician) and Sylvia Emily (a modern dance teacher) Bodmer; married Julia Gwynaeth Pilkington (a research scientist), August 11, 1956; children: Mark William, Helen Claire, Charles Walter. *Education:* Cambridge University, B.A., 1956, Ph.D., 1959. *Home:* Manor House, Mill Lane, Old Marston, Oxford, England. *Office:* Imperial Cancer Research Fund, Lincoln's Inn Fields, London WC2A 3PX, England.

CAREER: Stanford University, Stanford, Calif., fellow and visiting assistant professor, 1961-62, assistant professor, 1962-66, associate professor, 1966-68, professor of genetics, 1968-70; Oxford University, Oxford, England, professor of genetics, 1970-79; Imperial Cancer Research Fund, London, England, director of research, 1979—. *Member:* Royal Society (fellow; member of council, 1978-80), British Association Working Party on Social Concern and Biological Advances (chairman, 1972-80).

WRITINGS: (With L. L. Cavalli-Sforza) *The Genetics of Human Populations,* W. H. Freeman, 1971; (with Alan Jones) *Our Future Inheritance: Choice or Chance?,* Oxford University Press, 1974; (with Cavalli-Sforza) *Genetics, Evolution, and Man,* W. H. Freeman, 1976. Associate editor of *American Journal of Human Genetics,* 1968-70; member of editorial board of *American Naturalist,* 1969-71; associate editor of *Tissue Antigens,* 1970; editor of *British Medical Bulletin,* 1977.

SIDELIGHTS: Bodmer commented to *CA:* "The two books with Cavalli-Sforza arose from my professional work as a geneticist, while the book with Alan Jones reflects an interest in writing about science for the more general public. The latter was stimulated by involvement with the British Association Working Party on Social Concern and Biological Advances. This group has also been responsible for stimulating Magnus Pike to write *Long Life.*"

*   *   *

BOESIGER, Willi 1904-

PERSONAL: Born in 1904, in Bern, Switzerland; son of Jacob and Hermina (Segesser) Boesiger. *Education:* Attended technical school in Bern, Switzerland. *Home:* Limmatquai 16, Zurich 1, Switzerland.

CAREER: Editor.

WRITINGS: (Editor) Charles Edouard Jeanneret-Gris (pseudonym, Le Corbusier), *Oeuvre complete* (title means "Complete Works"; parts in English) Volume I (with Oscar G. Stonorov): *1910-29,* 9th edition (in French, English, and German), Editions d'architecture Artemis, 1967, Volume II: *1929-34,* 8th edition, Editions d'architecture Artemis, 1967, Volume IV (Boesiger was not associated with Volume III): *1938-46,* Editions d'architecture, 1946, 5th edition (in French and English), Editions d'architecture Artemis, 1967, Volume V: *1946-52* (in French, English, and German), Girsberger, 1953, Volume VI: *1952-57: Le Corbusier et son atelier rue de Sevres 35* (in French, English, and German), Girsberger, 1957, 4th edition, Editions d'architecture Artemis, 1966, Volume VII: *1957-65* (in French, English, and German), Editions d'architecture Artemis, 1965, Volume VIII: *Les Dernieres Oeuvres: The Last Works* (in French, English, and German), Editions d'architecture Artemis, 1970, published as *Oeuvre complete: Complete Works,* Volume I, Wittenborn, 8th edition, 1964, Volume II, Wittenborn, 7th edi-

tion, 1964, Volume IV, Wittenborn, Volume V, Wittenborn, Volume VI, Wittenborn, 1957, 4th edition, 1964, Volume VII, Wittenborn, 1966, Volume VIII: *Le Corbusier: Last Works,* translated by Henry A. Frey, Praeger, 1970, Volumes I-VII published in one volume as *Le Corbusier, 1910-1960,* translated by William B. Gleckman, Praeger, 1967, Volumes I-VIII reprinted in nine volumes as *Le Corbusier: Complete Works,* published by Museum Books, abridged edition (with Hans Girsberger) published as *Le Corbusier,* Praeger, 1972 (published in England as *The Complete Architectural Works,* Thames & Hudson, 1964, Volume VIII published as *Le Corbusier, 1910-60,* Timani, 1960, new edition published as *Le Corbusier, 1910-65,* Thames & Hudson, 1967, abridged edition, 1972); (editor) Richard Joseph Neutra, *Buildings and Projects* (in English, French, and German), three volumes, Girsberger, 1950, 6th edition, Thames & Hudson, 1966.

BIOGRAPHICAL/CRITICAL SOURCES: New Yorker, December 30, 1967.

*   *   *

BOGGS, Bill
See BOGGS, William III

*   *   *

BOGGS, William III 1942-
(Bill Boggs)

PERSONAL: Born July 11, 1942, in Philadelphia, Pa.; son of William, Jr. (an electrical appliance dealer) and Helene (a U.S. Navy purchasing agent; maiden name, Schmidt) Boggs; married Leslie Bennetts (a newspaper reporter), May 19, 1970 (divorced). *Education:* University of Pennsylvania, B.A., 1963, M.A., 1964. *Residence:* New York, N.Y. *Office:* WNEW-TV, 205 East 67th St., New York, N.Y. 10021.

CAREER: Armstrong Cork Co., writer, 1964-65; Patchett & Tarses, manager of comedy team, 1966-69; KYW-TV, Philadelphia, Pa., writer and producer of "McLean & Co.," 1970-72; host and producer of talk show, "Southern Exposure," 1972-74; WNEW-TV, New York, N.Y., host of "Midday With Bill Boggs." Member of advisory board of Ballet Hispanico, Juvenile Diabetes, and Humane Society. *Member:* New York Athletic Club. *Awards, honors:* Award from U.S. Rubber, for "Midday With Bill Boggs"; public service awards.

WRITINGS—Under name Bill Boggs: *At First Sight* (novel), Grosset, 1980. Author of comedy scripts. Contributor to *Diversion.*

WORK IN PROGRESS: Of All the Possibilities, a sequel to *At First Sight.*

SIDELIGHTS: As a television personality, Boggs's interviews include talks with William Buckley, Gore Vidal, Margaret Mead, Sidney Sheldon, Norman Mailer, Rona Jaffe, Isaac Asimov, and Neil Simon.

Boggs commented: "My novel was motivated by an intense relationship, and the desire to tell the story of love from a man's point of view."

*   *   *

BOHNET, Michael 1937-

PERSONAL: Born June 10, 1937, in Berlin, Germany; married Adelheid von der Thuesen, October 14, 1970; children: Philipp Max, Johannes. *Education:* Attended Technical University of Karlsruhe, 1958-59, and Free University of

Berlin. *Religion:* Evangelic. *Home:* Leibnitstrasse 67, 53 Bonn 2, West Germany. *Office:* Ministry for Economic Cooperation, Karl-marstrasse 4-6, 53 Bonn 2, West Germany.

CAREER: Free University of Berlin, Berlin, West Germany, lecturer in economic theory, 1962-67; Planungagruppe Ritter, Koenigstein/Taunus, West Germany, colleague, 1967; Ifo-Institute for Economic Research, Munich, West Germany, researcher and acting director of African Studies Center, 1968-73, director, 1974-78; Ministry for Economic Cooperation, Bonn, West Germany, head of planning department, 1978—. Member of scientific council of Ministry for Economic Cooperation, 1974-78. *Member:* European Association of Development Research Institutes (director, 1974-77), Verein fuer Social Politik.

WRITINGS—In English translation: (With Hans Reichelt) *Applied Research and Its Impact on Economic Development: The East African Case,* Weltforum Verlag, 1972; *Development Research and Development Theory,* Weltforum Verlag, 1973; *Entwicklungsforschung und Entwicklungspolitik: Eine Bilanz des Afrika-Forschunsprogramms des Ifo-Instituts,* two volumes, Weltforum Verlag, 1973, translation published as *Developing Countries, Research, and Policies: Results of the African Research Program of the Ifo-Institute,* 1974.

Other writings: *Die Konzepte der "external economies" unter besonderer Beruecksichtigung ihrer Bedeutung fuer Entwicklungslaender: Zum Problem der binnenwirtschaftlichen Integration,* Duncker & Humblot, 1968; (editor) *Das Nord-Sued-Problem: Konflikte zwischen Industrie und Entwicklungslaendern,* R. Piper, 1971, 5th edition, 1975; (with Rupert Betz) *Einkommensverteilung in Entwicklungslaendern: Income Distribution in Developing Countries* (with summary in English), Humanities, 1976; (with Winfried von Urff) *Wachstum: Einkommensverteilung und Beschaeftigung in Entwicklungslaendern,* Duncker & Humblot, 1978.

Contributor to scholarly journals.

* * *

BOON, Francis
    See BACON, Edward

* * *

BOOTH, Ken   1943-

PERSONAL: Born January 29, 1943, in Featherstone, England; son of Fred (an engineer) and Phyllis (Chesham) Booth; married Eurwen Jones (a magazine and television editor), July 29, 1967; children: Robert, Thomas. *Education:* University College of Wales, University of Wales, Aberystwyth, B.A. (with first class honors), 1964. *Home:* 18 Maesyfelin, Penrhyncoch, Aberystwyth, Dyfed SY23 3EN, Wales. *Office:* Department of International Politics, University College of Wales, University of Wales, Aberystwyth, Dyfed SY23 3DB, Wales.

CAREER: University of Wales, University College of Wales, Aberystwyth, lecturer, 1967-79, senior lecturer in international politics, 1979—. Scholar-in-residence at Naval War College, Newport, R.I., 1977; senior research fellow at Centre for Foreign Policy Studies, Dalhousie University, 1979-81. *Member:* International Institute for Strategic Studies, Royal United Services Institute for Defence Studies, British International Studies Association.

WRITINGS: The Military Instrument in Soviet Foreign Pol-

icy, 1917-1972 (monograph), Royal United Services Institute for Defence Studies, 1974; (editor with Michael MccGwire and John McDonnell) *Soviet Naval Policy: Objectives and Constraints,* Praeger, 1975; (with John Baylis, John Garnett, and Phil Williams) *Contemporary Strategy: Theories and Policies,* Holmes & Meier, 1975; *Navies and Foreign Policy,* Crane, Russak, 1977; (editor with Moorhead Wright, and contributor) *American Thinking About Peace and War,* Barnes & Noble, 1978; *Strategy and Ethnocentrism,* Holmes & Meier, 1979; *The Study of Naval Strategy,* Harvester Press, 1982; *Law, Force, and Diplomacy at Sea,* Allen & Unwin, 1982.

Contributor: MccGwire and McDonnell, editors, *Soviet Naval Influence: Domestic and Foreign Dimensions,* Praeger, 1971; MccGwire, editor, *Soviet Naval Developments: Capability and Context,* Praeger, 1973; John King Gamble, editor, *Law of the Sea: Neglected Issues,* University Press of Hawaii, 1979. Contributor of articles and reviews to military journals.

WORK IN PROGRESS: Regional Navies in the Indian Ocean, with Lee Dowdy and Jane Davis, Macmillan, 1983.

SIDELIGHTS: Booth wrote: "Most of my published work began as mind-clearing exercises which I then hoped would be useful for a wider audience. In principle, I believe academics should be free to pursue their interests without any guidance: that is their privilege and also their responsibility. In practice, I think that if they are going to throw their brains at something, it might as well be the big questions rather than the trivial. My own work and interest involves the study of war and peace in international politics, a subject which is as frustrating as it is fascinating, and as remote from our control as it is relevant to our everyday lives. Throughout the 1980's, issues of security and survival will be at the forefront of the agenda of most nations in the world."

* * *

BORN, Ernest Alexander   1898-

PERSONAL: Born in 1898, in San francisco, Calif. *Education:* University of California, A.B., 1922, M.A., 1923; American School at Fontainebleau, certificate, 1928; studied at Paris Painting Galleries, 1928. *Home:* 2020 Great Highway, San Francisco, Calif. 94116. *Office:* 730 Montgomery St., San Francisco, Calif. 94111.

CAREER: Designer with John Reid, Jr., 1924-25, John Galen Howard, 1926, George Kelham, 1927, Gehron Ross, 1928-30, Shreve, Lamb & Harmon, 1930-31; private practice of architecture in San Francisco, Calif., 1937—. Consulting architect with H. E. Fletcher Co., 1930-63. Professor at University of California, 1953-57. Member of San Francisco Art Commission, 1947-50.

MEMBER: American Institute of Architects (fellow), San Francisco Planning and Housing Association (member of board of directors, 1945), San Francisco Art Association (president, 1951), Tau Beta Pi, Tau Sigma Delta. *Awards, honors:* Burch Burdette Long Prize from Architectural League of New York, 1930; C. Valentine Kirby Award from northern California chapter of American Institute of Architects, 1951, award of high honor, 1954; Guggenheim fellowship, 1960-61.

WRITINGS: (With John S. Bolles) *A Plan for Fisherman's Wharf Comprising the Fisherman's Wharf-Aquatic Park Area,* San Francisco Port Authority, 1951; (with Walter William Horn) *The Barns of the Abbey of Beaulieu-St. Leonards,* University of California Press, 1965; (with Horn)

The Plan of St. Gall: A Study of the Architecture and Economy and Life in a Paradigmatic Carolingian Monastery, three volumes, University of California Press, 1979. Also author of *The New Architecture in Mexico,* 1937.

BIOGRAPHICAL/CRITICAL SOURCES: Washington Post Book World, February 17, 1980.*

*   *   *

BORRAS, Frank Marshall   (?)-1980

OBITUARY NOTICE: Died after a long illness, December 11, 1980, in England. Educator and author. A self-taught scholar of Russian, Frank Borras was professor and head of the Russian department at Leeds University in England. He was co-author of a book about the Russian language entitled *Russian Syntax.* He also wrote *Maxim Gorky: The Writer.* Obituaries and other sources: *London Times,* December 17, 1980.

*   *   *

BOSSERMAN, (Charles) Phillip   1931-

PERSONAL: Born October 9, 1931, in Hutchinson, Kan.; son of Harry O. (in sales) and Pearl (Shively) Bosserman; married Sue Moyer, January 29, 1954 (died, 1971); married Carol Pokrant (an academic dean), August 15, 1971; children: Marjorie Sue, Beth Christine, Phillip Marc, Kathleen Jeannet. *Education:* Baker University, B.A. (with honors), 1952; Boston University, S.T.M. (cum laude), 1955, Ph.D., 1963; attended University of Paris, 1956-57. *Home:* 300 Whitman Ave., Salisbury, Md. 21801. *Office:* Department of Sociology and Anthropology, Salisbury State College, Salisbury, Md. 21801.

CAREER: Ordained United Methodist minister, 1955; pastor of United Methodist churches in Norwell, Mass., 1957-60, and Kansas City, Kan., 1960-61; Baker University, Baldwin, Kan., assistant professor of political science and history, 1961-63; U.S. Peace Corps, Washington, D.C., deputy director for Gabon, 1963-64; Boston University, Boston, Mass., assistant professor of social sciences, 1964-66; University of South Florida, Tampa, professor of sociology, 1967-72; University of Paris, Paris, France, senior Fulbright professor of sociology, 1972-73; University of South Florida, professor of sociology, 1973-75, deputy director of leisure studies program; Salisbury State College, Salisbury, Md., professor of sociology and anthropology and head of department, 1975—, co-founder of leisure studies department. Director of Peace Corps programs and assistant dean at Dartmouth College, 1965-67; lecturer at University of Sussex, 1972-73; consultant to White House Conference on Youth.

MEMBER: International Sociological Association (president of research committee on sociology of leisure, 1974), Association Internationale des Sociologues, African Studies Association, American Alliance for Health, American Sociological Association, National Recreational Park Association, Physical Education and Recreation, Alpha Delta Sigma. *Awards, honors:* Danforth associate, 1969—; Danforth Foundation grant, 1978-79; National Endowment for the Humanities fellow, 1981-82.

WRITINGS: (Editor and translator, with Myrtle Korebaum) Georges Gurvitch, *The Spectrum of Social Time,* D. Reidel, 1964; *Dialectical Sociology: An Analysis of the Sociology of Georges Gurvitch,* Sargent, 1968; *A Survey of the United Methodist Church Education System of Liberia,* United Methodist Church, 1969; (editor with Max Kaplan, and contributor) *Technology, Human Values, and Leisure,* Abing-

don, 1971; *Technology and the Arts,* United Nations Education, Scientific and Cultural Organization, 1974.

Contributor: Georges Balandier, editor, *Perspectives de la Sociologie Contemporaine* (title means "Perspectives on Contemporary Sociology"), Presses Universitaires de France, 1968; David H. Smith and other editors, *Voluntary Action Research, 1972,* Lexington Books, 1972; Margaret S. Archer, editor, *Current Research in Sociology,* Mouton, 1974; *The American Issues Forum,* Voice of America, 1976. Contributor of articles and reviews to sociology and leisure studies journals. Member of editorial board of *Loisir et Societe/Society and Leisure,* 1978—, guest editor, 1980.

WORK IN PROGRESS: Leisure and Recreation in America, with Gerald Fein, publication by Allyn & Bacon expected in 1982; *Leisure and Labor in Post-Industrial Society,* with Joffre Dumazedier, publication by Allen & Unwin expected in 1983.

SIDELIGHTS: Bosserman wrote: "I started out in political science and history, moved to philosophy and theology, then on to sociology studies in France. These experiences were layered with a sojourn in Gabon and other regions of West Africa. I shifted to the study of leisure and work while in Florida. The shape of an emerging post-industrial society intrigues me. Such societal changes require the widest possible approach to understand them; hence, the catholicity of my interests seems appropriate for trying to undertake such a task."

*   *   *

BOSSOM, Naomi   1933-

PERSONAL: Born August 26, 1933, in Brooklyn, N.Y.; daughter of Irving J. (in business) and Tessie G. Feinfeld; married husband (a musician), 1954 (marriage ended); children: Jack, Lucy, Ciaron. *Education:* Columbia University, B.F.A., 1954; also attended Art Students' League, 1947-50, Bard College, 1950-52, Pratt Graphic Center, 1971, Brooklyn Museum Art School, 1974, Fashion Institute of Technology, 1975, New York School of Visual Arts, 1976, and Pratt Institute, 1978. *Home:* 284 Garfield Pl., Brooklyn, N.Y. 11215. *Agent:* Anne Brody, 55 Bethune St., New York, N.Y. 10014.

CAREER: Free-lance artist, 1954-64; teacher of adult education art classes in Rockville, Md., 1964-65; free-lance artist, 1965-68; Universal Color Slide Co., New York City, researcher for art education filmstrips, 1968; free-lance artist, 1968-71; assistant to business manager at school in New York City, 1971-73; Packer Collegiate Institute, Brooklyn, N.Y., instructor in art, 1973-78; free-lance artist, 1978—. Artwork exhibited in the East, including solo shows in New York City and Boston. Member of advisory committee of Brooklyn Museum's Community Gallery. Visiting artist at Long Island University, 1977.

WRITINGS: A Scale Full of Fish (self-illustrated juvenile), Morrow, 1979.

Art work represented in anthologies, including *National Anthology of Drawings,* Regina Publishing, 1974.

WORK IN PROGRESS: Another self-illustrated children's book.

SIDELIGHTS: Bossom told *CA:* "My pictures have always had a strong element of movement or action—sometimes even inanimate objects seem animated—so illustrating comes naturally. I have always enjoyed words, puns, and playing with words, although I am not a storyteller. I said to myself one day 'I must have a children's book!' The first idea that came to mind was 'a fish full of scales, a scale full of fish.' I thought up a large number of reversals that could be done in pictures. Two versions of this manuscript went the rounds of a number of publishers who were interested but wanted revisions. The manuscript was set aside for five years while I taught art to children of all ages. I returned to it and did twenty-four woodcuts which I felt deserved to be printed. This time it was accepted. Subsequent revisions cut out all but four of the original pictures.''

* * *

BOSTICCO, (Isabel Lucy) Mary
(Isabelle Bey)

PERSONAL: Born in Birmingham, England; daughter of Renato Agostino and Jessie (Watson) Bosticco. *Education:* Attended University of Madrid, New York University, Los Angeles City College, and Institut Francais d'Etudes Superieures, Buenos Aires, Argentina. *Home:* Oasis, 7-A Telston Close, Bourne End, Buckinghamshire, England. *Office:* Bracknell Development Corp., Farley Hall, Bracknell, Berkshire, England.

CAREER: Cement and Concrete Association, Wexham Springs, England, staff writer and editor, 1968-71; Commonwealth War Graves Commission, Maidenhead, England, editor, 1972; *International Management,* Maidenhead, associate editor, 1973-74; Bracknell Development Corp., Bracknell, England, press officer, 1974—. Guest on television and radio programs. *Member:* International Wine and Food Society, National Trust, Classical Association, Cats Protection League, Maidenhead Archaeological and Historical Society.

WRITINGS: Modern Personnel Management, Business Publications, 1964; *Personal Letters for Businessmen,* Business Publications, 1965; *Etiquette for the Businessman: At Home and Abroad,* Business Publications, 1967; *Instant Business Letters,* Business Books, 1968; *Top Secretary,* Business Books, 1970; (translator) Giuseppe Continolo, *Modern Filing Methods and Equipment,* Business Books, 1970; *Creative Techniques for Management,* Business Books, 1971; *The Businessman's Wife,* Mercury House Books, 1972. Contributor to magazines, sometimes under pseudonym Isabelle Bey.

WORK IN PROGRESS: Two nonfiction books; a series of short stories with a common character.

SIDELIGHTS: Mary Bosticco told *CA:* "I was determined to become a writer even before I reached my teens, but circumstances were such that it was many many years before I attained my ambition. First I became a linguist, fluent in Italian, French, and Spanish. I traveled extensively and lived in South America and the United States before returning to settle in the United Kingdom in 1960. I did not originally intend to write management books, but my first breakthrough happened to be in this subject, so I decided to heed the Wall Street dictum and follow up my success.''

* * *

BOURLIAGUET, Leonce 1895-1965

PERSONAL: Surname is pronounced *Boor*-li-a-gay; born January 6, 1895, in Thiviers, France; died March 26, 1965; married twice; children: (first marriage) Andre, Pierre, J. Jacques; (second marriage) Bruno. *Education:* Attended public schools in France.

CAREER: Rural schoolmaster in Mialet, Dordogne, France, 1919-20; school inspector for Saone et Loire, Arieze, and Correze departments, 1929-60. Author; began free-lance

work c. 1930. *Military service:* French Army, 49th infantry regiment, served in World War I. *Awards, honors:* Prix Jeunesse; Prix Enfance du Monde; Prix Olivier de Serres; Prix Fantasia; Prix de l'Academie Francaise; European Prize of the City of Caorle and Hans Christian Andersen Award honor roll, both 1966, both for *Les Canons de Valmy.*

WRITINGS—In English translation; all for children: *Pouk et ses loups-garous,* Magnard, 1955, translation by Monica Burns published as *Pouk's Gang,* University of London Press, 1962; *Contes de l'ile lumineuse,* Editions Bias, 1959, translation by Sheila Gettings published as *The Island of Light,* Ward, Lock, 1966; *Le Cluseau de bois-brun,* Magnard, 1962, translation by Philippa C. Gerry published as *Tunnel Under Brown Wood,* Ryerson Press, 1965; *Les Canons de Valmy,* Societe Nouvelle des Editions, 1964, translation by John Buchanan-Brown published as *Guns of Valmy,* Abelard, 1968; *The Giant Who Drank From His Shoe, and Other Stories* (contains stories from *Le Marchand de nuages*), translated by J. Buchanan-Brown, Abelard, 1968.

Other writings: *Quatre du cours moyen,* Bourrelier, 1934; *La Foret sereine,* Nelson, 1937, new edition, Magnard, 1952; *Les Aventures du petit Rat Justin,* Societe Universitaire d'Editions et de Librairie, 1939; *Sept Peaux de betes,* Societe Universitaire d'Editions et de Librairie, 1939; *Contes de mon pere le jard,* Hachette, 1944; *Par monts et par vaux,* Societe Universitaire d'Editions et de Librairie, 1945; *La Guerre des demoiselles,* Les Ouevres Francaises, 1946; *Le Moulin de catuclade,* Hachette, 1946.

Mitou les-yeux-verts, Hachette, 1950; *La Maison qui chante,* Hachette, 1952; *Hototogisu, le rossignol de minuit,* Magnard, 1953; *Castandour,* Magnard, 1954; *La Villa des grillons,* Hachette, 1954; *D'un veau, d'un saint, d'un poete,* Rougerie, 1956; *La Montagne endormie,* Magnard, 1957; *La Dette d'Henri,* Hachette, 1958; *Les Compagnons de l'arc,* Magnard, 1959.

L'Ami des sirenes, Hachette, 1960; *Contes de la chevillette,* Editions Bias, 1960; *Le Berceau limousin,* Magnard, 1961; *Contes de l'epi d'orge,* Editions Bias, 1961; *Journal vert de silette,* Hachette, 1961; *La Longue Eau verte,* Desclee, De Brouwer, 1961; *Clarinet le patagon,* Magnard, 1963; *De sel et de poivre,* Magnard, 1963; *Un Village au bord de la mer,* Magnard, 1963; *Les Contes du fileur de verre,* Desclee, De Brouwer, 1964; *Marie Mon-Homme,* Association des Amis du Nord-Perigord, 1966; *Le Franzmann,* Magnard, 1967; *L'Homme et le vent,* Presses de la Cite, 1968.

Also author of *Le Perigourdin,* Lavauzelle; *Le Marquis de la mardondon,* Lavauzelle; *La Nuit des deux roses,* G. P.; *Le Parc aux preles,* Lanore; *Propos pedagogiques matinaux de Monsieur Sabahu,* Lavauzelle; *Tambourin d'argile,* Lavauzelle.*

* * *

BOURNEUF, Alice E. 1912-1980

OBITUARY NOTICE: Born October 2, 1912, in Haverhill, Mass.; died after a long illness, December 7, 1980, in Boston, Mass. Educator, economist, and author. Alice Bourneuf was the first woman to hold a tenured professorship on the arts and sciences faculty at Boston College. She served as a senior economist for the Marshall Plan in Norway and France from 1948 to 1953. After teaching at the University of California at Berkeley and Mt. Holyoke College in South Hadly, Mass., Bourneuf joined Boston College's economics department. Her writings include *Norway: The Planned Revival.* Obituaries and other sources: *American Men and Women of Science: The Social and Behavioral Sciences,*

12th edition, Bowker, 1973; *Chicago Tribune,* December 10, 1980.

* * *

BOWERS, William 1916-

PERSONAL: Born January 17, 1916, in Las Cruces, N.M.; son of Henry M. (a doctor) and Dorothy (Nelson) Bowers; married Marjorie Wilson (a fashion and costume designer and a teacher), December 11, 1959; children: Tony, Andy, Amanda. *Education:* University of Missouri, B.J., 1937. *Politics:* Independent. *Home:* 1150 Linda Flora Dr., Los Angeles, Calif. 90049. *Agent:* Major Talent Agency, 12301 Wilshire Blvd., Los Angeles, Calif. 90025.

CAREER: Worked as reporter and feature writer for *New York World-Telegram* and for United Press, and as Hollywood correspondent for Newspaper Enterprise Association, all 1937-38; screenwriter, 1938—. *Military service:* U.S. Army Air Forces, 1942-44. *Member:* Writers Guild (West). *Awards, honors:* Writers Guild award nominations, 1949, for "The Gunfighter," and 1952, for "The Gal Who Took the West" and "The Sheepman"; Academy Award nominations from Academy of Motion Pictures Arts and Sciences, 1950, for "The Gunfighter," and 1958, for "The Sheepman."

WRITINGS—Screenplays: "Seven Day's Leave," RKO, 1942; "My Favorite Spy," RKO, 1942; "Higher and Higher," RKO, 1944; "Adventures of a Rookie," RKO, 1943; "Sing Your Way Home," RKO, 1945; "Ladies' Man," Paramount, 1946; "Night and Day," Warner Bros., 1946; "The Fabulous Suzanne," Republic, 1946; "The Wistful Widow of Wagon Gap," Universal, 1947; "Something in the Wind," Universal, 1947; "The Web," Universal, 1947; "River Lady," Universal, 1948; "Black Bart," Universal, 1948; "Jungle Patrol," Twentieth Century-Fox, 1948; "The Countess of Monte Cristo," Universal, 1948; "Larceny," Universal, 1948; "Abandoned," Universal, 1949; "The Gal Who Took the West," Universal, 1949.

"The Gunfighter," Twentieth Century-Fox, 1950; "Convicted," Columbia, 1950; "Cry Danger," RKO, 1951; "Mrs. O'Malley and Mr. Malone," Metro-Goldwyn-Mayer, 1951; "The Mob," Columbia, 1951; "Assignment—Paris," Columbia, 1952; "Split Second," RKO, 1953; "She Couldn't Say No," RKO, 1954; "Five Against the House," Columbia, 1955; "Tight Spot," Columbia, 1955; "The Best Things in Life Are Free," Twentieth Century-Fox, 1956; "My Man Godfrey," Universal, 1957; (with James Edward Grant) "The Sheepman," Metro-Goldwyn-Mayer, 1958; "The Law and Jake Wade," Metro-Goldwyn-Mayer, 1958; "Imitation General," Metro-Goldwyn-Mayer, 1958; "-30-" Warner Bros., 1959; "Alias Jesse James," United Artists, 1959; "The Last Time I Saw Archie," United Artists, 1961; "Advance to the Rear," Metro-Goldwyn-Mayer, 1964; "Way . . . Way Out," Twentieth Century-Fox, 1966; "The Ride to Hangman's Tree," Universal, 1967; "Support Your Local Sheriff," United Artists, 1969.

Plays: "Where Do We Go From Here?" (three-act), first produced in Los Angeles, Calif., at Hollytown Theatre, April, 1938; "Back to Eden" (three-act), first produced in Los Angeles at Wilshire Ebel Theatre, 1939.

WORK IN PROGRESS—Screenplays: "Ghosts"; "Language of Love," for Columbia; "Barnaby Jones Saves Jed Clampett," for Columbia Broadcasting System, Inc. (CBS-TV); "No Man's Land," for American Broadcasting Companies, Inc. (ABC-TV).

CA INTERVIEW

CA interviewed William Bowers by phone on June 24, 1980, at his office in Hollywood, Calif.

CA: You've always loved the movies. Do you still feel as enthusiastic about them as you did when you first started writing screenplays?

BOWERS: Yes, more so these days because you don't have as much censorship, outside supervision. I don't know if you remember the days of the Hays Office and the Johnston Office, but they were the censory board. God, we could say that a girl was going to have a baby, but we couldn't say she was pregnant. They decided "pregnant" was a dirty word. It was really ridiculous. You couldn't show a married couple in bed together; they had to sleep in twin beds. You notice it in the old pictures.

CA: You started with a stage play you wrote and produced in California, "Where Do We Go From Here?"

BOWERS: Yes. Oscar Hammerstein's nephew was in the cast, and he got Hammerstein to come. Opening night he came to me and asked if I was the one who wrote the play, and I said yes. He said, "My name is Oscar Hammerstein and I'd like to take it to New York," and I said, "O.K." He said, "I'll be in touch with you," and then I went backstage and asked them, "Who is Oscar Hammerstein?"

We ran it here [California] until Oscar wanted to close it because he didn't want it to get a reputation as a West Coast show. He got the whole cast together and said that this would not be a production with enough money in it to take them all to New York and pay their expenses during rehearsals. But he said, "You're all so good in your parts that any of you who can get to New York can have your parts in the New York show." They hitchhiked and everything else. Eight of them showed up, including Don Defore, and we got the rest of the cast in New York. While in New York I was signed to come out here [Hollywood, Calif.] right away by RKO.

When I got here, all the writers were so impressed that I had a play on Broadway, and I was so impressed by them that I couldn't see straight. They had written pictures that I thought were the greatest. You see, I grew up thirty miles from Hollywood, and pictures had always been a big thing in my life. To find myself actually on a lot was tremendous.

CA: You had wanted to be a newspaper man, hadn't you?

BOWERS: Sure. I was working for United Press when I wrote the play.

CA: You went to the University of Missouri from 1933 to 1937 and worked your way through. What kind of jobs did you have?

BOWERS: Oh, hashing in the fraternity house. I pledged the fraternity simply because they offered me a job. That made the whole thing possible. And then I got a play out of it; the play was about my fraternity house.

A couple of years ago, I was in Chasen's restaurant here. A guy tapped me on the shoulder. I turned around and it was Richard Widmark, and he said, "Bill, you don't know me," and I said, "Sure I do, you're Richard Widmark, the movie star." He continued, "Well, aside from that . . . I don't know if you know how much I wanted to get in that play of yours in New York." I said, "You were up for it?" and he said, "Bill, you had parts for twenty-two guys. Every actor who was in New York at that time tried out for that show." I asked him how he came out, and he said, "I got through two readings and then I was knocked out." I asked, "By who?" and he said, "By you!"

CA: What about John Wayne?

BOWERS: I liked him. One time when I was having lunch with him (we were doing a picture together) I said, "You know, Duke, everything you stand for just appalls me, but I kind of like you. Why is that?" He said, "Well, you're a f—— liberal; you're supposed to like people, aren't you?" It was impossible to dislike that man, but I disagreed with his politics.

CA: When you were under contract to a studio, you would often dig up your own material and ideas to work on. Was that unusual?

BOWERS: No, it wasn't at all. We had contracts then that were for forty weeks out of the year. They could lay you off for three months, and most of us never saved any money, so the prospect of layoff was like an ax over our heads. The guys who saved their money were delighted; they'd go to Europe. But the suckers like me—I'd be digging up everything I could think of to try and have an idea when and if layoff came. I usually managed. They kept me pretty busy; I'd sometimes write four or five pictures a year.

CA: You've written so many different kinds of movies—Westerns, musicals, comedies, straight drama. Has there ever been anything you were afraid to try or haven't done?

BOWERS: No, it's not that tough. I also did some tough-guy pictures with Dick Powell that were a lot of fun.

CA: You got a reputation somehow of being an expert on Westerns, which you've denied. Did the reputation come from "The Gunfighter"?

BOWERS: Yes, it's turned into a kind of classic now. People seem to think I research the West, but I never did a bit of research because they had research departments in those days. You just wrote the story. "The Gunfighter" actually wasn't a Western. The whole thing took place in a saloon. I could have written it as a play, and I don't know why I didn't. At the time, I remember they said, "The first adult Western," and I didn't know what in the hell they were talking about. The only reason I wrote it that way was, I guess, because I didn't know how to write a Western. I didn't have any action in it. I wrote a lot of Westerns after that. I always loved to do them. They're fun.

CA: You've also done comedy Westerns, and you've said to students that all the elements of a Western have to be there, and then you put in the humor.

BOWERS: Yes, I think so anyway. Westerns are as classic as Greek drama, and you must have certain elements in them. I told a class one time, "There's no use writing about the second-fastest gun in the West because nobody cares; they're only interested in the first."

I did two comedy Westerns, one called "The Sheepman," with Glenn Ford and Shirley MacLaine, and then I did one a few years ago called "Support Your Local Sheriff," with James Garner. They were actually Westerns, with all the elements of a Western in them; it was just that the characters were entirely different and they were funny. They were doing the same things that the others did, but for example in

"Support Your Local Sheriff," Walter Brennan pulled a gun on Jim Garner, who was the sheriff, and said, "I think you got one of my children in your jail," and Jim just stuck his finger in the end of the gun. You already knew that Garner was the fastest guy with a gun around and could kill Brennan, but he didn't and you liked him for it. Brennan was just outraged, saying, "Get your finger out of the end of my gun!"

CA: You've lectured at UCLA [University of California, Los Angeles] and USC [University of Southern California]. Where else?

BOWERS: The Motion Picture Academy sent me to the University of Kansas for a week. I lecture on screenwriting around here [California] and wherever they invite me.

CA: Do you find that it's possible actually to teach people much about screenwriting?

BOWERS: No. They just have to do it, that's all. There aren't many tips you can give them. There are technical things you have to know, such as the difference between a dissolve and a fade. There are maybe four things that can be taught. What you have to do is get hold of a script and see how to put it down.

CA: Is discipline the biggest problem in writing?

BOWERS: Yes. Self-discipline is absolutely the most important thing, and it's the thing that I have the least of and have always had the least of.

CA: You must have had a great deal to have written all of the screenplays you've done.

BOWERS: You did that because you needed the money! There are some guys that go to work like miners and never waste a minute, but the great majority of us are awful goof-offs. I'll wait until the last possible moment, and I hate myself for it because it just gets grinding then. Now I'm doing some rewriting that Francis Coppola asked me to do on a script they're going to start shooting in two weeks.

CA: Is that harder than starting from scratch?

BOWERS: Yes. They already have a production board set up, showing what scene is going to be shot on what date, and the sets are already built, so I have to work right within the framework of the script. I can change all the dialogue, but I can't change the locale because they've already got it set up. I've done this a lot of times, and it's always murder.

CA: How do you feel about the auteur theory?

BOWERS: It's ridiculous. When they say "a film by———," that always gets me, because that indicates that everything in it—the photography, the set designing, the costumes, the writing, everything—was done by one person. How can it be "a film by" if you don't do all those things? And there never has been a business that's so much a cooperative effort as pictures are. But they'll say "film by so-and-so, produced by so-and-so, directed by so-and-so," all the same guy; he'll get his name up three or four times.

I had a friend who did this one terrible picture. He invited me to a running, and it was the worst thing I'd ever seen. It had his name up there for four credits. When it was over, he said, "What do you think?" and I said, "You wanted all the credit, I'm going to give you all the credit for it. It bombed."

CA: Do you ever have a script that you think is good, but once the director starts on it, it somehow goes wrong?

BOWERS: Yes, I have. Usually, these days, I work more closely with the director because I try and produce the scripts I like. Then I've got control.

CA: Are you directing any of your own material now?

BOWERS: I should have, but it's too late now; I'm sixty-four.

CA: Do you try your ideas out on your family?

BOWERS: Sure, all the time. They read everything I do as I'm doing it. I've got a twenty-eight-year-old son, who directed his first feature last year, I've got a sixteen-year-old son, and I've got a twelve-year-old daughter.

CA: Do the other children have movie ambitions?

BOWERS: Both my younger children are already taking acting. It's impossible for them to escape. They're delighted when I invite them over for lunch and take them down on the set, just like any kids are.

CA: In his book, The Screenwriter Looks at the Screenwriter, *William Froug mentions your contact with a great many students and people who come to see you for various reasons.*

BOWERS: Froug's book has practically become the definitive work in screenwriting classes in film schools. I get calls from kids in the East who say, "Mr. Bowers, I read that interview of yours, and I'm going to be in California next summer. Could I see you?" and I say, "Sure." I don't know how they get my number. I talk to a lot of students. It's fun; they're nice kids. I met Francis Coppola when he was still a student at UCLA; he asked me to read a script he had written that had just won the Goldwin Award.

Anybody who comes to the Coast stays with us. When I went back to the University of Kansas, I met an English professor there named James Gunn, and I found out he was one of the top science-fiction writers in the country. My wife is a science-fiction nut! So when I came back and told her that I had met Jim Gunn, she said, "You mean James Gunn?" and I said, "Yes. Look, he's coming out. Do you want him to come and stay with us?" So Jim came out. At that point he was president of the Science Fiction Writers Association, so he said to my wife, "Margie, if you want to give a dinner, I'll get a lot of the top guys to come." She gave a dinner for 100 people, and many top science-fiction writers were there—everyone except Isaac Asimov, who never travels over a few hundred miles from home—and so I thought we ought to have some movie stars here for them. I called up Ralph Bellamy, and he said, "Oh God, I'd love it. I'm the biggest science-fiction fan around. I'd *love* to meet those guys." And I said, "Well, let me tell you something: we're going to have a chili dinner." And he said, "So what? I'm president of the Beverly Hills Chili Club." Harry Morgan also joined us, as did George Pal and others.

CA: Are you still writing for television?

BOWERS: Yes, sure. I did six two-hour movies in a row before I came here to work for Francis Coppola. I'd rather be in features for the main and simple reason that you get more time.

CA: How do you like television writing as opposed to screenwriting?

BOWERS: There's no difference. It's just a matter of time, and it seems that in television, because of the time factor, everything is a compromise from the first day, particularly for the director. How those guys do those things in the time they do them I don't know. They just finished one of mine. Remember the old show, "The Wild, Wild West," with Robert Conrad and Ross Martin? It's been off the air for ten years. We brought the two guys back from retirement, out of shape, and gave them one more job to do. We dug up an old heavy that they had, and it worked out great. They got a tremendous rating on it, so they asked me to do another one, and they just shot that. Now they're going to do one of them a year.

CA: You mentioned liking the fact that censorship of movies has been greatly relaxed. What other things do you think are better about movies?

BOWERS: Well, they don't make so many of them. You know, we used to make four hundred pictures a year; every major studio made fifty to fifty-two pictures a year, and that employed a lot of people. But obviously not all of them could be very good, and they weren't. The shows you see now that were done in the thirties and forties and fifties are the classics—they have lived on—but the majority of them weren't good. The studios owned their own theatres then, and they had to keep them filled, so they would change every week.

CA: Did you go to the movies a lot when you were a kid?

BOWERS: Oh, sure. I grew up on movies.

CA: Where did you get the idea of being a newspaper man?

BOWERS: I just liked it. I worked on the school paper in high school, and I loved it. I found out that Missouri had the best journalism school in the country, so I went there. I got out and went right to work for the United Press, which was unusual in the height of the Depression. I got thirty dollars a week. I was making twice as much money as anybody I knew, and I got ten dollars a week for expenses, too. You could live well on that. Then I got the play on; that brought about five hundred dollars a week, and the friends I had grown up with out here simply did not believe that. You couldn't spend it. I lived in the most expensive place in town. The rent was $140 a month. Most apartments were forty or fifty dollars. The people in pictures were doing well. It was great. I've been terribly lucky. I've been a lucky guy all my life. And don't kid yourself; luck plays an awful big part in it.

They'd bring novelists out, big novelists. Scott Fitzgerald I knew very well, and William Faulkner, and they weren't screenwriters. They were *never* good screenwriters. It's an entirely different form.

CA: Why were such good novelists unable to write screenplays?

BOWERS: They didn't have the ability to visualize things, to imagine how it was going to play. They never had to confront that in writing novels. The novelists I knew in the 1930's and 1940's mostly considered screenwriting whoring and looked on the business with a great deal of contempt, which didn't make them good screenwriters to begin with. You can't be contemptuous of what you're doing and do a good job. Then some of the guys started coming into the business who thought screenwriting was a marvelous profession and just kicked them out. Faulkner did good screenplays when he worked with Howard Hawks, because Hawks was the ultimate picture maker, and he loved Faulkner, and he would guide him. Then Faulkner would do wonderful things, but never alone.

CA: Were you around Faulkner when he was working?

BOWERS: Yes, I had the office next to his at Warner Brothers.

CA: Is it true that Faulkner asked the studio, "Would it be all right if I worked at home?" and, when they said OK, he went back to Mississippi?

BOWERS: That was not the truth. I asked him about that, and he said, "Well, I loved the story, so I never denied it." He didn't want to go home because he had a mistress out here. She was a script girl for Howard Hawks, and Faulkner was madly in love with her. His wife was an alcoholic, and he couldn't get her to divorce him, so every chance he got to come out here, he would. But he kept drinking so badly here. He'd started at $1500 a week, and when I met him, I was absolutely horrified to find out I was making $200 a week more than he was. He was getting $300 a week, and I was getting $500 at that point. It was Jack Warner just being nice and hiring him, and also because Hawks insisted on it. They did "The Big Sleep" and "To Have and Have Not," but I'm sure most of that was Howard's work.

CA: Is there anything you haven't written that you would like to try writing?

BOWERS: No. I've just written another original screenplay, and I'm trying to talk Coppola into doing it. I don't think they're making enough comedies now. I think everybody is starved for them. We used to do crazy-girl comedies out here. Carol Lombard would do them and Jean Arthur. There were lots of women that could play them—Irene Dunne, Claudette Colbert. They haven't made one of those for a long time, so I've got one. I just haven't made a deal on it yet.

CA: Is there anything that you would do differently if you had to do it over?

BOWERS: Sure, I'd direct. I remember when Francis [Coppola] was first starting out here, he spent a lot of time at my house. He married my wife's best friend, so we have seen a lot of each other over the years. He said, "Bill, I think you've got it figured all wrong. I think you've got to direct if you want to get your stuff done the way you want it done." He was absolutely right, and I had turned down three chances to direct when they begged me, and I said that I didn't want to sit around a moldly set all day. I was stupid.

CA: Some screenwriters don't seem to have the patience that directing takes. Nunnally Johnson was probably a good example.

BOWERS: Nunnally wasn't a particularly good director. He was a good friend of mine. He produced "The Gunfighter." He directed two or three films. They just weren't terribly good. Nunnally was a marvelous writer and a genuine wit. I'll tell you a story about Nunnally. He was going to drive to New York with his family, so he had the map out, and we were all standing around while he showed us where he was going to go. One of the guys said, "Hey, you're going to go right through my hometown. Do me a favor. When you get there, look in the telephone book. There's a woman named Giselle Worbicek Piffle. She's a friend of mine, and I'm going to write her and tell her that Mr. Johnson from Hollywood is going to come through there, and she will be really excited." And Nunnally says, "Giselle Worbicek Piffle?" So Nunnally gets to the town, and looks, and, sure enough,

there is a Giselle Worbicek Piffle in the phone book. He calls her up and says, "May I speak to Miss Piffle, please?" and the boy asks, "Who's calling?" and Nunnally replies, "Mr. Johnson from Hollywood." There's this long pause, and he comes on and says, "Miss Piffle says she doesn't know a Mr. Johnson from Hollywood." And Nunnally asks, "Could it be that I have the wrong Giselle Worbicek Piffle?"

CA: If you got the chance to direct one of your films, would you do it now?

BOWERS: I don't know. I just might if I get the chance to get this new screenplay made.

BIOGRAPHICAL/CRITICAL SOURCES: William Froug, *The Screenwriter Looks at the Screenwriter,* Macmillan, 1972.

—*Interview by Jean W. Ross*

*   *   *

BOWICK, Dorothy Mueller
See MUELLER, Dorothy

*   *   *

BOWIE, Janetta (Hamilton) 1907-

PERSONAL: Born August 16, 1907, in Greenock, Scotland; daughter of Duncan (a marine engineer) and Lilias (a dressmaker; maiden name, Scott) Bowie. *Education:* University of Glasgow, M.A., 1928; Glasgow Training College for Teachers, teaching diploma, 1929. *Home:* 32 Fox St., Greenock, Renfrewshire PS16 8SY, Scotland.

CAREER: Assistant teacher at primary school in Port Glasgow, Scotland, 1929-47; head infants mistress at primary school in Port Glasgow, 1947-64, and academy in Greenock, Scotland, 1964-70; Finnart High School, Greenock, principal teacher of remedial subjects, 1970-73; writer, 1966—. Teacher in Borstal section of Greenock Prison, 1945-59; lecturer on local history, education, and foreign travel. *Member:* Scottish Association of Writers (honorary vice-president, 1977-80), Greenock Writers Club (president, 1967-74), Greenock Camera Club (vice-president, 1970).

WRITINGS: Bi-Centenary of Port Glasgow, 1775-1975, Port Glasgow Town Council, 1975; *Penny Buff* (memoirs) Constable, 1975; *Penny Boss* (memoirs), Constable, 1976; *Penny Change* (memoirs), Constable, 1977.

Radio plays; juvenile: "The Witch of Diera," broadcast by British Broadcasting Corp. (BBC), 1966; "The Treasure of Diera," BBC, 1964; "The House That Ran Away," BBC, 1966; "The Queen and the Grumley," BBC, 1967; "The Tale of the Two Engines," BBC, 1968.

Contributor of articles, poems, and stories to Scottish magazines and newspapers.

WORK IN PROGRESS: Finwal (tentative title), a historical novel of eighteenth-century Jura and Greenock, completion expected in 1982.

SIDELIGHTS: Janetta Bowie told *CA:* "My motivation is some inner compulsion that was generated in earlier life, particularly in school. I have a great delight in life, the lightsome side of it, and a talent for words, both in prose and poetry. I had an encouraging home background, a thoroughly good education, a need to make money because my early years were not affluent, and a profound interest in education and the new educational ideas. Now quite affluent, I spend every penny on riotous living while I am still alive!

"I abhor obscure, wordy writing. Many modern authors

seem to me to fail in communication in this way. I have a passion for clarity, readability, and easy flow of words, perhaps because of having to make myself clear when teaching children. I admire facts, skillful use of words, euphony, and a good use of dramatic situations, even in memoirs. I find romantic novels distasteful, boring, unnatural, and generally immature, unless based on adequate research, good vocabulary, and knowledge of the realities of human nature. I find many modern authors lacking in style, that individualistic expression associated with authors of the past.

"Humor is a feature of most of my writing, even in articles. *Penny Buff* owed most of its success to this. My adventures in the world of education appealed to readers through the humor eternally associated with children. My philosophy is summed up in *Penny Buff*: 'There is one thing psychology never seems to consider—the rare sweet springs of laughter. . . . I feel that in the classroom there should be more of it.' And, 'In a school it is not the children who present the problems. It's the grown-ups.'"

AVOCATIONAL INTERESTS: Photographic processing of prints and slides, gardening, reading, attending plays.

BIOGRAPHICAL/CRITICAL SOURCES: Scotsman, April 27, 1970; *Glasgow Herald,* March 28, 1975; *Times Educational Supplement,* April 4, 1975; *Greenock Telegraph,* April 9, 1975.

* * *

BOWMAN, Derek 1931-

PERSONAL: Born January 13, 1931, in Liverpool, England; son of Edward (a factory supervisor) and Edith Minnie (a milliner; maiden name, Trunks) Bowman; married Marianne Margarete Recktenwald (a book shop assistant), August 6, 1958; children: Elisabeth Jane, Catherine Anna. *Education:* University of Liverpool, B.A., 1953, M.A., 1963; Cambridge University, certificate in education, 1957. *Home:* 75 Cluny Gardens, Edinburgh EH10 6BW, Scotland. *Office:* Department of German, University of Edinburgh, David Hume Tower, George Sq., Edinburgh EH8 9JX, Scotland.

CAREER: Modern languages master at schools in Southampton, England, 1957-62, and Elstree, England, 1962-64; University of Edinburgh, Edinburgh, Scotland, lecturer in German, 1964—. *Military service:* British Army, Royal Education Corps, 1953-55; served in Germany and Austria; became sergeant. *Awards, honors:* Felicia Hemans Prize Medal for Lyrical Poetry from University of Liverpool, 1969, for "Easter Snow-Streaks."

WRITINGS: (Editor and translator) Ulrich Braeker, *The Life Story and Real Adventures of the Poor Man of Toggenburg,* Edinburgh University Press, 1970; *Life Into Autobiography: A Study of Goethe's "Dichtung und Wahrkeit,"* Peter Lang, 1971; *Out of My System* (poems), Tamarind Press, 1976, 2nd edition, 1978; (contributor of translations) John Willett and Ralph Manheim, editors, *Bertolt Brecht: Poems, 1913-56,* Eyre Methuen, 1976; (editor) Ethel Bassin, *The Old Songs of Skye,* Routledge & Kegan Paul, 1977; *Tam: The Life and Death of a Dog,* Gordon Wright, 1978; (editor and translator) Braeker, *A Few Words About William Shakespeare's Plays,* Oswald Wolff, 1979.

WORK IN PROGRESS: Research on eighteenth-century German and Swiss autobiography and on the works of Ulrich Braeker.

SIDELIGHTS: Bowman wrote: "Poetry and autobiography have long been burning interests for me, because they go to the heart of the matter, individual consciousness, the per-

son. However, of late I've gotten interested again in novels and novel writing, and intend producing a trilogy about the sense of life in the twentieth century in Britain."

* * *

BOXER, Charles Ralph 1904-

PERSONAL: Born March 8, 1904; son of Hugh and Jane (Patterson) Boxer; married Emily Hahn, 1945; children: two daughters. *Education:* Attended Wellington College and Royal Military College, Sandhurst, England. *Home:* Ringshall End, Little Gaddesden, Hertfordshire HP4 1NF, England.

CAREER: University of London, London, England, Camoens Professor of Portuguese, 1947-51, professor of history of the Far East, 1951-53, Camoens Professor of Portuguese, 1953-67, professor emeritus, 1968—, fellow of King's College, 1967; Yale University, New Haven, Conn., professor of history of expansion of Europe overseas, 1969-72, professor emeritus, 1972—. Lecturer at colleges and universities, including Johns Hopkins University, Bryn Mawr College, University of Virginia, and University of Wisconsin. Trustee of National Maritime Museum, 1961-68; visiting research professor at Indiana University, 1967-76; honorary fellow of School of Oriental and African Studies, 1974. *Military service:* Served, 1939-47; Japanese prisoner of war, 1941-45; became major. *Member:* British Academy (fellow), Royal Netherlands Academy of Sciences. *Awards, honors:* Received honorary degrees from universities of Utrecht, 1950, Lisbon, 1952, Bahia, 1959, Liverpool, 1966, and Hong Kong, 1971; Order of Santiago da Espada (Portugal); Grand Cross of the Order of the Infante Dom Henrique (Portugal); Knight of the Order of St. Gregory the Great, 1969.

WRITINGS—In English: (Editor and translator) Goncalo de Siqueira de Sousa, *A Portuguese Embassy to Japan, 1644-1647,* K. Paul, Trench, Truebner, 1928, published as *The Embassy of Captain Goncalo de Siqueira de Sousa to Japan in 1644-1647,* Oficinas Graficas da Tipografia Mercantil, 1938; *The Affair of the Madre de Deus: A Chapter in the History of the Portuguese in Japan,* K. Paul, Trench, Truebner, 1929; (editor and author of introduction) Paul Craesbeeck, *Commentaries of Ruy de Andrada,* George Routledge & Sons, 1930; (editor and translator) *The Journal of Maerten Hampertszoon Tromp, Anno 1639,* Cambridge University Press, 1930; (author of introduction and notes) Frans Caron, *A True Description of the Mighty Kingdoms of Japan and Siam,* Argonaut Press, 1935; *Jan Compagnie in Japan, 1600-1817: An Essay on the Cultural, Artistic, and Scientific Influence Exercised by the Hollanders in Japan From the Seventeenth to the Nineteenth Centuries,* M. Nijhoff, 1936, 2nd edition, 1950.

The Topasses of Timor, Indisch Instituut, 1947; *Fidalgos in the Far East, 1550-1770: Fact and Fancy in the History of Macao,* M. Nijhoff, 1948, 2nd edition, Oxford University Press, 1968; *The Christian Century in Japan, 1549-1650,* University of California Press, 1951; *Salvador de Sa and the Struggle for Brazil and Angola, 1602-1686,* Athlone Press, 1952, reprinted, Greenwood Press, 1975; (editor) *South China in the Sixteenth Century: Being the Narratives of Galeote Pereira, Friar Gaspar da Cruz, and Friar Martin de Rada,* Hakluyt Society, 1953; *The Dutch in Brazil, 1624-1654,* Clarendon Press, 1957; *The Great Ship From Amacon: Annals of Macao and the Old Japan Trade, 1555-1640,* Centro de Estudos Historicos Ultramarinos, 1959; (editor and translator) Bernardo Gomes de Brito, editor, *The Tragic History of the Sea, 1589-1622: Narratives of the Shipwrecks of the Portuguese East Indiamen Sao Thome (1589), Santa Alberto (1593), Sao Joao Baptista (1622), and the Journeys of the Survivors in South East Africa*, Cambridge University Press, 1959.

(With Carlos de Azevedo) *Fort Jesus and the Portuguese in Mombasa, 1593-1729*, Hollis & Carter, 1960; *The Golden Age of Brazil, 1695-1750: Growing Pains of a Colonial Society*, University of California Press, 1962; (with J. S. Cummins) *The Dominican Mission in Japan, 1602-1622, and Lope de Vega*, Archivum Fratrum Praedicatorum, 1963; *Race Relations in the Portuguese Colonial Empire, 1415-1825*, Clarendon Press, 1963; *The Dutch Seaborne Empire, 1600-1800*, Knopf, 1965; *Portuguese Society in the Tropics: The Municipal Councils of Goa, Macao, Bahia, and Luanda, 1510-1800*, University of Wisconsin Press, 1965; *An African Eldorado: Monomotapa and Mocambique, 1498-1752*, Central African Historical Association, 1966; *Francisco Vieira de Figueiredo: A Portuguese Merchant-Adventurer in South East Asia, 1624-1667*, M. Nijhoff, 1967; (editor and translator) de Brito, editor, *Further Selections From the Tragic History of the Sea, 1559-1565: Narratives of Shipwrecks of the Portuguese East Indiamen*, Cambridge University Press, 1968; *Four Centuries of Portuguese Expansion, 1415-1825: A Succinct Survey*, Witwatersrand University Press, 1961, University of California Press, 1969; *The Portuguese Seaborne Empire, 1415-1825*, Knopf, 1969.

The Anglo-Dutch Wars of the Seventeenth Century, 1652-1674, Her Majesty's Stationary Office, 1974; *Women in Iberian Expansion Overseas, 1415-1815: Some Facts, Fancies, and Personalities*, Oxford University Press, 1975 (published in England as *Mary and Misogyny: Women in Iberian Expansion Overseas, 1415-1815; Some Facts, Fancies, and Personalities*, Duckworth, 1975); *The Church Militant and Iberian Expansion, 1440-1770*, Johns Hopkins University Press, 1978.

Other writings: (Editor) *A aclamacao del Rei D. Joao IV em Goa e um Macau: Relacoes contemporaneas reeditados e anotadas*, Lisboa, 1932; (editor) *Embaixada de Macau ao Japao em 1640*, Imprensa de Armada, 1933; (editor) Caetano de Sousa Pereira, *O plano da reconquista da provincia do Norte*, Tipografica Rangel, 1936; *O coronel Pedro de Mello e a sublevacao geral de Timor em 1729-1731*, Escola Tipografica do Orfanato Salesiano, 1937; *Sisnando Dias Bayao: Conquistador da "Mae de Ouro,"* Lisboa, 1938; (with J. M. Braga) *Algumas notas sobre a bibliografia de Macau*, Escola Tipografica Salesiana, 1939.

Antonio Coelho Guerreiro, e as relacoes entre Macau e Timor, no comeco do secule XVIII, Tipografica do Orfanato da Imaculada Conceicao de Macau, 1940; *Breve relacao da vida e feitos de Lopo e Inacio Sarmento de Carvalho*, Imprensa Nacional, 1940; *As viagens de Japao e os seus capitaes mores, 1550-1640*, Escola Tipografica do Oratorio de S.J. Bosco, 1941; (editor) *Macau na epoca da restauracao*, Imprensa Nacional, 1942; *Subsidios para a historia dos capitais gerais e governadores de Macau, 1557-1770*, [Macau], 1944; *A proposito dum livrinho xilografico dos Jesuitas de Pequim (secolo XVIII): Ensaio historico*, Imprensa Nacional, 1947; *"Adonde hay valor hay honor": Esboco biografico do almirante Luis Velho, 1624-1669*, Lisboa, 1948; (editor) Joao Rodrigues Girao, *Antes quebrar que torcer; ou, Pundonor portugues em Nagasaqui, 3-6 de Janeiro de 1610*, Imprensa Nacional, 1950; (with Frazao de Vasconcelos) *Andre Furtado de Mendonca, 1558-1610*, Diviso de Publicacoes Biblioteca, Angencia Geral do Ultramar, 1955.

Contributor of articles to numerous scholarly journals.

SIDELIGHTS: An authority on European territorial expansion, Charles Ralph Boxer has written numerous books on the Dutch and Portuguese colonization in Brazil, Angola, Japan, and China. *The Dutch in Brazil*, for example, is an account of Holland's rise to power in the early 1600's. Because the Portuguese closed their ports to Dutch trade, the Dutch were forced to obtain salt, sugar, and other necessities from friendlier ports such as Africa and America. Unintentionally, this act was the catalyst that brought Holland fame and glory as it rose to become the most powerful maritime and colonial faction of the early seventeenth century.

The Dutch continued their expansion into both Brazil, where they commandeered the profitable sugar industry, and Angola, where they obtained slaves to work the mills. Ironically, it was the Portuguese, then under Spanish domination, who were finally able to drive the Dutch out of Brazil. In a review of *The Dutch in Brazil* for the *New Statesman and Nation*, H. R. Trevor-Roper compared it to Boxer's earlier work, *Salvador de Sa and the Struggle for Brazil and Angola*. Whereas the earlier book presented new information and fresh insights into the Dutch occupation of Brazil, Trevor-Roper maintained that the newer work, "just as scholarly, just as well-written, is more squarely built, and sheds its light directly on the central problem." A writer for the *Times Literary Supplement* concluded: "The merit of Professor Boxer's accomplishment rests on the clear and methodical ordering of the subject-matter, on his proved impartiality and, not least, on the assurance of his historical judgment."

Another of Boxer's works, *The Dutch Seaborne Empire*, details the development, prosperity, and subsequent decay of the Dutch empire between 1600 and 1800. Boxer rationalized in this book that wide-spread political squabbling, racism that held back colonization and expansion, and insufficient supplies of coal required to carry Holland into the industrial nineteenth century were all factors that contributed to its decline. Reviewer E. K. Welsch commended the author for "skillfully [introducing] the reader not to kings and battles but to the people who lived [through that time]." A writer for *New Yorker* likewise praised Boxer's presentation as "far more than just theories of history; he offers an astonishing amount of statistical information, and uses it to give us a sense of the quality of life in the Netherlands' golden age."

In addition to the history of Dutch expansion, Boxer wrote of Portugal and her colonial activities from 1415 to 1825. In *The Portuguese Seaborne Empire* he discusses the motivations behind Portuguese colonization. Portugal, he explains, was not interested in finding a new route to the Far East by sailing west, as her native son Christopher Columbus was, but wished instead to round the Cape of Good Hope in order to open up trade from the Indian Ocean. Spurred on by fantastic tales of an enormously wealthy priest-king residing in splendor somewhere in the vast expanse of Africa, the Portuguese pursued colonization in hopes of obtaining for themselves the riches of that world.

The Portuguese Seaborne Empire was highly praised for its portrayal of four centuries of expansion and motivations that inspired it. A reviewer for the *Times Literary Supplement* commented that "the author's familiarity with the onion-and-garlic side of Portuguese idealism, and perhaps also a temperamental scepticism, makes his tribute to the achievements of Portuguese Christianity all the more impressive." Robert Rea hailed the book as "a magnificent new study." He added that "this volume is a great work of synthesis, an illuminating introduction packed with challenging interpretations and insights.''

Consisting of a series of lectures given by Boxer at the University of Wisconsin, *Portuguese Society in the Tropics* is an examination of the character and composition of the municipal councils of Portugal in Gao, Macao, Bahia, and Luanda in the period between 1510 and 1800. One of the major points Boxer discusses in the book is the high degree of local autonomy enjoyed by the councils due to the lack of qualified Portuguese statesmen to fill the seats of administration. As with his many other books, Boxer was again commended for presenting keen insights into previously slighted issues. The *Times Literary Supplement*, for instance, declared, ''Treading once more on virgin soil, Professor Boxer gives an admiringly succinct and readable account of the functions and importance of these municipal councils.''

In *Race Relations in the Portuguese Colonial Empire* Boxer attacked the popular notion that Portugal refrained from promoting racial superiority during its era of colonization. He argues that this was simply not the case, that the Portuguese were in fact no worse, yet no better, than the other European colonizing powers. According to the author, they engaged in slave trade, mistreatment of black subjects, and other common practices of the time. Although the work was considered controversial in Portugal, it was well received in other European countries and in the United States as well. A writer for the *Virginia Quarterly Review* assessed that ''this sincere, scholarly book restores a much needed authenticity to the study of Portuguese global conquest and colonization.'' The *Times Literary Supplement* concurred: ''Professor Boxer writes with refreshing directness. If only all works of learning were as sensible, pungent and sparing of verbiage.''

Related to Boxer's studies on Portuguese colonization, *Women in Iberian Expansion Overseas* probes the role of women during that era. The book was praised for revealing a long-ignored portion of the historical record, for as one writer pointed out, ''exploration of the role of women has much to say about culture, society, religious and intellectual history, and the economy.'' Reviewer John Lynch deemed the work ''a bibliographical and narrative masterpiece'' and added: ''Scholarship allied to lucid narrative and a sense of humour—these are the qualities we have come to expect from the prolific pen of Professor Boxer.''

BIOGRAPHICAL/CRITICAL SOURCES: New Statesman and Nation, February 23, 1957; *Times Literary Supplement*, April 12, 1957, June 4, 1964, June 2, 1966, December 18, 1969, October 3, 1975; *Virginia Quarterly Review*, summer, 1964; *Library Journal*, October 15, 1965, November 1, 1969, November 1, 1970; *New Yorker*, November 6, 1965, April 11, 1970; *Spectator*, November 8, 1969; *Choice*, December, 1975.

—*Sketch by Kathleen Ceton Newman*

* * *

BOYCE, Joseph Nelson 1937-

PERSONAL: Born April 18, 1937, in New Orleans, La.; son of John and Sadie (Nelson) Boyce; married Carol Hill, December 21, 1968; children: Leslie, Nelson, Joel. *Education:* Attended Roosevelt University, 1955-65, and John Marshall Law School, 1965-67. *Religion:* Episcopalian. *Residence:* East Point, Ga. *Office: Time*, 233 Peachtree St. N.W., Atlanta, Ga. 30303.

CAREER/WRITINGS: Chicago Police Department, Chicago, Ill., patrolman and academy instructor, 1961-66; *Chi-*

cago Tribune, Chicago, reporter, 1966-70; *Time*, New York City, correspondent, 1970-73, San Francisco bureau chief, 1973-79, Atlanta bureau chief, 1979—. Chairman of Marin County Black Leadership Forum, 1974-75; member of Marin Justice Council, 1976-78; lecturer at numerous colleges and universities. Professional vibraharpist, 1956—. *Military service:* U.S. Naval Reserve, 1954-62. *Member:* National Association for the Advancement of Colored People, American Federation of Musicians. *Awards, honors:* Outstanding Black Achiever Award from Metropolitan Young Men's Christian Association (New York City), 1975; Unity in Media Award from Lincoln University, 1975.

* * *

BOYLE, Andrew Philip More 1919-

PERSONAL: Born May 27, 1919, in Dundee, Scotland; son of Andrew (a public servant) and Rose (an artist; maiden name, McCann) Boyle; married Christina Galvin (a publisher), November 20, 1943; children: Edmund C., Diana. *Education:* Attended Sorbonne, University of Paris, 1937-40. *Religion:* Roman Catholic. *Home:* 16 Deodar Rd., Putney, London S.W.15, England. *Agent:* Curtis Brown Ltd., 1 Craven Hill, London W2 3EP, England.

CAREER: British Broadcasting Corp. (BBC-Radio), London, England, scriptwriter, 1947-50, producer, 1950-55, assistant editor, 1955-64, editor of ''The World at One,'' ''PM,'' and ''The World This Weekend,'' 1965-75, head of television and radio news in Glasgow and Edinburgh, Scotland, 1976-77. *Military Service:* Royal Air Force Volunteer Reserve, 1941-43. British Army, 1943-46; served in the Far East; became major. *Member:* Society of Authors. *Awards, honors:* Whitbread Literary Award for the outstanding biography of the year, 1974, for *Poor, Dear Brendan: The Quest for Brendan Bracken.*

WRITINGS: No Passing Glory: The Biography of Leonard Cheshire, V.C., Collins, 1959; (with others) *Heroes of Our Time*, Gollancz, 1961; *Trenchard: Man of Vision*, Collins, 1962; *Index to the Annuals*, Volume I: *The Authors, 1820-50*, privately printed, 1967; *Montagu Norman: A Biography*, Cassell, 1968; *Only the Wind Will Listen: John Reith of the B.B.C.*, Hutchinson, 1972; *Poor, Dear Brendan: The Quest for Brendan Bracken*, Hutchinson, 1974; *The Riddle of Erskine Childers*, Hutchinson, 1977; *The Climate of Treason: Five Who Spied for Russia*, Hutchinson, 1979. Contributor to newspapers.

WORK IN PROGRESS: ''A portrait of Baroness Moura Budhess, a remarkable Russian emigree who was the mistress, in turn, of Sir Robert Bruce Lockhart, H. G. Wells, and Maxim Gorky. She was also involved in film production with the Korda brothers, in translation, and in espionage.''

SIDELIGHTS: Boyle told *CA:* ''Subjects that mainly attract this biographer and contemporary historian are great individualists and eccentrics, whether positive persons of achievement, like Trenchard, Cheshire, and Childers, or negative and destructive figures like Blunt, Burgess, and Maclean, who spied for Soviet Russia.''

* * *

BOYUM, Keith O(rel) 1945-

PERSONAL: Born August 20, 1945, in Lakota, N.D.; son of Orel Archibald (in small business) and Doris (Craig) Boyum; married Renae Pieri (a teacher), June 19, 1971; children: Nicole. *Education:* University of North Dakota, B.A., 1967; University of Minnesota, M.A., 1971, Ph.D., 1974. *Politics:*

Democrat. *Religion:* Lutheran. *Home:* 32 Birdsong, Irvine, Calif. 92714. *Office:* Department of Political Science, California State University, Fullerton, Calif. 92634.

CAREER: California State University, Fullerton, assistant professor, 1972-75, associate professor, 1975-80, professor of political science, 1980—. Research study director for National Academy of Sciences, 1977-79; consultant to National Institute of Justice and National Institute of Juvenile Justice and Delinquency Prevention. *Military service:* U.S. Army Reserve, 1971-79; became captain. *Member:* American Political Science Association, Law and Society Association, Phi Beta Kappa, Blue Key.

WRITINGS: (Editor with Samuel Krislov, Jerry N. Clark, Roger Schaefer, and Susan O. White) *Compliance and the Law: A Multidisciplinary Approach,* Sage Publications, 1972; (editor with Krislov, Clark, and Harold Chase) *Biographical Dictionary of the Federal Judiciary,* Gale, 1976; (editor with Krislov) *Forecasting the Impact of New Legislation on Courts,* National Academy of Sciences, 1980; (editor with Lynn Mather) *Empirical Theories About Courts,* Longman, 1981. Contributor to professional journals.

WORK IN PROGRESS: Scholarly research.

SIDELIGHTS: Boyum wrote: "If there is an underlying theme to my writings, it is that questions about (or problems of) courts and legal institutions are not open to easy answers, but that careful, theoretical understanding is a necessary requisite. That theme is present in my analyses of problems of caseload and delay in trial courts: a search for 'quick fixes' is chimerical. The theory-building enterprise is central in reviewing the social composition of the federal judiciary and in considering compliance and obedience to the judicial command. The theme predominates my work on empirical theories about courts."

*   *   *

BRACE, Edward Roy   1936-

PERSONAL: Born January 4, 1936, in Towanda, Pa.; son of Kenneth LeRoy and Dorothy (a professor; maiden name, Patterson) Brace; married Barbara Ann Myers (a secretary), December 19, 1978. *Education:* Attended University of Vermont, 1953-56, and Harvard University, 1961-62. *Home and office:* 201 Chestnut St., Towanda, Pa. 18848.

CAREER: WTHS-Radio, Miami, Fla., radio announcer and engineer, 1950-51; radio personality on poetry programs in Burlington, Vt., 1952-56; affiliated with U.S. Air Force Office of Information Services, Winooski, Vt., 1956-61; Lahey Clinic and Foundation, Boston, Mass., associate medical editor and writer, 1961-63; National Drug Co., Philadelphia, Pa., medical editor and writer, 1963-65; Sterling Winthrop International, New York, N.Y., medical editor and writer, 1965-70; Laurence Urdang Associates Ltd., London, England, medical editor and writer, 1970-75; Wellcome Foundation, London, medical editor and writer, 1976-78; Independent Editorial Services, Towanda, Pa., head of company, 1979—. Writer and editor for Mixter Laboratories for Electron Microscopy, at Massachusetts General Hospital, and for World Health Organization. *Member:* American Association for the Advancement of Science, American Medical Writers Association (fellow), Authors League of America, Authors Guild, Medical Journalists Association (England).

WRITINGS: Parasites and the Human Heart, Wellcome Foundation, 1976; *Hamlyn Home Medical Guide,* Hamlyn Group, 1976; *An Illustrated Dictionary of Chess,* McKay,

1978; (with Robert R. Costello) *Nelson's New Compact Medical Dictionary,* Thomas Nelson, 1978; *150 Commonly Prescribed Drugs: A Guide to Their Uses and Side Effects,* World Book-Childcraft International, 1980.

Contributor: Edwin Riddell, editor, *Lives of the Stuart Age,* Osprey, 1976; Jack Tresidder, editor, *Living Well: The People Maintenance Manual,* Mitchell Beazley, 1977; William Gould, editor, *Lives of the Georgian Age,* Osprey, 1978.

Author of "The Exciting World of English Dictionaries," a column in *AMWA Bulletin,* and "Dateline England, "a column in *Meriden Journal;* medical editor and author of "Biological and Medical Science Review," in *Associated Press Almanac,* 1973-75, *CBS News Almanac,* 1976-78, and *Hammond Almanac,* 1979-80. Contributor to *Encyclopaedia Britannica.* Contributor of articles, poems, and reviews to journals and newspapers. Medical editor of *Good Housekeeping Family Health and Medical Guide* and *Collins Dictionary of the English Language* (also contributor).

WORK IN PROGRESS: Medical reference books and lexicons.

SIDELIGHTS: Brace told *CA:* "Being a writer was the most important goal for me from the very beginning—so much so that I was unmindful of what I put down on paper. For example, while attending junior high school I wrote a notebook full of all sorts of wonderful observations, mostly concerned with the world about me. This was submitted for approval to the teacher of journalism, who returned it a few days later with the stark comment: 'I can think of no useful purpose for this writing!'

"Two months later I got my first break as a writer. I was fortunate enough to interview Florence Chadwick (the first woman to swim the English Channel from England to France), and my article appeared in the *Trailer News.* It was my first by-line, at the age of 15. Not only was I thrilled, but I had learned a valuable lesson: readers are rarely interested in autobiographical details from an unknown writer.

"Poetry was in my soul—deeply from the age of sixteen and hopelessly from the age of nineteen. During this period I published two chapbooks. Gradually, my approach to poetry shifted, especially after absorbing the works of e. e. cummings and Dylan Thomas. I made the most of my newly-gained knowledge and never told another living soul. It seemed to have something to do with levels of consciousness and awareness of the shadows of the mind. No academic spotlight could get far enough into the corners. By writing within those corners I could be safe. And not found out. Take an idea, I thought, and attack it simultaneously from all angles. Sweep down from above; jab upward into its center. Dance around it. The idea was to leave something in the poem that would stimulate new thoughts upon subsequent readings.

"With great passion and purpose I continued to read as many poets as I could. I learned that some poets were *wet* (e.g., Dylan Thomas and Gerard Manley Hopkins) and some were *dry* (e.g., T. S. Eliot and W. H. Auden). The wordplay was exciting. The experiments of James Joyce were also exciting, although confusing. At long last, the comment of Archibald MacLeish was clear: 'A poem should not mean/ But be.'

"Poetry is fine, but it doesn't pay the bills. Even Robert Frost had to teach to supplement his income. Thus, I soon decided that in order to survive I had to write about subjects that would be of both commercial and personal interest.

Since the function of the human brain had always excited me, it was a short hop, skip, and jump to my new avocation and vocation: medical writing.

"Preparing to be a good medical writer involves many years of apprenticeship (or 'woodshedding,' as jazz musicians say). In my case, I had the good fortune to study with Charlotte Thompson White at the world-famous Lahey Clinic and Foundation in Boston. There, in my eventual role as associate medical editor, I learned that physicians and surgeons don't always write the way they mean to write. That is, they make slips, even of medical fact. In order to help them, I had to learn their special language. Then I could help them to say exactly what they really wanted to say, in the most meaningful and moving manner. Of course, this I am still learning—even after twenty years as a professional medical writer and editor. Learning never stops.

"Samuel Johnson, the famous lexicographer of the eighteenth century, once said that if a person wants to be an expert atheist he must first master theology. Know your enemy on his own ground, and only then attempt to defeat him! In my own case the situation is not so violent. But it became clear that patients are often in the dark. They know very little about the drugs they are given, and they often misunderstand what their physicians tell them about their specific disease or disorder. I have tried to bridge this gap in essential communications between doctors and their patients. My only reward is a new understanding between them both."

AVOCATIONAL INTERESTS: Modern poetry, chess, amateur radio (W3ETQ), classical music, modern jazz, "singing badly and loudly," discussion, sleep.

BIOGRAPHICAL/CRITICAL SOURCES: Towanda Daily Review, April 26, 1979.

* * *

BRADWELL, James
See KENT, Arthur William Charles

* * *

BRADY, Darlene A(nn) 1951-

PERSONAL: Born August 4, 1951, in Fort Hood, Tex.; daughter of Egbert Leo Brady (an engineer) and Eleanor (Langmaier) Wollenhaupt; married William M. Serban (head of a university library documents department, researcher, and stained glass artist), May 19, 1979. *Education:* Attended Ohio State University, 1969-71; Ohio University, B.F.A. (summa cum laude), 1976; University of Pittsburgh, M.L.S. (summa cum laude), 1978, M.A. (summa cum laude), 1980. *Home and office:* 609 Eastland Ave., Ruston, La. 71270.

CAREER: Ohio University, Athens, assistant curator of Fine Arts Slide Library, 1973-77, instructor in art history, winter, 1976; University of Pittsburgh, Pittsburgh, Pa., intern at Frick Fine Arts Library, winter, 1978, guest curator, autumn, 1979; artist (painting and stained glass), 1979—. Lecturer on stained glass; art work has been exhibited and commissioned. *Member:* American Library Association, College Art Association of America, Stained Glass Association of America (associate member representative, 1980—), Glass Arts Society, Beta Phi Mu, Phi Kappa Phi.

WRITINGS: (Editor with husband, William Serban) *Stained Glass Index, 1906-77,* Stained Glass Association of America, 1979; (editor with Serban) *Stained Glass: A Guide to Information Sources,* Gale, 1980. Contributor to *Stained Glass.*

WORK IN PROGRESS: A History of American Stained Glass.

SIDELIGHTS: Darlene Brady's current research focuses on the iconology of "Frick's *Fortune,*" the stained glass window by John La Farge, and on contemporary aesthetics and philosophy of the repair, restoration, and conservation of American stained glass.

She wrote, "I have been involved with stained glass research and production for the past six years. My interest in stained glass is an extension of my painting concerns about design and color. Stained glass provides another medium for expression. However, it was the absence of an adequate bibliography on stained glass that led to further research. Publication seemed a logical way to share the much-needed information with others, especially in light of the renewed interest in stained glass by historians, artists, and craftspeople alike.

"The strongest motivation behind my work is the belief that art is not created in isolation, but in context, and that it operates at many levels—aesthetic and intellectual, intuitive and rational, from the individual's psyche and that of the collective society. Therefore, when I research and write about art, I examine its social and historical implications as well as that of the individual artistic statement. And when I create my own art, I draw from a pool of cumulative sources that reflect a knowledge of the history and role of art, contemporary society, and personal impulses and aesthetics. My art and research are interwoven supportive elements essential to each other."

BIOGRAPHICAL/CRITICAL SOURCES: Stained Glass, spring, 1979.

* * *

BRANDEL, Arthur Meyer 1913(?)-1980

OBITUARY NOTICE: Born c. 1913, in New York, N.Y.; died of cancer, November 26, 1980, in Washington, D.C. Editor and journalist. Arthur Brandel was best known as the founder and editor of *Post*Age,* a publication related to developments in the postal field. For nearly two years he served in Yugoslavia as a news correspondent for the *New York Times* until he was expelled by the Yugoslavian Government for writing articles that it considered detrimental to Yugoslavian-U.S. diplomatic relations. He was also news editor at a Washington television station, reporter for the *American Metal Market,* and public relations director of the National Council of Senior Citizens. Obituaries and other sources: *Washington Post,* December 3, 1980.

* * *

BRANDON, S(amuel) G(eorge) F(rederick) 1907-1971

PERSONAL: Born in 1907, in Portsmouth, England; died, October, 1971; married Ivy Ada; children: one son. *Education:* Received M.A. and D.D. from University of Leeds.

CAREER: British Army, Royal Army Chaplains Department, chaplain, 1939-51; Victoria University of Manchester, Manchester, England, professor of comparative religion, 1951-71, pro-vice-chancellor, 1967-71.

WRITINGS: Time and Mankind: An Historical and Philosophical Study of Mankind's Attitude to the Phenomena of Change, Hutchinson, 1951, reprinted, Gordon Press, 1977; *The Fall of Jerusalem and the Christian Church: A Study of the Effects of the Jewish Overthrow of A.D. 70 on Christianity,* S.P.C.K., 1951, 2nd edition, 1957; (translator and author of introduction) Martin Werner, *The Formulation of Christian Dogma,* Harper, 1957.

Man and His Destiny in the Great Religions: An Historical

and Comparative Study Containing the Wilde Lectures in Natural and Comparative Religion in the University of Oxford, 1954-1957, Manchester University Press, 1962; *Creation Legends of the Ancient Near East,* Hodder & Stoughton, 1963; (editor) *The Saviour God: Comparative Studies in the Concept of Salvation, Presented to Edwin Oliver James,* Barnes & Noble, 1963; *Time as God and Devil,* John Reynolds Library, Victoria University of Manchester, 1964; *History, Time and Deity: A Historical and Comparative Study of the Conception of Time in Religious Thought and Practice,* Barnes & Noble, 1965; *Jesus and the Zealots: A Study of the Political Factor in Primitive Christianity,* Scribner, 1967; *The Judgment of the Dead: An Historical and Comparative Study of the Idea of a Post-Mortem Judgment in the Major Religions,* Weidenfeld & Nicolson, 1967, Scribner, 1969; *The Trial of Jesus of Nazareth,* Stein & Day, 1968; *Religion in Ancient History: Studies in Ideas, Men, and Events,* Scribner, 1969.

(With others) *The Fourth Dimension of Warfare,* edited by Michael Elliott-Batemann, Volume I: *Intelligence, Subversion, Resistance,* Manchester University Press, 1970; *Dictionary of Comparative Religion,* Scribner, 1970; (editor) *Milestones of History,* Volume I: *Ancient Empires,* Volume II: *The Fires of Faith,* Volume III: *The Expanding World of Man,* Volume IV: *Twilight of Princes,* Volume V: *Age of Optimism,* Volume VI: *Our Twentieth-Century World,* Weidenfeld & Nicolson, 1970; (editor) *Ancient Empires,* Newsweek, 1970, 2nd edition, 1973; (editor with Friedrich Heer) *Forty Centuries: From the Pharoahs to Alfred the Great,* Britannica Society, 1972; *Man and God in Art and Ritual: A Study of Iconography, Architecture and Ritual Action as Primary Evidence of Religious Belief and Practice,* Scribner, 1975.

Contributor to *Encyclopaedia Britannica* and *Dictionary of the History of Ideas.* Contributor to journals, including *History Today.*

BIOGRAPHICAL/CRITICAL SOURCES: Eric J. Sharpe and John R. Hinnells, editors, *Man and His Salvation: Studies in Memory of S.G.F. Brandon,* Manchester University Press, 1973, Rowman & Littlefield, 1974.*

*   *   *

BRANDT, Nat
   See BRANDT, Nathan Henry, Jr.

*   *   *

BRANDT, Nathan Henry, Jr. 1929-
   (Nat Brandt)

PERSONAL: Born May 24, 1929, in Brooklyn, N.Y.; son of Nathan Henry (a building contractor) and Della (Guterman) Brandt; married Patricia Flynn, 1950 (divorced, 1954); married Yanna Maria Kroyt (a television producer and writer), April 5, 1955; children: (first marriage) Kevin; (second marriage) Anthony, Ariane. *Education:* University of Rochester, B.A., 1951. *Home and office:* 1349 Lexington Ave., New York, N.Y. 10028. *Agent:* Jean Naggar, 420 East 72nd St., New York, N.Y. 10021.

CAREER/WRITINGS: Columbia Broadcasting System (CBS) News, New York City, newswriter, 1951-55; *Plainville News,* Plainville, Conn., reporter, 1955-56; *Bayonne Times,* Bayonne, N.J., reporter, 1956-57; *Newark Star-Ledger,* Newark, N.J., reporter, 1957-59; *New York Times,* New York City, copy editor, 1959-66; Cowles Book Co., New York City, senior editor, 1968; American Heritage Pub-

lishing Co., New York City, executive editor of magazine division, 1969-77; *Publishers Weekly,* New York City, managing editor, 1977-78, editor in chief, 1978-80. Some writings have appeared under name Nat Brandt. Adjunct professor at St. John's University, 1974-75 and 1980-81.

*   *   *

BRAUN, Eric 1921-

PERSONAL: Born March 31, 1921, in London, England; son of Hugo and Gertrude (Robertson) Braun. *Education:* Christ's College, Cambridge, M.A., 1941. *Politics:* "Socialist—Monarchist." *Religion:* Roman Catholic. *Home and office:* 36 Michelham Gardens, Strawberry Hill, Twickenham TW1 4SB, England. *Agent:* Doreen Montgomery, Rupert Crew Ltd., King's Mews, London WC1N 2JA, England.

CAREER: Associated with theatrical and motion picture productions, 1943-51, including "Cleopatra," "I See a Dark Stranger," and "The Calendar." Press and publicity agent and owner of Eric Braun Enterprises, Twickenham, England, 1951—. *Military service:* British Army, Royal Artillery, gunner, 1941-45. *Member:* British Film Institute, Cyclists Touring Club.

WRITINGS: Deborah Kerr, St. Martin's, 1977. Contributor to magazines, including *Picturegoer, Playgoer,* and *Easy Listening;* critic for *Films and Filming, Plays and Players, Stage and Television Today,* and *Films.*

WORK IN PROGRESS: Ruby Murray: The Ruby Trap, publication expected in 1981; *Play It as It Stands,* an autobiography, publication expected in 1981; a biography of Gracie Fields and a biography of Joan Bennett.

SIDELIGHTS: Braun wrote: "My determination to write on matters pertaining to the entertainment field persisted exclusively from my school days until the sixties. In order to gain insight and experience in other fields of human endeavor, I took jobs with building firms as a laborer, with the Inner London Education Authority as a schoolkeeper, and with a factory as a cleaner-upper. All were rewarding except the last.

"My aversion to motorized transportation and my devotion to physical fitness led me to take up bicycling as my sole means of transportation. Since 1951 I have traveled well over a quarter of a million miles in Great Britain and on the continent for both work and pleasure."

AVOCATIONAL INTERESTS: Weight lifting, running, swimming, roller skating.

*   *   *

BRAY, J(ohn) J(efferson) 1912-

PERSONAL: Born September 16, 1912, in Adelaide, Australia; son of Harry M. (a sharebroker) and Gertrude E. (a trainee nurse; maiden name, Stow) Bray. *Education:* University of Adelaide, LL.B., 1932, LL.B. (with honors), 1933, LL.D., 1937. *Home:* 39 Hurtle Sq., Adelaide, South Australia.

CAREER: Writer. Worked as barrister and solicitor, 1933-57; Queen's Counsel, 1957-67; chief justice of Supreme Court of South Australia, 1967-78; writer, 1978—. Chancellor of University of Adelaide, 1968—; member of board of directors of State Library of South Australia, 1944—. *Member:* University of Adelaide Club. *Awards, honors:* Companion of Order of Australia, 1979.

WRITINGS: Poems, F. W. Cheshire, 1962; *For Service to Classical Studies,* F. W. Cheshire, 1966; *Poems, 1961-71,*

Jacaranda Press, 1972; *Poems, 1972-1979,* Australian National University Press, 1979.

Plays: ''Papinian'' (one-act), first produced in Adelaide, Australia, 1955. Also author of ''Not Without Honour'' (three-act), and '' A Word in Your Ear'' (two-act). Contributor of articles and reviews to academic periodicals and law and literary journals.

WORK IN PROGRESS: Research for a book ''on a theme from Roman history''; poems.

SIDELIGHTS: Bray wrote: ''I continue to write poetry when so moved. I have no quarrel now with free verse but I prefer to write in traditional forms, as did every poet in the West (or nearly every poet) from Homer to Hardy. To me the form provides a framework and a challenge.

''I am interested in ancient history and classical themes. This is not antiquarianism. The present cannot be understood without some knowledge of the past which made it what it is. Both past and present are illuminated when each is seen in the perspective of the other.''

AVOCATIONAL INTERESTS: Travel (Europe, Japan).

BIOGRAPHICAL/CRITICAL SOURCES: Adelaide Law Review, January, 1980.

*   *   *

BREARS, Peter C(harles) D(avid)   1944-

PERSONAL: Born in 1944, in Wakefield, England; son of Charles and Mary (Fett) Brears. *Education:* Leeds College of Art, diploma, 1968. *Residence:* Leeds, England. *Agent:* Laurence Pollinger Ltd., 18 Maddox St., Mayfair, London W1R 0EU, England. *Office:* City Museum, Municipal Buildings, Leeds LS1 3AA, England.

CAREER: Curtis Museum, Alton, England, curator, 1967-69; Shibden Hall, Halifax, England, keeper, 1969-72; Clarke Hall, Wakefield, England, curator, 1972-75; Castle Museum, York, England, curator, 1975-79; City Museums, Leeds, England, director of city museums department, 1979—. Chairman of Group for Regional Studies in Museums. *Member:* Museums Association (fellow), Society of Antiquaries (fellow), Society for Post-Medieval Archaeology (vice-president).

WRITINGS: The English Country Pottery, David & Charles, 1971; *The Collector's Book of English Country Pottery,* David & Charles, 1971; *Yorkshire Probate Inventories, 1542-1689,* Yorkshire Record Series, 1972; *Horse Brasses,* Country Life Books, 1981.

Illustrator: J. G. Jenkins, *Nets and Coracles,* David & Charles, 1974; Jenkins, *Life and Tradition in Rural Wales,* Dent, 1976. Author of booklets and museum information sheets. Contributor of more than fifteen articles to periodicals, including *Connoisseur, Folk Life,* and *York Historian.*

WORK IN PROGRESS: History of Post-Medieval Food and Cooking Utensils in England, publication expected in the mid 1980's; research on English folk life and history of museums.

SIDELIGHTS: Brears commented: ''Today the quality of life in material terms is as high as it has ever been, but increasing industrialization and international trade are causing a great breach to develop between consumers and producers of food, clothing, furniture, etc. The consumer's appreciation and enjoyment of these items is greatly enlarged if he has a deeper knowledge of their origins and development. It is this interpretative role that forms the basis for my research and didactic promotions, both in museums and in publications.''

BREEN, Dana
See BIRKSTED-BREEN, Dana

*   *   *

BRESLAUER, Samuel Daniel   1942-

PERSONAL: Born April 23, 1942, in San Francisco, Calif.; son of Daniel Joseph (in sales) and Lynette Myrtle (a teacher; maiden name, Goldstone) Breslauer; married Frances Gurian (a teacher), June 23, 1968; children: Don Howard, Tamar Beth. *Education:* University of California, Berkeley, B.A., 1963; Hebrew Union College, M.H.L., 1969; Brandeis University, Ph.D., 1974. *Home:* 2702 University Dr., Lawrence, Kan. 66044. *Office:* Department of Religion, University of Kansas, Lawrence, Kan. 66045.

CAREER: Ordained rabbi, 1969; assistant rabbi at synagogue in New York, N.Y., 1968-69; Colgate University, Hamilton, N.Y., instructor in religion and chaplain, 1971-75; University of Nebraska, Omaha, visiting lecturer in Judaic studies, 1975-76; Princeton University, Princeton, N.J., assistant professor of religion, 1976-78; University of Kansas, Lawrence, assistant professor of religion, 1978—. Director of department of Jewish education, of Jewish Federation of Omaha, 1975-76. *Member:* American Academy of Religion, National Association of Professors of Hebrew, Society for the Scientific Study of Religion, Association for Jewish Studies. *Awards, honors:* National Endowment for the Humanities fellow, 1976—.

WRITINGS: The Ecumenical Perspective and the Modernization of Jewish Religion, Scholars' Press, 1978; *The Chrysalis of Religion: A Guide to the Jewishness of Buber's ''I and Thou,''* Abingdon, 1980. Contributor to theology journals.

WORK IN PROGRESS: Charisma and Jewish Religion: A Sociological and Historical Study, a monograph; *Toward a New Jewish Ritualism; Toward a New Jewish Theology; Spinoza and the Modernization of Jewish Thought;* ''New Images of Sinai,'' an essay.

SIDELIGHTS: Breslauer wrote: ''*Charisma and Jewish Religion* looks at Jewish religion from the biblical period to the present to see how charismatic innovation remained nonpolitical even while changing the shape of Jewish social and religious life. *Toward a New Jewish Ritualism* examines ways in which Jews express their Jewishness. One chapter will deal with personal rituals celebrating life-cycle events, and a final chapter will concern prayer and worship. The singular aspect of this book will be its utilization of modern American Jewish literature—works by Philip Roth, Saul Bellow, Bernard Malamud, and other writers of fiction—to exposit a modern theology of Jewish practice.

''*Toward a New Jewish Theology* will begin by looking at the challenges modernity presents to Jewish covenant theology, Jewish ethics, Jewish education, and Jewish self-identification. It will review what contemporary thinkers have said and then make suggestions for developing a new approach. *Spinoza and the Modernization of Jewish Thought* will take Spinoza's philosophy seriously as the most important challenge facing a modern Jewish theology.

''My interest in Jewish studies grows out of a humanistic as well as parochial concern. I am concerned with how human beings express their religious convictions, cope with the problems and disappointments of life, anticipate and imagine the future and the ideal, and mobilize talents and energies to communicate with other people. As a Jew I have long been fascinated by Jewish history as well as challenged by the attempt to continue being Jewish despite the problems of modernity. My studies tend to combine the analytic skills of sociology that enable me to locate problems and identify their shape and dimensions with the use of imaginative materials—whether by philosophical writers, theologians, poets, or novelists—that enable me to capture the human spirit struggling with those issues and problems.

"My knowledge of both Hebrew and Arabic has enabled me to shed some light on the relationship between the Jewish and Islamic tradition; my concern with the 'ecumenical perspective' has led to dialogue with Christians. My written work remains within the field of Jewish scholarship, since I feel my contribution to dialogue is best made as a Jew speaking from within my own tradition.

"I have studied those thinkers who took the challenge of modernity most seriously—Martin Buber, Mordecai Kaplan, Abraham Heschel, Robert Gordis, and Jacob Agus. While I do not identify myself as a Conservative Jew, I find the writings of Conservative Jews most helpful, since they struggle to maintain the tension between tradition and modernity at its highest level. I find the more traditionalist writers useful in gaining a perspective on the ways Jews can address a general audience and yet remain distinctively Jewish. I find Reform Jewish writers very helpful in their insightful recognition of the problems of the modern world and of the tradition."

*   *   *

BRIER, Bob   1943-

PERSONAL: Born December 13, 1943, in New York, N.Y.; son of Louis and Clara (David) Brier; married Henie Rosenberg, January 5, 1962 (divorced, 1970); married Barbara Benton (a writer), December 22, 1972; children: Elaine, Robin, Ian. *Education:* Hunter College of the City University of New York, B.A., 1964; University of North Carolina, Ph.D., 1970. *Office:* Department of Philosophy, C. W. Post College, Long Island University, Greenvale, N.Y. 11548.

CAREER: Long Island University, C. W. Post College, Greenvale, N.Y., assistant professor, 1971-74, associate professor of philosophy, 1974—, chairman of department, 1980—. *Member:* American Philosophical Association, American Association for the Advancement of Science, Philosophy of Science Parapsychological Association, Australasian Philosophy of Science Association, Egypt Exploration Society.

WRITINGS: Precognition and the Philosophy of Science, Humanities, 1973; *Ancient Egyptian Magic,* Morrow, 1980. Contributor to philosophy and Egyptian studies journals.

WORK IN PROGRESS: Research in Egyptian studies.

SIDELIGHTS: Brier told *CA:* "For years I was just an academician, writing articles for scholarly journals. I became bored with this and decided to write a fun book for laymen. Egyptology is such a rich and exciting subject that I was sure there would be a market for such a book. Years back, I was on the research staff of the Duke University Parapsychology Laboratory, so the topic of ancient Egyptian magic was a natural one.

"The book is selling remarkably well and is now being translated into foreign languages. It was easy to write; the big problem was for my publisher to find a printer with a hieroglyphic font!"

AVOCATIONAL INTERESTS: Long distance running, leading student groups to Egypt.

BRIGGS, Katharine Mary   1898-1980

OBITUARY NOTICE—See index for *CA* sketch: Born November 8, 1898, in London, England; died October 15, 1980, in Kent, England. Free-lance writer best known as a scholar of folklore. Her books on folklore include *The Anatomy of Puck, Folktales of England, The Fairies in English Tradition and Literature,* and *A Dictionary of British Folktales in the English Language.* Briggs also wrote several plays and novels. Obituaries and other sources: *London Times,* October 25, 1980; *Publishers Weekly,* November 7, 1980.

*   *   *

BRIN, David   1950-

PERSONAL: Born October 6, 1950, in Glendale, Calif.; son of Herbert (an editor) and Selma (a teacher; maiden name, Stone) Brin. *Education:* California Institute of Technology, B.S., 1972; University of California, San Diego, M.S., 1980, Ph.D., 1981. *Home and office:* Heritage Press, 2130 South Vermont Ave., Los Angeles, Calif. 90007. *Agent:* Richard Curtis Associates, Inc., 156 East 52nd St., New York, N.Y. 10022.

CAREER: Hughes Aircraft Research Laboratories, Newport Beach and Carlsbad, Calif., electrical engineer in semiconductor device development, 1973-77; Heritage Press, Los Angeles, Calif., book reviewer and science editor, 1980—. Managing editor of *Journal of the Laboratory of Comparative Human Cognition. Member:* British Interplanetary Society (associate fellow).

WRITINGS: Sundiver (novel), Bantam, 1980. Contributor of articles and stories to scientific journals and popular magazines.

WORK IN PROGRESS: Four novels, "which I would hope will be acknowledgeable as literate and interesting science-fiction mysteries"; continuing research on the nature and origins of the solar system.

SIDELIGHTS: Brin commented to *CA:* "People are often surprised to find that Huxley wrote nothing but science fiction, though sometimes he kept it a secret until the last five pages of a book. All of the best writers play with reality. They ask the questions that are normally asked only, and inefficiently, by college sophomores, and they do it in a manner that illuminates a self or a world. I'd trade a pound of flesh to be able to do that. Maybe someday I will."

*   *   *

BRINKLEY, Joel   1952-

PERSONAL: Born July 22, 1952, in Washington, D.C.; son of David McClure (a television commentator) and Ann (Fischer) Brinkley. *Education:* University of North Carolina at Chapel Hill, A.B., 1975. *Home:* 1334 Cherokee Rd., Louisville, Ky. 40204. *Office: Courier-Journal,* 525 West Broadway, Louisville, Ky. 40202.

CAREER/WRITINGS: Associated Press (AP), Charlotte, N.C., reporter, 1975; *Richmond News Leader,* Richmond, Va., reporter, 1975-78; *Louisville Courier-Journal,* Louisville, Ky., reporter, 1978—. Notable assignments include coverage of the Cambodian crisis and a year-long investigation of Kentucky's nursing home industry that prompted major reforms. *Awards, honors:* Pulitzer Prize for international reporting, 1980, for *Courier-Journal* series, "Living the Cambodian Nightmare."

SIDELIGHTS: On his first overseas assignment, Brinkley was sent to report on the catastrophies in Cambodia. Shortly after returning to the United States, he was stricken with typhoid fever; nevertheless, he continued to work on "Living the Cambodian Nightmare," a series of articles describing the war in Cambodia and the desperate plight of hundreds of thousands of refugees. Brinkley, the son of NBC news commentator David Brinkley, won the 1980 Pulitzer Prize for international reporting with his four-part series.

Brinkley told *CA:* "My stories from Cambodia contained few revelations; most of what I wrote had already been reported elsewhere. The stories were successful, I think, because of vivid writing. And that's a point journalists everywhere ought to note. Fewer and fewer people are inclined to read newspapers these days. So newspaper writing has to improve. It will have to become more creative and entertaining, if newspapers are to keep their readers."

* * *

BRISTOW, Gwen   1903-1980

OBITUARY NOTICE—See index for *CA* sketch: Born September 16, 1903, in Marion, S.C.; died after a lengthy illness, August 16, 1980, in New Orleans, La. Journalist and writer. Bristow was best known for *Plantation Trilogy,* a collection of three tales about plantation life. Her other writings include three mysteries written in collaboration with her husband, Bruce Manning. Obituaries and other sources: *Chicago Tribune,* August 19, 1980.

* * *

BRITCHKY, Seymour   1930-

PERSONAL: Born August 4, 1930, in New York, N.Y.; divorced. *Education:* Syracuse University, A.B., 1950. *Residence:* New York, N.Y. *Agent:* Lynn Nesbit, International Creative Management, 40 West 57th St., New York, N.Y. 10019.

CAREER: Author.

WRITINGS: The Restaurants of New York, Random House, 1974, *1976-1977 Edition,* 1976, *1977-1978 Edition,* 1977, *1978-1979 Edition,* 1978, *1979-1980 Edition,* 1979, *1980-1981 Edition,* 1980. Publisher of *Seymour Britchky's Restaurant Letter.*

* * *

BRODIE, Fawn M(cKay)   1915-1981

OBITUARY NOTICE—See index for *CA* sketch: Born September 15, 1915, in Ogden, Utah; died of cancer, January 10, 1981, in Santa Monica, Calif. Writer and editor. Brodie was best known for *Thomas Jefferson: An Intimate History,* a book about Jefferson's thirty-eight year love affair with a mulatto slave. Brodie also wrote biographies of Joseph Smith, the founder of the Mormon Church; Thaddeus Stevens, leader of post-Civil War reconstruction; and Sir Richard Burton, the poet and explorer of the Nile. At the time of her death, Brodie had just completed *Richard Nixon: The Child and the Man.* Obituaries and other sources: *Chicago Tribune,* January 13, 1981; *New York Times,* January 13, 1981; *Time,* January 26, 1981; *Newsweek,* January 26, 1981.

* * *

BRODSKY, Michael Mark   1948-

PERSONAL: Born August 2, 1948, in New York, N.Y.; son of Martin (an executive) and Marian (a clerical worker; maiden name, Simon) Brodsky; married Laurence Lacoste (a writer), November 28, 1976; children: Joseph Matthew. *Education:* Columbia University, B.A., 1969; attended Case Western Reserve University, 1970-72. *Religion:* Jewish. *Home:* 40 Columbia Pl., Brooklyn, N.Y. 11201. *Office:* Institute for Research on Rheumatic Disease, 2025 Broadway, New York, N.Y. 10023.

CAREER: Teacher of mathematics and science at school in New York City, 1969-70; teacher of French and English in Cleveland, Ohio, 1972-75; Institute for Research on Rheumatic Disease, New York City, editor of arthritis newspaper, 1976—. *Member:* International P.E.N. *Awards, honors:* Citation from Ernest Hemingway Foundation, 1979, for *Detour.*

WRITINGS: Detour (novel), Urizen Books, 1978; *Wedding Feast,* Urizen Books, 1980. Author of "Terrible Sunlight" (three-act play), first produced in New York, N.Y., at South Street Theatre, April 2, 1980. Contributor to *Partisan Review* and *Journal of Existential Psychology and Psychiatry.*

WORK IN PROGRESS: A novel; a play "exploring further the principles and possibilities staked out in 'Terrible Sunlight.'"

SIDELIGHTS: Brodsky told *CA:* "My interest in contemporary writers is minimal. I think there is a great void at the heart of contemporary American writing and feel no kinship with it. There is an inability to reexamine worn forms, and there is no unappeasable craving to follow the unfolding of thought to its outermost reaches where it is almost imperceptible, unseizable.

"The reviews of my work so far have nothing incisive about them. They merely underline the appalling stupidity of reviewers who, in order to earn their bread, pour out their dubious insights merely to cover a few pages. Fortunately, the writing of my novels, stories, and plays is independent of the reaction of the 'contemporary scene.'

"I write because I have something absolutely unique to say, never said before. The true writer takes the quantum leap out of the common plane. The only real motivating factor and circumstance in my writing life (I detest the word 'career') is my incessant collision with phenomena that force me to think."

* * *

BRODY, Jane E(llen)   1941-

PERSONAL: Born May 19, 1941, in New York, N.Y.; daughter of Sidney (an attorney and civil servant) and Lillian (a teacher; maiden name, Kellner) Brody; married Richard Engquist (a writer), October 2, 1966; children: Lee Erik and Lorin Michael (twins). *Education:* Cornell University, B.S., 1962; University of Wisconsin (now University of Wisconsin—Madison), M.A., 1963. *Residence:* Brooklyn, N.Y. *Agent:* Wendy Weil, Julian Bach Literary Agency, Inc., 747 Third Ave., New York, N.Y. 10017. *Office: New York Times,* 229 West 43rd St., New York, N.Y. 10036.

CAREER: Minneapolis Tribune, Minneapolis, Minn., reporter, 1963-65; *New York Times,* New York, N.Y., science writer, 1965—, author of column, "Personal Health," 1976—.

WRITINGS: (With husband, Richard Engquist) *Secrets of Good Health,* Popular Library, 1970; (with Arthur Holleb) *You Can Fight Cancer and Win,* Quadrangle, 1978; *Jane Brody's Nutrition Book,* Norton, 1981.

BROOKS, Gregory   1961-

PERSONAL: Born March 18, 1961, in Mount Kisco, N.Y.; son of William Joseph (an accountant) and Rosemary (in real estate sales; maiden name, Keller) Brooks. *Education:* Attended Parsons School of Design, 1979—. *Religion:* Catholic. *Home:* 74 Gregory Ave., Mount Kisco, N.Y. 10549.

CAREER: Writer and illustrator, 1979—. Member of New Youth Performing Theatre. *Member:* 4H Club of Mount Kisco. *Awards, honors:* New York State Summer School of the Visual Arts Scholarship, 1977; New York Regents Scholarship, 1979; Elaine Lindenberg Art Scholarship, 1979.

WRITINGS: Monroe's Island (juvenile), self-illustrated, Bradbury, 1979.

WORK IN PROGRESS: Several children's books.

SIDELIGHTS: Brooks's book, *Monroe's Island,* was written while he was taking a course in children's book writing at Parsons School of Design in White Plains. Geared for children from four to six years of age, *Monroe's Island* is about a young boy and his fanciful imagination which takes him to an island complete with trees that grow chocolate-chip cookies.

Long interested in art and drawing, Brooks created *Monroe's Island* because of his desire to illustrate a book. He told *CA:* "I guess technically I am an author, but in my heart I am an illustrator. I wrote *Monroe's Island* so I would have something to illustrate—I didn't actually expect to see it published."

AVOCATIONAL INTERESTS: Photography, theatre, music, biking, camping, paddle tennis, running, singing.

BIOGRAPHICAL/CRITICAL SOURCES: Patent Trader (Mount Kisco, N.Y.), October 24, 1979.

*   *   *

BROOKS, Tim(othy Haley)   1942-

PERSONAL: Born April 18, 1942, in Exeter, N.H.; son of John (in business) and Olive (a teacher; maiden name, Bradbury) Brooks. *Education:* Dartmouth College, B.A., 1964; Syracuse University, M.S., 1969; graduate study at Russell Sage College, 1967-68, and New School for Social Research, 1971-73. *Residence:* Floral Park, N.Y. *Office:* NBC-TV, 30 Rockefeller Plaza, New York, N.Y. 10020.

CAREER: WTEN-TV, Albany, N.Y., assistant production and promotion director, 1966-68; co-founder and business manager of TV spot production service in Syracuse, N.Y., 1968-69; WCBS-TV, New York City, research and sales promotion supervisor, 1969-70; NBC-TV, New York City, senior research analyst, 1970-72, manager of daytime research, 1972-74, manager of nighttime research, 1975-76, manager of audience measurement analysis, 1977-78, director of television network research, 1978—. Associate director of research and marketing for Television Advertising Representatives, Inc., New York City, 1976-77. Adjunct professor of communication arts at Long Island University, C. W. Post Center, 1980—. *Military service:* U.S. Army, Signal Corps, 1964-66, served in Vietnam. U.S. National Guard, 1966-74; became captain. *Member:* International Radio-Television Society, Association for Recorded Sound Collections (vice-president, 1979—). *Awards, honors:* American Book Award for best general reference-paperback, 1979, for *The Complete Directory to Prime Time Network TV Shows, 1946-Present.*

WRITINGS: (With Earle Marsh) *The Complete Directory to Prime Time Network TV Shows, 1946-Present,* Ballantine, 1979, 2nd edition, 1981. Frequent contributor to *Antique*

Phonograph Monthly, 1974—; author of "Current Bibliography" column for *Journal of the Association for Recorded Sound Collections,* 1979—; contributor to *Merit Student's Encyclopedia;* contributor of numerous articles to popular and professional publications.

WORK IN PROGRESS: A textbook on television audience research; research for a book on the history of the U.S. recording industry.

SIDELIGHTS: Brooks commented: "As a sometime book reviewer and teacher, I can only urge those who seek to codify our history in print to do so with a sense of perspective, a sense of humor, and an absolutely fanatic determination to *get it right.* There is no substitute for excellence."

*   *   *

BROSNAHAN, Leonard Francis   1922-

PERSONAL: Born September 15, 1922, in Wellington, New Zealand; son of Leonard T. (an engineer) and Isabella J. (a secretary; maiden name, James) Brosnahan; married Elisabeth S. Gerbracht, December 11, 1945; children: Janet Elisabeth Brosnahan Nairn. *Education:* Otago University, M.A., 1948; University of Leiden, D.Litt. et Phil., 1953. *Home and office address:* c/o University of the South Pacific, P.O. Box 1168, Suva, Fiji.

CAREER: University of Ibadan, Ibadan, Nigeria, lecturer, 1951-59, senior lecturer in English, 1959-62; Victoria University of Wellington, Wellington, New Zealand, professor of English language, 1963-69; University of the South Pacific, Suva, Fiji, professor of English, 1969—, deputy vice-chancellor, 1972-79. *Military service:* Royal New Zealand Air Force, 1941-45; served in England and Europe; became flight lieutenant. *Member:* Australasian Universities Language and Literature Association, Linguistic Society of New Zealand (president, 1965), Linguistic Society of America, National Council of Teachers of English.

WRITINGS: Some Old English Sound Changes, Heffer, 1953; *Genes and Phonemes,* Ibadan University Press, 1957; *The Sounds of Language,* Heffer, 1961; (with Bertil Malmberg) *Introduction to Phonetics,* Heffer, 1970; *Grammar and the Teacher,* New Zealand Council for Educational Research, 1973. Contributor to language and literature journals.

WORK IN PROGRESS: A book on language and thinking.

SIDELIGHTS: Brosnahan wrote: "A very heavy administrative load over the last few years—including the acting deanship of the University of the South Pacific—has restricted my writing largely to letters, memoranda, and reports."

*   *   *

BROTHERTON, Manfred   1900(?)-1981

OBITUARY NOTICE: Born c. 1900; died of a heart ailment, January 23, 1981, in Morristown, N.J. Physicist and author. Brotherton began his thirty-seven year career with Bell Laboratories as a research scientist; he later became a writer of textbooks, advertisements, and various articles for professional journals. Brotherton wrote several books, including *Capacitors: Their Use in Electronic Circuits; Masers and Lasers: How They Work, What They Do;* and *The Bellcomm Story.* Obituaries and other sources: *New York Times,* January 25, 1981.

*   *   *

BROUGHTON, Geoffrey   1927-

PERSONAL: Born in 1927, in Navenby, England; son of

Albert (a port missioner) and Ivy Laura (Taylor) Broughton; children: Philippa, Imogen, Vivian. *Education:* University of London, B.A. (with honors), 1948, M.Phil., 1966, Ph.D., 1972. *Home:* Eaton Hall International, Retford, Nottinghamshire, England.

CAREER: Schoolteacher, 1950-55; Malayan Teachers' Training College, Kirkby, England, lecturer, 1955-60; Alsager College of Education, Alsager, England, senior lecturer in English, 1960-62; University of London, Institute of Education, London, England, senior lecturer in education, 1962-80; Eaton Hall International, Retford, England, director, 1980—. Radio broadcaster. Gives lecture tours all over the world, including Brazil, Venezuela, China, Japan, Nigeria, and most countries in Europe. *Military service:* British Army, 1948-50; became second lieutenant. *Member:* International Association of Teachers of English as a Foreign Language, Royal Society of Arts (fellow), Society of Authors.

WRITINGS: (Editor) *A Technical Reader*, Macmillan, 1965; (editor) *Let's Go*, Armand Colin-Longman, 1976; *Know Your English*, Hutchinson, 1976; *Know the British*, Hutchinson, 1977; *Teaching English as a Foreign Language*, Routledge & Kegan Paul, 1978. General editor of ''Success With English,'' a series published by Penguin, 1968-70. Contributor to academic journals.

SIDELIGHTS: Broughton told *CA:* ''Eaton Hall International is a unique, public sector residential college for international education and training.''

*   *   *

BROWER, Charles Hendrickson   1901-
   (Charlie Brower)

PERSONAL: Born November 13, 1901, in Asbury Park, N.J.; son of Charles Hendrick and Mary Amelia (Hendrickson) Brower; married Mary Elizabeth Nelson, July 8, 1930; children: Brock Hendrickson, Charles Nelson, Anne Clayton (Mrs. James Culver). *Education:* Rutgers University, B.Sc., 1925. *Politics:* Independent. *Religion:* Episcopalian. *Home:* 914 Cole Dr., Brielle, N.J. 08730. *Agent:* Candida Donadio & Associates, Inc., 111 West 57th St., New York, N.Y. 10019.

CAREER: High school teacher in Bound Brook, N.J., 1925-26; Batten, Barton, Durstine & Osborne (advertising agency), New York, N.Y., writer, 1928-46, vice-president and director, 1940-46, executive vice-president in charge of creative services, 1946, member of executive committee, 1951, general manager and vice-chairman of executive committee, 1957, president, 1957-64, chairman of executive committee, 1957-71, chairman of board of directors, 1964-71; free-lance writer, 1971—. Life member of board of trustees and past chairman of board of governors of Rutgers University. National chairman of United Way, 1966. *Member:* Alpha Chi Rho, University Club, Manasquan River Country Club. *Awards, honors:* L.H.D. from Pace College (now University), 1962; LL.D. from Rutgers University, 1966, and Monmouth College, 1967.

WRITINGS—Under name Charlie Brower: *Me and Other Advertising Geniuses*, Doubleday, 1974. Contributor to *Reader's Digest.**

*   *   *

BROWER, Charlie
   See BROWER, Charles Hendrickson

BROWN, Deaver David   1943-

PERSONAL: Born December 30, 1943, in Toronto, Ontario, Canada; U.S. citizen born abroad; son of Edward Killoran (a professor of English) and Margaret (Deaver) Brown; married Julia Wilson Prewitt (a professor of English), June 15, 1968; children: Elizabeth Prewitt. *Education:* Harvard University, A.B. (magna cum laude), 1966, M.B.A. (with distinction), 1968. *Home:* Millbrook Valley, Thornton, N.H. 03223. *Office:* Sales and Marketing Resources, Inc., 29 Commonwealth Ave., Boston, Mass. 02116.

CAREER: General Foods Corp., White Plains, N.Y., product manager, 1968-70; Cross River Products, Rochester, N.Y., founder, president, and chief executive officer, 1971-75; Sales and Marketing Resources, Inc., Boston, Mass., president and chief executive officer, 1976—. General partner and chief executive officer of General Sound Co., 1978—. *Member:* Harvard Club.

WRITINGS: The Entrepreneur's Guide, Macmillan, 1980; *The Management Guide*, Macmillan, 1981.

SIDELIGHTS: Brown commented: ''*The Entrepreneur's Guide* was written because I was appalled by the quantity of books on the subject of starting and managing a new business that emphasized excessively technical information or get-rich-quick possibilities. The field of new business start-ups is, in my opinion, both personally fulfilling (which few enough jobs are these days) and necessary to counterbalance the influence of the multinationals in our society. As a trained executive and practicing entrepreneur, I thought I could make an important contribution to the field. Fortunately, my reviewers have been sympathetic to my book and its ideas.''

BIOGRAPHICAL/CRITICAL SOURCES: New York Times, January 7, 1973; *Time*, November 5, 1973; *Rochester Times Union*, August 23, 1974; *Venture*, November, 1979; *Boston Globe*, January 7, 1980.

*   *   *

BROWN, John Buchanan
   See BUCHANAN-BROWN, John

*   *   *

BROWN, Marel   1899-

PERSONAL: Legal name, Margaret Elizabeth Brown, began using name Marel Brown in 1938; born December 17, 1899, in Carroll County, Ga.; daughter of George B. and Olive S. Snow; married Alex B. Brown, October 8, 1919 (died December, 1975). *Education:* Attended public schools in Atlanta, Ga. *Politics:* ''Democrat (if the right candidate is nominated!).'' *Religion:* Baptist. *Home:* 1938 North Decatur Rd. N.E., Atlanta, Ga. 30307.

CAREER: Christian Index, Atlanta, Ga., secretary and assistant to editor, 1924-30, editor of ''Page for Boys and Girls,'' 1924-49; writer, 1938—. Chairman of Georgia's State Poetry Day, 1957-59; member of Dixie Council of Authors and Journalists and member of its workshop faculty; speaker at schools, clubs, and churches. *Member:* International Biographical Association, International Academy of Poets, Poetry Society of America, National League of American Pen Women (president, 1950-52), Georgia State Poetry Society, Poetry Society of Georgia, Atlanta Writers Club. *Awards, honors:* Dixie Council of Authors and Journalists poet of the year award for Georgia, 1968, for *The Shape of a Song*, and special award, 1980, for ''contributions to literature and poetry in the South''; first prize from National League of

American Pen Women, 1972, for *Three Wise Women of the East.*

WRITINGS: Red Hills (poems and essays), Broadman, 1941; *Hearth Fire* (poems and essays), Broadman, 1943; *Lilly May and Dan* (juvenile), Southern Baptist Home Mission Board, 1946; *The Greshams of Greenway* (juvenile), Southern Baptist Home Mission Board, 1952; *Fence Corners* (poems and essays), Broadman, 1952; *The Cherry Children* (juvenile), Southern Baptist Home Mission Board, 1956; *The Shape of a Song: Poetry and Essays,* Baker Book, 1968; *Three Wise Women of the East* (fiction), Upper Room, 1970; *Presenting Georgia Poets,* Harvey Dan Abrams, 1979. Contributor of articles, poems, and stories to magazines for adults and children, including *Home Life, Nature, Progressive Farmer, Georgia Life,* and *Christian Herald,* and newspapers.

WORK IN PROGRESS: Another book.

SIDELIGHTS: Marel Brown commented: "My feeling is that a person's writing, like a person's life, should contribute to the up-beat and betterment of the era in which it is lived. Writing is hard work—so is living—and to be successful a writer must be as dedicated to what is produced and published as anyone in any of the arts or professions. My special love is poetry, and in my older years I love to have the privilege of sharing with younger poets what I have learned about how to *say* the poems, which each of us feels before the words are put onto paper."

BIOGRAPHICAL/CRITICAL SOURCES: DeKalb News/Sun, October 17, 1979.

* * *

BROWN, Raymond Kay 1936-

PERSONAL: Born March 11, 1936, in Pocatello, Idaho; son of Raymond and Jeanne (Caldwell) Brown; married Marilyn Renner Ratcliffe, June 10, 1958 (divorced December, 1977); married Suzanne McMakin (a community senior center director), March 4, 1978; children: Steve, Mitch, Kevin, Deena, Jay. *Education:* Whitworth College, B.A., 1958; San Francisco Theological Seminary, B.D., 1962, D.Min., 1978. *Home:* West 5311 Shawnee, Spokane, Wash. 99208. *Office:* Office of Alumni Relations, Whitworth College, Spokane, Wash. 99251.

CAREER: Ordained United Presbyterian minister, 1962; assistant pastor of Presbyterian church in Fremont, Calif., 1962-65; pastor of Presbyterian church in Pender, Neb., 1965-68; associate pastor of Presbyterian church in Omaha, Neb., 1968-71; pastor of Presbyterian church in Tacoma, Wash., 1971-77; Whitworth College, Spokane, Wash., director of alumni relations, 1977—, seminar director at Whitworth Institute of Ministry, 1980. President of Whitworth College Alumni Council, 1975-78; chairman of single adult ministries task force of Greater Seattle Council of Churches, 1977; seminar director at Ghost Ranch National Adult Study Center, 1978-79.

WRITINGS: Reach Out to Singles: A Challenge to Ministry, Westminster, 1979.

SIDELIGHTS: Brown commented: "*Reach Out to Singles* is a revision of my doctoral dissertation. It is a product of my research and concern to help the church find ways of ministering to the one-third of the adult population who are not married. It is an attempt to raise the consciousness of the church to the needs of single adults and to develop more inclusive ways of involving singles in the life of the church and society.

"The book explores some of the 'pairing pressures' that singles face in our culture; defines some of the questions that need to be addressed by the church as it explores a ministry to single adults; describes needs that are common to singles, as well as specific needs of never-married, separated, widowed, divorced, young singles, and single parents. I feel that one of the particular contributions of *Reach Out to Singles* is a biblical-theological basis for affirming singleness. The final portion of the book discusses possible ways in which churches can be more inclusive of singles in their lives and programs."

* * *

BROWN, Rosel George 1926-1967

OBITUARY NOTICE: Born March 15, 1926, in New Orleans, La.; died November 26, 1967. Author. Brown wrote numerous fantasy and science-fiction short stories and books. Her writings include *Galactic Sibyl Blue, A Handful of Time,* and *The Waters of Centaurus.* She was also co-author of *Earthblood.* Obituaries and other sources: *Science Fiction and Fantasy Literature,* Volume 2, Gale, 1979.

* * *

BROWN, Terence 1944-

PERSONAL: Born January 17, 1944, in Loping, China; son of Henry Montgomery (a minister) and Elizabeth (a teacher; maiden name, Cully) Brown; married Suzanne Marie Krochalis (a teacher), 1969; children: Michael, Carolyn. *Education:* Trinity College, Dublin, B.A., 1966, Ph.D., 1970. *Office:* Department of English, Trinity College, University of Dublin, Dublin 2, Ireland.

CAREER: University of Dublin, Trinity College, Dublin, Ireland, lecturer in English, 1968—, fellow, 1976—, director of modern English, 1976—, registrar, 1980—. *Member:* International Association for the Study of Anglo-Irish Literature, Royal Irish Academy.

WRITINGS: (Editor with Alec Reid) *Time Was Away: The World of Louis MacNeice,* Humanities Press, 1974; *Louis MacNeice: Sceptical Vision,* Harper, 1975; *Northern Voices: Poets From Northern Ulster,* Roman & Littlefield, 1975; (editor with Patrick Rafroidi) *The Irish Short Story,* Humanities Press, 1979; *Ireland: A Social and Cultural History, 1922-79,* Fontana, 1981. Contributor to scholarly journals.

WORK IN PROGRESS: Editing a collection of critical essays on twentieth-century Irish writing in English, publication by Academy Press expected in 1982.

SIDELIGHTS: Brown wrote that his current interests include "exploring the field of Irish cultural history, a vital area to contemporary Irish self-understanding; continuing to produce critical essays on Irish writing; and, in due course, attempting a literary biography."

AVOCATIONAL INTERESTS: Collecting Irish paintings, the arts in general, travel, most sports (especially squash racquets).

* * *

BROWNE, Harry
See BROWNE, Henry

* * *

BROWNE, Henry 1918-
(Harry Browne)

PERSONAL: Born August 28, 1918, in Birmingham, England; son of James (a mail carrier) and Kate (a children's nurse; maiden name, Tidmarsh) Browne; married Anita Evelyn Goldschmidt (a charity organizer), October 22, 1949; children: Jessica, Simon, Martin, Nicholas. *Education:* Emmanuel College, Cambridge, B.A., 1948, M.A., 1951. *Politics:* "Labour party; supporter of European nuclear disarmament." *Religion:* None. *Home:* 4 Kentings, Camerton, Cambridge CB3 7DT, England. *Office:* Cambridgeshire College of Arts and Technology, Cambridge CB1 2AJ, England.

CAREER: Cambridgeshire College of Arts and Technology, Cambridge, England, lecturer in history, 1949-69, head of faculty of arts and languages, 1969—.

WRITINGS—All under name Harry Browne: *World History II,* Cambridge University Press, 1970; *Suez and Sinai,* Longman, 1971; *Joseph Chamberlain: Radical and Imperialist,* Longman, 1974; *World History I,* Cambridge University Press, 1974; *The Rise of British Trade Unions,* Longman, 1978; *Spain's Civil War,* Longman, 1981. General editor of "Flashpoints," Longman, 1970.

WORK IN PROGRESS: Victorian Worthies, publication by Longman expected in 1983.

SIDELIGHTS: Browne commented: "My writing and teaching is concerned with reconciliation. Our basic problem is to find a means of survival for a species committed to self-destruction. As a historian I am anxious to show by analysis how conflict developed, to point out what the fundamental problems are, and to stress the common humanity of those involved.

"I am also interested in languages (French, German, Spanish, Italian) and have advised all my students to study at least one foreign language to provide a comparative approach to their own culture."

* * *

BROWNING, John S.
See WILLIAMS, Robert Moore

* * *

BROY, Anthony   1916-

PERSONAL: Born February 20, 1916, in New York, N.Y.; son of Peter and Nascia (Kozlowski) Broy; married wife, Alma (a teacher); children: Steven, Laurel. *Education:* Columbia University, B.S., 1950, M.S., 1951, M.A., 1953. *Religion:* Unitarian-Universalist. *Home and office:* 857 57th Rd., Elmhurst, N.Y. 11373.

CAREER: Sydney Morning Herald, New York City, correspondent and reporter, 1951-58; Doremus & Co., New York City, in public relations, 1961-68; free-lance writer and public relations consultant, 1969—. *Military service:* U.S. Army Air Forces, 1942-45; became staff sergeant. *Member:* National Association of Science Writers, American Society of Journalists and Authors.

WRITINGS: Managing Your Money: How to Make the Most of Your Income and Have a Financially Secure Future, F. Watts, 1979. Contributor of several hundred articles to magazines.

WORK IN PROGRESS: Interpreting the Business and Financial News; Anxiety.

* * *

BRUEMMER, Fred   1929-

PERSONAL: Born June 26, 1929, in Riga, Latvia; married Maud Van Den Berg; children: two sons. *Education:* At-

tended high school in Germany. *Home and office:* 5170 Cumberland Ave., Montreal, Quebec, Canada H4V 2N8.

CAREER: Free-lance writer and photographer, 1950—. *Member:* Royal Canadian Academy of Art. *Awards, honors:* Queen's Jubilee Medal, 1977, for writing and photography.

WRITINGS: The Long Hunt, McGraw, 1969; *Seasons of the Eskimo,* McClelland & Stewart, 1971; *Encounters With Arctic Animals,* McGraw, 1972; *The Arctic,* Optimum, 1974; *The Life of the Harp Seal,* Times Books, 1978; *Children of the North,* Optimum, 1979. Contributor of about five hundred articles to magazines and newspapers in the United States, Canada, and Europe, including *Audubon, Natural History,* and *International Wildlife.*

SIDELIGHTS: Bruemmer has spent twenty years in the Far North, in Alaska, the Canadian Arctic, Greenland, and Lapland. All his books deal with the North, its people, wildlife, and history. He spends six months of every year in some remote spot in the North, the rest of the year at home in Montreal, writing."

* * *

BRUNET, Michel   1917-

PERSONAL: Born July 24, 1917, in Montreal, Quebec, Canada; son of Leo and Rose (DeGuise) Brunet; married Berthe Boyer, May 7, 1945 (died, 1974); married Leone Dussault, December 5, 1975. *Education:* University of Montreal, B.A., 1939, licentiate's degree in social sciences, 1946, M.A. (history), 1947; Clark University, Ph.D., 1949. *Home:* 1790 rue Dauphin, Laval, Quebec, Canada H7G 1N3. *Office:* Department of History, University of Montreal, C.P. 6128, Montreal, Quebec, Canada H3C 3J7.

CAREER: Commission des Ecoles Catholiques de Montreal, Montreal, Quebec, teacher, 1941-47; University of Montreal, Montreal, assistant professor, 1949-50, associate professor, 1950-59, professor of history, 1959—, head of department and member of council, 1959-67, secretary, 1962-66, vice-dean of Faculty of Arts, 1966-67. Visiting professor at Centre de Recherches d'Histoire Nord-Americaine, Sorbonne, University of Paris, 1972, and University of Poitiers, 1976.

MEMBER: Academie Canadienne-Francaise, Societe Historique du Canada, Academie des Sciences d'Outre-Mer de France (foreign member), Institut d'Histoire de l'Amerique-Francaise (president, 1970-72), Societe Historique de Montreal, Association des Professeurs de l'Universite de Montreal (president, 1965-66). *Awards, honors:* Rockefeller Foundation fellowship for study in the United States, 1947; Prix Duvernay from Societe Saint Jean Baptiste de Montreal, 1969; Laureat de Prix Litteraire from the Governor-General of Canada and Prix France-Quebec, both 1970, both for *Les Canadiens apres la conquete, 1759-1775;* medal from Societe Historique de Montreal, 1978, for contributions to Canadian historiography.

WRITINGS—In English translation: *Les Canadiens et les debuts de la domination britannique, 1760-1791,* Societe Historique du Canada, 1962, 3rd edition, 1970, translation by Naomi E. S. Griffiths published as *French-Canada and the Early Decades of British Rule, 1760-1791,* Canadian Historical Association, 1965, 4th edition, 1971; (editor with J. Russell Harper) William Henry Bartlett, *Un Essai de gravures romantiques sur le pays du Quebec au dix-neuvieme siecle: A Nineteenth-Century Romantic Sketch of Quebec;* "Quebec, 1800" (text in French and English), Editions de l'Homme, 1968.

Other writings: *Histoire du Canada par les textes*, Fides, Volume I (with Guy Fregault and Marcel Trudel): *1534-1939*, 1952, Volume II: *1855-1960*, 1963, revised edition, 1966; *Canadiens et Canadiens: Etudes sur l'histoire et la pensee des deux Canadas*, Fides, 1954; *La Presence anglaise et les Canadiens*, Beauchemin, 1958; *L'Universite dit non aux Jesuites*, Editions de l'Homme, 1961; *La Crise de l'enseignement au Canada francais: Urgence d'une reforme*, Editions du Jour, 1961; *Quebec-Canada anglais: Deux Itineraires, un affrontement*, HMH, 1968; *Les Canadiens apres la conquete, 1759-1775: De la revolution canadienne a la revolution americaine*, Fides, 1969.

Contributor: Peter Russell, editor, *Nationalism in Canada*, McGraw, 1966; *Les Investissements universitaires: Planification et coordination*, Editions du Jour, 1968; *L'Histoire et son enseignement*, Presses de l'Universite du Quebec, 1970; Dale C. Thomson, editor, *Quebec Society and Politics: Views From Inside*, McClelland & Stewart, 1973. Contributor of numerous articles to scholarly journals, popular magazines, and newspapers, including *Queen's Quarterly*, *Canadian Forum*, and *Maclean's*.

WORK IN PROGRESS: Les Canadiens apres la conquete, 1775-1795; research on relations between Quebec's and New England's entrepreneurs between 1880 and 1930.

SIDELIGHTS: Brunet told *CA:* "I received a Rockefeller fellowship in order to become the first teacher of American history at the University of Montreal. I have taught U.S. history since 1949, but I soon realized that there were few French-Canadian university teachers doing research on Canadian history. I felt that the Americans did not need me to learn their history, so I decided to do my research on Canadian and Quebec history. My book, *Canadians et Canadiens*, established the whole orientation of my career."

BIOGRAPHICAL/CRITICAL SOURCES: Canadian Historical Review, Volume XLV, number 4, 1964; Eleanor Cook, editor, *The Craft of History*, Canadian Broadcasting Corp. (CBC), 1973.

*   *   *

BUCHANAN-BROWN, John 1929-
(John Warland)

PERSONAL: Born April 2, 1929, in Bangalore, India; son of Maurice (an army officer) and Laura Mary (Warland) Buchanan-Brown; married Maisie Lydia Brazier Curtis, November 19, 1955; children: John Curtis, George, Mary Victoria, Jane. *Education:* King's College, Cambridge, B.A., 1952, M.A., 1968. *Politics:* Tory. *Religion:* Roman Catholic. *Home:* Highwood Lodge, 85 Fortis Green, London N2 9HU, England. *Agent:* Bolt & Watson Ltd., 8-12 Old Queen St., Storgy's Gate, London S.W.1, England.

CAREER: Bookseller in Leamington Spa, Warwickshire, England, 1952-55; editor in London, England, with Bodley Head, Putnam, and Abelard-Schuman (publishers), 1955-63; Cassell & Co. (publisher), London, manager of reference book department, 1964-76; editorial consultant to Brassey's Publishers Ltd., 1977—. Partner in Richard Sadler & Brown (publisher), 1964-66. *Military service:* Royal Artillery, 1947-49. *Member:* Society of Authors, Bibliographical Society of London.

WRITINGS: (Editor) *The Remains of Thomas Hearne*, Southern Illinois University Press, 1966; (editor) John Aubrey, *Three Prose Works*, Southern University Press, 1972; (editor and contributor) *Cassell's Encyclopaedia of World Literature*, 3rd edition (Buchanan-Brown was not associated

with earlier editions), three volumes, Cassell, 1973; *Phiz!: Illustrator of Dicken's World*, Scribner, 1978 (published in England as *Phiz!: The Book Illustrations of Hablot Knight Brown*, David & Charles, 1978); *The Illustrations of William Makepeace Thackeray*, David & Charles, 1979; *The Book Illustrations of George Cruikshank*, David & Charles, 1980.

Translator, sometimes under the pseudonym John Warland, of more than thirty books from French and Italian.

Contributor to *Library* and *Notes and Records of the Royal Society of London*.

WORK IN PROGRESS: The Romantic Book, a study of European book illustration from 1820-1860, publication by David R. Godine expected in 1981 or 1982.

SIDELIGHTS: Buchanan-Brown told *CA:* "As a member of the new book trade all my adult life, I feel that the insights so acquired have been of peculiar value in my work on publishing history and graphic art."

*   *   *

BUCK, Doris P(itkin) 1898(?)-1980

OBITUARY NOTICE: Born c. 1898, in New York, N.Y.; died of a pulmonary embolism, December 4, 1980, in Hyattsville, Md. Science-fiction writer and poet. In addition to writing poetry, Buck wrote numerous science-fiction short stories for the *Magazine of Fantasy and Science Fiction*. She also wrote newspaper and magazine articles on travel, gardening, remodeling, and landscaping. Obituaries and other sources: *Who's Who of American Women*, 2nd edition, Marquis, 1961; *Washington Post*, December 8, 1980.

*   *   *

BUDD, Mavis
(Sully Denham)

PERSONAL: Born in Trotton, West Sussex, England; daughter of Frederick Arthur (a builder) and Ivy Edith (Back) Budd. *Education:* Educated privately. *Religion:* "Completely unorthodox." *Home and office:* Mill Cottage, Hawkley, Liss, Hampshire GU33 6NU, England. *Agent:* Bolt & Watson, 8/12 Old Queen St., Storey's Gate, London SW1H 9HP, England.

CAREER: Free-lance writer and painter. Assistant therapist at King Edward VII Sanatorium (now Hospital); painter and model at theatre workshop of John Lee. Laboratory assistant, working on high fired refractories for furnaces and spacecraft.

WRITINGS: Dust to Dust (autobiography), Dent, 1966; *A Prospect of Love* (autobiography), Dent, 1968; *Fit for a Duchess* (autobiography), Dent, 1970. Contributor of articles and poems to journals, sometimes under pseudonym Sully Denham.

WORK IN PROGRESS: Research on family history of her eighteenth-century ancestor, Henry Lidgbird Wilding; research on the experiences of an English woman who worked in the Resistance in occupied Holland.

SIDELIGHTS: Mavis Budd told *CA:* "I am interested in 'uncultivated' gardening, in the conservation of wild plants and creatures. I enjoy cooking the weeds and I make most of my toiletries with what I gather in the countryside. I spend as much time in other countries as I am able, renting an isolated cottage where I can sketch the local flowers and plants and study the wildlife of the areas, which I record in a series of journals and notebooks.

"I am interested in music, and once hoped to be a concert

pianist. Although I began to play the piano at the age of three, I gave it up in favor of writing and painting. I am especially interested in current trends in music, in traditional jazz, 'the blues,' and all Greek music.

"I collect treasures of the past, particularly old knitting needles, needlework boxes and their contents, Victorian greeting cards, early carpenters' tools, old recipes, diaries, journals, and letters.

"I like solitude, walking by myself, and silence. But I am also fond of the theatre, opera, and entertaining one or two friends at a time. I am by nature an 'anti-joiner,' rather unconventional. Because there is so much of interest in the world, I'd really like to live forever."

*   *   *

BUELL, Jon A. 1939-

PERSONAL: Born December 20, 1939, in Oak Park, Ill.; son of Alfred L. and Ruth Buell; married Sandra Wheat, June 9, 1952; children: Wendy, Shelley, Jon. *Education:* University of Miami, Coral Gables, Fla., B.A., 1961; Institute of Biblical Studies, certificate, 1964. *Home:* 606 East Spring Valley Rd., Richardson, Tex. 75081. *Office:* Probe Ministries, 12011 Coit Rd., Suite 107, Dallas, Tex. 75251.

CAREER: Ordained minister; Campus Crusade for Christ, director at University of Miami, Coral Gables, Fla., 1962-65, director of central Texas district in Austin, 1965-68, director for southeastern region in Birmingham, Ala., 1968-72, associate minister with Christian Family Life, 1972-73, vice-president of Probe Ministries in Dallas, Tex., 1973—. Member of faculty of Institute of Biblical Studies, 1970; guest lecturer at universities. Member of board of directors of Scope Ministries. *Member:* Creation Research Society (associate member), American Scientific Affiliation (affiliate member).

WRITINGS: (With Quentin Hyder) *Jesus: God, Ghost, or Guru?*, Zondervan, 1979. Contributor to *Collegiate Challenge.* Editor-in-chief of Christian Free University Curriculum.

SIDELIGHTS: Buell commented that his lecturing and writing "address a number of tension points that exist between the academic curriculum of the university world and biblical Christianity in order to provide a broader perspective for students who struggle with their reconciliation."

*   *   *

BUREAU, William H(obbs) 1913-

PERSONAL: Born July 16, 1913, in Moscow, Ohio; son of William Lemar and Lulu Raechel Bureau; married Jule Taylor Wright, June 16, 1945; children: Judith Ann (Mrs. William Mamay), William Edward, Karen Louise, George Evans, Grace Wright. *Education:* Attended Purdue University, 1932-34; Illinois Institute of Technology, B.S., 1948. *Politics:* Republican. *Religion:* Episcopalian. *Home:* 237 Frederick St., Hanover, Pa. 17331.

CAREER: Butler Paper Co., Chicago, Ill., vice-president in research and development, 1934-63, manager of sales and technical services, 1963-65; P. H. Glatfelter Co., Spring Grove, Pa., product manager, 1965-78, product consultant, 1978—. *Military service:* U.S. Army, 1942-45. *Member:* Technical Association of the Pulp and Paper Industry, Hanover Historical Society, Community Concert Association. *Awards, honors:* Golden Keys Award from International Association of Printing House Craftsmen, 1973, for distinguished journalism.

WRITINGS: Paper From Pulp to Printing, Graphic Arts Publishing, 1968; *What the Printer Should Know About Paper,* Graphic Arts Technical Foundation, 1981. Contributor to *Encyclopedia of Science and Technology.* Contributor to trade journals. Contributing editor of *Graphic Arts Monthly,* 1956—.

WORK IN PROGRESS: "The Paper Industry and Its Products," an audio-visual series, completion expected in 1984.

*   *   *

BURKE, James 1936-

PERSONAL: Born December 22, 1936, in Londonderry, North Ireland; son of John James (a businessman) and Mary (Gallagher) Burke. *Education:* Oxford University, B.A. and M.A., both 1961. *Residence:* London, England. *Address:* c/o British Broadcasting Corp., Broadcasting House, London W. 1, England.

CAREER: British School, Bologna, Italy, teacher of English and director of studies, 1961-63; English School, Rome, Italy, dean and teacher of English, 1963-65; Granada Television, Rome, reporter for "World in Action" current affairs program, 1965-66; British Broadcasting Corp. (BBC-TV), London, England, 1966—, writer for television series, including "Tomorrow's World" and "The Burke Special," writer and television host for documentaries, including "The Inventing of America" and "Connections," chief reporter for the Apollo missions to the moon. *Awards, honors:* Silver medal, 1973, and gold medal, 1974, from Royal Television Society for achievements in television.

WRITINGS—Television documentaries: "The Inventing of America," first aired on British Broadcasting Corp. (BBC-TV), July 4, 1976, aired on National Broadcasting Co., Inc. (NBC-TV), July 3, 1979; "Connections," first aired on BBC-TV, autumn, 1979, aired on Public Broadcasting Service (PBS-TV), autumn, 1979.

Other: (With Raymond Baxter) *Tomorrow's World* (based on the BBC-TV series), British Broadcasting Corp., 1970; *Connections: An Alternative View of Change,* Macmillan, 1978, published as *Connections,* Little, Brown, 1979.

WORK IN PROGRESS: A ten-part television series, "The Day the Universe Changed," to be aired in 1983.

SIDELIGHTS: James Burke has earned a reputation as one of British television's finest writers. In order to prepare his celebrated documentary, "Connections," he traveled to twenty-three countries and spent more than two years researching and filming the program. "Connections" was immensely popular when it was shown in Great Britain and also scored a great success when it was aired in the United States.

A companion volume to this series, also entitled *Connections,* goes into greater detail about the history of technology than the television series. In this book Burke examines eight recent technological achievements—the computer, the production line, telecommunications, jet aircraft, the atom bomb, plastics, the guided rocket, and television—and traces the long sequence of events that gave rise to these inventions. For example, he explains how the waterwheel led to the invention of the computer and how the chimney prepared the way for the airplane. Burke's thesis is that technological progress is not usually the result of the work of a few brilliant individuals, but rather is brought about by the creative adaptations and combinations of many people. "Innovation happens bit by bit," contends Burke. "No one man does it all. It's only when all the bits come together that the final form comes into existence; and when it does, it causes worldwide change to occur.''

The book, which proved to be as popular as the television series, made the best seller list. A few reviewers expressed some reservations about *Connections*. Malcolm W. Browne objected to Burke's lack of scientific training (Burke has a degree in English literature), and pointed out that a number of famous scientists and scientific movements are ignored in the book. He concluded that "the promise of 'Connections' to satisfy real curiosity about science and technology seems no likelier to succeed than Laetrile as a cancer cure." By and large, however, critics greeted *Connections* with enthusiasm. A reviewer for the *Los Angeles Times* described it as "marvelously illustrated and written with a lively wit." Burke's ability to take a dry subject and make it interesting aroused Joseph McLellan's admiration. "There is a deep fascination in the way Burke traces the process and relates technology to everyday life," McLellan wrote in the *Washington Post*.

Burke told *CA*: "I am interested in trying to explain in a very limited way some aspects of why the world is as it is, and I believe that science has the most profound effect on it. Understanding science—even in the most general way—is a step toward understanding the social systems we live by. The derivation of those systems, their history, and their interaction with the scientific community is the subject of my next book.

"Some critics mistake my intentions, which are *not* to write definitively, but to provide access to the lay reader to subjects that are closed by nature of their very vocabulary."

BIOGRAPHICAL/CRITICAL SOURCES: Christian Science Monitor, September 5, 1979; *Washington Post*, September 20, 1979; *Los Angeles Times*, November 2, 1979; *New York Times Book Review*, December 30, 1979; *Best Sellers*, January, 1980.

*   *   *

BURNETT, Alfred David   1937-

PERSONAL: Born August 15, 1937, in Edinburgh, Scotland; son of Alfred Harding (a railway superintendent) and Jessica Millar (a teacher; maiden name, Scott) Burnett. *Education:* University of Edinburgh, M.A. (with honors), 1959; University of Strathclyde, A.L.A., 1964. *Religion:* Presbyterian. *Home:* 33 Hastings Ave., Merry Oaks, Durham DH1 3QG, England. *Office:* University Library, Palace Green, Durham DH1 3RN, England.

CAREER: University of Glasgow, Glasgow, Scotland, library assistant, 1959-64; University of Durham, Durham, England, assistant librarian, 1964—. *Member:* International Academy of Poets, Committee of International and Comparative Librarianship Group, Amnesty International, Bibliographical Society, Library Association, Private Libraries Association, National Council for Civil Liberties, Durham Union Society, Colpitts Poetry. *Awards, honors:* Patterson Bursary in Anglo-Saxon from University of Edinburgh, 1958; Kelso Memorial Prize in bibliography from University of Strathclyde, 1964; essay prize from Library Association, 1966, for "Problems of Older Material in British University Libraries and Some Suggested Solutions"; Sevensma Prize from International Federation of Library Associations, 1971, for *Studies in Comparative Librarianship*.

WRITINGS—Poetry: *Mandala*, Magpie Press, 1967; *Diversities*, Magpie Press, 1968; *A Ballad Upon a Wedding*, Magpie Press, 1969; *Columbaria*, London Literary Editions,

1971; *Shimabara*, Pointing Finger Press, 1972; *Thirty Snow Poems*, North Gate Press, 1973; *Fescennines*, Tragara Press, 1973; *Hero and Leader: A Poem*, privately printed, 1975; *The True Vine*, Hedgehog Press, 1975; *He and She*, Tragara Press, 1976; *The Heart's Undesign*, Tragara Press, 1977; *Figures and Spaces*, Pointing Finger Press, 1978; *Jackdaw*, Tragara Press, 1980.

Nonfiction: *Cataloguing Policy Objectives and the Computer*, [Durham], 1966; *Report of the North-East Libraries and Computers Group Working Party on the Operational Data Requirements of Different Kinds of Library*, [Durham], 1968; (with R. K. Gupta and S. Simsova) *Studies in Comparative Librarianship: Three Essays Presented for the Sevensma Prize, 1971*, Library Association, 1973; *Wood and Type: An Exhibition of Books*, [Durham], 1977; *Five Hundred Years of Science: Descriptive Catalogue of an Exhibition in the University Library, Palace Green, Durham*, Durham University Library, 1978; (editor with E. E. Cumming) *International Library and Information Programmes: Proceedings of the Tenth Anniversary Conference of the International and Comparative Librarianship Group of the Library Association*, Library Association, 1979; (editor and author of introduction, with D.F.C. Surman) *Henri Gaudier-Brzeska and Ezra Pound: A Display of Printed Material and Related Items Arranged to Accompany the Fourth International Ezra Pound Conference*, [Durham], 1979; (editor with S. P. Green) *The British Commitment Overseas: A Transcript of Seminary Discussions Held at the Library Association Study School and National Conference, Brighton, I.C.L.G.*, 1979. Contributor of more than twenty-five articles, poems, and reviews to scholarly journals and literary magazines, including *Journal of Librarianship, Universities Quarterly, Northern Notes, Annals of Science, Notes and Queries, Libri*, and *Focus*.

WORK IN PROGRESS: Poems and articles.

SIDELIGHTS: Burnett wrote: "'Homo sum; humani nil a me alienum puto.' ['I am a man; I consider nothing human foreign to me.']—Terence *(Heauton Timarumenos*, 77).''

*   *   *

BURNS, Alan Cuthbert   1887-1980

OBITUARY NOTICE: Born November 9, 1887, in St. Kitt, West Indies; died September 29, 1980. Colonial administrator and author. Burns held many posts in Africa during the 1920's and 1930's, including assistant secretary in Southern Nigeria and adjutant of the Nigeria Land Continent. He also served in the Bahamas and the British Honduras. From 1941 to 1947 he was governor of the Gold Coast. During those years, he was also enlisted as governor of Nigeria. A staunch proponent of British colonialism, Burns nonetheless favored constitutional progress for the territories, but he cautioned against dramatic constitutional revision in the colonies and warned that constitutional license must be balanced with cultural advancement. Burns retired in 1947 to become permanent United Kingdom representative on the Trusteeship Council of the United Nations. He then detailed his experiences and beliefs in *In Defence of Colonies*. In addition, he wrote *History of the British West Indies* and *History of Nigeria*. Burns was consulting editor of *New Commonwealth*. Obituaries and other sources: *The Writers Directory, 1980-82*, St. Martin's, 1979; *Who's Who*, 131st edition, St. Martin's, 1979; *London Times*, October 1, 1980.

BURNS, Robert M(ilton) C(lark), Jr. 1940-
(Scott Burns)

PERSONAL: Born November 9, 1940, in Cambridge, Mass.; son of Robert Milton Clark and Joanne (Mahoney) Burns; married Allegra Wendy Eames (a designer), December 17, 1965; children: Jasper, Oliver. *Education:* Massachusetts Institute of Technology, B.S., 1962. *Home:* 78 Monmouth St., Brookline, Mass. 02146. *Office:* Boston Herald American, 300 Harrison Ave., Boston, Mass. 02106.

CAREER: Arthur D. Little, Inc., Cambridge, Mass., management consultant, 1970-74; independent management consultant, 1974-76; *Boston Herald American*, Boston, Mass., editor and syndicated columnist, 1977—. Member of board of directors of Blasius Industries, Inc. and National Taxpayers Union.

WRITINGS—Under name Scott Burns: Squeeze It Till the Eagle Grins, Doubleday, 1972; *Home, Inc.,* Doubleday, 1975, reprinted as *The Household Economy,* Beacon Press, 1977. Contributor to magazines, including *New England Business.*

WORK IN PROGRESS: How to Finance the Rest of Your Life, applying the life cycle hypothesis to personal finance; research on technologies driving for resource conservation, or for less consumption.

SIDELIGHTS: Burns wrote: "Reaching an audience—a *large* audience—is a vital concern. That's why I'm delighted to be writing for a major newspaper. I also sense that the attention given to books—or any particular book—is declining rapidly as the public attention span shrinks and more and more material becomes highly time sensitive."

*   *   *

BURNS, Scott
See BURNS, Robert M(ilton) C(lark), Jr.

*   *   *

BURT, Robert Amsterdam 1939-

PERSONAL: Born February 3, 1939, in Philadelphia, Pa.; son of Samuel M. and Esther (a guidance counselor; maiden name, Amsterdam) Burt; married Linda Rose, June 14, 1964; children: Anne, Jessica. *Education:* Princeton University, B.A. (summa cum laude), 1960; Oxford University, B.A. (with first class honors), 1962, M.A., 1968; Yale University, J.D. (cum laude), 1964. *Home:* 66 Dogwood Circle, Woodbridge, Conn. 06525. *Office:* School of Law, Yale University, 127 Wall St., New Haven, Conn. 06520.

CAREER: Admitted to the Bar of Washington, D.C., the Bar of Michigan, and the Bar of the U.S. Supreme Court; U.S. Court of Appeals, Washington, D.C., clerk to chief judge, 1964-65; Office of the President's Special Representative for Trade Negotiations, Washington, D.C., assistant general counsel, 1965-66; U.S. Senate, Washington, D.C., legislative assistant, 1966-68; University of Chicago, Chicago, Ill., associate professor of law, 1968-70; University of Michigan, Ann Arbor, associate professor, 1970-72, professor of law, 1972-76, psychotherapist at Children's Psychiatric Hospital, 1974-76; Yale University, New Haven, Conn., professor of law, 1976—, co-chairman of program in law and medicine. Member of National Academy of Sciences-National Research Council Board on Maternal, Infant, and Family Health Care Research, 1975—, member of its Institute of Medicine, 1976—. *Member:* Institute for Society, Ethics, and the Life Sciences (fellow). *Awards, honors:* Fulbright fellow at Oxford University, 1962-68.

WRITINGS: (With M. Wald) *Standards Relating to Abuse and Neglect,* Ballinger, 1977; *Taking Care of Strangers: The Rule of Law in Doctor-Patient Relations,* Free Press, 1979.

Contributor: A. Milunsky and G. Annas, editors, *Genetics and the Law,* Plenum, 1975; Michael Kindred and others, editors, *The Mentally Retarded Citizens and the Law,* Free Press, 1976; Margaret K. Rosenheim, editor, *Pursuing Justice for the Child,* University of Chicago Press, 1976; G. Berment, C. Nemeth, and N. Vidmar, editors, *Psychology and the Law,* Lexington Books, 1976; S. Feinstein and P. Giovacchini, editors, *Adolescent Psychiatry,* Volume V: *Developmental and Clinical Studies,* Jason Aronson, 1977; P. A. Vardin and I. N. Brody, editors, *Children's Rights: Contemporary Perspectives,* Teachers College Press, 1979. Also contributor to *Legal Rights of the Mentally Handicapped,* edited by B. J. Ennis and P. R. Friedman, 1973. Contributor of articles and reviews to law and psychology journals.

SIDELIGHTS: Burt wrote: "My special interests in law and psychiatry led to my court appointment as counsel to the potential experimental subject in the Detroit psychosurgery case in 1973. I was subsequently invited to deliver the Ohio State Law Forum Lectures for 1974, where I reflected on that case in 'Biotechnology and Anti-Social Conduct: Controlling the Controllers.' My interests in legal aspects of medical sciences generally have also been pursued beyond psychiatry. From 1974 to 1976 I served as co-reporter of the volume on child abuse, neglect, and dependency of the American Bar Association-Institute for Judicial Administration Juvenile Justice Standards Project. In 1975 and 1976 I served as a member of the University of Michigan committee to evaluate the propriety of research at the university into recombinant DNA technology, and in 1974 and 1975 was a member of the National Academy of Sciences and National Research Council committee for the study of inborn errors of metabolism (genetic screening)."

*   *   *

BURTON, S(amuel) H(olroyd) 1919-
(Sam Holroyd)

PERSONAL: Born November 30, 1919, in Caverswall, England; son of Samuel Burton (a farmer) and Annie (a teacher) Holroyd. *Education:* Queen's College, Cambridge, M.A., 1945. *Home:* 51 Newport Rd., Stafford ST16 1DA, England. *Agent:* Peter Janson-Smith, 31 Newington Green, London N16 9PU, England.

CAREER: King Edward VI School, Stafford, England, schoolmaster, 1942-45; Blundell's School, Tiverton, England, schoolmaster, 1945-64; writer, 1964—. *Military service:* Served with Royal Berkshire Regiment. Visiting lecturer at schools and colleges.

WRITINGS—Travel books: Tiverton to Exmoor, Gore Allen & Co., 1951, 2nd edition, 1952; *Tiverton to Exeter,* Gore Allen & Co., 1952, 2nd edition, 1952; *Exmoor,* Westaway, 1952, 3rd edition, R. Hale, 1978; *Official Guide to Porlock and District,* Gore Allen & Co., 1953; *The North Devon Coast: A Guide to Its Scenery and Architecture, History, and Antiquities,* Laurie, 1953; *The South Devon Coast: A Guide to Its Scenery and Architecture, History, and Antiquities,* Laurie, 1954; *The Coasts of Cornwall,* Laurie, 1955; (with Arthur Elliott-Cannon) *Exmoor Companion: Illustrated Guide,* Cider Press, 1968, 2nd edition, 1969; *The West Country,* R. Hale, 1972; *Devon Villages,* R. Hale, 1973.

Textbooks; all published by Longmans, Green, except as noted: *The Criticism of Poetry,* 1950, 2nd edition, 1974;

Comprehension Practice, 1951; *English Study and Composition*, 1952; *English Appreciation*, 1953, 2nd edition, 1954; *Comprehensive English Course*, 1954; *Modern Precis Practice*, 1955; *Exercises in Criticism*, 1956; *Great Men of Devon*, Bodley Head, 1956; *A First English Course*, 1958; *Handbook of English Practice*, three volumes, Hutchinson, 1959-61; *A Second English Course*, 1959; *A Third English Course*, 1961; *A Fourth English Course*, 1962; *A Fifth English Course*, 1963; *Writing and Reading in English*, 1966; *The Criticism of Prose*, Longman, 1973; *Using English: Language Course for Advanced Students*, Longman, 1976; *African Poetry in English*, Macmillan, 1979; *People and Communication*, Longman, 1980; *Mastering English Language*, Macmillan, 1981.

Editor; All published by Longmans, Green, except as noted: John E. Masefield, *Martin Hyde* (abridged edition), 1953; Ernest Walter Parker, *A Pageant of Longer Poems*, 1956; (also author of introduction) Charles Dickens, *A Tale of Two Cities*, 1958; Hilda Van Stockum, *Andries*, 1959; Slavomir Rawicz (pseudonym), *The Long Walk* (abridged edition), 1960; David W. Bone, *The Brassbounder* (abridged edition), 1960; Felice Benuzzi, *No Picnic on Mount Kenya* (abridged edition), 1960; (also author of introduction) Dickens, *The Adventures of Oliver Twist*, 1961; (also author of introduction) Dickens, *David Copperfield*, 1964; *Modern Short Stories*, 1965; Samuel Butler, *The Way of All Flesh*, 1966; *Science Fiction*, 1967; Edward Morgan Forster, *The Machine Stops and Other Stories* (abridged edition), Longman, 1974; Aldous Huxley, *Brave New World* (abridged edition), Longman, 1975; *A West Country Anthology*, R. Hale, 1975; (also author of introduction) William Shakespeare, *King Henry V*, Longman, 1975; *Strike the Father Dead*, Longman, 1978; (also author) *Eight Ghost Stories*, Longman, 1980.

Under name Sam Holroyd: *Ghosts Three* (anthology), Topliners, 1974.

SIDELIGHTS: Burton told *CA:* "I was disabled and released from active army duty in 1942 and I've lived dangerously ever since! As a soldier, my economic future was secure, however dangerous the physical circumstances. As an author I have known only insecurity. Conditions are now worse than any before. However, I still get commissions, so I must count myself fortunate, and *somehow* I live. What keeps me going? Hope—and the pleasure of exercising my craft, which (I like to think) gets a little better with each book I write. I hope to be remembered as a versatile craftsman who turned his work in on time.

"My writing interests have been (and are) wide-ranging, but I suppose I could claim to have been influential in four areas: increasing my readers' awareness of England's rural heritage; enlarging my readers' understanding of criticism and literature; establishing the true role of grammar and linguistic drill in English language teaching; and pioneering the use of science fiction and super-natural stories to quicken interest in reading. As I read that statement I seem to be making large claims for myself, but the products of my thirty years of writing do, I hope, afford some justification of my belief."

*   *   *

BURY, Frank
See HARRIS, Herbert

*   *   *

BUTHELEZI, Gatsha   1928-

PERSONAL: Born August 27, 1928, in Mahlabatini, South Africa; son of Mathole B. (a Zulu chief) and Princess Ma-

gogo Buthelezi; married Irene Audrey Thandekile Mzila, 1952; children: seven. *Education:* Attended Adams College and Fort-Hare University. *Home:* Private Bag X01, Ulundi 3838, KwaZulu, South Africa.

CAREER: Chief of Buthelezi tribe in South Africa, beginning 1953; prime minister of KwaZulu, South Africa, 1972—. Chief member of executive council of KwaZulu Legislative Assembly. Assistant to King Cyprian as administrator of the Zulu people, 1953-68; leader of Zululand Territorial Authority, 1970, and South African Black Alliance, 1978—. *Awards, honors:* LL.D. from University of Zululand; knight commander of Liberia's Star of Africa.

WRITINGS: (With Leon Sullivan) *Power Is Ours: Buthelezi Speaks on the Crisis in South Africa*, Books in Focus, 1979. Also author of *Remarks on My British and German Tours of 1971, Together With Selected Speeches Delivered During 1972.*

BIOGRAPHICAL/CRITICAL SOURCES: Ben Temkin, *Gatsha Buthelezi, Zulu Statesman: A Biography*, Purnell Library Service, 1976.*

*   *   *

BUTLER, Marilyn (Speers)   1937-

PERSONAL: Born February 11, 1937, in Kingston-on-Thames, England; daughter of Trevor (a journalist) and Margaret Speers (Gribbin) Evans; married David Butler (a university teacher), March 3, 1962; children: Daniel, Gareth, Edmund. *Education:* St. Hilda's College, Oxford, B.A. (with first class honors), 1958, D.Phil., 1966. *Agent:* Curtis Brown Academic Ltd., 1 Craven Hill, London W2 3EP, England. *Office:* St. Hugh's College, Oxford University, Oxford, England.

CAREER: British Broadcasting Corp., London, England, trainee and talks producer, 1960-63; part-time university teacher in Oxford, England, and Canberra, Australia, 1966-70; Oxford University, Oxford, research fellow at St. Hilda's College, 1970-73, lecturer in English literature and fellow of St. Hugh's College, 1973—. *Awards, honors:* Rose Mary Crawshay Prize from British Academy, 1973, for *Maria Edgeworth.*

WRITINGS: Maria Edgeworth: A Literary Biography, Oxford University Press, 1972; *Jane Austen and the War of Ideas*, Oxford University Press, 1975; *Peacock Displayed: A Satirist in His Context*, Routledge & Kegan Paul, 1979; *Romantics, Rebels, and Reactionaries: English Literature in Its Context*, Oxford University Press, 1981. Contributor to magazines, including *London Review of Books.*

WORK IN PROGRESS: Research on mythology and English literature, 1812-22, and Walter Scott.

SIDELIGHTS: Marilyn Butler told *CA:* "I am fascinated by people's opinions and prejudices. The Romantic age is the period when 'public opinion' became recognized as a factor bearing immediately upon politics, even in societies with a restricted franchise. I collect those direct expressions of popular opinion, the caricatures of Gillray, Rowlandson, and others. I also like contemplating modern misapprehensions—the fruit of our prejudices—about opinions then. No subject has attracted a finer crop of critical myths than mythology."

AVOCATIONAL INTERESTS: Reading and collecting books and political caricatures, 1790-1820.

BUTTEL, Robert (William) 1923-

PERSONAL: Surname is pronounced Boo-*tell;* born June 10, 1923, in Brooklyn, N.Y.; son of Louis Otten and Helen (Reese) Buttel; married Helen Thwaits (a teacher), June 10, 1947; children: Robert Jeffrey, Steven Putnam (deceased). *Education:* Williams College, A.B., 1947; Columbia University, A.B., 1949, Ph.D., 1962. *Office:* Department of English, Temple University, Philadelphia, Pa. 19122.

CAREER: New York University, New York City, instructor in English, 1949; Williams College, Williamstown, Mass., instructor in English, 1949-51; Columbia University, New York City, lecturer, 1951-58, instructor in English, 1958-59; University of Cincinnati, Cincinnati, Ohio, instructor in English, 1959-62; Temple University, Philadelphia, Pa., assistant professor, 1962-65, associate professor, 1965-67, professor of English, 1967—, chairman of department, 1968-71. *Military service:* U.S. Army Air Forces, 1942-45; became first lieutenant; received Air Medal. *Member:* Modern Language Association of America.

WRITINGS: Wallace Stevens: The Making of Harmonium, Princeton University Press, 1967; *Seamus Heaney,* Bucknell University Press, 1975; (editor with Frank Doggett) *Wallace Stevens: A Celebration,* Princeton University Press, 1980.

WORK IN PROGRESS: Irish Poetry Since Yeats.

*   *   *

BUYS, Donna 1944-

PERSONAL: Born August 25, 1944, in Austin, Minn.; daughter of Melvin E. and Dorothy (Hjelman) Onstad. *Education:* University of Colorado, B.S., 1968. *Office:* 14006 Palawan Way, Marina del Rey, Calif. 90291.

CAREER: RN, Oradell, N.J., associate editor, 1968-71; National Multiple Sclerosis Society, New York City, science information director, 1974-75; free-lance writer, 1975—; Physicians Radio Network, New York City, Los Angeles correspondent, 1976—. *Member:* American Society of Journalists and Authors, National Association of Science Writers.

WRITINGS: Readings in Psychology 77/78, Dushkin, 1977. Contributor to medical journals, popular magazines, and newspapers, including *Cosmopolitan, Family Health, Family Circle, Glamour, Parents, Chic, Penthouse, American Baby,* and *TravelScene.* Editor of *Nursing Careers.*

WORK IN PROGRESS: A novel on female sexuality.

SIDELIGHTS: Donna Buys wrote: "My interests are in writing about divorce, female sexuality, and travel to foreign lands. I started out writing because I did not want to work as a registered nurse. I am one of thousands who leave nursing shortly after graduation, usually because of the dichotomy between what nurses learn as students and what they are able to practice within the bureaucratic structure of the physician-dominated hospital. I use my education to write about health and advances in medicine."

*   *   *

BYKAU, Vasilii Uladzimiravich
See BYKOV, Vasily Vladimirovich

*   *   *

BYKOV, Vasily Vladimirovich 1924-

PERSONAL: Born June 19, 1924, in Charaposchina, Vitebsk Oblast, U.S.S.R. *Education:* Attended Vitebsk Art School. *Office:* Redaktsiya zhurnala Maladosts, Leninsky prospekt 79, Minsk, Soviet Union.

CAREER: Member of editorial staff of *Grodnenskaya Pravda,* U.S.S.R.; member of editorial staff of *Redaktsiya zhurnala Maladosts,* Minsk, Belorussia. *Military service:* Service beginning in 1949; became commander. *Member:* Union of Soviet Writers, Byelorussian Writers Union (member of board of directors; member of board of presidium, 1966—).

WRITINGS—In English translation: *Tret'ia raketa: Povest' i rasskasy* (stories; translated from Byelorussian by Mikhaila Gorbacheva), Molodaia gvardiia, 1963, English translation by Robert Daglish included in *The Third Flare: Three War Stories,* Foreign Languages Publishing House, 1963; *Al'piiskaia ballada: Povesti* (translated from Byelorussian by Gorbacheva), Sovetskii pisatel, 1964, English translation by George Hanna published as *Alpine Ballad,* Progress Publishers, 1966; *Sotnikov* (novel), Mastatskaia literatura, 1972, translation by Gordon Clough published as *The Ordeal,* Dutton, 1972.

In Russian: *Zhurauliny kryk: Apovests' i apaviadanni,* [Minsk, Belorussia], 1960; *Tretsiaia raketa: Zdrada,* Red. mastatskai lit-ry, 1962; *Al'piis'ka balada: Povist',* translated from Byelorussian by Halyna Vihurs'ka, Molod', 1965; *Mertvym ne bolyt,* translated from Byelorussian by Ivan Koshelivtsya, Prolog, 1966; *Voennye povesti,* Voeni izd-vo, 1966; *Frontovye stranitsy: Povesti,* Byeloruss, 1966; *Apovesti,* Byeloruss, 1969.

Zhuravlinyi krik: Tretsiaia raketa–Alpiniskaya balada, Mastatskaia literatura, 1972; *Tret'ia raketa: Alpinskaya ballada,* translated from Byelorussian by I. L. Rabenau, Molodaia gvardiia, 1972; (editor) *Voprosy gidrodinamicheskogo kratkosrochnogo prognoza pogody i mezometeotologii,* Gidrometeoizdat, 1972; *Obelisk: Dozhit' do rassveta,* Molodaia gvardiia, 1973; *Obelisk: Povest',* translated from Byelorussian by Galiny Kurenevoi, Pravda, 1973; *Vybranyia tvory,* two volumes, Mastatskaia literatura, 1974; (editor) *Gidrodinamicheskie kratkosrochnye prognozy pogody i mezometeorologiia,* Gidrometeoizdat, 1974; *Obelisk,* translated from Byelorussian by Kurenevoi, Sov Rossiya, 1975; *Povesti,* Xhdozh lit-ra, 1975; *Volch'ia staia: Povest,* Pravda, 1975; *Ego batal'on: Povesti,* Molodaia gvardiia, 1976. Also author of *Mertvym ne bol'no.**

*   *   *

BYRNE, John Keyes 1926-
(Hugh Leonard)

PERSONAL: Born November 9, 1926, near Dublin, Ireland; son of Nicholas Keyes (a gardener) and Margaret (Doyle) Byrne; married Paule Jacquet, May 28, 1955; children: Danielle. *Education:* Educated in Dun Laoghaire, Ireland. *Politics:* "I detest politics and politicians." *Religion:* "Lapsed Catholic." *Home:* Theros, Coliemore Rd., Dalkey, County Dublin, Ireland. *Agent:* Harvey Unna, 14 Beaumont Mews, Marylebone High St., London W1N 4HE, England.

CAREER: Writer. Department of Lands, Dublin, Ireland, civil servant, 1945-59; Granada Television, Manchester, England, script editor, 1961-63; free-lance writer in London, England, 1963-70; Abbey Theatre, Dublin, literary editor, 1976—. *Member:* Dramatists' Club (London), The Players (New York). *Awards, honors:* Italia Prize from International Concourse for Radio and Television, 1967, for "Silent Song"; award of merit from Writers Guild of Great Britain, 1967, for "Silent Song"; Antoinette Perry ("Tony") Award for best play, New York Drama Critics' Circle Award for best play, Drama Desk Award for outstanding new play, Outer Critics Circle Award for outstanding play, all 1978, all for "Da"; Harvey Award for "A Life."

WRITINGS—All under pseudonym Hugh Leonard; *Leonard's Last Book* (essays), Tansy Books, 1978; *A Peculiar People* (essays), Tansy Books, 1979; *Home Before Night* (autobiography), Deutsch, 1979, Atheneum, 1980.

Plays: "The Italian Road" (two-act), first produced in Dublin, Ireland, 1954; "The Big Birthday," first produced in Dublin at Abbey Theatre, January 25, 1956; "A Leap in the Dark" (two-act), first produced in Dublin, 1957; "Madigan's Lock" (two-act), first produced in Dublin, 1958, produced in London, 1963, produced in Olney, Md., at Olney Theatre, June 23, 1970; "A Walk on the Water," first produced in Dublin, 1960; "The Passion of Peter McGinty" (two-act), first produced in Dublin, 1961; *Stephen D.* (two-act; adaptation of *A Portrait of the Artist as a Young Man* and *Stephen Hero* by James Joyce; first produced in Dublin, 1962; produced on the West End at St. Martin's Theatre, February, 1963; produced in New York, 1967), M. Evans, 1962; "Dublin One" (two-act; adaptation of *Dubliners* by Joyce), first produced in Dublin, 1963; *The Poker Session* (first produced in Dublin, 1963; produced on the West End at Globe Theatre, 1964; produced in New York, 1967), M. Evans, 1964; "The Family Way" (two-act), first produced in Dublin, 1964, produced in London, 1966; *The Late Arrival of the Incoming Aircraft* (one-act; adaptation of Leonard's television play), M. Evans, 1968; "When Saints Go Cycling In" (two-act; adaptation of *The Dalkey Archives* by Flann O'Brien), first produced in Dublin, 1965.

"Mick and Nick" (two-act), first produced in Dublin, 1966, also produced as "All the Nice People"; "The Quick, and the Dead" (two-act), first produced in Dublin, 1967; *The Au Pair Man* (three-act; first produced in Dublin, 1968; produced on the West End at Duchess Theatre, April 23, 1969; produced in New York, 1973), S. French, 1974; "The Barracks" (two-act; adaptation of novel by John McGahern), first produced in Dublin at Olympia Theatre, October 16, 1969; *The Patrick Pearse Motel* (two-act; first produced in Dublin at Olympia Theatre, March, 1971; produced on the West End at Queen's Theatre, June 17, 1971; produced in Washington, D.C., 1972), S. French, 1971; *Da* (two-act; produced in Dublin, 1973; produced in Olney, Md., at Olney Theatre; produced on Broadway at Morosco Theatre, May 1, 1978), Proscenium Press, 1975; "Summer" (two-act), first produced in Dublin, 1974; produced in Olney, Md., at Olney Theatre, produced Off-Broadway, September, 1980; "Irishmen: A Suburb of Babylon" (contains "Nothing Personal" and "The Last of the Last Mohicans"), first produced in Dublin, 1975; "Some of My Best Friends Are Husbands" (two-act; adaptation of play by Eugene Labiche), first produced in London, 1976; "Liam Liar" (two-act; adaptation of "Billy Liar" by Keith Waterhouse and Willis Hall), first produced in Dublin, 1976; *Time Was* (two-act), Penguin, 1981; *A Life* (two-act; produced in London at Old Vic Theatre; produced on Broadway, October, 1980), Penguin, 1981.

Screenplays: "Great Catherine," 1968; "Interlude," 1968; "Whirligig," 1970; "Percy" (adaptation of novel by Raymond Hitchcock), Metro-Goldwyn-Mayer (MGM), 1971; "Our Miss Fred," 1972.

Television plays: "The Irish Boys" (trilogy), 1962; "A Kind of Kingdom," 1963; "The Second Wall," 1964; "A Triple Irish," 1964; "Realm of Error," 1964; "My One True Love," 1964; "The Late Arrival of the Incoming Aircraft"; "Second Childhood," 1964; "Do You Play Requests?," 1964; "The View From the Obelisk," 1965; "I Loved You Last Summer," 1965; "Great Big Blond," 1965; "The Lodger" and "The Judge," 1966; "Insurrection," 1966;

"The Retreat," 1966; "Silent Song," 1966; "A Time of Wolves and Tigers," 1967; "Love Life," 1967; "Great Expectations" (adaptation of novel by Charles Dickens), 1967; "Wuthering Heights" (adaptation of novel by Emily Bronte), 1967; "No Such Thing as a Vampire," 1968; "The Egg on the Face of the Tiger," Independent (ITV), 1968; "The Corpse Can't Play," 1968; "A Man and His Mother-in-Law," 1968; "Assassin," 1968; "Nicholas Nickleby" (adaptation of novel by Dickens), 1968; "A Study in Scarlet" (adaptation of story by Arthur Conan Doyle), 1968; "The Hound of the Baskervilles" (adaptation of story by Doyle), 1968; (with H. R. Keating) "Hunt the Peacock," 1969; "Talk of Angels," 1969; "The Possessed" (adaptation of novel by Dostoevsky), 1969; "Dombey and Son" (adaptation of novel by Dickens), British Broadcasting Corp (BBC-TV), 1969; "P and O" (adaptation of story by Somerset Maugham), 1969; "Jane" (adaptation of story by Maugham), 1970; "A Sentimental Education" (adaptation of story by Gustave Flaubert), 1970; "White Walls and Olive Green Carpets," 1971; "The Removal Person," 1971; "Pandora," Granada Television, 1971.

"The Virgins," 1972; "The Ghost of Christmas Present," 1972; "The Trugh Game," 1972; "The Moonstone" (adaptation of novel by Wilkie Collins), 1972; "The Sullen Sisters," 1972; "The Watercress Girl" (adaptation of the story by H. E. Bates), 1972; "The Higgler," 1973; "High Kampf," 1973; "Milo O'Shea," 1973; "Stone Cold Sober," 1973; "The Bitter Pill," 1973; "Another Fine Mess," 1973; "Judgment Day," 1973; "The Travelling Woman," 1973; "The Hammer of God," 1974; "The Actor and the Alibi," 1974; "The Eye of Apollo," 1974; "The Forbidden Garden," 1974; "The Three Tools of Death," 1974; "The Quick One," 1974; "The Little World of Don Camillo," BBC-TV, 1980.

Writer for television series "Saki," "Jezebel Ex-UK," "The Hidden Truth," "Undermind," "Blackmail," "Public Eye," "Simeon," "The Liars," "The Informer," "Out of the Unknown," "Conan Doyle," "Somerset Maugham," "The Sinners," "Me Mammy," "Tales From the Lazy Acre," "Pandora," "Sweeney," "Country Matters," and "Father Brown."

Author of column, "Hugh Leonard on Sunday," in *Sunday Independent Ireland*. Drama critic for *Plays and Players* magazine, 1964-72.

SIDELIGHTS: Jeremy Kingston called Byrne's play, "The Au Pair Man," a "witty social parable" in which the author pokes fun at the British. The comedy revolves around Mrs. Elizabeth Rogers, whose initials indicate she is a parody of Queen Elizabeth (Elizabeth Regina). Her poverty-stricken but royal residence is soon invaded by a gauche young Irish debt collector endeavoring to reclaim a wall-unit. Considering how valuable this unit is to her, Mrs. Rogers seduces the young man and gradually transforms him into a personage possessing social grace. A *Variety* critic noted that the play "shows the British Empire crumbling but defiantly clinging to its outworn past, arrogant, broke, but still loftily trying to ignore the new world and control 'the peasants.'" He added: "Some of Leonard's [Byrne's] dialog has the air of second-hand Oscar Wilde, but he provides . . . many splendid flights of fancy and airy persiflage."

A later play, "The Patrick Pearce Motel," met with an enthusiastic reception. Critics praised the work for its artful combination of farce and satire. A *Plays and Players* critic observed that the play "is both an act of conscious homage to Feydeau and a pungent, witty, acerbic attack on the Irish *nouveau riche*—in particular on their exploitation of their country's political and folk heritage as a tourist attraction." The two principle characters are prosperous Irish business partners whose new venture, a motel, has recently been constructed. In an effort to attract customers, the entrepreneurs name each room after a famed Irish hero. The story begins at the celebration of the motel's opening and rapidly becomes a farcical comedy of misunderstanding and sexual innuendo involving the businessmen, their discontented wives, a rambunctious television personality, the nymphomaniac motel manager, and the night watchman. *Stage*'s R. B. Marriott hailed Byrne's efforts, asserting that while he "creates vivid personalities among his bizarre characters, he also creates strong, smoothly progressive farcical situations with rich trimmings." Marriott continued that Byrne's "wit can be sharp, his humour splendidly roudy [sic]."

The author's next play received rave reviews and won several drama awards. "Da" is an autobiographical comedy-drama about a bereaved son, Charlie, on his return to Ireland and the scene of his boyhood. Charlie's father, Da, has recently died and the son tries to exorcise himself of the painful memory of his parent while sitting in his father's vacant cottage discarding old papers. Da returns, however, in the form of a ghost, and the father and son remember the past together. "'Da' is a beguiling play about a son's need to come to terms with his father—and with himself," disclosed Mel Gussow of the *New York Times*. "Warmly but unsentimentally, it concerns itself with paternity, adolescence, the varieties of familial love and the tricks and distortions of memory." He concluded that "'Da' is a humane and honest memory play in which, with great affection and humor, we are invited to share the life of a family." Similarly complimentary, John Simon of *New York* remarked: "A charming, mellow, saucy, and bittersweet boulevard comedy, but from a boulevard whose dreams are not entirely housebroken and have a bit of untamable Hiberian wilderness left fluttering in them."

Byrne told *CA*: "I am not an Irish writer, but a writer who happens to be Irish. This is not hair-splitting: I find that the former is usually categorized as someone who writes quaint, charming, witty, idiomatic dialogue, but whose work has no real validity outside of Ireland. The people I write about are those in the small seaside town I was born in and in which I now live, ten miles from Dublin. I use them as a means of exploring myself, which is what I believe writing is about. I usually pick an emotional or biological crossroads: the realization of middle age ('Summer'), the death of a parent ('Da'), or the onset of death ('A Life'). The themes are weighty, but I treat them in terms of comedy—serious comedy, that is. I write without knowing where I am going; it is a journey for me as well as the audience, and I write about recognizable human beings. If a play of mine does not evoke recognition in Buffalo, Liverpool, Lille, or Melbourne, then it is an utter failure. I try not to repeat myself; life is too short to chew the same cabbage twice. I think that basically I am that unfashionable thing: an optimist. My work says that life may be bad, but we can change it by changing ourselves, and of course my best play is always the next one."

CA INTERVIEW

John Keyes Byrne was interviewed by phone on May 13, 1980, while at his home in Dalkey, Ireland.

CA: You began writing professionally when you were in your early thirties?

BYRNE: In 1959, so I would have been thirty-two.

CA: Was your writing a clean break from the work you were doing with the civil service?

BYRNE: Yes, it was a clean break. I'd been writing during my time with the civil service: I'd done four plays that were professionally produced, and I was doing some radio soap opera at the time. I went over to Granada Television, which is an independent company in Manchester, and I worked there for two years as story editor. But in the meantime I was still doing one play a year for the Dublin Theatre Festival.

CA: How did the television job open up?

BYRNE: Somebody came over to Dublin to see a play of mine called "A Walk on the Water" and asked me to drop in when I was in London. When I was in London a couple of months later, they said, "Look, why don't you come work for us?" I thought that would be a good idea; it would give me some training in television. So I went over to them for two years. I commuted for the first year, flying home at weekends. Then for the next seven years I went down to London and free-lanced.

CA: You've written television scripts, screenplays, stage plays, drama criticism, essays, autobiography. Do you prefer one kind of writing to the others?

BYRNE: I think basically I prefer writing for the theatre. I'd like to try a novel, which I haven't done yet.

CA: Are you working on that, or is it something for the future?

BYRNE: No; at the moment I'm trying to give myself a couple of months off. I'm sort of waiting for something to happen, in the sense that I'm going to start something major in the next two months, but I'm not sure whether it will be a play or a novel.

CA: Do you have any problem switching from one kind of writing to another?

BYRNE: Basically it's all writing. It's just that I find narrative prose, as I did in my autobiography, a whole new ball game. It took me a long time to get into it, to get used to the freedom that narrative gives you against the tightness of theatre. You know, if you've been writing to a particular discipline for many years, it's very difficult suddenly to relax and realize that you can write about whatever you like at any length you like.

CA: What are your writing habits?

BYRNE: What I'm inclined to do usually is to work from about half-one of the day until about 5:30; then I start again at half-eleven at night and work until about 3:15.

CA: You sound like a night person.

BYRNE: It's not really that. It's because the edge goes off after four hours. I find that it helps to rest and renew myself. So it's a question of living twelve-hour days rather than twenty-four-hour days.

CA: You've said that a play takes you a long time to write and that your methods involve "various subterranean levels." Could you elaborate on that?

BYRNE: I didn't mean to say that it took me a long time to write. I think what happens is it's a long time in one's subconscious mind before the writing starts. And I never know where I'm going when I start. But I write very tightly—I don't do drafts. I do a page over and over, and if I finish a page today, that's finished. I find that if you write in this particular way, what happens is that quite subconsciously there are sublevels in your work, and that these usually pop up on reading or, more especially, in performance. So that kind of writing gives you a multistrata thing, a kind of depth.

CA: Are there any dramatists who have influenced your work?

BYRNE: I think early on Kaufman and Hart, who were brilliant technicians. They taught me a great deal about technique. And of course being Irish, I was influenced early on by O'Casey.

CA: What about writers other than dramatists?

BYRNE: None, really. When I did my autobiography, I felt that my book might be very close to Frank O'Connor's book *An Only Child,* so I very deliberately veered away from his style and his kind of mood. I didn't want my book to seem like an echo of it. Generally one uses other writers in that way: you say, "I admire that book, therefore I musn't fall into the trap of being influenced by it."

CA: You have commented that playwriting in Ireland these days is not in a very good state. Do you have any favorites among Irish playwrights writing now, or playwrights from any country?

BYRNE: I think that Alan Ayckbourn is quite a brilliant writer, but I think he'll probably be written out quite soon, because he's writing up a one-way street. I think the best contemporary playwright alive is Beckett, certainly. There are very few of us Irish playwrights, and I think this is because we have such a small theatre-going population that it's very, very difficult for any playwright to write professionally here. He must be sure his work is done outside the country, if he's to live by it. This is why most of our playwrights are part-timers; they don't really have a chance to develop their work, doing a job for most of the day.

CA: Your plays have been produced in Dublin, London, New York, Washington. How do the audiences differ in each country?

BYRNE: They only differ in one significance: the Dublin audiences are inclined to laugh more. They seem to like to laugh. Outside Dublin the plays seem to get a kind of uniform reaction. In London an Irish play is regarded as slightly parochial. This doesn't happen in America. My play "Summer," which opens Off-Broadway in September [1980], was produced in Philadelphia and in Olney, outside Washington, D.C. It got exactly the same marvelous reaction in both places. In fact, we did quite a business. It was very enjoyable for me to see the same reaction, to see that I wasn't writing a parochial play—it meant as much to a non-Irish audience.

CA: Do you think the London audiences are warming up to your writing?

BYRNE: Well, there's no such thing really, basically, as a London audience. But my last play, "A Life," which I think is due on Broadway in October [1980], was put on for a limited season in the Old Vic by the Abbey Theatre, and we packed the house. We've picked up an award for it, in fact—it's the first of the Irish version of the Tonys. It was very encouraging to see these particular London audiences loving the play. I don't honestly know how it would have run if it had moved into the West End; that's usually a different

kettle of fish. The audiences are very cosmopolitan there, and they usually like plays about cities, or plays which are catered to them.

CA: How do you feel about theatre in the United States?

BYRNE: I don't know enough about it, really. I think it's terrifically healthy in a way. It's unfortunate that there's a kind of snobbish division made between Broadway, Off-Broadway, and Off-Off-Broadway. And also there's the feeling that all the writing talent is bounded by the East River and the Hudson River. So if you do a play in Olney, say, or in Chicago, and it gets rave notices, it's almost impossible to get a producer to come down from New York to see the play. Their attitude is, "When it gets to New York, I'll have a look at it." The standard of production and acting is quite superb. I suppose this can't be helped, but there's the old thing of the *New York Times* controlling, even though they might not want to, the public reaction to a play; if you get a bad notice in the *New York Times,* you really may close down. The people don't seem to go along of their own accord; they take the notice at its face value. They go if it's a rave, and they don't go if it's a bad notice.

CA: How much have you been involved in the actual stage productions of your plays in the United States?

BYRNE: I try to keep out of it. I think the real trick is picking a sympathetic cast and a good director. My feeling is that I know my job and I let him get along with his. I'm always available if there's a question of interpretation of a line; if there's an ambiguity, I'm certainly happy to clear it up. But I like to leave them to get on with it and do their own thing without being bothered by me.

CA: Have you been disappointed in any of the productions?

BYRNE: Very rarely; only a couple of times, I think. There was a production of "Da" in London which was directed by an actor. I feel that, with rare exceptions, actors don't make great directors, because they're inclined to indulge in a kind of love affair with the others and not pass on any notes; and this was what happened in this case in London. The performance just went over the top, and the whole thing was rather painful. But generally speaking, I've been very lucky. I've been working with very talented people.

CA: Have you been actively involved in the productions of your television scripts?

BYRNE: There's much more a sense of collaboration in a television thing, because it's much more mechanical. You go along to a read-through to see if you are overlength or if there are scenes that are not particularly working. In the latter case, you rewrite to a greater extent because you're crafting rather than writing. So it's more or less actors, director, designer, script editor, writer all mucking in together.

CA: You won several top awards in the United States for "Da." Was there a lot of personal response to the play, letters from people who really liked it?

BYRNE: People hardly ever write to a playwright. They write to you if you write a book—a book's a private experience. I think I've only had about four letters out of "Da." This is quite exceptionally high for stage writing. The main response was here, because the play had been existing here for three or four years before it went on; and suddenly the reaction was that I was a much better playwright than I had been a fortnight ago.

CA: Did you get a lot of personal response to Home Before Night?

BYRNE: Yes. Not from America yet, because it's only out a couple of weeks. But I've had many letters saying thank you and it's a lovely book; people saying, I can find echoes of my own growing up in your book.

CA: Why do you choose to write under a pseudonym?

BYRNE: I sent a play to the Abbey many years ago when I was a beginner, a play called "The Italian Road," and the Abbey turned it down. It was for a play competition. Then I got married, and my wife suggested that I send in an earlier play called "The Big Birthday." I don't know why, but out of a whim I took the name of the hero of "The Italian Road," a fellow called Hughie Leonard, and I stuck it onto the script. It was accepted and I got rather superstitious about it. By then things had got rather involved, and I was unable really to drop the name. I never really wanted it; I just did it as a gag.

CA: I've read that you don't particularly even like it.

BYRNE: I don't like the name Hugh. I'm usually known as Jack Leonard.

CA: You did the play "Stephen D" about the young James Joyce. Was Joyce an early love?

BYRNE: He never was really a love. I admired him very much, and I thought that would be a good vehicle for an actor friend of mine called Norman Rodway. I studied *A Portrait of the Artist as a Young Man* and *Stephen Hero* for about four months, and then I sat down and wrote the play in three weeks. There's nothing of me in it, because there's hardly a word that isn't Joyce's. But unfortunately it gave me the reputation here of being an adapter of other people's work. I like adapting, but I eventually had to give it up, because I had quite a fight to become accepted as a playwright in my own right. I enjoy adapting. When you finish a play, you've got to lie fallow for a while, and adapting isn't using the same juices, as it were; it's a completely different kettle of fish. Rather than sitting around the house, you can fill in the time adapting and do it quite well. But I don't usually do it except for a television thing every year, because it's too easy to do and there's always this danger that one is accepted as a kind of artisan rather than as an artist.

CA: You've adapted for television Joyce, Dickens, Emily Bronte, Flaubert, Dostoevsky, and other serious writers. How do you approach real literature to serialize it for television?

BYRNE: I think first you have to be able to look at it and say, "I wish I'd written that." Then you must ask yourself the question if it will adapt; not all great literature will adapt for television. Then you try to write it as if the author had written it for television in the first place. I think you must honor the writer's story and the writer's intentions. I don't believe in changing an author's work.

CA: What are the greatest difficulties in adapting the work of such writers for television or the stage?

BYRNE: It changes from writer to writer. Emily Bronte's *Wuthering Heights* is very difficult because of the texture of the book. Dickens is very easy because he depends a great deal on dialogue. The main difficulty, I think, when you're approached in the first instance, is to be sure that you've got the right number of chapters, that you're not stretching the book and making it flatter and, on the other hand, that you're

not compressing it to the point where you leave out things that should really be in the script.

CA: Are you still writing drama criticism?

BYRNE: Not really criticism, no. I gave that up because it became a question of dog eating dog. I still do my column for the *Sunday Independent of Ireland.* It's a column of general comment, satirical.

CA: Does the critical approach differ among the countries your work has appeared in?

BYRNE: The approach is a bit different between England and America. In America they have all this space to write in, and so many pressures: they have pressures for quotes and such things. They're all invisible pressures, such as producers and deadlines. This is not quite so important in England. Criticism in England is less polarized. In America the show is terrible or it's great—there's not much in between. In England it's much more careful. It's not as good reading, but it's probably fairer to the play.

CA: You've said that your best play is always your next one. Leaving your next one out, which of your plays do you like the best?

BYRNE: I'm of two minds, because I've always regarded "Summer" as my best play. But people have been telling me that "A Life" is. I finished writing "A Life" last September only four days before it went into rehearsal, so I haven't really been able to stand back and take a decent look at it yet. It's a more considerable play than "Summer." I still don't know if "Summer" is the better play or not.

CA: How does "A Life" differ from Home Before Night?

BYRNE: *Home Before Night* is biography, autobiography. "A Life" is not autobiography at all. There is a character in it called Drum who appears in *Home Before Night,* and he also appears in "Da" in a minor role. He was my boss; he was a man called Mulligan in the civil service when I worked there. He had a wife and two daughters, and that was all I knew. I knew what *kind* of man he was, but I didn't know the facts of his life. So I invented a kind of life for him, and I set it on the day before "Da" takes place. All the other characters there are quite fictitious, so it really doesn't compare at all with *Home Before Night.*

CA: What prompted your move from England back to Ireland?

BYRNE: We have this tax-exemption law for writers living and working in Ireland, exemption from income tax. It meant that instead of working for television so much in England, which is a bit of a treadmill, I was able to come back here, earn less money, and concentrate largely on theatre. So I only do one large television undertaking a year. For example, I've just finished "The Little World of Don Camillo" for the BBC; that's my television chore for this year. So I'm able actually to concentrate on what I want to do now. The financial element of it enabled me to do what I want to do. It wasn't to earn more money; it was because by earning less I could live properly.

CA: You're living now very close to where you grew up, aren't you?

BYRNE: Yes, I'm about two hundred yards away. I'm sitting in a room at the moment that looks out on the sea, which is twenty-five yards away, and an island opposite it; and about sixty miles away, out of sight, is Wales.

CA: That sounds like several scenes from Home Before Night.

BYRNE: I'm living at the harbor in which the father tried to drown the dog in *Home Before Night;* that's what I'm over-looking.

CA: What prompted you to move to that particular place?

BYRNE: We like the sea, my wife and I, and we don't like living in a city. We decided that we'd live either south of Dublin or north, and we just rooted around for a house. Eventually we found a house, and it just happened to be in a place we like. Lots of the people we know I grew up with or I was friends with in the civil service, and they live around here. So it suits us very well.

CA: Do you find that your goals are changing as you write more, or as you get older?

BYRNE: I don't really have a particular goal apart from the work in hand. I think it's very pretentious to think of work in the long range. What I try to do is not start a job unless I feel I've absolutely got to do it. I think the compulsion gives value to the work. Then you've got anything between three to six months of very difficult work on your play, and that's enough to look forward to. When you're writing it, you look forward to the day you finish it; and when it's finished, you look forward to the day you write something else.

CA: You've mentioned that you'd like to do a novel. Is there any other kind of work you haven't tried that you'd like to try?

BYRNE: Not in terms of writing, there isn't. I'd like to do a couple more plays. I *would* like to try a novel, and that's quite a challenge, because I haven't done it.

CA: Do you think you'll ever want to stop writing and do something else?

BYRNE: I would hope not, because I really don't have any-thing else I want to do full time. I have a boat which is in the middle of Ireland on the river Shannon. We visit that at weekends. It's a seven-berth cruiser. That much for leisure. But if I stopped writing, I'd say I would be very, very bored.

CA: You're careful not to be categorized as an Irish writer. Would you comment on that?

BYRNE: The general concept of Ireland is of either a rather O'Casey world of picturesque slums and swirling fogs and the "Troubles," or else it's a very pastoral scene, all thatched cottages and colorful peasants—"Quiet Man"-ish. I think this is what many Americans come over expecting to find. There *was* an element of truth in this, and now we're turning into—outside Dublin, anyway—a great conurbation which isn't so different from an American or an English city, with our industries. And we watch television a lot, and we've got this completely new way of life. It's a very drastic change in one generation from a spiritual, intensely Catholic kind of life. Suburbia, in the American sense, as we have it here, is a very new thing. Most of my plays are caught up in

this dichotomy between past and present—people with one leg in one kind of world and another foot in another. I like to write about people in the changing society and the problems they go through. So I'm not really an Irish writer; I'm an Irishman who happens to write plays.

BIOGRAPHICAL/CRITICAL SOURCES: Variety, April 30, 1969; *Punch,* April 30, 1969; *Stage,* June 10, 1971, June 24, 1971; *Observer Review,* June 20, 1971; *Plays and Players,* August, 1971; *New York Theatre Annual,* Volume 2, Gale, 1978; *New York,* April 10, 1978; *New York Times,* March 14, 1978, May 2, 1978, May 14, 1978, November 10, 1978, March 25, 1979, April 23, 1980; *Washington Post,* June 6, 1978.

—*Interview by Cynthia H. Rogers and Jean W. Ross*

*   *   *

BYRNE, Stuart J(ames)   1913-
(Rothayne Amare, John Bloodstone)

PERSONAL: Born October 26, 1913, in St. Paul, Minn.; son of Christopher J. (in advertising) and Grace H. (McLean) Byrne; married Joey A. Adamo, September, 1935; children: Joanne R., Richard I. *Education:* Received B.A. and M.A. from University of California, Los Angeles. *Address:* 19414 Joan Leigh Dr., Spring, Tex. 77373. *Agent:* Forrest J. Ackerman, Ackerman Sci-Fi Agency, 2495 Glendower Ave., Hollywood, Calif. 90027.

CAREER: Douglas Aircraft Co., Santa Monica, Calif., special assistant to manufacturing manager, 1940-43; Pan American-Grace Airways, Lima, Peru, systems store manager, 1943-47; Brown Pacific-Maxon, Guam, administrative assistant, 1948-50; Adamo Co., Los Angeles, Calif., purchasing agent, merchandise manager, and presidential staff assistant, 1950-57; screenwriter and producer in Hollywood, Calif., 1957-59; Engineering Industries, Hollywood, senior writer, 1959-61; Lehigh Engineering, Denver, Colo., chief writer, 1961; Litton Industries, Data Systems Division, Van Nuys, Calif., senior project engineer and materials control manager, 1961-67; Scientific Data Systems, El Segundo, Calif., materials control manager, 1967-68; Litton Industries, Data Systems Division, member of administrative staff, 1968-69, senior engineering writer, 1977-78; writer, 1969—. *Member:* Science Fiction Writers of America, Writers Guild of America (West), American Federation of Astrologers.

WRITINGS—Science fiction novels, except as noted: *God Man,* Powell, 1970; *Ambush Country,* Powell, 1970; *The Alpha Trap,* Major, 1976; (under pseudonym Rothayne Amare) *The Visitation* (gothic novel), Major, 1977.

"Star Man" series; all under pseudonym John Bloodstone; published by Major, except as noted: *Thundar: Man of Two Worlds,* Leisure Books, 1971; *Superman of Alpha,* 1977; *Interstellar Mutineers,* 1977; *The Cosmium Raiders,* 1977; *Slaves of Venus,* 1977; *Lost in the Milky Way,* 1977.

Author of screenplays, including "The Deserter," "The Doomsday Machine," "Monster in My Blood," and "Journey Into Fear." Contributor to magazines, including *Amazing Stories, Other Worlds, Authentic Science Fiction,* and *Science Stories.*

WORK IN PROGRESS: World's Answer, three volumes; *Star Quest,* a science-fiction novel.

C

CAHALAN, (John) Don(ald) 1912-

PERSONAL: Born October 3, 1912, in Lewistown, Mont.; son of Daniel Emmett and Emma Cecelia (Robinson) Cahalan; married Ellen Margaret Johnson, August 18, 1933; children: Carolyn Jane (Mrs. Richard N. Cooper), Michael D. *Education:* Iowa State University, B.A., 1937, M.A., 1938; George Washington University, Ph.D., 1968. *Home:* 1338 Grizzly Peak Blvd., Berkeley, Calif. 94708.

CAREER: University of Denver, Denver, Colo., associate professor of psychology and social science, 1946-49, director of Opinion Research Center, 1947-49; U.S. Army, civilian director of attitude assessment in Germany and Washington, D.C., 1949-52; director of national surveys for government agencies and businesses in Washington, D.C., and New York City, 1952-57; W.R. Simmons & Associates, New York City, chief project director, 1957-59; ARB Surveys, Inc., New York City, president, 1959-62; Nowland & Co., Greenwich, Conn., executive vice-president, 1962-64; George Washington University, Washington, D.C., program director of social research group working on alcohol studies, 1964-70; University of California, Berkeley, adjunct professor, 1970-72, professor of behavioral sciences, 1972-78, director of social research group at School of Public Health, 1970-78, professor emeritus, 1978—. Visiting scholar at University of Hawaii, 1978-79. Member of Denver mayor's Commission on Human Relations, 1947-48. Survey research consultant. *Military service:* U.S. Naval Reserve, active duty, 1943-46; became lieutenant junior grade.

MEMBER: American Psychological Association, American Sociological Association, American Public Health Association, American Association for Public Opinion Research, Society for the Psychological Study of Social Issues, Society for the Study of Social Problems, Sigma Xi. *Awards, honors:* National Institute of Mental Health grant, 1970.

WRITINGS: (With Ira H. Cisin and Helen M. Crossley) *American Drinking Practices,* Center for Alcohol Studies, Rutgers University, 1969; *Problem Drinkers: A National Survey,* Jossey-Bass, 1970; (with Robin Room) *Problem Drinking Among American Men,* Center for Alcohol Studies, Rutgers University, 1974. Contributor to professional journals.

WORK IN PROGRESS: The Sure Cure, a satirical novel; *Striking It Poor,* a biographical novel about his Irish ancestors in Ireland and the United States.

SIDELIGHTS: Cahalan told *CA:* "My writings thus far have been primarily for the purpose of presenting and interpreting the result of quantitative national surveys on human behavior, attitudes, and aspirations on a wide variety of subject matters, including intergroup and race relations, issues of national policy, and health issues. I hope that in my writings on the topic of drinking behavior and problems (the work for which I am probably best known), I have made some contribution toward a more complete understanding (a) that environmental factors such as sex, age, ethnic background, and socio-economic status are generally much more influential in determining adjustment to behavioral norms than are such primarily individual factors as personality and heredity; and (b) that habits of healthy or unhealthy living related to the use of alcohol, drugs, tobacco, and to nutrition, exercise, and rest and recreation are highly interrelated. As such, health-related human behaviors should be studied together rather than singly.

"While I am very grateful for the substantial support for alcohol studies by the National Institute on Alcohol Abuse and Alcoholism over a good many years, I would hope that the future funding of research in the behavioral sciences will encourage dealing with a broader range of behavioral problems in each study. Congress and the federal bureaucracy has tended to divide the behavioral world into separate compartments—for example, one compartment for alcohol studies and a completely separate one for drug studies—because this tactic makes it easier to find funding through appealing for the support of special-interest lobbies whose interests tend to be narrow. I think that only a strong counter-lobbying effort on the part of professional societies can reverse this trend toward overspecialization in governmentally-funded behavioral science research, so that future years will see more studies of a wide range of human behaviors within an integrated framework. For if it is true in biology that 'de neck-bone is connected to de back-bone,' the behaviors of the human organism should also be studied so as to recognize the interdependence of our health-related habits and attitudes."

*   *   *

CAHILL, Kevin Michael 1936-

PERSONAL: Born May 6, 1936, in New York, N.Y.; son of John D. and Genevieve (Campion) Cahill; married Kathryn McGinity, March 4, 1961; children: Kevin Michael, Sean C.,

Christopher P., Brendan H., Denis D. *Education:* Fordham University, A.B. (cum laude), 1957; Cornell University, M.D., 1961; University of London, diploma in tropical medicine and hygiene, 1963. *Office:* 850 Fifth Ave., New York, N.Y. 10021.

CAREER: St. Vincent's Hospital, New York City, intern, 1961-62; U.S. Naval Medical Research Unit, Cairo, Egypt, director of tropical medicine, 1963-65; private practice of tropical medicine in New York City, 1965—. Diplomate of American Board of Preventive Medicine and American Board of Microbiology. Lecturer at University of Cairo and University of Alexandria, 1963-65; associate professor at New York Medical College, 1965—, director of its Tropical Disease Center, 1966—; professor and director of tropical medicine at Royal College of Surgeons, Dublin, Ireland, 1969—; professor at New Jersey College of Medicine, 1974—. Member of attending staff at Lenox Hill Hospital and Flower Fifth Avenue Hospital; member of scientific advisory board of American Foundation for Tropical Medicine, 1966—; chairman of New York State Health Planning Commission and Health Research Council, 1975—; consultant to U.S. Public Health Service and International Longshoremans Association. *Military service:* U.S. Naval Reserve, active duty, 1963-65.

MEMBER: American College of Chest Physicians (fellow), American College of Preventive Medicine (fellow), American Public Health Association, American Society of Tropical Medicine and Hygiene, American Irish Historical Society, Royal Society of Tropical Medicine and Hygiene, New York Society of Tropical Medicine, Friendly Sons of Saint Patrick, Knights of Malta.

WRITINGS: Tropical Diseases in Temperate Climates, Lippincott, 1964; *Health on the Horn of Africa: A Study of the Major Diseases of Somalia,* Spottiswoode, Ballantyne, 1969; *Medical Advice for the Traveler,* Holt, 1970; (editor) *Symposia in Clinical Tropical Medicine,* Tropical Disease Center, New York Medical College, 1970; *The Untapped Resource: Medicine and Diplomacy,* Orbis, 1971; *Clinical Tropical Medicine,* Volume I: *Schistomiasis, Hepatitis: American Contributions to Tropical Medicine,* Volume II: *Malaria, Amebiasis, Cholera,* University Park Press, 1972; *Teaching Tropical Medicine,* University Park Press, 1973; (editor) *Health and Development,* Orbis, 1976; *Tropical Diseases: A Handbook for Practitioners,* Technomic, 1976; *Health in New York State: A Progress Report,* Health Education Services, 1977; *Irish Essays,* John Jay Press, 1980; *Somalia: A Perspective,* State University of New York Press, 1980. Contributor to medical journals.

BIOGRAPHICAL/CRITICAL SOURCES: New York, July 24, 1978.*

*   *   *

CALKIN, Ruth Harms   1918-

PERSONAL: Born August 16, 1918, in McClusky, N.D.; daughter of Abraham John (a Baptist minister and professor) and Luella (Paul) Harms; married Rollin Calkin (a Baptist minister), September 3, 1944. *Education:* Attended Linfield College, 1938-39, and University of Oregon, 1940. *Politics:* Republican. *Religion:* Baptist. *Home and office:* 1539 Ganesha Pl., Pomona, Calif. 91768.

CAREER: Commercial Credit Corp., Eugene, Ore., secretary, 1941; piano teacher, composer, and author of hymns in Eugene and Pomona, Calif., 1945-75; writer, 1975—. Substitute teacher at public schools in Eugene, 1945-46.

WRITINGS: I Know a Joy (religious songs), Harmony House, 1952; (with husband, Rollin Calkin) *Just for Today With Kandy Kaye* (poems and cartoons), Harmony House, 1955; *Tell Me Again, Lord, I Forget,* David Cook, 1974; *Lord, You Love to Say Yes,* David Cook, 1976; *Two Shall Be One,* David Cook, 1977; *Lord, I Keep Running Back to You,* Tyndale, 1979; *Love Is So Much More, Lord: A Celebration of Marriage,* David Cook, 1979; *Lord, Could You Hurry a Little?* (prayers and poems), Tyndale, 1981. Co-author of musical plays for local churches.

WORK IN PROGRESS: An autobiography tentatively entitled *Because of God,* publication by Tyndale expected in 1982.

SIDELIGHTS: Ruth Calkin wrote that her books are collections of "private dialogues with God," reflections on daily living dealing with the everyday experiences of men and women, Christian and non-Christian alike. She began her collections when she was still a child, in a notebook she called "God's Secrets." She continued writing songs and letters as a teenager, from a sanitarium where she was recovering from tuberculosis.

BIOGRAPHICAL/CRITICAL SOURCES: Today's Christian Women, fall, 1980.

*   *   *

CALLADINE, Andrew G(arfield)   1941-

PERSONAL: Born April 6, 1941, in Toronto, Ontario, Canada; came to the United States in 1964; son of Andrew (in business) and Audrey (Phillips) Calladine; married Carole Ingraham (a social worker and writer), May 29, 1967; children: Patrick, Gregory, Michael, Brendan. *Education:* Assumption University, Windsor, Ontario, B.A., 1964; Case Western Reserve University, M.S.S.A., 1966. *Home:* 17400 Hilliard Rd., Lakewood, Ohio 44107. *Agent:* Rhoda A. Weyr, William Morris Agency, 1350 Avenue of the Americas, New York, N.Y. 10019. *Office:* Center for Human Services, 3929 Rockey River Dr., Cleveland, Ohio.

CAREER: Cleveland Christian Home, Cleveland, Ohio, supervisor of group work program, 1966-78; Center for Human Services, Cleveland, administrator of community aftercare program, 1978—. Assistant hockey coach at high school in Lakewood, Ohio. Member of board of trustees of Kamm's Area Development Corp.; chairman of Lakewood mayor's advisory committee on youth. *Member:* National Association of Social Workers (member of board of directors, 1970), Academy of Accredited Social Workers.

WRITINGS: (With wife, Carole Calladine) *Raising Siblings,* Delacorte, 1979. Contributor to *Family Circle.*

SIDELIGHTS: Calladine wrote: "Essentially, I attempt to maintain a balanced lifestyle—my family, my self, and my work all receiving attention. Early on, in order to survive with four active, growing sons, my wife and I determined that our lifestyle would be one of sharing—sharing the parenting role and sharing the work. That has proven to be a satisfying way of life for all concerned.

"Our writing developed from our shared interest in and concern for families—ours and others'. My wife is the true writer. I'm the talker. We make a great team, and together we hope to write, teach, talk, and experience family-life education for many years to come. Together we're committed to our sons and the sons and daughters of others. We feel we have helpful, practical suggestions to give to others and will do so, while still having time for our family, each other, and ourselves."

CALLADINE, Carole E(lizabeth)   1942-

PERSONAL: Born May 21, 1942, in Clinton, Iowa; daughter of John Robert (a principal) and Naomi (a teacher; maiden name, Thuresson) Ingraham; married Andrew Garfield Calladine (a social worker and writer), May 20, 1967; children: Patrick, Gregory, Michael, Brendan. *Education:* University of Iowa, B.A. (with honors), 1964; Case Western Reserve University, M.S.S.A., 1966. *Religion:* Protestant. *Home and office:* 17400 Hilliard Rd., Lakewood, Ohio 44107. *Agent:* Rhoda A. Weyr, William Morris Agency, 1350 Avenue of the Americas, New York, N.Y. 10019.

CAREER: Lake County Mental Health Center, Mentor, Ohio, psychiatric social worker, 1966-68; Center for Human Services, Cleveland, Ohio, social worker and coordinator of West Site's family-life education program, 1973-79; private practice of social work, specializing in family counseling and parenting workshops, in Lakewood, Ohio, 1979—. Part-time teacher at local community college, 1973-79. *Member:* Academy of Accredited Social Workers, Westshore Writers Club.

WRITINGS: (With husband, Andrew G. Calladine) *Raising Siblings,* Delcorte, 1979. Contributor to magazines, including *Family Circle, True Romance, Essence, Parents' Magazine, Lady's Circle,* and *Lutheran Women.*

WORK IN PROGRESS: A second book on parenting.

SIDELIGHTS: Carole Calladine wrote: "Parenting is important work. It requires discipline, skill, love, and humor. As a mother of four sons, I feel the love and humor wane when skill and discipline are in short supply. *Raising Siblings* is a combination of what I have learned personally as a parent and professionally as a counselor leading parent education groups. Hopefully, this book passes along parenting skills and an understanding of children and sibling rivalry to parents. My husband and I wrote this book together, as we lead parenting groups together.'

*   *   *

CALLAHAN, Philip Serna   1923-

PERSONAL: Born August 29, 1923, in Fort Benning, Ga.; son of Eugene C. (a colonel) and Enid (Ainso) Callahan; married Winnie McGee, August 27, 1949; children: Catherine, Margaret Ann, Kevin, Colette. *Education:* University of Arkansas, B.A. and M.S., 1953; Kansas State College of Agriculture and Applied Science (now Kansas State University), Ph.D., 1956. *Office:* University of Florida, Gainesville, Fla. 32604.

CAREER: Louisiana State University, Baton Rouge, 1956-63, began as assistant professor, became associate professor of entomology; Southern Grain Insects Research Lab, Agricultural Research Service, Tifton, Ga., entomologist, 1962-69; University of Georgia, Tifton, professor of entomology, 1963-69; entomologist at University of Florida, Gainesville, and U.S. Department of Agriculture Behavior and Basic Biology Research Lab. Insect Attractants, Gainesville, 1969—. *Member:* Entomological Society of America, American Ornithological Union, North American Falconers Association, New York Academy of Sciences, Explorers Club (fellow).

WRITINGS—Nonfiction: *Insect Behavior* (juvenile; self-illustrated), Four Winds Press, 1970; *Insects and How They Function* (juvenile; self-illustrated), Holiday House, 1971; *The Evolution of Insects* (juvenile; self-illustrated), Holiday House, 1972; *The Magnificent Birds of Prey* (juvenile), Holiday House, 1974; *Bird Behavior* (juvenile), Four Winds Press, 1975; *Tuning in to Nature: Solar Energy, Infrared Radiation and the Insect Communication,* Devin-Adair,

1975; *Birds and How They Function* (juvenile), Holiday House, 1979; *The Soul of the Ghost Moth* (autobiography), Devin-Adair, 1980; *Exploring the Spectrum,* Devin-Adair, in press. Also author of *Insect Molecular Bioelectronics,* for Entomological Society of America, 1967, and other reports for governmental agencies and national organizations.

WORK IN PROGRESS: The Mysterious Round Towers of Ireland.

SIDELIGHTS: Callahan told *CA:* "I have demonstrated in scientific journals that organic molecules are stimulated to emit low energy infrared maser energy and that such frequencies are probably the communication system of life."

A member of the North American Falconers Association, Callahan is a master falconer.

BIOGRAPHICAL/CRITICAL SOURCES: Philip Serna Callahan, *The Soul of the Ghost Moth,* Devin-Adair, 1980.

*   *   *

CAMERON, Allan Gillies   1930-

PERSONAL: Born in 1930, in Kuala Lumpur, Malaysia; son of Donald (an iron foundry manager) and Kathleen (Bradshaw) Cameron; married Heather Cocks (a ward sister), March 21, 1964; children: Ruth, Anne. *Education:* University of St. Andrews, B.Sc., 1951. *Home:* 2 Beauchamp Rd., Solihull B91 2BX, England.

CAREER: Huddersfield College of Technology, Huddersfield, England, assistant lecturer in chemistry, 1954-58; College of Technology, Kingston-on-Thames, England, lecturer in chemistry, 1958-63; National College of Food Technology, Weybridge, England, lecturer in food science and chemistry, 1963-70; College of Food and Domestic Arts, Birmingham, England, head of department of applied sciences and food technology, 1970-78; elder of local church in Solihull, England, 1978—. *Military service:* Royal Air Force, 1951-54; served as flying officer. *Member:* Royal Institute of Chemistry (fellow), Institute of Food Science and Technology (fellow).

WRITINGS: (With Brian Anthony Fox) *A Chemical Approach to Food and Nutrition,* Hodder & Stoughton, 1961, 2nd edition published as *Food Science: A Chemical Approach,* 1970, 3rd edition, 1977; *Food and Its Functions,* Edward Arnold, 1964, new edition published as *The Science of Food and Cooking,* 1973, 2nd edition, 1978, tropical edition (with Yvonne Collymore), 1979; *Food: Facts and Fallacies,* Faber, 1971; (with Gordon Gerard Birch and Michael Spencer) *Food Science,* Pergamon, 1972, 2nd edition, 1977; (with Margaret Brown) *Experimental Cooking,* Edward Arnold, 1977; (with Ethel Chong) *Towards Understanding Food and Cooking,* Federal (Singapore), 1978.

WORK IN PROGRESS: Preparing a new edition of *Food Science* with a chemical approach.

SIDELIGHTS: Cameron told *CA:* "The general intention in all my writings has been to deal with the scientific aspects of food, diet, and cooking. The increasing public awareness of the relationship between diet and health has made this approach very topical and relevant. There is an increasing realization that many people are too fat and that obesity is a threat to health—hence the growing interest in dieting. The recent evidence linking diet with heart disease has encouraged a reappraisal of the place of animal fats in the diet. The harmfulness of an excessive intake of sugar and the effects of fiber in the diet are matters of current concern."

AVOCATIONAL INTERESTS: Music, walking.

CAMERON, Angus de Mille 1913-

PERSONAL: Born June 9, 1913, in Sussex Corner, New Brunswick, Canada; son of James Logan and Harriett Bernice (de Mille) Cameron; married Esther Cary Horner, November 9, 1942; children: Jean, Sheila, James, Bruce. *Education:* Attended University of New Brunswick; Acadia University, B.A., 1934; attended University of Chicago, 1935-37; Meadville Theological School, B.D., 1937. *Home:* Lochiel, Clifton Royal, New Brunswick, Canada E0G 1N0.

CAREER: Ordained Unitarian minister, 1937; pastor of churches in Dunkirk, N.Y., 1937-41, and Montreal, Quebec, 1941-59; First Unitarian Church of Philadelphia, Philadelphia, Pa., pastor, 1963-67; writer. Member of board of governors of Montreal Council of Social Agencies, 1942-46. *Member:* American Unitarian Association (Canadian member of board of directors; vice-president, 1948-51), Montreal Indoor Tennis Club, Riverside Country Club.

WRITINGS: Nightwatchers, Scholastic Book Services, 1971; (author of introduction) *The Magic of Owls,* Walker & Co., 1977.

Contributor to *Voices of Liberalism,* Volume I, 1947. Contributing editor of *Christian Register.*

AVOCATIONAL INTERESTS: Tennis, hunting, fishing.*

*　　*　　*

CAMP, Candace P(auline) 1949-
(Lisa Gregory, Kristin James)

PERSONAL: Born May 23, 1949, in Amarillo, Tex.; daughter of Grady W. (a newspaper business manager) and Lula Mae (Irons) Camp; married Pete Hopcus (a counselor), August 11, 1979. *Education:* Attended University of Texas, 1967-70; West Texas State University, B.A., 1971; University of North Carolina, J.D., 1977. *Politics:* Democrat. *Religion:* Roman Catholic. *Home and office:* 2714 Pecan Dr., Temple, Tex. 76501. *Agent:* Kathryne Walters, 1714 Church St., Rahway, N.J.

CAREER: Teacher at secondary public school in Eureka Springs, Ark., 1972-73; Wachovia Bank, Winston-Salem, N.C., administrative assistant in trust department, 1973-74; First City National Bank, Paris, Tex., lawyer in trust department, 1977-78; private practice of law in Paris, 1979; writer, 1979—. Actress and director in amateur theatre; member of board of directors of Paris Community Theatre. *Member:* Texas Bar Association.

WRITINGS—Novels; under pseudonym Lisa Gregory: *Bonds of Love,* Jove, 1978; *Rainbow Season,* Jove, 1979; *Analise,* Jove, 1981.

Under pseudonym Kristin James: *Windswept* (novel), Richard Gallen, 1981.

WORK IN PROGRESS: A sequel to *Windswept,* a contemporary romance novel, publication by Richard Gallen expected in 1982.

SIDELIGHTS: Candace Camp wrote: "Fantasy has been my mainstay since I was a child. I wrote my first book at age eleven, and the only time I did not write was when I taught school for a year. I wrote my first novel when I was in law school. My problem in writing was discipline, and I credit law school with giving me that. I then quit my law practice to write full time. I found that my practice did not allow enough time to write, and writing is my first love."

AVOCATIONAL INTERESTS: Live theatre, travel.

CAMP, Roderic (Ai) 1945-

PERSONAL: Born February 19, 1945, in Colfax, Wash.; son of Ortho O. (in small business) and Helen (a counselor; maiden name, Eknoyan) Camp; married Emily Ellen Morse (a librarian), October 1, 1966; children: Christopher, Alexander. *Education:* George Washington University, B.A., 1966, M.A., 1967; University of Arizona, Ph.D., 1970. *Home:* 1002 Monroe St., Pella, Iowa 50219. *Office:* Department of Political Science, Central College, Pella, Iowa 50219.

CAREER: Central College, Pella, Iowa, assistant professor, 1970-75, associate professor of political science, 1975—, chairman of department, 1973-76, 1980—, director of study program in Yucatan, Mexico, 1973, chairman of Council on International Programs, 1975-76, director of Latin American studies, 1976—, assistant to academic dean and director of institutional research, 1978-79. Visiting professor at Grand Valley State Colleges, 1974-75; visiting researcher at Centro de Estudios Internacionales, Colegio de Mexico, 1978; associate member of Center for Latin America, University of Wisconsin—Milwaukee, 1978—; professor at University of Arizona's program in Guadalajara, Mexico, summer, 1980, visiting professor at university, spring, 1981. *Military service:* U.S. Marine Corps, 1970; became sergeant.

MEMBER: Latin American Studies Association, American Historical Association (Conference on Latin America), Instituto Mexicano de Cultura, Midwest Association of Latin American Studies, Midwest Political Science Association (member of executive council, 1978-81), Rocky Mountain Council of Latin American Studies, North Central Council of Latin Americanists. *Awards, honors:* U.S. State Department scholar, 1971; National Science Foundation grant, 1974-75; American Philosophical Society grants for Mexico, 1974, 1975, 1980; National Endowment for the Humanities fellow, 1977; Earthwatch fellow in Peru, 1977; Fulbright-Hays grant for Mexico, 1978; grant from National Endowment for the Humanities and Iowa Humanities Board, 1979; University House fellow at University of Iowa, 1980.

WRITINGS: Latin American Civilization (textbook), Grand Valley State College, 1975; *Mexican Political Biographies, 1935-1975,* University of Arizona Press, 1976, revised edition, 1981; *The Role of Economists in Policy-Making: A Comparative Study of Mexico and the United States,* University of Arizona Press, 1977; (contributor) James W. Wilkie and Kenneth R. Ruddle, editors, *Quantitative Latin American Studies: Methods and Findings,* Volume VI, Latin American Center, University of California, Los Angeles, 1977; *Mexico's Leaders: Their Education and Recruitment,* University of Arizona Press, 1980.

In Spanish: *Politicos Mexicanos, 1935-1976: Diccionario Biografico* (title means "Mexican Politics: A Biographical Dictionary"), two volumes, Fondo para la Historia de las Ideas Revolucionarias, 1980; *La Formacion de un Politico: La Socializacion de los Functionarios Publicos en Mexico Post-Revolucionario* (title means "The Formation of a Politician: The Socialization of Public Men in Post Revolutionary Mexico"), Fondo de Cultura Economica, 1980. Also contributor to *Sociologia de la Paz y de la Guerra* (title means "The Sociology of Peace and War"), edited by Lucio Mendieta Nunez, 1979. Contributor of more than seventy articles, photographs, and reviews to education and Latin American studies journals.

WORK IN PROGRESS: A book on twentieth-century intellectual life in Mexico, publication expected in 1982.

SIDELIGHTS: Camp wrote: "I am interested in directing scholarly work to a much larger, non-scholarly audience. I have published numerous black-and-white photographs, and recently have begun to combine scholarly writing with photography.'' *Avocational interests:* Reading, sailing.

BIOGRAPHICAL/CRITICAL SOURCES: Excelsior, December 10, 1976, December 11, 1976; *El Sol de Mexico,* April 29, 1977; *Proceso,* May 15, 1978.

*   *   *

CAMPBELL, Carlos Cardozo 1937-

PERSONAL: Born July 19, 1937, in New York, N.Y.; son of Fred and Thelma (Waters) Campbell; married Sammie Marye Day, February 21, 1964; children: Kimberly Marie, Scott Kevin. *Education:* Michigan State University, B.S., 1959; U.S. Naval Postgraduate School, certificate in engineering science, 1965; Catholic University of America, M.C.R.P., 1968. *Home:* 11530 Links Dr., Reston, Va. 22070. *Office:* U.S. Department of Housing and Urban Development, 451 Seventh St., Room 7112, Washington, D.C. 22040.

CAREER: U.S. Navy, career officer. Worked as director of urban affairs of Corporation for Economics and Industrial Research, 1968-69; U.S. Department of Housing and Urban Development, Washington, D.C., special assistant to assistant secretary for metropolitan planning and development, 1969—. *Member:* American Society of Planning Officials, American Institute of Planners (associate).

WRITINGS: New Towns: Another Way to Live, Reston, 1976. Contributor to professional journals.

BIOGRAPHICAL/CRITICAL SOURCES: Contemporary Sociology, March, 1977.*

*   *   *

CAMPBELL, Maria 1940-

PERSONAL: Born in April, 1940, in Saskatchewan, Canada; married; children: four.

CAREER: Writer.

WRITINGS: Half-Breed (autobiography), Saturday Review Press, 1973; *People of the Buffalo,* Douglas & McIntyre, 1976; *Little Badger and the Fire Spirit,* McClelland & Stewart, 1977.

Author of "The Red Dress," a film released by National Film Board, 1977. Author of radio plays. Contributor to magazines, including *Maclean's,* and newspapers.*

*   *   *

CAMPBELL, Michael Mussen 1924-

PERSONAL: Born in 1924, in Dublin, Ireland; *Education:* Trinity College, Dublin, B.A. and B.L. *Office: Irish Times,* 39 Kendal St., London W.2, England.

CAREER: Writer. Worked for *Irish Times,* London, England.

WRITINGS: Peter Perry (novel), Heinemann, 1956, Orion Press, 1960; *Oh, Mary, This London* (novel), Heinemann, 1959, Orion Press, 1962; *Across the Water* (novel), Orion Press, 1961; *The Princess in England,* Orion Press, 1964; *Lord Dismiss Us,* Heinemann, 1967, Putnam, 1968; *Nothing Doing* (novel), Constable, 1970, Putnam, 1971. Contributor to magazines, including *Punch, Spectator,* and *Books and Bookmen,* and newspapers.*

*   *   *

CAMPBELL, Patrick Gordon 1913-1980

OBITUARY NOTICE: Born June 6, 1913; died November 9, 1980. Author, editor, and performer best known for his numerous volumes of humor, including *A Long Drink of Cold Water, Come Here Till I Tell You,* and *The Course of Events.* Campbell's wit was a key ingredient of British television programs such as "Call My Bluff." Campbell also worked for *Lilliput* and *Irish Times.* He wrote his autobiography, *My Life and Easy Times,* in 1967. Obituaries and other sources: *London Times,* November 11, 1980.

*   *   *

CANTOR, Norman F(rank) 1929-

PERSONAL: Born in 1929 in Winnipeg, Manitoba, Canada; naturalized U.S. citizen, 1968; married, 1957; children: two. *Education:* University of Manitoba, B.A. (with honors), 1951; Princeton University, M.A., 1953, Ph.D., 1957; attended Oxford University, 1954-55. *Office:* Faculty of Arts and Science, New York University, New York, N.Y. 10012.

CAREER: Princeton University, Princeton, N.J., assistant professor of history, c. 1958-60; Columbia University, New York City, 1960-66, began as associate professor, became professor of history, chairman of department, 1963-65; Brandeis University, Waltham, Mass., professor, 1966-68, Leff Professor of History, 1968-70, director of graduate program in comparative history, 1966-69; State University of New York at Binghamton, distinguished professor of history, 1970-76, chairman of department, 1970-74, provost for graduate studies and research, 1974-75, vice-president for academic affairs, 1975-76; University of Illinois at Chicago Circle, Chicago, professor of history and vice-chancellor for academic affairs, 1976-78; New York University, New York City, professor of history, 1978—, dean of faculty of arts and science, 1978—. Visiting professor at Johns Hopkins University, 1950, Yeshiva University, 1960-61, 1963-64, and Brooklyn College of City University of New York, 1972-74; public speaker. Member of Doctoral Council of the State of New York, 1979—. *Member:* Royal Historical Society (fellow), New York University Society of Fellows. *Awards, honors:* Rhodes scholar, 1954-55; American Council of Learned Societies fellow, 1960; LL.D. from University of Winnipeg, 1973.

WRITINGS: Church, Kingship and Lay Investiture, Princeton University Press, 1958; (contributor) V. Mudroch and G. Crouse, editors, *Essays on the Reconstruction of Medieval History,* McGill University Press, 1964; *Medieval History* (History Book Club selection), Macmillan, 1963, 2nd edition, 1969; (with R. Schneider) *How to Study History,* Crowell, 1967; *The English,* Simon & Schuster, 1968; *Western Civilization,* two volumes, Scott, Foresman, 1969; *The Age of Protest,* Hawthorn, 1969; *Perspectives on the European Past,* Macmillan, 1971; *The Meaning of the Middle Ages,* Allyn & Bacon, 1973.

Editor: *The Medieval World,* Macmillan, 1963, 2nd edition, 1968; *William Stubbs on the English Constitution,* Crowell, 1966; *Structure of European History,* six volumes, Crowell, 1968; *History of Popular Culture,* two volumes, Macmillan, 1968; *The English Tradition,* two volumes, Macmillan, 1968; *Monuments of Western Thought,* four volumes, Blaisdell, 1969-70; *Problems in European History,* three volumes, Crowell, 1970.

Editor of series, "General Studies in History," General Learning Press; "Crosscurrents in World History," Dial; "New Dimensions in History," Wiley; "Ideas and Institutions," Macmillan, 1963, 2nd edition, 1968. Contributor of articles and reviews to history and political science journals. Member of editorial board of *American Journal of Legal History,* 1971-75.

CAPSTICK, Peter Hathaway 1940-

PERSONAL: Born January 11, 1940, in Orange, N.J.; son of Thomas, Sr. and Ruth Hathaway (Connor) Capstick; married Gwendolyn Ann Willey, December 15, 1962 (divorced); married Mary Catharine Thompson (an owner of a women's store), April 16, 1971; children: Joshua Howard Thompson Simonton (stepson), Shirley Elizabeth (stepdaughter; Mrs. Frank Joseph McMackin III). *Education:* Attended University of Virginia, 1957-61. *Politics:* Conservative. *Religion:* Atheist. *Home and office:* 4000 Gulf Shore Blvd. N., Naples, Fla. 33940. *Agent:* Robert P. Mills Ltd., 156 East 52nd St., New York, N.Y. 10022.

CAREER: Sportsmen International Inc., New York City, president, 1964-67; Winchester Adventures, New Haven, Conn., hunting and fishing director, 1967-68; professional hunter and game officer in Zambia, Botswana, and Rhodesia, 1968-78; *Outdoor Life,* New York City, editor-at-large, 1980—. President of Venetian Villas Condominium, 1979-80. *Member:* International Professional Hunters Association (professional life member), Outdoor Writers of America, Explorers Club.

WRITINGS: Death in the Long Grass (nonfiction), St. Martin's, 1978; *Death in the Silent Places* (nonfiction), St. Martin's, 1981. Adventure editor of *American Hunter.*

WORK IN PROGRESS: An African novel.

SIDELIGHTS: Capstick wrote: "I specialize largely in Africana, normally with an adventure or hunting overtone. I have traveled most of the world, except the Far East, and speak KiSwahili, Chenyanja, Fanagalo, Sindebele, Spanish, and, questionably, English. Basically I champion the 'old' values of man, criticizing modern lack of reality in man's view of himself."

AVOCATIONAL INTERESTS: Archaeology, paleontology, African and South American history, ethology, vodka and tonic.

*　　*　　*

CARD, Orson Scott 1951-

PERSONAL: Born August 24, 1951, in Richland, Wash.; son of Willard Richards (a teacher) and Peggy Jane (a secretary and administrator; maiden name, Park) Card; married Kristine Allen, May 17, 1977; children: Michael Geoffrey, Emily Janice. *Education:* Brigham Young University, B.A. (with distinction), 1975; graduate study at University of Utah. *Politics:* Conservative Democrat. *Religion:* Church of Jesus Christ of Latter-day Saints (Mormons). *Residence:* Orem, Utah. *Agent:* Barbara Bova, Barbara Bova Literary Agency, 32 Gramercy Park S., New York, N.Y. 10003.

CAREER: Brigham Young University Press, Provo, Utah, editor, 1974-76; *Ensign,* Salt Lake City, Utah, assistant editor, 1976-78; free-lance writer and editor, 1978—. Local Democratic precinct chairman. *Awards, honors:* John W. Campbell Award, 1978, and short story finalist for Hugo Award, 1978-80, all from World Science Fiction Convention; short story finalist for Nebula Award from Science Fiction Writers of America, 1979, 1980.

WRITINGS: Listen, Mom and Dad, Bookcraft, 1978; *Capitol* (science fiction short stories), Ace Books, 1979; *Hot Sleep* (science fiction novel), Baronet, 1979; *A Planet Called Treason* (science fantasy), St. Martin's, 1979, revised edition, Dell, 1980; *Songmaster* (science fantasy), Dial, 1980; *Unaccompanied Sonata and Other Stories* (short stories), Dial, 1981; *Saints* (historical saga of Mormons), Berkley Publications, 1982.

Plays: "Stone Tables" (five-act), first produced in Provo, Utah, at Brigham Young University, 1973; "Father, Mother, Mother, and Mom" (two-act musical), first produced in Provo, 1974.

Contributor of articles and reviews to magazines, including *Washington Post Book World, Science Fiction Review, Destinies,* and *Eternity.*

WORK IN PROGRESS: The Hundred Horns of Inwit, a fantasy/allegory; *Gulag America,* a near-future thriller; *Wingmaker,* a historical fantasy set in fourteenth-century France.

SIDELIGHTS: Card wrote: "My work has been markedly shaped by my upbringing and current membership in the Church of Jesus Christ of Latter-day Saints. My early plays were all on Mormon themes; the moral viewpoint and cosmology underlie all my work; most of my relationships with other people have been within the church. I served a two-year mission for the church in Brazil a few years ago, and even now consider volunteer work for the church to be an important part of my (and my family's) life.

"While I gradually move away from science fiction, primarily because the conventions of the field no longer provide the tools I need to accomplish what I want to accomplish, I still can't feel comfortable with what passes for literary fiction in the English language today. The inward-turning, reflective novel seems to have degenerated into narcissism; with the more ancient tools of allegory, romance, and ritual I am able to bring off effects much closer to those I want to achieve. With any luck, I'll be able to change without losing the ability to support myself with my writing."

BIOGRAPHICAL/CRITICAL SOURCES: Washington Post Book World, August 24, 1980; *Chicago Tribune Book World,* October 12, 1980.

*　　*　　*

CARDOZO, Arlene Rossen 1938-

PERSONAL: Born January 12, 1938, in Minneapolis, Minn.; daughter of Ralph (a doctor) and Beatrice (an actress; maiden name, Cohen) Rossen; married Richard Nunez Cardozo (a professor), June 29, 1959; children: Miriam, Rachel, Rebecca. *Education:* University of Minnesota, B.A., 1958, graduate study. *Religion:* Jewish. *Residence:* Minneapolis, Minn. *Agent:* David Hull, James Brown Associates, 25 West 43rd St., New York, N.Y. 10036. *Office:* 1955 East River Rd., Minneapolis, Minn. 55414.

CAREER: University of Minnesota, Minneapolis, teacher in Department of Continuing Education for Women, 1976-77. Teacher of courses on family life in continuing education programs throughout Minnesota, 1974-80; conductor of seminars throughout the United States, 1974-80; lecturer on family issues, 1974—. Author. *Member:* National Book Critics Circle, Authors Guild, Minnesota Press Club.

WRITINGS: The Liberated Cookbook: How To Be a Guest at Your Own Table, McKay, 1972; *Woman at Home,* Doubleday, 1976. Contributor of articles to periodicals, including *Chicago Sun-Times, Redbook,* and *U.S. Information Agency Publications.*

WORK IN PROGRESS: The Jewish Family Sourcebook, completion expected in 1981.

SIDELIGHTS: Although Arlene Cardozo is, as a writer for *Time* noted, "no anti-feminist," she identifies some of the pitfalls in feminist ideology and counsels women to beware of the more extreme forms of feminist rhetoric. Feminists have urged women who are "just housewives" to seek fulfilling careers outside their homes; Cardozo admonishes women that working outside the home is no guarantee of fulfillment. She tells women something many men have learned: that the majority of jobs are unsatisfying and monotonous and serve not to liberate but to restrict personal development.

According to the writer for *Time,* Cardozo also objects to the feminist practice of "lumping housework and child care together and dismissing them as something that women must escape in order to achieve 'selfhood.'" She believes that the rhetoric of the women's movement has "deluded women about both the pleasures and the problems of commercial work and about the ease of being a responsible parent and pursuing a career at the same time."

Cardozo told *CA:* "Over the past ten years I have concentrated on researching and writing about family life in this and other cultures. I'm particularly interested in watching the ways in which changes in male/female relationships in this society affect family life and ways in which other social observers report (or rationalize) these changes.

"I've made three separate trips to Israel over the past two years and spent a total of five months living in Jerusalem. I write articles for American media about Israeli issues and lecture frequently on contemporary Israeli concerns. I've also spent some time recently in London, Paris, and Amsterdam."

AVOCATIONAL INTERESTS: Tennis, swimming, modern philosophy.

BIOGRAPHICAL/CRITICAL SOURCES: Chicago Daily News, September 4, 1976; *St. Paul Dispatch,* October 12, 1976; *St. Paul Pioneer Press,* October 15, 1976; *Time,* March 14, 1977; *Minneapolis Star,* November 18, 1977.

*   *   *

CARELESS, J(ames) M(aurice) S(tockford) 1919-

PERSONAL: Born February 17, 1919, in Toronto, Ontario, Canada; son of William Roy Stockford and Ada Josephine (de Rees) Careless; married Elizabeth Isobel Robinson, December 31, 1941; children: five. *Education:* University of Toronto, B.A., 1940; Harvard University, A.M., 1941, Ph.D., 1950. *Home:* 121 Ranleigh Ave., Toronto, Ontario, Canada M4N 1X2. *Office:* Department of History, University of Toronto, Toronto, Ontario, Canada.

CAREER: Royal Canadian Navy, Naval Service Headquarters, Ottawa, Ontario, assistant to naval historian, 1943; Canadian Department of External Affairs, Ottawa, wartime assistant, 1944-45; University of Toronto, Toronto, Ontario, 1945-59, began as lecturer, became professor of history, 1959—, chairman of department, 1959-67. Visiting professor at University of Victoria, 1968-69. Co-chairman of Archaeological and Historical Sites Board of Ontario, 1965—; member of Ontario Commission on Post-Secondary Education, 1969-72, and Historical Sites and Monuments Board of Canada, 1972—; member of board of trustees of Ontario Science Centre, 1963-73, and board of directors of Ontario Heritage Foundation, 1975—; consultant to Canadian Broadcasting Corp. *Wartime service:* Diplomatic officer on exchange ship *Gripsholm.*

MEMBER: Royal Society of Canada (fellow), Canadian Historical Association (president, 1967-68), Ontario Historical Society (president, 1959). *Awards, honors:* Governor General's Medal from governor-general of Canada, 1953, for *Canada: A Story of Challenge,* nonfiction award, 1964, for

Brown of the Globe; Rockefeller Foundation grant for England, 1955-56; medal for popular biography from University of British Columbia, 1960, for *Brown of the Globe;* Tyrrell Medal from Royal Society of Canada, 1962; Cruickshank Medal from Ontario Historical Society, 1968.

WRITINGS: Canada: A Story of Challenge, Cambridge University Press, 1953, St. Martin's, 1964, 3rd edition, Macmillan of Canada, 1970; (editor with George Williams Brown) *Canada and the World,* Dent, 1954; *Brown of the Globe,* Macmillan of Canada, Volume I: *The Voice of Upper Canada, 1818-1859,* 1959, Volume II: *Statesman of Confederation, 1860-1880,* 1963; *The Union of the Canadas: The Growth of Canadian Institutions, 1841-1857,* McClelland & Stewart, 1967; (co-editor with Robert Craig Brown) *The Canadians, 1867-1967,* Part I, St. Martin's, 1967; *The Pioneers: The Picture Story of Canadian Settlement,* McClelland & Stewart, 1968, revised edition published as *The Pioneers: An Illustrated History of Early Settlement in Canada,* 1973; (editor) *Colonists and Canadiens, 1760-1867,* Macmillan of Canada, 1971; (editor) *The Pre-Confederation Pioneers: Ontario Government Leaders, 1841 to 1867,* University of Toronto Press, 1980. Also co-author of *Canada and the Commonwealth,* 1953, and author of *Canada and the Americas,* 1953, and *Limited Identities in Canada,* 1969.

Contributor: *Canadian Business History, 1497-1971,* McClelland & Stewart, 1972; *Prairie Perspectives,* Volume II, Holt, 1973. Also contributor to *Nationalism in Canada,* edited by Peter Russell, 1966, and *The New Romans,* edited by Al Purdy, 1968.*

*   *   *

CARKEET, David 1946-

PERSONAL: Surname is accented on second syllable; born November 15, 1946, in Sonora, Calif.; son of Ross Albert (a judge) and Mary (Hill) Carkett; married Barbara Lubin (a social worker), August 16, 1975; children: Anne, Laurie. *Education:* University of California, Davis, A.B. (cum laude), 1968; University of Wisconsin—Madison, M.A., 1970; Indiana University, Ph.D., 1973. *Home:* 435 Westgate, St. Louis, Mo. 63130. *Office:* Department of English, University of Missouri, St. Louis, Mo. 63121.

CAREER: University of Missouri, St. Louis, assistant professor, 1973-79, associate professor of English, 1979—. *Member:* Authors Guild, Authors League of America. *Awards, honors:* James D. Phelan Award in literature from San Francisco Foundation, 1976, for *Double Negative.*

WRITINGS: Double Negative (novel), Dial, 1980. Contributor to language and literature journals.

WORK IN PROGRESS: A novel, *Cornish Diggings.*

SIDELIGHTS: Carkeet wrote: "The first obstacle a young writer faces is the industry's hostility to unknowns. It took me six years to land my first novel. Along the way I was encouraged at crucial moments by my family, a few editors, and the San Francisco Foundation. The second obstacle he or she faces is one of identity: now that I am a writer, what kind of writer am I? The best way to answer that question is by writing."

*   *   *

CARPENTER, John Jo
See REESE, John (Henry)

*   *   *

CARR, J(ames) L(loyd) 1912-

PERSONAL: Born May 20, 1912, in Thirsk, England; son of

Joseph and Elizabeth (Welbourn) Carr; married Sally Sexton; children: Robert Duane. *Education:* Attended grammar school in Castleford, England. *Home:* 27 Mill Dale Rd., Kettering, Northamptonshire, England.

CAREER: Teacher in Hampshire, England, 1933-35, and Birmingham, England, 1935-40; high school teacher in Huron, S.D., 1938-39; teacher of English grammar in South Dakota, 1956-57; writer. *Military service:* Royal Air Force, 1940-46; became flight lieutenant.

*WRITINGS—*Nonfiction; *The Old Timers,* privately printed, 1957; *Dictionary of Extra-Ordinary English Cricketers,* Milldale Press, 1977; *Dictionary of English Queens,* Milldale Press, 1977; *Dictionary of English Kings,* Milldale Press, 1979. *Sydney Smith: The Smith of Smiths,* Milldale Press, 1980.

Novels: *A Day in Summer,* Barrie & Rockliff, 1964; *A Season in Sinji,* London Magazine Editions, 1967; *The Harpole Report,* Secker & Warburg, 1970; *How Steeple Sinderby Won the F.A. Cup,* London Magazine Editions, 1975; *A Month in the Country,* Harvester Press, 1980.

Children's books: *The Dustman,* Macmillan, 1969; *The Red Wind Cheater,* Macmillan, 1971; *Red Foal's Coat,* Macmillan, 1973; *The Old Cart,* Macmillan, 1973; *An Ear-Ring for Anna Beer,* Macmillan, 1976; *The Green Children,* Longman, 1977; *Gone With the Whirlwind,* Macmillan, 1980.

* * *

CARROLL, Joseph T(homas) 1935-

PERSONAL: Born in 1935, in Castlebar, Ireland; married Katherine Leonard; children: two daughters. *Education:* University College, Dublin, National University of Ireland, M.A. *Home:* Rockfield, Hyde Park Ave., Blackrock, County Dublin, Ireland.

CAREER: Worked as sub-editor of *Irish Independent* in Ireland, 1962-63; Paris correspondent for *Sunday Telegraph,* 1965-68; foreign editor of *Irish Press.*

Assistant correspondent for *Guardian,* 1965-68.

WRITINGS: The French: How They Live and Work, David & Charles, 1968, 4th edition, 1977, Praeger, 1969, revised edition, 1970; *Ireland in the War Years, 1939-1945,* Crane, Russak, 1975.*

* * *

CARROLL, Joy 1924-

PERSONAL: Born July 8, 1924, in Melfort, Saskatchewan, Canada; daughter of John Robert and Elsie (Lee) Holroyd; married John Alexander Carroll, May 17, 1952; children: Anne Elizabeth, Barbara Evelyn, Scott Alexander, Angus John Gregory. *Education:* Attended Royal Conservatory of Music. *Religion:* Anglican.

CAREER: Writer. Worked as women's editor of *Prince Albert Daily Herald,* scriptwriter for Canadian Broadcasting Corp., scriptwriter for Claire Wallace, feature editor of *New World,* executive editor of *National Home Monthly,* Canadian editor of *Better Living,* editor for Harlequin Books, and travel editor of *Chatelaine.*

WRITINGS: God and Mrs. Sullivan, Simon & Schuster, 1974; *The Moth,* Dell, 1974; *Fire Over Eden,* Simon & Schuster, 1976; *Satan's Bell,* Simon & Schuster, 1976; *Pioneer Days, 1840-1860,* Natural Science, 1979; *Proud Blood,* Dell, 1980; *Pride's Court,* Dell, 1980. Also co-author with Claire Wallace of *Canadian Etiquette,* and author of *Night of Terror, Murdered Mistress, The Restless Lovers, Weekend,*

and *Soul's End.* Contributor of articles and stories to Canadian and American magazines and newspapers.

AVOCATIONAL INTERESTS: Music, swimming.*

* * *

CARROLL, Peter N(eil) 1943-

PERSONAL: Born October 26, 1943, in New York, N.Y.; son of Louis and Bessie Carroll; children: Matthew. *Education:* Queens College of the City University of New York, B.A., 1964; Northwestern University, M.A., 1967, Ph.D., 1968. *Home:* 2505 Casa Bona Ave., Belmont Calif. 94002. *Agent:* Fred Hill Associates, 2237 Union St., San Francisco, Calif. 94123.

CAREER: University of Illinois at Chicago Circle, Chicago, assistant professor of history, 1968-69; University of Minnesota, Minneapolis, associate professor of history, 1969-74; San Francisco State University, San Francisco, Calif., lecturer in history, 1975—. *Awards, honors:* Fellow of National Endowment for the Humanities, 1972-73.

WRITINGS: Puritanism and the Wilderness, Columbia University Press, 1969; (editor) *Religion and the Coming of the American Revolution,* Blaisdell, 1970; (with David Noble) *The Restless Centuries,* Burgess, 1973, 2nd edition, 1979; (with Noble) *The Free and the Unfree,* Penguin, 1977; *The Other Samuel Johnson,* Fairleigh Dickinson University Press, 1978; (with Noble and David Horowitz) *Twentieth Century Limited,* Houghton, 1980; *A History of America in the 1970's,* Holt, 1982. Book editor of *San Francisco Bay Guardian,* 1976-80.

SIDELIGHTS: Carroll told *CA:* "After having written several books about early American history, I'm now working on a contemporary project, *A History of America in the 1970's,* and am finding new types of challenges. One of these is the widespread assumption that the seventies were *not* a significant time period, what with all the narcissism and nostalgia. I'm trying to counter that impression by emphasizing the more lasting trends that began to emerge in this decade."

* * *

CARRUTHERS, Malcolm Euan 1938-

PERSONAL: Born February 9, 1938, in London, England. *Home:* 5 Makepeace Ave., London N6 6EL, England.

CAREER: Writer. Worked as lecturer at Middlesex Hospital; St. Mary's Hospital, London, senior lecturer in chemical pathology, 1972—. *Member:* Society of Psychosomatic Research, Royal Society of Medicine.

WRITINGS: The Western Way of Death: Stress, Tension, and Heart Attacks, Pantheon, 1974 (published in England as *The Western Way of Death,* David-Poynter, 1974); (with Alistair Murray) *F40: Fitness on Forty Minutes a Week,* Futura Publications, 1976; (editor with R. Priest) *The Psychosomatic Approach to Prevention of Disease,* Pergamon, 1977; *The Coming of Age of Psychosomatics,* Pergamon, 1979. Also editor of *Psychosomatic Research: Annual Proceedings,* and co-author with Murray of *Fitness for All.**

* * *

CARTER, Martin (Wylde) 1927-

PERSONAL: Born in 1927 in Georgetown, British Guiana. *Education:* Attended Queen's College, Georgetown.

CAREER: Writer. United Nations, New York, N.Y., representative for Guyana. Also worked as minister of information for Republic of Guyana.

WRITINGS: *The Hill of Fire Glows Red* (poems), Miniature Poets, 1951; *To a Dead Slave* (poems), privately printed, 1951; *The Kind Eagle* (poems), privately printed, 1952; *The Hidden Man* (poems), privately printed, 1952; *Poems of Resistance From British Guiana*, Lawrence & Wishart, 1954; *Poems of Resistance*, University of Guiana, 1964; (editor) *New World: Guyana Independence Issue*, New World Group Associates, 1966; *Creation: Works of Art*, Cariana Publishers, 1977; *Poems of Succession*, New Beacon Books, 1977. Contributor to magazines, including *Kyk-over-al* and *New World Fortnightly*.*

* * *

CASEY, Edward Scott 1939-

PERSONAL: Born February 24, 1939, in Topeka, Kan.; married, 1962; children: two. *Education:* Yale University, B.A., 1961; Northwestern University, M.A., 1964, Ph.D., 1967. *Office:* Department of Philosophy, Yale University, New Haven, Conn. 06520.

CAREER: University of California, Santa Barbara, assistant professor of philosophy, 1967-68; Yale University, New Haven, Conn., assistant professor, 1968-73, associate professor of philosophy, 1973—. *Member:* American Philosophical Association, American Society of Aesthetics, Society for Phenomenology and Existential Philosophy. *Awards, honors:* Woodrow Wilson fellowship, 1962-64; Fulbright fellowship, 1964-66; Morse fellowship, 1972-73.

WRITINGS: (Translator) *The Notion of the A Priori*, Northwestern University Press, 1966; (translator) *Phenomenology of Aesthetic Experience*, Northwestern University Press, 1973; (editor) *Explorations in Phenomenology*, Nijhoff, 1973; *Imagining: A Phenomenological Study*, Indiana University Press, 1976. Contributor to philosophy journals.*

* * *

CASH, Anthony 1933-

PERSONAL: Born November 21, 1933, in Leeds, England; son of Michael Patrick (a teacher) and Eileen (Mundy) Cash; married Judith Marie Carr, June 25, 1955 (divorced, 1971); married Gillian Mary Clark, May 14, 1971; children: Nicholas J., Thomas A., Sophia L., Amy L. *Education:* St. Edmund Hall, Oxford, B.A. (with honors), 1957, diploma in education, 1958, M.A., 1960. *Home:* 7 Lilyville Rd., London S.W.6, England. *Agent:* A. D. Peters & Co. Ltd., 10 Buckingham St., London WC2N 6BU, England. *Office:* London Weekend Television, Upper Ground, London S.E.1, England.

CAREER: Assistant Russian master at grammar schools in London, England, 1958-63; British Broadcasting Corp., London, television program assistant in Russian section of External Service, 1963-68, television producer and director, 1968-77; London Weekend Television, London, producer and director, 1977—. *Military service:* Royal Navy, coder, 1952-54.

WRITINGS: (Translator with Gordon Clough) General A. V. Gorbatov, *Years of My Life*, Constable, 1966; *The Russian Revolution*, Doubleday, 1967; *Lenin*, J. Cape, 1972. Also author of *Great Neighbours: The U.S.S.R.*, 1965. Author of radio scripts for British Broadcasting Corp.'s World Service. Contributor to *Listener, New Society,* and *Encounter*.

WORK IN PROGRESS: Television programs on Milos Forman, music in Venice from the sixteenth to the eighteenth centuries, Lytton Strachey and Dora Carrington, and Berg's opera "Lulu."

SIDELIGHTS: Cash told *CA:* "I have a wide-range knowledge of French and Russian culture. In 1977 I interpreted for the National Youth Jazz Orchestra and presented the orchestra on stage in Moscow and Leningrad. All aspects of broadcasting are my major concern.

"As a television producer/director working for Great Britain's major arts program, 'The South Bank Show,' I am in the privileged position of being able to make film documentaries on an extraordinarily wide range of subjects. During the last two years I have made programs on subjects as diverse as Mozart's 'The Marriage of Figaro,' the novels of Francoise Sagan, the work of the great Scottish comedian Billy Connolly, and the way British television drama reflects the conflict in Northern Ireland. I am very conscious of the advantages I enjoy over my colleagues in arts broadcasting in France, the Soviet Union, and even, I suspect, the United States. Arts broadcasting in Britain is happily free from both governmental interference and commercial pressure. Long may it continue."

* * *

CATALANO, Joseph S(tellario) 1928-

PERSONAL: Born October 16, 1928, in Brooklyn, N.Y.; son of Charles and Frances Catalano. *Education:* St. John's University, Jamaica, N.Y., B.A., 1950, M.A., 1956, Ph.D., 1962. *Home:* 1733 Second Ave., New York, N.Y. 10028. *Office:* Department of Philosophy, Kean College, Union, N.J. 07083.

CAREER: St. John's University, Jamaica, N.Y., instructor, 1959-63, assistant professor of philosophy, 1963-65; Kean College, Union, N.J., associate professor, 1965-73, professor of philosophy, 1973—. Adjunct associate professor at C. W. Post College, Long Island University, 1965, and New School for Social Research, 1968—. *Member:* American Philosophical Association, Association for Symbolic Logic, Society for Phenomenology and Existentialism. *Awards, honors:* National Endowment for the Humanities grant, 1978.

WRITINGS: *A Commentary on Jean-Paul Sartre's "Being and Nothingness,"* Harper, 1974, revised edition, University of Chicago Press, 1980. Contributor to philosophy journals.

WORK IN PROGRESS: *The Philosophy of Jean-Paul Sartre.*

* * *

CAVENEY, Philip (Richard) 1951-

PERSONAL: Born December 30, 1951, in Prestatyn, Wales; son of Alexander and Betsy Caveney. *Education:* Attended grammar school in Peterborough, England. *Politics:* "Ecology party." *Religion:* "None recognized." *Home:* Flat 3, Carlogie House, 365 Wilmslow Rd., Fallowfield, Manchester, England. *Agent:* Janet Freer, MBA Associates, 118 Tottenham Court Rd., London W.1, England.

CAREER: Writer, 1956—; worked as graphic designer, 1971. Worked as singer in rock music band. *Member:* Mystery Writers of America.

WRITINGS: *The Sins of Rachel Ellis* (mystery novel; Doubleday Book Club selection), St. Martin's, 1979.

WORK IN PROGRESS: *Storm*, a novel; poems.

SIDELIGHTS: Caveney told *CA:* "I am fascinated by the concept of myths and legends and how these things can be related to contemporary times, something I achieve (hopefully) by writing fiction. I am deeply concerned that the fiction market these days is ruled by overt trends and fashions that care little for the writer's integrity ... but anyway, I keep on trying.

"I think the medium of horror is a fine area for creative writing. To tap the streams of age-old fears and superstitions, to breathe new life, new credence into them is a difficult but tremendously rewarding task. In a world constantly battered by *real* horrors (war, famine, murder, rape, political assassination, man's everyday inhumanity to his fellow man), how refreshing, how delightfully uncomplicated to experience a chill manufactured by more simple evils. A dark corridor, a cobweb brushing against flesh, the tortured ghost of a child from an earlier time.

"At heart, I'm basically an entertainer and that's how I envision the role of a writer. I know myself that I hate to be pounded with 'heavy' thought-provoking intellectualism. Of course, stories needn't be complete mush either. Information should be there on a secondary level, for *those who wish to seek it*, but should never be allowed to intrude on the flow of the narrative. In my view, a book which requires 'application' or is 'heavy going' is simply badly written. Fiction should be un-put-down-able, whatever its literary merits.''

*   *   *

CAZELLES, Brigitte Jacqueline 1944-

PERSONAL: Born January 9, 1944, in Rabat, Morocco; came to the United States in 1970; daughter of Bernard Louis Paul and Francoise (Bouteron) Cazelles. *Education:* Sorbonne, University of Paris, Lic. es lettres, 1966, Diplome d'etudes supenrieures, 1967; University of California, Riverside, Ph.D., 1975. *Office:* Department of French and Italian, Stanford University, Stanford, Calif. 94305.

CAREER: National Center of Scientific Research, Paris, France, research assistant, 1964-69; College of the Paupi, assistant professor of French, 1975-77; Stanford University, Stanford, Calif., assistant professor of French, 1977—. *Member:* American Association of Teachers of French, Medieval Association of America.

WRITINGS: La Faiblesse chez Gautier de Coinci (title means "The Concept of Feebleness in Gautier de Coinci"), Anma Libri, 1978; (with P. A. Johnson) *Le Vain Siecle Guerpir: A Literary Approach to Sainthood Through Old French Hagiography of the Twelfth Century*, University of North Carolina Press, 1979. Contributor to *Romance Philology*. Editor of *Stanford French Review*.

WORK IN PROGRESS: Il etait une fois des saints ... (title means "Once Upon a Time, a Saint ..."), completion expected in 1982.

SIDELIGHTS: Cazelles told *CA:* "My research is on French didactic literature in the Middle Ages and in particular on the versified saints' lives. These vernacular poems are an enriching source of information on popular mentality and popular religious practices. Medievalists have given us a detailed picture of important personages and thinkers of the time; my present work attempts to draw, through these vernacular texts, a profile of the common man."

*   *   *

CECIL, R. H.
See HEWITT, Cecil Rolph

*   *   *

CELORIA, Francis (S. C.) 1926-

PERSONAL: Born in 1926 in London, England. *Education:*

Attended University of Edinburgh and University of London. *Home:* 154 Kensington Park Rd., London W.11, England.

CAREER: Geographical, member of editorial staff, 1952-53; worked for Rainbird McLean Ltd., 1953-54, and for *Encyclopaedia Britannica,* 1955-60; Islay Archaeological Survey, research secretary, 1959—. Member of Thames Basin Archaeological Observers, 1958-62. *Member:* Royal Geographical Society (fellow), Society of Antiquaries (Scotland; fellow).

WRITINGS: Teach Yourself Local History, English Universities Press, 1958; *Field Officer,* London Museum, 1960; (editor and author of notes and introduction) *Edward Dobson's "A Rudimentary Treatise on the Manufacture of Bricks and Tiles,"* George Street Press, 1971; *Archaeology,* Hamlyn, 1971, published in the United States as *Archaeology,* Grosset, 1973; (with J. H. Kelly) *A Post-Medieval Pottery Site With a Kiln Base Found off Albion Square, Hanley, Stoke-on-Trent, Staffordshire, England, SJ 885 474,* City of Stoke-on-Trent Museum Archaeological Society, 1973. Contributor to *Encyclopaedia Britannica.* Contributor to journals, including *People, Places, and Things* and *Journal of Ceramic History.**

*   *   *

CENDRARS, Blaise
See SAUSER-HALL, Frederic

*   *   *

CERAVOLO, Joseph 1934-

PERSONAL: Born April 22, 1934, in New York, N.Y.; son of John and Millie (DeNardo) Ceravolo; married Rosemary Biondo, September 25, 1961; children: Paul, Anita, James. *Education:* City College (now of the City University of New York), B.C.E., 1959. *Home:* 65 Spruce St., Bloomfield, N.J. 07003.

CAREER: New York State Department of Public Works, New York, N.Y., junior engineer, 1959-60; Jersey Testing Laboratories, Newark, N.J., design engineer, 1961-64; Porter & Ripa Associates, Newark, design engineer, 1964-69; Town of Bloomfield, N.J., principal engineer, 1969-71; Purcel Associates, East Orange, N.J., design engineer, 1971-72; Engelhard Enterprises, South Plainfield, N.J., design engineer, 1972; Porter & Ripa Associates, Inc., Morristown, N.J., hydraulic engineer, 1972—. *Military service:* U.S. Army, 1956. *Awards, honors:* Awards from Poets Foundation, 1962, 1963, 1965, and 1967; grants from National Endowment for the Arts, 1966, 1972; Frank O'Hara Award from Columbia University Press, 1968; grant from American Academy of Arts and Letters, 1970.

WRITINGS: Fits of Dawn (poems), ''C'' Press, 1965; *Wild Flowers Out of Gas* (poems), Tibor de Nagy Gallery, 1967; *Spring in This World of Poor Mutts: The Frank O'Hara Award Series* (poems), Columbia University Press, 1968; *Transmigration Solo,* Toothpaste Press, 1979.

Work represented in anthologies, including *Out of This World,* edited by John Perreault, Poetry Project (New York, N.Y.), 1973.

BIOGRAPHICAL/CRITICAL SOURCES: Poetry, May, 1967, autumn, 1969.*

*   *   *

CHAKRAVARTY, Birendra Narayan 1904-1980(?)

PERSONAL: Born December 20, 1904, in Bogra, Bangladesh; died c. 1980; son of Harendra Narayan and Jagdiswari (Sanyal) Chakravarty; married Indira Sanyal, September 8, 1931; children: Anita Chakravarty Benerji, Subrata Narayan. *Education:* University of Calcutta, B.S., 1926; attended School of Oriental and African Studies, London, 1926-29.

CAREER: Joined Indian Civil Service, 1929; appointed finance secretary of Bengal, 1944; secretary to governor of West Bengal, 1947; charge d'affaires at Indian embassy in Nanking, China, 1948; minister and head of Indian liaison mission in Tokyo, Japan, and political adviser to Supreme Commander of Allied Powers, 1948-49; joint secretary of Ministry of External Affairs in New Delhi, 1949-51; secretary of commonwealth relations, 1951-52; ambassador to the Netherlands, 1952-54; senior alternate chairman of Neutral Nations Repatriation Commission in Korea, 1953; acting high commissioner to the United Kingdom in London, England, 1954; high commissioner to Ceylon, 1955-56; special secretary of Ministry of External Affairs, 1956-60; high commissioner to Canada, 1960-62; permanent representative to the United Nations in New York, N.Y., 1962-65; governor of Haryana State, India, 1967-76. *Awards, honors:* LL.D. from Panjab University, 1972.

WRITINGS: India Speaks to America, John Day, 1966; *The Governor Speaks,* Director of Public Relations (Chandigarh, India), Volume I, 1970, Volume II, 1971; *Australia's Military Alliances,* Sterling, 1977.*

*   *   *

CHALMERS, Eric Brownlie 1929-

PERSONAL: Born September 29, 1929, in Glasgow, Scotland; son of James McDonald and Anne (McGill) Chalmers; married Rosemary Anne Folkes, September 20, 1980. *Education:* University of Edinburgh, M.A. (with honors), 1952. *Politics:* None. *Religion:* Church of Scotland. *Home:* Oak House, Brook St., Moreton Pinkney, Northamptonshire, England. *Office:* E. B. Savory Milln & Co., 20 Moorgate, London E.C.2, England.

CAREER: Ford Motor Corp., Dagenham, England, financial analyst, 1955-57; Marconi Marine, London, England, management statistician, 1957-59; Cyanamid of Great Britain, London, research manager, 1959-61; de Zoete & Bevan (stockbrokers), London, England, economic adviser, 1961-71; E. B. Savory Milln & Co. (stockbrokers), London, economic adviser, 1971—. Broadcaster for British Broadcasting Corp. *Military service:* Royal Air Force, flying officer, 1952-55. *Member:* Society of Business Economists.

WRITINGS: (Editor) *Readings in the Euro-Dollar,* Griffith, 1969; (editor) *Forward Exchange Intervention,* Hutchinson, 1971; *Economics for Executives,* J. Murray, 1971; *International Interest Rate War,* Macmillan, 1972; *The Money World,* Macmillan, 1974. Contributor to *Banker.*

SIDELIGHTS: Chalmers told *CA:* "As a city economist, I have naturally tended to specialize in monetary and international economics and most of my published work has been in this area. My personal philosophy stance is to be firmly opposed to inflation and to any policies that may contribute to it."

*   *   *

CHANCE, John Newton 1911-
(Jonathan Chance, John Lymington)

PERSONAL: Born in 1911 in London, England; son of Richard Newton Chance (a comic strip editor); married Shirley

Savill; children: three sons. *Education:* Attended secondary school in London, England.

CAREER: Writer. *Military service:* Royal Air Force.

WRITINGS—All novels, except as noted; published by Gollancz: *Wheels in the Forest,* 1935; *Murder in Oils,* 1935; *The Devil Drives,* 1936; *Rhapsody in Fear: A Crime Novel,* 1937; *Maiden Possessed,* 1937; *Death of an Innocent,* 1938; *The Devil in Greenlands: A Small Matter of Life and Death,* 1939; *The Ghost of Truth: A Scandal in Two Parts,* 1939.

Published by Macdonald & Co., except as noted: *Screaming Fog,* 1944, published as *Death Stalks the Cobbled Square,* R. M. McBride, 1946; *The Red Knight,* 1945; *The Knight and the Castle: A deHavilland Story,* 1946; *The Eye in Darkness,* 1946; *The Black Highway: A deHavilland Story,* 1947; *Coven Gibbet,* 1948; *The Brandy Pole,* 1949.

Other novels: *The Night of the Full Moon,* Macdonald & Co., 1950; *Bunst the Bold,* Oxford University Press, 1950; *Bunst and the Brown Voice,* Oxford University Press, 1950; *Aunt Miranda's Murder,* Macdonald & Co., 1951; *Bunst and the Secret Six,* Oxford University Press, 1951; (with wife, Shirley Newton Chance) *The Jennifer Jigsaw,* Oxford University Press, 1951; *The Man in My Shoes,* Macdonald & Co., 1952; *The Twopenny Box,* Macdonald & Co., 1952; *The Randy Inheritance,* Macdonald & Co., 1953; *The Jason Affair,* Macdonald & Co., 1953, published in the United States as *Up to Her Neck: A Novel of Suspense,* Popular Library, 1955; *Bunst and the Flying Eye,* Oxford University Press, 1953; *The Jason Murders,* Macdonald & Co., 1954; *Jason and the Sleep Game,* Macdonald & Co., 1954; *Jason Goes West,* Macdonald & Co., 1955; *A Shadow Called Janet,* Macdonald & Co., 1956; *The Last Seven Hours,* Macdonald & Co., 1956; *Dead Man's Knock,* R. Hale, 1957; *The Little Crime,* R. Hale, 1957; *Man With Three Witches,* R. Hale, 1958; *Affair With a Rich Girl,* R. Hale, 1958; *The Fatal Fascination,* R. Hale, 1959; *The Man With No Face,* R. Hale, 1959; *Yellow Belly* (nonfiction), R. Hale, 1959.

Lady in a Frame, R. Hale, 1960; *Alarm at Black Brake,* R. Hale, 1960; *The Night of the Settlement,* R. Hale, 1961; *The Crimes at Rillington Place: A Novelist's Reconstruction* (nonfiction), Hodder & Stoughton, 1961; *Import of Evil,* R. Hale, 1961; *Triangle of Fear,* R. Hale, 1962; *The Forest Affair,* R. Hale, 1963; *The Man Behind Me,* R. Hale, 1963; *Commission for Disaster,* R. Hale, 1964; *Death Under Desolate,* R. Hale, 1964; *Stormlight,* R. Hale, 1965; *The Double Death,* R. Hale, 1966; *The Affair at Dead End,* R. Hale, 1966; *The Case of the Death Computer,* R. Hale, 1967; *The Case of the Fear Makers,* R. Hale, 1967; *The Death Women,* R. Hale, 1967; *The Hurricane Drift,* R. Hale, 1967; *The Mask of Pursuit,* R. Hale, 1967; *The Thug Executive,* R. Hale, 1967; *The Rogue Aunt,* R. Hale, 1968; *Mantrap,* R. Hale, 1968; *The Halloween Murders,* R. Hale, 1968; *Fate of the Lying Jade,* R. Hale, 1968; *Death of the Wild Bird,* R. Hale, 1968; *Dead Men's Shoes,* R. Hale, 1968; *The Abel Coincidence,* R. Hale, 1969; *The Ice Maidens,* R. Hale, 1969; *Involvement in Austria,* R. Hale, 1969; *The Killer Reaction,* R. Hale, 1969; *The Killing Experiment,* R. Hale, 1969.

Published by R. Hale: *Three Masks of Death,* 1970; *A Ring of Liars,* 1970; *The Mists of Treason,* 1970; *The Mirror Train,* 1970; *The Faces of a Bad Girl,* 1971; *A Wreath of Bones,* 1971; *The Cat Watchers,* 1971; *A Bad Dream of Death,* 1972; *The Dead Tale-Tellers,* 1972; *Last Train to Limbo,* 1972; *The Man With Two Heads,* 1972; *The Love-Hate Relationship,* 1973; *The Grab Operators,* 1973; *The Farm Villains,* 1973; *Canterbury Killgrims,* 1974; *Girl in the Crime Belt,* 1974; *The Starfish Affair,* 1974; *Hill Fog,* 1975;

The Shadow of the Killer, 1975; *The Monstrous Regiment,* 1975; *A Fall-Out of Thieves,* 1976; *The Devil's Edge,* 1976; *The Murder Makers,* 1976; *Return to Death Valley,* 1976; *Motive for a Kill,* 1977; *The House of the Dead Ones,* 1977; *The Frightened Fisherman,* 1977; *End of an Iron Man,* 1978; *Ducrow Folly,* 1978; *Drop of Hot Gold,* 1979; *The Guilty Witness,* 1979; *Thieves' Kitchen,* 1979; *A Place Called Skull,* 1980; *The Death Watch Ladies,* 1980.

Under pseudonym Jonathan Chance: *The Light Benders,* R. Hale, 1968.

Under pseudonym John Lymington; science fiction novels, except as noted: *Night of the Big Heat,* Hodder & Stoughton, 1959, Dutton, 1960; *The Giant Stumbles,* Hodder & Stoughton, 1960; *The Grey Ones,* Hodder & Stoughton, 1960, Macfadden-Bartell, 1970; *A Sword Above the Night,* Hodder & Stoughton, 1961; *The Coming of the Strangers,* Hodder & Stoughton, 1961, Macfadden-Bartell, 1971; *The Screaming Face,* Hodder & Stoughton, 1963, Macfadden-Bartell, 1970; *The Sleep Eaters,* Hodder & Stoughton, 1963, Macfadden-Bartell, 1969; *Froomb!,* Hodder & Stoughton, 1964, Doubleday, 1966; *The Night Spiders* (stories), Corgi, 1964, Doubleday, 1967; *The Green Drift,* Hodder & Stoughton, 1965; *The Star Witches,* Hodder & Stoughton, 1965; *Ten Million Years to Friday,* Hodder & Stoughton, 1967, Doubleday, 1970; *The Nowhere Place,* Hodder & Stoughton, 1969, Doubleday, 1971; *Give Daddy the Knife, Darling,* Hodder & Stoughton, 1969; *The Year Dot,* Hodder & Stoughton, 1972; *The Hole in the World,* Hodder & Stoughton, 1974; *A Spider in the Bath,* Hodder & Stoughton, 1975; *The Laxham Haunting,* Hodder & Stoughton, 1977; *Starseed on Gye Moor,* Hodder & Stoughton, 1978; *The Waking of the Stone,* Hodder & Stoughton, 1978; *A Caller From Overspace,* Hodder & Stoughton, 1979.

Contributor of several hundred articles to newspapers.

BIOGRAPHICAL/CRITICAL SOURCES: Best Sellers, February 15, 1970.*

* * *

CHANCE, Jonathan
See CHANCE, John Newton

* * *

CHANDLER, Robert Wilbur   1921-

PERSONAL: Born May 12, 1921, in Maryville, Calif.; son of Wilbur Ray and Grace Helena (Johnson) Chandler; married Nancy Jane Renne, September 7, 1946; children: Janet, Margaret (Mrs. Gregory F. Cushman), Mary Jean (Mrs. David D. Jordan), Patricia Ann (Mrs. Gary A. Moss), Elizabeth Jane, Robert Wilbur, Jr. *Education:* Stanford University, B.A., 1942. *Home:* 1810 Northeast Neff Rd., Bend, Ore. 97701. *Office: Bulletin,* Bend, Ore. 97701.

CAREER/WRITINGS: San Francisco Chronicle, San Francisco, Calif., reporter, 1941; United Press, reporter and bureau manager in Portland, Ore., Helena, Mont., Phoenix, Ariz., and Boise, Idaho, 1941-43; *Denver Post,* Denver, Colo., reporter and copyreader in business office, 1946-50; worked for William Kotka & Associates, Denver, 1950-52; *Stanford University Review,* Stanford, Calif., editor, 1952-53; *Bulletin,* Bend, Ore., editor, 1953-60; *Los Angeles Mirror,* Los Angeles, Calif., general manager, 1960-62; *Bulletin,* editor, 1962—. President of Western Communications, Inc., 1966—; member of board of directors of Central Oregon Community College, 1962-66, Hawaii Newspaper Agency, Inc., 1974—, and American Press Institute. Member of Ore-

gon Constitutional Revision Commission, 1961-63, Judicial Council, 1966-69, State Board of Education, 1966-69, Judicial Fitness Commission, 1967—, Criminal Law Revision Commission, 1967-73, and Law Enforcement Council, 1974-75. *Military service:* U.S. Army, 1943-46. *Member:* American Society of Newspaper Editors (member of board of directors, 1972-79), Society of Professional Journalists (national president, 1970-71), Arlington Club.*

* * *

CHANDLER, Tertius   1915-

PERSONAL: Born February 6, 1915, in Dedham, Mass.; son of Theophilus (a farmer) and Sarah (Chase) Chandler; married Margot Mueller Tegelstroem, September 18, 1961. *Education:* Harvard University, B.A. (cum laude), 1937. *Politics:* Republican. *Religion:* None. *Home:* 2500 Buena Vista, Berkeley, Calif. 94708.

CAREER: Columbia University Encyclopedia, New York, N.Y., researcher, 1939-42; Lassen Junior College, Susanville, Calif., night school teacher of history, 1949-50; freelance researcher, 1950-69; University of California, Berkeley, researcher at Institute for Population and Urban Research, 1969-70; writer, 1970—. Occasional guest lecturer at Wesleyan University, University of California, and Harvard University. Candidate for U.S. Congress, 1980. *Awards, honors:* Athletic awards.

WRITINGS: Chandler's Half-Encyclopedia, privately printed, 1956; (with Gerald Fox) *Three Thousand Years of Urban Growth,* Academic Press, 1974; *Godly Kings and Early Ethics,* Exposition Press, 1976; *Remote Kingdoms,* Exposition Press, 1976; *Progress,* Exposition Press, 1976. Editor of *Digsig,* 1977—, and *Current Problems,* 1978—.

WORK IN PROGRESS: The Tax We Need.

SIDELIGHTS: Chandler told *CA:* "My motivation from the age of ten was to learn about all the great men who ever lived, and to make lists of cities. From the age of eighteen I've sought out the size of cities in the past, and this quest has led to my only successful book.

"The Depression made me a democratic Marxian socialist and led eventually to my residence in Sweden, 1956-67, where I met my wife.

"The rise of Howard Jarvis horrified me into the study of economics, and I swiftly became a Henry Georgist, believing in the need to tax land so high that no one will hold it off the market for speculative profit, and believing too that buildings should not be taxed at all. Five countries are prospering with this kind of tax. I have lived in one of them: New Zealand. Other countries in which I have resided are Mexico, England, Germany, Denmark, Austria, and Switzerland.

"For me the greatest man ever was Moses, for many reasons, including his creation of democracy and the weekly day of rest. I see the Greek gods as men and have placed them in history. I think I have found out which great man built Stonehenge, and which one built Zimbabwe. I reach these conclusions by combining legends with archaeology. Perhaps these conclusions of mine will someday be as well known as my findings on the past populations of cities.

"I see economic justice as the surest way to lasting peace, the land tax as the key to that justice, and politics as the way to get it. Hence my recent try for Congress."

AVOCATIONAL INTERESTS: Long-distance running (including marathons).

CHAPPELL, Mollie

CAREER: Writer.

WRITINGS—Novels: *Little Tom Sparrow*, E. J. Arnold, 1950; *Rhodesian Adventure*, Collins, 1950; *Tusker Tales*, E. J. Arnold, 1950; *The House on the Kopje*, Collins, 1951; *The Gentle Giant*, E. J. Arnold, 1951; *The Sugar and Spice*, Collins, 1952; *The Fortunes of Frick*, Collins, 1953; *Cat With No Fiddle*, Collins, 1954; *The Mystery of the Silver Circle*, Collins, 1955; *The Widow Jones: A Romance*, Collins, 1956; *Kit and the Mystery Man*, Collins, 1957; *Endearing Young Charms*, Collins, 1957; *Bachelor Heaven*, Collins, 1958; *A Wreath of Holly: A Romance*, Collins, 1959.

Novels; published by Collins: *One Little Room: A Romance*, 1960; *The Measure of Love*, 1961; *A Lesson in Loving: A Romance*, 1961; *Caroline*, 1962; *Come by Chance: A Romance*, 1963; *The Garden Room*, 1964; *The Ladies of Lark*, 1965; *Bright Promise*, 1966; *Since Summer*, 1967; *Bid Me Live*, 1967; *The Wind in the Green Trees*, 1969.

Novels, except as noted: *Great Horse Stories by Rene Guillot* (stories), Collins, 1970; *The Hasting Day*, Collins, 1970; *Tales of the Wild*, Collins, 1971; *Valley of Lilacs*, Collins, 1972; *Summer Story*, Collins, 1972; *Family Portrait*, Collins, 1973; *Cressy*, Collins, 1973; *Five Farthings*, Collins, 1974; *A Letter From Lydia*, Collins, 1974; *Seton's Wife*, Collins, 1975; *In Search of Mr. Rochester*, Collins, 1976; *The Loving Heart*, Collins, 1977, Fawcett, 1979; *Country Air*, Collins, 1977; *Romantic Widow*, Collins, 1978, Fawcett, 1979; *Wintersweet*, Collins, 1978.*

*   *   *

CHARLESTON, Robert Jesse   1916-

PERSONAL: Born April 3, 1916, in Upsala, Sweden; son of Sidney James (a high school teacher) and Katherine S. (Jesse) Charleston; married Joan Randle, December 17, 1941; children: Jennifer Ann, Robin Randle. *Education:* New College, Oxford, B.A., 1938, M.A. *Home:* 1 Denbigh Gardens, Richmond, Surrey TW9 1JA, England.

CAREER: Bristol Museum, Bristol, England, museum assistant, 1947; Victoria and Albert Museum, London, England, assistant keeper, 1948-59, deputy keeper, 1959-63, keeper of department of ceramics, 1963-76; writer. *Military service:* British Army, Royal Army Pay Corps, 1940-46; became major. *Member:* Museum Association (fellow).

WRITINGS: (Translator) Frederic Neuburg, *Glass in Antiquity*, Art Trade Press, 1949; *An Exhibition of Glass or Glass-Making as a Creative Art Through the Ages*, Temple Newsam House, 1961; (editor of revision) W. B. Honey, *English Pottery and Porcelain*, 5th edition (Charleston was not associated with earlier editions), A. & C. Black, 1962, 6th edition, 1969; *English Porcelain, 1745-1850*, Benn, 1965; (editor) *World Ceramics: An Illustrated History*, McGraw, 1968; *English Glass*, Victoria and Albert Museum, 1969; (editor with Wendy Evans and A. E. Werner) *Studies in Glass History and Design*, Society of Glass Technology, 1970; *Meissen and Other European Porcelain* (bound with *Oriental Porcelain* by John Ayers), National Trust, 1971; (editor) *Glass Circle: Papers for Collectors*, Unwin Brothers, Volume I, 1972, Volume II, 1975; *The Glass Circle*, Orion Press, 1973; (with Donald Towner) *English Ceramics, 1580-1830: A Commemorative Catalogue to Celebrate the Fiftieth Anniversary of the English Ceramic Circle, 1927-1977*, Sotheby Parke Bernet, 1977; *Illustrated Dictionary of Glass*, Thames & Hudson, 1977; (editor with Michael Archer and Madeleine Marcheix) *Glass and Stained Glass*, National Trust, 1978.

Editor of "Faber Monographs on Glass," Faber, 1961—. Contributor of articles and reviews to professional journals, popular magazines, and newspapers, including *Connoisseur*, *Burlington*, and *Apollo*.

AVOCATIONAL INTERESTS: Foreign travel, music.*

*   *   *

CHARNEY, Ann

PERSONAL: Born in Poland. *Education:* Attended McGill University and Sorbonne, University of Paris.

CAREER: Writer.

WRITINGS: Dobryd (novel), New Press, 1973.

Work represented in anthologies, including *Power Corrupted*, New Press, 1971.

Author of films "The Old Man's Fire," released by National Film Board, and "Elisabeth," released by Rohar Productions.

Author of "A View From Quebec," a column in *Maclean's*, 1971-72. Contributor to magazines and newspapers, including *Canadian*, *Ms.*, and *Canadian Forum*.

WORK IN PROGRESS: Elisabeth's Exile, a novel, for Doubleday.*

*   *   *

CHASE, Loriene Eck

PERSONAL: Born in Sacramento, Calif.; daughter of Walter and Genevieve (Bennetts) Eck; married Leo Goodman-Malamuth, 1946 (divorced, 1951); married Allen Chase, March 4, 1960 (divorced); married Clifton W. King, 1974; children: (first marriage) Leo. *Education:* University of Southern California, A.B., 1948, M.A., 1949, Ph.D., 1953. *Home:* 4925 Tarzana Woods Dr., Tarzana, Calif. 91356.

CAREER: Spastic Children's Foundation, Los Angeles, Calif., psychologist, 1952-55; private practice of psychology, 1955-57; Institute for Group Psychotherapy, Beverly Hills, Calif., psychologist, 1957-59; private practice of psychology, 1959—. Presenter of "Dr. Loriene Chase Show," on ABC-TV, 1966—. Member of board of directors of president's circle of University of Southern California and Chase-King Personal Development Center; member of executive board of Los Angeles Cancer Research Center; founding member of Achievement Rewards for Collegiate Scientists. *Military service:* U.S. Navy Women's Reserve, Women Accepted for Volunteer Emergency Service (WAVES). *Member:* National Art Association, Les Dames de Champagne, Dame de Rotisseur, Lakeside Country Club.

WRITINGS: (With husband, Clifton W. King) *The Human Miracle: Transcendent Psychology*, Hawthorn, 1974. Author of "Casebook of Dr. Chase," a newspaper column, and "Coming From Dr. Chase," a column in *Editor and Publisher*.*

*   *   *

CHEN, Anthony   1929-
(Tony Chen)

PERSONAL: Born January 3, 1929, in Kingston, Jamaica; came to the United States, 1949; naturalized U.S. citizen, 1956; son of Arthur and Maud Marie Chen; married Pura de Castro (a nurse supervisor), March 2, 1957; children: Richard, David. *Education:* Attended Art Careers School; Pratt Institute, B.F.A. (cum laude), 1955. *Religion:* Roman Catholic. *Home:* 53-51 96th St., Corona, N.Y.

CAREER: Newsweek, New York City, began in 1959, art director, 1968-70; free-lance artist and writer, 1970—. Instructor at Nassau Community College, 1969-71. Work featured in art exhibitions in New York City. *Awards, honors:* Citation of merit from Society of Illustrators, 1969, for *Cat Cousins,* 1970, for *House of Exiles,* and 1971, for *Hello, Small Sparrow;* award of excellence from Society of Illustrators and award from American Institute of Graphic Arts, both 1972, both for *Run, Zebra, Run;* award from Children's Book Showcase, 1973, for "Honshi"; citation of merit from Society of Illustrators, 1975, for illustrating cover for recording "The Yellow River Concerto"; award from Children's Book Showcase, 1975, for "About Owls"; citation of merit from Society of Illustrators, 1976, for "A Day in the Woods," and 1979, for "Land of Small Dragon."

WRITINGS—Under name Tony Chen; self illustrated: *Run, Zebra, Run* (juvenile verse), Lothrop, 1972; *Little Koala* (juvenile natural history), Holt, 1979. Illustrator of numerous books, including Helen B. Buckley, *Too Many Crackers,* Lothrop, 1966; Ruth Dale, *Do You Know a Cat?,* 1968; Isabelle C. Ching, *Tales From Old China,* 1969; and Edith Thacher Hurd, *The White Horse,* 1970. Work represented in anthologies, including *Timeless Voyage* (poems), Harcourt, 1979.

WORK IN PROGRESS: Little Racoons, for Holt; *The Cozy Book,* for Viking.

BIOGRAPHICAL/CRITICAL SOURCES: American Artist, May, 1972.

*   *   *

CHEN, Tony
See CHEN, Anthony

*   *   *

CHENEY, Sheldon Warren   1886-1980

OBITUARY NOTICE: Born July 29, 1886, in Berkeley, Calif.; died of a stroke, October 10, 1980, in Berkeley, Calif. Author, art historian, and theatre critic. Best known for his contributions in the areas of art and theatre, Cheney was a pioneer in the modernist movement in American drama during the 1920's and 1930's. Cheney's definition of American theatre influenced playwright Eugene O'Neill and set designer Robert Edmond Jones. In 1916 Cheney founded the magazine *Theatre Arts.* In addition to serving as an art and drama critic for numerous periodicals, he wrote thirteen books on the theatre and art. Some of his most highly acclaimed books include *New Movement in the Theatre; The Theatre: 3000 Years of Drama, Acting, and Stagecraft; Art and the Machine;* and *The Story of Modern Art.* Obituaries and other sources: *The Biographical Encyclopaedia and Who's Who of the American Theatre,* James Heineman, 1966; *Who's Who in American Art,* Bowker, 1978; *Who's Who in America,* 40th edition, Marquis, 1978; *New York Times,* October 14, 1980; *Time,* November 3, 1980; *AB Bookman's Weekly,* December 15, 1980.

*   *   *

CHESHER, Kim   1955-

PERSONAL: Born August 7, 1955, in Carshalton, England; daughter of Remington Charles (a publisher) and Betty (Read) Chesher. *Education:* Attended secondary school in Ewell, England. *Religion:* Christian. *Residence:* North Cheam, Surrey, England. *Agent:* c/o Hamish Hamilton Ltd., 90 Great Russell St., London WC1, England.

CAREER: Hamish Hamilton Ltd., London, England, editorial trainee in children's books, 1974-76; free-lance writer, 1976-78; Evans Brothers Ltd., London, plays assistant, 1978—.

WRITINGS—All juvenile: *The Fifth Quarter,* Hamish Hamilton, 1976; *Cuthbert and the Thingamabob,* Evans Brothers, 1976; *The Carnford Inheritance,* Hamish Hamilton, 1977; *Cuthbert and the Seamonster,* Evans Brothers, 1977; *The Finn Bequest,* Hamish Hamilton, 1978; *Cuthbert and the. Long Winter Sleep,* Evans Brothers, 1979; *Cuthbert and the Voyage of the Thingamabob,* Evans Brothers, 1981. Contributor to *Jointline.*

WORK IN PROGRESS: The Trouble With Magic (tentative title), a juvenile; *Kate's War,* a novel for older children.

SIDELIGHTS: Kim Chesher commented: "My writing is principally a form of escapism. My first published book was written after I had a brain hemorrhage in 1972 and wasn't able to do anything else. I've no pretension of being a 'great writer', but I believe I can write a good swashbuckling yarn, a belief which my father shared and encouraged.

"I write out of my own experiences, and *The Trouble With Magic* is about a family that has to come to terms with the death of a father, something I'm trying to do at the moment. I'm an optimistic pessimist trying hard to live up to my father's adage, 'Don't let the bastards grind you down!'"

*   *   *

CHESTER, Deborah   1957-

PERSONAL: Born April 25, 1957, in Chicago, Ill.; daughter of Kern E. (a chiropractor) and Ann (a receptionist; maiden name, Hatcher) Chester. *Education:* University of Oklahoma, B.A. (with honors), 1978. *Religion:* Church of Christ. *Agent:* Robbin Reynolds, 501 Madison Ave., New York, N.Y. 10022. *Office:* 506 West Kings Highway, Paragould, Ark. 72450.

CAREER: Writer, 1978—.

WRITINGS: A Love So Wild (novel), Coward, 1980; *The Sign of the Owl* (juvenile), Four Winds Press, 1981.

WORK IN PROGRESS: A romantic novel, tentatively titled "French Slippers," to be published in 1981, by Coward; a romantic novel set in nineteenth-century England.

SIDELIGHTS: Deborah Chester wrote: "I firmly believe that writers are born, not made. Training may be necessary to harness that talent, but the spark has to be there and it has to be recognized by the would-be writer. I started my first writing around the age of nine, and wasn't published until age twenty-one. No one ever grabbed me and said, 'You ought to be a writer!' I was the one who had the idea. The people around me thought it a highly impractical one, but by the time I finished high school I was fortunate enough to come across the information that the University of Oklahoma had a professional writing department in its journalism school, and that if I so wished I could major in writing fiction.

"That is what I did, and it's one of the smartest things I have ever done. My senior year I took two simultaneous classes on writing novels, and for each class wrote a different book. Both instructors are established novelists. One of them introduced me to his agent. She accepted me as a client, and a few months after my graduation she sold one of the novels I had written for class. Then she sold the other one and my third novel. With such a start, I haven't had time to consider any other career besides writing, nor would I wish to. Nothing is more suited to me than sitting alone in a room with paper and a pen for companions, and my imagination whisking me anywhere in the world or in time.

"My goal in writing is to provide readers with books that are vibrant, colorful, and fun to read. When I start a new book, it's with the intention to create one which I myself would enjoy reading. I think a fiction writer is doing something very wrong and harmful to himself when he tries to write something he hates. A writer has to be honest, with himself as well as with others. I can't see myself ever sitting down to produce some universally profound book, so laden with symbols and avant-garde images that everyone is kept guessing as to what it means. I couldn't write that because I never read that type of book, no matter what sort of prestige may be attached to it. And if I can't stay interested in something I'm writing, I won't be able to interest a reader in it either.

"I like characters who are doers. I like to give them spunk and courage. They charge out and make mistakes and get hurt, but they learn something from the experience and are better for it. That's a pretty simplistic formula, but life is so complicated these days I find simplicity refreshing.

"But I also throw in romanticism and melodrama because those things are fun and not to be taken too seriously. I want to try and produce a glow in a reader that will keep him inspired for a while after the book is over, that will keep him thinking about the characters and taking satisfaction in their failures or successes.

"My principal aim is to provide escape and entertainment, and I think it's an honorable one. It's the reason many of the great classics were written and why they are still read generation after generation. They are enjoyable and somehow capture that glow of elusive gloriousness.

"My first novel has been sold to British and German publishers. It has provided the means for me to visit England for the first time and obtain first-hand experience of the research which provides the basis for most of my books. At the moment I am concentrating on English history during the Napoleonic Wars, but I want to write more novels about the Middle Ages and possibly the Renaissance as well. I have a modern story in mind, but right now it is more interesting and fun for me to stick with historical settings. I find past times more flamboyant and colorful than ours."

AVOCATIONAL INTERESTS: Tennis, riding horses, photography, collecting Indian rocks, raising crossbred cattle.

* * *

CHETWODE, Penelope 1910-

PERSONAL—Home: New House, Cusop, Hay-on-Wye, Hereford, England.

CAREER: Writer and lecturer.

WRITINGS: Two Middle-Aged Ladies in Andalusia, J. Murray, 1963, Transatlantic, 1966; *Kulu: The End of the Habitable World,* Transatlantic, 1972.*

* * *

CHISHOLM, Roderick Milton 1916-

PERSONAL: Born November 27, 1916, in North Attleboro, Mass.; son of Alpin and Irma (Gardner) Chisholm; married Eleanor Parker, October 18, 1943; children: Yeddy, Roderick M., Jonathan Parker. *Education:* Brown University, A.B., 1938; Harvard University, A.M., 1940, Ph.D., 1942. *Home:* 170 Adams Point, Barrington, R.I. 02806. *Office:* Department of Philosophy, Brown University, Providence, R.I. 02912.

CAREER: Barnes Foundation, Merion, Pa., instructor in philosophy, 1946; University of Pennsylvania, Philadelphia, assistant professor of philosophy, 1946-47; Brown University, Providence, R.I., 1947—, began as assistant professor, became professor of philosophy, 1953—, Romeo Elton Professor of Natural Theology, 1953-73, Andrew W. Mellon Professor of Humanities, 1973—, chairman of department, 1951-64. Visiting lecturer at Harvard University, 1950, 1960, 1969, and University of Southern California, 1955; visiting professor at University of Graz, 1959-60, 1974, 1975, 1976, Princeton University, 1961-62, University of California, Santa Barbara, 1964, University of Atlanta, 1965, University of Illinois, 1966, University of Chicago, 1967, University of Massachusetts, 1970, 1971, 1972, 1973, University of Salzburg, 1972, University of Pittsburgh, 1973, and University of Heidelberg, 1977; Nellie Wallace Lecturer at Oxford University, 1967. Executive director of Franz Brentano Foundation. *Military service:* U.S. Army, 1942-46.

MEMBER: Institut International de Philosophie, Sociedad Interamericana de Filosofia, American Philosophical Association (member of executive committee, 1953-56; vice-president of Eastern Division, 1962; division president, 1968), Association for Symbolic Logic (member of executive committee, 1950-53), American Academy of Arts and Sciences, Metaphysical Society of America (member of council; president, 1972-73), American Association for the Advancement of Science, Phi Beta Kappa. *Awards, honors:* Fulbright grant for University of Graz, 1959-60, and Yugoslavia, 1975; Ph.D. from University of Graz, 1972.

WRITINGS: Perceiving: A Philosophical Study, Cornell University Press, 1957; (editor) *Realism and the Background of Phenomenology,* Free Press, 1961; *Philosophy,* Prentice-Hall, 1964; *Theory of Knowledge,* Prentice-Hall, 1966, 2nd edition, 1977; (editor) Franz Clemens Brentano, *The True and the Evident,* Humanities, 1966; (editor) Brentano, *The Origin of Our Knowledge of Right and Wrong,* Humanities, 1969.

(Editor) Alexius Ritter von Handschuchsheim Meinong, *Uber Moeglichkeit und Wahrscheinlichkeit: Beitrage zur Gegenstandstheorie und Erkenntnistheorie,* Akademische Druck und Verlagsanstalt, 1972; (editor with Robert J. Swartz) *Empirical Knowledge: Readings From Contemporary Sources,* Prentice-Hall, 1973; *The Problem of the Criterion,* Marquette University Press, 1973; (editor) Meinong, *Uber philosophische Wissenschaft und ihre Propaedeutik: Uber die Stellung der Gegenstandstheorie im System der Wissenschaften, uber die Erfahrungsgrundlagen unseres Wissens, zum Erweise des allgemeinen Kausalgesetzes,* Akademische Druck und Verlagsansalt, 1973; *Person and Object: A Metaphysical Study,* Open Court, 1976; (editor and translator with Rolf George) Franz Clemens Brentano, *Aristotle and His World View,* University of California Press, 1978; (editor with Rudolf Haller) *Die Philosophie Franz Brentanos* (title means "The Philosophy of Franz Brentano"), Rodopi, 1978. Contributor to philosophy journals. Associate editor of *Philosophy and Phenomenological Research* and *Meinong Gesamtausgabe.*

BIOGRAPHICAL/CRITICAL SOURCES: Keith Lehrer, editor, *Analysis and Metaphysics: Essays in Honor of R. M. Chisholm,* D. Reidel, 1975; *Times Literary Supplement,* August 26, 1977.*

* * *

CHODOROV, Edward 1904-

PERSONAL: Born April 17, 1904, in New York, N.Y.; son

of Harry (an actor and businessman) and Lena (Simmons) Chodorov; married Marjorie Roth (divorced); married Rosemary Pettit, June 16, 1954; children: Stephen; two daughters. *Education:* Attended Brown University.

CAREER: Playwright, screenwriter, producer, and director. Began as stage manager for "Abie's Irish Rose," 1922; traveled to South Africa as stage manager for "Is Zat So," 1928; worked as publicity writer for Columbia Pictures; writer of screenplays for Warner Bros., First National, Columbia Pictures, Metro-Goldwyn-Mayer (MGM), and Twentieth Century-Fox, 1933-57; producer of motion pictures, including "Rich Man, Poor Girl," 1938, "Woman Against Woman," 1938, "Spring Madness," 1938, "Tell No Tales," 1939, "The Man From Dakota," 1940, and "Road House," 1948; writer and director of stage plays, including "Those Endearing Young Charms," 1943, "Decision," 1944, "Common Ground," 1945, and "Monsieur Lautrec," 1959; American Broadcasting Co. (ABC-TV), New York, N.Y., writer for "Billy Rose Show," 1952; writer, director, and producer for Horizon Pictures, 1961-63, A.C.E. Productions, London, 1964, Columbia Pictures, 1965, and Twentieth Century-Fox, 1966-67; writer and producer for Warner-7 Arts, 1968-69; writer and director for Dowling, Whitehead & Stevens, 1971-72, Cheryl Crawford Productions, 1973, Universal Pictures, 1974-75, and Theatre Guild, 1976. Lecturer at California State University, 1977. *Member:* Dramatists Guild.

WRITINGS—Plays: (With Arthur Barton) "Wonder Boy," first produced on Broadway at Alvin Theatre, October 23, 1931; *Kind Lady* (adapted from the short story by Hugh Walpole, "The Silver Mask"; first produced on Broadway at Booth Theatre, April 23, 1935), Samuel French, 1936 (also see below); (with H. S. Kraft) *Cue for Passion* (three-act; first produced on Broadway at Royale Theatre, December 19, 1940), Samuel French, 1941; *Those Endearing Young Charms* (three-act; first produced on Broadway at Booth Theatre, June 16, 1943), Samuel French, 1943; *Decision* (three-act; first produced on Broadway at Belasco Theatre, February 2, 1944), Samuel French, 1946; *Common Ground* (three-act; first produced on Broadway at Fulton Theatre, April 25, 1945), Samuel French, 1946; "Signor Chicago," first produced in 1947.

Oh, Men! Oh, Women! (three-act; first produced on Broadway at Henry Miller's Theatre, December 17, 1953), Samuel French, 1955 (also see below); *The Spa* (adapted from a play by Ferenc Molnar; first produced in 1955), Dramatists Play Service, 1957; *Listen to the Mocking Bird* (adapted from the novel by Arnold Ridley and Mary Cathcart Borer, *Tabitha*; first produced in Boston, Mass., at Colonial Theatre, December 27, 1958), [New York, N.Y.], 1958; "Monsieur Lautrec," first produced in Coventry, England, at Belgrade Civic Theatre, 1959. Also author of unproduced plays, including "Erskine," "The Clubwoman," and "Irrational Knot." Work represented in anthology, *Three Plays About Crime and Criminals* (contains "Arsenic and Old Lace," "Detective Story," and "Kind Lady"), edited by Freedley, Pocket Books, 1979.

Screenplays: "The Mayor of Hell," Warner Bros., 1933; "Captured" (adapted from a short story by Philip Gibbs), Warner Bros., 1933; "The World Changes" (adapted from a story by Sheridan Gibney), First National, 1933; "Madame Du Barry," Warner Bros., 1934; (with Mary C. McCall) "Craig's Wife" (adapted from the play by George Kelly), Columbia, 1936; (with F. Hugh Herbert and Brown Holmes) "Snowed Under" (adapted from the novel by Lawrence Saunders), First National, 1936; "Yellow Jack" (adapted from the play by Sidney Howard and Paul de Kruif), Metro-

Goldwyn-Mayer (MGM), 1938; "Woman Against Woman" (adapted from the short story by Margaret Chulkin Banning, "Enemy Territory"), MGM, 1938; "Spring Madness" (adapted from the play by Philip Barry, "Spring Dance"), MGM, 1939.

"Undercurrent" (adapted from the novel by Thelma Strabel, *You Were There*), MGM, 1946; (with Luther Davis and George Wells) "The Hucksters" (adapted from the novel by Frederic Wakeman), MGM, 1947; (with Margaret Gruen, Oscar Saul, and David Hertz) "Road House," Twentieth Century-Fox, 1948; (with Jerry Davis and Charles Bennett) "Kind Lady" (adapted from own play), MGM, 1951; "Oh, Men! Oh, Women!" (adapted from own play), Twentieth Century-Fox, 1957.*

*   *   *

CHOWDER, Ken 1950-

PERSONAL: Born October 11, 1950, in New York, N.Y. *Education:* Attended Reed College, 1968-70; Stanford University, B.A., 1971. *Politics:* "Unlikely." *Religion:* "Impossible." *Agent:* Maxine Groffsky, 2 Fifth Ave., New York, N.Y. 10011. *Office:* 1023 Southeast 31st St., Portland, Ore. 97214.

CAREER: Shiver Mountain Press, Washington, Conn., pressman, 1972-76; National Center of Scientific Research, Paris, France, English language editor, 1976-77; Association Marzio, Istres, Bouches-du-Rhone, France, teacher of English as a foreign language, 1977-78; writer. Free-lance editor. Bottle-smashing director of Washington, Conn. *Awards, honors:* Harper-Saxton fellowship, 1978; Syracuse University fellowship, 1978 (declined); Mary Roberts Rinehart Foundation fellowship, 1980; Ingram Merrill Foundation fellowship, 1980.

WRITINGS: Blackbird Days (novel), Harper, 1980; *Delicate Geometry,* (novel), Harper, 1982.

SIDELIGHTS: Chowder told *CA:* "Ever since discovering, at the age of eleven, that I did not possess the proper talents to become a minor-league baseball player, I have considered myself to be a writer. My original motivation to write was caused by that self-depiction: I was a writer, I ought to write. More recently, my motivation has been twofold: the first fold is habit, persistent habit; the second fold is the difficulty of the thing, and the ever-increasing desire to produce, against all odds, a good novel. My goal is that rare bird itself."

With *Blackbird Days,* a novel about three brothers of the sixties generation and their struggles with imminent middle-age, Chowder appears to have beaten the odds against the success of a first novel. Carole Cook of *Saturday Review* wrote of Chowder, "He is a tremendously satisfying writer, bringing good news, for a change, of the people who used to be called the Woodstock generation." Scott Spencer of *New York Times Book Review,* however, indicated that though *Blackbird Days* is a good first novel, Chowder still has room for improvement. "Chowder can describe nearly anything and make it live," Spencer commented. "Still, the novel lacks power in the end. My guess is that 'Blackbird Days' is the warm-up exercise of a strong writer."

BIOGRAPHICAL/CRITICAL SOURCES: Los Angeles Times, July 29, 1980; *Saturday Review, July, 1980;* New Yorker, *August 4, 1980;* New York Times Book Review, *September 7, 1980.*

CHRISTESEN, Clement Byrne 1911-

PERSONAL: Born October 28, 1911, in Townsville, Australia; son of Patrick and Susan Stewart (Byrne) Christesen; married Nina Maximoff, 1942. *Education:* Attended Kings College, University of Queensland. *Home:* Stanhope House, Eltham, Victoria 3095, Australia. *Office:* Baillien Library, University of Melbourne, Parkville, Victoria 3052, Australia.

CAREER: Worked as journalist and broadcaster; *Meanjin Quarterly,* Melbourne, Australia, founder and editor, 1940-75; University of Melbourne, Parkville, Australia, Lockie fellow, 1966-75, honorary curator at Meanjin Archive at Baillieu Library, 1975—. *Member:* Australian Society of Authors (vice-president), Fellowship of Australian Writers (vice-president), Australian Academy of the Humanities (honorary fellow), Association for the Study of Australian Literature (life member), Rationalist Association (member of board of directors). *Awards, honors:* Officer of Order of the British Empire, 1961; Crouch Gold Medal, 1965; Britannica award for humanities, 1970; D.Litt. from Monash University, 1975; Priestley Gold Medal from James Cook University, Townsville, 1980, for literature.

WRITINGS: (Editor) *Australian Heritage,* Longmans, Green, 1949, 2nd edition, 1967; (editor) *Coast to Coast: Australian Stories, 1953-1954,* Angus & Robertson, 1955; (editor) *On Native Grounds: Australian Writing From Meanjin Quarterly,* Angus & Robertson, 1967; *The Hand of Memory: Selected Stories and Verse,* Meanjin Press, 1970; (editor) *The Gallery on Eastern Hill* (art criticism), Victorian Artists' Society, 1971; *Having Loved* (poetry), Stanhope Press, 1979; (translator) *Six Poems by Anna Akhmatova,* Stanhope Press, 1980.

WORK IN PROGRESS: The Generous Sun, an autobiography; a book of collected verse entitled *From the Desert's Edge.*

* * *

CHRISTOPHER, Robert Collins 1924-

PERSONAL: Born March 3, 1924, in Thomaston, Conn.; son of Gordon Newton and Ruth (Mignon) Christopher; married June Wiles, 1948 (divorced, 1969); married Rita Joan Goldstein (a journalist), May 17, 1970; children: (first marriage) Ulrica, Thomas, Valerie, Nicholas; (second marriage) Alistair, Gordon. *Education:* Yale University, B.A. (with exceptional distinction), 1948. *Religion:* Episcopalian. *Home:* 941 Bloomfield St., Hoboken, N.J. 07030. *Office: GEO,* 450 Park Ave., New York, N.Y. 10022.

CAREER/WRITINGS: Investment Dealers Digest, New York City, staff writer, 1949-50; *Time,* New York City, member of staff, 1950-56, associate editor, 1956-61, senior editor of U.S. and world business sections, 1961-63; *Newsweek,* New York City, foreign editor, 1963-69, executive editor, 1969-72, editor of international edition 1972-78; *GEO,* New York City, managing editor, 1979—. Contributor of articles to newspapers and magazines, including *Foreign Affairs, New York Times Sunday Magazine, Sunday Times of London, Horizon,* and *GEO.* Member of board of trustees of Corning Glass Works Foundation, African American Institute, and Correspondents Fund. *Military service,* U.S. Army, 1942-46, 1950-52; became captain. *Member:* Century Club, Elizabethan Club. *Awards, honors:* Overseas Press Club citation, 1966; Front Page Award, 1969.

CHURCHILL, Caryl 1938-

PERSONAL: Born September 3, 1938, in London, England; married David Harter, 1961; children: three sons. *Education:* Lady Margaret Hall, Oxford, B.A., 1960. *Home:* 12 Thornhill Sq., London N.1, England. *Agent:* Margaret Ramsay Ltd., 14a Goodwin's Court, London WC2N 4LL, England.

CAREER: Writer. Resident dramatist at Royal Court Theatre, 1974-75. *Awards, honors:* Richard Hillary Memorial Prize, 1961.

WRITINGS—Published plays: *Owners* (first produced in London, England, at Royal Court Theatre Upstairs, 1972; produced in New York, N.Y., 1973), Eyre Methuen, 1973; *Light Shining in Buckinghamshire* (first produced in London, 1975), Pluto Press, 1978; *Vinegar Tom* (first produced in 1976), TQ Publications, 1978; *Traps* (first produced in 1977), Pluto Press, 1978; *Cloud Nine,* Pluto Press, 1979.

Unpublished plays: "Downstairs," first produced in Oxford, England, 1958, produced in London, England, 1959; "Having a Wonderful Time," first produced in London, 1960; "Easy Death," first produced in Oxford, 1962; "Schreber's Nervous Illness," first produced in London at King's Head Theatre, 1972; "Perfect Happiness," first produced in London, 1974; "Moving Clocks Go Slow," first produced in London, 1975; "Objections to Sex and Violence," first produced in London, 1975.

Television plays: "The Judge's Wife," first broadcast in 1972; "Turkish Delight," first broadcast in 1974; "The After Dinner Joke," first broadcast in 1978; "The Legion Hall Bombing," first broadcast in 1978.

Radio plays: "Lovesick," first broadcast in 1967; "Identical Twins," first broadcast in 1968; "Abortive," first broadcast in 1971; "Not, Not, Not, Not, Not Enough Oxygen," first broadcast in 1971; "Schreber's Nervous Illness," first broadcast in 1972; "Henry's Past," first broadcast in 1972; "Perfect Happiness," first broadcast in 1973.

Work represented in anthologies, including "The Ants" (first broadcast on radio, 1962) in *Penguin New English Dramatists Twelve,* Penguin, 1968.

BIOGRAPHICAL/CRITICAL SOURCES: Cue, May 26, 1973.*

* * *

CIPRIANO, Anthony (John) 1941-

PERSONAL: Born May 12, 1941, in New York, N.Y.; son of John (a foreman) and Nancy (Daino) Cipriano; married Vikki Bachmann, September 23, 1971; children: Jillian, Valerie. *Education:* Attended Rutgers University, 1959-62; University of Pennsylvania, D.D.M., 1966. *Home and office:* 260 Godwin Ave., Ridgewood, N.J. 07450.

CAREER: Private practice of dentistry in Ridgewood, N.J., 1973—. Member of New Brunswick Planning Board, 1971-73. Guest on television programs. *Military service:* U.S. Air Force, Dental Corps, 1966-68; became captain. *Member:* American Dental Association, National Space Institute, American Bonsai Society, American Institute of Aeronautics and Astronautics (chairman of public policy of Greater New York section), British Interplanetary Society, New Jersey Dental Society, Space Studies Institute (fellow), Bergen County Dental Society. *Awards, honors: America's Journeys Into Space* was named outstanding science book for children by National Science Teachers Association-Children's Book Council Joint Committee, 1979.

WRITINGS: America's Journeys Into Space: The Astronauts of the United States (juvenile), Messner, 1979.

WORK IN PROGRESS: My Two Weeks as an Astronaut, a fictional biography of the first civilian to prepare for a ride on a space shuttle, for juveniles, publication expected in 1981; *High Flight: The History of the X-15 Experimental Rocket Plane;* "Breaking the Earth Barrier," a film tracing the ascendency of man from the cave to space.

SIDELIGHTS: Cipriano wrote: "Mankind's emergence into the environs of space constitutes a new and critical stage in the evolutionary process. The risks are high, but greater still is the opportunity to experience, for the first time, the full force of the universe beyond Earth's protective barriers. I can think of no other endeavor in the annals of human history that portends higher drama, greater challenge, or greater dividends—the unfolding of the secret of existence itself. The conquest of space is magical. Herein lies the ultimate answer, the ultimate truth. I am fascinated and cannot resist exploring the topic further."

*   *   *

CLAIR, Bernard (Eddy) 1951-

PERSONAL: Born May 13, 1951, in New York, N.Y.; son of Joseph A. (in sales) and Eleanor (Neuwirth) Clair. *Education:* Adelphi University, B.A., 1973; St. John's University, Jamaica, N.Y., J.D., 1976. *Religion:* Jewish. *Home:* 417 East 64th St., New York, N.Y. 10021. *Agent:* Goodman Associates, 500 West End Ave., New York, N.Y. 10024. *Office:* Clair & Daniele, 551 Fifth Ave., New York, N.Y. 10017.

CAREER: Admitted to New York Bar, 1977; Clair & Daniele (law firm), New York, N.Y., founder and partner, 1977—. *Member:* New York County Lawyers Association.

WRITINGS: (With Anthony R. Daniele) *Love Pact: A Layman's Complete Guide to Legal Living Together Agreements,* Grove, 1980.

WORK IN PROGRESS: "An exploration of the aftermath of divorce from a legal and emotional viewpoint that will put forth the notion that divorce merely ends the *marriage;* however, in many instances a continuation of the relationship occurs," publication expected in 1981.

SIDELIGHTS: Clair wrote: "Clair & Daniele is a firm specializing in matrimonial law. It is obvious that cohabitation is increasing to the point of gaining public acceptance as a legitimate social institution. Our book strives to inform readers of the legal repercussions of their decision to live together, and seeks to offer the best solution to the problem of protecting their rights and ensuring fairness if the relationship ends, which is for the couple to execute a written living together agreement."

*   *   *

CLARK, Eric 1937-

PERSONAL: Born July 29, 1937, in Birmingham, England; son of Horace Ernest (a television engineer) and Hilda (Mitchley) Clark; married Frances Grant, 1959 (divorced); married Marcelle Bernstein (a writer), April 12, 1972; children: Rachael, Charlotte, Daniel. *Education:* Attended secondary school in Birmingham, England. *Politics:* "Fluctuating." *Religion:* Christian. *Home:* 74 Osborne Villas, Hove, Sussex, England. *Agent:* Jonathan Clowes Ltd., 19 Jeffrey's Pl., London NWI 9PP, England.

CAREER: Daily Mail, London, England, reporter, 1961-63;

Guardian, London, staff writer, 1963-64; *Observer,* London, staff writer, 1964-72; free-lance writer, 1972—. *Member:* International P.E.N., Society of Authors, National Union of Journalists, Crime Writers Association.

WRITINGS: Diplomat: The World of International Diplomacy, Taplinger, 1973 (published in England as *Corps Diplomatique,* Allen Lane, 1973); *Black Gambit* (spy novel), Morrow, 1978; *The Sleeper* (spy novel), Atheneum, 1980; *Send in the Lions* (spy novel), Atheneum, 1981. Contributor to magazines, including *Observer* and *New Statesman,* and newspapers.

WORK IN PROGRESS: Another spy novel, publication by Atheneum expected in 1982.

SIDELIGHTS: Clark told *CA:* "I was a staff journalist for nearly twenty years before becoming a free-lance writer. I started on weekly newspapers in the Midlands of England, where I was born, and gradually worked my way southwards to London. In my last staff position, on the *Observer,* I was variously home affairs correspondent, chief writer of the magazine section, and writing-editor of a news-background unit.

"I was lucky in that my work had enormous variety and scope—from the escape of George Blake, the spy, and its signifigance, to the way the world's grand hotels were surviving the twentieth century. (One series of features, on London's casinos, was publicly credited by the then home secretary, Roy Jenkins, for making him decide to enact the United Kindom's present gaming laws). The variety lay not only in the stories, but the people—policemen to foreign leaders, minor bureaucrats to cardinals—and places. This meant not just a variety of countries, but also a diversity of lodgings from the George VI in Paris to some fly-blown place on the edge of the desert.

"What I didn't know at the time, because I had no plans in that direction, was how much material I was absorbing and laying down for when I came to write fiction. As far as specifically spy fiction is concerned, one other thing helped. I spent four years researching diplomats (along with my *Observer* job), spoke to several hundred at length, and stayed in many of their homes. Not all of them were the diplomats they were meant to be. When I came to write about spies I had a background of people whose company, and sometimes homes, I had shared.

"*Black Gambit,* the first, emerged seemingly by accident. I had broken off from writing an ordered feature article for some magazine, switched on the radio, and heard a piece about the Panovs, then still not being allowed to leave the U.S.S.R. During the afternoon the idea grew—why not get them out. I interrupted the feature again and began jotting down what was basically the plot of the book (though it was not the Panovs but a scientist who had to be spirited away in the book). Gradually the book took me over. I devoted more and more time to it, less to journalistic free lancing.

"The idea for *The Sleeper* came halfway through the writing of *Black Gambit.* Reading some research notes, I came across a factual mention of a Soviet spy who had been told by his Russian masters to 'lie low, do nothing' until they activated him. What, I wondered, would happen if this was done to a man who heard nothing for many, many years, and if—as is likely—he changed in the meantime. This became the basis of the plot. *Send in the Lions* was also triggered by a factual instance—or something at least I believe to be factual. During some research I came across claims from intelligence men that the British Secret Service masterminded a prison break in Uruguay in 1971 to free Tupamaro terrorists who were currently being demanded for the freedom of the kidnapped British ambassador. This resulted in my playing around with the idea of what would a country do if it had to satisfy the demands of a terrorist group for a reason unknown to others, but at the same time could not have been seen to give way.

"In *Send in the Lions* the country involved in the dilemma is the United States, and it 'solves' the problem by using an ex-CIA man as a mercenary. The journalistic influence extends in another way: after the idea and the outline (which I find I have to write in detail even though much of it changes later) I research in depth the specifics of the book—places, technical expertise (how do you best infiltrate gas into an air conditioning system?). That said, I reckon to discard seventy-five percent of the research, forcing myself to remember that what I should be writing is not a collection of all facts I have discovered, but a readable and, hopefully, exciting book in which specific interesting facts belong.

"And although I do try to use factual detail, my primary concern, apart from telling a story, is how people react in certain circumstances. This, to me, is one of the special interests of the espionage novel: it places people in situations of great stress.

"Being a journalist does present some specific working problems. Perhaps the greatest is staying glued to a desk for the whole time. Journalists are a bit like stage performers: they put on their act, get instant applause or not, as the case may be, and then move on to the next one. A book means eighteen months working in a vacuum of a sort before any kind of input from outside. Not surprisingly, the research is always the fun part—the discipline comes in knowing when to stop. It helps that my wife, Marcelle Bernstein, is a writer, and that we usually work in the same room.

"Writing, I sometimes think, is a lonely and almost unnatural pursuit. But at the same time it's a drug. As I look back over the few years and the few books so far, I *think* I see it's getting better. And getting better, getting closer to what you really want to say, is the biggest spur to keeping on writing."

*   *   *

CLARK, Mary T(wibill)

PERSONAL: Born in Philadelphia, Pa.; daughter of Francis S. (a lawyer) and Regina (Twibill) Clark. *Education:* Manhattanville College, B.A., 1939; Fordham University, M.A., 1952, Ph.D., 1955; postdoctoral study at Yale University, 1968-69. *Politics:* Independent Democrat. *Office:* Department of Philosophy, Manhattanville College, Purchase, N.Y. 10577.

CAREER: Entered Society of the Sacred Heart (R.S.C.J.), 1939, became Roman Catholic nun, 1941; teacher of English, Latin, and religion at Convents of the Sacred Heart in Albany, N.Y., 1945-49, and Philadelphia, Pa., 1947; supervisor of studies and English and religion teacher in Rochester, N.Y., 1949-51, and New York, N.Y., 1952-53; Manhattanville College, Purchase, N.Y., instructor, 1951-52, assistant professor, 1953-57, associate professor, 1957-61, professor of philosophy, 1961—, chairman of philosophy department, 1962-64, 1966-68, and 1972-79. Visiting professor at Villanova University, autumn, 1980, Fordham University, spring, 1981, and University of San Francisco. Adviser to Manhattanville Social Action Secretariat, 1960-66; worked with Anti-Defamation League, National Council of Christians and Jews, and Southern Leadership Conference.

MEMBER: International Patristic Association, North Amer-

ican Patristic Association, American Catholic Philosophical Association (president, 1976-77), Society for Medieval and Renaissance Philosophy, Conference of Philosophical Societies (member of steering committee, 1975—), American Philosophical Association (chairperson of Conference of Chairpersons, 1975-77), Metaphysical Society. *Awards, honors:* Interracial Justice Award from Catholic Interracial Council of the Bronx, 1966, for *Discrimination Today;* D.H.L. from Villanova University, 1977.

WRITINGS: Augustine: Philosopher of Freedom, Desclee, 1959; (with Helen Casey) *Logic,* Regnery, 1963; *Discrimination Today,* Hobbs/Context, 1966; *Augustinian Personalism,* Villanova University Press, 1970; (editor and translator) *An Aquinas Reader,* Doubleday, 1973; (editor) *The Problem of Freedom,* Appleton, 1973; (translator and author of introduction and notes) *Theological Treatises of Marius Victorinus,* Consortium, 1980; *The Spirituality of St. Augustine,* Paulist/Newman, in press. Member of advisory board of *Dionysius,* 1977—. Contributor to philosophy journals.

WORK IN PROGRESS: Continuing research on philosophical sources of fourth-century writer Marius Victorinus.

SIDELIGHTS: Mary Clark wrote: "My priority as an educator has been to enable students to gain as much self-understanding as possible so that they may appreciate their own uniqueness and dignity. I believe that although thinking is no substitute for living, philosophical knowledge can enhance human life. Therefore my books and articles try to make available to the general public those great philosophical and religious insights which can free people from cultural captivity and open them to good, to a participation in wisdom.

"I also believe that a clarification of the reality and the meaning of freedom is one of our great contemporary needs. We talk a great deal today about personal responsibility but do we really educate people to assume it? Contrary to the opinion of humanists, personal responsibility is not lessened but increased through the possibility of friendship with God, who brings out the best in persons who have a right understanding of God and of themselves."

*   *   *

CLARKE, Anna 1919-

PERSONAL: Born April 28, 1919, in Cape Town, South Africa; daughter of Fred (an educator) and Edith Annie (an educator; maiden name, Gillams) Clarke. *Education:* London External, B.Sc., 1945; Open University, B.A., 1973; Sussex University, M.A., 1975. *Politics:* Social Democrat. *Religion:* Unitarian. *Home:* 12 Franklin Rd., Brighton BN2 3AD, England.

CAREER: Writer. Victor Gollancz (publisher), London, England, private secretary, 1947-50; Eyre & Spottiswoode (publisher), London, private secretary, 1951-52; administrative secretary for British Association for American Studies, 1956-62. *Member:* British Federation of University Women, Crime Writers Association, Society of Authors.

WRITINGS: (Co-editor and translator) Karl Abraham, *Clinical Papers and Essays on Psychoanalysis,* Hogarth, 1955; *The Darkened Room,* John Long, 1968; *A Mind to Murder,* Chatto & Windus, 1971; *The End of a Shadow,* Chatto & Windus, 1972; *Plot Counter-Plot,* Collins, 1975; *Legacy of Evil,* Collins, 1976; *The Deathless and the Dead,* Collins, 1976; *This Downhill Path,* McKay, 1977; *The Lady in Black,* Collins, 1977, McKay, 1978; *One of Us Must Die,* Collins, 1978, Doubleday, 1980; *The Poisoned Web,* Collins, 1979; *Poison Parsley,* Collins, 1979; *Last Voyage,* Collins, 1980.

WORK IN PROGRESS: Two crime novels.

SIDELIGHTS: Anna Clarke told *CA:* "Originally I had planned a career in mathematics (which I am now taking up again after forty years), but was interrupted by a long and severe illness followed by the need to earn a living without further delay. I started writing late in life, had no success with straight novels, so I turned to mystery stories. I think my main motivation was to find in my own imagination a release both from the restrictions on life left by my illness, and from the frustration of office jobs that I disliked but which were the only ones I could do. And since I never plan a story, but feel as if it is being told to me as I write, there is the excitement of not knowing how it will end!"

*   *   *

CLARKE, Ernest George   1927-

PERSONAL: Born June 16, 1927, in Varna, Ontario, Canada; son of Melvin E. and Eva (Epps) Clarke; married Ruth Hunt, 1951; children: Paul, Margaret, Patricia, David. *Education:* University of Toronto, B.A., 1949, B.D., 1952, M.A., 1953; University of Leiden, D.Litt., 1962. *Office:* Department of Near Eastern Studies, University of Toronto, Toronto, Ontario, Canada M5S 1A1.

CAREER: Ordained by United Church of Canada, 1952; Queen's University, Kingston, Ontario, lecturer at Theological College, 1956-58, professor of Old Testament, 1958-61; University of Toronto, Toronto, Ontario, associate professor at Victoria College, 1961-64, professor of Near Eastern studies, 1964—, chairman of department, 1970—. Member of British School of Archaeology; member of Jerusalem excavation, summers, 1965-66. Member of governing council of University of Toronto, 1979—. Visiting fellow at Cambridge University, 1969-70. *Member:* American Oriental Society, Society of Biblical Literature, Canadian Society for Biblical Studies (president, 1967-68), Arts and Letters Club. *Awards, honors:* Canadian Council fellowship, 1969-70.

WRITINGS: The Selected Questions of Isho Bar Nun on the Pentateuch, E. J. Brill, 1962; *The Wisdom of Solomon,* Cambridge University Press, 1973. Contributor to theology journals.

WORK IN PROGRESS: A computer-generated concordance to Targum Pseudo-Jonathan to the Pentateuch, with J. C. Hurd and W. E. Augrecht, publication expected in 1982.

*   *   *

CLARKE, Henry Charles   1899-
(Hockley Clarke)

PERSONAL—Home: 79 Surbiton Hill Park, Surbiton, Surrey, England.

CAREER: Writer. Founder and editor of *Birds and Country Quarterly,* 1948—.

*WRITINGS—*Under pseudonym Hockley Clark: (Editor) *Birds Annual,* Ducimus Books, 1974; *Blackie and Company: Blackbirds in My Garden,* Gordon & Cremonesi, 1978; *Bird Watching for Everyone,* Gresham Books, 1979. Also author of *Country Commentary,* 1940, *The Unfolding Year,* 1948, *Bird Watching,* 1968, *Bird Watching for Everyman,* 1973, and *A Garland of Nightingales,* 1979.

Author of introduction: Gilbert White, *The Natural History of Selbourne,* 1976; James E. Harting, *Ornithology of Shakespeare,* 1977; Richard Jefferies, *Nature Near London,* 1980.

CLARKE, Hockley
See CLARKE, Henry Charles

*   *   *

CLARKE, Hugh Vincent   1919-

PERSONAL: Born November 27, 1919, in Brisbane, Australia; son of Patrick John (a publican) and Catherine (a secretary; maiden name, Goggin) Clarke; married Mary Patricia Ryan (a journalist), June 6, 1961; children: David, Bryan, John, Justin, Brigid. *Education:* Attended Teachers Training College, Brisbane, Australia, 1937, and Melbourne Technical College, 1947-48. *Home and office:* 14 Chermside St., Deakin, Australian Capital Territory, Australia.

CAREER: Worked as assistant surveyor for Old Main Roads Commission, 1945-46; Department of the Interior, Australia, senior survey computer, 1947-56; Department of External Territories, Canberra, Australia, director of information and publicity, 1966-73; Department of Aboriginal Affairs, Canberra, director of information and public relations, 1973-75; writer, 1975—. *Military service:* Australian Imperial Forces, bombardier, 1940-45; served in Malaya and Singapore; prisoner of war, 1942-45, in Singapore, Thailand, and Japan. *Member:* Australian Journalists Association, Society of Australian Authors, Canberra Historical Society.

WRITINGS: The Tub (novel), Jacaranda, 1963; (with Takeo Yamashita) *Breakout* (nonfiction), Horwitz, 1965; (with Yamashita) *To Sydney by Stealth* (nonfiction), Horwitz, 1966; *The Long Arm* (biography), J. S. Cumpston, 1974; *Fire One!* (contains "Breakout" and "To Sydney by Stealth"), Angus & Robertson, 1978.

Work represented in anthologies, including *Australia Writes,* 1953; *Australia at Arms,* 1955. Contributor of articles and stories to magazines and newspapers.

WORK IN PROGRESS: The Broke and the Broken, on the Depression years, 1926-39.

SIDELIGHTS: Describing his books, Clarke told *CA* that *The Tub* is a "factual novel about P.O.W. life in Singapore, Thailand, and Japan. *The Breakout* is the story of the biggest mass escape of P.O.W.s in British military history. Some one thousand Japanese prisoners broke out of a camp at Cowra, New South Wales, Australia, on August 5, 1944, and by morning, 231 of the escapees were shot dead. My next book, *To Sydney by Stealth,* details the episode of the Japanese midget submarine raid on Sydney Harbor on May 31, 1942. Three submarines entered the harbor and fired on the U.S.S. *Chicago,* but missed. Two of the enemy subs were then sunk, while one escaped, although it was never seen again. *The Long Arm* is the biography of a mounted policeman in Arnhem Land and elsewhere in the Northern Territory before World War II. *The Broke and the Broken* is the story of a family living in the country towns of Owensland and Brisbane between 1926 and 1939."

*   *   *

CLAYRE, Alasdair   1935-

PERSONAL: Born October 9, 1935, in Southampton, England; son of John (a physician) and D.E.M. (Findlay) Clayre. *Education:* Attended Christ Church, Oxford, 1956-59; Nuffield College, Oxford, B.A., 1959, M.A., 1973. *Home:* c/o All Souls College, Oxford University, Oxford OX1 4AL, England. *Agent:* A. D. Peters & Co. Ltd., 10 Buckingham St., London WC2N 6BU, England. *Office:* Antelope Films, 23 Alma Sq., London NW8 9QA, England.

CAREER: Oxford University, Oxford, England, fellow of

All Souls College, 1959—. British Broadcasting Corp. (BBC) television producer and member of arts faculty at Open University, 1970-76. Television and radio presenter, 1976—; producer and director for Antelope Films, 1980—. Gives poetry readings. *Military service:*British Army, Grenadier Guards, 1954-56. *Member:* Association of Cinematography, Television, and Allied Technicians, Association of Broadcasting and Allied Staff. *Awards, honors:* Shared Richard Hillary Award, 1963, for writing; Japan Prize for Radio, 1973, for "English Consort Music."

WRITINGS: The Window (novel), J. Cape, 1961; (editor) *A Hundred Folk-Songs and New Songs,* Wolfe, 1968; *A Fire by the Sea and Other Poems,* Compton Russell, 1974; *The Impact of Broadcasting,*Compton Russell, 1974; *Work and Play* (political science), Harper, 1974; *Adam and the Beasts and Other Songs,* Faber, 1976; (editor) *Nature and Industrialization,* Oxford University Press, 1977; (editor) *The Political Economy of Cooperation and Participation,* Oxford University Press, 1980. Political correspondent for *Economist,* 1977.

WORK IN PROGRESS: Television series for Antelope Films; documentary programs for BBC-Radio; a book on the foundations of political economy; songs.

SIDELIGHTS: Clayre has made record albums, "A Cold Wind Blows," released by Elektra in 1966, "Songs," released by Elektra in 1967, and "Adam and the Beasts," released by Acorn in 1976 and Folkways in 1977. He has translated songs from French, German, Greek, and other languages for Judy Collins, Joan Baez, Francoise Hardy, and other singers. He gives concerts and poetry readings, particularly with folk musicians and renaissance musicians, and has recorded his songs and poems for the Harvard Poetry Room collection. For the Open University he has made a number of records, including "The Rhythms of Poetry," tracing the European origins of the main rhythms of English verse.

*   *   *

CLEATOR, P(hilip) E(llaby)   1908-

PERSONAL: Born June 7, 1908, in Wallasey, England; son of Samuel Ellaby (a constructional design engineer) and Catherine (Phillips) Cleator; married Madelon Bermingham, February 3, 1940. *Education:* Attended grammar school in Wallasey, England. *Politics:* None. *Religion:* None. *Home:* Crosswinds, Budworth Rd., Oxton, Birkenhead, Merseyside L43 9TW, England.

CAREER: Constructional design engineer, 1926—; writer and illustrator, 1930—. Lecturer on space travel, 1932—. *Member:* British Interplanetary Society (fellow; president, 1933-36), Mencken Society.

WRITINGS: Rockets Through Space, Simon & Schuster, 1936; *Into Space* (Scientific Book Club selection), Allen & Unwin, 1953, Crowell, 1954; *The Robot Era,* Crowell, 1955; *The Past in Pieces* (Scientific Book Club selection), Allen & Unwin, 1957; *Lost Languages,* R. Hale, 1959, John Day, 1961; *Treasure for the Taking,* R. Hale, 1960; *Architectural Draughtsmanship,* Leonard Hill, 1960; *Archaeology,* Muller, 1960; *An Introduction to Space Travel,* Pitman, 1961; *Ancient Rome,* Muller, 1963; *Castles and Kings,* R. Hale, 1963; *Metals,* Muller, 1964; *Exploring the World of Archaeology,* Childrens Press, 1968; *Weapons of War,* R. Hale, 1967, Crowell, 1968; *Let's Look at Archaeology* (juvenile), Muller, 1969; *Underwater Archaeology,* St. Martin's, 1973; *Archaeology in the Making* (Scientific Book Club selection), St. Martin's, 1978; *Letters From Baltimore,* Associated University Presses, 1981.

Contributor: John Blair, editor, *The Second Meteor Book,* W. & R. Chambers, 1949; D. R. Bates, editor, *Space Research and Exploration,* Eyre & Spottiswoode, 1957, William Sloane, 1958; Arthur C. Clarke, editor, *The Coming of the Space Age,* Meredith Press, 1967; Joseph Jobe, editor, *Guns,* New York Graphic Society, 1971.

Author of "Ad Astra," a column in *Science Review,* "Interplanetary Parade," a column in *Tomorrow,* and "Satanic Soliloquy," a column in *Freethinker.* Contributor to scientific journals, popular magazines, and newspapers. Founder and editor of *Journal* of British Interplanetary Society, 1934.

WORK IN PROGRESS: An account of the early history of the British Interplanetary Society, publication expected in 1983.

SIDELIGHTS: Cleator told *CA:* "I began my career as a constructional design engineer, and thereafter decided to augment this activity by becoming a writer, a vocation in the pursuance of which I also undertook commissions as an illustrator (line drawings) and acted as a reader for various publishing houses.

"In the mid-twenties, meanwhile, I became interested in the prospect of space travel, and in 1932 wrote a pioneer thesis on the subject. I also published an appeal for members of a British Interplanetary Society and was elected first president. I visited and conferred with members of the Verein fuer Raumschiffahrt on the outskirts of Berlin, and later became British delegate of the E.V. Fortschrittliche Verkehrstechnik. I lectured on the problems of space travel at home and abroad, and undertook discussions about its prospects in live radio transmissions from stations as far apart as London and South Africa.

"I long ago proclaimed myself to be an 'agnostic, sceptic, and pacifist—a onetime idealist whose disillusionment is now complete.' My steadfast opposition to human conflict, and to those who wage and engage in it, was maintained throughout World War II, notwithstanding the prospect of imprisonment which I faced from 1942 onwards, a threat ultimately averted only by my being pronounced medically unfit to engage in the slaughter. As for my no less outspoken advocacy of agnosticism, also discernible in my writings over the past half-century, I have consistently dismissed the tenets of theology, the so-called science of God as a time-dishonored make-believe, and as consisting of a collection of unfounded assumptions which it is hoped will not be found out.

"These were views I shared and exchanged, over a period of twenty years, with my friend, Henry Mencken. Throughout this time, despite several unavailing attempts to do so, we two did not manage to meet. There now remains one final assignation, thanks to an arrangement we made to rendezvous in the confines of the sub-terrestrial Hell of the Christians. Here, by all pontifical accounts, the warmth attending our long-delayed encounter promises to be considerable."

AVOCATIONAL INTERESTS: "Visiting foreign parts and establishing amicable relations with the natives, be the color of their skin black, white, or khaki."

BIOGRAPHICAL/CRITICAL SOURCES: Eric Burgess, *Rocket Propulsion,* Chapman & Hall, 1951; Heinz Gartmann, *The Men Behind the Space Rockets,* Weidenfeld & Nicolson, 1955; Gartmann, *Man Unlimited,* Pantheon, 1957; Willy Ley, *Rockets, Missiles, and Space Travel,* Chapman & Hall, 1957; Beryl Williams and Samuel Epstein, *The Rocket Pioneers,* Lutterworth, 1957; Patrick Moore, *Space Exploration,* National Book League, 1958; Andrew D.

Haley, *Rocketry and Space Exploration,* Van Nostrand, 1958; Ursula Bloom, *He Lit the Lamp,* Burke Publishing, 1958; Werner von Braun and Frederick I. Ordway III, *History of Rocketry and Space Travel,* Thomas Nelson, 1967; Esther C. Goddard and G. Edward Pendray, *The Papers of Robert H. Goddard,* McGraw, 1970; Carl Bode, *The New Mencken Letters,* Dial, 1977.

*   *   *

CLEMOES, Peter Alan Martin   1920-

PERSONAL: Born January 20, 1920, in Southend-on-Sea, England; son of Victor Charles and Mary Williamson (Paton) Clemoes; married Jean Elizabeth Grew, April 2, 1956; children: Robin Aldred, Martin Richard. *Education:* Queen Mary College, London, B.A. (with first class honors), 1950; King's College, Cambridge, Ph.D., 1956. *Religion:* Church of England. *Home:* 14 Church St., Chesterton, Cambridge, England. *Office:* Emmanuel College, Cambridge University, Cambridge CB2 3AP, England.

CAREER: University of Reading, Reading, England, research fellow, 1954-55, lecturer in English, 1955-61; Cambridge University, Cambridge, England, lecturer, 1961-69, Elrington and Bosworth Professor of Anglo-Saxon, 1969—, fellow of Emmanuel College, 1962-69, professorial fellow, 1969—, director of studies in English, 1963-65, tutor, 1966-68, assistant librarian, 1963-69. Fellow of Queen Mary College, London, 1975—. *Military service:* British Army, Signal Corps, 1940-46. *Member:* Royal Historical Society (fellow), Early English Text Society (member of council, 1971—).

WRITINGS: (Editor) *The Anglo Saxons: Studies in Some Aspects of Their History and Culture,* Bowes & Bowes, 1959; (author of supplementary introduction) Bruno Assmann, editor, *Angelsaechsische Homilien und Heiligenleben* (title means "Anglo-Saxon Homilies and Saints' Lives"), Wissenschaftliche Buchgesellschaft, 1964; (author of supplementary introduction) Bernhard Fehr, editor, *Die Hirtenbriefe Aelfrics* (title means "Aelfric's Pastoral Letters"), Wissenschaftliche Buchgesellschaft, 1966; (editor with Norman Eliason) *Aelfric's First Series of Catholic Homilies: B.M. Royal Seven c. XII, Volumes 4-218,* Rosenkilde og Bagger, 1966; *Rhythm and Cosmic Order in Old English Christian Literature,* Cambridge University Press, 1970; (editor with Kathleen Hughes) *England Before the Conquest: Studies in Primary Sources,* Cambridge University Press, 1971; (editor with C. R. Dodwell) *The Old English Illustrated Hexateuch: British Museum Cotton Claudius B. IV,* Rosenkilde og Bagger, 1974. General editor of "Early English Manuscripts in Facsimile," Rosenkilde og Bagger, 1963-74. Contributor to scholarly journals. Founder and chief editor of *Anglo-Saxon England,* 1972—.

WORK IN PROGRESS: An edition of *Aelfric's First Series of Catholic Homilies* for Early English Text Society; a book on Old English poetry for Cambridge University Press.

*   *   *

CLEVELAND, Leslie   1921-

PERSONAL: Born September 21, 1921, in Adelaide, Australia; son of Francis Harold (a printer) and Viola Gladys (a musician; maiden name, Veitch) Cleveland; married Mary Lenore Sears (a teacher), May 5, 1967; children: Edward Roy, Peter Leslie. *Education:* Victoria University of Wellington, B.A., 1961, M.A., 1963, Ph.D., 1979. *Home:* 38 Havelock St., Wellington, New Zealand. *Office:* School of Political Science and Public Administration, Victoria University of Wellington, Private Bag, Wellington, New Zealand.

CAREER: Christchurch Press, Christchurch, New Zealand, journalist, 1946-48; *Wellington Evening Post,* Wellington, New Zealand, journalist, 1948-50; bush contractor in South Westland, 1951-55; *Truth,* Wellington, journalist, 1955-62; Technical Publications Ltd., Wellington, assistant editor, 1962-63; free-lance journalist, 1963-66; Victoria University of Wellington, Wellington, teaching fellowship, 1966-69, lecturer in politics, 1969-70, senior lecturer, 1970-79, reader, 1979—. Technical liaison officer of New Zealand Institute of Welding, 1966—. *Military service:* New Zealand Army, Territorial Force, 1941-42, Expeditionary Force, 1942-45; served in Italy; became staff sergeant. *Member:* International Institute of Communication, New Zealand Association of Radio Transmitters, New Zealand Association of University Teachers, Photo Forum.

WRITINGS: The Songs We Sang (poems and songs), Editorial Services, 1959; *The Silent Land* (poems), Caxton Press, 1966; *The Anatomy of Influence,* Hicks Smith, 1972; (with A. D. Robinson) *Readings in New Zealand Government,* A. H. & A. W. Reed, 1972; *The Politics of Utopia,* Methuen, 1979; *The Iron Hand* (poems), Victoria University Press, 1979. Editor of *Political Science Journal,* 1969-75.

WORK IN PROGRESS: A book on soldiers' songs of World War II; research on the folksong as social and political protest, early New Zealand newspapers, the mass media as instruments of social control, and early New Zealand photographers.

SIDELIGHTS: Cleveland wrote: "Writing is a means of finding out more about oneself and what one makes of experience. My work is driving me increasingly to speculate about the problems of national identity and survival of New Zealanders as a whole.

"I seem to be going through a 'stock-taking' phase at the moment. I keep thinking about my own personal situation. I can see a novel and perhaps some more poetry taking shape, probably because of my preoccupation with dead men's voices and far-off events. I'm compiling what is turning out to be an informal social history of what happened to some of us from 1939 to 1945. It was a strange time. Millions of words have been written about it, but not much seems to me to have the raw bite of actuality as the ordinary, individual soldier saw it. Some of the stuff I'm collecting is full of angry, youthful protest, summed up in the one great song of World War II: 'F—— 'em All!' How we laughed at each other and cursed and laughed at authority. We put on a comic face to mask fear, boredom, and anxiety about the unknown. Soldiers' songs and doggerel verse are a form of whistling in the dark as well as an uninhibited commentary on all authority. New Zealanders accept it and fight well, but they also know how to play the fool. It could be their salvation."

*   *   *

CLINE, Joan
See HAMILTON, Joan Lesley

*   *   *

CLUYSENAAR, Anne (Alice Andree Jackson)   1936-

PERSONAL: Born March 15, 1936, in Brussels, Belgium; daughter of John (a painter) and Sybil (a painter; maiden name, Fitzgerald) Cluysenaar; married Walter Freeman Jackson (an engineering surveyor), October, 1976; stepchildren: Mark, Gena, Tim. *Education:* Trinity College, Dublin, B.A. (with honors), 1957; University of Edinburgh, diploma in general linguistics, 1963. *Office:* Department of English, Totley Site, Sheffield City Polytechnic, Sheffield, Yorkshire, England.

CAREER: Manchester University, Manchester, England, assistant lecturer, 1957-58; Trinity College, Dublin, Ireland, assistant lecturer, 1961-62; Aberdeen University, Kings College, Aberdeen, Scotland, lecturer in English literature, 1963-65; Lancaster University, Bailrigg, Lancaster, England, lecturer in linguistics and literature, 1965-71; Huddersfield Polytechnic, Huddersfield, England, senior lecturer in language and literature, 1972-73; Birmingham University, Birmingham, England, lecturer in linguistics and literature, 1973-76; Sheffield City Polytechnic, Sheffield, England, senior lecturer in communication studies, 1976—.

WRITINGS: A Fan of Shadows (poems), Manchester Institute of Contemporary Arts, 1967; *Nodes: Selected Poems, 1960-1968,* Dolmen Press, 1971; *Introduction to Literary Stylistics: A Discussion of Dominant Structure in Verse and Prose,* Batsford, 1976; (editor) Burns Singer, *Selected Poems,* Carcanet New Press, 1977; (editor) *Selected Poems,* Dufour, 1977; *Bill Morey,* Bally Knocken Press, in press.

Work represented in anthologies, including *New Poets of Ireland,* Alan Swallow, 1963, and *Poetry Introduction Four,* Faber & Faber, 1978. General editor of *Sheaf.* Contributor to magazines and newspapers, including *Stand, Dublin, Poetry Review, Icarus, Hibernia, Poetry Nation Review, Poetry Ireland,* and *Aberdeen University Review.*

WORK IN PROGRESS: "Meditative documentary poems, including letters dating from 1860, in facsimile, and my mother's memoirs of a Victorian and post-Victorian childhood"; a long poem, including documentary prose pieces, for Faber & Faber.

SIDELIGHTS: Cluysenaar told *CA:* "After writing lyric poems, often rhymed, I have moved—after several years of seeking a style that would incorporate more varied experience—into a series of meditative poems whose claim not to be prose rests more on narrative and thematic interconnections than on details of phrasing. I want the focus to be on communication rather than the language drawing attention to itself for its own sake. These poems will, I hope, be published along with photographs, drawings, facsimile letters, and memoirs written by my mother, the intention being to relate poetry very closely to life, to the marks left by other people in other forms. The focus of interest is not this or that specific individual—myself or another—but on *the* individual and the value his or her life can be thought and felt to have in the 'dark backward and abysm of time.'

"Just as I want my poems to stand naturally beside other people's experience recorded in other ways, so I am engaged in teaching creative writing because I believe that many people can explore their sense of life through language and that there are aspects of writing, of fitting a medium to individual intention, that can be learned by discussion and practice, as in the case of other arts such as music, pottery, architecture, and painting. It seems very odd that literature alone is commonly taught without the inclusion of courses in 'production' to complement the analytical and theoretical courses.

"The study of linguistics and of stylistics is also a natural accompaniment to the study of verbal art, since the most advanced thinking about the medium is being done in these areas. A literary critic should, I feel, be able to approach a poem with an understanding of language capable of matching that of the writer, both through some experience of practical 'working with words' and through theoretical understanding of *how* language works."

BIOGRAPHICAL/CRITICAL SOURCES: Choice, December, 1976.

COATES, Austin 1922-

PERSONAL: Born in 1922 in London, England; son of Eric (a composer) and Phyllis (an actress; maiden name, Black) Coates. *Education:* Attended Royal Academy of Dramatic Art. *Home:* 80 Macdonnell Rd., Hong Kong.

CAREER: Colonial Administrative Service, Hong Kong, assistant colonial secretary, 1949-52, district officer and magistrate in New Territories, 1953-55, member of secretariat, 1955-56, Chinese affairs officer and magistrate in Sarawak, 1957, chairman of Kuching Rural Council, 1957-58, secretary to governor of Sarawak, 1958-59; British High Commission, Malaya, first secretary, 1959-62; writer, 1962-65; Singapore Tourist Promotion Board, Singapore, director, 1965-66; writer, 1966—. *Military service:* Royal Air Force, 1942-47. *Member:* Royal Asiatic Society (fellow). *Awards, honors:* Knight commander of Philippine Order of Rizal.

WRITINGS: Invitation to a Chinese Feast, Hutchinson, 1953, Harper, 1954; *Personal and Oriental,* Harper, 1957; *The Road,* Harper, 1959.

Basutoland, H.M.S.O., 1966; *Prelude to Hong Kong,* Routledge & Kegan Paul, 1966; *City of Broken Promises,* Muller, 1967, John Day, 1968; *Myself a Mandarin,* Muller, 1968, John Day, 1969; *Rizal: Philippine Nationalist and Martyr,* Oxford University Press, 1968.

Western Pacific Islands, H.M.S.O., 1970; *China, India, and the Ruins of Washington,* John Day, 1972; *Islands of the South,* Pica Press, 1974; *Numerology,* Muller, 1974, Citadel, 1975; *A Mountain of Light: The Story of the Hongkong Electric Company,* Heinemann, 1977; *A Macao Narrative,* Heinemann, 1978; *Whampoa Ships on the Shore,* South China Morning Post, 1980.

Translator, with Tan Kok Seng, of books by Seng; all published by Heinemann: *Son of Singapore: The Autobiography of a Coolie,* 1972; *Man of Malaysia: Tan Kok Seng,* 1974; *Eye on the World,* 1975; *Three Sisters of Sz,* 1979.

Contributor to magazines, including *Optima.*

*   *   *

COCHRANE, Jennifer (Ann Frances) 1936-

PERSONAL: Born May 2, 1936, in Southampton, Hants, England; daughter of Lionel (a naval officer) and Beatrice Rosalind Cochrane. *Education:* Attended University of Leicester, 1955-59. *Home:* La Vieille Tuisainne, La Seigneurie, Sark, Channel Islands, Great Britain.

CAREER: British Museum (Natural History), London, England, experimental officer, 1960-63; school teacher and personal assistant to senior research officer in market research, 1963-65; Science in General Management Ltd., London, head of production, 1965-67; Macdonald Educational, London, managing editor of encyclopedic section, 1968-75; writer, 1975—. *Member:* Zoological Society (associate).

WRITINGS—For children: Prehistoric Life, Macdonald Educational, 1968; *Fishes,* Macdonald Educational, 1969; *Amphibians and Reptiles,* Macdonald Educational, 1969; *Mammals,* Macdonald Educational, 1969; *Plants Without Flowers,* Macdonald Educational, 1969; *Life in Fresh Water,* Macdonald Educational, 1969; *Life on the Sea Shore,* Macdonald Educational, 1969.

Life in the Open Sea, Macdonald Educational, 1970; *Time and Timepieces,* Macdonald Educational, 1970; *The Theatre,* Macdonald Educational, 1970; *By the Sea,* Macdonald Educational, 1970; *Snakes and Lizards,* Macdonald Educational, 1971; *Mushrooms and Toadstools,* Macdonald

Educational, 1971; *Dinosaurs*, Macdonald Educational, 1971; *Birds and Migration*, Macdonald Educational, 1972; *The River*, Philograph Publications, 1972; *The Farm*, Philograph Publications, 1972; *The Zoo*, Philograph Publications, 1972; *The Market*, Philograph Publications, 1972; *The Street*, Philograph Publications, 1972; *The Funfair*, Philograph Publications, 1972; *Animals With Shells*, B.P.C. Publishing, 1972; *Looking at Living*, Macdonald & Co., 1974; *Exploring Ecology*, Macdonald & Co., 1974; *A Place to Live*, Macdonald & Co., 1975; *The Food We Eat*, Macdonald & Co., 1975; *The Amazing World of the Sea*, Angus & Robertson, 1976; *Animals and Their Homes*, Purnell, 1979, Grosset, 1980; *The Secrets of Nature*, Piper Books, 1979; *Piccolo Guide to Sea Shells*, Piper Books, 1979. Author of "Safari Cards," Edito Service, 1977-79. Contributor to *Journal of Bombay Natural History Society*.

WORK IN PROGRESS—For children: *A History of English Food; What to Do on Holiday*, publication expected in 1981; *Birds in Town* for Warne; "point of view" books.

SIDELIGHTS: Jennifer Cochrane commented: "I am interested in presenting information to children of all ages in an attractive fashion, although I have also written for adults. Most of my books are illustrated. My main interests are natural history and ecology, because of my training, but I am also interested in theatre and ballet.

"I live on Sark, the last feudal state in the world. I left London in 1975 because I was dissatisfied with urban life, a sedentary way of living, and the unceasing non-cooperation of modern society. Sark retains a community spirit and is in touch with the bases of living. It is a very small island, only three miles long and one and a half miles across, with five hundred fifty inhabitants. It is unusual in the modern world because there are no cars on the island, and pesticides and herbicides are not used on a large scale. We, therefore, live in pollution-free surroundings, drinking untreated, but quite pure, water. Thus we are made very conscious of the necessity for keeping our small world clean. It is an idyllic place in which to live, despite the dependence on good weather for communications. Sark is one of the British Isles, but not of the United Kingdom, having its own parliament and laws."

*   *   *

COCKBURN, (Francis) Claud   1904-
(James Helvick, Frank Pitcairn)

PERSONAL: Born April 12, 1904, in Peking, China; son of Henry (a diplomat) and Elizabeth (Stevenson) Cockburn; married second wife, Patricia Arbuthnot (a journalist and writer), 1940; children: (second marriage) three sons. *Education:* Attended Keble College, Oxford, University of Budapest, and University of Berlin. *Home:* Brook Lodge, Yougal, County Cork, Ireland.

CAREER: London Times, London, England, correspondent in New York, N.Y., and Washington, D.C., 1929-32; *The Week*, London, editor, 1933-46; *Daily Worker*, diplomatic and foreign correspondent writing under pseudonym Frank Pitcairn, 1935-46; writer. *Awards, honors:* Traveling fellow of Queen's College, Oxford, in Berlin, Germany.

WRITINGS: Nine Bald Men, Hart-Davis, 1956; *A Discord of Trumpets* (first volume in autobiography; also see below), Simon & Schuster, 1956 (published in England as *In Time of Trouble*, Hart-Davis, 1956; *Aspects of English History*, MacGibbon & Kee, 1957; *Crossing the Line* (second volume in autobiography; also see below), MacGibbon & Kee, 1958, Monthly Review Press, 1960; *View From the West* (third volume in autobiography; also see below), MacGibbon &

Kee, 1961, Monthly Review Press, 1962; *I, Claud: The Autobiography of Claud Cockburn* (contains updated editions of *A Discord of Trumpets, Crossing the Line*, and *View From the West*), Penguin, 1967.

Ballantyne's Folly (novel), Weidenfeld & Nicolson, 1970; *Bestseller: The Books That Everyone Read, 1900-1939*, Sidgwick & Jackson, 1972; *The Devil's Decade*, Mason & Lipscomb, 1973; *Jericho Road*, Cassell, 1974; *Mr. Mintoff Comes to Ireland*, Mercier Press, 1975; *Union Power: The Growth and Challenge in Perspective*, Kimber, 1976. Also author of *High Low Washington*, 1933.

Under pseudonym James Helvick; novels: *Beat the Devil*, Lippincott, 1951; *Overdraft on Glory*, Lippincott, 1955; *The Horses*, Walker & Co., 1963.

Under pseudonym Frank Pitcairn: *Reporter in Spain*, Lawrence & Wishart, 1936.

Contributor to newspapers and magazines, including *New Statesman, Daily Telegraph, Private Eye, Saturday Evening Post*, and *Punch*.

SIDELIGHTS: "Above everything, Cockburn is a journalist; perhaps the most perfect specimen of the genus ever to exist, certainly the most accomplished I have known," Malcolm Muggeridge once remarked about Claud Cockburn. "He loves the trade, and has practised it in the manner of a maestro, realising that news is life's drama, not its data; that stories really are stories, not ticker-tape." This virtuoso journalist got his start in the field in the 1920's, when he worked as an unofficial correspondent for the *London Times* in Berlin. Later Cockburn served, with much acclaim, as the paper's official correspondent in New York and Washington.

In 1933 Cockburn's career took an unexpected turn. In that year he joined the Communist party. Having resigned from the staff of the *London Times*, he founded a leftist newsletter, *The Week*. This periodical attracted widespread attention at home and abroad. "*The Week*," explained a reviewer for *Books*, "published news and near-rumour about the Establishment and its creatures, made them shake a little, look over their shoulders, and have nightmares about exposure to the truth." Frankly pro-Soviet and anti-Nazi, *The Week* was opposed to the policy of appeasement. The signing of the nonaggression pact between Hitler and Stalin in 1939 was a major setback for the newsletter; it was never again to achieve its former level of influence.

During the 1930's and 1940's Cockburn also worked as a correspondent for the Communist newspaper, *Daily Worker*. In this capacity he went to Spain during the civil war, where he wound up fighting on the Republican side. His experiences in that war-torn land are recounted in his book, *Reporter in Spain*.

The end of World War II marked another dramatic change in Cockburn's career. Having grown increasingly discontented with both his political and literary ventures, Cockburn moved with his family to an old country house in Ireland. In 1948 he broke with the Communist party, and since that time he has supported himself chiefly by free-lance journalism. He has contributed to a wide variety of magazines and newspapers, ranging from *Private Eye* to the *London Sunday Telegraph*.

During the 1950's Cockburn contributed regularly to the famous British humor magazine, *Punch*. He and Malcolm Muggeridge, who was serving as editor of *Punch* at that time, became close friends. A commentator for the *Times Literary Supplement* compared the two newsmen: "Mr.

Cockburn is almost alone among modern British journalists in riding his seriousness on so light a rein that he can be amusing and disquieting in the same breath. Though Malcolm Muggeridge is probably the nearest to a fellow spirit they differ in one essential. Mr. Cockburn takes an equally disenchanted view of the antics of collective humanity and of the power of journalists to influence the brutal processes of history, yet he never abandons hope. He keeps trying to lend a hand in the messy old world."

Since taking up a new life in Ireland, Cockburn has produced several novels. Under the pseudonym James Helvick he wrote three suspense novels—*Beat the Devil, Overdraft on Glory,* and *The Horses.* More recently he published a comic novel, *Ballantyne's Folly,* about a hotel proprietor who wants to purchase an old house to use as a local youth center. Trying to secure the help of the townspeople, he discovers that nearly all of them are corrupt. A commentator for the *Observer Review* found the book to be "little more than a pretext for some hobbyhorse-riding"; but a reviewer for the *Times Literary Supplement* was more positive. "Every cupboard, to Mr. Cockburn, has a built-in skeleton," the reviewer noted. "The pattern of deception is so complete that this dark comedy achieves a quite uncommon integrity."

Cockburn's nonfiction books have also met with critical acclaim. Although some critics objected to the Marxist viewpoint of *The Devil's Decade,* Cockburn's account of the 1930's, they nonetheless found it entertaining. "Cockburn not only knows both his decade and his devil, but has a writing manner of singularly stylish wit and irony; I believe it is called 'mordant' in the trade," James Cameron observed in the *New York Times Book Review.* "He treats of nothing that he does not illumine, at least for those who value journalism at its shrewd and elegant best." In another history book, *Union Power: The Growth and Challenge in Perspective,* Cockburn covers the British trade union movement in the twentieth century. Janet Montefiore commended the volume: "With a characteristic mixture of knowledgeable wit, deeply felt commitment, and sharp quirky realism, Cockburn attacks and entertains. *Union Power* is not only instructive, it is a very enjoyable book."

Although he has experimented with a number of genres, Cockburn is probably best known for his autobiography. His life story, which was initially published in three volumes, was later revised and condensed into one volume, *I, Claud.* In their reviews of the autobiography, many critics took the occasion to praise both the book and the man who had written it. Kingsley Amis, for example, wrote in a review of the first volume: "Let us be thankful that we have A Discord of Trumpets, the most brilliantly amusing and invigorating modern autobiography that any of us is likely to get his hands on. And let us be grateful, too, that all the disillusionments one can read behind these witty and high-spirited pages left Cockburn as they found him, hard-headed but never cynical, sensitive but never soft."

BIOGRAPHICAL/CRITICAL SOURCES: New York Herald Tribune, August 26, 1951, July 29, 1956, September 4, 1960; *New York Times,* August 28, 1955, May 20, 1956, March 2, 1974; *Spectator,* February 24, 1956; *Manchester Guardian,* February 24, 1956; *Times Literary Supplement,* March 2, 1956, September 7, 1967, May 28, 1970, October 12, 1973, June 14, 1974; *Nation,* June 16, 1956; *New Republic,* June 25, 1956; *Christian Science Monitor,* July 18, 1956; *New Yorker,* September 22, 1956; June 18, 1960; *New Statesman,* September 29, 1961, September 8, 1967; Malcolm Muggeridge, *Tread Softly, for You Tread on My Jokes,* Collins, 1966; Claud Cockburn, *I, Claud: The Autobiogra-*

phy of Claud Cockburn, Penguin, 1967; *Observer Review,* September, 24, 1967, May 31, 1970; Patricia Arbuthnot Cockburn, *The Years of "The Week,"* Macdonald & Co., 1968; *Books,* February, 1970; *Punch,* September 26, 1973; *New York Times Book Review,* March 10, 1974; *Books and Bookmen,* November, 1976.*

—*Sketch by Ann F. Ponikvar*

*　　*　　*

COFFMAN, Charles DeWitt 1909-

PERSONAL: Born July 10, 1909, in Richmond, Va.; son of William Harnsberger and Rosina (Brennan) Coffman; married Katharine Luttrell, January 10, 1933 (deceased); married Suzanne Gregoire, February 11, 1961; children: (first marriage) Michael. *Education:* Georgetown University, Ph.B., 1931. *Religion:* Roman Catholic. *Home:* 511 Almeria St., Coral Gables, Fla. 33134. *Office:* Coffman Corp., 100 North Biscayne Blvd., Miami, Fla. 33132.

CAREER: Mayflower Hotel, Washington, D.C., sales manager, 1938-47; C. DeWitt Coffman, Washington, D.C., president in Washington and New York City, 1947-52; Philadelphia Convention and Visitors Bureau, Philadelphia, Pa., executive director, 1952-54; Woodner Hotel, Washington, D.C., general manager, 1954-55; president of Hotel Sales Engineering, 1955-56; McAllister Hotel, Miami, Fla., general manager, 1956-60; Futterman Corp., New York City, vice-president, 1960-65; International Hotel Management Co., Miami, president, 1965-71; president of Treadway Inns Corp., 1971-72; Coffman Corp., Miami, president, 1972—. Vice-president of Schine Hotels, 1956-60; manager of Hotel Division of Keyes Co., 1976—; consultant to hotel developers all over the world. *Military service:* U.S. Naval Reserve, active duty, 1942-45; became lieutenant commander. *Member:* Hotel Sales Management Association (president, 1949), American Hotel and Motel Association (chairman of marketing committee, 1972), Kiwanis (president, 1952). *Awards, honors:* Member of Hotel Sales Management Association Hall of Fame.

WRITINGS: Profits Through Promotion, Ahrens Publishing, 1950; *The Full House: A Hotel/Motel Promotion Primer,* School of Hotel Administration, Cornell University, 1964; *Marketing for a Full House: A Complete Guide to Profitable Hotel/Motel Operational Planning* (edited by Helen J. Recknagel), School of Hotel Administration, Cornell University, 1970; (with John Keasler) *Keyhole Inn-Sights: An Uninhibited Peek Into the Hotel World,* Prentice-Hall, 1972. Also author of *Hospitality for Sale,* 1978. Contributor to professional journals. Management editor of *Hospitality.**

*　　*　　*

COGHILL, Nevill (Henry Kendall Aylmer) 1899-1980(?)

OBITUARY NOTICE—See index for *CA* sketch: Born April 19, 1899, in England; died c. 1980, in Cheltenham, England. Author and educator. A Chaucer scholar, Coghill wrote numerous books on the fourteenth-century writer and translated Chaucer's *The Canterbury Tales* and *Troilus and Criseyde* into modern English. Coghill was a teaching fellow in English for over forty years at Oxford University. While at Oxford, he directed dramatic plays, among them "Doctor Faustus," starring Elizabeth Taylor and Richard Burton. Obituaries and other sources: *Time,* November 24, 1980.

COHEN, Sara Kay Sherman   1943-

PERSONAL: Born April 10, 1943, in Baltimore, Md.; daughter of Charles and Charlotte Sherman; married Stanton N. Smullens (a medical doctor), December 14, 1979; children: Elizabeth, Kathyanne; stepchildren: Elizabeth, Douglas. *Education:* Goucher College, B.A., 1962; University of Pennsylvania, M.S.W., 1965. *Home and office:* 17th and Pine Sts., Philadelphia, Pa. 19103.

CAREER: Society to Protect Children, Philadelphia, Pa., caseworker, 1964-66; Philadelphia Psychiatric Hospital, Philadelphia, family therapist, 1966-68; Jewish Family Service, Philadelphia, director of family life education, 1968-72; private practice of psychiatric counseling in Philadelphia, 1972—. Instructor at Hahnemann College, Philadelphia, 1976, and Temple University, 1978. *Member:* National Association of Marriage and Family Counselors, National Association of Social Workers, American Association of Sex Educators and Counselors, National Organization for Women (NOW), Philadelphia Society of Clinical Social Work.

WRITINGS: Whoever Said Life Is Fair?, Scribner, 1980. Author of column, "Relationships," in *Philadelphia Inquirer,* 1976.

SIDELIGHTS: In her book, *Whoever Said Life is Fair?,* Cohen explores the injustices in life as both a woman and a psychotherapist. She sketches unfair incidents she has known herself and watched others endure. In her book (which began as a journal to be a gift to her two young daughters), she explores the unfairness in life that is unavoidable as well as those injustices that can be avoided by learning to be attracted to personal and professional experiences and relationships that fulfill rather than deplete. She emphasizes that life's injustices are salved by love, dignity, hope, and compassion.

*   *   *

COHEN, Sherry Suib   1934-

PERSONAL: Born October 17, 1934, in Brooklyn, N.Y.; daughter of David (an attorney) and Jane (in real estate; maiden name, Goldman) Suib; married Lawrence A. Cohen (an attorney), November 25, 1956; children: Jennifer Beth, Adam Moss. *Education:* Syracuse University, B.S., 1955. *Home and office:* 715 Crescent, Mamaroneck, N.Y. 10543. *Agent:* Connie Clausen Associates, 250 East 87th St., New York, N.Y. 10028

CAREER: Writer. Teacher of handicapped children at school in Roosevelt, N.Y., 1955-59; Mamaroneck High School, Mamaroneck, N.Y., teacher of English, 1970-80. Lecturer on teenagers, writing, and feminist activities. *Member:* American Society of Journalists and Authors.

WRITINGS: Tough Gazoobies on That! (prose and poetry), Ashley Books, 1974; (with Jean DuCoffe) *Making It Big: A Guide to Health, Success, and Beauty for Women Size Sixteen and Over,* Simon & Schuster, 1980. Contributor to magazines, including *Seventeen, Playgirl, Family Circle, Reader's Digest, Boating, Mademoiselle, Westchester,* and *Of Nassau.*

WORK IN PROGRESS: A book on alternative life styles.

SIDELIGHTS: Sherry Cohen commented: "Writing is my key to immortality. Someday, somewhere, some very-much-in-love couple will be browsing in a bookstore in Paris (my fantasy always says it's Paris) and will come across *my* books with *my* picture and hear ME . . . years after I'm dust. Now why else would anyone write? I mean, I could be schlepping around Thailand sipping something good, instead of being behind my Smith-Corona. Writing also gives a person points with surly teenagers who couldn't notice you around the house otherwise."

*   *   *

COHN, Jan Kadetsky   1933-

PERSONAL: Born August 9, 1933, in Cambridge, Mass.; daughter of Allan Robert and Beatrice (Goldberg) Kadetsky; married William Henry Cohn (a historian), March 9, 1969; children: Cathy Rebecca, David Seth. *Education:* Wellesley College, B.A., 1955; University of Toledo, M.A., 1961; University of Michigan, Ph.D., 1964. *Politics:* Democrat. *Religion:* Jewish. *Home:* 12100 Stirrup Rd., Reston, Va. 22091. *Office:* Department of English, George Mason University, Fairfax, Va. 22030.

CAREER: University of Toledo, Toledo, Ohio, instructor, 1963, assistant professor of English, 1964-68; University of Wisconsin, Whitewater, associate professor of English, 1968-70; Carnegie-Mellon University, Pittsburgh, Pa., associate professor of English, 1970-79, director of graduate studies in English, 1973-79; George Mason University, Fairfax, Va., professor of English and chairman of department, 1979—. *Member:* National Council of Teachers of English, Modern Language Association of America, Modern Humanities Research Association, Popular Culture Association. *Awards, honors:* National Endowment for the Humanities junior fellow, 1972-73; fellow of American Council of Learned Societies, 1973; associate of Danforth Foundation, 1974—.

WRITINGS: The Palace or the Poorhouse: The American House as a Cultural Symbol, Michigan State University Press, 1979; *Improbable Fiction: The Life of Mary Roberts Rinehart,* University of Pittsburgh Press, 1980. Contributor to language and literature journals.

WORK IN PROGRESS: A biography of George Horace Lorimer, editor of the *Saturday Evening Post* from 1898 to 1935, for University of Pittsburgh Press.

SIDELIGHTS: Jan Cohn told *CA:* "The research and writing that I have been doing over the past few years has taken me far afield from the new critical studies of literature that I was trained in. The questions that now interest me are those that ask about the relationship between literature and society in America. As a result, I find myself increasingly interested in popular literature.

"In studying the American house, I read hundreds of written documents of all kinds to discover what Americans thought about their own and other people's houses. Letters, histories, guide books, architects' writings, magazine articles, and novels all reveal attitudes toward the house as much more than a physical structure; they reveal the house to be a complex symbol of economic, aesthetic, political, and domestic values.

"In my book on Mary Roberts Rinehart I turned this process around. Rather than looking at one phenomenon through many writers' work, I looked at one writer whose work commanded an enormous audience during most of her long career. What in her fiction made her so significant to so many readers? What values did her novels reinforce for them? The same kind of questions will concern me in my study of Lorimer and the *Post*; what did he provide for Americans in the first third of the century that made his magazine probably the most important mass medium of his time?

"As a literature teacher I am concerned with the cultural distance between our students and the great writers we teach. Many factors have created that distance, but among them must be the closed world of scholarly literary study. With both popular and elite works of literature, I'd like to see increased attention paid to the interaction of writing and the 'real world.' I think that is what my own work is about and why I hope that it is written for a wider audience than other academics."

*   *   *

COHN, Nik   1946-

PERSONAL: Born in 1946 in London, England; married Jill Waddell; children: one daughter. *Education:* Attended secondary school in Londonderry, Northern Ireland. *Home:* Orchard Cottage, Wood End, Ardeley, Hertfordshire, England.

CAREER: Free-lance writer.

WRITINGS: Market (novel), Secker & Warburg, 1965; *I Am Still the Greatest Says Johnny Angelo* (novel), Secker & Warburg, 1967; *Pop From the Beginning* (nonfiction), Weidenfeld & Nicolson, 1969, reprinted as *A Wop Bopa Loo Bop a Lop Bam Boom: Pop From the Beginning,* Paladin, 1970; *Rock From the Beginning* (nonfiction), Stein & Day, 1969; *Arfur: Teenage Pinball Queen* (novel), Weidenfeld & Nicolson, 1970, Simon & Schuster, 1971; *Today There Are No Gentlemen: The Changes in Englishmen's Clothes Since the War,* Weidenfeld & Nicolson, 1971; (with Guy Peellaert) *Rock Dreams,* Popular Books, 1973; *King Death,* Harcourt, 1975. Contributor to magazines and newspapers in England and the United States, including *Queen, Mademoiselle,* and *Esquire.*

BIOGRAPHICAL/CRITICAL SOURCES: National Observer, July 21, 1969; *Punch,* August 27, 1969.*

*   *   *

COLBERT, Evelyn S(peyer)   1918-

PERSONAL: Born July 6, 1918, in New York. *Education:* Barnard College, A.B., 1938; Columbia University, A.M., 1939, Ph.D., 1947. *Office:* U.S. Department of State, Washington, D.C. 20520.

CAREER: Office of Strategic Services, Washington, D.C., research analyst, 1943-45; U.S. Department of State, Washington, D.C., research analyst, 1945-50, acting chief of China Branch, Division of Research for the Far East, 1951, division coordinator of National Intelligence Survey, 1951-61, chief of Southeast Asia Division, 1962-68, deputy director of Office of Research and Analysis for East Asia and the Pacific, 1968—, national intelligence officer for Japan and the Pacific area (assigned to Central Intelligence Agency), 1974-77, special assistant in policy planning for Bureau of East Asian and Pacific affairs, 1977—. Federal fellow of Brookings Institution, 1972-73. *Awards, honors:* Superior service awards from U.S. Department of State, 1964, 1974.

WRITINGS: Retaliation in International Law, King's Crown Press, 1948; *The Left Wing in Japanese Politics,* International Secretariat, Institute of Pacific Relations, 1952, reprinted, Greenwood Press, 1973; *Southeast Asia in International Politics,* Cornell University Press, 1977.

BIOGRAPHICAL/CRITICAL SOURCES: Choice, November, 1977; *Pacific Affairs,* summer, 1978; *Annals of the American Academy of Political and Social Science,* July, 1978.*

COLE, Andrew Thomas, Jr.   1933-

PERSONAL: Born August 22, 1933, in Chilhowie, Va.; son of Andrew Thomas Cole; married, 1965; children: two. *Education:* Harvard University, B.A., 1954, Ph.D., 1960. *Office:* Department of Classics, Yale University, New Haven, Conn. 06520.

CAREER: Harvard University, Cambridge, Mass., instructor in Latin and Greek, 1959-62; Stanford University, Stanford, Calif., assistant professor of Latin and Greek, 1962-65; Yale University, New Haven, Conn., associate professor, 1965-71, professor of Greek and Latin, 1971—. *Military service:* U.S. Army, 1956-57. *Member:* American Philological Association.

WRITINGS: Democritus and the Sources of Greek Anthropology, Press of Case Western Reserve University, 1967; (editor) *Studies in Latin Poetry,* Cambridge University Press, 1969; (editor) *Studies in Latin Language and Literature,* Cambridge University Press, 1973.*

*   *   *

COLE, Edmund Keith   1919-

PERSONAL: Born October 16, 1919, in Sydney, Australia; son of Charles Richard (a clerk) and Florence Anne (Gough) Cole; married Grace Merle Newell (a librarian), August 19, 1944; children: Ruth Elizabeth Goddard, Wendy Patricia Hall, Peter Edmund. *Education:* University of Sydney, M.A., 1949, B.D., 1949, Th.D., 1966, M.A.C.E., 1974. *Home:* 28 Woodbury Ave., Bendigo, Victoria 3550, Australia.

CAREER: Ordained Anglican priest, 1944; curate of Anglican churches in Sydney, Australia, 1944-50; Church Missionary Society, London, England, missionary in Kenya, 1950-63, member of staff at Kahuhia Normal School in Fort Hall, 1950-52, supervisor of schools in Embu, 1953, principal of St. Paul's United Theological College in Limuru, 1954-60, archdeacon of central Kenya in Fort Hall, 1961-63; University of Melbourne, Parkville, Australia, vice-principal of Ridley College, 1963-73; Nungalinya College, Darwin, Australia, founding principal, 1974-78; Diocese of Bendigo, Bendigo, Australia, director of theological education, 1978—. Lecturer at Moore Theological College, 1944-50. Australian commissary for bishop of Mount Kenya South. *Member:* Church Missionary Society (historian, 1968—), Australian and New Zealand Association of Theological Schools, Australian College of Theology (fellow), Australian College of Education, Australian Institute of Aboriginal Studies.

WRITINGS: Mau Mau Mission, Church Missionary Society, 1954; *After Mau Mau,* Church Missionary Society, 1956; *Kenya: Hanging in the Middle Way,* Church Missionary Society, 1959; *Roper River Mission,* Church Missionary Historical Publications, 1968; *Commissioned to Care,* Mission of St. James and St. John, 1969.

The Cross Over Mount Kenya, Church Missionary Historical Publications, 1970; *Sincerity My Guide,* Church Missionary Historical Publications, 1970; *Groote Eylandt Mission,* Church Missionary Historical Publications, 1971; *Groote Eylandt Pioneer,* Church Missionary Historical Publications, 1971; *A History of the Church Missionary Society of Australia,* Church Missionary Historical Publications, 1971; *Groote Eylandt Stories,* Church Missionary Historical Publications, 1972; *Oenpelli Pioneer,* Church Missionary Historical Publications, 1972; *Perriman in Arnhem Land,* Church Missionary Historical Publications, 1973; *Totems and Tam-*

arinds, Nungalinya Publications, 1973; *Groote Eylandt,* Nungalinya Publications, 1975, revised edition, Keith Cole Publications, 1982; *A History of Oenpelli,* Nungalinya Publications, 1975; *Oenpelli Jubilee,* Nungalinya Publications, 1975; *Outlines of Christian Belief,* Nungalinya Publications, 1976; *The Life of Jesus Christ,* Nungalinya Publications, 1976; *Winds of Fury,* Rigby, 1977; *Nungalinya College,* Nungalinya Publications, 1978; *Cole Family History,* Keith Cole Publications, 1979; *The Aborigines of Arnhem Land,* Rigby, 1980; *Arnhem Land: Places and People,* Rigby, 1980; *Dick Harris: Missionary to the Aborigines,* Keith Cole Publications, 1980; *Seafarers in the Groote Archipelago,* Keith Cole Publications, 1980; *Numbulwar (Rose River Mission),* Keith Cole Publications, 1981; *Aborigines: Towards Dignity and Identity,* Keith Cole Publications, 1981.

SIDELIGHTS: Nungalinya College, the Combined Training and Resource Center, Inc., is a training place for aborigines in theological education and community development, managed by Anglican and Uniting churches. Cole has been engaged in research on aborigines since 1966.

He wrote: "I am as vitally concerned now for aboriginal advancement and dignity as I was for that of Africans in Kenya. I have had the very great privilege of working among African people in Kenya as they moved towards independence in 1963. Since then I have returned to Africa, including Kenya, and I have seen how the Kenyans are coping. They have a new dignity and have grown in stature with their added responsibility.

"In contrast the Australian Aborigines lack dignity and identity. This is due almost entirely to the aggressive activities and expansion of white Australians since 1788. Aborigines were a dying race until missions and governments intervened in the 1920's and 1930's. Initial policies of protection and assimilation have now given way to self-management. They are now able to decide what culture and life-style they wish to opt for. In several states they have just been given communal freehold title to much of their land. They still have a long way to go, however. I am trying through my contacts and writings as a non-Aboriginal to explain to non-Aborigines my understanding of Aboriginal ways and our responsibilities to them."

*   *   *

COLEMAN, Felicia Slatkin   1916(?)-1981

OBITUARY NOTICE: Born c. 1916; died January 11, 1981, in Manhattan, N.Y. Author. Felicia Coleman wrote books on how to help children prepare for surgery. Obituaries and other sources: *New York Times,* January 15, 1981.

*   *   *

COLES, Susan Vaughan Ebershoff
See EBERSHOFF-COLES, Susan Vaughan

*   *   *

COLLARD, Edgar Andrew   1911-

PERSONAL: Born September 6, 1911, in Montreal, Quebec, Canada; son of Gilchrist and Florence May (Luttrell) Collard; married Henrietta Elizabeth Forde, August 23, 1947. *Education:* McGill University, B.A., 1935, M.A., 1937. *Politics:* Independent Conservative. *Religion:* United Church of Canada. *Home:* 400 Stewart St., Apt. 22, Ottawa, Ontario, Canada K1N 6L2.

CAREER: Writer. *Gazette,* Montreal, Quebec, associate editor, 1944-53, editor, 1953-70. *Member:* University Club.

Awards, honors: National newspaper awards, 1949, 1950, 1959, and 1969; D.Litt. from McGill University, 1962; certificate of merit from Canadian Historical Association, 1967; member of Order of Canada, 1976.

WRITINGS: *Oldest McGill,* Macmillan of Canada, 1946; *Canadian Yesterdays,* Longmans, Green, 1955, 2nd edition, 1963; *Montreal Yesterdays,* Longmans, Green, 1962, 2nd edition, 1963; *Call Back Yesterdays,* Academic Press, 1965; *The Story of Dominion Square: Place du Canada,* Longman, 1971; *The Montreal Board of Trade, 1822-1972,* Montreal Board of Trade, 1972; *The Art of Contentment,* Doubleday, 1974; *The McGill You Knew: An Anthology of Memories, 1920-1960,* Academic Press, 1975; *Montreal: The Days That Are No More,* Doubleday, 1976.*

*   *   *

COLLINS, Barry   1941-

PERSONAL: Born September 21, 1941, in Halifax, England; married wife, Anne, 1963; children: three. *Education:* Attended Queen's College, Oxford. *Home:* 7 Golf Cres., Highroad Well, Halifax, Yorkshire, England. *Agent:* Sheila Lemon, Spokesmen, 1 Craven Hill, London W2 3EW, England.

CAREER: Writer. Teacher at school in Halifax, England, 1962-63; *Halifax Evening Courier,* Halifax, England, journalist, 1963-71. *Awards, honors:* Arts Council grant, 1974.

WRITINGS—Published plays: *Judgement* (first produced in Bristol, England, at Old Vic, 1974; produced in London, England, 1975), Faber, 1974; *The Strongest Man in the World,* Faber, 1978.

Unpublished plays: "And Was Jerusalem Builded Here," first produced in Leeds, England, at Leeds Playhouse, 1972; "Beauty and the Beast" (for children), first produced in Leeds, 1973; "The Lonely Man's Lover," first broadcast on television, 1974; "The Witches of Pendle," first broadcast on television, 1976.*

*   *   *

COLLINS, Jackie

PERSONAL: Married Oscar Lerman. *Home:* Roebuck House, Apt. 121, Stag Place, London S.W. 1, England.

CAREER: Novelist and screen actress.

WRITINGS—Novels: *The World Is Full of Married Men,* World Publishing, 1968; *The Stud,* W. H. Allen, 1969, World Publishing, 1970; *Sunday Simmons and Charlie Brick,* W. H. Allen, 1971, published as *The Hollywood Zoo,* Pinnacle Books, 1975; *Lovehead,* W. H. Allen, 1974; *The World Is Full of Divorced Women,* W. H. Allen, 1975; *Lovers and Gamblers,* W. H. Allen, 1977, Grosset, 1978; *The Bitch,* Pan Books, 1979.

SIDELIGHTS: "The Stud" and "The World Is Full of Married Men" have both been released as feature films.*

*   *   *

COLLINS, Thomas Hightower   1910-
(Paul Hightower)

PERSONAL: Born November 26, 1910, in Cedartown, Ga.; son of Clifford Augustus and Fannie Lou (Hightower) Collins; married Beulah Blagden Stowe, April 6, 1946; children: Carol, Kent, Paul, Todd. *Education:* Attended University of Georgia, 1929-31, and University System Center (now Georgia State University), 1931-35. *Religion:* Episcopalian. *Home:* 15 Lake Shore Dr., Chapel Hill, N.C. 27514.

CAREER: DeKalb New Era, Decatur, Ga., reporter, 1932-35; *Atlanta Journal,* Atlanta, Ga., copyreader and picture editor, 1935-40; *Louisville Courier-Journal,* Louisville, Ky., copyreader and staff writer, 1940-42; *Chicago Daily News,* Chicago, Ill., 1942-62, feature editor, 1946-59, assistant managing editor, 1959-60, managing editor, 1960-61, executive editor, 1961-62. *Military service:* U.S. Naval Reserve, active duty, 1944-46; became lieutenant senior grade.

WRITINGS: The Golden Years: An Invitation to Retirement, John Day, 1956, reprinted as *The Golden Years of Retirement,* Doubleday, 1963; *The Complete Guide to Retirement,* Prentice-Hall, 1970, revised edition, 1977. Author (under pseudonym Paul Hightower) of "The Golden Years," a column in *Senior Forum,* 1952—.

BIOGRAPHICAL/CRITICAL SOURCES: Time, May 15, 1956.*

*   *   *

COLQUHOUN, Keith   1927-

PERSONAL: Surname is pronounced *Co*-hoon; born August 5, 1927, in London, England; son of Archibald (a customs officer) and Grace (a musician; maiden name, Humphreys) Colquhoun; married Maureen Smith; (marriage ended, 1980); children: Andrew, Mary, Edward. *Education:* Attended grammar school in Torquay, England. *Home:* 7 Andrewes House, Barbican, London EC2, England.

CAREER: Reporter on various provincial newspapers in England, 1945-59; *London Daily Herald/Sun,* London, England, chief sub-editor, 1959-70; *Observer,* London, managing editor, 1970-77; *Far Eastern Economic Review,* Hong Kong, news editor, 1977-80; *Economist,* London, writer, 1980—.

WRITINGS—Novels: *The Money Tree,* Hamish Hamilton, 1959; *Point of Stress,* Hamish Hamilton, 1961; *The Sugar Coating,* Chatto & Windus, 1973; *St. Petersburg Rainbow,* Chatto & Windus, 1975; *Goebbels and Gladys,* J. Murray, 1981.

WORK IN PROGRESS: Filthy Rich (tentative title), a novel set in Hong Kong, publication by J. Murray expected in 1982.

SIDELIGHTS: Colquhoun told *CA:* "Several of the writers I most admire are French: Maupassant, for example, and more recently, Marguerite Duras, Roger Vailland, and Albert Camus. I seek to work in a spare style, considering what can be left out as well as what should be put in. I avoid physical description, confining it to what I consider to be significant detail. My books tend to be shortish and I think of them as being read in one or perhaps two sittings: the time that you would give to a film or a play or a piece of music."

*   *   *

COLSON, Charles W(endell)   1931-

PERSONAL: Born October 16, 1931, in Boston, Mass.; son of Wendell Ball (a lawyer) and Inez (Ducrow) Colson; married Nancy Billings, June 3, 1953 (divorced); married Patricia Ann Hughes, April 4, 1964; children: (first marriage) Wendell Ball II, Emily Ann, Christian Billings. *Education:* Brown University, A.B. (with distinction), 1953; George Washington University, J.D., 1959. *Religion:* Baptist. *Home address:* P.O. Box 40562, Washington, D.C. 20016. *Office:* Prison Fellowship, P.O. Box 40562, Washington, D.C. 20016.

CAREER: Admitted to the Bar of Virginia, 1959, the Bar of

Washington, D.C., 1961, and the Bar of Massachusetts, 1964; assistant to assistant secretary of Navy, 1955-56; administrative assistant to Senator Leverett Saltonstall, 1956-61; Gadsby & Hannah, Boston, Mass., senior partner, 1961-69; president of the United States, White House, Washington, D.C., special counsel, 1969-73; Colson & Shapiro, Washington, D.C., partner, 1973-74; Fellowship House, Washington, D.C., associate, 1975—; Prison Fellowship, Washington, D.C., president, 1976—. *Military service:* U.S. Marine Corp, 1953-55; became captain; served during Korean conflict. *Member:* Beta Theta Pi. *Awards, honors:* Order of Coif; Religious Heritage of America award, 1977; *Born Again* was named outstanding evangelical book of 1976 by *Eternity.*

WRITINGS: Born Again (nonfiction), Chosen Books, 1976; *Life Sentence* (nonfiction), Chosen Books, 1979; (contributor) John Stott and Nicholas Miller, editors, *Crime and the Responsible Community,* Hodder & Stoughton, 1980, Eerdmans, 1981.

SIDELIGHTS: As a special counsel to President Nixon, Charles Colson earned a reputation as an "arrogant" and "ruthless" hatchet man. He has been described as one of the "original back room boys—the operators and brokers, the guys who fix things when they break down and do the dirty work when necessary." Devoted to Nixon, Colson willingly carried out these unpleasant duties. "I rarely questioned a Presidential order," he explained. Colson, who supposedly established Nixon's "enemies list," was also reported as saying, "I would walk over my grandmother if necessary to get Nixon re-elected." One of Colson's tasks was to discredit Daniel Ellsberg, the man who supplied the "Pentagon Papers" to the *New York Times* and *Washington Post* during his trial in 1971. Colson's smear tactics indirectly led to the burglary of the office of Ellsberg's ex-psychiatrist in an effort to obtain damaging information.

When the Watergate scandal broke, which brought Nixon and his advisers under fire, Colson was charged with conspiracy for allegedly concealing evidence about the Watergate break-in. While awaiting trial, Colson met an old business associate who had been converted to Christ and also read C. S. Lewis's book, *Mere Christianity.* Under these influences, he soon became a born-again Christian. Buoyed by the support of members of his prayer group, Colson decided to offer a plea of guilty to the obstruction of justice in the trial of Daniel Ellsberg if all other charges against him were dropped. The bargain was accepted, and Colson was convicted and sentenced in 1974. "I have watched with a heavy heart the country I love being torn apart these past months," he said, explaining his actions. "The prompt and just resolution of other proceedings, far more important than my trial, is vital to our democratic process. I want to be free to contribute to that resolution no matter who it may help or hurt—me or others."

After spending seven months in prison, Colson began working with the Christian ministry organization known as Fellowship House. He also published his first book, *Born Again,* which details his spiritual conversion. Many people were skeptical about Colson's convenient change of heart in 1974. Molly Ivins of the *New York Times Book Review* conceded that when "his conversion was made public in mid-Watergate, it produced a spell of coast-to-coast sniggering." But Ivins judged that Colson in *Born Again* "is not only serious, but also . . . manages to make his conversion entirely credible." She added: "There is no doubting his sincerity."

Colson told *CA:* "In 1976 I founded Prison Fellowship,

which is today the largest evangelical outreach into prisons in America. It has spread to England, Australia, New Zealand, and Canada.''

BIOGRAPHICAL/CRITICAL SOURCES: New York Times, March 29, 1973, March 2, 1974; *Time,* June 17, 1974, July 8, 1974, February 2, 1976; *Newsweek,* June 17, 1974, July 1, 1974, September 9, 1974, February 17, 1975, October 25, 1976; *New York Times Book Review,* March 28, 1976; *Commonweal,* July 1, 1976; *National Review,* August 6, 1976.

*   *   *

CONNELLY, Marc(us Cook)   1890-1980

OBITUARY NOTICE—See index for *CA* sketch: Born December 13, 1890, in McKeesport, Pa.; died December 21, 1980, in New York, N.Y. Playwright, producer, director, and actor, best known for his Pulitzer Prize-winning play ''The Green Pastures.'' Connelly was a prolific writer of lightly satirical plays for the stage, screen, and radio. He wrote dozens of plays, often collaborating with the eminent playwright George S. Kaufman. On his ninetieth birthday, Connelly was presented with a certificate of appreciation for his contributions to the theatre by New York mayor Edward Koch. Connelly's plays include ''Dulcy,'' ''Merton of the Movies,'' and ''Helen of Troy, New York.'' Among his screenplays are ''The Cradle Song,'' ''Captains Courageous,'' and ''I Married a Witch.'' Obituaries and other sources: *New York Times,* December 21, 1980; *Washington Post,* December 23, 1980; *London Times,* December 23, 1980; *Chicago Tribune,* December 23, 1980; *Newsweek,* January 5, 1981; *Publishers Weekly,* January 9, 1981; *Time,* January 12, 1981.

*   *   *

CONVERSE, John Marquis   1909-1980

OBITUARY NOTICE: Born September 29, 1909, in San Francisco, Calif.; died of a heart attack, December 27, 1980. Educator, plastic surgeon, and author of works in his field. Converse founded the Institute of Reconstructive Plastic Surgery. Obituaries and other sources: *American Men and Women of Science,* 14th edition, Bowker, 1979; *Who's Who in America,* 41st edition, Marquis, 1980; *Chicago Tribune,* January 2, 1981.

*   *   *

COOK, Ramsay   1931-

PERSONAL: Born November 28, 1931, in Alameda, Saskatchewan, Canada; son of George Russell and Lillie Ellen (Young) Cook; married Margaret Eleanor Thornhill; children: Margaret Michele, Markham Glen. *Education:* University of Manitoba, B.A., 1954; Queen's University, Kingston, Ontario, M.A., 1955; University of Toronto, Ph.D., 1960. *Home:* 65 Woodlawn Ave. W., Toronto, Ontario, Canada M4V 1G6. *Office:* York University, Toronto, Ontario, Canada.

CAREER: University of Toronto, Toronto, Ontario, professor of history, 1958-68; Harvard University, Cambridge, Mass., visiting professor of Canadian studies, 1968-69; York University, Toronto, professor of history and social science. Television commentator. *Member:* Royal Society of Canada (fellow), Canadian Historical Association, University League for Social Reform (past president). *Awards, honors:* President's medal from University of Western Ontario, 1966 and 1968; Tyrrell Medal from Royal Society of Canada, 1975.

WRITINGS: (With Kenneth McNaught) *Canada and the United States,* Clarke, Irwin, 1963; *The Politics of John W. Dafoe and the Free Press,* University of Toronto Press, 1963; (with John T. Saywell and John C. Ricker) *Canada: A Modern Study,* Clarke, Irwin, 1963, 3rd edition, 1977; *Canada and the French-Canadian Question,* Macmillan, 1966; *Provincial Autonomy: Minority Rights and the Compact Theory, 1867-1921,* Queen's Printer, 1969; (with Kenneth D. MacRae, Jeremy Boissevain, and others) *Royal Commission on Bilingualism and Biculturalism: Studies,* Queen's Printer, 1969; (author of introduction) Eleanor Cook, editor, *The Craft of History,* Canadian Broadcasting Corp., 1973; (with Robert Craig Brown) *Canada, 1896-1921: A Nation Transformed,* McClelland & Stewart, 1974; *The Maple Leaf Forever: Essays on Nationalism and Politics in Canada,* Macmillan, 1977.

Editor: *The Dafoe-Sifton Correspondence, 1919-1927,* D. W. Friesen, 1966; *Politics of Discontent,* University of Toronto Press, 1967; *Confederation,* University of Toronto Press, 1967; *Constitutionalism and Nationalism in Lower Canada,* University of Toronto Press, 1969; *French-Canadian Nationalism: An Anthology,* Macmillan, 1970; (with Michael Behiels) Andre Laurendeau, *The Essential Laurendeau* (translated from the original French by Joanne L'Heaureaux and Richard Howard), Copp, Clark, 1976; (with Carl Berger) *The West and the Nation: Essays in Honour of W. L. Morton,* McClelland & Stewart, 1976; (with Wendy Mitchinson) *The Proper Sphere: Woman's Place in Canadian Society,* Oxford University Press, 1976.

Contributor to scholarly journals and popular magazines, including *Canadian Forum* and *Saturday Night.* Editor of *Canadian Historical Review,* 1963-68.

AVOCATIONAL INTERESTS: Theatre, music, movies, bird-watching.

BIOGRAPHICAL/CRITICAL SOURCES: Canadian Forum, April-May, 1970.*

*   *   *

COOKE, John Fletcher
See FLETCHER-COOKE, John

*   *   *

COOPER, Colin Symons   1926-
(Daniel Benson)

PERSONAL: Given names are pronounced *Col*-lin *Sim*-mons; born July 5, 1926, in Birkenhead, England; son of Frederick Arthur and Clara (Symons) Cooper; married Maureen Elizabeth Goodwin (a lecturer in art), September 4, 1966; children: Daniel, Ben. *Education:* Attended private school in Bridgwater, England. *Home:* 25 Warner Rd., London N8 7HB, England. *Agent:* David Higham Associates Ltd., 3-5 Lower John St., Golden Sq., London W1R 4HA, England.

CAREER: Crypton Equipment, Ltd., Bridgwater, Somerset, England, 1948-52; John Lysaght, Ltd., Bristol, England, assistant sales manager, 1952-59, London representative, 1959-62; full-time writer, 1962-63; National Temperance Hospital, London, part-time administrative assistant, 1963-65; Center for the Study of Human Development, London, part-time statistics assistant, 1965-70; full-time writer, 1970-72; *Guitar* (magazine), co-founder and features editor, 1972-73; Society for Research Into Higher Education, offset lithography machine operator, 1973-75; Guarnerius (print and design business), owner and operator, 1976—. *Military service:* British

Army, Royal Corps of Signals, 1944-47. *Member:* Writers Guild of Great Britain, Writers Action Group, Defence of Literature and Arts Society, Save Our Space Action Group. *Awards, honors:* Awards from Somerset Rural Community Council, 1952, for "Good Neighbours," 1953, for "Laertes for a Night," 1954, for "Rediscovery," and 1956, for "Riches and Rags"; awards from *Observer* and *London Weekend Television,* both 1969, both for "The Funeral of H.M. Queen Victoria."

WRITINGS—All science-fiction novels: *The Thunder and Lightning Man,* Faber, 1968; *Outcrop,* Faber, 1969; *Dargason,* Dobson, 1977; *The Epping Pyramid,* R. Hale, 1978.

Under pseudonym Daniel Benson: *The Argyll Killings* (crime novel), R. Hale, 1980.

Plays: "Honeymoon in Paris" (one-act), first produced in Weston-Super-Mare, England, 1950; "Good Neighbours" (three-act), first produced in Somerset, England, 1953; "Laertes for a Night" (one-act), first produced in Glastonbury, England, 1953; "Rediscovery" (one-act), first produced in 1954; "Hands of Memory" (one-act), first produced in Kingston, England, 1956; *Riches and Rags* (one-act; first produced in Bridgwater, England, 1956), Deane, 1957; *The Diamond Tooth* (one-act; first produced in Kingston, England, 1958), Deane, 1960.

Television plays: "The Funeral of H.M. Queen Victoria," first broadcast by London Weekend Television, August 2, 1969.

Radio plays; all first broadcast by British Broadcasting Corp. (BBC): "Design for Danger," February 14, 1957; "Soldier With a Squeezebox," October 5, 1964; "Two Steps Forward," June 2, 1965; "Rough Music," April 30, 1966; "A Leap Into Darkness," 1967; "The Private Patient," May 29, 1970.

Co-author of "Host Planet Earth," a series on BBC-Radio, 1966. Author of "Letter From London," a monthly column in *Gendai Guitar,* 1975—. Contributor of articles and reviews to magazines and newspapers, including *Times Literary Supplement, Guardian* and *Music Teacher.*

WORK IN PROGRESS: Two novels, *Third Party* and *Deuce.*

SIDELIGHTS: Cooper told *CA:* "As a writer of fiction I am as much interested in what people say as in what they do. Writing of mine that does not contain a high proportion of dialogue appears to me to have a vital element missing. I am concerned with the rhythm of words within the sentence: at the back of my mind, as I write, is the feeling that someone may read my words aloud. As in music also, I find that dissonance and consonance—or conflict and its resolution into peace—are important ingredients without which good fiction can barely survive. With these simple tools a storyteller may still practice his age-old craft and gain an audience.

"A writer should have more than one string to his bow. I have discovered the ideal supplementary labor: printing. I am still involved with words, but in a different, more physical way that is refreshing after a long morning at the typewriter. The danger is that the words become more important than the truth, and that must be guarded against. When Benjamin Franklin signed the Declaration of Independence he gave his occupation as Author and Printer. Without claiming any other comparison at all, I am proud to claim the same occupations for myself—though without the capital letters."

* * *

COOPER, Derek Macdonald 1925-

PERSONAL: Born May 25, 1925; son of Stephen George

and Jessie (Macdonald) Cooper; married Janet Feaster (an architect), September, 1953; children: Penelope Jane, Nicholas. *Education:* Wadham College, Oxford, M.A. (with honors), 1950. *Home:* 1 Clement Rd., London SW19 7RJ, England; and Seafield House, Portree, Isle of Skye. *Agent:* Hilary Rubinstein, A. P. Watt Ltd., 26/28 Bedford Row, London WC1R 4HL, England.

CAREER: Radio Singapore, Singapore, 1950-60, began as writer, became controller of programs; writer and broadcaster, 1960—. Narrator for "World in Action," 1962-65, and "Tomorrow's World," 1962-80. Interviewer, presenter, and broadcaster for radio programs, including "Today," "Ten O'Clock," "Newstime," "World at One," "Women's Hour," "Start the Week," "Outlook," "New Worlds," and "Frankly Speaking." *Awards, honors:* Glenfiddich Gold Medal, 1972, 1980; Scottish Arts Council Award, 1980, for *Road to the Isles.*

WRITINGS: The Bad Food Guide, Routledge & Kegan Paul, 1967; *The Beverage Report,* Routledge & Kegan Paul, 1971; *Skye,* Routledge & Kegan Paul, 1971; *The Gullibility Gap,* Routledge & Kegan Paul, 1974; *The Hebridean Connection: A View of the Highlands and Islands,* Routledge & Kegan Paul, 1977; *The Road to the Isles: Travellers in the Hebrides,* Routledge & Kegan Paul, 1979; *A Guide to the Whiskies of Scotland,* Pitman, 1979. Also author of *Wine With Food,* 1980, *Enjoying Scotch,* with Dione Pattulo, 1980, and *The Whisky Roads of Scotland,* with Fay Godwin, 1981.

Writer and presenter of programs, including "Breathing Space," BBC-TV (Scotland), 1970-76, "I Am an Engineer," "Spotlight," "Twentieth Century Focus," "Science Session," "What Are the Facts," "Men and Materials," "Knowhow," "Twenty-Four Hours," "Horizon," "Blue Peter," "Adventure," "Odd World," "Release," and "Made in Britain." Script writer and commentator of documentary films for British and American firms, including Rolls Royce, British Leyland, Ferranti, Marconi, and Vickers.

Food and wine correspondent for *World Medicine;* war correspondent for *Observer;* contributor to magazines and newspapers, including *Wine and Food* and *New Statesman.*

* * *

COPP, E. Anthony 1945-

PERSONAL: Born September 8, 1945, in San Antonio, Tex.; son of Nelson Gage and Aurora Copp; married wife, Monica Linda, November 10, 1972 (marriage ended, 1980); children: Tara Linda, Jacqueline Aurora. *Education:* St. Mary's University, San Antonio, Tex., B.A. and M.A.; Texas A & M University, Ph.D. *Home:* 7707 Fall Meadow, Dallas, Tex. 75248. *Office:* Hunt Oil Co., 2900 First National Bank Building, Dallas, Tex. 75202.

CAREER: American Petroleum Institute, Washington, D.C., senior economist, 1970-74; Salomon Brothers, New York, N.Y., vice-president and manager of energy resource and development, 1974-80; Hunt Oil Co., Dallas, Tex., vice-president in corporate finance, 1980—. *Military service:* U.S. Army, Military Intelligence, until 1970; became captain. *Member:* American Economic Association, Society of Petroleum Engineers, New York Society of Security Analysts. *Awards, honors:* All-American Award in Journalism from American Association of Newspapers, 1965.

WRITINGS: Regulating Competition in Oil: Government Intervention in the U.S. Petroleum Refining Industry, 1948-1975, Texas A & M University Press, 1976. Contributor to professional journals.

COPPOCK, John Terence 1921-

PERSONAL: Born June 2, 1921, in Cardiff; Wales; son of Arthur Leslie and Valerie Margaret (Phillips) Coppock; married Sheila Mary Burnett, 1953; children: one son, one daughter. *Education:* Queen's College, Cambridge, B.A., 1949, M.A., 1954; University of London, Ph.D., 1960. *Home:* 57 Braid Ave., Edinburgh EH10 6EB, Scotland. *Office:* Department of Geography, University of Edinburgh, High School Yards, Edinburgh EH1 1NR, Scotland.

CAREER: Lord Chancellor's Department, Bargoed, Wales, clerical officer, 1938-39; Ministry of Works, Cardiff, Wales, executive officer, 1946-47; Board of Customs and Excise, Cardiff, officer of customs and excise, 1947; Cambridge University, Cambridge, England, demonstrator for department of geography, 1949-50; University of London, London, England, assistant lecturer, 1950-52, lecturer, 1952-64, reader in geography, 1964-65; University of Edinburgh, Edinburgh, Scotland, Ogilvie Professor of Geography, 1965—. Member of Scottish Sports Council, 1976—, and Ordnance Survey Review Committee, 1978-79. *Military service:* British Army, Welch Regiment, 1939-46. *Member:* British Academy (fellow), Royal Society of Edinburgh (fellow).

WRITINGS: (With Robin Hewitson Best) *The Changing Land Use in Britain,* Faber, 1962; *An Agricultural Atlas of England and Wales,* Faber, 1964, 2nd edition, 1976, Merrimack Book Service, 1976; *An Agricultural Geography of Great Britain,* G. Bell, 1971; (with Brian Snowden Duffield) *Recreation in the Countryside: A Spatial Analysis,* St. Martin's, 1975; *An Agricultural Atlas of Scotland,* J. Donald, 1976; *Land Use* (bound with *Town and Country Planning* by L. F. Gebbett) Pergamon, 1978; *Land Assessment in Scotland,* Aberdeen University Press, 1980.

Editor: (With Hugh C. Prince) *Greater London,* Faber, 1964; (with Christopher Barrie Wilson) *Environmental Quality: With Emphasis on Urban Problems,* Halsted, 1974 (published in Scotland as *Environmental Quality,* Scottish Academic Press, 1974); (with W. R. Derrick Sewell) *The Spatial Dimensions of Public Policy,* Pergamon, 1976; (with Sewell) *Public Participation in Planning,* Wiley, 1977; *Second Homes: Curse or Blessing?,* Pergamon, 1977.

Contributor to geography, agriculture, and history journals. Editor of more than forty reports of the Tourism and Recreation Unit and contributor to several.

WORK IN PROGRESS: Water Management in Scotland, with Sewell and Alan S. Pitkethly; *Nature Conservation and Tourism,* with Charles Rye-Smith and Jonathan Blackie.

SIDELIGHTS: Coppock told *CA:* "My interest in land use was stimulated both by my love of the British countryside and by lectures by Sir Frank Engeldow, then Drapers' Professor of Agriculture at Cambridge University. In my view it was necessary to establish and measure the scale of changes in rural land use in Great Britain, an approach that involved a careful evaluation of official statistics. On the basis of this experience and because of a conviction that geographers ought to contribute in a practical way to policies for the wise use of resources, I became increasingly involved with public agencies with responsibilities in these fields, notably in my appointment as a special advisor to the Select Committee on Scottish Affairs in its investigation into land resource use in Scotland (1971-72). My interest in recreation and tourism also arose from these studies of land use when it became clear to me in the early 1960's that these major uses of land had been largely neglected in Great Britain; this interest led to the formation of the Tourism and Recreation Research Unit and the undertaking of a major program of multi-disciplinary research under my guidance."

AVOCATIONAL INTERESTS: Listening to music, natural history.

*   *   *

COPPOLA, Raymond T(homas) 1947-

PERSONAL: Born March 28, 1947, in New York, N.Y.; son of Chris and Ida Coppola. *Education:* St. John's University, Jamaica, N.Y., B.A., 1968, Ph.D., 1974; New York University, M.A., 1972. *Home:* 114-12 85th Ave., Richmond Hill, N.Y. 11418.

CAREER: Teacher of mentally retarded children at school in Brooklyn, N.Y., 1968-74; Board of Education, New York City, administrator and supervisor, 1974-77; writer, lecturer, and owner of fast-food business in New Jersey, 1977-79; E. W. Williams Publications, New York City, advertising manager, 1979—.

WRITINGS: Successful Children, Walker & Co., 1978; *T.V.: A Learning Experience for Children,* TV Guide, 1978.

SIDELIGHTS: Coppola commented: "The education field is in great need of a complete revamp which would replace political nepotism with accountability and educational administrators with businessmen."

*   *   *

CORBETT, Elizabeth (Frances) 1887-1981

OBITUARY NOTICE—See index for *CA* sketch: Born September 30, 1887, in Aurora, Ill.; died January 24, 1981, in Manhattan, N.Y. Novelist, poet, and author. Corbett wrote historical novels that were often set during the Civil War. Among her writings are *Puritan and Pagan, The Graper Girls, She Was Carrie Eaton, Out at the Soldiers Home* (her autobiography), and *Sunday at Six.* Obituaries and other sources: Elizabeth Corbett, *Out at the Soldiers Home,* Appleton-Century, 1941; *New York Times,* January 31, 1981.

*   *   *

CORNER, George W(ashington) 1889-

PERSONAL: Born December 12, 1889, in Baltimore, Md.; son of George Washington and Florence (Evans) Corner; married Betsy Lyon Copping, December 28, 1915 (died, 1976); children: George Washington, Hester Ann (deceased). *Education:* Johns Hopkins University, A.B., 1909, M.D., 1913. *Home:* 104 South Fifth St., Philadelphia, Pa. 19106.

CAREER: Johns Hopkins Hospital, Baltimore, Md., resident house officer, 1914-15; assistant professor of anatomy at University of California, 1915-19; Johns Hopkins University, Baltimore, associate professor of anatomy, 1919-23, became professor emeritus of embryology; University of Rochester, Rochester, N.Y., professor of anatomy, 1923-40, curator of Medical Library, 1938-40; Carnegie Institution of Washington, Washington, D.C., director of department of embryology, 1940-56; Rockefeller Institute, New York, N.Y., historian, 1956-60. Medical assistant at Grenfell Laborador Mission, summers, 1912-13. Vicary Lecturer at Royal College of Surgeons, 1936; Vanuxem Lecturer at Princeton University, 1942; Terry Lecturer at Yale University, 1944; Commonwealth Fund research professor at University of Louisville, 1946; George Eastman Visiting Professor at Oxford University, 1952-53. Trustee emeritus of Samuel Ready School. U.S. delegate to International Congress of Endocrinology, 1941, president, 1964, president of International Congress of Anatomists, 1960.

MEMBER: American Association of Anatomists (president, 1946-48), American Philosophical Society (vice-president, 1953-56), National Academy of Sciences (vice-president, 1953-57), American Association for the History of Medicine (president, 1954-55), Society for Experimental Biology and Medicine, Royal Society of Edinburgh (fellow), Royal College of Obstetrics and Gynecology (fellow), Royal Society (foreign member), Anatomical Society of Great Britain (honorary member), Phi Beta Kappa, Sigma Xi, Century Club, Franklin Inn Club. *Awards, honors:* Squibb Award from Society for the Study of Internal Secretions, 1940; presidential certificate of merit, 1948; honorary degrees include D.H.C. from Catholic University of Chile, 1942; D.Sc. from University of Rochester, 1944, Boston University, 1948, University of Chicago, 1958, Thomas Jefferson University, 1971, and Rockefeller University, 1975; D.Sc. from Oxford University, 1950, M.A., 1952; LL.D. from Tulane University, 1955, Temple University, 1956, and Johns Hopkins University, 1975; M.D.S. from Women's Medical College, 1958, and D.Litt. from University of Pennsylvania, 1965; fellow of Rochester Museum of Arts and Sciences, 1943, and Balliol College, Oxford, 1952-53; award from Passano Foundation, 1958; Dale Medal from British Society of Endocrinology, 1964; Marshall Medal from British Society for the Study of Fertility, 1973; Welch Medal from American Association for the History of Medicine, 1975.

WRITINGS: Anatomical Texts of the Earlier Middle Ages: A Study in the Transmission of Culture, Carnegie Institution, 1927, reprinted, AMS Press, 1977; *Anatomy,* Hoeber, 1930, reprinted, AMS Press, 1978; *Attaining Manhood: A Doctor Talks to Boys About Sex,* Harper, 1938, revised edition, Harper, 1952; *Attaining Womanhood: A Doctor Talks to Girls About Sex,* Harper, 1939, revised edition, 1952; *The Hormones in Human Reproduction,* Princeton University Press, 1942, revised edition, 1947; *Ourselves Unborn: An Embryologist's Essay on Man,* Yale University Press, 1944, reprinted, Shoe String, 1972; (editor and author of introduction and notes) *The Autobiography of Benjamin Rush: His "Travels Through Life" Together With His Commonplace Book for 1789-1813,* Princeton University Press, 1948.

Anatomist at Large: An Autobiography and Selected Essays, Basic Books, 1958; *George Hoyt Whipple and His Friends: The Life-Story of a Nobel Prize Pathologist,* Lippincott, 1963; *A History of the Rockefeller Institute, 1901-1953: Origins and Growth,* Rockefeller Institute Press, 1964; *Two Centuries of Medicine: A History of the School of Medicine, University of Pennsylvania,* Lippincott, 1965; *Doctor Kane of the Arctic Seas,* Temple University Press, 1972.

Contributor to *Contributions to Embryology,* Carnegie Institution, 1915-57; contributor to journals. Co-editor of *American Journal of Anatomy,* 1939-41; editor for American Philosophical Society, 1977—.

BIOGRAPHICAL/CRITICAL SOURCES: George W. Corner, *Anatomist at Large: An Autobiography and Selected Essays,* Basic Books, 1958.*

*   *   *

CORNFORTH, Maurice   1909-1980

OBITUARY NOTICE—See index for *CA* sketch: Born October 28, 1909, in London, England; died December 31, 1980. Philosopher, editor, and author. As a member and organizer of the Communist party, Cornforth wrote several books promoting communist doctrine and explaining communist philosophy. As a managing director of Lawrence & Wishart Ltd., a London publishing company, Cornforth oversaw the publication in English of *Collected Works,* a fourteen volume set of writings by Karl Marx and Friedrich Engels. Cornforth's books include *Science Versus Idealism, Dialectical Materialism, Philosophy for Socialists, Marxism and the Linguistic Philosophy,* and *Communism and Philosophy.* Obituaries and other sources: *London Times,* January 8, 1981.

*   *   *

COSTELLO, Anne   1937-

PERSONAL: Born January 30, 1937, in Washington, D.C.; daughter of Thompson Brooke (a major) and Landon Priscilla (a lab technician; maiden name, Bunker) Maury; married David Raymond Costello (a professor of history), January 21, 1967; children: David, Elizabeth, Brooke Joseph, Sarah. *Education:* Goucher College, B.A., 1959. *Home:* 89 Woodward Ave., Buffalo, N.Y. 14214.

CAREER: U.S. Information Agency, Washington, D.C., assistant editor of "Voice of America," 1959-62; free-lance copy editor for various publishing houses in New York, N.Y., 1962-63; Wiltwick (boy's home), Esopus, N.Y., counsellor, 1963-64; Roger Spencer Real Estate, Rockville, Md., clerk, 1964-65; Montgomery County Welfare Board, Rockville, social worker, 1965-66; Booth Memorial Home, Buffalo, N.Y. social worker, 1966-67. Novelist. Docent at Albright-Knox Art Gallery, Buffalo, 1976—; member of Albright-Knox, Hallwalls.

WRITINGS—Novels: *Bittergreen,* Ballantine, 1980; *The Woman Who Wanted It All,* Ballantine, 1981. Also author of unpublished memoir, *To Harbour a Life.*

WORK IN PROGRESS: Women of Experience, "an intricate exploration of the relations among versions of events"; *All Those Starry Knights,* about West Point and the subject of honor.

SIDELIGHTS: After finishing the manuscript for *Bittergreen,* Anne Costello needed only to find a publisher. Her first contact, Houghton, Mifflin, told her that "editorial tastes differed widely" and suggested she try elsewhere. She did, figuring "fifty rejection slips down the road, something good would happen." Costello's dream came true much sooner than expected when Ballantine's Pamela Strickler called, saying "I'd like to publish *Bittergreen.*"

"I was delirious," Costello recalled in an article for the *Goucher Quarterly.* "Six years' work. Ten minutes here, fifteen minutes there, snatched to write down what was working in my mind as I pursued the standard life of any married woman not rich who has had four children in five and a half years. Fragments of time, splinters of time, turned into a 400 page manuscript that had been accepted. The children were using the worn kitchen floor as a trampoline."

Costello gave this description of her book to *CA:* "*Bittergreen* is my first novel, actually my first publication. Like Stendahl, I seem to have lived first. *Bittergreen* contains a death scene (in battle), a death scene (at home), an interracial wedding (in a park, gloveless), a divorce, folks from two to seventy-two (including cads, gentlemen, and would-be members of the haute bourgeoisie), more lists than *Ulysses,* more alliteration than *Beowulf,* make-up advice, four houses (five if you count the one in England), two apartments, and a screened porch in Connecticut. It has jellyfish, parrots, a California funeral, and someone getting fired from government service." An early reviewer of *Bittergreen,*

Spencie Love, said that the book "holds promise through the author's sheer individuality."

Though Costello did not publish her first book until she was forty-three, she had been working at her fiction long before that. She did some writing in college, but afterwards the demands of raising four children allowed her little more than time to write in her mind. "I've always thought novels through," she told the *Buffalo News.* Now Costello has the time to write, spending 9:30 to 2:00 every day in her private "cubby" at Buffalo's Canisius College library. That part of the day, she says, is her "happiest time."

BIOGRAPHICAL/CRITICAL SOURCES: Goucher Quarterly, summer, 1980; *Buffalo News,* July 6, 1980; *Washington Post Book World,* August 3, 1980.

* * *

COULLING, Sidney Baxter   1924-

PERSONAL: Born February 13, 1924, in Bluefield, W.Va.; son of Louis Roberdeau and Eva (Steger) Coulling; married Mary Price Stirling, June 23, 1958; children: Margaret Howard, Anne Baxter, Philip Price. *Education:* Washington and Lee University, A.B., 1948; University of North Carolina, M.A., 1949, Ph.D., 1957. *Home:* 604 Marshall St., Lexington, Va. 24450. *Office:* Department of English, Washington and Lee University, Lexington, Va. 24450.

CAREER: Florida State University, Tallahassee, instructor in English, 1949-52; University of Maryland, College Park, instructor in English, 1955-56; Washington and Lee University, Lexington, Va., 1956—, professor of English, 1965—. *Military service:* U.S. Army, 1943-46. *Member:* Modern Language Association of America, Phi Beta Kappa.

WRITINGS: Matthew Arnold and His Critics: A Study of Arnold's Controversies, Ohio University Press, 1974.

BIOGRAPHICAL/CRITICAL SOURCES: Times Literary Supplement, August 8, 1975.*

* * *

COUNCIL, Norman Briggs   1936-

PERSONAL: Born November 13, 1936, in Pensacola, Fla.; married, 1963; children: one. *Education:* University of the South, B.A., 1958; Stanford University, M.A., 1964, Ph.D., 1967. *Office:* Department of English, University of Utah, Salt Lake City, Utah 84112.

CAREER: University of Vermont, Burlington, instructor in English, 1964-67; University of California, Santa Barbara, assistant professor of English, 1967-76; University of Utah, Salt Lake City, associate professor of English and chairman of department, 1976—. Member of faculty at National Humanities Institute, 1967-68; visiting member of faculty at Claremont Graduate School, summer, 1972. *Member:* Modern Language Association of America.

WRITINGS: When Honour's at the Stake: Ideas of Honour in Shakespeare's Plays, Barnes & Noble, 1973. Contributor to literature journals.*

* * *

COURTNEY, William J(ohn)   1921-

PERSONAL: Born May 22, 1921, in Indianapolis, Ind.; son of William J. (a railroad official) and Bertha (Cosgrove) Courtney; married Constance Campion, June 16, 1948; children: six. *Education:* University of San Francisco, B.S., 1949, M.A., 1956. *Politics:* Democrat. *Religion:* Roman Catholic. *Home:* 224 Westbrook Ave., Daly City, Calif.

94015. *Office:* George Washington High School, 600 32nd Ave., San Francisco, Calif. 94121.

CAREER: San Francisco Community College, San Francisco, Calif., instructor in social studies, 1951—; George Washington High School, Daly City, Calif., teacher of social studies, 1970—. *Military service:* U.S. Army, field medical clerk, 1942-45; served in Europe and Africa. *Member:* San Francisco Federation of Teachers, San Francisco Press Club.

WRITINGS: San Francisco's Anti-Chinese Ordinances, 1850-1900, R & E Research Associates, 1974, William J. Courtney, 1975.

SIDELIGHTS: Courtney commented: "I was motivated to publish and copyright my 1956 dissertation because it had been pirated in 1974 by adventurers who sold numerous copies to university and law college libraries in this country and abroad before they were cautioned by our attorneys that a common law copyright had been infringed upon."

* * *

COWAN, Charles Donald   1923-

PERSONAL: Born November 18, 1923, in London, England; son of W.C. and Minnie Ethel (Farrow) Cowan; married Mary Evelyn Vetter, 1945 (divorced, 1960); married Daphne Eleanor Whittam, 1962; children: (first marriage) two daughters. *Education:* Peterhouse, Cambridge, M.A., 1948; University of London, Ph.D., 1956. *Office:* School of Oriental and African Studies, University of London, London W.C.1, England.

CAREER: Raffles College, Singapore, lecturer in history, 1947-48; University of Malaya, Singapore, Kuala Lumpur, lecturer in history, 1948-50; University of London, School of Oriental and African Studies, London, England, lecturer, 1950-60, professor of Southeast Asian history, 1961-80, professor of Oriental history, 1980—. Chairman of Centre for Southeast Asian Studies, 1966-72, director of School of Oriental and African Studies, 1976—. Visiting professor at Cornell University, 1960-61. *Military service:* Royal Navy, 1941-45.

WRITINGS: (Editor and author of introduction) *Early Penang and the Rise of Singapore, 1805-1832: Documents From the Manuscript Records of the East India Company,* Malaya Publishing House, 1950; *Nineteenth-Century Malaya: The Origins of British Political Control,* Oxford University Press, 1961; (editor) *The Economic Development of China and Japan: Studies in Economic History and Political Economy,* Praeger, 1964; (editor) *The Economic Development of Southeast Asia: Studies in Economic History and Political Economy,* Praeger, 1964; (editor with O. W. Wolters, and contributor) *Southeast Asian History and Historiography: Essays Presented to D.G.E. Hall,* Cornell University Press, 1976; (with P. L. Burns) *Sir Frank Swettenham's Malayan Journals, 1874-1876,* Oxford University Press, 1976. Contributor to scholarly journals.

BIOGRAPHICAL/CRITICAL SOURCES: Times Literary Supplement, March 11, 1977.

* * *

COWAN, George McKillop   1916-

PERSONAL: Born February 23, 1916, in Kelwood, Manitoba, Canada; married Florence Hansen, November 21, 1943; children: Paul, Esther, Ruth. *Education:* McMaster University, B.A., 1936; Dallas Theological Seminary, Th.M., 1941; University of North Dakota, M.A., 1963.

Home: 2218 West Edinger St., Apt. 3, Santa Ana, Calif. 92704.

CAREER: Director of Canadian Summer Institute for Linguistics, 1944-53; Wycliffe Bible Translators, director of language course in England, 1953-59, president, 1957—, deputy general for Europe and Asia, 1963-71. Member of board of directors of Summer Institute for Linguistics at University of Oklahoma, 1956—; director of Seminar Sprachmethodik, 1966-72; director of phonology at Gordon College's Summer Institute for Linguistics, 1970-72. *Member:* Linguistic Society of America, American Society of Missiology. *Awards, honors:* LL.D. from Biola College, 1970.

WRITINGS: Some Aspects of the Lexical Structure of a Mazatec Historical Text, Summer Institute for Linguistics, University of Oklahoma, 1965; (contributor) *Maria Sabina and Her Mazatec Mushroom Velada,* Harcourt, 1975; (contributor) *Speech Surrogates: A Reader,* Volume I, Mouton, 1976; *The Word That Kindles,* Christian Herald, 1979. Contributor to anthropology and linguistic journals.*

*   *   *

COWIE, Hamilton Russell   1931-

PERSONAL: Born May 9, 1931, in Invercargill, New Zealand; son of Hamilton (a farmer) and Adelaide (Lindsay) Cowie; married Kaye Hodges (a research assistant), April 5, 1958; children: David Hamilton, Susan Margaret, Anna Elizabeth. *Education:* University of Otago, B.A., 1951, M.A. (with honors), 1953; University of Queensland, B.Ed., 1973. *Religion:* Presbyterian. *Home:* 26 McIlwraith St., Auchenflower, Brisbane, Queensland 4066, Australia. *Office:* Department of Education, University of Queensland, St. Lucia, Brisbane, Queensland 4067, Australia.

CAREER: Teacher at high schools in New Zealand, 1954-56; teacher at grammar schools in England, 1957-58, and Australia, 1959-64; senior housemaster at grammar school in Brisbane, Australia, 1965-69; assistant to headmaster of grammar school in Brisbane, 1969-72; University of Queensland, Brisbane, lecturer, 1972-75, senior lecturer in education, 1975—. *Member:* Queensland History Teachers Association (member of executive committee, 1969-80), Old Presbyterian and Methodist Schools Association (member of council).

WRITINGS: (With J. H. Allsopp) *Challenge and Response: A History of the Modern World,* Thomas Nelson, Volume I, 1969, Volume II, 1970, revised edition, 1976; (editor and contributor) *Heritage* (high school textbook), Thomas Nelson, Volume I: *The First Fifty Thousand Years,* 1974, Volume II: *Australia and the Modern World,* 1975; *Frankfurt to Fra Mauro: A Thematic History of the Modern World,* Thomas Nelson, 1975, revised edition, 1981.

(Editor and contributor) *Foundations* (high school textbook), Thomas Nelson, 1976; (contributor) N. Little and J. Mackinalty, editors, *A New Look at History Teaching: Ideas on the Theory and Practice of Teaching History in Secondary Schools,* New South Wales History Teachers Association, 1977; (editor) *Horizons* (high school textbook), Thomas Nelson, 1978; *Revolutions in the Modern World,* Thomas Nelson, 1979; *Crossroads,* Thomas Nelson, Volume I: *Nationalism and Internationalism in the Modern World,* 1979, Volume II: *Economic Trends in the Modern World and Their Social Effects,* 1980, Volume III: *Asia and Australia in World Affairs,* 1980, Volume IV: *Historical Background to Problems of Contemporary Society,* 1981; *Discovering Brisbane,* Rigby, 1980; *Dictionary of Australian History,* Longmans Cheshire, 1981; (editor and co-author) *Outcomes* (high

school textbook), Thomas Nelson, 1981. Editor of *History Teacher,* 1970-75, and *Australian History Teacher,* 1974.

SIDELIGHTS: Cowie commented: "History books for schools should be collections of both evidence and expository writing, oriented toward the encouragement of a capacity to interpret events and trends. They should be offered as 'base-books' from which further studies from other resources can be launched."

*   *   *

COX, Edith Muriel
(Muriel Goaman)

PERSONAL: Born in Bideford, Devonshire, England; married Cyril H. Cox; children: one son, one daughter. *Education:* Attended West Bank School and Gloucester Training College of Domestic Science. *Home:* Willow Barn, Lower Cleave, Bideford, Devonshire, England.

CAREER: Free-lance writer, 1948—. Mayor, member of council, alderman, and justice of the peace in Devonshire, England, 1948-64; member of British Broadcasting Corp. advisory council. *Member:* National Book League, Society of Authors, Devonshire Association for the Advancement of Science, Literature, and Art. *Awards, honors:* Named honorary freeman of the Borough of Bideford.

WRITINGS—All under name Muriel Goaman: Anyone Can Cook!, Faber, 1952; *Thomas Guy: Friend of the Poor,* Macmillan, 1959; *Your Book of Camping,* Faber, 1960; *English Clocks,* M. Joseph, 1967; *Old Bideford and District,* E. M. & A. G. Cox, 1968; *Your Book of Knitting and Crochet,* Faber, 1968; *Fun With Chess,* Pelham Books, 1968; *Food,* Wills & Hepworth, 1968; *Fun With Time,* Pelham Books, 1970; *Picture Signs and Symbols,* Chatto & Windus, 1970; *Touch Wood!: A Book of Everyday Superstitions,* Chatto & Windus, 1973; *Chess Made Easy: An Introductory Guide to the Manoevers of Winning Chess,* Modern Canadian Library, 1973; *Never So Good; or, How Children Were Treated,* Pelham Books, 1974.

Children's books: *Judy's Book of Sweet-Making,* Faber, 1941; *Judy's Book of Housework,* Faber, 1947; *Judy's Cookery Book,* Faber, 1947; *Judy's Book of Parties,* Faber, 1949; *Judy's Book of Sewing and Knitting,* Faber, 1950; *Judy's and Andrew's Puppet Book,* Faber, 1952, 2nd edition, 1963, Plays, 1967; *Judy's and Andrew's Book of Bees,* Faber, 1954; *Judy's and Andrew's Book of the Seashore,* Faber, 1956; *Judy's Book of Flower Arrangement,* Faber, 1957; *Judy's Next Cookery Book,* Faber, 1958.

Your Book of the Year, Faber, 1963; *How Writing Began,* Faber, 1966, *Transport,* Ladybird Books, 1970; *News and Messages,* David & Charles, 1972; *Fun With Travel,* Pelham Books, 1972.

AVOCATIONAL INTERESTS: Chess, oil painting, reading.

*   *   *

CRAIG, Webster
See RUSSELL, Eric Frank

*   *   *

CRAMER, Richard L(ouis)   1947-

PERSONAL: Born April 5, 1947, in Los Angeles, Calif.; son of Martin M. (a corporate president) and Charlotte (Kessel) Cramer; married Arlene Renee Jacobs (in real estate sales), June 15, 1969; children: Matthew Hunter, Brandon Lloyd. *Education:* California State University, Northridge, B.S.,

1969. *Residence:* Sherman Oaks, Calif. *Office:* FourWay Communications, 9201 Wilshire Blvd., Suite 105, Beverly Hills, Calif. 90210.

CAREER/WRITINGS: Environmental Quality (magazine), Los Angeles, Calif., editor, 1970-73; East/West Network, Los Angeles, editor of in-flight magazines, 1973-74; free-lance writer and editor, 1974-75; *Denver* (magazine), Denver, Colo., editor, 1975-76; *Los Angeles* (magazine), Los Angeles, senior editor, 1976-77; *Playboy,* Los Angeles, West Coast editor, 1977; *Oui,* Los Angeles, editor and assistant publisher, 1977-80; FourWay Communications, Beverly Hills, Calif., owner and president, 1980—. West Coast correspondent for *Prevention* (magazine), 1974; contributor of articles to newspapers and magazines, including *Chicago Tribune, Playgirl,* and *Writer's Digest.* Speaker at civic, trade, journalistic, and professional organizations; member of Town Hall. *Military service:* U.S. Air Force Reserve, 1966-70. *Member:* American Society of Journalist and Authors, Los Angeles Ad Club.

SIDELIGHTS: For three years Richard Cramer was the editor and assistant publisher of *Oui* magazine, a subsidiary of Playboy Enterprises. His work included mapping out budgets and editorial policy, directing a staff of forty-two people, and deciding which of thousands of beautiful women should appear in the magazine. In his dual role as editor and publisher he was especially concerned with *Oui*'s competitive strength in the crowded field of men's magazines. During his time with the company, Cramer tried to develop a personality for *Oui* that distinguished it from *Playboy* and *Penthouse, Oui*'s principal competitors. "*Playboy* has the girl next door," he explained, "*Penthouse* has the girl across town. I tried not to have either. It's the real lifeness of women that I tried to bring to *Oui* with a little bit of exotica." In his comments to *CA* Cramer discusses his early career as a magazine editor, the evolution of *Oui* magazine, and his current occupation as president of his own consulting company, FourWay Communications.

"I was a business major in college and heir to the throne of my father's manufacturing company," Cramer remarked. "After I graduated with a Bachelor of Science in marketing, I told my father that I hated his business. I hated business per se, and I had designs to be a writer. I went back to Cal State and told the dean of admissions that I would like to get a degree in journalism. 'No, no, no,' he said. 'We have too many people who want their first bachelors, but you can enroll in the M.B.A. program.' I said, 'I don't want to be in the business world. I want to be a writer. I have written poems.' He said, 'That's nice, Mr. Cramer. Go away.'

"I left the building, dejected, and ran into an elderly woman who was selling the premier edition of an ecology magazine called *Environmental Quality.* I bought it, took it home, and read it. It was probably the first magazine in my life that I read cover to cover. I wrote that night to the editor and told him I thought the magazine was marvelous. I also sent him three poems about ecology that I had written a month or two earlier. He called me two days later and said, 'Your poems are terrific, Mr. Cramer. Do you have any more?' I told him I had hundreds, and he asked me to bring them in the next day. So that night I wrote hundreds. True, absolutely true. I wrote hundreds of poems that night. I probably wrote about a dozen, anyhow.

"The next day I went to see the editor and showed him my poems. We talked, I told him I was an aspiring writer, and then I mustered the courage and asked, 'Do you have any openings here?' He said, 'Well, we do and we don't. I need some people here who want to work hard and are talented, like you are. On the other hand, we don't have any money, so it's sort of voluntary for a while.' I was out of work and collecting unemployment, so I decided to go for it. He said, 'Fine. You're hired. You're an editorial assistant.' Well, I danced, I was so excited. I didn't know what the hell an editorial assistant was. I had even less an idea what an editor was.

"Four months later I became the editor of the magazine. It wasn't so much a power coup because I was much too naive to know what I was doing. It was simply a matter of survival. People couldn't afford to stay there for free. I was just so excited to learn the craft that I simply found myself in a position where I was the editor of the magazine. And I never looked back. Eighteen months later I got my first check.

"After the magazine folded in 1973 I went to East/West Network, which publishes in-flight magazines for various airlines, the magazines that are right next to the throw-up bags in the seat pockets. I edited four in-flight magazines for a couple of years. They were all monthlies—United Air Lines' magazine, Continental's, Ozark's, and Allegheny's. It wasn't exactly class stuff, but I took a certain amount of pride in the job because East/West Network is one of the major in-flight publishers in the country. The alumni of that august body are all over the place. They have been at *Rolling Stone,* at *Harper's,* at a variety of places. It's sort of the dues one pays. At East/West I learned discipline and tight editing and how to do the job quickly, which is critical.

"Then I was fired. I tried to explain to the publisher that things could be much more efficient if he restructured certain staff and let others go, hired more support help, and had a super editor or editorial director—me, naturally. I had ambitions even then. He liked the idea, but he didn't like me as the one to do it, so I was terminated, along with several of my colleagues. I then had my first experience at free lancing, which was petrifying because by then I had two children and my wife was not working.

"I free lanced for almost a year. For six months we starved. Then it all happened at once. I became the West Coast correspondent for *Prevention,* a terrific company. They pay very well. They are generous on expenses. Then I was a free-lance book editor for a while. All of a sudden I had too much to do. Just when I was thinking, 'Hey! This free-lance business can work,' I was offered a job in 1975 as the editor of a new city magazine called *Denver.*

"I took the job at *Denver,* and it was a disastrous experience. The magazine was run like a mom-and-pop store, and suffice to say that my publisher was not a very rational person. He was nuts is what he was. After a year I was fired. I told him that the cover lines I had just written for the new issue were very saleable and very good. He told me that I was stupid. Then he began fondling a baretta he liked to carry in his belt, at which point I said, 'I never quite looked at it your way. These *are* terrible cover lines.' I went home that night and said, 'I have just had an argument with my publisher and was almost shot!' I sent my wife and kids back to Los Angeles the next day, packed up the house over the weekend, and drove a twenty-three-foot Ryder truck home from Denver.

"I next worked as senior editor of *Los Angeles* magazine, and it was a very, very pleasurable experience for me. It's a terrific magazine, certainly, and probably one of the two or three best city magazines in the country. I once again learned certain disciplines and honed my writing. I wrote the gossip column and worked on several things at one time, but for the first time I was not in charge. I had a managing editor, an editor, and a publisher that I worked for, so there was a certain humility I had to learn. Then eighteen months later, the editor of *Playboy* hired me as the West Coast editor.

"I was, I think, the shortest-term West Coast editor of *Playboy* in history, and probably the shortest-term editor of any magazine. I was the West Coast editor for six weeks. Then the publisher of *Playboy* said to me, 'We would like you to become the editor and publisher of *Oui* magazine. We would like you to move the magazine from Chicago to Los Angeles. We'll give you another couple of dollars a year.' I thought, 'Jesus Christ! I don't know anything about *Oui* magazine. I don't even know about men's magazines.' I had come from ecology, in-flight, and city magazines, and all of a sudden they wanted me to get into this. It concerned me, but you don't turn those things down. I said, 'O.K. Sure,' and immersed myself in an entire new level of madness.

"Although I am certainly financially oriented, I am much more success oriented, and I have set certain standards for myself. I insisted that I make *Oui* magazine a screaming success. Originally, *Oui* was started to challenge the impending threat in 1972 of *Penthouse*. *Penthouse* had come from Britain and invaded America rather successfully because it was a little hotter (more sexually explicit, pictorially), or a lot hotter, than *Playboy* was at the time. *Oui* was a very, very good magazine the first couple of years, but it was very much ahead of its time. It was too hip, too cool, too slick. It simply had very little effect on *Penthouse*, which continued to increase in circulation. *Oui* went through several renaissances over the years, but I think its latest incarnation might be the best.

"At the end of 1980 *Oui* magazine was financially successful, way ahead of where it had been years before. We repositioned the magazine in the marketplace to sell as a men's *Ms.* or *Cosmo*, as a sexual-service magazine that offered advice for the young guy. The reader we aimed at was under thirty, certainly, somewhere in his early to mid-twenties. We tried to run as many articles as we could with a certain attitude, one which was not gonzo, madness, irreverence, and coolness, although that was certainly a part of it, a small part of it. It was oriented more towards sexual and sociological information. During my last year with the magazine we were selling slightly under one million issues a month, making *Oui* the fourth largest men's magazine in the world.

"One of my strengths is that I am a rather commercial animal. I think the sales of the magazine were such that I do indeed pride myself on understanding what might sell. I always tried to have as many things as I could that were extremely saleable, that interested as many people as possible. Things that you didn't read about elsewhere, but things that were of interest, especially to a young guy: what's it like to date a bitchy woman, what's terrific about this woman, how women differ, what this all means in the scheme of your life. Lots of advice about life, sexual and otherwise.

"If you took a look at *Oui* I think you saw a certain sophistication. We featured very attractive women, both dressed and undressed, because they were attractive, they were pretty. You bought *Oui* magazine to appreciate a beautiful woman and to read a lot of interesting things. I also tried to introduce to a young guy a certain sensitivity in his attitude and approach towards life, towards women, which is a function of maturity. I have an antagonism to this machismo ethic that finally seems to be going away. Can you imagine what it would be like to flatter a woman again without being a macho jerk? Just flatter a woman. That's a very nice thing

to think about, but it's a tricky thing to write about because you can come out sounding phony.

"There is a fine line one walks between saying what you want to say as an editor and still leaving intact what the writer has said. When I edited a piece I always worked with the writer so that he knew what I had done, in case he said I changed his work and completely blew it. It was rare that happened. I didn't want to change the writer's meaning. I didn't want to change his syntax or his verbage or his style of writing, but all of those things had to adhere to my editorial standards and the magazine's standards. When I edited I tried to leave exactly what was said, but I shifted things around slightly to say this sooner, this later, reemphasize this, de-emphasize that. But I was always very cautious and very cognizant of changing what the writer had said.

"I did very little writing for *Oui* magazine. I wrote the house copy, the gloss, the cover lines, the headlines, the subheads, the introduction, the snappy part that got you into the substance that I bought. Basically, I'm an editor. Writing is very solitary and painful. Editing, on the other hand, is only painful. Editors are like symphony conductors: they may not play any instruments well (or at all), but they know how each one should sound.

"I departed *Oui* in the fall of 1980 and spent a glorious three months doing nothing. No shaving, no writing, no reading, almost no breathing, knowing all along that I wouldn't accept any job offer, nor would I seek new employ. I knew it was time to do things all by myself.

"What I established was FourWay Communications, a multidimensional communications consultancy. It exists for the express purpose of advising publishers (and editors) in both startup and ongoing publications. I direct their energies and provide expertise on every facet of publishing—editing, writing, design, advertising, circulation, printing, typesetting, promotion, direct mail, and more. I am, after years of doing this at magazines I edited, rather well versed in all these fields. In addition, I have begun an agency to represent a handful of writers, artists, and photographers in the marketplace as well as a speaker's bureau for the further propagation of half-truths and bold-faced lies about how to sell what one has created."

BIOGRAPHICAL/CRITICAL SOURCES: Daily Variety, February 8, 1978; *Los Angeles Herald Examiner*, February 21, 1978; *San Francisco Examiner and Chronicle*, April 9, 1978; *Advertising Age*, July 2, 1979.

*   *   *

CREETH, Edmund Homer 1928-

PERSONAL: Born April 11, 1928, in Oakland, Calif.; son of Edmund G. and Alice Creeth; married wife, December 31, 1973; children: three. *Education:* University of California, Berkely, A.B., 1951, M.A., 1953, Ph.D., 1956. *Office:* Department of English, University of Michigan, Ann Arbor, Mich. 48109.

CAREER: University of California, lecturer, 1954, lecturer in English, 1955-56; Pomona College, Claremont, Calif., instructor in English, 1956-58; University of Michigan, Ann Arbor, instructor, 1958-61, assistant professor, 1961-64, associate professor, 1964-73, professor of English, 1973—. Visiting lecturer at University of Essex, 1968.

WRITINGS: (Editor and author of introduction) *Tudor Plays: An Anthology of Early English Drama*, Doubleday, 1966; (editor and author of introduction) *Tudor Prose, 1513-1570*, Doubleday, 1969; *Mankynde in Shakespeare*, University of Georgia Press, 1976. Contributor to language journals. Associate editor of *Michigan Quarterly Review,* 1975—.

SIDELIGHTS: Creeth told *CA:* "I hope to be able to devote myself to the writing of fiction and, for a few years till retirement, to the teaching of that art."

*   *   *

CRICK, Donald Herbert 1916-

PERSONAL: Born July 16, 1916, in Sydney, Australia; son of Herbert Taylor (a builder) and Pearl (Settree) Crick; married Iris King (a teacher), December 25, 1944; children: Madeleine Crick Pathe. *Education:* Educated in Sydney, Australia. *Home:* 1/1 Elamang Ave., Kirribilli, New South Wales 2061, Australia.

CAREER: Writer, 1936—. *Member:* Australian Society of Authors (member of board of management). *Awards, honors:* Mary Gilmore Award from Australasian Book Society, 1966, for *Period of Adjustment;* fellowships from Literature Board of Australia Council, 1971 and 1973-75; novel award from Rigby (publisher), 1980, for *The Moon to Play With.*

WRITINGS: Bikini Girl (novel), Horwitz, 1963; *Martin Place* (novel), Australasian Book Society, 1964; *Period of Adjustment* (novel), Australasian Book Society, 1966; *A Different Drummer* (novel), Gold Star, 1972; *The Moon to Play With* (novel), Rigby, 1980. Contributor to magazines, including *Australian, Overland, Realist,* and *Australian Author,* and newspapers.

WORK IN PROGRESS: A book of short stories.

SIDELIGHTS: Crick commented: "I have been employed as a farm worker, factory worker, clerk, insurance salesman, and shopkeeper. For years my concern was to find occupations I could forget at five o'clock, then to graduate to part-time work before realizing the ultimate distinction of being able to afford to be unemployed—at last.

"My writing career was motivated by the Great Depression of the thirties. Like William Saroyan, I took to writing as 'a defense against uselessness,' and to interpret my experience in the socially critical literary tradition that began with Defoe and *Moll Flanders,* and to which I am happy to have made a small contribution. A highlight of my writing career was a translation of *Martin Place* in the U.S.S.R., and a month's visit to Russia, Georgia, and Latvia in 1972 as a guest of the Soviet Writers Union.

"Incidentally, I have been a consistent critic of censorship, official and unofficial, and of the victimization of writers of dissent in the many countries where it occurs. To illustrate, I mention *A Different Drummer* which, to my knowledge, is the only published novel to deal, in its entirety, with the theme of absolute conscientious objection to war from the objector's standpoint. Literature's emotional appeal is transmitted by the author's feeling for his subject, and I wrote the novel from the kind of conviction that motivated Thoreau when he wrote his essay on civil disobedience, an espousal of the right of the individual to obey the dictates of his conscience. Predictably, I found it extremely difficult to obtain publication.

"Correlative to this theme is another, the mass manipulation of the public mind in the interests of power. It is the essential ingredient in *The Moon To Play With,* a satire based on a delusion of grandeur, with particular relevance to such sects as the Moonies."

CRITES, Ronald W(ayne) 1945-

PERSONAL: Born December 30, 1945, in Gridley, Calif.; son of Marvin A. (a farmer and agricultural engineer) and Beulah (a realtor; maiden name, Fillmore) Crites; married Pamela Osbourn, June 15, 1968; children: Stacie. *Education:* Chico State College, B.S.C.E., 1967; Stanford University, M.S.C.E., 1968, Engineers C.E., 1970. *Home:* 38 Meadowbrook, Davis, Calif. 95616. *Office:* Metcalf & Eddy, Inc., 106 K St., Suite 200, Sacramento, Calif. 95814.

CAREER: Metcalf & Eddy, Inc., Sacramento, Calif., project engineer, 1969-76, project manager, 1976—. Member of Greater Willowbank Improvement Association. *Member:* American Society of Civil Engineers, Water Pollution Control Federation.

WRITINGS: (Editor with George Tchobanoglous and Robert G. Smith) *Wastewater Management: A Guide to Information Sources,* Gale, 1976; (contributor) Tchobanoglous, editor, *Wastewater Engineering: Treatment, Disposal, Re-Use,* McGraw, 1979; *Land Treatment of Municipal and Industrial Wastewaters,* USEPA, 1981. Contributor to engineering and environmental studies journals.

*   *   *

CROFT-MURRAY, Edward 1907-1980

OBITUARY NOTICE: Born September 1, 1907, in Chichester, England; died September 18, 1980. Museum worker and author. Croft-Murray was keeper of the Department of Prints and Drawings at the British Museum from 1954 to 1973. His field of expertise was the drawings of the British School. He wrote the two-volume *History of Decorative Painting in England From 1537 to 1837.* Obituaries and other sources: *Who's Who,* 131st edition, St. Martin's, 1979; *London Times,* September 24, 1980.

*   *   *

CRONIN, A(rchibald) J(oseph) 1896-1981

OBITUARY NOTICE—See index for *CA* sketch: Born July 19, 1896, in Dumbarton, Scotland; died of bronchitis, January 6, 1981, in Glion, Switzerland. Surgeon and novelist. Cronin turned from a successful medical practice to writing bestselling novels in 1931. Among his novels are *Hatter's Castle, The Stars Look Down, The Keys of the Kingdom, The Citadel,* and *Shannon's Way.* Obituaries and other sources: *Chicago Tribune,* January 10, 1981; *New York Times,* January 10, 1981; *Washington Post,* January 10, 1981; *Newsweek,* January 19, 1981; *Time,* January 19, 1981; *AB Bookman's Weekly,* January 26, 1981.

*   *   *

CROOK, William 1933-

PERSONAL: Born November 2, 1933, in London, England; son of William Charles and Mary (Green) Crook; married Jane Kelly (a solicitor), January, 1975. *Education:* Attended Royal Military Academy, Sandhurst, 1952-53. *Politics:* Conservative. *Religion:* Church of England. *Home:* Spring House, Lymington Rise, Four Marks, Alton, Hampshire GU34 5BA, England. *Agent:* Campbell Thomson & McLaughlin Ltd., 31 Newington Green, London N16 9PU, England. *Office:* Reader's Digest, 25 Berkeley Sq., London W1X 6AB, England.

CAREER: British Army, infantry and parachute officer in Suez, Cyprus, Malaya, Borneo, Northern Ireland, and Brunei, 1952-76, retiring as major; insurance broker and consultant in England, 1976-77; partner and export executive in

London, England, 1977-78; *Riding,* London, staff feature writer, 1978-79; *Reader's Digest,* London, internal public relations officer and editor of house magazine, 1979—. Riding instructor for British Horse Society and British Army. *Member:* British Institute of Management (associate member), Special Forces Club, Lansdowne Club, Mounted Infantry Club. *Awards, honors*—Military: Member of Order of the British Empire; Bisley light machine gun champion. Other: Holder of English Channel canoe racing record.

WRITINGS: Four Days, Eyre Methuen, 1979, Atheneum, 1980. Contributor to British magazines. Founder and editor of *Army Housing Journal,* 1970-73.

WORK IN PROGRESS: "Pro Patria," a five-volume saga of a British and American dynastic military family, 1850-1980; *Gurkha,* a history of the Brigade of Gurkhas.

SIDELIGHTS: Crook wrote: "My ultimate aim is to become a full-time fiction writer, preferably of modern historical novels with a military bias, in the manner of Herman Wouk." *Avocational interests:* Canoe racing, judoka (black belt), free-fall parachuting, scuba diving, jungle navigating.

*   *   *

CROPPER, Margaret 1886-1980

OBITUARY NOTICE: Born in 1886 in South Westmoreland, England; died September 27, 1980, in South Westmoreland, England. Poet best known for her affinity for country life. Cropper's last collection of poetry, *Something and Everything,* was published in 1978. Obituaries and other sources: *London Times,* October 2, 1980.

*   *   *

CROSS, (Alan) Beverley 1931-

PERSONAL: Born April 13, 1931, in London, England; son of George (a theatrical manager) and Eileen (an actress; maiden name, Williams) Cross; married Elizabeth Clunies-Ross, 1955 (divorced); married Gayden Collins, 1965 (divorced); married Maggie Smith (an actress), 1974; children: five. *Education:* Attended Balliol College, Oxford, 1952-53. *Agent:* Curtis Brown Ltd., 1 Craven Hill, London W2 3EW, England.

CAREER: Seaman in Norwegian Merchant Marine, 1950-52; Royal Shakespeare Company, Stratford-upon-Avon, England, actor, 1953-56; British Broadcasting Corp., production assistant for children's television drama, 1956; playwright, 1956—. Consultant to Stratford Festival Theatre, Stratford, Ontario. *Military service:* Royal Naval Reserve, 1944-48. British Army, 1948-50. *Member:* Dramatists Club, Societe des Auteur et Compositeur Dramatique, Royal Ocean Racing Club, Marylebone Cricket Club. *Awards, honors:* Arts Council grant, 1957, for "One More River"; Arts Council award, 1960, for "Strip the Willow."

WRITINGS: Mars in Capricorn: An Adventure and an Experience (novel), Little, Brown, 1955; *The Nightwalkers* (novel), Hart-Davis, 1956, Little, Brown, 1957; *Haworth: A Portrait of the Brontes,* Theatrebooks, 1978.

Published plays: *One More River* (three-act; first produced in Liverpool, England, at New Shakespeare Theatre, 1958; produced on the West End at Duke of York's Theatre, 1959; produced on Broadway at Ambassador Theatre, March 18, 1960), Hart-Davis, 1958, Samuel French, 1960.

Strip the Willow (first produced in Nottingham, England, at Playhouse Theatre, 1960; produced in London at the Hippodrome, 1960), M. Evans, 1961; (translator) Marc Camolet-

ti, *Boeing-Boeing* (two-act comedy; first produced in Oxford, England, at New Theatre, 1961; produced on the West End at Apollo Theatre, 1962; produced on Broadway at Cort Theatre, February 2, 1965), Evans Brothers, 1965, Samuel French, 1967; *Half a Sixpence* (two-act libretto; adapted from the novel, *Kipps,* by H. G. Wells; first produced on the West End at Cambridge Theatre, 1963; produced on Broadway at Broadhurst Theatre, 1965), Chappell, 1963, Dramatic Publishing, 1966; "The Mines of Sulphur" (three-act opera; first produced in London at Sadlers Wells Theatre, 1965; produced in New York City at Juillard Theatre, 1968), published in *Plays of the Year Thirty,* Elek, 1965; *Jorrocks* (two-act musical; adapted from novels by R. S. Surtees; first produced on the West End at New Theatre, 1966), Chappell, 1968.

Victory (three-act opera libretto; based on the novel by Joseph Conrad; first produced in London at Covent Garden Theatre, April, 1970) Universal Editions, 1970; *The Rising of the Moon* (three-act opera libretto; first produced in Glyndebourne, England, 1970), Boosey & Hawkes, 1971, revised edition, 1976; *Catherine Howard* (first broadcast on television, 1970; revised version produced in York, England, at Theatre Royale, 1972), Samuel French, 1973, also published in *The Six Wives of Henry VIII,* edited by J. C. Trewin, Elek, 1972; *The Crickets Sing* (first produced in Devizes, England, at Civic Theatre, 1971), Hutchinson, 1970; *Happy Birthday* (two-act; first produced on the West End at Appolo Theatre, 1979), Samuel French, 1980.

Published children's plays: *The Singing Dolphin: A Christmas Play for Children in Two Acts* (first produced in Oxford, England, at Playhouse Theatre, 1959; produced in London, at Hampstead Theatre, 1963), Samuel French, 1973; *The Singing Dolphin and The Three Cavaliers: Two Plays for Children* (the latter first produced in Birmingham, England, at Birmingham Repertory Theatre, 1960), Hart-Davis, 1960; *All the King's Men* (musical; first produced in Coventry, England, 1969; produced in London, 1969), Universal Editions, 1969.

Unpublished plays: "Belle; or, The Ballad of Dr. Crippen" (two-act), first produced on the West End at Strand Theatre, 1961; "Wanted on Voyage" (two-act; adapted from the play by Jacques Deval), first produced in Canterbury, England, at Marlowe Theatre, 1962; "The Pirates and the Inca Gold," first produced in Sydney, Australia, at Phillip Street Theatre, 1966; (co-author) "Phil the Fluter" (two-act musical), first produced on the West End at Palace Theatre, 1969; "The Great Society" (two-act), first produced in London at Mermaid Theatre, 1974.

Unpublished children's plays: "The Owl on the Battlements" (two-act), first produced in Nottingham at Nottingham Theatre, 1971; "Where's Winkle?" (two-act), first produced in Liverpool at Playhouse Theatre, 1972; "Hans Andersen" (two-act musical), first produced on the West End at Palladium Theatre, 1974.

Screenplays: (With Jan Read) "Jason and the Argonauts," Columbia, 1963; (with Berkley Mather) "The Long Ships" (adapted from the novel by Frans Bengtsson), Columbia, 1964; (with Clarke Reynolds) "Genghis Khan," Columbia, 1965; "Half a Sixpence" (based on own play), Paramount, 1968; (co-author) "Mussolini: The Last Act," Paramount, 1972; "Sinbad and the Eye of the Tiger," Columbia, 1976; "Clash of the Titans," Metro-Goldwyn-Mayer, 1981.

Television plays; all broadcast by British Broadcasting Corp.: "The Nightwalkers," 1960; "The Dark Pits of War," 1960; "Catherine Howard," 1970; "March on, Boys!," 1975; "A Bill of Mortality," 1975.

AVOCATIONAL INTERESTS: Reading history, travel, cooking.

BIOGRAPHICAL/CRITICAL SOURCES: John Russell Taylor, *Anger and After,* Methuen, 1962.

* * *

CROSS, (Alfred) Rupert (Neal) 1912-1980

OBITUARY NOTICE: Born June 15, 1912; died September 12, 1980. Educator, expert in the field of law, and writer. Cross became a major authority on criminal law and evidence and was a popular lecturer at Magdalen College, Oxford. Among Cross's numerous writings on law is *Precedent in English Law,* a landmark analysis of evidence and its use in criminal law. He was knighted in 1973. Obituaries and other sources: *The Writers Directory, 1980-82,* St. Martin's, 1979; *Who's Who,* 131st edition, St. Martin's, 1979; *London Times,* September 15, 1980.

* * *

CROW, C(harles) P(atrick) 1938-

PERSONAL: Born July 14, 1938, in Jonesboro, Ark.; son of Judson L. and Lorene (Gibson) Crow; married Elizabeth Smith (a magazine editor), March 2, 1974; children: Samuel Harrison, Rachel Venture. *Education:* University of Missouri, B.A.,1960. *Residence:* New York, N.Y. *Agent:* Theron Raines, Raines & Raines, 475 Fifth Ave., New York, N.Y. 10017. *Office: New Yorker,* 25 West 43rd St., New York, N.Y. 10036.

CAREER: Arkansas Gazette, Little Rock, reporter and editor, 1960-62; *New York Times,* New York City, copy editor, 1963-65; *New York Herald Tribune,* New York City, assistant city editor, 1965-66; Expo '67, Montreal, Canada, and New York City, American radio and television editor, 1966-67; *New Yorker,* New York City, nonfiction editor, 1967—.

WRITINGS: No More Monday Mornings (novel), Viking, 1980.

WORK IN PROGRESS: Two novels, one about the Central Intelligence Agency, publication expected in 1981, the other "about hunting of a peculiar sort."

SIDELIGHTS: Crow told *CA:* "I enjoy trying to write what Graham Greene calls 'entertainments,' and I feel strongly that such works should be well written—not mere half-literate toss-offs."

* * *

CROW, Francis Luther
See LUTHER, Frank

* * *

CRYSTAL, John C(urry) 1920-

PERSONAL: Born September 18, 1920, in New York, N.Y.; son of Thomas Leslie and Isabelle Mary (Curry) Crystal; divorced; children: Barbara Ann. *Education:* Columbia University, B.A., 1942. *Residence:* Great Neck, N.Y. *Office:* John C. Crystal Center, Inc., 894 Plandome Rd., Manhasset, N.Y. 11030.

CAREER: Sears, Roebuck & Co., assistant to manager of foreign trade division in Philadelphia, Pa., 1947, manager of catalogue sales in Bogota, Columbia, 1948, field representative of foreign trade division in Egypt, Saudi Arabia, Bahrain, Kuwait, and Iraq, 1948-49, manager for Europe, North Africa, and Middle East, 1949-55; Warner Lambert International, Morris Plains, N.M., assistant to vice-president of

overseas marketing, 1955-56; William John Mindlin & Co., Inc., New York, N.Y., executive vice-president, 1956-58; Crystal Management Services, Inc., McLean, Va., president, 1959-75; writer and consultant, 1975-78; John C. Crystal Center, Inc., Manhasset, N.Y., founder, 1978—. Member of advisory council of National Institute of Education project; lecturer at universities, corporations, professional and women's groups, and churches; consultant to organizations, including General Motors Corp., World Bank, U.S. Department of State, U.S. Forest Service, and National Aeronautics and Space Administration (NASA). *Military service:* U.S. Army, Military Intelligence, 1942-46; served in Europe and Africa; became major; received Bronze Star.

WRITINGS: (With Richard N. Bolles) *Where Do I Go From Here With My Life?,* Seabury, 1974. Author of "Job Guidance," a column syndicated by Army Times Publishing Co., 1961-68.

WORK IN PROGRESS: A book tentatively entitled *Be Yourself: No One Else is Qualified,* which is "designed to teach people the benefit of applying unconventional thinking to planning, not just their working careers, but their whole lives along any lines they may care to choose, and how to apply the same kind of unconventional thinking to institutional, organizational, and business problems, too."

SIDELIGHTS: Crystal told *CA:* "My most vital concern is the fact that each of us is our own greatest untapped resource, but we not only do not know this, our culture tends in many subtle ways to discourage us from even trying to discover the tremendous power that lies within each of us. Thus my major area of vocational interest is quite simply my effort to persuade people that each of them is of great value and then to teach them how to benefit fully from the treasures that lie within them.

"My experience as an intelligence officer during World War II has been invaluable. It not only taught me to think clearly, it taught me to avoid conventional thought patterns. Thus I have been able to 'think the unthinkable,' especially with regard to orthodox procedures and institutions. This has allowed me to foment a revolution in the whole life/career planning field."

BIOGRAPHICAL/CRITICAL SOURCES: Washington Star News, December 6, 1974; Laille E. Barlett, *New World/New Life,* Harper, 1976; *New York Times,* November 16, 1975, August 9, 1978, October 14, 1979; *Christian Science Monitor,* October 25, 1978; *U.S. News & World Report,* March 12, 1979; *Working Woman,* May, 1979; *Washington Post,* January 24, 1980; *San Francisco Chronicle,* July 11, 1980.

* * *

CULLEN, George Francis 1901-1980

OBITUARY NOTICE: Born June 6, 1901, in Jersey City, N.J.; died November 28, 1980, in Washington, D.C., after a stroke. Journalist. Cullen joined the Bureau of National Affairs as a reporter in 1943 and subsequently worked for the organization as an editor and editorial consultant before his retirement in 1979. He was president of the National Press Club in 1962. Obituaries and other sources: *Who's Who in America,* 41st edition, Marquis, 1980; *Washington Post,* November 30, 1980.

* * *

CURLING, Bill
See CURLING, Bryan William Richard

CURLING, Bryan William Richard 1911-
(Bill Curling; Hotspur, Julius, pseudonyms)

PERSONAL: Born November 15, 1911, in Bilterne, England; son of Bryan (a military general) and Lillian (Wells) Curling; married Elizabeth Mary Bonham, June 1, 1940; children: Belinda, David, Christopher, Jonathan. *Education:* Attended private boys' school in Windsor, England. *Politics:* Conservative. *Religion:* Church of England. *Home:* Fullerton Manor, near Andover, Hampshire SP11 7LA, England. *Agent:* Andrew Hewson, John Johnson, Clerkenwell House, 45-47 Clerkenwell Green, London EC1R 0HT, England.

CAREER: Southern Echo, Southampton, England, reporter, 1931-35; *Yorkshire Post,* Leeds, England, racing correspondent under pseudonym Julius, 1936-39; *Daily Telegraph,* London, England, racing correspondent under pseudonym Hotspur, 1946-65; Jockey Club, London, public relations officer, 1965-69; free-lance writer, 1969—. *Military service:* Royal Navy, 1939-45; became lieutenant commander. *Member:* Naval Club.

WRITINGS—Under name Bill Curling: *British Racecourses,* illustrations by Lionel Edwards, H. F. & G. Witherby, 1951; *The Captain: The Biography of Sir Cecil Bond-Rochfort, Royal Trainer,* Barrie & Jenkins, 1970; (with Clive Graham), *The Grand National: Illustrated History of the Greatest Steeplechase in the World,* Barrie & Jenkins, 1972; *Derby Double: The Story of Trainer Arthur Budgett,* W. Luscombe, 1977; *All the Queen's Horses,* Chatto & Windus, 1978; *Royal Champion: The Story of Steeplechasing's First Lady,* M. Joseph, 1980.

SIDELIGHTS: Curling wrote: "I was born and spent most of my life in Hampshire. I am a Christian and strongly opposed to Marxism. I am much in favor of youth movements like Scouts and Girl Guides. I believe strongly that sports, such as sailing, shooting, stalking, tennis, and racing, bring people of all habits together and keep harmony in the world."

*   *   *

CURRIE, Ann (Brooke Peterson) 1922(?)-1980

OBITUARY NOTICE: Born c. 1922 in Dallas, Tex.; died of cancer, November 30, 1980, in Washington, D.C. Intelligence worker and writer. Currie served with the Office of Strategic Services during World War II, then joined the Central Intelligence Agency upon its inception in 1947. She was stationed in Uruguay, Argentina, and Panama. *Natalya,* her novel of Russia during the reign of Catherine the Great, was published posthumously. Obituaries and other sources: *Washington Post,* December 3, 1980.

*   *   *

CUTLER, Roland 1938-

PERSONAL: Born May 28, 1938, in New York, N.Y.; son of Charles (an artist and musician) and Rose (Shapiro) Cutler; married Ruth Truran (an administrative assistant), April 14, 1979; children: (from previous marriage) Cary (son), Morgan (daughter). *Education:* Hunter College (now of the City University of New York), B.A., 1960; Brooklyn Law School, LL.B., 1964. *Residence:* Brooklyn, N.Y. *Agent:* Elaine Markson Literary Agency, Inc., 44 Greenwich Ave., New York, N.Y. 10011.

CAREER: Commercial artist, 1960-61; art and history teacher at public schools in New York, N.Y., 1961-64; filmmaker, 1965-68; free-lance comedy writer, 1969-72; free-lance screen writer, 1972-77; writer, 1977—. Practicing attorney. *Member:* Writers Guild of America (East), Authors Guild. *Awards, honors:* Special jury award from Edinburgh Film Festival, 1966, for "The Next to Last Man"; gold medal from Atlanta Film Festival, 1972, for "The Locusts"; Porgie Award from *West Coast Review,* 1979, for *The First Born.*

WRITINGS: The First Born (novel), Fawcett, 1978; *The Gates of Sagittarius* (novel), Dial, 1980; *Precious* (novel), Jove, 1980.

Films: "The Next to Last Man," released independently, 1966; "The Locusts," released by Avco Embassy, 1972; "The Corner Bar," first broadcast by American Broadcasting Co. (ABC-TV), 1972; "Willie Dynamite," released by Universal, 1973.

WORK IN PROGRESS: The Valkyrie Cipher, a novel, publication expected in 1981; two plays, "Exit to Another Kingdom" and "The Tiger in Hiding."

SIDELIGHTS: Cutler told *CA:* "Development as a writer is a continuous struggle to make one's work have greater meaning to all the centers of experience—heart, mind, and body. This can be accomplished no matter what the vehicle. Once the author lights the reader's imagination he has the opportunity to go where he will in exploring the totality of the human condition. But he owes his best. That is, to discover, invent, and reinvent always.

"While I don't require Balzac's famous monks' habit to keep me before the typewriter, the discipline required offers unique personal satisfactions. Learning the craft brings one closest to the life of a medieval guildsman. One begins as an apprentice—even if it is to oneself—rises to journeyman, then strives to fulfill his vision through the mastery of form and content. What all that means is best said by some words of Conrad: 'No I don't like work. I had rather laze about and think of all the fine things that can be done. I don't like work—no man does—but I like what is in the work—the chance to find yourself. Your own reality—for yourself, not for others—what no man can ever know.'"

*   *   *

CUTLIFFE, Stephen H(osmer) 1947-

PERSONAL: Born January 17, 1947, in Melrose, Mass.; son of Woodrow A. and Elizabeth (Hosmer) Cutliffe; married Katie Fekula, August 29, 1980. *Education:* Bates College, A.B., 1968; Lehigh University, M.A., 1973, Ph.D., 1976. *Office:* Science, Technology, and Society Program, Lehigh University, 9 Maginnes Hall, Bethlehem, Pa. 18015.

CAREER: Lehigh University, Bethlehem, Pa., administrative assistant in science, technology, and society program, 1976—. Adjunct assistant professor at Lafayette College, 1980; consultant to Historic Bethlehem, Inc. *Military service:* U.S. Army, 1968-70; became sergeant. *Member:* Organization of American Historians, Institute of Early American History and Culture, Society for the History of Technology, Lawrence Henry Gipson Institute for Eighteenth-Century Studies, Phi Alpha Theta.

WRITINGS: (Editor with Judith A. Mistichelli and Christine M. Roysdon) *Technology and Human Values in American Civilization,* Gale, 1980. Contributor to history and technology journals. Editor of *Curriculum Development Newsletter.*

WORK IN PROGRESS: Research on public responsibility for technology.

SIDELIGHTS: Cutliffe wrote: "I have long been interested

in environmental concerns, partly instigated by early camping, hiking, and other outdoor activities—interests in which I
continue to be active. This has led me to try to understand
historically the impact of technology upon society and, in
turn, the effect of societal values upon technology.''

D

DAGLISH, Eric Fitch   1892-1966

PERSONAL: Born August 29, 1892, in London, England; died April 5, 1966; son of James and Kate (Fitch) Daglish; married Alice Leslie Mary Archer, 1918 (marriage ended); married Esther Lena Rutland, 1933; children: (first marriage) twin sons, one daughter; (second marriage) one son, one daughter. *Education:* Attended Hertford County College and University of London; earned Ph.D. from University of Bonn. *Home:* The Old Farmhouse, Darvills Hill, Speen, Aylesbury, England.

CAREER: Naturalist, author, and illustrator. *London Evening Standard,* London, England, scientific correspondent, 1923-25; J. M. Dent & Sons Ltd. (publishers), London, editor and illustrator of thirteen-volume Open Air Library, 1932-38; illustrator for works by authors, including Fabre, Thoreau, and Walton. Woodcuts exhibited at Redfern Gallery, 1925 and 1927; wood engravings appear in permanent collections of British Museum, Victoria and Albert Museum, Metropolitan Museum of New York, and many other museums and galleries. *Military service:* British Army, 1916-22; officer in charge of education, Woolwich Garrison, 1918-22. Royal Air Force, 1940-48; became captain. *Member:* Society of Wood Engravers.

WRITINGS: Our Butterflies and Moths, and How to Know Them, T. Butterworth, 1923; *Our Wild Flowers, and How to Know Them,* T. Butterworth, 1923; *Marvels of Life,* T. Butterworth, 1924; *Our Birds' Nests and Eggs, and How to Know Them,* T. Butterworth, 1924; *Woodcuts of British Birds* (self-illustrated), E. Benn, 1925; *Animals in Black and White* (juvenile; self-illustrated), six volumes, Morrow, 1928, published in one volume, 1938; *The Book of Garden Animals,* Chapman & Hall, 1928; *The Life Story of Birds* (juvenile; self-illustrated; American Literary Guild selection), Morrow, 1930; *The Life Story of Beasts* (self-illustrated), Morrow, 1931; *A Nature Calendar* (self-illustrated), Dent, 1932; *The Dog Owner's Guide* (self-illustrated), Morrow, 1933, 3rd revised edition, Dent, 1967; *Name This Bird,* Dent, 1934, revised edition, 1948; *The Junior Bird-Watcher* (self-illustrated), G. Routledge, 1936; *The Book of the Dachshund,* Our Dogs Publishing Co., 1937.

Birds of the British Isles (self-illustrated), Dent, 1948; *The Dog Breeder's Manual,* Dent, 1951; *The Popular Dachshund,* Popular Dogs, 1952, 6th revised edition published as *The Dachshund,* 1967, 9th edition, Merrimack Book Service,

1979; *Name This Insect,* Dent, 1952, revised edition, 1960; *Enjoying the Country* (self-illustrated), Faber, 1952; *The Seaside Nature Book,* Dent, 1954; *The Pet-Keeper's Manual,* Dent, 1958; *Dog Breeding and Management,* Arco Publications, 1962; (translator and contributor) Erich Schneider-Leyer, *Dogs of the World,* Popular Dogs, 1964, Arco Publications, 1970; (translator) Friederun Stockmann, *My Life With Boxers,* Coward, 1968.

"The Children's Nature Series"; all self-illustrated: *How to See Birds,* Morrow, 1932; *... Plants,* Morrow, 1932; *... Flowers,* Dent, 1933; *... Beasts,* Morrow, 1933; *...Insects,* Dent, 1934; *...Pond Life,* Dent, 1934.

"Foyles Handbooks for Dog Lovers" series; all originally published by W. & G. Foyle: *Dachshunds,* 1956, Arco, 1976; *Dog Breeding,* 1961, Arco, 1976; *The Beagle,* 1961; *Pugs,* 1962, Arco, 1976; *Training Your Dog,* 1963, Arco, 1976; *The Basset Hound,* 1964; *Whippets,* 1964; *Caring for Your Puppy,* 1966, revised edition published as *Care and Training of Your Puppy,* Arco, 1972.

"Open Air Library" series; editor and illustrator; Samuel Reynolds Hole, *Book About Roses,* Dent, 1932; Edward Thomas, *Heart of England,* Dent, 1932, Dutton, 1933; William Henry Hudson, *Nature in Downland and An Old Thorn,* Dutton, 1932; William Cobbett, *Rural Rides,* Dent, 1932; Ivan Sergeevich Turgenev, *Sportsman's Sketches,* translated by C. Garnett, Dutton, 1932; Henry David Thoreau, *Week on the Concord and Merrimac Rivers,* Dutton, 1932; W. H. Hudson, *Afoot in England,* Dent, 1933; Joseph Conrad, *Mirror of the Sea,* Dent, 1933; Arthur Stanley Megaw, *Out of Doors Book,* Dent, 1933; Edward Grey, *Fly Fishing,* Dent, 1934; Richard Jefferies, *Out of Doors With Richard Jefferies,* Dent, 1935; Samuel Smiles, *Life of a Scottish Naturalist: Thomas Edward,* Dent, 1936; William Gershom Collingwood, *Lake Counties,* Dent, 1938.

Illustrator: Jean Henri Casimir Fabre, *Animal Life in Field and Garden,* translated by Florence Bicknell and Kate Murray, T. Butterworth, 1925; Edward Max Nicholson, *Birds in England: An Account of the State of Our Bird Life and a Criticism of Bird Protection,* Chapman & Hall, 1926; Isaak Walton, *The Compleat Angler,* T. Butterworth, 1927; Henry David Thoreau, *Walden,* Houghton, 1927; Douglas Dewar, *Game birds,* Chapman & Hall, 1928; Gilbert White, *The Natural History of Selborne,* T. Butterworth, 1929; Harold John Massingham, *Birds of the Seashore,* T. W. Laurie, 1931; W. H. Hudson, *Far Away and Long Ago,* Dent, 1931;

Philip E. Thomas, *The South Country,* Dent, 1932; Arthur George Street, *Wheat and Chaff,* Faber, 1950.

SIDELIGHTS: At an early age, Eric Fitch Daglish became interested in natural history. A favorite childhood pastime was studying the insects, birds, and small animals to be found near his home. Fascinated by the creatures he observed, young Daglish wished to know as many facts about them as possible and cared little for the sentimental fantasies to be found in children's books on the subject.

Daglish's books are all factual texts dealing with the habitat, life cycle, and behavior patterns of birds, insects, or animals. Whether for children or adults, his books exhibit qualities of straightforward veracity and conciseness. In a review of *Animals in Black and White,* M. G. Bonner of the *New York Times* commented: "The writing in these books is meticulous in its natural history accuracy and is presented with a nice economy for the essentials. The beasts are treated with dignified, intelligent comment—something beasts do not always receive, and the pictures are really quite thrilling." Another critic makes a similar observation in *Saturday Review:* "The text is admirably simple and accurate and Mr. Daglish deserves special credit for striking the right note without slipping into the easy vice of 'writing down' to his audience."

Daglish illustrated most of his own work and several books by other authors. Although he had no formal art training, the inclusion of his woodcuts in a number of prestigious collections attests to his skill as an illustrator. His work has been admired by many critics for its lucidity and beauty. As Anita Moffet suggests in her *New York Times* review of *Life Story of Beasts,* "The woodcuts of Mr. Daglish should serve as a refutation of the doctrine so frequently expressed, that artistic expression in its highest form should be divorced from specific meaning. He has something of value to record, and his recording of it is marked by a perfect fusion between subject-matter and execution. To a superb craftsmanship and a sense of decorative design which would convey a powerful emotional effect through its rhythm and pattern even apart from its meaning is added a truthfulness of observation which seizes both accurately and imaginatively upon the personality of the animal depicted."

BIOGRAPHICAL/CRITICAL SOURCES: New York Times, December 2, 1928, May 18, 1930, October 25, 1931; *Saturday Review,* December 8, 1928.*

*   *   *

D'AMBROSIO, Richard A(nthony) 1927-

PERSONAL: Born April 2, 1927, in Sommerville, Mass.; son of Nunzio (an artist) and Louisa (Sosero) D'Ambrosio; married Vinnie Aguanno, January 26, 1952 (divorced November, 1962); children: Cynthia. *Education:* Brooklyn College (now of the City University of New York), B.A., 1950, M.A., 1955; New York University, Ph.D., 1958. *Home:* 10 Plaza St., Brooklyn, N.Y. 11238.

CAREER: Italian Board of Guardians, Brooklyn, N.Y., senior clinical psychologist, 1952-57; St. Vincent's Hall, Brooklyn, senior clinical psychologist, 1957-60; St. John's Home, Rockaway, N.Y., director of division of psychiatry and psychology, 1958-72; St. Vincent's Guidance Institute, Brooklyn, clinical director, 1960—; private practice of psychoanalysis in Brooklyn, 1960—; Long Island University, Brooklyn, associate professor of psychology, 1964—. Clinical consultant at Catholic Youth Organization, Brooklyn, 1966—; member of board of directors at Psychology Services Institute, 1968—. *Military service:* U.S. Naval Reserve, 1946-48;

became ensign. *Awards, honors:* Founders Day award from New York University, 1959; humanitarian award, 1972, and distinguished service award, 1978, both from St. Vincent's Hall.

WRITINGS: No Language but a Cry, Doubleday, 1970; *Leonora,* McGraw, 1978. Also author with Rod Steiger of a screenplay, "Leonora" (based on own book).

SIDELIGHTS: No Language but a Cry is Richard D'Ambrosio's story of his years of professional and personal devotion to Laura, one of his psychiatric patients. D'Ambrosio first came in contact with Laura when she was twelve years old. Abused, schizophrenic, and withdrawn, Laura had been diagnosed as possibly being retarded. Through D'Ambrosio's care and dedication, however, she eventually triumphs over her battered past. A critic for *Saturday Review* commented that "the moment when Laura first responds to her doctor, after months of patient therapy, is infinitely moving, her progress after that an affirmation of hope."

The author's second book, *Leonora,* is also an account of his attempt to save a victim of child abuse. D'Ambrosio's narrative describes his arduous task of reaching Leonora and his success in bringing her to normalcy. Colman McCarthy of the *Washington Post Book World* declared that *Leonora* is "a well-written and powerful account of a rescue mission that only a daring analyst would risk." The reviewer pointed out that D'Ambrosio's goal in treating Leonora "was never to provide a happy ending to Leonora's therapy—only an open ending, through which she could take herself to sounder feelings and new commitments. He met his goal, and in the process wrote of it movingly and clearly."

D'Ambrosio told *CA:* "I have always been fascinated by the agony and frustration faced by people who cannot express what they feel or are not in touch with their feelings. These individuals seem literally cut off from one of the most essential joys of living.

"I have tried, through my writings, to put into simple language my experience in helping these people learn to communicate, with the hope that it would increase understanding of the human drama behind closed lips. Writing made me aware of how much I had not expressed or was not aware of, and the more I articulated and described the characters in my books, the clearer my own thoughts and feelings became and the more I came to know myself."

BIOGRAPHICAL/CRITICAL SOURCES: Saturday Review, February 20, 1971; *Washington Post Book World,* December 1, 1978.

*   *   *

DANGERFIELD, Rodney 1922(?)-
(Jack Roy)

PERSONAL: Birth-given name Jacob Cohen; name legally changed; born in Long Island, N.Y.; married Joyce Indig (a singer), c. 1951 (divorced); children: Brian, Melaine. *Agent:* Estelle Endler, 3920 Sunny Oak Rd., Sherman Oaks, Calif. 91403. *Office:* c/o Dangerfield's, 1118 First Ave., New York, N.Y.

CAREER: Comedian and writer. Performer in nightclubs under pseudonym Jack Roy, 1941-51. Worked as businessman, c. 1951-63. Actor in motion pictures, including "The Projectionist" and "Caddyshack," 1980. Appeared on numerous television shows, including "The Ed Sullivan Show," "Tonight," and "Saturday Night Live." Founder of Dangerfield's (a nightclub), 1969. Commencement speaker at Harvard University, 1978.

WRITINGS: I Couldn't Stand My Wife's Cooking So I Opened a Restaurant (humor), Jonathan David, 1972; *"I Don't Get No Respect"* (humor), Price, Stearn, 1973. Also author of recordings, including "I Don't Get No Respect," for Bell, and "Rodney Dangerfield—The Loser," for Decca.

SIDELIGHTS: Dangerfield is best known for the phrase "I don't get no respect," with which he prefaces each of his self-deprecating recollections. Seemingly ill at ease before the spotlight, he struggles constantly with his necktie and wipes perspiration from his brow. It is all part of his act, though, for Dangerfield's persona is that of an individual denied dignity in even the most banal situations. "I tell you I don't get no respect," he complains to the audience. "When I step into an elevator, the attendant looks at me and says, 'Basement?'" While dining in a Chinese restaurant, he discovers that his fortune cookie contains another table's bill. He reveals that he's been suffering this persecution since birth. "When I was born, I was so ugly the doctor slapped my mother." There is also the time a policeman failed to reassure him when he was separated from his parents at the beach. "I don't know," confessed the officer. "There's so many places they could hide."

Perseverance is the key to Dangerfield's success. After enjoying reasonable success as a comedian during his twenties, he married singer Joyce Indig and decided to pursue a less demanding profession. "I dropped out of show business," he now jokes, "but nobody noticed." Working as a businessman, Dangerfield realized that he hadn't brought any more stability into his life. "It wasn't show business that was crazy," he concluded. "It was me."

Dangerfield's marriage ended, and he decided to resume his career as a comedian. Unfortunately, Dangerfield found himself unwanted by television producers who considered him, at forty-three, too old to begin establishing himself as a performer. He decided to work in resorts. "I played one club," he cracks; "it was so far out, my act was reviewed in *Field & Stream.*"

Unable to obtain television bookings, Dangerfield finally convinced his agents to arrange a mere dress rehearsal for him with television mogul Ed Sullivan. The rehearsal was successful in convincing Sullivan that Dangerfield, despite his age, might become a popular comedian. Sullivan signed him to appear on his variety show, and he was a huge success. He appeared on "The Tonight Show" and struck such a rapport with host Johnny Carson that he has since returned more than sixty times.

Dangerfield was reluctant to perform outside New York City, however, because he wished to remain with his children. In 1969 he opened his own nightclub, Dangerfield's, which enabled him to continue performing on stage. During the 1970's his career blossomed even further, with books, records, and films, allowing him to reach a variety of audiences. He is undaunted by his success, however, and steadfastly refuses to leave the stage. "I don't want to spend my time poring over scripts and memorizing," he insists. "When you do stand-up, *you* are the guy on. Live entertainment is the only real medium."

BIOGRAPHICAL/CRITICAL SOURCES: Time, July 28, 1980.

* * *

DANIEL, Emmett Randolph 1935-

PERSONAL: Born April 15, 1935, in Richmond, Va.; married, 1960; children: two. *Education:* Davidson College,

A.B., 1958; Union Theological Seminary, Richmond, Va., B.D., 1961; Harvard University, Th.M., 1964; University of Virginia, Ph.D., 1966. *Office:* Department of History, University of Kentucky, Lexington, Ky. 40506.

CAREER: Southeast Institute of Medieval and Renaissance Study, fellow, 1966; University of Kentucky, Lexington, assistant professor, 1966-73, associate professor of history, 1973—. *Member:* American Historical Association, American Society of Church History, Mediaeval Academy of America, Southern Historical Association, Midwest Medieval History Conference.

WRITINGS: The Franciscan Concept of Mission in the High Middle Ages, University Press of Kentucky, 1975. Contributor to theology journals.*

* * *

DANZIGER, Edmund J(efferson), Jr. 1938-

PERSONAL: Born February 10, 1938, in Newark, N.J.; son of Edmund Jefferson Danziger; married, 1961. *Education:* College of Wooster, B.A., 1960; University of Illinois, M.A., 1962, Ph.D., 1966. *Office:* Department of History, Bowling Green State University, Bowling Green, Ohio 43402.

CAREER: State University of New York College at Cortland, instructor in history, 1962-63; Bowling Green State University, Bowling Green, Ohio, assistant professor, 1966-71, associate professor, 1971-77, professor of history, 1977—. *Member:* Organization of American Historians, Western History Association.

WRITINGS: Indians and Bureaucrats: Administering the Reservation Policy During the Civil War, University of Illinois Press, 1974; *The Chippewas of Lake Superior,* University of Oklahoma Press, 1979.*

* * *

DARCY, Clare

PERSONAL—Address: c/o Walker & Co., 720 Fifth Ave., New York, N.Y. 10019.

CAREER: Writer.

WRITINGS—Novels; all published by Walker & Co., except as noted: *Georgina,* 1971; *Cecily; or, A Young Lady of Quality,* 1972; *Lydia; or, Love in Town,* 1973; *Victoire,* 1974; *Allegra,* 1974; *Lady Pamela,* 1975; *Elyza,* 1976; *Regina,* G. K. Hall, 1977; *Cressida,* 1977; *Eugenia,* 1977; *Gwendolen,* G. K. Hall, 1978; *Rolande,* 1978; *A Clare Darcy Trilogy,* 1979; *Letty,* 1980.*

* * *

DAS, Deb Kumar 1935-

PERSONAL: Born December 22, 1935, in Calcutta, India. *Education:* University of Calcutta, B.A. (with honors), 1955; Queen's College, Cambridge, B.A., 1958, M.A., 1962. *Home:* 3105½ Eastlake Ave. E., Seattle, Wash. 98102. *Agent:* P. Lal, Writers Workshop, 162-92 Lake Gardens, Calcutta 45, India.

CAREER: I.C.I., Calcutta, India, member of management staff, 1959-61; S.O.I.C., Seattle, Wash., 1967-70, began as instructor in mathematics and economics, became superintendent; State Board for Community College Education, Seattle, 1970-72, began as deputy director, became director of research and planning; U.S. National Utilization Project for Post-Secondary Education, Seattle, director, 1972—. Broadcaster for "Viewpoint," on radio. Artist; paintings shown in exhibitions in India and the United States. Co-founder of Writers Workshop, Calcutta.

WRITINGS—Books of poems: *The Night Before Us: Poems*, Writers Workshop (Calcutta, India), 1960, 2nd edition, 1968; *Through a Glass Darkly: Poems*, Writers Workshop (Calcutta, India), 1965, InterCulture Associates, 1975; *The Eyes of Autumn: An Experiment in Poetry*, Writers Workshop (Calcutta, India), 1968, InterCulture Associates, 1975; *The Four Labyrinths*, Writers Workshop (Calcutta, India), 1969, reprinted as *The Labyrinths*, 1969, published as *The Labyrinths: A Long Poem*, InterCulture Associates, 1975; *The Fire Canto*, Writers Workshop (Calcutta, India), 1971; *Always Once Was: Experiments in Metapoetics*, InterCulture Associates, 1977.

Nonfiction: *Navbharat Papers: A Political Programme for a New India*, San Vito Press, 1968; *Freedom and Reality*, six volumes, privately printed, 1968; *The First Philosopher: Yajnavalka*, San Vito Press, 1971; *The Agony of Arjun and Other Essays*, privately printed, 1971; *Svatvavada: Towards a Theory of Property, 2000 B.C.—1800 A.D.; An Essay in Three Parts*, privately printed, 1972. Also author of *An Essay on the Forms of Individualism*, 1973, *What Final Frontier?; or, The Future of Man in Space*, 1973, and *Beginnings of Human Thought: The Rig Vedas*, 1973.

Translator from Sanskrit: *Two Upanisads: Isa and Kena*, Writers Workshop (Calcutta, India), 1969, published as *Isa and Kena Upanisads*, by InterCulture Associates; *Sankaracharya: A Discourse on the Real Nature of Self*, Writers Workshop (Calcutta, India), 1970, InterCulture Associates, 1977; *Jabala and Paingaba Upanisads*, Writers Workshop (Calcutta, India), 1974.*

* * *

d'AULAIRE, Ingri (Mortenson) 1904-1980

OBITUARY NOTICE—See index for *CA* sketch: Born December 27, 1904, in Kongsberg, Norway; died of cancer, October 24, 1980, in Wilton, Conn. Illustrator and author. With her husband, Edgar, d'Aulaire, she wrote and illustrated dozens of books for children, including the Caldecott Medal-winning *Abraham Lincoln*. Among their books are *The Magic Rug*, *Children of the Northlights*, *East of the Sun and West of the Moon*, *Pocahontas*, *Buffalo Bill*, and *The Magic Meadow*. Obituaries and other sources: *New York Times*, October 28, 1980.

* * *

DAVENPORT, Elaine 1946-

PERSONAL: Born June 26, 1946, in Fullerton, Calif.; daughter of William J. and Velma (Vanscoy) Davenport; married Paul Eddy (a journalist). *Education*: University of Oregon, B.A., 1968. *Residence*: Surrey, England. *Agent*: Robert Ducas, 201 East 42nd St., Suite 2900, New York, N.Y. 10017. *Office*: 30 Baker St., London W.1, England.

CAREER: *Medford Mail Tribune*, Medford, Ore., reporter, summer, 1966; Associated Press (AP), Portland, Ore., on news desk and radio desk, 1967; free-lance writer, 1969-71; *Time*, Rio de Janeiro, Brazil, assistant to correspondent, 1971-73; *Newsweek*, Rio de Janeiro, stringer, 1973; Reuters News Agency, San Francisco, Calif., correspondent, 1974; *London Sunday Times*, New York, N.Y., reporter and researcher, 1975; free-lance writer, 1975—. Free-lance reporter for Canadian Broadcasting Corp. (CBC) and National Public Radio (NPR), 1974. *Member*: Phi Beta Kappa.

WRITINGS: (With husband, Paul Eddy) *The Hughes Papers* (on the last years of Howard Hughes), Ballantine, 1976; (with Eddy, Bruce Page, and Elaine Potter) *Destination Di-*

saster, Quadrangle, 1976; (with Eddy and Peter Gillman) *The Plumbat Affair*, Lippincott, 1978. Contributor to magazines and newspapers, including *New Statesman* and *International Herald Tribune*.

SIDELIGHTS: *The Plumbat Affair* details the way Israel clandestinely acquired the two hundred tons of uranium oxide that made possible the development of nuclear weapons there.

Elaine Davenport told *CA*: "As an American working in foreign parts, I am ever mindful of how much more difficult it is, on the whole, to acquire basic information outside the United States than in it. Soundly assessing that extra difficulty—calling on interviewees instead of acquiring information by phone is just one of the time consumers—can mean the difference between doing a good or a bad job as a journalist."

* * *

DAVIDSON, Hugh M(acCullough) 1918-

PERSONAL: Born January 21, 1918, in Lanett, Ala.; son of Robert Calvin and Anne Della (Stripling) Davidson; married Loretta Miller, June 15, 1951; children: Anne Stripling. *Education*: University of Chicago, A.B., 1938, Ph.D., 1946. *Religion*: Episcopalian. *Office*: Department of French, University of Virginia, Charlottesville, Va. 22903.

CAREER: University of Chicago, Chicago, Ill., instructor, 1946-48, assistant professor of French, 1948-53, chairman of college French staff, 1951-53; Dartmouth College, Hanover, N.H., assistant professor, 1953-56, professor of romance languages, 1956-62, chairman of department, 1957-59; Ohio State University, Columbus, professor of French, 1962-73; University of Virginia, Charlottesville, professor of French literature, 1973—, member of Center for Advanced Studies, 1973-75. Visiting professor at University of Michigan, summer, 1967; fellow of Downing College, Cambridge, 1979-80; director of National Endowment for the Humanities seminar, summer, 1975. *Military service*: U.S. Army Air Forces, 1942-46; became captain.

MEMBER: International Society for Philosophy and Literature, International Society for the History of Rhetoric (member of council, 1979—), Association Internationale des Etudes Francaises (member of council, 1976—), North American Society for Seventeenth Century Literature, Modern Language Association of America, American Association of Teachers of French, American Society for Eighteenth Century Studies, Phi Beta Kappa. *Awards, honors*: Carnegie fellow, 1948-49; M.A. from Dartmouth College, 1956; Fulbright fellow in France, 1959-60; senior fellow of National Foundation for Arts and Humanities, 1967-68; fellow of Downing College, Cambridge, 1979-80.

WRITINGS: (Editor with others) *The Idea and Practice of General Education*, University of Chicago Press, 1950; (editor and contributor) *A General School Survey for the Northern Area Joint School System*, Educational Research Service, 1960; (contributor) J. J. Demorest, editor, *Studies in Seventeenth-Century French Literature*, Cornell University Press, 1962; *Audience, Words, and Art: Studies in Seventeenth-Century French Rhetoric*, Ohio State University Press, 1965; (with Pierre H. Dube) *A Concordance to the Pensees of Pascal*, Cornell University Press, 1975; *The Origins of Certainty: Means and Meanings in Pascal's "Pensees"*, University of Chicago Press, 1978; (with Dube) *A Concordance to the "Provinciales" of Pascal*, Garland Publishing, 1980. Contributor to language, literature, and education journals. Member of board of publications of Modern Language Association of America, 1967-72.*

DAVIDSON, Julian M. 1931-

PERSONAL: Born April 15, 1931, in Dublin, Ireland; came to the United States in 1956, naturalized citizen, 1969; son of Aaron (a manufacturer) and Bunie (Cohen) Davidson; married Ann Gelber (a language clinician), August 20, 1960; children: Benjamin, Karen, Jeffrey. *Education:* Hebrew University of Jerusalem, M.S., 1955; graduate study at University of California, Davis; University of California, San Francisco, Ph.D., 1959. *Politics:* "Democratic socialist." *Office:* Department of Physiology, Stanford University, Stanford, Calif. 94305.

CAREER: Research fellow at University of California, Los Angeles, 1959-60, Hebrew University, 1961-62, and University of California, Berkeley, 1963; Stanford University, Stanford, Calif., assistant professor, 1963-69, associate professor, 1969-80, professor of physiology, 1980—. Visiting scholar at Battelle Seattle Research Center, 1974-75; visiting professor at University of Illinois, 1976, and University of Athens, 1978-79. *Member:* International Brain Research Organization, International Academy of Sex Research, International Society of Psychoneuroendocrinology, Endocrine Society, American Physiological Society, Society for the Study of Reproduction, Society of Endocrinology (England). *Awards, honors:* National Institutes of Health fellow at University of California, Los Angeles, 1960-61, University of California, Berkeley, 1962, and Oxford University, 1970-71; Guggenheim fellow, 1970.

WRITINGS: (With Gordon Bermant) *Biological Bases of Sexual Behavior,* Harper, 1974; (editor with Richard J. Davidson) *The Psychobiology of Human Consciousness,* Plenum, 1980. Contributor to about thirty books. Contributor of more than one hundred articles to scientific journals. Editor of *Hormones and Behavior;* member of editorial board of *Biology of Reproduction* and *American Journal of Physiology.*

SIDELIGHTS: Davidson commented: "I started my work life as a farm worker in England, lived for a year in a kibbutz in Israel, and studied agriculture there. I came to the United States to study animal physiology before moving into the specific areas of endocrinology and reproduction. My major areas of vocational interest now include human sexuality and reproductive physiology and relationships between the brain, hormones, and behavior.

"My academic 'hobby' is the study of altered states of consciousness and their biological correlates. I am currently developing a program of laboratory research in the physiological bases of human sexuality."

* * *

DAVIE, Ian 1924-

PERSONAL: Born April 5, 1924, in Edinburgh, Scotland; son of T. M. (a physician) and L. T. (Henderson) Davie. *Education:* St John's College, Oxford, M.A., 1950. *Religion:* Roman Catholic. *Home:* Alba, Acklam, Malton, North Yorkshire, England. *Agent:* Bolt & Watson Ltd., 8/12 Old Queen St., Storey's Gate, London SW1H 9HP, England.

CAREER: Assistant master at Jesuit school in Stonyhurst, Lancashire, England, 1950-55; associated with Commonwealth Relations Office, 1960-62; senior English master at school in Hampshire, England, 1962-65; English teacher and department head at Marlborough College, England, 1964-68; Ampleforth College, York, England, English teacher and director of theatre, 1968—. *Military service:* British Army, Gordon Highlanders, 1943-46; became captain. *Member:*

National Association for the Teaching of English, Society for the Study of Theology.

WRITINGS: (Editor) *Oxford Poetry,* Basil Blackwell, 1943; *Piers Prodigal* (poems), Collins, 1961; *A Play for Prospero: Shakespearean Parable,* Collins, 1965; *Roman Pentecost* (poems), Hamish Hamilton, 1970; *A Theology of Speech,* Sheed, 1973.

WORK IN PROGRESS: Formulating a Hindu Christology.

SIDELIGHTS: Davie wrote that, in 1946, he participated in a British Army expedition to Tibet, and has also traveled in India, Burma, Thailand, and Cambodia. "My main influences have been T. S. Eliot, Edward Thomas, G. M. Hopkins, early Wittgenstein, and Anselm. My main interests are William Blake, Hindu scriptures, the Fourth Gospel, and the Gospel of Thomas."

* * *

DAVIES, Martin Brett 1936-

PERSONAL: Born November 26, 1936, in Pudsey, England; son of Tom Brett (a minister) and Helen (Moat) Davies; married Judith Bainbridge Thomas (a nurse), October 31, 1964; children: Andrew Brett, Paul Brett. *Education:* University of Liverpool, B.A., 1959; Bedford College, London, Ph.D., 1971. *Politics:* Labour. *Religion:* Unitarian-Universalist. *Home:* Herons Hall, The Street, Brundall, Norfolk, England. *Office:* School of Social Studies, University of East Anglia, Norwich, England.

CAREER: Probation officer in London, Middlesex, and Berkshire, England, 1959-64; Home Office, London, research officer, 1964-71; Victoria University of Manchester, Manchester, England, senior lecturer in social administration, 1971-75; University of East Anglia, Norwich, England, professor of social work, 1975—. Past member of Council of Europe commission on rehabilitation of former prisoners.

WRITINGS: Social Work in the Environment, H.M.S.O., 1969; *Probationers in Their Social Environment,* H.M.S.O., 1969; *Financial Penalties and Probation,* H.M.S.O., 1971; *An Index of Social Environment,* H.M.S.O., 1973; (with Andrea Knopf) *Social Enquiries and the Probation Service,* H.M.S.O., 1973; *Prisoners of Society,* Routledge & Kegan Paul, 1974; *Support Systems in Social Work,* Routledge & Kegan Paul, 1977; *The Role of Social Workers in the Rehabilitation of Ex-Prisoners,* Council of Europe, 1979; *The Essential Social Worker,* Heinemann, 1981. Editor of series of community care practice handbooks, Heinemann, 1977—. Contributor to social work journals and popular magazines, including *New Society.* Editor of *British Journal of Social Work,* 1977—; editorial adviser for *Community Care,* 1975—.

WORK IN PROGRESS: Swapping the Elderly in Residential Care; research on the role of sociology in social work.

SIDELIGHTS: When Davies left active civil service for university teaching, he created research programs that focused on intermediate treatment, youth work, penal policy, and work with the elderly. His own view of the role of social work in today's world includes both the pastoral and political components of the discipline, but Davies is more drawn toward the pastoral, because in his own experience that has been what most clients want.

* * *

DAVIES, (Claude) Nigel (Byam) 1920-

PERSONAL: Born September 2, 1920, in Hendon, England;

son of Claude (an army officer) and Nellie (Cheka) Davies. *Education:* Attended University of Aix en Provence, 1937; University of London, Ph.D., 1970. *Politics:* Conservative. *Religion:* Church of England. *Home:* Gelati 80, Mexico City 18, Mexico.

CAREER: Windolite Ltd., Harlow, England, managing director, 1947-61; British Parliament, London, England, Conservative member of Parliament for Epping Division of Essex, 1950-51; writer. *Military service:* British Army, Grenadier Guards, 1942-46; served in Europe and the Middle East; became captain.

WRITINGS: The Aztecs: A History, Macmillan, 1973, Putnam, 1974; *The Toltecs: Until the Fall of Tula,* University of Oklahoma Press, 1977; *The Toltec Heritage: From the Fall of Tula to the Rise of Tenochtitlan,* University of Oklahoma Press, 1979; *Voyagers to the New World: Fact or Fantasy,* Morrow, 1979; *Human Sacrifice: In History and Today,* Morrow, 1981.

In Spanish: *Los senorios independientes del Imperio Azteca* (title means "The Independent Principalities of the Aztec Empire"), Instituto Nacional de Antropologia e Historia, 1968; *Los mexicas: Primeros pasos hacia el imperio* (title means "The Mexicas: First Steps to Conquest"), Instituto de Investigaciones Historicas, Universidad Nacional Autonoma de Mexico, 1973.

AVOCATIONAL INTERESTS: Travel.

BIOGRAPHICAL/CRITICAL SOURCES: Choice, February, 1978; *Science,* September 15, 1978; *American Historical Review,* October, 1978; *Economist,* April 21, 1979; *Best Sellers,* September, 1979.

*   *   *

DAVIS, Fitzroy K.   1912-1980

OBITUARY NOTICE—See index for *CA* sketch: Born February 27, 1912, in Evanston, Ill.; died of cancer, October 2, 1980, in Putnam, Conn. Actor, novelist, director, playwright, singer, and author. In addition to writing plays for the stage and screen, Davis wrote novels, including *Quicksilver,* about actors and the lives they lead. Obituaries and other sources: *New York Times,* October 2, 1980.

*   *   *

DAVIS, J(ames) William   1908-

PERSONAL: Born December 21, 1908, in Anderson, Tex.; son of James Thomas and Uta (Willson) Davis; married Edwena Barnes, August 15, 1933; children: James Thomas, Carolyn Davis Mahon, Donald Bruce. *Education:* Tarleton State University, A.S., 1926; Texas Agricultural and Mechanical College (now Texas A & M University), B.A., 1928; University of Texas, M.A., 1931, Ph.D., 1940. *Politics:* Democrat. *Religion:* Methodist. *Home:* 2830 23rd St., Lubbock, Tex. 79410.

CAREER: High school teacher of mathematics in Coleman, Tex., 1929-32; high school principal and teacher of mathematics in Lometa, Tex., 1932-36; University of Texas, Austin, instructor in government, 1936-38; Texas Tech University, Lubbock, instructor, 1938-40, assistant professor, 1940-42, associate professor, 1942-44, professor of political science, 1944-74, head of department of government, 1944-71. Member of Texas Economic Commission, 1950-52, social science commission of Texas Education Agency, 1957-58, and Texas Advisory Commission on Constitutional Revision, 1957-61; member of Lubbock City Charter Commission; consultant to Texas Research League. *Member:* Amer-

ican Political Science Association, National Collegiate Athletic Association.

WRITINGS: The Abortive Movement for Constitutional Revision, Crowell, 1966; *There Shall Also Be a Lieutenant Governor,* Institute for Public Affairs, 1967; *Essentials of Texas Government,* Kendall/Hunt, 1969; (with Ruth Wright) *Texas: Political Practice and Public Policy,* Kendall/Hunt, 1976, 2nd edition, Kendall/Hunt, 1978.

*   *   *

DAVIS, Margaret Thomson   1926-

PERSONAL: Born May 24, 1926, in Bathgate, Scotland; daughter of Samuel (a railway employee) and Christina (a cashier; maiden name, Watt) Thomson; married George Baillie, March 28, 1951 (divorced); married Graham J. Davis, July 15, 1958; children: (first marriage) Kenneth; (second marriage) Calvin Royce (stepson). *Education:* Attended secondary school in Glasgow, Scotland. *Religion:* Society of Friends (Quakers). *Home:* 18 Botanic Crescent, North Kelvinside, Glasgow G20 8QJ, Scotland.

CAREER: Writer, 1967—. Also worked as nursery nurse and nanny. Lecturer. *Military service:* Royal Navy, Voluntary Aid Detachment, nurse, 1948-50. *Member:* International P.E.N., Penn Club.

WRITINGS—All novels, except as noted; all published by Allison & Busby: *The Breadmakers* (first in trilogy), 1972; *A Baby Might Be Crying* (second in trilogy), 1973; *A Sort of Peace* (third in trilogy), 1973; *The Prisoner,* 1974; *The Prince and the Tobacco Lords* (first in trilogy), 1976; *Roots of Bondage* (second in trilogy), 1977; *Scorpion in the Fire* (third in trilogy), 1977; *The Dark Side of Pleasure,* 1981; *The Making of a Novelist* (autobiography), 1981; *A Very Civilised Man,* 1982.

WORK IN PROGRESS: Research for a novel set in 1916.

SIDELIGHTS: Margaret Davis wrote: "My new novel (or novels) will be based on material that belonged to my late father. I was cleaning out my writing room and found an old wooden chest. I had once glanced inside it and only saw old newspapers. I thought this was all it held. To my astonishment I found diaries and love letters and other papers dating back to 1913, when my father's mother died, his home broke up, and he had to go into lodgings in another town and start work on the railway at the age of fourteen. This material gives me a wonderful insight into the mind of a sensitive man, as well as a detailed record of his time. There are official papers, like the ones in connection with the time he ran away to the army but was discharged when they found out he was underage. My father seemed to have kept every piece of paper that ever came into his possession—even old train tickets! Needless to say, this is a real treasure trove for a novelist.

"I've still had to do the usual stint of research and have been traveling around, interviewing old railway men (some fascinating old men with wonderful stores of anecdotes), and searching out old steam locomotives and trying to understand how they work. Nevertheless, I hope my book will concentrate more on the human angles and the love story that unfolded in the diaries and letters.

"I believe writing is first and foremost about feeling. I believe that writers must care about individuals and be intensely interested in what motivates them and what goes on beneath the surfaces of their lives. Anyone who wants to write should have or should try to develop this curious and caring attitude and should convey with absolute honesty his or her own vision of life. As Katherine Mansfield said: 'Here are the inevitables—the realization that Art is absolutely self-development. The knowledge that genius is dormant in every soul—that that very individuality which is at the root of our being is what matters so poignantly.'"

BIOGRAPHICAL/CRITICAL SOURCES: Milngavie and Bearsden Herald, May 26, 1972; *Glasgow Herald,* October 12, 1972; *Scotsman,* October 14, 1972; *London Evening News,* October 18, 1972; *London Evening Standard,* October 18, 1972; *Guardian,* October 20, 1972; *Scottish Sunday Express,* December 10, 1972; Margaret Thomson Davis, *The Making of a Novelist,* Allison & Busby, 1981.

*   *   *

DAVIS, Michael Justin   1925-

PERSONAL: Born February 9, 1925, in Oxted, England; son of David Leopold and Eileen (Benjamin) Davis; married Elaine Johnson, April 7, 1951; children: Margaret Davis West, Anne Davis Hastings, Robert William. *Education:* Pembroke College, Cambridge, B.A. (with honors), 1949. *Religion:* Church of England. *Home:* Hyde Lodge, Hyde Lane, Marlborough, Wiltshire SN8 1JN, England.

CAREER: Marlborough College, Marlborough, England, teacher of English, drama, and religious education, 1949—, head of English department, 1958-62, housemaster, 1962-75. Guest lecturer at Victoria University of Wellington, University of Canterbury, University of Otago, City Art Gallery of Auckland, Art Gallery of New South Wales, National Book League, and Foreign Literary Library (Moscow, U.S.S.R.). *Military service:* Royal Naval Volunteer Reserve, 1943-46; became sub-lieutenant. *Awards, honors:* St. Cecilia Poetry Prize from Bournemouth Festival, 1976, for "A Sestina for St. Cecilia."

WRITINGS: The Harrap Book of Humorous Prose, Harrap, 1962; *Milton: Areopagitica and Of Education,* Macmillan, 1963; (editor) *Shakespeare: Macbeth,* Edward Arnold, 1964; (editor) *Shakespeare: Twelfth Night,* Edward Arnold, 1966; (editor) *Milton: Samson Agonistes,* Macmillan, 1968; (editor with Christopher Campling) *Words for Worship,* Edward Arnold, 1969; (editor with Laurie Christie) *Shakespeare: A Midsummer Night's Dream,* Edward Arnold, 1969; (editor) *Shakespeare: Hamlet,* Edward Arnold, 1974; *William Blake: A New Kind of Man,* University of California Press, 1977; (editor) *More Words for Worship,* Edward Arnold, 1980. Also editor of *Tennyson: In Memoriam,* 1956, and supervisory editor of "The Kennet Shakespeare" series.

Author of television scripts "Winchester Christmas," first broadcast by Southern-TV, December 30, 1979, and "Come Sunday," a series on Southern-TV, 1980.

WORK IN PROGRESS: Editing works of Alfred Williams, 1877-1930, publication by Alan Sutton expected in 1981; lyric and narrative poems; research on dramatic aspects of folk tale in group theatre.

SIDELIGHTS: Davis told *CA:* "My writing and editing have grown out of my teaching and play producing. Because I have been dissatisfied with available editions of Shakespeare, Milton, and Tennyson for teaching purposes, I have developed my own editions. In these I have tried to refine the work of scholars and to present only those glosses and comments likely to be needed by students.

"'The Kennet Shakespeare' concentrates on the theatrical nature of plays written for performance. My experience as director of school productions has molded my attitude toward school editions of Shakespeare. In a practical man of

the theatre, stage designer Colin Winslow, I found the illustrator I needed. We have emphasized the fact that Shakespeare wrote scripts that can be brought to life in many different sorts of performances. The only firm basis of interpretation, however, is a true understanding of Shakespeare's language, so in my editions I have tried to clarify the meaning of all words likely to puzzle students. My experience in the classroom suggests that some language presents more difficulty than is generally acknowledged.

"For use in assemblies, schoolmasters need prayers that a young congregation can accept. Few of the published prayers seemed right in house assemblies, so I took to writing my own. I kept them, and from this collection I developed more ambitious anthologies, *Words for Worship* and *More Words for Worship,* intended to provide words for a wide range of religious services. I am particularly interested in the devotional use of contemporary secular writings, and I aim to anthologize extracts from all sorts of writing.

"My book about Blake is an attempt to make that astonishingly creative man accessible to the common reader. I have long been fascinated by his versatility and helped by his spiritual perceptiveness. His visual art and his writings reveal different facets of the same vision; I have attempted to present both manifestations, using a biographical framework for my account of the man and his work. Lavish use of quotations and illustrations is intended to bring Blake close to the reader. My own intrusions, as narrator and interpreter, are minimal. At the Edinburgh Festival Fringe in 1980, the world premiere of Blake's brief play, 'The Ghost of Abel,' was presented under my direction.

"In my work as a teacher I try to break down curricular distinctions between English, religious education, and drama. These three subjects are primarily concerned with the awareness of eternal issues in everyday affairs. Consequently, all sorts of literature seem to me to be appropriate vehicles of religious education. I introduce drama, with its strong pull toward involvement and its immense power to liberate those who participate in it, as much as I can into all my teaching. I am very keen on the use of words and movement to present folk tales. I favor a style of rehearsed reading that is dramatic but very simple and can be used with adults as well as children. Many folk tales, especially the Indian, Persian, Turkish, and Armenian, convey spiritual insights through sharp and witty narrative. Lively translations of such tales have an immediate appeal. Students working with these ancient, simple narratives rapidly lose their inhibitions and give group performances of remarkable richness. In adult classes, the effect on some of the individuals involved is startlingly therapeutic. At the moment, I am working on a sequence of folk tales for a full-length dramatic performance.

"Through my quest for good translations of Indian folk tales, I came across the writings of the neglected Wiltshire poet Alfred Williams, who worked as a hammerman in the Swindon railway factory and died in 1930. I am now engaged in editing his writings about village life."

AVOCATIONAL INTERESTS: The arts, making pots, designing embroidery, gardening, theatre.

*   *   *

DAVIS, Polly Ann   1931-

PERSONAL: Born November 11, 1931, in Pittsboro, Miss.; daughter of Robert Sidney (a farmer) and Olive Marie (Flanagan) Davis. *Education:* Blue Mountain College, B.A., 1953; University of Mississippi, M.A., 1954; University of Kentucky, Ph.D., 1963. *Politics:* Democrat: *Religion:* Baptist. *Home:* 4301 John Reagan, Marshall, Tex. 75670. *Office:* Department of History and Political Science, East Texas Baptist College, Marshall, Tex. 75670.

CAREER: Bethel College, Hopkinsville, Ky., instructor in social studies, 1954-57; Western Kentucky University, Bowling Green, instructor in history, 1961-62; East Texas Baptist College, Marshall, associate professor, 1963-68, professor of history and political science, 1968—, chairman of department, 1963—, chairman of Division of Social Studies, 1964-79. *Member:* American Historical Association, Society of History Education, Kentucky Historical Society, Phi Alpha Theta, College Women's Club.

WRITINGS: Alben W. Barkley: Senate Majority Leader and Vice-President, Garland Publishing, 1979. Contributor to history journals, including *Southern Quarterly* and *Filson Club History Quarterly.*

WORK IN PROGRESS: Researching political history of United States.

*   *   *

DAVIS, Walter Richardson 1928-

PERSONAL: Born August 17, 1928, in Middletown, Conn.; son of Walter Young (an insurance clerk) and Helen (Klopstein) Davis; married Yolanda Leiss, June 21, 1951 (marriage ended August 7, 1974); married Cynthia Connell (a writer), August 9, 1974; children: (first marriage) Mark, Alison, Peter, Catherine, Elizabeth, Heidi. *Education:* Trinity College, Hartford, Conn., B.A. (with honors), 1950; Yale University, M.A., 1951, Ph.D., 1957. *Politics:* Democrat. *Religion:* Lutheran. *Home:* 628 Park Ave., South Bend, Ind. 46616. *Office:* Department of English, University of Notre Dame, Notre Dame, Ind. 46656.

CAREER: University of Rochester, Rochester, N.Y., instructor in English, 1954-55; Dickenson College, Carlisle, Pa., instructor in English, 1956; Williams College, Williamstown, Mass., instructor in English, 1956-59; Massachusetts Institute of Technology, Cambridge, assistant professor of humanities, 1959-60; University of Notre Dame, Notre Dame, Ind., assistant professor, 1960-64, associate professor, 1964-68, professor of English, 1968—. Visiting professor at Harvard University, summer, 1972. *Member:* Modern Language Association of America, University of Chicago Renaissance Seminar. *Awards, honors:* Grant from Huntington Library, summer, 1975; first annual award from International Porlock Society, 1979.

WRITINGS: A Map of Arcadia: Sidney's Romance in Its Tradition, Yale University Press, 1965; (editor) *The Works of Thomas Campion,* Doubleday, 1967; (editor) *Twentieth Century Interpretations of "Much Ado About Nothing,"* Prentice-Hall, 1969; *Idea and Act in Elizabethan Fiction,* Princeton University Press, 1969; (contributor) Stanley E. Fish, editor, *Seventeenth Century Prose,* Oxford University Press, 1971. Contributor of more than twenty-five articles and reviews to language and literature journals.

WORK IN PROGRESS: Editing *The Ripley Scroll,* an alchemical manuscript, publication expected in 1984; short stories; poems; research on John Donne, Henry Smith, Edmund Spenser, and Jeremy Taylor.

SIDELIGHTS: Davis commented: "I have always thought of scholarly writing as an act of friendship for the beloved dead: presenting older literature in such a way as to help modern readers create their own relation to it. In the past five years, I have turned from scholarly writing toward people, in administrative work, and toward mining my own creativity, in dream analysis, poetry, and fiction."

*   *   *

DAWISHA, Adeed Isam 1944-

PERSONAL: Born November 2, 1944, in Baghdad, Iraq; son of Isam (an air force officer) and Najma (a teacher; maiden name, Daddy) Dawisha; married Karen Lea Hurst (a university professor), January 1, 1972. *Education:* University of Lancaster, B.A., 1971; London School of Economics and Political Science, London, Ph.D., 1974. *Office:* Royal Institute of International Affairs, 10 St. James's Sq., London SW1Y 4LE, England.

CAREER: University of Lancaster, Bailrigg, England, lecturer in international relations, 1974-76; University of Southampton, Southampton, England, visiting fellow, 1976-77; International Institute for Strategic Studies, London, England, senior research associate, 1977-78; University of Keele, Keele, England, lecturer in international relations, 1978-79; Royal Institute of International Affairs, London, England, assistant director of studies, 1979—.

WRITINGS: Egypt in the Arab World: The Elements of Foreign Policy, Macmillan, 1976; *Saudi Arabia's Search for Security,* International Institute for Strategic Studies, 1979; *Syria and the Lebanese Crisis,* Macmillan, 1980.

WORK IN PROGRESS: Foreign Policy in the Middle East: A Comparative Analysis, publication expected in 1982.

SIDELIGHTS: Dawisha told *CA:* "I write because I am good at it, and I write on Middle East politics because others are so bad at it."

*   *   *

DAWLISH, Peter
See KERR, James Lennox

*   *   *

DAY, Dorothy 1897-1980

OBITUARY NOTICE—See index for *CA* sketch: Born November 8, 1897, in Brooklyn, N.Y.; died of congestive heart failure, November 29, 1980, in New York, N.Y. Catholic activist and writer best known for founding the Catholic Workers movement. A convert from agnosticism to Catholicism, Day led the Workers movement, a group that took literally the phrase from the Bible, "Go, sell what you have, and give to the poor." The group espouses voluntary poverty and cares for the destitute with free housing, food, and clothing. Because of their radical stance against hunger and war, Day and her followers often took part in demonstrations against government policy. Day was arrested twelve times for her participation in these protests, the first time in 1918, when she picketed the White House with other suffragettes. In 1933 Day started the *Catholic Worker* with Peter Maurin, a French philosopher and laborer. A monthly paper, the *Worker* is a forum for the doctrines of the Workers movement. Her writings include *House of Hospitality, Therese, Loaves and Fishes,* and *On Pilgrimage: The Sixties.* Obituaries and other sources: Dorothy Day, *The Long Loneliness: The Autobiography of Dorothy Day,* Harper, 1952; *Chicago Tribune,* December 1, 1980; *Time,* December 15, 1980.

*   *   *

DAY, M(ichael) H(erbert) 1927-

PERSONAL: Born March 8, 1927, in London, England; son

of Herbert Arthur and Amy Julienne (Brodwin) Day; married Jose Ashton Hankins (a doctor), 1952; children: Jeremy Paul. *Education:* Royal Free Hospital School of Medicine, London, M.B., B.S., 1954, Ph.D., 1962. *Home:* 26 Thurlow Rd., Hampstead, London NW3 5PR, England. *Office:* Department of Anatomy, St. Thomas's Hospital Medical School, Lambeth Palace Rd., London SE1 7EH, England.

CAREER: University of London, Royal Free Hospital School of Medicine, London, England, assistant lecturer in anatomy, 1958-63; Middlesex Hospital Medical School, London, lecturer, 1964-66, senior lecturer, 1966-69, reader in physical anthropology, 1969-72; St. Thomas's Hospital Medical School, London, professor of anatomy, 1972—. *Military service:* Royal Air Force, 1945-48. *Member:* American Association of Physical Anthropology, Anatomical Society of Great Britain and Ireland (president), Royal College of Surgeons, Royal College of Physicians (licenciate), Royal Anthropological Institute, Society for the Study of Human Biology, Linnean Society, Zoological Society of London.

WRITINGS: Guide to Fossil Man: A Handbook of Human Palaeontology, World Publishing, 1965, 3rd edition, University of Chicago Press, 1978; *Fossil Man,* Hamlyn, 1969, Grosset, 1970; (editor) *Human Evolution,* Barnes & Noble, 1973; *Fossil History of Man,* Carolina Biological Supply, 1977. Writer for British Broadcasting Corp. (BBC). Contributor to medical journals and popular magazines, including *Nature, Listener,* and *Impulse. Avocational interests:* Golf, chess, fly fishing.

* * *

DEACON, Ruth E.   1923-

PERSONAL: Born June 4, 1923, in Bellaire, Ohio; daughter of Floyd T. (a teacher and farmer) and Madge (Brawley) Deacon. *Education:* Ohio State University, B.S., 1944; Cornell University, M.S., 1948, Ph.D., 1954. *Politics:* Republican. *Religion:* United Presbyterian. *Home:* 311 North Dakota Ave., Ames, Iowa 50010. *Office:* College of Home Economics Administration, Iowa State University, 123 MacKay Hall, Ames, Iowa 50011.

CAREER: Teacher of vocational home economics at high school in West Carrollton, Ohio, 1944-45; Cooperative Extension Service of Ohio State University, home demonstration agent in Cadiz, Ohio, 1945-47; Cornell University, Ithaca, N.Y., instructor, 1948-54, assistant professor, 1954-57, associate professor of home economics, 1957-58; associate professor of home economics at Ohio Agricultural Experiment Station, 1958-65; Ohio State University, Columbus, associate professor, 1962-65, professor of home economics, 1965-74, chairman of Division of Home Management, Housing, and Equipment, 1962-74; professor of Ohio Agricultural Research and Development Center, 1965-74; Iowa State Universtiy, Ames, professor of family environment, 1974—, head of department, 1974-75, dean of College of Home Economics Administration, 1975—. Chairman of North Central Region Technical Committee, 1963-65; member of U.S. Department of Agriculture human nutrition and consumer use research advisory committee, 1964-69; member of Ohio governor's task force on income of the aging, 1971-72; consultant to United Nations Food and Agriculture Organization and U.S. Agency for International Development; member of advisory committee for governors White House conference on families, 1979-80.

MEMBER: American Home Economics Association (first vice-chairman of agency member unit, 1977-80), American Association for the Advancement of Science, National Council on Family Relations, Association of State Universities and Land-Grant Colleges (chairman of family economics concepts committee, 1962-65), National Council for Administrators of Home Economics, Phi Upsilon Omicron, Omicron Nu, Phi Lambda Theta, Phi Kappa Phi.

WRITINGS: (With Francille M. Firebaugh) *Home Management Context and Concepts,* Houghton, 1975; (with Firebaugh) *Family Resource Management: Principles and Application,* Allyn & Bacon, 1981. Contributor to journals in home economics and the behavioral sciences. Member of editorial board of *Home Economics Research Journal,* 1971-75.

SIDELIGHTS: Ruth Deacon commented: "Rapid changes in our social and economic systems have provided not only many opportunities for families, but complexities as well. There has been a tendency to minimize areas outside the mainstream such that fundamental and meaningful activities, such as housework and volunteer work, have been undervalued. I have been working to help interpret the nature of positive interaction between families and society. In the process, I have been concerned with the special roles of women and the need for recognition of the value of their nonpaid activity.

"As women have sought paid work, their contributions have often been undervalued. Also, the demands of their dual roles have often been excessive where limited sharing occurs.

"Many more people are currently aware of the issues than was the case twenty-five years ago. Actual or reciprocal role shifts have barely begun, however. Recognition of the value of worthwhile activity, wherever it occurs, is needed if deep-rooted ideas about sex roles are ever to change. My writing is directed toward that recognition."

* * *

DeBENEDETTI, Charles Louis   1943-

PERSONAL: Born January 27, 1943, in Chicago, Ill.; son of Louis and Tina (Deiro) DeBenedetti; married Sandra Kisala, August 29, 1964; children: Laura, David. *Education:* Loyola University, Chicago, Ill., B.S., 1964; University of Illinois, M.A., 1965, Ph.D., 1968. *Office:* Department of History, University of Toledo, 2801 West Bancroft, Toledo, Ohio 43606.

CAREER: University of Toledo, Toledo, Ohio, assistant professor, 1968-73, associate professor, 1973-78, professor of history, 1978—. *Member:* American Historical Association, Organization of American Historians, Conference on Peace Research in History (president). *Awards, honors:* National Endowment for the Humanities fellow, 1976; Rockefeller Foundation fellow, 1978-79.

WRITINGS: Origins of the Modern American Peace Movement, KTO Press, 1978; *The Peace Reform in American History,* Indiana University Press, 1980. Contributor to history journals and current affairs magazines, including *Progressive.*

WORK IN PROGRESS: The Anti-War Movement in America, 1961-1975.

* * *

de BEUS, Jacobus Gysbertus   1909-

PERSONAL: Born October 19, 1909, in Batavia; son of Willem Louis and Johanna Frederica (van Kooten) de Beus; married Louise G. Broussard, August 17, 1960; children:

Marjolyn. *Education:* Received Dr. International Law from University of Leyden. *Home:* Claire Fontaine, 1297 Founex, Switzerland. *Office:* United Nations Fund for Drug Abuse Control, Palais des Nations, Geneva, Switzerland.

CAREER: Netherlands Diplomatic Service, diplomat in Brussels, Belgium, 1936-38, Copenhagen, Denmark, 1938-39, Berlin, Germany, 1939-40, secretary to Foreign Office and Prime Minister in London, England, 1940-45, counselor in Washington, D.C., 1945-49, permanent delegate to United Nations in New York City, 1948-49, head of Far East office, 1949, deputy high commissioner in Djakarta, Java, 1950, minister in Washington, D.C., 1950-54, ambassador to Pakistan, 1955-57, ambassador to U.S.S.R., 1957-60, ambassador to Australia, 1960-63, permanent representative of the Netherlands to the United Nations in New York City, 1964-67, ambassador to West Germany, 1967-74, assistant secretary-general of United Nations in New York City, 1975—, executive director of United Nations Fund for Drug Abuse Control in Geneva, Switzerland, 1975—. *Awards, honors:* LL.D.; knight of Order of the Netherlands Lion; commander of Order of Orange Nassau; grand cross and order of merit from German Verdienst Order.

WRITINGS: The Jurisprudence of the General Claims Commission, Nijhoff, 1938; *The Future of the West,* Harper, 1953; *Tomorrow at Dawn,* Norton, 1979.

Other: *De Wedergeboorte van het Koninkryk,* 1942; *In Rusland,* 1963; *Morgen by het aanbreken van de dag,* 1977.

AVOCATIONAL INTERESTS: Tennis, squash, skiing.*

*   *   *

de COSTA, (George) Rene   1939-

PERSONAL: Born November 22, 1939, in New York, N.Y.; married Serpil Emre (a librarian), August 9, 1964; children: Alev. *Education:* Rutgers University, A.B., 1964; Washington University, St. Louis, Mo., Ph.D., 1970. *Office:* Department of Romance Languages, University of Chicago, 1050 East 59th St., Chicago, Ill. 60637.

CAREER: University of Chicago, Chicago, Ill., assistant professor, 1970-76, associate professor, 1976-80, professor of Spanish, 1980—, director of Center for Latin American Studies. *Member:* Modern Language Association of America, American Association of Teachers of Spanish and Portuguese, Latin American Studies Association. *Awards, honors:* Grant from American Council of Learned Societies and Social Science Research Council, 1971; fellow of National Endowment for the Humanities, 1974-75; Social Science Research Council grant, 1978-79.

WRITINGS: (Editor) *Vicente Huidobro y el Creacionismo* (title means "Vincent Huidobro and Creationism"), Taurus, 1975; *The Poetry of Pablo Neruda,* Harvard University Press, 1978; *En pos de Huidobro* (title means "In Pursuit of Huidobro"), Editorial Universitaria, 1979. Contributor to language and Latin American studies journals.

WORK IN PROGRESS: A literary biography of Huidobro, publication expected in 1981; research on Latin American theatre.

*   *   *

DEEGAN, Paul Joseph   1937-

PERSONAL: Born March 19, 1937, in Mankato, Minn.; son of Ray C. and Ellen G. (Coughlin) Deegan; married Dorothy A. Schreiner (a registered nurse), September 24, 1960; children: Lisa, Michael, John. *Education:* University of Minne-

sota, B.A., 1959. *Religion:* Christian. *Home:* 139 Eastwood Dr., Mankato, Minn. 56001. *Office:* P.O. Box 113, Mankato, Minn. 56001.

CAREER: Reporter and editor with newspapers in Austin, Mankato, and St. Paul, Minn., 1960-69; Creative Education, Inc., Mankato, editorial director, 1969-72; Children's Book Co., Mankato, president, 1973—. Chairman of Mankato Human Rights Commission.

WRITINGS—Juvenile; all published by Creative Education, except as noted: *The Monastery: Life in a Religious Community,* 1970; *Animals of East Africa: Our Vanishing Wildlife,* 1971; *A Hospital: Life in a Medical Center,* 1971; *The Kibbutz: Life on an Israeli Commune,* 1971; *Tom Seaver,* 1973; *Jerry West,* 1973; *Jack Nicklaus, The Golden Bear,* 1973; *Bill Russell,* 1973; *Kareem Abdul Jabbar,* Amecus Street, 1974; *O. J. Simpson,* 1974; *Hank Aaron,* 1974; *The Team Manager,* Amecus Street, 1974; *Almost a Champion,* Amecus Street, 1975; *Hitting,* 1975; *Important Decision,* Amecus Street, 1975; *The Jump Shot and Lay-Up,* 1975; *Close But Not Quite,* Amecus Street, 1975; *Dan Moves Up,* Amecus Street, 1975; *Catching the Football,* 1975; *Bunting and Baserunning,* 1975; *Passing the Football,* 1975; *Placekicking and Punting,* 1975; *The Set Shot,* 1975; *Shooting in a Game,* 1975; *The Tournaments,* Amecus Street, 1975; *Pitching,* 1975; *Skates and Skating,* 1976; *Stickhandling and Passing,* 1976; *Tennis,* 1976. Also author of *Serving and Returning Service* and *Volleying and Lobs;* co-author, with Gary Libman, of *Bjorn Borg, Catfish Hunter,* and *Reggie Jackson.* Contributor of articles and reviews to newspapers.

WORK IN PROGRESS: A book series for teenagers, on medicine; biographies of sports personalities; sports instructional books.

*   *   *

DEGANI, Meir H(ershtenkorn)   1909-

PERSONAL: Born January 4, 1909, in Warsaw, Poland; came to the United States in 1928, naturalized citizen, 1944; son of Dov and Haya (Goldman) Hershtenkorn; married Edith Schumacher, December 23, 1948; children: Vivian, Lynne Degani Mochon. *Education:* Massachusetts Institute of Technology, B.S., 1932, M.S., 1941, Sc.D., 1942. *Home:* 549 West 123rd St., New York, N.Y. 10027.

CAREER: Pennsylvania State University, University Park, assistant professor of geophysics, 1942-43; American Export Airlines, Flushing, N.Y., chief instructor in meteorology, 1943-44; State University of New York Maritime College, Fort Schuyler, assistant professor, 1946-47, professor of physics, 1946-79, professor emeritus, 1979—, chairman of science department, 1947-73, acting dean, 1966-67. Chairman of National Board of Histadruth Ivrith, 1973-75, vice-president, 1977—. *Military service:* U.S. Navy, 1944; became aerographer; received Bronze Star. *Member:* American Physical Society, American Association of University Professors, American Geophysical Union, American Technion Society, Labor Zionist Organization of America, Hebrew Circle of Manhattan, American Friends of Hebrew University. *Awards, honors:* Stratton Medal from Massachusetts Institute of Technology, 1931; Chancellor's Award for excellence in teaching from State University of New York, 1975.

WRITINGS: Astronomy Made Simple, Doubleday, 1955, 3rd edition, 1976. Contributor to scientific journals.

DeKALB, Lorimer
See KNORR, Marian L(ockwood)

*   *   *

DeLANEY, Joseph Lawrence 1917-

PERSONAL: Born December 9, 1917, in Sheridan, Wyo.; son of Edward J. and Mary Rose (Reuter) De Laney; married Gladys Boget, June 1, 1964; children: Virginia, Elizabeth, Deborah, Rebecca, Susan, Lawrence. *Education:* Muskingum College, B.A., 1954; California State University, Los Angeles, M.A., 1958; University of Southern California, B.Mus., 1959. *Religion:* Unitarian-Universalist. *Home address:* P.O. Box 4703, Stockton, Calif. 95204. *Agent:* Dmitri Ybroski, c/o New York Writers Guild, New York, N.Y.

CAREER: Member of KFBB string ensemble, 1936-38; played background music for Columbia Pictures, 1938-41; teacher in Georgia, Arizona, and New Mexico, 1947-64; Orange Coast College, Costa Mesa, Calif., instructor in creative writing, 1964-72; San Joaquin Delta College, Stockton, Calif., instructor in creative writing, 1972-77; Lodi Unified School District, Lodi, Calif., teacher, 1977—. Instructor at Golden West College, 1964-72; director of education at military academy in Lake Elsinore, Calif., 1968-72; director of Parapsychology Research Institute of Northern California, 1972—, and California Institute for Creative Education. Political speechwriter; public relations consultant. *Military service:* U.S. Army, paratrooper, 1941-47; became major.

MEMBER: National Teachers Association, Adult Education Association, Psychical Research Institute, Royal Photographic Society (fellow), Social-Psychology Association of England, Society for Psychical Research of England, New York Writers Guild. *Awards, honors:* Received honorary Ph.D.

WRITINGS: Writing Is a Business, Pierian, 1969, revised edition, 1979; *Cosmogenics,* Pierian, 1977; *The Realized Man* (novel), Pierian Press, 1980; *The Handicapped Learner: My Fourteen Years With Wards of the Court,* Pierian Press, 1981. Also author of *Symbols* and *Guide to Transpersonal Therapy.* Contributor of articles, stories, and poems to magazines. Editor of *Graphomania,* 1963—.

WORK IN PROGRESS: A book about teaching the learning handicapped; *New Mind, Unlimited,* a science fiction novel.

SIDELIGHTS: De Laney commented: "My interest is in seeking ways to develop latent mental power and psionic power. I use my research as a basis for my fiction. I am also interested in helping young people to find their individual expression and future—to allow them the opportunity to grow into themselves, not copies of people around them."

*   *   *

DELANO, Anthony 1930-

PERSONAL—Office: Daily Mirror, 220 East 42nd St., Suite 3103, New York, N.Y. 10017.

CAREER: Daily Mirror, London, England, Rome correspondent, 1956-60, Paris correspondent, 1960-63, American correspondent, 1963-70, editor of "London Diary" and roving correspondent, 1970-74, chief American correspondent, 1975-79, managing editor, 1980—. Director of Mirror Vision.

WRITINGS: Breathless Diversions (novel), Mayflower, 1975; *Slip Up* (nonfiction), Deutsch, 1976. Also author of *Joyce McKinney and the Manacled Mormon* (nonfiction), 1978.

WORK IN PROGRESS: Hesitation Waltz, a novel, publication expected in 1981.

*   *   *

DeLAPP, George Leslie 1895-

PERSONAL: Born November 4, 1895, in East Delavan, Wis.; son of Lawson LeGrand and Carrie Elizabeth (West) DeLapp; married Ardyce Lucile Case, July 25, 1926; children: Cicely Anne, Patricia Lucille, George Leslie. *Education:* Attended University of Minnesota, American Institute of Bankers, and Graceland College. *Home:* 16200 East 23rd St., Independence, Mo. 64055. *Office:* Auditorium, Independence, Mo. 64051.

CAREER: First National Bank, Minneapolis, Minn., clerk, 1913-17; associated with F. A. Bean Properties, Inc. (farm operators), 1918-28; Reorganized Church of Jesus Christ of Latter Day Saints, Independence, Mo., bishop of Minnesota district, 1926-28, bishop in Lamoni, Iowa, 1928-31, counselor to presiding bishop at headquarters in Independence, 1931-40, presiding bishop and trustee in trust, 1940-66, bishop in Independence, 1966—. Member of Independence Heritage Commission, 1973-77; past member of board of trustees of Kansas City General Hospital and Medical Center; consultant to Zionic Research Institute. *Military service:* U.S. Army, 1917-18.

WRITINGS: In the World, Herald House, 1973. Author of religious periodicals.*

*   *   *

DELORT, Robert 1932-

PERSONAL: Born September 21, 1932, in Agen, France; son of Jean (a customs inspector) and Marguerite (a professor; maiden name, Ginestet) Delort; married Annette Morel, September 27, 1958 (died July 8, 1975); children: Pierre, Isabelle, Yves. *Education:* Universite de Paris, agrege d'histoire, 1957; Ecole Normale Superieure, docteur es lettre, 1975; Ecole Francaise de Rome, licence es suine, 1980. *Home:* 137 rue de Grenelle, 75007 Paris, France. *Office:* Universite de Paris, 8 route de la Tourelle, 75012 Paris, France.

CAREER: Writer. Professor at Universite de Paris, Paris, France, and at Ecole Normale Superieure; director of "L'Aventure Humaine" collection for Editions Albin Michel. *Military service:* French Navy, 1957-60. *Member:* Institut d'Etudes Slaves, Hansischer Geschichtsverein (Hamburg, Germany).

WRITINGS: La Moscovie au XVIe siecle, Calmann Levy, 1965; *Introduction aux sciences auxiliares de l'histoire,* Armand Colin, 1969; *Le Moyen Age,* three volumes, Armand Colin, 1969-71, translation by Robert Allen published as *Life in the Middle Ages,* Edita Lausanne, 1972, Phaidon Press, 1974; *Venise: Portrait historique d'une cite,* Seuil, 1971; *Le Commerce des fourrures a la fin du moyen age,* two volumes, Ecole Francaise de Rome, 1978-80; *Histoire des animaux,* Seuil, 1981; *A la recherche du moyen age,* Seuil, 1981.

WORK IN PROGRESS: Histoire de animaus, publication by Seuil expected in 1981 or 1982.

SIDELIGHTS: Delort is a specialist on the history of the Middle Ages in Europe.

*   *   *

DEMETILLO, Ricaredo 1920-

PERSONAL: Born June 2, 1920, in Dumangas, Philippines;

son of Querobin (a farmer) and Rebecca Demetillo; married Angelita de la Riarte, 1944; children: Darnay, Rebecca, Lester, Weston. *Education:* Silliman University, A.B., 1947; University of Iowa, M.F.A., 1952. *Home:* 38 Bulacan St., West Ave., Quezon City, Metro Manila, Philippines. *Office:* Department of Humanities, University of the Philippines, Diliman, Quezon City, Philippines.

CAREER: University of the Philippines, Quezon City, assistant professor, 1959-70, associate professor, 1970-75, professor of humanities, 1975—, head of department, 1961-62. *Awards, honors:* Rockefeller Foundation fellow, 1952; Golden Jubilee Award from University of the Philippines, 1958, for epic poem "Barter in Panay"; Jose Rigal Centennial Award, 1963; Philippine Republic Cultural Heritage Award, 1968, for poetry and criticism; Art Association of the Philippines criticism award; distinguished alumnus award from Silliman University and from Central Philippine University; Palanca Memorial Award first prize for drama.

WRITINGS: No Certain Weather: A Collection of Poetry, Guinhalinan Press, 1956; *La Via: A Spiritual Journey* (poems), Diliman Review, 1958; *Daedalus and Other Poems,* Guinhalinan Press, 1961; *Barter in Panay* (poems), Office of Research Coordination, University of the Philippines, 1961; *The Authentic Voice of Poetry,* Office of Research Coordination, University of the Philippines, 1962; *Masks and Signature* (poems), University of the Philippines Press, 1968; *The Scare-Crow Christ* (poems), University of the Philippines Press, 1973; *The City and the Thread of Light and Other Poems,* Diliman Review, 1974; *Lazarus, Troubador* (poems), New Day Publishers, 1974; *The Heart of Emptiness Is Black: A Tragedy in Verse* (one-act play; first produced in Quezon City, Philippines, at Abelardo Hall, University of the Philippines, 1973), University of the Philippines Press, 1975; *The Genesis of a Troubled Vision* (novel), Diliman Review, 1976.

WORK IN PROGRESS: The Late Boughs of Summer, lyric poems; critical essays on painting and literature.

SIDELIGHTS: Demetillo told *CA:* "The Second World War released my poetic gifts. But it was not until 1950-52 that I really trained professionally as a creative artist, under the able teaching of Robert Lowell and Paul Engle at Iowa. Writing poetry has been the most rewarding experience in my life. I am privileged to be chosen by a gift."

* * *

DENDEL, Esther (Sietmann Warner) 1910-
(Esther S. Warner)

PERSONAL: Born February 2, 1910, in Laurel, Iowa; daughter of Louis P. and Grace (Stanton) Sietmann; married Gerald F. Dendel (an artist), December, 1950. *Education:* Iowa State University, B.S., 1938; Columbia University, M.A., 1939. *Politics:* Democrat. *Religion:* "Influenced by Zen." *Home and office:* 236 East 16th St., Costa Mesa, Calif. 92627. *Agent:* Paul R. Reynolds, Inc., 12 East 41st St., New York, N.Y. 10017.

CAREER: Artist, specializing in fiber art, 1946—. Member of Denwar Craft Fellowship.

WRITINGS—Under name Esther S. Warner: *New Song in a Strange Land* (autobiographical), Houghton, 1948; *Seven Days to Lomaland* (autobiographical), Houghton, 1954; *The Silk-Cotton Tree* (novel), Doubleday, 1958; *Art: An Everyday Experience,* Harper, 1963; *The Crossing Fee* (autobiographical), Houghton, 1968.

Under name Esther Dendel: *Needleweaving,* Doubleday,

1971; *Fingerweaving,* Simon & Schuster, 1974; *African Fabric Crafts,* Taplinger, 1974; *Basic Book of Twining,* Van Nostrand, 1978; *Designing From Nature,* Taplinger, 1978.

WORK IN PROGRESS: Ancient Textile Techniques for Today.

SIDELIGHTS: Esther Dendel commented: "I am interested in the crafts as an aid to international understanding. I have conducted nine craft tours to other nations, taking groups to Europe, Africa, Afghanistan, Japan, Turkey, and the People's Republic of China.

"I believe that the creative potential of each individual is one of America's greatest undeveloped resources."

* * *

DeNEEF, Arthur Leigh 1942-

PERSONAL: Born April 16, 1942, in Newton, N.J.; married, 1964; children: two. *Education:* Iowa Wesleyan College, B.A., 1964; Pennsylvania State University, M.A., 1965, Ph.D., 1969. *Office:* Department of English, Allen Building, Duke University, Durham, N.C. 22706.

CAREER: Pennsylvania State University, University Park, instructor in English, 1968-69; Duke University, Durham, N.C., assistant professor, 1969-75, associate professor of English, 1975—. *Member:* Modern Language Association of America, Renaissance Society of America, Southeastern Renaissance Conference.

WRITINGS: (Contributor of translations) Paulene Aspel, *Traversees: Crossings* (poems in French and English), Stone Wall Press, 1966; *"This Poetick Liturgie": Robert Herrick's Ceremonial Mode,* Duke University Press, 1974. Co-editor of "Renaissance Papers," Southeastern Renaissance Conference, 1970—. Contributor to literature journals.

BIOGRAPHICAL/CRITICAL SOURCES: Times Literary Supplement, July 25, 1975.*

* * *

DENGLER, Dieter 1938-

PERSONAL: Born May 22, 1938, in Wildberg, Germany; came to the United States in 1957, naturalized citizen, 1960; son of Reinhold and Maria (Schnuerle) Dengler. *Education:* College of San Mateo, A.A., 1963. *Religion:* Protestant. *Home and office:* 790 Panoramic Highway, Mill Valley, Calif. 94941.

CAREER: Journeyman tool and die maker in Germany, 1954-57; Trans-World Airlines, New York, N.Y., pilot and flight engineer, 1968—. *Military service:* U.S. Air Force, pilot, 1957-61; received Air Medal and Purple Heart. U.S. Navy, pilot, 1963-68; became lieutenant; received Navy Cross, Distinguished Flying Cross, Purple Heart, and Air Medal.

WRITINGS: Escape From Laos, Presidio Press, 1979.

SIDELIGHTS: Dengler's book describes his own experiences as a carrier pilot shot down in Laos. He told *CA:* "I crash-landed and was caught the following day. I lived and traveled with the Pathet Laos. I escaped and was recaptured. After several beatings and interrogations, I finally arrived two and one-half weeks later at a POW camp. There, with six others who had been POWs for three years, I planned and executed an escape. The group separated. Duane Martin was caught and beheaded. I burnt down a village and made air contact a few days later. I was rescued delirious and near death and weighed eighty-two pounds."

BIOGRAPHICAL/CRITICAL SOURCES: Saturday Evening Post, December 3, 1966.

DENGLER, Marianna (Herron) 1935-

PERSONAL: Born November 19, 1935, in Tulsa, Okla.; daughter of Clarence Richard and Edna Mae Herron; married Ben H. Dengler (an architect), August 25, 1956; children: Patti Diane, Amy Durene. *Education:* University of Oklahoma, B.S., 1957; graduate study at University of California, Los Angeles, San Fernando Valley State College, and California State University, Northridge, 1958-65. *Home and office:* 32119 Beachlake Lane, Westlake Village, Calif. 91361. *Agent:* Henriette Neatrour, Bill Berger and Associates, Inc., 444 East 58th St., New York, N.Y. 10022.

CAREER: English teacher at public schools in Los Angeles, Calif., 1957-59 and 1963-73; Viewpoint School, Calabasas, Calif., teacher, 1976-77; writer, 1977—. *Member:* International P.E.N., International College of Applied Nutrition (honorary member), Society of Children's Book Writers, Women's National Book Association, Southern California Council on Literature for Children and Young People. *Awards, honors:* Award for excellence in nutrition research and practices from International College of Applied Nutrition, 1980, for *A Pebble in Newcomb's Pond.*

WRITINGS: Catch the Passing Breeze (young adult novel), Holt, 1977, reprinted as *Vicki*, Scholastic Book Services, 1980; *A Pebble in Newcomb's Pond* (young adult novel), Holt, 1979.

WORK IN PROGRESS: Two contemporary novels for young adults; an adult novel.

SIDELIGHTS: Dengler told *CA:* "Eleven years of working with teenagers in the classroom and a concern for these young lives has made me acutely aware of the problems they face in this chaotic and shifting world. The old saws that would have us believe the world today is no worse and no better than it has always been begin to pale. The world is not the same.

"These young people struggle with the drug culture, the wars that threaten their lives and their futures without patriotic cause, the sexual revolution, the breakdown of the family unit, and the welcome but baffling emerging equality of women. Along side this is an ever more complex technological society demanding more highly specialized and more intense knowledge and skill juxtaposed against an eroding educational system that prepares them less well to face these demands. At the same time and for the first time in history, girls are faced with the challenge and the responsibility of directing and supporting their own lives and perhaps those of their children. Welcome as this is, it is also frightening, for there are few role models. Most women in their middle years today began with a different premise, and many of them (mothers of these girls) are struggling now with their own identities and transitions. Boys, too, are caught up in this transition, their traditional roles changed and their fathers are of little help.

"Compound all this with the threat of economic disaster, rising inflation that makes self-starting nearly out of reach for all but the most enterprising, a diminishing job market, and you have a bushel basket full of complexities that, if not worse than those of the past, are, at least, totally unique. Superimposed upon all of this is the pollution of air, water, and food supplies, a disaster that I believe is crippling these young bodies and minds at a pace far greater than we realize and rendering them less capable of meeting these difficult challenges.

"These young people are the future. Their lives are precious. No matter how jaded and disillusioned the adult world becomes, youth still believes it can change the world. Youth is worthy, and it deserves no less than our best effort. The contemporary 'problem' novel for young adults is a phenomenon of recent years, and it is one way of exposing to the light some of the seemingly unsolvable and often terrifying problems these young people face. It is a way of probing and exploring avenues of survival, and it is a way of saying, 'you are not alone; others feel as you feel, face what you face, and together we will find a way to prosper.'

"The writer of the contemporary 'problem' novel bears a great responsibility. Within the framework of the story, he or she must present all aspects of life with courage, honesty, and integrity, but he must never cross that gossamer line into exploitation. Sex, violence, cruelty, all play a part, as they are part of the human condition, but violence for the sake of a sale, sex for the sake of titillation, cruelty for the sake of shock is a betrayal of the reader. The contemporary novel, then, holds the author accountable not only for accurate and careful research but for responsible, non-exploitive handling of the story, for searching and sensitive probing of the problems, and for a denouement that, while not always 'happy,' offers the reader hope.

"*Catch the Passing Breeze* is the story of a struggle to reach out and capture an ephemeral joy, and it is a challenge to dare, to risk, to reach for that which nourishes the human spirit, lest it be lost forever. *A Pebble in Newcomb's Pond* is the story of a young girl's terrifying descent into mental illness, and it offers as hope one of the most exciting miracles of modern science in the past several decades."

* * *

DENHAM, Sully
See BUDD, Mavis

* * *

DENNEY, Myron Keith 1930-

PERSONAL: Born April 28, 1930, in Detroit, Mich.; son of William B. (a laborer) and Dorothea (Rosen) Denney; married Leonie Donegan (an actress), December 25, 1975. *Education:* University of Michigan, M.D., 1959. *Home and office:* 330 East 79th St., New York, N.Y. 10021. *Agent:* Sterling Lord Agency, Inc., 660 Madison Ave., New York, N.Y. 10021.

CAREER: Wayne County General Hospital, Eloise, Mich., intern, 1959-60; associated with North Atlantic Treaty Organization (NATO) and Chrysler Corp., 1960-62; Wayne County General Hospital, Eloise, Mich., surgeon, 1962-64; Detroit General Hospital, Detroit, Mich., surgeon, 1964-67; Wayne State University, Detroit, assistant professor of surgery, 1967-69; University of California, Davis, assistant professor of surgery, 1969-70; University of California, San Diego, clinical assistant professor of surgery, 1970-75; private practice of surgery in La Jolla, Calif., 1970-75; private practice of surgery and emergency medicine in San Francisco, Calif., 1975-80; writer, 1980—. Co-founder of Crisis Clinic and Beach Area Free Clinic and medical director of San Diego Council of Free Clinics, all 1972-74. *Military service:* U.S. Army, 1952-54. *Member:* Authors Guild, American College of Surgeons, American Association of Academic Surgery, American College of Emergency Physicians, Royal College of Medicine. *Awards, honors:* Fredrick Coller Award from American College of Surgeons, 1964, for "Experimental Studies in Barotraums."

WRITINGS: Second Opinion, Grosset, 1979. Editor with Health Communications, Inc., 1973-74. Contributor to scientific journals and popular magazines, including *Off-Road Vehicle* and *Pan American Clipper.*

WORK IN PROGRESS: A general nonfiction book about ethics in modern medical practice, publication by New American Library expected in 1980.

SIDELIGHTS: Denney wrote: "I gave up active suburban surgical practice and my academic appointments to write full time because I am disillusioned about the quality and the ethics of modern medical practice. I intend to improve medical care in the United States by writing candidly and forcefully so that average persons can learn all they need to know in order to make their own decisions about their medical care. I believe the medical profession belongs to people, not to doctors."

* * *

DENNIS, James M(unn) 1932-

PERSONAL: Born May 21, 1932, in New Philadelphia, Ohio; married, 1955; children: two. *Education:* Ohio State University, B.A., 1954, M.A., 1957; University of Wisconsin (now University of Wisconsin—Madison), Ph.D., 1963. *Office:* Department of Art History, Elvehjem Art Center, University of Wisconsin, Madison, Wis. 53706.

CAREER: University of Pittsburgh, Pittsburgh, Pa., instructor in art history, 1962; Kent State University, Kent, Ohio, instructor in art history, 1962-64; University of Wisconsin—Madison, 1964—, began as assistant professor, became associate professor of art history. *Member:* College Art Association. *Awards, honors:* Alexander von Humboldt fellow at Cent Institute of Art History, Munich, West Germany, 1968-69; distinguished service award from Society of Midland Authors, 1976.

WRITINGS: Karl Bitter: Architectural Sculptor, 1867-1915, University of Wisconsin Press, 1967; *Grant Wood: A Study in American Art and Culture,* Viking, 1975. Contributor to scholarly journals.

BIOGRAPHICAL/CRITICAL SOURCES: New York Times Book Review, December 7, 1975; *Best Sellers,* January, 1976.*

* * *

DER NERSESSIAN, Sirarpie 1896-

PERSONAL: Born September 5, 1896, in Constantinople, Turkey; came to the United States in 1930; daughter of Mihran and Akabie (Ormanian) Der Nersessian. *Education:* Sorbonne, University of Paris, lic. es lettres, 1920, dipl. d'etudes superieures, 1921, Dr. es lettres, 1936; Ecole des Hautes Etudes, diploma, 1926. *Home:* 3245 S St. N.W., Washington, D.C. 20007. *Office:* 1703 32nd St. N.W., Washington, D.C. 20007.

CAREER: Ecole des Hautes Etudes, Paris, France, in charge of temporary conference, 1926-29; Wellesley College, Wellesley, Mass., visiting lecturer, 1930-34, associate professor, 1934-37, Clara Bertram Kimball Professor of Art, chairman of department, and director of Farnsworth Museum, 1937-46; Harvard University, Cambridge, Mass., member of faculty in arts and sciences, 1946-67, professor emeritus, 1967—. Professor at Dumbarton Oaks; visiting lecturer at New York University, 1931 and 1936, and Ecole Libre des Hautes Etudes, 1942.

MEMBER: Mediaeval Academy of America (fellow), Archaeological Institute of America, College Art Association, Societe National des Antiquaires de France, Society of By-

zantine Studies (Greece). *Awards, honors:* Litt.D. from Wilson College, 1948; L.H.D. from Smith College, 1957; Prix Fould from Institut de France and Academie des Inscriptions et Belles Lettres; prize from Association des Etudes Grecques.

WRITINGS: Armenia and the Byzantine Empire: A Brief Study of Armenian Art and Civilization, Harvard University Press, 1945; (author of introduction) Alfred Chester Beatty, *A Catalogue of the Armenian Manuscripts,* two volumes, Hodges Figgis & Co., 1958; *Etudes byzantines et armeniennes: Byzantine and Armenian Studies* (in English and French), two volumes, Impr. Orientaliste, 1973; *Armenian Manuscripts in the Walters Art Gallery,* Walters Art Gallery, 1973; *Aght'amar* (in English and Italian), Ares, 1974; *L'Art armenien,* translation by Sheila Bourne and Angela O'Shea published as *Armenian Art,* Thames & Hudson, 1979. Also author of *The Armenians,* Praeger.

Other writings: *L'Illustration du roman de Barlaam et Joasaph: D'Apres les cliches de la Frick Art Reference Library et de la Mission Gabriel Millet au Mont-Athos,* E. de Boccard, 1936; *Manuscrits armeniens illustres des douzieme, treizieme, et quatorzieme siecles de la Bibliotheque des peres Mekhitharistes de Venise, d'apres les photographies de la Frick Art Reference Library,* E. de Boccard, 1936. Contributor to academic journals.

BIOGRAPHICAL/CRITICAL SOURCES: Best Sellers, March 1, 1970.*

* * *

de ST. JORRE, John 1936-

PERSONAL: Born in 1936. *Agent:* Deborah Rogers Ltd., 5-11 Mortimer St., London W1N 7RH, England.

CAREER: Associated with *Observer,* in England.

WRITINGS: Fernand Fleuret et ses amis, P. Bellee, 1958; *The Nigerian Civil War,* International Publications Service, 1972; *The Brothers' War: Biafra and Nigeria,* Houghton, 1972; (with Brian Shakespeare) *The Patriot Game,* Houghton, 1973; *A House Divided: South Africa's Uncertain Future,* Carnegie Endowment for International Peace, 1977.*

* * *

DeSALVO, Louise A(nita) 1942-

PERSONAL: Born September 27, 1942, in Jersey City, N.J.; daughter of Louis B. (a machinist) and Mildred (Calabrese) Sciacchetano; married Ernest J. DeSalvo (a physician), December 21, 1963; children: Jason, Justin. *Education:* Rutgers University, B.A., 1963; New York University, M.A., 1972, Ph.D., 1977. *Home:* 1045 Oakland Court, Teaneck, N.J. 07666. *Office:* Department of Education, Fairleigh Dickinson University, Teaneck, N.J. 07666.

CAREER: High school English teacher in Wood-Ridge, N.J., 1963-67; Fairleigh Dickinson University, Teaneck, N.J., coordinator of English education, 1977—. *Member:* Modern Language Association of America, National Council of Teachers of English, Assembly on Literature for Adolescents, Bronte Society, Virginia Woolf Society, Women's Ink, Northeast Victorian Studies Association. *Awards, honors:* National Endowment for the Humanities grant, 1980; seal from Committee on Scholarly Editions from Modern Language Association of America, 1980, for *Melymbrosia;* distinguished achievement award from Educational Press Association of America, 1980, for "Writers at Work."

WRITINGS: Virginia Woolf's First Voyage: A Novel in the

Making, Rowman & Littlefield, 1980; (contributor) Jane Marcus, editor, *Criticism on Virginia Woolf,* Macmillan, 1980; *Melymbrosia: Early Version of The Voyage Out,* New York Public Library, 1980. Contributor to literature journals. Contributing editor of *Media and Methods.*

WORK IN PROGRESS: Collecting essays by feminists about their research on the lives of women, with Sara Ruddick, publication expected in 1981; research on the literary friendship between Virginia Woolf and Vita Sackville-West and on literary explorations of the relationship between mothers and sons.

SIDELIGHTS: Louise DeSalvo wrote: "Reconstructing the earlier version of Virginia Woolf's first novel was extremely exciting. Knowing that I would be making an earlier version of a novel available that no one but Virginia Woolf herself might have seen carried me through the years that the work was in progress.

"Virginia Woolf is an endlessly fascinating subject for research. I have been working on Woolf for close to ten years and believe that I have just begun to scratch the surface. There is now an enormous amount of interest in the reasons why Woolf developed the views she did. Researchers such as Jane Marcus are looking at the earlier political views of her family members—people like Sir James Fitzjames Stephen, who was one of the great codifiers of English law.

"We are beginning to look at the intellectual climate in which Woolf moved and we are learning that she did not develop her feminist views, her pacifist views, in a vacuum, but, instead, in response to views held by members of her very own family. Unlike many of us, she was not protesting the way *society* thought about issues such as women's rights, she was revising views held by her very own forebears.

"I have spent some time reconstructing Woolf's life at sixteen and I was amazed to learn that in that year Woolf read no less than fifty weighty volumes and even at that early age she was concerned with matters of English history. I am beginning to think that Woolf was primarily a historian of English manners and morals who happened to write fiction. When I began my research, I had believed that she was simply a storyteller. And I believe that the direction that I have taken is the direction that many contemporary critics of Woolf are now taking—we are now interested in seeing how this woman connected with the most important issues of her time; we no longer see her as a dreamer spinning self-indulgent fictions.'

*   *   *

DEUTSCH, Marilyn Weisberg   1950-

PERSONAL: Born May 26, 1950, in Philadelphia, Pa.; daughter of George J. (in sales) and Celia Feldman (a bookkeeper; maiden name, Braverman) Weisberg; married Henri Deutsch (a psychologist), May 23, 1971; children: Jonathan. *Education:* Temple University, B.A., 1971; Ohio State University, M.A., 1975, Ph.D., 1978. *Politics:* Democrat. *Religion:* Jewish. *Home:* 6181 Middlebury Dr. E., Worthington, Ohio 43085. *Office:* Franklin County Program for Mental Retardation, 2572 Cleveland Ave., Columbus, Ohio 43214.

CAREER: Columbus Children's Psychiatric Hospital, Columbus, Ohio, milieu therapist, 1971-73; Ohio State University, Columbus, developmental disabilities psychologist at Nisonger Center, 1973-80; Franklin County Program for Mental Retardation, Columbus, chief of psychology, 1980—. *Member:* International Neuropsychology Society, American Association on Mental Deficiency, American Psychological Association, Professional Association on Retardation, Ohio Psychological Association.

WRITINGS: (Editor with Henry Leland) *Abnormal Psychology: A Guide to Information Sources,* Gale, 1980. Contributor to *Forum* and *Mental Retardation.*

WORK IN PROGRESS: Play Diagnosis: A Process of Assessing the Psychological Functioning of Emotionally Disturbed/Mentally Retarded Children.

SIDELIGHTS: Marilyn Deutsch wrote: "My major area of research is the development of the psychological assessment process designed for children with severe disabilities (mental retardation, emotional disorders, and brain damage). This assessment device is particularly exciting to me because it combines, by observing a child's play, areas which are not normally combined—normal development, abnormal development, behavior, and neuropsychology. It will also be used (hopefully) as a regular supplement to traditional I.Q. tests."

*   *   *

De VET, Charles V(incent)   1911-

PERSONAL: Born October 28, 1911, in Fayette, Mich.; son of John (a steamboat engineer) and Lucille (Feastre) De Vet; married Elenore Derwin, November 10, 1935; children: Annette, Charles F. *Education:* Ferris State College, B.S., 1938; attended University of Michigan, 1938-40. *Agent:* Robert P. Mills Ltd., 156 East 52nd St., New York, N.Y. 10022.

CAREER: Teacher at schools in Brampton, Mich., 1934-38, Ida, Mich., 1938-39, and Manistee, Mich., 1939-40; U.S. Postal Service, transport worker, 1940-68; writer, 1968—. *Member:* Science Fiction Writers of America.

WRITINGS: (With Katherine MacLean) *Cosmic Checkmate* (science-fiction novel), Ace Books, 1962; *Special Feature,* Avon, 1975. Contributor to science-fiction magazines, including *Amazing Stories.**

*   *   *

De VOS, Karen Helder   1939-

PERSONAL: Born September 2, 1939, in Lansing, Mich.; daughter of Harry and Mildred (Boeve) Helder; married Peter De Vos (a college dean), June 3, 1960; children: Michelle Mildred, Peter Scott. *Education:* Calvin College, B.A., 1960; Brown University, M.A.T., 1963. *Religion:* Protestant. *Home:* 1011 Worden S.E., Grand Rapids, Mich. 49507. *Office:* Christian Reformed World Relief Committee, 2850 Kalamazoo, Grand Rapids, Mich. 49560.

CAREER: Barrington College, Barrington, R.I., instructor in English, 1964-65; Calvin College, Grand Rapids, Mich., instructor in English, 1965-73; Christian Reformed World Relief Committee, Grand Rapids, director of communications, 1975—. Board member of Association for Public Justice.

WRITINGS: A Woman's Worth and Work, Baker Book, 1976. Author of a film column in *Eternity.* Editor of *Reformed Journal.*

*   *   *

DEWHIRST, Ian   1936-

PERSONAL: Born October 17, 1936, in Keighley, England; son of Harold (a news agent) and Mary F. (a shorthand typist; maiden name, Slater) Dewhirst. *Education:* Victoria University of Manchester, B.A. (with honors), 1958. *Poli-*

tics: "Used to be fairly neutral, but have gradually moved to the right." *Religion:* "Lapsed Congregationalist." *Home:* 14 Raglan Ave., Fell Lane, Keighley, West Yorkshire BD22 6BJ, England. *Office:* Keighley Public Library, North St., Keighley, West Yorkshire BD21 3SX, England.

CAREER: Keighley Public Library, Keighley, England, library assistant, 1960-65, lending librarian, 1965-57, reference librarian, 1967—. *Military service:* British Army, Royal Army Educational Corps., 1958-60; became sergeant. *Member:* Library Association (associate), Bronte Society, Yorkshire Dialect Society, Pennine Poets, Keighley Civic Society (vice-chairman, 1977—).

WRITINGS: The Handloom Weaver and Other Poems, Ridings Publishing, 1965; (editor) *Old Keighley in Photographs,* Hendon Publishing, 1972; *Gleanings From Victorian Yorkshire,* Ridings Publishing, 1972; (editor) *More Old Keighley in Photographs,* Hendon Publishing, 1973; *A History of Keighley,* Keighley Corp., 1974; *Gleanings From Edwardian Yorkshire,* Ridings Publishing, 1975; *Yorkshire Through the Years,* Batsford, 1975; *The Story of a Nobody: A Working-Class Life, 1890-1939,* Mills & Boon, 1980. Contributor to magazines, including *Yorkshire Ridings, Dalesman,* and *Yorkshire Life.* Member of editorial board of *Orbis,* 1970-75.

WORK IN PROGRESS: Research on an unsolved poisoning case in a workhouse in 1857.

SIDELIGHTS: Dewhirst wrote: "As a reference librarian working with archive material, and having lived most of my life in the locality where my forebears and I were born, I have become deeply aware both of the atmosphere and the ephemeral detail of past generations. It seems to me that the close study of one's local history, wherever one may be, holds the key to human nature and experience. To build up, through a scattered and accidental hotchpotch of letters, jottings, minute-books, clippings, old photographs, and ephemera, a sense of the lives of forgotten people can be moving indeed."

*   *   *

DIAMOND, Solomon   1906-

PERSONAL: Born September 18, 1906, in New York, N.Y.; married, 1938; children: one. *Education:* New York University, B.S., 1927; Columbia University, M.A., 1928, Ph.D., 1936. *Home:* 800 North Kenter Ave., Los Angeles, Calif. 90049.

CAREER: California State University, Los Angeles, 1949-71, began as assistant professor, became professor of psychology, professor emeritus, 1971—. *Member:* International Society of History of the Behavioral and Social Sciences, American Association for the Advancement of Science, American Psychological Association, Society for the Psychological Study of Social Issues.

WRITINGS: Personality and Temperament, Harper, 1957; *Information and Error: An Introduction to Statistical Analysis,* Basic Books, 1959; (with Richard S. Balvin and Florence Rand Diamond) *Inhibition and Choice: A Neurobehavioral Approach to Problems of Plasticity in Behavior* (edited by Gardner Murphy), Harper, 1963; *The World of Probability: Statistics in Science,* Basic Books, 1964; *Roots of Psychology: Psychology Recollected,* Basic Books, 1973; (editor) *The Roots of Psychology: A Sourcebook in the History of Ideas,* Basic Books, 1974. Contributor of more than twenty articles to journals in the behavioral sciences.*

DIAMOND, Stanley   1922-

PERSONAL: Born January 4, 1922, in New York, N.Y.; married, 1945; children: two. *Education:* Columbia University, Ph.D., 1951. *Office:* Graduate Faculty of Political and Social Science, New School for Social Research, 66 West 12th St., New York, N.Y. 10011.

CAREER: University of California, Los Angeles, visiting assistant professor of anthropology, 1953-54; Brandeis University, Waltham, Mass., assistant professor of anthropology, 1956-58; research associate in Nigeria, 1958-59; Brandeis University, assistant professor of anthropology, 1959-60; National Institute of Mental Health, Maryland, research anthropologist, 1960-67; New School for Social Research, New York, N.Y., research anthropologist, 1967-71, professor of anthropology, 1971—. Lecturer at Brooklyn College (now of the City University of New York), summer, 1950; assistant professor at Columbia University, 1954; consultant to Mayer & Whittlesey. *Wartime service:* American Field Service, 1942-43.

MEMBER: American Association for the Advancement of Science (fellow), American Anthropological Association (fellow), American Ethnological Society. *Awards, honors:* Social Science Research Council fellow in Israel, 1951-53; grants from Committee for the Study of Mental Illness and Health, 1956-57, Ford Foundation, 1958-59, and Bollingen Foundation, 1959-60.

WRITINGS: (Editor) *Culture in History: Essays in Honor of Paul Radin,* Columbia University Press, 1960, reprinted, Octagon, 1980, also reprinted as *Primitive Views of the World: A Critique of Civilization,* Columbia University Press, 1964; (editor with Fred G. Burke) *The Transformation of East Africa: Studies in Political Anthropology,* Basic Books, 1966; (with Simon Obi Anekwe and Obafemi Awolowo) *Nigeria: Model of a Colonial Failure,* American Committee on Africa, 1967; (editor with Murray L. Wax and Fred O. Gearing) *Anthropological Perspectives on Education,* Basic Books, 1971; (editor) *Toward a Marxist Anthropology: Problems and Perspectives,* Mouton, 1979.

BIOGRAPHICAL/CRITICAL SOURCES: American Anthropologist, September, 1975.*

*   *   *

DICKINSON, Peter A(llen)   1926-

PERSONAL: Born August 23, 1926, in Detroit, Mich.; son of Julian (an attorney) and Ruth (a museum curator; maiden name, Wilkinson) Dickinson; married Brigitte Wallerstein (a librarian), November 16, 1958; children: Ralph Henry. *Education:* Wayne State University, B.A., 1949. *Home and office:* 47 Chestnut Ave., Larchmont, N.Y. 10538. *Agent:* Pat Loud, 175 East 79th St., New York, N.Y. 10021.

CAREER: Pacific Factory, San Francisco, Calif., editor, 1952-54; *Western Industry,* San Francisco, editor, 1954-60; *Harvest Years* (now *Fifty Plus*), New York, N.Y., editor-in-chief, 1960-73; *Retirement Letter,* Washington, D.C., editor, 1973—. *Military service:* U.S. Army, Infantry, 1944-46; served in Okinawa and Japan. *Member:* American Society of Journalists and Authors, Gerontological Society. *Awards, honors:* Awards from National Press Club for excellence in consumer reporting, 1975 and 1976.

WRITINGS: The Fires of Autumn, Drake, 1974; *The Complete Retirement Planning Book,* Elsevier-Dutton, 1976; *Getting Your Share,* Publications International, 1977, 5th edition, in press; *Sunbelt Retirement,* Elsevier-Dutton, 1978, revised edition, 1980; *Retirement Edens,* Elsevier-Dutton,

1981; *Retirement Edens Abroad*, Elsevier-Dutton, 1982. Contributor to magazines and newspapers.

WORK IN PROGRESS: How to Make Money During Inflation/Recession, publication expected in 1980; *Investments for Singles*, publication expected in 1981; *Retirement Planning Guide*, publication expected in 1981.

SIDELIGHTS: Dickinson wrote: "I specialize mainly in the retirement field, with emphasis on finance, location, health, and leisure, and travel extensively to do field work. I edit a financial newsletter with a circulation of some twenty thousand relatively affluent older people, conduct seminars on retirement planning and related subjects, and contribute articles to magazines and newspapers. Also, I am teaching a graduate course on retirement planning at the College of New Rochelle and I am frequently a guest speaker at seminars, conferences, and programs on all aspects of retirement planning and living. This is a growing market, and I'm growing along with it."

*   *   *

DICK-LAUDER, George (Andrew)   1917-
(George Lauder)

PERSONAL: Born November 17, 1917, in Poona, India; son of Sir John North Dalrymple (an army officer) and Phyllis Mary (Iggulden) Dick-Lauder; married Hester Marguerite Sorel-Cameron, 1945; children: Piers Robert, Georgina Jane, Mark Andrew, Selina Rose. *Education:* Attended Royal Military College, Sandhurst. *Home:* 6-A Succoth Gardens, Edinburgh EH12 6BS, Scotland. *Agent:* John Farquharson Ltd., Bell House, 8 Bell Yard, London WC2A 2JU, England.

CAREER: British Army, career officer with Black Watch, 1937-60, served with Commandos, 1939-45, prisoner of war on Crete, served in Palestine, Somaliland, and Sudan, served with 52nd Commandos in the Middle East, retiring as major; writer, 1960—. Chancellor of Commandery of Lochore, 1974. *Member:* Puffins Club. *Awards, honors:* Knight of Grace of Military and Hospitaller Order of St. Lazarus of Jerusalem, 1977.

WRITINGS: (Under name George Lauder) *Let Soldiers Lust* (novel), P. Davies, 1963; *Our Man for Ganymede* (science-fiction novel), Dobson, 1969; *Skull and Two Crystals* (science-fiction novel), Dobson, 1972. Contributor of stories to magazines, including *Blackwood's Magazine*.*

*   *   *

DICKS, Henry V(ictor)   1900-

PERSONAL—Home: 26 Frognal Lane, London NW3 7DT, England.

CAREER: Tavistock Clinic, London, England, consultant psychiatrist, 1928-45, assistant medical director, 1934-45; University of Leeds, Leeds, England, Nuffield Professor of Psychiatry, 1946-48; Tavistock Clinic, consultant psychiatrist, 1948—, training secretary, 1948-65. Senior research officer at Columbus Centre, University of Sussex, 1966-70. *Military service:* British Army, Medical Corps, psychiatric adviser to Psychological Warfare Division of Supreme Headquarters, Allied Expeditionary Force, 1942-45; became lieutenant colonel.

WRITINGS: Clinical Studies in Psychopathology: A Contribution to the Aetiology of Neurotic Illness, Edward Arnold, 1939, 2nd edition, 1947; (contributor) John Rawlings Rees, editor, *The Case of Rudolf Hess: A Problem in Diagnosis and Forensic Psychiatry*, Norton, 1948; *Marital Tensions:*

Clinical Studies Towards a Psychological Theory of Interaction, Basic Books, 1967; *Fifty Years of the Tavistock Clinic*, Sage Publications, 1970; *Licensed Mass Murder: A Social-Psychological Study of Some S.S. Killers*, Heinemann, 1972, Basic Books, 1973.

BIOGRAPHICAL/CRITICAL SOURCES: Times Literary Supplement, March 21, 1968.*

*   *   *

DIECKMANN, Ed(ward Adolph), Jr.   1920-

PERSONAL: Surname is pronounced Deekman; born February 20, 1920, in San Diego, Calif.; son of Edward Adolph (a police detective and crime writer) and Martha Susan (Agnew) Dieckmann; married Charlotte L. Peltcher (a tax technician), March, 1943; children: Christopher M. *Education:* San Diego State College (now University), degree in English (with distinction), 1960. *Religion:* Unitarian. *Home and office:* 3120 East Third St., Long Beach, Calif. 90814. *Agent:* Howard Moorepark, 444 East 82nd St., New York, N.Y. 10028.

CAREER: San Diego Police Department, San Diego, Calif., patrolman, 1945-54, deputy marshal, 1954-56; State of California, Huntington Park, parole agent in charge of Downey Parole and Probation Employment Project, 1962-68; writer and public speaker, 1969—. *Military service:* U.S. Army, paratrooper, 1939-45; served in Pacific theater. *Member:* Mystery Writers of America (honorary member), Gamma Psi. *Awards, honors:* Shared award from *Argosy*, 1943, for essay, "What Kind of America Do I Want to Come Back To?"

WRITINGS: Volcano Mondo, Pinnacle Books, 1977; *The Secret of Jonestown: The Reason Why*, Historical Review Press, 1981. Contributor to history journals and popular magazines, including *Esquire, True, Coronet, American History Illustrated*, and *Civil War Times*. Contributing editor of *American Mercury*.

WORK IN PROGRESS: Research for a novel on Bacon's Rebellion of 1676.

SIDELIGHTS: Dieckmann wrote: "My interest has always been in little-known characters and/or incidents of historical fact, fictionalized to bring them to life. The fiction is not, however, in what *happened*, but of necessity in the recreation of dialogue, sometimes conjecture from available evidence, as to what really occurred and why. This is especially evident in the book on Jonestown and the People's Temple, where it is overwhelmingly demonstrated that the incorrect use of so-called 'sensitivity (human relations) training' was the cause and the tool, the very instrument of death.

"*Volcano Mondo* is the recreation of the 1902 eruption of the volcano Mont Pelee onto the city of St. Pierre on the island of Martinique. The book shows that it was the pressure of politics and ruthless men that kept forty thousand people in the city to die, even though it was obvious the volcano would erupt. Both political parties and the chief newspaper conspired to keep them there to vote!

"The book also shows the presence of nuclear energy, to an undetermined extent, in the eruption itself. Many of the same symptoms and damage were created by the recent eruption of Mount St. Helens in Washington and uncanny similarities were observed with the death-blasts at Hiroshima and Nagasaki and the eruptions of Mont Pelee and Mount St. Helens."

DILKE, Caroline (Sophia)   1940-

PERSONAL: Born May 28, 1940, in London, England; daughter of Christopher Wentworth (a novelist) and Alice Mary (a story editor; maiden name, Best) Dilke; married Timothy Dilke (a physician), September 4, 1965; children: Felix Wentworth, Rosemary Frances. *Education:* Open University, B.A., 1977. *Home:* 15 Wemyss Rd., London SE3 0TG, England. *Agent:* A. M. Heath & Co. Ltd., 40-42 William IV St., London WC2N 4DD, England.

CAREER: Science teacher at secondary school in London, England, 1978-80. *Member:* Asssociation for Science Education.

WRITINGS: The Sly Servant (novel), Chatto & Windus, 1975. Contributor of stories to *Woman's Journal* and *Woman's Realm.*

WORK IN PROGRESS: A story about an incestuous relationship.

SIDELIGHTS: Caroline Dilke wrote: "Some day I may write another novel, but in the meantime the only writing anyone sees are long, provocative, and sometimes mischievous personal letters to friends."

*   *   *

DILLON, George Lewis   1944-

PERSONAL: Born September 26, 1944, in Pittsburgh, Pa.; children: two. *Education:* Yale University, B.A., 1965; University of California, Berkeley, M.A., 1966, Ph.D., 1969. *Office:* Department of English and Linguistics, Indiana University, 2101 Coliseum Blvd. E., Fort Wayne, Ind. 46805.

CAREER: Southern Methodist University, Dallas, Tex., assistant professor of English, 1969-71; Indiana University, Fort Wayne, assistant professor, 1971-77, associate professor of English and linguistics, 1977—. *Member:* Modern Language Association of America, Linguistic Society of America.

WRITINGS: (Translator) *Three Plays: Phaedra, Andromache, Britannicus,* University of Chicago Press, 1961; *Introduction to Contemporary Linguistic Semantics,* Prentice-Hall, 1977; *Language Processing and the Reading of Literature: Toward a Model of Comprehension,* Indiana University Press, 1978. Contributor to language and linguistic journals.*

*   *   *

DIMOCK, Edward Cameron, Jr.   1929-

PERSONAL: Born March 18, 1929, in Boston, Mass.; son of Edward Cameron Dimock; married, 1952; children: five. *Education:* Yale University, B.A., 1950; Harvard University, S.T.B., 1953, S.T.M., 1954, Ph.D., 1959. *Office:* Department of Southeast Asian Languages, University of Chicago, Chicago, Ill. 60637.

CAREER: University of Chicago, Chicago, Ill., assistant professor, 1959-61, associate professor, 1961-66, professor of Bengali, 1966—, director of South Asian Language and Area Center, 1972—. *Member:* American Institute for Indian Studies, American Oriental Society, Association for Asian Studies. *Awards, honors:* Specialist grant from U.S. State Department, 1961; senior fellow of American Institute for Indian Study, Calcutta, India, 1963-64; fellow of U.S. Office of Education, 1965.

WRITINGS: (Editor and translator) *Thief of Love: Bengali Tales From Court and Village,* University of Chicago Press, 1963; (with Somdev Bhattacharji and Suhas Chatterjee) *An Introduction to Bengali,* Part I, East-West Center Press, 1965, reprinted as *An Introduction to Bengali: A Basic Course in Spoken Bengali, With Emphasis Upon Speaking and Understanding the Language,* Manohar Book Service, 1976; (editor and translator) Gangarama, *The Maharashtra Purana,* East-West Center Press, 1965; *The Place of the Hidden Moon: Erotic Mysticism in the Vaisnava-Sahajiya Cult of Bengal,* University of Chicago Press, 1966; (translator, with Denise Levertov, and editor) *In Praise of Krishna: Songs From the Bengali,* Doubleday, 1967; (editor) *Bengal: Literature and History,* Asian Studies Center, Michigan State University, 1967; (contributor) David Kopf, editor, *Bengal Regional Identity,* Asian Studies Center, Michigan State University, 1969; (with others) *The Literatures of India: An Introduction,* University of Chicago Press, 1975. Contributor to Asian studies journals.

BIOGRAPHICAL/CRITICAL SOURCES: Poetry, March, 1968.*

*   *   *

Di SCALA, Spencer M(ichael)   1941-

PERSONAL: Born April 15, 1941, in New York, N.Y.; son of Antonio and Nancy (DiCostanzo) Di Scala. *Education:* Queens College of the City University of New York, B.A., 1962; Columbia University, M.A., 1963, Ph.D., 1969. *Residence:* Boston, Mass. *Office:* Department of History, University of Massachusetts, Boston, Mass. 02125.

CAREER: University of Kentucky, Lexington, instructor, 1967-69, assistant professor of history, 1969-70; University of Massachusetts, Boston, assistant professor, 1970-75, associate professor of history, 1975—. Member of Italian committee of Festival Bostonian; lecturer to Italian-American cultural societies. *Member:* Society for Italian Historical Studies, Columbia University Seminar on Modern Italy. *Awards, honors:* Fulbright grants for Italy, 1965-67; Kentucky Research Foundation grant, summer, 1969; University of Massachusetts Faculty Growth grant, summer, 1972.

WRITINGS: Dilemmas of Italian Socialism, University of Massachusetts Press, 1980. Contributor to *Historical Dictionary of Italian Fascism.* Contributor to history journals.

Editor of *Italian Quarterly,* 1974-78, associate editor, 1978—.

WORK IN PROGRESS: Terrorism in Italy: From Fascism to the Present, publication expected in 1984.

SIDELIGHTS: Di Scala told *CA:* "I was always struck by the similarity between contemporary Italian politics on the left and during the Giolitton period. It is time the Left either stopped arguing or at least think up new problems."

*   *   *

DIXON, Christa Klingbeil   1935-

PERSONAL: Born December 8, 1935, in Essen, Germany (now West Germany); married, 1962; children: two. *Education:* University of Heidelberg, Staatsexamen I, 1959; attended Pittsburgh Theological Seminary, 1959-60; University of Bonn, Staatsexamen II, 1962, Ph.D., 1965. *Home:* 202 West Orlando, Normal, Ill. 61761.

CAREER: La Salle College, Philadelphia, Pa., assistant professor of German language, literature, and philosophy, 1969-74; Illinois State University, Normal, associate professor of German, 1978—. Adjunct associate professor at Western Illinois University, 1976-77. *Member:* Modern Language Association of America, American Association of Teachers of

German, American Association of University Professors. *Awards, honors:* Scholarships for the United States from World Council of Churches and Fulbright Foundation, 1959-60; grant from Illinois Humanities Council, 1975-76.

WRITINGS: Negro Spirituals: From Bible to Folk Song, Fortress, 1976.

In German: *Wesen und Wandel geistlicher Volkslieder: Negro Spirituals,* Wuppertal Jugenddienst-Verlag, 1967; *Peter Handke: Die Angst des Tormanns beim Elfmeter: Ein Beitrag zur Interpretation,* Sprachkunst, 1972. Contributor to scholarly journals.*

*   *   *

DOBBS, Kildare (Robert Eric) 1923-

PERSONAL: Born October 10, 1923, in Meerut, India; son of William Evelyn Joseph (a colonial civil servant) and Maud Clifford (Bernard) Dobbs; married Patricia Marjorie Agnes Parsons, 1944 (divorced September, 1955); married Mary McAlpine, March 1, 1958 (divorced December, 1973); children: (first marriage) Kildare John Evelyn, Christian Tracey Allan; (second marriage) Lucinda McAlpine, Sarah McAlpine. *Education:* Jesus College, Cambridge, B.A., 1947, M.A., 1952; Institute of Education, London, diploma, 1948. *Politics:* Liberal. *Home:* 28 Bracken Ave., Toronto, Ontario, Canada.

CAREER: British Colonial Service (now Overseas Civil Service), London, England, education officer in Moshi, Tanganyika, 1948-50, district officer in Iringa, Tanganyika, 1950-52; high school teacher in Florence, Ontario, 1952-53; Macmillan Co. of Canada Ltd., Toronto, Ontario, editor of trade books, 1953-61; *Saturday Night,* Toronto, associate editor, 1961-62; *Star Weekly,* Toronto, staff writer, 1962-65; *Saturday Night,* managing editor, 1965-67, associate editor, 1965-71; *Toronto Star,* Toronto, books editor, 1971-74; free-lance writer, 1974—. Member of Canada Council advisory arts panel, 1965-67, and literary awards jury, 1971; member of Governor General's Literary Awards Jury, 1972; consultant to Canadian Privy Council and Secretary of State. *Military service:* Royal Naval Volunteer Reserve, active duty, 1942-46; became sub-lieutenant. *Member:* Bookmen's Club. *Awards, honors:* Governor General's Award, 1963, for *Running to Paradise;* Canada Council senior arts fellow, 1964, 1968, and 1970; Centennial Medal, 1970.

WRITINGS: Running to Paradise (autobiographical sketches), Oxford University Press, 1962; *Canada* (travel book; illustrated by Peter Varley) Macmillan, 1964, revised edition, 1969; (contributor) *Ontario/66,* Ontario Department of Economics and Development, 1965; *Reading the Time* (literary essays), Macmillan, 1968; *The Great Fur Opera: Annals of the Hudson's Bay Company, 1670-1970* (humor; illustrated by Ronald Searle), McClelland & Stewart, 1970; (author of captions with Charles P. Stacey) Ken Bell, *Not in Vain* (photographs), University of Toronto Press, 1973.

Work represented in anthologies, including *The Oxford Book of Canadian Verse,* Oxford University Press. Author of a column in *Toronto Star,* 1968—. Co-founder of *Tamarack Review,* 1956; member of editorial board of *Canadian Forum.*

AVOCATIONAL INTERESTS: Music, walking.

BIOGRAPHICAL/CRITICAL SOURCES: Canadian Forum, May, 1968; *Saturday Night,* May, 1968.*

*   *   *

DOBINSON, Charles Henry 1903-1980

OBITUARY NOTICE: Born October 7, 1903; died December 26, 1980. Educator and writer. Dobinson was professor of education at the University of Reading from 1951 to 1968. His contributions to the field of education include *Technical Education for Adolescents.* He also edited *Education in a Changing World* and wrote the monograph *Rousseau.* Obituaries and other sources: *Who's Who,* 131st edition, St. Martin's, 1979; *London Times,* January 6, 1980.

*   *   *

DOBSON, Richard Barrie 1931-

PERSONAL: Born November 3, 1931, in Stockton on Tees, England; son of Richard Henry (a railway director) and Mary Victoria (Kidd) Dobson; married Narda Leon (a teacher), June 19, 1959; children: Mark, Michelle. *Education:* Wadham College, Oxford, M.A., 1954, D.Phil., 1961. *Home:* 121 Stockton Lane, York YO3 0JA, England. *Office:* Department of History, University of York, Heslington, Yorkshire YO1 5DD, England.

CAREER: University of St. Andrews, St. Andrews, Scotland, lecturer in medieval history, 1958-64; University of York, Heslington, England, lecturer, 1964-68, senior lecturer, 1968-71, reader, 1971-76, professor of history, 1976—. *Military service:* British Army, 1950-51; served in Malaya. *Member:* Society of Antiquaries (fellow), Royal Historical Society (fellow).

WRITINGS: Durham Priory, 1400-1450, Cambridge University Press, 1973; *The Jews of Medieval York and the Massacre of March, 1190,* University of York, 1974; (with John Taylor) *Rymes of Robyn Hood: An Introduction to the English Outlaw,* Heinemann, 1976; *York City Chamberlains' Accounts, 1396-1500,* Surtees Society, 1980.

WORK IN PROGRESS: Research on medieval English towns and cathedrals.

*   *   *

DODER, Dusko 1937-

PERSONAL: Born July 22, 1937, in Yugoslavia; son of Vaso and Maria (Giurhu) Doder; married Karin Weberg Rasmussen, March 6, 1964; children: Peter. *Education:* Washington University, St. Louis, Mo., B.A., 1962; attended Stanford University, 1962-63; Columbia University, M.S., 1964, M.A., 1965, certificate, 1966. *Home:* 2719 36th Place N.W., Washington, D.C. 20007. *Agent:* Julian Bach Literary Agency, Inc., 737 Third Ave., New York, N.Y. 10017. *Office: Washington Post,* Washington, D.C. 20071.

CAREER: Worked for Associated Press in New York and New Hampshire, 1964-68; United Press International, Moscow correspondent, 1968-70; currently with *Washington Post,* Washington, D.C., began as assistant foreign editor, 1971, became State Department correspondent, chief of East European Bureau, 1973-76, and Moscow correspondent, 1978. *Awards, honors:* Ford Foundation fellow; Woodrow Wilson fellow.

WRITINGS: The Yugoslavs, Random House, 1978.

WORK IN PROGRESS: A novel, completion expected in 1981.

BIOGRAPHICAL/CRITICAL SOURCES: New York Times Book Review, July 2, 1978.

*   *   *

DOEZEMA, Linda Pegman 1948-

PERSONAL: Surname is pronounced *Doo*-ze-ma; born May 25, 1948, in Hammond, Ind.; daughter of John Evert (a manager) and Florence (a secretary; maiden name, Clausing) Pegman; married William Reynold Doezema (a professor of history), August 8, 1970. *Education:* Calvin College, A.B., 1970; Kent State University, M.L.S., 1975, M.A., 1979. *Residence:* Houghton, N.Y. 14744. *Office:* Library, Houghton College, Houghton, N.Y. 14744.

CAREER: Junior high school teacher in Redlands, Calif., 1970-72; Kent State University, Kent, Ohio, library assistant, 1972-75, reference librarian, 1975-79; Houghton College, Houghton, N.Y., reference librarian, 1980—. *Member:* American Library Association, Beta Phi Mu.

WRITINGS: (Editor) *Dutch Americans: A Guide to Information Sources,* Gale, 1979.

SIDELIGHTS: Linda Doezema wrote: "As the 1970's experienced a surge of interest in ethnic studies, my interest was roused concerning my own ethnic background. Although a survey of the writings about Dutch Americans revealed a long-standing interest in this group, a comprehensive listing of publications appeared to be lacking. Thus, the object of my efforts was to provide a tool for researchers and others interested in Dutch Americans for locating information about Dutch immigrants and their communities and culture in the United States."

                              *   *   *

DOHERTY, Dennis J.   1932-

PERSONAL: Born November 22, 1932, in Indianapolis, Ind. *Education:* St. Meinrad Seminary, B.A., 1956; Pontifical University of St. Anselm, S.T.B., 1957; University of Wuerzburg, D.Th., 1966. *Office:* Department of Theology, Marquette University, Milwaukee, Wis. 53233.

CAREER: St. Meinrad Seminary, St. Meinrad, Ind., instructor in theology, 1964-67; Marquette University, Milwaukee, Wis., assistant professor, 1967-70, associate professor of theology, 1970—. *Member:* American Society of Christian Ethics, Catholic Theological Society of America, Institute of Society, Ethics, and Life Science.

WRITINGS: (With Charles Riker) *Marriage Instructions: A Guide for Priests,* Abbey Press, 1966; (translator) *Open to the World: Lay Spirituality for Today,* Gill & Son, 1966; *The Sexual Doctrine of Cardinal Cajetan,* Pustet, 1966; (contributor) *Absolutes in Moral Theology?,* Corpus Books, 1968; *Divorce and Remarriage: Resolving a Catholic Dilemma,* Abbey Press, 1974; (editor) *Dimensions of Human Sexuality: A Critical Response,* Doubleday, 1979. Contributor to theology journals.

BIOGRAPHICAL/CRITICAL SOURCES: America, January 19, 1980.*

                              *   *   *

DOLGOFF, Sam   1902-
(Sam Wiener)

PERSONAL: Born October 10, 1902, in Vitebsk, Russia (now U.S.S.R.); came to the United States in 1906, naturalized citizen, 1973; son of Max (a house painter) and Anna (Hanans) Dolgoff; married Esther Judith Miller, July 15, 1944; children: Abraham, Anatole. *Education:* Attended elementary school in New York City. *Home:* 208 East Broadway, New York, N.Y. 10002.

CAREER: Housepainter, 1922-65; writer, 1972—. *Member:* Industrial Workers of the World, Brotherhood of Painters and Allied Trades.

WRITINGS: (Editor and translator) *Bakunin on Anarchy,*

Knopf, 1972, 2nd edition, Black Rose Books, 1980; *The Anarchist Collective in Spain,* Free Life Editions, 1974; *The Cuban Revolution: A Critical Perspective,* Black Rose Books, 1976; *The American Labor Movement: A New Beginning,* Resurgence Press, 1980; *"Third World" Nationalism and the State,* Black Cat Press, 1980. Author of anarchist pamphlets, until 1970 under pseudonym Sam Wiener.

WORK IN PROGRESS: Memoirs; a survey of American labor history.

SIDELIGHTS: Dolgoff started his career as a hobo, working his way across the country on waterfronts, and at lumber camps, and factories. His earlier belief in socialism changed to a commitment to anarchism while he was still a teenager. He became a speaker for labor movements, lecturing all over the United States, from union halls to college campuses. His books have been translated into Spanish, Italian, Swedish, and German.

Dolgoff told *CA:* "I've been a manual worker all my life, not a professional writer, but I am contemplating my autobiography, stressing my relations with outstanding social revolutionaries here and abroad. At age seventy-eight, my future is *behind* me, but in the little time left to me perhaps I will leave at least a little fingerprint on the sands of time."

                              *   *   *

DOLLARD, John   1900(?)-1980

OBITUARY NOTICE: Born c. 1900; died October 8, 1980, in New Haven, Conn. Social psychologist, educator, and author of works in his field. Dollard is best known for his controversial analysis of black repression in *Caste and Class in a Southern Town.* His account of economic and social conditions in "Southerntown" was banned in Georgia after its publication in 1937. Dollard also co-wrote *Social Learning and Imitation, Personality and Psychotherapy,* and *Scorning Human Motives.* He was professor of psychology at Yale University for seventeen years before retiring in 1969. Obituaries and other sources: *New York Times,* October 11, 1980; *Newsweek,* October 20, 1980.

                              *   *   *

DOLSON, Hildegarde
See LOCKRIDGE, Hildegarde (Dolson)

                              *   *   *

DOMINGUEZ, Jorge Ignacio   1945-

PERSONAL: Born June 2, 1945, in Havana, Cuba; came to the United States in 1960, naturalized citizen, 1966; son of Jorge J. (a business executive) and Lilia (De La Carrera) Dominguez; married Mary Alice Kmietek (a teacher), 1967; children: Lara, Leslie. *Education:* Yale University, B.A., 1967; Harvard University, M.A., 1968, Ph.D., 1972. *Office:* Center for International Affairs, Harvard University, 1737 Cambridge St., Cambridge, Mass. 02138.

CAREER: Harvard University, Cambridge, Mass., assistant professor, 1972-77, associate professor, 1977-79, professor of political science, 1979—, member of Center for International Affairs, 1972—, and Latin American Scholarship Program of American Universities. Member of Council on Religion and International Affairs. *Member:* American Political Science Association, Council on Foreign Relations, Latin-American Studies Association (chairman of national convention program, 1977-79; president, 1980—), New England Council on Latin-American Studies (president), Pan American Society of New England (member of board of governors).

WRITINGS: Cuba: Order and Revolution, Harvard University Press, 1978; (with N. S. Rodley, B. Wood, and R. Falk) *Enhancing Global Human Rights,* McGraw, 1979; *Insurrection or Loyalty: The Breakdown of the Spanish-American Empire,* Harvard University Press, 1980. Contributor to *Handbook of Political Science.* Contributor to political science and law journals.

WORK IN PROGRESS: Co-writing *The Politics of U.S.–Latin American Economic Relations* and *The International Implications of Mexico's Internal Affairs.*

SIDELIGHTS: Dominguez told *CA:* "I like to vary my work from internal to international affairs and from historical to contemporary. My books and articles reflect this range."

* * *

DOMINGUEZ, Richard H(enry) 1941-

PERSONAL: Born September 13, 1941, in Chicago, Ill.; son of Samuel and Louise (McCorkle) Dominguez; married Judith Wickware; children: Jennifer, Heather, Sam, Matthew, Nathan, Benjamin, Megan. *Education:* Attended Houghton College, 1959-62; University of Chicago, M.D., 1966. *Residence:* Glen Ellyn, Ill. *Office:* Wheaton Orthopaedics Ltd., 501 Thornhill Dr., Carol Stream, Ill. 60187.

CAREER: University of Washington, Hospitals and Clinics, Seattle, surgical intern, 1966-67; University of Chicago, Hospitals and Clinics, Chicago, Ill., junior assistant resident, 1967-68, in private practice, 1968-70, resident in orthopedic surgery, 1970; Cook County Hospital, Chicago, senior resident in orthopedic surgery, 1971; Shriners' Hospital for Crippled Children, Chicago, resident surgeon, 1971; University of Chicago, Hospitals and Clinics, chief orthopedic resident, 1972; Wheaton Orthopaedics Ltd., Carol Stream, Ill., orthopedic surgeon, 1972—. Certified by American Board of Orthopaedic Surgery, 1973. Clinical instructor at Loyola University, Chicago. Chief of surgery at Central DuPage Hospital. Member of board of directors of B. R. Ryall Young Men's Christian Association. *Military service:* U.S. Air Force, orthopedic surgeon, 1970-72.

MEMBER: Federation Internationale de Natation Amateur, American Medical Association, American Academy of Orthopaedic Surgeons, American College of Surgeons, American College of Sports Medicine, Illinois State Medical Society, DuPage County Medical Society.

WRITINGS: (Contributor) Wendy Rieder and A. Paul Mouw, editors, *Swimming Medicine IV,* University Park Press, 1978; *The Complete Book of Sports Medicine,* Scribner, 1979. Contributor to medical journals.

WORK IN PROGRESS: A book on exercise and rehabilitation methods of sports injuries, for the lay person, athlete, coach, and physical therapist, publication expected in 1981.

SIDELIGHTS: Dominguez told *CA:* "I wrote *The Complete Book of Sports Medicine* as a guide for parents, coaches, and athletes themselves because there seemed to be very little basic advice available for the amateur sports participant of any age, or for coaches and parents of children involved in sports. I see a large number of athletic complaints and injuries in my mainly sports medicine orthopedic practice in the Chicago suburban area. On a personal level, my family is very involved in competitive swimming. This had convinced me of the need for such a book for some time, and finally I was able to set aside the necessary time to complete it.

"Several of my seven children are competitive swimmers, and my wife and I travel around the country whenever my practice will allow, to attend meets. I had the privilege in the summer of 1979 to serve as one of the team physicians for the Olympic Training Center in Colorado Springs, and was also team physician for the United States versus Great Britain meet in Nashville, Tenn., in August of 1979.

"I am very enthusiastic about my new manuscript. The successful rehabilitation of an athlete after any injury often determines whether he can return to a successful career (if he is a professional), further competition (if he is an amateur), or merely return to an enjoyable recreation (if he is a weekend enthusiast). There appears to be a great need for a book about exercise and sports injury rehabilitation among trainers, physical therapists, and athletes themselves.

"The value of sports participation for physical and emotional well-being cannot be overemphasized. However, especially in coaching young children, a commonsense approach is needed so that their participation will be a positive experience for them. Being pushed into a sport they dislike or really can't do well because of an over-zealous mother or because dad excelled in it at college can be a very painful experience for a child. It is this commonsense philosophy I ascribe to and wish to 'beat the drum' for in the contacts I make with people as an orthopedic surgeon and as an author."

* * *

DONAHUE, Kenneth 1915-

PERSONAL: Born January 31, 1915, in Louisville, Ky.; son of Samuel J. and Ida (Walton) Donahue; married Daisy Cain, August 13, 1940; children: L. Nicaea, Craig R. *Education:* University of Louisville, A.M., 1942, further graduate study, 1946-47. *Home:* 245 South Westgate, Los Angeles, Calif. 90049. *Office:* Los Angeles County Museum of Art, 5905 Wilshire Blvd., Los Angeles, Calif. 90036.

CAREER: University of Louisville, Louisville, Ky., art librarian, 1936-38; Museum of Modern Art, New York City, staff lecturer, 1938-43; Frick Collection, New York City, lecturer and curatorial assistant, 1949-53; John and Mabel Ringling Museum of Art, Sarasota, Fla., curator, 1953-57, director, 1957-64; Los Angeles County Museum of Art, Los Angeles, Calif., deputy director, 1964-66, director, 1966—. Member of art advisory panel of Internal Revenue Service, 1970-74. *Military service:* U.S. Army, 1943-45. *Member:* American Council of Museums (member of council, 1968-78; vice-president, 1969-72), Association of Art Museum Directors (vice-president, 1971-72), College Art Association (member of board of directors, 1966-70). *Awards, honors:* American Council of Learned Societies fellow in Rome, Italy, 1947-49.

WRITINGS: (Editor) Terisio Pignatti, *The Golden Century of Venetian Painting,* Braziller, 1979. Contributor to *Enciclopedia degli Italiani.* Contributor to art journals. Member of board of directors of *Gazette Beaux-Arts.**

* * *

DONNELLY, James S(tephen), Jr. 1943-

PERSONAL: Born January 19, 1943, in New York, N.Y.; son of James Stephen and Evelyn (Kunar) Donnelly; married Joan Murphy, September 5, 1964; children: Jennifer, Eileen, Elizabeth. *Education:* Fordham College (now University), A.B., 1964; Harvard University, M.A., 1965, Ph.D., 1971. *Politics:* Liberal Democrat. *Religion:* Roman Catholic. *Home:* 532 East St., Stoughton, Wis. 53589. *Office:* Department of History, University of Wisconsin, 3211 Humanities Building, 455 North Park St., Madison, Wis. 53706.

CAREER: University of Tennessee, Chattanooga, assistant professor of history, 1969-72; University of Wisconsin—Madison, assistant professor, 1972-75, associate professor, 1975-80, professor of history, 1980—. Member of executive committee of United Faculty, American Federation of Teachers. Member: American Historical Association, American Committee for Irish Studies, Conference on British Studies, Economic History Society, Past and Present Society, Irish Historical Society, Economic and Social History Society of Ireland, Phi Beta Kappa. Awards, honors: Herbert Baxter Adams Prize from American Historical Association, 1975, for The Land and the People of Nineteenth-Century Cork; Guggenheim fellowship, 1980-81.

WRITINGS: Landlord and Tenant in Nineteenth-Century Ireland, Gill & Macmillan, 1973; The Land and the People of Nineteenth-Century Cork: The Rural Economy and the Land Question, Routledge & Kegan Paul, 1975; Agrarian Violence and Secret Societies in Ireland, 1760-1845, Volume I, Oxford University Press, 1982. Contributor to Irish studies and history journals.

WORK IN PROGRESS: Volume II of Agrarian Violence and Secret Societies in Ireland, 1760-1845, publication by Oxford University Press expected in 1983.

*　　*　　*

DORIS, John Lawrence 1923-

PERSONAL: Born April 12, 1923, in New York, N.Y.; married, 1955; children: five. Education: City College (now of the City University of New York), B.Sc., 1951; Yale University, M.A., 1953, PhD., 1957. Office: Department of Human Development and Family Studies, Cornell University, Ithaca, N.Y. 14850.

CAREER: Yale University, New Haven, Conn., chief psychologist at Child Study Center, 1958-63; Cornell University, Ithaca, N.Y., associate professor, 1963-68, professor of child development and family relations, 1968—. Member: American Association for the Advancement of Science, American Psychological Association.

WRITINGS: (Contributor) Modern Perspectives in Child Development, International Universities Press, 1963; (editor with Seymour B. Sarason) Psychological Problems in Mental Deficiency, Harper, 4th edition, 1968; (with Sarason) Educational Handicap, Public Policy, and Social History: A Broadened Perspective on Mental Retardation, Free Press, 1979. Contributor to psychology and education journals.*

*　　*　　*

DORLAND, Michael 1948-

PERSONAL: Born March 16, 1948, in London, Ontario, Canada; son of Albert Arthur (an economist) and Janine (an educator; maiden name, Grumbach) Dorland; married Anna Antonopoulos (a writer), June 26, 1975; children: Christopher Alexander. Education: McGill University, B.A. (with honors), 1969, M.A., 1971. Politics: "On the left, like the heart." Religion: "Generally agnostic." Home and office: 4640 Hutchison, Montreal, Quebec, Canada H2V 4AZ. Agent: Susan P. Urstadt, Inc., 125 East 84th St., New York, N.Y. 10028.

CAREER: Writer. Awards, honors: Fellow of Government of Quebec, 1972-73; finalist for Books in Canada best first novel of the year award, 1978, for The Double-Cross Circuit.

WRITINGS: The Double-Cross Circuit (novel), Grosset, 1978; The Assassination of Leon Trotsky, Methuen, 1981. Contributor to newspapers.

SIDELIGHTS: Dorland told CA: "The only career of mine that I choose to give significance to is my writing. As for the rest, I went from university teaching of Asian and Russian history straight into the seventh circle of hackdom, tapping my way upward into the higher circles such as public relations or daily newspapers. But I've never considered this anything more than alimentary.

"Philosophers have hitherto only interpreted the world. The task of the novelist is to do the same thing in a manner that people can understand."

BIOGRAPHICAL/CRITICAL SOURCES: Weekend, autumn, 1978.

*　　*　　*

DORRIS, Michael Anthony 1945-

PERSONAL: Born January 30, 1945, in Dayton, Wash.; son of Jim and Mary Besy (Burkhardt) Dorris; children: Reynold Abel, Jeffrey Sava, Madeline Hannah. Education: Georgetown University, B.A., 1967; Yale University, M.Phil., 1970. Home address: R.F.D.2, Windsor, Vt. 05089. Office: Department of Native American Studies, Dartmouth College, Box 6152, Hanover, N.H. 03755.

CAREER: Franconia College, Franconia, N.H., assistant professor, 1971-72; Dartmouth College, Hanover, N.H., associate professor of native American studies and chairman of department, 1972—. Visiting assistant professor at University of New Hampshire, 1973-74; consultant to Public Broadcasting Service and National Endowment for the Humanities. Member: American Anthropological Association, National Congress of American Indians, Explorers Club, Phi Beta Kappa. Awards, honors: Woodrow Wilson fellow, 1967 and 1980; Guggenheim fellow, 1978.

WRITINGS: Native Americans: Five Hundred Years After, Crowell, 1975. Also author of Native Americans Today, Man in the Northeast, and A Sourcebook for Native American Studies. Contributor to professional journals.

WORK IN PROGRESS: A book on the Alaska Native Claims Settlement Act of 1971; comparing history of Maori-English and American Indian-English culture contact.

SIDELIGHTS: Dorris, a member of the Modoc Tribe, told CA: "I speak French and Tanaina, and am studying Maori. I came to cultural anthropology by way of an undergraduate program in English and classics and a master's degree in history of the theatre. I write poetry primarily for myself—to record feelings and people in the ways and at the times I knew them best."

*　　*　　*

DOTY, Robert McIntyre 1933-

PERSONAL: Born December 23, 1933, in Rochester, N.Y. Education: Harvard University, A.B.; University of Rochester, M.A. Office: Currier Gallery of Art, 192 Orange St., Manchester, N.H. 03104. Career: Writer. Worked as director of Akron Art Institute, Akron, Ohio; currently director of Currier Gallery of Art, Manchester, N.H. Arranges art and photographic exhibitions.

WRITINGS: Photo Secession: Photography as a Fine Art, George Eastman House, 1960, reprinted as Photo-Secession: Stieglitz and the Fine-Art Movement in Photography, Dover, 1978; (with Diane Waldman) Adolph Gottlieb, Praeger, 1968; Human Concern/Personal Torment: The Grotesque in American Art, Praeger, 1969; Contemporary Black Artists in America, Whitney Museum of American Art, 1971;

Lucas Samaras, Whitney Museum of American Art, 1972; *Extraordinary Realities,* Whitney Museum of American Art, 1973; (editor) *Photography in America,* Random House, 1974; *American Folk Art in Ohio Collections,* Dodd, 1976. Also editor with Melvin Watts of *Eagles, Urns, and Columns: Decorative Arts in the Federal Period,* Godine. Author of exhibition catalogs.*

*　　*　　*

DOUGLAS-HOME, Alec
　　See HOME, Alexander Frederick

*　　*　　*

DOUGLAS HOME, William
　　See HOME, William Douglas

*　　*　　*

DOWLING, Harry Filmore   1904-

PERSONAL: Born November 11, 1904, in Washington, D.C.; son of William Alexander and Mae (Krause) Dowling; married Edith Laine, June 27, 1931; children: Harry Filmore, William Laine, John Nelson. *Education:* Franklin and Marshall College, A.B., 1927; George Washington University, M.D., 1931. *Home:* 13801 York Rd., Apt. N-10, Cockeysville, Md. 21030.

CAREER: Baltimore City Hospital, Baltimore, Md., intern, 1931-32; Johns Hopkins University, Baltimore, research assistant in medicine, 1932-33; Harvard University, Cambridge, Mass., research fellow in medicine, 1933-34; George Washington University, Washington, D.C., clinical instructor, 1934-40, clinical professor of medicine, 1940-50, director of central laboratory at university hospital, 1934-41; University of Illinois at Chicago Circle, Chicago, professor of preventive medicine and head of department, 1950-51, professor of medicine and head of department, 1951-69, professor emeritus, 1969—; University of Delaware, Newark, special assistant to president, 1969-70; scholar-in-residence at National Library of Medicine, 1971—. Diplomate of American Board of Internal Medicine; research assistant at Thorndike Memorial Laboratory, Boston City Hospital, 1933-34; chief of George Washington Medical Division at Gallinger Municipal Hospital, 1940-50. Member of medical advisory board of U.S. Food and Drug Administration, 1965—.

MEMBER: American College of Physicians (master; fellow), American Society for Clinical Investigation, American Medical Association (chairman of Council on Drugs, 1963-65), National Institute of Allergy and Infectious Diseases (member of advisory council, 1960-63), American Federation for Clinical Research, Association of American Physicians, American Association for the History of Medicine, Central Society for Clinical Research, Chicago Medical Society, Chicago Society of Internal Medicine, Phi Beta Kappa, Sigma Xi, Alpha Omega Alpha. *Awards, honors:* Sc.D. from Franklin and Marshall College, 1953.

WRITINGS: (With Lewis K. Sweet and Harold L. Hirsch) *The Acute Bacterial Diseases: Their Diagnosis and Treatment,* Saunders, 1948; *Tetracycline* (monograph), Medical Encyclopedia, 1955; (with Tom Jones) *That the Patient May Know: An Atlas for Use by the Physician in Explaining to the Patient,* Saunders, 1959; *Medicines for Man: The Development, Regulation, and Use of Prescription Drugs,* Knopf, 1970; *Fighting Infection: Conquests of the Twentieth Century,* Harvard University Press, 1977.

BIOGRAPHICAL/CRITICAL SOURCES: Washington

Post, May 22, 1970; *New York Times Book Review,* January 8, 1977; *New Yorker,* November 14, 1977; *American Historical Review,* June, 1978.*

*　　*　　*

DRABBLE, Phil   1914-

PERSONAL: Born in 1914, in Bloxwich, England. *Education:* Attended Oxford University and University of London. *Home:* Goat Lodge, Abbots Bromley, Rugeley, Staffordshire, England.

CAREER: Television and radio broadcaster; writer.

WRITINGS: Staffordshire, R. Hale, 1948; *Black Country,* R. Hale, 1952; *A Weasel in My Meatsafe,* Collins, 1957, revised edition, M. Joseph, 1978; *The Penguin Book of Pets,* Penguin, 1964; *Of Pedigree Unknown: Sporting and Working Dogs,* Cassell, 1964, Transatlantic, 1977; *Badgers at My Window,* Pelham Books, 1969, Taplinger, 1970.

My Beloved Wilderness, Pelham Books, 1971, Transatlantic, 1972; *Design for a Wilderness,* Pelham Books, 1973, Transatlantic, 1974; *Phil Drabble's Country Scene,* Pelham Books, 1974, reprinted as *Country Scene,* Sphere Books, 1978; *Pleasing Pets,* Luscombe, 1975, Transatlantic, 1976, reprinted as *Phil Drabble's Book of Pets,* Fontana, 1977; *Country Seasons,* M. Joseph, 1976; (with C. Gordon Glover) *Tom Forrest's Country Calendar* (edited by Charles Lefeaux), BBC Publications, 1978; *One Man and His Dog,* M. Joseph, 1978; *No Badgers in My Wood,* M. Joseph, 1980.

Also author of *A Country Book for Children,* Collins, and *Animal Magic,* David & Charles; contributor to *The Book of the Dog,* Nicholson & Watson. Contributor to newspapers.*

*　　*　　*

DRISKELL, David Clyde   1931-

PERSONAL: Born June 7, 1931, in Eatonton, Ga.; son of George W. and Mary L. (Clyde) Driskell; married Thelma G. DeLoatch, January 9, 1952; children: Daviryne Mari, Daphne Joyce. *Education:* Skowhegan School of Painting and Sculpture, M.E., 1953; Howard University, A.B., 1955; Catholic University of America, M.F.A., 1962; Rijksbureau voor Kunsthistorisches Documentatie, certificate, 1964. *Home:* 4206 Decatur St., Hyattsville, Md. 20781. *Office:* Department of Art, University of Maryland, College Park, Md. 20742.

CAREER: Talladega College, Talladega, Ala., associate professor of art, 1955-62; Howard University, Washington, D.C., associate professor of art and acting chairman of department, 1963-64; Fisk University, Nashville, Tenn., professor of art and chairman of department, 1966-76, director of Division of Cultural Research 1968-76; University of Maryland, College Park, professor of art, 1976—. Visiting professor at University of Ife, 1970, Bowdoin College and Bates College, 1973; visiting lecturer for U.S. State Department, 1972. Guest curator of Smithsonian Institution, 1973, and Los Angeles County Museum of Art, 1974; curator of Aaron Douglas Collection of AMA Museum Collaborative, 1977—. Work exhibited widely in group and solo shows in the United States and abroad, including Rhodes National Gallery, Smithsonian Institution, White House, and National Academy of Design, and represented in private collections. Member of museum advisory panel of National Endowment for the Arts, 1974-77, and board of advisers of Museum of African Art, 1967—, Frederick Douglass Institute of Negro Arts and History, and Colby College Art Museum; member of Tennessee Arts Commission visual arts panel, 1969—, and museum advisory board, 1974—; co-chairman of Tennessee College Art Council, 1968-71. Member of board of directors of Barnett Aden Gallery, Washington Fine Arts Center, and Tennessee Fine Arts Center, and board of governors of Skowhegan School of Painting and Sculpture, 1975—.

MEMBER: College Art Association of America, American Association of Museums, National Conference of Artists, American Federation of Art (member of board of trustees, 1969—), Southeastern Museum Conference, Maine Arts and Crafts Association, Nashville Artist Guild. *Awards, honors:* Museum donor award from American Federation of Art, 1962; Rockefeller Foundation fellow, 1964; fellow of Government of the Netherlands, 1964; graphic art award from Corcoran Gallery of Art, 1965; purchase awards from Birmingham Museum of Art, 1972, and Tougaloo College, 1973.

WRITINGS: (Editor) *Amistad II: Afro-American Art*, Department of Art, Fisk University, 1975; *Two Centuries of Black American Art*, Los Angeles County Museum of Art, 1976; (with Earl J. Hooks) *The Afro-American Collection, Fisk University*, Department of Art, Fisk University, 1976. Also author of *Black Dimensions in Contemporary Art*, 1971. Author of exhibition catalogs.

BIOGRAPHICAL/CRITICAL SOURCES: *New Yorker*, June 20, 1977.*

*   *   *

DRUMMOND, John Dodds   1944-

PERSONAL: Born September 11, 1944, in Lancaster, England; son of James Dodds and Joyce Mary Drummond; married Susan Elizabeth Cockayne (a music teacher), September 4, 1972. *Education:* University of Leeds, B.A. (with first class honors), 1966, B.Mus., 1967; University of Birmingham, Ph.D., 1972. *Home:* 146 Glenpark Ave., Dunedin, New Zealand. *Office:* Department of Music, University of Otago, Dunedin, New Zealand.

CAREER: University of Otago, Dunedin, New Zealand, Blair Professor of Music, 1976—. Musical performer. *Member:* Australasian Musicological Society, Composers Association of New Zealand.

WRITINGS: *Opera in Perspective*, University of Minnesota Press, 1980. Translator of operas.

WORK IN PROGRESS: *Mozart's Vienna; Opera Production Techniques.*

*   *   *

DUBOIS, M.
See KENT, Arthur William Charles

*   *   *

DuBOIS, Paul M(artin)   1945-

PERSONAL: Born October 14, 1945, in New York, N.Y.; son of Donald A. and Nancy J. (a teacher; maiden name, Grenell) DuBois; married Kristy J. Roberson, December 31, 1979; children: Kara, Jonathan, Caleb. *Education:* Cornell University, Ph.D., 1977. *Residence:* Nashville, Tenn. *Office:* Department of Public Administration, Tennessee State University, Downtown Campus, Nashville, Tenn. 37203.

CAREER: University of Tennessee, Knoxville, assistant professor, 1979-80; Tennessee State University, Nashville, associate professor of public administration, 1980—. Executive director of FIGHT, 1966-74; management and training consultant. *Member:* American Society for Public Adminis-

tration, National Association for the Advancement of Colored People, Urban League, Planned Parenthood, Alive Hospice.

WRITINGS: *The Hospice Way of Death*, Human Sciences Press, 1979; *Modern Administrative Practices in Human Services*, C. C Thomas, 1980.

WORK IN PROGRESS: A book on life and career planning, publication expected in 1981; a book on thanatology, 1981.

SIDELIGHTS: DuBois told *CA:* "I am very interested in organizational life: how we exist in many organizations and how they exist as organic entities in their own right. The impact of organizational life upon the delivery of all human services (which all of us need and use from time to time) is an unexplored subject which deserves attention if we are all to become humane and compassionate."

*   *   *

DUGUID, John Bright   1895-1980

OBITUARY NOTICE: Born May 5, 1895, in Behelvie, Scotland; died December 21, 1980. Pathologist, educator, and author of *The Dynamics of Atherosclerosis*, the summarization of his study of the arterial system. Duguid devoted his entire professional life to atherosclerosis and made numerous discoveries in the field. He taught at Durham University. Obituaries and other sources: *Who's Who*, 131st edition, St. Martin's, 1979; *London Times*, January 5, 1981.

*   *   *

DUMMETT, Michael Anthony Eardley   1925-

PERSONAL: Born June 27, 1925, in London, England; son of George Herbert and Iris (Eardley-Wilmot) Dummett; married Ann Chesney, 1951; children: Christopher, Andrew, Susanna, Tessa, Paul. *Education:* Christ Church, Oxford, B.A. (with first class honors), 1950, M.A., 1954. *Home:* 54 Park Town, Oxford, England. *Office:* New College, Oxford, England.

CAREER: Oxford University, Oxford, England, fellow of All Souls College, 1950-79, senior research fellow, 1974-79, sub-warden, 1974-76, Wykehan Professor of Logic and fellow of New College, 1979—, emeritus fellow, 1980—, reader in philosophy of mathematics, 1962-74. Assistant lecturer at University of Birmingham, 1950-51; visiting lecturer at University of Ghana, 1958; visiting professor at Stanford University, 1960-66, University of Minnesota, 1968, Princeton University, 1970, and Rockefeller University, 1973; William James Lecturer in Philosophy at Harvard University, 1976. Founding member of Oxford Committee for Racial Integration, 1965, chairman, 1966; member of executive committee of Campaign Against Racial Discrimination, 1966-67; member of legal and civil affairs panel of National Committee for Commonwealth Immigrants, 1966-68; vice-chairman of Joint Council for the Welfare of Immigrants, 1967-69, 1973-75, chairman, 1970-71, chairman of unofficial committee of enquiry into Southall disturbances, 1979-80. *Military service:* British Army, Intelligence Corps, 1943-47; served in India and Malaya; became sergeant. *Member:* British Academy (fellow). *Awards, honors:* Commonwealth Fund fellow at University of California, Berkeley, 1955-56.

WRITINGS: (Editor with J. M. Crossley) *Formal Systems and Recursive Functions: Proceedings*, Humanities, 1965; (contributor) Lewis Donnelly, editor, *Justice First*, Sheed & Ward, 1969; *Frege: Philosophy of Language*, Harper, 1973; (with Robert Minio) *Elements of Intuitionism*, Oxford University Press, 1977; *Truth and Other Enigmas*, Harvard

University Press, 1978; *Catholicism and the World Order: Some Reflections on the 1978 Reith Lectures,* Catholic Institute for International Relations, 1979; *The Game of Tarot,* Duckworth, 1980; *Twelve Tarot Games,* Duckworth, 1980; *The Interpretation of Frege's Philosophy,* Harvard University Press, 1981. Contributor to *Encyclopedia of Philosophy.* Contributor to learned journals.

WORK IN PROGRESS: The Logical Basis of Metaphysics, for Harvard University Press; *Frege: Philosophy of Mathematics,* for Duckworth; *What Is a Theory of Meaning?,* for Duckworth; *Voting Procedures,* for Duckworth.

SIDELIGHTS: Dummett told *CA:* "Twenty years ago, philosophy as practiced at Oxford was very different from the style prevalent in the universities of the United States. Now, no such difference is apparent. This is largely due to the influence of American philosophy; but I myself feel much more at home in the present Oxford philosophical climate than I used to do, without having the impression that my own approach has changed very much. For the general public, the change is no great improvement. They suspected the earlier style of Oxford philosophy of triviality; they now find themselves repelled by excessive technicality. I have long believed that the analysis of thought is the starting point of all philosophy and that the only possible approach to that is via a theory of linguistic meaning. No doubt philosophers of the 'ordinary language' school once dominant in Oxford would agree with that general formulation; but they would have differed in not thinking a systematic theory either possible or desirable. It is the attempt to construct a systematic theory of meaning that gives to current philosophy its appearance of severe technicality; no doubt some of this can be avoided, but not all. Philosophy must be either anecdotal or systematic; if one rejects the anecdotal as trivial, one will have to put up with the laboriousness of the systematic.

"Tarot cards, my other interest, would be interesting in themselves, as instruments of a range of excellent games and as objects of beauty with a sometimes perplexing history, even if they had not been seized by fortune tellers and occultists. I have been concerned to record an aspect of culture which, like many others, is now at risk from the ever growing cultural uniformity which obliterates local customs that have survived for centuries, but I should also be glad if my researches into this subject helped to discredit the irrational theories and pseudo-history of the occultists."

*   *   *

DUNCAN, Dougal 1921-

PERSONAL: Born December 23, 1921, in Buxton, England; son of Donald (a soldier) and Doris (a farmer; maiden name, Cawley) Duncan; married Anne Margaret Ross (a teacher), September 7, 1946. *Education:* St. Edmund Hall, Oxford, B.A., 1941, M.A., 1948. *Politics:* None. *Religion:* Church of England. *Home and office:* Beaumont Place, New St., Wells, Somerset BA5 2LH, England.

CAREER: Ministry of Labour, Southampton, England, secretary of district manpower board, 1941-46; housemaster, senior history master, and careers master at Wells Cathedral School in Wells, England, and tutor at Millfield School in Street, England, 1946-55; Oakley School, Wells, headmaster, 1955-67; Home Office, London, England, adviser to Fire Service, 1968-77; writer, 1977—. Mayor of Wells, 1961-63. Lecturer at University of Bristol, Workers' Educational Association, Royal Institute of Public Administration, Bristol Technical College, Bath Technical College, South Dorset Technical College, and Aims of Industry. *Member:* Navy

League, Sikorski Institute, Wells Rotary Club (president, 1961-62), Wells City Chamber of Commerce (chairman, 1961-62). *Awards, honors:* Civil Defence Long Service Medal, 1963; member of Order of the British Empire, 1964; Defense Medal.

WRITINGS: My Sons, My England (novel; first volume of trilogy), Scribner, 1980. Contributor to magazines and newspapers, including *New Commonwealth, Somerset, West, Oxford,* and *Gates of Zion.*

WORK IN PROGRESS: The last two volumes of trilogy beginning with *My Sons, My England.*

SIDELIGHTS: Duncan wrote: "My main interests lie in the social and military history of the last two centuries, and I suppose it was partly these which led me to write books of the kind that I am writing. The other part of my motivation was financial. Having retired from civil service, I had to find some way (hopefully) of making money.

"As far as my viewpoints are concerned, as I grow older my viewpoint narrows or crystallizes—according to the beholder. I am sure, however, that much of humanity is as dull as hell and that the most important thing in life was said by the founder of one of England's earliest public schools centuries ago, 'Manners makyth man.'"

*   *   *

DUNDEE, Robert
See KIRSCH, Robert R.

*   *   *

DUNNING, Brad 1957-

PERSONAL: Born May 6, 1957, in Memphis, Tenn.; son of William J. and Doris J. (Noland) Dunning. *Home:* 7508 Fountain Ave., Los Angeles, Calif. 90046. *Agent:* Jet Literary Associates, Inc., 124 East 84th St., Suite 4A, New York, N.Y. 10028.

CAREER: Carnival ride operator, 1977; *National Enquirer,* Lantana, Fla., tape transcriber, 1978; Acme Firework Stands, Los Angeles, Calif., in sales, 1979; Gun Club (rock music band), Los Angeles, drummer, 1980—. Publisher of Contempo Trends. *Member:* Los Angeles Conservancy.

WRITINGS: (With Bart Andrews) *The Official Star Trek Quiz Book,* New American Library, 1977; (with Andrews) *The Super Sixties Quiz Book,* New American Library, 1978; (with Andrews) *The Fabulous Fifties Quiz Book,* New American Library, 1978; (with Andrews) *The Worst TV Shows—Ever,* Dutton, 1980. Author of "Dear Brabby," a column in *Lobotomy.* Contributor to *Los Angeles Weekly.*

WORK IN PROGRESS: A biography of evangelist Ernest Angely; *Veg-All,* a novel "of life in a southern suburb and how it affects an adolescent boy who is a human vegetable."

SIDELIGHTS: Dunning told *CA:* "One of the most amazing feats of my life has been my ability to actually 'eek' out a living from my writing. My talent lies not in the creation of beautiful prose or the revealing of truthful insight, but in being able to cash in on the 'knowledge' I inadvertently possess. I refer, of course, to the volumes of useless trivia I have at my mind's fingertips simply because I was so alienated growing up that television became my best friend, my fidus Achates, as it were. I was a vacuum for TV's babbling brook of wisdom to fill, to teach, to enlighten in its own inimitable style. And with the advent of new cable TV systems, enabling the subscriber to have at his fingertips over one hundred channels, my career is looking rosier every minute."

DUPRE, J(osef) Stefan 1936-

PERSONAL: Born November 3, 1936, in Quebec, Quebec, Canada; son of Maurice and Anita Arden (Dowd) Dupre; married Anne Louise Willson, July 6, 1963; children: Daphne, Maurice. *Education:* University of Ottawa, B.A., 1955; Harvard University, A.M., 1957, Ph.D., 1958. *Religion:* Roman Catholic. *Home:* 422 Glencairn, Toronto, Ontario, Canada M5N 1V5. *Office:* Department of Political Economy, University of Toronto, Toronto, Ontario, Canada M5S 1A1.

CAREER: Harvard University, Cambridge, Mass., instructor, 1958-61, assistant professor of government, 1961-63; University of Toronto, Toronto, Ontario, associate professor, 1963-66, professor of political economy, 1966—, chairman of department, 1970—, director of Centre for Urban and Community Studies, 1966-69, associate dean of graduate studies, 1969-70. Editorial director of Ontario Committee on Taxation, 1964-67; member of Ontario Civil Service Arbitration Board, 1965-68; member of National Research Council of Canada, 1969-77, and Ontario Council on University Affairs (chairman, 1974-77).

MEMBER: Institute of Public Administration of Canada (national vice-president, 1967-69; president, 1969-70), Social Sciences and Humanities Research Council of Canada (member of council of trustees), Institute for Research on Public Policy, Canadian Political Science Association, Canadian Tax Foundation. *Awards, honors:* Fellow of Brookings Institution, 1957-58; D.Sc.Soc. from Laval University, 1976; LL.D. from McMaster University, 1977; D.U. from University of Ottawa, 1977.

WRITINGS: (With Sanford A. Lakoff) *Science and the Nation: Policy and Politics,* Prentice-Hall, 1962; *Intergovernmental Finance in Ontario: A Provincial-Local Perspective,* Queen's Printer, 1968; (co-author) *Federalism and Policy Development: The Case of Adult Occupational Training in Ontario,* University of Toronto Press, 1973. Also author of *The Role of the Federal Government in the Support of Research in Canadian Universities,* 1969. Contributor to scholarly journals.

*   *   *

DURBAHN, Walter E. 1895(?)-1981

OBITUARY NOTICE: Born c. 1895; died February 3, 1981, in Chicago, Ill. Educator and author. Durbahn was the host of the television show "Walt's Workshop" and author of many works on carpentry and related do-it-yourself fields. Obituaries and other sources: *Chicago Tribune,* February 4, 1981.

*   *   *

DWOSKIN, Charles 1922(?)-1980

OBITUARY NOTICE: Born c. 1922; died August 11, 1980, in New York, N.Y. Editor at G. P. Putnam's Sons and author of the novel *Shadow Over the Land.* At Putnam's, Dwoskin's specialty was illustrated works. Obituaries and other sources: *Publishers Weekly,* August 29, 1980.

*   *   *

DYER, Esther R(uth) 1950-

PERSONAL: Born August 30, 1950, in Albany, N.Y.; daughter of Luther Hungerford (an engineer) and Ruth (a director of National Society for Autistic Children; maiden name, Lindheimer) Dyer. *Education:* State University of New York College at New Paltz, B.A. (cum laude), 1972;

State University of New York at Albany, M.L.S., 1973; Universidad de Salamanca, Certificate, 1974; Columbia University, Ph.D., 1976. *Politics:* Liberal. *Religion:* Lutheran. *Home:* 15 Gramercy Park, New York, N.Y. 10003. *Office:* Graduate School of Library and Information Science, Rutgers University, New Brunswick N.J. 08903.

CAREER: Troy Public Library, Troy, N.Y., head of children's department, 1972-73; media specialist at elementary school in Suagerties, N.Y., 1973-74; University of Maryland, College Park, lecturer in library and information services, 1975; St. John's University, Jamaica, N.Y., assistant professor of library and information science, 1976-77; Rutgers University, New Brunswick, N.J., assistant professor of library and information studies, 1977—. Member of adjunct faculty at Catholic University of America, 1975; director of summer institute in San Miguel de Allende, Mexico, 1977; lecturer at University of Paraiba, 1979. Member of New York Council for Children's Television; member of board of advisers of Video Rainbow Ltd.; consultant to Peruvian airlines and tour operators.

MEMBER: International Federation of Library Associations, International Association of School Librarians, American Library Association, American Association of School Librarians, American Association of Library Schools (founder of International Library Education Interest Group; chairperson of international library education coorperation with Latin America committee), National Society for Autistic Children, Association of Children's Literature in Spanish, Library Research Roundtable (chairperson of information exchange suite, 1978), International Relations Roundtable, Educational Media Association of New Jersey, New York Library Club (chairperson of research and scholarship committee, 1977-78), New York Junior Chamber of Commerce (member of board of directors, 1977-80), Beta Phi Mu, Kappa Delta Pi, National Arts Club (resident member). *Awards, honors:* Charles Scribner Award from Charles Scribner Publishing, Inc., 1974; grant from Rutgers University for travel to Czechoslovakia, 1978, and to Brazil, 1980.

WRITINGS: (Editor and contributor) *Cultural Pluralism and Children's Media,* American Association of School Librarians, 1978; *Cooperation in Library Service to Children,* Scarecrow, 1978; (editor and Pam Berger) *Public School and Academic Media Centers: A Guide to Information Sources,* Gale, 1980. Member of editorial board of "Libraries and Librarianship," a monograph series, Ablex Publishers, 1978. Contributor to library and education journals. Member of editorial board of *Emanations,* 1978-79, and *Newsletter* of International Association of School Librarians.

WORK IN PROGRESS: Librarianship in Developing Countries, publication expected in 1982; research on Latin America and on contributions of consultants to library development.

SIDELIGHTS: Esther Dyer has lectured in Brazil, Mexico, Germany, Czechoslovakia, and the Phillipines. She conducted a study tour of England, France, and Denmark, and has visited much of Europe, South America, Egypt, Greece, Hong Kong, India, and Thailand.

She wrote: "The majority of my professional interests lie in the area of international librarianship and the development of information systems in Latin America. Many of my writings and professional activities have a Latin American or Spanish-language focus, and I have served as a consultant and curriculum coordinator for the design and development of programs relating to bilingual education in this country.

"I combine my interest in international librarianship with my desire for travel, and frequently combine business and pleasure. In addition, I have started a partnership with Dr. Karl W. Neubauer of West Germany to provide consulting services to developing countries. It is my ambition to move out of the university and academic structure within the next few years and to devote myself full-time to information consulting.

"In New York I live in the National Arts Club, a private membership club situated on historic Gramercy Park. The buildings once belonged to Samuel Tilden, in an appropriate location for a librarian. It is the club's designation as a national historic landmark and its active cultural and community programs that keep me interested."

AVOCATIONAL INTERESTS: Horseback riding, cooking, dancing.

* * *

DYER, James (Frederick) 1934-

PERSONAL: Born February 23, 1934, in Luton, England; son of Frederick and Rose (Stevens) Dyer. *Education:* St. John's College, York, England, teaching certificate, 1958; University of Leicester, M.A., 1964. *Home:* 6 Rogate Rd., Cassel Park, Luton, Bedfordshire LU2 8HR, England.

CAREER: School teacher in Luton, England, 1958-66; Putteridge Bury College of Education, Luton, principal lecturer in archaeology, 1966-76; Harlington Upper School, Bedfordshire, England, teacher of archaeology and head of department, 1976—. Archaeological editor for Shire Publications, 1968—. *Military service:* Royal Air Force, 1953-56. *Member:* Society of Antiquaries, Prehistoric Society (member of council, 1972-76), Royal Archaeological Institute, Society of Authors.

WRITINGS: The Story of Luton, White Crescent Press, 1967; *Archaeology in Denmark,* Shire Publications, 1972; *Southern England: An Archaeological Guide,* Faber, 1973; *Your Book of Prehistoric Britain* (juvenile), Faber, 1974; (editor) *From Antiquary to Archaeologist: William Cunnington, 1754-1810,* Shire Publications, 1974; *Discovering Archaeology in England and Wales,* Shire Publications, 1980; *Penguin Guide to Prehistoric England and Wales,* Penguin, 1981; *Hillforts of England and Wales,* Shire Publications, 1981. Editor of *Bedfordshire,* 1965-74.

WORK IN PROGRESS: A book on teaching archaeology in schools.

SIDELIGHTS: Dyer commented: "I am particularly interested in the upstanding remains of the past in Western Europe and have traveled extensively to examine and record prehistoric material in museums and the countryside from Norway to Austria. I am especially involved in making my material available to children and in methods of teaching archaeology in English schools. I believe that I teach more archaeology to young people of fourteen to eighteen years than any other school in Britain. This has made me something of an authority, and I am constantly being asked to lecture and write articles about my methods. I suppose I would describe myself as a 'popularizer,' but I hope in the best sense of the word—introducing young people to a fascinating subject that can provide a lifelong interest and hobby!"

E

EARLE, Marilee
See ZDENEK, Marilee

*   *   *

EARLY, Richard E(lliott) 1908-

PERSONAL: Born August 7, 1908, in Witney, England; son of James Harold (a blanket maker) and Alice Kate (a teacher; maiden name, Elliott) Early; married Gerda Orlandi Madsen, August 15, 1940; children: Alice Inger Early Edwards, Charles Albert. *Education:* Pembroke College, Oxford, M.A. (with honors), 1930. *Politics:* Liberal. *Religion:* Wesleyan Methodist. *Home:* Mount House, Church Green, Witney, Oxfordshire OX8 6AZ, England. *Office:* Charles Early & Marriott (Witney) Ltd., Witney Mills, Witney, Oxfordshire OX8 5EB, England.

CAREER: Charles Early & Marriott (Witney) Ltd., Witney, England, blanket maker, 1930—, chairman, 1959-73, honorary president, 1973-81. President of Witney and District Chamber of Trade; past member of board of directors of West Oxfordshire Technical College. Guest on television and radio programs. *Wartime service:* Friends Ambulance Unit, 1939-45, prisoner of war in Greece and Germany. *Member:* Worshipful Company of Woolmen (past master), Worshipful Company of Weavers (past upper bailiff), Witney and District Historical and Archaeological Society (president).

WRITINGS: (With Alfred Plummer) *The Blanket Makers, 1669-1969: A History of Charles Early & Marriott (Witney) Ltd.,* Augustus Kelley, 1969; *Apprentice* (historical novel), Routledge & Kegan Paul, 1977; *Master Weaver* (historical novel), Routledge & Kegan Paul, 1980. Contributor to magazines, including *Boy's Brigade Gazette.*

WORK IN PROGRESS: Looking In, a wartime story.

SIDELIGHTS: Early's family has been making blankets in Witney for eight generations. He began his career on the shop floor and worked his way up to chairman of the family company. One of his novels tells the story of his ancestor, Thomas Early, who was apprenticed in Witney in 1669, and later presented a gift of gold-fringed blankets to King James II.

Early told *CA:* "Blanket making has been my life's work, and most of what I write has a bearing upon that subject. Since retiring from full-time blanket making, I have been able to give more attention to writing."

AVOCATIONAL INTERESTS: Rugby, cricket.

*   *   *

EBER, Irene 1929-

PERSONAL: Born December 29, 1929, in Halle, Germany (now East Germany); came to the United States in 1947, naturalized citizen, 1952; daughter of Yedidiah (a merchant) and Helen (Ganger) Geminder; married, 1948; children: Jonathan Michael, Miriam Alisa. *Education:* Pomona College, B.A., 1955; Sacramento State College, M.A., 1961; Claremont Graduate School and University Center, Ph.D., 1966. *Office:* Institute of Asian and African Studies, Hebrew University of Jerusalem, Jerusalem, Israel.

CAREER: Whittier College, Whittier, Calif., assistant professor of history, 1966-69; Hebrew University of Jerusalem, Jerusalem, Israel, senior lecturer in Chinese history, 1969—. *Member:* Association for Asian Studies, American Oriental Society, Phi Beta Kappa. *Awards, honors:* Social Science Research Council grant, 1968-69; grant from University of Michigan Center for Chinese Studies, 1973-74.

WRITINGS: (Contributor) *Modern Literature and Its Social Context,* Malmqvist, 1977; (contributor) Merle Goldman, editor, *Modern Chinese Literature in the May Fourth Era,* Harvard University Press, 1977; (editor) *Lectures on the I Ching: Constancy and Change,* translated by Richard Wilhelm, Princeton University Press, 1979; *Voices from Afar: Modern Chinese Writers on Oppressed People and Their Literatures,* Center for Chinese Studies, University of Michigan, 1980. Also author of *Hu Shih and Chinese History,* 1968. Contributor to Asian studies journals.

WORK IN PROGRESS: Research on Hu Shih's contribution to the modernization of Chinese scholarship; a book; an article on the translating of Western literature in China.

SIDELIGHTS: Eber told *CA:* "Over the years I have been increasingly interested in men and women who either directly or in their works can speak from within one culture to another, and who thereby contribute to human understanding. In *Voices From Afar* I tried to understand why Chinese writers looked to the literary works of peoples whose lives were very remote: Poles, Jews, Irish, and Black Americans. I tried to understand why the stories of H. Sienkiewicz and Sholem Aleichem or the poetry of W. B. Yeats and Langston Hughes would appeal to Chinese readers. In what ways can a literary work engage a reader across time and space and evoke in him or her the deepest feelings?

"A similar interest brought me to Wilhelm and his essays. He was deeply rooted in Western and German culture. And yet, an uncommon intellectual and emotional capacity allowed him to become steeped in Chinese history, scholarship, and culture. Wilhelm was one of those rare individuals who could interpret and articulate to a Western audience some of the most complex and profound insights of the Chinese sages. I look forward to writing his biography some day.

"My study of Hu Shih continues to deal with similar questions. Hu Shih was still thoroughly versed in Chinese tradition. When he turned to the study of Western philosophy, literature, and history it was with the profound conviction that within Western tradition he would find the tools for elucidating China's past in a rapidly changing present. He was, above all, concerned with cultural continuity in a world where both China and the West had to make sense to one another.

"Meanwhile, I keep an eye on translations of Western literature in China. For it will not be only politicians or occasional visitors but also often repeated literary images that will form the Chinese people's understanding of ourselves."

*　　*　　*

EBERSHOFF-COLES, Susan Vaughan 1941-

PERSONAL: Surname is pronounced *Ee-ber-shoff-Coles*; born August 28, 1941, in Lafayette, Ind.; daughter of Richard Vaughan (a company president) and Sarah (Schaaf) Ebershoff; married Wayne Edward Coles (a greenhouse operator), January 12, 1974. *Education:* Purdue University, B.A., 1963; Indiana University, M.L.S., 1965. *Politics:* Republican. *Religion:* Roman Catholic. *Home address:* R.R.1, Box 72-C, Pittsboro, Ind. 46167. *Office:* Indianapolis-Marion County Public Library, P.O. Box 211, Indianapolis, Ind. 46206.

CAREER: Milwaukee Public Library, Milwaukee, Wis., librarian, 1965-67; Indianapolis-Marion County Public Library, Indianapolis, Ind., librarian, 1967-70, assistant supervisor of technical services, 1970-75, supervisor, 1976—. *Member:* American Automobile Racing Writers and Broadcasters Association, U.S. Automobile Club, Sports Car Club of America, Indiana Library Association (member of executive board of Technical Services Round Table; chairperson of Technical Services Division, 1977), Hendricks County Ark Humane Society (member of board of directors, 1975—; chairperson of education committee, 1977-79), Sigma Kappa.

WRITINGS: (With Charla Ann Leibenguth) *Motorsports: A Guide to Information Sources,* Gale, 1979; (with Charla Ann Leibenguth Banner and Barbara Howes) *Bibliography of Alternative Sources of Energy,* Libraries Unlimited, 1981. Contributor of articles and reviews to library journals. Past editor of *Ad Lib.*

WORK IN PROGRESS: Guide to Endangered Species (tentative title), with Leibenguth Banner; a gothic novel, with Leibenguth Banner.

SIDELIGHTS: Susan Ebershoff-Coles wrote: "I am an active official with the U.S. Automobile Club in timing and scoring, and an active competitor in Formula Vee racing with the Sports Car Club of America. I am also an avid reader. I have a particular fascination with the Middle Ages and hope eventually to do a historical novel about medieval England. I am very interested in humane society work and wildlife/habitat conservation. Writing fits in well with this interest as it gives me the opportunity to educate and contribute to the available information.

"Wise use of our natural resources and protection of all forms of life is becoming increasingly important. I feel strongly that I, as a writer, have an opportunity to contribute to the debate and help educate others. As technology expands so must the awareness of the impact of that technology. Society has changed a great deal since the Middle Ages and many of those changes were the result of the Industrial Revolution. Technology continues to change our lives and we can learn much from history. I hope that whatever I am able to do with my historical writing in the future will contribute to an understanding of some of the historical reasons of current problems."

*　　*　　*

ECCLI, Sandra Fulton 1936-

PERSONAL: Born March 14, 1936, in Davenport, Iowa; daughter of James Sheppard (a safety engineer) and Mary (a secretary; maiden name, Sanders) Fulton; married Eugene Peter Eccli (an energy specialist and writer), May 25, 1969; children: John Julian. *Education:* University of Florida, A.A., 1956; University of Miami, Coral Gables, Fla., A.B. (cum laude), 1957; Virginia Polytechnic Institute and State University, M.A. (with high honors), 1975. *Politics:* Liberal. *Religion:* Unitarian Universalist. *Home:* 3515 North 14th St., Arlington, Va. 22201. *Office:* Design Alternatives, Inc., 1312 18th St. N.W., Washington, D.C. 20036.

CAREER: U.S. Navy, line officer in Naval Reserves, 1957-60, served as lieutenant senior grade, 1960-68; Bureau of Children's Services, Newark, N.J., social worker, 1969-70; *Alternative Sources of Energy,* Kingston, N.Y., co-editor and associate publisher, 1971-75; free-lance writer and editor, 1975-77; Design Alternatives, Inc. (energy consulting firm), Washington, D.C., vice-president, 1977—. Singer with Alan-a-Dale Singers, 1977—. Co-founder of Hudson Valley Women's Coalition. Member of policy board of Arlington County Human Resources Department, Status of Women Commission of Arlington County, and energy committee of United Community Ministries.

MEMBER: Zonta International, International Solar Energy Society, National Organization for Women, Unitarian Universalist Advance, Unitarian Universalist Women's Federation, Unitarian Universalist Christian Fellowship, Phi Alpha Theta. *Awards, honors:* Best science book award from *Library Journal,* 1974, for *Producing Your Own Power.*

WRITINGS: Power Unlimited, or P.U.!, Ecology Action East, 1970; *Alternative Sources of Energy: Practical Technology and Philosophy for a Decentralized Society,* Seabury, 1973; (editor with husband, Eugene Eccli, and Carol Hupping Stoner, and contributor) *Producing Your Own Power,* Rodale Press, 1974; *Odyssey Four, Part Two: The Path of Knowledge,* Unitarian Universalist Association, 1980.

Author of energy pamphlets for Department of Energy, ACTION/Peace Corps, and Community Services Administration. Contributor of articles, stories, poems, and illustrations to magazines, including *Organic Gardening and Farming, Catalyst, Spark, Folio,* and *Unitarian Universalist Christian.* Editor of *Naval War College Review,* 1963-65.

WORK IN PROGRESS: The Medieval Roots of Liberal Religion, publication expected in 1981; *The Pride of Man,* a series of novels, containing *The Wren, The Pain and the Need, Look to the Stronghold,* and *The Ringing of the Bell,* based on the life of fourteenth-century English radical John Ball.

SIDELIGHTS: Sandra Eccli commented: "My vocational interest is energy policy, concentrating on the effects of energy shortages on the poor and middle class, and on practical solutions.

"I look back on my forty-four years with some wonderment. Emerging out of the Midwest lower-middle-class 'WASP' culture, I wouldn't have been able to attend college had I not been lucky enough to get a scholarship. Our 'Fulton Family History,' compiled about one hundred years ago by my great-grandfather, James Jackson Fulton, a stone-dirt farmer, which is full of pioneer tales and adventures of poor Irish immigrants in the eighteenth-century wilderness, settled me on a life-study of history and other human studies. My own predilections—toward art, music, writing, and speaking—turned me toward the life of imagination at an early age.

"As for energy—after being forced out of a warm Chicago apartment in 1946 because of the severe inflation of rent, we moved to the only home we could afford, a fishing shack in rural northern Illinois, with no inside plumbing, electricity, or other amenities. The little heat we had was provided by a coal cook stove in the kitchen and a coal fireplace in the living room—but the heat was sucked out of the house immediately through the holes in the walls, floor, and ceiling. If you ever experience winter mornings with frozen wash-basins and even frozen chamber pots from the night before, you become obsessed with the effects of heat shortages on the poor.

"Later, after my marriage, my husband and I lived in a 'cockroach heaven' apartment in Newark, New Jersey, with *no* heat for an entire winter, since the coal furnace blew up the second time we used it. We rented a seven-room farmhouse two years later. The only heat came from a Franklin stove in the living room and a small propane burner in the workroom where we co-edited *Alternative Sources of Energy* and did our books.

"These experiences confirmed not only a lifelong desire to use energy wisely—reflected in the purchase of my first 'car,' in 1958, a Messerschmitt that got sixty-five miles to the gallon!—but also my desire to address practical solutions that ordinary people, even lower-income people, might use within their budgets. Thus, the greater part of my writings have been handbooks that are designed for training through local co-ops, community action groups, etc. I also helped organize one of the first community low-income weatherization programs (1973-74), following hard upon the first 'energy crunch'—'Project Energy Save' in Roanoke, Virginia.

"A particular concern of mine has been the effect of high energy costs on elderly women. A long-time feminist (I joined the Navy in 1957 in large part because it promised equal pay and promotions to women and men, which turned out *not* to be entirely true), I've helped organize a variety of women's coalitions, women's centers, and related activities. Simply because there are more elderly single women than there are elderly men or elderly couples, these women suffer disproportionately from heavy-handed government and oil company decisions to make the energy economy 'free.' Of course, anyone who believes that little jingle is hopelessly naive. In the context of the multinational oil companies, 'free' means the freedom of the strong to eradicate the weak.

"I've kept myself involved in history, too, for it seems to me that too many who call themselves 'liberals' or 'radicals' are condemned (in Clarence Darrow's phrase) to repeat all the mistakes of the past because they do not know their roots.

"In 1974 I went to England for a two-month walking tour, to conduct research on a subject that had long fascinated me—Medieval radicalism, concentrating on the English peasants' revolt of 1381. This trip, and continual research in American libraries from 1974 until the present, has had several felicitous results. First, I achieved an M.A. in medieval and intellectual history in 1975, working with three professors whose wisdom and guidance will always be valued. I've also produced some published writings in the field of history, the latest of which is a twelve-booklet modular packet for the Unitarian Universalist Association, *Odyssey Four, Part Two: The Path of Knowledge,* which I also illustrated. The booklets are designed for self-study or group-study of the varied and honorable roots of liberal and radical thought, arranged historically from ancient times to the present.

"I'm also continuing my writing of what I hope will be a magnum opus, a four-volume fictional biography of the life and times of John Ball, the fourteenth-century religious, social, economic, and political radical—England's first practical 'congregationalist,' democrat, and socialist.

"All of this leads me to surmise that *religion* is at the very core of whatever drive and ability I possess. Like many other Unitarian Universalists, I am obsessed with religion in an old-fashioned, 'committed' sense. I must look at every human action (or inaction) by comparing it against the ethical and moral standards of my faith. I am continually redefining 'God,' 'science,' 'ethics,' and all other profound questions of existence from the standpoint of my liberal religious inquiries. And I am eternally, profoundly grateful for the existence of a faith, Unitarian Universalism, which gives me the unbounded freedom to go where my mind directs, through whatever doors I'm capable of opening."

AVOCATIONAL INTERESTS: Music (building musical instruments, playing piano, composing choral and chamber works), carpentry, cabinet making, building prototypes and models of energy conservation and solar devices, electronics, lay service in social action, creative worship.

*   *   *

ECKLEY, Mary M.

PERSONAL: Born in Dayton, Ohio; daughter of Alexander Munn and Clara (Hoskinson) Eckley. *Education:* Simmons College, B.S., 1943; graduate study at Vassar College, 1949; Columbia University, A.M., 1952. *Home:* 55 East End Ave., New York, N.Y. 10028. *Office:* McCall's, 230 Park Ave., New York, N.Y. 10017.

CAREER: Everywoman's, New York City, assistant editor, 1952-53; *Good Housekeeping,* New York City, associate editor, 1953-58; *McCall's,* New York City, associate editor, 1960-64, senior editor of food section, 1964—. Worked with American Red Cross in Washington, D.C., France, and Germany, 1944-49.

WRITINGS: (Editor) Catherine Cambier, *The Young French Chef* (juvenile), Platt, 1969; (editor) *The New McCall's Cookbook,* Random House, 1973; (with Mary J. Norton) *McCall's Cooking School: Step-by-Step Directions for Mistake-Proof Recipes,* Random House, 1976; (editor) *McCall's Superb Dessert Cookbook,* Random House, 1978; (editor with Jean B. Read) *McCall's Book of Entertaining,* Random House, 1979.*

*   *   *

EDELMAN, Lily (Judith) 1915-1981

OBITUARY NOTICE—See index for *CA* sketch: Born September 2, 1915, in San Francisco, Calif.; died after a brief illness, January 22, 1981, in New York. Translator, editor, and author. Edelman was active in B'nai B'rith, serving as director of adult Jewish education for more than fifteen years, and editing the organization's monthly *Anti-Defamation League Bulletin.* She was a former editor of the Jewish Heritage Classics Service and book editor of *National Jewish Monthly.* Edelman's writings include travel books about Hawaii, Japan, and Israel, and English translations of Elie Wiesel's *A Beggar in Jerusalem* and *One Generation After.* Obituaries and other sources: *New York Times,* January 27, 1981.

* * *

EDMONDSON, Clifton Earl 1937-

PERSONAL: Born May 14, 1937, in Shreveport, La. *Education:* Mississippi College, B.A., 1959; Duke University, M.A., 1962, Ph.D., 1966. *Office:* Department of History, Davidson College, Davidson, N.C. 28036.

CAREER: University of North Carolina, Chapel Hill, 1962-70, began as instructor, became assistant professor of history; Davidson College, Davidson, N.C., assistant professor, 1970-77, associate professor of history, 1977—. *Member:* American Historical Association, American Association of University Professors, Conference Group on Central European History, Southern Historical Association.

WRITINGS: The Heimwehr and Austrian Politics, 1918-1936, University of Georgia Press, 1978. Contributor to history journals.

BIOGRAPHICAL/CRITICAL SOURCES: American Historical Review, December, 1979.*

* * *

EDWARDS, Jaroldeen 1932-

PERSONAL: Born February 23, 1932, in Raymond, Alberta, Canada; daughter of Charles Owen (a rancher) and Julia (a teacher; maiden name, Russell) Asplund; married Weston Eyring Edwards (an executive), March 23, 1954; children: Marianna Edwards Richardson, Julia Edwards Pratt, Catherine Edwards Tryon, Charles, Christine, Robin, Carolyn, Weston, Robert, William, Jaroldeen, Patricia. *Education:* Brigham Young University, B.A., 1954. *Politics:* Republican. *Religion:* Church of Jesus Christ of Latter-day Saints (Mormons). *Home:* 95 Ferris Hill Rd., New Canaan, Conn. 06840. *Agent:* Meredith Bernstein, 58 West 10th St., New York, N.Y. 10011.

CAREER: Writer, 1980—.

WRITINGS: A Woman Between (novel), Avon, 1980; *Bitterroot* (novel), Dell, 1981.

WORK IN PROGRESS: In Abraham's Grave (tentative title).

SIDELIGHTS: Jaroldeen Edwards wrote: "I consider myself a storyteller, and there is within me a great drive to create and communicate. In my twenty-five years as a wife and mother of twelve remarkable children, I have been impressed and delighted with the varied and exciting life experiences of women such as myself. Somehow in my writing I want to communicate both the challenges and the joys of a woman's life. I feel a crying need for women to rediscover themselves and the essential nature of their ability to love men, to bear children, and to nurture and sustain. It is this part of womanhood that I wish to celebrate and to reveal to the women of today. Triumph, sacrifice, pain, and delight, self-knowledge and the strength to give to others—these are

the attributes I strive to portray—and I want to uplift and enliven the human spirit.''

* * *

EDWARDS, Tilden Hampton, Jr. 1935-

PERSONAL: Born September 21, 1935, in Austin, Tex.; son of Tilden Hampton and Marie (Babare) Edwards; married Ann Austin, October 22, 1966; children: Jeremy Austin, Jennifer Gabrielle. *Education:* Stanford University, B.A., 1957; Harvard University, M.Div., 1961; Union Graduate School, Cincinnati, Ohio, Ph.D., 1979. *Home:* 1961 Biltmore St. N.W., Washington, D.C. 20009. *Office:* Shalem Institute for Spiritual Formation, Mount St. Alban, Washington, D.C. 20016.

CAREER: Ordained Episcopal priest, 1962; associate pastor of Episcopal church in Washington, D.C., 1962-67; Metropolitan Ecumenical Training Center, Washington, D.C., director, 1967-77; Shalem Institute for Spiritual Formation, Washington, D.C., director, 1978—. *Member:* Phi Beta Kappa.

WRITINGS: Living Simply Through the Day, Paulist/Newman, 1977; *Spiritual Friend,* Paulist/Newman, 1980; *Journey in Faith,* Abingdon, in press. Contributor to *American Quarterly of Theological Education.*

WORK IN PROGRESS: The Christian Sabbath.

SIDELIGHTS: Edwards has studied and worked in Europe, South America, and Japan.

* * *

EELLS, Robert J(ames) 1944-

PERSONAL: Born March 14, 1944, in Walton, N.Y.; son of Walter E. (a doctor) and Katherine (Henderson) Eells; married wife, Janice J. *Education:* Geneva College, B.S., 1966; Union College, Schenectady, N.Y., M.A., 1969; University of New Mexico, Ph.D., 1976. *Home:* 937 South Robb Way, Denver, Colo. 80226.

CAREER: Geneva College, Beaver Falls, Pa., instructor in history, 1969-70; executive secretary of Christian Government Movement, 1972-74; Rockmont College, Denver, Colo., professor of history and political science, 1977—.

WRITINGS: Lonely Walk: The Life of Senator Mark O. Hatfield, Christian Herald Books, 1979.

WORK IN PROGRESS: The Hatfield Project, "a revision and expansion of my doctoral dissertation.''

SIDELIGHTS: Eells told *CA:* "An interest in the 'mixing' of religion and politics has brought me to the Hatfield Project. I consider Senator Mark Hatfield to be one of the best (if not *the* best) examples of a Christian politician in America today.''

* * *

EFRON, Edith Carol 1922-

PERSONAL: Born in 1922, in New York, N.Y.; daughter of Alexander E. and Rose (Kunitz) Efron; divorced; children: Fortune Leonard Bogart. *Education:* Barnard College, B.A., 1942; Columbia University, B.S., 1943. *Office: TV Guide,* 1290 Avenue of the Americas, New York, N.Y. 10019.

CAREER: New York Times, New York City, in magazine section, 1944-47; Time, Inc., New York City, Central American reporter for *Time* and *Life,* 1948-54; *Look,* New York City, managing editor of special editorial departments, 1954-56; in public relations at Farley-Manning Co., 1956-58; staff writer for "Mike Wallace Show," 1958-60; *TV Guide*, New York City, staff writer, 1961—. *Member:* American Women in Radio and Television.

WRITINGS: The News Twisters, Nash Publishing, 1971; (with Clytia Chambers) *How CBS Tried to Kill a Book,* Nash Publishing, 1972.*

*   *   *

EFROS, Israel (Issac)   1891-1981
   (Efrot)

OBITUARY NOTICE—See index for *CA* sketch: Born May 28, 1891, in Ostrog, Poland; died January 4, 1981, in Tel Aviv, Israel. Translator, educator, poet, and author. Efros was a professor of Hebrew and Jewish literature and philosophy at universities in the United States and Israel. He wrote, edited, and translated numerous books on Judaism, including a definitive Hebrew-English dictionary. Obituaries and other sources: *New York Times,* January 13, 1981.

*   *   *

EFROT
   See EFROS, Israel (Issac)

*   *   *

EGAN, David R(onald)   1943-

PERSONAL: Born September 28, 1943, in Endicott, N.Y.; son of John A. and Patricia E. (LaStella) Egan; married Melinda A. Evanick (a psychologist and writer), December 3, 1971. *Education:* State University of New York College at Cortland, B.S., 1965; Colgate University, M.A.T., 1966; State University of New York at Binghamton, Ph.D., 1970. *Home:* 361 West Hills Rd., Huntington, N.Y. 11743.

CAREER: Cold Spring Harbor High School, Cold Spring Harbor, N.Y., teacher of history, 1970—. Associate director of Cold Spring Harbor Whaling Museum, 1972-74. Adjunct associate professor at C. W. Post College of Long Island University, 1972-79. *Member:* American Association for the Advancement of Slavic Studies.

WRITINGS: (With wife, Melinda A. Egan) *Leo Tolstoy: An Annotated Bibliography of English-Language Sources to 1978,* Scarecrow, 1979.

WORK IN PROGRESS: A multi-volume *Russian Biographical Index* of pre-1980 English-language sources on noteworthy Russians, with wife, Melinda A. Egan.

SIDELIGHTS: Egan commented to *CA:* "My research goal is to systematize and annotate the English-language sources on tsarist Russia and the Soviet Union. My bibliography on Tolstoy was a small step in this direction, whereas my current work will constitute a more significant step. The publication of the *Russian Biographical Index* will be followed by a series of bibliographies on major events in Russian history.

"My other interests include foreign travel. I have led student groups on tours of the Soviet Union five times since 1972."

*   *   *

EGAN, Melinda A(nne)   1950-

PERSONAL: Born June 29, 1950, in Binghamton, N.Y.; daughter of Michael and Margaret (Pollak) Evanick; married David R. Egan (an educator and writer), December 3, 1971. *Education:* State University of New York at Stony Brook, B.S., 1972; St. John's University, Jamaica, N.Y., M.S., 1973, diploma, 1974. *Home:* 361 West Hills Rd., Huntington, N.Y. 11743.

CAREER: Youth counselor for public schools in Suffolk County, N.Y., 1973-76, special education teacher, 1976-77, psychologist, 1977-79; Adelphi University, Garden City, N.Y., adjunct assistant professor of psychology, 1979—. Associate director of Cold Spring Harbor Whaling Museum, 1972-74. Adjunct assistant professor at C. W. Post College of Long Island University, 1976-78. School psychologist in Northport, N.Y., 1979—. *Member:* New York State Psychological Association, Suffolk County Psychological Association.

WRITINGS: (With husband, David R. Egan) *Leo Tolstoy: An Annotated Bibliography of English-Language Sources to 1978,* Scarecrow, 1979.

WORK IN PROGRESS: A multi-volume *Russian Biographical Index* of pre-1980 English-language sources on noteworthy Russians, with husband, David R. Egan.

SIDELIGHTS: Melinda Egan told *CA:* "My career interests include research in neuropsychology and development of appropriate psychological tests. However, I share my husband's enthusiasm for bibliographical research, which has proven to be intriguing and personally gratifying. I have also enjoyed accompanying him on his five student tours to the Soviet Union."

*   *   *

EGBUNA, Obi B(enue Joseph)   1938-

PERSONAL: Born in 1938 in Nigeria.

CAREER: Writer.

WRITINGS: Wind Versus Polygamy: Where "Wind" Is the "Wind of Change" and "Polygamy" Is the "Change of Eves" (novel), Faber, 1964; *The Anthill,* Oxford University Press, 1965; *Daughters of the Sun and Other Stories,* Oxford University Press, 1970; *Destroy This Temple: The Voice of Black Power in Britain,* Morrow, 1971; *Menace of the Hedgehog,* Barrie & Jenkins, 1973; *Emperor of the Sea and Other Stories,* Fontana, 1974; *The Minister's Daughter,* F. Watts, 1975; *Elina,* Fontana, 1978.

Unpublished plays: "Wind Versus Polygamy," first produced in Dakar, Senegal, 1966; "Theatre of Power," first produced in Copenhagen, Denmark, 1969; "The Agony," first produced in London, England, 1970.

Radio plays: "Divinity," 1965; "Wind Versus Polygamy," 1966; "Daughters of the Sun," 1970.*

*   *   *

EHRENBOURG, Ilya (Grigoryevich)
   See EHRENBURG, Ilya (Grigoryevich)

*   *   *

EHRENBURG, Ilya (Grigoryevich)   1891-1967

PERSONAL: Born January 27, 1891, in Kiev, Ukraine (now Ukrainian Soviet Socialist Republic); died of a heart attack, September 1, 1967, in Moscow, U.S.S.R.; married Lyuba Kozintsova (an artist), c. 1919; children: Irina. *Education:* Educated in Moscow, Russia (now U.S.S.R.). *Residence:* Moscow, U.S.S.R.

CAREER: Bolshevik revolutionary in Russia, 1906-09; imprisoned for five months in 1908; exiled in 1909; tour guide in Paris, France, c. 1909; poet in Paris, 1909-c. 1916; worked as freight packer in Paris, c. 1914-16; World War I correspondent on Western front for newspapers, *Birzhevye Vedemosti* ("Stock Market Gazette") and *Utro Rossii* ("Russia's Dawn"); returned to Russia, 1917; worked as supervisor of juvenile delinquents, lecturer in Russian literature, and organizer of nurseries for children and theatre groups in Kiev, Kharkov, the Crimea, and Moscow, U.S.S.R., 1917-21; writer in Belgium, 1921-24, and in Paris, 1924-32; regular correspondent for newspaper *Izvestia,* 1932-40; war correspondent in Russia for newspapers *Krasnaya zvezda* (''Red Star'') and *Pravda,* 1941-c. 1946; member of Supreme Soviet of the Union of Soviet Socialist Republics (U.S.S.R.), 1946-67, member of Foreign Affairs Commission of its Council of the Union, 1954-67. Vice-president of World Peace Council; deputy chairman of Soviet Committee for the Defense of Peace, 1955-67. Presidium member of Union of Soviet Writers and member of Lenin Peace Prize Committee. Delegate to Congress of Soviet Writers, Moscow, 1934; delegate to international peace congresses in Paris, Helsinki, Stockholm, Warsaw, and Wroclaw.

AWARDS, HONORS: Stalin Prize for literature, 1942, for *The Fall of Paris,* 1947, for *The Storm;* Cross of the Legion of Honor from the government of General Charles de Gaulle, during World War II; International Stalin Prize, 1952; Lenin Peace Prize, 1960; received Order of Lenin in 1944 and another at a later date; Order of the Red Banner of Labor; Order of the Red Star; also awarded several medals.

WRITINGS—In English translation: *Neobychainyia pokhozhdeniia Khulio Khurenito* (novel), [Moscow], 1922, translation by Usick Vanzler published as *The Extraordinary Adventures of Julio Jurenito and His Disciples,* Covivi, Friede, 1930, revised edition translated by Anna Bostock and Yvonne Kapp published as *Julio Jurenito,* MacGibbon & Kee, 1958, Dufour, 1963; *Liubov Zhanny Nei* (novel), Volume I, 1925, Volume II, 1926, translation by Helen Chroushoff Matheson published as *The Love of Jeanne Ney,* P. Davies, 1929, Doubleday, 1930, reprinted, Greenwood Press, 1968; *V Protochnom pereulke* (novel), 1927, translation by Sonia Volochova published as *A Street in Moscow,* Covici, Friede, 1932, reprinted, Hyperion Press, 1977; *Burnaia zhizn Lazika Roltshvanetsa* (novel), 1928, translation by Leonid Borochowicz and Gertrude Flor published as *The Stormy Life of Lasik Roitschwantz,* Polyglot Library, 1960; *Desiat loshadinykh sil,* 1929, translation by Joachim Neugroeschel published as *The Life of the Automobile,* Urizen, 1977.

Den' vtoroi (novel), [Paris], 1934, translation by Alexander Bakshy published as *Out of Chaos,* Holt, 1934, reprinted, Octagon, 1976; *Padenie Parizha* (novel), three volumes, [Moscow], 1942, translation by Gerard Shelley published as *The Fall of Paris,* Hutchinson, 1942, Knopf, 1943; *Voina, iiun 1941-aprel 1942* (nonfiction), [Moscow], 1942, translation by Shelley published as *Russia at War,* Hamish Hamilton, 1943, published as *The Tempering of Russia,* translated by Alexander Kaun, Knopf, 1944; *We Will Not Forget,* [Washington], 1944; (with others) *The Russians Reply to Lady Gibb,* [London], 1945; *We Come as Judges,* [London], 1945; *Dorogi Evropy* (nonfiction), [Moscow], 1946, translation by Anya Markov published as *European Crossroad: A Soviet Journalist in the Balkans,* Knopf, 1947; *Buria* (novel), [Moscow], 1948, translation by J. Fineberg published as *The Storm: A Novel in Six Parts,* Foreign Languages Publishing House, 1948, published as *The Storm,* edited by Isidor Schneider and Anne Terry White, Gaer Associates, 1949.

Deviatyi vai (novel), [Moscow], 1953, translation by Tatiana Shebunina and Joseph Castle published as *The Ninth Wave,* Lawrence & Wishart, 1955, Greenwood Press, 1974; *Ottepel,* [Moscow], 1954, translation by Manya Harari published as *The Thaw,* Regnery, 1955 (see below); *Frantsuzskie tetradi* (title means ''French Notebooks''), [Moscow], 1958,

translation by Bostock and Kapp published in part with *Perechityvaia Chekhova* in *Chekhov, Stendhal, and Other Essays,* MacGibbon & Kee, 1962, revised edition with additional translations by Shebunina, Knopf, 1963 (see below); *Perechityvaia Chekhova,* Gos. izd-vo khudozh lit-ry, 1960, translation by Bostock and Kapp published in part with *Frantsuzskie tetradi* in *Chekhov, Stendhal, and Other Essays* (see above); *The Spring,* translated by Humphrey Higgins, MacGibbon & Kee, 1961 (see below).

Liudi, gody, zhizn (memoirs), six volumes, [Moscow], 1961-c. 1967, translation published as *Men, Years, Life,* MacGibbon & Kee, Volume I: *People and Life: Memoirs of 1891-1917,* translated by Bostock and Kapp, 1961, 2nd edition published as *Childhood and Youth, 1891-1917,* 1962, Volume II: *First Years of Revolution, 1918-1921,* translated by Bostock and Kapp, 1962, Volume III: *Truce: 1921-1933,* translated by Shebunina and Kapp, 1963, Volume IV: *Eve of War: 1933-1941,* translated by Shebunina and Kapp, 1963, Volume V: *The War, 1941-1945,* translated by Shebunina and Kapp, 1964, Volume VI: *Post-War Years, 1945-1954,* translated by Shebunina and Kapp, 1966, also published as *Men, Years, Life,* Volume I: *People and Life, 1891-1921,* translated by Bostock and Kapp, Knopf, 1962, Volume II: *Memoirs: 1921-1941,* translated by Shebunina and Kapp, World Publishing, 1964, Volume III: *The War: 1941-1945,* translated by Shebunina and Kapp, New American Library, 1964, Volume IV: *Post-War Years, 1945-1954,* translated by Shebunina and Kapp, World Publishing, 1967; *A Change of Season* (contains ''The Thaw'' and ''The Spring''; see above), translated by Harari and Higgins, Knopf, 1962; *Selection From ''People, Years, Life,''* edited by C. Moody, Pergamon, 1972.

In Russian: *Stikhi o Kanunakh* (title means ''Verses on the Eve''; poetry), 1916; *Lik voiny* (title means ''Face of War''; nonfiction), 1920; *Nepravdopodobnye istorii,* c. 1920, reprinted, Flegon, 1972; *Kanuny,* 1921; *Razdumiia* (title means ''Reflections''), [Riga], 1921, reprinted, Prideaux, 1976; *Opustoshaiushchaia liubov* (title means ''Wasted Love''), Ogon'ki, 1922, reprinted, Prideaux, 1976; *A vse-taki ona vertitsia,* 1922; *Portrety russkikh poetov,* 1922, reprinted, W. Fink, 1972; *Shest poviestel o legkikh kontsakh,* Kn-vo Gelikon, 1922; *Poeziia revoliutsionnoi Moskvy* (poetry), 1922; *Zolotoe serdtse,* [Moscow], 1922; *Trest D.E.: Istoriia gibeli Evropy* (title means ''The D.E. Trust: The History of the Downfall of Europe''; novel), 1923; *Zhizn gibel Nikolaia Kurbova* (title means ''Life and Downfall of Nikolai Kurbov''; novel), [Moscow], 1923; *Chetyre povesti o legkikh kontsakh,* [Moscow], 1923; *Trinadtsat trubok* (title means ''Thirteen Pipes''; short stories), Gelikon, 1923; *Trubka,* [Moscow], 1924; *Rvach* (title means ''The Self Seeker''; novel), 1925; *Leto 1925 goda v Parizhe* (title means ''The Summer of 1925 in Paris''), 1926; *Zagovor ravnykh* (title means ''Conspiracy of Equals''; novel), 1928; *Skornyak* (title means ''The Furrier''), 1928; *Belyi ugol,* 1928.

Viza vremeni (title means ''Visa of Time''), 1930; *Edinyl front,* 1930; *Ispaniia* (travel), [Paris], 1930; (editor with Ovadii Savich) *My i oni: Frantsiia,* 1931; *Fabrika snov* (title means ''The Dream Factory''), 1931; *Moskva slezam ne verit* (title means ''Moscow Does Not Believe in Tears''; novel), [Paris], 1933; *Zatianuvshaiasia razviazka,* [Moscow], 1934; *Khronika nashikh dnei,* [Moscow], 1935; *Ne perevodia dykhaniia* (title means ''Without Stopping for Breath''; novel), Sovetskii pisatel, 1935, reprinted, Prideaux, 1976; *Kniga diia vzroslykh,* [Moscow], 1936; *Chetyre trubki,* [Moscow], 1936; *Granitsy nochi,* [Moscow], 1936; *Vne peremiriia,* [Moscow], 1937; *Chto cheloveku nado* (title means "What a Man Needs"; novel), [Moscow], 1937; *Ispanskii zakal* (short stories), [Moscow], 1938.

Vernost, [Moscow], 1941; *Fashistskie mrakobesy*, 1941; *Beshenye volki*, 1941; *Za zhizn*, [Moscow], 1942; *Solntsevorot*, [Moscow], 1942; *Svoboda* (poetry), [Moscow], 1943; *Stikhi o voine*, [Moscow], 1943; *Padenie duche*, [Moscow], 1943; *Rasskazy etikh let*, [Moscow], 1944; *Put k Germanii*, [Moscow], 1944; *Lev na ploshadi* (title means "Lion in the Square"), 1947; *Nadezhda mira*, [Moscow], 1950; *Za mir!* (essays), [Moscow], 1950, enlarged edition, 1952; *Sochineniia*, five volumes, [Moscow], 1952-54; *Volya noradnov* (title means "Will of the People"; speeches), 1953; *Liudi khotiat zhit*, [Moscow], 1953; *O rabote pisatelya* (title means "On the Labor of a Writer"; essays), 1953; *Sovest nardov* (addresses, essays, and lectures), [Moscow], 1956; *Indiiskie vpechatieniia* (travel), [Moscow], 1958; *Severnaya vesna* (title means "Northern Spring"), 1959; *Stikhi*, Sovetskii pisatel, 1959; (translator) Petros Anteos, *Rasskazy grecheskikh pisatelei*, Izd-vo inostrannoi lit-ry, 1959; *Putevye zapisi* (travel), Iskusstvo, 1960; *Sobranie sochinenii*, nine volumes, [Moscow], 1962-67; (contributor) *"The Actress"* (akterka) by Ilyo Ehrenburg and *"Petya the Cock"* (Petia-petel) by Vsevolod Ivanov, edited by G. A. Birkett, Appleton-Century-Crofts, 1966; (with Mikhail Vladimirovich Alpatov) *Grafika Pikasso*, [Moscow], 1967; *Den druhy*, Odeon, 1968; *Ten' derev'ev* (poetry), edited by L. Zonina, [Moscow], 1969; *Stikhotvoreniia*, [Moscow], 1972; *Letopis muzhestva* (addresses, essays, and lectures), [Moscow], 1974.

Member of board of *V zash chitu mira* (magazine), 1956-67. Contributor to magazines and periodicals, including *Severnye zori*.

WORK IN PROGRESS: The final volumes of *Men, Years, Life*, left unfinished at time of death.

SIDELIGHTS: Referred to by his critics as a perfidious maneuverer, Ehrenburg simply labeled himself a survivor. He was among the few Jews and "cosmopolitans" who escaped Stalin's purges during the late 1930's. One of Stalin's favorite writers and propagandists while many of his colleagues were killed or imprisoned, Ehrenburg admitted that he made compromises and once observed: "My life resembles a vaudeville act with many changes of costume, but I am not a ham. I am only trying to be obedient." He qualified this statement by revealing that in his writing he has "told the truth, but not all the truth." Ultimately, Ehrenburg attributed his survival in a perilous age to chance. He reflected, "I lived in an era when the fate of man resembled not so much a chess game as a lottery."

Ehrenburg was born into a middle-class Jewish family. His parents frequently entertained prominent guests, one being writer Maxim Gorky. The young Ehrenburg, though, far from exhibiting evidence of his future writing career, was a difficult child who was finally restrained by a special tutor proficient in hypnotism. Ehrenburg's irregular political involvement began in 1906 when he joined the Bolsheviks. In 1907 he was expelled from his school for inciting a student strike. He was arrested two more times by the police and after spending five months in jail in 1908, was exiled.

The future author arrived in Paris in 1909. While living predominately in the Montparnasse section of the city, Ehrenburg began associating with the many artists, painters, and writers who also lived there. He briefly fell under the influence of a number of Roman Catholic writers and for a time toyed with the idea of joining a Benedictine monastery. He wrote poetry, but it generally went unnoticed. During World War I Ehrenburg volunteered to fight for France but was found unfit for such duty. Instead, he toiled as a freight packer of war supplies and later worked as a reporter for the newspapers *Birzhevye Vedemosti* and *Utro Rossii*.

In 1917 the Bolshevik revolution broke out and Ehrenburg returned to Russia. Working at a number of occupations during this time of intense political confusion, he served as a supervisor of juvenile delinquents and lectured on Russian literature. He also founded nurseries for children. Ehrenburg, however, could not adjust to the revolutionary conditions existing in his native land and so departed once again in 1921. He tried to return to his beloved Paris, but officials thought he was a Bolshevik spy and refused him permission. He settled in Belgium instead and there wrote his first novel, *The Extraordinary Adventures of Julio Jurenito and His Disciples*.

This satirical work relates the tale of a Mexican prophet, Julio, who preaches anarchy and nihilism during his travels through Europe. The character Julio is supposedly fashioned after the Mexican artist Diego Rivera, a friend of Ehrenburg. In the novel the hero is accompanied by a group of unlikely companions that includes a French pacifist, an American entrepreneur, an illiterate Italian, and a German realist. *Julio Jurenito* appeared in English in 1930 and received generally favorable reviews. Clinton Simpson of the *Saturday Review of Literature* asserted: "Parts of . . . [Ehrenburg's] book are excellent satire—biting, fresh, derisive. Other parts, including much of the extravagant nonsense which binds the narratives together, fall pretty flat." M. Crobaugh in *Books Abroad* remarked that Ehrenburg "turns society upside down, and sardonically reveals the sham or hollowness of its structure." Crobaugh added that the author "leaves untouched little of the social fabric of pre-war, war time, and revolutionary Europe and Russia. . . . Compared to Hurenito, the criticisms of [Sinclair] Lewis and company appear as pleasant fables for children." Lenin, too, is said to have admired the book.

Ehrenburg was permitted to reenter Paris in 1924. Soon, the writer resumed his active social life. Living on the West Bank, Ehrenburg hobnobbed with such well-known figures as Pablo Picasso, Henri Matisse, Marc Chagall, Paul Eluard, Andre Malraux, Louis Aragon, Albert Einstein, and Pablo Neruda. During this time he also wrote several more novels.

In 1925 *Rvach* was published. The novel bitterly criticizes the speculators that surfaced during the time of Lenin's New Economic Policy (NEP) in the Soviet Union. This was followed by a melodramatic romance, *The Love of Jeanne Ney*, in the same year. The book met with good reviews. A *New York Times* critic observed that although "as art, except to the most thorough-paced fatalist, 'The Love of Jeanne Ney' fails to reach a level it might have achieved . . . it is important to repeat that here, often, is masterly story-telling, creative imagination and a mind that is almost always interesting." Arthur Ruhl of the *Saturday Review of Literature* was more fulsome in his praise: "It is difficult to give, in a word, much notion of a talent so vivid and versatile, so fluid and flamelike; of a writer who can be as concrete and even topical as you please, and in his style is always simple and restrained, and yet so completely makes his own world."

A Street in Moscow appeared in Russian in 1927 but not in English until 1932. The volume depicts the sordid life on Protochny Street in Moscow. Alexander Nazaroff commented in the *New York Times* that "the novel reeks with physical and moral dirt, fist blows, tears, tragedies, and yet through it all there is a thirst for life and for human love in even the most degraded and embittered human hearts." Ehrenburg followed this endeavor with *The Stormy Life of Lasik Roitschwantz* in 1928. A satire of the misadventures of a poor Jewish tailor, the novel was not translated into English until 1960 and then without the author's permission. Ivor Spectar maintained that "although this novel is, in many respects, a stark tragedy, there is an undercurrent of humor, strongly reminiscent of the late Jewish writer, Sholom Aleichem." A *Time* reviewer commented that "the book shows, despite uneven translation, what a considerable comic talent has been squandered on the gloomy chores of propaganda." *The Life of the Automobile,* written in 1929, did not appear in translation until 1977. When it did, Edwin Morgan of the *Times Literary Supplement* was both critical and complementary in his review of the volume. He asserted: "Although it is easy to be unfair to Ehrenburg, nothing he wrote was absolutely first-rate. He remains an extremely interesting and tantalizing 'case' rather than a great writer." Morgan went on to state, however, that *The Life of the Automobile* "is undoubtedly one of Ehrenburg's best things. It is both a period piece, and yet amazingly fresh and relevant."

With the rise of fascism in the 1930's, the focus of Ehrenburg's writing began to change. He was virulently anti-fascist and resolved to take his "place in the fighting ranks." Consequently, he forsook his satirical style, which earned the displeasure of many Soviet authorities who looked unkindly on such works as *Julio Jurenito, Rvach,* and *A Street in Moscow.* Instead, the author adopted the official Soviet policies and with them, the official communist school of art, social realism. Although Ehrenburg remained in Paris, he became a faithful adherent to Soviet dogma and in 1932, started reporting for the government's newspaper, *Izvestia.*

Ehrenburg's novels also reflected his shift in ideology. *Out of Chaos,* published in 1934, chronicles the lives of Soviet workers contructing a steel mill in Siberia. Critics were generally impressed with Ehrenburg's effort. "This pro-Soviet, but unregimented Russian novelist maintains a clearer perspective than do most of the Bolshevik novelists writing from the inside," exclaimed F. T. March of the *New York Herald Tribune Books.* "No phase of life in the U.S.S.R. is left wholly neglected. And one finds oneself again and again marking passages that are specially illuminating, preceptive or otherwise significant." Similarly, Lewis Gannett cited: "There is nothing in this gigantic, sprawling, clumsy, eager young country called Soviet Russia which Ehrenbourg refuses to face. This man is no propagandist, pro or con; he is mature, witty and compassionate, and a born story teller." A *Springfield Republican* reviewer disagreed, contending "that at bottom . . . [*Out of Chaos*] is not literature, but propaganda, and therefore at bottom as dishonest as a news report intentionally written with bias to mislead and pervert the public opinion of its community."

During the 1930's, much of the writer's time was spent reporting for *Izvestia.* He traveled about Europe covering such events as the Spanish civil war and the Saar popular vote of 1938. Ehrenburg observed some of the Spanish civil war in the middle of actual combat. His vivid dispatches describing the conflict helped elevate him to the position of one of Soviet Russia's leading correspondents.

After the fall of Paris to the Nazis in 1940, Ehrenburg moved to Moscow. Although he strongly opposed Stalin's ruthless purges and the Nazi-Soviet pact of 1939, the writer did not voice his opinions. Instead, he wrote *The Fall of Paris,* which mirrored his hate of the Nazis and his love of the French capital. Consequently, Ehrenburg could not find a publisher for the book in Russia, as it was blantantly hostile to the Soviet agreement with the Germans. Then Stalin tele-

phoned the writer one day and told him he liked the book. It went to press a few days later. Stalin's change of attitude regarding the volume was precipitated by Germany's invasion of the U.S.S.R. in June of 1941.

Outside Russia, *The Fall of Paris* met with a lukewarm reception. Many Western critics felt the book was just another propagandist tract. "'The Fall of Paris,' even though it has won the 100,000-ruble Stalin literary prize, can hardly, be called a creative work of art," noted Virgilia Sapieha of the *Weekly Book Review.* "For all its occasional moving moments, it must be judged, along with many other diatribes, as a harshly brilliant prosecution for a political doctrine." Similarly, Saul Bellow pointed out: "One can forgive a nation at war for not producing good novels. It is not so easy to forgive it for singling out one so specious for special honors as art and history." On the other hand, a *Times Literary Supplement* critic praised Ehrenburg as "an uneven writer, fluent and adroit almost to excess, but at his best he exhibits a bold, pointed imagination and a mordant and deftly reasoned irony." He continued that Ehrenburg "knows France, knows and loves Paris in particular, and love has given him a clarity, a comprehension, an intuitive tolerance to temper the scorn he feels."

At this time, Ehrenburg also began writing for two Soviet newspapers, *Krasnaya zvezda* and *Pravda.* He worked as a war correspondent covering the Soviet struggle against the invading German forces. His bitter hatred of the Nazis permeated his stories. Focusing on German atrocities and injustices, Ehrenburg's dispatches aroused such feeling against the Nazis in Russia that Soviet military leaders admitted they could not have won the conflict without Ehrenburg's rabble-rousing. Edward Crankshaw of the *Observer* recalled his impressions of Ehrenburg during World War II: "When I knew him in Russia during the war it seemed to me that the vitriolic hatred of the Germans that came pouring out in that extraordinary flow of daily articles which made him a popular hero was nourished not only by his rage and horror at what the Germans were doing to his country but also by his pent-up hatred of Stalin and himself." Ehrenburg received his first Order of Lenin for his wartime contributions.

After the conflict the writer continued to steadily churn out books. *The Tempering of Russia* details the battle between Russia and Germany using many of Ehrenburg's wartime articles. Leland Stowe of the *Weekly Book Review* proclaimed that "in every sense Ehrenburg is the prophet of Russian victory. He has inspired it and helped shape it, and he has done it with a moral voice. No more revealing book has been written about Russia at war." The *Springfield Republican*'s R. S. Scott concurred in his approval: "Ehrenburg is a keen interpreter of events, writes in a clear, crisp style; and has a fund of knowledge, gained through wide experience, to portray capably what he sees and feels."

European Crossroad: A Soviet Journalist in the Balkans followed a few years later. The volume was greeted by less than enthusiastic critics. According to John DeWitt in the *Christian Science Monitor,* Ehrenburg's "assessment of the aspirations of the people of eastern Europe is—in view of many facts of postwar history, present politics, and the reports of many other competent observers—open to most serious question." Also disapproving, the *Saturday Review of Literature*'s Leigh White declared that Ehrenburg "writes, as usual, in words of two syllables, and in a style that is perfectly adapted to the demands of Soviet censorship. His book, as a result, is superficial, inaccurate, maudlin, and unenlightening."

The Storm met with a similar appraisal in 1948. Ernest Pisko upheld that "as a literary work, 'The Storm' is infinitely inferior not only to the author's earlier writings but also to Russian war novels written and published before 1946." Philip Burnham of the *New York Times* conjectured that "Ehrenburg, the very official Russian reporter and culture delegate, needs all his tireless pages to work into one novel the propaganda points he appears bursting to remake all at once. By now the points are well rehearsed, outrageously clear, and neatly classified in pungent little thumbnail sketches."

Stalin died in 1953, and a year later Ehrenburg made an abrupt political about-face in his novel *The Thaw*. Whereas he had been one of Stalin's favorite party-line propagandists, he became an advocate for more liberal policies and called for greater creative freedom for artists than that allowed under social realism. Although reviewers questioned the book's literary value, its political implications caused an international brouhaha. Harrison E. Salisbury of the *New York Times* scoffed that "as a novel 'The Thaw' is not worth the paper it is written on." He added that "as a political event, however, it proved a minor bombshell. For the first time Ehrenburg mentioned a whole series of subjects which long had been [taboo]." Indeed, Ehrenburg mentioned such topics as "the horrible effects of the purges . . . ; squalid housing conditions among workers; shortages of consumer goods; cyncism among artists and writers; toadyism and careerism; the use of slander and smear." *New Republic*'s Jeri Laber concurred: "Although its significance as literature is slight, as social commentary it is outstanding."

Despite the fact that the author was roundly censured for this volume by the Soviet Writers Congress, Ehrenburg continued to support liberalization of Soviet artistic standards. In 1963, Nikita S. Khrushchev publicly disapproved of the aging writer's stance. Ehrenburg persisted, though, and in the spring before his death, refused to attend the congress of the Union of Soviet Writers in protest. His absence prompted a scolding from the novelist Mikhail Sholokhov. Untroubled, Ehrenburg remarked that Sholokhov "always says something at a congress to wake up the members."

Ehrenburg's autobiography, *Men, Years, Life*, is one of his last works and the most extensive of his career. *People and Life, 1891-1921*, the combined first two volumes of the six-volume set, received generally good reviews. Pisko in the *Christian Science Monitor* claimed that the author's sketches of his artist and writer friends in Paris "establish Ehrenburg as a superior cultural historian." Salisbury agreed in the *Saturday Review:* "In the guise of a literary memoir Ehrenburg is writing one of the most powerful political testaments of his day. And in the process he is creating as important and fascinating a document as has emerged from the U.S.S.R." Irving Howe, though, felt differently: "Ehrenburg's book of memoirs is one of the saddest books I have ever read. It is written with journalistic skill: he knows how to compose a sketch that will bristle with half-visible suggestion, he knows how to drop a telling phrase, he knows how to draw the external likeness of a famous writer. But what he cannot do, or thinks it wise not to do, is tell the whole truth."

Memoirs: 1921-1941, the combined third and fourth volumes of the set, provoked many critics to comment on the compromises Ehrenburg made during the Stalin era. *Nation*'s Isaac Deutscher theorized: "Ehrenburg's misfortune was not so much that he lacked the character to resist Stalinism, but that he submitted to it so completely and even zealously that he thereby corrupted his own work and nearly destroyed himself as novelist and poet. . . . The writing of the

Memoirs was for Ehrenburg an opportunity to cleanse himself, test his wasted talent, and regain something of his artistic quality. To a very limited extent, he has succeeded." Similarly, Marc Slonim disclosed that "unfortunately, Ehrenburg does not limit his plain talk to general judgments and startling examples but wants to use his memoirs for self-justification. This is probably the least pleasant part of his recollections; it does not sound right or convincing." Andrew Field of *Book Week* concluded: "The demands of history were more complicated for Ehrenburg, though. He met them, not as well as some, but better than most. His memoirs are an uneven but carefully polished mirror of those flawed times."

Volume V of *Men, Years, Life* received favorable reviews. "As a whole," reflected L. P. Slater, *The War: 1941-1945* "is exceptionally well-informed, clear-sighted and sincere." The reviewer also noted that "from these memoirs the author convincingly emerges as a man of deep conscience and humanity." The sixth and final volume, *Post-War Years: 1945-1954*, was published a year before Ehrenburg's death. Critics were for the most part disappointed in the work. *Post-War Years* is, according to a *Times Literary Supplement* reviewer, "the longest and least satisfactory" volume of the set. "A little more candour and less self-censorship (or was it simply *the* official censorship?) would have made it a better book." A *New Yorker* critic judged, however, that Ehrenburg was "a slightly better-than-average fellow trying to cope with unspeakable circumstances." He mused that "these sad memoirs are permeated by the bewilderment, relief, and guilt of a survivor."

BIOGRAPHICAL/CRITICAL SOURCES: Saturday Review of Literature, January 25, 1930, July 26, 1930, July 23, 1932, May 26, 1934, August 9, 1944, March 29, 1947, December 24, 1949; *New York Herald Tribune Books*, January 26, 1930, April 17, 1932, May 27, 1934; *New York Times*, February 16, 1930, April 17, 1932, June 3, 1934, June 6, 1943, August 13, 1944, March 23, 1947, December 4, 1949, October 9, 1955, December 29, 1965, January 28, 1966; *Books Abroad*, spring, 1930; *New York Herald Tribune*, May 24, 1934; *Springfield Republican*, June 17, 1934, August 20, 1944; *Spectator*, December 25, 1942; *Times Literary Supplement*, January 2, 1943, October 22, 1964, December 29, 1966, April 15, 1977; *New Statesman and Nation*, January 9, 1943; *Weekly Book Review*, June 6, 1943, August 20, 1944; *New Republic*, September 13, 1943, October 10, 1955, May 18, 1963, March 16, 1968; *Book Week*, August 20, 1944, November 8, 1964, July 11, 1965.

Christian Science Monitor, February 25, 1947, January 7, 1950, November 22, 1955, December 14, 1962; *New York Herald Tribune Weekly Book Review*, March 9, 1947; *San Francisco Chronicle*, October 9, 1955; *Saturday Review*, October 22, 1955, November 5, 1960, May 5, 1962, November 10, 1962, December 5, 1964, June 19, 1965, November 18, 1967; *Time*, August 22, 1960, November 13, 1964; *New Statesman*, September 15, 1961; *New York Times Book Review*, April 15, 1962, November 1, 1964, July 25, 1965, December 31, 1967; *Commentary*, February, 1963; *Newsweek*, November 16, 1964, October 23, 1967; *Nation*, December 21, 1964, January 22, 1968; *Commonweal*, January 8, 1965; *New York Review of Books*, November 9, 1967; *New Yorker*, November 25, 1967; *Contemporary Review*, July, 1970; Helen Muchnic, *Russian Writers*, Random House, 1971.

OBITUARIES: New York Times, September 2, 1967; *Observer*, September 3, 1967; *Time*, September 8, 1967; *Newsweek*, September 11, 1967; *Antiquarian Bookman*, September 18, 1967; *Publishers Weekly*, September 18, 1967; *Books Abroad*, spring, 1968.*

—*Sketch by Anne M. Guerrini*

* * *

EHRENBURG, Ilyo (Grigoryevich)
See EHRENBURG, Ilya (Grigoryevich)

* * *

EHRLICH, Leonard Harry 1924-

PERSONAL: Born April 2, 1924, in Vienna, Austria; married, 1944; children: two. *Education:* Roosevelt University, B.S., 1947; Yale University, Ph.D., 1960. *Home:* 122 Bay Rd., Hadley, Mass. 01035. *Office:* Department of Philosophy, University of Massachusetts, Amherst, Mass. 01002.

CAREER: University of Massachusetts, Amherst, instructor, beginning 1959, associate professor of philosophy, 1969—. Visiting professor at Mount Holyoke College, 1972, and University of Massachusetts at University of Freiburg, 1973-74. *Member:* American Philosophical Association, American Metaphysical Society.

WRITINGS: Philosophy as Faith: Studies in the Thought of Karl Jaspers, University of Massachusetts Press, 1974; *Karl Jaspers: Philosophy as Faith*, University of Massachusetts Press, 1975. Contributor to literature, philosophy, and theology journals.*

* * *

EICHELBERGER, Rosa Kohler 1896-

PERSONAL: Born April 28, 1896, in Baltimore, Md.; daughter of Jacob George and Mary Elizabeth (Condon) Kohler; married Clark Mell Eichelberger, October 6, 1924. *Education:* Attended Sorbonne, University of Paris, 1930. *Home:* 139 East 33rd St., New York, N.Y. 10016.

CAREER: Children's Playground Association, Baltimore, Md., playground director, 1916-20; storyteller and superintendent of national tour at Radcliffe Chautauqua, 1920-28; Hull House, Chicago, Ill., storyteller, 1931-32; Greenwich House, New York City, storyteller, 1936-38; writer. Leader of League of Women Voters Freedom Forums, 1941-45; member of emergency welfare division of Citizens Welfare Corps, New York City, 1942-45; member of county Democratic Committee, 1954-72.

MEMBER: Women's National Book Association (representative to United Nations Non-Governmental Organizations), American Association for the United Nations, League of Women Voters, United Nations Association of the United States of America, Women United for the United Nations, East Lynne Historical Society.

WRITINGS: Bronko (juvenile), Morrow, 1955; *Big Fire in Baltimore* (juvenile), Stemmer House, 1979. Contributor of articles and stories to children's magazines. Book review editor for *League of Nations Chronicle* (became *Publication of the American Association for the United Nations,*) 1930-55.*

* * *

EKEH, Peter P(almer) 1937-

PERSONAL: Born August 8, 1937, in Okpara Inland, Nigeria; son of Eghwujovwo (a farmer) and Eririomare (a farmer; maiden name, Eriomala) Ekeh; married Helen Emuobohwo Akarue (a university teacher), May 1, 1966; children: Onome, Akpofure, Onoriode, Onovughe, Ome-jevwe. *Education:* University of Ibadan, B.Sc., 1964; Stanford University, M.A., 1967; University of California, Berkeley, Ph.D., 1970. *Religion:* Christian. *Home:* 8 Crowther Lane, University of Ibadan, Ibadan, Nigeria. *Office:* Department of Political Science, University of Ibadan, Ibadan, Nigeria.

CAREER: University of California, Riverside, assistant professor of sociology, 1970-73; Ahmadu Bello University, Zaria, Nigeria, fellow at Centre for Social and Economic Research, 1973-74; University of Ibadan, Ibadan, Nigeria, lecturer, 1974-75, senior lecturer, 1975-78, professor of political science, 1978—. *Member:* International Sociological Association, Nigerian Political Science Association, American Sociological Association. *Awards, honors:* Rockefeller Foundation fellow in the United States, 1965-70; John Cadbury fellow at University of Birmingham, 1978.

WRITINGS: Social Exchange Theory: The Two Traditions, Harvard University Press, 1974.

WORK IN PROGRESS: Colonialism and Social Structure, publication by University of Ibadan Press expected in 1982.

SIDELIGHTS: Ekeh commented: "Although I began my writing career in the area of sociological theory, I am now attracted to the nature of African intellectual problems. In the midst of the excitement of ever-changing events and sour experiences in social development, it seems to me that African scholars have increasingly become concerned with the problems of the here-and-now, leaving undeveloped issues of lasting intellectual importance. For instance, in the study of colonialism attention has been focused on the visible actors in the colonial scene, namely the colonizers and the colonized. I believe there is need for the discernment of the more subtle processes and latent structures that have developed in Africa. In the area of colonialism I seek to delineate the supra-individual social formations in colonialism. More broadly, it is my intention to highlight the African genre of the human condition in the light of our unique emergence into the world system in the twentieth century."

* * *

ELGAR, Frank 1899-

PERSONAL: Born in 1899, in Blaye, France; married Marguerite Galliot; children: one daughter. *Education:* Sorbonne, University of Paris, lic. es lettres and L.L.L. *Home:* 25 rue Lamarck, Paris 18e, France.

CAREER: Writer. Worked as art critic of *Carrefour*, France, 1952—.

WRITINGS—In English: (With Robert Maillard) *Picasso: Etude de l'oeuvre et etude biographique*, F. Hazan, 1955, translation by Francis Scarfe published as *Picasso: A Study of His Work*, Praeger, 1956, revised edition, Tudor, 1972; *Van Gogh*, F. Hazan, 1958, translation by James Cleugh published as *Van Gogh: A Study of His Life and Work*, Praeger, 1958, revised edition, Thames & Hudson, 1966; (with Joseph-Emile Muller) *La Peinture moderne de Manet a Modrian*, [France], 1960, reprinted as *Peinture moderne*, five volumes, F. Hazan, 1965, revision published as *Un siecle de peinture moderne*, 1967, translation published as *One Hundred Years of Modern Painting*, Tudor, 1960, reprinted as *A Century of Modern Painting*, 1972; *Mondrian*, translated by Thomas Walton, Praeger, 1968; (with Eric Newton, James W. Lane, and Hans Maria Wingler) *Jean de Botton* (in French, English, and German), G. Fall, 1968; *Cezanne*, A. Somogy, 1968, translation published as *Cezanne*, Abrams, 1969; (with Raymond Cogniat and Jean Selz)

L'Impressionnisme (juvenile), F. Hazan, 1972, translation published as *Dictionary of Impressionism*, Eyre Methuen, 1973, Barron's, 1979; *Greene Mercier* (text in English, French, and German), Musee de Poche, 1978; *The Post-Impressionists*, Phaidon, 1977, Dutton, 1978; *Modern Painters*, Barron's, 1980.

In French: *Picasso et Leger: Deux Hommes, deux mondes*, Les Amis de l'art, 1954; *Reynold Arnould: Forces et rythmes de l'industrie*, Les Presses artistiques, 1959; *Montanier*, Le Musee de poche, 1973; *Picasso*, F. Hazan, 1974; *Van Gogh*, Leonard Amiel, 1975. Author of exhibition catalogs.

Contributor to magazines, including *Parisien Libere*.

BIOGRAPHICAL/CRITICAL SOURCES: Times Literary Supplement, October 16, 1969.*

*   *   *

ELKINS, Stanley Maurice   1925-

PERSONAL: Born April 27, 1925, in Boston, Mass.; son of Frank and Frances (Reiner) Elkins; married Dorothy Adele Lamken, June 22, 1947; children: Susan Roselyn, Robert Joel, Barbara Marion, Sara Ann. *Education:* Harvard University, A.B., 1949; Columbia University, M.A., 1951, Ph.D., 1959. *Home:* 17 Kensington Ave., Northampton, Mass. 01060. *Office:* Department of History, Smith College, Northampton, Mass. 01060.

CAREER: Teacher at private school in New York, N.Y., 1951-54; University of Chicago, Chicago, Ill., assistant professor of history, 1955-60; Smith College, Northampton, Mass., assistant professor, beginning 1960, professor of history, 1964—. Fellow of Institute for Advanced Study, 1970-71, 1976-77. *Military service:* U.S. Army, 1943-46. *Member:* American Historical Association, American Studies Association, New England American Studies Association (president, 1968-69). *Awards, honors:* Rockefeller Foundation grant, 1959-60; Social Science Research Council fellowship, 1963-64; Humanities Foundation grant, 1967-68; Guggenheim fellowship, 1976-77.

WRITINGS: Slavery: A Problem in American Institutional and Intellectual Life, University of Chicago Press, 1969, 3rd edition, 1976; (with Eric McKitrick) *The Hofstadter Aegis: A Memorial*, Knopf, 1974. Contributor to history and political science journals.

BIOGRAPHICAL/CRITICAL SOURCES: American Scholar, summer, 1975; *American Historical Review*, April, 1976.*

*   *   *

ELLEDGE, Jim   1950-

PERSONAL: Born August 28, 1950, in Granite City, Ill.; son of Richard M. (a millwright) and Mary L. (Heath) Elledge; married Diane Kay Dean, June 13, 1970 (divorced, 1972). *Education:* Eastern Illinois University, B.A., 1971, M.S., 1973; further graduate study at University of Illinois at Chicago Circle. *Home and office:* 2008 North Fremont St., Chicago, Ill. 60614.

CAREER: Mundelein College, Chicago, Ill., reference librarian, 1974-77; Columbus-Cuneo-Cabrini Medical Center, Chicago, assistant medical librarian, 1977—. Member of poetry workshop faculty at Norris Center, Northwestern University, spring, 1980. *Member:* Illinois Writers. *Awards, honors:* Literary award from Illinois Arts Council, 1980, for poem, "Voudouienne to Voudouienne."

WRITINGS: James Dickey: A Bibliography, 1947-1974,

Scarecrow, 1979; (contributor) Vivian Stein, editor, *Literary Bookstores in the U.S.*, 2nd edition (Elledge was not included in 1st edition), Poets and Writers, 1980. Contributor of poems, articles, and reviews to magazines, including *Berkeley Poetry Review, St. Andrews Review, Spoon River Quarterly, Journal of Popular Film, Sunrise, NewsArt*, and *Small Press Review*.

WORK IN PROGRESS: Hometown, a poetry chapbook, *Old Friends Our Fathers, the Earth*, a poetry chapbook; *Putting a Dog to Sleep*, poems; compiling a supplement to *James Dickey*, covering works by and about Dickey, 1975-80.

SIDELIGHTS: Elledge commented: "Although I've published work in genres other than poetry, I consider myself primarily a poet, and the reviews, essays, and bibliographies only sidelights.

"My poetry is anchored in experience, but the experiences written about are not necessarily mine, being derived from, or 'inspired by,' a variety of events, individuals, and demons from sources as diverse as newspaper articles (as in my poem 'Sitting With Serpents') and the memories of relatives and friends ('Greens'). Of course, some poems even spring from my own experience, although in such cases I tend to distort the lived experience—by adding imaginary details to all but one or two actual details of the experience ('Unwed Mothers'), by combining two or more actual experiences in one poem ('Putting a Dog to Sleep'), or by using personae (as in 'Voudouienne to Voudouienne'). I'm learning the value of exploring my own background (midwestern with southern ties) which, until relatively recently, I'd always ignored.

"The expansiveness of the long poem is extremely attractive to me and, like *vers libre*, is not as 'free' as it seems to be at first glance. My long poems are almost exclusively rooted in historical events or conditions, although I've never consciously brought the two together. 'Klondike' is about two prospectors during the gold rush era. 'The Piasa Bird' combines the experiences of a photographer—who's taking pictures of a replica of an ancient painting by the Illinois Indians—with images depicting the Illinois' actual extinction.

"A few of my basic themes are alienation, in all its various possibilities, the darkness that, day or night, floods the human heart, the secret life which each of us leads and keeps hidden from all others, and love—whole and in shambles."

*   *   *

ELLINGTON, Richard   1915(?)-1980

OBITUARY NOTICE: Born c. 1915 in West Virginia; died December 5, 1980, in Fort Lauderdale, Fla. Writer. Ellington wrote mystery scripts for radio shows, including "The Shadow" and "The Fat Man." He also wrote five novels, including *Exit for a Dame* and *Just Killing Time*. Obituaries and other sources: *New York Times*, December 9, 1980.

*   *   *

ELLIOTT, Alan C(urtis)   1952-

PERSONAL: Born July 10, 1952, in Dallas, Tex.; son of Tom S. (a postal employee) and Ida (a postal employee; maiden name, Scirratt) Elliott; married Annette Bertrand (a teacher), January 3, 1974. *Education:* Dallas Baptist College, B.A., 1974; Southern Methodist University, M.A.S., 1976; further graduate study at Emory University, 1976-80. *Religion:* Methodist. *Home:* 1028 North Madison Ave., Dallas, Tex. 75208. *Office:* Health Science Center, University of Texas, Dallas, Tex. 75235.

CAREER: University of Texas, Health Science Center, Dallas, programmer and analyst, 1979—. *Member:* American Scientific Affiliation, American Statistical Association.

WRITINGS: On Sunday the Wind Came, Morrow, 1980.

* * *

ELLIS, Keith Stanley 1927-

PERSONAL: Born in 1927, in Sheffield, England; married Myfanwy Rose Williams; children: two daughters. *Education:* St. John's College, Cambridge, B.A. *Home:* 3 Belmont Hill, St. Albans, Hertfordshire, England.

CAREER: Staff writer for *John Bull,* England, 1950-60; freelance writer, 1960—.

WRITINGS: How to Make Money in Your Spare Time: A Complete Guide, Harrap, 1967; *Warriors and Fighting Men* (juvenile), Wayland Publishers, 1971; *The American Civil War,* Putnam, 1971; *Prediction and Prophecy,* Wayland Publishers, 1973; *Man and His Money,* Priory Press, 1973; *Man and Measurement,* Priory Press, 1973; *The Making of America,* Wayland Publishers, 1973; *Thomas Edison: Genius of Electricity,* Priory Press, 1974, Crane, Russak, 1976; *Thomas Telford, Father of Civil Engineering,* Priory Press, 1974; *Science and the Supernatural,* Wayland Publishers, 1974; *Critical Approaches to Ruben Dario,* University of Toronto Press, 1975; *Number Power: In Nature, Art, and Everyday Life,* Heinemann, 1977, St. Martin's, 1978. Also author of *Health and Happiness in Retirement,* British Medical Association. Contributor to magazines.

AVOCATIONAL INTERESTS: Reading, gardening.

BIOGRAPHICAL/CRITICAL SOURCES: Choice, July-August, 1975.*

* * *

ELMER, Carlos Hall 1920-

PERSONAL: Born July 22, 1920, in Washington, D.C.; son of Charles Percival and Dorothy Winslow (Hall) Elmer; married Wilma Virginia Hudson, January 29, 1943; children: Frank Hudson, Elizabeth Anne. *Education:* University of California, Los Angeles, A.B., 1947. *Religion:* Presbyterian. *Office address:* P.O. Box 4005, Scottsdale, Ariz. 85258.

CAREER: Writer, 1939-47; U.S. Naval Ordnance Test Station, China Lake, Calif., superviser in photography and presentations function, 1947-57; Traid Corp., Encino, Calif., sales engineer in photographic instrumentation, 1957-65; free-lance writer, 1965—. Chairman and delegate to international congresses on high speed photography. Member of Brookings Institution Seminar on Alternative Futures, 1971-72. *Military service:* U.S. Army, 1942-46; became captain. *Member:* Society of Motion Picture and Television Engineers (fellow; vice-president in photographic instrumentation, 1970-71), Society of Photo-Optical Instrumentation Engineers, Theta Xi.

WRITINGS: Arizona: The Color Panorama of Carlos Elmer's Arizona, [Scottsdale, Ariz.], 1967, 6th edition published as *Carlos Elmer's Arizona,* KC Publications, 1976; *London Bridge in Pictures,* [Scottsdale], 1971; *The Glorious Arizona in Color,* Hastings House, 1973; *Grand Canyon Country,* Elmer, 1975. Also author of *Seasons of Arizona,* 1971; *Colorful Northern Arizona,* 1977; *Hoover Dam, Lake Mead, and Lake Mohave,* 1978. Contributor of articles and photographs to *Arizona Highways.**

ELPHINSTONE, Murgatroyd
See KAHLER, Hugh (Torbert) MacNair

* * *

ELYTIS, Odysseus 1911-

PERSONAL: Original name, Odysseus Alepoudelis; born November 2, 1911, in Heraklion, Crete, Greece. *Education:* Attended University of Athens, 1930-35, and Sorbonne, University of Paris, 1948-52. *Home:* 23 Skoufa St., Athens, Greece.

CAREER: Poet and writer. Hellenic National Broadcasting Institution, Athens, Greece, broadcasting and program director, 1945-46 and 1953-54; art and literary critic for *Kathimerini* (newspaper) in Greece, 1946-48. Adviser to Art Theatre, 1955-56, and to Greek National Theatre, 1965-68; represented Greece at Second International Gathering of Modern Painters, in Geneva, Switzerland, 1948, and at Congress of International Association of Art Critics, in Paris, France, 1949; president of governing board of Greek Ballet, 1956-58. *Military service:* First Army Corps, 1940-41; served in Albania; became second lieutenant. *Member:* International Union of Art Critics, Societe Europeenne de Culture. *Awards, honors:* National Poetry Prize and National Book Award, both 1960, both for *To axion esti;* Order of the Phoenix, 1965; Nobel Prize for literature, 1979.

WRITINGS—Poetry, except as noted; in English translation: *To axion esti* (title means "Worthy It Is"), Ikaros, 1959, translation by Edmund Keeley and George Savidis published as *The Axion Esti of Odysseus Elytis,* University of Pittsburgh Press, 1974; *O ilios o iliatoras,* Ikaros, 1971, translation by Kimon Friar published as *The Sovereign Sun: Selected Poems,* Temple University Press, 1974; *Maria Nefeli: Skiniko piima* (title means "Maria the Cloud: Dramatic Poem"), [Athens, Greece], 1978, 3rd edition published as *Maria Nefeli,* 1979, translation by Athan Anagnostopoulos published as *Maria Nephele,* Houghton, 1981.

In Greek: *Prosanatolizmi* (title means "Orientations"), first published in *Makedhonikes Imeres,* 1936, published under same title, Pirsos, 1939; *Ilios o protos, mazi me tis parallayies pano se mian ahtidha* (title means "Sun the First Together With Variations on a Sunbeam"), O Glaros, 1943; *Iroiko kai penthimo asma ghia ton hameno anthypolohagho tis Alvanias* (title means "A Heroic and Elegiac Song of the Lost Second Lieutenant of the Albanian Campaign"), first published in *Tetradhio,* August-September, 1945, published under same title, Ikaros, 1962; "I kalosini stis likopories" (title means "Kindness in the Wolfpasses"), published in *Tetradhio,* December, 1946.

Hexe kai mia typheis gia ton ourano (title means "Six and One Regrets for the Sky"), Ikaros, 1960; "Alvaniadha. Piima yia dhio phones. Meros proto." (title means "Albaniad. Poems for Two Voices. First Part."), published in *Panspoudhastiki,* December 25, 1962; *Ho helios ho protos,* Ikaros, 1963; *To fotodhendro ke i dhekati tetarti omorfia* (title means "The Light Tree and the Fourteenth Beauty"), Ikaros, 1971; *Thanatos ke anastasis tou Konstandinou Paleologhou* (title means "Death and Resurrection of Constandinos Paleologhos"), Duo d'Art, 1971; *Ta ro tou erota* (title means "The Ro of Eros"), Asterias, 1972; *To monograma* (title means "The Monogram"), first published in *L'Oiseau,* 1971, published under same title, Ikaros, 1972; *Ho zographos Theophilos* (art criticism; title means "The Painter Theophilos"), Asterias, 1973; *O fillomandis* (title means "The Leaf Diviner"), Asterias, 1973; *Anihta hartia* (essays; title means "Open Book"), Asterias, 1974; *Ta eterothali* (title means "The Stepchildren"), Ikaros, 1974; *I mayia tou papadhiamandhi* (essays), Ermias, 1978.

Work represented in anthologies, including *Six Poets of Modern Greece,* edited and translated by Edmund Keeley and Philip Sherrard, Knopf, 1961; *Modern Greek Poetry: From Cavafis to Elytis,* edited by Kimon Friar, Simon & Schuster, 1973.

SIDELIGHTS: Odysseus Elytis was relatively unknown outside his native Greece when he was awarded the Nobel Prize for literature in 1979. Although the Swedish Academy of Letters has in recent years bestowed the honor upon other previously little-known writers—notably Eugenio Montale, Vicente Aleixandre, and Harry Martison—their choice of Elytis came as a surprise nonetheless. The academy declared in its presentation that his poetry "depicts with sensual strength and intellectual clearsightedness modern man's struggle for freedom and creativeness. . . . [In] its combination of fresh, sensuous flexibility and strictly disciplined implacability in the face of all compulsion, Elytis' poetry gives shape to its distinctiveness, which is not only very personal but also represents the traditions of the Greek people."

To be a Greek and a part of its twenty-five-century-old literary tradition is to Elytis a matter of great pride. His words upon acceptance of the Nobel Prize give evidence of this deep regard for his people and country: "I would like to believe that with this year's decision, the Swedish Academy wants to honor in me Greek poetry in its entirety. I would like to think it also wants to draw the attention of the world to a tradition that has gone on since the time of Homer, in the embrace of Western civilization."

Elytis was born Odysseus Alepoudelis in the city of Heraklion on the island of Crete. To avoid any association to his wealthy family of soap manufacturers, he later changed his surname to reflect those things he most treasured. Frank J. Prial of the *New York Times* explained that the poet's pseudonymous name is actually "a composite made up of elements of Ellas, the Greek word for Greece; elpidha, the word for hope; eleftheria, the word for freedom; and Eleni, the name of a figure that, in Greek mythology, personifies beauty and sensuality."

Elytis first became interested in poetry around the age of seventeen. At the same time he discovered surrealism, a school of thought just emerging in France. He soon became absorbed in the literature and teachings of the surrealists and worked to incorporate aspects of this new school into the centuries-old Greek literary tradition. Elytis has since explained the motivations behind his embracing of the French ideals: "Many facets of surrealism I cannot accept, such as its paradoxical side, its championing of automatic writing; but after all, it was the only school of poetry—and, I believe, the last in Europe—which aimed at spiritual health and reacted against the rationalist currents which had filled most Western minds. Since surrealism had destroyed this rationalism like a hurricane, it had cleared the ground in front of us, enabling us to link ourselves physiologically with our soil and to regard Greek reality without the prejudices that have reigned since the Renaissance."

Thus, Elytis adapted only selected principles of surrealism to his Greek reality. Free association of ideas, a concept he often made use of, allowed him to portray objects in their "reality" but also in their "surreality." This is shown in various poems, as when a young girl is transformed into a fruit, a landscape becomes a human body, and the mood of a morning takes on the form of a tree. "I have always been preoccupied with finding the analogies between nature and language in the realm of imagination, a realm to which the surrealists also gave much importance, and rightly so," claims Elytis. "Everything depends on imagination, that is, on the way a poet sees the same phenomenon as you do, yet *differently* from you."

Prosanatolizmi ("Orientations"), published in 1936, was Elytis's first volume of poetry. Filled with images of light and purity, the work earned for its author the title of the "sun-drinking poet." Edmund Keeley, a frequent translator of Elytis's work, observed that these "first poems offered a surrealism that had a distinctly personal tone and a specific local habitation. The tone was lyrical, humorous, fanciful, everything that is young." In a review of a later work, *The Sovereign Sun,* a writer for the *Virginia Quarterly Review* echoed Keeley's eloquent praise: "An intuitive poet, who rejects pessimism and engages in his surrealistic images the harsh realities of life, Elytis is a voice of hope and naked vigor. There is light and warmth, an awakening to self, body, and spirit, in Elytis."

The poet, however, bridles at such descriptions of his work. He has suggested that "my theory of analogies may account in part for my having been frequently called a poet of joy and optimism. This is fundamentally wrong. I believe that poetry on a certain level of accomplishment is neither optimistic nor pessimistic. It represents rather a third state of the spirit where opposites cease to exist. There are no more opposites beyond a certain level of elevation. Such poetry is like nature itself, which is neither good nor bad, beautiful nor ugly; it simply *is*. Such poetry is no longer subject to habitual everyday distinctions."

With the advent of the second world war Elytis interrupted his literary activities to fight with the First Army Corps in Albania against the fascists of Benito Mussolini. His impressions of this brutal period of his life were later recorded in the long poem *Iroiko kai penthimo asma ghia ton maneno anthypolohagho tis Alvanias* ("A Heroic and Elegiac Song of the Lost Second Lieutenant of the Albanian Campaign"). Regarded as one of the most touchingly human and poignant works inspired by the war, the poem has since become one of the writer's best-loved works.

Elytis's next work, *To axion esti* ("Worthy It Is"), came after a period of more than ten years of silence. Widely held to be his *chef d'oeuvre,* it is a poetic cycle of alternating prose and verse patterned after the ancient Byzantine liturgy. As in his other writings, Elytis depicts the Greek reality through an intensely personal tone. Keeley, the translator of the volume into English, suggested that *To axion esti* "can perhaps be taken best as a kind of spiritual autobiography that attempts to dramatize the national and philosophical extensions of the poet's personal sensibility. Elytis's strategy in this work . . . is to present an image of the contemporary Greek consciousness through the developing of a persona that is at once the poet himself and the voice of his country."

After the overwhelming success of *To axion esti,* questions were raised regarding what new direction Elytis would pursue and whether it would be possible to surpass his masterpiece. When *Maria Nefeli* was first published in 1978, it met with a curious yet hesitant public. M. Byron Raizis related in *World Literature Today* that "some academicians and critics of the older generations still [wanted] to cling to the concept of the 'sun-drinking' Elytis of the Aegean spume and breeze and of the monumental *Axion Esti,* so they [approached] *Maria Nefeli* with cautious hesitation as an experimental and not-so-attractive creation of rather ephemeral value."

The reason behind the uncertainty many Elytis devotees felt toward this new work stemmed from its radically different presentation. Whereas his earlier poems dealt with the almost timeless expression of the Greek reality, "rooted in my own experience, yet ... not directly [transcribing] actual events," he once stated, *Maria Nefeli* is based on a young woman he actually met. Different from the women who graced his early work, the woman in Elytis's poem has changed to reflect the troubled times in which she lives. "This Maria then is the newest manifestation of the eternal female," noted Raizis, "the most recent mutation of the female principle which, in the form of Maria, Helen and other more traditional figures, had haunted the quasi-idyllic and erotic poems of [Elytis's youth]." Raizis explained further that Maria is the "attractive, liberated, restless or even blase representative of today's young woman. ... This urban Nefeli is the offspring, not the sibling, of the women of Elytis's youth. Her setting is the polluted city, not the open country and its islands of purity and fresh air."

The poem consists of the juxtaposed statements of Maria Nefeli, who represents the ideals of today's emerging woman, and Antifonitis, or the Responder, who stands for more traditional views. Through Maria, the Responder is confronted with issues which, though he would like to ignore them, he is forced to come to terms with. Rather than flat, lifeless characters who expound stale and stereotyped maxims, however, "both are sophisticated and complex urbanites who express themselves in a wide range of styles, moods, idioms and stanzaic forms," maintained Raizis.

Despite the initial reservations voiced by some critics, *Maria Nefeli* has come to be regarded as the summa of Elytis's later writings. Gini Politi, for example, announced: "I believe that *Maria Nefeli* is one of the most significant poems of our times, and the response to the agony it includes *is written;* this way it saves for the time being the language of poetry and of humaneness." Kostas Stamatiou, moreover, expressed a common reaction to the work: "After the surprise of a first reading, gradually the careful student discovers beneath the surface the *constants* of the great poet: faith in surrealism, fundamental humanism, passages of pure lyricism."

In an interview with Ivar Ivask for *Books Abroad,* Elytis summarized his life's work: "I consider poetry a source of innocence full of revolutionary forces. It is my mission to direct these forces against a world my conscience cannot accept, precisely so as to bring that world through continual metamorphoses more in harmony with my dreams. I am referring here to a contemporary kind of magic whose mechanism leads to the discovery of our true reality. It is for this reason that I believe, to the point of idealism, that I am moving in a direction which has never been attempted until now. In the hope of obtaining a freedom from all constraint and the justice which could be identified with absolute light, I am an idolater who, without wanting to do so, arrives at Christian sainthood."

BIOGRAPHICAL/CRITICAL SOURCES: Books Abroad, spring, 1971, autumn, 1975; *Virginia Quarterly Review,* spring, 1975; *Hudson Review,* winter, 1975-1976; *Chicago Tribune,* October 19, 1979; *New York Times,* October 19, 1979; *Washington Post,* October 19, 1979; *Publishers Weekly,* October 29, 1979; *Odysseus Elytis: Analogies of Light,* University of Oklahoma Press, 1980; *World Literature Today,* spring, 1980; *Contemporary Literary Criticism,* Volume 15, Gale, 1981.*

—*Sketch by Kathleen Ceton Newman*

EMENEGGER, Bob
See EMENEGGER, Robert

*   *   *

EMENEGGER, Robert   1933-
(Bob Emenegger)

PERSONAL: Born January 13, 1933, in Whittier, Calif.; son of Ernest and Bernadine (Burnham) Emenegger; married Margaret McLean (an artist), December 31, 1964; children: Ashley McLean. *Education:* University of California, Los Angeles, B.A., 1957. *Home:* 330 South Irving Blvd., Los Angeles, Calif. 90020. *Office:* 7447 Melrose, Hollywood, Calif.

CAREER: Grey Advertising, Inc., Los Angeles, Calif., vice-president and creative director, 1965-79; Robert E. Emenegger Ltd. (motion picture producers and writers), Hollywood, Calif., president, 1979—. Musical composer, 1965—. *Military service:* U.S. Air Force, 1952-53. *Member:* Broadcast Music, Inc. *Awards, honors:* Numerous awards from film festivals and advertising associations, including some for commercials.

WRITINGS—Under name Bob Emenegger: *U.F.O.'s: Past, Present, Future,* Ballantine, 1974. Also author of television documentaries, including "UFO's: Past Present, and Future," "Death, the Ultimate Mystery," and "Is Everybody Happy But Me?"; science fiction teleplays, including "Zeta," "Captive," "Ultimate Being," "Psi Factor," and "Laboratory"; television specials, including "Hypnosis and Beyond"; teleplays, including "Perfect Woman"; and short films, including "The Day the Silence Came."

WORK IN PROGRESS: Three science fiction films for television, and five additional films for television and film.

AVOCATIONAL INTERESTS: Collecting sixteenth- and seventeenth-century armor.

*   *   *

EMERSON, Mary Lee
See KENNEDY, Mary

*   *   *

EMETT, Rowland   1906-

PERSONAL: Born October 22, 1906, in London, England; married wife, Mary, 1941; children: one daughter. *Education:* Attended Birmingham College of Arts and Crafts. *Home:* Wild Goose Cottage, 113 East End Lane, Ditchling, Hassocks, West Sussex BN6 8UR, England; and Nell Gwynn House, Sloane Ave., London SW3 3AX, England.

CAREER: Siviter Smith Ltd., Birmingham, England, commercial artist, c.1939; free-lance artist, illustrator, inventor, and writer, c.1939—. Humourous mechanical inventions have been exhibited at Festival of Britain, Smithsonian Institution, Chicago Museum of Science and Industry, and in the film "Chitty Chitty Bang Bang." *Member:* Society of Industrial Artists (fellow). *Awards, honors:* Member of Order of the British Empire, 1978.

WRITINGS—Self-illustrated: *Anthony and Antimacassar* (juvenile), Faber, 1943; *Engines, Aunties, and Others: A Book of Curious Happenings,* Faber, 1943; *Sidings and Suchlike, Explored by Emett,* Faber, 1946; *Home Rails Preferred,* Faber, 1947; *Saturday Slow,* Faber, 1948.

High Tea, Infused by Emett, Faber, 1950; *The Emett Festival Railway,* Penguin, 1951; *Nellie Come Home,* Faber, 1952; *New World for Nellie,* Harcourt, 1952; *The Forgotten*

Tramcar, and Other Drawings, Faber, 1952; *Emett's Domain: Trains, Trams, and Englishmen; The Best of Rowland Emett,* Harcourt, 1953.

The Early Morning Milk Train: The Cream of Emett Railway Drawings, J. Murray, 1976, Stephen Greene Press, 1977; *Alarms and Excursions and Other Transports Transfixed by Emett,* J. Murray, 1977, Transatlantic, 1979.

Illustrator: *Hobby Horses,* Guinness Son & Co., 1958.

Contributor to magazines, including *Punch, Life, Vogue, Cosmopolitan, Mademoiselle,* and *Harper's Bazaar.*

BIOGRAPHICAL/CRITICAL SOURCES: New York Times, September, 28, 1947; *Popular Mechanics,* February, 1960; *Life,* December 2, 1966; *Time,* November 1, 1976.*

* * *

ENGELKING, L. L. 1903(?)-1980

OBITUARY NOTICE: Born c. 1903; died of cancer, October 19, 1980, in Cooperstown, N.Y. Editor and journalist. Engelking, who was once labeled "the greatest school of journalism ever invented," was formerly the city editor of and an editorial writer for the *New York Herald Tribune.* Obituaries and other sources: *Newsweek,* November 3, 1980.

* * *

ENGELS, Donald (W.) 1946-

PERSONAL: Born May 15, 1946, in Rockville Centre, N.Y.; son of Donald W., Sr., and Alice F. Engels. *Education:* University of Florida, B.A., 1969; University of Texas, M.A., 1972; University of Pennsylvania, Ph.D., 1976. *Politics:* "Anti-totalitarian." *Home:* 666 Washington St., Wellesley, Mass. 02181. *Office:* Department of History, Wellesley College, Wellesley, Mass. 02181.

CAREER: University of Pennsylvania, Philadelphia, instructor in history, 1977; Brandeis University, Waltham, Mass., visiting assistant professor of classics, 1977-78; Wellesley College, Wellesley, Mass., assistant professor of history, Greek, and Latin, 1978—. *Member:* American Philological Association, Association of Ancient Historians, Society for Ancient Medicine.

WRITINGS: Alexander the Great and the Logistics of the Macedonian Army, University of California Press, 1978. Contributor to history and classical studies journals.

WORK IN PROGRESS: The Social and Economic History of Roman Corinth, a history of science, demography, urbanization, social and economic history, the study of moral values and systems of belief and their cultural impact.

* * *

ENNES, James Marquis, Jr. 1933-

PERSONAL: Born April 26, 1933, in Newark, N.J.; son of James Marquis (a manufacturing executive) and Margaret Elizabeth (Lemkau) Ennes; married Teresa Ellen Latshaw, September 3, 1955; children: Mark Theodore, Julie Ann, Carolyn Teresa. *Education:* San Francisco State College, B.A., 1961. *Home:* 19009 194th Ave. N.E., Woodinville, Wash. 98072. *Agent:* Robert Lescher, 155 East 71st St., New York, N.Y. 10021.

CAREER: U.S. Navy, in communications, 1951-54, assigned to fleet activity in Yokosuka, Japan, 1951-53, and to U.S.S. *General George M. Marshall,* 1953-54; Retail Credit Co., San Francisco, Calif., investigator, supervisor, and trainer, 1955-61; U.S. Navy, cryptologist in communications, 1962-78, assigned to U.S.S. *Westchester County,* 1962-63, to naval security in Washington, D.C., 1963-66, to U.S.S. *Newport News,* 1966-67, to U.S.S. *Liberty,* 1967, to naval security in Bremerhaven, Germany, 1968-71, and to naval security in Washington, D.C., 1971-78, retiring as lieutenant commander; writer, 1978—. *Member:* Authors Guild, U.S. Naval Institute, Seattle Free Lances. *Awards, honors*—Military: Purple Heart, Navy Achievement Medal, and Presidential Unit Citation.

WRITINGS: Assault on the Liberty (nonfiction), Random House, 1980. Contributor to *U.S. Naval Institute Proceedings* and newspapers.

WORK IN PROGRESS: The Monkey Problem (tentative title), a suspense novel, publication expected in 1982.

SIDELIGHTS: Ennes was an officer on the bridge of the U.S.S. *Liberty* when the American intelligence collection vessel was attacked by Israeli aircraft and motor torpedo boats during the Six Day War. After 34 American crewmen were killed and 171 others (including Ennes) were wounded, Israeli officials apologized for what they claimed was a case of mistaken identity. Israel ultimately paid more than six million dollars to the injured and to families of the dead.

In his first book, Ennes claims that the attack on the *Liberty* was no mistake, but a deliberate attempt to sink an American ship in order to prevent the United States from detecting Israel's secret preparations to capture the Golan Heights from Syria. Although American government officials explained the attack as a plausible mistake because of limited reconnaissance and insufficient wind to hold the ship's American flag aloft, Ennes presents evidence that the flag was clearly displayed in a strong breeze and that Israeli reconnaissance aircraft flew directly over the ship at low level and were heard reporting the ship's identification by radio to their headquarters before the attack commenced. Although American government officials claimed that the ship was only under attack for about six minutes, Ennes presents evidence that she was actually under fire for seventy-five minutes and received no support from the United States Navy even though she called for help by radio for more than two hours. Ennes argues that, beyond the details of the attack itself, the incident reveals a serious failure of American command and control in the Navy's inability to convey orders to the ship or to respond to the *Liberty*'s repeated calls for help.

Ennes's version is supported by several members of Congress and by two retired chiefs of naval operations, Admiral Arleigh Burke and Admiral Thomas H. Moorer. In a signed statement for the dust cover Admiral Moorer said, "Every American should read *Assault on the Liberty*. . . . The attack could not possibly have been a case of mistaken identity." Senator Adlai Stevenson published a review of the book in the *Congressional Record* (S 13136 9-22-80) and urged the members to read it; in a statement for the dust cover Senator Stevenson said, "If this book received more attention, U.S. policies in the Middle East might be better balanced and more successful. It is well worth reading."

Ennes told *CA:* "I had always intended to pursue writing as a second career, although nonfiction and expose writing was not necessarily part of the plan. *Assault on the Liberty,* however, came first simply because I felt the story needed to be told. With that behind me, I am moving on to other things such as suspense fiction.

"One theme that has long fascinated me is the conflict between government need to protect its legitimate interests and the people's need in a democracy for free expression. That struggle can be seen in *Assault,* as the ship's officers and crew attempt to tell a story that their government does not want told, and in the author's battle to learn the truth about the affair. A somewhat similar struggle will be seen in my forthcoming book.

"For all the implied criticism of government, however, one should not overlook the fact that very few nations are sufficiently free and confident to allow such a book as *Assault on the Liberty* to be published, and even fewer allow citizens access (albeit restricted access) to government documents, as I was, to prove the case."

BIOGRAPHICAL/CRITICAL SOURCES: People, March 10, 1980; *Everett Herald,* May 3, 1980; *Washington Post,* May 18, 1980, May 25, 1980, May 28, 1980, June 10, 1980; *Florida,* June 1, 1980; *Christian Science Monitor,* October 2, 1980.

* * *

ERENBURG, Ilya (Grigoryevich)
See EHRENBURG, Ilya (Grigoryevich)

* * *

ETCHEBASTER, Pierre 1894-1980

PERSONAL: Born May, 1894, in the Basque Provinces, Spain; died March 24, 1980; married wife, Jeanne.

CAREER: Court tennis professional, c. 1925-1954; instructor. *Military service:* French Army, served in World War I; received two Croix de Guerre citations. *Awards, honors:* World court tennis champion, 1928-54.

WRITINGS: (With George Plimpton) *Pierre's Book,* Barre, 1971.

SIDELIGHTS: Pierre Etchebaster dominated the game of "real" tennis for twenty-six years. He won the world championship title in 1928 and successfully defended it seven times before he retired as champion in 1954. He was known for his speed, accuracy, endurance, and grace on the court.

OBITUARIES: New York Times, March 26, 1980; *London Times,* April 3, 1980.*

* * *

ETRA, Jonathan 1952-

PERSONAL: Born March 31, 1952, in New York, N.Y.; son of Harry (an attorney) and Blanche (an attorney; maiden name, Goldman) Etra. *Education:* Yale University, B.A., 1973, M.A., 1975, M.Phil., 1976. *Religion:* Jewish. *Home:* 35 East 84th St., New York, N.Y. 10028.

CAREER: Writer.

WRITINGS: Junk Food, Delta, 1980. Assistant book critic for *Soho Weekly News,* 1977-78.

WORK IN PROGRESS: A collection of humor, "all the delightful, morose, offensive, opinionated pieces magazines have been unwilling to publish. Topics include 'Why I Hate Bright Young People' and 'In Praise of Boredom' "; a novel.

SIDELIGHTS: Etra told *CA:* "There is no reason why, with careful thought and attention to overall patterns and trends, the general direction of the New York Stock Exchange cannot be predicted with accuracy. Options, though not the most secure investment, represent the only interesting market strategy available to the small investor. I give them a lot of my time and they, in turn, provide more excitement than most of the people one has the misfortune to associate with an a day-to-day basis. Everything is junk food, though this is not necessarily bad. It forces you to acquiesce to insignificance. Humor is what you can get away with."

EUROPEAN
See MOSLEY, Oswald (Ernald)

* * *

EUSTIS, Alvin Allen, Jr. 1917-

PERSONAL: Born June 17, 1917, in Coeur D'Alene, Idaho; son of Alvin Allen and Blanche (Kruse) Eustis; married Helen Sarah Lathrop, May 16, 1942; children: Anne Dorothy. *Education:* University of California, Berkeley, A.B., 1938, M.A., 1939, Ph.D., 1947. *Home:* 945 Euclid Ave., Berkeley, Calif. 94708. *Office:* Department of French, University of California, Berkeley, Calif. 94720.

CAREER: University of California, Berkeley, 1947—, began as instructor, became professor of French, 1962—. *Military service:* U.S. Naval Reserve, active duty, 1941-45. *Member:* Modern Language Association of America, American Association of Teachers of French, American Association of University Professors, Philological Association of the Pacific Coast, Phi Beta Kappa, Sigma Chi, Pi Delta Phi. *Awards, honors:* Ordre des Palmes Academiques; Fulbright grant for France, 1953-54.

WRITINGS: Hippolyte Taine and the Classical Genius, University of California Press, 1951; *Marcel Arland, Benjamin Cremieux, Ramon Fernandez: Trois critiques de la Nouvelle revue francaise,* Nouvelles Editions Debresse, 1961; (translator) Francois Chevalier, *Land and Society in Colonial Mexico: The Great Hacienda* (edited by Lesley B. Simpson), University of California Press, 1963; (editor) *Seventeenth Century French Literature: Poetry, Theater, Novel: A Critical Anthology,* McGraw, 1969; (contributor) *Modern French Criticism,* University of Chicago Press, 1972; *Moliere as Ironic Contemplator,* Mouton, 1973. Contributor to philology journals.*

* * *

EVANS, Christopher (Riche) 1931-1979

PERSONAL: Born May 29, 1931, in Aberdovey, Wales; died October, 1979; son of Herbert Riche (a civil engineer) and Kathleen (Gorst) Evans; married Nancy Jane Fulmer, August, 8, 1963; children: Victoria Amelia, Christopher Samuel. *Education:* University of London, B.A., 1960; University of Reading, Ph.D., 1963. *Agent:* Patrick Seale Books Ltd., 2 Motcomb St., Belgrave Sq., London SW1X 8JU, England.

CAREER: National Physical Laboratory, England, head of Man-Computer Interaction Section, Computer Science Division, 1963—. *Member:* British Psychological Society, British Association of Behavioral Psychology, Ergonomics Research Society, Brain Research Association.

WRITINGS: (Editor with Anthony Daniel James Robertson) *Brain Physiology and Psychology,* University of California Press, 1966; (editor with Robertson) *Cybernetics,* University Park Press, 1968; (editor with T. B. Mulholland) *Attention in Neurophysiology,* Appleton, 1969; (editor) *Mind at Bay: Eleven Horror Stories,* Panther, 1969; (editor) *Mind in Chains: Fourteen Horror Stories,* Panther, 1970; *Cults of Unreason,* Harrap, 1973, Farrar, Straus, 1974; (author of introduction) *Understanding Yourself,* A & W Visual Library, 1977; *Psychology: A Dictionary of The Mind, Brain, and Behaviour,* Arrow Books, 1978; *The Mighty Micro: The Impact of the Computer Revolution,* Gollancz, 1979; *The Micro Millennium,* Viking, 1980.

Recordings; "An Interview With . . ." series; all published by Harper, 1973: "An Interview With D. E. Berlyne," ". . .

Noam Chomsky," "... Sir John Eccles," "... I. J. Good," "... Richard Gregory," "... R. Melzack," "... George Miller," "... Peter Milner," "... Karl Pribram," "... B. F. Skinner," "... Montague Ullman," "... Patrick Wall," and "... Leon Festinger."*

* * *

EVANS, Ilona 1918(?)-1980

OBITUARY NOTICE: Born c. 1918 in Providence, R.I.; died of congestive heart failure, September 23, 1980, in Wellesley, Mass. Doctor, educator, and author of works in her field. Evans co-wrote and co-edited *Legal Aspects of International Terrorism.* She was the first woman president of the American Society of International Law and was a professor at Wellesley College for thirty-five years. Obituaries and other sources: *New York Times,* September 26, 1980.

* * *

EVANS, Jean 1939-
(Ruth Graham)

PERSONAL: Born August 20, 1939, in Leicester, England; daughter of Fred Ghent (a carpenter) and Elizabeth (Woolley) Williamson; married Eifion Evans (a senior nursing officer); children: Leonie Evans Middleton, Beverley Evans Rolfe. *Home:* 1 Tiptree Close, Boyatt Wood, Eastleigh, Hampshire, England.

CAREER: Writer. *Member:* Society of Women Writers and Journalists, Romantic Novelists Association.

WRITINGS—Novels; published by R. Hale except as noted: *Nine Days a Queen,* 1970, reprinted as *Lady Jane Grey,* Sphere Books, 1972; *Rival Queens,* 1970; *Jane, Beloved Queen,* 1971; *Rebel Stuart,* 1971; *Royal Widow,* 1971, reprinted as *Katherine Parr,* Sphere Books, 1972; *The Divided Rose,* 1972; *Suffolk's Queen,* 1972; *The Tudor Tragedy,* 1972; *The White Rose of York,* 1972; *An Heir for the Tudor,* 1973; *Katherine, Queen Dowager,* 1973; *The Scottish Tudor,* 1973; *Henrietta Maria, the Unhappy Queen,* 1974; *The Rose and the Ragged Staff,* 1974; *Essex, Traitor Earl,* 1976; *The Phoenix Rising,* St. Martin's, 1976; *A Brittle Glory,* 1977; *The King's Own,* 1977; *Maria d'Este, the Second Duchess,* 1978; *The Notorious Fanny Howard,* 1978; *Uncrowned King,* 1978; (under pseudonym Ruth Graham) *The Mimosa Spring,* 1979; *King's Puritan,* Mills & Boon, 1981; *Yukon Bride,* Mills & Boon, 1981. Contributor to magazines, including *Writer.*

WORK IN PROGRESS: Hospital in the Mountains (tentative title), for publication by Mills & Boon; a novel on the American Civil War.

SIDELIGHTS: Evans told *CA:* "I was married at the age of sixteen and by the age of thirty had two rapidly growing chil-

dren aged ten and twelve. I desperately needed some interests outside my home and family, despite loving them all dearly, so I decided to fulfill my lifelong ambition to write. Though my first book was never seriously intended for publication, it was accepted by Robert Hale and now I find myself caught up and producing usually three books a year.

"I still find that my family takes a huge amount of time, especially now that there are also grandchildren. My life is even more hectic and enjoyable than before, but I still feel the need for other interests. I recently joined a group of other women who had careers which they left in order to raise families. The informal group meets twice monthly just to discuss general topics, ambitions, anything but babies! It gives us all a feeling of having a real identity for a while, outside that of mother and general dogsbody (though we all revert happily to that role as required).

"I am not a women's liberationist as such, but I do feel that women have a growing and important role to play in society, while society, though professing to encourage this, still lags behind in many ways. I am a firm believer in the 'feminine female' but feel it is time it was recognized that we have minds of our own!"

* * *

EVANS, Lawrence Watt 1954-
(Lawrence Watt-Evans)

PERSONAL: Born July 26, 1954, in Arlington, Mass.; son of Gordon Goodwin (a professor of chemistry) and Doletha (a secretary; maiden name, Watt) Evans; married Julie Frances McKenna (a chemist), August 30, 1977. *Education:* Attended Princeton University, 1972-74, 1975-77. *Politics:* Independent. *Home:* 1637 Lindy Lane, Lexington, Ky. 40502.

CAREER: Writer, 1977—. *Member:* Lexington Fantasy Association.

WRITINGS—Under name Lawrence Watt-Evans; "Garth" science-fiction series: *The Lure of the Basilisk,* Ballantine, 1980; *The Seven Altars of Dusarra,* Ballantine, 1981; *The Sword of Bheleu,* Ballantine, 1982.

WORK IN PROGRESS—Under name Lawrence Watt-Evans: The fourth novel of the "Garth" science-fiction series, tentatively titled *The Book of Silence,* for Ballantine; *Slant,* a science-fiction novel.

SIDELIGHTS: Evans commented: "I became interested in fantasy and science fiction as a child, and took up writing it for lack of any more promising line of work (I have never held a full-time job more than twelve weeks; the longest was a summer job in a ladder factory in 1973). I regard myself, at least so far, as a beginning hack. I expect to turn out reams of passable fantasy in the years ahead. I hope they'll be slightly more original than the average."

F

FAGEN, Stanley Alan 1936-

PERSONAL: Born November 13, 1936, in Brooklyn, N.Y.; son of Percy (a mechanic) and Rae (a secretary; maiden name, Kaplowitz) Fagen; married Val Robinson (a teacher), 1962; children: Claire, Lenore, Sharon. *Education:* Brooklyn College (now of the City University of New York), B.S., 1957; University of Pennsylvania, M.A., 1959, Ph.D., 1963; Washington School of Psychiatry, certificate in group therapy, 1971. *Home:* 1605 Lemontree Lane, Silver Spring, Md. 20904. *Office:* Montgomery County Public Schools, 850 Hungerford Dr., Rockville, Md. 20850.

CAREER: Walter Reed General Hospital, Washington, D.C., staff psychologist, 1963-64, chief child psychologist, 1964-66; Hillcrest Children's Center & Children's Hospital, Washington, D.C., chief child psychologist, 1964-66, training director in psychology, 1966-69, psychoeducational research director, 1969-70; Montgomery County Public Schools, Rockville, Md., supervisor of professional development, 1970-76, staff development consultant, 1976—. Training director in psychology at Children's Hospital of the District of Columbia, 1966-69, psychoeducation research director, 1969-70; consulting clinical child psychologist at Walter Reed Hospital, 1969-73. Assistant research professor at George Washington University, 1967-70, assistant clinical professor, 1968-70; adjunct professor at American University, 1968-71; consultant to Maryland State Department of Education. Vice-president of Tamarack Civic Association; member of executive committee of Page School P.T.A. *Military service:* U.S. Army, Medical Service Corps, 1961-66; became captain. *Member:* American Psychological Association (member of executive committee, 1967-69), Council for Exceptional Children. *Awards, honors:* U.S. Public Health Service fellowship, 1960-62; Psi Chi research award.

WRITINGS: (With Nicholas J. Long and Donald J. Stevens) *Teaching Children Self-Control: Preventing Emotional and Learning Problems in the Elementary School,* C. E. Merrill, 1975; *Organization Manual for a School-Based Internship Model,* Montgomery County Public Schools, 1977; (with Jeffery M. Hill) *Behavior Management: A Competency-Based Manual for In-Service Training,* Psychoeducational Resources, 1977; (with Leonard J. Guedalia) *Individual and Group Counseling: A Competency-Based Manual for In-Service Training,* Psychoeducational Resources, 1977. Contributor to journals in the behavioral sciences, including *Pointer, Instructor, Behavior Disorders,* and *Focus on Exceptional Children.* Executive editor of *Pointer,* 1979—.

WORK IN PROGRESS: Handbook for School In-Service Coordinators for Mainstreaming, publication expected in 1981; *Activities for Teaching Self-Control in the Classroom,* with others.

SIDELIGHTS: Fagen told *CA:* "Over the years I have gained increasing admiration and empathy for the classroom teacher who is asked to take on society's responsibility for molding young people into contributing adults. Early in my training I wanted to help 'repair' mentally ill people, but gradually I began to see the greater importance of creating healthy youth, equipped to cope with life stresses. For the past ten years I have worked to help teachers build resilience and strength in their students—I hope to continue in this endeavor through my career."

* * *

FAGG, William Buller 1914-

PERSONAL: Born April 28, 1914; son of William Percy and Lilian Fagg. *Education:* Magdalen College, Cambridge, B.A. (classics), 1936, B.A. (archaeology and anthropology), 1937, M.A., 1939. *Home:* 6 Galata Rd., Barnes, London SW13 9NQ, England.

CAREER: British Museum, London, England, assistant keeper in department of ethnography, 1938-40; Board of Trade, England, worker in department of industries and manufactures, 1940-45; British Museum, deputy keeper, 1955-69, keeper of department of ethnography, 1969-72, and Museum of Mankind, 1972-74; writer, 1974—. Consulting fellow in African Art at Museum of Primitive Art, New York, N.Y., 1957—; chairman of United Kingdom committee for First World Festival of Negro Arts, Dakar, Senegal, 1966; member of board of trustees of United Kingdom African Festival Trust, 1973-77; chairman of African Fine Art Gallery Trust, 1974—. Conducted fieldwork in Nigeria, the Congo, Cameroon, and Mali; organized loan exhibitions all over the world, including National Gallery of Art, Washington, D.C., and Brooklyn Museum.

MEMBER: International African Institute, Royal Institute of International Affairs, Royal Anthropological Institute (member of council, 1966-69, 1972-75, and 1976—; vice-president, 1969-72; honorary librarian, 1976—), Royal Society of Arts (fellow), Reindeer Council of the United Kingdom, Royal

African Society, Museums Association, African Studies Association, Institute of Contemporary Arts, Association of Art Historians. *Awards, honors:* Silver medal from Royal Society of Arts, 1951; P. A. Talbot Prize, 1964, and grand prize from World Festival of Negro Arts, 1966, both for *Nigerian Images;* patron's medal from Royal Anthropological Institute, 1966; companion of Order of St. Michael and St. George, 1967.

WRITINGS—In English: (With Eliot Elisofon) *The Sculpture of Africa*, Praeger, 1958, reprinted, Hacker, 1978; *Afro-Portuguese Ivories*, Batchworth Press, 1959; *Nigerian Images: The Splendor of African Sculpture*, Praeger, 1963 (published in England as *Nigerian Images*, Lund, Humphries, 1963); *Africa: Hundert Staemme, Hundert Meisterwerke: Ausstellung; Africa: One Hundred Tribes, One Hundred Masterpieces* (in German and English), Hochschule fuer Bildende Kuenste, 1964 (published in French and English as *Afrique: Cent tribus, cent chefs-d'oeuvre*, Congres pour la liberte de la culture, 1964); (editor with Margaret Plass) *African Sculpture: An Anthology*, Studio Vista, 1964, revised edition, 1966, Dutton, 1966; *Tribes and Forms in African Art*, Tudor, 1965; *African Tribal Sculptures*, Volume I: *The Niger Basin Tribes*, Volume II: *The Congo Basin Tribes*, Tudor, 1966; *The Art of Western Africa: Sculpture and Tribal Masks*, New American Library, 1967; *The Art of Central Africa: Tribal Masks and Sculptures*, New American Library, 1967; *African Tribal Images: The Katherine White Reswick Collection*, Cleveland Museum of Art, 1968.

The Tribal Image: Wooden Figure Sculpture of the World, British Museum, 1970, 2nd edition, 1978, Farrar, Straus, 1978; *Miniature Wood Carvings of Africa*, Adams & Dart, 1970, New York Graphic Society, 1971; *African Sculpture*, International Exhibitions Foundation, 1970, revised edition, Studio Vista, 1974; *Divine Kingship in Africa*, British Museum, 1970; (editor with Michael Foreman) *The Living Arts of Nigeria*, Studio Vista, 1971, Macmillan, 1972; (editor) *Sir Hans Sloane and Ethnography*, British Museum, 1971, Farrar, Straus, 1978; *African Sculpture From the Tara Collection*, Art Gallery, University of Notre Dame, 1971.

Other: *Nigeria: Zweitausend Jahre Plastik*, Staedtische Galerie (Munich, West Germany), 1961; *Sculptures africaines: Les univers artistiques des tribus d'Afrique noir*, F. Hazan, 1965. Author of exhibition catalogs. Contributor to magazines. Honorary editor of *Man: A Monthly Record of Anthropological Science*, 1947-65.

SIDELIGHTS: Fagg's books have been translated into French, German, and Spanish. *Avocational interests:* Photography (especially of art and ancient churches), listening to music, cycling, travel, geopolitics.

BIOGRAPHICAL/CRITICAL SOURCES: Times Literary Supplement, July 7, 1966.*

*   *   *

FAINSTEIN, Norman Ira   1944-

PERSONAL: Born June 11, 1944, in New York, N.Y.; married, 1969; children: two. *Education:* Massachusetts Institute of Technology, B.S., 1966, Ph.D., 1971. *Home:* 808 South First Ave., Highland Park, N.J. 08904.

CAREER: Queens College of the City University of New York, Flushing, N.Y., lecturer in political science, 1969-70; Columbia University, New York City, assistant professor of sociology, 1970—, research associate at Bureau of Applied Social Research, 1973—. Research associate at Center for

Public Policy Research, New York City, 1970—; consultant to Russell Sage Foundation. *Member:* American Sociological Association, American Political Science Association, Society for the Study of Social Problems. *Awards, honors:* Woodrow Wilson fellowship.

WRITINGS: (editor with Susan S. Fainstein) *The View From Below: Urban Politics and Social Policy*, Little, Brown, 1972; (contributor) D. B. James, editor, *Outside Looking in: Critiques of American Politics and Institutions, Left and Right*, Harper, 1972; (with S. S. Fainstein) *Urban Political Movements: The Search for Power by Minority Groups in American Cities*, Prentice-Hall, 1974. Contributor to journals in the behavioral sciences.

BIOGRAPHICAL/CRITICAL SOURCES: Annals of the American Academy of Political and Social Science, January, 1975.*

*   *   *

FAIRFAX-BLAKEBOROUGH, Jack
See FAIRFAX-BLAKEBOROUGH, John Freeman

*   *   *

FAIRFAX-BLAKEBOROUGH, John Freeman   1883-1978(?)
(Jack Fairfax-Blakeborough; Hambletonian, a pseudonym)

PERSONAL: Born January 16, 1883, in Guisborough, England; died c. 1978; son of Richard (a playwright) and Margaret Ellen (Sanderson) Fairfax-Blakeborough; married Doris Purvis, January 12, 1928; children Richard Noel John. *Education:* Attended grammar school in Stockton on Tees, England. *Religion:* Roman Catholic.

CAREER: Writer. Official turf judge at North Country race meetings, 1920-33; racecourse official. *Military Service:* British Army, Cavalry and Artillery; became major; received Military Cross. *Member:* Cleveland Bay Horse Society of Great Britain and Ireland (past president). *Awards, honors:* Officer of Order of the British Empire.

WRITINGS: Cleveland and Its Hunt, T. Woolston, 1902; *Life in a Yorkshire Village: With Special Reference to the Evolution, Customs, Folklore, and Legends of Carlton-in-Cleveland*, Yorkshire Publishing, 1912; *Malton Memories and l'Anson Triumphs: Being the Sporting History of Malton From Earliest Times to the Present Day, Together With the Lives and Times of the Scotts, l'Ansons, and Other Trainers, Jockeys, and Gentleman Riders*, Truslove & Bray, 1925; *Sporting Days and Sporting Stories of Turf and Chase*, Philip Allan, 1925; *Country Life and Sport*, Philip Allan, 1926; *The Analysis of the Turf; or, The Duties and Difficulties of Racing Officials, Owners, Trainers, Jockeys*, Philip Allan, 1927; *Sykes of Sledmere: The Record of a Sporting Family and Famous Stud*, Philip Allan, 1929.

Humours of Village Life: Tales From Yorkshire, Heath, Cranton, 1932; *Beating the Nobblers*, Philip Allan, 1933; *The Disappearance of Cropton*, Philip Allan, 1933; *Nat Wedgewood, Jockey: Tales of Turf Plots and Villainy*, Philip Allan, 1933; *A Non-Trier Wins*, Philip Allan, 1933; *A Rank Outsider*, Philip Allan, 1933; *Who Maimed Spurto?: A Turf Mystery and Romance*, Philip Allan, 1933; *Robin the Racer: The Life Story of a Horse*, Burns & Oates, 1934; *Warned Off*, Philip Allan, 1934; *Yorkshire Days and Yorkshire Ways*, Heath, Cranton, 1935; *Paddock Personalities: Being Thirty Years' Turf Memories*, Hutchinson, 1935; *English Wild Animals: Tales From A Woodland*, Burns & Oates, 1935; *A*

Last Gamble, Philip Allan, 1936; *Letters From a Yeoman to His Son in Society*, Heath, Cranton, 1936; *Queen of the Gangsters: A Tale of the Turf*, Philip Allan, 1936.

(With J.H.B. Bell and E. F. Bozman) *British Hills and Mountains*, Batsford, 1940, 3rd edition, 1950; *Lizzie Leckonby an' Mary Thompson*, Castleton, 1947; *Lizzie Leckonby, Mary Thompson, and Matty: Sketches of Village Life, Told in Cleveland Dialect*, Horne & Son, 1948; *Nothern Turf History*, J. A. Allen, Volume I, 1949, Volumes II-III, 1958; *A Short History of York Racecourse*, Reid-Hamilton, 1950; *More Village Gossip From Lizzie Leckonby, Mary Thompson, and Matty*, Horne & Sons, 1950; *Yorkshire: East Riding*, R. Hale, 1951; *Racecourses of Yorkshire*, Reid-Hamilton, 1953; (with R. Fairfax-Blakeborough) *The Spirit of Yorkshire*, Batsford, 1954; *Racecourses of Scotland: A Short History of Ayr, Bogside (Irvine), Edinburgh, Hamilton Park, Kelso, Lanark, Perth Racecourses*, Reid-Hamilton, 1955; *Yorkshire Village Life, Humour, and Characters*, Brown, 1955, new edition, EP Publishing, 1977; *Foxhunting in Yorkshire: History of Twenty-One Packs*, Reid-Hamilton, 1957; *Canon J. L. Kyle, M.A.: Vicar of Carlton-in-Cleveland and Faceby, 1894-1943*, privately printed, 1968; (under name Jack Fairfax-Blakeborough) *"J.F.B.": The Memoirs of Jack Fairfax-Blakeborough, O.B.E., M.C.*, edited by son, Noel Fairfax-Blakeborough, J. A. Allen, 1978.

Also author of *Bits of West Cleveland, England's Oldest Hunt*, 1907, *Northern Sport and Sportsmen*, 1913, *The Badger*, 1913, *Life in a Training Stable, Flat Racing Since 1900, Steeplechasing, The Winning Post, Hunting in the North, Northern Racing Records, The Yorkshireman and the Horse*, and *Gipsy's Luck*.

Editor: *The Hunting and Sporting Reminiscences of H. W. Selby Lowndes, M.F.H.*, Philip Allan, 1926; *The Turf Who's Who*, Mayfair Press, 1932. Also editor of *The Cleveland Bay Stud Book*, Volume XV (Fairfax-Blakeborough was not associated with earlier volumes), Maud I. Harvey's *Hunting on Foot With Some Yorkshire Packs*, 1913, Richard Blakeborough's *The Hand of Glory and Further Grandfather's Tales*, 1924, R. Blakeborough's *Yorkshire Dialect Readings*, 1924, Jack Molyneux's *Thirty Years a Hunt Servant*, 1935, and John MacGuigan's *A Trainer's Memories*, 1946. Past editor of *Mudhook*.

Contributor to *A Dictionary of the Dialect of the North Riding of Yorkshire*, edited by Alfred E. Pease, 1928.

Contributor to country and sporting journals, popular magazines, and newspapers, including *Sports Pictures* and *Yorkshire Post* (under pseudonym Hambletonian), *Sportsman, Spectator, Country Life*, and *Tatler*.*

*   *   *

FAIRLEY, James Stewart   1940-

PERSONAL: Born August 12, 1940, in Belfast, Northern Ireland; son of William John (a garage proprietor) and Mary (Law) Fairley. *Education:* Queen's University, Belfast, Northern Ireland, B.Sc., 1962, Ph.D., 1965. *Politics:* "Laissez-faire conservative." *Religion:* Presbyterian. *Office:* Department of Zoology, University College, National University of Ireland, Galway, Ireland.

CAREER: Queen's University, Belfast, Northern Ireland, research fellow, 1966-68; National University of Ireland, University College, Galway, lecturer in zoology, 1968—. *Member:* Mammal Society, Zoological Society, British Ecological Society.

WRITINGS: *Irish Wild Mammals: A Guide to Literature*,

privately printed, 1972; *An Irish Beast Book*, Blackstaff Press, 1975; (editor) *The Experienced Huntsman*, Blackstaff Press, 1976; *Irish Whales and Whaling*, Blackstaff Press, 1980. Contributor of nearly one hundred articles to scientific journals. Sectional editor of *Irish Naturalists' Journal*.

SIDELIGHTS: Fairley commented: "I write for fun and through a love of English. My research interest—Ireland's wild mammals—happens to be one about which accurate books can be written that will sell reasonably well to the general public. So I write books because they will be published. Apart from my research topic I am generally interested professionally in mammalogy and in the Irish fauna generally."

AVOCATIONAL INTERESTS: Music (especially classic jazz).

*   *   *

FALB, Lewis W(illiam)   1935-

PERSONAL: Born August 8, 1935, in New York, N.Y. *Education:* Cornell University, B.A., 1952; attended Sorbonne, University of Paris, 1957-58; Yale University, M.A., 1959, Ph.D., 1967. *Home address:* Carpenter Rd., Hopewell Junction, N.Y. 12533. *Office:* Department of French, Boston University, Boston, Mass. 02215.

CAREER: Yale University, New Haven, Conn., acting instructor in French, 1962-66; Vassar College, Poughkeepsie, N.Y., 1966-73, began as instructor, became assistant professor of French; Hunter College of the City University of New York, New York, N.Y., associate professor of French, 1973-74; Briarcliff College, Briarcliff Manor, N.Y., associate professor of French, 1974-77; Boston University, Boston, Mass., visiting professor of French, 1977—. *Military service:* U.S. Army, Signal Corps, 1960 and 1961-62; became sergeant. *Member:* Modern Language Association of America, American Association of Teachers of French. *Awards, honors:* Fulbright scholar in France, 1957-58.

WRITINGS: *American Drama in Paris, 1945-1970: A Study of Its Critical Reception*, University of North Carolina Press, 1972; *Jean Anouilh*, Ungar, 1977. Contributor to French studies journals.

BIOGRAPHICAL/CRITICAL SOURCES: *Choice*, April, 1978; *Modern Language Journal*, April, 1978.*

*   *   *

FALWELL, Jerry   1933-

PERSONAL: Born August 11, 1933, in Lynchburg, Va.; son of Cary H. (an entrepreneur) and Helen V. (Beasley) Falwell; married Macel Pate, April 12, 1958; children: Jerry, Jr., Jeannie, Jonathan. *Education:* Attended Lynchburg College, 1950-52; Baptist Bible College, Springfield, Mo., B.A., 1956. *Politics:* Conservative. *Religion:* "Non-affiliated Baptist." *Home address:* Tall Oaks, Lynchburg, Va. 24502. *Agent:* Nelson Keener, Old-Time Gospel Hour, Lynchburg, Va. 24514. *Office:* Old-Time Gospel Hour, Lynchburg, Va. 24514.

CAREER: Ordained Baptist minister, 1954; Thomas Road Baptist Church, Lynchburg, Va., founder and senior pastor, 1956—. Founder and chancellor of Liberty Baptist College, 1971—; founder and president of Moral Majority Inc., 1979—. *Member:* National Religious Broadcasters (member of board of directors). *Awards, honors:* D.D. from Tennessee Temple University, 1968; LL.D. from California Graduate School of Theology, 1973; named clergyman of the year by Religious Heritage of America, 1979.

WRITINGS: (With Elmer Towns) *Church Aflame*, Impact Books, 1971; (with Towns) *Capturing a Town for Christ*, Revell, 1973; *Listen, America!*, Doubleday, 1980.

WORK IN PROGRESS: Inner Peace and Strength (tentative title), publication by Doubleday expected in 1982.

SIDELIGHTS: Falwell told *CA:* "When I began the Thomas Road Baptist Church in June, 1956, with thirty-five adults and their children, I never dreamed this nucleus would one day grow into a church of seventeen thousand members. As the church has grown, my vision has broadened geographically. Today the Thomas Road Baptist Church sponsors worldwide missions and oversees a Christian academy, a liberal arts college, and a seminary. We also sponsor the 'Old-Time Gospel Hour' radio and television ministry that reaches into thousands of homes in the Unites States, Canada, and several foreign countries."

Falwell attributes his own conversion largely to the effectiveness of media ministry. Every Sunday morning while he was growing up, he listened to the "Old-Fashioned Revival Hour" on the radio. Its message had lasting influence on Falwell and helped shape his belief that he could reach more souls through the media than by any other means. Today his daily radio program can be heard on 304 stations nationwide, and his weekly television program can be seen on 386 stations. He expects these numbers to continue to grow and with them the number of conversions to Christianity.

As he is ambitious for Christ, so also is he ambitious for America, Falwell explained to *CA.* He fears for the decay of American morality and calls for a hasty return to decency, morality, and traditional family values. "Today America is turning her back on her biblical heritage and thus precipitating her downfall," Falwell insists. "Because I believe we are in a fateful decade of destiny, I wrote *Listen, America!* to awaken apathetic Americans to the fact that our beloved nation can only be saved if moral Americans will act quickly."

In recent years Falwell has become active on the American political scene. His political message is based on a fundamentalist morality, and he speaks out on behalf of Judeo-Christian principles.

Falwell is also founder and president of Moral Majority, Inc., an organization dedicated to "influencing legislation which is beneficial to the moral health of society. It is pro-life, pro-family, pro-moral, and pro-American." He added that he sees his "responsibility as a gospel preacher as one of influence" and uses the influence to educate, inspire, and inform fellow Americans and leaders regarding moral precepts.

BIOGRAPHICAL/CRITICAL SOURCES: Esquire, October 10, 1978; Gerald Strober and Ruth Tomczak, *Jerry Falwell: Aflame for God,*Thomas Nelson, 1979; *Time*, October 1, 1979; *Newsweek,*September 15, 1980; *People*, October 13, 1980; *Penthouse*, March, 1981.

* * *

FARAGO, Ladislas 1906-1980

OBITUARY NOTICE—See index for *CA* sketch: Born September 21, 1906, in Csurgo, Hungary; died after a brief illness, October 15, 1980, in New York, N.Y. Journalist and author best known for his biographies of General George Patton. In 1964 Farago wrote *Patton: Ordeal and Triumph*, the book on which the Academy Award-winning film "Patton" was based. He also penned *The Broken Seal*, which later was made into the motion picture "Tora! Tora! Tora!" Farago's other writings include *The Game of the Foxes* and

The Last Days of Patton. Obituaries and other sources: *Chicago Tribune*, October 18, 1980; *Washington Post*, October 20, 1980; *Time*, October 27, 1980; *Newsweek*, October 27, 1980.

* * *

FARBER, Norma 1909-

PERSONAL: Born August 6, 1909, in Boston, Mass.; daughter of G. Augustus and Augusta (Schon) Holzman; married Sidney Farber, July 3, 1928; children: Ellen, Stephen, Thomas, Miriam. *Education:* Wellesley College, A.B., 1931; Radcliffe College, M.A., 1932. *Home:* 1010 Memorial Dr., Cambridge, Mass. 02138.

CAREER: Musician, poet, and author. Appeared as a soprano singer in solo recitals and with small ensemble groups and orchestras, 1940—. *Member:* Phi Beta Kappa. *Awards, honors:* Premier prix in singing from Jury Central des Etudes Musicales (Belgium), 1936; Borestone Award, 1957, 1973, 1975, and 1976; Children's Book Showcase award from Children's Book Council, 1976, for *As I Was Crossing the Boston Common;* National Book Award from American Academy and Institute of Arts and Letters, 1976, for *As I Was Crossing the Boston Common;* choice of best illustrated children's books of the year from *New York Times*, 1978, for *There Once Was a Woman Who Married a Man;* Golden Rose Award from New England Poetry Club, for poetry; prizes for poetry from Poetry Society of America.

WRITINGS—All poetry collections: *Hatch*, Scribner, 1955; *Look to the Rose*, privately printed, 1958; *A Desperate Thing: Marriage Is a Desperate Thing*, Plowshare Press, 1973, also published as *A Desperate Thing: Marriage Poems*, Plowshare Press, 1973; (translator with Edith Helman) Pedro Salinas, *To Live in Pronouns: Selected Love Poems*, Norton, 1974; *Household Poems*, Hellric, 1975; *Small Wonders: Poems* (juvenile), Coward, 1979; *Something Further: Poems*, Kylix Press, 1979.

For children: *Did You Know It Was the Narwhale?*, Atheneum, 1967; *As I Was Crossing the Boston Common* (illustrated by Arnold Lobel), Dutton, 1973; *I Found Them in the Yellow Pages* (illustrated by Marc Brown), Little, Brown, 1973; *Where's Gomer?* (illustrated by William Pene du Bois), Dutton, 1974; *This Is the Ambulance Leaving the Zoo* (illustrated by Tomie de Paola; Junior Literary Guild selection), Dutton, 1975; *A Ship in a Storm on the Way to Tarshish* (illustrated by Victoria Chess), Greenwillow Books, 1977; *Six Impossible Things Before Breakfast: Stories and Poems*, Addison-Wesley, 1977; *How the Left-Behind Beasts Built Ararat* (illustrated by Antonio Frasconi), Walker, 1978; *There Once Was a Woman Who Married a Man* (illustrated by Lydia Dabcovich), Addison-Wesley, 1978; *Three Wanderers from Wapping* (illustrated by Charles Mikolaycak), Addison-Wesley, 1978; *How Does It Feel to be Old?*, Dutton, 1979; *Never Say Ugh! to a Bug* (illustrated by Jose Aruego), Greenwillow Books, 1979; *There Goes Feathertop!* (illustrated by M. Brown), Dutton, 1979; *Up the Down Elevator*, Addison-Wesley, 1979; *How the Hibernators Came to Bethlehem*, Walker, 1980.

Contributor of poetry to periodicals, including *America, Christian Century, Horn Book, Nation, New Catholic World, New Republic, New Yorker, Poetry*, and *Saturday Review.*

SIDELIGHTS: Norma Farber has published several types of books for children, including nonsense ballads and instructional alphabet and counting stories. All of her books are written in rhyme, making them especially appropriate for reading aloud.

As I Was Crossing the Boston Common, for which Faber received the Children's Book Showcase Award and the National Book Award, is narrated by a turtle. He relates his experiences one day as he crossed the Boston Common, encountering beasts, fish, and fowl along the route. The unusual creatures parade before him in alphabetical order, from the angwantibo, boobook, and coypu to the zibet.

A number of Farber's story lines are taken from biblical or classical tales. Such is the case in her nonsense ballad, *How the Left-Behind Beasts Built Ararat,* which is a spoof on the story of Noah and his ark. As the great flood is overtaking the land, Noah finds to his dismay that there is no more room on the ark and many animals will have to stay behind. A cow directs the left-behind animals as head of the "Committee for Staying Alive," and the group begins to literally make a mountain out of a molehill. They save themselves from the floodwaters and are eventually joined by their friends on the ark.

Another of Farber's nonsense stories is *There Once Was a Woman Who Married a Man.* The man never says a word, although the woman makes every attempt to break the silence. She tries nearly drowning him, jumping on the bed, and doing a fandango dance, but all to no avail. Finally, the town carnival solves her problem. As she and her silent husband go up the Loop-the-Loop roller coaster, she hears him mumble, "I'm sick."

BIOGRAPHICAL/CRITICAL SOURCES: New York Times Book Review, November 11, 1979; *Christian Science Monitor,* February 11, 1980; *Brookline Chronicle Citizen,* April 17, 1980; *Chicago Tribune Book World,* December 7, 1980.

* * *

FARIA, A(nthony) J(ohn) 1944-

PERSONAL: Born December 29, 1944, in Highland Park, Mich.; son of Anthony (an electrician) and Barbara (Hemeli) Faria; married Marilyn Ann Gaylord, June 9, 1968 (divorced July, 1980); children: Lara Marie, Robert Gordon. *Education:* Wayne State University, B.S., 1967, M.B.A., 1969; Michigan State University, Ph.D., 1974. *Politics:* Republican. *Religion:* Roman Catholic. *Home:* 211 Crawford, Windsor, Ontario, Canada N9A 5C3. *Office:* Department of Marketing, University of Windsor, Windsor, Ontario, Canada N9B 3P4.

CAREER: Chrysler Corp., Centerline, Mich., buyer, 1969; Georgia Southern College, Statesboro, assistant professor of marketing, 1973-75; University of Windsor, Windsor, Ontario, chairman of marketing department, 1975—. President of Marcon Marketing Consultants, 1978—. *Member:* North American Simulation and Gaming Association, Canadian Association for Administrative Studies, American Marketing Association, Association for Business Simulation and Experiential Learning, National Gaming Council, Academy of Marketing Sciences, American Institute for the Decision Sciences, Windsor Advertising and Sales Club.

WRITINGS: Creative Selling, Southwestern Co., 1966, 3rd edition, 1980; *Compete: A Dynamic Marketing Simulation,* Irwin, 1974, revised edition, 1979. Contributor to marketing, management, and business journals.

WORK IN PROGRESS: "The Retail Management Game," a retail computer-scored simulation game.

* * *

FARMER, Herbert Henry 1892-1981(?)

OBITUARY NOTICE: Born November 27, 1892, in London, England; died c. 1981. Presbyterian minister, educator, and author of religious works. Farmer wrote *The World and God* and *The World of Reconciliation.* His lectures were collected in *Towards Belief in God, The Servant of the Word, God and Man,* and *Revelation and Religion.* He was Norris-Hulse Professor at the University of Cambridge. Obituaries and other sources: *The Author's and Writer's Who's Who,* 6th edition, Burke's Peerage, 1971; *Who's Who,* 131st edition, St. Martin's, 1979; *London Times,* January 19, 1981.

* * *

FARRELL, John Philip 1939-

PERSONAL: Born November 19, 1939, in New York, N.Y.; son of Patrick John and Catherine (Monaghan) Farrell; married Judith Murphy (a teacher), January 25, 1964; children: Sheridan, Marcy. *Education:* Fordham University, B.A., 1961; Indiana University, Ph.D., 1967. *Office:* Department of English, University of Texas, Austin, Tex. 78712.

CAREER: University of Kansas, Lawrence, assistant professor, 1966-72, associate professor of English, 1972-74; University of Texas, Austin, associate professor of English, 1974—. *Member:* Modern Language Association of America. *Awards, honors:* Younger humanist fellow of National Endowment for the Humanities, 1972-73; American Council of Learned Societies fellow, 1981.

WRITINGS: Revolution as Tragedy: The Dilemma of the Moderate From Scott to Arnold, Cornell University Press, 1980. Contributor to language and literature journals.

WORK IN PROGRESS: The Fiction of Community.

SIDELIGHTS: Farrell told *CA:* "*The Fiction of Community* will attempt to see how the image of community in several nineteenth-century novels displays the same uncertainties about the nature and meaning of community as can be found in works on the subject by several of the great nineteenth-century founders of sociological thought. This book, like *Revolution as Tragedy,* derives from my basic scholarly interest, which is the interdisciplinary study of Victorian culture."

* * *

FARRIMOND, John 1913-

PERSONAL: Born August 9, 1913, in Hindley, England; son of Thomas (a miner) and Jane (a house servant; maiden name, Hill) Farrimond; married Margaret Johnson, January 3, 1942; children: Brian Thomas. *Education:* Attended high school in Hindley, England. *Politics:* Labour. *Religion:* Roman Catholic. *Home:* 102 Algernon St., Hindley, near Wigan, Lancashire, England.

CAREER: Writer, 1939—. Miner, 1928-68; school caretaker, 1968-78.

WRITINGS: Dust in My Throat (novel), Harrap, 1963; *The Hollow Shell* (novel), Harrap, 1964; *Kill Me a Priest* (novel), Harrap, 1965; *Pick and Run* (novel), Harrap, 1966; *No Friday in the Week* (novel), Harrap, 1967; *Dust Is Forever* (novel), Harrap, 1969; *The Unending Track* (novel), Harrap, 1970; *The Hills of Heaven* (juvenile), BBC Publications, 1978; *The Weather Makers* (juvenile), BBC Publications, 1980.

Author of "Round Trip" (radio play), first broadcast by British Broadcasting Corp., June 28, 1980.

Work represented in anthologies, including *Never Till Now,* Oxford University Press, 1968; and *Hero,* Ginn, 1973.

WORK IN PROGRESS: "Hasbeens," a play for radio.

SIDELIGHTS: Hills of Heaven was made into a film, released by British Broadcasting Corp. in 1978; *The Weather Makers* was made into a television program, first broadcast by BBC-TV in March, 1980, as a five-part Jackanory story.

Farrimond wrote: "I was a deprived kid, brought up in George Orwell's *Road to Wigan Pier* country, where I still live. I was one of the ever-hungry kids in Orwell's book. I spent most of my childhood picking coal from the local slagheaps. The experience has stayed with me, and it has colored my writings. My adult and juvenile books are mostly about Lancashire of the 1930's.

"I have started writing for children. Though I'm now sixty-six I'm still a kid at heart. I love writing, so I write. I need to tell people things, and what better way than to involve myself with fictional characters who can fire the bullets I make?"

*   *   *

FAULK, John Henry   1913-

PERSONAL: Born August 21, 1913, in Austin, Tex.; son of John Henry and Martha Cynthia (Miner) Faulk; married Elizabeth Peake, May 29, 1965; children: (from previous marriage) Tannehill, Johanna, Evelyn, Frank Dobie; (from present marriage) John Henry III. *Education:* University of Texas, B.A., 1936, M.A., 1940. *Politics:* Democrat.

CAREER: Associated with University of Texas, Austin, 1942; American Red Cross, Cairo, Egypt, field director, 1942-44; Columbia Broadcasting System (CBS), New York, N.Y., star of radio programs, 1946-48; star of "John Henry Faulk Show," 1951-57. Star of CBS-TV programs, "It's News to Me," "Leave It to the Girls," and "Walk a Mile for a Camel," 1953-55; writer and performer on "Pear Orchard, U.S.A.," 1970-71; appeared in feature films "All the Way Home," 1963, and "The Best Man," 1964. Lecturer on humor and the American heritage, 1949-65. *Military service:* U.S. Army, 1944-46. *Member:* International Platform Association (member of board of governors, 1967—), American Federation of Television and Radio Artists (past vice-president), Screen Actors Guild. *Awards, honors:* Fellow of Julius Rosenwald Foundation, 1941-42.

WRITINGS: Fear on Trial, Simon & Schuster, 1964, revised edition, Grosset, 1976. Author of "Take It Easy," a column, 1971-72.

SIDELIGHTS: Faulk was accused of pro-Communist activities by Aware, Inc., during the 1950's. *Fear on Trial* describes his libel suit against Aware and its associates. He also made a sound recording, "Blacklist: A Failure in Political Imagination," released by the Center for the Study of Democratic Institutions, at University of California, Berkeley, in the 1960's.

BIOGRAPHICAL/CRITICAL SOURCES: Newsweek, December 29, 1952; *Look,* May 7, 1963; Louis Nizer, *The Jury Returns,* Doubleday, 1966; *Reader's Digest,* March, 1967; *TV Guide,* September 27, 1975.*

*   *   *

FAULKNER, Trader   1930-

PERSONAL: Born September 7, 1930, in Sydney, Australia; son of John (a silent film actor) and Sheila (a ballerina; maiden name, Whytock) Faulkner; married Ann Minchin (a television performer and journalist under name Bobo Faulkner), May 31, 1963 (divorced, 1973); children: Sasha (daughter). *Education:* Attended religious secondary school in Sydney, Australia. *Home:* Flat 15, 21 Lexham Gardens,

London W8 5JJ, England. *Agent:* Andrew Mann Ltd., 1 Old Compton St., London W.1, England; and Hope Leresche & Sayle, 11 Jubilee Pl., Chelsea, London SW3 3TE, England.

CAREER: Professional actor on stage, television, radio, and in motion pictures, 1948—; flamenco dancer, 1956-62; member of Royal Shakespeare Co., 1970—. Broadcaster for British Broadcasting Corp. (BBC). *Member:* Society of Authors, British Actors Equity.

WRITINGS: (Translator) Ramon Maria del Valle Inclan, *Divine Words* (play), Heinemann, 1977; *Peter Finch: A Biography,* Taplinger, 1979.

Radio scripts: "The Anguish of a Poet" (on Garcia Lorca), first broadcast by BBC-Radio Three, August 19, 1976; "A Musical Journey" (on Isaac Albeniz), first broadcast by BBC-Radio Four, September 26, 1979. Contributor to periodicals, including *Observer, Opera, Dancing Times, Australian, Financial Times, Theatre Australia,* and *Europa.*

WORK IN PROGRESS: A biography of a well-known musician; a radio feature on Manual de Falla, for British Broadcasting Corp.; a television script on Peter Finch.

SIDELIGHTS: Faulkner commented: "My mother danced at the old Met in 1919-21. Dad was a silent screen star in Australia, so I go in many directions—actor, director, dancer, translator, and writer.

"I trained as an actor under Peter Finch at his Mercury Theatre in Sydney, 1947-48. I left Australia under the aegis of Sir Tyrone Guthrie in 1950. I replaced Richard Burton on Broadway in Gielgud's production of 'The Lady's Not for Burning' in 1951 at the Royale Theatre in New York; later I played Malcolm to Olivier's Macbeth, and Sebastian to Vivian Leigh's Viola, both at Stratford-on-Avon.

"I have been guest artist with the greatest living Spanish dancer, Antonio, at the London Coliseum and Royalty Theatre, and have played leading roles in British theatre, television, motion pictures, and radio.

"I started writing articles and broadcasts in the early 1970's. I will only write about subjects that I feel are really worthwhile and of interest to the reading public, subjects that I am perhaps in a better position to write about than most."

*   *   *

FAWCETT, Brian   1906-

PERSONAL: Born May 26, 1906, in Cobh, Ireland; son of P. H. (an explorer and lieutenant colonel) and Nina Agnes (Paterson) Fawcett; married Charlotte Emily Heil (a diplomatic secretary), 1940 (died, 1944); married Lily Ruth Glass (a diplomatic secretary), May 4, 1946. *Education:* Attended high school in Los Angeles, Calif.; and technical school in England. *Politics:* "Social Crediter." *Religion:* "Agnostic (Pagan)." *Home:* 36 Durdar Rd., Carlisle, Cumbria CA2 4SB, England.

CAREER: Central Railway of Peru, Callao, assistant chief mechanical engineer, air brake specialist, and worker in design, production, and operations, 1924-47; free-lance artist, technical translator, writer, and lecturer, 1947—. Chartered engineer. Participated in Diarios Associados expedition to Brazil, 1952, and archaeological expedition to Mato Grosso, 1955. Principal bassoon player with Cumberland Symphony Orchestra; soloist with Carlisle Light Orchestra. *Member:* Institute of Mechanical Engineers (fellow). *Awards, honors:* Gold medal from Instituto de Bellas Artes, Lima, Peru, 1946, for "Chupaca," a landscape painting.

WRITINGS: Lost Trails, Lost Cities, Funk, 1953 (published

in England as *Exploration Fawcett,* Hutchinson, 1953); *The Proudest Llama,* Hutchinson, 1954; *A Skeleton Named George,* Hutchinson, 1958; *Ruins in the Sky,* Hutchinson, 1958; *Railways of the Andes,* Allen & Unwin, 1963; *Steam in the Andes,* Bradford Barton, 1973. Contributor to periodicals, including *Railroad* and *Blackwood's Magazine.*

WORK IN PROGRESS: A series of paintings on historical industrial subjects in northeastern England.

SIDELIGHTS: Fawcett wrote: "My writing activities have now been replaced largely by painting. I specialize in acrylics."

*   *   *

FAY, Thomas A(rthur) 1927-

PERSONAL: Born July 18, 1927, in Utica, N.Y.; son of Thomas A. and Theresa (Miller) Fay. *Education:* Catholic University of America, B.A., 1952; Laval University, M.A., 1963; Fordham University, Ph.D., 1970. *Home:* 83-53 Manton St., Jamaica, N.Y. 11435. *Office:* Department of Philosophy, St. John's University, Jamaica, N.Y. 11439.

CAREER: Affiliated with St. Bernard College, Cullman, Ala., 1963-64; St. John's University, Jamaica, N.Y., instructor, 1967-71, assistant professor, 1971-74, associate professor, 1974-77, professor of philosophy, 1977—, chairman of department. Visiting professor at Drew University, 1969; lecturer at universities throughout the world. Member of Joint Committee of Catholic Learned Societies and Scholars, 1976—. First violinist with Forest Hills Symphony Orchestra. *Military service:* U.S. Army, 1945-46.

MEMBER: International Society for Metaphysics, Societe Thomiste Internationale, Societe Internationale pour l'Etude de la Philosophie Medievale, Societe Internationale des Etudes Neoplatoniciennes, International Thomistic Society of North America (vice-president, 1977-78), American Catholic Philosophical Association (member of executive council, 1976-79; president, 1975—), American Philosophical Association, American Society for Value Inquiry, Maritain Academy of America, Mediaeval Academy of America, Metaphysical Society of America, Institute of Society, Ethics and the Life Sciences, Society for Health and Human Values, Heidegger Conference, New Jersey Philosophical Association, Long Island Philosophical Society (member of executive council).

WRITINGS: Heidegger: The Critique of Logic, Nijhoff, 1977; *And Smoking Flax Shall He Not Quench: Reflections on New Testament Themes,* Paraclete Books, 1979. Contributor of more than thirty-five articles and reviews to philosophy journals. Contributing editor of *Centro Internazionale di Cultura,* 1977—; member of editorial board of *Guidebook for Publishing Philosophy,* 1977—.

WORK IN PROGRESS: Philosophy of Law.

*   *   *

FAYE, Jean Pierre 1925-

PERSONAL: Born July 19, 1925, in Paris, France; married Marie-Odile Demenge; children: Gisele, Emmanuel. *Education:* Received licence, agregation, and doctorat d'etat from Sorbonne, University of Paris; received licence from Faculte de Droit et Sciences Economiques; also studied at Musee de l'Homme. *Agent:* Editions Seghers-Laffont, 6 St. Suplice, Paris 6, France.

CAREER: Lycee de Reims, Reims, France, teacher, 1951-54; University of Lille, Lille, France, assistant professor,

1955-56; University of Paris, Sorbonne, Paris, France, assistant professor, 1956-60; Centre National de la Recherche Scientifique, France, researcher, 1960-79; writer, 1979—. Founding member of poetry group, Set International; member of Russell Tribunal on Human Rights, 1978-79, and French delegation to Prague trials, 1979. *Awards, honors:* Exchange fellow at University of Chicago, 1954-55; Prix Renaudot, 1964.

WRITINGS—In English translation: *Le Portugal d'Otelo: La Revolution dans le labyrinthe,* J. C. Lattes, 1976, translation published as *Portugal: The Revolution in the Labyrinth,* Spokesman Books, 1976.

In French: *L'Hexagramme,* six volumes, Editions du Seuil, 1958-70; *Entre les rues* (novel), Editions du Seuil, 1958; *Fleuve renverse* (poems), GLM, 1960; *La Cassure* (novel), Editions du Seuil, 1961; *Battement* (novel), Editions du Seuil, 1962; *Theatre: Hommes et pierres,* Editions du Seuil, 1964; *Analogues,* Editions du Seuil, 1964; *L'Ecluse* (novel), Editions du Seuil, 1964; *Couleurs pliees,* Gallimard, 1965; (editor) *Epicure: Doctrines et maximes,* Hermann, 1965; (editor and translator) Friedrich Hoelderlin, *Poemes,* GLM, 1965; *Le Recit hunique,* Editions du Seuil, 1967; (with Claude Ollier and Maurice Roche) *Sorbonne,* Editions Fata Morgana, 1968; (with Leon Robel) *Le Cercle de Prague,* Editions du Seuil, 1969.

(With others) *Le Dessin du recit,* Editions du Seuil, 1970; *Les Troyens,* Editions du Seuil, 1970; *Langages totalitaires,* Hermann, 1972; *Theorie du recit: Introduction aux langages totalitaires,* Hermann, 1972; *Iskra, suivi de cirque,* Editions Seghers/Laffont, 1972; (editor) *Lutte de classes a Dunkerque: Les Mortes, les mots, les appareils d'etat,* Editions Galilee, 1973; *Inferno* (novel), Seghers/Laffont, 1973; *La Critique du langage et son economie,* Editions Galilee, 1973; (with others) *Change,* Seghers/Laffont, 1974; *Migrations du recit sur le peuple juif,* P. Belfond, 1974; (with others) *Mouvement du change des formes,* Editions Seghers/Laffont, 1974; *L'Ovale,* R. Laffont, 1975; (with Jacques Roubaud) *Changement de forme, revolution, langage,* Union Generale d'Editions, 1975; (contributor) Noam Chomsky, *Bains de sang constructifs,* Seghers/Laffont, 1975; *Verres,* Seghers/Laffont, 1977; *Les Portes des villes du monde,* P. Belfond, 1977; *Prague: La Revolution des conseils ouvriers, 1968-69,* Laffont, 1978.

Editor of *Change,* 1968—.

WORK IN PROGRESS: Les Grandes Journees du pere Duchesne.

*   *   *

FEATHERSTONE, Helen 1944-

PERSONAL: Born July 29, 1944, in Baltimore, Md.; daughter of Francis Haynes (an architect) and Elizabeth (Pleasants) Jencks; married Joseph Luke Featherstone (a teacher and writer), August 27, 1966; children: Elizabeth, Joseph, Caitlin. *Education:* Radcliffe College, A.B., 1966; Harvard University, M.Ed., 1967, Ed.D., 1973. *Politics:* Democrat. *Religion:* "No." *Office:* Hudson Institute, 123 Mount Auburn St., Cambridge, Mass. 02138.

CAREER: Harvard University, Cambridge, Mass., lecturer in education, 1976-78; Radcliffe College, Cambridge, fellow at Bunting Institute, 1978-79; Wellesley College, Wellesley, Mass., director of student teaching, 1980; Huron Institute, Cambridge, research associate, 1980—.

WRITINGS: A Difference in the Family (nonfiction), Basic Books, 1980. Contributing editor of *Working Papers.*

WORK IN PROGRESS: Research on the impact of special legislation on children, teachers, families, and school systems.

SIDELIGHTS: Featherstone told *CA:* "I'm interested in the way families shape children and adults and in the evolving relationships between families, professionals, and institutions."

* * *

FEINBERG, Mortimer R(obert) 1922-

PERSONAL: Born August 26, 1922, in New York, N.Y.; son of Max and Frieda (Siegel) Feinberg; married Gloria Granditer, June 22, 1947; children: Stuart Andrew, E. Todd. *Education:* City College (now of the City University of New York), B.S., 1944; Indiana University, M.S., 1945; New York University, Ph.D., 1950. *Religion:* Jewish. *Home:* 34 Brook Lane, Peekskill, N.Y. 10566. *Office:* 666 Fifth Ave., New York, N.Y. 10103.

CAREER: New York University, New York City, instructor in psychology, 1945-50; chief psychologist for Research Institute of America, 1953-58; Bernard M. Baruch College of the City University of New York, New York City, professor of psychology, 1958—, director of advanced management and assistant dean, 1974—. Diplomate of American Board of Examiners in Industrial Psychology. President of BSF Psychological Associates, 1960-74, chairman, 1974—. Professor at Brooklyn College (now of the City University of New York), 1959-60, and Columbia University, 1961-62; principal lecturer for American Management Association; lecturer for Young President's Organization. Publisher of *Interaction.* Research adviser to City of New York executive training program, 1959—; consultant to U.S. Marine Corps, General Electric Corp., and Amstar. *Military service:* U.S. Army, 1944-45; became captain. *Member:* American Psychological Association (fellow), American Association for the Advancement of Science (fellow), American Association of University Professors, New York Sales Executives (member of board of directors, 1974-76), Yale Club, New York University Club.

WRITINGS: (Co-author) *Development of Training,* Harper, 1955; *Effective Psychology for Managers,* Prentice-Hall, 1965; (with Robert Tanofsky and John J. Tarrant) *The New Psychology for Managing People,* Prentice-Hall, 1965; "Self-Discovery for the Manager" (sound recording), American Management Association, 1973; (with Tarrant and wife, Gloria Feinberg) *Leavetaking: When and How to Say Goodbye,* Simon & Schuster, 1978; (with Richard F. Dempewolff) *Corporate Bigamy: How to Resolve the Conflict Between Career and Family,* Morrow, 1980. Also author with D. Fryer of *Developing People in Industry,* 1956. Contributor to psychology journals.

AVOCATIONAL INTERESTS: Photography, golf, gardening.

* * *

FELDKAMP, Phyllis

PERSONAL: Born in Chicago, Ill.; daughter of Charles and Anna (Martony) Dubsky; married Fred Feldkamp; children: Phoebe Ann. *Education:* Attended Bryn Mawr College. *Office:* Philadelphia Bulletin, 30th and Market Sts., Philadelphia, Pa. 19101.

CAREER: Philadelphia Record, Philadelphia, Pa., reporter, 1942-44; *Life,* New York, N.Y., researcher and reporter, 1944-51; free-lance writer in Paris, France, 1956-58; *Philadelphia Bulletin,* Philadelphia, fashion editor, 1968—.

WRITINGS: (With husband, Fred Feldkamp) *The Good Life, Or What's Left of It: Being a Recounting of the Pleasures of the Senses That Contribute to the Enjoyment of Life in France,* Harper's Magazine Press, 1972. Contributor to national magazines.*

* * *

FENTON, James Martin 1949-

PERSONAL: Born April 25, 1949, in Lincoln, England. *Education:* Magdalen College, Oxford, B.A., 1970.

CAREER: Writer. *New Statesman,* London, England, assistant literary editor, 1971, member of editorial staff, 1972-73. *Awards, honors:* Eric Gregory Award, 1973.

WRITINGS: Our Western Furniture (poems), Sycamore Press, 1968; *Put Thou Thy Tears Into My Bottle* (poems), Sycamore Press, 1969; *Terminal Moraine* (poems), Secker & Warburg, 1972. Also author of *A Vacant Possession.**

* * *

FENTON, Thomas Trail 1930-

PERSONAL: Born April 8, 1930, in Baltimore, Md.; son of Matthew Clark (a salesman) and Beatrice (Trail) Fenton; married Simone France Marie Lopes-Curval, January 10, 1959; children: Ariane France, Thomas Trail. *Education:* Dartmouth College, A.B., 1952. *Religion:* Episcopalian. *Home:* 68 Eaton Place, London SW1X 8AT, England. *Office:* Columbia Broadcasting Service News, 100 Brompton Rd., London SW3, England.

CAREER/WRITINGS: Baltimore Sun, Baltimore, Md., member of staff, 1961-70, chief of Rome, Italy, bureau, 1966-68, chief of Paris, France, bureau, 1968-70; Columbia Broadcasting Service (CBS) News, Rome correspondent and producer, 1970-73, Tel Aviv correspondent, 1973-77, Paris correspondent, 1977-79, chief European correspondent in London, England, 1979—. Notable assignments include coverage of Indo-Pakistan War and Middle East War. *Military service:* U.S. Navy, 1952-61. *Member:* Anglo-American Press Association, Society of Cincinnati, Delta Upsilon, Reform Club. *Awards, honors:* Citation from Overseas Press Club, 1968, for articles from Paris; award for coverage of Indo-Pakistan War, 1971; award for coverage of Middle East War, 1973; award for "Sunday Morning, A Tale of Two Cities," 1980.

* * *

FENWICK, (Ian Graham) Keith 1941-

PERSONAL: Surname is pronounced *Fen*-nick; born May 17, 1941, in Derbyshire, England; married Jean McCormack (a teacher), 1964; children: Ian Patrick, Daniel Fitzgerald. *Education:* King's College, London, B.A., 1963; Victoria University of Manchester, Ph.D., 1967. *Office:* School of Education, University of Leeds, Leeds LS2 9JT, England.

CAREER: British College, Messina, Italy, teacher of English, 1963-64; British Council, London, England, officer in England, Spain, and Malawi, 1967-70; University of Leeds, Leeds, England, lecturer, 1971-80, senior lecturer in education, 1980—, adviser to overseas students, 1975-79. Member of Leeds City Council, 1973-80. Vice-chairman of United Kingdom Council for Overseas Student Affairs, 1979-80, 1980-81.

WRITINGS: The Comprehensive School, 1944-1970, Methuen, 1976; (with P.D. McBride) *The Government of Education,* Martin Robertson, 1980.

WORK IN PROGRESS: Research on local politics and education.

* * *

FENYVESI, Charles 1937-

PERSONAL: Born November 23, 1937, in Debrecen, Hungary; came to the United States in 1956, naturalized citizen, 1963; son of Aladar and Anna Fenyvesi; married Elisabeth Kelemen (a weaver), December 20, 1965; children: Shamu, Daniel, Malka. *Education:* Harvard University, B.A. (cum laude), 1960; Madras University, M.A. (with honors), 1962. *Office:* 1640 Rhode Island Ave. N.W., Washington, D.C. 20036.

CAREER: Jerusalem Post, Jerusalem, Israel, Washington correspondent, 1966-69; *Ha'aretz,* Tel Aviv, Israel, diplomatic correspondent, 1969-75; *National Jewish Monthly,* Washington, D.C., editor, 1972—. Commentator for Voice of America and Israel Radio.

WRITINGS: Splendor in Exile: The Ex-Majesties of Europe, New Republic, 1979. Contributor to magazines and newspapers, including *New Republic, Psychology Today, New York Times,* and *Washington Post.*

SIDELIGHTS: Fenyvesi commented to *CA:* "I write reports and essays on superpower relations and stray seeds, on the craft of building stone walls and the survival of master weavers of deception like Stalin. I am drawn to losers and dissidents; I am fascinated by the effect time has on character and inherited obligation. I am compulsive about meeting deadlines and I am spreading the rumor that time can be defeated."

* * *

FERBER, Ellen 1939-

PERSONAL: Born June 5, 1939, in New York; daughter of Louis (a physician) and Lena (a psychiatrist, gynecologist, writer, and marriage counselor; maiden name, Levine) Ferber; married William G. Walker, December, 1962 (died January, 1975). *Education:* Swarthmore College, B.A. (magna cum laude), 1961; University of Connecticut, M.A., 1962, Ph.D., 1971. *Home:* 5218 Scottwood Rd., Paradise, Calif. 95969. *Office:* Department of English, California State University, Chico, Calif. 95926.

CAREER: University of Connecticut, Storrs, instructor in English literature, 1966-67; University of Puerto Rico, San Juan, instructor in English literature, 1967-68; Central Connecticut State College, New Britain, instructor in English literature, 1968-69; Trinity College, Hartford, Conn., lecturer in English literature, 1972; California State University, Chico, associate professor of English literature, 1973—. Editor-in-chief of Small Press Book Club; associate editor of Dustbooks. Member of board of directors of Paradise Area Arts Council. *Member:* Modern Language Association of America, Feminist Writer's Guild, Association for the Advancement of the Humanities.

WRITINGS: (Contributor) R. E. Conot, editor, *American Odyssey,* Dustbooks, 1975; (editor with Len Fulton) *The International Directory of Little Magazines and Small Presses,* Dustbooks, Volumes XIII-XVI, 1977-80; (editor with Fulton) *Directory of Small Magazine Press Editors and Publishers,* Dustbooks, Volumes VIII-XI, 1977-80; (contributor) Bill Henderson, editor, *The Art of Literary Editing,* Pushcart Book Press, 1980. Associate editor of *Small Press Record of Books in Print,* Volumes V-VIII, 1977-80. Executive editor and contributor to *Small Press Review.*

WORK IN PROGRESS: A book on women characters in Shakespeare's comedies; research on small presses in the 1980's, Orlando's encounter with the lion and Rosalind's fainting in Shakespeare's "As You Like It," and the comedy of dialogue in Eudora Welty's *Losing Battles.*

SIDELIGHTS: Ellen Ferber commented: "The two most important influences on my career were my mother and Shakespeare: the former as a model of strength, work, integrity, a model for life; the latter as a molder of language, an illustrator of the 'negative capability,' a forger of words. Although for some language is a dying behemoth, it remains salvation for me. The writer's relationship to it is both aesthetic and moral. The best current analogy is the planet, our so-called 'environment.' Thus, one subject I consider vital is care of the natural world, the need to treat it with the same passion and delicacy with which it treats us. I speak French and am a different person when I do; a constructive schizophrenia. I value beautiful language, walking in the open air, trees, old houses, and knowing that other people are, by and large, on your side as you are on theirs. I am a citizen of New York, and a child of the urban east and college-town New England, trying to survive the vastness of California, subtlely unadaptable to western ways."

* * *

FERGUSON, Annabelle Evelyn 1923-

PERSONAL: Born June 17, 1923, in Duquesne, Pa.; daughter of John and Anna (McWilliams) Ferguson. *Education:* University of Pittsburgh, B.S., 1944, M.Ed., 1948; University of Maryland, Ph.D., 1970. *Politics:* Republican. *Religion:* Methodist. *Home:* 803 Pin Oak Rd., Severna Park, Md. 21146. *Office:* Prince George's County Central Area Office, Landover, Md. 20785.

CAREER: Teacher at public schools in Titusville, Pa., 1947-50; guidance counselor at public schools in Ellicott City, Md., 1950-58, and Severna Park, Md., 1958-59, supervisor of instruction in Severna Park, 1959-62; supervisor of guidance at public schools in Annapolis, Md., 1962-65, and Baltimore, Md., 1965-69; Prince George's County Board of Education, Upper Marlboro, Md., director of pupil services, 1969-73, director of central area, 1973-74, assistant superintendent at central area office in Landover, 1974—. Lecturer at Western Maryland College, Towson State College, and Bowie State College. *Military service:* U.S. Navy Women's Reserve, Women Accepted for Volunteer Emergency Service (WAVES), 1944-46; became lieutenant junior grade.

MEMBER: American Association of School Administrators, National Association of Pupil Personnel Administrators, Association for Supervision and Curriculum Development, American School Counselors Association, Association for Counselor Education and Supervision, American Personnel and Guidance Association (member of senate, 1967-69), Maryland Personnel and Guidance Association (president, 1956-58), Delta Kappa Gamma (president, 1956-58), Phi Delta Kappa. *Awards, honors:* Named administrator of the year by American School Counselors Association, 1971.

WRITINGS: (With Robert J. Shockley) *The Teenager and Homework* (juvenile), Richards Rosen, 1975.*

* * *

FERGUSSON, Bernard Edward 1911-1980

OBITUARY NOTICE—See index for CA sketch: Born May 6, 1911, in London, England; died January 28, 1980, in London, England. Military officer and author. Fergusson served in the British Army beginning in 1931 as second lieutenant in the Black Watch regiment and retired in 1958 as a brigadier. He was appointed governor-general of New Zealand in 1961, a position held earlier by his father and grandfather. He was made a life peer as Lord Ballantrae in 1972. Fergusson wrote numerous books about the British military, including *The Wild Green Earth, The Black Watch and the King's Enemies, The Wattery Maze: The Story of Combined Operations, Return to Burma,* and an autobiography, *The Trumpet in the Hall, 1930-58.* Obituaries and other sources: Bernard Edward Fergusson, *The Trumpet in the Hall, 1930-58,* Collins, 1970; *London Times,* January 29, 1980.

* * *

FERLAND, Carol 1936-

PERSONAL: Born August 21, 1936, in Schenectady, N.Y.; married Donald Ferland (a judge), June, 1958 (deceased); children: David, Catherine, James, Thomas, Peter. *Education:* University of Vermont, B.A., 1958. *Religion:* Episcopalian. *Home and office address:* R.D.3, Middlebury, Vt. 05753.

CAREER: Writer, 1974—. Member of board of directors of Community Mental Health Center. *Member:* Vermont Writers Association.

WRITINGS: The Long Journey Home, Knopf, 1980.

WORK IN PROGRESS: A book on single women, widowhood, death, and life, completion expected in 1985.

BIOGRAPHICAL/CRITICAL SOURCES: Newsweek, June 12, 1980.

* * *

FERREIRA de CASTRO, Jose Maria 1898-1974

PERSONAL: Born May 24, 1898, Salguerios, Portugal; died June 29, 1974.

CAREER: Writer. Worker on rubber plantation in Amazonia, Brazil, 1911-15; journalist in Para, Brazil, 1915-18.

WRITINGS—In English translation: *Emigrantes* (novel), [Portugal], 1928, reprinted, Guimaraes Editores, 1972, translation by Dorothy Ball published as *Emigrants,* Macmillan, 1962; *A selva* (novel), [Portugal], 1930, 24th edition, Guimaraes Editores, 1970, translation by Charles Duff published as *Jungle: A Tale of the Amazon Rubber-Tappers,* L. Dickson, 1934; *A missao: Tres novelas* (contains "A missao," "A experiencia," and "O senhor das navegantes"), Guimaraes Editores, 1954, 7th edition, 1972, title story published separately as *A missao,* Publicacoes Europa-America, 1971, translation by Ann Stevens published as *The Mission,* Hamilton, 1963.

Other writings: *Ferreira de Castro: A peregrina do mundo novo,* Edicao do ABC, 1926; *Eternidade* (novel; title means "Eternity"), [Portugal], 1933, 12th edition, Guimaraes Editores, 1970; *Terra fria* (novel; title means "Cold Earth"), Editorial Seculo, 1934, 10th edition, Guimaraes Editores, 1966; *Pequenos mundos e velhas civilizacoes* (nonfiction), [Portugal], 1937-38, 6th edition, Guimaraes Editores, 1963; *A tempestade* (novel; title means "Tempest"), Editorial Inquerito, 1941, reprinted, Guimaraes Editores, 1968; *A volta ao mundo* (nonfiction; title means "Voyages Around the World"), three volumes, Nacional de Publicidade, 1942-44; *A la e a neve* (novel; title means "The Wool and the Snow"), Guimaraes Editores, 1947, 11th edition, 1972; *A curva da estrada* (fiction; title means "The Bend in the Road"), Guimaraes Editores, 1950, 8th edition, 1968; *As maravilhas ar-*

tisticas do mundo (nonfiction), three volumes, [Portugal], 1957-61, 3rd edition, Guimaraes Editores, 1970; *Ferreira de Castro,* edited by Jaime Brasil, Arcadia, 1961; *Livro do cinquentenario da vida literaria,* Portugalia, 1967; *O instinto supremo,* Guimaraes Editores, 1968, 4th edition, 1970.

SIDELIGHTS: "Ferreira de Castro is generally credited with having introduced a social conscience into the Portuguese novel," disclosed William L. Grossman of the *New York Times.* The author recorded the plight of underprivileged people in Brazil and Portugal in his works. He left his native Portugal for Brazil in 1911, and worked in the Amazon jungle for four years. His experiences as an emigrant and laborer on a rubber plantation fueled his two most successful books, *Emigrants* and *Jungle.*

Emigrants relates the story of a Portuguese farmer who travels to Brazil in search of a better life. Instead, he encounters the same poverty he thought he left behind. "Everywhere the author's compassion and indignation come through, despite the restraint that keeps them fairly free of excess and sentimentality," Grossman noted. In agreement, *New York Herald Tribune*'s Vernon Hall, Jr., appraised the novel as "almost classical in the restrained presentation of . . . [the] social tragedy." *Jungle,* a novel about the life rubber-tappers lead in the Amazon, was highly praised by critics. Arthur Ruhl of the *Saturday Review of Literature* complimented Ferreira de Castro on realistically describing "that appalling wilderness of the Amazon's headwaters, its vastness, isolation, impersonal cruelty, as they gradually wear down and break—swallow, so to say—the courage, pride, sense of identity, even, of the occasional white man condemned to stay there, year in and year out, and to fight for existence with his own hands against that hideously hostile natural exuberance." Marguerite Harrison commented: "Its literary quality is singularly unequal. Some of the descriptive passages are extraordinarily vivid, almost epic."

BIOGRAPHICAL/CRITICAL SOURCES: New York Herald Tribune, February 3, 1935, October 28, 1962; *New York Times,* February 3, 1935, November 18, 1962; *Saturday Review of Literature,* February 16, 1935; *Books Abroad,* spring, 1957.

OBITUARIES: New York Times, July 2, 1974.*

* * *

FERSTER, C(harles) B(ohris) 1922-1981

OBITUARY NOTICE—See index for *CA* sketch: Born November 1, 1922, in Freehold, N.J.; died of a heart attack, February 3, 1981, in Washington, D.C. Psychologist, educator, and author best known for his development of the psychotherapeutic procedure of behavior modification. An experimental psychologist, Ferster did extensive research on human behavior. While an assistant professor at the Indiana University School of Medicine, he researched human verbal behavior by studying language communication between people and chimpanzees. As a result of his experiments, Ferster gained insight into the treatment of infantile autism. With behavioral psychologist B. F. Skinner, Ferster wrote *Schedules of Reinforcement,* a widely used textbook in the area of experimental psychology. He co-authored and edited numerous books on behavior and wrote more than eighty scientific papers and articles. Obituaries and other sources: *Washington Post,* February 5, 1981; *New York Times,* February 8, 1981.

FEUER, Kathryn Beliveau 1926-

PERSONAL: Born July 4, 1926, in Brooklyn, N.Y.; married in 1946; children: one. *Education:* Vassar College, B.A., 1946; Columbia University, M.A., 1954, Ph.D., 1965. *Office:* Department of Slavic Languages and Literatures, University of Toronto, 21 Sussex Ave., Toronto 181, Ontario, Canada.

CAREER: University of Vermont, Burlington, instructor in Russian, 1955-56; University of California, Berkeley, lecturer, 1960-65, associate professor of Slavic languages and literatures, 1965-66; University of Toronto, Toronto, Ontario, professor of Slavic languages and literatures, 1966—, chairman of department, 1966-71. *Member:* American Association for the Advancement of Slavic Studies.

WRITINGS: (Editor) *Solzhenitsyn: A Collection of Critical Essays,* Prentice-Hall, 1976. Contributor to *Russia: Essays in History and Literature,* E. J. Brill, 1972, Contributor to Slavic studies journals.*

*   *   *

FIBER, Alan

PERSONAL—Home: 9 Park Grove, Edgware, Middlesex HA8 7SH, England.

CAREER: Tack Retail Consultants, London, England, managing director, 1960-65; Business Management Advisory Services, London, managing director, 1965—. Editorial director of Tack Publications, 1960-65; program adviser and broadcaster for British Broadcasting Corp. (BBC) Radio and Independent Television. *Member:* Institute of Arbitrators (fellow), Society of Authors.

WRITINGS: The Independent Retailer: How to Buy, Manage, and Improve the Smaller Shop, Heinemann, 1964, 2nd edition published as *The Complete Guide to Retail Management,* Penguin, 1972; *Be Your Own Boss: How to Start and Successfully Run Any Business, Full or Part Time, Including a Classified Guide to One Thousand Possible Occupations, for Men and Women,* Management Books, 1967; *Quick and Easy Business Accounts,* Management Books, 1967. Scriptwriter for television and films. Contributor to business journals. Associate editor of *Stockholders Journal,* 1965-67.*

*   *   *

FILIPOVITCH, Anthony J(oseph) 1947-

PERSONAL: Born September 5, 1947, in Chicago, Ill.; son of Anthony J. (a foundry engineer) and Valerie (Kurtzweil) Filipovitch; married Kathleen Ann Brynaert (a philosopher), May 25, 1968; children: Alexandra Brynaert. *Education:* University of Michigan, B.A., 1968; Duquesne University, M.A., 1970; Portland State University, Ph.D., 1975. *Home:* 1416 Carney, Mankato, Minn. 56001. *Office:* Urban and Regional Studies Institute, Mankato State University, Mankato, Minn. 56001.

CAREER: Social studies teacher at adult education center in Pittsburgh, Pa., 1970-72; University of Tulsa, Tulsa, Okla., assistant professor of urban studies, 1975-78; Mankato State University, Mankato, Minn., associate professor of urban and regional studies, 1978—. Consultant. *Member:* Society for the Psychological Study of Social Issues, American Planning Association, Environmental Design Research Association, Council of University Institutes of Urban Affairs.

WRITINGS: (Editor) *Proceedings of the Floodplain Management Symposium,* University of Tulsa, 1976; (with Earl Reeves) *Urban Community: A Guide to Information Sources,* Gale, 1978. Contributor to professional journals.

WORK IN PROGRESS: Research on children's perceptions of the urban environment.

*   *   *

FINDLEY, Carter Vaughn 1941-

PERSONAL: Born May 12, 1941, in Atlanta, Ga.; son of John C. (a merchant) and Elizabeth (a merchant; maiden name, Steed) Findley; married Lucia LaVerne Blackwelder (a researcher), August 31, 1968; children: Madeleine Vaughn, Benjamin Carter. *Education:* Yale University, B.A., 1963; Harvard University, Ph.D., 1969. *Home:* 1617 Essex Rd., Columbus, Ohio 43221. *Office:* Department of History, Ohio State University, 230 West 17th Ave., Columbus, Ohio 43210.

CAREER: Ohio State University, Columbus, assistant professor, 1972-79, associate professor of history, 1979—. Consultant to National Endowment for the Humanities, 1977-78. *Military service:* U.S. Army, 1969-71; became captain; received Bronze Star. *Member:* Middle East Institute (fellow), Middle East Studies Association of North America (fellow), American Historical Association, American Oriental Society. *Awards, honors:* National Endowment for the Humanities fellowship, 1971-72; Social Science Research Council fellowship, 1976-77.

WRITINGS: Bureaucratic Reform in the Ottoman Empire: The Sublime Porte, 1789-1922, Princeton University Press, 1980. Contributor to Middle East and Far East studies journals.

WORK IN PROGRESS: Studies in the Social History of the Late Ottoman Bureaucracy, completion expected in 1981; articles.

SIDELIGHTS: Findley told *CA:* ``A career of teaching and research about the Islamic world, embarked on with some hesitation in the early sixties, has proven enormously exciting and increasingly worthwhile. I was attracted to this subject by a combination of feelings and needs: the lure of the exotic, a desire for a career in an underworked field, the hope of doing something of practical, contemporary utility, and curiosity to see if I could learn languages more difficult than French and German. Opportunities to study Arabic, to immerse myself deeply in Ottoman and modern Turkish, to do extensive reading and teaching in Islamic history and civilization, to travel widely, and to study in some of the richest manuscript repositories of the Middle East have done a lot to satisfy my original motivations. These experiences have also added to my initial sense of the exotic new ones of familiarity and affection; and it is these feelings, almost as much as substantive knowledge, that I try to convey to my readers and students. To study another civilization, one must empathize with its people; to write effectively about another civilization, one must convey understanding of it with the clarity and immediacy needed to elicit this empathy in one's readers. My major professional goal is to stimulate this kind of awareness in both scholarly and popular audiences.''

*   *   *

FINDLING, John Ellis 1941-

PERSONAL: Born March 16, 1941, in South Bend, Ind.; son of Willard F. (an engineer and contractor) and Ruth (a social worker; maiden name, Bransky) Findling; married Carol Nobis (a solar power advocate), May 31, 1968; children: Jamey Justin. *Education:* Rice University, B.A., 1963; University of Texas, M.A., 1965, Ph.D., 1971. *Residence:* Floyds Knobs, Ind. *Office:* Division of Social Sciences, Indiana University Southeast, 4201 Grant Line Rd., New Albany, Ind. 47150.

CAREER: American Nicaraguan School, Managua, teacher of English, 1965-67; Indiana University Southeast, New Albany, assistant professor, 1971-75, associate professor of history, 1975—, acting chairman of Division of Social Sciences, 1980—. *Member:* North American Society for Sport History, American Historical Association, Organization of American Historians, Society for Historians of American Foreign Relations, Popular Culture Association.

WRITINGS: Dictionary of American Diplomatic History, Greenwood Press, 1980. Contributor to history journals.

WORK IN PROGRESS: A work on turn-of-the-century Nicaragua; research on popular culture and sports history.

*　　*　　*

FINE, Estelle
　See JELINEK, Estelle C.

*　　*　　*

FINLATOR, John Haywood 1911-

PERSONAL: Born October 4, 1911, in Louisburg, N.C.; married Florence Boon, March 16, 1940; children: Florence, Marcia. *Education:* North Carolina State University, B.S., 1934; American University, M.A., 1944. *Home:* 2710 North Beechwood Pl., Arlington, Va. 22207. *Office:* 1405 I St. N.W., Washington, D.C. 20537.

CAREER: General Services Administration, Washington, D.C., director of administration, 1960-66; Federal Drug Administration (FDA), Washington, D.C., director of Bureau of Drug Abuse Control 1966-68, deputy director of Bureau of Narcotics and Dangerous Drugs, 1968—. Lecturer. *Member:* International Narcotics Enforcement Officers Association, International Association of Chiefs of Police, Association of Federal Investigators. *Awards, honors:* Distinguished service award from U.S. Department of Health, Education, and Welfare.

WRITINGS: The Drugged Nation: A "Narc's" Story, Simon & Schuster, 1973. Contributor to professional journals.*

*　　*　　*

FISCHETTI, John 1916-1980

OBITUARY NOTICE: Born September 27, 1916, in Brooklyn, N.Y.; died of heart disease, 1980, in Chicago, Ill. Political cartoonist and author of autobiography *Zinga, Zinga, Za!* Fischetti was best known for his keen criticism of powerful politicians and for his sympathetic portrayals of the downtrodden. His work was featured in the *Chicago Sun-Times.* Obituaries and other sources: *Who's Who in the World,* 4th edition, Marquis, 1978; *Chicago Tribune,* December 1, 1980; *Newsweek,* December 1, 1980.

*　　*　　*

FISHER, Allen J. 1907(?)-1980

OBITUARY NOTICE: Born c. 1907 in Camden, N.J.; died of cancer, November 23, 1980, in York, Pa. Economist, educator, and expert and author of works in the field of business management. Aside from his professorial duties, Fisher was a consultant on national and international economics. In 1973 he received the Albert Gallatin Award from the U.S. Treasury Department. Obituaries and other sources: *Washington Post,* November 25, 1980.

FISHER, Douglas 1934-

PERSONAL: Born July 2, 1934, in Pittsburgh, Pa.; son of Henry Clayton (a teacher) and Dorothea (a testing specialist; maiden name, Smith) Fisher; married Lois Anne Hamilton (a writer), June 11, 1959; children: Leslie Erika. *Education:* University of Pittsburgh, B.A., 1957, M.A., 1958; further graduate study at Brown University, 1960-61, and London School of Economics and Political Science, London, 1963-64; University of Chicago, Ph.D., 1965. *Office:* Department of Economics, North Carolina State University, Raleigh, N.C. 27650.

CAREER: University of Pittsburgh, Pittsburgh, Pa., teaching assistant in economics, 1958-60; Carnegie-Mellon University, Pittsburgh, instructor in economics, 1959-60; Brown University, Providence, R.I., teaching assistant in economics, 1960-61; University of Illinois at Chicago Circle, Chicago, instructor in economics, 1965; Queens College of the City University of New York, Flushing, N.Y., assistant professor of economics, 1965-66; State University of New York at Albany, assistant professor of economics, 1966-67; Queens College of the City University of New York, associate professor of economics, 1967-69; University of Essex, Colchester, England, senior lecturer in economics, 1969-71, chairman of department, 1970-71; Pomona College, Claremont, Calif., visiting professor of economics, 1971-72; University of Durham, Durham, England, visiting professor of economics, 1972-73; Claremont Graduate School, Claremont, Calif., visiting professor of economics, 1973-74; Concordia University, Sir George Williams Campus, Montreal, Quebec, professor of economics, 1974-77, director of graduate studies, 1977; North Carolina State University, Raleigh, professor of economics, 1977—. *Member:* American Economic Association, Southern Economic Association, Order of Artus.

WRITINGS: Money and Banking, with teacher's manual, Irwin, 1971; *Monetary Policy,* Halsted, 1976; *Monetary Theory and the Demand for Money,* Halsted, 1978; *Money, Banking, and Monetary Policy,* Irwin, 1980; *Macroeconomic Theory,* Volume I: *A Survey of the Literature on the Basic Macro Model,* Macmillan, in press.

Contributor: Bert F. Hoselitz, editor, *The Role of Small Industry in the Process of Economic Growth,* Mouton, 1968; J. M. Parkin and A. R. Nobay, editors, *Contemporary Issues in Economics,* Manchester University Press, 1973; R. S. Thorn, editor, *Monetary Theory and Policy,* 2nd edition (Fisher was not associated with 1st edition), Praeger, 1976; Nobay and M. J. Artis, editors, *Contemporary Economic Analysis,* Croom Helm, 1978. Contributor of articles and reviews to economic journals.

WORK IN PROGRESS: A Literary Pub Crawl, with wife, Lois H. Fisher; *Macroeconomic Theory,* Volume II: *A Survey of the Literature on the Macropolicy Debate,* publication by Macmillan expected in 1984; a study "of the locations in the literature on King Arthur and the locational associations of the Robin Hood legend," with wife, L. Fisher.

SIDELIGHTS: Fisher told *CA:* "In my books on economics I have generally tried to bridge the gap between the hard-to-read front-line journal articles and the audience of undergraduate and graduate students. I suspect my books are considered difficult by the users, but I have tried to help by bringing uniformity of outlook and notation to bear on a very heterogeneous literature. My subject area, broadly, is macroeconomics, and I tend to treat this as a topic best approached by means of theoretical models which have strong empirical implications. In addition, while a monetarist by training, I have tried to downgrade the often counter-productive disputes between Keynesians and monetarists in favor of the substantial body of consensus results."

*   *   *

FISHER, Nigel   1913-

PERSONAL: Born July 14, 1913, in Cosham, England; son of Sir Thomas (a naval commander) and Aimee (Loveridge) Fisher; married Lady Gloria Vaughen, 1935 (divorced, 1952); married Patricia Smiles, August 28, 1956; children: (first marriage) Amanda, Mark. *Education:* Eton College and Trinity College, Cambridge, B.A., 1934, M.A. *Religion:* Church of England. *Home:* 16 North Court, Great Peter St., Westminster, London S.W.1, England; and Portavo Point, Donaghadee, County Down, Northern Ireland; and St. George's Court, St. George's Bay, Malta. *Office:* House of Commons, London SW1A 0AA, England; and Winthrop House, Surbiton, Surrey, England.

CAREER: Assistant general manager of Associated London Properties, 1935-36, and of Earls Court Ltd., 1936-38; partner in firm of surveyors, 1938-39; stood for Parliament for Chiselhurst Division of North Kent, 1945; Conservative candidate for Hitchen, 1947; British Parliament, London, England, Conservative member of House of Commons for Hitchin, 1950-55, and Surbiton, 1955—, Parliamentary private secretary to minister of food, 1951-54, and to home secretary, 1954-57, under-secretary of state for colonies, 1962-63, and for commonwealth affairs and colonies, 1963-64, opposition spokesman for commonwealth affairs, 1964-66, treasurer of Commonwealth Parliamentary Association, 1966-68, and its United Kingdom Branch, 1977-79, vice-chairman, 1975-76, deputy chairman, 1979—. Member of executive of Conservative party, 1960-62, 1969—, and national executive committee, 1945-47, 1971—. Member of council and executive committee of Save the Children Fund and of council of Churchill Memorial Trust; member of board of management of London Heritage Trust and a director of Sterling-Winthrop Group of Pharmaceutical Companies. *Military service:* British Army, Welsh Guards, 1939-45; served in Europe; became major; received Military Cross, mentioned in dispatches. *Member:* British-Caribbean Association (president), Building Societies Association (vice-president), Society of Authors, Marylebone Cricket Club. *Awards, honors:* Knighted, 1974.

WRITINGS: Iain Macleod, Deutsch, 1973; *The Tory Leaders,* Weidenfeld & Nicolson, 1977; *Harold Macmillan,* Weidenfeld & Nicolson, 1981.

SIDELIGHTS: Sir Nigel wrote: "My first book was motivated by my close personal friendship with Iain Macleod, who had just died. The second was motivated by an interest in politics and political personalities. I would like to write a political novel, but doubt if I have the creative imagination. Biographies are harder work but easier. I write every word in longhand, because I think better through my pen and there is less revising necessary by this method.

"I have traveled extensively, especially in the Commonwealth. My political interests include foreign affairs, the Commonwealth and colonies, race relations, Northern Ireland, and constitutional reform."

*   *   *

FISHER, Welthy Honsinger   1879-1980

OBITUARY NOTICE—See index for *CA* sketch: Born September 18, 1879, in Rome, N.Y.; died December 16, 1980, in Southbury, Conn. Missionary, educator, and author. Fisher spent much of her life promoting education in underdeveloped countries. In 1953 she founded Literacy House, a training center for teachers in Lucknow, India. Its graduates have educated millions of villagers in impoverished India. Until she was ninety-two years old, Fisher was president of Literacy House and World Education, a group that supports the worldwide development of centers like Literacy House. In her one hundredth year, Fisher received an honorary Doctor of Letters degree from Delhi University and was honored on a commemorative stamp by India's government. Among her writings are *Beyond the Moon Gate; The Top of the World; A String of Chinese Pearls; Frederick Bohn Fisher, World Citizen;* and her autobiography, *To Light a Candle.* Obituaries and other sources: Welthy Honsinger Fisher, *To Light A Candle,* McGraw, 1962; *New York Times,* December 17, 1980.

*   *   *

FLECK, Richard Francis   1937-

PERSONAL: Born August 24, 1937, in Philadelphia, Pa.; son of J. Keene (a librarian) and Anne M. (a legal secretary; maiden name, DeLeon) Fleck; married Maura McMahon, 1963; children: Richard Sean, Michelle Marie, Ann Maureen. *Education:* Rutgers University, B.A., 1959; Colorado State University, M.A., 1962; University of New Mexico, Ph.D., 1970. *Politics:* Democrat. *Religion:* Roman Catholic. *Home:* 912 Mitchell, Laramie, Wyo. 82070. *Agent:* Lambert Wilson, 8 East 10th St., New York, N.Y. 10003. *Office:* Department of English, University of Wyoming, Laramie, Wyo. 82071.

CAREER: Princeton University, Princeton, N.J., bibliographical assistant at library, 1962-63; North Adams State College, North Adams, Mass., instructor in French and English, 1963-65; University of Wyoming, Laramie, instructor, 1965-70, assistant professor, 1970-75, associate professor, 1975-80, professor of English, 1980—. *Military service:* U.S. Navy, 1961-63. *Member:* Thoreau Society, Sierra Club, Rocky Mountain Modern Languages Association. *Awards, honors:* Summer research grants from University of Wyoming, 1967 and 1971; grant from Wyoming State Historical Society, 1973; grants from Wyoming Council for the Humanities, 1978 and 1979.

WRITINGS: Palms, Peaks, and Prairies (poetry), Golden Quill, 1967; *The Indians of Thoreau,* Hummingbird Press, 1974; *Cottonwood Moon* (poetry), Jelm Mountain Press, 1979; *Clearing of the Mist* (novel), Dustbooks, 1979; (author of preface) John Muir, *Our National Parks,* University of Wisconsin Press, 1981. Contributor to scholarly journals. Editor of *Thoreau Quarterly Journal,* 1975-77; member of editorial board of *Paintbrush.*

WORK IN PROGRESS: A novel, *Rebels of the Sage, Rebels of the Heather,* publication expected in 1981; a John Muir handbook, publication expected in 1982.

SIDELIGHTS: Fleck commented: "The most significant events in my life were my marriage to my Irish wife, Maura, and our frequent visits to and six-month residence in Ireland. My experience in Ireland has linked together with my knowledge of American Indians to inspire two novels connecting Irish and Indian struggles for cultural liberation. My interest in Muir and Thoreau has led to scholarly investigations of their sources of inspiration which are similar to my own. Their sense of place has been particularly important to me."

BIOGRAPHICAL/CRITICAL SOURCES: Walter Harding, *A New Thoreau Handbook,* New York University Press, 1980.

FLEISCHHAUER-HARDT, Helga 1936-

PERSONAL: Born July 19, 1936, in Konz, Germany; daughter of Jakob and Anna (Elenz) Hardt; married Joerg Fleischhauer (a medical director), June 6, 1962; children: Johannes, Anna Maria, Rafael. *Education:* Attended University of Freiburg, 1956-57, and University of Tuebingen, 1957-59; University of Munich, M.D., 1961; postdoctoral study at Zurich Psychoanalytic Institute, 1961-69. *Politics:* "Pacifist." *Religion:* Roman Catholic. *Home:* Chlosterweg 2, 4915 St. Urban/Lucerne, Switzerland. *Office:* Psychiatric Clinic, St. Urban/Lucerne, Switzerland.

CAREER: Psychiatric Clinic, Wil, Switzerland, medical assistant, 1961-63; worked at school in Reinach-Basel, Switzerland, 1969-77, president of school, 1974-77; in private practice of psychotherapy in Salem, West Germany, 1977-79; Psychiatric Clinic, St. Urban/Lucerne, Switzerland, teacher at psychiatric school, 1979—. Public speaker. *Awards, honors:* Silver Award from Art Directors Club of New York, 1975, for *Show Me!*

WRITINGS—In English: (With Will McBride) *Zeig Mal!: Ein Bilderbuch fuer Kinder und Eltern,* Jugenddienst, 1974, translation by Hilary Davis published as *Show Me!: A Picture Book of Sex for Children and Parents,* St. Martin's, 1975.

Other writings: (With R. Ammann) *Sexualerzrehnugrader Schule* (title means "Sex Education in School"), Haupt-Verlag, 1972. Author of radio scripts, including one on sex education in early childhood, first broadcast by Radio Saarbruecken, 1967. Correspondent for *Basel Nationalzeitung.* Contributor to Swiss journals and newspapers.

WORK IN PROGRESS: A book on behavioral disturbances and mental illness in childhood, publication by Jugenddienst Verlag Wuppertal expected in 1981.

SIDELIGHTS: Helga Fleischhauer-Hardt commented: "I want to contribute to the development of really human practices in bringing up children, such as avoiding punishment and avoiding divorce, in order to give children a fair chance for growing up in a natural loving family atmosphere. My special interest is 'friedenspaedagogik,' which means 'education for peace.' I try to be a good mother to my children and a good wife to my husband. I consider this to be my most important duty and the center of my life."

*　　*　　*

FLEMING, Joan Margaret 1908-1980

OBITUARY NOTICE—See index for *CA* sketch: Born March 27, 1908, in Horwich, Lancastershire, England; died November 15, 1980, in England. Novelist and author. Fleming wrote numerous witty crime and gothic novels, as well as many short stories. She also penned a travel guide, *Shakespeare's Country in Colour.* The author won the Crime Writers Association critics award in 1962 for *When I Grow Rich* and in 1970 for *Young Man, I Think You're Dying.* Her other writings include *He Ought To Be Shot, Malice Matrimonial, The Man From Nowhere, Nothing Is the Number When You Die, Screams From a Penny Dreadful, The Gallows in My Garden,* and *Too Late! Too Late the Maiden Cried.* Obituaries and other sources: *London Times,* November 21, 1980; *AB Bookman's Weekly,* January 26, 1981.

*　　*　　*

FLETCHER-COOKE, John 1911-

PERSONAL: Born August 8, 1911, in Burnham, Buckinghamshire, England; son of Charles Arthur (an army captain) and Gwendolen May Fletcher-Cooke; married Alice Egner, 1949 (divorced, 1971); married Marie-Louise Fournier de la Bare; children: (first marriage) two sons, one daughter. *Education:* University of Paris, diplome (degre superieur), 1928; St. Edmund Hall, Oxford, M.A. (with first class honors), 1929. *Politics:* Conservative. *Religion:* Church of England. *Address:* c/o Lloyds Bank, Finsbury Circus Branch, 3 Broad Street Place, London EC2M 7JQ, England.

CAREER: Oxford University, Oxford, England, economic researcher, 1933; United Kingdom Civil Service, Colonial Office, London, England, private secretary to successive permanent under secretaries of state for the colonies, 1934-37; Malayan Civil Service, Kuala Lumpur, officer, 1937, assistant secretary at Federated Malay States Secretariat, 1938, on special duty to Klang, 1939, magistrate in Singapore, 1939, deputy controller of Foreign Exchange Control in Singapore, and district officer of Cameron Highlands, 1939-42; United Kingdom Civil Service, on special duty in Colonial Office, London, 1946, on special duty with constitutional commissioner to Malta, 1946, under secretary to government of Palestine, 1946-48, member of executive council, 1947, special representative for Palestine at United Nations, 1948, United Kingdom representative on special committee and trusteeship council at United Nations, 1948-50, counselor for colonial affairs and permanent delegate from the United Kingdom at United Nations, 1949-51, colonial adviser to United Kingdom delegation to General Assembly of United Nations, 1948-50, colonial secretary and sometime governor of Cyprus, 1951-55, on special duty for Colonial Office, 1956, minister for constitutional affairs in Tanganyika, 1956-59, chief secretary to government of Tanganyika, 1959-60, special representative of Tanganyika to Ghana Independence Celebrations, 1957, Economic Commission for Africa, 1959, and Trusteeship Council of United Nations, 1957-61, sometime governor of Tanganyika, deputy governor, 1960-61. Visiting professor of African affairs at University of Colorado, 1961-62 and 1972-74; Conservative member of British Parliament for Southampton West, 1964-66; director of programs in diplomacy at Carnegie Endowment for International Peace, 1967-68; undertook various missions for United Kingdom to Nigeria, Kenya, and New Hebrides, 1966-69; chairman of various Civil Service selection boards in United Kingdom, 1966-79. *Military service:* Royal Air Force, 1942-45; became flying officer; prisoner of war in Java and Japan. *Member:* Society of Authors, Royal Commonwealth Society (member of council), Country Gentlemen's Association, Travellers Club. *Awards, honors:* Companion of Order of St. Michael and St. George, 1952; knighted, 1962.

WRITINGS: (Contributor) *Parliament as an Export,* Allen & Unwin, 1966; *The Emperor's Guest, 1942-45* (autobiography), Allen & Unwin, 1971, 2nd edition, Leo Cooper, 1972. Contributor of articles, stories, and reviews to periodicals in England, the United States, Canada, and Germany, including *Blackwood's.*

SIDELIGHTS: Sir John wrote: "I have been fortunate enough to live and work in various parts of the world, and I have a vast amount of material on which to base future books and short stories. I do not think I shall ever attempt to write fiction. My major work so far has been *The Emperor's Guest,* an account of my three-and-a-half years as a prisoner of war in Japanese hands. This was based on secret diaries which I managed to keep while in captivity. It was written after I had returned to Japan in 1969 to visit two of the three camps in which I was confined—and to entertain to dinner two of my less objectionable gaolers.

"The first edition of *The Emperor's Guest* was sold out within nine months, and the second edition has been out of print now for nearly a year. One of the publishers tried to negotiate a U.S. edition (as many of my fellow POW's were Americans), but he chose a bad moment to do this. The approach to American publishers was made just as the U.S. Government was negotiating for the release of American POW's in the hands of the North Vietnamese. I was told that a 'whisper' had emanated from the White House urging publishers not to publish books about POW's in Asian hands while these delicate negotiations were going on. So the chance was missed, though I have had many communications from fellow POW's in the U.S.A. asking *when* the book will appear in the U.S.A.

"Having taught myself Japanese while in captivity, I was called on to interpret for the camp commandant at the remote coalmining camp which I was in when the atomic bomb was dropped on Hiroshima. He made a long speech at a midnight parade of officer POW's (as described in the book). I had (with many others) been badly beaten up before I started interpreting, and I made a mistake in the interpretation of the commandant's speech. As a result I was beaten unconscious. The sequel to this was a serious operation on my head and eyes some thirty-two years later, in 1977, following which I was awarded a war service disability pension."

*   *   *

FLORMAN, Samuel C(harles) 1925-

PERSONAL: Born January 19, 1925, in New York, N.Y.; son of Arthur M. and Hannah (Weingarten) Florman; married Judith Hadas (a teacher), August 19, 1951; children: David, Jonathan. *Education:* Dartmouth College, B.S., 1944, C.E., 1973; Columbia University, M.A., 1947. *Home:* 55 Central Park W., New York, N.Y. 10023. *Office:* Kreisler Borg Florman, 97 Montgomery St., Scarsdale, N.Y. 10583.

CAREER: Associated with Hegeman Harris Co. in Venezuela, 1948, Thompson-Starrett Co. in New York City, 1949-53, and Joseph P. Blitz, Inc., in New York City, 1953-55; Kreisler Borg Florman Construction Company, Scarsdale, N.Y., principal, 1955—. *Military service:* U.S. Navy, 1944-46. *Member:* American Society of Civil Engineers, American Society for Engineering Education, National Society of Professional Engineers. *Awards, honors:* Stevens Award from Stevens Institute of Technology, 1976, for articles and books dealing with the relationship of technology to the general culture.

WRITINGS: Engineering and the Liberal Arts, McGraw, 1968; *The Existential Pleasures of Engineering,* St. Martin's, 1976. Contributing editor of *Harper's.*

*   *   *

FLYNT, Candace 1947-

PERSONAL: Born March 12, 1947, in Greensboro, N.C.; daughter of Ralph M. Lambeth (a radio station owner and manager) and Dorothea (Patterson Lambeth) Bray; married Chris Johnson, April 4, 1969 (divorced, 1972); married Charles Homer Flynt (a textile manufacturer), April 13, 1974; stepchildren: Chip, Elizabeth. *Education:* Greensboro College, B.A., 1969; University of North Carolina at Greensboro, M.F.A., 1973. *Politics:* Democrat. *Religion:* Episcopalian. *Home:* 2005 Madison Ave., Greensboro, N.C. 27403. *Agent:* Rhoda Weyr, William Morris Agency, 1350 Avenue of the Americas, New York, N.Y. 10019. *Office:* Sternberger Artists Studio, 712 Summit Ave., Greensboro, N.C. 27405.

CAREER: Greensboro News Co., Greensboro, N.C., reporter, 1969-73. Novelist and author of short stories. *Awards, honors:* Recipient of several awards for newspaper feature stories; first prize in fiction from *This End Up,* 1974, for "The Waiting Room"; distinctive short story citation from *Best American Short Stories,* 1975, for "The Creak," and 1977, for "Honey," and roll of honor citation, 1978, for "Best Friend"; third prize in fiction from *Carolina Quarterly,* 1976, for "Honey"; first prize from Norfolk Arts Society, 1977, for "Best Friend."

WRITINGS: Chasing Dad (novel), Dial, 1980.

Short stories: "The Creak," published in *Greensboro Review,* winter, 1973-74; "The Waiting Room," published in *This End Up,* summer, 1974; "On the Way to Brazil," published in *Greensboro Review,* winter, 1974-75; "Honey," published in *Carolina Quarterly,* spring-summer, 1976, and in *More Than Magnolias* (anthology), Green River Press, 1978; "Their Day Off," published in *Redbook,* August, 1977; "Best Friend," published in *Carolina Quarterly,* fall, 1977.

WORK IN PROGRESS: A novel, tentatively titled *Between Us,* publication by Dial expected in 1982.

SIDELIGHTS: Scott Spencer of the *New York Times Book Review* reported that Flynt's first novel, *Chasing Dad,* "in no way" announces itself as such. "Flynt's prose is rich and well-balanced," said Spencer, "and she knows exactly when to step forward and when to disappear. Her narration is objective, relentless, perfectly modulated. She describes seriously wayward lives with a strange, ultimately devastating tranquility—the tranquility of true art. . . . There is an accuracy here that takes the place of melodrama and infuses everyday events with a terrifying intensity."

"I am trying to write about the modern South," Flynt told *CA,* and her main character in *Chasing Dad* is a Southern carpenter, Merle Mitchell. After the suicide of Mitchell's oldest son, his younger son, Craig, searches for his father's love. Craig's quest is made difficult by the impenetrable nature of his father. "I don't know if it's possible to portray a more unreliable, conflicted, arrogant, self-hating and dangerous man and still make it possible for us to see ourselves in him," declared Spencer.

Flynt commented: "As a child I fell under the spell of my local library whose shelves regularly produced more excitement than my preteen years did. My life changed as I grew up, providing a fair amount of adventure, but my love of living vicariously, through characters in books, remains the same. The only difference is that now I am actively involved in creating characters of my own, along with reading those of other writers. For me the great reward of writing is learning about life through characters whose perspectives are different than mine. That can be achieved simply by reading. But when you also create the characters, you have embarked on an even more intimate experience. Merle Mitchell, in my novel *Chasing Dad,* is a lower middle-class Southern carpenter (I am Southern, but neither lower middle class nor a carpenter), a man wild and outrageous both before and after he loses his older son, Jay, to suicide. In creating Merle and the family that surrounds him, I was able to experience a way of life that I had never known. I spent four sobering, but exhilarating, years with the Mitchell family. Writing, then, educates me in the most intimate way. My hope is that my readers will be able to learn what I have learned."

BIOGRAPHICAL/CRITICAL SOURCES: Greensboro Sun, May, 1980; *Figaro,* July 7, 1980; *Greensboro Daily News,* July 13, 1980; *Cleveland Plain Dealer,* July 27, 1980; *Washington Post,* July 31, 1980; *Dallas Morning News,* August 3,

1980; *Greensboro Record,* August 8, 1980; *Los Angeles Times Book Review,* August 10, 1980; *Washington Star,* August 17, 1980; *New York Times Book Review,* September 7, 1980; *Chicago Tribune Book World,* September 21, 1980.

* * *

FOLADARE, Joseph 1909-

PERSONAL: Born July 9, 1909, in Los Angeles, Calif.; son of Henry (a merchant) and Mary (Josephson) Foladare; married Mabel Lee, July 14, 1935; children: Elise. *Education:* California Institute of Technology, B.S., 1930; Claremont Colleges, A.M., 1931; Yale University, Ph.D., 1936. *Home:* 2825 Clinton Ter., Santa Barbara, Calif. 93105. *Office:* Department of English, University of California, Santa Barbara, Calif. 93106.

CAREER: Iowa State College (now University), Ames, instructor, 1935-37, assistant professor of English, 1937-40; University of California, Santa Barbara, assistant professor, 1940-41, associate professor, 1941-49, professor of English, 1949—, chairman of department, 1947-51. Director of publications for Office of Scientific Search and Development, California Institute of Technology, 1941-46. *Member:* Modern Language Association of America. *Awards, honors:* Presidential Certificate of Merit, 1948, for writing, editing, and directing publications on artillery rockets at California Institute of Technology.

WRITINGS: (With Frederick A. Pottle) *Index to the Private Papers of James Boswell,* Oxford University Press, 1937; *Ballistics of Artillery Rockets,* California Institute of Technology, 1946; *Boswell's Paoli,* Shoe String, 1979. Contributor to language and literature journals.

WORK IN PROGRESS: Research on Boswell, Johnson, and Paoli.

SIDELIGHTS: Foladare commented: "I am continuing to develop an account of the Corsican general Pasquale Paoli past the time of Boswell's death. On Johnson, I have for some time been interested in illuminating and analyzing his comic sense, revealed abundantly in his own writings as well as in much that was written by his friends."

* * *

FOLB, Edith A(rlene) 1938-

PERSONAL: Born August 12, 1938, in Los Angeles, Calif.; daughter of Alex (in business) and Ruth (Esacove) Folb. *Education:* University of California, Los Angeles, A.B. (summa cum laude), 1960, M.A., 1963, Ph.D., 1972; post-doctoral study at University of California, San Diego, 1972-73. *Politics:* Independent. *Religion:* Jewish. *Office:* Department of Speech and Communication Studies, San Francisco State University, 1600 Holloway Ave., San Francisco, Calif. 94132.

CAREER: Department of Civil Service, Los Angeles, Calif., personnel analyst, 1965-70; University of California, Los Angeles, instructor in communication, 1971-72, fellow at Afro-American Studies Center, 1973-75; Feminist Studio Workshop, Los Angeles, instructor in arts and humanities, 1975-76; San Francisco State University, San Francisco, Calif., lecturer, 1976-78, assistant professor in speech and communication studies, 1978—. Instructor at East Los Angeles Junior College, 1966; lecturer at University of California, Irvine, 1974, 1975; teacher of adult education classes at public schools in Los Angeles, 1967-70; conducts workshops.

MEMBER: International Communication Association, Speech Communication Association (member of Women's Caucus), Society for the Anthropology of Visual Communication, Maledicta Society, Western Speech Communication Association (chairman of intercultural interest group, 1980-81), Phi Beta Kappa. *Awards, honors:* Woodrow Wilson fellow, 1967-68; Ford Foundation grant, 1973-75; American Council of Learned Societies grants, 1973, 1974; National Endowment for the Humanities grant, 1980, and fellowship, 1981-82.

WRITINGS: (Contributor) David Spain, editor, *The Human Experience: Readings in Sociocultural Anthropology,* Dorsey, 1975; (contributor) Larry Samovar and Richard Porter, editors, *Intercultural Communication: A Reader,* 2nd edition (Folb was not included in 1st edition), Wadsworth, 1976, 3rd edition, 1981; (contributor) Samovar and Robert Cathcart, editors, *Small Group Communication: A Reader,* 3rd edition (Folb was not included in earlier editions), W. C. Brown, 1979; *Runnin' Down Some Lines: The Language and Culture of Black Teenagers,* Harvard University Press, 1980. Contributor to academic journals.

WORK IN PROGRESS: An *Annotated Dictionary of Black Teenage Usage,* publication expected in 1981; *Covert Communication in Women's Folk Art Forms; The Handwriting Is on the Wall: An Ethnographic-Critical Study of Women's Graffiti; A Handbook for Field Research in Communication Studies; The Field Work Experience: A Personal Accounting.*

SIDELIGHTS: Edith Folb commented: "Both the black power movement and the women's movement have been instrumental in my life, my work, and my teaching. In all my writing, I want to reach beyond the dry pages of the academic journal. Good writing needn't be passionless or obscure. I have long been fascinated by the uses and abuses of language and ways to encourage students and colleagues to speak well and write clearly.

"Scholars often separate the spoken word from the written word in their teaching and in their approach to writing. I think this is a mistake and limits the richness of 'voice' that can be found in the best writers. Most of my own writing reflects a process of 'speaking the lines' to myself as I compose. Of course, the structure and content of the spoken lines are worked with, refashioned in subsequent drafts, but the author must hear the words, quite literally, as she or he sets them down. We dichotomize too much in this Western culture of ours; we need to look for connections, to seek to unify and integrate our lives, our experiences, and our oral and written language.

"Clyde Kluckhohn, the anthropologist, has noted that the analysis of vocabulary is a most important and illuminating way of looking at a culture and at cultural history. It is also a potent vehicle for understanding the world of experience shared by a given culture, or microculture, such as that of the urban black teenager. It is a key to interpreting the values, attitudes, and beliefs emerging from that world view. For most residents of the United States, entering a unique language community with its own special brand of talk—such as the world of the black youth who lives in what is euphemistically called 'the inner city'—is akin to being a visitor in a foreign land. And like the foreign visitor, a person does not (cannot) learn the language of the residents in a few days or a few months. It takes involvement with the life and experiences of those residents and a grasp of the values, beliefs, and attitudes that underscore their lives. My deepest wish for my writing and research on black teenage language use is to provide educators, scholars, and concerned lay people with an increased contact with and understanding of the black youth's world through a more thorough and sensitive awareness of the words and phrases that inform and give meaning to that world view. Then, perhaps, the so-called 'inner city' will become a bit less alien to the outsider.

"Historically, women have been forced to, or chosen to, hide, conceal, or suppress their thoughts and feelings, whether it be the concealment of body and face, as in Islamic culture, or the suppression of ideas and intellect in the face of societal displeasure with such 'unseemly' displays. In recent years I have become increasingly aware of and interested in looking at the covert in women's communication. The National Endowment for the Humanities has just awarded me a year-long fellowship to explore the nature, form, and function of covert communication outside my discipline to enrich my work within my teaching area. The project will concentrate on women's folk art in the United States, especially the needlework arts (i.e., embroidery, sampler stitchery, quilting, knitting). The needlework arts seem, from my initial reading and experience, to be an abundant source of both form language (e.g., pictographic symbols, 'alphabets' of stitchery, etc.) and written language (e.g., sampler literature, 'memory quilts,' and embroidered messages).

"I believe the study of the covert, the hidden, the disguised communicative act—whether it be the coded messages of enslaved Africans struggling to survive in an alien landscape, or the socially proscribed outpouring of female literature penned under the male nom de plume, or the unnamed 'anonymous'—is of vital concern to those who would know and understand the human spirit. The presence of the covert often alerts us to the fact, time, and place of oppression in a culture as well as the ingenious and undaunted ways humankind has contended—and continues to contend—with oppressive forces. And the study of 'artists in aprons' promises to be, I believe, an eloquent addition to our knowledge of that undaunted spirit. I hope to illuminate that collective 'voice' in perhaps a creative mode or a nonfictional narrative mode that will do some justice to their story."

AVOCATIONAL INTERESTS: Dance, politics, theatre, ballet, swimming, gardening, "good conversation, food, friends, and drink."

*   *   *

FOLEY, Mary Mix   1918-

PERSONAL: Born October 14, 1918, in Muncie, Ind.; daughter of Charles Melvin (a surgeon) and Margaret (an artist; maiden name, Tracy) Mix; married Justin Foley (an army information officer); June 4, 1949; children: Stephen Prescott. *Education:* Attended Skidmore College, 1936-37; Syracuse University, B.A., 1940; also attended Columbia University, 1943-44. *Religion:* Congregational. *Home and office:* 288 N St. S.W., Washington, D.C. 20024. *Agent:* Shirley Fisher, McIntosh & Otis, Inc., 475 Fifth Ave., New York, N.Y. 10017.

CAREER: McCall's, New York City, assistant editor, 1940-43; *Architectural Forum*, New York City, associate editor, 1943-49; American Institute of Architects, Washington, D.C., member of staff, 1950-54; writer, 1954—. *Member:* Society of Architectural Historians, Society for the Preservation of New England Antiquities.

WRITINGS: (With Nelson Foote, Janet Abu-Lughod, and Louis Winnick) *Housing Choices and Housing Constraints*, McGraw, 1960; (with Albert Christ-Janer) *Modern Church Architecture*, McGraw, 1962; *The American House*, Harper, 1980. Contributor to magazines and newspapers, including *Architectural Forum* and *Washington Star*.

WORK IN PROGRESS: Another book on American houses.

SIDELIGHTS: Mary Foley told *CA:* "After fourteen years, primarily in the field of architectural journalism, I resigned to remain at home as the traditional housewife and mother. Though no longer a staff member of a magazine, I continued to write, taking the opportunity offered by freedom from a job to undertake a major piece of work. *The American House*, begun when my son was in fourth grade, was published the year that he graduated from law school, rather longer than I had expected it to take.

"The book exemplifies the evolutionary approach to architecture that I could only have developed over many years of uninterrupted effort. Undertaken as a guide to style, and including drawings and descriptions of 320 houses from the early seventeenth century through 1979, *The American House* is not merely a catalogue of colonial, Georgian, Greek Revival, Victorian, modern, and solar houses. My unique approach shows how architecture happens.

"*The American House* illustrates how the basic house forms of the earliest settlers (English, Dutch, Scandinavian, German, French, and Spanish) persisted through the centuries, adopting each succeeding period style as trim; conversely, how the same traditional English house was remodeled by climate in New England and the South to produce new American regional types; how a modest French-West Indian cottage developed into the pillared plantation mansion of southern tradition; how Victorian concepts of family life and nature produced a new and uniquely American house, the 'picturesque villa,' with its spacious, functional rooms, cozy inglenooks, tower retreats, and encircling verandahs.

"This book also sorts out the complexities of style, showing, for example, the way in which Victorian revivals were broken apart and recombined, as in the 'Shingle Style,' that includes elements of Romanesque, Colonial, and Queen Anne. It shows how this typically Victorian process actually had its roots in the Federal period, when the simplification and combination of elements transformed the Adam Style into Regency; how this same process, at the other end of the time scale, was used by Frank Lloyd Wright to create modern architecture from Victorian styles such as 'Shingle,' Georgian Revival, Tudor Revival, and Italian Renaissance.

"Such derivations and connections tie the entire history of American domestic architecture into a continuous, interlocking story—something not done before in architectural writing."

BIOGRAPHICAL/CRITICAL SOURCES: Cleveland Plain Dealer, March 2, 1980; *Lewiston Daily Sun*, March 5, 1980; *Detroit News*, March 9, 1980; *Old-House Journal*, April, 1980; *Miami Herald*, April 6, 1980; *Chicago Tribune*, April 27, 1980; *Atlantic Monthly*, May, 1980.

*   *   *

FOLEY, Richard N.   1910(?)-1980

OBITUARY NOTICE: Born c. 1910 in Danville, Ky.; died September 22, 1980, in Washington, D.C. Educator and authority on American drama and on the works of Henry James. Foley was associated with Georgetown University for thirty-four years before his retirement in 1974. He wrote *Criticism in American Periodicals of the Works of Henry James*. Obituaries and other sources: *Washington Post*, September 25, 1980.

FOLEY, Winifred 1914-

PERSONAL: Born July 23, 1914, in England; daughter of Charles and Margaret Mason; married Sydney John Foley (a wood machinist), December 25, 1938; children: Christopher, Richard, Nicholas, Jennifer (Mrs. Nicholas Townsend). *Education:* Attended village school in Glousestershire, England. *Home:* Pear Tree Cottage, The Row, Cliffords Mesne, near Newent, Gloucestershire, England.

CAREER: Domestic servant, 1928-39; land worker, 1955-65; writer.

WRITINGS: A Child in the Forest (autobiography), BBC Publications, 1974, revised edition published as *As the Twig Is Bent,* 1978; *No Pipe Dreams for Father* (autobiography), Futura, 1977; *Back to the Forest* (autobiography), Macdonald & Co., 1980. Co-author of ''Hard Cheese,'' with Julian Mitchell, first broadcast by BBC-TV.

WORK IN PROGRESS: A children's book.

SIDELIGHTS: Winifred Foley told *CA:* ''I write now that I have time to spare in late middle age to look back and re-member. My motivation is the sheer fascination of exis-tence.

''I have no religion. I believe man's multiple gods are the invention of man's imagination, from the need to find a rea-son for his existence, and a future solace for the hell he must sometimes bear on earth. Darwin and his followers have log-ically proved the theory of evolution. It adds to man's spiri-tual dilemma—I have enough ego to get moods of depres-sion—frustration and deprivation at the thought of dying in ignorance of how matter began!

''Politically, my sympathies tend to be with the humanists. Despite man's incredible achievements, I believe we are on the road to self-destruction—by dividing ourselves by coun-try, religion, economic injustices, and ego-based ideas of national superiority. Aware of at least some of the flaws in my own character, my hopes are diminishing!

''As Shakespeare said, 'All the world's a stage.' I suppose if we blow up our 'theatre' with atomic warfare, our role will be over.''

* * *

FORD, Elaine 1938-

PERSONAL: Born December 12, 1938, in New York; daughter of John H. and Ruth (Palmer) Ford; married Gerald Bunker (divorced, 1977); married Arthur Boatin (a writer), December 27, 1977; children: Mark, Geoffrey, Lisa, An-drew, Anne-Elizabeth. *Education:* Radcliffe College, A.B., 1964; Simmons College, M.L.S., 1979. *Politics:* Democrat. *Religion:* Protestant. *Home:* 16 Illinois Ave., Somerville, Mass. 02145. *Agent:* Ellen Levine, 370 Lexington, Suite 906, New York, N.Y. 10017. *Office:* Somerville Public Library, Somerville, Mass. 02143.

CAREER: Somerville Public Library, Somerville, Mass., reference librarian, 1979—. *Member:* American Library Association, Massachusetts Library Association.

WRITINGS: The Playhouse (novel), McGraw, 1980.

WORK IN PROGRESS: Beware of Limbo Dancers (tenta-tive title), a novel set in Somerville, Mass.

SIDELIGHTS: Elaine Ford told *CA:* ''I'm interested in fate as a manifestation of character, and also as the consumma-tion of a linked series of choices. A strong sense of place is important to me, too. I think that credibility for the reader has a lot to do with the specific detail of the setting, but I like to be very selective about detail and to write as sparely as possible.''

* * *

FORMAN, Joan
(Pamela Greene)

PERSONAL: Born in Louth, Lincolnshire, England; daugh-ter of Henry Percy and Isabel Forman. *Education:* Attended grammar school in Louth, England. *Home address:* Taver-ham, near Norwich, Norfolk NR8 6QE, England. *Agent:* Bolt & Watson Ltd., 8-12 Old Queen St., Storey's Gate, London SW1H 9HP, England.

CAREER: Washington Hall Training College, Chorley, Lan-cashire, England, educational administrator and bursar, 1949-53; youth employment officer in Hertfordshire, En-gland, 1953-58; *John o' London's,* London, England, poetry page editor, 1958-62; *Time and Tide,* London, poetry page editor, 1962-63; writer, 1963—. Conference organizer at University of East Anglia, 1971-72. Lecturer and guest on radio and television. *Member:* Society of Authors, League of Dramatists, Educational Writers Group, Royal Overseas League (London).

WRITINGS: See for Yourself (nonfiction), Books 1-2, Cas-sell, 1964; (editor) *Galaxy,* Books 1-4, Pitman, 1967; *The End of a Dream* (drama), Holt, 1969; *The Freedom of the House* (drama), Holt, 1971; *The Turning Tide* (drama), Holt, 1971; *Look Through a Diamond* (poetry anthology), Holt, 1971; *Westward to Canaan* (drama), Holt, 1972; *The Princess in the Tower* (juvenile), Faber, 1973; *Haunted East Anglia* (nonfiction), R. Hale, 1974; *The Romans* (history), Macdon-ald & Co., 1975; *The Mask of Time* (nonfiction), Macdonald & Co., 1978; *The Haunted South* (nonfiction), R. Hale, 1978.

One-act plays: *Maid in Arms,* Evans, 1960; *The Accusers,* Evans, 1961; *Night of the Fox,* Evans, 1961; *Midwinter Jour-ney,* Evans, 1961; *Portrait of the Late,* Kenyon-Deanes, 1961; *Ding Dong Belle,* Kenyon-Deanes, 1962; *The Pilgrim Women,* Epworth Press, 1962; *The Wise Ones,* Cassell, 1968.

Contributor of short stories, articles, and reviews to maga-zines and newspapers, occasionally under pseudonym Pa-mela Greene.

WORK IN PROGRESS: A book on the subject of death sur-vival, its possible process and form; research on ''a special-ized aspect of the Pilgrim fathers.''

SIDELIGHTS: Joan Forman wrote: ''I find the need to communicate my particular view of the world to be totally compulsive, as though the individual vision were a filter or a concentrator of experience, and the consequent focusing would enlighten the segment of life with which it is con-cerned. Of all the aspects of literature, I believe I prefer playwriting, again for its unique capacity to illuminate hu-man experience and make sense of it. However, certain as-pects of writing books are also deeply rewarding, if the con-clusions arising from a nonfiction subject throw some light on life problems. I enjoy writing fiction and nonfiction about equally.''

BIOGRAPHICAL/CRITICAL SOURCES: Radio Times, June, 1978; *Eastern Daily Press,* June, 1978.

* * *

FORSBERG, (Charles) Gerald 1912-

PERSONAL: Born June 18, 1912, in Vancouver, British Columbia, Canada; son of Charles (a shipmaster) and Nellie

(Wallman) Forsberg; married Joyce Whewell Hogarth, April 16, 1952; children: Frederick Charles Whewell, Tessa Elinor Vega. *Education:* Sir John Cass College, London, Master Mariner, 1938; also attended Polytechnic School, London. *Agent:* c/o Barclay's Bank International Ltd., 1 Cockspur St., London SW1Y 5BG, England.

CAREER: British Merchant Marine, served in tramp steamers worldwide, 1928-38, leaving service as chief officer; Royal Navy, career officer, 1938-62, wartime service in Norway, Malta convoys, Greece, Crete, Tobruk, Atlantic Ocean, and North Sea, and commander of destoyers, 1943-49, retiring as commander; Ministry of Defence, London, England, deputy director of marine services in London and Bath, 1958-72, assistant director, 1972-75; writer, 1975—. Freeman of City of London. *Member:* Honourable Company of Master Mariners (liveryman), Nautical Institute (fellow), Channel Swimming Association (president, 1963—). *Awards, honors*—Military: Mentioned in dispatches. Other: Member of Marathon Swimming Hall of Fame, 1965—; Davids-Wheeler Award from Davids-Wheeler Foundation (Boston), 1971, for outstanding service to marathon swimming; younger brother in Trinity House.

WRITINGS: Long Distance Swimming, Routledge & Kegan Paul, 1957; *First Strokes in Swimming,* Routledge & Kegan Paul, 1961; *Modern Long Distance Swimming,* Routledge & Kegan Paul, 1963; *Salvage From the Sea,* Routledge & Kegan Paul, 1977; *Pocket Book for Seamen,* Brown, Son & Ferguson, 1981. Contributor of articles, stories, and reviews to magazines.

SIDELIGHTS: Forsberg wrote: "I have published round about half a million words on the sport of swimming and the profession of seafaring. A publisher, who had read one of my short stories in *Blackwood's* magazine, persuaded me to write my first book, or I might have forever thought the size of a bookwriting task was beyond my capability and patience. I love the preliminary thinking, the research and collection of material, and the final arrival of the book from the printers. I only dislike the 'writing bit' in between.

"Now, I am doing nothing other than leisurely thinking about two or three possible book projects, when not engaged in the monthly journalistic slog which never stops."

*   *   *

FOSKETT, Daphne 1911-

PERSONAL: Born December 23, 1911, in Kimpton, England; daughter of J.W.C. (a military colonel) and Maude Agnes (Haynes) Kirk; married Reginald Foskett (a bishop), April 3, 1937 (died, 1973); children: Patricia Anne Foskett Middleton, Margaret Helen Foskett Godfrey. *Education:* Attended private school in Bexhill, England. *Religion:* Church of England. *Home:* Field Broughton Pl., Field Broughton, Grange-over-Sands, Cumbria, England.

CAREER: Writer, 1963—. Governor of St. Anne's School, Windermere, England, 1971—. *Member:* Royal Society of Arts (fellow), Royal Overseas League, Theta Sigma Phi.

WRITINGS: British Portrait Miniatures: A History, Methuen, 1963; *John Smart: The Man and His Miniatures,* Adams & Mackay, 1964, October House, 1965; *A Dictionary of British Miniature Painters,* two volumes, Praeger, 1972; *Samuel Cooper, 1609-1672,* Faber, 1974; *John Harden of Brathay Hall, 1772-1847,* Abbot Hall Art Gallery, 1974; *Samuel Cooper and His Contemporaries,* H.M. Stationery Office, 1974; *Collecting Miniatures,* Antique Collectors' Club, 1979; *Elizabethan Miniatures,* Orbis, 1981. Author of

exhibition catalogs. Contributor to periodicals, including *Apollo, Connoisseur,* and *Antique Dealer and Collector's Guide.*

SIDELIGHTS: Daphne Foskett told *CA:* "I have a great interest in people, historical research, and all art contacts. It is important to keep up with current thought.

"In collecting antiques, I have traveled extensively, including visits to Persia, Greece, Africa, the United States, the Netherlands, Denmark, Norway, Turkey, and France and to their museums. I maintain contact with numerous private collections and a working knowledge of all current sales in London and abroad where miniatures are offered."

*   *   *

FOSTER, Doris Van Liew 1899-

PERSONAL: Born November 9, 1899, in Bellaire, Mich.; daughter of Leon Gray (a grocer) and Georgia (Knapp) Van Liew; married June 24, 1922 (marriage ended, June, 1946); children: Virginia Van Liew Foster Springer, Eleanor Van Liew Foster Vloedman. *Education:* Western State Normal School (now Western Michigan University), certificate, 1920. *Religion:* Methodist. *Home:* 7421 Southwest 53rd Pl., Miami, Fla. 33143.

CAREER: Teacher at public elementary school in Jackson, Mich., 1921; Indianapolis Day Nursery, Indianapolis, Ind., teacher and supervisor, 1945-64; writer, 1964—. *Awards, honors: A Pocketful of Seasons* was named outstanding children's book by *New York Times,* 1961; citation from Indiana University Writer's Conference, 1962, for *A Pocketful of Seasons.*

WRITINGS—Children's books: *Tell Me, Little Boy,* Lothrop, 1953; *Tell Me, Mr. Owl,* Lothrop, 1957; *A Pocketful of Seasons* (Junior Literary Guild selection), Lothrop, 1961; *Honker Visits the Island,* Lothrop, 1962; *Feather in the Wind,* Lothrop, 1972.

SIDELIGHTS: Doris Van Liew Foster commented: "Teaching in a day care center was living with children during most of their waking hours. To be trusted by children is the greatest compliment. It has to be earned. It is forever. In return for that I made up stories for them which eventually became words on paper and, behold, I was an author.

"I presume every author views the happenings about him as story material. Here discrimination must play a part. A half-hearted effort has no place in literature. I am alarmed by the current trend of mass production of books for children. Why cannot there be a place for the special book to meet the needs of a child who hears a different drummer? Why? Too expensive. What a pity."

*   *   *

FOSTER, Frederick
See GODWIN, John (Frederick)

*   *   *

FOWLER, Elizabeth Millspaugh 1921-

PERSONAL: Born May 24, 1921, in Newburgh, N.Y.; daughter of Anson J. and Hazel (Osterhoudt) Fowler; married Philip Livingston Azoy, November 10, 1950; children: Katrina, Cynthia. *Education:* Smith College, B.A., 1942; New York University, M.B.A., 1953. *Religion:* Episcopalian. *Home address:* Mount Kemble Ave., Morristown, N.J. 07960. *Office: New York Times,* 229 West 43rd St., New York, N.Y. 10036.

CAREER: Buffalo Evening News, Buffalo, N.Y., reporter, 1942-44; *Wall Street Journal,* New York City, copy editor, 1944-46; Merrill, Lynch, Pierce, Fenner & Smith, New York City, financial writer, 1946-56; *New York Times,* New York City, financial reporter, 1956—. Lecturer on investment and economics. *Member:* Morristown Junior League, York Club.

WRITINGS: Ninety Days to Fortune, Obolensky, 1965; (contributor) C. J. Rolo and G. J. Nelson, editors, *Anatomy of Wall Street,* Lippincott, 1968; *How to Manage Your Money: A Woman's Guide to Investment,* Little, Brown, 1973; *Your Estate, Retirement, and Will,* Dreyfus Publications, 1973. Contributor to magazines.*

*   *   *

FOX, James M.
(Grant Holmes)

PERSONAL: Born in The Hague, Netherlands; came to the United States in 1946, naturalized citizen, 1949; married. *Education:* Attended University of Leiden and University of Utrecht. *Residence:* Palm Springs, Calif. *Agent:* Blanche C. Gregory, Inc., 2 Tudor City Pl., New York, N.Y. 10017.

CAREER: Practiced foreign commercial law in Europe and New York, N.Y.; legal adviser to minister of war of Netherlands Government-in-Exile during World War II; writer, 1946—. *Member:* Writers Guild of America (West), Dramatists Guild.

WRITINGS—Novels: The Lady Regrets, Coward, 1947; *Death Commits Bigamy,* Coward, 1948; *The Inconvenient Bride,* Coward, 1948; *The Gentle Hangman,* Little, Brown, 1950; *The Wheel Is Fixed,* Little, Brown, 1951; *The Aleutian Blue Mink,* Little, Brown, 1951; *The Iron Virgin,* Little, Brown, 1951; *The Scarlet Slippers,* Little, Brown, 1952; *A Shroud for Mr. Bundy,* Little, Brown, 1952; *Bright Serpent,* Little, Brown, 1953; *Code Three,* Little, Brown, 1953; *Dark Crusade,* Little, Brown, 1953; *Free Ride,* Popular Library, 1957; *Dead Pigeon,* Hammond, 1967; *The Exiles,* Weybright, 1970; *Operation Dancing Dog,* Walker & Co., 1974.

Novels under pseudonym Grant Holmes: *Surabaya,* Cassell, 1956, Universal, 1958; *Courier to Marlborough,* R. Hale, 1971.

Screenplays: "Free Ride," released by Columbia Broadcasting System in 1958; "The Asphalt Commandos," released by United Productions in 1966; "Surabaya," released by Wray Davis Productions in 1968; "Tarots," released by Orfeo Productions in 1973; (co-author) "Reflections in a Fountain," released by Orfeo Productions, 1973. Author of television plays.

*   *   *

FOXON, David Fairweather 1923-

PERSONAL: Born January 9, 1923, in Paignton, England; son of Walter (a minister) and Susan Mary (Fairweather) Foxon; married Dorothy June Jarratt, 1947 (marriage ended, 1963); children: one daughter. *Education:* Magdalen College, Oxford, B.A., 1948, M.A., 1953. *Home:* 7 Fane Rd., Marston, Oxford 0X3 0RZ, England. *Office:* Wadham College, Oxford University, Oxford, England.

CAREER: Worked in Foreign Office, London, England, 1942-45; British Museum, London, assistant keeper in department of printed books, 1950-65; Queen's University, Kingston, Ontario, professor of English, 1965-67; Oxford University, Oxford, England, fellow of Wadham College, 1968—, Lyell Reader in Bibliography, 1975-76. Sandars

Reader in Bibliography at Cambridge University, 1977-78. Fellow of British Academy, 1978—. *Member:* Bibliographical Society (president, 1980-81). *Awards, honors:* Guggenheim fellow, 1967-68.

WRITINGS: T. J. Wise and the Pre-Restoration Drama, Bibliographical Society, 1959; *Libertine Literature in England, 1660-1745,* Book Collector, 1964, University Books, 1965; (author of introduction) John Wilford, editor, *The Monthly Catalogue, 1723-1730,* Gregg Press, 1964; (editor and author of introduction) *The Monthly Catalogue, 1714-1717,* three volumes, Gregg Press, 1964; (author of introduction) Edward Kimber, editor, *The Gentleman's Magazine, 1731-51,* Gregg Press, 1966; *English Verse, 1701-1750: A Catalogue of Separately Printed Poems With Notes on Contemporary Collected Editions,* Volume I: *Catalogue,* Volume II: *Indexes,* Cambridge University Press, 1975. Contributor to academic journals. Editor of *English Bibliographical Sources,* 1964-67.

WORK IN PROGRESS: Pope and the Early Eighteenth-Century Book-Trade; The Stamp Act of 1712.

BIOGRAPHICAL/CRITICAL SOURCES: Times Literary Supplement, September 5, 1975.

*   *   *

FOX-SHEINWOLD, Patricia
(Patricia Sheinwold)

PERSONAL: Born in Maryland; daughter of Morton Henry and Cornelia (Briscoe) Fox; married Julian Adler (divorced, 1958); married Alfred Sheinwold (a syndicated columnist; divorced, 1972); children: (first marriage) Elinor Fox Pynes, Judith Morton Thomas, John Rayner. *Residence:* New York, N.Y.

CAREER: Writer. Founding member of board of directors of Brandeis University Women's Division; co-founder of Southern California Politically Oriented Women; past member of board of directors of National Council of Jewish Women and Vista Del Mar Children's Center; past chairman of United Service for New Americans; member of board of Baltimore Symphony Orchestra. *Member:* American Contract Bridge League (past member of board of directors), Middle Atlantic Bridge League (past member of board of directors; tournament chairperson), California Young Musician's Association. *Awards, honors:* More than two hundred local, regional, and national bridge championships, including national novice championship, 1951, and national women's team championship, 1964.

WRITINGS—Under name Patricia Sheinwold: Husbands and Other Men I've Played With, Houghton, 1976; *Jolly Time Party Book for Children,* Dorson House, 1977; *Crossword Puzzle Dictionary,* Ottenheimer, 1978; *Too Young to Die,* Crown, 1979; *All Appliance Cookbook,* Ottenheimer, 1980; *Gone But Not Forgotten* (nonfiction), Crown, 1981. Contributor to magazines, including *Synergy, Be Alive,* and *Sports Illustrated,* newspapers, and Field Syndicate.

WORK IN PROGRESS: Double Edge Dream, a novel, publication expected in 1983; films for television; a weekly television series.

SIDELIGHTS: In addition to studying ballet for seventeen years, Patricia Fox-Sheinwold studied drama with Maude Adams, piano at the Peabody Conservatory in Baltimore, Md., and graphic design. She has won athletic championships in tennis, golf, riding, bowling, and swimming. Music is now her most important activity, and she is interested in helping young musicians and dancers.

She told *CA:* "My interest as a writer is in people—what makes them work, act, interact, their feelings, thoughts, and in some cases, what makes them die. The greatest influence on my work was my friend, Henry Miller."

AVOCATIONAL INTERESTS: Collecting modern art.

*   *   *

FRANCA, Jose-Augusto 1922-

PERSONAL: Born November 16, 1922, in Tomar, Portugal; son of Jose Maria (in business) and Carmen (Rodrigues) Franca; married Marie-Therese Mandroux (an art history researcher), February 19, 1972; children: (from previous marriage) Maria Manuela (Mrs. R. Perroud). *Education:* University of Lisbon, M.A., 1945; University of Paris, D.Hist., 1962, D. es L., 1969; Ecole des Hautes Etudes, diploma, 1963. *Home:* Rua Escola Politecnica 49/4, 1200 Lisbon, Portugal. *Office:* Department of Art History, Universidad Nova de Lisboa, Avenue Berne, 1100 Lisbon, Portugal.

CAREER: Art critic, 1946—; film critic, 1948—; Editorial Confluencia, Lisbon, Portugal, publisher and manager, 1949-59; Universidad Nova de Lisboa, Lisbon, professor of cultural history and art history and director of department of art history, 1974—. Founder and director of Galeria de Marco, 1952-54. Member of Lisbon City Council, 1974-75.

MEMBER: International Association of Art Critics (vice-president, 1971-73), International P.E.N. (chairman of Portuguese section), International Committee of Art History, International Association for Cultural Freedom, Academia Nacional de Belas Artes (president, 1976—), Academia Portuguesa de Historia, Instituto de Cultura Portuguesa (president, 1976—), Academia dos Ciencias de Lisboa. *Awards, honors:* Chevalier of French Ordre des Arts et Lettres; commander of Brazil's Ordem Rio Branco.

WRITINGS—In English translation: *Millares,* Poligrafia, 1977, translation by Kenneth Lyons published under same title, Rizzoli International, 1979.

Other writings: *Natureza morta* (novel; title means "Still Life"), Livros Horizonte, 1949; *Charles Chaplin: Le "Self-Made Myth",* Inquerito, 1954; *Amadeo de Souza-Cardoso,* four volumes, Editorial Sul, 1956-57; *Azazel: Peca em actos,* Editorial Sul, 1956; *Situacao da pintura occidental,* Edicoes Atica, 1958; *Despedida breve e outros contos* (stories), Publicacoes Europa-America, 1958.

Une Ville des lumieres: La Lisbonne de Pombal, SEVPEN, 1965; *A arte em Portugal no seculo XX,* Livraria Bertrand, 1966; *Oito ensaios sobre arte contemporanea,* Publicacoes Europa-America, 1967; *A arte e a sociedade portuguesa no secula XX,* Livros Horizonte, 1972; *As "Conferencias do Casion" no parlamento,* Livros Horizonte, 1973; *A arte em Portugal no seculo XX: 1911-1961,* Livraria Bertrand, 1974; *O romantismo em Portugal: Estudo de factos socioculturais,* Livros Horizonte, 1974; (author of introduction and notes) Joaquim Machada de Castro, *Descricao analytica de execucao da Real Estatua equestre do Senhor Rei fidellissimo D. Jose I.,* Academia Nacional de Belas Artes, 1975. Also editor of *Pentacornio: Antologia de ineditos de autores portugueses contemporaneos,* 1956.

Editor of *Unicornio,* 1951-56, *Pintura e nao,* 1969-70, and *Coloquio artes,* 1970—; co-editor of *Cadernos de poesia,* 1951-53.

WORK IN PROGRESS: Research on Portugal in the 1920's.

AVOCATIONAL INTERESTS: Travel, detective stories.

FRANCIS, Dennis S. 1943(?)-1980

OBITUARY NOTICE: Born c. 1943; died of a brain tumor, September 7, 1980, in New York, N.Y. Educator and authority in the field of architectural history. Francis wrote *Architects in Practice: New York City, 1840-1900.* Obituaries and other sources: *New York Times,* September 11, 1980.

*   *   *

FRANCIS, Richard H. 1945-

PERSONAL: Born May 14, 1945, in Shawford, England; son of Leslie (a civil servant) and Marian (Rennie) Francis; married Jo Watson (a teacher), January 14, 1967; children: William Rennie, Helen Elizabeth. *Education:* Magdalene College, Cambridge, B.A. (with honors), 1967; attended Harvard University, 1970-72; University of Exeter, Ph.D., 1976. *Politics:* None. *Religion:* None. *Home:* Wing Holding, Marchamley Wood, Shrewsbury, Shropshire, England. *Agent:* A.D. Peters & Co. Ltd., 10 Buckingham St., London WC2N 6BU, England. *Office:* Department of American Studies, Victoria University of Manchester, Manchester, England.

CAREER: Victoria University of Manchester, Manchester, England, lecturer in American literature, 1972—. Lecturer at Al-Fateh University, 1976-77. *Awards, honors:* American Council of Learned Societies fellowship, 1970-72.

WRITINGS: *Blackpool Vanishes* (novel), Faber & Faber, 1979; *Daggerman* (novel), Pantheon, 1980. Contributor to *American Quarterly, Critical Quarterly,* and *Studies in the American Renaissance.* Member of editorial board of Peterloo Poets.

WORK IN PROGRESS: A novel, *The Enormous Dwarf; After Baudelaire and Other Poems.*

SIDELIGHTS: Francis told *CA:* "In my published works, as in the recently completed novel *The Enormous Dwarf,* the central issue is the same—an attempt to reveal the implications of an alien perspective in the 'normal' world, in effect to explore the possibilities of transcendentalism. In *Blackpool Vanishes* the perspective is provided by the presence of what might be called interterrestrial life, beings who come not from other worlds but from interstices in what we complacently think of as the continuum of reality. In *Daggerman,* the alien vision belongs to the deranged consciousness of a mass-murderer and is formulated into a religion of the 'third alternative.' In *The Enormous Dwarf* the problem is seen as one of accommodating in the present an event which took place in the past, an event which was so horrific that it challenges imaginative reconstruction.

"I think that my doctoral research into New England transcendentalism has a bearing on my concerns as a novelist. What interested me about the transcendentalists was the peculiarly practical manner with which they undertook a task that is usually regarded as an essentially mystical one. They searched for a formula—I eventually decided to call it the 'Law of Series'—which would unite the one and the many, the relative perspective of the individual and the total viewpoint that we traditionally consign to God. The fact that my own cast of mind is not transcendentalist in either the philosophical or the popular sense does not diminish my admiration for this sort of enterprise. Even though the required synthesis proves unavailable in my own novels (so far, at least!) my belief in the importance of the theme continues unabated; after all, the very word fiction implies that one says 'This is not so' while doing one's utmost to convince the reader that in fact it is."

AVOCATIONAL INTERESTS: "My other interests include twentieth-century American poetry, music (especially Mozart's operas), travel (particularly to the Mediterranean region), and collecting the works of such contemporary painters as Bevis Sale and Gaylord Treat Meech. I brew my own beer, but this should perhaps be regarded not so much as a hobby as a financial necessity."

*   *   *

FRANK, Morton 1912-

PERSONAL: Born June 14, 1912, in Pitcairn, Pa.; son of Abraham and Goldie (Friedenberg) Frank; married Agnes Dodds, June 2, 1944 (divorced, 1957); married Elizabeth Welt Pope, December 31, 1963; children: (first marriage) Allan Dodds, Michael Robert, Marilyn Morton. *Education:* University of Michigan, A.B., 1933; postgraduate study at Carnegie Institute of Technology, University of Pittsburgh, and Duquesne University. *Home:* 534 Rock House Rd., Easton, Conn. 06425; and 115 East 67th St., New York, N.Y. 10021. *Office:* Family Weekly, 641 Lexington Ave., New York, N.Y. 10022.

CAREER/WRITINGS: Braddock Daily News-Herald, Braddock, Pa., advertisement manager, 1933-34; *Braddock Free Press,* Braddock, editor, 1934-35; *Pittsburgh Press,* Pittsburgh, Pa., rotagravure manager, 1935-42; commentator on radio stations in Pennsylvania, 1935-42; *Arizona Times,* Phoenix, Arizona, vice-president and business manager, 1946; *Canton Economist,* Canton, Ohio, editor, 1946-58; *Lorain Sun News,* Lorain, Ohio, editor, 1949-50; *Inter County Gazette,* Strasburg, Ohio, editor, 1950; *Stark County Times,* Canton, editor, 1950-58; *Farm and Dairy,* Salem, Ohio, editor, 1952; Tri-Cities Telecasting, Canton, president, 1956-58; president of Printype, 1956-58; president of Property Development Corp., 1956-58; *Family Weekly and Suburbia Today,* New York City, vice-president and director of publisher relations, 1958-65; *Family Weekly,* New York City, publisher and executive vice-president, 1966-71, president, 1971—. Member of board of directors for Canton Symphony Orchestra, 1950-56; chairman of the Commission of Corresponding Independent Higher Education, 1976—; trustee of Alfred University. *Military service:* U.S. Navy, 1942-45; became lieutenant.

MEMBER: International Circulation Managers Association, International Newspaper Advertising Executives Association, International Newspaper Promotion Association, International Press Institute, Controlled Circulation Newspapers of America (director, 1948-56), Tri-State Federation of Non-Commercial Theatres (president, 1936-38), Newspaper Advertising Bureau (member of plans committee, 1974—), Pittsburgh Foreign Policy Association (director, 1940-42), Overseas Press Club (founder and trustee), Deadline Club (president, 1974-75, chairman, 1975-76), Sigma Alpha Mu, Sigma Delta Chi. *Awards, honors:* Community service award from Accredited Hometown Newspapers of America, 1954; first prize for feature writing from Newspaper Enterprise Association, 1954; LL.D. from Alfred University, 1979.

*   *   *

FRANKLIN, Jerome L(ee) 1943-

PERSONAL: Born February 7, 1943, in Milwaukee, Wis.; son of Allen Jerome (a consultant) and Libby (a secretary; maiden name, Mishlove) Franklin; children: Lisa Anne, Michael Steven. *Education:* University of California, Berkeley, A.B., 1965; attended California State University, San Francisco, 1967-69; University of Michigan, M.A., 1970, Ph.D., 1973. *Home:* 4289 Caminito Pintoresco, San Diego, Calif. 92108. *Office:* 444 Camino del Rio S., No. 121, San Diego, Calif. 92108.

CAREER: University of Michigan, Ann Arbor, project director at Institute for Social Research, 1973-77; Rensis Likert Associates, San Diego, Calif., vice-president, 1977—. Consultant to U.S., Canadian, and South American organizations. *Member:* American Psychological Association, Academy of Management.

WRITINGS: (With A. L. Wissler and G. J. Spencer) *Survey Guided Development III: A Manual for Concepts Training,* University Associates, 1977; (editor) *Developing Organizations,* Gale, 1978; (with David G. Bowers) *Survey Guided Development I: Data Based Organizational Change,* University Associates, 1978. Contributor to journals in the behavioral sciences.

WORK IN PROGRESS: Survey of Organizations Questionnaire Users Manual, with Bowers, 1981; research on evaluation of organizational change projects.

*   *   *

FRANKLIN, Olga 1912-

PERSONAL: Born July 29, 1912, in Birmingham, England; daughter of Henry Israel (in business) and Becky (a hospital nurse; maiden name, Bernstein) Davis; married Norbert Frenkel-Franklin (a leather manufacturer), September 5, 1934 (deceased). *Education:* Attended high school in Birmingham, England. *Home address:* Caterham, Surrey CR3 6SE, England. *Agent:* Sheila Watson, Bolt & Watson Ltd., 8-12 Old Queen St., Storey's Gate, London SW1H 9HP, England.

CAREER: Austin Motors (now British Leyland Motors), Birmingham, England, German-English translator and shorthand typist for Sir Herbert Austin, 1930-39; Imperial Chemical Industries, England, secretary on special war material mission (in liaison with Bethlehem Steel) in Warsaw, Poland, 1939-41; Reuters News Agency, London, England, sub-editor at news desk, 1941-43; *Oxford Mail,* Oxford, England, reporter, 1943-44; *Daily Sketch and Graphic,* London, reporter, 1944-56; *London Daily Mail,* London, author of column "Frankly Yours," 1956-71; free-lance writer, translator, broadcaster, and lecturer, 1971—. *Member:* National Union of Journalists, National Trust.

WRITINGS: Born Twice (nonfiction), Garnett, 1952; *Oh That Spike!* (nonfiction), Hammond Hammond, 1957; *Biography of Dr. Anna Aslan,* Arthur Barker, 1963; *Steppes to Fleet Street* (autobiography), Gollancz, 1968; *Only Uncle* (nonfiction), Hutchinson, 1970; *Making Money at Home,* Macdonald & Co., 1977; (translator) Larissa Vassilyeva, *Lara in London* (nonfiction), Pergamon, 1978; *Living-on-Less,* Macdonald Futura Ltd., 1979, revised edition, 1981.

Author of "The Twilight of Old Warsaw," a radio script, first broadcast by British Broadcasting Corp. (BBC), December 3, 1975; "Chekhov Women in a Soviet World," a radio play, first broadcast by BBC-Radio, April 1, 1976; "Tolstoy in London," a radio script, first broadcast by BBC-Radio, 1981. Contributor of articles to journals and newspapers, including *London Times, Daily Telegraph,* and *London Daily Mail.*

WORK IN PROGRESS: What Are We to Do?, translation of a novel by N. Chernyshevsky, for Virago; a biography of Nikolai Platonovich Ogarev; *Rylka,* a novel.

SIDELIGHTS: Olga Franklin told *CA:* "I am writing the

first-ever biography of Nikolai Platonovich Ogarev, Czarist exile and friend of Alexander Herzen. He was a poet and journalist. His bones were dug up by Soviet officials from Woolwich cemetery in London in 1966 and flown to Moscow for ceremonial burial. Whilst researching his life and also the previously unknown visit of Tolstoy to London in 1861 for my script 'Tolstoy in London,' I made what I see as a 'literary' discovery, that Tolstoy's unknown three weeks in London were spent at the Herzen-Ogarev household in Marylebone, London, observing the tragic menage-a-trois whereby Nick Ogarev's wife, Natalie, was already pregnant with Herzen's twins. Tolstoy returned home to Tula, near Moscow, to continue *War and Peace* and then, several years later, *Anna Karenina*. I intend my biography to show that Anna was based on the character of the unhappy Natalie, as seen by the observant young Tolstoy, then thirty-three, because this until now unknown piece of evidence will explain to worldwide literary critics just why Lev Tolstoy 'punished' his Anna Karenina with suicidal death.

"My special interest is nineteenth-century British immigration, mainly because in Britain there are no reference books on the subject. This is in contrast with the United States, where immigrants of all nationalities published autobiographies. No such works have been written by British immigrants, except for a small number of Irishmen and Jews who use postgraduates to do research in cemeteries, archives, and parish records. However, their work is obviously limited. For this reason no historian in Britain or elsewhere has been able so far to write a properly documented work on Britain's immigrants—French, German, Christian Poles, Hungarian, Italian, Greek, Russian, Jewish, Armenian, or any other—although between 1848 and 1870 these emigrants or trans-migrants actually outnumbered those in the United States!

"It was while I was researching in the Reading Room of the British Museum that I found that this wide gap in history was only one of many unknown errors and inaccuracies, especially in encyclopedias and works of reference. I found, for instance, that no details had so far been published about Tolstoy's stay in London or of the fact that *War and Peace* might never have been published if Tolstoy's estranged friend, Ivan Turgenev, had not 'flogged' his own French translation to Paris publishers in 1865. Much biographical detail about him was inaccurate; *Encyclopaedia Britannica* had a photograph of Ivan Turgenev purporting to be the photograph of Lev Tolstoy until I wrote them and they made the necessary correction. So many biographies (Russian in particular) are false or inaccurate because the material had been translated several times, not from the original but from other translations.

"I long to get a true, documented picture of that life and that period because it was in the early 1870's that my father's family left their Russian-occupied Lithuanian village of Utyan, near Kaunas, and sailed to Grimsby, England. Perhaps one day some unknown reader in America will be able to tell me their real names, to give me a description of my grandfather's life in that forgotten stetl, now wiped from the map by a history untold, unknown, undocumented. Then I can write a definitive biography at last."

*   *   *

FRASER, Dorothy May   1903(?)-1980
  (Maxwell Fraser)

OBITUARY NOTICE: Born c. 1903 in London, England; died December 25, 1980. Travel writer. Fraser's writings in-

clude *Holiday Haunts;* a two-volume tour of Wales, *West of Offa's Dyke;* and *Welsh Border Country, Surrey.* Obituaries and other sources: *The Author's and Writer's Who's Who,* 6th edition, Burke's Peerage, 1971; *London Times,* January 8, 1981.

*   *   *

FRASER, Douglas   1910-
  (David Hope)

PERSONAL: Born January 12, 1910, in Edinburgh, Scotland; son of John Barclay (a law clerk) and Christina (McAlpine) Fraser; married Eva Nisbet Greenshields, March 30, 1940; children: Heather Joyce Fraser Moncur, Robin Stewart, Donald Neil. *Education:* Attended secondary school in Edinburgh, Scotland. *Politics:* Scottish National party. *Home:* 2 Keith Ter., Edinburgh EH4 3NJ, Scotland.

CAREER: Standard Life Assurance Co., Edinburgh, Scotland, clerk, 1927-71. *Wartime service:* National Fire Service, 1941-46. *Member:* International P.E.N. (member of committee, 1973-79), Scottish Association for the Speaking of Verse (vice-chairman, 1979), Scots Language Society, Scottish Mountaineering Club. Edinburgh Poetry Club. *Awards, honors:* Queen's Silver Jubilee Medal, 1977.

WRITINGS: Landscape of Delight (poems), Macdonald & Co., 1967; *Rhymes o' Auld Reekie* (poems), Macdonald & Co., 1973; *Where the Dark Branches Part* (poems), Macdonald & Co., 1977. Contributor of poems to magazines, including *Scots, Burns Chronicle, Friendship Book* (under pseudonym David Hope), *Lines Review, Lallans,* and *Fireside Book.*

SIDELIGHTS: Fraser commented: "Writing poetry has probably been a reaction against a rather humdrum life. I have lived in Edinburgh all my life and spent all my working life (since age seventeen) in one office. Writing poetry has not been an escape from reality, but perhaps an escape into reality. My main themes have been love, the Scottish Highlands, and the Edinburgh environment. I write in Scots and English, the subject matter usually dictating the medium used."

*   *   *

FRASER, Maxwell
  See FRASER, Dorothy May

*   *   *

FRASER, Morris   1941-

PERSONAL: Born July 4, 1941, in Inverness, Scotland; son of Roderick (a minister) and Elizabeth (Morrison) Fraser. *Education:* Queen's University, Belfast, Northern Ireland, M.B., B.Ch., and B.A.O., 1966, M.D., 1980; Royal College of Physicians and Surgeons, London, D.P.M., 1969; Royal College of Psychiatrists, London, M.R.C.Psych., 1971. *Politics:* None. *Religion:* Church of England. *Home:* 36-A Navarino Rd., London E8 1AD, England. *Agent:* A. D. Peters & Co. Ltd., 10 Buckingham St., London WC2N 6BU, England.

CAREER: Royal Belfast Hospital for Sick Children, Belfast, Northern Ireland, senior registrar in child psychiatry, 1971-73; Springfield Hospital, London, England, psychiatrist, 1973-76; London Hospital, London, senior registrar in psychiatry, 1976-79; University College Hospital, London, consultant psychiatrist, 1979—.

WRITINGS: Children in Conflict, Secker & Warburg, 1973;

The Death of Narcissus, Basic Books, 1977. Contributor to *New Statesman* and *New Society.* Editor of *International Journal of Social Psychiatry.*

WORK IN PROGRESS: A book on electro-convulsive therapy.

SIDELIGHTS: Fraser wrote: "People have been fed or have absorbed haphazard, gross misconceptions about mental health and ill-health, about psychiatry and its practitioners. My main job is to make my profession, and the writing about it, rational and coherent. I set great store by painstakingly constructed work and try to use it to present the treatment of mental ill-health as a science with status equivalent to the other branches of medicine."

AVOCATIONAL INTERESTS: European languages, travel, playing the organ, "real ale."

*   *   *

FREAS, Frank Kelly   1922-

PERSONAL: Born August 27, 1922, in Hornell, N.Y.; son of Francis Matthew and Miriam Eudora (Sylvester) Kelly; married Pauline H. Bussard (a business manager and publisher), March 26, 1952; children: Jacqueline Deborah, Jeremy Patrick. *Education:* Pittsburgh Art Institute, graduated, 1951. *Home and office:* 4216 Blackwater Rd., Virginia Beach, Va. 23457.

CAREER: Illustrator, 1947—, including commercial, science fiction, and religious work. Vice-president of Environmental Research Associates, 1970—. Work exhibited in solo shows. *Military service:* U.S. Army Air Forces, 1941-46. *Member:* Graphic Artists Guild, Science Fiction Writers Association, Association of Science Fiction Artists, Southern Fandom Confederation, Dorsai Irregulars. *Awards, honors:* Art awards include Hugo Awards from World Science Fiction Society, annually 1955-59, 1970, 1972-76; Nicholas van Rijn Award from Deep South Confederation, 1970; award from American Institute of Graphic Arts, 1971; named dean of science fiction artists by Eastern Science Fiction Association, 1971; awards from Printing Industries of the Virginias, 1972, and Society of Publication Designers, 1972; named grand master of science fantasy illustration by Creation '72, 1972; awards from International Science Fantasy Art Exhibition, 1973, for "Skylab Study," "Testament XXI," and "Symbiotes"; Frank R. Paul Award from Kwintus Khublius, 1977; Deep South Con (DSC) Art Award from Southern Fandom Confederation, 1978; ROVA Award from Nelson Bond Society, 1978; Inkpot Award from San Diego Comics Convention, 1979.

WRITINGS: The Astounding Fifties, privately printed, 1971; *Six to Go* (space posters), Chesapeake Public Schools, 1971; *Science Fiction Art Prints* (portfolios), five volumes, privately printed, 1972-78; *Officers of the Bridge,* New York Star-Trek, 1976; *Frank Kelly Freas: The Art of Science Fiction,* Donning Co., 1977. Co-editor with wife, Pauline Freas, and illustrator of "Starblaze Editions," a series, Donning Co., 1977-78. Contributor of articles to *Analog* and illustrations (including covers) to a wide variety of magazines, including *Mad.*

WORK IN PROGRESS: Frank Kelly Freas: The Art of Science Fiction, publication expected in 1981; *Painting for Pleasure,* expected in 1982; *Painting for Pay;* expected in 1983; *Painting for Profit,* expected in 1984.

SIDELIGHTS: Freas wrote: "As a professional science fiction illustrator I work for pay, and feel that any appearance of my work warrants a fee, however nominal. Thus, there is little of my work to be found in the usual histories of science fiction art. Obviously, then, it was necessary for me to write my own.

"My basic feeling toward my work is that of illustrator rather than artist. I regard story and illustration as a package in which each adds meaning and dimension to the other. In science fiction this means careful reading and careful research. That gives me an excuse to get into the backrooms (such as the Vehicle Assembly Building at Kennedy Spaceport and the nuclear hunter submarine on which I spent a week) where the fantastic becomes routine. My Deep Dive Certificate gives me as much pleasure as knowing that my posters (pushing the space program) were the first such to be hung in the Smithsonian Institution.

"I am not interested in painting (or writing) per se. I prefer story-telling pictures, and picture-generating stories. It may be momentarily out of fashion, but it's still fun, and to me the fun has always been as important as the fee.

"I have naturally been deeply interested in promoting the space program. There is no question that the destiny of mankind lies in space—and I would like someday to make a trip to Mars or Ganymede without the need to make the voyage bearable by learning Chinese, or even Russian.

"My wife, Polly, is as popular at science fiction conventions as I, and we attend as many as possible, sometimes as many as twenty-five in a year. In combination with television appearances and speaking engagements, it makes for a full schedule."

AVOCATIONAL INTERESTS: Martial arts, history, culture and art of Japan, music (classical and modern).

BIOGRAPHICAL/CRITICAL SOURCES: Newport News Times Herald, April 12, 1971, October 4, 1977; *Virginian Pilot,* September 10, 1972; *Virginia Beach Beacon,* September 14, 1972; *Newport News Daily Press,* April 22, 1973; Emil Petaja, *The Hannes Bok Memorial Showcase of Fantasy Art,* SISU, 1974; *Industrial Art Methods,* October, 1974; Lester del Ray, editor, *Fantastic Science Fiction Art,* Ballantine, 1975; *Delaps Fantasy and Science Fiction Review,* December, 1975; *San Francisco Monthly,* Volume III, number 2, 1976; *The Liberated Quark: Journal of the Hampton Roads Science Fiction Association,* September, 1977; *New Norfolk: Tidewater,* February, 1977; *Commonwealth: Magazine of Virginia,* December, 1977; *Virginia Beach Sun,* December 28, 1977; *Tidewater After Dark,* March, 1978; *Metro: Magazine of Southeastern Virginia,* July, 1978; Colin Lester, *The International Science Fiction Yearbook,* Big O, 1979.

*   *   *

FREDERICK, Pauline   1908-

PERSONAL: Born February 13, 1908, in Gallitzin, Pa.; daughter of Matthew Philip (a state government official) and Susan (Stanley) Frederick; married Charles Robbins (a lecturer and consultant on energy), March 31, 1969. *Education:* Received A.B. and A.M. from American University. *Residence:* Westport, Conn.

CAREER: Writer. Radio editorial assistant for H. R. Baukhage, Blue Network, and American Broadcasting Co. (ABC); American Broadcasting Co., news commentator and United Nations correspondent, 1946-53; National Broadcasting Co. (NBC), news correspondent and United Nations correspondent, 1953-74; National Public Radio (NPR), news analyst, 1975—. Member of board of directors of American University and Save the Children Foundation.

MEMBER: Society of Professional Journalists (fellow), United Nations Correspondents Association (president, 1959), Council on Foreign Relations, Association of Radio and Television Analysts, United Nations Association (member of board of directors). *Awards, honors:* Twenty-three honorary degrees from colleges and universities; Headliner Award from Theta Sigma Phi; Alfred I. DuPont Award; George Foster Peabody Award from School of Journalism at University of Georgia; Golden Mike award from *McCall's;* medal from School of Journalism at University of Missouri; citation from National Federation of Women's Clubs for United Nations coverage; award from East-West Center at University of Hawaii; journalism achievement award from University of Southern California; First Pennsylvania Journalism Achievement Award; Carr Van Anda Award from School of Journalism at Ohio University; member of New York Professional Journalists Society Hall of Fame; Paul White Award from Radio Television News Directors Association.

WRITINGS: Ten First Ladies of the World, Meredith Corp., 1968. Contributor to *Georgia Review.*

* * *

FREDMAN, Alice G(reen) 1924-

PERSONAL: Born October 24, 1924, in New York, N.Y.; married in 1950; children: two. *Education:* Swarthmore College, A.B., 1945; Smith College, M.A., 1946; Columbia University, Ph.D., 1953. *Home:* 30 Harbour Rd., Kings Point, N.Y. 11024. *Office:* Department of English, Columbia University, New York, N.Y. 10027.

CAREER: Smith College, Northampton, Mass., instructor in English, 1946-47; Hobart and William Smith Colleges, Geneva, N.Y., instructor in English and humanities, 1949-51; Queens College (now of the City University of New York), Flushing, N.Y., lecturer in English, 1952; Columbia University, New York, N.Y., instructor, 1953-55, assistant professor, 1955-60, associate professor, 1961-72, professor of English and comparative literature, 1972—. *Member:* Modern Language Association of America, Keats-Shelley Association of America. *Awards, honors:* American Council of Learned Societies fellow, 1962-63; Carl and Lily Pforzheimer Foundation travel grant, 1969.

WRITINGS: (Contributor) O. E. Fellows and N. L. Torrey, editors, *Diderot Studies,* Volume I, Syracuse University Press, 1950; *Diderot and Sterne,* Columbia University Press, 1954; *Anthony Trollope,* Columbia University Press, 1971; (contributor) John H. Middendorf, editor, *English Writers of the Eighteenth Century,* Columbia University Press, 1971.*

* * *

FREEDEMAN, Charles E(ldon) 1926-

PERSONAL: Born November 3, 1926, in Alliance, Ohio; married in 1956. *Education:* Mount Union College, A.B., 1949; Columbia University, A.M., 1950, Ph.D., 1957. *Office:* Department of History, State University of New York at Binghamton, Binghamton, N.Y. 13901.

CAREER: University of Maryland, College Park, instructor, 1955-56, lecturer in history, 1956-59; Wisconsin State College (now University of Wisconsin—Stevens Point), assistant professor of history, 1959-62; Northern Illinois University, DeKalb, 1962-68, began as assistant professor, became associate professor of history; State University of New York at Binghamton, associate professor of history, 1968—. *Member:* American Historical Association, Society for

French Historical Studies, Economic History Society, Agricultural History Society, Society of Modern History (France).

WRITINGS: The Conseil d'Etat in Modern France, Columbia University Press, 1961; (contributor) Charles K. Warner, editor, *From the Ancien Regime to the Popular Front,* Columbia University Press, 1969; *Joint-Stock Enterprise in France, 1807-1867: From Privileged Company to Modern Corporation,* University of North Carolina Press, 1979. Contributor to history journals.*

* * *

FREEMAN, Dave
See FREEMAN, David

* * *

FREEMAN, David 1922-
(Dave Freeman)

PERSONAL: Born August 22, 1922, in London, England; son of Joseph (a soldier) and Hilda Mary (a police officer; maiden name, Horton) Freeman; married Alberta Norma Allen, February 6, 1946; children: Ailsa Christine, Deborah Carolyn, Gregory William. *Education:* Attended elementary school in London, England. *Politics:* None. *Religion:* Methodist. *Home:* Pedlars Farm, Mockbeggar Lane, Biddenden, Kent, England. *Agent:* Richard Stone, 18-20 York Buildings, London WC2N 6JU, England.

CAREER: Electrician's helper, 1936-38; theatre electrician, 1938-40; Metropolitan Police, London, England, member of force, 1947-51, detective constable attached to Scotland Yard, 1952-53; U.S. Air Force Officers Club, London, civilian club officer, 1953-54; journalist with *Ruisup Weekly Post* and *London Star Sunday Express,* 1955; free-lance writer for television, 1955—. *Military service:* Royal Navy, 1940-47 and 1951-52; served in Indian and Pacific Oceans. *Member:* Writers Guild of Great Britain. *Awards, honors:* Grand Prix from Cannes Film Festival, 1961; awards for television commercials.

WRITINGS—Plays; under name Dave Freeman: (With Benny Hill) "Fine Fettle" (revue), first produced in London, England, at Palace Theatre, September, 1959; (with Leslie Bricusse) "Swinging Down the Lane" (revue), first produced in London, at London Palladium, May, 1960; "Deep and Crisp and Stolen" (three-act), first broadcast by Associated Rediffusion Television, December, 1965; "Solo for the Banker" (three-act), first broadcast by Associated Rediffusion Television, October, 1966; "A Bedfull of Foreigners" (two-act), first produced in London, at Ashcroft Theatre, February 19, 1974; "Murder in a Bad Light" (two-act), first produced in Guildford, England, at Yvonne Arnaud Theatre, November 28, 1978.

Films: "Rocket to the Moon" (released in the U.S. as "Those Fantastic Flying Fools," American International Pictures, 1967), Anglo Amalgamated, 1967; "Bless This House," Rank, 1973; "Carry on Behind," Rank, 1976. Writer for about three hundred television comedy programs; comedy writer for Benny Hill, 1955-65.

WORK IN PROGRESS: A stage comedy with John Chapman; contributing to "Terry and June," broadcast by British Broadcasting Corp. (BBC).

SIDELIGHTS: Freeman commented: "Since 'Bedfull of Foreigners' opened, it has played in South Africa, Rhodesia, Hong Kong, Spain, Germany, Denmark, and Belgium. It has also played at many theatres throughout the United States and Canada. As long as the royalties keep trickling in I don't intend doing any more work . . . ever. This of course doesn't apply to woodwork, which I enjoy, only to writing, which I detest. I can't tell you how much I loathe writing. My main literary ambition is to earn so much money that I don't ever have to write again. I tried farming for awhile, but found it even worse than writing. My motto is: 'All time not spent in sleep is time wasted.' I have read extensively and can now tackle words of three syllables and over.''

AVOCATIONAL INTERESTS: Woodwork, wood turning, collecting old woodworking tools (especially Stanley planes), Oriental meditation.

*   *   *

FREEMAN, James Montague   1936-

PERSONAL: Born December 1, 1936, in Chicago, Ill.; married in 1968. *Education:* Northwestern University, B.A., 1958; Harvard University, M.A., 1964, Ph.D., 1968. *Office:* Department of Anthropology, California State University, San Jose, Calif. 95114.

CAREER: California State University, San Jose, assistant professor of humanities, 1966, assistant professor of anthropology, 1966—. *Member:* American Anthropological Association, Association for Asian Studies.

WRITINGS: Manners and Customs of the Bible, Logos International, 1973; *Scarcity and Opportunity in an Indian Village,* Cummings, 1976; *Untouchable: An Indian Life History,* Stanford University Press, 1979. Contributor to *Monist.*

BIOGRAPHICAL/CRITICAL SOURCES: Times Literary Supplement, September 5, 1980.*

*   *   *

FRENCH, Alfred   1916-

PERSONAL: Born July 12, 1916, in Wolverhampton, England; son of Percy and Susan (Parsonage) French; married Lidmila Stolova, June 15, 1939 (died March 28, 1979); children: Philip David. *Education:* Selwyn College, Cambridge, B.A., 1938, M.A., 1944. *Home:* 27 Woodfield Ave., Fullarton, South Australia 5063. *Office:* Department of Classics, University of Adelaide, Adelaide, South Australia 5001.

CAREER: Caroline University, Prague, Czechoslovakia, lecturer in English, 1938-39; University of Sydney, Sydney, Australia, assistant lecturer in Latin, 1948-50; University of Adelaide, Adelaide, Australia, lecturer in classics, 1950-63, reader in classics, 1964—. Fellow of University College, Cambridge, 1968-69, and of Australian Academy of the Humanities, 1977—.

WRITINGS: (Contributor) H. B. Segel, editor, *Modern Slavic Literature,* Ungar, 1946; *A Book of Czech Verse,* Macmillan, 1958; (translator) Vitezslav Nezval, *Sunset Over Atlantis,* Dilia, 1960; *The Growth of the Athenian Economy,* Routledge & Kegan Paul, 1964; *The Poets of Prague,* Oxford University Press, 1969; (contributor) *Czechoslovakia, Past and Present,* Volume II, Mouton, 1970; *The Athenian Half-Century,* Sydney University Press, 1971; (editor) *Czech Poetry,* Volume I, Michigan Slavic Studies, University of Michigan, 1973; (contributor) M. Rechcigl, editor, *Baroque Poetry,* Doubleday, 1974; *Czech Writers and Politics,* Australian National University Press, 1981. Contributor to history, literature, and classical journals.

FREUD, Clement (Raphael)   1924-

PERSONAL: Born April 24, 1924; son of Ernst and Lucie Freud; married Jill Flewett, 1950; children: three sons, two daughters. *Home:* 22 Wimpole St., London W.1, England.

CAREER: Apprentice at Dorchester Hotel in London, England; trainee at Martinez Hotel in Cannes, France; Royal Court Theatre Club, London, proprietor, 1956-62; Southern Television, England, writer and performer for ''Sweet and Sour,'' 1962-64; Parliament, London, Liberal member of Parliament for Isle of Ely, 1973—, party spokesman on education and science, 1973-74, education and the arts, 1974-77, Northern Ireland and broadcasting and the arts, 1977—, member of services committee, 1973-76, and subcommittees on broadcasting, security, and catering, 1973-76. Chairman of finance and administration board of Liberal party. Director of Genevieve Restaurants; director and member of board of trustees of Playboy Club of London and Berkeley Hotel. Writer-performer for ''Freud on Food,'' Tyne Tees Television, 1968-71; guest on ''Frost Shows,'' ''Braden Shows,'' ''Jackanory,'' ''Late Late Show,'' and ''Tonight Show.'' Rector of University of Dundee, 1974—. *Military service:* British Army, Royal Ulster Rifles, liaison officer, 1946; served in Germany. *Member:* Savile Club, Marylebone Cricket Club, Lord Taverners' Club. *Awards, honors:* Won *Daily Mail*'s London-to-New York air race, 1969; award for pet food commercial, 1967.

WRITINGS: (Translator with Aidan Philip) Marie Paule Pomaret and Helene Cingria, *Be Bold in Your Kitchen,* Parrish, 1956; *Grimble* (juvenile), Collins, 1968, reprinted with other stories as *Grimble at Christmas,* Puffin Books, 1974; *Freud on Food,* Dent, 1978.

Sports writer for *Observer,* 1956-64. Author of columns in *Sun,* 1964-69, *Financial Times,* 1964—, *News of the World,* 1965, *Daily Telegraph,* 1968—, and *Daily Express,* 1973-75. Contributor to magazines, including *New Yorker, Punch, Queen,* and *Town.* Cookery editor of *Observer,* 1956-64, *Time and Tide,* 1961-63, and *Daily Telegraph,* 1968—.

AVOCATIONAL INTERESTS: Racing, cricket, backgammon, golf.

BIOGRAPHICAL/CRITICAL SOURCES: Time, August 20, 1973.*

*   *   *

FRIDAY, Peter
See HARRIS, Herbert

*   *   *

FRIEDMAN, Elizabeth   1893(?)-1980

OBITUARY NOTICE: Born c. 1893; died of arteriosclerosis, October 31, 1980, in Plainfield, N.J. Cryptanalyst and author best known for her work with her husband in refuting the theory that decoding specifics in William Shakespeare's canon would reveal Francis Bacon as the actual author. Their findings were published as *The Shakespearean Ciphers Examined.* Friedman also helped capture a ring of drug dealers by breaking a Chinese code despite her ignorance of the language. Obituaries and other sources: *Newsweek,* November 17, 1980; *Time,* November 17, 1980.

*   *   *

FRITH, H(arold) J(ames)   1921-

PERSONAL: Born April 16, 1921, in Kyogle, Australia; son of Richard (a farmer) and Elizabeth (Marshall) Frith; married

Dorothy Marion Killeen, November 20, 1943; children: Diana Gay Frith Sweetman, Richard David, Marion Elizabeth Frith Constantine. *Education:* University of Sydney, B.Sc. Agr., 1941, D.Sc.Agr., 1961. *Politics:* None. *Religion:* Presbyterian. *Home:* 20 Brown St., Yarralumla, Australian Capital Territory 2600, Australia. *Office:* Commonwealth Scientific Industrial Research Organization, Lyneham, Australian Capital Territory 2602, Australia.

CAREER: Commonwealth Scientific Industrial Research Organization, Canberra, Australia, researcher in horticulture at Irrigation Research Station in Griffith, 1946-53, associated with Wildlife Survey Section, 1953-61, chief of Division of Wildlife Research in Lyneham, 1962—. Member of permanent executive committee of International Ornithological Committee; member of state and territory fauna authorities. *Military service:* Citizen's Military Force, 1939-41 and 1950-56; became captain. Australian Imperial Force, 1941-46; served in the Middle East and New Guinea; became lieutenant.

MEMBER: Royal Australasian Ornithological Society (fellow), Australian Academy of Science (fellow), Australian Academy of Technological Science (fellow), American Ornithologists Union (corresponding member), Societe Ornithologique Francaise (honorary member), Deutsche Ornithologen Gesellschaft, (fellow), Commonwealth Scientific Industrial Research Organization Officers Association. *Awards, honors:* Whitley Medal from Royal Zoological Society of New South Wales, 1979, for second edition of *Wildlife Conservation;* officer of Order of Australia, 1980.

WRITINGS: The Mallee Fowl, Angus & Robertson, 1962; *Waterfowl in Australia,* Angus & Robertson, 1967, revised edition, A. H. & A. W. Reed, 1977, 2nd revised edition, Angus & Robertson, 1981; (editor and contributor) *Birds in the Australian High Country,* A. H. & A. W. Reed, 1969, revised edition, 1976, 2nd revised edition, Angus & Robertson, 1981; (with J. H. Calaby) *Kangaroos,* Humanities, 1969; *Wildlife Conservation,* Angus & Robertson, 1973, revised edition, 1979; (editor with A. B. Costin, and contributor) *Conservation,* Penguin, 1971, revised edition, 1974; (editor and contributor) *The Murray Waters,* Angus & Robertson, 1974; (editor with Calaby) *Proceedings of the Sixteenth International Congress,* Australian Academy of Science, 1976; (editor with B. S. Hetzel, and contributor) *The Nutrition of Aborigines,* Commonwealth Industrial Research Organization, 1978; *Pigeons and Doves in Australia,* Rigby, 1981. Contributor of about one hundred articles to scientific journals.

WORK IN PROGRESS: The Nature of Naturalists.

SIDELIGHTS: Frith wrote: "I am born and bred a naturalist with no wish to do anything else. I was stimulated by my father and uncles, typical backwoodsmen of their day, and drifted into professional ornithology almost accidentally after the war.

"I have been able to work in every region of Australia, from the central deserts to the lush jungles and icy alps, and in New Guinea and Antarctica. I have made study tours in Europe, the United Kingdom, North America, Japan, and most parts of the Pacific, Malaysia, Thailand, and Indonesia.

"In 1981 I intend to retire, return to a small farm in the backwoods district of my origin (now, of course, it is over-cleared and over-populated, but still it will do), watch birds, grow native plants, and perhaps write a book or two.

"Many scientists cannot communicate with the lay public, which is a pity. I have tried to bring the conservation mes-

sage directly to the book-reading public, so that people can press the government with solid facts to back their arguments, and it seems to work. If scientists cannot learn to drop their jargon and write simple prose that simple people like politicians can understand, then the cause is lost. So far Australia has been lucky, but development is now so active that nature will be lost if there is not a concerted effort. People with hard data must lay it on the line!"

BIOGRAPHICAL/CRITICAL SOURCES: Commonwealth Scientific Industrial Research Organization Officers Association Bulletin, autumn, 1980.

*   *   *

FRITSCH, Albert Joseph 1933-

PERSONAL: Born September 30, 1933, in Maysville, Ky.; son of Albert Anthony and Mary (Schumacher) Fritsch. *Education:* Xavier University, Cincinnati, Ohio, B.S., 1955, M.S., 1956; attended West Baden College, 1959-61; Fordham University, Ph.D., 1964; Loyola University, Chicago, Ill., S.T.L., 1968. *Agent:* William Adler, 110 East End Ave., New York, N.Y. 10028. *Office:* Center for Science in the Public Interest, 1346 Connecticut Ave. N.W., Room 812, Washington, D.C. 20036.

CAREER: Entered Society of Jesus (S.J.; Jesuits), 1956, ordained Roman Catholic priest, 1967; University of Texas, Austin, research fellow, 1969-70; Center for the Study of Responsive Law, Washington, D.C., technical consultant, 1970-71; Center for Science in the Public Interest, Washington, D.C., co-founder and director, 1971-77, executive director of Appalachia-Science in the Public Interest, 1977—. President of Technical Information Project, 1974—, Appalachian Coalition, 1978—, and Sun-Rep, 1980—; president of board of directors of Solar Lobby, 1980—. *Member:* American Chemical Society, American Association for the Advancement of Science. *Awards, honors:* Scholar at University of Miami, Coral Gables, Fla., 1976.

WRITINGS: A Theology of the Earth, CLB Publishers, 1972; *Gasoline,* Center for Science in the Public Interest, 1972; (with John W. Egan) *Big Oil: A Citizen's Factbook on the Major Oil Companies,* Center for Science in the Public Interest, 1973; (with Barbara Hogan and Susan Guhl) *How Aerosol Sprays Can Affect Your Safety and Health,* Center for Science in the Public Interest, 1973; (with Barry I. Castleman) *Asbestos and You,* Center for Science in the Public Interest, 1973, 3rd edition, 1975; *The Contrasumers: A Citizen's Guide to Resource Conservation,* Praeger, 1974; (with Castleman) *Lifestyle Index,* Center for Science in the Public Interest, 1974; (with Ralph Gitomer) *Major Oil: What Citizens Should Know About the Eight Major Oil Companies,* Center for Science in the Public Interest, 1974; (editor) Angus Henry McDonald, *Shale Oil: An Environmental Critique,* Center for Science in the Public Interest, 1974.

(With Linda W. Dujack and Douglas A. Jimerman) *Energy and Food: Energy Used in Production, Processing, Delivery, and Marketing of Selected Food Items,* Center for Science in the Public Interest, 1975, revised edition (with Anne Pierotti and Andrew G. Keeler), 1977; (editor) Keeler, *A Citizen's Oil Factbook: What Every Citizen Should Know About the Eighteen Largest Oil Companies,* Center for Science in the Public Interest, 1975; (editor) McDonald, *Solar Energy: One Way to Citizen Control,* Center for Science in the Public Interest, 1976; (editor with Alan Okagaki) *Ninety-Nine Ways to a Simple Lifestyle,* Doubleday, 1977; (with Dennis Darcey, Gerald McMahon, and Elaine Burns) *Strip Mine Blasting,* Appalachia-Science in the Public Interest

(ASPI), 1977; (with Jerome Nardt) *Harlan County Flood Report*, ASPI, 1978; (with Mark Morgan) *Citizen's Blasting Handbook*, ASPI, 1978; (with John Clemens and Francis Kazemek) *Citizen's Coal Haul Handbook*, ASPI, 1978; *Toxic Substances and Trade Secrecy*, Technical Information Project, 1978; (editor with Darcey and Hogan) *The Household Pollutants Guide*, Doubleday, 1978; (with Burns, Thomas Conry, and David Fry) *Environmental Ethics*, Doubleday, 1979; (with Robert Schemel) *Citizen's Resource Handbook*, ASPI, 1979; *Toxic Substances: Decisions and Values*, four volumes, Technical Information Project, 1979-80; (with McMahon, Okagaki, and William Millerd) *Environmental Ethics: Choices for Concerned Citizens*, Doubleday, 1980.

WORK IN PROGRESS: Land Use Ethics, completion expected in 1981.

* * *

FRY, Earl H(oward)   1947-

PERSONAL: Born May 19, 1947, in Oakland, Calif.; son of Harvey W. (a contractor) and Alice (Horlacher) Fry; married Elaine Fisher, May 29, 1971; children: Christopher Alain, Lisa Michelle, Leanna Christine, Kimberly Anne. *Education:* Attended University of California, Berkeley, 1965-67; Brigham Young University, B.A., 1971, M.A., 1972; University of California, Los Angeles, Ph.D., 1976. *Politics:* Independent. *Religion:* Church of Jesus Christ of Latter-Day Saints (Mormons). *Residence:* Morrisonville, N.Y. *Office:* Center for the Study of Canada, State University of New York College at Plattsburgh, Plattsburgh, N.Y. 12901.

CAREER: University of Paris I, Sorbonne, Paris, France, Fulbright lecturer in political science, 1974-75; Boise State University, Boise, Idaho, assistant professor, 1976-79, associate professor of political science, 1979—; State University of New York College at Plattsburgh, Plattsburgh, associate professor of political science and director of international education and Canadian studies, 1979—. President of E. H. Fry & Associates (consulting firm). *Member:* International Political Science Association, Association for Canadian Studies in the United States, French Conference Group, Western Social Science Association. *Awards, honors:* Fellowship from government of Canada, 1977.

WRITINGS: Canadian Government and Politics in Comparative Perspective, University Press of America, 1978; *Financial Invasion of the U.S.A.: A Threat to American Society?*, McGraw, 1980; (with Gregory Raymond) *The Other Western Europe: A Comparative Analysis of the Smaller Democracies*, ABC Clio, 1980. Contributor to political science journals.

WORK IN PROGRESS: A book on the politics of international investment, publication by McGraw expected in 1982; co-editing a series on managing global problems, publication by ABC Clio expected in 1982.

SIDELIGHTS: Fry wrote: "Although I am a professor of political science and must deal with the jargon of the discipline, I enjoy writing in a style which will be easily understood by a general audience. Too often books in my discipline are caught up in the academic fad of the month or are couched in jargonese, meaning that important subject matter may be incomprehensible to a large section of the reading audience."

AVOCATIONAL INTERESTS: Travel.

FUNT, Marilyn   1937-

PERSONAL: Born December 8, 1937, in New York, N.Y.; daughter of Stanley (a pharmacist) and Charlotte Laron; married Allen Funt (a television producer), September, 1964 (divorced); children: Juliet, William. *Education:* City College (now of the City University of New York), B.A., 1959. *Religion:* Jewish. *Home and office:* 65 Central Park W., New York, N.Y. 10023.

CAREER: Columbia Broadcasting System (CBS), worked in daytime programming, 1960-62, worked for "Candid Camera," 1962-66; associated with *Womensweek* (newspaper) in New York, N.Y., 1977-78; founder and partner of Bookbound, Inc., 1980—.

WRITINGS: Are You Anybody? (interviews), Dial, 1980.

WORK IN PROGRESS: Behind Every Successful Woman. . . .

SIDELIGHTS: Marilyn Funt wrote: "I have several other interview books in mind. One is *Men in Special Situations*, such as married to a famous woman, married to a sex symbol, or married to an older woman. But publication of my first book has begun a career in publishing, and my energy is directed toward the company I have formed with my partner, a company which will concentrate on packaging book projects, all the way through to television and movie deals."

* * *

FURST, Lilian Renee   1931-

PERSONAL: Born June 30, 1931, in Vienna, Austria; came to the United States in 1971, naturalized citizen, 1976; daughter of Desider (a physician and dental surgeon) and Sarah (a physician and dental surgeon; maiden name, Neufeld) Furst. *Education:* Victoria University of Manchester, B.A., 1952; Cambridge University, Ph.D., 1957. *Home:* 7654 Royal Lane, Dallas, Tex. 75230. *Agent:* Curtis Brown Ltd., 1 Craven Hill, London W2 3EP, England. *Office:* School of Arts and Humanities, University of Texas at Dallas, P.O. Box 688, Richardson, Tex. 75080.

CAREER: Queen's University of Belfast, Belfast, Northern Ireland, assistant professor, 1955-59, associate professor of German, 1959-66; Victoria University of Manchester, Manchester, England, associate professor of comparative literature and head of department, 1966-71; Dartmouth College, Hanover, N.H., visiting professor of comparative literature and German, 1971-72; University of Oregon, Eugene, professor of comparative literature and Romance languages and director of graduate program, 1972-75; Univeristy of Texas at Dallas, Richardson, professor of comparative literature, 1975—. Research associate at Harvard University, 1974-75; Mather Visiting Professor of English and Foreign Languages at Case Western Reserve University, 1978-79. *Member:* International Comparative Literature Association, American Comparative Literature Association, Modern Language Association of America, Modern Humanities Research Association. *Awards, honors:* American Council of Learned Societies fellow, 1974-75.

WRITINGS: Romanticism in Perspective, Humanities, 1969, 2nd edition, 1979; *Romanticism*, Barnes & Noble, 1969, 2nd edition, 1976; (with Peter N. Skrine) *Naturalism*, Barnes & Noble, 1971; (contributor) Ulrich C. Finke, editor, *French Nineteenth-Century Painting and Literature*, Manchester University Press, 1972; (editor with J. D. Wilson) *The Anti-Hero*, Georgia State University, 1976; *Counterparts: The Dynamics of Franco-German Literary Relationships, 1770-1895*, Wayne State University Press, 1977; *The*

Contours of European Romanticism, Macmillan (England), 1979, University of Nebraska Press, 1980; *European Romanticism: Self-Definition,* Methuen, 1980.

WORK IN PROGRESS: Perspective on Irony in the European Narrative, 1760-1857, publication by Macmillan expected in 1985.

SIDELIGHTS: Lilian Furst wrote: "I was born in Vienna of a Hungarian father and a Polish mother, grew up in England, and have recently chosen to work in the United States. I am bilingual in English and German and have a thorough knowledge of French, some Italian, and a little Hebrew. I am naturally committed to the comparative study of literature.

"I regard the study of European romanticism as a vital base for the understanding of modern literature and art. The romantic movement marks a decisive turning point in the history of Western civilization. The concepts elaborated by the romantics on the role of the artist, on the creative process, on the function of art, on freedom to experiment—all these are still of central relevance to our thinking and our experience today. The tragic-comic figure of the anti-hero, for instance, is a descendant of the romantic hero at odds with the world and ambivalent about himself."

G

GAJDUSEK, Robert Elemer 1925-
(Robin Gajdusek)

PERSONAL: Born April 18, 1925, in Yonkers, N.Y.; son of Karl Aloysius and Mahtil (Debrosky) Gajdusek; married Julia Lee Terry, December 27, 1949 (divorced, 1950); married Betty-jo Sode, January 3, 1951 (divorced, 1966); married Linda Carol Nusbaum, October 20, 1967; children: (first marriage) Mark Robert; (third marriage) Karl Lawrence. *Education:* Princeton University, B.A. (magna cum laude), 1949; Columbia University, M.A., 1959; also attended University of Lausanne, 1948, University of California, Berkeley, 1950-52, University of Kansas, 1952-54, and University of London, 1960. *Home:* 137 Granada Dr., Corte Madera, Calif. 94925. *Office:* Department of English, San Francisco State University, 1600 Holloway Ave., San Francisco, Calif. 94132.

CAREER: University of Kansas, Lawrence, instructor in English, 1952-54; George Washington University, Washington, D.C., instructor, 1954-56, assistant professor, 1956-58, associate professor of English, 1958-64, director of creative writing program, 1960-64; Hunter College of the City University of New York, New York, N.Y., assistant professor, 1964-65; San Francisco State University, San Francisco, Calif., assistant professor, 1965-67, associate professor, 1967-69, professor of English, 1969—. *Military service:* U.S. Army, Combat Infantry, 1943-46; prisoner of war.

WRITINGS: (Contributor) Harry T. Moore, editor, *A D. H. Lawrence Miscellany,* Southern Illinois University Press, 1959; *Hemingway's Paris,* Scribner, 1978. Contributor of more than fifty articles and poems to scholarly journals and little magazines (sometimes under name Robin Gajdusek), including *American Imago, D. H. Lawrence Review, American Scholar, Alchemy, Arcade, Beloit Poetry Journal, Buffalo Spree, Factotum, Epos, Berkeley Poets Cooperative, Neo, Psyclone,* and *Villager.*

WORK IN PROGRESS: A booklength study of metaphor as meaning in the works of Ernest Hemingway; *The King, the Queen, and the Celluloid Throne,* on myth and metaphor in contemporary film; *Traveling,* a collection of short stories; *Set Pieces,* a second collection of short stories; thirty books of poems, including *Ground Clearing, Green Song, Far Stranger, Alder Creek Eclogues, Belated Recognitions, Intervals of Silence, Madrid, Disappearance and Return of Wild Duck Island, A Disgrace of Seasons, Ritual Burial,* *Profane Adorations, Songs and Quatrains, Panels for the Stained Glass Windows of the Virgin in the Church of Maguelone by the Sea, A Defection of Shadows, Dark Dance: Mask Figure, Llinaritx-Nou, Italian Notebooks, The Girl in the Table, Night Jump, Songs of Dis, The Cross of Bone, The Drowned Child, Dark Dancer, Europe 1969, Portraits, Songs of the Unrecognized and Dispossessed, The Time, the Place, the Spirit of Love;* photographic recording for books on the early Romanesque sculpture of the Saintonge and the feudal chateaux of the Dordogne.

SIDELIGHTS: Robert Gajdusek told *CA:* "Hemingway's *Paris* is more a tribute to than a study of Hemingway. But we have scarcely begun to read him and to discover the depth and basis of his art or the intricate strategies of his technique. No American writer better understood our psychosexual dynamics and the fine and precise terms of the structuring of the sensibility/psyche. He is a poetic symbolist, all of whose images are metaphors. There are no topical or historical references in his work that are not primarily metaphors, and *Green Hills of Africa* and *A Moveable Feast* are more novels than ninety percent of works so designated. In time we will come to see as true—what we now refuse to believe—that Hemingway learned his techniques and art more from James Joyce than from Anderson, Stein, or Pound, and that his work is the successful exemplification of his unstated but conscious attempt—through style and delicate manipulation of the reader's sensibility—to forge the uncreated conscience of his race. We have had no modern prose writer since who has labored as hard or to as good effect as Hemingway to achieve a consummate style, one totally, sensitively answerable to the aesthetic-intellectual needs of its author and his time.

"My poetry is another thing. I write and have written all my life because I must. What is done emerges from necessities; the necessity of love restructures its world: the need for freedom. The roots of the Lombardy poplar travel far for water, heave up the sidewalk, transgress. What is sacrificed is always the existing landscape, where we are, the words we already have; the future rests on such casual murder: 'If we move, the blood rises in our footsteps,' says Lawrence. All of this means my eyes are wounded by living (and fulfilled) and I try to keep 'quiet eyes,' to be able to see and assess without malice or anger the simple and necessary exchanges; I try to hear the deeper rhythms: Ecce homo, I Caligula. If I am not seeing but rather reacting-exclaiming, that too is a (lyrical) necessity, but I don't necessarily judge it respectable: simply Nature as I perform it. Good, bad don't matter there. Certainly, apart from all the nonsense we say when we talk about ourselves, the poem is secretion, act, therapy, exorcism, momentary pacification and redefinition; it is purgation and revalidation, a way of becoming guiltless again, how to be uncommitted committed; and it is itself achieved through me—and goes beyond me and abandons me without guilt or gratitude or memory. And then, since all these may be true *in spite of* what we mean by shaping space like God—trying to arrive at a form or order that is its own meaning, and according to an order of being, a spiritual poise we believe in—it is a humbling before the solid presence of whatever includes us: our words that are being shaped as we shape with them let us know who we are and something of the conditions in which we move.

"In my short stories I like to force fiction hard against reality. I like to sense the humiliation of abstractions judged by facts; I like to acknowledge the way facts, walking at the center of myth and rite, like a hero costumed and endowed with multiple and complex purpose, are both neutral and fatal. Consequently, the interface between art and life is where I work, like a climber using the counter-thrust of the mountain to guarantee my center of gravity as I ascend my dream.

"Notice these many entries by many authors interpreting how/what/why we write: these postures. It doesn't really matter what we say, but rather what we do, which is *how* we say. Writing is doing—the act and the fact of it."

* * *

GAJDUSEK, Robin
See GAJDUSEK, Robert Elevier

* * *

GALSTON, Arthur William 1920-

PERSONAL: Born April 21, 1920, in New York, N.Y.; son of Hyman and Freda (Saks) Galston; married Dale Judith Kuntz, June 27, 1941; children: William Arthur, Beth Dale. *Education:* Cornell University, B.S., 1940; University of Illinois, M.S., 1942, Ph.D., 1943. *Home:* 307 Manley Heights, Orange, Conn. 06477. *Office:* Department of Biology, Yale University, New Haven, Conn. 06520.

CAREER: California Institute of Technology, Pasadena, research plant physiologist for emergency rubber project, 1943-44; Yale University, New Haven, Conn., instructor in botany, 1946-47; California Institute of Technology, senior research fellow, 1947-50, associate professor of biology, 1951-55; Yale University, professor of plant physiology, 1955-65, and biology, 1965-72, Eaton Professor of Botany, 1973—, chairman of department of botany, 1961-62, director of Division of Biological Sciences, 1965-66. Member of National Research Council Division of Biology and Agriculture, 1963-66 (member of national council, 1964-76), and National Science Foundation metabolic biology panel, 1959-60; former consultant to E. I. duPont de Nemours & Co; Albert Einstein fellow and visiting professor at Hebrew University, 1980. *Military service:* U.S. Naval Reserve, active duty, 1944-46; served in Okinawa.

MEMBER: American Academy of Arts and Sciences, American Association for the Advancement of Science (fellow), American Society of Plant Physiologist (vice-president, 1957-58; president, 1963-64), Botanical Society of America (president, 1967-68), Federation of American Scientists (member of council, 1973-76), American Society of Biological Chemists, Society of General Physiologists, Society for

Social Responsibility in Science (president, 1973-75), Growth Society (member of executive board, 1959), Scandinavian Society of Plant Physiologists. *Awards, honors:* Guggenheim fellow in Sweden, France, and England, 1950-51; M.A. from Yale University, 1955; Fulbright fellow in Australia, 1960-61; National Science Foundation fellow in England, 1967-68; merit award from Botanical Society of America, 1969; Phi Beta Kappa national visiting scholar, 1972-73; award from New York Academy of Sciences, 1979; LL.D. from Iona College, 1980.

WRITINGS: (With J. Bonner) *Principles of Plant Physiology,* W. H. Freeman, 1952; *The Life of the Green Plant,* Prentice-Hall, 1961, 3rd edition (with Peter J. Davies and R. L. Satter), 1980, reprinted as *The Green Plant,* 1968; (with Davies) *Control Mechanisms in Plant Development,* Prentice-Hall, 1970; (with Jean S. Savage) *Daily Life in People's China,* Crowell, 1973; *Green Wisdom,* Basic Books, 1981. Contributor to scientific journals. Member of editorial board of *American Journal of Botany,* 1959-61, 1972-76; member of editorial advisory board of *World Book Science Year,* 1976-78, *Chemical Engineering News,* 1977-78, *Pesticide Physiology and Biochemistry,* 1978—, and *Environment,* 1979—.

SIDELIGHTS: Galston participated in the first American scientific visit to the People's Republic of China in 1971.

* * *

GALVIN, Patrick Joseph 1927-

PERSONAL: Born in 1927, in Cork City, Ireland; son of Patrick Galvin; married Diana Ferrier; children: two sons. *Education:* Attended state schools in Cork, Ireland. *Agent:* Patrick Newley, 71 Moring Rd., London S.W.17, England.

CAREER: Writer, 1949—. Worked as bookseller, 1947, war correspondent in Korea, ballad singer in England and the United States, 1955-60, and film critic, 1961. Editor of Tone Press, 1972-74. Writer in residence of West Midlands Arts Association, 1979-80; gives lectures and readings in Europe and the United States. Freeman of City of Cork, 1974. *Military service:* Royal Air Force, 1940; served in Palestine and Jordan. French Foreign Legion, 1945. *Awards, honors:* Leverhulme fellow, 1976-80.

WRITINGS: Irish Songs of Resistance, Folklore Press, 1956; *Heart of Grace* (poems), Linden Press, 1957; *Christ in London* (poems), Linden Press, 1960; *The Woodburners* (poems). New Writers Press, 1973; *Three Plays by Patrick Galvin* (contains "Nightfall to Belfast," "The Last Burning," and "We Do It for Love"; also see below), Threshold, 1976; *Man of the Porch* (collected poems), Martin Brian & O'Keefe, 1980.

Plays: "And Him Stretched" (two-act), first produced in Dublin, Ireland, at Eblana Theatre, September, 1960, produced in London, England, at Unity Theatre, November, 1961; "Cry the Believers" (three-act), first produced in Dublin at Eblana Theatre, February, 1961, produced in London at Unity Theatre, March, 1961; "Boy in the Smoke" (three-act), first broadcast by BBC-TV, March, 1965; "Nightfall to Belfast" (three-act), first produced in Belfast, Northern Ireland, at Lyric Theatre, July, 1973; "The Last Burning" (three-act), first produced in Belfast at Lyric Theatre, July, 1974; "We Do It for Love" (two-act), first produced in Belfast at Lyric Theatre, March, 1976, produced in London at Young Vic Theatre, May 31, 1976, and New York, N.Y., at Olney Theatre, August, 1976; "The Devil's Own People" (two-act), first produced in Dublin at Gaiety Theatre, May, 1976. Editor of *Chanticleer,* 1955-60, and *Threshold,* 1976-78.

WORK IN PROGRESS: A musical commissioned by Lyric Theatre; a radio play for British Broadcasting Corp.

SIDELIGHTS: Galvin's sound recordings include "Irish Humour Songs," released by Riverside, 1960; "Irish Drinking Songs," Riverside, 1960; "Irish Love Songs," Riverside, 1960; "Irish Street Songs," Riverside, 1960; and "The Mad Woman of Cork: Poems, 1960-80," Audio Arts, 1980.

Galvin lives and works for most of the year in Belfast, Northern Ireland, although he does visit the United States frequently for lecture tours and readings of his own work. He told *CA:* "Many of my plays are set in the Belfast of today, and they are dedicated to the people of that city, a people I have grown to love in the short time that I have lived here. The songs spring from daily occurrences, tragic and comic, of Belfast, and their texts are centered on the sad adventures of a middle-aged Hamlet who runs a mythical merry-go-round. The trouble with myths, however, is that the more we talk about them the more real they become. In Belfast today the merry-go-round has become a nightmare of reality, and the only way off appears to be death. Many people have died, but the merry-go-round goes on.

"All writers are 'committed' in one way or another. The only way not to be committed is to say nothing and write less. I am committed to life and social justice. I am also committed against death and the merry-go-round of slaughter and decadence that has become the symbol of Belfast. A writer writes about what is happening to him. My plays happen to me, an Irish poet/dramatist living in Belfast and sharing the merry-go-round of its people."

Galvin is one of Ireland's most controversial writers, and critical opinion of him is diverse. Robert O'Donahue, writing of Galvin's plays in the *Cork Examiner,* said that they were of "a vividly imaginative dimension, both in the Genet-like rhetoric and the daring use of the real and super real. The result is always fascinating theatre, poised on a structure made up of uninhibited melodrama and a contemporary language, touching, as one might expect from such a fine poet, memorably effective imagery and sheer word power." In *Patrick Galvin and the Lady Devil,* Augustus Young commented, "To hear Patrick Galvin read out his ballad poems is one of the rare rewards left to those few survivors in England still interested in what has happened to Irish poetry."

AVOCATIONAL INTERESTS: Travel, films.

BIOGRAPHICAL/CRITICAL SOURCES: Augustus Young, *Patrick Galvin and the Lady Devil,* Lace Curtain Press, 1974; Sean Lucy, *The Poems of Patrick Galvin,* University of Cork, 1974; *Cork Examiner,* August 21, 1974; Patrick Newley, *A Select Bibliography of Works by Patrick Galvin,* Tone Press, 1980.

*   *   *

GAMOW, George   1904-1968

PERSONAL: Born March 4, 1904, in Odessa, Russia (now U.S.S.R); came to United States, 1934, naturalized citizen, 1940; died August 19, 1968, in Boulder, Colo.; son of Anthony M. and Alexandra (Lebedinzeva) Gamow; married Loubov R. Wochminzewa, November 1, 1931 (divorced, 1956); married Barbara Perkins, October 11, 1958; children: (first marriage) Igor Rustem. *Education:* University of Leningrad, Ph.D., 1928. *Home:* 758 Sixth St., Boulder, Colo. 80302.

CAREER: University of Copenhagen, Copenhagen, Denmark, assistant in physics research, 1930-31; Academy of Sciences, Leningrad, U.S.S.R., master in physics research,

1931-33; George Washington University, Washington, D.C., professor of theoretical physics, 1934-56; University of Colorado, Boulder, professor of physics, 1956-68. Lecturer at Universities of Paris and London, 1933-34, University of Michigan, 1934, Stanford University, 1936, and Venzuelian Association for the Advancement of Science, 1956; Sigma Xi lecturer, 1950-51; visiting fellow at Churchill College, Cambridge, 1965. *Wartime service:* Consultant to several U.S. Navy and Air Force boards, Los Alamos Scientific Laboratory, Johns Hopkins University, and RAND Corp.

MEMBER: International Astronomical Union, American Astronomical Society, American Geophysical Society, American Physical Society, National Academy of Sciences of the United States, Royal Danish Academy of Sciences, New York Academy of Sciences, Washington Philosophical Society. *Awards, honors:* Fellowship from University of Goettingen, 1928; Carlsberg fellowship for study at University of Copenhagen, 1928-29; Rockefeller fellowship for study at Cambridge University, 1929-30; Kalinga Award for popularization of science from UNESCO, 1956.

WRITINGS: Constitution of Atomic Nuclei and Radioactivity, Clarendon, 1931, 2nd edition published as *Structure of Atomic Nuclei and Nuclear Transformation,* 1937, 3rd edition, written with C. L. Critchfield, published as *Theory of Atomic Nucleus and Nuclear Energy Sources,* 1949; *Mr. Tompkins in Wonderland; or, Stories of c, G, and h,* Cambridge University Press, 1939, Macmillan, 1940; (self-illustrated) *The Birth and Death of the Sun: Stellar Evolution and Subatomic Energy* (first volume in cosmological trilogy; also see below), Viking, 1940; *Biography of the Earth: Its Past, Present, and Future* (second volume in cosmological trilogy; also see below), Viking, 1941, revised edition, 1959; *Mr. Tompkins Explores the Atom,* Macmillan, 1944; *Atomic Energy in Cosmic and Human Life: Fifty Years of Radioactivity,* Macmillan, 1946; (self-illustrated) *One, Two, Three . . . Infinity: Facts and Speculations of Science,* Viking, 1947, revised edition, Bantam, 1967; (translator) Alexander I. Khinchin, *Mathematical Foundations of Statistical Mechanics,* Dover, 1949.

The Creation of the Universe (third volume in cosmological trilogy), Viking, 1952, revised edition, Bantam, 1970; *The Moon,* H. Schuman, 1953, revised edition, Abelard, 1971; (self-illustrated) *Mr. Tompkins Learns the Facts of Life,* Cambridge University Press, 1953; (contributor) G. A. Baitsell, editor, *Science in Progress,* Yale University Press, 1953; *Matter, Earth, and Sky,* Prentice-Hall, 1958, 2nd edition, 1965; (with Marvin Stern) *Puzzle-Math,* Viking, 1958.

(With John M. Cleveland) *Physics: Foundations and Frontiers,* Prentice-Hall, 1960, 3rd edition, 1976; *The Atom and Its Nucleus,* Prentice-Hall, 1961; *Biography of Physics,* Harper, 1961; (self-illustrated) *Gravity: Classic and Modern Views,* Anchor Books, 1962; *A Planet Called Earth,* Viking, 1963; *A Star Called the Sun,* Viking, 1964; (also co-illustrator) *Mr. Tompkins in Paperback,* Cambridge University Press, 1965, revised edition, 1967; (self-illustrated) *Thirty Years That Shook Physics: The Story of Quantum theory,* Anchor Books, 1966; (with Martynas Ycas; self illustrated) *Mr. Tompkins Inside Himself: Adventures in the New Biology,* Viking, 1967; *My World Line: An Informal Autobiography,* Viking, 1970.

Contributor of articles on nuclear physics and astrophysics to various periodicals and scientific journals, including *Time, Newsweek, Science Digest,* and *Scientific Monthly.*

SIDELIGHTS: In the course of his career, Gamow made several significant contributions to the field of nuclear physics. His research on atomic nuclei and the processes of natural radioactivity permitted further development of the quantum theory of atomic structure and greatly advanced man's knowledge of nuclear fusion and fission. His calculation of the energy required to split the nucleus of an atom with artificially accelerated protons was instrumental in the first successful experiment on nuclear fission. In addition, his research with Edward Teller led to the formulation of the "Gamow-Teller" selection rule for beta emission.

Gamow is also credited with spearheading research in the field of astrophysics, especially in the development of theories on stellar energy production. He was also one of the most ardent and articulate supporters of the "Big Bang" theory of cosmology.

Putting his knowledge to work in another direction, Gamow became a skillful popularizer of science. In his writings he explained such esoteric and abstruse subjects as quantum theory, relativity, stellar evolution, and the human circulatory system. His books have been admired as reliable sources of scientific information for the general reader; they have been translated into many languages.

AVOCATIONAL INTERESTS: Reading and memorizing poetry, traveling, working on model electric railroads, collecting photographs and other memorabilia.

BIOGRAPHICAL/CRITICAL SOURCES: Time, July 1, 1940, July 12, 1948; *Science Illustrated,* May, 1947; *Science Digest,* June, 1947; *Nature,* October 20, 1956; *Physics Today,* February 3, 1968; Gamow, *My World Line: An Informal Autobiography,* Viking, 1970; Frederick Reines, editor, *Cosmology, Fusion, and Other Matters: George Gamow Memorial Volume,* Colorado Associated University Press, 1972.

OBITUARIES: New York Times, August 22, 1968; *Time,* August 30, 1968; *Newsweek,* September 2, 1968; *Publishers Weekly,* September 9, 1968; *Nature,* November 18, 1968.*

* * *

GANTT, William Andrew Horsley 1893-1980

PERSONAL: Born October 18, 1893, in Wingina, Va.; died of cancer, February 26, 1980, in Baltimore, Md.; son of Thomas Perkins and Anna Maria Perkins (Horsley) Gantt; married Mary G. Richardson, June 23, 1934 (died July, 1964); married Anna Rebecca Esler, August 8, 1965; children: (first marriage) William Andrew Horsley II, Emily Perkins Gantt Kahn. *Education:* University of North Carolina, B.S., 1917; University of Virginia, M.D., 1920; further graduate study at University College, London, 1923-24.

CAREER: Intern at University of Maryland Hospital, beginning in 1920; American Relief Administration, Petrograd, U.S.S.R., chief of medicine, 1922-23; affiliated with Research Institute of Experimental Medicine in Petrograd, 1924-29; Johns Hopkins Hospital, Baltimore, Md., psychiatrist, beginning in 1930; Johns Hopkins University, Baltimore, director of Pavlovian Laboratory, 1930-64, director emeritus and associate professor emeritus, 1964-80; University of Maryland, professor of psychiatry at Medical School, beginning in 1973. Member of Foreign Policy Association, beginning in 1935, secretary, 1935-44, chairman, 1944-46, member of executive board, 1945-50; vice-chairman of Russian War Relief, 1942-46. Visiting professor of pharmacology at University of Puerto Rico, 1954-55; senior scientist at Pavlovian Laboratory at Veterans Administration Hospital in Perry Point, Md., beginning in 1959.

MEMBER: International Collegium of Psychosomatic Medi-

cine, International Brain Research Organization, Collegium Internationale Activitatas Nervosae Superioris (president, beginning in 1966), American Psychiatric Association (life member), American Psychopathological Association (president, 1960), American Psychosomatic Society, American Medical Association, American College of Psychiatrists (fellow), American Physiological Society, American Neurological Association, American Society of Pharmacology and Experimental Therapeutics, American Academy of Arts and Sciences, Pavlovian Society of America (founder; president, 1955-65), Argentine Association of Biological Psychiatry (honorary member), Purkinje Society of Prague (honorary member), Society of Biological Psychiatry (vice-president, 1958, president, 1959), Southern Medical Association (life member), Fulton Neurological Society, Pavlovian Society for Investigation of the Causes of Mental Illness (founder), Sigma XI. *Awards, honors:* Lasker Award, 1946, for research in nervous diseases; award from American Heart Association, 1950, for research in hypertension; gold medal from Society of Biological Psychiatry, 1971; Ira Van Giesen Award from New York Psychiatric Institute, 1974; distinguished scientist citation from Karolinska University (Prague), 1975.

WRITINGS: Russian Medicine, P. B. Hoeber, 1937, reprinted, AMS Press, 1978; *Experimental Basis for Neurotic Behavior: Origin and Development of Artificially-Produced Disturbances of Behavior in Dogs,* American Society of Research in Psychosomatic Problems, 1944; (editor) *Physiological Bases of Psychiatry,* Thomas, 1958; (translator and editor) Aleksandr Romanovich Luria, *The Nature of Human Conflicts; or, Emotion, Conflict, and Will,* Washington Square Press, 1967; (compiler with Lothar Pickenhain and Charles Zwingmann) *Pavlovian Approach to Psychopathy: History and Perspectives,* Pergamon Press, 1970. Also translator of *Pavlov's Lectures on Conditioned Reflexes,* Volume I, 1928, Volume II, 1941.

Editor of *American Lectures in Objective Psychiatry,* beginning in 1955, *Pavlovian Journal of Biological Science,* beginning in 1966, and *Soviet Neurology and Psychiatry,* beginning in 1968.

Contributor of numerous articles to scholarly journals.

WORK IN PROGRESS: An autobiography, left unfinished at time of death.

SIDELIGHTS: William Horsley Gantt was the leading American authority on the Pavlovian principles of conditioned reflexes. The last American to study under the eminent Soviet physiologist Ivan Pavlov, Gantt furthered the Russian's experiments, proving that psychological disorders could be caused by environmental factors and not only by trauma experienced in childhood or sexual frustrations, as Sigmund Freud had maintained. Gantt was also instrumental in demonstrating that the heart, like any other muscle in the human body, is capable of being conditioned and thus strengthened. This discovery led directly to a better understanding of heart rate and the causes of high blood pressure.

OBITUARIES: New York Times, February 28, 1980; *Washington Post,* February 28, 1980; *Newsweek,* March 10, 1980.*

* * *

GARDNER, Jack Irving 1934-

PERSONAL: Born October 7, 1934, in Seattle, Wash.; son of Irving (a cab driver) and Florence (a nurse; maiden name, Morgan) Gardner; married Carroll Sutherland (a librarian),

June 12, 1963. *Education:* University of Washington, Seattle, B.A., 1958, M.Lib., 1960. *Politics:* Republican. *Religion:* Agnostic. *Home:* 3358 Saddleback Court, Las Vegas, Nev. 89121. *Office:* Clark County Library District, 1726 East Charleston, Las Vegas, Nev. 89104.

CAREER: Brooklyn Public Library, Brooklyn, N.Y., librarian, 1960-62; University of Nevada, Reno, librarian, 1963-65; Nevada State Library, Carson City, librarian, 1965-72; Clark County Library District, Las Vegas, Nev., administrator and librarian, 1972—. *Military service:* U.S. Army, 1954-56. *Member:* California Library Association, Nevada Library Association (president).

WRITINGS: Gambling (nonfiction), Gale, 1980. Contributor to library journals.

SIDELIGHTS: Jack Gardner wrote: "The true gamble is a compulsion, contrived to socially, economically, and psychologically ruin its participants, but is so intently cosmic in its interpretation that most cannot resist its lure. Gambling writers attempt to explore its mystery and succumb to the conical spiral and uncharted whims into which infinite odds send them spinning. My listing [*Gambling*] touched a few existent titles and sorted out their impact upon the world. None fully explain or solve that mystery; that is why it is gambling."

*   *   *

GARNETT, Bill
See GARNETT, William John

*   *   *

GARNETT, William John   1941-
(Bill Garnett)

PERSONAL: Born December 17, 1941, in Los Angeles, Calif.; son of Tay and Helga (Moray) Garnett; married Catriona Stewart, 1970 (divorced, 1978); children: Theresa, Tessa-Jane. *Education:* Attended University of Fribourg; Lincoln College, Oxford, earned diploma (with honors). *Politics:* Conservative. *Religion:* None. *Home and office:* 29 Stanhope Gardens, London S.W.7, England. *Agent:* Irene Josephy, 35 Craven St., London WC2N 5NG, England.

CAREER: Associated with Batten, Barton, Durstine & Osborn; worked as advertising copywriter; free-lance writer. *Member:* Oxford Union (life member). *Awards, honors:* M.A. from Oxford University.

WRITINGS—All under name Bill Garnett: *Paris,* Cavendish, 1979; (translator) *Animal Atlas,* Phoebus, 1980. Also author of *Down-Bound Train,* Doubleday.

Screenplays: "Horus," Metro-Goldwyn-Mayer; "Man of Qadr," Moram Productions. Contributor of stories, articles, and poems to magazines.

WORK IN PROGRESS—All under name Bill Garnett: Three novels, *Fadgway, Freak Show,* and *Slime,* a horror novel.

SIDELIGHTS: Garnett commented: "I have traveled almost everywhere and write because it is the only thing I can do well."

*   *   *

GAROOGIAN, Rhoda   1933-

PERSONAL: Born February 15, 1933, in Bronx, N.Y.; daughter of David (a manufacturer) and Rose (Fried) Lillian; married Andrew Garoogian (a librarian), February 19, 1954; children: David, Neill. *Education:* Brooklyn College of the City University of New York, B.A. (cum laude), 1961, M.A., 1970; Pratt Institute, M.L.S., 1973, further graduate study, 1973-74. *Home:* 477 East 16th St., Brooklyn, N.Y. 11226. *Office:* Graduate School of Library and Information Sciences, Pratt Institute, Brooklyn, N.Y. 11205

CAREER: Pratt Institute, Brooklyn, N.Y., part-time assistant professor, 1975-76, assistant dean of Graduate School of Library and Information Sciences, 1977—. Reference librarian at Medgar Evers College of the City University of New York, 1975-76; adjunct reference librarian at Brooklyn College of the City University of New York, 1976—. *Member:* American Library Association, Special Libraries Association, American Society for Information Science, Association of Information Managers, Association of American Library Schools, New York Library Association.

WRITINGS: (With husband, Andrew Garoogian) *Child Care Issues for Parents and Society,* Gale, 1977; (contributor) Daniel Ring, editor, *Studies in Creative Partnership: Federal Aid to Public Libraries,* Scarecrow, 1980; *How to Obtain Alternative Careers,* American Library Association, 1981; (contributor) *New Options for Librarians: Applying Your Skills in New Careers,* Neal-Schuman, 1981; (contributor) D. Ring, editor, *American Imprints Survey,* Scarecrow, 1981. Contributor to scholarly journals.

WORK IN PROGRESS: A book on alternative careers for librarians, with Theresa Maylone, publication by American Library Association expected in 1981.

SIDELIGHTS: Rhoda Garoogian commented: "I am very interested in promoting the field of information studies, which is one of the most exciting and rewarding areas that one can work in."

*   *   *

GARY, Romain
See KACEW, Romain

*   *   *

GEESLIN, Campbell   1925-

PERSONAL: Born December 5, 1925, in Goldthwaite, Tex.; son of Edward and Margaret Lee (Gaddis) Geeslin; married Marilyn Low (a teacher of English as a second language), 1951; children: Seth, Meg, Ned. *Education:* Columbia University, A.B., 1949; University of Texas, M.S., 1950. *Home:* 209 Davis Ave., White Plains, N.Y. 10605. *Agent:* Amanda Urban, International Creative Management, 40 West 57th St., New York, N.Y. 10019. *Office: Life,* Time-Life Building, Rockefeller Center, New York, N.Y. 10020.

CAREER: Houston Post, Houston, Tex., assistant managing editor, 1950-64; worked for Gannett Newspapers in Cocoa Beach, Fla., White Plains, N.Y., and Rochester, N.Y., 1964-68; *This Week,* New York City, managing editor, 1968-71; *Parade,* New York City, managing editor, 1970-71; *New York Times Syndicate,* New York City, editor, 1971-73; *Cue,* New York City, editor, 1973-75; *People,* New York City, senior editor, 1975-78; *Life,* New York City, text editor, 1978—. *Military service:* U.S. Navy, 1943-46.

WRITINGS: Whatever Became of the Bonner Boys (novel), Simon & Schuster, 1981.

SIDELIGHTS: Campbell Geeslin commented: "One of my earliest memories is of playing with the discarded spools under a frame-stretched quilt as it was being quilted by the ladies of the First Methodist Church in Brady, Texas. The light came through in tiny color patches like a stained glass ceiling, and I remember those moments held a special happiness.

"Along with my editing jobs on newspapers and magazines, I have always been a book reviewer—mostly of novels. Currently, I read five or six every week and write reviews on three or four of them. I enjoy mysteries, spy yarns, historical epics, novels about struggling artists, the multi-generational sagas. I like especially those books in which the writer has found some fresh way of handling a familiar and much-used genre.

"For years, my memories of growing up in a small west Texas town and the feelings that were evoked when I returned to visit, collected in my mind like colorful scraps of cloth. All I had to do, I thought, was find a pattern that would let them be fitted together into a novel. I wanted to do it just the way my mother turned her sewing scraps into a quilt top.

"There are, of course, some familiar devices in *The Bonner Boys*—Mama couldn't make a quilt without squares or triangles or diamond shapes. But I like to think that the pattern I finally found for this novel about five brothers is fairly original. And I hope that, like one of my mother's quilts, it will make its readers feel comforted and warm."

*   *   *

GEFFEN, Maxwell Myles   1896-1980

OBITUARY NOTICE: Born May 31, 1896, in Brooklyn, N.Y.; died October 11, 1980, in Manhasset, N.Y. Founder of magazines, including *Medical World News, Family Health,* and *1001 Decorating Ideas.* Geffen also founded several organizations, including Scientific Book Club and Religious Book Club. Obituaries and other sources: *Publishers Weekly,* October 31, 1980.

*   *   *

GENEVOIX, Maurice Charles Louis   1890-1980

OBITUARY NOTICE: Born November 29, 1890, in Decize, France; died September 8, 1980, in Spain. Author of more than sixty books. Most of Genevoix's writings reflect his deep concern for nature and the French language. His literary career began with a five-volume series about World War I called *Sous Verdun.* His novel about a gamekeeper, *Raboliot,* won the Prix Goncourt in 1925. The real hero of his books from that time on was the forest. According to the *London Times,* Genevoix was "a deeply thinking and feeling man, able to use his immense vocabulary to commit his feelings to paper." At age eighty-three he began a series of lectures on radio and television that made Genevoix a household name in France. Among his later works are *Un Jour* (1976), called "one of his most profound books," and the autobiographical *30,000 Jours* (1980). Obituaries and other sources: *Encyclopedia of World Literature in the Twentieth Century,* updated edition, Ungar, 1967; *The Oxford Companion to Canadian History and Literature,* Oxford University Press, 1967; *Everyman's Dictionary of European Writers,* Dent & Sons, 1968; *Cassell's Encyclopaedia of World Literature,* revised edition, Morrow, 1973; *London Times,* September 10, 1980.

*   *   *

GENN, Calder
See GILLIE, Christopher

*   *   *

GENTIL, Richard   1917-

PERSONAL: Born February 2, 1917, in Wimbledon, England; son of John Anthony Barnary Gentil; married Helen Martron. *Education:* Magdalen College, Oxford, B.A., 1937. *Politics:* Liberal. *Home:* 10 Stanford Rd., Kensington, London W.8, England.

CAREER: Worked in government service, 1948-57; manager of retail photography business, 1957—. *Military service:* Royal Air Force, pilot, 1940-46. *Member:* Huguenot Society (fellow), Royal Air Force Reserves Club.

WRITINGS: Trained to Intrude (autobiography), Bachman & Turner, 1974.

WORK IN PROGRESS: Romance and Intrigue of Old Houses, publication expected in 1981.

SIDELIGHTS: Gentil wrote: "The publishing trade in this country is going through a bad phase, and, according to literary agents, there is not much point in writing at all at the moment. Many first-class books are unable to find a market, and authors are pulling out. Secondly, editions in this country are not large enough to afford the writer a reasonable return for perhaps a year's work.

"The overriding problem at the moment is not the economy or unemployment, but the serious international situation which does not improve and, therefore, affects every facet of life and endeavor. In eighteen months I am semi-retiring, then I shall go back to photography and photo-journalism. Even so it is only possible to write these days on very ordinary subjects. The media are not prepared to publish anything that is fact or liberal if it conflicts with the propaganda machine.

"For example, my hobby is military strategy and tactical warfare. This is a subject that I have studied for forty years. From extensive travel and unique contacts in eastern Europe, I find that I cannot agree with any of the experts. I think the experts are wrong and living in a dream world while becoming more involved in conflict when they should be able to resolve their problems by political means. The door is open, but the hawks do not want to see this. A pity, because I might have written a book on the subject."

AVOCATIONAL INTERESTS: Painting in oils and water colors, photography, socializing.

BIOGRAPHICAL/CRITICAL SOURCES: Richard Gentil, *Trained to Intrude,* Bachman & Turner, 1974.

*   *   *

GERAS, Norman (Myron)   1943-

PERSONAL: Surname is pronounced *Gehr*-as, with hard "g"; born August 25, 1943, in Bulawayo, Zimbabwe; son of Jack (in business) and Beryl (Salis) Geras; married Adele Weston (a writer), August 7, 1967; children: Sophie, Jenny. *Education:* Pembroke College, Oxford, B.A. (with honors), 1965; graduate study at Nuffield College, Oxford, 1965-67. *Politics:* Socialist. *Religion:* None. *Home:* 14 Mayville Dr., Manchester M20 9RB, England. *Office:* Department of Government, Victoria University of Manchester, Manchester M13 9PL, England.

CAREER: Victoria University of Manchester, Manchester, England, lecturer in government, 1967—.

WRITINGS: The Legacy of Rosa Luxemburg, NLB, 1975; *Masas, partido y revolucion* (title means "Masses, Party, and Revolution"), Fontamara, 1980.

Contributor: Geraint Parry, editor, *Participation in Politics,* Manchester University Press, 1972; Robin Blackburn, editor, *Ideology in Social Science,* Fontana, 1972; Blackburn, editor, *Revolution and Class Struggle: A Reader in Marxist*

Politics, Fontana, 1977; Gareth Stedman Jones and others, editors, *Western Marxism: A Critical Reader*, NLB, 1977; Justin Wintle, editor, *Makers of Modern Culture*, Routledge & Kegan Paul, 1981. Member of editorial committee of *New Left Review*, 1976—.

WORK IN PROGRESS: An article on Marx and human nature.

SIDELIGHTS: Geras told *CA:* "My book on Rosa Luxemburg attempts to clear away certain common misconceptions about her (regarding, in particular, 'spontaneism,' the collapse of capitalism, socialist democracy) and to show that she was an important Marxist teacher. At present I am concerned to combat the prejudice amongst Marxists that Marx believed that there is no such thing as human nature."

AVOCATIONAL INTERESTS: Watching films (especially American ones), collecting books on the game of cricket, jogging twenty miles a week.

*   *   *

GERBER, John C(hristian)   1908-

PERSONAL: Born January 31, 1908, in New Waterford, Ohio; son of Christian G. and Leonora (Hauptmann) Gerber; married Margaret E. Wilbourn, September 3, 1941; children: Barbara Page Gerber Barrett, Ann Wilbourn. *Education:* University of Pittsburgh, A.B., 1929, M.A., 1932; University of Chicago, Ph.D., 1941. *Office:* Department of English, State University of New York at Albany, 1400 Washington St., Albany, N.Y. 12222.

CAREER: University of Pittsburgh, Pittsburgh, Pa., instructor in English, 1931-36; University of Chicago, Chicago, Ill., instructor in English, 1938-42, and meteorology, 1942-44; University of Iowa, Iowa City, assistant professor, 1944-47, associate professor, 1947-49, professor of English, 1949-76, Carpenter Professor emeritus, 1976—, chairman of department, 1961-76, director of School of Letters, 1967-76; State University of New York at Albany, Albany, professor of English, 1976—, and chairman of department, 1976-81. Visiting associate professor at University of Southern California, summer, 1944; visiting professor at University of New Mexico, summers, 1952, 1957, Trinity College, summers, 1960, 1963, University of California, Berkeley, 1960-61, University of Colorado, summer, 1965, American University of Cairo, 1970, Korean universities, summer, 1972, and Chinese universities, summer, 1979. Chairman of editorial board of Windhover Press, 1968-72; member of editorial board of University of Iowa Press, 1963-67.

MEMBER: National Council of Teachers of English (president, 1955; member of board of trustees of research foundation, 1962-65), Conference on College Composition and Communication (chairman, 1950), Modern Language Association of America (chairman of American literature section, 1969; member of executive council, 1972-75), Association of Departments of English (chairman, 1964), Midwest Modern Language Association (president, 1966), Northeast Modern Language Association, Phi Beta Kappa. *Awards, honors:* Hatfield Award and executive committee award from National Council of Teachers of English, 1964, for distinguished service; Founders Award from Conference on College Composition and Communication, 1976, for distinguished service; Doctor of Letters from Morningside College, 1979.

WRITINGS: (Editor with Walter Blair) *Better Reading*, Scott, Foresman, 1945, 5th edition, 1963; (editor) Henry James, *The Ambassadors*, Harper, 1948; (editor with Blair) *The College Anthology*, Scott, Foresman, 1949, revised edi-

tion, 1955; (editor with Kenneth Houp) *The Writer's Resource Book*, Scott, Foresman, 1953, revised edition, 1957; (with Jeffrey Fleece and D. E. Wylder) *Toward Better Writing*, Prentice-Hall, 1958.

(Editor with Walter Blair) *Repertory: Introduction to Essays and Articles, Biography and History, Short Stories, Drama, and Poetry*, Scott, Foresman, 1960; *The Evaluation of the 1962 Summer English Institutes*, Modern Language Association of America, 1964; (editor) *The College Teaching of English*, Appleton, 1965; (editor with Carroll C. Arnold) *The Speaker's Resource Book*, Scott, Foresman, 1960, 2nd edition, 1966; (editor) *Twentieth Century Interpretations of The Scarlet Letter: A Collection of Critical Essays*, Prentice-Hall, 1968; (editor) *The Merrill Studies in Huckleberry Finn*, C. E. Merrill, 1971; *American Humor*, Arete Publications, 1977; (editor) Samuel Clemens, *Tom Sawyer*, University of California Press, 1979.

Chairman of editorial board of "The Works of Mark Twain," 1965—; editor of "Key Editions," Scott, Foresman. Contributor to literature journals. Member of editorial board of *College English*, 1947-48 and 1965-71, and *American Quarterly*, 1963-68; editorial adviser for *Philological Quarterly*, 1951-57; editor of *Teaching College English*, 1965; member of editorial advisory board of *Resources for American Literary Study*, 1971—.

WORK IN PROGRESS: A book about Mark Twain, for Twayne.

*   *   *

GERSHATOR, Phillis   1942-

PERSONAL: Born July 8, 1942, in New York, N.Y.; daughter of Morton (an artist) and Mimi Green (an artist; maiden name, Honixfeld) Diamondstein; married David Gershator (a poet, professor, and editor), October 19, 1962; children: Yonah, Daniel. *Education:* Attended University of California, Berkeley, 1959-63; Rutgers University, B.A., 1966; Pratt Institute, M.L.S., 1975. *Residence:* Brooklyn, N.Y. *Office:* Downtown Poets, G.P.O. Box 1720, Brooklyn, N.Y. 11202.

CAREER: St. Thomas Public Library, St. Thomas, U.S. Virgin Islands, documents librarian, 1970-72; George Braziller, Inc., New York, N.Y., in library promotion, 1975-76; Brooklyn Public Library, Brooklyn, N.Y., children's librarian, 1977—. Co-editor of Downtown Poets, 1976—.

WRITINGS: A Bibliographic Guide to the Literature of Contemporary American Poetry, 1970-1975, Scarecrow, 1976; *Bang Bang Lulu: West Indies-Brooklyn* (poetry), Downtown Poets, 1977; *Honi and His Magic Circle* (juvenile), Jewish Publication Society, 1979.

Work represented in anthologies, including *Local*, edited by Jay Heller, Zone Press, 1977; *For the Time Being*, edited by Marianne Goldsmith and Jean Loria, Biel Press, 1978. Contributor of articles and poems to magazines, including *Home Planet News*, *Confrontation*, and *Judaica Book News*.

WORK IN PROGRESS: Spot Recordings, poems, publication expected in 1982; several stories and legends for children.

*   *   *

GESTON, Mark S(ymington)   1946-

PERSONAL: Born June 20, 1946, in Atlantic City, N.J.; son of John C. (a teacher) and Mary (a teacher; maiden name, Symington) Geston; married Gayle Howard, June 12, 1971 (divorced, 1972); married Marijke Havinga, August 14, 1976; children: Camille, Robert, Emily. *Education:* Kenyon College, A.B., 1968; New York University, J.D., 1971. *Home:* 1829 Edgecliff Terr., Boise, Idaho 83702.

CAREER: Eberle, Berlin, Kading, Turnbow & Gillespie (law firm), Boise, Idaho, partner, 1971—. *Member:* American Bar Association, Idaho Bar Association, Phi Beta Kappa, Delta Tau Delta. *Awards, honors:* Fiction achievement award from *Kenyon Review,* 1968.

WRITINGS—Science-fiction novels: *Lords of the Starship,* Ace Books, 1967; *Out of the Mouth of the Dragon,* Ace Books, 1969; *The Day Star,* DAW Books, 1972; *The Siege of Wonder,* Doubleday, 1976.

WORK IN PROGRESS: The Gifted, a novel.

* * *

GIBSON, H(amilton) B(ertie) 1914-

PERSONAL: Born October 15, 1914, in Romford, England; son of Hugh Young (a banker) and Christine (Simpson) Gibson; married Beatrice Elizabeth Cummings; children: Peter Hamilton, Jennifer Elizabeth. *Education:* London School of Economics and Political Science, London, B.Sc., 1956; Institute of Psychiatry, London, Ph.D., 1961. *Politics:* "Anti-authoritarian." *Religion:* None. *Home:* 10 Manhattan Dr., Cambridge CB4 1JL, England.

CAREER: Teacher at progressive school in London, England, 1945-53; University of London, Institute of Psychiatry, London, research psychologist, 1958-61; Cambridge University, Institute of Criminology, Cambridge, England, research psychologist, 1961-69; Hatfield Polytechnic, Hatfield, England, principal lecturer and head of psychology, 1970-75, senior research fellow, 1975-79. *Member:* International Society of Hypnosis, British Psychological Society (associate member), British Society of Experimental and Clinical Hypnosis (chairman), British Society of Medical and Dental Hypnosis (honorary member).

WRITINGS: The Gibson Spiral Maze, Hodder & Stoughton, 1965; (with W. P. Furneaux) *The New Junior Maudsley Personality Inventory,* Hodder & Stoughton, 1966; *Hypnosis: Its Nature and Therapeutic Uses,* P. Owen, 1977, Taplinger, 1980; *Hans Eysenck: The Man and His Work,* P. Owen, 1981; *Pain and Its Conquest,* P. Owen, 1981. Contributor of more than fifty articles to learned journals and political magazines.

WORK IN PROGRESS: Research on hypnosis and the control of pain.

SIDELIGHTS: Gibson commented: "I am the modern version of a nineteenth-century radical, and hence a scientist in outlook. I am old enough to be strongly influenced by the aftermath and legacy of the 1914-1918 war, hence my commitment to pacifism and a form of anarchism. I am greatly interested in psychology, and see it as the key science, for while many of those in the allegedly 'hard' sciences remain babes in their superstition and credulity, psychology can lead to a more realistic view of life.

"It was perhaps fortunate that economic circumstances forced me to earn a living by manual work until middle age, as I think that such experience has given me a view of life broader than that of many academics. Now that I approach old age, I am conscious of the wastefulness of the life of the thinker and the scientist which is expressed in the tag *ars longa, vita brevis.* A lifetime may be spent in gaining knowledge and acquiring fresh insights, but there is the certainty that it will be largely obliterated by the fact of human mortal-

ity. By writing, one commits to posterity a tiny fraction of a unique contribution to knowledge, and hence a sort of immortality is achieved. The carver in stone, the painter, the builder of buildings also achieves a sort of immortality, not in the artifacts of his hands which will eventually crumble, but in the creation of a new way of looking at things, a novel way of man relating to his environment.

"Thus my writing is the human extension of the process of all living creatures achieving immortality by propagating their unique being genetically. Yet being a thinking reed I recognize the nature of the winds that sway me, and have never doubted that my individuality is other than a brief spark of fire in the wilderness of an eternity I may not know. But I rejoice in the brightness of the spark."

* * *

GIBSON, Miles 1947-

PERSONAL: Born February 10, 1947, in New Forest, England; son of John and Marjory (Hunt) Gibson; divorced. *Education:* Attended secondary school in Somerford, Dorset, England. *Home:* 17 Abercorn Pl., London N.W.8, England. *Agent:* David Higham Associates Ltd., 5-8 Lower John St., Golden Sq., London W1R 4HA, England.

CAREER: J. Walter Thompson, London, England, copywriter, 1968-72; free-lance writer, 1972—. *Awards, honors:* Young Writer of the Year Award from *Daily Telegraph,* 1969, for magazine feature.

WRITINGS: The Guilty Bystander (poems), Methuen, 1970; *Permanent Damage* (poems), Eyre Methuen, 1973. Contributor to magazines, including *Telegraph,* and newspapers.

WORK IN PROGRESS: The Life and Work of Angus McBean, with Jake Wallis; *The Voyeurs,* a novel.

SIDELIGHTS: Gibson commented: "I am fascinated by the visual appearance of words, and this fascination often leads me into collage and painting. I am addicted to the idea of fiction as pure invention, and dream of a novel that will finally prove that the world itself is merely an invention."

* * *

GIBSON, Walter Samuel 1932-

PERSONAL: Born March 31, 1932, in Columbus, Ohio; son of Walter Samuel (an engineer) and Grace B. (a secretary; maiden name, Wheeler) Gibson; married Sarah Scott (a college educator and administrator), December 16, 1972. *Education:* Ohio State University, B.F.A. (cum laude), 1957, M.A., 1960; Harvard University, Ph.D., 1969. *Home:* 3057 Washington Blvd., Cleveland Heights, Ohio 44118. *Office:* Department of Art, Mather House, Case Western Reserve University, Cleveland, Ohio 44106.

CAREER: Case Western Reserve University, Cleveland, Ohio, assistant professor, 1966-71, associate professor, 1971-78, Andrew W. Mellon Professor of the Humanities, 1978—, chairman of department of art, 1971-79. *Military service:* U.S. Army, Finance Corps, 1952-54. *Member:* International Center of Medieval Art, Art Libraries Society of North America, College Art Association of America, Renaissance Society of America, Rowfant Club. *Awards, honors:* Fulbright scholar in Europe, 1960-61; Guggenheim fellow, 1978-79.

WRITINGS: Hieronymus Bosch, Praeger, 1973; *The Painting of Cornelius Engebrechtsz,* Garland Publishing, 1977; *Bruegel,* Oxford University Press, 1977. Contributor of articles and reviews to European and American journals.

WORK IN PROGRESS: A bibliography of Hieronymus Bosch, publication by G. K. Hall expected in 1981; *The Flemish Cosmic Landscape of the Sixteenth Century; Theatrum Mundi: The Netherlandish Proverbs of Pieter Bruegel the Elder;* research on sixteenth-century Netherlandish painting.

SIDELIGHTS: Gibson told *CA:* "My current research interests include Bosch, Bruegel, and sixteenth-century landscape painting. A first draft exists of my book on the Flemish cosmic landscape of the sixteenth century. I hope to complete it while on sabbatical next year. My long-range plans include a general survey of sixteenth-century Netherlandish painting."

* * *

GIDLEY, (Gustavus) M(ick) 1941-

PERSONAL: Born March 1, 1941, in Southampton, England; son of Gustavus (a lathe worker) and Doris Florence (a shop assistant; maiden name, Boulton) Gidley; married Nancy Rebecca Gordon (a teacher), October 17, 1964; children: Ruth Mayen, Benjamin Peter. *Education:* Victoria University of Manchester, B.A., 1963; University of Chicago, M.A., 1966; University of Sussex, D.Phil., 1976. *Residence:* Exeter, England. *Office:* American and Commonwealth Arts, University of Exeter, Exeter EX4 4QH, England.

CAREER: Senior English teacher at secondary school in Arochuku, Nigeria, 1963-65; University of Sussex, Brighton, England, research fellow in American studies, 1969-70; University of Exeter, Exeter, England, lecturer, 1971-78, senior lecturer in American literature, head of American and Commonwealth arts, and director of American Arts Documentation Centre, 1978—. *Member:* European Society for the History of Photography, British Association for American Studies. *Awards, honors:* American Council of Learned Societies fellow, 1976-77.

WRITINGS: A Catalogue of American Paintings in British Public Collections, University of Exeter, 1974; *The Vanishing Race: Selections From E. S. Curtis' "The North American Indian,"* David & Charles, 1976, Taplinger, 1977; *With One Sky Above Us: Life on an Indian Reservation at the Turn of the Century,* Putnam, 1979; *Kopet: A Documentary Narrative of Chief Joseph's Last Years,* University of Washington Press, 1981. Editor of "American Arts Pamphlet Series," University of Exeter, 1972—. Contributor to American studies, literary, and photography journals in England, Canada, and the United States.

WORK IN PROGRESS: American Photography, publication by British Association for American Studies expected in 1983; *Edward S. Curtis and the North American Indian,* University of Washington Press, 1983.

SIDELIGHTS: Gidley wrote: "Borders, edges, perimeters offer opportunities for revitalization by what lies just over the (shifting) other side. Trading takes place across them; new ideas, entities, unities come into being. I am interested in borders and frontiers, both in subject matter (principally Indians) and in method (making ideas meet images, feeling out photography and fiction). After all, in the deepest sense, at the heart of the self—for all of us, not just for writers—the periphery is the place we meet others: in those meetings the marginal becomes central."

* * *

GILIOMEE, Hermann (Buhr) 1938-

PERSONAL: Born April 4, 1938, in Sterlistroom, South Af-

rica; son of Gerhardus A. (a teacher) and Catharine (a teacher; maiden name, Buhr) Giliomee; married Anna Evan Coller (an architect and university lecturer), April 3, 1965; children: Francine, Adrienne. *Education:* University of Stellenbosch, M.A., 1962, D.Phil., 1972; postdoctoral study at Yale University, 1973. *Home:* Dennerand 5, Stellenbosch, Cape Province, South Africa 7600. *Office:* Department of History, University of Stellenbosch, Stellenbosch, Cape Province, South Africa.

CAREER: University of South Africa, Pretoria, lecturer in history, 1964-65; University of Stellenbosch, Stellenbosch, South Africa, senior lecturer in history, 1967—. Visiting research fellow at Yale University, 1977-78.

WRITINGS: Die Kaap tydens die Eerste Britse Bewind (title means "The Cape Colony During the First British Occupation"), Hollandsch Afrikaansche Uitgevers Maatschappij, 1975; (editor with Richard Elphick) *The Shaping of South African Society, 1652-1820,* Longman, 1979; (with Heribert Adam) *Ethnic Power Mobilized: Can South Africa Change?,* Yale University Press, 1979; *In the Same Strange Land: Afrikaner Political Thought, 1770-1980,* University of California Press, 1981.

SIDELIGHTS: Giliomee commented: "I want to change South Africa. The only way I can do it is to give South Africans (in particular my own ethnic group, the Afrikaners) a clearer understanding of how the present situation came about: to understand racial privilege and prejudice, and ethnic consciousness, both historically and sociologically."

* * *

GILL, Ronald Crispin 1916-

PERSONAL: Born March 10, 1916, in Plymouth, England; son of Joseph Henry (a builder) and Margaret Jane (Crispin) Gill; married Mary Beatrice Foot (died, 1971); married Betty Theed; children: Jane Gill Parks, Crispin Owen, Sarah Gill Mitchell. *Education:* Attended secondary school in Plymouth, England. *Religion:* Church of England. *Home:* No. 1, The Grey House, Kingsand, Torpoint, Cornwall PL10 1NP, England. *Office: Countryman,* Sheep St., Burford, Oxfordshire OX8 4LH, England.

CAREER: Western Morning News, Plymouth, England, reporter, 1934-38, sub-editor, 1939, chief sub-editor, 1946-47, news editor, 1948-49, assistant editor, 1950-70; *Countryman,* Burford, England, editor, 1971-81. *Military service:* British Army, Royal Army Service Corps Motor Boat Companies, 1940-46. *Member:* Society for Nautical Research, Royal Institution of Cornwall, Devonshire Association, Royal Western Yacht Club, Farmers Club.

WRITINGS: The West Country, Oliver & Boyd, 1962; (with Frank Booker and Tony Soper) *The Wreck of the Torrey Canyon,* David & Charles, 1967; *Plymouth: A New History,* David & Charles, Volume I, 1966, Volume II, 1979; *Mayflower Remembered: The Story of the Plymouth Pilgrims,* David & Charles, 1970; *Sutton Harbour,* Sutton Harbour Improvement Co., 1970; (editor) *Dartmoor: A New Study,* David & Charles, 1970; *The Isles of Scilly,* David & Charles, 1975; (editor) *The Countryman's Britain,* David & Charles, 1976; *Dartmoor,* David & Charles, 1977; *The Countryman's Britain in Pictures,* David & Charles, 1977.

WORK IN PROGRESS: Research on the early history of Burford.

* * *

GILLAN, Garth J. 1939-

PERSONAL: Born February 14, 1939, in Washington, D.C.;

son of James (a journalist) and Lolita (Jackson) Gillan; married Martene McCormick, December 28, 1964; children: Johanna, Rebecca, Daniel, Susannah. *Education:* St. John's University, Collegeville, Minn., A.B., 1962; attended St. Louis University, 1962-63; Duquesne University, M.A., 1964, Ph.D., 1966. *Office:* Department of Philosophy, Southern Illinois University, Carbondale, Ill. 62901.

CAREER: Seton Hill College, Greensburg, Pa., assistant professor of philosophy, 1965-66; Canisius College, Buffalo, N.Y., assistant professor of philosophy, 1966-69; Southern Illinois University, Carbondale, associate professor of philosophy, 1969—. Permanent deacon in Diocese of Belleville, Belleville, Ill., 1980—. *Member:* American Philosophical Association, Society of Phenomenology and Existential Philosophy.

WRITINGS: (Editor) *Horizons of the Flesh: Critical Perspectives on the Thought of Merleau-Ponty,* Southern Illinois University Press, 1973. Contributor to philosophy journals.

WORK IN PROGRESS: Michel Foucault, with Charles Lement, for Columbia University Press; *From Sign to Symbol,* for Harvester Press.

SIDELIGHTS: Garth Gillan told *CA:* "My research is focused preeminently upon the development of the relationship between language and desire as that relationship has been conceived by psychoanalysis, critical theory, critical semiotics, and political theology."

*   *   *

GILLAN, Patricia Wagstaff 1936-

PERSONAL: Born November 13, 1936, in Chester, England; daughter of Fred and Ettie (Wagstaff) Jones; married Richard Urquhart (an artist and psychiatrist), January 9, 1961. *Education:* Victoria University of Manchester, B.A., 1960; University of London, M.A., 1965, Ph.D., 1971. *Office:* 7 Upper Harley St., London N.W.1, England.

CAREER: University of London, London, England, researcher in department of psychology, 1962; Rockford General Hospital, Rockford, England, senior clinical psychologist, 1965-77; University of London, lecturer in physiology, 1978—. Co-organizer of Marital and Sexual Problem Clinic at Maudsley Hospital, 1974; honorary principal psychologist at Guys Hospital, 1977, and Maudsley Hospital, 1980. *Member:* World Association of Sexology (member of advisory committee), Rose Society for Research on Sex Education (co-president), Royal Asiatic Society (fellow).

WRITINGS: Sex Therapy Today, Open Books, 1976.

WORK IN PROGRESS: Research on group sex therapy, pornography, vaginal responses to sexual arousal, transcultural problems, and sex education for young people.

SIDELIGHTS: Patricia Gillan wrote: "In the sixties I worked as a behavior therapist specializing in phobic disorders, and I helped many people who possessed a fear of sex. In the seventies I became interested in the work of Masters and Johnson. I did research on stimulation therapy and on the effect of pornography on low sex drive. Now I am most keen on cultural problems in the field of sex and on the prevention of sex problems.

"I have always been fascinated by Africa (I once worked in the Sudan and crossed the Sahara), by the Caribbean, and by South America. I usually work every year in Venezuela."

GILLIE, Christopher 1914-
(Calder Genn)

PERSONAL: Born January 22, 1914, in London, England; son of Robert Calder (a minister) and Emily (Japp) Gillie; married Margery Beaumont (a counselor), July 8, 1947; children: Jane, Damian, Clarissa and Imogen (twins). *Education:* Trinity Hall, Cambridge, M.A., 1935. *Politics:* Liberal. *Religion:* Agnostic. *Home:* 1 Barton Close, Cambridge, England.

CAREER: Free-lance teacher and writer, 1945-67; Cambridge University, Trinity Hall, Cambridge, England, lecturer in English literature, 1967-80. Tutor at Open University. *Military service:* British Army, Infantry, 1939-45; became captain.

WRITINGS: Character in English Literature, Chatto & Windus, 1964; *Longman's Companion to English Literature,* Longman, 1972; *Jane Austen: A Preface Book,* Longman, 1974; *English Literature, 1900-1939,* Cambridge University Press, 1975; *E. M. Forster: A Preface Book,* Longman, in press. Contributor under pseudonym Calder Genn to *Underdogs,* Weidenfeld & Nicolson, 1961.

WORK IN PROGRESS: Research on Shakespeare and the idea of politics.

SIDELIGHTS: Gillie commented: "Every period, including our own, is blinkered by its own limitations. The study of literature is the breaking of such blinkers. Reading for escape is legitimate if 'escape' means release into larger dimensions. My books are introductions to literature, written in the hope of helping readers achieve this release. They are not merely for 'students' in the narrower sense: no book is truly read until it is studied—that is to say read with thought and an open mind—and in that sense the common reader is a student. I write for the common reader."

*   *   *

GILLOTT, Jacky 1939-1980

PERSONAL: Born September 24, 1939, in Bromley, England; died by her own hand in Somerset, England, September 19, 1980; daughter of William (a company director) and Irene Rose Gillott; married John Pervical (a television director), October 10, 1963; children: Matthew Edward, Daniel John. *Education:* University College, London, B.A. (with honors), 1960. *Home:* Stonecroft, Pitcombe, Bruton, Somerset, England. *Agent:* A. D. Peters & Co. Ltd., 10 Buckingham St., Adelphi, London WC2N 6BU, England.

CAREER: Associated with *Sheffield Telegraph* as a reporter. British Broadcasting Corp. (BBC), London, England, television and radio reporter on current affairs and arts, 1963—. News reporter for Independent Television, 1968-73. Also affiliated with "Kaleidoscope," BBC-Radio. *Member:* Society of Authors. *Awards, honors:* Scholarship from Society of Authors, 1980.

WRITINGS: Salvage (novel), Doubleday, 1971; *War Baby* (novel), Gollancz, 1974; *A True Romance* (novel), Hodder & Stoughton, 1975; *Crying Out Loud* (novel), Hodder & Stoughton, 1976; *Providence Place: Animals in a Landscape,* Hodder & Stoughton, 1977; *The Headcase* (novel), Hodder & Stoughton, 1979; *Intimate Relations* (short stories), Hodder & Stoughton, 1980. Contributor to periodicals, including *Punch, Cosmopolitan, Listener, Sunday Telegraph,* and *London Times.*

WORK IN PROGRESS: A Trip Around the Ruins, a novel, unfinished at time of death.

SIDELIGHTS: Jacky Gillott commented: "As somebody who is not a League Division One writer, I feel my license to write depends on my ability and obligation to entertain, and I am anxious that entertainment should be regarded as a perfectly respectable and worthwhile aim in the novel. Though frivolous, it can be a very serious pursuit."

BIOGRAPHICAL/CRITICAL SOURCES: Times Literary Supplement, August 1, 1980.

OBITUARIES: London Times, September 22, 1980; *AB Bookman's Weekly,* December 15, 1980.

*   *   *

GILLULY, James 1896-1980

OBITUARY NOTICE: Born June 24, 1896, in Seattle, Wash.; died December 29, 1980, in Denver, Colo. Geologist who challenged the accepted theory about the formation of mountains. In his 1948 presidential address to the Geological Society of America, Gilluly disputed the view that mountains developed over a long period of time. A spokesman for the U.S. Geological Survey commented, "[Gilluly's] 1948 address has had profound influence on scientific thinking and theorists on the development and structure of the Earth." Gilluly was awarded the Penrose Medal from the Geological Society in 1958 for his research and contributions to his field. He was the co-author of *Principles of Geology,* a standard college textbook. Obituaries and other sources: *Who's Who in the World,* 2nd edition, Marquis, 1974; *American Men and Women of Science,* 14th edition, Bowker, 1979; *Chicago Tribune,* January 1, 1981; *Washington Post,* January 1, 1981.

*   *   *

GILMORE, Maeve

PERSONAL: Born in London, England; daughter of Owen Eugene (a physician) and Matty Lascelles (Carr) Gilmore; married Mervyn Peake (a writer), December 1, 1937 (died, 1968); children: Sebastian, Fabian, Clare Peake Penate. *Education:* Attended Westminster School of Art and Bonn School of Art. *Religion:* Roman Catholic. *Home:* 1 Drayton Gardens, London SW10 9RY, England. *Agent:* Maurice Michael, Partridge Green, Horsham, Sussex RH13 8EJ, England.

CAREER: Artist, with exhibitions of paintings. *Member:* Mervyn Peake Society (honorary president).

WRITINGS: A World Away (memoirs), Gollancz, 1970; (editor) *A Book of Nonsense: Poems of Mervyn Peake,* P. Owen, 1972; (editor with Hilary Spurling) *Drawings of Mervyn Peake,* Davis-Poynter, 1974; (editor with Sheelagh Johnson) *Writings and Drawings of Mervyn Peake,* Academy Editions, 1974; (editor) *Peake's Progress,* Allen Lane, 1978, Overlook Press, 1981; (with Kenneth Welfare) *Magic Adventures of the House People* (juvenile), Methuen, 1981.

Work represented in anthologies, including *Arts Council Book Two,* 1977.

SIDELIGHTS: "Although I am primarily a painter," Maeve Gilmore wrote, "I have written since childhood. Writing and the world of books have become a much bigger force in my life since the death of my husband who was virtually unable to work for ten years due to a progressive illness. Because he was immensely productive during his creative life, he left behind a very great deal of unpublished material. Since his death in 1968 and the publication of *Titus Groan, Gormenghast,* and *Titus Alone,* his reputation has grown accordingly, and his work is being translated into many languages.

"Before he died, I began to write of our life together, to try not to let it be lost in the sadness of his slow, progressive illness. And although I had not written with a view to publication, one or two friends suggested I should send it to a publisher when it was finished. It was published as *A World Away* and dramatized by BBC-Radio 4 a year or two later. From this have sprung most of the other books I have edited, which are the works my husband had not published during his lifetime. However, I do have exhibitions of my own paintings, and I write a good deal."

BIOGRAPHICAL/CRITICAL SOURCES: Maeve Gilmore, *A World Away,* Gollancz, 1970; John Watney, *Mervyn Peake,* St. Martin's, 1976; *Observer,* January 28, 1979.

*   *   *

GILSON, Etienne Henry 1884-1978

PERSONAL: Born June 13, 1884, in Paris, France; died September 19, 1978, in Cravant, France; son of Paul Anthelme (a businessman) and Caroline (Rainaud) Gilson; married Therese Ravise, February 10, 1908; children: Jacqueline, Cecile, Bernard. *Education:* Sorbonne, University of Paris, degree, 1907, Ph.D., 1913. *Religion:* Roman Catholic.

CAREER: University of Lille, Lille, France, professor, 1913-19; University of Strasbourg, Strasbourg, France, professor, 1919-21; University of Paris, Paris, France, professor of medieval philosophy, 1921-32; College de France, Paris, professor of history of medieval philosophy, 1932-50; University of Toronto, Pontifical Institute of Medieval Studies, Toronto, Ontario, founder and director of studies, 1928-56. Visiting professor or lecturer at Harvard University, 1926-29 and 1936, University of Aberdeen, 1929-30, University of Virginia, 1937, and University of Notre Dame, 1950. Technical adviser to French delegation at San Francisco Conference, 1945; member of French delegation to UNESCO. *Military service:* Served in French Army Machine Gun Company at Verdun during World War I; became lieutenant.

MEMBER: French Academy, British Academy, Royal Academy of Denmark, Royal Academy of the Netherlands, Polish Academy, American Academy of Arts and Sciences, Medieval Academy of America, Roman Academy of St. Thomas Aquinas, Academy of Moral Sciences. *Awards, honors:* Croix de guerre; Grand Officier de la Legion d'honneur, 1935; named counseiller de la Republique, 1947-48; received honorary doctorate degrees from University of Paris, Oxford University, University of Aberdeen, St. Andrews University, University of Glasgow, University of Montreal, Harvard University, University of Pennsylvania, Columbia University, Laval University, and Milan College; Christian Culture Medal for Italian Studies from Assumption College, 1949; Serena Medal for Italian Studies from British Academy, 1952; Cardinal Spellman Thomas Aquinas Medal, 1952.

WRITINGS—In English translation: *Le Thomisme: Introduction au systeme de saint Thomas d'Aquin,* Vrin, 1922, 6th revised edition, 1965, translation by Edward Bullough published as *The Philosophy of St. Thomas Aquinas,* Heffer, 1924, B. Herder, 1929, 2nd revised edition, 1937, reprinted, Books for Libraries Press, 1971, translation by L. K. Shook published as *The Christian Philosophy of St. Thomas Aquinas,* Random, 1956; *La Philosophie de Saint Bonaventure,* Vrin, 1924, 2nd revised edition, 1943, translation by Illtyd Trethowan and Frank J. Sheed published as *The Philosophy of St. Bonaventure,* Sheed, 1938, reprinted, St. Anthony Guild Press, 1965; *Saint Thomas d'Aquin,* 4th edition, Lecoffre, 1925, 2nd revised edition published as *Saint Thomas moraliste,* Vrin, 1974, translation by Leo Richard Ward published as *Moral Values and the Moral Life: The Ethical Theory of St. Thomas Aquinas*, B. Herder, 1931, reprinted, Shoe String, 1961.

Introduction a l'etude de Saint Augustin, Vrin, 1931, 4th revised and enlarged edition, 1969, translation by L.E.M. Lynch published as *The Christian Philosophy of Saint Augustine*, Random, 1960; *L'Esprit de la philosophie medieval*, Vrin, 1932, 2nd revised edition, 1944, translation by A.H.C. Downes published as *The Spirit of Medieval Philosophy*, Scribner, 1936; *La Theologie mystique de Saint Bernard*, Vrin, 1934, 3rd edition, 1969, translation by Downes published as *The Mystical Theology of Saint Bernard*, Sheed, 1940; *Christianisme et philosophie*, Vrin, 1936, translation by Ralph MacDonald published as *Christianity and Philosophy*, Sheed, 1939; *Medieval Universalism and its Present Value*, Sheed, 1937; *The Unity of Philosophical Experience*, Scribner, 1937, reprinted, 1965; *Reason and Revelation in the Middle Ages*, Scribner, 1938; *Heloise et Abelard*, Vrin, 1938, 3rd revised edition, 1964, translation by L. K. Shook published as *Heloise and Abelard*, Regnery, 1951; *Dante et la philosophie*, Vrin, 1939, translation by David Moore published as *Dante the Philosopher*, Sheed & Ward, 1949, reprinted under title *Dante and Philosophy*, P. Smith, 1968.

God and Philosophy, Yale University Press, 1941; *History of Philosophy and Philosophical Education*, Marquette University Press, 1948; *Being and Some Philosophers*, Pontifical Institute of Medieval Studies, 1949, 2nd revised and enlarged edition, 1952; *Wisdom and Love in Saint Thomas Aquinas*, Marquette University Press, 1951; *L'Ecole des muses*, Vrin, 1951, translation by Maisie Ward published as *Choir of Muses*, Sheed, 1953; (contributor) *Disputed Questions in Education*, Doubleday, 1954; (editor) *The Church Speaks to the Modern World: The Social Teachings of Leo XIII*, Image Books, 1954; *History of Christian Philosophy in the Middle Ages*, Random, 1955; *A Gilson Reader: Selected Writings*, Hanover House, 1957; *Painting and Reality*, Pantheon, 1957.

Elements of Christian Philosophy, Doubleday, 1960; *Le Philosophie et la theologie*, Fayard, 1960, translation by Cecile Gilson published as *The Philosopher and Theology*, Random, 1962; *Saint Thomas Aquinas and Philosophy*, Saint Joseph College, 1961; (with Thomas Langan) *Modern Philosophy: Descartes to Kant*, Random, 1963; *Matieres et formes: Poetiques particulieres des arts majeurs*, Vrin, 1964, translation by Salvatore Attanasio published as *Forms and Substances in the Arts*, Scribner, 1966; *The Spirit of Thomism*, P. J. Kennedy, 1964; *The Arts of the Beautiful*, Scribner, 1965; (with Langan and Armand A. Maurer) *Recent Philosophy: Hegel to the Present*, Random, 1966; *In Search of Saint Thomas Aquinas*, Saint Joseph College, 1966.

Other writings: *Index scolastico-cartesian*, Alcan, 1913, Franklin, 1963; *La Liberte chez Descartes et la theologie*, Alcan, 1913; *Etudes de philosophie medieval*, Strasbourg, Commission des Publications de la Faculte des Lettres, 1921; *La Philosophie au moyen age*, two volumes, Payot, 1922, 2nd revised edition, 1976; (editor) Rene Descartes, *Discours de la methode*, Vrin, 1925, 4th edition, 1967.

Etudes sur le role de la pensee medievale dans la formation du systeme cartesian, Vrin, 1930, 4th edition, 1975; *Les Idees et les lettres*, Vrin, 1932; *Pour un Ordre catholique*, Desclee, de Brouwer, 1934; *Le Realisme thomiste et critique de la connaissance*, Vrin, 1939; (editor) *Existentialisme chretien: Gabriel Marcel*, Plon, 1947; *Philosophie et incarnation selon saint Augustin*, Institut d'Etudes Medievales, Universite de Montreal, 1947; *L'Etre et l'essence*, Vrin, 1948.

Les Metamorphoses de la Cite de Dieu, Publications Universitaires de Louvain, 1952; *Jean Duns Scot: Introduction a ses positions fondamentales*, Vrin, 1952; *Melanges offerts a Etienne Gilson, de l'Academie francaise*, Vrin, 1959; *Introduction a la philosophie chretienne*, Vrin, 1960; *Introduction aux arts du beau*, Vrin, 1963; (editor and compiler) *Saint Bernard*, Les Editions de Cerf, 1964; *Les Tribulations de Sophie*, Vrin, 1967; *La Societe de masse et sa culture*, Vrin, 1967; *Linguistique et philosophie: Essai sur les constantes philosophiques du langage*, Vrin, 1969; *D'Aristote a Darwin et retour: Essai sur quelques constantes de la biophilosophie*, Vrin, 1971; *Dante et Beatrice: Etudes dantesques*, Vrin, 1974.

SIDELIGHTS: In 1955 Reinhold Niebuhr remarked that "Etienne Gilson is the most authoritative living exponent and interpreter of the philosophy of the Middle Ages." As a neo-Thomist scholar, Gilson believed that faith and reason were not irreconcilable opposites, but had found a successful synthesis in the writings of Thomas Aquinas. Gilson's work includes studies not only of Christian philosophy, but also of music, painting, and literature. In Niebuhr's opinion, "he probably has no contemporary peer in the lucidity of his mind and the balance of his historical judgments."

BIOGRAPHICAL/CRITICAL SOURCES: Times Literary Supplement, May 30, 1936, July 6, 1940, November 15, 1941, April 23, 1949, May 2, 1958; *America*, October 17, 1936, April 2, 1938, June 26, 1965; *Books*, October 25, 1936, December 3, 1939; *American Review*, November, 1936; *New York Times*, November 8, 1936, January 30, 1938, January 29, 1939, January 23, 1955, January 27, 1957; *Yale Review*, winter, 1937; *Commonweal*, January 22, 1937, July 27, 1951, October 30, 1953, June 10, 1955, April 14, 1961; *Forum*, March, 1938; *Saturday Review of Literature*, April 23, 1938, October 15, 1949; *Christian Century*, October 1, 1941, February 13, 1957; *Journal of Philosophy*, December 18, 1941; *Newsweek*, February 7, 1955; *Saturday Review*, January 11, 1958; *New Statesman*, June 9, 1961; Etienne Henry Gilson, *The Philosopher and Theology*, Random House, 1962; *Catholic World*, July, 1962; *New York Times Book Review*, July 22, 1962; *Best Sellers*, May 1, 1965.*

*   *   *

GITTER, A. George 1926-

PERSONAL: Born July, 1926, in Poland; son of Arthur and Kalina Gitter; married Sofia E. (an artist); children: Natasha A., S. Alexei. *Education:* University of Virginia, B.A., 1949; American University, M.A., 1961, Ph.D., 1964. *Home:* 204 Pleasant St., Brookline, Mass. 02146. *Office:* Communication Research Center, Boston University, Boston, Mass. 02215.

CAREER: U.S. Navy, Bureau of Personnel, Washington, D.C., research psychologist, 1962; Lehigh University, Bethlehem, Pa., lecturer in psychology, 1962-63; Sweet Briar College, Sweet Briar, Va., assistant professor of psychology, 1963-65; Boston University, Boston, Mass., professor of communication research, 1965—, chairman of Communication Research Division and director of Communication Research Center, 1969-75, associate director interdisciplinary doctoral program. *Member:* American Psychological Association, American Statistical Association, American Association for the Advancement of Science, American Association of University Professors, Massachusetts Psychological Association, Phi Beta Kappa.

WRITINGS: (Contributor) Ernst Timaeus, editor, *Reader on Social Psychology*, Verlag Kiepenheuer & Witsch, 1973;

(with Robert Grunin) *Communication,* Gale, 1980. Contributor to journals in the behavioral sciences.

* * *

GLADDEN, Vivianne Cervantes 1927-

PERSONAL: Born October 8, 1927, in Brookhaven, Miss.; daughter of Thomas James (a realtor) and Douglas (an executive secretary; maiden name Jarrey) Guillemy; married Garnett Lee Gladden (a professor and writer), June 22, 1958; children: Mark Lee, Jean Sue. *Education:* Attended Oakwood College, 1956, Riverside City College, 1957-58, University of Southern California, 1966-67, Mount St. Mary's College, Westwood, Calif., 1967, California State University, Northridge, and University of California, Los Angeles, 1976-77; Golden State University, Ph.D., 1980. *Residence:* Culver City, Calif. *Agent:* Aaron M. Priest Literary Agency, Inc., 150 East 35th St., New York, N.Y. 10016. *Office:* Center for Health and Healing, Cedars Sinai Hospital, 8631 West Third St., Suite 1140E, Los Angeles, Calif. 90048.

CAREER: Worked as professional model, concert singer, and professional actress; writer. Associated with Center for Health and Healing, Cedars Sinai Hospital; academic field adviser for Golden State University; private practice as nutrition consultant. *Member:* Screen Actors Guild. *Awards, honors:* D.Litt. from Union University, 1978.

WRITINGS: (With husband, Lee Gladden) *Heirs of the Gods: A Space Age Interpretation of the Bible,* Rawson-Wade, 1979; (with L. Gladden and Gary L. Couture) *How to Win the Aging Game,* Harbour House, 1979.

WORK IN PROGRESS: A scholarly version of *Heirs of the Gods; The Decline and Fall of an Eagle,* with Lee Gladden.

AVOCATIONAL INTERESTS: Travel (Japan, Singapore, Manila, England, France, Germany, the Netherlands, West Indies, Mexico, Italy, Scandinavia), meditation, running, t'ai chi.

* * *

GLASSCO, John 1909-1981
(Miles Underwood)

OBITUARY NOTICE—See index for *CA* sketch: Born December 15, 1909, in Montreal, Quebec, Canada; died of a heart attack, January 29, 1981, in Montreal, Quebec, Canada. Editor, translator, poet, and author of *Memoirs of Montparnasse,* a book about his life as a young man in Paris during the late 1920's and early 1930's. Glassco served as councillor and mayor of the village of Foster in Quebec. He translated the poems and novels of French Canadian authors, thus gaining them a wide English-speaking audience. Glassco also finished artist Aubrey Beardsley's novel, *Under the Hill.* The author's other works include *The English Governess, Conan's Fig,* and *The Deficit Made Flesh.* Obituaries and other sources: John Glassco, *Memoirs of Montparnasse,* Oxford University Press, 1970; *Toronto Globe and Mail,* January 31, 1981.

* * *

GLAZEBROOK, G(eorge) P(arkin) de T(wenebrokes) 1899-

PERSONAL: Born in 1899, in London, Ontario, Canada; son of Arthur James (an exchange broker) and Lucy (MacLauchlan) Glazebrook. *Education:* University of Toronto, B.A., 1922; Oxford University, M.A., 1930. *Home:* 45 Glen Rd., Toronto, Ontario, Canada M4W 2V2.

CAREER: University of Toronto, Toronto, Ontario, began as lecturer, became associate professor of history, 1924-41; Department of External Affairs, Ottawa, Ontario, special wartime assistant, 1942-46; University of Toronto, professor of history, 1946-48; Department of External Affairs, head of External Affairs Division, 1949-53, minister to the United States, 1953-56, head of division, 1956-59, assistant undersecretary, 1956-63; University of Toronto, special lecturer in history, 1963-67; writer, 1967—. *Awards, honors:* J. B. Tyrrell Medal for historical writing; Canada Council fellowship, 1963-64.

WRITINGS: Sir Charles Bagot in Canada, Oxford University Press, 1929; *Sir Edmund Walker,* Oxford University Press, 1933; (editor) *The Hargrave Correspondence,* University of Toronto Press, 1938; *A History of Transportation in Canada,* Ryerson, 1938, reprinted, two volumes, McClelland & Stewart, 1964; *Canada at the Paris Peace Conference,* Oxford University Press, 1942; *History of Canadian External Relations,* Oxford University Press, 1950, revised edition, two volumes, McClelland & Stewart, 1966; *A Short History of Canada,* Oxford University Press, 1950; *A History of Canadian Political Thought,* McClelland & Stewart, 1966; *Life in Ontario: A Social History,* University of Toronto Press, 1968; (editor with Katharine B. Brett and Judith McErval) *A Shopper's View of Canada's Past: Pages From Eaton's Catalogues, 1886-1930,* University of Toronto Press, 1969; *The Story of Toronto,* University of Toronto Press, 1974.

WORK IN PROGRESS: The Church of England in Upper Canada; History of Ontario Schools.

SIDELIGHTS: Glazebrook wrote: "My first book was written as an alternative to a Ph.D. which I couldn't afford. The others were undertaken either by request or as a matter of interest. Most of the subjects I've written about were chosen because exploration in them seemed needed. Since I am invited to give advice to young writers it would be: (1) The job of a teacher is to teach, and this is more difficult and more important than writing; (2) work regular hours and don't get emotional."

* * *

GLENNY, Michael Valentine 1927-

PERSONAL: Born September 26, 1927, in London, England; son of Arthur Willoughby Falls (an air force officer) and Avice Noel (Boyes) Glenny; married Juliet Mary Crum (divorced, 1974); married Valerie Forbes Hartley-Brewer (a physician), August 23, 1975; children: three sons, one daughter. *Education:* Christ Church, Oxford, B.A., 1951; St. Anthony's College, Oxford, M.A., 1970. *Residence:* Bath, England. *Agent:* Deborah Rogers Ltd., Literary Agency, 5-11 Mortimer St., London W1N 7RH, England.

CAREER: Writer and translator. Worked as correspondent for *Observer,* London, England, 1964-67. *Military service:* British Regular Army, 1945-54; became captain. *Member:* Society of Authors, Translators Association.

WRITINGS—Editor: *Three Soviet Plays,* Penguin, 1966; (with George R. Urban) *Can We Survive Our Future?* (symposium), Bodley Head, 1972; (with Robert Clifton) *Options in Soviet Government and Politics,* Open University Press, 1976.

Translator: (With Eustace Wareing) Heinz Gartmann, *The Men Behind the Space Rockets,* Weidenfeld & Nicholson, 1955; Gartmann, *Space Travel,* B. T. Batsford, 1962; Johanna Moosdorf, *Next Door,* Gollancz, 1963; Willi Heinrich,

The Crumbling Fortress, Macdonald & Co., 1963; Hermann Eich, *The Unloved Germans,* Macdonald & Co., 1965; Joseph Carl Benedict von Eichendorff, *The Life of a Good-for-Nothing,* Blackie & Son, 1966; Bernhard Grzimek, *Wild Animal, White Man: Some Wildlife in Europe, Soviet Russia, and North America,* Thames & Hudson, 1966; Michail Afans'evich Bulgakov, *The Master and Margarita,* Collins & Harvill, 1967; (and editor) Anatoly Nasil'evich Lunacharsky, *Revolutionary Silhouettes,* Penguin, 1967; Hugo Portisch, *Eyewitness in Vietnam,* Bodley Head, 1967; Valery Yakovelvich Tarsis, *The Pleasure Factory,* Collins & Harvill, 1967; Bulgakov, *The Heart of a Dog,* Collins & Harvill, 1968; Vitaly Syomin, *Seven in One House,* Joseph, 1968; Yury Dombrovsky, *The Keeper of Antiquities,* Longmans, 1969; Fritz Novotny, *Toulouse-Lautrec,* Phaidon, 1960; (with Betty Ross) Helmut Schoeck, *Envy: A Theory of Social Behaviour,* Secker & Warburg, 1969.

Bulgakov, *Black Snow: A Theatrical Novel,* Penguin, 1971; Bulgakov, *The White Guard,* Collins, 1971; Vladimir Nabokov, *Mary,* Weidenfeld & Nicolson, 1971; Aleksandr Solzhenitsyn, *Stories and Prose Poems,* Bodley Head, 1971; Solzhenitsyn, *August 1914,* Bodley Head, 1972; (and editor) *Novy Mir: A Selection, 1925-1967,* J. Cape, 1972; Bulgakov, *A Country Doctor's Notebook,* Collins, 1975; David Markish, *The Beginning,* Hodder & Stoughton, 1976; Solzhenitsyn, *Matryona's House, and Other Stories,* Penguin, 1976; *Selected Readings in Soviet Literature,* Open University Press, 1977; Vladimir Maximov, *Farewell From Nowhere,* Collins, 1978; Georgi Vladimov, *Faithful Ruslan,* J. Cape, 1979.

Contributor to newspapers and periodicals, including *London Times, Guardian, Observer, Spectator, Survey, Journal of Contemporary History, Drama Review,* and *Studies in Comparative Communism.*

WORK IN PROGRESS: A screenplay based on Georgi Vladimov's *Faithful Ruslan;* a translation of an experimental, avant-garde novel by Vassily Aksyonov.

BIOGRAPHICAL/CRITICAL SOURCES: Publishers Weekly, September 25, 1972.

*   *   *

GLESS, Darryl James 1945-

PERSONAL: Born December 4, 1945, in Columbus, Neb.; son of Frank A. (a watchmaker) and Vivian (a nurse; maiden name, Herbrich) Gless; married Ruth M. Saunders (an architect), July 12, 1969. *Education:* University of Nebraska, B.A., 1968; Oxford University, B.Phil., 1971; Princeton University, Ph.D., 1974. *Home:* 208 Celeste Circle, Chapel Hill, N.C. 27514. *Office:* Department of English, University of North Carolina, Chapel Hill, N.C. 27514.

CAREER: University of Virginia, Charlottesville, assistant professor of English, 1974-80; University of North Carolina, Chapel Hill, associate professor of English, 1980—. *Member:* Modern Language Association of America, Spenser Society, Association of American Rhodes Scholars. *Awards, honors:* Rhodes scholar at Oxford University, 1968-1971; National Endowment for the Humanities fellow, 1979-80.

WRITINGS: "*Measure for Measure*": *The Law and the Convent,* Princeton University Press, 1979. Contributor to literature journals, including *English Literary Renaissance.*

WORK IN PROGRESS: A book on Edmund Spenser's *Faerie Queene,* completion expected in 1981.

GLICKMAN, Beatrice Marden 1919-

PERSONAL: Born December 31, 1919, in Winthrop, Mass.; daughter of Louis and Rose (Ruskin) Marden; married Harold Glickman (an advertising executive), August 30, 1942; children: Lizbeth Ann. *Education:* Lesley College, B.S., 1965; Wheelock College, Ed.M., 1968. *Politics:* Independent. *Religion:* Jewish. *Home:* 26 Russell Circle, Natick, Mass. 01760.

CAREER: Teacher of early childhood and director of schools for young children, 1958-62; Children's Hospital, Boston, Mass., in adolescent programming, 1972-74; writer and researcher, 1974—. *Member:* Lesley College Alumnae Association (president, 1966-68).

WRITINGS: (With Nesha Springer) *Who Cares for the Baby?: Choices in Child Care,* Schocken, 1978. Contributor to *Baby Care* and *Expecting.*

WORK IN PROGRESS: Articles about child care and divorce.

SIDELIGHTS: Beatrice Glickman wrote: "My main concern continues to be the care of infants and young children. Day care is *not* the complete answer, and no one asks children what they prefer. Group care will make different kinds of future citizens."

*   *   *

GLYN, Richard Hamilton 1907-1980

OBITUARY NOTICE: Born October 12, 1907, in Dorset, England; died October 24, 1980, in London, England. Lawyer, politician, and authority on pedigree dogs. Glyn was called to the bar in 1935 and eventually undertook a career in politics. He served as a member of parliament for North Dorset from 1957 to 1970. A noted expert on the breeding of pedigree dogs and other livestock, Glyn wrote *Bull Terriers and How to Breed Them* and *Champion Dogs of the World,* among several other books. Sir Richard succeeded his father in 1960 as ninth Baronet of Ewell and fifth Baronet of Gaunts. Obituaries and other sources: *Who's Who,* 126th edition, St. Martin's, 1974; *London Times,* October 29, 1980.

*   *   *

GOAMAN, Muriel See COX, Edith Muriel

*   *   *

GODDEN, Geoffrey 1929-

PERSONAL: Born in 1929, in Worthing, England; son of Leslie (an antique dealer) and Molly (Brown) Godden; married Jean Maghess, January 8, 1965; children: Jonathan. *Education:* Educated in Worthing, England. *Home:* 19 Crescent Rd., Worthing, Sussex, England.

CAREER: Godden of Worthing Ltd. (antique business), Worthing, England, managing director, 1970—. *Military service:* British Army during 1940's. *Member:* Rotary International (president, 1979-80),

WRITINGS—Published by Barrie & Jenkins, unless otherwise noted: *Victorian Porcelain,* 1961; *Encyclopaedia of British Pottery and Porcelain Marks,* 1964; *An Illustrated Encyclopaedia of British Pottery and Porcelain,* 1966; *The Handbook of British Pottery and Porcelain Marks,* 1968; *Minton Pottery and Porcelain of the First Period,* 1968; *Caughley and Worcester Porcelain, 1775-1800,* 1969; *The Illustrated Guide to Lowestoft Porcelain,* 1969.

Coalport and Coalbrookdale Porcelains, 1970; *The Illus-*

trated Guide to Mason's Patent Ironstone China, 1970; *Stevengraphs and Other Victorian Silk Pictures,* 1971; (editor of revision) *Jewitt's Ceramic Art of Great Britain, 1800-1900,* 1972; *The Illustrated Guide to Ridgway Porcelains,* 1972; *British Porcelain: An Illustrated Guide,* 1974; *British Pottery: An Illustrated Guide,* 1974; *Godden's Guide to English Porcelain,* Granada Publishing, 1978; *Oriental Export Market Porcelain and Its Influence on European Wares,* Granada Publishing, 1979; *Godden's Guide to Mason China and Ironstone Wares,* Antique Collectors Club, 1980; *Chamberlains: Worcester Porcelains,* 1981; *Staffordshire Porcelains,* Granada Publishing, 1982.

SIDELIGHTS: Godden, an antique dealer who specializes in English porcelains, is managing director of the family business established in 1900.

* * *

GODWIN, John (Frederick) 1922-
(Frederick Foster)

PERSONAL: Born December 4, 1922, in Hednesford, England; son of Frederick John (a colliery purchases manager) and Grace (Foster) Godwin; married Elizabeth Walsh (a teacher), December 22, 1952; children: Helen Elizabeth, Philip John. *Education:* County of Stafford Training College, teaching certificate, 1946; Leicester College of Education, certificate in education of the handicapped, 1969. *Politics:* Conservative. *Religion:* Church of England. *Home:* Lark Rise, 10 Church Lane, Etching Hill, Rugeley, Staffordshire, England. *Office:* St. Michael's Primary School, Sturgeons Hill, Lichfield, Staffordshire, England.

CAREER: Worked as clerk and cashier at Midland Bank Ltd., in Bloxwich, Hednesford, and Cannock, Staffordshire, England, 1940-46; assistant teacher at residential school in Rugeley, Staffordshire, 1948-55; headmaster of village school in Mawnan, England, 1955-58; deputy headmaster at residential school in Corley, England, 1958-61; headmaster at primary school in Stamford, England, 1961-69; St. Michael's Primary School, Lichfield, England, headmaster, 1970—. *Military service:* British Army, served in Radio Security Service of Royal Observer Corps, 1942-45. *Member:* National Association of Head Teachers, Society of Authors.

WRITINGS: Battling Parer (aviation history), Angus & Robertson, 1967; *Wings to the Cape* (aviation history), Tafelberg Uitgewers Beperk (Cape Town, South Africa), 1970; *Give Your Child a Better Start: Manual of Information for Preschool Education,* Cressrelles Publishing, 1973; *Lives to Inspire* (religious education textbook), Moorley's Bible and Book Shop, 1978; *More Lives to Inspire,* Moorley's Bible and Book Shop, 1980; *Lessons From Life and Legend,* Moorley's Bible and Book Shop, 1981. Contributor to history, education, and religious journals, including *Christian,* and newspapers; also contributor under pseudonym Frederick Foster to *Mother* (magazine).

WORK IN PROGRESS: Research on Staffordshire history.

SIDELIGHTS: Godwin told *CA:* "My first and second books are factual accounts of early long-distance flights. 'Battling Parer' was the first man to fly in a single-engined airplane from England to Australia (1920). *Wings to the Cape* is a story of endeavor and adventure as several airplane crews from England tried to be first to reach the Cape of Good Hope (1920).

"Preschool education is the theme of my third book. It was published with a kit of apparatus and is designed to show parents (particularly mothers) how a child can be profitably

employed at home in the important formative years before he comes to school.

"My latest three books are for use in connection with Christian education. I see evidence around me, in many aspects of life, of moral and spiritual decadence while I read of the appalling rise in crime statistics. It seems reasonable to me to suppose that this decadence and the increasing crime figures are connected. In the course of my work as a teacher I see many children and young people who obviously have no standards of thought or of action set before them at home, and I suspect that even at school in some instances the standards set are little better. Many young people (and, indeed, grown ups) seem to be preoccupied much more about their rights rather than about their responsibilities and with what they can grab from life rather than with what they can give. I feel that adults must accept a large share of the blame for such attitudes in the younger people.

"From what I have seen, I believe that the education of many of our children lacks a spiritual dimension and is concerned exclusively (or nearly so) with material things and material values. Many who leave school find themselves adrift on the ocean of life without a pilot to show them the way. They seem to have little idea of right and wrong. Many are without any real purpose in life and, worst of all, without any hope for the future.

"I feel that children must be given anew a set of permanent, eternal values by which to live. They must be taught that true fulfillment does not come from the acquisition of material things. They must be given an appreciation of the Force which can take command of their lives and make them want to do things for the good of others rather than for themselves. They must be guided to see that in pursuing selflessness they will, not by deliberate searching but incidentally, achieve a happiness which transcends anything that comes from a life of self-seeking.

"What better way is there to teach children to think of others than to give them stories of inspiration of men and women who have given their lives, regardless of cost, to the service of God and their fellow men? Youth is a time when minds can be fired with ideas which can profoundly affect the hearts and minds of the rising generation. It was this consuming desire to give children a glimpse of the eternal that prompted me to write *Lives to Inspire, More Lives to Inspire,* and *Lessons From Life and Legend,* for use at school morning assemblies in schools where Christian teaching is given."

AVOCATIONAL INTERESTS: Listening to short-wave radio.

* * *

GOLDBECK, Frederick E(rnest) 1902-

PERSONAL: Born February 13, 1902, in The Hague, Netherlands; son of Bernard (a British consul) and Celine (a violinist; maiden name, Bles) Goldbeck; married Yvonne Lefebure (a concert pianist), October 25, 1947. *Education:* Attended University of Frankfurt; studied music privately. *Politics:* Liberal. *Religion:* Protestant. *Home:* 12 rue Emile Duclaux, Paris XV, France.

CAREER: Conductor and lecturer, 1923-45; Radio France, Paris, producer and broadcaster, 1945—. Music adviser for Congress for Cultural Freedom, 1951-60.

WRITINGS: The Perfect Conductor, Pellegrini & Cudahy, 1951; *Twentieth-Century Composers,* Volume IV: *France, Italy, and Spain,* Weidenfeld & Nicolson, 1974.

GOLDWATER, Eleanor Lowenstein   1909(?)-1980

OBITUARY NOTICE: Born c. 1909; died of leukemia, December 1, 1980, in New York, N.Y. Bookstore proprietor, collector, and bibliographer. Goldwater worked as a social worker during the Depression. In 1940 she started the Corner Book Shop with a six hundred dollar investment. Her store, located on Fourth Avenue in New York City, was only a few blocks away from the University Place Book Shop owned by her husband Walter Goldwater, an eminent rare-book dealer. Eleanor Goldwater's special field of interest became the collection of cookbooks, and her *Bibliography of American Cookery Books, 1742-1860* has been called "the definitive work in the field." Obituaries and other sources: *Publishers Weekly,* December 19, 1980; *AB Bookman's Weekly,* January 19, 1981.

* * *

GOLDWIN, Robert Allen   1922-

PERSONAL: Born April 16, 1922, in New York, N.Y.; son of Alexander (a restaurateur) and Sed (a restaurateur; maiden name, Applebaum) Goldwin; married Daisy Lateiner (a private school administrator), October 13, 1944; children: Nancy Goldwin Harvey, Jane Goldwin Bandler, Elizabeth, Seth. *Education:* St. John's College, Annapolis, Md., B.A., 1950; University of Chicago, M.A., 1954, Ph.D., 1963. *Politics:* Republican. *Home:* 1565 44th St. N.W., Washington, D.C. 20007. *Office:* American Enterprise Institute, 1150 17th St. N.W., Washington, D.C. 20036.

CAREER: American Foundation for Political Education, Chicago, Ill., director of research, 1951-60; University of Chicago, Chicago, lecturer in political science and director of public affairs conference center, 1960-66; Kenyon College, Gambier, Ohio, associate professor of political science and director of public affairs conference center, 1966-69; St. John's College, Annapolis, Md., dean of college and Richard Hammond Elliott Tutor, 1969-73; U.S. Government, Washington, D.C., special adviser to ambassador of mission to the North Atlantic Treaty Organization (NATO), Brussels, Belgium, 1973-74, special consultant to President Gerald R. Ford, 1974-76, adviser to the secretary of defense, 1976; American Enterprise Institute, Washington, D.C., resident scholar and director of constitutional studies, 1976—. Member of the board of trustees of the Woodrow Wilson International Center for Scholars, Smithsonian Institution, 1975-76; member of the board of Overseers' Committee to Visit the Department of Government, Harvard University, 1975—; member of the Board of Foreign Scholarships, (vice-chairman, 1979—), 1977—; member of consulting group, Executive Council on Foreign Diplomats, Inc., 1977—; member of board of governors, St. John's College, Annapolis, Md., 1980—.

Moderator of "Dialogue of the Western World," fifteen one-hour televised seminars produced by Maryland Center for Public Broadcasting, 1972. Guest professor, lecturer, or consultant at many institutions, including British Broadcasting Corp., Hebrew University (Jerusalem), Harvard University, Smithsonian Institution, Cornell University, Aspen Institute for Humanistic Studies, Georgetown University, Sana'a University (Yemen Arab Republic), and Kenyon College. *Military service:* U.S. Army, 1942-46; became first lieutenant. *Member:* American Political Science Association. *Awards, honors:* Guggenheim fellow, 1966; D.L., Kenyon College, 1976; Department of Defense distinguished public service medal, 1977.

WRITINGS—Editor; all published by Rand McNally, ex-

cept as noted: *Readings in World Politics,* Oxford University Press, 1959, 2nd edition, 1970; *Readings in American Foreign Policy,* Oxford University Press, 1959, 2nd edition, 1971; *Readings in Russian Foreign Policy,* Oxford University Press, 1959; *A Nation of States,* 1963, 2nd edition, 1974; *America Armed,* 1963; *Why Foreign Aid?,* 1963; *Political Parties, USA,* 1964; *Beyond the Cold War,* 1964; *100 Years of Emancipation,* 1965; *Left, Right, and Center* 1967; *Higher Education and Modern Democracy,* 1967; *Representation and Misrepresentation,* 1968; *A Nation of Cities,* 1968; *On Civil Disobedience,* 1969; *How Democratic Is America?,* 1971; *How Democratic Is the Constitution?,* American Enterprise Institute, 1980; *How Capitalistic Is the Constitution?,* American Enterprise Institute, 1981.

Contributor: Leo Strauss and Joseph Cropsey, editors, *History of Political Philosophy,* Rand McNally, 1963; Robert H. Horwitz, editor, *The Moral Foundations of the American Republic,* University Press of Virginia, 1977, 2nd edition, 1979; Sidney Hook, Paul Kurtz, and Miro Jodorovich, editors, *The Ethics of Teaching and Scientific Research,* Prometheus Books, 1977; Hook, Kurtz, and Jodorovich, editors, *The University and the State: What Role for Government in Higher Education?,* 1978. Contributor to *Educational Record* and *Western Political Quarterly.*

WORK IN PROGRESS: Researching human rights and their relationship to the Constitutions of countries, including the United States.

SIDELIGHTS: Goldwin told *CA:* "All of my edited works present the best and most persuasive spokesmen I can find who disagree on the great political issues. The intention is to give the reader a solid basis of fact and opinion for thinking the question through for himself."

* * *

GONZALES, John
See TERRALL, Robert

* * *

GOODACRE, Elizabeth Jane   1929-

PERSONAL: Born February 24, 1929, in Sydney, Australia; daughter of Robert William (an accountant) and Jo (a teacher; maiden name, Anderson) Standish; married David Meakin Goodacre (an architect), April 10, 1960; children: Catherine, Stephen, Sarah. *Education:* Balmain Teachers Training College, Teaching Certificate, 1948; University of London, B.Sc. and Child Development Diploma, both 1958, Ph.D., 1965. *Home:* 24 Brookside Cres., Cuffley, Potters Bar, Hertfordshire EN6 4QN, England. *Office:* Middlesex Polytechnic, Trent Park, Cockfosters, Barnet, Hertfordshire, England.

CAREER: Teacher in Australia, 1948-51, and England, 1952-57; National Foundation for Educational Research, Slough, England, research psychologist, 1958-65; University of Reading, Reading, England, part-time lecturer in education, 1965-73; Middlesex Polytechnic, Barnet, England, principal lecturer, 1973-78, reader in education, 1978—. Consultant to Centre for the Teaching of Reading, University of Reading, 1969—, Nelson/Young World (publishers), 1972-75, and British Broadcasting Corporation, 1976-80. *Member:* International Reading Association, British Psychological Society, British Educational Research Association, Society of Authors, American Educational Research Association.

WRITINGS: Reading in Infant Classes, National Foundation for Educational Research, 1966; *Teachers and Their*

Pupils' Home Background, National Foundation for Educational Research, 1968; *Home and School,* National Foundation for Educational Research, 1971; *Provision for Reading,* University of Reading, 1971; *Children and Learning to Read,* Routledge & Kegan Paul, 1971; *Pictures and Words,* Blackie & Son, 1971; (with Fred Schonell) *The Psychology and Teaching of Reading,* Oliver & Boyd, 1974; (editor with Allan Blackwood) *Beanstalk Books,* Young World Publications, 1974; *Reading Tests,* Macmillan, 1981; *Miscue Analysis: Informal Diagnosis,* Wheatons, 1982.

WORK IN PROGRESS: Research on speech segmentation and the teaching of reading.

SIDELIGHTS Elizabeth Goodacre commented: "As an Australian teaching in English schools, I became very interested in teachers' ways of classifying and describing pupils' home backgrounds. Most of my work is concerned with how children learn to read and write and the influences on their progress and attitudes to literacy. I have learned a lot about children's progress and the complexity of the reading process from my own three children, who are all very different!"

*　　*　　*

GOODE, William Josiah 1917-

PERSONAL: Born August 30, 1917, in Houston, Tex.; son of William J. and Lillian Rosalie (Bare) Goode; married Josephine Mary Cannizzo, December 22, 1938 (divorced, 1946); married Ruth Siegel, October 20, 1950 (divorced, 1971); children: (first marriage) Brian, Erich, Rachel (deceased), Barbara Nan; (second marriage) Andrew Josiah. *Education:* University of Texas, B.A., 1938, M.A., 1939; Pennsylvania State University, Ph.D., 1946. *Office:* Department of Sociology, Stanford University, 147 Herbert Hoover Memorial Bldg., Stanford, Calif. 94305.

CAREER: Pennsylvania State University, University Park, instructor in sociology, 1941-43; Inter-American Statistics Institute, Washington, D.C., analyst, 1943-44; Wayne State University, Detroit, Mich., assistant professor of sociology, 1946-50; Columbia University, New York, N.Y., associate director of research, 1950-52, associate professor, 1952-56, professor of sociology, 1956-77, Franklin H. Giddings Professor of Sociology, 1975-77; Stanford University, Stanford, Calif., professor of sociology, 1977—. Visiting professor at Free University of Berlin; visiting scholar at Centre for Sociolegal Studies, Wolfson College, Oxford, 1980; lecturer at colleges and universities. Member of behavioral sciences training committee of National Institutes of General Medical Sciences; member of board of governors and associate director of Bureau of Applied Social Research, 1956-70, and board of directors of Social Science Research Council, 1962-68; U.S. delegate to United Nations Educational, Scientific & Cultural Organization's international seminar on the family in Yugoslavia, 1960, Japan, 1965, and France, 1973, and to United Nations conference on the application of science and technology for the benefit of less developed areas, in Switzerland, 1961; consultant to Government of Peru. *Military service:* U.S. Naval Reserve, active duty as radar operator on attack transport vessel, 1945-46; served in Pacific theater.

MEMBER: National Academy of Arts and Sciences (fellow), Sociological Research Association (member of executive council; president, 1967—), American Sociological Association (member of executive committee and council, 1959-62; president, 1971-72), American Civil Liberties union, Eastern Sociological Society (president, 1959-60; member of execu-

tive committee, 1959-61). *Awards, honors:* Guggenheim fellow, 1965-66; MacIver Prize from American Sociological Association, 1965; Burgess Award from National Council on Family Relations, 1969; National Institute of Mental Health senior scientist award, 1969-74; D.Sci. from Upsala College, 1972.

WRITINGS: Religion Among the Primitives, Free Press, 1951; (with Paul K. Hatt) *Methods in Social Research,* McGraw, 1952; *After Divorce,* McGraw, 1956, reprinted as *Women in Divorce,* Free Press, 1965; *Die Struktur der Familie,* Westdeutscher Verlag, 1960; *World Revolution and Family Patterns,* Free Press, 1963; *The Family,* Prentice-Hall, 1964; (editor) *Readings on the Family and Society,* Prentice-Hall, 1964; (editor) *The Dynamics of Modern Society,* Atherton, 1966.

(With L. Mitchell and F. Fursterberg) *Willard Waller: On the Family, Education, and War,* University of Chicago Press, 1970; (with Elizabeth Hopkins and H. M. McClure) *Social Systems and Family Patterns: A Propositional Inventory,* Bobbs-Merrill, 1971; (editor with Cynthia Fuchs Epstein) *The Other Half,* Prentice-Hall, 1971; (editor with Nicholas Tavuchis) *The Family Through Literature,* Oxford University Press, 1973; *Explorations in Social Theory,* Oxford University Press, 1973; *Principles of Sociology,* McGraw, 1977; *The Celebration of Heroes,* University of California Press, 1978.

Contributor: Robert K. Merton, L. Broom, and L. S. Cottrell, editors, *Sociology Today,* Basic Books, 1959; *Trends in American Living and Outdoor Recreation,* U.S. Government Printing Office, 1962; Berthold F. Hoselitz and Wilbert E. Moore, editors, *Industrialization and Society,* United Nations Educational, Scientific & Cultural Organization, 1963; R. Bendix and S. M. Lipset, editors, *Class, Status, and Power,* revised edition (Goode was not included in 1st edition), Free Press, 1966; Mayer N. Zald, editor, *Community Welfare,* Quadrangle, 1967; Merton and R. A. Nisbet, editors, *Social Disorganization,* 3rd edition (Goode was not included in earlier editions), Harcourt, 1967; Moore and Elanor B. Sheldon, editors, *The Indicators of Social Change,* Russell Sage Foundation, 1968; Amitai Etzioni, editor, *The Semi-Professions and Their Organization,* Free Press, 1969; D. J. Mulvihill and M. Tumin, editors, *Crimes of Violence,* U.S. Government Printing Office, 1969; Reuben Hill and Rene Konig, editors, *Families in East and West,* Mouton, 1970; Jean Cuisenier, editor, *The Family Life Cycle in European Societies,* Mouton, 1977.

General editor of sociology series for Dryden, 1953. Contributor of about forty articles to academic journals, including *Annals of the American Academy of Political and Social Science.* Associate editor of *Marriage and Family Living.*

AVOCATIONAL INTERESTS: Tennis.

*　　*　　*

GOODMAN, Joseph Irving 1908-

PERSONAL: Born March 2, 1908, in Cleveland, Ohio; son of Max and Belle Goodman; married Louise Weil, February 19, 1938; children: Carol Goodman Hopkins, Andrew J. *Education:* Case Western Reserve University, M.D., 1932. *Home:* 2865 Manchester Rd., Shaker Heights, Ohio 44122. *Agent:* Wieser & Wieser, Inc., 60 East 42nd St., Room 902, New York, N.Y. 10017. *Office:* 2460 Fairmount Blvd., Cleveland Heights, Ohio 44106.

CAREER: Private practice of medicine in Cleveland Heights, Ohio; writer. *Military service:* U.S. Army, Medical

Corps, 1942-46; became major. *Member:* American College of Physicians (fellow), American Diabetes Association, Cleveland Diabetes Association (past president), Phi Beta Kappa, Alpha Omega Alpha. *Awards, honors:* Certificate of merit from U.S. Army for nutritional research.

WRITINGS: Diet and Live, World Publishing, 1962; *Diabetes Without Fear,* Arbor House, 1977. Also author of *Diabetic Neuropathics,* C. C. Thomas. Contributor to *Clinical Nutrition,* edited by Norman Joliffe, 1960. Contributor of about seventy-five articles to medical journals.

* * *

GOODMAN, Richard Merle 1932-

PERSONAL: Born July 31, 1932, in Cleveland, Ohio; son of Edwin and Florence (Grossman) Goodman; married Audrey Rosenberg, June 26, 1955; children: Jeff, Daniel, David. *Education:* University of Cincinnati, B.S., 1954; Ohio State University, M.D., 1958. *Home:* 22 A Hahagana St., Ramat Hasharon, Israel. *Office:* Sheba Medical Center, Tel Hashomer Government Hospital, Tel Hashomer, Israel.

CAREER: Cook County Hospital, Chicago, Ill., intern, 1958-59, resident in medicine, 1959-61; Johns Hopkins University, Baltimore, Md., fellow in medicine, 1961-64; Ohio State University, Columbus, assistant professor of medicine and head of medical genetics, 1964-69; Tel Aviv University, Tel Aviv, Israel, professor of human genetics at Sheba Medical Center, 1970—. *Member:* Israel Exploration Society. *Awards, honors:* Batsheva de Rothschild Award from Rothschild Foundation, 1970.

WRITINGS: (With Robert J. Gorlin) *The Face in Genetic Disorders,* Mosby, 1970, 2nd edition published as *Atlas of the Face in Genetic Disorders,* 1977; (editor) *Genetic Disorders of Man,* Little, Brown, 1970; *Genetic Disorders Among the Jewish People,* Johns Hopkins Press, 1979; (editor with Arnold G. Motulsky) *Genetic Disorders Among Ashkenazi Jews,* Raven Press, 1979. Contributor to medical journals.

WORK IN PROGRESS: The Illustrated Pocketbook of Genetic and Congenital Human Malformations, with Robert J. Gorlin.

SIDELIGHTS: Goodman told *CA:* "In order for man to maintain a proper perspective on man he must know what he does not know." *Avocational interests:* Israel archaeology, poetry.

* * *

GORDON, Alan F. 1947-

PERSONAL: Born December 30, 1947, in Biddeford, Me.; son of Benjamin M. and Sara (Israelson) Gordon; married Betty L. Rockman (a nurse), December 29, 1972. *Education:* Dartmouth College, A.B., 1969. *Religion:* Jewish.

CAREER/WRITINGS: Patriot Ledger, Quincy Mass., reporter, 1969-71, associate editor of editorial page and author of weekly column, 1971-75; *Congressional Quarterly,* Washington, D.C., reporter, 1975-76; free-lance writer, Washington, D.C., 1976—; press secretary to U.S. Representative Joseph S. Ammerman (Democrat from Pennsylvania), 1977. American Political Science Association Congressional fellow, 1974-75. Contributor of articles to newspapers and periodicals, including *Washington Post, Los Angeles Times,* and *Nation. Member:* Washington Independent Writers.

SIDELIGHTS: Gordon told *CA:* "I specialize in writing about politics and government, especially Congress, but I have also written about energy, science, economics, social

welfare policies, law, environment, and other social issues. I have visited and written about Canada and the United Kingdom."

* * *

GORDON, Barry (Lewis John) 1934-

PERSONAL: Born February 16, 1934, in Sydney, Australia; son of Allan Lewis (a wool classer) and May (in retailing; maiden name, Brown) Gordon; married Moira Gallagher (a regional economist), May 19, 1956; children: Clare, Allan, Justin, Mark, Hugh, Ian, Ruth, Frances. *Education:* University of Sydney, M.Ec., 1958; University of Newcastle, Ph.D., 1968. *Politics:* "Apolitical." *Religion:* Roman Catholic. *Home:* 28 Helen St., Merewether, New South Wales 2291, Australia. *Office:* Department of Economics, University of Newcastle, Newcastle, New South Wales, 2308, Australia.

CAREER: University of Newcastle, Newcastle, Australia, lecturer, 1956-66, senior lecturer, 1966-68, associate professor of economics, 1968—, chairman of economics departmental board, 1974, chairman of industrial relations studies, 1976-78, editor of research publications series in economics, 1974-78, 1980—. Visiting lecturer at Massachusetts Institute of Technology and research associate at Harvard University, both 1965-66; academic visitor at London School of Economics and Political Science, London, 1972-73; visiting fellow at Magdalen College, Oxford, 1979. Director of Datex Research Cooperative, 1976—. *Military service:* Royal Australian Air Force, 1953-54. *Member:* History of Economics Society, Industrial Relations Society.

WRITINGS: Non-Ricardian Political Economy, Kress Library, Harvard University, 1967; (editor with Kevin Lindgren and Edward Mason) *The Corporation in Australian Society,* Law Book Co. (Sydney, Australia), 1974; *Economic Analysis Before Adam Smith: Hesiod to Lessius,* Barnes & Noble, 1975; *Political Economy in Parliament, 1819-1823,* Barnes & Noble, 1976; *Economic Doctrine and Tory Liberalism, 1824-1830,* Macmillan, 1979; *The Economic Problem in Biblical Thought,* Macmillan, 1982.

SIDELIGHTS: When asked about his motivation and viewpoint, Gordon responded with a quotation from *Syriac Baruch:* "'Long ago when the world with its inhabitants was not yet in existence, You conceived the thought, and commanded with a word, and at once the works of creation stood before You. You said you would make for Your world man an administrator of Your works, that it might be known that he was not made for the sake of the world, but the world for his sake.'"

AVOCATIONAL INTERESTS: "Be-bop, death and redemption, rugby, Stravinsky, Britten."

* * *

GORDON, Mary (Catherine) 1949-

PERSONAL: Born December 8, 1949, in Long Island, N.Y.; daughter of David (a writer and publisher) and Anna (a legal secretary; maiden name, Gagliano) Gordon; married James Brian (an anthropologist), 1974 (marriage ended); married Arthur Cash (a professor of English), 1979; children: Anna Gordon Cash. *Education:* Barnard College, B.A., 1971; Syracuse University, M.A., 1973. *Religion:* Catholic. *Residence:* Poughkeepsie, N.Y. *Agent:* Peter Matson, 32 West 40th St., New York, N.Y. 10023.

CAREER: Dutchess Community College, Poughkeepsie, N.Y., teacher of English, 1974-78; Amherst College, Amherst, Mass., teacher of English, 1979. Novelist and author of short stories.

WRITINGS—Novels: *Final Payments* (Literary Guild selection), Random House, 1978; *The Company of Women,* Random House, 1981.

Short stories: "Now I Am Married," published in *Virginia Quarterly Review,* summer, 1975; "The Other Woman," published in *Redbook,* August, 1976; "The Thorn," published in *Ms.,* January, 1977; "Sisters," published in *Ladies' Home Journal,* July, 1977; "A Serious Person," published in *Redbook,* August, 1977; "Kindness," published in *Mademoiselle,* October, 1977; "The Writing Lesson," published in *Mademoiselle,* April, 1978; "Delia," published in *Atlantic,* June, 1978; "More Catholic Than the Pope: Archbishop Lefebre and the Rome of the One True Church," published in *Harper's,* July, 1978.

SIDELIGHTS: Mary Gordon has made a name for herself after only two novels, *Final Payments* and *The Company of Women.* By showing some adept use of language and a willingness to probe unfashionable themes, she has already been acclaimed "one of the most gifted writers of her generation."

Final Payments is the story of Isabel Moore, a woman of thirty who is about to leave home for the first time. For eleven years she has nursed her domineering and devoutly Catholic father through a series of strokes, and upon his death she sets out to live a life of her own. Isabel finds a social service job, develops friendships, and involves herself with married men, but eventually feels remorse for her "self-indulgence." To atone for her presumptuousness, she steps back into the caretaker's role, devoting herself to a woman she despises, Margaret Casey, her father's former housekeeper. Finally, Isabel is saved from self-torment by an alcoholic priest.

Critics found Gordon's treatment of the theme of sacrifice both surprising and compelling. "All of a sudden," said Nan Robertson, "this first novel . . . has surged up out of the 'me generation' of self-absorbed, navel-contemplating, dropout American children, and has knocked the critics for a loop." Certain paradoxes, however, surround Isabel's life of devotion. To Wilfred Sheed, the book was "about such matters as the *arrogance* of loving the unlovable, and the resourcefulness of the latter in breaking their saviors." Doris Grumbach saw Isabel "caught in a web of Christian virtues: the need for sacrifice, the desirability of celibacy." Altogether, said Sheed, *Final Payments* "gives a picture of certain Catholic lives . . . more ambiguous than anything either a loyalist or a heretic would have had a mind to produce a few years ago."

One unambiguous aspect of the novel, critics seem to agree, is Gordon's strength as a writer. "From the opening rites of burial," remarked Martha Duffy, "the reader relaxes, secure in the hands of a confident writer." *Sewanee Review* critic Bruce Allen praised "Gordon's spectacular verbal skill [which] allows her heroine to express complex emotional and intellectual attitudes with great precision." And Pearl K. Bell contended that "it is no small thing, at twenty-nine, to write with Mary Gordon's phenomenal assurance and metaphoric authority."

Comparisons have already been made between Gordon and other masters of fiction. Critics Sheed and John Leonard both cited similarities between Gordon and Jane Austen. "It is no accident that her model is Austen, the patron writer of the cloistered," noted Sheed. Leonard, meanwhile, added that Gordon is "as good on friendship as Jane Austen."

Washington Post reviewer Edmund White paid further tribute to Gordon when he said, "It is the most intelligent and convincing first novel I have read in years, one that combines the high moral seriousness of Doris Lessing and the stylistic elegance of Flannery O'Connor."

Along with the abundance of praise for *Final Payments* has come some criticism. Isabel's "sojourn in the big world is a lot less interesting than her bondage," said Maureen Howard, and her ensuing "lightning conversion" to caring for the despised Margaret Casey has been called unconvincing. Others have objected to the book's "forced" cleverness and its "too schematic" plot. James F. Rawley and Robert F. Moss, too, had doubts about the story line, but still labeled the book "a sturdy hybrid: a relatively trashy plot, marked by contrivance and sensationalism, but handled with the tools of high art, specifically a technical sophistication and an allusive, savagely ironic tone."

In her second novel, *The Company of Women,* Gordon tells the story of Felicitas Taylor and the circle of Catholic women around her: Felicitas's widowed mother, two spinsters, and two women who have lost their husbands to alcohol and an asylum. At the center of their lives is a "fiercely conservative" priest, Father Cyprian, who has abandoned parish work because "he detests the permissiveness of the contemporary church." Similar in many ways to *Final Payments, The Company of Women* has reinforced Gordon's reputation as a penetrating writer of Catholic life. "If there was any doubt that Mary Gordon was her generation's preeminent novelist of Roman Catholic mores and manners when she published her remarkable first novel," contended Francine du Plessix Gray of the *New York Times Book Review,* "it is dispelled by her new book."

As the novel opens, the worldly hope for the circle of women is Felicitas, an exceptionally bright girl of fourteen. Her mother "could see Felicitas only among elders, the child in the temple, amazing the scribes with learning," writes Gordon. The story moves on in part two to cover Felicitas's life after she leaves a Catholic college to attend Columbia University. There, according to du Plessix Gray, Felicitas "rebels against the idols of her childhood. . . . [and] shacks up with a trendy, philandering Columbia professor and lets her classical studies fall by the wayside." She becomes pregnant, returns to the company of women, and, as *Time*'s R. Z. Sheppard pointed out, "pursues a career in ordinariness with a grudging acceptance." Seven years later, seeking a father for her child, Felicitas marries a hardware store owner. The women, meanwhile, see in Felicitas's daughter their hope for the future.

A question raised by du Plessix Gray is typical of the response to *The Company of Women:* "Is Miss Gordon's craft as a novelist keeping up with the grand and virginal boldness of her vision?" Du Plessix Gray cited Gordon's "problems creating fully fleshed, noncelibate male characters"; she complained about "frequent lapses into solemnity and self-righteousness"; she argued that Gordon's prose "in this novel is as prodigiously uneven as are her characterizations." But, du Plessix Gray continued, "If I've been harsh with 'The Company of Women' it is because of my enormous admiration for Miss Gordon's earlier book, for the purity, ambition and grandeur of vision offered in both her books."

Christopher Lehmann-Haupt, too, had reservations about some of Gordon's prose, but the *New York Times* critic felt that the clearness of Gordon's insight made her second novel a significant achievement. "The problem is simply that the new novel is technically more ambitious than the earlier one,'' thought Lehmann-Haupt. ''For in telling her story from at least seven different points of view, Miss Gordon is trying to achieve a narrative far more complex and modulated than she did in 'Final Payments.''' Lehmann-Haupt concluded by saying, '''The Company of Women,' for all its intelligence and moral insight, remains a disappointment. Next to the incandescence of 'Final Payments,' it merely glows.''

AVOCATIONAL INTERESTS: Theology, musical comedy.

CA INTERVIEW
CA interviewed Mary Gordon on May 29, 1980, in New York City.

Mary Gordon doesn't compose her fiction at a typewriter; she writes it out longhand, in bound notebooks from England with narrow rules. ''I have a fetish about my writing tools,'' she says. ''I cannot work without those notebooks and my special fine-point, felt-tipped pens.'' She approaches her writing as if it were more important and compelling than anything else; and, in fact, it is—''ever since I could hold a pencil.''

Gordon is first, and perhaps ultimately, a poet, though she has never published her poetry and has no impulse to do so. This she attributes to laziness. Yet there is nothing lackadaisical about her writing. ''Electric prose'' is how *New York Times* critic John Leonard described her use of language in her first novel, *Final Payments.*

Gordon is considered an intellectual writer by some, yet she feels she is not clever enough. ''It never occurs to me, for example, to use flashback as a matter of course. I'm on the level of the village taleteller for the first couple of drafts.... I'm like a little ox in terms of narrative.''

She is careful to point out that her first published novel was preceded by years of devotion to language in other forms. In addition to short stories published in a number of journals and magazines, her many years of writing poetry have given her a sensitivity to the rhythm of language, to pacing, and to how words sound. ''Perhaps more than anything else, poetry has given me a sense of metaphor as being centrally important,'' she says. ''Metaphor and simile do some of the work of explanation in a more efficient and profound way than other narrative techniques,'' she explains. ''I include them when something needs to be made more concrete, more physical.''

Some examples: ''The smell of sickness and medication still hung in the air like smoke in a barroom''; ''Her feet were flat as a fish, except where the bunions developed like small crops of winter onions''; ''The valley spread out from the kitchen like a lap.''

Many of the metaphors and similes come, she says, in the revising. *Final Payments* had two endings and went through three drafts before completion. Initially, she wrote in the third person to guard against a prejudice she says she picked up in graduate school, a notion that women write too personally and don't have a sense of detachment. ''This,'' she says, ''is pure nonsense.'' On the advice of writer Elizabeth Hardwick, her professor at Barnard College at the time, she switched to the first person in the final draft. In addition to this advice, Hardwick instilled into her student a ''terrific sense of what is interesting and worthwhile, and what is frivolous.''

This quality Gordon considers her own strong point: ''I don't think I write about things that are trivial. I had a fortu-

nate background in that I was exposed in a real sense to the 'complicatedness' of peoples' lives. On the other hand, the working-class people around me in my Long Island community led seemingly straightforward lives, yet they had a rich inner religious life,'' she says. ''It taught me to look a little below the surface.''

Religion, the Catholic religion in particular, is as surely a part of her fiction as of her background. Raised in a devoutly Catholic home (her father converted from Judaism), Gordon was immersed in church tenets as a child, only to rebel as a teenager and then come home again as an adult. ''Though certain realities of the church—such as its refusal to ordain women—appall me, it is a caretaker of a kind of spirituality that matters a lot to me,'' she explains.

Even as *Final Payments* dealt with the Catholic themes of devotion, piety, and the nature of goodness, so her second novel, *The Company of Women,* has as a pivotal character a priest. ''I'm fascinated by priests,'' she admits. ''They seem to have a hidden magical potency that is powerful, because it is both sexually inaccessible and directly connected to spiritual ritual and the mystical.''

With a priest as the primary male voice, the novel revolves around the lives of seven major women characters and the nature of their relationship to the priest and to other men. Gordon reveals a fascination with that paradoxical reality of the feminist era—''an age-old problem, really''—of independent and capable women who willingly give up the authority for their own inner lives to the men around them.

''It was a more demanding book in terms of craftsmanlike challenge than *Final Payments,* primarily in the juggling of several characters over a period of fourteen years,'' she explains. ''Most challenging was pinpointing the ticks of speech and peculiar mannerisms that distinguished the characters from each other and revealed their definite ways of looking at the world.''

In other authors, Gordon looks for a ''richness and generosity mixed with a real control of language.'' She is particularly drawn to Virginia Woolf, Jane Austen, and Ford Maddox Ford, because they have ''a depth of understanding of their characters combined with a poetic use of language.'' One special writer for her is Frenchman Georges Bernanos, author of her favorite book, *Diary of a Country Priest.*

BIOGRAPHICAL/CRITICAL SOURCES: Mary Gordon, *Final Payments,* Random House, 1978; *Saturday Review,* March 4, 1978; *New York Times,* April 4, 1978, May 31, 1978, February 13, 1981; *Washington Post Book World,* April 9, 1978, February 22, 1981; *Newsweek,* April 10, 1978, February 16, 1981; *New York Times Book Review,* April 16, 1978, February 15, 1981; *Time,* April 24, 1978, February 16, 1981; *New York Review of Books,* June 1, 1978; *Times Literary Supplement,* September 1, 1978; *Commentary,* September, 1978; *Sewanee Review,* fall, 1978; *Commonweal,* October 27, 1978; *Spectator,* January 13, 1979; *Feature,* March, 1979; *Contemporary Literary Criticism,* Volume 13, Gale, 1980; *Dictionary of Literary Biography,* Volume VI: *American Novelists Since World War II,* second series, Gale, 1980; *Publishers Weekly,* February 6, 1981; *Chicago Tribune Book World,* February 22, 1981; *Detroit News,* March 15, 1981.

—*Sketch by David Versical*
—*Interview by Trisha Gorman*

*   *   *

GORDY, Berry, Sr. 1888-1978

PERSONAL: Born July 10, 1888, in Oconee, Ga.; died November 21, 1978; son of Berry (a farmer) and Lucy (Hellum) Gordy; married Bertha Ida Fuller, January 18, 1918 (deceased); children: Fuller, Esther Gordy Edwards, Anna, Loucye, George, Berry, Jr., Robert, Gwendolyn. *Education:* Attended high school in Sandersville, Ga. *Politics:* Democrat. *Religion:* Protestant. *Office:* c/o E. G. Edwards, 2648 West Grand Blvd., Detroit, Mich., 48208.

CAREER: Berry Gordy Plastering, Detroit, Mich., contractor, 1940-65. Consultant to Motown Records Corp., 1965-78. *Military service:* U.S. Army, served in World War I.

WRITINGS: Movin' Up: Pop Gordy Tells His Story (young adult), Harper, 1979.

SIDELIGHTS: The father of Motown executive Berry Gordy, Jr., the elder Gordy told his own success story in *Movin' Up.* Inspired by the thriftiness his father, a former slave, exhibited, Gordy saved enough money to bring himself and his family north to Detroit. There his children learned the lessons of industriousness and sound money management by running a grocery store while Gordy prospered as an independent plaster and carpentry contractor.

Gordy's reminiscences, taped just before his death at the age of ninety, reveal his ability to turn adversity to his own advantage. He lived, said Mary Helen Washington, in a world "where just circumventing all the roadblocks set up for the poor and the black could consume all his energy." One such roadblock was constructed by a real estate agent who duped Gordy into buying a condemned house. Without paying the mortgage, Gordy managed to live in that house until evicted and, in the meantime, saved enough money to make a down payment on a different home.

According to Washington, "there is more than a little of the old bootstrap mentality" in *Movin' Up.* "The Gordys are able to do for themselves 'the same as white folks do' without depending on anybody to do special favors for them." But, Washington added, "the best story in this memoir is not about 'movin' up' at all; it is the story of Gordy's relationship with his stiff, authoritarian father and his deep sense of loss over his father's sudden death."

BIOGRAPHICAL/CRITICAL SOURCES: Washington Post Book World, January 13, 1980; *Kirkus Reviews,* February 1, 1980.

[Information provided by daughter Esther G. Edwards]

*   *   *

GOREAU, Angeline 1951-

PERSONAL: Surname is pronounced "Go-row"; born September 12, 1951, in Wilmington, Del.; daughter of Theodore Nelson (a businessman) and Eloise (a professor; maiden name, Keaton) Goreau. *Education:* Attended Princeton University, 1968-69; Barnard College, B.A., 1973. *Home:* 463 West St., No. 401, New York, N.Y. 10014; and 146 Nassau St., Princeton, N.J. 08540. *Agent:* Berenice Hoffman, 215 West 75th St., No. 16A, New York, N.Y. 10023.

CAREER: Worked as a literary agent, 1973-75; writer, 1974—. Consultant to Currier Fund, Paris, France, 1978-80. *Member:* Authors Guild. *Awards, honors:* National Endowment for the Humanities research grant, 1976-77; fellowship for Ossabaw Island project, 1980.

WRITINGS: Reconstructing Aphra: A Social Biography of Aphra Behn, Dial, 1980; *The Whole Duty of a Woman: The Roots of Feminism,* Dial, 1981. Contributor to journals, including *Communications.*

WORK IN PROGRESS: A novel; a biography.

SIDELIGHTS: Critics were impressed with *Reconstructing Aphra,* a "social biography" of the first female writer to earn her living by her craft. Dwelling in England during the Restoration, Aphra Behn's life was unconventional. She traveled to Surinam as a young woman, spied for Charles II during the second Anglo Dutch War, and spent some time in a debtors prison. When she began writing plays and books under her own name, Behn's contemporaries, men and women alike, were scandalized. Marcy Moran Heidish of the *Washington Star* complimented Goreau for bringing "color to this intricate life" and delineating "the era that in part determined its aspects." Heidish also noted that Goreau "shows us the process of rediscovering a lost historical figure; her technique seems almost archeological, as if she were lifting Behn, fragment by fragment, from the rock." *Newsweek's* Jean Strouse described *Reconstructing Aphra* as "a useful and impressive piece of work," while Julia Epstein of the *Manchester Guardian* called it "a well written and riveting book, one which firmly places the myth of the 'lewd widow' Aphra Behn within the history of feminist struggle and the history of literary women."

Goreau told *CA:* "My first book, *Reconstructing Aphra: A Social Biography of Aphra Behn,* attempts to come to terms with the experience of the first Englishwoman to make a living as a writer, the first to take a place among equals in the jealous literary world of Restoration England. I was initially attracted to Aphra Behn because her life resisted writing: settled firmly into obscurity for more than two hundred years, Mrs. Behn's history has grown into a shambles of contradiction and mystery. Describing her experience forced me to expand my idea of what biography might encompass; in the end I wrote a kind of archaeology of the passed-over, a reconstruction of the material possibilities, symbolic structures, and mentalities that determined the lives of women in Aphra Behn's time. *Reconstructing Aphra* is in this sense a 'social' biography.

"Out of my work on Behn, three years' research in the British Museum and a year's writing in Paris, grew a second book, *The Whole Duty of a Woman: The Roots of Feminism.* It discusses the evolution of the debate over women in cyclical rather than linear terms and attempts to describe the manner in which ideas about 'the feminine sphere' exercised influence over early women writers. The complex interaction between concrete and abstract censorship is also studied.

"I have, in addition to my work in biography and theory, been working on a novel for some time. It traces the history of an American family from mid-seventeenth-century Virginia to the present. I feel it is very necessary to write both fiction and nonfiction at the same time, I suppose because it allows me to grapple with the questions that preoccupy me from every possible angle."

BIOGRAPHICAL/CRITICAL SOURCES: Washington Star, July 27, 1980; *Washington Post,* August 3, 1980; *Newsweek,* August 11, 1980; *Boston Globe,* August 17, 1980; *Manchester Guardian,* August 24, 1980; *New York Times,* November 9, 1980.

*   *   *

GOULD, Ronald 1904-

PERSONAL: Born October 10, 1904, in Midsomer Norton, England; son of Frederick (a shoemaker and member of Parliament) and Emma (Gay) Gould; married Nellie Denning Fish, December 26, 1929 (deceased); children: Terence, Derek. *Education:* Attended training college in Westminster,

England. *Politics:* "Attached to no party." *Religion:* Methodist. *Home:* 12 St. John's Ave., Goring by Sea, Worthing, Sussex BN12 4HU, England.

CAREER: Teacher in England, 1924-40, head master, 1940-46; general secretary of National Union of Teachers, England, 1946-70; deputy chairman of Independent Television Authority, England, 1967-72; writer, 1972—. Chairman of Norton Radstock Urban League, 1935-45, and Central Bureau of Education Visits and Exchanges, 1946-70. Justice of the peace, 1935-45. *Member:* World Confederation of the Organizations of the Teaching Profession (president, 1952-70). *Awards, honors:* Fellow of Education Institute of Scotland, 1955; knight bachelor, 1955; LL.D. from University of British Columbia, 1962, McGill University, 1964, St. Francis Xavier University, 1969, and University of Leeds, 1971; officer of Ordre des palmes academiques, 1970; D.Univ. from University of York, 1972; Das Verdienstkreuz 1 Klasse, 1979.

WRITINGS: The Changing Pattern of Education, Epworth Press, 1965; *Chalk up the Memory,* G. Philip, 1976. Also author of *Linking Home and School* (with others), 1967; *World Trends in Education* (with others), 1967; *Looking Forward to the Seventies* (with others), 1968; and *The Education of Teachers in Britain* (with Donald Lomax, Brian Holmes, and others), 1973. Contributor to education journals and newspapers.

SIDELIGHTS: Sir Ronald wrote: "I came from a poor home, in material terms, but rich in every other way. My father left school at twelve, but he educated himself with the aid of his own extensive library. No one ever said I would make a successful career; it was simply assumed. For such success as has come my way I am indebted to loving, wise parents and later a devoted wife. Perhaps, too, because my father always acted as if religion should premeate all aspects of life, I have somewhat inadequately followed his example."

*   *   *

GOULDNER, Alvin W(ard)   1920-1980

OBITUARY NOTICE—See index for *CA* sketch: Born July 29, 1920, in New York, N.Y.; died of a heart attack, December 15, 1980, in Madrid, Spain. Educator, sociologist, editor, and author. Gouldner taught at Washington University as the Max Weber Research Professor of Sociology. He promoted the controversial theory that held objective sociological studies in contempt as efforts to maintain social inequality and escape moral obligations. Gouldner argued that sociologists should attempt to alleviate such injustices. The author founded and edited two journals, *Trans-Action* and *Theory and Society.* Gouldner also wrote several books, including *The Coming Crises of Western Sociology, Patterns of Industrial Bureaucracy,* and *For Sociology: Renewal and Critique in Sociology Today.* Obituaries and other sources: *New York Times,* January 10, 1981.

*   *   *

GRAHAM, Don   1940-

PERSONAL: Born January 30, 1940, in Lucas, Tex.; son of Willie (a merchant) and Joyce (a clerk; maiden name, Ballew) Graham; married Lois Volpone (an educator), May 10, 1980. *Education:* North Texas State University, B.A., 1962, M.A., 1964; University of Texas, Ph.D., 1971. *Office:* Department of English, University of Texas, Austin, Tex. 78704.

CAREER: Southwest Texas State University, San Marcos, instructor in English, 1965-69; University of Pennsylvania, Philadelphia, assistant professor of English, 1971-76; University of Texas, Austin, associate professor of English, 1976—. *Member:* Western American Literature Association.

WRITINGS: The Fiction of Frank Norris: The Aesthetic Context, University of Missouri Press, 1978; (editor with Will T. Pilkington) *Western Movies,* University of New Mexico Press, 1979; (editor) *Critical Essays on Frank Norris,* G. K. Hall, 1980.

WORK IN PROGRESS: A critical study of Texas fiction, completion expected in 1983.

*   *   *

GRAHAM, Gerald (Sandford)   1903-

PERSONAL: Born April 27, 1903, in Sudbury, Ontario, Canada; son of Henry Sandford (a minister) and Florence Marion Graham; married Winnifred Emily Ware, 1929 (marriage ended); married Constance Mary Greey, 1950; children: (first marriage) John Ware; (second marriage) James Robert Gerald, Laura Elizabeth, Constance Mary. *Education:* Queen's University, Kingston, Ontario, M.A., 1925; attended Harvard University, 1926-27; Trinity College, Cambridge, Ph.D., 1929; postdoctoral study at University of Freiburg and University of Berlin, 1929-30. *Religion:* Protestant. *Home:* Hobbs Cottage, Beckley, Rye, Sussex, England.

CAREER: Harvard University, Cambridge, Mass., instructor in history, 1930-36; Queen's University, Kingston, Ontario, assistant professor, 1936-42, associate professor, 1942-46, professor of history, 1946; University of London, London, England, reader in history at Birkbeck College, 1946-48, Rhodes Professor of Imperial History, 1949-70, professor emeritus, 1970—. Member of Institute for Advanced Study, Princeton, N.J., 1952. Kemper Knapp Visiting Professor at University of Wisconsin, Madison, 1962; visiting professor at University of Hong Kong, 1966, and University of Western Ontario, 1970-72; Montague Burton Visiting Professor of International Relations at University of Edinburgh, 1974. *Military service:* Royal Canadian Naval Volunteer Reserve, active duty, 1942-45.

MEMBER: Royal Historical Society (fellow), Athenaeum Club, Royal Commonwealth Society. *Awards, honors:* Queen's fellow at Harvard University, 1926-27; Rockefeller Foundation fellow in Germany, 1929-30; Guggenheim fellow, 1941; D.Litt. from University of Waterloo, 1973; LL.D. from Queen's University, Kingston, Ontario, 1976.

WRITINGS: British Policy and Canada, 1774-1791: A Study in Eighteenth-Century Trade Policy, Longmans, Green, 1930, reprinted, Greenwood Press, 1974; *Sea Power and British North America, 1783-1820: A Study in British Colonial Policy,* Harvard University Press, 1941, reprinted, Greenwood Press, 1969; (contributor) R. A. MacKay, editor, *Newfoundland: Economic, Diplomatic, and Strategic Studies,* Oxford University Press, 1946; *Empire of the North Atlantic: The Maritime Struggle for North America,* University of Toronto Press, 1950, 2nd edition, 1958; *Canada: A Short History,* Hutchinson, 1950; (editor and author of introduction) *The Walker Expedition to Quebec, 1711,* Champlain Society, 1953.

(Editor with Robert Arthur Humphreys) *The Navy and South America, 1807-1823: Correspondence of the Commanders-in-Chief on the South American Station,* Navy Records Society, 1962; *The Politics of Naval Supremacy:*

Studies in British Maritime Ascendancy, Cambridge University Press, 1965; *Bilan du monde en 1815: Rapport* (title means "The British Empire in Relation to the European Balance of Power at the End of the Napoleanic Wars"), Editions du Centre national de la recherche scientifique, 1966; *Great Britain in the Indian Ocean: A Study of Maritime Enterprise, 1810-1850*, Clarendon Press, 1967; *A Concise History of Canada*, Viking, 1968; *A Concise History of the British Empire*, Thames & Hudson, 1970, Viking, 1971; (editor, and author of introduction) *The Hamlyn History of the World in Colour*, Volume XII: *New Worlds to Conquer*, Hamlyn, 1971; *Tides of Empire: Discursions on the Expansion of Britain Overseas*, McGill-Queen's University Press, 1972; *The China Station: War and Diplomacy, 1830-1860*, Oxford University Press, 1978.

Editor of "Imperial Studies Series," Royal Commonwealth Society, 1958-70; general editor of "West Africa History Series," Oxford University Press, 1956-70. Contributor to *Cambridge History of the British Empire*. Contributor to history journals.

WORK IN PROGRESS: A memoir.

BIOGRAPHICAL/CRITICAL SOURCES: Times Literary Supplement, May 9, 1968; John E. Flint and Glyndwr Williams, editors, *Perspectives of Empire: Essays Presented to Gerald S. Graham*, Barnes & Noble, 1973; *Pacific Affairs*, autumn, 1979; *American Historical Review*, October, 1979.

*   *   *

GRAHAM, Ruth
See EVANS, Jean

*   *   *

GRANADOS, Paul
See KENT, Arthur William Charles

*   *   *

GRANT, Gordon   1875-1962

PERSONAL: Born June 7, 1875, in San Francisco, Calif.; died May 6, 1962; son of George (a bank officer) and Grace Adelaide (Griffin) Grant; married Violet Maude Goodall (an actress), February 19, 1901. *Education:* Attended Heatherly and Lambeth Art Schools, London, England. *Politics:* Republican. *Religion:* Presbyterian. *Residence:* New York, N.Y.

CAREER: Artist. *San Francisco Examiner*, San Francisco, Calif., staff artist, 1895; *New York World*, New York, N.Y., staff artist, 1896; artist on Boer War front for *Harper's Weekly;* staff artist for *Puck*, 1901-09. Work exhibited in permanent collections at the Metropolitan Museum of Art, the White House, and numerous other museums and public buildings. *Military service:* U.S. National Guard, until 1918; became captain. *Member:* American Society of Graphic Artists, American Watercolor Society, National Academy of Design, National Arts Club, Allied Artists of America, Chicago Society of Etchers, Audubon Artists, Ship Model Society (founder and former president), Salmagundi (life member), Dutch Treat, Amateur Comedy (life member). *Awards, honors:* Ranger Purchase Award from National Academy of Design; Chauncey F. Ryder Prize from American Watercolor Society; Shaw Prize from Salmagundi, 1931 and 1936; award from Chicago Society of Etchers, 1936; Silver Medal for Etching from Paris Exposition, 1937; Anonymous Members' Prize from Allied Artists of America, 1943; United States Honor Certificate granted by President John F. Kennedy.

WRITINGS—Self-illustrated: The Story of the Ship, McLaughlin, 1919; *Sail Ho!*, Payson, 1931; *Greasy Luck: A Whaling Sketch Book*, Payson, 1932, reprinted, Caravan Maritime Books, 1970; (with Harold Platt) *Ship Ahoy!*, Doubleday, 1934; *New Story of the Ship*, McLaughlin, 1936; *The Secret Voyage*, Morrow, 1942; *Sketchbook*, Watson-Guptill, 1960; *Wilderness* (poems), Noel Young, 1965; *Journey* (poems), Capricorn, 1969.

Illustrator: Willis J. Abbot, *Panama and the Canal in Picture and Prose*, Syndicate Publishing, 1913; Henry Brundage Culver, *The Book of Old Ships*, Doubleday, 1924; Booth Tarkington, *Penrod: His Complete Story*, Doubleday, 1931; Culver, *Forty Famous Ships*, Doubleday, 1936; Wilbert Snow, *Before the Wind* (poem), Gotham House, 1938; Arthur H. Baldwin, *Sou'wester Victorious*, Random House, 1939; Robert Carse, *There Go the Ships*, Morrow, 1942; Alexander Kinnan Laing, *Sea Witch*, Farrar, Straus, 1944; William Martin Williamson, editor, *The Eternal Sea: An Anthology of Sea Poetry*, Coward, 1946; Bruce Grant, *Eagle of the Sea*, Rand McNally, 1949; Herman Wouk, *The City Boy*, Doubleday, 1952; Leonard Outhwaite, *Unrolling the Map: The Story of Exploration*, John Day, 1972.

SIDELIGHTS: Gordon Grant, noted painter of ships and the sea, was born of Scottish parentage in the port city of San Francisco. Grant's father, an officer with Wells Fargo Nevada National Bank, decided that his son should be educated in Scotland, and it was during his four-and-one-half-month passage aboard a Glasgow sailing ship that images of the sea became firmly implanted in young Grant's imagination. His illustrations, then, grew out of continuous observation of the nautical world.

After receiving his early education at Kirkcaldy School in Tifeshire, Scotland, Grant studied art in London. He began his career by returning to San Francisco, where he spent one year as staff artist for the *Examiner*. After working for several other publications and after serving in the military the artist took up painting and etching as a full-time career.

Grant's pictures of ships, harbors, and the sea proved to be immensely popular with the public and critics as well. He gained respect not only for his artistic merit, but also for his technical knowledge. Much of the appeal of Grant's paintings lies in the mysterious quality that his use of lighting and shadow evoked.

Grant's depictions of ships were regarded as so accurate that he was commissioned by Congress to do the official portrait of the U.S.S. *Constitution*. The original painting of "Old Ironsides" now hangs in the President's office, and over a quarter of a million prints were sold to finance the restoration of the ship.

Grant's work began to be exhibited yearly at New York's Grand Central Gallery in 1928. His pictures have since become part of collections in major museums and galleries throughout the country. His painting "Eternal Sea," the focal point of the Chapel of the Seaman's Church Institute in New York, is one of his better-known works.

Model shipbuilding and amateur theatre were among Grant's avocational interests. In addition to acting and writing for the theatre, he designed props and sets.

BIOGRAPHICAL/CRITICAL SOURCES: St. Nicholas, October, 1934; *Design*, September 11, 1953; *American Artist*, September, 1960.

OBITUARIES: New York Times, May 8, 1962; *American Annual*, 1963.*

GRAVES, Eleanor MacKenzie   1926-

PERSONAL: Born in 1926 in New York, N.Y.; daughter of Luther Burns (a physician) and Rena (Glogaw) MacKenzie; married William W. Parish, 1949 (marriage ended); married Ralph Graves, 1958; children: William W. Parish, Jr., Alexander M. Parish, Sara E., Andrew D. *Education:* Barnard College, B.A. (cum laude), 1948. *Home:* 1158 Fifth Ave., New York, N.Y. 10029. *Office: Life,* 1271 Sixth Ave., New York, N.Y. 10021.

CAREER: Life, New York, N.Y., worked as assistant fashion editor and modern living editor, became senior editor, 1968. *Member:* American Society of Interior Designers (press associate), Women in Communications, Fashion Group, Phi Beta Kappa.

WRITINGS: Great Dinners From Life, Time-Life, 1969; *Best of Everything Cookbook,* Chicago Tribune Syndicate, 1970; (editor) *Life Goes to War,* Little, Brown, 1977. Also editor of a twenty-two volume series based on the television series, "Wild, Wild World of Animals," Time-Life, 1976.

*   *   *

GRAY, Dorothy Kate   1918-

PERSONAL: Born October 12, 1918, in Lanark, Scotland; daughter of Edward Oliver (a factory warehouse worker) and Kate (Griffin) Haynes; married John S. Gray (a clerk), February 2, 1946; children: Leonard Alisdair, Ian Edward. *Education:* Attended secondary school in Aberlour, Scotland. *Religion:* Scottish Episcopal. *Home:* 14 Quarryknowe, Lanark ML11 7AH, Scotland.

CAREER: Writer, 1939—. Also worked as library assistant, market research investigator, and teacher of English as a foreign language. Past member of Lanark Town Council. *Member:* Society of Authors. *Awards, honors:* Tom Gallon Award from Society of Authors, 1947, for story, "The Head"; Constable Trophy from Scottish Association of Writers Clubs, 1979, for *Revival at St. Greta's.*

WRITINGS: Winter's Traces (novel), Methuen, 1947; *Robin Ritchie* (novel), Methuen, 1949; *Thou Shalt Not Suffer a Witch* (short stories), Methuen, 1973; *Peacocks and Pagodas* (stories), Paul Harris, 1981. Also author of *Revival at St. Greta's* (novel), 1947, and *Haste Ye Back* (autobiography), 1973.

Work represented in anthologies, including *Pick of Today's Short Stories,* edited by John Pudney, Putnam, 1959, and *Scottish Ghost Stories,* edited by J. F. Hendry, Penguin, 1970.

Writer for British Broadcasting Corp. Contributor to magazines, including *Scots* and *Good Housekeeping,* and newspapers.

WORK IN PROGRESS A novel set in New Lanark.

SIDELIGHTS: Dorothy Gray commented: "I write mainly to get things out of my system. I prefer short stories and find them easier to write than novels—many people don't agree. I hope I don't preach in my stories. If I feel angry enough to preach, I write articles instead. I think many gossips are frustrated writers, but lack the polish and perfection for which all writers should strive. I hate sloppy or gimmicky writing, and the modern habit of not correcting grammar, spelling, and punctuation in schools. These are writers' tools and should be used properly."

*   *   *

GREEN, Frederick Pratt   1903-

PERSONAL: Born September 2, 1903, in Liverpool, England; son of Charles (a manufacturer of leather goods) and Hannah (Greenwood) Green; married Marjorie Mildred Dowsett. *Education:* Attended Didsbury Theological College, Manchester, England, 1924-28. *Home:* 96 Hillcrest Rd., Thorpe Saint Andrew, Norwich NR7 0JR, England.

CAREER: Ordained Methodist minister, 1931; pastor of Methodist churches in Bradford, London, and Brighton, England, 1931-57; bishop of York and Hull district in England, 1957-64; pastor of church in Sutton, Surrey, England, 1964-69; writer, 1950—. Member of Royal School of Church Music. Guest on media programs. *Member:* International P.E.N., Hymn Society of Great Britain (vice-president), Hymn Society of America, Norwich Writers Circle (past president). *Awards, honors:* Greenwood Prize for Poetry from Poetry Society of Great Britain, 1964; his hymn, "It Is God Who Holds the Nations," was chosen for the official celebration in all churches of the Silver Jubilee of Queen Elizabeth II, 1977.

WRITINGS: This Unlikely Earth (poems), Hand and Flower Press, 1952; *The Skating Parson* (poems), Epworth, 1963. *Twenty-Six Hymns,* Epworth, 1971; *The Old Couple* (poems), H. Chambers, 1976; (editor with Bernard A. Braley) *Partners in Praise,* Stainer & Bell, 1979.

Regular reviewer for *Expository Times,* 1970-78. Contributor of poems to many anthologies, including *Oxford Book of Twentieth Century Verse,* Oxford University Press, 1973. Contributing translator to *Cantate Domino,* World Council of Churches, 1974. Contributor of hymns to numerous modern hymn books and supplements, including *Galliard Book of Carols,* Stainer & Bell, 1980. Contributor of articles on literary and religious subjects to journals.

WORK IN PROGRESS: Secular lyrics for traditional and folk singing groups.

SIDELIGHTS: Green commented: "My aim has been (and is) to help meet the need for hymns that express traditional and contemporary religious insights in the language of today. What pleases me is that my hymns have proved acceptable to all the major Christian denominations. Coming to hymn-writing late in life, I have found my experience as a poet invaluable."

BIOGRAPHICAL/CRITICAL SOURCES: Worship, April, 1975; *Hymn,* July, 1979.

*   *   *

GREEN, Michael Frederick   1927-

PERSONAL: Born January 2, 1927, in Leicester, England; son of Jack (a store manager) and Winifred (a secretary; maiden name, Smeath) Green. *Education:* Open University, B.A. (with honors), 1978. *Home:* 78 Sandall Rd., London W5 1JB, England. *Agent:* Curtis Brown Ltd., 1 Craven Hill, London W2 3EW, England.

CAREER: Leicester Mercury, Leicester, England, reporter, 1943; *Northampton Chronicle and Echo,* Northampton, England, reporter, 1943-50; *Birmingham Gazette,* Birmingham, England, sub-editor, 1950-53; *Star,* London, England, sub-editor, 1953-56; free-lance writer, 1956—. *Military service:* British Army, 1944-48; became sergeant. *Member:* National Union of Journalists, Incorporated Society of Authors, Playwrights & Composers.

*WRITINGS—*Humor; published by Hutchinson, except as noted: *The Art of Coarse Rugby,* 1960; *The Art of Coarse Sailing,* 1962; *Even Coarser Rugby,* 1963; *Don't Print My Name Upside Down* (novel), 1963; *The Art of Coarse Acting,* 1964, Drama Book Specialists, 1980; *The Art of Coarse*

Sport, 1965; *The Art of Coarse Golf,* 1968; *The Art of Coarse Moving,* 1969; *Rugby Alphabet,* Pelham, 1971; *The Art of Coarse Drinking,* 1973; *Squire Haggard's Journal* (novel), 1975; *The Art of Coarse Cruising,* 1976; *Even Coarser Sport,* 1978; *The Art of Coarse Sex,* 1980.

Plays: *Four Plays for Coarse Actors* (first produced in Edinburgh, Scotland, at Cathedral Hall, August 22, 1977, under title "The Coarse Acting Show"; contains "Streuth" ["a murder mystery"]; "Il Fornicazione" ["the adulterer"; an opera]; "A Collier's Tuesday Tea" ["a mining epic"]; "All's Well That Ends As You Like It" ["a hitherto undiscovered Shakespeare comedy"]), Samuel French, 1978; *The Coarse Acting Show 2* (first produced in Edinburgh at George Square Theatre, August 20, 1979; produced in London, England, at Shaftesbury Theatre, October 1, 1979; contains "Moby Dick" ["a new adaptation of the novel by Herman Melville which condenses the whole thing into a quarter of an hour"]; "Last Call for Breakfast" ["an avant garde play so avant garde the cast does not know how it is going to end"]; "The Cherry Sisters" ["after Chekhov, some way after"]; "Henry the Tenth: Part Seven" ["an all-purpose Coarse Shakespearean history"]), Samuel French, 1980.

Other writings: *Stage Noises and Effects,* Jenkins, 1958. Contributor of articles to newspapers, including *News Chronicle, London Observer, Sunday Times, Daily Telegraph, London Times, Punch,* and *Spectator.*

WORK IN PROGRESS: The Coarse Acting Show 3; an adaptation of *The Art of Coarse Acting* for television.

SIDELIGHTS: Green wrote: "My books, *The Art of Coarse* . . . , deal with various human activities (sports such as golf or sailing, or social affairs such as drinking and sex) and are largely devoted to the way things are done in reality as distinct from theory. In theory, for instance, yachtsmen are bold, alert experts, braving the storm and tempest. In *The Art of Coarse Sailing,* I pointed out that, in reality, most people who own small boats are suburban cowards who, in a crisis, forget all nautical language and shout, 'For God's sake, turn left before we're all killed!'

"From this there is a natural transition to a 'coarse' golfer, who goes from tee to green without touching the fairway; and a 'coarse' amateur actor, who is defined as one who can remember the lines but not in the order in which they come; not to mention the 'coarse' lover, who always hopes it will be better next time. In the desperately competitive modern world, my books are about those who don't quite measure up to the theoretical standards of achievement expected in life and in sport. The majority of us, in fact the vast army of sportsmen hacking their way around the great golf course of life, can never hope to break 100, let alone reach par."

Green's *The Art of Coarse Moving* was serialized by BBC-TV as "A Roof Over My Head" in 1977.

*   *   *

GREENBERG, Joseph Harold 1915-

PERSONAL: Born May 28, 1915, in Brooklyn, N.Y.; son of Jacob (a pharmacist) and Florence (Pilzer) Greenberg; married Selma Berkowitz, November 23, 1940. *Education:* Columbia University, B.A., 1936; Northwestern University, Ph.D., 1940. *Home:* 860 Mayfield Ave., Stanford, Calif. 94305. *Office:* Department of Anthropology, Stanford University, Stanford, Calif. 94305.

CAREER: University of Minnesota, Minneapolis, instructor, 1946-47, assistant professor, 1947-48; Columbia University, New York, N.Y., assistant professor, 1948-52, asso-

ciate professor, 1953-58, professor of anthropology, 1959-62; Stanford University, Stanford, Calif., professor of anthropology, 1962—, Ray Lyman Wilbur Professor of the Social Sciences in Anthropology and chairman of department of anthropology, 1971-74. Haynes Foundation lecturer at University of California, Riverside, 1972; inaugural lecturer of Harry Hoijer Memorial Lectures at University of California, Los Angeles, 1979. *Military service:* U.S. Army, Signal Corps and Intelligence Corps, 1940-45; became first lieutenant. *Member:* Linguistic Society of America (president, 1976), African Studies Association (president, 1964-65), National Academy of Sciences, American Academy of Arts and Sciences, American Philosophical Society, West African Linguistic Society (president, 1955-70). *Awards, honors:* Haile Selassie Prize for African Research, 1967, in recognition of research on African languages; first distinguished lecturer of American Anthropological Association, 1970; award in behavioral sciences from New York Academy of Sciences, 1980.

WRITINGS: The Influence of Islam on a Sudanese Religion, J. J. Augustin, 1946; (editor) *Universals of Language,* M.I.T. Press, 1963, 2nd edition, 1966; *Languages of Africa,* Indiana University Research Center in Anthropology, Folklore, and Linguistics, 1963; *Essays in Linguistics,* University of Chicago Press, 1963; *Language Universals: With Special References to Feature Hierarchies,* Mouton, 1966; *Anthropological Linguistics: An Introduction,* Random House, 1968; *Language, Culture, and Communication: Essays by Joseph H. Greenberg* (edited by A. S. Dil), Stanford University Press, 1971; *Typology: A Historic and Analytic Overview,* Mouton, 1973; *A New Invitation to Linguistics,* Doubleday, 1977; (editor with Edith Moravcsik and Charles Ferguson) *Universals of Human Language,* Volume I: *Method and Theory,* Volume II: *Phonology,* Volume III: *Word Structure,* Volume IV: *Syntax,* Stanford University Press, 1978.

WORK IN PROGRESS: A monograph on American Indian languages, publication by Stanford University Press expected in 1982; research on pronoun systems of the world's languages, completion expected in 1983.

SIDELIGHTS: Greenberg commented: "I came into anthropology as an undergraduate, partly through auditing a course of Franz Boas. From my earliest years I was fascinated by language and, therefore, after my first work in Africa on religion, I concentrated on linguistics within anthropology. I was also very attracted to music and almost went into professional piano study."

AVOCATIONAL INTERESTS: Playing piano.

*   *   *

GREENE, Hugh Carleton 1910-

PERSONAL: Born November 15, 1910, in Berkhamsted, Hertfordshire, England; son of Charles Henry (a private school headmaster) and Marion (Raymond) Greene; married Helga Guinness, 1934 (divorced, 1948); married Elaine Gilbert Shaplen, September 24, 1951 (divorced); married Tatjana Sais, 1970; children: (first marriage) Graham Carleton, James Carleton; (second marriage) Christopher Louis, Timothy Charles. *Education:* Merton College, Oxford, B.A., 1935, M.A., 1958. *Home:* Earls Hall, Cockfield near Bury St. Edmunds, Suffolk, England. *Office:* 9 Bow St., London WC 2E 7AL England.

CAREER: New Statesman and *London Daily Herald,* newspaper correspondent in Germany, 1933-34; *London Daily Telegraph,* staff member in Berlin, 1934-38, Warsaw correspondent, 1936, chief Berlin correspondent, 1938-39; British Broadcasting Corporation (BBC), Warsaw correspondent, 1939, head of German service, 1940-46, controller of broadcasting, British zone of Germany, 1946-48, head of Eastern European services, 1949-50; Emergency Informational Services, Malaya, head of services, 1950-51; BBC, assistant controller of overseas services, 1952-55, controller of overseas services, 1955-56, director of administration, 1956-58, director of news and current affairs, 1958-59, director general, 1960-69, member of the board of governors, 1969-71; European Broadcasting Union, vice-president, 1963-68; Bodley Head (publishers), chairman, 1969—; Greene, King & Sons, Ltd. (brewers), Suffolk, chairman, 1971-78. *Military service:* Served with the Royal Air Force Volunteer Reserve, 1940. *Awards, honors:* Order of the British Empire, 1950; Knight Commander of the Order of St. Michael and St. George, 1964; D.C.L., University of East Anglia, 1969.

WRITINGS: (Editor, with brother Graham Greene) *The Spy's Bedside Book,* Hart-Davis, 1957; *The Third Floor Front: A View of Broadcasting in the Sixties,* Bodley Head, 1969; (compiler) *The Rivals of Sherlock Holmes: Early Detective Stories,* Pantheon, 1970; (compiler) *Cosmopolitan Crimes: Foreign Rivals of Sherlock Holmes,* Pantheon, 1971 (published in England as *More Rivals of Sherlock Holmes: Cosmopolitan Crimes,* Bodley Head, 1971); (compiler) *The Further Rivals of Sherlock Holmes,* Pantheon, 1973 (published in England as *The Crooked Counties: Further Rivals of Sherlock Holmes,* Bodley Head, 1973); (editor) William Wymark Jacobs, *Selected Short Stories,* Bodley Head, 1975; (editor) *The American Rivals of Sherlock Holmes,* Pantheon, 1976; (editor) *The Pirate of the Round Pond, and Other Strange Adventure Stories,* Bodley Head, 1977. Also author of several published essays on broadcasting.

SIDELIGHTS: Sir Hugh Greene, editor and compiler of several anthologies of detective stories, is probably best known for his contributions to British journalism and broadcasting. A foreign correspondent for the *London Daily Telegraph* prior to the outbreak of World War II, Greene worked in Berlin and Warsaw. In September of 1939, he was expelled from Germany in reprisal for the ousting of Germans from Britain. During the next several months, Greene covered events in Poland, Bulgaria, France, the Netherlands, Turkey, Romania, and Belgium.

After a brief stint in the Royal Air Force, Greene began his long and successful career with the British Broadcasting Corporation. He spent most of the war years as the head of the German Service. In 1946, he was assigned by the Foreign Office to rebuild a peacetime radio service in the British zone of Germany. Greene's experience prompted an assignment from the government to apply his knowledge of psychological warfare and serve as head of the Emergency Informational Services in Malaya.

From 1960 to 1969, Greene was director general of the British Broadcasting Corporation. These were changing years for the corporation, largely in response to the introduction of its first competitor in video programming, the Independent Television Authority, in 1954. In addition, color television was introduced in the mid-1960's. Greene reportedly rejuvenated the corporation, encouraging controversial programming. Although the government had the power to veto any program, Greene tested the theoretical restraint at every corner. Formerly taboo subjects and attitudes became commonplace, and even the revered institutions of religion, parliament, and the royal family were occasionally touched with satiric witticisms. Greene's years in broadcasting produced a book entitled *The Third Floor Front: A View of Broadcasting*

in the Sixties. A collector of first editions of early detective novels and other writings, Greene drew upon his personal library to produce a number of compilations of detective tales. He compiled thirteen stories written by Arthur Conan Doyle's contemporaries for his *The Rivals of Sherlock Holmes.* The detectives in all these tales have a common denominator: they are residents of London. The anthology was intended to bring to light mystery writers who may have become obscure under the shadow of Conan Doyle. He later published anthologies of the works of foreign mystery writers and a compilation of the work of American detective storytellers. The work of his brother, Graham Greene, appears in *The Pirate of the Round Pond.*

AVOCATIONAL INTERESTS: Wine-tasting.

BIOGRAPHICAL/CRITICAL SOURCES: London Observer, January 10, 1960; *Illustrated London News,* December 31, 1966; *Times Literary Supplement,* October 9, 1970; *New York Times Book Review,* November 8, 1970; *New Republic,* March 19, 1977; *Times Literary Supplement,* July 15, 1977.

*   *   *

GREENE, Pamela
See FORMAN, Joan

*   *   *

GREENLEAF, Stephen (Howell)   1942-

PERSONAL: Born July 17, 1942, in Washington, D.C.; son of Robert Wendell (a business executive) and Patricia (Howell) Greenleaf; married Ann Garrison (an artist), July 20, 1968; children: Aaron Howell. *Education:* Carleton College, B.A., 1964; University of California, Berkeley, J.D., 1967; studied creative writing at University of Iowa, 1978-79. *Home:* 1210 Franklin St., Iowa City, Iowa 52240.

CAREER: Admitted to the Bar of California, 1968, and the Bar of Iowa, 1977; Multnomah County Legal Aid, Portland, Ore., researcher, 1969-70; Thompson & Hubbard, Monterey, Calif., associate attorney, 1970-71; Sullivan, Jones & Archer, San Francisco, Calif., associate attorney, 1972-76; University of Iowa, Iowa City, adjunct professor of trial advocacy, 1979-80. *Military service:* U.S. Army, 1967-69. *Member:* Authors Guild, State Bar of California, Iowa State Bar.

WRITINGS: Grave Error (novel), Dial, 1979; *Death Bed* (novel), Dial, 1980; *Child Proof* (novel), Dial, 1981.

SIDELIGHTS: In an issue of *Library Journal,* Greenleaf revealed that he first became interested in detective novels in the fifth grade when he was sent home from school "for bringing one of Perry Mason's adventures to class." With this background, as critics have noticed, Greenleaf writes his novels in the tradition of Raymond Chandler and Ross MacDonald. Though typically hard-boiled, Greenleaf's detective, John Marshall Tanner, is likeable. To entertain his audience is Greenleaf's sole objective.

Greenleaf told *CA:* "My work can and will have to speak for itself. My personal life is of interest, if at all, only because, after finding myself at age thirty-four devoting most of my life to a profession I didn't enjoy, I wrote a novel and was able, without an agent or a 'contact' in publishing, or anything else but a manuscript and some stamps, to get it published and to be successful at least to the extent that someone was willing to pay me to do it again. I say this simply to inform and to encourage those who might be in a similar circumstance."

BIOGRAPHICAL/CRITICAL SOURCES: Library Journal,
June 15, 1979; *New Yorker,* August 27, 1979.

* * *

GREENSPUN, Roger (Austin) 1929-

PERSONAL: Born December 16, 1929, in Bridgeport,
Conn.; son of David Stovin and Belle (Schlossberg) Green-
spun; married Joanne Freeman (an editor), September 30,
1967. *Education:* Yale University, B.A., 1951, M.A., 1958.
Home: 320 West 89th St., New York, N.Y. 10024. *Agent:*
Joseph Spieler, 26 Bank St., New York, N.Y. 10014. *Office:*
Penthouse, 909 Third Ave., New York, N.Y. 10022.

CAREER/WRITINGS: Connecticut College, New London,
instructor in English, 1959-62; Macmillan Publishing Co.,
New York City, encyclopedia editor, 1963-68; *New York
Times,* New York City, film critic, 1969-73; Rutgers University, New Brunswick, N.J., associate professor of English,
1971—; *Penthouse,* New York City, film critic, 1973—. Col-
umnist for *New York Free Press,* 1968, *Rolling Stone,* 1970,
Changes, 1973-74, *Soho News,* 1975-76, and *New York
Guide,* 1978-79. Contributor to periodicals, including *Movie-
goer, Sight and Sound, On Film, Film Comment, American
Film, Film Society Review, Village Voice, New York Times
Book Review,* and *Cahiers du Cinema in English.* Film panelist for New York State Council for the Arts, 1974-77, and
National Endowment for the Arts, 1978-79; member of New
York Film Festival selection committee, 1975-78; participant
in National Endowment for the Humanities seminar in film
criticism at Rutgers University, summer, 1978.

WORK IN PROGRESS: A collection of essays on major
filmmakers; essays on the practice of film criticism.

* * *

GREER, Ben 1948-

PERSONAL: Born December 4, 1948, in Spartanburg, S.C.;
son of Bernard Eugene (in television news) and Margaret
(Philips) Greer. *Education:* University of South Carolina,
B.A., 1971; Hollins College, M.A., 1973. *Religion:* Roman
Catholic. *Agent:* c/o Macmillan Publishing Co., Inc., 866
Third Ave., New York, N.Y. 10022.

CAREER: South Carolina Correctional Institution, Columbia, prison guard, 1967-71; worked on fishing boat and in
construction in York Harbor, Me., 1973-74; worked at a
number of odd jobs in South Carolina, Savannah, Ga., and
on Cape Cod, Mass., 1973-79; associated with University of
South Carolina, Columbia, beginning in 1979. Novelist.

WRITINGS: Slammer (novel), Atheneum, 1975; *Halloween*
(novel), Macmillan, 1978.

SIDELIGHTS: When Ben Greer wrote *Slammer,* he was
able to draw on his experiences as a prison guard at the
South Carolina Correctional Institution. The resulting book
offers an authentic account of the inner workings of a prison;
it is this authenticity that critics have found most admirable.
A writer for the *New York Times Book Review* noted, "He
can tell us precisely how contraband drugs find their way
into prison and how a new inmate gets broken in as a scented
doxy for the other men."

Greer writes "with amazing economy of means . . . without
any slighting of the sensuous affective surface," noted
George Garrett. Greer details the inner conflict of his characters as the novel's pace accelerates toward the climactic
prison riot. At one point Father Breen, the prison chaplain,
realizes that he has compassionate feelings for the child mo-
lesters, the most despised inmates in the prison hierarchy.

"That it is possible to imagine, as Breen does, [such human
beings] . . . with charity and compassion, yet without an in-
hibiting loss of implacable morality, is one of the themes of
Slammer, where men, already in extreme situations, are
pushed to and beyond their limits," Garrett observed.

The prison explodes in a bloody riot as those limits of endurance are exceeded. Greer uses the riot to convey his larger
message, which Benjamin Dunlap interpreted to be that
"prison is symptomatic of society at large and. . . . human
society is by necessity . . . a precarious balance of good and
evil."

Given the fact that *Slammer* enjoyed both critical and financial success, Garrett found it admirable that Greer, instead
of writing "another novel on a timely and controversial subject," chose to write an almost entirely different kind of
story. *Halloween,* his second novel, tells of a son's rescue of
his mother from a killer on Halloween night and his attempt
to free her from the tyranny of their own family. What *Halloween* shares with *Slammer* is that in both novels the characters are pushed into extreme situations beyond their capacity to cope.

Although some critics agreed that Greer succeeded in creating a richly developed sinister atmosphere in *Halloween,*
they found the story difficult to believe at times. In fact,
when critics have found fault with Greer's work, a frequent
complaint has been that both his stories and his characters
occasionally border on the incredible. A writer for *Kirkus
Reviews* called *Halloween* a "stagy novel"; Benjamin Dunlap of *New Republic* felt that the characters in *Slammer* were
too neatly matched against one another to be entirely believ-
able. In *Commonweal* John Druska wrote that each character is "an exaggerated figure who's never allowed . . . to assume real dimensions."

However "exaggerated" Greer's characters may be, critics
agree that he is a promising novelist. The writer for *Kirkus
Reviews* declared that *Halloween* is written "with wonderful
authority, strong, cadenced, and projective." Both novels,
wrote Garrett, "have succeeded beyond anyone's expectations." In Greer, he concluded, "there is great promise for
the future."

AVOCATIONAL INTERESTS: Drawing, painting, cooking,
fishing, weightlifting, impersonating, playing folk guitar.

BIOGRAPHICAL/CRITICAL SOURCES: Newsweek, July
21, 1975; *New Republic,* August 16 & 23, 1975; *New York
Times Book Review,* September 14, 1975; *Commonweal,*
January 2, 1976; *Sandlapper,* February, 1977; *Kirkus Reviews,* October 1, 1978; *Dictionary of Literary Biography,*
Volume 6: *American Novelists Since World War II,* 2nd series, Gale, 1980.*

* * *

GREGG, Hubert 1916-

PERSONAL: Born July 19, 1916, in London, England; son
of Robert Joseph and Alice (Bessant) Gregg; married Zoe
Gail (divorced); married Pat Kirkwood (divorced); married
Carmel Lytton, 1980; children: Stacey Elizabeth. *Education:*
Attended St. Dunstan's College and Webber-Douglas School
of Singing and Dramatic Art. *Office:* British Broadcasting
Corp., Broadcasting House, London W1A 1AA, England.

CAREER: Professional actor and director, 1933—, working
in New York, N.Y., and England, on stage, in repertory, on
tour, in films and television; BBC-TV, co-star in series,
"From Me to You," 1956; BBC-Radio, London, England,
presenter of "A Square Deal," 1964-71, "Hubert Gregg

Says Thanks for the Memory,'' 1972—, ''Hubert Gregg at the London Theatre,'' 1973-75, ''I Call It Genius,'' 1980-81, and ''I Call It Style,'' 1981-82. Producer of more than three hundred commercial radio programs. Member of faculty at theatre schools, including Royal Academy of Dramatic Art. Performed with Birmingham Repertory Company, 1933, Croydon Repertory Company, 1936, Chantecleer Company, 1936, and Repertory Players, 1975. *Military service:* British Army, Lincolnshire Regiment and King's Royal Rifle Corps, 1942-43, Intelligence, 1943. *Member:* Concert Artists Association (president, 1979-81), Boys Book Club (president), Garrick Club.

WRITINGS: April Gentleman (novel), Museum Press, 1951; *A Day's Loving* (novel), Bachman & Turner, 1974; *Agatha Christie and All That Mousetrap* (memoirs of Christie), William Kimber, 1980.

Author of ''After the Ball,'' a film biography of Vesta Tilley, 1957; co-author of ''Three Men in a Boat,'' a film, released by Rank, 1961.

Plays: ''We Have Company'' (three-act), first produced in Blackpool, England, at Grand Theatre, 1952; ''The Great Little Tilley,'' first broadcast by BBC-TV, September, 1955; ''Cheque Mate'' (three-act), first produced in London, England, at Globe Theatre, 1957; ''From the French,'' first produced in London at Strand Theatre, 1959; ''Villa Sleep Four'' (three-act), first produced in Windsor, England, at Theatre Royal, 1961; ''Who's Been Sleeping . . .?,'' first produced in London at Bromley Theatre, 1965; ''The Rumpus'' (two-act), first produced in London at Wimbledon Theatre, 1970.

Composer of music and lyrics for revues and musicals, including ''Strike a New Note'' (two-act), first produced in London at Prince of Wales Theatre, 1943; ''The Love Racket'' (two-act), first produced in London at Victoria Palace, 1944; ''Sweet and Low'' (two-act), first produced in London at Ambassadors' Theatre, 1944; ''Strike It Again'' (two-act), first produced in London at Prince of Wales Theatre, 1945; ''Leslie Henson's Gaities'' (two-act), first produced in London at Winter Garden Theatre, 1945; ''Better Late'' (two-act), first produced in London at Lyric Theatre, 1947; ''Sauce Tartare'' (two-act), first produced in London at Cambridge Theatre, 1949. Composer of more than one hundred songs, including ''I'm Going to Get Lit Up When the Lights Go Up in London'' and ''Maybe It's Because I'm a Londoner.''

WORK IN PROGRESS: An autobiography; solo presentations for ''An Evening With Hubert Gregg,'' for television.

SIDELIGHTS: Gregg is noted for his versatility as an actor. He has played Hamlet and light comedy. He performed with John Gielgud in George Bernard Shaw's ''Caesar and Cleopatra,'' and with Sir Alec Guinness in ''The Cocktail Party.'' He also appeared in such films as ''High and Dry'' and the Walt Disney production of ''Robin Hood.'' The melody of his song, ''I'm Going to Get Lit Up When the Lights Go Up in London'' was used as a D-Day signal to the European resistance movement during World War II. On BBC-Radio he has given Bible and poetry readings, and performed in revues. Gregg has also made three solo record albums: ''Hubert Gregg as Jerome K. Jerome,'' released by Decca Records in 1960; ''The World of Hubert Gregg,'' released by Decca Records in 1978; and ''Hubert Gregg Says Thanks for the Memory—in Song,'' released by BBC Records in 1978.

BIOGRAPHICAL/CRITICAL SOURCES: Times Literary Supplement, February 27, 1981.

GREGORY, Lisa
See CAMP, Candace P(auline)

*   *   *

GREIG, Maysie   1902-
(Jennifer Ames, Ann Barclay, Mary Douglas Warren)

PERSONAL: Born in 1902, in Sydney, Australia; married Jan Sopoushek (marriage ended); married Delano Ames; children: one son. *Education:* Attended Presbyterian girls' secondary school in Australia.

CAREER: Writer, 1924—. *Member:* International P.E.N., Women Writer's Club.

WRITINGS—Novels: Peggy of Beacon Hill, Small, Maynard & Co., 1924; *The Luxury Husband,* John Long, 1926; *Ragamuffin,* John Long, 1929; *Satin Straps,* Longmans, Green, 1929.

A Nice Girl Comes to Town, Longmans, Green, 1930; *The Man She Bought,* Dial, 1930; *Lovely Clay,* Benn, 1930, reprinted, 1953, Doubleday, 1933; *Jasmine, Take Care!; or, A Girl Must Marry,* Benn, 1930, reprinted, 1953, published as *A Girl Must Marry,* Dial, 1931; *The Women Money Buys,* Dial, 1931; *This Way to Happiness,* John Long, 1931, Dial, 1932; *One-Man Girl,* Dial, 1931, reprinted, Collins, 1972, also reprinted in collection, *Hearts of Gold* (see below); *Faint Heart, Fair Lady,* John Long, 1932; *Cake Without Icing,* Dial, 1932, revised edition published as *Marriage Without a Ring,* Collins, 1972, reprinted in collection, *Hearts of Gold* (see below); *Little Sisters Don't Count,* Benn, 1932, Doubleday, 1934; *Laughing Cavalier,* John Long, 1932; *Professional Lover,* Doubleday, 1933, revised edition published as *Screen Lover,* Collins, 1969; *Parents Are a Problem,* Hodder & Stoughton, 1933; *Men Act That Way,* Doubleday, 1933; *Love, Honour, and Obey,* Doubleday, 1933; *A Bad Girl Leaves Town,* Doubleday, 1933.

Good Sport, Doubleday, 1934, revised edition published as *Love Will Win,* Fontana, 1969; *Romance for Sale,* Doubleday, 1934, revised edition, Collins, 1970, reprinted in collection, *Romance Under the Sun* (see below); *She Walked Into His Parlour,* Hodder & Stoughton, 1934; *Ten-Cent Love,* Doubleday, 1934; *Women Are Difficult: A Kent Wilburn Romance,* Doubleday, 1934; *Sweet Danger,* Doubleday, 1934; *Romance on a Cruise,* Doubleday, 1935; *Rich Man, Poor Girl,* Doubleday, 1935; *Marry in Haste,* Doubleday, 1935; *Love Me and Let Me Go,* Doubleday, 1935, revised edition published as *Love Me,* Collins, 1971; *I'll Get Over It,* Hodder & Stoughton, 1935, Doubleday, 1936, revised edition published as *Jilted,* Collins, 1968, 3rd edition, Fontana, 1969; *I Lost My Heart,* Hodder & Stoughton, 1935, Doubleday, 1936, revised edition (under pseudonym Jennifer Ames) published as *This Sinister Island,* Collins, 1968, 3rd edition, 1970; *Heart Appeal,* Doubleday, 1935, reprinted in collection, *Hearts of Gold* (see below); *Don't Wait for Love,* Doubleday, 1936; *Odds on Love,* Doubleday, 1936, revised edition, Collins, 1970; *Touching the Clouds,* Doubleday, 1936; *Workaday Lady,* Doubleday, 1936.

Retreat From Love, Doubleday, 1937, reprinted, Collins, 1965; *The Pretty One,* Doubleday, 1937, reprinted, Collins, 1968; *New Moon Through a Window,* Doubleday, 1937, reprinted, Collins, 1968; *Dreams Get You Nowhere,* Doubleday, 1937; *Doctor's Wife,* Doubleday, 1937; *Challenge to Happiness,* Doubleday, 1937; *Debutante in Uniform,* Doubleday, 1938; *Elder Sister,* Hodder & Stoughton, 1938, Doubleday, 1939, reprinted, Collins, 1971; *Honeymoons Ar-*

ranged, Doubleday, 1938; *Other Women's Beauty*, Hodder & Stoughton, 1938; *Stepping Under Ladders*, Hodder & Stoughton, 1938, Doubleday, 1939, reprinted as *Girl in Jeopardy*, Collins, 1967; *Stopover in Paradise*, Doubleday, 1938 (published in England as *The Girl Men Talked About*, Hodder & Stoughton, 1938); *Strange Beauty*, Doubleday, 1938, revised edition (under pseudonym Jennifer Ames) published as *Another Girl's Life*, Collins, 1971; *Young Man Without Money*, Hodder & Stoughton, 1938; *Not One of Us*, Doubleday, 1939, reprinted, Collins, 1973; *A Man to Protect You*, Doubleday, 1939, reprinted, Collins, 1966; *Girl on His Hands*, Doubleday, 1939; *Ask the Parlourmaid*, Hodder & Stoughton, 1939, reprinted as *Unmarried Couple*, Doubleday, 1940, revised edition, Collins, 1967.

Dangerous Cruise, Doubleday, 1940; *A Fortune in Romance*, Doubleday, 1940, revised edition published as *A Girl and Her Money*, Collins, 1971; *Grand Relations*, Hodder & Stoughton, 1940; *Honeymoon Alone*, Hodder & Stoughton, 1940, Doubleday, 1941, revised edition published as *Honeymoon for One*, Collins, 1971; *Make the Man Notice You*, Doubleday, 1940; *The Man Is Always Right*, Doubleday, 1940; *Rich Twin, Poor Twin*, Doubleday, 1940, reprinted, Fontana, 1969; *This Desirable Bachelor*, Doubleday, 1941; *Too Many Women*, Doubleday, 1941, reprinted, Collins, 1969; *Heaven Isn't Here*, Doubleday, 1941; *Girl Without Credit*, Doubleday, 1941; *The Girl From Nowhere*, Doubleday, 1942, revised edition published as *The Girl Who Wasn't Welcome*, Collins, 1969; *Diplomatic Honeymoon*, Doubleday, 1942; *Heartbreak for Two*, Doubleday, 1942; *No Retreat From Love*, Doubleday, 1942; *Pathway to Paradise*, Doubleday, 1942; *Salute Me Darling*, Hodder & Stoughton, 1942; *Professional Hero*, Doubleday, 1943; *I've Always Loved You*, Doubleday, 1943; *One Room for His Highness*, Collins, 1944; *Reluctant Millionaire*, Collins, 1944, reprinted, 1970, Random House, 1945; *I Loved Her Yesterday*, Collins, 1945, reprinted, Lythway Press, 1976; *Girl With a Million*, Collins, 1945; *Darling Clementine*, Collins, 1946, published as *Candidate for Love*, Random House, 1947; *Table for Two*, Random House, 1946; *Take This Man*, Collins, 1947; *The Thirteenth Girl*, R. & L. Locker, 1947; *Castle in the Air*, Collins, 1947; *I Met Him Again*, Collins, 1948; *Yours Ever*, Random House, 1948.

Dark Carnival, Random House, 1950; *It Happened One Flight*, Collins, 1951; *Date With Danger*, Random House, 1952; *Reluctant Cinderella*, Collins, 1952; *This Fearful Paradise*, Random House, 1953; *Passport to Happiness*, Avalon Books, 1954 (published in England as *Lovers Under the Sun*, Collins, 1954, reprinted as *Ship's Doctor*, 1966); *Cloak and Dagger Love*, Collins, 1955; *Kiss in the Sunlight*, Collins, 1956, Avalon Books, 1957; *Winds of Fear*, Avalon Books, 1956; *Romance Under the Sun*, Benn, 1957; *No Dowry for Jennifer*, Avalon Books, 1957; *Girl Without Money*, Collins, 1957; *Hearts of Gold* (contains *One-Man Girl*, *Cake Without Icing*, and *Heart Appeal*), Benn, 1957; *Love Is a Gambler*, Collins, 1958; *Send for Miss Marshall*, Collins, 1959; *Love Is a Thief*, Collins, 1959; *Follow Your Love*, Avalon Books, 1959.

Doctor in Exile, Collins, 1960, Avalon Books, 1961; *Every Woman's Man*, Collins, 1961; *Cherry Blossom Love*, Collins, 1961; *The Doctor Is a Lady*, Collins, 1962; *Nurse at St. Catherine's*, Collins, 1963; *French Girl in Love*, Collins, 1963; *Every Woman's Doctor*, Collins, 1964; *Married Quarters*, Collins, 1964; *Nurse in Danger*, Collins, 1964; *The Doctor and the Dancer*, Collins, 1965; *Doctor on Wings*, Collins, 1966; *The Girl Men Talked About*, revised edition published

as *The Golden Garden*, Collins, 1968, 3rd edition, Fontana, 1970; *Never the Same*, Collins, 1970.

Under pseudonym Jennifer Ames: *Pandora Lifts the Lid*, Longmans, Green, 1932; *Anything But Love*, Hodder & Stoughton, 1933, abridged edition, Mellifont Press, 1944; *Cruise*, Hodder & Stoughton, 1934; *Sweet Peril*, Hodder & Stoughton, 1935; *I Seek My Love*, Hodder & Stoughton, 1936; *Tinted Dream*, Hodder & Stoughton, 1936, revised edition published as *Doctor Brad's Nurse*, Collins, 1966, 3rd edition, Fontana, 1968; *Her World of Men*, Hodder & Stoughton, 1937, Doubleday, 1938; *Stranger Sweetheart*, Hodder & Stoughton, 1938; *Dangerous Holiday*, Hodder & Stoughton, 1939; *Bury the Past*, Doubleday, 1939.

Ring Without Romance, Hodder & Stoughton, 1940, Doubleday (under name Maysie Greig), 1941; *The Impossible Marriage*, Collins, 1943; *Dark Sunlight*, Collins, 1943; *At the Same Time Tomorrow*, Doubleday, 1944; *Restless Beauty*, Collins, 1944; *Journey in the Dark*, Collins, 1945; *I Married Mr. Richardson*, Collins, 1945; *Lovers in the Dark*, Collins, 1946; *Take Your Choice, Lady*, Collins, 1946; *Heart in Darkness*, Arcadia House, 1947; *Fear Kissed My Lips*, Collins, 1947; *Shadow Across My Heart*, Collins, 1948, Arcadia House (under pseudonym Mary Douglas Warren), 1952; *She'll Take the High Road*, Collins, 1948; *Whispers in the Sun*, Random House, 1949, reprinted as *The Reluctant Cinderella*, Bouregy, 1952; *Danger Wakes My Heart*, Collins, 1949; *Lips for a Stranger*, Collins, 1949.

Danger in Eden, Bouregy, 1950; *Flight to Happiness*, Bouregy, 1950; *My Heart's Down Under*, Collins, 1950, Bouregy, 1951; *Too Much Alone*, Collins, 1950; *London, Here I Come*, Collins, 1951, published as *Assignment to Love*, Avalon Books, 1953; *After Tomorrow*, Bouregy, 1951; *The Frightened Heart*, Collins, 1952; *Wagon to a Star*, Collins, 1952, Bouregy, 1953; *The Fearful Paradise*, Collins, 1953; *Flight Into Fear*, Avalon Books, 1954; *Love Is a Gamble*, Avalon Books, 1954 (published in England as *That Girl in Nice*, Collins, 1954); *Shadow Across the Sun*, Collins, 1955; *Rough Seas to Sunrise*, Collins, 1955; *Night of Seas to Sunrise*, Collins, 1956; *Night of Carnival*, Collins, 1956; *Love on Dark Wings*, Collins, 1957; *Follow Your Dream*, Avalon Books, 1957; *Beloved Night*, Collins, 1958; *Love on Wings*, Avalon Books, 1958; *Doctor's Nurse*, Collins, 1959.

Love in a Far Country, Collins, 1960; *Love in the East*, Collins, 1960; *It Started in Hong Kong*, Collins, 1961; *Her Heart's Desire*, Avalon Books, 1961; *Diana Goes to Tokyo*, Collins, 1961; *Honeymoon in Manila*, Collins, 1962; *The Timid Cleopatra*, Collins, 1962; *Sinners in Paradise*, Collins, 1963; *Geisha in the House*, Collins, 1963; *Happy Island*, Collins, 1964; *The Two of Us*, Collins, 1964; *Nurse's Story*, Collins, 1965; *Nurse's Holiday*, Collins, 1965; *Doctor Ted's Clinic*, Collins, 1967; *The Doctor Takes a Holiday*, Collins, 1969; *Write From the Heart*, R. Hale, 1972.

Under pseudonym Ann Barclay: *Swing High, Swing Low*, Collins, 1936; *Other Men's Arms*, Collins, 1936; *Men as Her Stepping Stones*, Collins, 1937, Doubleday, 1938.

Under pseudonym Mary Douglas Warren: *Reunion in Reno*, Carlton House, 1941; *The Rich Are Not Proud*, Carlton House, 1942; *The Wishing Star*, Doubleday, 1942; *Southern Star*, Arcadia House, 1950; *The Manor Farm*, Arcadia House, 1951; *The Sunny Island*, Arcadia House, 1952; *Salt Harbor*, Arcadia House, 1953; *The High Road*, Arcadia House, 1954; *Shadow Over the Island*, Arcadia House, 1955; *Moon Over the Water*, Arcadia House, 1956. Contributor to magazines and newspapers.*

GREMILLION, Joseph 1919-

PERSONAL: Born March 11, 1919, in Moreauville, La.; son of J. Ben Gremillion (a planter and sheriff) and Netti Rabalais (Nelson) Gremillion. *Education:* Attended Louisiana State University, 1935-37, and St. Benedict's College, Covington, La., 1937-38; Notre Dame Seminary, New Orleans, La., M.Phil., 1942; attended Catholic University of America, 1942-43; Gregorian University of Rome, D.S.S., 1958-1960. *Home address:* P.O. Box 7213, Shreveport, La. 71107. *Office:* Muslim Jewish Christian Conference, 3700 13th St. N.E., Washington, D.C. 20017.

CAREER: Ordained Roman Catholic priest, 1943, named monsignor, 1962; assistant pastor of Roman Catholic church in Alexandria, La., 1943-47; pastor of Roman Catholic churches in Lake Providence, La., 1947-49, and Shreveport, La. (also founder), 1949-58; U.S. Bishops' Conference, Washington, D.C., director of Catholic Relief Services' socio-economic development in New York, N.Y., 1960-67, executive secretary of Pastoral Aid Fund to Latin America, 1964-67; Pontifical Commission on Justice and Peace, Vatican City, founding secretary, 1967-74; Muslim Jewish Christian Conference, Washington, D.C., coordinator and secretary, 1975—. Lecturer at University of California, Berkeley, spring, 1976; fellow at University of Notre Dame, 1974-78. Officer of Committee for Inter-American Cooperation, 1964-67; co-chairman of Pope Paul VI's and World Council of Churches' committee on society, development, and peace (Sodepax) in Geneva, Switzerland, 1968-75; director of Roman Catholic social and ecumenical ministry in Alexandria and Shreveport, 1978—.

WRITINGS: The Journal of a Southern Pastor, Fides, 1957; *The Catholic Movement of Employers and Managers,* Gregorian University Press, 1960; *The Other Dialogue,* Doubleday, 1965; *Continuing Christ in the Modern World,* Pflaum, 1967; *The Gospel of Peace and Justice: Catholic Social Teaching Since Pope John,* Orbis, 1976; (with William Ryan) *World Faiths and the New World Order,* Interreligious Peace Colloquium, 1978; *Food/Energy and the Major Faiths,* Orbis, 1978; *Report and Interpretation of Harvard Seminar on Muslim Jewish Christian Faith Communities as Transnational Actors for Peace and Justice* (monograph), Muslim Jewish Christian Conference, 1979; *John Paul II, the Church, and the World,* Orbis, in press.

Contributor: Louis Putz, editor, *The Catholic Church, U.S.A.,* Fides, 1956; John Miller, editor, *Vatican II: An Interfaith Appraisal,* University of Notre Dame Press, 1966; Ralph Bucy, editor, *The New Laity: Between Church and World,* World Books, 1978; John Eagleson and Philip Scharper, editors, *Puebla and Beyond,* Orbis, 1980. Contributor to magazines, including *America, Commonweal,* and *Catholic World,* and newspapers.

WORK IN PROGRESS: An autobiography, *From Bayou Home to Rome and Back;* a book on the pastoral need for a North American theology; a book on Muslim, Jewish, and Christian relations; a book on regional Christian churches as a basic world ecclesial structure.

SIDELIGHTS: Gremillion told *CA:* "My first book, *The Journal of a Southern Pastor,* began as reflections I wrote to help me understand 'Who am I?' as pastor of an upper middle-class, white, suburban parish in the early 1950's, and 'Who comprises this community-in-faith?' which I attempt to lead and serve. With my people, I address especially the issue of justice and love for the blacks of our city. From this local concern, I attended my social ministry focus to migrant workers, the South, Latin America, and the world. During the Second Vatican Council, I worked with others to legislate the establishment of a Vatican department to promote justice, development, human rights, and peace. Pope Paul VI called me to direct this body when he created it in 1967. During my eight years in the Vatican, I worked closely with the World Council of Churches in Geneva and came to know the Jewish and Islamic faith communities in a global sense. This led me to my interfaith focus, since 1974, when I completed my term in the Vatican.

"While continuing these global connections two-thirds of the time, I purposely returned in 1978 to make my home amid my cultural and spiritual roots in Louisiana after twenty years 'in the stratosphere.' Here I devote about one-third of my time to parish and local church-secular relations. With some hundred pastors, rabbis, and lay leaders of Shreveport, we have formed the Interfaith Committee for Human Dignity and Justice. We form a city-wide coalition, forum, and front on local issues such as prison reform, Vietnam and Cuban resettlement, bussing of students, housing, etc. We aim at animating each of our congregations toward social ministry as a 'constitutive dimension' of the law, the prophets, and the gospel—and to work and 'conscientize' ourselves together—projecting among Christians the next generation of church unity and witness. My writings now relate such local experiences to the wider areas of the nation, North America and other regions, other faiths, and all humankind."

AVOCATIONAL INTERESTS: "Researching, questing, agog with the wonder of it all!"

* * *

GRIBBLE, Harry Wagstaff (Graham) 1891(?)-1981

OBITUARY NOTICE: Born c. 1891 in Sevenoaks, Kent, England; died January 28, 1981, in New York, N.Y. Playwright, producer, and director. Gribble was an actor for a brief time in England before coming to New York City in 1914. Shortly after his arrival in America, he was engaged as stage manager of Shaw's "Pygmalion." Gribble branched out as a playwright during World War I, when he wrote and produced what was called the Army's most successful play, "You Know Me, Al." Among the many other plays that he wrote, produced, or directed are "The Outrageous Mrs. Palmer," "March Hares," "Johnny Belinda," and "Anna Lucasta." Gribble became known as a versatile writer and director, with successes in comedy, farce, melodrama, drama, and musicals, and his writings also included the screenplays for "Stella Dallas," "A Bill of Divorcement," and "A Silent Witness." Obituaries and other sources: *Current Biography,* Wilson, 1945; *The Biographical Encyclopaedia and Who's Who of the American Theatre,* James Heineman, 1966; *New York Times,* January 30, 1981.

* * *

GROPPER, William 1897-1977

PERSONAL: Born December 3, 1897, in New York, N.Y.; died January 6, 1977, in Manhasset, N.Y.; son of Harry (a factory worker) and Jenny (a seamstress; maiden name, Nidel) Gropper; married Gladys Oaks (marriage ended); married Sophie Frankle (a bacteriologist), 1925; children: (second marriage) Gene, Lee. *Education:* Attended Ferrer School of Art, 1912-13, National Academy of Design, 1913-14, and New York School of Fine and Applied Art, 1915-18. *Religion:* Jewish. *Residence:* Croton-on-Hudson, N.Y.

CAREER: New York Herald Tribune, New York City, staff artist, 1919-21; affiliated with *Pravda* in U.S.S.R., c. 1924; *New York World,* New York City, staff artist, 1925-27; book illustrator, free-lance cartoonist, and artist, 1927-77. Ford Foundation artist-in-residence for American Federation of Arts, 1965; instructor and artist-in-residence at various workshops and institutions. Work represented in collections at Metropolitan Museum of Art (New York City), Museum of Modern Art (New York City), Museum of Western Art (Moscow, U.S.S.R.), Art Institute (Chicago, Ill.), and many others. Work exhibited in one-man shows in New York City, Los Angeles, Calif., London, England, and Prague, Czechoslovakia. *Member:* National Institute of Arts and Letters, Society of American Graphic Artists, Artists Equity Association, Society of Mural Painters. *Awards, honors:* Collier Prize for illustration, 1920; Harmon Prize, 1930; Young Israel prize, 1931; Guggenheim fellowship, 1937; Artists for Victory lithograph prize, 1944; prize for lithography from John Herron Art Institute, 1944; purchase award from Los Angeles County Museum, 1945; third prize from Carnegie Institute, 1946; *Uncle Ben's Whale* was selected by *New York Times* as one of the best-illustrated books of the year, 1955; artist-in-residence award from Ford Foundation, 1966; Tamarind lithographic fellowship, 1967; Carnegie International award, 1969, for ''Don Quixote''; Thomas B. Clark Prize from National Academy of Design, 1973; purchase award from Albrecht Gallery (St. Louis, Mo.), 1973.

WRITINGS—Self-illustrated: *Alay-Oop* (juvenile), Coward, 1930; *America: Its Folklore,* Associated American Artists, 1946; (with Melvin Howard Fast) *Never to Forget: The Battle of the Warsaw Ghetto,* Book League of Jewish Peoples' Fraternal Order, 1946; *The Little Tailor* (juvenile), Dodd, 1955.

Illustrator: Berges Johnson, *More Necessary Nonsense,* Harper, 1931; Josef Berger, *Bowleg Bill, the Sea-Going Cowboy; or, Ship Ahoy and Let 'Er Buck!,* Viking, 1938; Gale T. Parks, *Here Comes Daddy,* Scott, 1951; Walter Dumaux Edmonds, *Hound Dog Moses and the Promised Land,* Dodd, 1954; George Bernard Shaw, *The Crime of Imprisonment,* Citadel, 1961.

Work represented in collections: Herman Baron, *Gropper,* A.C.A. Gallery, 1938; August L. Freundlich, *William Gropper: Retrospective,* Ritchie Press, 1968; *William Gropper: Fifty Years of Drawing, 1921-1971,* Worldwide Books, 1971. Work also represented in *The Golden Land,* 1927, *Fifty-Six Drawings of the U.S.S.R.,* 1928, *Your Brother's Blood Cries Out,* 1945, *Caucasian Studies,* 1950, *American Folklore,* 1953, *The Lost Conscience,* 1955, *Twelve Etchings,* 1965, *Capricious,* and *Lest We Forget.*

Contributor to periodicals, including *Fortune, Life, Nation, Time,* and *Newsweek.*

SIDELIGHTS: William Gropper's cartoons and paintings often reflected his working-class background. The son of a factory worker, Gropper began to take part in the support of his family as a young boy by toting bundles of clothing for his seamstress mother. He received his artistic education at the New York School of Fine and Applied Art. It was during the twenties, when Gropper began his career as a cartoonist for the *New York Herald Tribune,* that he developed left-wing sympathies and became active in labor organizations such as the Industrial Workers of the World.

After leaving the *Herald Tribune,* Gropper worked at a variety of jobs while free-lancing for several left-wing publications. As his work became more widely publicized by conservative magazines such as *Life, Time,* and *Fortune,* his talents as a creative artist came to be more highly regarded. In addition to painting murals for businesses such as New York's Schenley Corporation, the artist received commis-

sions for murals in public buildings in Washington, D.C., New York City, and Detroit, Mich. Gropper never ceased to supply politically sympathetic publications with illustrations, however, often doing so without pay.

A thread of social comment binds much of Gropper's work. His paintings, whose bold colors and clean lines reveal his background as a cartoonist, are often depictions of working-class people and are touched with pathos. His books, namely, *The Little Tailor,* his best-known work for children, deal with the labor class and the promise of the American dream.

Gropper's art also reflects his Jewish faith. He has done cartoons and illustrations for Jewish publications such as *Freiheit* and has illustrated several books written in Hebrew. Among his most impressive commissions are five stained glass windows created for Temple Har-zion in Illinois.

BIOGRAPHICAL/CRITICAL SOURCES: Life, June 12, 1944; *Newsweek,* April 2, 1951; *Time,* December 8, 1961; *Art & Artists,* September, 1977.

OBITUARIES: New York Times, January 8, 1977; *Art in America,* March, 1977.*

*   *   *

GROSMAN, Ladislav   1921-

PERSONAL: Born February 4, 1921, in Czechoslovakia; son of Jakub and Ester (Sommer) Grosman; married Edita Friedman, December 3, 1949; children: Jiri. *Education:* Attended Political and Social Science University, Prague, Czechoslovakia; Charles University, Ph.D., 1958. *Office:* Bar Ilan University, Ramat Gan, Israel.

CAREER: Editor and literary adviser with State Publishing House; chief editor of *Magazin Usebni pmucky;* scenarian and dramatist with Barrandow Street Film Studio in Prague, Czechoslovakia; Bar Ilan University, Ramat Gan, Israel, research associate, 1969—. *Wartime service:* Served with Slovak State, 1941-43. *Awards, honors:* Academy Award from Academy of Motion Picture Arts and Sciences, 1966, for screenplay, ''The Shop on Main Street''; Blue Ribbon Award, 1966; Musa Melphoeme Literature Award, 1967; film critics award, 1967.

WRITINGS: Obchod na korze, Mlada fronta, 1965, 3rd edition bound with *Nevesta,* MF t. Mir 6, 1970, translation by Victor Ambrus published as *The Shop on Main Street,* Doubleday, 1970; *The Bride,* translated by Iris Urwin, Doubleday, 1970.

Not in English: *Hlavou proti zdi* (stories), Konfrontace, 1976; *Nevesta,* MF t. Rude pravo, 1969, 2nd edition bound with *Obchod na korze,* MF t. Mir 6, 1970.

Work represented in anthologies, including *New Writing in Czechoslovakia,* edited by George Theiner, Penguin, 1969. Author of short stories.*

*   *   *

GROSS, David C(harles)   1923-

PERSONAL: Born June 9, 1923, in Antwerp, Belgium; came to the United States in 1927, naturalized citizen, 1932; son of Milton (a furrier) and Menya (Weissman) Gross; married Esther Pearl (a teacher), June 25, 1944; children: Laura Gross Strumingher, Joel, Marc. *Education:* Attended Brooklyn College (now of the City University of New York), 1940-43; Herzliah Hebrew Teachers Seminary, B.H.L., 1944. *Politics:* Independent. *Religion:* Jewish. *Home:* 2901 Sylvan Court, Oceanside, N.Y. 11572.

CAREER: New York Post, New York City, reporter, 1943-44, copy editor, 1944; Jewish Telegraphic Agency, New York City, 1945-49; United Jewish Appeal, New York City, in publicity department, 1950-52; Palestine Economic Group, New York City, director of public relations, 1953-55; American Technion Society, New York City, director of public relations and yearbook editor, 1956-67; American-Israel Book Co., New York City, president and chief editor of Sabra Books, 1967-70; Keter, Inc., New York City, vice-president of *Encyclopedia Judaica,* 1970-72; Jewish Publication Society of America, Philadelphia, Pa., executive vice-president, 1972-74; free-lance writer, editor, and consultant, 1974-80; *Jewish Week,* New York City, associate editor, 1974—, associate publisher, 1980—. Founder of Blue Star Book Club (for children), 1970. *Member:* Authors Guild, B'nai Zion.

WRITINGS: (Editor and translator) Tuvia Friedman, *The Hunter,* Doubleday, 1961; (editor and translator) Lena Kuchler-Silberman, *One Hundred Children,* Doubleday, 1961; (editor) *Love Poems From the Hebrew,* Doubleday, 1976; *1001 Questions and Answers About Judaism,* Doubleday, 1978; (editor) Ben Isaacson, *Dictionary of the Jewish Religion,* Bantam, 1979; *Pride of Our People: The Stories of One Hundred Outstanding Jewish Men and Women* (young adults), Doubleday, 1979; *The Jewish People's Almanac,* Doubleday, 1981.

Films: "They Call It Left," Pan-Israel Oil Co., 1957; "A City Called Technion," American Technion City, 1965.

Created "Shalom Calendar for Young People," Random House, 1977. Editor of *Pioneer Woman,* 1975—.

WORK IN PROGRESS: A comprehensive, one-volume encyclopedia of Jewish knowledge of young people, publication expected in 1982.

SIDELIGHTS: "I came to the United States as a small child," Gross wrote, "not quite four. Yiddish was my mother tongue, and I did not really master English for a number of years. At about the age of eleven I discovered books, and would borrow a dozen at a time from the library, read them all, and go back for more to the library, a hike of some two miles each way. We owned some prayer books, but there were no other books at home. My family's poor immigrant status, as well as the depression era, precluded any such extravagance.

"Something still inexplicable led me to want to write, to put words on paper and share them. At thirteen I wrote and published a neighborhood weekly; it lasted for a month. A year later, my parents bought me a battered, fifth-hand typewriter for five dollars and I learned to type.

"My reading continued to be voracious, and ranged across history, current affairs, and finally fiction. It occurred to me at an early age that a novelist was almost divine, for he could create a whole world, or people, places, and events, comparable to the story of creation of Genesis.

"At sixteen, I began to write a weekly column for the Jewish Telegraphic Agency, which was syndicated to more than a hundred Jewish newspapers all over the world. I alternated between factual pieces and short fictional pieces, often tied to events of the day.

"In my late teens, I planned to become a rabbi, always having had a strong religious bent and commitment, but changed my mind when I discovered printer's ink at the *New York Post,* where I began as a copy boy and later became a reporter and copy editor.

"My prime interests all my life have been good writing and

the welfare of the Jewish people. The Holocaust in Europe and the establishment of Israel have had a profound effect on me and, I believe, on all Jews. I have been to Israel more than fourteen times, carrying out public-relations programs, doing editorial work, and writing and producing documentary films, most of them dealing with the Technion, Israel's engineering university in Haifa.

"Although all my writing in recent years has been nonfiction, I hope to try a novel in the not too distant future. I believe that a good work of fiction very often can reveal more truth and shed more light on people and places and events than many works of nonfiction. In all of my work I seek to demonstrate, to Jews and non-Jews, that the ancient truths of the Jewish lifestyle, if properly understood and faithfully adhered to, can bring about a society founded on genuine social justice, compassion, and brotherly love. I hope to be able to produce books, for children and adults, which will replace ignorance and hatred with understanding and love."

*   *   *

GROSSMAN, Martin A. 1951-

PERSONAL: Born December 5, 1951, in New York, N.Y.; son of Joseph Louis (an attorney) and Theresa (a secretary; maiden name, Goldsmith) Grossman. *Education:* New York Institute of Technology, B.A., 1976. *Home:* 144-23 78th Ave., Flushing, N.Y. 11367. *Office:* Consumers' Research, Bowerstown Rd., Washington, N.J. 07882.

CAREER/WRITINGS: Consumers' Research (magazine), Washington, N.J., tester and researcher, 1976—. *Member:* International Motor Press Association, Society of Automotive Engineers.

SIDELIGHTS: Grossman told *CA:* "My work at *Consumers' Research* consists of testing products of consumer interest and writing the reports on these tests for the publication. The products vary from shampoos to new cars to washing machines to pencil sharpeners." *Avocational interest:* Cars, photography, planning trips.

*   *   *

GROUT, Donald Jay 1902-

PERSONAL: Born September 28, 1902, in Rock Rapids, Iowa; son of John Jay and Gertrude (Woodworth) Grout; married Margaret Lavina Dunn, April 12, 1928; children: Martha Margaret. *Education:* Syracuse University, A.B., 1923; Harvard University, A.M., 1932, Ph.D., 1939. *Home:* Cloudbank, Bacher Rd., R.D.3, Skaneateles, N.Y. 13152.

CAREER: Mills College, Oakland, Calif., visiting lecturer in music history, 1935-36; Harvard University and Radcliffe College, Cambridge, Mass., instructor and tutor in music, 1939-42; University of Texas, Austin, associate professor of music, 1943-45; Cornell University, Ithaca, N.Y., professor of music, 1945-70, Given Foundation Professor of Musicology, 1962-70, professor emeritus, 1970—, chairman of department of music, 1947-49 and 1952-58, university organist, 1945-47, director of Sage Chapel Choir, 1945-47. Visiting professor at Carleton College, 1955, University of Utrecht, 1959-60, and University of Louvain, 1965-66. Ernest Bloch Professor of Music at University of California, Berkeley, 1975-76. Member of board of trustees of Accademia Monteverdiana; member of Institute of Comparative Music Studies and Documentation, Berlin, West Germany, and Central Institute for Mozart Research, Salzburg, West Germany.

MEMBER: International Musicological Society (president, 1961-64), American Academy of Arts and Sciences (fellow),

American Musicological Society (president, 1952-54 and 1960-62), Royal Academy of Belgium, Societe Francaise de Musicologie, Musicological Society of Italy, British Academy (corresponding fellow), Phi Beta Kappa, Harvard Club (New York). *Awards, honors:* Paine traveling fellow at Harvard University, 1933-35; Guggenheim fellow, 1951-52; Fulbright grants, 1951-52, 1959-60, senior grant for Belgium, 1965-66; Arents Pioneer Award from Syracuse University, 1965.

WRITINGS: A Short History of Opera, two volumes, Columbia University Press, 1947, 2nd edition, 1965; *A History of Western Music,* Norton, 1960, abridged edition, 1964, 3rd edition, 1980; (general editor) *The Operas of Alessandro Scarlatti,* Harvard University Press, Volume I: *Eraclea,* edited by Grout, 1974, Volume II: *Marco Attilio Regolo,* edited by Joscelyn Godwin, 1975, Volume III: *Griselda,* edited by Grout, 1975, Volume IV: *La princepessa fedele,* edited by Grout, 1977, Volume V: *Massimo Puppieno,* edited by H. Colin Slim, 1979, Volume VI: *La Caduta dei de' decemviri,* edited by Williams, 1980; *Alessandro Scarlatti: An Introduction to His Operas,* University of California Press, 1979. Contributor to magazines and musicological journals. Editor of *Journal of the American Musicological Society,* 1949-51.

BIOGRAPHICAL/CRITICAL SOURCES: William W. Austin, editor, *New Looks at Italian Opera: Essays in Honor of Donald J. Grout,* Cornell University Press, 1968.

*   *   *

GRUMET, Robert Steven   1949-

PERSONAL: Surname is pronounced *Groo*-met; born September 19, 1949, in Bronx, N.Y.; son of Samuel C. (a bus mechanic) and Sybel (Greenfield) Grumet; married Mary Lou Ganim, July, 1974 (divorced, July, 1980). *Education:* Attended Borough of Manhattan Community College, 1967-70; City College of the City University of New York, B.A. (with honors), 1972; Rutgers University, Ph.D., 1979. *Religion:* Jewish. *Residence:* Cottondale, Ala. *Office:* Office of Archaeological Research, University of Alabama, 1 Mound ite Monument, Moundville, Ala. 35474.

REER: Rutgers University, New Brunswick, N.J. insstuctor in anthropology and teaching assistant in anthropology and history, 1972-76; Blackwells Mills Canal House Restoration, Belle Mead, N.J., curator, 1974-78; College of Staten Island, St. George, N.Y., adjunct assistant professor of psychology, sociology, and anthropology, summer, 1979; Grinnell College, Grinnell, Iowa, lecturer in anthropology, spring, 1980; University of Alabama, Office of Archaeological Research, Moundville, senior research ethnohistorian, 1980-81. Laboratory assistant for Sandy Ground Archaeological Project, 1970-72; research associate of Museum of the American Indian, Heye Foundation, 1973-77, and Old Missouri Research Institute, 1980—; crew chief for Archaeological Services, Laramie, Wyo., 1979; conducted archival and archaeological research on Middle Atlantic and Northwest Coast native peoples in Alaska, British Columbia, Washington, New York, Wyoming, Iowa, Alabama, New Jersey, and Pennsylvania.

MEMBER: American Association for the Advancement of Science, American Anthropological Association, American Ethnological Society, American Society for Ethnohistory, Society for Historical Archaeology, Society for American Archaeology, Society of Professional Archaeologists, Organization of American Historians, Champlain Society, Algonquian Conference, Northwest Coast Studies Conference, New York Academy of Sciences. *Awards, honors:* Fellow at

Center for the History of the American Indian, Newberry Library, 1981.

WRITINGS: (Contributor) William Cowan, editor, *Papers of the Ninth Algonquian Conference,* Carleton University Press, 1978; *Native Americans of the Northwest Coast: A Critical Bibliography,* Indiana University Press, 1979; "We Are Not So Great Fools": Changes in Upper Delawaran Socio-Political Life, 1630-1758* (doctoral dissertation), Rutgers University Press, 1979; *Native American Place Names in New York City,* Museum of the City of New York, 1980; (contributor) Mona Etienne and Eleanor Burke Leacock, editors, *Women and Colonization: Anthropological Perspectives,* Praeger, 1980. Contributor to *Encyclopedia Americana* and *Encyclopedia of the Indians of the Americas.* Contributor of articles and reviews to academic journals.

WORK IN PROGRESS: A book on the resistance of the Ohio River Valley Delaware to white invasion between 1754 and 1794.

*   *   *

GUILLET, Jacques   1910-

PERSONAL: Born April 3, 1910, in Lyon, France; son of Jules (an engineer) and Alice (Collard) Guillet. *Education:* Universite de Paris, licence es lettres, 1931; Institut Biblique Pontifical (Rome), licence es sciences bibliques, 1950; Faculte de Theologie de Lyon-Fourviere, doctorat en theologie, 1971. *Religion:* Roman Catholic. *Home:* 128 rue Blomet, Paris, France 75015. *Office:* Centre Sevres, 35 rue de Sevres, Paris, France 75006.

CAREER: Entered order of Society of Jesus (Jesuits), 1927, ordained Roman Catholic priest, 1945; Faculte de Theologie de Lyon-Fourviere, Lyon, France, professor of Holy Scripture, 1951-72, dean of the Jesuit theology faculty, 1953-65; Centre Sevres, Society of Jesus, Paris, France, professor of Holy Scripture, 1972—. Professor at Ecole de la Foi, Fribourg, Switzerland, 1969—. *Military service:* French Army, 1939-45; became lieutenant; received Croix de Guerre and Legion of Honor. *Member:* Association Catholique Francaise Pour L'Etude de la Bible (president, 1973—), Association des Ecrivains Croyants d'Expression Francaise, Amities Judeo-Chretiennes.

WRITINGS: Themes Bibliques: Etudes sur l'expression et le developpement de la revelation, Aubier, 1951, second edition, 1962, translation by Albert J. LaMothe, Jr., published as *Themes of the Bible,* Fides Publishers, 1960; *Jesus-Christ hier et aujourd'hui,* Desclee de Brouwer, 1963, translation by John Duggan published as *Jesus Christ Yesterday and Today: Introduction to Biblical Spirituality,* Franciscan Herald Press, 1965; *La Generosite de Dieu: Grace, justice, et verite* (title means "The Generosity of God: Grace, Righteousness, and Truth"), Editions Montaigne, 1966; (contributor) *Discernment of Spirits,* translated from original French by Mary Innocentia Richards, Liturgical Press, 1970; *Jesus devant sa vie et sa mort,* Aubier Montaigne, 1971, third edition, 1976, translation by Edmond Bonin published as *The Consciousness of Jesus,* Newman Press, 1972; (contributor) *Dictionnaire de spiritualite,* volume 8, Beauchesne, 1973, translation by Richards of Guillet's article published as *The Religious Experience of Jesus and His Disciples,* Abbey Press, 1975; *Jesus Christ dans notre monde,* Desclee de Brouwer, 1974, translation by Matthew J. O'Connell published as *Jesus Christ in Our World,* Abbey Press, 1977; (author of commentary) *L'Evangile de Jesus-Christ selon les quatre evangelistes,* Editions du Cerf, 1976; *Les Premiers Mots de la foi: De Jesus a l'eglise* (title means "The First

Words of the Christian Faith''), Centurion, 1977; *Un Dieu qui parle,* Desclee de Brouwer, 1977, translation by Bonin published as *A God Who Speaks,* Paulist Press, 1979; *La Foi de Jesus-Christ* (title means "The Faith of Jesus Christ''), Desclee et Cie, 1980. Contributor to *Recherches de science religieuse,* 1947—.

WORK IN PROGRESS: Des Gestes de Jesus aux sacrements de l'eglise.

SIDELIGHTS: Guillet told *CA:* "My writing career, the choice of subjects and styles, was greatly determined by my captivity in Germany from 1940 to 1942. I have been struck by the fact that the usual language of religious writings was unintelligible and incomprehensible to the vast majority of people. Convinced, on the other hand, that Jesus had made himself understood to his listeners, and that the Gospel was intended for all men, and first of all to the most simple, I was resolved to try to tell the Christian faith in a language accessible to all.''

*　　*　　*

GUIN, Wyman (Woods) 1915-
(Norman Menasco)

PERSONAL: Born March 1, 1915, in Wanette, Okla.; son of Joel and Marie (Menasco) Guin; married Jean Adolph, 1939 (died, 1955); married Valerie Carson, 1956; children: Joel, Jennifer, Cynthia, Kevin, Kristen. *Education:* Riverside City College, J.C., 1934.

CAREER: Lakeside Laboratories, Milwaukee, Wis., technician in pharmacology then advertising writer, 1938-45, advertising manager, 1945-60, vice-president in marketing, 1960-62; Medical Television Communications, Chicago, Ill., vice-president, 1962-64; L. W. Frohlich & Co./Intercon International Inc. (advertising agency), New York, N.Y., planning administrator and creative director, c. 1964-69; freelance writer, 1969—.

WRITINGS: Living Way Out (science fiction stories), Avon, 1967 (published in England as *Beyond Bedlam,* Sphere Books, 1973); *The Standing Joy* (science fiction novel), Avon, 1969. Contributor of stories to science fiction magazines, including *Astounding Science Fiction* (under pseudonym Norman Menasco) and *Galaxy.**

*　　*　　*

GUINNESS, Bryan (Walter) 1905-

PERSONAL: Born October 27, 1905, in London, England; son of Lord Walter (a colonel and First Lord Moyne of Bury St. Edmunds) and Lady Evelyn (Erskine) Guinness; married Diana Freeman-Mitford, 1929 (marriage ended, 1934); married Elisabeth Nelson, September 21, 1936; children: (first marriage) Jonathan Bryan, Desmond; (second marriage) Rosaleen Guinness Mulji, Diarmid (deceased), Fiona, Finn, Thomasin, Kieran, Catriona, Erskine, Mirabel. *Education:* Christ Church, Oxford, M.A., 1927. *Home:* Knockmaroon House, Castleknock, County Dublin, Ireland; and Biddesden House, Andover, Hampshire, England.

CAREER: Called to the Bar, 1930, practiced law, 1930-33; Arthur Guinness Son & Co. Ltd. (brewers), Dublin, Ireland, and London, England, member of board of directors, 1934-79, vice-chairman, 1949-79, joint vice-chairman, 1967-79; writer, 1930—. Member of House of Lords. Barrister-at-law. Trustee and former chairman of Iveagh Charitable Housing Trust; trustee of Guinness Charitable Housing Trust, London. Member of board of governors of National Gallery of Ireland, 1955. *Military service:* British Army, Royal Sussex Regiment, 1940-45; became captain. *Member:* Irish Academy of Letters, Royal Society of Literature (fellow), Athenaeum Club, University Club, Kildare Street Club, Carlton Club. *Awards, honors:* LL.D. from Trinity College, Dublin, 1958, and National University of Ireland, 1961; fellow of Trinity College, Dublin, 1979.

WRITINGS: Twenty-Three Poems, Duckworth, 1931; *Singing Out of Tune* (novel), Putnam, 1933; *Landscape With Figures* (novel), Putnam, 1934; *Under the Eyelid* (poems), Heinemann, 1936; *A Week by the Sea* (novel), Putnam, 1936; *Lady Crushwell's Companion* (novel), Putnam, 1938; *Reflexions* (poems), Heinemann, 1947; *Collected Poems,* Heinemann, 1956; *A Fugue of Cinderellas* (novel), Heinemann, 1956; *Leo and Rosabelle* (novel), Heinemann, 1961; *The Giant's Eye* (novel), Heinemann, 1964; *The Rose in the Tree* (poems), Heinemann, 1964; *The Girl With the Flower* (short stories), Heinemann, 1966; *The Engagement* (novel), Rampant Lions Press, 1969; *The Clock* (poems), Dolmen Press, 1973; *Diary Not Kept* (biographical essays), Compton Press, 1973; *Hellenic Flirtation* (novel), Compton Press, 1978.

Children's books: *Johnny and Jemima,* Heinemann, 1936; *The Children in the Desert,* Heinemann, 1947; *The Animal's Breakfast,* Heinemann, 1950; *Story of a Nutcracker,* Heinemann, 1953; *Catriona and the Grasshopper,* Heinemann, 1957; *Priscilla and the Prawn,* Heinemann, 1960.

Plays: "The Fragrant Concubine" (five-act), first produced in London, England, at Little Theatre, 1938; "A Riverside Charade" (three-act), first produced in Dublin, Ireland, at Abbey Theatre, 1954. Also author of plays as yet unproduced, including "A Fugue of Cinderellas" (three-act), 1949; "Paralysed Princess" (puppet play for children), c. 1950; "Hero and Leander" (verse play), 1966; "Faithful Rosa" (children's play), c. 1970.

WORK IN PROGRESS: Poems; autobiographical essays.

SIDELIGHTS: Bryan Guinness, Second Lord Moyne of Bury St. Edmunds, wrote: "I have been a writer all my life. I had a non-executive appointment on the board of Arthur Guinness Son & Co. Ltd. and became vice-chairman from 1949 till my retirement in 1979. I came from Ireland and still partly live there in our family house in Dublin. I live mainly at Biddesden House in Wiltshire where I and my family own a 1200-acre farm. I try to do my duty in the House of Lords, but am not very active politically. I am probably best known as a poet and better known as such in Ireland.''

AVOCATIONAL INTERESTS: Travel.

*　　*　　*

GUNTON, Sharon R(ose) 1952-

PERSONAL: Born January 10, 1952, in Detroit, Mich.; daughter of Frank Anthony (an engineer) and Carolyn Catherine (Erb) Cillette; married Thomas Eugene Gunton (an editor), December 29, 1978; children: Thomas Eugene, Jr., Patrick Michael. *Education:* Attended University of Michigan, 1970-72; University of Michigan, Dearborn Campus, B.A. (magna cum laude), 1974; graduate study at University of Michigan, 1974-78. *Religion:* Roman Catholic. *Home:* 9328 Appleton, Redford, Mich. 48239. *Office:* Gale Research Co., Book Tower, Detroit, Mich. 48226.

CAREER: Transcontinental Travel Agency, Harper Woods, Mich., travel agent, 1974; Gale Research Co., Detroit, Mich., standing order representative, 1975, editorial assistant, 1976-77, assistant editor, 1977-78, production editor, 1977-80, associate editor, 1978-80, editor, 1980—.

WRITINGS: (Research assistant) *Contemporary Literary*

Criticism, Gale, Volume 6, 1976, Volume 7 (assistant editor), 1977, Volume 8 (production editor), 1978, Volume 9, 1978, Volume 10, 1979, Volume 11, 1979, Volume 12 (associate editor and production editor), 1980, Volume 13 (production editor), 1980, Volume 15 (editor with Laurie Lanzen Harris), 1980, Volume 16 (sole editor), 1981, Volume 17, 1981.

SIDELIGHTS: Sharon Gunton commented: "I consider my work on *Contemporary Literary Criticism* very important, but I also recognize the fact that a publication of this sort is a group effort, and I have a great respect for my staff. To a large extent, it is their hard work and dedication that has made *CLC* a valuable, accurate, and interesting reference work."

AVOCATIONAL INTERESTS: Reading (novels), films, sharing my time with my family.

*   *   *

GUPTA, Pranati Sen
   See SEN GUPTA, Pranati

*   *   *

GUTMAN, Naham   1899(?)-1981

OBITUARY NOTICE: Born c. 1899; died in January, 1981, in Israel. Author. Gutman wrote children's books, but he also worked as a painter and sculptor. Obituaries and other sources: *AB Bookman's Weekly,* January 26, 1981.

H

HACKES, Peter Sidney 1924-

PERSONAL: Born June 2, 1924, in New York, N.Y.; son of John R. and Ruth (Misch) Hackes; married Mary Ellen Propper, March 30, 1954 (divorced, 1979); children: Pamela Townsend Hackes Thurston, Carole Austin, Peter Quinn. *Education:* Grinnell College, B.A., 1948; University of Iowa, M.A., 1949. *Office:* 4001 Nebraska Ave. N.W., Washington, D.C. 20016.

CAREER/WRITINGS: Affiliated with radio stations WELM in Elmira, N.Y., WSUI and KXIC in Iowa City, Iowa, WAKR in Akron, Ohio, and WHAS in Louisville, Ky.; Columbia Broadcasting System, Inc. (CBS), New York City, Washington correspondent, 1952-55; National Broadcasting Co. (NBC), New York City, Washington correspondent, 1955—, defense department correspondent, 1956-67, anchorman of "World News Roundup," 1957-61. Member of board of directors of Cheshire Foundation; member of board of governors of National United Service Organizations; member of trustees council of Young Men's Christian Association (YMCA) of Metropolitan Washington; member of board of directors of Wolf Trap Farm Park for the Performing Arts, 1975-78; member of National Commission on Fire Prevention and Control. Consultant in public affairs, communications, media, congressional, and community relations for numerous organizations, including United States Fire Administration, National United Service Organizations, Cheshire Foundation, United Way of America, and YMCA of Metropolitan Washington, D.C. Notable assignments include coverage of national political conventions, Capital Hill, White House, Cuban missile crisis, Army-McCarthy hearings, Nixon impeachment hearing and Watergate cover-up trial, and Three Mile Island accident; presentation and indepth analyses for television and radio programs, including "Today," "Meet the Press," "Second Sunday," "Monitor," "World News Roundup," "Emphasis," "Nightly News," "Today in Washington," and "News Program Service." Contributor of articles to periodicals, including *Parade, Quill, Direction, Data,* and *Historic Preservation. Military service:* U.S. Naval Reserve, 1943-54, 1971—; currently captain; received Meritorious Service Medal.

MEMBER: American Federation of Television and Radio Artists, Radio-Television Correspondents Association, Society for the Preservation and Encouragement of Barbershop Quartet Singing in America, Academy of Independent Scholars. *Awards, honors:* D.Litt. from Newberry College, 1967;

L.H.D. from Grinnell College, 1967; Emmy Award from National Academy of Television Arts and Sciences, 1969, for coverage of *Apollo* space flights; George Foster Peabody Radio and Television Award from University of Georgia, 1971, for "Second Sunday" series.

SIDELIGHTS: Peter Hackes commented to *CA:* "Throughout my career as a journalist/broadcaster I have found much satisfaction in immersing myself in additional outside volunteer work, such as assisting voluntary agencies like the United Service Organizations (USO) and the United Way. My contribution to the local YMCAs has been most rewarding to me, as has my limited effort to help the Cheshire Foundation, an organization devoted to helping handicapped citizens lead normal lives in special housing facilities. The same can be said for my work with the Wolf Trap organization.

"My point is that no one is too busy to contribute some time, expertise, and general assistance to community organizations. It is such outside 'extracurricular' work that I find has given my life more meaning than it would otherwise have had. My small efforts, I believe, have rewarded me far more in the doing than I have given to these groups.

"I cannot recommend too highly that people in every walk of life make a point to devote some time—even a few hours a week or month—to some outside endeavor. It's a most broadening experience to help others, and the organizations can use all the help they can get."

*   *   *

HADINGHAM, Evan 1951-

PERSONAL: Born in 1951 in England. *Home:* West Lodge, Ridgemead Rd., Englefield Green, Surrey TW20 0YD, England.

CAREER: Archaeologist and writer.

WRITINGS: The Fighting Triplanes, Hamish Hamilton, 1968, Macmillan, 1969; *Youth Now,* Youth Now, 1971; *Ancient Carvings in Britain: A Mystery,* Garnstone Press, 1974; *Circles and Standing Stones: An Illustrated Exploration of Megalith Mysteries of Early Britain,* Walker & Co., 1975; *Secrets of the Ice Age: The World of the Cave Artists* (edited by Richard Winslow), Walker & Co., 1979.*

*   *   *

HAGGIN, B(ernard) H. 1900-

PERSONAL: Born December 29, 1900, in New York, N.Y.

Residence: New York, N.Y.

CAREER: Writer. Music and record critic for *Brooklyn Daily Eagle,* 1934-37, *New Republic,* 1934-35, 1957-66, and 1975-78, *Nation,* 1936-37, *Hudson Review,* 1958-72, and *Yale Review,* 1958—.

WRITINGS: A Book of the Symphony, Oxford University Press, 1937; *Music on Records,* Oxford University Press, 1938, Knopf, 1941; *Music for the Man Who Enjoys "Hamlet,"* Knopf, 1944; *Music in the Nation,* Sloane, 1949, reprinted, Arno Press, 1971; *The Listener's Musical Companion,* Rutgers University Press, 1956; *Conversations With Toscanini,* Doubleday, 1959, 2nd enlarged edition, Horizon Press, 1979; *Music Observed,* Oxford University Press, 1964, reprinted as *Thirty-Five Years of Music,* Horizon Press, 1974; (editor) *The Toscanini Musicians Knew,* Horizon Press, 1967; *The New Listener's Companion and Record Guide,* Horizon Press, 1967, 5th edition, 1978; *Ballet Chronicle,* Horizon Press, 1970; *A Decade of Music,* Horizon Press, 1973; *Violette Verdy,* Dance Horizons, 1975. Author of column, "Music on the Radio," in *New York Herald Tribune,* 1946-49. Contributor of articles to periodicals, including *Commentary, Encounter, American Scholar, Sewanee Review,* and *Ballet News.*

*   *   *

HALBERSTAM, Michael J(oseph)   1932-1980

OBITUARY NOTICE—See index for *CA* sketch: Born August 9, 1932, in Bronx, N.Y.; died of gunshot wounds, December 5, 1980, in Washington, D.C. Physician, editor, novelist, and author. Halberstam specialized in cardiology and internal medicine in private practice after serving as a doctor with the Public Health Service and on an Indian reservation in New Mexico. He was senior medical editor of *Modern Medicine* magazine in addition to writing newspaper columns and articles. The author was shot when he surprised an intruder in his home. Wounded, Halberstam started to drive himself to the hospital when he spotted his assailant fleeing the scene. The physician swerved into the man and incapacitated him, thus enabling the police to arrest him. Halberstam, however, died hours later while undergoing surgery. His works include *The Pills in Your Life* and *A Coronary Event,* and a novel, *The Wanting of Levine.* Obituaries and other sources: *Chicago Tribune,* December 7, 1980; *New York Times,* December 7, 1980; *Newsweek,* December 15, 1980; *Publishers Weekly,* December 19, 1980; *Time,* December 22, 1980; *AB Bookman's Weekly,* January 26, 1981.

*   *   *

HALE, John (Barry)   1926-

PERSONAL: Born February 5, 1926, in Woolwich, England; son of Alfred John (a soldier) and Ethel (Barr) Hale; married Valerie June Bryan (an artist), August, 1950; children: Simon John, Felicity Joanna. *Education:* Attended Royal Naval College, Greenwich, England. *Residence:* Margate Kent, England. *Agent:* Stephen Durbridge, Harvey Unna & Stephen Durbridge Ltd., 14 Beaumont Mews, Marylebone High St., London W1N 4HE, England.

CAREER: Stage hand, stage manager, and electrician in variety, touring, and repertory companies, 1952-55; Lincoln Repertory Theatre, Lincoln, England, founder and artistic director, 1955-58; Arts Theatre, Ipswich, England, artistic director, 1958-59; Bristol Old Vic Theatre, Bristol, England, artistic director, 1959-61; free-lance director, 1961—; free-lance writer, 1965—. Director of television dramas for independent television companies, 1961-64; directed Shakes-

pearean plays on record for EMI, 1962-64. Greenwich Theatre, London, member of board of governors, 1963-71, associate artistic director, 1968-71, 1975-76, resident playwright, 1975-76. *Military service:* Royal Navy, 1941-51.

WRITINGS—Novels: *Kissed the Girls and Made Them Cry,* Collins, 1963, Prentice-Hall, 1966; *The Grudge Fight,* Collins, 1964, Prentice-Hall, 1967; *A Fool at the Feast,* Collins, 1966; *The Paradise Man,* Bobbs-Merrill, 1969; *The Fort,* Quartet, 1973; *The Love School,* BBC Publications, 1974, St. Martin's, 1975; *Lovers and Heretics,* Gollancz, 1976, Dial, 1978.

Plays: "The Black Swan Winter" (two-act; first produced in Hampstead, England, at Hampstead Theatre Club, 1968), published in *Plays of the Year,* Volume XXXVII, edited by J. C. Trewin, Elek, 1970; "Spithead" (three-act; first produced in Greenwich, England, at Greenwich Theatre, 1969), published in *Plays of the Year,* Volume XXXVIII, edited by J. C. Trewin, Elek, 1971; "The Lion's Cub" (one-act; first broadcast by British Broadcasting Corp, [BBC-TV], 1971), published in *Elizabeth R.,* Elek, 1971; "Decibels" (one-act; first produced in Liverpool, England, at Liverpool Everyman Theatre, 1969), published in *Prompt Three,* edited by Alan Burband, Hutchinson, 1976.

Unpublished plays: "It's All in the Mind" (two-act), first produced at Hampstead Theatre Club, 1968; "Here Is the News" (one-act), first produced in Beaufort, England, at Beaufort Theatre, 1970; "Lorna and Ted" (two-act), first produced at Greenwich Theatre, 1970; "In Memory of . . . Carmen Miranda" (one-act), first produced at Greenwich Theatre, 1975; "Love's Old Sweet Song" (two-act), first produced at Greenwich Theatre, 1976; "The Case of David Anderson Q.C." (two-act), first produced in Manchester, England, at Library Theatre, 1980.

Screenplays: (With Bridget Boland) "Anne of the Thousand Days" (adapted from the play by Maxwell Anderson), Universal, 1969; (with Edward Simpson) "The Mind of Mr. Soames" (adapted from a novel by Charles Eric Maine), Columbia, 1970; "Mary, Queen of Scots," Universal, 1971.

Television plays: "The Rules That Jack Made," 1965; "The Noise Stopped," 1966; "Light the Blue Touch Paper," 1966; "The Queen's Traitor" (five-part series), 1967; "Retreat," 1968; "The Picnic," 1969; "The Distracted Preacher," 1969; "The Lion's Cub," 1971 (also see above); "The Bristol Entertainment," 1971; "Anywhere but England," 1972; "Ego Hugo: A Romantic Entertainment," 1973; "The Brotherhood," 1975; "An Impeccable Elopement," 1975; "Goodbye America," 1976. Also writer for "Thirteen Against Fate" (television series) and "Micah Clarke" (radio series).

WORK IN PROGRESS: "A book about my childhood," *Islands of Childhood,* publication by Gollancz expected in 1982; two plays on Arthur Koestler for BBC-TV; a dramatization of own novel *The Grudge Fight* for BBC-TV; a screenplay.

SIDELIGHTS: Although John Hale has written a number of novels and plays, he has perhaps received most attention in America for his television script "The Lion's Cub" (first in the "Elizabeth R." series), his screenplay for "Mary, Queen of Scots," and his contribution to the screenplay for "Anne of the Thousand Days." Critics have applauded Hale's ability to portray the complexities of Elizabethan England and to present a coherent plot and an engaging drama. In a review of "Mary, Queen of Scots," a writer for *Variety* said Hale "has fashioned a good original screenplay which alternates dramatically between the quicksand fortunes of Mary Stuart in Scotland and the well-organized court of Elizabeth."

Richard Mallett, a writer for *Punch*, found the dialogue of "Anne of the Thousand Days" to be "unobtrusively modern, without being out of key."

"The Lion's Cub," which tells the story of Elizabeth I in the years before she assumed the throne, was well received by critics. James Preston of *Stage and Television Today* praised Hale's "ability to untangle the intricacies of Tudor politics, underscore the religious faith and fervour of the age and characterise dead names from history books." A writer for *Variety* noted that the "path to the throne was a tortuous one for Elizabeth the girl and John Hale's script gave ... [Glenda] Jackson ample opportunities to reveal how intrigues, environment and eventual imprisonment were the crucible that formed her character in those early days."

Hale's play "Lorna and Ted" is a drastic departure from the majestic courts of Elizabethan England. Set in rural Suffolk, it is the story of a lonely, aging bachelor and his equally lonely housekeeper. Through a series of various comic maneuverings Ted persuades Lorna to marry him, but once they are married, their relationship decays rapidly. Although Robert Cushman of *Plays and Players* praised Hale for writing with "insight, intelligence, [and] a mournful humour," he wrote that the "long duologues punctuated by blackouts during which the actors visibly rearranged themselves, are really the stuff of television." In a more favorable review, *Stage's* R. B. Marriott commented that the "success of the play ... is in the effect of everyday detail, personal and domestic, and the creation of an air of relentless aloneness."

"Black Swan Winter," which Hale wrote as a requiem for his father, is about a man who, though he is a "success," senses that something vital is missing from his life. He journeys to his childhood home in an effort to learn what he can from his father, who counsels his son that the only way he can hope to avoid disappointment is to give up his dreams and adhere to a strict course of duty and discipline. The dialogue, wrote Jeremy Kingston of *Punch*, is "at its best in the heart to heart talks."

Kingston had previously praised Hale's skill at writing dialogue when he reviewed "It's All in the Mind." He called it an "alert, suspenseful play" and observed that Hale "has a keen ear for the edgy, slightly kidding talk that goes on between friends." This play, like "Black Swan Winter," deals with disillusionment as its heroine is confronted with the knowledge that both her husband and an old friend have been manipulating her for their own (in her eyes, dishonorable) ends.

The principal characters in Hale's novel *The Grudge Fight* are two teenage apprentices in the Royal Navy who, in an attempt to settle their multiple disputes, stage a "grudge fight." Hale, a Royal Navy veteran and the son of a career soldier, draws on his military background to create what David Sharpe of *Best Sellers* called a "confusing yet compelling story about the life of a young apprentice during the first hectic months of naval training." A writer for *New York Times Book Review* called *The Grudge Fight* "an action story that concentrates effectively on the immediate moment." Sharpe praised Hale's ability to "get into the mind of a boy, his thoughts, his feelings, his language, and his ambitions."

In *The Fort*, Hale again uses a military setting. The novel is set on the Mediterranean island of Dragut, "which, in the best traditions of fiction, is anywhere and everywhere," wrote Peter Ackroyd of *Spectator*. In 1807 the island had been the scene of a mutiny; over a century and a half later the descendants of those original mutineers attempt to

avenge the unjust execution of their ancestors. A *Times Literary Supplement* reviewer praised Hale for allowing his characters to develop fully: "None of the characters is trotted out for the convenience of the plot; each one comes with its own cloud of existence about it, a felt and complex past." Ackroyd called the novel "innovative" and went on to say that "this is no naive forward narrative, but the continual spinning of past and present into ... a web."

When asked to comment on his writing, Hale told *CA*, "I don't want to address my readers directly, I want to speak to them through my work!"

BIOGRAPHICAL/CRITICAL SOURCES: New York Times Book Review, September 10, 1967; *Best Sellers*, October 1, 1967; *Punch*, October 16, 1968, May 21, 1969, March 4, 1970; *Stage*, September 10, 1970; *Plays and Players*, October, 1970; *Stage and Television Today*, February 25, 1971; *Variety*, December 22, 1971, February 23, 1972; *Spectator*, September 29, 1973; *Times Literary Supplement*, November 23, 1973.

—*Sketch by Mary K. Sullivan*

*   *   *

HALE, John Rigby 1923-

PERSONAL: Born September 17, 1923, in Ashford, Kent, England; son of E.R.S. (a physician) and Hilda (Birks) Hale; married Rosiland Williams, 1953 (marriage ended); married Sheila Haynes, 1965; children: (first marriage) one son, two daughters; (second marriage) one son. *Education:* Jesus College, Oxford, B.A., 1948, M.A., 1953; also attended Johns Hopkins University and Harvard University, 1948-49. *Home:* 26 Montpelier Row, Twickenham, Middlesex, England. *Office:* Department of Italian, University of London, University College, Gower St., London WC1E 6BT, England.

CAREER: Oxford University, Jesus College, Oxford, England, fellow and tutor, 1949-64; University of Warwick, Coventry, England, professor of history, 1964-69; University of London, University College, London, England, professor of Italian, 1970—. Visiting professor at Cornell University, 1959, and University of California, Berkeley, 1969-70. Member of Advisory Committee of Royal Mint. Trustee of National Gallery in London, 1973-80, and chairman, 1974—. Public orator at University of London, 1980—. *Member:* British Academy (fellow), British Society for Renaissance Studies (chairman, 1973-78), Royal Historical Society (fellow), Royal Society of Arts (fellow), Society of Antiquaries (fellow). *Awards, honors:* Bronze Plaque of Academia Medicea for Italian edition of *Florence and the Medici*.

WRITINGS: Great-Uncle Toby (story), Faber, 1951; *England the Italian Renaissance: The Growth of Interest in Its History and Art*, Faber, 1954, revised edition, Arrow Books, 1963; *Napoleon: The Story of His Life*, Faber, 1954, Roy, c. 1957; (translator) Niccolo Machiavelli, *Mandragola: A Comedy*, Fantasy Press, 1956; *Machiavelli and Renaissance Italy*, Macmillan, 1960; *The Art of War and Renaissance England*, Folger Shakespeare Library, 1961; (with the editors of Time-Life Books) *Renaissance*, Time, Inc., 1965; (with the editors of Time-Life Books) *Age of Exploration*, Time, Inc., 1966; *Renaissance Exploration*, British Broadcasting Corp. (BBC), 1968, Norton, 1972; *Renaissance Europe, 1480-1520*, Fontana, 1971, published as *Renaissance Europe: Individual and Society, 1480-1520*, Harper, 1972; *The Hamlyn History of the World in Colour*, Volume IX: *Renaissance and Reformation* (Hale was not associated with earlier volumes), Hamlyn, 1971; (with Denys Hay) *The Renaissance* (phonotape), Holt Information Systems, 1972; *Florence and the Medici: The Pattern of Control*, Thames & Hudson, 1977; *Italian Renaissance Painting From Masaccio to Titian*, Dutton, 1977; *Renaissance Fortification: Art or Engineering?*, Thames & Hudson, 1977; *A Concise Encyclopaedia of Renaissance Italy*, Thames & Hudson, 1981.

Editor: *Settlers: Being Extracts From the Journals and Letters of Early Colonists in Canada, Australia, South Africa, and New Zealand*, Faber, 1950; *The Italian Journals of Samuel Rogers*, Faber, 1956; (and translator) Machiavelli, *Literary Works: Mandragola, Clizia, A Dialogue on Language and Balfagor; With Selections From the Private Correspondence*, Oxford University Press, 1961, published as *The Literary Works of Machiavelli: With Selections From the Correspondence*, Greenwood Press, 1979; John Smythe, *Certain Discourses Military*, Cornell University Press, 1964; *The Evolution of British Historiography From Bacon to Namier*, Meridian Books, 1964; Francesco Guicciardini, *History of Italy and History of Europe*, Washington Square Press, 1964; (with J.R.L. Highfield and B. Smalley) *Europe in the Late Middle Ages*, Northwestern University Press, 1965; *Renaissance Venice*, Rowman & Littlefield, 1973; *The Travel Journal of Antonio de Beatis*, Hakluyt Society, 1979.

Author of television scripts for "One Hundred Great Paintings," British Broadcasting Corp. (BBC-TV). Contributor to *The New Cambridge Modern History*, Volumes I, II, and III, and *The History of the King's Works*, Volume IV.

WORK IN PROGRESS: War and Society in Renaissance Italy, publication by Fontana expected in 1982.

SIDELIGHTS: In his book *Florence and the Medici: The Pattern of Control*, John Rigby Hale studies the three centuries in Italian history of Medici reign. For each of the more significant members of this powerful family, noted J. K. Hyde of the *Times Literary Supplement*, the author discusses "character and personal interests, . . . the pattern of control over Florence, . . . and the ways in which the Medici acted and were regarded outside Florence." In a review of the book for *Best Sellers*, S. A. Stussy complained that the work gets lost in detail and that the author seems not to know his own views on the subject: "He cannot decide whether he is a political or cultural historian, and this flaw drastically weakens his otherwise fine effort." John Porteous of the *New Statesman*, however, commended *Florence and the Medici* as "an impressive demonstration of a real historian's control over the full range of his sources and his discernment of a significant pattern in the material on which he is working."

Hale told *CA:* "My general books are as good as I can make them, but my main pleasure lies in the process of research and in writing up (mainly for learned journals) the immediate results. As an academic I believe my main usefulness is in making information (sometimes ideas and points of view) available for the authors of secondary works. The Renaissance is the period and Italy the place I feel most at home in imaginatively, and the topic I keep coming back to as the greatest stimulus to thinking about the past is warfare.

"Extra-curricularly, my greatest pleasure is derived from looking at works of art. My style of writing tends to be convoluted, and, to correct this, I find the writing of television scripts a thoroughly enjoyable discipline. I've just made seven programs for the BBC's current series, "One Hundred Great Paintings." At the moment I am hacking eighty thousand words out of a monograph on *The Military Organization of Renaissance Venice* in the hope of making it publishable."

BIOGRAPHICAL/CRITICAL SOURCES: Economist, November 26, 1977; *New Statesman,* December 9, 1977; *Observer,* December 11, 1977; *Best Sellers,* April, 1978; *Times Literary Supplement,* July 28, 1978.

* * *

HALL, Anthony Stewart 1945-
(Tony Hall)

PERSONAL: Born October 26, 1945, in Thorne, Yorkshire, England; son of Albert Hall (a Methodist minister); married Phoebe Katharine Souster (a social work service officer), December 28, 1968; children: Simon, Katharine. *Education:* London School of Economics and Political Science, London, B.Sc., 1968, graduate study, 1968-71. *Politics:* Socialist. *Religion:* "Devout atheist." *Home:* 12 Fernwood Ave., Streatham, London S.W.16, England. *Office:* British Agencies for Adoption and Fostering, 11 Southwark St., London S.E.1, England.

CAREER: National Institute for Social Work, London, England, lecturer in organization and management, 1971-73; University of Bristol, Bristol, England, lecturer in social administration, 1973-78; British Agencies for Adoption and Fostering, London, England, director, 1978—.

WRITINGS: (With Jimmy Algie) *A Management Game for the Social Sciences*, Bedford Square Press, 1974; *The Point of Entry: A Study of Client Reception in the Social Services*, Allen & Unwin, 1975; (contributor) M. Fitzgerald, editor, *Welfare in Action*, Open University, 1977; (contributor) M. Wicks, editor, *The Old and the Cold*, Heinemann, 1978.

Under name Tony Hall: (With wife, Phoebe Hall) *Part-Time Social Work*, Heinemann, 1980; (editor) *Access to Birth Records: The Impact of Section 26 of the Children Act 1975*, British Agencies for Adoption and Fostering, 1980. Contributor to professional journals and *New Society*.

SIDELIGHTS: Hall wrote: "I have always been fascinated by the organization of social service organizations and in particular by how they affect the clients and users of such services. Much of my research and writing develops this theme. More recently (since 1978) I have suspended my academic research in favor of a more practical contribution to relieving social problems. The Association of British Adoption and Fostering Agencies (since 1980 British Agencies for Adoption and Fostering) is an influential voluntary organization which aims to improve the quality of life of children in public care."

* * *

HALL, Fernau

PERSONAL: Born in Victoria, British Columbia, Canada; son of Henry Charles (a chief magistrate) and Elena (Fernau) Hall. *Education:* University of British Columbia, B.Comm., 1932; also attended Military College of Science, Watchet, England. *Home:* 44 South Hill Park, London NW3 2SJ, England. *Agent:* Christopher Busby Ltd., 44 Great Russell St., London W.C.1, England. *Office:* Daily Telegraph, 135 Fleet St., London E.C.4, England.

CAREER: Professional dancer, 1937-39 and 1945-50; stage and lighting director for dance companies, 1946-65; Rediffusion Television, London, England, producer of schools programs, 1957-63; Thames Television, London, producer of schools programs, 1963-72; writer and critic, 1937—. *Military service:* British Army, radar scientist, 1940-46. *Member:* Institute of Choreology (co-founder; member of council), British Society of Aesthetics, Critic's Circle.

WRITINGS: Ballet, Bodley Head, 1949; *Modern English Ballet*, Melrose, 1950; *An Anatomy of Ballet*, Melrose, 1953, published in the United States as *World Dance*, A. A. Wyn, 1954; *The World of Ballet and Dance*, Hamlyn, 1970, revised 2nd edition, 1971; (with Elvira Rone) *Olga Preobrazhenshaya: A Portrait*, Dekker, 1978. Chief critic for *Ballet Today*, 1962-71; dance critic for *New Statesman*, 1967-68; dance, mime, and puppetry critic for *Daily Telegraph*, 1969—. Contributor of articles and reviews to *Dancing Times*.

WORK IN PROGRESS: Antony Tudor: Choreographer of Genius.

SIDELIGHTS: Hall wrote: "I went to the university as a child prodigy, came to London, and began training as a dancer. I began writing criticism in 1937 while still a dance student, driven to it because existing London critics failed to recognize the importance of Antony Tudor's ballet 'Dark Elegies.' My training was interrupted by war service as a radar scientist, after which I had a short career as a dancer (beginning with an appearance in an Indian dance-drama while awaiting demobilization). I then moved on to stage and lighting direction.

"I worked with a wide variety of companies: ballet, modern dance, classical East Indian, Spanish, Indonesian, Kabuki, and No. And I helped to form Ballets Negres, a company of Black African and West Indian dancers. I performed the white roles in this company's productions. My work as a dancer was invaluable in later work as lighting director. It was also invaluable to my work as critic and writer.

"Having spent so much of my life on the active side of the proscenium arch, I remain very well aware of the feelings of the artists who read my criticism. When I criticize adversely, I try to do so in a constructive way. I feel that I have a responsibility to readers, dancers, choreographers, stage designers, lighting designers, composers, conductors, and the art of dance.

"My work for the *Daily Telegraph* covers three main fields: all forms of dance (including Flamenco, folk dance, and the classical dances of the East, which to me are just as much in need of expert and serious appraisal as ballet and modern dance), mime, and puppetry. Both mime and puppetry go well with dance, for they too are arts of stylized movement. In the classical theatre of the East dance and mime are part of one art form, along with singing, chanting, and instrumental music; in Japan the Bunraku puppets have always been regarded as a major branch of the theatre; and in Java the Wayang Kulit shadow puppets are the major theatrical form.

"I was one of the founding fathers of schools television in the United Kingdom. I helped establish the principle that these programs should not be didactic in the narrow sense. They should be fascinating for children, and they should have the same qualities as imaginative television programs for adults, good actors and skilled scriptwriters. In fourteen years I devised a large number of series, revised the scripts of programs with which I was associated, wrote a good many of the scripts, presented a number of the programs, and became very familiar with the techniques of television and film."

BIOGRAPHICAL/CRITICAL SOURCES: Ed Peter Noble, *British Ballet*, Sketon Robinson, 1948; G.B.L. Wilson, *A Dictionary of Ballet*, Penguin, 1957; Ed A. Chujoy and P. W. Manchester, *The Dance Encyclopedia*, Simon & Schuster, 1967; Horst Koegler, *The Concise Oxford Encyclopedia of Ballet*, Oxford University Press, 1977.

HALL, Frederic Sauser
See SAUSER-HALL, Frederic

*   *   *

HALL, James 1918-

PERSONAL: Born July 18, 1918, in Letchworth, Hertfordshire, England. *Home and office:* 19 Milton Rd., Harpenden, Hertfordshire AL5 5LA, England. *Agent:* David Higham Associates Ltd., 5-8 Lower John St., Golden Sq., London W1R 4HA, England.

CAREER: Worked in book publishing in London, England, 1946-72; proprietor of book production services company, 1972—.

WRITINGS: Dictionary of Subjects and Symbols in Art, Harper, 1974, new edition, 1979; (editor of revision) Julia M. Ehresmann, *The Pocket Dictionary of Art Terms*, J. Murray, 1980. Contributor to *Academic American Encyclopedia* and to art journals.

WORK IN PROGRESS: A History of Images: The Story of Art and Ideas in Italy, written from the standpoint of iconography, publication by J. Murray expected in 1982.

SIDELIGHTS: James Hall told *CA:* "I study and write about art history from the point of view of an amateur, in the original sense of the word: 'One who cultivates a particular study or art for the love of it, and not professionally.'"

*   *   *

HALL, Phil 1953-

PERSONAL: Born September 18, 1953, in Lindsay, Ontario, Canada; son of Cecil (a laborer) and Dorothy Agnes (Kimble) Hall; married Catharine Jo-anna Douglass, August 30, 1976 (divorced, 1980); children: D'Arcy Andrew. *Education:* University of Windsor, B.A. (with honors), 1976, M.A., 1978. *Home:* 4375 Prince Albert, Vancouver, British Columbia, Canada V5V 4J8.

CAREER: St. Clair College, Windsor, Ontario, instructor in creative composition, 1977-79; University of Windsor, Windsor, instructor in English composition, 1979; writer, 1979—. Editor of Flat Singles Press. *Member:* League of Canadian Poets, Vancouver Men Against Rape. *Awards, honors:* Alex Pavlini Memorial Award from Canadian Broadcasting Corp. (CBC), 1975; Ontario Arts grants, 1975 and 1976; first prize from short story contest sponsored by Essex County Arts Foundation, 1979, for "Cathedral"; Canada Council grant, 1979-80.

WRITINGS: Eighteen Poems, Cyanamid Press, 1973; *Homes* (poetry), Black Moss Press, 1979; *The Crucifiction* (poem), Flat Singles Press, 1980.

Work represented in anthologies, including *The Ontario Experience* and *Going for Coffee*. Contributor of poems to magazines, including *Echo, Poetry Toronto, Canadian Forum, Fiddlehead, Tamarack Review*, and *Ontario Review*. Past editor of *Generation*.

WORK IN PROGRESS: Shooting at the Dead Father, "a poem/xerox sequence"; *The Pedestrian Archives*, a poem sequence.

SIDELIGHTS: Hall wrote: "Poems that are created for us by the cross-hatching of coincidental events, poems as outlines to actions or indications of where the poetry (underrunning current of elegant truth) exists in the lives we lead, writing that is useful, words that recognize the ethnopoetic necessity for change: all of these preoccupy my mind and its efforts at this time."

HALL, Tom T. 1936-

PERSONAL: Born May 25, 1936, in Olive Hill, Ky.; son of Virgil L. (a brick plant worker and minister) and Della Lena (Henderson) Hall; married Dixie Dean (original name, Iris Violet May Lawrence; a dog breeder), March 19, 1968; children: (previous marriage) Dean Todd. *Education:* Attended Roanoke College, 1962-63. *Residence:* Fox Hollow, Franklin, Tenn. *Office address:* P.O. Box 40209, Nashville, Tenn. 37204.

CAREER: Performer with musical group Tom Hall and the Kentucky Travelers, 1952-54; WMOR, Morehead, Ky., disc jockey, 1952-57; Newkeys Music, Inc., songwriter, 1962-69; Hallnote Music (publishing firm), Brentwood, Tenn., founder, 1969—; performer with The Storytellers at Carnegie Hall, New York, N.Y., 1973; regular performer with The Grand ʾle Opry, Nashville, Tenn., 1980—; recorder of albums with Mercury Records, including "In Search of a Song," 1971, "We All Got Together and . . . ," 1972, "The Storyteller," 1972, "Songs of Fox Hollow," 1974, "Magnificent Music Machine," 1976, "Faster Horses," 1976, and "About Love," 1977; recorder of albums with RCA, including "New Train, Same Rider," 1978, "Places I've Done Time," 1978, "Saturday Morning Songs," 1979, "Ol' T's In Town," 1979, and "Soldier of Fortune," 1980. Instructor in songwriting at Middle Tennessee State University, 1978. Director of Harpeth National Bank, Franklin, 1981. *Military service:* U.S. Army, 1957-61.

MEMBER: Country Music Association, American Lung Association of Tennessee, Tennessee Heart Association, Veterinary Medical Association of Tennessee (chairman of education fund, 1978-79), Nashville Songwriter's Association, Nashville Humane Association, Rotary Club. *Awards, honors:* Cover award from Music City News, 1967, for most promising male artist; Country Music Association award, 1968, for "Harper Valley PTA"; eight Songwriter's Achievement awards from Nashville Songwriter's Association, including songwriter of the year, 1972; inducted into the Songwriter's Hall of Fame, 1978. Broadcast Music awards, 1964, for "D.J. for a Day," 1965, for "Mad," 1966, for "Artificial Rose," "Hello Viet Nam," and "What We're Fighting For," 1968 and 1969, for "Harper Valley PTA," 1970, for "Margie's at the Lincoln Park Inn," "One More Mile," "Homecoming," and "A Week in a County Jail," 1971, for "The Pool Shark," "That's How I Got to Memphis," and "If I Ever Fall In Love With a Honky Tonk Girl," 1972, for "The Year That Clayton Delaney Died," 1973, for "Old Dogs, Children, and Watermelon" and "Me and Jesus," 1974, for "I Love" and "Ravishing Ruby," 1975, for "Country Is" and "That Song Is Driving Me Crazy," 1976, for "Deal," "I Like Beer," and "Sneaky Snake," 1976 and 1977, for "Faster Horses," and 1978, for "Your Man Loves You."

WRITINGS: How I Write Songs, Why You Can, Chappell, 1976; *The Storyteller's Nashville,* Doubleday, 1979. Author of songs, including "Harper Valley PTA," "The Monkey Who Became President," "Homecoming," "I Washed My Face in the Morning Dew," and "A Week in a County Jail."

WORK IN PROGRESS: A novel tentatively entitled *The Laughing Man,* publication by Doubleday expected in 1981.

SIDELIGHTS: Tom T. Hall, author of "Harper Valley PTA," a tune which sold more than 4.5 million copies, began writing songs as a boy. He explained: "I wrote songs as a kid and it was like being able to wriggle my ears. Not to sound immodest, but I never had to bust ass to make a living at it." After years of work, Hall's career skyrocketed with the re-

cording of the popular song about an angry, outspoken mother who excoriates the stodgy and hypocritical PTA of Harper Valley. "I like to think there was a direct line from 'Spoon River Anthology' to 'Babbit' to, God forgive me, 'Harper Valley PTA,'" Hall contended. "I don't mean to compare it to the first two—but it did get a message across that I'm proud of."

In his music, Hall writes about subjects with which most people could identify. "I try to make people hear my songs and say, 'God damn, I thought I was the only one who knew that,'" the performer asserted. Hall also endeavors to be as genuine as possible in his songs. "You won't fool these folks for long," he remarked. "When country people sit down to eat ham, they don't try to remember which fork; they want to know which hog. Everything's simple and up front—and you'd better be honest with them. That's the most important thing—and probably the best thing—about our kind of music."

Hall's book *The Storyteller's Nashville* received a favorable review from Molly Ivins in the *New York Times Book Review.* Claiming he is indeed "a good storyteller," Ivins went on to explain that Hall's "stories . . . about his early years in Nashville as a songwriter are often raunchy and hilarious." She also added that he "has none of the saccharine piety that often mars country music."

CA INTERVIEW

Tom T. Hall was interviewed by phone on May 8, 1980.

CA: What do you think accounts for the growing popularity of country music among people in varied economic and social groups?

HALL: It's part of the general evolution of human beings, I think. We've become more tolerant of a lot of things. Country music for a long time had a stigma attached to it that it was illiterate, that it was unworthy of serious consideration. It used to be called hillbilly music, and the connotation hung around with it for so many years that people thought that if they listened to it and enjoyed it there might be a flaw in their characters. All of that's gone by the board, the mass media being largely responsible for the acceptance of a number of things of that sort. Country music has grown along with a lot of other cultural aspects of American society. It's grown along with the acceptance of Southern politics and Southern politicians. The Dallas Cowboys won the Superbowl—that has a lot to do with it. It was part of the New South. The music was thought by the national media to be somehow of Southern origin. Of course folk music is not of Southern origin; it's of European origin.

CA: Is there one person you think of as the greatest in country music?

HALL: No. I think country music has grown with the help of a lot of people. The Country Music Foundation has done a great deal. In the short span of twelve years the Country Music Foundation has changed the name of hillbilly music to *country.* That in itself is a public relations phenomenon. People in the business preferred to be called country, but the nation at large referred to it as *hillbilly.* I performed and entertained some in the military, and it was then legally labeled hillbilly music. We took that to be derogatory. Before John Kennedy's administration, country music was referred to in all governmental correspondence and records as hillbilly —that had been the official word—but Kennedy instructed all government bureaus to change it to country.

CA: In The Storyteller's Nashville *you wrote about the kind of paradoxical way that success sometimes breeds misery instead of happiness. Why do you think this happens?*

HALL: I think what I said was that people associate success with happiness; and not only do they not run around together, they probably don't even know one another. They don't have anything to do with one another. Material gain or public acclaim or anything of that sort has nothing to do with personal happiness, and people counting on that are often disappointed. Of course the average person will tell you that success is where it's at; the man on the street still believes that. They can't imagine any such person as Tom T. Hall would have any problems, or not be deliriously happy at every instant of his life.

CA: Also in that book you touched on drug use by musicians. Can you comment on the causes of such drug use?

HALL: In entertaining, you try to attain what's called "getting up" for a show. People use all sorts of devices, but the shortest route is drugs. It's also the most dangerous route. So some people, instead of trying to find an emotional high or find it in the music or find it in themselves, find it in drugs. It's that simple. It's not complicated at all. But then, of course, when the show is over, you're still high. Therein lies the danger. Once a show is over, you hopefully become a private citizen again, but a lot of people never get offstage for the simple reason that they never get off drugs. It's a dangerous little business. If a fellow had a way of getting high for a show and then coming right back down, he'd be a hell of an entertainer. The sad thing is that drugs work if you're onstage with them. Because you're high, the music sounds a little brighter and a little clearer and you can really entertain. But then it's not worth it, because once you get offstage, you go back to your room and, hell, you're still flying.

CA: Do you find it hard to switch from songwriting to prose writing?

HALL: No. You know, songs are the ultimate in communicative brevity. You have to get a lot done in just a little bit, because you have the restrictions of a melody. I've always written, but never published a lot. Lately I've done some things for magazines, and there are a couple of little books that I did, and that sort of thing. I had the feeling in the beginning that I would somehow have to take these ideas and enlarge on them. But that sort of writing bores me, so I decided just to write my books like I write my songs. If I'm finished talking about something, I go on to something else. I remember what Hemingway did in *The Old Man and the Sea.* His description of the main character in the opening line was, "He was an old man." Now a lot of writers would have described his eyes and his hair and his stature for a good twenty minutes, you know, because he was the main character. But that suited me when Hemingway said he was an old man; I've seen old men. I try to remember that. But I have stopped on occasion and said, "I've got to say more about this." Then I may leave it alone for a week, and when I go back to it I say, "Let's get on to something else. Maybe that's all I wanted to say about that."

CA: Have you been pleased with the reception of The Storyteller's Nashville?

HALL: Oh, yeah. It made money. I'm not writing for money, because I don't need it, but I wanted the people who invested money in it, like Doubleday, to be happy. And it's in the third printing, so they're very satisfied with it. I would

have hated for them to lose money on it; that would have been sad.

CA: What are your writing habits?

HALL: I only write in the winter. Well, I do some magazine pieces and things like that in the summer, but when I'm working on a book, I do that in the winter. I don't tour on the road and fool with the music business in the wintertime. From December to April, I write. And I write from about three in the morning until maybe nine or ten.

CA: Do you get any sleep?

HALL: Oh, yeah. I'm an early riser, but I haven't seen Johnny Carson in years.

CA: You've described yourself as self-educated. Other than Hemingway, whom you mentioned earlier, what writers have influenced you?

HALL: As a Southern writer, I'm supposed to be big on Southern writers, but I get bored with Tennessee Williams and Faulkner and all those dudes. I grew up in that, so to go back and read about it kinda bores me. But I like Sinclair Lewis and I like Hemingway. Sinclair Lewis, I think, will come back around. I think people will read him again. I know he was out of fashion there for a while.

What I would do was pick an author and read everything he had written. Then I would read a biography or an autobiography. This was just a scheme I hit on for myself. I was a disc jockey for a number of years and a bachelor, and I usually had a little apartment somewhere. So I would just find the local library and read completely through an author, then read his biography or autobiography. That way I had a good clear picture of what he did.

CA: Do you have any particular favorites you read now?

HALL: About the only thing I read now is current-events magazines and William Saroyan. I've read just about everything of his—well, not the old stuff. I don't know about *The Daring Young Man on the Flying Trapeze* and "My Heart's in the Highlands." But he's really written some good things lately. But I think mostly writers would enjoy it. I enjoyed *Obituary* tremendously. All his books are hard to find. You damn near have to go to Fresno to get one.

CA: Why does Saroyan appeal to you particularly?

HALL: He's straightaway, he's honest, and he really seems to enjoy writing. I also liked *The World According to Garp;* I thought that was the best book of the last five or six years. And for some reason or other I keep reading Joseph Heller. He's the fellow who said, "I'm leaving the rest of my life open in case something comes up." That endeared him to me.

CA: Would you talk about your library and how it came about?

HALL: As a child, I always wanted a house with a library. A neighbor of mine had a library, and I would get books from him. We didn't have a library in my hometown. The school had a limited one, but I read most of the things in there. And when I grew up, I wanted to have a house with a library. So I have paneled walls and huge shelves and it's all full of books. I go in there and it's sort of like sitting in the shade of a tree, sitting in the atmosphere of all those books. It's just a thing that I like to do—sometimes I just go in there and sit.

CA: Do you have first editions, collector's items?

HALL: No. I have some very old books I've bought. I really don't collect first editions or anything. A lot of times authors will send me autographed copies of their books. I love autographed books. I got a nice letter the other day from Herman Wouk, of all people. He had heard my music and read my book, and he wrote me a note to say he liked it. That was quite an endorsement. I was shocked. I've got a lot of authors who've given me autographed books: Peter Benchley, Joseph Wambaugh, people like that.

CA: You have an unusual circle of friends, I believe. Would you talk about them?

HALL: I have, I guess, a lot of characters for friends—a lot of poets, some very wealthy people, and some destitute people. I don't select them from any segment of society. I belong to a black church, too. I live near, and I'd hear them singing. So I went up there and visited with them. They needed a little help and I helped them out. Then they made me a member of the church. The junior choir made a record with me. And I'm a big fan of carpenters; people who build things. I know a lot of people who are carpenters; I find out where they're working and I go watch them work. I enjoy watching construction.

CA: Have you done any of it?

HALL: Oh, I'm sort of a decent carpenter, I guess. I couldn't build a house or anything like that. Mainly I just watch. I sit around on a bench or something and tell them stories while they're hammering. I'm a sidewalk superintendent.

CA: You've had some poetry readings in your home, haven't you?

HALL: I had Miller Williams. You know, when guitar players go somewhere, they take their guitars and they sing some songs. I called Miller and told him I was going to get some people together in Nashville, asked him if he'd come and read some poetry at my house, and he said sure. So we got a few jugs of white wine and got some people who like poetry and got the lights just right, and he was sitting in the library on a stool. And he read, I guess, an hour and a half. He had people crying and applauding. When it was over, I took him around Nashville and introduced him as my poet friend. Miller has a beret and a beard and a cane—he looks like a stereotype. I showed him off quite a bit, and everybody was impressed. Then I found out that he had never done that before; nobody had ever asked him to read in a house. We had a tremendous turnout; I think we had a hundred people there, and they were all very impressed. It's such great entertainment, and it's free. I can't imagine people not doing that more, but I may be the only guy here who's ever had a poetry reading in his house.

I have several real good poet friends, and I admire them. Jim Whitehead is a good poet. There's a guy named William Mills who's awfully good. He's got a collection of poetry called *Watch for the Fox* that's got some great stuff in it. It's published by Louisiana State University in Baton Rouge, but Mills teaches out West. It's unfortunate that these poets are so overshadowed by James Dickey. Although I did like *The Strength of Fields*. I like a poem called "The Rain Guitar." He's sitting there about half drunk, I suppose, and playing his guitar in the rain—it's raining on the wood of his good Martin guitar. And all these people come by from out of the past to haunt him, and he's picking away on the old guitar, and it's raining to beat hell. Sitting here in Georgia someplace drunker'n a monkey. It's a damn good poem.

CA: Your wife raises basset hounds. Is that a joint hobby, or just hers?

HALL: That's her hobby. My wife raises bassets, shows them and everything, which is a kind of phenomenon because I don't understand the dog business. They weep and moan and stomp their feet if they don't win a ribbon, those dogs. It's beyond me. But then trying to explain golf to somebody who doesn't play would be just about as difficult. So I just leave all that alone. You try to explain to people who don't write why you want to write, to go to all the trouble, and they don't understand that either. John Henry said one time, "That's just the way things is."

CA: What kind of advice would you give to aspiring country songwriters?

HALL: Not to take themselves too seriously, I guess. Just to write down what they want to write. I started writing songs because people weren't writing what I wanted to hear about. I don't think I would write for anybody's amusement but my own in the beginning. And it's as good a hobby as it is a profession, maybe a better hobby. You can write a song about your little niece or your daughter or your wife and sing it for them and almost be guaranteed that they'll like it. Songs serve a better purpose than to be put on records; that's not what songs were originally about. It's just that we'd made a commerce out of everything else, so why not make a commerce out of music? But young writers ought to understand that that's not what songs are about. When you're writing a song, you shouldn't see it on a record. That has nothing to do with the song.

CA: Would you advise people to keep trying, but to work at something to keep them fed in the meantime?

HALL: There's an old expression in Nashville: "Don't give up your day job." But I don't discourage adventurism, because I've been one of the most adventurous characters in the world. I never asked anybody what to do. And if anybody had told me, I'd have done what I pleased anyway. Maybe all this advice we're giving these writers, they probably don't want it.

CA: You've been doing some political campaigning lately, haven't you?

HALL: I've been traveling around the country for Jimmy Carter. I've campaigned in New Hampshire, Iowa, Wyoming, Alabama, Tennessee, Maryland. Partly for the experience. You know, there's golf and football and politics, and they're all great games. And they're widely divergent in their application of talent. But I enjoy campaigning. I get out on the streets and shake hands, go into department stores, all that, I guess, for the hell of it. And I believe in President Carter. My friend Tom Connelly (a writer and history professor at the University of South Carolina) and I were talking about the Southern mind. And I told him that the first thing we'd have to do was find out what the Northern mind is like to see what we were up against. Which disturbed him, because that doubled his research. It comes back to "as opposed to what?"

CA: Are you interested in writing in any genre you haven't tried yet?

HALL: I'm halfway through a novel. Doubleday has it, they like it, and they're going to see if they can con somebody into picking up a few copies.

CA: Do you want to talk about it?

HALL: I can't talk about it. It's kind of involved. I'm forty-three, see, so what I've gotta do is get busy and write some classics right away. I don't have time for police novels and *Jaws* and things like that. I've got to go straight to the classics.

BIOGRAPHICAL/CRITICAL SOURCES: Newsweek, June 18, 1973; Bill C. Malone and Judith McCulloch, editors, *Stars of Country Music,* University of Illinois Press, 1975; *New York Times Book Review,* October 21, 1979.

—Interview by Jean W. Ross

*   *   *

HALL, Tony
See HALL, Anthony Stewart

*   *   *

HALLIDAY, Brett
See TERRALL, Robert

*   *   *

HALPERN, Barbara Kerewsky
See KEREWSKY-HALPERN, Barbara

*   *   *

HAMBLETONIAN
See FAIRFAX-BLAKEBOROUGH, John Freeman

*   *   *

HAMILTON, Joan Lesley   1942-
(Joan Cline)

PERSONAL: Born April 17, 1942, in Hollywood, Calif.; daughter of John Leslie (an actor, director, and broadcaster) and Isabella Vara (an actress and writer; maiden name, Rozenfeld) Hamilton; married Charles Cline (a teacher of science and mathematics), April 6, 1963; children: Dorothy Joan, John Charles. *Education:* Attended high school in Hollywood, Calif. *Home:* 6334 Ben Ave., North Hollywood, Calif. 91606.

CAREER: Los Angeles Griffith Park Zoo, Los Angeles, Calif., assistant to supervisor and veterinarian, 1961-63; free-lance writer and independent editor, 1959—. Co-founder and past director of San Fernando Valley Audubon Society's "Suburban Safari" for children; director of Environmental Educational Curriculum. Public speaker. *Awards, honors:* Conservation education award from National Audubon Society, 1973.

WRITINGS: The Lion and the Cross: A Novel of Saint Patrick and Ancient Ireland, Doubleday, 1979. Contributor to magazines, including *Phainopepla* (under name Joan Cline).

WORK IN PROGRESS: The Lion in Darkness, a sequel to the first novel, publication by Doubleday expected c. 1985; *Refuge,* a novel of early California, the secularization of its missions, the last days of the sea otter trade, and the extinction of the Indians of coastal California.

SIDELIGHTS: Joan Hamilton wrote: "I suppose that there are many writers who write well and easily about themselves. As a native Hollywoodian, product of a family of thespians, one would assume that I would have inherited my share of bombast. Not so. I am the ordinary, run-of-the-mill shrinking violet, a shy seed sprung up out of generations of wild ancestors. If one follows the family name back to its

beginnings, one finds a mad Scottish earl, several generations of Irish patriots, and a fierce Pole who fled the tyranny of his homeland to become a Yankee brigadier general in the Civil War and the first unofficial governor of the Territory of Alaska. There were Texans. Classical painters. And grandparents who, at the turn of the century, thrilled and scandalized northern California with their own traveling circus in which, as aeronauts, they performed as stars of the high trapeze while floating aloft in hot-air balloons. It was only natural that their eldest son, my father, would become a stuntman and actor and double for Errol Flynn. And so I was born in Hollywood, where everything is possible and daydreams are marketable commodities.

"I do not remember ever consciously wanting to be a writer. I am simply one of those people who has never been able to look at a blank piece of paper without having my fingers twitch with the need to write upon it. And I have always been a dreamer. Even as a child, if asked to choose my preference for a Sunday outing, I would invariably beg to be taken far from the city. To lonely places. To wild places. Places free of concrete and city noise. Places where, I understand now, the soul can run free and the senses soar to dimensions impossible to find within the confines of an urban environment. I would imagine myself to be in other times. In far and mystical lands. On the seas of Melville and Stevenson and Sabatini. On the wide plains of Dorothy Johnson. On the torturous hills of John Steinbeck. Within the jungles and mountain vastnesses of Rudyard Kipling. I would create stories to fill the fancies of my imagination. It was by far the best game. The game of make-believe. It very often still is, although now, since I prefer to be considered a rational and sane adult by my family and peers, I have learned to channel my flights of fancy through the vehicle of my typewriter. And so, like many a grown-up child ill-content with the boundaries of the everyday world, I have become a writer.

"My first short story was published in *American Girl* when I was seventeen. I was accepted as a client of the Jaffe Literary Agency when I was eighteen. I was research editor on *Hunza Health Secrets,* a 1963 nonfiction best seller. Over the years, until the publication of my first novel, my career has been mainly as a ghost writer. My last such project has had eleven reprintings and has been published in five foreign languages.

"In 1963, I married. Our summers were spent traveling and exploring the Pacific Northwest and the wilds of rural Hawaii. After the birth of our children we built a mountain retreat high in the San Bernardino mountains. Since I am at heart an old-fashioned soul who believes that raising children is not only an art, but a full-time occupation, I gave up my job to pursue the home arts. Turn me loose on Walton's Mountain and I will out-Walton any female there, baking bread, putting up preserves, bottling homemade root beer, growing my own table garden, and designing my own quilts.

"Through my children I became active in the local conservation scene, contributing often to local conservation newsletters. In 1974 I wrote an article on the California gray whale. It appeared in a local newsletter and brought such a positive response from readers that I began once again to think of 'serious' writing. One reader wrote: 'I have never been so moved by anything I have read! I never write fan letters, but why haven't I seen more of your work? You must be a professional writer. If not—why the hell not?'

"Needless to say, that was enough to make any self-respecting ghost writer come out of the closet. It was time for me to begin my first novel. But what to write?

"My family and I are members of North Hollywood's Saint Patrick's parish. Set into the east wall of the church, there is a stained glass window portrait of Saint Patrick. On Sunday mornings the sun streams through the multi-colored facets of that window and seems to bring the face of that man, dead now some fifteen hundred years, to life. It is an arresting face. Somehow silently angry. Bearded. Blue-eyed. Stern-lipped. Reproving and infinitely sad. It seems to stare out of time, reminding those who have read his *Confessio* of his simple life's wish: 'that men might know and understand my heart's desire . . .' that the people of Ireland, indeed of all the world, might dwell in the 'peace of Christ.'

"As one whose ancestors have lived and died in Ireland, I was inspired to write Patrick's story. After nearly five years of intensive research and writing, *The Lion and the Cross* was complete. Those who first read it were less than encouraging. Where were the leprechauns? Where were the cute, sotted little men sipping poteen on every corner? Where were the rainbows and the pots of gold? Nowhere to be found. At all, at all. In the structuring of the book, in the reconstruction of pre-Dark Age Ireland, I had shattered many a myth and stereotype, writing not of a psalm-singing, quaint-little-saint with a shillelagh, but of a man among men, and of Ireland in her Golden Age, before her warrior kings had tasted the bitter wine of defeat. In 1979 it was published and glowingly reviewed by critics.

"Through *The Lion and the Cross,* and through my future projects, I hope to share with my readers my sense of joy in the living land, my ever-increasing awe of the resilience of the human soul, and my sense of the great, ever-onrushing tide of a predestination of which we may only dare to dream."

*   *   *

HAMILTON, William B(aillie)   1930-

PERSONAL: Born March 31, 1930, in Brule Point, Nova Scotia, Canada; son of Allister and Christene (Baillie) Hamilton; married Marian L. Banks, July 13, 1963; children: Brian. *Education:* Acadia University, B.A., 1949, B.Ed., 1950, M.A., 1953; University of Western Ontario, Ph.D., 1970. *Home:* 44 Tangmere Cres., Halifax, Nova Scotia, Canada B3M 1K1. *Office:* Atlantic Institute of Education, 5244 South St., Halifax, Nova Scotia, Canada B3J 1A4.

CAREER: High school teacher of history in Nova Scotia, 1950-56; principal of secondary school in Pugwash, Nova Scotia, 1956-64; Commonwealth Institute, London, England, lecturer in Canadian Studies, 1964-65; University of Western Ontario, London, assistant professor, 1965-70, associate professor and chairman of department of history and comparative education, 1970-75; Atlantic Institute of Education, Halifax, Nova Scotia, professor and director, 1975—. Visiting professor at University of New England, Australia, 1980. *Member:* Canadian Historical Association, Canadian Society for Studies in Education, Champlain Society (member of board of directors, 1980—).

WRITINGS: A Bibliography of the History of Canadian Education, University of Western Ontario Press, 1968; (contributor) J. D. Wilson, R. M. Stamp, and L. P. Audet, editors, *Canadian Education: A History,* Prentice-Hall, 1970; *Canadian Education and the Future,* University of Western Ontario Press, 1971; (with J. L. Granatein and Paul Stevens) *Canada: Bibliographic Guide,* Hakkert Press, 1974, 2nd edition, 1977; *Local History in Atlantic Canada,* Macmillan, 1974; *The Macmillan Book of Canadian Place Names,* Macmillan, 1978, second edition, 1982; *The Nova Scotia*

Traveller, Macmillan, 1981. Contributor to *Profiles of Canadian Educators,* Heath, 1974. Contributor to educational and historical journals.

SIDELIGHTS: Hamilton told *CA:* "My writing, largely an 'extracurricular' activity, has a strong historical bias. Each book seems to be a spin-off from the previous one. Thus, a chapter on place names in *Local History in Atlantic Canada* led to the publication of *The Macmillan Book of Canadian Place Names.* My most recent book, *The Nova Scotia Traveller,* integrates historical accounts of travel with the contemporary scene."

*   *   *

HAMMER, Signe

PERSONAL: Given name is pronounced *Sig*-na; born in Indianapolis, Ind.; daughter of John Jacob (a railway executive) and Agnes (an artist; maiden name, Hammer) Clutz. *Education:* Wellesley College, B.A., 1962. *Politics:* "Feminist, Democrat." *Residence:* New York, N.Y. *Agent:* Sandra Elkin, 161 West 15th St., No. 7E, New York, N.Y. 10011.

CAREER: Atlantic Monthly Press, Boston, Mass., reader and editorial assistant, 1963-65; Harper & Row Publishers, Inc., New York City, assistant editor in trade department, 1965-69; Metropolitan Applied Research Center, New York City, consulting editor and writer for urban affairs publications program, 1970-72; St. Ann's School, Brooklyn, N.Y., teacher of English and theatre, 1972-73; free-lance writer, 1973—. Adjunct assistant professor of creative writing at New York University, 1976—; guest lecturer at New School for Social Research and State University of New York; workshop lecturer at Womanschool, 1976-78, and at colleges and for women's groups. Gives poetry readings; performer in dance theatre with Meredith Monk and the House, 1968-71; guest on television and radio programs, including "Today Show," "Phil Donahue Show," and "American Women at the Crossroads." *Member:* Women's Ink, Authors Guild, National Society of Journalists and Authors. *Awards, honors:* Fellow at MacDowell Colony, 1979.

WRITINGS: Daughters and Mothers: Mothers and Daughters (Literary Guild alternative selection; Women Today Book Club selection), Quadrangle, 1975; (editor) *Women: Body and Culture; Essays on the Sexuality of Women in a Changing Society,* Harper, 1975; *Passionate Attachments,* Rawson, Wade, 1981. Contributor of articles and poems to periodicals, including *Mademoiselle, Parade, Harper's Bazaar, Ms., Fiction, Rapport,* and *Village Voice.*

WORK IN PROGRESS: Identity Papers, a memoir/fiction, publication expected in 1982.

SIDELIGHTS: In *Identity Papers,* Signe Hammer wrote: "Most lives are better lived than recorded; if I record some events in mine it is because my life has been, until now, impossible to live.

"You could say my life ended in the middle of a May night in 1950. I was nine years old. I was awakened by an explosion that entered my sleep as a sentence: 'The books fell on the floor' . . . I heard my brothers pounding down the spiral back stairs from their third floor rooms . . . Chris was out in the driveway yelling, 'fire!' I walked into the kitchen doorway and saw Richard standing over a body lying on what I have since learned was an ironing board. He had his hand on the wrist, feeling for a pulse. The body was my mother. . . .

"What I have been trying to find out all these years is, where did I disappear to?"

Hammer told *CA*: "My preoccupation in writing is identity—what you make up out of all the people and experiences and general chaos of your life. This has led me to an interest in psychology and to writing about women and family relationships. In *Identity Papers* I am writing about my own life, and in *Passionate Attachments,* my book on fathers and daughters, I am exploring my relationship with my own father and the relationships of a lot of other fathers and daughters I have talked to. The father part of women's identities is powerful, and it is time to sort out what is constructive and usable from what has been destructive and confusing."

BIOGRAPHICAL/CRITICAL SOURCES: New England Review, summer, 1980.

* * *

HANDY, Edward Smith Craighill 1893(?)-1980

OBITUARY NOTICE: Born c. 1893 in Roanoke, Va.; died of pneumonia, December 26, 1980, in Dunn Loring, Va. Ethnologist, anthropologist, and author. Handy was a noted authority on the peoples and cultures of the Pacific islands. Among those who sought out his assistance was the well-known anthropologist Margaret Mead. After making several expeditions to the Pacific islands in the 1920's, Handy worked as a visiting professor at Yale University during the Depression. In 1936 he became a farmer in his native Virginia. Among his writings are *Native Culture in the Marquesas* and *Polynesian Religion*. Obituaries and other sources: *Washington Post,* December 28, 1980.

* * *

HARBISON, Robert 1940-

PERSONAL: Born September 6, 1940, in Baltimore, Md.; son of Dale Howard and Lucile Lester (Meeks) Harbison; married Esther Menell (an editor), 1972. *Education:* Amherst College, B.A., 1962; Cornell University, Ph.D., 1969. *Home:* 84 Harmood St., London N.W.1, England. *Agent:* Knox Burger Associates Ltd., 39½ Washington Sq. S., New York, N.Y. 10012.

CAREER: Washington University, St. Louis, Mo., assistant professor of English, 1966-71; St. Louis Musuem, St. Louis, visiting lecturer, 1973-74; University of Maryland, College Park, lecturer in English in Munich, West Germany, and London, England, 1974-77; Architectural Association, London, England, lecturer at School of Architectur , 1978—. *Awards, honors:* Guggenheim fellow, 1977; National Endowment for the Arts fellow, 1977-78; Society for the Humanities fellow, 1980-81.

WRITINGS: Eccentric Spaces, Knopf, 1977; *Deliberate Regression*, Knopf, 1980.

* * *

HARBURY, Colin (Desmond) 1922-

PERSONAL: Born December 21, 1922, in London, England; son of Henry Walter (a stock jobber) and Esther May (an actress; maiden name, Haysack) Harbury; married Hana Lomosova, August 30, 1948 (marriage ended); married Janette Mathilde Powell, January 1, 1980; children: (first marriage) Claire Harbury Gough, Neil. *Education:* London School of Economics and Political Science, London, B.Com., 1950; University of Wales, Ph.D., 1957. *Home:* 154 Bromley Rd., Beckenham, Kent, England. *Office:* Department of Social Science and Humanities, City University, St. John's St., London E.C.1, England.

CAREER: University of Wales, Aberystwyth, Cardiganshire, lecturer in economics, 1950-57; University of Birmingham, Birmingham, England, senior lecturer in economics, 1957-68; Monash University, Clayton, Australia, senior lecturer in economics, 1968-69; Civil Service College, London, England, director of economic studies, 1969-71; City University, London, professor of economics, 1971—. Professor at San Diego State College (now University), 1962-63, and Trent University, 1977-78. *Member:* Economic Association (president, 1976-79; vice-president, 1979—).

WRITINGS: Descriptive Economics, Pitman, 1957, 6th edition, 1981; (with A.D. Smith) *Industrial Efficiency of Rural Labour*, University of Wales Press, 1958; *Workbook in Introductory Economics*, Pergamon, 1969, 2nd edition, 1974; *Workbook in Economics for Australian Students*, Pergamon, 1969; *Introduction to Economic Behaviour*, Fontana, 1972; (with D. M. Hitchens) *Inheritance and Wealth Inequality in Britain*, Allen & Unwin, 1979; *Economic Behavior: An Introduction*, Allen & Unwin, 1980. General editor of series, "Fontana Introduction to Modern Economics," Collins, 1970-73, and "Economics and Society," Allen & Unwin, 1975—.

WORK IN PROGRESS: Revising *Workbook in Introductory Economics* for a third edition, publication expected in 1982; a book on income and wealth distribution, publication expected in 1983.

SIDELIGHTS: Harbury commented to *CA:* "My books and articles fall mainly into two classes: economics education and research in applied economics. I have written both textbooks and papers on the teaching of economics and have been interested in several applied areas, including competition policy, economic efficiency, international trade, and the distribution of wealth."

He added that one of his ambitions is "to find the originator of the statement, 'It is easier to measure than know what it is you are measuring.'"

* * *

HARDIN, Tim 1941(?)-1981

OBITUARY NOTICE: Born c. 1941; died in January, 1981, in Hollywood, Calif. Singer and songwriter. Hardin's folk songs included "If I Were a Carpenter" and "Find a Reason to Believe." Although he recorded his own compositions and performed them onstage, Hardin never achieved the commercial success that his songs provided for other performers, such as Bobby Darin and Rick Nelson. His ballads became standard folk-rock selections in the 1960's. Obituaries and other sources: *Time,* January 12, 1981.

* * *

HARDT, Helga Fleischhauer
See FLEISCHHAUER-HARDT, Helga

* * *

HARDY, Melissa Arnold 1952-

PERSONAL: Born April 26, 1952, in Durham, N.C.; daughter of William Marion (a professor) and Martha Nell (a professor; maiden name, Zant) Hardy; married James Miller (a professor), May 17, 1977. *Education:* University of North Carolina, B.A., 1974; University of Toronto, M.A., 1976. *Politics:* Democrat. *Religion:* Roman Catholic. *Home:* 7 Beckwith Cres., No. 4, Somerville, Mass. 02143. *Office:* Mediaeval Academy of America, 1430 Harvard Sq., Cambridge, Mass. 02138.

CAREER: Mediaeval Academy of America, Cambridge, Mass., editor's assistant, 1979—.

WRITINGS: Cry of Bees (novel), Viking, 1970. Also author of another novel, *Greenhouse Effect.*

WORK IN PROGRESS: Translation of *De occulta philosophia* by Henricius Cornelius Agrippa.

SIDELIGHTS: Melissa Hardy told *CA:* "I stopped writing for ten years because I was in graduate school studying late antique history. I stopped attending graduate school because I'm a born liar and this is disapproved of by historians, though applauded in artists. I started writing again chiefly because there's no other way to understand or impose order, however fictive, on my life."

*   *   *

HARLOW, Enid 1939-

PERSONAL: Born May 26, 1939, in New York, N.Y.; daughter of Jacob (a business executive) and Enid (a dancer and interior decorator; maiden name, Robinson) Hoppenfeld; married Michael Harlow, April 21, 1961 (divorced, 1966); children: Michael. *Education:* Attended Smith College, 1956-57, and University of Michigan, 1957-58; New York University, B.A., 1960, M.A., 1968. *Politics:* Democrat. *Residence:* New York, N.Y. *Agent:* Alfonso Tafoya, 655 Sixth Ave., No. 212, New York, N.Y. 10010.

CAREER: Harper's Bazaar (magazine), New York, N.Y., literary editor, 1969-72; writer, 1972—.

WRITINGS: Crashing (novel), St. Martin's, 1980. Contributor of short stories to *New Voices, Ontario Review, Transatlantic Review, Small Pond, Short Story International, Roanoke Review, Boundary 2,* and *Southwest Review.* Freelance editor and writer for *Working Woman,* 1978-80.

WORK IN PROGRESS: Novels and short stories.

SIDELIGHTS: Enid Harlow commented to *CA:* "*Crashing,* my first novel, was begun some seven years ago when I first took up the writing of fiction on a daily basis. The self-doubt, paralyzing fears, and lack of any real sense of self exhibited by the novel's central character, Sara, a wife and mother of four, are what interested me about the book and propelled me to write it. These are, I believe, psychological struggles with which most women and many men can identify. Sara's amphetamine addiction was always to me a secondary consideration, a metaphor, really, for a woman who has lost control of her life. It therefore surprised me to find, upon publication, that the drug aspect of the novel was the one seized upon by reviewers and that the book is becoming known as a book about a woman with a drug problem."

Crashing, which has been optioned by singer-actress-producer Julie London for a feature film, was described by Joyce Carol Oates, writing in *Mademoiselle,* as a "disturbing, engrossing and completely convincing study of what might be called a representative drug addiction in an American housewife of the upper middle class. Harlow's heroine Sara is presented with an intelligent compassion that avoids sentimentality but does not palliate the tragic—indeed, horrendous—consequences of Sara's predicament."

AVOCATIONAL INTERESTS: Traveling (Europe, Hawaii, and Cuba), scuba diving.

BIOGRAPHICAL/CRITICAL SOURCES: Mademoiselle, July, 1980.

HARMON, H. H.
See WILLIAMS, Robert Moore

*   *   *

HARRINGTON, (Peter) Ty(rus) 1951-

PERSONAL: Born August 28, 1951, in Manhattan, N.Y.; son of Don and Gerry Harrington. *Education:* Union College, Schenectady, N.Y., B.A. and M.A., both 1973. *Residence:* Wilton, Conn.

CAREER: New York State Assembly, Albany, administrative director, 1970-73; *National Geographic,* Washington, D.C., staff writer, 1974-76; free-lance writer and photographer in Washington, D.C., and Wilton, Conn., 1976—. Partner of Don Harrington Associates (advertising firm). President of Wilton Summer Playshop, 1971. *Member:* Authors Guild, Authors League of America, National Press Club, Washington Independent Writers.

WRITINGS: The Sailing Chef, Walker & Co., 1978; *The Last Cathedral,* Prentice-Hall, 1979; *Never Too Old,* New York Times Books, 1980. Contributor of articles to newspapers and magazines, including *Smithsonian* and *Discovery.*

WORK IN PROGRESS: Newspaper and magazine articles.

*   *   *

HARRIS, Charles 1923-

PERSONAL: Born January 7, 1923, in New York, N.Y.; son of Leon (a physician) and Rae Harris; married wife, Rachel, November 24, 1947; children: Hana, Susan, Leon. *Education:* Cornell University, B.A., 1943; Long Island College of Medicine, M.D., 1946. *Home address:* P.O. Box C, Island Heights, N.J. 08723. *Office:* 20 Hospital Dr., Toms River, N.J. 08733.

CAREER: Fels Research Institute, Philadelphia, Pa., pathologist, 1954-62; Temple University, School of Medicine, Philadelphia, associate pathologist, 1954-62; Gerontology Research Institute, Philadelphia, staff member, 1962-69, director of clinical laboratories, beginning 1969; private practice of medicine in Toms River, N.J., 1970—. *Military service:* U.S. Army, 1951-53. *Member:* American Association for the Advancement of Science, American Society for Experimental Pathology, American Society of Hematology, American Association of Pathologists and Bacteriologists, Ocean County Medical Society (president). *Awards, honors:* National Institute of Health fellow, 1950-51.

WRITINGS: One Man's Medicine, Harper, 1974. Author of column appearing in *Ocean County Times-Observer.* Contributor of articles to scientific publications.

SIDELIGHTS: Harris told *CA* that he would like to see both a deregulated country and an accountable bureaucracy.

*   *   *

HARRIS, Herbert 1911-
(Frank Bury, Peter Friday, Michael Moore)

PERSONAL: Born August 25, 1911, in London, England; son of Edwin (a butcher) and Clara (Makemson) Harris; married Bonney Genn, April 20, 1944. *Education:* Educated in England. *Religion:* Church of England. *Home:* 26 Castle Ct., Ventnor, Isle of Wight PO38 1UE, England. *Agent:* John Gibson, 70 Windsor Rd., Bexhill-on-Sea, Sussex TN39 3PE, England.

CAREER: Navy, Army, and Air Force Institutes, Claygate, Surrey, England, press officer and deputy chief press officer, 1941-46; Harrogate International Toy Fair, Harrogate,

Yorkshire, England, press officer, 1950-74. *Member:* London Press Club, Crime Writers Association (honorary anthology editor, 1965—; chairman, 1969-70). *Awards, honors:* Dagger of special merit from Crime Writers Association, 1965.

WRITINGS: Who Kill to Live, Herbert Jenkins, 1962; (editor) *John Creasey's Mystery Bedside Book,* ten volumes, Hodder & Stoughton, 1966-76; *Serpents in Paradise,* W. H. Allen, 1975; *The Angry Battalion,* W. H. Allen, 1976; (editor) *John Creasey's Crime Collection,* five volumes, Gollancz, 1977-81; (editor) *A Handful of Heroes,* Reader's Digest Press, 1978. Also author of a reported thirty-five hundred short stories, many under pseudonyms Frank Bury, Peter Friday, and Michael Moore. Work represented in anthologies, including: *Choice of Weapons,* Hodder & Stoughton, 1958; *Crime Writers Choice,* Hodder & Stoughton, 1964; *Best Underworld Stories,* Faber, 1969; *Tales of Unease,* Pan Books, 1969; *Gourmet Crook Book,* Everest, 1976.

SIDELIGHTS: Since 1969 Herbert Harris has been listed yearly in the *Guinness Book of Records* as the most prolific short-story writer in the United Kingdom. His reported thirty-five hundred short stories have been published in thirty countries and in sixteen languages.

Harris told *CA:* "The writing of novels demands a disciplined working day (so many hours or words per diem), but short-story writing is largely inspirational. For example, the muse obliges you with a good pay-off line or 'sting in the tail'—the *ending* of the short story—whereupon you start to write all the preliminaries leading up to that final surprise twist, a bit like building the roof before you build the walls. As editor of many anthologies, I can confirm that few novelists can write short stories. Conversely, short-story writers like myself lack the stamina for writing novels, so that I have written only a few. Journalists make good short-story writers, having been trained to use words with the utmost economy."

*   *   *

HARRIS, John (Wyndham Parkes Lucas) Beynon 1903-1969
(John Beynon, Lucas Parkes, John Wyndham)

PERSONAL: Born July 10, 1903, in Knowle, Warwickshire, England; died March 11, 1969; son of George Beynon (a barrister) and Gertrude (Parkes) Harris; married Grace Wilson, 1936. *Education:* Educated in England. *Residence:* Petersfield, Hampshire, England.

CAREER: Writer. Worked in advertising and farming. *Military service:* Royal Signal Corps, served in World War II.

WRITINGS—Science-fiction novels: (Under pseudonym John Beynon) *The Secret People,* Newnes, 1935, Lancer Books, 1967; (under Beynon pseudonym) *Foul Play Suspected,* Newnes, 1936; *Sleepers of Mars,* Coronet, 1973.

Under pseudonym John Wyndham, except as noted; science-fiction novels: *Planet Plane,* Newnes, 1936, reprinted as *Stowaways to Mars,* Fawcett, 1972; *The Day of the Triffids,* Doubleday, 1951; *Out of the Deeps,* Ballantine, 1953 (published in England as *The Kraken Wakes,* M. Joseph, 1953, abridgment by G. C. Thornley published under same title, Longmans, Green, 1959, abridgment by S. S. Moody published under same title, Longmans, Green, 1961); *Re-birth,* Ballantine, 1955 (published in England as *The Chrysalids,* M. Joseph, 1955); *Village of the Damned,* Ballantine, 1957 (published in England as *The Midwich Cuc-*

koos, M. Joseph, 1957); (and under pseudonym Lucas Parkes) *The Outward Urge,* Ballantine, 1959; *The Trouble With Lichen,* Ballantine, 1960; *The Infinite Moment,* Ballantine, 1961; *The John Wyndham Omnibus* (contains *The Day of the Triffids, The Kraken Wakes,* and *The Chrysalids*), Simon & Schuster, 1966; *Chocky,* Ballantine, 1968.

Collections of short stories: *Jizzle,* Dobson, 1954; *The Seeds of Time,* M. Joseph, 1956; *Tales of Gooseflesh and Laughter,* Ballantine, 1956; *Consider Her Ways, and Others,* M. Joseph, 1961; *The Best of John Wyndham,* Sphere Books, 1973; *The Man From Beyond and Other Stories,* M. Joseph, 1975; (as John Beynon Harris) *Wanderers of Time,* Coronet, 1973.

Work represented in anthologies, including *The Year's Best Science Fiction,* edited by Harry Harrison and Brian Aldiss, Severn House, 1977; and *The Zeitgist Machine,* edited by Damien Broderick, Angus & Robertson, 1977.

Contributor to periodicals, including *Wonder Stories.*

SIDELIGHTS: Harris is probably best known for *Day of the Triffids,* his novel in which the human race, blinded during a meteor shower, is threatened by carnivorous plants. A reviewer for the *Times Literary Supplement* wrote, "The language is excellent, and the description of London filled with the groping blind . . . has all the qualities of a vividly-realized nightmare."

Harris's *The Midwich Cuckoos* depicted a small village whose women are mysteriously impregnated by aliens from outer space. H. H. Holmes declared that "the impact of these infant invaders upon tiny Midwich, where nothing of importance has happened in all the previous centuries, is carried out not only with honesty and absolute credibility, but with humor, charm and a strong touch of terror, in one of the most inescapably readable of modern imaginative novels."

AVOCATIONAL INTERESTS: Leatherworking, bookbinding.

BIOGRAPHICAL/CRITICAL SOURCES: New York Times, July 22, 1951; *New York Herald Tribune Book Review,* August 19, 1951, December 27, 1953, March 16, 1958; *Times Literary Supplement,* August 31, 1951, August 14, 1953; *Spectator,* September 7, 1951, September 27, 1957; *New Statesman,* September 28, 1957; *Time,* March 10, 1958.

OBITUARIES: New York Times, March 12, 1969.*

*   *   *

HARRIS, Mary Law   1892(?)-1980

OBITUARY NOTICE: Born c. 1892 in Willsonia, W.Va.; died September 27, 1980, in Washington, D.C. Journalist. Harris was a reporter for the old *Washington Herald* both before and after World War I. She later became a Washington publicist for private clubs, hotels, and individual clients, among others. In 1954 she joined the *Washington Post* as the newspaper's restaurant and night club editor, a position she left ten years later to resume her work as a publicist. Her feature articles appeared in several New York publications, including the *New York World* and the *New York Telegram.* Obituaries and other sources: *Washington Post,* September 28, 1980.

*   *   *

HARRISON, Brian Fraser   1918-

PERSONAL: Born September 6, 1918, in Liverpool, England; son of James Fraser (a judge) and Betty (Broadhurst)

Harrison; married Constance Kathleen Bennion (a company director), December 9, 1939; children: James Fraser. *Education:* Studied law privately. *Religion:* None. *Home:* Mouldsworth House, Mouldsworth, Chester CH3 8AP, England. *Office:* Mace & Jones, 19 Water St., Liverpool L2 0RP, England.

CAREER: Mace & Jones (solicitors), Liverpool, England, qualified assistant, 1945-48, partner, 1948—, senior partner, 1973—. Member of Lord Chancellor's Liverpool Circuit Advisory Committee, 1972—. *Military service:* British Army, Territorial Army, Royal Service Corps, 1939-44; became captain. *Member:* Law Society, British Legal Association, Justice Society.

WRITINGS: Advocacy at Petty Sessions, Sweet & Maxwell, 1952, revised edition, 1959; *The Work of a Magistrate,* Shaw & Sons, 1964, 3rd edition, 1975; *A Business of Your Own,* World's Work, 1968; *A Business of Your Own Today,* World's Work, 1973.

WORK IN PROGRESS: A book on the selection of professional advisers, private publication expected in 1981.

SIDELIGHTS: Harrison commented: "I am vitally interested in humorous art and cartooning. In 1983 I retire from active practice of law. I have already sold cartoons, and I hope, within the next three years, to establish myself as a professional humorous artist. And I am on the way to doing so."

* * *

HARRISON, Helen P(atricia) 1935-

PERSONAL: Born July 11, 1935, in Durham, England; daughter of Joseph and Mary (Carr) Harrison. *Education:* University of Sydney, B.A. (with honors), 1957. *Home:* 6 Barnhill Rd., Marlow, Buckinghamshire, England. *Office:* Walton Hall, Open University, Milton Keynes MK7 6AA, England.

CAREER: National Film Archive, London, England, senior cataloguer, 1960-61; Visnews (television news film agency), London, librarian, 1963-69; Open University, Milton Keynes, England, media librarian, 1969—. Member of board of directors of British Universities Film Council. *Member:* Library Association (fellow), Aslib (chairman of audiovisual group).

WRITINGS: Film Library Techniques, Focal Press, 1973; (editor) *Handbook of Picture Librarianship,* Library Association, 1981. Contributor to library journals.

WORK IN PROGRESS: Research on archives in audiovisual librarianship, sound archives, video materials, and television.

SIDELIGHTS: Helen P. Harrison told *CA:* "In previous posts I have worked with film material, and this led to my particular interest in the indexing of this material for easy retrieval by possible users. The thesis for the fellowship of the Library Association of Great Britain was a result of this interest and was one of the first works to concentrate on news-film libraries and the particular problems involved. The book *Film Library Techniques* grew out of this work and extended the range to include other types of film libraries.

"In 1969 I began work at the new Open University, an institution which demands no academic qualifications from students and which educates through an integrated system of correspondence booklets, national radio and television broadcasts, summer schools, and tutorial sessions in local study centers. Students number about eighty thousand. The

Media Library forms part of the general resources center of the Open University, and, as well as providing a reference service for the academic staff, we aim to supply a detailed indexing service of all Open University Broadcast productions and form an archive of these programs.

"The Open University Library is responsible for audiotapes, videotapes, photographs, illustrations, slides, and any other materials not in book or periodical format. This multi-media aspect of the work presents its own challenges, and the constant battle to keep up to date with technology has its own rewards. There has to be a constant balancing of technical materials and librarianship principles which adds savor to existence and an interest in the job at hand. The materials can be transitory, but the techniques for dealing with the materials represent a slower process, and therein lies the concern."

AVOCATIONAL INTERESTS: European travel (especially Greece), skiing.

* * *

HARRISON, Marcus 1924-

PERSONAL: Born August 29, 1924, in Melbourne, Australia; son of Vivian Heyward (a tailor) and Charlotte-Eliza (Busby) Harrison. *Education:* Educated privately. *Politics:* Liberal. *Religion:* "Free thinker." *Residence:* London, England. *Address:* c/o Williams and Glyn Bank, 29 Old Brompton Rd., London S.W.7, England.

CAREER: Worked as photographer's apprentice, 1938-42; J. C. Williamson Musical Comedy Co., Sydney, Australia, singer and dancer in stage productions, including "Viktoria and Her Hussar," "The Maid of the Mountains," and "Katinka," 1944-45; studio and darkroom manager in Sydney, 1945-47; Roosevelt Club, Sydney, nightclub photographer, 1947-51; free-lance photographer and newspaper correspondent, 1952-59; photographer, specializing in architectural and interior design, 1959—. Consultant on production publicity for motion pictures, 1961-64. *Military service:* Royal Australian Air Force, 1942-44. *Member:* Society of Authors.

WRITINGS: The Memoirs of Jesus Christ (novel), Arlington Books, 1975, Ballantine, 1977; (photographer) *Topolski's Buckingham Palace Panoramas,* Quartet Books, 1977. Contributor of articles and photographs to architectural and interior design journals.

WORK IN PROGRESS: The Memoirs of an Irish Orphan, a novel in three volumes, publication expected in 1982.

SIDELIGHTS: Harrison told *CA:* "I began to write ten years ago in an attempt to enlarge my consciousness. I have succeeded in doing that, but I have not so far succeeded in enlarging my bank account. I have always been an omnivorous reader and have learned much through reading the world's great books. It was natural that sooner or later I would try my hand at writing. I think that 'witness' is perhaps the most important function of literature. Style is important in providing a satisfactory vehicle, but a writer should reflect the time he lives in, and eventually I hope to do that.

"I have been influenced by many writers and am still discovering writers who were unknown to me, but who provide me with a positive thrill. I don't read a lot of contemporary work because of its note of dogged pessimism, which may be justified enough, but does not provide me with air I can breathe. The contemporary literary scene seems to me to be inbred and academic. It inhabits a region that is neither aristocratic nor vulgar, but lies on a lowland somewhere in between."

"*The Memoirs of Jesus Christ* was not conceived or written as a religious book, but rather as a kind of speculation and exploration of the narrative gaps in the New Testament. However, certain views imposed themselves on me after the work was done, which I might have had in mind subconsciously while it was being written, and some of these are as follows. The figure of Jesus plays an enormous part in the Western psyche both in an absolute and relative sense; that is, he is both a Platonic ideal and a relative accomplishment for the individual who can succeed in approaching in his own way to that kind of moral excellence. The most important message in the New Testament, as I am able to discern it, is that the unforgivable sin is to neglect one's own portion of divinity in favor of a purely material existence—but everything is relative to the individual.

"At the moment my working method is as follows. Something gives me the idea for a story—a newspaper cutting, or a history book, or a personal observation—and I write out some notes which, as time goes on, accumulate until there is enough material to start a new book. The opening paragraph is crucial, the seed from which the work develops. It is important not to limit the development of the work by a too-close plan, but I do sometimes write out work points before starting a chapter: what the characters are trying to achieve in it, how the plot is to be advanced, and so on. This often enables me to break through a writer's roadblock. I write standing at a typewriter. I begin with a rough draft, which is laid aside for a few days, and then the holes in the structure are filled. The superfluous matter is then trimmed away. This leaves other holes which again need to be filled. After several drafts the material assumes a more or less satisfactory shape.

"If I were to write *The Memoirs of Jesus Christ* again it would be rather different, myself having developed in some regions of the mind since then, but I am fairly satisfied with it as it is. Aspiring writers should choose subjects that are congenial and then follow their noses, realizing that their first efforts may result only in dross or slag. If they persist, though, the true metal will follow.

"Apart from my published work I have an unpublished novel, *Theodora*, and two 'entertainments': 'The Naturalist,' a story in the form of a film script, and 'Alcestis in Ireland,' a political adventure story which is also cast in the form of a film script. I am in no hurry to have these unpublished works printed, but I am content to wait for the right place and time."

Publishers Weekly noted that in *The Memoirs of Jesus Christ* Harrison has Jesus "telling the story of his life as it really happened. He was, to begin with, the child of Nicodemus by Mary, who had been drugged and ravished. Later, he was called upon by his father to play the role of a militant Messiah in a plan designed to bring Nicodemus the kingship." It is throughout a very different version of the Biblical story. In her review of the book, Myrna Blumberg, writing in the *London Times,* remarked that "simple, modern language (sometimes disconcertingly) is used in most of this novel; the narrative skill and all-affiliating warmth make it compulsive reading, yet I value it most for vividly making reverence so human. Whatever one feels about the fresh controversies of its plot, this book is too good to miss."

BIOGRAPHICAL/CRITICAL SOURCES: Australian, February 22, 1975; *Daily Express,* September 29, 1975; *Coventry Evening Telegraph,* October 2, 1975; *Scotsman,* October 11, 1975; *London Times,* October 16, 1975; *New Humanist,* March, 1976; *Publishers Weekly,* September 27, 1976.

HARRISON, Rosina 1899-

PERSONAL: Born December 11, 1899, in Aldfield, England; daughter of William (a stonemason) and Rosina (a laundry maid) Harrison. *Education:* Attended elementary school in Aldfield, England. *Politics:* Conservative. *Religion:* Church of England. *Home:* 2 Homefield Rd., Worthing, Sussex BN11 2HZ, England. *Agent:* Desmond Elliott, 2 Clifford St., Mayfair, London, England.

CAREER: Ladies' maid to daughters of Major John and Lady Tufton of Appleley Castle, 1918-22, to Viscountess Cranborne, 1923-28, to Phyllis Astor, 1928, and to Viscountess Astor, 1929-64; writer, 1975—. Guest on television and radio programs.

WRITINGS: Rose: My Life in Service, Cassell, 1975; *Gentlemen's Gentlemen: My Friends in Service,* Arlington Books, 1976.

SIDELIGHTS: Rosina Harrison told *CA:* "I was born in Yorkshire. I went to an ordinary elementary school and learned all I could. I was good at writing, mathematics, and reading. In 1916 I had private lessons in French. My mother was very ambitious for her children and encouraged us to learn all we could.

"As a family we all had to work. We lived off the land and had a big garden. This work was a help in later life. Nothing came as hardship to us, and we were able to turn our hands to anything we were asked to do.

"I had always wanted to travel and the only way to do that in those days was to be a lady's maid, so I was trained for that work from the bottom rung of the ladder to the top. I achieved my ambition through hard work and unselfishness. It was important to have a good sense of humor and to be pleasant and helpful, quick in one's actions, to be a conscientious worker, accept responsibility, to be trustworthy and able to mind one's own business.

"Writing a book stayed in the back of my mind while I served Lady Astor, and her children prompted and encouraged me to write as I spoke, with Yorkshire accent and brogue. I had collected postcards of every place I went to and wrote notes on the back, kept cuttings from the papers, and Lord Astor gave me press photographs. I had plenty of reference material, and had not to go out researching.

"But I could not write my book as well as look after Lady Astor. My work demanded forty-eight hours of the day, so to speak, and I could not do two jobs conscientiously, so I looked after my lady's maid situation until 1964.

"I have enjoyed every moment of my life. I am an avid sightseer. I can't sit still, and I am not lazy. I am retired now, with peace of mind, and am still enjoying myself."

BIOGRAPHICAL/CRITICAL SOURCES: Margaret Pringe, *Dance, Little Ladies, Dance,* Orbis, 1977; John Grigg, *Portrait of a Pioneer,* Sidgewick & Jackson, 1980.

*   *   *

HARRISON, Sarah 1946-

PERSONAL: Born August 7, 1946, in Exeter, England; daughter of Anthony (in British Army) and Jean (Laird) Martyn; married Jeremy Harrison (a charity director), June 7, 1969; children: Laurence, Fanny, Thea. *Education:* University of London, B.A. (with honors), 1967. *Religion:* Church of England. *Home and office:* Holmcrest, 17 Station Rd., Steeple Mordon, Royston, Hertfordshire, England. *Agent:* Carol Smith, 25 Hornton Court E., Kensington High St., London W8 7RT, England.

CAREER: International Publishing Corp., London, England, magazine journalist, 1967-70; free-lance writer, 1970-77.

WRITINGS: *The Flowers of the Field* (novel), Coward, 1980; *In Granny's Garden* (children's book), Holt, 1980. Contributor of stories to magazines.

WORK IN PROGRESS: *Foxtrot*, a sequel to *The Flowers of the Field*, for Coward.

SIDELIGHTS: Sarah Harrison told *CA:* "Having never anticipated writing a historical novel, I found the research for and the writing of *The Flowers of the Field* a joyous and rewarding experience. I come from an army background and was able to draw on my grandfather's battalion histories."

* * *

HARSCH, Joseph C(lose) 1905-

PERSONAL: Born May 25, 1905, in Toledo, Ohio; son of Paul Arthur and Leila Katherine (Close) Harsch; married Anne Elizabeth Wood, December 11, 1932; children: J. William Wood, Jonathon Hannum, Paul Arthur III. *Education:* Williams College, A.B., 1927; Corpus Christi College, Cambridge, B.A., 1929. *Religion:* Christian Scientist. *Home:* Highland Dr., Jamestown, R.I. 02835. *Office:* Christian Science Monitor, 1 Norway St., Boston, Mass. 02115.

CAREER: Christian Science Monitor, Boston, Mass., 1929-43, correspondent from Washington, D.C., 1931-39, and from Rome, Italy and Berlin, Germany, 1939-41; Columbia Broadcasting System, Inc. (CBS), commentator, 1943-49; National Broadcasting Co., Inc. (NBC), news commentator, 1953-67, senior European correspondent, 1957-65, diplomatic correspondent, 1965-67; American Broadcasting Co., Inc. (ABC), commentator, 1967-71; Christian Science Monitor, chief editorial writer, 1971-74, author of column, 1974—. Assistant director of Intergovernmental Commission, 1939. *Member:* National Press Club, Chi Psi, Cosmos Club, Metropolitan Club, St. Botolph Club, Century Club, Garrick Club, St. James Club. *Awards, honors:* M.A. from Williams College; decorated Commander of the Order of the British Empire.

WRITINGS: *Pattern of Conquest*, Doubleday, 1941; *The Curtain Isn't Iron*, Doubleday, 1950. Also author of *Germany at War: Twenty Key Questions and Answers*, 1942, and *Does Our Foreign Policy Make Sense?*, 1948.

* * *

HART, Barry
See BLOOM, Herman I.

* * *

HART, Ernest H(untley) 1910-

PERSONAL: Born October 2, 1910, in Manhattan, N.Y.; son of Asher (a postal clerk) and Sarah (Rodriguez-Miranda) Hart; married first wife, Louise R., 1934 (divorced, 1959); married Katherine Severence (in hospital management), December 31, 1962; children: Allan H., Lance R., Keith P. *Education:* Studied at Art Students League of New York, 1931-34. *Home and office:* 1800 Magnolia Dr., Clearwater, Fla. 33516. *Agent:* Raines & Raines, 475 Fifth Ave., New York, N.Y. 10017.

CAREER: Practical Science Publishing Co., New Haven, Conn., editor and art director, 1938-40; Goodman Publications, Inc., New York, N.Y., editor, 1941-43; Charleton Publications, Inc., Derby, Conn., managing editor, 1959-63;

T.F.H. Publications, Inc., Neptune, N.J., managing editor and art director, 1965-67. Civilian consultant to Super Dog Program of U.S. Armed Forces, Aberdeen Proving Grounds, Md. *Member:* German Shepherd Dog Club of America (director), Vereins fuer deutsche Schaferhunde (S.V.) of Germany, Authors Guild, Gulf Coast Budgerigar Society (honorary member), Club Canino Colombiana (honorary member). *Awards, honors:* Recipient of awards for painting and for dog-show judging.

WRITINGS—All published by T.F.H. Publications, except as noted: *This Is the German Shepherd*, Practical Science Publications, 1955, 3rd edition, 1967; *This Is the Puppy*, 1962; *This Is the Weimeraner*, 1965; *The Poodle Handbook*, 1966; *Dog Breeders' Handbook*, 1966; *How to Raise and Train a Pointer*, 1966; *How to Raise and Train an American Foxhound*, 1967; *How to Raise and Train a Fox Terrier*, 1967; *Your German Shepherd Puppy*, 1967; *Your Poodle Puppy*, 1967; *This Is the Great Dane*, 1967; *How to Train Your Dog*, 1967; *The Cocker Spaniel Handbook*, 1968; *The Encyclopedia of Dogs*, 1968; *How to Raise a Vizsla*, 1968; *How to Raise and Train a Spitz*, 1969; *The Budgerigar Handbook*, 1970; *Saint Bernards*, 1973; *This Is the Bassett Hound*, 1974; *Living With Pets*, Vanguard, 1977; *The Complete Guide to All Cats*, Scribner, 1980. Contributor of columns and short stories to newspapers and periodicals, including *Real West*, *Sportsman*, *True Confessions*, and *Clearwater Sun*.

WORK IN PROGRESS: Research for *The Association of Man and Dog Throughout the Ages*, publication expected in 1982; *The Black Ledgers*, a book of fiction.

SIDELIGHTS: Hart told *CA:* "I do in-depth research on the evolution of species, and I am interested in the obvious influence animals have had on the evolution of man and his genetic complexity. Mankind's reaching out to other animalistic life forms in an attempt to find rapport with them eternally piques my interest and understanding. I also find the life-styles and philosophies of the various races of man intriguing. To this end I have traveled to most of the cities, byways, and jungles of this and other continents to gather data for my writings."

BIOGRAPHICAL/CRITICAL SOURCES: *St. Petersburg Times*, June 5, 1976; *Clearwater Sun*, June 6, 1976; *New Haven Register*, June 13, 1976; *Memphis Commercial Appeal*, November 2, 1977; *Clearwater Sun*, June 4, 1978; *New York Times Magazine*, October 1, 1978.

* * *

HART, Sue
See HART, Susanne

* * *

HART, Susanne 1927-
(Sue Hart)

PERSONAL: Born May 19, 1927, in Vienna, Austria; daughter of Edward and Thekla Widrich; married A. M. Harthoorn, April, 1965 (divorced, 1973); children: Gail Laura (Mrs. Michael Strong), Guy. *Education:* Royal Veterinary College, London, M.R.C.V.S., 1949. *Religion:* Methodist. *Home and office address:* P.O. Box 727, White River, Eastern Transvaal 1240, South Africa.

CAREER: Practiced veterinary medicine in South Africa and Kenya, 1951-63; writer, broadcaster, lecturer, and conservationist, 1963—. *Member:* Wild Life Society of Rhodesia, East Africa, and Southern Africa, South Africa Veterinary

Association, Zoological Society of South Africa, British Veterinary Association.

WRITINGS—Under name Sue Hart: *Spider's Tales* (children's book), Voortrekkerspers, 1960; *Too Short a Day: A Woman Vet in Africa*, Bles, 1966, Taplinger, 1967, reprinted as *The Tame and the Wild: A Woman Vet in Africa*, Fontana, 1969; *Life With Daktari: Two Vets in East Africa*, Atheneum, 1969; *Listen to the Wild*, Taplinger, 1972; *In the Wild*, Africana Book Society, 1974; *Back in the Wild*, Harvil Press, 1977; *Tales of the Full Moon* (children's book), Via Africa, 1979; *Nature's A.B.C.* (children's book), Via Africa, 1981.

Author of "Our Wilderness," a film released by TEBA, 1979. Author of weekly column, "In the Wild," in *Rand Daily Mail*, 1975-77, and monthly column, "Nature Note Book," in *Cape Times*, 1980—.

WORK IN PROGRESS: Touch of the Wilderness, an autobiography, publication expected in 1981 or 1982.

SIDELIGHTS: Susanne Hart wrote that her motivation is "communication of wildlife conservation activities—the people involved and my personal experiences—to bring the amazing African fauna and flora right into the home and the school. Man cannot exist without nature in some form. My aim is to strengthen the link, to create awareness of our natural environment.

"I hope, in my work, to show something of the remarkable fauna and flora to be found in the glorious, undisturbed regions of southern Africa, some of which have been set aside as permanent refuges of the wild. I want to look at them in depth, rather than from the surface, and try to search out some of the mysteries of the complex, ever-changing natural system which can be likened to a many-dimensioned giant jigsaw.

"In the past years, as the quest for deeper knowledge has increased, this ecosystem, as it has come to be called, which perfectly blends all components into one whole, has become the essential focus in wildlife research and discovery. There is so much to find out that one hardly knows where to begin, and yet one cannot achieve anything in a hurry. Those who work in the wild have learnt that they must take their time. Though nothing in nature is random, be it sound, movement, scent, or shape, only patient years of research will provide the answers in the end.

"Looking into nature with wide-open eyes is like looking through a window of your own soul. Suddenly you view the world with new clarity and begin to comprehend the power of the creative force which governs every living thing."

In his introduction to Hart's *In the Wild*, Robert Ardrey wrote: "Here is the magic, the eternal, authentic magic of the African bush. Who but Sue Hart could have captured it, like some precious torch, to hand down to the rest of us? The dawns and the stirring of birds, the dusks and prowling dark menace, the quiet noons. In the bush we are most of us observers. She, like some rare species, is an inhabitant. And she writes of wild Africa, eastern or southern, as another might write of her house and her garden, with affectionate memories, long insights, grace, elegance, poetic passion. With her book she invites us to enter her home, and I for one shall never forget her hospitality."

BIOGRAPHICAL/CRITICAL SOURCES: George Adamson, *A Lifetime With Lions*, Doubleday, 1968; Joy Adamson, *The Spotted Sphinx*, Harcourt, 1969; Cynthia Moss, *Portraits in the Wild*, Houghton, 1975; Iain Douglass-Hamilton, *Among the Elephants*, Harvil, 1976.

HARTHAN, John Plant 1916-

PERSONAL: Born April 15, 1916, in Evesham, Worcestershire, England; son of George Ezra (a physician) and Winifred May (Slater) Harthan. *Education:* Jesus College, Cambridge, degree in history (with first class honors), 1938, M.A., 1944; also attended University College, London, 1938-39. *Home:* 20 Pelham St., London S.W.7, England.

CAREER: University of Southampton, Southampton, England, assistant librarian, 1940-43; Royal Society of Medicine, London, England, assistant librarian, 1943-44; Cambridge University, Cambridge, England, assistant under-librarian, 1944-48; Victoria and Albert Museum, London, assistant keeper of library, 1948-62, keeper of library, 1962-76; writer, 1950—. *Member:* Library Association (fellow).

WRITINGS: Bookbindings in the Victoria and Albert Museum, London, Her Majesty's Stationery Office, 1951, 2nd edition, 1962; (editor) Francis Donald Klingender, *Animals in Art and Thought: To the End of the Middle Ages*, Routledge & Kegan Paul, 1971; (editor with Evelyn Antal) *The Francis Williams Bequest: An Exhibition of Illustrated Books, 1967-1971*, National Book League, 1972; *Books of Hours: Illuminated Pages From the World's Most Precious Manuscripts*, Corwell, 1977 (published in England as *Books of Hours and Their Owners*, Thames & Hudson, 1977); *The History of the Illustrated Book*, Thames & Hudson, 1981. Contributor to periodicals, including *Apollo* and *Music and Letters*.

WORK IN PROGRESS: A revised 3rd edition of *Bookbindings in the Victoria and Albert Musuem, London*.

SIDELIGHTS: John Harthan wrote: "*Books of Hours* was the first general, non-specialist study of the largest surviving group of late medieval illuminated manuscripts—the personal prayerbooks of the laity—and appeared in American, English, French, and German editions. In my writings on the artistic aspects of books I attempt to convey specialized information in a quasi-popular manner and thus reach an audience which may be unaware of the treasures to be found both in manuscript and printed books."

AVOCATIONAL INTERESTS: Music, architecture, botany.

*   *   *

HARTOG, Joseph 1933-

PERSONAL: Born May 18, 1933, in Jersey City, N.J.; son of Gabriel (a diamond cutter) and Regina (Langer) Hartog; married Elizabeth Ann Bowden (a registered nurse), September 3, 1961; children: Rebecca, Leah, Deborah. *Education:* City College (now of the City University of New York), B.S., 1955; State University of New York Downstate Medical Center, M.D., 1959; trained in psychiatry at Stanford University, 1960-62, 1964-65. *Religion:* Jewish. *Residence:* San Francisco, Calif. *Office:* 3241 Sacramento St., San Francisco, Calif. 94115.

CAREER: Psychiatrist in San Francisco, Calif., 1960—. University of California, San Francisco, researcher and teacher of trans-cultural psychiatry, 1966—, associate clinical professor of psychiatry, 1975—. *Military service:* U.S. Army, Medical Corps, 1962-64; became captain; received Army Commendation Medal. *Member:* American Psychiatric Association, Union of American Physicians and Dentists, Northern California Psychiatric Society, Society for the Study of Psychiatry and Culture. *Awards, honors:* American Psychiatric Association fellow, 1979.

WRITINGS: (Editor with J. R. Audy and Y. Cohen) *The*

Anatomy of Loneliness, International Universities Press, 1980. Contributor of articles to professional journals, including *American Journal of Psychiatry, Mental Hygiene,* and *Ethnomedicine.*

WORK IN PROGRESS: A textbook on trans-cultural psychiatry; journal articles on neuro-anthropology and Valium withdrawal psychosis.

SIDELIGHTS: Hartog remarked: "My major academic interest in cross-cultural psychiatry developed with two years of research in Malaysia, from 1966 to 1968. The late Professor J. R. Audy deserves credit for his encouragement and support of that work and for recruiting me into the writing and lecturing on loneliness and into other frontier behavioral science areas such as human ecology and psychiatric geography."

*   *   *

HARVEY, Joan M(argaret)   1918-

PERSONAL: Born August 29, 1918, in Bradford, England; daughter of Frank (a master dairyman) and Dorothy (Illsley) Harvey. *Education:* Loughborough University of Technology, M.A., 1974. *Home:* 42 Hall Gate, Diseworth DE7 2QJ, England.

CAREER: Board of Trade, London, England, executive civil servant, 1941-57, librarian, 1957-66; Loughborough Technical College, Loughborough, England, lecturer, 1966-70, senior lecturer in librarianship, 1970-78; writer, 1978—. Visiting lecturer at Loughborough University of Technology. *Member:* Library Association, Aslib.

WRITINGS: Statistics—Europe: Sources for Social, Economic, and Market Research, CBD Research, 1968, 4th edition, 1981; *Sources of Statistics,* Linnet Books, 1969, 2nd edition, 1971; *Statistics—Africa: Sources for Social, Economic, and Market Research,* CBD Research, 1970, 2nd edition, 1978; *Statistics—America: Sources for Social, Economic, and Market Research (North, Central, and South America),* CBD Research, 1973; *Statistics: Asia and Australasia,* CBD Research, 1974, 2nd edition, 1981; *Specialised Information Centres,* Linnet Books, 1976; *Herbert Schofield and Loughborough College,* privately printed, 1977; *Introduction to Business Librarianship,* Clive Bingley, 1981.

WORK IN PROGRESS: Assisting A. J. Walford with the fourth edition of Volume II of *Guide to Reference Material,* publication expected in 1981.

SIDELIGHTS: Harvey told *CA:* "Now officially retired, I am devoting much of my time to the compilation of reference books and the writing of textbooks, all of which I hope will be of value to researchers, searchers for information, students, etc. In particular, the 'Statistics' series is unique, and the content improves with each edition; for instance, the fourth edition of *Statistics—Europe* will include a much greater number of non-official titles from earlier editions."

*   *   *

HARVEY, Paul
See AURANDT, Paul Harvey

*   *   *

HARVEY, Ruth C(harlotte)   1918-1980

*OBITUARY NOTICE—*See index for *CA* sketch: Born March 3, 1918, in Durham, England; died November 10, 1980. Educator, medievalist, and author. Harvey taught at several universities, including the University of London, St.

Andrews University, and Oxford University. Her book, *Moriz von Craun and the Chivalric World,* was published in 1961. Obituaries and other sources: *London Times,* November 14, 1980.

*   *   *

HASKELL, Arnold L(ionel)   1903-1981(?)

*OBITUARY NOTICE—*See index for *CA* sketch: Born July 19, 1903, in London, England; died c. 1981 in Bath, England. Journalist, editor, critic, and author of numerous books on ballet. Haskell worked as a dance critic for the *London Daily Telegraph,* the *Melbourne Herald,* and the *Sydney Daily Telegraph.* He also served as honorary director and governor of the Royal Ballet School and edited the *Ballet Annual.* Haskell was in part responsible for the revival of ballet in England. His works include *Balletomania, The Making of a Dancer, The Russian Genius in Ballet,* and *Heroes and Roses.* Obituaries and other sources: *AB Bookman's Weekly,* January 19, 1981.

*   *   *

HASS, Eric   1905(?)-1980

OBITUARY NOTICE: Born c. 1905; died of a heart attack, October 2, 1980, in Santa Rosa, Calif. Politician, free-lance writer, and editor. Hass was the Socialist Labor party's presidential candidate four times between 1952 and 1964. He was the editor of the party newspaper, the *Weekly People,* and a free-lance writer specializing in gardening. Obituaries and other sources: *Newsweek,* October 20, 1980.

*   *   *

HASTINGS, Philip Kay   1922-

PERSONAL: Born August 27, 1922, in Worcester, Mass.; son of Rowland and Eunice (Leach) Hastings; married Elizabeth Frances Hann, March 11, 1950; children: Pamela Dillenback, Elizabeth Leach, Ann Upton, Mary Florence. *Education:* Williams College, A.B., 1944; attended Yale University, 1944-45; Princeton University, M.A., 1949, Ph.D., 1950. *Home address:* Bulkley St., Williamstown, Mass. 01267. *Office:* Department of Psychology and Political Science, Williams College, Williamstown, Mass. 01267.

CAREER: University of Massachusetts, Amherst, instructor in psychology, 1946-47; Williams College, Williamstown, Mass., instructor in psychology, 1947-48; Princeton University, Princeton, N.J., senior research assistant at Office of Public Opinion Research, 1949-51, instructor in psychology and research associate of Human Resources Division of Navy Department, both 1950-51; Williams College, lecturer, 1951-52, assistant professor, 1952-57, associate professor, 1957-61, professor of psychology and political science, 1961—. Member of teaching staff of Salzburg Seminar in American Studies, 1957. Director of Roper Public Opinion Research Center, 1951-76; research associate of Psychological Corporation of New York, 1952-58; primary investigator of family planning and fertility research for U.S. Agency for International Development, 1972-74; chairman of board of directors of Survey Research Consultants International, 1980—. Member of advisory board of Inter-University Council of Social Science Data Archives, 1966-71, International Social Science Council, 1968—, National Council of Churches, 1970-72, and National Data Program for the Social Sciences, 1971—; consultant to American Telephone & Telegraph Co., Social Science Research Council, and Cable Arts Foundation. *Military service:* U.S. Naval Reserve, active duty as operations officer, 1945-46; became lieutenant junior grade.

MEMBER: World Association for Public Opinion Research (member of executive council, 1965—; president, 1970-72), American Association for Public Opinion Research, American Psychological Association (fellow), American Sociological Association (fellow), Sigma Xi. *Awards, honors:* Grants from U.S. State Department, 1969, and from Spencer Foundation.

WRITINGS: (With Warren F. Ilchman and Alice S. Ilchman) *The New Men of Knowledge and Developing Nations,* Institute of Governmental Studies, University of California, Berkeley, 1968; (editor) *Survey Data for Trend Analysis,* Social Science Research Council and Russell Sage Foundation, 1975; (editor) *Index to International Public Opinion, 1978-1979,* Greenwood Press, 1980; (editor) *Index to International Public Opinion, 1979-1980,* Greenwood Press, 1981.

Contributor: F. P. Kilpatrick, editor, *Human Behavior From the Transactional Point of View,* Institute for Associated Research, 1952; J. R. Fiszman, editor, *Reader in American Politics,* Little, Brown, 1960; S. M. Lipset and Neil J. Smelser, editors, *Sociology in Action,* Prentice-Hall, 1961. Contributor to *Encyclopaedia Britannica.* Contributor of about twenty articles to academic journals and popular magazines, including *Nation.* Member of editorial board of *Public Opinion Quarterly,* 1962-64, and *International Research Documents Journal,* 1964—.

* * *

HAWKE, David Freeman 1923-

PERSONAL: Born December 14, 1923, in Philadelphia, Pa.; son of Edward Lukens and Helen (Freeman) Hawke. *Education:* Attended Amherst College, 1941-43; Swarthmore College, B.A., 1948; University of Wisconsin (now University of Wisconsin—Madison), M.A., 1951; University of Pennsylvania, Ph.D., 1955. *Religion:* Protestant. *Home:* 61 Liberty St., Madison, Conn. 06443.

CAREER: Long Island University, Brooklyn, N.Y., assistant professor of history, 1957-58; Pace University, New York, N.Y., assistant professor, 1958-60, associate professor, 1960-62, professor of history, 1962-72, Herbert H. Lehman College of the City University of New York, Bronx, N.Y., professor of history, 1972—. *Military service:* U.S. Navy, Air Corps., 1943-46.

WRITINGS: In the Midst of a Revolution, University of Pennsylvania Press, 1961; (editor with Leonard Lief) *American Colloquy,* Bobbs-Merrill, 1963; *Transaction of Free Men,* Scribner, 1964; *The Colonial Experience,* Bobbs-Merrill, 1966; (editor) *U.S. Colonial History: Readings and Documents,* Bobbs-Merrill, 1966; *Benjamin Rush,* Bobbs-Merrill, 1971; *Paine,* Harper, 1974; *Franklin,* Harper, 1976; *Honorable Treason: The Declaration of Independence and the Men Who Signed It,* Viking, 1976; *John D.: The Founding Father,* Harper, 1980.

WORK IN PROGRESS: A book, tentatively titled *A House for the Afflicted,* about "medicine in eighteenth-century Philadelphia as seen through the surviving records of the Pennyslvania Hospital, the first in British America and still flourishing."

SIDELIGHTS: Hawke told *CA:* "I seek as a historian to meet the standards of my profession and thus satisfy colleagues but at the same time to arouse the interest of laymen in my subject. Seldom do I triumph over the challenge—one audience or the other generally raises objections—but the daily act of confronting it has been one of the large delights of life the past twenty years.

"I am, apparently, of that rare breed that likes to write. The demands of a chapter pull me from bed in the morning, and regardless of how well I think I know the day's road ahead there are always surprises. But the pleasures that come from writing about the American past, of discovering what I hope no one has seen before, are of course balanced by rough, often tedious stretches. Writing does not come easily for me; I work slowly, much like a sculptor with a chisel, only words rather than stone or wood are my medium. But when at the end of the day I have a page or two that seem right, I pull away from the desk certain that all is right in the world, regardless of what the evening news might tell me later."

* * *

HAWKE, Gary Richard 1942-

PERSONAL: Born August 1, 1942, in Napier, New Zealand; son of Vyvyan N. (a clerk) and Jean (Carver) Hawke; married Helena Joyce Powrie (a teacher), August, 1965; children: Richard Michael, Andrew Gilbert. *Education:* Victoria University of Wellington, B.A. (with honors), 1964, B.Com., 1965; Oxford University, D.Phil., 1968. *Politics:* "Swinging voter." *Religion:* None. *Home:* 7 Voltaire St., Karori, Wellington 5, New Zealand. *Office:* Department of Economics, Victoria University of Wellington, Private Bag, Wellington, New Zealand.

CAREER: Victoria University of Wellington, Wellington, New Zealand, lecturer, 1968-70, reader, 1971-73, professor of economic history, 1974—, Tawney Lecturer, 1978. Visiting fellow at Stanford University, 1972-73, and All Souls College, Oxford, 1977-78. Member of economic monitoring group of New Zealand Planning Council, 1980—. *Member:* Economic History Society of Australia and New Zealand, New Zealand Association of Economists, Public Service Investment Society (member of board of management, 1978-79), Economic History Association (United States), Economic History Society (United Kingdom).

WRITINGS: Railways and Economic Growth in England and Wales, 1840-1870, Clarendon Press, 1970; *The Development of the British Economy, 1870-1914,* Heinemann, 1970; *Between Governments and Banks: A History of the Reserve Bank of New Zealand,* Government Printer, 1973; *The Evolution of the New Zealand Economy,* Heinemann, 1977; *Economics for Historians,* Cambridge University Press, 1980.

Contributor: R. C. Floud and D. N. McCloskey, editors, *A New Economic History of Britain Since 1750,* Cambridge University Press, 1981; W. H. Oliver, editor, *The Oxford History of New Zealand,* Oxford University Press, 1981.

Contributor to economic and history journals. Editor of *New Zealand Economic Papers,* 1974-77.

WORK IN PROGRESS: Research on New Zealand economic history up to the nineteenth century.

SIDELIGHTS: Hawke commented: "I am concerned with the past and present development of New Zealand society and with the international world of economic history, seldom finding it necessary to choose between these. My first book was concerned with the role of technical change in economic growth, a topic much wider than Britain, even when London was at the center of the international economy. *Railways and Economic Growth* also has some methodological interest in its combination of economic theory and quantification with the traditional skills of historians. And that is followed up in my most recent book.

"My current interest is more directly associated with the

process of economic growth in New Zealand, its origins and consequences. With privileged access to the Reserve Bank's files, I found the writing of *Between Governments and Banks: A History of the Reserve Bank of New Zealand* to be an opportunity to deal with the period since the 1930's from the viewpoint of an organization intimately concerned with economic policy. I am now exploring the earlier period where even the main outlines of the economic experience remain to be constructed.

"The building of a new identifiable society in the South Pacific is a theme of perennial interest, and it also raises many economic questions which are close to those about which my colleagues in other countries are writing. I rarely feel isolated and can quickly conquer moments of doubt with the thought that the international economy is itself gradually moving south."

* * *

HAYES, Mary-Rose   1939-

PERSONAL: Born April 24, 1939, in Kent, England; came to the United States in 1956; daughter of Kenneth J. R. (a naval officer and writer) and Enid (Sutcliff) Langmaid; married Patrick Robert Hayes (a management consultant), January 14, 1961; children: Juliette Sarah, Nicholas Desmond. *Education:* Attended College of Marin, 1971-72, and San Francisco State University, 1979. *Residence:* San Francisco, Calif. *Agent:* Curtis Brown Ltd., 575 Madison Ave., New York, N.Y. 10022; and A. P. Watt Ltd., 26 Bedford Row, London WC1, England.

CAREER: Writer. Worked as in-hospital teacher in Bath, England; production assistant for Medical Radio and Television Institute, Inc., in New York, N.Y.; medical secretary at Peter Brent Grigham Hospital in Boston, Mass.; production assistant for Associated Television Ltd., in London, England; free-lance fashion model in London and San Francisco, Calif.; social secretary at dude ranch in Tucson, Ariz.; free-lance graphic designer in San Francisco; and deckhand. *Awards, honors:* Silver medal for literature from Royal Society of Arts, 1956, for collegiate creative writing.

WRITINGS: The Neighbors (novel), Pinnacle Books, 1977; *The Caller* (novel), Pinnacle Books, 1979; *The Yacht People* (novel), Pinnacle Books, 1979.

WORK IN PROGRESS: Overpass, a psychological suspense novel, set in England during the 1940's and in contemporary California; *The Second Staircase,* an occult suspense novel concerning an unexplained outbreak of fires in an old San Francisco apartment house.

SIDELIGHTS: Mary-Rose Hayes commented: "I gravitated into writing, after pursuing an enormous number of career blind alleys, because logically writing is about the only thing I am qualified for. I don't mind in the least working on my own and doing it every day, as I can't imagine what else I would do. Since I have worked in all kinds of widely different jobs, I know a little about quite a lot of things. I frequently find myself in bizarre situations. I am invariably confided in by total strangers. It's amazing what comes in useful from all of this rat-pack of unrelated information. I never take notes, and I never write plot outlines. If the book is going to be any good at all, the characters themselves dictate to *me* how the story will develop."

BIOGRAPHICAL/CRITICAL SOURCES: San Francisco Examiner, February 22, 1979.

HEATH, Sandra
See WILSON, Sandra

* * *

HEATON-WARD, William Alan   1919-

PERSONAL: Born December 19, 1919, in Durham, England; son of Ralph (a schoolmaster) and Mabel (a schoolmistress; maiden name, Orton) Heaton-Ward; married Christine Edith Fraser, March 28, 1945; children: Nicola Christine Heaton-Ward Kennedy, Lindsay Heaton-Ward Maldini. *Education:* University of Bristol, M.B., Ch.B., 1944, D.P.M., 1948. *Religion:* "Humanist." *Home and office:* 75 Pembroke Rd., Bristol BS8 3DP, England.

CAREER: Bristol Royal Infirmary, Bristol, England, house physician, 1944-45; Littlemore Mental Hospital, Oxford, England, assistant medical officer, 1945-46; St. James Psychiatric Hospital, Portsmouth, England, senior registrar, 1948-50; Brentry Hospital, Bristol, deputy medical superintendent, 1950-54; University of Bristol, Bristol, clinical teacher in department of mental health, 1954-78; Lord Chancellor's medical visitor for Southwestern Circuit, 1978—. Blake Marsh Memorial Lecturer at Royal College of Psychiatrists, 1976. Medical superintendent of Stoke Park Hospital Group, 1954-61, consultant psychiatrist, 1963-74; consultant psychiatrist for National Health Service, 1954-78. *Military service:* Royal Navy, neuropsychiatrist, 1946-48; became surgeon lieutenant commander.

MEMBER: Royal College of Psychiatrists (fellow; vice-president, 1976-78), British Medical Association, British Society for the Study of Mental Subnormality (president, 1979-80), American Society of Physician-Analysts (honorary member), Anglo-Zimbabwe Society (chairman of Bristol-Bath branch, 1980—), Bristol Medico-Chirurgical Society. *Awards, honors:* Burden Research Gold Medal and Prize from Burden Trustees, 1978, for published research in the field of the mentally handicapped.

WRITINGS: (With J. F. Lyons) *Notes on Mental Deficiency,* John Wright, 1953, 3rd edition, 1955; *Mental Subnormality,* John Wright, 1960, 4th edition, 1974; *Left Behind,* Macdonald & Evans, 1977. Contributor to medical journals and popular magazines.

WORK IN PROGRESS: Revising *Mental Subnormality,* publication by John Wright expected in 1982.

SIDELIGHTS: Heaton-Ward wrote: "I attribute whatever success I may have achieved throughout my career to being lucky enough to be in the right place at the right time. I believe that all human motivation is fundamentally selfish and that circumstances govern people, rather than the reverse.

"My main concern as a consultant psychiatrist was with the care of the mentally subnormal, and my attitude to the problem was presented by a comment I made as long ago as 1958 when the British mental health bill was being debated in Parliament: 'The problem of mental subnormality will never be solved by pretending it doesn't exist.'

"The choice of *Left Behind* as the title of my third book was intended to describe the position of the mentally subnormal in society and in the National Health Service and also to be an antithesis to what I regarded as the pejorative title of Pauline Morris's book, *Put Away.*

"I am concerned at the delusion of the present decade, steadfastly held, I believe, by all political parties and sociologists in the face of overwhelming evidence to the contrary, that any change is bound to represent progress. And I am concerned at the tendency for their committees to believe that they are about to give birth to a new Messiah, in the face of the best available advice that it will be the inevitable camel!''

*   *   *

HEBERT, Ernest 1941-

PERSONAL: Born May 4, 1941, in Keene, N.H.; son of J. Elphege (a mill weaver) and Jeannette (a nurse; maiden name, Vaccarest) Hebert; married Medora Lavoie (a photographer), March 22, 1969; children: Lael Scott. *Education:* Keene State College, B.A., 1969; attended Stanford University, 1969-70. *Politics:* Democrat. *Religion:* Roman Catholic. *Home:* 42 Elliot St., Keene, N.H. 03431. *Agent:* Rita Scott, Inc., 25 Sutton Pl. S., New York, N.Y. 10022. *Office: Keene Sentinel,* 60 West St., Keene, N.H. 03431.

CAREER: Telephone installer in Keene, N.H., 1960-63; worked as taxi driver in Keene, c. 1969; manager of gas station, Keene, 1970-72; *Keene Sentinel,* Keene, reporter, 1972-78, editor, 1978—, author of column, 1979—. *Military service:* U.S. Army, 1959-60 and 1961-62. *Awards, honors:* Journalism awards from New England United Press International, 1973, for humor and spot news; judge's citation from Ernest Hemingway Foundation, 1980, for novel, *The Dogs of March.*

WRITINGS: The Dogs of March (novel), Viking, 1979.

WORK IN PROGRESS: Another novel.

SIDELIGHTS: Hebert commented: ''Since I discovered writing at age twenty-three, I've believed it was the only thing I could do with some distinction. I feel as though I was put here to write; therefore I am obligated to write. It is a good way of finding out what's on my mind.''

*   *   *

HEIMLICH, Henry Jay 1920-

PERSONAL: Born February 3, 1920, in Wilmington, Del.; son of Philip and Mary (Epstein) Heimlich; married Jane Murray, June 3, 1951; children: Philip, Peter, Janet and Elizabeth (twins). *Education:* Cornell University, B.A., 1941, M.D., 1943. *Home:* 17 Elmhurst Pl., Cincinnati, Ohio 45208. *Office:* Department of Advanced Clinical Sciences, Xavier University, Cincinnati, Ohio 45207.

CAREER: Boston City Hospital, Boston, Mass., intern, 1944; Veterans Administration Hospital, Bronx, N.Y., resident, 1946-47; Mount Sinai Hospital, New York City, resident, 1947-48; Bellevue Hospital, New York City, resident, 1948-49; Triboro Hospital, Jamaica, N.Y., resident, 1949-50; Montefiore Hospital, New York City, attending surgeon, 1950-69; Jewish Hospital, Cincinnati, Ohio, director of surgery, 1969-77; Xavier University, Cincinnati, professor of advanced clinical sciences, 1977—. Diplomate of American Board of Surgery and American Board of Thoracic Surgery. Associate clinical professor at University of Cincinnati, 1969—. Member of board of directors of National Cancer Foundation, 1960-70, president of board, 1963-68; founder and president of Dysphagia Foundation; member of board of directors of Community Development Foundation, 1967-70, Save the Children Federation, 1967-68, and United Cancer Council, 1967-70. Member of President's Commission on Heart Disease, Cancer, and Stroke, 1965. Film producer. *Military service:* U.S. Naval Reserve, active duty, 1944-46; became lieutenant senior grade.

MEMBER: Collegium International Chirurgiae Digestive, Pan American Medical Association, American College of Surgeons (fellow; president, 1964), American College of Chest Physicians (fellow), American College of Gastroenterology (fellow), Society of Thoracic Surgeons (founding member), American Medical Association, Society of Surgery of the Alimentary Tract, American Gastroenterological Association, Central Surgical Association, New York Society of Thoracic Surgery, Cincinnati Society of Thoracic Surgery. *Awards, honors:* Award from Chinese Nationalist Government, 1944; Medaglione Di Bronze Minerva from Fourth International Festival of Medical-Scientific Films, 1961, for producing film, ''Esophageal Replacement With a Reversed Gastric Tube''; Sachs Award for outstanding achievement in the field of medicine, 1976; Ohio State Governors Award, 1980; Service Award Blue Cross of Massachusetts, 1980; humanitarian award from National Paramedics, 1980.

WRITINGS: Postoperative Care in Thoracic Surgery, C. C. Thomas, 1962; *Dr. Heimlich's Guide to Emergency Medical Situations,* Simon & Schuster, 1980. Also author of *Surgery of the Stomach, Duodenum, and Diaphragm: Questions and Answers,* with M. A. Cantor and C. H. Lupton, 1965. Contributor to medical journals. Member of editorial board of *Emergency Medicine* and Reportes Medicos.

WORK IN PROGRESS: An autobiography.

SIDELIGHTS: Heimlich developed the operation reversed gastric tube esophagoplasty, invented the Heimlich chest drain valve, and originated the ''Heimlich Maneuver,'' an easy technique designed to save victims choking on food. He also founded the international program, Computers for Peace.

Heimlich told *CA:* ''I have never been satisfied with existing methods and seek to simplify and improve them. After devising an operation for replacement of the esophagus, I became aware that one such discovery helps more people than is possible in a lifetime in the operating room. The 'Heimlich Maneuver' saves thousands of choking victims annually. My ultimate goal is to prevent death and promote well-being for the largest number of people by establishing a philosophy that will eliminate war.''

*   *   *

HEINS, Ethel L(eah) 1918-

PERSONAL: Born April 9, 1918, in New York, N.Y.; daughter of Herman E. (a pharmacist) and Rose M. (a pianist; maiden name, Marshak) Yaskin; married Paul Heins (a lecturer on children's literature), June 27, 1943; children: Peter S., Margery E. *Education:* Rutger's University, B.A., 1938; graduate study at Columbia University and Harvard University. *Home:* 29 Hope St., Auburndale, Mass. 02166. *Office:* The Horn Book, Inc., Park Square Bldg., Boston, Mass. 02116.

CAREER/WRITINGS: New York Public Library, New York, N.Y., children's librarian, 1938-43; Boston Public Library, Boston, Mass., children's librarian, 1955-62; Lexington Public Schools, Lexington, Mass., librarian and instructional materials specialist, 1962-74; *Horn Book* (magazine), Boston, member of book reviewing staff, 1962-74, editor, 1974—. Contributor to *Crosscurrents of Criticism,* edited by Paul Heins, Horn Book, Inc., 1977, and *Book Reviewing,* edited by Sylvia Kamerman, Plays, Inc., 1978; contributor of editorials and book reviews to several magazines, including *Horn Book, Harvard Magazine, Today's Education.* Lecturer in children's literature at Boston College, Chestnut Hill, Mass., 1968-71, and at Simmons College, Boston, 1975—; lecturer at numerous seminars on children's literature in the United States and Europe. Chairman of the first American commission at the Conference on Children's Literature in Education, Exeter, England, 1973; chairman of the book evaluation committee of the Association for Library Service to Children, May Hill Arbuthnot Memorial Lecture Committee, and Mildred L. Batchelder Awards Committee; member of New Round Table of Children's Librarians Hewins-Melcher Lecture Committee and Newbury-Caldecott Awards Committee; judge for the *Boston Globe-Horn Book* award, 1970, *Washington Post-Chicago Tribune Book World* Spring Book Festival Award, 1971, and National Book Awards, 1976.

MEMBER: International Research Society for Children's Literature, American Library Association, National Council of Teachers of English, New England Library Association, Children's Literature Association, Douglass Society. *Awards, honors:* Alumnae citation from Rutgers Graduate School of Library and Information Science for outstanding service to children's books, 1979.

WORK IN PROGRESS: Continued research on illustrated books for children and the criticism of children's literature.

SIDELIGHTS: Heins told *CA*: "Bringing good books and children together has been the inspiration behind all the work I have done for the past forty years—as librarian, reviewer, teacher, lecturer, and editor. My own fervid convictions and concerns have gathered strength through my years of public and school library service and through my work as a critic of children's literature. I have always felt a need to enlist teachers and parents as allies in my cause. Now, more than ever—as economic crises whittle away library services and as television and other electronic facts of life lure young people away from a preoccupation with reading—I feel that the adult must act as a human link between the child and the book. My hope for *Horn Book* is that it will continue to be a lively journal of criticism and commentary in which we can convince our readers of the humanizing power of children's literature. These aims, interestingly enough, are entirely compatible with the ideals of Bertha Mahony Miller, who founded the magazine in 1924."

*   *   *

HEIZER, Robert Fleming   1915-1979

PERSONAL: Born July 13, 1915, in Denver, Colo.; died July 18, 1979, in Berkeley, Calif.; son of Ott Fleming and Martha (Madden) Heizer; married Nancy Elizabeth Landwehr, July 31, 1940 (divorced); children: Stephen Rodney, Michael Madden, Sydney Alison (daughter). *Education:* University of California, Berkeley, A.B., 1936, Ph.D., 1941. *Residence:* California.

CAREER: University of Oregon, Eugene, instructor, 1940-41; University of California, Los Angeles, instructor, 1945-46; University of California, Berkeley, assistant professor, 1946-48, associate professor, 1949-52, professor of archaeology, 1952-75, professor emeritus, 1975-79, director of California archaeological survey, 1948-60, director of Archaeology Research Facility, head of department, and curator of North American archaeology at Lowie Museum of Archaeology, all 1950-75. *Member:* American Association for the Advancement of Science (fellow), American Anthropological Association, National Academy of Sciences, Society for American Archaeology (vice-president, 1959-60), Societe des Americanistes de Paris, Association for Topical Biogeography, Prehistoric Society, Institute of Andean Research. *Awards, honors:* Grants from American Philosophical Society, 1945-49, Wenner Gren Foundation for Archaeology, 1955-60, National Geographic Society, 1955,

1957, and 1965, and National Science Foundation, 1958-60, 1963-64, and 1968-69; Guggenheim fellow, 1963 and 1972; D.Sc. from University of Nevada, 1965; Center for Advanced Study in Behavioral Sciences fellow, 1972.

WRITINGS: Francis Drake and the California Indians, 1579, University of California Press, 1947, reprinted, Kraus Reprints, 1971; (with Sherburne F. Cook) *The Archaeology of Central California: A Comparative Analysis of Human Bone From Nine Sites,* University of California Press, 1949, reprinted, Kraus Reprints, 1976; *Archaeology of the Uyak Site, Kodiak Island, Asaska,* University of California Press, 1956; (contributor) William E. Ver Planck, *Salt in California,* [San Francisco], 1958.

(With Martin A. Baumhoff) *Prehistoric Rock Art of Nevada and Eastern California,* University of California Press, 1962; (contributor) *Aboriginal California: Three Studies in Culture History,* University of California, 1963; (with Frank Hole) *An Introduction to Prehistoric Archaeology,* Holt, 1965, 3rd edition, 1977; (with Cook) *Studies on the Chemical Analysis of Archaeological Sites,* University of California Press, 1965; *Languages, Territories, and Names of California Indian Tribes,* University of California Press, 1966; (with J. N. Bowman) *Anza and the Northwest Frontier of New Spain,* Southwest Museum, 1967; (with Philip Drucker) *To Make My Name Good: A Reexamination of the Southern Kwakiutt Potlatch,* University of California Press, 1967; (with Theodora Kroeber) *Almost Ancestors: The First Californians,* edited by F. David Hales, Sierra Club, 1968.

(With Lewis K. Napton and others) *Archaeology and the Prehistoric Great Basin Lacustrine Subsistence Regime as Seen From Lovelock Cave, Nevada,* Archaeological Research Facility, University of California, 1970; (with Albert B. Elsasser and C. William Clewlow, Jr.) *A Bibliography of California Archaeology,* Department of Anthropology, University of California, 1970; (with Kroeber and Elsasser) *Drawn From Life: California Indians in Pen and Brush,* Ballena Press, 1971; (with Alan J. Almquist) *The Other Californians: Prejudice and Discrimination Under Spain, Mexico, and the United States to 1920,* University of California Press, 1971; *The Eighteen Unratified Treaties of 1851-1852 Between the California Indians and the United States Government,* Archaeological Research Facility, University of California, 1972; (with Adan E. Treganza) *Mines and Quarries of the Indians of California,* reprint of original 1944 edition, Ballena Press, 1972; (with Thomas R. Hester) *Bibliography of Archaeology,* Addison-Wesley, 1973; (with Clewlow) *Prehistoric Rock Art of California,* two volumes, Ballena Press, 1973.

Elizabethan California: A Brief, and Sometimes Critical, Review of Opinions on the Location of Francis Drake's Five-Weeks' Visit With the Indians of Ships Land in 1579, to Which Are Added Reprintings of Two Papers Comprising an Ethnographic Analysis of Indian Customs and Language Recorded on the Drake Expedition, June 17, 1579 to July 23, 1579, Ballena Press, 1974; (with Karen M. Nissen and Edward D. Castillo) *California Indian History: A Classified and Annotated Guide to Source Materials,* Ballena Press, 1975; *The Indians of California: A Critical Bibliography,* Indiana University Press, 1976; (with Frank Hole) *Prehistoric Archaeology: A Brief Introduction,* Holt, 1977; (with George E. Anderson and W. H. Ellison) *Treaty Making and Treaty Rejection by the Federal Government in California, 1850-1852,* Ballena Press, 1978.

Archaeological survey reports: *Archaeological Evidence of Sebastian Rodriquez Cermeno's California Visit in 1595,*

California Historical Society, 1942; (with Edwin M. Lemert) *Observations on Archaeological Sites in Topanga Canyon, California,* University of California Press, 1947, reprinted, Kraus Reprints, 1971; (with Sherburne F. Cook and others) *The Physical Analysis of Nine Indian Mounds of the Lower Sacramento Valley,* University of California Press, 1951; (with Albert B. Elsasser) *Archaeological Investigators on Santa Rosa Island in 1901,* University of California Press, 1956; (with Alex Dony Krieger) *The Archaeology of Humboldt Cave, Churchill County, Nevada,* University of California Press, 1956.

Notes on Some Paviotso Personalities and Material Culture, Nevada State Museum, 1960; (contributor) *The Archaeology of Two Sites at Eastgate, Churchill County, Nevada,* University of California Press, 1961; (with Cook) *Chemical Analysis of the Hotchkiss Site,* Department of Anthropology, University of California, 1962; (with Elsasser) *The Archaeology of Bowers Cave, Los Angeles County, California,* Department of Anthropology, University of California, 1963; (with Elsasser) *Archaeology of Hum-67, the Gunther Island Site in Humboldt Bay, California,* Archaeological Research Facility, University of California, 1964; (with Henry Reichlen) *The Scientific Expedition of Leon de Cessae to California, 1877-1879,* Department of Anthropology, University of California, 1964; (with Cook) *The Quantitative Approach to the Relation Between Population and Settlement Size,* Department of Anthropology, University of California, 1965; (with Elsasser) *Excavation of Two Northwestern California Coastal Sites,* Department of Anthropology, University of California, 1966; (with John A. Graham) *Notes on the Papalhuapa Site, Guatemala,* Department of Anthropology, University of California, 1968; (with others) *Papers on Mesoamerican Archaeology,* Archaeological Research Facility, University of California, 1968.

(With Graham) *Observations on the Emergence of Civilization in Mesoamerica,* Department of Anthroplogy, University of California, 1971; *California's Oldest Relic?,* Museum of Anthropology, University of California, 1972; (with Thomas R. Hester) *The Archaeology of Bamert Cave, Amador County, California,* Department of Anthropology, University of California, 1973; (with Karen M. Nissen) *The Human Sources of California Ethnology,* University of California, 1973; (with Hester) *Review and Discussion of Great Basin Projectile Points: Forms and Chronology,* University of California, 1973, published as *Projectile Points: Forms and Chronology,* Ballena Press, 1978.

Editor: *A Manual of Archaeological Field Methods,* National Press, 1949, 3rd edition published as *A Guide to Archaeological Field Methods,* 1958, revised edition (edited with John A. Graham) published as *A Guide to Field Methods in Archaeology: Approaches to the Anthropology of the Dead,* 1967, 6th edition (edited with Thomas R. Hester) published as *Field Methods in Archaeology,* Mayfield, 1975; (with Mary Anne Whipple) *The California Indians: A Source Book,* University of California Press, 1951, 2nd edition, 1971; (with John E. Mills) *The Four Ages of Tsurai: A Documentary History of the Indian Village on Trinidad Bay,* University of California Press, 1952; *The Archaeology of the Napa Region,* University of California Press, 1953; *The Mission Indian Vocabularies of H. W. Henshaw,* University of California Press, 1955; *The Archaeologist at Work: A Source Book in Archaeological Method and Interpretation,* Harper, 1959.

(With Sherburne F. Cook) *The Application of Quantitative Methods in Archaeology,* Quadrangle Books, 1960; *Catalogue of the C. Hart Merriam Collection of Data Concerning*

California Tribes and Other American Indians, Archaeological Research Facility, University of California, 1961; (with Albert B. Elsasser) *Original Accounts of the Lone Woman of San Nicolas Island,* University of California, 1961; *Man's Discovery of His Past: Literary Landmarks in Archaeology,* Prentice-Hall, 1962, 2nd edition, Peek Publications, 1969; *The Indians of Los Angeles County: Hugo Reid's Letters of 1852,* Southwest Museum, 1968.

An Anthropological Expedition of 1913; or, Get It Through Your Head; or, Yours for the Revolution: Correspondence Between A. L. Kroeber and L. L. Loud, Department of Anthropology, University of California, 1970; *Collected Documents on the Causes and Events in the Bloody Island Massacre of 1850,* Archaeological Research Facility, University of California, c. 1970; *George Gibb's Journal of Redick McKee's Expedition Through Northwestern California in 1851,* Archaeological Research Facility, University of California, 1972; *Notes on Northern Paiute Ethnography: Kroeber and Marsden Records,* Archaeological Research Facility, University of California, 1972; *Reprints of Various Papers on California Archaeology, Ethnography, and Indian History,* Department of Anthropology, University of California, 1973; *Notes on the McCloud River Wintu and Selected Excerpts From Alexander S. Taylor's "Indianology of California,"* Archaeological Research Facility, University of California, 1973.

(With Karen M. Nissen and E. D. Castillo) *A Bibliography of Canadian Indian History,* Department of Anthropology, University of California, 1974; *The Costanoan Indians: An Assemblage of Papers on the Language and Culture of the Costanoan Indians Who in Aboriginal Times Occupied San Francisco, San Mateo, Santa Clara, Alameda, and Parts of Contra Costa, Monterey, and San Benito Counties,* California History Center, 1974; *The Destruction of California Indians: A Collection of Documents From the Period 1847 to 1865 in Which Are Described Some of the Things That Happened to Some of the Indians of California,* Pregrine Smith, 1974; *Indians of California: A Collection of Maps on Tribal Distribution,* Garland Publishing, 1974; *They Were Only Diggers: A Collection of Articles From California Newspapers, 1851-1866, on Indian and White Relations,* Ballena Press, 1974.

Seven Early Accounts of the Pomo Indians and Their Culture, Department of Anthropology, University of California, 1975; *A Collection of Ethnographical Articles on the California Indians,* Ballena Press, 1976; *Some Last Century Accounts of the Indians of Southern California,* Ballena Press, 1976; (with others) *Sources of Stones Used in Prehistoric Mesoamerican Sites,* Ballena Press, 1976; *The California Indians vs. the United States of America (HR 4497): Evidence Offered in Support of Occupancy, Possession, and Use of Land in California by the Ancestors of Enrolled Indians of California,* Ballena Press, 1978; (with Theodora Kroeber) *Ishi, the Last Yahi: A Documentary History,* University of California Press, 1979; C. Hart Merrimam, *Indian Names for Plants and Animals Among Californian and Other North American Tribes,* Ballena Press, 1979; *Federal Concern About Conditions of California Indians, 1853 to 1913: Eight Documents,* Ballena Press, 1979.

Contributor to numerous periodicals in his field.

SIDELIGHTS: Robert Fleming Heizer was a leading authority on the Indian tribes and archaeology of California and on the emergence of civilization in the New World. In 1976 he and John A. Graham announced new findings to support their hypothesis that the celebrated Mayan civilization began, not in the tropical Guatemalan lowlands where their magnificent architecture has been unearthed, but rather in the highlands of the Pacific Coast. At one point, the two anthropologists maintained, the ancient Mayans made a two-hundred-mile trek across volcanic mountains and settled in the lowlands. This revolutionary new data forced other anthropologists to reassess their interpretation of the rise of civilization in Mesoamerica.

BIOGRAPHICAL/CRITICAL SOURCES: American Anthropologist, December, 1959; *Washington Post,* October 25, 1978.

OBITUARIES: New York Times, July 20, 1979.*

*   *   *

HELMS, Roland Thomas, Jr.   1940-
(Tom Helms)

PERSONAL: Born October 13, 1940, in Concord, N.C.; son of Roland Thomas and Nadine (Kindley) Helms. *Education:* University of Georgia, B.B.A., 1963. *Home:* 186-1 Crosscreek Dr., Athens, Ga. 30605.

CAREER: Cabarrus Memorial Hospital, Concord, N.C., statistician, 1969-72; State of North Carolina, Raleigh, personnel administrator, 1972-78; writer, 1978—.

WRITINGS: (Under name Tom Helms) *Against All Odds* (autobiography), Crowell, 1978.

WORK IN PROGRESS: A novel, in which "two men return to a small Southern town to bury a childhood friend and, in the process of remembering their childhoods, find their lives are changed," publication expected in 1981.

SIDELIGHTS: Helms told *CA:* "I write out of desperation, a desperate need to touch someone, to tell someone that inside this broken body is a man. I write in an attempt to aquire those material things which will bring some comfort to my life. I write in an attempt to change some people's perceptions of those around us. But most important, I write because I love it so."

*   *   *

HELMS, Tom
See HELMS, Roland Thomas, Jr.

*   *   *

HELVICK, James
See COCKBURN, (Francis) Claud

*   *   *

HENAGHAN, Jim   1919-
(Archie O'Neill)

PERSONAL: Born December 16, 1919, in Liverpool, England; son of James Ambrose and Mary Ellen (O'Neill) Henaghan; married Gwen Verdon (an entertainer), December 25, 1940 (divorced December, 1941); married Mary Frances Le Roi (a fashion designer), June 2, 1960; children: Jim Henaghan, Jr. *Home:* 2170 Century Park E., Los Angeles, Calif. 90067.

CAREER: Writer. *Military service:* U.S. Army, 1941-45; received Distinguished Service Medal and Purple Heart. *Member:* Century City World War II Hero Luncheon Group. *Awards, honors:* Oarsman of the Month Trophy from Marina del Rey Rowing Club, June, 1977.

WRITINGS: The Da Vinci Rose, Bantam, 1973; *The Duplicate Stiff,* Bantam, 1974; *High Bid for Murder,* Bantam, 1974; (under pseudonym Archie O'Neill), *The Ginzburg Circle,* 1974; (under O'Neill pseudonym), *Azor!,* St. Martin's, 1977. Contributor to periodicals.

WORK IN PROGRESS: Memories of a Man, a biography of John Wayne; *Khadish,* a novel of three women after World War II; two more novels featuring Jeff Pride as the protagonist.

SIDELIGHTS: Henaghan told *CA:* "I was born in Liverpool, England, raised in an orphan asylum, ran away at age ten, didn't finish tenth grade in school, was a bum from age ten to sixteen, and educated myself reading everything in public libraries. When it came time to work, I knew only one thing—words—so I went to work as a reporter, got fired, fired, fired, and fired until I learned to write. I've never had a rejection in my career. I became a millionaire."

*   *   *

HENDERSON, Jean Carolyn Glidden   1916-

PERSONAL: Born May 22, 1916, in New York, N.Y.; daughter of Edgar (an engineer) and Mary (a teacher; maiden name, Fischer) Glidden; married William Natzroth (divorced, 1958); married Algo D. Henderson, April 6, 1963; children: Carol Natzroth Viole; (stepchildren) Philip, Joanne (Mrs. James Pratt). *Education:* New York University, B.S., 1951, M.A., 1954; University of Michigan, Ph.D., 1967. *Politics:* Independent. *Religion:* Unitarian-Universalist. *Home:* 239 Glorietta Blvd., Orinda, Calif. 94563.

CAREER: Long Island University, C.W. Post College, Greenvale, N.Y., director of admissions and registrar, 1955-59; University of Michigan, Ann Arbor, department assistant at Center for Study of Higher Education, 1959-61; Finch College, New York, N.Y., dean of women, 1961-63; California College of Arts and Crafts, Oakland, associate professor of psychology, counselor, and director of research on student characteristics, 1969-71; University of California, Cowell Hospital, Berkeley, counselor with student health services, 1975-78. Member of council of University of California Art Museum, 1968-71; member of International Hospitality Center of the San Francisco Bay Area, 1968-71; treasurer and member of board of directors of Kennedy-King Memorial College Scholarship Fund, 1971-80; consultant to Montgomery College, Rockville, Md., 1978; member of advisory board on county Health Maintenance Organization to board of supervisors of Contra Costa County, Calif., 1980—. *Member:* National Association of Women Deans and Counselors, National Organization for Women, American Association for Higher Education, American Association of University Women, American Personnel and Guidance Association, American Civil Liberties Union, League of Women Voters, Kappa Delta Pi, Pi Lambda Theta, Pi Omega Pi.

WRITINGS: (With husband, Algo D. Henderson) *Higher Education in America,* Jossey-Bass, 1974; *Ms. Goes to College,* Southern Illinois University Press, 1975. Also author of *Women as College Teachers,* 1967. Contributor to professional journals.

WORK IN PROGRESS: Women in Higher Education; Status of Women in America.

*   *   *

HENDIN, Josephine   1946-

PERSONAL: Born December 21, 1946, in New York, N.Y.; daughter of Charles and Florence Gattuso; married Herbert Hendin (a psychoanalyst and writer), June 7, 1968; children:

Neil, Erik. *Education:* City College of City University of New York, B.A., 1964; Columbia University, M.A., 1965, Ph.D., 1968. *Home:* 1045 Park Ave., New York, N.Y. 10028. *Agent:* Georges Borchardt, Inc., 136 East 57th St., New York, N.Y. 10022. *Office:* Department of English, New York University, 19 University Pl., New York, N.Y. 10003.

CAREER: Yale University, New Haven, Conn., instructor, 1968-69; New School for Social Research, New York City, member of faculty, 1969-79; New York University, New York City, instructor of American literature, 1979—. *Member:* Modern Language Association of America, National Book Critics Circle. *Awards, honors: The World of Flannery O'Connor* was named an outstanding academic book of 1970 by *Choice;* Guggenheim fellowship, 1975-76; *Vulnerable People* was named one of fifty notable books of 1980 by American Library Association.

WRITINGS: The World of Flannery O'Connor, Indiana University Press, 1970; *Vulnerable People: A View of American Literature Since 1945,* Oxford University Press, 1979; (contributor) Daniel Hoffman, editor, *The Harvard Guide to Contemporary Literature,* Harvard University Press, 1980. Contributor to magazines, including *Harper's, Saturday Review, New Republic, Ms., Psychology Today,* and *Esquire.* Fiction editor of *Savvy,* 1979-80.

WORK IN PROGRESS: The Right Thing to Do, a novel; *Violence in American Literature.*

SIDELIGHTS: Josephine Hendin wrote: "I am interested in the relation of cultural themes and the literary imagination."

* * *

HENDRA, Tony

PERSONAL—Agent: c/o Jennifer Roders, Workman Publishing Co., 231 East 51st St., New York, N.Y. 10022.

CAREER: Writer.

WRITINGS: (With Dean Fuller and Matt Dubey) *Smith: A Musical,* Samuel French, 1972; (editor with Christopher Cerf and Peter Ebling) *The Eighties: A Look Back at the Tumultuous Decade, 1980-89,* Workman Publishing, 1979.

SIDELIGHTS: The Eighties is a collection of humorous essays depicting life in the 1980's. The book laughingly lists the notable events of this decade from the perspective of the 1990's. Thus Hendra and his collaborators reveal that there was an oil glut in 1985 that rocked the financial world. Other incidents include the merger between the *New York Times* and *Variety* that created such headlines as "Afghan War Is Held Over for 6th Big Week"; the great slide in California that juxtaposed Los Angeles and San Francisco; the bankruptcy of the National Broadcasting Co. (NBC) in 1983; and the transformation of the magazine *Life,* which switched to exclusively covering nuclear power and became *Half Life.* Jean Strouse commented in *Newsweek* that "some of the jokes go on too long, others aren't funny. But the gems outnumber the duds." The *Washington Post's* reviewer Michael Gross disagreed and forebodingly quipped that *The Eighties* "is hardly cheerful reading, rather a prime example of history as 'the great dust heap.' But it should be widely read," he added, "otherwise, as the philosophers have warned, we run the danger of repeating it."

BIOGRAPHICAL/CRITICAL SOURCES: Washington Post, October 26, 1979; *Newsweek,* December 31, 1979.*

* * *

HENDY, Philip (Anstiss) 1900-1980

OBITUARY NOTICE: Born September 7, 1900, in Carlisle,

England; died September 20, 1980, in Oxford, England. Museum curator and art historian. Hendy was the director of Britain's prestigious National Gallery from 1946 to 1967. Following World War II, he reorganized the museum's collection of paintings which had been dispersed for safety during the war years. Prior to undertaking his post at the National Gallery, Hendy had been a lecturer and keeper at the Wallace Collection in London. He was also curator of the Boston Museum of Fine Arts. His writings include *Hours in the Wallace Collection* and a highly-regarded catalog of the Isabelle Stewart Gardner collection in Boston. Obituaries and other sources: *Who's Who in America,* 38th edition, Marquis, 1974; *Who's Who,* 126th edition, St. Martin's, 1974; *The International Who's Who,* Europa, 1978; *Washington Post,* September 23, 1980.

* * *

HENLEY, Karyn 1952-

PERSONAL: Born September 12, 1952, in Austin, Tex.; daughter of Ray (an investments adviser) and Kay (Dollar) McGlothlin; married Ralph D. Henley (a transportation analyst), August 12, 1974; children: Raygan Thomas. *Education:* Abilene Christian College (now University), B.S.Ed., 1974. *Religion:* Church of Christ. *Home:* 756 Kenwood, Abilene, Tex. 79601.

CAREER: Writer. Blevens & Blevens Insurance, Los Angeles, Calif., office manager, 1975; teacher in Sherman Oaks, Calif., 1975-76; Data Products, Inc., Woodland Hills, Calif., secretary, 1976-77. *Member:* Society of Children's Book Writers.

WRITINGS: Hatch! (juvenile), Carolrhoda, 1980. Contributor of articles to *Reflection* and *Discoveries;* contributor to activities page of *Bible Weekly Reader.*

WORK IN PROGRESS: Several children's books, both fiction and nonfiction; a how-to book on the craft of batiking.

SIDELIGHTS: Henley wrote: "I've always loved to read. As a child I found reading opened the doors to many experiences that I'd never otherwise hoped to have. As I was reading stories to the children in my classroom, it occurred to me that I could write books, too. That's where it all began—and who knows where it will end?"

* * *

HENRIQUES, Veronica 1931-

PERSONAL: Born May 10, 1931, in England; daughter of Robert (a writer) and Vivien (an artist; maiden name, Levy) Henriques; married Robert Gosling (a carpenter), December 6, 1957; children: Jonathan, Louisa, William, Samuel, Roland. *Education:* Educated in Cheltenham, England. *Home:* Hay Farm, Cliffords Mesne, Newent, Gloucestershire, England. *Agent:* Richard Scott Simon, 32 College Cross, London N.1, England.

CAREER: Writer, 1952—.

WRITINGS—All published by Secker & Warburg: Love From a Convict, 1954; *Home Is the Heart,* 1955; *Man in a Maze,* 1957; *The Face I Had,* 1965; (editor) Robert Henriques, *From a Biography of Myself,* 1968; *Tom's Sister,* 1975.

Author of radio play "By Air," first broadcast by British Broadcasting Corp. (BBC), 1956.

WORK IN PROGRESS: In Absence of Receptionist Please Ring Bell, a novel, publication expected in 1982.

SIDELIGHTS: Veronica Henriques told *CA:* "I write compulsively in order to discover sense in things and hope somehow, sometime to come across it while writing. What would then occur to me I don't know. Maybe there would be no need to write anymore. I write during moments snatched from a life of domesticity and of making practical objects out of once useful and now redundant good-looking metal things. Art, painting, and sculpture are most valuable to me; I would not wish to live in a world without them."

*   *   *

HERMAN, Esther 1935-

PERSONAL: Born February 22, 1935, in Baltimore, Md.; daughter of Harry H. (in sales) and Anna (Union) Mandelberg; married Gilbert Herman (a merchant; in automobile business), September 28, 1955; children: Betsy Herman Taubman, Mindy. *Education:* University of Maryland, B.A., 1955, M.L.S., 1968. *Politics:* Democrat. *Religion:* Jewish. *Home:* 10202 McGovern Dr., Silver Spring, Md. 20903. *Office:* College of Library and Information Services, University of Maryland, College Park, Md. 20740.

CAREER: St. Paul Public Library, St. Paul, Minn., library aide, 1955-56; teacher at public schools in Baltimore, Md., 1956-57; University of Maryland, College Park, director of publications and publicity for College of Library and Information Services, 1968—.

WRITINGS: (Editor with Derek Langridge) *The Universe of Knowledge,* College of Library and Information Services, University of Maryland, 1969; (editor with C.D. Needham) *The Study of Subject Bibliography,* College of Library and Information Services, University of Maryland, 1970; (editor with T. D. Wilson) *Fundamentals of Documentation,* College of Library and Information Services, University of Maryland, 1973; (editor with Paul Wasserman) *Museum Media,* Gale, 1973, 2nd edition published as *Catalog of Museum Publications and Media,* 1980; (editor with Wasserman) *Library Bibliographies and Indexes,* Gale, 1975; (editor with Wasserman) *Festivals Sourcebook,* Gale, 1977.

*   *   *

HESS, John L(oft) 1917-

PERSONAL: Born December 27, 1917, in New York, N.Y. *Home:* 285 Riverside Dr., New York, N.Y. 10025.

CAREER: Worked as farmhand, factory worker, and seaman, 1934-45, and as reporter in Arizona, California, and New York, 1945-54; *New York Times,* New York, N.Y., sub-editor, investigative reporter, critic, and foreign correspondent, 1954-78. Radio and television commentator. *Awards, honors:* French Order of Merit, 1970; Mike Berger Award from Columbia University, 1974, for feature writing; eight awards, including award from U.S. Department of Health, Education and Welfare and Front Page Award, all 1975, for nursing-home investigation.

WRITINGS: The Case for DeGaulle, Morrow, 1968; *The Grand Acquisitors,* Houghton, 1974; *Vanishing France,* Quadrangle, 1975; (with wife, Karen Hess) *The Taste of America,* Viking, 1977. Author of a column syndicated three times a week by United Features, 1979—. Contributor to magazines.

SIDELIGHTS: Hess commented to *CA:* "I have been accused of being a moralist. Guilty. All my writing has been dedicated to exposing folly and striving to further peace and justice, and to protect the quality of life."

HEWITT, Cecil Rolph 1901-
(R. H. Cecil, Oliver Milton, C. H. Rolph)

PERSONAL: Born August 23, 1901, in London, England; son of Frederick Thompson (a chief inspector of police) and Edith Mary Hewitt; married Anne Jennifer Wayne (a writer); children: Brenda Hewitt Biram, Deborah Hewitt Bowen, Thomas Michael Jonathan, Julia Miranda. *Education:* Attended state schools in London, England. *Politics:* "Recently nil." *Religion:* Church of England. *Home and office address:* Rushett Edge, Rushett Common, Bramley, Guildford, Surrey GU5 0LH, England.

CAREER: City of London Police, London, England, constable, 1921-25, sergeant, 1925-28, subinspector, 1928-30, inspector, 1930-38, chief inspector, 1938-46; *New Statesman,* London, staff writer, 1946-70; Statesman Publishing Co., London, director, 1965-80. Narrator of "Outside Contracts," broadcast by British Broadcasting Corp., 1946-75. Vice-president of New Bridge (for friends of released prisoners); member of Justice (British section of International Commission of Jurists); member of Parole Board for Great Britain, 1967-69. *Member:* National Union of Journalists (life member), Society of Authors, Howard League for Penal Reform (vice-president).

WRITINGS—Under pseudonym C. H. Rolph: *A Licensing Handbook,* Police Review Publishing, 1937; *Crime and Punishment,* Gollancz, 1950; *Towards My Neighbour,* Longmans, Green, 1950; *On Gambling,* Bureau of Current Affairs, 1951; *Personal Identity,* M. Joseph, 1956; (editor) *The Human Sum,* Heinemann, 1957; *Mental Disorder,* National Association for Mental Health, 1958.

Commonsense About Crime and Punishment, Gollancz, 1961; *The Trial of Lady Chatterley,* Penguin, 1961; (with Arthur Koestler) *Hanged by the Neck,* Penguin, 1961; *All Those in Favour?: The ETU Trial,* Deutsch, 1962; *The Police and the Public,* Heinemann, 1962; *Law and the Common Man,* C. C Thomas, 1967; *Books in the Dock,* Deutsch, 1969; *Kingsley,* Gollancz, 1973; *Believe What You Like,* Deutsch, 1973; *Living Twice* (autobiography), Gollancz, 1974; *Mr. Prone,* Oxford University Press, 1977; *The Queen's Pardon,* Cassell, 1978; *London Particulars* (autobiography), Oxford University Press, 1979; *The Police* (juvenile), Wayland Publishers, 1980.

Contributor to magazines and newspapers, including *Spectator* (under pseudonym R. H. Cecil) and *Time Literary Supplement* (under pseudonym Oliver Milton). Editor of *Author,* 1956-60.

WORK IN PROGRESS: A novel, publication expected in 1981.

SIDELIGHTS: Hewitt wrote: "I have a kind of itch to write, which most people have but mercifully control. For me, it is now many years since it was an excitement to see my name and work in print, but it is still a pleasure and is now recognized as a huge responsibility.

"In criminological matters, I am committed to the view (and to its propagation) that punishment is NOT reformative but purely retributive. I believe that imprisonment serves absolutely no purpose other than containment and the protection of society against villains (for which purpose, of course, it is indispensable). And I feel that all countries spend far too much money on prohibitions and punishments and far too little on the succor of individual victims of crime and on the *prevention* of crime (in which two last respects the United States and, to a lesser extent, Britain are now beginning to give a world lead).

"I am at work on my first novel, the nature and plot of which I would not divulge under torture, but a publisher is already interested."

AVOCATIONAL INTERESTS: "I am deeply involved in music and poetry (mainly eighteenth-century) and cannot envisage a world without either. I'm a reluctant and mutinous gardener on what seems to me a big scale, and in the garden I fight year by year a losing battle. I am enthusiastic to the verge of besottedness about American literature, about which I am almost certainly insufficiently critical because I am what is known as a sucker for everything American except pop and rock music."

BIOGRAPHICAL/CRITICAL SOURCES: Police Review, August 18, 1978.

*   *   *

HEXT, Harrington
See PHILLPOTTS, Eden

*   *   *

HICKEY, Michael 1929-

PERSONAL: Born September 16, 1929, in Burton-on-Trent, England; son of Brian (a soldier and schoolmaster) and Evelyn (Wright) Hickey; married Bridget Cullum, July 9, 1960; children: Miles, James. *Education:* Attended Royal Military Academy, Sandhurst, 1948-49, Staff College, Camberly, 1961, Joint Services Staff College, Latimer, 1967, and Royal Naval College, Greenwich, 1976. *Religion:* Church of England. *Home:* Pipersmead, Springvale Ave., King's Worthy, Winchester, England.

CAREER: British Army, career officer, 1947—, served in Korea, 1950-52, Malaya, 1953-55, Korea, 1955-56, East Africa, 1962-63, Aden, 1963-65, and Singapore and Malaya, 1967-70, aviator, 1952—, helicopter pilot, 1956—, member of general staff of Ministry of Defence, 1979—, present rank, colonel. *Member:* Royal Aeronautical Society (charter member), Royal United Services Institute (member of council), Leander Rowing Club, London Rowing Club, Army Rowing Clubs Association (chairman), Winchester Cathedral Choral Society (member of Wayneflete Singers). *Awards, honors*—Military: Perak distinguished conduct medal, 1955. Other: George Knight Clowes Memorial Prize from *Army Quarterly*, 1965, for essay "The Value of Military History As Part of an Officer's Educational Curriculum"; defense fellow of King's College, London, 1973-74.

WRITINGS: Out of the Sky (history of airborne warfare), Scribner, 1979. Contributor of articles and reviews to military journals.

WORK IN PROGRESS: A history of aviation in the British Army, publication expected in 1982.

SIDELIGHTS: Hickey wrote: "I took my first parachute jump (on a bet) at the age of forty-seven and survived, unharmed, two major aircraft accidents—in Malaya in 1954 and Uganda in 1962. I am active as a veteran oarsman at the international level, including Amsterdam in 1975 and Berlin in 1976.

"I am a committed member of the Anglican church, to which I returned in 1956 after some years of spiritual starvation. For many generations my family has produced priests for the Church of England, and my cousin is currently bishop of the Transkei in South Africa.

"As I am addicted to history of all types, I count myself fortunate to live in a village whose fields have been tilled for two thousand years, near the ancient city of Winchester—the real capital of old England—where the spirit of King Alfred the Great, founder of the Royal Navy, savior of his people, is justly revered to this day.

"I have just made my first visit to the U.S.A. and was knocked sideways by the energy, warmth of hospitality, and kindliness of all I met. I found New England, as might be expected, totally in sympathy and was profoundly moved by a detailed visit to the battlefield of Antietam. I have every intention of returning again and again to see more of this astonishing country and its peoples.

"I started writing professionally some years ago when given some books to review. Here is a literary form which concentrates the mind wonderfully. When writing any other type of article or book, I tend to look at what I have written through the critic's detached eye. This can make for an uneasy and self-conscious style and needs to be watched.

"I do not use a typewriter. Everything is drafted and redrafted in longhand and often revised drastically in its first typed draft. I write very early in the morning and late at night, often with background music, which has to be *absolute* music; Bach is easily the best, and his solo instrumental suites are good friends (I couldn't take them in cold blood in a recital room, though).

"Long solitary walks—twenty-five miles at a time—are an excellent tonic for the naturally gregarious. So is painting in water colors. I envy the Buddhist who can leave the world temporarily and be a monk; the nearest equivalent in the Western churches is retreat, but this is difficult to fit in. Pilgrimage, in the medieval sense, is an admirable goal; I realized what impelled our forefathers when I, too, stood in the holy places during a visit to Israel in 1978."

AVOCATIONAL INTERESTS: Travel in undeveloped countries (east and central Africa, Arabia, and the Far East), music (especially choral singing), painting, rowing, cooking (especially Asian cuisine).

*   *   *

HIERS, John Turner 1945-

PERSONAL: Born July 15, 1945, in Pensacola, Fla.; son of Emory Mitchell (an attorney) and Margaret (a professor; maiden name, Hanes) Hiers; married Phyllis Romita (a teacher), 1968; children: Leslie, Kevin, Meg. *Education:* Emory University, B.A., 1967, Ph.D., 1974; University of Georgia, M.A., 1968. *Home:* 2409 Meadowbrook Dr., Valdosta, Ga. 31601. *Office:* Department of English, Valdosta State College, Valdosta, Ga. 31601.

CAREER: Valdosta State College, Valdosta, Ga., assistant professor, 1968-71, associate professor, 1971-74, professor of English, 1974—. *Member:* Society for the Study of Southern Literature, South Atlantic Modern Language Association.

WRITINGS: (With Floyd C. Watkins and William R. Dillingham) *Practical English Workbook*, Houghton, 1978; (with Watkins and Dillingham) *English Workbook*, Houghton, 1979; (editor with Watkins) *Robert Penn Warren Talking: Interviews, 1950-1978*, Random House, 1980; (with J. O. Williams and A. L. Jacobs) *Today's Language*, Heath, 1981. Contributor to literature journals and literary magazines.

WORK IN PROGRESS: Religious Miracles in the Fiction of Willa Cather.

BIOGRAPHICAL/CRITICAL SOURCES: Washington Post Book World, April 13, 1980.

HIGGINS, Judith Holden 1930-

PERSONAL: Born September 5, 1930, in White Plains, N.Y.; daughter of John Francis and Grace (Galloway) Holden; married James Delaney Higgins, January 16, 1961 (divorced, 1965); children: James Edward. *Education:* Simmons College, B.S., 1951; Columbia University, M.L.S., 1967, D.L.S., 1977. *Home:* 83 Greenridge Ave., White Plains, N.Y. 10605. *Office:* Valhalla High School, Valhalla, N.Y. 10595.

CAREER: Life, New York City, reporter, 1951-61; Time-Life Books, New York City, free-lance researcher, 1961-66; Mamaroneck Free Library, Mamaroneck, N.Y., young adult and reference librarian, 1967-69; Valhalla High School, Valhalla, N.Y., director of Learning Resource Center, 1969—. *Member:* International Association of School Librarians, American Library Association, American Association of School Librarians, Special Libraries Association, School Library Media Specialists of Southeastern New York (president, 1972-73), Westchester Library Association (president of children's-young adult section, 1968-69), Beta Phi Mu (Nu chapter), White Plains College Club (member of executive board), Westchester County Simmons College Club (past president), Woman's Club of White Plains. *Awards, honors:* Award from American Heart Association, 1956, for "Heart Attack"; award from National Association for Mental Health, 1957, for "What Drugs Can Do for the Mentally Ill."

WRITINGS: Energy: A Multimedia Guide for Children and Young Adults, Neal-Schuman, 1979. Author of "Paperbacks," a column in *Teacher,* 1968—. Contributor to library journals and other magazines, including *Publishers Weekly* and *PTA.* Contributing editor of *Teacher,* 1968—.

WORK IN PROGRESS: Work on crucial issues for school libraries, children's and young adult book publishing, reference resources for secondary and community college students, library instruction, library education, and the impact of computers and videodisc on secondary education.

*   *   *

HIGH, Monique Raphel 1949-

PERSONAL: Born May 3, 1949, in New York, N.Y.; daughter of David (a film executive) and Dina (an agent; maiden name, Cornfield) Raphel; married Robert Duncan High (an advertising executive), June 6, 1969; children: Nathalie Danielle. *Education:* Barnard College, A.B., 1969. *Politics:* Independent Democrat. *Religion:* "Jewish." *Home and office:* 419 Redwood Dr., Pasadena, Calif. 91105. *Agent:* Roberta Pryor, International Creative Management, 40 West 57th St., New York, N.Y. 10019.

CAREER: Thomas More College, Fort Mitchell, Ky., assistant public relations director, 1969-70; writer, 1970—. *Member:* Authors Guild, Alliance Francaise of Pasadena, League of Women Voters of Pasadena.

WRITINGS: The Four Winds of Heaven (novel), Delacorte, 1980; *Encore* (novel), Delacorte, 1981.

WORK IN PROGRESS: The Eleventh Year, a novel about the destruction of a marrriage in the Paris of the 1920's, publication by Delacorte expected in 1982.

SIDELIGHTS: High told *CA:* "Storytelling has always been a part of me. As an only child who was reared all over Europe, I told myself stories as a way to entertain myself and to ward off loneliness. Later, entertaining other people became a natural outgrowth of this habit. More than anything, I want to connect myself to my readers, and whenever I receive a letter from someone who has read me, I feel touched and grateful: a bond has been created.

"My work habits are rather rigid: I write every day for at least six hours. *The Four Winds of Heaven* was motivated by the diaries of my paternal grandmother, a Russian Jewish baroness at the turn of the century. I was fascinated by the fact that her family was in a most unusual position: they were members of the rarified nobility, and they were Jews, the most maligned outcasts of their nation. The story of the Gunzburgs needed to be told, not only for Jewish history, but for everyone interested in Russia before, during, and after the Revolution.

"I personally do not believe that a writer needs writing classes. The classics are the best teachers a beginning novelist can find. But discipline and impeccable research are a must. Therein lies the difference between literature and *good* literature. Any number of people may have talent: few have perseverance, which is almost more important! My 'heroes' are Shakespeare, Boccaccio, Tolstoy, Henri Troyat, Fitzgerald, and John Fowles. A varied assortment.

"My background is French. English was only the fourth language I learned, and so for me, it is a never ending challenge to write it. My style, because of this, is more precise, perhaps more 'stylized' than that of other women writers of my generation. I therefore look for settings that will 'fit' my language."

*   *   *

HIGHTOWER, Paul
See COLLINS, Thomas Hightower

*   *   *

HILL, Mary A. 1939-

PERSONAL: Born September 7, 1939, in Fayetteville, N.C.; daughter of Thomas English (a professor) and Sara Prather (a teacher; maiden name, Armfield) Hill; married David Porter, August 25, 1962 (divorced, 1974); children: David Lewis, Noelle Jamila. *Education:* Oberlin College, B.A., 1961; attended London School of Economics and Political Science, London, 1959-60; University of Minnesota, M.A., 1962; further graduate study at Columbia University, 1963-65; McGill University, Ph.D., 1975. *Home:* 930 Market St., Lewisburg, Pa. 17837. *Office:* Department of History, Bucknell University, Lewisburg, Pa. 17837.

CAREER: Lecturer in history in Montreal, Quebec, 1967-68; University of Montreal, Loyola College, Montreal, instructor in history, 1968-70; Bucknell University, Lewisburg, Pa., instructor, 1973-75, assistant professor, 1975-79, associate professor of history, 1979—. Member of faculty at Macalester College, summer, 1966. *Awards, honors:* Canada Council grant, 1972-73; grant from Government of Quebec, 1972-73; National Endowment for the Humanities grant, 1980-81.

WRITINGS: Charlotte Perkins Gilman: The Making of a Radical Feminist, 1860-1896, Temple University Press, 1980. Contributor to *Massachusetts Review.*

WORK IN PROGRESS: The second volume of the biography of Charlotte Perkins Gilman, publication by Temple University Press expected in 1982.

SIDELIGHTS: Mary Hill wrote: "Professional commitments date back to a period of active involvement in the peace movement and civil rights movements of the 1960's, to a confrontation with Third World politics through an extended stay in Algeria, and to personal involvement with the feminist campaigns of the early 1960's. Already a college teacher in American history and also a divorced mother with two small children by 1970, I was amazed at the poverty of understanding of women's past obstacles and achievements. My biography of Charlotte Perkins Gilman, along with my commitment to teaching women's history, stems from my realization of the need for models from our past, for a vision of alternate approaches to conventional male-female roles.''

* * *

HILL, Mary V. 1941-

PERSONAL: Born January 28, 1941, in Norwalk, Conn.; daughter of Bruno (a biochemist) and Mary Erety (a musician; maiden name, Elmer) Vassel; married Keith K. Hill (a religious educator), June 28, 1963; children: Keith, Lewis, Arnetta, Marety, Bruno, Stephen, Christian, Bryce, Elisabeth. *Education:* Attended Brigham Young University, 1959, 1961, and Idaho State University, 1961, 1963-64. *Religion:* Church of Jesus Christ of Latter-day Saints (Mormons). *Home:* 4785 West Harman Dr., Salt Lake City, Utah 84120.

CAREER: Writer, 1973—.

WRITINGS: Angel Children (nonfiction), Horizon, 1973. Contributor to *Guideposts Daily Devotionals.*

WORK IN PROGRESS: A book on "finding peace in this life, even amid turmoil, through yielding one's life unto God," publication by Horizon expected in 1981.

SIDELIGHTS: Mary Hill wrote: "When we lost our fifth child after three-and-a-half brief but love-filled months, I yearned to understand many of life's great questions. Through the help of a number of wonderful people with far more experience than myself, I found many truly satisfying answers. Having known only too well the pain in the hearts of parents who have suffered the loss of a little child, I compiled the answers which had helped me so very much in the hopes that they might also be of some help to others. Thus was born *Angel Children.*''

* * *

HILLMAN, Barry L(eslie) 1942-

PERSONAL: Born August 18, 1942, in London, England; son of Leslie Frederick (a bus conductor) and Evelyn Annie (a shoe worker; maiden name, Morgan) Hillman. *Education:* Attended East Fifteen Acting School. *Politics:* "No belief in politics or *any* dogma." *Religion:* "Agnostic (of course!)." *Home:* Lynry, 48 Louise Rd., Northampton, England. *Office:* Northamptonshire County Council, Northampton House, Wellington St., Northampton NN1 3RR, England.

CAREER: Worked as proofreader with *Northampton Chronicle and Echo,* as postman, and as solicitor's clerk; Northamptonshire County Council, Northampton, England, local government officer, 1974—. Professional actor in repertory in Scotland and northern England. *Member:* National Association of Local Government Officers, Theatre Writers Union. *Awards, honors:* O. Z. Whitehead Award from Dublin Theatre Festival, 1971, for "Partly Furnished"; second prize from Bristol Old Vic and Harris Trust new play contest, 1980, for "The Amazing Dancing Bear."

WRITINGS—Poetry: Endymion Rampant, Golden Head Press, 1964; *These Little Songs,* Outposts Publications, 1979.

Plays: "Castle on the Rocks" (three-act), first produced in Northampton, England, at Thornton Park Theatre, 1964; *Happy Returns* (three-act; first produced at Thornton Park Theatre, 1962), Galloway Gazette, 1970; *Partly Furnished* (one-act; first produced in Dublin, Ireland, at Eblana

Theatre, 1971, produced in the West End at Haymarket Theatre, 1979), Hub Publications, 1971; *Roly-Poly* (one-act), Samuel French, 1973; *The Dispossessed* (one-act), Hub Publications, 1975; *Face the Music* (one-act), Samuel French, 1975; *Two Can Play at That Game* (three-act), Hub Publications, 1975; (co-author) *Bibs and Bobs,* Hub Publications, 1975; (co-author) *Odds and Sods,* Hub Publications, 1977; *Six for the Charleston* (three-act; first produced at Thornton Park Theatre, 1973), New Playwrights' Network, 1977; *The Queen and the Axe* (three-act; first produced in Northampton at Carnegie Hall, 1976), New Playwrights' Network, 1978; "The Guests" (one-act), first produced in 1978; "The Amazing Dancing Bear" (two-act), first produced in London, England, at Questors Theatre, 1981. Also author of "A Few Minor Dischords" (one-act), 1979.

WORK IN PROGRESS: Full-length plays about "the wild wolf-boy of Aveyron" and Dr. Marie Stopes.

SIDELIGHTS: Hillman commented to *CA:* "The literary subjects I favor most are the dangerous nature and undesirability of all beliefs, factual historical incidents which pose moral dilemmas (as in "The Amazing Dancing Bear"), female carnality (as in 'Partly Furnished'), and sexuality in general. I am still into the amateur theatre scene, and toured France in 1980 with a youth theatre. I am a great admirer of Edward Bond and Jacobean dramatists."

* * *

HILLSTROM, Tom 1943-

PERSONAL: Born May 11, 1943, in Chicago, Ill.; son of M. K. (a banker) and Margel (Johnson) Hillstrom; married Martha Carter (a fashion executive), December 20, 1975; children: Carter Thomas. *Education:* Northwestern University, B.S., 1965, M.S., 1966. *Residence:* Tallahassee, Fla. *Agent:* Karen Hitzig Agency, 34 Gramercy Park E., New York, N.Y. 10007.

CAREER: United Press International reporter and editor in New York, N.Y., 1968-72 and 1974-80, Los Angeles, Calif., 1972-73, and Tallahassee, Fla., 1980—. *Military service:* U.S. Army, 1966-68. *Awards, honors:* Investigative reporting award from New York Silurians, 1976.

WRITINGS: Coal (novel), Morrow, 1980.

WORK IN PROGRESS: Two novels, one concerning a couple caught up in the criminal justice system and the other involving the space program.

SIDELIGHTS: Hillstrom told *CA:* "*Coal* is an attempt to document, in human, economic, and social terms, the recent dramatic changes in the coalfields of West Virginia."

* * *

HINCHLIFF, Peter Bingham 1929-

PERSONAL: Born February 25, 1929, in Hermanus, South Africa; son of Samuel Bingham (a minister) and Brenda (Bagshaw) Hinchliff; married Constance Whitehead, April 16, 1955; children: Nicholas, Susan, Richard, Jeremy. *Education:* Rhodes University, B.A., 1948, Ph.D., 1958; Trinity College, Oxford, B.A., 1950, M.A., 1954, B.D., 1962, D.D., 1964. *Office:* Balliol College, Oxford University, Oxford OX1 3BJ, England.

CAREER: Ordained Anglican minister, 1952; assistant at Anglican church in Uitenhage, South Africa, 1952-55; subwarden at seminary in Grahamstown, South Africa, 1955-59; Rhodes University, Grahamstown, professor of ecclesiastical history, 1960-69; Church of England Missionary and

Ecumenical Council, London, England, secretary, 1969-72; Oxford University, Oxford, England, chaplain and fellow of Balliol College, 1972—. Hulsean Lecturer at Cambridge University, 1975; Bampton Lecturer at Oxford University, 1982. *Member:* Ecclesiastical History Society, Society for the Study of Theology, Oxford Society for Historical Theology (president, 1977-78).

WRITINGS: The South African Liturgy, Oxford University Press, 1959; *The Anglican Church in South Africa,* Darton, Longman & Todd, 1963; *John William Colenso,* Thomas Nelson, 1964; *The One-Sided Reciprocity,* Darton, Longman & Todd, 1966; (editor) *Calendar of Cape Missionary Correspondence,* South African Council for Social Research, 1967; *The Church in South Africa,* S.P.C.K., 1968; (editor) *The Journal of John Ayliff,* Rhodes University, 1971; *Cyprian of Carthage,* Geoffrey Chapman, 1974; (with David Young) *The Human Potential,* Darton, Longman & Todd, 1981.

WORK IN PROGRESS: The Morality of Politics (tentative title), publication by Darton, Longman & Todd expected in 1982; research on the relationship between missionary theology and imperial politics in the nineteenth century.

SIDELIGHTS: Hinchliff commented: "My belief is that religion is only worthwhile if it 'works' in terms of ordinary, everyday, commonsense reality. My interest in theology is, therefore, a practical one, and my teaching and pastoral duties provide the issues which provoke me to write. My concern about the relationship between religion and society is one aspect of this. No doubt it is colored by my South African experience, but it seems to me that this is also the area where religious truth is most sharply tested."

*   *   *

HINES, Barry (Melvin)   1939-

PERSONAL: Born June 30, 1939, in Barnsley, England; son of Richard Laurence (a miner) and Annie (Westerman) Hines; divorced; children: Sally, Thomas. *Education:* Attended Loughborough College of Education, 1958-60, 1962-63. *Politics:* Socialist. *Home and office:* 101 Cowley Lane, Chapeltown, Sheffield, Yorkshire, England. *Agent:* Sheila Lemon Ltd., 74 Forthbridge Rd., London SW11 5NY, England; and Curtis Brown Ltd., 1 Craven Hill, London W2 3EP, England.

CAREER: Teacher at schools in London, England, 1960-62, and Barnsley, England, 1963-68; West Riding County Council Education Authority, Wakefield, England, teacher, 1968-72; writer, 1972—. *Member:* Royal Society of Literature (fellow), East Midlands Arts Association (fellow, 1975-77). *Awards, honors:* Best British screenplay award from Writers Guild of Great Britain, 1970, for "Kes"; fellow of Yorkshire Arts Association, 1972-74; fellow of University of Wollongong, 1979.

WRITINGS—Novels: *The Blinder,* M. Joseph, 1966; *A Kestrel for a Knave,* M. Joseph, 1968; *First Signs,* M. Joseph, 1972; *The Gamekeeper,* M. Joseph, 1975; *The Price of Coal,* M. Joseph, 1979; *Looks and Smiles,* M. Joseph, 1981.

Co-author of "Kes," a screenplay released by United Artists, 1970.

Television plays: "Billy's Last Stand," first broadcast by British Broadcasting Corp. (BBC), 1970; "Speech Day," first broadcast by BBC, 1973; "Two Men From Derby," first broadcast by BBC, 1976; "The Price of Coal" (two films), first broadcast by BBC, 1977; "The Gamekeeper," first broadcast by Associated Television Ltd., December 10,

1980; (co-author) "A Question of Leadership" (documentary), first broadcast by Associated Television Ltd.

*   *   *

HIRSCH, Phil   1926-
(Norman Lemon Peel, Bob Vlasic)

PERSONAL: Born August 18, 1926, in New York, N.Y.; son of Leo and Clara (Gemeiner) Hirsch; married Joy Senft; children: Hope Lisa, Lee. *Education:* New York University, B.S., 1949. *Religion:* Jewish. *Home:* 27 Wedgewood Dr., Westbury, N.Y. 11590. *Office:* Ideal Publications, 2 Park Ave., New York, N.Y. 10016.

CAREER: Keystone Pictures, Inc., New York City, news editor, 1950-52; *Magazine Management,* New York City, associate editor, 1952-53; Allen Stearn Publications, New York City, editor, 1953-55; Pyramid Communications, Inc., New York City, vice-president, 1955-75; Phi Publishing Corp., New York City, president and publisher, 1976-77; Ideal Publishing, New York City, president and publisher, 1977—. Lecturer at New York University, 1968-71. *Military service:* U.S. Army Air Forces, 1944-46. *Member:* Overseas Press Club of America.

WRITINGS: How to Be a Jewish President, Kanrom, 1966; (with Paul Laikin) *One Hundred and One Watch Jokes,* Pyramid Publications, 1971; (with Laikin) *GVRAB Bag of Humor,* Pyramid Publications, 1974; (with Laikin) *Vampire Jokes and Cartoons,* Pyramid Publications, 1974; (under pseudonym Bob Vlasic) *One Hundred and One Pickle Jokes,* Pyramid Publications, 1974; (with Laikin) *Ghouling Around,* Pyramid Publications, 1975; (with Laikin) *Athlete's Feat,* Pyramid Publications, 1975; (with Laikin) *Classic Corny Joke Book,* Pyramid Publications, 1975; *Gorilla Jokes,* Grosset, 1976; *Behind the Ape Ball,* Scholastic Book Services, 1978; *One Hundred and One Hamburger Jokes,* Scholastic Book Services, 1978; *Santa Claus Jokes,* Grosset, 1978; *Chicken Jokes,* Grosset, 1979; *The Jogging Joke Book,* Xerox Education Publications, 1979; *Grinner's Book of Funny Facts,* Xerox Education Publications, 1979; *Phil Hirsch: Madman at Large,* Scholastic Book Services, 1980; *Pet Jokes,* Scholastic Book Services, 1980.

Editor of anthologies; all published by Pyramid Publications: *Men Behind Bars,* 1957; *The Death Dealers,* 1957; *Fighting Generals,* 1960; (with Edward Hymoff) *The Kennedy War Heroes,* 1960; *Fighting Eagles,* 1961; *The War Between the Mates,* 1961; *Business With Pleasure,* 1962; *Something for the Boys: Girls,* 1962; *Open Your Mouth and Say Ha,* 1962; *Mister and Mistress,* 1963; *Spy and Counterspy,* 1963; *By the She,* 1963; *One Against the Enemy,* 1963; (under pseudonym Norman Lemon Peel) *The Power of Positive Drinking,* 1963; *She Drives 'Em Crazy,* 1963; *Great Unknown Stories of World War II,* 1963; *War,* 1964; *Laugh 'Til You Bust,* 1964; *Fighting Marines,* 1964; *Two on the Isle,* 1964; *World War I,* 1964; *P.O.W.,* 1964; *Ghoul Days,* 1964; *Man and Strife,* 1965; *The Cursed,* 1965; *Fighting Aces,* 1965; *Hollywood Uncensored,* 1965; *Death House,* 1965; (with Hymoff) *The Kennedy Courage,* 1965; *Killer Subs,* 1965; *Come on 'a My House,* 1965.

Grin and Bare It, 1966; *Underwater,* 1966; *Pettin' Place,* 1966; *Good for What Jails You,* 1966; *A Mad Passion for Murder,* 1966; *Beastly Humor,* 1967; *Wedding and Bedding,* 1967; *Once Over Nightly,* 1967; *Vietnam Combat,* 1967; *Brass in Battle,* 1967; *Medal of Honor,* 1967; *Cop,* 1967; *Dirty Little Wars,* 1967; *Hitler and His Henchmen,* 1967; *Hollywood Confidential,* 1967; *The Tormented,* 1967; *Can You Topless This?,* 1967; *Through Enemy Lines,* 1967; *Alley of the Dolls*, 1968; *Sports Before Your Eyes*, 1968; *A Man for All Squeezin's*, 1968; *Gay Divorcees*, 1968; *Never on Freud Day*, 1968; *Kidding Around*, 1968; *Supernatural*, 1968; *Hooked*, 1968; (with Laikin) *One Hundred and One Hippie Jokes*, 1968; *Great Combat Stories of the Korean War*, 1968; *Jungle Belles*, 1969; *Great Adventures in Daredevil Sports*, 1969; *From Here to Maternity*, 1969; *Listen, White Man, I'm Bleeding*, 1969; *Medical Miracles*, 1969; *From Bed to Worse*, 1969; *Out to Launch*, 1969; *Survival*, 1969.

Teen Power, 1970; *Too Funny for Words*, 1970; *The Racketeers*, 1970; *Man Cannot Live by Broad Alone*, 1970; *More Teen Power*, 1970; *Courtoons*, 1970; *New Yock, New Yock*, 1970; *The Comedians*, 1970; *The Young Toughs*, 1970; (with Laikin) *How Sick Can You Get?*, 1970; *The World's Greatest Lovers*, 1970; *Everything's Relative*, 1970; *Disasters*, 1971; *Fires*, 1971; *The Mafia*, 1971; *The Age of Hilarious*, 1971; *Armed Farces*, 1971; *Adam's Ribs*, 1971; *The Killers*, 1971; *Great Stories of the Wild West*, 1971; *The Infernal Revenue Service*, 1972; *Kid's Lib*, 1973; *Ghosts, Monsters, and Witches*, 1973; *More Kids' Lib*, 1974; (with Laikin) *Good and Sick*, 1974; *The Copulation Explosion*, 1974; (with Laikin) *Sick of the Crop*, 1975.

*　　　*　　　*

HITCHCOCK, Susan Tyler　1950-

PERSONAL: Born March 30, 1950, in Ann Arbor, Mich.; daughter of Hugh Wiley (a musicologist) and Helene (a research administrator; maiden name, Jarvis) Hitchcock; married David W. Watkins III (a mechanical engineer), May 24, 1980. *Education:* University of Michigan, B.A., 1970, M.A., 1971; University of Virginia, Ph.D., 1978. *Home address:* Route 1, Box 31, Charlottesville, Va. 22901.

CAREER: Harper & Row Publishers, Inc., New York City, editorial assistant, 1972; Media Projects, Inc., New York City, editor and writer, 1972-73; writer, 1975—.

WRITINGS: Gather Ye Wild Things: A Forager's Year, Harper, 1980.

WORK IN PROGRESS: Wildflowers on the Windowsill; Eek! A Bug, a children's book; an imaginative biography of Shelley; research on wildflowers as house plants.

SIDELIGHTS: Hitchcock commented: "I began writing *Gather Ye Wild Things* as an antidote to the discouraging job market for college teachers of English. And now I find myself embarking on an adventure—challenging, sometimes scary, all my own."

*　　　*　　　*

HIX, Charles (Arthur)　1942-

PERSONAL: Born August 20, 1942, in Michigan; son of Arnold E. (a factory worker) and Helen (a factory worker; maiden name, Fleischman) Hix. *Education:* University of Michigan, B.A., 1963. *Politics:* Liberal Democrat. *Religion:* None. *Home and office:* 301 East 22nd St., New York, N.Y. 10010.

CAREER: Doubleday Book Shops, New York City, paperback manager, 1964-65; *Home Furnishings Daily*, New York City, 1966-68, began as reporter, became floor coverings editor; Monsanto Textiles, New York City, manager of home furnishings publicity, 1968-70; writer, 1970—. Conducts men's fashion seminars; guest on local and national television programs, including "Good Morning America," "The Today Show," and "The Merv Griffin Show." *Member:* Authors Guild, Phi Beta Kappa. *Awards, honors:* Jule and

Avery Hopwood Award from University of Michigan, 1962; Lulu Awards from Men's Fashion Association and Menswear Retailers of America, 1976, 1977, and 1978.

WRITINGS: Looking Good: A Guide for Men, Hawthorn, 1977; *Dressing Right: A Guide for Men*, St. Martin's, 1978; *Male Model: the World Behind the Camera*, St. Martin's, 1979.

Author of columns, "Imagery" and "Looking Good," both in *Gentlemen's Quarterly* and distributed by United Feature Syndicate, 1979—, and a column in *Playboy*. Feature writer for Newspaper Enterprise Association, 1975-79. Contributor to magazines and newspapers.

WORK IN PROGRESS: The Last Hunter (tentative title), a suspense novel.

SIDELIGHTS: Hix told *CA:* "Although I tried to write a play while I was in the third grade, it wasn't until high school that I became hooked on writing. In college I took a creative writing course, primarily as an acceptable alternative to a course on Chaucer (whom I've still never read). I was floored when I won the Jule and Avery Hopwood Award for Creative Fiction in 1963. Arthur Miller presented me with the check, noting that the cash value had increased since he'd won the award. I nodded speechlessly. Because the university stretched a few rules, I was able to take graduate courses in creative writing while still an undergraduate.

"New York's literary circle didn't welcome me with open arms when I fled Michigan after graduation. I had planned to enter Columbia University's Contemporary Literature Proseminar as a graduate student in 1964, but New York seduced me and I never did. Without success, I tried to get a job in publishing; instead I sold books. Eventually I happened into a writing job as a reporter at *Home Furnishings Daily*, a poor cousin to *Women's Wear Daily*. Writing about floor coverings was not exactly scintillating, but at least I stopped writing in longhand and learned to compose at a typewriter. Then I moved on to a public relations job, which I loathed. I quit that job impulsively in 1970, and I've been supporting myself since then by writing, principally for magazines.

"'Haunted' is too strong a word, so let's say throughout this time I was beseiged by a desire to write 'serious' fiction. My attempts were mostly laughable. I wouldn't write for months, then I'd leap into a story, and jump out of it within days. I took a few courses in short-story writing at the New School for Social Research. I only had the confidence to submit two stories to the *New Yorker*. Both were promptly and perfunctorily rejected. I've never tried again, and it's unlikely I'll ever again attempt the arduous task of writing a short story.

"I just happened into magazine writing. A friend would suggest I call so-and-so. Or I would fortuitously meet such-a-person at a cocktail party. I was lucky. And my luck held. I developed a reputation as an expert in covering men's grooming and fashion. I was approached by an editor to write what became the first book totally devoted to men's grooming to make the *New York Times* bestsellers list—*Looking Good*. My next two books were not as successful, but at least they gave the financial security (for the time being) to pursue fiction again. Most people—of the small number of people who have any idea who I am—think of me as the author of *Looking Good*. I'm not courting fame, but I hope in time that will change. I hope someday people will think of me as a writer of novels. I don't know if that day will ever arrive. I'll be frustrated if it doesn't.

"It isn't that I want to write. I *need* to write. I think the hardest part of being a writer is simply finding the time to write without interruption and distraction. I admire the people who work at nine-to-five jobs and still produce books. I don't know how they do it; I couldn't."

* * *

HOADLEY, Walter E(vans) 1916-

PERSONAL: Born August 16, 1916, in San Francisco, Calif.; son of Walter Evans and Marie Howland (Preece) Hoadley; married Virginia Alm, May 20, 1939; children: Richard Alm, Jean Elizabeth (Mrs. Richard A. Price, Jr.). *Education:* University of California, Berkeley, B.A., 1938, M.A., 1940, Ph.D., 1946. *Office:* World Headquarters, Bank of America Center, San Francisco, Calif. 94137.

CAREER: University of California, Berkeley, research economist, 1938-41, supervisor of industrial management war training office, 1941-42; Federal Reserve Bank, Chicago, Ill., senior economist, 1942-49; Armstrong World Industries, Inc., Lancaster, Pa., economist, 1949-54, treasurer, 1954-66, vice-president, 1960-66, member of board of directors, 1962—. Deputy chairman of Federal Reserve Bank, Philadelphia, Pa., 1960-61, chairman, 1962-66, chairman of Conference of Federal Reserve Chairmen, 1966; chief economist for Bank of America National Trust and Savings Association, 1966—, senior vice-president, 1966-68, executive vice-president, 1968—, member of managing committee, 1966—, member of management advisory council, 1968—, chairman of Bank of America Investment Management Corp. and BankAmerica Foundation.

Member of faculty at University of Wisconsin (now University of Wisconsin—Madison), 1945-49, 1955, and 1958-66; economic adviser to University of Chicago's Civil Affairs Training School, 1945; adviser to national commission to study nursing and nursing education, 1968-73. Collaborator with U.S. Bureau of Agricultural Economics, 1938-39; member of White House task force on U.S. economic growth, 1969-70, presidential task force on land utilization, presidential task force on U.S. foreign economic policy, and presidential conference on inflation, 1974; member of public advisory board of U.S. Department of Commerce, 1970-74; special adviser to U.S. Congressional Budget Office, 1975—, and Presidential Cabinet Committee on Innovation, 1978-79; past member of White House review committee on U.S. balance of payments and national citizen's advisory committee on environmental quality task force on land utilization and urban growth. Research economist with California governor's reemployment commission, 1939, and planning board, 1941; chairman of governor's Council on Economic and Business Development, 1978—; member of San Francisco Fiscal Advisory Committee, 1977—; chairman of San Francisco mayor's committee, 1978—; general chairman of San Francisco's Japan Week.

Member of Methodist Church Commission on World Service, 1957-64, chairman of investment committe, 1964-66; chairman of investment committee of California-Nevada United Methodist Foundation, 1968-75, member of committee, 1976—. Member of board of directors and executive committee of International Management and Development Institute (and its Corporate Strategic Planning Council), 1976—, and board of directors of National Bureau of Economic Research (member of economic advisory council, 1976-78); member of board of trustees of Pacific School of Religion, Duke University, 1968-73, Golden Gate University, 1974— (chairman of investment committee, 1977—),

Conservation Foundation, 1974—, Hudson Institute, 1979—, and Foundation for Teaching Economics; member of board of overseers of Harvard University, 1969-74. Delegate to United States-Japan Shimoda Conference, 1977.

MEMBER: International Chamber of Commerce (member of board of trustees; vice-chairman of commission on international monetary relations; chairman of U.S. Council's committee on international monetary affairs), International Conference of Commercial Bank Economists (member of steering committee, 1977—; chairman, 1978—), American Statistical Association (fellow; vice-president and member of board of directors, 1952-54; president, 1958), American Finance Association (member of board of directors, 1955-56; president, 1969), American Economic Association, American Marketing Association, American Bankers Association (chairman of urban and community affairs committee, 1972-73; member of economic advisory council, 1976-78; member of task force on inflation, 1979-80), U.S. Business Council (chairman, 1963-66), National Association of Business Economists (fellow), Conference of Business Economists (chairman, 1962), Chamber of Commerce of the United States, Conference Board Economic Forum, Western Finance Association (member of board of directors and steering committee), Western Economic Association, Financial Analysts of San Francisco, Phi Beta Kappa (vice-president of western region), Kappa Alpha, St. Francis Yacht Club, Commonwealth Club, Pacific Union Club, San Francisco Bankers Club, Silverado Country Club. *Awards, honors:* D.C.S. from Franklin and Marshall College, 1963; LL.D. from Golden Gate University, 1968, and University of the Pacific, 1979; honorary degree from Instituto Tecnologico Autonomo de Mexico, 1974; Berkeley fellow of University of California, 1979.

WRITINGS: International Interdependence Versus Protectionism, Center for International Business, 1978; *The Emerging International Economic Environment,* Kansai, University of Hawaii, 1979; *Economic Rearmament for the United States and Japan,* Institute of East Asian Studies, University of California, Berkeley, 1979; (editor) *The Economy and the President: 1980 and Beyond,* Prentice-Hall, 1980.

Author of "The Economy," a column in *Dun's Review.* Contributor to *Treasurer's Handbook.* Contributor to scholarly journals and newspapers.

WORK IN PROGRESS: Research on worldwide economic and financial outlook, government-business relationships, economic literacy, and the North-South problem.

SIDELIGHTS: Hoadley told *CA:* "The driving force behind my writing has been to help improve U.S. and global understanding of complex issues, especially economic, social, and political. I have tried to find common ground between thinking in the public and private sectors and to promote and demonstrate the importance of confidence in effective decision-making. Frequently my writing has been aimed for further use on radio and television, with a resultant emphasis on a brief, to-the-point, conversational style.

"Increasingly, I have noted public deficiency in economic literacy, but also the evident growing public interest in economic developments and ideas. The importance of improving adult economic understanding is high, but in my view there is also a great urgency to strengthen economic comprehension among youth. Therefore, my next book will focus on economics for children."

HOBSON, Julius W(ilson) 1922(?)-1977

PERSONAL: Born c. 1922, in Birmingham, Ala.; died of cancer, March 23, 1977, in Washington, D.C.; married first wife, 1947 (divorced, 1966); married Tina Lower, 1969; children: (first marriage) one son, one daughter; (second marriage) two stepsons. *Education:* Attended Tuskegee Institute and Howard University. *Politics:* Marxist. *Residence:* Washington, D.C.

CAREER: Civil rights activist and writer. Social Security Administration, Washington, D.C., economist and statistician, c. 1950-70. Member of Washington, D.C., school board, 1968; head of Washington Institute for Quality Education until 1971; political candidate, 1971 and 1972; member of District of Columbia City Council, 1974-77.

WRITINGS: (With Janet Harris) *Black Pride: A People's Struggle,* McGraw, 1969; *The Damned Children: A Layman's Guide to Forcing Change in Public Education,* Washington Institute for Quality Education, 1970; *The Damned Information: Acquiring and Using Public Information to Force Social Change,* Washington Institute for Quality Education, 1971.

SIDELIGHTS: Hobson was a civil-rights activist who spearheaded a number of successful reform movements in Washington, D.C., including some with nationwide implications. He sponsored litigation that led to reforms in the District of Columbia's school system and improved conditions for urban blacks. In the mid-1960's, he amassed collections of data proving that the school system was still operating under segregative guidelines more than a decade after the Supreme Court had ruled against such practices. Hobson also won the 1967 *Hobson v. Hansen* case in which a U.S. Court of Appeals decision invalidated the school district's student tracking program, a system that channeled students into certain types and levels of classes based on overall performances. The court ruled that the system perpetuated the segregation of blacks. Another of Hobson's victories came in 1970 when U.S. District Judge J. Skelly Wright upheld Hobson's complaint that the District of Columbia was spending more money per capita at predominantly white schools than at black schools.

Hobson is also credited with winning employment and promotion opportunities for blacks. He sued the Washington, D.C., police department to end discriminatory practices and secure promotions for blacks on the force. He also organized picketers to demonstrate against merchants who had refused to hire blacks. And a threatened boycott engineered by Hobson also resulted in the city's prompt hiring of black bus drivers.

Hobson also served on the Washington, D.C., school board and city council. His 1974 campaign was conducted from a wheelchair because he was suffering from cancer. Nonetheless, he was a strident supporter of reform measures, including the adoption of a citizen's initiation and referendum ordinance that allowed the public to draft legislation and place it on the ballot for popular vote.

In *Black Pride: A People's Struggle* Hobson and co-author Janet Harris recount the black individual's struggle for freedom and equality from the days of slavery to the 1960's militancy. Focusing on the development of pride in black culture and achievement, the book includes studies of black leaders such as Marcus Garvey, W.E.B. DuBois, Malcolm X, and Martin Luther King, Jr.

BIOGRAPHICAL/CRITICAL SOURCES: Ebony, May, 1965; *Saturday Evening Post,* April 20, 1968; Stanton L. Wormley and Lewis Fenderson, editors, *Many Shades of Black,* Morrow, 1969; *New York Times Book Review,* May 4, 1969; *Time,* December 4, 1972.

OBITUARIES: New York Times, March 25, 1977; *Newsweek,* April 4, 1977.*

*   *   *

HOCKING, Anthony 1938-

PERSONAL: Born August 26, 1938, in Worthing, England; son of Harold (a retailer) and Rena (Sutcliffe) Hocking; married Helen Ashford (a research officer), June 11, 1962; children: Catherine, Lucy Elizabeth. *Education:* University of Southampton, B.Sc., 1960, M.Sc., 1962. *Office:* Department of Economics, University of Tasmania, Hobart, Tasmania, Australia.

CAREER: University of Tasmania, Hobart, Australia, lecturer, 1962-69, senior lecturer, 1970-77, reader in economics, 1978—, acting head of department, 1980. Chairman of Tasmanian Apple and Pear Marketing Committee; consultant to Tasmanian Consumer Affairs Council. *Member:* Agricultural Economics Society, Economic Society of Australia and New Zealand.

WRITINGS: (With J. M. Grant and A. J. Hagger) *Economic Institutions and Policy: An Australian Introduction,* F. W. Cheshire, 1969; *United Kingdom Demand for Southern Hemisphere Apples,* University of Tasmania, 1969; *Outcome of Income: Economics and Society,* Longman Cheshire, 1972; *Investigating Economics,* Longman Cheshire, 1975, 2nd edition, 1980; *Teaching Economics: A Guide to Investigating Economics,* Longman Cheshire, 1975; (with C. B. Hewitt, R. J. Shield, and others) *Shaping the Apple Industry: The Hocking Report,* Tasmanian Government Printer, 1979; (with R. P. Rutherford) *Consumer Economics,* Longman Cheshire, 1981; *Consumer Society,* Longman Cheshire, 1981.

WORK IN PROGRESS: Agricultural marketing research.

SIDELIGHTS: Hocking told *CA:* "My academic work has developed in three directions: first, the development of the problems approach to economics education, integrating problem-solving with contemporary economic analysis; second, work in consumer economics in developing a state and national consumer complaints analysis system; and third, research and advice to the government on agricultural marketing."

AVOCATIONAL INTERESTS: Chess, royal tennis, farming.

*   *   *

HODGKIN, Robert Allason 1916-
(Robin A. Hodgkin)

PERSONAL: Born February 12, 1916, in Banbury, England; son of George Lloyd and Mary (Wilson) Hodgkin; married Elizabeth Mary Hodgson, December, 1947; children: Adam, Christopher, Catherine. *Education:* Queen's College, Oxford, B.A. (with honors), 1937, M.A., 1939. *Religion:* Society of Friends (Quakers). *Home:* Barepppa House, near Falmouth, Cornwall TR11 5EG, England. *Agent:* Curtis Brown Academic Ltd., 1 Craven Hill, London W2 3EP, England.

CAREER: Teacher at government school in Khartoum, Sudan, 1937-45; principal of Sudan Institute of Education, 1949-55; headmaster of private boys' school in Uttoxeter, England, 1956-67; free-lance writer, 1967-69; Oxford University, Oxford, England, lecturer in educational studies, 1969-77. Chairman of Friends Service Council's Asia committee, 1968-77. *Member:* Alpine Club (vice-president, 1974-75).

WRITINGS—Under name Robin A. Hodgkin: *Sudan Geography,* Longmans, Green, 1951; *Education and Change,* Oxford University Press, 1957; *Reconnaissance on an Educational Frontier,* Oxford University Press, 1970; *Born Curious: New Perspectives in Educational Theory,* Wiley, 1976. Writer for BBC-Radio 3. Contributor to *Friend.*

WORK IN PROGRESS: Writing on education and theology.

SIDELIGHTS: Hodgkin wrote: "My interest over many years has been mountaineering in the Alps, the Caucasus, and the Karakoram Himalaya. I am also interested in the problems of developing countries. I have worked in India, Indonesia, West Africa, and the Sudan."

*   *   *

HODGKIN, Robin A.
See HODGKIN, Robert Allason

*   *   *

HODGSON, Ralph   1871-1962

PERSONAL: Born March 12, 1871, in Yorkshire, England; died November 3, 1962, in Minerva, Ohio; married wife, Aurelia (a missionary teacher and clerk).

CAREER: Poet. Worked as journalist, draftsman, artist, publisher, and breeder of bull terriers. Lecturer in English literature at Sendai University, Sendai, Japan, and at Imperial University, Tokyo, Japan. *Awards, honors:* Edward de Polignac Prize from Royal Society of Literature, 1914, for *The Bull;* Order of the Rising Sun from the Japanese Government, 1938, for meritorious services to the country; award from National Institute of Arts and Letters, 1946, for distinguished achievement; Queen's Gold Medal for Poetry (Great Britain), 1954.

WRITINGS—Poetry: *The Last Blackbird, and Other Lines,* G. Allen, 1907, Macmillan, 1917; *The Bull,* A. T. Stevens, 1913; *The Mystery, and Other Poems,* A. T. Stevens, 1913; *The Song of Honour,* A. T. Stevens, 1913; *Poems,* Macmillan, 1917; *The Silver Wedding, and Other Poems,* privately printed, 1941; *The Muse and the Mastiff,* privately printed, 1942; *The Skylark, and Other Poems* (edited by Colin Fenton), privately printed, 1958, Macmillan, 1959; *Collected Poems,* St. Martin's, 1961; *Poets Remembered,* privately printed, 1967. Editor of *Key's* magazine. Contributor of poems to periodicals, including *Living Age, Literary Digest, Current Opinion, Scholastic, Dial,* and *Saturday Review of Literature.*

SIDELIGHTS: "He is not much to be met, being something of a recluse, but when you do meet him he is usually in the company of a bull terrier. He says little, but says that little with enthusiasm." This description of Hodgson is from a 1914 article by E. V. Lucas, written with the purpose of introducing the British poet to American readers. Lucas praised highly the "magic" of Hodgson's verse, especially "'Eve,' which I fearlessly call the most fascinating poem of our time."

Reading Hodgson's work, Lucas was instantly reminded of mystic poet William Blake. "But," he said, "the comparison so soon breaks down that there is no need to even set it up. His [Hodgson's] poetry proceeds peculiarly from himself—his passion for life, his championship of helpless things, his love of beauty, his rage at oppression."

When Hodgson published *Poems* in 1917, fellow poets acclaimed the collection "as one of the best works of the young century," *Time* magazine reported. Conrad Aiken, for example, said: "Mr. Hodgson is that rarity in these times, a poet of very small production and of production on a uniformly high level.... There are two arts in poetry: the art of precisely saying what is on one's mind; and, even more important (though less regarded), the art of excluding from one's conception all that is not of pure value. It is particularly in this latter respect that Mr. Hodgson excels."

The volume was lauded by other critics as well. A reviewer from *Athenaeum* stated: "Mr Hodgson has a place of his own among the minor poets of today. None writes more naturally; none has such an objective, simple, and direct style, or aims less at mere literary effects. His is the poetry, not of ideas, but of sights, sensations, raptures."

Soon after Hodgson published *Poems* he began teaching English literature in Japan. It was not until 1946, when the National Institute of Arts and Letters awarded him a one-thousand dollar prize that Hodgson's poetry returned to vogue in American literary circles. As *Time* put it, "those who had thought him long dead were surprised."

After 1940 Hodgson lived in near seclusion in a farmhouse near Minerva, Ohio. There, *Time* stated, he enjoyed "a long life of deeper privacy than most poets ever dream of." He was attracted to the place because "the birds seemed just as interesting as in England, and I'd never seen a hummingbird. It took my mind."

The simplicity of Hodgson's lifestyle is reflected in his literary style. *Time* noted: "A 'cumulative' poet interested in a flowing effect, Hodgson shuns brilliant images that grasp the eye. His life is the same way. Passersby are shocked at the disrepair of the farm that he has never worked.... His real work is [to] wonder about the energy of anything that grows, moves, breathes, or flies: 'I don't try to reconcile anything. It's a damned strange world.'"

BIOGRAPHICAL/CRITICAL SOURCES: Nation, September 17, 1914; *Times Literary Supplement,* June 14, 1917, February 13, 1959, October 6, 1961; *Boston Transcript,* July 11, 1917; *Athenaeum,* August, 1917; *Literary Digest,* August 11, 1917; *Dial,* August 30, 1917; *New York Times,* February 10, 1918; *New Statesman,* February 7, 1959, August 18, 1961; *Time,* March 30, 1959; *Canadian Forum,* March, 1962.*

*   *   *

HOEVELER, Diane Long   1949-

PERSONAL: Born April 9, 1949, in Chicago, Ill.; daughter of Vincent L., Jr. (a lawyer) and Constance (Puglise) Long; married J. David Hoeveler, Jr. (a professor), January 29, 1972; children: John David III. *Education:* University of Illinois, B.A., 1970, M.A., 1972, Ph.D., 1976. *Home:* 3004 East Hampshire, Milwaukee, Wis. 53211.

CAREER: Teacher of English and history at private school in Madison, Conn., 1973-74; Alverno College, Milwaukee, Wis., instructor in English, 1976-78; University of Louisville, Louisville, Ky., assistant professor of English, 1978—. Consultant to National Endowment for the Humanities. *Member:* Modern Language Association of America.

WRITINGS: (With Harris Wilson) *English Prose and Criticism in the Nineteenth Century,* Gale, 1979; *Milwaukee Women Yesterday,* Board of Regents, University of Wisconsin, 1979; *Milwaukee Women Today,* Board of Regents, University of Wisconsin, 1979. Contributor to literature journals.

WORK IN PROGRESS: The Apocalyptic Self: Androgynous Imagery in Romantic Poetry; Composition: A Guide to Theories and Methodologies.

SIDELIGHTS: "My writing, whether on English romanticism or modern drama, tries to convey some of the excitement I feel while reading literature," commented Diane Hoeveler. "I am most interested in the pattern of meaning that emerges when one studies the images and symbols in a work. Those deep structures, myth and psychosexual obsessions, express the universal fears and desires we all experience and yet never have the luxury to analyze. Although the mechanics of writing an annotated bibliography, such as the one I did for Gale, are far from exciting, I consider the task to have been valuable for all of the many things I learned and skills I developed. Of course, I also have a greater appreciation for the use of bibliographies in scholarly research."

*   *   *

HOGAN, Desmond 1950-

PERSONAL: Born December 10, 1950, in Ballinasloe, Ireland; son of William (a draper) and Christina (Connolly) Hogan. *Education:* National University of Ireland University College, Dublin, B.A., 1972, M.A., 1973. *Residence:* London, England. *Agent:* Harold Schmidt, William Morris Agency, 1350 Avenue of the Americas, New York, N.Y. 10019.

CAREER: Children's Theatre Co., Dublin, Ireland, actor, 1975-77; Inner London Education Authority, London, England, free-lance teacher, 1978-79; writer, 1979—. *Awards, honors:* Hennessy Award from Irish Press Ltd., 1971, for "Marigold Fire"; Rooney Prize from Pittsburgh Steelers, 1974; grant from Irish Arts Council, 1977; grant from United States, 1981.

WRITINGS: The Ikon Maker (novel), Irish Writers Cooperative, 1976, Ballinger, 1979; *The Diamonds at the Bottom of the Sea* (stories), Hamish Hamilton, 1979, Braziller, 1980; *The Leaves on Grey* (novel), Braziller, 1980; *Children of Lir* (stories), Hamish Hamilton, 1981.

Plays: 'A Short Walk to the Sea" (one-act), first produced in Dublin, Ireland, at Abbey Theatre, October, 1975; "Sanctified Distances" (two-act), first produced in Dublin at Abbey Theatre, December, 1976; "Jimmy" (one-act), first broadcast by BBC-Radio 3, August, 1978; "The Ikon Maker" (two-act), first produced in England, at Bracknev Arts Centre, September, 1980.

SIDELIGHTS: Hogan told *CA:* "My plays, stories, and novels are an extension of the plays I produced about Our Lady of Fatima and Dracula in the back yard when I was eight or nine. At the moment I can't stop writing; is it that Lady still?—Our Lady of Fatima, Mother Ireland, the visionary Ireland that compels so much pain and yet makes me write to alleviate that pain?"

*   *   *

HOGE, Warren McClamroch 1941-

PERSONAL: Born April 13, 1941, in New York, N.Y.; son of James Fulton (a lawyer) and Sarah Virginia (a teacher; maiden name, McClamroch) Hoge. *Education:* Yale University, B.A., 1963; graduate study at George Washington University, 1964-65. *Home:* 118 Riverside Dr., New York, N.Y. 10024. *Agent:* Sterling Lord Agency, Inc., 660 Madison Ave., New York, N.Y. 10022. *Office: New York Times,* 229 West 43rd St., New York, N.Y. 10036.

CAREER/WRITINGS: Washington Star, Washington, D.C.,

trainee and reporter, 1964-66; *New York Post,* New York City, Washington correspondent, 1966-70, night city editor, 1970-73, metropolitan editor, 1973-76; *New York Times,* New York City, regional editor and deputy metropolitan editor, 1976-79, chief of bureau in Rio de Janeiro, Brazil, 1979—. *Military service:* U.S. Army, 1964. U.S. Army Reserve, 1965-70.

*   *   *

HOLBROOK, Jennifer Kearns 1931-

PERSONAL: Born January 15, 1931, in Hale, Cheshire, England; daughter of John Lomas (a sports outfitter) and Phyllis (Kearns) Holbrook. *Education:* Manchester Training College, Teacher's Certificate (with distinction), 1953; Laban Art of Movement Studio, graduated, 1964; attended Dartington College of Arts, 1966-67; Victoria University of Manchester, Advanced Diploma in Education (with distinction), 1975. *Home:* Sodyllt Hall, Ellesmere, Shropshire, England. *Office:* West Sussex Institute of Higher Education, Bognor Regis, Sussex, England.

CAREER: High school teacher of physical education in Manchester, England, 1953-58; physical education teacher and department head at Wythenshawe Technical High School in Manchester, 1958-63; Crewe College of Education, Crewe, England, senior lecturer in physical education, 1964-69; Chelsea College of Physical Education, Eastbourne, England, senior lecturer in dance, 1970-71; West Sussex Institute of Higher Education, Bognor Regis, England, principal lecturer in movement and dance, 1972—. Visiting lecturer at University of Calgary, 1969-70. *Member:* National Association of Teachers in Further and Higher Education, (member of executive committee of dance section, 1971-77, 1980—), Dolmetsch Historical Dance Society, Laban Art of Movement Guild.

WRITINGS: Gymnastics: A Movement Activity, Macdonald & Evans, 1973.

WORK IN PROGRESS: Research on "Rudolf Laban from a later Wittgenstein perspective," and on the male dancer, including "attitudes, historical perspectives, and the aesthetics of the male dancer's role."

SIDELIGHTS: Jennifer Holbrook wrote: "My book arose from discussions with Canadian colleagues who found that my work in gymnastics made more sense than existing texts. It was also my belief that such texts misunderstood Laban's work on movement. My real interest is in dance in all its manifestations, and my special interest in the aesthetics of dance arose from my course of study in American modern dance in 1966 and 1967 at Dartington College of Arts and from subsequent courses in philosophy."

AVOCATIONAL INTERESTS: Visual arts, painting, listening to music, gardening.

*   *   *

HOLDER, Ray 1913-

PERSONAL: Born November 27, 1913, in Lucedale, Miss.; son of Allen Glover, Jr. (a mining engineer) and Katharine (a musician; maiden name, Weldy) Holder; married Virginia Lee Smart (a teacher of Latin), July 20, 1937; children: Allen Glover III, John Fleming (deceased), Ray, Jr., Katharine Lavinia. *Education:* University of Mississippi, B.A., 1935, M.A., 1936; Duke University, B.D., 1942. *Home and office:* 5890 East Sedgwick Court, Jackson, Miss. 39211.

CAREER: Ordained Episcopal priest, 1943; North Carolina State University, Raleigh, assistant dean of students, 1941-

43; rector of Episcopal churches in Raleigh, 1945-51, and Los Angeles, Calif., 1951-55; Episcopal Theological Seminary, Lexington, Ky., professor of preaching and pastoral theology, and dean, 1955-58; rector of Episcopal church in Highland Park, Ill., 1958-68; researcher, lecturer, and preacher, 1968-76; writer, 1976—. Lecturer at University of Southern California, 1951-55. Broadcaster on WPTF-Radio, KABC-Radio, "The Episcopal Hour," and "Columbia's Church of the Air." *Military service:* North Carolina National Guard, chaplain in Infantry, 1951-55; became captain. *Member:* Mississippi Historical Society, Mississippi Institute of Arts and Letters, Society of Mississippi Archivists. *Awards, honors:* D.D. from Episcopal Theological Seminary, 1955.

WRITINGS: William Winans: Methodist Leader in Antebellum Mississippi, University Press of Mississippi, 1977. Contributor of articles to history journals, including *Journal of Mississippi History* and *Louisiana History,* and poems to *Living Church.*

WORK IN PROGRESS: The Rise of Methodist Seminaries, 1769-1939; God Bless "Prodigal Sons," for Harper; *Mississippi: Citadel of Southern Methodism, 1799-1979,* for Louisiana State University Press; "Theocratic Natchez: A Critical Inquiry," a two-part article; *William Winans: Letters on Slavery, Politics, Religion, 1810-1857.*

SIDELIGHTS: Holder commented: "I preached and taught for nigh on to forty years all over this country. Several years ago I retired, came home to Dixie after persuading my Old Dominion spouse, Virginia, that my kith and kin were 'civilized,' and sat down to write something about my native land, its people, its passions, its enigmas, its virtues, its hopes.

"I'd published a lot of verse over the years, but the thought of doing a book was beyond me. But the manuscripts of an old Natchez County circuit rider named William Winans had intrigued me since graduate school days, so I began to scribble a profile of his life. After three changes of eyeglasses expended in reading his handwriting, I had a brief biography on my hands. When I saw the galley proof it was a shocker, like a misfitted hull chine or joint. No nail was firmly set; no corner was square; my pride died. Following the example of Saint Peter, I went fishing in other waters and came back determined to start all over again. Now I have five new studies on the hook, but like the coho, they fight back hard.

"Maybe the good Lord, who built boats and preached but never wrote a book, will graciously give me another day to see at least one galley proof in which the crooked pieces will be made straight and the rough paragraphs smoothed out. Hopefully, these efforts will contribute, however modestly, to the serious study of southern culture and what D. W. Brogan has called 'the American character.'"

*   *   *

HOLFORD, Ingrid   1920-

PERSONAL: Born January 10, 1920, in Kingston upon Thames, England; daughter of Vincent Charles (an accountant) and Elna (Sebelien) Bianchi; married Garth Holford, July 24, 1948; children: Lynn Baker, John. *Education:* University of London, B.Sc. (with first class honors), 1941. *Home:* 5 Oberfield Rd., Brockenhurst, Hampshire SO7 7QF, England.

CAREER: Associated with Outdoor Publicity Ltd., London, 1947-48; free-lance writer, 1960—. Substitute weather fore-

caster for Southern Television, 1979—. *Military service:* Royal Air Force, Women's Auxiliary Air Force, weather forecaster, 1942-46; became section officer. *Member:* Society of Authors, Royal Meteorological Society (fellow), Thames Sailing Club (past rear commodore), Royal Lymington Yacht Club.

WRITINGS: A Century of Sailing on the Thames, Weston Publications, 1968; *Interpreting the Weather,* David & Charles, 1973; *British Weather Disasters,* David & Charles, 1976; *The Guinness Book of Weather Facts and Feats,* Guinness Superlatives, 1978, 2nd edition, 1982; *The Yachtsman's Weather Guide,* Ward, Lock, 1979. Contributor to magazines, including *Yachting Monthly, Yachts and Yachting,* and *Amateur Gardening.*

SIDELIGHTS: Ingrid Holford commented: "I write specifically to try to bridge the gap in understanding between the lay person and the professional meteorologist. Today there are many new sports, from hang gliding to orienteering, which are strongly dependent on the weather and eagerly taken up by relatively inexperienced people. It is essential that everyone understand that weather can turn nasty and that everyone learn to avoid tragedy."

AVOCATIONAL INTERESTS: Sailing.

*   *   *

HOLLAND, Laurence B(edwell)   1920-1980

OBITUARY NOTICE—See index for *CA* sketch: Born October 21, 1920, in Lincoln, Neb.; died by accidental drowning, July 11, 1980, in Ripton Gorge, Vt. Educator, editor, and author. Holland taught English at Princeton University and Johns Hopkins University, where he also served as chairman of the English department. For several years, the author was an instructor each summer at the Bread Loaf School of English of Middlebury College. He wrote *The Expense of Vision: Essays on the Craft of Henry James* and edited *Who Designs America.* Holland, in addition, was an editor of *The Norton Anthology of American Literature.* Obituaries and other sources: *Washington Post,* July 15, 1980.

*   *   *

HOLLINGDALE, R(eginald) J(ohn)   1930-

PERSONAL: Born October 20, 1930, in London, England; son of Frederick (a store manager) and Ethel (a clerk; maiden name, Clutton) Hollingdale; married Judith Robertson (a journalist); children: Frances, James. *Education:* Attended secondary school in London, England. *Religion:* None. *Residence:* London, England. *Office: Guardian,* 119 Farringdon Rd., London EC1R 3ER, England.

CAREER: Croydon Times, London, England, reporter and news editor, 1950-60; free-lance writer, 1960-64; *Richmond Herald,* London, assistant editor, 1964-65; Europese Werkgroep, Amsterdam, Netherlands, editor, 1965-67; *Guardian,* London, sub-editor, 1968-75; Fondation Europeene de la Culture, Amsterdam, editor of English-language publications in Brussels, Belgium, and Amsterdam, 1975-76; *Guardian,* sub-editor, 1976—. *Military service:* Royal Air Force, 1949-50. *Member:* Society of Authors, National Union of Journalists.

WRITINGS: Nietzsche: The Man and His Philosophy, Louisiana State University Press, 1965; *Western Philosophy: An Introduction,* Kahn & Averil, 1966, revised edition, Taplinger, 1980; (editor of English text) B. de Gaay Fortman, *Theory of Competition Policy,* North-Holland Publishing, 1966; (editor with F. Alting von Geusau) *Economic Rela-*

tions After the Kennedy Round, Sijthoff, 1969; (editor of English text) P. C. Bos, *The Functions of Money,* Rotterdam University Press, 1969; *Thomas Mann: A Critical Study,* Bucknell University Press, 1971; *Nietzsche,* Routledge & Kegan Paul, 1973; (editor with Gabriel Fragniere) *Education Without Frontiers,* Duckworth, 1976; (editor) *Between School and Work,* Institut d'Education (Paris, France), 1976; (editor with Peter Hall) *Europe Two Thousand,* Duckworth, 1977.

Translator: (Also author of introduction and notes) Friedrich Nietzsche, *Thus Spoke Zarathustra,* Penguin, 1961, revised edition, 1969; Marielis Hoberg, *One Summer on Majorca* (juvenile novel), Abelard, 1961; Hoberg, *The Voyage to Africa* (juvenile novel), Abelard, 1964; (with Walter Kaufmann) Nietzsche, *The Will to Power,* Random House, 1967; (with Kaufmann) Nietzsche, *On the Genealogy of Morals,* Random House, 1967; (also author of introduction and notes) Nietzsche, *Twilight of the Idols and The Anti-Christ,* Penguin, 1968; (also editor and author of introduction) *Essays and Aphorisms of Schopenhauer,* Penguin, 1970; (also author of introduction) Johann Wolfgang von Goethe, *Elective Affinities,* Penguin, 1971; (also author of introduction and notes) Nietzsche, *Beyond Good and Evil,* Penguin, 1973; Joost Elffers, *Tangram: The Ancient Chinese Shapes Game,* Penguin, 1976; (also editor and author of introduction) *A Nietzsche Reader,* Penguin, 1977; (also author of introduction and notes) Nietzsche, *Ecce Homo,* Penguin, 1979; Fritz Loeffler, *Otto Dix,* Holmes & Meier, 1981; E.T.A. Hoffmann, *Tales of Hoffmann,* Penguin, 1982. Contributor to *Grove's Dictionary of Music and Musicians.*

WORK IN PROGRESS: Translating *The Life of Nietzsche,* by Curt Paul Janz, for Knopf.

*   *   *

HOLLOWELL, John 1945-

PERSONAL: Born February 18, 1945, in Los Angeles, Calif.; son of Glen D. and L. Virginia (Aldridge) Hollowell; married Eileen White, July 27, 1968; children: Daron, Keith. *Education:* Columbia University, A.B., 1967; Johns Hopkins University, M.A.T., 1971; University of Michigan, Ph.D., 1974. *Home:* 2010 East Ninth St., Tucson, Ariz. 85719. *Office:* Department of English, University of Arizona, Tucson, Ariz. 85721.

CAREER: U.S. Peace Corps, Washington, D.C., teacher in school gardens program in Ivory Coast, 1967-69; English teacher at public schools in Baltimore, Md., 1969-71; University of Arizona, Tucson, assistant professor of English, 1974—. Copy editor of *Baltimore News American,* summers, 1970-71. Consultant to Bureau of Indian Affairs. *Member:* National Council of Teachers of English, Arizona English Teachers Association (member of board of directors), Southern Arizona Council of English Teachers (president).

WRITINGS: Inventing and Playing Games in the English Classroom, National Council of Teachers of English, 1977; *Fact & Fiction: The New Journalism and the Nonfiction Novel,* University of North Carolina Press, 1977. Contributor to language and education journals.

WORK IN PROGRESS: A book on writing games for the English classroom; a critical study of novels and nonfiction of Joan Didion, completion expected in 1982.

SIDELIGHTS: Hollowell wrote: "One of the best things I did after graduating from Columbia was not to go to graduate school immediately. I entered the Peace Corps and was sent to the Ivory Coast. Being twenty-two years old, defenseless,

and in a foreign country teaches one many things about one's inner resources.

"As far as I can remember my interest in the new journalism began with a piece in *Esquire* by Tom Wolfe, 'Why They Aren't Writing the Great American Novel Anymore.' Wolfe made such outrageous claims about the 'death' of fiction in our time and the power of journalism that I began to get very interested in researching the accuracy of his claims and attempting to place the whole phenomenon in some perspective.

"Many commentators seem to think that the new journalism was a thing of the 1960's whose time has passed. Clearly such recent works as Gay Talese's *Thy Neighbor's Wife,* Tom Wolfe's *The Right Stuff,* and particularly Norman Mailer's *The Executioner's Song,* are continuations of the form of nonfiction reporting characterized in my book. At the moment I am most interested in Joan Didion's career in fiction and nonfiction, particularly such works as *A Book of Common Prayer* and her nonfiction book, *The White Album.*

"I also think Christopher Lasch's *Culture of Narcissism* is an important book. Lasch examines what Tom Wolfe has dubbed 'the Me decade' and documents the abundance of cults, religious fads, and personal therapies. Like Lasch, I worry about the possibilities for collective action and social progress in such a period. I think that as consumers of journalism we have to be very wary of the cult of personality. We have to be watchful to separate news from notoriety, and personality from genuine importance. The media coverage of the 1980 Republican National Convention illustrated practically all of the points I am making—lots of pseudo-events, such as the Reagan-Ford 'deal,' and very little *news.*"

*   *   *

HOLMES, Grant
See FOX, James M.

*   *   *

HOLMGREN, Norah 1939-
(Nancy Walter)

PERSONAL: Original name, Nancy Hagberg, name legally changed, 1978; born June 28, 1939, in St. Paul, Minn.; daughter of Martin B. (a house painter) and Alvina (a cook; maiden name, Holmgren) Hagberg; married Marlow Hotchkiss, 1959 (marriage ended); married Sydney Walter, 1968 (marriage ended); children: (first marriage) Marina, Lily; (second marriage) Daniel. *Education:* Attended University of Minnesota, 1957-61; Antioch College West, B.A., 1980. *Home and office:* Firehouse Theatre, 220 Redwood Hwy., Mill Valley, Calif. 94941.

CAREER: Firehouse Theatre, Minneapolis, Minn., founding member and producer, 1963-69; Firehouse Theatre, San Francisco, Calif., founding member and producer, 1969—. Founder of Heartwork Press, 1980. *Awards, honors:* Fellow of Office for Advanced Drama Research, 1969-72.

WRITINGS—Under name Nancy Walter: *Rags* (two-act play; first produced in Minneapolis, Minn., at Firehouse Theatre, December, 1967; produced Off-Broadway at La Mama Experimental Theatre Club, March, 1968), University of Minnesota Press, 1971.

Unpublished plays: "Trinity" (one-act), first produced in Minneapolis, Minn., at Firehouse Theatre, November, 1967; "Blessings" (one-act), first produced in San Francisco, Calif., at Firehouse Theatre, March, 1970; "The Window" (two-act), first produced in San Francisco at Firehouse

Theatre, April, 1972; "Traveling Light" (two-act), first produced in San Francisco at Firehouse Theatre, September, 1972; "Stab and Dance" (two-act), first produced in San Francisco at Firehouse Theatre, March, 1974; "Something Funny" (three-act), first produced in San Francisco at Firehouse Theatre, December, 1976; "His Voice" (one-act), first broadcast by KQED-Radio, 1980.

Work represented in anthologies, including "Still Falling" (two-act; first produced in San Francisco, Calif., April, 1971) in *Radical Theater Notebook,* edited by Arthur Sainer, 1975.

WORK IN PROGRESS: Two novels, *Driving North* and *Out in the Open,* both expected to be published in 1981; a play, "City Nights."

*   *   *

HOLROYD, Sam
See BURTON, S(amuel) H(olroyd)

*   *   *

HOLT, Thomas J(ung)   1928-

PERSONAL: Born May 4, 1928, in Hong Kong; came to the United States in 1947, naturalized citizen, 1956; son of Ting Jen and Aileen (Chu) Holt; married Deborah Wong, December 20, 1951; children: Evelyn. *Education:* St. John's University, Shanghai, China, B.A., 1947; New Bedford Textile Institute, B.S., 1950. *Politics:* Independent. *Religion:* Episcopalian. *Residence:* Westport, Conn. *Office:* T. J. Holt & Co., Inc., Holt Building, 290 Post Rd. W., Westport, Conn. 06880.

CAREER: Arnold Bernhard, New York City, securities analyst, 1955-62; Research Institute of America, New York City, senior research editor, 1963-66; T. J. Holt & Co., Inc. (investment advisory firm), Westport, Conn., president, 1967—. *Member:* New York Society of Security Analysts.

WRITINGS: Tactical Guide to Building Capital in the Soaring Seventies, T. J. Holt & Co., 1971; *Total Investing,* Arlington House, 1976; *How to Survive and Grow Richer in the Tough Times Ahead,* Rawson, Wade, 1981. Editor of *Holt Investment Advisory,* 1967—, and *Holt Executive Advisory,* 1976—.

SIDELIGHTS: Holt commented to *CA:* "Before coming to the United States in 1947, I personally witnessed the collapse of the Chinese currency. That experience has led me to believe firmly that no government should be allowed to print fiat money, lest it court destruction of the economy. Because of my engineering training, I am also convinced that economic and investment research should be based more on logic than on empirical evidence. Finally, I believe strongly that free-market forces are far more powerful than any artificial efforts by politicians in shaping the economic prospect."

BIOGRAPHICAL/CRITICAL SOURCES: Barron's, April, 1980.

*   *   *

HOLTZMAN, Will   1951-

PERSONAL: Born June 26, 1951, in St. Louis, Mo.; son of Donald (a retail furniture merchant) and Evelyn (a travel agent; maiden name, Goldman) Holtzman; married Sylvia Shepard (a college textbook editor), June 18, 1977. *Education:* Wesleyan University, Middletown, Conn., B.A. (magna cum laude), 1974. *Religion:* Jewish. *Residence:* Wilton, Conn. *Agent:* Mel Berger, William Morris Agency, 1350 Avenue of the Americas, New York, N.Y. 10019.

CAREER: Piano mover, 1974; *Real Paper,* Cambridge, Mass., film critic, 1975; free-lance writer, 1976—. *Member:* Amnesty International, Writers Guild of America, Dramatists Guild, National Organization for Women.

WRITINGS: William Holden, Harcourt, 1976; *Jack Lemmon,* Harcourt, 1977; *Seesaw: A Dual Biography of Anne Bancroft and Mel Brooks,* Doubleday, 1979; *Judy Holliday,* Putnam, 1982.

Plays: "Snap" (two-act for children), first produced in New York, N.Y., at Fashion Institute, August, 1977; "The Housewives' Cantata" (two-act), first produced in New York, at Theatre Four, February 18, 1980; "Hurrah Boys, Hurrah!" (two-act), first produced in East Haddan, Conn., at Opera House, 1981. Writer for children's television programs and entertainers Stiller and Meara. Contributor to newspapers.

WORK IN PROGRESS: A screenplay in collaboration with Ira Wohl; a play about Judy Holliday.

SIDELIGHTS: Holtzman told *CA:* "The world's oldest profession is not prostitution but writing, though it's sometimes hard to tell the two apart. There are writing writers and talking writers. The difference is probably that between painting and photography. For me, writing is visual before it is verbal. I imagine, then I caption the image.

"As for categories: television writing is piecework; critical writing is mostly masturbation, a substitute for experience; theatre writing is elemental and demands interpretation like a strong melody in the hands of a good jazz musician; nonfiction is flight to or from fiction; fiction, as Stanley Elkin reminded us in 'The Living End', is hubris; screenwriting is best summed up by the joke about the actress who came to Hollywood and was so dumb she went to bed with the writer. So much for generalizations. In the end, good writing, like good jazz, is best defined: if you have to ask what it is, it ain't."

BIOGRAPHICAL/CRITICAL SOURCES: St. Louis Globe-Democrat, December 25, 1979; *Showbill,* February, 1980.

*   *   *

HOME, Alexander Frederick   1903-
(Alec Douglas-Home; Lord Home)

PERSONAL: Born July 2, 1903, in London, England; son of Charles (the thirteenth Earl of Home) and Lilian (Lambton) Home; married Elizabeth Alington, October 10, 1936; children: Caroline, Meriel (Mrs. Adrian Darby), Diana (Mrs. J. Wolfe Murray), David. *Education:* Attended Christ Church, Oxford, 1922-26. *Religion:* Church of England. *Home:* The Hirsel, Coldstream, Berwickshire, Scotland; and Castlemams, Douglas, Lanarkshire, Scotland.

CAREER: British Parliament, London, England, Conservative member of Parliament for South Lanark, 1931-45, Parliamentary private secretary to Neville Chamberlain, 1935-40, joint under-secretary of state for foreign affairs, 1945, Conservative member of Parliament for Lanark, 1950-51; House of Lords, London, member of House of Lords as fourteenth Earl of Home, 1951-63, minister of state in Scottish Office, 1951-55, secretary of state for commonwealth relations, 1955-60, and foreign affairs, 1960-62, leader of House of Lords and Lord President of Council, 1957-60, Prime Minister and First Lord of the Treasury, 1963, disclaimed peerages for life, 1963; British Parliament, Conservative member of Parliament for Kinross and West Perthshire, 1963-74, leader of the opposition, 1964-65, opposition spokesman on foreign affairs, 1965-70, secretary of state for foreign and commonwealth affairs, 1970-74; House of Lords, member, 1974—. Chancellor of Heriot-Watt University, 1966—. *Awards, honors:* Chancellor of Order of the Thistle, 1973—; created life peer, 1974.

WRITINGS—Under name Alec Douglas-Home: *Britain's Place in the World,* Conservative Political Centre, 1969; (with others) *Britain and the International Scene and Other Lectures,* Heriot-Watt University, 1972.

Under name Lord Home: *The Way the Wind Blows* (autobiography), Collins, 1976; *Border Reflections,* Collins, 1979.

*   *   *

HOME, William Douglas   1912-

PERSONAL: Surname is pronounced Hume; born June 3, 1912, in Edinburgh, Scotland; son of Charles Cospatrick Archibald (an earl) and Lilian (Lambton) Home; married Rachel Brand, July 26, 1951; children: Jamie, Sarah (Mrs. Nicholas Dent), Gian, Dinah. *Education:* New College, Oxford, B.A., 1935; attended Royal Academy of Dramatic Art, 1935-37. *Politics:* "Floating voter." *Religion:* Episcopalian. *Home and office:* Drayton House, East Meon, Hampshire, England. *Agent:* Laurence Evans, International Creative Management, 22 Grafton St., London W. 1, England.

CAREER: Playwright, 1937—. Actor in stage plays, 1935-60, including "Bonnet Over the Windmill," 1937, "Plan for a Hostess," 1938, "The Chiltern Hundreds," 1948, and "The Reluctant Debutante," 1955. Progressive Independent candidate for Parliament, Cathcart Division, Glasgow, 1942, Windsor Division, Berkshire, 1942, and Clay Cross Division, Derbyshire, 1944. Chairman of Farnham Repertory Theatre Trust, beginning 1971. *Military service:* Royal Armoured Corps, 1940-44; became captain. *Member:* Garrick Co. Traveller's Club, Beefsteak. *Awards, honors:* Named playwright of the year, 1973, by Variety Club of Great Britain.

WRITINGS: Home Truths (poems), Lane, 1939; *Half-Term Report: An Autobiography,* Longmans, Green, 1954; *Mr. Home Pronounced Hume: An Autobiography,* Collins, 1979.

Plays: *Now Barabbas* (three-act; produced in London, England, at Boltons Theatre, February 11, 1947), Longmans, Green, 1947 (also see below); *The Chiltern Hundreds* (three-act comedy; produced on the West End at Vaudeville Theatre, August 26, 1947; produced on Broadway as "Yes, M'Lord" at Booth Theatre, October 4, 1949), Samuel French, 1949 (also see below); "The Thistle and the Rose" (first produced in London, 1949; produced on the West End at Vaudeville Theatre, 1951), published in *The Plays of William Douglas Home,* Heinemann, 1958 (also see below).

Master of Arts (three-act comedy; first produced in Brighton, England, 1949; produced on the West End at Strand Theatre, 1949), Samuel French, 1950; *The Bad Samaritan* (three-act; first produced in Bromley, England, 1952; produced on the West End at Criterion Theatre, June 24, 1953), Evans Bros., 1954 (also see below); *The Manor of Northstead* (three-act comedy; first produced on the West End at Duchess Theatre, April 28, 1954), Samuel French, 1956; *The Reluctant Debutante* (two-act; first produced on the West End at Cambridge Theatre, May 24, 1955; produced on Broadway at Henry Miller's Theatre, October 10, 1956), Evans Bros., 1956 (also see below); *The Iron Duchess* (two-act; first produced in Brighton, 1957; produced on the West End at Cambridge Theatre, March 14, 1957), Evans Bros., 1958; *The Plays of William Douglas Home* (contains "Now Barabbas," "The Chiltern Hundreds," "The Thistle and the Rose," "The Bad Samaritan," and "The Reluctant Debutante"), Heinemann, 1958.

Aunt Edwina (comedy; first produced in Eastbourne, England, 1959; produced on the West End at Fortune Theatre, November 3, 1959), Samuel French, 1960; *The Bad Soldier Smith* (first produced on the West End at Westminster Theatre, 1961), Evans Bros., 1962; *The Reluctant Peer* (three-act comedy; first produced on the West End at Duchess theatre, January 15, 1964), Evans Bros., 1965; *A Friend Indeed* (comedy; first produced in Windsor, England, 1965; produced on the West End at Cambridge Theatre, April 27, 1966), Samuel French, 1966; *Betzi* (first produced in Salisbury, England, at Salisbury Playhouse, March 23, 1965; produced on the West End at Haymarket Theatre, 1975), Samuel French, 1977; *The Secretary Bird* (three-act; first produced in Manchester, England, 1968; produced on the West End at Savoy Theatre, October 20, 1968; produced in Fairfield, Conn., at Candlewood Theatre, July 14, 1970), Samuel French, 1968.

The Jockey Club Stakes (two-act; first produced on the West End at Vaudeville Theatre, September 30, 1970; produced on Broadway at Cort Theatre, January 24, 1973), Samuel French, 1971; *Lloyd George Knew My Father* (two-act; first produced in Boston, England, as "Lady Boothroyd of the By-Pass," 1972; produced on the West End as "Lloyd George Knew My Father," July 4, 1972; produced in Washington, D.C., at John F. Kennedy Center, July 2, 1974), Samuel French, 1973.

Unpublished plays: "Great Possessions" (three-act), first produced in London at "Q" Theatre, 1937; "Passing By" (three-act), first produced in London at "Q" Theatre, April 29, 1940; "Ambassador Extraordinary" (three-act), first produced on the West End at Aldwych Theatre, 1948; "Caro William" (three-act), first produced in London at Embassy Theatre, October 22, 1952; "Up a Gum Tree" (three-act), first produced in Ipswich, England, 1960; "The Cigarette Girl" (three-act), first produced on the West End at Duke of York's Theatre, 1962; "The Drawing Room Tragedy" (three-act), first produced in Salisbury, 1963.

"Two Accounts Rendered: The Home Secretary and Lady M.P." (two one-act plays), first produced on the West End at Comedy Theatre, September 15, 1964; "The Grouse Moor Image" (three-act), first produced in Plymouth, England, 1968; "Uncle Dick's Surprise" (three-act), first produced in Salisbury, 1970; "The Douglas Cause" (two-act), first produced in Nottingham, England, at Nottingham Playhouse, August 31, 1971; produced on the West End at Duke of York's Theatre, November 10, 1971; "The Bank Manager" (two-act), first produced in Boston, England, 1972; "At the End of the Day" (two-act), first produced in Guildford, England, 1973; produced on the West End at Savoy Theatre, October 3, 1973; "The Dame of Sark" (two-act), first produced in Oxford, England, 1974, produced on the West End at Wyndhams Theatre, 1974; "The Lord's Lieutenant" (two-act), first produced in Farnham, England, 1974; "The Kingfisher" (two-act), first produced on the West End at Lyric Theatre, 1978, produced on Broadway at Biltmore Theatre, December 6, 1978.

Television plays: *The Bishop and the Actress* (first broadcast by British Broadcasting Corp. [BBC], 1968), Samuel French, 1969; "The Editor Regrets," first broadcast by BBC, November 27, 1970; "On Such a Night," first broadcast by BBC, April 15, 1973.

Screenplays: "Now Barabbas" (based on own play), De Grunwald, 1949; "The Chiltern Hundreds" (based on own play), Rank, 1949; (author of dialogue) "The Colditz Story," Republic, 1957; "The Reluctant Debutante" (based on own play), Metro-Goldwyn-Mayer, 1958.

WORK IN PROGRESS: More plays.

SIDELIGHTS: Known as the "king of light comedy" during the 1950's, Home is still considered a master of the genre. His reputation, however, has not always guaranteed him an audience. Following a number of post-World War II West End hits, Home's drawing room comedies suffered against a new climate of theatre: the theatre of relevance, as introduced in 1956 by John Osborne's "Look Back in Anger." Yet Home survived that period as well as other droughts in his career, and he remains an active force in British theatre.

As Home comes from an aristocratic family—his father was an earl and his mother an earl's daughter—his plays naturally focus on the English upper class. The highly popular "Chiltern Hundreds" and "The Manor of Northstead" satirize British political attitudes while featuring the eccentric Earl of Lister and his family. Another major work of the postwar era was "The Reluctant Debutante," about an eager mother's attempts to find a husband for her uncooperative daughter.

Home is not exclusively a writer of the upper class, however, as two of his earlier plays demonstrate. "Now Barabbas" studies life in prison in between the time of a condemned murderer's arrival and his execution. The play is based on Home's own prison experience; serving in the Royal Armoured Corps in World War II, he refused to take part in an Allied attack on Le Havre. A German officer had requested an evacuation of the city's civilians before the attack was to be made, but the invading forces denied the request. Home consequently refused to participate in the attack, receiving a court martial and a prison term for his defiance. His play left a lasting impression on a number of critics, including Ronald Bryden, who in 1968 called it "the best play yet written about life and sex in prison."

Home's other "serious" success of the time was a historical drama "The Thistle and the Rose." Focusing on the end of the age of chivalry and the beginning of power politics, the play chronicles the destruction of James IV and his Scottish Army at the Battle of Flodden.

The effects of the late 1950's call to purpose in British theatre are evident in the response to Home's work of that era. Two of his plays released after Osborne's "Look Back in Anger" suffered terribly at the hands of critics and audiences. Home sacrificed his own savings and even sold his car to keep the unpopular "Aunt Edwina" on stage in 1959. He spared the expense on "The Cigarette Girl" in 1962—and the play closed after six performances.

Among Home's complaints during this time was that critics had an automatic disregard for anything resembling "establishment" drama. But Bryden offered another explanation: "Believing himself a member of an oppressed, derided minority, Mr. Home sacrificed his art to protest, proclaiming the misfortunes, the persecutions, the superior beauty, virtue and sexuality, of the class into which he was haplessly born—the aristocracy." Home defended his choice of subject matter by saying that as long as an "eccentric landed gentry" existed, he believed it should be written about.

With the production of "The Secretary Bird" in 1968, Home proved that the drawing-room comedy could still be a theatrical force. The story of a sexually inadequate husband who wins his straying wife back with "humor and kindness," the play showed Home a master at making a simple plot work.

"The Secretary Bird" received warm praise in London while faring less well with American critics. Marilyn Stasio remarked that, though "based on the flimsiest plot material,

... the comedy is buoyed by the wit, charm, and attractiveness of its stock characters and sustained by its literate humor and flawless construction." Another London critic, Jeremy Kingston, at first admired Home's "skill at making this simple, almost hackneyed plot so very entertaining. At a second viewing what also impressed me was the civilised nature of his story and his hero." The play's possibilities for a Broadway run were erased, however, when *New York Times* critic Clive Barnes panned the popular London production. Broadway promoters then labeled the play a box-office risk and scrapped all performance plans.

The cancellation of "The Secretary Bird" merely postponed Home's return to Broadway. "The Jockey Club Stakes" opened in 1973, bringing to New York Home's story about "a breach of racing and betting rules involving family interests of the despotic Jockey Club stewards." The show, which played on the tradition of the "one-dimensional but slyly endearing carricature" in British productions, was a "nostalgic delight," said *Time*'s T. E. Kalem. To London critics the play proved that Home knew his audience. "He perceives unerringly that a certain section of the British middle-class is fascinated by people who live several social strata above them," commented Stanley Price.

Home offered another hit to American audiences with "The Kingfisher." After making its U.S. debut on Broadway, Home's play moved to Washington, D.C., in 1980. There it proved to critic James Lardner that indeed "they do make 'em like they used to." The story of an old bachelor attempting to win the hand of a woman who had refused him fifty years earlier, "The Kingfisher" was described by Lardner as "a 'vehicle.' As such, it may be a trifle rickety and it probably won't win any engineering awards, but it does what a vehicle should do: It delivers the goods."

Among those goods were the play's cast. Both the Broadway and Washington, D.C., productions starred Rex Harrison and Claudette Colbert, with George Rose playing the manservant. Walter Kerr assessed the New York performance as a "doodle" and "a jungle-gym composed of practically nothing but holes." But, he added, if it weren't such a play, would the players "have so many empty spaces to fill with their impertinent, infinitely polished, presences? ... The author is really very honest about what he's up to."

Reactions to Home's work depend largely upon the expectations viewers bring to the theatre. According to Price, "Home's appeal appears to lie with those "well-to-do commuters whose theatrical ideal is a good, uncomplicated night-out, and who prefer to believe that nothing has happened in the British theatre since the death of A E Matthews." With such an audience to depend on, Home will likely remain a lively "last gasp of Edwardian theatre."

Home's brother Alec was prime minister of the United Kingdom from 1962 to 1963.

BIOGRAPHICAL/CRITICAL SOURCES: William Douglas Home, *Half-Term Report: An Autobiography,* Longmans, Green, 1954; *Theatre Arts,* December, 1956; *Time,* July 6, 1962, September 18, 1972, February 5, 1973; *National Review,* December 31, 1963; *New York Times,* October 18, 1968, October 24, 1969, December 7, 1978, December 17, 1978; *Observer Review,* May 5, 1968, October 20, 1968; *Cue,* September 20, 1969; *Punch,* January 4, 1970; *Variety,* October 14, 1970, December 1, 1971; *Plays and Players,* November, 1970; *London Times,* July 9, 1972, October 4, 1973, October 7, 1973, September 22, 1974, April 9, 1977; *Washington Post,* October 21, 1978, February 2, 1980; Home, *Mr. Home Pronounced Hume: An Autobiography,* Collins, 1979.

—Sketch by David Versical

HOOVER, Thomas 1941-

PERSONAL: Born May 3, 1941, in Temple, Tex.; son of Orrin Garnett (a rancher) and Nettie (Landrum) Hoover; married Julie Hetrick (an urban planner), October 15, 1975. *Education:* University of Texas, B.A., 1962; Texas A & M University, Ph.D., 1966. *Home:* 109 Waverly Pl., New York, N.Y. 10011. *Agent:* Virginia Barber, Virginia Barber Literary Agency, Inc., 44 Greenwich Ave., New York, N.Y. 10011.

CAREER: United Technologies Research Laboratory, East Hartford, Conn., senior researcher, 1967-71; Parsons Brinckerhoff, Inc., New York, N.Y., vice-president, 1971-80; writer, 1980—. *Member:* Authors Guild, Authors League of America.

WRITINGS: Zen Culture, Random House, 1977; *The Zen Experience,* New American Library, 1980; *The Mogul* (historical novel), Doubleday, 1982. Contributor to magazines, including *Omni.*

SIDELIGHTS: Hoover told *CA:* "My historical novel, set in seventeenth-century India and England, is intended to explore the sensuality in the classic culture of India, through the dramatized experiences of the first Englishman to visit the Mogul court of India. I have traveled widely in India, and for my first two books I traveled in Japan and China. I live in Greenwich Village and am a confirmed New Yorker, although I still maintain a ranch in Texas."

*   *   *

HOPE, David
See FRASER, Douglas

*   *   *

HOPKINS, J(ohn) F(eely) 1922-

PERSONAL: Born April 5, 1922, in Philadelphia, Pa.; son of Joseph P. (a merchant seaman) and Marie (a secretary; maiden name, Feely) Hopkins; married Mary Louise Turner, July 1, 1950. *Education:* West Chester State College, B.S., 1946; Temple University, M.Ed., 1949; Drexel University, M.L.S., 1960. *Home:* 20 West Lucerne Circle, No. 817, Orlando, Fla. 32801.

CAREER: Philadelphia Naval Shipyard, Philadelphia, Pa., instructor, 1948-56; Free Library of Philadelphia, Philadelphia, librarian, 1957-68; Orlando Public Library, Orlando, Fla., librarian, 1973-80; writer. *Military service:* U.S. Army, 1943-46; became sergeant. *Member:* Authors Guild.

WRITINGS: McEckr'n (novel), St. Martin's, 1980. Contributor of stories to magazines, including *Folio, Four Quarters, Quartet,* and *Kansas Quarterly.*

WORK IN PROGRESS: A novel, completion expected in 1981 or 1982.

BIOGRAPHICAL/CRITICAL SOURCES: Los Angeles Times, March 20, 1980; *Baltimore News American,* May 4, 1980; *Pittsburgh Press,* June 16, 1980.

*   *   *

HOSKIN, Cyril Henry 1911(?)-1981
(Tuesday Lobsang Rampa)

OBITUARY NOTICE: Born c. 1911 in England; died of heart trouble, January 25, 1981, in Calgary, Alberta, Canada. Writer. Hoskin was best known as the author of *The Third Eye,* a bestseller which was exposed as a literary hoax. Purporting to be a Tibetan lama named Tuesday Lobsang Rampa, Hoskin claimed to have gained mystical powers through a surgical procedure opening the "third eye" in the center of his forehead. After the hoax was revealed, Hoskin declared that his body had been taken over by a mystic spirit. He published several other books on occultism and psychic themes, including *Cave of the Ancients, The Saffron Robe, My Visit to Venus, The Rampa Story,* and *The Thirteenth Candle.* Obituaries and other sources: *Encyclopedia of Occultism and Parapsychology,* Gale, 1978; *Chicago Tribune,* February 1, 1981.

*   *   *

HOTCHNER, Tracy 1950-

PERSONAL: Born March 1, 1950, in New York, N.Y.; daughter of A. E. (a writer) and Geraldine H. (a journalist; maiden name, Mavor) Hotchner. *Education:* Attended University of Pennsylvania; received degree from New York University, 1971. *Politics:* None. *Religion:* Atheist. *Agent:* Owen Laster, William Morris Agency, 1350 Avenue of the Americas, New York, N.Y. 10019.

CAREER: Worked as actress; free-lance journalist and writer for motion pictures and television. *Member:* Writers Guild of America, American Horse Shows Association, Authors Guild, Screen Actors Guild, Pacific Coast Hunter/Jumper Association, Tri-Valley Horse Shows Association, Los Angeles County Horse Shows Association. *Awards, honors:* Nomination for a National Book Award for *Pregnancy and Childbirth,* 1980.

WRITINGS: Pregnancy and Childbirth: The Complete Guide for a New Life, Avon, 1979; *Made in Heaven* (novel), Morrow, 1980. Author of screenplays, "Chinese Checkers" for Paramount and "Mommie Dearest." Creator of television series "Big Shamus, Little Shamus." Contributor of articles to periodicals, including *New West, Self, Redbook, Los Angeles Times,* and *Playgirl.*

WORK IN PROGRESS: "Blue Satin," a screenplay; *Simple Crimes of Passion,* a novel.

SIDELIGHTS: Hotchner's *Pregnancy and Childbirth* is a seven-hundred page guidebook that covers every aspect of pregnancy from the decision to get pregnant to the birth of the baby. Alice Digilio of *Washington Post Book World* wrote of *Pregnancy and Childbirth,* "Most of Hotchner's data is sound, objective and helpful." However, Digilio expressed concern that Hotchner might cause unnecessary anxiety in expectant couples with her elaborate discussions of rare complications such as fetal death in utero and ectopic pregnancy. "Such information," Digilio commented, "should present no problem for the 'rational' audience Hotchner envisions for her book; however, for those who might tend, during pregnancy, to manufacture anxiety hormones along with the others, Hotchner could compound the problem."

Hotchner told *CA:* "The intention of *Pregnancy and Childbirth* is to offer complete information about every aspect of pregnancy and childbirth without bias. By soft-pedaling upsetting information I would have performed the same censorship as if I hadn't included negative information about medical care during pregnancy or the dangers of certain drugs or foods. It is up to each individual to do what she wants with the thorough, nonjudgmental, consumer-oriented information in the book. She can use it for her protection and enhancement, or she can hide from it, as this reviewer thinks some may want to do. I don't believe that any intelligent, caring woman, nor her mate, will want to do that (as was common ten years ago, when people wanted the doctor to play God)."

BIOGRAPHICAL/CRITICAL SOURCES: Washington Post Book World, March 4, 1979.

*   *   *

HOTSPUR
See CURLING, Bryan William Richard

*   *   *

HOWARD, Stanley E.   1888(?)-1980

OBITUARY NOTICE: Born c. 1888; died October 28, 1980, in Neshanic, N.J. Educator. Howard taught economics at Princeton University for thirty-nine years, serving as chairman of the economics department from 1934 to 1948. He was the author of *The ABC of Accounting,* a popular textbook, and a frequent contributor to scholarly journals. Obituaries and other sources: *New York Times,* October 31, 1980.

*   *   *

HOWARTH, Pamela   1954-
(Pamela Barrow)

PERSONAL: Born April 30, 1954, in Bolton, England; daughter of Stanley (a joiner) and Joan (Hatchman) Barrow; married Stephen F. Howarth (a television engineer), September 21, 1974. *Religion:* None. *Home:* 45 Ashdene Cres., Harwood, Bolton BL2 3LW, England.

CAREER: Chloride Lorival Ltd., Little Lever, England, dispatch clerk, 1970—.

WRITINGS—Under name Pamela Barrow: *Traitor Queen* (novel), R. Hale, 1974; *Affair Royal* (novel), R. Hale, 1978.

SIDELIGHTS: Howarth told *CA:* "My chief interest is history, a subject I find utterly absorbing and fascinating. In my writing, I find it more important to seek out the motives and characters of the people concerned rather than merely chronicle their actions. Today, I feel historical fiction is often undervalued, but to my mind the historical novel can serve a useful purpose in bringing the past vividly alive."

*   *   *

HOWLAND, Harold Edward   1913-1980

OBITUARY NOTICE: Born August 18, 1913, in Pittsburgh, Pa.; died of a heart attack, November 30, 1980, in Tampa, Fla. Educator and Foreign Service officer. Howland was a school teacher in Pittsburgh for many years before he joined the State Department in 1951. He specialized in cultural and educational exchange programs and served as a cultural attache in Vienna and Tel Aviv. From 1965 to 1967 he was the deputy assistant secretary of state for international cultural affairs. He then served as consul general in Amsterdam until his retirement in 1972. Howland was the author of *American Life and Literature,* an English-language textbook used in the Austrian school system. Obituaries and other sources: *Who's Who in America,* 40th edition, Marquis, 1978; *Washington Post,* December 5, 1980.

*   *   *

HUDDLESTON, Eugene L(ee)   1931-

PERSONAL: Born January 29, 1931, in Ironton, Ohio; son of James Earl and Bernice (McClave) Huddleston; married Mary Lou Fishbeck, June 17, 1961; children: John R. *Education:* Marshall University, A.B., 1953; Ohio University, M.A., 1956; attended Indiana University, 1956-57; Michigan State University, Ph.D., 1965. *Politics:* Democrat. *Home:* 3926 Raleigh Dr., Okemos, Mich. 48864. *Office:* Department of American Thought and Language, Michigan State University, East Lansing, Mich. 48824.

CAREER: Tri-State College, Angola, Ind., instructor in technical writing, 1957-60; Kellogg Community College, Battle Creek, Mich., instructor in English, 1960-61; Indiana State University, Terre Haute, assistant professor of English, 1962-66; Michigan State University, East Lansing, assistant professor, 1966-70, associate professor, 1970-77, professor of American thought and language, 1977—. *Member:* Modern Language Association of America, Popular Culture Association, Chesapeake and Ohio Historical Society. *Awards, honors:* Norman Foerster Award from American literature section of Modern Language Association of America, 1966, for article, "Topographical Poetry in the Early National Period."

WRITINGS: (With Philip Shuster and Alvin Staufer) *C & O Power: Steam and Diesel Locomotives of the Chesapeake and Ohio Railway, 1900-1965,* privately printed, 1965; (contributor) Marshall Fishwick, editor, *The World of Ronald McDonald,* Bowling Green Popular Press, 1978; (with Douglas A. Noverr) *The Relationship of Painting and Literature: A Guide to Information Sources,* Gale, 1978; *Thomas Jefferson: A Reference Guide,* G. K. Hall, 1982. Contributor of more than twenty-five articles and reviews to academic journals.

WORK IN PROGRESS: Thomas Jefferson in American Literature, with publication expected to result; research on the relationship of railroads and geology.

SIDELIGHTS: Huddleson told *CA:* "As a railroad photographer I try mainly to please myself by giving the world as I know it some permanence as it recedes into nothingness. As a scholar of American thought and writing, I try to make some sense out of the flux of events as I perceive them. Gratification for the former activity comes from seeing the finished photograph or color slide; for the latter, only in seeing my work in print or having an audience for it. The work I am just starting on includes the relationship of land forms to railroading (an illustrated essay) and Thomas Jefferson in American literature."

BIOGRAPHICAL/CRITICAL SOURCES: Henry Doering, editor, *The World Almanac Book of Buffs, Masters, Mavens, and Uncommon Experts,* World Almanac, 1980.

*   *   *

HUDSON, Wilson Mathis   1907-

PERSONAL: Born December 26, 1907, in Flatonia, Tex.; son of Wilson M. (an oil man and rancher) and Ann Byrd (Brown) Hudson; married Mildred Ruckman, January 1, 1932 (died June 19, 1949); married Gertrude C. Reese (a professor), October 11, 1951. *Education:* University of Texas, Main University (now University of Texas at Austin), A.B., 1929, A.M., 1930; University of Chicago, Ph.D., 1947. *Home:* 2401 Ridgeview, Austin, Tex. 78704. *Office:* Department of English, University of Texas, Austin, Tex. 78712.

CAREER: Rice Institute, Houston Tex., instructor in English, 1930-37; G. & C. Merriam Co., Springfield, Mass., traveling representative, 1937-38; University of Chicago, Chicago, Ill., instructor in English, 1939-42; University of Texas, Main University, (now University of Texas at Austin), instructor, 1946-47, assistant professor, 1947-53, associate professor, 1953-64, professor, 1964-74, professor emeritus, 1974—. Visiting professor at Columbia University, summers, 1966 and 1968. *Military service:* U.S. Army Air Force, 1942-46; became captain. *Member:* Texas Institute of

Letters (secretary-treasurer, 1958-60), Texas Folklore Society (associate editor, 1951-64; editor and secretary, 1964-72), South-Central Modern Language Association.

WRITINGS: Andy Adams: His Life and Writings, Southern Methodist University Press, 1964; *Andy Adams: Storyteller and Novelist of the Great Plains,* Steck, 1967.

Editor: *The Healer of Los Olmos and Other Mexican Lore,* Southern Methodist University Press, 1951; Andy Adams, *Why the Chisolm Trail Forks and Other Tales of the Cattle Country,* University of Texas Press, 1956, revised edition published as *Andy Adams' Campfire Tales,* University of Nebraska Press, 1976; George D. Hendricks, *Mirrors, Mice, and Mustaches,* Texas Folklore Society, 1966; Paul Patterson, *Pecos Tales,* Encino Press, 1967; *Tire Shrinker to Dragster,* Southern Methodist University Press, 1968; Andy Adams, *The Corporal Segundo,* Encino Press, 1968; Emma Wilson Emery, *Aunt Puss and Others: Old Days in the Piney Woods,* Encino Press, 1969; Martha Emmons, *Deep Like the Rivers,* Encino Press, 1969; John Q. Anderson, *Texas Folk Medicine,* Encino Press, 1970; *Hunters and Healers: Folklore Types and Topics,* Texas Folklore Society, 1971; (and author of introduction) *Diamond Bessie and the Shepherds,* Texas Folklore Society, 1972.

Co-editor; all published by Southern Methodist University Press: *Folk Travelers: Ballads, Tales, and Talk,* 1953; *Texas Folk and Folklore,* 1954; *Mesquite and Willow,* 1957; *Madstones and Twisters,* 1958; *And Horns on the Toads,* 1959; *Singers and Storytellers,* 1961; *The Golden Log,* 1962; *A Good Tale and a Bonnie Tune,* 1964; (with Allan Maxwell) *The Sunny Slopes of Long Ago,* 1966.

Contributor of articles and reviews to *Texas Observer.*

WORK IN PROGRESS: A book on the role of the concept of myth in humanistic studies, completion expected in 1985.

SIDELIGHTS: Hudson told *CA:* "The fact that I edited or co-edited eighteen books for the Texas Folklore Society seems to point to folklore as my primary interest, but my chief effort was directed to the study and teaching of comparative literature and, in later years, the methodology of literary criticism. My own articles in the field of folklore were all comparative, and I added tale type and motif numbers to the articles I edited. It is my view that the comparative approach to literature, to which I was oriented by C. H. Slover in my undergraduate years, and the analytical approach, in which I was trained in graduate school by R. S. Crane, are not contradictory but complementary. I believe that a literary scholar should try to transcend the nationality and language into which he was born, and for this reason I have visited Europe almost every year since 1964, and I have studied other languages (Italian, Russian, and Swedish) besides those which were part of my program in college (Spanish, French, and German). In retrospect, I can say that I disregarded the half-serious advice of one of my teachers: 'Get in a good rut and stay there.' "

*   *   *

HUFFMAN, James Lamar   1941-

PERSONAL: Born October 17, 1941, in Plymouth, Ind.; son of Robert L. (a teacher) and Wilma June (a teacher; maiden name, Dumph) Huffman; married Judith C. Smith (a teacher), August 29, 1964; children: James Lamar, Jr., Kristen Suzanne. *Education:* Marion College, A.B., 1963; Northwestern University, M.S.J., 1964; University of Michigan, M.A., 1967, Ph.D., 1972. *Religion:* Presbyterian. *Home:* 362 Terrace Dr., Springfield, Ohio 45503. *Office:* Department of History, Wittenberg University, Springfield, Ohio 45501.

CAREER: Minneapolis Tribune, Minneapolis, Minn., reporter, 1964-66; University of Nebraska, Lincoln, assistant professor of history, 1972-75; Marion College, Marion, Ind., assistant professor of history, 1975-77; Wittenberg University, Springfield, Ohio, assistant professor, 1977-80, associate professor of history, 1980—. Senior translator and editorial adviser for *Japan Interpreter,* 1974-75. Chairman of Marion mayor's task force on police-fire merit system, 1976. *Member:* International House of Japan, Association for Asian Studies, Conference on Faith and History, Conference on Peace Research in History, Japan Media Workshop, Midwest Japan Seminar (chairman, 1978-81). *Awards, honors:* Fulbright-Hays grants, 1970-71, 1974-75; National Endowment for the Humanities grant, 1977.

WRITINGS: Politics of the Meiji Press: The Life of Fukuchi Gen'ichiro, University Press of Hawaii, 1980.

Contributor: *An Introductory Bibliography for Japanese Studies,* Volume II, Japan Foundation, 1975; Victor Koschmann, editor, *Authority and the Individual in Japan,* University of Tokyo Press, 1978; F. Gilbert Chan, editor, *Nationalism in East Asia: An Annotated Bibliography of Selected Works,* Garland, 1980.

Author of "Modernization of Japan," first broadcast by University of Mid-America, Lincoln, Neb., 1978.

Contributor to scholarly journals.

WORK IN PROGRESS: A study of press-government relations in late nineteenth-century Japan; a general political-social history of Meiji Japan (1868-1912), focusing on the work of foreign correspondent Edward J. House.

SIDELIGHTS: Huffman commented: "I am especially interested in the effects of political change on the quality of life of the 'common person'—on such issues as economic well-being, environment, justice, and minority conditions. I believe that institutional transformation that ignores these areas is, in the long run, self-destructive. As is obvious, my main focus is Japan, a country where the effects of change have been dramatic."

*   *   *

HUME, Paul Chandler   1915-

PERSONAL: Born December 13, 1915, in Chicago, Ill.; son of Robert Woolsey and Katherine English (Rockwell) Hume; married Ruth Fox, December 29, 1949 (deceased); children: Paul, Michael, Ann, Peter. *Education:* University of Chicago, degree, 1937. *Home:* 3625 Tilden St. N.W., Washington, D.C. 20008. *Agent:* Anita Diamant, Writers' Workshop, Inc., 51 East 42nd St., New York, N.Y. 10017. *Office: Washington Post,* 1150 15th St. N.W., Washington, D.C. 20071.

CAREER: Washington Post, Washington, D.C., music editor, 1947—; Georgetown University, Washington, D.C., professor, 1950-77. Visiting professor at Yale University, 1975—. Radio commentator on WGMS-Radio, 1947—, presenting weekly program, "A Variable Feast," and a weekly opera program; guest commentator for Metropolitan Opera intermission broadcasts. *Member:* American Association of University Professors, Music Critics Association (member of executive committee, 1962-63), Cosmos Club. *Awards, honors:* D.Mus. from Thiel College, 1968; Peabody Award, 1977; L.H.D. from Rosary College, 1977, and Georgetown University, 1979; prolific achievement award from University of Chicago Alumni Association, 1978.

WRITINGS: Catholic Church Music, Dodd, 1956; (with wife, Ruth Fox) *The Lion of Poland: The Story of Paderew-*

ski, Hawthorne, 1962; (with R. Hume) *King of Song: The Story of John McCormack,* Hawthorne, 1964; *Verdi: The Man and His Music,* Dutton, 1977; (with William Weaver) *Puccini: The Man and His Music,* Dutton, 1977. Also editor with Clifford Bennett of *Hymnal of Christian Unity,* 1964.

WORK IN PROGRESS: Music on Page One; Paderewski; Critical Letters (tentative title).

* * *

HUNKIN, Timothy Mark Trelawney 1950-

PERSONAL: Born December 27, 1950, in London, England; son of Oliver John Wellington (a television producer) and Frances Elizabeth (an artist; maiden name, Holmes) Hunkin. *Education:* Caius College, Cambridge, B.Sc., 1971. *Politics:* Socialist. *Home:* Bulcamp House, Blythburg, Suffolk, England.

CAREER: Phlegethon Fireworks (display contractors), London, England, boss, 1969-80; *Observer,* London, England, cartoonist and author of cartoon strips, "Rudiments," 1973—. Creator of animation for television.

WRITINGS: Mrs. Gronkwonk and the Post Office Tower (juvenile), Angus & Robertson, 1971; *Rudiments of Wisdom* (juvenile), Hutchinson, 1974.

WORK IN PROGRESS: Making Plastics, a book for juveniles, publication expected in 1981; an encyclopedia of cartoons from "Rudiments," publication by Longmans expected in 1984; research on microelectronics and minicomputers.

SIDELIGHTS: Hunkin commented: "Although I make most of my income from the 'Rudiments' and miscellaneous illustration and animation work, I spend most of my time making things, mostly furniture and wooden sculptures. I am currently working on a series of mechanical figures activated by putting coins in a slot. However, both the 'Rudiments' and the sculpture are just different ways of learning (which is what I really enjoy), the 'Rudiments' by reading, and sculptures by doing.

"I think that it is sad that engineering (how things work and are made) is not taught to younger children. It should be a subject like nature—children are surrounded by as many man-made objects as natural objects. Such books as there are on the subject are mostly boring and condescending. I feel some missionary zeal to improve the standard."

* * *

HUNT, David (Wathen Stather) 1913-

PERSONAL: Born September 25, 1913, in Durham, England; son of Bernard Patteson Wathen Slather (a canon) and Elizabeth Graham (Milner) Hunt; married Iro Ioannou Myrianthous; children: John, Richard. *Education:* Wadham College, Oxford, M.A., 1936; attended Magdalen College, Oxford, 1937-39. *Religion:* Church of England. *Home:* Old Place, Lindfield, Sussex RH16 2HU, England.

CAREER: British Diplomatic Service, London, worked in Defense and Atomic Energy Department, 1947-48, first secretary in Pretoria, South Africa, 1948-50, private secretary to Prime Minister, 1950-1952, assistant secretary, 1952, head of Economic Affairs Department, 1952-54, deputy high commissioner to Pakistan, 1954-56, head of Central African department, 1956-69, assistant under-secretary of state in Commonwealth Relations Office, 1959-60, deputy high commissioner to Nigeria, 1960-62, high commissioner to Uganda, 1962-65, Cyprus, 1965-66, and Nigeria, 1967-69,

ambassador to Brazil, 1969-73; Commonwealth Institute, London, chairman of board of governors, 1974—. Deputy chairman of Export-Import Credit Management and Consultants Ltd., 1974-78. Visiting professor at University of Edinburgh, 1980. Member of Press Council. *Military service:* British Army, 1940-47; became colonel; named officer of Order of the British Empire, received U.S. Bronze Star. *Member:* Royal Overseas League (member of council, 1975—), Society for the Promotion of Hellenic Studies (member of council, 1976—), Athenaeum Club. *Awards, honors:* Fellow of Magdalen College, Oxford, 1937-39; Knight Commander of the Order of St. Michael and St. George, 1963; named honorary citizen of Limassol, Cyprus, 1980.

WRITINGS: A Don at War, W. Kimber, 1966; *On the Spot,* P. Davies, 1975. Contributor of articles and reviews to classical journals and newspapers.

WORK IN PROGRESS: Studies in Cypriot history and archaeology.

SIDELIGHTS: Hunt told *CA:* "My main purpose in writing is to expound, after making discoveries, on what happened and why. The principal influence I would acknowledge is Herodotus." *Avocational interests:* Travel, military history, rose gardening.

* * *

HUNTER, Stephen 1946-

PERSONAL: Born March 25, 1946, in Kansas City, Mo.; son of Charles Francis (a professor) and Virginia (an executive; maiden name, Ricker) Hunter; married Lucy Hageman (a teacher), September 13, 1969; children: James H., Amy E. *Education:* Northwestern University, B.S.J., 1968. *Home:* 10013 Cape Anne Dr., Columbia, Md. 21046. *Office:* Baltimore Sun, 501 North Calvert, Baltimore, Md. 21203.

CAREER: Baltimore Sun, Baltimore, Md., copy reader, 1971-73, book review editor, 1973—. *Military service:* U.S. Army, Infantry, 1968-70.

WRITINGS: The Master Sniper, Morrow, 1980. Contributor to *Crawdaddy.*

BIOGRAPHICAL/CRITICAL SOURCES: Baltimore Evening Sun, May 27, 1980.

* * *

HUNTLEY, Timothy Wade 1939-

PERSONAL: Born June 20, 1939, in Florida; son of John David and Margaret (Ridges) Huntley. *Education:* Received B.A. from Kent State University; graduate study at University of California, Los Angeles. *Politics:* "Extreme Middle." *Religion:* "Devout Agnostic." *Home and office:* 22½ Thornton Ave., Venice, Calif. 90291. *Agent:* Henry Morrison, Inc., 58 West 10th St., New York, N.Y. 10011.

CAREER: Free-lance filmmaker, 1968—. *Awards, honors:* Nominated for Academy Award from Academy of Motion Picture Arts and Sciences, 1973; nominated for Emmy Award from Academy of Television Arts and Sciences.

WRITINGS: One of Me, DAW Books, 1980. Contributor to magazines, including *Evergreen Review,* and to newspapers.

WORK IN PROGRESS: "A short nonfiction (though humorous) book, offering unscrupulous advice to would-be cult leaders who are in it for the money, power, and fame (the latter third of the book will take the form of a shopper's guide that lists and briefly describes existing cults and religions for potential followers who have not yet committed themselves)."

SIDELIGHTS: Huntley commented to CA: "I have been a free-lance filmmaker since 1968, holding various positions on and in everything from feature films to industrials, all the way down to network television. Most of my recent work has been for the networks, including the American Everest expedition, 'Real People,' and 'Speak Up America.'

"I'm told there are only six science fiction novelists who write intending to be funny (though there are several dozen who succeed), which is to say, it's an open field. Humorous science fiction appeals to me for that reason. I'm a coward who can't face the competition in the mainstream. There's very little science to my fiction. I seem to be moving off toward religious and metaphysical humor. There's not a great deal of competition there, for sure. A fairly compact readership, too."

* * *

HURSTFIELD, Joel 1911-1980

OBITUARY NOTICE—See index for CA sketch: Born November 4, 1911, in London, England; died November 29, 1980, in California. Educator, historian, and author. Hurstfield taught history at the University of London for more than thirty years. He then became a senior research associate at Huntington Library in California. Specializing in the Elizabethan period, Hurstfield wrote several history books, including The Queen's Wards: Wardship and Marriage Under Elizabeth I, Elizabeth I and the Unity of England, and Freedom, Corruption, and Government in Elizabethan England. Obituaries and other sources: London Times, December 1, 1980; AB Bookman's Weekly, January 19, 1981.

* * *

HUTCHCROFT, Vera 1923-
(Vernon Richter)

PERSONAL: Born December 11, 1923, in Rosalia, Wash.; daughter of Ben F. (a farmer) and Laura (Zimmerman) Richter; married Norwin C. Hutchcroft (a minister), September 27, 1944; children: Wayne, Ronald, Donnelyn Hutchcroft Ham, Joyce Hutchcroft LeBret, Melonie Hutchcroft Salinas. Education: Attended Northwest Bible Institute (now Northwest College of the Assembly of God), 1943-44. Religion: Assembly of God. Home and office: 817 Empire Way, Seattle, Wash. 98122.

CAREER: Licensed minister of Assembly of God, 1980. Farm worker in Rosalia, Wash., 1940-44, and tack welder at Bremerton Navy Yard, 1942.

WRITINGS: Nature Stories for Children, Baker Book, 1967; Visual Talks for Children's Groups, Standard Publishing, 1972; Object Lesson Programs for Young People, Baker Book, 1973; Object Lessons for Church Groups, Baker Book, 1975; Number Quizzes on the Bible, Baker Book, 1975. Author of church school curriculum material. Contributor of articles and stories to religious magazines, including Child Life, Sunday School Counselor, Storymates, Partners, and under name Vernon Richter, to Brigade Leader.

WORK IN PROGRESS: Nature Devotionals, for children; That Mysterious Door, a novel for children.

SIDELIGHTS: Vera Hutchcroft wrote: "I believe the most important part of 'man' is the spirit. If the spirit is alive and ministered to through God—the only one who can minister in this way—other things will fall into place.

"I have been a teacher of children from my early teens, in Sunday school, children's church, youth groups, and kids' crusades. My concern for children has motivated me to

teach children through stories and in other interesting ways, so they will live a happier life here and be ready for the hereafter. Since becoming a licensed minister and co-pastor, my main avenue of contact and teaching children is through writing.

"My writing has also been an avenue of combat against the theory of evolution. The God that has created such an interesting, unusual, and outstanding world certainly deserves to receive credit and glory.

"As to the future, I think I shall begin including more inspirational articles for adults. When Christ fulfills so many needs in my life, I'd like to pass it on; he's able to do the same for others."

* * *

HUTCHINSON, William K(enneth) 1945-

PERSONAL: Born August 10, 1945, in Cortland, N.Y.; son of Kenneth W. and Fern Elizabeth Hutchinson; married wife, Dianne Carla (a speech clinician), November 25, 1965; children: Bryan William, Jennifer Anne. Education: State University of New York College at Geneseo, B.A., 1967; University of Iowa, M.A., 1969, Ph.D., 1975. Religion: Episcopal. Home: 150 Hilltop Rd., Oxford, Ohio 45056. Office: Miami University, 208 Laws Hall, Oxford, Ohio 45056.

CAREER: Miami University, Oxford, Ohio, assistant professor of economics, 1975—. Visiting scholar in economics at Harvard University, 1980. Researcher for Small Business Administration, 1979; member of board of trustees of United Cerebral Palsy of Butler County (vice-president, 1974-75). Member: American Economic Association, Economic History Association, History of Economics Society, Association for Evolutionary Economics.

WRITINGS: History of Economic Analysis, Gale, 1976; American Economic History, Gale, 1980. Contributor to economic journals.

WORK IN PROGRESS: A book on money and banking, with J. D. Ferguson, publication by Wadsworth expected in 1982; research on nineteenth-century interregional trade patterns in the United States.

SIDELIGHTS: Hutchinson wrote: "I have a desire to read about a variety of topics in addition to economics, but in general I wish to learn as much as I can about people and why they are the way they appear to be. I feel that economics, in one way or the other, has a great deal to do with this." Avocational interests: Jogging.

* * *

HUTTON, Harold 1912-

PERSONAL: Born May 12, 1912, near Mariaville, Neb.; son of Fred (a rancher) and Ethel (La Rue) Hutton; married Lucille Harman, June 30, 1933. Education: Attended high school in Rock County, Neb. Home address: R.R.1, Bassett, Neb. 68714.

CAREER: Ranch hand in Rock County, Neb., 1930-40; heavy equipment operator and mechanic in Washington, 1940-50; rancher in Rock County, 1950—.

WRITINGS: Doc Middleton (nonfiction), Swallow Press, 1974; Vigilante Days (nonfiction), Swallow Press, 1978.

WORK IN PROGRESS: History and Genealogy of the Hutton Family, publication expected in 1982; another book on the early Niobrara Valley country.

SIDELIGHTS: Hutton commented to CA: "My books cover topics never before written about; I thought someone should do it. They were worthy subjects. I had no training, and had to develop techniques as I progressed. It was twenty years from the time I commenced research until I had a book in print.

"As to why I have embarked upon this writing career, I can say only that there is a large area of north central Nebraska which had been overlooked by writers. We had these subjects which I thought deserved being written up."

*   *   *

HYMAN, Alan   1910-

PERSONAL: Born January 15, 1910, in London, England; son of Aubrey (a stockbroker) and Florence (Freeman) Hyman; married Noreen Gypson, April 4, 1942; children: Nicholas, Anthony, Timothy, Miranda Hyman Miller. *Education:* Attended language school near Fontainbleau, France. *Politics:* Conservative. *Religion:* Jewish. *Home:* 51 Cadogan Gardens, London S.W.3, England. *Agent:* Bolt & Watson Ltd., 8-12 Old Queen St., Storey's Gate, London SW1H 9HP, England.

CAREER: Daily Sketch, London, England, reporter and sub-editor, 1929-31; Gaumont-British Studios, London, production assistant and film writer, 1931-35; Herbert-Wilcox Productions, Elstree, England, film writer, 1935-37; G. S. Productions (now Rank), Pinewood, England, film writer, 1938-39; writer, 1939-41 and 1946-53; Shell Petroleum, London, producer of films and filmstrips, 1953-61; writer, 1961—. Member of Chelsea Conservative Ward Committee, 1962-70. Guest on radio programs. *Military service:* Royal Navy, script writer in Film Unit, 1941-46. *Member:* Writers Guild of Great Britain (member of council, 1954-58), Society of Authors, Cinema and Television Veterans, British Film Institute.

WRITINGS: The Rise and Fall of Horatio Bottomley (biography), Cassell, 1972; *The Gaiety Years* (biography), Cassell & Collier, 1975; *Sullivan and His Satellites* (biography), Chappell, 1978.

Screenplays: "Sunshine Susie," Oaumont, 1932; "Falling in Love," Vogue-Pathe, 1934; "The Three Maxims," Herbert Wilcox Productions, 1936; "Victoria the Great," Herbert Wilcox Productions, 1937; (co-author) "The Arsenal Stadium Mystery," G & S Films, 1939. Also author of "Funk-Hole Follies" and "Daily Express," both 1939, and co-author of "Dear Murderer."

Stage plays: "The Reluctant Winner," 1979.

Writer for series, "Pioneers of Jazz," on BBC-Radio, 1940, and "Spotlight on a Tunesmith," on BBC-Radio, 1940-41. Reporter and sub-editor for *Sunday Graphic,* 1929-31. General editor of "Chappell's Operetta Series," Chappell, 1977-78.

WORK IN PROGRESS: Education for Sons of Gentlemen; Remember Me to Wardour Street, completion expected in 1981; a television adaptation of work by Trollope.

SIDELIGHTS: Hyman wrote: "The fact that I had learned to type got me my first job on a Sunday newspaper. The fact

that British films almost collapsed soon after World War II led me to take a job with Shell Petroleum and gave me a useful insight into the workings of a major international company. I am now concentrating on writing books, although it is not bringing me a fortune."

BIOGRAPHICAL/CRITICAL SOURCES: West Sussex Gazette, May 3, 1979.

*   *   *

HYMAN, Sidney   1917-

PERSONAL: Born July 30, 1917, in Benton Harbor, Mich.; son of Schumm David (a rabbi) and Esther Rachel Hyman; married Fredda Herzmark (a ballet teacher), August 5, 1960; children: David, Joshua. *Education:* University of Chicago, B.A., 1936, M.A., 1938. *Politics:* Democrat. *Religion:* Jewish. *Home:* 4900 South Kimbark Ave., Chicago, Ill. 60615. *Office:* University of Illinois at Chicago Circle, Chicago, Ill. 60680.

CAREER: U.S. Senate, Washington, D.C., assistant to Senator Paul H. Douglas, 1949-53; *Washington Post,* Washington, D.C., assistant to publisher, 1954-59; staff consultant to *Encyclopaedia Britannica,* 1960-65; U.S. Department of State, Washington, D.C., American specialist, 1966; Johns Hopkins University, Bologna Center, Bologna, Italy, professor, 1966-68; senior research fellow at Adlai Stevenson Institute, 1968-70; University of Chicago, Chicago, Ill., professorial lecturer, 1970-72; currently affiliated with University of Illinois at Chicago Circle, Chicago. Member of Illinois Arts Council, 1975-76. European representative of McCall Publications, 1968-70; editorial adviser to International Institute for Educational Planning, of United Nations Educational, Scientific, and Cultural Organization, 1966-68. Commissioner of Illinois Racing Board, 1973-75. *Military service:* U.S. Army, Armored Division, 1942-45. *Member:* American Political Science Association, American Historical Association, American Criminal Justice Association, Quadrangle Club, Arts Club.

WRITINGS: The American President, Harper, 1954; *The Politics of Consensus,* Random House, 1969; *The Lives of William Benton,* University of Chicago Press, 1970; *Youth in Politics,* Basic Books, 1972; *The Aspen Idea,* University of Oklahoma Press, 1975; *Marriner S. Eccles: Public Servant and Private Entrepreneur,* Graduate School of Business, Stanford University, 1976. Special editor of *Annals of the American Academy of Political and Social Science;* contributing editor of *New Republic* and *Bulletin of Atomic Scientists.*

WORK IN PROGRESS: The Politics of Banking; The Foundations of Criminal Justice; The Discretionary Power of the Presidency.

SIDELIGHTS: Hyman commented to *CA:* "My interest in being a professional writer dates from 1945, when I was engaged by Harry Hopkins to assist him in the preparation of the books he had contracted to write. With his death I carried on the research work that culminated in *Roosevelt and Hopkins,* for which the author, Robert L. Sherwood, won the Pulitzer Prize and National Book Award in 1948."

I

IBUKA, Masaru 1908-

PERSONAL: Born April 11, 1908, in Nikko, Japan; son of Tasuku and Sawa (Furuta) Ibuka; married Sekiko Maeda, December 20, 1936 (marriage ended); married Yoshiko Kurosawa, August 31, 1966; children: (first marriage) Shizuko, Taeko, Makoto. *Education:* Waseda University, B.S., 1933. *Religion:* Protestant. *Home:* 7-1-702 Mita 2-chome, Minato-ku, Tokyo, Japan. *Office:* Sony Corp., 7-35 Kitashinagawa 6-chome, Shinagawa-ku, Tokyo, Japan.

CAREER: Photo-Chemical Laboratory Ltd., research engineer, 1933-37; Japan Optico-Acoustical Engineering Co., Ltd., chief of radio section, 1937-40; Japan Measuring Instruments Co., Ltd., managing director and chief engineer, 1940-45; Tokyo Telecommunication Laboratory, Tokyo, Japan, founder, 1946, company name changed to Tokyo Telecommunication Engineering Co., Ltd., senior managing director, 1946-50, president, 1950-58, company name changed to Sony Corp., president, 1958-71, chairman, 1971-76, honorary chairman. President of Japan Institute of Invention and Innovation; director of National Welfare Foundation for Handicapped Children; chairman of executive committee of Japan Committee for Economic Development and of board of directors of Sony Foundation of Science Education. Member of Japanese panel of U.S.-Japan Conference on Cultural and Educational Interchange; member of liaison committee of UNESCO.

MEMBER: Electronics Industries Association of Japan (executive director), Invention Association of Japan (president), Japan Electronic Industry Development Association (member of board of directors), National Academy of Engineering (foreign associate), Royal Swedish Academy of Engineering Science (foreign member), National Association for the Mentally Handicapped (director), Japan Audio Society (president), Institute of Television Engineers (fellow), Institute of Electrical and Electronic Engineers (fellow), Early Development Association, Talent Education Research Association. *Awards, honors:* Award from Director-General of Science and Technology, 1959, for conducting research in the tunnel diode and other new technology; medal of honor with blue ribbon from the emperor of Japan, 1960, for work in the development of the electronics industry; Prime Minister's Award, 1962, for contributions to exports; distinguished contribution award from Institute of Telecommunication Engineers, 1964, for contributions to the progress of electronics; Twenty-First Mainichi Industrial Technology Award, 1969; founders medal from Institute of Electrical and Electronic Engineers, 1972; Gold Mercury Award from Italy, 1973, for contributions to progress in electronics, science, and technology; Niwa-Takayanagi Award from Institute of Television Engineers of Japan, 1973, for the development of unique color television technology; D.Sc. from Plano University, 1974; honorary doctor of engineering from Sophia University, 1976; NHK Award, 1977, for the development of tape recording and television technology; decorated with First Class Order of the Sacred Treasure by emperor of Japan, 1978; honorary doctor of science from Waseda University, 1979.

WRITINGS—In English translation: *Yochien dewa Ososugiru,* Gomo Shobo, 1971, translation published as *Kindergarten Is Too Late!,* Simon & Schuster, 1977.

In Japanese: *Kikai ga Sensei ni Katta* (title means "A Machine Won Against the Teacher"), Shoden-sha, 1976; *Zerosai kara no Hahaoya Sakusen* (title means "Tactics for Mothers With Babies From Age Zero"), Goma Shobo, 1978. Also author of *Ibuka Kajinosuke to sono jidai,* 1969, *Watakushi no yoji kaihatsu ron,* 1970, *Oya no sekinin,* 1976, and *Oya no yorokobi,* 1976.

SIDELIGHTS: As president and chairman of the Sony Corp., Ibuka became a pioneer in the field of electronics. He directed the development and production of the first tape recorder to appear in Japan in 1950 and five years later, did the same for the transistor radio. The development of various types of semiconductor devices under his leadership accelerated the miniaturization of electronic components such as resistors, capacitors, loud-speakers, and transformers. In addition, Ibuka is responsible for managing the development and production of numerous inventions, including the all-transistor television receiver, the transistorized videotape recorder, the home videotape recorder, the U-matic videocassette system, the Betamax videocassette system, and the video projection systems. The Trinitron color television receiver system was also created under his guidance. These innovations enabled Ibuka to expand the Sony Corp. into a multi-billion-dollar concern, with manufacturing and marketing complexes all over the world.

BIOGRAPHICAL/CRITICAL SOURCES: Newsweek, June 13, 1966; *New York Times,* September 10, 1967.

INGRAM, Anne (Whitten) Bower 1937-

PERSONAL: Born October 18, 1937, in Manilla, Australia; daughter of John (a watchmaker and jeweler) and Mary (a bookseller; maiden name, Rowland) Bower; married Clark Morris Ingram, March 30, 1964; children: Nicholas Morris Bower. *Education:* Attended girls' school in Brisbane, Australia. *Office:* William Collins (Australia), 55 Clarence St., Sydney, New South Wales 2000, Australia; and John Ferguson Publisher, Ltd., History House, 133 Macquarie St., Sydney, Australia.

CAREER: Thomsons Bookstore, Brisbane, Australia, bookseller, 1953-58; Times Bookshop, London, England, bookseller, 1959; Thomsons Bookstore, bookseller, 1960-64; Children's Book Centre, London, bookseller, 1964-65; Thomsons Bookstore, bookseller, 1966-69; Wentworth Books, Sydney, Australia, editor, 1969-71; William Collins (Australia), Sydney, children's book editor, 1971-80, consulting editor on children's books, 1980—. Free-lance editor of children's books, 1980—. Member of literature board, Australian Council for the Arts. *Member:* Children's Book Council of Australia.

WRITINGS: It's Reading Time: Books for the Under Fives, Hodder & Stoughton, 1972; (editor) *Shudders and Shakes: Ghostly Tales From Australia,* Collins, 1972; (editor) *Too True: Australian Tall Tales,* Collins, 1974. Contributor to newspapers and journals. Editor of *Reading Time,* 1970-78.

WORK IN PROGRESS: Cockatoo Pie, a children's book of humor, expected in 1982; *The Min-Min;* two fantasy books.

SIDELIGHTS: Ingram told *CA:* "I'm an idealist and believe in introducing a tolerance of race, color, creed, and sex to children. I have been responsible in my role as a children's book editor for the growth and development of the full color picture book in Australia." *Avocational interests:* Reading, theatre, music, art, swimming, boating, gardening, camping, bush walking.

*   *   *

INNES, Jean
See SAUNDERS, Jean

*   *   *

IRWIN, Inez Haynes 1873-1970

PERSONAL: Born March 2, 1873, in Rio de Janeiro, Brazil; died September 25, 1970; daughter of Gideon and Emma Jane (Hopkins) Haynes; married Rufus Hamilton Gillmore, August 30, 1897 (marriage ended); married Will Irwin (a writer), February 1, 1916 (died, 1948). *Education:* Attended Radcliffe College, 1897-1900. *Residence:* New York, N.Y.; and Scituate, Mass. (summer).

CAREER: Writer. Correspondent for several magazines in France, England, and Italy, 1916-18. Member of American committee of Prix Femina, 1931-33; chairman of board of directors of Directors World Centre for Women's Archives, 1936-38. *Member:* Authors League of America (vice-president, 1930-31; president, 1931-33), National Collegiate Equal Suffrage League (co-founder), National Advisory Council of National Women's Part, P.E.N. (president of New York chapter, 1941-44), Authors Guild (president, 1925-27), Cosmopolitan, Heterodoxy, Query. *Awards, honors:* O. Henry Memorial Prize, 1924, for short story.

WRITINGS: June Jeopardy, Huebsch, 1908; *Phoebe and Ernest,* Holt, 1910; *Janey,* Holt, 1911; *Phoebe, Ernest, and Cupid,* Holt, 1912; *Angel Island,* Holt, 1914, reprinted, Arno, 1978; *The Ollivant Orphans,* Holt, 1915; *The Califor-*niacs, A. M. Robertson, 1916; *The Lady of Kingdoms,* Doran, 1917; *The Happy Years,* Holt, 1919; *The Native Son,* A. M. Robertson, 1919; *Out of the Air,* Harcourt, 1921; *The Story of the Woman's Party,* Harcourt, 1921, published as *Up Hill With Banners Flying,* Traversity Press, 1964, original edition reprinted, Kraus Reprint, 1971; *Gertrude Haviland's Divorce,* Harper, 1925; *Gideon,* Harper, 1927; *P.D.F.R.: A New Novel,* Harper, 1928.

Family Circle, Bobbs-Merrill, 1931; *Youth Must Laugh,* Bobbs-Merrill, 1932; *Angels and Amazons: A Hundred Years of American Women,* Doubleday, 1933, reprinted, Arno, 1974; *Strange Harvest,* Bobbs-Merrill, 1934; *Murder Masquerade,* H. Smith & R. Haas, 1935; (self-illustrated) *Little Miss Redhead,* Lothrop, 1936; *The Poison Cross Mystery,* H. Smith & R. Haas, 1936; *Good Manners for Girls,* Appleton-Century, 1937; *A Body Rolled Downstairs,* Random House, 1938; *Many Murders,* Random House, 1941; (self-illustrated) *Peter and Cynthia,* Lothrop, 1941; *The Women Swore Revenge,* Random House, 1946; *Adventures of Yesterday* (autobiography), General Microfilm, 1973.

"Maida" series; all published by Grosset, except as noted: *Maida's Little Shop,* Huebsch, 1910; *... House,* 1921; *... School,* Viking, 1926; *... Island,* 1939; *... Camp,* 1940; *... Village,* 1942; *... Houseboat,* 1943; *... Theater,* 1946; *... Cabins,* 1947; *... Zoo,* 1949; *... Lighthouse,* 1951; *... Hospital,* 1952; *... Farm,* 1953; *... House Party,* 1954; *... Treasure Hunt,* 1955.

Contributor of articles and stories to periodicals including *Atlantic Monthly, Cosmopolitan, McClure's, Harper's Bazaar, Collier's, Ladies' Home Journal, Woman's Home Companion.*

SIDELIGHTS: Inez Irwin was an ardent supporter of women's suffrage and co-founded the National Collegiate Equal Suffrage League. She was also a member of the National Advisory Council of the National Women's party. Irwin's book, *The Story of the Women's Party,* is an account of the history and activities of this political organization.

The author expressed her views on feminism in her writing. At a time when such subjects were generally considered taboo, Irwin confronted the issues of divorce, single-parenthood, unwed motherhood, and women in the work force. Her first novel, *Lady of Kingdoms,* centers around two young women who are the victims of a repressive small-town society. Seeking to change their lives, the women move to New York where one eventually marries and the other becomes an unwed mother. Gertrude, in *Gertrude Haviland's Divorce,* must face life without the security of marriage and ultimately emerges triumphant. *Angels and Amazons* is Irwin's nonfiction account of the lives and contributions of several American women.

For young people, Irwin wrote the popular "Phoebe and Ernest" series that was originally serialized by *American Magazine.* The story of this "typical" high-school couple, who eventually marry, was condensed in the books *Phoebe and Ernest* and *Phoebe, Ernest, and Cupid.* Irwin's "Maida" series was written for younger children and centers around Maida and her latest "little" possession.

Irwin also wrote mystery fiction including *Murder Masquerade* and *A Body Rolled Downstairs.* In addition to her other works of nonfiction, she wrote *The Californiacs*—a travel book—and an etiquette book for girls.

OBITUARIES: New York Times, October 1, 1970; *AB Bookman's Weekly,* October 26, 1970.*

ISKANDER, Fazil 1929-

PERSONAL: Born March 6, 1929, in Suhumi, U.S.S.R.; son of Abdul and Zely (Mishelia) Iskander; married Antonina Hlebnikova (an economist and editor), August 18, 1960; children: Marina. *Education:* Attended Literature Institution, 1948-54. *Home:* Krasnoarmejskaja h. 23, f. 104, Moscow, U.S.S.R. 125-319. *Agent:* Carl Proffer, 2901 Heatherway, Ann Arbor, Mich. 48104.

CAREER: Writer and journalist in Brjansk, Suhumi, and Moscow, U.S.S.R. *Member:* Union of Soviet Writers.

WRITINGS—In English translation: *Forbidden Fruit and Other Stories,* translated by Robert Daglish, Progress Publishers, 1972; *The Goatibex Constellation,* translated by Helen Burlingame, *Sozvezdie koxlotura,* Ardis, 1975; *Sandro iz Chegema,* Sovpis, 1974, translation published as *Sandro iz Chegema: Sandro From Chegem,* Ardis, 1979.

Other writings; poetry: *Gornii tropi,* Abgiz, 1956; *Dobrota zeml,* Abgiz, 1958; *Deti Chernomoria,* Abgiz, 1960; *Zeljoni dogd,* Sov. pisatel, 1961; *Molodost moria,* Molodaia gvardiia, 1964; *Letnii les,* Sov. pisatel, 1969.

Prose: Aervojedelo, Detgiz, 1965; *Trinadtsatyi podvig Gerakla,* Sovetskaia Rossiia, 1966; *Zapretnyi plod,* Molodaia gvardiia, 1966; *Vremia schastilivykh nakhodok,* Molodaia gvardiia, 1969; *Derevo detstva* (also see below), Sov. pisatel, 1970; *Pod sen iu gretskogo orekha: Povesti* (contains "Den' i noch' Chika," "Morskoi Skorpion," and "Derevo detstva"), Sov. pisatel, 1970. Also author of *Bogatyi Portnoi i Drugie* (title means "The Rich Tailor and Others").

SIDELIGHTS: Iskander told *CA:* "I think our world is in a heavy depression. My books are an attempt to break this depression and excite a vital force in my readers."

*   *   *

ISOGAI, Hiroshi 1940-
(Kanzein Ko)

PERSONAL: Born February 25, 1940, in Hiroshima, Japan; son of Isamu and Shigeko Isogai; married Yasuko Kato, March 31, 1975; children: Shirohi. *Education:* Sophia University, B.A., 1967; also attended University of Madrid. *Home:* 506 Shuwa-Seinan Residence, 4-18-3 Minamiaoyama Minato-ku, Tokyo, Japan. *Office:* Group Pam, 606 Shuwa-Seinan Residence, 4-18-3 Minamiaoyama Minato-ku, Tokyo, Japan.

CAREER: Group Pam (publishing company), Tokyo, Japan, chief director and producer, 1965—. Art director for Asahi Camera. Illustrator, under pseudonym Kanzein Ko. *Member:* Japan Balloon Club (president), Tokyo Designers Space Association, Sophia University Alumni Explorers Society (president).

WRITINGS: (With Shunjiro Marsushima) *Marketplaces of the World,* Kodansha, 1972; (photographer) Arthur S. Harris, *New York,* Kodansha, 1973; (photographer) Harris, *Boston,* Kodansha, 1973.

In Japanese: *Yoroppa o Hitchiru* (title means "Hitchhiking Through Europe"), Asahishinbunsha, 1963; *Yama no Otoko Shikkaku Monogatari* (title means "Story of a Mountain Climber Who Failed"), Hobundo, 1963; (with Matsushima; and photographer) *Meruhen no tabi* (title means "Fairy-Tale Journey"), Asahishinbunsha, 1971; (with Matsushima; and photographer) *Tansai bo-teki Gendai Tanken-ron* (title means "Contemporary Exploration as Viewed With a One-Track Mind"), Jiyu-Kokuminsha, 1971; (editor and photographer) *Subarashiki chikyu* (title means "This Wonderful World"), Yamatokeikokusha, 1974; (with Matsushima; and photograher) *Fusengaleu Nyuman* (title means "A Guide to Balloon"), Heibonsha, 1975; (photographer) Torahiko Tamiya, *Nihonsanka* (title means "Nippon Seen From the Air"), Yamatokeikokusha, 1979; (illustrator) Matsushima, *Minna de Tsukini ikumaeni* (title means "Before We Go to the Moon"), Yamatokeikokusha, 1980.

Contributor of articles and photographs to magazines.

WORK IN PROGRESS: A sequel to *Nippon Seen From the Air* entitled *The World Seen From the Air.*

SIDELIGHTS: Isogai told *CA:* "During my youth, I lived as a vagabond traveling all around the world. When I was in the university, I started to hitchhike through more than a hundred countries and I continued to do so until the end of my twenties. I was a hippie and visited Greenwich Village in New York City, Schwaben in Munich, Germany, and the Rue Huchette in Paris, France. I met a lot of young artists from America and Europe and felt the roundness of the earth inside myself. As everyone else, I learned that the earth is round in my school textbooks, but I wanted to feel it by actually using my feet. As a result, any language is useful to express myself. Some of my writings are published in foreign languages, but most of them are in Japanese, simply because I usually speak and write Japanese. But basically I have the round earth inside myself when I write, take pictures, and illustrate to express what all the people on the earth understand. So, it really doesn't matter whether I use Japanese or any other foreign language.

"I do not limit the opportunities to express myself, for the writer should express himself in every situation. In this sense I like Ernest Hemingway, who lived and wrote with his body. I would not say I respect him, but I do like him. I like his life and feel sympathy toward him. I'm proud of myself for living in the same way as a writer.

"Now, I hear the footsteps of the earth moving toward ruin. Many people have to move against this ruin in many ways. Hearing these footsteps, I feel that one of the writer's duties is to make people hear these footsteps so as to make the time of ruin come later or not at all. For this I have my paper and pen."

*   *   *

ITERSON, S(iny) R(ose) Van
See VAN ITERSON, S(iny) R(ose)

J

JACKSON, Karl (Dion) 1942-

PERSONAL: Born October 30, 1942, in Salem, Mass.; son of Walter T. and Jeannette (Dion) Jackson; married Virginia Hutton (a teacher), August 8, 1964; children: Colin, Andrea, Katharine. *Education:* Princeton University, B.A., 1965; Massachusetts Institute of Technology, Ph.D., 1971. *Home:* 1586 LeRoy Ave., Berkeley, Calif. 94708. *Office:* Department of Political Science, University of California, Berkeley, Calif. 94720.

CAREER: University of California, Berkeley, assistant professor, 1972-79, associate professor of political science, 1980—. *Member:* American Political Science Association, Association of Asian Studies.

WRITINGS: (Editor with Lucian W. Pye and contributor) *Political Power and Communication in Indonesia,* University of California Press, 1978; *Traditional Authority, Islam, and Rebellion,* University of California Press, 1980; (editor and contributor) *Rendezvous With Death: Democratic Kampuchuea, 1975-1979,* University of California Press, 1981.

WORK IN PROGRESS: "A comparison of elite perceptions and the role of substantive information in foreign policy decision-making in Thailand and the United States."

SIDELIGHTS: Jackson told *CA:* "I spent ten months in Thailand during 1977-78 conducting a research project entitled 'U.S.-Southeast Asian Relations After the Vietnam War.' This involved conducting in-depth interviews with a random sample of the Thai foreign policy elite. During the summer and fall of 1978 a comparable sample was drawn from the American foreign policy elite in Washington, D.C.

"*Rendezvous With Death* is a symposium of original essays on the economic, social, and political life of Democratic Kampachea (1975-79). Emphasis is on a) the day-to-day functioning of economic and social life; b) the political function of the terror; c) the ideology of the Kmer Rouge; and d) the Vietnam-Cambodia War."

*   *   *

JACOB, Francois 1920-

PERSONAL: Born June 17, 1920, in Nancy, France; married Lysiane Bloch (a pianist), November 27, 1947; children: Pierre, Laurent, Odile, Henri. *Education:* Lycee Carnot, Docteur en Medicine, 1947, Doctor es Sciences, 1954. *Of-*fice: Institut Pasteur, 25 rue du Dr. Roux, Paris 75015, France.

CAREER: Institut Pasteur, Paris, France, laboratory director, 1956-60, head of Department of Cell Genetics, 1960—; College de France, Paris, professor of cell genetics, 1964—. *Military service:* Free French Forces, 1940-45. *Member:* National Academy of Sciences, American Academy of Arts and Sciences, American Philosophical Society, Royal Society (London), Royal Academy of Medicine (Belgium), French Academy of Sciences, Danish Royal Academy of Arts and Sciences (foreign member). *Awards, honors:* Nobel Prize for medicine, 1965.

WRITINGS: Les Bacteries lysogenes et la notion de provirus, Masson, 1954; (with Elie L. Wollman) *La Sexualite des bacteries,* Masson, 1959, translation published as *Sexuality and the Genetics of Bacteria,* Academic Press, 1961; (with Wollman) *Viruses and Genes,* Freeman, 1961; *La Logique du vivant: Une Histoire de l'heredite,* Gallimard, 1970, translation by Betty E. Spillman published as *The Logic of Life: A History of Heredity,* Pantheon, 1974 (published in England as *The Logic of Living Systems,* Allen Lane, 1974).

*   *   *

JACOBS, Jill
See BHARTI, Ma Satya

*   *   *

JAGENDORF, Moritz (Adolf) 1888-1981

OBITUARY NOTICE—See index for *CA* sketch: Born August 24, 1888, in Czernowitz, Austria; died after a brief illness, January 8, 1981, in Ithaca, N.Y. Folklorist, children's playwright, dentist, editor, and author. Jagendorf worked as a dentist in New York City for forty years while he pursued his interest in the folklore of America, Europe, and the Orient. He transformed many folktales into plays and stories for children. Jagendorf also founded the Free Theatre in 1914 and served as director of the Children's Playhouse. He was editor of *French Folklore* magazine and wrote numerous books on folklore, including *Upstate, Downstate: Folk Stories of the Middle Atlantic States; The Priceless Cats, and Other Italian Folk Stories; The Gypsies' Fiddle and Other Gypsy Tales; Stories and Lore of the Zodiac;* and most recently *The Magic Boat,* a collection of Chinese folk stories. Obituaries and other sources: *New York Times,* January 13, 1981; *Publishers Weekly,* January 30, 1981.

JAMES, Kristin
   See CAMP, Candace P(auline)

*   *   *

JAMES, Naomi 1949-

PERSONAL: Born March 2, 1949, in Gisborne, New Zealand; daughter of Charles Robert (a farmer) and Joan (a farmer; maiden name, Doherty) Power; married Rob James (a yachtsman and author), May 29, 1976. *Education:* Attended girls' high school in Rotorua, New Zealand. *Home:* Tramore, R.D.1, Ngongotaha, Rotorua, New Zealand.

CAREER: Worked as hair stylist, 1965-71, and as language teacher, 1972-75; lecturer and writer, 1976—. *Member:* Royal Dart Yacht Club, Royal Lymington Yacht Club, Royal Western Yacht Club, Royal Southern Yacht Club. *Awards, honors:* Dame commander of Order of the British Empire, 1979; named New Zealand yachtsman of the year, 1979; Chichester Trophy, 1979.

WRITINGS: Woman Alone, Daily Express (London), 1978; *Alone Around the World,* Coward, 1979 (published in England as *At One With the Sea,* Hutchinson, 1979); *At Sea on Land: Homecoming 78 to Ostar 80,* Hutchinson, 1981. Contributor to magazines.

WORK IN PROGRESS: Freedom at Sea, "about the building and progress of the revolutionary yacht *Freedom 75,*" with husband Rob James.

SIDELIGHTS: Naomi James's second book is based on her own experiences in a fifty-three-foot sailing yacht while sailing singlehanded around the world in 1977-78. Her third book describes her participation in a 1980 single-handed transatlantic race and the events leading up to that race." *Avocational interests:* Travel, boardsailing, skiing, antiques.

*   *   *

JARVIS, E. K.
   See WILLIAMS, Robert Moore

*   *   *

JASPERSOHN, William 1947-

PERSONAL: Born October 4, 1947, in New Haven, Conn.; son of Paul (a manufacturing engineer) and Dorothy (a teacher; maiden name, Daley) Jaspersohn; married Pamela Cunningham (a potter), September 13, 1969; children: Andrew Godfrey. *Education:* Dartmouth College, A.B., 1969. *Agent:* Scott Meredith Literary Agency, Inc., 845 Third Ave., New York, N.Y. 10022.

CAREER: Waterville High School, Waterville, Maine, teacher of English, 1969-71; free-lance writer, 1971—. *Awards, honors:* Fanfare Honor Award from *Boston Globe* and *Horn Book,* 1980, for *How the Forest Grew.*

WRITINGS—Children's books: A Day in the Life of a Veterinarian, Little, Brown, 1978; *How the Forest Grew,* Greenwillow Books, 1980; *The Ballpark: One Day Behind the Scenes at a Major League Game,* Little, Brown, 1980; *A Day in the Life of a Television News Reporter,* Little, Brown, 1981; *A Day in the Life of a Marine Biologist,* Little, Brown, 1982. Contributor to magazines, including *Harper's Bookletter* and *Maine Times,* and newspapers.

WORK IN PROGRESS: The Golden Door, a novel.

SIDELIGHTS: Jaspersohn commented: "My ultimate motivation for writing is self-understanding. The books I write for children are the ones I wish had been there when I was a child. I have a keen and abiding interest in the movies, and

regard my photograph books for children as documentary films in book form."

BIOGRAPHICAL/CRITICAL SOURCES: Burlington Free Press, April 23, 1980; *New Haven Register,* June 10, 1980; *Washington World Weekly,* June 11, 1980.

*   *   *

JELINEK, Estelle C.   1935-
   (Estelle Fine)

PERSONAL: Born January 24, 1935, in Philadelphia, Pa.; daughter of Samuel (a tailor) and Sarah (a tailor) Cohen. *Education:* University of Pennsylvania, B.S., 1956, M.A., 1959, doctoral study, 1959-61; State University of New York at Buffalo, Ph.D., 1977. *Home:* 1301 Bonita Ave., Berkeley, Calif. 94709. *Agent:* Amy Rennert, c/o Michael Larsen/ Elizabeth Pomada, 114 Beaumont Ave., San Francisco, Calif. 94118.

CAREER: Holiday, Philadelphia, Pa., editor, 1961-63; Chilton Book Co., Philadelphia, editor, 1963-64; Random House, Inc., New York City, editor, 1965-67; *Southern Courier,* Jackson, Miss., reporter (under name Estelle Fine) in Jackson and Selma, Ala., 1967-68; *Dock of the Bay,* San Francisco, Calif., reporter, 1969; W. H. Freeman & Co., San Francisco, editor, 1970-72; free-lance writer and editor, 1972—. Instructor in English at Chabot College, 1972-75, 1977-79, and San Francisco State University, 1975, 1977-79. *Member:* Modern Language Association of America (Women's Caucus), National Women's Studies Association, Women's International League for Peace and Freedom, Agenda, Americans for Progressive Israel, Friends of Domestic Animals, Breira. *Awards, honors:* National Endowment for the Humanities fellowship, 1975-76.

WRITINGS: (Contributor) Cheryl Brown and Karen Olson, editors, *Feminist Criticism: Essays on Theory, Poetry, and Prose,* Scarecrow, 1978; (editor, author of introduction, and contributor) *Women's Autobiography: Essays in Criticism,* Indiana University Press, 1980. Contributor to *College English* and of book reviews to *Oakland Tribune.*

WORK IN PROGRESS: The Josephine Herbst Reader.

SIDELIGHTS: Jelinek told *CA:* "I consider myself a free-lance writer and editor on women's literature. I am just beginning to develop this phase of my life, after vacillating between college teaching and in-house editing. I left college teaching of my own choice since I find a free-lancer's life more flexible and liberating than I found academia."

*   *   *

JENKIN, A(lfred) K(enneth) Hamilton 1900-1980

OBITUARY NOTICE: Born in 1900 in Redruth, England; died August 20, 1980. Author, Jenkins grew up in England's mining country, where his family had lived for many generations. His books reflect his lifelong interest in mines and miners, beginning with *The Cornish Miner* in 1927. Among his several other books are *Cornwall and the Cornish, The Story of Cornwall, Cornwall and Its People, Mines and Miners of Cornwall,* and *Mines of Devon.* Obituaries and other sources: *London Times,* September 17, 1980.

*   *   *

JENNINGS, Lane (Eaton) 1944-

PERSONAL: Born September 4, 1944, in Wilmington, Del.; son of Robert Kimmel (a scientist) and Edith (Eaton) Jennings; married Margaret Stone (an editor and writer), September 12, 1970. *Education:* Williams College, B.A. (cum laude), 1966; Harvard University, M.A., 1968, Ph.D., 1970. *Politics:* Independent. *Religion:* Quaker. *Home:* 6373 Barefoot Boy, Columbia, Md. 21045. *Office:* World Future Society, 4916 St. Elmo Ave., Bethesda, Md. 20014.

CAREER: U.S. Department of State, Washington, D.C., escort-interpreter, 1970-71; National Savings and Loan League (trade association), Washington, D.C., writer, editor, and assistant director in international department, 1971-76; World Future Society, Bethesda, Md., research director, 1976—. Volunteer campaign worker and speaker for John Anderson, 1980. *Member:* Modern Language Association, World Future Studies Federation, U.S. Chess Federation, Writer's Center (Glen Echo, Md.), Peter Warlock Society. *Awards, honors:* Fulbright scholar at University of Munich, 1966-67; Harvard University traveling fellow, 1969.

WRITINGS: (Editor with Sally Cornish) *Education and the Future,* World Future Society, 1980; (contributor) Frank Feather, editor, *Through the '80s,* World Future Society, 1980. Book reviewer for *Futurist,* 1976—. Assistant editor of *Communications Tomorrow* and *Habitats Tomorrow,* 1976-78, and *Future Survey,* 1979—; editor of *World Future Society Bulletin,* 1977—. Contributor of articles, poems, and translations to magazines, including *Bitterroot, Smith, Nebula, Futurist, Bogg, Visions,* and *Little Patuxent Review.*

WORK IN PROGRESS: Satisfaction, a novel; *Werewords,* a book of poems; gathering material for an anthology of poems concerning space life and exploration, tentatively entitled *Prospects;* research on human interaction with computers and on the future of communication.

SIDELIGHTS: Lane Jennings told *CA:* "Growing up an only child, I learned most from adults and books; my family had no television until I was in high school. You might call me a radio child. Music in particular came to me by radio and on records borrowed from school and public libraries.

"I write poems to create effects; prose to convey information; and fiction to play with dreams. The writers whose work I've most often admired are George Bernard Shaw, Bertolt Brecht, Philip Larkin, and Robert Graves.

"What counts, in writing about the future, is not how accurate your predictions may be, but whether you offer your readers one or more persuasive visions they can build on or react to. Beware of believing yourself an authority on anything that hasn't happened yet."

* * *

JOHANSSON, Thomas (Hugo) B(ernard) 1943-

PERSONAL: Born September 10, 1943, in Karlshamn, Sweden; son of Goesta E. (a sales manager) and Anna-Lisa (a secretary; maiden name, Jeppsson) Johansson; married Lena Orrling (a lawyer), April 11, 1968; children: Peter, Staffan. *Education:* Lund Institute of Technology, civilingenjoer, 1968, Ph.D., 1974. *Home:* Tornagaarden, 24012 Torna-Haellestad, Sweden. *Office:* Environmental Studies Program, University of Lund, Gerdagatan 13, 22362 Lund, Sweden.

CAREER: University of Lund, Lund, Sweden, co-founder of joint environmental studies program with Lund Institute of Technology and member of its board of directors and executive committee, 1968-78, research associate, 1973-75, professor of environmental studies, 1975—. Research associate at Florida State University, 1972-73, visiting scientist, 1974; member of Swedish Energy Commission expert group on safety and environment, 1977-78; Swedish Nuclear Power

Inspectorate, member of board of directors, 1977-78 and 1979—, vice-chairman, 1978-79; member of Gorleben International Review, 1978-79; expert for Secretariat for Future Studies, Committee on Natural Resource and Environmental Policy, and Swedish Energy Research and Development Commission; consultant to Princeton University's Center for Energy and Environmental Studies. *Awards, honors:* Australian-European Award from Government of Australia, 1980.

WRITINGS—In English: (With Maans Loennroth and Peter Steen) *Energi och handlingsfrihet,* Secretariat for Future Studies, 1977, translation by Rudy Fiechtoner published as *Energy in Transition,* University of California Press, 1980; (with Steen) *Kaernkraftens radioaktiva avfall: Jufoer Ringhals-3 beslutet,* Ministry of Industry [Sweden], 1978, published as *Radioactive Wastes,* University of California Press, 1981; (with Loennroth and Steen) *Sol eller Uran,* [Sweden], 1978, translation by P. C. Hogg published as *Solar or Nuclear: To Choose an Energy Future,* Pergamon, 1980.

In Swedish: (With Steen) *Sol-Sverige* (title means "Solar Sweden"), Liberfoerleg, 1978; (with Stellan Atterkvist) *Sol-Norge* (title means "Solar Norway"), Universitetsfoerlaget, 1980.

Contributor to books and periodicals.

WORK IN PROGRESS: Energy future studies focused on energy demand.

* * *

JONES, Gareth (Elwyn) 1939-

PERSONAL: Born January 30, 1939, in Abergavenny, Wales; son of Henry Haydn (a minister) and Nellie Muriel (Morgan) Jones; married Katherine Scourse (a university tutor), August 16, 1963; children: Bethan Mari, Matthew Owain. *Education:* University College of Swansea, University of Wales, B.A., 1960, M.A., 1963, Ph.D., 1979; University College, Cardiff, University of Wales, M.Ed., 1972. *Religion:* United Reformed. *Home:* 130 Pennard Dr., Pennard, Gower, West Glamorganshire, Wales. *Office:* Department of Education, University College of Swansea, University of Wales, Hendrefoilan, Swansea, Wales.

CAREER: Second history master at grammar school in Croydon, England, 1963-65; Cardiff College of Education, Cardiff, Wales, lecturer in history, 1965-69; Swansea College of Education, Swansea, Wales, senior lecturer in history, 1969-72; University of Wales, University College of Swansea, Swansea, lecturer in history of education, 1972—. *Member:* Royal Historical Society (fellow), Glamorgan History Society (member of council).

WRITINGS: The Gentry and the Elizabethan State, Christopher Davies, 1977; (editor with Lionel Ward) *New History, Old Problems: Studies in History Teaching,* Faculty of Education, University College of Swansea, University of Wales, 1978. Contributor to education and history journals. Coeditor of *Morgannwg: Journal of Glamorgan History.*

WORK IN PROGRESS: Controls and Conflicts in Welsh Secondary Education, 1889-1944, publication by University of Wales Press expected in 1982.

SIDELIGHTS: Gareth Jones told *CA:* "As a Welshman and a historian I have been singularly fortunate to have spent most of my career teaching in Wales and writing about its history. My first interest was in the history of the Tudor period, and *The Gentry and the Elizabethan State* deals with the politics and government of Wales in the sixteenth century. I found it easy to be dispassionate on this subject; not so with my recent work on twentieth-century Welsh education.

"It is impossible for any Welsh person to be unaffected by the human consequences of, at best, inadequate British government policies as they affected Wales in the depressed twenties and thirties. Paradoxically, depopulation of industrial areas, particularly, greatly increased the percentage of secondary/grammar school attendance and contributed to the idealized picture of Welsh devotion to education. I nearly wrote 'myth,' yet throughout the century the Welsh secondary system has been more egalitarian, more open to talent, than the English. As a result it has helped create and cement class differences in Wales. And that is only one of those paradoxes of Welsh education which consolidate the schizophrenia of being Welsh in Great Britain."

*   *   *

JONES, Joseph L.   1897-1980

OBITUARY NOTICE: Born June 18, 1897, in Moody, Mo.; died December 7, 1980, in Hershey, Pa. Journalist. Among those who helped build the old United Press into United Press International, Joseph Jones was a managerial executive with the news agency for twenty-seven years. Between 1924 and 1937 he was an editor of foreign news, with bureau management experience in London, Lima, Santiago, and Caracas. When Jones became general foreign manager for the United Press in 1937, the agency was serving forty-eight countries. By the time he retired in 1964 as vice-president in charge of international divisions, the UPI had subscribers in 114 countries and territories. Obituaries and other sources: *Who's Who in America,* 39th edition, Marquis, 1976; *Chicago Tribune,* December 9, 1980.

*   *   *

JONES, Kathleen Eve   1944-
(Kathleen Adler)

PERSONAL: Born October 8, 1944, in Cape Town, South Africa; daughter of Hugo (a business manager) and Hilde (Weinstein) Adler; married Patrick Jones (an architect and manager), July 12, 1974; children: Daniel. *Education:* University of the Witwatersrand, B.A. (with first class honors; art history and English literature), 1965, B.A. (with first class honors; art history), 1966; Courtauld Institute of Art, London, M.A., 1969. *Home:* 19 Mountview Rd., London N4 4SS, England.

CAREER: University of Durban-Westville, Durban, South Africa, lecturer in art history, 1969-72; University of Natal, Durban, lecturer in history of architecture and related arts, 1970-76; North Staffordshire Polytechnic, Stoke-on-Trent, England, lecturer in art history and complementary studies, 1977; Middlesex Polytechnic, London, England, lecturer in art history and history of architecture and design, 1978—.

WRITINGS—Under name Kathleen Adler: (Contributor) Andrew Verster, editor, *Some Aspects of the Modern Movement,* Natal College for Advanced Technical Education (South Africa), 1971; (contributor) Frieda Harmsen, Cecily Sash, and Shirley Kossick, editors, *Festschrift in Honour of Professor Martienssen,* A. A. Balkema, 1973; *Camille Pissarro: A Biography,* Batsford, 1978. Contributor to journals, including *Plan.* Art critic for *Sunday Tribune,* Durban, South Africa, 1969-70, *Durban Daily News* and *Natal Witness,* 1974, and *Natal Mercury,* 1975.

WORK IN PROGRESS: Research on mirrors in paintings, especially of the late nineteenth century; research on Pissarro, especially urban paintings of the 1890's.

SIDELIGHTS: Kathleen Jones commented to *CA:* "I am returning to research and writing following an interval after the birth of my son. During the interval I continued teaching, but hope now to be able to extend my interest in late nineteenth-century French and English painting."

*   *   *

JONES, Philip Howard   1937-

PERSONAL: Born April 27, 1937, in Marion, Ind.; son of Thomas Howard and Charline (Shugart) Jones; married Patricia Ann Powell, June 4, 1961; children: Pamela Lynn, Paul Howard. *Education:* Indiana University, B.S., 1959. *Home:* 5014 Westport Rd., Chevy Chase, Md. 20015. *Office:* CBS News, 2020 M St. N.W., Washington, D.C. 20036.

CAREER/WRITINGS: WTHI-TV, Terre Haute, Ind., news director, 1960-61; WCCO-TV, Minneapolis, Minn., political correspondent, 1961-69; Columbia Broadcasting System (CBS) News, Washington, D.C., White House correspondent, 1974-76, Capitol Hill correspondent, 1977—. *Military service:* U.S. Air Force, 1961-62. *Member:* Masons. *Awards, honors:* International News award from Radio-Television News Directors Association, 1965; award, 1966, for Vietnam War reporting; Emmy Award from National Academy of Television Arts and Sciences, 1971, for Indochina air war coverage.

*   *   *

JONES, Sally Roberts   1935-
(Sally Roberts)

PERSONAL: Born November 30, 1935, in London, England; daughter of Iorwerth (a publican) and Joan Edith (a clerical worker; maiden name, Grew) Roberts; married Alwyn Bowen Jones (an industrial engineer), June 2, 1969; children: Huw, Gareth, Owain. *Education:* University College of North Wales, University of Wales, B.A. (with honors), 1957; North-Western Polytechnic, A.L.A., 1964. *Religion:* "Nonconformist." *Home:* 3 Crown St., Port Talbot, West Glamorgan SA13 1BG, Wales.

CAREER: Borough of Havering, London, England, senior assistant at reference library, 1964-67; Borough of Port Talbot, Port Talbot, Wales, reference librarian, 1967-70; writer, 1970—. Publisher of Alun Books, 1977—. Member of Welsh Arts Council children's book panel. *Member:* Yr Academi Gymreig, Cymmrodorion Society, West Wales Association for the Arts, Glamorgan Historical Society, Port Talbot Historical Society. *Awards, honors:* Literature award from Welsh Arts Council, 1970, for *Turning Away;* second prize from *Liverpool Daily Post,* 1979, for play, "A Game of Truth."

WRITINGS: (Under name Sally Roberts) *Turning Away* (poems), Gomer Press, 1969; (under name Sally Roberts) *Romford in the Nineteenth Century,* I. G. Sparks, 1969; (editor) *About Welsh Literature,* Welsh Arts Council, 1970; *Elen and the Goblin* (juvenile), Alun Books, 1977; *The Forgotten Country* (poems), Gomer Press, 1977; (editor) *Books of Welsh Interest: A Bibliography,* Welsh Books Council, 1977; *Allen Raine,* University of Wales Press, 1979; *Women Writers in Wales in the English Language,* English Language Section, Yr Academi Gyreig, 1979; *Welcome to Town: The Story of Pat Talbot's Inns* (history), Alun Books, 1980.

Plays: *Strangers and Brothers* (first broadcast by British Broadcasting Corp., April 4, 1975), Alun Books, 1977; "A Waste of Heroes" (verse play), first broadcast by British Broadcasting Corp., January 20, 1979. Also author of "A Game of Truth" (three-act).

Contributor of stories, poems, and articles to history and Anglo-Welsh literary magazines. Member of editorial committee of Port Talbot Historical Society.

WORK IN PROGRESS: Editing *A Bibliography of Anglo-Welsh Children's Books; The Fair Folk,* a study of Welsh fairy legends; research on Anglo-Welsh literature.

SIDELIGHTS: Sally Jones wrote: "Twenty per cent of the population of Wales speaks the Welsh language; eighty per cent does not, and therefore exists in a limbo neither Welsh nor English. My goal is to give the eighty per cent the opportunity to discover their heritage as Welsh men and women, and hence to have a place and purpose of their own. My interest in Anglo-Welsh writing (writing in English by writers of Welsh origin) is partly curiosity, but mainly a concern for the definition of roots and the healing of past conflicts.

"Alun Books is an attempt to fill gaps, and help other writers to have their work published; also, possibly, one day to provide jobs in an area that needs them badly. As Anglo-Welsh writers, we are unable to draw on official support to anything like the extent that Welsh language writers can; and the Welsh element can cause problems with London publishers. No doubt our position as Anglo-Welsh writers will seem more than a little obscure outside Wales, but it's exciting—rather like the discovery and fight for the independence of American literature though on a much smaller scale.

"I believe that, where possible, a writer should remain in and be part of his or her community, whatever or wherever that may be. One must, of course, remain faithful to one's original inspiration, but to withdraw to some ivory tower in order to do this impoverishes both the community and the writer."

* * *

JOY, Thomas Alfred 1904-

PERSONAL: Born December 30, 1904, in Oxford, England; son of Alfred George and Ann (Carpenter) Joy; married Edith Ellis. *Education:* Attended school in Oxford, England. *Home:* 13 Cole Park Gardens, Twickenham, Middlesex, England. *Office:* Hatchards', Booksellers, 187 Piccadilly, London, England.

CAREER: Oxford University, Oxford, England, junior assistant at Bodleian Library, 1919; J. Thornton & Son (university booksellers), Oxford, indentured apprentice, 1919-25; A. & F. Denny (booksellers), London, England, head of mail orders, 1926; J. Thornton & Son, buyer and cataloger, 1927-35; Harrod's, London, manager of Circulating Library, 1935-45, manager of book department, 1942-46; Army and Navy Stores, London, manager of book department and founder of library, 1946-56, merchandise manager, 1956, deputy managing director, 1956-66; Hatchards', Booksellers, London, managing director, 1965—. Employer's representative of Bookselling and Stationery Trade Wages Council, 1946-79, leader of employers' side, 1957; member of National Chamber of Trade and Wholesale Trades Advisory Committee, both 1946-51, and 1948 Book Trade Committee; member of Arts Council working party on obscene publications, 1968-69, and working party sub-committee on Public Lending Rights, 1970; president of Book Trade Charity of Book Trade Provident Society, 1974—; past deputy chairman of Buyers Benevolent Institution; past committee member of Drapers Cottage Homes.

MEMBER: Royal Society of Arts (fellow), Booksellers Association of Great Britain and Ireland (member of council, 1947-58; national president, 1957-58; chairman of London branch, 1946), Society of Bookmen (honorary life member), Oxford Booksellers and Assistants Association (chairman, 1934-35). *Awards, honors:* Silver Jubilee Medal from Queen Elizabeth II, 1977; member of Royal Victorian Order, 1979.

WRITINGS: The Right Way to Run a Library Business, Elliott, 1949; *Bookselling,* Pitman, 1953; *The Truth About Bookselling,* Pitman, 1964; *Mostly Joy* (autobiography), M. Joseph, 1971; *The Bookselling Business,* Pitman, 1974. Contributor to trade journals.

WORK IN PROGRESS: A textbook on bookselling.

SIDELIGHTS: Joy commented: "Bookselling is an art and I have devoted my life to mastering that art and to encouraging others in it by writing textbooks. It is also a business and to be successful one must be able to combine the two."

Joy's mastery of the art has earned him many honors. He has the distinction of being the nominee on the four Royal Warrants: bookseller to Queen Elizabeth, the Queen Mother, the Duke of Edinburgh, and the Prince of Wales. He was the prime mover for the establishment of the National Book Sale and it was Joy who inaugurated Hatchards' annual authors of the year party, a private function for England's notable celebrities in literature and the arts.

BIOGRAPHICAL/CRITICAL SOURCES: American Bookseller, July, 1980.

* * *

JUDSON, Margaret Atwood 1899-

PERSONAL: Born November 5, 1899, in Winsted, Conn.; daughter of George W. and Minnie (Atwood) Judson. *Education:* Mount Holyoke College, B.A., 1922; Radcliffe College, M.A., 1923, Ph.D., 1933. *Home:* 8 Redcliffe Ave., Highland Park, N.J. 08904.

CAREER: Rutgers University, Douglass College, New Brunswick, N.J., instructor, 1928-33, assistant professor, 1933-42, associate professor, 1942-48, professor of history, 1948-67, professor emeritus, 1967—, chairman of department of history and political science, 1955-63, acting dean, 1966-67. Alice F. Palmer Visiting Professor at University of Michigan, 1959. *Member:* American Historical Association, American Association of University Professors, Royal Historical Society (fellow), Berkshire Historical Conference (president, 1948-50), Phi Beta Kappa. *Awards, honors:* Guggenheim fellowship, 1954-55; LL.D. from Rutgers University, 1968; fellow of Bunting Institute, 1968-69; Litt.D. from Mount Holyoke College, 1972.

WRITINGS: (Contributor) Carl Wittke, editor, *Essays in History and Political Theory in Honor of Charles Howard McIlwain,* Harward University Press, 1936; *The Crisis of the Constitution: An Essay in Constitutional and Political Thought in England, 1603-1645,* Rutgers University Press, 1949, reprinted, Octagon, 1971; *The Political Thought of Sir Henry Vane, the Younger,* University of Pennsylvania Press, 1969; *From Tradition to Political Reality: A Study of the Ideas Set Forth in Support of the Commonwealth Government in England, 1649-1654,* Shoe String, 1980.

WORK IN PROGRESS: "An essay on my professional career as a woman professor and historian before the Women's Liberation Movement."

SIDELIGHTS: Judson told *CA:* "*The Crisis of the Constitution* is my most important book, and I am happy that thirty years after its publication, it is still used in many universities in the United States and England."

JULIUS
   See CURLING, Bryan William Richard

*   *   *

K

KACEW, Romain 1914-1980
(Romain Gary)

OBITUARY NOTICE: Born May 8, 1914, in Vilna, Lithuania (now U.S.S.R.); died December 2, 1980, in Paris, France, of a self-inflicted gunshot wound. Diplomat and writer best known for his novels, including *The Roots of Heaven,* for which he received the Prix Goncourt in 1956. After receiving decorations for his actions during World War II, Gary began converting his wartime experiences into fiction. Among his better-known works from the 1940's are *Education europ'eenne,* which dealt with Polish partisans, and *The Dance of Genghis Cohn,* which concerned a Jewish comedian's experiences in Auschwitz. Gary also wrote short stories, plays, and an autobiography entitled *Promise at Dawn.* In 1963 he married actress Jean Seberg, whom he divorced in 1970. Some journalists have suggested that Gary's suicide may have been a result of depression over Seberg's suicide in 1979. Gary served as French consul general in the United States during the early 1960's. Obituaries and other sources: *Encyclopedia of World Literature in the Twentieth Century,* updated edition, Ungar, 1967; *Twentieth Century Writing: A Reader's Guide to Contemporary Literature,* Transatlantic, 1969; *The Author's and Writer's Who's Who,* 6th edition, Burke's Peerage, 1971; *Cassell's Encyclopaedia of World Literature,* revised edition, Morrow, 1973; *New York Times,* December 3, 1980; *Washington Post,* December 3, 1980; *Time,* December 15, 1980; *Publishers Weekly,* December 19, 1980; *AB Bookman's Weekly,* January 26, 1981.

* * *

KAHLER, Hugh (Torbert) MacNair 1883-1969
(Murgatroyd Elphinstone)

PERSONAL: Born February 25, 1883, in Philadelphia, Pa.; died July 10, 1969; son of Frederick A. and Margaret Torbert (MacNair) Kahler; married Louise Kingsley, October 15, 1907; children: Kingsley (Mrs. F. W. Hubby, III.). *Education:* Princeton University, A.B., 1904. *Residence:* Princeton, N.J.

CAREER: Editor and writer. *Ladies' Home Journal,* fiction editor, 1943-60. *Member:* Nassau Club (president, 1931), Players Club (New York).

WRITINGS: Babel (short stories), Putnam, 1921; *The East Wind and Other Stories,* Putnam, 1923, reprinted, Arno, 1978; (under psendonym Murgatroyd Elphinstone, with Booth Tarkington under pseudonym Cornelius Obenchain Van Loot, and Kenneth Lewis Roberts under pseudonym Milton Kilgallen) *The Collector's Whatnot: A Compendium, Manual, and Syllabus of Information and Advice on All Subjects Appertaining to the Collection of Antiques, Both Ancient and Not So Ancient,* Houghton, 1923, abridged edition, American Life Foundation, 1969; (with Donald Grant Herring) *MacIvor's Folly* (novel), Appleton, 1925; *Father Means Well* (novel), Farrar & Rinehart, 1930; *Hills Were Higher Then* (short stories), Farrar & Rinehart, 1931; *The Big Pink,* Farrar & Rinehart, 1932; *Bright Danger* (novel), Triangle Books, 1941. Contributor of over one hundred stories to periodicals, including *Collier's, American, Saturday Evening Post,* and *Country Gentleman.*

SIDELIGHTS: Kahler's first novel, *MacIvor's Folly,* fared well with reviewers. A mixture of romance, drama, and adventure, the story revolves around a valuable stretch of North Carolina timberland called "MacIvor's Folly," its owner, and a beautiful married woman who befriends him. A *Saturday Review of Literature* critic asserted that the novel is "a very competently done study in the development of constrasting personalities."

The author's next work, *Father Means Well,* deals with the generation gap between a father and his daughter. He wants her to marry an ambitious young businessman, but she remains uninterested. "There is wisdom and a deep understanding of character in this novel," claimed a *Boston Transcript* reviewer. A *New York Times* critic praised it as "an extraordinarily amusing and complicated comedy."

A journey from Florida to California with a friend resulted in another novel. Midway during this intended vacation, Kahler visited his traveling companion's oil wells in the Louisiana-Texas-Arkansas part of the United States. The wells interested the author and he later commented that he "had an absolute rest from writing except for taking about six hundred pages of notes and making rough-outs for two books and maybe half a dozen stories." *Bright Danger,* about oil-well fires, emerged from this activity.

Two of Kahler's short stories have been adapted into motion pictures. "The Six Best Cellars" was released by Paramount in 1920 and "Fools First" was released by First National in 1922.

AVOCATIONAL INTERESTS: Football at Princeton,

grandchildren, Booth Tarkington, Strauss waltzes, Webster's cartoons.

BIOGRAPHICAL/CRITICAL SOURCES: New York Times, March 20, 1921, January 21, 1923, June 14, 1925, July 20, 1930; *New York Tribune,* January 28, 1923; *Literary Digest International Book Review,* March, 1923; *New York World,* March 11, 1923; *Literary Review of the New York Evening Post,* April 14, 1923; *Saturday Review of Literature,* April 18, 1925; *Boston Transcript,* August 13, 1930; *New York Herald Tribune Books,* November 22, 1931; *Saturday Evening Post,* December 28, 1935, April 17, 1937, April 16, 1938, November 15, 1941; *Ladies' Home Journal,* April, 1937, November, 1943.

OBITUARIES: New York Times, July 11, 1969.*

*   *   *

KAHN, Sholom J(acob)   1918-

PERSONAL: Born October 5, 1918, in New York, N.Y.; son of Harry and Sophie (Begun) Kahn; married Chava Gafni, October 11, 1951; children: (previous marriage) David; Tamar, Uri. *Education:* Columbia University, B.A., 1938, M.A., 1939, Ph.D., 1950; Seminary College of Jewish Studies, New York, N.Y., B.H.L., 1950. *Home:* 46 Nayoth St., Jerusalem, Israel. *Office:* Department of American Studies, Hebrew University of Jerusalem, Jerusalem, Israel.

CAREER: Columbia University, New York, N.Y., lecturer in general studies, 1948-50; Brooklyn Polytechnic Institute, Brooklyn, N.Y., instructor in English, 1948-49; Hebrew University of Jerusalem, Jerusalem, Israel, instructor, 1951-57, lecturer, 1957-65, senior lecturer, 1965-72, associate professor of American studies, 1972—, chairman of department, 1973-76. Distinguished visiting professor at San Fernando Valley State College, 1966-67; visiting professor at University of California, Davis, 1973, and Simon Fraser University, 1976-77. *Military service:* U.S. Army Air Forces, 1943-46; became sergeant. *Member:* University Teachers of English (Israel), Israel Association for American Studies (member of executive committee, 1977—), Modern Language Association of America, College English Association, American Philosophical Association, American Society for Aesthetics. *Awards, honors:* Fellow of Rockefeller Foundation, 1957-58.

WRITINGS: Science and Aesthetic Judgment: A Study in Taine's Critical Method, Columbia University Press, 1953; (editor) *A Whole Loaf: Stories From Israel,* Grosset, 1957; (translator with Eisig Silberschlag) *Saul Tschernichowsky: Poet of Revolt,* Cornell University Press, 1968; *Mark Twain's Mysterious Stranger: A Study of the Manuscript Texts,* University of Missouri Press, 1978.

In Hebrew: *Halutsiyut ve-haye ha-sefar* (title means "Pioneering and Frontier Life in American Literature"), Yachdav, 1962. Contributor to scholarly journals. Honorary foreign member of editorial board of *Journal of Aesthetics and Art Criticism.*

WORK IN PROGRESS: Walt Whitman's Poetry; Mark Twain and Vienna, 1896-1900; The Tragedy of Ahab.

BIOGRAPHICAL/CRITICAL SOURCES: American Literature, January, 1979.

*   *   *

KAIRYS, Anatolijus   1914-

PERSONAL: Surname is accented on second syllable; given name is accented on third syllable; born August 28, 1914, in St. Petersburg (now Leningrad), Russia (now U.S.S.R.);

came to the United States in 1947, naturalized citizen, 1953; son of Justinas (a farmer) and Monika (Juodvalkyte) Kairys. *Education:* Attended University of Kaunas, 1938-40; University of Vilnius, M.A., 1942. *Politics:* None. *Home:* 4304 West 55th St., Chicago, Ill. 60632.

CAREER: High school principal and teacher of psychology and logic in Siauliai, Lithuania, 1942-44; high school teacher of psychology and logic in Germany, 1946-47; writer. *Military service:* Lithuanian Army, 1935-36. *Member:* National Writers Club, Lithuanian Writers Association. *Awards, honors:* First prize from Lithuanian Theatre Association (Chicago, Ill.) for satirical comedy, 1964, for *Visciuku ukis;* first prize for *Sviesa, kuri uzsidege* and second prize for "Eldorado," both 1965, both from Lithuanian Scouts of Chicago; second prize from Los Angeles Drama Association, 1970, for "Ku-Ku"; second prize from Lithuanian Regeneration Association, 1971, for *Istikimoji zole;* prize from *Draugas* novel contest, 1978, for *Po damoklo kardu.*

WRITINGS—In English translation: *Curriculum vitae* (two-act play; first produced in Chicago, Ill., May 18, 1968), published in *Pradalge* (magazine), 1966, translation by Anthony Milukas published under same title in *Lithuanian Days* (magazine), 1971; *Po damoklo kardu* (novel), Draugas Lithuanian Book Club, 1978, revised translation by Nijole Grazulis published as *Under the Sword of Damocles,* Lithuanian Literary Associates, 1980.

In Lithuanian; poems, except as noted: *Blaskomi lapai* (title means "Scattered Leaves"), [Germany], 1946; *Auksine seja* (title means "The Golden Sowing"), Nemunas, 1954; *Istikimoji zole* (novel; title means "Faithful Grass"), Lithuanian Rejuvenation Association, 1971; *Laisves sonata* (title means "Sonata of Freedom"), Dialogas, 1979.

Plays: *Diagnoze* (three-act comedy; title means "Diagnosis"; first produced in Detroit, Mich., 1959; produced in New York, 1964), Terra, 1956; *Visciuku ukis* (three-act satire; title means "The Chicken Farm"; first produced in Chicago, May 15, 1965), Terra, 1965; *Sviesa, kuri uzsidege* (three-act; title means "The Light Which Kindled"; first produced in Chicago, December 1, 1968), Terra, 1968; *Palikimas* (one-act; title means "The Legacy"; first produced in Australia, May 17, 1970), Laiskai Lietuviams, 1969; *Du broliukai* (three-act; title means "Two Little Brothers"; first produced in Chicago, March 23, 1969), Amerikos Lietuviu Vaiko Ugdymo Draugija, 1970; *Sidabrine diena* (libretto for three-act operetta; title means "Silvery Day"; first produced in Chicago, December 11, 1971), Lietuviu Meno Ansamblis Dainava, 1972; *Karuna* (nine-act; title means "The Crown"), Dialogas, 1974; *Trys komedijos* (title means "Three Comedies"; contains "Ku-Ku" [three-act; first produced in Los Angeles, Calif., December 19, 1970], "The Good Friday" [five-act; first produced in Chicago, February 3, 1974], and "Boys and Girls" [three-act]), Dialogas, 1975; *Gintaro saly* (libretto for one-act opera; title means "In the Land of Amber"; first produced in Chicago, May 8, 1976), Chicago Lithuanian Opera, 1976; "Eldorado" (three-act), first produced in Sao Paulo, Brazil, August 6, 1978; *Trys dramos* (title means "Three Plays"; contains "Rutele" [four-act; title means "The Flower"], "Saules rumai" [title means "The Palace of the Sun"], and "Zmogus ir tiltas" [three-act; title means "The Man and the Bridge"; first produced in Cleveland, Ohio, May 4, 1974]), Dialogas, 1978; "Emilija plateryte" (libretto for three-act opera; title means "Emilia Plateris"), first produced in Chicago, 1979; "Cicinskas" (libretto for three-act opera), first produced in Chicago, November 8, 1980; *Vyskupo sodas* (three-act; title means "The Garden of the Bishop"), Lithuanian Literary

Associates, 1980; *Kryzkele* (three-act; title means "Crossroad"), Lithuanian Literary Associates, 1980.

WORK IN PROGRESS: The Danube, Not Necessarily Blue, a three-act drama; a novel.

SIDELIGHTS: Kairys told *CA:* "This question is really unnecessary. There is nothing new under lights in front, rear, or sides. Many noted writers give their views, reviews, and interviews on this subject without revealing anything of importance. As for me, my fate as a writer will be even worse than that of Sisyphus because forty years ago 'red marauders' stole my mountain and I have no way to roll my stone up. So I'm fighting with pen and paper to get it back. Or maybe I'm sick of hearing the broken 'Human Rights' record and writing is only medicine to stay alive."

BIOGRAPHICAL/CRITICAL SOURCES: Kazys Bradunas, editor, *Lithuanian Literature Abroad, 1945-1967,* Freedom Fund for Lithuanian Culture, 1968; Pranas Naujokaitis, editor, *Lithuanian Literature,* Volume IV, Council of Lithuanian Culture, 1976.

*   *   *

KALTER, Joanmarie 1951-

PERSONAL: Born September 19, 1951, in Mineola, N.Y.; daughter of Henry Hirsch (a physician) and Rose (a school principal; maiden name, Dorrance) Kalter. *Education:* Cornell University, B.A., 1972; Columbia University, M.S., 1981. *Home and office:* 53 Spring St., New York, N.Y. 10012.

CAREER: Belmont-Tower Books, Inc., New York City, editor, 1973-74; Manor Books, Inc., New York City, managing editor, 1974-76; free-lance writer, 1976—. Editor for Leisure Books, 1973-74.

WRITINGS: Actors on Acting: Performing in Theatre and Film Today, Sterling, 1979. Writer for cable television program, "Bookcase." Contributor to *After Dark.*

SIDELIGHTS: Joanmarie Kalter told *CA* that her book consists of interviews with such entertainers as Geraldine Page, Rip Torn, Lynn Redgrave, Imogene Coca, Estelle Parsons, and Bruce Dern.

*   *   *

KANAHELE, George Sanford 1930-

PERSONAL: Born October 17, 1930, in Kahuku, Hawaii; son of Clinton J. (a principal) and Agnes (Sanford) Kanahele; married Jeanne H. Sakakihara, June 4, 1972; children: George Sanford, Jr., Kauana Margaret, Joannah Leiko. *Education:* Brigham Young University, B.A., 1958, M.A., 1960; Cornell University, Ph.D., 1967. *Religion:* Church of Jesus Christ of Latter-day Saints (Mormons). *Home:* 5079 Poola Pl., Honolulu, Hawaii 96821. *Office:* 1164 Bishop, Suite 415, Honolulu, Hawaii 96813.

CAREER: Worked as administrator for Hawaii International Services Agency, 1968-71; Hawaii Corp., Honolulu, vice-president, 1971-73; George S. Kanahele & Associates, Honolulu, owner, 1973—. Partner of Hawaii Consulting Group, 1979—; president of Entrepreneurship Development Corp., 1980—. President of Hawaiian Music Foundation, 1971—; member of board of governors of East-West Center, 1975—, and board of directors of Hawaii Public Radio, 1979—; consultant to New Zealand Department of Maori Affairs. *Military service:* U.S. Army, Intelligence, 1954-57. *Member:* Hawaiian Businessmen's Association (president, 1976-77), Phi Kappa Phi. *Awards, honors:* Bachman Award from Asian-Pacific Affairs Council, 1970, for contributions to East-West relations; named outstanding Hawaiian of the year by Association of Hawaiian Civic Clubs, 1973; named public speaker of the year from Pacific Speech Association, 1973; Freedom Award from Sertoma, 1980, for contributions to development of Hawaiian music.

WRITINGS: A Native's Guide to Honolulu and Oahu, Topgallant, 1976; *Indonesia ni Okeru Nihon no Senryo* (title means "Prelude to Independence: Indonesia"), Obun, 1976; (editor) *Hawaiian Music and Musicians,* University Press of Hawaii, 1979. Contributor to scholarly journals and newspapers. Editor of *Hawaiian Business Digest,* 1976-79, and *Ha'ilono Mele,* 1978-79, 1980—.

WORK IN PROGRESS: The Business Plan, publication by Prentice-Hall expected in 1981 or 1982; research on the emergence of a "Pacific Community" and on entrepreneurship development in the United States and Asia.

SIDELIGHTS: Kanahele wrote: "*Hawaiian Music and Musicians* is an encyclopedic study, the first of its kind, of Hawaiian music. It has been critically acclaimed and is a model for other studies of ethnic music in the Pacific.

"As a tourist mecca, Hawaii has been the subject of countless visitor guidebooks. All of these books, ever since the first was written one hundred years ago, have been written by outsiders; that is, non-Hawaiians. As a native Hawaiian, I wanted to write about Hawaii as seen through the eyes of one born to the blood and *aina* (land) of the islands. *A Native's Guide to Honolulu and Oahu* is, then, a plea to the newcomer to appreciate and understand the essence of Hawaii—its Hawaiian people, its culture, and its history.

"Although more waves are being made today about the Pacific Community—more articles, more discussions, more planning among scholars, economists, businessmen, policymakers in Asia-Pacific regions—still a lot of people think of the Pacific Community as an abstraction, an ideal. The fact of the matter is the Pacific Community already exists. It exists in the form of many organized 'communities' that function on behalf of the complex of interests that represent the diversity of the Pacific world. These are the countless pan-Pacific organizations that have been operating for many years, some as long as half a century, in almost every conceivable field. Why not consider and work through these organizations as a general framework in which to pursue the formation of the Pacific Community at large? The twenty-first century will be the Century of the Pacific, and we ought to usher it in with a well-conceived and well-organized community of pacific interests.

"Entrepreneurship appears to be coming back in vogue. The lack of the entrepreneurial spirit is one of the oft heard reasons for America's economic decline. Any vision of America's ''reindustrialization'' will evaporate unless this country restores and develops its entrepreneurial capacities to the utmost. Our economic system operates on the entrepreneurial imperative: no growth can take place without entrepreneurs. It is vital that we create a national entrepreneurship development policy and program that will lead to the revitalization of our economic well-being."

*   *   *

KAPELRUD, Arvid Schou 1912-

PERSONAL: Born May 14, 1912, in Lillehammer, Norway; son of Gustav and Ingeborg (Schou) Kapelrud; married Brynhild Bommen, April 11, 1940; children: Rannveig Eriksen, Jon Gunnar. *Education:* University of Oslo,

Cand.Theol., 1938; University of Uppsala, Dr.Theol., 1948; attended Yale University, 1949-50. *Religion:* Lutheran. *Residence:* Oslo, Norway. *Office:* Department of Biblical Studies, University of Oslo, Blindern, P.B. 1023, Oslo 3, Norway.

CAREER: University of Oslo, Oslo, Norway, assistant librarian, 1935-46, librarian, 1946-52, associate professor, 1952-54, professor of Old Testament, 1954—, dean of theological faculty, 1969-71. Member of Norwegian Council for Science and the Humanities, 1968-73. *Military service:* Norwegian Army, 1940. *Member:* Norwegian Library Association (president, 1953-55), Norwegian Academy for Science and Humanities, Nathan Soederblom Society. *Awards, honors:* Kohut grant for Yale University, 1949; Fridtjof Nansen Award from Det Norske Videnskapsn—academi, 1978, for "eminent books and studies in the Humanities"; D.D. from University of Aberdeen, 1979.

WRITINGS: The Question of Authorship in the Ezra-Narrative, Det Norske Videnskaps—akademi, 1944; *Joel Studies,* Almqvist & Wiksell, 1948; *Baal in the Ras Shamra Texts,* Gad, 1952; *Central Ideas in Amos,* Oslo University Press, 1956, 3rd edition, 1978; *The Ras Shamra Discoveries and the Old Testament,* translated by G. W. Anderson, Basil Blackwell, 1963; *Israel From the Earliest Times,* translated by J. M. Moe, Basil Blackwell, 1966; *The Violent Goddess: Anat in the Ras Shamra Texts,* Oslo Univerisity Press, 1969; *Lectures on Exodus,* Oslo University Press, 1975, revised edition, 1978; *The Message of the Prophet Zephaniah,* Oslo University Press, 1975; *God and His Friends in the Old Testament,* Oslo University Press, 1979.

Not in English: *Hammurapis lov* (title means "Code of Hammurapi"), Tanum, 1943; *Paa vakt i Gudbrandsdalen* (title means "On Guard"), Tanum, 1945; *Ras Shamra–funnene og Det gamle Testaments* (title means "The Ras Shamra Discoveries and the Old Testament"), Tanum, 1953; *Doedehavsrullene* (title means "Dead Sea Scrolls"), Oslo University Press, 1956, revised edition, 1971; *Gamle byer og nye stater* (title means "Old Cities and New States"), Oslo University Press, 1958; *Fra Israels profeter til de vise menn* (title means "From Israel's Prophets to the Wise Men"), Oslo University Press, 1961; *Et folk paa hjemferd* (title means "A People on Its Way Home"), Oslo University Press, 1964, revised edition, 1977; *Profetene i det gamle Israel og Juda* (title means "The Prophets in Ancient Israel and Juda"), Oslo University Press, 1966, revised edition, 1974; *Med spade i bibeljord* (title means "Digging in the Bible Earth"), Oslo University Press, 1967; *Job og hans problem* (title means "Job and His Problem"), Gyldendal, 1976; *Vaar konge er Baal* (title means "Our King Is Baal"), Oslo University Press, 1973.

Contributor: J. Philip Hyatt, editor, *The Bible in Modern Scholarship,* Abingdon, 1963; Douglas A. Knight, editor, *Tradition and Theology in the Old Testament,* Fortress, 1977.

Editor of series, "Studia Theologica," Oslo University Press, 1966—. Co-editor of *Norsk theologisk tidskrift* and *Temenos,* both 1965—.

WORK IN PROGRESS: Research on Ugaritic texts from Ras Shamra, Syria.

SIDELIGHTS: Kapelrud told *CA:* "My travels in the Middle East have meant much for my writing. I visited the site of ancient Uruk in Iraq when temples and graves were dug out by masters in their field like Lenzen and Falkenstein. There I also experienced 'the creation of the world' when heavy rain covered the Babylonian lowland, then damped away so that

'the dray land appeared.' I met Bedu groups on their way to better pastures, I visited the marsh land in south. I saw Tigris flooding in the north and met Sir Max Mallowan and Dame Agatha Christie at the diggings at Nimrud and have been wandering in Jordan, Syria, and Israel. The ancient past came alive to me; it was part of a great, great connection in which we are still standing, and where the problems of life and death as met by Gilgamesh, Abraham, and Job are still actual—in spite of all our knowledge, all our technology."

*   *   *

KAPLAN, Helen Singer 1929-

PERSONAL: Born February 6, 1929, in Vienna, Austria; came to United States, 1940; naturalized U.S. citizen, 1947; daughter of Phillip Sigmund and Sophie (Lanzi) Singer; married Harold I. Kaplan, June 20, 1953 (divorced, 1970); married Charles P. Lazarus (in business), November 2, 1979; children: (first marriage) Phillip, Peter, Jennifer. *Education:* Syracuse University, B.F.A. (magna cum laude), 1951; Columbia University, M.A., 1952, Ph.D., 1955; New York Medical College, M.D., 1959. *Home:* 912 Fifth Ave., New York, N.Y. 10021. *Office:* 65 East 76th St., New York, N.Y. 10021.

CAREER: New York Medical College, Valhalla, N.Y., instructor in pharmacology and physiology, 1959-61; Bronx Hospital, Bronx, N.Y., intern, 1960-61; fellow in psychiatry at Bellevue Hospital, 1961-62; New York Medical College-Metropolitan Hospital Center, fellow in psychiatry, 1962-64, assistant to director of psychiatric training and education, 1964-66, assistant professor, 1966-68, associate professor of psychiatry, 1968-70, chairman of behavioral science topic teaching block for Medical College, 1969; Cornell University, Medical College, Ithaca, N.Y., associate clinical professor of psychology, 1970—. Associate attending psychiatrist at Metropolitan, Flower, and B.S. Coler Hospitals, 1966-70, and at Payne Whitney Clinic, Cornell Medical Center, 1970—. Chairperson of National Medical Committee on Planned Parenthood and World Population, 1976-77; diplomate of American Board of Psychiatry and Neurology.

MEMBER: American Psychological Association, American Medical Association, American Psychiatric Association (fellow; member of task force of nomenclature and statistics, section of psychosexual disorders, 1978-79), American Group Psychotherapy Association, Association for the Advancement of Behavior Therapy, Psychosomatic Association, Academy of Psychoanalysis, Eastern Association of Sex Therapy, New York Academy of Medicine, New York Academy of Science. *Awards, honors:* American Women's Medical Association scholastic achievement award.

WRITINGS: (Editor with C. J. Sager) *Progress in Group and Family Therapy,* Volume I, Brunner, 1972; (with Sager) *Group Therapy and Psychoanalysis,* Academy of Psychoanalysis, 1973; *The New Sex Therapy,* Brunner, Volume I, 1974, Volume II: *Disorders of Sexual Desire,* 1979; *An Illustrated Manual of Sex Therapy,* Quadrangle, 1975; *Making Sense of Sex* (young adult), Simon & Schuster, 1979. Also editor with Sager and H. Lear of *The Journal of Sex and Marital Therapy,* Behavioral Publications, and co-author of *The Psychiatric and Medical Evaluation of Sexual Disorders,* Brunner.

Contributor: *Comprehensive Textbook of Psychiatry,* Williams & Wilkins, 1967; Louise Rose, editor, *The Menopause Book,* Hawthorn, 1977; Benjamin Wolman, editor, *Psychological Aspects of Gynecology and Obstetrics,* Medical Economics Co., 1978; Gene Usdin and Jerry M. Lewis, editors,

Psychiatry in General Medical Practice, McGraw, 1979; *Better Homes & Gardens Women's Health and Medical Guide*, Meredith Corp., 1979; Judd Marmor and Sherwyn M. Woods, editors, *The Interface Between the Psychodynamic and Behavioral Therapies*, Plenum, 1980. Also contributor to *Sexuality Revisited*, Brunner, and *Psychotherapies and Therapeutic Techniques*, edited by E. Wick, 1978. Contributor of numerous articles to journals and periodicals, including *Family Process* and *American Journal of Psychiatry*.

WORK IN PROGRESS: Enduring Love, a study of successful romantic relationships, for Simon & Schuster.

SIDELIGHTS: A feature article in the *Washington Star-News* focused on Kaplan's involvement with the Payne Whitney Clinic of New York Hospital. Kaplan and her staff are trained in solving patients' problems with sex, and recommend a number of "specific sexual exercises" as a primary step toward solutions. According to Kaplan, "these sexual exercises involve intense and human reactions; they involve deeply emotional issues. . . . They are very revealing of psychological factors and enable us to work psychoanalytically with patients."

Kaplan brought her expertise on sex to a young adult audience with her book *Making Sense of Sex*. Her work "will smooth some anxious young brows," reported reviewer Mary Breasted. It "is written in quite clinical terms, using the tone of a confident scientist. It gives detailed, illustrated explanations of sexual responses, sexual development, male and female orgasm and the range of available contraceptive devices. The illustrations are tastefully done, with a clear effort to avoid prurience."

BIOGRAPHICAL/CRITICAL SOURCES: Washington Star-News, September 8, 1974; *Authors in the News*, Volume 1, Gale, 1976; *Washington Post Book World*, November 11, 1979.

* * *

KAPLAN, Hymen R. 1910-

PERSONAL: Born March 5, 1910, in Paterson, N.J.; son of Alexander Gregory (a manufacturer) and Yetta (Bernstein) Kaplan. *Education:* University of Pennsylvania, B.A.; Rutgers University, LL.B.; also attended Columbia University and Montclair State Teachers College. *Politics:* Independent. *Home and office:* 2020 F St. N.W., Washington, D.C. 20006.

CAREER: Worked as conference writer for War Production Board, 1942-44; Department of the Interior, Washington, D.C., information specialist, 1944-50; information specialist for National Production Authority, 1950-52; editor for Office of Armed Forces and Education, 1952-55; U.S. Coast Guard, Washington, D.C., public information officer, 1955-70; editor and public relations consultant for American Logistics Association, 1970-77. Public relations consultant for Columbia Lighthouse for the Blind. *Member:* National Press Club. *Awards, honors:* Meritorious Service Award from United States Treasury Department, 1966, for furthering understanding of functions and operations of the U.S. Coast Guard.

WRITINGS: A Guide to Sunken Ships in American Waters, Compass Publications, 1964; *Voyager Beware*, Rand McNally, 1966; *Immortal Bear*, Putnam, 1970; *This Is the Coast Guard*, Cornell Maritime Press, 1972. Also author of "A Letter to Linda" (screenplay), 1965. Contributor to periodicals, including *Parade, Ladies' Home Journal*, and *Washington Post*. Contributing editor of *Review*.

WORK IN PROGRESS: Voyage Into Hell, for Compass Publications; *The Devil's Ship*.

SIDELIGHTS: Kaplan wrote: "After more than thirty years of professional writing, I have found that the writing gives me a sense of identity and self-respect. In a world of clamoring voices, writing is the best way for mine to be heard. For me, it is an assertion of will and an affirmation of life—at least the only way that I can affirm it. Writing has been the one continuous and consistent thread of my life and, as such, has given it meaning. But it is not an easy life. It requires discipline, enormous tenacity, and the capacity to go on in spite of pain and disappointment. Not many can pay the price. But for those who can, the reward comes from a deep inner satisfaction and not solely from applause and money, pleasurable though these are. For me, this lonely passion for words has been the most precious thing in my life."

* * *

KARL, Barry D(ean) 1927-

PERSONAL: Born July 24, 1927, in Louisville, Ky.; married, 1957; children: two. *Education:* University of Louisville, B.A., 1949; University of Chicago, M.A., 1951; Harvard University, Ph.D., 1960. *Office:* Department of History, University of Chicago, 1126 East 59th St., Chicago, Ill. 60637.

CAREER: Washington University, St. Louis, Mo., assistant professor, 1962-63, professor of history, 1963-68; Brown University, Providence, R.I., professor of history, 1968-71; University of Chicago, Chicago, Ill., professor of American history, 1971—, Norman and Edna Freehling Professor of Social Science and American History, 1977—, chairman of department of history, 1976—. Member of Joint Committee for Research of Philanthropy, 1975—.

WRITINGS: Executive Reorganization and Reform in the New Deal: The Genesis of Administrative Management, 1900-1939, Harvard University Press, 1963; (contributor) *Philosophers and Kings: Studies in Leadership*, Braziller, 1970; *Charles E. Merriam and the Study of Politics*, University of Chicago Press, 1974. Also contributor to *New Aspects of Politics*, 1970. Contributor to learned journals.

BIOGRAPHICAL/CRITICAL SOURCES: Annals of the American Academy of Political and Social Science, July, 1975; *Political Science Quarterly*, summer, 1975; *Journal of Higher Education*, September-October, 1975.*

* * *

KARMI, Abdul Karim 1907(?)-1980
(Abu Salma)

OBITUARY NOTICE: Born c. 1907 in Tulkarm, Palestine; died of sepsis, October 11, 1980, in Washington, D.C. Attorney, government official, and poet. Karmi practiced law in Jerusalem before immigrating in 1948 to Syria, where he continued to practice law and became a judge. He was also a government official in Syria's Ministry of Information. In the mid-1970's he left Syria and settled in the United States. Karmi wrote four volumes of poetry under the pen name Abu Salma, including *The Homeless*, published in 1964, and *Songs From Home, From Palestine My Pen*, and *The Collected Works of Abu Salma*, all published in 1971. Obituaries and other sources: *Washington Post*, October 11, 1980; *New York Times*, October 14, 1980.

KAROL, Alexander
  See KENT, Arthur William Charles

*   *   *

KATZ, Michael Ray 1944-

PERSONAL: Born December 9, 1944, in New York, N.Y.; son of Louis M. (a teacher) and Alice (a nurse; maiden name, Gordon) Katz; married Mary Dodge (a professor), November, 1978; children: Rebecca. *Education:* Williams College, B.A., 1966; Oxford University, M.A., 1968, D.Phil., 1972; attended University of Leningrad, 1971-72. *Home:* 17 Chapin Court, Williamstown, Mass. 01267. *Office:* Department of Russian, Williams College, Williamstown, Mass. 01267.

CAREER: Williams College, Williamstown, Mass., assistant professor, 1972-78, associate professor of Russian, 1978—. *Member:* American Association for the Advancement of Slavic Studies, American Association of Teachers of Slavic and East European Languages. *Awards, honors:* National Endowment for the Humanities grant, 1980-82.

WRITINGS: The Literary Ballad in Early Nineteenth-Century Russian Literature, Oxford University Press, 1976.

WORK IN PROGRESS: Dreams in Russian Literature, publication expected in 1981; translating A. Herzen's *Who Is to Blame?*, publication expected in 1983.

*   *   *

KAYE, Phyllis Johnson

PERSONAL: Born in New Brunswick, N.J.; daughter of Harry (in business) and Jenny (Field) Johnson; married Robert G. Kaye, June 18, 1950; children: Steven, Amy. *Education:* Attended University of Connecticut. *Home:* 17 Riverside Dr., Waterford, Conn. 06385. *Office:* O'Neill Theater Center, 305 Great Neck Rd., Waterford, Conn. 06385.

CAREER: Associated with Eugene O'Neill Theater Center, Waterford, Conn., 1965—. Program coordinator of National Playwrights Conference, 1971-75; head of reception and guest relations at Playwrights Conference, 1975—. Member of board of directors of O'Neill Playwrights, 1972-75; consultant to International Theatre Institute.

WRITINGS: (Editor) New Playwrights Catalogue, O'Neill Theater Center, Volume II (Kaye was not associated with Volume I), 1969, Volume III, 1971; (editor) National Playwrights Directory, O'Neill Theater Center, 1977, 2nd edition, 1981.

*   *   *

KAZICKAS, Jurate C(atherine) 1943-

PERSONAL: Born February 18, 1943, in Vilnius, Lithuania; came to the United States in 1947, naturalized citizen, 1951; daughter of Joseph and Alexandra (Kalvenas) Kazickas. *Education:* Trinity College, Washington, D.C., B.A., 1964; attended University of Neuchatel, 1962, University of Exeter, 1962-63, and Columbia University, 1966. *Home:* 1518 26th St. N.W., Washington, D.C. 20007. *Office: Washington Star*, 225 Virginia Ave. S.E., Washington, D.C. 20061.

CAREER: Teacher of English at teacher training college in Nyeri, Kenya, 1964-66; *Look*, New York City, researcher, 1966-67; free-lance writer in Vietnam, 1967-68; Associated Press, New York City, feature writer, 1969-75; free-lance writer, 1975-77; Associated Press, Washington, D.C., feature writer and White House correspondent, 1977-79; *Washington Star*, Washington, D.C., feature writer, 1979—. Vol-

unteer teacher at schools in New York City, 1965-66; volunteer for Emmaus Services for the Aging, 1979—. *Member:* Washington Press Club. *Awards, honors:* Merit award from *Sports Illustrated*, 1965, for leading Mount Kenya expedition; Headliner Award from National Women's Press Club, 1973, for feature writing.

WRITINGS: (With Lynn Sherr) The American Woman's Gazetteer, Bantam, 1976. Also author with Sherr of *The Woman's Calendar*, published yearly by Universe Books from 1970-80, and by Dutton beginning in 1981. Contributor to *Working Woman* and *Ms*.

WORK IN PROGRESS: A screenplay; a romantic comedy.

SIDELIGHTS: Jurate Kazickas's assignments for the Associated Press included covering the Mideast War from Cairo in 1973 and covering the American Bicentennial Mount Everest Expedition. In 1973 she led an African women's expedition to Mount Kenya.

She told *CA*: "I had the good fortune from the years 1970 to 1975 to cover the social revolution in America—the alternative life styles, new-left politics, the anti-Vietnam movement, and most importantly, the women's movement, the most profound revolution of our decade. Things will never be the same again. *The Woman's Calendar* is a very thorough record of all the most important events in women's history, from colonial days through the suffrage movement to the present. I have very much enjoyed writing about the second wave of feminism and truly believe it is women who are affecting the most lasting changes in our society."

"As a journalist," she added, "I have always strived to be 'where the action is'—or at least as I perceived it. Although Vietnam was a difficult experience personally—I was wounded during the siege of Khe Sanh in March, 1968—I could not have been anywhere else during those years. Coming back to a country divided by the war only confirmed the importance of my having experienced the war.

"Jimmy Carter's victory in 1976 held out such promise to the country. I was sitting on the slopes of Mt. Everest those final days of his campaign knowing that if he won, Washington was where I had to be. I covered the White House, primarily First Lady Rosalynn Carter, and got to see government work from a unique vantage point. The world looks very different from Washington and, I may add, the view is often distorted."

*   *   *

KAZMER, Daniel (Raphael) 1947-

PERSONAL: Born February 10, 1947, in Chicago, Ill.; son of Edward R. (in business) and Josephine (Zolner) Kazmer; divorced. *Education:* University of Illinois at Chicago Circle, B.S., 1969; Massachusetts Institute of Technology, Ph.D., 1973. *Politics:* None. *Religion:* None. *Home:* 976 North Madison, Arlington, Va. 22205.

CAREER: Eastern Michigan University, Ypsilanti, assistant professor of economics, 1973-74, fellow of Center for the Study of Contemporary Issues, 1974-75; Central Intelligence Agency, Washington, D.C., economic analyst, 1975-78; SRI International, Arlington, Va., senior research associate at Center for Economic Policy Research, 1978-79; University of Maryland, College Park, lecturer in economics, 1980; Catholic University of America, Washington, D.C., lecturer in economics, 1980—; Wharton Econometrics Forecasting Associates, Inc., Washington, D.C., senior economist, 1980—. Economic analyst for Central Intelligence Agency, 1979-80; associate professorial lecturer at George Washington University, 1979. *Member:* International Association of Energy Economists, American Economic Association, Association for Comparative Economic Studies, American Association for the Advancement of Slavic Studies.

WRITINGS: (Contributor) *Soviet Economy in a New Perspective: A Compendium of Papers,* U.S. Government Printing Office, 1976; (with Vera Kazmer) *Russian Economic History: A Guide to Information Sources,* Gale, 1977; (contributor) Holland Hunter, editor, *The Future of the Soviet Economy, 1978-1985,* Westview Press, 1978. Contributor of articles and reviews to scholarly journals.

WORK IN PROGRESS: Modeling and analysis of centrally planned economics and of fuels and power consumption in major industrial economies.

SIDELIGHTS: Kazmer wrote that his particular interests are "analysis of how various economies respond to energy constraint on growth; the trade-offs among capital, labor, and energy inputs; and the impact of energy constraint on productivity."

*   *   *

KEAN, Edmund (Stanley) 1915-

PERSONAL: Born February 24, 1915, in Vienna, Austria; came to the United States in 1951, naturalized citizen, 1956; son of Eugen I. and Tova R. Kahan; married Doris Reiser (a receptionist), September 21, 1938; children: Ilana, Michael. *Education:* University of Basel, M.D., 1939. *Politics:* Liberal. *Religion:* Jewish. *Home:* 2327 Fifth St., East Moline, Ill. 61244. *Office:* 2500 Kennedy Dr., East Moline, Ill. 61244.

CAREER: In private practice of family medicine in East Moline, Ill. Clinical assistant at Lincoln Medical School, Peoria branch. *Military service:* British Army, Royal Medical Corps, 1941-46; served in the Near East and Africa; became captain. *Member:* American Medical Association, American Academy of Family Medicine (fellow), Rock Island Medical Society, B'nai B'rith. *Awards, honors:* Painting awards from Mississippi Valley Art Association.

WRITINGS: Marriage and Memo Lesson, Westminster, 1976. Contributor to *Rotary* and newspapers.

WORK IN PROGRESS: How to Survive a Heart Attack; a timely novel.

SIDELIGHTS: Kean told *CA:* "To me, writing is a conglomerate of facts and imagination, the development of characters into which readers, while they read, can comfortably slip to temporarily escape the everyday. It is the inner world of a writer bared to entertain and inform."

*   *   *

KEMPER, Rachel H. 1931-

PERSONAL: Born October 5, 1931, in Morristown, Ind.; daughter of Jasper Joseph (a farmer) and Mazie (a teacher; maiden name, Bennett) Kemper. *Education:* Attended John Herron Art Institute, 1949-53; Indiana University, B.A., 1955, M.A., 1957, M.A., 1960; also attended Columbia University, 1957-63. *Home:* 77 East 12th St., New York, N.Y. 10003. *Office:* Fashion Institute of Technology, 227 West 27th St., New York, N.Y. 10001.

CAREER: Fashion Institute of Technology, New York, N.Y., began association in 1962, associate professor, 1971-77, professor of art history, 1977—. *Member:* Archaeological Institute of America.

WRITINGS: (Contributor) Joseph L. Gardner, editor, *Sculpture,* Newsweek, 1975; *A Short History of the Western*

World, Kendall/Hunt, Volume I, 1975, Volume II, 1976; *Costume,* Newsweek, 1978.

WORK IN PROGRESS: A Lurid History of Cosmetics; A History of Textile Design.

SIDELIGHTS: Rachel Kemper commented: "I have traveled extensively to major and minor archaeological sites in Mexico and to Peru. I am interested in Pre-Columbian art and culture, primarily Mexican, and in traditional and tribal African art and culture. I am a collector (on a minor scale) of African tribal sculpture."

AVOCATIONAL INTERESTS: Cats.

*   *   *

KENNEDY, Mary
(Mary Lee Emerson)

PERSONAL: Born in Claxton, Ga.; daughter of Foster and Josephine (McMahon) Kennedy; married Joseph Deems Taylor, July 11, 1921 (divorced, 1934); children: Joan Kennedy. *Education:* Educated in convents in Georgia and Florida; attended Radcliffe College. *Home address:* Church St., Box 395, Stockbridge, Mass. 01262. *Agent:* Audrey Wood, International Creative Management, 40 West 57th St., New York, N.Y.

CAREER: Newspaper journalist; actress in films with Cosmopolitan Film Co., 1920; actress in Broadway plays, including "Lucky O'Shea," 1917, "A Young Man's Fancy," 1919, "The Love Habit," 1923, "The Blue Peter," 1925, "A Man with Red Hair," 1928, "The Camel Through the Needle's Eye," 1929, "The Barretts of Wimpole Street," 1931, and "The Joyous Season," 1934; writer, 1925—. *Member:* International P.E.N., American Society of Composers, Authors, and Publishers, Poetry Society of America, Authors Guild, Dramatists Guild, Actors' Equity Association, New York Women Poets. *Awards, honors:* Award from *Saturday Review;* William Rose Benet Award; lyric award from Poetry Society of America, prizes from *Lyric* and New York Women Poets.

WRITINGS—Plays: (With Ruth Hawthorne) *Mrs. Partridge Presents* (three-act comedy; first produced in 1925), Samuel French, 1925; "Jordan," first produced in London by the Venturers Society, 1928. Also author of "One Day of Spring."

Other: *A Surprise to the Children* (juvenile), Doubleday, 1933; *Question the Night* (novel), Dodd, 1938; *River Secret: A Mystery of Florida* (juvenile), Dodd, 1941; (with Helen Hayes) *Star on Her Forehead,* Dodd, 1949; *Violets Are Blue,* Lothrop, 1951; *Jenny,* Lothrop, 1954; *Come and See Me* (juvenile), Harper, 1966; (adapter) *I Am a Thought of You: Poems by Sie Thao (Hung Tu) Written in China in the Ninth Century,* Gotham Book Mart, 1968; *Ride Into Morning* (poems), Gotham Book Mart, 1969; (contributor) Evelyn Sybil Mary Eaton, editor, *Go Ask the River,* Harcourt, 1969; *Behind the Day* (poems), Gotham Book Mart, 1972; *The Bourrichon* (poem), Gotham Book Mart, 1974, second edition, 1976. Also author of *"So Many Butterflies, A Present for Miguel: A Story of Mexico,* and (with Cornelius Skipper) *Captain Fury of the Holy Innocents.* Contributor of stories (sometimes under pseudonym Mary Lee Emerson) and reviews to magazines.

WORK IN PROGRESS: An autobiography and a play.

*   *   *

KENNEDY, Richard 1910-

PERSONAL: Born April 9, 1910, in Cambridge, England;

son of John Pitt and Norah (Baddeley) Kennedy; married Olive Mary Johnstone (a librarian), October 8, 1937; children: Elizabeth Kennedy Stacey, John Pitt, Rachel Kennedy Ansari. *Education:* Attended Regent Street Polytechnic and Royal College of Art. *Home:* Woodcote, Ray Lea Rd., Maidenhead, Berkshire, England.

CAREER: Free-lance illustrator of children's books, 1940—; writer. *Military service:* Royal Air Force, ground staff, 1940-46.

WRITINGS: A Boy at the Hogarth Press (nonfiction), Whittington Press, 1972; *A Parcel of Time* (nonfiction), Whittington Press, 1977. Illustrator of more than two hundred books.

WORK IN PROGRESS: A Step in Time, nonfiction.

SIDELIGHTS: Kennedy wrote: "The chief influence on my creative powers as an artist and writer has been the work of the Italian painters from the age of Titian and the development of their style through the Baroque painters to Rubens and Watteau. I was drawn to them through my association with Virginia Woolf, who made many visits to the National Gallery, regarding these artists as having like minds to herself. She adapted their spiral methods of composition to her novels, weaving together two contrasting spirals, rather than adopting the logical structural method of the story teller. After a visit to India I was able to develop the spiral method of composition to its full in illustrations. I also adapted it to my prose autobiographical books, giving them a Proustian and comic flavor.

"In *A Boy at the Hogarth Press* I endeavored to contrast the intellectual Bloomsberries with the ordinary people with whom I came in contact. In *A Parcel of Time* I used the same method to contrast my upper class highly intellectual grandmother, proud of her social station and courageous and stoical, with the maids in the house.

"The artist Felix Topolski showed me in the thirties how the spiral method of composition could be adapted to ordinary life, and to the various books I illustrated, mainly for children, and numerous stories of myths and legends from various cultures.

"My Irish background has, I believe, been a formative influence, especially the poetry of W. B. Yeats and the painting of his brother, Jack Yeats. Travel to Venice, Florence, and Rome was also a source of inspiration, and my journeys in the Middle East led to an interest in Islamic decoration."

BIOGRAPHICAL/CRITICAL SOURCES: Books and Bookmen, May, 1972; *San Diego Union,* February 17, 1980.

*   *   *

KENT, Arthur William Charles 1925-
(James Bradwell, M. Dubois, Paul Granados, Alexander Karol, Alexander Stamper, Brett Vane)

PERSONAL: Born January 31, 1925, in London, England; son of Frederick Charles (a factory worker) and Hilda (Rixon) Kent; married Eileen Vickery, 1950 (separated, 1960); children: Margaret, Juliette. *Education:* Attended City Literary Institute, London. *Home:* 26 Verulam Ave., London E17 8ES, England. *Agent:* Maximilian Becker, 115 East 82nd St., New York, N.Y. 10028; and Ronald Copeman Agency, Bedford Row, London, England.

CAREER: News Chronicle, London, England, editorial assistant, 1943-46; reporter and feature writer for *Australian Daily Mirror,* 1947-53; associated with Beaverbrook Newspapers, London, 1969-70; associated with British Broadcasting Corp., London, 1970; free-lance writer.

WRITINGS—Novels, except as indicated: *The Kansas Fast Gun,* R. Hale, 1958; *Broken Doll,* Brown, Watson, 1961; *Action of the Tiger,* World Distributors, 1961; *Long Horn, Long Grass,* R. Hale, 1964; *Black Sunday,* R. Hale, 1965; *Red—Red—Red,* Compact Books, 1966; *Plant Poppies on My Grave,* Brown, Watson, 1966, Avon, 1967; *Corpse to Cuba,* Mayflower, 1966, Macfadden-Bartell, 1967; *Deadly Medicine: Doctors and True Crime* (nonfiction), Taplinger, 1974 (published in England as *The Death Doctors,* New English Library, 1974); *Maverick Squadron,* Futura Publications, 1975.

Under pseudonym James Bradwell: *Land of the Giants: The Mean City,* World Distributors, 1969; (with Zena Gunther de Tyras) *A Life in the Wind,* W. H. Allen, 1971.

Under pseudonym M. Dubois: *El Tafile,* Hamilton & Co., 1954; *Legion etrangere* (title means "Foreign Legion"), Hamilton & Co., 1954; *March and Die,* Hamilton & Co., 1954.

Under pseudonym Paul Granados: *Broadway Contraband,* Hamilton & Co., 1954.

Under pseudonym Alexander Karol: *Sword of Vengeance,* New English Library, 1973, Belmont-Tower, 1977. Also author of *Dark Lady,* 1974, *The King's Witchfinder,* 1975, and *The Nowhere War,* 1975.

Under pseudonym Alexander Stamper: *Revolt at Zaluig,* Fleetway, 1954; *Inclining to Crime,* Fleetway, 1957; *Special Edition Murder,* Fleetway, 1957; *Stairway to Murder,* Fleetway, 1958; *Wake Up Screaming,* Fleetway, 1958; (with Gordon Thomas) *The Camp on Blood Island,* Ballantine, 1958; *Last Action,* Fleetway, 1959; *The Weak and the Strong,* Fleetway, 1962; *The Counterfeiters,* Fleetway, 1962; (with Ivan Simson) *The Fall of Singapore: Too Little Too Late,* Leo Cooper Ltd., 1970.

Under pseudonym Brett Vane: *Sunny,* Hamilton & Co., 1953; *Gardenia,* Hamilton & Co., 1953.

Contributor to magazines in England, Australia, and the United States.

WORK IN PROGRESS: Nowhere War and *The Trouble With Pink,* novels; *Gallery of Eccentrics,* nonfiction.

SIDELIGHTS: Kent told *CA:* "I have been mainly studying over the last five years, catching up on education. I have also been traveling extensively. I have been mainly a journalist in my working life who turns to fiction for a break or to pay for vacations. I have been influenced more by American writers than those of my own country—Hemingway and Chandler are two that spring to mind. I am intending to do less journalism from now on and strive to be more serious in my fiction.

"I am impressed by the quality of American novels, less so by the quality of British. I am impressed by the quality of British television, but American television, at the moment for me, is so bland and slick that it's a turn off."

*   *   *

KEREK, Andrew 1936-

PERSONAL: Born April 12, 1936, in Budapest, Hungary; came to the United States in 1957, naturalized citizen, 1962; son of Michael (a doctor) and Leona (Szarvassy) Kerek; married Yvonne Richardson (a teacher), August 4, 1963; children: Michael, Viki Ann. *Education:* University of Michigan, B.A., 1962, M.A., 1963; further graduate study at University of California, Los Angeles, and University of Texas; Indiana University, Ph.D., 1968. *Residence:* Oxford, Ohio. *Office:* Department of English, Miami University, 368 Bachelor Hall, Oxford, Ohio 45056.

CAREER: Miami University, Oxford, Ohio, instructor, 1963-65, assistant professor, 1968-72, associate professor, 1972-77, professor of English and linguistics and director of linguistics, 1977—. Visiting professor at Ohio State University, summer, 1970; visiting lecturer at University of Illinois, summers, 1971, 1975; guest professor at University of Cologne, 1972-73; senior Fulbright lecturer at Al Azhar University, Cairo, 1979-80.

MEMBER: Linguistic Society of America, National Council of Teachers of English, American-Hungarian Educators' Association, American Association for Applied Linguistics. *Awards, honors:* Grants from American Council of Learned Societies, 1975, Exxon Education Foundation, 1976, 1978, and Commission for Educational and Cultural Exchange Between the United States of America and the United Arab Republic, 1979-80.

WRITINGS: Hungarian Metrics: Some Linguistic Aspects of Iambic Verse, Research Center for the Language Sciences, Indian University, 1971; (with Donald A. Daiker and Max Morenberg) *The Writer's Options: College Sentence Combining,* with instructor's manual, Harper, 1979; (editor with Daiker and Morenberg, and contributor) *Sentence Combining and the Teaching of Writing,* University of Akron Press, 1979.

Contributor: Denis Sinor, editor, *Studies in Finno-Ugric Linguistics in Honor of Alo Raun,* Indiana University, 1977; Gerhard Nickel, editor, *Contrastive Linguistics,* Heider HochschulVerlag, 1978; John Odmark, editor, *Language, Literature, and Meaning: Literacy Theory and Criticism in Poland, Hungary, and Czechoslovakia,* Volume II: *Current Trends in Literary Research,* John Benjamin Press, 1980. Contributor of about twenty-five articles and reviews to scholarly journals.

WORK IN PROGRESS: Sentence Combining and College Composition, a monograph, with Donald A. Daiker and Max Morenberg.

AVOCATIONAL INTERESTS: Travel (Europe, the Middle East).

*   *   *

KEREWSKY-HALPERN, Barbara   1931-

PERSONAL: Born December 23, 1931, in Mount Vernon, N.Y.; daughter of Samuel A. (a businessman) and Rose (an editor; maiden name, Schwartz) Kerewsky; married Joel M. Halpern (a professor of anthropology), 1952; children: Kay, Susannah, Carla. *Education:* Barnard College, B.A. (with honors), 1953, graduate study, 1953-54; further graduate study at University of Freiburg, 1970-71; University of Massachusetts, M.A., 1974, Ph.D., 1979. *Home address:* Market Hill Rd., Amherst, Mass. 01002. *Office:* Department of Anthropology, University of Massachusetts, Amherst, Mass. 01003.

CAREER: American Museum of Natural History, New York, N.Y., collector of ethnographic materials from Yugoslavia and Laos, 1953-54; researcher in Yugoslavia, 1954-56; American Museum of Natural History, collector of ethnographic materials from Yugoslavia and Laos, 1956-57; lecturer, 1957-68; University of Massachusetts, Amherst, adjunct professor of anthropology, 1979—, graphic designer for Fine Arts Council, 1973. Field cartographer and illustrator, 1953-54, 1961-62, 1964, 1966; field coordinator of summer research program at Brandeis University, 1964. Lecturer at University of Belgrade, 1978; lecturer for WGBH-TV, 1965-66, and World Affairs Council, Boston, Mass., 1966-68;

onboard lecturer for study cruises to Greece, Yugoslavia, and Brazil; guest on television programs.

MEMBER: American Anthropological Association, American Association for the Advancement of Slavic Studies, Modern Language Association of America, Association of Asian Studies, Bulgarian Studies Association. *Awards, honors:* Fulbright-Hays Award, 1978; grant from International Research and Exchanges Board for Yugoslavia, 1978; National Science Foundation fellowship, 1980-81.

WRITINGS—With husband, Joel M. Halpern: *Yugoslavia,* Doubleday, 1956; *A Serbian Village in Historical Perspective,* Holt, 1972; *The People of Serbia* (elementary school textbook), Addison-Wesley, 1972; (editor) Josip Obrebski, *Change From Peasant to Citizen: An East European Case Study,* Schenkman, 1976; (editor) *Ritual and Social Structure in a Macedonian Village,* Department of Anthropology, University of Massachusetts, 1977; (editor and contributor) *Selected Papers on a Serbian Village: Social Structure as Reflected by History, Demography, and Oral Tradition* (monograph), Department of Anthropology, University of Massachusetts, 1977.

Contributor: Mary Durkin and Patsy Tanabe, editors, *Teachers' Guide to People in States,* Addison-Wesley, 1973; Peter Morley and Roy Wallis, editors, *Anthropological Perspectives on Traditional Beliefs and Practices,* University of Pittsburgh Press, 1979; Jean Cuisenier, editor, *Europe as a Culture Area,* Aldine, 1979; John Foley, editor, *Oral Traditional Literature,* Slavia Publishers, 1980.

Illustrator: Joel M. Halpern, *A Serbian Village,* Columbia University Press, 1958; Walter Fairservis, Jr., *Costumes of the East,* Chatham Press, 1971. Contributor to *American People's Encyclopedia.* Contributor of articles, translations, and reviews to anthropology journals in the United States and Europe.

WORK IN PROGRESS: Pathways: The Coming of Age of an Anthropologist.

SIDELIGHTS: Barbara Kerewsky-Halpern speaks Serbo-Croatian, Bulgarian, Russian, French, German, and Lao. More than twenty-five years of field research have taken her to Serbia, India, Laos, Thailand, Cambodia, Japan, Poland, Romania, Bulgaria, the Soviet Union, including Soviet Central Asia, Germany, Switzerland, Brazil, and Greece. She wrote that her interests are "areal concerns in Southeast Europe and Southeast Asia, plus academic interests in the ethnography of communication, process in oral tradition, transition and change in peasant societies, and medical anthropology." Kerewsky-Halpern is also a member of the FeldenKrais Guild, and uses methods of "Awareness Through Movement and Functional Integration." She specializes in working with people with multiple sclerosis.

*   *   *

KERR, Catherine   1945-

PERSONAL: Born January 12, 1945, in Vancouver, British Columbia, Canada; daughter of George Earle (an agricultural consultant) and Eleanor Katherine (a teacher) Kerr. *Education:* University of British Columbia, B.Ed., 1972. *Residence:* Vancouver, British Columbia. *Office:* Open Learning Institute, P.O. Box 94000, Richmond, British Columbia, Canada V6Y 2A2.

CAREER: High school teacher of English and French in Kelowna, British Columbia, 1972-73; Douglas & McIntyre Ltd. (publishers), Vancouver, British Columbia, editor, 1973-79; Open Learning Institute, Richmond, British Columbia, coordinator of course editing, 1979—. *Awards, honors:* British Columbia Book Award from T. Eaton Co., 1980, for *Coast of Many Faces.*

WRITINGS: Coast of Many Faces (nonfiction), Douglas & McIntyre, 1979. Contributor to *Priorities.*

SIDELIGHTS: Catherine Kerr wrote: "I enjoy collaborating with artists—photographers, musicians—who are sensitive to language but like to rely on others to generate or synthesize scripts for them. *Coast of Many Faces* is the product of such a collaboration. It documents the life of working people in the rural towns and villages on the Canadian west coast. The photographer Ulli Steltzer, who established her reputation in Princeton during the sixties and seventies, traveled with me (and sometimes without me) to every coast settlement, interviewing residents informally in such a way that their comments and Ulli's photographs would complement each other in representing the texture of each community. I rough-edited the tape transcript while she developed her film and studied her contact sheets, sometimes consulting me on a printing decision. Then we fine-tuned the text and the photograph selection together before delivering them to Sally Mennell, who is a poet and illustrator as well as a favorite book designer for our publishers. The reviews all comment on the rich, sensitive realism of our result, and all three of us ended up thinking that the other two were wonderful.

"Another interest of mine is restoring inventive rhetoric to public life in the service of 'New Age' politics, a subject of great importance to me. By 'New Age' politics I mean leadership for a North America that may be ready to depart from the swashbuckling mentality of a frontier culture—selfishly competitive, restless, plunderous and ethnocentric—and move towards a society that husbands all its resources, (human and natural) not by making its institutions serve and promote privilege as in Europe but by making them responsive to its most creative democratic groups."

*   *   *

KERR, James Lennox   1899-1963
(Peter Dawlish)

PERSONAL: Born July 1, 1899, in Paisley, Renfrewshire, Scotland; died March 11, 1963; son of John and Sarah (Mathers) Kerr; married Elizabeth Lamorna Birch, 1932; children: one son. *Education:* Educated in Paisley, Renfrewshire, Scotland. *Home:* Lamorna, near Penzance, Cornwall, England.

CAREER: Writer. Worked as gold prospector; member of British Mercantile Marine, 1919-29 and 1939-42. *Military Service:* Royal Naval Volunteer Reserve, 1915-19 and 1942-46.

WRITINGS: Back Door Guest, Bobbs-Merrill, 1930, reprinted, Arno, 1974; *Old Ship* (novel), Constable, 1930, Macmillan, 1931; *Glenshiels* (novel), John Lane, 1932; (editor) *On, and Under, the Ocean Wave* (juvenile), Thomas Nelson, 1933; *Ice, a Tale of Effort* (novel), John Lane, 1933; *The Young Steamship Officer,* Thomas Nelson, 1933; *The Blackspit Smugglers* (novel), Thomas Nelson, 1935; *Woman of Glenshiels* (novel), Collins, 1935; *The Fool and the Tractor* (novel), Collins, 1936; *The Eye of the Earth* (juvenile), Thomas Nelson, 1936; *Cruising in Scotland: The Log of the Migrant,* Collins, 1938; *The Eager Years: An Autobiography,* Collins, 1940; (editor) Aylward Edward Dingle, *A Modern Sinbad,* Harrap, 1948; (editor with David James) *Wavy Navy by Some Who Served* (nonfiction), Harrap, 1950; (editor) *Touching the Adventures of Merchantmen in the Second World War* (nonfiction), 1953; *The Great Storm, Being the*

Authentic Story of the Loss at Sea of the Princess Victoria and Other Vessels Early in 1958, Harrap, 1954; (with Wilfred Granville) *The R.N.V.R.: A Record of Achievement,* Harrap, 1957; *Wilfred Grenfell: His Life and Work,* Dodd, 1959; *The Unfortunate Ship: The Story of H. M. Troopship Birkenhead,* Harrap, 1960.

All under pseudonym Peter Dawlish; for children; published by Oxford University Press, except as noted: *The First Tripper,* 1947; *North Sea Adventure,* 1949; *Aztec Gold,* 1951; *MacClellan's Lake,* 1951; *The Bagodia Episode,* 1953; *Young Drake of Devon,* 1954; *He Went With Drake,* Harrap, 1955; *Way for a Sailor,* 1955; *Martin Frobisher,* 1956; *The Sea Story Omnibus,* Collins, 1956; *Sailors All,* Basil Blackwell, 1957; *The Race for Gowrie Bay,* 1959; *Johnno, the Deep-Sea Diver: The Life Story of Diver John Johnstone,* Watts, 1960; *The Boy Jacko,* 1962; *The Royal Navy,* 1963; *The Seas of Britain,* Benn, 1963; *The Merchant Navy,* 1966.

"Peg-Leg" series: *Captain Peg-Leg's War,* 1939; *. . . and the Fur Pirates,* 1939; *. . . and the Invaders,* 1940: *. . . Swaps the Sea,* 1940.

"Dauntless" series: *Dauntless Finds Her Crew,* 1947; *. . . Sails Again,* 1948; *. . . and the Mary Baines,* 1949; *. . . Takes Recruits,* 1950; *. . . Sails In,* 1952; *. . . in Danger,* 1954; *. . . Goes Home,* 1960.

SIDELIGHTS: James Kerr drew from his experiences as a professional sailor to create many of his books for adults and children. His tales of the sea and ships are filled with adventure and humor and provide much practical information on boating.

The author's popularity was established with the publication of his "Dauntless" series of children's books. These stories relate the various adventures encountered by schoolboys who recondition a fishing boat. Another series of sea stories featured the burly skipper, Captain Peg-Leg. Kerr also became one of the first authors to market a career book for young people with the publication of *The First Tripper.*

For adults, Kerr wrote biographies in addition to his usual nautical fare. His biographies include a detailed account of the life of Wilfred Grenfell, a medical missionary who served in Labrador and Newfoundland, and the story of Johnno, a deep-sea diver from Liverpool who finds adventure on the seas near Australia and the East Indies.

BIOGRAPHICAL/CRITICAL SOURCES: New York Evening Post, March 22, 1930; *New York Times Book Review,* March 30, 1930, March 1, 1931; *New York Herald Tribune Books,* August 3, 1930; *Bookman,* March, 1931; *New York Herald Tribune Book Review,* December 27, 1959.*

*   *   *

KERTESZ, Louise   1939-

PERSONAL: Born May 23, 1939, in Ludlow, Mass.; daughter of Felice (a jute mill laborer) and Annetta (a jute mill laborer; maiden name, Merli) Cristina; married Christopher Kertesz (a newspaper editor), April 3, 1965; children: Nina, Sara. *Education:* Anna Maria College, B.A., 1960; Columbia University, M.A., 1963; University of Illinois, Ph.D., 1970. *Home:* 1300 Joliet Pl., Detroit, Mich. 48207.

CAREER: Forbes, New York, N.Y., editorial researcher, 1961-63; teacher of English in Lutry, Switzerland, 1963-64, and French at public school in Rushville, N.Y., 1965; Hobart College, Geneva, N.Y., instructor of English, 1965-66; *Daily Hampshire Gazette,* Northampton, Mass., book reviewer, 1974; teacher of English in Easthampton, Mass., 1976-78; artist-in-residence at elementary school in Farmington Hills,

Mich., 1980; Wayne State University, Detroit, Mich., instructor in composition, 1980-81, assistant professor, 1981—. Member of board of directors of Poetry Resource Center of Michigan, 1980—.

WRITINGS: The Poetic Vision of Muriel Rukeyser, Louisiana State University Press, 1980. Contributor to poetry magazines, including *New Orleans Review, Spirit, Sou'wester, Images, Sackbut Review, Earth's Daughters,* and *Scree.*

WORK IN PROGRESS: A book of poems; narrative poetry about the lives of immigrant jute mill laborers in Massachusetts.

SIDELIGHTS: Kertesz told *CA:* "I think of writing as a way to explore and clarify my perception of the world—my personal sphere of relationships, work, place, and sometimes, through these, the larger world as well. In writing, I seek what I truly know; I find it best when image, meaning, and my own voice happily unite in a poem. I am trying to write as simply as possible, and I admire the language of poets such as Paul Goodman, David Ignatow, and Jane Kenyon.

"I was drawn to Muriel Rukeyser's work because she achieved a positive vision of the human condition, though her writing reflects personal suffering and that of war victims, political prisoners, the poor, the exploited. In increasingly direct poems she sang the marvels of science, cities, and the fertile human spirit without ignoring the ugliness and the horror in our midst. As a writer whose habitat is the city, my own deepest urge is to celebrate, with both eyes open."

*   *   *

KESLER, (William) Jackson (II)   1938-

PERSONAL: Born July 15, 1938, in Roanoke, Va.; son of William Jackson (a merchandiser) and Eunice (a merchandiser; maiden name, Thrasher) Kesler; married Betty Wilson (a professor), August 19, 1960; children: Sara Elizabeth, Andrew Wilson. *Education:* Randolph-Macon College, B.A., 1959; George Peabody College, M.A., 1960; University of Texas, Ph.D., 1968. *Politics:* Independent. *Religion:* Methodist. *Home:* 1348 State St., Bowling Green, Ky. 42101. *Office:* Department of Communication and Theater, Western Kentucky University, Bowling Green, Ky. 42101.

CAREER: High school teacher of English, German, and theater in Richmond, Va., 1960-62; University of Georgia, Athens, assistant professor of drama and theatre, 1968-76; Western Kentucky University, Bowling Green, associate professor of theater, 1976—. Free-lance designer and director in the United States and Norway; member of Foutain Square Players. *Member:* American Theater Association, Puppeteers of America, Costume Society of Great Britain, Southeastern Theater Association, Kentucky Theater Association, Bowling Green Landmark Association, Pi Delta Epsilon, Alpha Psi Omega, Phi Delta Theta.

WRITINGS: Theatrical Costume, Gale, 1979. Contributor to theater, education, and communication journals.

WORK IN PROGRESS: The Howard-Aiken-Fox Theatrical Dynasty; a textbook on fundamentals of theater.

SIDELIGHTS: Kesler wrote: "I have studied and had experience in all phases of theater, from historical research to directing; however, my chief interests have been costume designing and directing. In addition, I have taught stagecraft, scene design, research methodology, and theater history and criticism. A great asset to my professional practice and teaching effectiveness has been involvement in summer theater since I first designed costumes for 'Drumbeats in Geor-

gia' in 1973. I have served as costumer, theater, administrator, and director at two other summer theaters: The McIntosh Trail and Discoveryland Outdoor Musical Dramas. These professional outlets have afforded me the opportunities to practice my craft and skills in the summertime and to approach the teaching of them with renewed insight and enthusiasm. It has also been an excellent source for employment for my students.

"In addition to my theatrical activities, I have a strong interest in the field of American pressed glass, and operate an informal antique business specializing in glass and American regional primitives. The consuming interest since 1977 has been the salvation and restoration of an 1883 Victorian house in the downtown area of Bowling Green. It has been returned from three apartments to a single-family dwelling, with many hours of toil and trial and error. I have traveled extensively in the United States, and served as tour guide for two theater tours of London, and have led a student theatrical troupe to Norway."

*   *   *

KILLINGER, George G(lenn)   1908-

PERSONAL: Born March 13, 1908, in Marion, Va.; son of James Peter and Lena (Kelly) Killinger; married Grace Davis, June 29, 1935; children: Robert Peter, Evangeline, George Evan. *Education:* Wittenberg College (now University), A.B. (with honors), 1930; University of North Carolina, Ph.D., 1933. *Politics:* Democrat. *Religion:* Lutheran. *Home:* 6504 East Hill Sr., Austin, Tex. 78731. *Office:* Texas Board of Pardons and Paroles, Austin, Tex.

CAREER: Worked as assistant personnel director of Mathieson Alkali Works, 1933-34; Tennessee Valley Authority, Knoxville, psychologist and special assistant to director of personnel, 1934-36; Southwestern State Hospital, Marion, Va.; director of social services and out-patient departments, 1936-37; U.S. Public Health Service, Federal Reformatory, Chillicothe, Ohio, psychologist, 1937-38; U.S. Penitentiary, Atlanta, Ga., director of education and assistant associate warden, in charge of individualized treatment, 1938-42; Bureau of Prisons, Washington, D.C., director of education, 1942-43; Pentagon, Washington, D.C., chairman of Army Clemency and Parole Board, 1946-48; U.S. Department of Justice, Washington, D.C., chairman of U.S. Board of Parole, 1948-58, member of board, 1958-60; Florida State University, Tallahassee, professor of criminology and corrections, 1960-65; Sam Houston State University, Huntsville, Tex., director of Institute of Contemporary Corrections and the Behavioral Sciences, 1965-77, Piper Distinguished Professor, 1968; Texas Board of Pardons and Paroles, Austin, chairman, 1977—. Diplomate of American Board of Examiners in Professional Psychology. Professorial lecturer at George Washington University, 1952-58; lecturer at New York University, 1950-68.

Member of National Advisory Council on Undergraduate and Graduate Accreditation of Colleges and Universities Offering Programs in Criminal Justice; member of task force on corrections of National Advisory Commission on Criminal Justice Standards and Goals, 1972-73; member of Texas Commission on Law Enforcement Standards and Education, 1965-77; member of advisory council of State of Texas Juvenile Corrections Plan and Texas Institute on Children and Youth; member of advisory committee on corrections of Texas Criminal Justice Council, and board of directors of Houston Regional Council on Alcoholism. Workshop leader; consultant to Texas Research League. *Military service:* U.S.

Public Health Service, chief of psychobiological activities with War Shipping Administration, 1943-46; became lieutenant commander. U.S. Public Health Service Reserve, 1946-66; became scientist director.

MEMBER: American Association for the Advancement of Science (fellow), American Psychological Association (fellow), American Society of Criminology, American Prison Association, American Correctional Association, National Probation and Parole Association (member of advisory council, 1952-54), National Council on Crime and Delinquency, American Association on Adult Education, Adult Education Association of the United States, American Association of University Professors, U.S. Public Health Service Reserve Officers Association, Southern Sociological Association, Texas Psychological Association, Texas Probation and Parole Association, Virginia Psychological Association, American Legion, Sons of the American Revolution, Wittenberg University Alumni Association (past president), Phi Mu Alpha Sinfonia (president, 1932-33), Psi Chi (co-founder; charter member; past president), Alpha Psi Delta, Phi Mu Delta, Pi Gamma Mu, Phi Alpha, Alpha Kappa Delta, Pi Kappa Alpha, Kiwanis, Advertising Club (New York, N.Y.), Kenwood Golf and Country Club, Touchdown Club, University Club (Washington, D.C.), Warwick Club, Huntsville Club. *Awards, honors:* LL.D. from Wittenberg University, 1953; named distinguished Virginian by governor of Virginia, 1957; grants from Florida Council on Research and Training in Mental Health, 1965, and U.S. Department of Labor, 1966; hall of honor award from Texas Corrections Association, 1975; special citation from Texas Senate and House of Representatives; national award from Society for Public Administration, 1976.

WRITINGS: Emotional Judgments of Music, University of North Carolina Press, 1934; *Gearing Federal Prisons to the War Effort,* U.S. Department of Justice, 1941; (contributor) Bernard Glueck, editor, *Personality Disorders,* Grune, 1947; *The Psychobiological Program of the War Shipping Administration,* Stanford University Press, 1947; *Prison Work as a Post-War Career,* Bureau of Prisons, U.S. Department of Justice, 1948; (contributor) Paul W. Tappen, editor, *Contemporary Corrections,* McGraw, 1951; *Series in Sociology and Anthropology,* McGraw, 1951.

Penology: The Evolution of the American Correctional System, West Publishing, 1973, 2nd edition, 1978; *Corrections in the Community,* West Publishing, 1974, 2nd edition, 1977; *Issues on Law Enforcement,* Holbrook, 1975; *Probation and Parole,* West Publishing, 1976; *Issues in Corrections and Administration,* West Publishing, 1976; *Introduction to Juvenile Delinquency,* West Publishing, 1977. Contributor to professional journals.

*   *   *

KIMBALL, Penn T(ownsend) 1915-

PERSONAL: Born October 12, 1915, in New Britain, Conn.; son of Arthur G. and Effie (Smallen) Kimball; married Janet Evelyn Fraser, April 8, 1947; children: Elisabeth K. Carlson. *Education:* Princeton University, B.A., 1937; Balliol College, Oxford, B.A. and M.A., 1939; further graduate study at University of Grenoble, 1939, Yale University, 1950-51, and Columbia University, 1951-59. *Politics:* Democrat. *Religion:* Congregationalist. *Home address:* P.O. Box 240, Chilmark, Mass. 02535. *Office:* Graduate School of Journalism, Columbia University, New York, N.Y. 10027.

CAREER: Washington Post, Washington, D.C., special correspondent from Europe, 1938-39; White House and con-

gressional correspondent for *U.S. News and World Report,* 1939-40; reporter for *PM* (newspaper), 1940-42; *Time,* New York City, contributing editor, 1945-46; *New Republic,* Washington, D.C., senior editor, 1947; administrative assistant to governor of Connecticut, 1948-49; executive secretary to U.S. senator, 1949-50; *New York Times,* New York City, assistant to Sunday editor and member of Sunday staff, 1951-54; affiliated with TV Radio Workshop of Ford Foundation, 1954-55; Columbia Broadcasting System (CBS), feature editor and writer for "Omnibus," 1954-55; senior editor of *Collier's* (magazine), 1955-56; Louis Harris & Associates, New York City, partner, 1957-58; administrative assistant to governor of New York, 1958; Columbia University, Graduate School of Journalism, New York City, professor of journalism, 1959—, member of administrative board of Bureau of Applied Social Research, 1963-67.

Member of faculty at Salzburg Seminar in American Studies, 1967; faculty adviser to National Urban Fellowship Program at Yale University, summers, 1969-70; visiting lecturer at Dartmouth College and University of California, Berkeley. University of Connecticut secretary of committee on appropriations of Connecticut General Assembly, 1949, member of citizen's commission, 1968-69; member of board of finance of City of Westport, Conn., 1953-55, member of charter commission, 1957, justice of the peace, 1959-60, representative at town meetings, 1959-63; member of Connecticut Constitutional Convention, 1965; director of public affairs of New York State Urban Development Corp., 1971-72; member of national advisory committee election systems project of National Municipal League and League of Women Voters, 1971-73. *Military service:* U.S. Marine Corps, 1942-45; became major. *Member:* American Association of Public Opinion Researchers, National Press Club, Phi Beta Kappa. *Awards, honors:* Rhodes scholar at Oxford University, 1937-39.

WRITINGS: (Contributor) *The U.S. and Latin America,* Columbia University Press, 1959; (contributor) *The Professions in America,* Houghton, 1965; *Bobby Kennedy and the New Politics,* Prentice-Hall, 1968; *The Disconnected,* Columbia University Press, 1972. Also contributor to books. Editor of *Louis Harris Public Opinion Survey,* 1963-74; member of board of editors of *Columbia Journalism Review,* 1963—.

*   *   *

KING, John Edward 1947-

PERSONAL: Born April 17, 1947, in London, England; son of Edward (a clerk) and Jessie (a hairdresser; maiden name, Stone) King; married Marian Dianna Austin, June 20, 1967; children: Cheryl Nichola, Victor John. *Education:* St. Peter's College, Oxford, B.A. (with honors), 1967. *Politics:* "Anarcho-Communist." *Religion:* None. *Home:* 4 The Grove, Lancaster, England. *Office:* Department of Economics, University of Lancaster, Lancaster, England.

CAREER: Oxford University, Oxford, England, assistant staff tutor in industrial relations, 1967-68; University of Lancaster, Lancaster, England, lecturer in economics, 1968—. Visiting fellow at La Trobe University, Melbourne, Australia, 1975-76, 1979-80.

WRITINGS: Labour Economics, Macmillan, 1972; (with Michael Charles Howard) *The Political Economy of Marx,* Penguin, 1975; (editor with Howard) *The Economics of Marx: Selected Readings,* Penguin, 1976; (with Philip Regan) *Relative Income Shares,* Macmillan, 1976; (editor) *Readings in Labour Economics,* Oxford University Press,

1980; (with Harry I. Dutton) *Ten Percent and No Surrender: The Preston Strike, 1853-54,* Cambridge University Press, 1981.

WORK IN PROGRESS: Research on British labor history and the history of economic heresies.

SIDELIGHTS: King told *CA:* "My interest in economic orthodoxy has declined as my interest in economic heresy (and its development in the British labor movement) has grown. I am equally opposed to Marxian economics as a counter-orthodoxy."

*   *   *

KING, Morton Brandon 1913-

PERSONAL: Born March 24, 1913, in Shelbyville, Tenn.; son of Morton Brandon and Margaret (Moody) King; married Joan Smith, 1965. *Education:* Vanderbilt University, A.B., 1934, A.M., 1936; University of Wisconsin (now University of Wisconsin—Madison), Ph.D., 1940; postdoctoral study at University of North Carolina and University of Michigan. *Religion:* Methodist.

CAREER: Davidson County Welfare Commission, Nashville, Tenn., case visitor, 1934-35; University of Mississippi, University, assistant professor of sociology, 1939-41; Mississippi State College (now University), Mississippi State, associate professor of sociology, 1941-43; University of Mississippi, professor of sociology and chairman of department, 1946-56; Southern Methodist University, Dallas, Tex., visiting professor of sociology, 1956-57; Northwestern University, Evanston, Ill., visiting professor of sociology, 1957-58; Southern Methodist University, professor of sociology, 1958-78, professor emeritus, 1978—, chairman of department, 1960-64, 1969-71, 1975-77, fellow of Graduate Council on Humanities, 1964-65. Chairman of Texas Committee on Population Study, 1960-62, and Southwest Faculty Conference, 1960-61; member of Methodist Council on Church-Related Colleges, 1966-72. *Military service:* U.S. Army, Adjutant General's Corps, 1943-46; became second lieutenant.

MEMBER: American Association for the Advancement of Science (fellow), American Sociological Association (fellow; member of council, 1966-67), Society for the Scientific Study of Religion (Southwestern president, 1975-78), Association for the Study of Religion, Religious Research Association, Association for the Sociology of Religion, Southwestern Sociological Association, Southern Sociological Association (president, 1954-55), Phi Beta Kappa, Sigma Alpha Epsilon, Alpha Kappa Delta.

WRITINGS: (With John N. Burrus and Harold A. Pedersen) *Mississippi Life Tables: 1950-51,* Bureau of Public Administration, University of Mississippi, 1954; (with John C. Belcher) *Mississippi's People,* Bureau of Public Administration, University of Mississippi, 1955; (with Harold A. Pedersen and John N. Burrus) *Mississippi's People, 1950,* Bureau of Public Administration, University of Mississippi, 1955; (with Lewis Rhodes) *Dallas Population Handbook: 1960,* Urban Studies Project, Southern Methodist University, 1962; (with Richard A. Hunt) *Measuring Religious Dimensions: Studies of Congregational Involvement,* Congregational Involvement Study, Southern Methodist University, 1972; (with Harry Hale, Jr., and Doris M. Jones) *New Witness: United Methodist Clergywomen,* United Methodist Board of Higher Education and Ministry, 1980. Contributor to sociology and related journals.

KIRSCH, Robert R. 1922-1980
(Robert Bancroft, Robert Dundee)

OBITUARY NOTICE—See index for *CA* sketch: Born October 18, 1922, in Brooklyn, N.Y.; died of cancer, August 16, 1980, in Santa Barbara, Calif. Journalist, columnist, editor, educator, and author. Kirsch was literary editor for the *Los Angeles Times* and wrote a daily column for more than twenty-five years. "There's no other writer who has sustained his level of productivity—or quality—as a book columnist in the United States," claimed the *Los Angeles Times.* Kirsch also taught journalism at the University of California. His works include *In the Wrong Rain, The Wars of Pardon, The Restless Lovers,* and *Knight of the Scimitar.* Obituaries and other sources: Roy Newquist, *Conversations,* Rand McNally, 1967; *Publishers Weekly,* August 29, 1980.

*   *   *

KNELMAN, Fred H. 1919-

PERSONAL: Born October 9, 1919, in Winnipeg, Manitoba, Canada; son of Morris J. and Betsy D. Knelman; married Pamela Fry (a writer and editor; divorced, 1960); children: Kevin M., Linda M. *Education:* Attended University of Manitoba, 1936-39; University of Toronto, B.A.Sc., 1943; McGill University, M.Eng., 1950; Imperial College of Science and Technology, London, diploma, 1953; University of London, Ph.D., 1961. *Home:* 3644 avenue du Musee, No. 22, Montreal, Quebec, Canada H3G 2C9. *Office:* 2010 Mackay, Montreal, Quebec, Canada H3G 1M8.

CAREER: Monarch Battery Co., Kingston, Ontario, chemical engineer in production control, 1945-46; McGill University, Montreal, Quebec, lecturer in chemical engineering, 1946-53; Stuart Brothers Ltd., Montreal, technical and research director, 1953-62; York University, Toronto, Ontario, associate professor of history of science, 1962-67; Concordia University, Montreal, professor of science and human affairs, 1967—, director of program. Director of Inovan Consulting Corp.; vice-president of Sollinger Industries. Chairman of United Nations Association, Montreal, 1978-80. Canadian delegate to World Conference on Human Environment, 1972; past chairman of Montreal Committee for Control of Radiation Hazards and Citizens for Social Responsibility in Science. Guest on Canadian radio and television programs, including "The Nature of Things"; consultant to Science Council of Canada, National Film Board, and Environment Canada.

MEMBER: International Epidemiological Association, Engineering Institute of Canada, Canadian Institute for Food Technology (chairman, 1958), American Association for the Advancement of Science, American Public Health Association, World Future Society, Mexican Institute of Chemical Engineers (honorary foreign member), New York Academy of Sciences. *Awards, honors:* Grant from World Wildlife Fund, 1970; peace essay prize for outstanding essay from World Federalists, 1971; White Owl Conservation Award for outstanding Canadian environmentalist from IMASCO, 1972.

WRITINGS: 1984 and All That, Wadsworth, 1970; *Nuclear Energy: The Unforgiving Technology,* Hurtig, 1976; *Anti-Nation: Transition to Sustainability,* Mosaic, 1979. Contributor of more than twenty articles to magazines and newspapers. Editor of *Flavour,* 1954-62. Author of more than fifty scholarly papers.

WORK IN PROGRESS: A biography of Cyrus Eaton, publication by Harvest House expected in 1982; *Occupational Health: The Politics of Cancer; Energy and Environment Policy Studies; The Information Society;* a book on the geopolitics of oil.

SIDELIGHTS: Knelman wrote that he is motivated by "a passion for poetry and justice." He added: "A Ph.D. in applied science and engineering sidetracked my career for a decade. I am an international opponent of nuclear power, having testified at dozens of formal hearings all over the world. I am also a critic of uncontrolled technology serving mindless and destructive growth. I have ecologized my thinking and life style to discover peace with myself, nonactively seeking world peace."

AVOCATIONAL INTERESTS: Music, tennis, card games.

*   *   *

KNIGHT, Thomas J(oseph)   1937-

PERSONAL: Born August 5, 1937, in Denton, Tex.; son of Thomas D. (in business) and Jo (in business; maiden name, Savage) Knight; married Barbara L. Jones, December 29, 1955; children: Russell Alan, Karen Jeanne. *Education:* North Texas State University, A.B., 1959; University of Texas at Austin, Ph.D., 1967. *Home:* 2023 North Oak Lane, State College, Pa. 16801. *Agent:* Gloria Stern, 1230 Park Ave., New York, N.Y. 10028. *Office:* Pennsylvania State University, University Park, Pa. 16802.

CAREER: Moore Business Forms, Denton, Tex., junior accountant, 1955-59; University of Minnesota, Minneapolis, teaching fellow, 1959-61; University of Nebraska at Lincoln, instructor in history, 1964-65; Michigan State University, East Lansing, assistant professor of humanities, 1966-68; Pennsylvania State University, Harrisburg, associate professor of social science and history, 1968-76; Pennsylvania State University, University Park, professor of American studies and history, 1976—, associate dean of College of Liberal Arts, 1976—. Technology assessment consultant to Pennsylvania Department of Commerce, 1973-74. Lecturer at Polish Academy of Sciences, Warsaw, 1979, and at National Polytechnic Institute, Mexico City, 1980. *Member:* American Historical Association, American Academy of Political and Social Sciences, Latin American Studies Association, Society for the History of Technology. *Awards, honors:* Woodrow Wilson fellowship, 1959-60; Southern Historical Association prize, 1962; James Jordan Teaching Excellence Award from Pennsylvania State University, Capitol Campus, 1974.

WRITINGS: Technology's Future, International Society for Technological Assessment, 1976, revised edition, Krieger Reprints, 1981; *Latin America Comes of Age,* Scarecrow, 1979. Contributor of about a dozen articles on European history, Latin American culture, and technology and society to journals and magazines, including *Journal of Modern History, Intellect,* and *Alternative Futures;* contributor of poems to *Poet Love, Gem,* and *Harpoon.*

WORK IN PROGRESS: Books on Third World and U.S. technology, and on Latin minorities in the United States; articles, short stories, poems, and translations on life in the southern and southwestern United States.

SIDELIGHTS: Knight told *CA:* "My major professional interest at the moment is in the effects of technology on society. Generally speaking, my methods are historical, although I occasionally use some of the quantitative methods of political science, sociology, and economics. In addition, I am doing some work on utopian visions of the technological society in the extensive utopian collection at Penn State. My creative work draws on my Texas origins and includes published poems and translations as well as yet unpublished short stories."

*   *   *

KNIGHTS, John Keell   1930(?)-1981

OBITUARY NOTICE: Born c. 1930; died of a heart attack, January 26, 1981, in Newport, Isle of Wight, England. Yachtsman and journalist. Knights was the yachting writer for the *London Daily Express* and, since 1973, the European correspondent for *Sail* magazine. His articles also appeared in sailing magazines around the world. Knights was the British Finn Class champion three times, a winner of North American Finn title, and an alternate on the British Olympic sailing team in 1956. Obituaries and other sources: *New York Times,* January 29, 1981.

*   *   *

KNORR, Marian L(ockwood)   1910-
(Lorimer DeKalb)

PERSONAL: Born December 2, 1910, in Long Island, N.Y.; daughter of Willard Datus and Louisa (Scofield) Lockwood; separated; children: Albert S. *Education:* Attended private girls' school in Philadelphia, Pa. *Religion:* Church of the Nazarene. *Residence;* Richmond Hill, N.Y. *Office:* Defense Contract Administration Services Management Area, U.S. Department of Defense, 60 Hudson St., New York, N.Y. 10013.

CAREER: Office worker, 1931-52; U.S. Department of Defense, New York, N.Y., secretary, 1952—. *Awards, honors:* Five superior sustained performance awards from U.S. Department of Defense.

WRITINGS: (Under pseudonym Lorimer DeKalb) *Stranger From the Past* (novel), Revell, 1975. Contributor of poems, songs and a skit to religious magazines, including *Herald of Holiness.*

SIDELIGHTS: Marian Knorr wrote: "Since I was saved in 1941, I have considered Christ the most important event in my life. I write Christian songs, poems, and stories and, when someone in my office leaves a job, I am asked to write a poem. I must have written and illustrated about three thousand.

"Several times in my own religious denomination, there have been people (mostly single men) who trail into a prayer meeting and 'prey' on innocent people, causing them to pray with them, give them money or a night's lodging, then get robbed. I finally said, 'I could write a book' and did. Including the three times I wrote it, the years it remained in file, and the winter I slashed it in half, it was fourteen years before I got it published. I have also written another novel, *Search for a Blueprint,* which has not been published."

AVOCATIONAL INTERESTS: Painting in oils and water colors, swimming, bicycling.

*   *   *

KNOWLES, Anne   1933-

PERSONAL: Born November 25, 1933, in Oxford, England; daughter of Walter (an army major) and Winifred (Dixon) Coleman; married Adam Knowles, December 21, 1957 (divorced January, 1979); children: Rachel, Simon, Matthew, Hannah, Gideon. *Education:* Bedford College, B.A., 1956. *Politics:* None. *Religion:* Church of England. *Home:* Clissold Farm, Sheepscombe, Stroud, Gloucestershire, England. *Agent:* Gina Pollinger, Murray Pollinger, 4 Garrick St., London WC2E 9BH, England.

CAREER: Part-time teacher, 1956—. Riding instructor; painter of landscapes.

WRITINGS: Flag (juvenile), Blackie & Son, 1976; *Sea Change* (juvenile), Blackie & Son, 1979; *Matthew Ratton* (adult novel), Eyre Methuen, 1980, St. Martin's, in press; *Halcyon Island* (juvenile), Blackie & Son, 1980, Harper, 1981; *The Raven Tree* (adult novel), Eyre Methuen, 1981.

WORK IN PROGRESS: A book on the Cotswolds; two novels.

SIDELIGHTS: Anne Knowles commented: "I run a small farm, ride, paint, and write because I can't stop writing—even without prospect of publication. I re-educate naughty ponies, have children to stay for riding holidays, and enjoy myself exploring the Cotswold countryside.

"I write, as far as possible, from my own knowledge and experience, but because these are limited, I must also see, with imaginative comparison, into the minds and lives of other people, in order to create believeable characters whose whole existence is credible, so that the reader feels that although the books are fiction—a presence of reality—yet things could and do happen in just such a way.

"When I write for children, I like to write a story that will tempt them to read, and then make them stretch to understand, because stretching makes you grow and that's what reading is for.

"I write what I enjoy writing. If I don't, the magic goes, and the whole timing fails; which is not to say the writing itself isn't very hard work, demanding, sometimes disappointing, constantly in need of drastic revision and painful pruning. It makes a full day on the farm seem easy by comparison!"

*   *   *

KO, Kanzein
     See ISOGAI, Hiroshi

*   *   *

KOENIG, John (Thomas) 1938-

PERSONAL: Born June 20, 1938, in Fort Wayne, Ind.; son of Melvin H. and Doris L. Koenig; married Elisabeth Kathleen Jameson, June 5, 1976. *Education:* Concordia Senior College, Fort Wayne, Ind., A.B., 1961; Concordia Seminary, St. Louis, Mo., B.D., 1965; Union Theological Seminary, New York, N.Y., Th.D., 1970. *Home and office:* General Theological Seminary, 175 Ninth Ave., New York, N.Y. 10011.

CAREER: Ordained Lutheran minister; Princeton Theological Seminary, Princeton, N.J., assistant professor of New Testament, 1971-76; Union Theological Seminary, New York City, associate professor of New Testament, 1976-78; General Theological Seminary, New York City, professor of New Testament, 1978—, director of graduate studies, 1980—. Member of summer faculty at St. John's University, Collegeville, Minn., 1976, 1978, and 1980. *Member:* Society of Biblical Literature (president of Delaware-Hudson region, 1978), Society for Values in Higher Education, Columbia Seminar for New Testament Studies, Biblical Theologians. *Awards, honors:* Kent fellow of German Academic Exchange Service.

WRITINGS: Charismata: God's Gifts for God's People, Westminster, 1978; *Jews and Christians in Dialogue: New*

Testament Foundations, Westminster, 1979; *Commentary on Philippians and Philemon,* Augsburg, in press.

WORK IN PROGRESS: The Wandering, Welcoming Christ: New Testament Hospitality and Contemporary Ministry.

SIDELIGHTS: Koenig told *CA:* "My consistent goal is to do New Testament studies so that they become resources for Christian ministry today." *Avocational interests:* Travel (Europe, South America, the Middle East).

*   *   *

KONNER, Linda 1951-

PERSONAL: Born February 16, 1951, in Brooklyn, N.Y.; daughter of Sol (a die-cutter) and Bernice (Mandell) Konner. *Education:* Brooklyn College of City University of New York, B.A. (magna cum laude), 1972; Fordham University, M.A.T., 1975. *Residence:* New York, N.Y. *Office: Seventeen,* 850 Third Ave., New York, N.Y. 10022.

CAREER: Henrietta (biweekly newspaper), New York City, founder, editor, and writer, 1972-74; *Brooklyn Courier-Life,* New York City, reporter and feature writer, 1975-76; *Seventeen,* New York City, staff writer and editor of "Mini-Mag," 1976—. Guest lecturer at New School for Social Research, 1978; instructor at Womanschool, 1979; lecturer at New York University, 1979—; conducts workshops. *Member:* Broadcast Music Inc. Musical Theatre Workshop, Phi Beta Kappa.

WRITINGS: The Lore and Lure of Birthstones (juvenile), Merrimack, 1977; *Roller Fever!* (young adult), Scholastic Book Services, 1979.

Work represented in anthologies, including *Sky Blue, Grass Green.*

Author of column, "Potpourri: People and Places in Brooklyn" in *Brooklyn Courier-Life,* a television review column in *Our Town,* and a theatre review column in *Brooklyn Today.* Contributor of stories and articles to magazines and newspapers, including *Ladies' Home Journal, Womensweek, Us, Soap Opera Digest,* and *Weight Watchers.*

WORK IN PROGRESS: The Book of Kids, publication expected in 1981; research on comedy and songwriting for cabarets.

SIDELIGHTS: Konner told *CA:* "In eighth grade, our English teacher, Mr. Berger, gave us the assignment to read and write a book review of Booth Tarkington's *Seventeen.* My 'review' was in the form of a synopsis for a musical comedy version of *Seventeen* and on it Mr. Berger wrote: 'A! This was even better than the original book!' That episode had a lot to do with my decision to become a writer. What a coincidence that, not only have I indeed pursued a writing career, but that I just happen to do much of my writing for *Seventeen* magazine."

AVOCATIONAL INTERESTS: Lyric writing, oriental cooking.

*   *   *

KORMAN, Keith 1956-

PERSONAL: Born May 12, 1956, in New York. *Education:* Hobart College, B.A. *Agent:* Theron Raines, Raines & Raines, 475 Fifth Ave., New York, N.Y. 10017. *Office:* Raines & Raines, 475 Fifth Ave., New York, N.Y. 10017.

CAREER: WECQ-Radio, Geneva, N.Y., disc jockey, 1977-78; Raines & Raines, New York, N.Y., literary agent, 1978—. *Member:* Authors Guild.

WRITINGS: Swan Dive, Random House, 1980. Contributor to *The Writers' Manual,* Beverly Hills Bar Association.

SIDELIGHTS: Korman wrote: "I have current interests in everything current and some things quite out of date. I get strange kicks from writing. The only thing harder than publishing is keeping yourself published, and the only thing harder than keeping yourself published is actually writing anything at all. I read a lot."

* * *

KOSYGIN, Alexei Nikolayevich 1904-1980

OBITUARY NOTICE: Born February 20, 1904, in St. Petersburg, Russia (now Leningrad, U.S.S.R.); died of a heart attack, December 18, 1980, in Moscow, U.S.S.R. Politician. Kosygin was the premier of the Soviet Union from 1964 to 1980. For a man whose political life began in 1927, years before the first of Stalin's purges, Kosygin's career was remarkably free of serious setbacks. He came to prominence in Soviet politics in the late 1930's, when he was named mayor of Leningrad, elected to the Central Committee of the Communist party, and placed in charge of the textile industry. In 1943 he became the premier of Russia, the largest of the republics in the Soviet Union. Kosygin's election in 1946 to the Politburo, the party's inner circle, significantly enhanced his influence in party affairs. Two years later Stalin unleashed the last of his purges in what became known as the "Leningrad Affair," a mass execution of leaders from that city. According to the memoirs of the late Nikita Khruschev, Kosygin's "life was hanging by a thread" during the time of terror, but he survived to become a deputy premier in Khruschev's government, in charge of the U.S.S.R.'s economy. In 1964 Kosygin joined with Leonid Brezhnev and Nikolai Podgorny in the so-called "troika" that wrested power away from Khruschev. He was from that time on the premier of the U.S.S.R. until illness obliged him to resign in October, 1980. He had remained at the top of the Soviet hierarchy for more than forty years, an achievement of note to many political analysts, among them former Secretary of State Henry Kissinger who attributed Kosygin's political longevity to his "undoubted competence." Russian dissident Andrei Sakharov has added that Kosygin was the "most intelligent and the toughest" of the Soviet leaders. Kosygin was the author of *Basic Guidelines of the Economic Development of the U.S.S.R. for 1976-1980.* Obituaries and other sources: *Who's Who,* 126th edition, St. Martin's, 1974; *The International Who's Who,* Europa, 1974; *Who's Who in Government,* Marquis, 1972; *New York Times,* December 20, 1980, December 21, 1980; *Washington Post,* December 20, 1980; *Time,* December 29, 1980.

* * *

KOULACK, David 1938-

PERSONAL: Born December 21, 1938, in New York, N.Y.; son of Isadore (a physician) and Annette (a bacteriologist; maiden name, Meretz) Koulack; children: Joshua, Daniel. *Education:* Brandeis University, B.A., 1960; Yeshiva University, M.S., 1961, Ph.D., 1967. *Office:* Department of Psychology, University of Manitoba, Winnipeg, Manitoba, Canada R3T 2N2.

CAREER: Brooklyn College of the City University of New York, Brooklyn, N.Y., lecturer in psychology, 1963-66; Washington State University, Pullman, assistant professor of psychology, 1966-68; University of Manitoba, Winnipeg, assistant professor, 1968-70, associate professor, 1970-77, professor of psychology, 1977—. *Member:* Canadian Psy-

chological Association, American Psychological Association, Association for the Psychophysiological Study of Sleep.

WRITINGS: Dream Research, Hoffman-La Roche, 1971; (editor with Daniel Perlman) *Focus on Canada,* Wiley, 1973; (with R. H. Gatley) *Single Father's Handbook: A Guide for Separated and Divorced Fathers,* Doubleday, 1979. Contributor of about thirty-five articles and reviews to psychology journals.

WORK IN PROGRESS: A book on sleep and dream research.

SIDELIGHTS: Koulack told *CA:* "I very much enjoy doing research in both sleep and dreams and social psychology, and I'm continuing work in those areas. I've also become interested in attempting to tie together loose threads in the research and the thrust of my work is becoming more theoretical. But most importantly, I've become interested in demystifying psychology for the lay person. To this end I've been writing newspaper and magazine articles on psychology topics."

* * *

KOVACS, Imre 1913-1980

*OBITUARY NOTICE—*See index for *CA* sketch: Born March 10, 1913, in Felsoegoeboeljaras, Hungary; died after a short illness, October 28, 1980, in New York. Politician, editor, and author. Kovacs was a political activist in his native Hungary in the 1930's and 1940's. He published his first book, *A Nema For radalom* (title means "The Silent Revolution"), in 1937. The volume, which severely criticized Hungary's inequitable social system, caused an immediate stir. As a result, Kovacs was imprisoned for three months. After his release, the author immersed himself in Hungarian politics, working as secretary-general with the Hungarian National Peasant Party and as a member of the Hungarian Parliament. When complete Soviet control of the country seemed inevitable, Kovacs immigrated to the United States. He then became president of the International Center for Social Research, Inc., and a senior editor of Free Europe, Inc. His other works include *Magyar Feudalizmus-Magyar Parasztsag* (title means "Hungarian Feudalism, Hungarian Peasantry"), *Elsullyedt Orszag* (title means "The Sunken Country"), and *The Ninety and Nine.* Obituaries and other sources: *London Times,* October 30, 1980.

* * *

KRAIG, Bruce 1939-

PERSONAL: Born September 23, 1939, in New York, N.Y.; son of Abe (a psychoanalyst) and Zaira (a physician; maiden name, Astafijew) Kraig; married Barbara Adams, November, 1960 (divorced, 1972); children: Robert A., Michael B., Theodore D. *Education:* University of California, Berkeley, B.A., 1962; University of Pennsylvania, M.A., 1963, Ph.D., 1969. *Home:* 45 Chicago Ave., Oak Park, Ill. 60302. *Agent:* Barbara Mullarkey, P.O. Box 946, Oak Park, Ill. 60303. *Office:* Department of History, Roosevelt University, 430 South Michigan Ave., Chicago, Ill. 60605.

CAREER: Eastern Illinois University, Charleston, assistant professor of history, 1968-70; Roosevelt University, Chicago, Ill., associate professor of history, 1971—, assistant to dean of faculties and director of university honors program. Curator and archaeologist at Pennsylvania State Museum, 1965; assistant director of archaeological projects in England, 1964, 1966-68. *Member:* American Historical Association, American Committee on Indo-European Studies, Society for Medieval Archaeology, Deserted Village Research Group, Royal Archaeological Institute, British Agricultural History Society, Yorkshire Archaeological Society.

WRITINGS: (With L. S. Stover) *Stonehenge: The Indo-European Heritage,* Nelson-Hall, 1978; *The Formation of Civilization* (monograph), Forum Press, 1979; *Mexican-American Cooking,* Nelson-Hall, 1981. Writer for WCEV-Radio. Author of "Cooking," a cooking column in *Wednesday Journal.* Contributor of articles and reviews to scholarly journals. Food editor of *Wednesday Journal,* 1979—.

WORK IN PROGRESS: Europe in the Barbarian Age; a textbook on world and Western civilization; collecting materials for a book on famous Chicago chefs; collecting materials for a book on ethnic restaurants.

SIDELIGHTS: Kraig wrote: "I have always been a teacher; that remains my primary interest whether I am working in a classroom or writing. But teaching is only part of a larger process of exploring the world and the people in it. Mainly, I want to find out how things (and people) work. Once I begin to get a handle on something of interest, then I try to work out the details and ramifications through the teaching process. That is, I end up talking about it—often to myself. My children regard such behavior as very eccentric, but I merely tell them that this is really a dialectical process.

"Whether the topic is European prehistory (this falls under the heading of 'how and why we got here') or food, my interests are much the same. As for the latter, food, I am not so much interested in recipes, though admitting to a certain gluttonous disposition, as in how food tells us something about the culture of a people. All of my newspaper articles deal with matters of popular culture, folklore, language—in short, all the elements that go to make up a people's culture. Without this, food writing tends to become fairly uninteresting, at least for me.

"I should add that I am endlessly interested in origins—how everything we see around us began. All of my work in history and archaeology, along with folklore, really moves toward that end. My teaching follows the same line, for if students and readers can understand the bases for their ideas then they are more apt to be able to criticize and change them when necessary. Our future and our present is made from what we conceive the past to have been. In a larger sense, knowing that is one of the major goals of the Liberal Arts."

*   *   *

KRAMER, Jane 1938-

PERSONAL: Born August 7, 1938, in Providence, R.I.; daughter of Louis (a physician) and Jessica (Shore) Kramer; married Vincent Crapanzano (professor and writer), April 30, 1967; children: Aleksandra. *Education:* Vassar College, B.A., 1959; Columbia University, M.A., 1961. *Residence:* New York, N.Y. *Agent:* Lynn Nesbit, International Creative Management, 40 West 57th St., New York, N.Y. 10019. *Office: New Yorker,* 25 West 43rd St., New York, N.Y. 10036.

CAREER: Morningsider, New York City, founder and writer, 1961-62; *Village Voice,* New York City, writer, 1962-63; *New Yorker,* New York City, writer, 1963—. Member of Council on Foreign Relations; member of Journalists Human Rights Committee; associate of Environmental Defense Fund. Consultant to German Marshall Fund, 1981. *Member:* Writers Guild of America (East; board member, 1963-65),

Authors League of America, Authors Guild, P.E.N., Book Critics Circle, Phi Beta Kappa. *Awards, honors:* Emmy award from National Academy of Television Arts and Sciences, 1966, for documentary, "This Is Edward Steichen"; named woman of the year by *Mademoiselle,* 1968; Front Page award from *New Yorker,* 1977, for best magazine feature, "The Invandrare."

WRITINGS—All nonfiction: *Off Washington Square: A Reporter Looks at Greenwich Village,* Duell, Sloan & Pearce, 1963; *Allen Ginsberg in America,* Random House, 1969 (published in England as *Paterfamilias,* Gollancz, 1970); *Honor to the Bride Like the Pigeon That Guards Its Grain Under the Clove Tree,* Farrar, Straus, 1970; *The Last Cowboy,* Harper, 1978; *Unsettling Europe,* Random House, 1980. Contributor to periodicals, including *New Yorker, New York Times Book Review* and *New York Review of Books.*

WORK IN PROGRESS: A nonfiction book on Europe.

SIDELIGHTS: Kramer's first widely reviewed book, *Allen Ginsberg in America,* met with a mixed reception. Many critics complained that Kramer's biographical portrait was too sketchy and admiring. Malcolm Muggeridge in the *Observer* called the author "sentimental, whimsical, sprawling" and explained that what the book "is lacking is any serious critical estimate of Ginsberg and his work." Similarly, Steve Lerner of the *Village Voice* observed "that while the book is an up, easy-flowing, often informative narrative about a colorful man, it lacks the tension and deep, often uncomfortable probing that a good biography requires in order to adequately depict a public figure." Lerner added, however, that even though Kramer in *Allen Ginsberg in America* "is repetitious of the flower-bedecked caricature we all know and love, she also manages to present enough new information, describe enough scenes that the television cameras missed, and hear enough good words that were inaudible to the masses to piece together a living Ginsberg. This, in itself, is enough of a recommendation to make the book worth reading for an audience of post beat-early hip generation who have missed the real article in person."

Honor to the Bride, Kramer's next book, is about the kidnapping and violation of a thirteen-year-old girl from her Arab family living in Meknes, Morocco. She is the family's most valuable asset, for her virginal state will bring in a substantial bride price. Therefore, when she is returned to her relatives, her family comically endeavors to legally reestablish her virginity. *Time*'s Martha Duffy highly praised *Honor to the Bride.* It "is an excellent example of the 'nonfiction novel,'" she commented. "Beyond its entertainment value, the book offers a remarkable glimpse into . . . Arab attitudes toward justice, money and women. . . . Thanks to the author's effortless narrative, the reader hurtles through an exotic world, not realizing until the end that he has been taken on a fascinating trip through the Arab mind."

A following book, *The Last Cowboy,* is the story of Henry Blanton, a cowboy who lives and works on a ranch in the Texas panhandle. With motion picture star Glen Ford as his model, Blanton has embodied the image of the proud cowboy to such a degree that he has become a caricature. Henry McDonald of the *Washington Post* explained that Blanton is seen "as an anomaly, not so much because he seems bigoted, chauvinistic and unpredictably violent. Rather, his oddity stems from his determination to live out a fantasy of himself as a rugged and heroic cowboy in a land which devalues such qualities." The *New York Times*'s John Leonard complimented the author on her portrait of Blanton and remarked: "It is a measure of Jane Kramer's immense skill that we come to like Henry almost in spite of himself. . . . We aren't poked in the tearducts; we merely watch and eavesdrop. . . . She [Kramer] is incapable of contempt, although the sadness has spurs.'' McDonald concurred and described *The Last Cowboy* as an ''insightful, unsentimental and handsomely crafted work.''

Unsettling Europe received favorable reviews from critics. Irving Howe of the *New York Times Book Review* explained that ''this accomplished book consists of four social-historical sketches—suavely but sturdily composed—about people in Europe who have been uprooted from their natural communities and thrust into alien, sometimes hostile settings.'' Featured are a Yugoslav family living in Sweden, French Algerians living in Provence, Ugandan Muslims dwelling in a London ghetto, and Italian Communists who feel their Party has forsaken them and the revolution. *Nation*'s Thomas Flanagan assessed that ''Kramer's intention is to break down the exhausted, conventional categories in which sociology and journalism solicit us to consider contemporary Europe, by creating for us the bitter, absurd, fractured lives of 'people who fell into the cracks of history.' '' James N. Baker of *Newsweek* agreed that Kramer's ''is no-nonsense journalism at its best: direct, finely detailed portraits of four troubled families . . . by a writer who combines the skills of a social historian with those of a novelist.''

CA INTERVIEW

CA interviewed Jane Kramer on October 20, 1980, at her home in New York City.

''What makes journalism so mediocre today is that journalists have stopped making connections between their stories and the intellectual data of the past.'' As Jane Kramer speaks, she is seated, appropriately, in front of a wall of books. A glance at the titles on the shelf behind her is illuminating. History. Philosophy. Anthropology. Politics. Her comment about the state of journalism stands in contrast to her own *New Yorker* pieces, which combine breadth of knowledge with a depth of analytical insight. ''I read a lot,'' she remarks unassumingly. A copy of *Economist* lies on the floor at her feet; today's air-delivered *Le Monde* is on her desk.

Although she is the *New Yorker*'s ''reporter in Europe,'' Kramer occasionally writes from other parts of the world such as the American West, in a series of articles that were eventually published in book form as *The Last Cowboy*, and Morocco, which she visited with her anthropologist husband, Vincent Crapanzano. Her pieces tend to fall into one of two categories: overview, analytical studies of the political and intellectual trends in the major European capitals; or intimate personality profiles of everyday people in out-of-the-way places. She is especially drawn to the ''marginal'' people in a society as a way of revealing the mainstream through contrast. ''I enjoy switching back and forth between two types of pieces, because each allows me to learn about a country and its people in different ways,'' she observes. ''While I enjoy the challenge of the theoretical pieces, I find it equally important to come back to the personal. In truth, I prefer the profiles. When I write them I am consciously creating; they are about real people, but I structure them as novels.''

Kramer initially writes a profile using the person's own name and later obscures the true identity in the final manuscript. ''I need to keep a sense of who the people are as I write,'' she explains. Profiles of an Italian Communist family, as well as a displaced Yugoslav family in Sweden, Ugandan Asians

in London, and French Algerians in France were collected into the highly-acclaimed *Unsettling Europe*.

A striking aspect of her work is the degree of intimacy she is able to develop with her subjects. She says she tries to go places where she has some personal connections so she is not perceived as a total stranger. On the other hand, she uses her status as an outsider to get closer to people than she might if she were a member of the community. She typically spends about six weeks with a family for a profile, often alternating a few days in their home with some time in a nearby town to do auxiliary research. Though Kramer speaks and reads French fluently, and speaks some Italian and Portuguese, she occasionally relies on interpreters in conducting interviews. Even when she cannot understand the language herself, she often spends time alone with the family members, observing their speech intonations, body language, and personal styles. ''I'm very much aware of rhythms of speech, and learn a lot even if I can't follow the words,'' she explains.

Asked what her strong points as a writer are, Kramer replies that she is able to gain insight into character, and then sketch that character for the reader. She also feels she has a knack for extracting from a large body of material the dramatic essence that holds its meaning. ''However, I'm terrible at abstraction,'' she admits. ''You'll notice that even my analytic pieces on Europe are grounded in observation and detail. I don't write well abstractly.'' The journalist who has most influenced her, she notes, is English writer Sybill Bedford, whose *The Faces of Justice* made a particularly strong impression.

Kramer works out of her home, using an enormous wooden Italian table as a writing desk, which nearly fills her small study. She is able to keep her working area uncluttered by filing past stories at the *New Yorker* offices. Her first drafts are triple-spaced, because, she says, they become ''indecipherable'' after her multiple editings. ''I spend as much time editing and reworking a piece as I do writing it the first time,'' she indicates. Kramer states that she knows she's working well when she loses all sense of time. Outlines are not written until she is well into a piece. ''And, they really aren't outlines in the usual sense of the word, but rather a list of several points I want to be sure to include.''

When she isn't brushing up on the current political and cultural trends in Paris or Berlin, she turns to her great love, poetry. She reads W. B. Yeats, John Donne, Gerard Manley Hopkins, Seamus Heaney, and Ted Hughes. Her favorite writer is George Eliot because the novelist ''writes about personal life in a moral universe. I like the moral rigor of Eliot's world. She is concerned with the ethical dimensions of personal and social behavior.'' Then, laughing, Kramer asks if she is sounding pretentious. Changing the mood, she adds: ''I *love* Proust, but can't stand Hemingway or Fitzgerald.''

BIOGRAPHICAL/CRITICAL SOURCES: New York Times Book Review, May 11, 1969, May 18, 1980; *New York Times*, May 17, 1969, January 24, 1978; *Christian Science Monitor*, July 17, 1969; *Village Voice*, September 4, 1969; *Time*, August 8, 1969, January 4, 1971; *Observer*, February 8, 1970; *New Statesman*, August 13, 1971; *Washington Post*, April 1, 1978; *Nation*, May 31, 1980; *Newsweek*, June 9, 1980; *New York Review of Books*, August 14, 1980.

—Interview by Trisha Gorman

KRAUS, Barbara 1929-1977

CAREER: United Nations Association of the United States of America, New York, N.Y., public relations director, 1957-66; owner of public relations firm, 1966-69; U.S. Peace Corps, Washington, D.C., special assistant to director, 1969-77.

WRITINGS: (Editor) *The Cookbook of the United Nations: Two-Hundred-Fifty Authentic Recipes From One-Hundred-Twelve Countries,* United Nations Association of the United States of America, 1964, revised edition, Simon & Schuster, 1970; *Calories and Carbohydrates,* Grosset, 1971, 2nd edition published as *The Dictionary of Calories and Carbohydrates,* 1973, 3rd edition published under original title, New American Library, 1979, excerpts published as *The Barbara Kraus 1974 Caloric Guide to Brand Names and Basic Foods,* New American Library, 1974, *The Basic Food and Brand-Name Calorie Counter,* Grosset, 1974, *The Barbara Kraus 1975 Carbohydrate Guide to Brand Names and Basic Foods,* New American Library, 1975, and *The Barbara Kraus 1976 Carbohydrate Guide to Brand Names and Basic Foods,* New American Library, 1975; (editor) *The Cookbook to Serve Two, Six, or Twenty-Four: America's Best Restaurant Recipes,* Quadrangle, 1973; *The Dictionary of Sodium, Fats, and Cholesterol,* Grosset, 1974; *The Barbara Kraus Dictionary of Protein: Over Eight-Thousand Brand Names and Basic Foods With Their Protein (and Caloric) Count,* Harper's Magazine Press, 1975; *The Barbara Kraus Guide to Fiber in Foods,* New American Library, 1975; *The Entertainer: Cookbook to Serve Two, Six, or Twenty-Four,* Times Books, 1975; *The Barbara Kraus Calorie Guide to Brand Names and Basic Foods,* New American Library, 1979; *The Barbara Kraus 1979 Carbohydrate Guide to Brand Names and Basic Foods,* New American Library, 1979; *The Barbara Kraus Caloric Guide to Brand Names and Basic Foods,* New American Library, 1980; *The Barbara Kraus Carbohydrate Guide to Brand Names and Basic Foods,* New American Library, 1980. Also author of *Compliments to the Chef.*

BIOGRAPHICAL/CRITICAL SOURCES: New York Times, December 22, 1977.*

*   *   *

KREISMAN, Marvin 1933(?)-1979(?)

OBITUARY NOTICE: Born c. 1933; died c. 1979 in Columbia, Mo. Photographer, collector, and historian. Kreisman taught photography at Stephens College for fourteen years. He and his wife helped found the Midwest Photo Historical Society in the early 1970's, as well as the American Photography Museum a few years later. A collector of photographs and cameras, Kreisman's own work was published by the Associated Press, United Press International, *Time, Life,* and other magazines. Obituaries and other sources: *AB Bookman's Weekly,* January 5, 1980.

*   *   *

KREN, George M. 1926-

PERSONAL: Born June 3, 1926, in Austria; came to the United States in 1940, naturalized citizen, 1943; son of Frank (a physician) and Gertrude (Bloch) Kren; married first wife, Claudia (divorced); married Margo Hemphill (an artist), June 1, 1968; children: Stefan. *Education:* Colby College, B.A., 1948; University of Wisconsin (now University of Wisconsin—Madison), M.A., 1949, Ph.D., 1960. *Home:* 823 Bertrand, Manhattan, Kan. 66502. *Office:* Department of History, Kansas State University, Manhattan, Kan. 66506.

CAREER: Research editor for *American People's Encyclopedia,* 1954-56; C. Bertelsmann Verlag, Munich, West Germany, research editor, 1956; Oberlin College, Oberlin, Ohio, instructor in history, 1958-59; Elmira College, Elmira, N.Y., assistant professor of history, 1959-60; Lake Forest College, Lake Forest, Ill., assistant professor of history, 1960-65; Kansas State University, Manhattan, associate professor, 1965-76, professor of history, 1976—. Visiting professor at University of New Mexico, summer, 1961; lecturer at Roosevelt University, 1964-65, and Menninger Foundation and Oxford University, 1978; public speaker; research associate of Institute for Psychohistory. *Military service:* U.S. Army, 1944-46.

MEMBER: International Society for the History of the Behavioral and Social Sciences, American Historical Association, Conference Group for Central European History, Group for the Use of Psychology in History, Conference Group on German Politics. *Awards, honors:* Grant from Kansas Committee on the Humanities, 1975; National Endowment for the Humanities grant, 1977.

WRITINGS: (With Leon Rappoport) *Varieties of Psychohistory,* Springer Publishing, 1976; (contributor) Marius Livingston, editor, *International Terrorism in the Contemporary World,* Greenwood Press, 1978; (with Rappoport) *The Holocaust and the Crisis of Human Behavior,* Holmes & Meier, 1980. Also contributor to *Psychology and Its Allied Disciplines,* edited by Marc H. Bornstein, Lawrence Erlbaum Associated. Contributor of about fifty articles and reviews to a wide variety of academic journals and popular magazines, including *Choice.* Contributing editor of *Childhood Quarterly* (now *Journal of Psychohistory*), 1975, issue editor, 1978; member of board of editors of *Psychohistory Review,* 1978.

AVOCATIONAL INTERESTS: Photography.

*   *   *

KRMPOTIC, Vesna 1932-

PERSONAL: Born June 17, 1932, in Dubrovnik, Yugoslavia; daughter of Mario (a physician) and Vera (Karlovsky) Krmpotic; married Radivoje Petkovic (a diplomat), April 8, 1964; children: Reya, Igor, Neven. *Education:* Received B.A. from University of Zagreb, and diploma from University of New Delhi. *Home:* Vuksanovica 4, 11090 Belgrade, Yugoslavia.

CAREER: Radio Television Zagreb, Zagreb, Yugoslavia, literary editor, 1960-62; Prosvjeta (publisher), Zagreb, literary editor, 1978—. *Member:* Association of Yugoslav Writers, Association of Yugoslav Literary Translators, Association of Psychologists of Croatia. *Awards, honors:* Prize from Nolit (publisher) for *Hiljadu Lotosa;* Nazer Prize for *Dijamantni faraon.*

WRITINGS—In English translation: *Eyes of Eternity: A Spiritual Autobiography,* Harcourt, 1979.

Other writings: *Poezija,* D.K.H., 1956; *Plamen i svijeca,* Prosvjeta, 1962; *Jama bica: Pesme,* Nolit, 1965; *Raskorak,* Bagdala, 1965; *Indija* (title means "India"), Epoha, 1965; *Krasna nesuglasja* (poems), Matica Hrvatska, 1969; *Hiljadu Lotosa* (title means "Thousand Lotuses"), Nolit, 1971; *Dijamantni faraon: Antologia sredisnjega glasa* (title means "Diamond Pharoah"), Znanje, 1975; *Cas je ozirise,* Nolit, 1976; *Ljevanica za Igora: Pesme,* Nolit, 1978.

WORK IN PROGRESS: Research on Oriental culture, especially Indian and old Egyptian.

KROTKOV, Yuri 1917-

PERSONAL: Born November 11, 1917, in Russia (now U.S.S.R.); son of Krotkov Vasiliy and Barannik Alexandra Krotkov; married Chabelski Adelle, 1975. *Education:* Attended Moscow Literary Institute. *Home:* 2657 Laurel Pass, Hollywood, Calif. 90046.

CAREER: Writer. News correspondent in Moscow, U.S.S.R., 1955-56; screenwriter and dramatist in Moscow, 1956-63. *Awards, honors:* Fellowships from McDowell Colony and Virginia Art Center.

WRITINGS: I Am From Moscow: A View of the Russian Miracle, translated by the author and Mark Barty-King from the original Russian, Dutton, 1967 (published in England as *The Angry Exile: A View of the Russian Miracle,* Heinemann, 1967); *The Red Monarch,* translated from the original Russian, Norton, 1979; *The Nobel Prize,* translated from the original Russian, Simon & Schuster, 1980.

WORK IN PROGRESS: A novel about Soviet life and America, tentatively entitled *Lights Over Moscow.*

SIDELIGHTS: In 1963 Yuri Krotkov requested political asylum in Great Britain during a visit there as a member of the Soviet film workers' delegation. Although he was a part of the "privileged new class" in the Soviet Union, "in the last analysis he left because he realized that he could never be an honest writer in Russia," explained Oscar Handlin of *Atlantic Monthly.* According to Bernard D. Williams, the individuals in this privileged class, which included artists, writers, scientists, government officials, and other notable personages, were able to better their standards of living considerably by way of their prominent positions. And yet Krotkov defected to the West because he wanted the freedom to express himself artistically.

Four years later Krotkov published *I Am From Moscow,* a chronicle of the thoughts and experiences that led him to leave his homeland. "Krotkov's account, indeed, renews our faith in the individual who is still willing to revolt against a government that attempts to make every citizen conform to every whim and wish of the state," declared Williams. A reviewer for the *Times Literary Supplement* stated that although the author is clearly a brave and sincere man, the book could have been "a very telling denunciation [of the Soviet system], had it been organized by a colder and more discriminating eye." Handlin, however, agreed with Williams's assessment and praised the book as a "simple, lucid, and convincing account."

In *The Nobel Prize* Krotkov depicts the last tumultuous year in the life of the famous Russian novelist and poet Boris Pasternak. Chosen to receive the Nobel Prize for literature in 1958, Pasternak fought desperately to accept the award for himself and for his people against the unrelenting Russian authorities forcing him to decline the honor. Krotkov includes in his narrative figures such as Nikita Khrushchev, the up-and-coming Leonid Brezhnev, and the novelist Konstantin Fedin, who was asked to betray Pasternak.

BIOGRAPHICAL/CRITICAL SOURCES: Times Literary Supplement, June 22, 1967; *Best Sellers,* October 1, 1967; *Atlantic Monthly,* November, 1967.

*   *   *

KUHLKEN, Ken(neth Wayne) 1945-

PERSONAL: Born September 4, 1945, in San Diego, Calif.; son of Charles Wayne (in business) and Ada (a teacher; maiden name, Garfield) Kuhlken; married Laura Lucille Steinhoff, October 7, 1967; children: Darcy, Cody. *Educa-*

tion: San Diego State University, B.A., 1968, M.A., 1971; University of Iowa, M.F.A., 1977. *Religion:* Christian. *Residence:* Tucson, Ariz. *Agent:* Keith Korman, Raines & Raines, 475 Fifth Ave., New York, N.Y. 10017. *Office:* 8641 Chevy Chase Dr., La Mesa, Calif. 92041.

CAREER: High school teacher of English in La Mesa, Calif., 1971-73, and Athens, Greece, 1973-74; Department of Public Welfare, El Cajon, Calif., welfare eligibility worker, 1974-78; San Diego State University, San Diego, Calif., instructor in creative writing, 1978-79; University of Arizona, Tucson, visiting assistant professor of creative writing, 1979—. Printer; operated import business.

WRITINGS: Midheaven (novel), Viking, 1980. Contributor of stories to magazines, including *Esquire, Fault, Virginia Quarterly Review,* and *Pacific Poetry and Fiction Review.*

WORK IN PROGRESS: The Gas Crisis, a novel, publication expected in 1982; another novel, publication expected in 1982; a film treatment; stories.

SIDELIGHTS: Kuhlken wrote: "I began writing fiction late, compared to some, at age twenty-five. I have done forty-some other jobs, but writing is the only one that gives me much satisfaction. I traveled a lot as a youth, but am currently slowing down. Grandma was important to my career, also my friend Eric, who died young, but in a couple years gave me confidence, knowledge that there was more to be written about than is often recognized, that the world is a microcosm of the WORLD. Eric (as did Grandma) made me think that I was smart and unique, God bless them.

"I used to be a musician, but was a bad one. I believe in hard labor but shy away from it. I like to read, like to try to do things well, like cars, boats, trains, things which move on the surface of the earth. I am currently trying to finance a truck and the time to spend in Mexico and border zones. Borders make me cringe so I'll be writing about them for awhile, until I don't cringe anymore.

"I believe in families, Jesus, responsibility, moderation, tolerance, freedom, but find all these things hard, and I'd rather live by the ocean than own a swimming pool."

*   *   *

KUHN, Edward, Jr. 1924(?)-1979

PERSONAL: Born c. 1924 in Cincinnati, Ohio; died after a long illness, December 20, 1979, in Mount Kisco, N.Y.; son of Edward and Esther Kuhn; married wife, Marianna; children: Andrew E., Eric W., Edward M. *Education:* Received degree from Dartmouth University, 1946; Columbia University, M.A.

CAREER: McGraw-Hill Book Co., New York City, assistant editor of trade books, 1947-59, editor in chief, 1959-64, general manager of trade department, 1964-65; New American Library, New York City, executive vice-president and editor in chief of paperback and hardcover programs, 1965-68; World Publishing Co., Cleveland, Ohio, specialist in Bibles, reference works, and children's books, 1968-70; Playboy Press and Playboy Book Club, Chicago, Ill., editorial director, 1970-77. *Military service:* U.S. Marine Corps, served in World War II; became lieutenant.

WRITINGS: The American Princess (novel), Simon & Schuster, 1971; *Ski Week* (novel), Doubleday, 1975.

SIDELIGHTS: In Kuhn's first novel, *The American Princess,* his mythical kingdom of Baktu provides a setting for political and sexual adventures. Martin Levin of the *New York Times Book Review* wrote that Kuhn "has contrived a cool hot-weather mixture of intrigue, satire, adventure and gynecology.'' According to Levin, all questions that are raised as the plot runs its course are answered by Kuhn ''in his own good time, with scholarly attention to the erotic rituals of his milieu.'' In *Ski Week* the action is focused on two characters: Alan Lang, an unscrupulous millionaire trying to buy his way to Washington, and a radical Jewish youth attempting to thwart Lang's efforts by destroying his reputation.

BIOGRAPHICAL/CRITICAL SOURCES: New York Times Book Review, June 27, 1971; *Harper's,* July, 1971.

OBITUARIES: New York Times, December 22, 1979; *Publishers Weekly,* January 11, 1980; *AB Bookman's Weekly,* January 14, 1980.*

*   *   *

KUPER, Yuri
   See KUPERMAN, Yuri

*   *   *

KUPERMAN, Yuri   1940-
   (Yuri Kuper)

PERSONAL: Born July 5, 1940, in Moscow, Soviet Union; son of Leonid Alexandrovich (a musician) and Judith (an engineer; maiden name, Burstein) Kuperman; married Ludmilla Romanowska (a journalist), May, 1971. *Education:* Attended Potemkin Art Institute, 1957. *Home:* 5 bis rue Schoelcher, 75014 Paris, France.

CAREER: Professional artist, 1963—.

WRITINGS: (Under name Yuri Kuper) *Holy Fools in Moscow,* Quadrangle, 1973.

WORK IN PROGRESS: Ditin, a novel.

*   *   *

KUSMER, Kenneth Leslie   1945-

PERSONAL: Surname is pronounced *Kooz*-mer; born June 19, 1945, in Cleveland, Ohio; son of Andrew L. (a machinist) and Dorthy (Brant) Kusmer. *Education:* Attended Ohio State University, Lakewood Branch, 1963-65; Oberlin College, A.B., 1968; Kent State University, M.A., 1970; University of Chicago, M.A., 1980, Ph.D., 1980. *Politics:* Democrat. *Home:* 327 Ashbourne Rd., Elkins Park, Pa. 19117. *Office:* Department of History, Temple University, Philadelphia, Pa. 19122.

CAREER: High school mathematics teacher in Mantua, Ohio, 1969; Cleveland State University, Cleveland, Ohio, instructor in history, 1969-71; Temple University, Philadelphia, Pa., assistant professor, 1976-80, associate professor of history, 1980—. *Member:* Amnesty International, Organization of American Historians, Southern Historical Association. *Awards, honors:* Louis Pelzer Prize from Organization of American Historians, 1973, for best essay; *A Ghetto Takes Shape* was named outstanding academic book by *Choice,* 1977.

WRITINGS: A Ghetto Takes Shape: Black Cleveland, 1870-1930, University of Illinois Press, 1976; *The Underclass: Tramps and Vagrants in American Society, 1865-1930,* Oxford University Press, 1982. Contributor to history journals and newspapers. Editor of *Temple University Historian,* 1978—.

WORK IN PROGRESS: Writing on the social and political history of the 1960's and 1970's.

SIDELIGHTS: Kusmer wrote: ''Although my work as a historian began with a strictly scholarly approach, I have recently published a number of newspaper articles and in the future would like to widen the scope of my writing to reach a more popular audience. I am very much inspired by a few historians like Carl Degler and Arthur Schlesinger, Jr., who have sought to combine sound scholarship with a popular writing style. I also believe that historians ought not to leave studies of the recent past to journalists alone, but should use their skills to cast light on the origins of contemporary problems.''

*   *   *

KYLE, Robert
   See TERRALL, Robert

L

LACH, Donald F(rederick) 1917-

PERSONAL: Surname is pronounced Lock; born September 24, 1917, in Pittsburgh, Pa.; son of Frederick Carl (in business) and Bertha (Hilberer) Lach; married Alma E. Satorius (a writer), March 18, 1939; children: Sandra Judith. *Education:* West Virginia University, A.B., 1937; University of Chicago, Ph.D., 1941. *Home:* 5750 Kenwood Ave., Chicago, Ill. 60637. *Office:* Social Sciences Building, University of Chicago, Chicago, Ill. 60637.

CAREER: Elmira College, Elmira, N.Y., 1942-1948, began as assistant professor, became professor of history; University of Chicago, Chicago, Ill., 1948-76, began as assistant professor, became professor of modern history, Bernadotte E. Schmitt Professor of Modern History, 1970—, resident master of Shoreland dormitory. Visiting professor at Cornell University, summers, 1942, 1952, 1963; distinguished visiting professor at Kent State University, summer, 1965; Rockefeller Professor of History at University of Delhi, 1967-68.

MEMBER: American Historical Association, Society for the History of Discoveries, American Association of University Professors, Association for Asian Studies, Hakluyt Society, Phi Beta Kappa, Quadrangle Club (member of governing board), Tavern, Wine, and Food Society. *Awards, honors:* Fulbright fellow in France, 1949-50; fellow of Social Science Research Council in Europe, 1952-53; Smith-Mundt fellow in Formosa and eastern Asia, 1955-56; American Council of Learned Societies fellow in Portugal, 1960; Doner fellow in Italy, 1965; Gordon J. Laing Prize from University of Chicago Press, 1967, for *Asia in the Making of Europe,* Volume I.

WRITINGS: (With Harvey F. MacNair) *Modern Far Eastern International Relations,* Van Nostrand, 1950, 2nd edition, 1955, reprinted, Octagon, 1976; *Europe and the Modern World,* Scott-Foresman, Volume I, 1951, Volume II, 1954; *The Preface to Leibniz Novissima Sinica,* University of Hawaii Press, 1957; *Asia in the Making of Europe,* University of Chicago Press, Volume I: *Century of Discovery,* Books 1-2, 1965, Volume II: *Century of Wonder,* Book 1: *The Visual Arts,* 1970, Book 2: *The Literary Arts,* 1978, Book 3: *The Scholarly Disciplines,* 1978; *China in the Eyes of Europe: The Sixteenth Century,* University of Chicago Press, 1968; *India in the Eyes of Europe: The Sixteenth Century,* University of Chicago Press, 1968; *Japan in the Eyes of Europe: The Sixteenth Century,* University of Chicago

Press, 1968; *Southeast Asia in the Eyes of Europe: The Sixteenth Century,* University of Chicago Press, 1968; (with Louis Gottschalk) *Toward the French Revolution: Europe and America in the Eighteenth-Century World,* Irvington Books, 1973; (with Edmund S. Wehrle) *International Politics in East Asia Since World War II,* Praeger, 1975; (author of introduction) Robert van Gulik, *The Chinese Gold Murders,* University of Chicago Press, 1977; (author of introduction) *The Chinese Nail Murders,* University of Chicago Press, 1977. Also author of *Asia on the Eve of Europe's Expansion,* 1965.

Member of editorial board of monograph series, "History of Cartography," Newberry Library, and "Europe in a Wider World." Contributor to *Encyclopaedia Britannica, Dictionary of the History of Ideas,* and *Hakluyt Handbook.* Contributor of articles and reviews to history journals. Member of editorial board of *Terrae Incognitae.*

WORK IN PROGRESS: Asia in the Making of Europe, Volume III, with Edwin Van Kley, publication by University of Chicago Press expected in 1984.

* * *

LACKS, Roslyn 1933-

PERSONAL: Born February 27, 1933, in New York, N.Y.; daughter of Charles J. (an accountant) and Goldie (a bookkeeper; maiden name, Dranoff) Lacks. *Education:* State University of New York at Albany, B.A., 1953, graduate study, 1955; attended Institute for Practicing Psychotherapists and Allied Professionals, 1964-65; Hunter College of the City University of New York, M.A., 1964; further graduate study at New York University, 1965-67. *Residence:* New York, N.Y.

CAREER: Goldman, Walter & Kenna Advertising Agency, Albany, N.Y., copywriter, 1952; WROW-Radio, Albany, N.Y., continuity writer, 1953; professional actress in summer stock and touring companies, on television, radio, and on stage in New York City, 1953-57; teacher of speech at high school in New York City, 1958; Lawrence Gumbinner Advertising Agency, New York City, writer in television and radio department, 1959; teacher of speech and English as a foreign language at high school in New York City, 1960-62; Adelphi University, Garden City, N.Y., lecturer in speech and drama, 1962-64; Charles Evans Hughes Senior High School, New York City, teacher of speech and English as a foreign language, 1964-71; free-lance writer, 1971—. Head of drama department at summer camp in Harrison, Me., 1959-64; speech therapist at Hunter College of the City University of New York, 1962-64; instructor at New York University, 1966-69; associate producer for WNYE-TV, 1969, producer, 1970; gives public lectures and dramatic readings from Hebrew and Yiddish literature. *Member:* Authors Guild, Authors League of America. *Awards, honors:* American Theatre Wing scholar, 1956.

WRITINGS: The New York Woman's Directory, Workman Publishing, 1973; *Women and Judaism: Myth, History, and Struggle,* Doubleday, 1980. Author of television scripts. Author of "The Feminist Postulate," a column in *Jewish Post,* 1976-77. Contributor of more than one hundred articles, reviews, and photographs to magazines, including *Present Tense, Psychiatric News,* and *Hadassah,* and newspapers.

BIOGRAPHICAL/CRITICAL SOURCES: Ms., April, 1980.

* * *

LADAS, Stephen P(ericles)   1898-1976

PERSONAL: Born July 11, 1898, in Grevena, Greece; died March, 1976, in New York, N.Y.; son of Pericles C. and Anastasia (Pattajo) Ladas; married Christine C. Douropulos, September 7, 1929; children: Natalie Elizabeth Ladas Arrigucci, Cornelia Ann Ladas Bauer. *Education:* University of Athens, LL.D.; Ecole des Sciences Politiques, M.A., 1923; Harvard University, LL.B., 1926, S.J.D., 1927.

CAREER: Greek Embassy, Paris, France, attache, 1921-22; Harvard University, Cambridge, Mass., secretary at Bureau of International Research, 1926-30; Ladas, Parry, von Gen, Goldsmith & Deschamps (foreign patents and trademarks law firm), New York, N.Y., began as partner, became senior partner, 1930-76. Chairman of Commission on Industrial Property, of national council of Chamber of Commerce of the United States, 1947-73; honorary chairman of Commission on Industrial Property of International Chamber of Commerce; member of board of trustees of American Friends of Greece, Athens College and Anatolia College. *Awards, honors:* Silver Cross of the Savior; commander of Royal Order of the Phoenix; Charles F. Kettering Award from Patents, Trademark, and Copyright Research Institute at George Washington University, 1968.

WRITINGS: The International Protection of Trademarks by the American Republics, Harvard University Press, 1929; *The International Protection of Industrial Property,* Harvard University Press, 1930; *The Exchange of Minorities: Bulgaria, Greece, and Turkey,* Macmillan, 1932, reprinted, AMS Press, 1977; *The International Protection of Literary and Artistic Property,* two volumes, Macmillan, 1938; *International Regime of Trademarks and Uniform Trademark Laws,* Nijhoff, 1950; *Patents, Trademarks, and Related Rights: National and International Protection,* three volumes, Harvard University Press, 1975. Contributor to law journals.

BIOGRAPHICAL/CRITICAL SOURCES: New York Times, March 15, 1976.*

* * *

LAITIN, Ken   1963-

PERSONAL: Born August 26, 1963, in Torrance, Calif.; son of Howard (a professor) and Liz (a teacher; maiden name, Watson) Laitin. *Education:* Educated in Torrance, Calif. *Religion:* Jewish. *Home:* 4916 White Court, Torrance, Calif. 90503.

CAREER: Writer, 1979—. *Awards, honors:* Athletic awards from American Youth Soccer Organization, California Youth Soccer Association, and Torrance City Council.

WRITINGS: (With brother, Steve Laitin) *The World's Number One Best-Selling Soccer Book* (juvenile), Soccer for Americans, 1979. Contributor of articles and stories to national magazines. Contributing editor of *Now.*

WORK IN PROGRESS: A book on guitar, publication by Youth Activities Institute expected in 1982.

SIDELIGHTS: Ken Laitin wrote: "As a young author, I want to help carry the message to youth and to parents that soccer is a great way to develop a positive self-image and to keep in good physical condition. I also want to encourage other young writers to attempt to publish, and hope that young readers will be stimulated by my stories and 'how-to-do' materials."

His father, Howard Laitin, added: "Acclaimed within soccer circles for its 'conciseness' and 'accuracy,' and by educators as 'an outstanding vehicle for encouraging children in the age range seven through twelve to read and play,' my sons' book carries a very important message to new young players: anyone can learn to play soccer.

"This is vividly illustrated by the authors' own development in the sport. Just a few years ago, Ken began his soccer career as a small and uncoordinated beginner in a world that appeared to be populated by 'skilled giants.' Soon Steve followed. Today, through steady practice, they are accomplished players. Since they had gained so much from soccer, the brothers wanted to relate their experiences to other young players. They began by teaching their little sister, Lindy, then age nine, and other children the skills of soccer.

"In their book they have described their feelings as beginning players and the problems that all new players face with themselves, teammates, opponents, officials, coaches, and parents. The result is challenging, exciting, and inspiring to the reader."

BIOGRAPHICAL/CRITICAL SOURCES: Soccer Now, December, 1978; *Gifted Child Quarterly,* fall, 1979; *Soccer America,* September, 1979; *American Soccer,* October, 1979; *Boy's Life,* March, 1980; *National Geographic World,* July, 1980; *Scholastic,* September, 1980; *Young Athlete,* December, 1980.

* * *

LAITIN, Steve   1965-

PERSONAL: Born April 15, 1965, in Torrance, Calif.; son of Howard (a professor) and Liz (a teacher; maiden name, Watson) Laitin. *Education:* Educated in Torrance, Calif. *Religion:* Jewish. *Home:* 4916 White Court, Torrance, Calif. 90503.

CAREER: Writer, 1979—. *Awards, honors:* Athletic awards from American Youth Soccer Organization and California Youth Soccer Association; California state championship for individual skills from National Skills Competition, 1975.

WRITINGS: (With brother, Ken Laitin) *The World's Number One Best-Selling Soccer Book* (juvenile), Soccer for Americans, 1979. Contributor of articles and stories to popular magazines.

WORK IN PROGRESS: A book on drums, publication by Youth Activities Institute expected in 1982.

SIDELIGHTS: Steve Laitin commented: "As a young writer, I want to carry the message to youth and their parents that all children, both boys and girls, can play soccer and have fun—all you have to do is try. Soccer helps every participant to develop himself physically, mentally, and socially. I hope to encourage other young people both to try sports and to try writing.

"The World's Number One Best-Selling Soccer Book is an introduction to the skills, tactics, language, and excitement of the fastest growing team sport in America. Ken, my sister Lindy, and I try to take the mystery out of the skills by telling how we first taught Lindy. If it worked on Lindy, then it went into the book.

"The language is conversational. We fully understand the problems that a new young player will face, whether it is from parents who get excited at games, opponents who are twice as big, teammates who won't pass the ball, or the unsportsmanlike player.

"We also tackled the 'tactics' of soccer, virtually unknown to players who just run and kick the soccer ball. The stories, which come from our own experience, complete the course in soccer for the seven- to twelve-year-old reader."

Steve's father, Howard Laitin, added: "The book and the authors have gained good acceptance within soccer circles. All of the major soccer magazines have liked the book. Other youth organizations have also given the book a very favorable reception. It has been well received by educational and children's magazines and by organizations specifically dedicated to promoting reading. The children are accepted as authors by the media, and the book is accepted commercially. It is now in more than one thousand schools and libraries."

BIOGRAPHICAL/CRITICAL SOURCES: Soccer Now, December, 1978; *Gifted Child Quarterly,* fall, 1979; *Soccer America,* September, 1979; *American Soccer,* October, 1979; *Boy's Life,* March, 1980; *National Geographic World,* July, 1980; *Scholastic,* September, 1980; *Young Athlete,* December, 1980.

*   *   *

LALLEY, Joseph M. 1897(?)-1980

OBITUARY NOTICE: Born c. 1897 in Philadelphia, Pa.; died of heart disease, August 16, 1980, in Baltimore, Md. Journalist. From 1937 to 1961 Lalley was an editorial writer and literary editor for the *Washington Post.* Among his columns for the newspaper was "Posting the Books," a weekly look at books that he found of special interest. Before coming to the *Post,* Lalley had worked for several newspapers in Philadelphia and then left journalism for a time to work in advertising. He was a contributor of book reviews to the *New Yorker* in the 1940's and the associate editor for book reviews of *Modern Age* magazine since 1963. Among his writings are *Our Jungle Diplomacy* and *Faith and Force: An Inquiry Into the Nature of Authority.* Obituaries and other sources: *Washington Post,* August 18, 1980.

*   *   *

LAMB, Charles Bentall 1914-
(Achilles)

PERSONAL: Born April 11, 1914, in Bolton, Lancashire, England; son of Arthur (a Congregational minister) and Violet Aubrey (Bentall) Lamb; married Josephine Frances Elgar, September 20, 1939; children: Jeremy, Jonathon. *Education:* Educated in England. *Politics:* Conservative. *Home:* Moat Cottage, Britford, Salisbury, Wiltshire SP5 4DX, England. *Agent:* Giles Gordon, Anthony Sheil, Associates, Ltd., 2-3 Morwell St., London, WC1B 3AR, England.

CAREER: Clan Line Steamers Ltd., England, apprentice at sea, 1930-34; Royal Navy, West Indies, midshipman, 1934; Royal Air Force, pilot, 1934-38, affiliated with Fleet Air Arm, 1938-58, commander of ship in charge of fishery protection for Scotland, Iceland, and the Faeroes, Orkney, and Shetland Islands, 1952-53; Joint School of Warfare, Old Sarum, England, assistant commandant, 1956-58; Royal Naval College, Greenwich, England, lecturer in finance, 1958-73; White Ensign Association, London, England, founder, secretary, and manager, 1958-73. Chairman of navy boxing and international boxing referee, 1947-53. *Awards, honors:* Navy lightweight boxing champion, 1934; Royal Air Force lightweight boxing champion, 1936 and 1939. Military: Distinguished Service Order, Distinguished Service Cross, mentioned in dispatches several times.

WRITINGS: War in a Stringbag, Cassell, 1977. Contributor to numerous naval journals, including *Mariner's Mirror* and *Aeroplane,* sometimes under pseudonym Achilles.

WORK IN PROGRESS: A book; a U.S. edition of *War in a Stringbag.*

SIDELIGHTS: Lamb told *CA:* "My book explains that I have had to undergo a lot of operations since World War II as a result of all that happened to me during it. My last operation was my thirty-fifth, so I think one could safely put down 'undergoing surgical operations' as my main occupation in peacetime. It certainly makes other writing more difficult and I am amazed that I managed to get one book published between 'ops'. The fourteen months I spent in a Vichy-French prison camp in the Sahara started the mess in 1941-42. We lived on pig swill, and an inadequate amount of that too, and it did none of us any good. I ended up with beriberi and hepatitis, and it took some time to recover in 1943 when we were released after the North African landings. Then in 1945 I was hit by an aircraft propeller off Japan in one of the five British fleet carriers operating with the U.S. fleet, and was dumped ashore in the Admiralty Islands at an American hospital base where I was the only Englishman for five months. The Americans saved my leg for me, but it was not until 1947 that I was able to walk again.

"My education began at a boy's prep school in Devon, England. Then I got a singing scholarship to Caterham School and had to sing all the treble solos in church on Sundays and in school concerts. Because I had to spend a lot of time on the stage dressed as a female—in order to sing the solos—I found it necessary to learn to box while at school, which stood me in very good stead later in life. (An ability to defend my honor as a small boy was absolutely essential in a boarding school.) As a result of learning how to use a straight left at school I was subsequently the lightweight champion of the navy and the Royal Air Force. So there were many advantages to be gained by becoming a choirboy in my teens.

"The urge to go to sea had become overwhelming by the time I was fifteen and so my father 'indentured' me to Clan Line Steamers Ltd. as an apprentice, and I began my four years training on my sixteenth birthday in 1930. The years were fascinating and I spent a lot of time in New York, Boston, and Philadelphia during Prohibition. In fact I joined in Mayor Walker's 'Beer Parade' (without knowing what was happening) and walked with the crowd the entire length of Broadway. I was also in New York when Lindbergh's baby was kidnapped and when General Balbo arrived over the Manhattan skyline with his huge nonstop formation of aircraft all the way from Italy. During those four years at sea in cargo ships I also crossed the equator precisely fifteen times, and went through the Suez Canal three times. I sailed to India, all the way around Africa more than once, and then went several times to South Africa.

"During the war I was given a permanent commission and after the war, when I had recovered from my injuries, I was promoted to commander and given command of the ship in charge of fishery protection. I had several jobs as a commander, the last one being assistant commandant of the Joint School of Warfare, teaching N.A.T.O. the intricacies of nuclear warfare. But in 1957-58 a government 'axe' was about to fall and many naval officers and sailors were to be laid off and given compensation for the loss of expected earnings. I listened to the conversation of some of these men and their wild plans, and it was clear to me that they were going to lose every penny, and so I wrote an article for a magazine with a wide circulation in London, appealing to the city to form an organization to advise these men on the wise investment of this money. In the end I was sent around London by Louis Mountbatten, the First Sea Lord, to follow up the various offers that were made, and after nine months had formed the White Ensign Association. It is now responsible for many millions of the Royal Navy's money and has done a magnificent job.

"After the war I became chairman of navy boxing, and an international referee, and once refereed the Golden Gloves match between America and Britain at Wembley. I had to give this up in the end because of my injured leg but it was fun while it lasted. Come to think of it, so was everything else!"

* * *

LAMBDIN, William 1936-

PERSONAL: Born December 14, 1936, in Yale, Okla.; son of Evan E. and Veta M. (Skeen) Lambdin; married Peggy Hunt, August 19, 1960; children: William W., Heidi. *Education:* Colorado State College, B.A., 1963, M.A., 1967; University of Northern Colorado, Ed.D., 1975. *Home:* 2513 14th Avenue Court, Greeley, Colo. 80631.

CAREER: Northeastern Junior College, Sterling, Colo., professor of English, 1966-72; University of Northern Colorado, Greeley, administrator for public information and funding programs for adults attending college, 1973—. Member of National Committee on Public Doublespeak. *Military service:* U.S. Air Force, technical writer, 1955-59; served in Europe. *Member:* International Society for General Semantics, Colorado Language Arts Society, Colorado Authors League, Greeley Press Club.

WRITINGS: Four-Legged Words, Western America Press, 1976; *Doublespeak Dictionary,* Pinnacle Books, 1979, revised edition, 1981. Author of a column in *Town and Country News,* 1973-77; editorial writer for *Greeley Tribune,* 1977—. Contributor to magazines and newspapers, including *Colorado West, English Journal, Washington Post, Los Angeles Times,* and *Denver Post.* Editor of *The Senior Voice.*

SIDELIGHTS: Lambdin wrote: "As an editorial writer for the *Greeley Tribune* and a former staff member at the University of Northern Colorado, I learned to speak several languages—journalese, educationese and officialese—all of them with ease.

"My childhood was spent on a farm, where I learned to like all animals—except chickens. They seemed to resemble bureaucrats, constantly feathering their nests, clucking importantly about nothing, and pecking aimlessly at the universe.

"As a young man, I was trained by the U.S. Air Force as a technical writer and have been writing for newspapers and

magazines since. I have never contributed a single, obscene graffito to a public wall. Nor have I felt the need to read such messages since I began listening carefully to political speeches.

"For a hobby, I collect words, as some men collect cars or women. Fortunately, my hobby is less expensive and safer than most amusements.

"I wrote *Doublespeak Dictionary* out of self defense, to counter assaults on sense that appear in official statements. Those who most influenced the work were Mark Twain, H. L. Mencken, and George Orwell. They still help me, as does my wife by seeing to it that I have so little money to spend I must write in order to have something to do.

"In fairness, I should say that my wife has been a great help, being a sensible, plain-speaking woman from a small Wyoming town. In fact, at times she speaks so plainly that I wonder where she learned such words."

* * *

LAMBERT, Betty
  See LAMBERT, Elizabeth (Minnie)

* * *

LAMBERT, Eleanor

PERSONAL: Born in Crawfordsville, Ind.; daughter of Henry Clay and Helen Houghton (Craig); married Seymour Berkson (a publisher), 1936 (died, 1959); children: William Craig Berkson. *Education:* Studied at John Herron Art Institute and Chicago Art Institute. *Religion:* Presbyterian. *Home:* 1060 Fifth Ave., New York, N.Y. 10028. *Office:* Eleanor Lambert Division, Creamer Dickson Basford, Inc., 1633 Broadway, New York, N.Y. 10019.

CAREER: Worked as reporter, free-lance artist for department stores, book jacket designer in New York City, consumer researcher in New York City, and owner of a public relations firm; president of Eleanor Lambert, Inc., in New York City; Creamer Dickson Basford, Inc., New York City, associated with Eleanor Lambert Division, 1980—. Producer of fashion shows, including one at American Exhibit in Moscow, U.S.S.R., 1959, Pageant of Fashion and the Arts at Kennedy Cultural Center, 1963, and American showing at International Clothing Exhibit, Moscow, 1967. Member of National Council on the Arts, 1965; member of advisory board of Costume Institute at Metropolitan Museum of Art and board of directors of Fashion Institute of Technology. *Member:* Council of Fashion Designers of America (cofounder; honorary charter member; member of board of directors). *Awards, honors:* Gold Medal from New York Board of Trade, 1960; named Indiana woman of the year by Theta Sigma Phi, 1963; awards from Girls Clubs of America, National Jewish Hospital, and New York League of the Association for the Help of Retarded Children.

WRITINGS: World of Fashion: People, Places, Resources, Bowker, 1976; *Quips and Quotes About Fashion,* Pilot Books, 1978. Author of "She," a column distributed by Hall Syndicate to about sixty newspapers in the United States and abroad, 1964—.

SIDELIGHTS: Arriving in New York City fresh from school, on the eve of the Depression and with only a hundred dollars, Eleanor Lambert found two part-time jobs: designing book jackets and doing consumer research. It was an emergency call from the publisher of the books for which she designed covers that gave her the opportunity to write a publicity release. Soon after that she set up her own small public relations business for creative artists. When the American Art Dealers Association was formed Lambert received her first official assignment. She was to do the organization's publicity, at ten dollars a week. Her business continued to grow and now she guides the press relations of creative talents at all levels of American fashion, as well as many of the important fashion events in the United States. She inaugurated the March of Dimes Fashion Shows and the Coty American Fashion Critics Awards and has taken large fashion shows to Australia and Europe. In 1967 she was assigned by the Chamber of Commerce of the United States and the U.S. State Department to organize the exporters of American fashion shows in several world capitals.

When the United States opened cordial relations with China through Richard Nixon, Lambert was the first member of the American fashion community to be invited to visit that country. She attended the Canton Fair in 1972 and offered advice on Chinese fabrics, furs, perfumes, and jewelry.

Lambert is also the coordinator of the annual International Best Dressed Women polls.

AVOCATIONAL INTERESTS: Collecting clothes, antique furniture, porcelain, and contemporary paintings, cooking, needlepoint, swimming, reading suspense novels, travel (including Outer Mongolia, Nepal, Amazon country of Brazil, and the Great Barrier Reef).

BIOGRAPHICAL/CRITICAL SOURCES: Biography News, Volume I, Gale, 1974.

* * *

LAMBERT, Elizabeth (Minnie) 1933-
(Betty Lambert, Betty Lee)

PERSONAL: Born August 23, 1933, in Calgary, Alberta, Canada; daughter of Christopher Thomas and Bessie Mildred (Cooper) Lee; married Frank Lambert, July 5, 1952 (divorced, 1960); children: Ruth Anne. *Education:* Attended Banff School of Fine Arts; University of British Columbia, B.A., 1957. *Politics:* New Democrat. *Religion:* None. *Home:* 12 North Grosvenor, Burnaby, British Columbia, Canada V5B 1J2. *Office:* Department of English, 6099AQ, Simon Fraser University, Burnaby, British Columbia, Canada V5A 1S6.

CAREER: Simon Fraser University, Burnaby, British Columbia, instructor, 1965-70, assistant professor, 1970-78, associate professor of English, 1978—. Theatre critic for CHQM-Radio, 1976. *Member:* Association of Canadian Television and Radio Artists, Playwrights Guild of Canada, Playwrights Canada, Association of Canadian University Teachers of English. *Awards, honors:* Scholarship from Banff School of Fine Arts, 1951, for "The Unloved"; award from Macmillan Publishers, Canada, 1956, for "A Woman in Love"; Nellie Award for radio drama from Association of Canadian Television and Radio Artists, 1980, for "Grasshopper Hill."

WRITINGS—Under name Betty Lambert; novels: *Crossings,* Pulp Press, 1979, published as *Bring Down the Sun,* Viking, 1980.

Plays: *The Song of the Serpent* (two-act juvenile; first produced in Vancouver, British Columbia, at Holiday Theatre, 1967), Playwrights Cooperative, 1973; *Sqrieux-de-Dieu* (two-act farce; first produced in Vancouver at Vancouver Cultural Centre, August 20, 1975), Talonbooks, 1976; *Clouds of Glory* (two-act; first produced in Vancouver at Vancouver East Cultural Centre, May, 1979), Playwrights Canada, 1979.

Unpublished plays: "The Visitor" (three-act), first produced

in Vancouver at Vancouver Playhouse Two, April, 1969; "World, World Go Away!" (two-act juvenile), first produced in Vancouver at Metro Theatre, March 27, 1970.

Teleplays: "The Annuity," 1960; "Return of a Hero," 1960; "This Side of Tomorrow," 1962; "Prescription for Love," 1966; "Tumult With Indians," 1967; "The Visitor" (adapted from the play by Lambert), 1970; "When the Bough Breaks," 1971; "Nobody Knows I'm Here," 1975; "The Infinite Worlds of Maybe," 1976; "Brooke," 1978.

Radio plays: "The Essentials," c. 1956; "The Lady Upstairs," 1958; "The Bequest," 1958; "The Death's Watch," 1959; "The Annuity," 1960; "The Dark Corner," 1960; "The Seagull" (adapted from the play by Anton Chekhov), 1960; "The Curious Bone," 1961; "The Sea Wall," 1962; "The Case of the Abominable Snowman," 1962; "The Doctor's Dilemma" (adapted from the play by George Bernard Shaw), 1962; "The Summer People," "And When the Nights Are Long . . . ," c. 1963; "Dr. MacGregor and the Case of the Persistent Poltergeist," 1963; "The Three Sisters" (adapted from the play by Chekhov), 1963; "The Good of the Sun," c. 1964; "Falconer's Island," c. 1964; "Once Burnt, Twice Shy," 1965; "Whoever Murdered Good Old Charlie?," 1965; "The Devil's Disciple" (adapted from the play by Shaw), 1966; "Portrait of a Lady" (adapted from the novel by Henry James), 1966; "The Best Room in the House," 1966; "Hamlet, Revenge!" (adapted from the work by Michael Innes), 1968; "The Encircling Island," 1972; "Grasshopper Hill," 1979.

Contributor to *Canadian Children's Drama and Theatre,* 1977, and *First Person.* Work anthologized in *New Voices,* Dent, 1956, and *Elbow Room,* Pulp Press, 1980. Contributor of poetry, under name Betty Lee, to *Canadian Girl, Legionnaire,* and other periodicals.

WORK IN PROGRESS: Guilt, a novel; "Fire People," a play; "Spare Change," a musical.

SIDELIGHTS: Lambert told *CA:* "I wish I could say I wrote for moral purposes, but I must say that I write, instead, to find out about things and, again, because it gives me such great joy. I'm like the executioner in a famous short story who explains to his son what a morally defensible thing it *is* to be an executioner and who, at the end, says with self-righteous indignation, 'So you see son, when people ask me if I enjoy it when I throw the switch on the electric chair, they just don't understand. Enjoy it? Enjoy it? My god, how could one not enjoy it?' Apologies to whoever wrote that story in the first place."

BIOGRAPHICAL/CRITICAL SOURCES: Canadian Literature, spring, 1980; *St. Louis Post-Dispatch,* June 1, 1980.

* * *

L'AMI, Charles Ernest 1896-

PERSONAL: Born September 24, 1896, in Kilkenny, Ireland; son of Frederick George and Elizabeth Jane (Campbell) L'Ami; married Christena Pearl Driscoll, May 22, 1926; children: Charles Francis Allan. *Education:* Attended University of Saskatchewan. *Religion:* Anglican. *Home:* 81 Deer Lodge Pl., St. James, Manitoba, Canada R3J 2B9.

CAREER: Reporter and city editor in Saskatoon, Saskatchewan, 1921-22; worked as magazine editor, as feature writer, and as Parliamentary correspondent in Canada, 1923-38; Canadian Broadcasting Corp. (CBC), press representative for prairie region, 1938-54, supervisor of information services, 1955-61, editor of *CBC Times,* 1938-61; free-lance writer, 1961—. Lecturer at University of Manitoba, 1945-51.

Military service: Canadian Army, 1915-18; served in France, Belgium, and Germany. *Member:* Canadian Authors Association. *Awards, honors:* Westminster Fiction Award from Westminster Press, 1952, for *The Green Madonna*.

WRITINGS: (Translator with Alexander Welikotny) Mikhail Lermontov, *Mtsyry* (poem; title means "The Novice"), University of Manitoba Press, 1945; (with Welikotny) *Lermontov: Biography and Translation,* University of Manitoba Press, 1949; *The Green Madonna* (novel), Westminster, 1952; *The Tipperary Stonethrowers* (poems), Carillon Press, 1975. Also translator of *Selected Minor Poems of Lermontov,* 1945, and author of *The Philosophy of Journalism,* 1949. Author of radio plays. Contributor of stories and articles to Canadian magazines.

WORK IN PROGRESS: God's Healing, a novel set in late sixteenth-century France and England, about a woman surgeon.

SIDELIGHTS: L'Ami told *CA:* "I was born in the village of Inistioge (pronounced Inisteeg) in the County Kilkenny, Ireland, a lovely place on the River Nore. I stayed there only a year and then went on with my family to another village, Dundrum in Tipperary, where we stayed for the next five years—long enough to make me think for the rest of my life of Tipperary as my spiritual home. I am, as you see, a late Victorian, having lived for five years in the reign of the old Queen.

"Schools in Dundrum were not wholly adequate, so before long we moved to Dublin. There I attended two private schools. When I was eleven, the family migrated to Canada, settling finally in one of the wildest parts of Saskatchewan, sixty miles from the nearest town, ten miles from the nearest neighbor. Since our principal companions there for the next three years were gophers, badgers, coyotes, and red foxes, we then moved seventy miles away to Saskatoon. There we went to school again, in grades lower than we should have been, and pretty well marked time for the next two years. After we got to high school, it was better and we struggled through to matriculation and were headed for the university when World War I began to get a bit hot. I joined up. When I came home I tried to resume at the university, made a little progress, but then gave up and went into the news game as a reporter on the Saskatoon paper. After that I moved to Winnipeg.

"In Winnipeg, two things especially began to attract my attention—radio, the new medium of communication, and the Russian classics. I wrote extensively about both.

"Some time about then I was invited to conduct a class in journalism and creative writing at Univerity of Manitoba's Evening Institute, and during that six years, since I had never written in the novel form, I turned out *The Green Madonna,* which won the award that enabled me to decorate and improve my house a bit.

"Not long after that, with Alexander Welikotny, I turned out *Lermontov: Biography and Translation,* which is now in use in more than two hundred Canadian and U.S. colleges and universities, as well as others in England, Ireland, Scotland, Wales, the Netherlands, Italy, South Africa, Australia, New Zealand, and Hong Kong. We have had many pleasant letters about this work from distinguished scholars.

"I have since published a small collection of verse, *The Tipperary Stonethrowers,* intending it merely as a souvenir for members of my family and friends, but a good many copies of it have been sold in Ontario, where there are several Irish settlements.

"A month or so ago, some representatives of the University Archives and Rare Books Department at University of Manitoba called on me and asked if they could have all my literary correspondence and records for their archives. They also catalogued my library, which will go to them in due course. I don't know whether you can get a singular out of 'archives' or not, or whether there is any sort of distinction in being an 'archive,' but there it is. When I have vanished, some poor Manitoba undergraduate may have to grub through that vast pile of dull stuff for an examination . . . the harm we do in the course of a lifetime!"

AVOCATIONAL INTERESTS: Music, basketweaving, hunting.

*   *   *

LAMME, Linda Leonard 1942-

PERSONAL: Born April 21, 1942, in Bay Shore, N.Y.; daughter of Harry Theodore (a civil engineer) and Laura (Watson) Leonard; married Ary J. Lamme III (a professor), December 15, 1962; children: Laurel Agnes. *Education:* Attended Principia College, 1960-62; University of Illinois, B.S., 1964, M.A., 1966; Syracuse University, Ph.D., 1974. *Religion:* Christian Scientist. *Home:* 3017 Northwest First Ave., Gainesville, Fla. 32607. *Office:* College of Education, University of Florida, Gainesville, Fla. 32611.

CAREER: Elementary school teacher in Fisher, Ill., 1964-65, Fayetteville, N.Y., 1965-68, and Brazil, Ind., 1968-69; Syracuse University, Syracuse, N.Y., lecturer in elementary education, 1969-74; University of Florida, Gainesville, assistant professor, 1974-79, associate professor of early childhood education, 1979—. Visiting professor at Syracuse University, summer, 1975. Chairman of parent involvement committee and member of board of directors of Alachua County Coordinated Child Care, 1975-79; vice-chairman of board of directors of Baby Gator Nursery, 1974-78. *Member:* International Reading Association, Association for Childhood Education International, National Council of Teachers of English (chairperson of committee on literature in the elementary language arts, 1977-80), National Association for the Education of Young Children, Southern Association for Children Under Six, Pi Lambda Theta. *Awards, honors:* Grants from Florida Education Research and Development Center, 1975, and State of Florida, 1977-78.

WRITINGS: (With Jane Matanzo, Miken Olson, and Vivian Cox) *Raising Readers,* Walker & Co., 1980; (editor and contributor) *Learning to Love Literature,* National Council of Teachers of English, 1981. Contributor of more than twenty articles to education and language journals.

WORK IN PROGRESS: Raising Writers.

SIDELIGHTS: Linda Lamme commented to *CA:* "Ten years ago a dear friend, a retired university professor, asked me why some people who can read, don't, while others read voraciously. He was referring to some of his fellow retirees who were bored and comparing their experiences with his. He claimed that he wouldn't be caught dead without something to read. His question sparked my interest in what has become a professional quest into how the reading habit is formed. As my own three-year-old has become a fluent reader, I have become convinced that part of the answer lies in learning to read and write naturally (as opposed to being taught)—that the most important things we can do, as parents and teachers, are to read aloud to young children, often and from a variety of literature, and to provide lots of opportunities for drawing and writing (or dictating) for real communication. This immersion in printed language helps raise readers."

LANE, Laura Gordon 1913-

PERSONAL: Born November 15, 1913, in Vernon, Tex.; daughter of William Allen III and Martha (Conner) Lane. *Education:* Texas Woman's University, B.S., 1933; also attended Columbia University, 1944. *Home:* 2018 Spruce St., Philadelphia, Pa. 19103. *Office: Farm Journal,* 230 West Washington Sq., Philadelphia, Pa. 19105.

CAREER: Texas A & M University, College Station, extension editor, 1939-47; *Country Gentleman,* Philadelphia, Pa., associate editor, 1947-55; *Farm Journal,* Philadelphia, associate editor, 1955-69, women's editor, 1969-70, contributing editor, 1970—. *Member:* Associated Country Women of the World (life member), Women in Communications, Washington Press Club. *Awards, honors:* Headliner Award from Women in Communications, 1950, for writing which contributed to better world understanding; Leaven Award from American Agri-Women, 1977, for excellence in general reporting.

WRITINGS: A Country Woman's Day, Curtis Publishing Co., 1949; (editor) *The United States of America: Its People and Its Home,* Stern, 1950, 5th edition, 1955; *Farm Journal's Estate Planning Idea Book,* Farm Journal, Inc., 1978.

WORK IN PROGRESS: Articles on changes in state and federal tax laws and sophisticated estate planning techniques, for possible inclusion in revised edition of *Farm Journal's Estate Planning Idea Book.*

SIDELIGHTS: Laura Lane commented: "For the last few years I have campaigned for changes in federal estate tax laws through the pages of *Farm Journal,* by speeches and by testimony before the U.S. House of Representatives Ways and Means Committee and the U.S. Senate Finance Committee. I have also written about discrimination against farm wives (who are nominal partners in the family business) by present property ownership laws. Hence, I am widely credited with having helped bring about changes in federal and state legal codes. I did coin the phrase 'widow's tax,' which is widely used by lawyers, legislators, and accountants.

"Farm women are not the only ones discriminated against by our present tax and inheritance laws. Any woman who works in a family business suffers the same bias, unless the business is incorporated. Presumably, under the law, her labor is given for love and affection; it has no financial worth, even if she takes over the work and management while her husband is ill or away from home. This notion goes back to the Blackstone (English common law) concept of 'woman as property or chattel.'

"In 1978 Congress did offer these women some token relief. A widow can 'earn' an amount equal to two percent of her husband's gross estate for every year she 'materially' participated in his business. The ceiling is twenty-five years and $500,000. She 'earns' no more by working thirty years than twenty-five, and the ceiling on her 'earnings' is half a million. Note the phrase 'materially' participates. The Internal Revenue Service is interpreting this phrase to mean the woman paid self-employment insurance (Social Security), although this was not written in the law. It is a rare occurrence for women to do this. In fact, in some states such as Illinois a woman may not legally contract with her husband for money for her services. Without that, she likely has no funds with which to pay the tax."

*   *   *

LANE, Rose Wilder 1887-1968

PERSONAL: Born December 5, 1887, in De Smet, S.D.; died October 30, 1968, in Danbury, Conn.; daughter of Almanzo James (a farmer) and Laura Elizabeth (a writer; maiden name, Ingalls) Wilder; married Gillette Lane, March 24, 1909 (divorced, 1918). *Education:* Attended public schools in Missouri and Louisiana. *Politics:* Independent. *Home:* c/o George T. Bye, 535 Fifth Ave., New York, N.Y.

CAREER: Writer. Western Union Telegraph Co., telegrapher, c. 1904-10; real estate agent in California, 1910-13; *San Francisco Bulletin,* San Francisco, Calif., reporter and feature writer, 1914-18; worked for American Red Cross in Europe and the Near East, 1918-21; National Economic Council, editor of *Review of Books,* 1943-45; *Woman's Day,* correspondent in Vietnam, 1965. *Member:* Missouri Writers Guild, Justamere Club of Mansfield. *Awards, honors:* O. Henry Prize, 1922, for "Innocence."

WRITINGS—Fiction: *Diverging Roads,* Century, 1919; *He Was a Man,* Harper & Brothers, 1925; *Hill-Billy,* Harper & Brothers, 1926; *Cindy: A Romance of the Ozarks,* Harper & Brothers, 1928; *Let the Hurricane Roar,* Longmans, Green, 1933, reprinted, 1957, published as *Young Pioneers,* McGraw, 1976; *Old Home Town* (short stories), Longmans, Green, 1935; *Free Land,* Longmans, Green, 1938, reprint published as *Young Pioneers: The Free Land,* Bantam, 1980.

Nonfiction: *Henry Ford's Own Story: How a Farmer Boy Rose to the Power That Goes With Many Millions, Yet Never Lost Touch With Humanity,* E. O. Jones, 1917; *The Making of Herbert Hoover,* Century, 1920; *The Peaks of Shala: Being a Record of Certain Wanderings Among the Hill-Tribes of Albania,* Chapman & Dodd, 1922, Harper & Brothers, 1923; *Give Me Liberty,* Longmans, Green, 1936, revised edition, Caxton, 1954; *The Discovery of Freedom: Man's Struggle Against Authority,* John Day, 1943, reprinted, Arno, 1972; *Woman's Day Book of American Needlework,* Simon & Schuster, 1963.

Other writings: (Author of prologue and epilogue; editor and author of setting) Laura Ingalls Wilder, *On the Way Home: The Diary of a Trip From South Dakota to Mansfield, Missouri, in 1894,* Harper, 1962; *The Lady and the Tycoon: Letters of Rose Wilder Lane and Jasper Crane,* Caxton, 1973; (with Roger Lea MacBride) *Rose Wilder Lane: Her Story,* Stein & Day, 1977. Also editor of *Art Smith's Story: The Autobiography of the Boy Aviator,* published serially in *San Francisco Bulletin,* c. 1915.

Contributor of short stories and articles to periodicals, including *Saturday Evening Post, Ladies' Home Journal, Redbook, Cosmopolitan, American Mercury, Good Housekeeping, Country Gentleman, Harper's, McCall's, National Geographic, Sunset,* and *Independent.* Also contributor of travel letters and articles to newspapers.

SIDELIGHTS: Rose Wilder Lane was born in a claim shanty to pioneering parents trying to carve a life in the Dakota Territory. Unable to make an adequate living, the family moved to the Ozark Mountains in Missouri. Later they moved to Crowley, Louisiana, where Rose attended high school. It was out of these homesteading experiences that her mother, Laura Ingalls Wilder, developed her classic "Little House" series.

Lane retained the pioneering spirit of her parents throughout her life. After graduation from high school, she left her family and moved to San Francisco, where she did odd jobs, including newspaper and telegraph work. In 1909 she married Gillette Lane, but the marriage ended in divorce about ten years later.

After the divorce, Lane went abroad with the American Red

Cross. Her position with the organization allowed her to travel widely, visiting such countries as Turkey, Iraq, and a number of European nations. In 1920 and again two years later, she made trips to Albania. These extended visits enabled her to learn the culture, language, and customs of the region, an education that she later drew upon in her writing. In keeping with her adventurous nature, Lane visited the dustiest corners of Albania, sometimes making the acquaintance of tribes never before exposed to a foreigner. One of Lane's most successful books, *The Peaks of Shala*, was based on her experiences in Albania.

Perhaps Lane's most prolific writing was done for magazines, although she has to her credit a lengthy list of fiction and nonfiction books. Among her publications is the best-seller *White Shadows in the South Seas*, but a controversy surrounds the book's authorship. Lane claimed to have ghostwritten the book for the presumed author, Frederick O'Brien, while O'Brien argued that she was merely his secretary. The controversy remained unresolved at the time of his death in 1932.

Lane's childhood provided the background for a number of her publications, which relate the difficulties of life as a pioneer. Some of these works are *Hill-Billy, Cindy,* and *Let the Hurricane Roar*. She wrote her autobiography with the assistance of Robert Lea MacBride, an heir to the family and the co-producer of the "Little House" television series.

AVOCATIONAL INTERESTS: Traveling, building, gardening.

BIOGRAPHICAL/CRITICAL SOURCES: Springfield Republican, February 13, 1917; *New York Times,* April 13, 1919, March 22, 1925, February 26, 1933; *Boston Transcript,* October 30, 1920, June 9, 1923, March 28, 1925, April 14, 1926; *New York World,* June 3, 1923; *New York Tribune,* March 22, 1925; *Literary Review,* March 28, 1925; *New York Herald Tribune Books,* April 14, 1925; *Saturday Review of Literature,* April 10, 1926, March 4, 1933, May 7, 1938; *Bookman,* March, 1933; *Weekly Book Review,* March 14, 1943; Rose Wilder Lane and Roger Lea MacBride, *Rose Wilder Lane: Her Story,* Stein & Day, 1977.

OBITUARIES: New York Times, November 1, 1968; *Publishers Weekly,* December 2, 1968.*

*   *   *

LANG, Derek   1913-

PERSONAL: Born October 7, 1913, in Guildford, England; son of Cecil Frederick (a soldier) and Jane (Forbes) Lang; married Morna Massy Dawson, October 9, 1942 (deceased); married Anita Shields, 1953 (deceased); married Elizabeth Harker, 1969; children: Simon, Sarah Lang Hunt. *Education:* Attended Royal Military College, Sandhurst, 1931-33. *Home:* 4 Belford Pl., Edinburgh EH4 3DH, Scotland. *Office:* P.A. Management Consultants, Hobart Ho Hanover St., Edinburgh, Scotland.

CAREER: British Army, Cameron Highlanders, career officer, served in Sudan, Palestine (now Israel), Egypt, and Scotland, 1934-39, and in France, Belgium, Holland, and Germany, 1939-41 and 1944-46, worked with Secret Operations Executive in Egypt and Palestine, 1942, instructor at Staff College, 1947-48, served in Australia, 1949-51, and in Canada, 1957-58, director of army training, 1964-66, commander-in-chief in Scotland, 1966-69, retiring as lieutenant general; University of Stirling, Stirling, Scotland, secretary, 1970-73; worked on private research project on youth service, 1973-75; P.A. Management Consultants, Edinburgh,

Scotland, associate, 1975—. *Member:* Army and Navy Club, New Club, Senior Golfers Society, Honourable Company of Edinburgh Golfers, Muirfield Club. *Awards, honors*—Military: Knight Commander of Order of the Bath, Distinguished Service Order, Military Cross, officer of the Order of St. John of Jerusalem.

WRITINGS: Return to St. Valery, Leo Cooper, 1974.

SIDELIGHTS: Sir Derek wrote: "My only book, and I am unlikely to write another, is a tribute to the simple French people in town and country who risked so much to help people like me escape from enemy-occupied territory in World War II.

"I was captured at St. Valery in Normandy in June, 1940, but escaped two weeks later. On the run in northern France, I was captured again after three weeks. I escaped a second time in Belgium, however, and worked my way back to France where I worked on a farm near Lille for a month. I then moved into Lille, hiding with various families for two months before traveling to Marseilles. I spent a month there until I was able to stow away on a ship headed to Beruit, Lebanon, from whence I walked across mountains to freedom in Palestine. My book title was chosen because I helped liberate St. Valery when commanding a battalion of my regiment in the Scottish Highland Division in 1944.

"Having spent much of my professional war career with part-time reserve soldiers and now working with consultants closely connected with industry, I am imbued with the need for closer cooperation between the armed services and civilian occupations. If I wrote another book it would be on the theme of how to use the managerial and leadership skills of the armed forces to better advantage in other walks of life both in one's own country and in developing countries overseas in a nonmilitary way."

AVOCATIONAL INTERESTS: International travel.

*   *   *

LANG, Maud
See WILLIAMS, Claerwen

*   *   *

LANGER, Walter Charles   1899-

PERSONAL: Born February 5, 1899, in Boston, Mass.; son of Charles Rudolph (a florist) and Johanna (Rockenbach) Langer; married Frances Merrick, August 7, 1941. *Education:* Harvard University, S.B., 1923, A.M., 1925, Ph.D., 1935; attended Vienna Psychoanalytic Institute, 1937-39, and Boston Psychoanalytic Institute, 1939-41. *Politics:* Independent. *Religion:* Christian. *Home and office:* 1441 Magellan Dr., Sarasota, Fla. 33580.

CAREER: Director of schools in Silver City, N.M., 1926-31, and Newton, Mass., 1931-33; Harvard Psychological Clinic, Cambridge, Mass., clinical assistant, 1933-35; private practice of psychoanalysis. Member of Rockefeller Foundation Commission on Human Relations, 1935-36; consultant to Office of Strategic Services, 1940-45. *Military service:* U.S. Army, Signal Corps, 1917-19. *Member:* National Audubon Society, Massachusetts Psychological Association, Boston Psychoanalytic Society and Institute, Harvard Club of Sarasota, Sara Bay Country Club.

WRITINGS: Psychology and Human Living, Appleton, 1943; *The Mind of Adolf Hitler,* Basic Books, 1971. Contributor to *Journal of the History of Behavioral Sciences.*

LANGLEY, James Maydon 1916-

PERSONAL: Born March 12, 1916, in Wolverhampton, England; son of Oswald (a barrister) and Muriel (Lewis) Langley; married Marguerite Vanlier, November 29, 1942; children: Michael, Christopher, Chantal, Peter, Roderick. *Education:* Attended Trinity Hall, Cambridge, 1934-36, and Harvard University, 1954. *Religion:* Church of England. *Home:* The Old Rectory, Alderton, Woodbridge, Suffolk IP12 3DE, England. *Agent:* A. D. Peters & Co. Ltd., 10 Buckingham St., London WC2N 6BU, England.

CAREER: Fisons Ltd. (fertilizer manufacturers), Ipswich, England, raw material research executive, 1947-67; Deben Bookshop, Woodbridge, England, assistant manager, 1967-70; Hatchards Ancient House (booksellers), Ipswich, book purchaser and publicity manager, 1970-74; writer, 1974—. *Military service:* British Army, Coldstream Guards, 1936-47; became lieutenant colonel; named member of Order of the British Empire, received Military Cross and French Croix de Guerre. *Member:* Brooks's Club.

WRITINGS: Fight Another Day (autobiography), Collins, 1974; (with M.R.D. Foot) *M.I. Nine* (history), Bodley Head, 1979, Little, Brown, 1980.

WORK IN PROGRESS: Research on escape and evasion organizations in France, Belgium, and the Netherlands, 1940-45; *That Thousands May Live,* a fictionalized account of an officer shot down over England in 1944.

SIDELIGHTS: Langley wrote: "I was wounded and captured as a platoon commander in the Coldstream Guards at Dunkirk in June, 1940. I escaped in November of the same year and returned to England via Paris, Vichy, Marseilles, Madrid, and Gibraltar. From 1941 until 1943 I was in charge of the escape and evasion organizations working in France, Belgium, and Holland. In 1944 I commanded jointly with an American colonel the unit under the command of the Supreme Headquarters of the Allied Expeditionary Force (S.H.A.E.F.) covering these activities from D-Day to V.E. Day (June 6, 1944, to May 8, 1945).

"Both of my books are devoted to escape and evasion incidents during World War II. *Fight Another Day* describes my personal experiences, including those during the retreat to Dunkirk in May, 1940. *M.I. Nine* is about the work of the British intelligence department and its American counterpart. It covers all the theaters of the war and includes many escape and evasion stories from official records and personal interviews.

"My first book was written at the behest of my children who said, 'Your stories are splendid and exciting, but when you are dead there will be no record of them.' *M.I. Nine,* however, endeavors to record the experiences of the men behind the lines before the truth becomes inextricably mixed with fiction and the official archives are lost or destroyed. The desire for self-justification and self-adulation often results in individuals recounting not what they did but what they know they ought to have done. If history is to be of any value to future generations it must be true and not fictionalized. Writers who were personally involved are more likely to detect such deviations from the truth. Thousands upon thousands of men and women of their own free will risked and often sacrificed their lives to help allied escapers and evaders. It is the duty of those soldiers for whom these sacrifices were made to ensure that the rescuers are not forgotten."

BIOGRAPHICAL/CRITICAL SOURCES: Airey Neave, *Saturday at M.I. Nine,* Hodder & Stoughton, 1969; *Sunday Times Weekly Review,* May 18, 1980.

LANGLEY, Lester Danny 1940-

PERSONAL: Born August 7, 1940, in Clarksville, Tex.; son of Lester L. (a carpenter) and Lona J. (Clements) Langley; married Wanda Dickson (a teacher), August 19, 1962; children: Charles, Jonathan. *Education:* West Texas State University, B.A., 1961, M.A., 1962; University of Kansas, Ph.D., 1965. *Office:* Department of History, University of Georgia, Athens, Ga. 30603.

CAREER: Texas A & M University, College Station, assistant professor of history, 1965-67; Central Washington State College, Ellensburg, assistant professor of history, 1967-70; University of Georgia, Athens, associate professor of history, 1970—. *Member:* American Historical Association, Organization of American Historians, Society of Historians of American Foreign Relations, Conference on Latin American History.

WRITINGS: The Cuban Policy of the United States: A Brief History, Wiley, 1968; (editor) *The United States, Cuba, and the Cold War,* Heath, 1970; (co-editor) *The United States and Latin America,* Addison-Wesley, 1971; *Struggle for the American Mediterranean: United States-European Rivalry in the Gulf Caribbean,* University of Georgia Press, 1976; *The United States and the Caribbean, 1900-1970,* University of Georgia Press, 1980. Contributor to journals.

*   *   *

LANGLEY, Noel 1911-1980

OBITUARY NOTICE—See index for *CA* sketch: Born December 25, 1911, in Durban, South Africa; died November 4, 1980, in Desert Hot Springs, Calif. Scriptwriter, playwright, director, and author. Langley wrote the screenplay for the motion picture "The Wizard of Oz," in addition to several others, including "They Made Me a Fugitive," "Tom Brown's School Days," and "Ivanhoe." He also directed a number of films. Langley penned successful stage plays such as "Edward My Son," "Little Lambs Eat Ivy," and "Cage Me a Peacock." Among his books are *Hocus Pocus, The Inconstant Moon,* and *Edgar Cayce on Reincarnation.* Obituaries and other sources: *London Times,* November 15, 1980.

*   *   *

LAPE, Fred 1900-

PERSONAL: Born August 20, 1900, in Holland Patent, N.Y.; son of Herman F. and Emma (Happe) Lape. *Education:* Cornell University, A.B., 1921. *Residence:* Esperance, N.Y. *Agent:* Agnes DeKay, Esperance, N.Y. 12066. *Office:* George Landis Arboretum, Esperance, N.Y. 12066.

CAREER: Free-lance writer. Cornell University, Ithaca, N.Y., instructor in English, 1921-23; Stanford University, Palo Alto, Calif., instructor in English, 1923-30; Rennselaer Polytechnic Institute, Troy, N.Y., instructor in English, 1936-40; farmer, 1940-57; George Landis Arboretum, Esperance, N.Y., founder and director, 1951—.

WRITINGS: Barnyard Year (poetry), Harper, 1950; *Bunch of Flowers* (poetry), Argus, 1960; *Garden and Trees and Shrubs* (nonfiction), Cornell University Press, 1965; *Along the Schoharie,* [Esperance, N.Y.], 1968; *Apples and Man* (nonfiction), Van Nostrand, 1979; *A Farm and Village Boyhood* (nonfiction), Syracuse University Press, 1980. Also author of poetry collections *At the Zoo,* 1966, *Hill Farm,* 1976, and *Poems From the Blue Beach,* 1976. Editor of *Trails,* 1932-50.

WORK IN PROGRESS: Stuff of Dreams, a book on dreaming and dreams.

SIDELIGHTS: Lape told *CA* that *Stuff of Dreams* is about the dream's "origin both in the body and in the mind. It includes the gradual development of the brain from the first mammal to man; how to interpret one's own dreams; a plea for the use of subjective as well as objective material in the study of dreams; and a general complaint against the limited subject matter of contemporary psychology.

"My poetry is probably influenced most by Robinson Jeffers."

AVOCATIONAL INTERESTS: Music, playing piano, collecting records.

*   *   *

LARGE, R(ichard) Geddes 1901-

PERSONAL: Born October 21, 1901, in Bella Bella, British Columbia, Canada; son of Richard Whitfield (a physician) and Isabella Matilda (a pianist; maiden name, Geddes) Large; married Annie Beatrice Wilson, September 18, 1923; children: F. Allan, Margaret, Richard D. *Education:* University of Toronto, M.B., 1923. *Politics:* Conservative. *Religion:* United Church. *Home address:* P.O. Box 487, Prince Rupert, British Columbia, Canada V8J 3R2. *Office:* Large Clinic, 219 Second Ave. W., Prince Rupert, British Columbia, Canada V8J 3R2.

CAREER: Private practice of surgery, 1923—; intern at Vancouver General Hospital, 1923-24; Hazelton Hospital, Hazelton, British Columbia, assistant medical officer, 1924-26; medical superintendent at Port Simpson General Hospital, 1926-31. Consulting surgeon at Miller Bay Indian Hospital. Past president of City of Prince Rupert Chamber of Commerce, chairman of school board, 1945-56, freeman, 1977, alderman, 1977—. President of Museum of Northern British Columbia. *Military service:* Canadian Army Reserve, active duty, 1940-45; became captain. *Member:* International College of Surgeons (fellow), Canadian College of Surgeons (fellow), American College of Surgeons (fellow), Canadian Medical Association (president of British Columbia division, 1953-54), Royal Geographical Society (fellow), British Columbia Medical Association (president, 1954-55), Prince Rupert Medical Association, Masons (past grand master).

WRITINGS: Soogiwilis (Indian legends), Ryerson, 1951; *Skeena: River of Destiny,* Mitchell, 1957; *Prince Rupert: Gateway to Alaska,* Mitchell, 1960, 2nd edition, 1973; *Drums and Scalpel* (history), Mitchell, 1968. Also author of *History of the Prince Rupert General Hospital,* 1971.

WORK IN PROGRESS: A genealogy of the Large family; an autobiography.

SIDELIGHTS: Large commented to *CA:* "With the exception of my first book, which was Indian legends illustrated with Indian art, all of my books have been historical, covering the area of northwestern British Columbia. *Avocational interests:* Music, yachting, civic affairs.

*   *   *

LARKIN, Maurice (John Milner) 1932-

PERSONAL: Born August 12, 1932, in Harrow-on-the-Hill, England; son of Terence John (a headmaster) and Winifred (Richards) Larkin; married Enid Lowe (a teacher of modern languages), December 17, 1958; children: John Stephen, Katharine Veronica. *Education:* Trinity College, Cambridge, B.A., 1954, M.A. and Ph.D., both 1958. *Home:* 5 St. Baldred's Cres., North Verwick, east Lothian EH39 4PZ, Scotland. *Office:* Department of History, University of Edinburgh, Edinburgh EH8 9JY, Scotland.

CAREER: University of Glasgow, Glasgow, Scotland, assistant lecturer, 1958-61, lecturer in modern history, 1961-65; University of Kent at Canterbury, Canterbury, England, lecturer, 1965-68, senior lecturer, 1968-75, reader in history, 1976; University of Edinburgh, Edinburgh, Scotland, Richard Pares Professor of History, 1976—. *Military service:* British Army, 1950-51; became lieutenant.

WRITINGS: Gathering Pace: Continental Europe, 1870 to 1945, Macmillan, 1969; *Church and State After the Dreyfus Affair: The Separation Issue in France,* Macmillan, 1974; *Man and Society in Nineteenth-Century Realism: Determinism and Literature,* Rowman & Littlefield, 1977. Contributor to history and literary journals.

WORK IN PROGRESS: France Since 1940, completion expected in 1984; research on political and religious discrimination in the French public services, 1879-1914.

AVOCATIONAL INTERESTS: Birdwatching, wildlife conservation, listening to music.

*   *   *

LASCH, Robert 1907-

PERSONAL: Born March 26, 1907, in Lincoln, Neb.; son of Theodore Walter (a bookkeeper) and Myrtle (Nelson) Lasch; married Zora Schaupp (a teacher), August 22, 1931; children: Christopher, Catherine, Allen. *Education:* University of Nebraska, A.B., 1928; attended Oxford University, 1930, and Harvard University, 1941-42. *Home address:* P.O. Box 728, 342 East El Pinon, Green Valley, Ariz. 85614.

CAREER: Omaha World Herald, Omaha, Neb., reporter and editorial writer, 1931-41; *Chicago Sun* (later *Chicago Sun-Times*), Chicago, Ill., chief editorial writer, 1942-50; *St. Louis Dispatch,* St. Louis, Mo., editorial writer, 1950-57, editor of editorial page, 1957-71. *Member:* Southern Arizona Watercolors Guild (president), Santa Cruz Valley Art Association. *Awards, honors:* Prize from *Atlantic,* 1944, for "For a Free Press"; Pulitzer Prize for distinguished editorial writing and St. Louis Civil Liberties Award, both 1966.

WRITINGS: Contributor to *Newsmen's Holiday,* 1942; *For a Free Press,* 1944, and *Breaking the Building Blockade,* 1946. Contributor to periodicals, including *Atlantic, American Oxonian, Progressive,* and *Newsweek.*

AVOCATIONAL INTERESTS: Watercolors, astronomy.

*   *   *

LATHROP, Dorothy P(ulis) 1891-1980

OBITUARY NOTICE—See index for *CA* sketch: Born April 16, 1891, in Albany, N.Y.; died December 30, 1980, in Falls Village, Conn. Illustrator and author. Lathrop won the first Randolph Caldecott Medal in 1938 for her illustration of *Animals of the Bible* by Helen Dean Fish. She illustrated numerous books by other authors as well as her own children's books. Lathrop's works include *The Fairy Circus, Hide and Go Seek, Puffy and the Seven-Leaf Clover,* and *Follow the Brook.* Obituaries and other sources: *Publishers Weekly,* January 23, 1981; *AB Bookman's Weekly,* January 26, 1981.

*   *   *

LAUDER, George
See DICK-LAUDER, George (Andrew)

LAUDER, George (Andrew) Dick
  See DICK-LAUDER, George (Andrew)

*   *   *

La VERDIERE, Eugene Armand   1936-

PERSONAL: Born April 7, 1936, in Waterville, Maine; son of Laurier Wilfred and Gladys Marie (Mathieu) La Verdiere. *Education:* Attended Blessed Sacrament Seminary, Cleveland, Ohio, 1958-64; John Carroll University, M.A., 1963; University of Fribourg, S.T.L., 1965; Pontifical Biblical Institute, S.S.L., 1967; further graduate study at Ecole Biblique, Jerusalem, Israel, 1967-68; University of Chicago, Ph.D., 1977. *Home:* 1335 West Harrison St., Chicago, Ill. 60607. *Office:* 5430 University Ave., Chicago, Ill. 60615.

CAREER: Entered Society of the Most Blessed Sacrament, 1958, ordained Roman Catholic priest, 1964; John Carroll University, Cleveland, Ohio, assistant professor of religious studies, 1969-76; Jesuit School of Theology, Chicago, Ill., assistant professor of New Testament theology, 1976-77, associate professor, 1977—. Director of Blessed Sacrament Seminary, Cleveland, 1969-74. Member of field archaeological staff of Mission de Tell Keisan, Jerusalem, Israel, 1973-75. Lecturer in the United States, South America, Africa, and Asia. *Member:* Society of Biblical Literature, Catholic Biblical Association, American Schools of Oriental Research.

WRITINGS: Introduction to the Pentateuch, Liturgical Press, 1971; *Trumpets of Beaten Metal,* Liturgical Press, 1974; *Finding Jesus Through the Bible,* Claretian, 1977; *The Year of Luke,* Celebration, 1979; *Acts of the Apostles,* Franciscan Herald, 1979; *Luke,* Michael Glazier, 1980; *The New Testament in the Life of the Church,* Ave Maria Press, 1980; *The Year of Matthew; The Year of Mark,* National Catholic Reporter, 1981. Associate editor of *Bible Today,* 1972—; member of editorial board of *Emmanuel,* 1973—, associate editor, 1975—.

WORK IN PROGRESS: Gospel and Culture, an interpretation of the New Testament through various cultural lenses.

SIDELIGHTS: La Verdiere told *CA:* "I'm particularly interested in showing how the New Testament can be interpreted in the process of communication and in the context of various ministries and cultures."

*   *   *

LAWRENCE, Alexander Atkinson   1906-1979

PERSONAL: Born December 28, 1906, in Savannah, Ga.; died August 20, 1979; son of Alexander Atkinson (a lawyer) and Isabel (Paine) Lawrence; married Margaret T. Adams, April 18, 1933; children: Alexander Atkinson, Margaret (deceased). *Education:* University of Georgia, A.B. (magna cum laude), 1929. *Religion:* Episcopalian.

CAREER: Admitted to Georgia Bar, 1930; lawyer in Savannah, Ga., 1930-68; chief judge in U.S. District Court, Southern District of Georgia, 1968-79. Member of Board of Bar Examiners, 1951-58; member of Judicial Conference of the United States, 1974-79. *Member:* Georgia Historical Society, Georgia Bar Association (past president), Phi Beta Kappa, Oglethorpe Club. *Awards, honors:* Thomas H. Gignilliat Trophy for outstanding contributions to cultural programs, 1968; plaque from Harvard Law School Association of Georgia, 1977, for outstanding contributions to the administration of justice.

WRITINGS: James Moore Wayne, Southern Unionist, University of North Carolina Press, 1943, reprinted, Greenwood

Press, 1970; *Storm Over Savannah: The Story of Count d'Estaing and the Seige of the Town in 1779,* University of Georgia Press, 1951, revised edition, 1979; *James Johnston, Georgia's First Printer,* Pigeonhole Press, 1956; *A Present for Mr. Lincoln: The Story of Savannah From Secession to Sherman,* Ardivan Press, 1961; *Johnny Leber and the Confederate Major,* Ashantilly Press, 1962; *Tongue in Cheek* (collected speeches), Cherokee, 1979.

*   *   *

LAWRENCE, David   1888-1973

PERSONAL: Born December 25, 1888, in Philadelphia, Pa.; died of a heart attack, February 11, 1973, in Sarasota, Fla.; son of Harris and Dora Lawrence; married Ellanor Campbell Hayes, July 17, 1918 (died June 13, 1969); children: David, Mark, Nancy (deceased), Etienne. *Education:* Princeton University, B.A., 1910. *Residence:* Washington, D.C.; and Sarasota, Fla.

CAREER: Buffalo Express, Buffalo, N.Y., reporter, 1903-06; Associated Press correspondent at Princeton University, 1906-10, member of Washington, D.C., staff, 1910-15; *New York Evening Post,* New York, N.Y., Washington correspondent, 1916-19; Consolidated Press Association, Washington, D.C., president, 1919-33; *United States Daily,* Washington, D.C., founder and president, 1926-33; *United States News,* Washington, D.C., president and editor, 1933-48; *World Report,* Washington, D.C., founder and president, 1946-48; *U.S. News and World Report,* Washington, D.C., editor, 1948-73, president, 1948-59, chairman of the board, 1959-73. *Member:* National Press Club, Metropolitan Club, Cosmos, Princeton Club, Sigma Delta Chi (fellow). *Awards, honors:* Presidential Medal of Freedom conferred by President Richard M. Nixon, 1970.

WRITINGS: The True Story of Woodrow Wilson, Doran, 1924; *The Other Side of Government,* Scribner, 1929; *Beyond the New Deal,* McGraw, 1934; *Stumbling Into Socialism and the Future of Our Political Parties,* Appleton-Century, 1935; *Nine Honest Men,* Appleton-Century, 1936; *Supreme Court or Political Puppets?,* Appleton-Century, 1937; *Who Were the Eleven Million?,* Appleton-Century, 1937; *Diary of a Washington Correspondent,* H. C. Kinsey, 1942; *The Editorials of David Lawrence,* six volumes, U.S. News and World Report, 1970. Contributor of articles to numerous magazines, newspapers, and journals.

SIDELIGHTS: David Lawrence began his journalistic career while still in high school as a reporter for the *Buffalo Express.* Upon entering Princeton University in 1906 he became campus correspondent for the Associated Press. His first big break came in 1908 when he was sent to report on the health of the seriously-ill President Grover Cleveland in his New Jersey home. Although he was forced to return to classes after only a few days on the scene, he had quickly become a friend of Mrs. Cleveland, who subsequently telegramed the young journalist upon the death of her husband. Lawrence immediately called in the story to the Associated Press and, because he was first with the information, "scooped" the other newspapers.

After leaving the Associated Press, Lawrence joined the *New York Evening Post* in 1916 as their Washington correspondent. He then presided over the Consolidated Press Association for more than a decade. In 1926 he founded the *U.S. Daily,* a magazine covering activities of the federal government, and began what would one day be a periodical referred to by millions of readers. The *U.S. Daily* ceased publication temporarily in 1933 to be reintroduced as the

U.S. News, a weekly report of national events. The year 1946 saw the founding of another Lawrence venture, *World Report.* This new magazine broadened the scope of his other periodicals by chronicling affairs of the entire world. Lawrence took the final step to complete the evolution in 1947 when he merged his two publications into the immensely successful *U.S. News and World Report.* This latest magazine has since grown steadily in popularity and presently enjoys a circulation of nearly two million.

BIOGRAPHICAL/CRITICAL SOURCES: Newsweek, February 26, 1973; *Time,* February 26, 1973; *U.S. News and World Report,* February 26, 1973, March 5, 1973, July 24, 1978.

OBITUARIES: New York Times, February 12, 1973; *Washington Post,* February 21, 1973; *U.S. News and World Report,* February 26, 1973; *Christianity Today,* March 2, 1973; *National Review,* March 2, 1973.*

*   *   *

LAWRENCE, Lesley
See LEWIS, Lesley

*   *   *

LAWSON, Michael
See RYDER, M(ichael) L(awson)

*   *   *

LAYTON, Andrea
See BANCROFT, Iris (Nelson)

*   *   *

LEACH, Barry Arthur   1930-

PERSONAL: Born June 27, 1930, in Addiscombe, England; son of Leslie Arthur and May Florence (Watts) Leach; married Dorothea Sophie Schneider (a director of Tibetan Refugee Aid Society), September 18, 1954; children: Corinna Marie, Markus Peter, Christopher Barry. *Education:* Attended Royal Military Academy, Sandhurst, 1949-50; University of London, B.A., 1962; University of British Columbia, Ph.D., 1968. *Home:* 13936 Terry Rd., White Rock, British Columbia, Canada V4B 1A2. *Office:* Institutes of International and Environmental Studies, Douglas College, P.O. Box 2503, New Westminster, British Columbia, Canada V3L 5B2.

CAREER: British Army, Royal Artillery, instructor of junior leaders' regiment, instructor in atomic, biological, and chemical warfare, instructor in army education, adjutant of Supreme Headquarters Allied Powers for Europe, liaison officer with West German Army, leaving service as captain, 1950-60; elementary school teacher in Surrey, British Columbia, 1961-64, adult education instructor in history, 1964-65, made historical and wildlife television programs, 1966-67; Vancouver City College, Vancouver, British Columbia, lecturer in modern history, 1967-70; Douglas College, New Westminster, British Columbia, chairman of department of liberal studies, 1970-71, founder and director of Institutes of International and Environmental Studies, 1971—. Lecturer at University of British Columbia, 1960-68; assistant professor at Western Washington State College, summer, 1968. Painter in oils and water colors. Producer for Canadian Broadcasting Corp., 1961, 1970. Trustee of Brett Vocational Training Fund, 1979—.

MEMBER: Save the Beaches Association (founding director, 1963), Tibetan Refugee Aid Society (member of board of

directors, 1972—), Spatsizi Association (member of board of directors, 1978—), Federation of British Columbia Naturalists (member of board of directors, 1976-79), British Columbia Waterfowl Society (founding director, 1961-67). *Awards, honors:* Canada Council fellow, 1966-68, grants, 1969, 1973.

WRITINGS: German Strategy Against Russia, Oxford University Press, 1972; *The German General Staff,* Ballantine, 1973; *Waterfowl of a Pacific Estuary* (natural history), Provincial Museum (Victoria, British Columbia), 1981.

Author of "Hitler Attacks Russia," first broadcast by CBC-TV, June 22, 1961, and "Dunkirk: The German Viewpoint," first broadcast by CBC-TV, June 2, 1970. Scriptwriter for "Klahanie," on CBC-TV, 1967-68. Contributor of articles and art work to *Times, Field, Wildfowl,* and *British Columbia Outdoors,* and newspapers.

WORK IN PROGRESS: Editing and translating *War Journal of Colonel General Franz Halder, Chief of the German General Staff, 1938-42,* publication by Clarendon Press expected in 1982.

SIDELIGHTS: Leach commented: "I have been fortunate to be able to direct my two major interests, military history and natural history, into publications and practical projects; the latter in the form of a system of wildlife sanctuaries and nature parks on the Lower Fraser River in British Columbia. In the field of international aid my wife and I work as a team to support rural development and refugee rehabilitation in India, and we have visited India on project inspection tours in 1974, 1976, 1977-78, and 1980."

*   *   *

LEE, Betty
See LAMBERT, Elizabeth (Minnie)

*   *   *

LEE, (Henry) Desmond (Pritchard)   1908-

PERSONAL: Born August 30, 1908, in Nottingham, England; son of Henry Burgass (a minister) and Ida (Pritchard) Lee; married Elizabeth Crookenden, March 23, 1935; children: one son, two daughters. *Education:* Corpus Christi College, Cambridge, M.A., 1930. *Politics:* Tory. *Religion:* Church of England. *Home:* 8 Barton Close, Cambridge, England.

CAREER: Cambridge University, Cambridge, England, fellow of Corpus Christi College, 1938-48, tutor, 1935-48, lecturer in classics, 1937-48; headmaster of secondary schools in Bristol, England, 1948-54, and Winchester, England, 1954-68; Cambridge University, fellow of Wolfson College, 1968-73, honorary fellow, 1974, president of Hughes Hall, 1974-78, honorary fellow, 1978. Life fellow of Corpus Christi College, Cambridge, 1948-68 and 1978—. Member of Cambridge Regional Commissioner's Office, 1941-44. Chairman of Headmasters Conference, 1959-60 and 1967. *Member:* Athenaeum Club. *Awards, honors:* Knighted, 1961; Litt.D. from University of Nottingham, 1963.

WRITINGS: (Translator and author of notes) *Zeno of Elea: A Text and Notes,* Cambridge University Press, 1936, reprinted, 1967; (translator) Aristotle, *Meteorologica,* Harvard University Press, 1952; (translator and author of introduction) Plato, *The Republic,* Penguin, 1955, 2nd edition, 1974; (editor) *The Winchester Book of Verse,* Harrap, 1959; (translator and author of introduction) Plato, *Timaeus,* Penguin, 1965; *Timaeus and Critias,* Penguin, 1972; (editor) *Wittgenstein Lectures, 1930-1932,* Basil Blackwell, 1979, published as *Wittgenstein's Lectures, Cambridge University, 1930 to*

1932: From the Notes of John King and Desmond Lee, Rowman & Littlefield, 1980. Contributor to classical studies journals.

WORK IN PROGRESS: "I continue to work on Wittgenstein and on *Plato's Republic,* but have no immediate publishing plans."

SIDELIGHTS: Lee told *CA:* "My interest in Wittgenstein goes back to a personal acquaintance with him from 1929 to 1931." *Avocational interests:* Carpentry, reading.

* * *

LEE, Leo Ou-fan 1939-

PERSONAL: Born April 9, 1939, in Honan, China; naturalized U.S. citizen, 1980; son of Lucas Y. (a professor) and Yuan (a teacher; maiden name, Chou) Lee. *Education:* National Taiwan University, B.A., 1961; Harvard University, M.A., 1964, Ph.D., 1970. *Home:* 715 South Mitchell St., Bloomington, Ind. 47401. *Office:* Department of East Asian Languages and Culture, Indiana University, Bloomington, Ind. 47401.

CAREER: Dartmouth College, Hanover, N.H., instructor in history, 1969-70; Chinese University of Hong Kong, Hong Kong, lecturer in history, 1970-71; Princeton University, Princeton, N.J., assistant professor of history, 1972-76; Indiana University, Bloomington, associate professor of Chinese literature, 1976—. *Member:* Modern Language Association of America, Association for Asian Studies.

WRITINGS: The Romantic Generation of Modern Chinese Writers, Harvard University Press, 1973; *Voices From the Iron House: A Study of Lu Xun,* Indiana University Press, 1981. Co-editor of series, "Chinese Literature in Translation," Indiana University Press.

WORK IN PROGRESS: Co-editing an anthology of modern Chinese stories and novellas with Joseph S. M. Lau and C. T. Hsia, publication by Columbia University Press expected in 1981; a study of urban popular literature and culture in modern China c. 1895-1911.

SIDELIGHTS: Lee told *CA:* "As a modern Chinese literature scholar and occasional 'writer' (in Chinese), I have a singular purpose—or 'cause': to introduce and promote more samples of Chinese creative writing in the recent period. It is my hope that in the near future Western readers will come to appreciate modern Chinese literature in the same way that they have accepted modern Japanese literature, by incorporating it as a vital part of world literature. If Mishima is a household word(?), can't we do the same with Lu Xun (who is regarded as a much more significant writer even in Japan)?"

* * *

LEE, Loyd Ervin 1939-

PERSONAL: Born July 16, 1939, in Broadway, Ohio; married, 1963. *Education:* Ohio State University, B.A., 1961; Cornell University, Ph.D., 1967. *Home:* 27 Maple Ave., Highland, N.Y. 12528. *Office:* Department of History, State University of New York College at New Paltz, New Paltz, N.Y. 12561.

CAREER: Arkansas Agricultural, Mechanical and Normal College, Pine Bluff, assistant professsor of history, 1965-67; State University of New York College at New Paltz, New Paltz, assistant professor, 1967-71, associate professor of history, 1971—, assistant dean for academic affairs, 1979—. *Member:* American Historical Association, American

Committee on the History of the Second World War, American Commission on Military History. *Awards, honors:* Woodrow Wilson fellow, 1963.

WRITINGS: The Politics of Harmony: Civil Service, Liberalism, and Social Reform in Baden, 1800-1850, University of Delaware Press, 1978. Contributor to history journals.

WORK IN PROGRESS: Research on European military social history.

* * *

LEEK, Sybil 1923-

PERSONAL: Born February 22, 1923, in England. *Religion:* Wicca. *Home address:* P.O. Box 158, Melbourne Beach, Fla. 32951. *Agent:* Mrs. Carlton Cole, Waldorf Towers, Park Ave., New York, N.Y. 10022.

CAREER: Astrologer and writer, 1939—. Editor and publisher of Twin World Publications, 1969-72.

WRITINGS: The Astrological Cookbook, Pyramid Books, 1968; *Diary of a Witch,* Prentice-Hall, 1968; *Numerology: The Magic of Numbers,* Collier Books, 1969; *The Tree That Conquered the World* (novel), Prentice-Hall, 1969; *Cast Your Own Spell,* Bee-Line, 1970; *The Sybil Leek Book of Fortune-Telling,* Macmillan, 1969; *Sybil Leek's Astrological Guide to Successful Everyday Living,* Prentice-Hall, 1970; *Phrenology,* Macmillan, 1970; *How to Be Your Own Astrologer,* New American Library, 1970; *Telepathy: The Respectable Phenomenon,* Macmillan, 1971; *The Complete Art of Witchcraft,* World Publishing, 1971; *Guide to Telepathy,* Macmillan, 1971; *Astrological Guide to Financial Success,* Grosset, 1972; *Astrological Guide to the Presidential Candidates,* Abelard, 1972; *ESP: The Magic Within You,* Abelard, 1972; *My Life in Astrology,* Prentice-Hall, 1972; (with son, Stephen B. Leek) *The Bicycle: That Curious Invention,* T. Nelson, 1973; *Sybil Leek's Book of Herbs,* T. Nelson, 1973; *The Story of Faith Healing,* Macmillan, 1973.

The Best of Sybil Leek, edited by Glen A. Hilken, Popular Library, 1974; *Reincarnation: The Second Chance,* Stein & Day, 1974; *Sybil Leek's Zodiac of Love,* Regnery, 1974; *Tomorrow's Headlines Today,* Prentice-Hall, 1974; *Driving Out the Devils,* Putnam, 1975 (published in England as *Sybil Leek on Exorcism: Driving Out the Devils,* W. H. Allen, 1976); *Herbs: Medicine and Mysticism,* Regnery, 1975; *The Night Voyagers: You and Your Dreams,* Mason/Charter, 1975; *Star Speak: Your Body Language From the Stars,* Arbor House, 1975; *Sybil Leek's Book of Curses,* Prentice-Hall, 1975; (with Bert R. Sugar) *The Assassination Chain,* Corwin, 1976; (with Hilken) *Inside Bellevue,* Mason/Charter, 1976; (with S. B. Leek) *A Ring of Magic Islands,* Amphoto, 1976; *Sybil Leek's Book of the Curious and the Occult,* Ballantine, 1976; *Moon Signs,* Berkley Publishing, 1977; *Astrology and Love,* Berkley Publishing, 1977. Also author of *Pictorial Encyclopedia of Astrology,* 1971, and *Astrological Guide to Love and Sex,* with R. V. Kaufman.

Author of "Sybil Leek Astrology," a column syndicated by Globe Communications. Contributor of articles and poems to magazines. Associate editor of MacFadden Women's Group.

SIDELIGHTS: Leek told *CA:* "I prefer to live very quietly these days doing research and assessing vast amounts of documentation on astrology, reincarnation, and politics."

* * *

LEHMBERG, Paul 1946-

PERSONAL: Born November 16, 1946, in Redwood Falls,

Minn.; son of F. G. (a dentist) and Henrietta (Hanson) Lehmberg; married Suzanne Smith (a histologist), November 27, 1968. *Education:* Concordia College, Moorhead, Minn., B.A., 1968; University of Utah, M.A., 1972, Ph.D., 1977. *Home:* 206 East Hewitt, Marquette, Mich. 49855. *Office:* Department of English, Northern Michigan University, Marquette, Mich. 49855.

CAREER: Milestone, Salt Lake City, Utah, feature editor, 1977; Northern Michigan University, Marquette, assistant professor of English, 1978—. *Military service:* U.S. Army, 1969-70.

WRITINGS: In the Strong Woods (nonfiction), St. Martin's, 1980.

WORK IN PROGRESS: "A meditative travelogue of a canoe trip down the Minnesota River."

SIDELIGHTS: Lehmberg commented: "*In the Strong Woods* is a group of seven reflective essays based on a summer I spent living alone at a remote cabin, called Nym, in the Minnesota/Ontario canoe country. Structurally the essays are discursive, and their purpose is simple: to make the reader 'see'—in the sense that Joseph Conrad used the term—what it was like to make the decision to live at Nym, and then to leave. I use Nym as both a tool and a base—a tool, because of the simplicities of living there, to aid me in forming order out of apparent disorder and meaning out of apparent meaninglessness; and a base from which to range back and forth between the local and concrete, and the general and more abstract. In the book I delve into subjects ranging from such lowly items as the purpose of pickles to such abstractions as Western man's concept of time. I try indirectly to present an image of man, whom I see as a creative/destructive man/animal of limited means and unlimited aspirations who is blessed and cursed with his own mind. These opposites cannot be fused, they can only be accepted and juggled, however precariously, and the book is an 'essay'—an attempt—at achieving this balance; as such it is also a search for ways of right living and for a path to wholeness and integrity."

*   *   *

LEHRMAN, Liza
See WILLIAMS, Liza

*   *   *

LEIGH, Spencer 1945-

PERSONAL: Born February 1, 1945, in Liverpool, England; son of Thomas (a paper merchant) and Ethel (Waugh) Leigh; married Anne Wolstenholme (a librarian), July 27, 1974. *Education:* Attended public school in Liverpool, England. *Politics:* Tory. *Religion:* Anglican. *Home:* 2 Westway, Hightown, Liverpool L38 0BT, England.

CAREER: Royal Insurance Group, Liverpool, England, pensions quotations officer, 1963—. *Member:* Institute of Actuaries (fellow), Chartered Insurance Institute (fellow).

WRITINGS: (With Richard Hill, Malcolm Barnes, and Tom Smirthwaite) *Collage Two,* Raven Books, 1972; *Paul Simon: Now and Then,* Raven Books, 1973, revised edition, 1976; *Presley Nation,* Raven Books, 1976; *Stars in My Eyes: Personal Interviews With Top Music Stars,* Raven Books, 1980. Contributor to magazines, including *Country Music Roundup* and *Not Fade Away.* Assistant editor of *Journal of the Institute of Actuaries.*

WORK IN PROGRESS: "I am currently preparing a documentary series for the British Broadcasting Corp. (BBC-

Radio) called 'Let's Go Down the Cavern,' which will feature over one hundred interviews. My intention is to put this into book form, probably to be published by Raven Books in 1982."

SIDELIGHTS: Leigh told *CA:* "My writings stem from a love of popular music and a desire to find out more about the people who make it. My book on Paul Simon tried to provide a reasoned analysis of his life and music, while *Presley Nation* was a look at Elvis Presley through the eyes of his admirers. In recent years I have been fortunate enough to meet many musicians and *Stars in My Eyes* was a collection of what I considered to be my best interviews. I believe that my strength as a writer is to prepare fully for each interview, and I am very proud of my profiles of Charles Aznavour, Burl Ives, and record producer George Martin, all of which are in the book."

*   *   *

LEITCH, Maurice 1933-

PERSONAL: Born July 5, 1933, in Muckamoke, Antrim County, Northern Ireland; son of Andrew (a linen worker) and Jean Leitch. *Education:* Attended Stran Millis Training College, 1950-53. *Agent:* Deborah Rogers Ltd., 5-11 Mortimer St., London W1N 7RH, England. *Office:* Drama Department, British Broadcasting Corp., Broadcasting House, Portland Pl., London W.1, England.

CAREER: Teacher of general subjects at Antrim Primary School in Northern Ireland, 1954-62; British Broadcasting Corp., features producer in Belfast, Northern Ireland, 1962-70, radio drama producer in London, 1970—. *Awards, honors:* Fiction prize from *Guardian,* 1969, for *Poor Lazarus.*

WRITINGS: The Liberty Lad (novel), MacGibbon & Kee, 1965, Pantheon, 1966; *Poor Lazarus* (novel), MacGibbon & Kee, 1969; *Stamping Ground* (novel), Secker & Warburg, 1975; *Silver's City* (novel), Secker & Warburg, 1981.

Plays: "A Little Bit of Heaven," first broadcast by BBC-Radio, May, 1978; "Rifleman," first broadcast by BBC-TV, November, 1980.

WORK IN PROGRESS: Short stories for a collection.

SIDELIGHTS: Leitch commented: "All my novels deal with Ulster's 'poor whites,' the Protestant working people. Thus, my influences are not Irish as such, but more Faulkner, Flannery O'Connor, and Eudora Welty, for obvious reasons. My ancestral links are very strong in the southern United States, culturally and ethnically speaking, because my forebears became the Scotch-Irish Americans of the eighteenth and nineteenth centuries. I'd like to pursue this thread, perhaps soon, in another book.

"For a Northern Irish writer at this time, it is important to take stock, to isolate oneself from the hysterical outpourings of the journalists and 'visiting firemen.' I tend more and more to shy away from the present situation, seeking an answer to our predicament in some other, oblique approach."

*   *   *

LELAND, Timothy 1937-

PERSONAL: Born September 24, 1937, in Boston, Mass.; son of Oliver Stevens (a businessman) and Frances Chamberlain (Ayres) Leland; married Natasha Bourso, September 26, 1964 (divorced). children: Christian Bourso, London Chamberlain. *Education:* Harvard University, A.B. (cum laude), 1960; Columbia University, M.S. (with honors),

1961. *Home:* 617 Tremont St., Boston, Mass. 02118. *Office: Boston Globe,* 135 Morrissey Blvd., Boston, Mass. 02107.

CAREER/WRITINGS: Boston Herald, Boston, Mass., medical editor, 1963-64; *Boston Globe,* Boston, science editor, 1965-66, State House bureau chief, 1966-67, assistant city editor, 1968-69, investigative reporter, 1970-71, assistant managing editor, 1972, managing editor of Sunday edition, 1976-81, managing editor of the daily paper, 1981—. *Member:* American Association of Sunday and Feature Editors (president, 1979-80), Harvard Club, Noble and Greenough Graduates Association (member of executive committee, 1972-74). *Awards, honors:* Columbia International Fellow, 1961; American Political Science Award, 1968, for "outstanding reporting in the area of governmental reform"; U.S. South African Leader Exchange program traveling grantee, 1969; Pulitzer Prize for investigative reporting and Sigma Delta Chi award for civic service (reporting), both 1972; Associated Press Managing Editors Award for public service and Sevellon Brown Award, both 1974.

SIDELIGHTS: Leland dealt with governmental reform and voter redistricting in Massachusetts in his prize-winning articles. In 1970, he formed a team to investigate municipal misconduct in Boston.

Leland told *CA:* "Journalism is a daily creation. Some days it goes well and leaves you feeling exhilarated. Others it goes poorly and leaves you feeling foolish. In either case, it's the process of instant history, a single frame of time. All writers are moviemakers, in a sense, and journalists, like others, take their satisfaction from watching the reel played back."

*   *   *

LEMIEUX, Marc 1948-
(Marc Best)

PERSONAL: Born January 2, 1948, in Fitchburg, Mass.; son of Joseph Albert (a lawyer) and Olivette (an office manager; maiden name, Lachance) Lemieux. *Education:* Attended high school in Arlington, Mass. *Home:* 3 Henmar Dr., Billerica, Mass. 01821. *Office:* Hanscom Air Force Base, Bedford, Mass.

CAREER: Worked at Firemen's Fund Insurance Co. and Shawmut County Bank, 1965-75; U.S. Department of Agriculture, Burlington, Mass., supply technician, 1975-79; Hanscom Air Force Base, Bedford, Mass., civilian research technician, 1979—. *Military service:* U.S. Army Reserve, Infantry, 1966-72.

WRITINGS—Under pseudonym Marc Best: *Those Endearing Young Charms* (nonfiction), A. S. Barnes, 1971; *Their Hearts Were Young and Gay* (nonfiction), A. S. Barnes, 1975.

WORK IN PROGRESS: Young Faces of the American Theatre, on juvenile actors and actresses.

SIDELIGHTS: Marc Lemieux told *CA:* "I have not made writing my career. I do not write for profit. For me writing has become a very rewarding hobby; rewarding not in a monetary sense but in the way I feel upon seeing my name in print. To all those readers who at one time may have harbored thoughts of writing a book, I say go to it. Do not be dismayed because you have no prior experience or useful credentials. I had none. Should your subject have any merit, you will be rewarded in the end. Perseverance always pays off."

*   *   *

LENNON, John (Ono) 1940-1980

PERSONAL: Original name, John Winston Lennon; name legally changed April 22, 1969; born October 9, 1940, in Liverpool, Lancashire, England; died of gunshot wounds, December 8, 1980, in New York, N.Y.; son of Alfred (a porter) and Julia (Stanley) Lennon; married Cynthia Powell, August 23, 1962 (divorced November 8, 1968); married Yoko Ono (an artist, vocalist, songwriter, and author), March 20, 1969; children: (first marriage) John Julian; (second marriage) Kyoko (stepdaughter), Sean Taro Ono. *Education:* Attended Liverpool College of Art. *Residence:* New York, N.Y.

CAREER: Composer, lyricist, performer (vocals, guitar, piano, organ, harmonica), writer. Member of the Nurk Twins, 1957; co-founder and member of the Quarrymen musical group, 1958; member of the Moondogs trio, 1959; member of the Silver Beatles, 1960; premiered with the Beatles in Liverpool, England, 1960; performed with the Beatles at clubs in Hamburg, West Germany, and Liverpool during early 1960's, in Sweden, 1963, with Royal Variety Show at Prince of Wales Theatre in London, England, 1963, in Paris, France, Denmark, Hong Kong, Australia, New Zealand, and the United States, 1964, in France, Spain, Italy, and the United States, 1965, in Japan, Greece, Canada, and the Far East during late 1960's; co-owner of Apple Boutique, London, 1967-68; Apple Corp, Ltd., London, partner, 1968—. Founder and member of the Plastic Ono Band, beginning in 1969. Guest on numerous television shows, including: "Juke Box Jury," British Broadcasting Corp. (BBC), December 7, 1963; "The Ed Sullivan Show," Columbia Broadcasting System (CBS), February 9, 1964, and February 23, 1964; "Magical Mystery Tour," BBC, 1967; "Not Only—But Also," BBC, c. 1967; "Rock and Roll Circus," 1968.

Actor in motion pictures, including: "A Hard Day's Night," United Artists, 1964; "Help!," United Artists, 1965; "How I Won the War," United Artists, 1967; "Let It Be," United Artists, 1970; "Dynamite Chicken," EYP Programs, 1972. Creator and director of film "Apotheosis," shown at Cannes Filmmaker Fortnight Festival, 1971; creator of short films "Erection," "Cold Turkey," and "The Ballad of John and Yoko," all shown with "Apotheosis" at Whitney Museum of American Art, New York City, 1971. Held one-artist exhibits of lithographs at London Arts Gallery and at Lee Nordness Galleries in New York City, 1970.

AWARDS, HONORS: Foyles Literary Prize, 1964, for *In His Own Write;* winner, with the Beatles, of Grammy Awards from National Academy of Recording Artists: for best new artists, 1964, for album of the year, best album cover, best contemporary rock and roll recording, and best engineered recording, all for "Sgt. Pepper's Lonely Hearts Club Band," all 1967, for best engineered recording for "Abbey Road," 1969, and for best original score for movie or television for "Let It Be," 1970; member of Order of the British Empire, 1965; Ivor Novello Award, 1970, for "Get Back" and "Ob-La-Di, Ob-La-Da"; platinum album awards for "Abbey Road," "Meet the Beatles," "Hey Jude," "Let It Be," "Sgt. Pepper's Lonely Hearts Club Band," "Rubber Soul," "A Hard Day's Night," "The White Album," "Magical Mystery Tour," "Revolver," and "Help"; gold album awards for "Imagine" and "John Lennon/The Plastic Ono Band."

WRITINGS: In His Own Write (humor), self-illustrated, Simon & Schuster, 1964; *A Spaniard in the Works* (humor), self-illustrated, Simon & Schuster, 1965; *The Penguin John Lennon* (contains *In His Own Write* and *A Spaniard in the Works*), Penguin, 1966, published as *In His Own Write* [and] *A Spaniard in the Works,* New American Library, 1967; (with Adrienne Kennedy and Victor Spinetti) *The Lennon*

Play (one-act; adapted from *In His Own Write* and *A Spaniard in the Works;* first produced in London at the National Theatre, June 27, 1968), J. Cape, 1968, Simon & Schuster, 1969; *Bag One: A Suite of Lithographs* (exhibit guide), [New York], 1971; *My Mummy's Dead,* Mini-Books, 1971; (with Jann Wenner) *Lennon Remembers,* Straight Arrow Books, 1971; (illustrator) Stanley Kapepa, *A Canoe for Uncle Kila,* Polynesian Voyaging Society, [Honolulu], 1976.

Songbooks: (With Paul McCartney) *Eine Kleine Beatlemusik,* Northern Songs Ltd., 1965; (with McCartney and George Harrison) *The Golden Beatles,* Northern Songs Ltd., 1966; (with McCartney) *The Music of Lennon and McCartney,* Hansen, 1969; (with McCartney) *Great Songs of Lennon and McCartney,* edited by Milton Okun, Dan Fox, and Victoria Heller, Quadrangle, 1973; (with McCartney and Harrison) *The Beatles Lyrics,* Futura, 1975, reprinted as *The Beatles Lyrics Illustrated,* Dell, 1975.

Author with wife, Yoko Ono, of television documentary film, "Rape," 1969. Contributor of poems and stories to periodicals.

Recordings; with the Beatles: "Please Please Me," Parlophone, 1963; "Introducing the Beatles," Parlophone, 1963; "Meet the Beatles!," Capitol, 1964; (with Tony Sheridan and others) "The Beatles With Tony Sheridan and Their Guests," MGM, 1964; (with Frank Ilfield) "Jolly What! The Beatles With Frank Ilfield on Stage," Vee Jay, 1964; (with Sheridan) "The Beatles' First," Polydor, 1964, reissued, 1967; "The Beatles' Second Album," Capitol, 1964; (with George Martin and Orchestra) "A Hard Day's Night," United Artists, 1964; "Something New," Capitol, 1964; (with the Four Seasons) "The Beatles Versus the Four Seasons," Vee Jay, 1964; (with Sheridan and the Swallows) "Ain't She Sweet?," Atxo, 1964; (with the Four Seasons) "Songs, Pictures, and Stories of the Fabulous Beatles," Vee Jay, 1964; "The Beatles' Story," Capitol, 1964; "Beatles '65," Capitol, 1964; "The Early Beatles," Capitol, 1965; "Beatles VI," Capitol, 1965; "Help!," Capitol, 1965; "Rubber Soul," Capitol, 1965.

"A Collection of Beatle Oldies," Parlophone, 1966; "Yesterday . . . and Today," Capitol, 1966; "Revolver," Capitol, 1966; (with Sheridan and others) "This Is Where It Started," Metro, 1966; (with the Swallows) "The Amazing Beatles," Clarion, 1966; "Sgt. Pepper's Lonely Hearts Club Band," Capitol, 1967; "Magical Mystery Tour," Capitol, 1967; "The Beatles" (two-record set; also known as "The White Album"), Apple, 1968; "Yellow Submarine," Apple, 1969; "Abbey Road," Apple, 1969.

"Hey Jude," Apple, 1970; "Let It Be," Apple, 1970; "The Beatles/1962-66," Apple, 1973; "The Beatles/1967-70," Apple, 1973; "Rock 'n' Roll Music," Capitol, 1976; "Love Songs," Capitol, 1979.

Other recordings: (With Y. Ono) "Unfinished Music No. 1—Two Virgins," Apple, 1968; (with Y. Ono) "Unfinished Music No. 2—Music With the Lions," Apple, 1969; (with Y. Ono) "Wedding Album," Apple, 1969; (with the Plastic Ono Band) "The Plastic Ono Band: Live Peace in Toronto," Apple, 1970; (with the Plastic Ono Band) "John Lennon/Plastic Ono Band," Apple, 1970; (with the Plastic Ono Band and the Flux Fiddlers) "Imagine," Apple, 1971; (with Y. Ono, the Plastic Ono Band, Elephant's Memory, and the Invisible Strings) "Sometime in New York City" (two-record set), Apple, 1972; (with the Plastic U.F. Ono Band) "Mind Games," Apple, 1973; (with the Plastic Ono Nuclear Band) "Walls and Bridges," Apple, 1974; "Rock 'n' Roll," Apple, 1975; "Shaved Fish," Apple, 1975; (with Y. Ono) "Double Fantasy," Geffen, 1980.

Lyricist and composer of songs, including: "Woman Is the Nigger of the World," "Sisters O Sisters," "Attica State," "Born in a Prison," "New York City," "Sunday Bloody Sunday," "The Luck of the Irish," "John Sinclair," "We're All Water," "Bring on the Lucie (Freda People)," "Nutopian National Anthem," "Mind Games," "Meat City," "Going Down on Love," "Whatever Gets You Through the Night," "Number Nine Dream," "Give Peace a Chance/Cold Turkey," "Instant Karma (We All Shine On)," "Remember Love," "Who Has Seen the Wind?," "Power to the People," "Beef Jerky," "Move Over Ms. L.," "Working Class Hero," "No Bed for Beatle John," "Oh Yoko!," "Starting Over," "Woman."

Lyricist and/or composer of songs with Paul McCartney, including: "I Saw Her Standing There," "Please Please Me," "Love Me Do," "Baby, It's You," "Do You Want to Know a Secret?," "A Taste of Honey," "There's a Place," "Twist and Shout," "P.S. I Love You," "It Won't Be Long," "All I've Got to Do," "Don't Bother Me," "All My Loving," "Little Child," "I Wanna Be Your Man," "I Want to Hold Your Hand," "This Boy," "Not a Second Time," "From Me to You," "Ask Me Why," "Thank You Girl," "I Call Your Name," "She Loves You," "A Hard Day's Night," "I'll Cry Instead," "I'm Happy Just to Dance With You," "I Should Have Known Better," "If I Fell," "And I Love Her," "Can't Buy Me Love," "Things We Said Today," "Anytime at All," "When I Get Home," "Slow Down," "Matchbox," "No Reply," "I'm a Loser," "Baby's in Black," "I'll Follow the Sun," "Mr. Moonlight," "I'll Be Back," "Everybody's Trying to Be My Baby," "She's a Woman," "I Feel Fine," "Eight Days a Week," "You Like Me Too Much," "I Don't Want to Spoil the Party," "The Word," "What You Doing?," "Dizzy Miss Lizzie."

"Tell Me What You See," "Every Little Thing," "I've Just Seen a Face," "Norwegian Wood," "You Won't See Me," "Michelle," "It's Only Love," "Girl," "I'm Looking Through You," "In My Life," "The Night Before," "Wait," "Run for Your Life," "Help!," "You've Got to Hide Your Love Away," "I Need You," "Another Girl," "Ticket to Ride," "You're Gonna Lose That Girl," "We Can Work It Out," "Yellow Submarine," "Bad Boy," "Day Tripper," "Paperback Writer," "Eleanor Rigby," "Drive My Car," "I'm Only Sleeping," "Nowhere Man," "And Your Bird Can Sing," "What Goes On," "She Said She Said," "Good Day Sunshine," "For No One," "Got to Get You Into My Life," "Tomorrow Never Knows," "Magical Mystery Tour," "The Fool on the Hill," "Your Mother Should Know," "I Am the Walrus," "Hello Goodbye."

"Strawberry Fields Forever," "Penny Lane," "Baby, You're a Rich Man," "All You Need Is Love," "Come Together," "Oh! Darling," "I Want You (She's So Heavy)," "Because," "You Never Give Me Your Money," "Sun King," "Mean Mr. Mustard," "Polythene Pam," "She Came in Through the Bathroom Window," "Golden Slumbers," "Carry That Weight," "The End," "Her Majesty," "Lady Madonna," "Hey Jude," "Rocky Raccoon," "Two of Us," "I Dig a Pony," "Across the Universe," "Dig It," "Let It Be," "Maggie Mae," "I've Got a Feeling," "One After 909," "The Long and Winding Road," "For You Blue," "Get Back," "Back in the U.S.S.R.," "Dear Prudence," "Glass Onion," "Ob-La-Di, Ob-La-Da," "Wild Honey Pie," "The Continuing Story of Bungalow Bill," "Happiness Is a Warm Gun," "Martha My Dear," "I'm So Tired," "Blackbird," "Why Don't We Do

It in the Road," "Julia," "I Will," "Birthday," "Yer Blues."

"Mother Nature's Son," "Everybody's Got Something to Hide Except Me and My Monkey," "Sexy Sadie," "Helter Skelter," "Revolution," "Honey Pie," "Cry Baby Cry," "Revolution No. 9," "Good Night," "Sgt. Pepper's Lonely Hearts Club Band," "With a Little Help From My Friends," "Lucy in the Sky With Diamonds," "Getting Better," "Fixing a Hole," "She's Leaving Home," "Being for the Benefit of Mr. Kite," "When I'm Sixty-Four," "Lovely Rita," "Good Morning Good Morning," "A Day in the Life."

Lyricist and composer, with McCartney, of original soundtrack for film, "All This and World War II," Twentieth-Century Records, 1976.

SIDELIGHTS: "The Beatles will be remembered not only for their considerable contribution as songwriters and recording artists," predicted Nicholas Schaffner, "but also as the most remarkable cultural and sociological phenomenon of their time. During the 1960's they seemed to transform, however unwittingly, the look, sound, and style of at least one generation." For example, Schaffner continued, "they were among the first major public figures of our time to break down the barriers dividing the sexes, with their long hair and vivid attire; champion the use of 'mind-expanding' drugs and the innovations in sound, language, design, and attitude these substances inspired; and, in general, show the way to a life style that defied so many of the conventions taken for granted in 1963."

The John Lennon/Paul McCartney partnership began in 1956, shortly after the two met at a Liverpool rock concert where they were both performing. Together they first performed as the Nurk Twins. Against some resistance from Lennon, McCartney introduced his schoolmate George Harrison into the group in 1958, and the three guitarists soon joined drummer Pete Best to form the Quarrymen. Slowly building a local following in Liverpool cellar clubs, the group evolved through several name changes—the Moondogs, the Moonshiners, the Silver Beatles—before settling on the Beatles in 1960. For a while the four were joined by guitarist Stuart Sutcliff, a friend of Lennon's from the Liverpool College of Art.

In 1959 the group took a tramp steamer to Hamburg, West Germany, where they got their first lucrative nightclub bookings. It was there they met Ringo Starr, who replaced Pete Best as the group's drummer. "The quick-witted, witheringly cynical Lennon was by all accounts the driving spirit behind the Beatles in those days," Schaffner commented. In Hamburg's Kaiserkeller Club, where the crowd consisted largely of gangsters, prostitutes, and transvestites, the band was often expected to play for eight-hour stretches. But, in Schaffner's opinion, the hard work greatly improved their music: "Their act grew livelier. The Beatles were encouraged to *Mak Schau* [put on a show] at all costs; so the sweating, leather-clad musicians learned to writhe, vamp, and mug for hours on end, punctuating their repertoire with obscene insults, food, and beer tossed at each other and at the audience. Lennon would often taunt the Germans with his impressions of Hitler, and was wont to appear on stage wearing nothing but a toilet seat and a pair of shorts." Schaffner also pointed out that "these stories, of course, did not come to light until long after the Beatles' later incarnation as cherubic moptops had won the hearts of millions."

Stuart Sutcliff decided to stay in Germany when Lennon, McCartney, Harrison, and Starr returned to Liverpool. It

was on their return to England that the Beatles were discovered by Brian Epstein, who became their manager. Epstein was impressed with what he saw: "I sensed that something was happening, something terribly exciting," he said. "There was this amazing communication with the audience and this absolutely marvelous humor." Epstein persuaded the four to stop their onstage swearing and food-fighting, to exchange their scruffy leather jackets for collarless Pierre Cardin suits, and to trim their shaggy hair. He also arranged prestigious engagements and a contract with Electrical and Musical Industries Ltd. (EMI). Schaffner reported that "Lennon [had] said he felt a few qualms about 'selling out' when the Beatles began to launder their once-raunchy image, but McCartney was always there to make sure his tie was straight."

The Beatles' first EMI recording in 1962 was the Lennon-McCartney composition "Love Me Do," which sold one hundred thousand copies. That record and the group's first British television appearance marked the beginning of a spectacular career. In the following years the group played a command performance for the British royal family and held sell-out concerts in other European countries as well as in the United States, Australia, New Zealand, Canada, and Japan.

Beatlemania became an international phenomenon. Hysterical fans filled auditoriums and sports stadiums to see their idols, even though the music was often drowned out by the din of screaming teens. Beatle boots, books, posters, and bubblegum cards sold as fast as they could be made. The sheets and towels the group used at one hotel were cut into one-inch squares and sold as souvenirs. Even the not-so-young celebrated the "Fabulous Four." "I think they are lovely boys, and I've been dying to meet them," the wife of British Prime Minister Harold Wilson told a reporter in 1964. "Harold and I are tremendous fans of the Beatles."

Part of the reason for the Beatles' universal appeal was their versatility. As Greg Shaw noted, "the Beatles weren't merely musicians; they were the first and foremost rock 'n' roll fans, and their knowledge of and devotion to the music made them something special." They had absorbed the "California sound" of the Beach Boys, the soul music sounds of Detroit, Chicago, and New Orleans, and the sounds of 1950's rock stars such as Buddy Holly, Chuck Berry, Elvis Presley, and Little Richard. "The Beatles just brought it all together," Shaw said.

The public had learned to expect a certain amount of outrageousness from the group, but Lennon's comments on religion in 1966 shocked and offended many people. "Christianity will go," he declared. "It will vanish and shrink. I needn't argue about that, I'm right and I will be proved right. We're more popular than Jesus Christ now. I don't know which will go first, rock 'n' roll or Christianity. Jesus was all right, but his disciples were thick and ordinary. It's them twisting it that ruins it for me." According to Schaffner, Lennon's comments caused such a scandal that "god-fearing disc jockeys, church leaders, and right wing politicians across the old Confederacy decided the time had come to stamp out the Beatles for good. Throughout the first two weeks of August, papers carried lurid reports that read like scenes from Ray Bradbury's *Farenheit 451*, of rallies around bonfires into which were dumped large quantities of Beatle records and memorabilia and sometimes even effigies of the Fab Four."

Protests were heard around the world, forcing Beatle manager Epstein to come to Lennon's defense. Lennon, Epstein explained, was merely expressing "deep concern" for modern society's lack of interest in religion. John himself made a public apology: "I suppose if I had said television was more popular than Christianity, I would have gotten away with it, I'm sorry I opened my mouth. I'm not anti-god, anti-christ, or anti-religion. I was not knocking it. I was not saying we are greater or better."

The anti-Beatles demonstrations prompted many fans to defend the group, and soon the controversy passed. Beatlemania continued, but the group members grew weary of having their clothes ripped and their hair pulled and clipped by hysterical admirers. Ringo told of a night when the band had been forced to climb a twenty-five story drain pipe to escape fans and the press. Exhausted, the Beatles decided that their 1966 concert at San Francisco's Candlestick Park would be their last live performance together. Ringo stated: "If it had gone on, I personally would have gone insane."

It was at this time that the group also began to tire of much of the music they had been putting out. Lennon complained: "I can't stand listening to most of our early stuff . . . songs like "Eight Days a Week" and "She Loves You" sound like big drags to me now. I turn the radio off if they're ever on." The Beatles began experimenting with compositions more sophisticated than their early four-four beat music had been. Lennon and Harrison had also been taking hallucinogenic drugs for several years by this time, and their new music reflected these experiences.

The release of the "Revolver" album in 1966 marked the Beatles' emergence as a studio band. "This almost flawless album," observed Roy Carr and Tony Tyler, "can be seen as the peak of the Beatles' creative career. . . . And it could probably have only been made at this particular juncture in the Beatles' career. Touring was, for them, a bar to music . . . the final assembly of all their influences in one place at one time, plus the growing infatuation with drug based ideology (and the drugs themselves) . . . all combined to create a pool of assets [that] was joyfully put to use in almost staggering fashion." Subsequent albums, most notably "Sgt. Pepper's Lonely Hearts Club Band," "The White Album," and "Abbey Road," illustrated the Beatles' maturation of musical style and achieved critical and commercial success.

As the music of the group developed, so did the individual styles and interests of each member. In 1967 Lennon made his solo acting debut in the motion picture "How I Won the War," and soon afterward the other Beatles followed in pursuing their separate ventures. Harrison parted for India to study transcendental meditation with Maharishi Mahesh Yogi; McCartney began work on a movie soundtrack; and Starr appeared in the film "Candy." The founding of Apple Records in 1968 helped keep the Beatles together for a few more recordings, but the bonds that once held the group together had begun to disintegrate.

A number of events contributed to the Beatles disbandment. Lennon traced the beginning of the split to the death of manager Epstein in 1967: "After Brian died, we collapsed." Lennon's 1969 marriage to artist Yoko Ono created further turmoil within the group. "I presumed that I would just carry on, and bring Yoko into our life," Lennon recalled. "But it seemed I had to either be married to them or to Yoko, and I chose Yoko, and I was right." Tension among the members of the group was evident again when the movie "Let It Be" was released in 1970. "I felt sad, you know," Lennon said. "I felt . . . that the film was set up by Paul for Paul. That is one of the main reasons the Beatles ended." One year after the release of "Let It Be," the Beatles officially announced their breakup.

By the time of the Beatles' separation, Lennon had already proven himself as a literary talent and a successful solo recording artist. His collections of satirical poems and stories, *In His Own Write* and *A Spaniard in the Works,* were compared with works of Lewis Carroll, James Joyce, and James Thurber. A *Virginia Quarterly Review* critic stated: "One shouldn't have been surprised at the wit and the intelligence of the leader of the Beatles considering the cleverness evident in their success, but the skill (one even toys with the word 'genius') which Lennon shows in this collection of comic poems and prose pieces places him in the great comic tradition of Twain, Perelman, the Marx brothers, and the best of the new seriously comic novelists of this country." The *London Times* deemed *In His Own Write* "worth the attention of anyone who fears for the impoverishment of the English language and the British imagination."

After forming the Plastic Ono Band in 1969, Lennon achieved his first commercial success outside the Beatles. The group's second release, the gold album-winning "John Lennon/Plastic Ono Band," earned praise from Stephen Holden as "a masterpiece that by its very nature could never be repeated." Throughout the early 1970's Lennon remained in the popular-music spotlight with such single recordings as "Instant Karma," "Imagine," "Power to the People," and "Mind Games." After the 1975 release of his album "Shaved Fish," however, Lennon withdrew from public life.

Lennon used the break to reassess himself as a person and as an artist. According to *Newsweek*'s Barbara Graustark, Lennon was calmer at this time, "showing no signs of the inner demons that once haunted his songs." Lennon attributed some of his newly found peace to the solitude that had allowed him "to re-establish me for myself." He recalled that his "actual moment of awareness" occurred while he was on a tour around the world, a trip he had made, at Ono's suggestion, by himself. "I wandered around Hong Kong at dawn, alone, and it was a thrill," reflected Lennon. "I thought—aha! *This* is the feeling that makes you write or paint . . . It was with me all my life! And that's why I'm free of the Beatles—because I took the time to discover that I was John Lennon before the Beatles and will be after the Beatles and so be it."

Beginning in 1975, Lennon lived quietly at home raising his son Sean. "My life revolves around Sean," he told interviewers in 1980. "Now I have more reason to stay healthy and bright . . . And I want to be with my best friend. My best friend's my wife. If I couldn't have worked with her, I wouldn't have bothered." Just before Lennon's fortieth birthday, he and Ono released a new album, "Double Fantasy." Lennon's contributions to the record, "simple, direct, and melodic, were celebrations of love and domesticity that asked for, and required, no apology," said *Time*'s Jay Cocks.

While returning home after a December 8, 1980, recording session, Lennon was shot and killed outside his New York City apartment. News of his death brought thousands of mourners to gather outside his home, and radio stations throughout the world played his music in tribute. For many, Lennon's death marked the end of an era. "It's the last nail in the coffin of the '60s," said one fan. But before his death, Lennon had spoken optimistically about his music and his personal life—"Starting Over" was the title of his latest single. "We had planned so much together," reflected Ono. "We had talked about living until we were 80. We even drew up lists of all the things we could do for all those years. Then, it was all over. But that doesn't mean the message should be over. The music will live on."

BIOGRAPHICAL/CRITICAL SOURCES—Books: Julius Fast, *Beatles: The Real Story*, Putnam, 1968; Hunter Davies, *The Beatles: The Authorized Biography*, McGraw, 1968; Jonathan Eisen, editor, *The Age of Rock*, Random House, 1969; John Lennon and Jann Wenner, *Lennon Remembers*, Straight Arrow Books, 1971; Richard DiLello, *Longest Cocktail Party: An Insider's Diary of the Beatles, Their Million-Dollar Apple Empire, and Its Wild Rise and Fall*, Playboy Press, 1972; Peter McCabe and Robert D. Schonfeld, *Apple to the Core*, Pocket, 1972; Wilfred Mellers, *Twilight of the Gods: The Beatles in Retrospect*, Faber, 1973; Roy Carr and Tony Tyler, *The Beatles: An Illustrated Record*, Harmony Books, 1975; Anthony Fawcett, *John Lennon: One Day at a Time*, Grove, 1976; George Tremlett, *The John Lennon Story*, Futura, 1976; Ron Schaumburg, *Growing Up With the Beatles*, Harcourt, 1976; *Rock Revolution*, Popular Library, 1976; Nicholas Schaffner, *Beatles Forever*, Cameron House, 1977; Cynthia Lennon, *A Twist of Lennon*, Avon, 1978; *Contemporary Literary Criticism*, Volume 12, Gale, 1980.

Periodicals: *Time*, November 15, 1963, February 21, 1964, October 2, 1964, February 19, 1965, December 31, 1965, September 2, 1966, March 3, 1967, June 16, 1967, September 22, 1967, January 5, 1968, September 6, 1968, December 6, 1968, January 18, 1971, January 25, 1971, April 2, 1973, March 25, 1974, November 11, 1974, January 13, 1975, March 17, 1975, October 20, 1975, August 9, 1976; *Newsweek*, November 18, 1963, February 17, 1964, February 24, 1964, February 15, 1965, June 28, 1965, October 4, 1965, March 21, 1966, August 22, 1966, June 26, 1967, May 27, 1968, August 19, 1968, September 30, 1968, November 25, 1968, December 9, 1968, October 20, 1969, September 7, 1970, January 18, 1971, April 2, 1973, March 17, 1975, October 6, 1975, October 20, 1975, September 29, 1980.

New York Times Magazine, December 1, 1963, February 23, 1964, September 6, 1964; *Vogue*, January 1, 1964, October 1, 1968, December 1, 1968, March 1, 1969; *Life*, January 31, 1964, February 21, 1964, August 28, 1964, October 31, 1964, May 21, 1965, July 15, 1966, June 16, 1967, April 24, 1970; *New Republic*, February 22, 1964; *Saturday Evening Post*, March 21, 1964, August 8, 1964, August 27, 1966; *Times Literary Supplement*, March 26, 1964; *Virginia Quarterly Review*, summer, 1964, autumn, 1965; *New York Post*, September 15, 1964; *Esquire*, July, 1965, December, 1967, November, 1980; *New York Times*, July 1, 1965, December 10, 1980; *Atlantic*, August, 1965; *Commonweal*, May 12, 1967, December 27, 1968; *Reader's Digest*, December, 1967; *Look*, January 9, 1968, March 18, 1969; *Saturday Review*, June 28, 1969; *New Yorker*, February 21, 1970, January 8, 1972, December 9, 1972; *Rolling Stone*, January 7, 1971; *New York Times Book Review*, February 2, 1972; *Chicago Tribune*, December 10, 1980, December 11, 1980; *Playboy*, January, 1981, April, 1981.

OBITUARIES: New York Times, December 9, 1980; *Chicago Tribune*, December 9, 1980; *Washington Post*, December 9, 1980; *Detroit Free Press*, December 9, 1980; *London Times*, December 10, 1980; *Time*, December 22, 1980; *Newsweek*, December 22, 1980; *Current Biography*, February, 1981.*

—*Sketch by Susan A. Stefani*

*   *   *

LENNOX-SHORT, Alan 1913-

PERSONAL: Born December 18, 1913, in Cape Town, South Africa; son of Alan (a journalist) and Susan Jane (Priest) Lennox-Short; married Shirley Isa Centlivres, December 23, 1946. *Education:* University of Cape Town, B.A. (with distinction), 1933, M.A. (with honors), 1934; Christ Church, Oxford, B.A. (with honors), 1937, M.A., 1965. *Home address:* P.O. Box 313, Claremont, Cape 7735, South Africa.

CAREER: Natal Witness, Pietermaritzburg, South Africa, editor, 1946-48; lecturer in English at Potchefstroom University for Christian Higher Education in Potchefstroom, South Africa, and at University of Natal in Durban, South Africa; senior lecturer in English and tutor for British Guiana and South America at University of the West Indies in Bridgetown, Barbados; University of Cape Town, Cape Town, South Africa, lecturer, 1962-66, senior lecturer, 1966-75, associate professor of English, 1975-79; writer, 1979—. Book critic for South African Broadcasting Corp. and past member of Cape advisory committee; past committee member of South African Council for English Education; past chairman of Pringle Award committee of English Academy of Southern Africa. *Military service:* South African Air Force, 1940-45, attached with Royal Air Force to British Ministry of Information, 1943-45; became captain. *Member:* Royal Society of Arts (fellow).

WRITINGS: Our English, South African Broadcasting Corp., 1964; *Language, Literature, and Life*, Purnell, 1965; *Third Thoughts on English*, Purnell, 1966; *Effective Expression: A Course in Communication*, M. Evans, 1970; (with F. Smith) *The Art of English*, ten volumes, Schofield & Sims, 1970-74; *Brief Candle*, Purnell, 1971; *Airing Your English*, South African Broadcasting Corp., 1971; *English Prose in Action*, Juta, 1975; *Idiomatic English*, Juta, 1977.

Editor: (With R. E. Lighton) *Stories South African*, Perskor, 1969, 2nd edition, 1976; *Stories From Seven Countries*, Juta, 1972; *English and South Africa*, Masou, 1973; *South African and Other Stories*, Juta, 1974; *Tales of Africa and Other Stories*, Juta, 1974; *The World in Verse*, Juta, 1974; *Paths to Poetry*, Juta, 1974; (with D. Welsh) *UCT at One Hundred Fifty: Reflections*, David Philip, 1979.

Editor of "ELTS Occasional Papers," of University of Cape Town's English Department, 1964-69. English-language editor of *Dictionary of South African Biography;* language adviser for *Standard Encyclopaedia of Southern Africa*. Book critic and literary leader-writer for *Cape Times*. Editor of *UTC*, journal of University of Cape Town, 1960-79.

WORK IN PROGRESS: A collection of comic verse about animals; an investigation of the background and history of some unusual English words.

SIDELIGHTS: Lennox-Short told *CA:* "My background is both literary and linguistic and, in consequence, my interests and convictions have taken two directions in my criticism and in my other writing.

"I have always insisted on the importance of reasonable adherence to a standard of written and spoken English in a multilingual South Africa. The official preference for Afrikaans has tended to undermine the adequate use of English, while the use of the language is being extended by the black preference for it, as Afrikaans is regarded by blacks as a symbol of apartheid. The black languages do, however, include dialects that deviate from standard English.

"In the ferment of a country passing through political, economic, and social changes and officially resisting international and African pressures, I have sympathized with the reasonable aspirations of the blacks, maintaining, however, that nobody should allow himself to be stampeded by prejudice, intolerance, and ignorance, and also that the white contribution to the country should not be obscured by fasionable hysterics or guilt phobias.

"It is also my contention that, in assessing South African literature in relation to international literature, sentimentality should not be allowed to inflate the quality—sometimes considerable—of South Africa's protest or dissident writing."

*   *   *

LEONARD, Hugh
See BYRNE, John Keyes

*   *   *

LERNER, Arthur 1915-

PERSONAL: Born January 10, 1915, in Chicago, Ill.; son of Samuel and Esther (Levin) Lerner; married Matilda T. Fisher (an artist). *Education:* Central Young Men's Christian Association College (now Roosevelt University), B.A., 1942; Northwestern University, A.M., 1946; University of Southern California, Ph.D., 1953, Ph.D., 1968. *Home:* 520 South Burnside Ave., Los Angeles, Calif. 90036. *Agent:* Bertha Klausner, International Literary Agency, Inc., 71 Park Ave., New York, N.Y. 10016.

CAREER: San Bernardino Valley College, San Bernardino, Calif., instructor in psychology, philosophy, and English, 1946-47; Homer Toberman Settlement House, San Pedro, Calif., counselor and director of boys' work, 1947-48; teacher at public schools in Los Angeles, Calif., 1948-57; Los Angeles City College, Los Angeles, joined faculty, 1957, became professor of psychology and humanities, 1968—. Poet-in-residence and director of Poetry Therapy Institute at Woodview Calabasas Hospital, 1971—; consultant for poetry therapy at Van Nuys Psychiatric Hospital, 1979—; conducts poetry therapy workshops. Visiting professor or lecturer at University of Southern California, Immaculate Heart College, Los Angeles, and University of California, Los Angeles, Extension Center. *Military service:* U.S. Army, 1942-44. *Member:* International P.E.N., Modern Language Association of America, American Psychological Association, American Association for Social Psychiatry, National Association of Social Workers, American Sociological Association, American Society of Group Psychotherapists and Psychodrama, Poetry Society of America, Authors League of America, Authors Guild, Poets and Writers. *Awards, honors:* Book award from International Poets Shrine, 1971, for *Psychoanalytically Oriented Criticism of Three American Poets.*

WRITINGS: Rhymed and unrhymed (poems), Swordsman, 1965; *follow-up* (poems), Swordsman, 1967; *Psychoanalytically Oriented Criticism of Three American Poets: Poe, Whitman, and Aiken,* Associated University Presses, 1970; *starting points* (poems), Swordsman, 1971; *Poetry in the Therapeutic Experience,* Pergamon, 1978. Member of editorial board of *Arts in Psychotherapy.*

SIDELIGHTS: Arthur Lerner told *CA:* "Craft, art, delight, wonder, respect for language, imagination, and, above all, hard work—this is what I find to be the enigma of writing well. As for poetry in therapy, poets have written about love, hate, greed, sorrow, joy, and all human emotions long before there was the discipline of psychology. Using poetry as a healing modality does not negate the rationale of poetry or make therapists of poets. Therapists do not automatically become poets because they employ poetry as part of their approach. Poets and psychologists are kinfolk from two distinct families."

Robert Kirsch, book critic for the *Los Angeles Times,* commented on Lerner's *Poetry in the Therapeutic Experience:* "There have been so many panaceas offered in the area of mental treatment that it is above all else refreshing to find no grandiose claims for poetry therapy in this collection of essays by people applying its techniques in a variety of circumstances, from private psychiatric practice and hospitals to group work and education. . . . The techniques are described and discussed, with examples and case histories by several of the writers out of their own experience."

Lerner calls poetry therapy "a tool and a bit, a school . . . presently composed of a wide variety of experiences and interests groping for a central theory or rationale." It is a technique available to all schools of thought, ranging from Jungian depth psychology to linguistic and semantic methodologies. In the therapeutic setting psychologists have used poetry to treat anxiety, shyness, timidity, and fear of criticism. It has also been used to help release unconscious data.

Although poetry therapy can be used successfully in some cases, Dr. Roger Lauer points out in his contribution to the book that the technique can be hazardous. Kirsch remarked, "Lauer discusses abuses of poetry therapy, warns against the panacea approach, gives some sobering case histories and concludes that poetry therapy is 'not altogether harmless,' 'presents special risks to schizophrenics' and can be used defensively against therapy by some patients."

BIOGRAPHICAL/CRITICAL SOURCES: Los Angeles Times, April 13, 1978.

*   *   *

LERNER, Carol 1927-

PERSONAL: Born July 6, 1927, in Chicago, Ill.; daughter of Edwin August (in sales) and Elsie (Harders) Drath; married Ralph Lerner (a teacher), October 30, 1954; children: Joshua, Jesse. *Education:* University of Chicago, B.A., 1950, M.A., 1954. *Residence:* Chicago, Ill. *Office:* c/o William Morrow & Company, Inc., 105 Madison Ave., New York, N.Y. 10016.

CAREER: Writer and illustrator, 1977—. *Awards, honors:* Award for special artistic merit from Friends of American Writers, 1979, for *On the Forest Edge.*

WRITINGS—Self-illustrated children's books: *On the Forest Edge,* Morrow, 1978; *Flowers of a Woodland Spring,* Morrow, 1979; *Seasons of the Tallgrass Prairie,* Morrow, 1980.

Illustrator: Glenda Daniel, *Dune Country,* Swallow Press, 1977; Robert M. McClung, *Peeper: First Voice of Spring* (for children), Morrow, 1977; McClung, *Green Darner,* Morrow, 1980; Daniel Sullivan and Jerry Sullivan, *A Naturalist's Guide to the North Woods,* Sierra Club, 1981; McClung, *Sphinx: The Story of a Caterpiller,* Morrow, 1981.

SIDELIGHTS: Carol Lerner studied botany, local flora, birds of the Midwest, and other nature subjects before enrolling in botanical illustration classes at Morton Arboretum. Her work is enhanced by the spring and summer months she spends at her Michigan cottage, where she photographs wild flowers, and by her passion for gardening.

AVOCATIONAL INTERESTS: Films.

*   *   *

LESLIE, Donald Daniel 1922-

PERSONAL: Born July 1, 1922, in London, England; son of Alfred (a shopkeeper) and Ada (Schneiderman) Leslie; married Helga Selz (a public servant), March 20, 1958; children: Michal Sharon, Gial Ilana, Jonathan David. *Education:* University of London, B.Sc. (with first class honors), 1943; Cambridge University, diploma in Chinese, 1951, M.Litt., 1943; Sorbonne, University of Paris, Dr. de l'Universite (with honors), 1962. *Home:* 18 Haines St., Curtin, Canberra, Australian Capital Territory 2605, Australia. *Office:* Canberra College of Advanced Education, Canberra, Australian Capital Territory 2614, Australia.

CAREER: Teacher of mathematics and English at high school in Haifa, Israel, 1956-57; Hebrew University of Jerusalem, Jerusalem, Israel, research fellow in Chinese studies, 1958-60; Australian National University, Canberra, research fellow, 1963-66, fellow in Far Eastern history, 1966-70; Tel-Aviv University, Tel-Aviv, Israel, associate professor of philosophy, 1970-71; Canberra College of Advanced Education, Canberra, Australia, senior lecturer in history, 1972—. *Military service:* British army, 1943-47; became lieutenant. *Awards, honors:* Honorary research fellow at Kyoto University, 1965; Tchernikowsky Prize from Tel-Aviv University, 1973, for translating *Maamarot;* prize from Academie francaise, 1981, for *Juifs de Chine.*

WRITINGS—In English (With Jeremy Davidson) *Author Catalogues of Western Sinologists,* Australian National University, 1966; (with Davidson) *Catalogues of Chinese Local Gazetteers,* Australian National University, 1967; (contributor) Hyman Kublin, editor, *Studies of the Chinese Jews,* Paragon, 1971; *The Survival of the Chinese Jews,* E. J. Brill, 1972; (editor with Colin Mackerras and Wang Gungwu) *Essays on the Sources for Chinese History,* Australian National University, 1973; (with Ludmilla Panskaya) *Introduction to Palladii's Chinese Literature of the Muslims,* Australian National University, 1977; *Islamic Literature in Chinese, Late Ming and Early Ch'ing: Books, Authors, and Associates,* Canberra College of Advanced Education, 1981; *A History of Islam in China,* E. J. Brill, 1982.

Other writings: (Translator with Amatzia Porat) *Maamarot* (title means "The Sayings of Confucius"), Bialik Institute, 1960; *Confucius* (in French), Seghers, 1962; (with Joseph Dehergne) *Juifs de Chine* (title means "Jews in China"), Institutum Historicum Societatis Iesu, 1980. Contributor of articles and reviews to Chinese studies journals.

SIDELIGHTS: Leslie wrote that his languages include Hebrew and French, Chinese, Japanese, and some Arabic. He has taught mathematics, physics, English, Chinese, Hebrew, philosophy, and history. Though he currently teaches modern Chinese and Japanese history, his only research interest is classical Chinese history.

He added: "I no longer research linguistics or philosophy. I believe the key to history is collation. One day I will tackle the problem of assimilation and survival of minorities in China."

Leslie's writings have been published in France, the Netherlands, Israel, Italy, Switzerland, Hong Kong, Singapore, India, and Portugal.

*   *   *

LESSER, Michael 1939-

PERSONAL: Born March 8, 1939, in Mitchell, S.D.; son of Samuel A. and Edith (Shapiro) Lesser; married Deborah Langman, April 6, 1969; children: Elijah Ben, Rebecca. *Education:* Washington University, St. Louis, Mo., A.B.; Cornell University, M.D. *Office:* 2340 Parker St., Berkeley, Calif. 94704.

CAREER: In private practice of psychiatry and nutrition in Berkeley, Calif., 1971—. *Military service:* U.S. Public Health Service, 1968-70; became lieutenant commander. *Member:* Alameda-Contra Costa Medical Society.

WRITINGS: Nutrition and Vitamin Therapy, Grove, 1980.

WORK IN PROGRESS: A novel.

*   *   *

LESTER, Richard A. 1908-

PERSONAL: Born March 1, 1908, in Blasdell, N.Y.; son of Garra K. (a physician) and Jessie I. (a teacher; maiden name, Holmes) Lester; married Doris M. Newhouse, June 19, 1937; children: Margaret Allyn (Mrs. Thomas E. Wing), Harriet Holmes (Mrs. Jackson Tarver, Jr.), Robert Allen. *Education:* Yale University, Ph.B., 1929; Princeton University, A.M., 1930, Ph.D., 1936. *Politics:* Democrat. *Home:* 32 Maclean Circle, Princeton, N.J. 08540. *Office:* Industrial Relations Section, Princeton University, Princeton, N.J. 08540.

CAREER: Princeton University, Princeton, N.J., instructor in economics, 1931-32, 1934-38; University of Washington, Seattle, assistant professor of labor, 1938-40; Duke University, Durham, N.C., assistant professor, 1940-42, associate professor of economics, 1942-45; Princeton University, associate professor, 1945-48, professor of economics, 1948—, Joseph Douglas Green 1895 Professor of Economics, 1948-68, chairman of economics and sociology, 1948-55, chairman of department of economics, 1961-66, associate dean and director of graduate program at Woodrow Wilson School of Public and International Affairs, 1966-68, dean of faculty, 1968-73. Visiting assistant professor at Haverford College, 1937-38. Member of editorial board and board of trustees of Princeton University Press, 1958-61, vice-president, 1969-72. Associate chief and branch chief in Labor Division of Office of Production Management, 1941, and War Production Board, 1942; branch chief for War Manpower Commission, 1942; referee and arbitrator for National War Labor Board and its regional board, 1942-45; chairman of Southern Textile Commission, 1945. Chairman of New Jersey Public Employer-Employee Relations Study Commission, 1974-75; member of New Jersey Employment Security Council (chairman, 1955-65), and Commission on the Airlines Dispute, 1961-62; vice-president of President's Commission on the Status of Women, 1961-63. Member of board of trustees of Center for Analysis of Public Issues, 1970—.

MEMBER: Teachers Insurance and Annuity Association of America (member of board of trustees, 1959-63), American Economic Association (vice-president, 1961), Industrial Relations Research Association (president, 1956), Royal Economic Society, Princeton Graduate Alumni (president, 1962-64).

WRITINGS: Monetary Experiments: Early American and Recent Scandinavian, Princeton University Press, 1939; *Economics of Labor,* Macmillan, 1941, 2nd edition, 1964; (editor with Joseph Shister) *Insights Into Labor Issues,* Macmillan, 1948; *Labor and Industrial Relations,* Macmillan, 1951; *As Unions Mature,* Princeton University Press, 1958.

The Economics of Unemployment Compensation, Industrial Relations Section, Princeton University, 1962; *Labor: Readings on Major Issues,* Random House, 1965; *Manpower Planning in a Free Society,* Princeton University Press, 1966; *Antibias Regulation of Universities: Faculty Problems and Their Solutions,* McGraw, 1974; *Reasoning About Dis-*

crimination, Princeton University Press, 1980. Contributor to academic journals and popular magazines, including *New Republic* and *Nation.*

WORK IN PROGRESS: Labor Relations in State and Local Governments.

*   *   *

LESURE, Thomas B(arbour) 1923-
(Thomas L. Barbour)

PERSONAL: Surname is pronounced Le-*sure;* born June 4, 1923, in Lawrence, Mass.; son of Harry L. and Mabel (Barbour) Lesure; married Nancy Carol Smith (a travel correspondent), May 19, 1949; children: Linda Lesure Elston, Wynn, Bonnie Lesure Perkins, Kim, Marc T. *Education:* Boston University, B.S. (cum laude), 1945, graduate study, 1945. *Religion:* Protestant. *Home:* El Rancho Nato, 6120 North 18th St., Phoenix, Ariz. 85016.

CAREER: Yankee Network, Boston, Mass., news editor, 1944-45; WCOP-Radio, Boston, news and travel editor, 1945-52; free-lance writer and travel consultant, 1952—. *Member:* American Society of Journalists and Authors, Authors Guild, Society of American Travel Writers, Arizona Press Club, Phoenix Press Club, Sigma Delta Chi, Kappa Tau Alpha, Dons Club of Phoenix. *Awards, honors:* Award from Pacific Area Travel Association, 1964, for best newspaper series; award from Trans World Airlines, 1959, for best Arizona story.

WRITINGS: Adventures in Arizona, Naylor, 1956; *Best in the West,* Harian, 1957; *All About Arizona: The State Where It's Great to Live and Vacation,* Harian, 1957, 13th edition, 1978; *Best in the East,* Harian, 1958; *Best in the South,* Harian, 1958; *The Heart of the Southwest,* Harian, 1959; *The Grand Tour of Europe,* Harian, 1960; *Pacific U.S.A.,* Harian, 1960; *All About California,* Harian, 1964; (under name Thomas L. Barbour) *Frommer's Dollar-Wise Guide to Arizona,* Frommer, 1965; (under name Thomas L. Barbour) *Frommer's Dollar-Wise Guide to Texas,* Frommer, 1967; *All the Southwest,* Harian, 1974, second edition, 1978.

Contributor: *Around the World With the Travel Experts,* Doubleday, 1970; *Explorers Guide to the West,* Gousha, 1972.

Author of radio scripts. Author of cruise column in *Travel/Holiday.* Contributor to *Encyclopedia of World Travel, Exxon Vacation Guide,* and *Fodor U.S.A. Guide.* Contributor of more than two thousand articles to magazines and newspapers.

SIDELIGHTS: Lesure has traveled in eighty-seven countries, specializing in cruising and the southwestern United States. He wrote: "My main aim is to give readers the complete feeling of an area, even if they've never been there, and to show travelers that no matter where they go, people are people, with similar problems. That is the greatest lesson travel offers."

AVOCATIONAL INTERESTS: Collecting arts, crafts, and coins.

*   *   *

LEVEN, Jeremy 1941-

PERSONAL: Born August 16, 1941, in South Bend, Ind.; son of Martin Paul (a publisher) and Marcia (a writer; maiden name, Obrasky) Levin; married Roberta Danza (a psychiatric nurse), August 8, 1980; children: (from previous marriage) Zoe Roberts, Zachary John. *Education:* St. John's

College, Annapolis, Md., B.A., 1965; Harvard University, M.Ed., 1973; doctoral study at Yale University and University of Connecticut, 1977—. *Politics:* Democrat. *Religion:* Jewish. *Home and office:* 105 Woodside Ter., New Haven, Conn. 06515. *Agent:* Elaine Markson Literary Agency, Inc., 44 Greenwich Ave., New York, N.Y. 10011; (films) Alain Bernheim, c/o Lorimar Productions, MGM Studios, Gable Bldg., West Washington Blvd., Culver City, Calif. 90230.

CAREER: WBZ-TV, Boston, Mass., director and producer, 1965-66; English teacher at public schools in Medford, Mass., 1967; Proposition (theatre group), Cambridge, Mass., founder, director, and writer, 1968-70; Harvard University, Cambridge, research associate, 1968-69; Cambridge Model Cities Program, Cambridge, director of education research and development, 1969-70; Newton College, Newton, Mass., assistant professor of psychology, 1971-72; Cambridge Psychological Associates, Cambridge, clinical director, 1972-74; Massachusetts Department of Mental Health, Northampton, principal psychologist, 1974-75, mental health center director, 1975-76, associate area director for children's and drug programs, 1976-77; writer and clinical psychologist, 1977—. *Member:* International Society for Developmental Psychobiology, Society for Neuroscience, American Association for the Advancement of Science, Writers Guild of America, Authors Guild, Authors League of America.

WRITINGS: Creator (novel), Coward, 1980. Author of "The Proposition" (satirical review), first produced in Cambridge, Mass., at Proposition Theatre, February 2, 1968, produced in New York, N.Y., 1970-73.

WORK IN PROGRESS: A novel dealing with the relationship between evil and human responsibility, publication expected in 1981 or 1982; a book on the neuropsychological development of the child, 1983; clinical research on the relationship of children's developing brain anatomy and brain chemistry, and how it relates to their psychological development.

SIDELIGHTS: "I have two careers," Leven told *CA,* "one as a clinician and neuroscientist; one as a writer of fiction and, more recently, of screenplays ('Creator'). With the exception of my next novel, which has much to do with brain and behavior, the two careers do not feed each other in any specific way. On an emotional level, however, they allow me to vary my life between the slower, highly structured, calmer analytic pursuits of science and clinical work, and the more highly charged, irregular, faster-paced synthetic work of fiction and film. I intend to pursue the two careers simultaneously until my own brain chemistry fails me."

BIOGRAPHICAL/CRITICAL SOURCES: Chicago Tribune Book World, April 27, 1980.

*   *   *

LEVERENCE, William John 1946-

PERSONAL: Born May 29, 1946, in Belvidere, Ill.; son of William John (in sales) and Dorothy Roberta (a legal secretary; maiden name, VanVleet) Leverence; married Margaret Kay Horn (a foundation administrator), May 28, 1965; children: Julie Ann. *Education:* University of Illinois at Chicago Circle, B.A., 1968; University of Chicago, M.A., 1969; Bowling Green State University, Ph.D., 1974. *Home:* 5253 Daggett St., Long Beach, Calif. 90815. *Office:* Academy of Television Arts and Sciences, 4605 Lankershim, Suite 800, North Hollywood, Calif. 90602.

CAREER: Bowling Green State University, Bowling Green,

Ohio, assistant professor of English, 1974-75; California State University, Long Beach, Calif., assistant professor of American studies and radio-television, 1975-78; consultant to American Film Institute, 1978-80; Academy of Television Arts and Sciences, North Hollywood, Calif., administrator of Emmy Awards, 1980. Free-lance graphic designer.

WRITINGS: Irving Wallace: A Writer's Profile, Bowling Green University, 1974. Contributor to scholarly journals. Associate editor of *Journal of Popular Culture.*

WORK IN PROGRESS: Family Life, a novel, completion expected in 1982.

SIDELIGHTS: Leverence commented: "Although I would like to make a living as a writer, I write mainly because my wife laughs at the funny parts and tells me I'm her favorite. The thesis of my fictional writing is that people are fundamentally clumsy. Good intentions and evildoing come and go, but clumsiness prevails forever. Even Baryshnikov gets gravy on his tie. If the truth were known, Lucifer probably did fall from grace. Stumbling and fumbling, dropping and slopping, the characters of my fictions do what they can to get what they want. Operating under misapprehensions and through garbled transmissions, stepping on one another's toes and sensibilities, they live as well as they can. I can't fault them for any of it."

*   *   *

LEVIN, Gail 1948-

PERSONAL: Born February 19, 1948, in Atlanta, Ga.; daughter of Barron W. and Shirley (Sunshine) Levin. *Education:* Attended Sorbonne, University of Paris, 1968; Simmons College, B.A. (with honors), 1969; Tufts University, M.A., 1970; Rutgers University, Ph.D., 1976. *Religion:* Jewish. *Office:* Whitney Museum of American Art, 945 Madison Ave., New York, N.Y. 10021.

CAREER: Rutgers University, New Brunswick, N.J., junior instructor, 1970-71, instructor in art history at Newark College of Arts and Sciences, 1972-73; New School for Social Research, New York City, instructor in art history, 1973-75; Connecticut College, New London, assistant professor of art history, 1975-76; Whitney Museum of American Art, New York City, associate curator of Hopper Collection, 1976—. Instructor at Drew University, spring, 1973, and Bernard M. Baruch College of the City University of New York, autumn, 1974; visiting assistant professor at Graduate Center of the City University of New York, 1979-80. Organizes panels, symposia, and art exhibitions. *Member:* College Art Association of America. *Awards, honors:* Citation of excellence from Art Libraries Society of New York, 1979, for *Synchromism and American Color Abstraction, 1910-1925.*

WRITINGS: Synchromism and American Color Abstraction, 1910-1925, Braziller, 1978; (with Robert C. Hobbs) *Abstract Expressionism: The Formative Years,* Whitney Museum of American Art, 1978; *Edward Hopper: The Complete Prints,* Norton, 1979; *Edward Hopper as Illustrator,* Norton, 1979; *Edward Hopper: The Art and the Artist,* Norton, 1980; *Edward Hopper: A Catalogue Raisonne,* four volumes, Norton, in press. Author of exhibition brochures. Contributor of more than twenty-five articles to art journals, including *Connoisseur, Museum, Woman's Art Journal, Arts,* and *Criticism.*

SIDELIGHTS: Levin told *CA:* "American art before World War II and the emergence of abstract expressionism has not yet received the attention it deserves. For years this art was overlooked, considered provincial and unimportant. Now

this unfair evaluation is changing and Americans are discovering their own aesthetic heritage.

"Art history can be at once scholarly and accessible to a general audience. I write about art and artists with the belief that I can explain important concepts and interpret essential ideas while making art more comprehensible to a larger public. The study of art offers insights into the cultural fabric of a society. Art history at its best investigates related developments in music, literature, theatre, popular art forms, and science."

AVOCATIONAL INTERESTS: International travel.

BIOGRAPHICAL/CRITICAL SOURCES: New York Times, June 26, 1976, January 27, 1978; *Chicago Tribune Book World,* December 7, 1980.

*   *   *

LEVINSON, Daniel Jacob 1920-

PERSONAL: Born May 28, 1920, in New York, N.Y.; son of Isaac David (a pharmacist) and Rose (Soshen) Levinson; married Maria Hertz (a psychologist), January 30, 1943; children: Mark E., Douglas F. *Education:* University of California, Los Angeles, B.A., 1940; University of California, Berkeley, M.A., 1942, Ph.D., 1947. *Home:* 21 Carriage Dr., Woodbridge, Conn. 06525. *Agent:* Donald R. Cutler, Sterling Lord Agency, Inc., 660 Madison Ave., New York, N.Y. 10021. *Office:* Department of Psychiatry, Yale University, 34 Park St., New Haven, Conn. 06519.

CAREER: Western Reserve University (now Case Western Reserve University), Cleveland, Ohio, assistant professor of psychology, 1947-50; Harvard University, Cambridge, Mass., assistant professor of social relations, 1950-55, research associate in social science and psychiatry, 1955-60, assistant professor of psychology and psychiatry, 1960-66; Yale University, New Haven, Conn., professor of psychology, 1966—. Visiting lecturer at Brandeis University, 1955-56, and University of Colorado, 1965. *Member:* American Psychological Association (fellow), American Sociological Association (fellow), American Association for the Advancement of Science (fellow), American Association of University Professors. *Awards, honors:* National Institute of Mental Health career investigator awards, 1955-60 and 1965-71, foundation fund fellowships, 1960-65.

WRITINGS: (With T. W. Adorno, E. Frenkel-Brunswick, and N. Sanford) *The Authoritarian Personality,* Harper, 1950; (with Eugene B. Gallagher) *Patienthood in the Mental Hospital,* Houghton, 1964; (with Richard L. Hodgson and Abraham H. Zaleznik) *The Executive Role Constellation,* Division of Research, Business School, Harvard University, 1965; (with C. N. Darrow, E. B. Klein, M. H. Levinson, and B. McKee) *The Seasons of a Man's Life,* Knopf, 1978.

WORK IN PROGRESS: Research on women's lives.

SIDELIGHTS: Levinson's fourth book, *The Seasons of a Man's Life,* has been translated into Swedish, German, Japanese, Spanish, and Dutch.

*   *   *

LEVY, Darline Gay Shapiro 1939-

PERSONAL: Born March 2, 1939, in New York, N.Y.; daughter of Aaron H. (a manufacturing executive) and Diana (Dymma) Shapiro; married Peter M. Levy (a professor), October 9, 1965; children: Eric Jacques Pierre, Serge Jacques-Francois. *Education:* Columbia University, A.B., 1960; Harvard University, Ph.D., 1968. *Office:* Department of History, New York University, New York, N.Y. 10003.

CAREER: Carnegie-Mellon University, Pittsburgh, Pa., instructor in history, 1965-66; Rutgers University, New Brunswick, N.J., assistant professor of history, 1970-71; Hunter College of the City University of New York, New York City, assistant professor of history, 1971-73; Columbia University, Barnard College, New York City, assistant professor of history, 1973-80; New York Univerisy, New York City, assistant professor, 1980—. Fellow at Radcliffe Institute, 1969-71. Member: International Society for the Study of the Eighteenth Century, American Historical Association, American Society for Eighteenth Century Studies, Society for French Historical Studies.

WRITINGS: (Editor, translator, and author of notes, with Harriet Branson Applewhite and Mary Durham Johnson) *Women in Revolutionary Paris, 1789-1795: Selected Documents,* University of Illinois Press, 1979; *The Ideas and Careers of Simon-Nicolas-Henri Linguet: A Study in Eighteenth-Century French Politics,* University of Illinois Press, 1980. Contributor to history journals.

WORK IN PROGRESS: A study of popular political participation and French revolutionary institutions, with H. B. Applewhite; a book on the correspondence of Simon-Nicolas-Henri Linguet; documentary studies of women in nineteenth-century French revolutionary movements in 1830, 1848, and 1870, with Applewhite.

*   *   *

LEVY, Eugene Donald   1933-

PERSONAL: Born December 4, 1933, in Los Angeles, Calif.; son of Samuel and Dorothy (Gewertz) Levy; married Lorraine Paul (an artist), June 26, 1960; children: Anna, Ella. Education: University of California, Riverside, A.B., 1956; Yale University, M.A., 1960, Ph.D., 1970. Office: Department of History, Carnegie-Mellon University, Pittsburgh, Pa. 15213.

CAREER: Yale University, New Haven, Conn., acting instructor, 1962-65, assistant professor of history and American studies, 1965-71; Carnegie-Mellon University, Pittsburgh, Pa., associate professor of history, 1971—. Member: Organization of American Historians, American Association for State and Local History. Awards, honors: National Endowment for the Humanities junior fellow, 1971-72; American Council of Learned Societies grant, 1972.

WRITINGS: (Editor with D. H. Fowler and J. W. Blassingame) *In Search of America,* two volumes, Holt, 1972; *James Weldon Johnson: Black Leader, Black Voice,* University of Chicago Press, 1973; (editor with J. R. Renaldo) *America's People,* Scott, Foresman, 1975; (with M. H. Brown and R. M. Smith) *The Faces of America,* Harper, 1981; (contributor) John Hope Franklin and August Meier, editors, *Black Leaders in the Twentieth Century,* University of Illinois Press, 1981. Contributor to journals, including *Journal of Popular Culture* and *Phylon.*

WORK IN PROGRESS: *Steel Valleys: A Social-Cultural Interpretation of Mill and Mining Towns of the Pittsburgh Region,* with David P. Demarest.

SIDELIGHTS: Levy told CA: "I feel the need at mid-career to speak to a broader audience than the handful who read academic publications. Writing about a region for the people of that region is to me a satisfying way of fulfilling that need."

BIOGRAPHICAL/CRITICAL SOURCES: *American Literature,* January, 1975; *American Historical Review,* March, 1975; *Journal of American History,* September, 1975.

LEWIS, John (Noel Claude)   1912-
(J. G. Venner, a joint pseudonym)

PERSONAL: Born in 1912, in Rhoose, Wales; son of Claude Pritchard (a bank manager) and Margaretta (Morris) Lewis; married Griselda Margaret Rideout (a writer and designer), 1940. Education: Attended Charterhouse and Goldsmiths' College School of Art, London, 1932-36. Home and office: 6 Doric Pl., Woodbridge, Suffolk IP12 1BT, England. Agent: A. D. Peters & Co. Ltd., 10 Buckingham St., London WC2N 6BU, England.

CAREER: Associated with Cowells of Ipswich in Ipswich, England, 1946-48; free-lance illustrator and designer, 1948-51; Royal College of Art, London, england, tutor in graphic design, 1951-64; free-lance writer and book designer, 1964—. Art director or design consultant for W. S. Cowell Ltd., 1948-72, S. H. Benson, Ltd, 1961-64, Evans Brothers, 1963-66, Studio Vista, 1964-72, Thomas Nelson & Sons, 1972-76, Barrie & Jenkins, 1975-80, and Dunlop Company, 1976—. External examiner for graphic design courses at British art colleges and polytechnics, 1963—. Lecturer in the United States, Canada, and United Kingdom. Military service: British Army, chief instructor at Camouflage School and commandant of Canadian Army Camouflage School, 1939-45. Member: Society of Industrial Artists and Designers (fellow), Double Crown Club, Garrick Club. Awards, honors: Award from National Book League, 1963, for *Printed Ephemera.*

WRITINGS: *Commercial Art and Industrial Design,* Robert Ross & Co., 1945; *A Ship Modeller's Logbook,* Percival Marshall, 1950; *Small Boat Conversion,* Hart-Davis, 1951; (with John Brinkley) *Graphic Design,* Routledge & Kegan Paul, 1954; *A Handbook of Type and Illustration,* Cowell, 1956; *Printed Ephemera,* Dover, 1962; *Typography: Basic Principles,* Reinhold, 1963, revised edition, 1966; (with Bob Gill) *Illustration: Aspects and Directions,* Reinhold, 1964; *The Twentieth-Century Book: Its Illustration and Design,* Reinhold, 1964; (with Edwin Smith) *The Graphic Reproduction and Photography of Works of Art,* Praeger, 1967; *A Taste for Sailing,* Adlard Coles, 1969.

Anatomy of Printing, Watson-Guptill, 1970; *Small Craft Conversion,* Adlard Coles, 1972; *Heath Robinson: Artist and Comic Genius,* Constable, 1973; *Restoring Vintage Boats,* International Marine, 1975; *Repair of Wooden Boats,* David & Charles, 1977; *John Nash: The Painter as Illustrator,* Pendomer Press, 1978; *Rowland Hilder: Painter and Illustrator,* Barrie & Jenkins, 1978; *Typography: Design and Practice,* Barrie & Jenkins, 1978; (with John O'Connor) *Illustration: Methods and Processes,* Barrie & Jenkins, 1982.

(With wife, Griselda Lewis, under joint pseudonym J. G. Venner) *The Three Spaniards,* W. & R. Chambers, 1949. Editor of "Studio Paperbacks," a series, Reinhold, 1964-72. Contributor to magazines, including *Blackwood's Magazine* and *Yachting Monthly.*

WORK IN PROGRESS: An autobiography in two volumes tentatively entitled *Character Count* and *Casting Off,* completion expected in 1982; *From Limehouse Reach,* on sailing, with Rowland Hilder, completion expected in 1983.

SIDELIGHTS: Lewis has been sailing for twenty years in *Patient Griselda,* a boat he designed and built in 1960. He has sailed in European waters and to Scotland and the Outer Hebrides. "This has provided me with material for books and articles in the yachting press," Lewis commented to CA. "This writing about boats and the sea is a healthy contrast to my other work, which is almost entirely about art and design. I thought that when I became a designer I would at least be able to be a Sunday painter. In fact I found I was a Sunday designer as well, so like a number of other typographers, I turned to writing as a more personal means of expression.''

AVOCATIONAL INTERESTS: Drawing, English pottery (eighteenth-century and modern), collecting pictures, illustrated books, and printed ephemera.

* * *

LEWIS, Lesley 1909-
(Lesley Lawrence)

PERSONAL: Born March 8, 1909, in Brentwood, England; daughter of James F.N. (a solicitor) and Kathleen (Pott) Lawrence; married David James Lewis (a medical entomologist), July 12, 1944. *Education:* Courtauld Institute of Art, London, B.A., 1935, M.A., 1938. *Religion:* Church of England. *Home:* 38 Whitelands House, Cheltenham Ter., London SW3 4QY, England. *Agent:* Anne Harrel, 32 Winsham Grove, London SW11 6NE, England.

CAREER: Called to the Bar at Lincoln's Inn, 1956; City and Guilds of London Art School, London, England, registrar, 1938-40; Lawrence, Graham & Co., Lincoln's Inn, England, managing clerk, 1940-44; Gezira Agricultural Research Institute, Wad Medani, Sudan, librarian, 1944-46; writer, 1946—. *Member:* Society of Antiquaries (vice-president, 1980—), Royal Archaeological Institute (vice-president, 1979—), Chelsea Society (chairman, 1980), Georgian Group (member of executive committee).

WRITINGS: Connoisseurs and Secret Agents in the Eighteenth-Century Rome, Chatto & Windus, 1961; *Hird's Annals of Bedale,* North Yorkshire County Record Office, 1975; *The Private Life of a Country House, 1912-39,* David & Charles, 1980. Contributor to magazines, including *Art Bulletin, Country Life, Burlington, Apollo, Jamaican Historical Review,* and *Journal of the Warburg Institute* (under name Lesley Lawrence).

SIDELIGHTS: "I was educated at home by governesses until the age of seventeen,'' Lesley Lewis told *CA.* "I spent a year (1926-27) in Paris to learn French and then pursued the social and sporting activities (in my case mainly tennis and riding) usual at that time for daughters of well-to-do families living in large country houses. When twenty-two I started myself on a formal education by qualifying for London University through a correspondence course. I joined the newly-founded Courtauld Institute of Art as one of its first undergraduates and later proceeded to a postgraduate degree there.

"My budding career in art history was checked by the outbreak of war, and in 1940 I joined my late father's firm of London solicitors to help take the place of men who had left to serve in the forces. In 1944 a friend and neighbor of my youth, David Lewis, came on leave from the Sudan. We married and lived in the Sudan until it became independent in 1955. I accompanied my husband to many parts of that country for his purpose of research into the insect transmission of diseases, often camping in very remote places and experiencing much that might be called adventure.

"At intervals during that time I read for the Bar, again by means of a correspondence course, and was called to the Bar in 1956. My husband continued his work, this time under the Medical Research Council, and we did a series of journeys to many parts of the tropics for fieldwork and attended conferences elsewhere.

"When in England I continued to study art history, but it became apparent that the old buildings which were my principal concern were increasingly threatened by modern developments, and that less and less might be left for study. I joined the committees of such societies as the Society for the Protection of Ancient Buildings, the Georgian Group, and Chelsea Society, gained experience in conservation matters, wrote reports, reviews, etc., and gave evidence at public inquiries in which my legal training was useful. I also lectured on art historical subjects at the Victoria and Albert Museum and elsewhere.

"The research on which I based my book, *Connoisseurs and Secret Agents in Eighteenth-Century Rome,* involved much reading in foreign archives, and, finding this difficult to fit in, I have tended since the book was published to concentrate on subjects in Britain. A life of varied occupations with outdoor and indoor interests has suited my tastes, and although my husband is very exclusively dedicated to his profession we both enjoy the same leisure pursuits, travel, and the company of a wide circle of friends.''

* * *

LEWIS, R(ichard) W(arrington) B(aldwin) 1917-

PERSONAL: Born November 1, 1917, in Chicago, Ill.; son of Leicester Crosby and Beatrix Elizabeth (Baldwin) Lewis; married Nancy Lindau, June 28, 1950; children: Nathaniel Lindau, Sophia Baldwin. *Education:* Harvard University, A.B., 1939; University of Chicago, M.A., 1941, Ph.D., 1953. *Home:* Litchfield Turnpike, Bethany, Conn. 06759. *Office:* Department of English, Yale University, New Haven, Conn. 06520.

CAREER: Bennington College, Bennington, Vt., teacher, 1948-50; dean of Salzburg Seminar in American Studies, 1950-51; Smith College, Northampton, Mass., visiting lecturer in English, 1951-52; Princeton University, Princeton, N.J., Hodder fellow in the humanities, 1952-53, resident fellow in creative writing, 1953-54; Rutgers University, Newark College, Newark, N.J., 1954-59, began as associate professor, became professor of English; Yale University, New Haven, Conn., professor of English and American studies, 1960—. Kenyon fellow in criticism, Florence, Italy, 1954-55; Indiana University, fellow of School of Letters, 1957—, senior fellow, 1964—, and chairman of English Institute, 1965; fellow of Calhoun College, 1960, and American Council of Learned Societies, 1962-63; Fulbright lecturer in American literature, University of Munich, 1957-58; literary consultant, Universal Pictures, 1966—. *Military service:* U.S. Army, 1942-46; became major. *Awards, honors:* National Institute of Arts and Letters award, 1958; Litt.D. from Wesleyan University, 1961; Pulitzer Prize, Friends of Literature award, National Book Critics Circle award, and Bancroft Prize, all 1976, all for *Edith Wharton: A Biography.*

WRITINGS: The American Adam: Innocence, Tragedy, and Tradition in the Nineteenth Century, University of Chicago Press, 1955; *The Picaresque Saint: Representative Figures in Contemporary Fiction,* Lippincott, 1959; *Trials of the Word: Essays in American Literature and the Humanistic Tradition,* Yale University Press, 1965; *The Poetry of Hart Crane: A Critical Study,* Princeton University Press, 1967; (with Cleanth Brooks and Robert Penn Warren) *American Literature: The Makers and the Making,* two volumes, St. Martins, 1973; *Edith Wharton: A Biography,* Harper, 1975.

Editor: *Herman Melville,* Dell, 1962; *The Presence of Walt Whitman,* Columbia University Press, 1962; Edith Wharton, *The House of Mirth,* Houghton, 1963; Herman Melville, *The*

Confidence Man, New American Library, 1964; *Malraux: A Collection of Critical Essays,* Prentice-Hall, 1964; Wharton, *The Collected Short Stories of Edith Wharton,* Scribner, 1968; Graham Greene, *The Power and the Glory,* Viking, 1970. Also co-editor of *Major Writers of America,* 1962.

Contributor of reviews and essays to a number of journals and periodicals.

SIDELIGHTS: R.W.B. Lewis is a literary critic, as Robert Martin Adams stated in the *New York Times Book Review,* with "formidable talents as historian of ideas and textual exegete." His approach to American literature has been for the most part thematic, explicating the works of various writers in terms of larger cultural patterns. Yet he is, as Sheridan Baker observed in the *Kenyon Review,* "a close reader" who seeks transcendent meaning in literature, but also examines "details, analogies, and techniques." Lewis explained his purpose in the prologue to his first book, *The American Adam:* "I am interested . . . in the history of ideas and, especially, in the representative imagery and anecdote that crystalized whole clusters of ideas."

The American Adam, he said, "has to do with the beginnings and the first tentative outlines of a native American mythology." According to Adams, the book is "a bold study in American ideas of innocence, tragedy and tradition," focusing on the basic theme of innocence versus experience in the work of such writers as Ralph Waldo Emerson, Henry David Thoreau, Walt Whitman, Nathaniel Hawthorne, Herman Melville, and Henry James.

From these nineteenth-century writings emerged what Lewis called the Adamic myth. The hero of this myth was "an individual emancipated from history, happily bereft of ancestry, untouched and undefiled by the usual inheritances of family and race; an individual standing alone, self-reliant and self-propelling, ready to confront whatever awaited him with the aid of his own unique and inherent resources." Like Adam before the Fall, "his moral position was prior to experience, and in his very newness he was fundamentally innocent."

As Lewis traced it, the Adamic myth arose from a "dialogue" among America's "chief intellectual spokesmen" of the nineteenth century who shared "the invigorating feeling that a new culture was in the making. . . . The American myth saw life as just beginning. It described the world as starting up again under fresh initiative, in a divinely granted second chance for the human race, after the first chance had been so disastrously fumbled in the darkening Old World. . . . America, it was said insistently from the 1820's onward, was not the end-product of a long historical process . . . ; it was something entirely new."

There were, on the one hand, figures like Emerson, Thoreau, and Whitman who saw this beginning with great hope and defined America in terms only of its present and future. On the other hand, there were also thinkers who, looking to an inescapable past, saw man's sinfulness and corruption as particularly rife in the New World. But Lewis defined as well a third group, writers with a sense of irony and "tragic optimism," who established an enduring pattern for American fiction by recognizing "the tragedy inherent in . . . innocence and newness." As illustrated in the works of Hawthorne and Melville, the *relation* between the past and the present, rather than the *distinction,* became a recurring theme.

In *The Picaresque Saint,* Lewis examined a similarly archetypal hero in the works of six modern novelists: Moravia, Silone, Camus, Graham Greene, Faulkner, and Malraux. The book's title, he explained in a prefatory note, "refers to

a number of things: to the paradoxical hero I see emerging from the works selected, implicit in some of them and explicit in others—a person who is something of a saint, in the contemporary manner of sainthood, but who is also something of a rogue; . . . and it refers to the kind or the genre of fiction—the old-fashioned picaresque novel, the episodic account of the rogue on his journeys—which has been revived and greatly modified for contemporary narrative purposes."

While the nineteenth-century American artist had to confront innocence and a new beginning, the twentieth-century artist, Lewis maintained, must confront death and absurdity. "Constantly seeking ways to confound death," he said, the writer must find grounds for living. In contrast to the earlier Proust, Mann, and Joyce, whom he labeled "artistic," Lewis saw the second generation of modern novelists as essentially "human," for whom human companionship became the new basis for living. Thus, embedded in an episodic plot, the new hero is one who shares with his fellow humans suffering and pain.

With *The Poetry of Hart Crane,* Lewis focused his attention on the work of a single writer. J. A. Bryant, Jr., in the *Sewanee Review,* called the study "probably the most consistently useful explication of Crane's work that has appeared in two decades." Once again, Lewis was concerned with "the tormentingly problematical relation between a subjective vision and an external historical reality." By illuminating phrases, lines, and extended passages in Crane's major works, Bryant explained, and by discerning the pattern of Crane's development, Lewis placed the author of *The Bridge* within the history of American literature—as part of a stream that began with Emerson and Whitman and continues through the present.

This tradition, Alan Trachtenberg pointed out in the *Kenyon Review,* is essentially Romantic. Not only was the world in Crane's vision basically good, he saw poetry, Trachtenberg observed, as more than a mode of expression: "It was a way of being—not the proof of having lived, a record of past moments, but the act of living itself. To achieve poetry, to win 'the bright logic,' was Crane's sufficient evidence that life is justified and redeemed."

By approaching Crane's opus chronologically, Lewis uncovered thematic patterns. From these emerges a view of the poet as, in John Unterecker's words, "American to the core": "a man fundamentally a product of the great 'ideas' that the English Romantics shared with the dominant thinkers and writers of nineteenth-century America, a man of 'visionary' nature who, without benefit of religious institutions, approached life in a 'religious' mood." Refuting the critical dismissal of Crane as "a death-haunted author of death-conscious poetry," Lewis upheld him rather as "the religious poet par excellence in his generation."

Lewis similarly revised the standard view of Edith Wharton in his prize-winning biography of that American novelist. He defined her old image as "too much of the *grande dame,* the aloof and fashionable woman of the world." In its place he offered what Robert F. Moss in the *Saturday Review* called "a new Edith Wharton": more than the proper if artistic matron of the upper class, she was "a connoisseur of friendship, struggling to create a 'republic of the spirit' among those she was most attracted to." Rather than "a sexually repressed Puritan," she was, as Lewis revealed, a woman with a libido.

In writing his *Edith Wharton,* Lewis made use of material never before available. For twenty years after her death, many of Wharton's papers, by her own request, had remained sequestered at Yale University. To these, as well as to the open collections and the papers in the possession of her heirs, Lewis was granted exclusive access. Further enriched by interviews with nearly all those still living who remembered her, the resultant volume is, as Millicent Bell acknowledged in the *New Republic,* "a work of inescapable importance."

Expanding upon the earlier portraits of a lady thoroughly, though perhaps uncomfortably, ensconced among the social elite, Lewis portrayed a woman whose ultimate sense of self derived from her art. "It was finally," he wrote, "her writing that constituted the life she most truly and deeply lived." By disclosing the facts of her one great love affair and by publishing as an appendix an uncovered piece of pornography, Lewis dispelled what Leon Edel defined in the *American Scholar* as "the 'society' image created by American criticism of a novelist who wrote in ladylike fashion about the adulteries and divorces of the rich."

As respected as his earlier criticism had been, the Wharton biography earned for Lewis much broader acclaim. Quentin Anderson in the *New York Times Book Review* called the work "one of the very best we have of an American writer." Peter Heinegg, in the *Nation,* wrote that "Lewis's monumental book on Edith Wharton now marks him as . . . a master of the rigorous, monkish art of literary history. . . . In the next few decades many readers who have never heard of Lewis's book will be reading Edith Wharton because of it." And Robert F. Moss concluded: "Exhaustive in its scholarship, discerning in its literary judgments, sensible in its theorizing, it merits the adjective all biographies aspire to: *definitive.*"

BIOGRAPHICAL/CRITICAL SOURCES: New York Times Book Review, November 21, 1965, October 22, 1967, August 31, 1975; *Kenyon Review,* June, 1966, November, 1967; *New York Review of Books,* November 19, 1967; *Yale Review,* spring, 1968; *Harper's,* July, 1968; *Poetry,* May, 1969; *Sewanee Review,* winter, 1969; *Saturday Review,* August 9, 1975; *Newsweek,* September 22, 1975; *New Republic,* September 27, 1975; *Nation,* November 22, 1975; *American Scholar,* winter, 1975-76.*

—*Sketch by Andrea Geffner*

*   *   *

LEY, Arthur Gordon   1911-1968
(Ray Luther, Arthur Sellings)

OBITUARY NOTICE: Author's name listed in some sources as Robert Arthur Ley; born May 31, 1911 (birthdate listed in some sources as 1921), in Tumbridge Wells, Kent, England; died September 24, 1968, in Worthing, Sussex, England. Scientist and science-fiction writer. From 1955 to 1968, Ley was a scientific researcher for the British Government. He began writing science-fiction short stories in the early fifties. His first novel, *Telepath,* was published in 1962, and his last novel, *Junk Day,* was published posthumously in 1970. Ley's other novels include *The Uncensored Man, The Quy Effect, The Power of X* and *Intermind.* Obituaries and other sources: *Science Fiction and Fantasy Literature,* Volume 2, Gale, 1979. (Author's name, Arthur Gordon Ley, and birthdate, May 31, 1911, provided by the author's widow.)

LEY, Robert Arthur
See LEY, Arthur Gordon

*   *   *

LIDDLE, Peter Hammond   1934-

PERSONAL: Born December 26, 1934, in Sunderland, England; son of Alan (a brewer) and Norah (Hammond) Liddle. *Education:* University of Sheffield, B.A. (with honors), 1956; University of Nottingham, teaching certificate, 1957; Loughborough University of Technology, diploma in physical education, 1958; University of Newcastle upon Tyne, M.Litt., 1975. *Politics:* "Opposition to Left Wing extremism." *Religion:* Church of England. *Office:* 1914-18 Personal Experience Archives, Sunderland Polytechnic, Chester Rd., Sunderland SR1 3SD, England.

CAREER: History teacher at secondary school in Sunderland, England, 1957-58; history teacher and department head at comprehensive school in Liverpool, England, 1958-67; Notre Dame College of Education, Liverpool, lecturer in history, 1967; Sunderland Polytechnic, Sunderland, lecturer, 1967-70, senior lecturer in history, 1970—. British Council tutor in Lesotho. *Member:* Historical Association, Navy Records Society, Royal United Services Institution, Cross and Cockade: Society of First World War Air Historians, Gallipoli Association, Salonika Association, Sunderland Industrial Archaeology Society (chairman, 1969). *Awards, honors:* Alton Nagel Prize from Northumbrian Universities Military Education Committee, 1979, for archival work on the 1914-18 war.

WRITINGS: Men of Gallipoli, Allen Lane, 1976; *World War I Archive: Personal Experience Material for Use in Schools,* Longman, 1977; *Testimony of War, 1914-18,* Michael Russell, 1979; *The Western Front, 1914-1918,* Michael Russell, 1981. Editor of filmstrip series on World War I, released by Common Ground in 1979. Contributor to history, education, and military journals.

WORK IN PROGRESS: Articles for *War Monthly* on the Ruhleben Experience, 1914-18, and on conscientious objection, 1916-18; research on conservation of original personal experience material related to World War I.

SIDELIGHTS: Liddle wrote: "The 1914-18 Personal Experience Archives were established in 1967 when I took up an appointment at Sunderland Polytechnic. The availability of the material has enriched the research experience of students working on the Great War. The purpose of the archive is to preserve evidence of personal experience in that war in order that this important aspect of British, Commonwealth, and European heritage shall never be lost.

"Over thirty-five hundred veterans have contributed documents and recollections by tape recording or by manuscript and typescript and, though the essential core of the archive must be the heritage of the 'ordinary man,' it is of rewarding significance that men of the highest military and civil eminence have contributed to the archives or are at this moment in active cooperation. The wonderful backing of old comrade organizations has also been a great source of inspiration and practical help: the old Contemptibles, the Gallipoli, Salonika, Royal Naval Division Associations, and the Old Comrades Associations of the Special Brigade. Special mention must also be made of men who served with Friends Ambulance Units and men who were interned in the camp at Ruhleben outside Berlin. Every aspect of the war is being thoroughly documented. It is unlikely that any archive in the world has comparable personal experience documentation on Gallipoli or conscientious objection, and it is not merely the Western and major fronts which are richly represented, but even the most obscure areas such as Tsing Tau are represented and of course women's service and domestic front experience.

"I have traveled extensively (France, Turkey, Australia, and New Zealand), not merely because of my work but because of my love of old buildings and unspoiled scenery."

AVOCATIONAL INTERESTS: Hockey, tennis, cricket.

*   *   *

LIEHM, Antonin J. 1924-

PERSONAL: Born March 2, 1924, in Prague, Czechoslovakia; came to the United States in 1970; son of Antonin and Marie (Langerova) Liehm; married Maria Skarkova, December 1, 1948 (divorced, 1963); married Drahomira Sisova (a writer), May 2, 1970; children: (first marriage) Alexandra (Mrs. Martin Urban). *Education:* Charles University, degree in political science, 1949. *Politics:* Democratic socialism. *Religion:* None. *Home:* 1530 Locust, Philadelphia, Pa. 19104. *Office:* Slavic Department, University of Pennsylvania, Philadelphia, Pa. 19104.

CAREER: University of Paris, Paris, France, associate professor, 1969-70; City University of New York, New York, N.Y., associate professor, 1970-76; National Film School, London, England, tutor, 1976-77; University of Pennsylvania, Philadelphia, visiting and adjunct professor, 1977—. Organizer and coordinator of Biennale on Dissident Culture in Eastern Europe, Venice, Italy, 1977. *Member:* International P.E.N., American Association for the Advancement of Slavic Studies, Society for Cinema Studies, Czechoslovak Society of Arts and Sciences. *Awards, honors:* Guggenheim fellowship, 1972; Theatre Library Award, 1978, for *The Most Important Art.*

WRITINGS: Interview (in Czech), Spisovatel, 1964, 2nd edition, 1968; *Generace,* Spisovatel, 1969, translation by R. Kussi published as *Politics of Culture,* Grove, 1972; *Closely Watched Films,* Mike Sharp, 1973; *The Milos Forman Stories,* Mike Sharp, 1973; *Le Passe Present* (title means "The Past of the Present"), Lattes, 1975; *The Most Important Art,* University of California Press, 1977. Member of editorial board of *Literarni Noviny,* 1961-69, and *Listy.*

WORK IN PROGRESS: A book on Czech writer Milan Kundera, publication by Gallimard expected in 1982; a history of postwar Italian cinema, with wife, Mira Liehm, publication by University of California expected in 1982.

SIDELIGHTS: Liehm wrote: "I am interested mostly in the relationship between politics and culture in general, in the Communist world in particular, with a special focus on film."

*   *   *

LIETAERT PEERBOLTE, Maarten 1905-

PERSONAL: Born July 3, 1905, in The Hague, Netherlands; son of Bert (a director general of a health department) and Adele Schagen (Van Soelen) Lietaert Peerbolte; divorced, 1957; children: Ellen, Machteld Lietaert Peerbolte Blom, Jolijn, Ewoud. *Education:* University of Leiden, M.D., 1932. *Home and office:* De Savornin Lohmanlaan 457, The Hague, Netherlands.

CAREER: Affiliated with psychiatric hospitals, 1932-35; private practice of psychoanalysis and psychotherapy, 1935—. Guest lecturer at University of Louvain. *Member:* International Study Association for Prenatal Psychology, Nederlandse Vereniging voor Psychiatrie, Nederlandse Vereniging voor Psychotherapie, Deutsche Akademie fuer Psychoanalyse, Masons.

WRITINGS: Prenatal Dynamics, Sythoff, 1954; *The Orgastical Experience of Space and Metapsychologic Psychagogy: An Outline of Practical Mental and Social Hygiene,* Sijthoff, 1955; *Psychic Energy in Prenatal Dynamics, Parapsychology, Peak-Experiences: A Paraphysical Approach to Psychoanalysis and Transpersonal Psycho-Dynamics,* Servire, 1975, Hunter House, 1979.

Other writings: *Peredur, de zoeker, zijn ontwikkeling in des levens tempel* (title means "Perdus, the Searcher, His Development Is the Temple of Life"), P. Leopold, 1945; *Psychocybernetica: Een psychisch-energetische inleiding* (title means "Psychocybernetics: A Psychic-Energetic Introduction"), De Bezige Bij, 1969; *Eros als bevrijding: Agressie en de twee sexen* (title means "Aggression and the Two Sexes"), De Driehoek, 1970; *De verschijning mens: Vanwaar, waarheen* (title means "The Appearance of Man: From Where, to Where"), De Bezige Bij, 1971; *Kosmisch bewustzijn: Terug naar de religieuze oerbron* (title means "Cosmic Consciousness: Backwards to the Religious Source"), De Bezige Bij, 1973; *Eu-topia* (title means "The Good Spot"), Nederlandse Boehandel, 1976; *Kosmisch existentialisme* (title means "Cosmic Existentialism"), Koan, 1978; *De foetal psyche* (title means "The Fetal Psyche"), Soethoudt, 1979; *Psychodynamische gezichtspunten over de toemost van de cultuur* (title means "Psychodynamic Views of Cultural Future"), Sirius & Siderius, 1981.

Contributor to academic journals.

WORK IN PROGRESS: The Imaginary Psychons and Psychic Energy in Man; The Book of Eupsychia: A Psychodynamical Approach to Maslow's Eupsychia; research on fertilization of the human ovum, in connection with research on schizophrenic processes and borderline cases.

SIDELIGHTS: Lietaert Peerbolte told *CA:* "The late philosopher, Professor Oliver L. Reiser of the University of Pittsburgh, and his books, *The Integration of Human Knowledge* and *Cosmic Humanism,* have been very strong supports for my concept of psychic energy as an energy, though 'imaginary' (the root of minus one), which I needed as a new phenomenology describing prenatal, thus extrasensory, psychic processes. Studies of modern views on energy and quantum mechanics were necessary, and I have added them to my psychoanalytical views.

"Psychic energy, like gravitons, belongs to the energies which exist in the unmanifested world of energy by the supraluminous velocities. The concept of this energy means that a) the recording and formation of engrams can be compared with the coming into existence of matter (psychic particles can be called "psychons"); b) consciousness (paying attention to something) means a relatively higher level of energy, just as an atom has a higher level of energy than an electron; and c) psychic energy as the ability of forming engrams exists already during conception.

"In my work in progress, *Psychodynamic Views of Cultural Future,* the emphasis is on cooperative structure of society together with a philosophical energism replacing the philosophical materialism which forms part of our present aggressive time with dominance and submission. From early youth I have never had any trust in such a mentality of dominance-submission. I chose for psychiatry and psychoanalysis to research what *is* the human mind."

LILIENTHAL, David E(li) 1899-1981

OBITUARY NOTICE—See index for *CA* sketch: Born July 8, 1899, in Morton, Ill.; died of a heart attack, January 14, 1981, in New York, N.Y. Government administrator and author. Lilienthal was a founding director and later the chairman of the Tennessee Valley Authority (TVA). He also served as the first chairman of the Atomic Energy Commission (AEC). As TVA chairman between 1941 and 1946, Lilienthal fought with private utility companies to sell the Authority's electricity at a lower rate. Eventually, he achieved this goal and the TVA became the largest power producer in the United States. As head of the AEC, Lilienthal supervised the transition of the atomic and nuclear energy programs from military control to civilian control. Despite harsh criticism, the administrator also sought to stockpile U.S. atomic arms. Lilienthal's works include *TVA: Democracy on the March*, *Big Business: A New Era*, and *Change, Hope, and the Bomb*. Obituaries and other sources: *London Times*, January 17, 1981; *Newsweek*, January 26, 1981; *Time*, January 26, 1981.

*   *   *

LIMERICK, Jeffrey W. 1948-

PERSONAL: Born May 1, 1948, in Lafayette, Ind.; son of Max D. (an electrical engineer) and Oralee (a teacher; maiden name, Huffman) Limerick; married Patricia L. Nelson (a professor), June 28, 1980. *Education:* University of California, Berkeley, B.Arch. (with honors), 1971; Yale University, M.Arch., 1974. *Politics:* Independent Democrat. *Residence:* Cambridge, Mass. *Office:* Cambridge Seven, 1050 Massachusetts Ave., Cambridge, Mass.

CAREER: BCR Architects, Sacramento, Calif., architect, 1971-72; Ulrich Franzen, New York, N.Y., architect, 1974; Meyers/Gravino, New Haven, Conn., architect, 1975-78; architect for Dehar-Buchanan Architects, 1978-80; Cambridge Seven, Cambridge, Mass., architect, 1980—. Lecturer at Yale University, 1975—.

WRITINGS: (With Nancy Ferguson and Richard B. Oliver) *America's Grand Resort Hotels*, Pantheon, 1979. Co-editor of *Perspecta Fifteen*.

WORK IN PROGRESS: The Residential Architecture of Bernard Maybeck.

SIDELIGHTS: Limerick describes himself as "a professional architect with a passionate interest in the history of architecture, both its cultural role in history and its beauty and emotional power."

*   *   *

LINDLEY, Hilda 1919(?)-1980

OBITUARY NOTICE: Born c. 1919; died of cancer, December 12, 1980, in New York, N.Y. Literary agent, editor, and advertiser. Lindley founded her own literary agency in 1978, representing such clients as Lewis Mumford, Herblock, and Karen Horney. She began her career as an editor and writer for *Tide* magazine and then worked for a number of publishing houses in promotion, sales, and advertising. In 1961 she joined Harcourt Brace Jovanovich in New York City, where she edited several writers, among them poet Carl Sandburg, and managed the company's promotion, advertising, and publicity. Obituaries and other sources: *Publishers Weekly*, January 2, 1981.

*   *   *

LINDSAY, Norman Alfred William 1879-1969

PERSONAL: Original name, Alfred William Norman Lindsay; born c. February 23, 1879, in Creswick, Victoria, New South Wales, Australia; died November 21, 1969; son of a physician; married Kate Parkinson, 1900 (divorced, 1920); married Rose Soady, 1920; children: (first marriage) Jack, Phillip, Raymond; (second marriage) two daughters. *Education:* Attended schools in Creswick, Australia. *Residence:* Springwood, New South Wales, Australia.

CAREER: Artist and writer. *Hawklet* (sporting paper), Melbourne, Australia, illustrator, 1896-99; *Tocsin*, Melbourne, illustrator, 1896-99; free-lance artist, 1899-1901; *Sydney Bulletin*, Sydney, Australia, cartoonist, illustrator, and writer, 1901-23 and 1932-58. Co-sponsor of Endeavor Press; co-founder of *Vision* (magazine), 1924. Art work exhibited in one-man shows in Sydney, 1898 and 1968, Melbourne, 1898, Adelaide, 1924, London, 1925, and New Castle, New South Wales, 1969; work exhibited in group shows, including Exhibition of Australian Art, London, 1923.

WRITINGS—Fiction: (self-illustrated) *A Curate in Bohemia*, New South Wales Bookstall, 1913, reprinted, Pacific Books, 1970; *The Magic Pudding* (for children), Angus & Robertson, 1918, Farrar & Rinehart, 1936, published in four volumes as *First Slice, Second Slice, Third Slice,* and *Fourth Slice,* 1977; *Redheap*, Faber, 1930, published as *Every Mother's Son*, Cosmopolitan Book Corporation, 1930, reprinted as *Redheap*, Ure Smith, 1966; (self-illustrated) *The Cautious Amorist*, Farrar & Rinehart, 1932, reprinted, Horwitz, 1969; *Miracles by Arrangement*, Faber, 1932; *Mr. Gresham and Olympus*, Farrar & Rinehart, 1932; (self-illustrated) *Pan in the Parlour*, Farrar & Rinehart, 1933; *Saturdee*, Endeavor Press, 1933, AMS Press, 1976; (self-illustrated) *The Flyaway Highway* (juvenile), Angus & Robertson, 1935; (self-illustrated) *Age of Consent*, Farrar & Rinehart, 1938.

The Cousin From Fiji, Angus & Robertson, 1945, Random House, 1946; *Halfway to Anywhere*, Angus & Robertson, 1947; *Dust or Polish?*, Angus & Robertson, 1950; *Rooms and Houses: An Autobiographical Novel*, Ure Smith, 1968; *Showdown at Iron Hill*, New English Library, 1969; *Puddin' Poems*, Angus & Robertson, 1977.

Other writings: (Self-illustrated) *Norman Lindsay's Book*, two volumes, New South Wales Bookstall, 1912-15; *The Pen Drawings of Norman Lindsay*, Angus & Robertson, 1918, published as *Norman Lindsay's Pen Drawings*, Art in Australia, 1931; (author of preface) *Poetry in Australia, 1923*, Vision Press, 1923; *Creative Effort: An Essay in Affirmation*, Cecil Palmer, 1924; *The Etchings of Norman Lindsay*, Constable, 1927; (self-illustrated) *Hyperborea: Two Fantastic Travel Sketches*, Fanfrolico Press, 1928; *Madam Life's Lovers: A Human Narrative*, Fanfrolico, 1929.

Pen Drawings, Argus, 1931; (contributor) G. Rayner Hoff, editor, *Work of Eileen McGrath*, privately printed, 1931; *Norman Lindsay Water Colour Book* (biographical sketch by Godfrey Blunden), Springwood Press, 1939, reprint published as *Norman Lindsay Watercolours*, Ure Smith, 1969; (with Douglas Stewart) *Paintings in Oil*, Shepherd Press, 1945; (author of foreword) Elioth Gruner, *Elioth Gruner: Twenty-Four Reproductions in Colour From Original Oil Paintings*, Shepherd Press, 1947; (compiler and author of introduction) Edward George Dyson, *The Golden Shanty: Short Stories*, Angus & Robertson, 1963.

Bohemians of the Bulletin, Angus & Robertson, 1965; *Norman Lindsay's Ship Models*, Angus & Robertson, 1966; *The Scribblings of an Idle Mind*, Lansdowne, 1966; *Selected Pen Drawings*, Angus & Robertson, 1968, Bonanza Books, c. 1970; *Norman Lindsay: His Books, Manuscripts, and Autograph Letters*, Wentworth Press, 1969; *Pencil Drawings*, Angus & Robertson, 1969.

My Mask: For What Little I Know of the Man Behind It (autobiography), Angus & Robertson, 1970; *Two Hundred Etchings,* Angus & Robertson, 1973; *Pen Drawings,* Ure Smith, 1974; *Norman Lindsay's Cats,* Macmillan, 1975; *Siren and Satyr: The Personal Philosophy of Norman Lindsay,* Sun, 1976; *Favourite Etchings,* Angus & Robertson, 1977; (editor) Ross Bott, *Study Guide for Human Information Processing,* 2nd edition, Academy Press, 1977.

Illustrator: (With others) Arthur Hoey Davis, *This Is the Book of Our New Selection,* Bulletin Newspaper Co., Sydney, 1903; Petronius Arbiter, *Petronius,* privately printed, 1910; Leon Gellert, *Songs of a Campaign,* 5th edition, Angus & Robertson, 1918; L. Gellert, *The Isle of San,* Art in Australia, 1919; Hugh Raymond MacCrae, *Colombine,* Angus & Robertson, 1920; W. C. Firebaugh, *The Inns of Greece and Rome,* F. M. Morris, 1923; Jack Lindsay, *The Passionate Neatherd,* Fanfrolico Press, 1925.

Aristophanes, *Lysistrata,* translated by Jack Lindsay, Fanfrolico Press, 1926, World Publishing Co., 1942; P. Arbiter, *The Complete Works of Gaius Petronius,* translated by J. Lindsay, Fanfrolico Press, 1927, published as *The Satyricon, and Poems,* Elek Books, 1960; Mad Tom, *Loving Mad Tom,* Fanfrolico Press, 1927; Propertius, *Propertius in Love,* translated by J. Lindsay, Fanfrolico Press, 1927; Friedrich Wilhelm Nietzsche, *The Antichrist,* translated by P. R. Stephensen, Fanfrolico Press, 1928; (and translator with J. Lindsay) Sappho, *A Homage to Sappho,* Fanfrolico Press, 1928; H. MacCrae, *Satyrs and Sunlight,* Fanfrolico Press, 1928; Aristophanes, *Women in Parliament,* translated by J. Lindsay, Fanfrolico Press, 1929; John Donne, *A Defence of Women for Their Inconstancy and Their Paintings,* Fanfrolico Press, 1930.

Charles Dickens, *Great Expectations,* Shepherd Press, 1947; Andrew Barton Paterson, *The Animals Noah Forgot,* Endeavor Press, 1933, reprinted, Lansdowne, 1970; Douglas Alexander Stewart, *Elegy for an Airman,* Frank C. Johnson, 1940; D. A. Stewart, *Ned Kelly,* Shepherd Press, 1946; Francis Webb, *A Drum for Ben Boyd* (poem), Angus & Robertson, 1948; Rachel Bidduoph Henning, *Letters,* Bulletin Newspaper Co., 1952, published as *The Letters of Rachel Henning,* Angus & Robertson, 1963; D. A. Stewart, *Fisher's Ghost,* Wentworth Press, 1960; D. A. Stewart, *The Garden of Ships,* Wentworth Press, 1962.

SIDELIGHTS: Norman Lindsay became a notable figure in several creative spheres, but especially in the areas of literature and art. At one time he was known as the leading artist in Australia, and he is credited with what some call the only children's classic in Australia.

In two generations, the Lindsay family produced a number of creative people. Norman Lindsay's brother and sister were both artists, and his three sons all became novelists. Lindsay and his sons, in a collaborative effort, founded *Vision,* a magazine that began publication in 1924.

Lindsay grew up in Creswick, a small town in Victoria, New South Wales. The town was used as a setting in several of his writings under the name Redheap. A series of books that relate events in the life of Australia's Huckleberry Finn, including *Redheap, Saturdee,* and *Halfway to Anywhere,* are set in Redheap and seem to be semi-autobiographical. Of these works, *Redheap* was banned in Australia, but was successful in the United States under the title *Every Mother's Son.*

The highly successful children's nonsense story, *The Magic Pudding,* was derived from Lindsay's belief that the most appealing factor of children's tales is food and not fairies or fantasy. The highlight of this story is in the character of Albert, a pudding that constantly replenishes itself, and that walks and talks when not being eaten. The hero of the tale is Bunyip Bluegum, a koala bear. Bunyip runs away from home and encounters Albert in the company of Bill Barnacle, a sailor, and Sam Sawnoff, a penguin. The plot livens when Albert is stolen by two pudding thieves, and a series of adventures results in the inexhaustible pudding being restored to the new trio of friends.

In his adult works, Lindsay is noted for a frankness and sarcastic tone bordering on the caustic. His writings are frequently humorous, and reviewers compliment his seemingly spontaneous use of language. One of these, *The Cautious Amorist,* is the story of three men shipwrecked with a young Australian woman, and the events before their rescue form a social satire. The novel was adapted for motion pictures and released as "Our Girl Friday" in England and "The Adventures of Sadie" in the United States.

In the area of art, Lindsay is best known for his black and white line drawings. He has also worked in a variety of other mediums, including oils, watercolors, lithography, and etching.

BIOGRAPHICAL/CRITICAL SOURCES—Books: Colin Arthur Roderick, *Twenty Australian Novelists,* Angus & Robertson, 1947; John Aikman Hetherington, *Norman Lindsay,* Lansdowne Press, 1961; Rose Lindsay, *Model Wife: My Life With Norman Lindsay,* Ure Smith, 1967; Norman Lindsay, *My Mask: For What Little I Know of the Man Behind It,* Angus & Robertson, 1970.

Periodicals: *New York Herald Tribune Books,* September 14, 1930, February 28, 1932, November 6, 1932, October 15, 1933, September 13, 1936, July 10, 1938; *New York Times,* September 28, 1930, February 28, 1932, November 13, 1932, October 29, 1933, September 13, 1936, July 10, 1938; *Bookman,* October, 1930, August, 1932; *Saturday Review of Literature,* November 19, 1932, October 21, 1933, April 6, 1946; *Time,* July 11, 1938; *New York Herald Tribune Weekly Book Review,* March 31, 1946; *Chicago Sun Book Week,* April 7, 1946.*

*   *   *

LITTLE, Ray 1918(?)-1980

OBITUARY NOTICE: Born c. 1918; died after a long illness, December 9, 1980. Publisher. In 1978 Ray Little retired from his position as vice-president and director of production of Bantam Books after thirty years with that company. He was known for having developed innovative techniques for the production of the "Bantam Extra," or instant book. Obituaries and other sources: *Publishers Weekly,* January 9, 1981.

*   *   *

LOCKRIDGE, Hildegarde (Dolson) 1908-1981 (Hildegarde Dolson)

OBITUARY NOTICE—See index for *CA* sketch: Born August 31, 1908, in Franklin, Pa.; died January 15, 1981, in Columbus, N.C. Author. Dolson wrote fourteen books, including *We Shook the Family Tree, Sorry To Be So Cheerful, My Brother Adlai,* and *Open the Door.* Obituaries and other sources: *New York Times,* January, 17, 1981.

*   *   *

LO-JOHANNSON, (Karl) Ivar 1901-

PERSONAL: Born February 23, 1901, in Osmo, Stockholm, Sweden; son of Gottfrid (a laborer) and Lovisa (a workwoman; maiden name, Ersson) Lo-Johannson. *Home:* Bastugatan 21, Stockholm, Sweden.

CAREER: Stonecutter, farmhand, journalist, and workman in France, England, and Hungary, 1925-29; writer, 1927—. *Awards, honors:* Ph.D. from University of Uppsala, 1964.

WRITINGS—In English translation: *Lyckan,* [Sweden], 1962, translation by Allan Tapsell published as *Bodies of Love,* Souvenir Press, 1971.

Other writings; published in Sweden, except as noted: *Vagabondliv i frankrike* (title means "Vagabondage in France"), 1927, Folket i Bilds Foerlag, 1950; *Kolet i vald* (title means "The Coal's Power"), 1928; *Maana aer dod* (novel; title means "Maana Is Dead"), 1932; *Godnatt, jord* (novel; title means "Goodnight, Earth"), 1933, reprinted, 1972; *Kungsgaten* (novel; title means "The King's Street"), 1935; *Statarna* (short stories; title means "The Farmers' Hands"), 1937, Bonnier, 1961; *Bara en mor* (novel; title means "Only a Mother"), Bonnier, 1939; *Statarliv* (title means "The Life of the Farmers' Hands"), Folket i Bilds Foerlag, 1941; *Traktorn* (novel; title means "The Tractor"), Bonnier, 1943, reprinted, Trevi, 1973; *Statarnoveller: Statarna I-II och jordproletaererna* (title means "Short Stories of the Farmers' Hands"), Bonnier, 1945; *Stridsskrifter* (title means "Polemical Pamphlets"), Bonnier, 1946; *Geniet: En roman om pubertet* (novel; title means "The Genius"), Bonnier, 1947; *Statarna i bild* (title means "Photo of the Farmers' Hands"), KFs Bokfoerlag, 1948; *Ungdomsnoveller: Ett lag historier; Tidiga noveller* (title means "Short Stories of the Youth"), Bonnier, 1948; *Aalderdom* (title means "Old Age"), KFs Bokfoerlag, 1949; *Vagabondliv* (title means "Vagabondage"; contains "Vagabondliv i frankriko," "Kolet i vald," "Nederstigen i doedsriket," "Zigenare," and "Mina staeders ansikten"), Bonnier, 1949.

Analfabeten: En beraettelse fraan min ungdom (title means "The Analphabet"), Bonnier, 1951; *Aalderdoms-sverige* (title means "Old Age in Sweden"), Bonnier, 1952; *Journalisten* (autobiography; title means "The Journalist"), Bonnier, 1956; *Att skriva en roman: Ett sjaelvbiografisk beraettelse* (autobiography; title means "Writing a Novel"), Bonnier, 1957; *Socialisten* (autobiography; title means "The Socialist"), Bonnier, 1958; *Ur klyvnadens tid* (title means "The Splitting Time"), FIBs Lyrikklubb, 1958; *Soldaten* (autobiography; title means "The Soldier"), Bonnier, 1959; *Proletaerforfattaren* (autobiography; title means "The Proletarian Writer"), Bonnier, 1960; *Noveller* (title means "Short Stories"), Svenska Bokfoerlaget, 1960; *Statarnas liv och doed* (title means "Life and Death of the Farmers' Hands"), Bonnier, 1963; *Astronomens hus* (title means "The House of the Astronomer"), 1966 (also see below); *Elektra* (novel), 1967, published as *Kvinna aar 2070* (title means "Woman of the Year 2070"), Oktoberfoerl, 1967; *Martyrerna* (title means "The Martyrs"), 1968; *Girigbukarna* (title means "The Misers"), 1969; *Karriaristerna* (title means "The Careerists"), 1969.

Statarskolan i litteraturen (title means "The Literary School of the Farmers' Hands"), Foerfattarfoerlaget, 1972; *Vishetslaerarna* (title means "The Teachers of Wisdom"), Bonnier, 1972; *Passionerna* (short stories; title means "The Passions"), seven volumes, 1968-1972; *Folket och herrarna* (title means "The People and the Husbands"), two volumes, Norstedt, 1973; *Nunnan i vadstena,* Bonnier, 1973; *Ordets makt* (title means "The Power of Words"), Bonnier, 1973; *Dagbok fraan tjugo-talet* (title means "Diary From the Twenties"), Corona, 1974; *Furstarna* (title means "The Rulers"), Bonnier, 1974; *Lastbara beraettelser* (title means

"Short Stories of Vice"), Bonnier, 1974; *Passionsnoveller* (title means "Short Stories of Passion"), Aldus, 1974; *Dagar och dagsverken: Debatter och memoarer* (title means "Days and Day's Work"), Bonnier, 1975; *Statarnoveller: Jordproletaererna* (sequel to *Statarnoveller: Statarna I-II;* title means "Short Stories of Farmers' Hands: The Proletarian of Earth"), Forum, 1975; *Romanen om Maana* (contains "Maana aer doed" and "Astronomens hus"; title means "The Novel About Maana"), Trevi, 1976; *Under de groena ekarna i Soermland* (title means "Under the Green Oaks in Soermland"), Forum, 1976; *Passioner i urval,* Bra Boecker, 1976; *Den sociala fotobildboken* (title means "The Social Photo Book"), Raben & Sjoegren, 1977; *En arbetares liv: Proletaernoveller* (title means "A Worker's Life"), Bonnier, 1977; *Pubertet* (memoirs; title means "Puberty"), Bonnier, 1978; *Asfalt* (memoirs; title means "Asphalt"), 1979.

WORK IN PROGRESS: A third book of memoirs.

SIDELIGHTS: Ivar Lo-Johannson has written numerous books on a wide variety of subjects, including travel, sports, politics, and Swedish social life, as well as books for young people. His writings on the "statare" ("farmers' hands") system of farm labor are credited by some Swedish scholars with contributing to the abolition of that system in 1935.

*   *   *

LONEY, Martin 1944-

PERSONAL: Born February 10, 1944, in Southport, England; son of James (a dentist) and Margaret (Parker) Loney; married Christine Poulter (a lecturer). *Education:* University of Durham, B.A. (with honors), 1966; Simon Fraser University, M.A., 1969. *Politics:* Socialist. *Religion:* None. *Office:* Faculty of Social Sciences, Open University, Walton Hall, Milton Keynes MK7 6AA, England.

CAREER: World University Services, Geneva, Switzerland, director of research, 1971-73; National Council for Civil Liberties in the United Kingdom, London, general secretary, 1973-74; Carleton University, Ottawa, Ontario, assistant professor of social work, 1974-76; South Bank Polytechnic, London, England, senior lecturer in community work, 1976-78; Open University, Milton Keynes, England, lecturer in social policy, 1978—. President of Canadian Union of Students, 1968-69. *Member:* Association of Community Workers of the United Kingdom.

WRITINGS: Rhodesia: White Racism and Imperial Response, Penguin, 1975; (editor) *The Crisis of the Inner City,* Macmillan, 1979. Contributor to magazines, including *Community Care, Maclean's, New Statesman, Monthly Review,* and *Canadian Dimension.* Member of editorial advisory board of *Community Development Journal* and editorial board of Association of Community Workers of the United Kingdom.

WORK IN PROGRESS: Research on community action and social change and on government policy making and the social sciences.

SIDELIGHTS: Loney commented: "My writings are primarily motivated by a desire to expose the gap between the rhetoric of politicians and the practice of governments." *Avocational interests:* Keeping fit, drinking wine.

*   *   *

LONGBEARD, Frederick
See LONGYEAR, Barry Brookes

LONGLEY, Michael 1939-

PERSONAL: Born July 27, 1939, in Belfast, Northern Ireland; married Edna Broderick. *Education:* Trinity College, Dublin, B.A. (with honors), 1963. *Home:* 18 Hillside Park, Stranmillis, Belfast 9, Northern Ireland.

CAREER: Poet. Worked as assistant master of school in Blackrock, Northern Ireland, 1962-63, high schools in Belfast and Erith, Northern Ireland, 1963-64, and Royal Belfast Academical Institution in Belfast, 1964-69; Arts Council of Northern Ireland, Belfast, assistant director, 1970—. *Awards, honors:* Eric Gregory Award from Society of Authors, 1965, for poetry.

WRITINGS—Poetry: *Ten Poems,* Festival Publications, 1965; (with Seamus Heaney and David Hammond) *Room to Rhyme,* Arts Council of Northern Ireland, 1968; *Secret Marriages: Nine Short Poems,* Phoenix Pamphlet Poets Press, 1968; (with Barry Tebb and Iain Crichton Smith) *Three Regional Voices,* Poet & Printer, 1968; *No Continuing City: Poems, 1963-1968,* Dufour, 1969; *Lares,* Poet & Printer, 1972; *An Exploded View: Poems, 1968-1972,* Gollancz, 1973; *Man Lying on a Wall,* Gollancz, 1976, Transatlantic, 1977; *The Echo Gate,* Secker & Warburg, 1979.

Other writings: (Editor) *Causeway: The Arts in Ulster,* Arts Council of Northern Ireland, 1971; (editor) *Under the Moon, Over the Stars: Young People's Writing From Ulster,* Arts Council of Northern Ireland, 1971. Also author of scripts for British Broadcasting Corp. (BBC-Radio). Contributor to magazines, including *Dublin, Encounter,* and *Phoenix.*

SIDELIGHTS: According to Alan Brownjohn of *New Statesman,* "*No Continuing City* shows the stubborn, interesting persistence of formal and intricate patterning in verse. Michael Longley, on this showing, is a deeply fastidious craftsman." Other reviewers, too, such as R. D. Spector of *Saturday Review,* have found "a clarity of expression, a sensitivity to language and rhythm" in Longley's poems. Robert Greacon in his *Books* review concluded that Longley "has obviously heeded Yeats' injunction to Irish poets to learn their 'trade' thoroughly."

Longley's careful attention to technique has sometimes meant "rather strenuous exercises in craftsmanship, models of determination which become exhausted," observed John Mole. At the same time, however, he calls Longley "a patient, properly ambitious poet who has worked hard to achieve a distinctive style without appearing to question his deep trust in the resources of formality and pattern." He reasoned that Longley's work demonstrates "the importance of learning the craft in order to release the imagination."

Longley's own comments on his work appeared in a *Poetry Book Society Bulletin* in 1979. "For a long time," he wrote, "I have been preoccupied with form—pushing a shape as far as it will go, exploring its capacities to control and its tendencies to disintegrate. Ideally this should be an inner adventure; plan and passion, improvisation and calculation should coincide." Mole considered these statements in his review of *The Echo Gate* and described Longley's chief strength as "that sudden lift from an immaculate ordering of particulars towards the numinous, a delighted 'waking into reason. . . .' The aim is a synthesis of sense and sensation, the vital concern being *balance*—to be achieved through the intelligent ordering of experience."

Andrew Motion claimed that Longley's most important theme is mutability. "Poem after poem deals with this in some form—usually by recording transformation within na-

ture." Overall, however, there is in Longley's work a tension between the change that he sees and the human need for constancy. Many of his poems "seek to define—in various geographical terms—the same sense of permanence that his love poems show him looking for in human relationships. . . . His imagination may be excited by flux, but his heart is set on stability." His work also encompasses a wide range of subjects, as Greacon observed: "Classical mythology, jazz, the Hebrides, John Clare, Emily Dickenson, Walter Mitty, the osprey—you name it and Mr. Longley has written a poem about it."

As an Ulsterman, Longley has considered the poet's peculiar circumstances in Northern Ireland: "I would insist that poetry is a normal human activity, its proper concern all of the things that happen to people. Though the poet's first duty must be to his imagination, he has other obligations—and not just as a citizen. He would be inhuman if he did not respond to tragic events in his own community, and a poor artist if he did not seek to endorse that response imaginatively."

BIOGRAPHICAL/CRITICAL SOURCES: New Statesman, December 5, 1969, February 18, 1977, January 11, 1980; *Books,* January, 1970; *Times Literary Supplement,* February 12, 1970, March 19, 1976, December 17, 1976, February 8, 1980; *Saturday Review,* December 26, 1970; *Poetry,* August, 1971; *Observer,* August 22, 1976, December 9, 1979, January 27, 1980; *Poetry Book Society Bulletin,* Number 103, 1979.

*   *   *

LONGYEAR, Barry Brookes 1942-
(Fan D. Ango, Frederick Longbeard, Tol E. Rant, Mark Ringdalh, Shaw Vinest)

PERSONAL: Born May 12, 1942, in Harrisburg, Pa.; married Regina Bedsun, May 4, 1967. *Education:* Attended Wayne State University, 1966-67. *Politics:* "Yes." *Religion:* "No." *Home and office:* 1 Wilton Rd., Farmington, Maine 04938.

CAREER: Madison Corp., Detroit, Mich., production manager, 1967-68; Sol III Publications, editor, publisher, and ghostwriter in Philadelphia, Pa., 1968-72, owner in Farmington, Maine, 1972-77; writer, 1977—. Conducts writer's workshops. *Member:* Authors Guild, Authors League of America, Science Fiction Writers of America, Association of Science Fiction and Fantasy Artists, New England Science Fiction Association. *Awards, honors:* Nebula Award from Science Fiction Writers of America, Hugo Award from World Science Fiction Convention, and Locus Award, all 1980, all for novella, "Every Mine"; John W. Campbell Award from World Science Fiction Association for best new writer.

WRITINGS: Science Fiction Writer's Workshop I: An Introduction to Fiction Mechanics, Owlswick Press, 1980; (contributor) Jack Williamson, editor, *Teaching Science Fiction: Education for Tomorrow,* Olswick Press, 1980; *Manifest Destiny* (science-fiction novel), Berkley Publishing, 1980; *City of Baraboo* (science-fiction novel), Berkley Publishing, 1980; *Circus World* (science-fiction novel), Berkley Publishing, 1980; (contributor) Terry Carr, *Carr's Best Science Fiction,* Del Rey, 1980; *Elephant Song* (science-fiction novel), Berkley Publishing, 1981; *The Tomorrow Testament* (science-fiction novel), Berkley Publishing, 1982. Author of "Salty," a monthly column in *Empire Science Fiction.* Contributor of about thirty-five stories, poems, and articles to science-fiction magazines, including *Analog* and *Isaac Asimov's Science Fiction Magazine* (sometimes under pseudonyms Fan D. Ango, Frederick Longbeard, Tol E. Rant, Mark Ringdalh, and Shaw Vinest).

SIDELIGHTS: Longyear wrote: "*Manifest Destiny* tells the story of Earth's early contacts and relations with alien cultures, and the movement to get the United States of Earth Planets to join the Ninth Quadrant Federation of Habitable Planets.

"*City of Baraboo* tells the story of John J. O'Hara and his efforts to preserve the institution of the canvas show. Toward this end he takes his moth-eaten circus show to an alien planet, then to other worlds on his circus starship, 'City of Baraboo,' against an enemy who grows more determined with each success O'Hara has.

"Momus is a planet inhabited by the descendants of O'Hara's Greater Shows some two hundred years before the story in *Circus World* takes place. In the intervening time, Momus has become strategically significant in a power struggle between two powerful forces in the galaxy. This forms the setting for Lord Ashly Allenby's efforts to inform the people of Momus, and then to protect and defend them against both forces.

"*Elephant Song* is a two-hundred-year epic tracing the generations of bullhands (elephant handlers) who took to the star road with O'Hara's Greater Shows. The novel begins on Earth, when O'Hara's show was little more than a carnival, and follows the success of the show until it is marooned on the planet Momus. The story continues, showing the development of Moman society, reaching the tensions and eventual war with the Tenth Quadrant, and concludes with the new mission of the Moman starshow: to get elephants.

"*The Tomorrow Testament* is set against the tense backdrop of delicate treaty negotiations between the United States of Earth Planets and the Dracon Chamber, when a translation of the hermaphroditic Drac's *Talman*, the alien's nontheistic bible, is widely spread among human-populated planets. Reactions vary from the formation of fanatical cults to religious outrage. The negotiations are to be held in a station orbiting a planet half populated by humans and half by Dracs—the original point of issue that brought about the recent war."

BIOGRAPHICAL/CRITICAL SOURCES: Detroit News, January 18, 1981.

*   *   *

LORD, Clifford L(ee)   1912-1980

OBITUARY NOTICE—See index for *CA* sketch: Born September 4, 1912, in Mount Vernon, N.Y.; died of cancer, October 22, 1980, in West Orange, N.J. Administrator, educator, historian, editor, and author. Lord taught at Columbia University for several years before moving to Hofstra University, where he served as president and chancellor. At Hofstra, the educator led the university through a period of great expansion, both in enrollment and building construction. Lord's field of interest was local history. After leaving Hofstra, he pursued this subject as the president of the Hudson Institute. Lord also edited the "Localized History Series," the *New York History* magazine, and the *Wisconsin Magazine of History.* His other works include *Handbook of the Museum and Art Gallery of the New York State Historical Association, History of United States Naval Aviation,* and *Teaching History With Community Resources.* Obituaries and other sources: *New York Times,* October 23, 1980; *Chicago Tribune,* October 24, 1980; *AB Bookman's Weekly,* December 15, 1980.

LORD HOME
See HOME, Alexander Frederick

*   *   *

LORENZ, J(ames) D(ouglas)   1938-

PERSONAL: Born March 23, 1938, in Dayton, Ohio; son of J. Douglas and Helen (Walper) Lorenz; children: Shanna, Aaron. *Home and office:* 16 Hillcrest Court, Berkeley, Calif. 94705.

CAREER: California Rural Legal Assistance, San Francisco, director, 1966-71; Lorenz, Greene & Kelley (law firm), San Francisco, partner, 1971-75; California Employment Development Department, Sacramento, director, 1975; Council for Public Interest Law, Washington, D.C., director, 1977-79; writer, 1979—. *Military service:* U.S. Army.

WRITINGS: Jerry Brown: The Man on the White Horse, Houghton, 1978.

WORK IN PROGRESS: A book on small business.

*   *   *

LORTZ, Richard   1930-1980

OBITUARY NOTICE—See index for *CA* sketch: Born January 13, 1930, in New York, N.Y.; died of a heart attack, November 5, 1980, in New York, N.Y. Playwright, editor, and author. Lortz began his career as an editor for Hoffman Publications. He then worked as managing editor of the magazines *Industrial Photography* and *Audio-Visual Communications.* Lortz penned several plays for the stage, including "A Journey With Strangers," "Voices," and "The Juniper Tree." Among his television plays number such productions as "Mr. Nobody," "M Is for Murder," and "Circle of Doom." The author's other works include the novels *A Crowd of Voices, A Summer in Spain, Children of the Night,* and *The Betrothed.* Obituaries and other sources: *New York Times,* November 11, 1980; *Publishers Weekly,* December 5, 1980; *AB Bookman's Weekly,* December 15, 1980.

*   *   *

LOZANO, Wendy   1941-

PERSONAL: Surname is pronounced Lothano; born September 23, 1941, in Evanston, Ill.; daughter of Jack C. (a market research analyst) and Gwen (a travel consultant; maiden name, Heilman) Griffin; married Enrique Lozano, September 8, 1962 (divorced December, 1971); children: Tauka (deceased). *Education:* University of California, Irvine, B.A. (magna cum laude), 1978, doctoral study, 1978—. *Home:* 22961 Lynda Lane, El Toro, Calif. 92630. *Agent:* Jane Jordan Browne Multimedia Product Development, Inc., 401 South Michigan Ave., Room 828, Chicago, Ill. 60605.

CAREER: Writer, 1980—. Also worked as puppeteer, diamond courier, legal interpreter, actress, and cabaret singer. *Member:* Mensa, California Women in Higher Education (vice-president, 1979-81).

WRITINGS: Sweet Abandon, Avon, 1980; *She Who Was King,* Ballantine, 1980.

WORK IN PROGRESS: A family saga set in Mexico, from the height of the Aztec rule in 1518 to the resignation of Diaz in 1911.

*   *   *

LUENING, Otto   1900-

PERSONAL: Born June 15, 1900, in Milwaukee, Wis.; son

of Eugene (a conductor and composer) and Emma (an amateur singer; maiden name, Jacobs) Luening; married Ethel Codd, April 19, 1927 (divorced, 1959); married Catherine Brunson (a music teacher), September 5, 1959. *Education:* Attended State Academy of Music, Munich, Germany, 1915-17, Municipal Conservatory of Music, Zurich, Switzerland, 1917-20, and University of Zurich, 1919-20; studied privately with Ferruccio Busoni and Philipp Jarnach. *Home:* 460 Riverside Dr., New York, N.Y. 10027. *Agent:* Curtis Brown Ltd., 575 Madison Ave., New York, N.Y. 10022.

CAREER: Flutist and conductor of opera and symphony orchestras in Munich, Germany, and Zurich, Switzerland, 1915-20; Chicago Musical Arts Studio, Chicago, Ill., director, 1920-25; Eastman School of Music, Rochester, N.Y., coach and executive director of opera department, 1925-28; Rochester American Opera Company, Rochester, coach and assistant conductor, 1925-26, conductor, 1926-28; University of Arizona, Tucson, associate professor, 1932-33, professor of music, 1933-34; Bennington College, Bennington, Vt., chairman of music department, 1934-44, director of music at School of Arts, 1940-41; Columbia University, Barnard College, New York, N.Y., professor of music, 1947-68, professor emeritus, 1968—, head of department, 1944-47, music chairman at School of Arts, 1966-70, director of opera projects, 1944-54, music director at Brander Mathews Theatre, 1944-59.

Guest conductor of American Opera Company, 1928, and New York Philharmonic Symphony Chamber Orchestra, 1937; professor at Joline Foundation, 1944-64; composer-in-residence and member of board of trustees at American Academy in Rome, 1958, 1961, 1965; member of faculty at Juilliard School, 1971-73; Distinguished Hadley Fellow at Bennington College, 1975, visiting composer at Peabody Institute of Music, 1977-78. Conducted first all-American opera performance in Chicago, Ill., 1922; co-founder of American Music Center, New York City, and chairman of center, 1940-60; co-founder of Composers' Recordings, Inc., and president, 1968-70, chairman of board of directors, 1970-75, co-president, 1975-77, member of board of directors, 1977—; co-director of Columbia-Princeton Electronic Music Center, 1959—. Member of board of directors of Vermont Symphony Orchestra, 1939, guest conductor, 1978. Performed as flutist in the United States, Canada, and Europe; U.S. delegate to international composers' conference, 1960.

MEMBER: National Institute of Arts and Letters (life member; vice-president, 1953), American Composers Alliance (co-founder; president, 1945-51), Composers Forum (member of board of directors), League of Composers (member of executive board, 1943), National Federation of Music Clubs (national chairman of American composition, 1943), Society for Publishing American Music, Music Educators National Conference, Phi Beta Kappa (honorary), Columbia University Faculty Club, Century Association. *Awards, honors:* Guggenheim fellowships, 1930-32, 1974-75; David Bispham Medal for American Opera from American Opera Society, 1933, for opera, "Evangeline"; D.Mus. from Wesleyan University, Middletown, Conn., 1963; citation from Wisconsin Senate and House of Representatives, 1965, 1976; citation from National Association of Composers and Conductors, 1966; Laurel Leaf Award from American Composers Alliance, 1970; award from Thorne Music Fund Foundation, 1972; National Endowment for the Arts grants, 1974, 1977; D.F.A. from University of Wisconsin, Madison, 1977; citation from Wisconsin Academy of Sciences, Arts, and Letters, 1977.

WRITINGS: (Contributor) Herbert Russcol, editor, *The*

Liberation of Sound: An Introduction to Electronic Music, Prentice-Hall, 1972; (Contributor) Jon H. Appleton, editor, *The Development and Practice of Electronic Music,* Prentice-Hall, 1975; *The Odyssey of an American Composer,* Scribner, 1980.

Musical compositions include "Synthesis," "Gargoyle," "Moonflight," "Fantasy in Space," "In the Beginning," and "Poems in Cycles and Bells." Contributor to music journals.

WORK IN PROGRESS: "Short Symphony"; "Canons for Two Flutes"; "Short Sonatas for Piano," Nos. 5, 6, and 7; "Potawatomi Legends for Chamber Orchestra"; "Songs," texts by William Blake.

SIDELIGHTS: Luening's more than one hundred seventy-five compositions for voice, solo instruments, and orchestra have been performed by American and foreign symphony orchestras and chamber music groups. A number of them have been published and recorded.

Luening told *CA:* "I believe that there are different kinds of music for different purposes, and they are all valid. In my own career I have composed quite a few pieces for children, some for beginners on various instruments and some that is music for amateurs. Many of my works were written for particular performers or for particular institutions that wanted a certain kind of composition for their programs. Another group of my works were very personal statements that I wanted to put down; some pieces in this group have been played widely, some have not yet reached an audience.

"I see no reason why a composer should not try his hand at popular music with its special requirements, but I also see no reason for the contemporary composer not to enter the field of research and development and compose music that is 'way out.' Experimenting with sound led me to electronic music. Obviously, production of electronic sound is here to stay. How it is used depends, of course, on the composers and on the reactions of audiences. It is like a new section in the orchestra, and there is no reason to fear that it will destroy other music, as long as people continue to sing and play individually and in groups and audiences listen to them. As always in music's history, the art has been carried forward by those Janus-like people who respect the past without fearing to explore the new and untried, and to peer into the future."

*   *   *

LUNIN, Lois F(ranklin)

PERSONAL: Born in Schenectady, N.Y.; daughter of Hyman and Sophie (Tauber) Frumkin; married Martin Lunin (a professor), June 22, 1947. *Education:* Radcliffe College, A.B., 1945; Drexel University, M.S., 1966. *Office:* Herner & Co., 1700 North Moore St., Arlington, Va. 22209.

CAREER: New Haven Hospital, Public Relations Department, New Haven, Conn., editorials assistant, 1945-46; C. V. Mosby Co., St. Louis, Mo., copy editor, 1947-48; Washington University School of Dentistry, St. Louis, editorial assistant, 1948-50; Columbia University, New York City, editorial assistant, 1950-55; William Douglas McAdams Inc., New York City, researcher in medical research department, 1955-56, research administrator, 1956-58; University of Texas, Houston, research associate at M. D. Anderson Hospital and Tumor Institute, 1959-64; Johns Hopkins University, Information Center for Hearing, Speech, and Disorders of Human Communication, Baltimore, Md., systems analyst, 1965-66, co-director and program director, 1966-76;

Environmental Programs, Inc., Baltimore, director of information science, 1977-78; Herner & Co. (consulting firm), Arlington, Va., vice-president, 1978—. Consultant to Pan American Health-World Health Organization, National Academy of Sciences-National Research Council, and Center for Bioethics at Kennedy Institute, Georgetown University.

MEMBER: American Association for the Advancement of Science (fellow), American Society for Information Science, Institute of Information Scientists (fellow), Association for Computing Machinery, Council of Biology Editors, Medical Library Association, Society for Scholarly Publishing, Phi Kappa Phi, Beta Phi Mu. *Awards, honors:* Watson Davis Award from American Society for Information Science, 1976.

WRITINGS: (With E. L. Worthington, M. T. Heath, and F. I. Catlin) *Index-Handbook of Ototoxic Agents,* Johns Hopkins Press, 1973; (Contributor) W. Sewell, editor, *Reader in Medical Librarianship,* Microcard Editions, 1973; (contributor) A. H. Rutscher, T. J. Fleming, and others, editors, *Communicating Issues in Thanatology,* MSS Information Corp., 1975; (editor) *Health Sciences and Services: A Guide to Sources of Information,* Gale, 1979. Contributor to medical and information science journals. Editor-in-chief of *Bulletin of the American Society for Information Science,* 1974-80; executive editor of *Digests of Environmental Impact Statements;* editor of Perspectives section of *Journal of the American Society for Information Science.*

WORK IN PROGRESS: A chapter for *Careers in Information.*

AVOCATIONAL INTERESTS: Crafts (especially fiber art).

BIOGRAPHICAL/CRITICAL SOURCES: Information Manager, July-August, 1949.

*   *   *

LUTHER, Frank   1905-1980

OBITUARY NOTICE: Born Francis Luther Crow, August 4, 1905, near Lakin, Kansas; died November 16, 1980, in New York, N.Y. Singer, composer, and writer. Frank Luther recorded over 3000 tapes and records, and his recordings of classic nursery rhymes and fairy tales made his voice a familiar one to children. He was well known for his book *Americans and Their Songs,* which contains 125 songs representative of American musical style. His songwriting credits include "Barnacle Bill the Sailor" and "Christmas is a Comin'." He also composed a folk opera production of *Tom Sawyer,* which appeared on television in 1956. Obituaries and other sources: *Who's Who in America,* 40th edition, Marquis, 1978; *New York Times,* November 20, 1980; *Publishers Weekly,* December 22-29, 1980.

*   *   *

LUTHER, Ray
See LEY, Arthur Gordon

LUTZ, Cora Elizabeth   1906-

PERSONAL: Born October 23, 1906, in Rockville, Conn.; daughter of George William and Cora (Townsend) Lutz. *Education:* Connecticut College, A.B., 1927; Yale University, A.M., 1931, Ph.D., 1933. *Home:* 24 Charlton Hill, Mount Carmel, Conn. 06518.

CAREER: Worked as high-school teacher of Latin and French, 1927-29; Judson College, Marion, Ala., associate professor of classics, 1933-35; Wilson College, Chambersburg, Pa., associate professor, 1935-50, professor of classics, 1950-69, professor emeritus, 1969—; Yale University, New Haven, Conn., cataloger of medieval manuscripts at Beinecke Library, 1969-75; writer, 1975—.

MEMBER: American Philological Association, Mediaeval Academy of America (fellow), American Association of University Women, Renaissance Society of America, Classical Association of New England, Connecticut Academy of Arts and Sciences, Phi Beta Kappa. *Awards, honors:* Kellogg fellowship for Yale University, 1943-44; Guggenheim fellowships, 1949-50, 1954-55; Lindback Award for distinguished teaching from Wilson College, 1962; Bollingen Foundation fellowship, 1966-67; Distinguished Alumni Award from Connecticut College, 1970.

WRITINGS: (Editor) *Iohannes Scotti: Glossae in Martianum,* Mediaeval Academy of America, 1939; *Dunchad: Glossae in Martianum,* American Philological Society, 1944; *Musonius Rufus: The Roman Socrates,* Yale University Press, 1947; *Remigius Autissiodorensis: Commentum in Martianum Capellam,* E. J. Brill, Volume I, 1962, Volume II, 1965; *Essays on Manuscripts and Rare Books,* Archon, 1975; *Schoolmasters of the Tenth Century,* Archon, 1977. Also author of *The Oldest Library Motto and Other Library Essays,* Shoe String. Contributor to classical studies journals.

WORK IN PROGRESS: Sidelights on Ezra Stiles.

SIDELIGHTS: Lutz told *CA:* "After many years of teaching Latin and Greek, at the same time doing research on medieval Latin manuscripts of texts that I felt were badly needed for an understanding of medieval scholarship, I undertook cataloging the pre-1600 manuscripts in Yale's Rare Manuscript Library. Just as that enterprise was nearing completion, a friend, a direct descendant of Ezra Stiles, presented me with a collection of rare books from the Stiles library. I eagerly welcomed the unusual opportunity to learn more about this most unusual scholar. Since his vast collection of manuscripts is now at Yale and at the New Haven Colony Historical Society I was in a most favored position to make a study of him. I have now completed a book of essays on his character and career. I have a great many more aspects of his life and accomplishments that I am exploring. I expect to be busied with this for a long time."

*   *   *

LYMINGTON, John
See CHANCE, John Newton

M

MAC

See MacMANUS, Seumas

*   *   *

MacAGY, Douglas G(uernsey)   1913-1973

PERSONAL: Born July 8, 1913, in Winnipeg, Manitoba, Canada; came to the United States, 1936, naturalized U.S. citizen; died September 6, 1973, in Washington, D.C.; son of Douglas Drillio and Elisabeth Beatrix (Guernsey) MacAgy; married Jermayne Smart, March 24, 1941 (divorced December, 1954); married Elizabeth Tillett, February 19, 1955; children: Ian Douglas, Caitlin Elisabeth. *Education:* Studied at University of Toronto, 1933-35, Barnes Foundation, 1936-39, and University of Pennsylvania, 1938-39; Western Reserve University (now Case Western Reserve University), A.B., 1940; also studied at Cleveland School of Art and Courtauld Institute of Art, London.

CAREER: Cleveland Museum of Art, Cleveland, Ohio, curatorial assistant in education department, 1939-40, and painting department, 1940-41; San Francisco Museum of Art, San Francisco, Calif., began as curatorial assistant, became curator, 1941-43; Office of War Information, Washington, D.C., propaganda analyst and chief of Japanese section of Propaganda Division, in Far East Bureau, 1943-45; California School of Fine Arts, San Francisco, director of aesthetics and modern art, 1945-50; Orbit Films, Seattle, Wash., vice-president, 1950-51; UNESCO, New York City, executive secretary of New York museums committee, 1951-52; Museum of Modern Art, New York City, consultant to director, 1953-56; Wildenstein & Co., Inc., New York City, director of research, 1956-57; Dallas Museum of Contemporary Arts, Dallas, Tex., director, 1959-63; independent consultant, 1963-68; National Endowment for the Arts and National Council on the Arts, Washington, D.C., deputy chairman, 1968-73, acting chairman, 1969. Curator and director of exhibitions for Joseph H. Hirshhorn Museum and Sculpture Garden at Smithsonian Institution, 1972-73. Tutor at University of Toronto, 1935-36; guest lecturer at University of Pennsylvania, 1965-66. Member of board of trustees of Tamarind Lithography Workshop, 1960-73, Four Winds Theatre, 1968-73, and International Foundation for Art Research, 1969-73; past member of National Council of Churches of Christ. *Awards, honors:* European fellow of Barnes Foundation.

WRITINGS: (Contributor) *Zeitschrift fuer aesthetik und allgemeine Kunst-Wissen Shaft: Index, 1906-1939,* Cleveland Museum of Art, 1940; (editor) *Western Round Table on Modern Art: Modern Artists in America,* Wittenborn & Schulz, 1951; *The Museum Looks in on TV,* Museum of Modern Art, 1955; (with wife, Elizabeth MacAgy) *Going for a Walk With a Line: A Step Into the World of Modern Art* (juvenile), Doubleday, 1959; *Art That Broke the Looking Glass,* Dallas Museum of Contemporary Arts, 1961; *One "i" at a Time,* Division of Fine Arts, Southern Methodist University, 1971. Author of exhibition catalogs. Contributor to journals, including *Canadian Forum, Magazine of Art, College Art Journal, Architect and Engineer,* and *Circle,* and newspapers. Past member of staff of *Gazette des Beaux-Arts.*

BIOGRAPHICAL/CRITICAL SOURCES: Harper's Bazaar, February, 1947; *Evergreen Review,* Volume I, number 2; Mary McChesney, *Was There a San Francisco School?,* Oakland Museum, 1972; *New York Times,* September 7, 1973; *Art America,* November, 1973.*

*   *   *

MacARTHUR-ONSLOW, Annette Rosemary   1933-

PERSONAL: Born March 21, 1933, in Sydney, Australia. *Education:* Attended East Sydney Technical College; Central School, London, England; Internationale Sommerakademie Fur Bildende Kunst; Alliance Francaise. *Residence:* Gloucestershire, England.

CAREER: Free-lance writer, designer, and illustrator. Worked with a marionette program in Sydney, Australia; production assistant for a London publisher; free-lance illustrator in Europe and Australia. *Awards, honors:* Australian Book of the Year Award, 1970, for *Uhu;* honorable mention, International Biennale of Illustration, Bratislava, Czechoslavakia, 1970.

WRITINGS—Author and illustrator: *Camden Park Estate: Australia's Oldest Pastoral Property,* Menagle, 1959; *Uhu* (juvenile), Ure Smith, 1969, Knopf, 1970; *Minnie* (juvenile), Rand McNally, 1971; *Round House,* Collins, 1975.

Illustrator: Ruth Manning-Sanders, *Animal Stories,* Roy, 1968; Hesba Fay Binsmead, *Pastures of the Blue Crane,* Oxford University Press, 1970; Sheena Porter, *Nordy Bank,* Oxford University Press, 1971; Andrew Barton Paterson, *The Man From Snowy River,* Collins, 1977; Mathew Flinders, *Trim,* Collins, 1978.*

MacDONALD, Malcolm John   1901-1981

OBITUARY NOTICE—See index for *CA* sketch: Born August 17, 1901, in Lossiemouth, Morayshire, Scotland; died January 11, 1981, near Sevenoaks, Kent, England. Diplomat, government administrator, editor, and author. MacDonald worked as an editor at the Reader's Library before going into politics. The son of England's first Labour party prime minister, he became a member of Parliament. During his career, MacDonald held a variety of governmental positions ranging from under-secretary in the Dominions Office to secretary of state of dominion affairs, secretary of state for colonies, minister of health, high commissioner in Canada, governor-general of the Malayan Union, Singapore, and British Borneo, high commissioner in India, and special representative in Africa. The diplomat also became England's youngest member of the British Cabinet in 1934. In addition, MacDonald was instrumental in helping to organize the Southeast Asia Treaty Organization. He was awarded the Order of Merit in 1969. The author's books, primarily about his travels and ornithology, include *Bird Watching at Lossiemouth, Birds in the Sun, Treasure of Kenya,* and *People and Places: Random Reminiscences.* Obituaries and other sources: *New York Times,* January 12, 1981; *Chicago Tribune,* January 12, 1981.

*　　　*　　　*

MACEY, Samuel L(awson)   1922-

PERSONAL: Born March 12, 1922, in London, England; married June Beryl Heape, 1954; children: Elizabeth, Caroline. *Education:* Institute of Work Study, Organization, and Methods, A.I.W.S.P., 1960, F.W.S.O.M., 1969; University of British Columbia, B.A. (with first class honors), 1964; University of Washington, Seattle, Ph.D., 1966. *Office:* Department of English, University of Victoria, Victoria, British Columbia, Canada V8W 2Y2.

CAREER: London Stock Exchange, London, England, office boy and clerk, 1938-40; owner of furniture and restaurant business in London, 1946-48, and wholesale importing business in Jersey, Channel Islands, 1948-57; University of Victoria, Victoria, British Columbia, assistant professor, 1966-72, associate professor of English, 1972—, associate dean of graduate faculty, 1975—. Member of board of governors of Open Learning Institute, 1978. *Military service;* Royal Naval Volunteer Reserve, active duty with Coastal Forces, 1940-46; became lieutenant.

MEMBER: International Society for the Study of Time (member of council, 1976-82), Johnson Society of the Northwest (president, 1973), American Society for Eighteenth Century Studies, British Horological Institute. *Awards, honors:* Canada Council fellow, 1967, 1972, and 1979-80; visiting fellow of Corpus Christi College, Cambridge, 1972.

WRITINGS: (Editor and author of introduction), "*A Learned Dissertation on Dumpling*" *and* "*Pudding and Dumpling Burnt to Pot,*" Augustan Reprint Society, 1970; (contributor) Ronald C. Rosbottom, editor, *Studies in Eighteenth Century Culture,* Volume V, University of Wisconsin Press, 1976; (contributor) J. T. Fraser, N. Lawrence, and D. Park, editors, *The Study of Time III,* Springer-Verlag, 1978; (editor and author of introduction and notes) *Henry Carey's Dramatic Works,* Garland Publishing, 1980; *Clocks and the Cosmos: Time in Western Life and Thought,* Archon Books, 1980; (editor with Robert Lawrence) *Studies in Robertson Davies' Deptford Trilogy,* E.L.S., 1980. General editor of monograph series, "English Literature Studies," University of Victoria, 1975—. Contributor of more than twenty-five articles to literary journals.

WORK IN PROGRESS: A monograph on clocks and chronology in the early English novel.

SIDELIGHTS: Macey commented: "My research focuses on the way in which technology affected literature and thought in the London of the period 1660-1800. This helps both me and my students to understand how Western technology today influences our lives in modern urban centers."

*　　　*　　　*

MacGORMAN, J(ohn) W(illiam)   1920-

PERSONAL: Born December 26, 1920, in Amherst, Nova Scotia, Canada; son of John R. (a minister) and Doris (Adams) MacGorman; married Ruth Stephens (a supervisor and diagnostician in special education), August 22, 1947; children: Donald Ray, Stephen Ross, Robert Scott, Linda Ruth, Deborah Kay, John Michael. *Education:* Attended Colby College, 1937-38; University of Texas, B.A., 1945; Southwestern Baptist Seminary, B.D., 1948, Th.D., 1956; attended Texas Christian University, 1956-59; Duke University, Ph.D., 1965; postdoctoral study at American University of Beirut, 1966-67. *Religion:* Baptist. *Home:* 34 Chelsea Dr., Fort Worth, Tex. 76134. *Office:* P.O. Box 22000-3A, Fort Worth, Tex. 76122.

CAREER: Ordained Baptist minister, 1943; pastor of Baptist church in Austin, Tex., 1943-45; Southwestern Baptist Seminary, Fort Worth, Tex., instructor, 1948-49, assistant professor, 1950-52, associate professor, 1953-56, professor of New Testament, 1957—, chairman of department, 1959-80, chairman of Biblical Division, 1980—. Pastor of Baptist church in Denton, Tex., 1957-58. Guest professor at Arab Baptist Theological Seminary, 1966-67; conducted lecture tours in South America, summer, 1958, the Bible lands, 1973, 1978, and the Philippines, Malaya, Thailand, Vietnam, Korea, Taiwan, and Hong Kong, 1974; lecturer at Baptist missions in the Bahamas, summer, 1950, West Africa, 1970, and Mexico, Costa Rica, Panama, and Guatemala, 1979. Interim pastor at Baptist church in Tokyo, Japan, 1973-74. *Member:* Society of Biblical Literature. *Awards, honors:* Grant from American Association of Theological Schools, 1959-60.

WRITINGS: Commentary on Galatians, Broadman, 1971; *The Gifts of the Spirit,* Broadman, 1974; *Romans: Everyman's Gospel,* Convention Press, 1976; *Romans and First Corinthians,* Broadman, 1980. Author of church school curriculum material. Contributor of articles and reviews to *Southwestern Journal of Theology.*

WORK IN PROGRESS: Reconstruction of the life and letters of Paul.

SIDELIGHTS: MacGorman told *CA:* "My Christian conversion took place during a twenty-five-month hospitalization in Maine between my freshman and sophomore years of college. At the end of the lengthy hospitalization I was pronounced inoperable (bronchiectasis in all lobes of both lungs). It was advised that I move from northern Maine, with its severe winters, to the southwest. I borrowed eighty-five dollars from a blacksmith deacon in my home church and left for Texas, arriving in October, 1941. It is now almost forty years, one wife, six children, and four grandchildren later, and I'm still inoperable, but thriving. God and Texas have been good to me."

*　　　*　　　*

MacGREGOR, Malcolm D(ouglas)   1945-

PERSONAL: Born February 21, 1945, in Oakland, Calif.; son of Gregor Donal (an accountant) and Bernice M. (Chadbourne) MacGregor; married Mary Margaret Little, February 8, 1964; children: Gregor D. II, George D., Margaret Mary, Gordon Dougall. *Education:* Portland State University, B.S., 1967. *Religion:* Christian. *Office:* Reality Ministries, P.O. Box 82, Gresham, Ore. 97030.

CAREER: Copeland Lumber Co., Portland, Ore., assistant credit manager, 1964; Standard Insurance Co., Portland, systems analyst, 1965-69; Stockman's Life (now American Guaranty), Portland, controller, 1969-70; Coopers & Lybrand, Portland, auditor, 1970-71; State of Oregon, Salem, chief examiner in Insurance Division, 1971-73; accountant with practice in Gresham, 1973—. Member of board of regents of L.I.F.E. Bible College and board of directors of Ministries Unlimited and Realities Ministries. National and international lecturer. Member of Oregon governor's Health Facilities Cost Review Commission. *Military service:* U.S. Naval Reserve, 1963-69.

WRITINGS—All published by Bethany Fellowship: Your Money Matters, 1977; *Financial Planning Guide for Your Money Matters,* 1978; *Training Your Children to Handle Money,* 1980; *Survival Plan for a Small Planet,* 1981; *Money Matters for the Single Parent,* 1982. Contributor to magazines and newspapers.

WORK IN PROGRESS: An elementary school curriculum for teaching money management.

* * *

MACKAY, Constance D'Arcy (?)-1966

PERSONAL: Born in St. Paul, Minn.; died August 21, 1966; daughter of Robert G. and Anne (D'Arcy) Mackay; married Roland Holt (a publishing executive), April 11, 1923 (died, 1931). *Education:* Attended Boston University, 1903-04.

CAREER: Writer. Director of theatrical events for War Camp Community Service, 1918-19; associated with various community theatres, including some presenting productions for children. *Member:* Festival Society of America, P.E.N., Society of American Dramatists and Composers, Pen and Brush Club (New York City), Town Hall Club.

WRITINGS: Costumes and Scenery for Amateurs, Holt, 1915; *How to Produce Children's Plays,* Holt, 1915; *The Little Theatre in the United States,* Holt, 1917; *Patriotic Drama in Your Town: A Manuel of Suggestions,* Holt, 1918; *Play Production in Churches and Sunday Schools,* Playground and Recreation Association of America, 1921; (editor) *Suggestions for the Dramatic Celebration of the Three-Hundredth Anniversary of the Purchase of Manhattan, 1626-1926,* Playground and Recreation Association of America, 1926. Also author of *Rural Drama Bibliography,* Playground and Recreation Association of America.

Published plays: *The House of the Heart, and Other Plays for Children,* Holt, 1909; *The Silver Thread, and Other Folk Plays for Young Children,* Holt, 1910; *The Pageant of Schenectady* (first produced in Schenectady, N.Y., at Union College, May 30, 1912), Gazette Press, 1912; *Patriotic Plays for Young People,* Holt, 1912; *The Historical Pageant of Portland, Maine* (first produced in Portland, 1913), Southworth, 1913; *The Beau of Bath, and Other One-Act Plays of Eighteenth Century Life,* Holt, 1915; *Plays of the Pioneers,* Harper & Brothers, 1915, reprinted, Core Collection Books, 1976; *The Forest Princess, and Other Masques,* Holt, 1916; *Memorial Day Pageant,* Harper & Brothers, 1916; *Franklin,* Holt, 1922; *America Triumphant,* D. Appleton, 1926; *Children's Theatres and Plays,* D. Appleton, *Midsummer Eve: An Outdoor Fantasy,* Samuel French, 1929; *Youth's High-*

way, and Other Plays for Young People, Holt, 1929; *Ladies of the White House,* Baker's Plays, 1948; *A Day at Nottingham: A Festival at Which All the Playgrounds of a City Can Take Part,* National Recreational Association of America, 1952.

Unpublished plays: "The Queen of Hearts" (three-act), first produced in Boston, 1904; "The Pageant of Patriotism," first produced in Brooklyn at Prospect Park, May, 1911; "William of Stratford: Shakespeare's Tercentenary Pageant," first produced in Baltimore, 1916; "Pageant of Sunshine and Shadow," first produced in New York City, 1916; "Patriotic Christmas Pageant," first produced in San Francisco, 1918; "Victory Pageant," first produced in New York City, 1918.

Contributor of plays and articles to periodicals, including *Woman's Home Companion* and *St. Nicholas.**

* * *

MACKAY, Ruddock F(inlay) 1922-

PERSONAL: Born November 15, 1922, in Auckland, New Zealand; son of James George H. and Madge Helena Mackay; married Alison Fairgrieve Allen, August 18, 1956; children: Gillian, Stanley Ruddock, Angus. *Education:* University of New Zealand, B.A., 1945; Oxford University, B.A., 1948, M.A., 1953; University of London, B.A., 1952. *Religion:* Church of England. *Home:* 5 Strathkinness High Rd., St. Andrews, Scotland.

CAREER: Schoolmaster at Sutton Valence School in England, 1949-50, and at Wanganni Collegiate School in New Zealand, 1951-54; lecturer in history at college in Dartmouth, England, 1954-65; University of St. Andrews, St. Andrews, Scotland, began as lecturer, became senior lecturer, 1965-74, reader in modern history, 1974—. *Military service:* Royal New Zealand Navy, 1942-46. *Member:* Historical Association, Navy Records Society. *Awards, honors:* D.Litt. from University of St. Andrews, 1975.

WRITINGS: Admiral Hawke, Clarendon Press, 1965; (contributor) Robin Higham, editor, *Sources of British Military History,* University of California Press, 1971; *Fisher of Kilverstone,* Clarendon Press, 1974; (contributor) Gerald Jordan, editor, *Naval Warfare in the Twentieth Century,* Croom Helm, 1977.

WORK IN PROGRESS: Balfour, Intellectual Statesman, publication by Oxford University Press expected in 1983.

SIDELIGHTS: Mackay wrote: "My motivation is my curiosity about the roles of certain individuals in history. Investigation of the documentary evidence is progressively enlightening and rewarding. Of special interest are the real reasons underlying important decisions."

* * *

MacKENZIE, Rachel 1909-1980

PERSONAL: Born December 2, 1909, in Shortsville, N.Y.; died March 28, 1980, in the Bronx, N.Y. *Education:* Wells College, graduated, 1930.

CAREER: Worked as teacher of English at Ginling College in Nanking, China, College of Wooster in Wooster, Ohio, Radcliffe College in Cambridge, Mass., Wellesley College in Wellesley, Mass., Tufts University, in Medford, Mass., and Breadloaf College in New York; *New Yorker,* New York, N.Y., fiction editor, 1956-79. *Awards, honors:* Blakeslee Award from American Heart Association, 1971.

WRITINGS: Risk (personal account), Viking, 1970; *The Wine of Astonishment* (novel), Viking, 1974.

SIDELIGHTS: Known as a patient and inspired editor of fiction, Rachel MacKenzie worked with such famous writers as Isaac Bachevis Singer, Philip Roth, Saul Bellow, Bernard Malamud, and Harold Brodkey. Upon hearing of her death in 1980 Singer spoke for many when he eulogized: "I consider her the greatest editor who ever lived. I think that American literature and literature generally has lost a giant, one of the last people who understood literature thoroughly from the beginning to the end."

In addition to her role as editor, MacKenzie was also an author in her own right. Her first book, *Risk,* is a personal account of her harrowing experience in undergoing open-heart surgery. A reviewer for *Harper's* declared the work to be "a perfect little piece, flawless in its prose, in its observations and its emotions." Jean Stafford of *Book World* also praised the book, claiming that the depiction of the operation itself "is all but impossible to label save in paradoxes: its understatement is resounding, its amorphous haze coruscates, its handling of the filth of fever and infection and of the multiformity of monstrous pain is regal and virtuous."

MacKenzie's next book, *The Wine of Astonishment,* centers on two spinster sisters living in a small New York community in the early 1920's. "The best thing about the book," commented a writer for the *New Yorker,* "is the author's sharp and touching evocation of the once fiercely binding conventions of American small towns." And a reviewer for *Newsweek* called it "a beautiful piece of work, useful and unpretentious as a fine quilt."

BIOGRAPHICAL/CRITICAL SOURCES: Harper's, May, 1971; *Book World,* May 16, 1971; *Newsweek,* May 27, 1974; *New Yorker,* June 3, 1974.

OBITUARIES: New York Times, March 30, 1980; *Publishers Weekly,* April 11, 1980; *New Yorker,* April 14, 1980; *AB Bookman's Weekly,* May 5, 1980.*

*   *   *

MacKETHAN, Lucinda Hardwick 1945-

PERSONAL: Born September 12, 1945, in Akron, Ohio; daughter of Lewis Eugene (in sales) and Mary E. (a nurse; maiden name, Downton) Hardwick; married John MacKethan (a certified public accountant), August 9, 1969; children: Alex, Karen. *Education:* Hollins College, B.A., 1967; University of North Carolina, M.A., Ph.D., 1974. *Politics:* None. *Religion:* Methodist. *Home:* 2904 Augusta Court, Raleigh, N.C. 27607. *Office:* Department of English, North Carolina State University, Raleigh, N.C. 27607.

CAREER: North Carolina State University, Raleigh, instructor, 1971-74, assistant professor, 1975-79, associate professor of English, 1980—. President of Raleigh Civic Council, 1978. *Member:* Modern Language Association of America, College English Association, South Atlantic Modern Language Association, Junior Women's Club of Raleigh (president, 1977), Phi Beta Kappa.

WRITINGS: The Dream of Arcady, Louisiana State University Press, 1980. Contributor to literature journals.

WORK IN PROGRESS: Freedom and Identity in the American Bildungsroman: Studies in Black and White Authors, completion expected in 1984.

SIDELIGHTS: Lucinda MacKethan wrote: "I am particularly interested in black writers and southern writers, partly because the works of both groups almost always stretch beyond self-concern and use history to illuminate experience. My greatest joy in teaching and studying literature is in the vitality of my subject; it is always new and open to fresh angles of seeing."

MACKIE, Margaret Davidson 1914-

PERSONAL: Born November 12, 1914, in Sydney, Australia; daughter of Alexander (a professor of education, principal of a teacher's college, and writer) and Annie Burnett (a lecturer; maiden name, Duncan) Mackie. *Education:* University of Sydney, B.A., 1937, diploma in education, 1937; Somerville College, Oxford, M.A., 1939. *Home:* 3 Fitzgerald Ave., Armidale, New South Wales 2350, Australia.

CAREER: Teacher of English, history, social studies, and French at state secondary schools in New South Wales, Australia, 1940-49; researcher in England, 1949-51; Armidale College of Advanced Education, Armidale, Australia, lecturer in education, 1951-78; writer, 1978—. *Member:* Australian College of Education (fellow).

WRITINGS: Education in the Inquiring Society, Australian Council for Educational Research, 1966; *Educative Teaching,* Angus & Robertson, 1969; (with Gwen Kelly) *What Is Right?,* Angus & Robertson, 1971; *The Beginning Teacher,* Angus & Robertson, 1973; *Philosophy and School Administration,* University of Queensland Press, 1977. Editor of *Chalk and Cheese.*

WORK IN PROGRESS: An autobiography; research on education in Fiji.

SIDELIGHTS: Margaret Mackie commented: "My parents encouraged me in creative writing from the age of four. My first book grew out of lecture notes I compiled for correspondence students.

"I have visited the United Kingdom five times since my undergraduate days at Oxford. I have visited Fiji four times recently and attended a conference on early childhood education in the South Pacific, where thirteen island countries were represented.

"I am currently studying the philosophy of Hegel and teaching Latin to a young, keen pupil who began his studies with me at the age of six."

*   *   *

MACLEAN, Norman 1902-

PERSONAL: Born December 23, 1902, in Clarinda, Iowa; son of John Norman (a minister) and Clara Evelyn (Davidson) Maclean; married Jessie Burns, September 24, 1931 (deceased); children: Jean Snyder, John Norman. *Education:* Dartmouth College, A.B., 1924; University of Chicago, Ph.D., 1940. *Home:* 5514 South Woodlawn Ave., Chicago, Ill. 60637.

CAREER: Dartmouth College, Hanover, N.H., instructor in English, 1924-26; worked in logging camps and U.S. Forest Service in Montana and Idaho, 1926-28; University of Chicago, Chicago, Ill., instructor, 1930-41, assistant professor, 1941-44, associate professor, 1944-54, professor of English, 1954-73, William Rainey Harper Professor of English, 1963-73, professor emeritus, 1973—, dean of students, 1941-46, chairman of Committee on General Studies, 1956-64. Member of board of directors of Southeast Chicago Commission. *Member:* Modern Language Association of America, Beta Theta Pi, Quadrangle Club. *Awards, honors:* Prize for excellence in undergraduate teaching from University of Chicago, 1932, 1940, and 1973; D.Letters from Montana State University, 1980.

WRITINGS: (Editor with R. S. Crane and others) *Critics and Criticism: Ancient and Modern,* University of Chicago Press, 1952; *A River Runs Through It and Other Stories,* University of Chicago Press, 1976. Contributor of articles and stories to magazines.

WORK IN PROGRESS: A long story based on the Mann Gulch fire of 1949.

SIDELIGHTS: Norman Maclean told *CA:* "At my retirement from teaching when I was seventy I started to write stories, most of them based on my early life in Montana. I was brought up in western Montana and have worked in the woods and have loved them and think I know something about them. I started to work in the U.S. Forest Service when I was fifteen, and I worked in it and in logging camps every summer until I started teaching English at the University of Chicago in 1928. A second part of me is that I continued to teach literature and writing until my retirement at seventy, although always returning for the summer to my cabin in Montana. All the reasons why I started to write stories about Montana are not clear to me, but an important one has to be connected with a lifetime of trying to make companion pieces of my love and knowledge of the woods and of my love and knowledge of literature and writing."

A River Runs Through It contains two novellas and a short story, all set in Montana. Each story is cast as a fictional memoir. John Cawelti commented in *New Republic,* "An older man looks back on some central experiences of his youth: how he learned to fish and how fishing was entangled in his relations with his father and younger brother . . . ; how he worked with a superhuman logger . . . ; and how he became part of a Forest Service crew's summer-end ritual of 'cleaning out the town' and learned something about life and art in the process."

"These stories are in part paeans to the harmonious unity of man and nature," wrote *Newsweek*'s James N. Baker, adding, however, that they are studded with "saloon brawls, foul-mouthed whores and back-alley murders." Maclean's stories "are like memories which have been revolved in the mind throughout a lifetime until their hidden truths have been brought to the surface and revealed," Cawelti noted. "[They] have that magical balance of the particular and the universal that good literature is all about and that so many attempts at Western fiction miss completely. . . . [These] stories are permeated with the monumental landscape of the 'Big Sky Country' observed with a keen documentary eye as well as a sense of the awesome beauty of mountains and rivers. [Maclean] writes brilliantly about work and sport. His pages describing logging, packing, mule-skinning, trail-cutting and fishing are full of precise images which convey as rich a sense of the spiritual form of these activities together that bear comparison with such classics as [Andy] Adams' *Log of a Cowboy.*"

James R. Frakes, writing in the *New York Times Book Review,* observed that Maclean's "voice—acerbic, laconic, deadpan—rings out of a rich American tradition that includes Mark Twain, Kin Hubbard, Richard Bissell, Jean Shepherd and Nelson Algren." Cawelti added: "Humor of the tall-tale variety abounds, side by side with an extravagant comedy of manners detailing the peculiar social rituals of loggers, fishermen and other Western types. Yet underneath the richness of particular details, there runs a wise and compassionate understanding of life and art forged through a lifetime of experience and learning."

BIOGRAPHICAL/CRITICAL SOURCES: Village Voice, March 29, 1976; *New Republic,* May 1, 1976; *New York Review of Books,* May 27, 1976; *Newsweek,* August 30, 1976; *New York Times Book Review,* September 19, 1976; *America,* October 9, 1976.

MACLEOD, Jennifer Selfridge   1929-

PERSONAL: Born November 26, 1929, in London, England; American citizen born abroad; came to the United States in 1940; daughter of H. Gordon (in retailing) and Charlotte (Dennis) Selfridge; married John Alexander Macleod, June 30, 1949 (divorced, 1972); children: Pamela J., Scott G. *Education:* Radcliffe College, B.A., 1949; Columbia University, M.A., 1952, Ph.D., 1958. *Home and office:* Jennifer Macleod Associates, 4 Canoe Brook Dr., Princeton Junction, N.J. 08550.

CAREER: Richardson, Bellows, Henry & Co., New York City, research assistant in psychological test development, 1950-52; McCann-Erickson, Inc., New York City, research assistant in marketing and advertising research, 1952-53, assistant research account executive, 1953-55; Ogilvy, Benson & Mather, Inc., New York City, project director in consumer research, 1955-57; Opinion Research Corp., Princeton, N.J., survey director of consumer and social research, 1958-64, research director, 1964-69, chief psychologist, 1969-71; Rutgers University, New Brunswick, N.J., director of Eagleton Institute of Politics Center for the American Woman and Politics, 1971; writer, lecturer, and consultant, 1972-75; Fidelity Bank, Philadelphia, Pa., vice-president and director of personnel, 1975-78; Jennifer Macleod Associates, Princeton Junction, N.J., founder and principal, 1978—. Vice-president of Fidelco Associates, 1978; founding trustee and chairman of board of directors of University-National Organization for Women Day Nursery, 1969-70; member of board of directors of E. L. Reilly Co., 1968-69, and Philadelphia Business Academy, 1976-78; member of advisory board of National Council for the Public Assessment of Technology, 1975-76.

MEMBER: American Psychological Association, American Society for Personnel Administration, American Civil Liberties Union (member of New Jersey state board of trustees, 1973-76), National Organization for Women (president of central New Jersey chapter, 1969-70), Women's Equity Action League, OD Network, New Jersey Association of Women Business Owners (member of board of directors, 1978-79), Phi Beta Kappa, Sigma Xi.

WRITINGS: Predicting the Responses to Advertising Themes From Sentence Completions or Direct Attitude Questions About an Advertised Product, Advertising Research Foundation, 1958; *"You Won't Do": What Textbooks on U.S. Government Teach High School Girls,* Know, Inc., 1973. Contributor to psychology, personnel administration, and public relations journals. Contributing editor of *EEO Today.*

SIDELIGHTS: Jennifer Macleod commented: "Jennifer Macleod Associates provides management consulting services related to human resources development and personnel matters, social and consumer research, and equal opportunity."

*   *   *

MacMANUS, James
See MacMANUS, Seumas

*   *   *

MacMANUS, Seumas   1869-1960
(Mac, James MacManus)

PERSONAL: Given name listed in some sources as James; born in 1869 in Mountcharles, County Donegal, Ireland; died October 23, 1960, in New York, N.Y. married Anna Johnston (a poet under pseudonym Ethna Carbery), 1901 (died 1902); married Catalina Violante Paez, 1911; children: (second marriage) Mariquita, Patricia. *Education:* Attended Teachers' Training School, Enniskillen, Fermanagh, Ireland. *Residence:* New York, N.Y.; and County Donegal, Ireland.

WRITINGS: The Humours of Donegal, Unwin, 1898; *A Lad of the O'Friels,* McClure, Phillips, 1903; *The Red Poocher,* Funk & Wagnalls, 1903; *Ballads of a Country-boy,* Gill, 1905; *Doctor Kilgannon,* Gill, 1907; *Yourself and the Neighbours,* Devan-Adair, 1914; *Ireland's Case,* Irish Publishing, 1917; *Lo, and Behold, Ye!,* F. Stokes, 1919; *Top o' the Mornin',* F. Stokes, 1920; (with others) *The Story of the Irish Race,* Irish Publishing, 1921, revised edition, Devan-Adair, 1945; *The Donegal Wonder Book,* F. Stokes, 1926; *Bold Blades of Donegal,* F. Stokes, 1935; *The Rocky Road to Dublin,* Macmillan, 1938; *Heavy Hangs the Golden Grain,* Macmillan, 1950; *The Little Mistress of the Eskar Mor,* Gill, 1960.

Story collections: *The Bend of the Road,* Downey, 1898; *In Chimney Corners,* Doubleday & McClure, 1899, reprinted, 1935; *Through the Turf Smoke: The Love, Lore, and Laughter of Old Ireland,* Doubleday & McClure, 1899, reprinted, Books for Libraries, 1969; *The Bewitched Fiddle and Other Irish Tales,* Doubleday & McClure, 1900; *Donegal Fairy Stories,* McClure, Phillips, 1900, reprinted, Dover, 1968; *O, Do You Remember?,* Duffy, 1926; *Dark Patrick,* Macmillan, 1939, reprinted, Books for Libraries, 1971; *The Well o' the World's End,* Macmillan, 1939; *Tales From Ireland,* Evans, 1949; *The Bold Heroes of Hungry Hill and Other Irish Folk Tales,* Pelegrini & Cudahy, 1951; *Hibernian Nights,* introduction by Padraic Colum, Macmillan, 1963.

Other: (Editor) Anna MacManus, *The Four Winds of Eirinn,* Gill, 1902, reprinted, 1927; (author of introduction) MacManus, *The Passionate Hearts,* Isbister, 1903; (editor) Mary Eva Kelly, *Poems,* Gill, 1909; (compiler with Alice Milligan) *We Sang for Ireland: Poems of Ethna Carbery,* Devin-Adair, 1950; *The Townland of Tamney* (one-act play, published together with *The Dream Physician* by Edward Martyn), De Paul University, 1972.

Also author of plays, including "Bong Tong Come to Balriddery," "The Lad from Largymore," "The Leadin' Road to Donegal," "Nabby Harren's Matching," "Orange and Green," "The Resurrection of Dinny O'Dowd," "Rory Wins."

Author of prose and verse under name Mac. Contributor to magazines, including *Harper's, Century, Lippincott's,* and *McClure's.*

BIOGRAPHICAL/CRITICAL SOURCES: New York Herald Tribune Book Review, October 7, 1951.

OBITUARIES: Publishers Weekly, November 7, 1960.*

*   *   *

MacNELLY, Jeff(rey Kenneth) 1947-

PERSONAL: Born September 17, 1947, in New York, N.Y.; son of Clarence Lamont and Ruth Ellen (Fox) MacNelly; married Marguerite Dewey Daniels, July 19, 1969; children: Jeffrey Kenneth, Jr., Frank Daniels. *Education:* Attended University of North Carolina, 1965-69. *Religion:* Episcopal. *Home:* 305 Old Oak Rd., Richmond, Va. 23229. *Office:* 333 East Grace St., Richmond, Va. 23219.

CAREER: Chapel Hill Weekly, Chapel Hill, N.C., cartoonist and staff artist, 1969-70; *Richmond News Leader,* Richmond, Va., cartoonist, 1970—. *Awards, honors:* Pulitzer Prize, 1972 and 1978, for editorial cartoons.

WRITINGS: The Best of Jeff MacNelly, Westover, 1973; *A Political Bestiary,* McGraw, 1979; *The Very First Shoe Book,* Avon, 1979; *The Other Shoe,* Avon, 1980.

SIDELIGHTS: In the three decades following World War II, the art of editorial cartooning was largely in the hands of three masters: Herb Block of the *Washington Post,* Bill Mauldin of the *St. Louis Post-Dispatch,* and Paul Conrad of the *Los Angeles Times.* During the 1970's, however, in the aftermath of Vietnam and Watergate, a new breed of editorial cartoonist came to the fore. According to *Newsweek* magazine, a sharper and more personal use of wit, together with a subtle, deft touch, distinguishes the work of the new generation. The best of these artists includes Jeff MacNelly, a two-time Pulitzer Prize winner whose cartoons appear in 450 newspapers across the country.

"MacNelly's are elaborate, finely drawn sketches," says *Newsweek* "with a distinctive goofy gracefulness, full of detail and humor." A cartoon that appeared at the close of the 1980 Democratic National Convention illustrates the MacNelly style. The personal and political differences between President Jimmy Carter and Senator Edward Kennedy were well publicized throughout the primaries and the convention. In MacNelly's cartoon a fiercely-grinning Carter is reaching out desperately to shake the hand of an aloof, disdainful Kennedy, who offers the president a limp index finger. Looming enormously behind the two antagonists is a sign proclaiming "UNITY."

Cruel or mean-spirited humor is generally not part of MacNelly's style. Some of his colleagues occasionally charge him with "excessive niceness," but MacNelly retorts that there are "many great cartoonists who if they couldn't draw would be hired assassins." Despite the profession's shortcomings, he believes that the cartoonist performs a vital function in American journalism: "Political cartoonists violate every rule of ethical journalism—they misquote, trifle with the truth, make science fiction out of politics and sometimes should be held for personal libel. But when the smoke clears, the political cartoonist has been getting closer to the truth than the guys who write political opinions."

BIOGRAPHICAL/CRITICAL SOURCES: Newsweek, October 13, 1980.

*   *   *

MacPHERSON, Malcolm Cook 1943-

PERSONAL: Born August 23, 1943, in Blackrock, Conn.; son of Andrew Claudot and Gladys (Cook) MacPherson. *Education:* Trinity College, Hartford, Conn., B.A., 1965. *Home and office:* 235 East 49th St., New York, N.Y. 10017. *Agent:* Knox Burger Associates Ltd., 39½ Washington Sq. S., New York, N.Y. 10012.

CAREER: Time, Inc., New York City, trainee, 1966-67; Fairchild Publications, New York City, reporter, 1967; *Seattle* (magazine), Seattle, Wash., associate editor, 1967-68; *Newsweek,* correspondent, 1968-78; free-lance writer, 1978—. *Military service:* U.S. Marine Corps Reserve, 1965-71. *Member:* New York Athletic Club, Muthiaga Country Club (Kenya), Mount Kenya Safari Club, Annabel's (London).

WRITINGS: Protege (novel), Dutton, 1980; *The Lucifer Key* (novel), Dutton, 1981.

WORK IN PROGRESS: The Resurrection of King Kong, an autobiographical novel, completion expected in 1982; *The Tunnel,* a historical novel based on the battle of Messines Ridge in Belgium, 1917, with consequences in the present, publication expected in 1983.

SIDELIGHTS: MacPherson told *CA:* "For ten years as a staff correspondent for *Newsweek,* based in Chicago, Los Angeles, Nairobi, Paris, and London, I covered a wide range of events in America, black Africa, the Middle East, and Europe. With that as training, what I set out to accomplish in starting a career in fiction was to rely heavily on narrative—more or less fictional extentions of my journalistic experience. Now after two novels, as my confidence in managing fiction grows, I am naturally turning more and more to intricate plotting and the development of character, with the hope of eventually replacing exotic setting and circumstance with credible and more interesting inhabitants, while at the same time keeping a practical eye on the commercial requirements of fiction. My choice of subjects—Africa in *Protege* and computers in *Lucifer*—will continue to range where fascination takes me, again drawing sustenance from the roots of my journalistic experience. About my goals, they are long term and include the expectation of a steady command of the medium and genre. Perhaps by my fifth or sixth novel I will approach something close to a work that satisfies me."

*   *   *

MADRUGA, Lenor   1942-

PERSONAL: Born March 22, 1942, in Ontario, Calif.; daughter of Ernest Calvine and Helen B. (Polick) Brawley; married Joseph Madruga (a farmer), February 21, 1965; children: Christianna, Daniella. *Education:* Attended San Francisco University. *Politics:* Republican. *Religion:* Roman Catholic. *Home:* 21790 South Naglee Rd., Tracy, Calif. 95376. *Agent:* John Brockman Associates, Inc., 200 West 57th St., New York, N.Y. 10019. *Office:* 807 Central Ave., Tracy, Calif. 95376.

CAREER: Writer, 1978—. Host of "The Lenor Madruga Show"; guest on radio and television programs. *Awards, honors:* Inspirational book of the year award from Religion in Media, 1979, for *One Step at a Time.*

WRITINGS: One Step at a Time: A Young Woman's Inspiring Struggle to Walk Again (selection of Literary Guild and Doubleday Book Club), McGraw, 1979. Author of "Inside the Inn," a column in *Tracy Press,* 1968-75.

WORK IN PROGRESS: "One Step at a Time," a screenplay; forming a national organization, One Step at a Time, for the benefit of amputees.

SIDELIGHTS: Lenor Madruga's book, *One Step at a Time,* describes her experiences after she discovered she would lose her leg in a hemi-pelvectomy. Her book covers her surgery and recovery, and her determination not to spend the rest of her life in a wheelchair. She has since re-learned how to swim, water ski, skin dive, and dance. Her next goal is to learn to use her artificial leg for running.

Lenor Madruga told *CA:* "At the suggestion of my stepmother, Dr. Muriel James, author of *Born to Win,* and my brother Ernest Brawley, author of *The Rap* and *Selena,* I wrote two chapters and a synopsis of *One Step at a Time* which were accepted by McGraw-Hill. Within six months time I had completed the manuscript. The book was published August 19, 1979.

"My personal reason for writing the book, aside from the fact that I felt it might be good mental therapy, was *outrage!* Outrage that most doctors amputate and then do not follow through with their patients' needs on what adjustments must be made. For example, how does one cope with phantom limb pain, a pain that most doctors do not recognize as a

principal pain? Its very name, 'phantom pain,' suggests delusion or apparition. Doctors prescribe morphine or powerful analgesics for their patients' pain. As a consequence most amputees become notorious dopers.

"Ultimately, how and where does an amputee buy a new leg? It isn't often we see legs displayed to sell in a Sears Roebuck catalog. After intensive research for my book I found that most amputees are almost totally incapacitated with a low self image. The cry is repeatedly heard, 'Who's going to want half a man (or woman) when they could have a whole man?' Hopefully, through my book, the feature film, and the national organization I am forming, we will be able to get every amputee 'back on his feet and back into life.'"

*   *   *

MAGGIN, Elliot S.   1950-

PERSONAL: Born November 14, 1950, in Brooklyn, N.Y.; son of Stanley and Sara (Herman) Maggin. *Education:* Brandeis University, B.A., 1972; Columbia University, M.S., 1974. *Politics:* Democrat. *Religion:* Jewish. *Home and office address:* P.O. Box 564, Campton, N.H. 03223. *Agent:* Felicia Eth, Writers House, Inc., 21 West 26th St., New York, N.Y. 10010.

CAREER: Waterville Valley Ski Educational Foundation, Waterville Valley, N.H., teacher of English, 1977—. Lecturer at Plymouth State College, 1979—. Candidate for New Hampshire House of Representatives, 1980.

WRITINGS: Superman: Last Son of Krypton, Warner Paperback, 1978; *Superman: Miracle Monday,* Warner Paperback, 1981. Editor of *Wig-Wag,* 1979—.

WORK IN PROGRESS: A novel about "a bank robber who was active in the 1970 national student strike"; a historical novel about Francis Parkman, publication by Dell expected in 1981.

SIDELIGHTS: Maggin wrote: "The writers who have probably had the greatest influence on me are Russell Baker, Homer, Thomas Jefferson, Mark Twain, and Kurt Vonnegut.

"I served my 'apprenticeship' writing kids' comic book stories. It generally seems that writers, like politicians, educators, and saints, are a pompous lot. One of the five or six most intelligent and accomplished men I ever knew well, Max Lerner, the historian, told me that no one has a right to be stuffy and he made a good case for this. I don't remember the case, but I do try to remember the lesson. I had lots of fun and learned most of what I know about writing to an audience when I was writing Superman, Batman, and Wonder Woman. Sometimes, if I get arrogant, somebody is likely to read this and remind me. I think having a favorite bubble burst every morning is a good way to stay young."

AVOCATIONAL INTERESTS: Skiing, horses.

*   *   *

MAGNUSON, Edward F.   1926-

PERSONAL: Born February 18, 1926, in St. Cloud, Minn.; divorced; children: two daughters, one son. *Education:* University of Minnesota, B.A. *Home:* 41 Perry St., Apt. 5A, New York, N.Y. 10014. *Office: Time,* Time-Life Bldg., Rockefeller Center, New York, N.Y. 10020.

CAREER/WRITINGS: Time, New York, N.Y., senior writer, 1960—. *Military service:* U.S. Navy, 1944-46 and 1950-51. *Member:* Phi Beta Kappa.

SIDELIGHTS: Magnuson has written more than eighty cover stories for *Time* magazine.

MAGORIAN, James 1942-

PERSONAL: Born April 24, 1942, in Palisade, Neb.; son of Jack and Dorothy (Gorthey) Magorian. *Education:* University of Nebraska, B.S., 1965; Illinois State University, M.S., 1969; attended Oxford University, 1971, and Harvard University, 1973. *Residence:* Helena, Mont. *Office:* 1225 North 46th St., Lincoln, Neb. 68503.

CAREER: Writer.

WRITINGS—Books of poems: *Almost Noon*, Ibis Press, 1969; *Ambushes and Apologies*, Ibis Press, 1970; *The Garden of Epicurus*, Ibis Press, 1971; *The Last Reel of the Late Movie*, Third Eye Press, 1972; *Distances*, Ibis Press, 1972; *Mandrake Root Beer*, Cosmic Wheelbarrow Chapbooks, 1973; *The Red, White, and Blue Bus*, Samisdat Press, 1975; *Bosnia and Herzegovina*, Third Eye Press, 1976; *Alphabetical Order*, Amphion Press, 1976; *Two Hundred Push-Ups at the Y.M.C.A.*, Specific Gravity Publications, 1977; *The Ghost of Hamlet's Father*, Peradam Publishing House, 1977; *Safe Passage*, Stone Country Press, 1977; *Notes to the Milkman*, Black Oak Press, 1978; *Phases of the Moon*, Black Oak Press, 1978; *Piano Tuning at Midnight*, Laughing Bear Press, 1979; *Revenge*, Samisdat Press, 1979; *The Night Shift at the Poetry Factory*, Broken Whisker Studio Press, 1979; *Spiritual Rodeo*, Toothpaste Press, 1980; *Ideas for a Bridal Shower*, Black Oak Press, 1980; *Tap Dancing on a Tightrope*, Laughing Bear Press, 1981.

Children's books: *School Daze*, Peradam Publishing House, 1978; *Seventeen Percent*, Black Oak Press, 1978; *The Magic Pretzel*, Black Oak Press, 1979; *Ketchup Bottles*, Peradam Publishing House, 1979; *Imaginary Radishes*, Black Oak Press, 1979; *Plucked Chickens*, Black Oak Press, 1980.

Contributor of poems to more than one hundred fifty literary magazines, including *American Poet*, *Ararat*, *Bitterroot Journal*, *Haiku Journal*, *Kansas Quarterly*, *New Earth Review*, and *Spoon River Quarterly*.

SIDELIGHTS: James Magorian told *CA:* "My children's stories and satirical poems deal with everyday obsessions and absurdities that I find both amusing and horrifying. My other poems reflect rural Nebraska and Montana where I have lived most of my life. These are simple poems of place."

* * *

MAIBAUM, Richard 1909-

PERSONAL: Born May 26, 1909, in New York, N.Y.; son of Jerome (an electrical engineer) and Claire (Friedman) Maibaum; married Sylvia Kamion (a teacher and musician), December 1, 1935; children: Matthew, Paul. *Education:* Attended New York University, 1927-29; University of Iowa, B.A., 1931, M.A., 1932. *Home:* 826 Greentree Rd., Pacific Palisades, Calif. 90272. *Agent:* Herb Tobias Associates, 1901 Avenue of the Stars, Los Angeles, Calif. 90067.

CAREER: Writer and producer. Worked as actor with New York Shakespearean Repertory Co., 1933; screenwriter and producer of motion pictures for Paramount Pictures, 1945-51. Visiting lecturer at University of Iowa, 1954-55. *Military service:* U.S. Army, 1942-46; became lieutenant colonel; head of Industrial Relations Film Division and chairman of Films for Defense; director of Signal Corps Photographic Center Combat Film Division. *Member:* Writers Guild of America, Screen Writers Guild, Phi Beta Kappa. *Awards, honors:* Emmy nomination for best original teleplay from Academy of Television Arts and Sciences, 1955, for "Fearful Decision"; Edgar Allen Poe Award from Mystery Writers of America, 1964, for "Goldfinger," and 1965, for "Thunderball"; Screen Writers Guild nomination for best comedy, 1977, for "The Spy Who Loved Me."

WRITINGS—Published plays: *Birthright* (three-act; first produced in New York at Forty-Ninth Street Theatre, 1933), Samuel French, 1934; *See My Lawyer* (first produced on Broadway at Biltmore Theatre, September, 1939), Dramatists Play Service, 1939; *Ransom*, Samuel French, 1963. Also author of *Addie Sails Away* (first produced in Evanston, Ill., 1934), Row Peterson.

Unpublished plays: "The Tree" (two-act), first produced in New York City at Parklane Theatre, 1932; "Tirade" (three-act), first produced in Putney, Vt., at A.R.P. Theatre, July, 1934; "Sweet Mystery of Life" (three-act), first produced on Broadway at Shubert Theatre, October, 1935; "A Moral Entertainment" (three-act), first produced in Iowa City, Iowa, at University Theatre, 1936; "Middletown Mural" (three-act), first produced in Cleveland, Ohio, at Cleveland Playhouse, 1941; "The Paradise Question" (three-act), first produced in New Haven, Conn., 1954.

Screenplays: (With Maurice Rapf) "We Went to College," Metro-Goldwyn-Mayer (MGM), 1936; (with Charles Brackett and Cyril Hume) "Live, Love, and Learn," MGM, 1937; (with Hume and Rapf) "They Gave Him a Gun," MGM, 1937; (with Hume) "The Bad Man of Brimstone," MGM, 1938; (with Leonard Praskins) "Stable Mates," MGM, 1938; (with Gertrude Purcell) "The Lady and the Mob," Columbia, 1939; (with Albert Duffy and Harry Segall) "Coast Guard," Columbia, 1939.

(With Sy Bartlett and Dwight Taylor) "The Amazing Mr. Williams," Columbia, 1940; (with Hume and E. E. Paramore) "Twenty Mule Team," MGM, 1940; (with Harry Ruskin) "The Ghost Comes Home" (adapted from the play by Georg Kaiser), MGM, 1940; (with Sig Herzig and Beirne Lay, Jr.) "I Wanted Wings" (adapted from the book by Lay), Paramount, 1941; "Ten Gentlemen From West Point," Twentieth Century-Fox, 1942; (with Hume) "The Great Gatsby" (adapted from the novel by F. Scott Fitzgerald), Paramount, 1949; "Song of Surrender," Paramount, 1949.

(With Bartlett and Frank Nugent) "The Paratrooper" (adapted from the novel by Hillary St. George Saunders, *The Red Beret*), Columbia, 1954 (released in England as "The Red Beret"); (with Hume) "Ransom" (adapted from the teleplay by Hume and Maibaum, "Fearful Decision"), MGM, 1956; (with Hume) "Bigger Than Life" (adapted from the nonfiction article by Berton Roueche), Twentieth Century-Fox, 1956; (with Bryan Forbes) "Cockleshell Heroes" (adapted from the story by George Kent), Columbia, 1956; "Zarak" (adapted from the novel by A. J. Bevan), Columbia, 1956; (with Terence Young) "Tank Force," Columbia, 1958; (with Willard Willingham) "The Battle at Bloody Beach," Twentieth Century-Fox, 1961.

Screenplays for "James Bond" series; all based on the character in novels by Ian Fleming; all released by United Artists: (With Johanna Harwood and Berkely Mather) "Dr. No," 1963; "From Russia, With Love," 1964; (with Paul Dehn) "Goldfinger," 1964; (with John Hopkins) "Thunderball," 1965; "On Her Majesty's Secret Service," 1969; (with Tom Mankiewicz) "Diamonds Are Forever," 1971; (with Mankiewicz) "The Man With the Golden Gun," 1975; (with Mankiewicz) "The Spy Who Loved Me," 1977.

Teleplays: (With Hume) "Fearful Decision," 1955; "Jarrett," 1975; "She," 1979.

Contributor to periodicals, including *Cosmopolitan*, *Esquire*, and *Playboy*.

WORK IN PROGRESS: Another James Bond screenplay, "For Your Eyes Only."

SIDELIGHTS: Maibaum is probably best known for his screenplays in the "James Bond" series. Bond is a British secret agent in possession of a double zero—007—agent number that grants him license to kill. As the film series has developed, Bond's assignments have grown into world-saving tasks. In "Goldfinger," Bond saves the American economy by thwarting Goldfinger's efforts to empty the Fort Knox gold supply. In "The Spy Who Loved Me," Bond must contend with both a neo-Nazi bent on destroying the world by initiating a nuclear war, and a vengeful Soviet agent whose lover was killed by Bond. As in most of the previous Bond films, "The Spy Who Loved Me" concludes with Bond saving the world, killing the villian, and seducing the once-dangerous woman. In its seventeen-year stretch, the Bond series has proven to be both one of the most durable and most popular continuing sagas on film.

CA INTERVIEW

CA interviewed Richard Maibaum on April 8, 1980, by phone at his home in Los Angeles, Calif.

CA: How did your career as a screenwriter evolve?

MAIBAUM: I was born in New York and went to New York University on a prep school prize scholarship. After that I studied dramatic art at the University of Iowa, where I was elected to the honorary drama society and Phi Beta Kappa. I owe a great deal to a man named E. C. Mabie, who was head of the speech and drama department at the University of Iowa. When I went out there from New York, I was about twenty years old, and I found him a very sympathetic man. He tore the curricula apart for me and I worked very hard. I was there for two and a half years getting my bachelor's and master's degrees, and in that time I wrote twelve plays, seven of which were put on there. One of them was "The Tree," one of the first anti-lynching plays ever written. Ira Marion put it on in New York, and that was my first Broadway play. I was a graduate student then.

Then I came back to New York and went with the Shakespearean Repertory Theatre and at the same time continued to write plays. I had two more Broadway plays at that time. One of them, "Birthright," was one of the first anti-Nazi plays. That was in 1933. I didn't wait until six million Jews were killed before I wrote an anti-Nazi play. I had been to Europe as a tutor and companion for two younger boys, and I had met in London the first refugees from Hitler's Germany. This was a composite of their stories. I wrote the play coming back on the boat. The other was "Sweet Mystery of Life," a comedy, a takeoff on the insurance business. It was produced by Herman Shumlin, and on the strength of it I got my first contract to come to Hollywood. I came in the December, 1935, batch of writers to Metro-Goldwyn-Mayer; at that time there were 110 writers under contract at MGM. For the next six or seven years I worked in Hollywood as a writer and also wrote the play "See My Lawyer," which was produced in New York by George Abbott and directed by Ezra Stone. Milton Berle played the lead. It ran all season and then was bought by Universal. "Sweet Mystery of Life" had been bought by Warner Brothers; they made "Golddiggers of 1937" out of it.

When the war came along I went into the army and was commissioned a captain. By the time I left I was a lieutenant colonel. I was head of the Industrial Relations Film Division, and chairman of the intragovernment agency, Films for Defense, which was marshaling all the motion-picture forces of the government to bring to the workers the message of their importance in producing the stuff to win the war. I worked out of Washington until I went to the Signal Corps Photographic Center on Long Island, where I became director of the Combat Films Division. One of my five sections was the Historical Films Branch. We made a six-hundred-reel history of the war. It's at West Point now. There was also the Special Projects Branch which made propaganda films and documentaries.

Toward the end of the war, Paramount asked me to become a writer-producer when I returned. And I did. I went back to Hollywood in 1945 and stayed at Paramount until 1951. I produced nine films there, three of which I wrote.

When I left, I kicked around for two years and then became associated with Albert R. Broccoli and Irving Allen. They had a company in England called Warwick, and for the next three or four years, off and on, I wrote films for them, including "Red Beret," "Cockleshell Heroes," and "Tank Force." It was funny, an American doing all these films about the British armed forces. I then came back to this country and worked in television. "Fearful Decision," which I wrote for television with Cyril Hume, was nominated for the Emmy Award for best screenplay. I also was executive producer of MGM-TV for two and a half years.

I left there because I've always considered myself basically a writer. There was a writers' strike in 1960. MGM had sold several series to various networks and had to get the scripts ready, but the only way to do that was to hire scabs under the table, and I refused to do it. I just had to make a choice. My heart still lay with the writers—always has and always will. I was on the board of directors that got them their first minimum basic contract from the producers. By then Cubby Broccoli had made a deal with Harry Saltzman to do the James Bond pictures together. He called me up from England and said, "How would you like to come over and write the first one for us?" We had talked about this five or six years earlier, but at that time the novels were more subject to censorship. And if you couldn't make them the way they were written, you lost a lot of the zap and the fun. But censorship had relaxed in the meantime. So I went back to England. After some legal problems with "Thunderball,' we decided to write "Dr. No," which was a very good thing, as it turned out. And the rest is history. The Bond films have grossed over a billion dollars; one out of every four people in the *world* has seen a Bond picture. I did most of them, writing other things here in Hollywood during that same period, and I'm now working on "For Your Eyes Only," my ninth job on a Bond picture. It's difficult, because we've used up all the novels. This one is based on bits and pieces of some of Ian Fleming's short stories.

CA: Why do you think the world was so ready for James Bond?

MAIBAUM: You have to go right back to the Fleming books. The first five or six were marvelous. Bond was a kind of anti-establishment guy, a villain-hero. He had a license to kill; he was a brutal man. And he fitted into the protest in a crazy kind of way—against the establishment, although he was very much establishment in his conspicuous consumerism, his love of luxuries. He was a universal escape figure. Incidentally, for Fleming, too, who fancied himself as James Bond, which was a complete sublimation of the life he was living. Then, too, the pictures were done very well. Broccoli and Saltzman were marvelous producers who put together a great team: the art direction, the special effects, casting, the writing, music—everything was top drawer.

One of the other great reasons for the success of the Bonds, I think, is the personality of Sean Connery. Fleming's choice of an actor for James Bond would have been David Niven, you see. But he was tried in "Casino Royale," the only Fleming novel that Broccoli and Saltzman didn't have the movie rights on, and it fell on its face. It was made as a kind of spoof of the Bond pictures, and you can't spoof a spoof. Connery has great talent as an actor and is an intelligent man. And he has a marvelous sense of irony, which gave the part depth and interest. As far as the American audiences are concerned, he wasn't a pukka sahib kind of Englishman. He was a Scotch Irishman, you know—tougher and rougher. We used to make seventy-five percent of our grosses in the United States when Sean was playing James Bond. Now we only make about thirty percent here, and seventy percent overseas. Most people think—and I agree with them—that it's because of Roger Moore, who is a skillful performer and a charming person, witty and so on, but Americans don't react to him as wholeheartedly as they did to Sean Connery.

Then the whole thing got a terrific boost with President Kennedy becoming a fan of Ian's novels. He loved the stories. The books had sold maybe two or three million worldwide, and there was a kind of Ian Fleming cult. But after about the fifth picture, they'd sold forty million. It was the pictures that brought such success for the books. We had to bring a lot more humor into the pictures than the books had. Fleming didn't quite understand what we were doing. He said to me once, "You know, the films are so much funnier than my books." He didn't quite understand why, and I didn't enlighten him. He took them very seriously, his books. But some of them are minor pop masterpieces, and they just coincided with what the public wanted at that time.

CA: Many of the critics didn't like the 1974 "The Great Gatsby." How would you compare it with the earlier version, for which you were the co-author of the screenplay and producer?

MAIBAUM: Well, I did the screenplay with Cyril Hume, who had been a 1920's writer and was a personal friend of Fitzgerald's. When we wrote the screenplay, we kept asking ourselves, "Would Scott approve?" I'd met Fitzgerald through Hume when we were writing together, and we came to an understanding of what Fitzgerald was all about. I'm not sure that the authorities on Fitzgerald would agree, but our concept was that Fitzgerald always wrote Faust. A man wants something and he makes a deal with the devil in some form to get it. He does and it turns to dust and ashes. I can draw you that parallel all through Fitzgerald's books. In *Tender Is The Night* Dick Diver is bringing a girl back to mental health, but he feels she'll never really be free until she's free of him, so he pushes her to another man. Then he discovers that she was his raison d'etre, his job in life, and he's the one that's left old and useless.

With the 1974 "Gatsby," nobody ever stopped to think, "What is this about?" All the trappings didn't mean a damn thing. Here's Robert Redford, a wonderful actor and a perfect choice for Gatsby, but nobody told him what the part was about. And poor Mia Farrow, whose father made a picture I produced called "The Big Clock" (one of my favorite films, with Charles Laughton and Ray Milland), didn't have a glimmer of an idea what it was all about. *The Great Gatsby? The Great Gatsby* is America selling out its soul for old Dan Cody's philosophy of get the money and you get

everything. It's as simple as that. Of course, we had to make great concessions at the time. For two years we fought the censors; they opposed the making of the picture. It dealt with illicit love, an unpunished murder, flaming youth, jazz, everything that they were against. We had to make certain concessions, and I bitterly regret that, but even so, enough was left to make the point. Fitzgerald was not a moralist; he told a story. But in the last part of the novel *The Great Gatsby,* when Nick is returning home and he looks out the window and thinks about the light on Daisy's dock—the green light that had beckoned Gatsby—and how it ever seemed to recede, there's a phrase: "where the dark fields of the republic rolled on under the night." You know a man who writes a phrase like that is thinking about America and what was happening to it. Everything has got to be about something; everything has got to make a point. And I just didn't know what the hell the point of the 1974 "Gatsby" film was.

CA: You've seen a lot of changes in movies over the years. Which ones do you like?

MAIBAUM: I wrote in a kind of straitjacket in the old days. For instance, I wrote a screenplay with Cyril Hume called "The Bad Man of Brimstone," which was one of the first funny Westerns, with Wallace Beery. Beery had been playing silly parts, parts in which he had to be a kind of childish bastard. He played a bandit in "The Bad Man of Brimstone," and the new sheriff was really his son and didn't know it. This gave Beery problems, because he couldn't be tough with his own son and run him off the way he had run everybody else off. He arranged to cook up a story that the son would come into a legacy if he went away to become a lawyer. Trigger Bill (the part that was played by Beery) was on the road waiting to say goodbye to him, and he gave him a Polonius speech in reverse, saying, "You know, son, before you go, I want to tell you, never stand up to a man in a fair fight—always go around and shoot him in the back. Never drink water; there's germs in it. Never have nothing to do with a decent woman; they hog-tie you somethin' terrible"—all of which was cut because Beery was too lazy to learn it. He said, "Aw, I can't say all that." Then, as the boy drove away, our stage direction indicated that Trigger Bill should wave a kind of "bye-bye" at him. Censorship came back and said, believe it or not, "Care must be taken that no homosexual relationship is indicated by this gesture." Those were the conditions under which people worked in 1937 or '38. You couldn't show a married couple in bed together; they had to be in separate beds. No reclining embraces or kisses. Everything was verboten.

It's good that we've broken through that and you can write about anything you want. Although I think it's abused artistically. People like Sam Peckinpah, I think, are way, way out with their excessive violence. You know, the Bond pictures, strangely enough, are not violent pictures and not very sexy. Never any frontal nudity or anything of that sort. We've said "hell" and "damn" and "crap" and stuff like that once or twice, but nothing worse. Everything is done indirectly. We never smash anybody in the face with a chain. The producers have the good taste to avoid that.

What I *don't* like is that, from a production standpoint, they pile so many people onto the upper echelon. And to a certain extent (now I'm going to say something that's going to get me in trouble) I think the directors have much too much power these days. They absolutely run the show. If you don't like what they do, the only alternative as a producer is to fire them. And if you do that, it costs a tremendous amount of money, you have to settle the contract, you've got to bring in somebody else, and the picture gets the reputation of going badly. There are many great directors, but there are also guys who are only traffic cops and keep the actors from running into each other. They have no way of evoking a real performance from somebody. The great ones can and do. But this is the age of the director. My only regret in life is that when John Farrow, who was originally going to direct "The Great Gatsby," walked off the job over a casting dispute, I could have said, "I'd like to direct this." At that time I was riding high and could have swung it, I think. But the thing that you need most as a director is what we used to call in the army a command presence. You have to be able to boss people around and make them do what you want them to do. I'm not that kind of person, really.

CA: Is there anything else you haven't tried that you'd like to try?

MAIBAUM: Well, we'll skip some of the obvious implications of that question! First of all, I'd like to break eighty in golf. I'm an avid golfer. And I'm afraid I won't, because I started the game too late—although I *did* have a hole in one. Yes, there are things I'd like to do, pictures I'd like to make, subjects I'd like to cope with. I don't know if I'd still like to direct. It's a terrible drain on one's energy, you know. And as I've said, being a director, you need lots of energy, guts, brass, and drive. There have been exceptions to that, such as Fred Zinneman. He's the sweetest man in the world and nothing like that. He prevails just by knowing better than anybody. That's the other way a director can get by. But usually they're pretty tough guys. When I started out, I wanted to write beautiful plays and make beautiful pictures. I still want to be associated with that sort of thing.

AVOCATIONAL INTERESTS: Golf, bridge.

—*Interview by Jean W. Ross*

*   *   *

MAIR, (Alexander) Craig 1948-

PERSONAL: Born May 3, 1948, in Glasgow, Scotland; son of George B. (a medical doctor and author) and Trudi (Clement) Mair; married Anne Olizar (a teacher), August 1, 1970; children: Lorna, George, Graeme. *Education:* University of Stirling, B.A., 1971. *Politics:* "I'm a patriotic Scot, but not necessarily a Nationalist." *Religion:* Church of Scotland. *Home:* Weaver Cottage, 10 Regent St., Kincardine-on-Forth, Fife FK10 4NN, Scotland.

CAREER: High school teacher of history in Falkirk, Scotland, 1972-80; Graeme High School, Falkirk, assistant principal teacher of history, 1980—. Archivist of local history group, Kincardine-on-Forth, 1977—. *Member:* British Institute of Archaeology, Scottish P.E.N., Scottish Lecture Agency.

WRITINGS—All published by John Murray: *A Time in Turkey,* 1973; *A Star for Seamen: The Stevenson Family,* 1978; *The Lighthouse Boy* (juvenile), 1981; *Britain at War 1914-19* (high school textbook), 1981.

WORK IN PROGRESS: Further historical novels for children; preparation of a biography of David Angus, a nineteenth-century Scottish railway engineer.

SIDELIGHTS: Mair told *CA:* "As a youth I had many stimuli to write. My father and uncle (Alistair Mair) were both well-known Scottish authors, columnists, contributors, and radio and television people. Through them I also met many more Scottish writers. They all encouraged me to write *something.*

"I also had plenty of travel all over Europe, and until my own family arrived I still had ideas of following in my father's very prolific travel-writer's footsteps. I lived in a remote Turkish village from 1967 to 1968 and described this in *A Time in Turkey;* but travel writing seems to have been killed by television recently.

"I've enjoyed a life of varying cultures, I suppose. A year in Turkey was obviously one example, but in addition, my mother is Dutch, which introduced me to a different culture, and my wife is half-Polish, which continues to open new interests for me. I speak fair French, German, Dutch, and Turkish, but Polish has defeated me so far, except for common phrases. The Scottish culture can be very insular, so these outside contributions to my life have enriched it and probably helped my writing.

"Another lasting enthusiasm has been music. I played for years in a Scottish pipe band, but also in a rock group, and more recently in a folk group. I still give lunchtime guitar lessons at the school where I teach history. I also enjoy most other kinds of music, including some opera and the more melodic classical composers. I find piano playing the best unwinder at the end of a day or when problems pile up. I don't smoke, so the piano relaxes me instead. I often break my writing to play some paino. This relaxes me when I can't find the right word, whereas walks with my dog help me to plan my work.

"If I live by a philosophy, it is a belief in developing your talents and finding your gifts. I help school pupils find what skills they may have in sports, or music, or in studying history. Hopefully I will stimulate my own children fully when they need it. And in writing I will hopefully find my own niche one day. Right now I'm still looking around for what I can do best, or enjoy most.

"My first book was a travel book, but I don't see this genre as a developing field. An interest in Scotland, history, and biography then led to my second book, *A Star for Seamen,* but finding another good biography subject has been difficult. Publishers only want sure-fire hits, but almost all well-known names have been covered, and mostly re-covered, too. I still research for biographical work, and I hope to produce the occasional book over the years, but I don't expect to become a full-time biographer.

"My most recent book is for children. *The Lighthouse Boy* is a historical novel set in Scotland, and offered me the chance to combine storytelling, history, research, some biography, and other varying stimuli all in one genre. I'm a father and a teacher, well used to telling tales from the past, especially those of my own heritage. I imagine I shall pursue this kind of writing in the future. It may not bring any critical acclaim or literary praise, but it will give me plenty of satisfaction. If I'm lucky I'll eventually develop into a regular teller of Scottish tales.

"My advice to young readers would be, 'Never let your imagination and your curiosity die.' Chidren should always ask questions, try new experiences, go places, do things, try things, absorb, listen, and always be ready to learn. The world is too full of unimaginative, uncreative, dull-witted, narrow-visioned, bored, and boring people."

AVOCATIONAL INTERESTS: Rugby, cricket, hill-walking, camping, swimming, sailing.

*   *   *

MALINA, Judith 1926-

PERSONAL: Born June 4, 1926, in Kiel, Germany (now

West Germany); daughter of Max (a rabbi) and Rose (an actress; maiden name, Zamora) Malina; married Julian Beck (a writer, director, producer, actor, and stage designer), October 30, 1948; children: Garrick Maxwell Beck, Isha Manna Beck. *Education:* Attended New School for Social Research. *Politics:* "Pacifist Anarchist." *Religion:* Jewish. *Home:* 800 West End Ave., New York, N.Y. 10025. *Office:* The Living Theatre, Via Gaeta 79, Rome, Italy 00185.

CAREER: Actress, producer, and director. Made acting debut in August, 1945; performer in plays, including "By Any Other Name," 1945, "The Flies," 1947, "The Dog Beneath the Skin," 1947, and "Ethan Frome," 1947; The Living Theatre, New York, N.Y., and Europe, co-founder, producer, actress, and director, 1947—; actress in plays for The Living Theatre, including "The Thirteenth God," 1951, "Beyond the Mountains," 1951, "Ladies Voices," 1952, "The Age of Anxiety," 1954, "Orpheus," 1954, "The Idiot King," 1954, "Tonight We Improvise," 1955, "Phaedra," 1955, "The Young Disciple," 1955, "Many Loves," 1959, "The Cave at Machpelah," 1959, "The Women of Trachis," 1960, "The Election," 1960, "The Mountain Giants," 1961, "In the Jungle of Cities," 1961, "Man Is Man," 1962, "Frankenstein," 1969, "Antigone," 1969, and "Prometheus," 1979; director of plays for The Living Theatre, including "The Thirteenth God," 1951, "Doctor Faustus Lights the Lights," 1951, "Ladies Voices," 1952, "Desire Trapped by the Tail," 1952, "Sweeny Agonistes," 1952, "The Age of Anxiety," 1954, "The Spook Sonata," 1954, "Orpheus," 1954, "The Connection," 1959, "The Devil's Mother," 1960, "The Marrying Maiden," 1960, "In the Jungle of Cities," 1960, "The Apple," 1961, "The Brig," 1963, "The Maids," 1965, "Frankenstein," 1965, and "Masse Mensch," 1980. Actress in motion pictures, including "Flaming Creatures," 1962, "Living and Glorious," 1965, "Amore, Amore," 1966, "Wheel of Ashes," 1967, "Le Compromis," 1968, "Etre Libre," 1968, "Paradise Now," 1969, and "Dog Day Afternoon," 1974.

MEMBER: American Federation of Television and Radio Artists, American Guild of Musical Artists, Actors' Equity Association, Screen Actors Guild. *Awards, honors:* Lola D'Annunzio Award, 1959, for outstanding contribution to Off-Broadway theatre; Page One award from Newspaper Guild, 1960; Obie Award from *Village Voice*, 1960, for "The Connection," 1964, for direction and production of "The Brig," 1969, for acting in "Antigone," 1969, for best production for "Frankenstein," and 1975, for sustained achievement; Creative Arts Theatre Citation from Brandeis University, 1961; Grand Prix de Theatre des Nations, 1961; Paris Critics Circle medallion, 1961; Prix de L'Universite, 1961; New England Theatre Conference award, 1962; Olympio Prize, 1967, for "Antigone."

WRITINGS: Conversations With Julian Beck and Judith Malina, edited by Jean-Jacques Lebel, Belfond, 1969; (with husband, Julian Beck, and Aldo Rostagno) *We, the Living,* Ballantine, 1970; (with Beck) *Paradise Now: A Collective Creation of the Living Theatre,* Random House, 1971; (with Beck) *The Legacy of Cain: Three Pilot Projects; A Collective Creation of The Living Theatre,* Belibaste, 1972; (with Beck) *Frankenstein: A Collective Creation of the Living Theatre,* La Fiacola, 1972; *The Enormous Despair* (memoirs), Random House, 1972; (with Beck) *Seven Meditations on Political Sado-Masochism: A Collective Creation of The Living Theatre,* Fag Rag, 1973; (contributor) John Lahr and Jonathan Price, editors, *The Great American Life Show,* Bantam, 1974; (with Imke Buchholz) *Theatre Means Living,*

Trikont, 1978. Also author of *Theatre Diaries: Brazil and Bologna,* Theatre Papers.

Co-author of plays with Beck, including "Frankenstein," "Paradise Now," "Six Public Acts," and "The Money Tower."

WORK IN PROGRESS: New York Diaries, 1947-1950, publication expected in 1982; *Living in the Streets,* with Beck, publication expected in 1982; *Brazil Diary, 1970-1971,* publication expected in 1983; *Antigone,* a translation of Brecht's play, Hoelderlin, for Random House.

SIDELIGHTS: The Living Theatre, founded by Malina and her husband, Julian Beck, in 1947, is the forerunner of avant-garde theatre in the United States. The company's use of unconventional methods, nudity, and profanity have made The Living Theatre a controversial group and has attracted the wrath of governments in the United States, Europe, and South America. While performing in Brazil in 1971, the entire company was arrested and jailed for more than a month. The Living Theatre's aim to heighten the "conscious awareness among the poorest of the poor" was not appreciated by the Brazilian dictatorship. Beck, however, did not view his incarceration as a total loss. He exclaimed in his cell that "this is theatre!" Malina disagreed: "We came to help the cause of liberation in the third world and got put into jail. We came to perform for the arts festival, and our only scene was our exit."

BIOGRAPHICAL/CRITICAL SOURCES: Yale/Theatre, spring, 1969; Renfreu Neff, *The Living Theatre USA,* Bobbs-Merrill, 1970; *The Living Book of The Living Theatre,* Greenich House, 1971; *Newsweek,* August 16, 1971; Pierre Biner, *The Living Theatre,* Horizon Press, 1972; Karen Malpede, *People's Theatre in Amerika,* Drama Books, 1972.

* * *

MANDEL, Sally Elizabeth 1944-

PERSONAL: Born June 20, 1944, in Oneida, N.Y.; daughter of Hamilton (a business executive) and Florence (Boyd) Allen; married Barry Mandel (a lawyer), August 17, 1967. *Education:* Attended University of Hull, 1964-65; University of Rochester, B.A., 1966. *Residence:* New York, N.Y. *Agent:* Peter Lampack Agency, Inc., 551 Fifth Ave., Suite 2015, New York, N.Y. 10017.

CAREER: McCall's, New York City, proofreader, 1966-67; D.C. Heath & Co., Boston, Mass., editorial assistant, 1967-68; Teradyne, Boston, secretary, 1968-69; Experiment in International Living, New York City, part-time secretary, 1969-71; secretary in law firm, 1971-73; secretary to soap opera writer, 1973-74; writer, 1974—. *Member:* Writers Room.

WRITINGS: Change of Heart (novel), Delacorte, 1980; *Quinn* (novel), Delacorte, 1981.

WORK IN PROGRESS: Book and lyrics for musical comedy, "Messages."

SIDELIGHTS: Sally Mandel told *CA:* "I began writing as a way to finance pet projects, and assumed I would never be able even to pay for my typewriter ribbons. But novel writing, much to my surprise, turned out to be fun (also agonizing, exhausting, and profoundly frustrating). Now that I am most of the way through novel number two, I can state that for me, writing is a cinematic experience, as if I am describing a movie spinning away inside my head. I hope to achieve the kind of writing that most satisfies me as a reader: writing with a sharp visual impact. I am not much interested in plot *per se.* Drama, for me, emerges out of the tension between carefully crafted layers: the things people say, what they actually mean, and finally, what they do. These elements are almost always in conflict with one another, and out of this conflict explodes enormous excitement. I want to write books that introduce the reader to lively, compelling people who will be remembered long after the last page.

"I am a descendant of the Oneida Community. I believe my connection with this experimental utopian society has had a substantial impact on me as a person and a writer. I grew up among people who had tried to achieve a paradise on earth. They were tragically disappointed, but they were also full of humor and a kind of nobility. Literature, art, and music were always considered more important than a new-model car or fashionable clothes. As children, we were encouraged to write plays and music to be performed regularly for the community.

"I was always a greedy reader, and most of the gobbling seemed to center on nineteenth-century novels. They are cinematic in the best sense. Characters and their environments are described with enormous clarity. I believe that my devotion to the Brontes, Jane Austen, and Trollope have directed my writing in a particular way, that for me, characterization will always be more important than plot, that visual detail will always hold more fascination than philosophical digressions.

"If I could write a modern *Wuthering Heights,* I might then feel free to throw my typewriter out the window and work in insurance sales."

* * *

MANDELSTAM, Nadezhda Yakovlevha 1899-1980

OBITUARY NOTICE: Born October 31, 1899, in Saratov, Russia (now U.S.S.R.); died of heart disease, December 29, 1980, in Moscow, U.S.S.R. Well-known member of Soviet intellectual world, translator, and author. Nadezhda Mandelstam struggled much of her life to preserve the work of her husband, Osip Mandelstam, a major Soviet poet whose outspokenly anti-Stalinist views eventually resulted in his arrest in 1934. After his death in a concentration camp in 1938, his wife wrote two books of memoirs, *Hope Against Hope* and *Hope Abandoned,* which contain detailed accounts of their lives together. Both books had to be smuggled out of the Soviet Union in order to be published. Mandelstam's efforts to preserve her husband's work led to the publication of a limited edition of his poems in Moscow in 1974. Obituaries and other sources: *World Authors, 1970-1975,* Wilson, 1980; *Chicago Tribune,* December 30, 1980; *Washington Post,* December 30, 1980; *Newsweek,* January 12, 1981; *Time,* January 12, 1981; *Publishers Weekly,* January 30, 1981.

* * *

MANNONI, Octave 1899-

PERSONAL: Born August 29, 1899, in Sologne, France; married Maud van der Spoel (a president of an experimental school). *Education:* Attended University of Paris. *Home:* 35 avenue Ferdinand Buisson, Paris, France.

CAREER: Writer. Director of Servuce General de l'Information, Tananarive, Madagascar, 1947-53. *Member:* Ecole Freudienne de Paris.

WRITINGS: Psychologie de la colonisation, Editions du Seuil, 1950, translation by Pamela Powesland published as *Prospero and Caliban: The Psychology of Colonization,* Praeger, 1956, 2nd edition, 1964; *Freud,* Editions de Seuil,

1968, translation by Renaud Bruce published as *Freud,* Pantheon, 1971 (published in England as *Freud: The Theory of the Unconscious,* New Left Books, 1971).

Other writings: *Lettres personnelles,* [France], 1951, reprinted as *La Machine,* Tchou, 1977; *Chefs pour l'imaginaire; ou, L'autre scene,* Editions du Seuil, 1969; *Sigmund Freud in Selbstzeugnissen und Bildokumenten,* Rowohlt, 1971; *Pouvoirs,* [France], 1973. Also author of *Fictions Freudiennes* and *Un Commencement qui n'en finit pas.* Contributor to scholarly journals.

* * *

MARAZZI, Rich(ard Thomas) 1943-

PERSONAL: Born November 20, 1943, in Derby, Conn.; son of Reno Anthony and Dorothy (Spagnola) Marazzi; married Loisann Kelly, July 3, 1971; children: Richard, Brian. *Education:* Quinnipiac College, A.A., 1963; State University of New York College at New Paltz, B.A., 1965; Southern Connecticut State College, M.A., 1971. *Home:* 105 Pulaski Hwy., Ansonia, Conn. 06401.

CAREER: Emmett O'Brien Regional Vocational Technical School, Ansonia, Conn., instructor in social studies, 1968-81, basketball coach, 1970-79. Host of weekly cable television program, "Sports Beat," in Seymour, Conn., 1979—; National Cable Television commentator for the 1980 World Series. Baseball umpire. *Member:* Valley Umpires Association (past president).

WRITINGS: The Rules and Lore of Baseball, Stein & Day, 1980; *The Stein & Day Baseball Date Book,* Stein & Day, 1981; (with Len Fiorito) *Aaron to Zuverink: A Nostalgic Look at Players in the Fifties,* Stein & Day, 1981. Columnist for *Diamond Report, Baseball Bulletin, Referee Magazine,* and *Evening Sentinel* (Ansonia, Conn.); contributor of articles to *Baseball Digest* and *Society for American Baseball Research Journal;* associate writer with sports commentator Mel Allen.

SIDELIGHTS: Marazzi wrote his first book because of his love and enthusiasm for the game of baseball. "Writing a book about baseball was what I've always wanted to do," Marazzi told the *New Haven Journal-Courier.* "First, I was trying to learn all I could about the sport. Then writing a book that would really explain the rules was a dream." *The Rules and Lore of Baseball* is a detailed description of baseball rules enhanced by anecdotes and baseball trivia.

Although he spent nine years compiling information for the book, Marazzi considers the work worthwhile. "I feel great about the success of the book and look back on the years of research, sometimes fruitless, sometimes gratifying, with satisfaction and pleasure," he commented. Marazzi's book has received acclaim from several baseball notables. New York Yankee broadcaster and former St. Louis Cardinal Bill White recommended the book as a rules guide, and American League umpire Nick Bremigan declared, "Rich Marazzi has authored a baseball masterpiece . . . a must for all baseball fans."

Marazzi told *CA:* "My literary career appears to be taking a natural course. I am a sports 'junkie' in general, and baseball has always been my first love. Writing about the game I love is utopia for me. It is my personal contribution to our national pastime. The satisfaction one gains in sharing knowledge is most fulfilling."

BIOGRAPHICAL/CRITICAL SOURCES: New Haven Journal-Courier, August 21, 1980; *New York Daily News,* August 24, 1980; *Bridgeport Post & Telegram,* August 31, 1980; *Yankee Magazine,* September, 1980.

MARCEL, Gabriel Honore 1889-1973

PERSONAL: Born December 7, 1889, in Paris, France; died of a heart attack, October 8, 1973, in Paris, France; son of Henri (a diplomat) and Laure (Meyer) Marcel; married Jacqueline Boegner; children: one. *Education:* University of Paris, Sorbonne, aggregation de philosophie, 1910. *Religion:* Roman Catholic. *Residence:* Paris, France.

CAREER: Writer. Teacher at lycees in Vendome, Condorcet, and Sens, France, 1911-23; reader at Grasset and Plon publishers and teacher at various schools, 1923-41; *Nouvelles Litteraires,* drama and music critic, 1945-73. Gifford lecturer at University of Aberdeen, 1949-50; William James lecturer at Harvard University, 1961. *Wartime service:* Served with the Red Cross during World War I. *Member:* Academie des Sciences Morales et Politiques. *Awards, honors:* Grand prix de litterature from Academy Francaise, 1948; Goethe Hanseatic Prize from Hamburg University, 1956; Grand Prix National des Lettres, 1958; Frankfurt peace prize, 1964; European Erasmus Prize, 1969; West German Booksellers peace prize; named officer of Legion of Honor, commander of arts and letters, and commander des Palmes Academiques.

WRITINGS—Books; all philosophy, except as noted: *Journal metaphysique,* Gallimard, 1927, 15th edition, 1958, translation by Bernard Wall published as *Metaphysical Journal,* Regnery, 1952; *Etre et avoir,* Aubier, 1935, translation by Katharine Farrer published as *Being and Having,* Dacre Press, 1949, Beacon Press, 1951, also published as *Being and Having: An Existentialist Diary,* Harper, 1965; *Du refus a l'invocation,* Gallimard, 1940, reprinted, 1964, also published as *Essai de philosophie concrete,* 1967, translation by Robert Rosthal published as *Creative Fidelity,* Farrar, Straus, 1964; *Homo viator: Prolegomenes a une metaphysique de l'esperance* (addresses, essays, and lectures), Aubier, 1945, translation by Emma Craufurd published as *Homo Viator: Introduction to a Metaphysic of Hope,* Regnery, 1951; *La Metaphysique de Royce,* Aubier, 1945, translation by Virginia Ringer and Gordon Ringer published as *Royce's Metaphysics,* Regnery, 1956; (editor and author of introduction) Marcelle de Jouvenel, *Au diapason du ciel,* Colombe, 1948; *The Philosophy of Existence,* translated by Manya Harari, Harvill, 1948, Philosophical Library, 1949; *Position et approches concretes du mystere ontologique,* Nauwelaerts, 1949, 2nd revised edition, 1967; (with others) *Recherche de la famille: Essai sur "l'etre familial,"* Editions Familiales de France, 1949.

Le Mystere de l'etre (lectures), Volume I: *Reflexion et mystere,* Volume II: *Foi et realite,* Auber, 1951, translation published as *The Mystery of Being,* Volume I: *Reflection and Mystery,* translated by G. S. Fraser, Volume II: *Faith and Reality,* translated by Rene Hague, Regnery, 1960; *Les Hommes contre l'humain,* La Colombe, 1951, translation by Fraser published as *Man Against Mass Society,* Regnery, 1952 (published in England as *Men Against Humanity,* Harvill, 1952); *Le Declin de la sagesse* (addresses, essays, and lectures), Plon, 1954, translation by Harari published as *The Decline of Wisdom,* Harvill, 1954, Philosophical Library, 1955; *L'Homme problematique,* Aubier, 1955, translation by Brian Thompson published as *Problematic Man,* Herder, 1967; *The Influence of Psychic Phenomena on My Philosophy,* Society for Psychical Research, 1956; (editor) *Un Changement d'esperance a la rencontre du rearmement moral: Des temoignages, des faits,* Plon, 1958, translation by Helen Hardinge published as *Fresh Hope for the World: Moral Re-armament in Action,* Longmans, 1960; *Presence et immortalite,* Flammarion, 1959, translation by Michael A. Machado published as *Presence and Immortality,* Duquesne University Press, 1967; *Theatre et religion,* E. Vitte, 1959; *L'Heure theatrale de Giraudoux a Jean-Paul Sartre* (criticism), Plon, 1959.

Philosophy of Existentialism, translated by Harari, Citadel, 1961, 7th edition, 1966; *Fragments philosophiques, 1909-1914,* Nauwelaerts, 1961, translation by Lionel A. Blain published in *Philosophical Fragments: 1904-1914; and the Philosopher and Peace,* University of Notre Dame Press, 1965; *The Existential Background of Human Dignity* (lectures), Harvard University Press, 1963; *Regards sur le theatre de Claudel,* Beauchesne, 1964; *Auf der Suche nach Wahrheit und Gerechtikeit* (lectures), J. Knecht, 1964, translation published as *Searchings,* Newman Press, 1967; *Der Philosoph und der Friede,* J. Knecht, 1964; *Paix sur la terre: Deux Discours, une tragedie,* Aubier, 1965; *Die Musik als Heimat der Seele* (addresses, essays, and lectures), Festungs-Verlag, 1965; *Gabriel Marcel et les niveaux de l'experience,* edited by Jeanne Parain-Vial, Seghers, 1966; *Pour une sagesse tragique et son au-dela* (addresses, essays, and lectures), Plon, 1968, translation by Stephen Jolin and Peter McCormick published as *Tragic Wisdom and Beyond,* Northwestern University Press, 1973; *Martin Buber: L'Homme et le philosophe,* l'Institut de Sociologie de l'Universite Libre de Bruxelles, 1968; (contributor) Andreas Resch, editor, *Im Kraftfeld des Christlichen Weltbildes,* Schoeningh, 1968; *Coleridge et Schilling* (title means "Coleridge and Schilling"), Aubier-Montaigne, 1971; *En chemin, vers quel eveil?,* Gallimard, 1971; (with others) *Plus decisif que la violence* (addresses, essays, and lectures), Plon, 1971; *Percees vers un ailleurs,* Fayard, 1973.

Plays: *Le Seuil invisible* (contains "La Grace" and "Le Palais de Sable"), Grasset, 1914; *Le Coeur des autres* (three-act), Grasset, 1921; "Le Regard neuf," 1922, published in *Trois Pieces* (see below); *L'Iconoclaste* (four-act; title means "The Iconoclast"), Stock, 1923; *Un Homme de Dieu* (four-act; first produced in Genoa, Italy, at Piccolo Teatro, May, 1946), Grasset, 1925, La Table Ronde, 1957, translation published as "A Man of God" in *Three Plays* (see below); *La Chapelle ardente* (three-act; first produced in Paris, France, at Theatre du Vieux-Colombier, September 25, 1925), L'Illustration, 1925, La Table Ronde, 1950, translation published as "The Funeral Pyre" in *Three Plays,* and as "The Votive Candle" in the revised edition of *Three Plays* (see below); *Le Quatuor en fa diese,* Plon, 1929.

Trois Pieces (contains "Le Regard neuf," "Le Mort de demain," "La Chapelle ardente"), Plon, 1931; *Le Monde casse* (four-act; title means "The Broken World"; first produced in Paris, 1930), Desclee de Brouwer, 1933, also published in *Cinq Pieces majeurs* (see below); *Le Fanal* (one-act; title means "The Beacon"), Stock, 1936; *Le Secret dans les iles* (first produced in Paris at Theatre des Arts, March 1, 1937), published in *Le Secret est dans les iles, theatre* (see below); *Le Dard* (three-act; title means "The Dart"; produced in Paris at Theatre des Arts, March 1, 1937), Plon, 1938, also published in *Le Secret est dans les iles, theatre* (see below); *La Soif* (three-act; title means "The Thirst"), Desclee de Brouwre, 1938, also published in *Cinq Pieces majeures* (see below), also published as *Les Coeurs avides* (title means "The Hungry Hearts"), La Table Ronde, 1952; "Les Pointes sur les I" (one-act) published in *Les Oeuvres libres,* [Paris], 1938, also published in *Theatre comique* (see below).

"L'Emissaire" (title means "The Emissary"; first produced in 1945), published in *Le Secret est dans les iles, theatre* (see below); *L'Horizon* (four-act; title means "The Horizon"), Editions aux Etudiants de France, 1945; *Theatre comique* (contains "Colombyre, ou le brasier de la paix," "La Double expertise," "Les Points sur les I," and "Le Divertissement posthume"), A. Michel, 1947; "La Fin des temps" (first produced by Radiodiffusion Francaise, June 17, 1950), published in *Le Secret est dans les iles, theatre* (see below); *Rome n'est plus dans Rome* (five-act; title means "Rome Is No Longer in Rome"), La Table Ronde, 1951; "Le Chemin de Crete" (first produced in Paris at Theatre du Vieux-Colombier, November 14, 1953), published in *Cinq Pieces majeures* (see below), translation published as "Ariadne" in *Three Plays* (see below); *Croissez et multipliez* (four-act; title means "Increase and Multiply"), Plon, 1955; *Mon Temps n'est pas le votre* (five-act; title means "My Time Is Not Yours"), Plon, 1955; *La Dimension florestan* (three-act), Plon, 1958; *Three Plays: A Man of God, Ariadne, The Funeral Pyre,* Hill & Wang, 1958, revised edition publshed as *Three Plays: A Man of God, Ariadne, The Votive Candle,* 1965.

Le Signe de la croix (three-act; title means "The Sign of the Cross"), Plon, 1961 (also see below); *Le Secret est dans les iles, theatre* (contains "Le Dard," "L'Emissaire," and "La Fon des temps"), Plon, 1967; *Cinq Pieces majeures* (contains "Un Homme de Dieu," "Le Monde casse," "Le Chemin de Crete," "La Soif," and "Le Signe de la croix"), Plon, 1973. Also author of "Le Palaise de sable" and "La Grace," both published in *Le Seuil invisible* (see above); "Le Mort de demain," published in *Trois Pieces* (see above); and "Le Divertissement posthume," "La Double expertise," and "Colombyre, ou le brasier de la paix," all published in *Theatre comique* (see above).

Contributor of articles to periodicals, including *L'Europe Nouvelle, Nouvelle Revue Francaise, Temps Present,* and *Vigile.*

SIDELIGHTS: According to Kenneth T. Gallagher, "nothing could be more uncustomary than the thought of Gabriel Marcel: there seems to be no direct precedent for it in the entire history of philosophy. Presenting elements of phenomenology, existentialism, idealism, and empiricism all consorting together in symbiotic bliss, it completely defies classification." Despite this, however, Marcel has been dubbed a "Christian existentialist," due to his deep commitment to Catholicism and the early influence of Soren Kierkegaard, the father of existentialism, on his philosophical thought. Marcel first introduced Kierkegaard's work to France in a 1925 article published by the *Revue de Metaphsique.* This article brought forth the philosophy of *existentialisme,* which became a prevalent school of thought through the works of Jean-Paul Sartre. Unlike Sartre, though, Marcel was not a pessimistic atheist, but a devout and optimistic Roman Catholic. He himself preferred to be called a "neo-Socratic" or a "Socratic Christian."

In common with atheistic existentialists, Marcel rejected the validity of philosophical systems and the search for abstract, universal truths. His interest lay with the real, individual human being; his approach is phenomenological, stressing experiences as they are actually encountered. Thus Marcel also called his theory "concrete philosophy." He concerned himself with the increasing dehumanization of man in twentieth-century society and with the means by which a human being can overcome the resulting sense of alienation and absurdity in order to live an authentic, meaningful existence. On the other hand, Marcel is distinguished from atheistic existentialists by his fundamental idealism; buoyed by his strong faith in God, he rejected the idea of an absurd uni-

verse. In this sense, Marcel most differed from the existentialists, for he lacked, as Marjorie Grene pointed out, "the terrible realization of dread as the core of human life," the concept, according to Grene, that sets existentialism apart from other schools of thought.

Nevertheless, Marcel does begin from what Grene called "the impassioned realization of the utter loneliness and dread of our being-in-the-world." A character in his play "Le Cour des autres" commented that "there is only one suffering, it is to be alone"; and, in fact, Marcel himself described his plays as dramas "of the soul in exile." Perhaps as a result, Francis J. Lescoe speculated, of a solitary childhood "literally starved for friendship, companionship and other spiritual values," Marcel came to regard the concrete experience of love, a relationship between oneself and an "other," as the key to an authentic, meaningful existence.

Marcel grew up in a generally nonreligious atmosphere. His mother died when he was four years old and Marcel never talked about the event with his father. His agnostic parent and the liberal Protestant aunt who helped raise him largely ignored the subject of religion. Discussions concerning death and the possibility of an afterlife were forbidden. As a result of the absence of spiritualism in Marcel's upbringing, the author took up the study of philosophy in school and eventually graduated with a degree in the subject in 1910.

Marcel, however, still entertained nagging questions regarding death and obsessively reflected on the probability of the existence of immortality. His perplexity was exacerbated by the work he did during World War I. Exempted from armed combat because of frail health, Marcel worked with the Red Cross as a liason officer dealing with the frantic relatives of soldiers missing in action. Often it was his duty to inform an unfortunate family of the death of their loved one. These wartime experiences left an indelible mark on Marcel's way of thinking. He became especially aware of the uselessness of abstract thought when one must confront human suffering. Marcel became convinced that man must be a participant in any philosophical theory and not a cold, objective observer.

The philosopher continued his quest for answers and began to record his thoughts in a diary that was published in 1927 as *Journal metaphysique.* Marcel experimented with Protestantism and other beliefs and attended seances, but gradually gravitated towards the Roman Catholic church. He was finally prompted to formally join the religion by the Catholic author Francois Mauriac, who in a letter asked, "Come, Marcel, why are you not one of us?" In 1929 Marcel converted to Catholicism at the age of thirty-nine, after which time, Lescoe noted, he "never wavered for a moment in his loyalty to the Catholic faith."

After his conversion, Marcel began to incorporate his previous thoughts and conclusions into his newly adopted religion. Thus he created the curious blend of spiritual elements that distinguished his philosophy. Marcel never sought to explain God or prove His existence. He found such proofs meaningless, believing that God could be known only through participation, not observation. Hence, in Marcel's philosophy, the relationship with another human being is all-important. Lescoe explained that Marcel "insists that to be genuine in our interpersonal relationships, we must be totally and unreservedly available to the other. We must sympathize with the afflicted, that we become the afflicted ones ourselves." Only through such concrete experiences, involving faith, love, and hope, Marcel proposed, could one know God.

Marcel felt his philosophy was especially important in view of the increasing alienation of modern man. Like Martin Buber and Karl Jaspers he was concerned with the "erosion of human values and human personality," which Marcel attributed to the denial of God's existence as well as to the growing importance of technology. The denial of God (and therefore of the existence of an afterlife) leaves man without hope and leading a meaningless existence while technology defines man purely in terms of his function, thus reducing him to an object and completely disregarding his human dignity. Only by being available to another human being and truly open to a genuine encounter can a person achieve freedom and identity. Through such an "I-Thou relationship," Lescoe asserted, Marcel thought one could find "authentic personhood."

The philosopher maintained that this "I-Thou" communion can then be expanded to communion with God. Faith in another will lead to a similar relationship with God. Conversely, it is faith in God that makes possible the relationship between two human beings. Lescoe reflected that "all true love of the other must ultimately be based on the love of God."

The majority of Marcel's books are not systematic explanations of his philosophy. Rather, the author recorded his thoughts unmethodically in either diary form or in collections of his talks and articles. Grene described Marcel's first book, *Journal metaphysique,* as "jotting of day-by-day reflections, sometimes interconnected, sometimes quite random." Consequently, his books did not receive great literary notice. His plays also did not enjoy much success as they were too heavily philosophical for the theatre. Dealing with alienation in some form, Marcel's plays study man "in his loneliness," noted Lescoe. "He examines man frustrated, alienated, bewildered and restless, when he cuts himself off from his fellow man and from God." The author summed up the philosopher's thought by disclosing that Marcel "underscores man's deepest longing for friendship, fidelity, interpersonal relationship and communion with others."

BIOGRAPHICAL/CRITICAL SOURCES: Marjorie Grene, *Introduction to Existentialism,* University of Chicago Press, 1959; J. B. O'Malley, *The Fellowship of Being,* Hague, 1966; Samuel Keen, *Gabriel Marcel,* John Knox, 1967; Francis J. Lescoe, *Existentialism With or Without God,* Alba House, 1973; Kenneth T. Gallagher, *The Philosophy of Gabriel Marcel,* Fordham University Press, 1975; Barbara Wall, *Love and Death in the Philosophy of Gabriel Marcel,* University Press of America, 1977; Francois Lapointe and Claire Lapointe, *Gabriel Marcel and His Critics: An International Bibliography,* Garland, 1977; Hilda Lazaron, *Gabriel Marcel the Dramatist,* Humanities, 1978; Joe McCowan, *Availability: Gabriel Marcel and the Phenomenology of Human Openness,* Scholars Press, 1978; Seymour Cain, *Gabriel Marcel,* Regnery, 1979; *Contemporary Literary Criticism,* Volume 15, Gale, 1980.

OBITUARIES: New York Times, October 9, 1973; *Time,* October 22, 1973; *Newsweek,* October 22, 1973.*

　　　　　　　　　　　　　　　　　　　—*Sketch by Andrea Geffner*

*　　　*　　　*

MARDER, Arthur Jacob 1910-1980

OBITUARY NOTICE: Born March 8, 1910, in Boston, Mass.; died of cancer, December 25, 1980, in Santa Barbara, Calif. Educator, historian, and author. A professor of history for more than thirty-five years, Arthur Marder was highly regarded as an authority on British naval history. Through-out his career, he received numerous academic distinctions, including a Guggenheim fellowship, a Fulbright fellowship, and a D.Litt from Oxford University. He made a significant contribution to the annals of British naval history with his work, *From the Dreadnought to Scapa Flow.* Marder was praised for this five-volume series that reflected extensive and painstaking research and demonstrated a remarkable understanding of his subject. Numbered among his other books are *Portrait of an Admiral, From the Dardanelles to Oran,* and *Operation Menace.* Obituaries and other sources: *Directory of American Scholars,* Volume I: *History,* 6th edition, Bowker, 1974; *Who's Who in America,* 40th edition, Marquis, 1978; *London Times,* December 29, 1980.

*　　　*　　　*

MARGOLIES, Luise 1945-

PERSONAL: Born September 7, 1945, in New York, N.Y.; daughter of Albert and June (Ackerman) Margolies; married Graziano Gasparini (an architect), August 7, 1970; children: Graziano Andrey. *Education:* Barnard College, B.A., 1966; Oxford University, diploma in anthropology, 1967; Columbia University, M.A., 1970, Ph.D., 1972. *Home and office:* Apartado 3305, Caracas, Venezuela.

CAREER: Instituto Venezolano de Investigaciones Cientificas, Caracas, Venezuela, research associate in anthropology and member of faculty, 1973-78; Ediciones Venezolanas de Antropologia, Caracas, director, 1978—. *Member:* American Anthropological Association (fellow), Society for Applied Anthropology (fellow), Latin American Studies Association, Latin American Anthropology Group (co-chairman, 1979-81). *Awards, honors:* Diploma from Instituto Nacional de Cultura, Peru, 1978, for *Inca Architecture.*

WRITINGS: Princes of the Earth: Subcultural Diversity in a Mexican Municipality, American Anthropological Association, 1975; (editor) *The Venezuelan Peasant in Country and City,* Ediciones Venezolanas de Antropologia, 1975; (with husband, Graziano Gasparini) *Inca Architecture,* Indiana University Press, 1980; (with Gasparini) *Essays on Inca Architecture,* Ediciones Venezolanas de Antropologia, 1980. Contributor to anthropology journals.

WORK IN PROGRESS: A book on the coffee economy in the Venezuelan Andes, expected in 1982.

SIDELIGHTS: Luise Margolies commented: "All of my writing is related to my professional interests in the anthropology of Latin America. It seems so important to me that the results of anthropological research be broadly disseminated that I have started a small publishing house in Venezuela dedicated to the publication of new manuscripts as well as important reprints on Latin America. I believe very strongly in the humanistic perspective in anthropology and strive for eloquence as well as scientific validity in this venture. Only by producing well-written books can we anthropologists hope to address ourselves to persons other than the small professional community."

*　　　*　　　*

MARKS, Sally (Jean) 1931-

PERSONAL: Born January 18, 1931, in New Haven, Conn.; daughter of Percy (a writer) and Margaret (a painter; maiden name, Gates) Marks. *Education:* Wellesley College, A.B. (with honors), 1952; University of North Carolina, M.A., 1961; University of London, Ph.D., 1968. *Residence:* Providence, R.I. *Office:* Department of History, Rhode Island College, Providence, R.I. 02908.

CAREER: U.S. Department of Defense, Washington, D.C., in policy planning, administration, and foreign liaison, 1953-57; teacher of history and geography at private school in Waterbury, Conn., 1957-58; teacher of history and current events at private school in Westport, Conn., 1958-59; University of North Carolina, Women's College, Greensboro, instructor in history, 1960-62; Rhode Island College, Providence, instructor, 1962-66, assistant professor, 1966-70, associate professor, 1970-77, professor of history, 1977—.

MEMBER: American Historical Association, Society of Historians of American Foreign Relations, American Association of University Women, American Association of University Professors (president, 1972-73; member of state executive board, 1973—), Conference on British Studies, Conference on Peace Research in History, Institut royal des relations internationales (Belgium; associate member), Centre interuniversitaire d'etudes europeenes (Quebec), Anglo-American Historical Conference (England), New England Historical Association, Rhode Island Historical Association, Phi Alpha Theta, Anglo-Belgian Club. *Awards, honors:* Woodrow Wilson fellow, 1960-61; American Council of Learned Societies fellow, 1977-78.

WRITINGS: The Illusion of Peace: International Relations in Europe, 1918-1933, St. Martin's, 1976, 4th edition, 1981; *Innocent Abroad: Belgium at the Paris Peace Conference of 1919,* University of North Carolina Press, 1981. Contributor of more than a dozen articles and reviews to history and European studies journals.

WORK IN PROGRESS: A monograph on the Western Entente (England, France, Belgium, and Italy) and its policy formulation toward Germany, 1920-26; research for a monograph on the Western Entente, 1926-36; several scholarly articles on the diplomacy of the 1920's.

AVOCATIONAL INTERESTS: Travel (France, Belgium, England).

*   *   *

MARNHAM, Patrick 1943-

PERSONAL: Born August 15, 1943, in Jerusalem, Palestine (now Israel); son of Sir Ralph (a surgeon) and Helena (Daly) Marnham. *Education:* Corpus Christi College, Oxford, degree in jurisprudence (with honors), 1965. *Agent:* Hughes Massie Ltd., 21 Southampton Row, London WC1B 5HL, England.

CAREER: Called to the Bar at Gray's Inn, 1966; *Private Eye* (magazine), London, England, 1966-68; *Daily Telegraph* (magazine), London, features editor, 1968-70; writer, 1970—.

WRITINGS: Road to Katmandu, Macmillan, 1971, Dell, 1972; *Nomads of the Sahel,* Minority Rights Group (London, England), 1977, revised edition, 1979; *Lourdes: A Modern Pilgrimage,* Heinemann, 1980; *Fantastic Invasion,* Harcourt, 1980. Contributor to magazines, including *Private Eye, Spectator, Books and Bookmen, Harper's,* and *New Republic.*

SIDELIGHTS: Marnham wrote: "I have traveled in the old way, overland, through Europe and Africa, the Indian subcontinent, and the Middle East. My books describe various journeys and events in those parts."

*   *   *

MARRIOTT, (Joyce) Anne 1913-

PERSONAL: Born November 15, 1913, in Victoria, British Columbia, Canada; daughter of Edward Guy (a civil engineer) and Catherine Eleanor (Heley) Marriott; married Gerald Jerome McLellan, December 16, 1947 (deceased); children: Marya Catherine McLellan Kosiancic, Celia Anne, Jerome Edward. *Education:* Attended University of British Columbia, 1942, 1956. *Religion:* Christian. *Home and office:* 3645 Skyes Rd., North Vancouver, British Columbia, Canada V7K 2A6.

CAREER: National Film Board of Canada, Ottawa, Ontario, script writer, 1945-49; *Prince George Citizen,* Prince George, British Columbia, reporter and women's editor, 1950-53; Prince George Public Library, Prince George, assistant librarian, 1953; assistant librarian for Squamish Public Library, 1958; writer, 1958—. Gives poetry workshops; broadcaster for Canadian Broadcasting Corp. Past director of North Vancouver Community Arts Council. *Member:* League of Canadian Poets, Literary Storefront, United Church Women. *Awards, honors:* Governor-General's Award for Poetry, 1941, for *Calling Adventurers;* shared drama award from Women's Canadian Club, 1943; Koerner Foundation scholarship, 1956; Ohio Award for Educational Broadcasting, 1958.

WRITINGS: The Wind Our Enemy (poems), Ryerson, 1939; *Calling Adventurers* (poems), Ryerson, 1941; *Salt Marsh and Other Poems,* Ryerson, 1942; *Sandstone and Other Poems,* Ryerson, 1945; *Countries,* Fiddlehead Poetry Books, 1971; (with Joyce Moller) *A Swarming in My Mind,* Curriculum Services Centre (North Vancouver, British Columbia), 1976; *The Circular Coast* (poems), Mosaic Press, 1980.

Work represented in anthologies, including *Book of Canadian Poetry,* University of Chicago Press, 1943; *British Columbia: A Centennial Anthology,* McClelland & Stewart, 1958; *Counterpoint in Literature,* Scott, Foresman, 1967. Contributor of stories and poems to magazines, including *Fiddlehead, Canadian Forum, Northern Review, Manitoba Arts Review,* and *Oregonian Verse.*

WORK IN PROGRESS: A children's novel set in the 1930's; an adult novel set in the 1930's.

SIDELIGHTS: Anne Marriott wrote: "My best-known poem, 'The Wind Our Enemy,' was written following a summer in the prairie drought area after an illness—the intense contrast with the green west coast was a traumatic experience resulting in a documentary poem.

"I particularly enjoy helping children to write, especially at the elementary school level. My feeling about the most important thing in writing—which I emphasize to young people—is *sincerity above all.* If what you write is not true to yourself, it can be of no lasting value in my opinion."

BIOGRAPHICAL/CRITICAL SOURCES: British Columbia Library Quarterly, January, 1959.

*   *   *

MARSHALL, Joyce 1913-

PERSONAL: Born November 28, 1913, in Montreal, Quebec, Canada; daughter of William Wallace and Ruth Winnifred (Chambers) Marshall. *Education:* McGill University, B.A., 1935. *Politics:* New Democrat. *Religion:* Agnostic. *Office:* Catherine Parr Traill College, Trent University, Peterborough, Ontario, Canada.

CAREER: Trent University, Peterborough, Ontario, writer-in-residence, 1980—. *Member:* Canadian Authors Association, Authors League of America. *Awards, honors:* Translation prize from Canada Council, 1976, for *Enchanted Summer.*

WRITINGS: Presently Tomorrow (novel), Little, Brown, 1946; *Love and Strangers,* Lippincott, 1957; *A Private Place,* Oberon Press, 1975. Also translator from French of Gabrielle Roy's *Enchanted Summer.*

Work represented in anthologies, including *Canadian Short Stories,* Series I, Series III, Oxford University Press; *Best Canadian Stories,* Hurtig; *Stories of Quebec,* Oberon Press. Contributor to literary magazines, including *Tamarack Review* and *Canadian Fiction.*

WORK IN PROGRESS: A Dream of Joe Brooke's (tentative title), a novel.

SIDELIGHTS: Joyce Marshall wrote: "I am a person who writes and leaves comments to others. I always wanted to write, even before I could spell, but I can't explain this and feel that any attempt to discuss my writing and desire to write would be ostentatious and somewhat ridiculous."

*   *   *

MARTIN, David C(lark) 1943-

PERSONAL: Born July 28, 1943, in Washington, D.C.; son of Joseph Walford and Norene (Dann) Martin; married Elinor Bond (a physician), September 24, 1966; children: Catherine Grosvenor, David Zachary. *Education:* Yale University, B.A., 1965. *Home:* 4700 Drummond Ave., Chevy Chase, Md. 20015. *Agent:* Theron Raines, Raines & Raines, 475 Fifth Ave., New York, N.Y. 10017. *Office:* Newsweek, 1750 Pennsylvania Ave. N.W., Washington, D.C. 20006.

CAREER: Associated Press, Washington, D.C., correspondent, 1973-77; *Newsweek,* New York, N.Y., Washington correspondent, 1977—. *Military service:* U.S. Navy, 1966-69; became lieutenant junior grade.

WRITINGS: Wilderness of Mirrors (nonfiction), Harper, 1980.

*   *   *

MARTIN, Earl S(auder) 1944-

PERSONAL: Born April 28, 1944, in New Holland, Pa.; son of Daniel H. and Elizabeth S. Martin; married Pat Hostetter (a writer), March 23, 1968; children: Lara Mai, Minh Douglas, Hans. *Education:* Hesston College, A.A., 1965; Stanford University, B.A., 1970, M.A., 1972. *Religion:* Mennonite. *Home address:* Rodano St., Malaybalay, Bukidnon, Philippines. *Office:* Mennonite Central Committee, Akron, Pa. 17501.

CAREER: Mennonite Central Committee, Akron, Pa., researcher in Vietnam (in fulfillment of alternative service as conscientious objector to military duty), 1966-69 and 1973-75; laborer in Pennsylvania, 1975-79; representative of Mennonite Central Committee in the Philippines, 1979—.

WRITINGS: Reaching the Other Side (nonfiction), Crown, 1978. Contributor to religious journals and newspapers.

*   *   *

MARTIN, John Henry 1915-

PERSONAL: Born August 14, 1915, in Paterson, N.J.; son of William Sylvester and Esther J. Martin; married Evelyn Doerflinger, August 23, 1937; children: Michael William, Susan Jane, Jane Alice. *Education:* University of Alabama, B.Sc., 1938; Columbia University, A.M., 1940, Ed.D., 1954. *Home:* CC207 Windjammer, Stuart, Fla. 33494.

CAREER: Teacher of English and history at public schools in New York, 1938; principal of public high and junior high schools in Oyster Bay, Kingston, and Manhasset, N.Y.,

1946-56; superintendent of schools in Wayne, N.J., and Freeport and Mt. Vernon, N.Y., 1956-66; ERC Corp., Englewood Cliffs, N.J., senior vice-president, 1966-69. Consultant to U.S. Joint Chiefs of Staff, U.S. Department of Health, Education and Welfare, Executive Office of the President, U.S. Department of Justice, Gerber Corp., and Edison Laboratories. *Military service:* U.S. Navy, 1942-46; became lieutenant commander. *Awards, honors:* Founders Gold Medal of Honor from Education Research Bureau, 1979, for distinguished service to education.

WRITINGS: Democracy in School Administration (monograph), Teachers College, 1954; (with Charles Harrison) *Free to Learn,* Prentice-Hall, 1972; *The Education of Adolescents,* U.S. Government Printing Office, 1976. Contributor to education journals and popular magazines, including *Look, Reader's Digest,* and *Saturday Review.*

WORK IN PROGRESS: I Am Your Friend, a children's book, publication expected in 1981; a reading program.

SIDELIGHTS: Martin wrote: "I have recently completed a three-year study of children learning to write and read."

*   *   *

MARTIN, Joseph George 1915-1981

OBITUARY NOTICE: Born May 9, 1915, in New York, N.Y.; died January 26, 1981, in Hyannis, Mass. Journalist. Martin, who spent his entire career with the *New York Daily News,* was co-recipient with Philip Santora of the 1959 Pulitzer Prize for international reporting. They received the award for a series of articles that documented the brutality of Fulgencio Batista's Cuban regime. Obituaries and other sources: *Who's Who in the World,* 2nd edition, Marquis, 1974; *New York Times,* January 27, 1981.

*   *   *

MARTIN, Marta San
See SAN MARTIN, Marta

*   *   *

MARTIN, Pete
See MARTIN, William Thorton

*   *   *

MARTIN, Robert K(essler) 1941-

PERSONAL: Born November 11, 1941, in Bryn Mawr, Pa.; son of Frank H., Jr. (a banker) and Margaret (Dever) Martin. *Education:* Wesleyan University, Middletown, Conn., B.A., 1963; Brown University, Ph.D., 1978. *Home:* 481 Prince Arthur St. W., Montreal, Quebec, Canada H2X 1T4. *Office:* Department of English, Concordia University, 7141 Sherbrooke St. W., Montreal, Quebec, Canada H4B 1R6.

CAREER: Concordia University, Montreal, Quebec, lecturer, 1967-69, assistant professor, 1969-76, associate professor of English, 1976—, director of graduate studies, 1980—. *Member:* Canadian Association for American Studies, Modern Language Association of America, American Studies Association, Phi Beta Kappa. *Awards, honors:* Pushcart Prize from Pushcart Press, 1975, for article, "Whitman's Song of Myself: Homosexual Dream and Vision."

WRITINGS: The Homosexual Tradition in American Poetry, University of Texas Press, 1979; (editor with Judith S. Herz) *E. M. Forster: Centenary Revaluations,* Macmillan, 1980. Contributor of articles and reviews to magazines and newspapers, including *Nation, Poetry,* and *Parnassus.* Contributing editor of *Christopher Street.*

WORK IN PROGRESS: A study of *The Bridge,* with emphasis on its structural coherence; a study of expressionism in England and the United States, including poetry, fiction, painting, theatre, film, and music; a study of the English homosexual literary tradition.

SIDELIGHTS: Martin told *CA:* "My work is the product of several disparate traditions: a training from childhood in American Protestant ethics and commitment to social justice and the moral life; a great love of words and in particular of poetry and its relationships to art and music; and an interest in the nature of American intellectual history and its connections with European social and intellectual history. My own work has taken its present form from a growing awareness of the need to speak out of my own experience as a gay man who can still hope to find significance through the creation of a viable artistic tradition. I try to combine the best of a New Critical sensitivity to the text and the power of language with a sense of engagement and an awareness of historical contest. I want to be moral but not moralistic."

BIOGRAPHICAL/CRITICAL SOURCES: Advocate, February 11, 1976; *Gay News,* June 12, 1980.

* * *

MARTIN, William Thorton 1901(?)-1980
(Pete Martin)

OBITUARY NOTICE: Born c. 1901; died of a heart attack, October 13, 1980, in Birchrunville, Pa. Journalist. Pete Martin, editor and staff writer for the *Saturday Evening Post,* was best known for his 'I Call On . . . '' interviews of show-business celebrities. Obituaries and other sources: *Newsweek,* October 27, 1980; *Time,* October 27, 1980.

* * *

MATHEWS, Arthur 1903(?)-1980

OBITUARY NOTICE: Born c. 1903; died after a brief illness, October 7, 1980, in Long Island, N.Y. Engineer, psychiatrist, and author. After a twenty-year career with the National Broadcasting Co. as an engineer in electronics, Arthur Mathews became a psychiatrist. He wrote a number of books, including *Take It Easy: The Art of Conquering Your Nerves* and *Start Living Today: A Guide to Positive Living.* Obituaries and other sources: *New York Times,* October 11, 1980.

* * *

MATTHEWS, Anthony
See BARKER, Dudley

* * *

MAURER, David J(oseph) 1935-

PERSONAL: Born June 9, 1935, in Canton, Ohio; son of Harry J. and Elizabeth (Fehn) Maurer; married Ellen Joyce Swan (a secretary), June 15, 1957; children: Elizabeth, William. *Education:* Beloit College, B.A., 1957; Ohio State University, M.A., 1958, Ph.D., 1962. *Religion:* Episcopal. *Home:* 8 Circle Dr., Charleston, Ill. 61920. *Office:* Department of History, Eastern Illinois University, Charleston, Ill. 61920.

CAREER: Eastern Illinois University, Charleston, assistant professor, 1962-67, associate professor, 1967-71, professor of history, 1971—, coordinator of faculty development, 1979—. Visiting professor at Ohio State University. Vice-president of Charleston Community Theater, 1970. *Member:* American Historical Association, American Association for

State and Local History, American Association of University Professors, Illinois Historical Society (vice-president, 1973-75; member of board of directors, 1975-78; president, 1980-81), Illinois Historic Sites Advisory Council.

WRITINGS: (Contributor) Donald F. Tingley, editor, *Essays in Illinois History,* Southern Illinois University Press, 1968; (contributor) John Braeman, David Brady, and Robert Bremner, editors, *The New Deal,* Volume II, Ohio State University Press, 1974; (contributor) Tingley, editor, *The Emerging University,* Eastern Illinois University Press, 1974; (contributor) Robert Sutton, editor, *The Prairie State: A Documentary History of Illinois,* Eerdmans, 1976; *United States Politics and Elections,* Gale, 1978. Contributor to history journals.

SIDELIGHTS: Maurer told *CA:* "Additional bibliographies are needed for the twentieth century on the subject of United States politics and elections. We need separate bibliographic aids that include reference to articles in professional journals and major national publications."

* * *

MAUZEY, Merritt 1897-1975

PERSONAL: Born September 16, 1897, in Clifton, Tex.; died in 1975 in Dallas, Tex. *Education:* Studied art in Dallas, Tex.

CAREER: Painter, lithographer, and illustrator, 1938-75. Work represented in collections, including Library of Congress, Metropolitan Museum, and New York Public Library; had group and solo shows in the United States and abroad, including the New York World's Fair, Art Institute of Chicago, and Whitney Museum. *Awards, honors:* Guggenheim fellowship, 1946; art awards include first prize in graphic arts from Arizona State Fair, 1946; first prize from Texas Print Annual, 1947; Belle Weedon Memorial Prize from Society of American Graphic Artists, 1956.

WRITINGS—Self-illustrated children's books: *Cotton-Farm Boy,* H. Schuman, 1953; *Texas Ranch Boy,* Abelard, 1955; *Oilfield Boy,* Abelard, 1957; *Rice Boy,* Abelard, 1958; *Rubber Boy,* Abelard, 1962; *Salt Boy,* Abelard, 1963.

Art work represented in anthologies, including *The Artist in America* and *Prize Prints of the Twentieth Century.* Designer of magazine covers.

BIOGRAPHICAL/CRITICAL SOURCES: Gordon Weaver, editor, *An Artist's Notebook: The Life and Art of Mauzey Merritt,* Memphis State Press, 1979.*

* * *

MAZUR, Paul M(yer) 1892-1979

PERSONAL: Born December 9, 1892, in Boston, Mass.; died July 30, 1979; son of Louis and Eva (Siskin) Mazur; married Adolphia Kaske, June 21, 1922; children: Peter, Ann Mazur Salkin. *Education:* Harvard University, A.B., 1914. *Home:* 1 Gracie Sq., New York, N.Y. 10028. *Agent:* Gerard McCauley Agency, Inc., 551 Fifth Ave., New York, N.Y. 10004. *Office:* Lehman Brothers, Kuhn, Loeb, Inc., 1 William St., New York, N.Y. 10017.

CAREER: Lehman Brothers (investment bankers), New York, N.Y., associate, 1924-27, partner, 1927-69, limited partner, 1969—, member of board of directors, 1929-69. Visiting professor at University of Pennsylvania, 1965-67. Member of board of directors of Allied Stores, 1929-59, Federated Department Stores, 1936-69, Western Union, 1943-57, Collins & Aikman, 1948-69, Radio Corp. of America,

1957-69, One William Street Fund, 1958-69, and National Broadcasting Co., 1958-69. *Military service:* U.S. Army, Ordnance, 1917-19; became captain. *Member:* Lotos Club, Wall Street Club, Harvard Club, Hopewell Valley Gold Club. *Awards, honors:* Tobe Award, 1959; D.C.S. from New York University, 1960; D.H.L. from Rutgers University, 1961.

WRITINGS: (With Myron S. Silbert) *Principles of Organization Applied to Modern Retailing*, Harper, 1927, reprinted, Guinn, 1966; *American Prosperity: Its Causes and Consequences*, Viking, 1928; *America Looks Abroad: The New Economic Horizons*, Viking, 1930; *New Roads to Prosperity: The Crisis and Some Ways Out*, Viking, 1931; *The Standards We Raise: The Dynamics of Consumption*, Harper, 1953, reprinted, Guinn, 1967; *The Dynamics of Economic Growth*, Prentice-Hall, 1965; *Unfinished Business: A Banker Looks at the Economy*, Nash Publishing, 1973. Contributor to *Harvard Business Review* and newspapers.

SIDELIGHTS: Mazur commented: "My lifework has consisted of a career as an investment banker, a writer, and a teacher of young people both in business and educational institutions in the subjects of economics, banking, and distribution. This guidance of younger people, exposition of economic factors, and the planning of organizational procedures have brought me a relative sense of fulfillment."

OBITUARIES: New York Times, August 2, 1979.

* * *

McBRIDE, Patricia
See BARTZ, Patricia McBride

* * *

McCLATCHY, Eleanor Grace   1895(?)-1980

OBITUARY NOTICE: Born c. 1895; died in 1980 in Sacramento, Calif. Publisher. Eleanor McClatchy, president of McClatchy Newspapers since the death of her father in 1936, was known for using the influence of her newspapers to support liberal candidates and their causes. She received a Pulitzer Prize in 1935 for exposing political corruption in Nevada. Obituaries and other sources: *Who's Who of American Women*, 11th edition, Marquis, 1979; *Time*, November 3, 1980.

* * *

McCOLLOUGH, Albert W.   1917-

PERSONAL: Born May 23, 1917, in Laramie, Wyo.; son of Albert Weede and Elsie Martha (Rogers) McCollough; married Helen Lorraine Harris, June 26, 1939; children: Marian Lorraine McCollough Siek, Kimberly Gay McCollough Thurler. *Education:* Attended Tarkio College, 1933-34; University of Wyoming, B.A., 1937. *Politics:* Independent. *Religion:* Presbyterian. *Home:* 60 Cliftwood Dr., Huntington, N.Y. 11743. *Office: Newsweek*, 444 Madison Ave., New York, N.Y. 10022.

CAREER: United Press Associations and United Press International (UPI), New York City, news desk editor, 1946-61; *Newsweek*, New York City, associate editor, 1961-65, chief of copy desk, 1965-80, general editor, 1969-79, senior editor, 1980—. Trustee of East Meadow Public Library, 1967-77, president, 1972, 1974, and 1975; trustee of Nassau library system, 1974-77, vice-president, 1977. *Military service:* U.S. Army, 1945-46; became staff sergeant. *Member:* Editorial Freelancers Association, Aircraft Owners and Pilots Association, Train Collectors Association, Toy Train

Operating Society, Long Island Early Fliers Club (executive secretary, 1979—), Sigma Nu. *Awards, honors:* Named distinguished alumnus of University of Wyoming, 1978, by University of Wyoming Alumni Association.

WRITINGS: The Complete Book of Buddy "L" Toys and Trains, Greenberg, 1981. Contributor to periodicals and newspapers, including *Newsweek, Train Collectors Association Quarterly*, and *T.T.O.S. Bulletin*.

SIDELIGHTS: McCollough told *CA:* "As a lifelong journalist, I have a deep interest in thorough and accurate news reporting and writing, and a strong support for, and profound belief in, the importance of the First Amendment to the U.S. Constitution as well as civil and human rights in general.

"I wish I had begun working on *The Complete Book of Buddy "L" Toys and Trains* thirty years earlier, when it probably would have been easier to find early employees of the Buddy "L" Company and obtain detailed and accurate information from firsthand sources. However, it has been fun tracking down the facts and obtaining pictures of what even many of the most ardent toy collectors do not realize was a varied and quite sizable line of steel toys. Accuracy in detail and completeness are my two goals. Besides collecting toys and toy trains, my hobbies include operating the trains and personal flying as a private pilot."

* * *

McCOMBS, Judith   1939-

PERSONAL: Born in 1939 in Virginia; daughter of Charles (a surveyor/geodicist) and Thelma (Sutterlin) McCombs; married Ernst Benjamin (a college professor); children: two. *Education:* University of Chicago, B.A., 1960, M.A., 1961. *Residence:* Farmington, Mich. *Office:* Department of General Studies, Center for Creative Studies, College of Art and Design, 245 East Kirby, Detroit, Mich. 48202.

CAREER: Center for Creative Studies, College of Art and Design, Detroit, Mich., instructor in English and creative writing, 1972—. Member of faculty at Wayne State University; participant in Poet-in-the-Schools program, Michigan Council for the Arts, 1976—; gives readings. *Awards, honors:* Juniper award finalist, University of Massachusetts Press, 1978; National Endowment for the Humanities grants, 1980; second place for NIMROD/Neruda second annual award for poetry, 1980; National Endowment for the Arts grants panelist, 1980.

WRITINGS: Sisters and Other Selves (poems), Glass Bell Press, 1976; *Against Nature: Wilderness Poems*, Dustbooks, 1979; (contributor) Arnold Davidson and Cathy N. Davidson, editors, *The Art of Margaret Atwood: Essays in Criticism*, House of Anansi Press, 1980.

Work represented in anthologies, including *We Become New*, Bantam, 1975; *I Hear My Sisters Saying*, Crowell; *Moving to Antarctica*, Dustbooks. Contributor of more than one hundred twenty-five poems and stories to literary journals, including *Poetry, Aphra, Prism, Poetry Northwest, Moving Out*, and *Fiddlehead*.

WORK IN PROGRESS: American Gothic: Mortal Songs and Other Stories; After the Surveyor's Death, a poetry chapbook; *Fifty-One Per Cent*, stories.

SIDELIGHTS: Judith McCombs writes poetry, fiction, criticism, and experimental visual poetry/display pieces. She teaches wilderness literature, gothics, science fiction, women's literature, and creative writing.

BIOGRAPHICAL/CRITICAL SOURCES: Thirteenth

Moon, Volume III, number 2, 1977; *Thoreau Quarterly Journal,* April, 1979; *Great Lakes Review,* summer, 1979; *Booklist,* November 15, 1979; *Snowy Egret,* spring, 1980, autumn, 1980.

* * *

McCULLOUGH, Bonnie Runyan 1944-

PERSONAL: Born January 6, 1944, in Denver, Colo.; daughter of Albert Roy (a carpenter) and Elda Mae (Almire) Runyan; married Robert Gale McCullough (an elementary school principal), January 28, 1964; children: Bobette, Laura, Wesley, Becky, Madison. *Education:* Attended Brigham Young University, 1962-64. *Religion:* Church of Jesus Christ of Latter-day Saints (Mormons). *Residence:* Lakewood, Colo. *Agent:* c/o St. Martin's Press, 175 Fifth Ave., New York, N.Y. 10010.

CAREER: Writer, 1978—.

WRITINGS: Bonnie's Household Organizer, St. Martin's, 1980; *Bonnie's Household Budget Book,* St. Martin's, 1980. Contributor to magazines, including *Family Circle* and *Brides.*

WORK IN PROGRESS: Four Hundred and Twenty Ways to Get Your Child to Work at Home (tentative title), with Susan Walker Monson, publication by St. Martin's expected in 1981.

SIDELIGHTS: Bonnie McCullough told *CA:* "As a young mother of three babies under three years old, I couldn't get beyond the dishes, beds, and diapers. I had majored in home economics in college. They had taught me to make ice cream without crystals, but not to manage a home. Because my career was in home economics and I had chosen to be a wife and mother, success at home was important to my feeling successful. I decided to attack my home chores the way I had my school work—improve my skill, become a professional rather than just a laborer.

"As I began my quest for ideas and answers, I found some of them in business situations and others from friends who had conquered similar home problems. As I found answers, I applied them to my home, and was able to get control and have time to do the other things I wanted to do. As my efforts showed results, I was asked to teach women at church and then in adult education classes. My thoughts turned to printing my lectures as a workbook. One letter someone wrote to Ann Landers cinched my goal. The letter was written by a husband whose wife paid to have most of the housework done and who still couldn't handle their two children or get the dinner dishes done before ten o'clock at night. I felt there was a need for a practical book on organization and home management. I worked on the material for two years, mostly during 'Sesame Street,' because my toddler would be entertained for that hour. My purpose was to help other people who have a struggle with clutter and confusion to know the freedom I have found with order.

"My publisher suggested I write my second book because I could draw on my practical experience of living on one salary (an educator's salary) with a family of seven people and because this was a topic that most authors had only passed over very quickly."

BIOGRAPHICAL/CRITICAL SOURCES: Rocky Mountain News, August 1, 1980; *Denver Post,* August 9, 1980.

* * *

McCUSKER, John J(ames) 1939-

PERSONAL: Born August 12, 1939, son of John J. (a fore-

man) and Helen I. (a telephone operator; maiden name, Esse) McCusker; married Diana E. Brandt (a biologist and teacher), April 17, 1964; children: John J. III, Patrick W., Margaret E. *Education:* St. Bernard's Seminary and College, Rochester, N.Y., B.A., 1961; University of Rochester, M.A., 1963; further graduate study at University College, London, 1966-67; University of Pittsburgh, Ph.D., 1970. *Home and office:* 5702 Ruatan St., Berwyn Heights, College Park, Md. 20740.

CAREER: St. Francis Xavier University, Antigonish, Nova Scotia, lecturer in history, 1965-66; Smithsonian Institution, Washington, D.C., intern, 1967-68, visiting research associate, 1969-70; University of Maryland, College Park, lecturer, 1968-69, assistant professor, 1969-76, associate professor of history, 1976—, lecturer in European division, London, England, 1971-72, 1976-77, member of department executive committee, 1974-76, and graduate committee, 1974-76, 1979—. Visiting lecturer at Mount Allison University, Sackville, New Brunswick, summer, 1963; visiting assistant professor of College of William and Mary, 1972-73. Consultant to U.S. Marine Corps Historical Division, 1973-74, Maryland Park Service, 1974-75, Canada Council, 1975-76, *Time,* 1975-76, and Institute of U.S. Studies, London, 1976. Coordinator of seminars; participant in workshops and symposiums in Canada, England, and United States.

MEMBER: American Historical Association, Organization of American Historians, Economic History Association, American Antiquarian Society (Fred Harris Daniels fellow, 1980-81), Economic History Society, British Association for American Studies, Royal Historical Society (fellow, 1976), Association of Caribbean Historians, Societe Francaise d'Histoire d'Outre-Mer, Societe d'Histoire de la Guadeloupe, New York Historical Society, Historical Society of Pennsylvania, Maryland Historical Society, Virginia Historical Society. *Awards, honors:* Grants from American Philosophical Society, 1969, 1970, 1972, 1975, Economic History Association, 1969, 1974, 1980, and American Council of Learned Societies, 1977; fellow of University College, London, and Institute of U.S. Studies, London, both 1971-72, 1976-77; University of Maryland faculty research award, 1971, 1974, 1980; fellowship from Institute of Early American History and Culture, 1971-73; Kress fellow, Harvard University, 1974; Leverhulme visiting fellow, University College of North Wales, 1975-76 (declined); National Endowment for the Humanities fellowship, 1976-77, 1978-79.

WRITINGS: Alfred: The First Continental Flagship, 1775-1778 (pamphlet), Smithsonian Institution Press, 1973; *Alfred: The First Flagship of the United States Navy* (pamphlet), R. R. Donnelley & Sons, 1975; (contributor) Eric P. Newman and Richard G. Doty, editors, *Studies on Money in Early America,* American Numismatic Society, 1976; *Money and Exchange in Europe and America, 1600-1775: A Handbook,* University of North Carolina Press, 1978.

Contributor of articles to historical magazines and journals, including *Journal of Economic History, William and Mary Quarterly,* and *Research in Economic History;* contributor of book reviews to numerous journals, including *American Historical Review, Journal of American History,* and *English Historical Review.* Member of advisory board of *Business History Review,* 1980-82.

WORK IN PROGRESS: The Price Currents, Money Currents, and Exchange Currents of Europe to 1776: A Survey, with Cora Gravesteijn, publication by Harvard University Library expected in 1982; *The Economy of British America, 1607-1790: Needs and Opportunities for Study,* with Russell

R. Menard, publication by University of North Carolina Press expected in 1982; a chapter for *The History of American Food Technology*, edited by G. Terry Sharrer, publication by Smithsonian Institution Press expected in 1982; *An Introduction to the British Colonial Naval Officer Shipping Lists, a Primary Source for the Study of Early American Economic History*, publication expected in 1984; other articles.

SIDELIGHTS: McCusker told *CA:* "I am a historian and teacher interested in the economy of early America. My research and writing has as its eventual goal an analysis of the production, trade and consumption of sugar, molasses, and rum in the North Atlantic world during the seventeenth and eighteenth centuries. If I do a good enough job of it, others might be able to delineate more clearly some of the other facets of life in the era."

*   *   *

McGARRY, Kevin J(ohn) 1935-

PERSONAL: Born June 14, 1935, in London, England; son of James and Stella (Meledy) McGarry; married wife Celia; children: Aidan James, Ruth Anna. *Education:* Ealing College of Higher Education, A.L.A.; University of London, diploma in sociology; University of Wales, M.A. *Politics:* Conservative. *Religion:* Roman Catholic. *Home:* 3 James Close, Llanon, Dyfed, Wales.

CAREER: Worked as tutor and librarian of Borough Road College of Education, 1960-65; principal lecturer in information system studies at College of Librarianship, Wales, 1967—.

WRITINGS: (With T. W. Burrell) *Logic in the Organisation of Knowledge*, Linnet Books, 1972; (with Burrell) *Semantics in the Organisation of Knowledge*, Linnet Books, 1972; (editor) *Mass Communications: Selected Readings for Librarians*, Linnet Books, 1972; (with Burrell) *Communication Studies*, Linnet Books, 1973; *Communication, Knowledge, and the Librarian*, Shoe String, 1975. Also author of *The West Riding of Yorkshire: County Handbook* (edited by John Cannon), County Associations.

*   *   *

McGARRY, Michael B(rett) 1948-

PERSONAL: Born March 4, 1948, in Los Angeles, Calif.; son of Thomas Joseph (an executive) and Rosemary (McDonald) McGarry. *Education:* St. Peter's College, Baltimore, Md., A.A., 1968; St. Paul's College, Washington, D.C., B.A., 1971; University of Toronto, M.Div., 1974, M.A., 1976. *Politics:* Democrat. *Home and office:* Paulist Center Community, 5 Park St., Boston, Mass. 02108.

CAREER: Entered Congregatio Sancti Pauli (Paulists), 1968, ordained Roman Catholic priest, 1975; Whitby Psychiatric Hospital, Whitby, Ontario, assistant chaplain, 1972-73; Interlink Productions, Toronto, Ontario, host of weekly television series, "Day by Day," 1973-75; University of Texas, Austin, campus minister at University Catholic Center and biblical studies faculty member, 1975-78; Paulist Center Community, Boston, Mass., director, 1978—. Lecturer at Boston College, 1979. Coordinator and director of workshops. Member of Boston Priests' Senate and Catholic-Jewish Committee.

WRITINGS: Christology After Auschwitz, Paulist/Newman, 1977; (contributor) Robert E. Moran, editor, *Technology, Faith, and Morality*, Part I, Paulist Institute for Religious Research, 1978. Contributor to religious magazines and newspapers.

SIDELIGHTS: McGarry commented: "As a Catholic priest in the Paulist community, I am interested in speaking to the religious uncommitted and doubtful. To this end, I work at the Paulist Center in downtown Boston, where we reach out to the alienated, the broken, and the tired. My published writing interests include pastoral care of psychiatric patients, American church history, and the meaning of being a single Christian."

*   *   *

McILWAIN, Charles Howard 1871-1968

PERSONAL: Born March 15, 1871, in Saltsburg, Pa.; died, 1968; son of William R. and Anne Elizabeth (Galbraith) McIlwain; married Mary B. Irwin, 1899 (deceased); married Kathleen Thompson, 1916 (deceased); children: two sons, two daughters. *Education:* Attended Princeton University and Harvard University; Oxford University, M.A.; also earned Ph.D.

CAREER: Miami University, Oxford, Ohio, professor of history, 1903-05; Princeton University, Princeton, N.J., preceptor, 1905-10; Bowdoin College, Brunswick, Maine, Thomas Brackett Reed Professor of History and Political Science, 1910-11; Harvard University, Cambridge, Mass., assistant professor, 1911-16, professor of history and government, 1916-25, Eaton Professor of the Science of Government, 1925-48; Princeton University, lecturer, 1947-49, emeritus member of board of trustees, 1949-68. George Eastman Visiting Professor at Oxford University, 1944; visiting professor at Yale University, 1930-31. *Awards, honors:* Honorary degrees include L.H.H., Litt.D., LL.D., and D.C.L.

WRITINGS: The High Court of Parliament and Its Supremacy: An Historical Essay on the Boundaries Between Legislation and Adjudication in England, Yale University Press, 1910, reprinted, Archon, 1962; (editor) *The Political Works of James I*, 1918, reprinted, Russell, 1965; *The American Revolution: A Constitutional Interpretation*, Macmillan, 1923, reprinted, Great Seal Books, 1958; *The Growth of Political Thought in the West: From the Greeks to the End of the Middle Ages*, Macmillan, 1932, reprinted, 1964; *Constitutionalism and the Changing World: Collected Papers*, Cambridge University Press, 1939, reprinted, 1969; *Constitutionalism: Ancient and Modern*, Cornell University Press, 1940, revised edition, 1947; (with Roscoe Pound and Roy F. Nichols) *Federalism as a Democratic Process: Essays*, Rutgers University Press, 1942, reprinted, Zenger, 1978; (editor) *An Abridgement of the Indian Affairs*, B. Blom, 1968. Also editor of *Wraxall's Abridgement of the New York Indian Records*, 1915, and with Paul L. Ward, of *Lambarde's Archeion*.

BIOGRAPHICAL/CRITICAL SOURCES: Carl Wittke, editor, *Essays in History and Political Theory in Honor of Charles Howard McIlwain*, 1936, reprinted, Russell, 1967.*

*   *   *

McINTOSH, Peter Chisholm 1915-

PERSONAL: Born November 25, 1915, in London, England; son of John and Winifred (Webb) McIntosh; married Josephine Mary Stevens, December 31, 1945 (died, 1966); married Eunice Irene Hodges, June 10, 1967; children: Solveig M., Angus P. J., Malcolm C., Patrick A.; Crispin M. Hodges (stepson). *Education:* Lincoln College, Oxford, B.A., 1938; University of Birmingham, M.A., 1952; attended Fredensborg College of Physical Education, Denmark, 1937; Carnegie College of Physical Education, diploma, 1939. *Poli-*

tics: "Of course." *Religion:* Society of Friends. *Home:* 12 Windmill Dr., Leatherhead, Surrey KT22 8PW, England.

CAREER: Head of physical education departments at schools in Malvern, England, 1939, and in Barnet, England, 1944-45; University of Birmingham, England, lecturer, 1946-59, deputy director of physical education, 1951-59, member of board of faculty of arts, 1955-58, member of university senate, 1956-59; Inner London Education Authority (formerly Greater London County Council), London, England, senior inspector of physical education, 1959-74; University of Otago, Dunedin, New Zealand, director and professor of physical education, 1974-78; University of Calgary, Calgary, Alberta, and University of Alberta, Edmonton, visiting professor of history, and sociology of sport, 1978-80. Member of International Committee for Sociology of Sport, 1964-76, executive board of International Council of Health, Physical Education, and Recreation, 1965-71, Great Britain Schools Council, 1966-73, Great Britain Sports Council, 1966-74, UNESCO Working Group on "Sport, Mass Media and International Understanding," 1971, 1973, New Zealand Minister of Education's committee on Health and Social Education, 1975-77, and planning committee of New Zealand Council for Recreation and Sport, 1975-78. *Wartime service:* Friend's War Relief Service, World War II; conscientious objector.

MEMBER: Physical Education Association of Great Britain and Northern Ireland (honorary member), New Zealand Physical Education Association (fellow), American Academy of Physical Education (fellow), University's Athletic Union (vice-president, 1958-74), Birmingham University Athletic Union (president, 1957-59). *Awards, honors:* North American Society for Sport History honor award, 1979.

WRITINGS: Physical Education in England Since 1800, G. Bell, 1952, revised edition, 1968; (with A. D. Munrow) *Britain in the World of Sport,* University of Birmingham, 1956; (editor and contributor) *Landmarks in the History of Physical Education,* Routledge & Kegan Paul, 1957, revised edition, 1981; *Games and Sports: How They Developed,* Ward, Lock, 1962; *Sport in Society,* C. A. Watts, 1963; (editor) *Mass Media, Sport, and International Understanding,* UNESCO, 1971; *Fair Play: Ethics in Sport and Education,* Heinemann, 1979.

Contributor: C. Lynn ven Dien and John E. Nixon, editors, *The World Today in Health, Physical Education and Recreation,* Prentice Hall, 1968; Bruce Bennett, editor, *History of Physical Education and Sport,* Athletic Institute (Chicago), 1972; J. E. Kane, editor, *Curriculum Development in Physical Education,* Crosby Lockwood Staples, 1976. Also contributor to *Sports Medicine,* edited by J.G.P. Williams and P. N. Sperryn, 1976.

Contributor of articles to journals, including *Journal of Physical Education, Olympic Review,* and *International Review of Sport Sociology;* contributor to *Encyclopaedia Brittanica.* Editor in chief of *Bulletin and Review of the International Council of Physical Education and Sport.*

WORK IN PROGRESS: A survey of "Sport for All" campaigns for UNESCO; research on H. Mercurialis's *De Arte Gymnastica 1569.*

SIDELIGHTS: McIntosh told *CA:* "At the invitation of the Sports Committee of the U.S.S.R., I presented a paper entitled 'Systems of Value and Competitive Sport' to the World Congress on Sports Science at Tbilisi in July, 1980. I regard ethical problems of sport, both in performance and administration, as being of the greatest importance. Of hardly less importance is the current power struggle between governments and non-governmental organizations for the control of sport."

*   *   *

McKEAN, Hugh Ferguson 1908-

PERSONAL: Born July 28, 1908, in Beaver Falls, Pa.; son of Arthur and Eleanor (Ferguson) McKean; married Jeannette Genius, June 28, 1945. *Education:* Rollins College, A.B., 1930; Williams College, M.A., 1940. *Home:* 930 Genius Dr., Winter Park, Fla. 32789.

CAREER: Rollins College, Winter Park, Fla., instructor, 1932-35, assistant professor, 1935-41, associate professor, 1941-45, professor of art, 1945—, director of Morse Gallery of Art, 1942—, acting president of college, 1951-52, president, 1952-69, chancellor, 1969-73, chairman of board of directors, 1969-75, president of Charles Hosmer Morse Foundation, 1976—. Member of Florida Fine Arts Council, 1970-74; member of board of trustees of Louis Comfort Tiffany Foundation, 1959—, and board of directors of Edyth Bush Charitable Foundation, 1973—. Art exhibited and represented in collections, including Toledo Museum of Art and University of Virginia. *Military service:* U.S. Naval Reserve, active duty, 1942-45; became lieutenant commander.

MEMBER: National Soccer Coaches Association, Omicron Delta Kappa, American Society of the Order of St. John, Century Association, Orlando Country Club. *Awards, honors:* Honorary degrees include L.H.D. from Stetson University, 1961, D.Space Education from Florida Institute of Technology, 1963, LL.D. from University of Tampa, 1970, and D.F.A. from Rollins College, 1972; art awards from Florida Federation of Art, 1931, 1949; Cervantes Medal from Hispanic Institute in Florida, 1952; John Young Award from Orlando Area Chamber of Commerce, 1967.

WRITINGS: The Lost Treasures of Louis Comfort Tiffany, Doubleday, 1980.

SIDELIGHTS: McKean commented: "I was a Tiffany fellow in 1930 while L. C. Tiffany was living. I knew him and admired him and his work. As a fellow I spent two months at Laurelton Hall. When it burned, my wife and I bought all the ruins and all surviving windows. Recently we gave the loggia from Laurelton Hall to the Metropolitan Museum in New York."

*   *   *

McKINNELL, Robert Gilmore 1926-

PERSONAL: Born August 9, 1926, in Springfield, Mo.; son of William Parks (a railroad claims agent) and Mary Catherine (a teacher; maiden name, Gilmore) McKinnell; married Beverly Walton Kerr, January 2, 1964; children: Nancy Elizabeth, Robert Gilmore, Susan Kerr. *Education:* University of Missouri, B.A., 1948; Drury College, B.S., 1949; University of Minnesota, Ph.D., 1959. *Politics:* "Democratic Farmer Labor." *Religion:* Presbyterian. *Home:* 2124 West Hoyt, St. Paul, Minn. 55108. *Office:* Department of Genetics and Cell Biology, University of Minnesota, St. Paul, Minn. 55108.

CAREER: Institute for Cancer Research, Philadelphia, Pa., research associate in embryology, 1958-61; Tulane University, New Orleans, La., assistant professor, 1961-65, associate professor, 1965-69, professor of biology, 1969-70; University of Minnesota, Minneapolis, professor of genetics and cell biology, 1970—. Visiting scientist at Dow Chemical, Freeport, Tex., 1976. Conference organizer of Third International Conference on Differentiation, Minneapolis, 1978;

participant in Princess Takamatsu cancer symposium, Tokyo, Japan, 1980; guest of Institute of Developmental Biology, Academia Sinica, Peking, China, 1980; guest of Department of Histopathology, Oxford University, Oxford, England, 1980. *Military service:* U.S. Naval Reserve, Supply Corps, 1944-47, 1951-53; became lieutenant.

MEMBER: International Society of Differentiation (secretary), American Association for Cancer Research, American Institute of Biological Sciences, Society for Developmental Biology, Environmental Mutagen Society, Linnean Society of London, Sigma Xi. *Awards, honors:* Excellence in teaching award from Tulane University, 1970; NATO senior science fellow, 1974; distinguished alumni award from Drury College, 1979.

WRITINGS: Cloning: Nuclear Transplantation in Amphibia, University of Minnesota Press, 1978; *Cloning: A Biologist Reports,* University of Minnesota Press, 1979; (editor with Marie A. DiBerardino, Martin Blumenfeld, and Robert D. Bergad) *Differentiation and Neoplasia,* Springer-Verlag, 1980. Contributor of more than fifty articles to scientific journals, including *Science, Cancer Research,* and *Journal of the National Cancer Institute.* Associate editor of *Gamete Research;* member of editorial board of *Differentiation.*

WORK IN PROGRESS: Research on the cell biology of aging, on genoclastic effects of environmental chemicals, and on cell biology of cancer with special interest in viral oncogenesis and metastasis.

SIDELIGHTS: McKinnell told *CA:* "I cherish the fact that I was born during the great American Depression in southwest Missouri, which was not a particularly affluent region at the time. Those circumstances, it seems to me, helped to provide an appreciation of lasting personal relationships and the capacity to endure the stress and difficult times that come to all people. I relied during that period on the joy of family and friends instead of plastic toys and the companionship of electronic devices. Placing value on human relationships instead of material goods freed me in later years to attempt biological research, which ultimately led to writing. The writing has been as much a source of satisfaction as the research which led to it, and I am grateful to my somewhat austere origins and the warm memories of family and friends that made it all possible."

* * *

McKINNON, Alastair Thomson 1925-

PERSONAL: Born May 25, 1925, in Hillsburgh, Ontario, Canada; son of Arnold Thomson and Ella McKinnon; married Mildred Mae Sutton, September 13, 1947; children: Catherine, Christine, Angus. *Education:* University of Victoria, B.A., 1947; University of Toronto, M.A., 1948; University of Edinburgh, Ph.D., 1950; McGill University, B.D., 1953. *Religion:* United Church of Canada. *Home:* 3005 Barat Rd., Montreal, Quebec, Canada H3Y 2H4. *Office:* Department of Philosophy, McGill University, Bronfman Building, 1001 Sherbrooke St. W., Montreal, Quebec, Canada H3A 1G5.

CAREER: McGill University, Montreal, Quebec, lecturer, 1950-53, assistant professor, 1953-60, associate professor, 1960-69, professor of philosophy, 1969—, MacDonald Professor of Moral Philosophy, 1971—, chairman of department, 1975—, member of university senate, 1976-79. *Military service:* Royal Canadian Navy, 1944-45.

MEMBER: Cercle International de Recherches Philosophiques Par Ordinateus (CIRPHO; president, 1973—), Canadian Theological Society (president, 1959-60), Canadian Philosophical Association (president, 1979-80), Canadian Federation for the Humanities (member of board of directors, 1979—), American Philosophical Association, Kierkegaard Akademiet (Denmark). *Awards, honors:* Canada Council grants, 1959—; Rockefeller Foundation grant for Europe, 1961-62; honorary fellow of Institute for Advanced Studies in the Humanities, at University of Edinburgh, 1972-73.

WRITINGS: (Contributor) J. H. Gill, editor, *Essays on Kierkegaard,* Burgess, 1969; *Falsification and Belief,* Mouton, 1970; *The Kierkegaard Indices,* Brill, Volume I: *Kierkegaard in Translation/en Traduction/in Übersetzung,* 1970, Volume II: *Fundamental Polyglot Konkordans til Kierkegaards Samlede Vaerker,* 1971, Volume III: *Index Verborum til Kierkegaards Samlede Vaerker,* 1973, Volume IV: *Computational Analysis of Kierkegaard's Samlede Vaerker,* 1975; (contributor) Roy A. Wisbey, *The Computer in Linguistic Research,* Cambridge University Press, 1971; *Ausgewaehlte Konkordanz zu Wittgensteins philosophischen Untersuchungen,* Blackwell, 1972; (contributor) Venant Cauchy, *La Communication,* Editions Montmorency, 1973; (with Hans Kaal) *Concordance to Wittgenstein's Philosophische Untersuchungen,* E. J. Brill, 1975; (contributor) John King-Farlow, *The Challenge of Religion Today,* Watson, 1976. Editor of "The Kierkegaard Monograph Series," Wilfred Laurier University Press. Contributor to periodicals, including *International Philosophical Quarterly, American Philosophical Quarterly, Journal of the History of Philosophy, McGill Reporter,* and *Revue Internationale de Philosophie.* Editor of *Revue CIRPHO Review,* 1972-77.

WORK IN PROGRESS: Several books on Kierkegaard.

SIDELIGHTS: McKinnon participated in scholarly exchange programs for France, 1973, and the Soviet Union, 1976.

* * *

McLIN, Jon (Blythe) 1938-

PERSONAL: Born October 18, 1938, in Memphis, Tenn.; son of James C. (a farmer) and Jessica (a bookkeeper; maiden name, Blythe) McLin; married Francoise Petitpierre, July 26, 1965; children: Valerie, Alexander. *Education:* Washington and Lee University, B.S., 1960; Oxford University, B.A., 1962; Johns Hopkins University, Ph.D., 1966. *Home:* 27 Oval Ave., Riverside, Conn. 06878. *Office:* Scallop Corp., 1 Rockefeller Plaza, New York, N.Y. 10020.

CAREER: University of Alabama, University, assistant professor of political science, 1965-68; American Universities Field Staff, Hanover, N.H., associate for international organizations, 1968-78; Scallop Corp., New York, N.Y., public affairs manager, 1978—. *Member:* American Association of Rhodes Scholars, Council on Foreign Relations. *Awards, honors:* Rhodes scholar at Oxford University, 1962; North Atlantic Treaty Organization fellowship, 1968; Social Science Research Council fellowship, 1968; fellow of Woodrow Wilson International Center for Scholars, 1976-77; Rockefeller Foundation fellowship, 1977.

WRITINGS: Canada's Changing Defense Policy, 1957-63, Johns Hopkins Press, 1967; (contributor) Harrison Brown and Alan Sweezy, editors, *Population Perspective, 1971,* Freeman, Cooper, 1972; (contributor) Brown and Sweezy, editors, *Population Perspective, 1972,* Freeman, Cooper, 1973; (contributor) Brown and others, editors, *Population Perspective, 1973,* Freeman, Cooper, 1973; *Mediterranean Europe and the Common Market,* University of Alabama

Press, 1976; (editor with Barbara Huddleston) *Political Investments in Food Production,* Indiana University Press, 1979. Contributor to scholarly journals.

* * *

McLUHAN, (Herbert) Marshall 1911-1980

OBITUARY NOTICE—See index for *CA* sketch: Born July 21, 1911, in Edmonton, Alberta, Canada; died after a long illness, December 31, 1980, in Toronto, Ontario, Canada. Educator, editor, and author. McLuhan is best known for his controversial theory of communication that proposed: "It is the medium that is the message because the medium creates an environment that is indelible and lethal." The author believed television to be the most influential medium of communication because it involves a majority of the viewer's senses. For this reason, McLuhan termed the television a "cool" medium, while books are "hot," for they require fewer senses. He contended that the world would become a "global village," united by television and other "cool" media. McLuhan's thoughts earned him a number of epithets such as "the High Priest of popcult," "an intellectual madhatter," and "a master of media mush." In acknowledgement of his impact, however, the word "McLuhanism" has been added to the Oxford English Dictionary. McLuhan taught at the University of Toronto for more than thirty years. His works include *The Mechanical Bride: Folklore of Industrial Man, Understanding Media: The Extensions of Man, War, and Peace in the Global Village,* and *Culture Is Our Business.* Obituaries and other sources: Harry H. Crosby and George R. Bond, editors, *The McLuhan Explosion,* American Book Company, 1968; Sidney Walter Finkelstein, *Sense and Nonsense of McLuhan,* International Publishers, 1968; Raymond Rosenthal, editor, *McLuhan: Pro and Con,* Funk, 1968; Donald F. Theall, *The Medium Is the Rear View Mirror: Understanding McLuhan,* McGill-Queens University Press, 1971; *New York Times,* January 1, 1981; *Chicago Tribune,* January 1, 1981; *London Times,* January 2, 1981; *Newsweek,* January 12, 1981; *Time,* January 12, 1981; *AB Bookman's Weekly,* January 19, 1981; *Publishers Weekly,* January 23, 1981; *Current Biography,* February, 1981.

* * *

McMILLAN, George 1913-

PERSONAL: Born March 11, 1913, in Knoxville, Tenn.; son of Horace and Mabel (Hitch) McMillan; children: Christopher. *Education:* Attended high school in Knoxville, Tenn. *Home address:* Coffin Point, Frogmore, S.C. 29920.

CAREER: Writer.

WRITINGS: The Old Breed: A History of the First Marine Division in World War II, Washington Infantry Journal Press, 1949; *The Golden Book of Horses,* Golden Press, 1968; *The Making of an Assassin: The Life of James Earl Ray,* Little, Brown, 1976.

WORK IN PROGRESS: The Death of the Confederacy, for Random House.

* * *

MEISEL, Perry 1949-

PERSONAL: Born January 26, 1949, in Shreveport, La.; son of I. S. and Rebecca Meisel. *Education:* Yale University, B.A., 1970, M.Phil., 1973, Ph.D., 1975. *Residence:* New York, N.Y. *Office:* Department of English, New York University, 19 University Pl., New York, N.Y. 10003.

CAREER: Wesleyan University, Middletown, Conn., visiting instructor in English, 1973; New York University, New York, N.Y., assistant professor, 1975-80, associate professor of English, 1980—. Fellow of New York Institute for the Humanities, 1978—. *Member:* Modern Language Association of America, Virginia Woolf Society, Popular Culture Association, Northeast Modern Language Association (chairman of literary criticism section, 1978-79). *Awards, honors:* Spencer Foundation grant, 1977-78.

WRITINGS: Thomas Hardy, Yale University Press, 1972; *The Absent Father: Virginia Woolf and Walter Pater,* Yale University Press, 1980; (editor) *Freud: A Collection of Critical Essays,* Prentice-Hall, 1981. Contributor of articles and reviews to magazines and newspapers.

* * *

MEISTER, Barbara 1932-

PERSONAL: Born January 25, 1932, in New York, N.Y.; daughter of David S. (in business) and Charlotte (Needell) Lewittes; children: Howard, Susan, Matthew. *Education:* Barnard College, B.A. (cum laude), 1953; attended American Conservatory, Fontainebleau, France, 1967. *Home:* 200 East 84th St., New York, N.Y. 10028. *Agent:* Denise Marcil Literary Agency, 316 West 82nd St., New York, N.Y. 10024.

CAREER: Horace Mann School, Riverdale and New York, N.Y., teacher of piano, 1972—. Pianist. *Member:* Phi Beta Kappa.

WRITINGS: Nineteenth-Century French Song, Indiana University Press, 1980; *An Introduction to the Art Song,* Taplinger, 1980.

WORK IN PROGRESS: A survey of the arts in the second half of the nineteenth century in France, publication expected in 1982.

SIDELIGHTS: Meister told *CA:* "Before my first book was published, most of my professional experience was that of a performer as a soloist in chamber-music ensembles. What a luxury it is to be able to polish and repolish a manuscript before the critics have a go at it, and not to rely on the vagaries of live appearances! On the other hand, what a disappointment to see that—despite painstaking proofreading by several people—nothing is ever totally free from error. Oh well, perhaps perfection would be a bore!"

* * *

MENASCO, Norman
See GUIN, Wyman (Woods)

* * *

MENDONCA, Susan 1950-
(Rose Sinclair)

PERSONAL: Born June 6, 1950, in Harrow, England; came to the United States in 1957; daughter of Vernon Leonard (a research engineer) and Phyllis (Hunt) Smith; married Victor Ronald Mendonca (a tanner and welder), April 21, 1971; children: Trina, Cory. *Education:* Attended Cabrillo College, 1967, and Patricia Stevens Secretarial College, 1968-69. *Politics:* None. *Religion:* Christian. *Home and office:* 1101 North Branciforte Ave., Santa Cruz, Calif. 95062. *Agent:* Amy Berkower, Writers House, Inc., 21 West 26th St., New York, N.Y. 10010.

CAREER: Richard Wilcox Manufacturing Co., San Francisco, Calif., secretary, 1968-69; O'Neill's Surf Shop, Santa

Cruz, Calif., designer and producer of wetsuits, 1969-70; writer, 1973—. Teacher of writing classes at Young Women's Christian Association, 1980—.

WRITINGS: Tough Choices (young adult novel), Dial, 1980.

Work represented in anthologies, including *Freedom Is An Inside Job,* Pacific Press, 1978, and *Discovery on a Summer-Ripe Day,* both edited by Pat Horning. Contributor of articles and stories to magazines (once under pseudonym Rose Sinclair), including *Guideposts* and *Parents' Magazine.*

WORK IN PROGRESS: The Laboratory, a young adult suspense novel dealing with building of nuclear weapons.

SIDELIGHTS: Susan Mendonca wrote: "I began writing seriously when my first child was ten months old. Possibly having an infant in the house made me realize the value of my time, and in that first year I sold twenty pieces to various magazines. The second year I earned over a thousand dollars at writing, which I thought was pretty good. Then I had another baby and wrote a book.

"Producing children seemed to have a positive effect on my writing (I think that attitude could work up to a point, but I didn't want to push it, so I stopped at two kids). I wrote another book, *Tough Choices,* which was inspired by a situation I found myself very close to.

"Too often we forget that we all started out as children, without sophistication, without masks and facades—a condition which is really quite refreshing. Childhood is an inherent part of adulthood—it doesn't fall away like dead skin once you 'grow up.' And because childhood and adulthood are actually inseparable and intertwined, they are together (or should be) in *all* writings, as the basis for character and motivation in fiction and reality.

"What I try to do is write that which can be enjoyed by just about everyone. If I've done it right, the reader should find it not too forgettable."

BIOGRAPHICAL/CRITICAL SOURCES: Santa Cruz Sentinel, October 10, 1980.

* * *

MERCER, David 1928-1980

OBITUARY NOTICE—See index for *CA* sketch: Born June 27, 1928, in Wakefield, Yorkshire, England; died of a heart attack, August 8, 1980, in Haifa, Israel. Playwright, screenwriter, and educator. Mercer taught school for several years before he started writing. An acclaimed author, he won the French Film Academy's "Caesar" for his screenplay "Providence," in 1977. His other screenplays include "Morgan!," "Wednesday's Child," and "A Doll's House." Among Mercer's plays for the stage number "Ride a Cock Horse," "After Haggerty," and "Flint." The author also wrote television plays such as "A Climate of Fear," "Let's Murder Vivaldi," and "On the Eve of Publication." Obituaries and other sources; *London Times,* August 9, 1980; *New York Times,* August 22, 1980.

* * *

MERCEY, Arch Andrew 1906-1980

OBITUARY NOTICE: Born December 18, 1906, in Mercer, Ky.; died after a stroke, October 30, 1980, in Silver Spring, Md. Publisher, editor, and writer. Arch Mercey was the director of information for the documentary films "The Plow That Broke the Plains" and "The River." He later held such positions as motion picture consultant to the president and chief information officer for the World Health Organization.

In 1948 he joined the staff of Ransdell, Inc., a precursor of Merkle Press, as editor and writer. He later became managing editor and vice-president of Merkle Press and senior vice-president of Publishers Co. Mercey wrote several books, including *Sea, Surf, and Hell* and *The Laborers' Story.* Obituaries and other sources: *Who's Who in Finance and Industry,* 18th edition, Marquis, 1973; *Washington Post,* November 1, 1980.

* * *

MERCHANT, Larry 1931-

PERSONAL: Born February 11, 1931, in New York, N.Y.; son of Emanuel (in business) and Anne Merchant; married Patricia Stitch (a television program moderator and actress), August 2, 1980; children: Jamie. *Education:* University of Oklahoma, B.A., 1951. *Home:* 1655 Marmont Ave., Los Angeles, Calif. 90069.

CAREER: National Broadcasting Co., New York, N.Y., reporter and editor, 1977-78; free-lance television reporter, commentator, host, and producer, 1978—. *Military service:* U.S. Army, 1952-53.

WRITINGS: And Every Day You Take Another Bite, Doubleday, 1971; *The National Football Lottery,* Holt, 1973; *Ringside Seat at the Circus,* Holt, 1976. Author of a sports column in *Philadelphia Daily News,* 1957-66, a sports column in *New York Post,* 1966-76, and a column in *Los Angeles Herald-Examiner,* 1979-80.

SIDELIGHTS: "My long-range goals are in producing quality, entertaining television shows and movies," Merchant told *CA.* "I have no writing projects in the works, but one day I will go back to writing, perhaps fiction."

* * *

MEREDITH, Don 1938-

PERSONAL: Born April 12, 1938, in Inglewood, Calif.; son of Clyde Lee and Grace (McGannon) Meredith; married Jane Hofer, April, 1960 (divorced, 1963); married wife, Jo Ann (an editor and typist), October 15, 1963. *Education:* Orange Coast College, A.A., 1959; also attended California Polytechnic State University, California State University, Long Beach, and California State University, San Francisco, all 1959-63. *Residence:* Montecito, Calif. *Agent:* Elaine Markson Literary Agency, Inc., 44 Greenwich Ave., New York, N.Y. 10011.

CAREER: Tides Bookstore, Sausalito, in sales, 1963-65; No Name Bar, Sausalito, bartender, 1965-69; writer, 1969-73; farm caretaker in Tuscany, Italy, 1973-79; writer, 1979—. *Military service:* California Army National Guard, 1960-66. *Member:* Authors Guild.

WRITINGS: Morning Line (novel), Avon, 1980; *Home Movies* (novel), Avon, 1981.

SIDELIGHTS: Meredith wrote: "A Western result of that migration which began in Puritan New England a few generations back, then continued slowly across the Great Plains until it burst westward between the wars, nesting finally in that last paradise of the homesteader, Los Angeles, I came from a background in which conversation wasn't fluid, words did not come easily. Hitching oxen to a Conestoga or stoking a reaper didn't give my forebears much opportunity to talk. And if you didn't have anything to say, you could always hitch up and move on again. A backhanded wave, a short nod of the head were sufficient goodbyes. Writing fiction has offered me a way out of this familial reticence.

"I was a slow starter. When I was thirty, my wife and I left the United States and moved to Korcula, an island off the coast of Yugoslavia. It was the migration in reverse, only we skipped the Great Plains, the wooded East, and plunged directly into Europe. I was forty-one and a resident of Italy when I published my first novel. Now, back in California, I am completing another.

"I work four hours each day, during which I complete one page or, on very good days, a page and a half of fairly polished prose. It is the slowness with which I work, the gradualness with which the phrases and sentences are crafted that allow them to come into being at all, that allow me, in some measure, to overcome those silences which still, inevitably, creep into the fabric of my life."

BIOGRAPHICAL/CRITICAL SOURCES: Library Journal, June 15, 1980.

*   *   *

MERNE, Oscar James   1943-

PERSONAL: Born November 6, 1943, in Dublin, Ireland; son of Oscar Sean (a bank manager) and Madelene (Patten) Merne; married Margaret Claridge (a librarian), April 17, 1968; children: Cian, Catherine, Jane. *Education:* Attended high school in Dublin, Ireland. *Politics:* "Nonpolitical, but probably slightly left of center." *Religion:* Roman Catholic. *Home:* 78 Clover Hill, Herbert Rd., Bray, County Wicklow, Ireland. *Office:* Forest and Wildlife Service, Sidmonton Pl., Bray, County Wicklow, Ireland.

CAREER: Wexford Wildfowl Reserve, North Slob, Ireland, head warden, 1968-77; Department of Fisheries and Forestry, Forest and Wildlife Service, Bray, Ireland, animal ecology, wildlife research, and conservation officer, 1977—. Guest on radio and television programs. *Member:* Irish Wildbird Conservancy, British Ornithologists Union (past member of council), British Trust for Ornithology, Royal Society for the Protection of Birds, Seabird Group, Wildfowl Trust, An Taisce (member of council).

WRITINGS: Wexford Bird Report, Irish Wildbird Conservancy, 1970; *Ducks, Geese, and Swans,* Hamlyn, 1974; *The Birds of Wexford,* Bord Failte Eireann, 1974; (with Richard Roche) *Saltees: Islands of Birds and Legends,* O'Brien Press, 1977; *Wading Birds,* Folens, 1978; (contributor) Sharon Gmelch, editor, *Irish Life,* O'Brien Press, 1979; (contributor) Fergus O'Gorman, editor, *The Irish Wildlife Book,* John Coughlan, 1979. Contributor to journals, including *British Birds, Irish Birds,* and *Irish Naturalists Journal.*

SIDELIGHTS: Merne told *CA:* "I usually write only when asked, and when pressed by deadlines. My main interests are birds (especially waterfowl and seabirds), wildlife conservation, and the natural environment. I have traveled to wildlife areas in Iceland and to remote uninhabited islands." *Avocational interests:* Photography, swimming, reading, travel, exploration, gardening, women.

*   *   *

MERRICK, Hugh
See MEYER, H(arold) A(lbert)

*   *   *

MERZER, Meridee   1947-

PERSONAL: Born September 22, 1947, in Chicago, Ill.; daughter of Philip S. (a dentist) and Rhea (a copywriter and editor; maiden name, Heyman) Merzer. *Education:* University of London, B.A. (with honors), 1967; University of Pennsylvania, M.A., 1970. *Home:* 3826 Enfield Ave., Skokie, Ill. 60076. *Agent:* Dorothy Pittman, Illington Rd., Ossining, N.Y. 10562.

CAREER: Executive and consultant to music industry in New York City and London, England, 1967-68; *Philadelphia Bulletin,* Philadelphia, Pa., reporter, 1969; *Philadelphia Daily News,* Philadelphia, reporter and reviewer, 1970; executive and consultant to music industry in New York City and London, 1971-76; free-lance writer, 1976—. Music director for RKO—General Broadcasting Corp., 1972-73. Fundraiser for Circle Repertory Company and BAM Theatre Company. *Member:* Authors Guild, Mensa, Chicago Council on Foreign Relations. *Awards, honors:* Grant from English-Speaking Union for study in England, 1966-67; feature writing award from Pennsylvania Women's Press Club, 1970; grant from Carrie C. Gunnison Foundation, 1976.

WRITINGS: Green Roses and Other Stories, Roundhouse Press, 1967; *Crazy Quilt* (novel), Roundhouse Press, 1968; *Winning the Diet Wars* (nonfiction), Harcourt, 1980. Contributor of more than two hundred articles and stories to popular magazines and newspapers in the United States and abroad, including *Cosmopolitan, People, Redbook, Ms., Esquire, Saturday Review, Self,* and *Rolling Stone.* Contributing editor of *London International Times,* 1966-68, *Viva,* 1973-76, *Penthouse,* 1973-78, *Gallery,* 1975—, and *New Dawn,* 1977-78.

WORK IN PROGRESS: A novel dealing with contemporary man-woman relationships, publication expected in 1982.

SIDELIGHTS: Meridee Merzer wrote: "By the age of twenty-one, I had traveled alone throughout Europe, Africa, the Middle East, and North and South America. For several years I was passionately active in the international music business. I thought we could somehow change the world through a music-spawned alternative culture. When that bright hope fizzled as my generation got co-opted, I returned to my first and most lasting love—writing."

*   *   *

MEYER, H(arold) A(lbert)   1898-1980
(Hugh Merrick)

OBITUARY NOTICE—See index for *CA* sketch: Born June 23, 1898, in New York, N.Y.; died July 23, 1980. Businessman, civil servant, editor, translator, and author. Meyer was in business at the beginning of his career and then went on to work for the British Government. While a civil servant, he began writing books under the name Hugh Merrick. His works, which are mainly about mountains and mountain climbing, include *Pillar of the Sky, Rambles in the Alps,* and *Out of the Night.* Meyer also translated many works into English and edited several volumes on track-and-field sports. Obituaries and other sources: *London Times,* July 31, 1980.

*   *   *

MEYER, Mary Keysor   1919-

PERSONAL: Born October 20, 1919, in Greenwich, Ohio; daughter of William C. (a farmer) and Grace (Allen) Keysor; married Christian C. Meyer III, February 3, 1939; children: Christian C. IV, Steven Keysor. *Education:* Attended high school in Cato, N.Y. *Home:* 297 Cove Rd., Pasadena, Md. 21122. *Office:* Maryland Historical Society, 201 West Monument St., Baltimore, Md. 21201.

CAREER: Maryland Historical Society, Baltimore, genealogical reference librarian, 1967—. Founder and chairman of

Maryland Genealogical Council, 1975—. Proprietor of Libra Publications, Pasadena, Md., 1976—. *Member:* National Genealogical Society, Maryland Historical Society, Maryland Genealogical Society, Pennsylvania Genealogical Society, Anne Arundel Genealogical Society (president, 1978-80), Ann Arrundell County Historical Society (member of board of directors), Auglaize County Genealogical Society. *Awards, honors:* Good citizenship medal from John Paul Jones chapter of Sons of the American Revolution, 1978.

WRITINGS: Keyser-Keysor Cousins, privately printed, 1959; *Cemetery Inscriptions of Madison County, New York,* Volume I, privately printed, 1959; *Divorces and Names Changed in Maryland, 1634-1854,* privately printed, 1970; *Directory of Genealogical Societies in the United States of America and Canada,* Libra Publications, 1976, 3rd edition, 1980; *Genealogical Research in Maryland: A Guide,* Maryland Historical Society, 1972, 2nd edition, 1976; (with P. William Filby) *Passenger and Immigration Lists Index,* Gale, 1980; (with Betty M. Key and Richard Cox) *Guide to Manuscript Collections of the Maryland Historical Society,* Maryland Historical Society, 1980; *Ships and Things: The Peopling of Maryland,* Libra Publications, 1981; (with Filby) *Who's Who in Genealogy and Heraldry,* privately printed, 1981; *Fehler Family History and Genealogy,* Libra Publications, 1982.

SIDELIGHTS: Mary Meyer wrote: "Genealogy is now the third most popular avocation in the United States. It not only commands interest for its sake alone, but it is called into use by the demographer, historian, psychologist, geneticist, social historian, biographer, and novelist. As such the study has taken on new dimensions. Due to the scholarly research of the genealogists, the early history of this country as well as of others is being rewritten. Great strides are being made in the field of medicine, especially in the areas of inherited diseases. We are realizing for the first time that the individual did not come full blown into this world, but is a product of his preceding generations, physically, medically, socially, and psychologically, with the option of altering some aspects and learning to cope with those he cannot alter."

* * *

MEYERS, Albert L.   1904(?)-1981

OBITUARY NOTICE: Born c. 1904 in North Tonawanda, N.Y.; died of pneumonia, January 31, 1981, in Takoma Park, Md. Educator and author. Albert Meyers, professor emeritus of economics at Georgetown University, served as chief economist of the American Farm Bureau and principal economist of the Department of Agriculture's Bureau of Agricultural Economics. His textbook, *Elements of Modern Economics,* was widely used in major universities in the 1930's, 1940's, and 1950's. Obituaries and other sources: *Washington Post,* February 5, 1981.

* * *

MICHELMAN, Herbert   1913-1980

OBITUARY NOTICE: Born March 26, 1913, in Harrisburg, Pa.; died of a heart attack, November 11, 1980, in New York. Editor, publisher, and author. Herbert Michelman joined the staff of Crown Publishers in 1943 as production manager and went on to become vice-president and editor-in-chief of that company. He edited the works of such authors as Albert Einstein, Clive Barnes, and Isaac Asimov, and was the American editor for the *Cambridge Encyclopedia of Archaeology* and the *Cambridge Encyclopedia of Astronomy.* In 1979 he began publishing for Crown under his own imprint, Herbert Michelman Books. Among the books published under his imprint are *How to Avoid Probate: Updated!,* a best-seller by Norman F. Dacey; *Explaining China,* by Steve Allen; and *Son of Adam,* by Frederick Manfred. Michelman was also co-author with Herman Gawer of an exercise book, *Body Control and Personal Fitness.* Obituaries and other sources: *Who's Who in America,* 40th edition, Marquis, 1978; *New York Times,* November 13, 1980; *Publishers Weekly,* November 28, 1980.

* * *

MIKESELL, John L(ee) 1942-

PERSONAL: Born October 23, 1942, in Bloomington, Ind.; son of R. M. (a college teacher) and Minnie (Shigley) Mikesell; married Karen Roberts (a librarian), June 13, 1964; children: Amy, Thomas, Daniel. *Education:* Wabash College, B.A., 1964; University of Illinois, M.A., 1965, Ph.D., 1969. *Home:* 5930 East Lampkins Ridge, Bloomington, Ind. 47401. *Office:* School of Public and Environmental Affairs, Indiana University, Bloomington, Ind. 47405.

CAREER: West Virginia University, Morgantown, assistant professor, 1968-72, associate professor of economics, 1972; Indiana University, Bloomington, associate professor, 1973-78, professor of public and environmental affairs, 1978—. *Member:* American Economic Association, National Tax Association, Municipal Finance Officers Association, Public Choice Society, Southern Economic Association, Phi Beta Kappa, Omicron Delta Epsilon.

WRITINGS: (With Jerry L. McCaffery) *Urban Finance and Administration,* Gale, 1980; (with John F. Due) *State and Local Sales Tax Administration,* Johns Hopkins Press, 1981; *Fiscal Administration: Analysis and Applications,* Dorsey Press, 1982. Contributor to finance and economic journals.

* * *

MILES, Gary Britten   1940-

PERSONAL: Born July 21, 1940, in St. Johns, New Brunswick, Canada; son of Oliver C. (a computer researcher) and Barbara (Schumaker) Miles; married Margaret J. Bone (a teacher of English as a second language), June 23, 1962; children: Britten, Melanee. *Education:* Colby College, B.A., 1962; Harvard University, A.M., 1964; Yale University, Ph.D., 1971. *Office:* Cowell College, University of California, Santa Cruz, Calif. 95064.

CAREER: Instructor in classics at private secondary school in Andover, Mass., 1964-66; University of Texas, Austin, assistant professor of history, 1970-71; University of California, Santa Cruz, associate professor of history, 1971—. *Member:* American Philological Association, Society for Values in Higher Education. *Awards, honors:* Associate of Danforth Foundation, 1977.

WRITINGS: Virgil's Georgics, University of California Press, 1980. Contributor to theology, history, and philology journals.

WORK IN PROGRESS: The Laws Behind the Laws: Concepts of Public Authority in Republican Rome (tentative title).

SIDELIGHTS: Gary Miles told *CA: "The Laws Behind the Laws* will focus on works of Cicero and Livy. It will be concerned not with the specific constitutional models endorsed by those authors but rather with the kinds of arguments they employ to justify their preferences."

MILLER, Bill D.   1936-

PERSONAL: Born May 24, 1936, in San Luis Obispo, Calif.; son of William H. (a farmer) and Elsie (Huse) Miller; married Virginia Weigel, April 6, 1963. *Education:* University of Missouri, B.A., 1962. *Politics:* Republican. *Religion:* Episcopalian. *Home:* 150 Lafayette Ave., Brooklyn, N.Y. 11238. *Office: Mechanix Illustrated,* CBS Publications, 1515 Broadway, New York, N.Y. 10036.

CAREER/WRITINGS: Toys (magazine), New York City, managing editor, 1970; *Mechanix Illustrated,* New York City, outdoors editor, 1971—. Contributor of articles to magazines, including *Toys* and *Popular Projects. Member:* International Motor Press Association, American Society of Magazine Editors, Overseas Press Club.

*   *   *

MILLER, Clarence H(arvey)   1930-

PERSONAL: Born August 4, 1930, in Kansas City, Mo.; son of Clarence C. and Theresa (Woess) Miller; married Jeanne Zimmer, September 5, 1959 (divorced December, 1971); children: Lucy, Paula, Christopher, Bartholomew. *Education:* St. Louis University, A.B., 1951; Harvard University, A.M., 1952, Ph.D., 1966. *Office:* Department of English, St. Louis University, St. Louis, Mo. 63103.

CAREER: St. Louis University, St. Louis, Mo., instructor, 1957-60, assistant professor, 1960-63, associate professor, 1963-66, professor of English, 1966—, Dorothy Orthwein Professor of English Literature, 1969. Fulbright professor at University of Wuerzburg, 1960-61; exchange professor at Ruhr University, 1976-77; visiting professor of English at Yale University, 1979—. *Military service:* U.S. Army, 1955-57. *Member:* Phi Beta Kappa, Alpha Sigma Nu. *Awards, honors:* American Council of Learned Societies grant, 1962; Guggenheim fellow, 1966-67; fellow of Southeastern Institute of Medieval and Renaissance Studies, Duke University, 1974.

WRITINGS: (Editor) Desiderius Erasmus, *The Praise of Folie* (translated by Thomas Chaloner), Oxford University Press, 1965; (editor) Thomas More, *De tristitia Christi* (title means "The Sadness of Christ"), two volumes, Yale University Press, 1976; (contributor) Michael J. Moore, editor, *Quincentennial Essays on St. Thomas More,* Albion Press, 1977; (contributor) Richard De Molin, editor, *Essays on the Works of Erasmus,* Yale University Press, 1978; (translator and author of introduction and commentary) Erasmus, *Praise of Folly and Letter to Dorp,* Yale University Press, 1979; (editor) Erasmus, *Moriae encomium, id est Stultitiae laus,* Volume III of *Opera omnia Desiderii Erasmi Roterodami,* North Holland Publishing Co., 1979.

Member of advisory board of "Collected Works of Erasmus," University of Toronto Press. Member of editorial board of *Moreana.* Contributor of articles and reviews to literature journals.

WORK IN PROGRESS: Editing and writing commentary for *Answer to the First Parte of the Poisoned Book,* by Thomas More, for Yale University Press; editing and writing commentary for the Latin poems of St. Thomas More.

SIDELIGHTS: Miller wrote: "Apart from editing and translating an important work of Thomas More from his own autograph manuscript (rediscovered in Valencia, Spain, in 1963), I suppose my principal achievement in writing has been to establish a sound text of the Latin of Erasmus's *Praise of Folly.* I found out long ago, while editing Thomas Chaloner's 1549 translation, that Erasmus's most famous work, though it had been translated scores of times into dozens of languages, did not exist in a reliable form—that in fact, he had augmented and revised it himself several times before his death. It was not difficult to see why there was no authoritative text: that required minute comparison of at least the thirty-six editions printed during Erasmus's lifetime. I did that, established the text, and wrote a fuller commentary than any done before. It took a long time to get the Latin edition in press, and in the meantime I thought I might as well make a new English translation based on what I had done."

*   *   *

MILLIN, Sarah Gertrude   1889-1968

PERSONAL: Born March 19, 1889, in Kimberly, Cape Province, South Africa; died July 6, 1968; daughter of Isiah and Olga Liebson; married Philip Millin (a judge; died, 1952). *Education:* Educated in South Africa. *Residence:* Johannesburg, South Africa.

CAREER: Writer. *Awards, honors:* D.Litt. from Witwatersrand University, 1952.

WRITINGS—Novels: *The Dark River,* W. Collins, 1919, T. Seltzer, 1920; *The Jordans,* Boni & Liveright, 1923; *God's Step-Children,* Boni & Liveright, 1924; *Mary Glenn* (adaptation as play first produced as "No Longer Mourn," in London, England, at Gate Theatre, 1935), Constable, 1925; *An Artist in the Family,* Boni & Liveright, 1928; *The Coming of the Lord,* H. Liveright, 1928; *The Fiddler,* H. Liveright, 1929; *Adam's Rest,* H. Liveright, 1930; *The Sons of Mrs. Aab,* H. Liveright, 1931; *Three Men Die,* Harper, 1934; *What Hath a Man?,* Harper, 1938; *The Dark Gods,* Harper, 1941 (published in England as *Bucks Without Hair,* Harper, 1941); *The Herr Witch Doctor,* Heinemann, 1941; *King of the Bastards,* Harper, 1949; *The Burning Man,* Putnam, 1952; *The Wizard Bird,* Heinemann, 1962; *Goodbye, Dear England,* Heinemann, 1965. Also author of *Middle Class,* 1921.

Other writings: *The South Africans* (nonfiction), Boni & Liveright, 1926; *Men on a Voyage* (essays), Constable, 1930; *General Smuts* (biography; adaptation as radio play first broadcast in 1943), Little, Brown, 1936; *Cecil Rhodes* (biography), Harper, 1938 (published in England as *Rhodes: A Life,* Harper, 1938, revised edition, Chatto & Windus, 1952); *The Night Is Long: The Autobiography of a Person Who Can't Sleep,* Faber, 1941; *War Diaries,* Faber, Volume I: *World Blackout,* 1944, Volume II: *The Reeling Earth,* 1945, Volume III: *The Pit of the Abyss,* 1946, Volume IV: *The Sound of the Trumpet,* 1947, Volume V: *Fire Out of Heaven,* 1947, Volume VI: *The Seven Thunders,* 1948; *The People of South Africa* (nonfiction), Constable, 1951, Knopf, 1954, reprinted, Greenwood Press, 1977; *The Measure of My Days* (autobiography), Faber, 1955, Abelard-Schuman, 1956; *Two Bucks Without Hair and Other Stories,* Faber, 1957; (editor) *White Africans Are Also People,* H. Timmins, 1966, 3rd edition, Bailey Bros. & Swinfen, 1966.

SIDELIGHTS: Of her many novels, South African writer Sarah Millin's *God's Step-Children* has proven most popular with American audiences. It is the story of the Reverend Andrew Flood, a missionary who comes to South Africa in the early nineteenth century to educate the natives. In his loneliness and desolation he marries a young girl from the village. By doing this he begins a new line of half-white, half-black children who belong to and are accepted by neither race. The novel follows the lives of four generations of the Flood family, depicting their struggle for self-respect and dignity.

"A remarkable piece of work," proclaimed L. M. Field of the *International Book Review,* "a book whose largeness of scope, whose excellence of construction and of characterization, whose vividness and terseness, balance and pervasive feeling of reality, make one long for space to comment on its every detail." J. W. Crawford, writing in the *New York Times,* declared *God's Step-Children* to be "a book to read and to treasure and fight over and to contend with. It cannot be laid aside, once it is started; it cannot be readily forgotten once it is finished. It is fertile incitement to endless and delightful discussion. It is thoughtful and witty and stimulating and exciting and profoundly stirring. It is apt to unsettle rooted convictions, to force a 'revaluation of old values,' and to increase, rather than to dispel, those disintegrating doubts which seem so much a spirit of this age."

BIOGRAPHICAL/CRITICAL SOURCES: New York Times, February 1, 1925; *Outlook,* February 25, 1925; *International Book Review,* March, 1925; Millin, *The Measure of My Days,* Faber, 1955, Abelard-Schuman, 1956; Martin Rubin, *Sarah Gertrude Millin: A South African Life,* Donker, 1977.

OBITUARIES: New York Times, July 13, 1968; *Publishers Weekly,* August 12, 1968; *Britannica Book of the Year,* 1969.*

*   *   *

MILTON, Oliver
See HEWITT, Cecil Rolph

*   *   *

MINTERS, Arthur Herman 1932-

PERSONAL: Born July 22, 1932, in Bronx, N.Y.; son of Herman (a designer) and Fira (Schwartzman) Minters; married Kathryanne M. Bakers, July 2, 1957 (divorced November, 1974); married Frances Caplan (a writer); children: (first marriage) Elizabeth Anne, Michele Anne. *Education:* New York University, B.A., 1960. *Home:* 121 East 31st St., New York, N.Y. 10016. *Office:* Arthur H. Minters, Inc., 84 University Pl., New York, N.Y. 10003.

CAREER: Art of the Synagogue Commission, Springfield, Mass., sculptor's assistant, 1952-53; Paul Gottschalk, Inc. (booksellers), New York City, assistant to president, 1953-56, secretary, 1955-62; Arthur H. Minters, Inc. (booksellers), New York City, founder, 1957, bookseller, 1957-69, president, 1969—. Artist and lecturer. *Member:* International League of Antiquarian Booksellers, Antiquarian Booksellers Association of America (chairman of mid-Atlantic chapter, 1966-67), New York University Club, Ephemera Society of America.

WRITINGS: Collecting Books for Fun and Profit, Arco, 1979. Contributor to *Antiquarian Bookman's Yearbook.* Contributor to magazines.

WORK IN PROGRESS: Two books, one fiction, the other nonfiction.

SIDELIGHTS: Minters told *CA:* "I wrote *Collecting Books for Fun and Profit* to help those who were unfamilar with the book trade and its jargon, and who loved books but were unable to buy them because of a feeling of inadequacy." *Avocational interests:* Painting, sculpting, drawing, photography.

*   *   *

MITCHELL, Allan 1933-

PERSONAL: Born March 28, 1933, in Pittsburgh, Pa.; son

of George A. and Janet R. Mitchell; children: Catherine, Alexandra. *Education:* Davidson College, A.B., 1954; Duke University, M.A., 1956; Middlebury College, M.A., 1958; Harvard University, Ph.D., 1961. *Office:* Department of History, University of California, San Diego, La Jolla, Calif. 92093.

CAREER: Smith College, Northampton, Mass., assistant professor, 1961-65, associate professor, 1965-69, professor of history, 1969-72; University of California, San Diego, La Jolla, professor of history, 1973—, chairman of department, 1978—. *Member:* American Historical Association, Society for French Historical Studies, Conference Group on Central European History. *Awards, honors:* Fulbright scholarship, 1954-55; French Government fellowship, 1958-59; Rockefeller Foundation fellowship, 1964-65; American Philosophical Society fellowships, 1971 and 1973; National Endowment for the Humanities grant, 1977.

WRITINGS: Revolution in Bavaria, 1918-1919, Princeton University Press, 1965; *Bismarck and the French Nation, 1848-1890,* Bobbs-Merrill, 1971; (editor with John Snell) *The Nazi Revolution,* Heath, 1973; (editor with Istvan Deak) *Everyman in Europe,* two volumes, Prentice-Hall, 1974, revised edition, 1981; *The German Influence in France After 1870: The Formation of the French Republic,* University of North Carolina Press, 1979. Contributor to history journals. Member of board of editors of *Journal of Central European History.*

WORK IN PROGRESS: The German Influence in France After 1870: The Army and the Church, publication by University of North Carolina Press expected in 1983.

*   *   *

MITTERLING, Philip Ira 1926-

PERSONAL: Born February 27, 1926, in Altoona, Pa.; son of Ira (a veterinarian) and Sara (Montelius) Mitterling; married Doris Davenport (an archivist), August 27, 1949; children: Martha Mitterling Potyondy, Philip. *Education:* Muhlenberg College, B.A., 1947; University of Illinois, M.A., 1948, Ph.D., 1952. *Religion:* Presbyterian. *Home:* 1455 King Ave., Boulder, Colo. 80302. *Office:* Center for Interdisciplinary Studies, University of Colorado, Boulder, Colo. 80309.

CAREER: U.S. Steel Corp., Pittsburgh, Pa., education specialist, 1952-55; University of Pittsburgh, Pittsburgh, instructor in history, 1954-57; Hobart and William Smith Colleges, Geneva, N.Y., assistant professor of American history, 1957-60; Thiel College, Greenville, Pa., professor of history and dean of college, 1960-63; University of Colorado, Boulder, professor of history and social science, 1963—, director of inter-university committee on the superior student, 1963-65. *Member:* American Culture Association, American Studies Association, Organization of American Historians, Popular Culture Association, Alpha Tau Omega, Omicron Delta Kappa, Phi Alpha Theta, Pi Gamma Mu, Sigma Delta Pi, Tau Kappa Alpha.

WRITINGS: America in the Antarctic to 1840, University of Illinois Press, 1959; (editor) *Proceedings of the Conference on Talented Women and the American College: Needed Research on Able Women in Honors Programs, College, and Society,* U.S. Office of Education, 1964; (with Frederick S. Allen and others) *The University of Colorado, 1876-1976,* Harcourt, 1976; (editor) *U.S. Cultural History: A Guide to Information Sources,* Gale, 1980.

WORK IN PROGRESS: Fin de Siecle America: Culture at the Beginning of Our Time.

SIDELIGHTS: Mitterling told *CA:* "My interests recently have turned to the history of American popular culture as an adjunct to social history. I am looking at history as the record of coping behavior, and I am particularly concerned with the means by which people coped with life as it became increasingly complex in the late nineteenth and early twentieth centuries."

*   *   *

MOBLEY, Tony Allen 1938-

PERSONAL: Born May 19, 1938, in Harrodsburg, Ky.; son of Cecil and Beatrice (Bailey) Mobley; married Betty Weaver; children: Derek Lloyd. *Education:* Georgetown College, Georgetown, Ky., B.S. (cum laude), 1960; Indiana University, M.S., 1962, Re.D., 1965; Southern Seminary, Louisville, Ky., M.R.E., 1963. *Office:* School of Health, Physical Education, and Recreation, Indiana University, Bloomington, Ind. 47405.

CAREER: Young Men's Christian Association (YMCA), Lexington, Ky., assistant physical director, 1957-60; Department of Parks and Recreation, Lexington, aquatic director, 1961; elementary school teacher, head teacher, and athletic coach in Unionville, Ind., 1964-65; Western Illinois University, Macomb, assistant professor, 1965-69, associate professor of recreation and park administration, 1965-72, chairman of department, 1968-72; Pennsylvania State University, University Park, associate professor, 1972-75, professor of recreation and parks, 1975-76, chairman of department, member of advisory committee of Center for Study of Environmental Policy; Indiana University, Bloomington, professor of recreation and park administration, 1976—, dean of School of Health, Physical Education, and Recreation. Director of recreation at Ridgecrest Assembly, summers, 1962-63; chairman of health advisory council, White River Park Commission.

MEMBER: American Alliance of Health, Physical Education, Recreation, and Dance, National Recreation and Park Association (member of board of trustees, 1976-79; vice-president, 1977-78; president, 1978-79; chairman of national awards committee, 1976-77, and national research committee, 1976-77; member of national council, 1973-76; chairman of national committee on professional development, 1970), National Council on Accreditation, Society of Park and Recreation Educators (member of board of directors, 1969-70 and 1972-73; president-elect, 1973-74; president, 1974-75), Indiana Association of Health, Physical Education, and Recreation, Indiana Park and Recreation Association, Phi Delta Kappa (president, 1968-69). *Awards, honors:* Fellow of American Council on Education, 1970-71; distinguished fellow award from Society of Park and Recreation Educators, 1978; special service citation from National Recreation and Park Association, 1978, and Academy of Leisure Science, 1980.

WRITINGS: (Editor) *An Integrative Review of Research and Church Recreation and Related Areas* (monograph), College of Health, Physical Education, and Recreation, Pennsylvania State University, 1975; (editor of revision) Charles K. Brightbill, *Educating for Leisure-Centered Living,* Wiley, 1977. Contributor of about thirty-five articles and reviews to professional journals.

WORK IN PROGRESS: Research on the status and attitudes of recreation and parks faculty members in universities throughout the United States.

SIDELIGHTS: Mobley told *CA:* "Leisure is assuming a major role in the lives of most Americans and this can be supported by almost every social indicator available today. Because of prevailing attitudes toward leisure and recreation, it is extremely difficult to interpret to the general public the importance and the potential of leisure for improving the quality of life. With almost everything I write, there is a major thrust toward interpreting the role of recreation, parks, and the leisure services in our lives."

*   *   *

MOCKER, Donald W(ilbur) 1935-

PERSONAL: Born October 18, 1935, in St. Louis, Mo.; son of Wilbur H. (in sales) and Bernice (Dexheimer) Mocker; married Carole L. Stites (a librarian), August 26, 1961; children: Jeffrey Scott, Amy Lynn. *Education:* Missouri Valley College, B.S., 1961; University of Missouri, M.S., 1967; State University of New York at Albany, Ed.D., 1974. *Home:* 1108 Hubach, Raymore, Mo. 64083. *Office:* School of Education, University of Missouri, Kansas City, Mo. 64110.

CAREER: University of Missouri, Kansas City, instructor, 1969-71, assistant professor, 1971-76, associate professor of education, 1976—, associate director of National Center for Resource Development in Adult Education, 1972-75. Visiting professor at University of Wisconsin—Madison, summer, 1975; conducts workshops. *Military service:* U.S. Army, 1958-65. *Member:* International Reading Association, Adult Education Association of the United States of America, National Association of Public Continuing Adult Education (chairperson of committee on professional standards of adult educators), Association of Professors of Adult Education, Phi Delta Kappa. *Awards, honors:* Achievement award from Missouri Association of Adult and Continuing Education, 1974, for general achievement in the field of adult education; grants from National Endowment for the Humanities, 1974, and National Institute of Education, 1979.

WRITINGS: (Contributor) *The Learning Center in ABE,* Iowa State Department of Education, 1974; (with George Spear) *Urban Education: A Guide to Information Sources,* Gale, 1978; (contributor) Laura S. Johnson, editor, *Reading and the Adult Learner,* International Reading Association, 1979; (contributor) M. Alan Brown and Harlan G. Copeland, editors, *New Directions for Continuing Education,* Jossey-Bass, 1979; (contributor) Philip D. Langerman and Douglas H. Smith, editors, *Managing Adult and Continuing Education Programs and Staff,* National Association for Public Continuing Adult Education, 1979; (contributor) Frances A. Karnes and other editors, *Issues and Trends in Adult Basic Education,* University of Mississippi Press, 1980. Contributor of articles and reviews to education journals.

WORK IN PROGRESS: Conducting a national study of nonformal learning for adults who have less than a high school education.

SIDELIGHTS: Mocker told *CA:* "Increasingly, public schools are failing in their basic function. Thus, adult basic education has been considered by many to be the last chance for persons who have been victims of that system, yet many adult basic education programs are also unsuccessful. Too often adults who enroll in them find a school which does nothing more than replicate standard public school philosophy. If this philosophy fails with children at an early stage and also with adults, then it seems that traditional curriculum and traditional teaching methods must be removed from adult education programs."

BIOGRAPHICAL/CRITICAL SOURCES: Adult Education, summer, 1975, March, 1976; *Adult Leadership,* December,

1975, March, 1976; *Convergence,* Volume VII, number 4, 1975; *Competency-Based Adult Education Report,* U.S. Department of Health, Education, and Welfare, 1976; *Administrators Swap Shop,* March, 1976.

* * *

MOENKEMEYER, Heinz 1914-

PERSONAL: Born September 16, 1914, in Hamburg, Germany (now West Germany); came to the United States in 1939, naturalized citizen, 1952; son of Heinrich and Martha Moenkemeyer; married Nancy Adams, 1945. *Education:* Attended University of Hamburg, 1934-35 and 1937-39; University of Pennsylvania, M.A., 1950, Ph.D., 1952. *Home:* 119 Ashby Rd., Upper Darby, Pa. 19082. *Office:* Department of German, 745 Williams Hall, University of Pennsylvania, Philadelphia, Pa. 19174.

CAREER: University of Pennsylvania, Philadelphia, instructor in German, 1952-55; Wilson College, Chambersburg, Pa., assistant professor, 1955-57, associate professor of German, 1957; University of Pennsylvania, assistant professor, 1957-62, associate professor, 1962-69, professor of German and general literature, 1969—. Visiting professor at State University of New York at Buffalo, summer, 1967. *Member:* American Association of University Professors, Modern Language Association of America, American Association of Teachers of German, American Comparative Literature Association, American Lessing Society, American Goethe Society (founding member), Deutsche Schiller-Gesellschaft, Theodor-Storm-Gesellschaft.

WRITINGS: Erscheinungsformen der Sorge bei Goethe, Giessen, 1954; (with Max Kirch) *Functional German,* American Book Co., 1959; *Francois Hemsterhuis,* Twayne, 1975. Contributor to academic journals.

WORK IN PROGRESS: Research on Klopstock and Lessing.

* * *

MOLLO, Terry (Madeline) 1949-

PERSONAL: Born December 26, 1949, in New York, N.Y.; daughter of Frank C. (a radio and television technician) and Anne (a legal secretary; maiden name, Cilia) Santino; married George Mollo (a retail executive), October 20, 1973; children: Lindsay Anne. *Education:* Pace University, B.A., 1971. *Home:* 32 Amarillo Dr., Nanuet, N.Y. 10954. *Office:* Knowledge Industry Publications, 701 Westchester Ave., White Plains, N.Y. 10604.

CAREER: Volunteers in Service to America (VISTA), Washington, D.C., volunteer in Putnam County, Fla., 1971-72; Council for the Arts in Westchester, White Plains, N.Y., assistant director, 1972-75; Knowledge Industry Publications, Inc., White Plains, manager of exhibits, workshops, and seminars, 1976, managing editor of Overseas Assignment Directory Service, 1977—, *Video Register,* 1978-79, and *Business With China,* 1979.

WRITINGS: (Senior editor) *U.S. Book Publishing Yearbook and Directory,* Knowledge Industry Publications, Volume I, 1980, Volume II, 1981.

SIDELIGHTS: Mollo told CA: "Professionally, I am an editor, researcher, and writer. The task of taking a publisher's concept and seeing it through from a cloudy idea to a finished, printed, bound product has always been a challenging and gratifying experience for me. The responsibility of communicating an idea (or group of ideas) to the reader in a clear, concise, organized, and artistically appealing manner

has always been the main objective behind my work. The organization and dissemination of valuable information, it seems to me, will always be important as long as people yearn to be more knowledgeable in any particular field."

* * *

MONNET, Jean (Omer Marie) 1888-1979

PERSONAL: Born November 9, 1888, in Cognac, Charente, France; died March 16, 1979, in Montfort-l'Amaury, France; son of J. G. (a distillery owner) Monnet; married Silvia de Mondini (a painter); children: Marianne, Anna. *Education:* Attended Cognac College, Cognac, France. *Residence:* Montfort-l'Amaury, France.

CAREER: J. & G. Monnet Co. (family distillery), Cognac, France, international salesman, 1904-16, manager, beginning 1923; French representative on Interallied Executive Committees, 1916-19; appointed member of Supreme Economic Council during World War I; deputy secretary-general of League of Nations, 1919-23; international banker with Blair & Co. (American investment firm), beginning c. 1925, and with Monnet, Murnane & Co., 1935-43; British Supply Council, Washington, D.C., member, 1940-43; French National Liberation Committee, Algiers, commander for armament, supply, and reconstruction, 1943-44; French Provisional Government, commissioner without portfolio, 1944-45, commissioner of National Economic Council, beginning 1945; president of Preparatory Conference of the Schuman Plan, 1950; president of European Coal and Steel Community, 1952-55; chairman of Action Committee for the United States of Europe, 1956-75.

AWARDS, HONORS: Honorary knight of the Order of the British Empire, 1947; Wateler Peace Prize, 1951; Charlemagne Prize from City of Aachen, West Germany, 1953; Grand Cross of Merit from West Germany, 1958; Freedom House freedom award, 1963; Foundation Gouverneur Emile Cornez Prize, 1963; U.S. Presidential Medal of Freedom, 1963; Family of Man award from Protestant Council of New York; Robert Schuman Prize. Honorary doctorates from Columbia University, 1953, Glasgow University, 1956, Princeton University, 1959, Yale University, 1961, Cambridge University, 1961, and Oxford University, 1963. Named a Citizen of Europe by the leaders of the nine Common Market governments, 1976.

WRITINGS: Dans le maquis de Haute-Savoie, Gardet et Gardin, 1946; *Les Etats-Unis d'Europe ont commence: La Communaute europeenne du charbon et de l'acier, discours et allocutions,* R. Laffont, 1955; *La Communaute europeenne et la Grande-Bretagne,* University of Lausanne, 1958; *Memoires,* Fayard, 1976, translation by Richard Mayne published as *Memoirs,* Doubleday, 1978.

SIDELIGHTS: Monnet is often quoted as having said, "There are two kinds of people in the world, those who want to do something, and those who want to be somebody." And Monnet, who never sought political office, was decidedly a doer. He was driven by a transcendent purpose, defined by George W. Ball in the introduction to Monnet's *Memoirs* as the transformation of Europe, the creation, in his own words, of "the United States of Europe." Because of his unflagging dedication to that purpose and his ultimate, if unfinished, success, he came to be known as the "Father of Europe."

More precisely, Monnet was the "Father of the European Community," for as Ball wrote, "Not only has he been the architect of the European Economic Community but also its master builder." His supranational career began when he went to Canada to sell his father's brandy and convinced the Hudson Bay Company to put it on the Canadian market. He also successfully marketed the brandy in the United States, England, and Egypt, where he lived for a time due to an extended illness.

Because of his business contacts, Monnet secured a position with the French Ministry of Commerce during World War I. In addition to arranging large advances from the Hudson Bay Company for the French Government, Monnet was also instrumental in creating interallied committees for the acquisition of food, arms, and raw materials. These agencies were officially recognized at the Paris Conference of December, 1917, as the Interallied Executive Committees; and for his role in their development, Monnet was appointed by Premier Clemenceau to the Supreme Economic Council. Later, as deputy secretary-general of the League of Nations, he was an active force in the reconstruction of Austria.

During the 1920's Monnet withdrew from public life to manage the family business. He also became involved in international banking, associated at first with Blair and Company, which eventually became the Bancamerica-Blair Corporation. He participated during these years in the reorganization of the Diamond Match Company, the liquidation of Kreuger and Toll (the Swedish match monopoly), the founding by the Chinese Government of the China Development Finance Corporation, and the refinancing of Poland and Rumania.

During World War II Monnet again worked for Allied cooperation. Following the fall of France, he worked closely with Winston Churchill and Franklin D. Roosevelt and is credited with the idea of lend-lease. The Lend-Lease Act, passed by the U.S. Congress in 1941, provided for the transfer of goods and services to allies of the United States during World War II. Initially he participated in armament and production projects, but eventually limited his role to relief and rehabilitation, arranging supplies for the liberated regions of France.

Toward the end of the war, he focused his energies on the Monnet Plan, a program for revitalizing French industry. His elaborate plans concentrated on the six basic industries of coal, electricity, steel, cement, agricultural machinery, and transportation. Specifically, Monnet recognized, as Alden Whitman pointed out in the *New York Times*, "that the production of coal and steel in Western Europe was a key to the successful rebuilding of French industry and that the problem was how to free that production from tariff and other national restrictions."

Years later Monnet said: "The idea was all so simple. After the war France had to rebuild. Italy was in a miserable condition. All the Benelux countries were defeated and the future was far from clear, so European union was a natural feeling." The first step toward the eventual European Common Market was the European Coal and Steel Community, which included France, Belgium, the Netherlands, Luxembourg, West Germany, and Italy.

Monnet, however, sought more than economic cooperation; he wanted political union. He wanted people as well as products to move freely across borders. With the establishment of the Common Market, including the admission of Great Britain in 1971, he worked for a European monetary reserve fund, with the long range goal of a single European currency. In his *Memoirs* he explained his hope for the future: "Like our provinces in the past, our nations today must learn to live together under common rules and institutions freely arrived at. The sovereign nations of the past can no longer solve the problems of the present: they cannot ensure their own progress or control their future. And the [European]

community itself is only a stage on the way to the organized world of tomorrow."

"Even after his retirement in 1975," John Nielsen wrote in *Newsweek,* "Monnet remained Europe's unofficial elder statesman and conscience," perhaps because his accomplishments had so often come out of influence rather than position. Whitman noted that he had "accumulated remarkable influence and the trust of an international circle of distinguished friends." Though ostensibly a financier, Whitman suggested, his chief role was as a persuader, "a merchandiser of economic change, a supersalesman," even an evangelical lobbyist.

George Ball said, "As a negotiator, he was without equal, in part because he applied to even the most marginal exchange excruciating efforts to achieve the right phrase, the precise nuance, so that, as I came to expect in working with him, even the simplest letter might have to be redrafted fourteen or fifteen times." He knew how to discover the seats of power, not always vested in political leaders; he knew how to induce men to action with a keen sense of timing; and, an "incorrigible optimist," he knew that the logic of events and of humanity would some day result in the fruition of his ideas.

When Monnet's *Memoirs* appeared a year before his death, James Reston wrote in the *New York Times,* "Monnet reminds us that there are still men of France, worthy successors of Alexis de Tocqueville and Paul Valery, who stick to the honor of the mind and believe in the ultimate unity of the Western nations." Among the many tributes paid him upon his death was this message sent to Madame Monnet by President Giscard d'Estaing: "The French will not forget what he did for the reconstruction of the French economy and French prestige, nor the Europeans what they owe him for his unceasing efforts toward mutual understanding and union on our continent." And, in the *Chicago Tribune,* George W. Ball wrote, "A man not for the hour but for ages, he altered the history of his time."

BIOGRAPHICAL/CRITICAL SOURCES: Merry Bromberger and Serge Bromberger, *Jean Monnet and the United States of Europe,* Coward, 1969; *Newsweek,* May 5, 1975; *Foreign Affairs,* April, 1977; *New York Times,* November 8, 1978; Jean Monnet, *Memoirs,* Doubleday, 1979.

OBITUARIES: New York Times, March 17, 1979; *Chicago Tribune,* March 23, 1979; *Newsweek,* March 26, 1979; *Time,* March 26, 1979.*

—*Sketch by Andrea Geffner*

*   *   *

MONTGOMERY, Vivian

PERSONAL: Born in Chicago, Ill.; daughter of Glenn A. and Emma (Broadfield) Blomquist; married James E. Montgomery (a director of training); children: James E., Jr., Clinton Linn. *Education:* Received B.S. from University of Illinois and M.S., 1953; attended Our Lady of the Lake University, 1968-69. *Religion:* Episcopalian. *Home and office:* 111 Moss Dr., Castle Hills, San Antonio, Tex. 78213.

CAREER: Worked as advertising copywriter and account executive with WDSU-Radio station, Grubb Advertising Agency, and *Champaign-Urbana News-Gazette,* all in Champaign, Ill., 1948-53; Deb 'n Heir Children's Shop, Gulfport, Miss., owner, 1956-60; school librarian and teacher in San Antonio, Tex., 1965-77; free-lance writer, 1978—. *Member:* American Library Association, Society of Children's Book Writers (regional adviser, 1980—), Women in

Communications, Authors Guild, Authors League of America, Texas State Teachers Association, San Antonio Writers Guild (president, 1980—), San Antonio Conservation Society, San Antonio Symphony Society, Castle Hills Women's Club (president, 1965-66), Castle Hills Garden Club, Gulfport Junior Auxiliary.

WRITINGS: Mr. Jellybean (juvenile), Shoal Creek Publishers, 1980. Contributor to *Highlights for Children, Ebony, Jr., Motorhome Life,* and *Trailer Life.*

WORK IN PROGRESS: Boy at Shiloh, a book on the Civil War, for children.

SIDELIGHTS: Vivian Montgomery told *CA:* "Reading and writing have been my favorite occupations since childhood. My interest in children grew naturally when I had children of my own. Through being a school librarian and writing for children, I hope I've been able to awaken an interest in books that will bring life-long pleasure to many youngsters. I'll continue to try.

"Meeting President Lyndon B. Johnson and watching him communicate with children inspired *Mr. Jellybean.* That was the name given him by children in the Head Start school near his ranch—he brought them jellybeans."

*   *   *

MOORE, Elizabeth
See ATKINS, Meg Elizabeth

*   *   *

MOORE, Kenneth Clark   1943-
(Kenny Moore)

PERSONAL: Born December 1, 1943, in Portland, Ore.; son of Melvin Clark (a salesman) and Marian Lois (Smith) Moore; married Roberta Conlan, November 22, 1968 (divorced, 1979). *Education:* University of Oregon, B.A., 1966, M.F.A., 1972; attended Stanford University, 1966-67. *Home:* 1570 Prospect Dr., Eugene, Ore. 97403. *Office: Sports Illustrated,* Rockefeller Center, New York, N.Y. 10020.

CAREER: Georgia Pacific Corp., Eugene, Ore., mill worker, 1962-66; free-lance writer, 1970-80; *Sports Illustrated,* New York, N.Y., senior writer, 1980—. Director of Oregon Track Club, 1971—; member of Athletes Advisory Council to U.S. Olympic Committee, 1973-80; member of International Competition Committee of Athletics Congress, 1977-80. Chairman of Steve Prefontaine Foundation, 1976-79. Consultant to Warner Brothers, 1980. *Awards, honors:* Journalism award from Road Runners Club of America, 1980, for career-long service to the sport.

WRITINGS: World Class, Doubleday, 1981. Contributor of news articles, features, and profiles, under professional name, Kenny Moore, to *Sports Illustrated.*

SIDELIGHTS: Kenneth Moore told *CA:* "Twice an Olympic marathoner, I found it important to make an athlete's experience understandable to a wider readership. With a marathoner's stubbornness, I still feel it important to try, but now have fewer illusions about the chances of success. I plan to wander farther afield (toward fiction, drama, film), probably writing with increasing self-centered eccentricity."

BIOGRAPHICAL/CRITICAL SOURCES: Runner, November, 1979.

MOORE, Kenny
See MOORE, Kenneth Clark

*   *   *

MOORE, Michael
See HARRIS, Herbert

*   *   *

MOORE, Robert
See WILLIAMS, Robert Moore

*   *   *

MORGAN, Jean (Werner)   1922-

PERSONAL: Born September 14, 1922, in Malverne, N.Y.; daughter of Charles A. (in business) and Gladys (Murrill) Werner; married Delbert Thomas Morgan, Jr. (a professor), August 20, 1947; children: Lucille Morgan Covey. *Education:* Wellesley College, B.A., 1944; Columbia University, M.A., 1948; University of Maryland, M.S.L.S., 1968. *Politics:* Independent. *Religion:* Protestant. *Home:* 4609 Fordham Rd., College Park, Md. 20740.

CAREER: U.S. Department of Agriculture, Beltsville, Md., editorial assistant in plant physiology, 1955-57; Vitro Laboratories, Silver Spring, Md., part-time librarian in cataloging, abstracting, and indexing, 1968-72; editor, 1973—. Member of Maryland International Friendship Families. *Member:* Wellesley College Alumnae Association, Washington Wellesley Club, Phi Beta Kappa, Sigma Xi, Beta Phi Mu.

WRITINGS: (Editor with Paul Wasserman) *Consumer Sourcebook,* Gale, 1974, 2nd edition, 1978; (editor with Wasserman) *Ethnic Information Sources of the United States,* Gale, 1976.

SIDELIGHTS: Jean Morgan wrote: "Editing reference books satisfied my quest and long-time campaign for a responsible, meaningful, fulfilling part-time position that could be pursued without neglecting family and home. Editing books provided an opportunity to do extensive reference work with the results recorded in print for widespread use."

*   *   *

MORLEY, Frank Vigor   1899-1980

OBITUARY NOTICE: Born in 1899; died October 8, 1980, in Buckinghamshire, England. Publisher, editor, and writer. Frank Morely was a co-founder of the British publishing company Faber & Faber and was vice-president and editor at Harcourt, Brace & Co. Included among his books is *Literary Britain.* Obituaries and other sources: *Publishers Weekly,* October 31, 1980.

*   *   *

MORRIS, Bernadine (Taub)   1925-

PERSONAL: Born June 10, 1925, in New York, N.Y.; daughter of Max and Sadie Taub; married Jesse Morris (a credit manager), June 5, 1947; children: Cara, Michael. *Education:* Hunter College (now of the City University of New York), B.A., 1945; New York University, M.A., 1949. *Home:* 375 Riverside Dr., New York, N.Y. 10025. *Office: New York Times,* 229 West 43rd St., New York, N.Y. 10036.

CAREER: Fairchild Publications, New York City, editor of *Women's Wear Daily,* 1947-63; currently journalist at *New York Times. Member:* Fashion Group.

WRITINGS: American Fashion, Times Books, 1975; (with

Barbara Walz) *The Fashion Makers*, Random House, 1977. Author of a fashion column in *Playbill*. Contributor to *RAM Reports*.

* * *

MORRIS, John 1895-1980

OBITUARY NOTICE: Born August 27, 1895, in Gravesend, Kent, England; died December 13, 1980. Soldier, anthropologist, educator, broadcaster, and author. While serving in the British Army, Morris traveled extensively to such places as Sikkim, Tibet, and Nepal. His ability to speak fluent Nepali made him an invaluable participant in the 1922 and 1936 Mt. Everest expeditions. From 1943 to 1952 he was head of the Far Eastern service for the British Broadcasting Corp., and while in Japan he wrote two books, *Traveller From Tokyo* and *The Phoenix Cup*. Among his other works is an autobiography, *Hired to Kill*. Obituaries and other sources: *Who's Who*, 126th edition, St. Martin's, 1974; *Who's Who in the World*, 2nd edition, Marquis, 1974; *International Who's Who*, 42nd edition, Europa, 1978; *London Times*, December 23, 1980.

* * *

MORTON, Gregory 1911-

PERSONAL: Original name George Kossoff, name legally changed in 1939; born November 30, 1911, in New York, N.Y.; son of Morris (in textiles) and Ida (a singer; maiden name, Kasdan) Kossoff; married Enid Breslaw (a teacher), January 2, 1962; children: three. *Education:* Attended public school and studied with private tutors. *Politics:* "Humanist." *Religion:* "The sun, the moon, and the stars!" *Home:* 134 Stonehaven Way, Los Angeles, Calif. 90049.

CAREER: Professional actor, 1936—. *Military service:* U.S. Army, 1939-40. *Member:* Screen Actors Guild, Actors Equity Association, American Federation of Television and Radio Artists.

WRITINGS: Family (novel), Citadel, 1980.

Author of screenplay, "The Adulteress," released by Cinema Overseas Ltd. in 1973. Writer for television programs, including "Lights Out," "Montgomery Presents," and "Danger."

WORK IN PROGRESS: Characters and Comedians, a novel.

SIDELIGHTS: Morton wrote: "I had basically a musical education, attending public school to the ninth grade, then private tutoring. I studied violin at age five and played my debut recital at New York Town Hall at eighteen. A year later my left forearm was fractured, terminating a possible career as a violinist. Eventually I could play, and I still play a good deal of chamber music with professional musicians, but concert pitch was out.

"In the early thirties I fiddled in the beer joints of Yorkville, in New York City, and observed the local Nazis taking their first steps. Six months of them was nausea enough. I then played on the streets of Greenwich Village and outside Carnegie Hall, picking up enough loot for bed and bread. This was in 1936, when my rent for one room was one dollar a week!

"One April morning I slouched down Fourteenth Street, and just beyond Eighth Avenue I noticed a cluster of people. Thinking it was a handout I joined the group. It turned out to be a theatre company auditioning for possible apprentices. I was accepted! I had literally stumbled into show business. I had found a beginning.

"Over a period of more than forty years, sixteen Broadway shows, radio shows, live television shows, summer stock, narrations, commercials, and a recording of Keats's poetry, now in the Library of Congress, I have worked with Basil Rathbone, Joan Blondel, Frederick March, Franchot Tone, Olivia de Havilland, and many others. An arch of time, and I am still in motion."

Morton's book, *Family*, is about a pack of coyotes that comes from the Santa Monica mountains to his neighborhood looking for food. Morton commented: "My novel was written as a protest against the piggishness of the world. Universally the poor are considered lesser creatures, no better than the coyotes. Considering the state of the world, I feel that every creative work should have social cognizance."

BIOGRAPHICAL/CRITICAL SOURCES: Variety, March 27, 1980; *Macon Telegraph and News*, April 27, 1980.

* * *

MOSKOWITZ, Ira 1912-

PERSONAL: Born March 15, 1912, in Turka, Poland; U.S. citizen born abroad; came to the United States in 1927; son of Israel (a rabbi) and Miriam (Yolles) Moskowitz; married Anna Barry (an artist), November 13, 1938; children: Diana Gordon. *Education:* Attended Art Students League. *Religion:* Jewish. *Home:* 390 West End Ave., New York, N.Y. 10024.

CAREER: Artist. Worked at batik and designed and painted on silk in shop in New York City, 1928-29, partner of shop, 1929; worked on farm in Woodstock, N.Y., 1930; painter, etcher, and lithographer for Works Progress Administration (WPA), 1933; worked in photoengraving and printing shops in New York City, 1938; tool and die designer, 1939-44; American Artists Group, New York City, designer of greeting cards, 1949-50; designer of greeting cards and booklets for United Nations in New York City, 1952-53; Moss Art Publishers, New York City, founder, 1953, director, 1953-55; Shorewood Publishers, New York City, founder, 1955, chief editor, 1955-62; writer, 1962—. *Awards, honors:* Guggenheim fellowship, 1943; American War Prize, 1944, for a lithograph; award from Library of Congress, 1945, for lithograph, "Storm in Toas Valley"; *Drawings of Berthe Morisot* was named one of the fifty best books of the year, 1961; award from Harvard University for *Great Drawings of All Time*.

WRITINGS: (Illustrator) John Collier, *Patterns and Ceremonials of the Indians of the Southwest*, Dutton, 1949; (editor) *The Drawings of Berthe Morisot*, Tudor, 1961; (editor) Maurice Serullaz, *French Impressionists*, Shorewood Publishers, 1962; (editor) *Great Drawings of All Time*, four volumes, Shorewood Publishers, 1962; *Pygmalion Suite* (lithographs; text by Vlademir Georges), Fernand Mourlot, 1964; *The Drawings of Ira Moskowitz*, Shorewood Publishers, 1967; *Torah Suite* (etchings; text by John Davis Hatch), A. Lublin, 1970; (illustrator) Collier, *American Indian Ceremonial Dances*, Crown, 1971; (with Isaac Bashevis Singer) *The Hadisim*, Crown, 1973; *Catalogue Raisonne*, Roten Galleries, 1975; (with Singer) *A Little Boy in Search of God*, Doubleday, 1976; *The Reaches of Heaven: The Life of the Bal Shem Tov* (etchings; text by Singer), Landmark Publishers, 1980; (illustrator) Singer, *Satan of Goray*, Sweetwater Editions, 1981.

WORK IN PROGRESS: The Penitent, drawings, with story by Isaac Bashevis Singer, for Farrar, Straus; *Mysticism and the Supernatural*, a portfolio, with text by Singer, for David R. Godine.

SIDELIGHTS: Moskowitz wrote: ''I was brought up in a Chassidic home in a family of Chassic rabbis. Until the age of fifteen I experienced the life of the *shtetl* (small Jewish town).

''I have always had a tremendous interest in the various aspects of religion—the emotional and spiritual life of men. I lived with American Indians on a Navajo reservation. I also lived in Palestine for three years, becoming involved with Mohammedism, Christianity, and Judaism.

''In recent years, since my association with Isaac Bashevis Singer, I've been very much absorbed in the history of the Eastern European peoples: the religions and superstitions, Jewish life, the peasantry, the Cabala and various mystical writings.''

*   *   *

MOSLEY, Oswald (Ernald) 1896-1980 (European)

OBITUARY NOTICE—See index for *CA* sketch: Born November 16, 1896, in London, England; died December 2, 1980, in Orsay, France. Politician and author. Mosley was a member of Parliament from 1918 to 1931, during which time he served alternately as a Conservative, Independent, and Labour representative. In the mid-1930's, though, Mosley became a follower of Hitler, Mussolini, and the fascists and organized the British Union of Fascists. He lead his fellow blackshirts, armed with rubber hoses, pipes, and brass knuckles, on raids of London's Jewish areas. Hitler himself attended Mosely's wedding in 1936. When war with Germany erupted, Mosely was imprisoned by the British as a security risk. After the Allied victory, the fascist went into voluntary exile in France. His works include *Blackshirt Policy; Mosely: What They Say, What They Said, What He Is;* and *Europe: Faith and Plan.* Obituaries and other sources: Oswald Mosley, *My Life,* Thomas Nelson, 1968; *New York Times,* December 4, 1980; *Newsweek,* December 15, 1980; *Time,* December 15, 1980; *Current Biography,* February, 1981.

*   *   *

MUELLER, Dorothy 1901- (Dorothy Mueller Bowick)

PERSONAL: Born April 15, 1901, in London, England; daughter of Gilbert (a mining engineer and explorer) and Louise (Wilson) Bowick; married Paul Mueller (a lawyer), October 10, 1929; children: Skye Moritt. *Education:* Attended University of Perugia. *Politics:* ''Fed up with them.'' *Religion:* Protestant. *Home:* Castell, 6926 Montagnola, Switzerland.

CAREER: Writer. Worked as secretary and foreign correspondent in 1920's. *Awards, honors:* First prize from Mountview Theatre, London, England, for play, ''Palazzo Albrizzi.''

WRITINGS: (Under name Dorothy Mueller Bowick) *Tapestry of Death* (thriller), R. Hale, 1973, Walker & Co., 1975; *The Monkey Wanderu* (nonfiction), Vantage, 1978. Also author of play, ''Palazzo Albrizzi.'' Writer for Swiss radio programs.

WORK IN PROGRESS: Old Maid; Past Forgetting.

SIDELIGHTS: Dorothy Mueller told *CA:* ''My husband has always considered me a gypsy, despite my upbringing in a Hampstead boarding school where a Victorian atmosphere permeated us. My daughter has often alluded to my habit, when abroad, of departing from any beaten track: 'What

about that time when you were prowling around the native quarter of Tangiers and landed up in a brothel?' Then she would drag up another episode when I was hunting for a present for my husband (an ardent collector of pottery) and was entertained by a family of Etruscan grave robbers.

''For Switzerland, where we live, my collection of foreign languages is not outstanding. When asked, I mention German, French, and Italian, and usually add 'a little English.' A knowledge of languages gives a great zest to traveling. You can make friends with a vast number of unusual people, get a deeper insight into their ideas and habits. This is invaluable to a writer. I was particularly impressed by many of the men and women I met on a lengthy stay in India, but Ceylon—Sri Lanka—entirely won my heart. *The Monkey Wanderu* commences in Ceylon.

''Dickens was the first author to arouse my early imagination. After reading how he told stories to his childhood friends I started in, was greatly in demand by classmates, and had to carry on with a continuous sequence of thrillers. When I was twelve I dramatized my first full-length play based on *Great Expectations.* I also produced and acted in it. This was followed by 'Ivanhoe.' I continued on these lines. I produced plays in Lugano, in English, which was something completely new for that city. I think it was due to repeated requests from my relations in England that I finally started writing novels.''

BIOGRAPHICAL/CRITICAL SOURCES: Jack-Pine Warbler, June, 1979.

*   *   *

MULLER, Dorothy
See MUELLER, Dorothy

*   *   *

MUNRO, Duncan H.
See RUSSELL, Eric Frank

*   *   *

MURARI, Timeri N(rupendra) 1941-

PERSONAL: Born July 29, 1941, in Madras, India; came to the United States in 1977; son of Timeri and Rajarnma (Vasu) Murari. *Education:* Attended Madras University, 1958-59, and McGill University, 1961-64. *Home and office:* 498 West End Ave., New York, N.Y. 10024. *Agent:* Dick Duane, 159 West 53rd St., New York, N.Y. 10019.

CAREER: Kingston-Whig Standard, Kingston, Ontario, journalist, 1964-65; *Guardian,* London, England, journalist, 1965-67; free-lance writer, 1967—. *Member:* Writers Guild, Marylebone Cricket Club.

WRITINGS: The Marriage (novel), Macmillan, 1973; *The New Savages* (documentary drama), Macmillan, 1975; *The Oblivion Tapes* (novel), Berkley Publishing, 1978; *Lovers Are Not People* (novel), Morrow, 1978; *Goin' Home* (nonfiction), Putnam, 1980; *Field of Honor* (novel), Simon & Schuster, 1981.

Author of ''Grenade'' (two-act play), first produced in London, England, at Hampstead Theatre, October 18, 1972. Author of ''Only in America,'' a documentary series on Thames Television.

WORK IN PROGRESS: A six-part drama series for Associated Television; research for a novel.

SIDELIGHTS: Murari commented: ''I write because I enjoy it and have been fortunate enough to earn a decent living from this act. My heroes are not mere individuals battling the world; but individuals who can, under harsh conditions, re-shape the world to their own images and impose an order on their immediate social relationships.

''Another part of my writing, the nonfiction side, deals continuously with those (both in the western world and the Third World) who are socially, politically, and economically deprived. I travel extensively, often to my country, India.''

AVOCATIONAL INTERESTS: Cricket, squash.

*   *   *

MURDOCH, Joseph S(impson) F(erguson)   1919-

PERSONAL: Born February 19, 1919, in Philadelphia, Pa.; son of Alexander J. M. (a merchant) and Agnes (a teacher; maiden name, Ferguson) Murdoch; married Elizabeth Gale (a registered nurse), April 5, 1947; children: Alexander J., Loraine E. *Education:* Charles Morris Price School of Advertising, A.A., 1947. *Religion:* Protestant. *Home:* 638 Wagner Rd., Lafayette Hill, Pa. 19444.

CAREER: *Philadelphia Inquirer,* Philadelphia, Pa., copy-writer in promotion department, 1947-51; Sun Oil Co., Philadelphia, special merchandising assistant, 1951-60, advertising specialist, 1960-68, advertising manager, 1968-76; Sun Petroleum Products Co., Philadelphia, advertising manager, 1976-80. *Military service:* U.S. Army, 1942-46; became master sergeant. *Member:* Golf Writer's Association of America, Golf Collectors' Society, St. Andrews Society of Philadelphia, Philadelphia Seniors Golf Association, Philadelphia Cricket Club.

WRITINGS: The Library of Golf, Gale, 1968; (with Janet Seagle) *Golf: Guide to Information Sources,* Gale, 1980; (contributor) Cecil Hopkinson, *Collecting Golf Books,* Grant Publications, 1980. Editor of *Golf Collectors' Society Bulletin.*

WORK IN PROGRESS: A History of Golf at Philadelphia Cricket Club, publication by Philadelphia Cricket Club expected in 1982; *Golf in Philadelphia and Suburbs,* Golf Association of Philadelphia, 1982.

SIDELIGHTS: Murdoch wrote: ''I spent a working lifetime in advertising, enjoying every minute of it. My avocation, golf, stems from a life-time interest in playing the game and, latterly, writing about it. While no game overrules life, the playing of a game adds to one's enjoyment of life. So golf is to me.''

BIOGRAPHICAL/CRITICAL SOURCES: U.S. Golf Association Journal, April, 1965; *South African Golf,* August, 1969; *Golf,* March, 1979, January, 1980; Larry Sheehan, editor, *The Whole Golf Catalog,* Atheneum, 1980.

*   *   *

MURPHY, Ed
See MURPHY, Edward Francis

*   *   *

MURPHY, Edward Francis   1914-
(Ed Murphy)

PERSONAL: Professional name, Ed Murphy; born January 27, 1914, in Tarrytown, N.Y.; son of James Francis and Mary Jane Murphy; married Patricia Clare Flynn, November 3, 1945; children: Maura (Mrs. Thomas Harding), Constance (Mrs. Joseph Mason), Brian, Dennis. *Education:* Attended National Academy of Design, 1937-38, Columbia University, 1939-40, Fordham University, 1944-45, and Art

Students League, 1952-54. *Politics:* Independent. *Religion:* Roman Catholic. *Home and office:* 24-20 146th St., Whitestone, N.Y. 11357.

CAREER/WRITINGS: Smith-Barney & Co., bond order clerk, 1932-39; radio vocalist and musician with Tex Ritter and others in New York City, 1939-40; Holyoke Publishing Co., editor and writer, 1940-42; free-lance writer, 1943-44; McFadden Publications, New York City, editor, 1944-45; Harle Publications, New York City, editor, 1946-50; Ziff-Davis Publications, New York City, editor, 1950-52; Kable News Co., editor, 1952-53; free-lance writer, 1953-55; Hearst Corp., New York City, began as editor of *Sports Afield,* became executive editor, 1955-79. Author of numerous articles on fishing and hunting for *Sports Afield;* contributor of confession stories to McFadden Publications and others. *Military service:* U.S. Army, 1942-43; became staff sergeant. *Member:* Outdoor Writers Association of America, Catholic War Veterans, Racquet Club International (Miami Beach, Fla., and Cap D'Antibes, France).

*   *   *

MYERS, Gay Nagle   1943-

PERSONAL: Born July 27, 1943, in New York, N.Y.; daughter of Richard Edward and Margaret (Trahue) Nagle; married Merrill Thompson Myers (a financial consultant), January 25, 1975; children: Jennifer Nagle. *Education:* University of Texas, B.J., 1965. *Home and office:* 14 East 74th St., New York, N.Y. 10021.

CAREER/WRITINGS: Worked as free-lance travel writer; *Travel and Leisure* (magazine), New York, N.Y., contributing editor, 1977—. *Member:* New York Travel Writers.

*   *   *

MYERSON, Joel   1945-

PERSONAL: Born September 9, 1945, in Boston, Mass.; son of Edward Yale (a theatre manager) and Gwenne (Rubenstein) Myerson. *Education:* Attended Case Institute of Technology (now Case Western Reserve University), 1963-64; Tulane University, B.A., 1967; Northwestern University, M.A., 1968, Ph.D., 1971. *Home:* 5879 Woodvine Rd., Columbia, S.C. 29206. *Office:* Department of English, University of South Carolina, Columbia, S.C. 29208.

CAREER: University of South Carolina, Columbia, assistant professor, 1971-76, associate professor, 1976-80, professor of English, 1980—. *Member:* Modern Language Association of America, American Studies Association, Association for Documentary Editing, Conference of Editors of Learned Journals, Bibliographical Society of America, Poe Society, Poe Studies Association, Thoreau Society, Thoreau Fellowship, Thoreau Lyceum, Nathaniel Hawthorne Society, Melville Society, South Atlantic Modern Language Association (chairman of textual and bibliographical section). *Awards, honors:* American Philosophical Society grant, 1972-73; National Endowment for the Humanities fellowship, 1976, grant, 1978-81; *Margaret Fuller: An Annotated Secondary Bibliography* was named an outstanding academic book of the year by *Choice,* 1977, as were *The American Renaissance in New England, Brook Farm: An Annotated Bibliography and Resources Guide,* and *Margaret Fuller: A Descriptive Bibliography,* both 1979; *The American Renaissance in New England* was designated outstanding reference book by *Library Journal* in 1979.

WRITINGS: (With Arthur H. Miller, Jr.) *Melville Dissertations: An Annotated Directory,* Melville Society, 1972; *Mar-*

garet Fuller: An Exhibition From the Collection of Joel
Myerson, University of South Carolina, 1973; *Margaret
Fuller: An Annotated Secondary Bibliography*, B. Franklin,
1977; (editor) *The American Renaissance in New England*,
Gale, 1978; *Brook Farm: An Annotated Bibliography and
Resources Guide*, Garland Publishing, 1978; *Margaret
Fuller: A Descriptive Bibliography*, University of Pittsburgh
Press, 1978; (editor) *Margaret Fuller: Essays on American
Life and Letters*, College & University Press, 1978; (editor)
Antebellum Writers in New York and the South, Gale, 1979.

(Editor) *Critical Essays on Margaret Fuller*, G. K. Hall,
1980; *The New England Transcendentalists and the "Dial":
A History of the Magazine and Its Contributors*, Fairleigh
Dickinson University Press, 1980; (editor with Philip Gura)
Critical Essays on American Transcendentalism, G. K. Hall,
1982; (editor with Robert E. Burkholder) *Critical Essays on
Ralph Waldo Emerson*, G. K. Hall, 1982; (editor) *The Brook
Farm Book: A Collection of First-Hand Accounts of the
Community*, AMS Press, 1982; (editor) *Emerson Centenary
Essays*, Southern Illinois University Press, 1982; (with Burk-
holder) *Ralph Waldo Emerson: An Annotated Secondary
Bibliography*, University of Pittsburgh Press, 1982; *Ralph
Waldo Emerson: A Descriptive Bibliography*, University of
Pittsburgh Press, 1982.

Series editor of "American Authors Logs Series," Twayne,
and "American Literary Manuscripts Series," Twayne;
member of editorial board of "Pittsburgh Series in Bibliography," University of Pittsburgh Press, and editorial associate
to "The Writings of Herman Melville," Northwestern University Press, 1970-77. Editor of *Studies in the American
Renaissance*, 1977—.

*WORK IN PROGRESS: Theodore Parker: A Descriptive
Bibliography*, publication by Garland Publishing expected in
1983; editing *The Transcendentalists: A Review of Research
and Criticism*, Modern Language Association of America,
1984; *Emily Dickinson: A Descriptive Bibliography*, University of Pittsburgh Press, 1984.

N

NAAR, Jon 1920-

PERSONAL: Born May 5, 1920, in London, England; came to the United States in 1946, naturalized citizen, 1956; son of Alfred A. (a politician) and Dorine (a dress designer and manufacturer; maiden name, Plater) Naar; married second wife, Beverly Russell (an editor), January, 1981; children: (previous marriage) Alex. Education: University of Paris, Certificat d'Etudes, 1937; University of London, B.A. (with honors), 1940; Columbia University, M.A. and Certificate of the Russian Institute, 1951. Home: 230 East 50th St., New York, N.Y. 10022.

CAREER: World Wide Medical News Service, New York City, managing editor, 1953-59; Seagram's, New York City, assistant scientific director, 1960; Pharmacraft Laboratories, New York City, director of international marketing, 1962-63; free-lance writer and photographer, 1964—. Military service: British Army, 1940-46; became major. Member: American Society of Magazine Photographers (member of board of directors, 1979-81), American Wind Energy Association.

WRITINGS: (With Norman Mailer) The Faith of Graffiti, Praeger, 1974; (with Molly Siple) Living in One Room, Random House, 1976; Design for a Limited Planet, Ballantine, 1977; (with Norma Skurka) Your Space, St. Martin's, 1980; The New Wind Power, Viking, 1981. Contributor of articles and photographs to magazines all over the world.

WORK IN PROGRESS: A series of books and articles on renewable energy.

SIDELIGHTS: Jon Naar is an international ecology-energy consultant. He also lectures on the uses of renewable energy. In 1979 his advice was responsible, in large part, for the establishment of an alternative energy center in a factory group at Poona, India. Design for a Limited Planet is a best-selling reportage on passive solar energy in residential applications. The New Wind Power is the first comprehensive report on the use of wind energy in the United States.

Naar's photographs have been exhibited at the Metropolitan Museum and the Museum of Modern Art in New York City.

*   *   *

NADEL, Ira Bruce 1943-

PERSONAL: Born July 22, 1943, in Rahway, N.J.; son of Isaac David and Francis (Sofman) Nadel; married Susan Matties, June 5, 1966 (died February 23, 1975); married Jose-phine Margolis (a lawyer), July 4, 1976. Education: Rutgers University, B.A., 1965, M.A., 1967; Cornell University, Ph.D., 1970. Home: 4208 Doncaster Way, Vancouver, British Columbia, Canada V6S 1V9. Office: Department of English, University of British Columbia, Vancouver, British Columbia, Canada V6T 1W5.

CAREER: University of British Columbia, Vancouver, assistant professor, 1970-76, associate professor of English, 1977—. Member: Canadian Association of University Teachers of English, Modern Language Association of America, Victorian Studies Association of Western Canada (president, 1980-82), Phi Beta Kappa. Awards, honors: Canada Council fellowship, 1975-76; leave fellowship from Social Sciences and Humanities Research Council, 1982.

WRITINGS: (Contributor) Norman A. Anderson and Margene E. Weiss, editors, Interspace and the Inward Sphere: Essays on the Romantic and Victorian Self-Essays in Literature Books, Western Illinois University, 1978; (editor with F. S. Schwartzbach, and contributor) Victorian Artists and the City, Pergamon, 1980; Jewish Writers of North America, Gale, 1980; (contributor) Judith Herz and Robert K. Martin, editors, E. M. Forster: Centenary Revaluations, Macmillan, 1981; (contributor) Gordon S. Haight and Rosemary Van Arsdel, editors, George Eliot: Centenary Essays, Macmillan, 1981. Contributor to literature journals.

WORK IN PROGRESS: Editing Victorian Fiction, for Dictionary of Literary Biography series, publication by Gale expected in 1982; a study of the literary forms of biography.

SIDELIGHTS: Nadel told CA: "My concern with the relationship between literature and society has recently been focused by my interest in the evolution of biography as a literary genre. Through various comparative studies I have been exploring the link between an actual and written life as well as the importance of imagination in writing the narrative of another. The crucial question, however, may not be why one writes a biography, but what use is it?''

*   *   *

NAGY, Gregory 1942-

PERSONAL: Born October 22, 1942, in Budapest, Hungary; came to the United States in 1953, naturalized citizen, 1959; son of Bela B. (a professor) and Martha (Falaky) Nagy; married Olga Merck Davidson, August 1, 1975. Education: Indiana University, A.B., 1962; Harvard University, Ph.D.,

1966. *Religion:* Roman Catholic. *Home:* 84 Revere St., Boston, Mass. *Office:* Department of Classics, Harvard University, Cambridge, Mass. 02138.

CAREER: Harvard University, Cambridge, Mass., instructor, 1966-69, assistant professor of classics, 1969-73; Johns Hopkins University, Baltimore, Md., associate professor, 1973-74, professor of classics, 1974-75; Harvard University, professor of Greek and Latin, 1975—. *Member:* American Philological Association, Linguistic Society of America, Phi Beta Kappa.

WRITINGS: Greek Dialects and the Transformation of an Indo-European Process (monograph), Harvard University Press, 1970; (with Fred W. Householder) *Greek: A Survey of Recent Work,* Mouton, 1972; *Comparative Studies in Greek and Indic Meter* (monograph), Harvard University Press, 1974; *The Best of the Achaeans: Concepts of the Hero in Archaic Greek Poetry,* Johns Hopkins Press, 1979. Associate editor of *American Journal of Philology,* 1973-75.

* * *

NAIFEH, Steven Woodward 1952-

PERSONAL: Surname is pronounced *Nay*-fee; born June 19, 1952, in Tehran, Iran; U.S. citizen born abroad; son of George Amel (a consultant) and Marion (a professor; maiden name, Lanphear) Naifeh. *Education:* Princeton University, A.B. (summa cum laude), 1974; Harvard University, J.D., 1977, M.A., 1978, doctoral study, 1978—. *Home:* 24 Peabody Ter., No. 1301, Cambridge, Mass. 02138. *Agent:* Connie Clausen, Connie Clausen Associates, 250 East 87th St., New York, N.Y. 10028. *Office:* Sabbagh, Naifeh & Associates, Inc., 4600 Reno Rd. N.W., Washington, D.C. 20008.

CAREER: National Gallery of Art, Washington, D.C., staff lecturer, summer, 1976; Milbank, Tweed, Hadley & McCloy (law firm), New York, N.Y., associate, summer, 1976; Sabbagh, Naifeh & Associates, Inc. (consulting and public relations firm), Washington, D.C., vice-president, 1980—. Work exhibited in solo shows in the United States, United Arab Emirates, Nigeria, and Pakistan; lecturer in art. *Member:* Phi Beta Kappa.

WRITINGS: Culture Making: Money, Success, and the New York Art World, Princeton University, 1976; (with Gregory White Smith) *Moving Up in Style,* St. Martin's, 1980; *Gene Davis,* Arts Publisher, 1981. Contributor to *Arts, Art International,* and *African Arts.*

WORK IN PROGRESS: From Primitive to Modern: One Hundred Years of Nigerian Art, publication expected in 1982; *The Arts Book,* with Gregory White Smith, publication expected in 1982; *Pillars of Wisdom: New Buildings for the World of Islam,* publication expected in 1982 or 1983.

* * *

NALTY, Bernard Charles 1931-

PERSONAL: Born June 13, 1931, in Omaha, Neb.; son of Richard B. (a letter carrier) and Madeline (Helmer) Nalty; married Barbara Kathryn Watke, December 30, 1954; children: Diane, Kathleen Nalty Lewis, Bernard Charles, Jr., Elizabeth, Richard. *Education:* Creighton University, B.A., 1953; Catholic University of America, M.A., 1957. *Politics:* Democrat. *Religion:* Roman Catholic. *Home:* 5905 15th Ave., Hyattsville, Md. 20782.

CAREER: U.S. Marine Corps, Headquarters, Washington, D.C., civilian historian, 1956-61; U.S. Joint Chiefs of Staff, Washington, D.C., historian, 1961-64; Office of U.S. Air Force History, Washington, D.C., historian, 1964—. *Mili-*

tary service: U.S. Army, 1953-55. *Member:* American Aviation Historical Society, Air Force Historical Foundation.

WRITINGS: (Contributor) Karl Schuon, editor, *The Leathernecks: An Informal History,* F. Watts, 1963; (with Henry Shaw and Ed Turnbladh) *Central Pacific Drive,* U.S. Government Printing Office, 1966; (contributor) Doris Condit and Bert Cooper, editors, *Challenge and Response in Internal Conflict: Experience in Africa and Latin America,* American University, 1968; (with Charles Hildreth) *1001 Questions Answered About Aviation History,* Dodd, 1969.

Air Power and the Fight for Khe Sanh, U.S. Government Printing Office, 1973; (editor with Morris MacGregor) *Blacks in the Armed Forces: Basic Documents,* thirteen volumes, Scholarly Resources, 1977; *Tigers Over Asia,* Dutton-Elsevier, 1978; (with Carl Berger) *The Men Who Bombed the Reich,* Dutton-Elsevier, 1978; (editor with Dennis Noble and Truman Strobridge) *Shipwrecks, Rescues, and Investigations,* Scholarly Resources, 1978; (contributor) Ray Bonds, editor, *The Vietnam War,* Crown, 1979.

WORK IN PROGRESS: An official account of aerial interdiction in southern Laos, 1968-72, publication by Office of Air Force History expected in 1985.

* * *

NEAL, Larry
See NEAL, Lawrence (P.)

* * *

NEAL, Lawrence (P.) 1937-1981
(Larry Neal)

OBITUARY NOTICE—See index for *CA* sketch: Born September 4, 1937, in Atlanta, Ga.; died of a heart attack, January 6, 1981, in Hamilton, N.Y. Poet, critic, and playwright best known as a major influence in the black arts movement of the 1960's. He served as the arts editor of *Liberator* during the sixties and acted as editor for other black publications. With Amiri Baraka, previously known as LeRoi Jones, he helped found the Black Arts Theatre in New York in 1965. Neal's writings include *Black Fire: An Anthology of Afro-American Writing, Black Boogaloo: Notes on Black Liberation, Trippin': A Need for Change, Hoodoo Hollerin' Bebop Ghosts,* and *Analytical Study of Afro-American Culture.* He also authored a screenplay and contributed to numerous periodicals. Obituaries and other sources: *New York Times,* January 9, 1981; *Washington Post,* January 12, 1981; *AB Bookman's Weekly,* January 26, 1981.

* * *

NELLIS, Muriel

PERSONAL: Born in New York; daughter of Abraham and Sarah (Fried) Gollon; married Joseph L. Nellis (a general counsel); children: Barbara, David, Adam, Amy. *Education:* Attended New School for Social Research and Hofstra University. *Politics:* "Yes." *Religion:* "Yes." *Home:* 3539 Albemarle St. N.W., Washington, D.C. 20008. *Agent:* Ann Buchwald, 4327 Hawthorne St. N.W., Washington, D.C. 20016. *Office:* National Research and Communications Associates, Inc., 4201 Connecticut Ave. N.W., Suite 301, Washington, D.C. 20008.

CAREER: WLNA-Radio, Peekskill, N.Y., director of continuity, traffic, and women's programs, 1949-50; WGNR-Radio, New Rochelle, N.Y., traffic manager and program personality, 1950; WIP-Radio, Philadelphia, Pa., continuity director, 1955-56; WDAS-Radio, Philadelphia, traffic director, 1956-57; worked in publishing, 1960-63; National Research and Communications Associates, Inc., Washington, D.C., president, 1974—. National coordinator of U.S. Department of Health, Education, and Welfare's Alliance of Regional Coalitions on Drugs, Alcohol, and Women's Health, 1972-78; member of women's task panel of President's Commission on Mental Health, 1978; manager of international conference of drugs, alcohol, and women, 1975. Consultant to National Institute on Mental Health, 1972, to U.S. House of Representatives' select committee on crime, 1977, to committee on substance abuse, in Hawaii, to WETA-TV in Washington, D.C., and to task force on drug abuse in Washington, D.C., schools. Director of community relations for Lionel Corp., 1947. *Member:* American Bar Association (administrative law associate), American Public Health Association. *Awards, honors:* Named honorary citizen of New Orleans, La., 1978.

WRITINGS: (Editor with Ruth Hargreaves) *Bibliography on Women and Health Concerns,* United Methodist Church, 1974; (editor and contributor) *Resource Book on Drug Abuse Education,* National Institute on Mental Health, 1972; (contributor) *Developments in the Field of Drug Abuse,* Schenkman, 1974; (editor) *Drugs, Alcohol, and Women,* privately printed, 1976; *The Female Fix,* Houghton, 1980.

Editor of "Let's Color in French (Spanish, Hebrew, German)," a series of coloring books for elementary school students of foreign languages, Murette Publications, 1962-65. Contributor to magazines, including *Harper's Bazaar, Ms., Engage—Social Action,* and *Women's Action Agenda.* Founder, publisher, and managing editor of *Ladies' Circle,* 1963.

WORK IN PROGRESS: "Treatment," a movie for television.

SIDELIGHTS: National Research and Communications Associates, Inc., is a human services consulting firm, specializing in health and education, including drug and alcohol issues, government, research, and specialized and mass communications.

Muriel Nellis commented to *CA:* "I have always been engaged by events and moods that signify the 'passions of my time,' especially those couched in Ralph Waldo Emerson's admonition, 'The public mind wants self respect.' I admire effectiveness in people and strategies alike. I savor the challenge of growth and am impatient with limited notions, horizons, or people."

AVOCATIONAL INTERESTS: Water skiing, reading, singing, dancing, ballet and theatre, painting and drawing, graphic design and layout.

BIOGRAPHICAL/CRITICAL SOURCES: San Francisco Examiner, May 8, 1977; *Christian Science Monitor,* May 9, 1977; *Seattle Times,* May 26, 1977; *New Orleans Times-Picayune,* July 10, 1977; *Chicago Sun-Times,* July 31, 1977, February 24, 1980, June 1, 1980; *People,* May 8, 1978; *Honolulu Advertiser,* August 20, 1979, August 8, 1980; *Saturday Review,* March 1, 1980; *Los Angeles Times,* March 23, 1980; *San Francisco Chronicle,* April 8, 1980; *Palm Springs Life,* June, 1980.

*   *   *

NEVELL, Dick
    See NEVELL, Richard (William Babcock)

NEVELL, Richard (William Babcock)   1947-
    (Dick Nevell)

PERSONAL: Born July 1, 1947, in Greenwich, Conn.; son of Thomas G. W. (an artist) and Raye (Babcock) Nevell. *Education:* Boston University, A.B., 1969. *Home:* 11494 East Yale Pl., Aurora, Colo. 80014.

CAREER: Choreographer, composer and musician, film and record producer, and singer. President of Nine Pines Music Co. in Hancock, N.H.; leader of Dick Nevell Dance Band in New York City. Free-lance editor and photographer. *Member:* American Society of Composers, Authors, and Publishers, Order of Flamingoes. *Awards, honors:* Award from Dance Film Association, 1978, for "Country Corners"; Ambassador Author Award from English-Speaking Union, 1979, for *A Time to Dance;* award from American Film Festival, 1979, for "Full of Life A-Dancin'."

WRITINGS: A Time to Dance: American Country Dancing From Hornpipes to Hot Hash, St. Martin's, 1980; "Rachel" (song), Nine Pines Music, 1980; "Woodland Dream" (song), Nine Pines Music, 1980; "Snooze" (recording), released by Nine Pines Records, 1981.

WORK IN PROGRESS: The Life and Times of Stephen Collins Foster: American Songwriter, publication expected in 1982.

SIDELIGHTS: Richard Nevell told *CA:* "All of my 'written' work, whether it be in the form of a book, a song, a play, or a film, is totally dependent upon the inspiration gained from the lives of other creatures on this planet, be they humans, animals, or plants. I am equally interested in the outer exploration of the universe and the inner exploration of the consciousness, for I believe the knowledge gained from these frontiers is the only way to save Earth from continued misery, war, and famine. The horror is that the answers to these problems have been made explicit many times in the Ten Commandments, the Koran, the songs and poems of countless writers, and in the 'scientific' work of people like Einstein and Lyall Watson. We simply have not yet learned to listen."

*   *   *

NEWCOMB, William W(ilmon), Jr.   1921-

PERSONAL: Born October 30, 1921, in Detroit, Mich.; son of William W. and Esther (Matthews) Newcomb; married Glendora E. Thielan, August 24, 1946; children: Mary Elaine (Mrs. Robert Kannenberg), William Andrew. *Education:* Attended Albion College, 1939-41; University of Michigan, A.B., 1943, M.A., 1947, Ph.D., 1953. *Politics:* Liberal independent. *Religion:* None. *Home:* 6206 Shoal Creek Blvd., Austin, Tex. 78757. *Office:* Department of Anthropology, University of Texas, Austin, Tex. 78712.

CAREER: University of Texas, Austin, instructor in anthropology, 1947-50, 1951-52; Colgate University, Hamilton, N.Y., visiting assistant professor of anthropology and sociology, 1953-54; University of Texas, research scientist at Texas Memorial Museum, 1954-57, director of museum, 1957-78, professor of anthropology, 1962—. Consultant to Wichita Indian tribe of Oklahoma. *Military service:* U.S. Army, Combat Infantry, 1943-46; received four battle stars.

MEMBER: American Anthropological Association (fellow), Texas State Historical Association (fellow), Texas Archaeological Society, Texas Institute of Letters. *Awards, honors:* Writers Roundup Award from Theta Sigma Phi and award from Texas Institute of Letters, both 1961, for *The Indians of Texas,* and 1967, both for *The Rock Art of Texas Indians;*

Presidio la Bahia Award from Kathryn Stoner O'Connor Foundation, 1969, for monograph, "A Lipan Apache Mission."

WRITINGS: The Indians of Texas: From Prehistoric to Modern Times, University of Texas Press, 1961; *The Rock Art of Texas Indians,* University of Texas Press, 1967; *North American Indians: An Anthropological Perspective,* Goodyear Publishing, 1974; *The People Called Wichita,* Indian Tribal Series, 1976; *German Artist on the Texas Frontier: Richard Friedrich Petri,* University of Texas Press, 1978. Contributor to museum journals.

WORK IN PROGRESS: A book about frontier Indians who played a central role as scouts, hunters, trackers, mediators, and interpreters in the opening of the American West.

* * *

NEWMAN, Adrien Ann 1941-
(Adrien Arpel)

PERSONAL: Born July 15, 1941, in Jersey City, N.J.; daughter of Samuel and Ada (Stark) Joachim; married Ronald Newman (a business executive), October 30, 1960; children: Lauren. *Education:* Attended Pace College (now University). *Home:* 14 Foxwood Rd., Kings Point, N.Y. 11024. *Agent:* R. Newman, 265 Great Neck Rd., Great Neck, N.Y. 11021. *Office:* 666 Fifth Ave., New York, N.Y. 10019.

CAREER: Adrien Arpel (cosmetic firm), New York, N.Y., president, 1965—.

WRITINGS—Under pseudonym Adrien Arpel: (With Ronnie Sue Ebenstein) *Adrien Arpel's Three-Week Crash Makeover/Shapeover Beauty Program,* Rawson Associates, 1977; (with Ebenstein) *How to Look Ten Years Younger,* Rawson Wade, 1980.

SIDELIGHTS: Adrien Arpel commented to *CA:* "My business career has been devoted solely to helping women look their best and in so doing feel their best. I've been able to do this by teaching women how to make themselves over creatively by using cosmetics and coordinating them with hair and clothing styles.

"My writing has been directed at many of these same women, informing them with factual and easy-to-read reference books on beauty, of how to do the best with what they have, and if they don't have it, where to get it."

BIOGRAPHICAL/CRITICAL SOURCES: People, July 3, 1978; *New York Times Book Review,* July 9, 1978.

* * *

NEWMAN, Barbara
See NEWMAN, Mona Alice Jean

* * *

NEWMAN, David 1937-

PERSONAL: Born February 4, 1937, in New York, N.Y.; son of Herman (a clothing manufacturer) and Rose (a bookkeeper; maiden name, Spatz) Newman; married Leslie Harris England (a writer), June 22, 1958; children: Nathan, Catherine. *Education:* University of Michigan, B.A., 1958, M.A., 1959. *Agent:* Sam Cohn, International Creative Management, 40 West 57th St., New York, N.Y. 10019. *Office:* Academy of Motion Picture Arts and Sciences, 8949 Wilshire Blvd., Beverly Hills, Calif. 90211.

CAREER: Esquire magazine, New York City, editor, 1960-64, contributing editor, 1964—; *Mademoiselle* magazine, New York City, author of column "Man Talk" with Robert

Benton, 1964-74; free-lance writer, 1964—. *Awards, honors:* Avery Hopwood Fiction Award from University of Michigan, 1957, for short stories; Avery Hopwood Drama Award from University of Michigan, 1958, for three plays; Writers Guild of America award for best drama, New York Film Critics Best Screenplay Award, and National Film Critics Best Screenplay Award, all 1967, all for "Bonnie and Clyde"; Writers Guild of America award for best comedy, 1972, for "What's Up Doc?"

WRITINGS: (Editor) *Esquire Book of Gambling,* Harper, 1962; *Esquire World of Humor,* Harper, 1964; (with Robert Benton) *Extremism: A Non Book,* Viking, 1964; "It's a Bird, It's a Plane, It's Superman" (two-act play), first produced on Broadway at Alvin Theatre, March, 1966; (contributor) "Oh! Calcutta" (one-act play), first produced Off-Broadway at Eden Theatre, 1969.

Screenplays: (With Robert Benton) "Bonnie and Clyde," Warner Bros., 1967; (with Benton) "There Was a Crooked Man," Warner Bros., 1969; (with Benton) "Hubba, Hubba; or, Will the Big Bands Ever Come Back," (based on play "The Play's the Thing" by Ferenc Molnar), 1968; (with Benton and Buck Henry) "What's Up, Doc?," Warner Bros., 1971; (with Benton) "Bad Company," Paramount, 1972; (with Benton, Mario Puzo, and wife, Leslie Newman) "Superman," Warner Bros., 1978; (with Benton) "Stab," 1981; (with L. Newman) "Superman II," Warner Bros., 1981.

WORK IN PROGRESS: Writing screenplay and directing film, "Letters to Michael."

CA INTERVIEW
CA interviewed David Newman by phone April 3, 1980, at his office in New York City.

CA: You and your sometime collaborator Robert Benton have written several movies in which outsiders, outlaws, "bad guys" are the protagonists. When you were a kid, did you always want the bad guys to win?

NEWMAN: I don't know if I always wanted the bad guys to win. Like everybody else, I probably thought the bad guys were the most interesting guys. They are certainly the most fun to write. But I think what we began doing was trying to turn the bad guys into good guys. Or to phrase it another way, we saw the bad guys as not being so bad.

CA: What attracted you so strongly to the western?

NEWMAN: What attracted me to the western was simply that I just loved the genre. I've loved westerns ever since I can remember. Two directors who've had a tremendous influence on my own work and my own thinking about film were John Ford and Howard Hawks, both of whom—Ford especially—did almost exclusively westerns. There's something about that larger-than-life myth that makes it kind of interesting to come up and play with bigger-than-life conflicts. They're played out on a kind of open, unsophisticated scale, so you can deal with a certain lack of sophistication in the western—you don't get caught up so much in the minutiae of everyday life. I also like the research. That was always a lot of fun with westerns because I like the way people talked and the way people lived. And you could go for a kind of eccentricity that may be imaginary, but that's almost Dickensian, and that you couldn't necessarily do in a contemporary piece.

Of all the things I've done, I think only two of them are westerns, but one of the things that I also like about not only westerns but anything that happens to be period—which I would say is maybe half of the things I've done—is that it has often seemed easier to me to make a comment on the way we live now by looking at it through a lens of the past, rather than to write a movie in which everybody says "Hey, man!" all the time. It's sometimes easier to talk about today by casting it in a time that's once or twice removed. I think, in fact, things really never change that much, but you can sometimes see attitudes a little more clearly when you have a certain distance from them.

CA: In an article called "David Newman's Guilty Pleasures" [Film Comment, November-December, 1978], you wrote about the old Hopalong Cassidy movies, how awful they were and how much you loved them—

NEWMAN: It's absolutely true.

CA: Which do you consider the really good westerns?

NEWMAN: There would be no surprises on my list. There would be an awful lot of Ford films—especially "The Searchers" and "The Man Who Shot Liberty Valance" and "She Wore a Yellow Ribbon" and the great Hawks westerns like "Red River" and "Rio Bravo." "Rio Bravo" is a movie that I've seen now thirty-four times by my last count, and it's just a continual source of delight and inspiration to me. I think probably a lot of filmmakers would put those on their lists of best westerns—or best films.

CA: The controversy about violence in the movies touched "Bonnie and Clyde" when it first came out. How do you feel generally about violence in movies?

NEWMAN: Violence to me is one color on the palette that I think filmmakers have to work with. And I find it absurd to be denied that color if it contributes to the picture I'm making. I don't like violence for violence's sake; I think only an idiot does. And I don't like karate movies where people are always getting their arms broken in half and screaming. "Bonnie and Clyde" seems rather mild now in comparison to some of the films that came afterward.

But the point that we were trying to make is that, unlike most earlier films dealing with crime which glossed over violence, we wrote in the introduction to the screenplay of "Bonnie and Clyde" that we wanted to make it quite clear to the audience that when a bullet enters somebody's body, that hurts a hell of a lot. And for years we'd been seeing movies where bad guys got gunned down and they would just go *ugh* and fall off a horse or keel over. It was always like playing.

Some people who mistakenly said "Bonnie and Clyde" glorified violence always seemed to me to be absurd; the thing about "Bonnie and Clyde" that made it so visceral and so upsetting to some people was that, far from being glorified, it was done realistically. The blood was bloody and people were screaming and pain was horrible. It was a movie about two people who, in a way, in the beginning of their career, were playing at cops and robbers; they were playing at being celebrities; they were playing at being outlaws. What they found out was, once you start shooting people, that isn't playing anymore. Bullets kill and bullets hurt, and pain is something that goes with that way of making a living. So we wanted to be quite moral and point that out, and the only way to do that was to be as realistic as possible about the violence. And of course just because it was done in such a kind of bold way, and so beautifully realized by Arthur Penn, who directed the film, it created an enormous controversy, because at the time people weren't used to seeing that.

Shortly after "Bonnie and Clyde," along came Sam Peckin-

pah, who began making bloodbath movies, and then after a while it got to be almost a cliche—to the point where the so-called realistic depiction of violence in films became just another convention. Those bullets no longer hurt; somehow you knew about the blood spurting because you'd seen that in every Clint Eastwood movie. And I think somewhere along the way we began seeing a lot of Vietnam on television. And people began to find out the difference between movie violence and real violence, so that the issue seems to me to be a slightly dated one now. Nobody's making a fetish out of it; people take it for granted, for the most part. They understand now that you can get an R-rating for violence as well as for sexual content. If you need it and it's part of your story, you have to use it.

CA: So much has been written about "Bonnie and Clyde." People have read meanings into it that you didn't intend, and a lot has been said about its impact on filmmaking. In retrospect, what do you feel its real importance has been?

NEWMAN: I think about that often, because I'm asked about it often. There's no question in my mind that in some way it was a watershed film: it seemed to be the beginning of a whole new kind of filmmaking in America—a new kind of subject matter, a kind of personal way of making films about fringe, marginal people—looking at them in another way—and a new way of talking about the underside of American life. I think you can make a direct line from "Bonnie and Clyde" to "Butch Cassidy and the Sundance Kid." I think you can make a direct line from "Bonnie and Clyde" to "Easy Rider." I think there were an enormous number of films in the five or six or seven years following "Bonnie and Clyde" that really bore the imprint of it and a new kind of filmmaking. Now I think maybe that cycle is over. I think it's been absorbed into the mainstream of the culture, but I don't see its having a specific influence on filmmaking now. I think we're into something else, whatever that is. Having just done "Superman," I know we're into blockbusters, which have always been a part of the business but now are almost too much of a part.

The meaning of the film, to us, was always very clear. It derived to a great extent from an *Esquire* [July, 1964] piece we had written called "The New Sentimentality," which had to do with the examination of attitudes that we felt were shaping American culture. A curious thing happened, as far as I was concerned, to "Bonnie and Clyde." Somewhere during the end of the sixties and in the early seventies, when the protest movement was going on and we began to have a tremendous amount of middle-class outlaws—dropouts, Weathermen, college graduates who were suddenly being hunted by the FBI for bombing draft centers and leading protests and so on—in some funny kind of a way, I always thought that "Bonnie and Clyde" was a little bit prophetic of that. Curiously enough, I've spoken to some people like Jerry Rubin, who was notorious during that period, and Jerry told me that "Bonnie and Clyde" had a great influence on him. So I think it did have something to do with our thinking that American life was about to undergo a kind of wrenching, and it *did*. And there was a long time there when I thought that the movie was quite dated because, in fact, real American life had now gone beyond it, in that people were literally embracing a kind of romantic outlaw life for themselves. That they were saying, it's kind of exciting and important to live in a way beyond the law, since many people were saying that the law was bad at the time, or the existing laws were. I think now the pendulum has swung back the other way, but that was one of the things it was about.

And the movie was about another thing. One of the things that attracted us to those characters in the first place was not the fact that they robbed banks so much and shot people, but the fact that they had a lot of bizarre stylistic qualities—the real Bonnie and Clyde. And we took that and we went with it even further—the fact that Bonnie wrote this poetry, the fact that they would get people tatooed. Again, it was all a kind of what I think in the sixties was called the underground. Benton and I both have a theory that things begin in the so-called underworld and work their way up into the under*ground*. I don't know how much of an underground culture we have anymore, or a counterculture. I think there are five punk rock bands and that seems to be it. But it was about that, about people who by the very virtue of their style, the aberrant nature of their style, put themselves outside the mainstream of their culture and I think, in our film, were persecuted as much for that as for any actual illegal activities that they did. One of the key things in the movie is that the guy who turns Clyde in at the end of the movie is outraged not that they're bank robbers, but that they've had his son tatooed. That's what upsets him—the fact that they're freaky. One of the things that movie was about for us was freakiness, or what we used to call freakiness back in the sixties.

CA: In his history, Talking Pictures, *Richard Corliss wrote of you and Benton: "Their modest ambition—to recapture, and then recast, the spirit of the great American movies—seems nothing less than heroic." Is that overstatement?*

NEWMAN: Corliss is very kind. I think it's an overstatement. But I think probably what he was talking about is that both Benton and myself have a great love of what people call genre films—westerns, screwball comedies, gangster movies, superheroes—and we respect those forms. We respect the heritage of films, of American films, and perhaps we try to work within those genres but somehow putting them in a new light or bending them to deal with material that they don't usually deal with—but still with some respect for the form. I think that's what Corliss meant.

CA: You also seem to have an unusually happy outlook on Hollywood, for a screenwriter—you don't begrudge the director his credit and you don't seem daunted by projects that don't turn out as well as you had hoped.

NEWMAN: I have to split that into two parts. It's quite true that I have never begrudged any director his credit, because I've never had a bad experience with a director. As far as being undaunted by projects that don't work out, that ain't necessarily so. I have been just recently dismayed about a couple of projects that haven't worked out and have been rather upset about them, so I can't say I view that with equanimity. I don't think anybody does, because it's disheartening for anybody to put in a lot of work and have a project come to naught. And that happens more and more in our business.

CA: Often there's no way to tell part-way along, is there?

NEWMAN: There really isn't, and projects often collapse for reasons that one never understands. What sometimes happens is that everybody loves it, and then because there's one actor that everybody wants and the actor's got something else to do, the studio loses interest. There are so many reasons why movies don't get made or why they sit around for a long time and then sort of revive themselves and become live projects again. But that's my least favorite part of this business.

CA: When you collaborate on a screenplay and one of you directs the movie, such as Benton did "Bad Company," does the other get actively involved in the production?

NEWMAN: That certainly was the case on "Bad Company." I was on the set for most of the shooting and sat in on the editing and was consulted all along the way. I was quite pleased about my involvement. I then directed a film in Europe that Benton did not write with me, that my wife wrote with me, so he wasn't involved in that. The film he's about to make, which is called "Stab," is a film we wrote together, and I think probably I will be involved in it—to the extent that my time and schedule allow, because I'm working on something of my own now.

CA: Does it get any easier to work out the details of plot?

NEWMAN: It's always difficult. Every time you start something new, you're beginning from scratch again. And each story and each film brings its own set of problems. Sometimes plot is the key; sometimes you have the plot and that's not where you're getting hung up. And sometimes plot isn't even terribly important. I'm working on something now that's not going to be a very plotted kind of film in the sense of a complicated story to tell. I don't know that plot is something I even think very much about; I guess structure is really what we're talking about. And that's always a chore, and it always changes a lot. And it always goes through so many revisions. None of this seems any easier to me now than it did when I started, but it doesn't seem any more difficult either.

CA: Is there any film criticism that you find helpful?

NEWMAN: There are some critics that I find helpful. I find Andrew Sarris helpful, personally, in that Andrew has written things about my work, or Benton's and my work, or Leslie's and my work, where I've actually learned something reading it. There are other film critics that I like, but I think probably Sarris is the only guy that has ever actually made me reconsider material or the way I approach it. I think no other critic has had that precise an influence on me, but I read a lot of film criticism, and there are a number of critics that I respect.

CA: Are there any problems that stem from having two writers in the same household?

NEWMAN: Yes and no. Leslie's always said that the studios think if they have a married couple writing together, that every time somebody rolls over in the middle of the night, they get an instant story conference. It is hard to leave your work in the office when you're with your collaborator day and night. You know, we just did "Superman II" together, which opens this Christmas [1980]. But since that, we've been working on separate projects. And we find it a kind of relief in a way.

It's not hard to have two writers in the same household, but it's hard to be with anybody twenty-four hours a day seven days a week. No matter how madly in love with each other we are, after a while you get a little claustrophobic. And we both found that, in fact, we have rather different ways of goofing off. I like to go for walks and stuff like that; Leslie likes to go in the kitchen and cook. Everybody has their own rhythms. And we also have our own writing rhythms. That was something that we had to learn how to solve. For example, there are long periods when I am seemingly inactive. I look like I'm goofing off and I'm not working; that's the way I am. My mind is working, but I don't just feel like I've got to get up at nine o'clock in the morning and sit there at the typewriter until five. I might have two or three days where no pages come out, and then suddenly in a great burst out will come fifteen pages. Leslie is one of those people that sit down at the desk every single day and write hour after hour. At the end of the three days we'll both have fifteen pages, except mine will all have come on the third day and hers will have come, let's say, five pages a day. One has to get used to that and not feel that somebody's working more than somebody else is. That's true about all collaborations.

There's one other thing. When we worked together again on "Superman II"—we had to rewrite the whole film this summer because there's a new director and there were many, many changes—we found that, in fact, what was better than the way we had worked together before was that I would go into my office and Leslie would stay at home, where her office is. And when we needed to consult each other, we had a wonderful instrument called the telephone. And it was a little easier for us not to physically be in the same room day and night. And then at night we would go over each other's stuff, rewriting and so on. Just the usual kind of collaborative problems, not unlike some of the ones that any kind of collaboration has, but I think when you're living with your collaborator there are some differences.

CA: Any problems with living in New York and writing for Hollywood?

NEWMAN: Not at all. That's something I've never regretted. The nice thing about writing, of course, is that you can write anywhere, as long as you have a typewriter or a pencil and a pad. You can write in the south of France or you can write at the North Pole. Whenever I have to, I go out to Hollywood for meetings; sometimes that's once a month and sometimes almost a full year will go by. Not all films come out of Hollywood. "Superman," for example, which occupied years of our life, has always been a European-based thing, in England and in Rome and in France, where the producers lived. We've never had to go to California on that project at all. So I've never felt it necessary to be in Hollywood. I don't very much like it out there. I mean I like it for a week, but I wouldn't want to live out there. I think if you're a television writer, you've practically got to be there, because that's where the business is, and it's a weekly kind of thing. But film's generally a project that takes six months, so you just don't have to be out there.

CA: Any big changes in the writing between "Superman I" and "Superman II"?

NEWMAN: No. The only big change is that the Marlon Brando character, the father of Superman, who was in part one and was supposed to be in part two, for all kinds of monetary and contractual reasons is not going to be in part two. So we had to take that character out and figure out a way for his function in the story to be given to other characters. It was a little complicated. That's the only *problem* problem. In a way I think I much prefer part two, because, first of all, it has a lot more of the love story in it, which was fun to do. I would say about half the movie is that. Also, in part one, we had perforce to spend a long period of time dealing with the so-called legend of Superman—the planet Krypton, the background, the baby coming to earth—all that stuff from the comic book. It took a lot of time and it was a lot of the movie. And it had to be done, because that's the famous story. But one of the nice things about part two was that we didn't have to worry about all that exposition. We could just open up, bang, and tell our own story this time. So it was

more fun. And I think it's probably less heavy going than parts of part one.

CA: I tend to forget that there are people around who don't already know all about "Superman," don't you?

NEWMAN: Yes! We grew up with it. When we first started doing this, some cynical person said, "What kind of a dopey project is that to do?" as if it was some kind of kids' comic book. And I said, and I meant it quite sincerely, that I think Superman is our King Arthur. If you were an English writer and you were writing about King Arthur and the Knights of the Round Table, everybody would treat it with great respect. I think Superman is about as close to that kind of a real mythological legend to come out of our popular culture. And I think it says a great deal about our culture, the fact that that character has been around for thirty-five years and is still as meaningful as he is.

—*Interview by Jean W. Ross*

*   *   *

NEWMAN, Mona Alice Jean (Barbara Newman, Jean Stewart)

PERSONAL: Born in Sydney, Australia; daughter of William (a financier) and Mary Elizabeth (Maunsell) Stewart; married John FitzGerald Newman (a military colonel), August 19, 1944; children: Patrick FitzGerald. *Education:* Prince Henry's Hospital, S.R.N., 1932. *Religion:* Church of England. *Home:* St. Fillans, 88 Shipton Rd., York YO3 6RJ, England. *Agent:* Rosemary Gould, Laurence Pollinger Ltd., 18 Maddox St., London W1R 0EU, England.

CAREER: Cedars Private Nursing Home, Sydney, Australia, theatre sister, 1931-34; D.M. Bembaron Ltd., London, England, industrial nurse, 1934-39; King James School, Knaresborough, England, tutor, 1974-79; writer, 1979—. Past nursing officer with St. John Ambulance Brigade; member and past county borough organizer for Women's Royal Volunteer Service; member of executive committee of Soldiers, Sailors, Air Force Association; past member of Yorkshire Area Mental Health Executive Committee. *Military service:* Queen Alexandra's Imperial Military Nursing Service, nurse, 1940-45; served in Africa, the Pacific, and Burma. *Member:* Romantic Novelists Association, Authors North, York Writers Circle (past chairman), York Ladies Luncheon Club (past president).

WRITINGS—Novels, except as noted: *History of Clifton and Clifton Parish Church* (nonfiction), Vicar & Parochial Church Council, 1967; *Centenary Souvenir*, [England], 1967; *Tenderly Touch My Cheek*, [England], 1967; *Night of a Thousand Stars*, [England], 1968, Aston Hall Publications, 1979; *The Faithful Heart*, [England], 1969, reprinted as *Two Faces of a Spy*, Fratelli Fabbri Editora, 1970; *Softly Shines the Moon*, R. Hale, 1970; *Harbour of Dreams*, R. Hale, 1970; *Stranger in the Wolds*, R. Hale, 1971; *Hills of the Purple Mist*, R. Hale, 1973; *Love Be Not Proud*, R. Hale, 1974; *Dr. Cherrill's Dilemma*, R. Hale, 1976; *The Surgeon's Choice*, R. Hale, 1976; *The Substance Not the Dream*, Woman's Weekly, 1976; *Conflict in Berlin*, R. Hale, 1979; *To Vienna With Love*, R. Hale, 1980; *Hong Kong Triangle*, R. Hale, 1981.

Under pseudonym Barbara Newman: *Military Hospital Nurse*, Mills & Boon, 1978.

Under name Jean Stewart: *Where Love Could Not Follow*, Woman's Weekly, 1977; *Nurse in Istanbul*, R. Hale, 1979; *Escape to Hong Kong*, Hamlyn, 1981. Contributor of articles and stories to magazines and newspapers, including *Lady* and *Woman's Story*.

WORK IN PROGRESS: In the Steps of the Emperor, under name Jean Stewart; a historical novel set in early nineteenth-century Australia.

SIDELIGHTS: Mona Newman wrote: "I have been extremely lucky to be able to do so much traveling and to actually live in so many foreign countries. This has helped my writing tremendously, not only with experiences, but in providing exotic backgrounds for my books. I lived in India three years, Nigeria three and a half years, Ghana three and a half years, and Egypt eighteen months. I have visited most western European countries, and the Far East, including Turkey, Ceylon, and Iraq.

"*Night of a Thousand Stars* was born years ago when I came down from a holiday in Darjeeling, having seen range upon range of the mighty Himalayas. That in itself was an experience, but the night I came down by the small mountain train along tortuous winding tracks from nine thousand feet to the plains at Siliguri was my night of nights. Above us the sky was peppered with large, shining stars, larger than ever seen in nontropical areas; below us on the ground were scattered thousands of glow worms and all around us fireflies, their lights flashing on and off in a constant rhythm. It was impossible to see where the sky finished and the earth began. I always remember that as my 'Night of a Thousand Stars' so, when I started writing several years later, a novel was born.

"Incidents in other countries have also inspired my novels. In the early fifties I had a weekly radio program in Nigeria. I wrote, produced, and presented it. It was great fun and brought me into contact with many Nigerians I would not otherwise have met. Some of these inspired my first novel, *Tenderly Touch My Cheek.*

"I enjoy my writing, but I will not write any form of pornography. I feel very strongly on this subject, as I think it does far more harm than good. Everyone has imagination, but no one is being asked to exercise it these days."

AVOCATIONAL INTERESTS: Travel, painting (oils), reading, photography, natural history, collecting stamps, public speaking.

*   *   *

NEWMAN, Oscar 1935-

PERSONAL: Born September 30, 1935, in Montreal, Quebec, Canada; came to the United States in 1964, naturalized citizen, 1970; son of Sam and Estelle (Malamud) Newman; married Irene Kopper Koning, July 31, 1964; children: Robert N. Paul, Jonathan David, Hinde Jill. *Education:* McGill University, B.Arch., 1959. *Agent:* Aaron M. Priest Literary Agency, Inc., 150 East 35th St., New York, N.Y. 10016. *Office:* Institute for Community Design Analysis, 853 Broadway, New York, N.Y. 10003.

CAREER: Nova Scotia Technical College, Halifax, assistant professor of architecture, 1960-62; University of Montreal, Montreal, Quebec, associate professor of architecture, 1962-64; Washington University, St. Louis, Mo., associate professor of architecture, 1964-68, director of Urban Renewal Design Center, 1967-68; Columbia University, New York City, associate professor of architecture, 1968-71; New York University, New York City, associate professor of city planning and director of Institute for Planning and Housing, 1970-73; Institute for Community Design Analysis, New York City, founder and president, 1972—. Principal in Oscar Newman & Associates (architectural and city planning firm), 1962—. *Awards, honors:* Grants from National Science Foundation, National Institute of Mental Health, U.S. De-

partment of Housing and Urban Development, National Institute of Law Enforcement and Criminal Justice, and Ford Foundation; documentary film award from Berlin's Prix-Futura Film Festival, 1975, for "The Writing on the Wall"; awards of excellence from Federal Design Council, 1975, and United Nations Conference on Human Habitat, 1976, both for film, "No Place to Rest His Head."

WRITINGS: New Frontiers in Architecture, Universe Books, 1961 (published in England as *C.I.A.M. '59 in Otterlo,* Tiranti, 1961); *Park Mall: Lawndale,* Department of Development and Planning (Chicago, Ill.), 1968; *Defensible Space: Crime Prevention Through Urban Design,* Macmillan, 1972 (published in England as *Defensible Space: People and Design in the Violent City,* Architectural Press, 1972); *Architectural Design for Crime Prevention,* U.S. Government Printing Office, 1973; *A Design Guide for Improving Residential Security,* U.S. Government Printing Office, 1973; (with Stephen Johnston) *A Model Security Code for Residential Areas,* Institute for Community Design Analysis, 1975; *Design Guidelines for Creating Defensible Space,* U.S. Government Printing Office, 1975; *Community of Interest,* Doubleday, 1980; *Unmasking of a King* (novel), Macmillan, 1981.

Contributor: J. Palen, editor, *Cities and Urbanization,* McGraw, 1974; J. Goldstein, editor, *Aggression and Crimes of Violence,* Oxford University Press, 1975; *Exploding Cities,* Sunday Times Publishing, 1975; T. Porter and B. Mikellides, editors, *Colour in Architecture,* Studio Vista, 1976; N. Kalt and S. Zalkind, editors, *Urban Problems: Psychological Inquiries,* Oxford University Press, 1976; *Manscape: The Human Environment,* Wadsworth, 1976; *Language Experience in Reading,* Encyclopaedia Britannica Education Corp., 1976; J. Hagen, editor, *The Disreputable Pleasures,* McGraw, 1976; D. Montero, editor, *Urban Studies,* Kendall/Hunt, 1977; P. Zimbardo, editor, *Psychology for Our Times: Readings,* Scott, Foresman, 1977; *The Practice of Local Government,* International City Management Association, 1979; *Justice and Corrections,* Wiley, 1979; R. J. Healy, editor, *Protection of Assets Manual,* Merritt, 1979; M. Labory, editor, *Urban Social Space,* Wadsworth, 1980; F. Jensen and G. Rojek, editors, *Delinquency in America,* Heath, 1980; B. Mikellides, editor, *Architecture for People,* Studio Vista, 1980.

Also contributor to *Deviance: Definition, Management, and Treatment,* edited by Simon Dinitz, Oxford University Press, *The Home of Man,* edited by Barbara Ward, 1975, and *Psychology: Understanding Behavior,* 1977.

Films: "The Writing on the Wall," first broadcast by British Broadcasting Corp. (BBC-TV), 1974; "No Place to Rest His Head," released by Institute for Community Design Analysis, 1975; "Home Is Where You Hang," first broadcast by National Broadcasting Co. (NBC-TV), 1978.

Contributor of about twenty articles to architecture and mental health journals and popular magazines, including *Society, Human Nature, Intellectual Digest,* and *Esquire.*

WORK IN PROGRESS: New York Village, Before the Fall, "the *fin de siecle* in New York, its characters and the buildings they inhabited," publication expected in 1982; *The Siege Manhattan, 1990,* publication expected in 1982; a study of crime and stability in residential communities; research on housing design and children's anti-social behavior.

SIDELIGHTS: Newman's Institute for Community Design Analysis is a not-for-profit research firm engaged in the study of the effects of the man-made environment on human behavior. His architectural and planning practice is primarily involved with design and modification of low and moderate income housing developments, including projects in New York, San Francisco, Columbus, Ohio, and Oklahoma City. Between 1964 and 1968, he developed a professional association with sociologists Irving Louis Horowitz and Lee Rainwater, which reinforced his interest in studying the effects of the man-made environment on behavior. Newman is best-known for the publications that followed his research on how the social and physical design of housing environments can be used to promote stability and help residents control and maintain the areas outside their dwelling units.

Newman told *CA:* "In my travels throughout this country and abroad in my professional capacity as an architect and city planner, I am continually surprised by the extent to which the ideas I helped develop in my books are being discussed and assimilated. From listening to people talk about them I conclude that I may just have been lucky to have set down early what everybody was already thinking about. The most often quoted line about *Defensible Space* is that it is just common sense. I find that flattering.

"My studies of the effects of the man-made environment on human behavior seem to have provided the vehicle that has caused people to express their views and concerns about how and where they want to live in urban settings.

"Despite the well-formed personalities we are born with, we are all creatures of our environment. (By environment I mean not only the physical setting, but its social and institutional framework as well.) In my research as a social scientist, in my design work as an architect and planner, and in both my scientific and fictional writing, I am interested in exploring how these environments affect our attitudes and behavior. I do not think that man has yet begun to perceive the extent to which he is influenced by the settings in which he finds himself. All my work is directed at communicating my insights on this subject to others."

BIOGRAPHICAL/CRITICAL SOURCES: Progressive Architecture, January, 1961, October, 1972, October, 1974; *Architectural Forum,* December, 1968, October, 1969, November, 1969; *New York Times,* December, 22, 1970, June 20, 1971, October 26, 1972, November 5, 1972, April 19, 1973, May 27, 1973, June 1, 1980; *Washington Post,* November 13, 1972; *Wall Street Journal,* November 17, 1972; *Time,* November 27, 1972; *Newsday,* December 29, 1972; *Christian Science Monitor,* January 5, 1973; *Fortune,* January, 1973; *HUD Challenge,* September, 1973; *Ekistics,* November, 1973; *U.S. News and World Report,* March 15, 1976; *London Times,* October 31, 1978; *Der Spiegel,* December 11, 1978; *German Tribune,* January 7, 1979; *Vrij Nederland,* July 14, 1979; *de Nieuwe Bijlmer,* August 9, 1979, August 30, 1979; *de Volkskrant,* August 18, 1979; *de Tijd,* February 1, 1980; *New Society,* February 28, 1980.

* * *

NICHOLS, Leigh [a pseudonym]

PERSONAL—Agent: c/o Mary Hall, Pocket Books, 1230 Avenue of the Americas, New York, N.Y. 10020.

CAREER: Writer.

WRITINGS: The Key to Midnight (novel), Pocket Books, 1979; (with Ann Patty) *The Eyes of Darkness* (novel), Pocket Books, 1980.*

* * *

NICHOLS, Marion 1921-

PERSONAL: Born March 20, 1921, in Foochow, China;

came to the United States in 1930; daughter of O. G. (a missionary) and Martha (a missionary; maiden name, Bourne) Reuman; married Roger Nichols (a company and county administrator), June 15, 1942; children: Jeffrey, Joyce, Randall. *Education:* Ohio Wesleyan University, B.F.A., 1942. *Home:* 946 Southwest Magnolia Bluff, Stuart, Fla. 33490.

CAREER: Free-lance artist, 1940—; professional worker for Girl Scouts of the U.S.A., 1955-62; teacher of painting and teacher/designer of embroidery, 1962—; Crewel School Art Center, Seaford, N.Y., owner and director, 1966-73.

WRITINGS: A Comprehensive Course in Crewel Embroidery, M. N. Needlework Originals, 1971; *Designs and Patterns for Embroiderers and Craftsmen,* Dover, 1974; *Encyclopedia of Embroidery Stitches, Including Crewel,* Dover, 1974. Also author of *Astrological Workbook,* 1980.

WORK IN PROGRESS: Collected Poems, publication expected in 1981; *Finger Embroidery,* publication expected in 1982.

SIDELIGHTS: Nichols wrote: "I am blessed (or cursed) by a compulsive drive to share (sun in Pisces) new and inventive ways (Aries ascendant) of creative, expressive living (moon in Leo); all these combine to force me to find the most efficient way (Saturn in Virgo) to share. Lacking effective teaching (sharing) tools, I developed my own 'how-to-do' books on crewel embroidery and astrology.

"Continuing with the flow of universal growth and awareness, we continue to express and expand our creative horizons. As we enter the new age, group-consciousness displaces the individual, and as new/old wisdoms are unveiled, each of us must share our awakening awareness of joyful living. I'm just sharing."

* * *

NIELSON, Ingrid
See BANCROFT, Iris (Nelson)

* * *

NIEMEYER, Eberhardt Victor, Jr. 1919-

PERSONAL: Born September 28, 1919, in Houston, Tex.; son of Eberhardt Victor and Elise (Shaffer) Niemeyer; married Dorothea Hasskarl, January 15, 1944 (died, 1956); married Lala Acosta (a teacher), May 31, 1958; children: Eberhardt Victor III, Ruth (Mrs. Edmundo Salvatierra), Stephen, Christopher. *Education:* University of Texas, B.A., 1941, M.A., 1951, Ph.D., 1958; Texas A & M University, B.S., 1948. *Politics:* Democrat. *Religion:* Episcopal. *Home:* 1413 Thaddeus Cove, Austin, Tex. 78746.

CAREER: Worked at Brenham Jersey Farms, Brenham, Tex., 1949-50, and at Borden Milk Co., Tyler, Tex., 1950; U.S. Foreign Service, director of Instituto Hondureno de Cultura Interamericana in Tegucigalpa, Honduras, 1953-55, Instituto Cultural Peruano Norteamericano in Lima, Peru, 1955-56, Instituto Guatemalteco Americano in Guatemala, Guatemala, 1958-60, and Philippine American Cultural Foundation, Manila, Philippines, 1961-63, assistant cultural affairs officer at American Embassy in Mexico City, Mexico, 1963-65, branch public affairs officer at American Consulate in Monterrey, Mexico, 1965-69, public affairs officer at American Embassy in Port of Spain, Trinidad and Tobago, 1969-70, deputy director of book program of U.S. Information Agency in Washington, D.C., 1970-72, writer and researcher in press section of U.S. Information Agency in Washington, D.C., 1972-73, director of Instituto Chileno Norteamericano de Cultura in Santiago, Chile, 1973-76, branch public affairs officer at American Consulate in Monterrey, 1976-79; University of Texas, Austin, assistant cooordinator of Office of Mexican Studies, 1980—. Assistant professor at Texas A & T College, 1957-58; visiting professor at University of Puerto Rico, 1958; guest professor at Catholic University of Chile, 1975-76; lecturer at St. Edward's University, 1980. *Military service:* U.S. Naval Reserve, active duty, 1942-45; became lieutenant senior grade; served in Atlantic and Pacific theaters.

MEMBER: International Good Neighbor Council, Latin American Studies Association, Conference on Latin American History, American Society of Chile (president, 1975), Sociedad Nuevoleonesa de Historia, Geografia y Estadistica, Southwestern Council on Latin American Studies, Texas State Historical Association, Rotary International, Common Cause. *Awards, honors:* Medalla de Acero al Merito Historico from Sociedad Nuevoleonesa de Historia, 1972.

WRITINGS: (With Charles Gibson) *Guide to the Hispanic American Historical Review, 1946-1955,* Duke University Press, 1958; *El General Bernardo Reyes,* Centro de Estudios Humanisticos, Universidad de Nuevo Leon, 1966; *Revolution at Queretaro: The Mexican Constitutional Convention of 1916-1917,* University of Texas Press, 1974; (contributor) Walter Sanchez, editor, *Panorama de la politica mundial,* Editorial Universitaria, 1977; (contributor) Sanchez and Christian Guerrero, editors, *La Revolucion Norteamericana, auge y perspectivas,* Editorial Universitaria, 1979.

WORK IN PROGRESS: Research on Mexican history of the revolutionary period.

*　　*　　*

NOER, Thomas John 1944-

PERSONAL: Born November 29, 1944, in Emmetsburg, Iowa; son of John (a sales manager) and Lucille Noer; married Linda S. O'Connor (a social worker), September 25, 1968; children: Jennifer Elizabeth, Derek Thomas. *Education:* Gustavus Adolphus College, B.A., 1966; Washington State University, M.A., 1968; University of Minnesota, Ph.D., 1972. *Home:* 6117 Fifth Ave., Kenosha, Wis. 53140. *Office:* Department of History, Carthage College, Kenosha, Wis. 53140.

CAREER: University of Minnesota, Minneapolis, assistant professor of history, 1972-73; Carthage College, Kenosha, Wis., associate professor of history, 1973—. Consultant to Wisconsin Humanities Committee. *Member:* American Historical Association, Organization of American Historians, Society for the History of American Foreign Relations. *Awards, honors:* Grants from American Philosophical Society, 1978, and Harry S Truman Institute, 1979; fellow of Charles Warren Center for American History, Harvard University, 1979-80.

WRITINGS: Briton, Boer, and Yankee: The United States and Southern Africa, 1870-1914, Kent State University Press, 1978; *Cold War and Black Liberation: The United States and White Africa, 1948-1968,* Oxford University Press, 1981. Contributor to academic journals.

WORK IN PROGRESS: America and the Third World, completion expected in 1982.

*　　*　　*

NORDOFF, Paul 1909-1977

PERSONAL: Born June 4, 1909, in Philadelphia, Pa.; died January 18, 1977, in Herdecke, West Germany; son of Paul

Bookmyer and Kathryn (Huntington) Nordoff; married Sabina Zay, 1945; children: Anthony, Sylvia Nordoff Meader, Guy. *Education:* Philadelphia Conservatory of Music, Mus.B., 1927, Mus.M., 1932; attended Juilliard School of Music, 1932.

CAREER: Philadelphia Conservatory of Music, Philadelphia, Pa., teacher of composition and department head, 1937-42; composer, 1942-45; Michigan State College (now University), East Lansing, assistant professor of music, 1945-49; Bard College, Annandale-on-Hudson, N.Y., professor of music, 1949-58; music therapist in the United States and abroad, 1958-61; University of Pennsylvania, Philadelphia, chief music therapist working with handicapped children, 1961-67; music therapist in the United States and abroad, 1967-77. Music therapist at schools in Devon, Pa., 1961, and Institute of Logopedics, Wichita, Kan., 1962-63; teacher at public schools in Philadelphia, 1962-67; lecturing research fellow of American-Scandinavian Foundation, 1967-68. *Awards, honors:* Guggenheim fellowships, 1933 and 1935; Bearns Prize from Columbia University, 1933; Pulitzer scholarship, 1940; Ford Foundation fellowship, 1954; Mus.D. from Combs College of Music, 1958, B. Music Therapy, 1960.

WRITINGS: (With Clive E. Robbins) *Music Therapy for Handicapped Children: Investigations and Experiences,* Rudolf Steiner, 1965, revised edition published as *Therapy in Music for Handicapped Children* (foreword by Benjamin Britten), St. Martin's, 1971; (with Robbins) *Music Therapy in Special Education,* Crowell, 1971; (with Robbins) *Creative Music Therapy: Individualized Treatment for the Handicapped Child,* Crowell, 1977; (with Robbins) *Therapy in Music for the Handicapped Child,* Humanities, 1979. Also author of *Songs for Children.*

Author of "The Masterpiece" (one-act opera), first produced in Philadelphia, Pa., January 24, 1941.

More than three hundred compositions include *Beautiful City,* Associated Music Publishers, 1948, *Fun for Drums: A Rhythmic Game for Children,* Presser, 1968, and such unpublished works as "Secular Mass," 1935, "Every Soul Is a Circus," 1939, "Tallyho," 1947, "Lost Summer," "Winter Symphony," "The Sea-Change," "Robert Burns: Poems and Songs," and "Spirituals for Children to Sing and Play."

SIDELIGHTS: During the early part of his career, Nordoff wrote scores for Martha Graham, Agnes de Mille, and Katharine Cornell. From 1959 until his death his work was devoted almost entirely to musical therapy with the handicapped, especially mentally-retarded and brain-damaged children. He worked with autistic children in the United States in the 1960's and with handicapped children in Scandinavia, including Finland, and in Germany and England, where the Goldie Leigh Hospital has named the Nordoff Music Therapy Center in his honor.

BIOGRAPHICAL/CRITICAL SOURCES: John Tasker Howard, *Our American Music,* Crowell, 1946; *New York Times,* January 19, 1977.*

*　　*　　*

NORMAN, Frank 1930-1980

OBITUARY NOTICE—See index for *CA* sketch: Born June 9, 1930, in Bristol, England; died December 23, 1980. Novelist and playwright best known for his play "Fings Ain't Wot They Used T'Be." Norman a small-time criminal, became recognized as a writer after he authored accounts of his incarcerations in various prisons, including a three-year sentence at Camp Hill Prison on the Isle of Wight. His writings include *Bang to Rights*, "A Kayf Up West," *The Monkey Pulled His Hair*, "Costa Packet," *Lock 'Em Up and Count 'Em*, and *The Dead Butler Caper*. Obituaries and other sources: Frank Norman, *Stand on Me* (autobiography), Simon & Schuster, 1961; Norman, *The Guntz* (autobiography), London, Secker & Warburg, 1962; Norman, *Banana Boy* (autobiography), London, Secker & Warburg, 1969; *London Times*, December 29 1980.

* * *

NORMAN, Lloyd H(enry) 1913-

PERSONAL: Born November 25, 1913, in Aurora, Ontario, Canada; son of Henry and Ida Norman; married Dorothy Hecht, November 21, 1937; children: Neil, Albert H. *Education:* Northwestern University, Evanston, Ill., B.S., 1934; graduate study at University of Chicago. *Home:* 4450 South Park Ave., Apt. 903, Chevy Chase, Md. 20015. *Office:* *Newsweek*, 1750 Pennsylvania Ave. N.W., Washington, D.C. 20006.

CAREER/WRITINGS: Social worker for Cook County Bureau of Public Welfare, 1934-36; City News Bureau, Chicago, Ill., reporter, rewriter, and night editor, 1936-38; *Chicago Tribune*, Chicago, reporter, 1938-58; *Newsweek*, Washington, D.C., Pentagon correspondent, 1958-78. Contributor of articles to periodicals, including *Army Magazine* and *Collier's*. *Military service:* U.S. Naval Reserve, 1944-46; became lieutenant junior grade. *Member:* Overseas Writers. *Awards, honors:* Book award from *Chicago Tribune*, 1955; editors' citation from Associated Press; distinguished and exceptional civilian service awards.

WORK IN PROGRESS: Research on the history of the U.S. joint chiefs and their role in U.S. strategic thinking and policies.

SIDELIGHTS: Lloyd Norman told *CA:* "I always wanted to be a newspaperman. When I was young a far-off goal was to be a news correspondent based in Russia. When I was finally offered such an assignment in 1951 by the *Chicago Tribune*, I had to turn it down because my two sons were too young to be exposed to the harsh climate and austerity of Moscow. I became a military correspondent purely by chance."

* * *

NORTHGRAVE, Anne
See TIBBLE, Anne

* * *

NORTON-TAYLOR, Duncan 1904-

PERSONAL: Born August 14, 1904, in East Orange, N.J.; son of Alfred and Florence Hannah (Goodwin) Norton-Taylor; married Margaret Scott, October 19, 1926; children: Nancy, Joan, Susan. *Education:* Brown University, Ph.B., 1926. *Residence:* Oxford, Md.

CAREER: Reporter for *Newark Star-Eagle* and *Brooklyn Times*, 1926-28; Frank A. Munsey Co., New York City, editor, 1928-36; free-lance writer, 1936-39; *Time*, New York City, member of board of editors, 1939-51; *Fortune*, New York City, member of board of editors, 1951-67, managing editor, 1959-65; editor and writer, 1965-67; free-lance writer, 1967—.

WRITINGS: With My Heart in My Mouth, Coward, 1944; *The Celts*, Time-Life, 1974; *God's Man: A Novel on the Life of John Calvin*, Baker Book, 1979.

WORK IN PROGRESS: Hebb's Crime, "a novel of contemporary things."

SIDELIGHTS: Norton-Taylor commented: "A writer never stops writing. I have been telling stories since I was a boy, writing professionally for more than fifty years. Along the way I have written hundreds of stories of people for *Time* and *Fortune*. But certainly no figure of this century has enlisted my interest so much as that towering figure of the sixteenth century, John Calvin—hated and maligned, admired and revered. Conflict always attracts authors."

* * *

NORWAY, Nevil Shute 1899-1960
(Nevil Shute)

PERSONAL: Born January 17, 1899, in Ealing, Middlesex, England; died January 12, 1960, in Melbourne, Australia; son of Arthur Hamilton (a post office official) and Mary Louisa (Gadsden) Norway; married Frances Mary Heaton, 1931; children: two daughters. *Education:* Balliol College, Oxford, B.A., 1922. *Religion:* Church of England. *Residence:* Langwarrin, Victoria, Australia.

CAREER: Aeronautical designer and engineer with De Havilland Aircraft Co., 1922-24; chief calculator with Airship Guarantee Co., 1924-28, deputy chief engineer, 1928-30; founder and managing director of Airspeed Ltd., 1931-38; writer, 1939-60. *Military service:* British Army, Infantry, 1918. Royal Naval Voluntary Reserve, 1940-45; became lieutenant-commander. *Member:* Royal Aeronautical Society (fellow), Yorkshire Aeroplane Club (managing director, 1927-30).

WRITINGS—All under name Nevil Shute; all novels except as noted: *Marazan* (also see below), Cassell, 1926, reprinted, Heinemann, 1966; *The Mysterious Aviator*, Houghton, 1928 (published in England as *So Disdained* [also see below], Cassell, 1928), reprinted, Ballantine, 1968; *Lonely Road*, Morrow, 1932, reprinted, Heinemann, 1965; *Kindling*, Morrow, 1938, reprinted, F. Watts, 1968 (published in England as *Ruined City* [also see below], Cassell, 1938, reprinted, Heinemann, 1965); *Ordeal* (Book-of-the-Month Club selection), Morrow, 1939 (published in England as *What Happened to the Corbetts*, Heinemann, 1939, reprinted, 1968).

An Old Captivity (Literary Guild selection; also see below), Morrow, 1940, reprinted, Heron Books, 1969; *Landfall: A Channel Story* (also see below), Morrow, 1940; *Pied Piper* (also see below), Morrow, 1942, reprinted, Ballantine, 1969; *Pastoral* (also see below), Morrow, 1944, reprinted, Greenwood Press, 1970; *Most Secret*, Morrow, 1945, reprinted, Queens House, 1976; *Vinland the Good* (drama), Morrow, 1946; *The Chequer Board* (also see below), Morrow, 1947, reprinted, F. Watts, c. 1967; *No Highway* (also see below), Morrow, 1948, reprinted, Heinemann, 1970.

The Legacy, Morrow, 1950 (published in England as *A Town Like Alice* [also see below], Heinemann, 1950); *Round the Bend*, Morrow, 1951, reprinted, Queens House, 1977; *The Far Country* (also see below), Morrow, 1952; *In the Wet*, Morrow, 1953; *Slide Rule: The Autobiography of an Engineer*, Morrow, 1954; *The Breaking Wave*, Morrow, 1955 (published in England as *Requiem for a Wren* [also see below], Heinemann, 1955); *Beyond the Black Stump*, Morrow, 1956; *On the Beach* (also see below), Morrow, 1957; *The Rainbow and the Rose*, Morrow, 1958; *Trustee From the Toolroom* (Book-of-the-Month Club selection), Morrow, 1960; *Stephen Morris*, Morrow, 1961.

Collections: *Three of a Kind: Requiem for a Wren, An Old*

Captivity, Pastoral, Heinemann, 1962; *Marazan* [and] *So Disdained*, Heron Books, 1969; *Ruined City* [and] *Landfall: A Channel Story*, Heron Books, 1969; *A Nevil Shute Omnibus* (contains *No Highway, A Town Like Alice*, and *On the Beach*), Heinemann, 1973; *A Town Like Alice, Pied Piper, The Far Country, The Chequer Board, No Highway*, Heinemann, 1976.

SIDELIGHTS: Roger Pippett once remarked in the *New York Times* that Nevil Shute's autobiography, *Slide Rule*, is a record "not so much of a writer's apprenticeship as of a man who has always liked to do two jobs at the same time." Shute even thought of himself as "an engineer who writes books." Some felt that he actually led a dual life: Nevil Norway, the aeronautical engineer, business executive, and lieutenant-commander of the Admiralty, storing up ideas for the novels of Nevil Shute, the author and storyteller.

Shute drew heavily from his own experiences and professional expertise in writing his novels. Several of his books, such as *An Old Captivity* and *Landfall*, cast aviators in compelling adventures of espionage or discovery. The credulity of these tales was enhanced by Shute's intimate knowledge of aviation that allowed him to incorporate technical data and detail into the fabric of the stories. Thus Shute, who had himself flown the Atlantic twice in the Airship Guarantee Company's *R 100* as their representative, was more than a textbook expert in the field. His knowledge of modern weaponry prompted him to write *Ordeal*, the story of a Southampton family driven from their home by enemy bombing raids.

One of Shute's highly successful novels, *No Highway*, concerns an aeronautical engineer sent to Labrador to investigate the wreck of a new aircraft that had become incapacitated by premature wearing of the metal, known as "metal fatigue." The engineer, however, finds himself on a plane of the same model that is approaching its own stress limit. Applying his knowledge of aircraft design, Shute dealt with the theme of metal fatigue long before it became known to the general public. This novel was adapted as a film by Twentieth Century-Fox in 1951 under the title "No Highway in the Sky." In negotiating the screen rights for the novel, Shute, apparently concerned with the image of the British aircraft industry, made the unusual stipulation that the manufacturer in the film not be identified as a British firm.

Shute is probably best remembered for *On the Beach*, a novel about a nuclear holocaust. Set in Melbourne, Australia, in 1963, *On the Beach* tells of the world's last few survivors of an atomic war. The novel was another of Shute's attempts to caution his readers against the unbridled proliferation of warfare technology. During the three years between the book's publication and Shute's death, *On the Beach* sold well in excess of two million copies. The novel was released as a film by United Artists in 1959.

Four other motion pictures have been adapted from Shute's novels. "Scotland Yard Commands," a film version of *The Lonely Road*, was released in 1937, and Twentieth Century-Fox produced "The Pied Piper," the story of an old man who leads a group of children out of German-occupied France, in 1942. "Landfall" was adapted for the screen by Associated British Film Distributors in 1948, and a J. Arthur Rank presentation of "A Town Like Alice" appeared in 1958.

About Shute's last novel, *Trustee From the Toolroom*, published posthumously in 1960, Edmund Fuller wrote in *Saturday Review:* "Nevil Shute will be missed. He was one of our most prolific and diversified storytellers. His twenty novels varied widely in tone and pace, as well as in scene, and time, ranging from his own Australia, where he lowered the curtain on the human race, to England and America, and from a little into the future back to the Vikings." As Fuller pointed out, Shute was similar to the mild-mannered hero of *Trustee From the Toolroom*. In this novel, Keith Stewart interrupts his orderly career as a designer of miniature machines and motors to recover the legacy of his niece lost off the Bermuda coast in the wreck of his sister's and brother-in-law's boat. Just as Mr. Stewart became trustee of his ward's inheritance, Fuller noted, Shute became "a trustee of some grand stories."

BIOGRAPHICAL/CRITICAL SOURCES: Time, March 27, 1939, June 26, 1950; *New York Herald Tribune*, September 14, 1952; Nevil Shute, *Slide Rule: The Autobiography of an Engineer*, Morrow, 1954; *New York Times*, May 30, 1954; *New Yorker*, August 17, 1957; *Saturday Review*, April 2, 1960; Julian Smith, *Nevil Shute*, Twayne, 1976; *Journal of British Studies*, spring, 1977.

OBITUARIES: New York Times, January 13, 1960; *Illustrated London News*, January 23, 1960; *Newsweek*, January 25, 1960; *Publishers Weekly*, January 25, 1960; *Time*, January 25, 1960; *Wilson Library Bulletin*, March, 1960; *Saturday Review*, April 2, 1960.*

*   *   *

NOVERR, Douglas A(rthur) 1942-

PERSONAL: Born May 13, 1942, in Battle Creek, Mich.; son of Joseph Louis (a politician and editor) and Loretta Irene (a secretary; maiden name, Heflin) Noverr; married Betty Jean Stoel (an elementary school teacher), August 17, 1968. *Education:* Central Michigan University, B.A., 1965, M.A., 1966; Miami University, Oxford, Ohio, Ph.D., 1972. *Politics:* Liberal Democrat. *Religion:* Roman Catholic. *Home:* 428 Butterfield, East Lansing, Mich. 48823. *Office:* Department of American Thought and Language, Michigan State University, 285 Bessey Hall, East Lansing, Mich. 48824.

CAREER: Central Michigan University, Mount Pleasant, instructor in English, 1966-67; Miami University, Oxford, Ohio, instructor in English, 1968-70; Michigan State University, East Lansing, instructor, 1970-72, assistant professor, 1972-77, associate professor of English, 1977—. Senior Fulbright lecturer at Marie Curie Sklodowska University, 1976-77. Guest on television programs. *Member:* Modern Language Association of America, American Studies Association, Popular Culture Association, Thoreau Society, Fulbright Alumni Association.

WRITINGS: (Contributor) David D. Anderson, editor, *MidAmerica IV*, Midwestern Press, 1977, *MidAmerica VII*, 1980; (with Eugene L. Huddleston) *The Relationship of Painting and Literature: A Guide to Information Sources*, Gale, 1978; (with Lawrence E. Ziewacz) *The Games They Played: American Sports and Culture, 1865-1980*, Nelson-Hall, 1981; (contributor) John M. Carroll and William Baker, editors, *American Sports in the Twentieth Century*, Rivercity Press, 1981; (contributor) Gerald R. Baydo, editor, *The Evolution of Mass Culture in America: 1877 to the Present*, Forum Press, 1981. Associate editor of *The Journalism of Walt Whitman*, Volume I, G. K. Hall, 1982. Contributor to academic journals. Co-editor of *American Examiner: A Forum of Ideas*, 1974-76, editor, 1977—.

WORK IN PROGRESS: A book on midwestern art and culture, publication expected in 1982; a history of American baseball, publication expected in 1982.

SIDELIGHTS: Noverr told *CA:* "Research and writing provide the center for my academic career and personal life. I enjoy the discipline and intellectual excitement that result from scholarly investigations, and my interests are wide-ranging and diverse. I hope that I bring a humanistic and interdisciplinary perspective to my research. I want to avoid narrow specialization, although nineteenth-century American art, literature, and culture are my special research interests. As a result of my travels I also have a special interest in Poland and the Soviet Union.

"As a teacher of composition and American culture studies, I am dedicated to conveying, in whatever ways I can, an appreciation for the craft, discipline, and beauty of good writing. My own writing has been a gradual search for a mature style as well as a personal investigation of various dimensions of American culture and its expression at many levels."

* * *

NOWAK, Mariette 1941-
(M. M. Ronsman)

PERSONAL: Born August 15, 1941, in Milwaukee, Wis.; daughter of Harry and Martha (Popp) Ronsman; married David Nowak (an advanced development engineer), August 7, 1965; children: Robert, Michael. *Education:* Alverno College, B.S. (magna cum laude), 1963; University of Wisconsin—Milwaukee, M.S., 1976. *Home:* 5998 Sycamore St., Greendale, Wis. 53129. *Office:* Wehr Nature Center, 5879 South 92nd St., Hales Corners, Wis. 53130.

CAREER: Teacher at public schools in Peoria, Wis., 1963-64, and Milwaukee, Wis., 1964-68; Milwaukee Area Technical College, Milwaukee, instructor in zoology, 1976-77; Wehr Nature Center, Hales Corners, Wis., naturalist, 1977-80, director, 1980—. *Member:* Authors Guild, National Audubon Society, Citizens for a Better Environment, National Organization for Women, Botanical Club of Southeastern Wisconsin (vice-president, 1980), Southeastern Wisconsin Naturalist Association (member of board of directors), Southeastern Wisconsin Coalition for Clean Air (citizen action chairperson, 1971-74), Greendale League of Women Voters (environmental quality chairperson, 1971-73).

WRITINGS: Eve's Rib (nonfiction), St. Martin's, 1980. Contributor to adult and juvenile magazines (once under name M. M. Ronsman), including *Ranger Rick's Nature* and *Wisconsin Trails.*

WORK IN PROGRESS: Research related to the female in various species and in contemporary cultures.

SIDELIGHTS: Mariette Nowak commented: "Why did I write *Eve's Rib*? Animal behavior studies had long fascinated me, but little was said of the female of the species. And what was said almost always reinforced the old stereotypes concerning sex roles. So I decided to ferret out what I could about the female in the belief that with the growing interest in animal behavior, more and more data would become available. The research was exciting. I found even more information than I had dared to hope for. Not only is there, today, an ever-growing body of information on animal behavior in general, but there are more and more women in the natural sciences and more male researchers aware of past sexual biases concerning the female. Together, these scientists have provided much rich and revealing material concerning the subject of my book—the female of the species."

O

OBERHOLZER, Emil, Jr. 1926(?)-1981

OBITUARY NOTICE: Born in Switzerland c. 1926; died of a heart attack, January 6, 1981, in Washington, D.C. Educator, historian, and writer. An expert on church history, Emil Oberholzer was the author of the book *Delinquent Saints: Disiplinary Actions in the Early Congregational Churches of Massachusetts.* Obituaries and other sources: *Washington Post,* January 14, 1981.

*   *   *

O'CONNELL, David 1940-

PERSONAL: Born November 27, 1940, in New York, N.Y.; son of James Anthony (an investment counselor) and Alice Cecelia (Fennon) O'Connell; married Cathleen Casey, September 30, 1967 (died April 27, 1978); married Kathleen Lavin (a Montessori teacher), May 31, 1980; children: (first marriage) David Tristan, Nathaniel Casey. *Education:* St. Peter's College, Jersey City, N.Y., B.A., 1962; University of Louvain, certificate, 1960; Princeton University, M.A., 1964, Ph.D., 1966; also attended University of Paris, 1964-65. *Religion:* Roman Catholic. *Home:* 1118 Monroe Ave., River Forest, Ill. 60305. *Office:* Department of French, University of Illinois at Chicago Circle, P.O. Box 4348, Chicago, Ill. 60680.

CAREER: University of Massachusetts, Amherst, assistant professor, 1968-73, associate professor of French, 1973-77; University of Illinois at Chicago Circle, Chicago, professor of French and head of department, 1977—. *Military service:* U.S. Army, 1966-68; served in Vietnam; became captain; received Bronze Star. *Member:* American Association of Teachers of French, Modern Language Association of America, Illinois Foreign Language Teachers Association, Fulbright Alumni Association. *Awards, honors:* Woodrow Wilson fellow, 1962 and 1964; Fulbright scholar, 1964; grants from American Philosophical Society, 1972, 1975, and 1980, and from American Council of Learned Societies, 1976.

WRITINGS: The Teachings of Saint Louis, University of North Carolina Press, 1972; *Les Propos de Saint Louis* (title means "The Sayings of Saint Louis"), Gallimard, 1974; *Celine,* Twayne, 1976; *The Instructions of Saint Louis,* University of North Carolina Press, 1979. Field editor of French collection for "Twayne World Authors Series," Twayne, 1978—. Contributing editor of *MLA Bibliography,* 1975—; review editor of *French Review,* 1975-77.

WORK IN PROGRESS: Catholic Writers in France Since 1945, publication expected in 1982.

SIDELIGHTS: O'Connell told *CA:* "In doing research in Paris for my doctoral thesis on the writings of Saint Louis, I discovered that he (Louis IX, 1214-1270) is quoted in the first person on hundreds of occasions by contemporary chroniclers. Thus, I proposed a book to France's most prestigious publishing house that would recover, translate into French, and present in a readable manner all these quotations. The result was *Les Propos de Saint Louis.* This 1974 book nearly won me a French prize and helped advance my career. Future work will be devoted to other major figures of the thirteenth century, notably Philippe de Beaumanoir, father of French law, and Vincent de Beauvais, the greatest encyclopedist of that century."

*   *   *

O'HARA, Mary
See ALSOP, Mary O'Hara

*   *   *

OLIPHANT, Robert (Thompson) 1924-

PERSONAL: Born October 25, 1924, in Tulsa, Okla.; son of Stephen Duncan (a steelworker) and Dorothy (a librarian; maiden name, Thompson) Oliphant; married Lois Millett, April 24, 1956 (divorced February 10, 1964); married Jane Johnson (a painter), July 26, 1965; children: Matthew, Jason. *Education:* Washington and Jefferson College, A.B., 1948; Stanford University, M.A., 1958, Ph.D., 1962. *Residence:* Woodland Hills, Calif. *Agent:* Clyde Taylor, Curtis Brown Ltd., 575 Madison Ave., New York, N.Y. 10022. *Office:* Department of English, California State University, Northridge, Calif. 91330.

CAREER: Professional musician, 1948-55; Stanford University, Stanford, Calif., acting instructor in English, 1955-59; California State University, Northridge, assistant professor, 1959-63, associate professor, 1963-67, professor of English, 1967—. Visiting associate professor at Stanford University, 1965-66. *Military service:* U.S. Army, 1942-46; served in European theater. *Member:* Linguistic Society of America, College English Association.

WRITINGS: The Harley Latin-Old English Glossary, Mouton, 1966; *A Piano for Mrs. Cimino* (novel), Prentice-Hall, 1980; *A Trumpet for Jackie* (novel), Prentice-Hall, 1982.

Plays: "The Importance of Being Earnest" (three-act opera), first produced in Northridge, Calif., at Studio Theatre of California State University, February 10, 1972; "Anatol, Anatol!" (two-act musical), first produced in Northridge at Studio Theatre, May 12, 1973; "Alice in Wonderland" (children's musical), first produced in Northridge at Campus Theatre of California State University, December 1, 1973; "Underground Man" (one-act monologue with songs), first produced in Canoga Park, Calif., at Unitarian Church, April 15, 1978. Also author of "Lost Boy" (musical), 1971.

Contributor of more than twenty articles and stories to magazines, including *Virginia Quarterly* and *Antioch Review*.

WORK IN PROGRESS: Two nonfiction books, *How to Fight Pre-Senility* and *Learning in the Lump;* revising and re-scoring his musical compositions.

SIDELIGHTS: Oliphant commented in *Library Journal:* "A few years ago the musician side of me began to clamor for a little more action, so I started writing tunes, then lyrics to fit the tunes, followed by two operas and a number of musical plays. In the process I learned something about structure and pacing, with the result that I found the writing of fiction congenial. My favorite authors are Chaucer, Trollope, and Proust. I feel a novelist should be interested in how his society actually works."

AVOCATIONAL INTERESTS: Travel, learning languages, looking at old manuscripts.

BIOGRAPHICAL/CRITICAL SOURCES: Library Journal, June 15, 1980.

* * *

O'NEILL, Archie
See HENAGHAN, Jim

* * *

O'NEILL, George   1921(?)-1980

OBITUARY NOTICE: Born c. 1921; died of complications following abdominal surgery, 1980, in New York, N.Y. Anthropologist and author. George O'Neill advocated candid and direct communication between spouses in his best-selling book *Open Marriage,* which he wrote with his wife Nena. The two also co-authored *Shifting Gears,* which is based on the premise that a healthy marriage is possible only when both members are free to change. Obituaries and other sources: *Authors in the News,* Volume 1, Gale, 1976; *Time,* October 20, 1980.

* * *

ONSLOW, Annette Rosemary MacArthur
See MacARTHUR-ONSLOW, Annette Rosemary

* * *

ORWELL, Sonia   1919(?)-1980

OBITUARY NOTICE: Born c. 1919; died after a long illness, December 11, 1980, in London, England. Editor and translator. Sonia Orwell, widow of author George Orwell, helped to edit the four-volume collection of her husband's articles, essays, and letters that was published in 1968. Her translation of "Days in the Trees," by French playwright Marguerite Duras, was produced in New York City at the Circle in the Square Theatre in 1976. She also worked with essayist and critic Cyril Connolly on the literary magazine *Horizon.* Obituaries and other sources: *Chicago Tribune,* December 13, 1980; *New York Times,* December 13, 1980; *Newsweek,*

December 22, 1980; *AB Bookman's Weekly,* January 19, 1981.

* * *

OSBORN, Frederick (Henry)   1889-1981

OBITUARY NOTICE—See index for *CA* sketch: Born March 21, 1889, in New York, N.Y.; died January 5, 1981, in New York, N.Y. Military officer, businessman, and author. As a temporary brigadier general during Wrold War II, Osborn was the director of the Morale Branch of the War Department and the director of the Army's Education and Information Division for the duration of the war. He became a temporary major general in 1943. After World War II, he served on the United Nations Atomic Energy Commission and concentrated on population and eugenics. Prior to the war, Osborn was influential in the railroad and investment-banking industries. His writings include *Heredity and Environment, Preface to Eugenics, Three Essays on Population,* and *The Human Condition: How Did We Get Here and Where Are We Going.* Obituaries and other sources: *Newsweek,* January 19, 1981.

* * *

OSBORNE, Maggie
See OSBORNE, Margaret Ellen

* * *

OSBORNE, Margaret Ellen   1941-
(Maggie Osborne)

PERSONAL: Born June 10, 1941, in Hollywood, Calif.; daughter of William Edward and Lucille Prather; married George M. Osborne II (an insurance company manager), April 29, 1972; children: (from previous marriage) Zane Carter. *Education:* Attended Fort Lewis Junior College. *Religion:* Protestant. *Home and office:* 7190 West David Dr., Littleton, Colo. 80123. *Agent:* Donald MacCampbell, Inc., 12 East 41st St., New York, N.Y. 10017.

CAREER: United Airlines, Denver, Colo., flight attendant, 1963-67; Welcome Service, Denver, owner and operator, 1970-72; State Farm Insurance, Denver, secretary, 1972-76; writer, 1977—. *Member:* Mensa, Rocky Mountain Writers Guild, Denver Woman's Press Club. *Awards, honors:* Named writer of the year by Rocky Mountain Writers Guild, 1980.

WRITINGS—Under name Maggie Osborne: *Alexa* (historical novel), Signet, 1980; *Salem's Daughter* (historical novel), Signet, 1981. Contributor to magazines, including *McCall's* and *Guideposts.*

WORK IN PROGRESS: Another historical romance, publication by Signet expected in 1982.

SIDELIGHTS: "I've been writing off and on for the last twenty years," Margaret Osborne told *CA,* "but have approached writing seriously only in the last three. In late 1976 I decided to devote myself to being published or finally getting this monkey off my back once and for all. I enrolled in a critique class sponsored by the Rocky Mountain Writers Guild and began learning the basics. Not long afterward, I sold my first article.

"The euphoria was, however, short lived. I quickly discovered my true interest lay in the realm of fiction. I think the competition is fierce in the short story market; it appears to me that the fiction market is dwindling as would-be readers depend more and more on television for fictional entertainment.

"With this in mind I turned to novels—to historical romance. Not having been a history buff in school, this area fascinated me. I found myself caught up in the research necessary for this genre. My aim is to present history (fictionalized) in such a manner as to inform and entertain the reader. The idea of inserting fictional characters into 'real' situations is a challenge.

"I've been very fortunate. Unlike many writers I have no first novel tucked into a desk drawer somewhere. My first novel sold, thankfully, and I feel as if I've lived a Cinderella existence since, with autographs and speaking engagements. It's been unforgettable. I've had the pleasure of addressing writers' groups (beginners mostly) and one question continually arises: 'What would you advise the beginner?' I think the key is never to give up. Finer writers than I continue to go unpublished. This is a tough business with a great deal of rejection, but those who develop discipline and determination will eventually make it.

"My own most difficult problem is confidence. For reasons I can't even guess, the more success I have, the less confident I become. I want each published effort to reflect the best work I can do, but I'm never satisfied.

"I love writing. It frustrates me, maddens me, drives me wild, but I love it. I'm amazed when I receive a check for doing something I would do if I never received another penny. I get paid for daydreaming in print. What could be lovelier?"

AVOCATIONAL INTERESTS: Travel (including Mexico, Monte Carlo, and the Bahamas), gardening, playing the organ, reading.

P

PANOV, Valery (Shulman) 1938-

PERSONAL: Original name, Valery Shulman; name legally changed, c. 1963; born March 12, 1938, in Vilnius, Lithuania, U.S.S.R.; came to Israel, 1974, naturalized citizen, 1973; son of Matvei and Elizaveta Petrovna (Charitonova) Shulman; married Liya Panov, December, 1958 (marriage ended); married Galina Ragozina (a ballerina), 1970; children: (first marriage) Andrei. *Education:* Attended Leningrad State Choreographic Academy, 1949-57. *Residence:* Jerusalem, Israel. *Office:* c/o The Carson Office, 119 West 57th St., New York, N.Y. 10019.

CAREER: Dancer and choreographer. Became professional ballet dancer, c. 1954; dancer with Maly Theatre Ballet Co., Leningrad, U.S.S.R., 1958-63, appearing in more than thirty productions, including "Swan Lake," "Seven Beauties," and "Scheherazade"; dancer with Kirov Ballet, 1963-72, appearing in more than twenty-five major productions, including "Don Quixote" and "The Sleeping Beauty"; artistic director and chief choreographer of Vilna Ballet Co.; dismissed from Kirov Ballet for political reasons, 1972; solo dancer in companies throughout the world, 1974—, including performances with the Berlin Ballet in "Cinderella," "The Rite of Spring," and "The Idiot." Principal guest choreographer and guest artist for Berlin Ballet; principal guest artist for Vienna Opera Ballet. *Awards, honors:* Honored Artist of Russian Republic, 1968; best male role award from Soviet Government, 1970, for "Hamlet"; recipient of other dancing awards.

WRITINGS: To Dance (autobiography), Knopf, 1978.

SIDELIGHTS: Known as "one of the few great male dancers in the world," Panov began dancing at the age of eight. Three years later he entered the Leningrad State Choreographic Academy, the prestigious training ground for such dancers as Vaslav Nijinsky, Rudolf Nureyev, and Natalia Makarova. By the age of fifteen he had turned professional, and in 1958 he joined the Maly Theatre Ballet Company. With that group Panov played more than thirty leading parts, including the title role in Igor Stravinsky's "Petrouchka." Stravinsky himself witnessed one performance and was reportedly "stunned" by Panov's dancing brilliance.

Panov accepted an invitation to become the principal dancer in the Kirov Ballet in 1963, but only after changing his name. "My real name is Shulman," he told Herbert Gold in 1974, "but I couldn't join the Kirov Ballet until I called myself

Panov. I managed to change my passport from Jew to Russian. Many dancers are Jewish, but they don't admit it. Even ballet is ruled by politics here, though it seems very far from ideology." Panov performed with the company for nine years, until political differences resulted in his dismissal.

Friction with Soviet authorities was nothing new to Panov. Once, one of his New York City bookings had to be canceled after a telegram informed him that his father had been struck by an illness. When he returned home Panov discovered the report to be false. Later he was prohibited from participating in any of the Kirov tours outside the U.S.S.R. Tensions increased when his unorthodox choreographic techniques fell under attack from cultural officials, and when his staging of "Pugachev" was banned for depicting the independent will of the peasantry.

In 1968, after years of trying to perfect his dancing, of trying "to make my body behave," Panov came to assess life as an artist in the Soviet Union. "I looked at what was happening outside me," he reflected in his autobiography. "The Soviet system was essentially the same. But the easing of my anxiety about my own problems allowed me to see it clearly. With 10 star-kissed years ahead of me, I realized that I was nothing as a person. I would never be able to do what I wanted even as a dancer, and this was no accident. . . . Now I recognized that the system was designed to kill real art."

Unwilling to suppress his art any longer, Panov announced plans to immigrate to Israel in 1972. Officials quickly denounced him as a traitor and prohibited him from any further work with the ballet. Two years of conflict with the Soviet system followed; the government refused to acknowledge Panov's and his wife's emigration petitions and for a time imprisoned him with a group of invalids. Later his mail and telephone services were canceled. Unable to dance outside their home, the Panovs converted their tiny apartment into a space to practice their art. "We try," Panov told visitor Herbert Gold in 1974. "Of course we lose some of our skills."

As the Panovs' plight continued, their case drew international attention. Sympathizers formed the Ad Hoc Committee for Valery and Galina Panov, petitioning the Soviet government for their release. Senator Henry Jackson wrote Soviet leader Brezhnev. Laurence Olivier, Beverly Sills, Clive Barnes, and Barbara Streisand spoke publicly on the Panovs' behalf. In December, 1973, Panov's request was finally granted, but his wife's was denied. As she was pregnant at the time, Panov refused to leave (she later miscarried). The *New York Times* furthered the Panov cause by editorializing, "No gesture would do more to promote genuine goodwill than for Moscow to cease its spiteful crime against marriage and art and permit the Panovs to dance again." They did dance again, in their new home, Israel, and throughout the world, after finally being allowed to leave the Soviet Union in June, 1974.

Four years later Panov published his autobiography, *To Dance. Washington Post Book World* reviewer Anthony Astrachan remarked that Panov "tells the story of his life up to his departure from the Soviet Union in very human terms, without the posturings that many dancers assume in prose and without the tinny note that many heroes strike when they recount their own battles. He provides more details than we have ever had before of the ways in which personal politics and party ideology deform the magnificent potential of Soviet ballet."

The Panovs' "escape to Israel and appearance now on the New York stage seem almost inconceivable," wrote Caroline Seebohm in 1978. "That the Panovs danced here at all says something awesome about the human spirit. What has been lost by their persecution is a tragedy for art. What continues to be lost by the existence of an inhuman political regime should make us choke over our uncensored books, our uncensored music, our uncensored trips and our uncensored work, in gratitude and shame."

BIOGRAPHICAL/CRITICAL SOURCES: New York Times, July 1, 1968, April 23, 1972, April 9, 1973, January 16, 1974, February 7, 1974, March 18, 1974, June 14, 1974, August 6, 1974, July 8, 1978; *Washington Post*, January 19, 1974; *Christian Science Monitor*, February 15, 1974, June 8, 1978; *Newsweek*, July 1, 1974; *New Republic*, August 24, 1974, June 17, 1978; Valery Panov, *To Dance*, Knopf, 1978; *Washington Post Book World*, May 15, 1978; *Harper's*, July, 1978; *Saturday Review*, July 22, 1978; *New York Times Book Review*, July 30, 1978; *New York Review of Books*, September 28, 1978; *Commonweal*, September 29, 1978.

—*Sketch by David Versical*

*   *   *

PANOVA, Vera (Fedorovna)   1905-1973
(Vera Veltman)

PERSONAL: Born March 20, 1905, in Rostov-on-Don, Russia (now U.S.S.R.). *Education:* Attended schools in Russia.

CAREER: Novelist, short story writer, and playwright. Worked as journalist, 1922-46. *Member:* Soviet Writers Union, Congress of Soviet Writers. *Awards, honors:* Stalin Prize, 1947, for *Sputniki*, 1948, for *Kruzhilikha*, and 1950, for *Yasni bereg*.

WRITINGS—In English translation: *Sputniki* (novel), [Moscow, U.S.S.R.], 1946, translation by Marie Budberg published as *The Train*, Knopf, 1949 (also see below); *Kruzhilikha* (novel), [Moscow], 1948, translation by Moura Budberg published as *The Factory*, Putnam, 1949, reprinted, Hyperion Press, 1977; *Vremena goda* (novel), [U.S.S.R.], 1954, translation by Vera Traill published as *Span of the Year*, Harvill, 1957; *Serezha* (novel), [Leningrad, U.S.S.R.], 1956, translation published as *Time Walked*, Harvill, 1957, Arlington Books, 1959, published as *A Summer to Remember*, T. Yoseloff, 1962, translation of original Russian by Rya Gabel published as *On Faraway Street*, Braziller, 1968 (also see below); *Selected Works* (contains "The Train," "Valia," "Volodia," and "Serezha"), translated by Olga Shartse and Eve Manning, Progress, 1976.

Other writings: *Yasni bereg* (novel), [U.S.S.R.], 1949; *Izbrannye sochineniya* (two-volume collection; contains "Sputniki," "Yasni bereg," "Serezha," "Kruzhilikha," and "Vremena goda"), [U.S.S.R.], 1956; *Metelitsa* (play; first produced in 1942), [U.S.S.R.], 1957; *Sentimental'nyi roman* (novel; title means "Sentimental Story"), [U.S.S.R.], 1958; *V staroi Moskve* (play; first produced in 1940), Iskusstvo, 1958; *Ilia Kosogor* (collection of plays; contains "Ilia Kosogor" [first produced in 1939], "V staroi Moskve," "Metelitsa," and "Devochki" [first produced in 1945]), [U.S.S.R.], 1958.

Valia [and] *Volodia* (two short stories), Pravda, 1960; *Evdokiia* (fiction), [U.S.S.R.], 1960; *Rabochii poselok* (collection; contains "Rabochii poselok," "Sasha," and "Rano utrom"), [U.S.S.R.], 1966; *Liki na zare*, [U.S.S.R.], 1966; *Povesti*, Lenizdat, 1966; *Pogovorim o strannostiakh liubvi* (collection of plays), [U.S.S.R.], 1968; *Skazanie ob Ol'ge* (juvenile), [U.S.S.R.], 1968; *Izbrannoe* [U.S.S.R.], 1972; *Zametki literatora* (addresses, essays, and lectures), [U.S.S.R.], 1972; *Nashi deti* [U.S.S.R.], 1973; *O moei zhizni, knigakh i chitateliakh* (biography), [U.S.S.R.], 1975. Also author of "Provody belykh nochei" (play), first produced in 1961, and "Skolko let, skolko zim!" (play; title means "It's Been Ages!"), first produced in 1966.

Author of humorous sketches under pseudonym Vera Veltman. Work represented in anthologies, including *Contemporary Russian Drama*, edited by Franklin O. Reeve, Pegasus, 1968.

SIDELIGHTS: Vera Panova, a noted Russian novelist, received little formal education. Her father was killed in a boating accident when she was only five, leaving the family in financial difficulties. Panova worked in a laundry as a child and, although unable to attend school, was an avid reader. At age seventeen, Panova began her writing career working for a Soviet newspaper. In the early 1930's, she published several plays. She found drama too confining, however, and soon turned to writing fiction.

During World War II, Panova was a correspondent on a hospital train, writing dispatches from interviews with wounded Soviet soldiers. She later drew from these experiences for her first novel, *The Train*. It was published in the Soviet Union in 1946 and became one of the most popular and successful novels about World War II.

The Train is a character study of a number of people who lived on a hospital train for several years during the war. The story explores how the war affected their lives and relates the adjustments to peacetime conditions. With a new national unity born out of the war, the Soviet people on Panova's train were forced to reassess their personal values and ethics.

The transition period from war to peace is the setting of Panova's second novel, *The Factory*. As in *The Train*, Panova again focuses on a group of people and how they are affected by external conditions, although this novel is set in a factory.

Panova received a public reprimand in 1954 following the publication of her next novel, *Span of the Year*. This novel concerns a corrupt Soviet official and a young criminal. Critics argued that such a thing would not exist or at least not escape punishment under their party system.

In these and later novels, Panova's style was decidedly feminine. She limited her themes to the human elements of a given situation and was commended for her characterizations of ordinary people and their lives. The major forces in her works are such things as love, compassion, the bringing up of children, and family relationships.

BIOGRAPHICAL/CRITICAL SOURCES: New Statesman and Nation, January 22, 1949; *New York Herald Tribune Weekly Book Review*, April 10, 1949; *New York Times*, April 10, 1949; *New Yorker*, April 16, 1949; *Time*, April 18, 1949; *Saturday Review of Literature*, April 30, 1949; *San Francisco Chronicle*, May 15, 1949; *Time*, May 11, 1959; *New York Herald Tribune Book Review*, June 28, 1959.

OBITUARIES: New York Times, March 6, 1973.*

*   *   *

PAOLUCCI, Henry 1921-

PERSONAL: Born February 4, 1921, in New York, N.Y.; son of Donato and Nancy Paolucci; married Anne Attura (a writer and university professor), September 5, 1949. *Education:* City College (now of the City University of New York), B.S.S., 1942; Columbia University, M.A., 1948, Ph.D., 1961; also attended University of Florence, 1948-49, and University of Rome, 1951-52. *Politics:* Conservative Democrat. *Home:* 166-25 Powells Cove Blvd., Beechhurst, N.Y. 11357. *Office:* St. John's University, Jamaica, N.Y. 11439.

CAREER: Columbia University, New York, N.Y., lecturer in comparative literature, 1954-55; Iona College, New Rochelle, N.Y., 1955-67, instructor in comparative literature, 1955-58, associate professor of history, 1958-65; St. John's University, Jamaica, N.Y., professor of government and politics, 1967—. Instructor at City College of City University of New York, 1955-64, and Brooklyn College (now of City University of New York), 1957-59; lecturer at conferences in the United States and abroad. Vice-chairman of Conservative Party of New York, 1968—; president of Walter Bagehot Research Council on National Sovereignty; member of Center for the Study of the Presidency. Theatrical producer at Spa Music Theatre, of Saratoga Springs Performing Arts Center, 1961-64; publications coordinator for Council on National Literatures. Guest on television and radio programs, including "Meet the Press," "The Today Show," and "Issues and Answers." *Military service:* U.S. Army Air Forces, aerial navigator, 1942-46; prisoner of war in Italy, 1945-46; served in Africa and Italy.

MEMBER: Hegel Society of America, American Political Science Association, Dante Society of America, Pirandello Society of America, American Historical Association, American Catholic Historical Association, Northeastern Political Science Association, Friends of Rhodesia (president, 1975-78), Friends of the Library of Columbia University. *Awards, honors:* Fulbright fellow, 1951-52.

WRITINGS: (Editor and author of introduction) *St. Augustine: Enchiridion*, Gateway, 1961; (with wife, Anne Paolucci) *Hegel on Tragedy*, Doubleday, 1962; *The Political Writings of St. Augustine*, Gateway, 1962; (with James Brophy) *The Achievement of Galileo*, Twayne, 1962; *War, Peace, and the Presidency*, McGraw, 1968.

Who Is Kissinger?, Griffon House, 1972; *F. W. Maitland: Justice and Police*, AMS Press, 1974; (editor and author of introduction) *Aldebaran: Nixon and the Foxes of Watergate*, Griffon House, 1974; *A Separate and Equal Station: Hegel, America, and the Nation-State System*, Griffon House, 1978; *The South and the Presidency*, Griffon House, 1978; *The Political Thought of G.W.F. Hegel*, Griffon House, 1978; *Hegel: On the Arts*, Ungar, 1979; *A Brief History of Political Thought and Statecraft*, Griffon House, 1979; (editor and author of introduction) Richard C. Clark, *Technological Terrorism*, Devin-Adair, 1980.

Translator: (With A. Paolucci, and author of introduction)

Machiavelli's Mandragola, Liberal Arts Press, 1957; (also author of introduction) *Beccaria: On Crimes and Punishments*, Bobbs-Merrill, 1963; (with A. Paolucci) Mario Apollonio, *The Apocalypse According to J. J. (Rousseau)*, Griffon House, 1980.

Contributor: (Author of introduction) *Dino Bigongiari: Essays on Dante and Medieval Culture*, Olschki, 1964; Frederick G. Weiss, editor, *Beyond Epistemology*, Nijhoff, 1974; James T. Curran and Austin Fowler, editors, *Police and Law Enforcement*, AMS Press, 1974; D. P. Verene, editor, *Hegel's Social and Political Thought*, Humanities, 1980. Also contributor to *Hegel and the Sciences*, edited by R. S. Cohen and M. W. Wartofsky, 1980.

Musical composer and lyricist. American correspondent for *Il Borghese*, 1969-72. Guest columnist for *New York Times*, 1971-73. Contributor to *Encyclopedia Americana*. Contributor of articles to magazines, including *Owl of Minerva*, *American Mercury*, and *National Review*, and newspapers. Editor of *State of the Nation*; contributing editor of *Review of National Literatures*, 1970—. Coordinator of *Avery Encyclopedia of American History*.

BIOGRAPHICAL/CRITICAL SOURCES: New York Times, September 1, 1964; *National Review*, February 25, 1969; *Congressional Record*, June 7, 1974.

*   *   *

PARKER, Bertha Morris 1890-1980

OBITUARY NOTICE—See index for *CA* sketch: Born February 7, 1890, in Rochester, Ill.; died November 14, 1980, in Chicago, Ill. Educator and author. Parker served as chair of the science department of the Laboratory School at the University of Chicago. She was also associate editor for science education for the National Association for Research in Science Teaching. Parker wrote more than eighty books, including *Book of Plants*, *The Golden Treasury of Natural History*, *Living Things*, *The Sea*, *Around the Year*, and *Aquariums*. Her books have been translated into nearly thirty languages. She also wrote teaching manuals and contributed to education and health journals. Obituaries and other sources: *Chicago Tribune*, November 16, 1980.

*   *   *

PARKER, Nathan Carlyle 1960-

PERSONAL: Born August 7, 1960, in Eureka, Calif.; son of John Carlyle (a librarian) and Janet C. Parker. *Education:* Attended Brigham Young University, 1978-79. *Home:* 2115 North Denair Ave., Turlock, Calif. 95380.

CAREER: Church of Jesus Christ of Latter-day Saints, Japan Tokyo North Mission, Tokyo, missionary, 1979—.

WRITINGS: (Editor) *Personal Name Index to the 1856 City Directories of California*, Gale, 1980.

*   *   *

PARKES, Lucas
See HARRIS, John (Wyndham Parkes Lucas) Beynon

*   *   *

PARKINSON, J(ohn) R(ichard) 1922-

PERSONAL: Born April 3, 1922, in Calverley, England; son of Alfred Wright (a wool merchant) and Ethel Ann (Rogers) Parkinson; married Nancy Bessie Giles (a civil servant), April 11, 1946; children: Richard Andrew, John Charles,

Elizabeth Annis Scothern, Sarah Gillian. *Education:* University of Leeds, B.Com. (with first class honors), 1942. *Home:* The Chestnuts, Clare, Valley, The Park, Nottingham NG7 1BU, England. *Office:* Department of Economics, University of Nottingham, University Park, Nottingham NG7 2RD, England.

CAREER: Prime Minister's Statistical Branch, London, England, assistant, 1942-45; University of Leeds, Leeds, England, lecturer in economics, 1946-48; Organization for European Economic Cooperation, Paris, France, counselor, 1948-51; Prime Minister's Statistical Branch, adviser, 1952-53; University of Glasgow, Glasgow, Scotland, senior lecturer in economics, 1954-62; Queen's University, Belfast, Northern Ireland, professor of economics, 1962-69; University of Nottingham, Nottingham, England, professor of economics, 1969—. Member of Northern Ireland Economic Council, 1965-69; consultant to World Bank. *Member:* Royal Economic Society (member of council), British Institute of Management, Royal Statistical Society.

WRITINGS: The Economics of Shipbuilding in the United Kingdom, Cambridge University Press, 1960; (with James Bates) *Business Economics,* Basil Blackwell, 1963, 2nd edition, 1970; *Agricultural Cooperation in Northern Ireland,* H.M.S.O., 1965; (with Anthony Gater, David Insull, and others) *Thrusters and Sleepers,* Allen & Unwin, 1965; (with Robert Matthew and Thomas Wilson) *Northern Ireland Development Programme, 1970-75,* H.M.S.O., 1970; (with Just Faaland) *Bangladesh: The Test Case of Development,* Hurst, 1976; (with Faaland and Nurul Islam) *Aid and Influence,* Macmillan, 1981. Contributor to economic and statistical journals.

WORK IN PROGRESS: A textbook on economic development, publication expected in 1982.

SIDELIGHTS: Parkinson has lived or worked in Bangladesh, Pakistan, Southern Rhodesia, Botswana, and Mozambique. He told *CA* that he "spends his time keeping his fingers crossed for Bangladesh and wondering why people have any use for economics." *Avocational interests:* Electronics.

*   *   *

PARKINSON, Thomas P(aul)
(Tom Parkinson)

PERSONAL: Born in Decatur, Ill.; son of N. P. (an insurance executive) and Florence (North) Parkinson; married Margaret Gill, December, 1947; children: Richard G., Ann (Mrs. John Meek). *Education:* Attended Millikin University, 1939-41; University of Illinois, B.A., 1943; Northwestern University, M.S., 1947. *Residence:* Savoy, Ill. *Office:* Assembly Hall, University of Illinois, Champaign, Ill. 61820.

CAREER: Shreveport Times, Shreveport, La., reporter, 1947-50; *Billboard,* Chicago, Ill., associate editor, 1950-61; University of Illinois, Champaign, director of Assembly Hall, 1961—. Consultant on arena management and design. *Military service:* U.S. Army, Infantry, 1944; served in Europe; became staff sergeant. *Member:* International Association of Auditorium Managers (president, 1972), International Society of Performing Arts Administrators (vice-president, 1977), National Academy of the Arts (member of board of directors), Circus Historical Society (president, 1977-81), Circus World Museum (member of board of directors), Champaign Rotary (member of board of directors).

*WRITINGS—*Under name Tom Parkinson: (With Charles Philip Fox) *The Circus in America,* Country Beautiful Corp., 1969, 2nd edition, 1972; (with Fox) *The Circus Moves by Rail,* Pruett, 1978. Contributor to magazines.

WORK IN PROGRESS: One book on the circus's influence on American life and another about circus advertising, both with Charles Philip Fox.

*   *   *

PARKINSON, Tom
See PARKINSON, Thomas P(aul)

*   *   *

PARR, John (Lloyd) 1928-

PERSONAL: Born June 18, 1928, in Chicago, Ill.; son of Lloyd Thomas (in sales) and Della (Napier) Parr; married Joan Asgeirson, January 9, 1954; children: Kristin Thora, Louise Joan. *Education:* University of Manitoba, B.A., 1950, certificate in education, 1960. *Home:* 102 Queenston St., Winnipeg, Manitoba, Canada R3N 0W5.

CAREER: Worked as usher, property assessor, and social worker, 1950-60; teacher of English at collegiate school in Winnipeg, Manitoba, 1960-67; free-lance writer and part-time teacher, 1968-70; Red River Community College, Winnipeg, instructor in communications, 1970—. *Member:* Writers Union of Canada. *Awards, honors:* Canada Council grants, 1967 and 1973.

WRITINGS: (Editor) *Speaking of Winnipeg,* Queenston House, 1974; (editor) *Selected Stories of Robert Barr,* University of Ottawa Press, 1977; *Jim Tweed* (novel), Queenston House, 1978. Writer for Canadian Broadcasting Corp. (CBC). Contributor of articles, stories, and reviews to literature journals and literary magazines, including *Journal of Canadian Fiction, Canadian Children's Literature, Brick, Plaintiff, Edge,* and *Fiddlehead,* and newspapers.

WORK IN PROGRESS: Passion in the North (tentative title), a satirical novel about Canadian literary politics and tangled love relationships, publication by Queenston House, expected in 1982.

SIDELIGHTS: Parr commented: "The present moment is an extremely exciting time for writers in Canada, what with the emergence of nationalism, government interest in the arts (including sponsored reading tours across Canada), and the advent of 'Women's Lib'—as indicated by the domination of Canadian fiction by our female authors. All of this would appear to deserve a literary treatment, of one sort or another. The great influence on my work (at least I hope some of his approach comes through) is the serio-comic writing of U.S. novelist Calder Willingham, who really showed how it all could be done. Current Canadian writers of great personal interest are: among the men, Fred Stenson and David McFadden, both of whom are carrying on in the Willingham tradition quite ably (although possibly unbeknownst to themselves); and among the women, Sylvia Fraser, spokesperson for the 'new,' and Carol Shields, spokesperson for the 'tried and true.' "

*   *   *

PARSONS, Ian (Macnaghten) 1906-1980

OBITUARY NOTICE—See index for *CA* sketch: Born May 21, 1906, in London, England; died October 29, 1980. Publisher. Parsons was chairman of Chatto & Windus Ltd. and director of several other publishing firms. His writings include *Shades of Albany, Men Who March Away, Poems of C. Day Lewis, The Collected Works of Isaac Rosenberg,* and *Bird, Beast, and Flower.* Obituaries and other sources: *London Times,* October 31, 1980.

PASCAL, John Robert 1932(?)-1981

OBITUARY NOTICE: Born c. 1932; died of cancer, January 7, 1981, in New York, N.Y. Educator, journalist, and author. John Rascal collaborated with his wife, Francine, on television scripts, including the daily serial "The Young Marrieds." They also co-authored *George M!,* a biography of singer-composer George M. Cohan, as well as the script for the Broadway musical of the same title. Pascal wrote for a number of newspapers, including the *New York Herald Tribune* and the *New York Times,* and was the author of several books, including *The Strange Case of Patty Hearst.* Obituaries and other sources: *New York Times,* January 9, 1981.

* * *

PATTERSON, Virginia 1931-

PERSONAL: Born January 23, 1931, in New Mexico; daughter of Edward Cecil (a rancher) and Edith Elizabeth (Roweton) Patterson. *Education:* Attended Draughons Business College, 1948-49, and Northeastern Oklahoma A & M College, 1949-50; University of Tulsa, B.A., 1953; attended Prairie Bible Institute, 1953-54; Columbia Bible College, Columbia, S.C., M.A., 1956; Oklahoma State University, M.S., 1963; Northern Illinois University, Ed.D., 1978. *Residence:* Winfield, Ill. *Office:* Pioneer Ministries, Inc., P.O. Box 788, Wheaton, Ill. 60187.

CAREER: Private tutor to handicapped child, 1954-56; high school teacher at girls' industrial school in Columbia, S.C., 1957-58; elementary school teacher at mission school for missionaries' children in Miango, Nigeria, 1958-68; substitute teacher at public schools in Tulsa, Okla., 1968-69; Pioneer Girls, Inc., Wheaton, Ill., publications director, 1969-70, president, 1970—. Adjunct professor at Gordon-Conwell Theological Seminary and Wheaton College, 1980; conducts seminars and workshops. Member of board of directors of Pioneer Girls of Canada. *Member:* Adult Education Association of the United States of America, Religious Research Association, Wheaton Chamber of Commerce, Phi Mu, Glen Ayre Tennis Club, Hanover Park Racquetball Club.

WRITINGS: A Touch of God, Abingdon, 1979; (contributor) Roy B. Zuck and Warren S. Benson, editors, *Youth and the Church,* Moody Bible Institute, 1979; *A Woman Succeeds,* Abingdon, 1981. Contributor to magazines, including *Christian Camping International, Standard,* and *His.* Member of editorial advisory board of *Leadership.*

WORK IN PROGRESS: Research on the developmental stages of women.

SIDELIGHTS: Virginia Patterson wrote: "I have always set many goals for myself. As I began my college career, I found it difficult to limit myself to one area of study when so many avenues were challenging. Once one goal was accomplished, I set another. As a Christian, I find that life has much more meaning when goals and accomplishments are being pursued. I love to learn, although my learning usually follows practical rather than theoretical avenues. Christian education and management are my two main professional interests."

AVOCATIONAL INTERESTS: Tennis, racquetball, skiing, entertaining, swimming, reading.

* * *

PEARSON, Michael

PERSONAL—Residence: Surrey, England. *Agent:* Julian Bach, 747 Third Ave., New York, N.Y. 10017.

CAREER: Writer and journalist.

WRITINGS—All nonfiction, except as noted: (With Bill Strutton) *The Secret Invaders,* Hodder & Stoughton, 1958, British Book Centre (New York), 1959; *The Millionaire Mentality,* Secker & Warburg, 1961; *The Million-Dollar Bugs,* Putman, 1969; *The L 5 Virgins,* Saturday Review Press, 1972 (published in England as *The Age of Consent: Victorian Prostitution and Its Enemies,* David and Charles, 1972); *Those Damned Rebels: The American Revolution as Seen Through British Eyes,* Putnam, 1972, revised edition published as *Those Yankee Rebels; Being the True and Amazing History of the Audacious American Revolution As Seen Through British Eyes and Being a Young People's Version of Those Damned Rebels,* 1974 (published in England as *Those Damned Rebels: Britain's American Empire in Revolt,* Heinemann, 1972); *The Sealed Train,* Putnam, 1975; *Tears of Glory: The Heroes of Vercors 1944,* Macmillan (London), 1978, Doubleday, 1979; *The Store* (novel), Macmillan, 1980, Simon & Schuster, 1981. Contributor to periodicals, including *American Heritage, Horizon, True, New York Times,* and *London Sunday Times.*

WORK IN PROGRESS: A novel in the same genre as *The Store.*

SIDELIGHTS: Pearson's first book, in collaboration with Bill Strutton, relates the story of the British secret beach reconnaissance force, the Combined Operations Pilotage Parties (COPP). "'The Secret Invaders' adds some new information to our knowledge of the development, training, and operations of the beach reconnaissance units," commented F. C. Pogue in *Saturday Review.* One of the examples of COPP's work cited in the volume is the daring, clandestine mission carried out by two men in 1944, five months before the Normandy invasion. These soldiers swam to the Normandy coast at night and while under the watch of unknowing German guards, measured the gradients of the beaches and collected sand samples. A *Times Literary Supplement* critic judged *The Secret Invaders* as "eminently worthwhile."

A later book, *The Million Dollar Bugs,* details the workings of the pharmaceutical industry during the period when "bugs" or microorganisms vital to the production of antibiotics were processed into useful drugs that included penicillin and sulfa. Pearson covers such topics as industrial espionage, drug proliferation, monopolization, price fixing, and patent protection. The author's next endeavor, *The L 5 Virgins,* is a social history of prostitution in Victorian England. Pearson details the efforts of W. T. Stead to prevent organized prostitution by the state and white slavery to the continent. The reformer attempted this through a series of newspaper articles that appeared in the *Pall Mall.*

Pearson's following book, about the American Revolution, received glowing reviews. Regarding *Those Damn Rebels,* Edward Weeks of *Atlantic* exclaimed that "I cannot remember reading anywhere a more vivid account of the action at Boston, Saratoga, or Long Island." Similarly, *Book World*'s Alan Pryce-Jones asserted: "Pearson sets the strong personalities in strong color. Lord George Germain, Banastre Tarleton, and General Clinton live as human beings, though it is Pearson's virtue throughout to set sober fact above the picturesque. . . . The whole story, as he tells it, is exemplary."

The Sealed Train also received favorable reviews. While outlining Lenin's famous journey across Germany and into Russia in a sealed train, Pearson puts forth his theory that in addition to financing Lenin's trip, Germany also funded the vast communist propaganda drive employed by the Bolsheviks. In this way, Germany successfully manipulated Russia into withdrawing from World War I. W. J. Parente praised the author, proclaiming that "Pearson deserves our thanks for a series of original and brilliant hypotheses intelligently argued with a good deal of intellectual balance and a minimum of scholarly certitude."

The author's next book, *Tears of Glory,* tells of the massacre of French Resistance fighters at Vercors' plateau in southern France. Basing his story on recently declassified information, Pearson relates how more than eight hundred French partisans were killed because of "bureaucratic betrayal" as Elizabeth Peer dubbed it in *Newsweek.* The Resistance was promised air coverage and backup troops when it launched its attack on the Germans after D-Day. Instead, it got lame excuses and as a result Nazi paratroopers slaughtered hundreds of partisans. Martin Sokolinsky of the *Christian Science Monitor* remarked: "Now, filling a 35-year historical gap for the American reader, 'Tears of Glory' has come to pay homage to their memory."

Pearson told *CA:* "*The Store,* my first novel, is a family saga of a young man who opens a small draper's shop in London in the 1860's and on this foundation builds a huge quality department store similar in character to Harrods, of which my father-in-law, the late Sir Richard Burbidge, was chief executive—the third member of the dynasty that directed it for sixty-eight continuous years.

"Although I shall probably write nonfiction from time to time, the main thrust of my work will now be in fiction—at least for my next few books—since it is an area which I enjoy particularly, though newly discovered in book form. (I wrote much short fiction at the beginning of my career.)"

BIOGRAPHICAL/CRITICAL SOURCES: *Times Literary Supplement,* June 20, 1958, November 3, 1972; *Saturday Review,* June 27, 1959, November 1, 1969; *Best Sellers,* December 15, 1969, April 1, 1972, March 1, 1975; *Atlantic,* March, 1972; *Book World,* April 9, 1972; *Newsweek,* July 30, 1979; *Christian Science Monitor,* August 1, 1979.

*   *   *

PEATTIE, Donald Culross   1898-1964

PERSONAL: Born June 21, 1898, in Chicago, Ill.; died November 16, 1964; son of Robert Burns (a journalist) and Elia (Wilkenson) Peattie; married Louise Redfield (a writer), May 23, 1923; children: Celia Louise (deceased), Malcolm Redfield, Mark Robert, Noel Roderick. *Education:* Attended University of Chicago, 1916-18; Harvard University, A.B. (cum laude), 1922, A.M., 1946. *Home:* 224 Buena Vista Rd., Santa Barbara, Calif.

CAREER: Nature writer, 1924-64. Worked as botanist at U.S. Department of Agriculture, Office of Foreign Seed and Plant Introduction, 1922-24; free-lance writer and author of nature columns for *Washington Evening Star* and *Chicago Daily News. Member:* National Institute of Arts and Letters, Society of American Historians, California Historical Society, California Academy of Sciences, Phi Gamma Delta. *Awards, honors:* Gold medal from Limited Editions Club, 1935, for *An Almanac for Moderns;* Guggenheim fellowship for creative writing, 1936-38; monetary prize from Houghton Mifflin Co., 1941, for *The Road of a Naturalist.*

WRITINGS—Nonfiction: (With wife, Louise Redfield Peattie) *Bounty of Earth,* illustrations by Margaret Evans Price, Appleton, 1926; *Cargoes and Harvest,* Appleton, 1926; (with L. R. Peattie) *Down Wind: Secrets of the Underwoods,* Appleton, 1929; *Flora of the Indiana Dunes,* Field Museum of Natural History, 1930; *Vence: The Story of a Provencal Town Through Two Thousand Years,* Imprimerie de l'Eclaireur de Nice, 1930; *Trees You Want to Know,* illustrations by Francois Andre Michaux and Ethel Bonney Taylor, Whitman, 1934; *Singing in the Wilderness: A Salute to John James Audubon,* Putnam, 1935; *An Almanac for Moderns,* illustrations by Lynd Ward, Putnam, 1935; *Green Laurels: The Lives and Achievements of the Great Naturalists* (Literary Guild selection), Simon & Schuster, 1935; *A Book of Hours,* illustrations by Ward, Putnam, 1937; *A Prairie Grove,* Simon & Schuster, 1938; *This Is Living: A View of Nature With Photographs,* Dodd, 1938; (editor) *A Gathering of Birds: An Anthology of the Best Ornithological Prose,* illustrations by Edward Shenton, Dodd, 1939; *Flowering Earth,* illustrations by Paul Landacre, Putnam, 1939, reprinted, Viking, 1965.

The Road of a Naturalist (autobiography), Houghton, 1941; *Journey Into America,* illustrations by Ward, Houghton, 1943; *Immortal Village,* illustrations by Landacre, University of Chicago Press, 1945, reprinted as *Vence: Immortal Village,* 1963; *American Heartwood,* illustrations by David Hendrickson, Houghton, 1949; (with Noel Peattie) *A Cup of Sky,* Houghton, 1950; *A Natural History of Trees of Eastern and Central North America,* illustrations by Landacre, Houghton, 1950; *Lives of Destiny* (biography), Houghton, 1954; *Parade With Banners,* World Publishing, 1957.

Fiction: (With L. R. Peattie) *Up Country: A Story of the Vanguard,* Appleton, 1928; *Port of Call,* Century, 1932; *Sons of the Martian,* Longmans, Green, 1932; *The Bright Lexicon,* Putnam, 1934; *Forward the Nation,* Putnam, 1942.

For children; all published by Grosset, except as noted; all illustrated by Naomi Averill, except as noted: *A Child's Story of the World From the Earliest Days to Our Own Time,* Simon & Schuster, 1937; *The Story of America,* 1937; *The Story of Ancient Civilization,* 1937; *The Story of the First Men,* 1937; *The Story of the Middle Ages,* 1937; *The Story of the Modern Age From the French Revolution to Now,* 1937; *The Story of the New Lands,* 1937; *The Rainbow Book of Nature,* illustrations by Rudolf Freund, World Publishing, 1957.

Contributor to periodicals; including *Saturday Evening Post, Nature, Ladies Home Journal, Good Housekeeping, Better Homes and Gardens,* and *Sunset.*

SIDELIGHTS: Although Donald Peattie wrote fiction and children's books, he was best known for his nature writing. His expertise in botany served as the basis for his nature columns in the *Washington Star* and the *Chicago Tribune* as well as his numerous nature books.

Peattie's most successful book, *An Almanac for Moderns,* was the culmination of his attempts to combine poetry with scientific fact. The book consisted of 365 short essays which, while grounded on the sound observations of a naturalist, were expressed in the language of a poet. The *Almanac,* which was chosen the book most likely to become a classic by the Limited Editions Club, reflected Peattie's belief in the need for books that combine sound science and literary excellence.

Peattie also wrote biographies on some of the great naturalists. His own autobiography, *The Road of a Naturalist,* earned him a monetary award from Houghton Mifflin.

BIOGRAPHICAL/CRITICAL SOURCES: *Atlantic,* January-March, 1938, May, 1941; *Saturday Review,* July 5, 1941, October 9, 1943; *Better Homes and Gardens,* December, 1943; *Christian Science Monitor Magazine,* September 23, 1950.

OBITUARIES: New York Times, November 17, 1964; *Newsweek,* November 30, 1964; *Publishers' Weekly,* November 30, 1964; *Time,* November 27, 1964.*

*   *   *

PEDERSON, Kern O(wen)   1910-

PERSONAL: Born September 23, 1910, in Westbrook, Minn.; son of Louis P. (a construction worker) and Miriam O. (Jacobsen) Pederson; married Evelyn M. Erickson, March 2, 1942; children: Steven Kern, Gary Bruce, Jeffrey Kern. *Education:* St. Olaf College, B.A., 1936; also attended University of Minnesota. *Politics:* Republican. *Religion:* Lutheran. *Home:* 7204 Del Pasado N.W., Albuquerque, N.M. 87120.

CAREER: Worked in store in Red Wing, Minn., 1937-38; State Training School, Red Wing, instructor in art and journalism, 1938-41; Navy Department, Washington, D.C., draftsman, 1941-43; *Catholic Digest* (monthly magazine), St. Paul, Minn., art director and production manager, 1946-60; Maplewood High School, St. Paul, art and history teacher, 1960-73. Free-lance writer and cartoonist. Member of Golf Executive committee and executive board, 1976-78. *Military service:* U.S. Navy, 1943-45; became petty officer. *Member:* National Cartoonists Society, Colonial Country Club (member of executive board, 1976-78).

WRITINGS—Self-illustrated: The Story of Fort Snelling, St. Paul Historical Society, 1966; *Makers of Minnesota,* Marric Publishing, 1971; *Leaders of America,* Country Beautiful Corp., 1976.

Author of "Little Farmer," a comic strip, 1951—, "Color This," a children's feature, 1977—, "It Just So Happened," an oddity feature, 1977—, and "Famous Americans," 1979—, all syndicated by Smith Feature Service. Contributor to *Milwaukee Journal.*

WORK IN PROGRESS: Research on New Mexico and the people who pioneered there and built the state; "California Hi-Lights," a series of drawings of famous Californians for weekly papers.

SIDELIGHTS: Pederson told *CA:* "I am an ardent student of art and history with majors in both fields. Combining the two mediums with the illustrations as the dominant part, my work is interesting for students studying American or state history. I feature the strong and determined men and women who built this country. I illustrate key scenes from their lives and basic facts about their backgrounds and careers, putting them all in chronological order. My conversations with my good friend of thirty years, Charles 'Sparky' Schultz, creator of 'Peanuts,' had a lot to do in motivating me to work in the writing field as well as with my comic feature work."

BIOGRAPHICAL/CRITICAL SOURCES: Hemet News (Hemet, Calif.), June 7, 1976; *Press Enterprise* (Riverside, Calif.), October 6, 1976; *Milwaukee Journal,* October 15, 1972.

*   *   *

PEEL, Norman Lemon
See HIRSCH, Phil

*   *   *

PEELE, David A(rnold)   1929-

PERSONAL: Born March 24, 1929, in New York, N.Y.; son of Wilfred Earle (a journalist) and Margaret (a high school teacher; maiden name, Harrison) Peele; married Marla Hamilton (a librarian), April 20, 1968. *Education:* Swarthmore College, B.A., 1950, M.A., 1954; Western Reserve University (now Case Western Reserve University), M.S.L.S., 1951. *Home:* 111 West 94th St., New York, N.Y. 10025. *Office:* Library, College of Staten Island, 715 Ocean Ter., Staten Island, N.Y. 10301.

CAREER: Swarthmore College, Swarthmore, Pa., member of library staff, 1951-55; City College of the City University of New York, New York, N.Y., member of library staff, 1955-62; Staten Island Community College, Staten Island, N.Y., member of library staff, 1962-76; College of Staten Island, Staten Island, member of library staff, 1976—. *Member:* American Library Association, Library Association of the City University of New York.

WRITINGS: Racket and Paddle Games: A Guide to Information Sources, Gale, 1980. Contributor of articles and reviews to library journals.

SIDELIGHTS: Peele wrote: "I am the owner of what is probably the largest collection by an individual of books on the racket sports—badminton, paddleball, platform tennis, squash, racquets, racquetball, table tennis, and tennis—in the United States.

"I spent time abroad as a participant and assistant leader of Experiment in International Living, and also worked at the library of the New York World's Fair, 1964-65."

*   *   *

PEERBOLTE, Maarten Lietaert
See LIETAERT PEERBOLTE, Maarten

*   *   *

PENNINGTON, John Selman   1924(?)-1980

OBITUARY NOTICE: Born c. 1924 in Andersonville, Ga.; died of cancer, November 23, 1980, in St. Petersburg, Fla. Journalist. John Pennington, a staff reporter for the *St. Petersburg Times,* was credited by President Jimmy Carter with having helped launch his political career. Pennington's exposure of a vote fraud during Carter's race for a Georgia state senate seat in 1962 afforded Carter his first political victory. Obituaries and other sources: *Washington Post,* November 25, 1980; *Time,* December 8, 1980.

*   *   *

PERKINS, Carl (Lee)   1932-

PERSONAL: Born April 9, 1932, in Lake County, Tenn.; son of Fonnie Arbor and Mary Louise Perkins; married Valda Crider, January 24, 1953; children: Carl Stanley, Debra Joyce (Mrs. James Barton Swift), Stephen Allen, Gregory Jay. *Education:* Attended elementary schools in western Tennessee. *Religion:* Methodist. *Home:* 459 Country Club Lane, Jackson, Tenn. 38301.

CAREER: Entertainer. *Member:* Masons (Scottish Rites, Shriners).

WRITINGS: Disciple in Blue Suede Shoes, Zondervan, 1978. Composer of musical score for "Little Fauss and Big Halsey," feature film released by Paramount, 1970.

SIDELIGHTS: Perkins commented: "My ambitions are to write more songs like 'Blue Suede Shoes,' 'Honey Don't,' 'Match Box,' and 'Daddy Sang Bass,' and to be of any help I can to the young people of our great country."

PERNOUD, Regine 1909-

PERSONAL: Born June 17, 1909, in Chateau-Chinon, France; daughter of Louis and Nelly (Fournier) Pernoud. *Education:* Cours Notre Dame de France, Marseilles, B.A., 1926; Faculte des lettres d'Aix-en-Provence, lience es lettres dessiques, 1928; Ecole Nationale des Chartes, diplome d'archiviste paleographe, 1933; attended Ecole du Louvre, 1946. *Religion:* Roman Catholic. *Home:* 17 rue Rousselet, 75007 Paris, France. *Office:* Centre Jeanne d'Arc, 24 rue Jeanne d'Arc, Orleans 45000, France.

CAREER: Faculte des Lettres d'Aix-en-Provence, Aix-en-Provence, France, head of conferences, 1945-46; Musee de Reims, Reims, France, curator, 1947-49; Musee de l'Histoire de France, Paris, France, curator, 1950-74; Centre Jeanne d'Arc, Orleans, France, founder and director, 1974—. History consultant to *Archeologia* revue, 1965-70. *Member:* Societe de Gens de Lettres, P.E.N. *Awards, honors:* Femina Prize, 1946, for *Lumiere du moyen age;* award from the city of Paris, 1978; officer of Legion of Honor, 1979; Docteur Honoris Causa from College Anna-Maria de Worcester.

WRITINGS—In English translation: *Lumiere du moyen age,* Grasset, 1944, translation by Joyce Emerson published as *The Glory of the Medieval World,* Dobson, 1950; *Vie et mort de Jeanne d'Arc: Les Temoignages du proces de rehabilitation, 1450-1456,* Hachette, 1953, translation by J. M. Cohen published as *The Retrial of Joan of Arc: The Evidence at the Trial for Her Rehabilitation, 1450-1456,* Harcourt, 1955; *Les Croises,* Hachette, 1959, translation by Enid Grant published as *The Crusaders,* Oliver & Boyd, 1963, Dufour, 1964; *Jeanne d'Arc,* Editions du Seuil, 1959, translation by Jeanne Unger Duell published as *Joan of Arc,* Grove, 1961; (contributor) Frederique Duran, *Dans les pas des croises,* Hachette, 1959, translation published as *In the Steps of the Crusaders,* Hastings House, 1959; *Les Croisades,* Julliard, 1960, translation by Enid McLeod published as *The Crusades,* Putnam, 1963; (with sister, Madeleine Pernoud) *Saint Jerome,* Mame, 1960, translation by Rosemary Sheed published as *Saint Jerome,* Macmillan, 1962; *Jeanne d'Arc par elle-meme et par ses temoins,* Editions du Seuil, 1962, translation by Edward Hyams published as *Joan of Arc by Herself and Her Witnesses,* Macdonald, 1964, Stein & Day, 1966; (contributor) *L'Histoire des rois mages,* Editions Trianon, 1964, translation published as *The Story of the Wise Men According to the Gospel of Saint Matthew,* Holt, 1964; *Alienor d'Aquitaine,* A. Michel, 1965, translation by Peter Wiles published as *Eleanor of Aquitaine,* Collins, 1967, Coward, 1968; *Heloise et Abelard,* A. Michel, 1970, translation by Wiles published as *Heloise and Abelard,* Stein & Day, 1973; *La Reine Blanche,* A. Michel, 1972, translation by Henry Noel published as *Blanche of Castile,* Coward, 1975.

Other writings: *Essai sur l'histoire du port de Marseille des origines a la fin du XIIIme siecle* (title means "An Essay About the History of Marseilles Harbor From Its Origins to the End of the Thirteenth Century"), Institut historique de Provence, 1935; (editor) *Un Guide du pelerin de Terre sainte au XVe siecle* (title means "A Guide for Holy Land Pilgrims in the Fifteenth Century"), Mantes, 1940; (editor) Pierre Andre de Suffren St. Tropez, *La Campagne des Indes* (title means "Indies Campaign"), Mantes, 1941; *L'Amerique du Sud au XVIIIe siecle* (title means "South America in the Eighteenth Century"), Mantes, 1942; *L'Unite francais,* Presses Universitaires de France, 1944, third edition published as *La Formation de France,* 1966; *Les Origines de la bourgeoisie,* Presses Universitaires de France, 1947, fourth edition, 1969; *Les Villes marchandes aux XIVe et XVe sie-*cles: *Imperialisme et capitalisme au moyen age,* Editions de la Table Ronde, 1948; *Les Statuts municipaux de Marseille* (title means "Municipal Laws and Statutes of Marseilles"), Archives du Palais de Monaco, 1949.

(Contributor) Louis Henri Parias, editor, *Histoire du peuple francais* (title means "A History of French People"), Nouvelle Librairie de France, 1951-53; (with Mireille Rambaud) *Telle fut Jeanne d'Arc* (title means "Such Was Joan of Arc"), Fasquelle, 1956; (author of text) Frederique Duran, *Dans les pas de Jeanne d'Arc* (title means "In the Steps of Joan of Arc"), Hachette, 1956; *Les Gaulois* (title means "The Celts"), Editions du Seuil, 1957; *Un Chef d'etat: Saint Louis de France* (title means "A King: St. Louis of France"), J. Gabalda, 1960; *Histoire de la bourgeoisie en France* (title means "A History of the Bourgeoisie in France"), two volumes, Editions du Seuil, 1960-62; (contributor) H. LeSourd, *Croyants et incroyants d'aujourd'hui* (title means "Believers and Unbelievers Today"), Editions du Cerf, 1962; *Moyen age* (title means "Middle Ages"), Armand Colin, 1965; *L'Histoire racontee a mes neveux* (title means "Recounting History to My Nephews"), Stock, 1969; *La Liberation d'Orleans, 8 Mai 1429* (title means "How Orleans Was Liberated, May 8, 1429"), Gallimard, 1969; *Jeanne devant les Cauchons* (essay; title means "Joan and the Cauchons"), Editions du Seuil, 1970; *Beaute du moyen age* (title means "Beauty of the Middle Ages"), Gantier-Languereau, 1971; (with M. Pernoud and M. M. Davy) *Sources et clefs de l'art roman* (title means "Sources and Keys of Romanesque Art"), Berg International, 1973; *Les Templiers* (title means "The Templars"), Presses Universitaires de France, 1974; *Pour en finir avec le moyen age* (title means "To Come to an End About the Middle Ages"), Editions du Seuil, 1976. Author of television script "La Memoire de papier," Archives Nationales, 1975.

WORK IN PROGRESS: La Femme au temps des cathedrales.

SIDELIGHTS: In her numerous books about the people and customs of the Middle Ages, Regine Pernoud has shown a special interest in the women of that era, including Joan of Arc, Heloise, Eleanor of Aquitaine, and Blanche of Castile. F. J. Gallagher of *Best Sellers* said that *Blanche of Castile* "is an interesting and informative reminder that women played an important part in the development of medieval civilization."

Although B. D. Hill noted that in some of Pernoud's books "the lack of historical evidence on several subjects tends to lead her into the realm of fantasy," other critics have pointed out Pernoud's careful research on the geography, philosophy, mores, and clothing of the Middle Ages. "If imaginative, she is also a scholar," wrote Roger Highfield in the *Times Literary Supplement.*

BIOGRAPHICAL/CRITICAL SOURCES: Observer Review, November 12, 1967; *Best Sellers,* April 1, 1968, June 15, 1973, May, 1975; *Commonweal,* May 24, 1968; *Times Literary Supplement,* May 18, 1973, April 25, 1975; *Encounter,* August, 1975.

*   *   *

PERRY, Grace 1926-

PERSONAL: Born January 27, 1926, in Melbourne, Australia; daughter of R. R. (a journalist) and Grace (Symes) Perry; married Harry Kronenberg, June 12, 1951; children: Ruth Anne, Coralie, Hugh. *Education:* University of Sydney, M.B. and B.S., both 1951. *Religion:* Church of England. *Home:* 1834 Magistrate's House, Berrima, New

South Wales 2577, Australia. *Office:* South Head Press, The Market Place, Berrima, New South Wales 2577, Australia.

CAREER: Worked as radio programmer, 1943-44, and piano teacher, 1944; general practice of medicine in Sydney, Australia, 1953-72; pediatrician in Sydney, 1953-65; *Poetry,* Sydney, editor, 1962-64; South Head Press, Australia, proprietor, 1964—. Director of writing schools and festivals. *Member:* Australian Society of Authors, Australian Breeders Association. *Awards, honors:* Australian Council fellowship, 1973, special grant, 1980.

WRITINGS—Books of poems: *I Am the Songs You Sing and Other Poems,* Consolidated Press, 1944; *Red Scarf,* Edwards & Shaw, 1964; *Frozen Section,* Edwards & Shaw, 1967; *Two Houses: Poems 66-69,* South Head Press, 1969; *Black Swans at Berrima,* South Head Press, 1972; *Berrima Winter,* South Head Press, 1974; *Journal of a Surgeon's Wife,* South Head Press, 1975; *Snow in Summer,* South Head Press, 1980. Editor of *Poetry Australia,* 1964—.

WORK IN PROGRESS: Poetry.

SIDELIGHTS: Grace Perry wrote: "The perception and the passion are the first requirements of a writer. I am unaware of any literary influence. The lion is the sum of the assimilated sheep and it is not necessary or desirable to remember their faces.

"I create my own environment and like the hermit crab change shells from time to time as I grow, and it is in these intervals that the flesh is exposed and most vulnerable."

BIOGRAPHICAL/CRITICAL SOURCES: Spirit, spring, 1970; *Hudson Review,* summer, 1973; *Poetry Australia,* June, 1980.

* * *

PETERKIN, Julia Mood   1880-1961

PERSONAL: Born October 31, 1880, in Fort Motte, S.C.; died August 10, 1961; buried at Peterkin Cemetery, Fort Motte, S.C.; daughter of Julius Andrew (a physician) and Alma (Archer) Mood; married William George Peterkin, June 3, 1903; children: William George. *Education:* Converse College, B.A., 1896, M.A., 1897. *Home:* Lang Syne Plantation, Fort Motte, S.C. 29050.

CAREER: Teacher in a country school, 1897-1903; full-time writer, 1903-1961. *Member:* P.E.N., Daughters of the American Revolution, Daughters of the Confederacy, Cosmopolitan Club, Afternoon Music Club (Columbia, S.C.). *Awards, honors:* Pulitzer Prize, 1929, for *Scarlet Sister Mary.*

WRITINGS—Novels: *Black April,* Bobbs-Merrill, 1927, reprinted, Norman S. Berg, 1972; *Scarlet Sister Mary,* illustrations by Julia Peterkin, Bobbs-Merrill, 1928, reprinted with illustrations by Charles Hamrick, Franklin Library, 1978; *Bright Skin,* Bobbs-Merrill, 1932, reprinted, Norman S. Berg, 1973.

Other writings: *Green Thursday* (short stories), Knopf, 1924; *Roll, Jordan, Roll,* photographs by Doris Ulmann, Ballou, 1933; *A Plantation Christmas,* illustrations by David Hendrickson, Houghton, 1934, reprinted, Books for Libraries, 1972; *Collected Short Stories of Julia Peterkin,* University of South Carolina Press, 1970.

SIDELIGHTS: Julia Peterkin is noted for her accurate depictions of the culture of Gullah blacks, inhabitants of the coastal South Carolina vicinity. She became acquainted with Gullah dialect and folklore at an early age through the Gullah nurse who raised her.

After graduation from college, Peterkin married the manager

of Lang Syne Plantation, thereby becoming mistress of one of South Carolina's most productive plantations. Here she and her husband were in daily contact with the nearly four hundred fifty black workers on the plantation.

Peterkin began writing seriously at age forty, with the Gullah culture as her main subject. Her first short stories are represented in H. L. Mencken's *The Smart Set* and in *O. Henry Memorial Prize Stories of 1930.* The pinnacle of Peterkin's career came with the publication of her Pulitzer Prize-winning novel, *Scarlet Sister Mary.* The book was praised for its characterization of its black heroine and for its representation of black culture. The very qualities which won it adulation, however, caused it to be condemned in several Southern cities.

In addition to her fiction, Peterkin wrote *Roll, Jordan, Roll,* a book of essays dealing with black culture, and *A Plantation Christmas,* describing life on a Southern plantation.

BIOGRAPHICAL/CRITICAL SOURCES: New York Times, September 28, 1924, March 6, 1927, October 21, 1928, April 10, 1932, January 7, 1934; *Boston Transcript,* November 1, 1924, November 10, 1928, April 30, 1932, December 30, 1933; *New York Tribune,* December 14, 1924; *Literary Review,* March 5, 1927; *New York Herald Tribune Books,* April 17, 1927, October 28, 1928; *New York Evening Post,* November 3, 1928; *New York World,* November 4, 1928; *Survey,* December 1, 1928; *New Republic,* December 26, 1928; *Nation,* January 9, 1929, January 24, 1934; *Times Literary Supplement,* February 7, 1929; *Bookmen,* June, 1929, October, 1929, December, 1929, April, 1932; *Literary Digest,* June 1, 1929; *Saturday Review of Literature,* April 9, 1932, April 16, 1927, November 3, 1928, April 9, 1932, December 30, 1933; *Theatre Arts,* July, 1932; *Better Homes and Gardens,* October, 1932; *Chicago Daily Tribune,* December 16, 1933; *Scholastic,* December 14, 1935; *Good Housekeeping,* May, 1938.

OBITUARIES: New York Times, August 11, 1961; *Time,* August 18, 1961; *Publishers Weekly,* August 28, 1961.*

* * *

PHILLIFENT, John Thomas   1916-1976
(John Rackham)

OBITUARY NOTICE: Born November 10, 1916, in Durham, England; died December 16, 1976, in England. Engineer and writer. Science-fiction writer John Phillifent wrote many of his books under the pseudonym John Rackham. In addition to several book spin-offs from the "Man from U.N.C.L.E." television series, Phillifent wrote *Watch on Peter* and *Genius Unlimited.* Obituaries and other sources: *Encyclopedia of Science Fiction,* Granada, 1979; *Science Fiction and Fantasy Literature,* Volume 2, Gale, 1979.

* * *

PHILLIPS, Billie M(cKindra)   1925-

PERSONAL: Born July 1, 1925, in St. Louis, Mo.; daughter of William D. (a landscape gardener) and Anne (Wilson) McKindra; divorced; children: LaMonte Hamilton Mays. *Education:* Attended Washington University, St. Louis, Mo.; Harris Stowe Teachers College (now Harris Teachers College), B.A., 1947; Webster College, M.A.T., 1972. *Religion:* Lutheran. *Residence:* St. Louis, Mo. *Office:* Visual and Performing Arts High School, 2516 South Ninth St., St. Louis, Mo. 63104.

CAREER: Teacher at nursery school in St. Louis, Mo., 1950; teacher at elementary schools in St. Louis, Mo., 1952-65, art teacher, 1965-72; high school art teacher and department head in St. Louis, 1972-75; Visual and Performing Arts High School, St. Louis, art teacher and head of department, 1975—. Artist, with exhibitions in Missouri; set designer for stage productions; workshop teacher. President of Las Amigas; member of board of directors of St. Louis Learning Center, 1976-79; consultant to Milton Bradley. *Member:* Pi Lambda Theta. *Awards, honors:* Literary achievement award from St. Louis's Crest House, 1967; distinguished achievement award from Educational Press Association of America, 1973, for professional journalism; plaque from Zeta Phi Beta, 1979.

WRITINGS: (With Virginia S. Brown) *New Discovery Techniques for Art Instruction,* Parker Publishing, 1976.

Children's books: (With Virginia S. Brown) *Who Cares,* McGraw, 1965; (with Brown) *The Hidden Lookout,* McGraw, 1965; (with Brown) *Watch Out for C,* McGraw, 1965; *Out Jumped Abraham,* McGraw, 1967; *Christmas Is When,* Concordia, 1969; *Love Is,* Concordia, 1970; *Easter Eggs,* Concordia, 1970; *Birthday Tract,* Concordia, 1970.

Co-author of "Early Educational Guide," a column in *Grade Teacher,* 1970, and "The Green Pages," in *Early Years,* 1970—. Contributor to *My Devotions.*

WORK IN PROGRESS: A book of children's poems, publication by Alan Raymond expected in 1981.

SIDELIGHTS: Billie Phillips told *CA:* "I believe that becoming is superior to being. Literature, poetry, and the visual and performing arts are aesthetically linked by an intrinsic multitude of invisible ties. I began to write because of a desire to utilize an art technique. To accomplish this I wrote my first story for children. Writing for children is rewarding and refreshing.

"I believe that the imagination must be equipped with 'wings for soaring.' The parent, teacher, artist, writer, dancer, musician, and all those involved in the creative process contribute to the aesthetic growth of individuals. The written word has a special place in this process. I have found that the mind is a memory bank for storing experiences and fleet impressions. These observations continue to shape and reshape as new experiences are added, and the experiences enhance aesthetic growth. When asked to explain the aesthetic sense I respond, 'It's all five senses working together to create a sixth sense, which allows us to enjoy moments. It is not necessary to explain or share these experiences. It's like a very secret smile. These experiences are very private moments that may last a lifetime or vanish in seconds. It is these kinds of experiences that tune us into life and living.'

"This sometimes invisible or transparent quality is a dominant influence in my writing and art instruction. For instance, in my poem, 'Summer Sauce,' I am reminded of my childhood: 'Lightning bugs / With yellow lights, / Sunny days / And starry nights, / Brown sandcastles, / Clear blue skies, / Green June bugs, / Pink butterflies, / Ice cream sherbet, / Orange and lime, / Make me think / Of summer time!' I realize that all the things I am and do relate to and become a part of some past, present, or future experience. The secret is to make them work for me creatively and positively.

"I am fascinated by the personality of cities. I marvel at the atmosphere and color created by the collages of people, buildings, textures, lights, movement, and sound. Each city is a collage that creates its own rhythm for the drummer.

"Everything is relevant! I continue to enjoy the challenge of designing a stage set or solving a problem in graphic art. Most of all I love sharing experiences with people of all ages who desire to 'create creatively.'"

AVOCATIONAL INTERESTS: Reading (novels and stories), dance (including modern ballet), Broadway productions, good music (especially jazz).

*   *   *

PHILLIPS, Keith W(endall) 1946-

PERSONAL: Born October 21, 1946, in Portland, Ore.; son of Frank C. and Velma (Black) Phillips; married Mary Katherine Garland, April 16, 1973; children: Joshua Keith and Paul Garland (twins), David John. *Education:* University of California, Los Angeles, B.A., 1968; Fuller Theological Seminary, M.Div., 1971, D.Min., 1972. *Religion:* Christian. *Office:* World Impact, Inc., 2001 South Vermont Ave., Los Angeles, Calif. 90007.

CAREER: Ordained Conservative Baptist minister, 1971; World Impact, Inc., Los Angeles, Calif., president, 1971—.

WRITINGS: Everybody's Afraid in the Ghetto (nonfiction), Regal Books (Ventura, Calif.), 1975; *They Dare to Love the Ghetto* (nonfiction), Regal Books (Ventura, Calif.), 1975, 2nd edition, 1978; *The Making of a Disciple* (nonfiction), Revell, 1981.

SIDELIGHTS: Keith W. Phillips told *CA:* "World Impact is a Christian missionary organization that is dedicated to bringing God's love to the ghettos. Our philosophy includes ministering to the total person in the name of Christ, living where we minister, and training indigenous leadership so well that they can join us in teaching others to teach others. We have found that the inner city is an area that is wide open to the gospel of Jesus Christ if men and women are willing to move into the community to minister. My books describe what it is like to live and minister as a Christian in the inner city. *The Making of a Disciple* focuses specifically on our philosophy of ministry."

*   *   *

PHILLIPS, Laughlin 1924-

PERSONAL: Born October 20, 1924, in Washington, D.C.; son of Duncan (a museum director and art critic) and Marjorie (Acker) Phillips; married Elizabeth Hood, March 17, 1956 (divorced, 1975); married Jennifer Stats Cafritz, August 13, 1975; children: (first marriage) Duncan Vance, Elizabeth Laughlin. *Education:* Attended Yale University, 1942-43; University of Chicago, M.A., 1949. *Home:* 3044 O St. N.W., Washington, D.C. 20007. *Office:* The Phillips Collection, 1600 21st St. N.W., Washington, D.C. 20009.

CAREER/WRITINGS: U.S. Department of State, Washington, D.C., foreign service officer, 1949-64, vice-consul in Hanoi, Vietnam, 1950-53, second secretary in Tehran, Iran, 1957-59; *Washingtonian* (magazine), Washington, D.C., co-founder, 1965, editor, 1965-74, editor-in-chief, 1974-79, president, 1965-79; Phillips Collection, Washington, D.C., president, 1966—, director, 1972—. Author of editor's notes in *Washingtonian,* 1965-74, and forewords to exhibition catalogs of Phillips Collection, 1972—. Trustee of National Committee for an Effective Congress, 1966—, and of Federal City Council, 1974—. *Military service:* U.S. Army, 1943-46; became technical sergeant; received Bronze Star. *Member:* Association of Art Museum Directors, Cosmos Club (Washington, D.C.).

SIDELIGHTS: Laughlin Phillips wrote: "The only thread through this somewhat disjointed career is an interest in finding, presenting, and interpreting talent. It is an interest shared by magazine editors and museum directors. It was very strong in my father, Duncan Phillips, who launched the

Phillips Collection in 1921 as the first American museum to focus on the work of contemporary artists.''

AVOCATIONAL INTERESTS: Salt water fishing, ornithology, tennis.

* * *

PHILLPOTTS, Eden 1862-1960
(Harrington Hext)

PERSONAL: Born November 4, 1862, in Mount Aboo, Rajputana, India; died December 29, 1960, at Broad Clyst, near Exeter, Devon, England; son of Henry (a political agent in India) and Adelaide (Waters) Phillpotts; married Emily Topham, 1892 (died, 1928); married Lucy Robina Webb, October 17, 1929; children: (first marriage) Mary Adelaide; one son. *Education:* Attended private school in Plymouth, England. *Religion:* "Rationalist."

CAREER: Novelist, playwright, poet, and author of short stories. Sun Fire Insurance Co., London, England, clerk, 1800-90. *Member:* Rationalist Press Association of Great Britain.

WRITINGS—Novels: My Adventure in the Flying Scotsman: A Romance of London and North-Western Railway Shares, 1888, reprinted, Aspen Press, 1975; *The End of Life,* Simpkin, Marshall, Hamilton, Kent, 1891; *Folly and Fresh Air,* Trischler, 1891, Harper & Brothers, 1892, revised edition, Hurst & Blackett, 1899; *A Tiger's Cub,* J. W. Arrowsmith, 1892; *Some Every Day Folks,* three volumes, Osgood, 1894, Harper & Brothers, 1895; *A Deal With the Devil,* Bliss, 1895, reprinted, Arno, 1976; *Lying Prophets,* two volumes, F. A. Stokes, 1896; *The Good Red Earth,* Doubleday, Page, 1901, published as *Johnny Fortnight,* J. W. Arrowsmith, 1904; *The American Prisoner,* Macmillan, 1903; *The Golden Fetich,* Dodd, 1903; *The Farm of the Dagger,* illustrated by R. M. Relyea, Dodd, 1904.

Daniel Sweetland, Authors and Newspapers Association, 1906 (published in England as *The Poacher's Wife,* Methuen, 1906); (with Arnold Bennett) *Doubloons,* McClure, Phillips, 1906 (published in England as *The Sinews of War: A Romance of London and the Sea,* Laurie, 1906), reprinted, Books for Libraries, 1975; (with Bennett) *The Statue,* illustrated by T. K. Hanna, Moffat, Yard, 1908, reprinted, Books for Libraries, 1975; *The Haven,* John Lane, 1909; *The Lovers,* Rand McNally, 1912; *The Joy of Youth,* Little, Brown, 1913; *Faith Tresilion,* Macmillan, 1914; *The Master of Merripit,* Ward, Lock, 1914; *Old Delabole,* Macmillan, 1915; *The Green Alleys,* Macmillan, 1916; *The Banks of Colne (The Nursery),* Macmillan, 1917; *The Spinners,* Macmillan, 1918; *Storm in a Teacup,* Macmillan, 1919.

The Bronze Venus, Grant Richards, 1921; *Eudocia,* Macmillan, 1921; *Cheat-the-Boys,* Macmillan, 1924; *Redcliff,* Macmillan, 1924; *George Westover,* Hutchinson, 1925, Macmillan, 1926; *A Cornish Droll,* Hutchinson, 1926; *The Jury,* Macmillan, 1927; *The Ring Fence,* Macmillan, 1928; *Tryphena,* Macmillan, 1929; *The Three Maidens,* R. R. Smith, 1930; *Stormbury,* Hutchinson, 1931, Macmillan, 1932; *The Broom Squires,* Macmillan, 1932; *The Captain's Curio,* Macmillan, 1933; *Nancy Owlett* (illustrated by C. E. Brock), Macmillan, 1933; *Minions of the Moon,* Macmillan, 1935; *The Oldest Inhabitant,* Macmillan, 1934; *Portrait of a Gentleman,* Hutchinson, 1934; *Ned of the Caribbees,* Hutchinson, 1935; *Physician Heal Thyself,* Hutchinson, 1935; *Farce in Three Acts,* Hutchinson, 1937; *The Owl of Athene,* Hutchinson, 1936; *Wood-Nymph,* Hutchinson, 1936, Dutton, 1937; *Lycanthrope: The Mystery of Sir William Wolf,* Butterworth & Co., 1937, Macmillan, 1938; *Dark Horses,* J. Murray,

1938; *Golden Island* (juvenile), illustrations by George Morrow, J. Joseph, 1938; *Portrait of a Scoundrel,* Macmillan, 1938; *Saurus,* J. Murray, 1938, reprinted, Hyperion Press, 1976; *Monkshood,* Macmillan, 1939; *Thorn in Her Flesh,* J. Murray, 1939.

Chorus of Clowns, Methuen, 1940; *Goldcross,* Methuen, 1940; *A Deed Without a Name,* Hutchinson, 1941, Macmillan, 1942; *Pilgrims of the Night,* Hutchinson, 1942; *Flower of the Gods,* Hutchinson, 1942, Macmillan, 1943; *A Museum Piece,* Hutchinson, 1943; *The Changeling,* Hutchinson, 1944; *The Drums of Dombali,* Hutchinson, 1945; *There Was an Old Woman,* Hutchinson, 1947; *Fall of the House of Heron,* Hutchinson, 1948; *Address Unknown,* Hutchinson, 1949; *Dilemma,* Hutchinson, 1949; *The Waters of Walla,* Hutchinson, 1950; *Through a Glass Darkly,* Hutchinson, 1951; *The Hidden Hand,* Hutchinson, 1952; *His Brother's Keeper,* Hutchinson, 1953; *The Widow Garland,* Hutchinson, 1955; *Giglet Market,* Hutchinson, 1957; *There Was an Old Man,* Hutchinson, 1959.

Dartmoor novel series: *Children of the Mist,* Putnam, 1899; *Sons of the Morning,* Putnam, 1900; *The River,* F. A. Stokes, 1902; *The Secret Woman,* Macmillan, 1905; *The Portreeve,* Macmillan, 1906; *The Virgin in Judgement,* P. R. Reynolds, 1907, abridged version published as *A Fight to a Finish,* Cassell, 1911; *The Whirlwind,* McClure, Phillips, 1907; *The Mother of the Man,* Dodd, 1908 (published in England as *The Mother,* illustrated by Gunning King, Ward, Lock, 1908); *The Three Brothers,* Macmillan, 1909; *The Thief of Virtue,* John Lane, 1910; *The Beacon,* John Lane, 1911; *Demeter's Daughter,* John Lane, 1911; *The Forest on the Hill,* John Lane, 1912; *Widecombe Fair,* Little, Brown, 1913; *Brunel's Tower,* Macmillan, 1915; *Miser's Money,* Macmillan, 1920; *Orphan Dinah,* Heinemann, 1920, Macmillan, 1921, reprinted, Chivers, 1975; *Children of Men,* Macmillan, 1923.

Human Boy series: *The Human Boy,* Methuen, 1899, Harper & Brothers, 1900, reprinted, Books for Libraries, 1971; *From the Angle of Seventeen,* J. Murray, 1912; *The Human Boy and the War,* Macmillan, 1916, reprinted, Books for Libraries, 1970; *A Human Boy's Diary,* Macmillan, 1924.

Mysteries: *The Three Knaves,* Macmillan, 1912; *The Grey Room,* Hurst & Blackett, 1921, Macmillan, 1931; (under pseudonym Harrington Hext) *Number 87,* Macmillan, 1922; *The Red Redmaynes,* Macmillan, 1922; (under Hext pseudonym) *The Thing at Their Heels,* Macmillan, 1923; (under Hext pseudonym) *Who Killed Cock Robin?,* Macmillan, 1923 (published in England as *Who Killed Diana?,* Butterworth & Co., 1924); (under Hext pseudonym) *The Monster,* Macmillan, 1925; *A Voice from the Dark,* Macmillan, 1925; *Jig-Saw,* Macmillan, 1926 (published in England as *The Marylebone Miser,* Hutchinson, 1926); *Found Drowned,* Hutchinson, 1930, Macmillan, 1931, reprinted, Garland, 1976; *Bred in the Bone* (first novel in trilogy; also see below), Macmillan, 1932; *A Clue From the Stars,* Macmillan, 1932; *Witch's Cauldron* (second novel in trilogy; also see below), Macmillan, 1933; *A Shadow Passes* (third novel in trilogy; also see below), Hutchinson, 1933, Macmillan, 1934; *Mr. Digweed and Mr. Lumb,* Hutchinson, 1933, Macmillan, 1934; *The Wife of Elias,* Hutchinson, 1935, Dutton, 1937; *The Book of Avis* (trilogy; contains *Bred in the Bone, Witch's Cauldron, A Shadow Passes*), Hutchinson, 1936; *The Anniversary Murder,* Dutton, 1936; *A Close Call,* Macmillan, 1936; *Awake Deborah!,* Macmillan, 1941; *Ghostwater,* Macmillan, 1941; *They Were Seven,* Hutchinson, 1944, Macmillan, 1945; *George and Georgina,* Hutchinson, 1952.

Short story collections: *Summer Clouds and Other Stories*, illustrations by Harrold Copping, R. Tuck, 1893; *Down Dartmoor Way*, Osgood, 1895; *Loup-Garou!*, Sands, 1899; *Fancy Free*, Methuen, 1901; *The Striking Hours*, F. A. Stokes, 1901; *The Transit of the Red Dragon, and Other Tales*, J. W. Arrowsmith, 1903; *Knock at a Venture*, Macmillan, 1905; *The Unlucky Number*, illustrations by Cyrus Cuneo, George Newnes, 1906; *The Folk Afield*, Putnam, 1907, reprinted, Books for Libraries, 1970; *The Fun of the Fair*, J. Murray, 1909; *Tales of the Tenements*, John Lane, 1910; *The Old Time Before Them*, J. Murray, 1913, revised edition published as *Told at "The Plume,"* Hurst & Blackett, 1921; *The Judge's Chair*, J. Murray, 1914; *The Chronicles of St. Tid*, Skeffington, 1917, Macmillan, 1918, reprinted, Books for Libraries, 1970; *Black, White and Brindled*, Macmillan, 1923, reprinted, Books for Libraries, 1970; *Up Hill, Down Dale*, Hutchinson, 1925, Macmillan, 1926, reprinted, Books for Libraries, 1971; *Peacock House and Other Mysteries*, Hutchinson, 1926, reprinted, Books for Libraries, 1970; *It Happened Like That*, Hutchinson, 1927; *The Torch and Other Tales*, Macmillan, 1929, reprinted, Books for Libraries, 1971; *Cherry Gambol and Other Stories*, Hutchinson, 1930; *They Could Do No Other*, Hutchinson, 1932, Macmillan, 1957; *Once Upon a Time*, Hutchinson, 1936; *The End of Count Rollo, and Other Stories*, Polybooks, 1946; *Quartet*, Hutchinson, 1946.

Fairy stories: *The Flint Heart* (illustrated by Charles Folkard), Dutton, 1910, revised edition, Chapman & Dodd, 1922; *The Girl and the Faun* (illustrated by Frank Brangwyn), Palmer & Hayward, 1916, Lippincott, 1917; *Evander*, Macmillan, 1919; *Pan and the Twins*, Macmillan, 1922; *The Lavender Dragon*, Macmillan, 1923; *The Treasures of Typhon*, G. Richards, 1924; *Circe's Island and The Girl and the Faun*, G. Richards, 1925; *The Miniature*, Watts & Co., 1926, Macmillan, 1927; *Arachne*, Faber & Gwyer, 1927; *The Apes*, Macmillan, 1929; *Alcyone*, Benn, 1930.

Essays: *In Sugar-Cane Land*, McClure, 1894; *My Laughing Philosopher*, Innes, 1896; *My Devon Year*, Methuen, 1904; *My Garden*, Scribner, 1906; *Dance of the Months* (illustrated by Annie T. Benthall), Gowans & Gray, 1911; *My Shrubs*, John Lane, 1915; *A Shadow Passes*, Palmer & Hayward, 1918; *A West Country Pilgrimage* (illustrated by Benthall), L. Parsons, 1920; *Thoughts in Prose and Verse*, Watts & Co., 1924; *A West Country Sketch Book*, Hutchinson, 1928; *Essays in Little*, Hutchinson, 1931; *A Year With Bisshe-Bantam*, Blackie & Son, 1934; *The White Camel* (illustrated by Sheikh Ahmed), Country Life, 1936, Dutton, 1938; *A Mixed Grill*, Watts & Co., 1940; *One Thing and Another*, Hutchinson, 1954.

Plays: *A Breezy Morning*, Lacy's Acting Edition of Plays, 1895; (with Jerome K. Jerome) *Prude's Progress* (three-act), Chatto & Windus, 1895; (with Charles Groves) *A Golden Wedding* (one-act), Lacy's Acting Edition of Plays, 1899; *A Pair of Knickerbockers*, Samuel French, 1900; *Curtain Raisers* (contains "The Point of View," "Hiatus," and "The Carrier Pigeon"), Duckworth, 1912; *The Mother* (four-act), Duckworth, 1913; *The Secret Woman* (five-act; adapted from own novel of the same name), Duckworth, 1912, revised edition, 1935; *The Shadow* (three-act), Duckworth, 1913; *Three Plays* (contains "The Shadow," "The Mother," and "The Secret Woman"), Duckworth, 1913; (with Basil M. Hastings) *The Angel in the House* (three-act), Samuel French, 1915; *The Farmer's Wife* (three-act; based on own novel *Widecombe Fair*; first produced in Birmingham, England, at Birmingham Repertory Theatre, 1916; produced on the West End at Royal Court Theatre, 1924), Brentano's,

1916; *St. George and the Dragons* (three-act), Duckworth, 1919.

The Market-Money (one-act), LeRoy Phillips, 1923; (with Hastings) *Bed Rock* (three-act), Stage Play Publishing, 1924; *A Comedy Royal* (four-act; adapted from own novel *Eudocia*), Laurie, 1925, revised edition, Duckworth, 1932; *Devonshire Cream* (three-act; first produced in Birmingham, England, at Birmingham Repertory Theatre, 1924), Macmillan, 1925; (with daughter, Adelaide Phillpotts) *Yellow Sands* (three-act; first produced in Birmingham, England, at Birmingham Repertory Theatre, November, 1926; produced on the West End at Haymarket Theatre), Duckworth, 1926, Samuel French, 1930; *The Blue Comet* (three-act), Duckworth, 1927; *Devonshire Plays* (contains "The Farmer's Wife," "Devonshire Cream," and "Yellow Sands"), Duckworth, 1927; *The Runaways* (three-act), Duckworth, 1928; *Three Short Plays* (contains "The Market-Money," "Something to Talk About," and "The Purple Bedroom"), Duckworth, 1928; *Buy a Broom* (three-act), Duckworth, 1929.

Jane's Legacy (three-act; first produced in Birmingham, England, at Birmingham Repertory Theatre, 1925), Duckworth, 1931, Samuel French, 1932; *Bert* (one-act), Samuel French, 1932, revised edition by Felix Fair published as *Geordie*, Samuel French, 1937; (with A. Phillpotts) *The Good Old Days* (three-act), Duckworth, 1932; *A Cup of Happiness* (three-act), Duckworth, 1933; *West Country Plays* (contains "Buy a Broom," "A Cup of Happiness," and "The Good Old Days"), Duckworth, 1933; *At the Bus Stop: A Duologue for Two Women*, Samuel French, 1943; (with Lilian N. B. Price) *The Orange Orchard*, Samuel French, 1951.

Poems: *Up-Along and Down-Along*, illustrations by Claude A. Shepperson, Methuen, 1905; *Wild Fruit*, John Lane, 1911; *The Iscariot*, John Lane, 1912; *Delight*, Palmer & Hayward, 1916; *Plain Song, 1914-1916*, Heinemann, 1917; *As the Wind Blows*, Macmillan, 1920; *A Dish of Apples*, illustrations by Arthur Rackham, Hodder & Stoughton, 1921; *Pixies' Plot*, G. Richards, 1922; *Cherry-Stones*, G. Richards, 1923, Macmillan, 1924; *A Harvesting*, G. Richards, 1924; *Brother Man*, G. Richards, 1926; *Brother Beast*, M. Secker, 1928; *Goodwill*, Watts & Co., 1928; *A Hundred Sonnets*, Benn, 1929; *A Hundred Lyrics*, Benn, 1930; *Becoming*, Benn, 1932; *Song of a Sailor Man*, Benn, 1933; *Sonnets From Nature*, Watts, 1935; *A Dartmoor Village*, Watts & Co., 1937; *Miniatures*, Watts & Co., 1942; *The Enchanted Wood*, Watts & Co., 1948.

Other: (Contributor) Edmund Christian, editor, *The Light Side of Cricket*, J. Bowden, 1898; *The Devil's Tight Rope*, D. Biddle, 1900; *Little Silver Chronicles*, D. Biddle, 1900; *The Mound by the Way*, D. Biddle, 1900; *Tabletop*, Macmillan, 1939; *From the Angle of 88* (autobiography), Hutchinson, 1951; *Connie Woodland*, Hutchinson, 1956; *Letters from Eden Phillpotts to Mrs. F. E. Hardy*, Toucan Press, 1968.

Collections: *Eden Phillpotts* (poems), Benn, 1926; *The Widecombe Edition of the Dartmoor Novels*, twenty volumes, Macmillan, 1927-28; *Eden Phillpotts* (short stories), Harrap, 1929; *The Complete Human Boy*, Hutchinson, 1930; *Dartmoor Omnibus* (contains *Orphan Dinah, The Three Brothers*, and *The Whirlwind*), Hutchinson, 1933.

Contributor of poetry and fiction to numerous periodicals.

SIDELIGHTS: During his seventy years as a writer, Eden Phillpotts proved to be both versatile and prolific. His more than two hundred fifty published works include at least one hundred fifty novels, plus poems, essays, plays, short stories, and mysteries. Of all his writings, Phillpotts is probably best known as author of the play "The Farmers's Wife," which ran for 1,329 performances in London. Despite the play's popularity, the introverted author once admitted that he had never seen it or any of his other plays performed on stage.

Although his name is unknown to most Americans, Phillpotts is highly regarded in England as a regional novelist. His works generally were based on the environment and rural life of west England, particularly Devon. The Dartmoor novel series and the "Human Boy" series were highly praised for their portrayal of the English character. Many critics have noted a similarity between Phillpotts's writing and that of his contemporary Thomas Hardy, who wrote mainly about Wessex, England.

The Mother of the Man from the Dartmoor series of novels was adapted as a motion picture, "A Mother Dartmoor," in 1917.

BIOGRAPHICAL/CRITICAL SOURCES: Outlook, February 24, 1912; *Bookman,* January, 1916; *London Mercury,* March, 1920; Mary Adelaide Eden Phillpotts, *Yellow Sands: The Story of the Play by Eden and Adelaide Phillpotts,* Chapman & Hall, 1930; Eden Phillpotts, *From the Angle of 88,* Hutchinson, 1951; Waveney Girvan, *Eden Phillpotts: An Assessment and a Tribute,* Hutchinson, 1953; *New York Herald Tribune Book Review,* December 1, 1957.

OBITUARIES: New York Times, December 30, 1960; *Britannica Book of the Year, 1961,* Encyclopedia Britannica, 1961; *Illustrated London News,* January 7, 1961; *Publishers Weekly,* January 9, 1961.*

* * *

PINCUS, Harriet 1938-

PERSONAL: Born October 13, 1938, in New York, N.Y. *Education:* Attended Art Students League.

CAREER: Illustrator and author of children's books. *Awards, honors:* Honor Book Award from Book World Children's Spring Book Festival, 1967, for *The Wedding Procession of the Rag Doll and the Broom Handle and Who Was in It;* first prize from Book World Children's Spring Book Festival, 1970, for *Tell Me a Mitzi;* Brooklyn Art Books for Children Citation, 1973, for *The Wedding Procession of the Rag Doll and the Broom Handle and Who Was in It.*

WRITINGS: Minna and Pippin, self-illustrated, Farrar, Straus, 1972.

Illustrator; all published by Harcourt, except as noted: Carl Sandburg, *The Wedding Procession of the Rag Doll and the Broom Handle and Who Was in It,* 1967, reprinted, 1978; Mae Durham, *Tit for Tat, and Other Latvian Folk Tales,* translated by Skaidrite Rubene-Koo, 1967; Elizabeth K. Cooper, *Who Is Paddy?,* 1967; Richard R. Livingston, *The Hunkendunkens,* 1968; Brothers Grimm, editor, *Little Red Riding Hood,* 1968; Lore Groszmann Segal, *Tell Me a Mitzi,* Farrar, Straus, 1970.

SIDELIGHTS: The first book Harriet Pincus illustrated was Carl Sandburg's *The Wedding Procession of the Rag Doll and the Broom Handle and Who Was in It.* She illustrated the book using a scene-by-scene approach to enhance the already descriptive story. With this book Pincus established a reputation as an artist who uses rich colors in an inventive way.*

PINTER, Walter S. 1928-

PERSONAL: Born June 15, 1928, in Milwaukee, Wis.; son of Stanley (a decorator) and Agnes K. (Kubelka) Pinter; married wife, Mira, December 10, 1949 (divorced September, 1978); children: Victoria, Mark. *Education:* Attended Layton School of Art, 1935 and 1949, and University of Wisconsin—Milwaukee, 1949 and 1950. *Home:* 409 East Willow Rd., Milwaukee, Wis. 53217. *Office:* Pinter Grafix Corp., 224 West Washington St., Milwaukee, Wis. 53204.

CAREER/WRITINGS: Pinter Grafix Corp., Milwaukee, Wis., owner and manager, 1978—. Author and illustrator of cartoon strips, "Lucky and Able," Transworld News Service, 1975—, and "Hausfrau Hannah," Los Angeles Times Syndicate, 1977—. *Military service:* U.S. Army, Engineers, 1944; became captain. *Member:* Screen Printing Association (president, 1965), Sokol Gymnastic Association, Milwaukee Ad Club.

* * *

PISANO, Ronald George 1948-

PERSONAL: Born December 19, 1948, in New York, N.Y.; son of Robert and Mildred (Wilhelmi) Pisano. *Education:* Adelphi University, B.A., 1971; graduate study at University of Delaware, 1971-73. *Residence:* East Setauket, N.Y. *Office:* 353 Riverside Dr., No. 4-A, New York, N.Y. 10025.

CAREER: Bernard M. Baruch College of the City University of New York, New York, N.Y., director of exhibitions, 1974-76; Parrish Art Museum, Southampton, N.Y., associate curator of William Merritt Chase Collection and Archives, 1976-78, curator of museum, 1978—. Guest curator at Museums at Stony Brook, 1977 and 1978. *Member:* College Art Association of America, American Federation of Arts, American Association of Museums, North East Museums Conference. *Awards, honors:* A. Conger Goodyear Award from Adelphi University, 1971, for special achievement in the field of art history; Stebbins family grant from Heckscher Museum, 1972-73; distinguished art historian award from Grand Central Art Galleries, 1979, for outstanding contributions to American art history.

WRITINGS: William Merritt Chase, Watson-Guptill, 1979; *An American Place,* Parrish Art Museum, 1981; *Long Island Artists, 1865-1919,* Parrish Art Museum, 1981. Author of exhibition catalogs. Contributor to art journals.

WORK IN PROGRESS: William Merritt Chase: Catalogue Raisonne.

* * *

PITCAIRN, Frank
See COCKBURN, (Francis) Claud

* * *

PLATT, Lyman De 1943-

PERSONAL: Born June 10, 1943, in Moab, Utah; son of Gordon Leavitt (an agricultural inspector) and Allie (an expediter in purchasing; maiden name, Lyman) Platt; married Bertha Paula Vega, September 30, 1965; children: Patricia, Bruce, David, Daniel, Julie, Don Carlos, Maria Elena, Debbie, Nicholle, John. *Education:* Brigham Young University, B.A., 1974. *Politics:* American Independent. *Religion:* Church of Jesus Christ of Latter-day Saints (Mormons). *Home address:* R.R. 2, Box 216, American Fork, Utah 84003. *Office:* Genealogical Society, 50 East North Temple, Salt Lake City, Utah 84150.

CAREER: Genealogical Society, Salt Lake City, Utah, senior reference consultant, 1969—. President of Highland Microdata Systems. *Military service:* U.S. Air Force, 1965-68; served in Vietnam; received Vietnamese Medal of Honor, second class, and two stars.

WRITINGS: The Perkins Family History, privately printed, 1975; (editor) *Edward Partridge,* privately printed, 1977; *Genealogical Historical Guide to Latin America,* Gale, 1978; *The Platt Family History,* privately printed, 1979; *Nauvoo, 1839-1846,* privately printed, 1980; *Military Records of Mexico,* Genealogical Society of Utah, 1980. Contributor to *Utah Genealogical Magazine.*

WORK IN PROGRESS: The Platte DeAlton Lyman Family History, publication expected in 1984; a fifteen-volume biographical index of early Mormon pioneers, 1830-46, completion expected in 1990; genealogical guides and indexes.

SIDELIGHTS: Platt commented: "I have been interested in genealogy since I was a child. I feel the past must be preserved in such a way as to instill in individual lives an appreciation of their heritage, and to give them a gauge against which to measure themselves.

"I speak Spanish and Portuguese, some Welsh, French, and Italian. I am interested in the preservation of historical documents throughout the world, but particularly in the United States and Latin America. I have traveled in all areas of Latin America and the Caribbean in the pursuit of this goal."

AVOCATIONAL INTERESTS: Farming, studying genetics in rabbits and plants, collecting stamps.

* * *

PLUMMER, William (Halsey Jr.) 1945-

PERSONAL: Born January 15, 1945, in Elizabeth, N.J.; son of William Halsey Plummer (a furniture restorer) and Geraldine (an antiques expert; maiden name, Vogel); married Molly McKaughan (a managing editor), May 13, 1978; children: Nicholas Fremont. *Education:* Colgate University, B.A., 1968; Rutgers University, Ph.D., 1978. *Home:* 924 West End Ave., New York, N.Y. 10025. *Agent:* Gail Hochman, Paul R. Reynolds Agency, 12 East 41st St., New York, N.Y. 10017. *Office: Quest,* 1133 Avenue of the Americas, New York, N.Y. 10036.

CAREER/WRITINGS: Bergen Record, Hackensack, N.J., reporter, 1969-70; *Daily Journal,* Elizabeth, N.J., reporter, 1970-71; *Star Ledger,* Newark, N.J., reporter, 1971-72; Rutgers University, New Brunswick, N.J., instructor in English, 1972-75; *Paris Review,* New York City, associate editor, 1975—; *Quest* (magazine), New York City, book review editor, 1976—. Contributor of more than one hundred essays and reviews to magazines, including *Hudson Review, New York Times Magazine, GEO,* and *Village Voice. Member:* National Book Critics Circle.

WORK IN PROGRESS: A book on Neal Cassady, the hero of Jack Kerouac's novel, *On the Road,* tentatively titled *The Holy Goof,* publication by Prentice-Hall expected in 1981; compiling a collection of critical essays on Gabriel Garcia Marquez; a novel.

SIDELIGHTS: Plummer told *CA:* "My current interests seem to lie in three or four general areas, though my head is easily turned: the 1960's, where all my changes were; the American literary experience, Edwards, Emerson, Faulkner, Pynchon, etc.; Spanish and Hispanic culture; and travel and travel writing."

PLUTSCHOW, Herbert Eugen 1939-

PERSONAL: Born September 8, 1939, in Zurich, Switzerland; came to the United States in 1966, naturalized citizen, 1977; son of Eugen Franz and Martha (Geiger) Plutschow; married Yoshiko Kogure, 1966; children: Patrick Taro, Nicol Jiro. *Education:* University of Paris, B.A., 1962; Waseda University, M.A., 1966; Columbia University, Ph.D., 1973. *Office:* Department of Oriental Languages, University of California, 405 Hilgard Ave., Los Angeles, Calif. 90024.

CAREER: University of Illinois, Champaign-Urbana, instructor in Japanese, 1971-73; University of California, Los Angeles, assistant professor, 1973-79, associate professor of Japanese, 1979—. Visiting professor at University of Zurich, 1979-80. *Member:* Association for Asian Studies.

WRITINGS: Nihon Kiko Bungaku Binran (title means "Handbook for the Study of Medieval Japanese Travel Diary Literature"), Musashino Shoin, 1976; *Introducing Kyoto,* Kodansha, 1979; *Introducing Nara,* Kodansha, 1981; *Four Japanese Travel Diaries of the Middle Ages,* Cornell University East Asia Papers, 1981.

WORK IN PROGRESS: Medieval Japanese Travel Diaries, publication expected in 1981; a history of the city of Nagasaki, expected in 1982.

SIDELIGHTS: Plutschow's languages include German, French, Spanish, Russian, Japanese, with some Chinese, Dutch, and Italian. *Avocational interests:* Travel.

* * *

POIRIER, Normand 1928(?)-1981

OBITUARY NOTICE: Born c. 1928; died after a lengthy illness, February 1, 1981. Journalist. Poirier was an assistant editor with *Newsday* at the time of his death. During his career he wrote for the *New York Post,* the *Saturday Evening Post, Life,* and *Esquire.* An article he wrote for *Esquire* was among the first to report on atrocities in the Vietnam War. Obituaries and other sources: *New York Times,* February 4, 1981.

* * *

POOLE, Roger 1939-

PERSONAL: Born February 22, 1939, in Cambridge, England; son of John Rea and Joan (Buttress) Poole; married Lise-Bente Wulff Knudsen (a medical researcher); children: Vincent, Magnus, Richard Victor. *Education:* Trinity College, Cambridge, B.A., 1961, M.A., 1965, Ph.D., 1965. *Religion:* Anglican. *Home:* 26 Parkside, Wollaton, Nottingham NG8 2NN, England. *Office:* Department of English, University of Nottingham, University Park, Nottingham NG7 2RD, England.

CAREER: University of Paris, Sorbonne, Paris, France, reader in English, 1965-67; University of Nottingham, Nottingham, England, member of faculty in department of English, 1968—. *Member:* British Comparative Literature Association (member of executive committee), Savile Club. *Awards, honors:* Commonwealth fellow at York University, 1976-77.

WRITINGS: (Author of preface) Claude Levi-Strauss, *Totemism,* Penguin, 1969; *Towards Deep Subjectivity,* Harper, 1972; (contributor) Jonathan Benthall and Ted Polhemus, editors, *The Body As a Medium of Expression,* Allen Lane, 1975; *The Unknown Virginia Woolf,* Cambridge University Press, 1978. Member of advisory panel of *New Universities Quarterly.*

WORK IN PROGRESS: A study of embodiment and text in Milton, Swift, and Joyce; a book on the indirect communication of Soren Kierkegaard.

SIDELIGHTS: Poole wrote: "Doing moral science at Cambridge gave me a deep distrust of logical positivism and unquestioned empiricism. This led in time to the writing of *Towards Deep Subjectivity.* Over the years my scepticism has continued to increase.

"Working in Paris in the late 1960's on structuralism and phenomenology, I became fascinated by the fact that the world is given entirely 'perspectively' and this led, in its turn, to the description of two 'perspectively' unharmonious worlds in a study of Leonard and Virginia Woolf (*The Unknown Virginia Woolf*). If a perspectively coherent 'world' is a function of 'embodiment' (the term is from phenomenology again) then this has very important literary consequences. The two books I am working on now are studies of the embodiment expressed in a text.

"This concern itself is a product of a more recent scepticism, a scepticism before the contentions of Jacques Derrida and 'the Yale School.' They have questioned whether a literary text relates to an 'outer world' at all, and suggested that its referentiality, its 'presence,' is just an illusion. While their writing has been extraordinarily thought-provoking and fruitful, it does seem to require some sort of answer. Hence my current writing tries to elicit ways in which authorial 'presence' is undeniably there in the text, since, as well as being a mere textual condition, the text is also the mediation of an 'embodiment' in particular. The task is as difficult as it is fascinating."

*   *   *

POOLE, Victoria (Simes) 1927-

PERSONAL: Born December 26, 1927, in Portland, Maine; daughter of Charles F. (in business) and Dorothy (Wright) Simes; married Parker Poole, Jr. (in business), April 15, 1950; children: Malcolm, Parker III, Charles, Christina, Talcott, Alexandra. *Education:* Connecticut College, B.A., 1949. *Residence:* Cape Elizabeth, Maine.

CAREER: Waynflete School, Portland, Maine, tutor, 1949-50; writer, 1977—. Member of board of trustees of Waynflete School, 1963-68 and 1975-78, and Kent School, 1976—. Assistant director of Portland's Children's Theatre, 1949-50, member of board of directors, 1952-60.

WRITINGS: Thursday's Child (nonfiction; Book-of-the-Month Club alternate selection), Little, Brown, 1980.

WORK IN PROGRESS: A book of poems about U.S. presidents; research on Ireland, 1840-49, Boston and Portsmouth, N.H., 1840-1900, and the New York City silk trade, 1830-60.

SIDELIGHTS: "Since childhood, English history has delighted me," Victoria Poole told *CA.* "If I have a dream of glory, it is to make U.S. history comparably entertaining, especially for children. I have been working for several years on a book of poems about the Presidents, which I fervently hope (but doubt) will compare with *Kings and Queens,* by Eleanor and Herbert Farjeon.

"I expect that *Thursday's Child* must be classified as a fluke. A friend thought the story of our seventeen-year-old son's heart disease and subsequent heart transplant interesting enough to introduce to a senior editor at Little Brown. The editor urged me to write a book, and after a couple of false starts, I did. The majority of reviews have been vastly more favorable than I expected and I have been delighted to find that, although I was dealing with 'tear-jerker' material, I have yet to be called mawkish, which I dreaded.

"I wrote the book in hopes that the story of Sam Poole's courage and refusal to accept death might help other people through despairing times. One reviewer (Katherine Frank, in *Miami Herald,* June 1, 1980) makes me feel that perhaps I may have succeeded: 'The book uplifts and consoles because Victoria Poole shows that suffering can have meaning and can be stopped, that people want to love and help each other, and that death can be vanquished and life regained.' Although I also stand accused (by reviewer Sylvia Sachs) of having 'an innately sunny view of life,' I do believe in all those things. Even more devoutly I believe in families and in giving of one's self. I am terrified at the prospect of a world populated by people all busily discovering 'ME.'"

AVOCATIONAL INTERESTS: Gardening, skiing, tennis, jogging, travel (the Caribbean, especially St. Kitts, England, Scotland, Ireland, France).

*   *   *

POPKIN, Jeremy D(avid) 1948-

PERSONAL: Born December 19, 1948, in Iowa City, Iowa; son of Richard and Juliet Popkin; married wife, Beate, 1980. *Education:* University of California, Berkeley, B.A., 1970, Ph.D., 1977; Harvard University, M.A., 1971. *Office:* Department of History, University of Kentucky, Lexington, Ky. 40506.

CAREER: University of Pittsburgh, Pittsburgh, Pa., visiting assistant professor, 1977-78; University of Kentucky, Lexington, assistant professor of history, 1978—.

WRITINGS: The Right-Wing Press in France, 1792-1800 (monograph), University of North Carolina Press, 1980.

WORK IN PROGRESS: Research on European history of the eighteenth and nineteenth centuries.

SIDELIGHTS: Popkin told *CA:* "My first book, *The Right-Wing Press in France, 1792-1800,* is a study of how communications media influence and are affected by political and social movements. I was interested to find that the conservative opponents of the French Revolution used the newspaper press extensively and effectively to combat the movement which had made a free press in France possible in the first place. I have been led to ask whether our traditional equation of freedom of the press with freedom and progress in general is correct."

*   *   *

POPOVSKY, Mark 1922-

PERSONAL: Born July 8, 1922, in Odessa, U.S.S.R.; came to the United States in 1977, naturalized citizen, 1980; son of Alexander (a writer) and Eugene (a biologist; maiden name, Lubarsky) Popovsky; married Vasilevskaya Tatiana, 1948 (divorced, 1968); married Lilya Grinberg (a clerk), November 4, 1969; children: Konstantin, Anna. *Education:* Moscow State University, B.A., 1950, M.A., 1952. *Home:* 2 Ellwood St., Apt. 3-Y, New York, N.Y. 10040.

CAREER: Free-lance journalist in Moscow, U.S.S.R., 1946-77; free-lance writer in New York, N.Y., 1978—. Founder of news agency, Mark Popovsky Press, 1977. Fellow of Kennan Institute for Advanced Russian Studies, at Woodrow Wilson International Center for Scholars, 1980. Lecturer on scientific subjects. *Military service:* Soviet Union Army, Medical Science, 1941-45; became lieutenant. *Member:* International P.E.N., Writers-in-Exile.

WRITINGS—In English translation: The Manipulated Science, translated from Russian by Paul Falla, Doubleday,

1979; *The Vavilov Affair,* translated by David Floyd, Doubleday, 1981.

In Russian: *Kogda vzach mechtaet* (essays on physicians; title means "When a Doctor Dreams"), Trudovye Rezervy Publishing House, 1957; *Put k serdtzu* (on military medicine; title means "The Road to the Heart"), U.S.S.R. Ministry of Defense Publishing House, 1960; *Khozyain solnechnogo tzvetka* (on plant breeding; title means "The Master of the Sunflower"), Molodaya Gvardia Publishing House, 1960; *Razorvannaya pautina* (about the helminthologist, Skryabin; title means "The Torn Spider's Web"), Soverskaya Rossia Publishing House, 1962; *Sudba Doktora Khavkina* (biography; title means "The Fate of Doctor Khavkin"), Vostochnaya Literatura Publishing House, 1963; *Po sledam otstupaushikh* (about epidemiologists; title means "Following in the Tracks of Retreat"), Molodaya Gvardia Publishing House, 1963; *Kormilzy planeti* (about agronomists; title means "Food Suppliers of the Planet"), Znaniye Publishing House, 1964; *Pyat dnei odnsi zhizni* (novel about Russian Jewish bacteriologist, Khavkin; title means "Five Days or a Life"), Detskaya Literatura Publishing House, 1964.

Dorozhe zolota (on plant breeders; title means "More Precious Than Gold"), Detskaya Literatura Publishing House, 1966; *Tisyacha dnei akademika Nikolaya Vavilova* (title means "A Thousand Days of the Academician Nikolai Vavilov"), Prostor Journal, 1966; *Nado speshit* (biography of geneticist, Nikolai Vavilov; title means "Let Us Hurry!"), Detskaya Literatura Publishing House, 1968; *Nad kartoi chelovecheskikh stradanii* (on infectious diseases and epidemiologists; title means "A Map of Human Suffering"), Detskaya Literatura Publishing House, 1971; *Ludi sredi ludei* (on Vavilov, Khavkin, and Isayev; title means "Men Among Men"), Detskaya Literatura Publishing House, 1972; *Panatzeya, doch Eskulapa* (on pharmacologists; title means "Panacea, Daughter of Aesculapius"), Detskaya Literatura Publishing House, 1973. Also author of books in Russian, *June News: Notes of a Non-Accredited Correspondent,* Posev-Verlag, 1978, and *The Blessed Life of Professor Voino-Yasenetzki, Archbishop and Surgeon,* Young Men's Christian Association Press, 1979.

Contributor of about five hundred articles to scientific journals in the U.S.S.R. and to *Samizdat.*

WORK IN PROGRESS: Research on the archive of peasants (Tolstoyans), which he brought with him from the Soviet Union; research on the topic "sex and socialism."

SIDELIGHTS: Popovsky wrote three other books that were scheduled to be published in the Soviet Union and were canceled just before his immigration to the United States—one on the ethics of Soviet scientists, another about the surgeon, Seppo, geneticist, Khadzhinov, and agronomist, Mazlumov, and a third book on sensory discoveries of the twentieth century.

He wrote: "I left medicine because I felt I was born to be a writer. For the last twenty-five years my major interest has fallen in the area of ethics of the Russian intelligentsia, particularly Russian scientists. I write nonfiction about those scientists. Unfortunately, I speak only Russian."

*   *   *

PORELL, Bruce 1947-

PERSONAL: Born July 16, 1947, in Fitchburg, Mass.; son of Leon (a sales representative) and Beatrice (a switchboard operator; maiden name, Reynolds) Porell; married Linda J. Yorton (a writer), October 18, 1975; children: Ian Yorton.

Education: Fitchburg State College, B.S.Ed., 1969, M.S.Ed., 1972. *Home address:* R.D.3, Goshen, Vt. 05733.

CAREER: Teacher at schools in Blackstone, Mass., 1969-70, New Epswich, N.H., 1970-71, in Rindge, N.H., 1971-72, and Sturbridge, Mass., 1972-77; Otter Valley Union High School, Brandon, Vt., teacher of biology and theatre arts, 1978—. Administrative assistant at Bread Loaf Writers' Conference, 1976-80.

WRITINGS: Digging the Past (juvenile), Addison-Wesley, 1979. Contributor to education journals and *Cobblestone History.*

WORK IN PROGRESS—Children's picture books: *The Most Beautiful Animal; Would You Kiss a Buffalo?; Guess What I Am; A.P. McFaddin McCatt; A Magic Afternoon,* a fantasy.

SIDELIGHTS: Porell commented to *CA:* "Right now I'm most interested in writing fiction that my young son will enjoy—using his words to create guessing games, stories, and poems, and writing fiction that will stimulate his imagination. I'm also trying fiction for children around eleven to fourteen years old since, as a teacher, I'm with this age group a lot. I have plans to try some plays for young people, plays that will portray some of the pains and pleasures of growing up."

*   *   *

POSTMAN, Neil

PERSONAL—Office: New York University, Shimkin Hall, 50 West Fourth St., New York, N.Y. 10012.

CAREER: Writer. Professor of media ecology at New York University in New York, N.Y.

WRITINGS: (With the Committee on the Study of Television of the National Council of Teachers of English) *Television and the Teaching of English,* Appleton-Century-Crofts, 1961; (with Harold Morine and Greta Morine) *Discovering Your Language,* Holt, 1963; (with Howard C. Damon) *The Uses of Language,* Holt, 1965; (with Damon) *Language and Systems,* Holt, 1965; (with Damon) *The Languages of Discovery,* Holt, 1965; *Exploring Your Language,* Holt, 1966; *Language and Reality,* Holt, 1966; (with Charles Weingartner) *Linguistics: A Revolution in Teaching,* Delacorte, 1966; (with Weingartner) *Teaching as a Subversive Activity,* Delacorte, 1969; (editor with Weingartner and Terence P. Moran) *Language in America: A Report on Our Deteriorating Semantic Environment,* Pegasus, 1969.

(With Weingartner) *The Soft Revolution: A Student Handbook for Turning Schools Around,* Delacorte, 1971; (with Weingartner) *The School Book: For People Who Want to Know What All the Hollering Is About,* Delacorte, 1973; (contributor) *The Politics of Reading: Point-Counterpoint,* International Reading Association, 1973; *Crazy Talk, Stupid Talk: How We Defeat Ourselves by the Way We Talk and What to Do About It,* Delacorte, 1976; *Teaching as a Conserving Activity,* Delacorte, 1979.

Contributor to magazines and periodicals, including *Atlantic* and *Nation.*

SIDELIGHTS: During the late 1960's and early 1970's, the names of Neil Postman and Charles Weingartner appeared beside those of John Holt and Jonathan Kozol as the most vocal figures in the call for radical education reform. The Postman/Weingartner team argued that "an educational establishment indentured students to 'years of servitude in a totalitarian environment' and disabled them for life in the era of mass communication.'' Schools needed change, the authors believed, and any effective changes would have to come from within, from teachers and students.

Postman first joined the movement towards radical education reform when he and Weingartner published *Teaching as a Subversive Activity* in 1969. Schools at that time, the authors contended, discouraged students from learning by barring them from the learning process—from asking meaningful questions, from recognizing the joy of learning. Instead of force-feeding trivial facts to disinterested students, schools should concentrate on fostering a ''new education.'' Its purpose would be to develop ''a new kind of person, one who—as a result of internalizing a different series of concepts—is an actively inquiring, flexible, creative, innovative, tolerant, liberal personality who can face uncertainty and ambiguity without disorientation, who can formulate viable new meanings to meet changes in the environment which threaten individual and mutual survival.''

Having explained the need for educational change in *Teaching as a Subversive Activity,* Postman and Weingartner followed with a book directed towards students, *The Soft Revolution.* Designed as a handbook for educational change, *The Soft Revolution* is not a guide to overthrowing the system. Rather, it's a conglomeration of ''advice, maxims, homilies, metaphors, models, case studies, rules, commentaries, jokes, sayings, and a variety of other things you may use now or in the years ahead to hasten educational change.''

The movement toward change, however, had no room for the self-righteous or those eager to destroy every icon of the establishment in their way. The soft revolutionary was to have as his purpose the renewal and reconstruction of educational institutions without the use of violence. Violence, Postman and Weingartner agreed, only avoids the subject.

Among the authors' examples of soft revolutionary gestures are the words of Deborah Jean Sweet. She had helped organize a fund-raising march for proverty stricken children and earned a Young American Medal for her efforts. As Richard Nixon was about to present the award to her, she softly said to the president, ''I can't believe your sincerity in giving these awards for service until you get us out of the Vietnam war.'' Earlier in the ceremony Nixon had spoken of ''a small minority of young Americans who have lost faith''; Sweet said she objected to being used ''as a symbol for satisfied youth.''

In their 1975 work, *The School Book,* Postman and Weingartner aimed away from students and teachers and directed their views towards those ''who want to know what all the hollering is about'': the parents. The book is primarily a source of information and includes a who's who of notable names in education, a summary of important court cases on education, and a glossary of educational terms. Though most of the information is straightforward, the authors' lexicography is sometimes less than neutral: ''Education research,'' they said, is ''a process whereby serious educators discover knowledge that is well-known to everybody, and has been for several centuries. Its principal characteristic is that no one pays any attention to it.''

Some skeptics may have thought Postman was joking again when he published *Teaching as a Conserving Activity.* But the author defends his newfound conservatism by arguing that in times of social stagnation, schools must direct change; in times of rapid social change, schools must conserve. What schools must specifically conserve now, Postman says, is a stable learning environment to counter the fragmented education offered by television and other electronic media. He calls for a policy directed toward ''the continuity of the human enterprise'' with an emphasis on, in critic Constance Horner's words, ''the virtues of intellectual inquiry, the rigorous and subtle use of language, . . . the arts, science, and religion—in other words, the attributes of a culture that is something more than media-created.''

Part of the schools' task, says Postman, is to reestablish school as an honored place for learning. He advocates dress codes for both students and teachers because ''a dress code signifies that school is a special place in which special kinds of behavior are required.'' He scoffs at calls to allow the poor and minorities to use their own language in school, dismissing them as arguments ''put forward by 'liberal' education critics whose children *are* competent in Standard English but who in some curious way wish to express their solidarity with those who are less capable. . . . Like the mode of dress, the mode of language in school ought to be relatively formal and exemplary, and therefore markedly different from the custom in less rigorous places.''

Despite his apparent reversal of philosophy, Postman has impressed critics with his new book. ''He has become an educational conservative since . . . *Teaching as a Subversive Activity,*'' said Leonard Kriegal of *Nation.* ''And I find this new book even more refreshing than its predecessors.'' Horner agreed, praising Postman for his ability to adapt to the changing needs of education. ''Now, when many anti-establishment academic intellectuals either lie low in a state of demoralized quietude or restlessly pace the groves searching for new causes, it is inspiring to find one who, like Mr. Postman, straightforwardly admits he has changed his mind.'' Postman himself would hardly contend that statement. As he says in his latest work, ''I suspect you will think . . . that I have turned my back on 20th-Century 'liberalism,' which would be entirely correct.''

BIOGRAPHICAL/CRITICAL SOURCES: English Journal, May, 1966, November, 1967, March, 1968, May, 1978, May, 1979; *Record,* November, 1967; *New York Times Book Review,* May 11, 1969, December 12, 1976, September 25, 1977, September 16, 1979; *Saturday Review,* July 17, 1969; *Commentary,* June, 1970; Neil Postman and Charles Weingartner, *The Soft Revolution: A Student Handbook for Turning Schools Around,* Delacorte, 1971; *Progressive,* September, 1971; *Observer,* November 7, 1971; *Washington Post Book World,* September 23, 1973, September 16, 1979; *Christian Science Monitor,* June 23, 1975; *Christian Century,* May 18, 1977; *Sewanee Review,* July, 1978; *Atlantic,* September, 1979; Postman, *Teaching as a Conserving Activity,* Delacorte, 1979; *Wall Street Journal,* October 5, 1979; *Nation,* October 6, 1979; *Best Sellers,* November, 1979.*

—*Sketch by David Versical*

*   *   *

POTASH, Robert A(aron) 1921-

PERSONAL: Born January 2, 1921, in Boston, Mass.; son of Philip and Sarah (Simes) Potash; married Jeanne Feinstein, June 9, 1946; children: Janet Ruth, Ellen Bess. *Education:* Harvard University, A.B. (magna cum laude), 1942, M.A., 1947, Ph.D., 1953. *Office:* Department of History, University of Massachusetts, Amherst, Mass. 01002.

CAREER: Boston University, Boston, Mass., visiting lecturer in regional studies, 1949; University of Massachusetts, Amherst, instructor in history, 1950-55; U.S. Department of State, Washington, D.C., foreign service reserve officer, 1955-57; University of Massachusetts, assistant professor, 1957-58, associate professor, 1958-61, professor of history,

1961—, head of department, 1968-69, chairman of Latin American studies committee, 1968-76. Visiting professor at Columbia University, summer, 1963, and Harvard University, summer, 1974. Past member of local Town Meeting. *Military service:* U.S. Army, 1942-46; served in Asiatic-Pacific theater; became master sergeant; received Bronze Star. *Member:* American Historical Association, Conference on Latin American History, Latin American Studies Association, New England Council on Latin American Studies (president, 1973-74). *Awards, honors:* Fellow of American Council of Learned Societies and Social Science Research Council, 1961-62, 1965, and 1970.

WRITINGS: El Banco de Avio de Mexico (title means "The Industrial Development Bank of Mexico"), Fondo de Cultura Economico, 1959; *The Army and Politics in Argentina, 1928-1945: Yrigoyen to Peron,* Stanford University Press, 1969; (with Lyle N. McAlister and Anthony Maingot) *The Military in Latin American Sociopolitical Evolution: Four Case Studies,* Center for Research in Social Systems, 1970; (contributor) Alberto Ciria and other editors, *New Perspectives on Modern Argentina,* Latin American Studies Program, Indiana University Press, 1972; *The Army and Politics in Argentina, 1945-1962: Peron to Frondizi,* Stanford University Press, 1980. Contributor to history and Latin American studies journals.

WORK IN PROGRESS: A pilot project to develop a computerized guide to notarial archives in Mexico.

SIDELIGHTS: Potash told *CA:* "I became interested in the political role of the Argentine military in the mid-1950's when President Juan Peron was overthrown by an armed revolt. Today, several books and twenty-five years later, I feel that my work has served two purposes: first, to illuminate to the non-Argentine reader the complexities of the Argentine political scene, and in particular to offset the simplistic notion that what is involved here is a two-sided struggle with all the civilians on the one side and the military on the other; and second, to provide Argentine readers with a dispassionate, documented account of their contemporary history to offset the partisan treatments that frequently appear from their presses. As an outsider, I have enjoyed numerous advantages, not the least of which has been the willingness of key Argentine personalities, civilian and military, to be interviewed about their activities and views. Working, thus, in the field of contemporary history has had its exhilarating aspects even though the lack of documentary sources is often frustrating."

*   *   *

POWELL, Adam Clayton, Jr.   1908-1972

PERSONAL: Born November 29, 1908, in New Haven, Conn.; died of cancer, April 4, 1972, in Miami, Fla.; son of Adam Clayton (a minister) and Mattie (Fletcher) Powell; married Isabel Washington (a dancer), March 8, 1933 (divorced, 1943); married Hazel Scott (a pianist and singer), 1945 (divorced, 1960); married Yvette Marjorie Flores Diago, 1960 (separated, 1965); children: Preston (adopted); (second marriage) Adam Clayton III; (third marriage) Adam Diago. *Education:* Colgate University, B.A., 1930; Columbia University, M.A., 1932. *Residence:* Bimini, Bahamas.

CAREER: Abyssinian Baptist Church, New York City, manager and assistant pastor, 1930-36, pastor, 1936-71; New York City councilman, 1941-45; United States congressman, 1945-67 and 1969-70, served as chairman of House Committee on Education and Labor, 1960-67. *Awards, honors:* Doctor of Divinity degree from Shaw University, 1938; LL.D.

from Virginia Union University; golden medallion from Ethiopia for relief work.

WRITINGS: Marching Blacks: An Interpretive History of the Rise of the Black Common Man, Dial, 1945, revised edition, 1973; *The New Image in Education: A Prospectus for the Future by the Chairman of the Committee on Education and Labor,* U.S. Government Printing Office, 1962; *Keep the Faith, Baby!,* Trident, 1967; *Adam by Adam,* Dial 1971. Editor of *People's Voice,* c. 1940.

SIDELIGHTS: According to Thomas A. Johnson in the *New York Times,* Powell was a man of many roles. "He was at once the leader of the largest church congregation in the nation, a political demagogue, a Congressional rebel, a civil rights leader three decades before the Montgomery bus boycott, a wheeler-dealer, a rabble-rouser, a grandstander, a fugitive, a playboy and a most effective chairman of the House Committee on Education and Labor." *Newsweek's* David M. Alpern described Powell's legacy: "Before black power, before black pride, before the civil rights movement took its first steps in the dusty streets of Montgomery, Ala., before any of it, there was Adam. For 30 years, Adam Clayton Powell Jr. did more than any other man to dramatize the quest of Negro Americans and, by an outrageous larger-than-life style, give his people a vicarious piece of the white man's action. He was New York's first black city councilman, Harlem's first black congressman—and the most celebrated black politician in the nation."

Shortly after his birth Powell's family moved to New York City where his father was made pastor of the Abyssinian Baptist Church. In 1923 the church and the Powells moved to Harlem where young Adam was exposed to the ideas of Marcus Garvey and attended sessions of the African Nationalist Pioneer Movement. "Marcus Garvey was one of the greatest mass leaders of all time," Powell later wrote. "He was misunderstood and maligned, but he brought to the Negro people for the first time a sense of pride in being black." During the Depression, Powell became a leader in his own right. He led a series of demonstrations against department stores, bus lines, hospitals, the telephone company, and other big businesses in Harlem, forcing them to hire blacks. He became chairman of the Coordinating Committee on Employment and organized picket lines outside the executive offices of the 1939-40 World's Fair, thereby gaining jobs at the fair for hundreds of black workers.

The activist also organized the social and welfare programs at the Abyssinian Baptist Church, including a vocational guidance clinic as well as a soup kitchen and relief operation that supplied food, clothing, and fuel for thousands of Harlem residents. He served as the leader of the militant Harlem People's Committee and quickly earned a reputation, *Ebony's* Simeon Booker noted, "for scrap, for agitation and for stinging rebuke." People began calling him "the Angry Young Man" and "Fighting Adam." Booker credited him with single-handedly changing the course of national Negro affairs. In 1941 Powell was elected to the New York City Council.

After serving four years on the council, Powell turned a voteless community into a "ballot kingdom," Booker observed, and went to Congress as the representative of central Harlem. In Washington the new legislator continued his fight against racial discrimination. Although unwritten prejudicial rules excluded him from such public places as dining rooms, steam baths, and barber shops, Powell defiantly made use of these facilities, often with his entire staff in tow. In Congress he debated furiously with Southern segregationists, challenged discrimination in the armed forces, and authored the Powell Amendment—an attempt to deny federal funds to projects that tolerated discrimination. Booker disclosed that Powell "upset tradition on Capitol Hill—against the wishes and combined efforts of many of his colleagues. Like no other Negro, except possibly the late Malcolm X, Adam knew how to anger, to irritate and to cajole his white counterparts."

Powell tackled a variety of causes. He fought for the admission of black journalists to the Senate and House press galleries. He introduced legislation to ban racist transportation, and he brought to the attention of Congress the discriminatory practices of such groups as the Daughters of the American Revolution (DAR). As chairman of the House Committee on Education and Labor, a position that made him perhaps the most powerful black in America, Powell's record was extraordinary. Under his direction the committee passed forty-eight major pieces of social legislation, including the 1961 Minimum Wage Bill, the Manpower Development and Training Act, the Anti-Poverty Bill, the Juvenile Delinquency Act, the Vocational Educational Act, and the National Defense Educational Act.

Booker asserted, however, that as Powell "became influential, powerful and dominating . . . he frequently clashed with Democrats, government officials, labor and educational leaders, and even the President on segregation and discrimination policies. While Southern chairmen blocked civil rights legislation at will, Adam tried to bottle major legislation whenever he felt it needed some anti-bias safeguards. This tactic brought him into open conflict with the 'white power structure.'" The resulting tense situation and Powell's record of high absenteeism brought upon him severe censure from his fellow legislators. This criticism was exacerbated by his reputation as a playboy and the accusation that he misused public funds by keeping on his payroll a receptionist with whom he was personally involved. His colleagues also charged him with tax evasion and junketeering. In response, Powell asserted: "The things other Congressmen try to hide, I do right out in the open. I'm not a hypocrite."

Powell's desire for public attention, though, also brought him into conflict with other black leaders. "He credited himself with being more powerful than the leaders and probably he was," explained Booker, "but the shortcoming was that the black teamwork he stressed, he never carried out." Still, it wasn't until a television interview in March, 1960, that his flamboyant and outspoken public image jeopardized his political effectiveness. A court case ensued after Powell had called a sixty-three-year-old Harlem widow, Ester James, a "bag woman" (a collector of graft for corrupt police). Powell ignored the libel case, refusing to make an apology or a settlement. After Mrs. James won and was awarded damages, the congressman still would not comply with the court ruling. Eventually, Powell was found guilty of civil contempt but avoided arrest by appearing in New York City only on Sundays when summonses could not be served. When the politician was convicted of criminal contempt in 1966, he took up residence on the Bahamian island of Bimini.

In response to this conviction and the other charges of misbehavior, a select committee of representatives investigated Powell and on March 1, 1967, the House voted 307 to 116 to exclude him from the ninetieth Congress. Powell thus became the first committee chairman to be expelled from the House in 160 years. Nevertheless, in a special election to fill his vacant seat two months later, Powell was overwhelmingly voted to his former position by his constituents. Ulti-

mately, he paid the damages to Mrs. James and was then reseated in Congress in January, 1969. Powell, however, was fined for misuse of funds and stripped of his seniority.

During this time, white liberals with whom Powell had worked abandoned him while black leaders rallied to his defense. The split marked a breach in the civil rights movement, which Francis E. Kearns analyzed in *Commonweal:* "The chief significance of Adam Clayton Powell's recent difficulties with Congress lies not in the state of the Congressman's personal fortunes or even in the constitutional question of whether the House may deny a district representation by its duly elected Congressman. . . . Clearly Powell's censurable behavior hardly approaches in gravity the misconduct of some other Congressmen who have escaped punitive action. . . . The unseating of one of the most powerful Negro politicians in American history at the very time when a battery of editorialists are urging the Negro to temper his militancy is hardly likely to demonstrate that legislative action offers a viable alternative to mob action in the streets."

Six months after Powell's return to Congress, the Supreme Court ruled that the 1967 House decision to exclude the errant politician had been unconstitutional. He told reporters at the time: "From now on, America will know the Supreme Court is the place where you can get justice." But Powell's political career was coming to an end. In 1969 he was defeated by Charles B. Rangel in a Democratic primary after having been hospitalized for cancer.

Powell's writing was as controversial as his lifestyle. In the *New York Times Book Review*, Frank Adams dwelled on the author's "intemperance" and "intransigence," calling the congressman's first book, *Marching Blacks*, "the battle cry of an embittered man who avows the hope that his cause will triumph without bloodshed, but warns that only the conscience of white America can prevent another civil war from being fought with all the fury of the war that freed the slaves." H. A. Overstreet of the *Saturday Review*, however, appraised the volume as "a non-violent fighting book," and the "story of Negro unification. . . . In few books is the ugliness of racial injustice so vividly and succinctly described; in few is the case so clearly stated for the fact that race prejudice is poison that kills dignity and decency in the souls of race haters."

Keep the Faith, Baby! is a collection of Powell's sermons and speeches. *Saturday Review*'s David Poling maintained that Powell "has to be considered above average in ability to relate scripture to the needs and problems of everyday life. There is a directness, an economy of words that eludes too many preachers." Powell's autobiography met with a mixed reception from reviewers. A *New Yorker* critic described *Adam by Adam*, as an "impenitent apologia," while Martin Kilsen of the *New York Times Book Review* found the book "deficient in serious self-analysis." Kilsen praised the author, at the same time, though, as "a discerning observer of American politics, both at the city and national levels, as well as of the pattern of cruel defeats and illustrations that surround the life of the ghetto Negro."

BIOGRAPHICAL/CRITICAL SOURCES: Time, January 12, 1942, June 15, 1942, January 10, 1969, June 27, 1969; *New York Times Book Review,* February 3, 1946, November 7, 1971; *Saturday Review,* February 9, 1946, April 22, 1967; *Nation,* February 16, 1946; *Commonweal,* January 27, 1967; *Life,* March 24, 1967; *Ebony,* March, 1967, January, 1971, June, 1972; *Newsweek,* April 1, 1968, December 2, 1968, January 13, 1969, June 30, 1969; *New Yorker,* November 13, 1971.

OBITUARIES: New York Times, April 5, 1972; Washington Post, April 6, 1972; L'Express, April 10, 1972; Newsweek, April 17, 1972; Time, April 17, 1972.*

—Sketch by Andrea Geffner

*   *   *

POWER-ROSS, Robert W.   1922-
(Robert W. Ross)

PERSONAL: Original name, Robert W. Ross; name legally changed in 1975; born January 19, 1922, in Yuma, Colo.; son of Albert M. (a carpenter) and Miriam (Bartlett) Ross; married Elizabeth Langeloh (died January 20, 1952); married Sally Jo Power (a university administrator), September 22, 1975; children: Rebecca E., David J. Education: Westmont College, B.A., 1948; attended University of Washington, Seattle, 1954-55 and 1962; Associated Colleges of Claremont, M.A., 1955; further graduate study at University of California, Berkeley, 1955-58; University of Minnesota, Ph.D., 1972. Politics: Independent Democrat. Home: 317 Eighth St. S.E., Minneapolis, Minn. 55414. Office: Department of Religious Studies, University of Minnesota, 107 TNA, 122 Pleasant St. S.E., Minneapolis, Minn. 55455.

CAREER: Ordained Christian minister, 1950; Christian Missionary Alliance, pastor in southern Pacific district, 1948-54; Simpson College, San Francisco, Calif., professor of religion and history, 1955-59; Wheaton College, Wheaton, Ill., visiting assistant professor of history, 1959-60; Northern Illinois University, DeKalb, assistant professor of history, 1960-61; Northwestern College, Minneapolis, Minn., assistant professor of history and chairman of department, 1962-64; pastor of Baptist church in Minnesota, 1965-66; University of Minnesota, Minneapolis, instructor, 1967-73, assistant professor, 1973, currently associate professor of religious studies, coordinator of religious activities, 1967-68. Assistant professor at Biola College, 1949-51; guest lecturer at United Theological Seminary and Luther Northwestern Seminaries, 1979. Member of board of directors of University Young Men's Christian Association, Greater Minneapolis Council of Churches, 1971-77, and Twin Cities Metropolitan Church Commission, 1971-77, advisory board of Parents Without Partners, and young adult ministry board of U.S. Catholic Conference; member of Ida M. Grossman Holocaust Commemoration Committee and Minneapolis Jewish Center. Lecturer; conducts workshops. Military service: U.S. Coast Guard, 1942-45. Member: American Academy of Religion, American Studies Association, American Church History Society, American Association of University Professors, Presbyterian Historical Society, Minnesota Historical Society, Phi Delta Kappa.

WRITINGS—Under name Robert W. Ross: The Church Through the Years, Gospel Light Press, 1958; Intercultural Sourcebook: Cross-Cultural Training Methods, Intercultural Communication Network, Society for Intercultural Education and Research, 1977; (contributor) The Christian Tradition, Argus Communications, 1978; (contributor) Lee Smith and Wes Bodin, editors, The Single Experience: A Resource, Department of Education, U.S. Catholic Conference, 1979; So It Was True: The American Protestant Religious Press and the Nazi Persecution of the Jews, 1933-1945, University of Minnesota Press, 1980. Author of "American Genesis," a filmscript, released by Argus Communications, 1978. Contributor to Wycliffe Bible Commentary and Baker's Dictionary of Theology. Contributor of articles and reviews to theology and education journals, Annals of the American Academy of Political and Social Science, and newspapers.

WORK IN PROGRESS: Were They Welcome?: The Protestant Press in America and the Jews as Refugees, publication expected in 1982; Minnesota Military Men Encounter the Concentration Camps, publication expected in 1982.

SIDELIGHTS: Power-Ross told CA: "I have a particular interest in the American religious press as a basis for ongoing research in American religions. I also believe that the Holocaust poses as many problems for Christians as for Jews. For this reason I continue to write on aspects of this problem. I write as a Protestant Christian, using the Protestant press as a base. Typically, teaching, writing, and research consume most of my time and interest.

"I am a bit further along in years than most to have published so late. I spent sixteen years in church-related colleges teaching history and religion, not planning an academic career that was traditional. I was fired from two and in trouble at a third for asking questions and advocating for students. In midcareer (at age forty-three) I shifted to university affiliation, taking an administrative position and reordering priorities around American studies, with an emphasis on American religions. When the religious studies program was established at the University of Minnesota I began to combine all my background into one course, 'Religions of the American People,' from which new interests have grown, such as writing."

*   *   *

PRESTON, John Hyde   1906-1980

OBITUARY NOTICE: Born in 1906; died of cancer, November 11, 1980, in Quebec City, Quebec, Canada. Writer. Preston was best known for Revolution, 1776, a book debunking the myths surrounding the birth of the United States. He also wrote two novels, The Liberals and Portrait of a Woman, and a biography, Mad Anthony Wayne, Gentleman Rebel. In the 1930's, while a writer-in-residence at Black Mountain College, he was awarded a grant from the Mellon Foundation. Preston was a contributor of articles to various magazines, including Atlantic Monthly, Holiday, and McCall's. Obituaries and other sources: New York Times, November 15, 1980.

*   *   *

PRIEST, Alice L.   1931-

PERSONAL: Born March 4, 1931, in Mount Vernon, N.Y.; daughter of Alfred and Beatrice Dorothy (Bierman) Lyons; married Richard N. Priest (an executive director), September 14, 1952; children: Andrea R., Adam R. Education: Columbia University, B.A., 1952; attended University of Connecticut, 1952-53. Home: 279 Farrington Ave., North Tarrytown, N.Y. 10591. Agent: Aaron M. Priest Literary Agency, Inc., 150 East 35th St., New York, N.Y. 10016. Office: Business Week, 1221 Avenue of the Americas, New York, N.Y. 10020.

CAREER: Commercial and Financial Chronicle, feature writer, 1973; Business Week, New York, N.Y., editor in companies department, 1974-77, corporate strategies department, 1977-78, and special projects department, 1978-79, associate editor, 1980—.

WRITINGS: Charles Coolidge Parlin, University of Pennsylvania Wharton School, 1975; Family Budget Book, Lorenz, 1978.

AVOCATIONAL INTERESTS: Travel (Far East).

PRUETT, John H(aywood) 1947-

PERSONAL: Born June 3, 1947, in Richmond, Va.; son of Haywood Cato and Anne Thornton (Weaver) Pruett. *Education:* University of Virginia, B.A., 1969; Princeton University, M.A., 1971, Ph.D., 1973. *Religion:* Episcopalian. *Home:* 1614 West Lock Raven Rd., Champaign, Ill. 61820. *Office:* Department of History, University of Illinois, Urbana, Ill. 61820.

CAREER: University of Illinois, Urbana, assistant professor, 1973-79, associate professor of history, 1979—. *Member:* Phi Beta Kappa. *Awards, honors:* Danforth fellowship, 1969-73.

WRITINGS: The Parish Clergy Under the Later Stuarts: The Leicestershire Experience, University of Illinois Press, 1978. Contributor to religious history journals.

WORK IN PROGRESS: Moderate Patriots of the American Revolution.

SIDELIGHTS: Pruett told *CA:* "I consider myself to be primarily a teacher. My research and publication efforts are aimed at furthering my understanding of the material I present to my students. Since I am presently engaged in teaching American history, I have shifted my research activities from early modern Britain to early America, and especially the period of the American Revolution."

*   *   *

PURCELL, Arthur Henry 1944-

PERSONAL: Born August 11, 1944, in Evanston, Ill.; son of Edward (an engineer) and Ethel (a librarian; maiden name, Lohman) Purcell; married Deborah Ross, February 2, 1973. *Education:* Attended Institute for European Studies, Vienna, Austria, 1965; Cornell University, B.S., 1966; Northwestern University, M.S., 1971, Ph.D., 1972. *Politics:* Democrat. *Home:* 4416 Fessenden St. N.W., Washington, D.C. 20016. *Office:* Technical Information Project, Inc., 1346 Connecticut Ave. N.W., Suite 217, Washington, D.C. 20036.

CAREER: U.S. Army, Environment Office, civilian environmentalist, 1971; American Association for the Advancement of Science, Office of Science and Government, Washington, D.C., associate director of Congressional scientific fellow program, 1973-74; Technical Information Project, Inc., Washington, D.C., co-founder and director, 1975—. Adjunct professor at George Washington University,

1975—, and American University, 1980—. Independent consulting engineer, 1974—. Member of President's Scientific Policy Task Force, 1976, and President's Commission on Scholars, 1978; staff principal of President's Commission on the Accident at Three-Mile Island, 1979. *Member:* American Institute of Mining, Metallurgy, and Petroleum Engineers, American Association for the Advancement of Science, Federation of Materials Societies, Sigma Xi. *Awards, honors:* Award from German Marshall Fund, 1980.

WRITINGS: Citizens and Waste, Technical Information Project, Inc., Volume I, 1976, Volume II, 1978; *Tin Cans and Trash Recovery,* Technical Information Project, Inc., 1980; *The Waste Watchers,* Doubleday, 1980. Contributor of about seventy-five articles to scientific journals and newspapers, including *Science Digest, National Development,* and *Technology Review.*

WORK IN PROGRESS: Materials, Energy, and the Environment, a textbook; research on future trends of materials consumption; research on compensation of victims of toxic substances and hazardous wastes.

SIDELIGHTS: Purcell wrote: "Travel is both a vocation and hobby. In 1976, for instance, I served as a member of the U.S. delegation to the first United Nations conference on non-waste technology held in Paris. Opportunities such as these give me the chance to meet people and observe what other cultures and nations are doing to conserve natural resources and to trim global largesse. The infusion of many perspectives and the 'energy' released by citizens across the country provide me with much material for my writing.

"The area of energy and resource waste is a good case in point. As I have opportunities to meet and work with individuals and organizations around the country and overseas, I learn the full meanings of such concepts as 'energy policy' and 'environmental policy.' The black-lunged coal miner in the depressed town of Welch, W.Va., tells me something about energy and environmental policy that is not in the textbooks or well understood in the marble halls of Washington. Our people know, just as this miner's life showed me, that we need both energy *and* a clean environment. Until we develop a conservation ethic that lets us optimize our use of limited resources, we will have—literally or figuratively—a lot of these 'miners' in our society. Victims of irresponsible resource use will grow in number until we learn how to properly use our energy and environmental resources."

R

RACKHAM, John
See PHILLIFENT, John Thomas

* * *

RADIN, George 1896-1981

OBITUARY NOTICE: Born January 29, 1896, in St. Nickolas, Austria-Hungary (now Rumania); died of a stroke, January 4, 1981, in Washington, D.C. Lawyer and author of two books on the Balkan region. A specialist in international law, Radin practiced in New York, Zurich, and Washington, D.C., before he retired in 1976. He was the recipient of the Carnegie Endowment for International Peace in 1946, and he founded the International Development Foundation in 1963 and the Serbian Research Foundation in 1972. Radin co-authored *The Balkan Pivot: Yugoslavia* with Charles A. Beard. He also wrote *Postwar Economic Reconstruction: A Practical Plan for the Balkans*. Obituaries and other sources: *Who's Who in America*, 39th edition, Marquis, 1976; *New York Times*, January 7, 1981; *AB Bookman's Weekly*, January 26, 1981.

* * *

RAKOFF, Alvin 1927-

PERSONAL: Born February 6, 1927, in Toronto, Ontario, Canada; son of Samuel (a shopkeeper) and Pearl (Himmelspring) Rakoff; married Jacqueline Hill (an actress), June 4, 1958; children: Sasha Victoria, John-Dmitri. *Education:* University of Toronto, B.A., 1948. *Home:* 1 The Orchard, London W4 1JZ, England.

CAREER: Journalist for *Northern Daily News*, Kirkland, Ontario, *Windsor Star*, Windsor, Ontario, *Toronto Globe and Mail*, Toronto, Ontario, and *Lakeshore "Advertiser,"* Toronto, 1949-52; British Broadcasting Corp. (BBC-TV), London, England, writer, director, and producer, 1953-57; free-lance film and television director in London, 1957—. Producer of television program "Waiting for Gillian." *Member:* Association of Cinema and Television Technicians, Directors Guild of Canada, Writers Guild of Great Britain. *Awards, honors:* National television award from *London Daily Mail*, 1955, for "Waiting for Gillian"; Emmy Award from Academy of Television Arts and Sciences, 1968, for "Call Me Daddy."

WRITINGS—Screen and television plays: "A Flight of Fancy," first broadcast by BBC-TV, July, 1952; (co-author) "The Troubled Air" (adaptation), first broadcast by BBC-TV, April, 1953; "Thunder in the Realms," first broadcast by BBC-TV, July 1, 1955; "Our Town" (adaptation), first broadcast by BBC-TV, April, 1957; "The Caine Mutiny Court Martial" (adaptation), first broadcast by BBC-TV, June, 1958; "Say Hello to Yesterday," released as a feature film by Cinerama, 1959.

"Summer and Smoke" (adaptation), first broadcast by BBC-TV, January, 1971; "A Kiss Is Just a Kiss" (adaptation), first broadcast by Anglia Television, 1971; "A Man About a Dog" (adaptation), first broadcast by Anglia Television, 1972; (co-author) "The Adventures of Don Quixote" (adaptation), first broadcast by BBC-TV, January, 1972; "Rooms," first broadcast by Thames Television, 1974; "O Canada," first broadcast by BBC-TV, August, 1974; "Mineshaft," first broadcast by BBC-TV, 1975; "Lulu Street" (adaptation), first broadcast by CBC-TV, 1975; "In Praise of Love" (adaptation), first broadcast by Anglia Television, 1975; "Romeo and Juliet" (adaptation), first broadcast by BBC-TV, September, 1978; (co-author) "City on Fire," released as a feature film by Avco Embassy, 1979.

SIDELIGHTS: Rakoff commented: "I came to England for three months in 1952, but fell in love with the warm beer and the gentle people. I now divide my time fairly evenly between Canada, the United States, and Europe."

* * *

RAMPA, Tuesday Lobsang
See HOSKIN, Cyril Henry

* * *

RAMSDEN, E. H.

Home: 30 Mallord St., Chelsea, London S.W.3, England.

CAREER: Writer. Worked as official censor in England, 1940-43 and 1944-47; museum assistant at London Museum; co-editor of *Eidos: Journal of Painting, Sculpture, and Design;* reviewer for *Apollo*, 1964—.

WRITINGS: *Introduction to Modern Art*, Oxford University Press, 1940, revised edition, 1949; *Twentieth-Century Sculpture*, Pleiades Books, 1949; *Sculpture: Theme and Variations*, Lund, Humphries, 1953; *The Letters of Michelangelo*, two volumes, Stanford University Press, 1963; *Michelangelo*, Phaidon, 1971.

WORK IN PROGRESS: *Come, Take This Lute*.

RANDALL, John Herman, Jr. 1899-1980

OBITUARY NOTICE—See index for *CA* sketch: Born February 14, 1899, in Grand Rapids, Mich.; died December 1, 1980, in New York, N.Y. Author and philosopher best known for *The Making of the Modern Mind*. His writings include *Religion and the Modern World, Nature and the Historical Experience, The Career of Philosophy in Modern Times,* and *The Philosophy of Darwin*. The second volume of *The Career of Philosophy in Modern Times* received the Ralph Waldo Emerson Award from the Phi Beta Kappa Senate in 1966. Randall was also the joint editor of two professional journals. Obituaries and other sources: John P. Anton, editor, *Naturalism and Historical Understanding: Essays on the Philosophy of John Herman Randall, Jr.,* State University of New York Press, 1967; *AB Bookman's Weekly,* December 22-29, 1980.

* * *

RANT, Tol E.
See LONGYEAR, Barry Brookes

* * *

RAWLINGS, John 1930(?)-1981(?)

OBITUARY NOTICE: Writer, choreographer, and educator. Rawlings wrote *Let Me Put It to You Another Way,* a book on education, and he was a contributor of poetry to several literary reviews. Obituaries and other sources: *AB Bookman's Weekly,* January 19, 1981.

* * *

RAYMOND, Patrick (Ernest) 1924-

PERSONAL: Born September 25, 1924, in Cuckfield, England; son of Ernest (a novelist) and Zoe (Doucett) Raymond; married Lola Pilpel (a designer), May 27, 1950; children: Christopher. *Education:* Attended University of Cape Town, 1941; Royal Air Force Staff College, graduated, 1962; Joint Services Staff College, graduated, 1965. *Politics:* "No formal politics." *Religion:* "Church of England, lapsed." *Home:* 24 Chilton Rd., Chesham, Buckinghamshire, England. *Agent:* A. P. Watt Ltd., 26/28 Bedford Row, London WC1R 4HL, England.

CAREER: Royal Air Force, career officer, 1942-77, served with heavy bomber squadron, 1944-45, staff officer with Air Ministry (now Ministry of Defence), 1945-47, 1949-51, 1959-61, 1965-68, and 1974-77, assigned to the Far East, 1953-56 and 1963-65, officer commanding RAF Uxbridge, 1972-74, retiring as group captain; writer, 1977—.

WRITINGS—Novels: *A City of Scarlet and Gold,* Cassell, 1963; *The Lordly Ones,* Cassell, 1965; *The Sea Garden,* Cassell, 1970; *The Last Soldier,* Cassell, 1974; *A Matter of Assassination,* Cassell, 1977; *The White War,* Cassell, 1978; *The Grand Admiral,* Cassell, 1980.

WORK IN PROGRESS: The Loyalist, a novel "of a military rebellion in Britain—the one that hasn't happened," publication expected in 1982; novels with a military background.

SIDELIGHTS: "Why do I write?" Raymond asked. "I suppose to make sense out of what seems chaotic and pointless, but can't be; to find the smothered harmonies. I have no fixed viewpoint and mistrust all theoretical solutions, which usually end in a bloodbath. To me, the best form of truth lies in poetry, and the things that spin from that, but I am an incurable novelist."

RAYWARD, W(arden) Boyd 1939-

PERSONAL: Born June 24, 1939, in Invernell, Australia; came to the United States in 1975; son of Warden B. and Ellie Dora Rayward. *Education:* University of Sydney, B.A. (with honors), 1960; University of New South Wales, diploma in library science, 1964; University of Illinois, M.S.L.S., 1965; University of Chicago, Ph.D., 1973. *Home:* 1455 North Sandburg Ter., Chicago, Ill. 60610. *Office:* Graduate Library School, University of Chicago, 1100 East 57th, Chicago, Ill. 60637.

CAREER: University of New South Wales, Sydney, Australia, lecturer in library science, 1971-73; University of Western Ontario, London, assistant professor of library science, 1973-74; University of Chicago, Chicago, Ill., assistant professor, 1975-78, associate professor of library science, 1979—, dean of Graduate Library School, 1980—. Member of national advisory board of Center for the Book, at Library of Congress; chairman of board of publications of Illinois Regional Library Council, 1976-78; consultant to National Endowment for the Humanities. *Member:* American Library Association, Association of American Library Schools, Special Libraries Association, Library Association of Australia (associate). *Awards, honors:* Council of Library Resources fellowship, 1978.

WRITINGS: Universe of Information: The Work of Paul Otlet for Documentation and International Organization, Federation International de Documentation, 1975; (editor) *The Variety of Librarianship: Essays in Honour of J. W. Metcalfe,* Library Association of Australia, 1976; (editor) *The Public Library: Circumstances and Prospects,* University of Chicago Press, 1978. Contributor of articles to U.S., Australian, and international journals. Editor of *Library Quarterly,* 1975-79.

WORK IN PROGRESS: Editing, translating, and writing annotations for *Essays of Paul Otlet,* publication by Libraries Unlimited expected in 1982; *The Work of the League of Nations for Libraries and Bibliography.*

SIDELIGHTS: Rayward told *CA:* "I have always been fascinated by the problem of organizing knowledge in such a way as to make it available between nations as well as locally. Paul Otlet was a great theorist, bibliographer, and internationalist and it seemed not inappropriate that a book about a Belgian, written by an Australian living in the United States, should be published for an international organization headquartered in the Hague. The work was also published in Russian by the U.S.S.R. Academy of Sciences. I plan to follow up earlier studies of the Royal Society of London and those of Otlet and the League of Nations by focussing on UNESCO and other more contemporary bodies. I might add that that uniquely Anglo-Saxon institution, the free public library, is a tremendously inventive way of making knowledge available to people."

* * *

REARICK, Charles Walter 1942-

PERSONAL: Born August 2, 1942, in St. James, Mo.; married Mary L. Waite; children: Ann, Deborah, Andrew. *Education:* College of Idaho, B.A., 1964; Harvard University, M.A., 1965, Ph.D., 1968. *Office:* Department of History, University of Massachusetts, Amherst, Mass. 01002.

CAREER: University of Massachusetts, Amherst, assistant professor, 1968-74, associate professor of modern European history, 1974—. *Member:* Society for French Historical Studies.

WRITINGS: Beyond the Enlightenment: Historians and Folklore in Nineteenth-Century France, Indiana University Press, 1974. Contributor to history journals.

WORK IN PROGRESS: A study of French thinking about leisure; "a history of popular amusements in *Belle Epoque.*"

* * *

REDWOOD, John (Alan) 1951-

PERSONAL: Born June 15, 1951, in Dover, England; son of William Charles and Amy (Champion) Redwood; married Gail Felicity Chippington (a barrister), April 12, 1974; children: Catherine Gail Acott. *Education:* Magdalen College, Oxford, B.A. (with honors), 1971; St. Antony's College, Oxford, D.Phil., 1975, M.A., 1975. *Politics:* Conservative. *Religion:* Church of England. *Office:* All Souls College, Oxford University, Oxford, England.

CAREER: Oxford University, Oxford, England, fellow of All Souls College, 1972—. Merchant banker, 1973—. Member of Oxfordshire County Council, 1973-77, and Centre for Policy Studies. Member of board of governors of Oxford Polytechnic, 1974-77, and Silverthorne School, 1980—.

WRITINGS: Reason, Ridicule, and Religion: The Age of Enlightenment in England, Thames & Hudson, 1976; (contributor) Lord Blake and John Patton, editors, *The Conservative Opportunity,* Macmillan, 1976; *Public Enterprise in Crisis,* Blackwell, 1980; (with Michael Grylls) *NEB,* Centre for Policy Studies, 1980. Contributor to banking journals.

WORK IN PROGRESS: Research on nationalized industries in the United Kingdom.

SIDELIGHTS: Redwood wrote: "My work on public enterprise in the United Kingdom is related to my political activities within the Conservative party and involves me in a number of policy questions concerning the future of government involvment in industry."

* * *

REED, Evelyn 1905-1979

PERSONAL: Born October 31, 1905, in Haledon, N.J., died March 22, 1979, in New York, N.Y.; married George Novack (a philosopher and writer). *Education:* Attended Parsons School of Design and Art Students League; studied painting with John Sloan, George Luks, and Grant Wood.

CAREER: Assistant in household of Leon Trotsky in Mexico, 1939-40; Civil Rights Defense Committee, executive director, 1940-45; *Militant,* staff writer, 1945-79. Lecturer at more than one hundred universities in the United States, Canada, New Zealand, Australia, Ireland, and Japan. Leader of Socialist Workers Party.

WRITINGS: Problems of Women's Liberation: A Marxist Approach, Merit Publishers, 1960, 5th edition, Pathfinder Press (N.Y.), 1970; (editor) *Writings of Leon Trotsky,* Merit Publishers, 1969; (editor) *Writings of Leon Trotsky, 1937-38,* Pathfinder Press (N.Y.), 1970; (with Ruthann Miller) *In Defense of the Women's Movement,* Pathfinder Press (N.Y.), 1970; *Women's Evolution From Matriarchal Clan to Patriarchal Family,* Pathfinder Press (N.Y.), 1975. Contributor to magazines, including *International Socialist Review* and *Fourth International.*

* * *

REED, James 1922-

PERSONAL: Born January 26, 1922, in Meldon, England; son of William Davison (a schoolmaster) and Hannah Isa-
bella (Davidson) Reed; married Bertha Carol Lockey (a high school English teacher), December 28, 1948; children: James William, Jonathan. *Education:* University of Durham, B.A. (with honors), 1950, teaching diploma, 1951. *Home:* 83 Raikes Rd., Skipton-in-Craven, Yorkshire BD23 1LS, England.

CAREER: Teacher of English at schools in Newcastle on Tyne, Northumberland, England, 1951-56, and Hemsworth, Yorkshire, England, 1956-64; Bingley College, Bingley, Yorkshire, England, 1964-78, teacher of English, 1964-68, head of humanities, 1974-78; writer, 1978—. Guest lecturer at University of Newcastle upon Tyne, University of Edinburgh, University of Leeds, and University of Bradford. *Military service:* Royal Air Force, 1941-46.

WRITINGS: The Border Ballads, Athlone Press, 1973; (contributor) Edward J. Cowan, editor, *The People's Past,* Edinburgh University Student Publications Board, 1979; *Sir Walter Scott: Landscape and Locality,* Athlone Press, 1980. Contributor of articles and reviews to magazines, including *Dickensian, Scotland's, Blackfriars,* and *Use of English.*

WORK IN PROGRESS: Research on the Scottish writings of Robert Louis Stevenson.

SIDELIGHTS: Reed told *CA:* "My main professional interest is writing about and teaching English literature in various spheres of adult education.

"In my writing I am particularly concerned with the way in which literature and environment interact. Because I am a native of Northumberland in the north of England, and descended from the border families of Davidson, Reed, and Rutherford, I have written in some depth about the literature of this region. Apart from this, my main literary studies have been in the Elizabethan/Jacobean period, and in the twentieth century, up to such contemporaries as Iris Murdoch, John Fowles, William Golding, and Seamus Heaney.

"Since 1950, as well as teaching in schools and colleges, I have been tutor in English literature for university extramural courses and for the Workers' Educational Association. In 1978 I left Bingley College to give my whole time to lecturing and writing."

* * *

REED, Walter Logan 1943-

PERSONAL: Born February 9, 1943, in New York, N.Y.; son of Stephen Winsor and Barbara (Logan) Reed; married Loreen Rogers (a writer and editor), June 20, 1964; children: Seth Logan, Melissa Alden, Catherine Rogers. *Education:* Yale University, B.A., 1965, Ph.D., 1969. *Religion:* Christian. *Home:* 7300 Lamplight Lane, Austin, Tex. 78731. *Office:* Department of English, University of Texas, Austin, Tex. 78712.

CAREER: Yale University, New Haven, Conn., assistant professor of English, 1969-76; University of Texas, Austin, associate professor of English, 1976—. *Awards, honors:* Guggenheim fellowship, 1977-78.

WRITINGS: Meditations on the Hero: The Romantic Hero in Nineteenth Century Fiction, Yale University Press, 1974; *An Exemplary History of the Novel: The Quixotic Versus the Picaresque,* University of Chicago Press, 1981.

* * *

REESE, John (Henry)
(John Jo Carpenter)

PERSONAL: Born in Sweetwater, Neb. *Education:* Educated in Kansas and Nebraska. *Residence:* Santa Maria, Calif.

CAREER: Writer. Worked variously for the U.S. Department of Internal Revenue and as a reporter for the *Los Angeles Examiner* in Los Angeles, Calif. *Member:* Western Writers of America. *Awards, honors:* Spur Award for best Western novel, 1977, for *Halter-Broke.*

WRITINGS—Published by Doubleday, except as noted: *Sheehan's Mill,* 1943; (under pseudonym John Jo Carpenter) *Signal Guns at Sunup,* Simon & Schuster, 1950; *Big Mutt,* Westminster, 1952; *The Shooting Duke: A Story Scientifically Calibrated to the Taste, Needs, and Emotional Development of the Nine to Ninety Age Groups,* Westminster, 1952; *The High Passes,* Little, Brown, 1954; *Three Wild Ones,* Westminster, 1963; *Dinky,* McKay, 1964; *Sunblind Range,* 1968; *Sure Shot Shapiro,* 1968; *The Looters,* Random House, 1968; *Pity Us All,* Random House, 1969, *Singalee,* 1969.

Horses, Honor, and Women, 1970; *Jesus on Horseback: The Mooney County Saga* (trilogy; contains *Angel Range, The Blowholers,* and *The Land Baron*), 1971; *Big Hitch,* 1972; *Springfield .45-70,* 1972; *The Wild One,* Fawcett, 1972; *They Don't Shoot Cowards,* 1973; *Weapon Heavy,* 1973; *The Sharpshooter,* 1974; *Texas Gold,* 1975; *Wes Hardin's Gun,* 1975; *Blacksnake Man,* 1976; *A Sheriff for All the People,* 1976; *Hangman's Springs,* 1976; *Omar, Fats, and Trixie,* Fawcett, 1976; *The Cherokee Diamondback,* 1977; *Halter-Broke,* 1977; *Sequoia Shootout,* 1977; *Dead Eye,* 1978; *A Pair of Deuces,* 1978; *Rich Man's Range,* New American Library, 1978; *Legacy of a Land Hog,* 1979; *Two Thieves and a Puma,* 1980.*

*   *   *

REICHL, Ernst   1900-1980

OBITUARY NOTICE: Born May 2, 1900, in Leipzig, Germany (now East Germany); died September 19, 1980, in New York, N.Y. Book designer and author. Reichl's career spanned almost sixty years. Before opening his own studio in 1946, he worked for various publishers and book manufacturers, including Knopf, Doubleday, H. Wolff, and Foote, Cone & Belding. He was best known for his unique, but practical, approach to the art of bookmaking, which involved continuous experimentation with new ideas and technology without any sacrifice of high standards. A Random House edition of *Ulysses,* and the *New International Version of the Holy Bible* published in 1973 by the New York Bible Society and Zondervan, were among his most famous book designs. Less then two weeks before he died, he delivered his last completed design layouts. He was the publisher of a line of calligraphic books, and he wrote *Legibility: A Typographic Book of Etiquette.* Obituaries and other sources: *Who's Who in America,* 40th edition, Marquis, 1978; *Publishers Weekly,* October 10, 1980; *AB Bookman's Weekly,* January 19, 1981.

*   *   *

REINER, Laurence E(rwin)

PERSONAL: Born in New York, N.Y.; son of Carl Sigmund (a machinist) and Edith (Singer) Reiner; married Karin Constance Grape, April, 1930. *Education:* Stevens Institute of Technology, M.E., 1927. *Politics:* Independent Republican. *Home and office:* 253 Middlesex Rd., Darien, Conn. 06820.

CAREER: Estimator, assistant superintendent, and superin-

tendent at J. H. Taylor Construction Co., 1927-34; district real estate manager at Irving Trust Co., 1934-38; regional mortgage supervisor at National Life of Vermont, 1938-40; Equitable Life Assurance Society, New York, N.Y., construction manager and second vice-president of real estate and construction, 1940-63, first vice-president of real estate and construction, 1964-69; writer and consulting engineer, 1970—. Member of Darien planning and zoning commission, zoning board of appeals, school building commission, architectural advisory commission, building code commission, and town hall commission; chairman of Darien Auditorium Building. *Member:* Professional Engineers, Country Club of Darien, Darien Boat Club.

WRITINGS: Methods and Materials of Construction, Prentice-Hall, 1970; *Handbook of Construction Management,* Prentice-Hall, 1972; *Buy or Build: The Best House for You,* Prentice-Hall, 1973; *Builders Guide to Construction Business Success,* McGraw, 1978; *How to Recycle Buildings,* McGraw, 1979; *Methods and Materials of Residential Construction,* Prentice-Hall, 1981; *Guide to Economic Housing,* McGraw, 1981; *Guide to Architectural Blueprint Reading,* McGraw, in press.

SIDELIGHTS: Reiner commented: "I would hope that my writings, which are somewhat of a synopsis of my long career in construction and real estate, will help readers to build better shelters. Shelter is one of the prime necessities of life, and it should be safe and tight against the elements. A house should be a home that provides comfort and some of the amenities of the good life."

AVOCATIONAL INTERESTS: Travel (safaris, Zanzibar, the Far East, Hong Kong, Singapore, Indonesia, Uganda, India, Ceylon, Europe, Egypt [archaeology]), reading (fiction, biography, science), painting (oils and watercolor), drawing.

*   *   *

REMLEY, Mary L(ouise)   1930-

PERSONAL: Born January 26, 1930, in St. Louis, Mo.; daughter of Aubrey J. (an ice and coal dealer) and Kate (a boarding house owner; maiden name, Clarida) Remley. *Education:* Southeast Missouri State University, B.S., 1951; Ohio University, M.Ed., 1960; University of Southern California, Ph.D., 1970. *Home:* 3695 Robin Rd., Bloomington, Ind. 47401. *Office address:* HPER 168, Indiana University, Bloomington, Ind. 47402.

CAREER: Instructor at high school in Harrisonville, Mo., 1951-52; Ohio University, Athens, teaching assistant, 1952-53; instructor at high school in Coronado, Calif., 1953-54; coordinator of elementary physical education at public schools in Hinsdale, Ill., 1954-56; Macalester College, St. Paul, Minn., instructor in physical education, 1956-58, 1961; Glendale College, Glendale, Calif., instructor in physical education, 1958-62; Macalester College, assistant professor of physical education, 1962-67; University of Southern California, Los Angeles, teaching assistant and motor learning laboratory assistant, 1967-69; University of Wisconsin—Madison, assistant professor of physical education and coordinator of professional program, 1969-76; Indiana University, Bloomington, associate professor of physical education, 1976—.

MEMBER: North American Society for Sport History (president, 1979—), American Alliance for Health, Physical Education, Recreation, and Dance, National Association for Physical Education of College Women, National Association for Physical Education in Higher Education, Midwest Association for Physical Education of College Women, Indiana Association of Health, Physical Education, Recreation, and Dance, Wisconsin Association for Health, Physical Education, and Recreation.

WRITINGS: Women in Sport, Gale, 1980. Contributor of articles to *Maryland Historian, Wisconsin Magazine of History, Journal of the West,* and *Journal of Physical Education and Recreation.*

WORK IN PROGRESS: Continuing research on women in sports and physical education.

SIDELIGHTS: Remley told *CA:* "Because I was particularly impressed with the number of prominent women physical educators who lived extremely long lives and with other women who were actively involved in sports at time when society looked askance at such participation, I became interested in the historical development of sports for women. The recent growth and development of high level sports programs for women also contributed to my interest. Most of my research and professional presentations are concerned with women's activities, and my special 'pet' is a graduate course which I developed and have taught for the past seven years, "Women in Sport: Historical Perspectives.""

*   *   *

RENSCH, Bernhard (Carl Emmanuel)   1900-

PERSONAL: Born January 21, 1900, in Thale, Germany; son of Carl and Lisette (Siebenhuner) Rensch; married Ilse Maier, May 20, 1926. *Education:* University of Halle, D.Phil., 1922. *Religion:* Protestant. *Home:* 16 Moellmannsweg, 44 Muenster, West Germany. *Office:* Zoological Institute, 9 Bade-Strasse, 44 Muenster, West Germany.

CAREER: University of Halle, Halle, Germany, research assistant at Institute for Plant Breeding, 1923-25; University of Berlin, Berlin, Germany, research assistant in zoology at museum and head of department, 1925-37; University of Muenster, Muenster, West Germany, reader, 1938-43, professor of zoology and director of Zoological Institute, 1947-68, professor emeritus, 1968—. Guest professor in Japan and Malaysia, 1963-64. Conducted biological expeditions in Lesser Sunda Islands, 1937, and India, 1953. *Military service:* German Army, 1917-20, 1940-42.

MEMBER: International Union of Biological Sciences (member of executive committee, 1955-61), Rheinisch-Westfael Akademie der Wissenschaften, National Academy of America (foreign member), American Academy of Arts and Sciences (honorary member), American Ornithologists Union (honorary member), American Zoological Society (corresponding member), Linnean Society (fellow), Society of Natural Sciences of Madrid (honorary member), Deutsche Zoologische Geseleschaft (honorary member), Physiographical Society of Lund. *Awards, honors:* Leibniz Medal from Prussian Academy of Science, 1938; D.Phil. from University of Uppsala, 1957; Darwin-Wallace Medal from Linnean Society, 1958; Darwin Plaque from Academy of Sciences of Germany, 1959; Vits-price from University of Muenster, 1974.

WRITINGS—In English translation: *Neuere Probleme der Abstammungslehre: Die transspezifische Evolution,* F. Enke, 1947, 3rd edition, 1972, translation by R. Altevogt published as *Evolution Above the Species Level,* Methuen, 1959, Columbia University Press, 1960; *Homo sapiens: Vom Tier zum Halbgott,* Vandenhoeck & Ruprecht, 1959, 3rd edition, 1970, translation by C.A.M. Sym published as *Homo Sapiens: From Man to Demigod,* Columbia University

Press, 1972; *Biophilosophie auf erkenntnistheoretischer Grundlage (Panpsychistischer Identismus),* G. Fischer, 1968, translation by Sym published as *Biophilosophy,* Columbia University Press, 1971.

In German: *Das Prinzip geographischer Rassenkreise und das Problem der Artbildung* (title means "The Principle of Complexes of Geographical Races and the Problem of Speciation"), Gebrueder Borntraeger, 1929; *Eine biologische Reise nach den Kleinen Sunda-Inseln* (title means "A Biological Voyage to the Lesser Sunda Islands"), Gebrueder Borntraeger, 1930; *Kurz Anweisung fuer zoologisch-systematische Studien* (title means "Brief Instruction for Zoological Systematical Studies"), Akademische verlagsgesellschaft, 1934; *Die Geschichte des Sundabogens: Eine tiergeographische Untersuchung* (title means "The History of the Sunda Islands: A Zoogeographical Investigation"), Gebrueder Borntraeger, 1936; *Psychische Komponenten der Sinnesorgane: Eine psychophysische Hypothese* (title means "Psychic Components of the Sense Organs: A Psychological Hypothesis"), G. Thieme, 1952.

(With Gerti Duecker) *Biologie II: Zoologie,* Taschenbuch Verlag, 1963; (editor) *Handgebrauch und Verstaendigung bei Affen und Fruehmenschen* (title means "Use of Hands and Communication in Apes and Early Man"), Huber, 1968; *Probleme der Gedaechtnisspuren* (title means "Problems of Memory Traces"), Westdeutscher Verlag, 1971; *Gedaechtnis, Abstraktion, und Generalisation bei Tieren* (title means "Memory, Abstraction, and Generalization in Animals"), Parey, 1973; *Lebensweg eines Biologen in einem turbulenten Jahrhundert* (title means "Way of Life of a Biologist in an Ambivalent Century"), G. Fischer, 1979; *Gesetzlichkeit, psychophysischen Zusammenhang, Willensfreiheit, und Ethik* (title means "Lawfulness, Psychophysical Relations, Freedom of Will, and Ethics"), Duncker & Humblot, 1979. Contributor to scholarly journals.

WORK IN PROGRESS: Research on animal learning and memory.

SIDELIGHTS: Rensch wrote that his scientific goal has not so much been to become a good specialist in evolution and animal behavior, but "to get a biologically and philosophically realistic picture of the world." He continued: "I hold the opinion that the development from the origin of the solar system and the earth to the origin of life, of a phylogenetic tree of plants and animals up to man, was a continuous, lawful process guided 'polynomistically,' that is to say by the laws of causality, universal laws of logic and probability, and microphysical constants and relations. This opinion supposes that matter and mind have a neutral, ambivalent basis (which was already assumed by Spinoza)."

*   *   *

REYNOLDS, Julia Louise   1883(?)-1980

OBITUARY NOTICE: Born c. 1883 in LaGrange, Tenn.; died November 30, 1980, in Richmond, Va. Philanthropist and poet. Reynolds was the widow of Richard Samuel Reynolds, founder of Reynolds Metals Co., one of the largest aluminum producers in the country. Best known for her philanthropic activities, she was the president of the R. S. Reynolds Foundation and a benefactress to the Union Theological Seminary to which she donated 465 acres of land in Goochland County, Va. She wrote three volumes of poetry. Obituaries and other sources: *Washington Post,* December 3, 1980.

REYNOLDS, Paul R(evere) 1904-

PERSONAL: Born July 21, 1904, in New York, N.Y.; son of Paul R. and Amelia (Stead) Reynolds; married Ruth Wood, March 21, 1940; children: Mary (Mrs. John W. Hawkins), Rebecca (Mrs. H. James Stahl), Jane (Mrs. Eric Swain). *Education:* Williams College, B.A., 1926. *Home:* 828A Heritage Village, Southbury, Conn. 06488.

CAREER: Paul R. Reynolds, Inc. (literary agents), New York, N.Y., president, 1956-70; writer, 1970—. *Member:* Society of Authors' Representatives (president, 1968-69, 1970-71, 1972-73), Century Association, Dutch Treat Club.

WRITINGS: The Writing Trade, Writer, Inc., 1949; *The Writer and His Markets,* Doubleday, 1959; *The Writing and Selling of Nonfiction,* Doubleday, 1963; *The Writing and Selling of Fiction,* Morrow, 1965; *A Professional Guide to Marketing Manuscripts,* Writer, Inc., 1968; *The Nonfiction Book,* Morrow, 1969; *The Middle Man,* Morrow, 1972; *Guy Carleton* (biography), Morrow, 1980.

SIDELIGHTS: A former literary agent, Paul R. Reynolds has penned how-to books for writers of fiction and nonfiction. Aimed at the novice writer, Reynolds's guidebooks offer advice about cultivating and researching ideas, preparing and revising manuscripts, and dealing with publishers and literary agents. All of Reynolds's instructional books have been praised for their straightforward answers to the questions raised by beginning writers. *Saturday Review* remarked of *The Nonfiction Book,* "In the how-to genre this is a well-nigh perfect work."

In *The Middle Man: The Adventures of a Literary Agent,* Reynolds discusses his years as an agent, expounding upon tricks of the trade and supplying anecdotes about his experiences in the publishing industry.

BIOGRAPHICAL/CRITICAL SOURCES: Saturday Review, March 14, 1970.

*   *   *

RICHARDS, Dennis L(ee) 1938-

PERSONAL: Born July 7, 1938, in Garland, Utah; son of Elmer Thomas (a farmer) and Mildred Elizabeth (Johnson) Richards; married Judy Hess, June 11, 1961; children: Denise, Galen H, Lori Kay, Sheldon Lee, Paul Quintin, Julie Anne, Vicki Elizabeth. *Education:* Utah State University, B.S., 1962; Florida State University, M.A.L.S., 1963. *Religion:* Church of Jesus Christ of Latter-day Saints (Mormons). *Home:* 2 Kasota Court, Missoula, Mont. 59801. *Office:* Mansfield Library, University of Montana, Missoula, Mont. 59812.

CAREER: Indiana State University, Terre Haute, assistant teaching materials librarian, 1963-65, documents librarian, 1965-67; University of Montana, Missoula, documents librarian, 1968—, professor of library science, 1980—. Librarian for Missoula branch of Montana Genealogical Library. *Member:* Montana Library Association, Western Montana Genealogical Society (member of board of directors).

WRITINGS: (Editor) *Montana's Genealogical and Local History Records,* Gale, 1981. Editor of *Western Montana Genealogical Society Bulletin,* 1981—.

WORK IN PROGRESS: A directory of Montana's church records from the beginning to 1980; a Montana cemetery directory.

SIDELIGHTS: Richards wrote: "I have taught genealogical research classes in the community and on campus. I have attended seminars in Provo, and on August 12, 1980, pre-

sented 'How to Use Indexes to U.S. Government Documents for Family History Data' at the World Conference on Records in Salt Lake City."

*   *   *

RICHLAND, W(ilfred) Bernard 1909-

PERSONAL: Born March 25, 1909, in Liverpool, England; came to the United States in 1925, naturalized citizen, 1932; son of Julius (a tailor, adventurer, and seaman) and Esther Richland; married Pauline Diamond, July 8, 1933; children: Robin Richland Silverton, Lisa Richland Maciejak. *Education:* Attended New York University, 1932-36. *Home:* 75 Henry St., Brooklyn, N.Y. 11201. *Agent:* Steve Axelrod, Curtis Brown Ltd., 575 Madison Ave., New York, N.Y. 10022. *Office:* 200 Park Ave., New York, N.Y. 10166.

CAREER: Admitted to Bars of New York, 1937, U.S. Supreme Court, and U.S. Court of Appeals; office boy, clerk, and law associate of Judge Samuel Seabury, in New York City, 1925-43; City of New York, Law Department, New York City, assistant corporation counsel and acting corporation counsel, 1943-58, chief of Opinions and Legislation Division, 1944-58; Baer Marks, New York City, partner, 1958-64; O'Dwyer & Bernstein, New York City, counsel, 1964-73; City of New York, general counsel to State Charter Revision Commission, 1973-75, corporation counsel, 1975-77; New York Supreme Court, Appellate Division, referee in attorney disciplinary proceedings, 1978—. Adjunct professor of local government law at New York Law School, 1978—. Member of New York City mayor's advisory committee on rent control, 1960-65, mayoralty transition team, 1973-74, committee on the judiciary, 1974-75, policy committee and board of ethics, 1975-77, member of executive committee of Public Development Corp. and Criminal Justice Coordinating Council, 1975-77; special counsel to New York World's Fair Corp., 1964-65. Counsel to Nassau County Commission on Governmental Revision, 1964-66, and Botein, Hays, Sklar & Herzberg, 1978—. Member of Commission on Home Rule, New York State Office for Local Government, 1960-64; member of technical advisory committee of New York-New Jersey-Connecticut Metropolitan Regional Council, 1960-65. Member of advisory board of Kings County Hospital, 1958-75, and board of trustees of National Institute of Municipal Law Officers, 1975-77. *Member:* National Municipal League, American Academy of Political and Social Science, Authors Guild, Authors League of America, New York County Lawyers Association (chairman of Committee on the City of New York), Association of the Bar of the City of New York.

WRITINGS: You Can Beat City Hall, Rawson, Wade, 1980. Contributor to magazines, newspapers, and law journals. Member of editorial board of *New York Law Journal,* 1980—.

WORK IN PROGRESS: A book about the New York City fiscal crisis of 1975; children's stories; recollections of Liverpool in the 1914-25 period.

SIDELIGHTS: Richland told *CA:* "I have been writing all my adult life and have a long string of credits. But I discovered that you don't officially become an 'author' until you publish in hardcover, get an advance, have your book issued by a commercial book publisher, and appear on television and radio in New York City and all over the land. *You Can Beat City Hall* is the only work of its kind. I hope to match its quality in my future books."

RICHTER, Vernon
   See HUTCHCROFT, Vera

* * *

RINGDALH, Mark
   See LONGYEAR, Barry Brookes

* * *

RINZEMA, Jakob 1931-

PERSONAL: Born May 26, 1931, in Groningen, Netherlands; son of Jan (a railroad worker) and Nauta (Berendina) Rinzema; married Geziena Schreuder, July 13, 1956; children: Jan, Reinout, Bernarda Gerdien. *Education:* Attended Free University, Amsterdam, 1949-56; Theological Seminary, Kampen, Ph.D., 1960. *Home:* Soesterbergsestraat 99, 3768 EC Soest, Netherlands. *Agent:* J. H. Kok B.V., Gildestraat 5, Kampen, Netherlands.

CAREER: Ordained pastor of Reformed Church of Netherlands; pastor of several churches in Aalten, Leeuwarden, and Soest, Netherlands, 1969. Advisor to the general assembly of Reformed churches in Netherlands, 1970; chairman of pastoral board of Reformed churches of Holland. *Member:* National Family Council of Churches, Ethical Society of Holland.

WRITINGS: Huwelijk en Echtscheiding (title means "Marriage and Divorce"), Graafschap, 1960; *De sexuele Revolutie,* Kok Kampen, 1972, translation by L. B. Smedes published as *The Sexual Revolution,* Eerdmans, 1973; *Over lief de gesproken* (title means "Spoken About Love"), Voorhoeve, 1977. Contributor of articles to newspapers.

WORK IN PROGRESS: Researching "the use of modern communication theories for pastoral practice."

SIDELIGHTS: Rinzema told *CA:* "My concern in writing books is to make the message of the gospel a strong influence in the field of human and social relations. I have received great inspiration from Dietrich Bonhoeffer and his work, *Widerstand und Ergebung,* in which he poses the question of what it means to be a believer in Jesus Christ. Another source of inspiration is the current developments in the Roman Catholic church and its search for 'aggiornamento' or renewal."

AVOCATIONAL INTERESTS: Music, literature, the problems of mass communication.

* * *

RITTS, Paul 1920(?)-1980

OBITUARY NOTICE: Born c. 1920; died of a heart attack, October 18, 1980, in Monroe, Mich. Producer, director, performer, and writer. Ritts was best known as a creator of children's television shows. He produced "The Big Top," a circus program, and with his wife, Mary, he created the Ritts Puppets for CBS-TV's "In the Park." The puppets achieved celebrity status by appearing regularly in two children's series and through appearances on the television variety shows of Ed Sullivan, Merv Griffin, Mike Douglas, and the "Tonight" shows. Ritts wrote *The TV Jeebies,* a humorous book about television. His plays include "The Quartet," "Oregon Bound," and "A Piece of Cake." He also wrote scripts for children's television series. Obituaries and other sources: *New York Times,* November 20, 1980.

* * *

RIVIERE, Claude 1932-

PERSONAL: Born December 24, 1932, in Curzon, France;

son of Joseph (a blacksmith) and Maria (a dressmaker; maiden name, Ageneau) Riviere; married Anne Chauvigne (a teacher); children: Siegfried, Annabelle. *Education:* University of Poitiers, lic., 1959, D.Phil., 1964; Sorbonne, University of Paris, Ph.D., 1975. *Religion:* Roman Catholic. *Home:* 7 Allee du Mali, 94260 Fresnes, France. *Office:* Department of Social Sciences, University of Paris V, 12 rue Cujas, 75005 Paris, France.

CAREER: University of Angers, Angers, France, lecturer in logic and sociology, 1960-64; Polytechnic Institute, Conakry, Guinea, senior lecturer in sociology and dean of faculty of social sciences, 1964-68; Sorbonne University of Paris, Paris, France, maitre assistant, 1968-76; University of Benin, Lome, Togo, maitre de conferences of sociology and anthropology and head of department of philosophy and social sciences, 1976-80; University of Paris V, Paris, professor of sociology and anthropology, 1980—. *Military service:* French transmission, 1955-58; served in Algeria. *Awards, honors:* Prix L. Marin from Academie des Sciences d'Outre Mer, 1978, for *Classes et stratifications sociales en Afrique.*

WRITINGS: Guinea: The Mobilization of a People, translated from the original French by Virginia Adloff and Richard Adloff, Cornell University Press, 1977.

In French: *L'Objet social: Essai d'epistemologie sociologique* (title means "The Social Object: Essay in Sociological Epistemology"), Marcel Riviere, 1969; *Mutations sociales en Guinee* (title means "Social Mutations in Guinea"), Marcel Riviere, 1977; *Classes et stratifications sociales en Afrique* (title means "Classes and Social Stratifications in Africa"), Presses Universitaires de France, 1978; *L'Analyse dynamique en sociologie* (title means "Dynamic Analysis in Sociology"), Presses Universitaires de France, 1978; *Anthropologie religieuse des Eve* (title means "Religious Anthropology of the Eve [Togo]"), Nouvelles Editions Africaines, 1980; *Politique et religion dans les nouveaux etats* (title means "Politics and Religion in the New States"), Presses Universitaires de France, in press.

Translator; with wife, Anne Riviere: Edward Evans-Pritchard, *La femme dans la societe primitive* (title means "The Position of Women in Primitive Societies"), Presses Universitaires de France, 1971; Evans-Pritchard, *Les Anthropologues face a l'histoire et a la religion* (title means "Essays in Social Anthropology"), Presses Universitaires de France, 1974; Karl Polanyi and Conrad Arensberg, *Les Systemes economiques dans l'histoire et dans la theorie* (title means "Trade and Markets in the Early Empires"), Larousse, 1974; Stanislas Andreski, *Les Sciences sociales, sorcellerie des temps modernes* (title means "Social Sciences as Sorcery"), Presses Universitaires de France, 1975.

Contributor to journals in the social sciences.

SIDELIGHTS: Riviere told *CA:* "The analysis of conflicts must be used as a preferential revealer in the study of any kind of social dynamics whose theoretical patterns of explanation I set out. One of the great social changes in modern Africa consists of borrowing language, value, and behavior paradigms from religion to transmit ideology and ritualize political life."

* * *

ROBERTS, Benjamin Charles 1917-

PERSONAL: Born August 1, 1917, in Leeds, England; son of Walter Whitfield (a grocer) and Mabel (Maclean) Roberts; married Veronica Lilian Vine-Lott, September 29, 1945; children: Richard Whitfield, David Charles. *Education:* Attended London School of Economics and Political Science, London, 1945-46; New College, Oxford, M.A., 1948. *Office:* Department of Industrial Relations, London School of Economics and Political Science, University of London, Houghton St., Aldwych, London WC2A 2AE, England.

CAREER: University of London, London School of Economics and Political Science, London, England, lecturer, 1949-56, reader, 1956-62, professor of industrial relations, 1962—, member of court of governors. Chairman of Economists' Bookshop. Member of council of Advisory Conciliation and Arbitration Service; member of National Reference Tribunal of the Mining Industry; consultant to European Economic Community and Organization for Economic Cooperation and Development. *Member:* International Industrial Relations Association (president, 1967-73), British Universities Industrial Relations Association (president, 1965-68).

WRITINGS: Trade Union Government and Administration in Great Britain, G. Bell, 1956; *The Trades Union Congress, 1868-1921,* Allen & Unwin, 1958; *National Wages Policy in War and Peace,* Allen & Unwin, 1958; *Unions in America,* Princeton University, 1959; *Trade Unions in a Free Society,* Hutchinson, 1959, 2nd edition, 1962.

(Editor) *Industrial Relations,* Methuen, 1962, 3rd edition, 1968; *Labour in the Tropical Territories of the Commonwealth,* Duke University Press, 1964; (with L. Greyfie de Bellecombe) *Collective Bargaining in African Countries,* Macmillan, 1967; (editor) *Industrial Relations: Contemporary Issues,* Macmillan, 1968; (with John Lovell) *A Short History of the Trades Union Congress,* Macmillan, 1968.

Trade Unions: The Challenge Before Them, Foundation for Business Responsibilities, 1971; (with R. D. Clarke and D. J. Fatchett) *Workers Participation in Management,* Heinemann Educational Books, 1972; (with Raymond Loveridge and John Gennard) *Reluctant Militants: A Study of Industrial Technicians,* Heinemann Educational Books, 1972; (editor) *Towards Industrial Democracy,* Croom Helm, 1979; (with H. Okomoto and George C. Lodge) *Collective Bargaining and Employee Participation in Western Europe, North America, and Japan,* Trilateral Commission, 1979. Editor of *British Journal of Industrial Relations,* 1963—.

WORK IN PROGRESS: Research on multinational enterprise, comparative industrial relations systems, and pay policies.

SIDELIGHTS: Roberts told *CA:* "The growth of multinational business has been the most important means of transfering capital, technology, and modern managerial methods from advanced to less developed countries. Without this evolution of multinational business, world economic development and world welfare would have developed much more slowly during the past half century. Trade union efforts to prevent this development would have been damaging to their members had they been successful. Attempts to develop international guidelines are only likely to work to the general advantage if they do not discriminate against multinationals."

*   *   *

ROBERTS, MacLennan
    See TERRALL, Robert

ROBERTS, Sally
    See JONES, Sally Roberts

*   *   *

ROBERTS, Sheila   1942-

PERSONAL: Born May 25, 1942, in Johannesburg, South Africa; came to the United States in 1977; daughter of Gideon P. and Claire M. (Freestone) Williamson; married Peter Roberts, January 17, 1963 (died April 19, 1971); married Philip C. McGuire (a professor), June 20, 1980; children: (first marriage) Sandra, Kelly. *Education:* University of South Africa, B.A. (with honors), 1967, M.A., 1972; University of Pretoria, Ph.D., 1977. *Home:* 6393 Reynolds Rd. W., Haslett, Mich. 48840. *Office:* Department of English, Michigan State University, East Lansing, Mich. 48824.

CAREER: Performing Arts Council, Transvaal, South Africa, literary consultant, 1974-75; University of Pretoria, Pretoria, South Africa, lecturer in English, 1975-77; Michigan State University, East Lansing, assistant professor of Commonwealth and African studies, 1977—. *Member:* Modern Language Association of America, Detroit Women Writers. *Awards, honors:* Olive Schreiner Award for prose from English Academy of South Africa, 1975, for *Outside Life's Feast;* Teacher-Scholar Award from Michigan State University, 1980.

WRITINGS: Outside Life's Feast (short stories), A. D. Donker, 1975; *Lou's Life and Other Poems,* Bateleur Press, 1976; *He's My Brother* (novel), A.D. Donker, 1977; *Johannesburg Requiem* (novel), Taplinger, 1980; *The Weekenders* (novel), Bateleur Press, 1981; *Don Jacobson,* Twayne, 1981.

Work represented in anthologies, including *On the Edge of the World,* Ad Donker, 1979, *Sudafrika* (German translation), Horst Erdmann Verlag, 1978, and *Modern South African Short Stories,* Ad Donker, 1981.

Contributor of stories to magazines, including *Cavalier, Fair Lady, New Nation, Contrast,* and *Short Story International.*

SIDELIGHTS: Sheila Roberts wrote: "The political situation in South Africa has strongly influenced my writing, as well as the existence of the 'underdogs'—blacks, women, children, failures. My interest still lies with Africa, even though I am now a resident in the United States, and my university research all centers on Africa. That continent still appears in most of my writing."

*   *   *

ROBERTSON, Mary D(emmond)   1927-

PERSONAL: Born November 9, 1927, in Savannah, Ga.; daughter of E. Carson (a physician) and Mary Choate (a registered nurse; maiden name, Baker) Demmond; married Mason Gordon Robertson (a physician), August 9, 1952; children: Mary Lynn Robertson Zirkle, William Preston, Susan Radford. *Education:* Hollins College, A.B., 1945; Armstrong State College, M.Ed., 1975. *Politics:* Democrat. *Religion:* Episcopalian. *Home:* 1221 Lawndale Rd., Savannah, Ga. 31406. *Office:* Department of History and Political Science, Armstrong State College, Savannah, Ga. 31406.

CAREER: Armstrong State College, Savannah, Ga., part-time instructor in history, 1975—. Vice-president of Hollins College Alumnae Board; past chairman of Help Our Public Education; past member of board of directors of Chatham Council on Human Relations and Greenbrier Children's Center. *Member:* Organization of American Historians, League of Women Voters (past president), Oral History Association, National Trust for Historic Preservation,

Southern Historical Association, Georgia Historical Society, Roanoke Valley Historical Society, Phi Alpha Theta (president of Sigma Theta chapter, 1974-75).

WRITINGS: (Editor) *Lucy Breckinridge of Grove Hill: Journal of a Virginia Girl, 1862-1864,* Kent State University Press, 1980. Contributor to history journals.

WORK IN PROGRESS: Editing family letters of the Breckinridge family, focusing on Lucy Breckinridge's mother, Emma Walker Gilmer Breckinridge, publication expected in 1982.

SIDELIGHTS: Mary Robertson wrote: "Although I am not a Grandma Moses, I am a late-bloomer in regard to my academic career and writing career, having returned to academia after an absence of twenty-two years. My advice to older women is: avoid the empty nest syndrome, seek personal fulfillment in a career of your own. It's never too late to develop interests and talents!"

*   *   *

ROBINSON, Jill   1936-
(Jill Schary, Jill Schary Zimmer)

PERSONAL: Born May 30, 1936, in Los Angeles, Calif.; daughter of Dore (a playwright, director, and film producer) and Miriam (a painter; maiden name, Svet) Schary; married Jon Zimmer (a stockbroker), January 8, 1956 (divorced, 1966); married Jeremiah Robinson (a computer analyst), April 7, 1968 (divorced, 1977); married Stuart Shaw (a consultant and writer), June 21, 1980; children: Jeremy Zimmer, Johanna Schary Robinson. *Education:* Attended Stanford University, 1954-55. *Politics:* "Left-wing eclectic." *Religion:* Jewish. *Home:* 6 Willow Rd., Weston, Conn. 06883. *Agent:* Lynn Nesbit, International Creative Management, 40 West 57th St., New York, N.Y. 10019.

CAREER: Foote, Cone & Belding, Los Angeles, Calif., advertising copywriter, 1956-57; free-lance journalist, 1964—; free-lance book reviewer, 1973—. Host of "The Jill Schary Show" on KLAC-Radio in Los Angeles, 1966-68. Writing teacher at Womanschool in New York, N.Y., 1975-77.

WRITINGS: (Under name Jill Schary Zimmer) *With a Cast of Thousands: A Hollywood Childhood* (autobiographical), Stein & Day, 1963; (under name Jill Schary) *Thanks for the Rubies, Now Please Pass the Moon,* Dial, 1972; *Bed/Time/Story* (autobiographical), Random House, 1974; *Perdido* (novel), Knopf, 1978; *Doctor Rocksinger and the Age of Longing* (novel), Knopf, 1981. Contributor to periodicals, including *Cosmopolitan, Vogue, House and Garden, New York Times, Los Angeles Times, Soho Weekly News, Chicago Tribune,* and *Village Voice.*

SIDELIGHTS: Robinson's first book, *With a Cast of Thousands,* is about her childhood in Hollywood as the daughter of Dore Schary, the head of production at Metro-Goldwyn-Mayer (MGM). Robinson relates anecdotes about such personalities as John F. Kennedy, Loretta Young, Adlai Stevenson, Elizabeth Taylor, Marlon Brando, and Humphrey Bogart. C. P. Collier of *Best Sellers* commented that *With a Cast of Thousands* "could easily have become over-the-backyard-fence gossip, but even the most barbed ... observations, while sometimes hilariously perceptive, are devoid of maliciousness." *Book Week*'s Joe Hyams similarly noted that Robinson tells "with astonishing frankness stories about her schoolmates, the multi-parented children of Hollywood's famous folk." He continued, however, that "the reader is never embarrassed for the people she so hilariously dissects, analyzes and pins down on paper with needle-sharp words."

Bed/Time/Story also met with a favorable reception. The book details the story of Robinson's second marriage to Jeremiah Robinson. "It is about two people whose love for each other slowly conquered their hatred for themselves," explained Annie Gottlieb of the *New York Times Book Review.* "It is, quite literally, about the lifesaving and healing power of love." With her husband's help, Robinson quit drinking and taking speed, acquired a good job, and began to piece her life together again. Gottlieb further stated: "Robinson portrays herself, with candor and humor, as having been so anxious to please, so terrified of rejection, so padded and propped by drugs, that she had no idea what she wanted or felt. The book tells about her discovery of herself, not as is currently fashionable, through lonely search, but through the unexpected, ferocious strength of her feeling for another." *Nation*'s Nancy Lynn Schwartz contended that "*Bed/Time/Story* ... [is] a beautifully written book which forces the reader to care about the characters and their fate."

Critics were also impressed with Robinson's next book. *Perdido* is about teenager Susanna Howard, the granddaughter of a Hollywood pioneer who founded his own film studios. Susanna narrates this story about Hollywood in the 1950's, during the cold war, blacklisting, and the rise of television. Tinged with an "epic, rather tragic flavor," as Schwartz described it, *Perdido* tells of things lost or soon to be lost. The heroine searches for her father, who left when she was still an infant. She is unhappy with her remote mother and stepfather and longs for the love of her missing parent. Constantly comparing real life to life in the movies, Susanna speculates that her grandfather "invented the happy American family and put it into the movies to drive everyone crazy." Reviewer Kevin Scott compared *Perdido* with F. Scott Fitzgerald's *The Last Tycoon,* because "it is the first 'Hollywood' novel [able] to stand the comparison." He asserted, though, that Robinson was less nostalgic in her portrayal than Scott: "*Perdido* is a realist's rebuttal of 'The Last Tycoon.' And in its own way, it's just as good."

CA INTERVIEW
Jill Robinson was interviewed by *CA* in New York City on August 1, 1980.

Jill Robinson does not have to look far to find her story ideas: she writes about her life. "Life is the rough draft," she explained. "When I step into precarious situations, I always have a sense I'll pull through, because I have to write about it later." For this reason, Robinson takes seeming tragedy—two failed marriages, alcoholism and drug addiction, the near-fatal stabbing of her son, Jeremy—and turns it into a frank appraisal of life in all its chaos. "It seems like there's always something, just when things seem to be going okay. But this is reality; it is up to the writer to notice, to attempt to make order, to find meaning, in the changes and losses all of us go through."

Her typical writing cycle is to take the material from recent periods of high drama and write about them during the peaceful lulls in between. *Bed/Time/Story,* Robinson asserted, is the autobiography of her second marriage, and her novel, *Doctor Rocksinger and the Age of Longing,* is a "fictionalized" account of an affair she had with a younger man after her second husband left her. "It was an engaging experience; it got me over the image of myself as an abandoned woman. I also tried in this book to begin to move outside of myself. Nothing is unsuitable to write about. As I'm living through it, I'm seeing it in words, shaping life into scenes.

Writers are fortunate: we get to explore and re-examine our experiences several times."

Robinson grew up in Hollywood, Calif., during the 1940's and 1950's. Daughter of the late MGM executive and playwright Dore Schary, she says the ambience of that period is something she will return to again and again in her work. "It interests me to write about the way it really was—that way *we felt* it was, anyway—and there is a difference between those two." Her novel, *Perdido*, depicts this world vividly. Robinson's childhood instilled in her the feeling that life was a movie that could be stopped during the bad parts and done better the next time. It also gave her a well-developed sense of fantasy, high drama, and romanticism, which has sometimes led her down dark alleys, such as her amphetamine habit during her Los Angeles radio talk show days. "I used speed to trigger discipline. I never thought I could write without it."

It was during this period she wrote *Thanks for the Rubies, Now Please Pass the Moon,* a book she adores and says is filled with "total lunacy. Only 119 people in the whole world ever bought that book. But I love it the very best of all my books. I have a fantasy someday of meeting a person who has actually finished it, and liked it, and will sit down with me and tell me what it was about."

The drug and alcohol abuse are behind Robinson now, and she works informally in treatment centers near her home in Weston, Conn., helping others with similar problems. "I used to be very committed to political action, but somehow today working for candidates doesn't seem as useful as working directly for people."

She has also instilled into her life the measure of discipline necessary for a professional writer. "Structuring your time, and having the ability to juggle family, work, and outside commitments, are essential to a writer. I'd say they're even more essential than insight, or overwhelming inspirations." Interestingly, it took Robinson two years as a salesclerk in a New York City department store—a period in which she did not write at all—to learn the discipline she needed to get back to her typewriter.

Her one abiding obsession—the passion that has followed her from the beginning—is a desire to be famous. "It's something I once wanted more than anything in the world, and it's something I still wrestle with now. I initially started writing as an escape that would lead to instant fame—if only I could finish the perfect novel. I just can't imagine anyone not wanting to be famous." Robinson believes the root of her desire goes back to her Hollywood days, when fame was considered the path to immortality. "Then again," she mused, "I don't understand the motivations behind my obsessions completely. I'm not certain I want to know. I used to feel that if I understood myself, perhaps I would not have anything to write about anymore. However, I also think that understanding myself will unleash me from self-involvement; I may move forward in my work and become a deeper, better writer with a richer style, a sounder purpose: the exploration of feelings, the dedication to words as the unique private code between a writer and his or her world."

BIOGRAPHICAL/CRITICAL SOURCES: Best Sellers, November 1, 1963; *Book Week,* December 22, 1963; *New York Times Book Review,* October 27, 1974, April 23, 1978; *Nation,* April 22, 1978; *Newsweek,* April 24, 1978; *Washington Post,* May 2, 1978; *Harper,* August, 1978; *Times Literary Supplement,* September 22, 1978; *Contemporary Literary Criticism,* Volume 10, Gale, 1979.

—*Interview by Trisha Gorman*

ROCH, John H(enry) 1916-

PERSONAL: Surname is pronounced "Rock"; born August 24, 1916, in Albany, N.Y.; son of Albert H. (a bookkeeper) and Matilda (Wood) Roch; married Katherine Anne Dwyer (a teacher), October 28, 1944; children: Joanne, John M., Joseph, Michael, Katherine. *Education:* Attended North Adams State College, 1939-41; University of Massachusetts, B.A. (cum laude), 1945; Columbia University, M.A., 1947, Ph.D., 1958. *Politics:* Democrat. *Religion:* Roman Catholic. *Home:* 130 North Woodbury Rd., Pitman, N.J. 08071. *Office:* Department of English, Glassboro State College, Glassboro, N.J. 08028.

CAREER: University of Maryland, College Park, instructor in English, 1948-50; Clarkson College of Technology, Potsdam, N.Y., instructor, 1952-54, assistant professor, 1954-58, associate professor of English, 1958-59; Glassboro State College, Glassboro, N.J., associate professor, 1959-62, professor of English, 1962—, chairman of department, 1968-74. Adjunct teacher for U.S. Department of Agriculture and Aluminum Co. of America. Member of National Endowment for the Humanities project on work, leisure, and rapidity of change. *Military service:* U.S. Army, 1943-46; served in European theater; became sergeant.

MEMBER: Modern Language Association of America, College English Association, American Federation of Teachers, American Association of University Professors (president, 1963-64), New Jersey Association of Teachers of English, Glassboro Faculty Association (president, 1970-71), Phi Kappa Phi.

WRITINGS: (Editor with Donald Yannella) *American Prose to 1820,* Gale, 1979. Contributor to *Writers' Forum.*

WORK IN PROGRESS: Research on character displacement in the work of Mark Twain.

SIDELIGHTS: John Roch told *CA*: "Having spent the middle years of my life teaching and participating fully in the academic life (administration of a department, consultations, committee work, leadership in professional organizations), I hope to be able to devote more of my time to my first love—writing. My expectations are modest—a few articles, a story or two, maybe a book."

AVOCATIONAL INTERESTS: European travel, camping, tennis, fishing, a summer home in Cape May, N.J.

*   *   *

ROCK, James M(artin) 1935-

PERSONAL: Born August 17, 1935, in Plymouth, Wis.; son of Carroll George (a farmer) and Lillian (Leverenz) Rock; married Bonnie Brown (a teacher), August 20, 1962; children: Jennifer, Peter, James, Sara. *Education:* University of Wisconsin (now University of Wisconsin—Madison), B.S., 1957, M.S., 1960; Northwestern University, Ph.D., 1966. *Home:* 2016 Laird Dr., Salt Lake City, Utah 84108. *Office:* Department of Economics, University of Utah, Salt Lake City, Utah 84112.

CAREER: Central Intelligence Agency, Langley, Va., economist, 1964-66; Wisconsin State University (now University of Wisconsin), Oshkosh, assistant professor of economics, 1966-67; University of Utah, Salt Lake City, assistant professor, 1967-72, associate professor of economics, 1972—. Member of board of trustees of Alberta Henry Education Foundation, 1967—, and board of directors of Salt Lake City Youth Hostel, 1972—. *Member:* American Economic Association, American Civil Liberties Union, Planned Parenthood, Delta Epsilon, Omicron Delta Epsilon, Phi Kappa Phi.

WRITINGS: The Wisconsin Aluminum Cookware Industry Prior to World War II, Metal Cookware Manufacturers Association, 1967; (editor) *Money, Banking, and Macroeconomics: A Guide to Information Sources*, Gale, 1977; *A Blend of the Two* (biography), University of Utah Press, 1978. Contributor of articles and reviews to professional journals and national magazines, including *Intellect*. Editor of *U.S.A. Today*.

WORK IN PROGRESS: Research on the symmetry between product and factor analyses, teaching macroeconomics with computer models, symmetry of neoclassical firms and households, evolution of house-staff market and institutional arrangements, and time-fine ratios and the welfare cost of inflation.

SIDELIGHTS: James Rock commented: "I believe the microeconomic foundations of macroeconomic economics are important in economic education. The circular-flow diagram of the economy (found in almost every principles-of-economics textbook) is a treasure trove of symmetries between firms and households and factor markets and product markets that have not been exploited for economic education. This is the main area of my current research."

* * *

ROGERS, Donald I(rwin) 1918-1980

OBITUARY NOTICE—See index for *CA* sketch: Born November 17, 1918, in New Hartford, Conn.; died November 4, 1980, in New York. Editor and author best known for his conservative economic views. Rogers was the economic editor of the Hearst newspapers. Prior to his association with the Hearst organization, he was a columnist and the business and financial news editor of the *New York Herald Tribune*. His writings include *Teach Your Wife to Be a Widow, The Trials of Jimmy Hoffa, How to Beat Inflation by Using It,* and *The Day the Market Crashed: October 24, 1929.* Obituaries and other sources: *New York Times,* November 6, 1980; *Chicago Tribune,* November 8, 1980.

* * *

ROGERS, Elyse M(acFadyen) 1932-

PERSONAL: Born September 28, 1932, in New Jersey; daughter of Frank H. and Silvia E. (Simms) MacFadyen; married Edward W. Rogers (a chemical company president), July 18, 1952; children: Pamela Rogers Dawson, Cynthia, Jenifer. *Education:* Indiana University, B.S.; Purdue University, M.A.; Mountainside Hospital School of Nursing, R.N. *Politics:* Republican. *Religion:* Episcopalian. *Agent:* Julian Bach Literary Agency, Inc., 747 Third Ave., New York, N.Y. 10017. *Office address:* P.O. Box 1425, Midland, Mich. 48640.

CAREER: Saginaw General Hospital, Saginaw, Mich., instructor in nursing, 1955-56; E.J. Meyer Memorial Hospital, instructor in nursing, 1956-57; Midland Hospital, Midland, Mich., staff nurse, 1975-77; Scientific Syntax Services, Midland, Mich., president, 1979—. Chairman of Midland County Board of Health, 1978—. Associate editor of Writer's Digest Schools, 1963-78. *Member:* American Medical Writers Association (fellow; member of executive committee, 1980—), American Society of Journalists and Authors, Michigan Association of Boards of Health (member of board of directors, 1978—).

WRITINGS: Health in the Home, American Red Cross, 1975. Also author of *Angelina* (historical novel), Berkley Publishing. Author of booklets. Contributor of more than one hundred fifty articles and stories to national magazines, including *Ski, Popular Mechanics, Family Health, Writer,* and *Highlights for Children.* Associate editor of *Medical Communications,* 1978—; past food and dining editor of *Valley.*

WORK IN PROGRESS: A contemporary novel.

SIDELIGHTS: Elyse Rogers wrote: "The largest share of my writing time currently is devoted to writing for business and industry, and my two largest corporate clients are Dow Chemical Co. and Dow Corning Corp. I have written booklets on cancer and life-style and epidemiology for Dow Chemical Co."

* * *

ROGERS, Henry C. 1914-

PERSONAL: Born April 19, 1914, in Irvington, N.J.; son of Maurice and Mildred (Harrison) Rogosin; married Rosalind Jaffe, June 16, 1937; children: Marcia Rogers Medavoy, Ron. *Education:* Attended University of Pennsylvania. *Home:* 130 South Cliffwood Ave., Los Angeles, Calif. 90049. *Office:* Rogers & Cowan, Inc., 9665 Wilshire Blvd., Beverly Hills, Calif. 90212.

CAREER: Founder and chairman of Rogers & Cowan, Inc., Beverly Hills, Calif. President of Center Theatre Group and Los Angeles County Music Center; member of board of trustees of Los Angeles County Art Museum and board of directors of Los Angeles County Music Center Performing Arts Council and Los Angeles International Film Exposition (Filmex). *Member:* Public Relations Society of America, Academy of Motion Picture Arts and Sciences, American Jewish Committee, Hillcrest Country Club. *Awards, honors:* Commendations from American Film Institute, 1979, and Motion Picture and Television Fund.

WRITINGS: Walking the Tightrope, Morrow, 1980.

* * *

ROLAND SMITH, Gordon 1931-

PERSONAL: Born March 6, 1931, in Westcliff-on-Sea, England; son of Stanley George (a builder) and Doris Ree (a teacher; maiden name, Geddes) Smith; married Marjory Gladys Bowen (a teacher), January 19, 1957; children: Hannah Lara, Daniel Marc. *Education:* Attended Southend-on-Sea College of Art, 1946-49, and Stockwell College of Education, 1964-66. *Politics:* "None particularly." *Religion:* "Swedenborgian." *Home and office:* Melilot, Well Hill Lane, Chelsfield, Orpington, Kent BR6 7QJ, England.

CAREER: Teacher at school in Kent, England, 1951-55; Marley Group, Sevenoaks, Kent, graphic designer, 1955-57; teacher in Kent, 1958-64 and 1966-68; Cannock School, Kent, teacher of art and head of department, 1968—. Freelance design consultant. *Military service:* Royal Air Force, 1949-51. *Member:* Society of Industrial Artists and Designers, College of Preceptors (associate), Society of Authors, British Film Institute (fellow), Ancient Monuments Society (fellow), Missionary Society of the New Church (president, 1970-77, 1979—), Swedenborg Society.

WRITINGS: First Models in Cardboard, Dryad Press, 1963; *Creative Crayon Craft,* Cosmic, 1964; *My Side of the Grave* (nonfiction), Seminar Books, 1970; *Making a Model Village,* Wolfe, 1970; *The Zebra Book of Papercraft,* Evans Brothers, 1974; *Make It From Paper,* Evans Brothers, 1975; *Paper for Play,* Evans Brothers, 1975; *Thinks* (philosophy), Seminar Books, 1980; *I Suppose I Shall Survive* (on philosophy of survival), Seminar Books, 1981; *The Educational Uses of*

Paper Fasteners, Evans Brothers, 1981. Contributor to magazines, including *Child Education, Art and Craft, School Arts, New Church,* and *Lifeline.*

SIDELIGHTS: Roland Smith commented: "My writing is of two kinds—practical material for education and religious ideas. They tend to be separate, but there are connections (as in the fields of symbolism and perception). My religious writing is largely inspired and informed by Emanuel Swedenborg, but I don't regard him as a holy oracle. I am interested in the practicalities of book production (such as typography and design) and am able to put such skills to use. I worked in advertising for a bit, but found it rather sordid. The exchange of human ideas about humanity is more imporant."

*　　*　　*

ROLFE, Sheila Constance 1935-

PERSONAL: Born January 4, 1935, in London, England; daughter of Wyndham R.C. (a marine architect) and Kathleen (Wright) Madden; married Marten Havelock Rolfe (a general insurance agent), September 1, 1956; children: Basil, Valerie. *Education:* University of British Columbia, B.A., 1955. *Home:* 3269 West 49th Ave., Vancouver, British Columbia, Canada V6N 3T5.

CAREER: Writer. *Member:* Vancouver Lawn Tennis and Badminton Club.

WRITINGS: Amulets and Arrowheads (juvenile), Burns & MacEachern, 1967; *Sasquatch Adventure* (juvenile), Hancock House, 1975. Writes book reviews for CHQM-Radio. Contributor of humorous articles and reviews to magazines and newspapers.

SIDELIGHTS: Sheila Rolfe told *CA:* "I care about grammar (many writer's don't), and I enjoy whatever is funny in life."

*　　*　　*

ROLL, Eric 1907-

PERSONAL: Born December 1, 1907. *Office:* 30 Gresham St., London EC2P 2EB, England.

CAREER: University of Hull, Hull, England, professor of economics and commerce, 1935-46; Civil Service, London, England, permanent under secretary of state in Department of Economic Affairs, 1964-66; S. G. Warburg & Co. Ltd., London, deputy chairman, 1967-74, chairman, 1974—. *Awards, honors:* Knight commander of St. Michael and St. George; companion of Order of the Bath.

WRITINGS: An Early Experiment in Industrial Organisation, Longmans, Green, 1930; *Spotlight on Germany,* Faber, 1933; *About Money,* Faber, 1934; *Elements of Economic Theory,* Oxford University Press, 1935; *A History of Economic Thought,* Faber, 1938, 4th edition, 1973; *The Combined Food Board,* Stanford University Press, 1957; *The World After Keynes,* Praeger, 1968; *The Uses and Abuses of Economics,* Faber, 1978.

*　　*　　*

ROLPH, C. H.
See HEWITT, Cecil Rolph

*　　*　　*

ROMNEY, Rodney Ross 1931-

PERSONAL: Born January 17, 1931, in Arco, Idaho; son of Daniel Gaskell and Lois Luella (Taylor) Romney; married Beverly Jean Wilcoxon (a homemaking teacher), August 22, 1964. *Education:* Linfield College, B.A., 1954; American

Baptist Seminary of the West, M.Div., 1960, D.Min., 1976. *Politics:* Democrat. *Home:* 1008 Northwest 132nd, Seattle, Wash. 98177. *Office:* First Baptist Church, 1111 Harvard Ave., Seattle, Wash. 98122.

CAREER: Ordained American Baptist minister, 1960; pastor of Baptist church in Oakland, Calif., 1961-79; First Baptist Church, Seattle, Wash., senior minister, 1980—. Broadcast "Hour of Prayer" on KFAX-Radio, 1961-80. Chairman of board of directors of Scandinavian Seamen's Mission, 1963-67; member of executive committee of American Baptist Churches of the West, 1965-68; member of Council of Churches Radio-TV Commission.

WRITINGS: Journey to Inner Space: Finding God in Us, Abingdon, 1980.

WORK IN PROGRESS: A novel for adults; animal parables for children.

SIDELIGHTS: Romney commented: "I wrote my first book in 1976, a spiritual autobiography. It was privately published by my church in Oakland, California, under the title *A Promise of Light* and had sold enough copies through advance sales to finance its first printing. The book has been marketed solely by the church and has had good success, considering its necessarily limited promotion. From there I moved to writing *Journey to Inner Space,* which was instantly accepted by Abingdon Press and is doing well since its release less than a year ago.

"When I can find the time to do so, I continue to write. My deepest interest is to write fiction, but I find it difficult to find long blocks of time to devote to the process of allowing the story to unfold in all its facets. I am the pastor of a large, prestigious church. My congregation has come to expect sermons and newsletter articles of high literary quality, and I try not to disappoint them. What writer could be more fortunate than I, to have a captive audience meet together once a week just to listen to the words you have written!"

*　　*　　*

RONAN, Margaret 1918-

PERSONAL: Born April 25, 1918, in Pueblo, Colo.; daughter of Charles William and Dolores (Worell) Sylvester; married Frank Ronan (a commercial artist and photographer); children: Gabrielle Ronan Streetman, Alan James, Eve. *Education:* Attended Columbia University. *Politics:* None. *Religion:* Society of Friends (Quakers). *Home:* 260-53 Union Turnpike, Floral Park, N.Y. 11004. *Office:* Scholastic Magazines, 50 West 44th St., New York, N.Y. 10036.

CAREER: Scholastic Magazines, New York, N.Y., switchboard operator and secretary, 1937-38, assistant editor of *Junior Scholastic,* 1938-44, associate editor of *Summertime,* 1959-62, and *Voice,* 1962-75, motion picture editor, 1964—. *Member:* American Film Institute.

WRITINGS—For children; all published by Scholastic Book Services, except as noted: All About Our Fifty States, Random House, 1962, revised edition, 1978; (editor) Thomas Hardy, *Tess of the d'Urbervilles,* Barnes & Noble, 1968; (editor) George Eliot, *The Mill on the Floss,* Barnes & Noble, 1969; *Faces on Film,* 1970; *Strange Unsolved Mysteries,* 1975; *The Hindenburg Is Burning,* 1976; (with daughter, Eve Ronan) *Astrology and Other Occult Games,* 1976; *House of Evil and Other Strange Unsolved Mysteries,* 1977; (with E. Ronan) *Death Around the World,* 1977; *Hunt the Witch Down,* 1978; (with E. Ronan) *Curse of the Vampires,* 1978; *Superstars,* 1978; *The Dynamite Monster Hall of Fame,* 1979; *The Dynamite Book of Movies and Movie-Making,*

1979; *Master of the Dead,* 1979; *Dark and Haunted Places,* 1981.

Author of motion picture study guides. Author of columns and regular features in magazines, including ''True UFO Mysteries'' in *Weird Worlds;* ''Weird Unsolved Mysteries'' in *Bananas;* ''Historical Mysteries'' in *Search;* ''True Tales of Terror'' in *Dynamite;* and ''Movies'' in *Senior, Weird Worlds, Search, Scope, Voice,* and *Science World.* Contributor of more than one thousand articles to magazines.

WORK IN PROGRESS: Research on a book about historical blunders and disasters; a book about great battles of World War II, publication by Action Books expected in 1981.

SIDELIGHTS: ''When I was still a child,'' Margaret Ronan told *CA,* ''my mother told me I would be a writer, and I never questioned her. She also insisted I learn stenography in case I couldn't live on writing. I made my first writing money winning second place in a Scholastic poetry contest, and from then on money has been a strong motivation, driving me to turn out three books and one hundred fifty articles in one year. I doubt that I could write if no reward were in view—but you never know.

''I have been lucky enough to be paid to cover the subjects in which I am interested—movies and the occult. My writing schedule is so full that I have no time for outside interests, but if I did it would be to pursue a passion of my youth—making marionettes. I once owned my own puppet theatre.''

*   *   *

RONSMAN, M. M.
See NOWAK, Mariette

*   *   *

ROOD, Karen Lane 1946-

PERSONAL: Born June 25, 1946, in Southampton, N.Y.; daughter of Norman R. (an electrical engineer) and Sheila (Waldron) Lane; married Robert M. Rood (a professor of political science), September 7, 1965; children: Jonathan. *Education:* Syracuse University, B.A. (summa cum laude), 1971; University of South Carolina, M.A., 1973, Ph.D., 1979. *Politics:* Democrat. *Home:* 4221 Blossom St., Columbia, S.C. 29205. *Office:* BC Research, 1210 Pickens St., Columbia, S.C. 29201.

CAREER: BC Research, Bruccoli Clark Publishing Co., Columbia, S.C., editor, 1978—. *Member:* Phi Beta Kappa.

WRITINGS: (Editor) *Dictionary of Literary Biography,* Volume IV: *American Writers in Paris, 1920-1939,* Gale, 1980.

WORK IN PROGRESS: A study of the literary and artistic friendships of Janet Flanner (Genet of *New Yorker*) and her role as a cultural historian of the 1920's and 1930's in Paris.

*   *   *

ROONEY, William Richard 1938-

PERSONAL: Born March 12, 1938, in New Brunswick, N.J.; son of William Richard (a credit manager) and Bernadette (Huether) Rooney; married Rita Ann Scherer, July 20, 1963; children: Karen, Kevin, Brian. *Education:* St. Peter's College, B.A., 1959. *Religion:* Catholic. *Home:* 7916 Carrie Lane, Manassas, Va. 22110. *Office:* American Forestry Association, 1319 18th St. N.W., Washington, D.C. 20036.

CAREER/WRITINGS: Marine Engineering/Log (magazine), New York City, assistant editor, 1960-64; *Outdoor Life,*

New York City, associate editor, 1964-72, managing editor, 1972-76, senior editor, 1976-77; *American Forests,* Washington, D.C., editor, 1977—. Contributor to *Complete Outdoors Encyclopedia,* Harper, 1975. *Military service:* U.S. Army Reserves, 1959-65, active duty, 1959-60. *Member:* Outdoor Writers Association of America.

*   *   *

ROPER, John Stephen 1924(?)-1980

OBITUARY NOTICE: Born c. 1924; died December 26, 1980, in Dudley, England. Historian, educator, and author. Roper is best known for his contributions to the recorded history of the West Midlands of England. His many publications include *Some Early Staffordshire Churches, The Mediaeval Town, The Early Town, The Seventeenth Century Town,* and *The Town in the Eighteenth Century.* Obituaries and other sources: *London Times,* December 30, 1980.

*   *   *

ROSE, James M. 1941-

PERSONAL: Born July 20, 1941, in Newport, R.I.; son of Manuel and Doris Rose; married wife, Brenda A. (a social worker), March 30, 1977. *Education:* Union Graduate School, Cincinnati, Ohio, Ph.D., 1980. *Home:* 29 Cedar St., Hempstead, N.Y. 11550. *Office:* Department of Urban Studies, Queens College of the City University of New York, Flushing, N.Y. 11337.

CAREER: Queens College of the City University of New York, Flushing, N.Y., assistant professor of urban studies, 1974—. *Military service:* U.S. Army, 1960-63.

WRITINGS: Black Genesis, Gale, 1978; *Tapestry: A Living History of the Black Family in Southeastern Connecticut,* New London Historical Society, 1979; *Black Roots in Southeastern Connecticut,* Gale, 1980; *Blacks in the Federal Census Records of New York, 1790-1830,* Gale, 1981.

WORK IN PROGRESS: Secret Roots, a novel, publication expected in 1982.

*   *   *

ROSEBORO, John 1933-

PERSONAL: Born May 13, 1933, in Ashland, Ohio; son of John Henry and Geraldine (Cecil) Roseboro; married Geraldine Fraime, August 17, 1956 (divorced, 1975); married Barbara Walker (an owner of a public relations firm), September 5, 1975; children: Shelley, Stacy, Jaime, Nicky. *Education:* Attended Central State College, Wilberforce, Ohio. *Home:* 1703 Virginia Rd., Los Angeles, Calif. 90019.

CAREER: Catcher with Brooklyn Dodgers, 1957, Los Angeles Dodgers, 1958-67, and Minnesota Twins, 1968-69; player-coach with Washington Senators, 1970. Owner of Fouch-Roseboro (public relations firm), Los Angeles, Calif. *Military service:* U.S. Army, 1953-55.

WRITINGS: Glory Days With the Dodgers (memoirs), Atheneum, 1978.

SIDELIGHTS: Roseboro commented: ''After going through a bankruptcy and divorce I decided I needed a new start, writing. My life in professional baseball was the subject I chose to write about.'' *Avocational interests:* Travel (Japan, Venezuela, Cuba, Jamaica, Germany, England, Mexico).

*   *   *

ROSENTHAL, Erwin Isak Jacob 1904-

PERSONAL: Born September 18, 1904, in Heilbronn, Germany; son of Moses (a merchant) and Amalie (Levis) Rosenthal; married Elizabeth Marx, July 25, 1933; children: Thomas G., Miriam A. Rosenthal Hodgson. *Education:* Attended University of Heidelberg and University of Munich; University of Berlin, D.Phil., 1929; Cambridge University, Litt.D., 1958. *Religion:* Jewish. *Home:* 199 Chesterton Rd., Cambridge CB4 1AH, England.

CAREER: University of London, London, England, Goldsmid Lecturer in Hebrew and head of department, 1933-36; Victoria University of Manchester, Manchester, England, lecturer in Semitic languages and literatures, 1936-44; Foreign Office, Political Intelligence Department, Cairo, Egypt, temporary officer, 1945-46, German Section, London, temporary officer, 1946-48; Cambridge University, Cambridge, England, lecturer in Hebrew, 1948-59, reader in Oriental studies, 1959-71, reader emeritus, 1971—, fellow of Pembroke College, 1962-71, fellow emeritus, 1971—, chairman of management committee of Middle East Centre, 1969-78. Visiting professor at Columbia University, 1967-68, and Colegio de Mexico, 1968; member of board of directors of Leo Baeck Institute. *Military service:* British Army, Royal Army Service Corps, 1944-45. *Member:* British Association for Jewish Studies (president, 1977), Society for Near Eastern Studies (president, 1957-59, 1972-74, 1979-80), Society of Old Testament Study. *Awards, honors:* Rockefeller Foundation grant, 1960-62; Leverhulme Trust emeritus fellowship, 1974-76.

WRITINGS: (Editor and contributor) *Law and Religion,* Sheldon Press, 1938; (editor and contributor) *Saadya Studies,* Manchester University Press, 1942; (editor and translator) *Averroes' Commentary on Plato's Republic,* Cambridge University Press, 1956, 3rd edition, 1969; *Political Thought in Medieval Islam,* Cambridge University Press, 1958, 3rd edition, 1968; *Judaism and Islam,* Yoseloff, 1961; *Islam in the Modern National State,* Cambridge University Press, 1965; (editor with A. J. Arberry, Max Warren, and Charles Beckingham) *Religion in the Middle East,* Cambridge University Press, 1969; *Studia Semitica,* Volume I: *Jewish Themes,* Volume II: *Islamic Themes,* Cambridge University Press, 1971; *Politics and Religion in Islam,* Cambridge University Press, in press.

Other writings: *Ibn Khalduns Gedanken ueber den Staat* (title means "The Political Thought of Ibn Khalduns"), Oldenburgh, 1932, *Griechisches Erbe in der Juedischen Religionsphilosophie* (title means "The Greek Legacy in Medieval Jewish Philosophy"), Kohlhammer, 1960. Contributor of articles and reviews to scholarly journals and newspapers.

WORK IN PROGRESS: Research on early and contemporary Islam.

SIDELIGHTS: Rosenthal wrote: "Specializing in political thought in medieval Islam and Judaism, I have always tried to understand Islam from within itself, seeing the Muslim's point of view. It is very important for understanding contemporary Islam in the modern national states of Iran, Pakistan, Malaysia, Egypt, and Turkey. I have also worked on Jewish-Christian relations in the Middle Ages and on Jewish commentaries on the Old Testament in Hebrew and Arabic."

Rosenthal's work has been published in Spanish and Japanese.

BIOGRAPHICAL/CRITICAL SOURCES: A.J.R. Information, September, 1979; A. J. Emerton and S. C. Reif, editors, *Interpreting the Hebrew Bible,* Cambridge University Press, 1981.

ROSS, Alan Strode Campbell   1907-1980

OBITUARY NOTICE—See index for *CA* sketch: Born February 1, 1907, in Brecon, Wales; died September 23, 1980. Philologist, professor, and author. A professor of linguistics since 1951, Campbell was primarily concerned with the history and the development of the English language. He established *English Philological Studies,* a journal dedicated to his interests in language. His writings include *The Dream of the Rood, The Lindisfarne Gospels, Ginger, A Loan-Word Study, The Durham Ritual,* and *U and Non-U Revisited.* Obituaries and other sources: *London Times,* September 26, 1980.

*   *   *

ROSS, Bernard H(arvey)   1934-

PERSONAL: Born March 29, 1934, in Brooklyn, N.Y.; son of Leonard S. (a business executive) and Nettie (Friedman) Ross; married Marlene Feldstein (an educational consultant), June 2, 1963; children: Jeffrey, Joanne, Carolyn. *Education:* University of Pennsylvania, B.S., 1955; New York University, M.A., 1966, Ph.D., 1971. *Home:* 4902 Rokeby Pl., Kensington, Md. 20795. *Office:* 305 Ward Circle Building, American University, Washington, D.C. 20016.

CAREER: American University, Washington, D.C., assistant professor, 1967-71, associate professor, 1971-77, professor of government, 1977—, director of urban affairs program, 1971—, National Center for State and Local Government, 1974-76, and Center for Urban Public Policy Analysis, 1977—. Consultant to business and government. *Military service:* U.S. Navy, 1955-57. *Member:* American Political Science Association, American Society for Public Administration, National Association of Neighborhoods, Council of University Institutes for Urban Affairs, National Association of Schools of Public Affairs and Administration (chairman of urban affairs section), White Flint Park Citizens Association (vice-president, 1978—).

WRITINGS: University-City Relations: From Coexistence to Cooperation, American Association for Higher Education, 1973; (contributor) Don Rowat, editor, *The Government of Federal Capitals,* University of Toronto Press, 1973; (with A. Lee Fritschler) *Urban Affairs Bibliography: An Annotated Guide to Literature in the Field,* American University, 1974, 3rd edition, 1974; (with Martin Jenkins) *The Urban Involvement of Higher Education in the 1970's,* U.S. Department of Housing and Urban Development, 1974; *Urban Management: A Guide to Information Sources,* Gale, 1979; (with Fritschler) *Business Regulation and Government Decision Making,* Winthrop Publishing, 1980. Contributor to education journals.

WORK IN PROGRESS: A textbook on urban politics, publication by Winthrop Publishing expected in 1982.

SIDELIGHTS: Bernard H. Ross wrote: "*Business Regulation and Government Decision Making* is the first book written for business executives explaining how the governmental system really works. It is written by authors who have taught government and public administration and have worked with both government and business executives. I believe business executives need to have a much better understanding of how government makes decisions if they are to be able to function effectively in the political system. The book is being used in many executive training programs around the country."

ROSS, Robert W.
See POWER-ROSS, Robert W.

* * *

ROSSABI, Morris 1941-

PERSONAL: Born December 5, 1941, in Alexandria, Egypt; came to the United States in 1950, naturalized citizen, 1958; son of Joseph (in business) and Corinne (Hakim) Rossabi; married Mary Jane Herrmann (a teacher), June 16, 1965; children: Amy, Tony. *Education:* Columbia University, M.A., 1964, Ph.D., 1970. *Home:* 175 Riverside Dr., New York, N.Y. 10024. *Office:* Department of History, Case Western Reserve University, Cleveland, Ohio 44106.

CAREER: Case Western Reserve University, Cleveland, Ohio, associate professor of history, 1970—. Consultant to National Endowment for the Humanities and Brooklyn Museum. *Member:* American Historical Association, Association for Asian Studies (chairman of development committee for Inner Asia, 1979-82), American Oriental Society, Middle East Studies Association. *Awards, honors:* Fulbright-Hays fellowship, 1969-70; National Endowment for the Humanities fellowship, 1974-75; American Council of Learned Societies fellowship, 1978-79.

WRITINGS: China and Inner Asia, 1400-1970, Thames & Hudson, 1975; *Cambridge History of Inner Asia,* Cambridge University Press, 1978; (contributor) Jonathan Spence, editor, *From Ming to Ch'ing,* Yale University Press, 1979; (contributor) John Langlois, editor, *China Under Mongol Rule,* Princeton University Press, 1980; (editor) *China Among Equals,* University of California Press, 1981. Contributor to Asian studies journals.

WORK IN PROGRESS: Khubilai Khan: A Biography, publication by University of California Press expected in 1982.

* * *

ROTHSCHILD, Kurt William 1914-

PERSONAL: Born October 21, 1914, in Vienna, Austria; son of Ernst (in sales) and Phillipine (Hollub) Rothschild; married Valerie Kunke (a secretary), August 10, 1938; children: Thomas, Elisabeth Rothschild Menzel. *Education:* University of Vienna, Dr.Juris, 1938; University of Glasgow, M.A. (with honors), 1940. *Home:* Doblinger Hauptstrasse 77A, A1190 Vienna, Austria. *Office:* Department of Economics, University of Linz, A4040 Linz, Austria.

CAREER: University of Glasgow, Glasgow, Scotland, lecturer in economics, 1940-47; Austrian Institute for Economic Research, Vienna, Austria, senior member of research staff, 1947-66; University of Linz, Linz, Austria, professor of economics, 1966—. Member of Supreme Court for Cartel Affairs, 1972-80; consultant to Austrian Institute for Economic Research. *Member:* American Economic Association, Royal Economic Society, Gesellschaft fuer Sozial- und Wirtschafts Wissenschaften, Gessellschaft fuer National-oekonomie, Club of Rome. *Awards, honors:* Award from city of Vienna, 1980, for distinguished work in the social sciences.

WRITINGS: Austria's Economic Development Between the Two World Wars, Muller, 1947; *The Austrian Economy Since 1945,* Royal Institute of International Affairs, 1950; *The Theory of Wages,* Basil Blackwell, 1954; *Lohntheorie* (title means "Wage Theory"), F. Vahlen, 1963; *Marktform, Leohne und Aussenhandel* (title means "Market Forms, Wages, and Foreign Trade"), Europa-Verlag, 1966; *Wirtschaftsprognose* (title means "Economic Forecasting"), Springer-Verlag, 1969; *Development of Income Distribution*

in Western Europe, Organization for Economic Cooperation and Development, 1971; (editor) *Power in Economics,* Penguin, 1971; (with Ewald Nowotny) *Bestimmungsgruende der Lohnbewegung* (title means "Determinants of Money Wage Movements"), Springer-Verlag, 1972; (with H. J. Schmahl) *Beschleunigter Gerdwertschwund* (title means "The Decline in the Value of Money"), Weltwirtschaftliches Institut, 1973; (with others) *The Utilization of Social Sciences in Policy Making,* Organization for Economic Cooperation and Development, 1977; *Arbeitsldsigkeit in Oesterreich, 1955-1975* (title means "Unemployment in Austria, 1955-1975"), Institute for Labour Market Studies, 1977. Contributor to economic journals.

WORK IN PROGRESS: Einfuehrung in die Ungleichgewichtstheorie (title means "Introduction to Disequilibrium Theory"), publication by Springer-Verlag expected in 1981 or 1982.

SIDELIGHTS: Rothschild wrote: "I have a strong interest in economic, social, and political development. I want to improve the economic situation of less privileged groups. I am critical of entrenched interest groups. On all these matters economic theory could make a greater contribution if it did not get lost—too often—in unrealistic problems and sophisticated detail. In my writings I hope to find ways of turning research toward relevant questions and extracting usable answers from theoretical results."

AVOCATIONAL INTERESTS: Walking, climbing, theatre, film.

* * *

ROTTENBERG, Daniel 1942-

PERSONAL: Born June 10, 1942, in New York, N.Y.; son of Herman and Lenore (Goldstein) Rottenberg; married Barbara Rubin (a music teacher), January 4, 1964; children: Lisa, Julie. *Education:* University of Pennsylvania, B.A., 1964. *Religion:* Jewish. *Home:* 1801 Kennedy Blvd., Philadelphia, Pa. 19103. *Agent:* McIntosh & Otis, Inc., 475 Fifth Ave., New York, N.Y. 10017. *Office:* 275 South 19th St., Philadelphia, Pa. 19103.

CAREER: Commercial Review, Portland, Ind., sports editor, 1964-66, editor, 1966-68; *Wall Street Journal,* Chicago, Ill., reporter, 1968-70; *Chicago Journalism Review,* Chicago, managing editor, 1970-72; *Philadelphia,* Philadelphia, Pa., executive editor, 1972-75; free-lance writer, 1975—. *Awards, honors:* Penney-Missouri Newspaper Award from J.C. Penney Co. and University of Missouri, 1976, for article, "Fernanda"; Clarion Award from Women in Communications, 1977, for article, "Edison's Nuclear Gamble."

WRITINGS: Finding Our Fathers, Random House, 1977. Author of monthly film column syndicated to city magazines, 1971—, and weekly column in *Philadelphia Inquirer,* 1978—. Contributor to *Chicago* and *Town and Country.*

SIDELIGHTS: Rottenberg described his areas of expertise as "business, the law, news media, movies, the super-rich, and Judaica."

* * *

ROY, Archibald Edmiston 1924-
(Archie E. Roy)

PERSONAL: Born June 24, 1924, in Yoker, Scotland; son of Archie Whyte (an engineer) and Magdalene (Hamilton) Roy; married Frances Helen Hall (a teacher), July 1, 1954; children: Archie, Ian, David. *Education:* University of Glasgow, B.Sc., 1950, Ph.D., 1954. *Home:* 40 Highburgh Rd., Glasgow G12 9EF, Scotland. *Agent:* Harvey Unna and Stephen Durbridge Ltd., 14 Beamount Mews, Marylebone High St., London W1N 4HE, England. *Office:* Department of Astronomy, University of Glasgow, Glasgow, Scotland.

CAREER: Science teacher at private academy in Glasgow, Scotland, 1954-58; University of Glasgow, Glasgow, lecturer, 1958-66, senior lecturer, 1966-73, reader, 1973-77, professor of astronomy, 1977—. Member of British National Committee on Astronomy. *Member:* International Astronomical Union, Royal Astronomical Society (fellow), British Interplanetary Society (fellow), Society for Psychical Research (member of council, 1980—), Brain Research Association, Royal Society of Edinburgh (fellow).

WRITINGS—Under name Archie E. Roy: *Great Moments in Astronomy,* Phoenix House, 1963; *The Foundations of Astrodynamics,* Macmillan, 1965; *Deadlight* (novel), John Long, 1968; (translator) Thomas de Galiana, *Concise Encyclopedia of Astronautics,* Collins, 1968; *The Curtained Sleep* (novel), John Long, 1969; *All Evil Shed Away* (novel), John Long, 1970; *Sable Night* (novel), John Long, 1973; *The Dark Host* (novel), John Long, 1976; (with David Clarke) *Astronomy, Principles and Practice,* Adam Hilge, 1977; (with Clarke) *Astronomy: Structure of the Universe,* Adam Hilge, 1977; *Orbital Motion,* Adam Hilge, 1978; *Devil in the Darkness* (novel), John Long, 1978. Contributor to scientific journals, popular magazines, and newspapers.

WORK IN PROGRESS—Under name Archie E. Roy: *The Waiting Future, the Persistent Past,* on the nature of time; *Object,* a novel about human contact with extraterrestrial life; *The Lamps of Atlantis,* on the origin of the constellations.

SIDELIGHTS: Roy commented: "My writing, both fiction and nonfiction, arises from my research, my absorbing interest in the dimensions of man's personality, his relationships with the universe and his fellow humans, and his 'cliffhanger' situation in the last part of the twentieth century."

*   *   *

ROY, Archie E.
See ROY, Archibald Edmiston

*   *   *

ROY, Jack
See DANGERFIELD, Rodney

*   *   *

ROYSTON, Olive   1904-

PERSONAL: Born February 10, 1904, in London, England. *Education:* Attended Bedford College, London, 1921-25; Birkbeck College, London, B.A., 1933. *Home:* Lewis Cottage, Chertsey Bridge, Surrey KT16 8JZ, England.

CAREER: Teacher at elementary schools in London, England, 1926-48; Geffrye Museum, London, teacher, 1948-67; Hatchford Park School, London, part-time teacher of typing, 1968-78.

WRITINGS: (Editor with Molly Harrison) *Picture Source Book for Social History: Late Nineteenth Century,* Allen & Unwin, 1961; (editor with Harrison) *How They Lived, 1485-1700,* Basil Blackwell, 1963; (editor with Harrison) *Picture Source Book for Social History: Twentieth Century,* Allen & Unwin, 1967; *Living Creatures of an English Home,* Routledge & Kegan Paul, 1971; *The Post Office,* Routledge & Kegan Paul, 1972; *The Town Hall,* Routledge & Kegan Paul, 1975.

SIDELIGHTS: Olive Royston told *CA:* "My interest in modern methods in education, and more particularly in informal education, stems from my own school days. In 1918 or so some of us went on a day's nature ramble—quite unusual in those days—and a little later a small group was taken to sit on the platform at the Queen's Hall concerts in order to learn to listen and to differentiate between the various musical instruments.

"From school I went on to study mathematics at Bedford College, the first university college for women, and was fortunate in my professor, who had very wide interests outside his subject, including all forms of sport. It was during these years that I took up Guiding in a slum London company, and later ran a Brownie pack in the same area, where I was among the first to organize a pack holiday adjusted to younger children.

"I went on to teach in what were then known as elementary schools, with the comment from my own headmistress that probably 'good people were more needed here than in secondary schools.' I was again fortunate in the headmistress of my first permanent school. She was a most enlightened and enthusiastic woman who had been a suffragette, and she ran her school on a modified form of the Dalton Plan.

"Throughout the 1939-45 war I was evacuated with my London school. As well as mathematics, geography, and physical training, I taught botany under near-perfect conditions, collecting my specimens on the way to school! On our return to London, this school was selected as one of the first to be used to try out the comprehensive system. This I think, while good in theory, comes down badly in practice owing to the enormous numbers of students needed to provide the necessary choice of subjects. The individual, in my experience, is swamped in the process, and it seems to me that the individual must be at the center of all true education.

"So I joined the staff of the Geffrye Museum as schools' organizer and member of the teaching staff. This is a small museum illustrating English homes from about 1600 to the present day and is well known in many countries of the world as the pioneer of the idea of encouraging children to visit in their leisure time. Here I had experience with groups from many different types of school, as well as the leisure-time children, and took small groups on visits to places of interest in or near London, and on week-long visits to such places as Bath, Norwich, and York. While the museum was closed in 1951-52 for war damage repairs, I assisted in running the Sayers Croft Rural Studies Centre at Ewhurst, Surrey. Groups of children from London secondary schools, with their teachers, spent a fortnight here gaining some experience of country life.

"In 1956 I spent a most enjoyable year on unofficial exchange with a teacher from the Dominion Museum in Wellington, New Zealand. With the help and encouragement of the museum staff, I was able to visit most of the other New Zealand museums and to see a great deal of the country—including Stewart Island, which was at that time just native 'bush' and unknown to many New Zealanders.

"After my retirement in 1967, I obtained the post of part-time teacher of typing at a residential school for physically handicapped children, most with dual handicaps. I taught children who, because of their handicaps, found writing difficult or impossible. I retired (not voluntarily, but because of age) from this school in 1978, and on a recent visit when I could view things from an outside standpoint, I realized afresh what a very worthwhile scheme this is."

AVOCATIONAL INTERESTS: "I am an out-of-doors person and have enjoyed courses in natural history, biology, and other subjects at centers of the Field Studies Council. I am keenly interested in animal welfare and have at present two dogs who would otherwise have had little chance of a happy life. Exercising them keeps me fit as well! Birds are encouraged to visit my small garden. Under the Action Aid scheme, I have sponsored a little girl in Burundi and a boy in Kenya.''

* * *

RUBIN, Joan 1932-

PERSONAL: Born June 7, 1932, in Detroit, Mich.; daughter of David and Ann (Meckler) Rubin. *Education:* University of Michigan, B.A., 1954, M.A., 1956; Yale University, Ph.D., 1963. *Home:* 2011 Hermitage Ave., Wheaton, Md. 20902. *Office:* National Center for Bilingual Research, 4665 Lampson, Los Alamitos, Calif. 90720.

CAREER: American University, Washington, D.C., assistant professor of anthropology, 1963-65; University of North Carolina, Chapel Hill, assistant professor of anthropology, 1965-66; George Washington University, Washington, D.C., assistant professor of anthropology, 1966-68; University of Hawaii, Honolulu, senior fellow in language planning, 1968-69; Stanford University, Stanford, Calif., research associate, 1969-72; University of Indonesia, Jakarta, research associate, 1969-70; Tulane University, New Orleans, La., associate professor of anthropology, 1970-73; Georgetown University, Washington, D.C., visiting professor of sociolinguistics, 1973-74; East-West Culture Learning Institute, Honolulu, visiting researcher, 1974-77; University of California, Berkeley, research associate, 1978-80; National Center for Bilingual Research, Los Alamitos, Calif., research scholar, 1980—. Consultant to U.S. Agency for International Development. *Member:* American Anthropological Association, Council for Anthropology and Education, Association of Teachers of English to Speakers of Other Languages. *Awards, honors:* National Science Foundation grant, 1965-67; grants from Wenner-Gren Foundation for Anthropological Research, 1965-67, 1973.

WRITINGS: Outline Report on the Position of English in India (monograph), Center for Applied Linguistics, 1966; *National Bilingualism in Paraguay*, Mouton, 1968; (editor with Bjorn H. Jernudd) *Can Language Be Planned?: Sociolinguistic Theory and Practice for Developing Nations*, East-West Center Press, 1971; (editor with Roger Shuy) *Language Planning: Current Issues and Research*, Georgetown University Press, 1973; (editor) *Sociolinguistics in Southeast Asia*, International Journal of the Sociology of Language, 1975; (editor) *Language Planning in the United States*, International Journal of the Sociology of Language, 1976; (with Jernudd and others) *Language Planning Processes*, Mouton, 1977; *References for Students of Language Planning*, University Press of Hawaii, 1979.

Contributor: J. A. Fishman, C. A. Ferguson, and Jyotirindra Das Gupta, editors, *Language Problems in Developing Nations*, Wiley, 1968; J. J. Honigmann, editor, *Handbook of Cultural and Social Anthropology*, Rand McNally, 1973; W. N. O'Barr and Jean O'Barr, editors, *Language and Politics: Their Interaction in Formal and Informal Arenas*, Mouton, 1976; Ben Blount and Mary Sanches, editors, *Sociocultural Dimensions of Language Change*, Academic Press, 1977; B. P. Sibayan and A. B. Gonzalez, editors, *Language Planning and the Building of a National Language*, Linguistic Society of the Philippines and Language Study Center, 1977; Bernard Spolsky and Robert Cooper, editors, *Fron-*

tiers of Bilingual Education, Newbury House, 1977; James Alatis, editor, *International Dimensions of Bilingual Education*, Georgetown University Press, 1978; Dorothy Danielson, Helen Hinze-Pocher, and other editors, *Readings in English: For Students of English as a Second Language*, Prentice-Hall, 1979; John Pride, editor, *Sociolinguistic Aspects of Language Learning and Teaching*, Oxford University Press, 1980; Juan Cobarrubias and Joshua Fishman, editors, *Progress in Language Planning: International Perspectives*, Mouton, 1981. Contributor to *New Catholic Encyclopedia*. Contributor of about twenty-five articles and reviews to scholarly journals.

WORK IN PROGRESS: Research on acquisition of a second language, language problems and development, and language communication problems in the fields of medicine, law, and education.

* * *

RUBINSTEIN, Daryl Reich 1938(?)-1981

OBITUARY NOTICE: Born c. 1938 in Washington, D.C.; died of cancer, January 28, 1981, in Washington, D.C. Critic, lecturer, and author. Rubinstein lectured on nineteenth- and twentieth-century prints and graphic arts at numerous institutions, including the National Collection of Fine Arts and Georgetown University. She wrote *Max Weber: A Catalogue Raisonne of His Graphic Work*. Obituaries and other sources: *Washington Post*, February 2, 1981.

* * *

RUDIN, Marcia Ruth 1940-

PERSONAL: Born September 28, 1940, in Pueblo, Colo.; daughter of Max (a college professor) and Elizabeth (a secretary; maiden name, Neu) Kaplan; married A. James Rudin (a rabbi), July 27, 1969; children: Eue Sandra, Jennifer Anne. *Education:* Attended University of Edinburgh, 1960-61; Boston University, B.A., 1962; Columbia University and Union Theological Seminary, joint M.A., 1965; attended New School for Social Research, 1967-69. *Religion:* Jewish. *Agent:* Berenice Hoffman Literary Agency, 215 West 75th St., New York, N.Y. 10023.

CAREER: William Paterson College, Wayne, N.J., assistant professor of philosophy and religion, 1965-69; free-lance writer, 1972—. Member of faculty at Friends school in Brooklyn, N.Y., 1966. Public speaker. *Member:* Phi Beta Kappa.

WRITINGS: (With husband, A. James Rudin) *Prison or Paradise?: The New Religious Cults*, Fortress, 1980. Contributor of articles and reviews to popular journals and religious magazines, including *Present Tense, Worldview, New Leader, Antigonish Review, Dialogue*, and *Keeping Posted*.

WORK IN PROGRESS: Children's books; novels; stories.

* * *

RUEVENI, Uri 1933-

PERSONAL: Born July 10, 1933, in Tel-Aviv, Palestine (now Israel); came to the United States in 1957, naturalized citizen, 1966; married wife, Miriam M. (a psychologist), May 19, 1957; children: Roni, Deena. *Education:* University of Pittsburgh, B.S., 1961, M.Ed., 1963; Michigan State University, Ph.D., 1966. *Religion:* Jewish. *Home:* 8501 Elliston Dr., Wyndmoor, Pa. 19118.

CAREER: Pittsburgh Child Guidance Center, Pittsburgh, Pa., research aid family therapist, 1960-61; counselor at St.

Francis Hospital in Pennsylvania, 1961-62; Pittsburgh Guild for the Blind, Pittsburgh, counselor, 1962-63; Southern Michigan State Correctional Institute, chief psychologist, 1963-66; Temple University, Philadelphia, Pa., assistant professor of counseling, 1966-67; Franklin Institute, research director of career motivation project at Research Laboratory, 1967-68; Hahnemann Medical College, Philadelphia, director of group dynamics program at mental health center, 1968-70; Eastern Pennsylvania Psychiatric Institute, Philadelphia, director of Division of Social and Community Intervention, 1970—. Lecturer at Philadelphia's State Correctional Institute, 1966-67, and Community College of Philadelphia, 1968—; lecturer for corporations. *Member:* American Psychological Association, American Association of Marriage and Family Therapists, American Orthopsychiatric Association, Pennsylvania Psychological Society, Family Institute of Philadelphia, Philadelphia Society of Clinical Psychologists.

WRITINGS: The Application of Sensitivity Training Techniques in the Development of Interpersonal Skills and Effective Teamwork Among Mental Health and Community Worker Students, National Association of Psychiatric Technicians, 1970; *Networking: Families in Crisis,* Human Science Press, 1979; *Interventions: Healing Human Systems,* Human Science Press, 1981. Contributor to psychology and health care journals.

SIDELIGHTS: Rueveni commented: "I write about the family system, in particular the families who are experiencing emotional and psychological as well as physical traumas and crises. I believe in strengthening the family system by improving its relationship of communication and trust with members of the extended family and the social system within which one lives and works."

* * *

RUNTE, Alfred 1947-

PERSONAL: Born April 16, 1947, in Binghamton, N.Y.; son of Paul and Erika (a secretary; maiden name, Brinkman) Runte. *Education:* State University of New York at Binghamton, B.A., 1969; Illinois State University, M.A., 1971; University of California, Santa Barbara, Ph.D., 1976. *Home:* 5505 27th N.E., Apt. 2, Seattle, Wash. 98105. *Office:* Department of History, DP-20, University of Washington, Seattle, Wash. 98195.

CAREER: University of California, Santa Barbara, lecturer in history and environmental studies, summer, 1973, spring, 1975, 1976-78; Smithsonian Institution, Washington, D.C., fellowship specialist at Woodrow Wilson International Center for Scholars, 1978-79; Baylor University, Waco, Tex., assistant professor of environmental studies and assistant director of Institute of Environmental Studies, 1979-80; University of Washington, Seattle, assistant professor of history, 1980—. Consultant to California Department of Transportation.

MEMBER: Organization of American Historians, Forest History Society, Western History Association, National Association of Railroad Passengers (member of board of directors, 1974-80), Phi Alpha Theta. *Awards, honors:* Frederick K. Weyerhauser Award from *Journal of Forest History,* 1978, for article, "The National Park Idea: Origins and Paradox of the American Experience."

WRITINGS: (Contributor) J. Wreford Watson and Timothy O'Riordan, editors, *The American Environment: Perceptions and Policies,* Wiley, 1976; *National Parks: The American Experience,* University of Nebraska Press, 1979; *Ameri-*

can Environmental History: Issues and Interpretations, Boyd & Fraser, 1982. Contributor to *Rolling Rivers: An Encyclopedia of America's Rivers.* Contributor to scholarly journals and popular magazines, including *Conservationist* and *American West.*

WORK IN PROGRESS: Wildlife in American Thought and Culture, a social and cultural history.

SIDELIGHTS: Runte told *CA:* "My basic interest in environmental studies and environmental history goes back many years to my boyhood in New York state, and to 1959, when my mother took my brother and me on a summer camping trip through the national parks of the West. The professional outgrowth of those experiences was my book, *National Parks.* Now, as a university professor, I am continuing my research and writing on numerous subjects, largely related to the environment of the American West and the changes wrought by westward expansion."

AVOCATIONAL INTERESTS: Public speaking, activism toward the re-establishment of rail passenger travel in the United States.

* * *

RUSSELL, Eric Frank 1905-1978
(Webster Craig, Duncan H. Munro)

OBITUARY NOTICE: Born January 6, 1905, at Sandhurst, Surrey, England; died February 28, 1978. Science-fiction writer. Russell wrote both short stories and novels and was a frequent contributor to *Astounding* and other science-fiction magazines. His works include *Dark Tides, Somewhere a Voice, Wasp, The Space Willies,* "The Saga of Pelican West," and "Allagamoosa." Obituaries and other sources: *Science Fiction and Fantasy Literature,* Volume 2, Gale, 1979.

* * *

RUSSELL, Gordon 1930(?)-1981

OBITUARY NOTICE: Born c. 1930 in Salem, Mass.; died of cancer, January 19, 1981. Writer. Russell was best known for his eighteen-year career as a writer of daytime television dramas. The shows he wrote for included "One Life to Live," "The Doctors," and "Dark Shadows." Russell also wrote a play, "Masterpiece," which was produced in London and which he later adapted for television. It earned him an award from the Writers' Guild of America. Obituaries and other sources: *New York Times,* January 22, 1981.

* * *

RUSSELL, Joan Mercedes 1921-

PERSONAL: Born September 26, 1921, in Birmingham, England; daughter of Roland (an engineer) and Annie Mercedes (a secretary and piano teacher; maiden name, Lane) Russell. *Education:* Studied at Laban Art of Movement Studio, 1949-50. *Religion:* Church of England. *Home:* Hawkhurst House, Cradley, near Malvern, Worcestershire, England. *Office:* Department of Dance, Worcester College of Higher Education, Henwick Grove, Worcester WR2 6AJ, England.

CAREER: Worcester College of Higher Education, Henwick Grove, England, lecturer, 1948-52, head of dance division, 1952-75, senior tutor in dance and head of department, 1975—. Chairman of Laban Art of Movement Guild, 1968-74, 1978—. Dance producer for religious broadcasting section of British Broadcasting Corp. (BBC) and for Worcester Cathedral; dance director for Laban Centenary Celebrations, 1978. Lecturer in England, Australia, the United States, Canada, Tanzania, and Uganda; dance education consultant. *Member:* Dance and the Child International, Association of Teachers in Colleges and Departments of Education (chairman of Dance section, 1958-68), West Midlands Arts Society.

WRITINGS: Modern Dance in Education, Macdonald & Evans, 1958; *Creative Dance in the Primary School,* Macdonald & Evans, 1965, revised edition published as *Creative Movement and Dance for Children,* Plays, 1975; *Creative Dance in the Secondary School,* Macdonald & Evans, 1969, revised edition, 1979.

WORK IN PROGRESS: Research on dance in education, dance in worship, and dance as recreation.

SIDELIGHTS: Russell wrote: "I am first and foremost a teacher and trainer of teachers rather than a writer. However, I began to write about dance in education because, despite the developing interest in this subject in postwar Britain, there was only one textbook, *Modern Educational Dance* by Rudolf Laban. As a practicing teacher and trainer of teachers, I realized the dearth of books on this aspect of art education. I, therefore, wrote my first book to deal with the philosophy underlying this area of the curriculum and to give practical help in drawing up a syllabus and planning lessons for students and teachers. Two further books gave greater detail for different age groups.

"Perhaps one reason for the success of the books is the fact that they are based on personal experience and on-going work with children and that they include action photographs of classes I taught. My books have been used in English-speaking countries throughout the world and have been responsible for invitations to present papers and to give workshops at international conferences overseas. My concern to give opportunities to everyone who wishes to dance has been given practical expression through my teaching of courses for leaders of recreation groups as well as through my own leadership for twenty-five years of the Worcestershire Dance Group."

*   *   *

RUSSELL, Ronald 1924-

PERSONAL: Born May 18, 1924, in Croydon, England; son of Alfred and Dora Russell; married Barbara Mary Lambert, January 5, 1952 (died, 1969); married Jill Elizabeth Healey Wilson (a librarian), July 27, 1970; children: Adrian J.; stepchildren: Simon, Margaret, Nicholas. *Education:* Merton College, Oxford, B.A., 1948, M.A., 1950. *Home:* 4 Maners Way, Cambridge CB1 4SL, England.

CAREER: Senior English master at school in Newcastle, England, 1948-56; head of English departments at schools in England, 1956-72; City of Ely College, Ely, Cambrigeshire, England, head of English department, 1972—, and director of studies, 1973—. *Military service:* Royal Air Force, 1943-46; became flying officer. *Member:* Railway and Canal Historical Society (keeper of photographic archives), Inland Waterways Association (founder and past chairman of local branch). *Awards, honors:* Leverhulme grant, 1973-74.

WRITINGS: Lost Canals of England and Wales, David & Charles, 1971; *Waterside Pubs,* David & Charles, 1974; *Discovering Lost Canals,* Shire Publications, 1975; (with John Boyes) *Canals of Eastern England,* David & Charles, 1977; *Rivers,* David & Charles, 1978; *Guide to British Topographical Prints,* David & Charles, 1979; *Britain's Lost Canals,* David & Charles, 1981.

WORK IN PROGRESS: Discovering Antique Prints, publication by Shire Publications expected in 1982.

SIDELIGHTS: Russell commented: "Because I am suspicious of 'progress,' and possibly also because I turned to writing for publication later in life than most, I tend to look to the past for my subjects, especially its more neglected corners. The challenge, then, is to find a way of sharing this information and interest using clear, plain English.

"My waterway books are mostly illustrated by my own photographs, which may help readers to see the way I look at things. I don't want the relics of the past labeled or put in museums, but I do want them recognized and protected. On the old inland navigations, much modern prosperity was founded; where it is possible for relics to be restored and used again, I want to see that done.

"Old prints of the sort I am concerned with tell us much about the way people were encouraged to see their environment. There are plenty of books on 'old master prints' or prints as art forms, but little has been done on the mostly unpretentious examples, the precursors of the photograph. So I am doing a little more."

*   *   *

RYALLS, Alan 1919-

PERSONAL: Born February 22, 1919, in Sheffield, England; son of Charles Vincent (in business) and Gertrude (a seamstress; maiden name, Rew) Ryalls; married Peggy Coole (a headmistress), June 15, 1941; children: Janet, Carolyn Ryalls Cookson, Steven, Paul. *Education:* Attended boys' grammar school in Sheffield, England. *Politics:* "Liberal, with a small 'l'." *Religion:* None. *Home and office:* Acres End, Field Way, Helmdon, Brackley, Northamptonshire NN13 5QN, England.

CAREER: Worked as civil servant and trade union officer in London, England, 1940-56; *Camping and Caravanning,* London, editor, 1956-75; *Motor Caravan and Motorhome,* London, overseas correspondent 1976—. *Member:* British Guild of Travel Writers. *Awards, honors:* Award from Bulgarian Ministry of Tourism, 1970, for article, "Beautiful Bulgaria."

WRITINGS: Enjoy Camping Holidays, Gollancz, 1963; *Your Guide to Hungary,* Redman, 1967; *Your Guide to Cyprus,* Redman, 1969; *Camping With B.P.,* Kenneth Mason, 1969; *Bulgaria for Tourists,* Kenneth Mason, 1971; (with Roger Marchant) *Better Camping,* Kaye & Ward, 1973; *Modern Camping,* David & Charles, 1975.

Author of educational television script, "Caravanning and Camping" (eight-part series), first broadcast by Independent Television, March/April, 1971. Contributor to *Encyclopaedia Britannica.* Contributor to magazines, including *Camping World.*

WORK IN PROGRESS: "An account of my life deep in the countryside of the Algarve, with many illustrations of the old country crafts still practiced there."

SIDELIGHTS: Ryalls commented: "The urge to travel (and to write about it) has taken me throughout Europe, west and east, as far north as North Cape, and to Iceland, Cyprus, Israel, and North Africa. I have camped in the game reserves of Tanzania and Kenya, and have made several extensive trips through the United States and Canada, including a Greyhound coast-to-coast trip from Los Angeles to New York. A recent trip to Sri Lanka, Singapore, Bali, Hong Kong, and around Thailand by bus, train, boat, rickshaw, and small plane has opened up new vistas. Travel to and from my cottage in the Algarve province of Portugal has given me a deep insight into and a great love of Iberia.

"My extensive travels in Eastern Europe led me to revise slightly idealistic opinions on life there, and a visit to the Soviet Union, camping and self-catering, confirmed my revised opinions very definitely. What a poor country, despite such magnificences as the Hermitage in Leningrad, and what a poor life, despite over sixty years of communism."

* * *

RYAN, Cheli Duran

PERSONAL: Born in New York. *Education:* Attended Trinity College, Dublin, and University of Barcelona.

CAREER: Editor and writer. *Awards, honors:* Finalist in National Book Award's children's book category, and honor book for Randolph J. Caldecott Medal, both 1972, both for *Hildilid's Night.*

*WRITINGS—*For children: *Hildilid's Night,* illustrations by Arnold Lobel, Macmillan, 1971; *Paz,* illustrations by Nonny Hogrogian, Macmillan, 1971; (editor and translator) *The Yellow Canary Whose Eye Is So Black* (poems), Macmillan, 1977.

BIOGRAPHICAL/CRITICAL SOURCES: New York Times Book Review, November 7, 1971; *Christian Science Monitor,* May 1, 1974.*

* * *

RYAN, Kathryn Morgan 1925-

PERSONAL: Born August 3, 1925, in Oskaloosa, Iowa; daughter of Eldon Monk (a legislator) and Zana (deWitt) Morgan; married Cornelius Ryan (a writer and historian), May 27, 1950 (died November 23, 1974); children: Geoffrey, Victoria. *Education:* University of Missouri, B.J., 1946. *Home and office:* Old Branchville Rd., Ridgefield, Conn. 06877. *Agent:* Paul Gitlin, 7 West 51st St., New York, N.Y. 10019.

CAREER: Conde Nast Publications, New York City, associate editor, 1946-55; *Time,* New York City, associate editor, 1955-60; writer. Adviser to Ohio University on Cornelius Ryan Memorial Foreign Correspondence Internships. *Member:* Authors Guild, Authors League of America. *Awards, honors:* Awards for best trade magazine reporting, 1958, 1959, and 1960, for articles in *Time;* special honor award from Ohio University College of Communications, 1977; honor awards of the 101st Airborne Division and 82nd Airborne Division; honorary lifetime member of British First Airborne Division and Polish Parachute Brigade.

WRITINGS: House & Garden's Book of Building, Conde Nast Press, 1960; (with Alan King) *Anyone Who Owns His Own Home Deserves It* (humor), Dutton, 1962; *The Betty Tree* (novel), Trident, 1972; *A Private Battle* (nonfiction), Simon & Schuster, 1979. Contributor to *Reader's Digest* and *New York Times.*

WORK IN PROGRESS: Two nonfiction books, including one "on more of *The Longest Day, The Last Battle,* and *A Bridge Too Far;* this work is currently shelved since time and travel priorities demand that the other book mentioned take precedence over World War II material."

SIDELIGHTS: As the wife of Cornelius Ryan, author of books on World War II such as *The Longest Day* and *A Bridge Too Far,* Ryan assisted him by interviewing subjects, collecting material, and editing his work. Ryan's husband died after a lengthy bout with cancer; *A Private Battle* is a documentation of his struggle.

Ryan told *CA:* "I cannot remember a time when I did not want to write, or a time when writing was not a vital part of my life. Certainly my husband's historical research, investigative reporting, and clear sightedness have largely influenced me. I find the novel in decline and find myself tending more and more to nonfiction in which the facts can be and usually are more dramatic and compelling than current works of fiction. I work usually an eighteen hour day, seven days a week—undoubtedly a slow thinker—and I cannot proceed on a work until each sentence is as perfect as I can make it. It all seems to revolve around pacing and making sure that each word says exactly what it is intended to say."

CA INTERVIEW

Kathryn Ryan was interviewed by *CA* at her home in Connecticut on July 14, 1980.

Discipline is the word that comes to mind when one considers the career of Kathryn Ryan, a journalist, researcher, and writer. Seven days a week she treks the short distance between her home and adjoining office to work at her desk from nine-thirty until six o'clock. There is no break for lunch. "Food makes me sleepy in the afternoon," Ryan confesses.

"If I didn't come out to my office every day, I might find a reason to stay away the next day," she says while sitting by the fireside. "I don't believe in taking walks when I get stuck on a sentence, or giving up for the day. If you go away, the problem will still be there when you get back. In the writer versus typewriter game, you can't let that typewriter intimidate you."

Ryan believes that free-lance writers should dress for work every day as if they were going to a typical office job. She usually wears a skirt and stockings. "I'm not a believer in the dressing gown school of free-lance journalism," she remarks.

Though Ryan has written four books, she feels her greatest skills are as an editor. "I can edit bad writing to the point where a second editor doesn't know what else to change," she contends. Unlike some writers, she is also able to edit her own work. "Perhaps that's why it takes me so long to finish anything," she muses.

She believes that the key components of writing and editing are concision and clarity. "This is the most important aspect of writing, and also the most difficult," she declares, "to make an absolutely clear, on-target sentence that anyone of any age can comprehend. At the same time, the language should make the reader feel what the writer was experiencing."

Ryan is uncomfortable writing fiction. "Fiction should have components of both fantasy and autobiography," she states, "but I don't feel I can delve that easily into fantasy, and as for true life experiences, I don't think the things that happen to me would interest other people."

As an editor, Ryan worked closely with her husband on his nonfiction World War II work. "I took out his purple prose," she said. She also coordinated research and conducted interviews with soldiers and civilians who witnessed the events in question. After her husband died of cancer, she delved into diaries and tape recordings he had made and fashioned them into *A Private Battle,* an account of his struggle with the disease. Interspersed with comments from the tapes and diaries are her thoughts and reactions to her husband's illness. Ryan acknowledges that the book has been an inspiration to cancer patients. "Many readers tell me that reading certain passages before seeing their doctors gives them the courage to ask questions about their own illnesses,'' she reveals. Although her husband's death drastically changed her life, Ryan insists that she will keep working. ''I cannot imagine not writing,'' she observes.

—*Interview by Trisha Gorman*

* * *

RYDEN, Ernest Edwin   1886-1981
(Ernest Augustson)

OBITUARY NOTICE: Born September 12, 1886, in Kansas City, Mo.; died January 1, 1981, in Providence, R.I. Lutheran minister, hymnologist, and author. Ryden served on the thirty-four member committee that unified four denominations to form the Lutheran Church in 1962. He was best known as the author and translator of more than forty hymns that have been published in Lutheran, Methodist, Episcopalian, and Presbyterian hymnals. Ryden's interest in Christian hymns continued long after his retirement from the ministry in 1961. His last project, which he began in his eighties, required that he learn Portuguese to edit a hymnal for the Presbyterian church in Brazil. He was the author of *The Story of Our Hymns* and *The Story of Christian Hymnody*. Obituaries and other sources: *Who Was Who Among North American Authors*, Gale, 1976; *New York Times*, January 3, 1981.

* * *

RYDER, M(ichael) L(awson)   1927-
(Michael Lawson)

PERSONAL: Born July 24, 1927, in Leeds, England; son of Cecil (a chemist) and Alice (Lawson) Ryder; married Mary Nicholson, September 6, 1952; children: Stephen Nicholas Lawson, Jonathan William Lawson. *Education:* University of Leeds, B.Sc., 1951, M.Sc., 1954, Ph.D., 1956. *Home:* 23 Swanston Pl., Edinburgh EH10 7DD, Scotland. *Office:* Animal Breeding Research Organisation, Agricultural Research Council, Kings Buildings, Edinburgh EH9 3JQ, Scotland.

CAREER: Wool Industries Research Association, Leeds, England, scientific officer, 1950-59; University of New England, Armidale, Australia, senior lecturer in rural science, 1960-62; Agricultural Research Council, Animal Breeding Research Organisation, Edinburgh, Scotland, principal scientific officer and press officer, 1962—. Honorary lecturer at University of Edinburgh. *Member:* International P.E.N., Institute of Biology (fellow), British Agricultural History Society, Society of Authors, Rare Breeds Survival Trust (founder; former member of council).

WRITINGS: (With Stuart Kimball Stephenson) *Wool Growth*, Academic Press, 1968; *Animal Bones in Archaeology*, Blackwell Scientific Publications, 1969; *Hair*, Edward Arnold, 1973; *Sheep and Wool for Handicraft Workers*, privately printed, 1978. Contributor to scholarly journals and popular magazines under name Michael Lawson, including *Antiquity, Countryman, History Today, New Scientist, Lady, Popular Archaeology,* and *Wool Record*.

WORK IN PROGRESS: A history of the association of man with sheep, publication by Duckworth expected in 1981 or 1982.

SIDELIGHTS: Ryder commented: ''Although a professional biologist, I am interested in archaeology and history, particularly the histories of animals and of other affects of my day-to-day research, such as textiles. I am pleased with the worldwide return of wool through handicrafts and feel that U.S. sheep numbers may soon be on the increase. But on the working front, I deplore the declining rate of pay for authors (particularly in the academic field). The author of a book may get only ten percent, yet the bookseller demands sixty percent merely for opening a parcel!''

AVOCATIONAL INTERESTS: Anthropology, food, cooking, travel.

S

SABATIER, Robert 1928-

PERSONAL: Born August 17, 1928, in France. *Home:* 64 Blvd. Exelmans, 75016 Paris, France.

CAREER: Writer. *Member:* Academie Goncourt. *Awards, honors:* Laureat of Societe des gens de lettres, 1961; Grand Prix de Poesie from Academie Francaise, 1969, for Chateaux de millions d'annees; Antonin-Artaud Prix and Prix Appollinaire, both for *Les Fetes solaires.*

WRITINGS—In English translation: *Alain et le negre* (novel), A. Michel, 1953, translation by Mervyn Savill published as *The Little Barrier,* Putnam, 1955; *Boulevard* (novel), A. Michel, 1956, translation by Lowell Bair published as *Boulevard,* McKay, 1958; *Les Allumettes Suedoises* (novel), A. Michel, 1969, translation by Patsy Southgate published as *The Safety Matches,* Dutton, 1972 (published in England as *The Match Boy,* Elek, 1974); *Trois sucettes a la menthe* (novel), A. Michel, 1972, translation by Southgate and Joan Wright Smith published as *Three Mint Lollipops,* Dutton, 1974.

In French; published by A. Michel, except as noted: *Le Marchand de sable* (novel), 1954; *Le Gout de la cendre* (novel), 1955; *Les Fetes solaires* (poems), 1955; (with Alain Bosquet and Charles Le Quintrec) *Trois poetes,* Seghers, 1956; *Canard au sang* (novel), 1958; *Bedicace d'un navire* (poems), 1959; *Saint Vincent de Paul,* La Table Ronde, 1959; *La Sainte farce* (novel), 1960; *L'etat princier: Art et creation poetiques,* 1961; (editor) *Les Plus belles lettres de Saint Vincent de Paul,* Calmann-Levy, 1961; *La Mort du figuier* (novel), 1962; *Dessin sur un trottoir* (novel), 1964; *Les Poisons delectables* (poems), 1965; *Le Chinois d'Afrique* (novel), 1966; *Dictionnaire de la mort,* 1967; *Les Chateaux de millions d'annees* (poems), 1968; *Les Noisettes sauvages* (novel), 1974; *Histoire de la poesie francaise,* Volume I: *La Poesie du moyen age,* Volume II: *La Poesie du XVIe siecle,* Volume III: *La Poesie du XVIIe siecle,* Volume IV: *La Poesie du XVIIIe siecle,* 1975; *Icare et autres poemes,* 1976; *Les Enfants de l'ete* (novel), 1977.

BIOGRAPHICAL/CRITICAL SOURCES: L'Express, November 10, 1969; *Variety,* January 14, 1970, May 13, 1970.

SAFIAN, Jill
See BHARTI, Ma Satya

*   *   *

SALGADO, Gamini 1929-

PERSONAL: Given name is accented on first syllable; born March 27, 1929, in Moratuwa, Ceylon; son of Aladdin (an accountant) and Florence (Gunasekera) Salgado; separated; children: Melanie Salgado Svenneby, Adrienne, Kumari, David. *Education:* University of Nottingham, B.A. (with first class honors), 1952, Ph.D., 1955. *Home:* 2 Kingsbridge Lane, Ashburton, South Devonshire, England. *Office:* Department of English, University of Exeter, Queen's Building, Exeter, Devonshire EX4 4QH, England.

CAREER: University of Singapore, Singapore, lecturer in English, 1957-60; Queen's University, Belfast, Northern Ireland, lecturer in English, 1960-63; University of Sussex, Brighton, England, lecturer, 1963-70, reader in English, 1970-76; University of Exeter, Exeter, England, professor of English, 1976—. Visiting professor of English at Earlham College, Richmond, Ind., 1965-66. *Member:* International Shakespeare Association, Malone Society. *Awards, honors:* Leverhulme fellow, 1975; fellow at Huntington Library, 1980.

WRITINGS: A Study of Sons and Lovers, Edward Arnold, 1965; *Eyewitnesses of Shakespeare,* Sussex University Press, 1975; *The Elizabethan Underworld,* Dent, 1977; *English Drama: A Critical Introduction,* Edward Arnold, 1980; *A Preface to D. H. Lawrence,* Longman, 1981.

Editor: *Three Jacobean Tragedies,* Penguin, 1965; *Three Restoration Comedies,* Penguin, 1968; *A Casebook on Sons and Lovers,* Macmillan, 1969; *Conycatchers and Bawdybaskets,* Penguin, 1972; *Othello,* Longman, 1975; *Four Jacobean City Comedies,* Penguin, 1975; *The Context of English Literature: Elizabethan and Jacobean,* Eyre-Methuen, 1981.

Contributor: G. R. Hibbard, editor, *Renaissance and Modern Essays,* Routledge & Kegan Paul, 1965; Christopher Ricks, editor, *Sphere History of English Literature: Drama 1570-1640,* Sphere Books, 1970; Stanley Wells, editor, *Shakespeare: Select Bibliographical Guide,* Oxford University Press, 1973; Gabriel Jasipovici, editor, *The Modern English Novel: The Reader, the Writer and the Book,* Open Books, 1975.

Contributor to magazines, including *Essays in Criticism, Critical Quarterly, Shakespeare Survey, Encounter,* and *New Statesman,* and newspapers. Critic for *British Book News.*

WORK IN PROGRESS: Everyman's Companion to the Theatre, with Peter Thomson Dent, publication expected in 1982; *Shakespeare and the Underworld,* publication expected in 1983.

SIDELIGHTS: Salgado commented: "As a product of the twilight of empire, I have always been drawn to my own literature (Sinhalese) and to that of England. I write and translate in, from, and into both.

"The particular attraction of Elizabethan society was the early and growing realization of parallels between it and the traditional yet changing society I myself experienced in early childhood. D. H. Lawrence just came as a bolt from the blue and stayed.

"Books fascinate me as physical objects as well as through their contents."

AVOCATIONAL INTERESTS: Bookbinding, collecting books.

* * *

SALMA, Abu
See KARMI, Abdul Karim

* * *

SALTZ, Donald 1933-

PERSONAL: Born January 9, 1933, in Salisbury, Md.; son of Louis (a merchant) and Goldye (Moffitt) Saltz; married Mozelle Barukh (a secretary), March 19, 1967. *Education:* Attended American University, 1949-50, Salisbury Teachers College, 1952-53, and American Institute of Banking, 1957-60. *Politics:* Republican. *Religion:* Jewish. *Home and office:* 4007 Connecticut Ave. N.W., Washington, D.C. 20008.

CAREER: Worked as assistant manager of a confectionery store in Crisfield, Md., 1954-56; *Washington Star,* Washington, D.C., copyboy, 1956-57; Munsey Trust Co. and Union Trust Co., Washington, D.C., commercial and head teller, 1957-60; associated with Republican National Finance Committee, 1960-63; National Draft Goldwater Committee/Goldwater for President Committee, assistant finance director, 1963-64; Republican National Finance Committee, assistant finance director, 1964-66; *Washington Daily News,* Washington, D.C., business editor, 1966-72; *Washington Star,* business writer, 1972—. Chairman of Adas Israel Chronicle Committee.

WRITINGS: The Trivia Quiz Book, privately printed, 1973; *The Trivia Quiz Book Number Two,* privately printed, 1974; *The Bantam Trivia Quiz Book,* Bantam, 1975; *The Bantam Trivia Quiz Book Number Two,* Bantam, 1976; *Check Your Knowledge,* privately printed, 1976. Author of two columns, "Daily Trivia Quiz," 1966—, and "Check Your Knowledge," 1971—, both syndicated by Quiz Features.

WORK IN PROGRESS: The Radiator Wasn't There, a book about the problems involved in having a house refurbished; a book tentatively entitled *How to Live Well Below Your Income and Retire Early.*

SIDELIGHTS: Saltz wrote: "I have been on dozens of radio shows, discussing quizzes and 'trivia' as well as other subjects with which I am familiar, including politics and business economy. I believe that the syndicated 'Trivia Quiz,' started in March, 1966, is the oldest such quiz in existence.

"My comments on the economy are that inflation is America's worst enemy and must be stopped. We must take pay cuts, if necessary, and taxes must be cut. Saving must be encouraged with tax benefits, and some of this can be made up by taxing instead of exempting interest paid, at least a substantial part of it. The federal budget *must* be balanced. Additionally, more firms should allow flexible hours and shorter work weeks for those who desire them at lower pay. This is a good way to ease people into partial or full retirement."

* * *

SAMUEL, Maurice 1895-1972

PERSONAL: Born February 8, 1895, in Macin, Rumania; died May 4, 1972, in New York, N.Y.; naturalized U.S. citizen, 1921; son of Isaac and Fanny (Acker) Samuel; married Gertrude Kahn, 1921 (divorced); married Edith Brodsky; children: Eva, Gershon. *Education:* Attended Victoria University, Manchester, England, 1911-14.

CAREER: Essayist, novelist, critic, and lecturer. Interpreter at World War I peace conference and reparations commission in Berlin and Vienna. Guest on numerous radio and television programs, including "Words We Live By," aired by National Broadcasting Co., Inc. (NBC-Radio), 1953-71. *Military service:* Served in U.S. Army during World War I; became sergeant. *Awards, honors:* Anisfield-Wolf Award, 1943, and annual award from *Saturday Review of Literature,* 1944, both for *The World of Sholom Aleichem;* Stephen B. Wise Award, 1956; B'nai B'rith Jewish Heritage award, 1967; honorary doctor of humane letters from Brandeis University, 1967; Manger Prize in English literature, 1972.

WRITINGS: You Gentiles, Harcourt, 1924; *I, the Jew,* Harcourt, 1927; *What Happened in Palestine: The Events of August, 1929, Their Background, and Their Significance,* Stratford, 1929; *On the Rim of the Wilderness: The Conflict in Palestine,* Liveright, 1931; *Jews on Approval,* Liveright, 1932; *The Great Hatred,* Knopf, 1940; *The World of Sholom Aleichem,* Knopf, 1943; *Harvest in the Desert,* Jewish Publication Society of America, 1944; *Prince of the Ghetto,* Knopf, 1948.

The Gentleman and the Jew, Knopf, 1950; *Level Sunlight,* Knopf, 1953; *Certain People of the Book,* Knopf, 1955; *The Professor and the Fossil: Some Observations on Arnold Toynbee's "A Study of History,"* Knopf, 1956; *Light on Israel,* Knopf, 1961; (editor) *Ten Commandments,* University of Chicago Press, 1963; *Little Did I Know: Recollections and Reflections,* Knopf, 1963; *Blood Accusations: The Strange History of the Beiliss Case,* Knopf, 1966; *In Praise of Yiddish,* Cowles, 1971; (with Mark Van Doren) *In the Beginning, Love: Dialogues on the Bible,* edited by wife, Edith Samuel, John Day, 1973; (with Van Doren) *The Book of Praise: Dialogues on the Psalms,* edited by E. Samuel, John Day, 1975; *The Words of Maurice Samuel,* Jewish Publication Society of America, 1977.

Novels: *The Outsider,* Duffield, 1921; *Whatever Gods,* Duffield, 1923; *Beyond Woman,* Coward, 1934; *The Web of Lucifer: A Novel of the Borgia Fury,* Knopf, 1947; *The Devil That Failed,* Knopf, 1952; *The Second Crucifixion,* Knopf, 1960.

Translator: Edmund Fleg, *The Jewish Anthology,* Harcourt, 1925; Shmarya Levin, *Childhood in Exile,* Harcourt, 1929; Levin, *Youth in Revolt,* Harcourt, 1930; Levin, *The Arena,* Harcourt, 1932; Sholem Asch, *The Nazarene,* Putnam, 1939; *Haggadah of Passover,* Hebrew Publishing, 1942; Israel Joshua Singer, *The Brothers Ashkenazi,* World Publishing,

1963; Singer, *Yoshe Kalb,* Harper, 1965; Alex Bein, *Theodore Herzl: A Biography of the Founder of Modern Zionism,* Atheneum, 1970; Chaim Nachman Bialik, *Selected Poems,* Union of American Hebrew Congregations, 1972; Singer, *East of Eden,* Vanguard, 1976; Singer, *The River Breaks Up,* Vanguard, 1976. Also translator of *Children of Abraham: The Short Stories of Sholem Asch,* 1942.

Also author of sound recording, *The Latest Period in Yiddish Literature,* McGraw, 1967.

Contributor of numerous articles to periodicals, including *Look* and *Saturday Review.*

SIDELIGHTS: Maurice Samuel was, as Robert Alter wrote in *Commentary,* "a kind of one-man educational movement in American Jewish life." His subjects ranged from anti-Semitism to Zionism and from the Bible to Sholom Aleichem, and his audience ranged "from sisterhood ladies to intellectuals ignorant of Judaism and curious non-Jews." Yet, as an expositor of Jewish values and culture, Samuel imbued the wide variety of his books with a unity of purpose: to explain an unfamiliar world to Western readers.

To achieve this purpose, Samuel sustained a dual perspective in his writings. On the one hand, Alter noted, he placed many of his books within an autobiographical framework. As a result, his subject often comes through, not as "a set of ideas, lives, or events," but as "his own discovery of them." On the other hand, Samuel "continually viewed the idea of being a Jew against the background of eternity." The basis of his work was religious, supporting the conviction, in Alter's words, "that the moral aspirations of Jewish tradition do reflect a divine will and purpose."

Although he was born into a traditional Jewish home in Rumania, it was not until his adulthood that he became absorbed in the Jewish culture. His understanding of Jewish life and letters was acquired both through study, including learning the Yiddish and Hebrew languages, and through extensive travels.

Alter suggested that Samuel's need "to reconstruct the past through painstaking effort qualified him perfectly to create it for others who had no knowledge of it." Even his novels are enriched by his ability to recreate older cultures. Ten years of research, for example, preceded *The Second Crucifixion,* which the *Times Literary Supplement* called "a notable and sober feat of historical reconstruction." *Christian Century* called the work "a vivid recreation of a dramatic period in the early history of the church." Set in Rome in the second century A.D., the novel is about a Jewish girl who is adopted by an aristocratic Roman family but then rejoins the Roman Jewish community after an ill-fated marriage.

Similarly, *The Web of Lucifer* was described in the *New Yorker* as "a brilliant closeup of life in the service of the Borgias during the reign of Alexander VI in Rome." The story of a young Italian peasant's search for his brother's murderer, the novel was especially praised for what R. E. Danielson in *Atlantic Monthly* called its "careful reconstruction and presentation of an amazingly rich and varied scene." As P. J. Searles wrote in the *New York Herald Tribune Weekly Book Review,* "the author, whose knowledge of the times seems prodigious, has woven a tapestry of history, complete and accurate in detail."

Alter observed that "the one thing [Samuel] can clearly do with words better than most writers is to make the past moment present in all its flow of emotional life." Perhaps even more effectively than in his novels, this skill is at work in his nonfiction, particularly in *The World of Sholom Alei-*

chem. Considered by a number of critics to be his best work, the book recorded the details and quality of life in the Russian and Polish Jewish Pale at a time when that life was being forever destroyed by Hitler's armies.

Sholom Aleichem, frequently labeled the "Jewish Dickens," was a Yiddish humorist and story writer. His tales, set in the small town of Kasrielevky, centered on the poverty and piety of its people, on what Clement Greenberg called "the disparity between the Jew's visions of heaven, space, security, and wealth on the one hand and his cramped and precarious confinement on the other." In his book, Samuel discussed not Aleichem and his writings, but his world. By depicting "how the Kasrielevkites lived, married, brought up children, earned their bread, sorrowed, rejoiced and died," as a *New York Times* reviewer put it, Samuel created not a critical work but a memorial to an entire people.

Thus Samuel is credited with introducing Sholom Aleichem to the English-speaking world, as he is similarly credited with doing for another great Yiddish humorist, Isaac Loeb Peretz. *Prince of the Ghetto,* a collection of Peretz's stories, contains in addition two essays on Yiddish in which Samuel discusses that language's unique characteristics. His insistence that Yiddish literature cannot be translated, but must be retold, brought disparaging comments from his critics.

Samuel tackled this problem in a later work, *In Praise of Yiddish,* whose appearance was called a capstone to Samuel's career "as translator and Jewish cultural mediator." According to Lucy S. Dawidowicz, the book goes beyond a study of the complexities of the Yiddish language for it "also constitutes, in effect, a kind of discursive Yiddish-English dictionary of over a thousand words, idioms, and phrases. These are not merely translated, but are also defined and fully explicated, with appropriate examples." Samuel's historical perspective is again brought to bear, Curt Leviant observed in the *Saturday Review,* as he analyzes the language "from its birth nearly a millenium ago."

Samuel's other works touched on most aspects of Jewish life. *Blood Accusations,* for example, recounts the story of Mendel Beiliss, a Russian Jew accused in 1911 of killing a Ukrainian boy and using his blood for a religious ritual. Although known to be innocent, Beiliss was framed in a conspiracy of the actual murderers, local officials, and, it was suggested, agents of the czar himself. Samuel's account emphasized the czar's purported role in the case and his ill-advised attempt to link the revolutionary movement in Russia with "the Jewish evil." As with his historical reconstructions, Samuel's version of the Beiliss case was praised for the fineness of its detail. Leonard Schapiro of the *New York Review of Books,* for example, called it "a scrupulous study" told with passion and dignity, "a most valuable book for the historian both of Russia and of the Jewish people."

Samuel's *Light on Israel* is a discussion of the history of Jewish-Arab relations in the twentieth century. In it the author maintained: "I'm not writing to persuade or convince anyone. I am writing to testify." In his review of the book for the *New York Times Book Review,* Chaim Potok noted not only the author's "keen and subtle insights" but also "the grace and wit and passion we have come to expect from Maurice Samuel." Curt Leviant, moreover, declared: "For the constant intelligence, urbanity, and grace of his writing, Maurice Samuel has earned an honored role in Jewish literature. American literary critics have been remiss in not properly evaluating the place in English letters of one of the master stylists in the language."

BIOGRAPHICAL/CRITICAL SOURCES: Commonweal,

March 19, 1943; *New York Times,* April 4, 1943, August 13, 1966; *New Republic,* June 21, 1943; *Nation,* October 16, 1943, October 17, 1966; *New Yorker,* March 1, 1947; *New York Herald Tribune Weekly Book Review,* March 2, 1947; *Atlantic Monthly,* May, 1947; *Christian Century,* January 11, 1961, May 26, 1971; *Times Literary Supplement,* May 26, 1961, April 6, 1967; Maurice Samuel, *Little Did I Know: Recollections and Reflections,* Knopf, 1963; *Commentary,* March, 1964, December, 1971; *New York Times Book Review,* September 18, 1966, June 2, 1968; *Harper's,* October, 1966; *New York Review of Books,* June 1, 1967; *Observer Review,* October 8, 1967; *Jewish Quarterly,* spring, 1968; *Saturday Review,* May 18, 1968; *New Leader,* August 26, 1968; Milton Hindus, editor, *The Words of Maurice Samuel,* Jewish Publication Society of America, 1977.

OBITUARIES: New York Times, May 5, 1972; *Washington Post,* May 6, 1972.*

—*Sketch by Andrea Geffner*

*   *   *

SAMUELS, Lesser 1894(?)-1980

OBITUARY NOTICE: Born c. 1894 in Pittsburgh, Pa.; died December 2, 1980, in New York. Writer. Samuels wrote the screenplays for several films, including "You're in the Navy Now," "The Silver Chalice," and "Great Day in the Morning." He received Academy Award nominations for "No Way Out," which he wrote in collaboration with Joseph L. Mankiewicz, and "Ace in the Hole," on which he collaborated with Billy Wilder. In 1958, Samuels went to New York and began writing for the stage. He wrote a musical comedy, "Greenwillow," with Frank Loesser. It was produced on Broadway in 1960. Obituaries and other sources: *International Motion Picture Almanac,* Quigley, 1979; *New York Times,* December 23, 1980.

*   *   *

SANDERS, Colonel
See SANDERS, Harland

*   *   *

SANDERS, Harland 1890-1980
(Colonel Sanders)

OBITUARY NOTICE: Born September 9, 1890, near Henryville, Ind.; died of pneumonia, December 16, 1980, in Louisville, Ky. Restaurateur and founder of fast-food chain. Sanders, best known as "the Colonel," was the founding-father of the Kentucky Fried Chicken fast-food eateries. A familiar figure in a white linen suit, string tie, and goatee, he was the living symbol of the corporation he created. Sanders began his culinary career by selling snacks to hungry travelers from the backroom of a gas station. The venture grew into a restaurant which he ran successfully for twenty-seven years. In 1956, when he was sixty-six years old, the Colonel set out to establish a franchise business by selling his secret recipe for "finger lickin' good" chicken. Eight years later he sold the franchise operation for $2 million to entrepreneurs Jack Massey and John Y. Brown. The number of franchises grew from six hundred in 1964 to thirty-five hundred in 1971, the year that Heublein, Inc., acquired the company for an estimated $287 million in stock. Sanders remained with the Kentucky Fried Chicken Corp. as a consultant and good-will ambassador until his death. He wrote *Life as I Have Known It Has Been Finger Lickin' Good.* Obituaries and other sources: *Current Biography,* Wilson, 1973, February, 1981; *Who's Who in America,* 40th edition, Marquis, 1978; *New York Times,* December 17, 1980; *Time,* December 29, 1980.

SANDOR, Bela I(mre) 1935-

PERSONAL: Born May 6, 1935, in Szombathely, Hungary; came to the United States in 1957, naturalized citizen, 1962; son of Bela B. and Augusta (Derfler) Sandor; married Ruth Godfrey (a librarian and demographic researcher), December 19, 1968; children: Margit J.; (stepchildren) Leigh, Christina, Susan. *Education:* University of Illinois, B.S., 1961, Ph.D., 1968; New York University, M.S., 1963. *Home:* 438 Hillington Way, Madison, Wis. 53705. *Office:* Department of Engineering Mechanics, University of Wisconsin, Madison, Wis. 53706.

CAREER: Bell Telephone Laboratories, Murray Hill, N.J., member of technical staff, 1961-64; University of Wisconsin—Madison, assistant professor, 1968-71, associate professor, 1971-77, professor of engineering mechanics, 1977—. *Member:* American Society for Testing and Materials, American Society for Engineering Education, Sigma Xi.

WRITINGS: Fundamentals of Cyclic Stress and Strain, University of Wisconsin Press, 1972; *Strength of Materials,* Prentice-Hall, 1978; *Experiments in Strength of Materials,* Prentice-Hall, 1980; *Statics,* Prentice-Hall, in press; *Dynamics,* Prentice-Hall, in press. Contributor to engineering and education journals.

WORK IN PROGRESS: A three-act play; research on fatigue and fracture of engineering materials.

SIDELIGHTS: Sandor told *CA:* "My work in engineering education has ranged from presentations to high-school students to advising Ph.D. candidates in thesis research. Helping young people develop their skills is as delightful as watching a cat stretch after a nap. And, of course, most students have been half napping before they get here.

"How is reveille called? By the notes of many different instruments: the sound of a bridge collapsing, a car overturning, a wing falling off, a surgical implant bending, a heart valve tapping, and Galileo slurping wine with his assistants. Also by personal challenges to discover, invent, swim, lift weights, jitterbug, and jump, all in good fun. The students in their ascent are also coaxed to read and write, read and write. In my own views of all this, classical dance serves as a perfect counterpoint for creative work based on discipline and structure."

When Bela Sandor was a student at the University of Illinois, he set an unofficial world record for swimming 125 yards underwater. He has studied dance since 1973, and has performed in major roles in local ballets.

*   *   *

SANDROFF, Ronni 1943-

PERSONAL: Born December 19, 1943, in Dobbs Ferry, N.Y.; daughter of Michael and Sylvia Sandroff; married Leonid Kulberg (a consultant), 1977; children: Samantha, Michael. *Education:* Hunter College of the City University of New York, A.B., 1964; University of Iowa, M.A., 1966. *Politics:* Radical. *Religion:* Jewish. *Home:* 117 Bellaire Dr., Dobbs Ferry, N.Y. 10522. *Agent:* Erica Spellman, William Morris Agency, 1350 Avenue of the Americas, New York, N.Y. 10019. *Office: RN,* Kinderkamack Rd., Oradell, N.J.

CAREER: Albert Einstein College of Medicine, Bronx, N.Y., medical writer, 1966-76; free-lance magazine writer, 1976-78; *RN,* Oradell, N.J., editor and writer, 1978—. Fellow at Bread Loaf Writers Conference, 1976, staff assistant, 1978. *Member:* Authors Guild, Authors League of America, Poets and Writers, Women's Ink.

WRITINGS: *Party Party/Girlfriends* (two short novels), Knopf, 1975; *Fighting Back* (novel), Knopf, 1978. Contributor of short stories to magazines, including *Redbook, McCall's, Cosmopolitan, Confluence,* and *Prairie Schooner.*

WORK IN PROGRESS: *Occasional Courage,* a novel about the son of a black marketeer from Odessa, Russia, who immigrates to the United States.

SIDELIGHTS: Roni Sandroff told CA: "In fiction I am most interested in how we influence each other, and how we're molded by the trends and fashionable ideas of our times. Dr. Drummond, a columnist for *Mother Jones* magazine, said it well: 'Instead of a red thread of personality, there are great cultural waves upon which our personal lives ride.'

"*Party Party* and *Girlfriends* are two short novels about male/female entanglements at the start of the women's movement era. *Fighting Back* is about how groups—a religious cult and a left-wing political organization—ensnare and develop people. The book I'm working on now concerns how nationality shapes character: the main characters are a Russian emigrant and an American woman who is immersed in Chinese politics.

"Of course I'm not aware of these themes until I stand back from the work. While I'm writing I worry more about keeping the action funny and fast-moving and letting the characters do and say what they choose. I work on my fiction in the early morning hours. The rest of the day is devoted to medical editing which pays the bills."

*   *   *

SANDS, Dorothy   1893-1980

OBITUARY NOTICE: Born March 5, 1893, in Cambridge, Mass., died September 11, 1980, in Croton-on-Hudson, N.Y. Actress. Sanders was a stage actress for nearly fifty years. She was best known as a diseuse and mimic. Her talent for mimicry was displayed early in the 1920's when she had starring roles in the annual "Grand Street Follies," which burlesqued the stars of Broadway. She produced and starred in her own one-woman shows, including "Styles in Acting" and "Our Stage and Stars." In 1959 Sands received a Tony Award for teaching in the American Theatre Wing's professional training program. Her last major role was in 1972. She wrote *Twenty-one Lessons in Acting* with Donald Keyes. Obituaries and other sources: *Who's Who in the Theatre,* 16th edition, Pitman, 1977; *New York Times,* September 17, 1980.

*   *   *

SAN MARTIN, Marta   1942-

PERSONAL: Born October 11, 1942, in Cuba; daughter of Julian (in business) and Isabel (in law; maiden name, Morejon) San Martin; married Ramon L. Bonachea IV (deceased); children: Ramon L. V. Education: Dubuque University, B.A. (cum laude), 1967; American University, M.A., 1968; Columbia University, M.A., 1976. Religion: Protestant. Office: North Hudson Regional Council of Mayors, 6914 Bergenline Ave., Guttenberg, N.J. 07093.

CAREER: Writer. North Hudson Regional Council of Mayors, Guttenberg, N.J., researcher and planner, 1978—. Adjunct instructor at Montclair State College, 1978—.

WRITINGS: (With Ramon Bonachea) *The Cuban Insurrection,* Transaction Books, 1975. Also contributor to *Cuban Communism,* edited by Irving Louis Horowitz, 1979.

WORK IN PROGRESS: *The Cuban Armed Forces: A Study of Militarization.*

SASS, Lorna Janet   1945-

PERSONAL: Born October 20, 1945, in New York, N.Y.; daughter of Alfred and Eleanor (Sailon) Sass. Education: Columbia University, Ph.D., 1979. Home and office: 46 West 83rd St., New York, N.Y. 10024.

CAREER: Queens College of the City University of New York, Flushing, N.Y., instructor in writing, 1974-79. Member of faculty at New School for Social Research, 1978, Columbia University, 1978-80, Bennington College, summers, 1979-80, and University of Pennsylvania, 1979—; gives workshops and lectures; consultant to Culinary Institute of America. Member: American Society of Journalists and Authors, Authors Guild.

WRITINGS: *To the King's Taste: Richard II's Book of Feasts and Recipes,* Metropolitan Museum of Art, 1975; *To the Queen's Taste: Elizabethan Feasts and Recipes Adapted for Modern Cooking,* Metropolitan Museum of Art, 1976; *Dinner With Tom Jones,* Metropolitan Museum of Art, 1977; *The Fourme of Cury: A Fourteenth-Century Cookbook in Middle English,* Garland, 1981. General editor of "Classics in the History of Gastronomy," Johnson Reprint and Walter Johnson. Contributor to *Grolier Children's Encyclopedia.* Contributor to magazines and newspapers, including *Gourmet, Ford Times, International Review of Food and Wine, Library Journal, Museum News,* and *New York Times.*

WORK IN PROGRESS: A major text on the history of gastronomy.

SIDELIGHTS: At her lectures, workshops, and cooking school, Lorna Sass teaches the history and literature of gastronomy, as well as cooking in a wide variety of historical cuisines, including Roman, medieval English, Italian, French, Arabic, Elizabethan, Italian Renaissance, early American, and the eighteenth century.

Sass commented: "I believe that the proper study of mankind is food."

*   *   *

SAUNDERS, Jean   1932-
(Sally Blake, Jean Innes, Rowena Summers)

PERSONAL: Born February 8, 1932, in London, England; daughter of John Alexander and Minnie (Wheatley) Innes; married Geoffrey Saunders (a lecturer), September 20, 1952; children: Barry Clive, Janet Saunders Underhay, Ann Lesley Saunders Bees. Education: Educated in Weston-Super-Mare, Avon, England. Home: 2 Kingfisher Rd., Worle, Weston-Super-Mare, Avon, England. Agent: Curtis Brown Ltd., 1 Craven Hill, London W2 3EP England.

CAREER: Writer. Medical Research Council, Clevedon, Avon, England, assay laboratory assistant, 1948-54; writer, 1965—. Member: Romantic Novelists Association, Society of Women Writers and Journalists, West Country Writers Association.

WRITINGS—Teenage novels: *The Fugitives,* Heinemann, 1974; *Only Yesterday,* Scholastic Book Services, 1975; *Nightmare,* Heinemann, 1977; *Roses All the Way,* Heinemann, 1978; *The Tally-Man,* Dreyers Forlag, 1979; *Anchor Man,* Heinemann, 1980.

Romantic novels: *The Tender Trap,* Woman's Weekly, 1977; *Lady of the Manor,* Woman's Weekly, 1979; *Cobden's Cottage,* Woman's Weekly, 1979; *Rainbow's End,* Woman's Weekly, 1979; *The Enchantment of Merrowporth,* Cameo, 1980; *The Kissing Time,* Simon & Schuster, 1981.

Under pseudonym Jean Innes; all published by R. Hale:

Ashton's Folly, 1975; *Sands of Lamanna,* 1975; *The Golden God,* 1975; *The Whispering Dark,* 1976; *White Blooms of Yarrow,* 1976; *Boskelly's Bride,* 1976; *The Wishing Stone,* 1976; *The Dark Stranger,* 1979; *Silver Lady,* 1981.

Other: (under pseudonym Rowena Summers) *Blackmaddie* (historical romance), Hamlyn, 1980; (under pseudonym Sally Blake) *The Devil's Kiss,* Macdonald/Futura, 1981.

Contributor of more than six hundred short stories to women's magazines, including *Woman's Story, Woman's Own, My Weekly, Hers, Love Affair, True,* and *Loving.*

WORK IN PROGRESS: Moon Child.

SIDELIGHTS: Saunders told *CA:* "I think 'staying power' is as vital as anything to an aspiring author. In fifteen years of writing, my determination to 'get there' has never wavered, despite rejections and setbacks. I give many talks to writers' groups and always emphasize this aspect of the job. And it *is* a job for me—not a little hobby!

"Although most of my fiction is of the light romance variety, when people tell me they couldn't put my book down, I know I've succeeded in what I set out to do. I have a great feel for backgrounds, and really live out my characters' lives as I write. At the end of my longest novel, *Moon Child,* I was emotionally drained. This book is set in the United States during the Civil War, and when I recently visited Washington, D.C., and actually took a boat trip on the Potomac River, I felt extremely emotional about being where my characters had lived.

"Every year I go to the Writers Summer School in England, and to various weekend conferences, both to listen and learn, and to give talks myself. I think it's the biggest mistake for a writer to believe there's nothing more to learn—and there's nothing so enjoyable as meeting other writers and talking 'shop.'

"I'm told I'm a prolific writer. I don't find it difficult to keep doing a job that I love, though I admit it takes self-discipline to sit at a desk when the sun is shining outside, and there are still blank moments when the ideas don't come, but fortunately not too many. The more I write, the more receptive I become to ideas, and to the way of communicating them on paper for other people's enjoyment as well as my own."

*   *   *

SAUSER-HALL, Frederic   1887-1961
(Blaise Cendrars)

PERSONAL: Born September 1, 1887, in Paris, France; died January 21, 1961, in Paris; married second wife (an actress); children: two sons. *Education:* University of Paris, B.A., 1907.

CAREER: Writer. Worked variously in business, horticulture, journalism, and motion pictures. *Military service:* Served with French Foreign Legion during World War I.

WRITINGS—All under pseudonym Blaise Cendrars; in English: *Le Panama; ou, Les Aventures de mes sept oncles,* [Paris], 1918, translation by John Dos Passos published as *Panama; or, The Adventures of My Seven Uncles,* Harper, 1931; (compiler) *L'Anthologie negre,* Editions de la Sirene, 1921, revised edition, Correa, 1947, reprinted, Le Livre de Poche, 1972, translation by Margery Bianco published as *The African Saga,* Payson & Clarke, 1927, reprinted, Negro University Press, 1969; *Kodak,* Stock, 1924, translation by Ron Padgett published under same title, Adventures in Poetry, 1976; *L'Or: La Merveilleuse Histoire du general Johann August Suter* (novel), B. Grasset, 1925, reprinted,

1964, translation by Henry Longan Stuart published as *Sutter's Gold,* Harper, 1926; *Moravagine* (novel), B. Grasset, 1926, reprinted, 1956, translation by Alan Brown published under same title, Owen, 1968, Projection Books, 1970; *Dan Yack,* Volume I: *Le Plan de l'aiguille,* Au Sans Pariel, 1927, Volume II: *Les Confessions de Dan Yack,* [Paris], 1929, published together in one-volume edition, [Paris], 1946, translation published as *Antarctic Fugue,* Pushkin Press, 1948; *Petite contes negres pour les enfants des blancs,* [Paris], 1928, translation by Bianco published as *Little Black Stories for Little White Children,* Payson & Clarke, 1929.

(Editor) Hans Bringolf, *I Have No Regrets: Being the Memoirs of Lieutenant Bringolf,* translated from the original French by Warre B. Wells, Jarrolds, 1931; *L'Homme foudroye* (autobiographical novel), Denoel, 1945, reprinted, Gallimard, 1973, translation by Nina Rootes published as *The Astonished Man,* Owen, 1970; *La Main Coupee* (title means "The Cut-off Hand"), Denoel, 1946, reprinted, Gallimard, 1973, translation by Rootes published as *Lice,* Owen, 1973; *Bourlinguer* (title means "Reminiscences"), Denoel, 1948, abridged translation by Rootes published as *Planus,* Owen, 1972; *Emmene-moi au bout du monde!,* Denoel, 1956, translation by Brown published as *To the End of the World,* Owen, 1967; *Selected Writings,* translated from the original French, edited by Walter Albert, New Directions, 1966; *Complete Postcards From the Americas: Poems of Road and Sea,* translated from the original French, University of California Press, 1976; *Pathe Baby,* translated from the original French, City Lights, 1980.

In French; all published in France: *La Legende de novgorode,* 1909; *Sequences,* 1912; *Les Paques a New York,* 1912; *La Prose du trans-siberien et la petite Jehanne de France* (title means "The Prose of the Trans-Siberian and of Little Jehanne of France"), 1913, reprinted as *Le Trans-siberien,* P. Seghers, 1957; *Profound aujourd'hui,* LaBelle, 1917; *J'ai tue,* 1918; *Du Monde entier au coeur du monde* (poems; title means "From the Entire World"), Editions de la Nouvelle revue francaise, 1919, reprinted, Denoel, 1957; (with Abel Gance) *J'accuse,* 1919; *Dix neuf poemes elastiques* (title means "Nineteen Elastic Poems"), 1919; *La Fin du monde,* Editions de la Sirene, 1919, reprinted, P. Seghers, 1949; *J'ai saigne,* 1920; (with Gance) *La Roue,* 1922; *Feuilles de route,* Au Sans Pareil, 1924; *ABC de cinema,* 1926; *L'Eloge de la vie dangereuse,* 1926; *Une nuit dans la foret,* 1929.

Rhum: L'Aventure de Jean Galmot, B. Grasset, 1930, reprinted, 1960; *Aujourd'hui,* B. Grasset, 1931; *Vol a voiles* (autobiographical), Payot, 1932; *Hollywood: La Mecque de cinema,* B. Grasset, 1936; (translator) O. Henry, *Hors la Loi!: La Vie d'outlaw american racontee par lui-ineme,* 1936; *Histoires vraies,* B. Grasset, 1938; *La Vie dangereuse* (title means "The Dangerous Life"), B. Grasset, 1938; *D'Oultremer a indigo,* B. Grasset, 1940; *Poesies completes,* Denoel, 1944; *Blaise Cendrars,* Nouvelle Revue critique, 1947; *Oeuvres choisies,* 1948; *La Banlieue de Paris,* La Builde du livre, 1949; *Le Lotissement du ciel* (title means "Heaven in Lots"), Denoel, 1949.

Blaise Cendrars vous parle, Denoel, 1952; *Le Bresil: Des Hommes sont venus,* Documents d'art, 1952; *Trop c'est trop* (title means "Too Much"), Denoel, 1957; *A L'Aventure,* Denoel, 1958; *Films sans images,* Denoel, 1959; *Saint Joseph de Cupertino,* Club de livre chretien, 1960; *Amours* (poems), P. Seghers, 1961; *Blaise Cendrars, 1887-1961,* Mercure de France, 1962; *Serajevo,* Theatre universitaire, 1963; *Oeuvres completes,* eight volumes, Club francais du livre, 1968-71; *Dites-nous, Monsieur Blaise Cendrars,* edited by Hughes Richard, Editions Recontre, 1969; *Ineduts secrets,* Club francais du livre, 1969.

SIDELIGHTS: When Blaise Cendrars ran away from home at age fifteen, he embarked on the first of many journeys that would span his lifetime and take him to such places as Siberia, Panama, China, Persia, Mongolia, North America, and the greater part of Europe. His novels and poems, celebrated for their rich images and striking effects, are largely autobiographical, evolved from his own experiences and travels.

BIOGRAPHICAL/CRITICAL SOURCES: Paris Review, April, 1966; *Times Literary Supplement,* February 16, 1967; *New York Times Book Review,* August 4, 1968; *Blaise Cendrars: Discovery and Re-Creation,* University of Toronto Press, 1978.

OBITUARIES: New York Times, January 22, 1961; *Publishers Weekly,* February 13, 1961.*

*   *   *

SAVITT, Todd Lee   1943-

PERSONAL: Born November 30, 1943, in New York, N.Y.; son of Arnold J. and Jane B. Savitt; married Carole Legon (a medical secretary), March 31, 1968; children: Allyson Beth, Jodey Rebecca. *Education:* Colgate University, A.B., 1965; graduate study at University of Rochester, 1965-68; University of Virginia, M.A., 1970, Ph.D., 1975; postdoctoral study at Duke University, 1974-76. *Religion:* Jewish. *Home:* 3922 Northwest 36th Ter., Gainesville, Fla. 32605. *Office:* Department of Community Health and Family Medicine, University of Florida, Box J-222, Gainesville, Fla. 32610.

CAREER: University of Florida, Gainesville, assistant professor of history of medicine and medical humanities, 1976—. Member of National Institutes of Health panel on history of life sciences, 1979-80; member of Hastings Center and Institute of Society, Ethics, and the Life Sciences, consultant to Center for the Study of Southern Culture. *Member:* American Association for the History of Medicine, Organization of American Historians, Southern Historical Association. *Awards, honors:* National Institutes of Health grants.

WRITINGS: Medicine and Slavery: The Diseases and Health Care of Blacks in Ante-Bellum Virginia, University of Illinois Press, 1978; (contributor) Ronald A. Carson, Richard C. Reynolds, and H. Gene Moss, editors, *Patient Wishes and Physician Obligations,* University Presses of Florida, 1978; (editor with Martin Kaufman and Stuart Galishoff) *Dictionary of American Medical Biography,* Greenwood Press, 1981. Contributor to history and medical journals.

WORK IN PROGRESS: Medicine After Emancipation, on health care of black people in the South after the Civil War, 1865-1900; an essay to be included in *The Health Professions,* edited by Marcia V. Boyles, Margaret K. Morgan, and Mary H. McCaulley, for Saunders; research on the social and medicial history of crib death and the history of sickle cell anemia.

SIDELIGHTS: Savitt wrote: "Providing a humanistic and historical perspective on medicine and health is a major goal of my involvement in the university. Health professional students often avoid or miss courses such as these as they prepare for their careers."

*   *   *

SAYEGH, Fayez A(bdullah)   1922-1980

OBITUARY NOTICE—See index for *CA* sketch: Born January 11, 1922, in Kharaba, Syria; died of a heart attack, December 9, 1980, in New York. Palestinian spokesman, political adviser, and author. At the time of his death, Sayegh was a political adviser at the Kuwaiti mission. Previously, he held that position at the Lebanese and Yemeni missions. He was a member of the Arab Information Office of the Arab League and, in 1965, he served on the Executive Committee of the Palestine Liberation Organization. Sayegh also founded the Palestine Research Center. His writings include *Nida al-a'mag, Ila ayn?, Arab Unity: Hope and Fulfillment, The Palestine Refugees,* and *Palestine, Israel and Peace.* Obituaries and other sources: *New York Times,* December 11, 1980.

*   *   *

SCAVULLO, Francesco   1929-

PERSONAL: Born January 16, 1929, in Staten Island, N.Y.; son of Angelo Carmelo (in manufacturing) and Margaret (Pavis) Scavullo; married Carol McCallson (a model), 1952 (divorced, 1956). *Education:* Educated in New York, N.Y. *Religion:* Roman Catholic. *Home and office:* 212 East 63rd St., New York, N.Y. 10021.

CAREER: Vogue Studios, New York City, apprentice photographer with Horst, 1945-48; Scavullo Studio, New York City, proprietor and photographer, 1948—; photographer in New York City with *Seventeen* (magazine), 1948-50, *Town and Country* (magazine), 1950, *Harper's Bazaar* (magazine), 1960, *Cosmopolitan* (magazine), 1965—, and *Vogue* (magazine), 1974—; photographs have appeared in numerous other magazines, including *Oui, Playboy, Viva, People, US, Good Housekeeping, Ladies Home Journal, New York, Rolling Stone, Time, Newsweek, Redbook,* and *Glamour.* Photographer for motion picture advertisements and of album covers. Actor and visual consultant in motion picture, "Lipstick," 1978. *Member:* Directors Guild of America. *Awards, honors:* Named photographer of the year, 1977.

WRITINGS: Scavullo on Beauty, Random House, 1976; *Scavullo on Men,* Random House, 1977.

WORK IN PROGRESS: A volume of Scavullo photographs from 1949 to 1980, publication by Harper expected in 1981; another beauty book, publication by Harper expected in 1981.

SIDELIGHTS: Ruth Kling of the *New York Daily News* called Francesco Scavullo "one of the world's best fashion photographers." For more than thirty years his photographs have graced the covers of such trend-setting magazines as *Cosmopolitan, Vogue, Seventeen, Town and Country,* and *Glamour.* In that time, he has firmly established the "Scavullo look" of simple elegance with no distracting frills or baubles. "I think women look better the more extra things they take off," he remarked. Apparently many agree. One of his photographic sessions costs in excess of five thousand dollars, and Scavullo does not lack customers. His subjects have included Martha Mitchell, Barbara Walters, Janis Joplin, Faye Dunaway, Barbara Streisand, Liza Minnelli, and Bianca Jagger. Scavullo also helped launch Burt Reynolds's career with his well-known nude photograph of the actor.

Scavullo started puttering in photography as a young boy. He experimented on his older sisters, making up their faces to resemble Dorothy Lamour and then snapping their pictures with the camera he borrowed from his father. "They were my guinea pigs," he asserted. Scavullo worked in a photographer's studio as a janitor and errand boy and then served an apprenticeship with the high-fashion *Vogue* photographer, Horst. By the age of nineteen, Scavullo had his first cover photo published on the front of *Seventeen*.

The photographer works in a stark white room with a large skylight in the roof to let in natural sunlight. Scavullo described his studio as "like a shell. I always work with music in the background. . . . Otherwise it would be like a tomb in there." When taking photographs, he endeavors to make his subject feel as relaxed and comfortable as possible. One of his techniques is to seat his customer on the floor with two huge white satin pillows. He explained: "We are all like children. We're comfortable on the floor or in bed." Another characteristic of a Scavullo sitting is that he always talks to his subject. Breathing such compliments as "you're perfect . . . you're silk . . . you're satin . . ." and "you're delicious," Scavullo aims to snap a beautiful portrait. "I coax and encourage and flatter, in fact I'll do anything to relax my model and get the best out of him or her."

Otherwise, Scavullo claims he has "no secrets. . . . I like to bring out the best in people. There's maybe a little too much realism today, with unflattering light and expressions. Photography can be an art because it can say everything or nothing." Scavullo added that "if I were to use the wrong lighting or camera angles I could even make the world's most beautiful woman look like s—."

Scavullo on Beauty, the photographer's first book, is a collection of interviews with fifty-nine female celebrities who reveal intimate details about their lifestyles. These interviews are supplemented by Scavullo photographs and beauty tips. The photographer's second book, *Scavullo on Men,* is similar in content and contains interviews with fifty well-known men also accompanied by photographs.

BIOGRAPHICAL/CRITICAL SOURCES: Newsweek, February 4, 1974, November 22, 1976; *New York,* December 16, 1974; *Biography News,* Volume II, Gale, 1975; *Philadelphia Inquirer,* January 9, 1975; *New York Daily Mail,* March 30, 1977; *New York Daily News,* November 20, 1977; *San Francisco Examiner,* November 23, 1977; *San Diego Union,* July 30, 1978; *New York Post,* October 20, 1978; *People,* May 1, 1980.

*   *   *

SCHACHTER, Michael 1941-

PERSONAL: Surname is pronounced *Shack*-ter; born January 15, 1941, in New York, N.Y.; son of Saul (a manufacturer) and Ann (a secretary; maiden name, Palestine) Schachter; married Margaret J. Kavanagh, July 22, 1967 (divorced March 29, 1978); children: Brian, Amy, Stefan. *Education:* Columbia University, B.A., 1961, M.D., 1965. *Residence:* Valley Cottage, N.Y. *Agent:* Barbara Lowenstein, 250 West 57th St., New York, N.Y. 10019. *Office:* Mountainview Medical Associates, Mountainview Ave., Nyack, N.Y. 10960.

CAREER: Hospital for Joint Diseases, New York, N.Y., intern, 1965-66; Kings County Hospital, Brooklyn, N.Y., resident in psychiatry, 1966-69; Rockland County Community Mental Health Center, Pomona, N.Y., director of emergency and admissions, 1971-72; Rockland County Mental Health Clinic, Pomona, director, 1972-74; Mountainview Medical Associates, Nyack, N.Y., private practice of medicine, 1974—. Associate attending physician at Good Samaritan Hospital; consultant to Bath Center for Brain-Injured Children. *Military service:* U.S. Air Force, co-director of Psychiatric Outpatient Clinic at Keesler Air Force Base, 1969-71; became captain.

MEMBER: International Academy of Preventive Medicine, International College of Applied Nutrition, American Academy of Medical Preventics (vice-president), American College of Nutrition, American Psychiatric Association, American Holistic Medical Association, Society of Clinical Ecology, Academy of Orthomolecular Psychiatry (third vice-president), New York State Medical Society, Rockland County Medical Society. *Awards, honors:* Appreciation award from National Health Foundation, 1979; Carlos Lamar Pioneer Memorial Award from American Academy of Medical Preventics, 1979, for research on chelation therapy.

WRITINGS: (With David Sheinkin and Richard Hutton) *The Food Connection,* Bobbs-Merrill, 1979, reprinted as *Food, Mind, and Mood,* Warner Books, 1980. Contributor to scholarly journals.

WORK IN PROGRESS: A book with David Sheinkin, *Helping Yourself Get Well: A Step by Step Program for Recovering From Illness.*

SIDELIGHTS: Schachter commented: "The group of holistically oriented physicians and assistants who work with me in an office setting strive to treat the 'whole' person. Our approach includes nutrition, orthomolecular psychiatry, orthomolecular medicine and preventive medicine. Patients range from those who are basically healthy and wish to achieve optimal health to those who are very ill. Psychological and medical problems include schizophrenia, severe depression, food allergies, hypoglycemia and degenerative diseases such as cancer, arthritis, and cardiovascular disease.

"Treatment programs are individualized and may consist of a detoxification program, specialized diet, nutritional supplements, an exercise program, any variety of stress reduction or psychological modalities, and specialized therapies such as chelation or metabolic therapies for cancer patients.

"I believe that many of the diseases and illnesses people suffer from today are a result of our lifestyle and the way we eat. Because of modernization and industrialization, many artificial elements and substances have been introduced into our previously 'natural' environment. Many of these are carcinogenic and downright life threatening. The whole food chain is contaminated by various toxic agents; thus, I stress eating the natural, organic foods as much as possible. I am also an outspoken opponent of artificial fluoridation of our water supplies. Drinking water is essential to life, and the people drinking it should have a choice whether or not they wish to drink water containing a prescription drug.

"I have incorporated much of what I have learned about nutrition and preventive medicine into my own life and that of my family. For example, my nine-year-old daughter, who is afflicted with a moderate case of cerebral palsy, has benefitted greatly from a holistic treatment program.

"Many people live a long life, but I am concerned with the quality of the life they lead. Do they feel as well physically, emotionally, and spiritually as they possibly can? Little do people realize that many of those chronic, nagging ailments or feelings they've 'learned to live with' can be modified or greatly improved with a few changes in life-style or eating habits.

"Research and self-education regarding new treatments and techniques constitute a large chunk of my life. As much as possible, I share my learning with my staff and colleagues; and now, through my writing, I am able to reach a greater number of people."

BIOGRAPHICAL/CRITICAL SOURCES: Prevention, December, 1976; *National Food Association Newsletter,* autumn, 1977.

SCHARY, Jill
See ROBINSON, Jill

*   *   *

SCHERMAN, David E(dward) 1916-

PERSONAL: Born March 2, 1916, in New York, N.Y.; son of William S. and Celia (Harris) Scherman; married Rosemarie Redlich (a writer and historian), June 11, 1949; children: John, Anthony. *Education:* Dartmouth College, B.A., 1936. *Home address:* Collaberg Rd., Stony Point, N.Y. 10980.

CAREER: Time, Inc., New York, N.Y., 1936-76, staff photographer for *Life*, 1939-47, associate editor of *Life*, 1947-66, senior editor of *Life*, 1966-72; free-lance writer, 1976—. War correspondent, 1941-46. *Member:* Willa Cather Pioneer Memorial Society (member of board of governors).

WRITINGS: Literary England, Random House, 1944; (with John R. McCrary) *The First of the Many* (nonfiction), Simon & Schuster, 1944; (with wife, Rosemarie Redlich Scherman) *Literary America*, Dodd, 1951; (with R. R. Scherman) *America: The Land and Its Writers*, Dodd, 1953; (editor) *The Best of Life*, Time-Life, 1973; (editor) *Life Goes to the Movies*, Time-Life, 1974; (editor) *Life Goes to War*, Little, Brown, 1976. Contributor to newspapers.

WORK IN PROGRESS: Research for a book on home construction.

SIDELIGHTS: Scherman told *CA* that he turned from a writer and photographer to a building contractor.

*   *   *

SCHLOBIN, Roger Clark 1944-

PERSONAL: Surname is pronounced *Slow*-bin; born June 22, 1944, in Brooklyn, N.Y.; son of James Henry (a financial analyst) and Virginia (a legal secretary; maiden name, Clark) Schlobin; married Melody A. Carlsen, August 30, 1969 (divorced July 11, 1975). *Education:* C. W. Post College, Long Island University, B.A., 1966; University of Wisconsin—Madison, M.A., 1968; Ohio State University, Ph. D., 1971. *Home:* 802 North Calumet Rd., Chesterton, Ind. 46304. *Office:* Department of English, Purdue University, North Central Campus, Westville, Ind. 46391.

CAREER: Ohio State University, Columbus, assistant to director of Center for Medieval and Renaissance Studies, 1969-71; Purdue University, North Central Campus, Westville, Ind., assistant professor, 1971-78, associate professor of English, 1978—, special assistant to chancellor, 1979—. Instructor at Ohio Dominican College, 1968-71; public speaker; chairman of science fiction and fantasy seminars. Film consultant. Youth basketball coach, 1972-76. *Member:* Early English Text Society, Science Fiction Research Association, Mediaeval Academy of America, Modern Language Association of America, Fantasy Association, Science Fiction Foundation (England), Midwest Modern Language Association. *Awards, honors:* National Endowment for the Humanities fellowship, 1978.

WRITINGS: (With Marshall B. Tymn and L. W. Currey) *A Research Guide to Science Fiction Studies: An Annotated Checklist of Primary and Secondary Sources for Fantasy and Science Fiction*, Garland Publishing, 1977; (with Tymn) *The Year's Scholarship in Science Fiction and Fantasy, 1972-1975*, Kent State University Press, 1978; *The Literature of Fantasy: A Comprehensive, Annotated Bibliography of Modern Fantasy Fiction*, Garland Publishing, 1979; *Andre Norton: A Primary and Secondary Bibliography*, G. K. Hall, 1980.

Contributor: Marleen S. Barr, editor, *The Future Females*, Bowling Green University Popular Press, 1980; Marshall B. Tymn, editor, *The Science Fiction Reference Book*, FAX Collector's Editions, 1981. Editor of series "The Reader's Guides to Contemporary Science Fiction and Fantasy Authors," Starmont House, 1978—, and "Classics of Fantasy Literature," Garland Publishing, 1980-81. Contributor to magazines, including *Extrapolation* and *Media and Methods*. Advisory editor of *Proceedings of the First International Conference on the Fantastic*, 1980-81.

WORK IN PROGRESS: Editing *The Aesthetics of Fantasy*, publication expected in 1981; *A Handbook to Fantasy*, with Gary K. Wolfe, publication expected in 1982 or 1983.

SIDELIGHTS: Schlobin wrote: "My approach to my teaching and scholarship has always concentrated on epistemology, focusing on my concern that people infrequently understand their own ways of knowing and reacting. Toward this end, I've always been interested in definitions that grow out of the issues at hand and that bring skills and insights that further insight and pleasure."

AVOCATIONAL INTERESTS: "Playing basketball (well) and racquetball (poorly) and living a quiet life with my sixteen-pound tomcat, Joshua Thunderpussy."

*   *   *

SCHNEIDER, John C(harles) 1945-

PERSONAL: Born March 15, 1945, in New York, N.Y.; son of Charles L. (an insurance office manager) and Josephine A. (a university administrative assistant; maiden name, Bolin) Schneider; married Suzanne Whiting (a property manager), August 24, 1968; children: Olivia, David. *Education:* Fordham University, B.A., 1966; University of Minnesota, M.A., 1968, Ph.D., 1971. *Home:* 3405 South 28th St., Lincoln, Neb. 68502. *Office:* Department of History, University of Nebraska, Lincoln, Neb. 68588.

CAREER: University of Nebraska, Lincoln, assistant professor, 1971-77, associate professor of history, 1977—. Member of Lincoln Historic Preservation Commission. *Member:* National Commission for Historic Preservation, Organization of American Historians.

WRITINGS: Detroit and the Problem of Order, 1830-1880, University of Nebraska Press, 1980. Contributor to history journals.

WORK IN PROGRESS: Research on homeless men in urban America, 1850-1940.

SIDELIGHTS: Schneider told *CA:* "My interest in the book on Detroit was in exploring the social and institutional consequences of spatial change, specifically the ways in which changing patterns in land use affected the levels and perception of crime and disorder among various elements of the population. My latest research is a spin-off from this: homeless men and bachelor subculture in the American city, 1850-1940."

*   *   *

SCHRAG, Philip G(ordon) 1943-

PERSONAL: Born April 12, 1943, in Chicago, Ill.; son of Louis P. (in business) and Lala (Fineman) Schrag; married Emily Shiling (a newsletter editor), June 7, 1964; children: David, Zachary. *Education:* Harvard University, A.B., 1964; Yale University, LL.B., 1967. *Residence:* Washington, D.C. *Agent:* Peter Matson, 32 West 40th St., New York, N.Y. *Office:* U.S. Arms Control and Disarmament Agency, Washington, D.C. 20451.

CAREER: National Association for the Advancement of Colored People (NAACP), Legal Defense and Education Fund, New York City, assistant counsel, 1967-70; New York City Department of Consumer Affairs, New York City, consumer advocate, 1970-71; Columbia University, New York City, associate professor of law, 1971-73, professor of law, 1973-77; U.S. Arms Control and Disarmament Agency, Washington, D.C., deputy general counsel, 1977—. Chairman of Consumers Advisory Council of the City of New York, 1968-70; member of board of directors of Municipal Employees Legal Services Fund of the American Federation of State, County, and Municipal Employees, 1974-77; member of Puerto Rico governor's advisory council, 1970; consultant to New York State Consumer Protection Board.

WRITINGS: Counsel for the Deceived, Pantheon, 1972; *Consumer Protection Law,* West Publishing, 1973; (with Michael Meltsner) *Public Interest Advocacy,* Little, Brown, 1974; (with Meltsner) *Toward Simulation in Legal Education,* Foundation Press, 1979. Contributor to law journals. Editor for Carter-Mondale Transition Planning Committee, 1976.

*   *   *

SCHREIBER, Jean-Jacques Servan
See SERVAN-SCHREIBER, Jean-Jacques

*   *   *

SCHWARTZ, Hillel 1948-

PERSONAL: Born April 27, 1948, in Chicago, Ill.; son of Harry Raymond (a chemist) and Frieda Leah (a nurse; maiden name, Levin) Schwartz. *Education:* Brandeis University, B.A. (summa cum laude), 1969; Yale University, Ph.D., 1974; University of California, Berkeley, M.L.S., 1975. *Religion:* "Amelist." *Home:* 129 10th St., Apt. F, Del Mar, Calif. 92014. *Office:* Department of English, San Diego State University, San Diego, Calif. 92182.

CAREER: University of Florida, Gainesville, adjunct assistant professor of history and humanities, 1975-77; University of California, San Diego, La Jolla, visiting assistant professor of history and humanities, 1977-78; San Diego State University, San Diego, lecturer in English, 1979—. Member of board of directors of Yale Cooperative, 1972; director of Del Mar Arts Cooperative, 1979—. *Member:* American Historical Association, Society for Values in Higher Education, American Society for Eighteenth Century Studies. *Awards, honors:* Abram L. Sachar traveling fellowship from Brandeis University for study in Europe, 1969-70; Danforth fellow, 1969; named president's scholar by University of Florida, 1977-78.

WRITINGS: Knaves, Fools, Madmen, and That Subtle Effluvium, University Presses of Florida, 1978; *The French Prophets: The History of a Millenarian Group in Eighteenth Century England,* University of California Press, 1980.

Plays: "Animal Park" (two-act), first produced in Del Mar, Calif., at Stratford Studio Theatre, May 25, 1979; "Krill" (one-act), first produced in Del Mar at Stratford Studio Theatre, January 18, 1980; "Leapghosts" (three-act), first produced in Del Mar at Stratford Studio Theatre, July 12, 1980.

Work anthologized in *1980 Anthology of Magazine Verse,* edited by Alan Pater, Monitor Book, 1980; and *Amorata,* edited by Elliot Fried, Deep River Press, 1981. Contributor of poems to periodicals in the United States and Canada, including *Prairie Schooner, Denver Quarterly, Southern*

Humanities Review, Chicago Review, Loon, Descant, and *Fiddlehead.*

WORK IN PROGRESS: Some Local Aristocracy, a poem-cycle; a history of the relationship between technology and kinesthetics; two plays.

SIDELIGHTS: Schwartz told *CA:* "I am most interested in how the world is going to end."

*   *   *

SCHWARTZMAN, Aaron 1900(?)-1981

OBITUARY NOTICE: Born c. 1900 near Kiev, Russia (now U.S.S.R.); died of cancer, February 3, 1981, in Washington, D.C. Physician, translator, farmer, and author. A practicing physician for fifty years, Schwartzman supported himself through medical school by translating Russian novels and medical journals into English. He also translated three volumes on chemotherapy from the German and wrote a book on cardiology directed toward a general audience. Concurrent with his activities as a medical doctor and translator, Schwartzman was a farmer and raised livestock for over forty years. Obituaries and other sources: *Washington Post,* February 9, 1981.

*   *   *

SEAGLE, Janet 1924-

PERSONAL: Born March 29, 1924, in Spokane, Wash.; daughter of Edgar Ray (in business) and Norma (Bills) Seagle. *Education:* Attended Ohio Wesleyan University, 1941-42; New York University, B.A., 1945. *Religion:* Christian Science. *Residence:* Morristown, N.J. *Office:* U.S. Golf Association, Golf House, Far Hills, N.J. 07960.

CAREER: Associated with Bachrach Studios, New York, N.Y., 1945-46; employed in own photography business, 1946-61; worked at a department store in Corpus Christi, Tex., 1962-63; U.S. Golf Association, Far Hills, N.J., member of staff, 1963—. *Member:* Special Libraries Association, Golf Collectors Society.

WRITINGS: Golf: A Guide to Information Sources, Gale, 1979. Contributor to *Golf Journal* and *Club Makers.*

SIDELIGHTS: Janet Seagle wrote: "As a librarian and museum curator, I see the need for reference books on information sources. I have just had printed a list of golf club makers, a museum publication to assist collectors."

*   *   *

SEEBOHM, Caroline 1940-

PERSONAL: Born September 14, 1940, in Nottinghamshire, England; came to the United States in 1971; daughter of Frederick and Evangeline (Hurst) Seebohm; married Walter H. Lippincott, Jr. (a publisher), June 8, 1974; children: Sophie Elizabeth. *Education:* Oxford University, earned degree (with honors), 1961. *Home:* 322 Central Park W., New York, N.Y. 10025. *Office:* Conde Nast Publications, 350 Madison Ave., New York, N.Y. 10017.

CAREER: British Broadcasting Corp. (BBC-TV) research assistant, 1962-63; assistant to film director in Hollywood, Calif., 1963-65; London, England, advertising copywriter, 1965-70; free-lance writer, 1970-74; *House and Garden,* New York, N.Y., senior writer, 1974—. President of American Friends of the Aldeburgh Festival, 1975-79.

WRITINGS: (Editor) *House and Garden's Book of Total Health,* Putnam, 1978; (editor and author of introduction) *Twentieth-Century Decorating, Architecture, Gardens,*

Holt, 1980; *The Man Who Was Vogue* (biography of Conde Nast), Viking, 1982.

Author of television play, "A Diamond Is Forever," first broadcast by Associated Television Ltd., 1969. Author of "New York," a monthly column in *New Statesman*, 1976-79, and "Nonfiction in Brief," a column in *New York Times*, 1978-80. Contributor to *Vogue, Quest, New York,* and *Savvy.*

WORK IN PROGRESS: A novel, tentatively entitled *The Last Romance.*

* * *

SEELYE, H(ugh) Ned 1934-

PERSONAL: Born February 4, 1934, in Kingston, Pa.; son of Hugh L. (in business) and Margaret Ann (a teacher; maiden name, Griffiths) Seelye; married Neyde Marques de Azevedo, December, 1955 (divorced, 1963); married Clara James Aldana, September 14, 1963; children: David, Alan, Michael. *Education:* Attended Mexico City College, 1952-54; Brigham Young University, B.A., 1956; attended Tulane University, 1962-64; Universidad de San Carlos de Guatemala, M.A., 1967; further graduate study at Northwestern University, 1971. *Home:* 138 North Waiola Ave., La Grange, Ill. 60525. *Office:* International Resource Development, Inc., P.O. Box 721, La Grange, Ill. 60525.

CAREER: Free-lance writer, 1954; high school teacher of Spanish and history in Coopersburg, Pa., 1956-57; Ursinus College, Collegeville, Pa., instructor in Spanish, 1959-62; high school teacher of social studies and literature at American school in Guatemala City, Guatemala, 1964-67; Illinois State Office of Education, Chicago, state foreign language supervisor, 1968-71, state director of bilingual and bicultural education, 1971-77; International Resource Development, Inc., La Grange, Ill., founder and chairman of board of directors, 1977—. Instructor at Universidad Rafael Landivar in Guatemala City, 1965; teacher of English as a second language at Instituto Guatemalteco Americano, summers, 1965-66; organized program on English as a second language at Universidad del Valle de Guatemala, 1967; instructor at Northern Illinois University, 1967-69; assistant professor at University of Hawaii, 1971; lecturer at Loyola University, Chicago, Ill., 1973—; senior Fulbright lecturer at Catholic University of Ecuador, 1975, visiting professor, 1976 and 1977; visiting associate professor at University of Miami, Coral Gables, Fla., 1979. Art work has been exhibited in Guatemala. *Military service:* U.S. Army, personnel specialist, 1957-59; served in Italy.

MEMBER: Society for Intercultural Education, Training, and Research (member of board of governors), American Association of Teachers of Foreign Languages, American Association of Teachers of Spanish and Portuguese. *Awards, honors:* First place in book review contest sponsored by southern European theatre of U.S. Army, 1958, for review of *Lolita,* by Vladimir Nabokov; first place in photography contest, 1959; Rockefeller Brother Foundation grant, 1967; Stephen A. Freeman Award from Northeast Conference on Teaching Foreign Languages, 1973, for "Penetrating the Mass Media: A Unit to Develop Skill in Reading Spanish Newspaper Headlines."

WRITINGS: (Editor) *A Handbook on Latin America for Teachers: Methodology and Annotated Bibliography,* Office of the Superintendent of Public Instruction (Springfield, Ill.), 1968; (contributor) Emma M. Birkmaier, editor, *Britannica Review of Foreign Language Education,* Volume I, Encyclopaedia Britannica, 1969; (editor) *Teaching Cultural Con-*

cepts in Spanish Class, Office of the Superintendent of Public Instruction (Springfield, Ill.), 1972; (contributor) G. R. Green, editor, *Foreign Language Education Research,* Rand McNally, 1973; *Culture Tests for Spanish, Levels I-IV,* Hawaii State Department of Education, 1973; (with J. Lawrence Day) *The Newspaper: Spanish Culture Units,* National Textbook Co., 1974; (editor) Raymond L. Gorden, *Living in Latin America: A Case Study in Cross-Cultural Communication,* National Textbook Co., 1974; *Teaching Culture: Strategies for Foreign Language Educators,* National Textbook Co., 1974; (with B. N. Navarro) *A Guide to the Selection of Bilingual Education Program Designs,* Bilingual Education Service Center, 1977; (contributor) Henan LaFontaine, Barry Persky, and L. H. Golubchick, editors, *Bilingual Education,* Avery Publishing, 1978; (contributor) M. D. Pusch, *Multicultural Education: The Cross-Cultural Training Approach,* Intercultural Network, 1979; (contributor), J. D. Arendt, D. L. Lange, and P. J. Myers, editors, *Foreign Language Learning, Today and Tomorrow,* Pergamon, 1979. Contributor of about fifty articles to education, social science, and language journals.

WORK IN PROGRESS: Research on the effect of biculturalism on individuals.

SIDELIGHTS: Seelye wrote: "After dropping out of high school as an undistinguished scholar at the end of my junior year in Sunbury, Pa., I hitchhiked to Mexico City, and spent half of the next thirty years in various countries abroad.

"To survive as a peripatetic youth, I worked as a veterinarian's helper in Hollywood, a pizza cook in an Italian restaurant in Key West, a counselor in a camp for 'nervous' children in New Jersey, a cherry picker in Utah and a peach swamper in California, a free-lance writer in Cuba, a fireman on the Southern Pacific Railroad the last year they ran steam engines, and a teacher. My ability to rationalize what I was doing in the face of questioning relatives was improved somewhat by a college education.

"My teaching career spans all levels from junior high school through graduate school—and ranges from teaching English to soldiers in an Army school in Italy and physical anthropology in a Jesuit university in Guatemala, to Spanish in a maximum security penitentiary in Illinois.

"After acquiring an impressive dossier of magazine rejection slips, I began publishing in scholarly journals on sundry aspects of intercultural communication. In 1977 I founded a corporation to provide educational institutions and businesses with international research."

AVOCATIONAL INTERESTS: Judo (brown belt), photography, oil painting.

* * *

SEIM, Richard K(nudt) 1928-

PERSONAL: Born September 5, 1928, in Marshalltown, Iowa; son of Knudt Olai (a farmer) and Dorothy (Kersey) Seim; married Alene Sloppy (a secretary), October 27, 1950; children: Becky Seim Owings, Arne. *Education:* Attended Marshalltown Junior College, 1948-49; Iowa State University, B.S., 1956. *Religion:* Methodist. *Home:* 2228 Clark, Ames, Iowa 50010. *Office:* Farm Journal, P.O. Box 768, Ames, Iowa 50010.

CAREER: Iowa State University, Ames, assistant extension editor, 1956-58; *Wallaces Farmer,* Des Moines, Iowa, assistant editor, 1958-59; *Farm Journal,* Philadelphia, Pa., regional editor for the Midwest, 1959—. *Military service:* U.S. Army, 1950-52. *Member:* American Agricultural Editors' Association.

WRITINGS: The American Farmer, Rand McNally, 1974.

WORK IN PROGRESS: A book "that I hope will add depth and humanity to the image of the American farmer (man or woman) today."

SIDELIGHTS: Seim commented: "I have been motivated in the past and present (beyond ego satisfaction) by a desire to present a realistic picture of farmers and farm life. Very little contemporary literature deals with commercial farmers. Yet these men and women lead vital, fascinating lives. And (most would be startled or puzzled by the term) they are romantics. And doers. Executive and staff in one. Many still feel used by government and money interests, frustrated by an inability to speak to the non-farm public. I guess I'm trying, in a modest way, to be a voice for them, to help interpret farm people to the general public, and perhaps to themselves."

* * *

SELL, Betty (Marie) H(aas)   1928-

PERSONAL: Born October 31, 1928, in Coplay, Pa.; daughter of William F. (a horticulturist) and Margaret L. (Wormick) Haas; married Kenneth D. Sell (a sociologptember 17, 1949; children: Peter, Rebecca. *Education:* Ursinus College, B.S., 1950; Lancaster Theological Seminary, M.R.E., 1953; Escuela de Idiomas, San Jose, Costa Rica, diploma, 1958; Florida State University, M.S., 1967, A.M.D., 1976, Ph.D., 1981. *Politics:* Democrat. *Religion:* United Church of Christ. *Home address:* Route 9, Box 112, Salisbury, N.C. 28144. *Office:* Library, Catawba College, Salisbury, N.C. 28144.

CAREER: United Church of Chirst, San Pedro Sula, Honduras, educational missionary, 1957-65; Florida State University, Tallahassee, assistant librarian and instructor in library science, 1966-68; Livingstone College, Salisbury, N.C., acquisitions librarian, 1968-70; Catawba College, Salisbury, library director and assistant professor of library science, 1970—.

MEMBER: American Library Association, Library Administration and Management Association, Association of College and Research Libraries, National Librarians Association, American Association of University Professors (chapter president, 1979-80, member of executive committee of North Carolina conference, 1980—), Groves Conference on the Family, Association of Couples for Marriage Enrichment (national co-treasurer, 1980-82), League of Women Voters, Historical Society of the Evangelical and Reformed Church (vice-president of southern chapter, 1973—), Southeastern Library Association, North Carolina Library Association, Documents Librarians of North Carolina (charter officer), North Carolina Family Life Council, Salisbury-Rowan Family Life Council (president, 1979-80), Delta Kappa Gamma, Beta Phi Mu. *Awards, honors: Divorce in the United States, Canada, and Great Britain* was named outstanding reference book by American Library Association and choice book of the year by *Family Relations,* both 1978.

WRITINGS: (Editor with husband, Kenneth D. Sell) *Divorce in the United States, Canada, and Great Britain: A Guide to Information Sources,* Gale, 1978; (editor with K. D. Sell and David Lester) *Suicide: A Guide to Information Sources,* Gale, 1980; (contributor) Neal Kaske, editor, *Library Effectiveness: A State of the Art,* Library Administration and Management Association, 1980. Co-editor of "Information Guides on Social Problems and Social Issues," a series, Gale.

WORK IN PROGRESS: A manual for academic library program evaluation, publication expected in 1982; a theoretical book on library management, publication expected in 1983; continuing research on library effectiveness in regard to management; research on measurement and evaluation of the effectiveness of complex service organizations.

SIDELIGHTS: Betty Sell wrote: "Along with my husband, I am active in marriage enrichment education. I am also very much interested in library management and research, and plan to become an academic library consultant, using a management model that I developed and tested.

"During eight years in Honduras as an educational missionary, my duties often simultaneously included the following: elementary school principal, professor at a secondary and normal school and at a theological school, leadership training, member of various governing boards of educational institutions, business manager of several institutions, literature production, founder and administrator of an audiovisual center which served church denominations, public health service, CARE, and Peace Corps programs. I designed a television spot and a widely distributed health poster during an epidemic. Both received recognition in the United States. All of the above was done in collaboration with Honduran colleagues, and in the Spanish language."

AVOCATIONAL INTERESTS: Gardening, poster design, music, disco dancing, travel in Central America and the Caribbean.

* * *

SELL, Kenneth D(aniel)   1928-

PERSONAL: Born April 29, 1928, in Littlestown, Pa.; son of Stanley R. (a real estate broker) and Mabel (Forry) Sell; married Betty Haas (a library director), September 17, 1949; children: Peter, Rebecca. *Education:* Ursinus College, B.S., 1950; Lancaster Theological Seminary, B.D., 1954; Escuela de Idiomas, San Jose, Costa Rica, Diploma, 1958; Pennsylvania State University, M.Ed., 1961; Florida State University, Ph.D., 1968. *Politics:* Democrat. *Home address:* Route 9, Box 112, Salisbury, N.C. 28144. *Office:* Department of Sociology, Catawba College, Salisbury, N.C. 28144.

CAREER: Ordained minister of United Church of Christ, 1954; pastor of United Church of Christ in New Bloomfield, Pa., 1954-57; teacher at United Church of Christ in San Pedro, Honduras, 1957-65; Florida State University, Tallahassee, instructor in sociology, 1967-68; Livingstone College, Salisbury, N.C., associate professor of sociology, 1968-72; Catawba College, Salisbury, professor of sociology and chairman of department, 1972—. Founder and president of Salisbury-Rowan Family Life Council, 1974-76.

MEMBER: National Council on Family Relations, Association of Couples for Marriage Enrichment, American Sociological Association, Groves Conference on the Family, Southern Sociological Society, Southeastern Council on Family Relations (treasurer, 1978-79), North Carolina Family Life Council (president, 1976-77), North Carolina Sociological Society, Alpha Kappa Delta, Elks. *Awards, honors: Divorce in the United States, Canada, and Great Britain* was named outstanding reference book by American Library Association and choice book of the year by *Family Relations,* both 1978.

WRITINGS: (Editor with wife, Betty H. Sell) *Divorce in the United States, Canada, and Great Britain: A Guide to Information Sources,* Gale, 1978; (with B. H. Sell and David Lester) *Suicide: A Guide to Information Sources,* Gale, 1980;

(with Sarah M. Shoffner, M. Cynthia Farris, and E. Wayne Hill) *Enriching Relationships: A Guide to Marriage and Family Enrichment Literature,* privately printed, 1980; *Divorce: A Systematic Subject Bibliography,* Oryx, 1981. Co-editor of "Information Guides on Social Problems and Social Issues," a series, Gale. Contributor to sociology and law journals. Associate editor of *Family Relations,* 1979—.

WORK IN PROGRESS: Research on marriage enrichment, assessing current and new programs in the field.

SIDELIGHTS: Sell wrote: "I am especially interested in comprehensive, multidisciplinary explorations of topics concerning the family. These studies require extensive use of libraries. In the past five years I have worked in sixty libraries of all types, from Boston to Tallahassee.

"My family interests include marriage enrichment programs for the enhancement of family functioning and intimacy as well as various aspects of divorce, including do-it-yourself divorce, joint custody, and step-parenting. I have also done some research on divorce and the law. For several years I have been involved in a divorce information network which involves supplying information to researchers, counselors, and educators to keep them current in their field.

"I enjoy counseling, teaching family relations and communications skills. I speak Spanish, and for several years taught chemistry and theology in Spanish."

AVOCATIONAL INTERESTS: Chinese cooking, disco dancing, gardening, travel (Mexico, Central America, the Caribbean).

*　　*　　*

SELLINGS, Arthur
See LEY, Arthur Gordon

*　　*　　*

SEN GUPTA, Pranati   1938-

PERSONAL: Born November 18, 1938, in Calcutta, India; daughter of Hirendra Nath (a manager of a German shipping company) and Hemlata (Sen) Gupta; married Joy Gopal Sen Gupta (a scientist), June 6, 1958; children: Sandip, Supriya. *Education:* University of Calcutta, B.A., 1957; Career Institute, Chicago, Ill., Certificate, 1968. *Religion:* Hindu. *Home:* 1852 Playfair Dr., Ottawa, Ontario, Canada K1H 5S1.

CAREER: Ottawa Board of Education, Ottawa, Ontario, instructor in cooking, 1971—. Workshop instructor in Canterbury Community; guest on television programs; lecturer on Indian culinary arts; gives cooking demonstrations.

WRITINGS: The Art of Indian Cuisine, Hawthorn, 1974. Food editor of *Canadian India Times,* 1974—.

SIDELIGHTS: Pranati Sen Gupta wrote: "My major areas of vocational interest include nutrition, diet, food additives, and obesity.

"I have been a resident of Ottawa for the past eighteen years, all of which I have spent working closely with different ethnic groups. I have been teaching Indian cooking and culture, gourmet cooking, cooking for entertaining, and basic cooking in the Adult Division of the Ottawa Board of Education.

"In 1968 I went to visit India and managed to learn a few more things about Indian cooking, and also learned a great deal about the vast differences between the diets of North and South India. In 1973 I went back to visit India from north to south and from east to west, gathering information for my book. In 1978 I visited Europe for five weeks, taking European cooking lessons and visiting restaurants and hotels for culinary information and skills."

AVOCATIONAL INTERESTS: Travel (England, France, Italy, Egypt, Lebanon, West Germany, Switzerland, Austria).

BIOGRAPHICAL/CRITICAL SOURCES: City Paper, November, 1972; *Ottawa Journal,* October 18, 1975, December 14, 1978, March 26, 1980; *Canadian India Times,* September 21, 1974, December 3, 1976, December 15, 1980; *Ottawa Citizen,* March 5, 1980.

*　　*　　*

SERBAN, William M(ichael)   1949-

PERSONAL: Born September 28, 1949, in Canton, Ohio; son of George Edward (a mechanical engineer) and Virginia (a registered nurse; maiden name, Shearer) Serban; married Darlene Brady (an artist and researcher), May 19, 1979. *Education:* Purdue University, B.A., 1971; Ohio University, M.A., 1973; University of Pittsburgh, M.L.S., 1978. *Home:* 609 Eastland Ave., Ruston, La. 71270. *Office:* Government Documents Department, Library, Louisiana Technical University, Ruston, La. 71272.

CAREER: Ohio University, Athens, library technical assistant in government documents department, 1974-77; Louisiana Technical University, Ruston, documents librarian in government documents librarian in government documents department, 1978—. *Member:* Stained Glass Association of America (associate member), Glass Art Society, Louisiana Library Association, Pi Sigma Alpha, Sigma Delta Chi.

WRITINGS: (Editor with wife, Darlene Brady) *Stained Glass Index, 1906-77,* Gale, 1979; (editor with Brady) *Stained Glass: A Guide to Information Sources,* Gale, 1980. Contributor to library and economic journals.

WORK IN PROGRESS: Stained Glass Repair and Restoration, publication expected in 1983; *Stained Glass Bibliographies;* "Online Bibliographic Retrieval" and "Use and Maintenance of Government Publications," articles.

SIDELIGHTS: Serban told *CA:* "My means of earning a living is that of a librarian. I oversee a collection of over six hundred thousand government publications. Each year I make sure that millions of published words about governments and their activities are systematically arranged so they can be easily found by people being governed.

"In the last six years I have never worked in an office with a window. I assume my infatuation with stained glass is some subconscious yearning for light, window space, and imagery. Consciously, over the past six years I helped produce reference sources so the millions of published words about stained glass can be easily found by the people governed by a similar yearning."

AVOCATIONAL INTERESTS: Gardening, refinished furniture.

*　　*　　*

SEREBRYAKOVA, Galina Iosifovna   1905-1980

OBITUARY NOTICE: Born in December, 1905, in Kiev, Russia (now U.S.S.R.); died in May, 1980, in Moscow, U.S.S.R. Writer. Serebryakova was imprisoned during the Stalin purges and spent twenty years in labor camps. After Stalin's death in 1953, she was freed and resumed her writing. In spite of the hardships she endured in the camps, Serebryakova maintained that she never lost faith in Communism. She is best known for her works on Marx and Engels, and her trilogy on the life of Karl Marx was widely respected in the Soviet Union. She also wrote *Sandstorm,* an autobiographical novel about her prison-camp experiences, which was smuggled abroad and printed without her permission. Obituaries and other sources: *Who's Who in the Socialist Countries,* 1st edition, K. G. Saur, 1978; *New York Times,* July 11, 1980; *AB Bookman's Weekly,* September 1, 1980.

* * *

SERRON, Luis A(ugusto) 1930-

PERSONAL: Born February 19, 1930, in Iquitos, Peru; came to the United States in 1948, naturalized citizen, 1957; son of Ladislao (a bookkeeper and French translator) and Ada (a seamstress; maiden name, Patow) Serron; married Adelia Pitcher (a secretary), May 10, 1952; children: Eric George, Sonya Katherine, Tanya Diane. *Education:* University of Illinois, B.S., 1955, M.A., 1957; graduate study at Tulane University, 1959-61; Washington University, St. Louis, Mo., Ph.D., 1974. *Politics:* "Socialist humanism." *Religion:* "Knowledge of human life and of human self-liberation." *Home:* 627 East Carlisle, Whitefish Bay, Wis. 53217. *Office:* Department of Sociology, University of Wisconsin, Milwaukee, Wis. 53201.

CAREER: Moorhead State College, Moorhead, Minn., instructor in sociology, 1957-59; East Tennessee State University, Johnson City, assistant professor, 1961-69, associate professor of sociology, 1969; Lawrence University, Appleton, Wis., lecturer in sociology, 1970-71; Blackburn College, Carlinville, Ill., teacher of sociology, 1971-74; University of Wisconsin—Milwaukee, assistant professor of sociology, 1974—, co-director of Cuba-Mexico study tour. *Military service:* U.S. Air Force, 1948-52. *Member:* American Sociological Association, Midwest Sociological Society.

WRITINGS: Scarcity, Exploitation, and Poverty: Marx and Malthus in Mexico, University of Oklahoma Press, 1980. Contributor to sociology journals.

WORK IN PROGRESS: A study dealing with the relations between poverty, revolution, and development.

SIDELIGHTS: Serron wrote: "The basic motivation behind the writing of *Scarcity, Exploitation, and Poverty* was the need to find a way to obtain knowledge despite the tendency of class-conditioned ideologies to influence perception. It was also an effort to come to terms with the tendency to neutralize intellectual activity as a political force within social science circles.

"The chief conditioning circumstance behind the book was an effort on the part of graduate school advisers to force a re-orientation of my thinking away from a focus on facts to a focus on the forms of thought through which human beings approach reality—this combined with a claim in Max Weber's essay on objectivity that the quality which makes economic events economic is not objective, but subjective, since it arises (so Weber claimed) out of our cognitive interests when we face the fact of scarcity of means for the satisfaction of our needs.

"My master's thesis on 'Institutional Developments in American Agriculture' made it impossible for me to accept 'scarcity of means' as a fact, since American agriculture had been producing surpluses for several decades, and hunger existed in the midst of plenty. The economy of action which made it possible to produce more and more with less and less human effort appeared to me to be largely taken for granted or kept out of sight, for reasons which appeared to bear systematic relations to labor exploitation under capitalism.

"The work on poverty itself led to the insight that knowledge is the intellectual form which justice takes in human affairs just as law, when legitimate, is its practical form. Hence, I am of the view that the effort to neutralize values taken as a methodological principle in sociology—a principle which obviates the logical necessity to draw the political implications which follow from sociological explanation—is self-deceptive and self-defeating. Just as freedom of thought, intellectual honesty, and humility before evidence are indispensable values in research, so is justice integral and indispensable to the process of thought. Throughout the process of research one is under a conscious obligation to do justice to this or that theorist, to this or that set of facts. To the extent that we fail to accomplish this task, our work fails.

"Thus, sociologists can no more continue to avoid coming to terms with the political implications of their research activities than they can avoid coming to terms with the consequences of intellectual repression, dishonesty, and arrogance. Therefore, I am of the view that we must abandon the shallow identification of value-free research with bias-free research, and that our intellectual activities should be carried out as if the fate of the future depended on them. It might! Who says 'justice' does not necessarily say 'bias,' although it might mean bias in the decisions of a racist judge, in the activities of a bribe-taking policeman, or in the research of an 'ethically neutral social scientist.'

"My vocational interests within sociology are about as wide as the field itself. During more than twenty years of university teaching I have taught practically every course in the catalogs, some of which, I might add, came to me unsolicited. My current interests are primarily in the areas of social classes, inequality, migration, poverty, revolution, and development. I am particularly interested in the interplay between Marxist criticism and Liberation Theology and with the implications of their interplay for the future of Latin America.

"The best and most important influence on my development was Professor Erich A. Ahrens of the University of Illinois. There is no way to sum up the richness of this man's work or the extent of my debt to him. He used to say, in the early fifties, that the reason there is no more radical thinking going on than there actually is, is that there is no thinking going on at all, because thinking *is* a radical activity. He worked in the tradition of Plato and Elijah Jordan. A second invaluable influence on my intellectual development was Professor Irving M. Zeitlin. Prior to my studies under Zeitlin, my chief exposure to the work of Marx had been in a course on contemporary philosophy. Zeitlin opened up Marx for me by placing his work at the center of sociological theory."

AVOCATIONAL INTERESTS: World literature, classical, folk, and Latin American music, writing poems.

BIOGRAPHICAL/CRITICAL SOURCES: American Association of University Professors Bulletin, spring, 1973.

* * *

SERVAN-SCHREIBER, Jean-Jacques 1924-

PERSONAL: Born February 13, 1924, in Paris, France; son of Emile (a newspaper publisher) and Denise (Bresard) Servan-Schreiber; married Madeleine Chapsal, September 18, 1947 (divorced); married Sabine Becq de Fouquieres, August 11, 1960; children: David, Emile, Franklin, Edouard. *Education:* Ecole Polytechnique, Paris, graduated in 1947. *Home:* 8 place de la Carriere, 54-Nancy, France. *Office:* Assemblee Nationale, Paris 7 eme, France.

CAREER: Writer and politician. Worked as reporter for *Le Monde,* 1947-53, diplomatic editor, 1953; European correspondent for *Reporter,* 1949; foreign affairs writer for *Paris-Press,* 1951-52; president and general manager of Group Express-Express Union, 1953-70; administrator for Societe francaise d'editions economiques, 1953; security general for Radical Socialist Party, 1969-71, president, 1971—; deputy from Lorraine, Nancy, to French National Assembly, 1970—, minister of reforms, 1974. Founder of *L'Express,* 1953, and *L'Expansion,* 1964. *Member:* National Federation of Algerian Veterans, Institute for Advanced Study's International Association for Cultural Freedom Seminar. *Military service:* Free French Air Force, 1943, received military cross for valor; French Army, 1956-57; became lieutenant.

WRITINGS—In English: *Lieutenant en Algerie,* Julliard, 1957, translation by Ronald Mathews published as *Lieutenant in Algeria,* Knopf, 1957; *Le Defi americain,* Denoel, 1967, translation by Ronald Steel published as *The American Challenge,* foreword by Arthur Schlesinger, Jr., Atheneum, 1968; *Le Reveil de la France, mai-juin 1968,* Denoel, 1968, translation by Steel published as *The Spirit of May,* Mc-Graw, 1969; (with Michel Albert) *Ciel et terre: Manifesto radical,* Denoel, 1968, published as *Le Manifeste radical,* Le Livre de Poche, 1970, translation by H. A. Fields published as *The Radical Alternative,* edited by Roy Pryce, Macdonald, 1970, new edition, with introduction by John Kenneth Galbraith, Norton, 1971.

In French: *Forcer le destin* (title means "Forcing Destiny's Hand"), Presses Pocket, 1970; *Le Pouvoir regional* (title means "Regional Power"), Grasset, 1971.

Also author of pamphlets. Contributor to periodicals, including *Time* and *New York Herald Tribune.*

SIDELIGHTS: Servan-Schreiber was born into the world of journalism, for his father and uncle were the co-founders of *Les Echos,* France's first financial newspaper. According to *Life,* however, he "turned newspaperman almost by accident." After World War II, Servan-Schreiber began life anew as a free-lance writer. On the basis of his work, he was offered a staff position on *Le Monde.* From the beginning, the focus of his work was international politics.

In 1953, along with Francoise Giroud, Servan-Schreiber founded *L'Express,* a left-wing weekly. In addition to serving as a platform for Pierre Mendes-France, a radical who served as the French premier briefly in 1954, *L'Express* frequently antagonized the French establishment with its leftist content. In 1954, the publication was temporarily halted after printing a top secret report. Some observers speculated that the induction of Servan-Schreiber into the French army was linked to governmental dissatisfaction with the controversial *L'Express.*

Servan-Schreiber's military service proved similarly newsworthy. Although his actions were distinguished, he was court martialed upon publication of *Lieutenant in Algeria.* In the book, he exposed atrocities committed by the French military. The minister of national defense subsequently charged Servan-Schreiber with "weakening the morale of the French Army." He was acquitted. Years later, his book was credited, as Melvin Kranzberg noted, with helping "to turn French opinion against the Algerian war and to bring about the negotiated settlement."

In the mid-1960's, Servan-Schreiber reorganized *L'Express.* Carolyn Morgan assessed the new *L'Express:* "This is a 'moderately leftist' weekly political magazine full of big-business advertising.... It is not beside the point, either, that this weekly is outwardly the most American-looking of

all such French weeklies. It uses a format like that of *Time* or *Newsweek* without losing the politically sophisticated French touch." As a reaction to Servan-Schreiber's changes, readers of the paper accused him of contradicting his socialist beliefs. A more favorable summation of Servan-Schreiber's new stance came from Arthur Schlesinger, Jr., who called him "a European of the Kennedy generation." David Caute agreed. "Servan-Schreiber does indeed embody all the self-conscious modern-mindedness of the Kennedy generation in America," he wrote. He added that Servan-Schreiber's political convictions are a combination of "the traditional attachment of the left to social justice and social mobility with an admirable grasp of modern economics and technological realities."

In *The American Challenge,* Servan-Schreiber wrote of his political and economic views. He began the book with a warning to his fellow Europeans regarding America's growing economic control of the continent, and proceeded to present a program of economic and social change. *Nation's* Harry Magdoff called the book "a manifesto designed to mobilize public opinion in support of a political federation of Europe ... a United States of Europe, one which will maintain national and cultural differences but will nevertheless have enough unity and central direction to enable it to compete with the United States." But Naomi Bliven observed that Servan-Schreiber "wants Western Europe not just to federate but to copy other features of American political organization." In the *Washington Post,* Alfred Friendly explained that "it is America's 'flexibility' of management, its systematic search for innovation, its technological devotion, its decentralization of decision making and, above all, its investment in the education of its people ... that accounts for America's present dominance." According to Kranzberg, Servan-Schreiber "wants American industrial technology; but he wants it to be European."

Some critics noted the irony of Servan-Schreiber's position in *The American Challenge.* Bliven wrote: "Servan-Schreiber is indeed baffling to Americans when he praises achievements of which many of us are not exactly proud; he praises, and urges Europeans to duplicate, the burst of American technological creativity, managerial innovation, and industrial expansion that ... has been achieved by cooperation between government, industry, and the universities. He politely calls this collaboration the 'industrial-intellectual complex'; we know it as the ':military-industrial complex,' and scarcely any American has a kind word for it." In the *Chicago Tribune Book World,* Anthony Hartly wrote that "it is ironic that the book should appear at the very moment when a rebellion is under way against the very nature of advanced industrial society."

In *The Spirit of May,* Servan-Schreiber offered an explanation of the 1968 student revolt consistent with his socioeconomic position. The volume is a collection of *L'Express* editorials written during the uprisings that caused the closing of universities and factories. In the *Christian Science Monitor,* Carlyle Morgan contended that "according to Mr. Servan-Schreiber, the student uprisings were directly linked to those features of French life which have been frustrating most Frenchmen for years." Peter Steinfels called these features "the centralization of all power in Paris and the oligarchic self-perpetuation of unqualified French elites." Most critics concluded that, as in *The American Challenge, The Spirit of May* called for the revitalization of French institutions in order to catch up with technologically advanced capitalism.

In 1970, Servan-Schreiber led an anti-Gaullist attempt to

decentralize the French government. The platform, published as *The Radical Alternative,* was summarized in *Atlantic:* "The aim was to give every Frenchman equal footing before he entered the battle of the marketplace: raise inheritance taxes, let everyone have a chance to go to college, provide cheap and decent housing for the poor, and so on. A second tenet was to denationalize industry, to get the government out of business and into what it should be doing better—welfare, transportation, and communication.... Finally ... he discussed how state power must be redistributed to local and regional governments."

Entering a by-election in Nancy, Lorraine, Servan-Schreiber resisted the Gaullist opposition by relentlessly reiterating his belief "that the economic problems of Lorraine were the fault of Paris planners and that the region, if it had the political means, would prosper on its own." He won on the second ballot. In 1974, newly elected President d'Estaing appointed Servan-Schreiber minister of reform. However, when France announced the resumption of nuclear testing in the Pacific Ocean, Servan-Schreiber spoke out in opposition. Consequently, he was dismissed from his post only twelve days after he began serving.

BIOGRAPHICAL/CRITICAL SOURCES: Times Literary Supplement, November 23, 1967, July 25, 1968; *New Yorker,* January 20, 1968, November 23, 1968; *Life,* May 17, 1968; *Books Abroad,* spring, 1968; *New York Review of Books,* June 20, 1968; *Chicago Tribune Book World,* July 7, 1968; *Atlantic,* July, 1968, February, 1971; *Time,* July 12, 1968, June 24, 1974; *Washington Post,* July 16, 1968; *New York Times,* July 16, 1968, December 1, 1968, December 2, 1968, December 3, 1968; *Newsweek,* July 22, 1968, June 24, 1974; *Listener,* July 25, 1968; *Christian Science Monitor,* July 25, 1968, August 7, 1969, February 2, 1970; *New Republic,* July 27, 1968; *New York Times Book Review,* July 28, 1968, March 16, 1969; *National Observer,* September 23, 1968; *New Leader,* October 7, 1968; *Canadian Forum,* November, 1968; *Books and Bookman,* November, 1968; *Virginia Quarterly Review,* autumn, 1968; *Nation,* December 30, 1968; *Best Sellers,* April, 1969; *Book World,* April 6, 1969; *Saturday Review,* April 19, 1969; *Variety,* February 18, 1970.*

—*Sketch by Andrea Geffner*

*   *   *

SEWELL, Winifred 1917-

PERSONAL: Born August 12, 1917, in Newport, Wash.; daughter of Harold A. (an engineer) and Grace (Vickerman) Sewell. *Education:* Washington State University, B.S., 1938; Columbia University, B.S.L.S., 1940; also attended other city universities in New York, 1940-46. *Home and office:* 6513 76th Place, Cabin John, Md. 20731.

CAREER: Wellcome Research Laboratories, Tuckahoe, N.Y., librarian, 1942-46; Squibb Institute for Medical Research, New Brunswick, N.J., senior librarian, 1946-61; National Library of Medicine, Bethesda, Md., subject heading specialist and deputy chief of Bibliographic Services Division, 1961-65, head of drug literature program, 1965-70; University of Maryland, School of Pharmacy, Baltimore, adjunct assistant professor of pharmacy, 1970—. Instructor at Columbia University, summer, 1959; adjunct lecturer at University of Maryland, 1969—. Member of International Federation of Pharmacy's Commission on Pharmaceutical Abstracts, 1958-60, and National Academy of Sciences committee on modern methods of handling chemical information, 1965-67; member of U.S. State Department exchange team on special libraries in the Soviet Union, 1966;

consultant to National Health Planning Information Center and Federal Library Committee.

MEMBER: American Society for Information Science (chairman of special interest group on classification research, 1974-75), American Chemical Society, American Society of Hospital Pharmacists, American Association of Colleges of Pharmacy (chairman of libraries/educational resources section, 1979-80), Drug Information Association (vice-president, 1966-67; president, 1970-71), Special Libraries Association (president, 1960-61), Medical Library Association (fellow; chairman of public health and health administration libraries section, 1979-80). *Awards, honors:* Publication award from Science-Technology Division of Special Libraries Association, 1966, for *Unlisted Drugs;* Ida and George Eliot Prize from Medical Library Association, 1977, for *Guide to Drug Information;* D.Sc. from Philadelphia College of Pharmacy and Science, 1979.

WRITINGS: (With Merle Harrison) *Using MeSH for Effective Searching: A Programmed Guide,* National Library of Medicine, 1975; *Guide to Drug Information,* Drug Intelligence Publications, 1976. General editor of "Gale Information Guides: Health Affairs," Gale, 1972—. Contributor of articles and reviews to pharmaceutical and library journals. Editor of *Unlisted Drugs,* 1949-59 and 1962-64.

BIOGRAPHICAL/CRITICAL SOURCES: San Francisco Examiner, October 15, 1960; *San Diego Union,* October 16, 1960; *Milwaukee Journal,* February 24, 1961; *Globe and Mail,* Toronto, Ontario, April 11, 1961; *Pittsburgh Post Gazette,* April 18, 1961.

*   *   *

SHAARA, Michael (Joseph) 1929-

PERSONAL: Born June 23, 1929, in Jersey City, N.J.; son of Michael Joseph, Sr. and Alleene (Maxwell) Shaara; married Helen Krumweide, September 16, 1950 (marriage ended, June, 1980); children: Lila Elise. *Education:* Rutgers University, B.A., 1951; graduate study at Columbia University, 1952-53, and University of Vermont, 1953-54. *Politics:* None. *Religion:* None. *Home and office:* 2074 Robinhood Dr., Melbourne, Fla. 32935.

CAREER: Writer. Worked as merchant seaman, 1948-49; St. Petersburg Police Department, St. Petersburg, Fla., police officer, 1954-55; short story writer, 1955-61; Florida State University, Tallahassee, associate professor of English, 1961-73. Guest lecturer at universities. *Military service:* U.S. Army, paratrooper in 82nd Airborne Division, 1946-49; became sergeant. U.S. Army Reserve, 1949-53. *Member:* International Platform Association, Authors Guild, Omicron Delta Kappa, Gold Key. *Awards, honors:* Award from American Medical Association, 1966, for article, "In the Midst of Life"; Pulitzer Price for fiction, 1975, for *The Killer Angels;* short story awards include Dikty's best science fiction of the year awards and citations from Judith Merrill.

WRITINGS: The Broken Place (novel), New American Library, 1968; *The Killer Angels* (novel), McKay, 1974; *The Herald* (novel), McGraw, 1981; *Collected Short Stories,* Simon & Schuster, 1981.

Author of screenplay, "Billy Boy," 1980. Contributor of stories to magazines, including *Saturday Evening Post, Playboy, Galaxy, Redbook, Cosmopolitan,* and *McCall's,* and newspapers.

WORK IN PROGRESS: A novel about William Shakespeare, publication by McGraw expected in 1982; an autobiography; a screenplay, "The Killer Angels."

SIDELIGHTS: Shaara told *CA:* "I have written almost every known type of writing, from science fiction through history, through medical journalism and *Playboy* stories, always because I wrote only what came to mind, with no goal and little income, always for the joy of it, and it has been a great joy. The only trouble comes from the 'market mind' of the editor when the work is done. I have traveled over most of the world, lived three years in South Africa, two years in Italy, speak some foreign languages, and love airplanes, almost as much as women. I enjoyed teaching, because it taught me a lot."

BIOGRAPHICAL/CRITICAL SOURCES: Authors in the News, Volume 1, Gale, 1976.

* * *

SHACKET, Sheldon R(ubin) 1941-
(Kehlog Albran, a joint pseudonym)

PERSONAL: Born April 3, 1941, in Chicago, Ill.; son of Ben (a locksmith) and Evelyn (a legal secretary; maiden name, Warshafsky) Shacket; married Jan Irene Lackey (a teacher), August 22, 1975. *Education:* Attended Art Institute of Chicago, 1958-64; University of Chicago, B.A., 1964. *Residence:* Chicago, Ill. *Agent:* Toni Mendez, Inc., 140 East 56th St., New York, N.Y. 10022. *Office:* Cohen & Greenbaum, Inc., 875 North Michigan Ave., Suite 1557, Chicago, Ill. 60611.

CAREER: Cohen & Greenbaum, Inc. (advertising agency), Chicago, Ill., executive art director and vice-president, 1968—. President of IBEX International, Inc. *Member:* Fox Valley Electric Vehicle Club.

WRITINGS: (With Martin A. Cohen under joint pseudonym Kehlog Albran) *The Profit* (humor), Price, Stern, 1973, revised edition, 1981; (with Faye Steiner and Barry Steiner) *Color Me Beautiful* (humor), Phase One, 1976, revised edition, 1977; *The Complete Book of Electric Vehicles,* Domus, 1978, 3rd edition, 1981. Also author of *Rich Means Never Having to Say* (humor), 1972. Author of film script, "Anokil," 1976.

WORK IN PROGRESS: Mr. Know-It-All's Encyclopedia, publication expected in 1982.

SIDELIGHTS: Shacket told *CA:* "Most recently I am the inventor of the Incredible IBEX, 'the force that defies gravity,' a mystifying new game/toy. I am in the process of marketing some and will become rich shortly. I also write country and western music, and am concluding negotiations for publication of my first two songs, 'It's a Fine Line' and 'Heaven on Earth.' I am occupying my spare time inventing new toys and finishing new songs, with a couple of books thrown in to break up the boredom."

BIOGRAPHICAL/CRITICAL SOURCES: Chicago Sun-Times, May 22, 1972; *Chicago Tribune,* November 9, 1980.

* * *

SHAEVITZ, Morton H(erbert) 1935-

PERSONAL: Born June 23, 1935, in New York, N.Y.; son of Arthur (a retail store owner) and Dorothy (a retail store owner; maiden name, Spievak) Shaevitz; married Marjorie Hansen (a counselor), March 11, 1972; children: Erica, Jonathon, Geoffrey, Marejka. *Education:* University of California, Los Angeles, B.A., 1957, M.A., 1961, Ph.D., 1963. *Home:* 2671 Greentree Lane, La Jolla, Calif. 92037. *Agent:* Julian Bach Literary Agency, Inc., 3 East 48th St., New York, N.Y. 10017. *Office:* Institute for Family and Work Relationships, 1020 Prospect St., Suite 400, La Jolla, Calif. 92037.

CAREER: University of Michigan, Ann Arbor, assistant professor of psychology, 1963-69; University of California, San Diego, La Jolla, director of counseling and psychological services, 1969-77, associate clinical professor of psychiatry, 1974—. Director of Morton H. Shaevitz (associates in clinical psychology), 1975—; clinical professor at University of San Diego, 1977—; co-director of Institute for Family and Work Relationships, 1977—; psychologist at Scripps Clinic Medical Group, 1978—. Member of San Diego Mental Health Advisory Board, 1970-72; chairman of manpower development and in-service training task force of Improving Mental Health Services on Western Campuses Program, 1971-74. *Member:* American Psychological Association, American Orthopsychiatric Association, California State Psychological Association (chairman of committee on consumer affairs, 1977-78), La Jolla Farms Association (co-president, 1977-78).

WRITINGS: (With Daniel Fader) *Hooked on Books,* Berkley Publishing, 1966; (with wife, Marjorie Hansen Shaevitz) *Making It Together as a Two-Career Couple,* Houghton, 1980.

SIDELIGHTS: Shaevitz wrote: "Much of my current and proposed writing is directed at translating behavioral science findings to lay audiences. The goal is that of primary prevention in mental health."

* * *

SHANAHAN, Eileen 1924-

PERSONAL: Born February 29, 1924, in Washington, D.C.; daughter of Thomas Francis and Vena (Karpeles) Shanahan; married John V. Waits, Jr., September 16, 1944; children: Mary Beth, Kathleen. *Education:* George Washington University, A.B., 1944. *Home:* 3608 Van Ness St. N.W., Washington, D.C. 20008. *Office:* 225 Virginia Ave. S.E., Washington, D.C. 20061.

CAREER/WRITINGS: United Press International (UPI), Washington, D.C., dictationist, 1944-45, reporter, 1945-47; Washington Radio News Bureau, Washington, D.C., reporter for Walter Cronkite, 1949-50; reporter for columnist Robert S. Allen, 1951; Research Institute of America, Washington, D.C., reporter and editor, 1951-56; *Journal of Commerce,* Washington, D.C., reporter, 1956-61; Department of the Treasury, Washington, D.C., special assistant to assistant to secretary of department, 1961-62; *New York Times,* Washington, D.C., reporter, 1962-77; Department of Health, Education, and Welfare (HEW; now Department of Health and Human Services), Washington, D.C., assistant secretary for public affairs, 1977-79; *Washington Star,* Washington, D.C., assistant managing editor, 1979—. Member of executive committee of Reporters' Committee for Freedom of the Press, 1972-76; member of advisory council of Woodrow Wilson School of Government, Princeton University, 1973-76; member of board of governors of Fund for Investigative Journalism, 1973-76; member of faculty at Summer Program for Minority Journalists, University of California, Berkeley, 1976—. *Member:* Washington Press Club. *Awards, honors:* Business Journalism award from University of Missouri School of Journalism, 1966; named newspaper woman of the year by New York Women in Communications, 1972.

* * *

SHAPIRO, Lillian L(adman) 1913-

PERSONAL: Born October 11, 1913, in New York; daughter of Julius (a merchant) and Manya (in business; maiden name, Duckerevitch) Ladman; married Herman Shapiro (an accountant), June 23, 1935; children: Judith, Susan Shapiro Skea. *Education:* Hunter College (now of the City University of New York), B.A., 1932; Columbia University, B.S.L.S., 1940, M.S.L.S., 1969; also attended Queens College of the City University of New York, St. John's University, Jamaica, N.Y., New School for Social Research, and C. W. Post College, Long Island University. *Politics:* Independent. *Religion:* "Deist." *Home and office:* 70 East 10th St., New York, N.Y. 10003.

CAREER: High school Latin teacher in Jamaica, N.Y., 1933-38, and New York City, 1938-40; library assistant at high school in Richmond Hill, N.Y., 1940-48; head librarian at high schools in Jamaica, 1948-61, and Flushing, N.Y., 1961-63; supervisor of academic and vocational high schools in New York City, 1963-65; head librarian at high school in Springfield Gardens, N.Y., 1965-67; St. John's University, Jamaica, assistant professor of library science, 1969-73; United Nations International School, New York City, director of media services, 1974-75; consultant to publishers of books for children and young adults, 1975—. Adjunct instructor at Queens College of the City University of New York and Drexel Graduate School of Library Science. Member of board of directors of Literacy Volunteers of New York; member of New York Public Library committee to support young adult services; member of annual booklist committee of National Conference of Christians and Jews.

MEMBER: American Library Association (chairman of nominating committee of Young Adult Services Division), Women's National Book Association (president), Booksellers League (member of board of managers), New York Library Association (second vice-president; president of library educators' section), New York City School Librarians Association (president), New York Library Club (president), Book League of New York, Eta Sigma Phi, Beta Phi Mu. *Awards, honors:* Certificate of merit from high school division of Catholic Library Association, 1976, for contributions as an author and keynote speaker at numerous conferences on librarianship.

WRITINGS: Serving Youth: Communication and Commitment in the High School Library, Bowker, 1975; *Teaching Yourself in Libraries: A Guide to the High School Media Center and Other Libraries,* H. W. Wilson, 1978; *Fiction for Youth: A Guide to Recommended Titles,* Neal-Schuman, 1980. Contributor to library journals.

SIDELIGHTS: Lillian Shapiro wrote: "My career in librarianship was accidental. Teaching had always been foremost among my professional choices. I enjoyed my years as a Latin instructor in the New York City school system but the declining enrollments and gradual disappearance of Latin from the high school curriculum forced me to retrain at Columbia University's Library School, although I deliberately chose *school* librarianship in order to stay connected with young people who are such a provocative mixture of fun and frustration.

"Until personal problems related to the health of my husband forced a change to a kind of work that could be done from my study at home, I took pleasure in the teaching aspect of school librarianship, and in the years spent as a library school professor. It remains a joy to hear—still—the successes of former students who are now librarians in public, college, and special libraries—and one who has just opened her own bookshop.

"Travel has been an annual treat for me, with Japan the farthest point to which I have ventured. It may reveal some provincialism in me if I confess that I have no strong urge to visit those places avidly sought by tourists these days, for example, China and Egypt. For me, sheer joy resides in going back again and again to Paris, London (with theatre every night), and Siena—or almost anywhere in Italy. I have not traveled widely on this continent except for conferences and speaking engagements, but this past year I enjoyed two wonderful weeks in the Canadian Rockies. That brief stay was the push that has propelled me to think of leaving New York City and relocating where there is space and peacefulness that might generate ideas for further writing.

"My ideas for a next project are still too inchoate to be given a definite name, but I am playing with the possibility of trying my hand at juvenile fiction, for which there has been a rather strong demand in recent years. I shall have to see how that goes, since all of my writing thus far has been in the form of criticism or professional essays."

AVOCATIONAL INTERESTS: Reading, walking, golf, needlepoint, playing piano, studying French.

* * *

SHAPIRO, Martin M(athew) 1933-

PERSONAL: Born November 13, 1933, in Pittsburgh, Pa.; son of Thomas and Marietta Shapiro; married Barbara Schuman (a professor), July 3, 1955; children: Eve. *Education:* University of California, Berkeley, B.A., 1955; Harvard University, Ph.D., 1961. *Office:* School of Law, University of California, Berkeley, Calif. 94720.

CAREER: Harvard University, Cambridge, Mass., instructor in government, 1960-62; Stanford University, Stanford, Calif., assistant professor of political science, 1962-65; University of California, Irvine, associate professor, 1965-67, professor of political science, 1968-70; University of California, Berkeley, professor of political science, 1970-71; Harvard University, professor of government, 1971-74; University of California, San Diego, La Jolla, professor of political science, 1974-77; University of California, Berkeley, professor of law, 1977—. Visiting professor at Harvard University, University of California, Los Angeles, and University of California, Riverside. *Military service:* U.S. Army, 1955-57; became first lieutenant. *Member:* Law and Society Association, American Academy of Arts and Sciences (fellow), Phi Beta Kappa, Pi Sigma Alpha. *Awards, honors:* Woodrow Wilson fellowship, 1957-58; Ford Foundation fellowship, 1969-70; Guggenheim fellowship, 1977-78.

WRITINGS: Law and Politics in the Supreme Court (monograph), Free Press, 1964; *Freedom of Speech: The Supreme Court and Judicial Review* (monograph), Prentice-Hall, 1966; *The Supreme Court and Administrative Agencies* (monograph), Free Press, 1968; (with Louis Koenig and others) *American National Government,* Scott, Foresman, 1971; (with Douglas Hobbs) *The Politics of Constitutional Law,* Winthrop Publishing, 1975; (with Hobbs) *Constitutional Law,* Winthrop Publishing, 1978; (with Rocco Tresolini) *American Constitutional Law,* 3rd edition (Shapiro was not associated with earlier editions), Macmillan, 1969, 4th edition, 1974, 5th edition, 1979; (with Raymond Wolfinger and Fred Greenstein) *Dynamics of American Politics,* Prentice-Hall, 1975, 2nd edition, 1979; *Courts* (monograph), University of Chicago Press, 1981.

Editor: *The Supreme Court and Constitutional Rights,* Scott, Foresman, 1967; *The Supreme Court and Public Policy,* Scott, Foresman, 1969; (with Joseph Palamountain) *Issues and Perspectives in American Government,* Scott, Foresman, 1971; *The Pentagon Papers and the Courts,* Chandler, 1972.

Contributor: (Author of introduction) *Constitution of the United States*, Crofts, 1966; S. Sidney Ulmer, editor, *Political Decision-Making*, Van Nostrand, 1970; Fred Greenstein and Nelson Polsby, editors, *The Handbook of Political Science*, Addison-Wesley, 1975; M. Judd Harmon, editor, *Essays on the Constitution*, Kennikat, 1978; Anthony King, editor, *The New American Political System*, American Enterprise Institute, 1978; S. M. Lipset, editor, *The Third Century*, Hoover Institution/University of Chicago Press, 1979; Ronald Collins, editor, *Constitutional Government in America*, University Presses, 1980; Mauro Cappelletti, editor, *The Prospects for Access to Justice*, Sijthoff, 1981; Vincent Blasi, editor, *Studies in Constitutional Law*, Yale University Press, 1981. Contributor to *Encyclopedia of the Social Sciences*. Contributor of more than twenty-five articles and reviews to scholarly journals and newspapers.

SIDELIGHTS: Shapiro told *CA:* "I seek to develop a view of the United States Supreme Court and other courts as essentially political institutions that play an important role in the policy-making process."

* * *

SHATTOCK, Ernest (Henry) 1904-

PERSONAL: Born October 22, 1904, in Colombo, Ceylon; son of Ernest Mark (in business) and Evelyn Mabel Shattock; married Oz Armstrong, January 24, 1958; children: (from previous marriage) Janice, Vanessa, Jonothan, Belinda. *Education:* Attended Royal Naval College, Osborne, and Royal Naval College, Dartmouth, 1918-22. *Home:* Mill House, Newark, Ripley, Surrey, England.

CAREER: Royal Navy, career officer, 1918-56, worked on various aircraft carriers, 1926-34, pilot of catapult aircraft incruisers, 1934-37, commander of squadron of amphibians in 2nd cruiser squadron, 1937-38, assigned to Admiralty, 1939-41, naval attache for air in Washington, D.C., 1941, commander of flying on H.M.S. *Illustrious*, 1942-44, chief of staff to flag officer of Naval Air Pacific, 1944-46, assigned to Admiralty, 1946-48, commander of H.M.S. *Glory* (aircraft carrier), 1948-50, director of Senior Officers War College, 1950-52, admiral in command of Malayan Area, 1953-56, retiring as rear admiral; European adviser for Guest, Keen & Nettlefold, 1957-60; partner in European Export and Investment Service, 1960-68; consultant on manufacturing licences, 1968—. Director of Filtration Specialists, 1975—. Member of Institute of International Licensing Practitioners (founding fellow) and Medical and Scientific Network. *Awards, honors:* Officer of Order of the British Empire, 1944; Companion of Order of the Bath, 1954.

WRITINGS: An Experiment in Mindfulness, Rider, 1958; *Mind Your Body*, Turnstone Press, 1979.

WORK IN PROGRESS: The Greatest of All Adventures: Discovery of Mind, publication by Turnstone Press expected in 1981; an autobiography; *A Course in Self-Healing*, Turnstone Press, 1981 or 1982; *Tools of the Mind*, completion expected in 1982.

SIDELIGHTS: Shattock commented: "I was interested in philosophy from my earliest days and in magic. I was a member of the Magic Circle for some twenty years.

"I specialized in flying in the Royal Navy. I learned to fly in 1926 on World War I aircraft and have qualified on all types, from jets to helicopters.

"The outstanding period and experience in my life, so far, was the four weeks spent in a Buddhist monastery training center for Satipatthana meditation under the venerable Ma-

hasi Sayadaw in 1956. This experience revolutionized my thinking and enlarged the scope of my awareness. Over the next twenty years there was a process of sifting and digestion that resulted in the experiment in mental control of the healing processes, which was related in *Mind and Body*. And I gained much knowledge of the mind's real place in man's development. This is the subject of *The Greatest of All Adventures: The Discovery of Mind*.

"After leaving the Royal Navy, I took a job with Guest, Keen & Nettlefold as their European adviser and adviser on the development of the Common Market. After four years of that I set up my own company to handle manufacturing licenses throughout the world. My company has now folded up, but I continue to handle selected licensing matters as a private consultant.

"I live in a lovely, but small, Georgian house some two hundred fifty years old, situated in the country near Guildford. Although the house is mine, I regard it as a trusteeship for a small bit of traditional England, and I hope that, some hundred years on, another will feel the same.

"I am a student of the Arcane School, and this study has taken over the highest priority of my life's activities. I intend to live to the age of eighty-eight. And, if my body and mind are not capable of coming up to what is required of them before that, I shall depart, not by an overdose of drugs or other forceful method, but by an effort of will."

* * *

SHEINWOLD, Patricia
See FOX-SHEINWOLD, Patricia

* * *

SHELBY, Graham 1940-

PERSONAL: Born in 1940 in England. *Agent:* Curtis Brown Ltd., 1 Craven Hill, London W2 3EP, England.

CAREER: Writer. Worked as copywriter and book reviewer.

WRITINGS—Novels: *The Knights of Dark Renown*, Weybright, 1969; *The Kings of Vain Intent*, Weybright, 1970; *The Oath and the Sword*, Weybright, 1972; *The Devil Is Loose*, Doubleday, 1973; *The Wolf at the Door*, Doubleday, 1975; *The Cannaways*, Doubleday, 1978; *The Cannaway Concern*, Doubleday, 1980; *Cannaway Drive*, Doubleday, 1982.

* * *

SHERWOOD, Martin (Anthony) 1942-

PERSONAL: Born January 10, 1942, in England. *Education:* University of Montreal, B.Sc., 1962; University of Exeter, Ph.D., 1965. *Agent:* Sheila Watson, Bolt & Watson Ltd., 8-12 Old Queen St., London SW1H 9HP, England. *Office:* Society of Chemical Industry, 14 Belgrave Sq., London SW1X 8PS, England.

CAREER: Royal Institute of Chemistry, London, England, senior assistant editor, 1966-71; *New Scientist*, London, science policy editor, 1971-76; *Chemistry and Industry*, London, editor, 1976—. *Member:* Association of British Science Writers (chairman, 1974-76).

WRITINGS: The New Chemistry, Basic Books, 1974, revised edition published as *New Worlds in Chemistry*, 1978; *Survival* (novel), New English Library, 1975; *Maxwell's Demon* (novel), New English Library, 1976.

SHONFIELD, Andrew Akiba 1917-1981

OBITUARY NOTICE: Born August 10, 1917, in Tadworth, England; died January 23, 1981, in Tooting, England. Economist, journalist, educator, and author. Shonfield was an economic journalist and editor with the *Financial Times* and *Observer* before moving in 1961 to the Royal Institute of International Affairs, which he directed from 1972 to 1977. He viewed economics from a practical perspective rather than from a theoretical one, and he was a leader in the development of an international and intellectual understanding of world affairs. As a professor of economics at the European University in Florence, Shonfield strove to raise the general level of understanding of economic events. He was knighted in 1978. He wrote *Attack on World Poverty, A Man Beside Himself, Modern Capitalism, Europe: Journey to an Unknown Destination,* and he was working on a second edition of *Modern Capitalism* at the time of his death. Obituaries and other sources: *The International Who's Who,* Europa, 1978; *Who's Who in the World,* 4th edition, Marquis, 1978; *London Times,* January 24, 1981; *New York Times,* January 28, 1981.

*   *   *

SHORT, Alan Lennox
See LENNOX-SHORT, Alan

*   *   *

SHOUP, Laurence H(enry) 1943-

PERSONAL: Born June 10, 1943, in Los Angeles, Calif.; son of David John (a jeweler) and Edna Ruth (a teacher; maiden name, Jaenke) Shoup; married Suzanne Marie Baker (an archaeologist), August 12, 1974; children: Daniel David. *Education:* Glendale College, A.A., 1963; California State College at Los Angeles (now California State University, Los Angeles), B.A., 1966, M.A., 1967; Northwestern University, Ph.D., 1974. *Home:* 1464 La Playa, San Francisco, Calif. 94122.

CAREER: U.S. Peace Corps, Tigre, Ethiopia, teacher of world history, 1967-69; Northwestern University, Evanston, Ill., instructor in U.S. history, 1971-74; University of Illinois, Urbana, assistant professor of U.S. history, 1974-75; writer. Lecturer at University of California, Berkeley, 1975 and 1980, and at San Francisco State University, San Francisco, Calif., 1976-77. Historical consultant to Archaeological Consultants, San Francisco, 1978—. Co-chairman of membership committee of Sunset Cooperative Nursery School, 1980-81.

WRITINGS: (With William Minter) *Imperial Brain Trust: The Council on Foreign Relations and U.S. Foreign Policy,* Monthly Review Press, 1977; *The Carter Presidency and Beyond: Power and Politics in the 1980s,* Ramparts, 1980. Contributor to *Insurgent Sociologist* and *Inquiry.*

WORK IN PROGRESS: Geopolitical Economics: A Documentary History of U.S. Foreign Policy 1940-80, publication expected in 1982.

SIDELIGHTS: In *The Carter Presidency and Beyond,* Shoup explored the forces that make and control the U.S. presidency. According to the author, the members of the American ruling class—the leading media, the corporate elite, and private policy planning organizations like the Council on Foreign Relations and Trilateral Commission—are the nation's "real power wielders." These "real sources of political power," Shoup contended, control the political parties and elections. He stated that the aim of the ruling class is to enhance its power and influence through selecting and financing favored candidates and controlling the process by which ideology is disseminated. For example, Shoup explained, "a key function of primaries from the point of view of far-sighted ruling class leaders is to determine which of several acceptable candidates can gain broad support from the American people."

Critics Michael Kinsley of the *Washington Post Book World* and Aaron Wildavsky of the *New York Times Book Review* objected to Shoup's definition of the ruling class. "The concept of a ruling class in America is not silly, but Shoup's treatment of it is," commented Kinsley. "Shoup's version is flexible enough to cover any contingency." Wildavsky also expressed doubts about some of Shoup's classifications. He questioned Shoup's statement that the members of the "Eastern establishment control the elite universities of America": "Why has a distinguished member of the Princeton faculty . . . been allowed to write a laudatory introduction to this book attacking the 'ruling class?'"

On the other hand, Harvey Bresler of the *Seattle Times Magazine* assessed that "the author gives a coherent, persuasive account of the damage to the public weal of a Carter administration whose primary concern is healthy company profits." The *Berkeley Graduate*'s Marian Kester complimented Shoup's work. "Whatever its theoretical shortcomings, *The Carter Presidency and Beyond* is full of highly useful and sometimes prophetic information." The author, she continued, "accurately predicted, writing in the summer of '79, that a Cold War II would be both the logical extension of administration policy, and a terrorist-style 'non-negotiable demand' for Carter's re-election."

Shoup told *CA:* "The aim of my intellectual work is to understand how the U.S. and world power system operates as a first step toward transforming this system into a cooperative commonwealth characterized by respect for nature, nonviolence, equality, economic democracy, world peace, and social justice."

AVOCATIONAL INTERESTS: Camping, hiking, fishing, Africa, gold panning, traveling.

BIOGRAPHICAL/CRITICAL SOURCES: Washington Post Book World, March 16, 1980; *Berkeley Graduate,* April, 1980; *New York Times Book Review,* April 27, 1980; *Seattle Times Magazine,* June 29, 1980; *Le Monde Diplomatique,* November, 1980.

*   *   *

SHRAGIN, Boris 1926-

PERSONAL: Born August 18, 1926, in Viazma, U.S.S.R.; came to the United States in 1974; son of Iosif and Revecca Shragin; married Valentina Paranitcheva, 1949 (marriage ended, 1968); married Natalia Sadomskaya (a university lecturer), 1968; children: Iliya. *Education:* Moscow University, M.A., 1949; Plechanov Institute, Ph.D., 1966. *Politics:* Liberal Democrat. *Religion:* Agnostic. *Agent:* Goodman Associates, 500 West End Ave., New York, N.Y. 10024.

CAREER: Associated with Arts History Research Institute, Moscow, U.S.S.R., 1959-68; Amherst College, Amherst, Mass., visiting lecturer in Russian philosophy, 1975-76; Queens College of the City University of New York, Flushing, N.Y., member of faculty, 1976-77; Hunter College of the City University of New York, New York, N.Y., member of faculty, 1977-78; University of Pittsburgh, Pittsburgh, Pa., visiting professor of Russian history, 1979. Scholar-in-residence at Harvard University, 1975; senior fellow in Russian literature at Columbia University, 1976. *Member:* American Association for the Advancement of Slavic Studies, Institute of Modern Russian Culture.

WRITINGS: (Editor with Albert Todd) *Landmarks: A Collection of Essays on the Russian Intelligentsia,* Karz Howard, 1977; (editor with Michael Meerson-Aksenov, and contributor) *The Political, Social, and Religious Thought of Russian "Samizdat",* Nordland, 1977; *The Challenge of the Spirit,* Knopf, 1978. Contributor of more than forty articles to Russian scholarly journals.

WORK IN PROGRESS: Editing and writing a chapter for *Russian Liberals About Solzhenitsyn: A Collection of Essays; A Muscovite in America.*

SIDELIGHTS: Shragin wrote: "In the Soviet Union I had published articles and essays on aesthetics, modern art, and cultural history. In 1968 I lost my academic position and was deprived of the opportunity to publish in my country for participating in protests against the Soviet violations of human rights. But my work on social and cultural problems appeared under a pseudonym in underground publications. I try to understand the state of contemporary Soviet society and its problems."

* * *

SHULMAN, David Dean 1949-

PERSONAL: Born January 13, 1949, in Waterloo, Iowa; son of Herbert (a physician) and Deana (Krantman) Shulman; married Eileen Lendman (a teacher and artist), January 3, 1972; children: Eviatar, Mishael. *Education:* Hebrew University of Jerusalem, B.A., 1971; London School of Oriental and African Studies, London, Ph.D., 1976. *Religion:* Jewish. *Office:* Department of Indian Studies, Hebrew University of Jerusalem, Jerusalem, Israel.

CAREER: Hebrew University of Jerusalem, Jerusalem, Israel, lecturer in Indian studies, 1976—. *Awards, honors:* Neuman Poetry Prize from Jerusalem Writers' House, 1973, for *Hamiqdash vehamayim.*

WRITINGS: Hamiqdash vehamayim (poems; title means "The Temple and the Water"), Neumann, 1974; *Tamil Temple Myths: Sacrifice and Divine Marriage in the South Indian Saiva Tradition,* Princeton University Press, 1980. Contributor to religious and Asian studies journals.

WORK IN PROGRESS: A book on symbolic types in medieval southern India; translating classical Tamil poetry into Hebrew; research on Kampan's Tamil version of the *Ramayana.*

SIDELIGHTS: Shulman commented: "I was first attracted to the Tamil area of southern India by translations of classical Tamil poetry. My interests center on the classical and medieval literatures of southern India and on the history of Hinduism in this region. I have lived for short periods of time in Madras, and have traveled extensively in India.

"The major influences on my work have been those of my teachers: John Ralston Marr (who is in the line of teachers stretching back to the great U.V. Caminataiyar, the founder of modern Tamil studies) and Wendy Doniger O'Flaherty."

* * *

SHUTE, Nevil
See NORWAY, Nevil Shute

* * *

SIDRAN, Ben H. 1943-
PERSONAL: Born August 14, 1943, in Chicago, Ill.; son of

Louis W. and Shirley G. Sidran; married Judith Lutrin (a weaver), July 10, 1969; children: Leo. *Education:* University of Wisconsin (now University of Wisconsin—Madison), B.S. (cum laude), 1966; University of Sussex, M.A., 1968, Ph.D., 1970. *Home:* 1305 Rutledge St., Madison, Wis. 53703. *Office:* P.O. Box 763, Madison, Wis. 53701.

CAREER: Musician and record producer. Lecturer at University of Wisconsin—Madison. Member of music panel of Wisconsin Arts Board; member of board of advisers on popular music and society at Bowling Green State University. *Member:* American Society of Composers, Authors and Publishers, National Academy of Recording Arts and Sciences, Musicians Federation.

WRITINGS: Black Talk, Holt, 1971. Contributor to *Rolling Stone.*

WORK IN PROGRESS: Research for a book on the recording industry in America, and the effects that industry has had on music and musicians.

SIDELIGHTS: Sidran commented: "Nobody has ever written a really first rate book about what it is like to be a musician in this country. I hope to write that book. I travel constantly (as a pianist and singer), performing for audiences large and small. I see this as my research as well as my current vocation."

* * *

SIEBER, Roy 1923-
PERSONAL: Born April 28, 1923, in Shawano, Wis.; son of Roy L. and Margaret (Collard) Sieber; married Sophia Yeran, June 10, 1950; children: Mark, Thyne, Ellen, Matthew. *Education:* New School for Social Research, B.A., 1949; Iowa State University, M.A., 1951, Ph.D., 1957. *Home:* 114 Glenwood Ave. E., Bloomington, Ind. 47401. *Office:* Department of Fine Arts, Indiana University, Bloomington, Ind. 47405.

CAREER: Iowa State University, Ames, instructor, 1950-57, assistant professor of art history, 1957-62; Indiana University, Bloomington, associate professor, 1962-64, professor of art history, 1964—, Rudy Professor of Fine Arts, 1974—, chairman of department of fine arts, 1967-70, curator of primitive art at Fine Arts Museum, 1962—, chairman of museum policy committee, 1971-79, curator of ethnic art at Museum of History and Anthropology, 1964—. Visiting lecturer at University of Arizona, summers, 1961-62, and University of Wisconsin—Madison, summer, 1963; visiting professor of University of Ghana, 1964 and 1967; visiting research professor at University of Ife, 1971; Baldwin Lecturer at Oberlin College, 1972; Sutphin Lecturer in Humanities at Indiana Central University, 1975; Benedict Distinguished Visiting Professor at Carlton College, 1976-77; Phi Beta Kappa visiting scholar at colleges and universities, 1979-80; U.S. Peace Corps lecturer. Organizes art exhibitions. Member of American Council of Learned Societies/Social Science Research Council joint committee on Africa, 1963-71, advisory committee of primitive collection at Metropolitan Museum of Art, and Smithsonian Institution's African Art Commission; member of board of trustees of Museum of African Art; consultant to Ford Foundation and museums.

MEMBER: American Association of University Professors, Royal Anthropological Institute of Great Britain and Ireland, College Art Association of America, African Studies Association (chairman of arts and humanities committee, 1963), Midwest Art Association. *Awards, honors:* Ford Foundation grant for England and Nigeria, 1957-58, for Ghana, 1964; grants from American Council of Learned Societies and Social Science Research Council, 1962-63, (for Ghana), 1962; grants from African Studies Association and American Council of Learned Societies for Senegal, 1966 and 1967; Wenner-Gren Foundation grant for Austria, 1967; senior scholar grants from National Endowment for the Humanities, 1971 and 1980-81; Social Science Research Council grant for Europe and North Africa, 1980-81.

WRITINGS: Sculpture of Northern Nigeria (monograph), Museum of Primitive Art, 1961; (with Arnold Rubin) *Sculpture of Black Africa: The Paul Tishman Collection,* Los Angeles County Musuem of Art, 1968, supplement (with Rubin and Robin Poynor), International Exhibitions Foundation, 1970-71; *African Textiles and Decorative Arts,* Museum of Modern Art, 1972; *African Furniture and Household Objects,* Indiana University Press, 1980.

Contributor: F. Rainey, editor, *Seven Metals in Africa,* University Museum, University of Pennsylvania, 1960; Robert A. Lystad, editor, *The African World: A Survey of Social Research,* Praeger, 1965; Creighton Gabel and Norman R. Bennett, editors, *Reconstructing African Culture History,* Boston University Press, 1967; Daniel Biebuyck, editor, *Tradition and Creativity in Tribal Art,* University of California Press, 1969; Charlotte Otten, editor, *Anthropology and Art,* American Natural History Press, 1971; Yehudi A. Cohen, editor, *Man in Adaptation: The Institutional Framework,* Aldine, 1971; J. H. Limpman, editor, *The Collector in America,* Viking, 1971; D. F. Fraser and H. M. Cole, editors, *African Art and Leadership,* University of Wisconsin Press, 1972; Warren L. d'Azevedo, editor, *The Traditional Artist in African Societies,* Indiana University Press, 1973; Anthony Forge, editor, *Primitive Art and Society,* Oxford University Press, 1973; Newell S. Booth, editor, *African Religions: A Symposium,* NOK Publishers, 1977; Phyllis M. Martin and Patrick O'Meara, editors, *Africa,* Indiana University Press, 1977. Also contributor to *Twenty-Five: A Tribute to Henry Radford Hope,* Indiana University Press, 1966.

Author of exhibition catalogs. Contributor to *Encyclopaedia Britannica* and *Encyclopedia Americana.* Contributor of articles and reviews to academic journals.

WORK IN PROGRESS: Studying museum collections of Islamic art.

*   *   *

SIEGAL, Mordecai 1934-

PERSONAL: Born July 25, 1934, in Philadelphia, Pa.; son of Abraham Jacob and Ida Siegal; married Victoria Blankenship (an actress), November 27, 1968; children: Thomas Jesse, Ida Justine, Jasper Charles. *Education:* Attended Hedgerow Theatre School, American Theatre Wing School, and Neighborhood Playhouse School of the Theatre. *Politics:* "Constitutional Democrat." *Religion:* Jewish. *Residence:* New York, N.Y. *Agent:* William Morris Agency, 1350 Avenue of the Americas, New York, N.Y. 10019.

CAREER: Writer. Commentator on "Morning Edition" for National Public Radio. Host of "Vets and Pets," a program on WNYC-Radio, 1979-81; pet authority on "Hour Magazine," Group W-TV, 1980—. Chairman of legal committee of Westbeth Artists Residents Council. *Military service:* U.S. Air Force, in Armed Forces Radio Service, 1952-56; served in Korea and Japan. *Member:* Authors Guild, Authors League of America, Dramatists Guild, Screen Writers of America (East), Dog Writers Association of America,

American Federation of Television and Radio Artists, Bide-a-Wee Home Association (member of advisory council). *Awards, honors:* Best Book Award from Dog Writers Association of America, 1977, for *The Good Dog Book;* four awards from Dog Writers Association of America, for articles.

WRITINGS: (With Matthew Margolis) *Good Dog, Bad Dog,* Holt, 1973; (with Margolis) *Underdog,* Stein & Day, 1974; *The Good Dog Book,* Macmillan, 1975; *Mordecai Siegal's Happy Pet/Happy Owner Book,* Rawson Associates, 1978; *The Good Cat Book,* Simon & Schuster, 1981; *Metropolitan Dog,* Viking, 1982.

Author of "Shayna" (three-act play), first produced in New York, N.Y., at Open Space Theater, May 10, 1977.

Author of screenplays, including "Buck Buck Number One" and "The Tenants." Author of "At Home With Pets," a column in *House Beautiful,* 1977—, "Pets by Mordecai Siegal," a column in *Sunday Woman,* 1978-80, and "People and Their Pets," a column in *Good Housekeeping,* 1979-81. Contributor to *Cat Catalog* and *Dog Owner's Bible,* and to periodicals, including *Cat Fancy* and *American Kennel Gazette.*

WORK IN PROGRESS: A Flood of Waters, a novel, publication expected in 1983; nonfiction books.

SIDELIGHTS: Siegal commented: "Theater is my primary discipline. Writing for films is an exciting prospect. Writing fiction is also very pleasant. But writing about pet animals not only affords me my writer's reputation and income, it also gives me great satisfaction. Helping animals live better by advising their human surrogates is most rewarding. It is as important a subject for writing as any I can think of. Having animals in the human environment is civilizing, while giving us a slight connection with what's left of the natural world. It is, to me, of vital importance. I shall always be glad I became involved with the subject."

*   *   *

SIEGEL, Esther 1949-

PERSONAL: Born January 12, 1949, in New York, N.Y.; daughter of David I. (a civic association president and writer) and Ada (a political analyst; maiden name, Steinberg) Siegel. *Education:* George Washington University, B.A., 1970. *Religion:* Jewish. *Home:* Beecher Cooperative, 2316 40th Pl. N.W., Apt. 301, Washington, D.C. 20007. *Office:* Metropolitan Washington Planning and Housing Association, 1225 K St. N.W., Washington, D.C. 20005.

CAREER: American Film Institute, Washington, D.C., cataloger, 1971-74; Circle Theatre, Washington, D.C., ticket seller and in advertising, 1974; free-lance writer, 1974-79; Metropolitan Washington Planning and Housing Association, Washington, D.C., assistant director of Cooperative Housing Services Program, 1979—.

WRITINGS: American Film Institute Catalog, Bowker, 1976; (with David L. Parker) *Guide to Dance in Films: A Guide to Information Sources,* Gale, 1978; *From Rental to Cooperative, A Tenant Initiative,* Metropolitan Washington Planning and Housing Association, 1980.

SIDELIGHTS: Siegel told *CA:* "I got involved in cooperative housing quite by accident. It was during my free-lance days in 1977 when I received a certified letter—not a raving review, but rather an eviction notice! I did not know then that that letter and the subsequent two year struggle to save my and my neighbors' homes was to be a dramatic turning point in my life.

"The tenants association that I led succeeded in buying our apartments cooperatively and forming a cooperative committed to providing decent, affordable housing to low and moderate income people. Washington, D.C., is in the midst of a condominium epidemic that is rapidly shrinking the availability of decent, affordable housing for such people. My experience in and commitment to protecting housing for low and moderate income people led me to my present job where I work with other tenant groups faced with losing their homes and make available literature on cooperative housing."

*   *   *

SINCLAIR, (Allan) Gordon   1900-

PERSONAL: Born June 3, 1900, in Toronto, Ontario, Canada; son of Alexander and Bessie (Eesley) Sinclair; married Gladys Prewett, May 8, 1926; children: Gordon, Jr., Donald, Jean (died, 1943), Jack. *Education:* Attended public schools in Toronto, Canada. *Religion:* None. *Home:* 35 Burnhamthorpe Park Blvd., Islington, Ontario, Canada M9A 1H8. *Office:* CFRB-Radio, 2 St. Clair Ave. W., Toronto, Ontario, Canada M4V 1L6.

CAREER: Writer, journalist, and radio commentator. Worked as clerk at Bank of Nova Scotia, Toronto, Canada; T. Eaton Co. (department store), Toronto, bookkeeper, c. 1917, cashier, 1919; worked at calendar factory, slaughterhouse, and rubber company, 1919-22; *Toronto Star,* Toronto, reporter, 1922-43; CFRB-Radio, Toronto, host of "Let's Be Personal," 1942—, and news broadcaster, 1944—. Host of traveling radio show, "Ontario Panorama," 1943; panelist on CBC-TV's "Front Page Challenge," 1957—; book reviewer and show business critic for CFRB-Radio. *Military service:* Canadian Army, 48th Highlanders Regiment, 1917-19. *Awards, honors:* Gordon Sinclair Award, 1970, for "outspoken opinions and integrity in broadcasting"; named to Canada's News Hall of Fame, 1972; H. Gordon Love News Trophy from Canadian Association of Broadcasters, 1974; distinguished service award from Radio and Television News Directors' Association, 1974, for "challenging and courageous commentary"; appointed officer of Order of Canada, 1979.

WRITINGS—All nonfiction: *Footloose in India,* Doubleday, Doran & Gundy, 1932, Farrar & Rinehart, 1933, reprinted, McClelland & Stewart, 1966; *Cannibal Quest,* Doubleday, Doran & Gundy, 1933, Farrar & Rinehart, 1934; *Loose Among Devils,* Farrar & Rinehart, 1935; *Khyber Caravan: Through Kashmir, Waziristan, Afghanistan, Baluchistan, and Northern India,* Farrar & Rinehart, 1936, reprinted, Simon & Schuster, 1975; *Signpost to Adventure,* McClelland & Stewart, 1947; *Bright Paths to Adventure,* McClelland & Stewart, 1952; *Will the Real Gordon Sinclair Please Stand Up* (autobiography), McClelland & Stewart, 1966; *Will Gordon Sinclair Please Sit Down* (memoirs), McClelland & Stewart, 1975.

Author of recording, "The Americans," Avco Records, 1973. Contributor of feature articles to magazines.

SIDELIGHTS: Gordon Sinclair has been described as "the unquiet Canadian," a colorful, often "wildly controversial" journalist whom "millions love to cuss." Many Canadians remember him as the reporter who traveled all over the world for the *Toronto Star* in the 1930's, sending back stories about his adventures in faraway lands. He is an institution in Toronto, where his opinion program and daily radio newscasts have been aired since World War II, and people across the country know him as a regular panelist on the weekly

quiz show "Front Page Challenge," the longest continuing program on Canadian television. In the United States, however, he is perhaps best known for a four-minute radio broadcast made in June, 1973, an opinion piece called "The Americans" that praised the country and its people.

Sinclair began his career at the *Toronto Star* in 1922. After what he called four "uneventful years" as a reporter, he was promoted to woman's editor, but found himself unsuited for the job. "Having never had a sister or a wife," he explained, "I knew little or nothing about women, and one day, in desperation, my editor told me to go and write some stories about hoboes." During the assignment he rode a boxcar from Toronto to New York City, signed on as a bootblack aboard the liner *Laurentic,* and sailed in the company of hoboes to England. He was soon after arrested in Germany for smuggling cigarettes.

"All of these adventures made entertaining reading," he wrote, and his editor decided that he should continue his journey, wandering where he pleased with no particular duties or assignments. From 1928 to 1940 Sinclair traveled around the world four times, crossing every continent and all but the Antarctic Ocean. Many of the places he visited became the subjects of books, including the best-selling *Footloose in India* and *Cannibal Quest.*

Among Sinclair's most memorable adventures was a trip to China in 1938. Along with adventurer-author Richard Halliburton, Sinclair was one of the first outsiders to enter the city of Canton after its fall to the Japanese. A few weeks later he was at the center of an international incident when he was stabbed by a Japanese sentry. Evacuated to Hong Kong aboard an American gunboat, he spent the next several weeks with Halliburton, who was building a sea-going junk. Sinclair notes that he is the last living man to have spoken with Halliburton. In March, 1939, Halliburton set out across the Pacific aboard his junk, the *Sea Dragon,* and was never seen again.

By the time Sinclair returned to Toronto in 1940, he was a well-known journalist and the author of four adventure books. A series of dramatic articles about the French penal colony on Devil's Island had been collected for *Loose Among Devils,* his third book, and his fourth, *Khyber Caravan,* described his travels along the remote borderland of Afghanistan, Pakistan, Kashmir, and India. According to Sinclair, *Khyber Caravan* was his "first attempt at a serious and literate book," and even though it failed financially, he still considers it his best.

At the outbreak of World War II Sinclair wrote a series of unflattering articles about Canada's military leaders. As a result the Canadian forces branded him a troublemaker and denied him accreditation as a war correspondent. The ban was never lifted, and Sinclair decided to go into radio broadcasting, beginning with a midday personality show, "Let's Be Personal." When the *Star* compelled him to choose one career or the other, Sinclair resigned from the paper and joined the news department of CFRB-Radio, Canada's largest privately-owned station.

Sinclair gained national exposure in 1957 when he became a charter member of CBC-TV's "Front Page Challenge." Similar in format to the old "What's My Line?" show on American television, "Front Page" features a panel of four interviewers who try to guess the identity of a notable person in the news. A round of interviews follows the game, and Sinclair has distinguished himself over the years by asking especially blunt or provocative questions. A writer for the *Detroit News* commented, "Sinclair is still one of the best television interviewers in Canada and no subject goes through his probing without facing the question: 'How much do you make?'"

Sinclair's comments have often caused a public commotion, but he contends that it is "an absolutely natural sort of thing to speak your mind." Listeners protested loudly when he asked an Olympic swimmer how she trained and competed during menstruation, and his publicly-proclaimed agnosticism has upset a number of people, including a group of young evangelists who once prayed for his conversion in the CFRB lobby. In another well-known incident, he complained that a rich man's will had left nothing to charity. His remarks sent lawyers scurrying back to their wealthy clients with a clause that protects them against such criticism, a provision that some lawyers call the Sinclair Clause.

Sinclair hasn't hesitated to criticize the United States when it interferes in Canadian affairs, but his popularity with Americans was assured after his radio broadcast of June 5, 1973. At that time the United States was beset with problems, including a shrinking dollar, escalating oil prices, the Watergate investigation, natural disasters, and mounting world criticism. When he heard that the American Red Cross was broke, Sinclair typed out an editorial that extolled the generosity of Americans and attacked the country's critics: "This Canadian thinks it is time to speak up for the Americans as the most generous and possibly the least-appreciated people in all the earth," he wrote. "I'm one Canadian who is damned tired of hearing them kicked around."

Sinclair read his editorial on "Let's Be Personal," then filed it away. "I didn't expect any reaction at all," he said, but by December his desk was buried under 100,000 pieces of mail, including letters of appreciation from John Wayne and President Richard Nixon. "The Americans" was recorded five times, read into the Congressional Record seven times, and distributed to U.S. Information offices in more than one hundred countries. Sinclair's own recorded version sold 500,000 copies in ten days and brought him hundreds of requests for personal appearances.

The whole affair bemused Sinclair, who preferred not to accept an invitation to read "The Americans" at a Seattle concert with the Mormon Tabernacle Choir singing "The Battle Hymn of the Republic" in the background. Nor did he want to appear on "The Tonight Show" or "The Mike Douglas Show," or fly with former spy pilot Francis Gary Powers aboard his traffic helicopter in Burbank, California. All the royalties he earned from "The Americans" were to be given to the American Red Cross, he decided, saying that he didn't "want anything for doing something he believes in."

CA INTERVIEW

CA interviewed Gordon Sinclair on May 1, 1980, at his office in Toronto, Ontario.

CA: When did you start making money as a writer?

SINCLAIR: The very first time I ever wrote something for which I was paid was when I was a sales clerk at Eaton's at Christmastime. At that time I was working in the office, but they sent office help down to the sales floor at Christmas for the rush. Well, I sold a necktie one day to Sir John Eaton, and I recognized him and gave him the necktie. I wrote a story about that, which I sold to the *Toronto Star Weekly* for three dollars. That gave me the big idea of getting started as a reporter. That would be about 1920, and I joined the *Toronto Star* about 1922.

CA: The earliest pieces by you that I saw were in the Border Cities Star *in Windsor. I saw them in the clipping file at the Windsor Star.* You weren't working for them, were you?

SINCLAIR: No, no, they were just buying the stuff from the *Toronto Star*. No, I started with the *Toronto Star* right from the start.

CA: I saw that you did a big expose on crime, prostitution, and gambling down in Windsor, though.

SINCLAIR: Yes, that's right. I guess that would be about 1927. I started on the first foreign assignment (for the *Toronto Star*) in 1928, and I think that was just before that. Yeah, it was kind of a loose-leaf kind of thing. I went to a few whorehouses, stuff like that. But that was for the *Toronto Star*.

CA: Did the Border Cities *do anything about it?*

SINCLAIR: No, and I was kind of disappointed they didn't. I was a little surprised, but I had the same experience in New Orleans. Huey Long was about to clean up New Orleans. I don't know why, but the papers down there were ignoring him, so my editor said: "Go down to New Orleans and go around with him. But make sure before you go that he'll see you!" So I phoned, and he said, "Sure, I'll see you." And I went down and spent a week with Long. In fact, the last three days of my week I lived with him in his own house. His wife had walked out on him. And on the very day that I left he was assassinated. The very day.

CA: In those early days at the Star *you met some interesting people—Morley Callaghan and Ernest Hemingway. What were they like?*

SINCLAIR: I disliked Hemingway because I thought he was patronizing. In terms of myself, he was a little older, maybe a year older, but I disliked him. Maybe it was just ego on my part. I was assigned to him on only one story as an assistant, and he made me damn well conscious of the fact that I was his assistant and he was the reporter. As a matter of fact, he didn't get a by-line on that story. The story appeared about a column and a half long, but Hemingway didn't get a by-line.

CA: What is the story about the cinnamon toast?

SINCLAIR: Hemingway corrected the proofs of *The Sun Also Rises* at Child's Restaurant across from the *Star* on King Street while eating cinnamon toast and drinking a lot of coffee. I put that in a book, and a reviewer for *Saturday Night* did a piece that said this couldn't have happened because of the dates. Well, he was wrong, and I was right.

CA: What did you think of Hemingway as a reporter?

SINCLAIR: I think he was a mood guy, he kind of set a mood. The one story I worked on with him was the return to Toronto of some people who had been in a big earthquake in Japan, and his story, if you had a lot of time to write it, was good, because it described how he'd met these people and the costumes they were wearing. They happened to be just unpacking with their Japanese clothes when Hemingway, Mary Lowry, and myself went up there to see this woman. She had just put on her Japanese garments, so it was quite a distinctive meeting. She opened the door, wearing a beautiful scarlet robe. That's what he wrote about. He probably was right to write the story like that, because the earthquake was far behind her.

I remember him writing in that story that when we went into the house, there was water running. It happened to be a bathtub upstairs. We could hear it. I remember him writing this. Looking back on it now, I think my assessment and his editor's assessment were wrong. Maybe that was the right way to write it—the presentation of the women in costumes, the water running, this and that; but anyway, he didn't get a by-line on it.

CA: What about your influences. Today kids go to school to become journalists. In your day, they didn't.

SINCLAIR: There were several influences. I worked personally for Sime Silverman, founder of *Variety,* and I was the *Variety* stringer in Ontario for a time in the mid-1920's. I also worked for Flo Ziegfeld and John Philip Sousa in publicity, and my *Toronto Star* editor, Harry Hindmarsh, was an influence, too. And I was a constant reader of the *New York World.* The *World* was considered at that time to be a very good newspaper, and it had a tremendous influence upon me.

CA: Your background, however, gives you an edge over many journalists today. You wrote in one of your books that you have spoken with every prime minister in Canada from Laurier to the present, and you have even spoken with people who fought in the U.S. Civil War.

SINCLAIR: I've told the anecdote about the Civil War several times, but it doesn't seem to strike a chord, which puzzles me. In 1914 there was not a mile of paved road in North America, but the first paved highway was being built between Toronto and Oakville. I had an uncle who drove from Indiana in his automobile, and he invited me to go back with him. No roads, remember, and he did go back. My mother said to keep a diary of this, and I did. I've kept a diary from that day in 1914 to now. Anyhow, we went first to Indiana to a place called College Corners, a little village, then to Dayton, Ohio. I had a different uncle there who had a house next door to a military hospital, and in that military hospital were maybe eighty men who had fought in the Civil War. This was 1914. The Civil War had ended in 1865, so they didn't have to be all that old. They were very talkative, and I used to go next door to the hospital day after day and talk to these men. I was fourteen.

CA: What was your method of approach in Footloose in India *and your last book,* Will Gordon Sinclair Please Sit Down? *How did you change?*

SINCLAIR: My method of approach with *Footloose in India* was to write it because I had a ready publisher, and I wrote the whole book in nineteen days, largely based on columns that had appeared in the *Star.* That sold well. Mind you, it was a slang book.

CA: But it doesn't sound like columns.

SINCLAIR: No, it doesn't. I went over it quite a bit. I wrote that up in Muskoka in nineteen days. I still get royalty checks from it. They're very small now.

CA: What about the last book?

SINCLAIR: In the last book, *Will Gordon Sinclair Please Sit Down,* or even in *Will the Real Gordon Sinclair Please Stand Up,* I found my attention span had been acclimated to radio and television. In other words, I could write an item and interest myself in an item up to eight hundred words, and then I'd lose interest. Then I'd start again. So that each of those books, in my view, run downhill. They start out alright, but I think they run downhill because of my own attention span.

Also because my radio experience tells me to make it short, make it punchy.

CA: Do you see yourself as a book writer, or do you see yourself as a journalist?

SINCLAIR: As a journalist.

CA: Do you see the books as a kind of higher journalism?

SINCLAIR: I don't, but most people who write books do. They're just journalism, and I think the best-selling books—take Harold Robbins as an example—they're a kind of journalism. Gay Talese is another.

CA: Where do you do most of your book writing?

SINCLAIR: I have written most of them in Muskoka, on Acton Island, four measured miles from Bala. I have a cottage there all my own. That is to say, there is a family cottage, but I had one built for me and me alone. It's not much bigger than this room, and I do my writing there.

CA: In the course of your journalism career you've met some very interesting people, like Gandhi and Adolph Hitler. What was Hitler like? How did you meet him anyway?

SINCLAIR: I met Hitler when he was leader of the Nazi party. He wasn't chancellor yet. I met him by strange circumstances. I was in Munich on a Sunday afternoon. I forget the year. I think it was 1932 or 1933. I was alone in Munich, and I was studying the language. I went to a restaurant that was partly indoors and partly outdoors, like some of them were in Paris. Well, I was seated outside, and it started raining, so I was moved inside. It was crowded, but I had a table for four all to myself.

Some men in brown-shirted uniforms came into the restaurant and put a Nazi flag on my table. They didn't say a word, and I was reading a German newspaper, so they must have thought I was German. Well, this was a signal that I was to get the hell up and out of there. They wanted that table. In a sense they were right. It was a table for four, the place was crowded, and I was alone. When I paid no attention they started to abuse me. Now I could read German, but at their speed of talking I couldn't understand them, and I was a little bewildered. So the proprietor came down and explained to them that I was a foreign journalist. I don't know how he knew I was a journalist, but anyhow they were full of apologies. They lifted the flag, then they got someone who could speak English to me, and they explained how they didn't mean to be nasty to a foreigner, and would I like to meet their leader. They arranged a meeting the following morning, in fact.

They supplied a little girl as an interpreter, and I had no difficulty with Hitler. I do remember the room he was in overlooked a large cemetery. Big high windows and a large cemetery. Then he began to talk, and I could follow him at first, but then I lost him. He began to talk about the terrible injustices his country had suffered, how Germany was in the center of Europe, and how it could move outward in any direction, and people could not keep such a brave and noble people down, and so on. It became his regular speech.

CA: Do you think it was all nonsense?

SINCLAIR: No. I was impressed by him.

CA: Did you think after meeting him that he would become Germany's leader?

SINCLAIR: I thought he would become a very strong force, and I tried to tell my people at home. The interview certainly didn't hit page one—no, it was in the inside. It was used.

CA: What about Gandhi?

SINCLAIR: Gandhi? I met him on various occasions. It was one of the biggest assessments that I ever made badly. I thought in the beginning that Gandhi was a fake, a fraudulent man, and I said so to him. But as I got to meet him afterwards—I met him many, many times—we got to know each other very well. I soon began to realize what a terrible mistake I had made about him.

CA: You seem always to be getting into trouble. I remember when you asked Elaine Tanner, the Olympic swimmer, how she trained and competed when she was menstruating, and how that caused such a furor. Then there was the broadcast in August, 1979, about the boat people (the Vietnamese fleeing to Canada), and you said they could just turn around and go back. Do you do that kind of thing out of conviction?

SINCLAIR: No, I'm a blurter. I sort of blurt these questions out. There's one upcoming that will get me in trouble. There's an astronomer who knows all about the heavens. I asked her, after her four-year examination of the heavens: "Have you ever come across Heaven? Do you believe in God?" She said, "I've never come across Heaven, but I believe in God," and I blurted, "Well, I don't, and I'll tell you why!"

CA: Some of your blurting has made you friends below the border in the United States. I remember the four-and-one-half-minute editorial on the radio which took you only twenty minutes to write.

SINCLAIR: That was in 1973.

CA: With Nixon having been thrown out and the Watergate episode behind us, what do you think of the American people now?

SINCLAIR: It doesn't change my view of the American people at all. They're a generous people, rather naive, perhaps, but a very generous people, and that was the idea of my piece. They have helped almost everybody, and who has helped them? That was my theme.

CA: There's a story about how you were one of the first to see the Dionne quintuplets in North Bay. You went up there with Fred Davis, the host of "Front Page Challenge." He was a photographer then with the Toronto Star.

SINCLAIR: I wasn't the first up there. There was another guy called Gordon. He was the first. But I went to see Dionne, and he said, "I'm the kind of man they should kill," or something like that, and then we went into the house. Madame Dionne was in the bed. We picked up the kids and took pictures and everything.

CA: With all the people you have ever met—Gandhi, Hitler, Laurier, and others—what would you ask Nixon if you met him in an interview?

SINCLAIR: That's a tough one. I've never given it a thought. I would have gone somewhere to the Shakespearean idea of "Methinks the Lady dost protest too much!" In other words, he had so often said he was not a thief, not a crook, not a this and that, why was he always on the defensive when he went on the television? The thing with the dog. I would have asked him about that. Why all this protesting of your innocence when you haven't been outwardly accused.

CA: You said in one of your books that your grandmother

was one of the greatest storytellers in the world.

SINCLAIR: She told me about the Scot heroes, especially the Black Douglas, and she romanticized Sir Walter Scott's Lochinvar, Bruce, and Wallace. She told them in different ways each time, never accurately. And I'm certainly not one of the most accurate reporters, but I make a good story, and her style did affect me. I think it came as a big surprise to me to be tripped up by accuracy, because I was out to tell a story, and it never occurred to me that newspapers had to have a measure of accuracy. Even now I exaggerate and embellish and add to stories. I don't see anything wrong with that. That is my major weakness: to make a good story rather than a factual one.

CA: Was there any turning point in your career, something that happened to you that you could peg as the beginning of something exciting for you?

SINCLAIR: The hobo story was the turning point of my career, if anything was. The story came when I was told there was a raid on the Toronto Jungle, as it was called. One hundred twenty-nine hoboes were scooped up, and I was to go with them, because they couldn't put all of them in jail—it was too costly. So I went with them. They were interesting people. Well, I came back. I didn't realize I had a story, and I didn't write one. A couple of days later my editor sent a memo: "Where's your story on the hoboes?" I told him I didn't think there was anything to it, that not much had happened. Well, one of the hoboes had hit me, and I had a black eye, and he said: "That's it! Write it!" So I wrote the story. I figured about nine hundred words. It didn't appear the next day or the next, but on the third day the story was returned to me saying this was very good, but could I break it down into two or three stories, and I did.

CA: It seemed like a big jump to go from that to traveling all over the world, didn't it?

SINCLAIR: It wasn't such a big jump. There's a lot left out. At the end of the four stories on the hoboes, I had said we were near New York City, and these bums I was with were hoping to get on a ship to England, to work their way to England. Whether they did or not, I don't know. But a memo came to me asking, "Why didn't you follow them?" Well, first I had no passport, secondly I had no money, and I had a family at home. "Go anyway!," they said. So I went to Montreal and got a job on the *Laurentic* on the White Star Line as a bootblack. But by the time I reached Quebec City the other guys found out I was a reporter and not a shoe shiner, so they got me tossed out. But I went anyway. I went to England.

CA: Harry Hindmarsh (editor of the Toronto Star*) was such a dynamo of a man. He sent you across the world to write stories. What an assignment. I wonder, are there any people like him today?*

SINCLAIR: No. It's a great regret today. There's no such newspaper and no such editor. It's a terrible thing. I think today there are two spots in the world which need exploring in the old-fashioned way—the Amazon Valley and the so-called Rooftop of the World, the golden road to Samarkand, as it was sometimes called. I was in those countries, and I wrote about them, but very little. Ian Fleming's brother, Peter, has done the best books about them.

CA: So you think it can still be done?

SINCLAIR: Let's put it this way. As I told you, I've kept a diary since I was fourteen, and I often check back to see what I did a year ago, or two years ago, on a certain day. Well, I looked at it this morning, and two years ago—that's usually as far back as I will go—I was asked by the *Toronto Star* to go around the world again, as I did five times. That was 1978, but I'm too old now to do that. I wish there was some young man or some young woman who could do that.

CA: Do you think journalism has become too slick?

SINCLAIR: No, too political! They're interested in politics, not in human interest, not in snake charmers or the old Indian rope trick. They're all interested in who's going to get elected here, what's the political meaning of this and that.

CA: Do you think people read that stuff?

SINCLAIR: I guess they have no alternative. I don't read it myself. I don't use it on the news here.

CA: Well, what are you doing here? What kind of work?

SINCLAIR: I'm doing the worst kind of journalism there is—scalping! That's all I'm doing. I get the stuff off the news ticker machines and write it in my style. But what kind of a life is that? It pays well, but you don't see anything.

AVOCATIONAL INTERESTS: Growing flowers, boating, fishing, bird watching.

BIOGRAPHICAL/CRITICAL SOURCES: Gordon Sinclair, *Will the Real Gordon Sinclair Please Stand Up,* McClelland & Stewart, 1966; *Biography News,* Volume I, Gale, 1974; *Detroit News,* January 6, 1974; *Newsweek,* January 7, 1974; *Time,* January 21, 1974; *Windsor Star,* February 15, 1974; *Saturday Night,* November, 1975; *Authors in the News,* Volume I, Gale, 1976; Yousuf Karsh, *Karsh Canadians,* University of Toronto Press, 1978.

—*Sketch by B. Hal May*
—*Interview by C. H. Gervais*

*   *   *

SINCLAIR, Rose
See MENDONCA, Susan

*   *   *

SINCLAIR-STEVENSON, Christopher 1939-

PERSONAL: Born June 27, 1939, in London, England; son of George (a lawyer) and Gloria (Gordon) Sinclair-Stevenson; married Deborah Susan Walker-Smith, June 10, 1965. *Education:* St. John's College, Cambridge, M.A., 1960. *Home:* 3 South Ter., London SW7 2TB, England. *Agent:* Richard Scott Simon, 32 College Cross, London N.1, England. *Office:* Hamish Hamilton Ltd., 57-59 Long Acre, London WC2E 9JZ, England.

CAREER: Hamish Hamilton Ltd. (publisher), London, England, editor, 1961-70, editorial director, 1970-74, managing director, 1974—. Member of literature panel of Arts Council of Great Britain, 1976-79. *Awards, honors:* Award from Scottish Arts Council, 1971, for *Inglorious Rebellion.*

WRITINGS: (Editor) *The Hamish Hamilton Book of Princes,* Hamish Hamilton, 1964; *The Gordon Highlanders,* Leo Cooper, 1968; *Inglorious Rebellion,* St. Martin's, 1971; *The Life of a Regiment,* Leo Cooper, 1974; *Blood Royal,* J. Cape, 1979, Doubleday, 1980.

WORK IN PROGRESS: Anatomy of the French, publication by J. Cape expected in 1983.

SIDELIGHTS: Sinclair-Stevenson commented: "I write basically to amuse myself, to entertain my readers, and to contribute to the studies of history and character.

"My previous books have covered military and social history of the eighteenth and early nineteenth centuries. My book in progress is quite different, far more personal, perhaps even egocentric in the real sense, in any case a mixture of history, topography, character evaluation, language, and literature. My main reason for writing such a book is that no one has even written a satisfactory or stimulating book on the French. The French themselves cannot do it and British or American attempts have been either purely critical or impossibly adulatory. The real trouble is that it will please no one—except conceivably the author."

*   *   *

SINGER, Burns
See SINGER, James Hyman

*   *   *

SINGER, James Hyman 1928-1964
(Burns Singer)

PERSONAL: Born August 29, 1928, in New York, N.Y.; died of heart disease, September 8, 1964, in Plymouth, England; son of Michael (a salesman) and Bertha (Burns) Singer; married Marie Battle (a psychologist), 1956. *Education:* Attended University of Glasgow, 1945 and 1949-51.

CAREER: Writer. Scottish Home Department, Aberdeen, Scotland, research assistant in marine laboratory, 1951-55; free-lance writer and reviewer in London, England, 1955-59, and Cambridge, England, 1959-64; in research at marine laboratory in Cambridge, 1964. *Awards, honors:* Leverhulme fellowship, 1964.

WRITINGS—Under name Burns Singer; poetry, except as noted: *The Gentle Engineer,* Botteghe Oscure, 1952; *Sonnets for a Dying Man,* Botteghe Oscure, c. 1957; *Still and All,* Secker & Warburg, 1957, Dufour, 1959; *Living Silver: An Impression of the British Fishing Industry* (documentary novel), Secker & Warburg, 1957, published as *Living Silver,* Houghton, 1958; (editor and translator with Jerry Peterkiewicz) *Five Centuries of Polish Poetry, 1450-1950,* Secker & Warburg, 1960, Dufour, 1962; *The Collected Poems of Burns Singer,* edited by Walter A. S. Keir, Secker & Warburg, 1970; *Selected Poems,* edited by Anne Cluysenaar, Carcanet New Press, 1977. Also author of television documentary film, "Between the Tides," first broadcast in 1956. Contributor to *Times Literary Supplement, Listener,* and *Encounter.*

SIDELIGHTS: Burns Singer's poetry has been praised as sparse, stoical, and tough-minded. J. W. Krutch commended the author's documentary novel, *Living Silver,* for its "plain, muscular, vigrorous and unself-conscious prose which is enormously effective without being in the slightest degree strained or fancy." It is the story of Jan, a young British boy who decides to become a fisherman. Through him the reader is exposed to the hardships of fishermen in their struggle to make an honest living. In the book, Singer criticizes the corrupt system that pays the men who deliver the catch to market twice as much as the fishermen who daily risk their lives to net the fish. V. S. Pritchett summarized in the *New Statesman* that the author "is a poet and a critic. He is perpetually alert for words. He has a close, simple, patient style that insinuates the unexpected verb or adjective, and excites the sense of the reader."

BIOGRAPHICAL/CRITICAL SOURCES: New Statesman, September 28, 1957; *Times Literary Supplement,* November 8, 1957; *New York Herald Tribune Book Review,* July 13,

1958; Michael Schmidt, editor, *Fifty Modern British Poets,* Carcanet New Press, 1979.*

*   *   *

SINGH, Amritjit 1945-

PERSONAL: Born October 20, 1945, in Rawalpindi, India; son of Kesar Singh (a teacher) and Balbir (Kaur) Uberoi; married Premjit Prem Lata Seth (a teacher), March 24, 1968; children: Samir Punit (son), Reshma (daughter). *Education:* Panjab University, B.A., 1963; Kurukshetra University, M.A., 1965; New York University, A.M., 1970, Ph.D., 1973. *Religion:* Sikh. *Home:* L-5A, University Campus, Jaipur, India. *Office:* Department of English, University of Rajasthan, Jaipur 302004, India.

CAREER: University of Delhi, Delhi, India, lecturer in English, 1965-68; Herbert H. Lehman College of the City University of New York, Bronx, N.Y., lecturer in English, 1970-71; New York University, New York, N.Y., instructor in English, 1971-72; Herbert H. Lehman College of the City University of New York, assistant professor of English, 1973-74; American Studies Research Centre, Hyderabad, India, research associate in American studies, 1974-77; University of Hyderabad, Hyderabad, reader in English, 1977-78; University of Rajasthan, Jaipur, India, professor of English, 1978—. Honarary visiting lecturer in English at Osmania University, Hyderabad, 1974-77. Lecturer at universities in Japan, South Korea, and Singapore. Life member of American Studies Research Centre, Hyderabad. *Awards, honors:* Fulbright fellow, 1968-69; graduate fellow at New York University, 1969-70; Ford Foundation fellow, 1972-73.

WRITINGS: The Novels of the Harlem Renaissance, Pennsylvania State University Press, 1976; (editor with William P. French) *Afro-American Poetry and Drama, 1760-1975,* Gale, 1979; (editor and author of introduction and notes) Richard Wright, *Native Son,* Oxford University Press, 1980; (editor with Rajiva Verma and Irene Joshi) *Indian Literature in English, 1827-1979,* Gale, 1981. Contributor of articles to journals, including *Studies in Black Literature, Southwest Review, Literary Criterion,* and *Indian Journal of English Studies.* Editor of *Indian Journal of American Studies,* 1974-77.

WORK IN PROGRESS: A bibliographic monograph on Afro-American fiction, publication by American Studies Research Centre expected in 1982; books on Commonwealth literature, including Indian literature in English, publication expected in 1983 or 1984.

SIDELIGHTS: Singh commented: "As a scholar, I am particularly intersted in the historical forces that lie behind literature and the relationship of the arts to their folk origins. Literature and society interact in a variety of ways, and I have little use for literary criticism that focuses purely on matters of technique or rhetoric with no concern for the quality of life around us. The job of the literary critic-scholar-historian (the differences in their functions are often exaggerated) is to bring literature alive to his readers. It is important, thus, to consider the living relationship between the work and economics, biography, psychology, or sociology. Even more important, however, is the interplay between the work and the critic's mind and personality. The value of his output is primarily determined by the extent of his immersion in the subject and the vitality of his own responses.

"As a native of India who has lived in the United States for several years and traveled extensively elsewhere, I find it hard to separate my consciousness of the world from my objectives in literary criticism. There are large chunks of life's experiences where the East and West meet in most interesting and illuminating syzygies. In interpreting the West to the East, or vice versa, one must draw attention to values and experiences that touch the core of humanity everywhere and attack tendencies that create artificial barriers. The literary critic, like the artist, must expose prejudice, hypocrisy, pomposity, provincialism, insensitivity, and complacency. Literature may be studied in conjunction with and in the light of contemporary forces—the rising nationalism of many third-world countries and its concomitant effects, for example. Comparative approaches are helpful when pursued without prejudgments or mechanical insistence. My knowledge of Panjabi, Hindi, and Sanskrit has increasingly involved me since 1977 in taking a closer look at Indian literatures and critically examining their shared artistic and cultural basis."

BIOGRAPHICAL/CRITICAL SOURCES: Minority Voices, spring, 1977; *Black American Literature Forum,* fall, 1977; *World Literature Today,* autumn, 1977; *New Letters,* December, 1977; *Southwest Review,* summer, 1978.

*   *   *

SIRKIS, Nancy 1936-

PERSONAL: Born August 22, 1936, in New York, N.Y.; daughter of Robert Benjamin (in business) and Sylvia (Landress) Sirkis; married Frank Horch, September 22, 1958 (died, 1975); children: Andrew, Daniel. *Education:* Rhode Island School of Design, B.F.A., 1958. *Home:* 310 Riverside Dr., New York, N.Y. 10025.

CAREER: Writer. International Center of Photography, New York, N.Y., member of staff, 1976—.

WRITINGS: Newport: Pleasures and Palaces, Viking, 1962; *Boston,* Viking, 1964; *One Family,* Little, Brown, 1971; *Reflections of 1776: The Colonies Revisited,* Viking, 1974; *Massachusetts: From the Berkshires to the Cape,* Viking, 1977.

WORK IN PROGRESS: Research on nineteenth-century printing processes and on American portraits and landscapes.

SIDELIGHTS: Sirkis told *CA:* "For twenty-two years I have been documenting all aspects of the American scene: people, architecture, and landscape."

*   *   *

SLATER, Nigel 1944-

PERSONAL: Born January 10, 1944, in Lahore, India; son of Richard Mercer and Barbara Janet Slater; married Jackie Deere, 1966 (divorced, 1969); married Hester Cameron (a secretary), 1974; children: (second marriage) Cameron. *Education:* Magdalene College, Cambridge, B.A. (with honors), 1965. *Home:* Shrimp's Cottage, Kilchrohane, Bantry, County Cork, Ireland. *Agent:* Richard Scott Simon Ltd., 32 College Cross, London N.W., England.

CAREER: Diplomatic Service, London, England, private secretary to ambassador in Rome, Italy, 1965-67; McCorqoudale & Co. Ltd., Basingstoke, England, print executive, 1967-73; Maurice Hawker Associates Ltd., Newbury, England, director of fundraising consultancy, 1973-77; writer, 1977—.

WRITINGS: Crossfire (novel), Collins, 1977, Atheneum, 1978; *Falcon* (novel), Atheneum, 1979. Contributor to *Shooting Times.*

WORK IN PROGRESS: The Mad Death, a novel.

SIDELIGHTS: Slater wrote: "The international canvas intrigues me, having traveled widely under the auspices of the Diplomatic Service; *Crossfire* and *Falcon* deal with Uganda and Italy respectively. However, *The Mad Death* is a fictional account of a rabies epidemic in England. I have a leaning towards writing predictive novels—a risky occupation if history proves one wrong!"

*   *   *

SLESSOR, Kenneth 1901-1971

PERSONAL: Born March 27, 1901, in Orange, New South Wales, Australia; died June 19, 1971, in Sydney, Australia; son of Robert (a mining engineer and metallurgist) and Margaret (McInnes) Slessor; divorced; children: one son. *Education:* Attended Sydney Church of England Grammar School, Australia.

CAREER: Began journalism career as cadet for *Sydney Sun,* Sydney, Australia, 1920; staff member of *Vision* magazine, 1923-24; worked for various newspapers in Melbourne, Australia, c. 1924-27; joined staff of *Smith's Weekly,* 1927, became editor; literary editor of *Sydney Sun,* beginning 1944; editor of literary quarterly *Southerly,* Sydney, 1956-61. Member of advisory board of Australian Commonwealth Literary Fund, beginning 1954. *Wartime service:* Official war correspondent for Australian Army, 1940-45. *Awards, honors:* Officer of the Order of the British Empire, 1959.

WRITINGS—Poetry: Earth Visitors, Fanfrolico Press, 1926; *One Hundred Poems, 1919-1939,* Angus & Robertson, 1944, revised edition published as *Poems,* 1957, new edition published as *Selected Poems,* 1978; (co-editor) *The Penguin Book of Australian Verse,* Penguin, 1958. Also author of *Thief of the Moon,* 1924, *Surf,* 1930, *Trio,* 1931, *Cuckoo Contrey,* 1932, and *Five Bells,* 1939.

Nonfiction: (Contributor) Gwen Spencer, editor, *Portrait of Sydney,* U. Smith, c. 1950; *Australian Profile,* Australian Government, 1964; *Life at the Cross,* Rigby, 1965; *Canberra,* Rigby, 1966; *Bread and Wine: Selected Prose,* Angus & Robertson, 1970.

SIDELIGHTS: Slessor, known as one of the first truly Australian poets, began publishing his poetry in the 1920's in *Vision.* These early poems illustrated a stylistic movement from Australian bush poetry to a Nietzschean unrestrained joy in beauty and life. The early poems revealed an anti-modernist, anti-intellectual paganism.

In his later works, Slessor applied technical innovations to Australian themes. He utilized unconventional rhyme, lyrical experiments, rich imagery, and dramatic techniques. His poetry vented verbal energy mollified by the use of irony. Though melancholy and disillusion were characteristic of Slessor's poetry, individualism and a zest for life were also prominent features. Slessor's favorite themes included time, the sea, and reflections on memory; his message was one of romantic renunciation.

BIOGRAPHICAL/CRITICAL SOURCES: Contemporary Literary Criticism, Volume 14, Gale, 1980.*

*   *   *

SLOBODIN, Richard 1915-

PERSONAL: Born March 6, 1915, in New York, N.Y.; naturalized Canadian citizen, 1970; son of Henry Leon (an attorney) and Selma (Goldstein) Slobodin; married Doris Lambert, 1944 (died, 1945); married Zelma Jane Smith, 1947 (divorced, 1951); married Elizabeth Archer Cannan, 1953 (died, 1969); married Eleanor Christine Warren, January 23, 1970; children: Jennifer Ruth, Catherine Ann, John Archer; (stepchildren) Elizabeth Miller Kjellberg, J. Roderick Miller, Rebecca Miller, Peter M. Miller. *Education:* City College (now of the City University of New York), B.A., 1936, M.S., 1938; Columbia University, Ph.D., 1959. *Politics:* New Democrat. *Religion:* "Raised in Jewish faith." *Home:* 196 Governor's Rd., Dundas, Ontario, Canada L9H 3J9. *Office:* Department of Anthropology, McMaster University, Hamilton, Ontario, Canada L8S 4L9.

CAREER: Teacher of English in high schools in New York, N.Y., 1938-41; ethnographic fieldwork in Canadian Subarctic and Alaska, 1938-39, 1946-47, and 1963-64; archaeological fieldwork in New Mexico, 1942; University of Southern California, Los Angeles, assistant professor of anthropology, 1947-49; Los Angeles State College (now California State University, Los Angeles), Los Angeles, assistant professor of anthropology, 1950-51; worked as a miner, truck driver, apprentice cabinet-maker, and social worker in California, 1951-58; Cornell University, Ithaca, N.Y., research associate in anthropology, 1959-60; Smith College, Northampton, Mass., lecturer in anthropology, 1960-62; Department of Northern Affairs and National Resources, Canada, senior research officer, 1962-64; McMaster University, Hamilton, Ontario, associate professor of anthropology, 1964-69, professor, 1969—.

Visiting associate of Scott Polar Research Institute, Cambridge; associate of Clare Hall, Cambridge. *Military service:* U.S. Army Air Forces, 1942-43. U.S. Naval Reserve, active duty, 1943-46; served in Pacific theater; became lieutenant senior grade; received five battle stars.

MEMBER: Canadian Ethnological Society, American Anthropological Association (fellow), Royal Anthropological Association (fellow). *Awards, honors:* National Science Foundation grant for the Yukon, 1961; National Museum of Canada grants, 1962-63 and 1966-67; Canada Council grants, 1968-72 and 1972-73.

WRITINGS: Band Organization of the Peel River Kutchin, National Museum of Canada, 1962; *Metis of the Mackenzie District,* Canadian Research Centre for Anthropology, 1966; *W.H.R. Rivers,* Columbia University Press, 1978. Contributor of articles and reviews to anthropology journals.

WORK IN PROGRESS: Research on reciprocal raiding among peoples of the western Subarctic, on the history of research among peoples of the western Subarctic, and on British and American folklore studies at the beginning of the twentieth century.

SIDELIGHTS: Slobodin told *CA:* "Use of the imagination is by no means interdicted to the scholar in collecting, organizing, and presenting material. However, the kind of imagination used in the production of good ethnographic work or of social or culture-historical theory is distinct from the kind drawn upon in imaginative poetry and fiction.

"One responsibility that should be shared by the imaginative writer, the journalist, and the scholarly writer is a tender and conscientious respect for language. If authors do not cherish language, who will?

"As for myself, in the 1950's I became one of the obscurer objects of the McCarthy Era witch-hunt in academia. As a result, I spent about eight years in a variety of pursuits. I look back on this period with mixed feelings; for me it was interesting and sometimes fun; for North American society, one may earnestly hope that what Dalton Trumbo called 'The Time of the Toad' may never recur. I count myself as quite lucky in spending my boyhood and youth in Manhattan and then spending years in the north of Canada in magnificent unspoiled country, among hunters and trappers, and in fairly close association with the wonderful fauna of the far north—all this before the metropolis and the far places had been subjected to drastic change.''

*   *   *

SLOTKIN, Richard S. 1942-

PERSONAL: Born November 8, 1942, in Brooklyn, N.Y.; son of Herman and Roselyn B. Slotkin; married Iris Shupack (a clinical social worker), June 23, 1963; children: Joel Elliot. *Education:* Brooklyn College of the City University of New York, B.A., 1963; Brown University, Ph.D., 1967. *Religion:* Jewish. *Home:* 708 Ridge Rd., Middletown, Conn. 06457. *Agent:* Carl D. Brandt, Brandt & Brandt Literary Agents, Inc., 1501 Broadway, New York, N.Y. 10036. *Office:* Department of English, Wesleyan University, Middletown, Conn. 06457.

CAREER: Wesleyan University, Middletown, Conn., assistant professor, 1966-73, associate professor, 1973-76, professor of English, 1976—. *Member:* American Studies Association, American Association of University Professors (president, 1979-80), Modern Language Association of America, Western History Association, Organization of American Historians, American Historical Association. *Awards, honors:* Beveridge Prize from American Historical Association, 1973, and nominated for National Book Award, both for *Regeneration Through Violence;* National Endowment for the Humanities fellow, 1973-74; Rockefeller Foundation fellow, 1977-78.

WRITINGS: Regeneration Through Violence: The Mythology of the American Frontier, 1600-1860, Wesleyan University Press, 1973; *So Dreadful a Judgment: Puritan Responses to King Philip's War,* Wesleyan University Press, 1978; *The Crater* (novel), Atheneum, 1980. Contributor of articles and reviews to magazines, including *American Quarterly, Popular Culture, Journal of the West,* and *Saturday Review,* and newspapers.

WORK IN PROGRESS: The Man With the Grey Eyes, a novel about William Walker; research on the myth of the frontier in the age of industrialization.

SIDELIGHTS: Slotkin commented: ''I see my recent work in fiction as an outgrowth of my scholarship. Both are concerned with American history, and the shape and meaning of American myths.''

AVOCATIONAL INTERESTS: Western travel, the guitar, photography.

BIOGRAPHICAL/CRITICAL SOURCES: Library Journal, October, 1980; *New York Times Book Review,* January 4, 1981; *Washington Post Book World,* March 22, 1981.

*   *   *

SLUNG, Michele (Beth) 1947-

PERSONAL: Born April 5, 1947, in Louisville, Ky.; daughter of Rafael (in business) and Dorothy (Miller) Slung. *Education:* Western College for Women, B.A., 1969. *Home:* 1765 P St. N.W., Washington, D.C. 20036. *Agent:* Sterling Lord Agency, Inc., 660 Madison Ave., New York, N.Y. 10021.

CAREER: Charles Sessler Bookshop, Philadelphia, Pa., clerk, 1969-70; Wakefield-Young Books, New York City, buyer and manager, 1971-73; David McKay Co., Inc., New York City, senior editor of McKay-Washburn novels of suspense, 1975-77; *Washington Post,* Washington, D.C., editor of "Book World," 1978—. *Member:* International Wizard of Oz Club, Mystery Writers of America, National Book Critics Circle.

WRITINGS: (Editor) *Crime on Her Mind: Fifteen Stories of Women Sleuths From the Victorian Era to the Forties,* Pantheon, 1975; (contributor) John Ball, editor, *The Mystery Story,* Penguin, 1978; (editor) *Women's Wiles: The 1979 MWA Anthology,* Harcourt, 1979; (author of introduction) Seeley Regester, *The Dead Letter,* Gregg, 1979; (contributor) John M. Reilly, editor, *Twentieth Century Crime and Mystery Writers,* St. Martin's, 1980; (author of introduction) C. L. Pirkis, *The Experiences of Loveday Brooke,* Dover, 1981. Contributor of articles and reviews to magazines, including *New Republic, Newsday, Publishers Weekly,* and *Ms.,* and newspapers.

WORK IN PROGRESS: Writing introduction for *The Leavenworth Case,* by Anna Katherine Green, for Dover.

SIDELIGHTS: Michele Slung commented: "From childhood I always intended to have a career 'in books.' Happily, I have accomplished what I set out to do. My first goal was to work in bookstores; having done that in the early seventies I can say, without reservation, that such a beginning is immeasurably useful to a career in publishing.

"As I moved on from those early jobs I found myself, without having planned it, turning into a free-lance writer and, later, editor. *Crime on Her Mind* was a delight to research and put together, and it has made me many valued friends since it first appeared.

"The time I put in at David McKay (unfortunately they stopped publishing fiction to concentrate on other sorts of books) was also remarkably worthwhile. I had the chance to discover and publish new authors in the genre—such as Clarissa Watson and Marcia Muller—and to introduce writers new to America, like Mignon Warner. Even better, I was able to pull Gladys Mitchell out of my hat (a trick of which that *grande dame* would approve); an honored novelist in her native England, Gladys had not been published here since the twenties.

"I am and always will be a passionate reader, surrounded by stacks of books and lists of book titles, and unable to pass a secondhand book store without going in to spend an hour or two. Certainly, I think anyone who surrounds herself with books qualifies as a detective of sorts: tracking down bibliographical information, identifying characters, remembering what was said where and by whom, and putting it all together, if possible.''

*   *   *

SMITH, A(rthur) J(ames) M(arshall) 1902-1980

OBITUARY NOTICE—See index for *CA* sketch: Born November 8, 1902, in Montreal, Quebec, Canada; died October, 1980, in East Lansing, Mich. Educator, editor, and poet. Smith helped establish Montreal as the hub of Canadian poetry for many years by co-founding the *McGill Fortnightly Review* in 1925. The poet went on to instruct at several colleges and universities until he began teaching at Michigan State University, where he remained for more than three decades. In 1961, the university appointed Smith its poet-in-residence. When the professor retired in 1972, Michigan State University's Committee of Canadian-American Studies established the A.J.M. Smith Award, an honor bestowed annually on the best volume of verse by a Canadian. Smith wrote several books of poetry, including *News of the*

Phoenix, A Sort of Ecstacy, and *Masks of Poetry*. The author also edited numerous poetry anthologies such as *The Book of Canadian Poetry, Seven Centuries of Verse,* and *The Oxford Book of Canadian Verse*. Obituaries and other sources: *Toronto Globe and Mail,* October 26, 1980.

* * *

SMITH, (Christopher) Colin 1927-

PERSONAL: Born September 17, 1927, in Brighton, England; son of Alfred Edward (a teacher) and Dorothy May (Berry) Smith; married Ruth Margaret Barnes (an editorial assistant), August 14, 1954; children: Jennifer Marion, Rebecca Frances, Jocelyn Clare. *Education:* St. Catharine's College, Cambridge, B.A., 1950, Ph.D., 1954. *Politics:* "Middling liberal with left-right deviations." *Religion:* "Darwinian humanist." *Home:* 56 Girton Rd., Cambridge CB3 0LL, England. *Office:* St. Catharine's College, Cambridge University, Cambridge CB2 1RL, England.

CAREER: University of Leeds, Leeds, England, lecturer, 1956-64, senior lecturer in Spanish, 1964-68; Cambridge University, Cambridge, England, lecturer, 1968-75, professor of Spanish, 1975—, fellow of St. Catharine's College. *Member:* Association of Hispanists of Great Britain and Ireland (president, 1977-79).

WRITINGS: Spanish Ballads, Pergamon, 1964; *Collins' Spanish-English, English-Spanish Dictionary,* Collins, 1971; *Ramon Menendez Pidal, 1869-1968,* Hispanic and Luso-Brazilian Councils, 1970; *English-Spanish Word List,* Harrap, 1964; (with A.L.F. Rivet) *Place-Names of Roman Britain,* Batsford, 1979; *The Making of the "Poema de mio Cid",* Cambridge University Press, 1981.

Other: (Editor) *Poema de mio Cid* (title means "Poem of the Cid"), Oxford University Press, 1972; *Estudios cidianos* (title means "Studies About the Cid"), CUSPA, 1977. Contributor of poems to journals. Hispanic editor of *Modern Language Review,* 1974-80, general editor, 1976-81.

WORK IN PROGRESS: Research on Hispanic subjects and place names.

SIDELIGHTS: Smith wrote: "I have had a placid, rather fortunate career in teaching, research, and administration. I have been lucky in friends and in invitations at the right time, perhaps regretting that early invitations to splendid posts in the United States could not be taken up; but I am totally European at heart."

AVOCATIONAL INTERESTS: Natural history, archaeology, gardening, chess, bridge, cricket, squash, "the fringes of college and university politics, antiwinemanship (the promotion of coarse drinking)."

* * *

SMITH, Edward E(lmer) 1890-1965

OBITUARY NOTICE: Born May 1, 1890, in Sheboygan, Wis.; died August 31, 1965, in Seaside, Ore. Chemist and author. An explosives expert and organic chemist, Smith began writing science fiction in 1927. His thirty years of science-fiction writing earned him recognition at the Second World Science Fiction Convention in 1940 and an award from the Fandom Hall of Fame in 1964. Among Smith's novels in the "Lensmen" and "Skylark" series are *Galactic Patrol, Skylark DuQuesne,* and *Masters of the Vortex*. Some of the author's fictional inventions have been used as bases for actual technological innovations. Obituaries and other sources: Ron Ellik and Bill Evans, *Universes of E. E. Smith,* Advent, 1966.

SMITH, Frank Kingston 1919-

PERSONAL: Born January 11, 1919, in Philadelphia, Pa.; son of Frank (an attorney and judge) and Marion (Owen) Smith; married Marianne Hiller, June 25, 1941; children: Frank Kingston, Jr., Douglas Hiller, Hugh Gregory. *Education:* Trinity College, Hartford, Conn., A.B., 1941; attended University of Pennsylvania, 1941-42; Temple University, LL.B., 1949. *Politics:* Republican. *Religion:* Protestant Episcopal. *Home and office:* 6 West Aberdeen Rd., Ocean City, N.J. 08226.

CAREER: Called to the bar; Philips, Faran & McKeag, Philadelphia, Pa., associate, 1950; Hamilton, Smith & Darmopray, Philadelphia, partner, 1952-63; National Aviation Trades Association, Washington, D.C., national president, 1964-73; writer, 1973—. Vice-president and director of Flying W Ranch, 1962-64. *Military service:* U.S. Naval Reserve, active duty with Office of Naval Intelligence and on motor torpedo boats, 1942-45; served in Pacific theater; became commander. *Member:* International Aviation Writers Association, Federal Bar Association, Aircraft Owners and Pilots Association, Aviation/Space Writers Association, Pennsylvania Bar Association, Philadelphia Bar Association, Crime Prevention Association of Philadelphia (past member of board of directors), Seaview Country Club, Pontra Vedre Club, Ocean Ridge Club, Lawyers Club of Philadelphia (past member of board of directors).

WRITINGS: Week-End Pilot, Random House, 1957; *Flights of Fancy,* Random House, 1959; *I'd Rather Be Flying!,* Random House, 1961; *How to Take Great Photos From Airplanes,* TAB Books, 1979; *Private Pilot's Survival Manual,* TAB Books, 1980; *Winging It,* Random House, 1981; *Mailwing to Whirlwing* (biography of Harold F. Pitcairn), Ziff-Davis, 1981. Contributor to aviation magazines. Contributing editor of *Flying,* 1958-68; editor-at-large of *AOPA Pilot,* 1978—.

WORK IN PROGRESS: A History of Aeronautics in Pennsylvania, publication expected in 1981.

SIDELIGHTS: Smith told *CA:* "While practicing law in Philadelphia I took up flying light planes as a hobby. I wrote a series of books on learning to fly, flying high-performance single-engine airplanes, and obtaining instrument and multi-engine ratings. I became involved with the Flying W Ranch, a western-style 'dude ranch' for light-plane pilots in Lumberton, N.J., then resigned from law practice and accepted the position of director of the Washington, D.C. office of the major aviation industry association. In 1973 I resigned and retired to follow a full-time writing career."

BIOGRAPHICAL/CRITICAL SOURCES: Today's Health, summer, 1958; *Holiday,* fall, 1960; *Private Pilot,* January 1972.

* * *

SMITH, Gordon Roland
See ROLAND SMITH, Gordon

* * *

SMITH, Gudmund J(ohn) W(ilhelm) 1920-

PERSONAL: Born January 29, 1920, in Lund, Sweden; son of Lennart (a professor) and Eva (a teacher; maiden name, Sylvander) Smith; married Margareta Aspegren, 1947 (divorced); married Maj Henriksson (a psychologist), September 30, 1955; children: Lennart, Henrik, Patrik. *Education:* University of Lund, M.S., 1943, Ph.D., 1949; postdoctoral study at Harvard University, 1951-53. *Religion:* Protestant.

Home: Kavallerigraenden 1, Lund, S-22239 Sweden. *Office:* Department of Psychology, University of Lund, Lund 1, S-22350 Sweden.

CAREER: University of Lund, Lund, Sweden, teaching assistant, 1943-49, assistant professor, 1949-55; New York University, New York, N.Y., visiting research professor, 1955-56; Medical Research Council, Sweden, senior research fellow, 1956-60; University of Lund, professor of psychology, 1960—. *Member:* American Psychological Association.

WRITINGS: (With Ulf Kragh) *Percept-Genetic Analysis,* Gleerup, 1970; (with Alf L. Andersson, Alt Nilsson, and Eqil Ruuth) *Visual Aftereffects and the Individual as an Adaptive System,* Gleerup, 1972; (with Anna Danielsson) *Anxiety and Defensive Strategies in Childhood and Adolescence,* International Universities Press, 1981; (with Uwe Hentschel) *Experimentelle Persoenlichkeitspsychologie* (title means "Experimental Personality Psychology"), Akademische Verlagsgesellschaft, 1980. Also author of several monographs.

WORK IN PROGRESS: Research on creativity.

SIDELIGHTS: Smith told *CA:* "My research on creativity is an extension of previous work on perceptual processes which are laid bare by means of various so-called percept-genetic techniques. Early stages of such a process (when not automatized by repetition) seem more closely related to deep-seated, archaic levels of functioning than middle or late stages, the latter becoming more and more adapted to outside reality. It is important, in creativity research, to uncover the lines of communication between deep-seated levels and reality-adapted ones. Current studies have focused on development problems and anxiety and have concerned many groups of subjects, including researchers, artists, young children, and psychiatric patients. The percept-genetic techniques are also used in other research areas to describe defense mechanisms and test theoretical concepts in clinical psychology."

BIOGRAPHICAL/CRITICAL SOURCES: Ladd Wheeler, editor, *Review of Personality and Social Psychology,* Volume I, Sage Publications, 1980.

* * *

SMITH, Margaret F(oltz) 1915-

PERSONAL: Born January 11, 1915, in Leipsic, Ohio; daughter of Parley J. (an educator) and Mary (Norris) Foltz; married Karl U. Smith (a professor and consultant), August 3, 1937; children: Thomas, Eric, Joanna Smith Stein, Sarah Smith de Ferron, Nicholas. *Education:* Oberlin College, A.B., 1936; University of Rochester, M.A., 1937. *Politics:* Democrat. *Religion:* Unitarian-Universalist. *Home:* 1001 Tower Blvd., Lake Wales, Fla. 33853.

CAREER: Writer.

WRITINGS: (With husband, Karl U. Smith) *Cybernetic Principles of Learning and Educational Design,* Holt, 1966; (with K. U. Smith) *Psychology: Introduction to Behavior Science,* Little, Brown, 1973.

* * *

SMITH, Michael A(nthony) 1942-

PERSONAL: Born December 15, 1942, in Ellsworth, Kan.; son of John Wesley (a railroad dispatcher) and Jean (Hardy) Smith; married Patricia Kay Giese (a realtor), February 28, 1964; children: Tim, Julie. *Education:* Kansas Wesleyan

University, B.A., 1965; graduate study at University of Kansas, 1965-67. *Home:* 48 Squires, Springfield, Ill. 62704. *Agent:* Dominick Abel Literary Agency, 498 West End Ave., No. 12-C, New York, N.Y. 10024.

CAREER: *Salina Journal,* Salina, Kan., reporter, 1968; *Great Bend Daily Tribune,* Great Bend, Kan., reporter, 1969; *Golden Daily Transcript,* Golden, Colo., editor, 1969-70; Lindsay-Schaub Newspapers, Decatur, Ill., editorial writer, 1970-73; Illinois Board of Higher Education, Springfield, associate director, 1973-78; free-lance writer, 1978—.

WRITINGS: *Legacy of the Lake* (novel), Avon, 1980; *Secrets* (novel), St. Martin's, 1981.

WORK IN PROGRESS: A novel.

* * *

SMITH, Robert G(ordon) 1947-

PERSONAL: Born May 11, 1947, in Reno, Nev.; son of Francis R. (in business) and Ethel (Hanson) Smith; married Toni Robustellini (a medical technician), August 22, 1970; children: Lindsay. *Education:* Stanford University, B.S., 1969, M.S., 1970; University of California, Davis, Ph.D., 1980. *Home:* 701 Hacienda Ave., Davis, Calif. 95616. *Office:* Department of Civil Engineering, University of California, Davis, Calif. 95616.

CAREER: Metcalf & Eddy Engineers (environmental consultants), Palo Alto, Calif., project engineer, 1970-75; University of California, Davis, lecturer and development engineer, 1978—. *Member:* Water Pollution Control Federation, Tau Beta Pi.

WRITINGS: (with George Tchobanoglaus and Ronald Crites) *Wastewater Management,* Gale, 1975; *Land Treatment of Wastewater,* Prentice-Hall, 1981.

* * *

SMYER, Richard 1935-

PERSONAL: Born August 6, 1935, in Dallas, Tex.; son of Richard Albert (a business executive) and Jean (Esperance) Smyer; married Virginia Thomas, July 21, 1960 (divorced June 30, 1970); children: Gretchen, Karen. *Education:* Southern Methodist University, B.A., 1957, M.A., 1960; Stanford University, Ph.D., 1966. *Home:* 2309 East First St., Tucson, Ariz. 85719. *Office:* Department of English, University of Arizona, Tucson, Ariz. 85721.

CAREER: U.S. Department of Health, Education and Welfare (HEW; now Department of Health and Human Services), Dallas, Tex., social security claims representative, 1960-62; University of Arizona, Tucson, instructor, 1966-68, assistant professor, 1968-72, associate professor of modern literature, 1972—. *Member:* Amnesty International (group leader, 1979-80), Parents Without Partners (member of board of directors, 1974-77; international president, 1974-75), Modern Language Association of America, American Association of University Professors, Phi Beta Kappa.

WRITINGS: *Primal Dream and Primal Crime,* University of Missouri Press, 1979. Contributor to literature and language journals.

WORK IN PROGRESS: Research on the fiction of V. S. Naipaul, on English-language fiction of the West Indies and Africa, and on the development of detective fiction.

SIDELIGHTS: Smyer wrote: "I am particularly interested in the relationship between imaginative literature and those social and historical processes influencing the writer's imagination. Especially intriguing is the fiction writer's response to historical events in the Third World countries."

SNELL, John Nicholas Blashford
See BLASHFORD-SNELL, John Nicholas

*   *   *

SONGE, Alice Heloise 1914-

PERSONAL: Born June 15, 1914, in Morgan City, La.; daughter of Ourlien J. (a contractor and builder) and Alice (Duplantis) Songe. *Education:* University of Southwestern Louisiana, B.A., 1936; Louisiana State University, B.S. in L.S., 1937; Catholic University of America, M.A., 1956. *Politics:* Independent. *Religion:* Roman Catholic. *Home and office:* 4500 Connecticut Ave. N.W., Apt. 608, Washington, D.C. 20008.

CAREER: High school librarian in Church Point, La., 1937-38, Lutcher, La., 1938-42, and Franklin, La., 1942-44; chief librarian of Pointe Coupee County, 1944, and Vermillion County, 1944-46; Oteen Veterans Administration Hospital, Oteen, N.C., librarian, 1946-47; head librarian at a junior college and academy, 1947-49 and 1950-52; Catholic University of America, Washington, D.C., chief of reference department, 1952-56; Library of Congress, Congressional Research Service, Washington, D.C., education bibliographer, 1956-63; U.S. Department of Health, Education and Welfare (HEW; now Department of Health and Human Services), Washington, D.C., education specialist, 1963-73; National Institute of Education, Washington, D.C., reference librarian, 1973-75; library and research consultant and writer, 1975—. *Member:* American Library Association, American Society of Indexers.

WRITINGS—Editor: *The Land-Grant Movement in American Higher Education: An Historical Bibliography of the Land-Grant Movement and the Individual Land-Grant Institutions,* National Association of State Universities and Land-Grant Colleges, 1962; *The National Defense Education Act of 1958: An Annotated Bibliography,* Library, U.S. Department of Health, Education and Welfare, 1964; *Vocational Education: An Annotated Bibliography of Selected References, 1917-1966,* U.S. Government Printing Office, 1967; *Vocational Education, 1967-1972: An Annotated Bibliography,* U.S. Government Printing Office, 1973; (with Josephine Fang) *Handbook of the National and International Library Association,* American Library Association, 1973; *American Universities and Colleges: A Dictionary of Name Changes,* Scarecrow, 1978; (with Fang) *International Guide to Library, Archival, and Information Science Associations,* Bowker, 1976, 2nd edition, 1980; (with Pauline Mangin) *Educator's Source Book on China: A Guide to Information Sources,* K. G. Saur, 1980; *The Land-Grant Idea in American Education: A Guide to Information Sources,* K. G. Saur, 1980. Contributor to library journals, including *IFLA Journal* and *Library Journal.*

WORK IN PROGRESS: Nonpublic Elementary and Secondary Education in the U.S.: An Annotated Bibliography, 1950-1980, publication by Scarecrow expected in 1981; other reference books in education and library science.

SIDELIGHTS: Alice Songe wrote: "My publications have been inspired by my work in the field of education librarianship, especially in reference. I have attempted to supply what is needed in certain areas. International librarianship is also a special interest and a subject that needs development through published information sources."

AVOCATIONAL INTERESTS: Painting in oils, pastels, and water colors.

SOSNA, Morton 1945-

PERSONAL: Surname is pronounced *Soz*-na; born April 26, 1945, in Chicago, Ill.; son of Aaron (a jeweler) and Rose (a secretary; maiden name, Ellis) Sosna; married Barbara Marie Moe (in public relations), December 17, 1971; children: Rachel, Emily. *Education:* University of Illinois at Chicago Circle, B.A., 1967; University of Wisconsin—Madison, M.A., 1968, Ph.D., 1973. *Home:* 2905 King St., Alexandria, Va. 22302. *Office:* Division of Fellowships, National Endowment for the Humanities, 806 15th St. N.W., Washington, D.C. 20506.

CAREER: National Endowment for the Humanities, Washington, D.C., program specialist on fellowships for ethnic minority studies and studies on the relationship between human values and science and technology, 1973-74, program specialist on fellowships for independent study and research, 1974-75, associate program officer for fellowships and seminars for non-academic professionals, 1975-78, program officer for summer stipends, 1979, program officer for fellowships at centers for advanced study and residential fellowships for college teachers, 1980—. Visiting assistant professor at University of Missouri, 1979-80. *Member:* American Historical Association, Organization of American Historians, Southern Historical Association. *Awards, honors:* William B. Hesseltine Award from State Historical Society, 1970-71, for "The South in the Saddle: Racial Politics During the Wilson Years." National Endowment for the Humanities fellow, 1972-73.

WRITINGS: In Search of the Silent South: Southern Liberals and the Race Issue, Columbia University Press, 1977. Contributor of more than a dozen articles and reviews to scholarly journals. Book review editor of *Wisconsin Magazine of History,* 1969-72; member of editorial board of *Journal of American History,* 1980—.

WORK IN PROGRESS: Social History of the Impact of the U.S. Space Program on the South; A Study of the Southern Industrialist, Andrew Jackson Higgins of New Orleans.

SIDELIGHTS: Sosna commented: "I became interested in the South as a Northerner whose principal views about the region had been shaped and informed by the civil rights movement. The more I examine the history of the South in relation to the history of the rest of the United States, the more I become convinced that the stereotypical images of the region that have been held by outsiders ever since antebellum times are either wrong or misleading. I feel that my study of southern liberalism demonstrated that, beneath the surface orthodoxy that characterized the South during the Jim Crow era, there ran a brisk and persistent current of dissent that contributed significantly to the arduous process of desegregation.

"I have also come to believe that, insofar as the social changes within the region that it brought about, World War II has had a far greater impact on the South than did the Civil War. My current interest in the coming of the space industry during the 1950's and 1960's to large areas of the Deep South, stretching from Florida to Texas, will emphasize both the magnitude and rapidity of social change since World War II. How a former sugar plantation becomes a site for building moon rockets may be a subject better suited to the talents of a poet rather than to those of a historian, but I hope that looking at the effects of a multibillion dollar federal program on the people whom it most immediately affected will convey the drama, trauma, and unanticipated consequences of the South's most recent, and most significant, transformation."

SPARKS, Jack Norman 1928-

PERSONAL: Born December 3, 1928, in Boone County, Ind.; son of Oakley (a farmer) and Geraldine Ruth (Edrington) Sparks; married Esther Lois Bowen, April 11, 1953; children: Stephen Michael, Robert Norman, Ruth Ann Sparks Sorensen, Jonathan Russell. *Education:* Purdue University, B.S., 1950; Iowa State University, M.A., 1951, Ph.D., 1960. *Home and office:* 885 Fortuna Lane, Isla Vista, Calif. 93117. *Agent:* Peter E. Gillquist, 6884 Pasado Rd., Isla Vista, Calif. 93117.

CAREER: High school teacher of mathematics, 1954-57; University of Iowa, Iowa City, research assistant, 1957-60; University of Northern Colorado, Greeley, assistant professor, 1960-63, associate professor of education and psychology, 1963-65; Pennsylvania State University, University Park, associate professor of education and psychology, 1965-67; director of direct mail and Bible Study follow-up programs for Campus Crusade for Christ, 1967-69; Christian World Liberation Front, Berkeley, founder and director, 1969-75; Academy of Orthodox Theology, Isla Vista, Calif., dean and chancellor, 1975—. Bishop of Evangelical Orthodox church, 1978—. Publisher of *Right On*, 1971-75. *Military service:* U.S. Army, Medical Service Corps, 1951-54; became first lieutenant.

WRITINGS: Letters to Street Christians, Zondervan, 1971; *God's Forever Family,* Zondervan, 1974; *The Mindbenders,* Thomas Nelson, 1977, revised edition, 1979; *Apostolic Fathers,* Thomas Nelson, 1978; *Resurrection Letters,* Thomas Nelson, 1979. Author of "Sage Sayeth," a column in *Again,* 1978—. Contributor to *Journal of Educational Psychology, Overview, Journal of Research Services, Arithmetic Teacher,* and *Reading Research Quarterly.* Editor of *Right On,* 1969-71.

WORK IN PROGRESS: With Christ in the School of Prayer (tentative title), on St. Cyril of Alexandria and his commentaries.

SIDELIGHTS: The Mindbenders examines seven religious cults that are currently popular. Those covered are the Unification Church, The Way, The Local Church, Transcendental Meditation (TM), Children of God, Divine Light Mission, and Hare Krishna. Sparks explains each cult, according to *Eternity*'s William J. Peterson, "in terms of its history, theology and method of operation . . . [and] then . . . presents a refutation of the cult." Peterson noted, however, that "in his refutations Sparks goes overboard in quoting church fathers and church creeds and councils." A *Moody* critic asserted that the book "gives not only a knowledgeable view of heresies, but also a better knowledge of the doctrines of orthodox Christianity."

Sparks's next book, *The Apostolic Fathers,* is a collection of new translations of and introductions to the works of "those writers who lived in the late first or early second century, near enough to the time of Our Lord to have talked with the last of the Apostles or at least to have heard someone who heard them," disclosed P. H. Hallett of *National Catholic Register.* The volume includes the works of Barnabas, Clement, Hermas, Polycarp, and Ignatius. *The Resurrection Letters,* Sparks's following book, is a compilation of the letters of St. Athanasius, Bishop of Alexandria, who wrote during the fourth century.

Sparks told *CA:* "My life and writing are geared to Christ and his church and prayer for the eventual unity of that church."

BIOGRAPHICAL/CRITICAL SOURCES: Eternity, November, 1977; *Christian Courier,* November, 1977; *Moody,* April, 1978; *National Catholic Register,* February 18, 1979; *Terre Haute Tribune-Star,* March 2, 1980; *Augusta Chronicle,* March 6, 1980; *Wisconsin Lutheran Quarterly,* April, 1980; *Mansfield News Journal,* April, 1980; *Wichita Falls Times Sunday Magazine,* April 6, 1980; *Spiritual Book News,* November, 1980.

* * *

SPEAR, George E(lliott) 1925-

PERSONAL: Born January 3, 1925, in St. Louis, Mo.; son of George E. (a publisher) and Florence (Maack) Spear; married Barbara Reyburn (an educational coordinator), September 9, 1972; children: Michael B., Brett M., Leslie. *Education:* Baker University, B.A., 1948; University of Missouri, Kansas City, M.A., 1965; University of Michigan, Ph.D., 1972. *Office:* School of Education, University of Missouri, Kansas City, Mo. 64110.

CAREER: Belton Star-Herald, Belton, Mo., editor, 1948-63; University of Missouri, Kansas City, public relations director, 1963-65, assistant professor of sociology, 1965-71, director of continuing education and associate dean, 1965-80, assistant professor of education, 1971-77, associate professor of education, 1980—. Member of Belton School Board. *Military service:* U.S. Navy, aviation radio operator, 1943-46. *Member:* Adult Education Association of the United States, National Association of Public Continuing Adult Education (chairman of research committee, 1975-76), Missouri Association of Adult and Continuing Education, Belton Chamber of Commerce, Phi Delta Kappa, Sigma Delta Chi.

WRITINGS: (Contributor) Thomas P. Murphy, editor, *Universities in the Urban Crisis,* Dunellen, 1975; (editor) *Adult Education Staff Development,* Center for Resource Development in Adult Education, University of Missouri, Kansas City, 1976; (with Donald Mocker) *A Study to Determine Competencies by ABE/APL Teachers,* University of Missouri, Kansas City, 1976; (with Mocker) *Urban Education,* Gale, 1978; (contributor) Philip D. Langerman and Douglas H. Smith, editors, *Managing Adult and Continuing Education Programs and Staff,* National Association of Public Continuing Adult Education, 1979.

WORK IN PROGRESS: Research on non-formal learning patterns of adults.

SIDELIGHTS: Spear commented: "It is a fact that the organized education of people in our society now occurs more outside than within formal and traditional educational institutions. Those who instruct are usually entirely competent in their knowledge, but are not prepared at all to teach. My own teaching, research, and writing are motivated by, and directed toward, improvement of this major area of learning and education."

* * *

SPENCER, LaVyrle 1943-

PERSONAL: Born August 17, 1943, in Browerville, Minn.; daughter of Louis Joseph (a carpenter) and Janet Adamek (Baughman) Kulick; married Daniel F. Spencer (an estimator for a general contractor), February 10, 1962; children: Amy Elizabeth, Beth Adair. *Education:* Attended high school in Staples, Minn. *Home and office:* 6701 79th Ave. N., Brooklyn Park, Minn. 55445.

CAREER: Seamstress in Minneapolis, Minn., 1969-72; Osseo Junior High School, Osseo, Minn., instructional aide, 1974-78; writer, 1978—.

WRITINGS: The Fulfillment (novel), Avon, 1979.

WORK IN PROGRESS: *Hummingbird,* a novel; *The Endearment,* a novel; a contemporary love story set in Minneapolis.

SIDELIGHTS: LaVyrle Spencer told *CA:* "I began writing because of author Kathleen Woodiwiss. After reading her first novel, I became obsessed by it, studied it as my idea of the perfect love story, one with sexual tension, tenderness, and the ability to move me deeply.

"Shortly after reading that book, I began dreaming about writing one of my own and did in fact dream its entire plot repeatedly. In June, 1976, I awoke from the dream again and decided to give it rein: I got up and started putting it on paper.

"I am an American of Polish-Bohemian descent, born in the town where my first novel is set. All of my grandparents were farmers, and although I myself have never lived on a farm, the memories of kerosene lanterns, feather ticks, and wood stoves were part of my youth. I spent part of each summer on the farm of my Bohemian grandparents, which still stands today much as it did then. I placed my story there because I'd always been told, 'Write about what you know about!' At first it seemed absurd to write a story set in such a mundane place. But I decided that since romance happens everywhere, why not? Many of the smaller settings in my book are memories, too: the general store in back of which my father sold produce, the restaurant, the outdoor plumbing, the feed store, the bakery.

"The movies of the fifties greatly influenced my writing. My parents' marriage was unhappy and I was allowed to go to the theatre any time I wanted. My many twelve-cent admissions allowed me to 'escape' from a home environment into the dreamworld of movies that still is the basis for many love scenes I write today.

"My last two years of high school were in Staples, Minn. I had plans to attend college and become an English teacher, but I fell in love and scrapped the whole college career—one of the wisest decisions of my life.

"*The Endearment* is the story of a Swedish immigrant to Minnesota in the mid-1850's and the mail order bride who writes a pack of lies to get out of a bad life in Boston, bringing her lies into the marriage in the wilderness. It depicts the life of the early settler here and the love story of a man and woman who learn to accept each other for what they really are.

"Having traveled on vacation to Colorado several years ago, I set *Hummingbird* there, in 1869. This is the story of a straitlaced moralist who gets taken down a notch when she falls in love with a teasing scoundrel of a train robber.

"As a writer, my goal is to entertain and to leave the reader feeling good. I feel that sexual anticipation is the most important element of a good romance and that a couple good love scenes are far more satisfying to the reader than countless poorly-written meaningless encounters between hero and heroine. The element of utmost importance in my novels is love.

"My transient youth made me an assertive person, I think. If I wanted a place in the school society of each new town I lived in, I had to make that place for myself. I attribute some of my success to that attribute: knowing what you want and going after it. I recently read a quote that struck a chord in me: 'It is not because a thing is difficult that we don't dare attempt it. It is because we don't dare attempt it that it is difficult.'

"My goal in writing was never to get rich. My first goal was to begin the book. Next to finish it. I set my goals one at a time, each one a little tougher than the one before.

"I abhor the violent, mundane, repetitive books that are so prevalent today under the section they call 'romance.' I prefer to be called a writer of 'love stories' rather than 'romances,' if that's what people call romance. Readers today pine for love in their books. They've had enough of violent rapes, angry heroes, and simpering heroines. They want the tenderness and sensitivity that has somehow been left by the wayside during the decades that spawned the books loosely called romances. My goal is to give the readers those missing elements: tenderness, sensuality, and love."

AVOCATIONAL INTERESTS: Reading, music ("My husband is a vocalist and guitarist. I play bass guitar and we sing together."), Gordon Lightfoot concerts, playing piano, composing and arranging music, movies, entertaining guests, gardening, flower arranging, calligraphy, photography, sewing, interior decorating, drawing, dancing, exploring old houses and cemeteries, travel, coaching summer softball teams, hunting partridge, league bowling, buying clothes, "visiting places where my ancestors lived, and talking to old-timers about the days gone by."

* * *

SPENGEMANN, William Charles 1932-

PERSONAL: Born August 11, 1932, in San Jose, Calif.; son of Walter Andrew (a mail carrier) and Phyllis (a medical secretary; maiden name, Gates) Spengemann; married Sycha Elisabeth Ansley, August 22, 1962; children: Joaquin Gates Ansley, Pascal Morgan. *Education:* San Jose State College, A.B., 1957; Stanford University, Ph.D., 1961. *Office:* Department of English, Claremont Graduate School, Claremont, Calif. 91711.

CAREER: Stanford University, Stanford, Calif., assistant instructor in English, 1958-60; University of Hawaii, Honolulu, assistant professor of English, 1961-62; University of Connecticut, Storrs, assistant professor, 1962-65, associate professor of English and assistant provost, 1965-67; Claremont Graduate School, Claremont, Calif., associate professor, 1967-70, professor of English, 1970—. *Military service:* U.S. Marine Corps, 1953-56; became first lieutenant. *Member:* Modern Language Association of America, Philological Association of the Pacific Coast. *Awards, honors:* Essay prize from *American Quarterly,* 1965, for "Autobiography and the American Myth"; National Endowment for the Humanities fellowship, 1969.

WRITINGS: *Mark Twain and the Backwoods Angel,* Kent State University Press, 1967; *The Adventurous Muse,* Yale University Press, 1977; *The Forms of Autobiography: Episodes in the History of a Literary Genre,* Yale University Press, 1980; (editor) Henry James, *The American,* Penguin, 1981. Contributor to literature journals. Member of editorial board of *Early American Literature.*

WORK IN PROGRESS: *The Literature of British America,* an anthology and bibliography.

SIDELIGHTS: Spengemann told *CA:* "My writing to date has attempted to organize more or less disparate but somehow related materials—Mark Twain's writings, American novels, autobiographies—into some sort of historical, evolutionary scheme by tracing the changes that take place in some recurring element—the idea of innocence, narrative technique, autobiographical form—over time. The more I have employed this strategy of explanation, the more I have come to realize how much these perceived patterns are in fact an invention of my own, how much historicism itself is—in all senses of the word—a fiction. Having drawn so much upon the deposits of earlier scholars, I now feel obliged to cover my overdraughts by making some scholarly deposits of my own. Hence, my present project, *The Literature of British America,* will be not so much a historical explanation of materials that others have turned up as a redefinition of the field called 'Colonial American Literature' and an introduction to the enormous and largely unread store of documents written in English before 1765 by persons who had been to the New World. If this project goes as planned, the next generation of scholars will have new materials upon which to construct new explanatory schemes, new fictions of the sort that have given me so much pleasure over the years.''

*   *   *

SPIELBERGER, Charles D(onald) 1927-

PERSONAL: Born March 28, 1927, in Atlanta, Ga.; son of A. R. and Eleanor W. Spielberger; married Carol Lee (a dancer), June 4, 1971; children: three. *Education:* Georgia Institute of Technology, B.S., 1949; University of Iowa, B.A., 1951, M.A., 1953, Ph.D., 1954. *Home:* 11313 Carrollwood Dr., Tampa, Fla. 33618. *Office:* Department of Psychology, University of South Florida, Tampa, Fla. 33620.

CAREER: University of Iowa, Iowa City, psychometrist in department of medical psychology, 1952-53, counselor at Student Counseling Office, 1953-54; Worcester State Hospital, Worcester, Mass., intern in clinical psychology, 1954-55; Duke University, Durham, N.C., assistant professor, 1955-61, associate professor of psychology, 1961-63, staff psychologist at Psychiatric Outpatient Clinic, 1955-58; Vanderbilt University, Nashville, Tenn., professor of psychology, 1963-67; Florida State University, Tallahassee, professor of psychology, 1967-72, director of doctoral training program in clinical psychology, 1967-70, member of London Study Center, 1972; University of South Florida, Tampa, professor of psychology and director of doctoral program in clinical and community psychology, 1972—. Diplomate of American Board of Professional Psychology; attending clinical psychologist at Psychiatric Service of Veterans Administration Hospital in Durham, 1956-63; training specialist at National Institute of Mental Health, 1965-67. Visiting distinguished professor at University of Puerto Rico, 1970. Scientific director of North Atlantic Treaty Organization Advanced Study Institutes in Munich, West Germany, 1973, Urbino, Italy, 1976, and Cambridge, England, 1978, conference director of national conference in Oslo, Norway, 1975; consultant to Federal Aviation Authority, Veterans Administration, and Social Security Administration. *Military service:* U.S. Naval Reserve, 1945-79; active duty as electronics technician, 1945-46; became commander.

MEMBER: American Psychological Association (fellow; president of Division of Community Psychology, 1974-75; member of national council, 1976-78), American Association for the Advancement of Science (fellow), American Academy of Political and Social Science, American Educational Research Association, American Association of University Professors, Interamerican Society for Psychologists (vice-president, 1976-79), Psychonomic Society, Society for Personality Assessment (fellow), Society for Psychophysiological Research, Midwestern Psychological Association, Southeastern Psychological Association (chairman of Universities and Colleges Division, 1970-71; member of executive council, 1971-74; president, 1972-73), Florida Psychological Association, Sigma Xi (fellow), Psi Chi (southeastern

vice-president, 1976-80; national president, 1980—).

Awards, honors: Grants from National Institute of Mental Health, 1959-62, 1968-73, and 1970-73, North Atlantic Treaty Organization, 1972-74, 1974-75, 1975-76, and 1977-78, and Law Enforcement Assistance Administration, 1975-77 and 1978-81; certificate from American Personnel and Guidance Association, 1962, for article, ''Group Counseling and the Academic Peformance of Anxious College Freshmen''; distinguished scholar award from University of South Florida, 1973; award from Florida Psychological Association, 1977, for distinguished contributions to psychology through theory and research; Netherlands Institute for Advanced Study fellow, 1979-80.

WRITINGS: (Editor and contributor) *Anxiety and Behavior,* Academic Press, 1966; (editor with R. B. Masterton and Robert Fox) *Contributions to General Psychology,* Ronald, 1968; *Student Workbook for Principles of General Psychology,* Ronald, 1968, 4th edition, 1970; (editor) *Current Topics in Clinical and Community Psychology,* Academic Press, Volume I, 1969, Volume II, 1970, Volume III, 1971.

(Editor with Ira Iscoe; and contributor) *Community Psychology: Perspectives in Training and Research,* Appleton, 1970; (with R. E. Lushene and R. L. Gorsuch) *The State-Trait Anxiety Inventory: Test Manual,* Consulting Psychologists Press, 1970; (with Eric Gaudry) *Anxiety and Educational Achievement,* Wiley, 1971; (editor and contributor) *Anxiety: Current Trends in Theory and Research,* two volumes, Academic Press, 1972; *State-Trait Anxiety Inventory for Children,* Consulting Psychologists Press, 1973.

(Editor with Irwin G. Sarason; and contributor) *Stress and Anxiety,* Wiley, Volumes I and II, 1975, Volume III, c. 1975, Volumes IV and V, 1976, Volume VI, 1979, Volume VII, 1980; (editor with Marvin Zuckerman, and contributor) *Emotions and Anxiety: New Concepts, Methods, and Applications,* Wiley, 1976; (editor with Rogelio Diaz-Guerrero, and contributor) *Cross-Cultural Research on Anxiety,* Wiley, 1976; (editor and contributor) *Police Selection and Evaluation: Issues and Techniques,* Praeger, 1979; *Understanding Stress and Anxiety,* Harper, 1979; (editor with Harold F. O'Neil, Jr.) *Cognitive and Affective Learning Strategies,* Academic Press, 1979; *The Test Anxiety Inventory: Test Manual,* Consulting Psychologist Press, 1980.

Contributor: C. W. Ericksen, editor, *Behavior and Awareness,* Duke University Press, 1962; Sheldon Rosenberg, editor, *Directions in Psycholinguistics,* Macmillan, 1965; E. L. Cowan, E. A. Gardner, and M. Zax, editors, *Emergent Approaches to Mental Health Problems,* Appleton, 1967; B. A. Maher, editor, *Progress in Experimental Personality Research,* Volume VI, Academic Press, 1972; S. E. Golann and Carl Eisdorfer, editors, *Handbook of Community Psychology,* Appleton, 1972; Lennert Levi, editor, *Emotions: Their Parameters and Measurement,* Raven Press, 1975.

Editor of series: ''Current Topics in Clinical and Community Psychology,'' Academic Press, 1968-72; (with I. G. Sarason, and contributor) ''Advances in Personality Assessment,'' LEA, 1981—; ''Centennial Psychology,'' 1981-82.

Contributor to *International Encyclopedia of Neurology, Psychiatry, Psychoanalysis, and Psychology.* Contributor of more than sixty articles to journals in the behavioral sciences.

Founder and editor-in-chief of *American Journal of Community Psychology,* 1972—; associate editor of *Personality and Individual Differences* and *Revue Internationale Psychologie,* both 1979—. Member of editorial boards of *Psychological Monographs,* 1962-66, *Journals of Abnormal Psychol-*

ogy, 1971-73, *Contemporary Psychology*, 1971-74, *Journal of Personality*, 1972-76, *Journal of Educational Psychology*, 1976—, *Journal of Personality Assessment*, 1976—, and *Archiv fuer Psychology*, 1977—.

* * *

SPITZER, John 1956-

PERSONAL: Born April 19, 1956, in Washington, D.C.; son of George Leroy and Dorothy Elizabeth (an interior decorator; maiden name, Simpson) Spitzer. *Education:* Attended Georgetown University, 1974-75, Northern Virginia Community College, 1976-80, and Washington International College, 1977. *Religion:* "Mystic." *Residence:* Arlington, Va. *Office:* Northstar Theatre, Inc., 3808 North 14th St., Arlington, Va. 22201.

CAREER: WGTB-FM Radio, Washington, D.C., playwright, 1976; Northstar Theatre, Inc., Arlington, Va., actor-in-residence, 1978—, playwright, 1979-80. Actor with Edwin Booth Players, Arlington Theatre Associates, and Silver Spring Stage.

WRITINGS: "Daggers of Mourning" (one-act play), first broadcast by WGTB-FM Radio, 1976; "Dracula" (three-act play), first produced in Washington, D.C., at Northstar Theatre, March 28, 1980.

WORK IN PROGRESS: "Room With the Smell of Cat Food," a "dada play in one act showing the worthlessness of everything, including itself; "Cultural Impotence," a two-act dialectic play; "Displaced," an autobiographical play, "embodying the scholarly life robbing the artist of life, the struggle to break free, and the subsequent progress through breakdown to socialization."

SIDELIGHTS: Spitzer told *CA:* "I feel theatrical form has been confined to the conventions of plot, character, time-space continuity, and plausibility since the days of the Greeks to the point of smothering it. It's time for a change, a change I see as taking a form similar to surrealism in modern art and photography. True, for a brief time we had expressionism in theatre, but no one paid any attention to it save for the intelligensia. We need surrealism, a form of surrealism that can filter down to the totality of our theatre-going audience. I don't feel the borrowing of concepts from other art forms is necessarily bad; the various art forms are segregated enough. I look forward to the day when authors, actors, artists, musicians, and photographers exchange knowledge among themselves and band together in the common goal of furtherance of art as a whole."

* * *

SPROUT, Harold 1901-1980

OBITUARY NOTICE—See index for *CA* sketch: Born March 14, 1901, in Benzonia, Mich.; died December 12, 1980, in Princeton, N.J. Educator, authority on international and environmental politics, and author. Sprout was the chairman of the politics department at Princeton University. After his retirement in 1969, he served as a research associate at that university's Center of International Studies. His writings include *The Rise of American Naval Power*, *Foundations of National Power*, *Toward a New Order of Sea Power*, *A War Atlas for Americans*, and *The Ecological Perspective on Human Affairs, With Special Reference to International Politics*. Obituaries and other sources: *New York Times*, December 15, 1980.

SPRUCH, Larry 1923-

PERSONAL: Surname is pronounced Spruck; born January 1, 1923, in Brooklyn, N.Y.; son of Joseph (an insurance agent) and Gussie (Friedlander) Spruch; married Grace Marmor (a professor of physics), January 8, 1950. *Education:* Attended City College (now of the City University of New York), 1939-41; Brooklyn College (now of the City University of New York), B.A., 1943; University of Pennsylvania, Ph.D., 1948. *Politics:* "Reasonable; that is, to the left of the Democratic party." *Religion:* "Agnostic, but pleased to have been born a Jew." *Home:* 14 East Eighth St., New York, N.Y. 10003. *Office:* Department of Physics, New York University, 4 Washington Pl., New York, N.Y. 10003.

CAREER: Massachusetts Institute of Technology, Cambridge, postdoctoral fellow in physics, 1948-50; New York University, New York, N.Y., assistant professor, 1950-55, associate professor, 1955-61, professor of physics, 1961—. *Member:* American Physical Society (fellow), American Civil Liberties Union. *Awards, honors:* Atomic Energy Commission fellowship, 1948-50; National Science Foundation senior postdoctoral fellowship for University of London and Oxford University, 1963-64.

WRITINGS: *The Ubiquitous Atom*, Scribner, 1974; (translator with wife, Grace Marmor Spruch, of Spruch's own book) *El atomo omnipresente* (title means "The Ubiquitous Atom"), Editores Associados, 1977. Correspondent for *Comments on Atomic and Molecular Physics*, 1972—. Co-author of "Quiz," a monthly science quiz column in *Sciences*, 1976—. Contributor of about one hundred twenty-five articles to scientific journals. Member of editorial board of *Zeitschrift fuer Physik*, 1975-79, and *Physical Review*, 1980—.

WORK IN PROGRESS: A book based on his science quiz column, with wife, Grace Marmor Spruch, publication by Barnes & Noble expected in 1981 or 1982.

SIDELIGHTS: Spruch wrote: "Having been advised, as a high school senior, that one could not make a living in physics (true then) and further advised that accounting enabled one to utilize mathematical skills (true neither then nor now), I entered college as an accounting major and became thoroughly miserable. Recognizing that I would never complete college as an accountant, I concluded that it would be better to be unable to earn a livelihood in a subject I loved than in a subject I hated, and I switched to physics.

"My doctoral thesis was in nuclear physics (the spelling is nucLEAr despite the pronunciation of several U.S. Presidents) and I worked in that area for awhile, but for some time my primary interest has been atomic physics. I have also been a camp follower of astrophysics. It is a reflection on our educational system, and a measure of the inability (unwillingness?) of scientists to communicate with the layman, that there isn't a much greater interest on the part of the public in the almost unbelievable recent developments in astrophysics, one of the few branches of physics for which the essential ideas are at least comprehensible to the layman. I do not know what to do about the situation, but feel strongly that the typical science writer, although he may write well, has little genuine understanding of the science, and can therefore not transmit the true meaning and excitement of developments in the field.

"One of the perquisites of being a physicist is that physics, through its international character, provides ready opportunities for travel. I have lectured not only in countries such as Canada, England, France, the Netherlands, and Mexico, but in more exotic spots, including India and the Soviet Union. These were individual colloquia at conferences or universities. In addition, I lectured for one month both at a summer school in Yugoslavia and a winter school in Poland. I've also had the opportunity to visit other countries as a physicist, including Czechoslovakia, Greece, Israel, Japan, and the Scandinavian countries, and to visit still more on side trips. Highlights of the last included a stop at the animal parks in Kenya and Tanzania and the sight of the Himalaya in Nepal.

"As physics has been dominated by U.S. physicists since World War II (the dominance is not as overwhelming now as it was a decade ago) almost all physicists everywhere know English. That, and a singular lack of linguistic facility, have left me, despite my travels, unable to communicate well in any foreign language.

"All in all, I find it a miracle and a blessing that society is willing to support me in teaching and doing research in one of the great intellectual areas at a time when it is in great ferment."

* * *

STAMPER, Alexander
See KENT, Arthur William Charles

* * *

STANFORTH, Deirdre 1924-

PERSONAL: Born May 14, 1924, in New Orleans, La.; daughter of Robert L. (a regional publisher) and Tess B. (an owner and manager of a bookshop; maiden name, Mayer) Crager; married James D. Stanforth, March 15, 1952; children: Jamie (daughter), Yancey (daughter). *Education:* Tulane University, B.A. (with honors), 1946; also attended Temple University. *Politics:* Democrat. *Religion:* None. *Home:* 8 West 83rd St., New York, N.Y. 10024.

CAREER: Writer and artist. Vice-president of Brownstone Revival Committee; lecturer on restoration of old American buildings. *Member:* Phi Beta Kappa.

WRITINGS: (Editor and illustrator) *The Art of Cooking With Spirits,* Doubleday, 1964; *The New Orleans Restaurant Cookbook,* Doubleday, 1967; *Creole!* (cookbook), Simon & Schuster, 1969; (with Martha Stamm) *Buying and Renovating a House in the City,* Knopf, 1972; *Restored America,* Praeger, 1975; *Romantic New Orleans,* Viking, 1977. Also editor and illustrator of *Brennan's New Orleans Cookbook,* with father, Robert L. Crager.

WORK IN PROGRESS: A television film series based on *Restored America.*

SIDELIGHTS: Stanforth told *CA:* "I fell into writing by accident. My mother, Tess Crager, proprietor of the Basement Bookshop, was a literary personage in New Orleans. Every important writer who came to the city visited our house and many were feted at her renowned bookshop parties. Among those passing through were Gertrude Stein and Alice B., Sherwood Anderson, Alexander Woollcott, Andre Maurois, and Sinclair Lewis. Regulars at her 'salon' were the local literati, publishers' representatives, and editors from New York who turned up fairly frequently. With such a background it was almost inevitable that I should be detoured from illustrating books into writing them."

* * *

STEELE, Gordon (Charles) 1892-1981

OBITUARY NOTICE: Born November 1, 1892, in Exeter, England; died January 4, 1981, in England. Naval officer, educator, and author. Steele received his early nautical training as a cadet on the H.M.S. *Worcester,* of the Nautical Training College, and after obtaining his master mariner's certificate was assigned a commission in the Royal Naval Reserve. His distinguished service in World War I was highlighted by several acts of skill and bravery. His highest honor was earned during the raid on the Soviet Union's Kronstadt Harbor on August 18, 1919, when he assumed command of a torpedo boat following the fatal wounding of his commander. Not only did Steele save the boat from the immediate danger of losing control, but he was able to torpedo two enemy battleships before guiding his boat through heavy fire to safety. He was later awarded the Victoria Cross for conspicuous gallantry, skill, and devotion to duty. He retired in 1957 as captain-superintendent of the Thames Nautical College, on the H.M.S. *Worcester.* His published works include *The Story of the Worcester, About My Father's Business,* and *In My Father's House.* Obituaries and other sources: *Who's Who,* 131st edition, St. Martin's, 1979; *London Times,* January 7, 1981.

* * *

STEELE, Jack 1914-1980

OBITUARY NOTICE: Born September 15, 1914, in North Manchester, Ind.; died of cancer, December 31, 1980, in Bennington, Vt. Journalist and editor. Called "the father of modern investigative reporting," Steele began his career as a newspaperman with the old *New York Herald Tribune.* In 1953 he joined the Scripps-Howard Newspaper Alliance where he eventually became managing editor and later editor of the Scripps-Howard News Service. Steele's forty-year career earned him many honors, including the Raymond Clapper Award for distinguished Washington correspondence, the Heywood Broun Award, the Sigma Delta Chi Award, and the Ernie Pyle Memorial Award for coverage of civil rights assertions in Mississippi and Alabama. Steele's other major coverage includes the Hindenberg dirigible disaster, the death of Franklin D. Roosevelt, a series of influence-peddling scandals during the Truman Administration, and the Vietnam conflict. Obituaries and other sources: *Who's Who in America,* 41st edition, Marquis, 1980; *New York Times,* January 2, 1981; *Washington Post,* January 2, 1981.

* * *

STELLMAN, Jeanne M(ager) 1947-

PERSONAL: Born May 27, 1947, in Bensheim, Germany; American citizen born abroad; daughter of Abraham (a tool and die maker) and Rosalie (in sales; maiden name, Shapiro) Mager; married Steven D. Stellman (a scientist), September 10, 1967; children: Andrew, Emma. *Education:* City College of the City University of New York, B.Sc., 1968; City University of New York, Ph.D., 1972. *Religion:* Jewish. *Home:* 117 St. Johns Pl., Brooklyn, N.Y. 11217. *Office:* School of Public Health, Columbia University, 60 Haven Ave., No. B-1, New York, N.Y. 10032.

CAREER: City College of the City University of New York, New York City, instructor in chemistry, 1969-72; Oil, Chemical, and Atomic Workers International Union, assistant to the president for health and safety, 1972-75; University of Pennsylvania, Philadelphia, clinical associate professor of research medicine, 1976-80; Columbia University, New York City, executive director of Women's Occupational Health Resource Center, 1977-80, associate professor of public health, 1980—. Adjunct professor at Rutgers University, 1971-76. Chief of American Health Foundation Division of Occupational Health and Toxicology, 1977-80; chairperson of task force on the workplace environment of Scientists' Institute for Public Information, 1975-76; committee member of March of Dimes and National Cancer Institute; consultant to U.S. Department of Labor, U.S. Surgeon General, and Coalition of Labor Union Women.

MEMBER: American Association for the Advancement of Science, American Chemical Society (chairperson of task forces on benzene, 1978-79, and safe laboratory practices), American Physical Society, American Industrial Hygiene Association, Society for Occupational and Environmental Health, New York Academy of Sciences, Sigma Xi. *Awards, honors:* Academic Career Development award; grants from National Cancer Institute and U.S. Department of Labor, 1979-84, National Institute of Mental Health, 1980-82, Environmental Protection Agency, 1980-82, and National Cancer Institute.

WRITINGS: (Contributor) K. D. Poe and other editors, *Advances in Polymer Science and Engineering,* Plenum, 1972; *Work Is Dangerous to Your Health: A Handbook of Health Hazards of the Workplace and What You Can Do About Them,* Pantheon, 1973; *Women's Work, Women's Health: Myths and Realities,* Pantheon, 1978; (contributor) Richard Egdahl, editor, *Industry and Health Care IX,* Springer-Verlag, 1980; (contributor) *Report of the Surgeon General,* U.S. Public Health Service, 1980; (contributor) William Rom, editor, *Environmental and Occupational Medicine,* Little, Brown, in press. Author of "Your Work, Your Health," a column in *Paperworker,* and "Saving Your Life," a column in *Service Worker.* Contributor of about twenty-five articles to scientific journals and *Civil Rights Digest.* Contributing editor of *Environment.*

WORK IN PROGRESS: Health Hazards in White Collar Work (tentative title), publication by Pantheon expected in 1982; scientific reports of on-going research, including studies on the effect microwaves, sterilizing agents, and welding have on health; research on the effects of Agent Orange on Vietnam veterans, with husband, S. D. Stellman.

SIDELIGHTS: Stellman told *CA:* "My work is a mixture of pure research and efforts to 'de-mystify' science and technology for those directly concerned. Thus *Work Is Dangerous to Your Health* represents the first, and still most popular, attempt at presenting occupational health to people in language they can understand and use. My new book, *Health Hazards in White Collar Work,* although not my main research interest, which remains chemical toxicity, endeavors to bridge the same science-technology/people gap. It is a particularly timely work because of the growing automation and indoor air pollution problems of people working in white collar jobs.

"Being a scientist and a public health information disseminator is a difficult path to follow because each role tends to discredit the other. One's scientific peers feel uncomfortable with someone who deals with workers and tries to break down technical jargon. Similarly, as I grow in my professional career, more and more workers call me 'doctor' rather than Jeanne. I believe this situation to be a microcosm of the larger problem of our society and its need to make technology relevant, to control its effects on our lives, and yet to allow scientists and technologists the freedom and latitude they need to be creative and productive.

"The lack of much needed research is obvious in women's occupational health, particularly reproductive health, where so little is understood about the implications of work on successful childbearing for women. And virtually nothing is known about the effects of working conditions on men, a situation that has not precluded policies excluding women from many jobs while allowing men to remain in most certainly dangerous conditions. I intend to continue to write about and study this serious inequity.

"We face trying times where the conflict between the *need* to work and the *right* to a safe and beautiful workplace will continue to grow and where the conditions of the general environment will be hostage to the economic pressures of productivity. It will not be easy. The need for public understanding of the technical factors in the lives of workers has never been greater."

*   *   *

STEPHEN, George 1926-

PERSONAL: Born March 15, 1926, in Aberdeen, Scotland; came to the United States in 1957, naturalized citizen, 1969; son of George and Mary Foss (Henderson) Stephen; married Veronika Rosenberger, July 8, 1949; children: Colin, David, Mark. *Education:* Aberdeen School of Architecture, D.A., 1952. *Home:* 191 Upland Rd., Newtonville, Mass. 02160. *Office:* National Park Service, 15 State St., Boston, Mass. 02109.

CAREER: General practice of architecture in Edinburgh, Scotland, and London, England, 1952-57; Shepley, Bulfinch, Richardson & Abbott, Boston, Mass., architect, 1957-60; Edwin T. Steffian & Associates, Boston, architect, designer, and project manager, 1960-63; Boston Redevelopment Authority, Boston, South End project design officer, 1963-65, director of rehabilitation design, 1965-74; National Park Service, Boston, North Atlantic regional architect, 1974—. Private practice as consulting architect. Lecturer at Boston University, 1966-74, Massachusetts Bay Community College, 1968-70, Boston Center for Adult Education, 1970-74, and Boston Architectural Center, 1974—; lecturer in the United States and Canada; guest on radio and television programs. Member of national advisory board of Back to the City, Inc.; member of Newton Historical Commission. *Military service:* British Army, 1944-47; served with Royal Engineers and Royal Army Education Corps.

MEMBER: National Trust for Historic Preservation, Royal Institute of British Architects. *Awards, honors:* Award from American Society of Registered Architects, 1971, for preservation work with Boston Redevelopment Authority; award from American Institute of Architects, 1974, for housing and neighborhood design; awards from U.S. Department of the Interior for work with National Park Service.

WRITINGS: Remodeling Old Houses Without Destroying Their Character (Book-of-the-Month Club selection), Knopf, 1972; (contributor) George C. Rogers, editor, *Handbook for Rehabilitation Specialists,* U.S. Department of Housing and Urban Development, 1973; *Revitalizing Older Houses in Charlestown,* Boston Redevelopment Authority, 1973; (contributor) *Boston Sign Design Code,* City of Boston, 1973; *Rehabilitating Old Houses,* National Trust for Historic Preservation, 1976; *This Old House,* National Educational Television, 1981.

WORK IN PROGRESS: Research for a book on architectural styles of the nineteenth century and their derivations.

SIDELIGHTS: Stephen wrote: "My major vocational interest has always been architectural preservation, most particularly in adapting existing buildings for new uses. My private practice has included the rehabilitation of Cleaves St., Roxbury, Mass., a unique collaborative project consisting of the rehabilitation of all the houses on the street and of the street itself, now a semi-private mall. It has also included much new work as well as the rehabilitation of buildings of all types and sizes, and the production of original art work for architectural publication.

"I feel very strongly that most architects do not communicate clearly with non-architects on matters of design and that only by having a better-informed public are we to get better architecture. My writings have always aimed, among other things, at stimulating a popular interest in architecture by openly discussing 'professional' design matters in a way that is intelligible to the average person.

"By concentrating mainly on nineteenth-century examples, I have tried to draw attention to the architectural virtues of many of these buildings and their tremendous potential for adaptation and re-use, something that until recently had not been taken too seriously by many architects and owners. The failure of much of our twentieth-century work in terms of simple human values and adaptability is now making us look more seriously at the buildings of the recent past. And we are surprised at how often they succeed in these respects. It seems that the term 'functional' is due for revaluation."

Reviews of *Remodeling Old Houses Without Destroying Their Character* were favorable. "No one should be allowed to purchase a Victorian House without being compelled to read this book and then pass a test on it," remarked L. J. Davis in the *New York* magazine. "Like anonymous gifts of mouthwash, this book ought to be sent to all homeowners guilty of permastone and naked aluminum," commented Maryann Ondovosik of *Woman's Wear Daily.* "It ought to be required reading for everyone who takes out a building permit."

AVOCATIONAL INTERESTS: Music and history of music (particularly nineteenth-century symphonic), drawing, painting, printmaking, designing and building furniture, model aircraft, building boats, sailing, walking and climbing.

BIOGRAPHICAL/CRITICAL SOURCES: Woman's Wear Daily, March 7, 1972; *New York,* March 13, 1972.

*   *   *

STERN, Paula 1945-

PERSONAL: Born March 31, 1945, in Chicago, Ill.; daughter of Lloyd and Fan (Wener) Stern; married Paul A. London (executive director of Coalition of Northeastern Governors); children: Gabriel Stern London. *Education:* Attended Brandeis University's Jacob Hiatt Institute, Jerusalem, Israel, 1965-66; Goucher College, B.A., 1967; Harvard University, M.A. (Middle East studies), 1969; Fletcher School of Law and Diplomacy, M.A. (international affairs) and M.A.L.D., both 1970, Ph.D., 1976. *Politics:* Democrat. *Religion:* Jewish. *Home:* 3314 Ross Pl. N.W., Washington, D.C. 20008. *Office:* U.S. International Trade Commission, 701 E St. N.W., Washington, D.C. 20436.

CAREER: New Republic, Washington, D.C., staff writer, summer, 1969; U.S. Senate, Washington, D.C., legislative assistant, 1972-74; Brookings Institution, Washington, D.C., guest scholar, 1975-76; U.S. Senate, senior legislative assistant, 1976; Carter-Mondale Transition Team, Washington, D.C., policy analyst, 1976-77; Council on Foreign Relations, Washington, D.C., international affairs fellow, 1977-78; U.S. International Trade Commission, Washington, D.C., commissioner, 1978—. Adjunct associate professor at State University of New York at Stony Brook, 1974-75; lecturer at National War College, Harvard University, and American University. Member of board of directors of Inter-American Foundation. *Awards, honors:* Alicia Patterson Foundation Award for the Middle East and North Africa, 1970-71.

WRITINGS: Water's Edge: Domestic Politics and the Making of American Foreign Policy, Greenwood Press, 1979. Contributor of articles and photographs to magazines and newspapers, including *Washington Post, Atlantic Monthly, Progressive, Middle East Journal, Open Forum,* and *Executive.*

WORK IN PROGRESS: Dollars and Diplomacy, about Kissinger and Nixon's use of U.S.-Soviet trade in pursuit of Vietnam peace as a case study in economic linkage.

SIDELIGHTS: Stern's book, *Water's Edge,* details how the United States endeavored to correct violations of Jewish human rights in the Soviet Union through an international trade agreement. The resulting 1974 Trade Reform Act was the product of heavy domestic political pressures. A compromise between Senator Henry Jackson, Congress, the President, and the Soviet Union, the act illustrates how domestic politics form American foreign policy.

*   *   *

STEVENS, Robert (Bocking) 1933-

PERSONAL: Born June 8, 1933, in Leicester, England; son of John Skevington and Enid (Bocking) Stevens; married Rosemary Anne Wallace (a professor), January 28, 1961; children: Carey Thomasine, Richard Nathaniel. *Education:* Oxford University, B.A., 1955, B.C.L., 1956, M.A., 1959; Yale University, LL.M., 1958. *Home:* 1 College Circle, Haverford, Pa. 19041. *Office:* Haverford College, Haverford, Pa. 19041.

CAREER: Yale University, New Haven, Conn., assistant professor, 1959-61, associate professor, 1961-65, professor of law, 1965-76; Tulane University, New Orleans, La., provost, 1976-78; Haverford College, Haverford, Pa., president, 1978—.

WRITINGS: (With B. S. Yamey) *The Restrictive Practices Court: A Study of the Judicial Process and Economy Policy,* Weidenfeld & Nicolson, 1965; (with Brian Abel-Smith) *Lawyers and the Courts: A Sociological Study of the English Legal System, 1750-1965,* Harvard University Press, 1967; (with Abel-Smith) *In Search of Justice: Society and the Legal System,* Allen Lane, 1968; (with Leonard William Doob) *The Fermeda Workshop,* Office of Advanced Political Studies, Yale University, 1969; (editor) *Income Security: Statutory History of the United States,* Chelsea House, 1970; (with wife, Rosemary Stevens) *Welfare Medicine in America: A Case Study of Medicaid,* Free Press, 1974; *Vain Hopes, Grim Realities,* F. Watts, 1976; *Law and Politics: The House of Lords as a Judicial Body, 1800-1976,* University of North Carolina Press, 1978.

WORK IN PROGRESS: A study of the rise of higher education and the professions between the Civil War and World War I, publication expected in 1981.

*   *   *

STEVENSON, Burton Egbert 1872-1962

PERSONAL: Born November 9, 1872, in Chillicothe, Ohio; died May 13, 1962; married Elizabeth Shepard Butler, June 12, 1895 (died, 1960). *Education:* Attended Princeton University, 1890-93.

CAREER: Correspondent for United Press and *New York Tribune,* c. 1891-1893; *Chillicothe Leader,* Chillicothe, Ohio; reporter, 1893-94; *Chillicothe Daily News,* Chillicothe, city editor, 1894-98; *Daily Advertiser,* Chillicothe, city editor, 1898-99; Chillicothe Public Library, Chillicothe, librarian, 1899-1957. Founder of American Library in Paris, France, 1918, director, 1918-20 and 1925-30. *Wartime service:* European director of American Library Association's Library War Service, 1918-25. *Member:* National Institute of Arts and Letters, Century Club (New York), Union Interalliee Club (Paris). *Awards, honors:* Ohioana grand medalist, Martha Kinney Cooper Ohioana Library Association, 1949; Litt.D., Marietta College, 1955.

WRITINGS: *At Odds With the Regent: A Story of the Cellamare Conspiracy* (historical novel), Lippincott, 1900; *A Soldier of Virginia: A Tale of Colonel Washington and Braddock's Defeat* (historical novel), Houghton, 1901; *The Heritage: A Story of Defeat and Victory,* Houghton, 1902; *Tommy Remington's Battle* (for children), Century, 1902; *The Holladay Case* (mystery novel), Holt, 1903; *Cadets of Gascony: Two Stories of Old France,* Lippincott, 1904; (editor) Henry Fielding, *The History of Tom Jones, a Foundling,* Holt, 1904; *The Marathon Mystery: A Story of Manhattan* (mystery novel), Holt, 1904; (editor) Theodore Winthrop, *Mr. Waddy's Return,* Holt, 1904; *The Young Section-Hand* (for children), L. C. Page, 1905; *Affairs of State,* Holt, 1906; (compiler with wife, Elizabeth Shepard Stevenson) *Days and Deeds: Book of Verse for Children's Reading and Speaking,* Baker & Taylor, 1906; *The Girl With the Blue Sailor,* Dodd, 1906; (compiler with E. S. Stevenson) *Days and Deeds: Prose for Children's Reading and Speaking,* Baker & Taylor, 1907; *That Affair at Elizabeth,* Holt, 1907; *The Young Train Dispatcher* (for children), L. C. Page, 1907; (editor) *Poems of American History,* Houghton, 1908, revised edition, Books for Libraries, 1970; *A Child's Guide to Biography: American Men of Action,* Baker & Taylor, 1909, published as *A Guide to Biography for Young Readers: American Men of Action,* 1910; *The Quest for the Rose of Sharon,* L. C. Page, 1909; *The Young Train Master* (for children), L. C. Page, 1909.

A Guide to Biography for Young Readers: American Men of Mind, Baker & Taylor, 1910; *The Path of Honor: A Tale of the War in the Bocage,* Lippincott, 1910; *Among Dutch Inns,* L. C. Page, 1911; (compiler) *Favorite Poems in English,* Holt, 1911; *The Spell of Holland: The Story of a Pilgrimage to the Land of Dykes and Windmills* (travel), L. C. Page, 1911; (compiler) *The Home Book of Verse, American and English, 1580-1920,* Holt, 1912; *The Mystery of the Boule Cabinet,* Dodd, 1912, reprinted, Arno, 1976; *The Young Apprentice,* L. C. Page, 1912; *The Destroyer: A Tale of International Intrigue,* Dodd, 1913; *The Gloved Hand: A Detective Story,* Dodd, 1913; *The Charm of Ireland* (travel), Dodd, 1914; *The Home Book of Verse for Young Folks,* Holt, 1915, reprinted, 1969; *Little Comrade: A Tale of the Great War,* Holt, 1915, published as *The Girl From Alsace: A Romance of the Great War,* Grosset, 1915 (published in England as *Little Comrade: The Romance of a Lady Spy in the Great War,* Hutchinson, 1915); *A King in Babylon,* Maynard Small, 1917, published as *A King in Babylon: A Romantic Melodrama in Three Acts,* Baker & Taylor, 1955.

The Kingmakers, Dodd, 1922; (editor) *Famous Single Poems, and the Controversies Which Have Raged Around Them,* Harcourt, 1923, reprinted, Books for Libraries, 1971; *The Storm-Center: A Romance,* Dodd, 1924; *The Home Book of Modern Verse,* Holt, 1925; *The Coast of Enchantment,* Dodd, 1926.

(Editor and compiler) *American History in Verse, for Boys and Girls,* Houghton, 1932; *The House Next Door: A Detective Story,* Dodd, 1932; (compiler and editor) *My Country: Poems of History for Young Americans,* Houghton, 1932, reprinted, Books for Libraries, 1970; *Villa Aurelia: A Riviera Interlude,* Dodd, 1932 (published in England as *Mystery of Villa Aurelia,* Rich & Cowan, 1933); (compiler and editor) *Great Americans as Seen by the Poets: An Anthology,* Lippincott, 1933; (editor) *The Home Book of Quotations, Classical and Modern,* Dodd, 1934 (published in England as *Stevenson's Book of Quotations, Classical and Modern,* Cassell, 1958); (editor) *The Home Book of Shakespeare Quotations,* Scribner, 1937, reprinted, 1965 (published in England as *Stevenson's Book of Shakespeare Quotations,* Cassell, 1969); *The Red Carnation: An Antony Bigelow Story,* Dodd, 1939 (published in England as *Death Wears a Carnation,* Cassell, 1940).

(Editor) *The Home Book of Proverbs, Maxims and Familiar Phrases,* Macmillan, 1948, reprinted as *The Macmillan Book of Proverbs, Maxims, and Familiar Phrases,* Macmillan, 1965 (published in England as *Book of Proverbs, Maxims, and Familiar Phrases,* Routledge & Kegan Paul, 1949); (compiler) *The Home Book of Bible Quotations,* Harper, 1949, reprinted, 1977; (compiler) *The Standard Book of Shakespeare Quotations,* Funk, 1953.

Contributor to periodicals, including *Bookman, Century, Delineator, Dial, Independent, Ladies' Home Journal, Lippincott's Magazine, McClure's Magazine, Munsey, Nation, Pictorial Review,* and *St. Nicholas.*

SIDELIGHTS: Burton Stevenson published over fifteen thousand pages during his life. He was as diverse as he was prolific, writing a number of mystery and detective novels, children's books, travel books, historical novels, and anthologies.

During World War I, Stevenson responded to requests from Camp Sherman servicemen for a library service. He initiated a statewide campaign for book donations and was appointed camp librarian. In the fall of 1917 he was called to Washington, D.C., to head a national campaign.

Stevenson's work in establishing libraries for servicemen led to his appointment as European director of the American Library Association's Library War Service. In Paris Stevenson supervised the distribution of two million books and at least twice as many magazines. After the war Stevenson saw a need in Europe for a center that would provide accurate information on the United States. He converted his Paris office into the American Library and became its director.

Stevenson is well known for his anthologies. His *Home Book of Proverbs, Maxims, and Familiar Phrases,* published in 1948, took nearly ten years to compile. Stevenson was also noted for his ability to weave a tale of intrigue. The most successful of his mystery tales, *The Mystery of the Boule Cabinet,* was adapted for film as "In the Next Room," produced by First National Pictures in 1930. *Little Comrade* was also adapted for film and was produced as "On Dangerous Ground" by World Film Corporation in 1916.

BIOGRAPHICAL/CRITICAL SOURCES: *New York Times Book Review,* November 3, 1906, January 26, 1913, October 5, 1913, March 21, 1913, November 17, 1913, December 9, 1934, November 7, 1948; *Literary Digest,* December 14, 1912; *Bookman,* March, 1913; *Times Literary Supplement,* July 31, 1924; *Outlook,* July 8, 1925; *New York Herald Tribune Books,* August 23, 1925, April 23, 1933, December 30, 1934, May 26, 1935, November 14, 1937; *International Book Review,* December, 1925; *New York Herald Tribune,* December 9, 1934; *Saturday Review of Literature,* December 15, 1934, November 27, 1937; *Christian Science Monitor,* July 3, 1935; *New York Herald Tribune Weekly Book Review,* December 5, 1948.

OBITUARIES: New York Times, May 15, 1962; *Time,* May 25, 1962; *Newsweek,* May 28, 1962; *Publishers Weekly,* May 28, 1962; *Library Journal,* July, 1962; *Wilson Library Bulletin,* September, 1962; *American Annual,* 1963.*

* * *

STEVENSON, Christopher Sinclair
See SINCLAIR-STEVENSON, Christopher

* * *

STEVENSON, Ian Ralph 1943-

PERSONAL: Born June 11, 1943, in Sydney, Australia. *Education:* Sydney Teachers College, teachers certificate, 1966; University of Sydney, B.A., 1970; University of New England, B.Ed., 1974, M.Ed., 1975. *Office:* Kindergarten Union of South Australia, 85 John St., Salisbury, South Australia 5108.

CAREER: High school teacher of modern languages in New South Wales, Australia, 1964-68, counselor, 1969; Wagga Teachers College, Wagga, New South Wales, lecturer in special education, 1970-71; Kuring-Gai College of Advanced Education, Sydney, New South Wales, lecturer in education, 1972-74; Darwin Community College, Darwin, Northern Territory, Australia, senior lecturer in educational psychology, 1975-78, acting head of faculty, 1979-80; Kindergarten Union of South Australia, Salisbury, principal adviser, 1980—. *Military service:* Australian Army Reserve, Psychology Corps, 1961—; present rank, captain. *Member:* Australian College of Education, Australian Psychological Society.

WRITINGS: Let's Explore Language, Jacaranda, 1968; *The Line That Led to Nowhere,* Rigby, 1979.

WORK IN PROGRESS: George Stevenson: Democrat or Demagogue?

SIDELIGHTS: Stevenson commented: "Cornelius Ryan, author of *The Longest Day* and *A Bridge Too Far,* wrote of 'academic historians . . . rewriting one another from year to year, including repeating the same mistakes.' Since I am not a historian, but an educator, I try to bring a fresh approach to writing about Australian history, correcting the mistakes and myths which too often pose as history.

"*The Line That Led to Nowhere* is the first definitive account of the North Australia railway and the part it played in the development of the Northern Territory. In my latest work, I seek to reassess the early years of European settlement in South Australia, especially the contribution of my pioneer ancestor George Stevenson, an increasingly contentious topic as the state prepares to celebrate its 150th anniversary in 1986."

* * *

STEWART, Jean
See NEWMAN, Mona Alice Jean

* * *

STIGWOOD, Robert C. 1934-

PERSONAL: Born April 16, 1934, in Adelaide, Australia; son of Gordon (an electrical engineer) and Gwen (a nursing home supervisor; maiden name, Burrows) Stigwood. *Educa-*

tion: Attended Catholic boarding school in Adelaide, Australia. *Residence:* Bermuda. *Office:* Stigwood Group of Companies, 1775 Broadway, New York, N.Y. 10019.

CAREER: Producer. Worked as copywriter for advertising agency in Adelaide, Australia, c. 1953-56; immigrated to London, England, 1956; held series of jobs, including manager of provincial theatre and manager of halfway house for delinquents in Cambridge, 1956-62; manager of talent agency, beginning 1962; independent record producer, beginning 1965; NEMS Enterprises (talent management firm), London, co-manager with Brian Epstein, 1967; founder and chairman of the board of Stigwood Group of Companies, 1967—; formed RSO Records, 1973—; co-founder of R & R Films, 1980—. Producer of stage plays in England and the United States, 1968—, including "Hair," "Oh! Calcutta!," "Sweeney Todd," "Pippin," "Jesus Christ Superstar," and "Evita"; producer of television programs, including "Steptoe and Son," "Till Death Do Us Part," and "The Prime of Miss Jean Brodie"; producer of motion pictures, 1973—, including "Jesus Christ Superstar," "Tommy," "Saturday Night Fever," "Grease," "Sgt. Pepper's Lonely Hearts Club Band," "Moment by Moment," and "Times Square." Co-founder of Music for UNICEF, 1979. *Awards, honors:* Named international producer of the year by ABC-TV, 1975, for "Tommy."

WRITINGS: (With Dee Anthony) *Official Sgt. Pepper's Lonely Hearts Club Band Scrapbook,* Pocket Books, 1978.

SIDELIGHTS: Robert Stigwood, a self-made, multi-millionaire producer of films, plays, rock concerts, records, and television shows, has been called "the Ziegfeld of the disco age." He heads a twenty-nine-division conglomerate of companies, the Stigwood Group, that includes RSO Records and superstar clients like the Bee Gees, Eric Clapton, Andy Gibb, and John Travolta. "Jesus Christ Superstar," "Tommy," "Saturday Night Fever," "Grease," "Sgt. Pepper's Lonely Hearts Club Band," and "Times Square," were all films produced by Stigwood, and their spin-off sound-track albums and tapes brought in additional millions of dollars. "He glides through his empire like a Rolls-Royce parting the crowd at a rock concert," wrote *Newsweek*'s David Ansen. "In the eye of the hurricane, the only sound is the ring of the cash register."

A convert to Catholicism at age fifteen, Stigwood had originally intended to become a priest. Disinterest in his studies at a Catholic boarding school convinced him to revise his plan, however, and he went to work as a copywriter for an Adelaide advertising agency. Three years later, in 1956, he set out for London promising his friends that he would return a millionaire.

Stigwood opened a London theatrical agency in 1962. Initially, he specialized in casting commercials for television, but then a young singer-actor, John Leyton, asked him to produce his new song, "Johnny Remember Me." Although major recording companies had already rejected the song, Stigwood persuaded EMI to market the single which soon topped the charts. It also made Stigwood the first independent record producer in Great Britain. After a brief partnership with Brian Epstein, the manager of the Beatles, Stigwood formed his own company and began producing records for the Bee Gees and Cream, among others.

In 1968 Stigwood brought the American musical "Hair" to the London stage, his first venture as a theatrical producer. The play was an enormous success on the West End, and Stigwood returned with a string of hits, including "Oh! Calcutta!," "Jesus Christ Superstar," "Pippin," "Sweeney

Todd,'' and ''Evita.'' Opening in June, 1978, ''Evita'' drew rave reviews in London and enjoyed record-breaking runs in London, New York, Los Angeles, Australia, Spain, and Austria. The show won several top honors, including both the Los Angeles and New York Drama Critics Circle Awards and the Tony Award for Best Musical of 1980.

As Ansen observed, ''Stigwood was the first to realize the phenomenal potential of merging rock music with theatre and movies.'' The rock opera became the producer's trademark. ''Jesus Christ Superstar,'' originally a rock album, was adapted for the stage in 1970 and then reworked again for Stigwood's debut as a motion picture producer in 1973. Two years later Stigwood produced the screen version of ''Tommy,'' another successful merger of rock music and film that made millions of dollars.

Stigwood's most spectacular combination of mediums came in 1978, the year of ''Saturday Night Fever'' and ''Grease.'' Together the films grossed more than $200 million and made John Travolta an instant superstar. ''Fever'' put the Bee Gees back on top of the music world, and ''Grease'' produced the same effect for singer Olivia Newton-John. Although ''Grease'' the stage musical had begun to lose its luster after a long run on Broadway, the film adaptation dazzled millions of younger moviegoers who were still dancing to the disco sounds of ''Saturday Night Fever.'' Stigwood's RSO label dominated the record charts week after week: the sound-track album from ''Fever'' alone grossed more than $285 million, and the sound track from ''Grease'' outpaced ''Fever'' in the rate of sales, climbing to first place on the Record World chart within weeks of its release.

''Fever'' and ''Grease'' demonstrated rock critic Henry Edward's claim that Stigwood is ''the first great crossover artiste.'' By 1978 the producer had perfected a marketing method that practically guaranteed success. Ansen wrote: ''Crossover: album sells theater ticket, play sells movie rights, sound-track album sells movie, movie sells soundtrack album. A cybernetic spiral of cross-selling that wrings a property of every last drop of profit.'' In 1978 the Stigwood Group had estimated earnings of between $300 million and $500 million.

Stigwood's empire is so thoroughly diversified that should any one division falter, twenty-eight others provide backup support. ''Sgt. Pepper's Lonely Hearts Club Band,'' for example, did not fare as well at movie theatres as expected, but the sound-track album was an amazing success, selling 3 million copies prior to the film's release. ''Moment by Moment,'' produced by Stigwood for $5 million, was a boxoffice flop for its distributor, Universal, but Stigwood had sold the distribution rights for $8 million. With companies active in television, talent management, concert tours, and music publishing, Stigwood has ''stamped his red-cow logo across the surface of American pop culture.''

Although his influence pervades the entertainment world, Stigwood has preferred to remain outside the show-business community. Business deals and opening-night parties may oblige him to visit Hollywood and New York City, but Stigwood conducts most of his business by phone from his twenty-four-acre estate in Bermuda. Between deals he escapes to the Mediterranean and Aegean aboard his 226-foot yacht. ''Not since the splashy days of the cigar-chomping Mike Todd has a producer made such waves,'' Ansen remarked. ''Or reveled in success with such flair.''

Stigwood's plans for the eighties call for four motion pictures to be filmed in New York City and a fifth based on the stage musical ''Evita.'' The producer has also joined with publishing tycoon Rupert Murdoch to form R & R Films. The two Aussies hope to establish Australia as a major international production center and to produce at least three features there each year.

BIOGRAPHICAL/CRITICAL SOURCES: Newsweek, July 31, 1978; Michael Pie, *Moguls,* Holt, 1980; *Bulletin,* May 20, 1980.

*   *   *

STODDARD, Richard   1942-

PERSONAL: Born September 28, 1942, in Salem, Mass. *Education:* Tufts University, B.A., 1967; Yale University, Ph.D., 1971. *Home and office:* 90 East 10th St., New York, N.Y. 10003.

CAREER: University of Georgia, Athens, assistant professor of drama and theatre, 1971-75; antiquarian bookseller, specializing in the performing arts, 1975—. Appraiser of performing arts materials. *Member:* American Society for Theatre Research, Theatre Library Association, Society for Theatre Research (England).

WRITINGS: (Editor) *Stage Scenery, Machinery, and Lighting,* Gale, 1977; (editor) *Theatre and Cinema Architecture,* Gale, 1978. Contributor to theatre, arts, and antiques journals.

*   *   *

STOLOROW, Robert D(avid)   1942-

PERSONAL: Born November 4, 1942, in Pontiac, Mich.; son of Sam L. (in business) and Mary (Fire) Stolorow; married Virginia Moy, October 30, 1971; children: Lisa, Benjamin, Stephanie. *Education:* Harvard University, B.A., 1964, M.A., 1967, Ph.D., 1970; postdoctoral study at Postgraduate Center for Mental Health, 1970-74. *Home:* 2 Horizon Rd., Apt. 802, Fort Lee, N.J. 07024. *Office:* Department of Psychology, Ferkauf Graduate School, Yeshiva University, 55 Fifth Ave., New York, N.Y. 10003.

CAREER: Massachusetts Mental Health Center, Boston, intern in clinical psychology, 1967-68, part-time psychotherapist, 1968-70; Solomon Mental Health Center, Lowell, Mass., staff psychologist, 1969-70, chief psychologist, 1970; Brooklyn College of the City University of New York, Brooklyn, N.Y., instructor in psychology, 1970-71; Rutgers University, New Brunswick, N.J., assistant professor of psychology, 1972-76; Yeshiva University, New York, N.Y., associate professor of psychology, 1976—. Diplomate of American Board of Professional Psychology; certified in psychotherapy and psychoanalysis by Postgraduate Center for Mental Health and National Accreditation Association for Psychoanalysis. Part-time child psychotherapist at private school in Framingham, Mass., 1968-69; associate member of staff at Postgraduate Center for Mental Health, 1970-74; private practice of psychoanalysis and psychotherapy, 1972—; member of Institute for Psychoanalytic Training and Research. Supervisor and senior member of faculty at National Institute for the Psychotherapies, 1975-78; training and supervising analyst and member of faculty at Training Institute of National Psychological Association for Psychoanalysis, 1976—.

MEMBER: American Psychological Association, National Psychological Association for Psychoanalysis (senior member), Council of Psychoanalytic Psychotherpists, National Accreditation Association for Psychoanalysis, Psychologists Interested in the Study of Psychoanalysis. *Awards, honors:* Essay awards from Postgraduate Center for Mental Health,

1972-73, 1973-74, and 1975-76, for best papers on therapeutic theory and technique.

WRITINGS: (With George E. Atwood) *Faces in a Cloud: Subjectivity in Personality Theory,* Jason Aronson, 1979; (with Frank M. Lachmann) *Psychoanalysis of Developmental Arrests: Theory and Treatment,* International Universities Press, 1980.

Contributor: Robert Cancro, editor, *Annual Review of the Schizophrenic Syndrome,* Volume II, Brunner, 1972; Arnold Goldberg, editor, *Advances in Self Psychology,* International Universities Press, 1980. Also contributor to *The Annual of Psychoanalysis,* 1980, *Psychoanalysis and Contemporary Thought,* 1980, and *Fathers: Observations and Perspectives,* edited by S. Cath, A. Gurwitt, and J. Ross, Little, Brown. Contributor of nearly fifty articles and reviews to journals in the behavioral sciences. Member of editorial board of *Psychoanalytic Review* and *Review of Psychoanalytic Books.*

WORK IN PROGRESS: Psychoanalytic Phenomenology: The Subjective World in Psychoanalytic Theory and Therapy, with Atwood, publication expected in 1983; contributing articles to appear in *Perspectives on Self Psychology* and *The Future of Psychoanalysis,* edited by Goldberg and E. Wolf.

SIDELIGHTS: Stolorow wrote that he is currently engaged in "construction of a new psychoanalytic theory of personality which rests on current human developmental principles, rather than on the biological assumptions prevailing in Freud's day." He continued: "This new framework, called 'psychoanalytic phenomenology,' takes the organizing structures of the personal subjective world of the individual as its central theoretical and therapeutic focus."

* * *

STOLZENBERG, Mark 1950-

PERSONAL: Born October 19, 1950, in New York, N.Y.; son of Seymour (in watch repair) and Arlene (Morganheim) Stolzenberg. *Education:* Brooklyn College of the City University of New York, B.A. (with honors), 1972; graduate study at New York University, 1973; studied at H.B. Studio. *Home and office:* 210 West 89th St., No. 4E, New York, N.Y. 10024.

CAREER: Special education teacher at public schools in New York City, 1973-75; clown with Ringling Brothers Barnum & Bailey Circus, 1975-76; clown, mime, and actor, 1976—. Artistic co-director and teacher at Hudson Street Studio and New York Variety Theatre; teacher at Brooklyn College of the City University of New York and New School for Social Research; performer on stage and television and in films. *Member:* American Guild of Variety Artists, Screen Actors Guild.

WRITINGS: "Silent Fantasies" (two-act mime play), first produced in New York, N.Y., at Open Eye Theatre, September 29, 1978; *Exploring Mime,* Sterling, 1979; *Clown for Circus and Stage,* Sterling, 1981. Co-author of a film, "Clowns."

WORK IN PROGRESS: A Clown in New York, a novel, publication expected in 1982.

SIDELIGHTS: The skills Stolzenberg uses as a clown include unicycling, fire juggling, stunt work, playing blues harmonica, and singing blues. His acting credits include a wide variety of stage plays, ranging from Shakespeare to "Zoo Story" and "Macreune's Guevera." He has appeared as a mime or clown at Amandis International Circus, Lincoln

Center, the United Nations, hotels, museums, cabarets, and college campuses. He has also performed on television programs "A.M.," "Channel Mime," and "The Joe Franklyn Show," and he has been featured on the cover of *New York.*

Stolzenberg wrote: "I believe in living fully, embracing life with action and commitment in spite of the absurdity. Positive action helps us believe in and respect ourselves and others. I learn from experiencing and observing, not from reading."

BIOGRAPHICAL/CRITICAL SOURCES: New York City News, October 5, 1978.

* * *

STONE, John (Timothy, Jr.) 1933-

PERSONAL: Born July 13, 1933, in Denver, Colo.; son of John Timothy (a minister, educator, and writer) and Marie (an educator; maiden name, Briggs) Stone; married Judith Bosworth (a medical executive), June 22, 1955; children: John Timothy III and George W. B. (twins). *Education:* Attended Instituto Allende, 1950-51, and Amherst College, 1951-52; University of Miami, Coral Gables, Fla., B.A., 1955. *Home and office:* 5508 Williamsburg Way, Madison, Wis. 53719. *Agent:* Conrad Johnson, 20 North Carroll St., Madison, Wis. 53701; and Art Aveilhe, 1211 Horh Ave., Hollywood, Calif. 90069.

CAREER: Associated with Household Finance Corp., Chicago, Ill., 1958-59; Janeff Credit Corp., Madison, Wis., vice-president, 1960-68, president, 1969-74; writer, 1974—. President of Lake Sport and Travel, 1970-74, Diamond J Companies, 1970-74, Compass Club, Inc., 1972-74, and Continental Royal Services and Recreation International, Inc., both 1973-74; founder of Wisconsin Lender's Exchange; director of Madison Credit Bureau; member of Madison Chamber of Commerce, Madison Community Center, and Madison Arts Center. *Military service:* U.S. Army, Counterintelligence Corps, 1956-58.

MEMBER: World Wildlife Fund, American Athletic Union African First Shotters, One Shot Antelope Hunt Club, University of Wisconsin Weigh-In Club, Omicron Delta Kappa, Sigma Alpha Epsilon. *Awards, honors:* Robert Bosch Award for Outstanding Athletic Achievement; leadership award from Omicron Delta Kappa; diplomatic award from government of Kenya, 1973; set East African big game fishing record for marlin, 1973; diplomatic award from Honduras, 1974; citation from attorney-general of Wisconsin, 1975.

WRITINGS: Going for Broke (nonfiction), Regnery, 1976; *The Minnesota Connection* (nonfiction), Warner Books, 1978; *Debby Boone So Far,* Zondervan, 1980; *He Calls Himself an Ordinary Man* (novel), Ralston, 1981. Contributor to magazines.

WORK IN PROGRESS: Assumption of Guilt, a novel; *Aroma,* a novel co-written with Ken Artis; two novels with Tim Malencon, *The Spinny Thing* and *The Switch; How to Be a Survivor, Hustling Junque,* and *On Falling From Grace,* all nonfiction.

* * *

STORM, Russell
See WILLIAMS, Robert Moore

* * *

STROBOS, Robert Julius 1921-

PERSONAL: Born July 2, 1921, in The Hague, Netherlands;

came to the United States in 1949, naturalized citizen, 1959; son of Harm (an Amsterdam postmaster) and Anna (Ritzen-hofer) Strobos; married, 1947 (divorced, 1964); married Virginia L. Gaskin (in nursing education), February 10, 1967; children: Semon, Jur, Carolyn, Katharine, Eben. *Education:* University of Amsterdam, B.A., 1941, M.D. 1945. *Religion:* None. *Home:* 253 West 99th St., New York, N.Y. 10025. *Office:* New York Medical College, Munger Pavilion, Valhalla, N.Y. 10595.

CAREER: University Hospital, Amsterdam, Netherlands, rotating intern, 1945-47; Lago Oil Co., San Nicolas, Aruba, staff physician, 1947-49; Montefiore Hospital, New York City, resident in neurology, 1950 and 1952-53; National Hospital, London, England, clinical clerk in neurology, 1950-51; Columbia University, Neurological Institute, New York City, research fellow in neurosurgery, 1951-52; New York Hospital, White Plains, resident in psychiatry, 1953-54; Bowman Gray School of Medicine, Winston-Salem, N.C., assistant professor, 1954-59, associate professor of neurology, 1959-60; New York Medical College, Valhalla, professor of neurology and chairman of department, 1960—. Diplomate of American Board of Neurology and Psychiatry, 1955. Attending neurologist at Lincoln Hospital, Metropolitan Hospital, Bird S. Coler Hospital, and Westchester County Medical Center.

MEMBER: American Academy of Neurology (fellow), American Epilepsy Society (member of New York chapter medical advisory board), American Electroencephalographic Society, Association for Research on Nervous and Mental Diseases, Association of University Professors of Neurology, Multiple Sclerosis Society (member of New York chapter medical advisory board).

WRITINGS: (Contributor) P. J. Vinken and G. W. Bruyn, editors, *Handbook of Clinical Neurology,* Volume XVII, North-Holland Publishing, 1974; *Treading Water* (novel), Louisiana State University Press, 1980. Contributor to medical journals.

WORK IN PROGRESS: The Annals of Failure, a novel; another novel.

SIDELIGHTS: Strobos wrote: "As a young man I hesitated between careers in writing, philosophy, psychoanalysis, and medicine, but settled on the last one. I managed nevertheless to write two novels in Dutch, which fell short of my standards (that could never have been met). After surviving the German occupation (I lost my two best friends, one in a concentration camp and the other to tuberculosis) and graduating from medical school, I traveled and worked in the West Indies, South America, England; then I came to the United States. I made my career neurology, but literature remained my great love (particularly certain works of Celine, Kafka, Sartre, Rilke, Stendhal, and Dostoevsky). I finally started to write again in my adopted second language.

"I am trying to portray, as tersely and honestly as possible, one protagonist's experience of his world, to encompass and pierce one situation until it is really felt and comprehended, to remain amusing in the face of existential despair, and to write with the tightness and the blues quality of early jazz."

*   *   *

SUMMERS, Rowena
See SAUNDERS, Jean

*   *   *

SUSS, Elaine
PERSONAL: Born in New York, N.Y.; daughter of Louis

D. (a silk merchant) and Birdie (Persky) Cusack; married Harold Suss (a teacher and stockbroker), December 24, 1941; children: Warren, Wendy. *Education:* Brooklyn College (now of the City University of New York), B.A., 1941. *Home:* 76 Meadow Woods Rd., Great Neck, N.Y. 11020. *Agent:* Harvey Klinger, Inc., 250 West 57th St., New York, N.Y. 10019.

CAREER: Writer. Executive in cosmetic industry, 1968-72. *Member:* Poetry Society of America, National League of American Pen Women.

WRITINGS: A Money Marriage (novel), Taplinger, 1980. Contributor of poems to magazines, including *Saturday Review, Plume and Sword, Snowy Egret,* and *Bitterroot,* and newspapers.

WORK IN PROGRESS: A novel.

*   *   *

SUTHERLAND, Fraser   1946-

PERSONAL: Born December 5, 1946, in Pictou, Nova Scotia, Canada; son of Russell (a farmer) and Mary (a teacher; maiden name, McHardy) Sutherland; married Alison Armour (a librarian), October 21, 1978. *Education:* Attended University of King's College, 1965-66; Carleton University, B.J. (with honors), 1969. *Religion:* Presbyterian. *Home address:* Scotsburn, Pictou County, Nova Scotia, Canada B0K 1R0.

CAREER: Halifax Chronicle-Herald, Halifax, Nova Scotia, reporter, 1966; *Wall Street Journal,* New York, N.Y., reporter from Parliamentary Press Gallery in Ottawa, Ontario, 1967; *Globe and Mail,* Toronto, Ontario, reporter, 1968; *Toronto Daily Star,* Toronto, reporter, 1969; Maclean-Hunter Business Publications, Toronto, staff writer, 1969-70; free-lance writer, 1970—. Part-time reporter for *Pictou Advocate,* 1965-68; Parliamentary Press Gallery reporter for Canadian Dow Jones News Service, 1967. Conducts creative writing workshops; gives public readings. Organizer of Scottish-Canadian Literary Celebration, 1979.

MEMBER: League of Canadian Poets (member of executive committee from Atlantic provinces, 1979-80), Writers Federation of Nova Scotia (member of executive committee, 1978-80; chairman of Nova Scotia Writers' Council, 1979-80). *Awards, honors:* Grants from Ontario Arts Council, 1975-76, and Canada Council, 1975-76.

WRITINGS: Strange Ironies (poems), Fiddlehead Poetry Books, 1972; *The Style of Innocence,* Clarke, Irwin, 1972; *In the Wake Of* (poems), Northern Journey Press, 1974; *Within the Wound* (poems), Northern Journey Press, 1976; *Madwomen* (poetry broadside), Dreadnaught Press, 1977; *Some Cases in Thought* (poetry broadside), Word, 1977; *Madwomen* (poems; edited and introduced by Al Purdy), Black Moss Press, 1978; *Scotland Here: A Checklist of Canadian Writers of Scottish Ancestry,* Scottish-Canadian Literary Celebration, 1979; *Dunrobin* (poetry broadside), Scottish-Canadian Literary Celebration, 1979; *The Last Words of the Reverend Jim Jones* (poems), League of Canadian Poets, 1980.

Work represented in anthologies, including *Nearly an Island: A Nova Scotian Anthology,* Breakwater Books, 1979; *A Pottersfield Portfolio,* Pottersfield Press, 1979; *Magic Realism,* Aya Press, 1980. Contributor of poems, stories, and articles to magazines, including *Canadian Literature, Quill and Quire, Fiddlehead, Poetry Toronto, Cross Country,* and *Modern Times.* Co-founder and editor of *Northern Journey,* 1971-76.

WORK IN PROGRESS: What We Do With the Dream: Gaston Bachelard and the Materials of the Imagination, a monograph; translating *The Dreams in Water,* by Gaston Bachelard; *The Night Season,* "a factual novel"; a long poem about the life and death of Norman Bethune; a bibliography of works by and about John Glassco, to be included in *Essays in Canadian Writing,* edited by Jack David, 1981; two novellas, "Fidelities" and "Big Steel Rail"; short stories; poems.

SIDELIGHTS: Sutherland commented: "When I began writing full time ten years ago, I was a convinced cultural nationalist. Although I still believe in the idea of a Canadian literature and the inescapability of cultural roots, specifically Nova Scotian, I have gradually realized that the artist's true subject matter is the discovery of self. I've long conducted a civil war between public and private selves. Doing so, I've come to react against many things, and, I hope, acquired the power to say no. No to the provincial society from which I emerged; no to journalism; no to the mainstream of Canadian literature. My travels—Bulgaria, Spain, England, New York, Mexico, Columbia, and Ecuador, and six years' residence in Montreal—have all contributed to that end. Cultural background, social forces are indispensable, but primarily as material to react against, and to shape artistically. Everything seems fiction; hence, I am writing more fiction, and being more careful about the choice between prose and poetry. I have more ideas than I know what to do with. That's the aesthetic, one may even say the moral, struggle; like most writers, I also struggle economically. Combining them, my obsessions are sex, religion, vocation, and money."

BIOGRAPHICAL/CRITICAL SOURCES: John Robert Colombo, editor, *Colombo's Canadian References,* Hurtig, 1978; Philip Milner, editor, *Nova Scotia Writes,* Formac, 1979.

* * *

SUTHERLAND, Zena Bailey 1915-

PERSONAL: Born September 17, 1915, in Winthrop, Mass.; daughter of Jacob and Lena (Baum) Karras; married Roland Bailey, December 19, 1937 (marriage ended, 1961); married Alec Sutherland (employed by British Broadcasting Corp.), July 30, 1964; children: Stephen, Thomas, Katherine (Mrs. Thomas Linehan). *Education:* University of Chicago, B.A., 1937, M.A., 1966. *Politics:* Independent. *Religion:* Unitarian-Universalist. *Home:* 1418 East 57th St., Chicago, Ill. 60637. *Office:* 1100 East 57th St., Chicago, Ill. 60637.

CAREER: Bulletin of the Center for Children's Books, Chicago, Ill., editor, 1958—; *Book Review Journal,* Chicago, editor, 1958—; University of Chicago, Chicago, lecturer, 1968-77, associate professor of library science, 1977—. Consultant to National Broadcasting Co. (NBC), 1968-71, and Museum of Science and Industry. *Member:* International Research Society for Children's Literature, International Reading Association, International Board on Books for Young People, Women's National Book Association, American Library Association (member of board of directors, 1977-80), National Council of Teachers of English, Authors League of America, Mensa, Children's Reading Round Table, Children's Literature Association, Society of Midwest Authors, Beta Phi Mu, Quadrangle Club (member of board of directors, 1976-79). *Awards, honors:* Phi Delta Kappa award, 1973, for *Children and Books;* annual award from Children's Reading Round Table, 1978, for contributions in the field of children's literature.

WRITINGS—For adults: *History in Children's Books,* McKinley Publishing, 1967; (with May Arbuthnot) *Children and Books,* Scott, Foresman, 1972, 6th edition, 1981; *The Best in Children's Books,* University of Chicago Press, 1973, 2nd edition, 1980; (editor) *The Arbuthnot Anthology,* Scott, Foresman, 1976; (editor) *Burning Bright,* Open Court, 1979; (editor) *Close to the Sun,* Open Court, 1979; (editor) *Spirit of the Wind,* Open Court, 1979; (editor) *The Arbuthnot Honor Lectures,* American Library Association, 1980; *Children and Libraries,* University of Chicago Press, 1981.

Contributor to *World Book Encyclopedia, Britannica Junior,* and *Compton Encyclopedia Yearbook.* Contributor to magazines for adults and children, including *Modern Realistic Stories for Children and Young People* and library journals. Contributing editor of *Saturday Review,* 1966-72; children's book editor of *Chicago Tribune,* 1972—.

WORK IN PROGRESS: Editing an anthology for young children, publication by Dutton expected in 1982; a history of American children's literature, Ab Raben & Sjoegren Bokforlag, 1982.

SIDELIGHTS: Zena Bailey told *CA:* "One of my major interests is making *good* films from *good* books; I am now consultant for a Britannica program to that end. I am also interested in the exchange and translation of international children's literature. I have served on international juries, traveling to many European countries and Iran. I consider *Children and Books* my major work. My co-author died many years ago and the book carries her name (always will), but it expresses all my passionate concern and my ideas about what ought to be taught at the college level about children's literature."

* * *

SWAIN, Roger (Bartlett) 1949-

PERSONAL: Born February 5, 1949, in Cambridge, Mass.; son of C. Gardner and Marguerite (Stay) Swain; married Elizabeth Ward (a professor), July, 1979. *Education:* Harvard University, A.B., 1971, M.A., 1972, Ph.D., 1977. *Office: Horticulture,* 300 Massachusetts Ave., Boston, Mass. 02115.

CAREER: Horticulture, Boston, Mass., science editor, 1978—.

WRITINGS: Earthly Pleasures: Tales From a Biologist's Garden, Scribner, 1981.

SIDELIGHTS: Washington Post critic Peggy Thomson commented that Swain's book *Earthly Pleasures: Tales From a Biologist's Garden* "is a nice mix of observation, glimpses into current research, and snippets of history."

BIOGRAPHICAL/CRITICAL SOURCES: New York Times Book Review, February 15, 1981; *Washington Post,* March 23, 1981.

* * *

SWARTLEY, David Warren 1950-

PERSONAL: Born July 12, 1950, in Sellersville, Pa.; son of G. Merrill (a music teacher) and Miriam K. (Landis) Swartley. *Education:* Goshen College, B.A., 1977; Indiana University, M.S., 1981. *Religion:* Episcopalian. *Home address:* 64712-12 C.R. 21, Box 286, Goshen, Ind. 46526.

CAREER: Bashor Children's Home, Goshen, Ind., child care worker, 1976; Jefferson Elementary School, Goshen, fourth grade teacher, 1977—. Private tutor. Church choir master. *Member:* International Reading Association.

Awards, honors: Nomination for Excellence in Eudcation award by Indiana University, 1980-81.

WRITINGS: My Friend, My Brother (young adult; fiction), Herald Press, 1980.

WORK IN PROGRESS: My Little George, a novel on foster care by a single parent.

SIDELIGHTS: Swartley is a single foster parent, active in the Big Brothers-Big Sisters Organization and has done extensive public speaking. He told *CA:* "In *My Friend, My Brother,* I wanted to give the age group from nine to fourteen years old the experience of reading about peer problems and some help in making decisions about these problems. The end of the book is a happy one, yet realistic in that adjustments do have to be made in the lives of everyone involved in the troubled situation."

*   *   *

SWAYZE, John Cameron   1906-

PERSONAL: Born April 4, 1906, in Wichita, Kan.; son of Jesse Ernest (a wholesale drug salesman) and Mary Christine (Cameron) Swayze; married Beulah Mae Estes, October 29, 1932; children: John Cameron, Suzanne Louise. *Education:* Attended University of Kansas, 1925-27, and Anderson-Milton Dramatic School, New York, N.Y., 1928-29. *Religion:* Presbyterian. *Home:* 491 Riversville Rd., Greenwich, Conn. 06830.

CAREER/WRITINGS: Kansas City Journal-Post, Kansas City, Mo., reporter and feature editor, 1930-40; WHB-Radio, Kansas City, news commentator, 1930-40; KMBC-Radio, Kansas City, news commentator, 1930-40, and member of news staff, 1940-45; National Broadcasting Co. (NBC), news and special events director of Western network in Hollywood, Calif., 1946-47, radio and news commentator in New York City, 1947-56, and anchorman of nightly network news program, "News Caravan," 1949-56; American Broadcasting Co. (ABC), New York City, producer of television news programs, 1956-57, and host of syndicated feature news radio program, "Swayze Notebook," 1959; commercial spokesman for Timex and other companies, 1956—. Host and narrator of travel programs, including "Sightseeing With the Swayzes," 1956-58. *Member:* Legion of Honor, Order De Molay, National Press Club (Washington, D.C.), Players Club (New York City), Greenwich Country Club (Greenwich, Conn.), Woodway Gun Club (Darien, Conn.), Lambs Club (New York City).

SIDELIGHTS: One of the most enduring commercials on American television features John Cameron Swayze for Timex. After a grueling test that demonstrates the shock or water resistance of a Timex watch, Swayze confidently assures consumers that a Timex "takes a licking, but keeps on ticking." Swayze has been so closely identified with the promotion over the years that many viewers know him solely as the watch company's spokesman. But for twenty-nine years Swayze worked as a full-time newsman, in both print and broadcast journalism, before taking on commercial accounts and other career projects.

Swayze trained as a journalist in Kansas City, Missouri, "a tough newspaper school in its boss-controlled, racket-ridden days." As a cub reporter at the *Kansas City Journal-Post* he was given a job no one else wanted, broadcasting news stories for the local radio station from a cubbyhole in one corner of the city room. Swayze, who had studied elocution with the hope of one day becoming a stage actor, welcomed the radio assignment, although the job was in addition to his

normal reportorial duties. In 1940, after ten years as a news-paperman, he left the *Journal-Post* to work exclusively as a broadcaster.

Following his move to Los Angeles in 1945, Swayze joined the National Broadcasting Company (NBC) and was made a director of news and special events. His transfer to New York City two years later returned him to the airwaves, and in 1948 he helped cover the national political conventions in Philadelphia. He then found himself among the pioneers of network television news.

Swayze contends that he was "pushed into television against my will because I was expendable." Television in 1949 was new to the broadcasting world, he explains, and NBC decided that its better-known personalities should remain in radio. His work in Philadelphia the previous year had impressed the network, and he was made anchorman of the "News Caravan," one of the first two network news programs on television. He continued in this post with an estimated nightly audience of 15 million until 1956.

After leaving NBC Swayze pursued other interests as a producer and commercial spokesman. Recalling his career in television, he tells the anecdote that he has been tongue-tied only twice in his life, once when President Eisenhower greeted him and again when he met Elia Kazan, but that his most trying experience on the air didn't cause him to fluff a word. "It happened during the live TV days on a Steve Allen show when the Timex watch I was demonstrating disappeared from an outboard motor propeller during a test," he says. "I ad-libbed my way through the spot, put on my hat, and went home untroubled and fluent."

*   *   *

SYED, Anwar H(ussain)   1926-

PERSONAL: Born December 17, 1926, in Batala, India; came to the United States in 1962, naturalized citizen, 1976; son of Muhammad Hussain and Rehmat Sultana Syed; married Shameem J. Khan (a librarian), January 1, 1960; children: Sarah (Mrs. Najam Wasty), Sameer, Amir. *Education:* Punjab University, B.A., 1946, M.A., 1951; University of Chicago, M.A., 1953; University of Pennsylvania, Ph.D., 1957. *Home:* 364 South East St., Amherst, Mass. 01002. *Office:* Department of Political Science, University of Massachusetts, Amherst, Mass. 01003.

CAREER: University of Karachi, Karachi, Pakistan, lecturer, 1957-59, reader in public administration, 1959-62; University of Pennsylvania, Philadelphia, assistant professor of political science, 1962-63; University of Massachusetts, Amherst, assistant professor, 1963-64, associate professor, 1964-68, professor of political science, 1969—. Member of executive committee of board of trustees of American Institute of Pakistan Studies. *Member:* American Political Science Association, Association of Asian Studies. *Awards, honors:* Ford Foundation grant for Pakistan, 1965; fellowship from Foreign Policy Research Institute at University of Pennsylvania, 1965-66 and 1973-74; grant from American Institute for Pakistan Studies, 1979-80.

WRITINGS: Walter Lippmann's Philosophy of International Politics, University of Pennsylvania Press, 1963; *Political Theory of American Local Government,* Random House, 1966; *China and Pakistan: Diplomacy of an Entente Cordiale,* University of Massachusetts Press, 1974. Contributor to political science journals.

WORK IN PROGRESS: Z. A. Bhutto: A Study in Political Leadership, completion expected in 1982.

SIDELIGHTS: Syed told *CA:* "During the last twenty-five years that I have been studying and teaching politics, I have met numerous heads of government (President Ayhb Khan and Prime Minister Bhutto of Pakistan, the late shah of Iran, and the king of Jordan, among others) and found that, not-withstanding the majesty with which protocol invests them, most rulers are in fact rather ordinary—one might say—mediocre. Prime Minister Bhutto, with whom I had several long interviews in 1974, was an exception. He was truly brilliant so far as capacities of mind and intellect were concerned. But in his actual conduct of statecraft he couldn't put aside the habits and biases of the feudal lord that he also was by way of family background."

T

TAGGART, Dorothy T(rekell) 1917-

PERSONAL: Born April 20, 1917, in Harper, Kan.; daughter of Emery (a physician) and Mae (Maple) Trekell; married James Howard Taggart (an attorney), March 8, 1941; children: Earl James II, Deanne (Mrs. Stephen Edward Curtis), David Marshall. *Education:* University of Kansas, B.A., 1938; received degree from University of Minnesota, 1940; graduate study at University of Washington, Seattle, 1967; Emporia State University, M.L.S., 1969; doctoral study at University of Colorado, 1970. *Politics:* Republican. *Religion:* Presbyterian. *Home:* 315 North C St., Wellington, Kan. 67152. *Office:* Wellington Senior High School, 605 North A St., Wellington, Kan. 67152.

CAREER: Teacher of English, journalism, and speech at schools in Kansas, 1938-61; Wellington Senior High School, Wellington, Kan., librarian, 1961—. Instructor at Northern Michigan University, 1970—. Presents workshops; public speaker. Member of study team for Biographical Center for Research; member of White House Conference on Libraries and Information Sources. *Member:* American Library Association, American Association of School Librarians, Association for Educational Communications and Technology, National Education Association, Kansas Library Association, Kansas Association of School Librarians, Kansas Association for Educational Communications and Technology, Kansas Education Association (vice-president), Mortar Board. *Awards, honors:* Recognition award from Mountain Plains Library Association, 1976, for notable contributions to the library profession.

WRITINGS: A Guide to Sources in Educational Media and Technology, Scarecrow, 1975; *Management and Administration of the School Library Media Program,* Shoe String, 1980. Contributor of articles and reviews to library journals.

WORK IN PROGRESS: Networking and the School Library Media Program.

SIDELIGHTS: Dorothy T. Taggart commented that "the Senior High Library Media Center was a Knapp Finalist and has served as a demonstration library for Kansas." She noted that her book *Management and Administration of the School Library Media Program* was described by one reviewer as "a much needed book devoted exclusively to school media program administrative problems at the school building level. The book addresses all aspects of the managerial and administrative functions of the media specialists. It describes in detail the decision-making process itself; budgeting and accounting; staff development and training; program evaluation and relationships with the community and library personnel."

The author told *CA:* "The library media field is a rapidly changing and expanding one with many possibilities for improvement of services and programs and for innovative approaches to problems and programs. The creative media specialist has the opportunity to build a program which is the center of the educational program of the school. Media administration in the school is changing with an emphasis on programs and services to the user rather than on the technical aspects of library operation. The library media center must serve the needs of students, teachers, and the community."

AVOCATIONAL INTERESTS: Watercolor painting, travel (London, Edinburgh, the Orient, the lakes of Minnesota, the mountains of California and Colorado), sewing, gardening.

*　　*　　*

TAMARIN, Alfred H. 1913-1980

OBITUARY NOTICE—See index for *CA* sketch: Born May 31, 1913, in Hudson, N.Y.; died after a long illness, August 18, 1980, in Manhattan, N.Y. Publicist and author. During the 1940's Tamarin was the director of advertising and publicity for the Theatre Guild. Later he held a similar position with United Artists until 1958, when he became vice-president of two of the corporation's subsidiaries, United Artists Record Corp. and United Artists Music Corp. Tamarin was also co-founder and vice-president of In Flight Motion Pictures, Inc. His writings include *Revolt in Judea: The Road to Masada; Benjamin Franklin: An Autobiographical Portrait; Japan and the United States: Early Encounters, 1791-1860;* and *Voyaging to Cathay,* which received a Boston Globe Horn Book award in 1976. Obituaries and other sources: *New York Times,* August 20, 1980.

*　　*　　*

TAPLIN, Oliver 1943-

PERSONAL: Born August 2, 1943, in Kent, England; married Kim Stampfer (a writer), 1964; children: Phoebe, Nat. *Education:* Oxford University, M.A., 1968, D.Phil., 1973. *Office:* Magdalen College, Oxford University, Oxford OX1 4AU, England.

CAREER: Center for Hellenic Studies, Washington, D.C., junior fellow, 1970-71; University of Bristol, Bristol, England, lecturer, 1972-73; Oxford University, Oxford, England, lecturer in classics and fellow of Magdalen College, 1973—. *Awards, honors:* Cromer Greek Prize from British Academy, 1971.

WRITINGS: The Stagecraft of Aeschylus, Oxford University Press, 1977; *Greek Tragedy in Action,* University of California Press, 1978. Contributor of articles and reviews to learned journals.

WORK IN PROGRESS: Research on Homer, the epic, and Greek drama.

*   *   *

TAUBER, Maurice F(alcolm)   1908-1980

OBITUARY NOTICE: Born February 14, 1908, in Norfolk, Va.; died after a short illness, September 21, 1980, in New York, N.Y. Librarian, educator, and author. Recognized as one of America's leading authorities on cataloguing, classification, and technical processes, Tauber was a professor at Columbia University's School of Library Service for more than thirty years. He was appointed Melvil Dewey Professor of Library Service in 1954, a seat named for the founder of the Columbia library school and creator of the widely used Dewey Decimal System. Tauber published numerous books, including surveys of libraries that extend as far as Australia, where he investigated the country's library resources while on a Fulbright scholarship. Obituaries and other sources: *A Biographical Directory of Librarians in the United States and Canada,* 5th edition, American Library Association, 1970; *Who's Who in America,* 40th edition, Marquis, 1978; *New York Times,* September 26, 1980; *AB Bookman's Weekly,* December 15, 1980.

*   *   *

TAYLOR, Duncan Norton
See NORTON-TAYLOR, Duncan

*   *   *

TAYLOR, George A(lbert)   1942-

PERSONAL: Born March 12, 1942, in Charleston, W.Va.; son of Britton Morton and Catherine (Gilbert) Taylor; married Susan Black, September 5, 1964; children: Melissa. *Education:* Attended Randolph-Macon College, 1960-62; Baptist College at Charleston, B.S., 1968; University of Georgia, M.A., 1970, Ph.D., 1975. *Home:* 2017 Fox Run Rd., Burlington, N.C. 27215. *Office:* Department of Political Science, Elon College, Elon College, N.C. 27244.

CAREER: Brooklyn College of the City University of New York, Brooklyn, N.Y., visiting professor of political science, 1972-73; Indiana University, Bloomington, assistant professor of public and environmental affairs, 1973-77; University of Kansas, Lawrence, research associate at Center for Public Affairs, 1977-78, assistant professor of political science, 1977-79; Elon College, Elon College, N.C., associate professor of political science and director of public administration program, 1979—. Management consultant. *Member:* American Society for Public Administration, American Political Science Association, Southern Political Science Association.

WRITINGS: (With Dennis Palumbo) *Urban Policy: A Guide to Information Sources,* Gale, 1978; Also author of *Public Sector Collective Bargaining,* 1981. Contributor of articles and reviews to journals in the social sciences, including *So-*cial Science Quarterly, American Journal of Political Science,* and *Journal of Politics.*

SIDELIGHTS: Taylor told *CA:* "I see the concept of collective bargaining as both a very important skill and tool for public sector management. As a skill, the manager must be able to get his ideas and points across and to lead his government (agency) toward a better employee-employer work situation. As a tool, the manager must be able to keep open the lines of communication with his employees in order to prevent a total breakdown of the work place. These two factors are just as important in communities where collective bargaining is legal as well as those where it is illegal. In essence, it is a process in which management allows the employees to have a say in those factors which affect their lives also.

"The concept of agenda setting is one of the strongest powers granted to mayors and city managers in local government. This concept allows those people to have control over what the council is doing. And with a part-time council, this power is even greater. This power is stronger than the veto power because the mayor can arrange what will and will not be discussed."

*   *   *

TAYLOR, Theodore Brewster   1925-

PERSONAL: Born July 11, 1925, in Mexico City, Mexico; American citizen born abroad; came to the United States in 1941; son of Walter Clyde (a general secretary of Young Men's Christian Association) and Barbara (Howland) Taylor; married Caro Dwight Arnim, June 13, 1948; children: Clare E. Taylor Hastings, Katherine W. Taylor Robertson, Christopher H., Robert P., Jeffrey J. *Education:* California Institute of Technology, B.S., 1945; Cornell University, Ph.D., 1954. *Politics:* Democrat. *Religion:* Protestant. *Home:* 10325 Bethesda Church Rd., Damascus, Md. 20750. *Office:* Appropriate Solar Technology Institute, 10325 Bethesda Church Rd., Damascus, Md. 20750.

CAREER: University of California, Berkeley, theoretical physicist at Radiation Laboratory, 1946-49; Los Alamos Scientific Laboratory, Los Alamos, N.M., nuclear weapon designer, 1949-56; General Dynamics Corp., General Atomic Division, San Diego, Calif., senior research adviser, 1956-64; U.S. Department of Defense, Defense Atomic Support Agency, Washington, D.C., deputy director of science, 1964-67; International Research and Technology Corp., McClean, Va., chairman of board of directors, 1967-76; Princeton University, Princeton, N.J., visiting lecturer in aerospace and mechanical engineering, 1976-79; Holosolar Corp., Damascus, Md., president, 1980—. President of Appropriate Solar Technology Institute, 1980—. Member of U.S. Army Scientific Advisory Panel, 1967-71; member of board of directors of Center for Renewable Resources, 1978—, and Jet Propulsion Laboratory, 1979—; member of advisory board of Solar Energy Research Institute, 1979—. Member of President's Commission on the Accident at Three Mile Island, 1979; expert witness at hearings of U.S. Congress; speaker for U.S. International Communications Agency in India, Indonesia, Singapore, Malaysia, Thailand, and Ghana, 1977-79; consultant to Rockefeller Foundation, 1977—, Los Alamos Scientific Laboratory, Aerospace Corp., and International Atomic Energy Agency. *Military service:* U.S. Naval Reserve, active duty, 1942-46.

MEMBER: International Solar Energy Society, American Association for the Advancement of Science, American Physical Society. *Awards, honors:* Ernest Orlando Lawrence Award from U.S. Atomic Energy Commission, 1965, for design of nuclear weapons and TRIGA research reactor; meritorious civilian service medal from U.S. Department of Defense, 1966, for director of U.S. nuclear weapons effects programs; award from Forum on Physics and Society, 1978.

WRITINGS: (Contributor) Robert Marshak, editor, *Perspectives in Modern Physics,* Interscience, 1966; (with Charles Humpstone) *The Restoration of the Earth,* Harper, 1973; (with Mason Willrich) *Nuclear Theft: Risks and Safeguards,* Ballinger, 1974; (with Ted Greenwood and Harold Feiveson) *Nuclear Proliferation,* McGraw, 1977; (contributor) O. K. Karidoglu, A. Perlmutter, and L. Scott, editors, *Nuclear Energy and Alternatives,* Ballinger, 1978; *Energy: The Next Twenty Years,* edited by Hans Landsberg, Ballinger, 1979. Contributor to scientific journals and magazines. Editor and publisher of *International Research and Technology Nuclear Journal,* 1968-69.

WORK IN PROGRESS: Prospects for Worldwide Use of Solar Energy.

SIDELIGHTS: Taylor wrote: "From 1946 to 1977 most of my career was devoted to military and peaceful uses of nuclear energy. Since 1966 I have pressed actively and publicly for effective national and international safeguards against the abuse of nuclear energy for destructive purposes by governments, terrorists, and criminals. In spring, 1977, I decided to devote the rest of my career primarily to stimulate as widescale use of solar energy as possible, to alleviate the environmental and security impacts of nuclear energy and fossil fuels. I am especially attracted by possibilities of enhancing self-sufficiency on a community or neighborhood scale by use of solar energy, greenhouse production of foods, and appropriate management of local water resources. I am convinced that widescale use of technologies for such possibilities will also encourage more political self-reliance, individual responsibility for community affairs, and individual self-fulfillment.

"My birth and childhood in Mexico City contributed to an interest in international affairs, especially in developing countries. I lived in Vienna, Austria, from fall, 1966, to summer, 1968, working as an independent consultant on nuclear safeguards."

BIOGRAPHICAL/CRITICAL SOURCES: New Yorker, December 3, 1973, December 10, 1973, December 17, 1973; John McPhee, *The Curve of Binding Energy,* Farrar, Straus, 1974.

* * *

TAYLOR, Wendell H(ertig) 1905-

PERSONAL: Born June 15, 1905, in Uniontown, Pa.; son of Frank Herbert (a physician) and Louise (a physician; maiden name, Hertig) Taylor. *Education:* Princeton University, B.S., 1926, A.M., 1930, Ph.D., 1933. *Politics:* Independent. *Religion:* Presbyterian. *Home:* 122 Patton Ave., Princeton, N.J. 08540.

CAREER: E.I. du Pont de Nemours, Wilmington, Del., research chemist, 1926-29; Princeton University, Princeton, N.J., instructor, 1933-37, assistant professor of chemistry, 1937-43; science teacher and head of department of Lawrenceville School, 1943-70; writer, 1970—. *Member:* American Chemical Society, Princeton Club of New York. *Awards, honors:* Princeton Award for Distinguished Secondary School Teaching, 1966.

WRITINGS: (Co-author) *General Education in School and College,* Harvard University Press, 1952; (with L. E. Strong and others) *Chemical Systems,* McGraw, 1964; (with

Jacques Barzun) *A Catalogue of Crime,* Harper, 1970; (editor with Barzun) *Fifty Classics of Crime Fiction, 1900-1950,* Garland Publishing, 1976. Also editor with Barzun of *Fifty Classics of Crime Fiction, 1950-1975,* 1981.

AVOCATIONAL INTERESTS: European travel, railroads, recorded music, detective fiction.

* * *

TCHOBANOGLOUS, George 1935-

PERSONAL: Surname is accented on second syllable; born May 24, 1935, in Patterson, Calif.; son of Christo (a farmer) and Penelope (Megdani) Tchobanoglous; married Rosemary Ash, June 16, 1957; children: Kathryn, Lynn Marie, Julianne. *Education:* University of the Pacific, B.S.C.E., 1958; University of California, Berkeley, M.S.C.E., 1960; Stanford University, Ph.D., 1969. *Home:* 662 Diego Pl., Davis, Calif. 95616. *Office:* Department of Civil Engineering, University of California, Davis, Calif. 95616.

CAREER: University of California, Davis, assistant professor, 1970-71, associate professor, 1971-76, professor of civil engineering, 1976—. *Member:* American Association for the Advancement of Science, Federation of American Scientists, American Water Works Association, Water Pollution Control Federation, California Water Pollution Control Federation, Sigma Xi.

WRITINGS: Wastewater Engineering: Collection, Treatment, Disposal, McGraw, 1972, revised edition published in two volumes as *Wastewater Engineering: Treatment, Disposal, Reuse,* 1979, and *Collection and Pumping of Wastewater,* 1981; (editor with Ronald Crites and Robert G. Smith) *Wastewater Management: A Guide to Information Sources,* Gale, 1976; (with Hilary Theisen and Rolf Eliassen) *Solid Wastes: Engineering Principles and Management Issues,* McGraw, 1977.

WORK IN PROGRESS: A three-volume series on environmental engineering, with E. D. Schroeder, publication by Addison-Wesley expected in 1981.

AVOCATIONAL INTERESTS: Hi-fidelity sound, photography, gardening (roses).

* * *

TEALE, Edwin Way 1899-1980

OBITUARY NOTICE—See index for *CA* sketch: Born June 2, 1899, in Joliet, Ill.; died October 18, 1980, in Norwich, Conn. Author, naturalist, illustrator, and photographer best known for chronicling the history of the seasons in America. Teale was a staff writer for *Popular Science* magazine. The author of nearly thirty books, his writings include *Dune Boy, North With the Spring, Autumn Across America, Journey Into Summer, A Walk Through the Year,* and *Insect Friends.* The fourth volume of his series on the seasons, *Wandering Through Winter,* received a Pulitzer Prize for general nonfiction in 1966. In 1943 Teale was awarded the John Burroughs Medal. Obituaries and other sources: Edward H. Dodd, Jr., *Of Nature, Time and Teale,* Dodd, 1960; *Washington Post,* October, 21, 1980; *New York Times,* October 21, 1980; *Time,* November 3, 1980; *Newsweek,* November 3, 1980; *Publishers Weekly,* November 7, 1980; *AB Bookman's Weekly,* January 5, 1981.

* * *

TEGA, Vasile 1921-

PERSONAL: Born May 20, 1921, in Baeasa, Greece; son of

George (in business) and Ecaterina (Zottu) Tega; married Filoteia Costelian, December 14, 1954; children: George, Katherine. *Education:* Academy of High Commercial and Industrial Studies, Bucharest, Romania, M.A., 1950; University of Montreal, B.L.S., 1969; McGill University, M.L.S., 1972. *Religion:* Greek Orthodox. *Home:* 12185 de Poutrincourt, Montreal, Quebec, Canada H3M 2A8. *Office:* Ecole des Hautes Etudes Commerciales, 5225 avenue Decelles, Montreal, Quebec, Canada H3T 1V6.

CAREER: Industria Usoara, Bucharest Romania, editor, 1951-64; *Industria Textila,* Bucharest, editor, 1951-64; Ecole Des Hautes Etudes Commerciales, Montreal, Quebec, head reference librarian, 1969—. *Member:* Corporation of Professional Librarians of Quebec. *Awards, honors:* Research prize from Ecole des Hautes Etudes Commerciales, 1978, for *Management and Economics Journals;* medal from Ecole Superieure des Sciences Economiques et Commerciales (Cergy, France), 1978, for "Journal Evaluation, Selection, and Ranking: A Review in Business and Economics."

WRITINGS: Human Resources Accounting, Ecole des Hautes Etudes Commerciales, 1972; *Franchising,* Ecole des Hautes Etudes Commerciales, 1972; *Flexible Working Hours and the Compressed Workweek,* Guerin, 1975; *Information et documentation: Facteurs de progres dans l'enterprise* (title means "Information and Documentation: Elements of Progress in the Enterprise"), Guerin, 1975; *Management and Economics Journals,* Gale, 1977; *Industrial Democracy,* Les Editions Agence d'ARC (Montreal), 1981. Contributor to business and library journals.

*   *   *

TERNER, Janet 1938-

PERSONAL: Born March 17, 1938, in Reading, Pa.; daughter of Edward I. (a pharmacist) and Irma R. (in sales; maiden name, Matzkin) Gibstein; married Benjamin B. Terner (an attorney), August 14, 1960; children: Jessica L., Michele A. *Education:* Shimer College, B.S., 1958; University of Wisconsin—Madison, M.S., 1960. *Religion:* Jewish. *Home and office:* 1523 Live Oak Dr., Silver Spring, Md. 20910.

CAREER: Library of Congress, Washington, D.C., science reference librarian, 1961-79; writer, 1979—. Consultant to National Bureau of Standards Library. *Member:* Cheiron: International Society for the History of the Behavioral Sciences, North American Society of Adlerian Psychology, History of Science Society, Individual Psychology Association (vice-president, 1980-81). *Awards, honors:* Meritorious service award from Library of Congress, 1978.

WRITINGS: (With Frank Marsden) *United States International Geophysical Year Bibliography, 1953-1960,* Library of Congress, 1963; (with W. L. Pew) *The Courage to Be Imperfect: The Life and Work of Rudolf Dreikurs,* Hemisphere Books, 1978. Contributor to *International Encyclopedia of Psychiatry, Psychology, Psychoanalysis, and Neurology.* Contributor to library science and psychology journals. News and notes editor of *Journal of Individual Psychology.*

WORK IN PROGRESS: Research on family life, history of psychology, democracy in family life and the workplace, and the role of women in today's world.

SIDELIGHTS: Janet Terner told *CA:* "Two major factors motivated me to write the Dreikurs biography. As a parent, I personally experienced the effective and rewarding results of his democratic child-rearing philosophy, which is based on Alfred Adler's holistic psychology. As a professional historian of science, I was also intrigued by the lack of acknowl-

edgement, indeed the ignorance of many psychologists, of the significant influence of Adler's psychology on contemporary thinking about human behavior."

AVOCATIONAL INTERESTS: Photography, travel.

*   *   *

TERRACE, Herbert S(ydney) 1936-

PERSONAL: Born November 29, 1936, in Brooklyn, N.Y.; son of Morris Abraham and Esther (Marsh) Terrace. *Education:* Cornell University, A.B., 1957, M.A., 1958; Harvard University, Ph.D., 1961. *Home:* 460 Riverside Dr., Apt. 91, New York, N.Y. 10027. *Office:* 418 Schermerhorn Hall, Columbia University, New York, N.Y. 10027.

CAREER: Columbia University, New York, N.Y., instructor, 1961-63, assistant professor, 1963-66, associate professor, 1966-68, professor of psychology, 1968—. Visiting professor at Harvard University, 1972-73. *Member:* American Psychological Association (fellow), American Association for the Advancement of Science, Society for Experimental Analysis of Behavior, Eastern Psychological Association. *Awards, honors:* Grants from National Institute of Mental Health, 1962—, National Science Foundation, 1963-76, and W. T. Grant Foundation, 1976-78; Guggenheim fellowship, 1969-70.

WRITINGS: (With Scott Parker) *Introduction to Statistics,* Individual Learning Systems, 1971; (with T. G. Bever) *Psychology and Human Behavior: Prediction and Control in Modern Society,* Warner Publications, 1973; (photographer and author of introduction) Anna Michel, *The Story of Nim: The Chimp Who Learned Language,* Knopf, 1979; (with C. Locurto and J. Gibbon) *Autoshaping,* Academic Press, 1980; *Language in Apes,* Academic Press, 1982. Associate editor of *Journal of Experimental Analysis Behavior,* 1966-74, *Learning and Motivation,* 1970-72, *Animal Learning and Behavior,* 1971-75, and *Behaviorism,* 1972—:

WORK IN PROGRESS: Serial learning in pigeons; *Introduction to Statistics,* publication by Random House expected in 1983.

SIDELIGHTS: In order to begin Project Nim, Herbert Terrace and his associates obtained a baby chimpanzee from the Institute for Primate Studies. Nim Chimpsky (named for linguist Noam Chomsky) was raised in a human home, attended nursery school five days a week at Columbia University, and in under four years learned to use 125 signs of American Sign Language. After the project was completed, Nim was returned to his birthplace to live with other chimpanzees.

*   *   *

TERRALL, Robert 1914-
(John Gonzales, Brett Halliday, Robert Kyle, MacLennan Roberts)

PERSONAL: Born December 6, 1914, in Neihart, Mont.; son of William (a lawyer) and Genevieve Terrall; married Joan Thomas (marriage ended); married Martha Porter; children: Susan Terrall Simon, Mary, James, Benjamin. *Education:* Harvard University, B.A., 1936. *Home address:* White Hollow Rd., Sharon, Conn. 06069. *Agent:* Knox Burger Associates Ltd., 39½ Washington Sq. S., New York, N.Y. 10012.

CAREER: Time, New York, N.Y., staff writer, 1937-40; free-lance writer, 1940—. *Military service:* U.S. Army, 1943-46.

WRITINGS: They Deal in Death (mystery novel), Simon & Schuster, 1943; *Madam Is Dead* (mystery novel), Duell, Sloan & Pearce, 1949; *A Killer Is Loose Among Us* (mystery novel), Duell, Sloan & Pearce, 1950; *The Steps of the Quarry* (novel), Crown, 1950; (editor) *Great Scenes From Great Novels*, Dell, 1956; *The Wow Factor* (novel), Fawcett, 1970; *Sand Dollars* (novel), St. Martin's, 1978; *Luck Be a Lady* (novel), Peter H. Wyden, 1979.

Novels under pseudonym John Gonzales: *Death for Mr. Big*, Fawcett, 1951; *The Magnificent Moll*, Fawcett, 1952; *End of a J.D.*, Fawcett, 1960; *Someone's Sleeping in My Bed*, Fawcett, 1962; *Follow That Hearse*, Fawcett, 1963; *The Art of Love*, Fawcett, 1965.

Novels under pseudonym Brett Halliday; all published by Dell: *Fit to Kill*, 1958; *Target Mike Shayne*, 1959; *Murder Takes a Holiday*, 1960; *Murder in Haste*, 1961; *The Violent World of Michael Shayne*, 1965; *Nice Fillies Finish Last*, 1966; *Murder Spins the Wheel*, 1966; *Armed Dangerous*, 1966; *Mermaid on the Rocks*, 1967; *Guilty as Hell*, 1967; *Violence Is Golden*, 1968; *So Lush So Deadly*, 1968; *Lady Be Bad*, 1969; *Six Seconds to Kill*, 1970; *Fourth Down to Death*, 1970; *I Come to Kill You*, 1971; *Count Backwards to Zero*, 1971; *Caught Dead*, 1972; *Kill All the Young Girls*, 1973; *Blue Murder*, 1974; *At the Point of a Thirty-Eight*, 1974; *Last Seen Hitchhiking*, 1974; *Million Dollar Handle*, 1976; *Win Some Lose Some*, 1976.

Novels under pseudonym Robert Kyle; all published by Dell unless otherwise noted: *The Crooked City*, 1954; *The Golden Urge*, 1954; *Nice Guys Finish Last*, 1955; *A Tiger in the Night*, 1955; *Blackmail, Inc.*, 1958; *Model for Murder*, 1959; *Kill Now Pay Later*, 1960; *Some Like It Cool*, 1962; *Ben Gates Is Hot*, 1964; *Venus Examined*, Geis, 1968.

Novels under pseudonym MacLennan Roberts: *Moses and the Ten Commandments*, Dell, 1956; *The Great Locomotive Chase*, Dell, 1956; *Sea Avenger*, Dell, 1957. Contributor of stories to magazines, including *Saturday Evening Post* and *Cosmopolitan*.

WORK IN PROGRESS: Wrap It in Flags, a novel under name Robert Terrall, publication expected in 1981.

* * *

TERRELL, Carroll Franklin 1917-

PERSONAL: Born February 21, 1917, in Richmond, Maine; son of Arthur L. (a shoemaker) and Eula (a teacher; maiden name, Spaulding) Terrell. *Education:* Bowdoin College, B.A., 1945; University of Maine, M.A., 1950; New York University, Ph.D., 1956. *Home:* 501 College Ave., Orono, Maine 04473. *Office:* Department of English, University of Maine, Orono, Maine 04473.

CAREER: University of Maine, Orono, instructor, 1948-52, assistant professor, 1952-56, associate professor, 1956-66, professor of English, 1966—. President of National Poetry Foundation. Managing editor of *Paideuma*. *Military service:* U.S. Army, 1941-45; became captain. *Member:* Modern Language Association of America, College English Association.

WRITINGS: A Companion to the Cantos of Ezra Pound, Volume I, University of California Press, 1980; (editor) *Basil Bunting: Man and Poet*, National Poetry Foundation, 1981; *A Companion to the Cantos of Ezra Pound*, Volume II, University of California Press, 1981. Editor of *Louis Zukovsky: Man and Poet*, 1979. Contributor to literature journals. Founder and editor of *Paideuma*, 1972—.

WORK IN PROGRESS: May Sarton: Woman and Poet, publication by National Poetry Foundation expected in 1982.

SIDELIGHTS: Terrell commented: "A conviction that poetry is the most valuable and human of the creative arts has motivated most of my activities for the last twenty-five years; along with this conviction is another one which has strengthened over the years: I believe Ezra Pound to be the great creative mind and seminal genius of the twentieth century as well as perhaps the greatest non-dramatic poet since Dante. His influence is everywhere apparent. Thus my concerns have grown to encompass the important poets who carried on his work, such as William Carlos Williams, Charles Olson, Louis Zukovsky, and George Oppen, as well as those among the young today who are following in their footsteps."

* * *

THATCHER, Floyd W(ilson) 1917-

PERSONAL: Born November 27, 1917, in Indianapolis, Ind.; son of Harold L. (a minister) and Edna (Curtis) Thatcher; married Harriett Hall, August 28, 1938; children: Sherrill Lynn Thatcher Colony. *Education:* Attended Ventura College, 1935-36, and Simpson College, San Francisco, Calif., 1945-48. *Religion:* Episcopalian. *Home:* 2716 Westbury Circle, Waco, Tex. 76710. *Office:* Word, Inc., 4800 West Waco Dr., Waco, Tex. 76710.

CAREER: Standard Brands, Inc., Los Angeles, Calif., in sales, 1939-43, manager of Pasadena branch, 1943-45; Cowman Publishing Co., Los Angeles, president and publisher, 1948-64; Zondervan Publishing House, Grand Rapids, Mich., vice-president in publishing, 1964-67; Word, Inc. (publisher), Waco, Tex., vice-president and editorial director, 1967—. *Member:* Authors Guild.

WRITINGS: Prophets With Pens, Baptist Standard, 1970; (with Gary Player) *Gary Player, World Golfer*, Word, Inc., 1974; *The Splendor of Easter*, Word, Inc., 1974; *The Gift of Easter*, Word, Inc., 1976; (with Charlie W. Shedd) *The Christian Writers' Seminar*, Word, Inc., 1976; *The Miracle of Easter*, Word, Inc., 1980; (with wife, Harriett Thatcher) *Long-Term Marriage*, Word, Inc., 1980.

SIDELIGHTS: Thatcher commented to *CA:* "I began writing after twenty years as a book publisher and editor. I am interested and primarily involved in the inspirational and religious writing field, with a strong interest in marriage and family relationships and a holistic view of life.

"The style of my writing has been strongly influenced by a variety of contemporary writers, including John Steinbeck, Morris West, and Adela Rogers St. John. Since I work entirely in the field of nonfiction, my goal is to write in a crisp, anecdotal style more generally associated with good fiction."

* * *

THERIAULT, Yves 1915-

PERSONAL: Born November 28, 1915, in Quebec City, Quebec, Canada; son of Alcide and Aurore (Nadeau) Theriault; married Michelle-Germaine Blanchet (a writer), April 21, 1942; children: Yves-Michel, Marie-Jose. *Education:* Educated in Montreal, Quebec. *Religion:* Roman Catholic.

CAREER: Novelist, playwright, and author of short stories. Worked as a trapper, cheese salesman, truck diver, nightclub host, and tractor salesman in early 1930's; radio announcer in Montreal, New Carlisle, Quebec City, Trois-Rivieres, and Hull, Quebec, 1935-39; director of a newspaper in Toronto, Ontario; publicity manager; National Film Board of Canada, Ottawa, Ontario, script writer and public relations staff member, 1943-45; script writer for Canadian Broadcasting Corp. (CBC-Radio), 1945-50; Department of Indian Affairs, Ottawa, cultural director, 1965-67. *Member:* International P.E.N., Canadian Authors Association (president), Royal Society of Canada (fellow), Societe des Ecrivains Canadiens (president, 1965), Societe des Auteurs Dramatiques, Societe des Gens de Letters, Syndicat National des Ecrivains de France. *Awards, honors:* First prize for best French radio play, 1952; Quebec Government prize, 1954, for *Aaron,* and first prize, 1958, for *Agaguk;* Canada Council senior arts fellowship and French language prize for fiction from French Academy, both 1961; Governor General's Literary Award from Canada Council, 1961, for *Ashini;* Prix France-Canada, 1961, for *Agaguk* and *Ashini;* Molson Prize from Canada Council, 1971; Prix Mgr Camille Roy for *Le Vendeur d'etoiles et autre contes.*

WRITINGS—In English translation: *Agaguk* (novel), Grasset, 1958, translation by Miriam Chapin published under same title, Ryerson, 1971; *Ashini* (novel), Fides, 1960, translation by Gwendolyn Moore published under same title, Harvest House, 1972; *N'Tsik* (novel), Editions de l'Homme, 1968, translation by Moore published under same title, Harvest House, 1972; *Oeuvre de chair,* Stanke, 1975, translation by Jean David published as *Ways of the Flesh,* Gage Publishing, 1977; *Agoak: L'Heritage d'Agaguk,* Quinz, 1975, translation by John David Allen published as *Agoak: The Legacy of Agaguk,* McGraw, 1979.

Other writings: *Contes pour un homme seul* (short stories), Editions de l'Arbre, 1944; *Trois Rivieres: Ville de reflet,* Editions de Bien Public, 1954; *Aaron* (novel), Grasset, 1957; *Amour au gout de mer* (novel), Beauchemin, 1961; *Cul-de-sac* (novel), Institut Litteraire du Quebec, 1961; *Le Vendeur d'etoiles et autres contes* (short stories), Fides, 1961; *Les Commettants de Caridad* (novel), Institut Litteraire du Quebec, 1961; *Sejour a Moscou* (nonfiction), Fides, 1961; *La Fille laide* (novel), Editions de l'Homme, 1962; *Si la bombe m'etait contee* (novel), Editions du Jour, 1962; *Le Grand Roman d'un petit homme* (novel), Editions du Jour, 1963; *Le Ru d'Ikoue* (prose poem), Fides, 1963, revised edition, 1977; *La Rose de Pierre: Histoires d'amour* (short stories), Editions du Jour, 1964; *Les Vendeurs du temple* (social satire), Editions de l'Homme, 1964.

Le Dompteur d'ours (social satire), Editions de l'Homme, 1965; *Les Temps du carcajou* (novel), Institut Litteraire du Quebec, 1965; *Le Dernier Rayon* (novel), Lidec, 1966; *L'Appelante* (novel), Editions du Jour, 1967; *Contes erotiques* (short stories), Ferron, 1968; *Kesten* (novel), Editions du Jour, 1968; *La Mort d'eau* (novel), Editions de l'Homme, 1968; *Le Marcheur: Piece en trois actes* (three-act play; produced in Montreal, 1950), Lemeac, 1968; *L'Ile introuvable: Nouvelles,* Editions du Jour, 1968; *Mahigan: Recit,* Lemeac, 1968; *Antoine et sa montagne* (novel), Editions du Jour, 1969; *L'Or de la felouque* (novel), Jeunesse, 1969; *Tayaout, Fils d'Agaguk,* Editions de l'Homme, 1969; *Textes et documents,* Lemeac, 1969; *Valerie,* Editions de l'Homme, 1969.

Fredange: Piece en deux actes (two-act play; includes "Les Terres neuves"), Lemeac, 1970; *Le Dernier Havre,* L'Actuelle, 1970; *La Passe-au-Crachin* (novel), Ferron, 1972; *Le Haut Pays* (novel), Ferron, 1973; *Moi, Pierre Huneau: Narration,* Hurtubise, 1976.

For children: *Alerte au camp 29,* Beauchemin, 1959; *La Revanche du Nascopie,* Beauchemin, 1959; *La Loi de l'Apache,* Beauchemin, 1960; *L'Homme de la Papinachois,* Beauchemin, 1960; *Le Roi de la Cote Nord: La Vie extraordinaire de Napoleon-Alexandre Comeau,* Editions de l'Homme, 1960; *La Montagne sacre,* Beauchemin, 1962; *Le Rapt du lac cache,* Beauchemin, 1962; *Nakika, le petit Algonquin,* Lemeac, 1962; *Avea, le petit Tramway,* Beauchemin, 1963; *Les Aventures de Ti-Jean,* Beauchemin, 1963; *Les Extravagances de Ti-Jean,* Beauchemin, 1963; *Maurice le moruceau,* Beauchemin, 1963; *Nauya, le petit esquimau,* Beauchemin, 1963; *Ti-Jean et le grand geant,* Beauchemin, 1963; *Zibou et Coucou,* Lemeac, 1964; *La Montagne Creuse,* Lidec, 1965; *Le Secret de Muffarti,* Lidec, 1965; *Le Chateau des petits hommes verts,* Lidec, 1966; *Les Dauphins de Monsieur Yu,* Lidec, 1966; *La Bete a 300 tetes,* Lidec, 1967; *Les Pieuvres,* Lidec, 1967; *Les Vampires de la rue Monsieur-le-Prince,* Lidec, 1968.

Also author of plays "Le Samaritain," 1952, and "Berengere ou la chair en feu," 1965.

Contributor to periodicals, including *Culture, Maclean's, Saturday Night, Nouveau Journal, Le Jour,* and *Revue de l'Universite Laval.*

SIDELIGHTS: Theriault is considered one of the leading French-Canadian writers of the twentieth century. The book that sealed his reputation was *Agaguk,* published in 1958. It gained him international recognition and has been translated into a number of languages, including German, Italian, Spanish, Japanese, and Portuguese.

Theriault explores a number of themes in his writings. Primitivism, exoticism, violence, and eroticism frequent his works, as do characters struggling against basic human passions and instincts or searching for self-identity. Several of his books, including *Les Vendeurs du temple* and *Le Dompteur d'ours,* are social satires. Theriault frequently involves oppressed groups in his works, examining the plights of immigrants, Jews, Eskimos, and Indians.*

*   *   *

THORNTON, Peter Kai 1925-

PERSONAL: Born April 8, 1925, in St. Albans, England; son of Sir Gerard (a microbiologist) and Gerda (Noerregaard) Thornton; married Mary Rosamund Helps (a bookbinder), August 22, 1950; children: Emma Bettina, Minna Thecla, Dora Frieda. *Education:* Attended De Havilland Aeronautical Technical School, 1943-45; Trinity Hall, Cambridge, degree in modern languages, 1950. *Home:* 15 Cheniston Gardens, London W.8, England. *Office:* Department of Furniture and Woodwork, Victoria and Albert Museum, London S.W.7, England.

CAREER: Fitzwilliam Museum, Cambridge, England, assistant keeper, 1950-52; National Art-Collections Fund, London, England, joint secretary, 1952-54; Victoria and Albert Museum, London, assistant keeper of textiles, 1954-62, assistant keeper of woodwork, 1962-66, keeper, 1966—. *Military service:* British Army, Intelligence Corps, 1945-48; served in Austria. *Member:* Society of Antiquaries (fellow).

WRITINGS: Baroque and Rococo Silks, Faber, 1965; (contributor) Helena Hayward, editor, *World Furniture,* Hamlyn, 1965; *Seventeenth-Century Interior Decoration,* Yale University Press, 1978; (with Maurice Tomlin) *The Furnishing and Decoration of Ham House,* History Society, 1980. Contributor to magazines, including *Burlington, Apollo, Antiques,* and *Connoisseur,* and *Times Literary Supplement.*

WORK IN PROGRESS: A book on the history of western interior decoration, 1620-1920; a contribution to a history of historic upholstery, publication by Boston Museum of Fine Arts expected in 1981.

SIDELIGHTS: Thornton commented: "I have been much

concerned with the restoration of historic interiors and country houses; I stress authenticity. I am engaged in conservation work, both technically and politically.''

BIOGRAPHICAL/CRITICAL SOURCES: Times Literary Supplement, January 9, 1981.

*   *   *

THUNDY, Zacharias Pontian 1936-
(Zacharias Pontian Thundyil)

PERSONAL: Original name Zacharias Pontian Thundyil, name legally changed in 1975; born September 28, 1936, in Changanacherry, India; came to the United States in 1964, naturalized citizen, 1975; son of Joseph Joseph and Mary Joseph (Palakunnel) Thundyil. *Education:* Pontificium Athenaeum, Poona, India, B.Ph. (cum laude), 1958, L.Ph. (cum laude), 1959, B.Th., 1961, S.T.L. (summa cum laude), 1963; DePaul University, M.A., 1966; University of Notre Dame, Ph.D., 1969. *Home:* 401 West Kaye, Marquette, Mich. 49855. *Office:* Department of English, Northern Michigan University, Marquette, Mich. 49855.

CAREER: Entered the Order of the Carmelites of Mary Immaculate, 1952, ordained Roman Catholic priest, 1963; Dharmaram College, Bangalore, India, instructor of philosophy, 1963-64; pastor of Roman Catholic churches in Chicago, Ill., 1964-65, and South Bend, Ind., 1965-68; Northern Michigan University, Marquette, assistant professor, 1968-72, associate professor, 1972-76, professor of English, 1976—. Member of American Studies Research Center.

MEMBER: International Society for the Comparative Study of Civilizations, International Arthurian Society, International Courtly Literature Society, North American Patristic Society, Modern Language Association of America, Linguistic Society of America, American Dialect Society, Modern Linguistic Society, Conference on Christianity and Literature, Mediaeval Academy of America, American Anthropological Association, American Ethnological Association, American Folklore Society, American Association of University Professors, American Comparative Literature Association, Dravidian Linguistics Association, Semiotic Society of America, Smithsonian Institution, Societe Rencesvals, Midwest Modern Language Association, Michigan Linguistic Society, Michigan Academy of Science, Arts, and Letters (founder of medieval studies section), Delta Tau Kappa (life member). *Awards, honors:* Senior fellow of American Institute of Indian Studies, 1974; fellow of Medieval Academy at Harvard University, summer, 1975; citation from Michigan Academy of Science, Arts, and Letters, 1976, for outstanding scholarship in State of Michigan; Fulbright-Hays fellow, 1978-79.

WRITINGS: (Under name Zacharias Pontian Thundyil) *Covenant in Anglo-Saxon Thought,* Macmillan, 1972; (editor with Robert Glenn and Stewart Kingsbury) *Language and Culture: A Book of Readings,* Northern Michigan University Press, 1975; (editor with Carol Scotton and Jane Hill) *Papers in Linguistics,* University of Michigan Press, 1977; (editor with Edward Vasta) *Chaucerian Problems and Perspectives,* University of Notre Dame Press, 1979; (editor with Ayyappa Panikkar) *Modern Malayalam Literature: An Anthology,* two volumes, Michigan State University Press, 1980; *South Indian Folktales of Kadar,* Folklore Institute, 1981; *The Origin and Religion of the Cheras and Cholas* (monograph), Dravidian Linguistics, 1982. Contributor of more than fifty articles to scholarly journals and popular magazines (until 1975 under name Zacharias Pontian Thundyil), including *Marian, Nature, Priest,* and *Thought,* and newspapers. Associate editor of *Journal of South Asian Literature.*

WORK IN PROGRESS: Editing, translating, and writing commentary for *Lamentations of Matheolus: A Fourteenth-Century Latin Anti-Feminist Work,* publication by University of Georgia Press, expected in 1983.

SIDELIGHTS: Thundy's languages include Malayalam, Tamil, Hindi, Kada, Kurumba, Cholanayikka, Sanskrit, German, French, Spanish, Old Norse, Latin, Greek, Hebrew, Aramaic, Old French, Chippewa Indian, Old English, Middle English, and Old High German. Recent research has taken him to England and western Europe, India and the Middle East, and Peru.

He wrote: ''My broad academic training in philosophy, religion, literature, and linguistics has helped me broaden my research interests. So much so, I can claim that I am classicist, medievalist, linguist, comparatist, and anthropologist. For me, to write is to explicate and to explicate is to connect. In my previous writings I have been able to connect ideas and realities that lie contiguously in a narrow space or live in a short span of time.

''In my current and future writings I am eager to make East meet West, North meet South, and Southeast meet Far East. First, the mythology and classical writings of ancient India are the best guide in understanding and explicating the myths and epics of the Greco-Roman world, since both cultures belong to the common Indo-European tradition; further, there is much in the Gospels of Christianity that can be better explained by a closer study of Buddhist-Hindu scriptures which were available to the early Christians through the ubiquitous Buddhist missionaries. Second, in my monograph on the ethnic and religious origins of the South Indian tribes, I show that the Cheras and Cholas of South India originally were Mundas—not Dravidians—who lived in the northwestern parts of India. Third, someday I would like to 'prove' that there is a 'Pacific connection' between some of the Indian tribes of South America and some of the tribes of South Asia, on the basis of linguistic and anthropological evidence.''

*   *   *

THUNDYIL, Zacharias Pontian
See THUNDY, Zacharias Pontian

*   *   *

TIBBLE, Anne 1912-1980
(Anne Northgrave)

OBITUARY NOTICE—See index for *CA* sketch: Born January 29, 1912, in Rounton, Yorkshire, England; died August 31, 1980. Literary critic, poet, and novelist best known for her autobiographical trilogy, *Greenhorn, One Woman's Story,* and *Alone.* Tibble, with her husband, J. W. Tibble, was instrumental in reviving the popularity of poet John Clare. Her writings include *John Clare: A Life, The Apple Reddens, The God Spigo,* and *African-English Literature: A Short Survey and Anthology of Prose and Poetry Up to 1965.* Obituaries and other sources: *London Times,* September 19, 1980.

*   *   *

TIMOTHY, Hamilton B(aird) 1913-

PERSONAL: Born April 13, 1913, in Irvine, Scotland. *Education:* University of Glasgow, M.A. (with distinction), 1934, B.D., 1941; University of London, B.A. (with honors), 1943; University of Edinburgh, Ph.D., 1958; University of Saskatchewan, Ph.D., 1974. *Home:* 18 McNiven Pl., Regina,

Saskatchewan, Canada S4S 3X2. *Office:* Philosophy/ Classics Department, University of Regina, Regina, Saskatchewan, Canada S4S 0A2.

CAREER: United College, Winnipeg, Manitoba, assistant professor of Near Eastern languages and literatures and lecturer in psychology of religion, 1958-63; University of Western Ontario, London, assistant professor, 1963-65, associate professor of classics, 1966-73; University of Utrecht, Utrecht, Netherlands, research assistant at Philosophy Institute, 1971-72; University of Regina, Regina, Saskatchewan, professor of humanities, 1973-80, associate dean of arts, 1973-75, acting chairman of religious studies program, 1975-77, lecturer in religious studies, 1975-80, emeritus professor of humanities, 1980—.

WRITINGS: Illustrated History of Wemyss Parish Church (*St. Mary's-by-the-Sea*), Dumfries & Galloway Standard Press, 1945; *One Increasing Purpose: The Galts and Their Contribution to the Making of Canada,* University of Western Ontario Press, 1968; (editor) *The Collected Poems of John Galt, 1779-1839,* privately printed, Volume I, 1969, Volume II, 1981; *The Early Christian Apologists and Greek Philosophy Exemplified by Irenaeus, Tertullian and Clement of Alexandria,* Van Gorcum, 1973; *The Tenets of Stoicism: Assembled and Systematized From the Works of L. Annaeus Seneca,* Adolph M. Hakkert, 1973; *The Galts, a Canadian Odyssey,* McClelland & Stewart, Volume I: *John Galt, 1779-1839,* 1977, Volume II: *Sir Alexander Tilloch Galt and Elliott Torrance Galt,* 1981. Contributor of articles, poems, cover designs, and reviews to journals and newspapers. Member of advisory editorial board of *Journal of Comparative Sociology and Religion,* 1979—.

WORK IN PROGRESS: Editing Marko Vovchok's *Ukrainian Folk Stories: A Selection* (translation into English by Nadiya Popil).

SIDELIGHTS: Timothy wrote: "My involvement with the Galts is a long story. It began with my paternal grandmother whose house I much frequented as a boy and who frequently, a propos of nothing in particular, remarked that she was 'related to John Galt.' Her saying so was beyond my comprehension at the time. It must have lodged, however, in my subconscious for it surfaced when, on my coming to Canada, I found myself amid the scenes of John Galt's enduring work as colonizer in western Ontario. My accidental meeting soon afterwards with his great-grandson in Winnipeg and with some of his present-day descendants in other parts of Canada led to their generous bestowal on me of much material relating to Galt family history of which my two-volume book on the Galts is the result."

*   *   *

TINKER, Ben (Hill) 1903-

PERSONAL: Born January 29, 1903, in Prescott, Ariz.; son of John George and Edna Grace (Hill) Tinker; married Violet Marie Martin, April 9, 1972. *Education:* Attended Columbia University and University of Arizona. *Politics:* Republican. *Religion:* Roman Catholic. *Home:* 1775 North Acacia Ave., Rialto, Calif. 92376.

CAREER: Writer. Worked as federal game guardian in Mexico, 1922-26; rancher in Sonora, Mexico, 1927—. Rancher in Tucson, Ariz., 1927-38, and Thermal, Calif., 1938-51.

WRITINGS: (Editor of reprint) George H. Tinker, *Arizona: A Land of Sunshine,* Arthur Clark, 1969; *Mexican Wilderness and Wildlife,* University of Texas Press, 1978. Author of column "Fish and Game" for *Tucson Daily Citizen,* 1927-

29. Contributor of more than two hundred fifty articles to magazines and newspapers, including *Outdoor Life, Gun World, Westways, Mexico This Month, Petersen's Hunting,* and *Western Out of Doors.*

WORK IN PROGRESS: The Trail; Baja California; Via con Dios (title means "Go With God"); *The Devil's Backbone; The Assassin.*

SIDELIGHTS: Tinker wrote: "I am motivated to record data concerning wildlife and wilderness in Mexico. The opportunity to observe the habits and habitats of the wildlife and study of the wilderness presented itself during the years I was a federal game guardian and engaged in cattle ranching in the Sierra Madres of northern Mexico.

"As a sportsman, I believe in promoting a sensible attitude toward the environment and conservation of wildlife.

"My major vocational interests are ranching and writing, including researching and developing data on historical events of the far west and Mexico. I have made personal hunting expeditions to Africa, Alaska, British Columbia, Mexico, and South America, and I speak Spanish, Papago Indian, and Yaqui Indian."

AVOCATIONAL INTERESTS: Music, the arts, outdoor life, hunting, trout fishing.

BIOGRAPHICAL/CRITICAL SOURCES: Tales of Nature's Wonderland, Scribner, 1924; *Status of the Pronghorn Antelope,* U.S. Government Printing Office, 1925; *Records of North American Big Game,* Derrydale Press, 1932; *Records of North American Big Game,* Scribner, 1939; *Auk,* January, 1940; *Palm Springs Desert Museum Annual,* 1952; *Flora and Fauna of Mexico,* University of California Press, 1965; *They Came to the Mountain,* Northland Press, 1976.

*   *   *

TISE, Larry Edward 1942-

PERSONAL: Born December 6, 1942, in Winston-Salem, N.C.; son of Russell Edward and Lena Irene (Norman) Tise; married, 1965; children: Larry Edward, Nicholas Allen. *Education:* Duke University, B.A., 1965, M.Div., 1968; University of North Carolina, Ph.D., 1974. *Religion:* Methodist. *Home:* 328 Wildwood Dr., Durham, N.C. 27712. *Office:* North Carolina Division of Archives and History, 109 East Jones St., Raleigh, N.C. 27611.

CAREER: John Fries Blair (publisher), Winston-Salem, N.C., part-time editor, 1969-71; University of North Carolina, Chapel Hill, instructor in history, 1972-73; North Carolina Bicentennial Committee, Raleigh, heritage coordinator and director of historical publications, 1973-74; North Carolina Division of Archives and History, Raleigh, assistant director, 1974-75, director and state historic preservation officer, 1975—. Chairman of U.S.S. Monitor Technical Advisory Committee and coordinator of research at Monitor Marine Sanctuary, 1976—; chairman of National Coordinating Committee for the Promotion of History's historic preservation task force and its North Carolina committee for the promotion of history, both 1977—; member of U.S. Advisory Council on Historic Preservation, 1979—. Secretary of North Carolina Historical Commission; corporate director of Friends of the North Carolina Archives, Historic Preservation Fund of North Carolina, Museum of History Associates, North Carolina Institute of Applied History, Stagville Center Corp., State Capitol Foundation, and Transportation History Corp. of North Carolina.

MEMBER: American Historical Association, Organization of American Historians, National Conference of State Historic Preservation Officers (president, 1979—), National Association of State Archives and Records Administrators (president, 1980—), American Association for State and Local History, Society of American Archivists, American Association of Museums, Association for Historians of the Early American Republic, Southern Historical Association, Federation of North Carolina Historical Societies, Historic Preservation Society of North Carolina, North Carolina Literary and Historical Association. *Awards, honors:* W.R. Davie Award from Society of Cincinnati, 1979, for *The Southern Experience in the American Revolution.*

WRITINGS: A House Not Made With Hands, Piedmont, 1966; *The Yadkin Melting Pot: Methodism and the Moravians in the Yadkin Valley, 1750-1850,* Henry Clay Press, 1968; *Building and Architecture in Winston-Salem History,* Historic Winston, 1976; *Winston-Salem in History: Government,* Historic Winston, 1976; *Winston-Salem in History: The Churches,* Historic Winston, 1976; *Winston-Salem in History: Publications,* Historic Winston, 1976; (with Manley Wade Wellman) *Winston-Salem in History: Education,* Historic Winston, 1976; (with Wellman) *Winston-Salem in History: A City's Culture,* Historic Winston, 1976; (with Wellman) *Winston-Salem in History: Industry and Commerce, 1766-1896,* Historic Winston, 1976; (with Jeffrey J. Crow) *The Southern Experience in the American Revolution,* University of North Carolina Press, 1978; *A Comprehensive Records Management Program for the United Methodist Church,* Commission on Archives and History, Lake Junaluska, N.C., 1978; (with Crow) *Writing North Carolina History,* University of North Carolina Press, 1979.

Contributor: *Three Forks of Muddy Creek,* Old Salem, Inc., 1976; O. Kelley Ingram, editor, *Methodism in North Carolina,* Duke University Press, 1976; *Plantation Society in the Americas,* University of New Orleans, 1979. General editor of "Winston-Salem in History," thirteen volumes, Historic Winston, 1976. Contributor to professional journals. Editor-in-chief of *North Carolina Historical Review* and *Carolina Comments,* both 1975—; member of editorial board of *Public Historian,* 1980—.

WORK IN PROGRESS: Proslavery Ideology, on the history of the defense of slavery in the United States, publication by University of North Carolina Press expected in 1982; editing *Travelers and Sojourners in North Carolina; The Philosophy and Practice of Public History,* essays, 1982.

SIDELIGHTS: Tise wrote: "I consider my career in religion, history, and public history administration to be one of seeking as concretely as possible to convert ideas, emotions, and insights into action, activity, project, program, and product. Midstream I also came into contact with material, and realized that materials are but three-dimensional expressions of man, and that those objects can bespeak the ideas, emotions, and insights of man. If I can, through writing on the one hand and programs to preserve and interpret documents, artifacts, buildings, and sites on the other hand, maintain the interplay of the abstract and the concrete, I will have felt successful. Perhaps that is why I spend my days prompting activities and establishing programs, my evenings writing and doing research, my nights thinking and feeling, and my weekends as a carpenter and cabinetmaker."

AVOCATIONAL INTERESTS: Carpentry and cabinetmaking, promoting canal preservation, collecting nineteenth-century American religious literature and antique American woodworking tools.

BIOGRAPHICAL/CRITICAL SOURCES: Raleigh News and Observer, September 2, 1979.

TOKAYER, Marvin 1936-

PERSONAL: Surname is pronounced Toe-*kay*-er; born September 4, 1936, in Brooklyn, N.Y.; son of Louis (a clerk) and Fanny (Rosenberger) Tokayer; married Mazal Ovadia, June 11, 1967; children: Shira, Amiel, Naama, Dan. *Education:* Yeshiva University, B.A., 1958, B.R.E., 1958; Jewish Theological Seminary of America, M.A., 1960, Rabbi, 1962. *Religion:* Jewish. *Home:* 425 West 44th St., Miami Beach, Fla. 33140.

CAREER: Rabbi in New York, N.Y., 1964-66, and in Great Neck, N.Y., 1966-68; Jewish Community of Japan, Tokyo, rabbi, 1968-76; Hebrew High School of Temple Israel, Great Neck, director, 1977-79; writer, 1979—. Instructor in classical Hebrew at Waseda University, Tokyo, 1969-70. Delegate to World Council of Religion and Peace, Kyoto, Japan, 1970; director of the Federation of Jewish Communities of Southeast Asia and the Far East, 1972-76; delegate to First Conference of Science and Religion, Kyoto, 1978. *Military service:* U.S. Air Force, 1962-64; became captain. *Member:* Asiatic Society, Japan Old Testament Society, Rabbinical Assembly. *Awards, honors:* Journalism award from U.S. Air Force, 1964, for chapel bulletin.

WRITINGS—In English: (With Mary Sagmaster Swartz) *The Fugu Plan: The Untold Story of the Japanese and the Jews During World War II,* Paddington, 1979, also published as *Desperate Voyagers,* Dell, 1980. Contributor of articles to *Encyclopedia Judaica.*

In Japanese: *Yudaya gosennen no chie,* Jitsu gyo no nippon, 1971; *Atama no tokun,* Jitsu gyo no nippon, 1972; *Yudaya hasso no kyoi,* Jitsu gyo no nippon, 1972; *Yudaya joku shu,* Jitsu gyo no nippon, 1973; *Yudaya kakugen shu,* Jitsu gyo no nippon, 1975; *Nihonginwa shinda,* Nisshin hodo, 1975; *Yudaya chie no hoseiki bako,* Sangyo noritsu tanki/Daigaku, 1975; *Nazo no kodaishi yudaya to nihon,* Sangyo noritsu tanki/Daigaku, 1975; *Nihon ni wa kyoiku gai nai,* Tokuma shoten, 1976; *Nihon kaimasenka,* Futabasha, 1976; *Nihonni mingshumingshugiwa nai,* Nisshin hodo, 1976; *Nihon byo ni tsuite,* Tokuma shoten, 1977; *Fugu keikak,* Brittanica Japan, 1979; *Yudaya shoseijitsu,* Tokuma shoten, 1980.

WORK IN PROGRESS: A book in Japanese, title means "Jewish Answers to Japanese Problems," publication expected in 1981; *Pepper, Silk, and Ivory: The Exotic Jews of the Far East,* publication expected in 1982; research on the sources of Jewish history in the Far East.

SIDELIGHTS: In 1968 Marvin Tokayer accepted an invitation to serve as rabbi to the Jewish Community of Japan. Shortly after his arrival he became curious about the history of Jews in Japan and about how they happened to settle in the Orient. One day a long-time resident supplied Tokayer with documents that revealed a Japanese plan to lure Jews to the Far East. The plan, which was recorded in multi-volume top-secret documents, had been devised between 1934 and 1940 by Japanese government officials and members of the military.

The goal of the plan was to fortify the Japanese empire and to enhance relations with America. By attracting millions of endangered Jews, whose technological expertise would aid in the development of Manchuria (a Japanese territory), it was argued that Japan would gain favor and possible financial support from the United States. The "fugu plan" was named for the Japanese blowfish that, though considered a delicacy, contains a poison center which must be carefully removed before being eaten. Proponents of the plan felt that it had to be activated with extreme caution lest it backfire and result in Jewish advancement at the expense of the Japanese.

Tokayer discovered that although the plan had been approved by the government, it had failed to achieve the results its creators had anticipated. This failure was due in part to the Japanese attack on Pearl Harbor, which crushed any hope of American financial support. Ultimately, however, several thousand Jews fled to Japan to avoid persecution by the Nazis. Tokayer interviewed some of those refugees while doing research for his book, *The Fugu Plan: The Untold Story of the Japanese and the Jews During World War II.* He also interviewed relatives of the fugu plan's original sponsors and several Japanese who had been involved in protecting the Jews. The book contains their account of this previously ''untold story.'' Raymond Sokolov, a writer for *New York Times Book Review,* praised Tokayer and co-author Mary Swartz for having written ''this wonderful saga . . . with the verve of a thriller.''

Tokayer told *CA:* ''My career as an author is a pure accident. While I was in Japan a book appeared, *The Japanese and the Jews,* which sold over one million copies. The author of the book posed as a Jew who was raised in Japan. In truth, the author was a Japanese who hid behind a Jewish mask. Many assumed that I was the author of the book and my name appeared in the Japanese press. Soon I was asked to write a book, for the Japanese, about the wisdom of the Talmud. To everyone's surprise, including my own, the book is now in its twenty-fourth printing and was the first of fifteen books so far in Japanese.

''My congregation in Japan was one of 'talking books' and I enjoyed listening to their unusual tales of life in the Orient. This led to *The Fugu Plan* and to my next book about untold and unknown tales of Jews in India, China, and Japan.''

BIOGRAPHICAL/CRITICAL SOURCES: New York Times, February 18, 1979, May 19, 1979; *Chicago Tribune,* July 10, 1979; *New York Times Book Review,* October 7, 1979.

* * *

TORREY, Norman Lewis 1894-1980

OBITUARY NOTICE—See index for *CA* sketch: Born November 6, 1894, in Newbury, Mass.; died December 12, 1980, in Peterborough, N.J. Educator, author, and authority on eighteenth-century French literature. A professor at Columbia University since 1937, Torrey was best known for his works on Voltaire and Diderot. His writings include *Voltaire and the English Deists, The Spirit of Voltaire, The Censoring of Diderot's Encyclopedia, Diderot Studies* and *The Age of Enlightenment.* Obituaries and other sources: *New York Times,* December 19, 1980.

* * *

TOTH, Robert Charles 1928-

PERSONAL: Born December 24, 1928, in Blakely, Pa.; son of John (a miner and painter) and Tillie (Szuch) Toth; married Paula Goldberg, April 12, 1954; children: Jessica, Jennifer, John. *Education:* Washington University, St. Louis, Mo., B.S., 1952; Columbia University, M.S., 1955; graduate study at Harvard University, 1960-61. *Home:* 21 Primrose St., Chevy Chase, Md. 20015. *Office:* 1875 Eye St. N.W., Washington, D.C. 20006.

CAREER/WRITINGS: U.S. Army, Picatinny, N.J., engineer in department of army ordnance, 1952-54; *Providence Journal,* Providence, R.I., reporter, 1955-57; *New York Herald Tribune,* New York City, science reporter, 1957-62;

New York Times, Washington, D.C., science reporter, 1962-63; *Los Angeles Times,* staff writer, 1963-65, bureau chief in London, England, 1965-70, diplomatic correspondent, 1970-71, White House correspondent, 1972-74, bureau chief in Moscow, U.S.S.R., 1974-77, staff writer in Washington, D.C., 1977—. Notable assignments include coverage of Arab-Israeli Six Day War, 1967, Soviet bloc invasion of Czechoslovakia, 1968, and dissident movement in Soviet Union, 1974-77. *Military service:* U.S. Marine Corps, 1946-48. *Awards, honors:* Pulitzer traveling scholar, 1955; Nieman fellow at Harvard University, 1960-61; Overseas Press Club award, 1977; Sigma Delta Chi award, 1977; George Polk Memorial Award from Long Island University, 1978, for foreign reporting; Columbia University Alumni award, 1978.

* * *

TRACY, James D. 1938-

PERSONAL: Born February 14, 1938, in St. Louis, Mo.; son of Leo W. (an accountant) and Marguerite (Meehan) Tracy; married Nancy Ann McBride, September 6, 1968; children: Patrick, Samuel, Mary Ann. *Education:* St. Louis University, B.A., 1959; Johns Hopkins University, M.A., 1960; University of Notre Dame, M.A., 1961; Princeton University, Ph.D., 1967. *Politics:* Democrat. *Religion:* Roman Catholic. *Home:* 934 Portland, St. Paul, Minn. 55104. *Office:* Department of History, University of Minnesota, Minneapolis, Minn. 55455.

CAREER: University of Michigan, Ann Arbor, instructor in history, 1964-66; University of Minnesota, Minneapolis, associate professor, 1966-77, professor of history, 1977—.

WRITINGS: Erasmus: The Growth of a Mind, Droz, 1972; *The Politics of Erasmus,* University of Toronto Press, 1979; *True Ocean Found,* University of Minnesota Press, 1980.

* * *

TRAER, James Frederick 1938-

PERSONAL: Born August 1, 1938, in Kalamazoo, Mich.; son of James K. (a business manager) and Effie J. Traer; married Maribeth Kay Esch (a registered nurse), January 28, 1964; children: Mary Christine, Anne Kathleen, Jeanne Ellen. *Education:* College of Wooster, B.A., 1960; University of Michigan, J.D., 1964, M.A., 1965, Ph.D., 1970. *Home:* 4083 Tipton Woods Dr., Adrian, Mich. 49221. *Office:* Adrian College, Adrian, Mich. 49221.

CAREER: Hamilton College, Clinton, N.Y., assistant professor, 1969-75, associate professor of history, 1975-79, associate dean of college, 1976-79; Adrian College, Adrian, Mich., vice-president of college and dean for academic affairs, 1979—. *Member:* American Historical Association, Society for French Historical Studies, American Society for Legal History, American Association of Academic Deans. *Awards, honors:* Fulbright fellowship, 1967-68; Margaret Bundy Scott fellow at Hamilton College, 1975-76; National Endowment for the Humanities grant, 1976.

WRITINGS: Marriage and the Family in Eighteenth-Century France, Cornell University Press, 1980. Contributor to history journals.

WORK IN PROGRESS Research on eighteenth-century French social, institutional, and legal history.

* * *

TRAVERS, Ben 1886-1980

OBITUARY NOTICE: Born November 12, 1886, in London,

England; died December 18, 1980, in London, England. Playwright, screenwriter, and author. A farceur compared to Ben Johnson, Travers was regarded as the twentieth century's master of stage farce. In 1922 he began to delight British audiences with his sometimes risque comedies about realistic, rational people reacting to absurd circumstances. After more than three decades, however, the author felt the audiences had changed and considered his career over, but in the 1970's he began once again to write new farces and revive old ones. In 1976, eighty-nine-year-old Travers enjoyed successful simultaneous runs of his most recent play and a 1928 revival. The author wrote more than twenty plays, thirty screenplays, five novels, and two autobiographies. Obituaries and other sources: Ben Travers, *Vale of Laughter*, Bles, 1957; *Who's Who in Theatre*, 16th edition, Pitman, 1977; Travers, *A-sitting on a Gate*, W. H. Allen, 1978; *The Writers Directory, 1980-82*, St. Martin's, 1979; *London Times*, December 19, 1980; *New York Times*, December 19, 1980; *Time*, December 29, 1980.

* * *

TRUSS, Jan 1925-

PERSONAL: Born May 3, 1925, in Stoke-on-Trent, England; daughter of William Edwin (a hawker, storekeeper, and poet) and Catherine (a storekeeper; maiden name, Spragg) Degg; married Donald Truss (an educator), July 6, 1946; children: Martin, Sally. *Education:* Goldsmiths' College, London, teacher's certificate, 1945; University of Alberta, B.Ed., 1961; graduate study at University of Calgary, 1965-68. *Politics:* "Socialist leanings." *Religion:* "Open." *Home address:* Water Valley, Alberta, Canada T0M 2E0. *Agent:* Bella Pomer Agency, 9 Ardmore Rd., Toronto, Ontario, Canada M5P 1V4.

CAREER: Teacher in schools in Midlands and southern England, 1945-57; teacher and administrator in schools in southern Alberta, 1957-64; art consultant to Alberta school system, 1964-65; University of Calgary, Calgary, Alberta, lecturer in drama, creative writing, art, and education, 1968-69 and 1975-78; reviewer of books, theatre, and music for Canadian Broadcasting Corp. (CBC), 1973-76; writer, 1978—. *Member:* Writers Union of Canada, Canadian Association of Writers and Illustrators for Children, Association of Canadian Radio and Television Artists, Guild of Canadian Playwrights, Playwrights Canada, Writers' Guild of Alberta. *Awards, honors:* First winner of Alberta Find a New Novelist Contest sponsored by government of Alberta, 1974, for *Bird at the Window*.

WRITINGS: Bird at the Window (novel), Macmillan, 1974, Harper, 1980; *A Very Small Rebellion* (juvenile novel), J. M. Lebel, 1977; *Oomerahgi Oh! and A Very Small Rebellion* (juvenile; contains "Oomerahgi Oh!," a one-act play, first produced in Calgary, Alberta, at University of Calgary, 1974; and "A Very Small Rebellion," a one-act play, first produced in Calgary at Alberta Theatre Projects, 1975), Playwrights Canada, 1978; *The Judgment of Clifford Sifton* (juvenile; one-act play; first produced in Calgary at Alberta Theatre Projects, 1978), Playwrights Canada, 1978. Author of several short stories broadcast by CBC and British Broadcasting Corp. (BBC). Contributor of articles and stories to education journals and popular magazines, including *Chatelaine*, *Woman*, and *Darling*.

WORK IN PROGRESS: The True Story of Jasmin Marie Antoinette Stalke, a juvenile novel, publication by Atheneum expected in 1981; a "middle-aged novel"; libretto for "Silver City," a chamber opera.

SIDELIGHTS: Jan Truss commented: "I came to writing when I thought I was a finished, burned-out teacher of forty-five. Teaching was a joy and a passion. In despair, my children grown and gone, the house deliciously empty, I taught myself to type and started selling stories about being an immigrant and about education. I was encouraged by a series of small successes to go on writing, but I still regard myself as an apprentice writer."

BIOGRAPHICAL/CRITICAL SOURCES: In Review (Ontario Ministry of Culture), June, 1980.

* * *

TUCKER, Anne 1945-

PERSONAL: Born October 18, 1945, in Baton Rouge, La.; daughter of Robert B. and Geraldine (Wilkes) Tucker. *Education:* Randolph-Macon Woman's College, B.A., 1967; Rochester Institute of Technology, A.A.S., 1968; State University of New York at Buffalo, M.F.A., 1972. *Home:* 4118 Bellfontaine St., Houston, Tex. 77025. *Agent:* Helen Merrill, 337 West 22nd St., New York, N.Y. 10011.

CAREER: International Museum of Photography, Rochester, N.Y., research assistant, 1968-70; Museum of Modern Art, New York City, curatorial intern in department of photography, 1970-71; Creative Artists Public Service Program, New York City, photography consultant, 1971-72; Cooper Union Forum, New York City, director of photography lecture series, 1973-75; Museum of Fine Arts, Houston, Tex., curator of photography, 1976—. Visiting lecturer at New School for Social Research, spring, 1973, and Philadelphia College of Art, 1973-75; affiliate artist at University of Houston, 1976-79. Director of photographic exhibitions; lecturer at museums, schools, and workshops. *Member:* Society for Photographic Education (member of national board of directors, 1976-80), College Art Association of America.

WRITINGS: (With William Burback) *Walker Evans: Photographs* (bibliography), Museum of Modern Art, 1971; (editor and author of introduction) *The Woman's Eye*, Knopf, 1973; (editor) *Suzanne Bloom and Ed Hill (Manual): Research and Collaboration*, Seashore Press, 1980; *The Photo-League, 1936-1951*, Knopf, 1981. Contributor to magazines, including *Afterimage, Ms.*, and *Harvard Advocate*. Editor of *Camera*, February, 1972.

SIDELIGHTS: Anne Tucker wrote: "My primary interest is twentieth-century American art, specifically photography. I am focusing on areas previously neglected and unrecognized and prefer to view them in the full context of their time: cultural, political, social."

* * *

TURKLE, Sherry 1948-

PERSONAL: Born June 18, 1948, in New York, N.Y.; daughter of Milton and Harriet (Bonowitz) Turkle; *Education:* Harvard University, A.B., 1970, M.A., 1973, Ph.D., 1976. *Office:* Program in Science, Technology, and Society, Massachusetts Institute of Technology, Room 20D-212, Cambridge, Mass. 02139.

CAREER: Harvard University, Cambridge, Mass., clinical intern in psychology at University Health Services, 1974-75; Massachusetts Institute of Technology, Cambridge, assistant professor, 1976-80, associate professor of sociology, 1980—. *Member:* American Psychological Association, American Sociological Association, American Association for the Advancement of Science. *Awards, honors:* Rockefeller Foundation fellowship, 1980; Guggenheim fellowship, 1981.

WRITINGS: (Contributor) Barbara Meyerhoff and Sally Moore, editors, *Symbol and Politics in Communal Ideology: Cases and Questions,* Cornell University Press, 1976; (contributor) Alan Roland, editor, *Psychoanalysis, Creativity, and Literature: A French-American Inquiry,* Columbia University Press, 1978; *Psychoanalytic Politics: Freud's French Revolution,* Basic Books, 1978; (contributor) David Ingleby, editor, *Critical Psychiatry,* Pantheon, 1980.

WORK IN PROGRESS: *Computers-to-Think-With* (tentative title), on the impact of the computer presence on values and modes of perception.

SIDELIGHTS: Sherry Turkle told *CA:* "I study the sociology of sciences of mind, a study of interactions among technical, literary, and popular discourses about the self as they develop in specific social contexts. In *Psychoanalytic Politics* I looked at the recent growth of a structuralist and politicized French psychoanalytic movement. Until the 1960's psychoanalysis was marginal to French medicine and psychiatry as well as to the dominant French intellectual culture. I studied the process by which this changed, leading to an 'infatuation with Freud' in intellectual and popular circles in the aftermath of the May-June, 1968, events. In doing so I had the opportunity to see how a set of technical ideas (in this case ideas borrowed from the writings of French psychoanalyst Jacques Lacan) were taken up as powerful metaphors by a non-technical public and used as building blocks in a discourse about politics, about education, and about the self, that is, as building blocks in the development of a psychoanalytic culture. These ideas took many shapes as they became integrated into advice-to-the-lovelorn columns as well as into academic theories of psychology. Living in a psychoanalytic culture meant that a language rich in terms like 'repression,' 'the unconscious,' and 'the Oedipus complex' made a difference to the ways in which many people thought about their problems, their pasts, and their possibilities for change, even for people who didn't 'believe in' psychoanalysis.

"My work on computation begins with the premise that we live in a nascent computer culture that will exert an analogous influence on the way we think. What I have found in my investigations of people who are currently involved with computation is that computers and a discourse about them are implicated in their ways of thinking about many other things, among these politics, religion, psychology, and education. There is good reason to believe that computational metaphors for thinking about the world and the self will not remain the province of the experts. There is a rapid spread of computational ideas into everyday language; there is the appropriation of information processing models in psychology as well as in behavioral and social sciences. And just as psychoanalytic ideas became culturally embedded through their embodiment in therapeutic practice, computational ideas are growing their own roots in education. My forthcoming book on computation looks at computers as carriers of culture, as objects that give rise to new metaphors, to new relationships between people and machines, between different people, and most significantly between people and their ways of thinking about themselves."

*   *   *

TVARDOVSKY, Alexandr Trifonovich   1910-1971

PERSONAL: Born June 21, 1910, in Zagorye, Russia (now U.S.S.R.); died of a stroke, December 18, 1971, in Krasnaya Pakhra, U.S.S.R.; son of Trifon Gordeyevich Tvardovsky (a blacksmith); married; children: one daughter. *Education:*

Moscow Institute of History, Philosophy, and Literature, graduated, 1939.

CAREER: Poet. Chief editor of *Novy Mir* ("New World") in U.S.S.R., 1950-54 and 1958-70. Member of Communist party, 1940-71, member of Central Committee, 1963-66. *Military service:* Russian Army, beginning in 1939; served in Belorussian campaign and as war correspondent. *Awards, honors:* Three Stalin Prizes, including 1941, for *Strana Muraviia,* and 1946, for *Vasily Tyorkin;* Order of Lenin Prizes, 1961, for *Za dalyu dal,* 1967, and 1971; Order of the Red Banner, 1970, for "services in the development of Soviet poetry."

WRITINGS—In English translation: *Pechniki,* Sovetskaia Rossiia, 1959, translation by R. Daglish published as *The Stovemakers; Terkin na tom svete,* [U.S.S.R.], 1963, translation by Leo Gruliow published as *Tyorkin in the Other World; Tyorkin and the Stovemakers: Poetry and Prose,* translated by Anthony Rudolf from the original Russian, Carcanet Press, 1974; *Vassili Tyorkin: A Book About a Soldier,* text in Russian and English, translated by Alex Miller from the original Russian, Progress (Moscow, U.S.S.R.), 1975.

In Russian; all published in U.S.S.R.: *Put k sotsializmu* (title means "The Path to Socialism"), 1931; *Dnevnik predsedateliya kolkhoza,* 1932; *Sbornik stikhov, 1930-1935,* 1935; *Strana Muraviia* (title means "The Land of Muravia"), 1936; *Doroga,* 1938; *Sel'skaya khronika,* 1939; *Izbrannye stikhi,* 1941; *Zagor'e,* 1941; *Vasilli Terkin: Kniga pro boitsa,* 1944; *Dom u dorogi* (title means "The House by the Roadside"), 1946; *Izbrannye stikhotvoreniia i poemy,* 1947; *Rodina i chuzhbina,* 1947; *Kniga liriki,* 1949; *O sebe* (autobiography; title means "On Myself"), 1949.

Izbrannoe, 1950; *Antologiia belorusskol poezil,* 1952; *Poslevoennye stikhi,* 1952; *Kak byl napisan "Vasilli Terkin,"* 1952; *Za dalyu dal* (poems; title means "Horizons Beyond Horizons"), 1953; *Poemy,* 1957; *Izbrannaia lirika,* 1958; *Stat'i i zametki o literature,* 1961; *Stikhi iz zapisnoi knizhki,* Molodaia gvardiia, 1961; *Aleksandr Tvardovskii,* 1964; *Lirika,* Molodaia gvardiia, 1964; *Lenin i pechnik,* 1966; *Sobranie sochinenii,* five volumes, 1966-71; *Iz liriki etikh let, 1959-1967,* 1967; *Poeziia Mikhaila Isakovskogo,* 1969; *Pisateli sovetskoi rossil,* c. 1971; *O samom glavnom,* 1974; *Proza, stat'i pis'ma,* Izvestiia, 1974.

SIDELIGHTS: In Russia, Alexandr Tvardovsky was regarded primarily as a gifted poet. He was also, however, the chief editor for more than fifteen years of the Soviet periodical *Novy Mir* ("New World"), a fact the Soviets chose to ignore. The reason behind this was that he published in *Novy Mir* controversial works of numerous writers, including those of Alexander Solzhenitsyn, and voiced his opposition to the views of the ultra-conservative literary establishment. Tvardovsky's first dismissal from the publication came in 1954 after four years of service. He was reinstated in 1958 and edited the periodical for twelve more years until 1970 when he was again forced to resign his post. Ironically, in that same year he was awarded the prestigious Order of the Red Banner for his "services in the development of Soviet poetry."

BIOGRAPHICAL/CRITICAL SOURCES: *Newsweek,* January 16, 1967, August 25, 1969, March 2, 1970, January 3, 1972; *New York Times,* January 19, 1970; *Time,* March 2, 1970; *Nation,* September 21, 1970; *Christian Science Monitor,* August 1, 1971; *Times Literary Supplement,* August 30, 1974; *Poetry,* November, 1976.

OBITUARIES: *Detroit News,* December 19, 1971; *New York*

Times, December 19, 1971; *Washington Post,* December 19, 1971; *London Times,* December 20, 1971; *Newsweek,* December 27, 1971; *AB Bookman's Weekly,* January 17, 1972.*

*   *   *

TWINAME, Eric   1942(?)-1980

OBITUARY NOTICE: Born c. 1942 in England; died October 14, 1980. Sailboat racer and writer. Twiname was a champion team and solo sailboat racer, as well as a contributor of innovative ideas to the yachting world. He served as an adviser to the British racing team at the Olympic Games in 1976. His three widely read books on sailing, *Dinghy Team Racing, Start to Win,* and *The Rules Book,* have become standard works in their field and are valued as fresh and effective guides. Obituaries and other sources: *London Times,* October 23, 1980.

U

UDEN, (Bernard Gilbert) Grant 1910-

PERSONAL: Born June 17, 1910, in Kent, England; children: two daughters.

CAREER: Writer. Teacher at Alwick Castle, Northumberland, England; lecturer and school inspector. *Awards, honors:* Kate Greenaway Medal from British Library Association, 1968, notable book award from American Library Association, 1969, Children's Spring Book Festival Award runner-up from *Book World,* 1969, and Carnegie Medal runner-up, all for *A Dictionary of Chivalry.*

WRITINGS: Strange Reading, George Newnes, 1936; *Farm History,* Methuen, 1946; *The Fighting Temeraire,* Basil Blackwell, 1961; *Life-Boats: A Survey of Their History and Present State of Development,* Basil Blackwell, 1962; *Collector's Casebook,* Constable, 1963.

The Knight and the Merchant, Faber, 1965, Roy, 1966; (compiler) *They Looked Like This: An Assembly of Authentic Word-Portraits of Men and Women in English History and Literature Over 1900 Years,* Basil Blackwell, 1965, Barnes & Noble, 1966; (compiler with Avril J. Pedley) *They Looked Like This: An Assembly of Authentic Word-Portraits of Men and Women in European History, Art and Literature Over 1900 Years,* Basil Blackwell, 1966, Barnes & Noble, 1967; (compiler) *Anecdotes from History: Being a Collection of 1000 Anecdotes, Epigrams, and Episodes Illustrative of English and World History,* Barnes & Noble, 1968; *A Dictionary of Chivalry* (juvenile), Longman Young, 1968, Crowell, 1969; *I, John Froissart* (juvenile), Longman Young, 1968, published as *Hero Tales From the Age of Chivalry,* World Publishing, 1969; *British Ships and Seamen,* Macmillan Volume I: *The Ships,* 1969, Volume II: *Naval Art and Science,* 1969; *Drake at Cadiz,* Macdonald & Co., 1969.

The Loss of the "Royal George," Macdonald & Co., 1970; *High Horses,* Kestrel Books, 1976; (editor) *Longman Illustrated Companion to World History,* Kestrel Books, 1977; (with Roy Yglesias) *Cabbages and Kings: A Book of Incidental History,* Kestrel Books, 1978; (with Richard Cooper) *A Dictionary of British Ships and Seamen,* Allen Lane, 1981.

SIDELIGHTS: Uden's *They Looked Like This* contains nearly four hundred verbal portraits of medieval characters. He describes the dress and, to a large extent, the personal habits of such personalities as kings and queens, musicians, artists, and highwaymen.

A book of the same order, *A Dictionary of Chivalry,* was highly commended. The volume reveals the world of English knighthood and chivalry, presenting definitions and descriptions of battles, different types of armor, buildings, books, sporting terms, and the dominant ideas of the times. Quotes from early documents and ballads are also included.

AVOCATIONAL INTERESTS: Collecting first editions, historical documents, letters, and pictures.

BIOGRAPHICAL/CRITICAL SOURCES: Times Literary Supplement, January 19, 1967, June 6, 1968, March 13, 1981; *Growing Point,* March, 1978.*

* * *

ULLMANN, Liv 1939-

PERSONAL: Born December 16, 1939, in Tokyo, Japan; Norwegian citizen; daughter of Viggo (an aircraft engineer) and Janna (Lund) Ullmann; married Gappe Stang (a psychiatrist), 1960 (divorced c. 1965); lived with Ingmar Bergman (a writer and director of stage productions and motion pictures), c. 1965-70; children: Linn. *Education:* Educated in Norway and England. *Religion:* Lutheran. *Home:* Drammensviens 91, Oslo, Norway. *Agent:* The Lantz Office, 114 East 55th St., New York, N.Y. 10022.

CAREER: Actress in stage productions, including "The Diary of Anne Frank," 1956, "A Doll's House," 1974, and "La Voix humane," 1978; and motion pictures, including "Persona," 1966, "The Passion of Anna," 1969, "Cries and Whispers," 1972, and "Autumn Sonata," 1978. Member of board of directors of International Rescue Committee; goodwill ambassador for United Nations International Children's Emergency Fund (UNICEF). *Awards, honors:* Best actress award from National Society of Film Critics, 1969, for "Hour of the Wolf," and 1970, for "Shame"; best actress award from New York Film Critics Circle, 1973, for "Cries and Whispers"; Golden Globe Award for best actress from Hollywood Foreign Press Association, and nomination for Academy Award for best actress from Academy of Motion Picture Arts and Sciences, both 1973, both for "The Emigrants"; nomination for Academy Award for best actress, 1977, for "Face to Face"; and numerous other awards.

WRITINGS: Changing (autobiography), Knopf, 1977.

SIDELIGHTS: Ullmann is probably best known for her performances under the direction of Swedish filmmaker Ingmar Bergman in films such as "Persona," "Hour of the Wolf," and "Cries and Whispers." Aside from appearing in a handful of Norwegian films during the early 1960's, Ullmann had devoted most of her acting career to portraying characters in the classic Scandinavian plays of Strindberg and Ibsen. But in 1965, a chance meeting with Ingmar Bergman while strolling with fellow actress Bibi Anderson ended with the famed director offering Ullmann a part in his next film. "I blushed terribly," she recalled, "and I was a little bit disappointed, too, because . . . that was too much like a book."

Bergman eventually contacted Ullmann and convinced her to appear with Anderson in his film "Persona." It concerns two women: Elizabeth, an actress whose sudden attack of stage fright has driven her into a self-imposed silence; and Alma, a talkative nurse whose attempts to spark a friendship with Elizabeth precipitate her own emotional destruction. Despite the fact that Ullmann, as Elizabeth, uttered only one word—"nothing"—in the film, she was hailed by impressed viewers as one of the most exciting actresses of recent years. Critics also praised Bergman's artistic triumph and applauded him for breaking free of the theological obsessions that plagued him during the early 1960's.

For Ullmann, Bergman's direction provided new insight into her craft. "It was the first time I met a film director who let me unveil feelings and thoughts no one else had recognized," she noted. "A director who listened patiently . . . , and who understood everything I was trying to express. A genius who created an atmosphere in which everything could happen—even that which I had not known myself."

"Persona" proved only the first in a series of films by Bergman that showcased Ullmann's talents. In 1967 she appeared in "Hour of the Wolf," a surreal voyage into the psyche of a hallucinatory artist as narrated by his similarly afflicted wife. Though some critics contested the film's coherence, they seemed unanimous in their praise of Ullmann's performance. "Hour of the Wolf" was quickly followed by "Shame," in which Ullmann played a musician who, together with her overly sensitive husband, reveals the often repugnant behavior that people resort to during wartime.

After her performance in two more films by Bergman, "The Passion of Anna" and "Cries and Whispers," Ullmann arrived in Hollywood in 1973 to expand her career and become an actress of international reknown. Unfortunately, her first two films, "Lost Horizon" and "40 Carats" were both critical and commercial disappointments. In "Lost Horizon," Ullmann was miscast as a schoolteacher in a role that called for singing and dancing. She was likewise misused in "40 Carats," a romantic comedy in which Ullmann played a divorcee pursuing a younger man.

Despite her initial American film failures, Ullmann's reputation remained intact due to powerful performances in Jan Troell's "The Emigrants" and its sequel, "The New Land." "The Emigrants" had sparked much of the initial interest in Ullmann from American producers. Its relentlessly realistic documentation of the struggles experienced by immigrant Swedes in America during the nineteenth century also proved moderately successful at American box-offices. Hollywood film moguls determined after the debacles of "Lost Horizon" and "40 Carats" to reunite Ullmann with Troell in "Zandy's Bride," a film about a mail-order bride that sought to duplicate the success of "The Emigrants" while broadening Ullmann's commercial appeal. However, most critics found the film inferior to "The Emigrants," and audiences largely ignored it.

Ullmann continued to excel in Bergman's films, though, throughout the 1970's. Her portrayal of a suicidal psychiatrist in "Face to Face" earned her an Academy Award nomination. Her next collaboration with Bergman, "The Serpent's Egg," was deemed by reviewers as an inferior enterprise for all concerned, but she recouped critical favor with "Autumn Sonata." That film featured Ullmann as a housewife who takes in her mother, a concert pianist, following the death of the mother's lover. The rigid affection exuded by the daughter eventually turns into ranting hysteria in one fateful evening during which she confronts her mother with her parental failings.

Throughout the late 1970's, Ullmann has also distinguished herself on the American stage. She repeated her highly regarded role of Nora in Henrik Ibsen's "A Doll's House," played the title character in "Anna Christie," and performed in Jean Cocteau's one-character play "The Human Voice." In another attempt to broaden her talents, Ullmann also appeared in the Broadway musical "I Remember Mama." But despite accolades, she has managed to keep her career in perspective. "All the time I am trying to change myself," she wrote in *Changing*. "For I do know that there is much more than the things I have been near. I would like to be on the way toward this. To find peace, so that I can sit and listen to what is inside me without influence."

BIOGRAPHICAL/CRITICAL SOURCES: Time, January 10, 1969, December 4, 1972; *Vogue*, February, 1973; *New York Times Magazine*, December 22, 1974; *Newsweek*, February 17, 1975; March 17, 1975; January 29, 1979; *Redbook*, September, 1975, August, 1977; *Parents' Magazine*, August, 1976; Liv Ullmann, *Changing*, Knopf, 1977; *Ms.*, March, 1977; *Ladies' Home Journal*, April, 1977.*

—*Sketch by Les Stone*

*   *   *

UNDERWOOD, Miles
See GLASSCO, John

*   *   *

URBANSKI, Marie M. Olesen   1922-

PERSONAL: Born March 12, 1922, in Pittsburgh, Pa.; daughter of Charles W. (an engineer) and Esther (Mitchell) Olesen; married Edmund Stephen Urbanski, 1952 (divorced, 1965); children: Jane Robbins, Wanda Urbanska. *Education:* University of Texas, B.A., 1944; Western Illinois University, M.A., 1963; University of Kentucky, Ph.D., 1973. *Home:* 17 Oak St., Orono, Me. 04473. *Office:* Department of English, University of Maine, 304 E-M., Orono, Me. 04469.

CAREER: University of Kentucky, Lexington, lecturer, 1965-71; University of Maine at Orono, assistant professor, 1974-77, associate professor of American literature, 1977—. *Member:* Phi Kappa Phi.

WRITINGS: Margaret Fuller's "Woman in the Nineteenth Century," Greenwood Press, 1980. Editor of *Thoreau Journal Quarterly.*

WORK IN PROGRESS: Research on Joyce Carol Oates, Anna Jameson, Margaret Fuller, and Henry David Thoreau.

SIDELIGHTS: In *Margaret Fuller's "Woman in the Nineteenth Century,"* Urbanski reevaluates criticism of Fuller and her work and offers her view to counter previous misrepresentations.

*   *   *

UREY, Harold C(layton)   1893-1981

OBITUARY NOTICE: Born April 29, 1893, in Walkerton, Ind.; died of a heart ailment, January 6, 1981, in La Jolla,

Calif. Physical chemist, educator, and writer. Urey's 1931 discovery of deuterium, or heavy hydrogen, was the first highlight in a long and fruitful career as a researcher and academician. For that discovery he was awarded the Nobel Prize for chemistry in 1934. His work with the separation of isotopes aided in making the first atomic bomb, which Urey also contributed to as a member of the War Research Atomic Bomb Project. With a colleague, Urey developed a model of primordial earth, which proposed that lightning striking a chemical "soup" formed the basic molecules of life. As a consultant with the National Aeronautics and Space Administration on the Apollo and Viking missions, Urey was a foremost lunar geologist. Honored many times over, Urey spoke out often on the dangers of atomic weapons and nuclear energy. He contributed to numerous magazines and journals, and authored or edited several books, including *The Planets*. Obituaries and other sources: *Current Biography*, Wilson, 1960; Shirley Thomas, *Men of Space*, Volume 6, Chilton, 1963; *The International Who's Who*, Europa, 1979; *American Men and Women of Science*, 14th edition, Bowker, 1979; *London Times*, January 7, 1981; *Washington Post*, January 7, 1981; *Newsweek*, January 19, 1981; *Time*, January 19, 1981.

*   *   *

URVATER, Michele 1946-

PERSONAL: Surname is pronounced *Er*-vah-ter; born March 23, 1946, in New York; daughter of Philip (a diamond dealer) and Judith (Dimenstein) Urvater; married Michael F. Cook (an elementary school teacher), September 5, 1974. *Education:* Barnard College, B.A., 1967; Columbia University, M.L.S., 1969. *Home and office:* 200 West 86th St., New York, N.Y. 10024.

CAREER: Bank Street College of Education, New York, N.Y., reference librarian, 1971-76; worked as cooking teacher and executive chef, 1976-79; writer and restaurant consultant, 1979—. *Member:* International Association of Cooking Schools, Les Dames d'Escoffier.

WRITINGS: (With David Liederman) *Cooking the Nouvelle Cuisine in America*, Workman Publishing, 1979; *Christmas Cookies and Candles*, Potpourri Press, 1981; *Fresh Food: Quick and Easy*, Irena Chalmers Cookbooks, 1981. Contributor to magazines and newspapers, including *Bon Appetit*, *Cook's*, and *Cuisine*.

SIDELIGHTS: Michele Urvater told *CA:* "I wrote my book in order to clarify misconceptions about the *nouvelle cuisine*, which has been misinterpreted as a diet cuisine. I also wanted to write recipes Americans could really use. Food and cooking have always been great passions of mine. Writing about these is one way of teaching a large group of people.

"In the next few years I intend to focus my energies and writing on glamorizing nutritious and healthful foods and menus. Americans have an enormous amount to learn about taste, nutrition, and eating well. I want to combine the esthetics and imagination of nouvelle cuisine with sound principles of nutrition. This does not mean dietetic food; it means simply good food, imaginatively and beautifully prepared."

BIOGRAPHICAL/CRITICAL SOURCES: New York Post, January, 1979; *Bon Appetit*, March, 1979; *House and Garden*, April, 1979.

*   *   *

USSHER, (Percival) Arland 1899-1980

OBITUARY NOTICE—See index for *CA* sketch: Born September 9, 1899, in London, England; died December 24, 1980, in Dublin, Ireland. Author and critic. Ussher was considered "Ireland's grand old man of letters." He was awarded the Gregory Medal of the Academy of Letters. His writings include *The Midnight Court, The Twilight of Ideas, Three Great Irishmen, The Magic People*, and *The Juggler*. Obituaries and other sources: *London Times*, December 31, 1980.

V

VAIRO, Philip Dominic 1933-

PERSONAL: Born August 4, 1933, in New York, N.Y.; son of Nicola and Rosana (Contino) Vairo; married Lillian Escalante, June 28, 1958; children: Mary E., Bonnie R. *Education:* Hunter College (now of the City University of New York), B.A., 1955; New York University, M.A., 1958; Duke University, Ed.D., 1963. *Home:* 2041 Carolwood Dr., Arcadia, Calif. 91006. *Office:* College of Education, California State University, Los Angeles, Calif. 90032.

CAREER: Social studies teacher, department chairman, and educational counselor at public schools in New York City, 1957-61; North Carolina Board of Higher Education, Raleigh, research associate, 1962-63; Hunter College of the City University of New York, New York City, instructor in education, 1963-64; University of North Carolina, Charlotte, associate professor of education and chairman of department, 1964-67; Fordham University, New York City, associate professor of education and chairman of Division of Curriculum and Teaching, 1967-69; University of Tennessee, Chattanooga, professor of education and dean of professional studies, 1969-73; California State University, Los Angeles, professor of education and dean of College of Education, 1973—. Visiting professor at St. Lawrence University, summer, 1961, College of New Rochelle, summer, 1968, Southern Illinois University, summer, 1968, and Rollins College, summer, 1969. *Military service:* U.S. Naval Reserve, active duty, 1955-57. *Member:* National Education Association, American Association of University Professors, Kappa Delta Pi.

WRITINGS: How to Teach Disadvantaged Youth, McKay, 1969; *Urban Education: Problems and Prospects,* McKay, 1969; *Urban Education: Opportunity or Crisis?,* Scarecrow, 1972; *Learning and Teaching in the Elementary School,* Scarecrow, 1973. Contributor to education journals.

*   *   *

VALLANCE, Elizabeth (Mary) 1945-

PERSONAL: Born April 8, 1945, in Glasgow, Scotland; daughter of William Henderson (an engineer) and Jean (Kirkwood) McGonnigill; married Iain David Thomas Vallance (a finance director), May 8, 1967; children: Rachel Emma, Edmund William Thomas. *Education:* University of St. Andrews, M.A. (with first class honors), 1967; London School of Economics and Political Science, London, M.Sc.

(with distinction), 1968; Queen Mary College, London, Ph.D., 1978. *Office:* Department of Political Studies, Queen Mary College, University of London, Mile End Rd., London E1 4NS, England.

CAREER: University of London, Queen Mary College, London, England, assistant lecturer in politics, 1968-70, lecturer in government and political studies, 1971-79, senior lecturer in government and political studies, 1980—. Governor of London Grammar School. Member of National Committee for Electoral Reform. *Member:* Political Studies Association of the United Kingdom, Association of University Teachers. *Awards, honors:* Leverhulme fellowship, 1977-78.

WRITINGS: (Contributor) R. J. Benewick and T. A. Smith, editors, *Direct Action and Democratic Politics,* Allen & Unwin, 1972; (editor and contributor) *The State, Society, and Self-Destruction,* Allen & Unwin, 1975; *Women in the House: A Study of Women Members of Parliament,* Humanities, 1979. Contributor of more than a dozen articles and many reviews to academic journals and newspapers.

WORK IN PROGRESS: A biographical study of early women members of Parliament, publication expected in 1982.

SIDELIGHTS: Elizabeth Vallance wrote: "Although much of my writing has been professionally inspired, I enjoy writing in an *ad hominem* way as much as in a formal style. My forays into journalism are therefore in many ways as indicative of my style and interests as the more extended works."

BIOGRAPHICAL/CRITICAL SOURCES: Scotsman, August 13, 1979; *Glasgow Herald,* November 6, 1979.

*   *   *

VAN der SPIEL, Luigi 1920-

PERSONAL: Born January 24, 1920, in Pottsville, Pa.; son of Emil Anthony (a proprietor of taco stands) and Eva Francesca (a bartender; maiden name, Martini) Van der Spiel; married Vianne Noralee Eta (a pest control expert), March 16, 1945 (divorced October 3, 1955); married Ramona Mary Catherine Quarles (an Amway representative), March 17, 1957 (marriage ended August 8, 1958); children: Lena Maria, Gilbert Finnagin, Patricia Georgia, Minnoe Carla, Trina Wilhemina, Marco Stefan, Jeanetta Krista, Benjamin Kenneth. *Education:* Attended high school in Pottsville, Pa. *Home:* 221 Lewiston Rd., Grosse Pointe Farms, Mich. 48236.

CAREER: Worked as bootblack and street cleaner in Poughkeepsie, N.Y., 1938-40; Utterville's Dairy Farms, Baraboo, Wis., milkman, 1940-45; Dagwood's Marina, New York, N.Y., barnacle scraper, 1945-47; Merchant Marines, S.S. *Sea Urchin*, deck hand, 1947-53, harpooner in North Sea, 1953-55, bilge pump operator, 1955-56, poop deck swabber, 1956-57; tar on S.S. *Ta-Tu* (tug boat) in Sea of Japan, 1957-62; dealer in quahogs in Bar Harbor, Me., 1962-68; Merchant Marines, S.S. *Anemone*, porter, 1968-73, watchman, 1973—. *Member:* National Association for Dramamine Research, Sailors United, Society of Land Lubbers and Haters. *Awards, honors:* Popeye Award from Sailors United, 1954, for *Salt Gets in Your Eyes;* silver swab award for outstanding dereliction of duty, 1957.

WRITINGS: Kelp, I'm Drowning (nonfiction), Square Knot Press, 1953; *Salt Gets in Your Eyes,* Nautical Non-Sense Press, 1954; *The Schooner, the Better* (historical), House of Ahab, 1956; *Three-Day Pass: Bombed Away* (autobiography), Albatross Books, 1957; *Low Budget Meals to Tide You Over* (cookbook), T. Driftwood, 1962; *The Art of Tatooing,* Guppy Guff Publishers, 1963; *Filet de Soul* (philosophy), Red Sky Press, 1965; *Whale, Let Me Tell You . . .* (short stories), Weatherbeaten Books, 1968; *All Decked Out and Nowhere to Go* (autobiography), Tidal Wave Press, 1971; *New Wave* (geography), Foam & Brine, Ltd., 1974; *Not on Porpoise, Just for the Halibut* (nonfiction), Crow's Nest Publications, 1979.

WORK IN PROGRESS: Cry Rope, "a novel about a castaway ship without any rope aboard due to a rare mold that rots hemp. The unfortunate sailors must improvise by tying fishing tackle and shoelaces together to survive the wrenching ordeal."

SIDELIGHTS: Van der Spiel told *CA:* "I ran away from home after graduating from high school. True to its name, Pottsville, Pa., is not the most stimulating place to dwell, so I escaped and worked at a number of menial, though to my young mind, liberating, occupations. After working at Dagwood's Marina as a barnacle scraper I realized I would never again be happy on land, much less Pottsville. The sea and her rich bounty beckoned me. I joined the Merchant Marines and began working on the S.S. *Sea Urchin*. It was while on this noble tub that I discovered I had an impossibly nervous stomach, susceptible especially to rolling swells. The ship's doctor gave me Dramamine and I have taken this lifesaving drug ever since. I am even a member of the National Association for Dramamine Research.

"I held several positions on the *Urchin* but proved to be an indifferent, although good-humored, sailor. I won an award in 1957 for my amazing capacity to shirk work. One of my favorite pastimes was sitting in the crow's nest contemplating the glorious watery horizon. Few of my colleagues would voluntarily brave the mast to retrieve me, so I generally did a lot of contemplating.

"Liberty, of course, continued to be my most enjoyable time. How we anxious tars used to wait for the gang plank to fall and liberty to begin! When it finally did, we launched off the ship in a mighty stream and flooded the hospitable port with our overflowing spirits. We joyously frolicked and cavorted with the wild abandon of children let out of school for the summer. Many of my most memorable experiences on liberty found their way into my books, *Three-Day Pass* and *Whale, Let Me Tell You. . . .* However, *All Decked Out and Nowhere to Go* describes the doldrums one experiences when at sea for seemingly interminable lengths of time. Such boring and uneventful periods can catapult one into the murky depths of depression. Many a young sailor has forsaken the sea for this reason. It takes a hearty lad to survive the vicissitudes of life on the ocean.

"I feel I have survived rather well. Even so, I did take a leave of absence from my true occupation in 1962 to sell quahogs in Bar Harbor, Me. I needed the rest, true, but the real reason for my sabbatical was that I just couldn't pass up the opportunity to reel in the enormous profits one is able to make in vending quahogs. It was a profitable venture, to be sure, but I tired of the ceaseless puttering over figures and fish. Hence, I returned to my only true love: the sea. Since then I have not left her comforting bosom and will never again."

*   *   *

VANE, Brett
See KENT, Arthur William Charles

*   *   *

VAN HASSEN, Amy
See WILES, Domini

*   *   *

VAN ITERSON, S(iny) R(ose)

PERSONAL: Born in Curacao, Netherlands Antilles; children: Foyita, Victor, Loretta, Marnix. *Residence:* Columbia, South America.

CAREER: Author of books for young people. *Awards and honors:* Dutch Juvenile Book Prize, 1969, Hans Christian Anderson honor list, 1970, American Library Association notable book citation, 1971, and Mildred L. Batchelder Award, 1973, all for *Pulga.*

WRITINGS—All for children: De smokkelaars van Buenaventura, Leopold, 1964, translation by Hilda van Stockum published as *The Smugglers of Buenaventura,* Morrow, 1974; *De adjudant van de vrachtwagen,* Leopold, 1967, translation by Alexander Gode and Alison Gode published as *Pulga,* Morrow, 1971; *Het gouden suikerriet,* Leopold, 1970, translation by Patricia Pitzele and Joske Smedts published as *Village of Outcasts,* Morrow, 1972; *Om de Laguna Grande,* Leopold, 1972, translation by van Stockum published as *The Curse of Laguna Grande,* Morrow, 1973; *Weerspiegel in de bron,* translation by van Stockum published as *In the Spell of the Past,* Morrow, 1975; *Schaduw over Chocamata,* translation by van Stockum published as *The Spirits of Chocamata,* Morrow, 1977.*

*   *   *

VAN VLECK, John Hasbrouck   1899-1980

OBITUARY NOTICE: Born March 13, 1899, in Middletown, Conn.; died November, 1980, in Cambridge, Mass. Physicist, educator, and author. A Nobel Prize-winning physicist, Van Vleck's research formed the basis for the development of computer memory systems. His work in magnetism established a new understanding of electron interaction; his 1932 book, *The Theory of Electric and Magnetic Susceptibilities,* on this theory, remains a standard text in the field. Obituaries and other sources: *The International Who's Who,* Europa, 1979, *American Men and Women of Science,* 14th edition, Bowker, 1979; *Who's Who,* 131st edition, St. Martin's, 1979; *Who's Who in the World,* 5th edition, Marquis, 1980; *Time,* November 17, 1980.

VELTMAN, Vera
See PANOVA, Vera (Fedorovna)

* * *

VENNER, J. G.
See LEWIS, John (Noel Claude)

* * *

VERNER, Gerald 1897(?)-1980

OBITUARY NOTICE: Born c. 1897; died September 16, 1980, in Broadstairs, England. Playwright and author of more than one hundred books, including the popular *The Embankment Murder.* Verner also wrote plays, including "Meet Mr. Callaghan" and "The Urgent Hangman." Obituaries and other sources: *The Men Behind Boy's Fiction,* Howard Baker, 1970; *London Times,* September 16, 1980; *AB Bookman's Weekly,* December 22, 1980.

* * *

VIKTORIA LUISE 1892-1980

OBITURAY NOTICE: Born September 13, 1892; died in 1980 in Hanover, West Germany. Member of the British royal family and author of a three-volume autobiography. The author, a great-granddaughter of Queen Victoria and the daughter of Kaiser Wilhelm of Germany, was herself the Duchess of Brunswick and Lueneburg and the Princess of Prussia. Her autobiography was published collectively as *The Kaiser's Daughter* in 1977. Obituaries and other sources: *London Times,* December 16, 1980.

* * *

VINCENT, Jack E(rnest) 1932-

PERSONAL: Born December 26, 1932, in Portland, Ore.; son of Ernest and Helen (Lang) Vincent; married wife, 1953; children: four. *Education:* Portland State College, B.S. (cum laude), 1957; University of Oregon, M.S., 1960, Ph.D., 1964. *Office:* Department of Political Science, Florida Atlantic University, Boca Raton, Fla. 33432.

CAREER: Oklahoma State University, Stillwater, instructor in political science, 1962-64; Central Michigan University, Mount Pleasant, assistant professor of political science, 1964-65; Florida Atlantic University, Boca Raton, assistant professor, 1965-68, associate professor of political science, 1968—, chairman of publications committee, 1967-68. Member of faculty at Chadron State College, summer, 1964, Maxwell Air Force Base, 1977-78, and University of Florida; lecturer at Canadian School of Peace Research, 1976-77; research associate at University of Hawaii, 1971.

MEMBER: International Peace Science Society (vice-president, 1973-74; president and program chairman, 1977-78), International Studies Association (chairman of international relations theory section, 1974; vice-president and program chairman, 1978-79; president, 1979-81), Interpolimetrics Society (member of governing council, 1974-75), American Political Science Association, American Association of University Professors (member of executive committee, 1972-73), United Nations Association (chairman, 1972-73), Open Ocean Association (member of board of directors, 1973), Florida Academy of Sciences (chairman of social science, 1970-71), United Faculty of Florida (first vice-president; president). *Awards, honors:* Grants from National Science Foundation, 1967-68, 1968-69, 1970-71, Institute of Transnational Studies at University of Southern California, 1974, Peace Research Institute, 1975-77, U.S. Air Force, 1977-78, and Florida Endowment for the Humanities, 1979.

WRITINGS: The Caucusing Groups of the United Nations: An Examination of Their Attitudes Toward the Organization, Oklahoma State University Press, 1965; *Statistical Concepts for Students of International Relations* (monograph), University Press of America, 1966, *The Handbook of International Relations,* Barron's, 1969; *United Nations Handbook,* Barron's, 1969, revised edition, 1976; *Factor Analysis in International Relations: Interpretation, Problem Areas and an Application,* University of Florida Press, 1971; *Predicting Conflict and Cooperation in the International System,* RFP Publishing, 1975; *Various Approaches in the Study of International Relations: Readings,* U.S. Air Force, 1977; *Attributes and National Behavior: A Series of Empirical Studies,* Peace Research Institute, Volume I, 1978, Volume II: *Conflict Studies,* 1978; (contributor) *Peace Research Reviews,* Peace Research Institute, Volume IV, 1978, Volume V, 1978; *Understanding International Relations,* University Press of America, 1979; *Project Theory: Interpretations and Policy Relevance,* University Press of America, 1979. Contributor to scholarly journals. Associate editor of *Review of Peace Research,* 1974-75.

* * *

VINEST, Shaw
See LONGYEAR, Barry Brookes

* * *

VLASIC, Bob
See HIRSCH, Phil

* * *

VOLKAN, Vamik D(jemal) 1932-

PERSONAL: Born December 13, 1932, in Nicosia, Cyprus; came to the United States in 1957, naturalized citizen, 1964; son of Ahmet (a teacher) and Fatma (a teacher) Cemal; married Elizabeth Palonen, September 30, 1967; children: Kevin, Susan, Alev (daughter), Kurt. *Education:* University of Ankara, M.D., 1956; Washington Psychoanalytic Institute, graduated, 1971. *Home:* 102 Smithfield Court, Charlottesville, Va. 22901. *Office:* Department of Psychiatry, University of Virginia, Charlottesville, Va. 22904.

CAREER: University of Ankara, Ankara, Turkey, resident in internal medicine at university hospital, 1956-57; Lutheran Deaconess Hospital. Chicago, Ill., rotating intern, 1957-58; North Carolina Memorial Hospital, Chapel Hill, resident in psychiatry, 1958-60, chief resident, 1960-61; Cherry Hospital, Goldsboro, N.C., staff physician, 1961-63; University of Virginia, Charlottesville, instructor, 1963-64, assistant professor, 1964-68, associate professor, 1968-72, professor of psychiatry, 1972—, supervisor of psychiatric inpatient ward at university medical center, 1963-68, director of psychiatric inpatient services, 1968-74, director of psychiatric outpatient activities, 1975-77, member of Gender Identity Clinic, 1970-76, coordinator of summer psychiatric externship program, 1966-70, acting chairman of department of psychiatry, 1977-78, medical director of Blue Ridge Hospital and chairman of management review committee and administrative coordinating committee, 1978—, member of Institute of Psychiatry, Law, and Public Policy. Staff physician at Dorothea Dix Hospital, 1961-63.

Clinical instructor at University of North Carolina, 1961-63; chairman of candidate's curriculum committee at Washington Psychoanalytic Institute, 1967, lecturer, 1971-73, instructor, 1973-74, teaching analyst, 1974—, chairman of psychopathological formations faculty, 1976-78; visiting professor at University of Ankara, 1974-75; member of faculty at Virginia Institute of Group Psychotherapy, 1976-78; conducts workshops. Member of board of directors of American Psychotherapy Center, 1978—, and Institute for Psychiatry and Foreign Affairs, 1979—; member of advisory council of Advanced Institute for Analytic Psychotherapy, 1979—, national advisory council of Middle East Educational Trust, 1979—, and professional advisory committee of Virginia Mental Health Foundation, 1970-76; consultant to U.S. Agency for International Development.

MEMBER: International Psychoanalytic Association, International Society of Political Psychology (charter member), American Psychiatric Association (fellow), American Psychoanalytic Association, Group for the Advancement of Psychiatry, Turkish-American Neuropsychiatric Society (charter member; president-elect, 1976; president, 1977), Turkish Mental Health Association of Cyprus, Royal Society of Medicine (fellow), Virginia Psychoanalytic Study Group (charter member), Virginia Psychoanalytic Society (charter member; president, 1980), Medical Society of Virginia, Neuropsychiatric Society of Virginia, Washington Psychoanalytic Society, Albemarle County Medical Society, Charlottesville Study Group for Psychoanalytic Psychotherapy (group head, 1975—). *Awards, honors:* National Institute of Mental Health grants, 1964, 1965; grants from New York Grant Foundation, 1972, 1973, 1974; first prize from Washington Psychoanalytic Society, 1977, for "The Introjection of the Therapist During the Treatment of Schizophrenia"; grants from U.S. Agency for International Development.

WRITINGS: Primitive Internalized Object Relations, International Universities Press, 1976; *Cyprus: War and Adaptation; A Psychoanalytic History of Two Ethnic Groups in Conflict,* University Press of Virginia, 1979; *Linking Objects and Linking Phenomenon: A Study of the Forms, Symptoms, Metapsychology, and Therapy of Mourning,* International Universities Press, 1981. Also co-author with Norman Itzkowitz of *Ataturk: A Psycho-History,* 1981.

Contributor: D. W. Abse, L. M. Nash, and L.M.R. Louden, editors, *Marital and Sexual Counseling in Medical Practice,* Harper, 1974; J. G. Howells, editor, *World History of Psychiatry,* Brunner, 1975; P. L. Giovacchini, Alfred Flarsheim, and L. B. Boyer, editors, *Tactics and Techniques in Psychoanalytic Psychotherapy,* Volume II, Jason Aronson, 1975; B. Shoenbey, I. Gerber, A. Wiener, and other editors, *Bereavement: Its Psycho-Social Aspects,* Columbia University Press, 1975; Paul Olsen, editor, *Emotional Flooding,* Behavioral Publications, 1975; Howells, editor, *Modern Perspectives in the Psychiatric Aspects of Surgery,* Brunner, 1976; L. C. Brown and Norman Itkowitz, editors, *Psychology and Near-Eastern Studies,* Princeton University Press, 1977; Simon Grolnick, Leonard Barkin, and Werner Muensterberger, editors, *Between Fantasy and Reality: Transitional Phenomena and Objects,* Quadrangle, 1978; Joseph LeBoit and Attilio Capponi, editors, *Advances in Psychotherapy of the Borderline Patient,* Jason Aronson, 1979; Lorelle Saretsky, G. D. Goldman, and D. S. Milman, editors, *Integrating Ego Psychology and Object Relations,* Kendall/Hunt, 1979.

Contributor to *Encyclopaedic Handbook of Medical Psychology.* Contributor of nearly fifty articles and reviews to medical journals. Member of editorial board of *Comprehensive Psychotherapy,* 1977, *Journal of Political Psychology,* 1978—, and *Review of Psychoanalytic Books,* 1980—.

SIDELIGHTS: Vamik Volkan told *CA:* "In my work regarding Ataturk with Professor Norman Itzkowitz, a Princeton historian, we are especially writing about historical developments and their intertwinement with the internal processes of a leader. In this instance, it is a leader who attempted to establish a 'fit' between himself and his followers, directed at the reinforcement of the cohesiveness of his grandiose self. This work and other works of mine apply the theory of internalized object relations to show the relationship between certain leaders' (Ataturk, for example) personalities and their followers and the effect this process has on historical developments.

"My research also deals with ethnic groups in conflict. Cyprus, being a small island where two ethnic groups in conflict have lived side by side for centuries, maintaining their very separate and distinct ethnic identities, was especially appropriate as a psycho-historical research laboratory. My contribution is to hopefully reemphasize that the resolution or understanding of such a conflict, or even the evaluation of partial solutions to such a conflict, is not possible without taking the emotional attitudes of the opposing groups into consideration."

                              *   *   *

von FURSTENBERG, Egon (Edvard) 1946-

PERSONAL: Born June 29, 1946, in Lausanne, Switzerland; came to United States, 1967; son of Tassilo and Clara (Agnelli) von Furstenberg; married Diane Helfin (a fashion designer), July 16, 1968 (separated, 1975); children: Alexandre, Tatiana. *Education:* University of Geneve, degree in economics, 1966; attended Parsons School of Design, 1971. *Home:* 955 Park Ave., New York, N.Y. 10028. *Office:* Egon von Furstenberg Ltd., 50 West 57th St., New York, N.Y. 10019.

CAREER: Peace Corps teacher in the African Congo, 1966-67; banker at Chase Manhattan Bank and Lazard Freres, New York City, 1967-71; E. J. Korvette's, New York City, men's wear buyer, 1971-73; Egon von Furstenberg Ltd., New York City, founder, designer, president, and chairman of the board, 1972—.

WRITINGS: (With Camille Duhe) *The Power Look,* Holt, 1978; (with Karen Fisher) *The Power Look at Home,* Morrow, 1980.

SIDELIGHTS: A prince by birth and husband of one of the foremost fashion designers for women, Egon von Furstenberg has devoted himself to helping other men gain the look and style he feels is necessary in order to have authority and success. He designs fashions for eighteen companies around the world. His designing resume includes costumes for the Broadway show "Don't Call Back," with Arlene Francis, and for the film "Chanel Solitaire," based on the life of Coco Chanel.

In *The Power Look,* von Furstenberg expounds on his belief that success in the business world greatly depends upon one's appearance and style of dress. "In the business world, discrimination by appearance is a fact of life," says von Furstenberg. "What man has time to waste in being passed over for opportunities because he 'looks wrong'?" To assist men in dressing to win, von Furstenberg advises them on clothing choices, fabric care, and personal grooming. Though written with highly motivated, success-oriented men in mind, *The Power Look* does not promote a uniform look for everyone; von Furstenberg stresses that the basic power look be individually tailored to suit one's personality and lifestyle.

Von Furstenberg's second book, *The Power Look at Home,* attempts to do for a man's home what *The Power Look* attempted for his body. Aimed primarily at single, prosperous, apartment-dwelling males, *The Power Look at Home* stresses that a man's lifestyle should be reflected in his home. This guide to decorating offers tips on achieving a successful look through furniture, accessories, lighting, and color.

BIOGRAPHICAL/CRITICAL SOURCES: West Coast Review of Books, November, 1978; *Esquire*, March, 1980.

W

WADDELL, Helen (Jane)   1889-1965

PERSONAL: Born May 31, 1889, in Tokyo, Japan; daughter of Hugh Waddell (a Presbyterian minister and missionary). *Education:* Queen's University, Belfast, B.A. (first class honors), 1911, M.A., 1912.

CAREER: Somerville College, Oxford University, Oxford, England, lecturer in Latin at Somerville College, 1920-22, Cassell Lecturer at St. Hilda's Hall, 1921; Bedford College, London University, London, England, lecturer, 1922-23; *Nineteenth Century,* London, assistant editor, from late 1930's until 1945; translator, lecturer, and free-lance writer. *Member:* Royal Society of Literature (fellow), Irish Academy of Letters, Medieval Academy of America (corresponding fellow). *Awards, honors:* Susette Taylor fellowship from Lady Margaret Hall, Oxford University, 1922-24; A. C. Benson Silver Medal from Royal Society of Literature, 1927, for *The Wandering Scholars;* D.Litt. from Columbia University, 1935, and from University of Belfast and Durham University; LL.D. from St. Andrews College.

WRITINGS: The Spoiled Buddha (two-act play), T. Fisher Unwin, 1919; *The Wandering Scholars,* Houghton, 1927, 7th edition, Collins, 1968; (editor) *A Book of Medieval Latin for Schools,* Constable, 1931, 3rd edition, 1962; *The Abbe Prevost* (play; first produced in London, England, at Arts Theatre Club, May, 1935), Bungay, 1931; *Peter Abelard* (novel; London Times Book Club selection), Holt, 1933, reprinted, Viking, 1970; *Poetry in the Dark Ages,* Jackson (Glasgow), 1948, Barnes & Noble, 1958; *Stories From Holy Writ* (juvenile), Constable, 1949, Macmillan, 1950, reprinted, Greenwood Press, 1975; *The Story of Saul the King* (juvenile; abridged by Elaine Moss from *Stories From Holy Writ*), David White, 1966; *The Princess Splendour, and Other Stories* (juvenile), edited by Eileen Colwell, Longmans, Green, 1969.

Translator: (And compiler) *Lyrics From the Chinese,* Constable, 1913, Houghton, 1914, reprinted, Roth, 1973; (and compiler) *Mediaeval Latin Lyrics,* Constable, 1929, R. R. Smith, 1930, reprinted, Norton, 1977; Antoine Prevost D'Exiles, *The History of the Chevalier Des Grieux and of Manon Lescaut,* Constable, 1931; Marcel Ayme, *The Hollow Field,* Constable, 1933; *Beasts and Saints,* Holt, 1934; *The Desert Fathers,* Constable, 1936, University of Michigan Press, 1957, reprinted, Barnes & Noble, 1974; Jacques, *A French Soldier Speaks,* Constable, 1941; John Milton,

Lament for Damon, privately printed, 1943; David Holbrook, compiler, *Plucking the Rushes: An Anthology of Chinese Poetry in Translations,* Heinemann, 1968; *Aphrodite: A Mythical Journey in Eight Episodes,* (poems), World's End Press, 1970; Felicitas Corrigan, editor, *More Latin Lyrics From Virgil to Milton,* Gollancz, 1976, Norton, 1977.

Contributor of articles to newspapers and magazines, including *London Times, Nineteenth Century,* and *Manchester Guardian.*

SIDELIGHTS: Known primarily for her expert translations of medieval Latin literature and her scholarship on the Middle Ages, Helen Waddell possessed the abilities to make that distant time accessible and alive for her readers. One of her earliest works to receive acclaim from critics and readers alike was *The Wandering Scholars.* A critical account of the classical Latin tradition in literature, it was the result of two years of research at the Bibliotheque Nationale in Paris. C. H. Haskins of *American Historical Review* called the book "fascinating" and noted that "with all its sophistication it has grace and charm as well, and its nimble wit and happy renderings of Latin verse draw the unfamiliar reader into some real touch with medieval life." Marie Shields Halvey echoed similar sentiments in her review of a later work, *Mediaeval Latin Lyrics:* "Enchantingly does [the book] open a door into a world forgotten by most readers of English literature; a door closed by the Reformation and the development of the Protestant tradition in English letters on a world of wandering scholars and lyric-voiced poets."

Waddell was also the author of three children's books and *Peter Abelard,* a novel about the medieval lovers Heloise and Abelard. She also wrote two plays, "The Spoiled Buddha" and "The Abbe Prevost." In her writing, as Peter Dronke noted, she "was able to convey much of the excitement, the profanities and the mystical heights of that world, with a vividness that purely scholarly works seldom attain. Her success was in large measure due to her being unafraid, in her writing, of expressing her own imaginative warmth: she both perceived the ardent emotions that were at play in the realm she studied and coloured that realm with ardent emotions of her own."

BIOGRAPHICAL/CRITICAL SOURCES: American Historical Review, October, 1927; *Commonweal,* January 5, 1934, September 17, 1937; Monica Blackett, *The Mark of the*

Maker: A Portrait of Helen Waddell, Constable, 1973; *Times Literary Supplement,* June 17, 1977.*

* * *

WAGNER, Philip Marshall 1904-

PERSONAL: Born February 18, 1904, in New Haven, Conn.; son of Charles Philip and Ruth (Kenyon) Wagner; married Helen Crocker, April 16, 1925 (marriage ended); married Jocelyn McDonough, September 4, 1940; children: Susan, Philip C. *Education:* University of Michigan, A.B., 1925. *Politics:* Democrat. *Home and office address:* Boordy Vineyard, P.O. Box 38, Riderwood, Md. 21139.

CAREER: General Electric Co., Schenectady, N.Y., in publicity department, 1925-30; *Baltimore Evening Sun,* Baltimore, Md., editorial writer, 1930-36, London correspondent, 1936-37, editor, 1938-43; *Baltimore Sun,* Baltimore, editor, 1943-64; free-lance writer, 1979—. Regents Lecturer at University of California, 1961 and 1964; American delegate to Federation Nationale de la Viticulture Nouvelle. *Member:* National Press Club, Overseas Press Club, Washington Fruit Testing Cooperative Association, Hamilton Street Club. *Awards, honors:* Officer of French Ordre du Merite Agricole.

WRITINGS: American Wines and How to Make Them, Knopf, 1933; *Wine Grapes and How to Grow Them,* Harcourt, 1937; *The Wine Growers Guide,* Knopf, 1945, revised edition, 1965; *American Wines and Wine Making,* Knopf, 1963; *H. L. Mencken,* University of Minnesota Press, 1966; *Grapes Into Wine: The Art of Wine-Making in America,* Knopf, 1976. Also editor with Sanford V. Larkey of *Turner on Wines,* 1941. Contributor to magazines.

WORK IN PROGRESS: Contribution to *Winemaking in America: The State of the Art* (tentative title), publication expected in 1981.

SIDELIGHTS: Wagner told *CA:* "With my wife I established Boordy Vineyards winery and nursery and pioneered the introduction of French hybrid wine grapes into American viticulture. Experimental work with new hybrids continues, and wine growing has been a lifelong avocation, an ideal foil for the tensions of newspaper editorial work."

* * *

WAGSCHAL, Peter H(enry) 1944-

PERSONAL: Born October 18, 1944, in New York, N.Y.; son of Rolf (a physician) and Grete (Hausmann) Wagschal; married Kathleen Lanpher (a child care center director), July 17, 1971; children: Adam, Colin. *Education:* Harvard University, B.A. (cum laude), 1966; Stanford University, M.A., 1967; University of Massachusetts, Ed.D., 1969. *Home:* 133 Fearing St., Amherst, Mass. 01002. *Office:* Department of Education, University of Massachusetts, Amherst, Mass. 01003.

CAREER: High school social studies teacher in Santa Clara, Calif., 1966-67, and Palo Alto, Calif., 1967; University of Massachusetts, Amherst, lecturer, 1968-69, assistant professor, 1969-75, associate professor of education, 1975—, director of teacher resources and improvement program, 1971—, and future studies program, 1975—. Psychometrician for International Educational Associates; conference speaker. *Member:* Phi Beta Kappa, Phi Delta Kappa.

WRITINGS: (Contributor) Daniel Levine, editor, *Farewell to Schools,* National Society for the Study of Education, 1972; (editor and contributor) *Learning Tomorrows: Commentaries on the Future of Education,* Praeger, 1978; (editor

with Robert D. Kahn) *R. Buckminster Fuller on Education,* University of Massachusetts Press, 1979. Contributor to *Teachers' Handbook.* Contributor of more than twenty-five articles and reviews to education journals and *Saturday Review.* Contributing editor of *Education Section Newsletter* (of World Future Society).

WORK IN PROGRESS: Tomorrow and Tomorrow and Tomorrow: An Informal Guide to the Future.

SIDELIGHTS: Wagschal wrote: "My interests center on the social, economic, and political institutions which make life so difficult for so many in the twentieth century. I write in the hope of illuminating the ways in which these institutions invade our lives and minds. Though I reside in academia, I am convinced that a basic understanding of complex human institutions is within anyone's grasp and, in fact, that the language of the Academy does more to obscure reality than to reveal it. Most importantly, we need writers who can show the workings of large-scale structures in American society in the day-to-day details of our lives."

* * *

WAJDA, Andrzej 1926-

PERSONAL: Born March 26, 1926, in Suwalki, Poland; son of Jakub (a cavalry officer) and Aniela (a schoolteacher; maiden name, Biaxowas) Wajda; married Beata Tyszkiewicz (an actress), 1967 (divorced); married Krystyna Zachwatowicz, 1975; children: one daughter. *Education:* Attended Fine Arts Academy, Cracow, 1946-49, and Lodz Film School, 1950-52. *Home:* 14 Haukego St., 01-540 Warsaw, Poland. *Office:* Film Polski, ul. Mazowiecka 6/8, Warsaw, Poland.

CAREER: Director of motion pictures and stage productions; screenwriter. Worked as assistant stage manager, 1953; assistant director to Aleksander Ford, 1953. Director of stage productions, including "Hamlet," 1960, and "The Devils," 1963. Scenographer for stage productions, including "A Hatful of Rain," 1959, and "The Devils," 1972. *Member:* Union of Polish Artists and Designers.

AWARDS, HONORS: State Prize (Poland), 1954, for "Pokolenie"; award from Cannes Film Festival, 1957, for "Kanal"; Fipresci Prize, 1958, for "Popiol i diament"; award from Milan Film Festival, 1970, and from Moscow Film Festival, 1971, both for "Brzezina"; award from Milan Film Festival, 1970, and Grand Prize from Colombo (Sri Lanka) Film Festival, 1973, both for "Krajobraz na much"; Bambi Prize, 1973, for "Pilatus und andere"; Silver Prize from San Sebastian Film Festival, 1973, for "Wesele"; State Prize (Poland), 1974, Golden Hugo from Chicago Film Festival, 1975, nomination for Academy Award for best foreign language film from Academy of Motion Picture Arts and Sciences, 1976, Gold Laceno Prize, 1978, and award from Cartanega Film Festival, 1978, all for "Ziemia obiecana"; Order of Banner of Labour, 1975; Luchino Visconti Prize, 1978, and Ecumenical Prize from Cannes Film Festival, 1979, both for "Bez Znieczulenia"; Fipresci Prize, 1978, for "Czlowiek z marmaru"; and other film awards.

WRITINGS—Published screenplays: (With others; and director) *The Wajda Trilogy* (contains "A Generation" by Bohdan Czeszko and adapted from his own novel, released in Poland as "Pokolenie," 1954; "Kanal" by Jerzy Stefan Stawinski and adapted from his own novel, released in Poland in 1956; and "Ashes and Diamonds" by Wajda and Jerzy Andrzejewski and adapted from Andrzejewski's own novel, released in Poland as "Popiol i diament," 1958), translation from the Polish by Boleslaw Sulik, Simon & Schuster, 1973.

Unpublished screenplays in Polish; and director: "Kiedy ty spisz" (short; title means "While You Sleep"), 1950; "Zly chlopiec" (short; title means "The Bad Boy"; adapted from the short story by Anton Chekhov), 1950; "Ceramika il-zecka" (documentary; title means "The Pottery of Ilza"), 1951; "Ide ku sloncu" (short; title means "I Walk to the Sun"), 1955; (with Wojceich Zukrowski) "Lotna" (adapted from the novel by Zukrowski), Film Polski, 1959; (with Kazimierz Brandys) "Samson" (adapted from the novel by Brandys), Film Polski, 1961; (with Sveta Lukic) "Sibirksa ledi magbet" (title means "Siberian Lady Macbeth"; adapted from the novel by Nikolay Leskov, *Lady Macbeth of Mtsensk District*), Avala Film, 1962; (with Stawinski) "Warsaw" (short), 1962; (with Andrzejewski) "Vrata raja" (released in the U.S. as "Gates of Paradise"; adapted from the novel by Andrzejewski), Jointex Films, 1967; "Wszystko no sprzedaz" (released in the U.S. as "Everything for Sale"), Film Polski, 1968.

(With Andrzej Brzozowski) "Krajobraz na much" (released in the U.S. as "Landscape After Battle"; adapted from short stories by Tadeusz Borowski), Film Polski, 1970; (with Andrzej Kijowki) "Wesele" (released in the U.S. as "The Wedding"; adapted from the play by Stanislaw Wyspianski), Film Polski, 1972; "Ziemia obiecana" (released in the U.S. as "Land of Promise"; adapted from the novel by Wladyslaw Reymont), Film Polski, 1974; "Czlowiek z marmaru" (released in the U.S. as "Man of Marble"), Film Polski, 1976; (with Agnieszka Holland) "Bez Znieczulenia" (released in the U.S. as "Without Anesthesia"), Film Polski, 1978; "Dziewka z Wilko" (released in the U.S. as "The Maids of Wilko"), Film Polski, 1979.

Teleplays; and director: "Pilatus und andere" (German; title means "Pilate and Others"; adapted from the novel by Mikhail Bulgakov, *The Master and Margarita*), Zweites deutsches Fernsehen, 1972.

SIDELIGHTS: Most of Wajda's films explore the disruptive effect of war. His first major film, "A Generation," deals with young Poles resisting Nazi oppression. Throughout the film, their actions are contrasted with those of the relatively ineffective organized Polish resistance, which seems incapable of evolving past the planning stage. The renegade young fighters, however, frequently exchange gunfire with Nazi troops. Wajda often seems to imply in "A Generation" that the young fighters were the salvation of Poland during World War II.

"A Generation" is the first of three films on war commonly referred to as "The Wajda Trilogy." The second work, "Kanal," depicts a group of Polish resistance fighters living in the sewers of their Nazi-occupied village. Each of the fighters meets a grim end: one exasperated member finally emerges from a manhole only to discover that he has interrupted a Nazi execution squad; a dying lieutenant and his lover come upon a forest that lies on the other side of an immovable iron grate; and two others are killed while trying to defuse a grenade-filled boobytrap.

In "Kanal," Wajda harbors little compassion for the resistance fighters. When the commander and a sergeant escape from the sewers, they find that the entire village has been destroyed by the Nazis. Overwhelmed with fury, the officer murders his comrade. He then returns to the sewers with his pistol waved defiantly over his head. David Austen later wrote, "In this gesture of futile defiance by a half-insane man is reflected the whole madness of war."

Wajda's best-known film is probably "Ashes and Diamonds," the third film of the trilogy. It details the mental anguish experienced by a young resistance fighter who tires of killing. After the soldier falls in love with a woman working at the hotel sheltering his next victim, he realizes that there is a moral issue involved even in the killing of the enemy. Nonetheless, he completes his assignment and murders an important Communist official. The following day, he unexpectedly witnesses the murder of another agent by a friend and fellow resistance fighter. Stunned by the persistant violence, he turns from the murder site and races past Russian soldiers. They notice his weapon and give chase. When he refuses to halt, they fire. Moments later he dies. "Throughout the trilogy violence breeds violence," noted Austen, "it gathers a momentum of its own, until finally the killer is himself killed."

Throughout most of the 1960's Wajda seemed unable to match the accomplishment of his war trilogy. In films such as "Siberian Lady Macbeth" and "Gates of Paradise," as Colin McArthur contended, Wajda appeared "trapped in a theme" of the "recurrent tragedy of Polish history." Stylistically, Wajda was deviating from the expansiveness of his earlier works with little success. Lacking the romantic symbolism and historical significance of his films during the late 1950's, Wajda's following works were deemed little more than "filmed screenplays" by some critics.

Considered past his prime by many observers, Wajda sparked his comeback in 1968 with "Everything for Sale." The film traces the life of an actor whose experiences and untimely death closely parallel that of Zbigniew Cybulski, the James Dean-like lead actor in "Ashes and Diamonds." In "Everything for Sale" Wajda blurs the distinction between the film and reality by retracing the actor's life via a film within the film. The movie being made within "Everything for Sale" concerns the actor's life. By studying the actor's life within the context of the interior film, Wajda details not only the actor's life but his influence on the people involved with the filming. As Krzysztof-Teodor Toeplitz noted, "The situation gives Wajda the occasion for confronting legend with reality. . . . The dead actor's legend persists among the living characters as a challenge." The film is thus much different than those preceding it. "'Everything for Sale'· introduces us into an entirely new world," wrote Toeplitz. "Instead of experiences dictated by the great storms of history, we face those stemming from the variety of human character; instead of tensions arising from military conflicts they come from individual needs, poses, ambitions; instead of pathos there is irony."

In 1970, Wajda made "Landscape After Battle," in which he fused pathos with irony. The film concerns the experiences of Tadeusz, a Jewish poet, who finds himself freed from his Nazi captors by Allies, only to be detained by them in a displaced persons camp. At the film's end, Tadeusz determines to escape the incompetently-managed camp and return to Poland.

Wajda's next major work was "Land of Promise," a three-hour expose on the evils of capitalism as revealed through the actions of a few Polish Jews and Germans during the turn of the century. Stanley Kauffmann complained that "Wajda plunges us into this almost unrelieved swamp of cynicism and greed to show us capitalism naked . . . ; but the result is *un*-naked, swaddled by his mannerisms."

Kauffmann was more restrained in his criticism of Wajda's "Without Anesthesia." The film details the sufferings endured by a highly successful, but complacent, journalist whose life is destroyed when his wife deserts him and he loses his job. Kauffmann called it "the best-directed film of

Wajda's that I know." He added: "Fairly subtly, many of the scenes of mere dailyness are composed to suggest closure, confinement. And the performances avoid the Wajda vein of broadness; for once his actors draw with fine lines, not with felt pens."

Wajda's 1978 effort, "The Man of Marble," resembles "Everything for Sale." In it he once again uses the device of a film within a film to reveal a deceased character's past. The subject is a bricklayer whose sculptings and paintings are discovered by a film student. Using newsreels and documentary footage, Wajda is able to reveal the social and political climate that the bricklayer worked in and was eventually destroyed by. By also detailing the unraveling of the man's life by the film student, Wajda is able to explore, as he already had in "Everything for Sale," the myth-making apparatus. "The poetic aspects of *Man of Marble* have no equivalent in Wajda's *oeuvre*," wrote Ryszard Koniczek. "Wajda has ... written a human drama about the relationship between the individual and society, the dialectics of history itself."

Wajda followed "The Man of Marble" with "The Maids of Wilko," which details a man's inability to understand and reciprocate the love he receives from his five sisters. Summing up the film, Jack Kroll declared that "Wajda seems to have reached the point of mastery where filmmaking is as natural and expressive as the shaping hand of Matisse or Hokusai."

BIOGRAPHICAL/CRITICAL SOURCES: Films and Filming, November, 1961, July, 1968; *Sight and Sound,* summer, 1969; *Film Quarterly,* winter, 1969-70; *Newsweek,* October 21, 1974, October 22, 1979; *New York Times,* February 10, 1978, October 9, 1979; *Village Voice,* October 15, 1979; *Nation,* November 3, 1979; *New Republic,* November 3, 1979; *Film Comment,* November/December, 1979; Peter Cowie, editor, *International Film Guide,* A. S. Barnes, 1979; *Contemporary Literary Criticism,* Volume 16, Gale, 1981.*

—*Sketch by Les Stone*

*   *   *

WALDO, Ralph Emerson III   1944-
(Terry Waldo)

PERSONAL: Born November 26, 1944, in Ironton, Ohio; son of Ralph Emerson (in insurance) and Lorna (Broom) Waldo; married Jane Y. Fong (divorced). *Education:* Ohio State University, B.A., 1967, M.A., 1970. *Home:* 504 South Lazelle St., Columbus, Ohio 43206.

CAREER: Independent filmmaker in Columbus, Ohio, 1967-71; professional musician and composer, 1971—. Producer and narrator of "This Is Ragtime," on National Public Radio, Athens, Ohio, 1974; producer and music director for QUBE-TV, Columbus, 1978-79. *Member:* American Society of Composers, Authors and Publishers, American Federation of Musicians. *Awards, honors:* Ohioana Award from Martha Kinney Cooper Foundation, 1976, for *This Is Ragtime.*

WRITINGS—Under name Terry Waldo: *This Is Ragtime,* Hawthorn, 1976.

Recordings: "Jazz Babies," Dirty Shame Records, 1979; "Terry Waldo: Wizard of the Keyboard," Stomp Off Records, 1980; "Waldo's Gutbucket Syncopators: Feelin' Devilish," Stomp Off Records, 1981. Has made nearly a dozen other recordings.

WORK IN PROGRESS: Composing music for a ragtime-jazz musical play based on the life of Warren G. Harding, to be produced on the Broadway stage.

SIDELIGHTS: Waldo wrote: "As a musical entertainer, I have toured the United States and Europe and have appeared on numerous television and radio shows. My mentor is the grand old man of ragtime, Eubie Blake, who considers me his protege. We have often appeared together, and I have transcribed a folio of Eubie's rags for Mark's Music.

"Since 1976 I have been performing with my partner, Susan LaMarche, and Waldo's Gutbucket Syncopators, which draws its membership from the country's top echelon of traditional jazz musicians."

*   *   *

WALDO, Terry
See WALDO, Ralph Emerson III

*   *   *

WALKER, Theodore J.   1922-

PERSONAL: Born January 7, 1922, in Great Falls, Mont.; son of Ira I. (a postal clerk) and Eva Pearl (a teacher; maiden name, Gailey) Walker; married Delphine Elizabeth Blondeau, September, 1943 (deceased); married Betty Jane Johnson (a registered nurse), December 7, 1974; children: (first marriage) Stephen D., Claudia C., Deborah, Priscilla. *Education:* Montana State University, B.A. (with honors), 1938; University of Oklahoma, M.S., 1940; University of Wisconsin—Madison, Ph.D., 1947. *Politics:* Democrat. *Home and office:* Natural History Consultants, Inc., 727 Balboa Court, San Diego, Calif. 92109.

CAREER: Scripps Institute of Oceanography, La Jolla, Calif., research oceanographer, 1948-69; H & M Sportfishing, San Diego, Calif., naturalist, 1969—. Naturalist with U.S. Park Service, 1948-65, on National Audubon Society tours, and in the Sea of Cortes, Alaska, Bali, and Antarctica, 1976—. President of Natural History Consultants, Inc.; founder of Gray Whale Observation and Cabrillo National Monument of San Diego; film lecturer in the United States and Canada. *Military service:* U.S. Navy, 1942-45; became lieutenant. *Awards, honors:* Nominated for Academy Award from Motion Picture Academy of Arts and Sciences, 1971, for film, "Lake Eva."

WRITINGS: Whale Primer, Cabrillo Historical Society, 1962; *Red Salmon, Brown Bear,* World Press, 1971. Also author of scripts "Lake Eva," "Wilderness Lake," and "The Sea and Shore of Baja." Contributor to *National Geographic.*

WORK IN PROGRESS: A documentary film about Antarctica.

SIDELIGHTS: Walker wrote: "My professional career has involved the dichotomy between science and the world of nature. I seriously considered the career of the naturalist, then became deeply involved in the natural history of the gray whale, in which field I am considered an expert by my peers. I am vitally concerned about the loss of the wilderness and contact with nature as a consequence of the population explosion."

AVOCATIONAL INTERESTS: Classical music, playing French horn, trumpet, and recorder, gourmet cooking.

*   *   *

WALLIS, Jim   1948-

PERSONAL: Born June 4, 1948, in Detroit, Mich.; son of James E. (in business) and Phyllis (in business) Wallis. *Education:* Michigan State University, B.S., 1970; attended

Trinity Evangelical Divinity School, 1970-72. *Office: Sojourners*, 1309 L St. N.W., Washington, D.C. 20005.

CAREER: Sojourners, Washington, D.C., editor, 1971—. Pastor at Sojourners Fellowship, 1975—.

WRITINGS: Agenda for Biblical People, Harper, 1976; *Called to Conversion*, Harper, 1981. Contributor to periodicals.

WORK IN PROGRESS: An edited anthology of Christian responses to nuclear armaments; a book in the ''Journeys in Faith'' series for publication by Abingdon in 1982.

* * *

WALSH, Raoul 1887-1980

OBITUARY NOTICE: Born March 11, 1887, in New York, N.Y.; died of a heart attack, December 31, 1980, in Simi Valley, Calif. Actor, motion picture director, and author. Walsh's fifty-year career in Hollywood produced some of the finest high-adventure films ever made. His more than one hundred films set impressive standards for action-filled genres such as westerns, war and gangster stories, and historical dramas. A sailor, cavalryman, and cowboy himself, Walsh was recovering from a riding accident when he met film director D. W. Griffith, an association that led to Walsh's role in Griffith's classic, ''Birth of a Nation.'' Walsh's ''tough guy'' films helped establish such stars as Humphrey Bogart, James Cagney, and John Wayne. Among the filmmaker's best-known motion pictures are ''High Sierra,'' ''White Heat,'' ''What Price Glory,'' ''They Died With Their Boots On,'' ''Gentleman Jim,'' ''They Drive by Night,'' and ''The Naked and the Dead.'' Obituaries and other sources: Raoul Walsh, *Each Man in His Time: The Life Story of a Director*, Farrar, Straus, 1974; William R. Meyer, *Warner Brothers Directors*, Arlington House, 1978; *International Motion Picture Almanac*, Quigley, 1979; *New York Times*, January 3, 1981; *Washington Post*, January 3, 1981; *Newsweek*, January 12, 1981; *Time*, January 12, 1981; *Detroit News*, January 18, 1981.

* * *

WALTER, Nancy
See HOLMGREN, Norah

* * *

WARD, William Alan Heaton
See HEATON-WARD, William Alan

* * *

WARLAND, John
See BUCHANAN-BROWN, John

* * *

WARNER, Esther S.
See DENDEL, Esther (Sietmann Warner)

* * *

WARREN, Mary Douglas
See GREIG, Maysie

* * *

WATSON, Roderick (Bruce) 1943-

PERSONAL: Born May 12, 1943, in Aberdeen, Scotland; son of Bruce (a professor of chemistry) and Johan (Angus) Watson; married Celia Hall Mackie, July 14, 1966; children:

Christopher, Joanna. *Education:* University of Aberdeen, M.A., 1965; Peterhouse, Cambridge, Ph.D., 1971. *Home:* 19 Millar Pl., Stirling FK8 1XD, Scotland. *Office:* Department of English, University of Stirling, Stirling, Scotland.

CAREER: University of Victoria, Victoria, British Columbia, lecturer in English, 1965-66; University of Stirling, Stirling, Scotland, lecturer in English, 1971—. *Member:* Association for Scottish Literary Studies. *Awards, honors:* Award from Scottish Arts Council, 1970.

WRITINGS: (With James Rankin) *Twenty-Eight Poems*, Aberdeen University Poetry Society, 1964; *Poems*, Akros, 1970; (contributor) Robin Fulton, editor, *Trio: New Poets From Edinburgh*, New Rivers Press, 1971; *True History on the Walls* (poems), William Macdonald, 1976; *Hugh MacDiarmid*, Open University, 1976; (editor with Angus Ogilvie and George Sutherland) *Birds* (poems), Stirling Gallery, 1977; (with Martin Gray) *The Penguin Book of the Bicycle*, Penguin, 1978; (editor with Ogilvie and Sutherland) *Stones* (poems), Stirling Gallery, 1980; *The Literature of Scotland*, Macmillan, 1981. Co-editor of *Scottish Poetry*, 1974-76.

WORK IN PROGRESS: Research on the poetry of Hugh MacDiarmid.

SIDELIGHTS: Watson wrote: ''Poetry is always an exploration of being—a way of understanding the world, an activity that seems to be important to me, and yet the sources of it are finally unknowable. Sometimes I find myself living out states of mind which I formulated imaginatively maybe two or three years earlier in a poem. So only now do I *really* know what I meant then: a healthy surprise for one who believes as I do in the importance of control and craft.''

BIOGRAPHICAL/CRITICAL SOURCES: Lines Review, September, 1972, February, 1973; *Akros*, March, 1973; *Aberdeen University Review*, Volume XLIV, number 3, 1973.

* * *

WATT-EVANS, Lawrence
See EVANS, Lawrence Watt

* * *

WATTS, Richard (Jr.) 1898-1981

OBITUARY NOTICE: Born January 12, 1898, in Parkersburg, W.Va.; died of a cardiac arrest, January 2, 1981, in New York, N.Y. Journalist and drama critic. Watts's career spanned forty years at the *New York Herald Tribune* and the *New York Post*. With brief interruptions as a correspondent in the Far East and South America, Watts continued as a discerning, gentle drama critic until his retirement in 1976. Obituaries and other sources: *The Biographical Encyclopaedia and Who's Who of the American Theatre*, James Heineman, 1966; *Who's Who in the East*, 14th edition, Marquis, 1974; *Who's Who in the Theatre*, 16th edition, Pitman, 1977; *New York Times*, January 3, 1981; *Newsweek*, January 12, 1981.

* * *

WEARING, J. P.

PERSONAL: Born in Birmingham, England; came to the United States in 1974. *Education:* University of Wales, B.A., 1967, Ph.D., 1971; University of Saskatchewan, M.A., 1968. *Office:* Department of English, University of Arizona, Tucson, Ariz. 85721.

CAREER: University of Alberta, Edmonton, lecturer in

English, 1971-74; University of Arizona, Tucson, assistant professor, 1974-77, associate professor of English, 1977—. Theatre critic on CKUA-Radio, 1973-74. *Member:* Modern Language Association of America, Society for Theatre Research (England). *Awards, honors:* Izaac Walton Killam memorial fellowship from University of Alberta, 1971-73; Guggenheim fellow, 1978-79.

WRITINGS: (Editor) *Collected Letters of Sir Arthur Pinero,* University of Minnesota Press, 1974; *The London Stage, 1890-1899: A Calendar of Plays and Players,* Scarecrow, 1976; (with L. W. Connolly) *English Drama and Theatre, 1800-1900,* Gale, 1978; *American and British Theatrical Biography,* Scarecrow, 1979; *The London Stage, 1900-1909,* Scarecrow, 1981. Contributor to literature and theatre journals. Editor of *Nineteenth Century Theatre Research,* 1973—.

WORK IN PROGRESS: Editing *George Bernard Shaw: An Annotated Secondary Bibliography,* publication by Northern Illinois University Press expected in 1983; *The London Stage, 1910-1919,* publication by Scarecrow expected in 1983.

SIDELIGHTS: Wearing commented: "My main ambition is to complete the calendar of plays and players on the London stage from 1890 to the end of 1999, which I hope will rank as one of the major scholarly works in English theatre history."

*   *   *

WEBER, James A(mbrose)   1932-

PERSONAL: Born September 22, 1932, in Evanston, Ill.; son of Philip H. and Marion P. Weber; married Shirley C. Krieter (a teacher), May 7, 1960; children: Christopher John, Theresa Marie. *Education:* Northwestern University, B.S., 1954; Loyola University, Chicago, Ill., M.A., 1969. *Religion:* Roman Catholic. *Home and office:* 6309 North Knox Ave., Chicago, Ill. 60646.

CAREER: James A. Weber & Associates (public relations consultants), Chicago, Ill., president, 1968—. President of Peterson Park Improvement Association, 1977-78. *Member:* Society of Midland Authors.

WRITINGS: Grow or Die (nonfiction), Arlington House, 1976; *Power Grab* (nonfiction), Arlington House, 1979.

WORK IN PROGRESS: Research for a book on morality in America.

SIDELIGHTS: Weber told *CA:* "My first book, *Grow or Die,* discusses the benefits of U.S. population growth. I wrote it in response to what I considered to be the vast outpouring of ideological propaganda concerning the supposed perils of population growth emitted in the media during the late 1960's and early 1970's. Based on what has happened since the book was published, I don't feel I have to change a word in it.

"My second book, *Power Grab,* had a similar birth. The book recommends rapid development of our domestic energy resources in contrast to the no-growth ideology concerning energy which surfaced in the late 1970's under the Carter Administration. Once again, I haven't seen anything since the book was published to indicate that its emphasis was misplaced.

"In writing a book, I first get interested in a subject because it, in my opinion, is being horribly distorted or misinterpreted in the media and by our so-called leaders and 'experts.' I then begin doing research by reading all the books

and articles I can get my hands on. Someplace along the way, I begin to feel dissatisfied with the material that's available and believe that no one has really said what I think should be said on the subject. It is then a short step to the notion that I can say what I think should be said better than anybody. I don't mean this to be egotistical. I just think that an author has to feel something along these lines in order to justify all the work required to write a book.

"Books, it should be said, are not necessarily an instant road to financial success. As a matter of fact, they can result—and in my case they have—in a net financial loss, including the lost time I might otherwise have spent in my regular business which puts the bread and butter on the table. However, although I might wish for a different result, I in no way begrudge the time and effort I've expended to write my books. Writing a book is, of course, a vast learning experience and worth at least several million dollars (inflation, you know) in ego, even if you can't buy groceries at the supermarket with them.

"Although my books address current subjects, I like to think that they include enough of a longterm view that they could be read ten years from now and still be applicable.

"I'm currently doing some limited research for a possible book on the subject of morality in America. Perhaps this next book, if I ever get it done (and that is always a big 'if'), will ring the bell. But, regardless, the answer that I like best to the question 'Why do you write books?' is similar to the answer mountain climbers give as to why they climb mountains: because the subject is there."

*   *   *

WEISS, Edna
See BARTH, Edna

*   *   *

WEITZ, Morris   1916-1981

OBITUARY NOTICE—See index for *CA* sketch: Born July 25, 1916, in Detroit, Mich.; died after a long illness, February 1, 1981, in Boston, Mass. Professor and author. Weitz, a Richard Koret Professor at Brandeis University, specialized in aesthetics and analytical philosophy. His writings include *Philosophy of the Arts, Hamlet and the Philosophy of Literary Criticism, The Beautiful Music,* and *Twentieth Century Philosophy: The Analytical Tradition.* Obituaries and other sources: *New York Times,* February 4, 1981.

*   *   *

WELLISCH, Hans H(anan)   1920-

PERSONAL: Born April 25, 1920, in Vienna, Austria; came to the United States in 1969; son of Fritz and Marianne (Fischer) Wellisch; married Shulamith Oberlaender, February 5, 1946; children: Tamar Seltzer, Ilana Hofmekler, Yuval. *Education:* University of Maryland, Ph.D., 1975. *Religion:* Jewish. *Home:* 5015 Berwyn Rd., College Park, Md. 20740. *Office:* College of Library and Information Services, University of Maryland, College Park, Md. 20742.

CAREER: TAHAL Consulting Engineers Ltd., Tel Aviv, Israel, head of Information Center and Library, 1956-69; University of Maryland, College Park, visiting lecturer, 1969-74, assistant professor, 1975-76, associate professor of library and information services, 1976—. *Member:* International Federation for Documentation, American Society of Indexers, Association for the Bibliography of History (member of council), Association for the Study of Jewish Languages, Israel Society of Special Libraries and Information Centres (founding member). *Awards, honors:* H. W. Wilson Award for Excellence in Indexing from American Society of Indexers, 1979, for index to *The Conversion of Scripts.*

WRITINGS: *Water Resources Development, 1950-1965: An International Bibliography,* Israel Program for Scientific Translation, 1967; *An International Centre for Standards Documentation,* Israel Society of Special Libraries and Information Centres, 1969; *The Universal Decimal Classification: A Programmed Instruction Course,* University of Maryland, 1970; *A Survey of Indexing and Abstracting Services for Water Resources Engineering,* Water Resources Research Center, University of Maryland, 1972; *Transcription and Transliteration: An Annotated Bibliography on the Conversion of Scripts,* Institute of Modern Languages (Silver Spring, Md.), 1975; *Nonbook Materials: A Bibliography of Recent Publications,* University of Maryland, 1975; (editor) *The PRECIS Indexing System: Principles, Applications, and Prospects,* H. W. Wilson, 1977; *The Conversion of Scripts: Its Nature, History, and Utilization,* Wiley, 1978; *Abstracting and Indexing: An International Bibliography,* ABC-Clio Press, 1980; *Conrad Gessner: A Bio-Bibliography,* Inter Documentation Co., 2nd edition, 1981.

In Hebrew: *Hasifriya hameyuhedet: Nihula veirguna* (title means "The Special Library: Its Management and Organization"), Library Department, General Federation of Jewish Labour, 1962; *Hamiyyun haesroni* (title means "Dewey Decimal Classification"), Israel Library Association, 3rd edition, 1965; *Kelale hasidur haalefbeti* (title means "Filing Rules, With Examples in Hebrew and Roman Characters"; introduction in English), Centre for Public Libraries (Jerusalem, Israel), 1966; (editor and translator) *Hamiyyun hesroni hauniversali* (title means "Universal Decimal Classification"), abridged Hebrew edition, Center of Scientific and Technical Information (Tel Aviv, Israel), 1970. Regional editor of "World Bibliographical Series," ABC-Clio Press, 1979—. Contributor to *World Encyclopedia of Library and Information Sciences.* Contributor of about thirty articles to library journals.

WORK IN PROGRESS: A history of bibliographic and library classifications; a manual on the organization of multiscript library catalogs; research on problems posed by different writing systems in bibliographic control; a translation of Rudolf Blum's *Kallimachos und die Literaturverzeichnung bei den Griechen* ("Kallimachos and Greek Bibliography"), publication expected in 1982.

SIDELIGHTS: Wellisch wrote: "The books I have written or edited seem to be concerned with technical matters only—what librarians now call 'bibliographic control'—that is, the cataloging of books and other media and the indication of their subject content. But beyond these purely technical aspects, I have always been concerned with the wants and needs of the end user, the person who seeks information in a book, a movie, a record, or a picture—be that a scientist and scholar, or a first-grader. More often than not, users cannot find what they are looking for in a library because librarians have made it so difficult. This is particularly true for books written in foreign languages and scripts, the readers of which are forced to look them up in a transmogrified form known as Romanization. *Conversion of Scripts* tries to point out the futility of this practice which is convenient for filers of catalog cards but denies, as it were, the immense cultural and intellectual values of works written in any script other than the Roman, such as Arabic, Chinese, Cyrillic, Greek, and Hebrew.

"On a closely related issue, I am concerned about the linguistic aspects of information retrieval systems that are much more important and much less amenable to facile solutions than the mechanical or electronic components of such systems. This pertains especially to indexing and abstracting services that seek to provide access to the ever-growing pool of recorded information. I have also become interested in the history of these tools that are not, as is often thought, recent inventions of the computer age but whose roots go back to the early days of classical antiquity."

AVOCATIONAL INTERESTS: Travel, photography, classical music.

*   *   *

WENDT, Lloyd 1908-

PERSONAL: Born May 16, 1908, in Spencer, S.D.; son of Leo L. and Marie (Nylen) Wendt; married Helen Sigler, June 16, 1932; children: Bette Joan. *Education:* Attended Sioux Falls College, 1928-29; Northwestern University, S.B., 1931, S.M., 1934. *Home:* 1623 Pelican Cove Rd., Sarasota, Fla. 33581.

CAREER: *Sioux Falls Press,* Sioux Falls, S.D., reporter and drama reviewer, 1927-28; publicity director for South Dakota Democratic Central Committee, 1928; reporter for *Daily Argus-Leader,* 1929, telegraph editor, 1932-33; *Chicago Tribune,* Chicago, Ill., 1934-61, worked as reporter, special feature writer for magazine section, editor of *Grafic,* and Sunday editor; *Chicago American,* Chicago, editor, 1961-69; *Chicago Today,* Chicago, editor and publisher, 1969-74; *Chicago Tribune,* associate Sunday editor and associate editor, 1975-77; free-lance writer, 1977—. Past member of faculty at Sioux Falls College; lecturer at Northwestern University, 1946, chairman of Fiction Division at Medill School of Journalism, 1950-53. *Military service:* U.S. Naval Reserve, active duty, 1942-46; became lieutenant commander. *Member:* Society of Midland Authors (president, 1947-50), Society of Journalists.

WRITINGS: (With Herman Kogan) *Lords of the Levee: The Story of Bathhouse John and Hinky Dink,* Bobbs-Merrill, 1943; *Bright Tomorrow,* Bobbs-Merrill, 1945; (with Kogan) *Bet a Million! The Story of John W. Gates,* Bobbs-Merrill, 1948; (with Kogan) *Give the Lady What She Wants! The Story of Marshall Field & Company,* Rand McNally, 1952; (with Kogan) *Big Bill of Chicago,* Bobbs-Merrill, 1953; (with Kogan) *Chicago: A Pictorial History,* Dutton, 1958; *Chicago Tribune: The Rise of a Great American Newspaper,* Rand McNally, 1979; *The Wall Street Journal,* Rand McNally, 1982. Also author of *Gunners Get Glory,* 1944.

*   *   *

WERICH, Jan 1905(?)-1980

OBITUARY NOTICE: Born c. 1905, in Czechoslovakia; died October 31, 1980, in Prague, Czechoslovakia. Actor and author. A comic performer and writer, Werich was known for his anti-authoritarian stance. He acted in the United States during World War II. After 1948, Werich was primarily a stage actor in Czechoslovakia. Obituaries and other sources: *Newsweek,* November 17, 1980.

*   *   *

WERTHEIMER, Marilyn L(ou) 1928-

PERSONAL: Born December 1, 1928, in Pueblo, Colo.; daughter of Louis Robert and Alice (Peck) Schuman; married Michael Wertheimer (a professor of psychology), September 12, 1970. *Education:* Stanford University, B.A., 1950; Columbia University, M.A. and Certificate of the Russian Institute, 1953; attended University of California, Berkeley, 1961-62; University of California, Los Angeles, M.L.S., 1967. *Home:* 546 Geneva Ave., Boulder, Colo. 80302. *Office:* University Libraries, University of Colorado, Boulder, Colo. 80309.

CAREER: Current Digest of the Soviet Press, New York City, proofreader, 1953; Free Europe Committee, New York City, secretary, 1953-54; Council on Foreign Relations, New York City, secretary, 1954-55; World Publishing Co., New York City, secretary, 1955-56; Rockefeller Brothers Fund, New York City, secretary, 1956-57; personal staff of Nelson A. Rockefeller, New York City, secretary, 1957-58; General Dynamics Corp., General Atomic Division, San Diego, Calif., legal secretary, 1959-60, secretary, 1961-63; University of California, San Diego, cataloger of Russian materials, 1965-66, cataloger of science materials, 1967-68; University of Colorado, Boulder, reference librarian and political science bibliographer, 1968—. *Member:* American Library Association, Women's Caucus for Political Science, Colorado Library Association.

WRITINGS: (Editor with husband, Michael Wertheimer, and Wayne Viney) *History of Psychology: A Guide to Information Sources,* Gale, 1979; (contributor) Carl M. White, *Sources of Information in the Social Sciences,* 3rd edition (edited by William H. Webb; Wertheimer was not included in earlier editions), American Library Association, 1981.

WORK IN PROGRESS: An annotated bibliography on psychology.

SIDELIGHTS: "My vocational interests are Russian studies, political science, and librarianship," Wertheimer told *CA.* "I have been teaching a seminar on Soviet civilization annually for many years. My interest in Russia was sparked by my mother who read excerpts to me from books about Russia while I was still a youngster. I was convinced then that inhumanity and war are stupid, and I still am. If we are ever to eliminate these evils I believe people must try to understand other cultures, particularly those very different from their own.

"As a reference librarian I recognize the importance of the availability of good bibliographies. For anyone aspiring to compile one, I recommend diligence, care, persistence, and patience—and awareness that it will take at least five to ten times as long as you first think.

"I love to travel and still find it a thrill to see places I've read about. No matter how much one has read about a country, though, nothing can replace the magic of being there and observing things through one's own eyes. One of the most exciting moments of my life was seeing Red Square for the first time lit up at night. Another was viewing the Iguassu Falls from a distance of a few feet in a small boat."

AVOCATIONAL INTERESTS: Recreational reading, photography, modern dance and ballet, art, listening to classical music, tennis, swimming, skiing, hiking, travel (Eastern and Western Europe, the Soviet Union, South America, Mexico, the Himalayas).

*   *   *

WERTS, Margaret F. 1915-

PERSONAL: Born July 18, 1915, in Washington, D.C.; daughter of Abner H. (a lawyer) and Ethel (Lyons) Ferguson; married Charles L. Werts (a rear admiral in the U.S. Navy), November 22, 1938 (died, 1965). *Education:* Welles-

ley College, B.A., 1936. *Politics:* Democrat. *Religion:* Episcopalian. *Home:* 5104 Allan Rd., Bethesda, Md. 20016. *Office:* Undersea Medical Society, 9650 Rockville Pike, Bethesda, Md. 20014.

CAREER: George Washington University, Washington, D.C., bibliographer at University Medical Center, 1965-73; Undersea Medical Society, Bethesda, Md., bibliographer and associate editor of *Pressure,* 1974—.

WRITINGS: (With C. W. Shilling) *Underwater Medicine and Related Sciences,* Volume I, Plenum, 1973, Volume II, Plenum, 1975, Volume III, Undersea Medical Society, 1977, Volume IV, Undersea Medical Society, 1979; (editor with Shilling and N. R. Schandelmeyer) *Underwater Handbook,* Plenum, 1976.

*   *   *

WEST, Mae 1893-1980

OBITUARY NOTICE—See index for *CA* sketch: Born August 17, 1893, in Brooklyn, N.Y.; died of complications after a stroke, November 22, 1980, in Hollywood, Calif. Actress, comedienne, author, composer, and sex symbol. West was best known for her role as "Diamond Lil." The actress became an American institution in the 1930's when she immortalized the blond bombshell image of swinging hips, silken walk, and listless gestures. She called herself "the first person to bring sex out in the open." By illustrating the humor in sex, the comedienne confronted the general public's inhibitions about the subject. West was a master of innuendo as was evidenced by her famous lines "Beulah, peel me a grape" and "Come up and see me sometime." She wrote in several media, including novels, plays, and screenplays. Her writings include *Babe Gordon, Diamond Lil,* "Sex," "Catherine Was Great," "She Done Him Wrong," and "My Little Chickadee." Obituaries and other sources: Mae West, *The Wit and Wisdom of Mae West,* edited by Joseph Weintraub, Putnam, 1967; West, *Goodness Had Nothing to Do With It* (autobiography), Macfadden-Bartell, 1970; *Washington Post,* November 23, 1980; *New York Times,* November 23, 1980, November 24, 1980; *Chicago Tribune,* November 24, 1980; *Newsweek,* December 1, 1980; *Time,* December 9, 1980.

*   *   *

WETHERBY, Terry (Lynne) 1943-

PERSONAL: Born January 3, 1943, in Louisville, Ky.; daughter of Sherman Henry and Evelyn (Durbin) Wetherby; divorced. *Education:* Attended University of Ghana, 1963-64; Centre College of Kentucky, B.A., 1965; San Francisco State University, M.A. (with honors), 1973; further graduate study at Golden Gate University, 1979—. *Politics:* Democrat. *Religion:* "Christian ethics." *Home:* 32 Josiah Ave., San Francisco, Calif. 94112.

CAREER: Writer. *Awards, honors: Conversations* was named a best book for young adults by American Library Association, 1979.

WRITINGS: Black Roses (poems), Aisling, 1975; (editor) *New Poets: Women,* Les Femmes, 1976; (editor) *I Love Radio,* Gloger, 1977; (editor) *Conversations: Working Women Talk About Doing a "Man's Job,"* Les Femmes, 1978.

WORK IN PROGRESS: Co-editing *Women Poets of North America: A Trilingual Anthology,* with Miriam de Uriarte and Judith Serin; co-editing *Dirty Linen* (tentative title), an anthology of first-person erotic accounts by women, with Ellen Cooney.

SIDELIGHTS: Terry Wetherby commented: "The purpose of the writer is to answer a high calling—to contribute to the understanding and growth of humanity through the written word. Another area of my life in which I strive to achieve such an objective is my work in traditionally male occupations—as a skilled welder, millhand, and as a member of two male-dominated blue-collar unions. My next and last profession, other than writing and editing, will be that of attorney. With the law as a vehicle I hope to achieve some of the goals writing has not realized."

*   *   *

WHELAN, James Robert   1933-

PERSONAL: Born July 27, 1933, in Buffalo, N.Y.; son of Robert J. (a police officer) and Margaret (Southard) Whelan; married Pamela Ewing, April 8, 1978; children: Robert J., Laura, Craig, Heather Elizabeth. *Education:* Attended University of Buffalo, 1951-53, and Harvard University, 1966-67; Florida International University, B.A., 1973. *Home:* 8155 Morningside Dr., Hidden Valley, Loomis, Calif. 95650. *Office: Sacramento Union,* 301 Capitol Mall, Sacramento, Calif. 95812.

CAREER: United Press International (UPI), correspondent in Buffalo, N.Y., Boston, Mass., Providence, R.I., and New York, N.Y., 1955-58, manager in Providence, 1955-57, foreign correspondent in Buenos Aires, Argentina, Caracas, Venezuela, and San Juan, Puerto Rico, 1958-68, country manager in Venezuela, 1961-66, division manager in San Juan, 1966-68; Scripps Howard Newspaper Alliance, Washington, D.C., correspondent, 1970-71; *Miami News,* Miami, Fla., managing editor, 1971-73; Hialeah Publishing Co., Hialeah, Fla., president and editor, 1974-77; Panax Newspapers, Washington, D.C., vice-president and editorial director, 1977-80; *Sacramento Union,* Sacramento, Calif., vice-president and editor, 1980—. *Military service:* U.S. Army, 1953-55. *Member:* National Press Club, Overseas Press Club (president of Caracas chapter, 1962-64, and San Juan chapter, 1967-68), University Club of Washington, Sigma Delta Chi. *Awards, honors:* Nieman fellowship to Harvard University, 1966-67; citation of excellence from Overseas Press Club, 1971, for best reporting on Latin America in any medium; Unity award in journalism from Lincoln University, 1975.

WRITINGS: Through the American Looking Glass: Central America in Crisis (monograph), Council for Inter-American Security, 1980; *Allende: Death of a Marxist Dream,* Arlington House, 1981. Contributor of articles to magazines, including *Saturday Review* and *Signature.*

WORK IN PROGRESS: The Marxist Road to Power, publication expected in 1981.

SIDELIGHTS: Whelan told *CA:* "Although I have not consciously set for myself the goal of debunking myths, all three of my major works to date do precisely that—or, at the minimum, take careful, considered aim at myths. The first of them, the subject of *Allende: Death of a Marxist Dream,* concerns Salvador Allende, the Chilean president whose death was as much a myth as was his public life. The book describes more fully, more thoroughly, more authoritatively, I believe, than any other, the last hours in the life of this Pirandellian figure—hours which saw him die by his own hand (and not as the martyred victim of some sordid assassin), and in a revolution instigated, plotted, and played out by Chileans acting alone, with neither the knowledge nor connivance of outsiders and for reasons of their own.

"The second book—in the hands of an academic house I hope will become the publishers—attacks still another myth of Chile: the myth, so long favored by American, Latin American, and European intellectuals (and/or political scientists) that Chile was, prior to 1973, the flowering of a political civilization with few rivals in the world. I argue and document that Chile was, in fact, a case study in the disintegration of the social, economic, and political framework needed to sustain a functioning democracy. The book is, then, a maverick (but entirely credible) political history of Chile from 1920 to 1970, the year of Allende's election.

"The third myth, considered in the monograph, involves the cliches about Central America that became the justification for the incredibly inept U.S. foreign policy in that region in recent years. For the most part, however, my professional endeavors center on the transmission of facts—the stock-in-trade of the journalistic craft."

*   *   *

WHITAKER, James W.   1936-

PERSONAL: Born July 15, 1936, in Spring Valley, Ill. *Education:* Oberlin College, B.A., 1960; University of Wisconsin, Madison, M.S., 1962, Ph.D., 1965. *Office:* Department of History, Iowa State University, Ross Hall, Ames, Iowa 50011.

CAREER: University of Wisconsin (now University of Wisconsin—Madison), instructor in history, 1964-65; Iowa State University, Ames, assistant professor, 1965-68, associate professor of history, 1968—. *Military service:* U.S. Army, 1954-56. *Member:* American Historical Association, Organization of American Historians, Agricultural History Society.

WRITINGS: (Contributor) Ernest Kohlmetz and others, editors, *The Study of American History,* Volume II, Dushkin, 1974; *Feedlot Empire: Beef Cattle Feeding in Illinois and Iowa, 1840-1900,* Iowa State University Press, 1975. Contributor to professional journals.

*   *   *

WHITEHEAD, Don(ald) F.   1908-1981

OBITUARY NOTICE—See index for *CA* sketch: Born April 8, 1908, in Inman, Va.; died of lung cancer, January 12, 1981, in Knoxville, Tenn. Journalist. During World War II, Whitehead served as a war correspondent for the Associated Press (AP). He was the first American reporter to send a dispatch telling of Paris's liberation. Later, in 1950, he was a war correspondent in Korea. Whitehead was awarded a Pulitzer Prize in 1951 for internal affairs reporting of the Korean War. He received a second Pulitzer Prize in 1953 for his coverage of President-elect Eisenhower's secret trip to Korea. Whitehead also received the Medal of Freedom from the U.S. Army and the Polk Award for wire service reporting. His writings include *The FBI Story: A Report to the People, Journey Into Crime, Border Guard: The Story of the United States Customs Service,* and *Attack on Terror: The FBI Against the Ku Klux Klan in Mississippi.* Obituaries and other sources: *Chicago Tribune,* January 14, 1981; *New York Times,* January 14, 1981.

*   *   *

WHITING, John (Robert)   1917-1963

PERSONAL: Born November 15, 1917, in Salisbury, Wiltshire, England; died of cancer, June 16, 1963, in London, England; son of Charles (a solicitor) and Dorothy (Herring) Whiting; married Asthore Lloyd Mawson; children: four. *Education:* Attended Royal Academy of Dramatic Art, 1935-37. *Residence:* Sussex, England.

CAREER: Playwright. *Military service:* Served with Royal Artillery during World War II. *Awards, honors:* Festival of Britain award from Arts Council, 1951, for "Saint's Day."

WRITINGS: John Whiting on Theatre, Alan Ross, 1966; *The Art of the Dramatist,* edited by Ronald Hayman, London Magazine Editorial, 1970.

Plays: "Conditions of Agreement" (two-act), 1946, revised one-act version produced as "A Walk in the Desert" in Bristol, England, at Mountview Theatre Club, 1964; *Saint's Day,* completed, 1947 (first produced in London, England, at Arts Theatre Club, September, 1951), Heinemann, 1963; *A Penny for a Song* (comic fantasy; first produced in England at Haymarket Theatre, 1951, produced on the West End, 1951), Heinemann, 1964; *Marching Song* (three-act; first produced in England at St. Martin's Theatre, 1954), Samuel French, 1954; "Gates of Summer," first produced, 1956; *Plays* (collection; contains "Saint's Day," "A Penny for a Song," and "Marching Song"), Heinemann, 1957; *The Devils* (adapted from the book, *The Devils of Loudon,* by Aldous Huxley; first produced in London at Aldwych Theatre, 1961, produced on Broadway, November 16, 1965), Heinemann, 1961, Hill & Wang, 1962; *No Why?* (one-act; first produced in London at Aldwych Theatre, July 2, 1964), Samuel French, 1961; *The Collected Plays of John Whiting* (contains "Conditions of Agreement," "Saint's Day," "A Penny for a Song," "Marching Song," "The Gates of Summer," "No Why?," "A Walk in the Desert," "The Devils," and "Norman and the Nomads"), edited by Hayman, two volumes, Theatre Art Books, 1969.

Radio plays: "Paul Southman," 1946, "Eye Witness," 1947, "The Stairway," 1949, "Love's Old Sweet Song," 1950.

Screenplays: "The Ship That Died of Shame," 1954, "Castle Minerva," 1955, "The Golden Fool," 1956, "Talk of the Devil," 1956, "The Captain's Table," 1957, "The Gypsum Flower," 1958, "The Reason Why," 1958, "Gentlemen of China," 1960, "Young Cassidy," 1960.

Translator of several plays by Andre Obey, Armond Salacrou, and Jean Anouilh.

Contributor of reviews to periodicals, including *London Magazine.*

SIDELIGHTS: An extremely underrated playwright during his lifetime, John Whiting has since been recognized as a leading voice in post-war theatre and the predecessor of such writers as Samuel Beckett and Harold Pinter. Although his first important play, "Saint's Day," was condemned by critics and audiences alike because they failed to understand much of the religious symbolism, it won the coveted Festival of Britain prize in 1951. The play centers on an aging poet, approaching senility, who has been hounded relentlessly by enraged critics and audiences throughout his life. When these detractors then throw a dinner party in his honor after so many years of abuse and attempt to force him to attend, the poet mistakenly believes they are really planning to kill him. This dark tragedy, which later was cited as a mirror of Whiting's own life, served as a forerunner to his later studies of self-destruction and alienation.

Like "Saint's Day," Whiting's next major play, "Marching Song," depicts the torment of an individual at the hands of cruel and contemptible strangers. The central character is a German officer, General Forster. After being imprisoned for seven years following the war, he is released only to learn that he is to be put on trial as a scapegoat for the loss of the war. It seems that while on an important campaign his tanks had been obstructed by a large group of children, unarmed

though determined not to let the troops pass. Infuriated, Forster shot one through the head. When his soldiers followed his lead and all four hundred children lay dead, he is appalled and outraged. So struck was he with the senselessness and brutality of the situation, he refused to advance his men in order to capture a bridge vital to the German strategy. Although this act alone was not the sole cause of the defeat, Forster was singled out to serve as a scapegoat to appease the angry mob. He is, however, offered an alternative to the humiliation of a public trial: suicide.

According to Benedict Nightingale of *New Statesman,* Whiting is pointing out in this drama that a man "is more than the product of other people's uninformed imaginations: he demands further exploration." Raymond Williams, in his book *Drama From Ibsen to Brecht,* noted that the play "is not penetrating: not the savagely exposing, disturbed and distorted action of the post-liberal collapse. It is a late compression, internally honest and serious and restrained, of an achieved structure of feeling and its essential conventions. The tension, that is to say, has all gone inward."

However unpopular with the general public, "The Devils" is considered Whiting's masterwork. Commissioned by director Peter Hall for the 1961 season of the Royal Shakespeare Company, the play was adapted from *The Devils of Loudon* by Aldous Huxley. It is the story of the martyrdom of Father Grandier, a seventeenth-century libertine priest whose escapades have long angered many of the townsfolk. The sexually-obsessed nuns of the neighboring convent, moreover, in order to excuse their own excesses, claim that the priest is possessed by the devil and they are powerless to resist his advances. Together they conspire against Grandier. Refusing to confess to being an agent of the devil even after agonizing torture, he is handed over to be burned at the stake.

Condemned by outraged Catholics, the play was considered a success only by the critics. One reason given for its failure was its inherent complexity: a tangle of plots and subplots, two dozen characters, and sixty changes of scenery. Another reason, and one that has been offered for the bulk of his works, is that after the harrowing experience of World War II the British public desperately craved light-hearted entertainment; Whiting insisted for the most part on presenting doleful and nihilistic drama.

Although he was writing about "The Devils," Richard Gilman of *Commonweal* summarized the art of John Whiting: "His drama is in the fullest sense a universal one: it is a complex, sometimes brutal and shocking but always beautifully passionate image of faculties and powers in collision with one another, of the body struggling against the spirit and becoming reconciled to it, of lust learning its own nature through sacrifice, and, on a different and more immediate level, of secular authority using religion for the consolidation of its control."

BIOGRAPHICAL/CRITICAL SOURCES: Commonweal, December 20, 1963; *Partisan Review,* spring, 1966; Raymond Williams, *Drama From Ibsen to Brecht,* Chatto & Windus, 1968; *Spectator,* November 8, 1969; *Listener,* March 26, 1970; *New Statesman,* April 3, 1970; *Times Literary Supplement,* August 21, 1970; *New York Times,* June 8, 1978; *Time,* June 26, 1978.

OBITUARIES: New York Times, June 17, 1963; *Drama,* autumn, 1963.*

WHITING, Robert 1942-

PERSONAL: Born October 24, 1942, in Long Branch, N.J.; son of Sheldon George (a businessman) and Josephine (Campbell) Whiting. *Education:* Attended Humboldt State University, 1960-61; Sophia University, Tokyo, B.A., 1969. *Home:* Ambassador Arms, No. 502, Roppongi 3-15-10, Tokyo, Japan.

CAREER: Encyclopaedia Britannica, Tokyo, Japan, editor, 1969-72; Grolier International, Tokyo, project editor, 1972-73; Kelly Girl, New York, N.Y., typist, 1974; Time-Life Books, Tokyo, project director, 1975-76; Creative Resources Group, Tokyo, president and co-owner, 1977—. Translator for FU51-TV, Tokyo, 1978. Consultant to *Encyclopaedia Britannica,* 1977, and British Broadcasting Corp., 1979. *Military service:* U.S. Air Force, 1961-65.

WRITINGS: The Chrysanthemum and the Bat (nonfiction), Dodd, 1977. Work represented in anthologies, *A Culture-and-Personality Approach to Human Relations in a Changing World,* edited by Stanley Stark, Ginn, 1979, and *Sport in the Socio-Cultural Process,* edited by Susan Birrell, Brown, 1980. Author of numerous documentary film scripts on Japan for Foreign Ministry of Japan; author of weekly column, "Kiku to Batto," in *Daily Sports.* Contributor to magazines, including *Sports Illustrated, Sport, Readers' Digest, California, Pacific, Playboy* (Japan), *Bungei Sports Graphic,* and *Winds.*

WORK IN PROGRESS: A sequel to *The Chrysanthemum and the Bat;* research on the foreigner as a "villain" in Japanese sports such as baseball, boxing, and pro-wrestling.

SIDELIGHTS: Whiting told *CA:* "I became a writer by accident. My original field was writing 'English as a second language' (ESL) learning materials for Asians. It was a field I had become involved in while going to school in Tokyo and a field I stayed in until 1977. On frequent trips back to the United States, I would of course try to 'explain' Japan to people. I'd talk about the country's nonmilitant unions that schedule limited strikes so as not to inconvenience anyone, the lifetime employment system, the 'hand-in-hand' relationship of government and big business, and all I got were blank stares 90 percent of the time. When I started talking about the Japanese approach to baseball (their adopted national sport in which 'spring training' starts in January and superstar players never hold out for more money and never criticize their manager or their teammates because it would disrupt team harmony), then people started to listen because there was a common ground of interest.

"It was while living in New York, out of work and subsisting as a Kelly Girl employee, that I decided to write a book about the Japanese national character through baseball. I wanted to address the man on the street in the hopes of increasing his understanding of Japanese thinking. I tried to write a book that didn't read like a doctoral thesis; one that described the 'real Japan' without resorting to academic analyses of socio-political-economic phenomena. I think I succeeded because the book has been critically acclaimed both as a sports book and as an introduction to Japan that a non-sports fan can understand. Ironically, the book is on reading lists in the Japanese departments of many U.S. universities. (The book was a minor-seller in the United States, but the translated edition was a best-seller in Japan.)

"I've lived in Japan for twelve of the past sixteen years and in that time it's become clear to me that a study of the games a given people play is one of the easiest and most effective ways to understand their culture. The bulk of my writing over the past three years (primarily for magazine publica-

tion) has been on the theme of cross-cultural understanding through sports.

"Since leaving the ESL field in 1977 I've become a full-time writer. That's a short time and I'm still learning. To me writing is still a lot of pain. (Oh, how I envy the 'one-draft' writers.) But the end result is worth it. I have also come to realize that if a writer has a good story to tell, he doesn't need a lot of style, as long as he has mastered the basic mechanics of his craft. All he has to do is let the story tell itself.

"In my opinion, Japan and America are not really designed to understand one another, so great are the respective differences in thinking of the two peoples. It is my hope that I will be able in some small way to help narrow the gap that separates them."

AVOCATIONAL INTERESTS: Reading, studying Chinese ideographs, drinking beer.

*   *   *

WHITMORE, George 1945-

PERSONAL: Born September 27, 1945, in Denver, Colo.; son of Lowell A. (an airline mechanic) and Irene D. (Davis) Whitmore. *Education:* MacMurray College, B.A., 1967; graduate study at Bennington College, 1967-68. *Agent:* Michael Powers, Hutto Management, 110 West 57th St., New York, N.Y. 10019.

CAREER: Planned Population-World Population, New York City, member of editorial staff, 1968-72; Citizens Housing and Planning Council, New York City, member of administrative staff, 1972—. *Awards, honors:* Woodrow Wilson fellowship and Bennington Masters fellowship, both 1967; grant from New York State Creative Arts Public Service, 1976.

WRITINGS: Getting Gay in New York (poems), Free Milk Fund Press, 1976; *The Confessions of Danny Slocum: Gay Life in the Big City,* St. Martin's, 1980; *Out Here: Fire Island Tales* (stories), Seahorse Press, 1981.

Plays: "The Caseworker" (two-act), first produced in New York City at Playwrights Horizons, May, 1976; "A Life of Gertrude Stein: Flight/The Legacy" (two one-acts), first produced in New York City at Eighteenth Street Playhouse, April, 1979; "The Rights" (two-act), first produced in New York City at The Glines, Network Theatre, January, 1980. Also author of unproduced plays "Secretaries," "Nebraska," and "Beloved Intruders" (radio play).

Author of "Literature," a biweekly column in *Advocate,* 1975-76. Contributor of stories, articles, poems, and reviews to magazines and newspapers, including *Alternate, New York Times, Journal of the Gay Academic Union, Washington Post, Drummer, Body Politics,* and *Boston Gay Review.* Contributing editor of *Advocate,* 1974-76.

WORK IN PROGRESS: Deep Dish, a serial; *The New York Native.*

SIDELIGHTS: Whitmore wrote: "I have been a gay activist since 1972, so it's only natural that my writing interests should center around the subjects of gay liberation and gay life. My first experience in writing was quite academic; but my professional life began with journalism, reporting on progress in gay-rights efforts for national publications. Concurrently, my first book of poetry was the first openly gay volume to be awarded a major grant, in 1976, and my play 'The Caseworker' is among the first 'post-Stonewall' gay dramas. 'The Caseworker' has been called a 'seminal work in gay theater.' With this and other work, I believe I helped develop a basis for modern gay literary criticism. I applied some of these principles to a study of Thoreau and his contemporaries in 'Friendship in New England,' which was well received by Thoreau critics and biographers.

"Recently, I've concentrated on playwriting and fiction. *The Confessions of Danny Slocum* elicited a remarkable reader response. The subject of the book is sex therapy—a fictionalized account of one man's treatment. But this only serves as the spine of the book; it's also an examination (humorous and wry, I should add) of gay life in urban America.

"A career in gay writing (merely being called and thinking of oneself as 'a gay writer' is a new development in the profession, I think) has many rewards. The first among those is the sense of building a minority literature that has in the past been repressed from the outside and often cryptic in its intentions and techniques. It has been very important for me to help to rescue gay works from the past and reassess what has been a fragmented tradition. This undertaking is hardly the kind of thing one can do alone. Gay criticism as such is a highly collaborative effort as many of us across the country (and internationally as well) pool our insights and information. Being a 'post-Stonewall' gay writer has been an exciting undertaking, too. The relationships between politics and journalism, politics and literature, are fascinating, and the influences of progressive movements and/or feminism to what we're doing as gay writers are profound.

"In practice, however, I'd have to say that politics is very distinctly separate from my creative work (though not my daily life) at this point. Unless I set out to write a parable or a broad satire, I've found that political concerns are beside the point in my fiction. Instead, I try to reflect gay life as it really is.

"The accusation always made against gay (or indeed, any minority) literature is that it's too hermetic. I'd say the most hermetic thing about it is how the commercial publishing scene limits it. Aside from the apartheid that exists between the gay world (often loose but sometimes highly ghettoized) and the general culture, gay writers have an uphill battle —first to be understood, then to be published.

"Currently, I'm getting great pleasure out of short fiction, of which I'm publishing a lot. The market for gay fiction, while not lucrative, is good in the magazine field—somewhat like the market for general fiction forty or more years ago—and the genre is strong and growing.

"After a decade or so of gay writing, I think I can say that this particular generation of gay writers will not disappear nor will our works be destroyed. Edmund White, Felice Picano, Armistead Maupin, Paul Monette and many others—not to mention scores of excellent poets—have created a very exciting and durable literature. I'm proud to be part of it."

*   *   *

WIAT, Philippa 1933-

PERSONAL: Born October 2, 1933, in London, England; daughter of Henry Edmund (a civil servant) and Anne (Turner) Wyatt; married Dennis Ferridge (an accountant); children: Elaine, Teresa, Francesca. *Education:* Attended grammar school in Wimbledon, England. *Religion:* Roman Catholic. *Residence:* Sussex, England. *Office:* 5 Orchard Ave., Chichester, Sussex PO19 3BE, England.

CAREER: Writer, 1972—.

WRITINGS—Novels; all published by R. Hale: *Like as the Roaring Waves,* 1972; *The Master of Blandeston Hall,* 1973;

The Heir of Allington, 1973; *The Knight of Allington,* 1974; *The Rebel of Allington,* 1974; *Lord of the Black Boar,* 1975; *Sword of Woden,* 1975; *Tree of Vortigern,* 1976; *The Queen's Fourth Husband,* 1976; *Lion Without Claws,* 1976, St. Martin's, 1977; *The Atheling,* 1977; *Sound Now the Passing-Bell,* 1977; *My Lute Be Still,* 1977; *Raven in the Wind,* 1978; *Maid of Gold,* 1978; *Yet a Lion,* 1978; *Westerfalca,* 1979; *The Golden Chariot,* 1979; *The Four-Poster,* 1979; *Lord of the Wolf,* 1980; *Shadow of Samain,* 1980.

WORK IN PROGRESS: Five Gold Rings, a historical novel about Katherine Grey, cousin and one-time heir to Queen Elizabeth I.

SIDELIGHTS: Philippa Wiat told *CA:* "From Sir Thomas Wyatt, the sixteenth-century poet, onward, my family has produced more than its fair share of writers and poets, though I myself did not start writing professionally until the youngest of my three daughters had reached school age. It did not occur to me until the day I started writing that I would be a writer, although many people find that difficult to believe. I simply woke up one morning with an urge to write. I can only assume that my writing genes had started working, for it was then I had the idea of writing a saga of my family, writing under my maiden name, but using the archaic spelling, Wiat.

"I had grown up with the knowledge that I came from a literary family, which included Sir Thomas, his grandson George Wyatt, who was the first biographer of Anne Boleyn, and his great-grandson, Sir Francis Wyatt, who became governor of Virginia in the early days of colonization, and also wrote poetry.

"I spent many days at the British Musuem, researching that large collection of family papers known as 'The Wyatt Manuscripts,' and at home I wrote and rewrote almost unceasingly until my first novel was completed.

"It is generally agreed amongst authors that everyone thinks writing is easy—except authors! In my experience nothing is more true. I next started writing my Allington trilogy and for the three years following worked with feverish intensity, making up for lost time as it were, writing for twelve hours a day, seven days a week.

"The Allington trilogy was centered around Sir Thomas Wyatt who, born at Allington Castle in 1503, became a favorite of Henry VIII and ambassador to Spain. Sir Thomas was reputedly the lover of Anne Boleyn, the second wife of King Henry VIII. Both research and family tradition have convinced me that, not only was Sir Thomas Anne's lover, he was moreover the father of her daughter, Queen Elizabeth I."

BIOGRAPHICAL/CRITICAL SOURCES: Eastbourne Herald, October 27, 1973, December 10, 1977, April 15, 1978; *Kent Messenger,* May, 1976; *Wimbledon News,* September 17, 1976; *Sunday Telegraph,* July 16, 1978.

*   *   *

WICKS, Harold Vernon, Jr. 1931-
(Harry Wicks)

PERSONAL: Born May 13, 1931, in Mineola, N.Y.; son of Harold Vernon and Anna C. Wicks; married Maureen Marlow (a court clerk), October 21, 1951; children: Ellen, Harold Vernon III (deceased), Patricia, James, John. *Education:* Pratt Institute, A.A.S., 1961. *Politics:* Republican. *Religion:* Roman Catholic. *Home:* 32 Rose Ave., Floral Park, N.Y. 11001. *Agent:* Bertha Klausner International Literary Agency, Inc., 71 Park Ave., New York, N.Y. 10016. *Office:*

Popular Mechanics, 224 West 57th St., New York, N.Y. 10019.

CAREER: Ran own home improvement and custom furniture business until 1967; National Association of Homebuilders, Long Island, N.Y., member of marketing committee, 1979—. Workshop director for *Woman's Day,* 1975-76; home and shop director and editor for *Popular Mechanics,* 1977—. Vice-president of South Side Civic Association of Floral Park, 1963-64. *Military service:* U.S. Army, 1950-53; became first lieutenant.

WRITINGS—Under name Harry Wicks: *How to Plan, Buy, or Build Your Leisure Home,* Reston, 1976; *Furniture Refinishing,* Grosset, 1977; (editor) *Simply Fix It,* Hearst Books, 1980; (editor) *Popular Mechanics: Five Hundred Hints,* Hearst Books, 1981. Associate editor of *Popular Science,* 1967-68; workshop editor of *Popular Mechanics,* 1969-75.

WORK IN PROGRESS: A series of craft books for Hearst Books.

SIDELIGHTS: Wicks commented: "To test my expertise and to gain insightful feedback from readers, I teach basic woodworking in an adult education course on Long Island. My aim is to present expert technical advice to readers in the area of home improvement, maintenance, and home workshop activities in a setting that is pleasing to the eye. The ideas must be sound, functional, and attractive. I prefer material to be prepared by experts in the field rather than by academic-type editors who never practice what they preach."

*   *   *

WICKS, Harry
    See WICKS, Harold Vernon, Jr.

*   *   *

WIDENOR, William C(ramer)   1937-
PERSONAL: Born December 15, 1937, in Easton, Pa.; son of Thornton C. and Florence R. (Freeman) Widenor; married Mary Helen Barrett (a lawyer), December 27, 1964 (divorced); children: Geoffrey, Victoria. *Education:* Princeton University, A.B. (with honors), 1959; graduate study at Harvard University Law School, 1959-60; University of California, Berkeley, M.A., 1969, Ph.D., 1975. *Religion:* Episcopalian. *Home:* 811 South Victor, Champaign, Ill. 61820. *Office:* Department of History, University of Illinois, 309 Gregory Hall, Urbana, Ill. 61801.

CAREER: U.S. Department of State, Foreign Service, Washington, D.C., consular officer in Munich, West Germany, 1961-63, and Zurich, Switzerland, 1963-64, United Nations development and human rights officer at Office of International Organization Affairs in Washington and U.S. observer on United Nations subcommission on the protection of minorities, 1964-66, consul and second secretary at embassy in Mexico City, Mexico, 1966-68; University of Illinois, Urbana, assistant professor of American diplomatic history, 1975—, fellow of Center for Advanced Study, 1978.

WRITINGS: Henry Cabot Lodge and the Search for an American Foreign Policy, University of California Press, 1980. Contributor to history and political science journals.

WORK IN PROGRESS: A critical analysis of U.S. planning for the United Nations, 1942-45.

SIDELIGHTS: "On the whole," wrote John Thompson of the *Times Literary Supplement,* Henry Cabot Lodge "has not had a good press." In *Henry Cabot Lodge and the*

Search for an American Foreign Policy, William Widenor is "clearly concerned to rehabilitate Lodge after his condemnation by ... historians," Thompson noted. Lodge, who was an American legislator, is most often remembered for leading the opposition against the Treaty of Versailles and the covenant of the League of Nations. Widenor explains the stands that Lodge took and argues that they were consistent with his conservative political beliefs and his pessimistic view of human nature. Thompson praised Widenor for writing an "impressive study of the development of Lodge's thought on foreign policy questions."

BIOGRAPHICAL/CRITICAL SOURCES: Times Literary Supplement, January 2, 1981.

*   *   *

WIENER, Harvey Shelby   1940-
PERSONAL: Born April 7, 1940, in Brooklyn, N.Y.; son of Jack (in sales) and Frieda (Grossman) Wiener; married Barbara Koster (a teacher), August 28, 1965; children: Melissa Grace, Joseph Micah, Saul Adam. *Education:* Brooklyn College of the City University of New York, B.S., 1961, M.A., 1968; Fordham University, Ph.D., 1971. *Home:* 309 Clearview Lane, Massapequa, N.Y. 11758. *Office:* Department of English, LaGuardia Community College of the City University of New York, Long Island City, N.Y. 11101.

CAREER: Queensborough Community College of the City University of New York, Bayside, N.Y., instructor in basic skills, 1970-71; LaGuardia Community College of the City University of New York, Long Island City, N.Y., assistant professor, 1971-73, associate professor, 1973-77, professor of English, 1978—. Adjunct assistant professor at Brooklyn College of the City University of New York, 1970-72; visiting assistant professor at State University of New York at Stony Book, 1974—; visiting associate professor at Pennsylvania State University, 1976-77. President of Council of Writing Program Administrators. *Member:* Modern Language Association of America, National Council of Teachers of English, Conference on College Composition and Communication, Phi Beta Kappa. *Awards, honors:* National Endowment for the Humanities fellow, 1972-73, 1974.

WRITINGS: Creating Compositions, McGraw, 1973, 3rd edition, 1981; (with Rose Palmer) *The Writing Lab,* Glencoe, 1974, 2nd edition, 1980; (with Charles Bazerman) *English Skills Handbook,* Houghton, 1977; (with Bazerman) *Reading Skills Handbook,* Houghton, 1978; *Any Child Can Write,* McGraw, 1978; (with Gilbert Muller) *The Story Prose Reader,* McGraw, 1979; *Total Swimming,* Simon & Schuster, 1980; *The Writing Room,* Oxford University Press, 1981. Contributor to scholarly journals.

WORK IN PROGRESS: The McGraw Hill College Handbooks with Richard Marius; *The Shadrach Mission,* a novel.

*   *   *

WIENER, Sam
    See DOLGOFF, Sam

*   *   *

WILDER, Alec
    See WILDER, Alexander Lafayette Chew

*   *   *

WILDER, Alexander Lafayette Chew   1907-1980
    (Alec Wilder)
OBITUARY NOTICE: Born February 16, 1907, in Roches-

ter, N.Y.; died of lung cancer, December 24, 1980, in Gainesville, Fla. Composer and author. Wilder, educated at the Eastman School of Music, was a versatile and individualistic composer of popular songs and orchestral and chamber music. His unique works often blended jazz and classical musical styles. Wilder is best known for his hundreds of popular songs, which are characterized by unusual, haunting melodies. Many of his pieces were commissioned by notables such as Frank Sinatra, Bing Crosby, and Mitch Miller. Wilder's 1972 book, *American Popular Song,* was highly acclaimed, and led to a weekly hour-long radio show in 1976, with Wilder as its witty, encyclopedic host. Obituaries and other sources: *The Biographical Encyclopedia and Who's Who of the American Theatre,* James Heineman, 1966; *Authors of Books for Young People,* 2nd edition, Scarecrow, 1971; Alec Wilder, *Letters I Never Mailed,* Little, Brown, 1975; *Who's Who in America,* 40th edition, Marquis, 1978; *Current Biography,* Wilson, 1980, February, 1981; *New York Times,* December 25, 1980; *Newsweek,* January 5, 1981; *Time,* January 12, 1981.

* * *

WILES, Domini 1942-
(Amy Van Hassen, Tina Williams)

PERSONAL: Original name Domini High-Smith; name legally changed in 1972; born August 10, 1942, in Bradford, England; daughter of Vernon Washington (a farmer) and Mary (Daynes) High-Smith; married three times (divorced); children: (first marriage) Tammy. *Education:* Attended secondary school in Bradford, England. *Home and office:* 952 Great Horton Rd., Bradford, West Yorkshire BO7 4AE, England. *Agent:* Murray Pollinger, 4 Garrick St., London WC2E 9BH, England.

CAREER: Printing assistant in Bradford, England, 1957-59; factory worker in Bradford, 1959-72; Lister's Mill (art and craft shop and gallery), Bradford, co-owner, 1972-74; Boardman & Smith (weavers), Bradford, wages clerk, 1975-77; writer, 1977—. *Awards, honors:* Small short story award from Mills & Boon (publisher), 1974, for "Someone for Sharon."

WRITINGS: Death Flight, Collins, 1977; *Skin Deep,* Collins, 1978; *The Betrayer,* Collins, 1979; (under pseudonym Amy Van Hassen) *Menace* (suspense novel), New England Library, 1980. Contributor of stories to *Fiesta,* under pseudonym Tina Williams.

WORK IN PROGRESS: Killers, short stories dealing with the psychology of killers; *White Trash,* a novel on distorted grievances in a multi-racial society; *Victim,* a novel about society's attitudes to the rape victim and her treatment within the family.

SIDELIGHTS: Domini Wiles told *CA:* "Inadequately educated, of mixed blood (my grandfather was a black American), and from a poor background, I am fascinated by the inner drives and outer pressures (real or imaginery) of other people. The personality of the 'outsider' intrigues me, as do the shifting attitudes of society and the family.

"I live alone, have few friends, and am striving to combine my flair for storytelling with the results of my private studies and experiences. My writing is compulsive. In order to 'rest' between novels, I write essays, short stories, and poetry —anything to keep the words flowing.

"My career began with my marriage to Brian Wiles (since divorced) who encouraged me to attempt publication of the stacks of work which took so much of my time and energy

only to be stored away in cupboards and suitcases. *Death Flight* was my first book to be published, and was an instant success.

"I wrote *Death Flight* while working full time as a wages clerk and tending a home and family, just to prove that I could do it. The first half of the book took six weeks to complete; the second only took one week due to the interest of a literary agent.

"Once an idea presents itself, I am driven to getting it down on paper whatever the cost in lost sleep, frayed tempers, and missed meals. While involved in a book, my diet deteriorates to bread, coffee, and cigarettes, friends are neglected, my social life ends, and I survive quite happily on nothing but inspiration and hard work. I am fascinated by the actual mental change that takes place once a book is under way.

"To aspiring writers I would say, 'Believe in yourself and never allow disappointment, criticism, or even downright ridicule to daunt your enthusiasm.'"

* * *

WILKIE, Jane 1917-

PERSONAL: Born March 30, 1917, in Philadelphia, Pa.; daughter of Donald W. (a writer) and Katharine (Einwechter) Wilkie; married Robert Botwinick, October 27, 1946 (divorced, 1967); children: Jan Botwinick Logan. *Education:* Attended high school in Philadelphia, Pa. *Home and office:* 820 Cookie Lane, Fallbrook, Calif. 92028. *Agent:* Barbara Lowenstein, 250 West 57th St., New York, N.Y. 10019.

CAREER: Secretary in Philadelphia, Pa., and Los Angeles, Calif., 1935-42; *Western Family,* Los Angeles, in advertising sales, 1940-42; *Movieland,* Los Angeles, West Coast editor, 1942-44; *Modern Screen,* Los Angeles, West Coast editor, 1944-46; free-lance writer, 1946—.

WRITINGS: (With Sally Struthers and Joyce Virtue) *The Sally Struthers Natural Beauty Book,* Doubleday, 1979; *The Divorced Woman's Handbook,* Morrow, 1980; *Confessions of an Ex-Fan Magazine Writer,* Doubleday, 1981. Contributor to magazines and newspapers, including *Life, Good Housekeeping, Ladies' Home Journal, TV Guide,* and *Cosmopolitan.*

WORK IN PROGRESS: Cop (tentative title), "limning day-to-day highlights and low life of a detective who is talking following his first kill"; *Patriot* (tentative title), "a biography of Lewis Cass, an ancestor who was governor of Michigan Territory, secretary of state, and candidate for U.S. president."

SIDELIGHTS: Jane Wilkie commented to *CA:* "I graduated from years of writing primarily for 'fan' magazines only after relief from the responsibility of raising a family. The recent freedom has allowed contributions to national magazines and, in the past two years, three books. My forte is putting people on paper. I consider myself a hack, although a good one, and an able ghost writer. Fiction is an unfulfilled dream, almost impossible without subsidization, but, like Grandma Moses, I may begin producing in my dotage."

* * *

WILLIAMS, Claerwen 1938-
(Maud Lang)

PERSONAL: Born September 23, 1938, in Melbourne, Australia; daughter of Samuel Owen and Jean Isobel Elizabeth (Sinclair) Jones; married Gordon Maclean Williams (a novelist), February 28, 1963; children: Harriet, Jessica, Samuel.

Education: Attended University of Sydney, 1955-58; Hammersmith College of Art, diploma, 1964. *Home:* 5 Horbury Crescent, London W.11, England. *Agent:* John Farquharson Ltd., Bell House, 8 Bell Yard, London WC2A 2JU, England.

CAREER: Sydney Morning Telegraph, Sydney, Australia, reporter, 1958-59; secretary for British Council, 1960-61; Her Majesty's Prison, teacher in Normwood Scrubs, England, 1966-67, and Exeter, England, 1968-69; part-time secretary, beginning 1969; writer, 1974—.

WRITINGS—Under pseudonym Maud Lang; novels: *Summer Station,* Coward, 1976; *The Moon Tree,* Coward, 1978.

WORK IN PROGRESS: A novel about the British penal colony of Van Diemen's Land, set around 1825.

AVOCATIONAL INTERESTS: Painting, gardening.

* * *

WILLIAMS, Liza 1928-
(Liza Lehrman)

PERSONAL: Born September 29, 1928, in New York, N.Y.; daughter of Alexander (a professor of chemistry) and Hattie (an artist; maiden name, Glass) Lehrman; married Robert Gold (an artist; divorced); married Mansell Williams (a travel agent; divorced); married Harold Julius Rubens (a concert pianist; divorced); children: (first marriage) Michael David. *Education:* Attended Reed College, 1948-49, New York University, 1949-51, La Grand Chaumier, 1951-52, and Central School of Art, London, England, 1952; also studied with Hans Hofmann. *Politics:* "Humanist/feminist." *Religion:* "Pantheist." *Residence:* New York, N.Y. *Agent:* Roslyn Targ Literary Agency, Inc., 250 West 57th St., Suite 1932, New York, N.Y. 10019.

CAREER: Radio broadcaster and artist in Cape Town, South Africa, 1952-63; broadcaster and editor for Pacifica Foundation in California, 1964-68; Capitol Records, Los Angeles, Calif., publicist, 1968-71; Island Records, Los Angeles, president, 1971-73; California State University, Long Beach, assistant professor of creative writing, 1973-76; Olivia Records, Los Angeles, publicist, 1976-78; Burning Sounds (recording company), London, England, publicist, 1979; St. Ann's School, Brooklyn Heights, N.Y., teacher, 1979—. *Awards, honors:* Named one of the "heavy eighty-nine of rock and roll" by *Esquire,* 1972.

WRITINGS: Up the City of Angels, Putnam, 1971; *Art Deco Los Angeles,* Harper, 1978.

Work represented in anthologies, including *Voices From the New Underground, The Hippie Papers,* and *Mixed Bag.* Author of "Liza Williams," a weekly column in *Los Angeles Free Press,* 1966-72. Contributor to magazines, including *Playgirl* (once under name Liza Lehrman), *Los Angeles, F.M. and Fine Arts,* and *City.*

WORK IN PROGRESS: A book on women in the "beat scene"; a fictionalized autobiography.

SIDELIGHTS: Liza Williams wrote: "I have traveled extensively in Mexico and lived for four years (off and on) in London and for eleven years in South Africa. I am constantly amazed by the variety of life. I hope for a world in which all human potential will be given the opportunity of manifesting itself. I am anti-classist/racist/sexist/agist and against anything that oppresses the human spirit, because to do so deprives the world of its true treasure, which is human creativity. I find it obscene that THINGS are valued more than beings."

AVOCATIONAL INTERESTS: Reading, walking, talking, making things.

* * *

WILLIAMS, Robert Moore 1907-1977
(John S. Browning, H. H. Harmon, E. K. Jarvis, Robert Moore, Russell Storm)

OBITUARY NOTICE: Born June 19, 1907, in Farmington, Mo.; died February, 1977. Novelist and author. Under his own name and various pseudonyms, Williams published more than one hundred fifty novels and works of short fiction in his forty-year career as a contributer to science-fiction magazines and paperback series. Among his works are *The Day They H-Bombed Los Angeles, The Second Atlantis,* the "Jongor" series, and the "Zanthor" series. Obituaries and other sources: *Who's Who in Science Fiction,* Taplinger, 1976; *The Encyclopedia of Science Fiction,* Granada, 1979; *Science Fiction and Fantasy Literature,* two volumes, Gale, 1979.

* * *

WILLIAMS, Strephon Kaplan 1934-

PERSONAL: Born April 2, 1934, in New York, N.Y.; son of Oscar (a poet) and Gene (a poet and painter; maiden name, Derwood) Williams; married wife, Laurie (divorced); married Helen Saul (divorced); children: Alison Elizabeth, Marya Sheila. *Education:* Los Angeles State University, M.A. (literature), 1962; San Francisco State University, M.A. (counseling), 1972; studied at Guild for Psychological Studies, 1966-76. *Politics:* "Universalist." *Religion:* "Mystical." *Home and office:* 1828 Virginia St., Berkeley, Calif. 94703.

CAREER: St. George Homes (residential treatment center), Berkeley, Calif., chief therapist and assistant director, 1972-76; Jungian-Senoi Institute, Berkeley, founder and director, 1978—. Instructor at John F. Kennedy University, 1980—. Public speaker on contemporary issues in psychology and religion. *Member:* Association for Humanistic Psychology, Association for Transpersonal Psychology.

WRITINGS: The Meditative Day, Journey Press, 1975; *The St. George Transformation Plan Manual,* St. George Homes Press, 1975; *Jungian-Senoi Dreamwork,* Journey Press, 1978; *Jungian-Senoi Dreamwork Manual,* Journey Press, 1980; *Transformations I: Meditations in a New Age,* Journey Press, 1980; (contributor) Adrian Kelly, editor, *Holistic Health Lifebook,* 2nd edition (Williams was not affiliated with 1st edition), And/Or Press, 1981; *The Seven Basic Archetypes Unified Field Theory,* Journey Press, 1981. Contributor to psychology journals.

WORK IN PROGRESS: The Transformation of Anger, publication expected in 1982; *The Psychological Teachings of Jesus,* 1983; *Jungian Personal Mythos Journal,* 1984; *Stories of the Journey for Children,* 1984; *Mythic Drama,* a new age novel.

SIDELIGHTS: Williams told *CA:* "Whenever possible I write from a prophetic and evolutionary point of view. My chief concern is the quest for meaning and new consciousness as it is still evolving in both the individual and collective life. My writing has its roots in both my professional work as a teacher and psychotherapist and in my own individual relation to a guiding inner source that empowers my life.

"My work as a teacher and psychotherapist revolves primarily around working with dreams and with creative choice-making. Underlying the work with others is a basic commitment on my part to write about the processes I teach. In addition, my own growth and dreamwork processes are vitally important to me.

"The consciousness focus of my work and writing leads me to write about the wholeness process in practical books such as the dreamwork manual. But I am also concerned and vitally interested in writing epic novels and plays that embody the values, visions, struggles, and life styles of a new age consciousness. I shall use my psychological knowledge, literary ability, and meditative focus in this challenge. Thus with my present writings I hope to establish myself as an author and get my approach before people. These works are preparation for even more exciting and meaningful possibilities."

AVOCATIONAL INTERESTS: Aikido.

*   *   *

WILLIAMS, Tina
See WILES, Domini

*   *   *

WILLIAMSON, Chilton, Jr.   1947-

PERSONAL: Born April 25, 1947, in New York, N.Y.; son of Chilton and Frances (Philpotts) Williamson. *Education:* Attended Bowdoin College, 1965-66; Columbia University, B.A., 1969, graduate study, 1969-73. *Politics:* Conservative. *Religion:* None. *Home address:* P.O. Box 695, Kemmerer, Wyo. 83101. *Agent:* Robin Straus, Wallace & Sheil Agency, Inc., 177 East 70th St., New York, N.Y. 10021. *Office: National Review,* 150 East 35th St., New York, N.Y. 10016.

CAREER: National Review, New York, N.Y., executive editor of books, arts, and manners, 1976—.

WRITINGS: Saltbound: A Block Island Winter, Methuen, 1980. Contributor of articles and reviews to magazines, including *Harper's, New Republic, Nation, Commonweal, Human Life Review,* and *American Spectator.*

WORK IN PROGRESS: Roughnecking It, nonfiction about life in the Overthrust Belt of southwest Wyoming.

SIDELIGHTS: Williamson wrote: "My books are part of a project which I hope will ultimately comprise many volumes. My idea is to put on paper a portrait of the United States that is not generally seen by writers anymore—rural, adventurous, unintellectual, outside the sphere of 'sophisticated,' educated, post-modern, middle class, urban-suburban, 'committed,' highly self-conscious people. What I want to show is that the so-called 'older America' is still very real, that what goes on in it remains of as much interest and importance as it was when Mark Twain, for instance, described it. I want to fill in and populate what Tom Wolfe calls the 'flyover zone'—that vast, dull, continental expanse that New Yorkers glimpse from thirty-nine-thousand feet on their way to Los Angeles.

"I have studied voice for ten years at the studio of William S. Hess in New York City, and for a time thought of becoming a professional opera singer. I loathe the cities, especially New York, and am planning to return to live in Wyoming, where I spent a year researching *Roughnecking It.* I have lived a year in England and visited France, but I have no interest in traveling to Europe again. When I have the time, I get in my jeep and roam around the American West. I have plans to visit Alaska and am considering eventually doing a book about life in Australia.

"I will read anything in print—literature, history, philoso-phy, biography, theology, the nonacademic products of sociology, but have no interest in painting, sculpture, dance, or winetasting. I love the opera, particularly Verdi and Wagner, most nineteenth-century music, and some eighteenth; earlier stuff bores me, and post-World War I music generally leaves me cold. I also enjoy country western music.

"My happiest moments when I am not working are probably spent in bars, especially Western bars, where I drink mostly beer, as I dislike the feeling of being intoxicated, except on special occasions. The best beer in the world is Wurzburger's Dark on tap at Luchow's."

*   *   *

WILLIAMSON, Moncrieff   1915-

PERSONAL: Born November 23, 1915, in East Linton, Scotland; son of James Watt and Gwendoline Pilkington (Jackson) Williamson; married Pamela Upton Fanshawe, September 30, 1948; children: Timothy Malcolm Moncrieff. *Education:* Attended Edinburgh College of Art. *Religion:* Anglican. *Home:* 14 Churchill Ave., Charlottetown, Prince Edward Island, Canada C1A 1Y8. *Agent:* Helene Hoffman, Authors' Marketing Services Ltd., 51 Spruce St., Toronto, Ontario, Canada M5A 2H8. *Office:* Confederation Art Gallery and Museum, Confederation Centre, Charlottetown, Prince Edward Island, Canada.

CAREER: Art Exhibitions Bureau, London, England, director, 1953-57; Glenbow Foundation, Calgary, Alberta, director of art department, 1960-63; Art Gallery of Greater Victoria, Victoria, British Columbia, curator, 1963-64; Confederation Art Gallery and Museum, Charlottetown, Prince Edward Island, director, 1964—. Assistant professor at Prince of Wales College and University of Prince Edward Island, 1966-71; consultant to Canadian Conference of the Arts. *Military service:* British Army, Intelligence Corps, 1943-46; served in Europe.

MEMBER: International Council of Museums, Canadian Art Museum Directors Organization (president, 1971-73), Canadian Museums Association (fellow), American Art Museum Directors Association, Royal Society of Arts (fellow). *Awards, honors:* Centennial Medal, 1967; Silver Jubilee Medal, 1977; LL.D. from University of Prince Edward Island, 1972; diplome d'honneur from Canadian Conference of the Arts, 1975; gold medal from Royal Canadian Academy, 1975; member of Order of Canada, 1976.

WRITINGS: Robert Harris, 1849-1919: An Unconventional Biography, McClelland & Stewart, 1971; *Robert Harris Portraits,* National Gallery of Canada, 1973; *Through Canadian Eyes,* Glenbow, 1976. Author of exhibition catalogs. Contributor of articles and poems to magazines in England, Germany, New Zealand, Canada, and the United States.

WORK IN PROGRESS: An autobiography; detective fiction.

AVOCATIONAL INTERESTS: Conversation, reading, swimming.

*   *   *

WILLIAMSON, Robin (Duncan Harry)   1943-

PERSONAL: Born November 24, 1943, in Edinburgh, Scotland; came to the United States in 1974; son of Walter and Elizabeth (Welsh) Williamson; married Janet Shankman (a manager and artist), December 20, 1970. *Education:* Educated in Scotland, England, and France. *Home and office address:* P.O. Box 27522, Los Angeles, Calif. 90027. *Agent:* Richard Curtis Associates, Inc., 156 East 52nd St., New York, N.Y. 10022.

CAREER: Writer and poet, 1961—. "Incredible String Band," United Kingdom, founding member, performer, and songwriter, 1966-74; "Robin Williamson and His Merry Band," California, founder, performer, songwriter, and record producer, 1977-79; solo performer and songwriter, 1980—. Owner of Pig's Whisker Music (publishing firm), 1977—. *Member:* British Academy of Songwriters, English Folk Song and Dance Society, Composers and Authors, Epigraphic Society. *Awards, honors:* Grammy Award nomination from National Academy of Recording Arts and Sciences, 1968, for "Hangman's Beautiful Daughter."

WRITINGS: Incredible String Band Song Book, Music Sales, 1968; *Home Thoughts From Abroad* (poetry), Deepdown Books, 1972; *Incredible String Band: A Second Songbook,* Music Sales, 1973; (with Dan Sherman) *Glory Trap* (novel), New English Library, 1976; *Fiddle Tunes: English, Welsh, Scottish, and Irish,* Oak Books, 1976; *The Penny Whistle Book,* Oak Books, 1977; *Five Denials on Merlin's Grave* (poetry), Pig's Whisker Music, 1979.

Work represented in anthologies, including *Poetry of Rock,* Bantam, 1969; *Poetry of Relevance,* Methuen, 1970; *Golden Horses,* Admiral Books, 1976; *Outlaw Visions,* Acrobat Books, 1977; *Beyond the Fields We Know,* Triskell Press, 1978.

Recordings: "Incredible String Band," Elektra, 1966; "Five Thousand Spirits; or, The Layers of the Onion," Elektra, 1967; "Hangman's Beautiful Daughter," Elektra, 1968; "Wee Tam" [and] "The Big Huge," two albums, Elektra, 1968; "Changing Horses," Elektra, 1969; "I Looked Up," Elektra, 1970; "U," two albums, Elektra, 1970; "Be Glad for the Song Has No Ending," Island, 1971; "Relics of the Incredible String Band," Elektra, 1971; "Liquid Acrobats as Regards the Air," Elektra, 1971; "Myrrh," Island, 1972; "Earthspan," Warner, 1972; "No Ruinous Feud," Warner, 1973; "Hard Rope and Silken Twine," Warner, 1974; "Seasons They Change," two albums, Elektra, 1977.

Recordings with musical group "Robin Williamson and His Merry Band"; all released by Flying Fish Records: "Journey's Edge," 1977; "American Stonehenge," 1978; "A Glint at the Kindling," 1979.

WORK IN PROGRESS: Research on early Celtic lore, music, and tales as a basis for a new book.

SIDELIGHTS: Williamson told *CA:* "In the early 1960's and during the period of the 'Incredible String Band,' I was involved in a search for the musical and poetic threads which would link East and West. I have since circled back to my Celtic roots and seek to create new music, songs, and stories to continue what might be called the 'bardic tradition' as drawn on by such authors as Yeats, Dylan Thomas, and Robert Graves.".

BIOGRAPHICAL/CRITICAL SOURCES: New York Times, March 10, 1968, May 10, 1970, August 28, 1974, March 23, 1977; *London Daily Telegraph,* October 22, 1970, December 5, 1978; *Billboard,* December 12, 1970; *London Sunday Times,* December 17, 1972; *Washington Post,* October 17, 1979; *Boston Globe,* December 20, 1979.

*   *   *

WILLIG, George 1949-

PERSONAL: Born June 11, 1949, in New York, N.Y.; son of George H. (a stereotyper) and Therese (in human resources; maiden name, Fortier) Willig. *Education:* State University of New York Junior College at Farmingdale, A.A.S., 1969; St. John's University, Jamaica, N.Y., B.S.

(cum laude), 1976. *Home address:* P.O. Box 1219, Studio City, Calif. 91604. *Agent:* William Morris Agency, 1350 Avenue of the Americas, New York, N.Y. 10019.

CAREER: Ark Research, Farmingdale, N.Y., modelmaker and designer, 1969-75; Ideal Toy Corp., Hollis, N.Y., modelmaker and inventor, 1976-77; American Broadcasting Co. (ABC), New York, N.Y., rock climber for live telecasts of "ABC Wide World of Sports," 1977-80; actor, lecturer, stuntman, and technical consultant, 1980—. Member of board of directors of Infinite Skye Alpinism, Inc. *Member:* Explorers Club, Omicron Delta Epsilon. *Awards, honors:* Sir Isaac Newton Award from Brooklyn Polytechnic Institute, 1977, for defying gravity by climbing the World Trade Center in New York City.

WRITINGS: (With Andrew Bergman) *Going It Alone* (autobiography), Doubleday, 1979.

WORK IN PROGRESS: Developing properties for television and film production.

SIDELIGHTS: Willig received public attention in 1977 when he climbed the World Trade Center in New York City. He devised a special climbing apparatus to scale the building's wall of windows and on May 26, 1977, made his ascent. His feat sparked the interest and curiosity of New Yorkers and Willig found himself being televised on the "Good Morning America" and "Today" shows. He became an instant celebrity. The *New York Daily News* ran an entire front-page photograph of him, adorned with the headline, "Human Fly. To the Top of the World!" Willig's stunt earned him commercial spots with Chapstick and Gamer's Pub Cider and a job with "ABC Wide World of Sports."

Willig told *CA:* "Writing for me has always been quite a chore; it doesn't come easily at all. When Doubleday approached me to write a book of an autobiographical nature, I decided to work with Andrew Bergman as a co-author. Because I was somewhat self-conscious about writing my story and because there was a deadline, collaborating was the perfect solution. Not being a writer by profession, I was able to learn how a book comes together and benefit from all that Andrew could teach me. The partnership was a learning experience and gave me a heightened appreciation of the trials and tribulations of a writer. Ironically, I find myself developing film and television projects on my own and doing more writing than ever before. One of these projects is a feature film adaptation of *Going It Alone,* which I will also be co-producing.

"Viktor Frankl's *Man's Search for Meaning,* Erich Fromm's *The Art of Loving,* David Robert's *The Mountain of My Fear,* and the poetry of Robinson Jeffers have been influences in my life and work."

BIOGRAPHICAL/CRITICAL SOURCES: San Francisco Examiner, May 26, 1977; *Washington Post,* May 27, 1977; *New York Times,* May 27, 1977, May 28, 1977; *Newsweek,* June 6, 1977, November 7, 1977; *Sports Illustrated,* June 6, 1977; *Los Angeles Times,* October 5, 1977; *Adventure Travel,* February, 1980; *Baltimore News American,* June 29, 1980.

*   *   *

WILMETH, Don B(urton) 1939-

PERSONAL: Born December 15, 1939, in Houston, Tex.; son of Perry D. (a minister and editor) and Pauline M. (Goodrum) Wilmeth; married Judy Eslie Hansgen (a secretary), June 10, 1966; children: Michael Tyler. *Education:* Abilene Christian University, B.A., 1961; University of

Arkansas, M.A., 1962; University of Illinois, Ph.D., 1964. *Home:* 525 Hope St., Providence, R.I. 02906. *Office:* Department of Theater Arts, Brown University, Box 1897, Providence, R.I. 02912.

CAREER: Eastern New Mexico University, Portales, assistant professor of drama and head of department, 1964-67; Brown University, Providence, R.I., assistant professor, 1967-70, associate professor, 1970-76, professor of theatre and English, 1976—, associate director of theatre, 1967-70, acting director, 1970, executive officer of theatre arts, 1973-78, chairman of department of theatre arts, 1979—. Member of board of directors of local Players, 1972-74, 1978-80.

MEMBER: International Federation for Theater Research, American Society for Theatre Research (member of board of directors, 1976-78 and 1980-83), American Theatre Association (chairman of publications committee, 1974-79), Society for the Advancement of Education (member of board of trustees, 1977—), Theatre Library Association (member of board of directors, 1978-83), Theatre Historical Society, National Collegiate Players, American Association of University Professors, Society for Theatre Research (England), New England Theater Conference, Providence Shakespeare Society, Phi Beta Kappa, Alpha Chi, Phi Kappa Phi, Alpha Psi Omega. *Awards, honors:* M.A. from Brown University, 1970.

WRITINGS: (Editor) *The American Stage to World War I*, Gale, 1978; *George Frederick Cooke: Machiavel of the Stage*, Greenwood Press, 1980; (editor) *American and English Popular Entertainment*, Gale, 1980; *The Language of Popular Entertainment: A Glossary of Argot, Slang, and Terminology*, Greenwood Press, 1981. Author of "Theatre Today," a column in *U.S.A. Today*, 1974-80. Contributor of more than a hundred articles and reviews to theatre and library journals, and *Choice*. Book review editor of *Theatre Journal*, 1977-80.

WORK IN PROGRESS: Editing plays of William Gillette, publication by Cambridge University Press expected in 1982; a book on stage entertainments and outdoor amusements (including the circus), Greenwood Press, 1982; editing plays of Augustin Daly, Cambridge University Press, 1983.

SIDELIGHTS: Wilmeth wrote: "I have long been a lover of books and have consequently collected large numbers in the area of theatre. I consider myself a theatre historian, director, and actor as well as an educator and writer. For the past decade I have served as juror or chairman of two prestigious book awards given by the Theatre Library Association. Within the last five years, my focus has turned to popular entertainments and my writing has begun to turn in that direction. Much of my energy has now turned to administration, a situation that is both satisfying and terribly frustrating in terms of time consumption."

*   *   *

WILMUT, Roger (Francis) 1942-

PERSONAL: Born June 9, 1942, in Stratford-upon-Avon, England; son of Harold Francis (a teacher) and Catherine (Tjaden) Wilmut. *Education:* Attended Warwick School. *Residence:* Surrey, England. *Agent:* Roger Hancock Ltd., 8 Waterloo Pl., London SWIY 4AW, England.

CAREER: Recording engineer and sound mixer, 1961—.

WRITINGS: (With Jimmy Grafton) *The Goon Show Companion: A History and Goonography*, St. Martin's, 1976; *Tony Hancock, Artiste: A Tony Hancock Companion*, Eyre Methuen, 1978; *From Fringe to Flying Circus*, Eyre Methuen, 1980.

SIDELIGHTS: Wilmut wrote: "I'm interested in the history of broadcasting; the three books to date are about British broadcast comedy. I believe in doing very thorough research, and the first two books contain 'broadcastographies'—very detailed listings of relevant broadcasts. If I have a philosophy about writing, it is that complex subjects don't have to be dealt with in complex language—I hope I write in plain English."

AVOCATIONAL INTERESTS: Hi-fi, music, old records, cinema, old films.

*   *   *

WILSON, Ethel Davis (Bryant) 1888-1980

PERSONAL: Born January 20, 1888 (listed in some sources as 1890), in Port Elizabeth, South Africa; came to Canada, 1898; died December 22, 1980, in Vancouver, British Columbia, Canada; daughter of Robert William (a missionary) and Lila (Malkin) Bryant; married Wallace Wilson (a physician), January 4, 1921 (died March 12, 1966). *Education:* Educated in England and Canada.

CAREER: Worked as public school teacher in Canada, 1907-1920; writer. *Awards, honors:* D. Litt., from University of British Columbia, 1955; Canada Council medal, 1961; Royal Society of Canada Lorne Pierce gold medal from Learned Societies, 1964; Order of Canada medal of service, 1970.

WRITINGS: *Hetty Dorval*, Macmillan, 1947, reprinted, 1967; *The Innocent Traveller*, Macmillan, 1949; *The Equations of Love: Tuesday and Wednesday and Lilly's Story* (two novellas; also see below), Macmillan, 1952, reprinted, 1974; *Lilly's Story* (novella; also see above), Harper, 1953; *Swamp Angel* (novel), Harper, 1954; *Love and Salt Water* (novel), St. Martin's, 1957; *Mrs. Golightly, and Other Stories* (short stories), Macmillan, 1961. Work represented in anthologies. Editor of *Red Cross*, 1940-45. Contributor of short stories and essays to periodicals, including *New Statesman and Nation, Canadian Forum*, and *Chatelaine*.

SIDELIGHTS: Born in South Africa, Wilson was taken to England by grandparents after the death of her mother. They then moved to Canada, where Wilson remained thereafter. During her marriage to Vancouver physician Wallace Wilson she and her husband took trips to the Middle East, the Mediterranean, and Europe.

Wilson came to writing late in life; her first story appeared when she was forty-nine, and her first novel was published ten years later. Thus as Desmond Pacey noted in *Ethel Wilson,* she was a contemporary of James Joyce and T. S. Eliot, though her novels were not written until after World War II. However, she was much less experimental than either Joyce or Eliot. Pacey wrote: "Her stories are almost always told in straightforward chronological order by an omniscient narrator who is not above commenting occasionally, in a very old-fashioned way, on the persons and events he is narrating.... Upon everything she writes is the mark of a fastidious and exigent craftsman: her art is quiet, gentle, controlled, exquisitely fashioned and finished."

Wilson strove to imbue her work with "incandescence." She wrote: "There is a moment, I think, within a novelist of any originality, whatever his country or his scope, when some sort of synthesis takes place over which he has only partial control. There is an incandescence, and from it meaning emerges, words appear, they take shape in their order, a fusion occurs. A minor writer, whose gift is small and canvas limited, stands away at last if he can and regards what he has done, without indulgence. This is a counsel of perfection which I myself am not able to take with skill, but I must try to take it. I am sure that the very best writing in our country will result from such an incandescence which takes place in a prepared mind where forces meet.''

Wilson has also been compared to Jane Austen and Daniel Defoe. Her sense of reality, as well as her devotion to the details of place and social behavior was similar to those earlier writers. And on a psychological level, Wilson has been compared to Marcel Proust and Virginia Woolf, for she enriched her characterizations by portraying the emotional reverberations of phenomena and the subtleties of human relationships.

Many critics have focused on Wilson's style and symbolism. Pacey listed her strengths as "economy, matter-of-fact-statement, limpid style, lack of pretentiousness, and a combination of involvement and detachment." Other reviewers described the quality of her prose in similar terms. Edith James, reviewing *Hetty Dorval* in the *San Francisco Chronicle,* declared that "Wilson's writing has the precision of Janet Lewis and the singing quality of the early Willa Cather." And V. P. Hass of the *Chicago Tribune* praised the "admirable economy of words" of *Lilly's Story.*

Beneath the finely crafted simplicity, however, is a complexity of meaning. Reviewing *Swamp Angel,* L.A.G. Strong wrote, "From the quiet but powerful opening to the last Excalibur flight of Swamp Angel the story troubles the mind with overtones and reticences, as if each chapter were a moon with a hidden side more important than the one which Mrs. Wilson shows us." Similarly, W. H. New wrote that *The Innocent Traveller* "has at its base a kind of symbolic structure." Pacey observed that "Wilson's chief themes are loneliness and love, human vulnerability and tenacity, the juxtaposition in the world of innocence and cruelty, beauty and fear, and she treats these themes in a style that is straightforward but also suggestive, realistic but also poetic and symbolic." He added that Wilson "sees human beings as lonely creatures who forever seek, and occasionally find, the comfort and sustaining power of mutual love, and nature as a setting which is at once beautiful and menacing."

BIOGRAPHICAL/CRITICAL SOURCES: San Francisco Chronicle, August 21, 1947, May 7, 1953; *New York Herald Tribune Book Review,* October 19, 1947, January 15, 1950, May 3, 1953, August 29, 1954; *Times Literary Supplement,* July 24, 1948, March 28, 1952; *Christian Science Monitor,* October 21, 1949; *Canadian Forum,* December, 1949; *Saturday Review of Literature,* December 10, 1949, May 16, 1953, September 4, 1954; *Saturday Night,* July 26, 1952; *Chicago Tribune,* May 3, 1953, August 29, 1954; *Queen's Quarterly,* spring, 1954; *Kirkus Review,* June 15, 1954; *Spectator,* September 3, 1954; *British Columbia Library Quarterly,* April, 1958; *Canadian Literature,* autumn, 1959, autumn, 1965; Desmond Pacey, *Ethel Wilson,* Twayne, 1967; *Contemporary Literary Criticism,* Volume 13, Gale, 1980.

OBITUARIES: Chicago Tribune, December 24, 1980.*

*   *   *

WILSON, John Dover   1881-1969

PERSONAL: Born July 13, 1881, in London, England; died January 15, 1969; son of Edwin (a scientific artist) and Elizabeth (Dover) Wilson; married Dorothy Baldwin, July 30, 1906 (died, 1961); married Elizabeth Emma Wintringham, August 17, 1963; children: (first marriage) one son (deceased), two daughters. *Education:* Gonville and Caius College, Cambridge, B.A., 1903, M.A., 1908. *Residence:* Midlothian, Scotland.

CAREER: Assistant master at headmaster's school in England, 1904-05; University of Helsingfors, Helsingfors, Finland, lecturer in English, 1906-09; University of London, Goldsmiths' College, London, England, instructor, 1909-12; inspector of adult education and continuation schools for British Government, 1912-24; University of London, King's College, London, professor of education, 1924-35; University of Edinburgh, Edinburgh, Scotland, Regius Professor of Rhetoric and English Literature, 1935-45. Trustee of Shakespeare's birthplace, 1931-69; trustee of National Library of Scotland, 1946-69, vice-chairman, 1951-57; member of general council of Friends of the National Libraries, 1949. *Member:* British Academy (fellow), Scottish Classical Association (president, 1950-51), Deutsche Shakespeare Gesellschaft (honorary member). *Awards, honors:* Companion of Honour of the Order of the British Empire, 1936; fellow of Gonville and Caius College, Cambridge; numerous honorary degrees include LL.D. from University of Natal and University of Edinburgh, D.Litt. from University of Durham, University of Leicester, and University of London, and D.-es-L. from University of Lille.

WRITINGS: John Lyly, Macmillan, 1905, reprinted, Folcroft Library Editions, 1970; (editor) *Life in Shakespeare's England: A Book of Elizabethan Prose,* Cambridge University Press, 1911, 2nd editon, 1956, reprinted, Folcroft Library Editions, 1976, abridged edition for junior readers published as *Through Elizabethan Eyes,* 1939; *Martin Marprelate and Shakespeare's "Fluellen": A New Theory of the Authorship of the Marprelate Tracts,* A. Moring, 1912, reprinted, Folcroft Library Editions, 1971; (editor) *The Poetry of the Age of Wordsworth,* Volume I: *An Anthology of the Five Major Poets,* Cambridge University Press, 1927, reprinted, Greenwood Press, 1970; (editor) *The Schools of England: A Study in Renaissance,* Sidgwick & Jackson, 1928, University of North Carolina Press, 1929; *Six Tragedies of Shakespeare: An Introduction for the Plain Man,* Longmans, Green, 1929, reprinted, Folcroft Press, 1970.

The Essential Shakespeare: A Biographical Adventure, Cambridge University Press, 1932, reprinted, Haskell House, 1977; *The Manuscript of Shakespeare's "Hamlet" and the Problems of Its Transmission: An Essay in Critical Bibliography,* two volumes, Macmillan, 1934, reprinted, Cambridge University Press, 1963; *What Happens in "Hamlet,"* Macmillan, 1935, 3rd edition, Cambridge University Press, 1951; *The Meaning of "The Tempest,"* Literary and Philosophical Society of Newcastle upon Tyne, 1936, reprinted, Folcroft Library Editions, 1974; *Leslie Stephen and Matthew Arnold as Critics of Wordsworth,* Cambridge University Press, 1939, reprinted, Haskell House, 1972.

The Fortunes of Falstaff, Cambridge University Press, 1943, Macmillan, 1944; (with T. C. Worsley) *Shakespeare's Histories at Stratford, 1951,* M. Reinhardt, 1952; *Shakespeare's Happy Comedies,* Northwestern University Press, 1962; *An Introduction to the Sonnets of Shakespeare for the Use of Historians and Others,* Cambridge University Press, 1963; (editor) Thomas Lodge, *The Wounds of Civil War,* Oxford University Press, 1965; (with A. W. Pollard) *Shakespeare's Problems,* reprint of original edition, Cambridge University Press, 1967; *Milestones on the Dover Road* (autobiography) Faber, 1969. Also author of *The War and Democracy,* 1914, *Shakespeare's Hand in the Plays of Sir Thomas More* (with Pollard and others), 1923, and *A. W. Pollard: A Memoir,* 1948. Also editor of *Matthew Arnold's "Culture and Anarchy,"* 1932.

Editor of plays by William Shakespeare; all published by Cambridge University Press: *All's Well That Ends Well,*

1929, 2nd edition, 1955; *Richard III*, 1954; (with George Ian Duthie) *Romeo and Juliet*, 1955; *Julius Caesar*, 1956; (with Arthur Quiller-Couch) *As You Like It*, 1957; (with Alice Walker) *Othello*, 1957; *Richard II*, 1957; (with Walker) *Troilus and Cressida*, 1957; *Coriolanus*, 1958, published as *The Tragedy of Coriolanus*, 1960; *The History of Henry IV*, two volumes, 1958; *Hamlet*, 1958; *Henry V*, 1958; *Macbeth*, 1958; (with Quiller-Couch) *Measure for Measure*, 1958; *The Merchant of Venice*, 1958; (with Quiller-Couch) *Twelfth Night; or, What You Will*, 1958; *Antony and Cleopatra*, 1959; (with Quiller-Couch) *Much Ado About Nothing*, 1959; *The Winter's Tale*, 1959; *Cymbeline*, 1961; *King Lear*, 1961; *The Life of Timon of Athens*, 1961; *King Henry VI*, three volumes, 1961-62; (with Quiller-Couch) *The Comedy of Errors*, 1962; *Love's Labour's Lost*, 1962; *Titus Andronicus*, 1963; (with Quiller-Couch) *The Merry Wives of Windsor*, 1965; (with Quiller-Couch) *The Taming of the Shrew*, 1965; *The Sonnets*, 1966.

Co-editor of *New Shakespeare*, 1921-30, general editor, 1930-69; editor of *Journal of Adult Education*, 1927-29.

OBITUARIES: New York Times, January 17, 1969; *Newsweek*, January 27, 1969; *America*, February 1, 1969; *Publishers Weekly*, February 3, 1969; *Britannica Book of the Year*, 1970.*

* * *

WILSON, Richard Lawson 1905-1981

OBITUARY NOTICE: Born September 3, 1905, in Galesburg, Ill.; died of cancer, January 18, 1981, in Washington, D.C. Journalist. Associated with the *Des Moines Register and Tribune* for almost fifty years, Wilson was the newspaper's Washington bureau chief from 1933 to 1970. He received the Pulitzer Prize for national reporting in 1954 for his three-part exclusive series about Soviet espionage in the United States. Wilson wrote a syndicated column and contributed to *Look* magazine as well. Obituaries and other sources: *New York Times*, January 19, 1981.

* * *

WILSON, Sandra 1944-
(Sandra Heath)

PERSONAL: Born August 10, 1944, in Pontypridd, Wales; daughter of Tom Edward (a Royal Air Force officer) and Betty Jean Machin; married Robin Wilson (an architectural draftsman), October 28, 1967; children: Sarah Jane. *Education:* Attended grammar school in Gloucestershire, Lincolnshire, and Nottingham, England. *Agent:* Bolt & Watson Ltd., 8-12 Old Queen St., Storey's Gate, London SW1H 9HP, England.

CAREER: Worked for British Civil Service, 1963-67; writer.

WRITINGS—All historical novels: Less Fortunate Than Fair, St. Martin's, 1973; *The Queen's Sister*, St. Martin's, 1974; *The Lady Cicely*, St. Martin's, 1974; *Wife to the Kingmaker*, St. Martin's, 1976; *Alice*, St. Martin's, 1977; *The Penrich Dragon*, St. Martin's, 1977; *Jessica*, R. Hale, 1979, Fawcett, 1980.

Under pseudonym Sandra Heath: *Mannerby's Lady*, New American Library, 1977; *The Whispering Rocks*, Hamlyn, 1978; *The Smuggler's Daughter*, New American Library, 1979; *Green Girl*, Hamlyn, 1979; *Lily of the Sun*, Hamlyn, 1980.

WORK IN PROGRESS: A saga concerning farm life in England's West Country during the Victorian era.

SIDELIGHTS: Sandra Wilson wrote: "I'm the happiest of women—with a marvelous husband and daughter, staying at home doing something I love doing just for the pleasure of it: writing. And then I have the further pleasure of seeing my books published. What more can I ask?"

Several of Wilson's books have been translated into Dutch, Swedish, and Norwegian.

* * *

WINCKLER, Paul A(lbert) 1926-

PERSONAL: Born May 17, 1926, in Brooklyn, N.Y.; son of Albert C. and Bernadette (Arnaud) Winckler; married Anne M. O'Regan, July 2, 1955; children: Mark, Christopher, Karen, Patrick, Pamela. *Education:* St. John's University, Jamaica, N.Y., B.A., 1948; Pratt Institute, M.L.S., 1950; New York University, M.A., 1953, Ph.D., 1968. *Religion:* Roman Catholic. *Home:* 49 Hammond Rd., Glen Cove, N.Y. 11542. *Office:* Palmer Graduate Library School, C. W. Post Center, Long Island University, Greenvale, N.Y. 11548.

CAREER: Brooklyn Public Library, Brooklyn, N.Y., librarian, 1950-51; St. John's University, Brooklyn Campus, Brooklyn, librarian, 1951-56; Bryant Library, Roslyn, N.Y., director, 1956-60; Suffolk County Community College, Selden, N.Y., librarian, 1960-62; Long Island University, C. W. Post Center, Greenvale, N.Y., associate professor, 1962-68, professor of library science, 1968—. Member of Center for Book Arts; member of executive board and treasurer of local Library Public Relations Council, 1959-60; member of fine arts committee of Long Island Arts Center, 1963-66.

MEMBER: Association of American Library Schools, American Printing History Association (chairperson of committee to study teaching methods and materials in the history of books and printing, 1976-79), Printing Historical Society (England), New York Printing History Association, Melvil Dui Chowder and Marching Association, Typophiles. *Awards, honors:* Grant from Grolier Foundation of New York, 1967; Founders Day Award from New York University, 1969.

WRITINGS: (Editor) *Reader in the History of Books and Printing*, Information Handling Services, 1978; (editor) *History of Books and Printing: A Guide to Information Sources*, Gale, 1979. Contributor to *Encyclopedia of Library and Information Science*. Contributor to library and education journals.

WORK IN PROGRESS: Editing *Bio-Bibliographical Dictionary in the History of Books and Printing*.

SIDELIGHTS: Winckler wrote: "My editing and writing reflect my areas of interest and are related to my professional work as a library educator. The areas include the history of books and printing, cultural history, the humanities, and the book arts, as well as library history."

* * *

WINDELER, Robert 1944-

PERSONAL: Born March 22, 1944, in Somerville, N.J.; son of Robert Rey (an educator) and Dorothy (DeVoe) Windeler. *Education:* Duke University, A.B., 1964; Columbia University, M.S., 1965. *Politics:* Democrat. *Religion:* Episcopalian. *Home:* 1438 North Beverly Dr., Beverly Hills, Calif. 90210. *Office: New York Times*, 5670 Wilshire Blvd., Los Angeles, Calif. 90036.

CAREER: Time, New York City, Beverly Hills correspondent, 1965-67; *New York Times*, New York City, Hollywood correspondent in Los Angeles, Calif., 1967-69; *Time*, New York correspondent, 1970-72; United Nations, New York City, consultant to UNICEF, 1972-73; *Time, Inc.*, New York City, Beverly Hills correspondent for *People*, 1974-79; New York Times Magazine Group, West Coast editor, 1979—. Member of faculty at University of Southern California, 1979—.

WRITINGS: Julie Andrews, Putnam, 1970; *Sweetheart: The Story of Mary Pickford*, Praeger, 1974; *The Films of Shirley Temple*, Citadel, 1978; (with Milton Williams) *The Party Book: The Complete Guide to Home Entertaining*, Doubleday, 1981; *Country Girls* (biography), Morrow, 1982. Contributor to magazines, including *TV Guide, Ladies' Home Journal, Good Housekeeping, Tennis*, and *Los Angeles*, and to newspapers. Contributing editor of *Stereo Review*, 1968-78; New York editor of *Entertainment World*, 1969-70.

WORK IN PROGRESS: A historical novel of middle nineteenth-century America; a contemporary novel set in Hollywood, New York City, Sydney, and London.

SIDELIGHTS: Windeler commented: "None of my career items would mean much of anything to me if I couldn't share the knowledge I've acquired working with some fascinating people in some fairly high-powered situations. The most important and rewarding thing I do is teach at the University of Southern California. It's a class I created, interviewing and reviewing for magazines, with particular emphasis on show business journalism. It's unique in the world, so far as we know. Writers are born, not created. But to those who are already inclined to develop their talents for perceiving people and situations and for putting words together well, I can provide some guidance—and a warning or two about the life of a writer."

*   *   *

WITHEFORD, Hubert   1921-

PERSONAL: Born March 18, 1921, in Wellington, New Zealand; son of Robert and Florence (Poynton) Witheford; married Noel Brooke Anderson (a teacher), November 27, 1941; children: Nicholas. *Education:* Victoria University of Wellington, M.A., 1943. *Home:* 88 Roxborough Rd., Harrow, Middlesex, England. *Office:* Central Office of Information, Hercules Rd., London S.W.1, England.

CAREER: Office of the Prime Minister, Wellington, New Zealand, member of staff, 1939-45; War History Branch, Wellington, member of staff, 1945-53; Central Office of Information, London, England, member of staff, 1954-67, head of overseas section, Reference Division, 1968-78, director of Reference Division, 1978—. *Awards, honors:* Jessie Mackay Prize from New Zealand State Literary Fund, 1963, for *The Lightning Makes a Difference.*

WRITINGS: Shadow of the Flame: Poems, 1942-47, Pelorus Press, 1949; *The Falcon Mask* (poems), Pegasus Press, 1951; *The Lightning Makes a Difference: Poems*, Paul's Book Arcade, 1962; *A Native, Perhaps Beautiful* (poems), Caxton Press, 1967; *A Possible Order* (poems), Ravine Press, 1980.

WORK IN PROGRESS: Illumination and Organisation, a study of the problems of transmitting esoteric teachings through organizations.

SIDELIGHTS: Witheford commented: "I am basically trying to wake up from confusions, and am now a Buddhist."

WITTENBERG, Judith Bryant   1938-

PERSONAL: Born May 28, 1938, in Binghamton, N.Y.; daughter of Stanley Reynolds (a business executive) and Eleanor (a teacher; maiden name, Stager) Bryant; married Jack Wittenberg (a physician), March 7, 1964; children: Derek, Keith, Mark. *Education:* Cornell University, B.A., 1960; Boston University, M.A., 1973; Brown University, Ph.D., 1977. *Home:* 146 Allerton Rd., Newton Highlands, Mass. 02161. *Office:* Department of English, Simmons College, 300 Fenway, Boston, Mass. 02115.

CAREER: J. Walter Thompson Co., New York, N.Y., advertising copywriter, 1960-64; free-lance writer in Boston, Mass., 1964-73; Brown University, Providence, R.I., lecturer in English, 1975-77; Tufts University, Medford, Mass., lecturer in English, 1977-78; Simmons College, Boston, assistant professor of English, 1978—. *Member:* Modern Language Association of America, Thomas Hardy Society, Northeast Modern Language Association, Phi Beta Kappa.

WRITINGS: Faulkner: The Transfiguration of Biography, University of Nebraska Press, 1979; (contributor) Fritz Fleischmann, *Feminist Perspectives on the American Novel*, G. K. Hall, 1982. Contributor of articles and reviews to scholarly journals, including *Mississippi Quarterly*.

WORK IN PROGRESS: A monograph on Thomas Hardy.

BIOGRAPHICAL/CRITICAL SOURCES: Boston Globe, March 9, 1980; *Choice*, June, 1980; *Sewanee Review*, fall, 1980; *Virginia Quarterly Review*, autumn, 1980; *Times Literary Supplement*, January 2, 1981.

*   *   *

WOBBE, R(oland) A(rthur)   1938-

PERSONAL: Surname is pronounced *Wo*-bee; born June 25, 1938, in Springfield, Ohio; son of Robert William (in business) and Mary Kathryn (Lytle) Wobbe; married Stirlene Strock, June 8, 1962. *Education:* Ohio State University, B.A., 1964; University of Iowa, M.F.A., 1966; University of Exeter, Ph.D., 1971. *Religion:* Roman Catholic. *Home:* 19 Douglas Dr., South Charleston, W.Va. 25309. *Office:* Department of Humanities, West Virginia College of Graduate Studies, Institute, W.Va. 25112.

CAREER: Muskingum College, New Concord, Ohio, instructor in English and creative writing, 1966-68; West Virginia State College, Institute, assistant professor, 1971-73, associate professor of English, 1974-79; West Virginia College of Graduate Studies, Institute, professor of English and humanities and program director in humanities, 1979—. *Military service:* U.S. Air Force, in radio maintenance, 1956-60. *Member:* American Association of University Professors, Shakespeare and Renaissance Society, West Virginia Association of College English Teachers (vice-president, 1979; president, 1980), West Virginia Humanities Association.

WRITINGS: Graham Greene: A Bibliography and Guide to Research, Garland Publishing, 1979.

WORK IN PROGRESS: Graham Greene and the Name of Power, publication expected in 1981; *A Graham Greene Companion*, publication by Garland expected in 1982.

SIDELIGHTS: Wobbe told *CA:* "I have several loves, one of them being the work of Graham Greene. Perhaps it is his use of cinematic structures that attracts me. Aside from teaching and research, I work occasionally as a free-lance photographer and cinematographer. I am a confirmed Anglophile."

WOLDIN, Beth Weiner 1955-

PERSONAL: Born April 18, 1955, in Philadelphia, Pa.; daughter of Irwin I. (president of a clothing manufacturing company) and Shirley (Corson) Weiner; married John J. Woldin (an advertising agency art director), May 22, 1977. *Education:* Rhode Island School of Design, B.F.A., 1977. *Residence:* New York, N.Y. *Agent:* Joan Raines, Raines & Raines, 475 Fifth Ave., New York, N.Y. 10022.

CAREER: Free-lance writer and illustrator, 1977—. *Member:* Authors Guild, Authors League of America.

WRITINGS—Self-illustrated children's books: *Benjamin's Perfect Solution*, Warne, 1978; *Ellie to the Rescue*, Warne, 1979; *Chipmunk Stew*, Warne, 1980; *Christmas in the Junkyard*, Warne, 1981.

Illustrator: Thomas P. Lewis, *Call for Mr. Sniff*, Harper, 1981; Jan Wahl, *Too Many Raccoons*, Warne, 1981.

WORK IN PROGRESS: Cyrus Pinchpenny, a self-illustrated children's book; illustrating a children's picture book entitled *Puppies Need Someone to Love.*

SIDELIGHTS: Beth Woldin commented: "I spend my time writing and illustrating books for children that I know I would have read as a child. I like to supply a moral and happy ending because I feel it's important for young people to have good role models. I try to give examples of how children should begin to nurture their own feelings of right and wrong, honesty, and magnanimity. In my first book, *Benjamin's Perfect Solution*, the main character felt out of place because he was different from everyone else. Who doesn't, at some point in life, feel different from everyone else?"

*   *   *

WOLFF, John U(lrich) 1932-

PERSONAL: Born November 1, 1932, in Berlin, Germany; came to the United States; naturalized citizen; son of Reinhold Paul (an economist) and Erna (Weber) Wolff; married Ida Operario (a librarian), March 9, 1963; children: Erna, Rebecca, Sarah, John. *Education:* Cornell University, A.B., 1954, M.A., 1955; Yale University, Ph.D., 1965. *Home:* 109 West Upland, Ithaca, N.Y. 14850.

CAREER: Cornell University, Ithaca, N.Y., associate professor of linguistics, 1963—. *Member:* Linguistic Society of America, American Orient Society, Association of Asian Studies.

WRITINGS: A Description of Cebuano Visayan: Texts, Analysis, and Vocabulary, four volumes, [Cebu City, Philippines], 1962; *Beginning Cebuano*, Yale University Press, 1966; (with wife, Ida Wolff) *Beginning Waray-Waray*, four volumes, Southeast Asia Program, Cornell University, 1967; *Beginning Indonesian*, two volumes, Southeast Asia Program, Cornell University, 1972; (editor) *A Dictionary of Cebuano Visayan*, two volumes, Southeast Asia Program, Cornell University, 1972; *Indonesian Conversation*, Southeast Asia Program, Cornell University, 1978; *Indonesian Readings*, Southeast Asia Program, Cornell University, 1978.

*   *   *

WOLFF, Robert Lee 1915-1980

OBITUARY NOTICE: Born December 22, 1915, in New York, N.Y.; died of a heart attack, November 11, 1980, in Cambridge, Mass. Historian, educator, and author. A Harvard University professor of history, Wolff was not only a specialist in Balkan and Byzantine history and European

East-West relations, but also an expert in Victorian literature. He spoke several languages and published widely in both of his fields of expertise. The author's work includes *A History of Civilization, A History of the Crusades*, and *Gains and Losses: Novels of Faith and Doubt in Victorian England*. Obituaries and other sources: *The Author's and Writer's Who's Who*, 6th edition, Burke's Peerage, 1971; *Directory of American Scholars*, Volume I: *History*, 7th edition, Bowker, 1978; *The Writer's Directory, 1980-82*, St. Martin's, 1979; *Who's Who in America*, 41st edition, Marquis, 1980; *New York Times*, November 13, 1980; *Chicago Tribune*, November 14, 1980; *A B Bookman's Weekly*, January 5, 1981.

*   *   *

WOODING, Dan 1940-

PERSONAL: Born December 19, 1940, in Vom, Nigeria; son of Alfred (a missionary) and Anne (a missionary; maiden name, Blake) Wooding; married Norma Knight, July 13, 1963; children: Andrew, Peter. *Education:* Attended Birmingham College of Commerce. *Religion:* Baptist. *Home and office:* 26 Trafalgar Dr., Walton-on-Thames, Surrey KT12 1NZ, England.

CAREER: Hill Farm (drug rehabilitation center), Besley, England, co-founder and warden, 1968; *Christian*, London, England, chief reporter, 1969-70; *Middlesex County Times*, London, chief reporter, 1970-76; *Sunday People*, London, senior reporter, 1976-79; *Sunday Mirror*, London, senior reporter, 1979-80; free-lance writer, 1980—. Chief reporter for *Christianity Today*, 1969-70. Chairman of Grenville Film Productions Ltd. *Member:* National Union of Journalists, Arts Center Group (head of journalists group, 1976-78).

WRITINGS: Junkies Are People Too, Scripture Union, 1969; *Stresspoint*, Lutterworth, 1969; *I Thought Terry Dene Was Dead*, Coverdale House, 1972; (with Trevor Dearing) *Exit the Devil*, Logos International, 1976; *Supernatural Superpowers*, Logos International, 1977; (contributor) Chris Spencer, editor, *Little Fat Buzz*, Hodder & Stoughton, 1977; (with Mini Loman) *Train of Terror*, New Life Ventures, 1978; *Rick Wakeman: The Caped Crusader* (foreword by Elton John), R. Hale, 1978; (with Maurice O'Mahoney) *King Squealer*, W. H. Allen, 1978; (with Salu Daka Ndebele) *Guerrilla for Christ*, Spire Books, 1979; (with Ray Barnett) *Uganda Holocaust*, Zondervan, 1980; (with Howard Cooper) *Miracles in Sin City*, C.R.A., 1980; (with Henry Hollis) *Farewell Leicester Square*, Diamond Books, 1981; (with Brother David) *God's Smuggler to China*, Tyndale, 1981. Contributor to newspapers.

SIDELIGHTS: Wooding wrote: "I left journalism so I could write about Christians who are being persecuted for their faith around the world. *Uganda Holocaust* was born out of the feeling that I should be doing something more worthwhile with my writing ability. The book on Brother David's work in China has the same motivation.

"I have no formal training as a journalist or writer. I have learned the hard way—doing the job. As a journalist I specialized in crime, religion, and show business for both the *Sunday People* and *Sunday Mirror*. (Both newspapers have circulations of four million.) I was often called upon to 'ghost' the stories of show business personalities in Britain. I wrote series with Diana Dors, Barbara Windsor, Larry Grayson, Eric Morcambe (Britain's most famous comic), as well as with the former wife of boxer Joe Bugner, Melody; and Maurice O'Mahoney, the notorious King Squealer, who lives in constant fear after informing on two hundred top criminals in London."

BIOGRAPHICAL/CRITICAL SOURCES: Crusade, July, 1979; *Woman's Home Companion*, July, 1980.

* * *

WUBBEN, Hubert H(ollensteiner) 1928-

PERSONAL: Born February 4, 1928, in Houston, Tex.; son of J. Hubert (a minister) and Neola A. (Hollensteiner) Wubben; married Shirley L. Griffith (a medical secretary), November 23, 1950; children: Nancy Lea, Thomas Craig. *Education:* Cornell College, Mount Vernon, Iowa, B.A., 1950; University of Iowa, M.A., 1958, Ph.D., 1963. *Office:* Department of History, Oregon State University, Corvallis, Ore. 97331.

CAREER: Teacher of English and journalism at high school in Oskaloosa, Iowa, 1950-51; teacher of English, journalism, and history at high school in Davenport, Iowa, 1951-52 and 1954-57; teacher of history at high school in Iowa City, Iowa, 1957-63; Oregon State University, Corvallis, assistant professor, 1963-68, associate professor, 1968-79, professor of history, 1979—. *Military service:* U.S. Army, Artillery, 1952-54; served in Korea; became sergeant. *Member:* Organization of American Historians, Iowa Historical Society.

WRITINGS: Civil War Iowa and the Copperhead Movement, Iowa State University Press, 1980. Contributor to history and social studies journals.

WORK IN PROGRESS: Research on combat actions during the Korean War and on the Civil War era.

SIDELIGHTS: Wubben told "My service in combat artillery in Korea sparked a continuing interest in the vast perceptual gulfs existing in wartime among and between line soldiers, upper echelon military commanders, civilian policy shapers, and the general public."

* * *

WULFFSON, Don L. 1943-

PERSONAL: Born August 21, 1943, in Los Angeles, Calif.; son of Charles Robin (an engineer) and Corinne (a real estate broker; maiden name, Lockwood) Wulffsohn; married wife, Pamela (a teacher), June 29, 1969; children: Jennifer, Gwendolyn. *Education:* University of California, Los Angeles, B.A., 1965, Teaching Credential, 1967. *Politics:* "Indifferent." *Religion:* "Confused." *Home:* 18718 Kirkcolm Lane, Northridge, Calif. 91326. *Office:* 11133 O'Melveny, San Francisco, Calif.

CAREER: San Fernando High School, Los Angeles, Calif., teacher of English, 1967—. *Member:* United Teachers of Los Angeles. *Awards, honors:* Leather Medal from New Directions Publishing Corp., 1971, for "You Too Can Be a Floorwax That Even Your Husband Could Apply"; distinguished achievement award from Educational Press Association of America, 1978, for *Writing You'll Enjoy.*

WRITINGS—Juveniles: Themes and Writers, McGraw, 1973; *Eyebrowse* (stories and essays), Economy Co., 1976; *Building Vocabulary* (workbook), Xerox Education Publications, 1976; *Writing You'll Enjoy* (workbook), Xerox Education Publications, 1977; *The Touchstone Series* (workbooks), three volumes, Steck, 1977; *Punctuation Errors You Hate to Make* (workbook), Xerox Education Publications, 1978; *The Wonderful Word Book* (workbook), Xerox Education Publications, 1978; *Strange, Extraordinary Stories Behind How Sports Came to Be,* Lothrop, 1980; *True Stories You Won't Believe,* Xerox Education Publications, 1980; *Supergrammar* (workbook), Pruett, 1980; *Mindgame: Experiences in Creative Writing* (workbook), Xerox Educational Publica-

tions, 1980; *Visions* (stories and essays), Globe Book, 1980; *Extraordinary Stories Behind the Invention of Ordinary Things,* Lothrop, 1981. Also author of "Skillmaster Series," Xerox Education Publications.

Plays for young people: "Heartbreak on the Beach" (one-act), published in *Read Magazine,* November 29, 1978; "Herbie's Comeuppance" (one-act), published in *Read Magazine,* April 11, 1979.

Work represented in anthologies, including *New Directions Twenty-Three,* New Directions, 1971; *Words and Beyond,* Ginn, 1973; *National Poetry Anthology,* National Poetry Press, 1975. Contributor of articles, poems, and children's plays to journals, including *Hyperion, Tangent Poetry Quarterly, Journal of Reading,* and *Read.*

WORK IN PROGRESS: Incredible Stories From the Unread Pages of History; The Strange Lives of Strange People; a book of science-fiction stories for teenagers; a book of supernatural stories for teenagers; a remedial reading workbook; a science-fiction novel for teenagers.

SIDELIGHTS: Wulffson told *CA:* "While in college I wanted to grow up to be Lawrence Ferlinghetti or a psychiatrist. Much to my dismay I ended up as an English teacher. In 1971 I published a surrealistic poem, 'You Too Can Be a Floorwax That Even Your Husband Could Apply.' It appeared in the New Directions annual that included works by Ferlinghetti. I was so impressed by my achievement that I decided to quit writing poetry. Over the last few years most of my writing has been for children—educational workbooks, short stories, and nonfiction books.

"I have always been intrigued by both the past and the future. I now aspire to be a second-rate novelist, indulging either in historical fiction or science fiction."

* * *

WYNDHAM, John
See HARRIS, John (Wyndham Parkes Lucas) Beynon

* * *

WYNNE, Ronald D(avid) 1934-

PERSONAL: Born October 19, 1934, in New Haven, Conn.; son of William Harris (an economist) and Evelyn (an artist and teacher; maiden name, Burman) Wynne; married Suzan Fischer (a community activist), August 27, 1967; children: Michael, Melanie. *Education:* University of Maryland, B.A., 1955; Catholic University of America, M.A., 1958, Ph.D., 1961. *Religion:* Jewish. *Home:* 3915 Livingston St. N.W., Washington, D.C. 20015. *Office:* 1314 18th St., N.W., Washington, D.C. 20036.

CAREER: Institute of the Pennsylvania Hospital, Philadelphia, research psychologist, 1961-62; New Jersey Bureau of Research in Neurology and Psychiatry, Princeton, research psychologist, 1962-64; researcher in psychiatric hospitals, 1956-64; Queens College of the City University of New York, Flushing, N.Y., assistant professor of psychology, 1964-65; Office of Economic Opportunity, Washington, D.C., director of center assessment branch of Job Corps, 1965-67; Volt Information Sciences, Washington, D.C., director of research and evaluation, 1968-70; private social science consultant, 1970—; Wynne Associates (social science consultants), Washington, D.C., director, 1973-77; private practice in clinical and community psychology in Washington, D.C., 1978—. Co-founder and member of board of directors of Citizens for City Living, 1971—; member of executive committee of Friendship Neighborhood Coalition, 1972-74; member of board of directors of Area A Community Mental Health Center, president, 1978-80; psychologist with For Love of Children, Inc.; Member of faculty at Washington School of Psychiatry; conducts workshops and seminars; guest on television and radio programs, including "The Baxters." Adjunct psychologist for public schools of Montgomery County, Md., 1978; member of District of Columbia mayor's committee on drug abuse, 1972-74; trainer and project director for U.S. Department of Justice, 1979; principal survey investigator for Committee on Consumer Affairs, Americans for Democratic Action; member of funding task force of North American Congress on Drug and Alcohol Problems, 1974-76; expert witness before Federal Trade Commission, 1977.

MEMBER: American Psychological Association, Association of Labor-Management Administrators and Consultants on Alcoholism, District of Columbia Psychological Association. *Awards, honors:* Certificate of recognition from District of Columbia Psychological Association, 1977, for directing a District of Columbia community planning project survey.

WRITINGS: (With Susan Wynne, and others) *Effective Coordination of Drug Abuse Programs: A Guide to Community Action,* U.S. Government Printing Office, 1973; (contributor) Edward Senay, Vernon Shorty, and Harold Alksne, editors, *Developments in the Field of Drug Abuse: National Drug Abuse Conference, 1974,* Schenkman, 1975; (contributor) Stephen J. Mule, editor, *Cocaine: Chemical, Biological, Clinical, Social, and Treatment Aspects,* CRC Press, 1976; (with J. L. Phillips) *Cocaine: Mystique and Reality,* Avon, 1980; (with Susan Wynne, Shoshana Churgin, and James Kendrick) *Community Organization of Alcoholism Services: A Technical Assistance Guide,* National Institute on Alcohol Abuse and Alcoholism, 1980; (with Margaret Blasinsky and Paddy Cook) *Community Action and Legal Responses to Drug Paraphernalia* (monograph), National Institute on Drug Abuse, 1980. Contributor to professional journals.

WORK IN PROGRESS: A study of drug dealers in psychotherapy; research on the impact of government bureaucracy on the practice of psychotherapy; a study of the effect of conservative political groups in the practice of family therapy.

Y

YANNATOS, James 1929-

PERSONAL: Born March 13, 1929, in New York, N.Y.; son of Gerry and Pauline Yannatos; married Nyia O'Neil (a teacher), September 3, 1959; children: Dion, Kalya. *Education:* Yale University, B.Mus., 1951, M.Mus., 1952; University of Iowa, Ph.D., 1961; also studied music with Nadia Boulanger in Paris, France, 1957-59. *Home:* 9 Stearns, Cambridge, Mass. 02138. *Office:* Department of Music, Harvard University, Cambridge, Mass. 02138.

CAREER: San Antonio Symphony Orchestra, San Antonio, Tex., violinist and assistant conductor, 1952-55; free-lance violinist, 1956-57; Grinnell College, Grinnell, Iowa, assistant professor, 1960-64; Harvard University, Cambridge, Mass., assistant professor, 1964-69, senior lecturer in music, 1969—, conductor of Harvard-Radcliffe Orchestra, 1964—. Musical director of Hanover Chamber Orchestra; guest conductor of Boston Pops, San Antonio Symphony Orchestra, Baltimore Symphony Orchestra, Winnipeg Symphony Orchestra, and Edmonton Symphony Orchestra; conductor of Young Artists Orchestra and member of faculty at Tanglewood, Berkshire Music Center; composer-in-residence at Saratoga Performing Arts Festival; conductor of Youth Orchestra and director of music school at Chautauqua Institution. Past member of Cambridge Arts Council. *Member:* Broadcast Music, Inc., American Composers Alliance. *Awards, honors:* Grant from Charles Ulrick and Josephine Bay Foundation, 1978-80.

WRITINGS: *Explorations in Musical Materials* (on composition), Prentice-Hall, 1978; *Silly and Serious Songs* (for elementary and high school students), four volumes, with teachers' manuals and cassettes, Sonory, 1980.

Musical compositions include *Five Epigrams* (for string quartet), Associated Music Publishers, 1966; *Three Choruses* (on poems by e. e. cummings), Associated Music Publishers, 1972; "To Form a More Perfect Union," an oratorio; "Cycles"; "American Rituals"; "Polarities" (for brass and percussion).

WORK IN PROGRESS: Editing his musical compositions, with publication expected to result.

SIDELIGHTS: Yannatos's goal in preparing his musical instruction series, *Silly and Serious Songs,* for school children, was to help them develop some musical taste. He wants children to enjoy the process of singing together while learning the fundamentals of musical theory and structure, and to encourage them to write their own music and poems. He told *CA:* "The songs are in a variety of musical forms and styles, in one to five parts. Part songs are employed from the *beginning,* a departure from most methods. The entire series is meant to supplement the songbooks now in use and can be adapted by the various systems (Orf, Kodaly, etc.). The unique feature of the collection is that all the songs are based on the words and poetry of children. In addition, all the songs are original—a deficiency in the songbooks in use, since there is little twentieth-century music in the existant collections in use."

His own compositions have been recorded on "Music of James Yannatos," released by Sonory Records in 1978.

BIOGRAPHICAL/CRITICAL SOURCES: *Harvard Gazette,* March 7, 1980.

* * *

YEAGER, Robert Cushing 1942-

PERSONAL: Born February 15, 1942, in Los Angeles, Calif.; son of Paul Webster and Elizabeth (Royde) Yeager; married wife, Judith Ann (a teacher), August 1, 1970. *Education:* Attended Columbia University, 1963; Whittier College, A.B., 1965; University of California, Berkeley, M.J., 1972. *Home and office:* 2147 Park Blvd., Oakland, Calif. 94606. *Agent:* Mitchell J. Hamilburg Agency, 292 South La Cienega Blvd., Suite 212, Beverly Hills, Calif. 90211.

CAREER: *Napa Register,* Napa, Calif., reporter, 1968-72; Associated Press, San Francisco, Calif., news writer, 1972-73; McGraw-Hill Publishing Co., San Francisco, correspondent for periodicals, including *Business Week,* 1973-78; free-lance writer, 1978—. Consultant to Electric Power Research Institute. *Military service:* U.S. Coast Guard, journalist, 1965-67. *Member:* Sigma Delta Chi, University of California Alumni Association (life member). *Awards, honors:* National environmental writing award, 1977.

WRITINGS: *Seasons of Shame: The New Violence in Sports,* McGraw, 1980; *Losing It: The Economic Fall of the Middle Class,* McGraw, 1980. Contributor to magazines, including *Reader's Digest,* and newspapers.

WORK IN PROGRESS: Fiction and nonfiction on energy, health care, education, violence in society, craft, and competition.

SIDELIGHTS: Yeager commented: "Anyone who attempts

to write a serious book must possess enormous courage, because to write a serious book usually—almost always—means sacrificing some secure and respectable aspect of life. I am a journalist by profession and am skilled in that area to, I hope, some degree of competence."

* * *

YEAZELL, Ruth Bernard 1947-

PERSONAL: Born April 4, 1947, in New York, N.Y.; daughter of Walter and Annabelle (Reich) Bernard; married Stephen C. Yeazell, 1969 (marriage ended, 1980). *Education:* Swarthmore College, B.A. (with high honors), 1967; Yale University, M.Phil., 1970, Ph.D., 1971. *Home:* 555 Midvale Ave., Los Angeles, Calif. 90024. *Office:* Department of English, University of California, Los Angeles, Calif. 90024.

CAREER: Boston University, Boston, Mass., assistant professor of English, 1971-75; University of California, Los Angeles, assistant professor, 1975-77, associate professor, 1977-80, professor of English, 1980—. *Member:* Modern Language Association of America, Phi Beta Kappa. *Awards, honors:* Woodrow Wilson fellow, 1967-68; Guggenheim fellow, 1979-80.

WRITINGS: Language and Knowledge in the Late Novels of Henry James, University of Chicago Press, 1976; (editor) *The Death and Letters of Alice James,* University of California Press, 1981. Associate editor of *Nineteenth-Century Fiction;* member of advisory board of *Publications of the Modern Language Association,* 1980—.

WORK IN PROGRESS: A book on marriage proposal scenes in English fiction from *Moll Flanders* to *Women in Love.*

BIOGRAPHICAL/CRITICAL SOURCES: Washington Post Book World, November 30, 1980.

* * *

YETTE, Samuel F(rederick) 1929-

PERSONAL: Surname is pronounced "yet"; born July 2, 1929, in Harriman, Tenn.; son of Frank Mack and Cora Lee (Rector) Yette; married Sadie Lee Walton (a teacher and librarian), December 27, 1958; children: Frederick Walton, Michael Lewis. *Education:* Attended Morristown College, 1947-48; Tennessee State University, B.S., 1951; Indiana University, M.A., 1959. *Politics:* Independent. *Religion:* Baptist. *Home address:* P.O. Box 2071, Silver Spring, Md. 20902. *Agent:* Lester Lewis Associates, Inc., 156 East 52nd St., New York, N.Y. 10022. *Office:* Department of Journalism, Howard University, Washington, D.C. 20059.

CAREER: Worked as schoolteacher in Tennessee, 1953-55; sportswriter for *Chattanooga Times,* Chattanooga, Tenn.; writer for *Afro-American* (newspaper); associate editor of *Ebony;* organizer and director of Information Bureau at Tuskegee Institute, Tuskegee Institute, Ala.; city hall reporter for *Dayton Journal Herald,* Dayton, Ohio; information officer for West Africa programs, U.S. Peace Corps, Washington, D.C.; organizer of Information Office and special assistant for civil rights at Office of Economic Opportunity, Washington, D.C.; Board of Education, New York, N.Y., study director, 1967; *Newsweek,* Washington correspondent, 1968-72; Howard University, Washington, D.C., professor of journalism, 1972—. Proprietor of Sam Yette Enterprises (photojournalism firm). Lecturer at colleges, including Oberlin College, Hampton Institute, and University of the District of Columbia; gives photographic exhibitions and lectures; guest on television programs, including "Meet the

Press," "Face the Nation," and "The Today Show." Delegate to Colloquium on Black Culture and Development, Dakar, Senegal, 1976. Member of board of trustees of Morristown College. *Military service:* U.S. Air Force, communications and information officer, 1951-53; became second lieutenant. U.S. Air Force Reserve, 1953-63; became captain.

MEMBER: Society of Professional Journalists (president, 1972-73), Capital Press Club (vice-president, 1967-68). *Awards, honors:* D.Hum. from Prentiss Institute, 1971; *The Choice* was named nonfiction work of distinction by Black Academy of Arts and Letters, 1972; book award from Capital Press Club, 1972.

WRITINGS: The Choice: The Issue of Black Survival in America, Putnam, 1971; (contributor) *Alienation and Violence in the North American Community,* University of Windsor Press, 1972. Author of "Washington Viewpoint," a weekly column in *Afro-American,* 1976-79. Contributor of articles and photographs to magazines and newspapers, including *People, Time,* and *National Geographic.* Member of editorial board of *Journal of Negro Education;* chairman of editorial advisory board of *New Directions.*

SIDELIGHTS: Yette wrote: "Although I had earlier worked as a sportswriter, my journalistic career was significantly boosted in the summer of 1956, when I teamed with photographer Gordon Parks to work on a four-part *Life* series on racial segregation in the United States. After that special assignment, I began work with *Afro-American,* covering such historic events as the Montgomery bus boycott, the organization meetings of the Southern Christian Leadership Conference, and the 1957 march on Washington for jobs and freedom.

"In September, 1977, I was a member of a small group of American journalists who toured the People's Republic of China. During the three-week tour of some five thousand miles, we visited numerous factories, farms, schools, and homes, and, in general, received warm hospitality from the Chinese people. During 1979, I traveled widely in the United States and abroad.

"Throughout my journalistic career, I have preferred to see events, whenever possible, with my own eyes. Thus, my 1979 sabbatical year included two overseas trips—a ten-day tour of the Soviet Union in the spring, and in September, a one-week visit to Lebanon, where I covered the historic meeting of Southern Christian Leadership Conference delegates with the Palestine Liberation Organization chairman, Yasser Arafat, and others.

"A major effort of my sabbatical, however, was the development and expansion of my interest in photojournalism, an increasingly important aspect of journalism in general. I pursued this interest with photographic excursions, exhibits, and lectures. My own photographic exhibitions have included a color-slide lecture in observance of the Chinese New Year at the University of Maryland, a color-slide lecture on the Middle East for journalists covering the U.S. Congress, and 'The Many Colors of Man,' a Howard University exhibition on Africa, tne Caribbean, China, the Soviet Union, and the United States."

* * *

YOUNG, I(sador) S. 1902-

PERSONAL: Born June 29, 1902; son of Samuel and Ida Young; married wife, Gertrude. *Education:* New York University, B.S., 1926, M.A., 1932. *Home:* 222 East Eighth St.,

Brooklyn, N.Y. 11218. *Agent:* James Seligmann Agency, 280 Madison Ave., New York, N.Y. 10016.

CAREER: Board of Education, New York, N.Y., assistant principal of a junior high school, 1947-72; writer, 1972—.

WRITINGS: Jadie Greenway (juvenile novel), Crown, 1947; *A Hit and a Miss* (juvenile novel), Follett, 1952; *The Two-Minute Dribble*, Follett, 1964; *Carson at Second*, Follett, 1966; *Quarterback Carson*, Follett, 1967; *Carson's Fast Break*, Follett, 1969; *Uncle Herschel, Dr. Padilsky, and the Evil Eye* (novel), Harcourt, 1973.

WORK IN PROGRESS: Two novels.

Z

ZALON, Jean E(ugenia) 1919-

PERSONAL: Born March 30, 1919, in New York, N.Y.; daughter of Irving (a dentist) and Rose (an interpreter; maiden name, Glick) Berlin; married Jules Zalon (a photographer), June 1, 1942; children: Paul, Michael. *Education:* Hunter College (now of the City University of New York), B.A., 1946. *Politics:* Liberal. *Religion:* Jewish. *Home:* 372 Central Park W., New York, N.Y. 10025. *Agent:* Regina Ryan, 1 West 85th St., New York, N.Y. 10024.

CAREER: Interviewer and research assistant for research organizations, 1955-64; Health Insurance Plan of Greater New York, New York, N.Y., research associate, 1964-74; writer and counselor to mastectomy patients, 1974—. Guest on television and radio programs. *Member:* American Cancer Society.

WRITINGS: I Am Whole Again: The Case for Breast Reconstruction After Mastectomy, Random House, 1978.

SIDELIGHTS: As a research associate for Health Insurance Plan of Greater New York, Jean Zalon worked with a breast cancer research program supported by the U.S. Public Health Service and National Cancer Institute. She interviewed patients and doctors, and coordinated a screening program at various New York City hospitals. While collecting material for her book, she interviewed medical and social science experts in the field and several hundred women. After her book was published, she made several tours across the United States and Canada. She also made a video film on the value of breast reconstruction and two-step mastectomy procedure.

Zalon wrote: "My primary motivation was to alert women to the availability of breast reconstruction after mastectomy, partly as an inducement not to procrastinate when they need treatment. There *is* an alternative to the mutilation of mastectomy."

BIOGRAPHICAL/CRITICAL SOURCES: New York Times, December 6, 1976; *People,* September 11, 1978.

* * *

ZDENEK, Marilee 1934-
(Marilee Earle)

PERSONAL: Born June 4, 1934, in Lampasas, Tex.; daughter of John Baylis (a building contractor) and Perla (an architectural designer; maiden name, Dickason) Earle; married Leonard S. Picker (an attorney), April 20, 1958 (died November 23, 1961); married Albert N. Zdenek (a physician), December 11, 1962; children: Gina Picker Zdenek, Tamara Picker Zdenek Fletcher. *Education:* Attended University of California, Los Angeles, 1951-53; studied privately with Robert Kirsch, 1979; International College, Los Angeles, B.A., 1979. *Residence:* Woodland Hills, Calif. *Agent:* Don Congdon, Harold Matson Co., 22 East 40th St., New York, N.Y. 10016.

CAREER: Worked as professional actress (under name Marilee Earle), 1952-58, in plays, including "Call Me Madam," "Carousel," and "The Male Animal," in motion pictures, including "Ambassador's Daughter," "Fearmakers," "Streets of Sinners," "Island Woman," and "Terror in a Texas Town," and on television in "Life of Reiley" and "The Brothers"; director of Creative Workshop, Bel Air Presbyterian Church, 1970; writer, 1970—. Sponsor of Los Angeles Music Center and member of its support groups, Center Theater Group and Amazing Blue Ribbon; past member of board of directors of Argyle Episcopal Academy and Ojai Community Hospital. *Member:* International P.E.N. (vice-president of Los Angeles Center, 1979-80 and 1980-81), Women's National Book Association, American Society of Composers, Authors, and Publishers. *Awards, honors:* Award for excellence in poetry from *Campus Life,* 1975, for *God Is a Verb!*

WRITINGS: (With Marge Champion) *Catch the New Wind,* Word, Inc., 1972; (with Champion) *God Is a Verb!,* Word, Inc., 1974; *Someone Special,* Word, Inc., 1977; *Splinters in My Pride,* Word, Inc., 1979. Also author of program, "Adventures From the Bible," first broadcast on KFVD-Radio, c.1953.

Work represented in anthologies, including *Hymns for the Family of God,* edited by Fred Bach, Paragon Associates, 1976. Contributor of articles and poems to national magazines.

WORK IN PROGRESS: The Severing, a suspense novel set in Los Angeles, London, and Jerusalem; *Clock Wise,* a book of poems and photographs about moving on; research for another suspense novel.

SIDELIGHTS: Marilee Zdenek wrote: "*Splinters in My Pride* begins: 'I've written miles of words; / placed end to end, / they stretch across the landscape of my years, / measuring feelings and moods, / changes of heart and mind. . . .'

"The feelings in this book are conveyed through poems, one-page stories, and photographs. It is the interior landscape that interests me. If I photograph a crevasse in a Canadian glacier, I use the picture to illustrate a poem about personal separation and feelings of abandonment. A photograph of a deserted and decaying boat in Alaska relates to a poem about talents that die from lack of use and care. I write about children, old people, lovers—and the pictures always have a tight relationship to the words.

"*Someone Special* was originally written as a theatre piece for Carol Lawrence, with music composed by Ron Harris. It is the story of Mary of Nazareth, portrayed first as a young Jewish girl, pregnant and scared, then as an old woman looking back on her life, dealing with the extraordinary events and feelings she encountered. The work was performed by Miss Lawrence on her concert tours and was presented with full orchestra at the Dorothy Chandler Pavilion in Los Angeles.

"*God Is a Verb!* combines prayer-poems with action-oriented photographs. I wrote the poems, and Marge Champion, using the talents of many photographers, collected the extraordinary action photographs that illuminate the theme of the words. Again, the emphasis is on the exploration of feelings.

"*Catch the New Wind* is about contemporary liturgy, creative worship, and the value of using the talents of the congregation for corporate worship. It was used as a text in many seminaries and universities. The book contains poetry, photographs of liturgical dance, banners, as well as a philosophy of worship and detailed explanations of how these celebrations are performed. We also included elements that *didn't* work, with comments about how future directors could avoid the same pitfalls.

"In 1967, I wrote the lyrics to 'The Morning Star,' an anthem composed by Paul Sjolund. It is considered a contemporary classic in choral music and has been recorded by various artists. In addition to my work with poetry, I have also been writing fiction for the last few years.

"In evaluating my career, it seems that any account of my professional life should contain some of the failures as well as the successes. To present only the winning side is misleading, especially to young writers who may not realize that most of us who publish frequently also have to deal with rejected manuscripts. In my case, I worked for over two years on a novel that made the publishing rounds and apparently isn't going to sell. I'll take a look at it again when I finish the novel I'm working on now. Perhaps a fresh approach will help. Or perhaps it should just stay in my drawer and serve as my 'training manuscript' for writing novels.

"I like the balance of writing poetry and fiction; both are hard work in my case. I enjoy the camera, too, though I've never taken myself seriously as a photographer. When the *Los Angeles Times* reviewed *Someone Special*, the reviewer liked the pictures better than the text; that was tough on my ego because I work hard at my writing—the camera is just for fun. It was a disquieting realization that, at least for one reviewer, my pictures had upstaged my words."

BIOGRAPHICAL/CRITICAL SOURCES: Newsweek, October 9, 1972; *Los Angeles Times,* November 5, 1972; *New York Daily News,* November 27, 1972.

*   *   *

ZELINKA, Sydney   1906(?)-1981

OBITUARY NOTICE: Born c. 1906 in New York, N.Y.; died of cancer, January 17, 1981, in Amagansett, N.Y. Screenwriter and television writer. Zelinka's career as a comedy writer began in Hollywood, where he wrote screenplays for the Marx Brothers, Jimmy Durante, and Sid Caeser. He returned to New York to write for Jackie Gleason's "The Honeymooners" and Phil Silvers's "Sergeant Bilko," for which he received an Emmy Award and an award from the Writers Guild of America. Zelinka's screenplays include "A Night in Casablanca" and "Copacabana." Obituaries and other sources: *New York Times,* January 19, 1981.

*   *   *

ZIEGLER, Ronald M(elvin)   1935-

PERSONAL: Born August 10, 1935, in Cuyahoga Falls, Ohio; son of Melvin Franklin (an engineer) and Elsie (a teacher; maiden name, Stokes) Ziegler; married Elli Resch (an accounting technician), July 25, 1963; children: Birgit, Christopher. *Education:* University of Miami, A.B., 1966; Florida State University, M.S., 1968. *Politics:* Independent. *Home:* Northeast 1025 B St., Pullman, Wash. 99163. *Office:* Library, Washington State University, Holland 120-G, Pullman, Wash. 99164.

CAREER: Cafe Maerchenpark, Lindau, West Germany, owner-operator, 1962-64; U.S. Army and Air Force Exchange Service, Colorado Springs, Colo., food service manager, 1966-67; Florida Atlantic University, Boca Raton, librarian and associate professor of library science, 1969-70; Washington State University, Pullman, librarian, 1970—. Owner and publisher of Outside Enterprise Press, 1980—. *Military service:* U.S. Army, 1957-60. *Member:* National Librarians Association, American Library Association, Western European Languages Specialists Group, Beta Phi Mu.

WRITINGS: Wilderness Waterways, Gale, 1979; *Ski Northwest/Canada West,* Outside Enterprise Press, 1981; *Boating Northwest: A Directory of Pleasure Boating Facilities in the Coastal and Inland Northwest,* Outside Enterprise Press, in press. Editor of "Sports, Games, and Pastimes," a series, Gale, 1975—.

SIDELIGHTS: Ziegler wrote: "In any season I try to find an excuse to head for the outdoors. The excuse can be flimsy at times, since around here, where I live, the outdoors is a thing of preposterous beauty found in sinful abundance. I like to share information about the outdoor places I know. To this end I've formed a company engaged in publishing regional directories of outdoor sports facilities."

AVOCATIONAL INTERESTS: Skiing, "spending the summer in a rubber raft on a free-flowing river."

*   *   *

ZIMMER, Jill Schary
See ROBINSON, Jill

*   *   *

ZIMMERMANN, Caroline A(nna)   1944-

PERSONAL: Born October 19, 1944, in New York; daughter of H. Paul (an industrial designer) and Frances (in real estate; maiden name, Short) Zimmermann. *Education:* Georgia State University, B.A., 1966. *Politics:* Republican. *Religion:* Methodist. *Residence:* New York, N.Y. *Agent:* Jeffrey Feinman, Ventura Associates, 200 Madison Ave., New York, N.Y. 10016. *Office:* Zimmermann Marketing, Inc., 342 Madison Ave., Suite 1916, New York, N.Y. 10017.

CAREER: Christian Herald Publishing Co., New York City,

book club manager, 1966-68; William Steiner Associates, New York City, vice-president, 1968-71; Zimmermann Marketing, Inc., New York City, president, 1971—. *Member:* Direct Mail Marketing Association, One Hundred Millimeter Club, Writers Club. *Awards, honors:* Echo Award from Direct Mail Marketing Association, 1980, for advertising campaigns.

WRITINGS: Laetrile: Hope or Hoax, Zebra Books, 1977; *The Super Sneaker Book,* Doubleday, 1978; *Your Child Can be a Model,* Hawthorn, 1980; *How to Break Into the Media Professions,* Doubleday, 1981.

SIDELIGHTS: Caroline Zimmermann told *CA:* ''The number of young people who wish to break into the media professions is astronomical. In my experience, it is not necessarily the 'brightest and the best' who break in; it is those who are willing to work hard and diligently pursue one of these careers. *How to Break In* was written to help every eager, earnest, and persevering young person to launch a career by providing them with a 'competitive edge.' ın fact, there are many tips, many 'secrets' that can help a person to land that first (and essential) job in media to get them on their way.

''Most parents who help their children get into child modeling do not understand the consequences of that decision until after they are in the business. *Your Child Can Be a Model* was written to help parents understand all the aspects of this career for their child. It is a guidebook with facts, figures, and plenty of insights, including an in-depth interview with an entire family (including the grandfather) that models.''

CONTEMPORARY AUTHORS

CUMULATIVE INDEX VOLUMES 1-102

This index includes references to all entries in the series listed below.
References in the index are identified as follows:

Volume number only—*Contemporary Authors* Original Volumes 1-102
R after number—*Contemporary Authors* Revised Volumes 1-44
CANR before number—*Contemporary Authors New Revision Series,* Volumes 1-3
CAP before number—*Contemporary Authors Permanent Series,* Volumes 1-2
CLC before number—*Contemporary Literary Criticism,* Volumes 1-16
SATA before number—*Something About the Author,* Volumes 1-21
AITN before number—*Authors in the News,* Volumes 1-2

A

A. A.
See Willis, (George) Anthony Armstrong
Aaker, David A(llen) 1938- ... 49-52
Aalben, Patrick
See Jones, Noel
Aalto, (Hugo) Alvar (Henrik)
1898-1976 Obituary ... 65-68
Aardema, Verna
See Vugteveen, Verna Aardema
See also SATA 4
Aaron, Benjamin 1915- ... 23-24R
Aaron, Chester 1923- ... 21-22R
See also SATA 9
Aaron, Daniel 1912- ... 13-14R
Aaron, James Ethridge 1927- ... 23-24R
Aaronovitch, Sam 1919- ... 13-14R
Aarons, Edward S(idney) 1916-1975 ... 93-96
Obituary ... 57-60
Aaronson, Bernard S(eymour) 1924- ... 29-32R
Aarsleff, Hans 1925- ... 21-22R
Aaseng, Rolf E(dward) 1923- ... 49-52
Abajian, James De Tar 1914- ... 65-68
Abarbanel, Karin 1950- ... 65-68
Abbaanano, Nicola 1901- ... 33-36R
Abbas, Khwaja Ahmad 1914- ... 57-60
Abbazia, Patrick 1937- ... 57-60
Abbe, Elfriede (Martha) 1919- ... 15-16R
Abbe, George (Bancroft) 1911- ... 25-28R
Abbey, Edward 1927- ... CANR-2
Earlier sketch in CA 45-48
Abbey, Merrill R. 1905- ... CANR-3
Earlier sketch in CA 1R
Abbot, Charles G(reeley) 1872-1973 ... 77-80
Obituary ... 45-48
Abbot, Rick
See Sharkey, John Michael
Abbott, Alice
See Borland, Kathryn Kilby
and Speicher, Helen Ross S(mith)
Abbott, Anthony S. 1935- ... 17-18R
Abbott, Carl (John) 1944- ... 65-68
Abbott, Claude Colleer 1889-1971 ... 7-8R
Obituary ... 89-92
Abbott, Freeland K(night) 1919-1971 ... CAP-2
Earlier sketch in CA 25-28
Abbott, George 1887- ... 93-96
Abbott, H(orace) Porter 1940- ... 45-48
Abbott, James H(amilton) 1924- ... 77-80
Abbott, Jerry (Lynn) 1938- ... 45-48
Abbott, John J(amison) 1930- ... 17-18R
Abbott, John Janisen ... 17-18R
Abbott, Manager Henry
See Stratemeyer, Edward L.
Abbott, Martin 1922-1977 ... 33-36R
Abbott, May L(aura) 1916- ... 9-10R
Abbott, R(obert) Tucker 1919- ... 9-10R
Abbott, Raymond H(erbert) 1942- ... 57-60
Abbott, Richard H(enry) 1936- ... 33-36R
Abbott, Rowland A(ubrey) S(amuel) 1909- ... 53-56
Abbott, Sidney 1937- ... 41-44R
Abbott, Walter M(atthew) 1923- ... 11-12R
Abbotts, John 1947- ... 73-76
Abboushi, W(asif) F(ahmi) 1931- ... 29-32R
Abbs, Peter 1942- ... 93-96
Abcarian, Richard 1929- ... 33-36R
Abdallah, Omar
See Humbaraci, D(emir) Arslan
Abdel-Malek, Anouar 1924- ... 29-32R
Abdelsamad, Moustafa H(assan) 1941- ... 53-56
Abdul, Raoul 1929- ... 29-32R
See also SATA 12
Abdullahi, Guda 1946- ... 93-96
Abdul-Rauf, Muhammad 1917- ... 101
Abe, Kobo 1924- ... 65-68
See also CLC 8
Abel, Alan (Irwin) 1928- ... 19-20R
Abel, Bob 1931- ... 65-68
Abel, Elie 1920- ... 61-64
Abel, Ernest L(awrence) 1943- ... 41-44R
Abel, Jeanne 1937- ... 19-20R
Abel, Lionel 1910- ... 61-64
Abel, Raymond 1911- ... SATA-12
Abel, Reuben 1911- ... 37-40R
Abel, Robert H(alsall) 1941- ... 102
Abel, Theodora M(ead) 1899- ... 57-60
Abel, Theodore 1896- ... 23-24R
Abell, George O(gden) 1927- ... CANR-3
Earlier sketch in CA 9-10R
Abell, Kathleen 1938- ... 49-52
See also SATA 9
Abell, Kjeld 1901-1961 ... CLC-15
Abella, Alex 1950- ... 93-96
Abella, Irving Martin 1940- ... 49-52
Abels, Jules 1913- ... 61-64
Abel-Smith, Brian 1926- ... 21-22R
Abelson, Raziel A. 1921- ... 11-12R
Abelson, Robert P(aul) 1928- ... 41-44R
Abend, Norman A(nchel) 1931- ... 33-36R
Aber, William M(cKee) 1929- ... 57-60
Aberbach, Joel D(avid) 1940- ... 45-48
Abercrombie, Barbara (Mattes) 1939- ... 81-84
See also SATA 16
Abercrombie, Nigel J(ames) 1908- ... 101
Aberg, Sherrill E. 1924- ... 21-22R
Aberle, David F(riend) 1918- ... 21-22R
Aberle, John Wayne 1919- ... 1R
Aberle, Kathleen Gough 1925- ... 13-14R
Abernathy, David M(yles) 1933- ... 53-56
Abernathy, (M.) Elton 1913- ... 17-18R
Abernathy, M(abra) Glenn 1921- ... 13-14R
Abernathy, William J(ackson) 1933- ... 93-96
Abernethy, Francis Edward 1925- ... 21-22R
Abernethy, George Lawrence 1910- ... 2R
Abernethy, Peter L(ink) 1935- ... 69-72
Abernethy, Robert G(ordon) 1927- ... 21-22R
See also SATA 5
Abernethy, Thomas Perkins 1890- ... CAP-1
Earlier sketch in CA 19-20
Abernethy, Virginia 1934- ... 93-96
Abisch, Roslyn Kroop 1927- ... 21-22R
See also SATA 9
Abisch, Roz
See Abisch, Roslyn Kroop
Abish, Walter 1931- ... 101
Able, James A(ugustus), Jr. 1928- ... 93-96
Ableman, Paul 1927- ... 61-64
Abler, Ronald F. 1939- ... 53-56
Abler, Thomas S(truthers) 1941- ... 101
Abodaher, David J. (Naiph) 1919- ... 17-18R
See also SATA 17
Abrahall, Clare Hoskyns
See Hoskyns-Abrahall, Clare (Constance Drury)
Abraham, Claude K(urt) 1931- ... 23-24R
Abraham, Gerald Ernest Heal 1904- ... 89-92
Abraham, Henry Julian 1921- ... CANR-2
Earlier sketch in CA 5-6R
Abraham, Willard 1916- ... 13-14R
Abraham, William E. 1934- ... 13-14R
Abraham, William I(srael) 1919- ... 25-28R
Abrahams, Gerald 1907-1980 ... 102
Obituary ... 97-100
Abrahams, Howard Phineas 1904- ... 57-60
Abrahams, Peter (Henry) 1919- ... 57-60
See also CLC 4
Abrahams, R(aphael) G(arvin) 1934- ... 25-28R
Abrahams, Robert David 1905- ... CAP-2
Earlier sketch in CA 33-36
See also SATA 4
Abrahams, Roger D. 1933- ... 11-12R
Abrahams, William Miller 1919- ... 61-64
Abrahamsen, Christine Elizabeth 1916- ... 101
Abrahamsen, David 1903- ... 65-68
Abrahamson, Mark J. 1939- ... 101
Abrahamsson, Bengt 1937- ... 97-100
Abram, H(arry) S(hore) 1931-1977 ... 29-32R
Abramov, Emil
See Draitser, Emil
Abramovitz, Anita (Zeltner Brooks) 1914- ... 97-100
Abramowitz, Jack 1918- ... 7-8R
Abrams, Alan E(dwin) 1941- ... 89-92
Abrams, Charles 1901-1970 ... CAP-2
Earlier sketch in CA 23-24
Abrams, George J(oseph) 1918- ... 61-64
Abrams, Harry N(athan)
1904-1979 Obituary ... 93-96
Abrams, Joy 1941- ... 77-80
See also SATA 16
Abrams, Linsey 1951- ... 102
Abrams, M(eyer) H(oward) 1912- ... 57-60
Abrams, Peter D(avid) 1936- ... 33-36R
Abrams, Richard M. 1932- ... 13-14R
Abrams, Sam(uel) 1935- ... 21-22R
Abramson, Doris E. 1925- ... 25-28R
Abramson, Harold Alexander
1889-1980 Obituary ... 102
Abramson, Harold J(ulian) 1934- ... 45-48
Abramson, Jesse P. 1904-1979 Obituary ... 89-92
Abramson, Joan 1932- ... 25-28R
Abramson, Martin 1921- ... 49-52
Abramson, Michael 1944- ... 69-72
Abramson, Paul R(obert) 1937- ... 61-64
Abrash, Merritt 1930- ... 23-24R
Abrecht, Mary Ellen (Benson) 1945- ... 69-72
Abreu, Maria Isabel 1919- ... 45-48
Abse, Dannie 1923- ... 53-56
See also CLC 7
Abse, David Wilfred 1915- ... 49-52
Abshire, David M. 1926- ... 23-24R
Abt, Clark C(laus) 1929- ... 69-72
Abt, Lawrence Edwin 1915- ... 33-36R
Abu Jaber, Kamel S. 1932- ... 21-22R
Abu-Lughod, Ibrahim Ali 1929- ... 5-6R
Abu-Lughod, Janet L(ouise) 1928- ... 65-68
Abun-Nasr, Jamil Miri 1932- ... 69-72
Academic Investor
See Reddaway, W(illiam) Brian
Accola, Louis W(ayne) 1937- ... 29-32R
Ace, Goodman 1899- ... 61-64
Achard, George
See Torres, Tereska (Szwarc)
Achard, Marcel
See Ferreol, Marcel Auguste
Achebe, Chinua 1930- ... 4R
See also CLC 1, 3, 5, 7, 11
Achenbaum, W(ilbert) Andrew 1947- ... 89-92
Acheson, Dean (Gooderham) 1893-1971 ... CAP-2
Obituary ... 33-36R
Earlier sketch in CA 25-28
Acheson, Patricia Castles 1924- ... 3R
Achilles
See Lamb, Charles Bentall
Achtemeier, Elizabeth (Rice) 1926- ... 17-18R
Achtemeier, Paul J(ohn) 1927- ... 17-18R
Achyut
See Birla, Lakshminiwas
Acker, Duane Calvin 1931- ... 33-36R
Acker, Helen ... 73-76
Acker, Robert Flint 1920- ... 89-92
Acker, William R. B.
1910(?)-1974 Obituary ... 49-52
Ackerley, J(oe) R(andolph) 1896-1967 ... 102
Obituary ... 89-92
Ackerman, Bruce A. 1943- ... 53-56
Ackerman, Carl W(illiam) 1890-1970 ... 73-76
Obituary ... 29-32R
Ackerman, Diane 1948- ... 57-60
Ackerman, Edward A.
1911-1973 Obituary ... 41-44R
Ackerman, Eugene (Francis) 1888-1974 SATA-10
Ackerman, Forrest J(ames) 1916- ... 102
Ackerman, Gerald M(artin) 1928- ... CANR-1
Earlier sketch in CA 45-48
Ackerman, J. Mark 1939- ... 53-56
Ackerman, James S(loss) 1919- ... 9-10R
Ackerman, Nathan W(ard) 1908-1971 ... CAP-2
Earlier sketch in CA 29-32
Ackerman, Robert E(dwin) 1928- ... 45-48
Ackerson, Duane (Wright, Jr.) 1942- ... 33-36R
Ackland, Rodney 1908- ... 57-60
Ackley, Charles Walton 1913-1975 ... 41-44R
Ackley, Hugh Gardner 1915- ... 61-64
Ackley, Randall William 1931- ... 53-56
Ackoff, Russell L(incoln) 1919- ... 41-44R
Ackroyd, Peter R(unham) 1917- ... 25-28R
Ackworth, Robert Charles 1923- ... 5-6R
Acland, Alice
See Wignall, Anne
Acland, James H. 1917-1976 ... 41-44R
Acomb, Evelyn Martha
See Acomb-Walker, Evelyn
Acomb Walker, Evelyn 1910- ... 85-88
Acorn, Milton 1923- ... CLC-15
Acquaviva, Sabino Samele 1927- ... 101
Acquaye, Alfred Allotey 1939- ... 25-28R
Acre, Stephen
See Gruber, Frank
Acred, Arthur 1926- ... 25-28R
Acton, Edward J. 1949- ... CANR-2
Earlier sketch in CA 45-48
Acton, Harold Mario Mitchell 1904- ... CANR-3
Earlier sketch in CA 4R
Acton, Jay
See Acton, Edward J.
Acton, Thomas (Alan) 1948- ... 57-60
Aczel, Tamas 1921- ... 49-52
Adachi, Barbara (Curtis) 1924- ... 49-52
Adair, Ian 1942- ... 69-72
Adair, James R. 1923- ... 19-20R
Adair, John G(lenn) 1933- ... 49-52
Adair, Margaret Weeks ?-1971 ... CAP-1
Earlier sketch in CA 13-14
See also SATA 10
Adam, Ben
See Drachman, Julian M(oses)
Adam, Cornel
See Lengyel, Cornel Adam
Adam, Helen 1909- ... 19-20R
Adam, Michael 1919- ... 53-56
Adam, Ruth (Augusta) 1907- ... 23-24R
Adam, Thomas R(itchie) 1900- ... CAP-1
Earlier sketch in CA 19-20
Adamczewski, Zygmunt 1921- ... 15-16R
Adamec, Ludwig W(arren) 1924- ... 23-24R
Adamov, Arthur 1908-1970 ... CAP-2
Obituary ... 25-28R
Earlier sketch in CA 17-18
See also CLC 4
Adams, A. Don
See Cleveland, Philip Jerome
Adams, A. John 1931- ... 33-36R
Adams, Adrienne 1906- ... CANR-1
Earlier sketch in CA 49-52
See also SATA 8
Adams, Alice (Boyd) 1926- ... 81-84
See also CLC 6, 13
Adams, Anne H(utchinson) 1935- ... 41-44R
Adams, Annette
See Rowland, D(onald) S(ydney)
Adams, Ansel (Easton) 1902- ... 21-22R
See also AITN 1
Adams, Arthur E(ugene) 1917- ... 7-8R
Adams, Arthur Merrihew 1908- ... 53-56
Adams, Arthur Stanton
1896-1980 Obituary ... 102
Adams, Bart
See Bingley, David Ernest
Adams, Betsy
See Pitcher, Gladys
Adams, Cedric M. 1902-1961 Obituary ... 89-92
Adams, Charles J(oseph) 1924- ... 17-18R
Adams, Christopher
See Hopkins, Kenneth
Adams, Chuck
See Tubb, E(dwin) C(harles)
Adams, Cindy ... 23-24R
Adams, Clifton 1919- ... 13-14R
Adams, Clinton 1918- ... 33-36R
Adams, Don(ald Kendrick) 1925- ... 33-36R
Adams, E(lie) M(aynard) 1919- ... 3R
Adams, Elsie B(onita) 1932- ... 69-72
Adams, F(rank) Ramsay 1883-1963 ... 7-8R
Adams, Florence 1932- ... 49-52
Adams, Francis A(lexandre)
1874-1975 Obituary ... 61-64
Adams, Frank C(lyde) 1916- ... 69-72
Adams, Franklin P(ierce)
1881-1960 Obituary ... 93-96
Adams, George Matthew
1878-1962 Obituary ... 93-96
Adams, George Worthington 1905- ... 41-44R
Adams, Georgia Sachs 1913- ... 37-40R
Adams, Graham, Jr. 1928- ... 17-18R
Adams, Harlen M(artin) 1904- ... CAP-1
Earlier sketch in CA 13-14
Adams, Harriet S(tratemeyer) ... 19-20R
See also SATA 1
See also AITN 2
Adams, Harrison
See Stratemeyer, Edward L.

INDEX

Anthony, John
See Beckett, Ronald Brymer
Anthony, John
See Roberts, John S(torm)
Anthony, John
See Sabini, John Anthony
Anthony, Katharine (Susan)
1877-1965 Obituary 25-28R
Anthony, Michael 1932- 19-20R
Anthony, Piers
See Jacob, Piers A(nthony) D(illingham)
Anthony, Robert N(ewton) 1916- 15-16R
Anthony, Susan B(rownell) 1916- 89-92
Anthony, William G. 1934- 17-18R
Anthony, William P(hilip) 1943- 77-80
Anticaglia, Elizabeth 1939- CANR-1
Earlier sketch in CA 45-48
See also SATA 12
Antico, John 1924- 29-32R
Antill, James Macquarie 1912- 33-36R
Antin, David 1932- 73-76
Antoine-Dariaux, Genevieve 1914- 57-60
Anton, Frank Robert 1920- 41-44R
Anton, Hector R(oque) 1919- 73-76
Anton, John P(eter) 1920- 21-22R
Anton, Michael J(ames) 1940- 57-60
See also SATA 12
Anton, Rita (Kenter) 1920- 9-10R
Antonacci, Robert J(oseph) 1916- 7-8R
Antoncich, Betty (Kennedy) 1913- 15-16R
Antoni
See Iranek-Osmecki, Kazimierz
Antonick, Robert J. 1939- 37-40R
Antoninus, Brother
See Everson, William (Oliver)
Antonioni, Michelangelo 1912- 73-76
Antoniutti, Ildebrando
1898-1974 Obituary 53-56
Antonovsky, Aaron 1923- 29-32R
Antony, Jonquil 1916- 15-16R
Antony, Peter
See Shaffer, Peter (Levin)
Antoun, Richard T(aft) 1932- 65-68
Antreasian, Garo Z(areh) 1922- 81-84
Antrim, Harry Thomas 1936- 33-36R
Antrim, William H. 1928- 69-72
Antrobus, John 1933- 57-60
Antschel, Paul 1920-1970 85-88
See also CLC 10
Anttila, Raimo (Aulis) 1935- 33-36R
Anvic, Frank
See Sherman, Jory (Tecumseh)
Anweiler, Oskar 1925- 65-68
Anyon, G(eorge) Jay 1909- 7-8R
Aoki, Haruo 1930- 49-52
Apel, Willi 1893- CANR-2
Earlier sketch in CA 2R
Apgar, Virginia 1909-1974 73-76
Obituary 53-56
Apitz, Bruno 1900-1979 Obituary 85-88
Apolinar, Danny 1934- 61-64
Apostle, Chris(tos) N(icholas) 1935- 21-22R
Apostolon, Billy (Michael) 1930- 97-100
App, Austin Joseph 1902- 101
Appadorai, A(ngadipuram) 1902- 102
Appel, Allan 1946- 77-80
Appel, Benjamin 1907-1977 .... 13-14R
Obituary 69-72
Appel, John J. 1921- 33-36R
Appel, Kenneth Ellmaker
1896-1979 Obituary 89-92
Appel, Martin E(liot) 1948- 85-88
Appel, Marty
See Appel, Martin E(liot)
Appelbaum, Judith 1939- 77-80
Appelbaum, Stephen A(rthur) 1926- 101
Appelman, Hyman (Jedidiah) 1902- 5-6R
Appiah, Peggy 1921- 41-44R
See also SATA 15
Appignanesi, Lisa 1946- 49-52
Applbaum, Ronald L. 1943- 57-60
Apple, Max (Isaac) 1941- 81-84
See also CLC 9
Apple, R(aymond) W(alter), Jr. 1934- 89-92
Applebaum, Samuel 1904- 65-68
Applebaum, Stan 1929- 85-88
Applebaum, William 1906- 11-12R
Applebee, Arthur N(oble) 1946- 81-84
Appleby, John T. 1909(?)-1974 Obituary .. 53-56
Appleby, Jon 1948- 33-36R
Appleby, Joyce Oldham 1929- 69-72
Applegarth, Margaret Tyson
1886-1976 Obituary 69-72
Applegate, James (Earl) 1923- 33-36R
Applegate, Richard
1913(?)-1979 Obituary 85-88
Appleman, John Alan 1912- CANR-2
Earlier sketch in CA 7-8R
Appleman, Mark J(erome) 1917- 29-32R
Appleman, Philip (Dean) 1926- 15-16R
Appleman, Roy Edgar 1904- CAP-1
Earlier sketch in CA 9-10
Appleton, Arthur 1913- 93-96
Appleton, James Henry 1919- CANR-2
Earlier sketch in CA 5-6R
Appleton, Jane (Frances) 1934- 102
Appleton, Jay
See Appleton, James Henry
Appleton, Sarah 1930- 37-40R
Appleton, Sheldon Lee 1933- 1R
Appleton, Victor CAP-2
Earlier sketch in CA 19-20
See also SATA 1
Appleton, Victor II 19-20R
See also SATA 1
Appleton, William S. 1934- 101
Applewhite, Cynthia 89-92
Applewhite, E(dgar) J(arratt, Jr.) 1919- 89-92
Applewhite, James W(illiam) 1935- 85-88
Appley, M(ortimer) H(erbert) 1921- 15-16R
Appleyard, Donald 1928- 5-6R
Appleyard, Reginald Thomas 1927- 17-18R
Applezweig, M. H.
See Appley, M(ortimer) H(erbert)
Apps, Jerold W(illard) 1934- CANR-1
Earlier sketch in CA 49-52
Apps, Jerry
See Apps, Jerold W(illard)
Apsler, Alfred 1907- CANR-3
Earlier sketch in CA 5-6R
See also SATA 10
Apt, (Jerome) Leon 1929- 53-56
Apted, M(ichael) R. 1919- 25-28R
Aptekar, Jane 1935- 81-84
Apter, David Ernest 1924- CANR-3
Earlier sketch in CA 1R
Apter, Michael J(ohn) 1939- 29-32R
Aptheker, Bettina 1944- 29-32R
Aptheker, Herbert 1915- 5-6R
Aquarius, Qass
See Buskirk, Richard H(obart)
Aquin, Hubert 1929-1977 .... CLC-15
Aquina, Sister Mary
See Weinrich, A(nna) K(atharina) H(ildegard)
Arafat, Ibtihaj Said 1934- 85-88
Aragon, Louis 1897- 69-72
See also CLC 3
Araki, James T(omomasa) 1925- 15-16R
Arango, Jorge Sanin 1916- 61-64
Aranow, Edward Ross 1909- 41-44R
Arapoff, Nancy 1930- 29-32R
Arata, Esther S(pring) 1918- 89-92
Arberry, A(rthur) J(ohn) 1905-1969 .... 4R
Arbib, Robert (Simeon, Jr.) 1915- 33-36R
Arbingast, Stanley A(lan) 1910- 17-18R
Arbogast, William F. 1908-1979 Obituary .. 89-92
Arbuckle, Dugald S(inclair) 1912- 13-14R
Arbuckle, Robert D(ean) 1940- 61-64
Arbuckle, Wanda Rector 1910- 41-44R
Arbuthnot, May Hill 1884-1969 .... 9-10R
See also SATA 2
Arbuzov, Alexei Nikolaevich 1908- 69-72
Arce, Hector 1935-1980 97-100
Arceneaux, Thelma Hoffmann Tyler AITN-1
Arch, E. L.
See Payes, Rachel C(osgrove)
Archambault, Paul 1937- 81-84
Archdeacon, Thomas J(ohn) 1942- 65-68
Archer, A. A.
See Joscelyn, Archie L.
Archer, Frank
See O'Connor, Richard
Archer, Fred 1915- 57-60
Archer, Fred C. 1916(?)-1974 Obituary 53-56
Archer, Gleason Leonard, Jr. 1916- 65-68
Archer, H(orace) Richard 1911-1978 .... 15-16R
Obituary 89-92
Archer, Jeffrey (Howard) 1940- 77-80
Archer, John H(all) 1914- 101
Archer, Jules 1915- 9-10R
See also CLC 12
See also SATA 4
Archer, Marion Fuller 1917- 5-6R
See also SATA 11
Archer, Myrtle (Lilly) 1926- 102
Archer, Peter Kingsley 1926- CANR-2
Earlier sketch in CA 7-8R
Archer, Ron
See White, Theodore Edwin
Archer, S. E.
See Soderberg, Percy Measday
Archer, Sellers G. 1908- 17-18R
Archer, Stephen H(unt) 1928- 19-20R
Archer, W(illiam) G(eorge) 1907- 57-60
Archibald, (Rupert) Douglas 1919- 101
Archibald, Joe
See Archibald, Joseph S(topford)
Archibald, John J. 1925- 5-6R
Archibald, Joseph S(topford) 1898- 9-10R
See also SATA 3
Archibald, William 1924-1970 Obituary . 29-32R
Arciniegas, German 1900- 61-64
Arcone, Sonya 1925-1978 .... 21-22R
Obituary 77-80
Ard, Ben N(eal), Jr. 1922- 33-36R
Ard, William (Thomas) 1922-1962(?) 5-6R
Ardagh, John 1928- 25-28R
Ardalan, Nader 1939- 69-72
Arden, Barbi
See Stoutenburg, Adrien (Pearl)
Arden, Gothard Everett 1905- CAP-1
Earlier sketch in CA 11-12
Arden, J. E. M.
See Conquest, (George) Robert (Acworth)
Arden, Jane 61-64
Arden, John 1930- 15-16R
See also CLC 6, 13, 15
Arden, William
See Lynds, Dennis
Ardener, Edwin (William) 7-8R
Ardies, Tom 1931- 33-36R
Ardizzone, Edward (Jeffrey Irving)
1900-1979 .... 5-6R
Obituary 89-92
See also SATA 1
Ardizzone, Tony 1949- 85-88
Ardmore, Jane Kesner 1915- 7-8R
Ardoin, John (Louis) 1935- 57-60
Ardrey, Robert 1908-1980 .... 33-36R
Obituary 93-96
Arecco, Vera Lustig
See Lustig-Arecco, Vera
Areeda, Phillip E. 1930- 23-24R
Arehart-Treichel, Joan 1942- 57-60
Arellanes, Audrey Spencer 1920- 33-36R
Arem, Joel E(dward) 1943- 89-92
Arena, John I. 1929- 45-48
Arendt, Hannah 1906-1975 .... 19-20R
Obituary 61-64
Arenella, Roy 1939- SATA-14
Arens, Richard 1921- 73-76
Arens, William 1940- 89-92
Arensberg, Conrad Maynadier 1910- 61-64
Arent, Arthur 1904-1972 .... CAP-2
Obituary 33-36R
Earlier sketch in CA 23-24
Areskoug, Kaj 1933- 29-32R
Aresty, Esther B(radford) 9-10R
Areta, Mavis
See Winder, Mavis Areta
Arey, James A. 1936- 41-44R
Argan, Giulio Carlo 1909- 65-68
Argenti, Philip 1891(?)-1974 Obituary 49-52
Argenzio, Victor 1902- 53-56
Argiro, Larry 1909- 5-6R
Argo, Ellen 1933- 73-76
Argow, Waldemar 1916- 23-24R
Arguedas, Jose Maria 1911-1969 89-92
See also CLC 10
Arguelles, Jose A(nthony) 1939- 45-48
Arguelles, Miriam Tarcov 1943- 45-48
Argus
See Osusky, Stefan
Argus
See Phillips-Birt, Douglas Hextall Chedzey
Argyle, Aubrey William 1910- CAP-1
Earlier sketch in CA 17-18
Argyle, Michael 1925- 21-22R
Argyris, Chris 1923- 2R
Arian, Alan (Asher) 1938- CANR-1
Earlier sketch in CA 49-52
Arian, Edward 1921- 33-36R
Arias-Misson, Alain 1936- 77-80
Ariel
See Moraes, Frank Robert
Aries, Philippe 1914- 89-92
Arieti, Silvano 1914- 21-22R
Arimond, Carroll 1909-1979 Obituary 89-92
Aring, Charles D(air) 1904- 49-52
Ariyoshi, Shoichiro
1939(?)-1979 Obituary 89-92
Arkell, Anthony John 1898-1980 102
Obituary 97-100
Arkhurst, Frederick S(iegfried) 1920- .. 29-32R
Arkhurst, Joyce Cooper 1921- 17-18R
Arkin, David 1906- 21-22R
Arkin, Frieda 1917- 65-68
Arkin, Herbert 1906- 7-8R
Arkin, Joseph 1922- 7-8R
Arkin, Marcus 1926- 53-56
Arkush, Arthur Spencer
1925-1979 Obituary 85-88
Arlandson, Leone 1917- 29-32R
Arlen, Michael J. 1930- 61-64
Arleo, Joseph 1933- 29-32R
Arley, Catherine 1935- CANR-2
Earlier sketch in CA 45-48
Arlott, (Leslie Thomas) John 1914- 9-10R
Arlotto, Anthony (Thomas) 1939- 33-36R
Arlow, Jacob A. 1912- 53-56
Armacost, Michael Hayden 1937- 101
Armah, Ayi Kwei 1939- 61-64
See also CLC 5
Armand, Louis 1905-1971 .... CAP-2
Obituary 33-36R
Earlier sketch in CA 29-32
Armatas, James P. 1931- 41-44R
Armbrister, Trevor 1933- 89-92
Armbruster, Carl J. 1929- 33-36R
Armbruster, F(ranz) O(wen) 1929- 49-52
Armbruster, Francis E(dward) 1923- 29-32R
Armbruster, Frank
See Armbruster, Francis E(dward)
Armbruster, Maxim Ethan 1902- 1R
Armens, Sven 1921- 21-22R
Armentrout, William W(infield) 1918- ... 33-36R
Armer, Alberta (Roller) 1904- 7-8R
See also SATA 9
Armer, Laura (Adams) 1874-1963 65-68
See also SATA 13
Armerding, George D. 1899- 85-88
Armerding, Hudson Taylor 1918- 23-24R
Armes, Roy 1937- 73-76
Armington, John Calvin 1923- 53-56
Armistead, Samuel (Gordon) 1927- 53-56
Armitage, Angus 1902- CAP-1
Earlier sketch in CA 13-14
Armitage, E(dward) Liddall 1887- CAP-1
Earlier sketch in CA 9-10
Armitage, Merle 1893-1975 Obituary 61-64
Armour, John
See Paine, Lauran (Bosworth)
Armour, Lloyd R. 1922- 29-32R
Armour, Richard 1906- 1R
See also SATA 14
Armour, Rollin Stely 1929- 33-36R
Arms, George (Warren) 1912- 5-6R
Arms, Johnson
See Halliwell, David (William)
Arms, Suzanne 1944- 57-60
Armstrong, (Walter) Alan 1936- 73-76
Armstrong, Ann Seidel 1917- 9-10R
Armstrong, Anne(tte) 1924- 13-14R
Armstrong, Anthony
See Willis, (George) Anthony Armstrong
Armstrong, Anthony C.
See Armstrong, Christopher J. R.
Armstrong, (Grace) April (Oursler) 1926- ... 89-92
Armstrong, Arthur Hilary 1909- 69-72
Armstrong, Benjamin Leighton 1923- 93-96
Armstrong, Brian G(ary) 1936- 69-72
Armstrong, Charlotte 1905-1969 .... CANR-3
Obituary 25-28R
Earlier sketch in CA 1R
Armstrong, Christopher J(ohn) R(ichard)
1935- 69-72
Armstrong, D(avid) M(alet) 1926- 25-28R
Armstrong, David M(ichael) 1944- 57-60
Armstrong, Douglas Albert 1920- 9-10R
Armstrong, Edward Allworthy 1900-1978 .. 7-8R
Armstrong, (Annette) Elizabeth 1917- ... 25-28R
Armstrong, Frederick H(enry) 1926- 33-36R
Armstrong, George D. 1927- SATA-10
Armstrong, Gerry (Breen) 1929- 15-16R
See also SATA 10
Armstrong, Gregory T(imon) 1933- 9-10R
Armstrong, Hamilton Fish 1893-1973 93-96
Obituary 41-44R
Armstrong, Henry H.
See Arvay, Harry
Armstrong, J(on) Scott 1937- CANR-1
Earlier sketch in CA 45-48
Armstrong, (A.) James 1924- 29-32R
Armstrong, John A(lexander, Jr.) 1922- . CANR-3
Earlier sketch in CA 4R
Armstrong, John Borden 1926- 33-36R
Armstrong, John Byron 1917-1976 .... 5-6R
Obituary 65-68
Armstrong, Joseph Gravitt 1943- 101
Armstrong, Judith Mary 1935- 102
Armstrong, Keith F(rancis) W(hitfield)
1950- 29-32R
Armstrong, (Daniel) Louis
1900-1971 Obituary 29-32R
Armstrong, Marjorie Moore 1912- 89-92
Armstrong, Martin 1882-1974 Obituary ... 49-52
Armstrong, O(rland) K(ay) 1893- 93-96
Armstrong, (Raymond) Paul 1912- 37-40R
Armstrong, Richard 1903- 77-80
See also SATA 11
Armstrong, Richard G. 1932- 73-76
Armstrong, Robert L(aurence) 1926- 29-32R
Armstrong, Robert Plant 1919- 41-44R
Armstrong, Roger D. 1939- 19-20R
Armstrong, Ruth Gallup 1891- CAP-1
Earlier sketch in CA 9-10
Armstrong, Terence Ian Fytton 1912-1970 . CAP-2
Obituary 29-32R
Earlier sketch in CA 17-18
Armstrong, Thomas 1899- 7-8R
Armstrong, Wallace Edwin
1896-1980 Obituary 97-100
Armstrong, William A(lexander) 1912- ... 13-14R
Armstrong, William A(rthur) 1915- 17-18R
Armstrong, William H(oward) 1914- 19-20R
See also SATA 4
See also AITN 1
Armstrong, William M(artin) 1919- 49-52
Armytage, Walter Harry Green 1915- 9-10R
Arnade, Charles W(olfgang) 1927- 33-36R
Arnason, H(jorvardur) H(arvard) 1909- 61-64
Arnaud, Saint Romain
See Aragon, Louis
Arndt, Ernst H(einrich) D(aniel) 1899- CAP-2
Earlier sketch in CA 23-24
Arndt, H(einz) W(olfgang) 1915- 21-22R
Arndt, Karl John Richard 1903- 17-18R
Arndt, Walter W(erner) 1916- 13-14R
Arnett, Caroline
See Cole, Lois Dwight
Arnett, Carroll 1927- 21-22R
Arnett, Harold E(dward) 1931- 21-22R
Arnett, Ross H(arold), Jr. 1919- CANR-2
Earlier sketch in CA 49-52
Arnez, Nancy Levi 1928- 29-32R
Arnheim, Daniel D(avid) 1930- 11-12R
Arnheim, Rudolf 1904- CANR-3
Earlier sketch in CA 4R
Arno, Peter 1904-1968 73-76
Obituary 25-28R
Arnold, Adlai F(ranklin) 1914- 33-36R
Arnold, Alan 1922- 7-8R
Arnold, Alvin L(incoln) 1929- 93-96
Arnold, Armin H. 1931- CANR-3
Earlier sketch in CA 9-10R
Arnold, Arnold (Ferdinand) 1921- 19-20R
Arnold, Bruce 1936- 93-96
Arnold, Carl
See Raknes, Ola
Arnold, Charles Harvey 1920- 65-68
Arnold, Charlotte E(lizabeth) Cramer 57-60
Arnold, Corliss Richard 1926- 49-52
Arnold, Denis Midgley 1926- CANR-2
Earlier sketch in CA 7-8R
Arnold, Edmund C(larence) 1913- CANR-3
Earlier sketch in CA 4R
Arnold, Elliott 1912-1980 .... 19-20R
Obituary 97-100
See also SATA 5
Arnold, Emmy (von Hollander) 1884- 23-24R
Arnold, Francena H(arriet Long) 1888- CAP-1
Earlier sketch in CA 17-18
Arnold, G. L.
See Lichtheim, George
Arnold, Guy 1932- 25-28R
Arnold, H(arry) J(ohn) P(hilip) 1932- CANR-2
Earlier sketch in CA 7-8R
Arnold, Herbert 1935- 37-40R
Arnold, Janet 1932- 93-96
Arnold, Joseph H.
See Hayes, Joseph
Arnold, June (Davis) 1926- 21-22R
Arnold, L. J.
See Cameron, Lou
Arnold, Lloyd R. 1906-1970 .... CAP-2
Earlier sketch in CA 25-28
Arnold, Magda B(londiau) 1903- 5-6R
Arnold, Margot
See Cook, Petronelle Marguerite Mary
Arnold, Mary Ann 1918- 65-68
Arnold, Milo Lawrence 1903- 57-60
Arnold, Olga Moore 1900-1981 Obituary ... 102
Arnold, Oren 1900- CANR-2
Earlier sketch in CA 5-6R
See also SATA 4

INDEX

INDEX

INDEX

INDEX

INDEX

INDEX

INDEX

INDEX

INDEX

INDEX

INDEX

INDEX

INDEX

INDEX

INDEX

INDEX

INDEX

INDEX

INDEX

INDEX

INDEX

INDEX

INDEX

INDEX

INDEX

INDEX

INDEX

INDEX

INDEX

INDEX

INDEX

INDEX

INDEX

INDEX

INDEX

INDEX

INDEX

INDEX

INDEX

INDEX

INDEX

INDEX

INDEX

INDEX

INDEX

INDEX

INDEX

INDEX

INDEX

INDEX

INDEX

INDEX

INDEX

INDEX

INDEX

INDEX

INDEX

INDEX

INDEX

INDEX

INDEX

INDEX

INDEX

INDEX

INDEX

INDEX

INDEX

INDEX

INDEX

INDEX

INDEX

INDEX

INDEX

INDEX

INDEX

INDEX

INDEX

INDEX

INDEX

INDEX

INDEX

INDEX

INDEX

INDEX

INDEX

INDEX